ENGLAND

Ostend
Bruges Antwerp
Ghent
Dunkirk
Calais Brussels
BELGIUM
Boulogne Lille Mons Charleroi Namur Liège
GERMANY
Le Touquet Etaples Douai
Arras Cambrai Solesmes
ENGLISH CHANNEL
Fécamp
Cuverville
Etretat
Dieppe
Amiens

Charleville Sedan
Luxembourg

Paris is shown at an
enlarged scale
inside the back cover

Laon
Cherbourg
Trouville
Deauville
Le Havre Croisset
Beauvais Villers- Soissons
Honfleur Rouen Auteuil Cotterets Senlis Reims
Verdun Metz
Pont l'Evêque Chantilly La Ferté-Milon
Caen Cabourg Royaumont
Evreux Meaux Château- Bar-le-Duc
Mantes-la-Jolie PARIS Thierry
Villeparisis Coulommiers Nancy Strasburg
Dreux Sceaux Cirey
Igny
Rambouillet Vaux-le- Nogent-sur-Seine Colmar
Vicomte
Chartres Fontainebleau Troyes Mulhouse
Alençon Sens
Fougères Langres Basle
Le Mans Pontigny
Vitré Laval Vendôme Orléans Auxerre SWITZERLAND
Chateaubriant La Flèche Blois Vézelay Dijon Besançon Neuchâtel
Le Lude Amboise Berne
Angers Bourgueil Tours Dôle
Loire Chenonceaux Saône
Saumur Chinon Chambord Bourges Nevers Châlons-sur-Saône Lausanne Vevey
Loudun Loches Loire Coppet
Richelieu Châtellerault Châteauroux Paray-le- Ferney Genèva Simplon
Nohant Monial Pass
Poitiers La Châtre Moulins Mâcon Chamonix
Fontenay-le- Ligugé Montluçon Saint Point Bourg-en-Bresse Annecy Great St Bernard Pass
Comte Niort Vichy Little St Bernard Pass
Vivonne Villefranche Belley Bourg Saint Maurice
La Rochelle Verteuil-sur- Limoges Clermont-Ferrand Lyons ITALY
Charente Chambéry
Rochefort La Rochefoucauld Grenoble Mont Cenis Turin
Angoulême Saint-Etienne Pass
Briançon
Périgueux Le Puy
Montaigne Sarlat Grignan
Bordeaux Dordogne Valence
Arcachon La Orange
Brède Cahors
Agen Alès Avignon Menton
Cayla Uzès Nice
Nérac Montauban Nîmes Tarascon Cannes
Garonne Albi Arles Aix
Toulouse Montpellier Marseilles
Pézenas Toulon Saint Tropez
Bayonne Orthez Béziers
Biarritz Pau Narbonne
Jean de Luz Tarbes Carcassonne
Lourdes
Cauterets Montségur Perpignan

MEDITERRANEAN

Perrott CartoGraphics

GUIDE TO

FRENCH LITERATURE
1789 to the Present

Guide to French Literature

Beginnings to 1789

1789 to the Present

GUIDE TO

FRENCH LITERATURE

1789 to the Present

ANTHONY LEVI

St-J

ST. JAMES PRESS
CHICAGO AND LONDON

© 1992 by St. James Press

For information write:
ST. JAMES PRESS
233 East Ontario Street
Chicago, Illinois 60611
U.S.A.

or

2–6 Boundary Row
London SE1 8HP
England.

British Library Cataloguing in Publication Data
Levi, Anthony, *1929–*
    Guide to French literature : 1789 to the present
    I. Title
    840.9

ISBN 1-55862-086-9

FOR

CLAUDIA and CLARISSA

CONTENTS

LIST OF ENTRIES

CHRONOLOGY

1775–83   American War of Independence

1778   France joins war against Britain

1783   Peace of Versailles

1788   Estates General in Brittany (December) leads to rioting (January 1789)

1789–99   Revolution

1789   5 May: Estates General opens at Versailles

17 June: Third Estate constitutes National Assembly

14 July: Storming of Bastille

27 August: *Declaration of the Rights of Man and of the Citizen*, modelled on American *Declaration of Independence* (1776)

5 October: Royal family brought back to Tuileries from Versailles

1791   May: adoption of guillotine as method of execution

June: Flight of royal family to Varennes, arrest and return to Paris

1792   War with Austria

Ascendancy of the Commune

Imprisonment of royal family

2–5 September: Massacre of more than 1200 political prisoners

21 September: Inauguration of National Convention

First Republic (until 1804)

1793   21 January: Execution of Louis XVI

6 April: Committee of Public Safety inaugurated

13 July: Marat assassinated by Charlotte Corday

16 October: Execution of the ex-queen, Marie Antoinette

1794   5 April: Execution of Danton

27 and 28 July (9 and 10 Thermidor): Fall and execution of Robespierre and 71 followers. End of Terror

October: Emergence of Napoleon Bonaparte as successful young General, defence of Paris against insurrection

Abolition of capital punishment

Famine

1795   The Directory (27 October 1795–9 November 1799)

1796   Successes of Revolutionary army continue

24 June: Crossing of Rhine at Kehl

1798   Egyptian campaign. French naval defeat at Aboukir (1 August)

1799   9 November (18 Brumaire): Napoleon's *coup d'état*

13 December: Napoleon (1769–1821), as First Consul, continues overseas wars

1801   Concordat with Vatican restoring Catholicism as state religion signed. Solemnly inaugurated 18 April 1802.

1802   Napoleon First Consul for life

1804   Kidnapping and execution (21 March) of duc d'Enghien, the last Condé to bear the title and a possible focus of future political opposition

18 May: Napoleon made emperor, crowned by himself on 2 December at Notre-Dame in presence of Pius VII

1804–14   First Empire. Napoleon's internal reorganization of France is radical and is much admired. Napoleon conquers or otherwise controls much of Europe, but does not establish naval supremacy, and after losing Battle of Trafalgar (21 October 1805) is obliged to renounce plans to invade England. Napoleon's ambitions to achieve dominion over England, Spain, and Russia eventually lead to his downfall.

1807   Slave trade abolished in British Empire

1812   Napoleon obliged to retreat from Moscow

1813   Napoleon defeated at Leipzig

1814   Allied invasion of France. Capitulation of Paris (31 March)

6 April: abdication of Napoleon. Restoration of Bourbons under Louis XVIII, younger brother of Louis XVI, whose son (born 1785) had been declared dead in a Revolutionary prison on 8 June 1795

12 April: entry into Paris of the comte d'Artois, "Monsieur," younger brother of Louis XVIII, to succeed him as Charles X

20 April: Napoleon exiled to Elba

4 June: Issue of *La Charte constitutionnelle* providing for a constitutional monarchy

1814–15   Congress of Vienna agrees new boundaries within Europe

1815   1 March: Napoleon escapes. After landing near Cannes he picks up support, and is carried in triumph to the Tuileries on arrival in Paris (20 March)

19 March: flight of Louis XVIII to Belgium

18 June: Napoleon routed at Waterloo. New abdication, banishment to St. Helena, and new restoration of Louis XVIII. Restored monarchy lasts until 1848.

1815–20   Political debate centres on disputes between

republicans, liberal supporters of a constitutional monarchy, and "ultra" royalists seeking a return to an absolutist as well as hereditary monarchy

1820   13 February: Assassination of the duc de Berry, son of the comte d'Artois, and potential heir presumptive to the throne. His posthumous son (1820–83), the comte de Chambord, becomes the "legitimist" claimant to the throne on the death of his exiled grandfather in 1836, and is known to his supporters as Henri V

1822   Declaration of Greek independence

1823   Ferdinand VII of Spain forcibly reinstated by France

1824   Death of Louis XVIII. Accession of Charles X, crowned with much ceremony at Reims, who announces his intention of ruling by divine right. Under his chief minister, Villèle, the *émigrés* are compensated, and repressive, anti-liberal policies pursued

1830   26 July: Charles X dissolves the Chamber and, by re-introducing formal press censorship, provokes a political upheaval

27–29 July: street rioting in Paris

2 August: abdication of Charles X and of his eldest son

The liberals rally round the duc d'Orléans (1773–1850), son of Philippe-Egalité, descended from the younger brother of Louis XIV, the focus of opposition in pre-Revolutionary France, executed in 1793

7 August: Orléans is proclaimed king as Louis-Philippe I. He accepts the charter, and his rule is known as "The July Monarchy"

1830–31 Failure of Polish uprising against Russian domination

1831   14 February: Archbishop's palace in Paris destroyed by rioters

21 November: First revolt of Lyons silk-weavers

1832   February–May: Cholera epidemic reaches Paris. At least 12,000 deaths

15 August: Papal Bull *Mirari vos* condemns Lamennais's *L'Avenir*

1833   Guizot's law formalizing the re-organization of primary education

1835   28 July: Joseph Fieschi's attempt to assassinate Louis-Philippe leads to repressive measures. Social unrest during the whole reign largely due to impact of mechanization on wages

1840–48 Guizot ministry

1842   Administrative measures for first main state-owned railway lines, to be operated by private companies. Seven out of nine to emanate from Paris

1847   The first "banquets" replace banned political meetings

1848   23–25 February: Revolution in Paris and proclamation of Second Republic (until 1852). Abdication of Louis-Philippe

December 10: After a summer of street fighting in Paris Louis Napoleon (Napoleon III), Bonaparte's nephew, is elected President

1851   1–2 December: After increasingly restrictive measures, Napoleon III's *coup d'état* establishes the Second Empire (until 1870). Both republican and royalist opponents are arrested

1852   20 and 21 November: plebiscite ratifying Napoleon III as emperor

1853   Baron Eugène-Georges Haussmann (1809–91) begins reconstruction of Paris

1854–56 France and Britain allies in Crimean War to protect Ottoman empire from Russian attack

1855   Universal Exhibition

1859   France helps Italy in war of independence against Austria

1860   Incorporation into France of Savoy and Nice

1867   Universal Exhibition

1869   Opening of Suez Canal

1870   19 July: France, alarmed at the possibility of a Prussian on the throne of Spain, declares war on Prussia

1 September: Prussia accepts unconditional French surrender at Sedan

4 September: Proclamation by Léon Gambetta (1838–82) and Jules Favre (1809–80) of Third Republic (until 1940)

18 September–28 January 1871: Siege of Paris

27 October: Capitulation of main French army

1871   29 January: Armistice signed.

National Assembly elected on 8 February meets in Bordeaux. The liberal Adolphe Thiers (1797–1877) leads the first government of the Third Republic

18 March–28 May: the commune uprising in Paris. The government at Versailles retakes Paris 21–28 May

1878   Third Universal Exhibition

1880   10 July: amnesty for communards

1882   Primary education becomes free, compulsory, and lay

1886   General Georges Boulanger (1837–91) heads popular movement for a military government. In 1889, when he might have seized power, he flees. Condemned for treason, and discredited, in December 1891 he commits suicide on his mistress's grave

1889   Failure of Panama Canal company helps to

discredit business ethics of Second Empire. Scandal reaches its height in 1892

Universal Exhibition, for which the Eiffel Tower is built

1894   Court martial of Alfred Dreyfus. Condemnation for betraying military secrets

1896   Colonel Picquart discovers and suppresses evidence pointing to guilt of Major Esterhazy. His deputy, Colonel Henry, forges evidence to support Dreyfus's guilt

1898   13 January: *L'Aurore* publishes Zola's *J'Accuse*

Colonel Henry admits to forgery, is imprisoned and commits suicide

1899   Dreyfus re-tried, found guilty, given reduced sentence, then pardoned. Reversal of verdict and re-instatement not until 1906. *L'Affaire Dreyfus* catalyst for appearance of deep splits in French social fabric

1900   Universal Exhibition

1902–05   Strongly anti-clerical government of Combes

1909   Blériot flies across the Channel

1914   Assassination of socialist leader Jean-Léon Jaurès (1858–1914)

1914–18   World War I, of which only the immediate occasion is the assassination of Archduke Ferdinand at Sarajevo on 28 June 1914. Trench warfare: continues throughout the war, which lasts from 3 August 1914 to 11 November 1918

1917   Bolshevik revolution in Russia

1918   Influenza epidemic responsible for an estimated 7,000,000 deaths throughout the world

1919   Treaty of Versailles

1925–35   Gradual emergence in Russia, Germany, and Italy of totalitarian power blocs based on the apparently conflicting philosophies of social organization of the "left" and the "right"

1929   Wall Street crash, followed by the depression

1936   German occupation of the Rhineland

1936–39   Spanish Civil War

1936–38   Front Populaire in power in France

1938   Annexation by Germany of Austria, the "Anschluss"

1939   Annexation by Germany of Czechoslovakia

August: Hitler–Stalin pact, supported by French communist party

1 September: German invasion of Poland

3 September: Formal outbreak of war between France and Germany

1940   14 June: Germans take Paris

16 June: Marshal Pétain takes over from Paul Reynaud and signs an armistice on 22 June

18 June: General de Gaulle appeals from London on behalf of Free French forces, of which on 28 June the UK acknowledges him to be the leader

French government moves to Vichy

1942   11 November: the free part of France is occupied

1944   26 August: de Gaulle enters Paris

1945   7 and 8 May: German surrender

10 August: Japanese surrender

1945–58   Fourth Republic

1954   Fall of Dien Bien Phu

Outbreak of Algerian war

1957   Rome Treaty for Common Market ratified

1958–61   Army revolt in Algeria

1958   De Gaulle made President of the Fifth Republic

1962   Independence of Algeria proclaimed

1968   Student riots in Germany and France

1969   Resignation of de Gaulle

INTRODUCTION

The Revolution has so often been regarded as a point of discontinuity in French cultural history that the decision to split the contents of this *Guide* at the end of the 18th century requires a prefatory comment. The positioning of the split was determined by convenience and convention rather than by more fundamental considerations about any discontinuity in French culture marked either by the Revolution of 1789 or by the Terror which followed it, and which lasted until the fall of Robespierre and his followers on 27–28 July 1794. The inception of French literature dates from what we call "the early middle ages," shortly after a recognizable vernacular emerged from a series of variants of low Latin. Any discontinuities discoverable in the waxing and waning of literary movements, styles, and fashions in the history of French literature since then can be seen to have occurred only on the surface of a deeper and apparently almost steadily continuous development in the evolution of the values informing the converging cultures of western European society.

Culturally speaking, the 1789 Revolution was like an exceptional wave, which suddenly broke under the weight of the water piled up behind it, but only momentarily interrupted the flow of the underlying tide. There is a clearly continuous development from the sensibility of such 18th-century writers as Jean-Jacques Rousseau (1712–1778) and Jacques-Henri Bernardin de Saint-Pierre (1727–1814) on the one hand, to that of such "pre-romantic" (q.v.) authors as François-René de Chateaubriand (1768–1848) and Benjamin Constant (1767–1830) on the other. By taking the Revolution as the starting point, generations of 19th- and even 20th-century French historians, wishing for religious or political reasons either to discredit it or to find in it the seedlings of all subsequent cultural development, have established a misleading base from which to measure the pace or the magnitude of 19th-century cultural phenomena of all kinds.

The development of the French school system, clearly relevant to the spread of literacy, and therefore of significance in the development of literature, also reflects the dispute about cultural continuity in a different way. Did the French school system date from the Revolution, which emancipated the population from the obscurantist tutelage of the Church under the ancien régime, or did the Revolution wreck especially the elementary school system which the Church had carefully built up? Both sides in that controversy, central to French political debate for almost a century, wrongly assumed that the Revolution marked a cultural discontinuity rather than a brief interruption in a relatively steady advance. As late as 1977 in their remarkable study of the history of literacy in France, *Reading and Writing. Literacy in France from Calvin to Jules Ferry* (Cambridge Studies in Oral and Literary Culture, No. 5, Cambridge 1982, p. 100), François Furet and Jacques Ozouf found it necessary to write: "We ought to stop taking the Revolution as our point of reference."

On the other hand it would be absurd to maintain that nothing at all changed in the organization of French cultural life on account of the tensions which erupted during the last decade of the 18th century. There are said to have been 180,000 émigrés, a fair proportion of whom must have come from Paris. In 1800 the population of Paris was about 550,000, that of France about 27,000,000. The relative concentration of the Terror in Paris clearly entailed the disappearance from the capital of a high enough proportion of the educated population, however briefly, to bring about a suspension of the ordinary mechanisms for ensuring the continuity of cultural change. It is clear from the contents of this *Guide* that both Napoleon and, after 1814, the restored Bourbons had some difficulty in re-establishing them.

However, the view taken here that the production and consumption of "literature" must be regarded as a principal mechanism both for ensuring the continuity of cultural change and for the inauguration of movements of social advance, necessarily entails a particular way of looking at literary texts. It is impossible to write even a reference guide to French literature without at least implied evaluative judgements, and such judgements must rest on critical procedures which presuppose at least elements of a theory of literature. The process of selecting great authors and significant movements presupposes a coherent idea of what literature is, and on what criteria its interest can be judged. Literary theory is notoriously controversial, but the principles by which authors are included within a literary canon or excluded from it, need to be made explicit even if, as in the present *Guide*, the operation of such principles is mitigated by respect for an established consensus of who the great French authors are, and which are the most important literary groupings and movements. Such a consensus emerges from the general functioning of the cultural and educational communities, and is, of course, constantly in the process of being revised. It is necessarily felt to be always obsolescent. It does, however, raise problems.

By what historical process do we change the canon of the great literature of the past? How far can the literary text be regarded as "self-referential," to be evaluated independently of any knowledge of its historical origins, its author, the circumstances of its production, or its cultural context? How far are the criteria by which it should be judged merely formal? Is literary criticism a branch of "semiotics" (see: structuralism), concerned with the tensions built up within a text without reference to any other than a no doubt socially conditioned but otherwise purely "aesthetic" reaction which the text itself is said to be capable of provoking, as even some Marxist critics have thought? Do literary critics speak with any authority other than their own, or do they objectively elucidate quantifiable qualities in texts, which justify the importance accorded to them? Can there be rigorous intellectual demonstrations of literary quality? In what sense might it be possible to accept Walter Benjamin's statement of 1961 that "Nowhere does a concern for the reception of a work of art or of an artform aver itself fruitful for its understanding… No poem is addressed to a reader, no painting to its beholder, no symphony to its listeners" ("Die Aufgabe des Übersetzers," in *Illuminationen*, Frankfurt 1961, p 56, translated by Harry Zohn in *Illuminations*, New York 1968, and quoted by Paul de Man in his Introduction to the collected essays of Hans Robert Jauss, translated as *Toward an Aesthetic of Reception*, Brighton 1982, p. xv).

How far on the other hand are both the production and the reception of literature culturally conditioned? According to what laws of cultural development does chronological distance affect the reception of a literary text and cause the value accorded to it to increase or diminish? How far does or should literature reflect the tensions within the society in which it is produced? By what mental processes can a competent literary historian date a text, even if its spelling and punctuation have been made to conform to contemporary usage? What are the relationships between literature, society, and the personal and social values which are the roots of any culture? Is it philistine to refer to the fact that masterpieces of painting, sculpture, music, or literature are traded commodities which are often produced and sold for money? How are aesthetic qualities related to marketplace valuations, since they quite clearly do not always accord with them? Yet the sums of money involved are so vast that the economics of the market must affect the nature of the product, and it is necessary for any literary guide to be aware of, and perhaps even guard against, what might be taken as the contamination of aesthetic values by market pressures. What finally distinguishes literature from non-literature, and great literature from literature which is less great?

The introduction to the first volume of this *Guide* will discuss in detail the methodological presuppositions of the whole work, the criteria used for the valuation of literary quality, for the *Guide*'s inclusions and exclusions, and its adoption of a "life-and-works" format. There are, however, matters specific to post-Revolutionary literature in France which should properly be presented here, and this introduction must at least touch on the methodological matters to be considered more extensively in the introduction to the volume devoted to pre-Revolutionary literature. Essentially the criterion of literary quality on which the *Guide* has sought to rely is "imaginative power," a concept to which recourse is not only necessary but also sufficient to answer all the questions of the two preceding paragraphs. It is sufficiently flexible to allow for differences of opinion, to account for changes of value with time, and it can be used to explain how the market value of a work of the imagination does not need to accord with its aesthetic merits. Yet, properly understood, it is objectively verifiable and quantifiable, and its establishment requires a combination of formal qualities and of criteria relative to the historical and social circumstances of both the production and the reception of literary texts. As a criterion of literary quality not the least virtue of imaginative power is its ultimate reliance on public acknowledgement as a touchstone, however historically and culturally conditioned, and however difficult to define that acknowledgement must be.

Greatness as an objective quality in any work of art depends virtually by definition on recognition, although that does not mean that public discernment is necessarily either immediate or infallible, or that the artist's creative imagination was necessarily conditioned by a quest for public recognition. Since the Revolution in France, admission to the canon of great literature has naturally depended on an elaborate system in which editors, publishers, critics, collectors, teachers, juries, journals, students, examiners, readers, and audiences all take their time and play their part. Collectively, in any literary context, they constitute "the general public," although with regard to particular authors and groups there will always be enthusiasts and doubters among them. The general public is a heterogeneous body. On the whole and in the end, their consensus on the presence and intensity of literary quality, while not of course constitutive of literary greatness, is at the highest level its indispensable indication. Sufficiently protracted, and widely enough based, public recognition

makes it possible to speak of great literature as virtually "timeless," even if, like the works of Dante and Shakespeare, it makes reference to dated events. Literature and its excellence can be timeless only when universal experiences are so powerfully explored as always and everywhere to challenge established assumptions, attitudes, and personal or social values. This is the sense in which Homer, Aeschylus, and in a different way Virgil are timeless.

The adoption of the criterion of "imaginative power" leads to the need to consider the links between literature and social history. Essentially, those links derive from the need which all Western societies have always experienced to understand the values they have been living by, to assess their appositeness, to examine possible alternatives to them, and continuously to change them. That is why great works of literature have normally been subversive of established attitudes. Works of the imagination, in whatever medium, have always been the testing bench on which society has sought to "understand, evaluate, and if necessary modify" systems of value, personal and social attitudes, and forms of behaviour, often focusing on whatever aspects and implications of its accepted attitudes society as a whole has at different dates found it easier to ignore.

Literature has the advantage that its investigation into society's values is imaginative. It can be tentative or aggressive, radical or reactionary in its thrust. For obvious reasons, the more radical its assessments, the more tentatively, like Flaubert's, they have often been put forward. Literary examination of the meaning of human experience, of the personal and social attitudes, political organization, domestic life, and rational and irrational forces bearing on behaviour of itself changes nothing. In investigating the implications of behaviour, attitudes, and values, literature has necessarily confined itself to exploring what is or could be the case, leaving the desirability of change implicit. The open advocacy of change belongs to the domain not of the literary author but of the pamphleteer or polemicist. Literature, however, in merely probing personal and social values, has always been able to call on a whole spectrum of literary registers, of which the epic, lyric, elegiac, tragic, comic, ironic, and fantastic are only a few. It can vary the style, tone, and intensity of its register. The function of criticism is chiefly to establish the text's mode of communication.

Whatever it does, the stature of a literary text depends on the imaginative vigour with which it does it. Dumas's *Antony* of 1831, however important a play in the history of romantic tragedy, is weakened by its failure to carry through the confrontation between two sets of incompatible values, for both of which Dumas has achieved the audience's sympathy. But romantic tragedy itself offers an excellent example of the way in which a new literary form had to be created to examine the implications of new actual and potential forms of social experience. Imaginative vigour has often demanded the creation of new literary forms and movements, requiring for instance the abandonment of formal constraints, as in Hugo, or their adoption, as in the Parnassians (q.v.). It has virtually forced literature to combine with other media of imaginative creation, like film, just as it enlisted typographical aid in addition to the semantic content of language when Mallarmé or Apollinaire insisted on incorporating layout on the printed page into the poetic structure of their work. No brilliance of formal execution can compensate for its absence. The result of its failure is most often the sentimentality of a Coppée or the pastiche of a Cocteau. The greatest danger in the adoption of imaginative power as the principal criterion of literary quality lies in the premium it puts on literature which is bleak, disturbing, or shocking in its vision, and therefore often tightly complex in its formal organization, as in the case of Racine, Pascal, Kafka, Camus, Perec, or Beckett.

Literature that is merely self-referential, in the sense that it justifies its own existence by demanding to be regarded as a metaphor of its own gestation, without reference to any experience other than that which it is itself capable of provoking cannot have either imaginative power, in the sense in which the term has been defined, nor any historically conditioned dimension. For this reason, even the strictest schools of literary formalists, like the "structuralist" (q.v.) school of Prague linguisticians as represented by the work of Jan Mukařovský and carried on by Felix Vodička, have been led to study literary structures specifically in their historical concretizations. Relatively recent debate in France on the subject of freeing the literary text from the association with which any reader must invest his understanding of it is the subject of the *Guide*'s entry under the title of the review *Tel Quel*. Virtually all the advocates of a purely formalist theory of criticism have now had recourse to some concept, like that of imaginative power, which in the jargon of literary theory links the two indispensable elements in any theory of literature, the "poetics," or the study of form, and the "hermeneutics," or the study of meaning.

In the period of French literary history with which this volume is concerned, literature started with only a quasi-monopoly of its all-important public social function. Less powerful and less public machinery impelling, not necessarily by imaginative activity, towards or against social change was still provided at first by the restored Bourbon Courts, and more importantly and lastingly by the salons, the educational and legal systems, the development of administrative practice, and of course discussion in private or semi-private groups. The role of literature itself was to be challenged by the invention of the popular press, the proliferation of periodicals, often fashion magazines or fascicules or manuals devoted to housekeeping, the serious reviews, and the introduction successively of cinema, radio, and then television.

On the other hand, the role of literature was boosted by the rise in the literacy rate, for social reasons higher among men than among women and for administrative reasons statistically better recorded for men, who were subject to conscription and compulsory testing. When the Guizot–Falloux laws on education started to be implemented in 1833, fewer than 50 per cent of young males were literate. By 1870, more than 80 per cent were. Private and public recitations and readings in salons, and then halls by authors, hostesses, and then actors, only gradually gave way to private reading, often in the "cabinets de lecture". Because public readings were also social occasions, they lasted until the dada (q.v.) manifestation-recitals in the early 1920s, which seem finally to have discredited them, but the number of libraries and bookshops lending for a fee increased steadily in the first half of the 19th century, peaking around 1844, when there were 215 in Paris alone.

Lending libraries started to decline with the appearance of really cheap editions, starting with the Bibliothèque Charpentier in 1838. Some novels were published as fascicules in serial form. By and large that meant that, while the amount of reading material available for entertainment or instruction increased enormously, the consumers even of serious literature came from

lower down the social scale, now more often and more easily, if at first still patchily, offered the possibility of schooling. As that happened, changes in the subject matter of literary works accelerated, and romantics, realists, and naturalists (qq.v.) progressively altered their conventions. In the late 1840s, when France underwent the 1848 revolution and Dickens's books were meeting with such overwhelming success in the UK, the best-selling volumes of fiction in France were reflecting a taste which, as might have been predicted, was both lowbrow and radical.

In the top 20 best-selling volumes between 1845 and 1850, fiction was represented by *The Arabian Nights*, followed by two Dumas novels, *Le Comte de Monte-Cristo* and *Les Trois mousquetaires*, Fénelon's *Télémaque* of 1699, Defoe's *Robinson Crusoe*, Bernardin de Saint-Pierre's *Paul et Virginie* of 1787, three novels by Sue, *Les Mystères de Paris*, *Le Juif errant*, and *Les Mystères du peuple*, the now forgotten novels of F.-G. Ducray-Dumenil (1761–1819), *Victor; ou L'Enfant de la forêt*, and M.-R.-L. Reybaud (1799–1879), *Jérôme Paturot à la recherche d'une position sociale*, and *Le Chevalier de la Maison-Rouge* by Dumas. Also in the list were Lamartine's *Histoire des Girondins* of 1847, and the *Physiologie du goût; ou, Méditations sur la gastronomie transcendante* of 1825 by Brillat-Savarin (1755–1826). The figures for five-year periods from 1810 to 1850 show the overwhelming popularity of the *Fables* of La Fontaine (1621–1695), with sales estimated at over 600,000, and of Fénelon's *Télémaque*, which sold over 500,000 copies and fell out of the list of the top five best-sellers only after 1845.

The links between literature and social history demand that, in spite of the increase in non-literary reading material, works which, on account of their imaginative power can be classified as literature of whatever grade had to reflect the real imaginative needs of the culture in which they were produced. If Balzac continues to be a great author, and to make us re-examine our assumptions about our attitudes and relationships, it is because, even if he had no solutions to the social problems of his own day, he retains an enduring power which derives from the intensity of the vision he developed to penetrate the values of the society in which he was himself living. He shared cultural horizons and expectations with his readers, but the vision which he developed, which made his work powerful then, and still accounts for its power today, was partly gestated by the focuses of imaginative concern imposed by his own youth.

A psychoanalytical understanding of an author's experience is no substitute for a critical evaluation of the work of literature although, like Marx, Freud established a framework which has subsequently aided gifted critics to understand the nature of the constraints working on a writer's imagination. It is frequently important to know something about a writer's own experience whose meaning the literary texts seek to elucidate or investigate.

The attitudes to life examined in the works of Flaubert, Gide, and Proust cannot properly be understood without reference to the dates and circumstances of the composition of their works. The focuses of interest in the imaginative writings of Stendhal and Beckett can be pinpointed only in the light of some knowledge of their childhoods. Why do Stendhal's male heroes so often love older women? What drove Beckett to his minimalist concentration on the meaningless circularity of all human experience? We very often need some knowledge of an author's background, as a host of biographies, catalogues, dust jackets, and programme notes testify, if we are to be able to answer the fundamental question "What is this work about?" Very often the authors themselves do not know, but anyone who has ever studied or taught a literary subject will know that this is the question which every examiner endlessly and annually has to rephrase. The most striking example of all is Perec, no part of whose work can be understood on any but the most superficial level without reference both to the totality of the work and to the terrifying experiences of Perec's extreme youth, as the entry devoted to him attempts to make clear.

These preliminary considerations about the nature of literature, the criteria to be adopted for assessing its quality, and its relationship to the circumstances of its production point towards the four principal ways in which literary history locks into social history. Firstly, the personal and social experience illuminated and the values explored by imaginative literature are specific to the constraints, attitudes and values, whether personal, social, economic, or political, operating at a definite moment within a given society. Secondly, however special the status of literature, it is also a commodity which has always been bought and sold, and has therefore to have been subject to economic mechanisms. Thirdly, the subject matter of French literature in the period since the Revolution has had to take account of major historical events, including the industrial and technological revolutions, two world wars, and radical changes in systems of transport and communication. Fourthly, technological advance, in affecting the production and dissemination of literature, must also have affected its content.

Because it is unlikely that young male Anglophone adults today will swoon over Lamartine's *Méditations poétiques* as once young Frenchmen did, it constitutes, as *Die Leiden des jungen Werthers* also does, what is perhaps virtually a limiting case. The slim anonymous volume of verse, like Goethe's novel, was felt on its publication in 1820 to be enormously powerful. Nobody reacts today to Lamartine's poetization of his experience as Lamartine expected that his contemporaries might react. Are the poems great literature? The answer of course is yes, and for much the same sort of reasons that Balzac's novels remain great literature. The power that generated the work somehow remains present within it, even if our sensibilities are quite different now from those of Lamartine then.

The power is recognizable partly from the courageous consciousness of audacity with which the author's sensitivity is paraded. The feelings are tentative, but their expression is not, and the decision to exhibit them is not far short of brazen. The systematized vagueness of the imagery is instantly arresting, and clearly announces an important statement. The romantic generation proper laughed at Lamartine, "le pleurard (crybaby)." It is not, however, the value of the sentiments themselves that is important, but the intensity of feeling which drove the poet into visibly daring to take them so seriously. The stylization with which the tenderness is laid bare suggests a strikingly tentative defiance of established norms comparable to Goethe's in *Werther*, and it invests even what we may well regard as an extreme expression of sensitivity to the beauties of scenery and the sorrows of loss and love with great power, in spite of using images of "the sublime" conventional even in 1820.

The proof is not in our emotional reaction, which may well be nil, but in an intellectually demonstrable imaginative power of a very considerable order of magnitude. Before Lamartine wrote the first line of "L'Isolement," "Souvent sur la montagne, à l'ombre du vieux chêne (Often on the mountain in the shade of the old oak)," who could have expressed his tenderest feelings with such evocative intensity by generalizing banal natural imagery with such systematically calculated vagueness? The power is quantifiable because the originality here is a measurable reflection of the intensity with which the poet felt the need to parade for inspection, communication, and comment feelings of whose intimate, refined, and highly cultivated nature he makes his awareness clear.

The authenticity of Lamartine's feeling that his innermost sentiments, which he protected with anonymity, needed to be paraded and examined is certified by the perfect musicality of tone, the meticulously balanced rhetoric, the absence of any hint of affectation, the obvious restraint of extreme emotion within the strictest prosody, the complex syntactical organization of the imagery, and the relegation of the imagery itself to a register of vague, fluid, and generalized banality. The point of the poems is not the landscape at all, but the importance to the poet of his own feelings. The lakes and woods, loves and sorrows are token stage properties denoting that which evokes the poet's quite possibly over-delicate feelings of harmony and consolation. After all, centuries of sweet sorrows have not extinguished the power of Petrarch's stylized posturings.

There was nothing very new about Lamartine's feelings, but the daring in writing about what was still normally taken for excessive sentiment in so personal a way would have been unachievable more than three or four years before the *Méditations poétiques* appeared and, three or four years later it was impossible to arouse the same response by writing more of the same. What had been real daring when Lamartine had began to write the poems of the *Méditations poétiques* in the winter of 1817–18 quickly became a tedious affectation. By 1823 Lamartine's verse had degenerated into pastiche. What locks the *Méditations poétiques* into social history is the fact that by 1823, the date of the *Nouvelles méditations poétiques*, what had taken everyone's breath away three years earlier already seemed trite. Lamartine had exactly satisfied the imaginative requirements of a generation who had been adolescents under Napoleon, who were still young adults when he fell, but who by 1820 were looking for something more from life than the entrepreneurial rewards the restored Bourbon monarchy had to offer.

The literary history of France from the final restoration after Napoleon's hundred days in 1815 until the 1830 revolution and the inauguration of the July monarchy was predictably animated. Entries in the *Guide* trace the successes of the boulevard theatre of Pixérécourt until even the educated theatre-going public were no longer prepared to endure the declamatory rhetorical delivery of the imaginatively impotent neoclassical verse tragedies on the legitimate stage. What we know as romantic tragedy was the result of something like a take-over bid to move the formal theatre down market, powerfully helped by the stage effects already being achieved by Daguerre on the boulevards, and the further possibilities afforded by the invention of gas lighting, already installed at Covent Garden, London, which allowed for dimming during the course of a scene and eventually also for the use of filters to project coloured lighting.

Voltaire's attempts at tragedy, like those of the 18th century generally, had lacked power because the underlying culture was fundamentally too optimistic to want a tragic exploration of life. When Shakespeare was rediscovered in France between 1820 and 1830, it was because he, too, satisfied a new imaginative need for drama which tragically explored human emotional experience more directly than French neoclassical convention allowed for. Penley's Paris Shakespeare season in 1822 had been a failure, partly because anti-English feeling was still running high after Waterloo, but the Shakespeare season of the Covent Garden troupe at the Odéon in 1827–28 came as a revelation. The Shakespeare known in France before 1820 had chiefly been that of Jean-François Ducis (1733–1816), who had trivialized him by giving *Othello* and the other major tragedies happy endings and cramming the actions into the unity of time. Even the unperformed version of *Romeo and Juliet* by Deschamps and Vigny in 1827 called for sorbets to be served after the principals had danced a quadrille at the ball given on stage by the Capulets. That of course subverts our understanding of what Shakespeare's play was about, but it does tell us something about the romantic movement in France. The literature produced by a society to explore the meaning of its experience can also be used by historians who correctly understand the nature of the relationship between literature and society as a guide to identifying the reasons for which particular attitudes required to be investigated in identifiable ways.

The link between literature and society observable in 1820 and again in the early days of the romantic movement is often subsequently reaffirmed. Technical innovation in literature, involving the abandonment of old conventions and recourse to new formal structures and genres, included the "automatic writing" of the surrealists (q.v.), a new way of looking into an experience itself felt to be new. The imaginative assimilation of the implications of both world wars in France was a huge undertaking, probably not yet seen in its proper perspective. There is a sense in which, after Proust's sustained examination of acts of indeliberate memory, surrealist attempts to snatch at whatever was contained in the pre-conscious psyche through self-induced hypnosis were not so very new or exciting. But World War I did not seem to have been the possible consequence of any rationally calculated decision. Whatever had happened appeared to have included a reversion to simply atavistic, destructive, and self-annihilatory instincts, clearly sub-rational in origin. Yet no investigation into the sub-rational component of human behaviour could convey the appropriate sense of devastation and urgency through the medium of ordered narrative fiction.

It may even be that the creative writers and painters had been giving notice before the outbreak of war. They had already felt the need to investigate experiences beyond rational control. The cubist (q.v.) painters had broken with convention by doing away with the creation in painting of mathematically calculated means of creating the illusion of depth in two dimensions. Max Jacob was innovating in poetry in a way analogous to one of several in which Picasso was innovating in painting. Orphism had tried in vain to substitute a new formal structure, the "section d'or" for the old perspective. Apollinaire decided, at the last moment, to take the punctuation out of *Alcools*, thereby disrupting the syntax when the text was in proof. Proust was portraying a society in the ultimate stages of interior decay, while delving into mental activity not subject to rational control. At every point in French literary history from the Revolution to the present day, it is possible to trace the link between the imaginative needs of French society and the values and attitudes incorporated into its daily life, to understand the history of literature in the light of social history, and to use literary history as a means of understanding the inner history of French society.

The second way in which the history of literature locks into social history, as a commodity, also confirms that it has always filled a real social need. Literature is finally produced only because there is public support for it, not necessarily manifested just through buying and selling. Perhaps only in France has the intricate network of arrangements for looking after creative artists been of quite such indescribable complexity, but it has actually functioned rather well. In the 19th century librarianships (see Index) that were little more than sinecures were bestowed on a host of authors including Nodier, Sandeau, Bouilhet, Gautier, and Sainte-Beuve, whose succession was thought to have been secured by Flaubert, Leconte de Lisle, and Heredia, with honorific appointments or small public pensions granted to many more, and memberships of commissions or political appointments to a few.

Mallarmé was a poor teacher of English, but was protected by the inspectorate on account of his literary reputation. Sartre and Beauvoir were posted near one another by some anonymous official at the ministry of education with his ear to the ground, acting in the best French administrative tradition, and at least three 20th-century French ambassadors have been major writers–Paul Claudel, Saint-John Perse, and Paul Morand. It is well known in French literary circles that Gaston Gallimard could generally be relied on to find a post in his publishing house for a promising young writer with good credentials in need of a job. Without the patronage of Jacques Doucet, the couturier, the French literary heritage of the years following World War I would be a great deal poorer.

France has always been justly proud of its record in publicly protecting artistic experiment even when creative artists have felt impelled to explore alleys leading towards self-annihilating conclusions. In the end the perfect poem cannot be a blank piece of paper, the ultimate musical experience cannot be silence, and the most meaningful form of drama is not a bare bulb flickering on an empty stage, but interest has often continued to be shown in creative artists whose work had begun to explore paths which led towards such possibilities. The extent of public patronage, and interest, may even have had the result of leaving France's cultural history studded with an unusually high proportion of failures, but it is also astonishing to see how often, admittedly with some exceptions and the occasional fluke, the French public's judgement has proved sound, even with regard to avant-garde works of art. Error has seemed to be on the side of generosity. It is difficult not to think that there are more writers with unwarrantedly inflated reputations than there are geniuses starving in garrets for want of public support. The rewards offered by the talent-spotting industry are such as to ensure that not much gets missed.

In achieving this situation, the key figures as far as literature is concerned have been the publishers, offshoots either of bookshops, like that of Lemerre, or of reviews, like Alfred Valette's *Mercure de France*, or the printers' cooperative run by Gaston Gallimard for the *Nouvelle Revue Française* (q.v.), and eventually taken over by him. The discernment of the publishers and editors, backed by the economic power they wielded, powerfully helped to determine the course of French literature. They acted as brokers, buying, investing in, finding consumers for, and sometimes warehousing the writers' products, "literature." They encouraged, bullied, and threatened their authors, took them to law, sold their products, sometimes went broke, and, less often, made their authors rich. They have been ill paid for their services to literature by a public perception of them, going back at least as far as the 17th century, as mere exploiters, battening on the other-worldly talent of impoverished geniuses, whom in fact they more often spotted, tended, nourished, and staked a great deal on. They were by and large committed defenders of the right to publish, connived at by the authorities, who vindicated their own sporadically draconian censorship measures by fining the publishers generally only affordable sums, and imprisoning them for only brief periods, often at dates to suit the publisher's convenience.

The greatest of them in the 19th century was François Buloz, who edited and controlled the *Revue des Deux Mondes* (*RDM*, q.v.), and for a while also controlled the *Revue de Paris*, which gave him a near monopoly of serious imaginative writing for serialized periodical production. For a period he was also director of what we now know as the Comédie-Française. Before he himself controlled the shares, he was paid a commission on the number of subscriptions to the *RDM*. A self-educated proofreader, perhaps marginally left of centre, but politically unaligned, he refused to publish anything he could not himself understand, and once returned a piece on Kant to Victor Cousin, at the time France's best-known philosopher, on the grounds that he could not follow it. Buloz was a litigious, lanky, bullying figure, who exploited his writers, lent them money, withheld advances from them, encouraged, tyrannized, guided, underpaid, and bestowed immense prestige on them. His judgements on his contemporaries, with the single exception of Balzac, about whom he felt bitter after losing a court case to him, have proved to be virtually infallible.

Unlike another colourful 19th-century broker of the arts, Louis Véron, who founded the *Revue de Paris* before taking over the Opéra and then acquiring *Le Constitutionnel*, Buloz paid his authors by the line. It is difficult not to reflect that, had Flaubert not had independent means at the time of writing his great novels, he could simply not have afforded to condense his enormous first drafts into his final meticulously wrought masterpieces. Payment by the line did nothing to discourage the prolixity of a Sue, a Sand, or a Dumas. Buloz, who favoured a rotund, oratorical style, probably did more than any other single figure to establish the norms of conservative literary taste and the acceptable boundaries in bourgeois society of the exploration of social attitudes and values in 19th-century France.

It was Buloz who reined in George Sand's utopian idealism and held Sainte-Beuve back in the attack on "industrial literature" and the notion of a writer's copyright, about which, by August 1838, when the first serious cases were brought for illegal publication, there was urgent need for action. In 1826 the young Emile de Girardin had started *Le Voleur*, so named because at the start it consisted solely of material reprinted from elsewhere without fresh payment. In 1835 Balzac had sued Buloz for sending the uncorrected proofs of *Le Lys dans la vallée* to St Petersburg without his authorization, and in 1838 the five papers successfully sued were *L'Estafette*, *L'Echo Français*, *La Quotidienne*, the *Cabinet de Lecture*, and the *Courrier Français*, followed the next year by *Le Mémorial de Rouen*.

It was, however, the alliance between journalists defending themselves against new competition from novelists looking for serialization and the press which wanted to protect its rights to the fiction it was serializing, rather than the novelists, who made the Société des Gens de Lettres into an effective organization for the defence of copyright. Even so, the critic Jules Janin and

Sainte-Beuve, who worked for Buloz and had long been jealous of Henriette de Castries's affection for Balzac, had some reason to satirize the early procedures and mercenary attitudes of the Société, especially under the presidency (1838–39) of Balzac, whose novels were pirated in up to a score of editions, and who himself resigned from the Société in 1841, after only three years of membership. George Sand was also to resign in order to sue the Société in defence of her own rights. In spite of Buloz's hostility to Balzac, it was he who finally refused to print the third part of Sainte-Beuve's attack on industrial literature.

On 1 July 1836 Girardin launched *La Presse* and Armand Dutacq *Le Siècle* at a subscription price of exactly half what was then normal for a daily newspaper, 40 francs instead of 80. The income was to be made up from mass circulation and advertising revenue. Not until four years later, in 1840, did Charles Havas launch the first reliable daily carrier pigeon service between Paris, Brussels, and London, so that what the cheap press created included an urgent demand for serialized fiction to fill the bottom of the front page. There was no guarantee that there would be any news, or even political debate, to report. Serialization filled a popular need, which it may also have created, and the demand for it increased even after the inauguration of the pigeon service.

It peaked in about 1846, and declined only slowly, having in effect been taxed by the raising of the stamp duty on advertisements. Downmarket the authors in chief demand were notoriously Dumas *père*, Sue, and Soulié. Although the pretext was a political squabble, it was on behalf of the new cheap press that, in a duel on 22 July 1836, Girardin fought and killed Armand Carrel, founder of the liberal *Le National*, who had been vainly defending the old order. Girardin, on crutches, incidentally insisted on speaking at the funeral. Even Buloz was forced to undertake the extensive serialization of fiction, although he did not cut his prices, and it was the economic pressure on writers to work with serialization, deadlines, and episodic structure in mind that created the form of the 19th-century French novel. In the general context of the broadening market for books, even guides to literature need also to note the success of the famous "Manuels Roret," handbooks at first for mayors and magistrates before being joined by manuals for lemonade makers (1822), cooks (1826), and "young ladies" (1826). By 1846 the new edition of *La Cuisinière bourgeoise*, a general handbook of housekeeping, was clearly intended to be read by the servants.

Prudery in 19th-century France did not extend to shame about discussing how much a line you could get paid for what you wrote. Michel Lévy paid Flaubert 10,000 francs for *Salammbô* and an assorted bundle of other rights, but made him connive for publicity purposes into admitting that he had been paid 30,000 francs, so boosting market demand for his wares. Ordinary novelists were paid from 75 centimes to 1 franc a line by ordinary newspapers. Buloz paid half as much again although, when he was taking her work at all, he paid George Sand over 12 times as much. In the middle of the 19th century only the top three per cent of Parisians earned more than 50,000 francs a year, and a top civil servant was paid about 22,000. When Nerval, halfway up the journalistic ladder, was given a job in 1836 by Alphonse Karr on *Le Figaro*, at that time a scandal sheet, he was able to earn 10,000 francs a year, being paid 5 francs a column.

The threshold of being well-to-do was passed at about 5,000 francs a year. An averagely successful novel brought in some 2,000 francs, a successful play about 40,000 francs, for which a novel, after the introduction of payment by royalty, would need to sell 80,000 copies. Until towards the end of the century publishers bought specific rights from authors, generally to sell a work for a given period, or to publish a given number of copies. About 10 per cent of writers could live by their pen. During the 19th century novelists began to earn rather more, relative to dramatists, but the real money was still to be made at the end of the century from royalties on stage performances. Sardou, Labiche, and Augier all died rich, as did Paul Hervieu (1857–1915) and Ludovic Halévy (1834–1908), who partnered Henri Meilhac (1831–1907) as Offenbach's librettist.

Most writers, other than successful dramatists, were also journalists. Many, for obvious reasons, lived unusually intense lives, and some preferred to undergo real hardship rather than seek more mundane employment. Balzac almost consciously fuelled his huge creative urge with heroic quantities of cultivated women, specially brewed coffee, and massive debt. It is impossible not to suppose that he needed to write, and used debt to keep up the steam. He was only just 51 when he died. George Sand wrote because she needed the money to sustain her charitable works rather than because she enjoyed it. Chateaubriand, who nearly succeeded in becoming prime minister, and Lamartine, who could have become president, or even emperor, in 1848, both earned enormous sums from their pens. Like those other huge earners Sue, Balzac, and Dumas, they both became bankrupt. An understanding of the conventions and content of 19th-century French literature still depends more than historians and critics suppose on a familiarity with the economic background of writing.

The third way in which literary history dovetails into general social history needs to be mentioned only briefly here, although fuller attention has been paid to it in appropriate entries in the *Guide*. It is, for instance, obvious that technology had to become the subject of the literary investigation into the human condition. The public needed a Zola to draw attention to the social consequences of the industrial revolution, but it had also much earlier needed a Sue. It took the cholera epidemic of 1832 with its 20,000 deaths to get piped water and proper sewage into Paris, and it was largely Sue who prepared the minds of his barely literate contemporaries for the investment which that required, as for what increasingly came to look like the necessity for the 1848 revolution, and the merciful clearances of the rat-infested slums by Haussmann, Paris without the great swathes cut across it by Haussmann might have been a more attractive town today, but it is difficult to see any programme less radical than Haussmann's as likely to have been nearly as effective. Sue died in 1857, but it is arguable that his *Les Mystères de Paris* of 1842–43 was a more powerful novel than Hugo's *Les Misérables* of exactly 20 years later, which examined the same probable relationship between destitution, crime, and prostitution, including child prostitution, but was documented from the records of 1817. His famous description of the sewers was written after Paris was well on the way to being rebuilt.

In the context of the effect of developments in French society on the content of literary works, a general awareness of the pace of change is clearly necessary. Unhappily, its magnitude in the most important respects was not recorded exactly, and there is no consensus. In the first half of the 19th century prices tended to rise, but overall only by about 10 per cent. Money wages kept steady in building, slowly increased in mining, but fell dramatically in the mechanizable industries. Some reputable sources put the fall in textile wages at 80 per cent between 1823 and 1840, others limit it for males to 40 per cent between 1810 and 1850. It is reasonable to assume that living standards were being pinched for all workers for the first half of the century, but very severely cut for some, and for all in some years, since food prices depended on harvests. Before 1860 cycles recurred when, because harvests were bad, food became dear and almost the whole of working-class budgets went on it, so depressing the demand for manufactured goods and increasing unemployment in the manufacturing industries.

At the worst moments, the probability is that about one Frenchman in four could not afford enough bread. Meat and wine were luxuries. A labourer could earn 2 francs a day, a woman 75 centimes, while a two-kilo loaf of bread cost on average 85 centimes. By 1847, out of just over a million factory workers, about two thirds were men, a quarter of a million were women paid not much more than half what the men got, and 130,000 were children of anything over six, working for derisory sums. In the 1840s, out of an adult population of 900,000 in Paris, only about a third earned their living in identifiable ways. Of 15,000 registered prostitutes, one in eight was under 12. One child in three was illegitimate, one in four abandoned, and one in two died before reaching the age of one.

If literary authors ignored this situation, they were marginalizing literature into trivial, if elegant, entertainment of however cultivated a sort. If they did not, they had to confront the problem of moving the imaginations of their literate public, who overwhelmingly had an interest in keeping themselves ignorant of the country's social problems. That had to affect both their subject matter and their way of treating it. By isolating the authors of French literature for discussion, we have already selected those writers who were not on the one hand simply entertainers, or on the other simply journalists or pamphleteers, but they were all necessarily subject to the generally conflicting constraints imposed on them by whatever caste they belonged to, by their childhood and education, social background, economic motivation, humanitarian impulse, and political instinct. A number of major authors were uncertain about whether to devote themselves to politics or pamphleteering rather than to imaginative literature. A few combined successful journalistic careers with major literary work.

In 1800 just over a fifth of the French population lived in towns, and that proportion scarcely increased until after 1850, when it was still less than a quarter. The growth of the Paris agglomeration, where just under 20 per cent of the French population now lives, came only late. About two per cent of the population of France lived in the Département of the Seine in 1800, three per cent in 1850, and in 1871 still only seven and a half per cent. Other towns had grown earlier, the administrative centres before the industrial ones. But in 1900 over 40 per cent of the French population was still engaged in agriculture, forestry, or fishing, and only 40 per cent lived in towns. For the content of works of literature, so largely static a 19th-century population entailed a huge demand for travelogues. Most of the major writers travelled, and the demand for their accounts of their travels, even round France, was voracious. It was even greater if they had been somewhere mountainous, like Switzerland, culturally important, like Italy, or exotic, like Egypt.

Rather as the cheap press was established before there was any way of ensuring a flow of news, so, analogously, did a demand for tourist guides begin to oust the demand for travelogues before there were any railways. The first proper railway line in France, Paris–Rouen, was opened in 1843. Six years later the demand for wooden rail sleepers was so great that Balzac dreamt of sending them home from Russia. By 1866 all the main railway lines had been laid, and the railway companies were employing over 100,000 people. But the guides had become popular much earlier. The old multi-volume descriptions were rapidly replaced. Richard's *Guide du voyageur en France* had 24 editions from 1823 to 1854. A guide to Italy followed, then one to the Pyrenees, with six editions from 1834 to 1855.

Louis Hachette (1800–1864) had founded his publishing house in 1826, and rapidly cornered the market in educational manuals and textbooks. He was a liberal and cultivated the university world, ultimately with important consequences for the French educational system. By the 1850s he had added major contemporary authors and a number of magazines to his list, but had attracted the hostility of Napoléon Chaix, who had obtained the monopoly of the railway timetables and route maps, but overlooked the potential profitability of station bookstalls, of which Hachette now acquired the virtual monopoly. An obvious outlet for the new guides, their prudish stocking policy later made them rather a joke, but Hachette had 43 railway bookshops by 1853 and his firm over 1,000 by 1900. The famous *Guides bleus* are the direct descendants of Hachette's first guides, themselves inaugurated when, in 1859, Hachette took over the publication of Adolphe Joanne's *Itinéraire descriptif et historique de la Suisse, du Jura français…du mont Blanc, de la vallée de Chamonix…* of as early as 1841.

Still with regard to the way in which the evolution of society has affected the subject matter of literature, it is important not to overlook the importance of the theatre of the Second Empire, not only on account of the "naturalistic" drama of Becque, whose real interest lies in the astringency of his social satire, but because it was on the stage that the values and attitudes of Second Empire French society were very largely examined. Partly, of course, this was because of the greater rewards offered to authors writing for the theatre, as already mentioned. Partly, too, however, it was because, even after the literacy level had risen, the public naturally continued to prefer the less demanding forum of the theatre for the imaginative investigation of the implications of its attitudes.

However, the theatre was expensive, at any given date roughly twice as expensive, relatively, as London or, in the 20th century, New York. By social convention it also involved at least relatively formal dress, and the social apparatus of an evening out. Even after World War II Beckett was criticized in New York for failing to provide a proper evening's entertainment, so entrenched had the convention become. The result, naturally, was that the overwhelmingly bourgeois Paris audiences had to be made aware of the often unconsidered but unpleasant implications of their own attitudes, while paying for it and enjoying it. That constraint not only created the skills behind what has been sneered at as the "well-made play," but also demands further consideration for the perhaps pompously undramatic treatment of social problems on the stage by Dumas *fils*, which may well be thought, however, to make up in power what it lacks in grace. It should also lead historians and critics to trawl again through Feydeau, Scribe, Sardou, and Labiche, whose wit, humour, and lightness of register can still touch important nerves without causing enough pain to damage the box office. None of those four dramatists is entirely trivial, and it could be

argued that the best work of each is as powerful as, if less pretentious than, Maeterlinck's *Pélleas et Mélisande*.

It is clear from the entries in the *Guide* that a great deal of French literature from 1870 has been devoted to the imaginative assimilation of the implications of both world wars, and indeed of the international tensions leading from the Franco-Prussian War of 1870–71 to the trauma of ending French colonial administration throughout the world. From 1914 it was no longer possible to look on war as simply the glorious patriotic enterprise it had once been thought to be. War had to be looked at in an altogether new way, and the means to do it, which included dada and surrealism, had yet to be invented. Obviously the events of both worlds wars have been examined from every angle in contemporary and subsequent literary works. Much later technical innovations like hypermarkets and one-way mirrors have been occupying powerful novelists like Le Clézio, whose place in any pantheon of 20th-century French writers is certainly assured. Aeroplanes, once symbols of aspiration for Apollinaire, have become commonplace and uncomfortable necessities. A week in the Transsiberian Express, which seemed romantic to the readers of Cendrars, is no longer anyone's idea of a holiday. Only Verne's exact mathematical calculations prove the rigour of his imagination. He knew to within two miles where a rocket returning from the moon would have to come down again on earth, if it could ever get between the two gravitational pulls in the first place.

What technological innovation has markedly done to the content of the literature of 20th-century France is to reinstate its preoccupation with rural life and regional roots. Communication and travel had become so easy that there was no longer any need to put up with the expense and discomfort of living in Paris in order to stay in contact with literary life. Not only Giono, Pagnol, and Bernanos stayed away from Paris, but even Mauriac and Gide took to living away from the capital. For the first time since Paris became the intellectual capital of Europe in the Middle Ages, it was no longer necessary for members of the intellectual and literary communities to live in its geographical proximity.

The fourth way in which literature and social history interlock is in the effect on the content of literary works of the manner of their production and marketing. The effect is noticeable before the middle of the 19th century. The changes in the system of production and distribution, particularly when electricity had taken over from steam power to drive machinery, and the installation of presses demanded in consequence very heavy new investment, meant a serious shift of emphasis towards profit-earning books that could be printed in large runs. By the 1870s quite small firms were advertising their telephone lines "direct to Paris" and their installation of the electrically operated machinery. The bookseller-publishers could only survive away from Paris if they specialized. Mame at Tours virtually monopolized the market for liturgical books. Balzac had never envisaged *La Comédie humaine* as a closed cycle of novels, although a closed cycle was what efficient marketing demanded, as Balzac himself was made to acknowledge, and that was how his novels were sold when published in volume form.

As long print runs became economically more and more necessary, the not inconsiderable consequence was that a larger number of writers, unless they could instantly establish themselves as journalists, had to start their careers by paying to have their first volumes of poems printed privately in the hope of attracting favourable reviews. The *Guide* entries make it clear how frequently that happened, but it is worth reflecting that we would never have heard of Rimbaud if his mother had not in the end scraped together sufficient funds and enough goodwill to put down a deposit for the printing of her rebellious son's *Une saison en enfer.*

By the end of the 19th century, the process which had imposed the title on Balzac's famous cycle had also created an identifiable canon of great authors. The "leisure, health, and education" proportion of middle-class family budgets was growing. Michel Lévy was regarded as having breached the rules of taste when, on 18 September 1897, he published a full-page advertisement in *Le Rire* offering 59 volumes with no down payment for 200 francs, payable at 10 francs a month with what, by modern standards, was a generous free gift, claimed to be worth 100 francs. Since Lévy was an astute judge of the market, his list of 19th-century authors for middle-class readers wishing to spend money on self-improvement is worth quoting. It comprised About, Balzac, Bourget, Coppée, Daudet, Dumas, Feuillet, Flaubert, Gautier, Goncourt, Halévy, Hugo, Loti, Maupassant, Mérimée, Murger, Musset, Ohnet, Sand, Sandeau, Sardou, Simon, Sue, Theuriet, Verne, Vigny, and Zola.

The final way which must be mentioned here in which technological development has affected the content of literature concerns the manner in which cinema, radio, and finally television have changed the subject matter and style of literary material. Pagnol's twin gifts for dialogue and narrative would never have excited comment if, after his first comedies, the commercial viability of synchronized sound in the cinema had not suddenly become apparent in 1930. Pagnol was 35. He knew Giono and Fernandel. The confluence of circumstances was exactly right, and the three much admired films of the Marseilles trilogy were the result, although they were originally also much criticized for merely "canning" stage performances for cinema presentation. Perhaps they did. It has clearly taken serious creative artists a long time to exploit the full potential of television as a medium. It is not unusual to hear criticisms that TV programmes with cultural pretensions, if not re-hashed films, are still not yet properly adapted to the medium. It took a long time before colour filters were used to change the colour of gas lighting in stage productions.

Radio came at exactly the right moment to provide the medium Beckett required for his no longer stageable dramatic dialogues. Whether the already existing medium just happened to suit his late style, or whether he adapted his style to suit the medium is not clear, and it is perhaps going too far to allege his radio plays as an instance of technological effect on the content of literature, but Beckett had begun to lose the ability to provide the night out demanded by theatre audiences and always provided, for instance, by Anouilh and Giraudoux, even at their most serious. It probably suited him to do without the visible support of staging if he could then be as briefly undramatic as he wished and needed to be.

Such close interlocking in at least the four indicated ways suggests that literature and social history have a symbiotic relationship. Through literature, if also otherwise, society examines its attitudes, assumptions, and values, and assesses the desirability of change, and through its literature the historian can discover the tensions at work in a given society. Literature, at any rate, cannot be properly understood or evaluated without reference to the circumstances and constraints under which it was written.

The *Guide*'s entries show certain other recurrent features which warrant comment in the context of this introduction to the literature of post-Revolutionary France, but which might also have a much wider reference. The most important of these features is undoubtedly the tendency of writers to group together, often with workers in other art forms, so that it is meaningful to speak of "movements," although virtually all the movements we do speak of are in urgent need of redefinition. To start with, however, it is essential to remember that the imaginative ways of examining our experience are the most tentative ones. Sociological analysis is part of a complex and often inexact discipline, dependent on the skilful interpretation of statistical data, and only with great difficulty capable of being made to yield evidence about the personal and social tensions within a society.

Imaginative enquiry is a more efficient way of discovering what is the quality of individual and social experience, but it is necessarily tentative. Its understanding is of its nature non-exact, a proposition for discussion, often merely an invitation to agreement that certain types of experience can or need to be looked at in this or that light, which is why the reception accorded to imaginative work is so important, and its power is the criterion of its value. Only when there is general agreement on the literary stature of a text can we be reasonably sure that the experience it investigates is in some generally agreed way illuminated. It is certainly because authors are undertaking what is necessarily a delicate task in proposing new ways of understanding experience that they feel the need to discuss their work with others inclined to view similar experience in a similar light. The phenomenon is striking.

Nodier believed in patronizing the young. His elegant receptions at the Arsenal from 1824 involved cards, dancing, pretty girls, book collectors, connoisseurs of the fantastic, scholars, and young writers. The writers then took to meeting in the famous drawing room of Hugo's apartment, where in 1829 they, and such senior members of the literary establishment as Baron Taylor, the newly appointed director of the Théâtre-Français, were invited to hear Hugo's brilliant declamations first of the play that was to become *Marion Delorme,* and then of *Hernani.* The Covent Garden Shakespeare season had overwhelmed all of them, and both Vigny, with his adaptation of *Othello,* and Dumas, with *Henri III et sa cour,* were to get in with their first great romantic tragedies before the famous opening of *Hernani,* whose claque was organized in the same drawing room.

Rivalry, especially between Hugo and Vigny, led to bitterness, but without the original coherence of the group it is doubtful whether any of them could have created romantic tragedy. It needed quite new dramatic techniques to examine radically new ways of looking at society's organization, and the individual's relationship with it. It is a not entirely fortuitous indication of the corporate hesitancy even of the group, on whose fringes Dumas was still to be found in 1829, that Dumas should have presented a tragedy in prose, normally still considered the vehicle for the less elevated forms of comedy, almost seeming to invite his play to be taken with less than total seriousness, while Vigny should have presented an adaptation of Shakespeare, holding back from the imaginative commitment a wholly original work would have entailed. The young romantic movement took almost two years to achieve critical mass. The result was *Hernani.*

Something analagous took place later in the century. A group of young writers started to meet in Lemerre's religious bookshop (see Le Parnasse). Some had known one another as members of the student society the Conférence La Bruyère, and they began to meet in various of their houses, their most prominent member for a time being Catulle Mendès. They began to accept the benign patronage of Leconte de Lisle, and it was from meetings in his drawing room, where poetry was read and aesthetic norms were discussed, that Mallarmé eventually took over. Again a radically new, if still developing, way of looking at human experience, often at first in epic, mythological forms, was taking shape. New literary forms were clearly required to understand man and his world in this new way, and here, too, the individual writers, with the possible exception of Leconte de Lisle himself, could not have achieved what they did without the confidence created by discussion within the group.

Again it was the more or less spontaneously discovered affinities between a group of writers and painters who decided to join one another in or around the Rue Ravignan in the second half of the first decade of the 20th century which enabled and encouraged them, as members of a coherent social grouping, to achieve things which almost none of them would have achieved in isolation. Picasso might be the exception but, for a period culminating in or soon after 1908, Vlaminck, Apollinaire, Derain, Jacob, Marie Laurencin, André Salmon, and Paul Fort were all dependent on one another as, later on, elsewhere in Paris, was the "surrealist" group surrounding Breton and including Eluard, Aragon, Péret, Soupault, and for a time Leiris. Here, too, what was achieved by individuals depended on contacts within the group. The concept of critical mass, borrowed from nuclear physics, offers a reasonably good metaphor of what took place in the four entourages of Hugo, Leconte de Lisle, Picasso, and Breton. It might even be argued that critical mass was what both the inchoate "symbolist" and the "existentialist" (qq.v.) movements, among so many others, failed to achieve. These groups, like the "naturalists" and the team cooperating on *Tel Quel* (q.v.), differed from the other four in grouping round a leading figure, respectively Mallarmé, Sartre, Zola, and Sollers, whose views were strongly enough held to demand adherence rather than discussion.

Ease of reference to these groupings of more or less likeminded creative writers and artists has inevitably led to the damaging use of pigeonholes for the convenience of critics, historians, and students. Most of the labels were repudiated, at least at first, by those on whom they had been stuck. "Cubism" like "impressionism," was originally a term of derision. It is clearly apt to be misleading when applied to literature, as "cubism" is essentially visual, just as "surrealism" is essentially literary and can be applied to painting only by analogy. "Realism" was a movement associated with Champfleury and Duranty. Flaubert, often considered its greatest figure, strongly repudiated the term. The word "surrealism" was created to mean something quite other than what it is now taken to denote, and Sartre, at least when the term was first used of him, denied that he knew what "existentialist" meant. There is no reasonable way in which the term can or ever could be applied to Camus. In no reasonable way can Foucault be considered to have been a "structuralist." He wrote a book to prove he was not one. "Symbolism" was defined for a newspaper in a hurry by Moréas, who understood only how to make the most of the platform he had been offered. The only obvious member of the movement known as "decadence" is the fictional character Des Esseintes from Huysmans's *A rebours*.

The French made fun of the vogue for creating "-isms," and invented about a score, usually less rather than more seriously,

between about 1890 and 1910. Clearly the use of terms for groupings and movements has some validity, and certainly points neophytes in a helpful general direction. The danger is that the individualities of members of such groupings and of those who have been said by others to belong to movements will be lost from sight, and that the names given to the movements may be taken to denote something that never really existed. It does not help to call Flaubert a "realist" unless it is explained how his practice differs from that of Champfleury and Duranty, and indeed from novel to novel within his own slender output.

Critics and readers have been deflected from a proper understanding of Zola's novels partly because they were marketed in a wrapping of untenable physiological theory. Had Zola really been as interested in demonstrating a theory of heredity as he said he was, he would have written less powerfully. Tzara issued so many dada manifestos as understandably to send up the whole dangerous belief that great authors have sets of beliefs, or are necessarily good either at defining their own aims or at adhering to them. The enunciation of a literary programme can be a useful exercise for a writer, but the power of his or her writing will not primarily depend on adherence to a set of stated intentions. References to groups, whose nature and existence is often a matter of recorded historical fact, or movements, whether defined by writers in their manifestos, or by historians, but which cannot be said to have existed other than as groups of individual creative writers, need to be treated with caution. Recourse to them too often covers slovenly critical analysis.

The *Guide* attempts to indicate in the appropriate entries how the major literary movements might helpfully be redefined. In order to understand a writer's works it is not, however, sufficient to interpret them in the light of any stated literary intentions or of the known attitudes of any particular group. Here again, but now for reasons less likely to be regarded as controversial, it is impossible to regard many of what are acknowledged to be major literary texts as in any serious sense self-referential, unless, of course, self-referentiality is itself made the criterion of literary excellence, in which case literature becomes a series of word games, a sophisticated entertainment with no bearing on who we are, or how we should live our lives, and with no more educative value than crossword puzzles. It is simply not the case that we can understand literary texts without bringing to them widespread cultural assumptions of our own, and without knowing how to de-code their registers of language and often "intertextually" implied allusions, that is without reference to the whole cultural background in which the texts arose.

A simple enough example of some importance for the *Guide* is the French word "littérature." When it occurs, the reader has to know whether the word is being used in the contemptuous sense in which Verlaine used it, or even whether there is an implied reference to Verlaine's famous line "Et tout le reste est littérature. (And all the rest is literature)." The difficulty arises because today's Anglophone readers cannot necessarily be expected to bring to a French text of perhaps a century ago the cultural background which its understanding demands. Often enough it is clear that even a contemporary French public was not able, or indeed intended to be able, to decode what was happening within a literary text. Just how many Parisians who went to see Colette playing at the Moulin Rouge in *Rêve d'Egypte* in 1907 knew that when she kissed the woman playing the male lead she was kissing her real-life lesbian partner?

In both Gide and Claudel the density of literary, religious, and cultural reference is too great even for the best-educated non-specialist reader with the most sophisticated literary tastes to be able to do without a guide. To understand virtually anything that either author published between 1900 and World War I, the reader or audience has to know about the familiarity of each author with the works of the other, the controlled limits of their spiritual hostilities, and the way in which each knew intimately Greek, Latin, and German literature. Understanding either author calls for the ability to recognize common and not so common liturgical forms and formulae, and for knowledge about the Catholic revival, Catholic and Protestant attitudes to lust, the demise of both scientism and symbolism, the total context of debates about freedom, and the reactions of the lower French aristocracy to the social policy of Leo XIII. The potential length of that token list no doubt reflects the fact that both Claudel and Gide were particularly lavish with implied as well as explicit allusions. The real difficulty comes when the allusions are hidden. Beckett's early poem *Whoroscope* can be understood only if you happen to know that Descartes really did have an egg for breakfast, and the sonnet by Jaccottet quoted in the entry under his name depends for its comprehension on knowing that the simple French "tu brûles (you are burning)" can refer not only to being physically on fire and burning with passion, but also to the "you're getting warm" of children playing hunt-the-thimble. That, of course, brings us to another difficulty, the need to avoid providing a literary text with excessive overlays of commentary.

The coded nature of literary texts and the cultural background the reader has to bring to their understanding also take us to the heart of what the *Guide* attempts, which is to say, on the basis of a prior decoding, of which never more than a tiny example can be printed, what it is that important authors are writing about, what experiences works regarded as important are examining, and in what light. The question always implicitly asked is what a given author or text is essentially about. What experience does it seek to illumine? To what attitudes does it explore alternatives? To what question does it look for or suggest an answer? It is in an attempt to answer these questions that the *Guide* has generally adopted a "life-and-works" format, since so much of the meaning of a text emerges only from some knowledge of the background of its composition. It is not at all clear, for instance, on a casual first reading what Proust was writing about. Here the Anglophone reader is particularly unfortunate because the title of the famous first translation was itself a mistranslation. *A la recherche du temps perdu* means "In pursuit of lost time," and not the "The remembrance of things past," a title to which Proust himself, incidentally, took vigorous exception. It is the analytic techniques of decoding which are passed on whenever literature is "taught" in the context of an academic discipline. It is in their ability to use them that students are examined. Historical background knowledge is generally essential, but always subsidiary.

It is, for instance, only by quite careful decoding that it is possible to understand what it was in 1857 that stung the authorities into prosecuting first Flaubert's *Madame Bovary,* where the charge was outrage against public and religious morality and against decency, and then, when that failed, Baudelaire's *Les Fleurs du mal* for similar offences against public morality. The charges were of course mere pretexts. What both writers had done was subversively, but with no discernible political intent, for different reasons and in different ways, to explore visions of the moral and social orders quite incompatible with the values on which the Second Empire was being built. The implication was that, after the revolution of 1848 had surrendered its temporary victory to the coup d'état of December 1851, the Second Empire was being erected on a set of illusory assumptions and values.

The *Guide* has respected the established canon of great French writers, but inevitably some reputations look as if they should be lower and some higher than is commonly assumed. Looking back over the literary history of France, it seems today as if we have allowed ourselves seriously to underestimate the power and interest of the "pre-romantic" authors, especially Germaine de Staël, Senancour, Constant, and Chateaubriand. Each in a different way played a powerful part in investigating and then in establishing the new attitudes to life, art, society, and nature required by the generation which had survived the Revolution and the Terror, and sought to continue in a changed and more liberal atmosphere to reaffirm confidence in a more liberal society, in the benignity of a "nature" which actually nearly killed three of them, and in the firm relationship between instinct, virtue, and happiness.

Of the romantic generation proper, we may have underestimated the interest of Alexis de Tocqueville. Of all his contemporaries he seems to have been the most clearly aware of the nature of the problem. A disillusioned aristocrat, half of whose family had been wiped out in the Terror, he was also a liberal and a lawyer. He had exactly the right credentials to discover where the liberalizing movement which had risen up in the late 18th century against a pretentious and inept monarchy had then gone wrong, to produce the horrific and arbitrary tyranny of the Terror. In search of a sane way to implement the Declaration of the Rights of Man, Tocqueville must have known what he was going to find before he ever campaigned to get his mission to go to America.

If a general comment had to be made about the critical evaluation of 19th-century French authors, it would have to concern the need for a high estimation of popular writers and genres, of Sue, Sand, the dramatists mentioned earlier, and also Maupassant, perhaps at the expense not of the over-ambitious writers with world views, like Taine and Renan, or visions, like Leconte de Lisle and Zola, or vast historical ambitions, like Lamartine and Michelet, but of the symbolists. The danger sign for the symbolists has long been flashing. It lies in the bias in the ratio of interest in their aesthetic discussions to that in their actual achievements. The aesthetic aims were too esoteric, the effects striven for too inexpressible, the achievements too slight, the posturing too dilettante, for the importance accorded to the group surrounding Mallarmé not to have become exaggerated. The most successful of the inheritors of the symbolist aesthetic, once Gide had abandoned it, must have been Claudel.

Much of the 20th century is still too close for the establishment of any definitive pantheon, but it has seemed in compiling this *Guide* that the work of Giraudoux has generally been both misunderstood and undervalued, and that the handful of most important imaginative authors to have published in French since World War II will include Beckett, Perec, and Le Clézio, although that is possibly because the vision of each of the three is mercilessly penetrating and remorselessly bleak about the prospects for our civilization. The list of writers whose imaginative power seems in fact to be slighter than their reputation suggests is actually quite long, but it must be headed by Barbey d'Aurevilly, a master of flamboyance and paradox, but without the intensity or fundamental seriousness of, for instance, a Lautréamont or a Roussel. It will one day be asked whether Anatole France left anything of lasting value, whether at his most successful Maeterlinck was not too precious, whether Alain was more than a very gifted teacher, and whether Cendrars's loss of an arm during World War I did not involve the abandonment of what might have developed into a quite outstanding poetic talent.

There is, however, one relatively recent development in French writing which may turn out to have been of overwhelming importance. It may be that insufficient attention has been paid to it as a unified phenomenon, possibly because its origins are engagingly buried in an apparently arcane anthropological dispute about the interpretation of ritual gift-giving on the occasion of Maori betrothals. The clash of visions about man which was opened up on the slender foundations of that dispute is of monumental significance, and constitutes easily the most important intellectual debate about the nature of man which France, and probably the Western world, has known in the 20th century. Details of the debate and of the works of its participants will be found in the *Guide*'s entries as indicated in the index, but there is a difficulty. The clash of imaginative visions derives largely from work not ordinarily regarded as imaginative at all, but belonging to different technical disciplines, in the sciences as well as the arts. Although, on account of its importance, the definition of imaginative writing has been stretched in the context of this dispute, it seemed finally impossible to include writers none of whose writing is normally considered to have been imaginative at all, without also adding a host of scientists, historians, scholars, and philosophers whose exclusion would have become illogical but whose inclusion in a guide to literature would have been impossible.

During World War II the anthropologist, Claude Lévi-Strauss, had got to know Roman Jakobson, the linguistician and earlier founder of the Russian formalist literary movement, and under Jakobson's impulsion Lévi-Strauss had started to apply linguistic categories to anthropological investigation (see structuralism). When invited by Georges Gurvitch to write a preface to Marcel Mauss's work on Maori gift-giving in *Sociologie et anthropologie,* for its reissue in 1950, Lévi-Strauss accepted, but effectively wrote that what Mauss should have said was that Maori gift-giving was essentially a form of communication, a view which presupposed that behavioural forms of communication were pre-consciously determined, as some linguisticians, notably Noam Chomsky, have thought language structures to be.

In 1948 Michel Leiris had published *Biffures,* extracts of which had already appeared in 1946 in *Les Temps Modernes* (q.v), of which he was literary editor. Leiris had assimilated literature, too, to gift-giving, although this time among north-west American Indians. The text, thrown out, comes back enriched like the tribal shields which increase in value according to the number of ceremonial exchanges of which they have been the object. Lévi-Strauss had also been closely associated with *Les Temps Modernes* since the end of the war, so it is difficult to know what is owed to his discussions with Jakobson, and what to those with Leiris, but by 1950 there was in embryo in France

a whole new "science de l'homme" linking all human behaviour in a general theory of communication, and the forum for its discussion was *Les Temps Modernes.*

In 1950 both Leiris and Lévi-Strauss were, or had very recently been, on terms of close friendship with Sartre, who had founded *Les Temps Modernes,* but the alarm was sounded in February 1951 in an article in the review by Claude Lefort. The view of literature and gift-giving as forms of pre-consciously conditioned communication conflicted with the view being defended by Sartre that man's existence was not only given meaning but actually constituted by his freedom. Personal friendships and political alliances covered up cracks, but political, as well as personal and academic positions did eventually diverge and, while the new Leiris–Levi-Strauss vision could call for support on Freud, whose psychoanalytical theories Sartre still wanted somehow to fit into his new non-Stalinist but still Marxist existentialism, it seemed clearly incompatible with Marxism, which demanded an economic and a social interpretation of the exchange of gifts. Their value and the relationships of oppression and submission which they created had to be taken into account. By the end of the 1950s the pot was bubbling over with ingredients, including Marxism, Freudian psychoanalytical theory, anthropological theory, the theory of language, and literary theory. "Structural" was spelled in French either "structurale" or "structurelle" according to whose side you were on, and it greatly mattered what you thought the difference was between ethnology and ethnography. What was at stake, however, was quite clear. It was a unified vision of man unifying his behavioural, linguistic, and literary codes of communication, a new "science de l'homme."

Looking back, it is now possible to see how a number of other major figures contributed to the elaboration of the new vision of man and society, not all of them normally considered imaginative authors at all. Michel Foucault and Roland Barthes have their own entries in the *Guide,* as do Lévi-Strauss, Leiris, and the Jesuit palaeontologist Pierre Teilhard de Chardin. All have contributed in significant ways to a new philosophy of man. Also, however, so have some other recent philosophers, literary theoreticians, and psychoanalytical theorists like Louis Althusser (born 1918), Jacques Derrida (born 1930), and Jacques Lacan (1901–1981), as well as such figures associated with a new school of historical writing as Fernand Braudel (1902–1985) and Emmanuel Le Roy Ladurie (born 1929). Perhaps significantly, almost all these figures have been sharply criticized by colleagues in the professional disciplines from which they at any rate started. It may well be the case that all of them have become so interested in the wider implications of discoveries or hypotheses from within their own disciplines as in the end to have transcended their limits. They may all now need some new corporate designation. They are all philosophers, critics, sociologists, psychologists, anthropologists, or historians, and most of them belong to more than one of those groups. The probability is that the elaboration and discussion of a unified theory of man and society is likely to dominate French intellectual debate for some time to come, and that it will leave in its path an exceedingly powerful literature.

PREFACE

The index to this *Guide* has been designed in such a way as to link the individual entries on authors and literary movements with conventional narrative literary history, and indeed cultural history generally. It is intended to enable users of the *Guide* to relate writers, including those without their own entries, as well as many editors, publishers, patrons, painters, and musicians, to other figures, movements, and groupings, including the important salons, restaurants and cafés, with which they were associated. Individual entries have in principle been reserved for authors of imaginative literature and for movements in the history of French literature, but the anomalies created by excluding authors who did not publish in the imaginative genres have at least to some degree been smoothed over by indexing references to them not only with a page number but, wherever appropriate, with some indication of the connection in which their name occurs in the body of the *Guide*. In this way virtually as much information is given about a critic like Gustave Planche (1808–1857) or an editor like François Buloz (1803–1876) as if they had written in an imaginative genre and individual entries had been devoted to them.

In the same way the index indicates which writers frequented which important salons and cafés, in addition to giving the page number to the relevant reference. It is possible from the index alone to discover which writers were published by the principal publishers and editors, as well as which publishers and editors took material from particular writers. The index itself also makes clear which literary figures played important political roles, or were involved in the revolutions of 1830 and 1848 and the Commune uprising of 1871 and on which side. Also in the index, and in what connection, are naturally all the painters and musicians associated with the literary world and therefore mentioned in the text. The role of Wagner as a catalyst in French literary life is of particular interest. Consultation of the index also reveals, for instance, that George Sand was an early anonymous reviewer of the first Paris performances of Beethoven symphonies.

Some indication of how the index is tended to be used is given under the heading "Dates and Discrepancies." Auguste Comte, as a pure philosopher not himself the subject of an individual entry, occurs in the index with his dates, and an indication of the entry Positivism in which he is principally treated, together with any mentions of his name which may occur elsewhere in the *Guide*. Under "Magny" in the index are references to all those who attended the famous literary dinners held in the restaurant, a rather poor 10 francs' worth according to George Sand, and under the names of the hostesses the index refers the user of the *Guide* to anyone mentioned in it as having attended a particular salon. The index is intended to provide important information about the social history of the literary world in France since the Revolution.

Since the length of individual entries had anyway to be dictated largely by the complexity and interest of available biographical details, and by the number of publications, and could

not therefore be made proportional to the literary importance of an individual writer, some entries have been artificially lengthened as the appropriate place to accommodate information important in contexts outside the entry in which they appear. Matters concerned with the cubist painters appear chiefly under the entry devoted to Apollinaire as well as under that devoted to Cubism. A detailed account of the events of the 1848 revolution will be found in the entry devoted to Lamartine, owing to the peculiarly important part he played in it, the entry on Cocteau deals with the relationships between Stravinsky, Satie, "Les Six," the Ballets Russes, and the literary world, as well as with Cocteau's own life and works. Other entries which are longer than the literary importance of their subject strictly warrants include those devoted to Jammes, on account of the religious polemic in France early in the 20th century, and Saint-Exupéry, partly on account of his popularity as a syllabus author, but also to recall the impact on French life of the early stages of the 20th-century revolution in systems of transport and communication.

However, some writers have been treated at greater length than their literary achievements may be thought to have warranted. Sometimes, as with the entry devoted to Simone de Beauvoir, that is simply on account of the amount of public comment which has been devoted to an author's work, or the amount of public interest which has been shown in an author's biography. None the less there are entries whose lengths do not so much reflect literary stature as the apparent urgency of the need to argue the case for a literary importance not, for instance, usually accorded to Sue, Sand, or even Chateaubriand. In all three cases the biographies are of exceptional interest, but all three wrote works of sufficient imaginative power to have contributed to changes in the ways in which whole generations looked at their personal experience or at the values incorporated into the political and social organization of the world they lived in. It therefore seemed appropriate to treat their careers at much greater length than users of the *Guide*, used to the established pantheon of great authors, might have expected.

Anomalies have occasionally been allowed to remain wherever the rigorous application of principle would have led to clearly unhelpful consequences. As the Introduction points out, there is at least a serious possibility that some recent apparently non-imaginative writing in France is actually of the greatest literary significance. It could be argued that *Tristes Tropiques* earns Lévi-Strauss a place as a "literary" writer. The claim would be justified, but specious, as would similar claims made for Barthes and Foucault. In fact the reason for including all three is that their technical work as anthropologist, sociologist/critic, and philosopher/historian respectively, whatever its merits or weaknesses in the professional field to which it was intended to contribute, has made an overwhelming contribution to a new vision of man centred on the complementary nature of linguistic and social means of communication. But because the line had to be drawn somewhere, the inclusion of Lévi-Strauss,

Barthes, and Foucault has not entailed entries devoted to scholars like Fernand Braudel and Emmanuel Le Roy Ladurie, whose professional historical work makes an only marginally slighter contribution to a new vision of man and the anthropology of his social relationships. The practice of other guides and histories has been closely scrutinized and sometimes regarded as normative, but the distinctions which included Merleau-Ponty while excluding Raymond Aron (1905–1983), and included Bergson, but not Maurice Blondel (1861–1949) are very fine ones.

The bibliographies attached to each author entry are normally as complete as they could be made, although there are occasional exceptions, notably when a writer of novels has turned out to have published works, for instance, on a hobby, like ornithology, or when formal speeches have received automatic publication, as on reception at the Académie Française. Where an author has used several names, the entry is under that by which he or she is principally known. Vian published different sorts of work under two separate names. Balzac's early publications used a number of pseudonyms. Simenon used about a dozen, and Stendhal at one time or another several score. All the names attached to published volumes are given, but the entry is always under the commonly known name—Stendhal, for instance, rather than the family name of Beyle. The aim has always been to make the *Guide* convenient to use, even if that has entailed the occasional sacrifice of consistency. On the increasingly sensitive subject of the private lives of authors, the *Guide* has felt free to draw on all published information, wherever it has appeared, but on nothing, of whatever potential interest, that has not already been subject to the scrutiny entailed by previous publication.

DATES AND DISCREPANCIES

On account of the needs of certain categories of potential user a much more exact system of dating has been employed in the *Guide* than is usual in works of reference. This has necessarily led to discrepancies, and other exceptions to the rules set out have been allowed in the interests of clarity, accuracy, convenience, and common sense. The overriding consideration has been to make the writers' intentions clear and the use of the *Guide* as helpful and as uncomplicated as possible, given what it undertakes to achieve.

The first authorized volume edition of Flaubert's *Madame Bovary* was published late in April 1857 by Michel Lévy. That is the universally accepted date of the first edition. It is, however, a "formal" or "conventional" date. A text, slightly cut, had actually appeared in six instalments in the *Revue de Paris* from 1 October to 15 December 1856. In January 1857 Flaubert, the editor and the publisher were prosecuted for "outrage to public decency" and acquitted, but not awarded costs. A pirated volume edition of the text, printed in Germany from the serialized text, was on sale in Paris early in 1857; Lévy published the more expensive "first edition" in late April, having restored the cuts, and the authorities decided, this time with more success, to prosecute Baudelaire for *Les Fleurs du mal*.

Users of the *Guide* knowing the title, and wanting only to know the name of the author of *Madame Bovary* and the date of its publication, will find the author from the title index, and the date, 1857, in the list of publications appended to the Flaubert entry. Other users, interested in the personal history of Flaubert, or the history of attempts to control the publishing trade, or of the concept of "public decency," may wish to know about the prosecution and its outcome, while yet others, interested in the economics of publishing, or the financial arrangements of authors, may need to know about the pirated edition. This note attempts to explain among other things why there has to be an apparent discrepancy of dates.

Volumes offered for sale, and for that matter newspapers and most periodicals, had to be registered with one or more of a variety of official bodies. "Formal" or "conventional" dates of publication are taken from those registers, or from the dates printed on title sheets, fly leaves, or under rubrics like "dépôt légal" or "achevé d'imprimer" in the volumes themselves. Publishers, who were often really only booksellers, did however have a strong financial incentive to keep the official date of publication as late as possible, since they had often bought from authors the right to publish only for a certain period. Their profits were obviously liable to increase the later the "publication date" was deemed to have occurred. The date of the public availability of a text, often recorded in the *Guide*'s text, is not therefore always the date of publication given in the list of publications at the end of the entry. The dates given in the list are those of the official date of first publication in volume form. Where a work has been translated, the year of the first dated translation has been given. The purpose with older books is to show how quickly they were translated rather than how often. Names of translators and places of publication are not normally given, but many early translations were anonymous and undated.

Where plays, film scenarios, and broadcasting scripts are concerned, dates of first performance have normally been given in the text, but occasionally also in the list of publications. Where only one date appears in the list of publications, it is that of the publication of the printed text, not that of performance or, in the case of films, of release. Matters have naturally been further much complicated by the difficulty in knowing what constitutes "volume publication." Some "volumes" are single, folded, uncut sheets. The definition of a "volume" changed in France in 1856. For 20 years volume publication had edged up by an average of 100 volumes a year to the 8,253 registered volumes published in 1855. In 1856 the number of registered titles suddenly jumped to 12,027.

Some material was published several times under different titles, and sometimes the same title was used several times for different material. Occasionally the use or omission of capitals or commas in a title was of clear importance to a writer, and sometimes the division of a writer's publications into different lists for drama, fiction, and verse is so arbitrary as to be misleading. Prose poems in particular go from something like fiction to what should clearly be regarded as poetry. Autobiography is often so heavily fictionalized as to belong with novels. Much that was written in dialogue form was not intended to be drama. Wherever it seemed more likely to confuse than to help, categorization in the lists of publications has not been attempted. Whenever, as so often in the 19th century, a novelist turned his novel into a play, the same title is likely to occur in both lists. Some very short poems have been published in a volume of their own, and their titles are normally italicized. Some long poems that were published only in collections have also been italicized where it seemed sensible to indicate in that way that they were major works. Consistency has been striven for, but the overriding consideration has always been the likely convenience of the *Guide*'s users.

General Principles

– Dates of publication given in the *Guide*'s text are actual dates at which texts were made publically available, in the manner indicated (serialization, broadcast, article) unless they are in brackets, in which cases they are "formal" or "conventional" dates as explained above

– Dates given in the lists of publications appended to each author entry are "formal" or "conventional" dates

– Titles of all separately published texts, "volume publications," and those of plays, paintings, films, and broadcast scripts are given in italics

– Titles of poems and short stories, unless they are also the titles of collections in volume form, titles of abandoned projects, fragments, and articles are given in roman type within double quotation marks

– Accents are omitted on upper case letters, except in the names of authors at the head of the entry (e.g. Éluard)

– Diphthongs are printed as double vowels (e.g. *oeuvre*)

– For the purposes of alphabetical arrangement, the *Guide* follows the usual convention in counting the prefixes "Le," "La," "Les," "Du," and "Des," as the opening part of a name, whether or not they are prefixes, as in "Des Esseintes," which precedes "Desfontaines." "De," "d'," "von," and "van" are ignored for purposes of placing within an alphabetical arrangement. Simone de Beauvoir is therefore placed under "B," but Maxime Du Camp under "D." "De la" is always split, so that an entry for François, duc de la Rochefoucauld would appear in an alphabetically ordered list as "La Rochefoucauld, François duc de." Since the Parnassian poets are normally sought under "P," they are treated under that letter in the *Guide*, in the entry "(Le) Parnasse"

A

ADAMOV, Arthur, 1908–1970.

Dramatist.

Adamov was born into a wealthy Armenian family, which owned a number of oil wells, but even during his childhood at Baku he suffered from chronic states of anxiety, which later developed into severely inhibiting neuroses. The family were in Germany when the war broke out, but escaped to Geneva, which Adamov did not like. In Geneva, however, he got to know the Pitoëffs, who helped to revitalize Parisian theatre between the wars. When the family returned to Germany in 1922, the oil wells had been confiscated and the family jewels sold. Adamov's father turned to gambling while Arthur went to the French lycée at Mainz, where he occasionally acted out the masochistic fantasies he had begun to write about.

In 1924 the family moved to Paris. Adamov was expelled from the well-known Lycée Lakanal for truancy, collaborated with a friend he had made in Mainz on an article, "Vive l'anarchie!" published in 1927, sent some poems to Eluard, became politically active, and was associated with the review *Discontinuité*. He drifted on the edges of avant-garde circles, meeting a number of surrealist writers, and also Giacometti, Roger Blin, and the already famous director Antonin Artaud, whose celebrated production of Strindberg's *The Dream Play* he attended.

We know from the ruthlessly self-revelatory autobiography *L'Aveu*, written in four parts between 1938 and 1943, that Adamov was impotent, needed to be humiliated by women, blamed himself for his father's suicide in 1933, and suffered from a paralysing sense of isolation. He had lived with a woman named Irène for a few months in 1928, and in 1933 published five short prose poems in the *Cahiers du Sud*. For a period during 1941 he was interned, an experience which bred in him the view that man's only dignity lay in a refusal to submit to the laws of the cosmos. On his mother's death from tuberculosis in 1942, by which time he had read Kafka and translated some Jung, the feelings of guilt had become overwhelming.

After the liberation Adamov co-founded a review, *L'Heure Nouvelle*, to which Artaud, René Char, and Jacques Prévert collaborated. In 1947 he met Jacqueline Trehet, whom he was finally to marry in 1961, and finished his first play, *La Parodie*, in which one of the characters, N, is run over by a car and swept up by the environmental health department—a fate reminiscent of the protagonist's in Kafka's most famous short story, *Die Verwandlung* (The Metamorphosis)—while the other character, the Employee, ends up in prison blind. In the winter of 1948–49 he finished *L'Invasion*, in which a scholar is torn between the demands of his work and his family. Jean Vilar of the Théâtre National Populaire (TNP), liked the "stark dramatic purity" of these two works and compared Adamov's drama favourably with Claudel's.

Adamov began writing prolifically, driven by the need to externalize his obsessions and resolve his fantasies. Later, his 20 or so plays, radio scenarios, translations, adaptations, study on Strindberg, dramatic theory, and autobiographical works were to be subsumed into his social commitment to the political left. Before any of the works was published or staged, Vilar recruited support for Adamov—from Gide, among others—and in 1948 he presented Adamov's adaptation of Büchner's *Dantons Tod* (Danton's Death), one of the only two "masterpieces of adaptation" that, according to Vilar, the TNP ever staged. In November 1950 Serreau staged *La Grande et la Petite Manoeuvre*, in which the figure of the universal victim is caught between rival factions and destroyed, at the Théâtre des Noctambules, while Vilar put on *L'Invasion* at the Studio des Champs-Elysées. In the following years, other great Parisian directors staged Adamov plays: Blin, Planchon in Lyons, Serreau again, and Mauclair. He also formed a brief friendship with Ionesco.

Adamov's subjects are generally ironic. In *Le Professeur Taranne* the chief character is arbitrarily humiliated by an accusation of indecent exposure and cannot convince anyone of his innocence. He ends up by undressing and so committing the crime of which he had been wrongly charged. *Tous contre tous* is about a war waged against people who limp by equally unfortunate antagonists. The early plays often deal with man's pain and suffering rather than with his metaphysical isolation, or, clearly drawing on Kafka, play out symbolically the clash of forces in Adamov's psychological complexes or deriving from his experience of internment. In *Le Sens de la marche* the son murders his father's grotesque companion, while in *Les Retrouvailles* the mother wheels the son away in a pram.

Generally unhelpful pigeonholing has linked the early Adamov with surrealism (q.v.), the theatre of the absurd, and the theatre of cruelty, although his style, thematic material, and dramatic sense differed from all three. After 1955 his theatre came to satirize the capitalist world of the pin-table society (*Le Pingpong*) or the refusal of the French to shake off corruption, represented by a trader in dead butterflies who destroys beauty for profit (*Paolo Paoli*). This is not quite the socialist art transformed by the techniques of German expressionism which it has been taken for. It is still too privately concerned with the victims of injustices, though the socialist element is strong in the anti-Gaullist sketches (*Intimité, Je ne suis pas Français, La Complainte du ridicule*), and in *Le Printemps 71*, set during the last days of the Commune uprising of 1871 and clearly influenced by Brecht.

Adamov signed the "Manifeste des 121" against the Algerian war in 1960 and taught briefly at Cornell in 1964. His wife joined the Communist Party, but he did not. His plays became more physically cumbersome and difficult to stage, so that productions were infrequent, although he had success in the US as well as in the UK, East Germany, Italy, and Czechoslovakia.

Adamov continued to make a living from his translations and adaptations from Russian (Gogol, Dostoyevsky, Gorky, Chekov) and his radio plays, but his unbalanced psychological state finally overcame him. He drank heavily, lost his memory and, as his mental and physical condition deteriorated, was no longer able to work. In his final plays—*La Politique des restes, M. le Modéré, Sainte Europe, Off Limits*, and *Si l'été revenait*, published in the year of his death from an overdose of barbiturates—Adamov did, however, achieve a synthesis of the personal and the political.

Until 1967 Adamov lived in hotels. He may well be remembered chiefly for the autobiographical *L'Aveu*. Like the German expressionists he realized that neurosis was an enlargement and exaggeration of a universal defect and that its stage portrayal could occasion a therapeutic resonance in an audience itself not subject to its abnormal or excessive form, a theatrical truth at least as old as Aeschylus' dramatization of the Oedipus legend.

PUBLICATIONS

Plays

La Parodie (produced 1952), with *L'Invasion*, 1950
L'Invasion (produced 1950), with *La Parodie*, 1950; as *The Invasion*, 1968
La Grande et la Petite Manoeuvre (produced 1950), 1950
Le Sens de la marche (produced 1953), 1953
Tous contre tous (produced 1953), 1953
Le Professeur Taranne (produced 1953), 1953; as *Professor Taranne*, in *Two Plays*, 1962
Comme nous avons été (produced 1954), in *La Nouvelle Nouvelle Revue Française 1*, 1953; as *As We Were*, in *Evergreen Review 4*, 1957
Théâtre I-IV, 1953–68
Le Ping-pong (produced 1955), 1955; as *Ping Pong*, 1959
Les Retrouvailles, 1955
Paolo Paoli (produced 1957), 1957; as *Paolo Paoli* (in English), 1959
Les Ames mortes (produced 1960), 1960
Le Printemps 71 (produced 1963), 1961
Sainte Europe, 1966
La Politique des restes (produced 1963), 1967
M. Le Modéré (produced 1968), *in Théâtre IV*, 1968
Off Limits (produced 1969), 1969
Si l'été revenait, 1970
En fiacre (radio play), 1959

Fiction

Je...ils..., 1969

Other

L'Aveu, 1946
Auguste Strindberg, dramaturge, with Maurice Gravier, 1955
Théâtre de société, 1958
Ici et maintenant, 1964
L'Homme et l'enfant, 1968

Editor, *Le Commune de Paris*, 1959

Translator

Le Moi et l'inconscient, by Jung, 1938
With Marie Geringer, *Le Livre de la pauvreté et de la mort*, by Rilke, 1941
With Marthe Robert, *Théâtre complet*, by Büchner, 1953
Crime et châtiment, by Dostoyevsky, 1956
Les Aventures de Tchitchikov, by Gogol, 1956
La Mère, Vassa Geleznova, and *Les Petits Bourgeois*, by Gorky, 3 vols., 1958
Théâtre, by Chekov, 1958
Le Père, by Strindberg, 1958
Le Revisor, by Gogol, 1958
Oblomov, by Goncharov, 1959
Cinq récits, by Gogol, 1961
With Claude Sebisch, *Le Théâtre politique*, by Erwin Piscator, 1962
Les Ennemis, by Gorky, 1970
With Jacqueline Autrusseau, *La Grande Muraille*, by Max Frisch, 1973

Critical studies

Chahine, Samia Assad, *Regards sur le théâtre de Adamov*, 1961
Gaudy, René, *Arthur Adamov*, 1971
Mélèse, Pierre, *Arthur Adamov*, 1973
Reilly, John H., *Arthur Adamov* (in English), 1973
McCann, John J., *The Theatre of Adamov*, 1975

Bibliography

Bradby, David, *Adamov* (in English), 1975

ALAIN (Pseudonym of Emile-Auguste CHARTIER), 1868–1951.

Philosopher, essayist, teacher, and journalist.

LIFE

Alain, as he signed his "Propos" from 1906, was born into a middle-class family on 3 March 1868 at Mortagne, about 80 miles due west of Paris. His mother was 23, and his father 32, a well-read and independent-minded veterinary surgeon, to whom Alain owes his early intellectual training. He was bored and inattentive at his primary school. From 1881 he attended the lycée at Alençon, where he was an outstanding pupil, invariably first in his class. Originally destined for a scientific education and an army career, he changed over to arts only at the age of 18. He was particularly attracted to Homer and Plato and, among French authors, Descartes, Balzac, and Stendhal. From 1886 to 1889 he attended the lycée at Vanves on the edge of Paris, and then for three years the Ecole Normale Supérieure, where he passed his agrégation. He was appointed as a teacher at Pontivy, where he wrote his first published article, the "Premier dialogue entre Eudoxe at Ariste," signing it "Criton." It appeared in the *Revue de Métaphysique et de Morale* for November 1892.

A year later Alain was posted to Lorient in Brittany, where he began his career as a journalist, writing for *La Dépêche de Lorient*. In 1894 his father died. Alain published a further "Dialogue," signed Criton, in the *Revue de Métaphysique et de Morale* each year from 1894 to 1897, and four other philosophical articles signed E. Chartier in 1898–99. He continued to publish philosophical articles alongside his journalistic "Chroniques" while teaching in Normandy, in particular at Rouen. In 1903 he was posted to the Lycée Condorcet in Paris, but that year he began to publish first the "Propos du dimanche" and then the "Propos du lundi" for *La Dépêche de Rouen*. The daily "Propos d'un Normand," signed Alain, started in that newspaper on 16 February 1906, and the first series of 101 was published in an edition of 150 copies in 1908. The fourth volume of 101 "Propos" was published in 1914 in a printing of 300 copies. Alain, now 40, was essentially a left-wing liberal, although he often aligned himself with the socialists. He had been heavily pro-Dreyfus, although his writings do not really warrant the radical reputation he has kept. In principle he was a pacifist.

Although he had loathed the idea of war, with its waste of so many promising young lives, Alain joined up at the outbreak of war. At this time his reflections show a sustained intellectual effort to think clearly about the complex issues raised by the prospect of war: death, violence, freedom, constraint, obligations, and rights. He served from October 1914 until October 1917, for two and a half years of that time in the artillery, was injured in the heel, and spent three months in hospital in 1916. Convalescence provided Alain with the opportunity to write at greater length than his usual 500 words. In 1915 he published the *Quatre-vingt-un chapitres sur l'esprit et les passions*, intended to be a manual and later reworked as *Eléments de philosophie*, and it was during 1917 that he wrote the *Système des beaux-arts*, published in 1920. The first version of *Mars; ou, La Guerre jugée* was written early in 1916. The work was then rewritten during the summer and autumn of 1919, and again in July 1920. This time Alain had allowed himself to make deletions. Only one chapter of the first version survives in the published volume of 1921.

On demobilization later in 1917 Alain bought a house and returned to his teaching post, one at least of the most important in the French secondary education system, as principal teacher of philosophy at what was regarded as the best school in Paris, the Lycée Henri IV. He also taught at a celebrated girls' school, the Collège Sévigné. Although he increasingly wanted to write for a wider public, Alain did not succeed in forcing an entry into the world of serious journalism, and remained confined to the "Propos" published in diary form in the *Journal* or gathered together in volumes under subject headings like "aesthetics," "Christianity," and "happiness." He also published reflections in various forms on philosophers, philosophical systems, and ideas, writing intelligently and lucidly, but always as a teacher, destroying assumptions, pointing out what had been overlooked, but with no attempt at intellectual profundity. As a teacher he was punctual, formal, and a believer in careful hand writing, always on the lookout for talent. He repeatedly turned down offers of a university post, and in his pupils he welcomed radical thought whenever it was clear. His own philosophy teacher had

been "the only God I have ever recognized." His pupils included Maurice Schumann, André Maurois, Simone Weil, Raymond Aron, and Maurice Merleau-Ponty. Sartre tried to avoid Henri IV to elude his influence, but did not succeed.

Alain married his secretary, Gabrielle Landormy, on his retirement. She was present at his death, just before midnight on 2 June 1951, after a short illness, in the house he had bought at Vésinet in 1917.

WORKS

Alain, the inventor of the "Propos" as a literary genre, used his assumed name from 1906, when he began contributing his "Propos d'un Normand" daily to *La Dépêche de Rouen*. By 1 September 1914 he had reached his 3,098th. He gained extraordinary influence not as a philosopher in the Anglo-Saxon sense, but as a teacher of "philosophie." It was in that role that he stimulated his pupils, and also his readers, by his occasionally penetrating reflections about the great philosophers, but also about literature, the arts, religion, politics, and the values and beliefs which underpinned the structure of society, as he knew, understood, and experienced it. His great strength was to strip away from discussion the everyday assumptions, often embedded in ordinary language, which blunted incisiveness of judgement. His short daily essays, written on two sheets of letter paper, contained no corrections, sustained arguments, or especially penetrating insights. They were unusually stimulating journalism and quickly gained for their author a reputation for clear-sightedness that extended well beyond Normandy.

The three-volume Pléiade edition devoted to Alain's work is a tribute to his reputation, but his anti-intellectualist humanism, stressing the role of the will and the emotions in human judgements, is little more than a civilized reflection in the cultivated French liberal tradition, anti-clerical, politically more radical in thought than in commitment, conservative in morals, and nourished by the great classics of antiquity and by those of France's own literature. Alain believed strongly in the corruptive influence of power. His gentle cynicism was grafted on to a classical taste, and he was particularly sceptical about anything too redolent of rank, hierarchy, or authority. He was especially critical of all positions, like so many of those held during World War I, whose defence involved intellectual obfuscation or even dishonesty.

Before the outbreak of war Alain was already writing about its social implications, the destruction of the generous, the heroic, and the risk-takers, the survival of a France rich "de prudents, de calculateurs, de thésauriseurs… de prêteurs et de rusés… de natures pauvres… de tyrans et d'esclaves (in the prudent, the calculating, the hoarders… the lenders and the schemers… the poor in nature… the tyrants and the slaves)." The *Système des beaux-arts* was intended to be "une réflexion sur ce qui est reconnu beau et nullement une recherche de belles oeuvres parmi les médiocres (a reflection on what is regarded as beautiful, and not a search for beautiful works among second-rate ones)."

Since the celebrated "Propos" are each so brief, it is most easily possible to convey an idea of them by taking a random week of five, for instance those published on consecutive days starting on 6 December 1921, which was a Tuesday. Alain starts with 700 words on Frazer's *The Golden Bough*. The reader's mind is not taxed, but his literary sophistication is flattered. The book is about the collective dreams of the childhood of all of us. The golden bough protects us from believing too much and not believing enough, and the reader is gently led, quite unnecessarily by way of Lucretius, to the series "magic, religion, science." This is a watered-down version of turn-of-the-century religious scepticism, uttered with a sang-froid which dates it to within half a decade of 1925. The piece could not have been written in that tone at any other time, or in any other guise. It was middle-class liberal-conservative continental west European journalism between the immediate reaction to the armistice and the radical change of attitude in the literate public towards the Church in about 1930.

Then comes a paragraph saying that ideas cannot be true. The perennial view, usually associated with the 13th century, that truth lies not in ideas but in the relationship of the mind with external reality is elegantly dressed up: "Ce qui est vrai c'est le mouvement qui va du rêve à la chose (What is true is the movement which goes from the dream to the reality)." Magic and childhood have similar places at the outset of a process of growth. The final paragraph is amusingly clever journalism. The word "law" is a metaphor, whether we are talking of the rules imposed on children or Newton's description of the action of physical forces.

For Wednesday Alain wrote a slightly shorter piece about Christianity and socialism. "A Christian who doesn't know that he is one." Is that what a socialist is? What Christians and socialists have in common is a value system. Othewise one has to do with politics, and the other with the individual, not society. The socialist says you avoid war by justly organizing production, and the Christian says you avoid war by being truly peaceable. Thursday's piece, also short, gives an intelligent account of Jarry's *Ubu Roi*, using Goethe, Machiavelli, and Rabelais to help make its point, which is again good journalism. King Ubu, like Machiavelli's prince, is still wearing clothes, even if Jarry pretends that he is an emperor without any. On Friday Alain published a little moral reflection about love and hate, starting from the love and hate of individuals, and moving on to relationships between states. It is a pity, he says, that states and individuals cannot both abstain from entanglements and just be polite to one another in the street. Saturday draws the reader's attention to how unpleasant Proust is to his characters, although the subject of the piece is not reached until its last three lines. The real difficulty is to square these elegant light-weight conversation pieces with Alain's formidable reputation as a thinker and a teacher.

PUBLICATIONS

Collections

Propos, Bibliothèque de la Pléiade, 1956
Les Arts et les dieux, Bibliothèque de la Pléiade, 1958
Les Passions et la sagesse, Bibliothèque de la Pléiade, 1960
Humanités, 1960
Propos sur des philosophes, 1961
Cahiers de Lorient, 2 vols., 1963
Esquisses d'Alain, 2 vols., 1963–64
Etudes, 1968
Salut et fraternité, 1969

Essays

Les Cent-un propos d'Alain:
    1st series, 1908
    2nd series, 1909
    3rd series, 1911
    4th series, 1914
Vingt-et-un propos d'Alain: méditations pour les non-combattants, 1915
Quatre-vingt-un chapitres sur l'esprit et les passions, 1915
Les Marchands de sommeil, 1919
Système des beaux-arts, 1920
Mars; ou La Guerre jugée, 1921; as *Mars; or, The Truth about War*, 1930
Jeanne d'Arc, 1925
Eléments d'une doctrine radicale, 1925
Souvenirs concernant Jules Lagneau, 1925
Le Citoyen contre les pouvoirs, 1925
Les Idées et les âges, 1927
Esquisses de l'homme, 1927
Les Sentiments familiaux, 1927
Visite au musicien (on Beethoven), 1927
Entretiens au bord de la mer, 1931
Vingt leçons sur les beaux-arts, 1931
Les Dieux, 1934
Stendhal, 1935
Histoire de mes pensées, 1936
Commentaires (on Valéry), 1936
Avec Balzac, 1937
Eléments de philosophie, 1941
En lisant Dickens, 1945

Bibliographical studies

Dewit, S., *Alain: essai d'une bibliographie*, 1954; revised edition, 1961
Drevit, A., "Bio-bibliographie d'Alain," in *Association des Amis d'Alain: Annuaire, 1966*

Critical and biographical studies

Pascal, G., *La Pensée d'Alain*, 1947
Maurois, André *Alain*, 1950
Maurois, André, *Hommage à Alain*, 1952
Mondor, H., *Alain*, 1953
Bénézé, G. *Généreux Alain*, 1962
Pascal, G. *Alain éducateur*, 1964
Halda, B., *Alain*, 1965
Miquel, J., *Les Propos d'Alain*, 1966

ALAIN-FOURNIER, 1886–1914.

Pseudonym of Henri-Alban Fournier, novelist.

Alain-Fournier's single complete novel, *Le Grand Meaulnes*, an expression of intense nostalgia for the innocent fantasies of a childhood pastoral paradise, must count among the more remarkable literary successes of the 20th century. In spite of the novel's enduring popularity, however, the attempts to elevate its author to a literary stature approaching that of Proust or Gide have never been critically justified.

Henri Fournier was the only son of a country schoolmaster, brought up at Epineuil, in the geographical heart of France. His closest companion was his sister Isabelle, born in 1889, who was to marry Jacques Rivière. After an idyllic but unremarkable country childhood, at the age of 12 Alain-Fournier, as he became, was sent to board with a family friend while attending the Lycée Voltaire in Paris. Although academically successful, he was miserable, but when in 1901 he went to the strict Brest lycée in order to prepare to enter the navy, he found its quasi-military discipline even more distasteful. He gave up after 16 months, and passed his baccalauréat as a boarder at Bourges, already ineluctably drawn towards his past: "Je ne veux pas connaître le monde en dehors de mon âme où il n'est que rappel de paysages désirés et d'histoires évoquées (I don't want to know the world outside my own head, where there are memories only of longed-for landscapes and of imagined events)."

He returned to Paris as a boarder, met Rivière, and spent some time in London preparing for his entry examination for the Ecole Normale Supérieure, which trained the elite of the teaching profession. His voracious appetite for modern literature was not enough to get him through his agrégation, which, like Rivière, he failed. He had been writing verse and, in September 1907, hurriedly finished an essay disputing the views of Pierre Louÿs on the female nude before departing for military service. He found life in the cavalry too harsh, transferred to the infantry, developed ways of avoiding the grosser chores against which his fastidiousness rebelled, and during his first leave discovered that *La Grande Revue* had published his essay. He had adopted his pseudonym to avoid confusion with a well-known admiral and a famous cyclist.

In 1905 he had a fleeting encounter with a girl whose image was to haunt him until his death and around whom he now planned a novel. This novel was also to incorporate elements from his childhood and a house in the country. He produced some fragments which endeavoured to convey his sense of the marvellous and inevitably centred on love and childhood. Rivière sent the first fragment to Gide, who turned it down for the *Nouvelle Revue Française* (*NRF*, q.v.).

Alain-Fournier graduated as an officer, and considered becoming a seriously committed, rather than nominal Roman Catholic. In 1909 he attended the wedding of his sister to Rivière, by now a close friend of his. He wrote some short prose pieces, four of which were published in 1910 and 1911, and during the winter of 1909–10 he began sketches for what was to be his great novel. It was to be clearly autobiographical and a novel of renunciation, still focusing on the vanished girl of five years before. Meanwhile he wrote a literary gossip column for a Paris daily and shared a house with the Rivières. He got to know some of the main figures of literary society, notably Giraudoux, Péguy, and the important names associated with the *NRF*. For a while he took T. S. Eliot as a private pupil. A tempestuous affair changed his plan for the novel: Meaulnes was to lose Yvonne not through renunciation but through guilt.

Isabelle gave birth to a daughter in 1911, and from 1912 Alain-Fournier worked for a wealthy young politician, which gave him more time to work on his novel. He finished it in December 1912, and it was serialized in the *NRF* from July to November 1913. Earlier that year he had contrived a meeting with its heroine, now married.

Le Grand Meaulnes, as we have it, is related by François Seurel, the son of village schoolteachers. The ungainly young Meaulnes arrives at the school, is not chosen to accompany François to the station to pick up his grandparents, takes a hired pony and trap to meet them farther up the line, and gets lost for several days, stumbling into a dream party and meeting a beautiful girl.

Meaulnes returns to school. Various adolescents from the party turn up in different guises. Meaulnes and Seurel try unsuccessfully to find their way to the ruined house where the party had been held and, while Meaulnes goes off in search of the girl, Seurel tells the other boys of his adventure. The plot is complex, full of autobiographical details, adolescent fantasy, medieval literary idealization of passion, nostalgia for childhood, for the country and gypsy freedom, innocent joys, loyalties, and quests for beautiful but inaccessible women and the ruined castles where they live. After a lengthy search Meaulnes finally meets up again with Yvonne and marries her.

Yvonne's brother, Frantz, had become engaged to a girl called Valentine. It was to celebrate this engagement that the party had been held. Thinking herself too poor for him, however Valentine, had run away and Frantz had tried to shoot himself. Frantz had then become friendly with Meaulnes, who had sworn to help him whenever called on to do so. In his quest for Yvonne, Meaulnes had become engaged to a girl who turned out to be Valentine, and whom he had then abandoned to prostitution. Meaulnes feels too guilty to be happy with Yvonne. Possession of the ideal makes it mundane. He goes off to find Valentine, reunites her with Frantz, but finds on his return that Yvonne has died while giving birth to their baby daughter. In the earlier sketches the ending was considerably more bitter.

All the dream elements in the novel have a normal explanation, even when they are clearly realized fantasies or come close to surrealism (q.v.). Elements of the narrative relate it to the romantic and symbolist (qq. v.) movements as well. The real and the imaginary, the ordinary and the miraculous, the mundane and the magic are treated with no distinction of register. The tone of the novel is lofty and poetic, but the characterization is patchy, the narrative uneven, the charm rather slight, and the emotional content at times sentimental. There is a lack of finesse, even of moral integrity, amounting to imaginative self-indulgence, and the psychoanalytical content is at best superficial. The book's immense success does not derive from its literary qualities so much as from its true subject, the quest for inaccessible joy, which, as Alain-Fournier himself pointed out, "n'est pas de ce monde (is not of this world)." The novel appeared as a book, dedicated to Isabelle, in October 1913.

Alain-Fournier was killed in action in September 1914. He left an unfinished second novel, *Colombe Blanchet*, and the two volumes of his correspondence with Jacques Rivière, published in 1948.

PUBLICATIONS

Fiction

Le Grand Meaulnes, 1913
Colombe Blanchet (fragment), *NRF*, 1922

Other

Correspondance 1905–1914, with Jacques Rivière, 2 vols., 1948

Critical studies

Rivière, Jacques, *Images d'Alain-Fournier par sa soeur Isabelle*, 1938
Rivière, Jacques, *Nouvelles études*, 1947
Gibson, R., *The Quest of Alain-Fournier*, 1953

_____

ANOUILH, Jean (-Marie-Lucien-Pierre), 1910–1987.

Dramatist.

LIFE

Jean Anouilh was born in Bordeaux on 23 June 1910. His father was a tailor and his mother a violinist who played in the casino orchestra in Arcachon. Anouilh was proud of his father's competence as an artisan and regarded himself as an artisan of the theatre—a play-"wright," not just a writer. As well as writing about 50 plays, he became increasingly involved in producing his own works, and occasionally other people's. Both his wives were actresses, and he always took a detailed interest in the technical aspects of staging his plays. Apart from one book of fables and one volume of memoirs, he wrote exclusively for or about the theatre.

Perhaps in reaction to the very public world of the theatre, Anouilh was extremely reticent about his private life. When asked to contribute details for an entry in *Crapouillot—Dictionnaire des contemporains* (1946), he wrote in a letter to its editor, Jean Galtier-Boissière: "Le reste de ma vie et tant que le ciel voudra que ce soit encore mon affaire personnelle, j'en réserve les détails (I would like the rest of my life, and whatever heaven sends, to remain my personal business, and I will keep the details to myself)." He went to school in Bordeaux and is known to have spent three months in Arcachon in 1919, listening to operettas every night. He moved to Paris in 1928 and started to study law, but gave up in 1929 and spent two years working in the advertising agency Publicité Damour. He admitted that this taught him accuracy and ingenuity. He also had a job in the complaints department of a Paris store, where the first complaint he had to deal with, "The Vicomtesse d'Eristal has not received her mechanical carpet sweeper," gave him the title for his memoirs, published in 1987.

In 1931 Anouilh was called up for military service but he was invalided out on the grounds of poor health. He then became secretary to Louis Jouvet, whose production of Giraudoux's *Siegfried* in 1928 he had greatly admired. *Siegfried* taught Anouilh "qu'on pouvait avoir au théâtre une langue poétique et artificielle qui demeure plus vraie que la conversation sténographique (in the theatre you can have an artificial poetic language which is more true to life than transcribed conversa-

tion)," and this revelation influenced his subsequent writing.

While working in the advertising agency, Anouilh met the actress Monelle Valentin, and they were married in 1931. Jouvet lent them the scenery from *Siegfried* to furnish their apartment but gave Anouilh no other encouragement in his attempts to establish a career in the theatre. Anouilh had been writing since about the age of 12, but his first two plays as an adult were not commercially successful. *L'Hermine*, produced by Lugné-Poë, folded after 37 performances in 1932, and *La Mandarine*, presented by Jouvet, after only 13 in 1933. Meanwhile, as assistant to the director Georges Pitoëff, Anouilh scraped a living by writing subtitles for silent films until his first commercially successful plays, *Le Voyageur sans bagage*, performed by the Pitoëffs in 1937, and *La Sauvage* of 1938. The marriage to Monelle Valentin produced a daughter, Catherine, but it was only when he sold the film script of *Y'avait un prisonnier* to Metro Goldwyn Mayer that Anouilh could afford to buy Catherine a pram. The bitter depictions of poverty and its effect on the spirit that characterize his early plays were clearly based on personal experience.

Steady success and popularity began with Anouilh's collaboration with the director André Barsacq in 1938. Barsacq produced *Le Bal des voleurs* in Paris, then took it to the French theatre in New York, along with *Le Voyageur sans bagage*, for the winter of 1938–39. He went on to direct *Le Rendez-vous de Senlis* in 1941, *Eurydice* in 1942, *Antigone*, starring Monelle Valentin, in 1944, *L'Invitation au château* in 1947, and *Colombe* in 1951. By the time Anouilh changed to a different director, Roland Piétri, in 1948, he was established as a leading playwright.

During the German occupation Anouilh was disdainful of the Resistance and political action and quietly continued his work in the theatre. He did become involved, however, in the Brasillach affair. Brasillach was the editor of the newspaper *Je Suis Partout*, which published Anouilh's *Léocadia* after it was first performed in November 1940. He was a known collaborationist, and his behaviour, particularly the fact that he dressed in German uniform, was regarded as evidence of treason after the liberation. He was condemned to death on 1 February 1945. Anouilh was among the many writers of left and right who signed the petition to spare Brasillach's life, but de Gaulle reneged on a promise to commute the sentence, and Brasillach was executed on 6 February. This episode confirmed Anouilh's hostility towards left-wing politicians and he expressed it searingly in *Pauvre Bitos*, which shocked French audiences in 1956 by appearing to be a right-wing attack on the left. It also antagonized the critics by its criticism of France.

In 1953 Anouilh's first marriage ended in divorce and on 30 July of that year he married the actress Nicole Lançon, whose stage name was Charlotte Chardon. They had three children: Caroline, Nicolas, and Marie-Colombe. Anouilh was so expert at guarding his privacy that *France-Dimanche* did not find out about his second marriage until October 1956. It has been suggested that the optimistic tone of *L'Alouette* was due to Anouilh's happier personal circumstances, since it coincided with his marriage to Nicole Lançon. But any assumption that he then settled down to a placid family life is at odds with the atmosphere of his later plays. Family life is consistently portrayed as acrimonious and destructive, and the central character is often a father figure surrounded by parasites. The fact that this figure is often called the Author, and graduates to being a playwright in

Cher Antoine and *Le Nombril*, indicates that Anouilh is commenting on his own experience of being a playwright responsible for a family. By 1981 Léon de Saint-Pé in *Le Nombril* is quite unable to work because of constant interruptions from his demanding relatives, mistress, housekeeper, and various workmen. His house is chaos, and he does not even have the freedom of escaping into creative work. But Anouilh himself was still writing and producing plays: he found a solution in presenting a character who could not.

WORKS

Certain themes recur throughout Anouilh's long and prolific career: the corrupting effect of poverty on character, the gulf between rich and poor, and the contrast between complacent superficial characters, who are usually middle-aged, and idealistic young ones who refuse to abandon their integrity. The earlier plays show a clear distinction between the purists and the compromisers, but as Anouilh matures the issues become less black and white and the atmosphere becomes more obviously theatrical and less realistic. As the count says in *La Répétition*, "C'est très joli la vie, mais cela n'a pas de forme. L'art a pour objet de lui en donner une précisément, et de faire par tous les artifices possibles plus vrai que le vrai (Life is a fine thing, but it has no form. The purpose of art is to give it one, and to use any artificial means available to create something more real than real life)."

The impression of a family likeness between Anouilh's plays is reinforced by the way he grouped them together for publication, and by the titles he chose for the collections. "Pièces noires," first published together in 1942, were *L'Hermine*, *Le Voyageur sans bagage*, *La Sauvage*, and *Eurydice*. They all present characters who reject their past but are unable to adapt to the reality offered by the present. Franz, in *L'Hermine*, has experienced severe poverty and knows how it can ruin human relationships. His fiancée Monime has a rich aunt, and Franz murders the aunt to protect Monime from suffering as he has in the past. But Monime interprets his obsession with poverty as a symptom of pride. She keeps her white ermine coat as symbolic insulation against reality, and Franz gives himself up to the police in despair. In *La Sauvage* it is the female character, Thérèse, who is familiar with poverty and obsessed with money. She is unable to be happy because she is constantly aware of other people's suffering. She is the first of several idealistic young heroines who refuse to compromise with the corrupt and careless adult world and who, like Antigone, reject the possibility of happiness.

The central character of *Le Voyageur sans bagage* has suffered amnesia for 18 years due to shell shock in World War I, and has therefore lost his past. Several families claim that he belongs to them, and during a visit to the Renaud family it becomes clear that Gaston must be Jacques Renaud, a thorough villain. Gaston is horrified, but Anouilh rescues him from having to resume his unwelcome identity by providing another family in which he can adopt a more congenial personality. *Eurydice* is a modern interpretation of the Orpheus myth, set in a railway waiting room and a seedy hotel. Eurydice is an actress in a touring repertory company and Orpheus is a travelling musician. Eurydice realizes that she cannot match up to Orpheus' ideal of her as pure and virtuous, so she runs away from him and dies in a road accident. Orpheus fails to bring her back from the Under-

world because he looks into her eyes to confirm his suspicion that she is impure, and he then commits suicide. The message is that love cannot survive once it is tainted by contact with real life.

The "Pièces roses" are predictably more optimistic, but also more remote from reality, with their characters escaping into a fantasy world. This collection contains *Le Bal des voleurs*, *Léocadia*, and *Le Rendez-vous de Senlis*. *Humulus le muet*, a short curtain-raiser, was written in 1929 and published in the review *La Nouvelle Saison*, but only added to the "Pièces roses" in 1958. In *Le Rendez-vous de Senlis* the unhappily married Georges creates a fictitious ideal family to impress his girlfriend Isabelle. When the truth comes out, the play gets a happy ending thanks to Isabelle's faith in Georges, and he is able to make a fresh start. In *Léocadia* an artificial world is also created by one of the characters for the benefit of another. Prince Albert once had a blissful relationship with an opera singer called Léocadia, but she died after they had spent only three days together. His aunt, the duchess, tries to preserve all the mementoes of her nephew's romance and finally resorts to "replacing" the lost Léocadia by Amanda, a "pure" Anouilh heroine. It is Amanda's goodness and simplicity that gives the prince hope of a happy future.

The "Nouvelles pièces noires" are *Antigone*, *Jézabel*, written in 1932 but not performed in France, *Roméo et Jeannette*, and *Médée*. The emphasis here is on death and the struggle between the inner world of a heroic individual and the outer world of reality. *Antigone* retains the features of the Greek myth and Sophocles' tragedy, and the Chorus ensures that the audience knows in advance what is going to happen. Antigone chooses to die because she stubbornly believes in her duty as an individual and would rather hold on to her childhood ideals than compromise with life by growing up: "Moi, je veux tout, tout de suite,—et que ce soit entier,—ou alors je refuse!... Je veux être sûre de tout aujourd'hui et que cela soit aussi beau que quand j'étais petite—ou mourir (I want everything, right now, and it has to be complete—or else I want nothing!... I want to be sure of everything today and I want it to be just as beautiful as it used to be when I was little. If I can't have that, I'd rather die)."

Roméo et Jeannette also has a heroine who refuses to grow up and accept that life is less beautiful than she thought. The play was not very successful on the stage. The attraction between the lovers is unconvincing, and their suicide by drowning is caused by fate rather than anything they brought upon themselves. The same emphasis on fate as opposed to decisions by the characters can be found in *Médée*, which was a failure when it was put on in 1953, although most critics thought this was the fault of the production.

The "Pièces brillantes" provide light relief in the shape of *L'Invitation au château*, *La Répétition; ou, L'Amour puni*, *Colombe*, and *Cécile; ou, L'Ecole des pères*. Anouilh is operating here as an entertainer and displays his highly developed talent for exploiting theatrical effects. *La Répétition* uses the device of a play within a play, where the characters are rehearsing an amateur production of Marivaux's *La Double Inconstance*. The plot of *L'Invitation au château* hinges on the fact that the main male characters are identical twins; they can never appear on stage at the same time since they have to be played by the same actor. The English version, *Ring round the Moon*, was particularly successful in London in 1950, possibly helped by its glittering fantasy atmosphere, which provided an antidote to the gloom of post-war rationing.

The post-war plays collected as "Pièces grinçantes" were *Ardèle; ou, La Marguerite, La Valse des toréadors, Ornifle; ou, Le Courant d'air,* and *Pauvre Bitos; ou, Le Dîner de têtes.* These were followed in 1970 by the "Nouvelles pièces grinçantes": *L'Hurluberlu; ou, Le Réactionnaire amoureux, La Grotte, L'Orchestre, Le Boulanger, la boulangère, et le petit mitron,* and *Les Poissons rouges; ou, Mon père, ce héros.* The tone of these plays is harsh and sombre, and many of them present family life as a failure. In *Ardèle* the central "pure" character is an old hunchbacked aunt who never appears on stage. The rest of the household try to persuade her through the keyhole to give up her romance with the children's tutor, who is also a hunchback. The other members of Ardèle's family are dishonest, coarse, and dominated by sensuality. Even childhood is contaminated for her nephew and niece, and Ardèle herself is driven to suicide.

Her brother, General Saint-Pé, reappears in *La Valse des toréadors*, along with his invalid wife. The play, like *Ardèle*, is a biting social satire. The waltz of the title was the general's one moment of ideal love many years before, but he failed to follow it up. The lady he danced with comes back into his life, but he loses her to his secretary, who turns out to be his own illegitimate son. This play received such hostile reviews from the Paris critics that Anouilh was stung into publishing a defence of it, maintaining that his plays were not intended to deal with philosophical ideas: "Monsieur Anouilh avoids general ideas… He uses our petty human miseries to try to make us laugh." He later said that *La Valse des toréadors* was the sort of play he would have liked to go on writing, but that its failure in Paris had made him change direction.

Pauvre Bitos caused a storm of protest because it was perceived as a condemnation of the "épuration," the largely left-wing backlash against collaborators. The subtitle, *Le Dîner de têtes*, refers to the setting of the play—an aristocratic dinner party where the guests wear wigs representing characters from the French Revolution—but it also has undertones of severed heads. Bitos is the odd one out, the only guest who is not an aristocrat. He is a deputy public prosecutor and the only one in full fancy dress, as Robespierre. His hosts intend to humiliate him as a punishment for having ordered a boyhood friend to be executed for collaboration. He faints when a gun is pointed at his face, and an entire act of the play shows his dream of himself as Robespierre. Although the aristocrats are portrayed as cruel and childish, Bitos himself is cold and unlikeable, and the play is antagonistic to political extremism from either end of the spectrum.

Two of Anouilh's best-known and most enduring successes are in the "Pièces costumées" collection, *L'Alouette* and *Becket; ou, L'Honneur de Dieu.* The other play in the group is *La Foire d'empoigne*, in which the same actor has to play Napoleon and Louis XVIII. Anouilh's treatment of the Joan of Arc story in *L'Alouette* is original and effective. The setting is Jeanne's trial, and scenes from her life are enacted on the empty stage by the characters who are already there. There are constant reminders that this is a play, not a portrayal of reality, and Anouilh even manipulates a happy ending. Instead of showing Jeanne being burnt at the stake, he sends one of the characters rushing on to remind the others that they still need to perform the coronation scene, and the play ends with a tableau of Jeanne leaning on her standard and smiling. "La vraie fin de l'histoire de Jeanne… ce n'est pas dans sa misère de bête traquée à Rouen, c'est l'alouette en plein ciel, c'est Jeanne à Reims dans toute sa gloire… La vraie fin de l'histoire de Jeanne est joyeuse (The real ending of Joan's story… is not as a miserable cornered animal in Rouen; it is when she is flying free as a lark in the sky; it is when she is in Rheims in all her glory…Joan's story has a happy ending)."

In *Becket* the story of Thomas à Becket provided Anouilh with inbuilt dramatic conflict between the characters and ambitions of King Henry II and his archbishop. He also exploited the theme of racial tension between the Anglo-Saxons and the Norman conquerors, although it was historically inaccurate to make Becket a Saxon. When Anouilh found out that this was a mistake, he decided not to change the play, on the grounds that he was writing theatre, not serious history. The subtitle, *L'Honneur de Dieu*, refers to the ethical value Becket discovers once he has reluctantly become archbishop of Canterbury. Although not a particularly devout Christian, he recognizes the honour of God as something worth dying for. The play shows this new loyalty making Becket remote from his friendship with the king, whose love progressively turns to hatred, to the point where he can allow his knights to murder Becket. Becket is Anouilh's most conventional hero, and in many ways the most satisfactory, as he appeals to the audience's sympathy on both the intellectual and the emotional level.

From the 1960s onwards Anouilh's plays tended to rework his established themes and even to repeat characters. He still bitterly attacked bourgeois hypocrisy and criticized the social upheaval caused by the war. His interest in emphasizing the performance aspect of the theatre continues in *L'Orchestre*, where all the cast are disillusioned musicians and the cellist commits suicide in the ladies' room at the end. In *Cher Antoine* the Antoine of the title was a successful playwright but is already dead. The other characters gather to hear the reading of his will. In their confrontations with each other they meet different reflections of Antoine's personality.

Apart from his own plays, Anouilh translated and adapted Oscar Wilde's *The Importance of Being Ernest* in collaboration with Claude Vincent as *Il est important d'être aimé*, and, also with Claude Vincent, Shakespeare's *As You Like It, The Winter's Tale,* and *Twelfth Night.*

PUBLICATIONS

Collections

Théâtre complet, 9 vols., 1968

Plays

L'Hermine (produced 1932), 1934; as *The Ermine* (produced 1955), in *Plays of the Year 13*, 1956; in *Five Plays*, 1958
La Mandarine (produced 1933)
Y'avait un prisonnier (produced 1935), in *La Petite Illustration*, 18 May 1935
Le Voyageur sans bagage (produced 1937), in *Pièces noires*, 1942; as *Traveller Without Luggage* (produced 1959), 1959; in *Seven Plays*, 1967
La Sauvage (produced 1938), 1938; as *The Restless Heart* (produced 1957), 1957; in *Five Plays*, 1958
Le Bal des voleurs (produced 1938), 1938; as *Thieves' Carnival* (produced 1952), 1952
Léocadia (produced 1940), in *Pièces roses*, 1942; as *Time*

Remembered (produced 1954), 1955

Marie-Jeanne; ou, La Fille du peuple, from a play by Dennery and Mallian (produced 1940)

Le Rendez-vous de Senlis (produced 1941), in *Pièces roses,* 1942; as *Dinner with the Family* (produced 1957), 1958

Eurydice (produced 1942), in *Pièces noires,* 1942; as *Point of Departure* (as *Eurydice,* produced 1948), 1951; as *Legend of Lovers* (produced 1951), 1952

Pièces roses (includes *Le Bal des voleurs, Le Rendez-vous de Senlis, Léocadia*), 1942; augmented edition (includes *Humulus le muet*), 1958

Pièces noires (includes *L'Hermine, La Sauvage, Le Voyageur sans bagage, Eurydice*), 1942

Antigone, from the play by Sophocles (produced 1944), 1946; as *Antigone* (in English; produced 1946), 1946

Roméo et Jeannette (produced 1946), in *Nouvelles pièces noires,* 1946; as *Romeo and Jeannette* (as *Fading Mansions,* produced 1949), in *Five Plays,* 1958

Nouvelles pièces noires (includes *Jézabel, Antigone, Roméo et Jeannette, Médée*), 1946

Médée (produced 1953), in *Nouvelles pièces noires,* 1946; as *Medea* (produced 1956), in *Plays of the Year 15,* 1956; in *Seven Plays,* 1967

L'Invitation au château (produced 1947), 1948; as *Ring round the Moon* (produced 1950), 1950

Ardèle; ou, La Marguerite, with *Episode de la vie d'un auteur* (produced 1948), 1949; as *Ardele* (as *Cry of the Peacock,* produced 1950), 1951; in *Five Plays,* 1958

Humulus le muet, with Jean Aurenche (produced 1948), n.d.; as *Humulus the Great* (produced 1976)

La Répétition; ou, L'Amour puni (produced 1950), 1950; as *The Rehearsal* (produced 1957), in *Five Plays,* 1958; published separately, 1961

Monsieur Vincent (screenplay), with Jean Bernard Luc, 1951

Colombe (produced 1951), in *Pièces brillantes,* 1951; as *Colombe* (in English; produced 1951), 1952; revised version, with music by T.M. Damaye (produced 1961)

Pièces brillantes (includes *L'Invitation au château, Colombe, La Répétition, Cécile*), 1951

Cécile; ou, L'Ecole des pères (produced 1954), in *Pièces brillantes,* 1951; as *Cecile; or, The School for Fathers,* in *Seven Plays,* 1967

La Valse des toréadors (produced 1952), 1952; as *Waltz of the Toreadors* (produced 1956), 1956

Trois comédies (includes adaptations of *As You Like It, A Winter's Tale,* and *Twelfth Night* by Shakespeare), 1952

La Nuit des rois, from the play *Twelfth Night* by Shakespeare (produced 1961), in *Trois comédies,* 1952

Le Loup (ballet scenario), with Georges Neveux, 1953

L'Alouette (produced 1953), 1953; as *The Lark* (produced 1955), 1955

Ornifle; ou, Le Courant d'air (produced 1955), 1956; as *Ornifle* (in English), 1970; as *It's Later Than You Think,* 1970

Il est important d'être aimé, with Claude Vincent, from the play *The Importance of Being Earnest* (produced 1964), in *L'Avant-scène 101,* 1955

Pauvre Bitos; ou, Le Dîner de têtes (produced 1956), in *Pièces grinçantes,* 1956; as *Poor Bitos* (produced 1963), 1964

Pièces grinçantes (includes *Ardèle, La Valse des toréadors, Ornifle, Pauvre Bitos*), 1956

Five Plays, 1958

L'Hurluberlu; ou, Le Réactionnaire amoureux (produced 1959), 1959; as *The Fighting Cock* (produced 1959), 1960

Becket; ou, L'Honneur de Dieu (produced 1959), 1959; as *Becket; or, The Honor of God* (produced 1960), 1961

Madame de... (in English; produced 1959), 1959

La Petite Molière, with Roland Laudenback (produced 1959), in *L'Avant-scène,* 15 December 1959

Le Songe du critique (produced 1960), in *L'Avant-scène 143,* 1959

Pièces costumées (includes *L'Alouette, Becket, La Foire d'empoigne*), 1960

La Foire d'empoigne (produced 1962), in *Pièces costumées,* 1960; as *Catch as Catch Can,* in *Seven Plays,* 1967

Tartuffe, from the play by Molière (produced 1960), in *L'Avant-scène,* 15 May 1961

La Grotte (produced 1961), 1961; as *The Cavern* (produced 1965), 1966

Victor; ou, Les Enfants au pouvoir, from the play by Roger Vitrac (produced 1962), in *L'Avant-scène,* 15 November 1962

L'Amant complaisant, with Nicole Anouilh, from the play *The Complaisant Lover* by Graham Greene (produced 1962), 1962

L'Orchestre (produced 1962), 1970; as *The Orchestra* (produced 1969), in *Seven Plays,* 1967; published separately, 1975

Richard III, from the play by Shakespeare (produced 1964), n.d.

L'Ordalie; ou, La Petite Catherine de Heilbronn, from a story by Heinrich von Kleist (produced 1966), in *L'Avant-scène,* 15 January 1967

Seven Plays, 1967

Le Boulanger, la boulangère, et le petit mitron (produced 1968), 1969; as *The Baker, The Baker's Wife, and the Baker's Boy* (produced 1972)

Cher Antoine; ou, L'Amour raté (produced 1969), 1969; as *Dear Antoine; or, The Love That Failed* (produced 1971), 1971

Le Théâtre; ou, La Vie comme elle est (produced 1970)

Ne réveillez pas Madame (produced 1970), 1970

Les Poissons rouges; ou, Mon père, ce héros (produced 1970), 1970

Nouvelles pièces grinçantes (includes *L'Hurluberlu; La Grotte; L'Orchestre; Le Boulanger, la boulangère, et le petit mitron; Les Poissons rouges*), 1970

Tu étais si gentil quand tu étais petit (produced 1971), 1972; as *You Were So Sweet* (produced 1974)

Le Directeur de l'Opéra (produced 1973), 1972; as *The Director of the Opera* (produced 1973), 1973

Pièces baroques (includes *Cher Antoine, Ne réveillez pas Madame, Le Directeur de l'Opéra*), 1974

L'Arrestation (produced 1975), 1975; as *The Arrest* (produced 1974), 1978

Le Scénario (produced 1976), 1976; as *The Scenario* (produced 1976)

Chers Zoizeaux (produced 1976), 1977

Pièces secrètes (includes *Tu étais si gentil quand tu étais petit, L'Arrestation, Le Scénario*), 1977

Vive Henri IV, 1977

La Culotte (produced 1978), 1978

La Belle Vie, suivi de Episode de la vie d'un auteur, 1980

Le Nombril, 1981

Oedipe; ou Le Roi boiteux, from the play by Sophocles, 1986

Screenplays: *Les Dégourdis de la onzième,* with Jean Aurenche,

1936; *Vous n'avez rien à déclarer*, with Jean Aurenche, 1937; *Les Otages*, with Jean Aurenche, 1939; *Cavalcade d'amour*, 1939; *Le Voyageur sans bagage (Identity Unknown)*, with Jean Aurenche, 1944; *Monsieur Vincent*, with Jean Bernard Luc, 1947; *Anna Karenina*, with Julien Duvivier and Guy Morgan, 1948; *Pattes blanches*, with Jean Bernard Luc, 1949; *Caroline chérie*, 1951; *Deux sous de violettes*, with Monelle Valentin, 1951; *Le Rideau rouge*, 1952; *Le Chevalier de la nuit*, 1953; *La Mort de belle (The Passion of Slow Fire)*, 1961; *La Ronde (Circle of Love)*, 1964; *A Time for Loving*, 1971

Television plays: *Le Jeune Homme et le lion*, 1976; *La Belle Vie*, 1979

Ballet scenarios: *Les Demoiselles de la nuit*, 1948; *Le Loup*, with Georges Neveux, 1953

Other

Michel-Marie Poulain, with Pierre Imbourg and André Warnod, 1953
Fables, 1962
La Vicomtesse d'Eristal n'a pas reçu son balai mécanique: souvenirs d'un jenne homme (autobiography), 1987

Bibliography

White, Kathleen, *Anouilh: An Annotated Bibliography*, 1973

Critical studies

Archer, Marguerite, *Anouilh*, 1951
Marsh, Edward O., *Anouilh, Poet of Pierrot and Pantaloon*, 1953
Pronko, Leonard C., *The World of Jean Anouilh*, 1961
Harvey, John, *Anouilh: A Study in Theatrics*, 1964
Thody, Philip, *Anouilh* (in English), 1968
della Fazia, Alba, *Anouilh* (in English), 1969
Falb, Lewis W., *Anouilh* (in English), 1977
McIntyre, H.G., *The Theatre of Anouilh*, 1981
Howarth, W.D., *Anouilh: Antigone*, 1983
Chaillet, Ned, *Anouilh: Five Plays*, 1987

APOLLINAIRE, Guillaume (-Albert-Wladimir-Alexandre-Apollinaire de Kostrowitzky), 1880–1918.

Poet, art critic, and journalist.

LIFE

Apollinaire delighted in the mystery surrounding the identity of his parents. For some years before and after his birth, his mother, Angélique-Alexandrine Kostrowitzka (1858–1919), was living in Rome with an Italian officer, Francesco Flugi d'Aspermont (born in 1835), who in spite of the uncertainty must be presumed to be Apollinaire's father. Angélique came from an aristocratic Polish family who took refuge from the Russians in Rome after the failure of the 1863 Polish rising. Apollinaire's maternal grandfather was honoured by Pius IX, and his mother was educated in a convent from 1868 until 1874, when, aged 16, she was removed for indiscipline. Her father had paid the fees for one term only. D'Aspermont's elder brother was the abbot primate of a congregation of Benedictine monasteries, but d'Aspermont himself was given to gambling and appears to have been an embarrassment to his family. They tried to ship him off to America in 1884, but had to prevail on him to disappear of his own accord the following year, since he had disembarked before leaving Europe.

Alternatively Apollinaire's father could have been Napoleon's grandson, conceived in Vienna, but born in Rome in 1831 to the 18-year-old Melanie Kostrowitzka, and brought up in and by the Vatican. Melanie was certainly known to Apollinaire's mother, and in 1959 Apollinaire's wife Jacqueline possessed a brooch which Apollinaire said had been given to his mother by Melanie. It is perfectly possible that his mother did not know which of her lovers was Apollinaire's father. She was known as Olga, and gave birth in 1882 to a second son, Albert, who emigrated to Mexico in 1913. In 1887 Olga was active as a professional hostess at the Monaco casino, but an expulsion order from the principality is recorded against her. It may not have been executed. Apollinaire did brilliantly at school in Monaco, Cannes, and then Nice. His education appears to have been paid for by the d'Aspermont family through the abbot primate, who died in 1904. Apollinaire recalled various "uncles," with one of whom, Jules Weil (born in 1869), his mother formed a steady liaison, which lasted until after Apollinaire's death. Weil was sometimes penniless, and occasionally very rich. Gambling had drawn him to Monaco, which had been the acknowledged gambling capital of Europe since the closure of the German casinos in the 1860s.

When Apollinaire left school in 1897 his first language was French, although his Italian was excellent, and his school records show good German. He had begun to write verse in French in the new symbolist (q.v.) manner and already felt a nostalgia for the religion of his upbringing. In 1899 Olga settled at Spa in eastern Belgium for the casino. Apollinaire and his brother were lodged nearby at Stavelot, where Apollinaire discovered the Ardennes and the rivers and forests which so impressed him. "Kostro" fell in love, wrote verse, and composed his first contes. Some work dating from this time and rewritten or incorporated into later material has subsequently been published. He and his brother had to leave Belgium and go and join their mother, who was living under an assumed name in Paris, when their hotel bill could not be paid, and the local paper noted that the two young men accomplished their disappearance with skill.

During that winter Apollinaire did odd jobs, helped a Monaco acquaintance with a novel entitled *Que faire?*, ending up writing most of the chapters himself, and borrowing the central character, Dr Peter of Prague, from Jarry's Doctor Faustroll. The novel was serialized in *Le Matin* from February until the paper closed down in May. Apollinaire finally found a job with a broker on the verge of bankruptcy. He also met the nephew of the manager of the Bouffes-Parisiens, got free tickets to that theatre, and even had a piece, *A la cloche de bois*, accepted, though it was never put on. He learnt to type, read widely, acquired some Hebrew, and continued to write. His first three signed poems appeared in *La Grande France* in September 1901. One of them was finally published as "Clair de lune" in Apollinaire's first important published volume of verse, *Alcools*, in 1913. It was not until 1901 that he started using the name "Apollinaire" rather than Kostrowitzky.

Apollinaire had written a pornographic novel, *Mirely ou le petit trou pas cher*, to earn some money, and had started another novel. He had various amorous adventures, and wrote verse to a friend's sister, Linda Molina da Silva. Another friend's mother presented him to the Vicomtesse de Milhau, the eccentric and pretty widow of a Norman who had committed suicide. She was German and engaged Apollinaire to teach French to her daughter, Gabrielle, who had an English governess. Apollinaire accepted an appointment for a year and the countess drove him in her de Dion-Bouton to her mother's villa at Honnef on the Rhine. The family, called Hölterhoff, is said to have grown rich through slave trading. While he was with them in their Rhineland houses, Apollinaire fell in love with the English governess, Annie Playden, whom he wanted to marry. He courted her and purported to be rich and aristocratic, ill-treated her and threatened to kill her if she did not accept him. Annie was frightened by him and turned him down.

During his year in Germany Apollinaire managed to visit Cologne, Berlin, Dresden, Prague, Vienna, Munich, and all the major Rhineland towns. He was writing a good deal, mostly contes, and in March 1902 published "L'hérésiarque" in the *Revue Blanche*, signing it "Apollinaire." A small stream of contes, articles, and poems appeared in 1902 in the *Revue Blanche, Tabarin*, which was run by a friend, and *La Grande France*. In August 1902 Apollinaire returned to his mother and brother in Paris and started work in a bank. Life was difficult and lonely, but he was now writing regularly for the *Revue Blanche* and starting to appear in *L'Européen*, a pacifist review. Early in 1903 he also began to attend the Saturday evening poetry readings held at the Café du Départ by the poetry magazine *La Plume*, founded in 1889. The soirees had been discontinued in 1895, but were restarted under the new editor as the focus of an avant-garde literary and artistic club in 1902. Apollinaire read his Rhine poems, some of which were to appear in *Alcools*, met Jarry and André Salmon, who read "Le banquet," and gradually became better known.

In October Apollinaire, with Salmon and three others, founded *Le Festin d'Esope*, a "revue des belles-lettres," nine issues of which appeared from November 1903 to August 1904. In November 1903 Apollinaire visited Annie again in London. She was living a sheltered life, but Apollinaire was allowed into the house even late in the evenings for fear that he would batter down the door. On his return to Paris he began his long poem "La chanson du mal-aimé," first published in 1909 in the *Mercure de France* and then in *Alcools*. By the winter of 1903–04 Apollinaire and his magazine were beginning to rebel against the relatively staid symbolism of *La Plume*, and Apollinaire's obscene fantasy was beginning to get the better of him.

It was probably money put into it by Jean Sève, a well-off journalist friend of Apollinaire from Monaco, that kept *Le Festin d'Esope* going. The magazine's manager was Jean Mollet, who became inseparable from Apollinaire and Salmon, and who spoke later of the long incubation of Apollinaire's poems before he wrote first the notes, and then finally a draft. The text would be allowed to rest before being rewritten up to a dozen times. Mollet remarks on Apollinaire's delightful company, wealth of fantasy, and desire to surprise. Apollinaire went to London again in 1904 in pursuit of Annie Playden, who invented a fiancé in the US. She did effectively emigrate there as a governess to escape from Apollinaire, saying goodbye to him on Waterloo station. On his return to Paris this time, Apollinaire wrote "L'émigrant de Landor Road," which was to appear in *Alcools*.

Sometime that year he also met the painters Maurice de Vlaminck (1880–1954), a former racing bicyclist and café violinist who had never been inside the Louvre, and who described himself as a gentle barbarian trying to express his emotions in pure colour, and André Derain (1876–1958), who shared the same plastic values, but was better educated and more reflective than Vlaminck. The two were firm friends. With Henri Matisse (1869–1954) and the first fauves they shared Apollinaire's quest for a new and more direct means of expression. They were reacting strongly against the limits, allusions, and draperies of symbolism, which sought to avoid direct expression in any aesthetic medium.

In the early summer of 1904 Jean Mollet had been introduced to a bohemian pair living in Rue Ravignan in Montmartre: Pablo Picasso (1881–1973), who was living with his mistress, Fernande Olivier, at no. 13, the wooden shack that came to be called the Bateau Lavoir, and Max Jacob. Apollinaire used to go to one of the English bars near the Gare Saint-Lazare between the end of his day at the bank and dinner with his mother. One evening Mollet brought Picasso to meet him, and a few days later Picasso brought Jacob. Accounts of the initial meetings of Apollinaire, his painter friends, and Jacob are plentiful and contradictory, but Apollinaire took to visiting the Bateau Lavoir, and Salmon moved in next door with Juan Gris. The extraordinary processes of self-selection had brought together the immensely talented avant-garde group associated with Montmartre in the first decade of the century until it reached critical mass. The resulting artistic explosion included fauvism and cubism (q.v.) and was to reverberate for decades throughout western Europe and the US.

It was Apollinaire who introduced Georges Braque (1882–1963) to Picasso in 1907, and it used to be generally agreed that his cultural activity within and on behalf of the group exceeded his personal achievement as a poet. His insensitivity to plastic values in all that he wrote about his friends' paintings while frankly posturing as an art critic was a commonplace among them, formally recorded certainly by Picasso, Braque, and the group's principal dealer, Apollinaire's friend and the first publisher of his poetry, Daniel-Henry Kahnweiler. Attempts to describe Apollinaire's poetry as cubist have also been strongly challenged, notably by Paul Reverdy (1889–1960), who wrote with distinction about the painters and was later to edit the avant-garde review *Nord-Sud*. Apollinaire was the painters' intellectually stimulating friend, a gifted poet, their indefatigable promoter and champion at a moment at which they needed their work to be brought to public attention. He was closest to Picasso, about whom he wrote most importantly in *LES PEINTRES CUBISTES* and *Chroniques d'art*; to Marie Laurencin, whom he included in his list of cubist painters in a famous article written for *Les Soirées de Paris*, perhaps in an attempt to woo her back; and later to Robert Delaunay.

The Montmartre group was very far from self-assured. Its famous harlequins and its general use of the fairground imagery of charlatans, mountebanks, and columbines were the clown's traditional symbols of insecurity. Like the group's antics, all of them came together finally—when the group as such had dissolved and neither Apollinaire nor Picasso was living any longer in Montmartre—in Diaghilev's *Parade* of 1917, for which Picasso designed the set and Apollinaire invented the term "surrealist" (q.v., and see Cocteau). Artistically, the group's unifying feature was to be a growing anti-symbolist reaction and a movement away from the fauves. It is always difficult to disentangle Apollinaire's personal loyalties and enthusiasms, however, from his aesthetic reactions. He was quite capable of deviating from symbolist practice while still relying in theory on a symbolist aesthetic when it suited him.

In July 1904 Apollinaire had published a long piece on Anatole France's *Thaïs* in the *Mercure de France*, and he had been seeing much of Jarry. In April 1905 he tried to revive *Le Festin d'Esope* as the *Revue Immoraliste*. He had found someone to finance the review, but since its headquarters were at the same address as that of a convent, its name was changed for its second and last number to *Les Lettres Modernes*. As well as work of his own, Apollinaire published verse by André Salmon and four of Jacob's poems.

Picasso was exhibiting at the Galerie Serrurier in April 1905, and Apollinaire, who had taken exception to what Charles Morice had said about Picasso in the preface to the exhibition catalogue, published a reply, "Picasso peintre et dessinateur," in the April number of the review. He also wrote his first essay in art criticism, "Picasso, peintre," for *La Plume* in May. That summer Apollinaire visited Amsterdam, and in December he published "L'emigrant de Landor Road" with two other poems in Paul Fort's *Vers et Prose*. Finding himself short of money, and eager to break away from his tedious bank job, in 1906 he wrote two more (anonymous) pornographic novels, *Les Onze mille verges* and *Les Exploits d'un jeune Don Juan*, both in fact unrecognized as parodies until much later.

From now on Apollinaire, whose anonymity remained transparent, made a sporadic living editing, translating, and writing pornography for the publishers Briffaut Frères. With the help of two friends and a little bribery he also managed to produce a catalogue of the erotica, access to which normally required special authorization, in the Bibliothèque Nationale, whose authorities were surprised and pleased in due course to receive a copy. Apollinaire wrote erotic verse, and is said to have introduced, edited, partly translated, supplied bibliographies for, or annotated 27 licentious texts. In April 1907 he moved into an apartment of his own, furnished by his mother, where he could receive Marie Laurencin, to whom Picasso had introduced him. He was to follow her when she and her mother moved house in 1911.

Meanwhile he continued to lunch on Sundays with his mother and his brother, who was now doing well as a banker. He would occasionally bring with him one of his Montmartre friends, and always his dirty linen for washing. His genius for self-advertisement, put to serious use when he became the virtual impresario of the Montmartre group, is clear from his challenge to Max Daireaux to a duel for a couple of innocuous, but now famous, lines in an unremarkable article, "Symbolistes et mi-carême," in *Le Censeur Politique et Littéraire* for 2 March 1907. Daireaux, whose misspelling of Apollinaire's name apparently went unnoticed, had maintained that Apollinaire used to draw attention to himself by drinking Apollinaris mineral water, claiming: "It's

my water, it's my water." The challenge is said to have been lost because the review's editor, André Billy, did not bother to open the mail, but the episode, which resulted in a comic bill from Jacob to Apollinaire for the discharge of his duties as a second, but not of course in a duel, grew its own legend, thereby perfectly serving its purpose. Later in 1907, after occasional pieces in *Le Soleil* and *Je Sais Tout*, Apollinaire began to write poetry and art criticism regularly for Jean Royère's neosymbolist *La Phalange*, maintaining in an important article on Matisse that there was "no relationship between literature and painting" and, even more surprisingly, that Royère's own poems "were more beautiful on account of their obscurity," which implies that by that time Picasso, in painting, and Jacob, in poetry, were emphatically rejecting the symbolist aesthetic.

Fernande Olivier, who disliked Marie Laurencin, has left an account of her liaison with Apollinaire. The pretty and mischievous Marie was still an art student at the Académie Julian when she met Apollinaire. She had Creole blood, and was illegitimate, although her mother had become highly respectable. She was dominated by her mother, disliked what she remembered of her father, and was not readily responsive to men. Apollinaire promoted her paintings with dealers, but was later spiteful about her in *Le Poète assassiné*, and she felt that she had been out of her depth in the brilliant but poverty-stricken company he kept, especially that of Picasso and Jacob. Apollinaire's sensitivity and charm do not seem to have extended to his relationships with women, who seldom found him attractive, and the affair, which lasted until 1912, was stormy and possibly even violent. Apollinaire was paranoid about having creases on his bed, even to the extent of conducting his liaison with Marie on the armchair, and when he entertained in his largest room, where the bed was the largest piece of furniture, no one was allowed to sit on it. His relationship with Marie finally came to an end, owing to pressure exercised by Marie's mother, after Apollinaire's imprisonment on suspicion of complicity in the *Mona Lisa* theft.

From 1908 Apollinaire became virtually a professional art journalist, doing odd promotional and journalistic jobs for the art world, such as prefaces for exhibition catalogues. On 25 April 1908 he gave an important but informal lecture on the new school of young French poets, the "Phalange nouvelle," at the Salon des Indépendants, and then wrote an account of the paintings there, praising the revolutionary styles of Braque, Derain, and Vlaminck. His preface to the catalogue of Braque's first exhibition at Kahnweiler's gallery started a controversy with the established art critic Louis Vauxcelles. Following a remark dropped by Matisse, in a review of the Braque exhibition in *Gil Blas* for 14 November 1908, Vauxcelles had derisively referred to "cubes" and "bizarreries cubiques" (cubic oddities).

As self-appointed spokesman for the conniving painters, who did not mind being grouped together in their reaction to the fauve reliance on broadly applied primary colours, Apollinaire semi-officially accepted on their behalf the group denomination of "cubist," the word having originally been intended in a derogatory sense, as had "impressionism". Like the term "existentialist" (q.v.) its appositeness was only subsequently recognized by some of those to whom it had been applied, but was used for convenience by critics looking for shorthand and enemies looking for broad but identifiable targets. The difficulty, as always, is to know how far Apollinaire had his tongue in his cheek. Did his acceptance of the term "cubism," or his praise of his patron's obscurity, start life as a joke that ended up by being taken seriously?

Apollinaire had moved to Montparnasse in 1909 and in the spring of 1910 took over from Salmon as art critic for *L'Intransigeant*. In 1911 he was taken on by the *Mercure de France* as a literary and artistic columnist, a position he kept until his death. Some consternation was caused by his satirical account, on April Fool's Day 1913, of the funeral of Walt Whitman, who had died in 1892 and become a cult figure. What he said about the all-day barbecue, Whitman's lovers of both sexes, and the drunken pallbearers on all fours reverberated in the *Mercure* for a year. At this period Apollinaire was also publishing more important work. The still unknown Kahnweiler published *L'Enchanteur pourrissant* on 28 November 1909 with woodcuts by Derain. It contained "Onirocritique," Apollinaire's most advanced prose poem to date. Only 100 copies were printed, of which 58 remained unsold after five years. *L'Hérésiarque et Cie* was published by P.V. Stock in 1910 and was at least considered for the Prix Goncourt. Apollinaire denied borrowing from a host of established authors he said he had not read, including some he must have. On the list were Poe, Nerval, Hoffmann, Baudelaire, and Barbey d'Aurevilly. His first volume of poetry, *Le Bestiaire; ou, Cortège d'Orphée* was published by Deplanche in 1911, with woodcuts by Raoul Dufy. About 50 copies were sold out of a printing of 120.

Apollinaire, who was touching 30, is universally described at this time as charming, sentimental, a touch vulgar, reassuring and talkative, always mock-serious, and a bit absent-minded. He loved fruit, all home pursuits, window-shopping, and walking round Paris, and was a knowledgable gourmet. His life, though anything but luxurious, was relatively carefree. Its flavour is concentrated in the not very serious banquet given in honour of the "Douanier" Henri Rousseau (1844–1910) in 1908, the year of Rousseau's portrait of Apollinaire and Marie Laurencin exhibited in 1909 at the Indépendants as *La Muse inspirant le poète*. Apollinaire had probably met Rousseau in 1907 through Jarry, who died that year, and used to attend Rousseau's soirees with a small crowd of painters, art dealers, and other inhabitants of Montmartre—Delaunay, Picasso, Braque, Jacob, and Vlaminck, but also Georges Duhamel, Jules Romains, Brancusi, Marie Laurencin, Soupault, and Fénéon.

The party was held by Picasso at the Bateau Lavoir, apparently to celebrate his acquisition, as old canvas from a rag dealer, of Rousseau's full-length *Portrait de Mlle M.* About 30 guests were invited to a meal at eight p.m. in the decorated and candlelit studio. A table had been improvised by placing planks on trestles, the chairs were rented, the crockery and glass borrowed, and the meal was partly ordered from a catering grocer. Apollinaire was to bring Rousseau, and the rest of Montmartre was invited for after dinner. Most of the guests had drunk too much before arriving. Even Marie Laurencin was tipsy, sang the songs her mother had taught her, fell on top of the pastries on the sofa, and quarrelled with Apollinaire, who sulked, wrote letters, and recited a toast in verse. Rousseau played his violin under a Chinese lantern which dripped hot wax on him all evening. Latecomers brought a donkey in with them, and the party went on until dawn. There are five eye-witness accounts, not surprisingly conflicting, and the evening has long been seen as a symbol of the exuberance of avant-garde Montmartre just before it disintegrated. Apollinaire's greatest achievements were its orchestration and promotion.

He experimented with opium and wrote for Eugène Montfort's *Les Marges* during 1909, first under the deliberately female pseudonym of Louise Lalanne, then later, under his own name, about his contemporaries in a column entitled "Les contemporains pittoresques." He was busy with appointments at newspaper and magazine offices, correcting proofs for his Briffaut series, giving readings, attending functions and exhibitions, and discussing literary matters. On 13 July 1909 André Salmon got married, and Apollinaire wrote a wedding poem, which appeared later in *Alcools*. In August 1911 he was imprisoned for a short time. A secretary-assistant of his called Gery Pieret had stolen two Iberian stone heads from the Louvre and sold them in 1907 to Picasso, who knew their provenance and was just entering on what is known as his Negro period. Then in 1911 an Italian stole the *Mona Lisa*. He took it to Florence two years later and it was, of course, recovered, but in the meanwhile there had been a huge fuss, involving a third statuette returned to the Louvre via *Paris-Journal*, which enjoyed enormous publicity while posing as the guardian of the public interest against lax officialdom.

Picasso and Apollinaire were too frightened of being seen to risk throwing the two stolen heads into the river, and one or other returned them via the newspaper offices. Somehow Apollinaire's connection with the heads through Pieret, although not Picasso's, was leaked, and the police were informed, probably on 7 August. It became evident that Apollinaire, while not condoning Pieret's thefts, had known about the statuettes—which the Louvre had either not missed, or whose loss its officials had concealed—and had helped him personally to get away from Paris. The Louvre had long been a joke with the avant-garde, and it took three or four days to clear Apollinaire. He was forced to spend at least three nights in prison, partly because the whole of officialdom had been made to look so foolish.

The whole incident caused Apollinaire much pain. The police had ransacked not only his flat, from which he subsequently moved, but his whole life, and they threatened to do as much to his friends, some of whom disclaimed close or even any acquaintance with him. Half Montmartre, knowing about Picasso's statuettes, could have been charged with conspiracy, and the police needed a conspiracy charge to compensate for the outrageously easy theft, in fact by a mad house painter, of the *Mona Lisa*. Apollinaire was not French, was terrified of deportation, and the police scattered charges until mud stuck. In 1912 the Briffaut brothers and he were nearly indicted for offences against public morality, and Marie Laurencin was forced by her mother to end her affair with him. The article linking Marie to the cubists was written in 1913, and her memory evoked the most poignant poems of *Alcools*. Apollinaire became the object of anti-semitic sentiment although he had no Jewish blood, and was attacked for his pornography. He wrote an account of his imprisonment for the publicity-avid *Paris-Journal*, which was seeking to prolong the incident, but the prison poems from *Alcools*, typically grouped under a punning title, and the reactions of his friends, all show how deeply unsettled Apollinaire was by the incident.

Picasso regarded Apollinaire as a great poet and was grateful to him for his promotional activities, but by 1912 he was fully aware that his friend lacked visual sensitivity and was perpetually drawn to what was new. Like Kahnweiler, Picasso was not surprised when Apollinaire made clear his allegiance to the "Section d'Or" painters who exhibited together that year, and had taken their name from the ratio between the length of a square's side and its diagonal. The group, whose focus was Jacques Villon's studio in Puteaux, comprised Villon and his brothers, Gleizes, La Fresnaye, Léger, Metzinger, Francis Picabia (see Dada) and his wife Gabrielle Buffet, Kupka, and Chagall. Apollinaire was unaware of their admiration for Cézanne, although he must have sensed the new lyricism they wished to introduce into what was already the cubist tradition. He also became the publicist of another subgroup, centred on Villon himself, Picabia, Delaunay, and Duchamp, which was moving at the same time towards further abstraction, and coined the term "orphic" to give them corporate identity.

In January 1912 Apollinaire became art critic of *Le Petit Bleu*, where he immediately defended the "futurists", whom he had already mentioned in the *Mercure* for November 1911. In February, largely to restore Apollinaire's self-confidence in the wake of the Louvre affair, André Billy and other close friends founded a new review, *Les Soirées de Paris*. Apollinaire wanted to use the magazine indiscriminately to promote all cubist painters, even Chirico, whose work none of them thought interesting, and ill-feeling was caused at the outset. When the review changed hands in September 1913, there was a three-month gap, and Apollinaire had much more editorial freedom to promote his favourite painters. He now chose Picasso, Rousseau, Derain, Matisse, and Vlaminck, a list which suggests that he was keeping a keen ear to the ground rather than indulging personal taste. He published the poem "Le pont Mirabeau" in his first number in February 1912, together with "Per te praesentit aruspex," which commemorates a brief affair entered into on the rebound from Marie Laurencin.

Apollinaire also published Cendrars, from whose poem about Easter in New York he was accused of borrowing too freely for his own "Zone." Later in 1912 he became friendly with Robert Delaunay, staying with him while waiting for preparations to be completed for a new flat. He probably wrote, or at least revised, his poem "Fenêtres" in Delaunay's studio, intending it to bear a relationship to Delaunay's non-figurative compositions. Apollinaire himself thought highly of the poem, regarding it as reflecting "a totally new aesthetic." It was published as a preface to the catalogue of Delaunay's exhibition in Berlin in December 1912, and André Billy has left an account of its apparently casual composition, which has subsequently been challenged by Robert and Sonia Delaunay.

Apollinaire had in fact been disparaging about Delaunay two years previously, but he was now beginning to regard cubism as old-fashioned, and was following his own taste in coming to admire Chirico and Chagall. His old liking for strong colour was reasserting itself, and "orphism" was extended to include Kandinsky and Mondrian. He met Picabia and Duchamp in October 1912 and in November he published his first unpunctuated poem, "Vendémiaire." *Alcools: poèmes 1898–1913* was published by the *Mercure de France* on 20 April 1913, with all punctuation removed from the poems in proof, a month after Apollinaire's *Méditations esthétiques: LES PEINTRES CUBISTES*, which contained reproductions of 40 cubist paintings. The typography of that title is important, as the capitalization of the second half rather than the first is the result of a commercial decision by the publisher, making it seem as if the book is unified in a way which Apollinaire neither intended nor claimed. Apollinaire paid for the printing of 60 copies of *Alcools* in articles, and the book sold only 350 copies in its first year, then four, seven, and five copies in the three succeeding years. By 1960

there had been well over 100 editions. Apollinaire's could have left a rich legacy. In fact his widow collected 36 francs in royalties in 1927. The reviews of *Alcools* were largely poor, with a particularly harsh piece from Duhamel, who spitefully threw in renewed allegations of plagiarism, mentioning Jacob and Salmon and raking up the old accusations against *L'Hérésiarque et Cie*. He was later forced to retract.

Under its new management *Les Soirées de Paris* was to be a distinguished review until its last issue in July-August 1914. The June number of that year contained the first of Apollinaire's "Calligrammes." Meanwhile he had written "L'antitradition futuriste, manifeste synthèse" for Marinetti, an iconoclastic but almost puerile release of fury no doubt occasioned by the hostile reviews of *Alcools*. He narrowly avoided having to fight two duels, and was dropped by *L'Intransigeant*, although within two months he was taken on by *Paris-Journal*, for which he wrote daily from May until the outbreak of war. An attempt to bring him together again with Marie Laurencin failed in the summer of 1913, and on 21 June 1914 she married a young German painter, Otto von Waëtjen. She spent the war in Spain and did not meet Apollinaire again. She was divorced after the war and never married again.

Apollinaire spent the summer of 1914 reporting on the Deauville season for *Comoedia*. Shortly after his return he tried to enlist although, as a foreigner, he was not obliged to. The application to enlist of 10 August was ignored, and Apollinaire made a second one, this time successfully, from Nîmes. He changed his name back to Kostrowitzky, was posted to the artillery but volunteered for much more arduous service with the infantry in the trenches, and rose to be a lieutenant. He was awarded French nationality on 9 March 1916, eight days before he was wounded in the head by shell splinters while reading a copy of the *Mercure*. The subsequent operation to relieve paralysis changed his appearance and left him open to the influenza which killed him on 9 November 1918.

In late 1914 Apollinaire had a very brief affair with Louise de Coligny-Châtillon ("Lou") after a 10-week courtship, and he received 76 love letters from October 1914 to September 1915. He also wrote a long series of often erotic letters (not all of which have been published) to Madeleine Pagès, whom he had met fleetingly on a train on 1 January 1915, referring to many of the principal incidents and relationships in his life. He spent two weeks leave with her and her family in December 1915, became engaged to her, but wrote letters to her similar to those he also wrote to Lou, and he later had another companion whom he did not mention to Madeleine. The posthumous *Ombre de mon amour* and *Tendre comme le souvenir* commemorate these relationships, as do many of the *Calligrammes* poems.

During the war Apollinaire continued to write short series of poems and his chronicle for the *Mercure*. The engagement with Madeleine was broken off after his injury in 1916, and Apollinaire attempted once again to lead a normal life in Paris. *Le Poète assassiné* was published on 26 October 1916. On 31 December some 90 of his friends gave a lunchtime banquet for him as the grand old man of the avant-garde. It was a reminiscence of those given for Zola, Verlaine, and Rousseau. The guests included Gide, Copeau, Romains, Cocteau, Salmon, Cendrars, Alfred Valette, Henri de Régnier, Paul Fort, Braque, Matisse, Vlaminck, Juan Gris, Picasso, Jacob, and Reverdy. Apollinaire was no longer eligible for active service and now worked in the censor's office. He published poems in the principal avant-garde magazines: Reverdy's *Nord-Sud*, whose first number appeared in March 1917 with a compliment to Apollinaire and contes by Tzara (see Dada) and Breton; Picabia's *391*, whose name was an allusion to Stieglitz's New York studio, where Rousseau's first ever one-man exhibition had been held in 1910, and Albert-Birot's *Sic* (see Cocteau).

In May 1917 Apollinaire wrote the programme for Cocteau's *Parade*, and on 24 June his "surrealist" *Les Mamelles de Tirésias* was given a stormy reception. When Apollinaire first coined the term he had considered "surnaturaliste (supernatural)" but had been unable to get round the theological connotations of the word. The programme note for *Parade* in which the word "surréaliste" first appeared was published in *Excelsior* on 18 May 1917. Cocteau, whom Apollinaire regarded as a dilettante, was mortified that the programme note barely mentioned him. The note was in fact chiefly devoted to the contributions of Satie, Picasso, and Massine. An important article on cubism appeared in the *Mercure* for 16 September 1917, and *Vitam impendere amori* was published on 10 November with illustrations by Rouveyre. *Calligrammes* appeared on 15 April 1918, and on 2 May Apollinaire married Jacqueline Kolb. His witnesses were Picasso and the art dealer Vollard. His final promotion to full lieutenant occurred on 28 July and he died on 9 November, four months before his mother. Shortly afterwards his brother died in Mexico.

WORKS

Apollinaire has been called "a ringmaster of the arts." His function was nearer to that of the showman beckoning passers-by into the fairground booth to watch the puppet charades. It is difficult to resist the image of the professional charlatan luring the bystanders inside to watch the poignantly comic harlequinades of Picasso's rose period canvases, or the openly sad gyrations of Marie Laurencin's clowns. Apollinaire was thrown off his balance by the affair of the Louvre statuettes, almost extinguished as a literary figure by his decision to enlist as a soldier in World War I, and virtually unknown as a poet until 1913. His reputation during his lifetime rested, as a result, on often perfunctory or sometimes posturing art journalism, pulp novels, and the promotion of artists, into which he could never inject the discernment of the connoisseur, but for which he had instead to rely on the thrusting skills of the impresario. Yet he presided over the launching of almost all the successive approaches to artistic innovation until the fracturing of western European culture by World War I, scarcely aware of the debris from which surrealism and dada (qq.v.) would emerge before art forms began to re-establish coherence and intelligibility.

Apollinaire came rightly to distrust his own taste. As an art critic, which is how he was chiefly known, he has had a bad press, especially from his painter friends. Few of the boisterous Montmartre circle, and few even of the readers of the little magazines in which his verse appeared, realized quite how clever it was, and how carefully the intentionally outrageous surface effects were polished to conceal the vulnerabilities, uncertainties, aspirations, and frustrations probed in the poems themselves. Apollinaire's strictly literary bequest is reducible to a couple of volumes of verse together with a number of further short cycles of poems written during the war. His art criticism has come to be regarded as merely of historical interest. Picasso

and Braque were right: for all his energetic thirst for experience, robust vitality, charm, and subtlety of wit, Apollinaire was not sensitive to plastic values. At its best, his art criticism combines a need for self-questioning with an effort to impose intelligibility on the types of innovation which he attempted to classify.

There is deliberate paradox, self-parody, perhaps even a touch of hoax in Apollinaire's writing about the "Douanier" Rousseau, so-called on account of the minor customs post he held from 1866, but as he came better to know and like Rousseau, so his enthusiasm for his work increased. The same is also true of his attitudes to Marinetti, Rouault, Delaunay, and Picabia. Marinetti's futurist manifesto was published in *Le Figaro* on 20 February 1909, but Apollinaire took no interest in the movement until he had met some of its adherents, like Umberto Boccioni and Gino Severini, in 1911. A revealing letter of 26 January 1912 to Ardengo Soffici, the Italian critic who had defended Baudelaire in *La Voce*, says of the futurists: "A vrai dire je ne connais pas encore leur peinture mais je me doute de ce qu'elle doit être (To tell the truth, I don't know their painting yet, but I can imagine what it must be like)." A fortnight later, on 7 and 9 February 1912, Apollinaire publicized the futurists' Paris exhibition, singled out the painters he had met, but attacked the new ideas of the new futurist manifesto of 11 April 1910. In almost all of what Apollinaire wrote on painting there was an amalgam of insight, punditry, and prejudice which sometimes descends into silliness, together with the potent ability to generate myths and communicate enthusiasms.

LES PEINTRES CUBISTES, published in 1913, a year after the *Du cubisme* of Gleizes and Metzinger, consists largely of reprinted articles from 1905–12, and has been the object of much disparagement. The real primary title, *Méditations esthétiques*, gives a much better view of the contents, which become more interesting when read as a poetic reflection rather than as a guide. Apollinaire was undoubtedly too categorical in his judgements, and his powers of intellectual analysis were also very limited, but he could feel sympathy not only for individual painters but also, once that was alight, for their aims and works. He therefore produced much promotional journalism which, while enthusiastic, was not intended to be as assertive on the level of artistic theory as it often reads.

The first section of the book, "Sur la peinture," concentrates on Picasso, and is a genuine, if metaphorical rather than analytical, reflection about painting. In a passage reprinted from 1908, for instance, flame is the "symbol of painting," and "the three plastic virtues," purity, unity, and truth, radiate from flame. This part of the book, not surprisingly, gives up to fortune the vulnerable hostage of a quite unsustainable classification of types of cubism. The second section contains nine vignettes of individual painters, and adds a sculptor, again giving Picasso the first place, but including Marie Laurencin as a cubist, which she was not and did not pretend to be. The insights are valuable, but there is also flamboyant cladding and intellectual flabbiness. Without Apollinaire's close personal association with the painters and his historical role in their promotion, the book would have been forgotten. It was in fact reprinted in 1922, but not again until 1950. Its failure as a collected volume lies chiefly in its presentation of cubism as merely a "necessary reaction" against impressionism. The *Chroniques d'art, 1902–1918* is entirely composed of reprinted journalism.

Apollinaire's critical writings on literature are limited to a few remarks on such subjects as the justification for republishing

Sade as the creator of sexual psychopathology, and Baudelaire's alleged inability to penetrate "the new spirit." In stating that the poet wanted to transform both nature and art into "something pernicious," Apollinaire's criticism of Baudelaire is clearly one-sided, if not actually wrong-minded. His dismissal of Claudel as a shadow of Rimbaud, creating a literature of images strung together like rosary beads, and of Laforgue as a poet with whom he is simply out of sympathy, together with his unbounded admiration for Nerval, confirm how great a part emotional sympathy played in the formation of Apollinaire's literary judgements.

He foresaw the importance that cinema and gramophone were to have for the cultural function of the printed word, but welcomed poetry's perpetual power to "surprise," implying the necessity for continuous innovation: "L'esprit nouveau est dans la surprise... *La surprise est le grand ressort nouveau* (The new spirit lies in surprise... *Surprise is the great new mechanism*)." In 1908 Apollinaire had written that the entirely new art "towards which we are moving" would relate to earlier painting as music does to literature: "Ce sera de la peinture pure, de même que la musique est de la littérature pure (It will be pure painting, just as music is pure literature)." That is simple rhetoric, snatched even at this date from some exaggerated distortion of the symbolist aesthetic, which merely replaces critical investigation with a pseudo-poetic expression of enthusiasm.

Yet Apollinaire was not quite an innovator at any price. He oscillates uncertainly between novelty and an ultimately conservative lyricism, such as that which overflows from his own poems, themselves revealingly often written in classical or even complex pre-classical metres. Even the most modernistic of Apollinaire's effects jostle with old-fashioned word and sound games. He seeks the impossibility of eternal lyrical feelings clothed in new artistic forms, created to express something different, or at any rate in forms put at the disposition of sensibilities attuned to the examination of sorts of experience which are anything but lyrical. He looks for the chimera in which shockingly modern means of expression are reconciled with new poetry's "quest for a lyricism which is both new and humanistic," as he said in his April 1908 lecture at the Salon des Indépendants. He wants both order and adventure, tradition and modernity, as impossible to combine as his sympathies, which are both internationally cosmopolitan and chauvinistically French, overcompensating for his foreignness of birth.

His fiction seldom surpasses the work of an agreeable raconteur, at his best when most relaxed and anecdotal. *L'Enchanteur pourrissant* may have been written as early as 1898. It first appeared as a serial in *Le Festin d'Esope* in 1904, before publication in volume form, with the addition of "Onirocritique," in 1909. The fable, developed from the 13th- century prose fiction *Merlin*, concerns a succession of visits paid to the wizard's tomb by the woman narrator, woven round the general theme of the division of the sexes. Both Merlin and the Lady of the Lake have an urge to possess which turns into rivalry and ends in a desire for death. The narrative overflows with fantasies and ideas, is episodic but monotonous, and could have been indefinitely prolonged. "Onirocritique" is a dream sequence whose images, conjured up rather than spontaneous, ambitiously evoke the apocalyptic vision of a form of creation put together out of what can be regarded as leftover pieces of the one we know.

L'Hérésiarque et Cie is a collection of stories, of which Apollinaire has left about 50, showing a slow diminution in the energy of his inventive fantasy. This volume was to have been called "Phantasmes" and in it some of the characters from *L'Enchanteur* return. The themes, again mythical and legendary, blend the mystical with the erotic, and are generally treated in traditional ways, displaying the fundamental psychological principles on which fairy tales and folklore narratives are generally based. Repentance is rewarded, trickery is successful, criminal behaviour can have virtuous motives, there is gratuitous violence, and there are gruesome fates. The contes are invariably the product of fantasy rather than imagination.

Le Poète assassiné of 1916, with interpolations made in the text after the break with Marie Laurencin, is longer but still episodic in form, a short self-parodying, half-poetic nouvelle. It adds a strongly autobiographical element to the mythologized fiction. The stories make a parade of erudition and show a fascination with the sound and sense of words, especially rare and foreign ones, which the poetry was to extend to an interest in their display on the page. The Rabelaisian hero Croniamantal gives an example of "poetry free from all fetters." It is one of Apollinaire's more extravagant linguistic fantasies, interesting only for its parody of the formal business card, with punctilious spacing and punctuation, and the inclusion in the nonsense of a number for the new-fangled telephone:

MAHÉVIDANOMI RENANOCALIPNODITOC
EXTARTINAP + v.s.
A. Z.
Tél.: 33–122 Pan : Pan
OeaoiiiioKTin
iiiiiiiiiiii

Les Mamelles de Tirésias is a boisterous mock-medieval piece of circus with Apollinaire's usual base of licentiousness. The play, written in 1903, is less interesting that the 1917 prologue, which uses the word "surrealism."

Apollinaire's chief claim to literary fame is his poetry. *Alcools: poèmes 1898–1913* is his most important monument. It is a collection of 55 poems carefully selected on the eve of World War I from Apollinaire's output over the 15 years since his 18th birthday. The order is neither haphazard nor chronological. "Zone" was written specifically to open the collection after "Vendémiaire" had been chosen to close it. There are 20 poems in the volume from Apollinaire's stay in Germany, but only nine are printed in the group "Rhénanes," and a dozen more are excluded altogether. The three poems commemorating the disappearance of Marie Laurencin from his life—"Le pont Mirabeau," in a complex medieval form, "Marie," and "Cors de chasse"—are scattered within the volume. In the proof the last stanza of "Le larron" overflowed on to a page of its own. Apollinaire simply cut it out and used the resulting free page for the one-line multiple pun poem "Chantre," which runs:

Et l'unique cordeau des trompettes marines

The literal meaning is "And the single string of marine trumpets," but the line could mean "And the solitary row of megaphones," while "cordeau" means a string, as of beads, or, as "corps d'eau," a stretch of water, or, as "cor d'eau," a sea horn, which would be a marine trumpet, although "trompette marine" is a one-stringed musical instrument as well as a shellfish. The line is a classical Alexandrine and the last word provides a rhythmic cadence which would not be out of place in the romantic (q.v.) poetry of Lamartine. The interplay of sound and meaning, and the visual effect of the one-line page, approach the sort of "simultaneity" which Apollinaire saw as the goal of the cubist movement, conquering duration as the cubists had conquered perspective.

The best poems are those which depend not on skilful verbal acrostics, but on disappointed love. They exhibit most poignantly the tension between aspiration and fulfilment running through the collection. "Zone" is a poem of immense hope and disappointment on many more planes than that of love. It is crammed with erudition, and builds on the paradox of regarding all that is most conventional and unimaginative, like the Catholic Church of Pius X, as united with all that is most modern, like the aeroplane. The result is a multiple resonance in which the new century soars like a bird, and Christ the aviator holds the world altitude record, while the poet, the "you" of the poem, goes back to Auteuil and sleeps surrounded by fetishes from Oceania or Guinea, "lower Christs of dimmer hopes." The last line expresses the bitterness of the poet's disillusion in the vision of a rising sun, communicated by the sound of the words as well as by the sense, but makes no explicit mention of red, the colour of sunrises and blood, which links the day's dawn, the hour of execution by guillotine, to the severed neck. In its entirety it reads:

Soleil cou coupé

Sun slit neck/throat)

The zone is itself situated somewhere on the margins of Paris and of life. The poem is a recollection which starts by repudiating what is old, and goes on to create in a second one-line stanza the striking image of the Eiffel Tower as a shepherdess herding her flocks of bleating bridges:

Bergère ô tour Eiffel le troupeau des ponts bêle ce matin

(Shepherdess, oh Eiffel Tower, the flock of bridges is bleating this morning).

The metre of the poem is complex, and the disruption of meaning within this line, as the poet switches between Paris and sheep, clashes with the conversational normality of its syntax and register. It is difficult to decide whether the line works better with punctuation, emphasizing the syntax, or without, emphasizing the dislocation of imagery. The poem, starting with dawn and ending with a new sunrise and the poet's death, incidentally affirms some episode of adolescent religiosity by referring to an all-night vigil in the college chapel as if it were a historical event. This is not only most unlikely, it also shows Apollinaire writing in registers of language which still bewilder his exegetes and biographers. Apollinaire generally uses statement as if it were a not even poetically enhanced statement of fact. He is often assumed to be affirming what he teasingly knows ought to be taken with a pinch of salt, although he offers no clues to his register, and indeed often simply lies with a straight face, for the fun of it, as when he gave a New York dateline to reports of happenings he had simply invented.

Calligrammes, subtitled *poèmes de la paix et de la guerre*, is about events less private than those of *Alcools* and, in particular, treats of the wartime theme of the absence of the soldier's loved one. There is greater stylistic unity and a more determined modernity than in the earlier volume, and Apollinaire is now aware of the challenge of combining staidly traditional emotions with stridently modern poetic forms. He closes the collection with a masterful and moving poem, "La jolie rousse," containing a clear premonition of death in a resumé of his life:

Je juge cette longue querelle de la tradition et de l'invention
De l'Ordre et de l'Aventure

(I sit in judgement on that long quarrel between tradition and innovation / Between Order and Adventure).

Apollinaire defended his "calligrammes"—witty little poems printed in the form of stylized doodles—as the brilliant apotheosis of free verse typography at a moment when typography seemed to him to be becoming unnecessary. He pretended to be unaware of earlier picturegrams, and was certainly unaware of the danger of overloading his verse with self-parody, successfully tempting solemn critics to miss his jokes and amused readers to overlook the poetry, both of them in hordes, so frequently did Apollinaire fall off his tightrope.

Almost all the poems, although not "La jolie rousse," were written before his transfer to the infantry and trench warfare on 22 November 1915. Only three were written after the trepanning operation which changed Apollinaire's physical appearance, and must have made him half-aware that he had not long to live. The order of the poems reflects Apollinaire's evolving experience. The accusation, by Breton and Aragon, that his poetry showed an inadequate response to the war is surely wrong, even if he did take some refuge in clever verbal frivolities. Even the refusal to avert to danger can be a form of courage, and political commitment is not the only form of human response apposite to the cultural trauma inflicted by war. Apollinaire was the brilliantly accomplished showman of the Montmartre school of painters and a great poet, but one whose achievement was seldom sustained, staccato in its successes and erratic in its taste. It was rarely balanced enough to create such perfect masterpieces as "Zone" or such brilliant miniatures as "Crépuscule," which, first sent on a postcard to Picasso in November 1905, with that slightest of final twists of self-parody, must be among the most accomplished poems in the French language.

PUBLICATIONS

Collections

Oeuvres poétiques, Bibliothèque de la Pléiade, 1956
Oeuvres complètes, edited by Michel Décaudin, 4 vols., 1965–66
Oeuvres en prose, Bibliothèque de la Pléiade, edited by Michel Décaudin, 1977

Verse

Le Bestiaire; ou, Cortège d'Orphée. 1911; as *Le Bestiaire* (in English), 1977
Alcools: Poèmes 1898–1913, 1913; edited by Tristan Tzara, 1953, and Garnet Rees, 1975; as *Alcools* (in English), 1964

Case d'armons, 1915
Vitam impendere amori, 1917
Calligrammes: Poèmes de la paix et de la guerre, 1918
Le Cortège priapique, 1925
Julie; ou, La Rose, 1927
Le Condor et le morpion, 1931
Ombre de mon amour, 1947; revised edition, as *Poèmes à Lou*, 1955
Le Guetteur mélancolique, 1952
Tendre comme le souvenir, 1952
Selected Poems, edited by Oliver Bernard, 1956

Plays

Les Mamelles de Tirésias (produced 1917), 1918
Couleur du temps (produced 1918), 1949
Casanova, 1952
La Température, with André Salmon (produced 1975), in *Oeuvres en prose*, 1977

Fiction

Les Exploits d'un jeune Don Juan, 1907
Les Onze mille verges, 1907; as *The Debauched Hospodar*, 1958; as *Les Onze Mille Verges* (in English), 1979
L'Enchanteur pourrissant, 1909
L'Hérésiarque et Cie, 1910; selection, as *Contes choisis*, 1922; as *The Heresiarch and Company*, 1965
La Fin de Babylone, 1914
Les Trois Don Juan, 1915
Le Poète assassiné, 1916; edited by Michel Décaudin, 1959; as *The Assassinated Poet*, 1923
La Femme assise, 1920
Les Epingles: contes, 1928
Que faire?, 1950
The Wandering Jew and Other Stories, 1965

Other

Méditations esthétiques: LES PEINTRES CUBISTES, 1913; edited by Leroy C. Breunig and J.-Cl. Chevalier, 1965; as *The Cubist Painters: Aesthetic Meditations 1913*, 1949
Le Flâneur des deux rives, 1918
Il y a, 1925
Anecdotiques, 1926
Contemporains pittoresques, 1929
Oeuvres érotiques complètes (verse and prose), 3 vols., 1934
L'Esprit nouveau et les poètes, 1946
Lettres à sa marraine, 1948
Selected Writings, edited by Roger Shattuck, 1950
Chroniques d'art, 1902–1918, edited by Leroy C. Breunig, 1961; as *On Art*, 1972
Correspondance, with André Level, edited by Brigitte Level, 1976
Editor, *Chronique des grands siècles de la France*, 1912

Critical studies

Adéma, Marcel, *Apollinaire*, 1954
Carmody, Francis J., *The Evolution of Apollinaire's Politics 1901–1914*, 1963

Steegmuller, Francis, *Apollinaire: Poet among Painters*, 1963
Davies, Margaret, *Apollinaire* (in English), 1964
Bates, Scott, *Apollinaire* (in English), 1967
Breunig, Leroy C., *Apollinaire* (in English), 1969
Shattuck, Roger, *The Banquet Years: The Origins of the Avant-Garde in France: 1885 to World War I*, revised edition, 1969
Stamelman, Richard Howard, *The Drama of Self in Apollinaire's Alcools*, 1975
Little, Roger, *Apollinaire*, 1976
Buckley, Harry E., *Apollinaire as an Art Critic*, 1981
Berry, David, *The Creative Vision of Apollinaire*, 1982

———

ARAGON, Louis, 1897–1982.

Poet, novelist, and political propagandist.

LIFE

Aragon's parents kept a "pension" in the bourgeois but not really smart 16th arrondissement of Paris. At 11 Aragon was given an anthology of Barrès as a school prize. It made him determined to become a writer, and he started reading widely, especially the great Russians, to whom he was introduced by his mother. She did, however, confiscate his Gorky, who thereafter held a fascination for him and, according to Aragon, directed his religious energies when, while still a child, he ceased to believe in God. He attended the Lycée Carnot until 1916, passed his baccalauréat, and started to study medicine, entering the army as a medical aide in 1917. He met Breton, also in the medical corps, and Soupault, and was awarded the Croix de Guerre for his part in the final operations of the war. He wrote a long autobiographical poem *Le Roman inachevé*, took part in the occupation of the Rhineland, and sided with the miners he was under orders to shoot for refusing to return to dangerous conditions underground. This experience gave rise to what was to be a life-long commitment to communism. Aragon came to hate the war, never mentioned it, and refused to be classified as a war veteran.

On his return to Paris Aragon, Breton, and Soupault co-founded *Littérature*, a review devoted to avant-garde poetry, whose first number contained some of the poems which Aragon was later to include in *Feu de joie*. The review became associated with Tristan Tzara's dada (q.v.) group. Aragon and his companions eventually abandoned dada, whose credo was totally destructive of established values, creating surrealism (q.v.) instead. At first politics and the Russian revolution held no particular significance for the surrealists, intent merely on the destruction of established ideas and conscious associations. The turning point was the Moroccan war of 1925, and henceforth the surrealist movement in France was increasingly committed to social change. In this way it became a movement of reconstruction, for Aragon necessarily socialist, aiming to ensure a better life for man. No political revolution was possible unless its ideology had previously been the subject of a sufficiently forceful imaginative investigation.

Surrealism, adopting what it took to be Freud's ideas, also regarded love as the agent which tapped the forces of the unconscious, a view which had a powerful effect on Aragon. For Aragon, love is conceived as opening the way to a synthesis of the real and the marvellous. His wife, Elsa Triolet, assumed the role for him of the mythical woman, inspiring his best poetry and providing him with his political initiation. As he moved beyond his surrealist phase, which he came to regard as part of the innocence and excitement of youth, Aragon found in love not the generalized mystical experience which the surrealists believed it to be, but commitment to another person and, as he put it, through her to mankind.

Before returning to poetry in the middle of the decade, Aragon published his first major prose works in the early 1920s, *Anicet; ou, Le Panorama roman*, *Les Aventures de Télémaque*, and a work inspired by his travels in Germany, *Les Plaisirs de la capitale*, published in Berlin in 1923. On 28 November 1928, while sitting in a Montparnasse café, Aragon was invited to join Mayakovsky at his table. The next day he met his future wife, Mayakovsky's sister-in-law Elsa. It was she who persuaded him of the significance of the Russian revolution, and it was Mayakovsky who encouraged him to adopt the view that it was a writer's duty to promote a better world. After initial hesitation on his part Aragon had already been admitted to the communist party with Breton and Eluard in 1927, but his political commitment and his growing disillusion with surrealism plunged him into a personal crisis in 1929, when he attempted to commit suicide.

In 1930 he made a number of journeys to the USSR and attended the congress of revolutionary writers in Karkov. While in the Soviet Union he wrote "Front rouge," a poem attacking the French government and calling for its dismissal. This earned him a five-year suspended sentence in 1932. The surrealists supported him, but on the grounds of principles which Aragon could not now accept, and he therefore repudiated their defence. He had broken with the group in 1931 and was now fully dedicated to prosecuting the communist cause, although he continued to look back on his surrealist years as his truly formative ones.

From 1932 until the war Aragon's activity was uniquely directed towards political ends, whether as poet, novelist, journalist for the communist *L'Humanité*, pamphleteer, or simply as political activist, and his publications reflect this dedication. This is true even of the novels *Les Cloches de Bâle* and *Les Beaux Quartiers* of 1936, which Aragon finished at sea while on his way to see Gorky in Russia before his death, and which won the Prix Renaudot. A year previously he had become joint secretary of the Association of Writers for the Defence of Culture. In 1937 Aragon and Elsa visited Spain, and Aragon became co-editor of the communist newspaper *Ce Soir*, for which he wrote a defence of the Nazi–Soviet pact in 1939, holding that it did nothing to invalidate the Franco-Soviet agreement. On account of this article he was forced to take refuge in the Chilean embassy.

In 1939 Aragon was called up and served in a medical brigade. He was taken prisoner, escaped, and received the Croix de Guerre twice and the Médaille Militaire. During the occupation, he lived in Nice, Lyons, and the Drôme, and epitomized for many in France and elsewhere the spirit of the Resistance movement. He published six volumes of poetry and wrote for a variety of clandestine publications the pieces later collected in *Servitude et grandeur des Français* and the two volumes of *L'Homme communiste* (1946 and 1953). In 1945 he signed the clemency petition for Brasillach, whom de Gaulle was to have shot for collaboration.

After the liberation Aragon again devoted himself to the communist cause, becoming director of the revived *Ce Soir* in 1947. He was deprived of his civil liberties for 10 years on account of one of his editorials. In 1949 he joined the staff of the newspaper *Les Lettres Françaises* and in 1953 became its director when *Ce Soir* closed. In 1950 he arranged with Gallimard for the publication of a number of contemporary Russian works, and in 1957 he received the Lenin peace prize. Honorary doctorates were conferred on him by Prague (1963) and Moscow (1965). Aragon condoned the Russian intervention in Hungary in 1956, but finally spoke out against the Soviet trials of Sinyavsky and Daniel in 1966, and condemned with the French Communist Party the Russian intervention in Czechoslovakia in 1968. Elsa died in 1970. The Soviet authorities reacted strongly to Aragon's break with them, denouncing Elsa Triolet's sister for her influence on Mayakovsky.

There is an ambivalence in Aragon, clearly revealed during the war but discernible before it, between his roots in French literary tradition, the source of his patriotism, and his writer's desire to create a better society for mankind, which led him from dada to a life devoted to communism. He was clearly a man of extraordinary charm.

WORKS

Feu de joie is a collection of only 25 poems associated with the dadaist aim to destroy all established systems of value, although the volume also displays a trust in beauty, an admiration for charm, and a nostalgia for the pure joys of childhood. It was followed by *Anicet; ou, Le Panorama roman*, a philosophical fable nearer to Diderot than to Voltaire. The fable, which is about personal freedom and love, involves a meeting between the poet Anicet, who is marked out by his inability to retain from his schooling anything except the laws of relativity and of the three dramatic unities, and Rimbaud, who teaches him the supreme value of love. The story is told by a narrator, and the "roman" of the title is a repudiation of the surrealists' total dismissal of the traditional novel. Anicet is initiated into the cult of Mirabelle, symbolizing both woman and urban beauty, by destroying ancient paintings to make way for modern beauty. Fellow members of the cult include ill-disguised versions of Breton, Cocteau, Chaplin, Valéry, Picasso, Vaché, and a blend of Jacob and Reverdy. The ultimate moral of the story is the interchangeability of aesthetic and ethical frames of reference.

Les Aventures de Télémaque of 1922 is modelled on the work of the same title by Fénelon, and marks Aragon's switch to surrealism. In Aragon's version of the story Télémaque's tutor, Mentor, now preaches dadaist nihilism, which is rejected by Télémaque, who hurls himself off a cliff to prove his freedom. Mentor says that Télémaque's death proves only his enslavement, but he himself is crushed by a loose rock, while "the Lord God" laughs uncontrollably. The work, clearly drawing on Gide's *Les Caves du Vatican*, simply touches on the possibility that man can never be free and that the forces shaping his destiny are evil, taking Fénelon's christianized version of the Greek fable and transposing it into an original Greek register. This book draws and demands from the reader an obviously wide philosophical and literary culture.

The second collection of poems, *Le Mouvement perpétuel*, published in 1926, was intended to be shocking and offensive and is devoted largely to surrealist themes, especially the problems of language, imagination, and consciousness. It includes the already published "Une vague de rêves," a manifesto containing a theory of the image. Aragon is clearly inspired by Apollinaire, and most of the poems are more carefully wrought than appears at first sight. In the same year Aragon published *Le Paysan de Paris*, the highpoint of Aragon's surrealistic effort to bathe in a new light the ordinary, even the sordid and especially the technical, but also routine inner-city objects and events of everyday experience, revealing the marvellous aspect which the imagination can show them to contain. Aragon appears here to have been using Baudelaire as a prototype. The fusion of dream and reality, often investigated by avant-garde writers at the turn of the century, is communicated through images. Love gives access to the absolute, and poetry to love.

Le Traité du style of 1928 includes an attack on orthodox contemporary writers, including Mauriac, Gide, and Valéry, on established classics, and on those Aragon saw as exploiting Einstein, Freud, and Rimbaud. The second part of the work elaborates surrealist theory, though Aragon now regards surrealism as offering insights which must be accepted only selectively. *La Peinture au défi* of 1930, Aragon's last surrealist work, maintains that the marvellous revealed by the imagination is always moral in nature. *La Grande Gaieté* of 1929 marks the crisis in Aragon's life which culminated in his attempted suicide. He emerged from this crisis not only a communist, but a writer devoted to the depiction of reality, and not to its destruction. The collection, which contains further satirical portraits, shifts towards a new type of imagery. Aragon now relies on images to reinforce the real, not to achieve surrealistic tensions by disrupting connecting links. *Persécuté persécuteur* of 1931 was still published by the Editions Surréalistes. It is the first politically committed volume of communist verse and contains the celebrated "Front rouge" on the class struggle and its economic basis, a satire with some revolutionary ardour, as well as Aragon's first love poem to Elsa, "Je ne sais pas jouer au golf."

In 1934 Aragon published *Les Cloches de Bâle*, the first in the series "Le monde réel," which was completed by *Les Beaux Quartiers, Les Voyageurs de l'Impériale*, and *Aurélien*. Aragon stated that he needed to read and subsequently to write novels in order to give outward form to the sort of imagination where "even the most miserable can find love, beauty, music, and everything that makes the greatness of dreams and the humanity of man." The result, of course, is novels which do not so much throw light on experience as fantasize about it. The tetralogy presents the history of the class struggle from 1880 to 1930. Elsa did not like the first part of *Les Cloches*, which is largely devoted to the double standards applied by bourgeois society as a means of protecting itself. The second part concerns a fictional Cathérine and the real Clara Zetkin, one of the founders of the German communist party. Cathérine is a rich woman who sympathizes too simplistically with the working class, breaks with her lover, who does not, and seeks to find meaning in her life through a group of Paris anarchists whose crippled leader is beaten to death by the police. Cathérine attempts suicide, meets an idealized communist worker, and gropes towards the strongly feminist pacifism personified in Clara.

Les Beaux Quartiers also mixes history and fiction and takes its principal characters from the well-off classes. Once again the characters stand for ideas, values, ways of looking at the world, showing at most signs of personal compromise rather than serious conflict. The third volume in the series, *Les Voyageurs de l'Impériale*, contrasts those who seek only to preserve their comforts with those who seek to become members of a true human community. Less and less interested in writing novels, Aragon now began his practice of interjecting personal comments into the narrative. *Aurélien* mixes autobiography and fiction. It concerns a well-off young man, a survivor of World War I, who finds himself unable to return the absolute love offered him by a young woman, Bérénice. Aragon adds an epilogue from World War II. Both Aurélien and Bérénice have married. Aurélien now discovers how much he still loves Bérénice, but in her quest for the absolute she has embraced a political ideal.

To the tetralogy can be added the six volumes of *Les Communistes*, a work which virtually abandons any pretence at being a novel. It avoids psychological analysis, and the characters' reactions are determined purely by class. The work is a glorification of the role of women in the proletariat's struggle and is dominated by party dogma. Aragon knew, and in his autobiographical *J'abats mon jeu* of 1959 admitted, that essentially he was not a novelist. The dangers of his approach are not only sentimentality and formlessness, both of which he failed to avoid, but also a lack of feeling for what the novel in all its forms does best, which is to explore the meaning of some part of human experience. The most highly praised of Aragon's novels, *La Semaine sainte*, recounts the events of Holy Week 1815 from the news of Napoleon's escape from Elba to the disintegration of the entourage of Louis XVIII on the Belgian border on Holy Saturday. Aragon's criticism of his own work here is that it includes too much verifiable historical detail, "This is not a historical novel, but an impudent exploitation of history." The novel contains the by now usual attempt at a moral paradigm and a hopeful ending—which nothing in the work itself justifies—in anticipation of man's transformation and radiant future.

Aragon's novelistic technique now included not only interpolated personal interjections but also flashbacks and visions of the future, devices to be used increasingly in the last two novels. *La Mise à mort* of 1965 is an ambitious work with passages of poetic prose, history, and personal reflection. It includes three short stories about the multiple personalities contained within a single individual. *Blanche; ou, L'Oubli* recounts the effort of its protagonist, Geoffroy Gaiffier, to regain the affections of his wife Blanche, who had left him 20 years earlier, by reading and writing about her. The book becomes, according to Aragon, a theory of the novel, which he regards as a means of communicating knowledge, particularly love. Like its predecessor, it shows Aragon's gradual disillusion with Marxism. Three books play as big a role in this novel as any of the characters.

As an author Aragon is best remembered as a late-developing poet whose best work belongs to World War II or later and is dominated by his love for his wife Elsa and by his feelings for France and the Resistance. He believed in using rhyme, although he adopted Apollinaire's new definition of masculine and feminine rhymes, and freely ran the rhymed lines beyond the end of the printed ones. This created a rhyme scheme impossible to translate, and Aragon much preferred his work to be translated into prose. His theory on rhyme appeared in *Le Rime en 1940*. The first war-time collection, *Le Crève-coeur*, reflecting the poet's patriotic feelings until just after the defeat of France, was published in London, Canada, and Algiers. *Les Yeux d'Elsa* contains poems written from December 1940 to February 1942 in the unoccupied zone. The preface continues the defence of rhyme, which Aragon considered especially important in the establishment of contact between the poet and the people, and the poems themselves extensively exploit images of darkness and night. *Le Musée Grévin* is a long poem full of irony and invective, modelled on Hugo's *Les Châtiments*, which ends with a note of hope and a panegyric on the France of the future. The popular *Brocéliande* contrasts the mythical heroes of Celtic legend with Nazi racial myth. The war-time alliance between Catholics and communists begins to be reflected in Aragon's poems as he assumes the charge of spokesman for those who fought or fell for France.

The Elsa poetry mourns Aragon's separation from his wife during the war and also the impossibility of true joy even together in the face of France's plight. *Cantique à Elsa* is a long autobiographical poem, while *Les Yeux d'Elsa* exalts Elsa to the ranks of the legendary objects of devotion, Petrarch's Laura and Helen of Troy. After the war Aragon wrote a further series of long autobiographical poems, all of them devoted to the praise of Elsa. *Les Yeux et la mémoire* is inspired by Elsa's novel based on the hydrogen bomb and intertwines references to Aragon's love with allusions to contemporary events. *Le Roman inachevé* is a verse romance, introspective rather than political, while the long *Elsa* is really a series of love poems, including a one-act play entitled "La chambre d'Elsa." In 1960 Aragon published *Les Poètes*, a work which exalts the function of poetry. The series of collections of poems ends with *Il ne m'est Paris que d'Elsa* and *Le Voyage de Hollande*, both published in 1964 and in each of which Elsa gives meaning to the poet's surroundings, and *Le Fou d'Elsa*. Written in six parts, with an epilogue containing some 200 passages of prose and verse, this last work deals with the fall of Granada in 1492 before switching to Elsa's own time.

Aragon wrote easily and prolifically. Both his early prose, written for a surrealist elite, and his late verse have caught the public imagination. It is noteworthy that even his love poetry was partly political, and that most of his literary energies were deployed in accordance with the rules and purposes of a group, dadaist, surrealist, or communist, within the confines of which he only gradually asserted his personal independence. He will be remembered as a leading communist of the Resistance, but it is as yet too early to say how well his literary reputation will survive, or on what works it will rest.

PUBLICATIONS

Feu de joie, 1920
Anicet; ou, Le Panorama roman, 1921
Les Aventures de Télémaque, 1922
Les Plaisirs de la capitale, 1923
Le Libertinage, 1924; as *The Mirror-Wardrobe one Fine Evening* (short play), 1964
Une vague de rêves, 1924
Le Mouvement perpétuel, 1926
Le Paysan de Paris, 1926
Le Traité du style, 1928
La Grande Gaieté, 1929
La Peinture au défi, 1930
Persécuté persécuteur, 1931
Les Cloches de Bâle, 1934; as *Bells of Basel*, 1936

Hourra l'Oural, 1934
Pour un réalisme socialiste, 1935
Les Beaux Quartiers, 1936; as *Residential Quarter*, 1938
Le Crève-coeur, 1941
Cantique à Elsa, 1941
Les Voyageurs de l'Impériale, 1942; as *The Century was Young*, 1941
Les Yeux d'Elsa, 1942
Brocéliande, 1942
En français dans le texte, 1943
Le Musée Grévin, 1943
Aurélien, 1944; as *Aurélien* (in English), 1947
La Diane française, 1945
Servitude et grandeur des Français, 1945
L'Enseigne de Gerseint, 1946
L'Homme communiste, vol.1, 1946; vol.2, 1953
Apologie du luxe, 1946
La Culture et les hommes, 1947
Chroniques du bel canto, 1947
Le Nouveau Crève-coeur, 1948
Les Communistes, 6 vols., 1949–51
L'Exemple de Courbet, 1952
Hugo, poète réaliste, 1952
Avez-vous lu Victor Hugo?, 1952
Le Neveu de M. Duval, 1953
Journal d'une poésie nationale, 1954
Mes caravanes et autres poèmes, 1954
La Lumière de Stendhal, 1954
Les Yeux et la mémoire, 1954
Littératures soviétiques, 1955
Le Roman inachevé, 1956
La Semaine sainte, 1958; as *Holy Week*, 1962
Elsa, 1959
J'abats mon jeu, 1959
Entretiens sur le musée de Dresde, with Jean Cocteau, 1959
Les Poètes, 1960
Histoire parallèle (URSS-USA), with André Maurois, 4 vols., 1962; Aragon's two volumes as *A History of the USSR from Lenin to Kruschev*, 1964
Le Fou d'Elsa, 1963
Il ne m'est Paris que d'Elsa, 1964
Le Voyage de Hollande, 1964
Entretiens avec Francis Crémieux, 1964
La Mise à mort, 1965
Les Collages, 1965
Élégie à Pablo Neruda, 1966
Blanche; ou, L'Oubli, 1967

Translator

La Chasse au snark, by Lewis Carroll 1928
Cinq sonnets de Pétrarque, 1947
Djamilia, by Tchinghiz Aitmatov, 1959

Critical studies

Josephson, Hannah, and Malcolm Cowley (editors), *Aragon: Poet of the French Resistance*, 1945
Caute, David, *Communism and the French Intellectuals*, 1964
Becker, Lucille F., *Louis Aragon* (in English), 1971

ART POUR L'ART, (L')

See also Gautier and Parnasse, (Le).

———

ARTAUD, Antonin, 1896–1948.

Actor, producer, and writer on and for the theatre.

Although Artaud's own theoretical and practical work is of only marginal significance in the context of the revitalization of Parisian theatre between the wars, his influence on its major dramatists, actors, and directors was profound, and his views were sufficiently radical to need serious consideration in the total context of dramatic writing between 1920 and the generation of Beckett and Ionesco.

His parents were first cousins, his grandmothers being sisters. They were Greek, and Artaud spent vacations with them during what was apparently a hauntingly unhappy childhood. At school he wrote poetry, painted, drew, and read, notably Baudelaire and Poe, but at 19 he underwent a serious depression, destroyed everything he had written, and got rid of both his library and his friends. After a spell in a clinic he was drafted for military service but was discharged, for sleep walking as he alleges, and spent further periods in sanatoriums, including two years at the Chanet clinic in Switzerland. On his return he wanted to open a theatre in a factory, and in 1920 his parents sent him to Paris to try and establish himself in an artistic career. He lived with a doctor who had his own review, *Demain*.

In Paris Artaud met Max Jacob and began to publish poems and essays in the more highly regarded reviews. Until 1924 he worked for the actor and producer Dullin, who now had his own company, with an outstanding reputation for experimental theatre, at the Théâtre de l'Atelier. There Artaud had his one and only love affair, broken off in 1927. He tried to alleviate his financial difficulties by taking small acting parts and working in film. In 1922 he had endeavoured to break his dependence on laudanum and opium, and from 1924, the year his father died, he lived with his mother in the suburb of Passy. Jacques Rivière had turned down some poems Artaud had submitted to the *Nouvelle Revue Française* (*NRF*, q.v.), but continued to correspond with him about poetry. Later in 1924 the *NRF* published this correspondence, which attracted considerable attention.

That same year Artaud also formed a close association with André Breton and the surrealist (q.v.) group, editing the third number of their official review, *La Révolution Surréaliste*. He remained fully committed to the surrealists, who were not interested in either Artaud's theatre or the serious problems occasioned by his health, only until 1926. During this period he wrote *L'Ombilic des limbes* and the less literary *Le Pèse-nerfs*, two collections of verse and prose with letters, a scenario, a play, and an assortment of fragments which develop the views expressed in the correspondence with Rivière and increasingly emphasize the intellectually debilitating effects of physical pain.

The first play in the first collection, *Le Jet de sang*, is almost wholly constituted by the absurd juxtaposition of unconnected objects accompanied by non-sequiturs in the dialogue. Nothing

has any logical link with anything else, and the "events" are both shocking and absurd. Physical metamorphoses occur without reason. The terse, abbreviated style accentuates the gap between object and perception, making the central surrealist point that the categories we impose on experience are themselves as demanding and incapable of justification as the arbitrary, haphazard proliferation and transformation of the objects themselves.

Artaud was not interested in demonstrating the absurdity of capitalist social and economic orders, and the surrealist commitment to communism irritated him. He obtained literary and financial backing to found the Théâtre Alfred Jarry, publishing its manifesto in the *NRF* for November 1926. The theatre put on plays by Artaud, Roger Vitrac, and Robert Aron in 1927. These were followed in January 1928 by a forbidden film and an attack on Claudel, and in June by a famous performance of Strindberg's *Dream Play*, which offended the surrealists. The company folded for lack of funds in 1929. Artaud had been living meanwhile on what he had earned from acting in films. Only one film script of his was ever produced and he considered the production a betrayal. He tried and failed to found a film company, continuing to seek an artistic forum he could control.

Much impressed by a Balinese troupe he had seen in 1931, Artaud became increasingly convinced of the theatrical importance of physical gesture. Drama, in his view, must be a primitive ritual concerned only with the most profound human feelings and the most implacable forces. The conventions of the modern theatre—scenes, acts, speeches, characters, plots, and proscenium arch—must give way to irrational "assemblages of sounds" and pantomime. Gestures must symbolize ideas, and strange objects hostile cosmic forces. The stage must surround the audience, whose feeling of security must be destroyed in order to revive a sense of the cosmic forces both within and without.

Artaud worked closely with Louis Jouvet, trying to free himself from financial dependence on films and working towards the foundation of a radically new theatre based on revolutionary dramatic principles. The result was the Théâtre de la Cruauté—which opened and closed in 1935 after 17 performances of the only play it staged, Artaud's *Les Cenci*—and the collection of articles, speeches, manifestoes, and lectures composed from 1931 to 1933 and appearing as *Le Théâtre et son double*, of which Gallimard printed 100,000 copies.

Artaud was now living off what he could scrape together from writing. Two further attempts to give up drugs in 1932 and 1935 had failed, and all his hopes were pinned on *Les Cenci*, an amalgam of texts from Shelley and Stendhal adapted into a play which he himself directed, designed, and in which he played the leading part. French society was blamed for the coolness of the play's reception, although some of the ideas embodied in it have powerfully influenced subsequent dramatic theory.

Artaud now succeeded in attracting support for a visit to Mexico, which turned out to be a disappointment. He was deeply changed, however, by his visit to the Tarahumara Indians, in whose traditional indigenous culture he saw the prospect of Europe's salvation. His apocalyptic ideas met with little enthusiasm on his return to Paris and, although he became engaged briefly to a Belgian woman, he dabbled more and more in the esoteric–tarot, astrology, and the occult in particular. He reestablished his friendship with Breton and must have enjoyed lucid intervals along with his paranoid delusions. One such delusion was his belief that a cane which had been given to him dated from the time of Jesus and was the one used by St Patrick to drive the snakes out of Ireland. He believed he was the prophet of a destruction and a renewal to come, a message he preached in Ireland in 1937 until he was deported and the cane had been confiscated.

On his return to France he was diagnosed as schizophrenic and confined to a series of asylums, where he wrote vividly about his misery, isolation, and virtual starvation. He was sent to Rodez and received art therapy, shock and chemical treatments. He translated and wrote essays as well as letters, and became a fervent Christian before ultimately repudiating Christianity. Arthur Adamov finally secured his release. In order to raise some funds for him a gala benefit was held at the Sarah Bernhardt Theatre and virtually every major French writer and painter, from Sartre to Picasso, gave work to an auction. Artaud's literary output now became a torrent. On 13 January 1947 he attempted a lecture, and the evening was only saved from being an embarrassing disaster by Gide's timely and well-calculated intervention.

Artaud was awarded the Sainte-Beuve prize for literature for an essay on Van Gogh accusing society of forcing genius to suicide, and in July 1947 he held an exhibition of his own paintings and drawings. He wrote incessantly. There is controversy surrounding the cause of his death. He may have been in intolerable pain and deliberately have taken an overdose. Through all his activities and projects he was the product, chronicler, and publicist of pain.

PUBLICATIONS

Collections

Oeuvres complètes, 16 vols., 1956–81; revised edition, 1970
Collected Works, 4 vols., 1968–75
Antonin Artaud: Selected Writings, 1976

Plays

Les Cenci (produced 1935), in *Oeuvres complètes 4*, 1967; as *The Cenci*, 1970
Pour en finir avec le jugement de Dieu, 1948; as *To Have Done with the Judgment of God*, in *Selected Writings*, 1976

Verse

Tric-trac du ciel, 1923
Artaud le mômo, 1947; as *Artaud the Momo*, 1976
Ci-gît, précédé de la culture indienne, 1947

Other

Le Pèse-nerfs, 1925; with *Fragments d'un journal d'enfer*, 1927
L'Ombilic des limbes, 1927
Correspondance, with Jacques Rivière, 1927
L'Art et la mort, 1929
Le Théâtre Alfred Jarry et l'hostilité public, with Roger Vitrac, 1930
Le Théâtre de la cruauté, 1933
Héliogabale; ou, L'Anarchiste couronné, 1934

Le Théâtre de Séraphin, 1936
Les Nouvelles Révélations de l'être, 1937
Le Théâtre et son double, 1938; as *The Theatre and Its Double*, 1958
D'un voyage au pays des Tarahumaras (essays and letters), 1945
Lettres de Rodez, 1946
Van Gogh, le suicidé de la société, 1947
Supplément aux Lettres de Rodez suivi de Coleridge le traître, 1949
Lettres contre la Cabbale, 1949
Lettres à Jean-Louis Barrault, 1952
La Vie et mort de Satan le feu, 1953; as *The Death of Satan and Other Mystical Writings*, 1974
Les Tarahumaras (letters and essays), 1955; as *The Peyote Dance*, 1976
Galapagos, les îles du bout du monde (travel), 1955
Autre chose que l'enfant beau, 1957
Voici un endroit, 1958
Mexico, 1962
Lettres à Anaïs Nin, 1965
Artaud Anthology, edited by Jack Hirschman, 1965
Poète noir et autres textes/Black Poet and Other Texts, edited by Paul Zweig, 1966
Lettres à Génica Athanasiou, 1969
Selected Writings, edited by Susan Sontag, 1976
Nouvelles écrits de Rodez, 1977
Lettres à Annie Besnard, 1978

Translator, *Le Moine*, by Matthew Gregory Lewis, 1931
Translator, with Bernard Steele, *Crime passionel*, by Ludwig Lewisohn, 1932

Bibliography

Virmaux, Alain, *Artaud et le théâtre*, 1970

Critical studies

Sellin, Eric, *The Dramatic Concepts of Artaud*, 1968
Greene, Naomi, *Artaud: Poet Without Words*, 1970
Knapp, Bettina, *Artaud: Man of Vision*, 1971
Esslin, Martin, *Artaud* (in English), 1976
Hayman, Ronald, *Artaud and After*, 1977
Costich, Julia F., *Artaud* (in English), 1978

———

AUGIER, Emile (Guillaume-Victor-), 1820–1889.

Dramatist

LIFE

Less given to light popular entertainment than Scribe, Labiche, Sardou, or Feydeau, Emile Augier has often been compared to Dumas *fils* on account of his defence of Second Empire bourgeois values. His approach to moral values is more robustly empirical and less pulpit-inspired than that of Dumas, however, and his characters are more memorable than Dumas's stage stereotypes. Augier is in fact a moralist in the best comic tradition, upholding a moral code by examining what happens when it is breached by complacency, philistinism, corruption, vulgarity, ostentatiousness, and social climbing. The moralist's skill comes into play in the reconciliation of personal morality with the satisfactorily entrepreneurial social order he believes in. Deviations from either are derided.

Augier was born in Valence on 17 September 1820, the son of a lawyer who wrote romantic (q.v.) novels and bought himself an official position in Paris, and of Anna-Honorine Pigault-Lebrun, the daughter of the riotously dissipated novelist, actor, and dramatist who adopted that name when his father published a notice of his death in disgust at his activities. He later became a customs inspector. Augier was taken to Paris in 1828, when his father acquired his position there, and attended the Lycée Louis-le-Grand, where he was a schoolfellow and friend of the Duc d'Aumale. His school career was academically distinguished, and in 1840 he began to study law, for which he had no taste, as became even clearer when, three years later, he joined a firm of lawyers. Both Augier's parents had come from literary families. He had started writing plays at school, and at the age of 20 had had his first rejection. He persevered, nevertheless, and in 1844 the Odéon took his classical verse fantasy, *La Ciguë*.

Augier later announced that nothing at all had happened in his life after this date. As far as we know, that is a fair statement of his career. He became librarian to his childhood friend the Duc d'Aumale in 1846, co-edited *Le Spectateur Républicain* with his fellow dramatist François Ponsard (1814–1867) from 1848, was elected to the regional assembly at Drôme in 1852, resigned in 1855, published a pamphlet on electoral reform entitled *La Question électorale* in 1864, became successively Chevalier, Officier, and Commandeur of the Légion d'Honneur in 1850, 1858, and 1868, and was elected to the Académie Française in 1857. He married Laure Lambert in Rome as late as 1873.

Apart from his theatre and his electoral pamphlet, Augier published only a small collection of verse, *Les Pariétaires*. His early plays, after *La Ciguë*, *L'Aventurière* of 1848, and *Gabrielle* of 1849, were in verse. The best known play is *Le Gendre de M. Poirier* of 1854, written in prose in collaboration with Jules Sandeau. Occasionally Augier makes allusions to Paris theatre life. Romantic drama had finally collapsed with the failure of Hugo's verse drama *Les Burgraves* of 1843, and Augier's *Diane* of 1852 has been regarded as a reply to Hugo's *Marion Delorme*, just as his *Le Mariage d'Olympe* of 1855 is a riposte against *La Dame aux camélias* of Dumas *fils*. In general Augier moved away from verse, and his dramatic production falls roughly into three chronological groups. After the romantic revolution against insipid neoclassicism and the exploration of human reactions under extreme conditions, generally between the individual and society, the Paris theatre-going public who were interested in more than light entertainment wanted an imaginative and intelligent examination of the values by which they actually lived. Given the new literacy of the bourgeois theatre-going public, the sympathies of the middle-to-well off who could afford to go to the theatre, generally twice as expensive in Paris as in London, were on the whole liberal. After the revolutionary menace seemed to have been lanced in 1848, what the public wanted was an exploration of the personal, family, commercial, and social values which were still being formed and which we can now see to have emerged from the revolution and the subsequent coup d'état of 1851.

Serious comedies for the bourgeois and in bourgeois settings were what Augier provided. He had the advantage of being a liberal and a provincial, which made him just enough of an outsider to take an objective view of the society off which in the end he had to make a living, and to which, like Monnier and Daumier, he held up the clear mirror it needed. He started by returning to the neoclassical norms of verse drama and, although that experiment failed, sneering references to the subsequent "well-made plays" sometimes betray in literary critics and dramatic historians an unfamiliarity with the social realities and imaginative needs of the theatre-going public of the period.

In the early 1850s Augier was chiefly concerned with the comedy of manners. *La Pierre de touche* deals with the problems posed by unearned wealth; *Le Gendre de M. Poirier* sets off an offensively arrogant aristocrat against an upstart draper; *Le Mariage d'Olympe* debunks the idealization of the courtesan in *La Dame aux camélias*; and *Les Lionnes pauvres* examines the disruptive effect on family life brought about by a wife's adultery. From about 1860 Augier, who was still inept at creating female characters and tended to end his plays with too facile an optimism even for his contemporaries, turned to social and even political comedy. The social upheaval of 1871 was beginning to announce its eventual arrival. *Les Effrontés* satirizes the speculative greed which was becoming a social pest; *Le Fils de Giboyer* is a hard-hitting satire of efforts to give politics a religious gloss and, with *Lions et renards*, attacks conservatives, Jesuits, and above all the ultra-conservative militant Catholic Louis Veuillot; and *Maître Guérin* invites a Paris audience to see itself in the guise of a country businessman and to scoff at dishonest lawyers. In his final period, after he had already veered towards the left in politics before the Second Empire gave way to the republic, Augier took up the big themes of patriotism in *Jean de Thommeray*, divorce in *Madame Caverlet*, and illegitimacy in *Les Fourchambault*, in which an illegitimate son saves his father, and his father's legitimate family, from ruin.

WORKS

Augier's plays are in fact less well constructed and much less inventive than those of Scribe and Sardou, but they are also less vulgar and meretricious, and they avoid the heavy moralizing of Dumas *fils*.

The early five-act verse play *L'Aventurière*, set in 16th-century Padua, concerns an elderly noble, Monte Prado, who insists on marrying the adventuress of the title, Clorinde, although to do so will disgrace his name and make it impossible for his daughter Célie to marry his nephew, Horace. Célie and Horace are in love, and the plot is standard commedia dell'arte, in which the happiness of young lovers is threatened by senile folly. Augier could have taken it from Molière or Beaumarchais, as well as from Plautus. Prado's son Fabrice returns in disguise after a long absence, takes pity on the lovers, and undertakes to open his father's eyes to Clorinde's real profession, of which Prado has hitherto been unwilling to learn.

Augier is not content with the standard happy ending, however. Clorinde shows depths of self-sacrifice which touch Fabrice, who sees in her attitude to his father an example of the only real love he has ever witnessed. It seems that perhaps she really wanted to make the old man happy, and was not just an adventuress after all.

In *Le Gendre de M. Poirier*, Poirier, a retired merchant in search of a title, manages to marry off his daughter Antoinette to a ruined and dissolute marquis, Gaston de Presles. Presles lives off his father-in-law while continuing to despise him, and Poirier, hurt, determines to cut off supplies and insists on a legal separation from Antoinette. In the end she allows her husband to fight a duel with her father, so showing acceptance of his vapid, corrupt system of values. The duel never takes place. Presles falls in love with his wife and is ready to reform, while Poirier only pretends to be cured of his ambition to become a peer of France. The structure of the plot is pure Molière, down to the preservation of Poirier's deluded ambition now that it can do no harm, but the content of the play is not Molière at all.

It contains not only satire of vulgar and philistine bourgeois aspirations to nobility, but also strong satire of a frivolous, arrogant, contemptuous aristocracy. Presles is quite prepared to treat his bourgeois wife badly while sponging off her father, whom he despises. The play's point is made clearer by the inevitable introduction of normative examples of both classes—the bourgeois Verdelet and the aristocratic Duc de Montmeyran, both of whom behave well. What we have is social satire grafted on to standard farce. Poirier is honest and hard-working, but vulgar, unimaginative, and deluded. Presles is trivial, shallow, arrogant, and dissipated. None the less, Augier does not attack the symbiosis in which the two classes live. Verdelet buys Antoinette the Presles family's ancestral home as a wedding present. Social subservience and the power of the bourgeois purse are both given their due.

What Augier sees most clearly and attacks most strongly is the corrosive power of money-grabbing. The class system is not really battered by the fun poked at in *Le Gendre de M. Poirier*, or in *Le Mariage d'Olympe*, where we can still sympathize with the old Marquis de Puygiron when he shoots dead a society whore, Olympe Taverny. Posing as the respectable daughter of a farmer, she had clandestinely married his nephew Henri, and the shooting is simple murder. As a matter of historical fact Augier got it wrong. In the eyes of the audience the old aristocrat did not seem to be justified in shooting off the acquisitive slut who had penetrated the aristocratic fortress, and the play caused a storm. Possibly the Puygiron's were too moribund and Olympe too warm-blooded for it to work as it was intended to in Paris in 1855. The quest for easy money is more successfully dealt with in *Ceinture dorée* of 1855, when the millionaire Roussel finds that the only acceptable suitor for his daughter is a young nobleman whose father he has ruined. The young man, with touchingly aristocratic scruple, apparently acceptable to the audience, will not marry Roussel's daughter until her father has lost his plundered wealth. Wisely, Augier hedged against the possibility that he had pitched his values too conservatively. Young de Trélan might be avenging his father rather than acting out of scruple. We are carefully not told.

Vernouillet in *Les Effrontés* of 1861 both manipulates the market and, as a result, controls the press. Augier acquiesces in the system, merely thwarting Vernouillet's exaggerated exploitation of it. He has been criticized for being insufficiently radical. It has been said that to be either a poet or a real moralist he ought to have been harsher on the bourgeois values and the aristocratic pretensions he satirized. There is undoubtedly substance in the criticism, but it must be remembered that Augier was a working playwright with a place to retain in a society he enjoyed. He had a sharp social sense, but he was not seeking to excoriate society like Bloy or Juvenal or John the Baptist. He undertook the less personally punishing but no less imaginatively delicate task of finding a decent accommodation between values often accepted as perennial and an existing society. In this he was unusually successful.

PUBLICATIONS

Collections

Poésies complètes, 1852
Théâtre complet, 7 vols., 1889

Plays

La Ciguë, 1844; as *The Love of Hyppolita*, 1881
Un homme de bien, 1845
L'Aventurière, 1848; as *Her Last Stake*, 1882; as *Home*, 1893
L' Habit vert with Alfred de Musset, 1849; as *The Green Coat*, 1914
Gabrielle, 1850; as *Good for Evil* (as *Home Truths*, produced 1860), 1860
Sapho (opera), with music by Gounod, 1851
Le Joueur de flûte, 1897
La Chasse au roman, with Jules Sandeau, 1851
Les Méprises de l'amour, 1852
Diane, 1852
Philiberte, 1853
La Pierre de touche, with Jules Sandeau, 1854
Le Gendre de M. Poirier, with Jules Sandeau, 1854; as *Monsieur Poirier's Son-in-Law*, 1915
Le Mariage d'Olympe, 1855; as *The Marriage of Olympe*, 1915
Ceinture dorée, 1855
Les Lionnes pauvres, 1858; as *A False Step*, 1879
La Jeunesse, 1858
Un beau mariage, 1859
Les Effrontés, 1861; as *Faces of Brass*, 1888
Le Fils de Giboyer, 1863
La Question électorale, 1864
Maître Guérin, 1865
La Contagion, 1866
Paul Forrester, 1868; as *Paul Forrester* (in English), 1871
Le Post-scriptum, 1869; as *The Post-Scriptum*, 1915
Lions et renards, 1870
Jean de Thommeray, with Jules Sandeau, 1874
Madame Caverlet, 1876
Le Prix Martin, with Eugène Labiche, 1876
Les Fourchambault, 1878; as *The House of Fourchambault*, 1915

Verse

Les Pariétaires, 1855

Critical and biographical studies

Morillot, P., *Emile Augier*, 1901
Gaillard, H., Emile Augier et la comédie sociale 1910

—————

AYMÉ, Marcel 1902–1967.

Novelist, dramatist, and author of short stories.

Aymé was born at Joigny in the Jura, the sixth and last child in his family. His mother died when he was two, and Aymé was brought up by his rather puritanical widowed grandmother until, soon afterwards, she too died, and Aymé was taken in by an uncle. In 1910 he was sent to boarding school in Dôle. Although his childhood was impoverished, in his later fiction he remembers with affection the accoutrements of rural life. The family was free-thinking and republican, although his grandmother had Aymé baptized and occasionally sent him to Mass. From 1911 he and his sister Suzanne lived with his Aunt Léa, who had just lost her husband.

By the age of 17 Aymé was semi-delinquent, partly no doubt on account of his wartime schooling, but he passed his baccalauréat and won a mathematics scholarship to Besançon. In 1922–23 he completed 18 months of military service, and then moved to Paris. He did a variety of ill-paid jobs as clerk, translator, and film extra, and was dismissed as an apprentice journalist for "not knowing how to write." He was ill in 1925, returned to Dôle to convalesce, and was urged by his elder sister, Camille, to write a book to save himself from despair. He apparently burnt his first novel, but Camille got *Brûlebois* published. Aymé returned to Paris, married a teacher, who bore him a daughter, and worked in an insurance office and as a journalist, while continuing to write at night. Gallimard published *Aller retour* and *La Table aux crevés* in 1927 and 1929, and Aymé decided to become a full-time writer, while also continuing his journalism. He had almost given up all hope of success when *La Jument verte* won him public acclaim.

He worked in the evenings, spent a great deal of time wandering the streets of Paris, meeting up with friends from the worlds of literature (notably Céline) and the performing and visual arts. He cultivated a dilettante image with the critics, was politically uncommitted, and, if Anouilh seriously overestimated him in calling him "the greatest French writer," he may at least have been "un des plus brillants classiques du XXe siècle," and was certainly more than the mere entertainer, the bucolic novelist in a whimsical context, which he made himself out to be.

From 1932 Aymé wrote occasional film scripts, and eventually devoted himself to more serious journalism. *Collier's* financed a trip to the US in 1949, but cancelled it when it did not like what it received. Aymé's literary aims are mostly to be found in the prefaces to the classical curriculum authors he edited. Politically he moved towards the right, but without muddying his populism. He continued to publish under the occupation and to write for various pro-German reviews, including

Drieu la Rochelle's *Nouvelle Revue Française* (*NRF*, q.v.), although he carefully distanced himself from anti-semitism and, in veiled allusions, supported the Resistance, to which he also lent his flat. However, his support for Brasillach and Céline was a political stance which later generations have not condoned.

After the early 1950s Aymé virtually stopped writing fiction and polemical works in order to devote himself to the theatre, a move he came to regard as a mistake. His later work contains diminishing gaiety and new traces of bitterness. In the late 1950s he was diagnosed as suffering from cancer and his face was partially paralysed. He died of a heart attack.

WORKS

Brûlebois is an ironic novel of uncertain touch concerning small town life. It evokes the atmosphere of Dôle, its inhabitants and their concerns, successes, failures, and conflicts. It includes a satire of the carefully graded caste system, ranging from the stupid and pretentious Reboudins through the crank Rodolphe to Brûlebois himself, the drunken station porter. *La Table aux crevés* is a bantering novel of country life gently satirizing a peasant Catholicism that accommodates pagan rites and culminates in a classical clash between the republican mayor and the Catholic priest. The third-person narrator is interrupted by much dialogue and reports the characters' interior monologues in their own speech idioms, raising implicit questions about the relationship between thought and language.

La Rue sans nom is a realistic novel in an urban setting featuring the animosities that exist between mutually dependent French and Italian working-class communities in the same street and the fantasies indulged in by their members as a means of escaping the sordidness of slum life. *Maison basse* lacks narrative tension but turns the lens of social realism towards the life of a lower-middle-class apartment building whose inmates cannot communicate with one another and are each undergoing some personal despair. *Le Vaurien* deals in an uncoordinated way with the disconnected series of Parisian misadventures experienced by a provincial youth who finally goes mad. *Aller retour* concerns Galuchey, a Paris clerk who revolts against his humdrum existence, replaces his superior at work, tries to reject his wife for the seductive Raymonde, but returns to his wife in despair when an uncle shows to Raymonde Galuchey's wedding photograph and she laughs.

Aymé later rejected *Les Jumeaux du diable*, which reads like a pastiche of Voltaire. In *Le Boeuf clandestin* a father, his daughter, and her fiancé seek to bring their relationship into equilibrium behind the formal social sham. *La Jument verte* is bawdily funny, a popularly successful tableau of country life, revolving once more round a clash between republicans and Catholics. Aymé's humour depends here on the deadpan style inspired by Voltaire and Kafka. "In the village of Claquebue," we read, "one day a green mare was born..." The green mare, her spirit distilled into a painting, comments on the at times ribald action in separate chapters. Aymé had to defend the salacious element of the novel, which, once it had been turned into a film, unfortunately lost much of the humour. *La Belle Image*, which has been criticized for being merely an expanded short story, is a comic treatment of a classic identity crisis.

Apart from the late and unsuccessful *Les Tiroirs de l'inconnu*, Aymé's final novels form a socio-political war trilogy, opening with *Travelingue*, a study of the 1936 Front Populaire in France as viewed by the bourgeoisie it threatens, and who are no longer able to impose their own order on society. *Le Chemin des écoliers* is a picture of the occupation published during the subsequent anti-collaborationist "épuration" and deals with the universal compromises, using footnotes to emphasize the authenticity of the account. *Uranus* evokes the post-war disillusion of both right and left in the face of centrist solutions to political problems. What reigns among the chaos is hypocrisy and opportunism.

Aymé's great literary virtue was his mastery of language. His fiction inclined him more and more towards drama as he came increasingly to rely on confrontation and dialogue. The fact that on the whole his short stories, with their dry narration and ironic asides, are on a higher literary plane than the more pretentious novels also seems to confirm the dramatic nature of his talent. In his novels he had found it difficult to sustain tension except by resorting to an irony which was at times vicious. By 1944 he had published 14 novels and five collections of short stories, and had already been writing plays for some time. His first play to be performed, *Vogue la galère*, was written eight years before its publication and 11 years before its premiere in 1947.

The plays generally contain social satire, together with political innuendoes, directed at justice, social structures, and the US, the profit motive, and racism. The best-known plays are probably *Les Maxibules*, written not in acts but in "parties," on the theme of the idealist who disrupts the lives of everyone around him, and the relaxed *Clérimbard*, which deals with a total conversion of attitudes, but is in fact also a reflection on the relationship between the real world and that of dream and fantasy. Other plays, too, exploit transformation themes, sometimes under the influence of Ionesco.

Aymé's plays were avoided by avant-garde producers, however. Their social satire does not really disconcert and their characters are not sufficiently universal. But the plays were easier to write than the novels and, on the whole, they were a box-office success. Aymé was an admirer of Andersen and Perrault, and wrote prefaces to the works of both.

PUBLICATIONS

Collections

Oeuvres Romanesques complètes, Bibliotheque de la Pléiade, 1989–

Novels

Brûlebois, 1926
Aller retour, 1927
Les Jumeaux du diable, 1928
La Table aux crevés, 1929
La Rue sans nom, 1930
Le Vaurien, 1931
La Jument verte, 1934
Maison basse, 1935
Le Moulin de la Sourdine, 1936

Gustalin, 1937
Le Boeuf clandestin, 1939
La Belle Image, 1941
Travelingue, 1941
La Vouivre, 1943
Le Chemin des écoliers, 1946
Uranus, 1948
Les Tiroirs de l'inconnu, 1960

Short story collections

Le Puits aux images, 1932
Le Nain, 1934
Derrière chez Martin, 1938
Les Contes du chat perché, 1939
Les Passe-muraille, 1943
Le Vin de Paris, 1947
En arrière, 1950
Enjambées (collection of mostly published contes), 1967

Plays

Vogue la galère, 1944
Lucienne et le boucher, 1947
Clérambard, 1950
La Tête des autres, 1952
Les Quatre vérités, 1954
Les Oiseaux de lune, 1956
La Mouche bleue, 1957
Louisiane, 1961
Les Maxibules, 1962
Le Minotaure, with *Consommation* and *La Convention Belzébir,* 1967

Adaptations

Les Sorcières de Salem, from Arthur Miller, *The Crucible,* 1955
Vu du pont, from Arthur Miller, *View from the Bridge,* 1958
La Nuit de l'Iguane, from Tennessee Williams, *The Night of the Iguana,* 1962

Essays

Silhouette du scandale, 1938
Le Trou de la serrure, 1946
Le Confort intellectuel, 1949
Images de l'amour, 1946

Critical studies

See the *Cahiers Marcel Aymé*
Cathelin, Jean, *Marcel Aymé: le paysan de Paris,* 1958
Vandromme, Pol, *Aymé,* 1960
Lord, Graham, *Marcel Aymé* (in English), 1987

B

BACHELARD, Gaston, 1884–1962.

*Philosopher of science and theoretician of aesthetics and
    literary criticism.*

LIFE

Bachelard was born at Bar-sur-Aube, about 200 kilometres
south-east of Paris, the son of shopkeepers and the grandson of
shoemakers. On leaving school he taught for a year before getting a job in the postal service, although what he really wanted
was to become a newspaper editor. He became interested in
telegraphy, did his military service as a telegraphist, and
resumed his work in the postal service from 1907 to the outbreak
of war. For three years he took evening classes in engineering at
the Lycée Saint-Louis. In 1912, at the age of 28, he obtained his
"licence" in mathematics and came third in the entrance examination for the Ecole Supérieure de Télégraphie, which was
offering only two places. He took leave of absence from the
postal service, obtained a scholarship from the Lycée Saint-
Louis, and prepared for the "concours", or competitive examination, for engineering students in telegraphy.

In July 1914 he married a schoolteacher from his own region,
but in August he was called up. After more than three years in
the trenches he returned home with the Croix de Guerre, and in
1919 began teaching physics and chemistry at Bar-sur-Aube.
His wife died in 1920, leaving him with a baby daughter. After
only a year Bachelard took his licence in philosophy and two
months later passed his agrégation. He insisted on keeping his
science courses going alongside his philosophy lectures. In 1927
he obtained a doctorate for his two theses—on knowledge by
approximation and on the history of the problem of heat transfer
in solids. They were published in 1928. At 44 Bachelard was
finally fully qualified.

Bachelard continued to teach at Bar-le-Duc but also gave
courses at the University of Dijon for three years. In 1930 he was
given the chair of philosophy there. In 1932 he moved beyond the
limits of his own disciplines by publishing *L'Intuition de l'instant*, and from 1940 to 1954 he held the chair of the history and
philosophy of science at the Sorbonne, publishing regularly on
both epistemology and the imagination. He was also director of
the Institute of the History of Science. In 1951 he was made an
Officier of the Légion d'Honneur and in 1955 he was elected to
the Academy of Moral and Political Sciences. Only now that he
was retired could Bachelard give full rein to his enquiries into the
mysteries of the literary imagination with *La Poétique de
l'espace, La Poétique de la rêverie*, and *La Flamme d'une chandelle*. He became a commander of the Légion d'Honneur and was
awarded the Grand Prix National des Lettres. After his death in
Paris three posthumous collections of articles and a colloquium at
Cerisy were devoted to his work.

WORKS

The most important question raised by Bachelard's work concerns the possible relationship between his rigorously philosophical, mainly epistemological studies and his theory of the
imagination. Critical opinion, generally convinced that there
must be a link, has not united in identifying it. After Bachelard's
death Georges Canguilhem presented, under the title *Etudes*,
five short essays from between 1931 and 1934 which demonstrate a broadening of Bachelard's epistemological concerns.
Canguilhem proceeded to put together a further 13 articles on
philosophical subjects, *L'Engagement rationaliste*, while Philippe Garcin collected some 26 previously published pieces, all
dealing with the imagination and the arts, in *Le Droit de rêver*.
It is Bachelard's work on the imagination and its consequences
for literary criticism that occasions most interest today. Georges
Poulet wrote in 1965 that "Bachelard made it impossible to
describe consciousness as anything but concrete and difficult to
perceive except through the layers of images covering it up."

Bachelard's first four books are narrowly concerned with the
means whereby we arrive at scientific knowledge: "approximation, induction, coherence." In 1932 and 1933 his interests
broadened as his epistemology was extended to include metaphysical considerations, and henceforward even the professedly
epistemological works incorporate discussions of the wider consequences of scientific enquiry for the emergence of "the new
scientific mind," conditioned by the historical philosophical
assumptions that lie behind the concepts it employs. It was
between 1940 and 1949 that Bachelard produced his major
works on the imagination, while in 1949 he returned to his
enquiry into the new scientific mind with a trilogy of books on
rationalism.

During the 1930s Bachelard had dealt, slowly and discontin-
uously, with space, time, matter, water, air, and earth as they are
experienced rather than known experimentally. He held that
objectivity does not necessarily result from studying objects,
which can elicit wonder and cloud the judgement—the phenomenon on which *La Psychanalyse du feu* is based. The shift from
epistemology to a study of the function of imagination derives
from an awareness that the poetry and the science of fire are
complementary. Bachelard's "psychoanalysis" draws more on
Jung than on Freud, and he is more interested in the semi-orga-
nized workings of what he calls "rêverie," working on archetypes, than in discrete elements of repressed material from the
subconscious. He freely uses "complexes" of any collection of
associated subjective attitudes towards the same object, such as
the "Prometheus," "Empedocles," and "Pantagruel" complexes
towards fire. From here it is not far to an analysis of the literary
imagination, divided first according to an orientation towards
earth, air, fire, or water. The phenomena themselves can only be
studied with scientific objectivity when the image can also be

studied objectively. This requires the process of "dialectical sublimation," which both joins and separates epistemology and the theory of the imagination. Literary criticism requires that one take account of the pre-reflexive elements of the creative process, the hesitations, and the ambiguities from which results the "syntax of metaphors." There are recognizable analogies between Bachelard's understanding of the work of the imagination, and Proust's, and the philosophy of Merleau-Ponty.

Lautréamont, which examines in detail that author's *Les Chants de Maldoror*, constitutes Bachelard's attempt at creating a model for his new form of literary criticism. "Rêverie" translates concrete, immediate reality subjectively, in terms of its means of expression, while scientific reason constructs an objective reality inseparable from the method of knowing. Merleau-Ponty's "body-subject" also took him towards a psychological analysis of what Bachelard calls "rêverie." Earth, air, and water are dealt with as imaginative archetypes in *L'Eau et les rêves, L'Air et les songes, La Terre et les rêvries de la volonté*, and *La Terre et les rêveries du repos*, before Bachelard returns in 1949 to straight epistemology. In his later *La Poétique de l'espace* he sets out to produce a phenomenology of the imagination, "apprehending the literary image without reference to its psychological causes or its role, but as it emerges into the consciousness." Only the phenomenological method allows the image to be apprehended without destroying its specific reality.

La Poétique de la rêverie suggests a poetics which would demand a non-reductive psychology and allow imaginative activity to be studied systematically. Bachelard himself contrasts critical reading—an activity of the "animus"—with creative reading—a process that continues the author's "rêverie" and demands the cooperation of the reader's "anima." The terms are again borrowed from Jung. Bachelard's great contribution to literary criticism is his warning against premature conceptualization, which can destroy the reverberation of the author's images in the reader's mind.

PUBLICATIONS

Works

Essai sur la connaissance approchée, 1928
La Propagation thermique dans les solides, 1928
La Valeur inductive de la relativité, 1929
L'Intuition de l'instant, 1932
Le Pluralisme cohérent de la chimie moderne, 1932
Les Intuitions atomistiques, 1933
Le Nouvel Esprit scientifique, 1934
La Dialectique de la durée, 1936
L'Expérience de l'espace dans la physique contemporaine, 1937
La Formation de l'esprit scientifique: contribution à une psychanalyse de la connaissance objective, 1938
La Psychanalyse du feu, 1938; as *The Psychoanalysis of Fire*, 1964
Lautréamont, 1939
La Philosophie du non, 1940; as *The Philosophy of No*, 1969
L'Eau et les rêves, 1942
L'Air et les songes, 1943
La Terre et les rêveries de la volonté, 1948
La Terre et les rêveries du repos, 1948

Le Rationalisme appliqué, 1949
L'Activité rationaliste de la physique contemporaine, 1951
Le Matérialisme rationnel, 1953
La Poétique de l'espace, 1957; as *The Poetics of Space*, 1964
La Poétique de la rêverie, 1960; as *The Poetics of Reverie*, 1969; as *The Poetics of Reverie: Childhood, Language and the Cosmos*, 1971
La Flamme d'une chandelle, 1961

Collections and excerpts of previously published work

Le Droit de rêver, 1970; as *The Right to Dream*, 1971
Etudes, edited by Georges Canguilhem, 1970
Epistémologie, edited by Dominique Lecourt, 1971
L'Engagement rationaliste, edited by Georges Canguilhem, 1972

Bibliography

Rummens Jean, "Gaston Bachelard: une bibliographie," in *Revue Internationale de Philosophie*, 17 (1963), pp. 492–504
Alden, Douglas W., and Richard B. Brooks (editors), *A Critical Bibliography of French Literature*, 1980, vol.6, part 3, pp. 1,423–31

Critical studies

Mansuy, Michel, *Gaston Bachelard et les éléments*, 1967
Pire, François, *De l'imagination poétique dans l'oeuvre de Gaston Bachelard*, 1967
Gagey, Jacques, *Gaston Bachelard ou la conversion à l'imaginaire*, 1969
Therrien, Vincent, *La Révolution de Gaston Bachelard en critique littéraire*, 1970
Smith, R. C., *Gaston Bachelard* (in English), 1982

BALZAC, Honoré de, 1799–1850.

Novelist.

LIFE

Balzac's father, Bernard-François Balssa (1746–1829), the eldest of 11 children, was born at Canezac of peasant stock, but was taught by the local priest to read and write. He became a clerk in a local notary's office, went while still young to Paris, with nothing more than the proverbial knapsack holding three shirts and a flowered waistcoat, and rose quickly as a legal clerk in the public service. He was private secretary to the naval minister for six months from 1791 to 1792 and was thereafter active in the administration of army supplies. From 1795 to 1814 he was director of the commissariat of the 22nd division, and in 1797, aged 51, he married the 19-year-old Anne-Charlotte-Laure Sallambier (1778–1854), the daughter of an affluent family of Paris drapers turned functionaries. She brought to the marriage a farm worth some 120, 000 francs as a dowry, and her husband promised her a settlement of 1,800 francs a year.

Balzac, as Balssa had been called since 1775, managed to retain his position through the Revolution, although suspected of royalist leanings. He had several salaries, though little capital, boasted of his stamina, and was obsessed by the state of his health, which was robust. He moved rapidly up the social scale, intrigued, sold his wife's farm, bought a house, and acquired authority in the community as deputy mayor. Laure had been brought up strictly and educated well. She was vain, supercilious, and prone to fits of nervous depression. A pretty young wife, she led an active social life and appears to have had little affection for her children. The first baby died. Balzac, born on 20 May 1799, was sent out to nurse, as was his sister Laure (born in late 1800), to whom he became deeply attached. On the baptism certificate of a second sister, Laurence, born in 1802, the father's name is preceded by the aristocratic "de." Laurence was to make an unhappy marriage in 1821 and to die in 1825. In 1807 Balzac's mother had a further child, Henri, the son of Jean de Margonne (1780–1858), who owned a château at Saché in Touraine, where Balzac was often to be a guest.

On returning from the nurse in 1803 the children were put in the charge of a governess and now saw their mother, of whom they were frightened, on Sundays. When Laure's father died in 1803, her mother came to live in the household, bringing 5,000 francs a year, but entrusting a further 40,000 francs of her capital to Bernard-François, who lost it all. Money, and the lack of it, played an unusually prominent part in Balzac's early life, which was also marked, to his later bitter reproaches, by his mother's emotional rejection. Her reputation for strict propriety sank, but she did take Balzac to church, and in 1804 he was sent to a local school. In 1807 he was sent to the boarding school at Vendôme, 35 miles away, run by laicized Oratorians. Discipline, while not military, was relatively strict, and during the six years Balzac was there he was never allowed to return home, and saw his mother only twice.

His father, whose congenial immediate superior had been replaced in 1806, prudently published four papers on social topics between 1807 and 1810. Balzac himself, with the connivance of the librarian, contrived to read avidly at school, and also wrote verse. About the time of his first Communion, now thin and pale, he experienced a crisis of mystical exaltation, and in 1813 his excessively cloistered existence led to symptoms of nervous exhaustion. He was accordingly taken home to Tours in the middle of the school year. By then his father's new superior, the district prefect, had charged him and other charity commissioners with financial irregularities. Although he was supported by the ministry, the atmosphere became sensitive. The upper levels of Tours society were split into hostile camps: the freemasons, to which Balzac's atheistic father belonged, and the Catholics, who maintained their opposition. Having lost his mother-in-law's money, in 1813 Balzac's father was forced to sell his house. Balzac's mother, meanwhile, continued to collect the writings of the mystics and, in spite of her illegitimate child, to preserve her attitude of moral severity.

In good health once more, Balzac had been sent to board in Paris, but was brought home on account of the political situation after Napoleon's abdication on 20 April 1814. He had private lessons and continued to read a great deal. At Tours as a dayboy from that year he suffered from his mother's parsimony, being

less generously provided for than his companions. Perhaps on that account he developed a fierce ambition which at first had no particular object. His school career was never distinguished, but he won occasional school prizes, got on well with his sisters, observed in precise detail everything that was going on around him, and developed a prodigious memory. Laure left a biographical account, printed in the 24th volume of the 1858 edition of her brother's works, the source of all domestic details about Balzac's early life, but one that necessarily relies chiefly on the letters he wrote and the very limited periods when he was at home.

His father, having rapidly unfurled his royalist affiliations again, succeeded in obtaining promotion to a post in Paris from 1814, and moved the family to the bourgeois Marais district. Balzac was now sent to board at the royalist and Catholic Institution Lepître, where he got into debt for the first time. It is generally assumed that he showed himself too Bonapartist during the hundred days of Napoleon's escape in 1815, and that it was for this reason that he was transferred back to his previous Paris boarding institution, while attending classes at the Lycée Charlemagne. He came 32nd in Latin, which earned him a scathing letter from his mother and a period of house detention. On Sundays he was taken to dancing classes. He showed some aptitude for writing but, having finished school in 1816, he became clerk to a lawyer and enrolled in law classes at the Sorbonne. He also attended lectures by Guizot and Cousin, and at the Muséum d'Histoire Naturelle, where he became aware of the difference between Cuvier's empirical approach to natural science and Saint-Hilaire's quest for philosophical conclusions. Balzac would later seek to apply some comparably unified theory to man's social behaviour. He also read the phrenological work of the family doctor, Nacquart, who regarded the soul as the expression of the chemical and physical forces within the body, effectively removing the basis on which it was possible to establish personal and social moral values.

Of most obvious use to him later on, however, was the knowledge of the legal codes governing civil law procedures in France which he gained in the lawyer's office, where his unsettling exuberance once caused the head clerk to ask him not to come that day "because there is a great deal of work to be done." Halfway through his course he moved from the advocate's office to work with the family notary. Laure tells us that at around this time Balzac had remarkable success with girls. He also became a favourite of his grandmother's, who would deliberately lose to him at cards to enable him to buy books. She also lost a bet of 100 crowns she had wagered that he could not win the favours of a particular girl.

In 1819 Balzac qualified as a lawyer, and his father was retired. His income dropped from 7,800 to 1,695 francs a year, plus what little his wife's investments brought in, and the family had to move out of Paris to Villeparisis, about 15 miles to the east, where a Sallambier relative bought a house for them to rent. Balzac rented an attic room for 60 francs a year and, resisting all attempts to make a notary of him, spent his time in libraries reading and making notes on philosophy. He also worked on projects for the theatre, including a comic opera whose title, *Le Corsaire*, was no doubt inspired by Byron, a tragedy, *Sylla*, and a verse tragedy, *Cromwell*, finished early in 1820. The family's life style was still middle-class. They had a housekeeper, cook, and gardener, and there is no mention in the family papers of the guillotining in 1819 of Bernard-François's younger brother, accused, perhaps wrongfully, of the murder of a farm girl he was alleged to have seduced. Appearances were being kept up.

Balzac now knew he wanted to write. His family regarded him as a last hope for the restoration of its fortunes, but Balzac's father promised him 1,500 francs a year, on which it was possible to live with care, for two years while he tried to establish himself. He could have lived at home, but we owe to his self-imposed poverty in Paris a lively correspondence with Laure, full of the family's private language. On 18 May 1820 she married an engineer, Eugène Surville (1790–1866), the illegitimate son of a provincial actress, who now revealed his father's name so that Eugène could enter into his inheritance and claim his right to use "de" before his name. In 1819 Balzac had contemplated a treatise on the immortality of the soul, setting out the reasons for not believing in it, and in 1820 he attempted two novels which remained unfinished, one of which was derived from Scott and had a medieval subject, and the other was in epistolary form. He was lucky in the draw for military service and became exempt. By the end of 1820 he had given up the attic and returned to Villeparisis, but frequently used a pied-à-terre in the Marais that the family had at their disposition. He found writing verse difficult, and *Cromwell* was not well received by an assembly of family and friends. Professional opinion, when sought, was even harsher.

Balzac's life, with its visits to Paris, to the old family friend Louis-Philippe de Villers-La Faye (1749–1822), mayor of L'Isle-Adam, and trips elsewhere, was not unpleasant. His grandmother's belief in clairvoyance and his mother's interest in the occult, together with his own studies and reflections, had bred in him a belief in quasi-magical powers contained within the personality which he was convinced he could release within himself. They had featured in the heroine of his medieval novel, and were clearly more easily adapted to exploitation in prose fiction than in drama. He accepted an invitation from a Paris friend, Auguste Le Poitevin de l'Egreville (1793–1854), to join a small recently formed team of novel writers he had formed. They mostly wrote to a formula of fantasy and horror, involving an innocent victim and an avenger of wrongs.

Balzac signed his work anagrammatically "Lord R'Hoone" or "Horace de Saint-Aubin," and published a series of five pseudonymous novels, a couple of them in collaboration. They were not unremunerative. The first brought the collaborators 800 francs, the second 1,200. Balzac drafted and began work on two short stories, three melodramas, and two novels. In 1821 his sister Laurence had unenthusiastically (and unwisely as it turned out) married the debauched and heavily indebted son of a recently ennobled family, Amand-Désiré de Michaut de Saint-Pierre de Montzaigle. Balzac himself stayed that year with Henri-Joseph de Savary, who owned a château at Vouvray and was Jean de Margonne's father-in-law. From 1825 to 1829 he published nothing important, and only what was published after that break is of any literary significance. Balzac himself later referred to his early publications as trash.

In 1822 he began a liaison with his "dilecta," Laure de Berny (1777–1836), daughter of a musician called Hinner and one of Marie-Antoinette's ladies-in-waiting. Laure's godparents had been Louis XVI and Marie Antoinette. When Hinner died, Laure's widowed mother married the model for Dumas's Chevalier de Maison-Rouge while she, at 16, was married speedily to the Comte de Berny. Only the fall of Robespierre saved them from the guillotine. Berny had been a colleague of Bernard-François in the commissariat, and he and Laure had nine children. Laure also had a daughter by a Corsican with whom she had lived from 1800 to 1805. The Bernys had come to live in Villeparisis and played the part of the village squirearchy, being present for instance when the child of the Balzacs' cook was baptized.

They hired Balzac as tutor, and Mme de Berny teased him about his coarse manners, his ambitions, and his energetic self-confidence. He fell in love with her and pleaded with her to become, significantly, "his mistress and his mother." She was 45, a year older than his own mother. Balzac was to write often to her, always keeping a draft of his letter. By May 1822 they were lovers. Balzac's mother, who had been spending a few weeks with the unhappy and insolvent Laurence, returned home, found out what was going on, and immediately forced Balzac to go to Bayeux to stay with the Survilles. He was away from 21 May until August. On his way back he stopped off in Paris and sold two novels for 2,000 francs, with the delivery deadline fixed for 1 October. In addition to being a lawyer, Balzac was by now a time-served writer of popular fiction, willing also, with Le Poitevin, or Horace Raisson, or Etienne Arago, to run up a melodrama for a good-looking actress, to write gossip or scandal for *Le Corsaire-Satan* when it was founded in 1823, to churn out facetious codes of behaviour or "physiologies," or even to devil for more affluent practitioners. The craze for physiologies was of course to lead to Brillat-Savarin's celebrated *La Physiologie du goût* of 1825 and to Balzac's own *La Physiologie du mariage*, whose first version dates from 1826.

Balzac's mother had taken in a 22-year-old nephew, Edouard Malus, a rich orphan who was dying of consumption. He died on 25 October, leaving her 90,000 francs. The Balzacs returned to the Marais, having found a suitable apartment at 730 francs a year. Balzac insisted on paying for his own board and lodging. Signed "Horace de Saint-Aubin," his *Le Vicaire des Ardennes*, the story of a marquise who falls in love with a vicar who turns out to be her son by a bishop, was published in November and seized by the authorities in December 1822. Another novel, this one ghoulish, appeared only a fortnight later under the same pseudonym. A melodrama, *Le Nègre*, was turned down the following month, when Balzac's grandmother, who had been passing his letters on to Mme de Berny, also died. In the summer of 1823, which Balzac spent at Vouvray, Saché, and Tours, he was still clearly thinking of an eventual literary career. He wrote a poem entitled "Foedora" and contemplated an *Alceste*.

In 1822, under Nacquart's influence, he became interested in Lavater, whose works he had had expensively bound. Lavater systematically categorized the relationship between outward human appearances and inner characteristics, and it is possible that Balzac's interest in him marked the beginnings of his own ambition to study human social groups. There is also ample evidence to confirm Balzac's continued interest in theories of personal magnetism, of the vital force which can be dissipated or conserved and projected by the power of the will. Although he was strongly inclined to the cynical atheism of his father, Balzac could not rid himself of a fascination for mysticism, the occult, the illuminism of Saint-Martin, or the visionary philosophizing of Swedenborg. He even thought of writing a treatise on prayer. Henri Monnier, the caricaturist, said of him that he looked like "a monk or a peasant." His primary concern, however, was with becoming rich. When, in 1824, they found they could afford it, the Balzacs moved out again to Villeparisis, buying for 10,000 francs the house which they had once rented. Bernard-François was still vigorous at 78 and continued to enjoy the country girls. Balzac himself rented a small room in Paris in order, he said, to work, but in fact, as his mother supposed, to be able to receive Mme de Berny, whose teasing affection had become a devouring passion. She had moved to Paris, and Balzac now saw her nearly every day.

Balzac's first commercial enterprise, undertaken in partnership with Horace Raisson and Urbain Canel, was for illustrated pocket editions of Molière and La Fontaine. He then began planning a series of novels which would constitute the "Histoire de France pittoresque," met Philarète Chasles, not yet the serious historian of European literature he was to become, and Hyacinthe de Latouche, from 1825 editor of the *Mercure de France*, set up as a printer, and with the help of Mme de Berny established a foundry for casting type. He helped Canel with his *Annales romantiques* of 1827–28, and cooperated in a whole series of subliterary ventures. The printing concern and the foundry became insolvent in 1828, leaving Balzac with debts of 60,000 francs, most of which he owed to his mother. Among the literary projects of that year historical novels predominate. One of them, originally entitled "Le gars" and published by Canel in March 1829 as *Le Dernier Chouan; ou, la Bretagne en 1800*, was to become the first signed novel and the first to be admitted to *La Comédie humaine*.

By this date Laurence, exhausted after the death of her second son, had died at her mother's home. Laure and her husband had moved to Versailles, where her daughter was at school with the daughter of the Duchesse d'Abrantès, who was to become Balzac's mistress. He used domineering language with her and demanded that she submit completely to his wild behaviour. Laure de Berny heard about the new liaison, presumably through Balzac's mother, who had been staying with the Survilles, and succeeded in putting a stop to it for two whole years. Balzac's father, now an octogenarian, was accused in Villeparisis gossip of having made a local girl pregnant. The Balzacs, who had become adept by now at keeping up appearances and had saved Balzac himself from formal bankruptcy, moved to Versailles to be near their surviving daughter, whose husband was now in charge of building the Essonne canal. His financial disaster of 1828 had left Balzac homeless. He was taken in by Latouche, and Surville found him an apartment, paying the first quarter's rent for him. Although the experience of insolvency had etched itself on his mind, Balzac proceeded to forget about his creditors and, installing himself elegantly in his new home, began to write, following the vogue for the historical novel in Scott's manner on which Hugo and Vigny were capitalizing.

Balzac felt the need to do his own documenting, as Flaubert and Zola were also to do, and went to Brittany to stay in the Chouan country with his father's patron's son, General Gilbert de Pommereul. His host relates that he offered to pay for his stay by entertaining them, and in fact his masterfully vivid narrative gifts gave his stories such authenticity that he was for ever being asked if they were true, to which he would reply: "Pas un mot de vrai! Du Balzac tout pur (Not a word of truth. Balzac pure and simple)." Latouche underwrote the publication of *Le Dernier Chouan*. Balzac was to receive 1,000 francs for an edition of 1,000 copies, with the rights then reverting to him. He was late with his copy, made extensive and expensive proof corrections, and demanded extra copies for friends. The novel, published in March 1829, attracted favourable attention among a small group

of literary specialists, but it sold only 450 copies in eight months. The coarse-grained Balzac then wrote an unenthusiastic review of the fastidious Latouche, and the two fell out.

On 19 June 1829 Balzac's father died at the age of 83, leaving his mother in serious financial straits. Laure d'Abrantès had introduced Balzac to the important literary salons, including that of Jeanne-Françoise "Juliette" Récamier, who was now receiving, among others, Chateaubriand, Constant, and Lamartine. Balzac's rapture at being invited to join such heady company was noted by the art critic Etienne Delécluze, friend of Stendhal, but in practice Balzac felt uneasy in salon company, for which he was too vulgar and ungainly. He fascinated but never dazzled, and Paris did not know what to make of him: "plump, bright-eyed…the bearing of a herbalist, the clothes of a butcher," as the minor romantic author Fontaney wrote in his *Journal*. He was "heavy and cumbersome," vain, unkempt, potbellied, but witty and full of energy, and had a magnetic presence. Balzac also frequented the atelier of François Gérard, the pupil of David, met Delacroix and the Dutch engraver Ary Scheffer, and in July 1829 was invited by Victor Hugo along with Mérimée, Vigny, Sainte-Beuve, Musset, and Dumas to the reading of *Marion Delorme*. That October he wrote *Gloire et malheur*, which was to become *La Maison du chat-qui-pilote*, and signed a contract for a collection of five novels intended for the *Scènes de la vie privée*. In December he published the successful *La Physiologie du mariage*. Between 1829, when he was 30, and 1848, he produced over 90 novels and short stories in addition to increasing amounts of journalism.

Balzac's initial intention was to write novels about middle-class life depicting the history of his own age, essentially what were to become the *Scènes de la vie privée*, the title under which Louis Mame published six novels in 1830, *El Verdugo, Gloire et malheur* (later *La Maison du chat-qui-pelote*), *La Femme vertueuse* (which was to become *Une double famille*), *Le Bal des Sceaux, La Paix du ménage*, and *Les Dangers de l'inconduite* (now *Gobseck*). Balzac received 3,750 francs for the volume after what he had earned from newspaper serialization. In 1830 *La Mode* published seven excerpts from Balzac's novels, the *Revue de Paris* four, and in December the *Revue des Deux Mondes* (q. v.) published an excerpt which *La Mode* had already published under a different title in May. In addition to the novels and episodes, not all of which were from novels in the Mame volume, in 1830 Balzac also published articles in *La Silhouette, Le Voleur*, which carried 19 "Lettres sur Paris" to keep provincial readers in touch with what was happening in Paris after the July revolution, and *La Caricature*. The first two of these newspapers had been established by Emile de Girardin, using the harsh, irreverent drawings of Gavarni and Henri Monnier, creator of "Monsieur Prudhomme," the caricature of the typical bourgeois. Since Girardin's journalists used interchangeable initials, no one can be sure what Balzac actually wrote unless it was published over his name.

After quarrelling with Latouche, Balzac became friendly with Girardin, who founded *La Presse* in 1836. Together with *Le Siècle*, it inaugurated the era of cheap newspapers in France by charging 40 francs a year, only half the usual price, and relying for the first time on advertisements for revenue. In January 1830 Balzac found time to publish a new newspaper with Girardin and Victor Varaigne, the *Feuilleton des Journaux Politiques*. In February he was part of the claque organized to support Hugo's *Hernani*, of which he also wrote a very harsh anonymous review. He spent three months during the summer with Mme de Berny in the Loire valley, so missing the street fighting in Paris, and got to know Eugène Sue. Both politically and artistically Balzac was non-aligned. He satirized the middle-class entrepreneurs of whom he was himself a notable example, but he was neither a revolutionary nor a reactionary, neither a Catholic nor a militant atheist, neither a romantic nor a slave to the classical tradition he cherished. He was in favour, however, of a strong central authority, whose job it would be to impose a middle way in the wake of the fierce social resentments created by the Industrial Revolution in France.

In 1830 Balzac had a short affair with Olympe Pélissier, the mistress of Eugène Sue, with whom he cooperated briefly on an abortive theatrical project. By 1831 there was considerable demand for Balzac's work. August of that year saw publication of the highly successful *La Peau de chagrin*, for which Balzac had received 1,135 francs from Canel and Charles Gosselin in January, and at the end of September came his *Romans et contes philosophiques*. *La Peau de chagrin*, with an introduction by Philarète Chasles, had a second edition in September. At around this time Balzac came to rely increasingly on his wealthy and high-minded republican friend Zulma Carraud, wife of the director of studies at Saint-Cyr, who was demoted and became director of a gunpowder factory at Angoulême in 1831. He met Rossini, the flamboyant Dr Véron, founder of the *Revue de Paris* in 1829 and director of the Opéra from 1831 to 1835, Jules Sandeau, George Sand, and the Marquise de Castries, and was a witness at the marriage of Delphine Gay, daughter of Sophie Gay, to Girardin on 1 June 1831. He thought of standing as a candidate in the 1831 elections, but found no support, and added *L'Artiste* to the list of reviews to which he contributed extensively, dropping only *La Caricature*. He entertained a great deal, abandoned numerous projects, mostly for the theatre, and signed contracts for others which never came to fruition.

Politically, while his reports for *Le Voleur* had been even-handed, he had moved towards a nominally monarchist position, probably to please Henriette de Castries (1796–1861). She had left her husband to live with Metternich's son, Victor, and in 1827 had had a son by him. She later had a riding accident. Victor Metternich died in 1829 and late in 1831 the marquise wrote Balzac an unsigned letter which nevertheless gave her address. It was not Balzac's fault if they did not become lovers when, after replying at length, he was invited to stay in March 1832. Meanwhile, although he had received a total of 10,125 francs from books and 4,166 francs for newspaper and review articles in 1831, his debts that year rose by 6,000 francs. He had bought three sets of the house gowns he worked in from his tailor Buisson, a tilbury and a couple of horses, and had spent a great deal on champagne, books, bindings, and a groom. He borrowed from friends, kept on the most intimate of terms with Laure de Berny and Laure d'Abrantès, and even contemplated marriage to a wealthy widow, the Baronne Deurbroucq.

The horses and groom had to go, but Balzac's mother managed to borrow 10,000 francs for him in 1832. That allowed him to leave the Carrauds' home at Angoulême, where he liked working but where Zulma Carraud was resisting his advances, and to visit Mme de Castries at Aix, although he had to borrow 150 francs from Major Carraud and get his mother to repay it and send him 300 more to be picked up at Lyons. The visit to Aix and then, still in the company of the coquettish Mme de Castries, to Geneva from 27 August to 18 October was frustrat-

ing for Balzac, who cancelled a visit to Italy with her when she refused ever to become his mistress, and went to stay with Mme de Berny until early December. By the end of the year his debts totalled 100,000 francs and the first volume of the collected, obscene *Contes drolatiques* had appeared. They were intended to read like a Rabelaisian pastiche, although Balzac's interest in the more spiritual aspects of love increased as he wrote them. They delighted Zulma Carraud and Delphine de Girardin, and Fontaney notes the pleasure they gave, although George Sand was disgusted. Véron of the *Revue de Paris* wrote suggesting that Balzac should take chaster themes "if only to show the full range of your talent." He published a chilly review, as did the *Revue des Deux Mondes* (q.v.). Balzac continued to publish copiously in both reviews, as in *L'Artiste*, but he had now added the legitimist *Le Rénovateur* to the list in deference to Henriette de Castries. He was also using as publishers Gosselin and Canel as well as Mame. The *Scènes de la vie privée* was now in its second four-volume edition containing *Le Curé de Tours*, and the original of *Le Colonel Chabert* had appeared in four consecutive editions of *L'Artiste* from 19 February to 11 March.

The most important event for Balzac in 1832 however, was, the arrival of a letter, posted in Odessa in February, from "L'Etrangère," who eventually turned out to be Evelina Hanska, née Countess Rzewuska (1805/6–1882), the rich wife of a land-owner from the Polish Ukraine. Her sister had left her husband to live openly with a Russian general for 15 years, during which time she had had affairs with the poet Adam Mickiewicz, and with Pushkin. The tsar, who distrusted the Polish Ukrainian aristocracy, thought the sisters dangerous. Evelina Hanska was 33 and her husband 55. A secure communication line with Balzac was established via the Swiss governess, "Lirette," in charge of Mme Hanska's only surviving child, Anna. Mme Hanska wrote again in November, and Balzac acknowledged receipt as requested, by an insertion in *La Quotidienne*.

He spent 1833 under great pressure. The almost autobiographical study of his own intellectual development, *L'Histoire intellectuelle de Louis Lambert*, later expanded into the 1835 *Louis Lambert* of *Le Livre mystique*, was a failure when it appeared in January. Literary commitments and debtors were pressing. Balzac began to shorten his life by extending his working hours and drinking black coffee reduced to the consistency of soup. He did take a rest with the Carrauds in the spring, but returned to furious publishers in Paris. He had contributed to a new review, *L'Europe Littéraire*, while unfulfilled contracts remained with old ones. He broke with the *Revue de Paris*. Mame took him to court and the critics rubbished some of his better thinking in *Le Médecin de campagne*. While waiting to meet Mme Hanska, Balzac had a liaison with Maria du Fresnay (1809–1892), by whom he had a daughter, born on 4 June 1834. He was entertained by the James de Rothschilds, met Marceline Desbordes-Valmore, set up a popular book club, which offered a book a month at one franc a volume, and signed a contract with Mme Charles Béchet (1800–1880) for 12 volumes, divided into three series, of his collected works for between 27,000 and 30,000 francs. When she needed another 80 pages, Balzac wrote *L'Illustre Gaudissart* in one night. The first parts to be published, five and six, contained *Eugénie Grandet*. At least five other projects were aborted, and Balzac's purely journalistic work ceased. Only parts of novels and stories were released to newspapers and reviews. Further *Contes drolatiques* appeared.

On 25 September Balzac met Mme Hanska for the first time

at Neuchâtel. He left on 1 October. On 24 December they met again in Geneva, and Balzac gave her the manuscript of *Eugénie Grandet* as a Christmas present. She had made enquiries and received all sorts of reports about him from Paris and found him vulgar but bewitching. They became lovers, chiefly at her instigation, in January 1834. Balzac left for Paris on 8 February. He spent a fortnight with the Carrauds, took a place in a box at the Opéra and at the Théâtre des Italiens, spent six weeks with Laure de Berny in July and part of the autumn at Saché. In October, at about the time he met Frances Sarah Lovell (1804–1833), Countess Guidoboni-Visconti, Jules Sandeau moved in with him in the Rue Cassini. He made his peace with the *Revue de Paris* under its new director, Achille Brindeau, who published two sections of *Séraphîta*, two of *Le Père Goriot*, and a "Lettre aux écrivains français du XIXe siècle." Balzac also wrote for Sophie Gay's new *Les Causeries du Monde*, and Vimont and Ollivier joined his list of publishers. In 1834 what was to become *La Comédie humaine* coalesced into a concrete literary project.

Zulma Carraud's father died and Balzac received a warm invitation from her to come and visit. She was in her second pregnancy, which was not proving easy. Laure de Berny was ill. Balzac's mother had lost the rest of her money, but *Eugénie Grandet* was selling well, and through Mme Hanska's cousin, Marie Potocka, Balzac was invited to the glittering assemblies at the Austrian embassy. He also dined with Vidocq, the criminal turned police chief, and the son of Sanson, the executioner of Louis XVI. His half-brother Henri returned home from Mauritius in 1834 with his considerably older wife, currently pregnant, and debts amounting to 150,000 francs. Balzac's mother sold her last property to help him, and now had only what Balzac paid her in interest to live on.

There seemed to be no means of smoothing over the quarrel with Gosselin, Canel's partner, and the contract for the whole expanded *Comédie* was about to go to Mme Béchet, who was already publishing the original *Etudes de mœurs au XIXe siècle* in three series of *Scènes de la vie privée*, when her publishing manager, Edmond Werdet, came to see Balzac and offered to put up his life savings of 3,500 francs for the contract. Balzac laughed, dismissed him, reflected, called him back, and accepted the offer. Rights were bought back with money that did not yet exist. Letters were constantly written to Mme Hanska. From now on Balzac's biography is the story of how the *Comédie* was written, with Balzac working himself to death to keep his creditors at bay. He probably had an affair with Countess Guidoboni-Visconti in 1835, after which he met Mme Hanska in Vienna, where he was received by Metternich. On leaving Mme Hanska on 4 June he would not see her again until 1843.

In October 1835 Balzac saw Laure de Berny for the last time before her death on 27 July 1836. Like Mme Hanska, who became his wife, and Zulma Carraud, who was in love with him but was never his mistress, Mme de Berny played something of a maternal role in Balzac's life. Most of Balzac's biographers have drawn attention to the touch of femininity in his sexual make-up. His mistresses noticed it, too, although it shows up only occasionally in the imaginative patterns of his work, above all in the lesbian plot of *La Fille aux yeux d'or* from the *Histoire des treize* trilogy. Philarète Chasles suggests in the unpublished part of his memoirs that there were more than just homosexual nuances in Balzac's relationships with Jules Sandeau and the

painter Auguste Borget, Sandeau's predecessor in the Rue Cassini. But even if the effects of his mother's withdrawal of affection during Balzac's childhood were not as far-reaching as Chasles suggests, it is possible to observe in the novels what amounts to almost feminine insight in some of the portrayals of men.

The pressure on Balzac to deliver during 1835 was extreme. He wrote *La Messe de l'athée* in one night, *L'Interdiction* in three. At the end of the year he quarrelled with François Buloz, the powerful new director of the *Revue de Paris*, director of the *Revue des Deux Mondes* since 1831, and director-to-be of the Comédie-Française, who had sent the uncorrected proofs of a novel to which Balzac attached much importance, *Le Lys dans la vallée*, to St Petersburg. Balzac refused to supply the rest of the novel and when he won a partial victory in the long-drawn-out lawsuit, Werdet sold 1,800 of his 2,000 copies in a few hours. The reviews had not been good, partly because Buloz saw to it that they were not, and partly because the book was an obvious challenge to Sainte-Beuve, long a literary enemy of Balzac, who was not above resenting the affection in which Sainte-Beuve was held by Mme de Castries.

Harassed on all sides, Balzac, whose silver Laure had pawned while he was in Vienna, now sold the right to republish the early Saint-Aubin novels, hired assistants to produce stage works, and acquired the *Chronique de Paris*, putting in editorial staff to run it. The editorial line-up included some of Buloz's other current enemies, such as the trenchant Gustave Planche, but also the young Gautier and Hugo himself, with Granville, Monnier, and Daumier for the cartoons. Balzac paid only 120 francs for the business, but he needed 45,000 francs of working capital to run it. He was still living well beyond his means and now had 46,000 francs of debts over and above those run up by his family. He bought silverware for a single dinner party to impress Rossini, pawning it after the meal, and could only work surrounded by comforts and elegant furnishings. The writers for the *Chronique* came to dine richly and hilariously every week, but the rent was owing, and Balzac had to do most of the writing himself. What he wrote under these pressures was of staggeringly high quality. It is difficult to avoid the suspicion that Balzac subconsciously needed and chose to subject himself to such intolerable pressures for the creative satisfaction he derived from the activities to which they impelled him.

There were periodic breakdowns and releases of tension, and there were further love affairs. Balzac may well have been the father of "Fanny" Guidoboni-Visconti's child. He moved from the Rue Cassini to Chaillot partly to evade creditors and partly to escape his turn of watch duty in the Garde Nationale, which cost him eight days of imprisonment in 1836. In prison he lived like a king, spending 575 francs (Werdet's) during that one week. The *Chronique* failed, leaving an additional debt of 47,217 francs. Balzac's business ventures invariably made a fortune for someone else, providing him meanwhile, like the clutter of people and places in his memory, with the raw material for his novels. Part I of *Illusions perdues*, generally rated among his best work, was written under threat of imminent bankruptcy.

Help generally came from somewhere. In 1836 it came from Fanny Guidoboni-Visconti. Her husband had inherited money from his mother and required someone to act on his behalf in Turin. Balzac was a qualified lawyer, and he needed to get away from his creditors. He was given power of attorney and offered a commission on whatever he could obtain of the disputed inheritance. He travelled with his "page," Caroline Marbouty (1803–1890), dressed in male attire. She had once replaced George Sand in the affections of Jules Sandeau, who had left Balzac at Chaillot, unable to stand the pace. Now, having captivated Balzac's affections, she paid her own fare in order to accompany him. It looks as though, while sharing a suite, they never became lovers. Werdet had gone bankrupt and sold the rights to Balzac's future works to a consortium for 63,000 francs. In November Balzac received an advance of 50,000 francs, which enabled him to pay off his most pressing debts, and was promised 1,500 francs a month together with half of the profits. He also dined with Talleyrand the year after dining with Metternich.

Balzac now became the first novelist ever to publish a novel in a French daily newspaper. *La Vieille Fille* appeared in Girardin's *La Presse* in 12 instalments from 23 October to 4 November. Balzac missed Laure de Berny, who had kept him away while she was ill and called for him only when she was dying and he was in Italy. She alone had made him rewrite his sentences before submitting his work for typesetting. His normal practice was to have everything set immediately in worn-out type, which he then totally smothered in additions, and the compositors complained about their "hour of Balzac." He sometimes had very great difficulty in actually starting a work. The first page of the manuscript of *Illusions perdues* shows dozens of false starts and doodles, and the first draft was often only a skeleton. That of *Le Médecin de campagne* was written in 72 hours. The subsequent rewriting took 60 nights.

In 1837 the Guidoboni-Viscontis sent Balzac to Italy again on the same terms to finish their business and, at considerable social risk, Fanny later took him into her house on the Champs-Elysées. He now owed 162,000 francs. Delayed at Genoa on his return from Venice, where he had been given the suite once occupied by Musset and George Sand, he was beguiled into visiting Sardinia, where the Romans had apparently left potentially lucrative silver-bearing slag heaps for lack of the means to refine the deposits. Unfortunately, although the assay proved the value of the slag, the rights had already been acquired by someone else. The mines yielded 1,200,000 francs. *Le Figaro* had bought *César Birotteau* for a sales promotion, to be given free to anyone who subscribed to the paper for three months. Balzac was offered 20,000 francs, with the delivery deadline set for 1 December 1837, and worked with his feet in a mustard bath. He spent some time with George Sand, who addicted him to pipe smoking at Nohant early in 1838, before revisiting Sardinia, only to discover the slag heaps already taken. On his return he found that Laure d'Abrantès had died on 7 June. Her career as a writer had failed, her belongings had been sold, and she had died in penury.

The Guidoboni-Viscontis agreed to finance Balzac's purchase of a dilapidated cottage and a plot of land called Les Jardies near Versailles and the new railway line. The plan was that Surville would run up a second house, and Balzac would then have two houses and four or five acres for 40,000 francs, which he was going to set about earning. He installed Fanny Guidoboni-Visconti and her children in the renovated and decorated cottage at Les Jardies, and moved his best furniture and books there as a precaution against seizure. He intended to make a fortune by building greenhouses to grow pineapples for the Paris market. He hired an assistant to cook an enormous meal at one a.m. and then take dictation until seven, working during the day on the notes for the stage successes Balzac never ceased to dream about. The assistant did not last long, but Balzac did find an excellent collaborator in the irredeemably bohemian Jean-Laurent, who was devoted to Balzac's affairs and managed them well. It was in 1838 that Balzac wrote an apologia in one of his prefaces for cutting literary material to the size and taste demanded by the public and by commercial requirements. He himself would surely have been quite unable to write had he, like some of those who despised him, had an inherited fortune to support his literary endeavours. He responded creatively to commercial constraints, and kept a stock of stories, sketches, drafts, rejected attempts, and ideas on which to draw as his paymasters demanded.

Balzac suffered a defeat in 1840 with his play *Vautrin*. In order to get it finished, he had been obliged to share out the writing, and Frédéric Lemaître in the title role looked like a caricature of Louis-Philippe. The Duc d'Orléans left the theatre and woke the king. The play was banned next day, and Lemaître refused to play any more Balzac roles. Dumas, Sue, and Frédéric Soulié were now challenging his supremacy in newspaper serialization, and the whole family was broke. Seeking to play the role of Voltaire in the Calas affair, in 1839 Balzac spent 10,000 francs in a vain effort to save a lawyer, Peytel, from the guillotine. By 1840 his debts stood at 262,000 francs, of which 115,000 was owing to his family or close friends, and another 37,000 was for the moment dormant. One creditor, Foulon, who had backed *Vautrin*, tried to seize Les Jardies. He had already got hold of the furniture Balzac had persuaded his tailor to hide for him.

Relations with Fanny were cooling, and even the correspondence with Evelina Hanska had lost some of its urgency. In 1840 Balzac did finally alight, however, on the title *La Comédie humaine* for the project unified in his mind since 1834. He also had a liaison with Hélène de Valette (1808–1873), who lent him 10,000 francs. On the model of Karr's *Les Guêpes* he founded the *Revue Parisienne*, a political and literary monthly review whose circulation started at 20,000 copies in 1839 and quickly climbed to 30,000. Balzac's venture lasted only three issues, long enough, however, to include the famous review of Stendhal's *La Chartreuse de Parme* of 25 September 1840 and to create or continue hostilities with Latouche, Sue, and Sainte-Beuve. Balzac now rented a house in Paris under an assumed name, even allowing his mother to live with him for the first time. Foulon pressed too hard and finally forced Balzac into the ultimate refuge of the debtor, liquidation. Les Jardies was worth perhaps 100,000 francs. A valuation on forced sale was obtained at 17,550 francs, for which sum Balzac bought it back, using his architect for the purpose. The creditors were forced to share the derisory sum between them. The new house at Passy had entrances on two levels. Balzac installed a housekeeper, known as "Mme de Brugnol" (1804–1874), whose guest he purported to be, but who was part mistress and part literary agent as well as cook-cum-housekeeper. Balzac worked a 16-hour day, interrupting his routine only very occasionally, although he visited the Girardins and George Sand. His mother soon found the presence of the housekeeper intolerable and from 1842 ceased to live with her son. Mme Hanska eventually forced Balzac to dismiss Mme de Brugnol, who finally married a wealthy industrialist and became the sister-in-law of a peer of France.

On 2 October 1841 Balzac signed a contract with four publishers, Furne, Hetzel, Dubochet, and Paulin, for the whole of the *Comédie*. He was to become a close friend of Hetzel. During

1841 Balzac published episodes and extracts in *Le Commerce, La Presse, Le Messager, L'Artiste*, and *Le Siècle*. No year in his life is quite typical, but this one saw the publication of a novel, *Le Curé de village*, by Souverain, two small illustrated "physiologies," which had taken over as a popular genre from the earlier "scènes," an extract from *Le Médecin de campagne* in volume form, and several texts in Hetzel's *Scènes de la vie publique et privée des animaux*. His illustrators included Gavarni, Monnier, Daumier, Meissonier, Trimolet, Lorentz, and Grandville. The Odéon took a play, *Les Ressources de Quinola*, in which Marie Dorval refused to play the part written for her. It was a failure, met by a hostile press and public, and only ran to 19 performances in March and April 1842. Balzac still wrote occasionally to Evelina Hanska, who was occupied with the strictly Catholic upbringing of her daughter and rarely replied. Her husband died on 10 November 1841, leaving her in a delicate situation since his family now intervened to prevent the transference to her of his vast and vastly underexploited estates, comprising not only the mansion at Wierzchownia but 21,000 acres inhabited by some 3,000 people. She warned Balzac to stay away. The High Court in Kiev refused to endorse the will. The tsar was not well disposed towards the Polish Ukrainian aristocracy, and the family was anti-Balzac, whoever got the estate. The last thing Evelina needed was an impecunious plebeian French author of doubtful orthodoxy knocking on her door, although Balzac was clearly intent on marrying her. He took a considerable risk by sending the notorious Liszt to call on her, and she clearly found him as attractive as his reputation suggested he would be.

La Comédie humaine was now taking its final shape. The prospectus appeared on 10 April 1842. Both Hippolyte Rolle, the critic of *Le National*, and George Sand refused invitations to write a preface, and Hetzel obliged Balzac to write his "Avant-propos" in July. The first volume was completed with delivery of its 10th part in June, the second with the 20th in September, and the third in November. Balzac sketched another novel, abandoned it, and wrote "Les fantaisies de la Gina," which did not appear until it was translated into Italian in 1848. Meanwhile, and all in 1842, he published three novels, the failed play, and episodes and extracts in *La Presse, Le Siècle, Le Musée des Familles*, and *La Législature*. While dining with Victor Hugo, he agreed to have his bust made by David d'Angers. In spite of lack of encouragement from Evelina, Balzac finally arrived in St Petersburg on 29 July 1843.

The visit was a great success and Balzac returned much heartened, travelling overland. He met Tieck and Humboldt, and visited Berlin, Leipzig, and Dresden. He had to abandon his ambitions to be elected to the Académie Française, however, largely on account of his chronic and much-talked-of indebtedness. He was awarded the Légion d'Honneur in 1845, but literary acknowledgement otherwise eluded him, as did success in writing for the stage and the political career he sporadically envisaged. There was now considerable hostility towards him in Parisian literary circles, led by Sainte-Beuve, and although he was given a contract to write two novels for the *Journal des Débats*, which had serialized Sue's greatest success, readers of *La Presse* found *Les Paysans* tedious and Balzac eventually repaid some of the advance on it.

Evelina Hanska won her case but, unable to get a passport to France, went to Dresden. She forbade Balzac to join her there, largely because his presence would have made it more difficult to arrange her daughter's marriage. He wrote almost every day, and was allowed to go in April 1845. Anna (1828–1915) was to be married to Count Georges Mniszech (1823–1881). The couple travelled with Balzac and Evelina to Hamburg, Cannstadt, and Strasburg. The trip was a happy one, and Balzac started collecting antique furniture with his habitual energy. Mme Hanska and her daughter were installed in Paris, and a new lawyer persuaded Balzac's creditors to settle for about 50 per cent of his debts, although Les Jardies finally had to be sold in October 1845. Balzac's health had been declining since 1844.

Evelina entrusted Balzac with 100,000 francs for furnishings, but he naturally invested it. The Guidoboni-Viscontis lent him a further 12,000 francs, and that summer Evelina and he visited the Loire valley, returned to Strasburg, and travelled downstream by Rhine steamer to Holland. Balzac visited her in Baden and then both of them, with Anna and Georges, travelled down the Saône and the Rhône by boat before leaving for Naples. Balzac returned by Pisa, and later in the year smoked hashish at the Hôtel Pimodan. On 26 December he went to Rouen by train. Early in 1846 Furne was able to announce the completion of the 16-volume edition of *La Comédie humaine*.

In March 1846 Balzac left to join Evelina in Italy, and they travelled through Italy and Switzerland together. Evelina, by now pregnant, was to have a miscarriage, which left Balzac so upset that he was unable to write for weeks. Balzac was Anna's witness at her marriage to Mniszech in Wiesbaden on 13 October. Evelina was brought incognito to Paris on 6 February 1847, and in May Balzac took her back to Germany. In September he joined her at Wierzchownia and stayed in the Ukraine until January 1848. Miscalculating the cost of transport, he immediately dreamt of exporting some of the 20,000 odd acres of oak forest to satisfy France's insatiable demand for railway sleepers. The estate was made over to Anna by her mother in exchange for an annuity, a condition specified by the tsar for granting her permission to marry Balzac.

The 1848 revolution upset all Balzac's plans. He arrived in Paris on 15 February after visiting various antique shops. Success in the theatre with *La Marâtre* was prevented by the political situation. Balzac, who was already suffering from a dangerous heart condition, visited Saché again and attended Chateaubriand's funeral. Jean-Laurent became his literary executor and his mother was put in charge of everything else when Balzac left again for Wierzchownia, where, apart from a visit to Kiev, he stayed until his marriage to Evelina Hanska on 14 March 1850 at seven a.m. The couple left for France on 24 April, arriving late in May. Balzac was now very ill. He died on 18 August 1850. The pall bearers were Hugo, Dumas, Sainte-Beuve, and the minister of the interior. Hugo gave the graveside oration.

WORKS

It was typical of Balzac's method of composition and way of life that he generally had several books on the go at once. Serialization imposed deadlines, and the need for money generated unpredictable urgencies which overtook one another. There were frequent setbacks, best overcome by shelving a work that might be taken up again later, to be developed to a different length or in a different direction or genre from that originally intended. Many projects were simply left in abeyance, or some were dropped altogether. If literary composition often demanded the feverish expenditure of creative energy, it was because the imposition of literary form on the seething raw materials within his mind required intense concentration. The difficulty always lay in the selection, development, and reduction to ordered patterns of materials taken from a simmering stockpot of ideas, experiences, and acutely observed phenomena of behaviour.

Despite the deplorable illegibility of his corrected proofs, Balzac was a surprisingly slow, painstaking, and fastidious author, who was never content until the sense of his sentences was perfectly clear. He rewrote the first page of *La Dernière Incarnation de Vautrin* 25 times. At no point did he intend never to add anything more to a closed cycle of novels which would complete a planned series. That we have a more or less neatly bundled corpus of novels to which we can legitimately refer as *La Comédie humaine* is a function of the economics of the publishing trade rather than of imaginative requirements. Balzac was active from 1841 on extending legal protection to author's copyright. There are 20 known pirated editions of *César Birotteau*, published within a little over a year of its first appearance. When in 1834 Balzac became aware of the general coherence of his work, it seemed to consist of a general study of human behaviour, which he intended to classify in an essay on human energy. He wrote to Mme Hanska emphasizing the comprehensiveness of what he planned: "the history of the human heart, traced thread by thread, social history in all its parts." Nothing would be imagined. "It will be what happens everywhere." Balzac envisaged the novels as almost scientifically depicting the social effects of human behaviour in the *Etudes de moeurs* (24 volumes), the causes in the *Etudes philosophiques* (15 volumes), and its nature or principles in the *Etudes analytiques* (9 volumes). Contemporary society would be not only depicted, but also judged. Balzac distanced himself from Scott's merely historical romances because he wanted to deal with every aspect of his own society and make fierce moral comments on what he observed.

By 1840 the collection of novels was enriched by a fund of material, some of which had already been formed into future projects to which Balzac was almost fully, or almost not at all, mentally or financially committed. It was to be called *La Comédie humaine*, rivalling Dante's *Divine Comedy* only in its comprehensiveness. The final contract was signed on 14 April 1841 and revised on 2 October, with the title *La Comédie humaine* used for the first time in October. It was for 16 octavo volumes to be published over two years. In fact publication took place over five years:

Volumes 1–3	*Scènes de la vie privée* i, ii, and iii	1842
Volumes 5,6,8	*Scènes de la vie de province* i, ii, and iv	1843
9	*Scènes de la vie parisienne* i	1843
Volume 7	*Scènes de la vie de province* iii	1843
10, 11	*Scènes de la vie parisienne* ii, iii	1844
Volume 4	*Scène de la vie privée* iv	1845
13	*Scènes de la vie militaire, Scènes de la vie de campagne*	1845
Volume 12	*Scènes de la vie parisienne* iv, *Scènes de la vie politique*	1846
14, 15	*Etudes philosophiques* i, ii (dated 1845)	1846
16	*Etudes philosophiques* ii and *Etudes analytiques*	1846
Supplementary volume 17, published by Furne,	*Les Parents pauvres*	1848

In fact by 1846 Balzac had written much more. He reclassified the novels in 1845, and we have his corrections on Furne's 1846 prospectus for a new edition. The classification would of course be of much greater interest if it had included works projected to complete a set of novels constituting a closed cycle, but such a project never really existed. Indeed, the evidence suggests that at several moments from 1845 onwards Balzac would gladly have exchanged his novelist's trade either for the theatre or for a more secure literary income, such as membership of the Académie Française would have brought, or even for wealth and leisure with Evelina Hanska. The likelihood is that in the end, and at whatever cost, Balzac chose almost exactly the life he wanted to lead, surrounded by luxury, driven by debt, loved by well-bred, cultivated, and beautiful women and, sustained by coffee, burning himself out in immensely satisfying creative activity.

There was a shifting vision of a corpus of novels. It is true that in 1847 Balzac still thought that he was only two thirds of the way through the *Comédie*, with the *Etudes analytiques* still to be written, that *Louis Lambert* was to have had a sequel, and that *Le Contrat de mariage* was to be balanced by "L'inventaire après décès." A list of 53 novels or stories projected but never written has been drawn up, and there are in addition sets of brief notes for countless more, some of which were plundered for pieces which were in fact written. If Balzac had married earlier and settled down happily, would he have had anything to write about? So many of the novels we have grow so obviously out of the unpleasantness of Balzac's situation at the time of writing them that it seems unlikely that he was ready for domestic bliss much before he was offered the real prospect of attaining it. The probability is that the exceedingly shrewd Mme Hanska realized this. At Wierzchownia in the winter of 1847 Balzac finished *L'Initié* and was working simultaneously on four other novels, of which one, *La Femme auteur*, presaged what could have amounted to as much again as the original *Comédie* had contained. We do not know what Balzac would have written, or how his vision, always depending on his changing experience, would have developed, or what raw materials of memory or fantasy he would have drawn upon.

In spite of what must therefore be regarded as its limited interest, the final classification, taking into account Balzac's markings on Furne's catalogue, as adopted by the 40-volume Conard edition (1912–1940), is given in an appendix to the bibliography. The dates refer to first publication and not, as in the bibliography itself, to publication in volume form. The bibliography needs to be used with exceptional care. *La Rabouilleuse* is not untypical. Conceived as a novel in 1833, it was referred to spasmodically by Balzac in 1835. Its first part, *Le Bonhomme Rouget*, was set in type in 1839 and, under the new title of *Les Deux frères*, appeared in *La Presse* from 24 February to 4 March 1841. The second part, *Un ménage de garçon en province*, appeared in October-November 1842. The two parts were not put together until 1843, and were only referred to as *La Rabouilleuse* in Balzac's posthumous notes.

Balzac's output is unified by the use of the same almost invariably middle-class characters in different books at different stages of their development. They play sometimes principal and sometimes subordinate roles, and they know other characters from different books. The element of observation is strong, so that Balzac writes at his best when he is dealing with situations, people, and places similar to those with which we know him to have been familiar. The often harsh moral comment is almost entirely implicit and frequently ambiguous. If the honest are often victims, it is because they are often also stupid. If the dominating members of society can be evil, they do not necessarily lack an admirable strength of purpose. This is the observation of a La Rochefoucauld, less aphoristically but more vividly presented. Double-dealers, timeservers, trimmers, and swindlers are contemptible, but can come out on top. They are none the less presented by Balzac with highly moral disdain. Implied condemnation can be tempered with admiration. Machiavelli fights with Rousseau for Balzac's soul, and neither wins.

The strength of the oeuvre is cumulative. Balzac very nearly portrays the way of life of a whole society, although he is stronger on its domestic and urban than on its rural or religious aspects. The characters are built up gradually, with shrewdness rather than subtlety. Balzac has been criticized for failing wholly to transpose his moral attitudes into aesthetic terms, for describing the moral qualities of his characters rather than embodying them in action, and it is true that his rumbustious style can lead him to abandon the restraint which greater artistic integrity might have imposed. But without the colossal energy and fertility of his imagination, we should not have the acutely perceptive panorama of his society which he has left us and for which occasionally overblown metaphors and idiosyncratic manifestations of personal philosophy are small prices to pay. Balzac only ever goes seriously wrong in his fiction when he is gratuitously bawdy, as in the *Contes drolatiques*, or resorts to overt statement, as in *Louis Lambert* which fails to make the moral comment through the narration itself of the action. The characters do not have the psychological complexities of Stendhal's, and the novels do not have the concentrated disillusion of Flaubert's, but they do display an intensity of social observation not again rivalled in French literature before Proust. Balzac neither overdramatizes like Dumas, nor trivializes and simplifies like Sue, his rivals in the feuilleton market, and he is far superior to either in his control of irony and his expert use of dialogue.

Occasionally Balzac wields his scalpel clumsily when morally dissecting specimens from the society he is depicting, but the scalpel can be very sharp, revealing nuances in moral and social constraints in such a way as to throw quite unexpected light on complexities of motivation. Personal behaviour can be linked to implied criticisms of public policy. The inadequacies of the transport and financial systems, for instance, are clear from *Le Médecin de campagne* and *La Maison Nucingen*, while some of the novels, like *Eugénie Grandet*, the *Histoire de la grandeur et de la décadence de César Birotteau*, and the unfinished *Les Paysans* are virtually devoted to public issues, economic, legal, and social. It has been pointed out that one of Balzac's frivolous and amusing codes of behaviour for persons of various social conditions, *Le Code des gens honnêtes* of 1825, leads to the recurrent idea that all moral principles can be violated respectably and legally. We are told in *La Maison Nucingen* "Il y a des actes arbitraires qui sont criminels d'individu à individu, lesquels arrivent à rien quand ils sont étendus à une multitude quelconque, comme une goutte d'acide prussique

devient innocente dans un baquet d'eau (There are deliberate acts which are criminal among individuals but which come to nothing when they are extended to any collectivity, as a drop of prussic acid becomes innocuous in a bath of water)." This is also Vautrin's view in *Le Père Goriot*: "Le secret des grandes fortunes sans cause apparente est un crime oublié, parce qu'il a été proprement fait (The secret of great fortunes without apparent foundations is a crime which has been forgotten because it was properly executed)." Balzac never forgot his legal background.

Some of Balzac's novels rely on the supernatural, usually some non-religious form of mesmerism, illuminism, second sight or phrenology, thereby impoverishing the psychological motivation of the characters, and these are often, like *Ursule Mirouët*, the weaker novels. At his weakest Balzac was liable to slip into the melodramatic retribution of a world for which he unconvincingly created supernatural dimensions. The best novels include a conflict of personal or social forces, often involving republicanism, monarchism, greed, or probity, and almost always social standing. The new social order is to be welcomed for its entrepreneurial openings, its receptivity to change, and its opportunities for the middle classes, but abhorred for its inhumanity, its immorality, and the destruction of so much that autocracy alone can produce in patronage, cultivation, and beauty. By relating his society to a larger moral framework Balzac none the less outstrips the merely realist (q. v.) authors, just as his own reliance on observed behaviour allows him to surpass the writers of romantic (q. v.) melodrama.

His famous descriptions of his characters' environments not only enhance the authenticity of the atmosphere, binding the characters to the physical surroundings which help to determine their actions. They also metaphorically communicate qualities of character. The description of the "maison Vauquer" in *Le Père Goriot* gives an insight into the moral qualities of the lives lived by its inhabitants, as does the description of Grandet's house in *Eugénie Grandet*. The furniture in the "maison Vauquer" is "one-eyed, sickly, dying." In *Le Curé de Tours* Balzac describes a house in the following terms: "cet endroit est un désert de pierres, une solitude pleine de physionomie, et qui ne peut être habitée que par des êtres arrivés à une nullité complète ou doués d'une force d'âme prodigieuse (this place is a desert of stones, a solitude full of character which can only be lived in by people who have reached complete nullity or who are endowed with an extraordinary strength of soul)." The environment and its inhabitants can challenge as well as mirror one another.

The realism often depends if not on recent documentation, then on accurate memories of places and dates which lend the novels the sort of authenticity that Balzac the story teller had shown himself able to create when first visiting the Pommereuls at Fougères in 1828. *La Cousine Bette* starts "Vers le milieu du mois de juillet de l'année 1828 (Towards the middle of July 1828)," as if the narrator were trying hard to remember the precise circumstances in which the events he wants to narrate actually took place. A similar effect is created in *Ursule Mirouët*: "En entrant à Nemours, du côté de Paris, on passe sur le canal du Loing…Depuis 1830 on a malheureusement bâti plusieurs maisons en deça du pont (On entering Nemours from the direction of Paris, you pass over the Loing canal…Unhappily they have built several houses beyond the bridge since 1830)." A reader instinctively trusts a narrator who has views about the siting of recent property developments.

There are said to be 2,472 named and 566 unnamed characters

in *La Comédie humaine* and endless attempts have been made to relate the characters in the novels to real people, and the situations to those experienced by Balzac himself. The novels certainly show recurrent imaginative patterns imposed by Balzac's own experiences, especially with women, and especially deriving from a psychological need to depict mother-substitutes. But it is profitless to try to identify real-life situations with those in the novels and otiose to attempt the psychological analysis of any author in other than the most general terms from his literary creations, even if Balzac's life is sufficiently well documented to make it perfectly possible to see the correspondence between his psychology and experiences and the pattern of relationships, obsessive manias, and financial preoccupations in his novels. There was always a Nucingen, a Goriot, a Grandet, a Rastignac struggling to get out of him. He was too much all of them for any one to have come near to resembling him.

Les Chouans is about the guerrilla warfare between revolutionaries and monarchists in 1799, interesting largely on account of the softening of Balzac's attitude both to love and to the legitimist cause between the 1829 and the 1834 versions, and for its obvious dependence on Scott. What distinguished it from Scott is what entitles it to later incorporation into the *Comédie*, the depiction of the active force of passion: "La femme porte le désordre dans la société par la passion: la passion a des accidents infinis. Peignez donc les passions (Woman introduces disorder into society through passion. Passion has an infinity of varieties. Go and paint the passions)." This advice, given by d'Arthez to Lucien de Rubempré in the second part of *Illusions perdues* and taken up by Balzac for himself, defines one intention of the *Comédie* and defies Scott's idea of women as purely passive objects caught up in the course of events. Love deflects a civil war in *Les Chouans*, but the loyal protagonist who deserts on account of love was fighting for a cause that is depicted as already lost. It is a romantic novel with a romantic ending, but it marks the emergence of Balzac the novelist from Balzac the hack.

La Physiologie du mariage still betrays its light-hearted derivation from the codes, giving only a foretaste of the novels to come. From 1830 to 1832 we have the six novellas from the first two volumes of the *Scènes de la vie privée*, *Le Curé de Tours* and *Le Colonel Chabert*, both still shorter than standard novels, the *Contes philosophiques*, and *La Peau de chagrin*, with its reliance on the supernatural. Raphaël de Valentin, broke after gambling, acquires a magic piece of wild ass's skin whose possessor's wishes will always be granted, but with the granting of each wish the skin will shrink, and its possessor's life will shorten. The novel has been likened to a poem. In fact it is an allegory of the self-destructive forces of life. In order to live we must destroy ourselves.

The first really important novel is commonly considered to have been *Eugénie Grandet*, a study of the conflict between a miser and his daughter in Saumur. Grandet is totally concentrated inside his master passion, avaricious beyond the point of caricature. We are startled into finding him convincing, and the social consequences of his operations alarming. It is a well-coordinated and well-proportioned novel which avoids the trap of making Eugénie too insipid to inherit her father's strength of will. *Le Médecin de campagne*, which reflects a change in Balzac's political views, is about rural economy and Catholicism as a socially beneficial force.

Le Père Goriot is another study of monomania, this time the perverted love bestowed by a widower on his daughters which becomes increasingly grotesque. Again the character is taken beyond caricature to a degree of distortion that is pathologically tragic. The work was taken out of the *Scènes de la vie parisienne*, although it was at home there, not least because it introduces us to the as yet uncorrupted Eugène de Rastignac. It was Balzac's meeting with Vidocq, the criminal who, from 1811 to 1827 and from 1831 to 1832, turned police chief, and whose ghosted memoirs had appeared in 1828–29, which persuaded him to turn a conte into the complex novel we now have, with Vautrin an inhabitant with Goriot of the Vauquer boarding house. This is the first novel to use recurrent characters and, in spite of the incredibility of Vautrin and Goriot, it is generally regarded as one of Balzac's best. Goriot's increasing seediness as he becomes demented with doglike devotion to his daughters is depicted against the luxuriously elegant salon to which one of them has automatic entrée and the other would give her soul to be admitted, making this novel a trenchant comment on contrasting traits of character as well as on contrasting ways of life and ambitions within the same society.

Le Lys dans la vallée has an extra-literary interest as a retake of Sainte-Beuve's *Volupté* and the basis for the life-long hostility that existed between Balzac and his pall bearer. *Illusions perdues* depicts the love of the 20-year-old Lucien for the 36-year-old Louise which disillusions both. The three parts were redesigned to fit into a scheme in which the middle one would take place in Paris. The first volume, *Les Deux poètes*, became a study of the atrocious workings of the class system in a provincial town. The *Histoire de la grandeur et de la décadence de César Birotteau*, its title parodying Montesquieu and Gibbon, was conceived in 1833, written at the Carrauds' in 1834, and finished at speed to meet its November 1837 deadline. Like *La Maison Nucingen*, which appeared in 1838, it is a study of commercial habits and values in the Parisian middle classes. *César Birotteau* brings to perfection the technique derived from Scott of starting in the middle of the story, flashing back, and resuming the central thread, taking up subordinate ones as the narrative progresses. It is a story of hubris: Birotteau can manage honest trading but not speculation. The novel contains much good-humoured satire of small tradespeople brilliantly observed, and Birotteau, while touching, is one of Balzac's great comic figures. The limitations of his mind and his imagination are masterfully drawn, and Balzac here reaches out towards the peaks attained by Flaubert. It cost him some anguish to find the key to the novel in Birotteau's integrity. The other side of that coin was Nucingen and *La Maison Nucingen* presents an excellent picture of brilliantly clever financial chicanery which concentrates on the victims. Balzac unleashes here his feelings about the journalists and newspaper proprietors against whom he had to struggle and whom he was inclined to regard as rapacious adventurers.

La Cousine Bette from 1846, near the end of Balzac's period of most intense activity, is the story of the poor relation who takes her revenge on the family that has patronized her. Her cousin Adeline has made a brilliant marriage and Bette encourages Adeline's husband Hulot in his infidelities, not satisfied until she has brought the whole family to shame and ruin. The novel is a story of rancour and hatred played off, as usual in Balzac, against the restraints imposed by the social proprieties, for the whole world depicted by the *Comédie* would simply dissolve if no one cared what anyone else thought of them. None even of the monomanias would have crystallized. In Hulot *La Cousine Bette* contains a study in geriatric eroticism. Balzac was dropping allusions for those who knew how to pick them up. When he made Hulot Valérie's lover he was probably alluding to Victor Hugo's well-known embarrassment at being caught as the lover of Mme Léonie Biard. He enjoys the victory of his fictional women, and Valérie is a spectacular example of hypocrisy and cunning, simultaneously persuading each of her four lovers that he is the father of the child she is carrying. Balzac was in fact outbidding his rival Sue as a purveyor of morality while simultaneously depicting prurience. Unlike Sue, he was not a socialist, although *La Cousine Bette* is also important for its insights into working-class Paris.

La Cousin Pons of 1847 is simpler and more concentrated. The poor relation is now not the villain but the victim. Pons is the gluttonous conductor of a theatre orchestra, a failed musician whose recreation consists in dining at the tables of his relatives long after he has ceased to be welcome. Compensating, like Bette, for his sexual unattractiveness, he has become dependent on the Camusot de Merville family, who humiliate him. However, he has also been a collector of bric-à-brac, and when he falls ill Mme Camusot makes moves to secure his valuable collection for herself. *Le Cousin Pons* is one of the saddest of Balzac's novels, but it is one which shows no coarseness of moral response or inelegance of execution. Its irony is exquisite and it ranks as one of the quite outstanding achievements by one of the half-dozen greatest 19th-century novelists writing in any language.

PUBLICATIONS

Collections

Oeuvres complètes, edited by Marcel Bouteron and Henri Longnon, 40 vols., 1912–40
La Comédie humaine, edited by Marcel Bouteron, Bibliothèque de la Pléiade, 11 vols., 1951–59; revised edition, edited by Pierre-George Castex and Pierre Citron, 12 vols., 1976–81
The Human Comedy, edited by George Saintsbury, 40 vols., 1895–98

Fiction

L'Héritage de Birague, with Le Poitevin de Saint-Alme and Etienne Arago, 1822
Jean-Louis; ou, La Fille trouvée, with Le Poitevin de Saint-Alme, 1822
Clotilde de Lusignan; ou, Le Beau Juif, 1822
Le Centenaire; ou, Les Deux Beringheld, 1822; as *Le Sorcier*, in *Oeuvres complètes de Horace de Saint-Aubin*, 1837
Le Vicaire des Ardennes, 1822
La Dernière Fée; ou, La Nouvelle Lampe merveilleuse, 1823
Annette et le criminel, 1824
Wann-Chlore, 1825; as *Jane la pâle*, in *Oeuvres complètes*, 1836
Le Dernier Chouan; ou, La Bretagne en 1800, 1829; revised edition, as *Les Chouans; ou, La Bretagne en 1799*, 1834; as *Le Chouan*, 1838; as *The Chouans*, 1893
Mémoires pour servir à l'histoire de la révolution française, with Lheritier de l'Ain, 1829
La Physiologie du mariage; ou, Méditations de philosophie éclectique, 1829; as *The Physiology of Marriage*, 1904
Scènes de la vie privée, 1830; augmented edition, 1832
La Peau de chagrin, 1831; edited by S. de Sasy, 1974; as *The Magic Skin*, 1888; as *The Wild Ass's Skin*, in *The Human Comedy*, 1895–98
Romans et contes philosophiques, 1831
Contes bruns, with Philarète Chasles and Charles Rabou, 1832
Les Salmigondis: contes de toutes les couleurs, 1832; as *La Comtesse à deux maris*, in *Scènes de la vie privée*, 1835; as *Le Colonel Chabert*, in *La Comédie humaine*, 1844
Les Cent contes drolatiques, 3 (of an intended 10) vols., 1832–37; *Quatrième dizaine* (fragments), 1925; as *Contes drolatiques* (in English), 1874
Nouveaux contes philosophiques, 1832
Le Médecin de campagne, 1833; excerpt, as *Histoire de Napoléon*, 1833; edited by Patrick Barthier, 1974
Etudes de moeurs au XIXe siècle, 12 vols., 1833–37; includes reprints and the following new works:
  La Fleur des pois, 1834
  La Recherche de l'absolu, 1834; as *Balthazar; or, Science and Love*, 1859; as *The Alchemist*, 1861; as *The Quest of the Absolute*, in *The Human Comedy*, 1895–98; as *The Tragedy of a Genius*, 1912
  Eugénie Grandet, 1833; as *Eugenie Grandet* (in English), 1859
  La Femme abandonnée, 1833
  La Grenadière, 1833
  L'Illustre Gaudissart, 1833
  La Vieille Fille, 1837
  Illusions perdues (part 1: *Les Deux poètes*), 1837
  Les Marana, 1834
  Histoire des treize, 1834–35; as *History of the Thirteen*, 1974; translated in part as *The Mystery of the Rue Soly*, 1894, *The Girl with the Golden Eyes*, 1928, and *The Duchess of Langeais*, 1946
Le Père Goriot, 1835; as *Père Goriot* (in English), 1886
Le Livre mystique (includes *Louis Lambert* and *Séraphîta*), 1835; as *Louis Lambert* and *Seraphita* (in English), 2 vols., 1889
Etudes philosophiques, 20 vols., 1835–40; includes reprints and the following new works:
  Un drame au bord de la mer, 1835
  Melmoth réconcilié, 1836
  L'Interdiction, 1836
  La Messe de l'athée, 1837
  Facino cane, 1837
  Les Martyrs ignorés, 1837
  Le Secret des Ruggieri, 1837
  L'Enfant maudit, 1837
  Une passion dans le désert, 1837
Le Lys dans la vallée, 1836; as *The Lily of the Valley*, 1891
L'Excommuniée, with Auguste de Belloy, in *Oeuvres complètes de Horace de Saint-Aubin*, 1837
La Femme supérieure, 1837; as *Les Employés*, 1865; as *Bureaucracy*, 1889
Histoire de la grandeur et de la décadence de César Birotteau, 1838; as *History of the Grandeur and Downfall of Cesar Birotteau*, 1860; as *The Bankrupt*, 1959
La Femme supérieure, La Maison Nucingen, La Torpille, 1838
Les Rivalités en province, 1838; as *Le Cabinet des antiques* (includes *Gamara*), 1839; as *The Jealousies of a Country*

Town, in *The Human Comedy*, 1895–98

Gambara; Adieu, 1839; as *Gambara*, in *The Human Comedy*, 1895–98

Une fille d'Eve (includes *Massimilla Doni*), 1839; as *A Daughter of Eve* and *Massimilla Doni*, in *The Human Comedy*, 1895–98

Un grand homme de province à Paris (*Illusions perdues 2*), 1839; as *A Great Man of the Provinces in Paris*, 1893

Beatrix; ou, Les Amours forcées, 1839; edited by Madeleine Fergeaud, 1979; as *Beatrix* (in English), 1895

Pierrette, 1840; as *Pierrette* (in English), 1892

Physiologie de l'employé, 1841

Physiologie du rentier de Paris et de province, with Arnould Frémy, 1841

Le Curé de village, 1841; as *The Country Parson*, in *The Human Comedy*, 1895–98

Oeuvres complètes: la comédie humaine, 20 vols., 1842–53; includes reprints and the following new works:
  Albert Savarus, 1842; as *Albert Savarus* (in English), 1892
  Autre étude de femme, 1842
  Illusions perdues (part 3), 1843; parts 1 and 3 translated as *Lost Illusions*, 1893
  Esquisse d'homme d'affaires; Gaudissart II; Les Comédiens sans le savoir, 1846
  Un épisode sous la terreur; L'Envers de l'histoire contemporaine; Z. Marcas, 1846; *L'Envers...* translated as *Love*, 1893

Ursule Mirouët, 1842; as *Ursula*, 1891

Scènes de la vie privée et publique des animaux, 1842

Mémoires de deux jeunes mariées, 1842; as *Memoirs of Two Young Married Women*, 1894

Une ténébreuse affaire, 1842; edited by René Guise, 1973; as *The Gondreville Mystery*, 1898; as *A Murky Business*, 1972

Les Deux frères, 1842; as *Un ménage de garçon en province*, in *La Comédie humaine*, 1843; as *La Rabouilleuse*, in *Oeuvres complètes*, 1912; edited by René Guise, 1972; as *The Two Brothers*, 1887; as *A Bachelor's Establishment*, in *The Human Comedy*, 1895–98; as *The Black Sheep*, 1970

Un début dans la vie (includes *La Fausse Maîtresse*), 1844

Catherine de Médicis expliquée; Le Martyr calviniste, 1845; as *Catherine de' Medici*, 1894

Honorine (includes *Un prince de la Bohème*), 1845

Splendeurs et misères des courtisanes: Esther, 1845; as *A Harlot's Progress*, in *The Human Comedy*, 1895–98; as *A Harlot High and Low*, 1970

La Lune de miel, 1845

Petites misères de la vie conjugale, 1845–46, as *The Petty Annoyances of Married Life*, 1861

Un drame dans les prisons, 1847

Le Provincial à Paris (includes *Gillette, Le Rentier, El Verdugo*), 1847

Les Parents pauvres (includes *La Cousine Bette* and *Le Cousin Pons*), 1847–48; as *Poor Relations*, 1880; as *Cousin Pons*, 1886; as *Cousin Betty*, 1888

La Dernière Incarnation de Vautrin, 1848

Le Député d'Arcis, completed by Charles Rabou, 1854; as *The Deputy of Arcis*, 1896

Les Paysans, completed by Mme Balzac, 1855; as *Sons of the Soil*, 1890; as *The Peasantry*, in *The Human Comedy*, 1895–98

Les Petits Bourgeois, completed by Charles Rabou, 1856; as

The Lesser Bourgeoisie, 1896; as *The Middle Classes*, 1898

Sténie; ou, Les Erreurs philosophiques, edited by A. Prioult, 1936

La Femme auteur et autres fragments inédits, edited by Spoelberch de Lovenjoul, 1950

Mademoiselle du Vissard, edited by Pierre-George Castex, 1950

Selected Short Stories, 1977

Plays

Vautrin (produced 1840), 1840; as *Vautrin*, in *Works*, 1901

Les Ressources de Quinola (produced 1842), 1842; as *The Resources of Quinola*, in *Works*, 1901

Paméla Giraud (produced 1843), 1843; as *Pamela Giraud*, in *Works*, 1901

La Marâtre (produced 1848), 1848; as *The Stepmother*, in *Works*, 1901

Le Faiseur (produced 1849), 1851; as *Mercadet*, in *Works*, 1901

L'Ecole des ménages, edited by Spoelberch de Lovenjoul (produced 1910), 1907

Other

Du droit d'aînesse, 1824

Histoire impartiale des Jésuites, 1824

Le Code des gens honnêtes; ou, L'Art de ne pas être dupe des fripons, 1825

Mémoires de Mme la Duchesse d'Abrantès, with the duchess, vol. 1 only, 1831

Maximes et pensées de Napoléon, 1838

Traité de la vie élégante, 1853

Lettres à l'étrangère (to Mme Hanska), 4 vols., 1899–1950

Cahiers balzaciens, edited by Marcel Bouteron, 8 vols., 1927–28

Le Catéchisme social, edited by Bernard Guyon, 1933

Traité de la prière, edited by Philippe Bertault, 1942

Journaux à la mer, edited by Louis Jaffard, 1949

Correspondance, edited by Roger Pierrot, 5 vols., 1960–68

Editor, *Oeuvres complètes*, by La Fontaine, 1826

Editor, *Oeuvres complètes*, by Molière, 1826

APPENDIX

See p. 53 of main entry

Etudes de moeurs

SCÈNES DE LA VIE PRIVÉE: *La Maison du chat-qui-pelote* (1830); *Le Bal de Sceaux* (1830); *Mémoires de deux jeunes mariées* (1841–42); *La Bourse* (1832); *Modeste Mignon* (1844); *Un début dans la vie* (1842); *Albert Savarus* (1842); *La Vendetta* (1830); *Une double famille* (1830); *La Paix du ménage* (1830); *Madame Firmiani* (1832); *Etude de femme* (1830); *La Fausse Maîtresse* (1841); *Une fille d'Eve* (1838–39); *Le Message* (1832); *La Grenadière* (1832); *La Femme abandonnée* (1832); *Honorine* (1843); *Béatrix* (1839); *Gobseck* (1830); *La Femme de trente ans* (1831–44); *Le Père Goriot* (1834–35); *Le Colonel Chabert* (1832); *La Messe de l'athée* (1836); *L'Interdiction* (1836); *Le Contrat de mariage* (1835); *Autre étude de femme* (1842)

SCÈNES DE LA VIE DE PROVINCE: *Ursule Mirouët* (1841); *Eugénie Grandet* (1833); *Les Célibataires*—(i) *Pierrette* (1840), (ii) *Le Curé de Tours* (1832), (iii) *La Rabouilleuse* (1841–42); *Les Parisiens en Province*—(i) *L'Illustre Gaudissart* (1833), (ii) *La Muse du département* (1843); *Les Rivalités*—(i) *La Vieille Fille* (1836), (ii) *Le Cabinet des antiques* (1836–38, 1839); *Illusions perdues*—(i) *Les Deux poètes* (1837), (ii) *Un grand homme de province à Paris* (1839), (iii) *Les Souffrances de l'inventeur* (1843)

SCÈNES DE LA VIE PARISIENNE: *Histoire des Treize*—(i) *Ferragus* (1833), (ii) *La Duchesse de Langeais* (1833–34), (iii) *La Fille aux yeux d'or* (1834–35); *Histoire de la grandeur et de la décadence de César Birotteau* (1837); *La Maison Nucingen* (1838); *Splendeurs et misères des courtisanes*—(i) *Comment aiment les filles*, (ii) *A combien l'amour revient aux vieillards*, (iii) *Où mènent les mauvais chemins*, (iv) *La Dernière Incarnation de Vautrin* (1838–47); *Les Secrets de la princesse de Cadignan* (1839); *Facino cane* (1836); *Sarrasine* (1830); *Pierre Grassou* (1840); *Les Parents pauvres*—(i) *La Cousine Bette* (1846), (ii) *Le Cousin Pons* (1847); *Un homme d'affaires* (1845); *Un prince de la Bohème* (1840); *Gaudissart II* (1844); *Les Employés* (1837); *Les Comédiens sans le savoir* (1846); *Les Petits Bourgeois* (posthumous); *L'Envers de l'histoire contemporaine*—(i) *Madame de la Chanterie* (1842), (ii) *L'Initié* (1848)

SCÈNES DE LA VIE POLITIQUE: *Un épisode sous la terreur* (1830); *Une ténébreuse affaire* (1841); *Le Député d'Arcis* (1847); *Z. Marcas* (1840)

SCÈNES DE LA VIE MILITAIRE: *Les Chouans* (1829); *Une passion dans le désert* (1830)

SCÈNES DE LA VIE DE CAMPAGNE: *Les Paysans* (1844); *Le Médecin de campagne* (1833); *Le Curé de village* (1839–1846); *Le Lys dans la vallée* (1835)

Etudes philosophiques

La Peau de chagrin (1830–31); *Jésus-Christ en Flandre* (1831); *Melmoth réconcilié* (1835); *Massimilla Doni* (1839); *Le Chef-d'oeuvre inconnu* (1831); *Gambara* (1837); *La Recherche de l'absolu* (1834); *L'Enfant maudit* (1831–36); *Adieu* (1830); *Les Marana* (1832–33); *Le Réquisitionnaire* (1831); *El Verdugo* (1830); *Un drame au bord de la mer* (1835); *Maître Cornélius* (1831); *L'Auberge rouge* (1831); *Sur Catherine de Médicis*—(i) *Le Martyr calviniste* (1841), (ii) *Le Secret des Ruggieri* (1836–37), (iii) *Les Deux rêves* (1831); *L'Elixir de longue vie* (1830); *Les Proscrits* (1831); *Louis Lambert* (1832); *Séraphîta* (1834–35)

Etudes analytiques

Physiologie du mariage (1829); *Petites misères de la vie conjugale* (1830, 1840, 1845)

Bibliography

Royce, W. Hobart, *A Balzac Bibliography* and *Index*, 1929–30

Critical studies

Rogers, Samuel G. A., *Balzac and the Novel*, 1953
Hunt, Herbert J., *Balzac: A Biography*, 1957
Hunt, Herbert J., *Balzac's Comédie Humaine*, 1959
Oliver, Edward J., *Balzac the European*, 1959
Maurois, André, *Prometheus: The Life of Balzac*, 1965
Hemmings, F. W. J., *Balzac: An Interpretation of the Comédie Humaine*, 1967
Schilling, Bernard N., *The Hero as Failure: Balzac and the Rubempré Cycle*, 1968
Pritchett, V. S., *Balzac* (in English), 1973
Kanes, Martin, *Balzac's Comedy of Words*, 1975
Pugh, Anthony, *Balzac's Recurring Characters*, 1975
Bellos, David, *Balzac Criticism in France (1850–1900)*, 1976
Prendergast, Christopher, *Balzac: Fiction and Melodrama*, 1978
Adamson, Donald, *Balzac: Illusions Perdues*, 1981
McCarthy, Mary Susan, *Balzac and His Reader*, 1983

BANVILLE, (Etienne-Claude-Jean-Baptiste-)Théodore Faullain de, 1823–1891.

Poet, dramatist, author of fiction, and essayist.

LIFE

Banville was born on 14 March 1823 at Moulins in the centre of France. His grandfather, Jean-Louis, was descended from an ancient Norman family and had settled in Moulins as a civil engineer in 1780. After 20 years in the navy Banville's father, Claude-Théodore, retired to Moulins to marry. He worked in the land registry, where he was known for his integrity and dignity. Banville's mother, Elisabeth-Zélie Huet, whose family had lived in the area for at least two centuries, and whose father had bought her a country property, La Font-Georges, near Moulins, complete with orchard, vineyard, meadows, and stream, had her first child, Zélie, in 1821. Banville himself adored his mother and dedicated his first volume of verse, *Las Cariatides*, to her, as well as *Roses de Noël* in the year of her death. He was brought up in a large house with a garden, a few yards away from the home of his mother's parents, with whom he spent much time. His mother's father died when he was two, and his grandmother devoted herself to the welfare of the two grandchildren. Banville's early childhood was exceptionally happy.

In 1830 his grandmother died, and Banville was sent to board at the Pension Sabatier in Paris, where he was less happy. His fellow pupils seemed to him to come from more monied families, and he said that he was made to feel that he did not fit in. He did however emerge in 1839 with his baccalauréat, deeply impressed by the acrobats, jugglers, clowns, tightrope walkers, and mimes he had seen. The family had moved to Paris in 1834, and Banville became a law student, although he abandoned his studies in 1842, publishing *Les Cariatides* that year with his mother's encouragement. The main source of Banville's early biography is his own *Mes souvenirs* of 1883. Like all autobiographical recollections, it must be treated with caution, but Banville tells us that he always wanted to be a poet. His reading had been unremarkable, although he had developed an admiration for Hugo, whose free treatment of verse forms was constantly to inspire him, not only in his poetic practice, but also in the treatise on versification of 1872, the *Petit traité de poésie française*. In 1842 Banville met Baudelaire, with whom he was to form a close friendship. Baudelaire wrote appreciatively about Banville's work, and it was Banville who later applied for state aid on Baudelaire's behalf, edited *Les Fleurs du mal*, and spoke at Baudelaire's funeral.

Les Cariatides came at the beginning of a decade which saw no major innovation in French poetry. The collection, some of whose contents date from Banville's 17th year, is therefore a predictable mixture of late romantic (q.v.) verse with tentative experiments in new styles. Only in retrospect is it possible to see it as anticipating the developments of Baudelaire and of the Parnassian and symbolist (qq.v.) poets. What is clear from the obviously youthful volume is the lingering inspiration of Lamartine, although now with a touch of ironic humour, the skill at verbal juggling, the preoccupation with clowns, and with the poet and the nature of poetry. Some of the verse forms are complex, using five or seven syllables to the line, and some of the poetic forms are built up according to the complicated medieval rules for the different genres codified, for instance, by Sebillet.

The early collection attracted some attention. Baudelaire and Gautier both liked it. Jules Janin wrote to Banville about it and both Verlaine and Mallarmé were to count among his admirers. He met Vigny and was admitted to Hugo's salon. Still living with his parents, he himself began to receive before he was 20. Between 1850 and 1891 Banville was to produce 17 volumes of verse in addition to 17 plays, eight volumes of fiction, and at least four other volumes of prose, as well as miscellaneous criticism and other journalism. The most important verse collections, for which alone he is remembered, are probably the *Odes funambulesques* of 1857 and *Les Exilés* of 1867. It is not without significance, however, that the volume called after the sculpted female figures used as pillars in architecture, *Les Cariatides*, should have been followed by *Les Stalactites* of 1846, dedicated to Banville's father. Taken with the difficult poetic forms chosen, the hard column-like shapes implied by the title announce a literary kinship with the Gautier of *Emaux et camées* (1852) and the "L'Art pour l'art" (q.v.) movement. The sometimes exotic contents of the volume derive inspiration from Hugo's *Les Orientales* of 1829 and look forward cautiously to Leconte de Lisle's *Poèmes antiques* (1853) and to the Parnassians, who were also preoccupied with hard physical objects. Reference in the preface to "half-light" and "the artifices of negligence" even suggests the inchoate formation of symbolist ideas.

In 1846 Banville's father died, and by 1850 his own health had begun to fail. He probably had tuberculosis and in 1852 himself came close to dying. Meanwhile, he had started to earn his living as a journalist and was short of money rather than destitute, working for *La Silhouette* from 1845, and within three years for *Le Pamphlet*, *Le Corsaire*, and *Le Pouvoir*. During the early years of the Second Empire he wrote for the revived *Revue de Paris* and *Le Figaro*. Much in his poems confirms the view that he had moderately republican sympathies but was not interested in politics or, in spite of his social satire, concerned about

reform. What he did greatly dislike was the greed and philistinism which had come to be associated with the monarchy of 1830, money-grabbing and the taste for sentimental romances and plastic prints, what Banville also referred to as "the apotheosis of the grocery and the glorification of sellers of rabbit skins." He was better disposed in his satirical verse to prostitutes than to politicians, financiers, and Eugène Scribe.

Two dozen poems from the previous decade were published in *Odelettes* in 1856, dedicated to Sainte-Beuve. In spite of its admitted technical mastery, however, the collection was heavily criticized in the *Revue de Paris* for the insubstantiality of its contents. It was in reply to one of Banville's "odelettes," addressed to him in this collection and dated May 1856, that Gautier wrote "L'art," which was first published in *L'Artiste* for September 1857, starts with the word "Oui" to indicate that it is a reply, and goes on to develop Banville's ideas. The work of art is better in hard material according to Gautier: "Vers, marbre, onyx, émail (Verse, marble, onyx, enamel)."

Many of the poems collected in the *Odes funambulesques* had been published in *La Silhouette* or other journals, some of them anonymously, and the earliest dating back to 1844. More than half are dedicated to prominent figures in the literary world, including Houssaye, Sainte-Beuve, Murger, Karr, Gavarni, Gautier, and the Goncourts. The sequel to this volume, *Nouvelles odes funambulesques* of 1869, consisted of odes published mostly in *Le Charivari*, then edited by Pierre Véron, to whom the volume was dedicated. The title of the second edition in 1875 was changed to *Les Occidentales*, parodying Hugo's more famous *Les Orientales*. Meanwhile, in 1857, the year of the *Odes funambulesques*, Banville had also published *Le Sang de la coupe*, some 30 more serious poems on the poet and on love.

Banville had been seriously ill again in 1857 and had to spend periods in a clinic for the next two years. His financial distress attracted government grants. During the winter of 1859 to 1860 he accompanied the actress Marie Daubrun to Nice, where she was working and he thought his health might improve. The trip was the occasion of a tiff with Baudelaire. In fact Banville was ill for much of the time, but thanks to his two poems celebrating France's annexation of Nice he obtained the Légion d'Honneur, and the dozen love poems of *Améthystes*, published in 1861, were dedicated to Marie Daubrun. His letters from Nice, published in *Le Moniteur Universel*, appeared in 1861 as *La Mer de Nice*.

In 1863 Banville met the widowed Marie-Elisabeth Rochegrosse, whom he was to marry in 1866, the year before the publication of his favourite and most personal collection, *Les Exilés*. It had taken a long time for personal emotion to break through into his poetry. He had been in financial difficulties since 1850 and had had intermittent bouts of severe illness. Many of his close friends had died. As a poet he had not attracted wide attention, although he did become one of the 37 contributors to *Le Parnasse Contemporain* of 1866. By that date his health had improved, so that things were beginning to look brighter when he married, although his sister Zélie was to die in 1867. His wife had a son, Georges (born in 1859), and the arrangement appears to have been a happy one, with Marie-Elisabeth acting also as nurse and mother to Banville. *Les Exilés* is dedicated to her. Banville returned to the practice of Catholicism. In about 1861 he had been at the centre of the group which gathered round Catulle Mendès and from which the Parnassians (q.v.) were to emerge. It was one of the sources of sadness of Banville's old age that the younger poets with whom he liked to associate began to lose interest in him.

His other principal collections are the *Rimes dorées* of 1869; the *Idylles prussiennes*, 65 poems mostly collected from *Le National*, for which Banville was the theatre critic from 1869, published as a volume in 1871 just after the Franco-Prussian War, and considered by Barbey d'Aurevilly to contain Banville's best poetry; and the *Trente-six ballades joyeuses à la manière de François Villon* of 1873, with the *Rondels à la manière de Charles d'Orléans* of 1875, *Les Princesses* of 1874, and *Roses de Noël* of 1878. In 1879–80 Banville published his *Poésies complètes*. In 1880 he started writing for *Gil Blas* and, from 1888, for *L'Echo de Paris*. His three remaining volumes of verse were *Nous tous*, containing poems from *Gil Blas*, *Sonnailles et clochettes*, containing the poems from *L'Echo de Paris*, and the posthumous *Dans la fournaise*.

From 1869 Banville had been a theatre critic. His own plays were all comedies and all except one in verse. The first, *Le Feuilleton d'Aristophane* of 1852, played for a fortnight at the Odéon from 26 December 1852. Many waited a long time before being staged, and many were not staged at all. None was particularly successful. After 1880 Banville published a dozen volumes of prose, most of which had appeared in *Gil Blas*. Seven volumes are contes; one is a novel, *Marcelle Rabe*; and the rest are collections of articles, sketches of Paris life, and recollections. The 1872 *Petit traité de poésie française*, which may have been written as a school textbook, had already been serialized in *L'Echo de la Sorbonne*. It is unlikely that it was intended to be a manifesto, although it has often been taken to represent the views of the Parnassian school.

From 1884, as Banville's health deteriorated, he spent more time in the country, in his home near Moulins. He died of lung disease on the night of 12 March 1891.

WORKS

Like many even of the major 19th-century French authors, Banville was a working journalist, and most of his poetry was not only published in newspapers and magazines but was written to a deadline. Until his marriage, he was short of money. The result was poetic overproduction and, even when poetic inspiration was clearly drying up and Banville diverted his energies to drama and prose, mental processes scarcely attuned to the production of more than diverting pieces of no imaginative power. He never wrote well for the theatre and, in spite of the interest of Baudelaire and Mallarmé, his advanced techniques and accomplished verbal juggling, the hints of symbolism (q.v.) and of the Parnassian aesthetic to come, and his connections in the newspaper, stage, and literary worlds, even Banville's poetic reputation will probably wane still further. He did not illuminate or even examine in depth any form of personal or social experience, and there is virtually no personal emotion, passion, or commitment in anything he wrote. Perhaps because his position there was never very elevated, historians have continued to put him in the pantheon of 19th-century French poets.

Banville did not write pastiche, but too much of his poetry is derivative. The first poem of his first collection starts with a "vague et lointain souvenir (vague and distant memory)" and a "rêve triste et moqueur (sad and mocking dream)," the language

of Lamartine without the substance. Too many of the characters in Banville's poems are drawn from literature or mythology, although a scattering is also chosen from Watteau, Paris, and the harlequinades of the boulevard sideshows. In the 12-part "Songe d'hiver" from *Les Cariatides* love is rejected in favour of poetry. Banville's treatment of love is almost always conventional, lacking personal emotion, an occasion for technical experimentation and the movement of images rather than the inspiration of any true lyricism.

The *Odes funambulesques* did attract attention, but it only confirmed Banville's reputation as a juggler with words who regarded poetry as a game in which ideas and feeling were superfluous. For Banville the poet was much closer to the clown or the harlequin with his wry tricks than to the solitary or outcast. Banville's own technical skills tempt him into parodies, as of Hugo, or of medieval forms, which may have amused the readers of the newspapers which printed them, but which do not really have a place in collections of serious verse. Even his satire is facetious. He can end a catalogue of the troubles of France with the lines:

Je pense alors sous mon tilleul
Songeant à nos peines secrètes,
Que l'Empereur n'est pas le seul
Qui fume trop de cigarettes!

(Then I think under my linden tree,/Reflecting on our secret woes,/That the Emperor is not the only one/Who smokes too many cigarettes!)

Banville's most successful play was the only one not in verse, *Gringoire* of 1866. In his drama generally there is little depth of characterization and little dramatic urgency. The characters who are not comic are noble dreamers in pursuit of a not very serious ideal. Chaste women love gifted poets with an affection which is pure and elevated. In the fiction some of the vignettes of Paris and its inhabitants are attractively drawn. The 300 contes are classified into their volumes of stories for women, fairy stories, heroic stories, and so on, but they are never more than merely diverting. The one novel, *Marcelle Rabe*, concerns a girl from Dijon who goes to Paris and becomes a prostitute. She sacrifices her love for a doctor because she does not wish to compromise him, but he has a sordid affair with someone else, a woman who is outwardly innocent and respectable but has a virtually split personality, so savage is her lovemaking. Near the end of the novel Marcelle sees the doctor again, but her admonition to him fails to be moving.

The treatise on versification is primarily of interest for the stress it lays on rich rhymes and its view of poetry as syntactically correct organization of sound patterns. Music rather than discourse is what is important, a view which brings Banville perceptibly nearer to the symbolists than might have been expected in 1872.

PUBLICATIONS

Collections

Poésies complètes, 3 vols., 1878–79
Oeuvres, 9 vols., 1972

Verse

Les Cariatides, 1842
Les Stalactites, 1846
Odelettes, 1856
Odes funambulesques, 1857
Le Sang de la coupe, 1857
Améthystes, 1861
Les Exilés, 1867
Rimes dorées, 1869
Nouvelles odes funambulesques, 1869; as *Les Occidentales*, 1875
Idylles prussiennes, 1871
Trente-six ballades joyeuses à la manière de François Villon, 1873; as *The Ballades of Théodore de Banville*, 1913
Les Princesses, 1874
Rondels à la manière de Charles d'Orléans, in *Poésies*, 1875
Roses de Noël, 1878
Nous tous, 1884
Sonnailles et clochettes, 1890
Dans la fournaise, 1891

Plays

Les Nations: ode (part of an entertainment staged by Paris), 1851
Le Feuilleton d'Aristophane, with Philoxène Boyer (produced 1852), 1852
Les Folies nouvelles: prologue (produced 1854), 1854
La Muse des chansons: prologue, 1854
Le Beau Léandre (produced 1856), 1856; as *Charming Léandre* 1915
Le Cousin du roi, 1857
Diane au bois: comédie héroïque (produced 1863), 1864
Les Fourberies de Nérine, 1864
La Pomme: comédie, 1865
Gringoire: comédie en prose (produced 1866), 1866; as *Gringoire* (in English), 1916
Florise: comédie, 1870
Adieu: scène lyrique (produced 1871), 1871
Deïdamia: comédie héroïque (produced 1876), 1876
Les Deux jardiniers: opéra-comique, with Charles de la Rounat, 1877
La Perle, 1879
Hymnis: comédie lyrique (produced 1879), 1880
Le Messager (produced 1880), 1880
Esope: comédie, 1881
Riquet à la houppe, 1884
Socrate et sa femme (produced 1885), 1885; as *Socrates and His Wife* 1889
Le Forgeron, 1887
Le Baiser: comédie, 1888

Other

Les Pauvres Saltimbanques, 1853
Paris et le nouveau Louvre, 1857
Esquisses parisiennes, 1859
La Mer de Nice, 1861
Les Parisiennes de Paris, 1866
Petit traité de poésie française, 1872

Contes pour les femmes
Contes féeriques, 1882
Mes souvenirs, 1883
Petites études (includes, "La lanterne magique," "Camées parisiens," "La Comédie française"), 1883
Petites études (includes "Paris vécu," "Feuilles volantes"), 1883
Contes héroïques, 1884
Petites études (includes "Lettres chimériques"), 1885
Contes bourgeois, 1885
Dames et demoiselles et fables choisies, 1886
Les Belles Poupées, 1888
Madame Robert
Petites études (includes "L'ame de Paris"), 1890
Marcelle Rabe (novel), 1891

Biographical and critical study

Harms, Alvin, *Théodore de Banville*, 1983

BARBEY D'AUREVILLY, Jules-Amédée, 1808–1889.

Critic, novelist, and poet.

LIFE

Jules-Amédée Barbey was the eldest of four sons born to André-Marie-Théophile Barbey and Ernestine-Eulalie-Théodose Ango (1787–1858). They were married on 4 January 1808, and Barbey was born at Saint-Sauveur- le-Vicomte in Normandy on 2 November of the same year. He had three brothers: Léon, Edouard, and Ernest, born in 1809, 1810, and 1811 respectively. The Barbey family was of peasant origin and can be traced back to the 14th century. It was ennobled by the purchase of an office in 1756. Barbey d'Aurevilly's father was a lawyer. His mother's bourgeois family came from Caen and can be traced back to the 16th century. Barbey d'Aurevilly's uncle, Jean- François, mayor of Saint-Sauveur, first started to use the "d'Aurevilly" suffix, deriving it from a property he is said to have owned at Aureville. On his uncle's death in 1829 Barbey refused to use it, although his brother Léon adopted it. Barbey only began signing himself "d'Aurevilly" at the height of his dandy period, in about 1837.

In 1816 his father and his uncle failed to get Barbey into a military school, and in 1818, probably after being tutored privately, he was sent to the college at Valognes. Here he lived until 1825 with a liberal, agnostic uncle, Dr Pontas-Duméril, with whose daughter Ernestine-Louise he experienced his first sentimental flutterings. In 1824, when Barbey was 15, he dedicated a poem, "Aux héros des Thermopyles," to the neoclassical dramatist Casimir Delavigne. It was published by a cousin of his. Barbey was sufficiently encouraged to put together a volume of verse, but when he failed to find a publisher for it he burnt it in a fit of pique. There is no clear record of his education until he entered the Collège Stanislas with his brother Léon in October 1827. There he was a co-pupil of Maurice de Guérin, who alerted him to the work of Scott, Byron, and Sterne. He returned to Saint-Sauveur with his baccalauréat in 1829, ardently hoping for a military career. He had become liberal and republican, breaking with the far right-wing legitimism of his family, from whom he was now independent after being left an annual income of 1,200 francs by his great-uncle and godfather. One of his younger brothers, Edouard, had broken with his parents and enlisted. Léon had adopted the "d'Aurevilly" suffix and, with financial help from his father, founded a small, satirical, royalist review. He was to become a missionary of the Order of St John Eudes. Barbey was still democratically signing himself "Jules Barbey," not yet even hyphenating his Christian names. He started to study law at Caen, where he founded a republican review financed by his cousin Edelstand, Ernestine's brother. Barbey remained on good terms with Léon despite the growing difference of outlook between them.

The purpose of the review was clearly for Barbey to publish his own work, and he printed his second short story, "Léa," in its only number on 30 October 1832. The promised finance had not come through, and his first short story, "Le cachet d'onyx," was not printed until 1919. At Caen Barbey developed a close friendship with the bookseller Guillaume Trebutien and fell in love with Louise Cautru des Costils, who had married his cousin Alfred du Méril in 1830. He was later to refer to the period from 1831 to 1833 as the stormiest and most unhappy of his life. It may be that the experience, of whose nature we know virtually nothing, but which Barbey never forgot, was at the root of his later fictional obsession with impossible love. There is an element of exaggeration in what he said about the everlasting nature of his relationship with Louise, since her husband died, and from 1856 she was free to marry him. Meanwhile, in 1833 he successfully graduated in law.

It looks as if Barbey exchanged his inherited annuity for a capital sum, which he spent. By 1840 he appears to have been financially ruined, and by 1843–44 he was certainly borrowing. In 1848 his literary earnings were still small enough for Barbey to have to live almost wholly from loans. Financial equilibrium was re-established when, in 1871, he liquidated his father's estate, paid his debts, and collected his inheritance of 30,000 francs. On the death of his cousin Edelstand du Méril he inherited a further 2,000 francs a year. His literary career was an apparently reluctant expedient to sustain a life style which Barbey could never really afford.

Meanwhile, a letter of August 1833 reports on his social successes in the literary world and makes clear his journalistic ambitions. He also aspired to a political career, became close to his school friend Guérin again, wrote fiction which he did not succeed in having published, and in 1834 founded the *Revue Critique de la Philosophie, des Sciences et de la Littérature* with Trebutien and Edelstand du Méril. Barbey published his first articles of literary criticism in this review, which lasted only a few months. *La Bague d'Annibal* was written in 1834, not serialized in *Le Globe* until October 1841, and published only in 1843 in an edition of 150 copies by Trebutien. It both uses a Byronic hero and takes an ironic stance towards him. "Germaine," finished in 1835 and also called "La pitié," was rewritten in 1845, but published only in 1884, when it was called *Ce qui ne meurt pas*. The prose poem "Amaïdée," inspired by George Sand and written for Guérin, was completed in 1835, then sent to Trebutien and eventually forgotten. Barbey also wrote some articles on law for the *Encyclopédie du XIX siècle*.

Barbey d'Aurevilly's critical judgements were hesitant. He disliked George Sand but at the same time imitated her. In 1836 he began to write his *Memoranda*. Part diary, part self-discovery, it was not free from attitudinizing and romantic poses of worldly cynicism and despairing passion. At this period Barbey d'Aurevilly started, but did not finish, several pieces of prose fiction, some of which he would take up again later. His notes show that he did not read very much, and almost nothing modern, and that he liked very little of what he did read. Relations with his family became strained in 1836, after which he stayed away from Normandy for 20 years, and in 1837 there came a break with Trebutien. There was a second sentimental entanglement with a woman called Paula, of which we know only that it ended in a rejection before her death at the end of 1839. Barbey d'Aurevilly could find neither publishers nor employment, although he did work for a year on *Le Nouvelliste*, which supported the republicanism of Thiers. He began to be interested in Stendhal and in Joseph de Maistre. He was certainly very short of money, although the dandyism was fast becoming something more than a mask as his interest in social advancement made him begin to look on his republicanism as shabbily bourgeois: "La démocratie est la souveraineté de l'ignoble (Democracy is the sovereignty of the ignoble)." In 1836 Barbey d'Aurevilly had become friendly with the well-known dandy Roger de Beauvoir. He later worked on a biography of Beau Brummel. His life in the meanwhile was conventionally dandified, involving a five o'clock promenade on Boulevard de Gand, ices at Tortoni's, a table at the Café Anglais, and up-market girls.

Maurice de Guérin had died in 1839. His elder sister, Eugénie, had looked after him following their mother's death. In 1841 she came to Paris with Mme de Maistre, who was married to a distant relation of the writer Joseph de Maistre and had been close to Maurice. It was partly on account of Mme de Maistre, who was a year younger than himself, that Barbey d'Aurevilly broke with Eugénie de Guérin, with whom he had had a close brotherly relationship and who had been counting on him to get Maurice's works into print. Mme de Maistre's interest in Barbey d'Aurevilly was certainly more than merely friendly, and he assiduously frequented her ultra-monarchical and Catholic salon. In 1841 he patched up the quarrel with Trebutien, now librarian at Caen, and started with him what he came to recognize as an important correspondence for the literary historian: "Je puis attendre la gloire, appuyé là-dessus (I can expect fame, resting on those letters)." Barbey d'Aurevilly wrote to Trebutien virtually every Sunday until 1858. In 1841 he also published *L'Amour impossible* and had a liaison with a mysterious "Vellini," probably the prototype of the heroine of *Une vieille maîtresse*.

By this date Barbey d'Aurevilly's career ambitions seemed to be making some progress. He had got to know a number of leading literary journalists—Hugo, Janin, Sainte-Beuve, Dumas, and Chasles—and an editor or two, but his letters show him living off promises and hopes. For a period during 1842 he wrote for *Le Globe*, and in 1845 he worked briefly again for Villemessant at *La Sylphide*, which published *Du dandyisme et de Georges Brummel*, before its volume publication by Trebutien. A long campaign to join the *Journal des Débats* ended in failure, plus two parts of a review separated by a year, and a third part left unpublished. Barbey d'Aurevilly's correspondence tells us that they did not like his material at *Le Moniteur de la Mode* either. His writing was too concerned with abstract issues of principle for anyone to want to buy it, or to be able to sell it. By the mid-1840s he was making voluminous notes, often on subjects from recent history, that were never turned into anything. Probably as a relief he turned back to fiction and *Une vieille maîtresse*, although he was the fashion critic for *Le Constitutionnel* in 1845.

Under the influence of Mme de Maistre and her salon, Barbey d'Aurevilly suddenly became a Catholic again, at least intellectually. It would take another 10 years before he started to practice once more, and the religious aspect of Catholicism never interested him as much as the panoply and the ceremonial. He could not understand, and disapproved of, his brother Léon's ecclesiastical career. He also disappeared on a mysterious business journey, and came back to help establish, with other frequenters of the salon, the *Revue du Monde Catholique*, of which he was editor. The first number appeared on 2 April 1847, and the last on 5 May 1848. The review was to be the organ of the "Société catholique" and was intended to promote the renewal of religious art. Barbey d'Aurevilly's articles are exceedingly orthodox. The most likely explanation of his return to Catholicism is that, emotionally, he had never really abandoned the religious and political alignments of his extreme youth, but only during a period of intellectual revolt wandered off in rationalist and republican directions. It is nevertheless difficult totally to discount the snobbish appeal of royalism and the religion of the ancien régime, to which his dandyism had led him back. Much of his later weakness as a critic becomes understandable in the light of his need to foist his monarchism and Catholicism on to Balzac, although Barbey d'Aurevilly's defence of Balzac in 1857, published in *Le Pays*, may have been prompted by his desire to spite Buloz, the editor of the *Revue des Deux Mondes* (*RDM*, q.v.), which had attacked Balzac and turned down his work.

He did not take fright at the 1848 revolution at first, although he published nothing from May 1848 until December 1849. Notes he kept on his reading reveal the disorder of his mind. His concerns encompassed literature, science, magic, religion, and history, which increased his contempt for democracy. In 1849 he began to write, although not yet to publish, more fiction. The *RDM* turned down "Le dessous de cartes d'une partie de whist," and the second part of *Une vieille maîtresse*—slights which Barbey d'Aurevilly did not forget—but the first article of *Les Prophètes du passé*, devoted to Joseph de Maistre, appeared in *L'Opinion Publique* for 29 December 1849. During 1850 Barbey d'Aurevilly wrote political articles for the legitimist *La Mode*, which also took "Le dessous de cartes." His political conviction sent him looking for a strongly led, hierarchical society in which an emperor could if necessary do service for a king, and he swiftly became a fervent supporter of the Second Empire and Napoléon III.

Veuillot took one article for *L'Univers* before dismissing Barbey d'Aurevilly, whose political opinions were by now too extreme even for the right-wing Catholic legitimist press, which was not infrequently suppressed on ecclesiastical authority for involving the Church in politics. Barbey d'Aurevilly did however write for the Orleanist, non-legitimist *L'Assemblée Nationale* in 1851, the year in which he published *Les Prophètes du passé* and *Une vieille maîtresse* in volume form, and in which he met his future fiancée at Mme de Maistre's salon. This was the Baronne de Bouglon, the 30-year-old widow of an officer, who, for 15 months, became Barbey d'Aurevilly's "white angel," although he never married her. By the end of 1852 he had been forced back to a career of literary journalism. He wrote to Trebutien that his projected marriage had been put off.

L'Assemblée Nationale had serialized *L'Ensorcelée*, and Barbey d'Aurevilly had supported Louis-Napoléon in *Le Public*. His first article of literary criticism appeared on 6 November 1852 in the Bonapartist *Le Pays*, for which Barbey d'Aurevilly had hoped to write on politics. He was to carry on writing literary criticism for it for 10 years. During the next few years he published *L'Ensorcelée* in volume form and his *Poésies*, formed a friendship with Baudelaire, and became a practising Catholic again. He also published Eugénie de Guérin's *Reliquiae* (1855), visited his parents again, stayed with Trebutien, and in 1856 wrote another *Memorandum*. He scarcely mixed in literary circles, irritated Flaubert by his piece on *Madame Bovary*, attacked Hugo's *Les Contemplations*, but tried to defend *Les Fleurs du mal*. He was already showing the qualities of ardour, passion, and prejudice that would characterize his literary criticism and make it, if not enlightening, at least readable: "Le Journalisme pour moi, vous le savez, c'est la vie, c'est les mémoires acquittés du tailleur et du bottier (Journalism for me, you know, is my life. It's the receipted bills of the tailor and the boot-maker)." The best that can be said for Barbey d'Aurevilly as a literary critic is that he was never a time-server. He was a master of invective, wielded his weapon without discrimination, and pierced sharply, but even for money he would not follow a party line.

By 1858 Barbey d'Aurevilly had begun to collect enemies. That year his mother died and he travelled in the South of France with Mme de Bouglon. He co-founded the literary, Catholic, and pro-government *Le Réveil* with Granier de Cassagnac, who came from *Le Constitutionnel* and was to return to *Le Pays* when *Le Réveil* folded in 1859. Barbey d'Aurevilly also broke definitively with Trebutien, although opinion has on the whole rallied to the view that the final quarrel was of Trebutien's making. However, Barbey d'Aurevilly also quarrelled with Sainte-Beuve, Veuillot, and the legitimist critic Pontmartin. He also wrote another *Memorandum*. His position at *Le Pays* was never very secure, but as a critic he managed to slip in attempts to appear superior at the expense of Pascal, the *Lettres portugaises*, Chateaubriand, Constant, Prévost, and Champfleury. Barbey d'Aurevilly very slowly became the principal literary critic of *Le Pays*, was not allowed to give free rein to his views, was constantly constricted in the allocation of space to different works, and could never be sure either of having his piece published or of being able to write about the books he wanted.

The financier Mirès had bought *Le Pays* along with *Le Constitutionnel*, and the paper was in full decline, with sales dropping from over 13,500 in 1855 to 7,000 in 1861 and 3,300 in 1866. At the same time its sister, *Le Constitutionnel*, which was where the major pro-government campaigns were waged by the common management, went from 24,000 in 1855 to 19,000 in 1861 and 12,000 in 1866. In 1855 the circulation of the *Gazette de France* was only 2,500 and that of *L'Univers* 3,500 but, if at the beginning Barbey d'Aurevilly had a reasonably large readership, the violence of his personal style clashed with the paper's moderate image. He spent 10 years fighting the management, which cautiously allowed him an article a week from March 1853. Within a fortnight editorial censorship was imposed, and by the end of 1853 the frequency of his articles was reduced.

Barbey d'Aurevilly was again being forced slowly back to fiction. In 1860 he moved into the small Paris lodgings where he would stay until his death and published the first volume of his critical writings, *Les Oeuvres et les hommes*. He was beginning to drink too much and from 1884 was to suffer from liver disease. His relationship with Mme de Bouglon was becoming looser. The definitive break with *Le Pays* came with an article against Sainte-Beuve after an attack on Hugo's *Les Misérables* in 1862, although Barbey d'Aurevilly was taken back in 1864. Mirès had been arrested in 1861, and the new director was hostile to Barbey d'Aurevilly, who could not refrain from taking part in the dangerous warfare over Veuillot's ecclesiastical position and the suppression of *L'Univers*. In *Le Figaro* for 30 April 1863 he had attacked the redoubtable Buloz, who had repeatedly refused to have anything to do with Barbey d'Aurevilly at the *RDM*, in spite of the siege to which Barbey d'Aurevilly had subjected him. Buloz sued, no doubt stung by Barbey d'Aurevilly's rancour, which had clearly been stoked by information from inside his own camp, and Barbey d'Aurevilly had to pay a 2,000-franc fine imposed jointly on himself and the newspaper. He was allowed only one more article for *Le Figaro* until he returned 10 years later and, although the final article was an attack on the *Journal des Débats*, there was a lot of editorial comment surrounding it to draw its sting.

From 1863 the contes began to appear regularly alongside the journalism, serialized before volume publication whenever Barbey d'Aurevilly could arrange it. He wrote for *Le Nain Jaune* in 1863, rejoining it in 1865 after definitively leaving *Le Pays*, although it had been bought by Gregory Ganesco and turned into an anti-clerical, democratic organ. Barbey d'Aurevilly remained for four years, during which he took on the review's political hue. Then in 1869 he rallied to the empire once more, before finally turning hostile to it again, although from that year he succeeded Sainte-Beuve as literary critic of *Le Constitutionnel*, a position he retained for the rest of his life. He was also drama critic for Ganesco's republican *Le Parlement* for a year, clearly willing, if necessary, to earn a living as a journalist irrespective of whether or not he agreed with the politics of the organ which employed him.

His father had died in 1868, but it was not until after the siege of Paris in 1871 that Barbey d'Aurevilly returned to Normandy to settle the family affairs. By 1872 he was again harshly attacking republicanism in *Le Figaro*, entering into a last phase of strong political reaction and unleashing his views also in *Le Gaulois*. At the same time he began to meet some of the younger writers beginning to be active in Paris during and after the Franco-Prussian War. He was to get to know Bloy, Coppée, Bourget, Cladel, Houssaye, and Huysmans. His major work, *Les Diaboliques*, went on sale in 1874, although it had to be withdrawn in 1875 to avoid prosecution. Mme de Bouglon had become prickly about her reputation, and Barbey d'Aurevilly was apparently made to destroy letters from former lovers, and to remove from poems the names of those who had inspired them. The relationship cooled into a placid friendship, fanned into jealousy on Mme de Bougeon's part when Louise Read, whom Barbey d'Aurevilly met in 1879, became his secretary, friend, and the companion of the last years of his life. She was a Protestant, and he referred to her as "Mademoiselle Magloire." In 1879 Barbey d'Aurevilly became drama critic of *Paris-Journal*.

The short novel *Le Chevalier des Touches* had been serialized in *Le Nain Jaune* in 1863 and published the following year. It was in 1866 during his collaboration with *Le Nain Jaune*, that Barbey d'Aurevilly was to attack the new poetic school known as the Parnassians (q.v.). In 1864 *Un prêtre marié* was serialized

in *Le Pays*, appearing as a volume the following year, but it was reworked in 1874, and in 1879 the archbishop of Paris forbade the new edition. Barbey d'Aurevilly was now working for several newspapers or reviews at once, in 1868 and 1869 for *L'Eclair, La Veilleuse, Le Constitutionnel, Dix Décembre, Le Gaulois*, and *Le Parlement*. In 1871 Edelstand du Méril died and Barbey d'Aurevilly inherited a further 2,000 francs a year. His financial situation now eased sufficiently for him to have an apartment at Valognes, where henceforward he spent several months a year. In 1876 his brother Léon died.

From 1877 Barbey d'Aurevilly was to be subjected to increasingly hostile criticism from the Catholic side, and in 1880 he changed his political affiliations yet again, at least in appearance, by breaking with the royalists. In fact, his association with the young royalist and Catholic newspaper *Triboulet*, which lasted only a year and must be distinguished from the weekly of the same name, which lasted a lot longer, made it clear that his political and religious positions had been becoming increasingly personal, and that the public alignments were almost factitious. Barbey d'Aurevilly liked the splendours and power of Catholicism and what he despised about democracy was its ordinariness. His alliance with Catholic religious discipline and practice, as with royalist political thinking, was on that account at best fragile. Any strong leader, not necessarily a legitimate king, would have satisfied him politically. The break with Catholics, royalists, and *Triboulet* came because his writing was becoming imprudent, provocative, and compromising, rather than because of any change in his opinions other than a radicalization of his positions.

In 1880 he published *Goethe et Diderot* and in 1882 serialized *Une histoire sans nom* in *Gil Blas*, for which he began to write regularly. Bourget wrote prefaces for two of the four volumes of *Memoranda*, and in 1884 *L'Artiste* published Barbey d'Aurevilly's poems, *Les Rhythmes oubliés*. Barbey d'Aurevilly continued to publish his collected essays in the *Les Oeuvres et les hommes* series and his first volume of the *Théâtre contemporain* appeared in 1887. In 1886 and 1887 he contributed to the symbolist *Revue Indépendante*. His white angel and Louise Read were quarrelling over him by now, and over his wills, of which he made three in succession. From April 1888 Barbey d'Aurevilly was permanently and gravely ill. He died on 23 April 1889.

WORKS

Although the case has often been made for taking seriously Barbey d'Aurevilly's literary and theatrical criticism, historians have yet to demonstrate that it shows perceptivity, subtlety, or sensitivity. It is difficult to defend it against accusations not only of prejudice, but also of philistinism and unintelligence. Barbey d'Aurevilly's critical writing scores zero for acumen. Seldom can such extreme positions have been so flamboyantly expressed in such apparently earnest forums of discussion, even if the mixture of adolescent petulance, superciliousness, quips, boisterousness, prejudice, spite, and unpretentiousness makes it entertaining reading, dangerous only if taken for what it does not in the end pretend very seriously to be.

Barbey d'Aurevilly delighted in flaunting before the public viewpoints which he knew to be not entirely defensible, and there was clearly a market for his material, if editors were prepared to take the risk of publishing it. Some were, but what evidence there is suggests that it did not help their circulations. Was the 19th-century public fooled by Barbey d'Aurevilly, or does the relegation to the little magazines, the slow start, the arm's length approach by the major editors and publishers mean that Barbey d'Aurevilly was understood to be at best semi-serious, ingenious in unmasking the fallacies in fashionable thinking, and expert at shoring up principles in which he did not genuinely believe? The evidence, if not Barbey d'Aurevilly's work as a critic, must be taken seriously.

To have survived for 20 years as the principal literary critic of *Le Constitutionnel*, even in its decline, is an achievement that cannot simply be written off, and 10 Paris publishers published 37 volumes of Barbey d'Aurevilly's assorted critical writings between them, 26 of the 37 in the three series of *Les Oeuvres et les hommes*. Seventeen of the 37 were published by Lemerre alone, although he is normally associated with the Parnassians, whom Barbey d'Aurevilly started by attacking, but with many of whom he later became friendly. Lemerre was admittedly a young publisher trying to corner a market in young poets, who referred to Barbey d'Aurevilly as "le connétable des lettres (the constable of letters)," and we know that Barbey d'Aurevilly's sales were notoriously weak. One must presume, however, that Lemerre, who is even better known for his highly successful cheap editions of popular classics, did not go on selectively publishing Barbey d'Aurevilly from 1889, the year of Barbey d'Aurevilly's death, to 1913 without an eye on his sales figures. The risks had been taken by the houses which published Barbey in his lifetime, Amyot, Palmé, Cadot, and, towards the end, Franzine and Lemerre, who became Barbey d'Aurevilly's official publisher.

Champfleury refers to the poor sales of *Une vieille maîtresse* as to a known fact in *Le Réalisme* when discussing the impact of the "cabinet de lecture" or reading library on the sale, and therefore also on the production, of literature. "Avant-garde" is a late 19th-century military metaphor, but it is clear that there is no sense in which the weak public rating of Barbey d'Aurevilly's reactionary publications, including the novels, was due to the normal underestimation by the public of something in advance of its understanding. It is still difficult to say more than that the prospective reader today needs a map and a chronology of Barbey d'Aurevilly's piques and friendships to know how seriously any particular piece should be taken. His peers in the 19th century did not take him at face value, but extracted the entertainment value, enjoyed the games he played, and only got really annoyed, as Buloz and Flaubert did, when Barbey d'Aurevilly broke the rules. He sometimes did, mostly by taking himself too seriously.

Barbey d'Aurevilly owes his place in the works of literary history chiefly to the documentation he left about the intellectual, artistic, and literary life of the capital in his letters, his *Memoranda*, and the guide to its cabals and conspiracies hidden behind the positions he takes in his criticism. It would however be wrong to neglect his importance as a novelist, historically interesting for the way in which, moving from the flamboyance of high romanticism (q.v.) towards the decadent cult of over-refined sensation, he almost bypasses realism (q.v.), which, like naturalism (q.v.), he disliked. Catholicism is never more than the backdrop, the excuse for sumptuousness of décor and ceremony, the inspiration for fervent spiritual commitment. Even those novels published on their own have the structure of contes, without the complexities of subplots and character relationships

which distinguish the true novel. If their roots in romantic characters in violent or picturesque historical settings separate Barbey d'Aurevilly's novels from those of the realists, like them he allows glimpses only of the surface of his characters.

L'Ensorcelée, Le Chevalier des Touches, and *Un prêtre marié* all deal with Normandy and local adventures and disasters set during the period of the Revolution. Barbey d'Aurevilly strives for extremes of colour, character, and plot, but also of contrast, cruelty, passion, religion, and anything to enliven jaded palates. He does not disguise the autobiographical nature of much of what the novels fictionalize. Indeed he not infrequently writes about it at considerable length in the letters or the *Memoranda*. He is also at pains to make the characters vivid, employing the usual devices of realism, particularly ordinarily conversational direct speech, to bring them to life. The narrative is brisk, and there is almost no irony. Even if the reader came quite fresh to the first major novel, *Une vieille maîtresse*, knowing nothing of its author or the circumstances of the composition of its two parts, it would soon be obvious that the novel was the elaboration of the author's personal experience with the shadowy "Vellini," recounted by a fictionalized alter ego, Ryno de Marigny. It would not be difficult to guess that the novel was written for serialization in an attempt to capitalize on personal experience by transforming it into saleable fiction.

In fact, this is essentially Champfleury's objection. Barbey d'Aurevilly had treated him with his habitual disdain since 1854, and in 1856 Champfleury hit back with a long article on Barbey d'Aurevilly's novel in the form of a letter to Veuillot complaining about the daring language and the style pushed beyond the tolerance of correct syntax, but above all about the indulgent titillation with which the passion is depicted before it meets with its merely perfunctory punishment. It is difficult not to agree with Champfleury's innuendo that Barbey d'Aurevilly has written a novel which would attract readers while pasting on to it, for form's sake, a conventionally moral retributive ending. Barbey d'Aurevilly himself was to say of its predecessor, *L'Amour impossible* of 1841: "It's scarcely a novel. It's a chronicle."

In the second part of *Une vieille maîtresse* Barbey d'Aurevilly had discovered his Norman inspiration. The personal memories were still a powerful source of inspiration, but now no longer enclosed the text. In his literary career, and indeed in everything except his cultivated dandyism, Barbey d'Aurevilly was still a failure when, in 1849, he began to think of *Le Chevalier des Touches*. We know that he made a serious effort at research, no doubt required to liberate his imagination, that the short novel took most of 1855 and 1856 to write, and that it was not published for another seven years, finally appearing in *Le Nain Jaune* from 18 July to 2 September 1863. Michel Lévy published it in volume form in 1864. It is a simple adventure story, episodically written, no doubt in the hope of serialization. Thirty years have elapsed since the narrated events took place, thereby transposing the work into a conte of disillusion, an epic receding into a simple memory of faded strength, courage, and beauty. It is perfectly possible to see the influence of Scott being superseded by that of the young Balzac, and even of Champfleury, in the long, slow, realistically described setting of the scene in the opening chapters. Mme de Bouglon made Barbey d'Aurevilly cut back the violence.

Les Diaboliques is a collection of six short stories, given that title after five had been written. Barbey d'Aurevilly's narrative skills are now much more developed, and he has learnt technical lessons from Balzac. The contes are set in appropriate milieus and often have historical sources as well as embroidering on Barbey d'Aurevilly's own reminiscences. Barbey d'Aurevilly is now more skilled in the use of named fictional narrators. We do not know the dates of composition with any accuracy, except that "Le dessous de cartes d'une partie de whist" dates from 1849 and was published in 1850 by *La Mode*, after Buloz had turned it down for the *RDM*, saying to Pontmartin: "He's got a lunatic talent, but I don't want him …ing around in my shop." What Buloz wrote was that he had the susceptibilities of his readership to consider. The title "Diaboliques" can scarcely have been intended to deflect attention from the volume.

Once again, the point is not whether devilries, naughtinesses, or even serious crimes are punished, but with what degree of complacency they are narrated. The danger of prosecution came from the light which Barbey d'Aurevilly let into psychological motivations, thoughts, and deeds generally left unexamined. The objections could finally be resolved into the single reproach that what was narrated was too realistic to be edifying. *Les Diaboliques* was published on 15 October 1874, but the volume was never put on public sale, although the newspapers and reviews had all received copies and discussed it at length. The seizure was ordered on 11 December and, although the prosecution dropped its case on 21 January 1875, the seized copies were destroyed and Barbey d'Aurevilly did not dare republish the book before 1882.

PUBLICATIONS

Collections

Oeuvres complètes, 17 vols., 1926–27
Oeuvres romanesques complètes, 2 vols., Bibliothèque de la Pléiade, 1964 and 1966

Fiction

L'Amour impossible, 1841
La Bague d'Annibal, 1843
Du Dandyisme et de George Brummel, 1845; as *The Anatomy of Dandyism with Some Observations on Beau Brummel*, 1928
Une vieille maitresse, 1851
L'Ensorcelée, 1854; as *The Bewitched*, 1928
Le Chevalier des Touches, 1864
Un prêtre marié, 1865
Les Diaboliques, 1874; as *Weird Women*, n.d.; as *The Diaboliques*, 1925
Une histoire sans nom, 1882; as *The Story Without a Name*, 1891
Ce qui ne meurt pas, 1883; as *What Never Dies*, translated by Sebastian Melmoth (Oscar Wilde), 1902
Une page d'histoire, 1886
Amaïdée, 1889
Le Cachet d'onyx, Lea, 1919

Criticism

Les Oeuvres et les hommes:
Series 1
  Les Philosophes et les écrivains religieux, 1860

  Les Historiens politiques et littéraires, 1861
  Les Poètes, 1862
  Les Romanciers, 1865
  Les Bas-bleus, 1878
  Les Critiques ou les juges jugés, 1885
  Sensations d'art, 1886
  Sensations d'histoire, 1887
Series 2
  Les Philosophes et les écrivains religieux, 1887
  Les Historiens, 1888
  Les Poètes, 1889
  Littérature étrangère, 1890
  Littérature épistolaire, 1892
  Mémoires historiques et littéraires, 1893
  Journalistes et polémistes, 1895
  Portraits politiques et littéraires, 1898
Series 3
  Les Philosophes et les écrivains religieux, 1899
  Le Roman contemporain, 1902
  Romanciers d'hier et d'avant-hier, 1904
  De l'histoire, 1904
  A côté de la grande histoire, 1906
  Femmes et moralistes, 1906
  Poésies et poètes, 1906
  Voyageurs et romanciers, 1908
Series 4
  Philosophes et écrivains religieux et politiques, 1909
  Critiques diverses, 1909
  Les Prophètes du passé, 1850; revised edition, 1880 *Les Ridicules du temps*, 1883
  Polémiques d'hier, 1889
  Les Vieilles Actrices, Le Musée des antiques, 1889
  Dernières polémiques, 1891
Goethe et Diderot, 1919
Victor Hugo, 1922
Les Quarante médaillons de l'Académie française, n.d.
Théâtre contemporain, i, ii, iii, 1887–89
Théâtre contemporain, nouvelle série, 1892
Théâtre contemporain, dernière série, 1896
Disjecta membra, 2 vols., 1925

Other

Memoranda, 1947
Poésies, 1889
Lettres à Léon Bloy, 1903
Lettres à une amie, 1907
Lettres à Trebutien, 1927
Lettres et fragments, 1958

Critical and biographical study

Bésus, R., *Barbey d'Aurevilly*, 1958
Rogers, B.G., *The Novels and Stories of Barbey d'Aurevilly*, 1967
Berthier, P., *Barbey d'Aurevilly et l'imagination*, 1978

BARRÈS, (Auguste-)Maurice, 1862–1923.

Novelist, essayist, and politician.

LIFE

Barrès's family came from Lorraine. His strong identification with that region underpins the French nationalism which he adopted in response to the German advance of 1870. The emotions of the eight-year-old boy, however respectably they would later be dressed up in political and social theory, were to remain at the heart of what Barrès came to stand for publicly. He disliked boarding school as an 11-year-old, was a "below average" pupil at the Nancy lycée he attended at 15, and took early in life to the Catholicism of flowers and incense. He suffered from depressions, generally accompanied by physical ailments, and as an adolescent developed a strong taste for reading. From 1883, in which year he visited Italy, he was allowed to settle in Paris and test himself in its literary life. He launched his own review, *Les Taches d'Encre*, and allowed it to fold after four issues, by which time it had already brought him the reputation he sought and sufficient invitations to write elsewhere. By 1887 he was living by his pen.

In 1889 he was elected to parliament as an anti-republican "Boulangist," so-called after General Georges Boulanger (1837–91), who had gained popularity as minister of war and whose platform was the military rehabilitation of France, the strengthening of the Franco-German frontier and an end to the abuses of parliamentary government. Barrès's first novels appeared in 1888 and 1889, with the third of the "Culte du moi (Cult of the self)" trilogy to follow, already reflecting the author's interest in the sources of creative energy.

The discredited Boulanger committed suicide on his mistress's grave in Brussels, and in 1893 Barrès lost his parliamentary seat. The voters of Nancy preferred a more strongly antisemitic candidate and Barrès's socialism started to shift towards the newly popular nationalism. He had helped to found La Ligue de la Patrie Française in 1889, although he was to resign from it in 1901 and could never accept the narrow monarchism of Maurras and the Action Française. He now founded another newspaper, the second since his election, *La Cocarde*, which lasted six months and attempted to build a socialist youth movement. Barrès's nationalistic commitment to a France dominated by military strength and its civilizing role by no means excluded a belief in social progress, which he considered inevitable, and in a developing society, which, in his view, needed only strong leadership. In 1893 he married, and from 1896 to the end of his life lived at Neuilly, where, although supported by Jaurès and the socialists, his later opponents, he failed to re-enter parliament. His multiple political defeats brought on a depression from which he was rescued by a passionate affair with Anna de Noailles.

The first novel of a new trilogy devoted to "L'énergie nationale," *Les Déracinés*, extolled an awareness of cultural heritage, and in 1906 Barrès was elected to the Académie Française and at last to parliament again, keeping the seat until his death. He began not so much to defend the Church as to attack the lay anticlerical educational establishment for what he considered as the vacuum it left by destroying traditional moral values. Jealous of losing her hold on Barrès, Anna de Noailles had taken his nephew under her wing. When she broke with him, he committed suicide, strengthening Barrès's view that French youth was being left in a moral void, unable to face up to its problems. Barrès now devoted his efforts to creating in Joan of Arc a focus of national feeling. He integrated his novel *La Colline inspiré*, which deals with the 19th-century rise and fall of two religious sites in Lorraine, into his defence of the Church. He visited the Middle East and, although his political position had polarized against that of the socialist leader, he wrote an impressive letter to Jaurès's daughter after his assassination.

Politically he admired the US for its classless society, industrialized for the benefit of all, and began to campaign with some success for French support for scientific research. He was an influential newspaper columnist and speaker at official occasions, collecting his most important articles in *Pour la haute intelligence française*. He thought that Prussians were more degenerate than other Germans on account of the Slav blood in their veins, and in 1920 he had given five lectures in Strasbourg on "Le génie du Rhin." His speeches promoting French influence in the Rhineland were collected in the posthumous *Les Grands Problèmes du Rhin*.

WORKS

As a literary figure, Barrès is sometimes over-rated, but he did display technical dexterity in his use of assertive and ironic rhetoric in his novels, as in his political tracts, and in the fusion of the two genres in which he specialized. It would be wrong to neglect the historical importance and popularity of Barrès's novels, even if there are few admirers today of either his literary achievement or his political attitudes. Barrès is best known for his mystical attachment to regional roots, and an unusually nationalistic loyalty which derided the idealistic internationalism he associated with both Kant and Bismarck. In extolling the cultural and racial supremacy of the French and the civilizing role of France in the world, he encouraged a belief in the importance of the Church and the army, urging his youthful admirers to demonstrate in war the true proof of their virility. His posthumously published *Cahiers* contain interesting reflections about the personal and social sources of creative energy.

Barrès's first novels, the "Culte du moi" trilogy, *Sous l'oeil des barbares*, *Un homme libre*, and *Le Jardin de Bérénice*, hold the reader's attention thanks to their ambivalence rather than their characters or their plot. Together they form a Bildungsroman, the story of a progression from youth to adulthood, written under the influence of Bergson and virtually proclaiming the development of the self as the supreme virtue, while testing, accepting, rejecting, and experimenting with various values on the way. There is much theoretical discussion here, and a fair display of the prejudices which were to win Barrès political acclaim. He aimed, dangerously, to sensitize his generation to needs bred by the processes of creative evolution which it was his ambition to satisfy.

The following trilogy, entitled collectively *Le Roman de l'énergie nationale* and comprising *Les Déracinés*, *L'Appel au soldat*, and *Leurs figures*, broadens the perspective by sketching the fortunes and misfortunes of a whole group of students as they enter the social world, insisting now on nationhood based on regional roots as a prerequisite of selfhood. There is still an underlying belief in progress, but the evolution of society clearly requires an educational process, just as the individual requires a proper personal formation. Barrès frequently refers to public events and ends by turning his central figure, Sturel, into his own spokesman. Sturel is portrayed as taking a route as long and circuitous to Barrès's positions as Barrès's own.

The link forged by Barrès between his instinctive nationalism and his belief in socialism was fortuitous but fruitful, and underpins much of his political writing. Barrès frequently has recourse to a popularization of philosophical thinkers as a means of constructing an intellectual foundation for his social and political convictions, but his passion for moral and social education linked to traditionalist patriotism proved a mixture heady enough for him to be able to advocate programmes of action without much regard for systems of thought. A grandiose rhetoric of the intellect runs through *De Hegel aux cantines du Nord*, which pits Taine against Marx, Bakunin against Hegel, and finds an open-ended French synthesis in Proudhon. The programme as it had developed by 1902 is incorporated into the speeches collected in *Scènes et doctrines du nationalisme* and in the essay *Les Amitiés françaises*.

To some extent the Dreyfus affair forced Barrès to choose between socialism and the nationalism which had come to take precedence for him, as in the matter of the treatment of foreign workers. Somehow a belief in the civilizing role of France, based on a frankly racial superiority together with the rights this conferred, had to be combined with a belief in cultural nourishment drawn from regional roots. Adherence to national order and authority was essential, but Barrès associated monotheistic Judaism, like Protestantism, with undesirable centralization, whereas Catholicism's proliferation of saints, ceremonies, and holy places fitted in with the regional roots Barrès was seeking for French nationalism.

During the war Barrès wrote daily patriotic articles in the *Echo de Paris*, later published in the 14 volumes of the *Chronique de la Grande Guerre*. The novel *Au service de l'Allemagne* examined and extolled the integrity of the culture of Alsace-Lorraine following the German invasion and unashamedly maintained the superiority of French civilization, the central theme of *Colette Baudoche*, which extends it even to the superiority of French cooking and of French wine over German beer. Colette's German suitor gradually submits to the refining influence of a French environment, but Colette remains too true to her upbringing to sacrifice her honour by marrying him.

Some of Barrès's literary output is exotic. *Du sang, de la volupté et de la mort*, *Amori et dolori sacrum*, *Le Voyage de Sparte*, and *Le Greco et le secret de Tolède* are clear attempts to exorcize the remaining attractions of romanticism and decadence. A further group of works is concerned with the importance of mysticism and of non-material values, which Barrès links with the fusion already existing in his own mind between religion and nationalism. *La Grande Pitié des églises de France* and *Le Mystère en plein lumière* are examples of the exploitation of religious loyalties for patriotic objectives. *Une enquête aux pays du Levant* and *Un jardin sur l'Oronte* reunite religious mysticism with sensual exoticism.

PUBLICATIONS

Collections

L'Oeuvre de Maurice Barrès, 20 vols., 1923–57, re-edited

1965–68
Chronique de la Grande Guerre, 14 vols., 1931–39
Mes cahiers, 11 vols., 1929–48

Bibliography

Zarach, H., *Bibliographie Barrèsienne*, 1951

Critical studies

Actes du Colloque Maurice Barrès organisé par la Faculté des lettres et des sciences humaines de l'Université de Nancy, 1963
Soucy, R., *Fascism in France: The Case of Maurice Barrès*, 1972
Ouston, P., *The Imagination of Maurice Barrès*, 1974
Greaves, Anthony A., *Maurice Barrès*, 1978
Chiron, Yves, *Barrès et la Terre*, 1987

———

BARTHES, Roland (Gérard), 1915–1980.

Critic and essayist.

LIFE

Apart from the setbacks imposed by his tuberculosis, Roland Barthes's career followed the stereotyped progress of French intellectuals of his age and dazzling skills. From a desire, clear from the tone of his early works, to tilt at established values and conventions, whether academic, social, or political, he moved to the point at which he was himself absorbed into the academic establishment, in which he made his career and whose honours he both deserved and accepted.

Barthes's father had died in a naval battle before he was one. He grew up deeply attached to his mother, was dominated by his desire to keep his homosexuality from her, and lost the will to live when she died. He was knocked down by a van in Paris and, though not seriously injured at the time, died three years later from the effect of the accident. In his autobiographical *Roland Barthes par Roland Barthes* he tells us that his childhood was serene but, when he wrote that, his mother was still alive. Louis-Jean Calvet's biography, *Roland Barthes*, shows that his life was bleak, with its emotional outlets confined to sauna baths and foreign brothels.

Barthes was born in Cherbourg and spent his early school years in Bayonne. In 1924 his mother took him to Paris, where he attended the Lycée Montaigne until 1930, and thereafter the Lycée Louis-le-Grand until 1934, when he passed his baccalauréat. He spent a year in the Pyrenees to recover from tuberculosis and went on to study classics at the Sorbonne, graduating in 1939. In 1938 Barthes visited Greece with the Groupe de Théâtre Antique, which he had founded. He had been excused military service on account of his health and had spent a year of his course as a French language assistant in Hungary. He went to Biarritz to teach for a year in 1939, then took two further degrees in Paris, the diploma in Greek tragedy in 1941, and the "licence" in grammar and philology in 1943. From 1940 to 1941 he also taught in two Paris lycées until he had a relapse of tuberculosis. His first article, on Gide's *Journal*, was published in the sanatorium newspaper. Ill health, cures, and convalescence kept Barthes from professional activity until 1948, although he did undertake pre-medical studies in the Alpine sanatorium where he was recovering. He went to Bucharest for a year in 1948 and then for a further year to Alexandria as a French language assistant. His first article, "Le degré zéro de l'écriture," appeared in *Combat* in 1947.

Barthes spent from 1950 to 1952 in Paris, attached to the teaching branch of the Direction Générale des Affaires Culturelles, and from 1952 to 1954 in an appointment by the Centre National de Recherche Scientifique to work on lexicography. From 1955 to 1959 he held a CNRS research post in sociology. He then moved to the social and economic sciences section of the Ecole Pratique des Hautes Etudes in Paris as chairman of section VI (1960–62) and professor of semiology ("the sociology of signs, symbols, and collective representations," as he defined it). He remained at the school for the rest of his life, becoming director of studies. He was made a member of the Collège de France, where he was professor of literary semiology from 1976. He visited Japan and the US in 1966 and spent the academic year 1967–68 at Johns Hopkins University, Baltimore. In Paris he was co-founder of *Théâtre Populaire* in 1953 and of *Arguments* in 1956.

Barthes's most celebrated and certainly most accessible book is *Mythologies*, a series of amusing and often acute pieces of journalism written mostly for *Les Lettres Nouvelles*, although the first and most famous, about wrestling, "Le monde où l'on catche," was published in *Esprit* in 1952. The "Le degré zéro" article, on what should really be translated as something like "the freezing point of literary style," had given its title to Barthes's first book, a short collection of critical essays published in 1953. It was academically irreverent and, like the journalistic essays, amusing and perceptive. Together with Sartre's *Qu'est-ce que la littérature?* of 1948, it is sometimes regarded as having established the "nouvelle critique."

Barthes's reputation was at first more firmly established, however by the publication of the widely applauded anthology and study of texts in a book belonging to a well-known series, *Michelet par lui-même*. This is neither historical narration nor literary analysis, but a dissection of the images used by Michelet, and what they signify. Real fame came with *Sur Racine*, an open attack on conventional academic criticism as brilliantly exhibited in Raymond Picard's *La Carrière de Jean Racine* of 1961. There ensued one of those furious, publicly conducted intellectual debates which seemed to put the whole of traditional culture into the melting pot, and which happen most easily, if not exclusively, in France. Barthes's participation in the debate culminated in *Critique et vérité*, his forceful defence of the view, to be developed in *S/Z*, that literature is primarily of importance for the way it uses language.

Even at its most technical, Barthes's writing is seldom obscure, or even difficult, and it is very frequently amusing, wittily exploiting paradox and making its most powerful points in the guise of unmasking "myths," conventions, half-truths, the nonsense of social assumptions and formally academic presuppositions. Apart from the 1975 autobiography, his most important book is the technically structuralist *Eléments de sémiologie*

of 1964, although *S/Z*, being less purely theoretical, gives easier access to the sociology of language for which Barthes is chiefly renowned.

WORKS

Barthes's starting point as a thinker was the contention of Ferdinand de Saussure in his *Cours de linguistique générale* (1913) that words are arbitrary linguistic signs, and that all communication, necessarily implying a social context, must rely on an often elaborate system of conventions. The analysis of these linguistic, literary, and social conventions, which we often, even normally, take for granted is the "semiology" to which Barthes devoted his life. The disentanglement and study of the purely linguistic conventions is the most technical part of his work and properly belongs to the academic discipline of linguistics. The analysis of the literary codes and the establishment of the "nouvelle critique" is still academic, but more accessible. It is the subject of *Le Degré zéro, Sur Racine*, and above all *S/Z*, a minute analysis of a passage from Balzac, dissolving it into the series of quite artificial codes upon which Barthes seeks to show that it depends. The unmasking of the codes underlying ordinary social, and especially middle-class, ways of thinking, speaking, and behaving is the subject of the amusing and sometimes dizzily brilliant literary output, which never surpassed what was achieved in *Mythologies*.

Because Barthes wished to popularize the already victorious battle against the view that linguistic, literary, and social signs were in some sense "natural," and because he believed that middle-class attitudes to linguistic, literary, and social conventions were contrary to his view, his work was generally "left-wing" in tone, although *Mythologies* scarcely goes beyond merely teasing the crustier defenders of middle-class propriety. If the controversy with Picard was conducted at a culturally more elevated level, the hostilities were sharper and Barthes had found a particularly staid defender of traditional academic historical and critical work against whom to make his most telling points. His love of paradox occasionally led him to defend extreme debating positions, and he both feared being pinned down in his turn as the proponent of any precise theory and relished his ability wittily to shock with structuralist (q.v.) or Freudian analysis. His own values, as demonstrated in *Le Plaisir du texte* and *Fragments d'un discours amoureux*, were largely hedonistic. Each of us, in Barthes's view, is an indefinite number of projected images rather than a unified personality.

Barthes regarded the *Système de la mode* of 1967 as unsuccessful, ineptly failing to be scientific in its categories. It analyses the way in which personality is communicated in dress, continuing and concentrating the inspiration of *Mythologies*. Barthes insists that the essay on wrestling is not about sport, like boxing or first-class wrestling itself, but about wrestling as entertainment, with its excessive gestures, like pounding the ring or lifting the arms, ritualized expressions or social "signs" of something which is not actually felt, or not to the degree which the gestures would indicate. Everything about the wrestling is coded communication, from the very appearance of the wrestlers to their expressions of intellectual stupidity or moral righteousness.

This is not great literature, or even particularly profound analysis, but it is forceful, witty, ingenious, and perceptive.

The subjects of many of the essays are ephemeral, but Barthes is at his cleverest and funniest in 800 words on, for instance, the advertising of soap powders on the occasion of the first Congrès Mondial de la Détergence, the conditions a woman writer has to satisfy to be acceptable as a public figure, or the launching of a new model by Citroën. *Mythologies* contains 53 such essays and a more serious reflection on "myth today." Barthes's analyses of language, literature, and society adopt approaches and come to conclusions which, in spite of their important differences, have often been compared to those of Lévi-Strauss's anthropological descriptions of social behaviour within primitive tribes.

PUBLICATIONS

Criticism/Semiology

Le Degré zéro de l'écriture, 1953; as *Writing Degree Zero and Elements of Semiology*, 1968
Michelet par lui-même, 1954
Mythologies, 1957; selections as *Mythologies* (in English), 1972
Sur Racine, 1963; as *On Racine*, 1964
Essais critiques, 1964; as *Critical Essays*, 1972
Eléments de sémiologie avec Le Degré zéro de l'écriture, 1964; as *Elements of Semiology*, 1968
Critique et vérité, 1966
Système de la mode, 1967; as *The Fashion System*, 1983
S/Z, 1970; as *S/Z* (in English), 1975
L'Empire des signes, 1970; as *The Empire of Signs*, 1982
Sade, Fourier, Loyola, 1971; as *Sade/Fourier/Loyola* (in English), 1976
Nouveaux essais critiques, 1972; as *New Critical Essays*, 1980
Le Plaisir du texte, 1972; as *The Pleasure of the Text*, 1975
Leçon inaugurale, 1977
Image, Music, Text (selected essays), 1977
Fragments d'un discours amoureux, 1977; as *A Lover's Discourse*, 1978
The Eiffel Tower and Other Mythologies, 1979
Le Chambre claire, 1980; as *Camera Lucida*, 1981
A Barthes Reader, edited by Susan Sontag, 1982
L'Obvie et l'obtuse, 1982; as *The Responsibility of Forms*, 1985
Le Bruissement de la langue, 1984; as *The Rustle of Language*, 1986

Other

Exégèse et herméneutique, with others, 1971
Analyse structurale et exégèse biblique, with others, 1973; as *Structural Analysis and Biblical Exegesis: Interpretation and Essays by Roland Barthes and Others*, 1974
Roland Barthes par Roland Barthes, 1975; as *Roland Barthes by Roland Barthes*, 1977
Le Grain de la voix: entretiens 1962–1980, 1981; as *The Grain of the Voice: Interviews 1962–1980*, 1985

Bibliography

Freeman, Sanford, and Carole Anne Taylor, *Roland Barthes: A Bibliographical Reader's Guide*, 1983

Critical and biographical studies

Picard, Raymond, *Nouvelle critique ou nouvelle imposture*, 1965; as *New Criticism or New Fraud?*, 1969
Heath, Stephen, *Vertige du déplacement: lecture de Barthes*, 1974
Thody, Philip, *Roland Barthes: A Conservative Estimate*, 1977
Fages, J.B., *Comprendre Roland Barthes*, 1979
Nordahl Lund, Steffen, *L'Aventure du signifiant: une lecture de Barthes*, 1981
Wasserman, Georges R., *Roland Barthes*, 1981
Lavers, Annette, *Roland Barthes, Structuralism and After*, 1982
Culler, Jonathan, *Barthes* (in English), 1983
Ungar, Steven, *Roland Barthes: The Professor of Desire*, 1983
Champagne, Roland A., *Literary History in the Wake of Roland Barthes: Re-Defining the Myths of Reading*, 1984
Calvet, Louis-Jean, *Roland Barthes*, 1990

———

BATAILLE, Henri, 1872–1922.

Poet and dramatist.

Bataille's poetry, *La Chambre blanche* and *Le Beau Voyage*, never went far beyond the false tones of a lyrical nostalgia. His early symbolist theatre was also immature. But his psychological melodramas have been found pleasantly redolent of the "belle époque," a mixture of daring and sentimentality. In spite of the derision of recent historians, they were undoubtedly popular at the time of their publication.

The best known is *Le Colibri*, in which a hysterical mother is in love with her son's best friend and caught up in a semi-erotic relationship with her own son. *La Marche nuptiale* is about a pretty girl who makes an untalented piano teacher sacrifice his family for her, whereas *Poliche* has a tawdrier and even less structured plot. Later plays, like *Le Scandale*, are written to successful formulas and often exploit notorious society scandals (*La Femme nue, Les Flambeaux, La Phalène*). *La Vierge folle* has been criticized for its unpleasant plot. Bataille's style changed with the war (*L'Amazone, Notre image*), but then reverted to the pre-war dramatic formula (*Les Soeurs d'amour, La Tendresse, La Possession, La Chair humaine*). He was adept only at giving the public what it wanted. *La Divine Tragédie*, on the other hand, contains mature and moving war poetry.

PUBLICATIONS

Collections

Théâtre complet, 12 vols., 1922–29

Verse

La Chambre blanche, 1895

Le Beau Voyage, 1905
La Divine Tragédie, 1916

Critical studies

Biondolillo, F., *Il teatro di Henri Bataille*, 1915
Blanchet, P., *Henri Bataille, son oeuvre*, 1922
Besançon, J.-B., *Essai sur le théâtre de Henri Bataille*, 1928

BAUDELAIRE, Charles (-Pierre), 1821–1867.

Poet, literary, music, and art critic.

LIFE

Baudelaire's mother, an orphan brought up in comfortable circumstances by a friend of her family, came from a royalist background and spent her early years in England as a refugee from the Terror. She was initiated into social life via the Paris salon kept by her foster mother, Mme Pérignon, where she met the widower François Baudelaire (1759–1827). He was a cultivated amateur painter and an ex-priest, 34 years her senior. He had a son, Alphonse (1805–1862), who was 14 when the couple married in 1819. When Baudelaire himself was born, his mother was 26 and his father 60. The age disparity between his parents may have contributed to Baudelaire's nervous instability, but he probably owed to his father his enthusiasm for the plastic arts and to his mother his command of English. His father died in 1827 when he was nearly six, leaving a house stuffed full of paintings and sculptures.

Baudelaire's mother, now reasonably provided for, was already pregnant when she remarried in 1828. His stepfather, Jacques Aupick (1789–1857), was an officer, later a general, ambassador to Constantinople, then Madrid, and ended his career a senator. Their one child, a daughter, was stillborn. Baudelaire later grew to hate his stepfather and compensated for these feelings by idealizing the father he had scarcely known. His early relationship with his mother was also unusually intimate. In 1830 and 1831, when he was nine, he spent 15 months alone with her while Aupick was serving with distinction in Morocco. She was to become over-ambitious for his academic success.

Baudelaire was educated first at a Lyons boarding school while Aupick was garrisoned in that town, and then, from 1835, at the Lycée Louis-le-Grand. He excelled at classics and won a Latin verse prize in 1837, but was finally expelled from the Lycée in 1839 for what was probably the culmination of a series of minor insubordinations. He passed his baccalauréat that August and determined on a literary career, so causing the first serious rift with his stepfather, who could have contrived an excellent start for him in a diplomatic career. As a compromise Baudelaire registered as a law student, living in lodgings from the autumn of 1839. He almost immediately contracted the syphilis that was practically universal at the time, and his half-brother, Alphonse, helped him obtain treatment. In 1840 he had an affair with a young prostitute, Sarah, for whom he wrote some verse, including at least one poem later to be included in *Les Fleurs du mal*. He became known for his dandyism and by early 1841 owed various tradesmen 2,370 francs, partly as a result of generous gifts to Sarah.

Baudelaire's half-brother clearly regarded debt as more serious than disease and informed his stepmother of the situation. As a result Baudelaire was sent off to Calcutta and the East Indies, the necessary 4,000 francs being raised against the 100,000 his father had left in trust until his majority in April 1842. Baudelaire, whose only interest was literature, had no part in the decision, and the money was entrusted to the captain of the small sailing ship in which he sailed. He left Bordeaux on 9 June 1841. However, following a storm in which but for Baudelaire's help the ship would probably have foundered, extensive repairs were required in Mauritius, where Baudelaire's social graces led to repeated invitations from a local solicitor. At this point Baudelaire refused to travel further, finally forcing the captain to arrange for his return to France from nearby Réunion. A sonnet to the solicitor's wife, "A une dame créole," appears in *Les Fleurs du mal*. After a delay, Baudelaire's even smaller ship home left on 4 November, and he arrived back in Bordeaux on 15 February, two months away from his 21st birthday and his legacy. Most of the accrued interest had been charged by Baudelaire's mother and stepfather for his upkeep and education from the date of their marriage. After the legal settlement, Aupick informed his wife that he did not wish to see her son again.

Baudelaire took a room on the not yet fashionable Ile-St-Louis in Paris, furnished it minimally, and acquired some cats. He was still writing verse and rapidly running through his legacy. By the end of 1843 a couple of dozen or so of the poems to be included in *Les Fleurs du mal* had been written, as well, apparently, as a good deal of other material, much of it morbid or macabre, which Baudelaire would occasionally recite to friends. After a brief stay elsewhere when his lease ran out, he returned to a two-room apartment at the top of a 17th-century house on the Ile, for which he paid 315 francs a year. Through the other tenants in the building, also Bohemian, Baudelaire met Banville, Gautier, and probably also Balzac. The "Club des Haschischins", which gave him the idea for *Les Paradis artificiels*, also had its home there. Baudelaire decorated his living room expensively, hiding away his few books, mostly Latin and Renaissance French in fine bindings, in a cupboard. He bought pictures, notably 13 lithographs of scenes from *Hamlet* by Delacroix, scented his carpet daily with musk, had frosted glass put in his windows to block out visual distractions, and hung among his other pictures his treasured portrait of his father. His taste was already riveted by Delacroix, Daumier, and the Spanish school, and Emile Deroy, who painted the carefully posed portrait of Baudelaire with his head resting on his left hand, forefinger on temple, introduced him to a number of art critics and helped further to educate his taste.

Soon after his return to France Baudelaire had begun what was to be an almost life-long love affair with Jeanne Duval, a beautiful part-African actress from a slave family who had been sold into prostitution. The relationship was only partly physical. Baudelaire was fascinated by the effect that Jeanne's sheer bodily beauty had on his senses but, perhaps as a result of his disease, seems almost to have resented actual physical contact, while Jeanne herself appears from his poems to have been sexually cool towards him. It is not unlikely that she was lesbian, and her physical charms, coupled with her unresponsiveness, could also inspire Baudelaire to embittered rage, which he expressed in some of his poems. Nor did his poetry avoid reminders of the physical decomposition that awaits even the most beautiful.

Baudelaire's taste in decoration, clothes, objets d'art, and entertainment and the financial support he gave Jeanne and her mother had been fast eroding his capital. He lost a lot of money buying fake paintings, paying for them with promissory notes and reselling them for pocket money, and was having little success in placing his work. He made little headway with literary friends like Sainte-Beuve, who was always reserved about him, and made himself a reputation for bizarre behaviour, wild jokes, and disturbing remarks which gave him a sinister unpredictability unlikely to endear him to editors. He tried in vain to reassure his mother with regard to his circumstances, but he had used up half his legacy in two years, had earned nothing, and steps were taken to get the court to appoint a legal administrator of his affairs from September 1844, a procedure more usually invoked for the insane than the improvident. The family lawyer, Ancelle, was appointed and he paid Baudelaire only interest on his remaining capital, refusing all advances not sanctioned by his mother, to whom Baudelaire would go on owing money while refusing to settle outstanding debts. His creditors had to wait for payment until after his death.

In 1845 Baudelaire issued warnings that he was going to commit suicide and did in fact make a somewhat half-hearted attempt. He convalesced at his mother's home, leaving it when the strain of being near his stepfather became too great. He spent the rest of his life living in cheap hotels. However, in the spring of 1845 he published at his own expense an account of the 1845 Salon, the now annual exhibition at the Louvre at which it was every artist's ambition to exhibit, and reviews of which were published in the newly fashionable newspapers and in all the magazines. The *Salon de 1845* allowed Baudelaire to contribute occasional pieces to *Le Corsaire-Satan* and *L'Esprit Public*. His article on an exhibition of French neoclassical painting shows excellent judgement, but went unnoticed at the time.

However intelligent the content of his work, he was writing in the context of popular journalism. It is noteworthy that in both the *Salon de 1845* and the *Salon de 1846*, Baudelaire refuses to denounce bourgeois taste or, in 1845 at least, the painters compelled to pander to it in order to earn a living. They needed to paint for a new market hungry for sharp portraits in oils and for "genre" paintings. Only in the body of the 1846 brochure does Baudelaire virulently attack their leader, Vernet. What he wanted was for artists and writers to educate public taste, leading it towards higher things. Within a few years, however, his tolerance of bourgeois values changed to contempt. He failed to penetrate the reserve of Delacroix, the artist he most admired, when he visited him before the 1846 Salon, but publication of his *Salon de 1846* in brochure form gained him admission to the Société des Gens de Lettres. By 1846 Baudelaire was also occasionally publishing without acknowledgement pieces he had translated from English, including short stories by Poe. At this date his forthcoming book of poems was to be entitled *Les Lesbiennes*.

In 1847 Baudelaire published a long short story, *Le Fanfarlo*, in the *Bulletin de la Société des Gens de Lettres*. It was partly inspired by Balzac but also partly a self-portrait, and the first draft probably dates from 1843–44. His debts mounted and his dandyism declined. He had his hair cropped to disguise the hair loss which was a side effect of his syphilis, and after 1846 he wore overalls on top of his elegant clothes whenever he went out in the street. By 1847 he was scrounging meals and changing lodgings to evade creditors. He took up a strongly reactionary position on political and social issues although, during the 1848 revolution, he joined the republican demonstrators on the barricades, apparently shouting that Aupick, who had recently been made commander of the Ecole Polytechnique for the training of officers, should be shot. We do not in fact know how serious he was. He was beginning to make a name for himself in artistic circles and was on friendly terms with Gautier, Nerval, the sculptor Préault, and the actor Lemaître. In 1847 he met Courbet and the actress Marie Daubrun, with whom he may have started a liaison immediately. He was certainly involved with her at a later date.

During the revolution Baudelaire witnessed the bayonetting of a demonstrator who had tripped while fleeing, wrote a number of violent articles for *Le Salut Public* and, after taking part in a raid on a gunsmith's shop, carried what must have been a double-barrelled sporting gun. His adoption of revolutionary attitudes may have been partly due to Proudhon, whom he got to know slightly, becoming secretary of *La Tribune Nationale*, which supported Proudhon. His revolutionary fervour may also have been kindled by his taste for the abnormal and the violent. It eventually faded and, later in 1848, Baudelaire became editor of the conservative *Représentant de la Loire*, although his paradoxical attitudes continued to shock his readers and his directors. His friendship with Courbet deepened and, in 1850, he got to know Poulet-Malassis, the future publisher of *Les Fleurs du mal*. The paradoxes in his behaviour began to suggest the feelings of self-loathing and the self-destructive tendencies which lie behind some of his poems.

By 1850, at which time his prospective volume of poems was to be called *Les Limbes*, Baudelaire was going to extraordinary lengths to find out all he could about Poe, who had died at the end of 1849, and whose works had been published in a three-volume set. He eventually found in Paris an obituary and a review article on the three-volume edition, which enabled him to write *Edgar Allan Poe, sa vie et ses ouvrages*. It was published in the *Revue de Paris* for March and April 1852, translated into Russian, and later reissued as the introduction to his translation of Poe's stories, the *Histoires extraordinaires* of 1856. Baudelaire changes Poe's physical appearance to accord with his own mental image, much as in his description of David's *The Death of Marat* the painting's content was modified to emphasize Baudelaire's affinity with the painter. By 1853 his destitution and indebtedness were becoming pitiable, as he indicated in his letters to his mother. Baudelaire's greatest fear, however, was that he might lose his grip on his mental faculties. He was translating Poe, having acquired the three-volume edition of his works in 1853, and again going to extraordinary lengths to render his translation accurate and idiomatic, searching out a tutor and even English jockeys and sailors for the purpose. The translation was enthusiastically received by the critics and went into several editions.

Baudelaire and his mother quarrelled over Jeanne Duval and he scarcely wrote to her while she was with her husband who was then Ambassador in Turkey. Mother and son were reconciled in 1851, when she returned briefly to Paris before Aupick took up his next post as ambassador to Madrid. Baudelaire was now clearly tired of Jeanne's constant presence. They got on one another's nerves and sporadically parted only to come together again. From 1851 Baudelaire had cultivated an idealized affection for the singer "Apollonie" Sabatier, until 1860 the established mistress of the banker Alfred Mosselman. She ran her own salon, where Baudelaire regularly met Flaubert, Gautier, the Goncourt brothers, and a host of painters and sculptors. Baudelaire regarded her as an object of almost religious veneration and, from 1852 to 1854, frequently sent her quasi-anonymous poems. They became lovers for a short time in 1857, although that was not strictly the relationship which Baudelaire wanted from her. In 1855, in anticipation of Marie Daubrun's return to Paris, he borrowed an advance of 500 francs from Ancelle in order to furnish lodgings for her. Marie did return, but went to live with Banville, and Jeanne Duval moved in with Baudelaire instead, only to walk out again a year later.

Baudelaire had had his poems copied in 1849. In 1851 he published 11 of them in *Le Messager de l'Assemblée*. Their collective title, *Les Limbes*, referred to the limbo of the theologians between hell and heaven, but also to Fourier's description of the period preceding the socialist utopia. A new title, "Les Fleurs du mal," was suggested casually by someone one evening in a café. It was intended to signify things of beauty which can be produced by something in itself physically unpleasant or morally evil, as well as the seductive but poisonous blossoms of certain plants. It also indicated a selection of particularly fine specimens the "Flower of." The title as we have it therefore has a triple meaning and was first used for 18 poems published in the *Revue des Deux Mondes* (q.v.) in 1855. Mostly love poems, they are characterized by self-reproach and a premonition of the physical decomposition that lies in wait for the syphilitic lover. The editor of the review added a cautious prefatory note.

The contract for the collected volume was signed on 30 December 1856 and stipulated a print run of 1,000 copies and a royalty of only 25 centimes a copy. The difficulty was to cut the volume down to 100 poems, selected from the considerable portfolio Baudelaire had by now built up. He later destroyed the surplus poems, excluded on the grounds of apparent audacity. In April 1857 Aupick died. The book was published on 21 June. Delation, prosecution, and seizure swiftly followed, the authorities possibly hoping to avenge the recent acquittal of Flaubert's *Madame Bovary*. Some reviews were deferred, some were eulogistic, some scandalized. When the case was heard, charges on account of the four poems impugned for offences against religion were dropped, as were three for offences against morality, leaving six poems condemned. The 350-franc fine was reduced to 50 francs on appeal.

In 1858 Baudelaire published an article on hashish in *La Revue Contemporaine*, to which in 1860 he added a digest of de Quincey, publishing both together as *Les Paradis artificiels*. Hashish was considered a delicacy at the time. Although known to produce hallucinations, no social stigma attached to its use. Baudelaire, like de Quincey, may also have used opium, in the form of laudanum, possibly as an anaesthetic or a palliative for hunger, but Baudelaire became addicted. In reasonable quantities it could be bought over the chemist's counter. It is probable that his secondary syphilis raised Baudelaire's alcohol consumption to the point at which gastritis set in, which he assuaged with laudanum, so slowly destroying his digestive system.

In 1859 *L'Artiste* published Baudelaire's study of Gautier,

later reprinted as a pamphlet with a preface by Hugo. This was also the year of the third and last *Salon*. Jeanne had a stroke and was admitted to a hospice. The *Revue Française* printed "La genèse d'un poëme." Translated by Baudelaire from Poe, it is the source of the theory which was to dominate French poetry from Valéry to Mallarmé. At this point a brother of Jeanne's suddenly appeared out of the blue and began living off what Baudelaire was able to send her and stealing from her. Baudelaire, uncharacteristically disgusted, henceforward sent Jeanne help only anonymously. One of his acquaintances apparently caught sight of her, now lame, after his death, and she almost certainly died in squalor.

In 1860, a year in which he again contemplated suicide, Baudelaire, determined to replace the six condemned poems, started a whole new series of poems, not all of which were ready for the well-received 1861 edition of *Les Fleurs du mal*. He also began writing more prose poems, mostly realistic street scenes, a score of which were published in *La Presse* during 1862, publishing another six under the title *Le Spleen de Paris* in *Le Figaro* of 7 February 1864, "spleen" in French being a romantic word for a mixture of nostalgia and disgust. The first examples of this new genre, of which Baudelaire was the true originator, had appeared in 1857 as *Poèmes nocturnes*. The prose poems sometimes have the same title as the verse poems, but the contents do not necessarily correspond, and the prose poems generally carry often perverse morals. At this time, too, Baudelaire must have been writing the posthumously published work we know as *L'Art romantique*, for which he had signed a contract with Poulet-Malassis in 1860.

The important *Richard Wagner et Tannhäuser à Paris* was published in 1861 in the *Revue Européenne* and later as a pamphlet. In a letter to his mother at this date Baudelaire informs her of his intention to write *Mon cœur mis à nu*, for which Poulet-Malassis, to whom Baudelaire sold all future rights to his works, written and unwritten, kept the notes. Nine prose poems were also published in Catulle Mendès's *Revue Fantaisiste* in 1861, the year in which Baudelaire was fortunately persuaded to withdraw his candidacy for the Académie Française. The next year his half-brother died, paralysed. Baudelaire was much encouraged by Swinburne's laudatory review of *Les Fleurs du mal* in the *Spectator*. He tried to resell the rights to his works already sold to the now bankrupt Poulet-Malassis, fleeing his creditors in Belgium. In 1864 Baudelaire, too, moved to Belgium, where he was invited to give a series of lectures. He was paid less than he had been promised and the lectures themselves were a disaster. Baudelaire stayed on in Belgium, only to become increasingly disillusioned with the country and what he regarded as the stolidity of its citizens, disliking everything about it except some of its buildings.

Baudelaire also published an important panegyric on Delacroix and an article fulsomely praising the painter Constantin Guys, giving today the impression that he was apt to overestimate artists with whom he felt a special affinity, such as Poe, de Quincey, and Guys, although posterity has endorsed his enthusiasm for Delacroix and Wagner. Baudelaire's own reputation was still unsettled. Mallarmé published a complimentary article on 1 February 1865 in *L'Artiste*, but a Belgian attack on him appeared in the same month. Poulet-Malassis, with whom Baudelaire had at first regularly dined, was now threatening him as a creditor, although he rallied to Baudelaire's support again as his health gave way. Verlaine wrote three pieces praising

Baudelaire in November and December, but Baudelaire does not appear to have appreciated his compliments. On his last visit to Paris, before his final return to a nursing home, he told Catulle Mendès, who had met him by chance and given him a bed for the night, that he had earned less than 16,000 francs during the whole of his working life. It was July 1865, and Baudelaire was again contemplating suicide. He refused in his confusion to believe that Nerval had killed himself.

He had been forced to tell his mother about his syphilis and in March 1866 fell seriously ill with hemiplegic paralysis, which deprived him of the power of speech. Shortly after this Mendès published a further 15 poems in *Le Parnasse Contemporain*. They also appeared in the 1868 posthumous edition of *Les Fleurs du mal*. Baudelaire's mother brought him back to Paris in July 1866, and he was able to receive visitors, including Sainte-Beuve, Banville, and Leconte de Lisle. He died a year later in his mother's arms, on the day the *Revue Nationale* published the final series of his prose poems.

WORKS

Although Baudelaire published relatively little, he seized on certain elements in the work of his contemporaries and by blending them with his own morbid obsession with corruption and decay, possibly born of fear regarding the consequences of the syphilis he had contracted in his mid-teens, virtually created a new sensibility, or way of seeing and feeling, which was to dominate Europe's artistic life for generations. Forced to confront the ordinary, the ugly, and the "natural," he defended himself against it not only through transient dandyism, but by transforming it in his poems into the marvellous, the ethereal, and the beautiful. His critical writings grope uncertainly towards the formulation of an aesthetic theory underlying his achievement. Baudelaire is sometimes regarded as bridging the gulf between late romanticism and the symbolism which was in some ways a reaction to it. He himself wrote that "romanticism" was simply "l'expression la plus récente, la plus actuelle du beau (the most recent, the most up-to-date expression of beauty)."

The artist, according to Baudelaire, transfigures experience by virtue of his aspiration to the infinite: "Qui dit romantisme dit art moderne, c'est-à-dire intimité, spiritualité, couleur, aspiration vers l'infini, exprimées par tous les moyens que contiennent les arts (To speak of romanticism is to speak of modern art, that is to say intimacy, spirituality, colour, aspiration towards the infinite, expressed by every means at the disposition of the arts)." The enemy of art is therefore that which inhibits the transformation of the ordinary and the everyday, "ennui"—not merely lassitude, but the positive attraction of the commonplace and the degrading—and "spleen," with its note of nostalgia for the sordid, the macabre, and the platitudinous. What distinguishes Baudelaire from the exaggerated late romanticism which these attitudes suggest is a meticulous striving for perfection of form, which is part of his legacy and which explains why he could never sustain his vision for more than brief moments of poetic intensity.

Baudelaire's first significant published writings were reviews of art exhibitions. There is some evidence that he later wished to disavow the *Salon de 1845*, perhaps because of its somewhat ironic prefatory refusal to attack bourgeois taste: "to despise the flocks of those who have got lost is not the best way of leading

them back to where they should be." It was signed, using his mother's maiden name, Baudelaire Dufaijs. The text itself starts with a ringing eulogy of Delacroix, praising his paintings for the subtlety of their colour, for the "intimate, mysterious, and romantic poetry" with which Delacroix could endow a simple head, and for the accuracy of the drawing, which Baudelaire compared to that of Daumier and Ingres. Baudelaire already attached importance to formal perfection and, in his remarks on Corot, to the artist's transformation of nature. The review of the winter exhibition which appeared in January 1846, *Le Musée classique du Bazar Bonne-Nouvelle* (the exhibition was held above a department store), contains the admiring description of David's *The Death of Marat*, insisting on the artist's imaginative idealization of an intrinsically horrifying scene.

The 1846 Salon, to which entry was free except on Saturdays, is said to have attracted more than a million visitors over a period of three months, at a date at which there were not quite a million adult inhabitants in Paris. Baudelaire's *Salon de 1846*, signed Baudelaire Dufaÿs, still using a variant of his mother's name, was published commercially and, breaking with tradition, no longer treats the paintings according to the categories "portrait," "landscape," "genre," and so on. It lectures the bourgeois on the importance of art and plays down the importance of Mme de Staël's distinction between colour—appropriate to cloudy northern climates—and line—more suited to the bright sunlight of Mediterranean countries. A beautiful painting is "nature reflected by an artist," but Baudelaire clearly prefers the artists of the north, among whom he has to include the Venetian Renaissance colourists, the modernists, the romantics, and especially their leader Delacroix, to whom almost a quarter of the text is devoted and of whom he clearly thinks more highly than he does of Hugo. Ingres is praised, and Vernet excoriated for his lack of poetry.

Baudelaire's next important publication, *Edgar Allan Poe, sa vie et ses ouvrages*, primarily sees in its subject a fellow writer also doomed by fate to misfortune and poverty. Baudelaire exaggerates his two sources, from which he took three quarters of his material, to make Poe's situation fit his image of his own. He does, however, find in Poe the principle that poetry is "human aspiration towards a superior beauty" and the purist aesthetic that poetry justifies itself by the creation of what is beautiful, a combination of his own idea of romanticism with the doctrine of "art for art's sake" (q.v.). Baudelaire's discovery of Poe, therefore, became a major supporting link in the bridge which, thanks to his own aesthetic theory and practice, connects late romanticism with both the Parnassian (q.v.) ideal and symbolism (q.v.). According to Baudelaire, the test of great poetry lies in the intensity of its ability to stimulate and uplift the mind. A long poem becomes a contradiction. Poetry contributes to the creation of joy through beauty, and only by inducing a necessarily transient emotional excitement can poetry impinge on the moral order. Mallarmé and Valéry were also to discover this aesthetic, which with modifications they made their own, through the Poe whom Baudelaire's essay had introduced to the French literary public.

Les Paradis artificiels consists of an essay entitled "Du vin et du Haschisch," published in four parts in *Le Messager de l'Assemblée* in March 1851, and a reworking of that piece with selected excerpts on opium, translated from de Quincey and published in the *Revue Contemporaine* in 1858 and 1860 before being issued in book form by Poulet-Malassis. Baudelaire scarcely even tried hashish but gives a convincingly analytic account of its effects based on the mostly controlled experiments at the Hôtel Pimodan, where the "Club des Haschischins" met. The final "Le poëme du haschisch" of 1858 is a considerable reworking of the 1851 text. "Un mangeur d'opium" blends Baudelaire's own penetrating reflections into de Quincey's account.

Les Fleurs du mal has only the loosest of structures. The work appeared in three important editions. The first, with 101 poems, was published in 1857. That of 1861 is extended, notably by the addition of the section "Tableaux parisiens," to 127 poems, but loses the six condemned ones, which were to be republished in Belgium with others in the 1866 *Les Epaves*. The 1868 edition, with 14 more poems, is the last not illegally to print the six condemned poems until the lifting of the ban in 1949. The volume contains love poems inspired by Jeanne Duval, Apollonie Sabatier, and Marie Daubrun. The poems on death are conventionally put last, but death for Baudelaire is equivocal, "le but de la vie… et le seul espoir (the end/purpose of life, and the only hope)." It is one of many symbols, like "l'azur," for an infinite which cannot be attained and to which penetration is impossible.

"Un voyage à Cythère," a poem inspired by a story of Nerval's, in the section of the work actually entitled "Fleurs du mal," celebrates the soul's free, joyous, and unfettered aspiration to reach the island of total bliss, with alternate stanzas showing the vision dissolving into disillusion. The island of infinite satisfaction becomes the "Eldorado banal," a bitter, rock-strewn desert containing, not the promised fulfilment, but a corpse hanging from a gibbet being picked by vultures, more ridiculous than disgusting. Many poems deal with ultimate romantic disillusion along the same lines, if using less polarized imagery. Baudelaire's poems contain no heroism, no attainable absolutes, but often frustration or the inescapable dreariness of what is sordid, contemptible, and ordinary, inspiring "ennui" or the revulsion of "spleen."

This is made clear from the prefatory "Au lecteur." The poet writes of "us" in the plural, associating the reader with himself. Nothing about us is heroic, neither our pettifogging failings, such as stupidity, error, and sin, nor our complacent remorse, which we feed like beggars "nourishing their vermin." We squeeze our pleasures from juiceless, dessicated fruit, incapable of the real villainy of rape, poison, murder, or arson. Among the jackals, panthers, scorpions, and vultures of vice, we have only "ennui," and the poet in his last couplet addresses the reader directly: "you… hypocrite reader, like me, my brother".

Some of the poems are crafted to achieve a formal perfection The first line of "La chevelure," for example, does not actually "mean" anything; it simply establishes associations to be worked into complex metaphors later in the poem:

O Toison, moutonnant jusque sur l'encolure!
(O fleece, swelling down to reach the collar!)

The title tells us the poem is about hair, presumably a woman's. This hair is like a sheep's fleece, which carries associations of softness and warmth. "Moutonner" (from "mouton," meaning "sheep") is what you might expect a fleece to do, but it in fact describes what the sea does when it swells. So in one line Baudelaire has established associations of a woman's hair, a fleece, the sea, a gentle motion, warmth, softness, and a neckline. In the poem's seven stanzas of five lines Baudelaire

appeals to all five senses, using words of smell, sight, sound, touch, and taste. There are three words for the sea's swelling, only the first of which carries the association with sheep/fleece, while the hair/sea itself is linked to the idea of port, haven, rest, harbour, and satisfaction. The poem works through a dense and rich build-up of mutually reinforcing or contradicting associations, so that when the woman's hair is said to be blue it becomes a sign of the infinite, like the "azur" to which the poet aspires or the ocean on which he sails. The poem's effect is also enhanced by assonance and alliteration, the abrupt or caressing sounds made by the repetition of consonants and vowels.

The most important recurring themes of the collection are the frustrated aspiration to self-transcendence, self-loathing, and the transformation of objects of disgust into symbols of infinite potentiality, as in "Une charogne," or "Les sept vieillards" and "Les petites vieilles," two poems dedicated to Hugo which he said gave him "un frisson nouveau (a shiver of fresh excitement)." These works display a restrained irony which disappears in the prose poems, where the transfiguration of the ordinary is continued into the marvellous in a series of vignettes which lack the concentration of verse as well as the narrative interest of the short story. The words addressed to Paris in the second edition of *Les Fleurs du mal* sum up the prose poems of *Le Spleen de Paris*, as the collection was entitled when posthumously published: "Tu m'as donné ta boue et j'en ai fait de l'or (You gave me your filth, and I have turned it into gold)."

Also published posthumously were *Journaux intimes*, comprising *Fusées, Mon cœur mis à nu*, and *Carnet*, the first two consisting of notes, ideas, private reminders, reactions of indignation, sometimes elaborated into passages of continuous prose, sometimes left aphoristic. *Fusées* contains Baudelaire's famous definition of the beautiful as "something ardent and sad, something rather vague, leaving scope for the imagination." Dreams belong to it, together with pleasure and sadness, melancholy, lassitude, and even repletion, a desire for life combined with a pent-up bitterness. Mystery and regret can also be its signs. Literature, for its part, must contain something supernatural and something ironic, in the French sense of paradoxical and cruel. Baudelaire uses the word "satanic."

Mon coeur mis à nu contains a reflection on Baudelaire's revolutionary experience of 1848 and, among the jottings, a note on the "identical sensations of cruelty and pleasure." Not all the notes represent Baudelaire at his best, and it is even possible to regret the fascination with the creative process and the personality behind it which leaves no inchoate thought unpublished and nothing private in the posthumously published papers of the great, not even Baudelaire's hostile, disjointed, and obscure notes on the Belgium he loathed. Baudelaire was, however, a very accomplished prose writer. *La Fanfarlo* appeared in 1847, complex in style, ironic and amused in tone, containing a barely veiled but fictionalized self-portrait. It was probably written in 1844 and portrays the more carefree Baudelaire of that time. La Fanfarlo herself is a clear reminiscence of Jeanne Duval.

During the last 10 or 12 years of his life Baudelaire expressed a deepening scepticism about the likelihood of moral progress in society based on scientific discovery. The *Exposition universelle de 1855* attacks the possibility not so much of scientific progress as of progress in the moral and especially the aesthetic orders. Baudelaire is scathing about the idea that artistic creation can build on what has gone before. Each artist, he thought, must depend on himself alone. The *Salon de 1859* restates Baudelaire's attitude to nature as the raw material of art. Nature is not to be copied, but transformed by imagination: "How mysterious a faculty is this queen of the faculties." The third and fourth parts of this essay contain Baudelaire's clearest statement of his whole aesthetic.

The panegyric on Delacroix published in three parts in the *Opinion Nationale*, starting on 13 August 1863, three weeks after the artist's death, and subsequently in *L'Art romantique*, repeats the passage from the *Salon de 1859* in which Baudelaire attributes to Delacroix the view that nature is a dictionary, not itself a work of art. Baudelaire rather puzzlingly compared Delacroix to Lebrun and David, the master of Delacroix's rival, Ingres, when he praised him for the dream-like quality and the power of suggestion in his paintings, and the passion that inspired them. It is possible that the true grounds for some of Baudelaire's aesthetic enthusiasms require further examination, especially in view of his final two great pronouncements on aesthetics, composed in 1860 or 1861, the essays on Guys and Wagner.

Le Peintre de la vie moderne, published in three parts in *Le Figaro* in 1863, was Constantin Guys, one of the last artist-illustrators soon to be replaced by professional photographers. His sketches of Parisian life had something in common with what Baudelaire was trying to achieve in *Le Spleen de Paris,* the transfiguration of the ordinary, "the daily transfiguration of external things." Losing himself in the crowd, the painter catches and fixes the fugitive moment, "le fantastique réel de la vie." The work contains a revealing attack on the 18th-century notion of "nature...as base, source, and type of all possible goodness and beauty." The 18th-century philosophers, according to Baudelaire, had forgotten original sin. His essay on Wagner was published in the *Revue Européenne* for 1 April 1861, when Paris knew only *Tannhäuser, The Flying Dutchman*, and *Lohengrin*. Baudelaire predictably praised the composer for his powers of suggestion, for his ability to plunge the individual into the "espaces infinis," in Pascal's famous phrase, and for the music's mystical, mysterious elements.

Baudelaire's literary output was slight and uneven, and his aesthetic theory uncertain in its expression and in its consistency. Yet the theory, as illustrated in practice by the best poems in *Les Fleurs du mal*, and by the prose poems, and as expounded in the *Salons* and the essays on Poe, Delacroix, Guys, and Wagner, revealed to Europe's advanced aesthetic elite the new sensibility it was looking for. As late romanticism was threatened by decadence, this new sensibility dominated the imaginative activity of that elite for almost a century.

PUBLICATIONS

Collections

Oeuvres complètes: Les Fleurs du mal; Curiosités esthétiques; L'Art romantique; Petits poèmes en prose, Les Paradis artificiels, La Fanfarlo, Le Jeune Enchanteur, with a foreword by Théophile Gautier, 4 vols., 1868–69
Oeuvres complètes, edited by Jacques Crepet and Claude Pichois, 19 vols., 1922–53

Oeuvres complètes, Bibliothèque de la Pléiade, 1961
Oeuvres complètes, edited by Claude Pichois, 2 vols., 1975–77

Verse

Les Fleurs du mal, 1861; revised editions, 1861, 1868 (in *Oeuvres complètes*); as *Flowers of Evil*, 1909; also translated by Richard Howard, 1982
Les Epaves, 1866
Le Parnasse contemporain (includes "Les Nouvelles Fleurs du mal"), 1866
Petits poèmes en prose, 1869; as *Paris Spleen*, 1869
Vers retrouvés, 1929
Selected Verse, translated by Francis Scarfe, 1961
Selected Poems, translated by Joanna Richardson, 1975

Other

Salon de 1845, 1845; edited by André Ferran, 1933
Salon de 1846, 1846; edited by David Kelley, 1975
Théophile Gautier, 1859
Les Paradis artificiels: opium et haschisch, 1860
Richard Wagner et Tannhäuser à Paris, 1861
Le Peintre de la vie moderne, 1863
L'Oeuvre et la vie d'Eugène Delacroix, 1863
Journaux intimes, 1920; as *Intimate Journals*, 1930
Selected Critical Studies, edited by D. Parmee, 1949
The Mirror of Art: Critical Studies, edited by J. Mayne, 1955
Baudelaire: A Self-Portrait (selected letters), edited by Lois Boe and F.E. Hyslop, 1957
Baudelaire as a Literary Critic, edited by Lois Boe and F.E. Hyslop, 1964
The Painter of Modern Life and Other Essays, edited by J. Mayne, 1964
Art in Paris 1845–1862: Salons and Other Exhibitions, edited by J. Mayne, 1965
Edgar Allan Poe, sa vie et ses ouvrages, edited by W.T. Bandy, 1973
Correspondance, edited by Claude Pichois and Jean Ziegler, 2 vols., 1973

Translator, *Histoires extraordinaires, Nouvelles histoires extraordinaires, Aventures d'Arthur Gordon Pym, Euréka, Histoires grotesques et sérieuses*, by Edgar Allan Poe, 5 vols., 1856–65

Critical studies and biographies

Mansell Jones, P., *Baudelaire* (in English), 1952
Fairlie, Alison, *Baudelaire: Les Fleurs du mal* (in English), 1960
Mossop, D.J., *Baudelaire's Tragic Hero*, 1961
Ruff, M.A., *Baudelaire*, 1966
Leakey, F.W., *Baudelaire and Nature*, 1969
Jonge, Alex de, *Baudelaire, Prince of Clouds*, 1976
Hemmings, F.W.J., *Baudelaire the Damned: A Biography*, 1982
Pichois, Claude, *Baudelaire* (in English), 1989

BEAUVOIR, Simone (-Ernestine-Lucie-Marie-Bertrand) de, 1908–1986.

Novelist and essayist.

LIFE

Simone de Beauvoir was born in Paris on 9 January 1908. Her father, Georges Bertrand de Beauvoir (1878–1941), came from a Catholic landowning family in the south-west, but lost his mother when he was 13 and developed into a religious sceptic. He would have liked to have become an actor but, because that was socially impossible, had to make do with amateur theatricals and constant theatre-going. He became a practising lawyer and a dandy. A suitable marriage was arranged with Françoise Brasseur (1887–1963) when Georges was 32 and she was 19. The Brasseur family were from the north-east and wealthier and more conservatively Catholic, but lacked the Beauvoir social pretensions, being bankers and functionaries rather than landowners. Françoise, the eldest child, had considered becoming a nun. Their families agreed that their children should meet at Houlgate in Normandy during the summer of 1906, and Georges and Françoise were married on 21 December. The families had so carefully laid their plans that the couple were by that time in love.

Rather like her husband's dead mother, Françoise would have been happy to lead a modest, pious life, but Georges, to whom she remained subservient, had more flamboyant tastes, even if his means were limited. As an infant, Simone was catered for by the cook-cum-housekeeper. Shortly after her birth, her father went bankrupt, though her mother did not know what was going on until the family lost their house and moved to Paris. Criminal charges were preferred, and Georges was jailed for just over a year. He was subsequently dismissed from a series of managerial posts and invented wild schemes for regaining his former wealth, none of which came to anything. Françoise's dowry meanwhile was never paid. Her brother, Hubert, married a girl without money. Her spinster sister Marie-Thérèse came to Paris with her parents, and eventually married without a dowry. Beauvoir said later that her father was the role model for her intellectual life, and her mother that for her quite separate spiritual life, although it is difficult to know at what stage she became even inchoately aware of these influences. She was treated from childhood as a miniature adult, and expected to sit still and keep quiet when in adult company, but that did not mean that she was not spoiled. A sister, Henriette-Hélène, was born in 1910.

From 1913 Beauvoir was educated at the Cours Désir, a private Catholic school that was not quite as high on the social scale as the better convents. Beauvoir's own later account of her education is too improbable to be relied on, but it was certainly conservative, upper middle-class, Catholic, and academically undistinguished. During the war her father's weak heart kept him from active service after a few weeks, and he worked at the Paris war ministry, where he was paid as a corporal. Beauvoir herself was discovered to have a curved spine, which resulted in a lack of grace in movement and of ability at athletic activities. She was a bright schoolgirl, however. Her mother took Beauvoir and her sister to daily Mass, supervised their schooling and reading, and led night-time prayers. When the war ended the family had little remaining money, since what they had had left had gone on investments in Russian railways and mining stocks.

At 40 Beauvoir's father had two heart attacks, and he could not afford to set up a legal practice again. Françoise's father was by now director of a shoe factory and Georges became an unenthusiastic co-director. When that venture failed, he drifted, got up late, appearing at his office just before or just after lunch, and then playing bridge until it was time to go to a café and drink until dinner. At the age of 10 Beauvoir had few treats, but she learnt fast how to keep up appearances. She recounts that the family had to move into a tiny flat with no lavatory and only one tap, although they still tried to keep a maid, who lived in one of the maid's rooms at the top of the building until they could no longer afford to retain her. Beauvoir shared a small room with her sister, and claims to have been jealous of her good looks, which attracted their father's favouritism.

By the time she was 14, in 1922, Beauvoir's belief in God had been eroded, and about a year later she thought she would like to become a writer. During the school year 1917–18, she had formed a close friendship with Elisabeth Mabille, Known as "ZaZa," the third of nine children, who was to die in 1929. ZaZa exercized a cynical, liberating influence on her, possessing a sense of humour Beauvoir herself never had. Her father was a wealthy engineer and a practising Catholic. ZaZa, also a firmly orthodox believer, had an audacity, an atheleticism, and a sharp tongue which made her more flirtatious than Beauvoir, who had never been to a public beach nor ridden a bicycle, and was proper to the extent of prudishness.

In 1925 Beauvoir, who by now wanted to be a philosophy teacher, moved on to the Institut Sainte-Marie at Neuilly, run by the fashionable and influential Mme Daniélou, who was known for her relatively advanced but none the less safe educational views. Beauvoir had started to keep a diary. Her relations with her parents were becoming strained, her mother being too intrusive, and her father's political views too far to the right. At 18, still sexually innocent and ignorant, she became quite fond of a cousin, Jacques Champigneulle, who had a car, taught her to smoke and drink, and gave her books of modern literature to read. Jacques failed his law examinations. Beauvoir passed both parts of her baccalauréat and, while studying Latin and literature at Neuilly, attended lectures first on mathematics at the Institut Catholique, and then on philosophy and literature at the Sorbonne.

In 1928 she was admitted to the Ecole Normale Supérieure (ENS,) to prepare for the agrégation in philosophy while finishing her licence at the Sorbonne, where she had come second in the philosophy exams the year before. (Simone Weil had come first and Maurice Merleau-Ponty third.) Meanwhile she joined the "Equipes sociales" founded by Robert Garric, her literature teacher at Neuilly, the aim of which was to bring together students and working-class youths, and taught literature to young women. She found her students unmotivated and the experience unrewarding, but none the less later thought that she had reacted against the conventional standards of the well-heeled Jacques. From 1927 her sister Hélène tried to establish herself as a painter after finishing at the Cours Désir, while Beauvoir was earning a little money as a teaching assistant at Neuilly. Her father had a job selling advertising space for the right-wing *Revue Française*, which he kept until his death, and seems to have partially maintained a number of women.

In 1927 Beauvoir, beginning to doubt whether she would ever have a fully satisfactory relationship with a man, was invited again by ZaZa to stay with her family. The pandemonium of the

Mabille household—generated by the presence of nine children, guests, and servants, and the absence of electricity—was further increased by the arrival of a new Polish governess for the summer, Estepha Awdykovicz or "Stépha," who was to become a lifelong friend of Beauvoir, and with whom she had lunch daily on returning to Paris. Stépha was to marry Fernando Gerassi. Through her sister, Beauvoir also met "GéGé," Geraldine Pardo, a vivacious designer with a working-class background. Beauvoir claimed that at this period ZaZa's family looked down on her with pity because of her poverty, and with distaste because of her unbelief, but many of these recollected feelings smack of mythologized autobiography. She later told of wild evenings with Stépha, and then with Hélène and GéGé, in bars and cafés, of mock fights and real ones with prostitutes, and of consorting with flashers and men who picked her up. If the recollections are not exaggerated, then Beauvoir was dangerously mixing public misbehaviour with the well-attested private prudery which was the result of her upbringing.

Her behaviour was at any rate obsessive. She wrote lists of tasks to be accomplished, books to be read, and how each day was to be split up. She never allowed Stépha and GéGé to meet. At the ENS she was friendly with Merleau-Ponty and might have been with Simone Weil and Georgette Lévy, had they not both been Jews, and had Simone Weil not snubbed her for putting her philosophical quest for her own identity before the need to find a way to feed the world's starving. ZaZa and Beauvoir played tennis every Sunday with Merleau-Ponty, who was still more or less a Catholic, and Gandillac, who was later to win fame as a Catholic philosopher. In the summer of 1929 Beauvoir struck up an acquaintanceship with René Maheu, who, with Nizan and Sartre, formed a tight trio of highly gifted students with a reputation for intellectual arrogance. Beauvoir, whose main aim was to get to know Nizan and, particularly, Sartre, succeeded in infiltrating the group, and formed a life-long intimacy with Sartre, its only unmarried member and her first sexual partner. That year he came first in the agrégation, and Beauvoir second.

Beauvoir spent a few days that summer with ZaZa's family, who were trying to head off Merleau-Ponty, with whom ZaZa had become very friendly, and went for a few weeks as usual to Meyrignac, her grandfather's property, which had passed to her father's elder brother, Gaston, and would be inherited by her cousin Jeanne. Here she was told one morning that a young man was waiting for her in a field nearby. It was Sartre. He received no invitation to stay, so Beauvoir at first smuggled lunch to him, then openly took a picnic. They became lovers. Beauvoir's father came one day and asked Sartre to spend the rest of the holidays elsewhere, as his presence was compromising the local standing of the whole family, in which two marriages had recently been arranged but had not yet taken place. Sartre explained that Beauvoir and he were working together on a project they hoped to publish, but left a week later. That September Beauvoir left home and rented a room in her grandmother's Paris flat. In the autumn ZaZa, who was about to be sent off to Berlin for a second year, used to call round, often in a distressed state. Before she could go to Berlin she caught a fever, possibly meningeal in origin, from which she died after four days in hospital. Only later did Beauvoir learn that ZaZa's family had investigated Merleau-Ponty's background and found him to be the child of his mother's lover.

Beauvoir knew quite early that she had found in Sartre a man to whom she could devote her life. She declared war on what she regarded as her parents' middle-class values, but her devotion to work and her fidelity to Sartre's needs and interests must have owed something to her religious upbringing, and she returned to those elements of a bourgeois life style that attracted her whenever there was enough money. For the moment Sartre had his military service to do, and Beauvoir kept herself by giving private lessons and undertaking part-time teaching. Sartre and she promised never to conceal anything from one another, and never to lie to each other. They greatly enjoyed analysing together the nature of their own relationship, and whether the extra money which marriage would bring was worth the abandonment of principle it would entail. They promised to be faithful to one another for two years. Sartre had hoped to go to Japan on demobilization, but he did not get the job, and was given a teaching post at Le Havre. Beauvoir herself was posted to Marseilles at the same time. She had managed to see a good deal of Sartre during his military service, and she continued to do so while they were at different ends of France. She took long walks in the country, and spent the summer of 1931 visiting Stépha and her husband in Madrid with Sartre.

All her attempts at writing were foundering. She abandoned a novel and a biography of ZaZa and began instead to fill the role she was to play for many years, reading everything Sartre wrote, commenting on it in detail, and generally attempting to be helpful with criticisms and suggestions. She rightly perceived that his real talent was not for philosophy but for fiction, and without her we should not have *La Nausée*, Sartre's one unchallenged masterpiece. Sartre meanwhile was encouraging her to write, but read only what she specifically asked him to and then not during his working day. All her life they used the formal "vous" to one another rather than the intimate "tu," an oddity that became a form of public affectation. In Marseilles Beauvoir had kept very much to herself, despising both her colleagues and her pupils.

In 1932 the ministry of education, aware of Beauvoir's liaison with Sartre, posted her to Rouen, scarcely an hour from Le Havre by train. She and Sartre spent the summer visiting Spain and Morocco, and drove back through Spain with Mme Morel and Pierre Guille with whom Beauvoir had a sporadic liaison. It was she who paid Sartre's and her joint expenses, and she was, predictably, bothered by Sartre's casual attitude to money, which meant giving it away rather than saving it, and keeping it in cash rather than in banks. Beauvoir's general slovenliness, on the other hand, shocked Sartre, who still took care of his appearance, if not of the tidiness of his workplace, and who linked Beauvoir's carelessness in such matters with an abdication of all worthwhile intellectual endeavour.

Neither Sartre nor Beauvoir was politically interested, even in what was happening in Germany, and Beauvoir later explained away her unenthusiastic teaching and unsuccessful attempts at writing at this period by the effort she was making to see everything in life through Sartre's eyes. She was sinking her whole personality into his, trying to reach the point where she could accommodate herself to his bewilderingly swift changes of opinion and his capriciously self-indulgent sexual infidelities. She became one of the few people whose agreement did not immediately alarm Sartre into changing his view. From 1933 to 1934 Sartre was on leave, studying Husserl in Berlin. Beauvoir did not even consider giving up her job and going with him. Instead she received from him long, detailed, and sexually explicit letters about an affair he was having with the wife of another member of the French Institute in Berlin. She herself cultivated one of her pupils, Olga Kosakiewicz, the first of a succession who were to have sexual liaisons with Sartre. In the summer of 1934 she toured Germany and Austria with him, after she had visited him in Berlin and he had come to Paris at Easter.

When Sartre returned to Le Havre in the autumn of 1934 his physical needs were increasingly satisfied by Olga, while Beauvoir herself had several brief affairs with Pierre Guille. Her relationship with Sartre became both more intense and more restricted to its intellectual and emotional dimensions, with Beauvoir's role as surrogate mother increasingly dominant. She started to lead the normal social life of a lycée teacher, at first resentful of Olga, but gradually able to see her through Sartre's own worshipping eyes. The one who suffered most in fact was Olga herself. Beauvoir was at last managing to write, and the five short stories of "La primauté du spirituel" were mostly written before she was posted to the Lycée Molière in Paris in 1936, when Sartre was moved to Laon, about an hour to the north-east.

Beauvoir and Sartre now spoke of their "family," a close group of friends, lovers, disciples, and mistresses to which Sartre controlled the entrée and from which he contrived the exclusions. It was an unknown little bohemian group still very much governed by middle-class convention, except for the complicated relationships it entailed, the sexual liaisons, and games of passion it played, and which none of its members seems to have enjoyed very much. The group included Olga's sister Wanda and Jacques-Laurent Bost, a pupil of Sartre's who was to be Beauvoir's occasional lover and eventually married Olga. At this time Beauvoir and Olga had rooms in a cheap hotel. Loose associates were the Nizans, Stépha and Fernando Gerassi, GéGé, Marc Zuorro, a French Algerian who flirted with members of both sexes within the group, and the well-off and outwardly respectable Mme Morel, who offered to bring up any child Sartre and Beauvoir might have together.

Early in 1937 Beauvoir was seriously ill with a collapsed lung. Sartre was closely attentive, and during her convalescence Beauvoir revised her short stories, adding the fifth and changing the collection's title to *Quand prime le spirituel*. It was turned down first by Gallimard and then by Grasset. This was the year of Sartre's first literary successes and of his obsession with Wanda Kosakiewicz. Beauvoir shared his excitements and received his accounts of other, briefer liaisons. She chain-smoked, drank a lot of champagne, and began an affair (which Olga knew about) with Bost while they were on a hiking trip together. After a holiday with Sartre in the summer and another hiking trip, Beauvoir started another novel, *L'Invitée*. On seeing the first third, Brice Parain, Gallimard's reader, rejected it. In 1939 Beauvoir's relationship with Sartre was forced to undergo further charges. Two other women had entered his life, Nathalie Sorokine and Bianca Bienenfeld. Beauvoir protected him from rejection by them, and allowed herself to be used as a pretext, in turn, for his rejection of them. Her own physical intimacy with him was now only occasional, but in 1939 they made a "pact" to remain together permanently.

Apart from taking Sartre away from her for a time, the outbreak of war did not much affect Beauvoir's life at first. She moved from a pacifism more absolute than his ("Anything is preferable to war") to an agreement with him on the need for a greater degree of political involvement, which was to lead also to social commitment. War thus became preferable to fascism.

She managed to visit Sartre for a few days in October 1939, although not without the intervention of luck, determination, coded letters, and bribery, since she was not supposed to know where he was. They talked for most of four days, and Sartre, having looked at Beauvoir's diaries, suggested to her that she should write about what it actually meant to be a woman. On two occasions Gallimard's Parain had thought her attitudes too innovative, and she herself, while continuing to play the triple female role of Sartre's mistress, elder sister, and substitute mother, was proud of the masculinity of her mind. For a while, however, she was too listless to write. She taught, looked after friends who needed identity documents or money, of which she herself had very little to spare, and put aside her novel to read Hegel and Heidegger in order to help Sartre with *L'Etre et le néant*. In 1940 she fled south to escape the invading Germans, but returned to Paris, partly for news and partly to pick up her salary. She was told to resume her teaching, and moved back into her grandmother's apartment. She finished *L'Invitée* early in 1941.

During the war Beauvoir discovered that the Café Flore, which was frequented by the Germans, always had adequate heating. Henceforward, that was where she wrote. To Sartre's later disapproval she signed the oath testifying that she was not Jewish although, when the war was over, Sartre and she were virtually alone among left-wing intellectuals in refusing to sign the petition for clemency for Brasillach, whose shooting for collaboration de Gaulle had authorized in 1945. The occupying forces wanted to emphasize cultural continuity with pre-war France, and Beauvoir helped them, having a good deal to do with them in their administrative capacities. The Germans certainly knew of her association with Sartre, an escaped prisoner-of-war writing plays and publishing in Paris whom they chose not to pick up. Like everyone else, she suffered from cold, hunger, and tiredness but, as long as she did not make trouble for the Germans, she was personally safe from molestation.

Beauvoir's father died on 1 July 1941. She joined with Sartre in a futile effort to organize resistance to the occupying powers, although others were doing the job more efficiently, as several of them pointed out when she went south with Sartre in 1941 and 1942. During the liberation of Paris in 1944, they went briefly into hiding. Beauvoir continued to be hurt by Sartre's infidelities, especially when he wanted to marry Wanda Kosakiewicz, for whom he wrote some of his best dramatic roles, and Nathalie Sorokine, who tried to make a living during the war by stealing the bicycles which had become invaluable, and who, along with Beauvoir's mother, Wanda, Olga, and Bost, she and Sartre partly supported. Restaurants had become so expensive that Beauvoir finally had to resign herself to learning to cook. She found a small room with cooking facilities in the Hôtel Mistral, where Sartre took a room one floor down. In spite of Sartre's strictures Beauvoir bought on the black market when she could afford to. Food and books came from Mme Morel at La Pouèze, near Angers, and after the war Beauvoir never cooked again.

L'Invitée was well received in August 1943, and in three months that year Beauvoir wrote the philosophical dialogue *Pyrrhus et Cinéas*. At La Pouèze in September, she also finished *Le Sang des autres*, and started *Tous les hommes sont mortels*. In 1944 she wrote the play *Les Bouches inutiles*, which was staged and published the next year. She immediately accepted Sartre's views on freedom and responsibility when she went through the manuscript of *L'Etre et le néant*, as she had earlier accepted the views on contingency finally fictionalized, largely at her insistence, in *La Nausée*. She was to maintain to the end of her life that she was not a philosopher, although she attached importance to *Pyrrhus* and to *Pour une morale de l'ambiguïté*, published in *Les Temps Modernes* (q.v.) in December 1946 and January 1947, and as a book in 1947. At her agrégation her examiners had thought her capable of producing original philosophical work of her own, but she preferred to help Sartre.

In 1942 Beauvoir and Sartre arrived back after the summer so late that Beauvoir's hotel room had been permanently relet, and they had to move. Beauvoir was dismissed as a teacher in 1943 on account of a complaint made by Nathalie Sorokine's mother, who wanted Beauvoir to intervene in a liaison between Nathalie and a wealthy Algerian Jew, Jean-Pierre Bourla, who was 19 and was in due course deported for extermination. Although reinstated in 1944, Beauvoir never actually taught again. Sartre and she worked virtually all day in the Café Flore, although the café was not serving food, so they had to eat in their hotel. Beauvoir was happy that Sartre and she were now not so much lovers as a "writing couple," and Sartre found her a job on the radio, where the salary was good, although the organization naturally collaborationist.

The couple were now meeting a much wider range of literary and artistic figures, including Mauriac, whom Sartre continued on and off to attack, but with whom he also occasionally cooperated, Cocteau, Zette and Michel Leiris, who often had Jews in his apartment and was running a Resistance cell, Queneau, and Salacrou, then Picasso, Lacan, and Bataille. Immediately after the war they also met the Giacomettis. Camus also came into their lives, although Beauvoir grew to dislike him in spite of his considerable kindness to her just after the war. He passed on news from Sartre in the US and affiliated her to *Combat* for a lecture tour of Spain and Portugal. It was actually Beauvoir who wrote the articles for *Combat* reporting on the liberation of Paris which appeared over Sartre's signature. Beauvoir regarded herself as not so much an individual writer as a member of a firm.

By 1945 she was drinking quite heavily. She arrived at the Flore early to work, and ended the day at a club or a party, often retiring to bed very late. She also started to travel outside France again. Sartre left her to visit the US soon after the launch of the first issue of his new review, *Les Temps Modernes*, and she had an affair with Michel Vitold, who directed her play, *Les Bouches inutiles*. The play's premiere was on 29 October 1945, and the reviews were mostly unfavourable. It ran for some 50 performances. Sartre went back to the US and Dolorès Vanetti early in 1946. By 1946 some of the editorial board of *Les Temps Modernes* were already veering away from the Marxism which was the review's unofficial orthodoxy. Beauvoir found Violette Leduc's increasing dependency on her difficult to endure and was cruel to her. She was also uncooperative with Natalie Sarraute, a Russian Jew who had shown much courage during the war and whom Sartre had wished to help, and she found Koestler arrogant. She frequently got drunk and continued to chain-smoke, allowing the quarrelsomeness to show through in her autobiographical writing, which was now aimed among others at former friends such as Merleau-Ponty and Aron.

From November 1945 to April 1946 Beauvoir published four essays on existentialism (q.v.) in *Les Temps Modernes*, which she regarded as the important prelude to *Les Mandarins* and the memoirs. One of them, "Littérature et métaphysique," was her only sustained piece of literary criticism. In 1946 she accompa-

nied Sartre to Switzerland and Italy, but felt as if he was slipping away from her intellectually. Three weeks of solitary walking in the Dolomites failed to restore her. Later that year Sartre again put to her the idea of writing about women's role in society. Then she was invited to spend four months on a lecture tour in the US, where she arrived on 24 January 1947.

She walked a great deal in New York, lectured in many parts of the US, and started her four-year liaison with Nelson Algren, "the only truly passionate love in my life," staying in the US for nearly five months. Meanwhile *Tous les hommes sont mortels*, first published in *Les Temps Modernes*, had received a bad press. Beauvoir returned to the US to see Algren in Chicago for a fortnight in September 1947, forewarning him that she would have very little money. On her return her activity in Paris was mostly concerned with Sartre's political initiatives. Merleau-Ponty was running the review and it published *L'Amérique au jour le jour* from January 1948. The Swiss publisher Nagel was collecting some of Beauvoir's essays in *L'Existentialisme et la sagesse des nations*. Politics, Sartre's new obsession, seems to have bored her. The result was a stream of reflections on herself and on women's place in society. Meanwhile she returned to the US in 1948 and travelled with Algren to Mexico, budget and route meticulously planned out in advance, although the stay from May to July was extended by a few days. Beauvoir's letters to Algren are written in the same style as that used to refer to Sartre in her memoirs, and for a period he meant as much to her as Sartre, or more. She told him that she and Sartre had stopped being lovers after eight or 10 years together, although their intellectual bond remained very strong,.

Both volumes of *Le Deuxième Sexe*, started in 1946, were published in 1949. Its success was phenomenal. It made Beauvoir's name in her own right overnight, ensured her financial security, was translated into a score of languages, and sold in all some 3- 4,000,000 copies worldwide. That year Algren came to Paris, arriving just before the book's serialization in *Les Temps Modernes* created a furore. In 1950 Beauvoir crossed the Sahara with Sartre, and they then spent two weeks in Morocco. Her relationship with Algren ended in 1951, partly because she had told him she was fictionalizing it in *Les Mandarins*, of which 1,200 typed pages existed by late 1953. Gallimard planned publication for April 1954. Algren, who had been having an affair with someone else who half supported him financially, had in the end forced Beauvoir to choose between living with him permanently or carrying on as Sartre's indispensable intellectual companion, which is the role she chose, defended, and in which she depicted her success in her memoirs. Algren was to remarry his first wife and later to divorce her again.

During a trip to the US by Merleau-Ponty, Beauvoir was left in effective charge of *Les Temps Modernes*. Gallimard himself supported de Gaulle and, when the review offended Malraux, it moved to Juillard. There were further fits and starts in Beauvoir's relationship with Algren. By chance she met her cousin Jacques Champigneulle again, now an alcoholic whose wife had left him. She would not help him when he refused to go on a cure, and he died at 46. In 1952 Beauvoir herself was frightened that she might have cancer, but the tumour turned out to be benign. She started to live with Claude Lanzmann, the film director now famous for *Shoah*, and the only man with whom Beauvoir ever shared a home. He joined the reconstituted board of *Les Temps Modernes* at 27 when Beauvoir was 44, and they became lovers almost immediately, staying together until 1959.

Les Mandarins, written from 1950 to 1953, was awarded the Prix Goncourt. Beauvoir bought herself a studio apartment in 1955 and Gallimard lent her the money to buy a small car. Her summers continued to be reserved for Sartre in Rome, and she also continued to travel with him. She went to Russia with him in 1954, and even put up the translator, Lena Zonina, with whom he had an affair, whenever she could get to Paris. Sartre had a further series of intimate liaisons at this time: with Michelle Vian from 1954, with Evelyne Rey, Lanzmann's beautiful sister, the actress who later committed suicide, and with Arlette Elkaïm, whom he was to adopt and to whom he left everything in his will. Beauvoir infringed the copyright interest in the letters Sartre had written to her by publishing them without Arlette's permission, although the copyright now belonged to Arlette, with whom Beauvoir had an acrimonious public dispute.

Beauvoir was now generally invited as Sartre's consort when they travelled together. She went with him to China in 1955, writing *La Longue Marche*, a book she was later to consider dishonest, and to Cuba, and later Brazil, in 1960. She was in the USSR with him again in 1962, 1964, and 1966, the year they also went to Japan, and she accompanied him to Israel and Egypt in 1967. She also visited Belgium and Holland several times, Yugoslavia, Czechoslovakia, and Sweden. In 1960 Algren was in Paris briefly, and their affair resumed momentarily. Beauvoir went to Spain, Turkey, and Greece with him. In 1960 she and Sartre signed the "Manifeste des 121," advocating civil disobedience in support of Algerian independence, although by this time Sartre was becoming politically isolated as well as exploited.

Immediately after publication of *Les Mandarins* Gallimard pressed Beauvoir to publish a collection of her articles from *Les Temps Modernes*. *Privilèges* contained "La pensée de droite aujourd'hui," "Merleau-Ponty et le pseudo-sartrisme," the reply to Merleau-Ponty's defence of himself against Sartre in *Les Aventures de la dialectique* (1955), and "Faut-il brûler Sade?" Beauvoir, who was still not particularly interested in philosophy or politics, later thought that *Privilèges* adequately explained her positions in both areas. From this period onwards she was principally occupied with the four volumes of memoirs, which emerged posthumously as her most enduring achievement.

Mémoires d'une jeune fille rangée was followed by *La Force de l'âge*, which was as much about Sartre as about herself and sold 45,000 pre-publication copies and 25,000 more in the first week of publication. Gallimard ordered a reprint of 200,000. *La Force des choses* and *Tout compte fait* ended the series, although *La Cérémonie des adieux*, the "official" version of Sartre's last 10 years, can be considered an epilogue. Beauvoir was on the whole hostile to the "nouveau roman" group of novelists, and as late as 1965 was still trying hard to uphold the image of the Sartre–Beauvoir couple. Sartre was secretive about his adoption of Arlette Elkaïm, but Beauvoir was more open about regarding her relationship with Sylvie le Bon, a young woman philosophy teacher to whom she was very close from 1964, as "the strongest and the most important" friendship in her life. Sartre and Beauvoir could go out with either Arlette or Sylvie, but not with both at once. In 1963 Beauvoir's mother died. From 1964 the final pattern of relationships was in place. A number of books were still to come: *Une mort très douce*, the collection of short stories *La Femme rompue*, comprising "La femme rompue," "Monologue," and "L'âge de discrétion," *La Vieil-*

lesse, and *Quand prime le spirituel*. Algren, who had been furious over *La Force des choses*, was to die in 1981.

In the 1970s Beauvoir was heavily involved in feminist activities, like the campaigns for easier abortion and free contraception. From about 1973 she needed cortisone to relieve severe arthritic pain. She distrusted the influence of Sartre's last secretary, Benny Lévy, who read to Sartre and tried to tease his missing autobiography out of him in conversation. It was she who found Sartre four hours after his final stroke. He had not been able to telephone for help as he had been cut off in consequence of an unpaid bill. After Sartre's death she had already had a first unseemly quarrel with Arlette Elkaïm over some of his effects left to Arlette but of which Beauvoir claimed part or whole ownership. Sartre's pet name, invented by René Maheu, for Beauvoir had been "Castor," meaning "beaver," and the *Lettres à Castor* (1983) were the Sartre letters to her published in breach of copyright. Sylvie took Beauvoir to New York in Concorde. She liked to stay at the Algonquin, famous for the literary associations of its Round Table. By 1985 the state of her liver was such that she could not expect to live long, and she died on 14 April 1986.

WORKS

Like that of so many other writers, Beauvoir's lasting importance derives from a chance circumstance in her life. The reflections on women's position in society for which she will be remembered caught almost by accident the cultural wave which brought her commercial success. They derive from her intelligent and perceptive meditation on her own commitment to a man to whom she deferred with the whole of her personality and intelligence. By turns passionate, possessive, jealous, realistic, and submissive, she settled down from being Sartre's mistress to vindicating her sole right to the title of his intellectual consort. She was not a great novelist, and contributed nothing more than elevated journalism to politics or philosophy. Her single play was badly written, and her best-remembered work, *Le Deuxième Sexe*, is prolix, repetitive, and not even particularly perceptive. She found the appropriate form in which to illuminate women's real social potential when she came to reflect on her own total and bourgeois self-subordination to one man, even when she had other lovers. The literary forum in which her "feminism" found its imaginative power was self-analysis, as encapsulated in the four volumes of her memoirs.

In spite of the number of times and the number of ways in which Sartre hurt her, it is not possible to regard, as some have done, even *La Cérémonie des adieux*, which details the day-to-day decline in his health over his last 10 years, as some sort of revenge for neglect or infidelity. Beauvoir genuinely believed that the world should be, indeed that it was, interested in every detail of Sartre's life, activity, thinking, and even finally physical decline. And so in the end it was, but more for what Beauvoir reveals about her own determination to keep alive a myth regarding Sartre's importance and her own role in his life than because of her subject itself. The world's curiosity about the details of Sartre's activities was less unassuageable than she imagined. Beauvoir was determined to vindicate her intellectual and emotional rights well after Sartre's death, and to defend her view of what Sartre believed. The all-important memoirs suggest that their writer was hurt more by not being taken on Sartre's first flight to the US than by his physical infidelities, even when these were protracted, emotional, and might have ended in marriage to someone else. The ones she resented were those which threatened to oust her as Sartre's life-long intellectual partner.

The events of the over-long and repetitive two parts of *L'Invitée* concern Françoise and Pierre, a Paris theatrical producer, who have lived together happily for eight years. Xavière Pagès, a young girl from Rouen whose life has reached an impasse, comes to join them. The story of the jealousies resulting from the ménage à trois is told principally from the point of view of Françoise, and is complicated by Pierre's quite ordinary sexual jealousy of a secondary character, Gerbert, with whom Xavière has an affair. What Françoise feels is a far more fundamental deprivation. Her self-affirmation demands nothing less than the extinction of Xavière's perception both of Françoise herself and of the events recounted, so that she ends by murdering Xavière.

It was on Sartre's advice that Beauvoir introduced two secondary characters into the plot and limited the narratorial point of view in each chapter to that of one character, mostly of Françoise, but also of Pierre's sister Elisabeth, and of Gerbert. The reader is therefore prevented from assuming that Françoise's perception of events represents the whole truth, while also being made to realize that the depictions of environments and of the passing of time depend on the characters and their various moods. The novel shows technical virtuosity, although the techniques derive manifestly from Flaubert, and is ultimately not about jealousy, but about something deeper. Françoise's motivation for the murder is described in the following terms: "C'était sa volonté qui était en train de s'accomplir, plus rien ne la séparait d'elle- même (It was her will which was being accomplished. Nothing separated her any longer from herself)."

Beauvoir herself thought that *Le Sang des autres* was too didactic and lacked depth of characterization, although its Resistance setting ensured a commercial success in 1945. Jean Blomart, the son of an industrialist, has become a communist. When a friend's brother is killed in a demonstration, he withdraws from political action to concentrate on merely social left-wing activity and, when Hélène Bertrand uses her influence to have him moved away from the front after war breaks out and he has joined up, he breaks with her and founds a Resistance group. Hélène then recognizes her responsibilities and joins the group, in the course of whose activities she is mortally wounded. At the end of the novel she dies, and Blomart carries on with the Resistance operation he was planning, having learnt that violence is after all sometimes a necessary means justified by the end. Here the chapters are narrated alternately from the viewpoint of each of the protagonists. *Tous les hommes sont mortels*, written just after *Le Sang des autres*, was not a success. Its main character, Fosca of Carmona, in seeking worldwide political power, drinks a potion to make himself immortal, only to discover that life without death to end it has no meaning. Immortality destroys Fosca's relationships with others, particularly with women. It also enables him to see how mankind has made no progress through the centuries. As in *Le Sang des autres*, the main events are narrated retrospectively.

The only really important fiction is *Les Mandarins*. It is a novel of disillusion, burying the hopes of the immediately postwar period, and traces the history of a group of left-wing Paris intellectuals. An editor, Henri Perron, aligns his hard-pressed daily paper, *L'Espoir*, behind Dubreuilh's left-wing political group in return for financial support, but against Dubreuilh's will publishes information about the Soviet labour camps.

Dubreuilh's psychiatrist wife, Anne, has an affair in the US which ends when she refuses to give up her life in Paris. She is tempted to kill herself but refrains, largely because of the effect her suicide would have on other people. The rift between Perron and Dubreuilh, in which Beauvoir saw the novel's unifying thread, is eventually healed. The novel is related alternately from the points of view of Henri and Anne. The characters are clearly driven by the pressures of post-liberation Paris into new and ill-considered relationships which mirror the ill-considered reconstruction of French society, whose breakdown is foreshadowed in theirs, but the plot is too complex and the novel too long. Its immense success in 1954 was due to its semi-autobiographical, panoramic account of life among the left-wing intelligentsia of post-war Paris. It is held together by its broad political framework, within which Beauvoir treats a variety of favourite themes, most of them pointing to what she will have to say in her memoirs.

Neither *Les Belles Images* nor the short stories in *La Femme rompue* are major works of fiction. *Les Belles Images* is narrated from the point of view of Laurence, a high-powered professional woman, and consists of a succession of scenes in which a series of relationships breaks up. It ends with a flicker of hope that there may be a way round conventional middle-class wisdom for her daughter, but its weakness lies in its characterization. Beauvoir is writing about characters with whose values, views, and life style she is unable to sympathize: "il s'agissait de faire parler le silence (the task was to make silence speak)." The three short stories are united by the theme of "la solitude et l'échec (isolation and failure)." "I wanted to have the voices of three women heard who were using words to fight in situations with no way out." "L'âge de discrétion" is a study of a couple growing old; "Monologue" is an incoherent monologue by Murielle, alone on Christmas Eve, and aware that her possessiveness has driven her daughter to suicide; and "La femme rompue" gives a diary account of Monique's self-deception up to the point at which she is left to face a bleak future alone. The recurrent themes are the subservience of women to husbands and their attempts to retain domination over their children.

The moral essays, while not substantial contributions to philosophical thinking, seemed important to a post-war generation concerned to reaffirm values which, although never based on a systematic philosophy, were heavily emphasized by Sartre. *Pyrrhus et Cinéas* attacks the question of the limits it is appropriate for human beings to set to their actions. Pyrrhus represents a spontaneous and adventurous way of life, Cinéas one that is wise, restrained, and passive. The message is that we have to choose our own self-definition in relation to the world and to other people, and while we must solicit ratification for our free choices, we may never impose them on others by force, a view which Beauvoir was later to jettison in theory as well as in her practical attitudes. The philosophical arguments are too weak, and the attempt to find a positive basis for ethical values, as distinct from affirming a belief in them, is postponed until *Pour une morale de l'ambiguïté*. Here again, however, Beauvoir does not get beyond an affirmation that freedom is the basic reality of human existence. Philosophically, the difficulty lies in supporting the view that we have an obligation to seek freedom for others, and in the exploitation of the confusion generated between the existential, political, and economic senses of the word "freedom." The argument is neither tight nor integrated, and it is not cogent.

Le Deuxième Sexe is certainly Beauvoir's most influential book, although it is not well constructed. In calling for a much-needed reassessment of women's potential in society, it inevitably calls for a reconsideration of attitudes to contraception and abortion. Certain ways of looking at women's status are so obviously the product of cultural stereotyping and prejudice that Beauvoir cannot help scoring important goals by drawing attention to women's commonly neglected affectivity, although her grasp of social history is unimpressive. There are some interesting passages about myths concerning women, but in the area in which the book has been regarded as most strikingly important it was sufficient to show, as Beauvoir has done, that women's role in history has been absurdly subordinate. What the book achieved was to say this at exactly the right moment, to make the statement in an intellectually fashionable idiom, and to be published in a place and at a time when all the conventions of Western society clearly required and were also open to radical restructuring. It is probable that the Anglo-Saxon cultures were much readier to receive and act on the message, as intellectually packaged by Beauvoir, than was the culture of her compatriots, but that the French intellectual tradition favoured its elaboration and original expression in the context of a powerful French cultural grouping such as that to which Beauvoir belonged.

More impressive as literary artefacts, and more effective as statements of position appealing neither to controversial philosophical theory nor to inadequately informed historical analysis, are the autobiographical works. The *Mémoires d'une jeune fille rangée* take Beauvoir's life, for which the work is an unreliable source, up to 1929. The point is not so much the accurate reconstitution of events as the attempt at self-understanding and self-vindication written from Beauvoir's point of view in 1956, and the possibly unconscious artistry of the obvious distortions she imposes on the story of her youth. The result is a trenchant criticism of well-observed forms of middle-class domestic repression, which widens into a more generalized assessment of the social system that leads to them. From the literary point of view the *Mémoires* is probably Beauvoir's most interesting work, although many critics do not look to it for what it most importantly contains, which is a generalized reflection about the bringing up of children.

La Force de l'âge is longer and deals with the reflections generated by Beauvoir's experiences as a student, as a school teacher, as an aspiring writer, and as a traveller. The book includes edited passages of Beauvoir's diary during the first months of the war, and considerations about her not untypical love life, her conversations, relationships, and reading. Most interesting is Beauvoir's retrospective awareness of the dangers she was running by becoming so clearly a satellite of Sartre, and the virtue now made of repenting what are presented as earlier "mistakes": "Nous nous trompions, à peu près en tout (We were wrong in just about everything)." Beauvoir now waited two and a half years before writing *La Force des choses*, which is ostensibly an account of her life from the liberation to the autumn of 1962 and contains a reflection on the vogue for existentialism, including the reasons why she felt it necessary to repudiate some of the views formed in the 1940s. The core material is less personal than it was in the earlier volumes, and Beauvoir was naturally less anxious here to repudiate political attitudes so recently forged. If this volume is inferior to its predecessors, it is on account of its concern to make political points. The fourth volume, *Tout compte fait*, was published in the autumn of 1972,

is no longer chronologically organized, and is too often anecdotal or banal. Like the rest of the volumes, it starts from a very limited range of relationships and experiences but, because it deals with the recent past, unlike them it does not generate a sufficiently general level of reflection and analysis.

PUBLICATIONS

Fiction

L'Invitée, 1943; as *She Came to Stay*, 1949
Le Sang des autres, 1945; edited by John F. Davis, 1973; as *The Blood of Others*, 1948
Tous les hommes sont mortels, 1946; as *All Men Are Mortal*, 1956
Les Mandarins, 1954; as *The Mandarins*, 1956
Les Belles Images, 1966; as *Les Belles Images* (in English), 1968
La Femme rompue (includes "L'âge de discrétion" and "Monologue" 1968; as *The Woman Destroyed*, 1969
Quand prime le spirituel, 1979; as *When Things of the Spirit Come First: Five Early Tales*, 1982

Play

Les Bouches inutiles (produced 1945), 1945

Other

Pyrrhus et Cinéas, 1944
Pour une morale de l'ambiguïté 1947; as *The Ethics of Ambiguity*, 1948
L'Amérique au jour le jour, 1948; as *America Day by Day*, 1952
L'Existentialisme et la sagesse des nations, 1948
Le Deuxième Sexe: Les Faits et les mythes and *L'Expérience vécue*, 2 vols., 1949; as *The Second Sex*, 1953; vol. 1 as *A History of Sex*, 1961, and as *Nature of the Second Sex*, 1963
Must We Burn de Sade? 1953; in *The Marquis de Sade*, edited by Paul Dinnage, 1953
Privilèges (includes "Faut-il brûler Sade?"), 1955
La Longue Marche: essai sur la Chine, 1957; as *The Long March*, 1958
Mémoires d'une jeune fille rangée, 1958; as *Memoirs of a Dutiful Daughter*, 1959
Brigitte Bardot and the Lolita Syndrome, 1960
La Force de l'âge, 1960; as *The Prime of Life*, 1962
Djamila Boupacha, with Gisèle Halimi, 1962; as *Djamila Boupacha* (in English), London, 1962
La Force des choses, 1963; as *Force of Circumstance*, 1965
Une mort très douce, 1964; as *A Very Easy Death*, 1966
La Vieillesse, 1970; as *Old Age*, 1972; as *The Coming of Age*, 1972
Toute compte fait, 1972; as *All Said and Done*, 1974
La Cérémonie des adieux, 1981; as *Adieux: A Farewell to Sartre*, 1984

Bibliography

Francis, Claude, and Fernande Gontier, *Les Ecrits de Simone de Beauvoir*, 1980

Critical studies

Marks, Elaine, *De Beauvoir: Encounters with Death*, 1973
Cottrell, Robert D., *De Beauvoir* (in English), 1975
Leighton, Jean, *De Beauvoir on Women*, 1976
Madsen, Axel, *Hearts and Minds: The Common Journey of de Beauvoir and Jean-Paul Sartre*, 1977
Bieber, Konrad, *De Beauvoir* (in English), 1979
Whitmarsh, Anne, *De Beauvoir and the Limits of Commitment*, 1981
Keefe, Terry, *Simone de Beauvoir: A Study of Her Writings*, 1983
Fallaize, Elizabeth, *The Novels of Simone de Beauvoir*, 1988
Bair, Deirdre, *Simone de Beauvoir: A Biography*, 1990

BECKETT, Samuel, 1906–1989.

Novelist, dramatist, and poet; winner of the Nobel prize for literature (1969)

LIFE

Beckett's insistence that he was born on a Good Friday which was also the 13th of the month is important because it is a circumstance in which he wryly rejoiced, and means that he was born in April, whereas his birth certificate says May. He took a delight in mythologizing himself, as he did in mystifying his audiences and his readers. He was born in Foxrock, a smart Dublin suburb, but lived permanently in Paris from 1937, and wrote largely in French. His father's family were originally Huguenot cloth merchants before moving into construction and property development, and his father, William Frank (1871–1933), known as "Bill," was born in the Dublin suburb of Ballsbridge, the eldest of four boys and a girl. Bill entered the family business when he was 15, borrowed money from his father to buy a partnership in a firm of surveyors, and prospered. His plans to marry were thwarted because the proposed bride was a Catholic, and he went to hospital with severe depression.

On 31 August 1901 he married Mary Roe (1871–1950), one of his nurses, from a family of landed Protestant gentry from County Kildare, and had a large house built at Foxrock. Beckett's parents entertained little and rarely went out together. Their marriage was companionable, but they used separate bedrooms. Beckett's mother was given to depressions and outbursts of cold rage, no doubt brought on by the tension generated in suppressing the affective, emotional, and fun-loving side of her nature. Beckett's father insisted on tough standards of physical performance and social conformity from his wife and family.

Beckett, the second of two boys, was happy as a child, but lonely. Both boys enjoyed outdoor activities, were good swimmers and tennis players, and liked having their friends round to tea. Beckett saw little of his father and engaged in a life-long battle of wills with his mother, who beat him and tried to bring him up to fill the role in life for which she was for ever casting him. He grew up emotionally inhibited, and his early relationship with his mother dominated his imagination throughout his adult life. When Beckett was eight, his mother's sister died, and the two boys were joined by three cousins, two girls and a boy. Beckett appears to have been both the tidiest and the most withdrawn of the five.

For Beckett religion was part of a social upbringing that was pro-English and well-to-do. He was sent to a disciplined kindergarten, followed by a Dublin preparatory school, and, from 1920, to a boarding school in Ulster, one of the two best Protestant schools in all Ireland. He excelled at cricket. In 1923 he entered Trinity College, Dublin, where he drifted into modern languages, played golf, and rode motorbikes, retreating into a world which he kept private from his family. He began to go to the theatre but also visited pubs, a habit which his family would have regarded, for social reasons, as unacceptable. He did well enough academically to be encouraged to think of a career teaching modern languages, and spent the summer of 1926 bicycling in France. In 1927 he went to Florence and, when he took his BA degree, it already seemed likely the he would join the Trinity teaching faculty. He was found a post teaching French in Belfast for nine months before going to the Ecole Normale Supérieure (ENS) as a lecteur from 1928 to 1930. He took to spending what time he could in Kassel, where he had cousins, and was known to be drinking quite heavily.

In Paris he met Joyce and formed what was to be a life-long friendship with another Trinity man, Thomas McGreevy, who knew both James and Nora Joyce well. According to Richard Aldington, another member of the Joyce entourage, Beckett arrived in Paris preoccupied with the idea of suicide. He became almost an amanuensis to Joyce, who was conscious of the lower social position to which his own Catholic culture entitled him. Their relationship, while intimate, remained formal. During his student years Beckett's relationships with women had been neither deep nor long-lasting, but he now fell in love with his cousin Peggy Sinclair in Kassel. Peggy was one of the five children of a Jewish art dealer and Bill Beckett's young sister, Cissie, who had become a painter. She was to die of tuberculosis in 1933.

Beckett spent the first months of 1929 writing his essay "Dante...Bruno. Vico...Joyce," one of 12 published in defence of punning polyglot language in *Our Exagmination Round His Factification for Incamination of Work in Progress*, which first appeared in an issue of *transition* that also carried Beckett's short story "Assumption." The title of Beckett's essay was Joyce's. Joyce had wanted to indicate his debt to the three Italian authors, their separation in time, and the position his own work occupied at the apex of the ascent. Beckett's place in the circle of Joyce's exiled adulators was by now assured. He was still preoccupied with the idea of suicide, and became increasingly interested in Schopenhauer. He met a "disdainful" Ezra Pound and with Valéry, Fargue, Romains, and Soupault, among others, attended the lunch to celebrate the publication of *Ulysses* in French on 27 June 1929. He spent the summer with the Sinclairs, visiting Ireland only briefly. During the 1929–30 academic year he translated for Joyce, read Descartes, wrote verse, made little progress with Peggy, and was pursued by Joyce's daughter Lucia. His unwillingness to respond caused a break with Joyce himself.

Some of Beckett's translations began to appear in little magazines, and he rather jokingly wrote a 98-line poem on Descartes entitled *Whoroscope* for a prize competition in 1930, which he won. The competition organizer, Nancy Cunard, had 300 copies printed. She was to become a close friend. Other friends got Beckett a commission to contribute a monograph on Proust to a series published by Chatto and Windus. He was short of money and stayed in Paris to write it. His position as Trinity's lecteur at the ENS obliged him to return to Trinity as an instructor for three years from 1930 to 1933 at £200 a year, rising to £350, after which a permanent appointment would have been customary. A suite of rooms was provided, although electricity and central heating had not yet been installed. Beckett remained withdrawn, forming close friendships only with a pupil from the ENS, now French lecteur at Trinity, and with Jack Yeats, the painter and brother of W.B. Yeats, who now filled for him the sort of function which Joyce had filled in Paris. Beckett disliked teaching, and by December he was physically run down. He took part in a disastrous skit on *Le Cid* and his spirits were not even raised by the publication of *Proust* on 5 March. That month he went to Paris, where he placed a number of his poems. During the summer he worked on a translation of Rimbaud and went on a walking tour with his brother Frank.

By the winter of 1931 he was unable to continue teaching and took permanently to bed. He finally went to Kassel, wired back his resignation to Trinity, and stayed until the summer of 1932, receiving from an uncomprehending father, who wanted him in the family business, an allowance that was not quite big enough to live on. The Sinclairs were in financial difficulties, saw racial tribulations ahead for the Jews, and were worried about Peggy, though as yet unaware that she was terminally ill. Beckett's emotional attachment to her had ebbed away by now. More of his short stories began to appear in Paris. Lucia Joyce was now in an asylum there, and Bechett did not receive an invitation to her father's 50th birthday celebrations. In March 1932 he visited Paris and before returning to Kassel was commissioned to translate some surrealist (q.v.) poems. By May he had finished, and with some poems of his own and an idea for a novel he went back to Paris. He was cautiously readmitted to Joyce's circle, and wrote the "Dream of Fair to Middling women," which was never published, but almost all of which except satirical references to friends was incorporated into subsequent works.

The clampdown on foreigners in Paris in 1932 meant that Beckett had to leave, since he had no residence permit. He slept a few nights on Lurçat's floor, finishing his translation of Rimbaud's "Le bateau îvre," for which he was paid 800 francs by a magazine which folded, and went to London to look for a publisher for the "Dream" before confronting his parents again. He could not find one and returned home, where his mother ensured that financial support, hitherto often surreptitiously supplied by his father, was limited to a pound a week, scarcely enough to keep him in drink and cigarettes. Beckett wrote the poem "Serena I" and adapted the short story "Dante and the Lobster" from the "Dream". It failed to win a prize he needed, but was published in December in *This Quarter*, one of the small Paris-based English-language reviews. Beckett's mother continued to humiliate him by pushing him into looking for jobs and arranging for him to take private French classes, which quickly collapsed. He was still managing to drink a good deal, and the correspondence with McGreevy in Paris acted as a safety valve, but despite this he became ill again. After more rejections of the "Dream," in the winter of 1932–33 he began to delete hurtful references to living people, and then to extract more short pieces from the text. Over Easter 1933, which he spent alone with his

mother, he went for a motorbike ride, following which he wrote "Sanies I."

He began to read again, now in Trinity library, and wrote seven stories, which he sent to Chatto and Windus together with the three earlier ones and "Dante and the Lobster." The short story "Echo's bones," not to be confused with the 1935 book of 13 poems of that title, was rejected and has never been published. The other 10, which Beckett later regarded as juvenilia, made up the 1934 *More Pricks than Kicks*. His allowance was reduced to 10 shillings after an incident when he returned home drunk and broke all the crockery. In May he heard of Peggy's death, and he began to suffer from panic dreams, and then severe headaches. On 21 June his father had a serious heart attack, and a second one on 26 June killed him. Beckett's mother went into a trance of stiff-lipped mourning. Peggy's mother and father returned destitute to Dublin from Hitler's Germany but would not receive him because of a story in *More Pricks than Kicks* which appeared to make fun of one of Peggy's letters. In September Beckett's father's estate, which was eventually to be divided between Beckett and his brother after their mother's death, was valued at £42,395. In the meanwhile Beckett was given an annuity of £200 a year. The advance on *More Pricks* went to pay a tax bill. The total payment was £25.

Beckett had often discussed his health with a friend from his student days, now a doctor, who had listened patiently as he had disclosed his emotional frustrations to him. He thought that the cure for Beckett's physical symptoms lay in psychoanalysis. Beckett's brother, who was running the business and studying in the evenings for his surveying exams, had to sleep in the same bed as Beckett to calm him at nights. Eventually his mother consented to send Beckett for analysis to London's Tavistock Clinic. McGreevy was in London eking out a living as a handyman and literary journalist, and late in 1933 Beckett found a furnished room off the King's Road. Even a short pre-Christmas stay had restored his health and, as the analysis began in 1934, more of the translations undertaken for Nancy Cunard began to appear in Paris. The acrostic "Home Olga," written for Joyce, appeared in the US, and *More Pricks* came out on 24 May. The reception was favourable, except in Ireland, where the work's blasphemous title, which ambiguously but obscenely alluded to the New Testament, ensured that it was banned there, but only 500 copies of the print run of 1,500 were sold. Beckett managed to secure a little reviewing, but his reviews were generally both stinging and self-revealing. He wrote a short story, "A Case in a Thousand," a disquieting fictionalization of repressed erotic feelings involving his mother

Beckett consented to pay for an edition of his poems in Paris, adding four to the original nine, returned to Dublin for the summer of 1934, and then spent the rest of the year lonely, poor, and out of work in London, where there were some casual episodes with women, and where he read Schopenhauer and Nietzsche. Returning to Dublin again for Christmas, he managed to patch up his friendship with Peggy's parents. He continued to work on a story started in the autumn, but was in a lamentable state early in 1935, well into his analysis, but feeling worthless, incapable, and, as a long letter to McGreevy shows, extremely confused. He called on Cyril Connolly, who, no doubt thinking of Orwell, suggested that he still needed a spell of dish-washing if he wanted to become a writer. Meanwhile he made no headway with literary projects or in the literary world, but continued to read and spent time in museums. In late April, against his analyst's advice, he went back to Ireland and put himself in thraldom to his mother again by borrowing from her. His condition improved when he discovered how much the Sinclairs needed him. They were short of money, and Cissie's husband was in hospital. Back in London Beckett thought of film making in Russia with Eisenstein, and had made some progress with his story, when his mother came over, which stopped all creative flow.

What started it again was a lecture by Jung at the Tavistock, the third of those published in *Analytical Psychology, Its Theory and Practice*, and in particular Jung's answer to a question about children's dreams in which he recounted how a 10-year-old's mythological dreams contained a premonition of early death, and resulted from an "improper birth." The lecture itself had stressed the autonomous nature of the characters a dramatist or a novelist thought he was creating with conscious control. Beckett broke off his analysis against his analyst's advice late in 1935, and was immediately ill when he arrived home. His analyst had correctly predicted how his mother would behave. Beckett recovered, but again became withdrawn, contemplating violence and suicide before very slowly adjusting to minor tasks. *Echo's Bones* had been published, but remained unsold and unreviewed. An article on censorship in Ireland was lost. Beckett was asked for another monograph similar to *Proust* on an author of his choice, and invited to do some more translating. He went back to the story begun in 1934, to be published in 1938 as *Murphy*. He had had over a score of rejections for it.

He spent most of 1936 waiting and doing odd literary jobs. As Beckett's health improved, so the pressure put on him by his mother increased. He applied or considered applying for various posts in various subjects and capacities in Capetown, Geneva, and at Harvard, and wondered about learning to fly. Then came an invitation out of the blue to edit, and eventually purchase, the *Dublin Magazine*, but Beckett did not want it. In September the over-charged tax was returned, and Beckett scraped together enough money to get to Germany, where he spent six miserable months. Almost all the modern paintings had been removed from display, and Beckett was too preoccupied with his own problems, particularly with the progress of *Murphy*, to enjoy even Dresden, where he met congenial company. A letter from his mother made him feel guilty enough to cut short his stay and return home, marking his sense of urgency by flying. His brother was about to get married, leaving him in sole charge of his mother. In Dublin he turned down literary chores, got openly drunk oftener than before, did not even try to write, crashed his mother's car, and fought and lost a prosecution for dangerous driving. His mother left the house without giving Beckett her address in a last effort to keep him in Dublin and get him gainfully employed, but in October 1937 he left for Paris and settled there for good, cautiously resuming contact with Joyce. On 9 December he received a telegram to say that, after 42 rejections, *Murphy* had been taken by Routledge. They paid him an advance of £25.

While walking home with friends in the early hours of 7 January 1938 Beckett was stabbed in the street by a pimp to whom he had refused money. He was seriously hurt, and his companions got help from a passer-by, Suzanne Deschevaux-Dumesnil. Suzanne, who was a piano student, was later to become Beckett's wife. Meanwhile Joyce had him put in a private hospital room. Peggy Guggenheim, the heiress with whom Beckett had had a brief liaison, called and agreed to give McGreevy a job in her London gallery. She also took a room in Beckett's hotel to help him during convalescence when he was released a fortnight later. Suzanne, who was seven years older than Beckett, was discreet and efficient in her attentions. Nancy Cunard organized distractions for him which he did not want, and his mother and brother flew over from Dublin. Various people offered lucrative occupations, and Beckett turned down an invitation to translate Sade. He had been disappointed by the lukewarm reception given to *Murphy*, although sales had been good, and he now tried to promote the book, while also writing poetry in French. Eventually he finished the translation of *Murphy* into French himself. He visited his mother from time to time, helped Joyce, played tennis, and went back to France at the outbreak of World War II. When the Germans occupied Paris he went south, but failed to get back to Ireland via Portugal, and returned to Paris.

Late in 1940 Beckett was recruited by Péron, the ENS lecteur with whom he had worked and developed a close friendship in Paris, to help with resistance activities, which involved collecting, collating, and transmitting information on microfilm. Suzanne was living with him and both were forced to flee when Péron was arrested. Beckett spent 10 days in Nathalie Sarraute's attic, then fled with Suzanne to Roussillon, which they reached after numerous adventures, and where they were to spend most of the war. Beckett began *Watt* in Roussillon, and undertook occasional jobs for the local maquis until the US army arrived on 24 August 1944, but the boredom of wartime life had brought him to the brink of a complete breakdown, avoided only by bringing some structure to the daily routine. After the war he was awarded the Croix de Guerre with gold star.

Suzanne and he returned to Paris as soon as they could, and Beckett took the only possible route to Dublin, which was via London, where he left the manuscript of *Watt*. He was furious to discover that 782 copies of *Murphy* had been remaindered in 1942 out of the printing of 1,500. His mother was now elderly and infirm, and his brother was prosperous, reliving his father's life. As an alien Beckett was not immediately allowed back into France and, as a Frenchwoman, Suzanne was not allowed out. Routledge turned down *Watt*, and Beckett heard that Péron had died on release from Mauthausen. His sense of guilt now bound him to France even more strongly than it had previously bound him to his mother, and he managed to return there with the Irish Red Cross.

From 1946 he tried again to write, at first occasional pieces or drafts of pieces later abandoned. His most fruitful period was beginning, but he was aware only that *Watt* was unpublished, and that the subject of all his writing was confined to his personal experiences and anxieties. It was in Dublin in 1946 that Beckett realized that his writing had to begin from his own unconscious, from the memories and dreams that surfaced, and that a narrator merely got in the way of communication. From now on, he used "I" as the narrative voice and found himself able to write fluently again. He still needed protection against the autonomous creations breaking into his articulate consciousness, and therefore found it easier to write in a non-maternal language, French. He started the novel "Mercier et Camier" and published "Suite" in *Les Temps Modernes* (q.v.). He eventually discarded the novel although, as usual, parts were salvaged for other works. "Suite," as "La fin," became the first of the four stories in *Nouvelles*. Beckett fell ill again, and Suzanne took him to the country, where he recovered. In Paris she earned a living for them both by dressmaking, and devoted herself to ensuring that Beckett should be able to write, preferring not to accompany him on social occasions.

Murphy came out in Beckett's French translation in 1947 but sold only six copies in 1948 and only 95 by 1951, partly because Beckett's obsessive need for privacy prevented him from taking part in publicizing the book, as was expected of authors in France. He was reduced to translating copy into French for *Reader's Digest* at two dollars a page. He finished the unpublished play *Eleutheria* in 1947, and *Molloy* by Christmas. It was to be published with *Malone meurt* and *L'Innommable* as a trilogy by the Editions de Minuit in 1951. The year 1948 was difficult financially. The Irish annuity was now worth practically nothing, and the French tax officials were inquisitive about money remitted from abroad. Beckett applied for a job as a translator and tried to give English lessons, but without success. He published three short stories in French with his own English translations in *transition 48*, as it was now called, and agreed to translate for the review, which, for a time, produced a substantial portion of his joint income with Suzanne. Cyril Connolly made overtures for something for *Horizon*, but nothing came of them.

En attendant Godot of 1952 was written from October 1948 to January 1949, and in the course of 1949 *transition 48* published Beckett's *Three Dialogues with Georges Duthuit*. Suzanne was collecting rejections from producers for *Godot*, and UNESCO finally offered Beckett some translating. Some pages from *Watt* were taken by *Envoy*. After further exasperating rounds of producers and publishers, Suzanne finally thought of taking *Godot* to Roger Blin, who was currently staging Strindberg "somewhere in Montmartre" (in fact *The Ghost Sonata* at the Gaité-Montparnasse). It was the relative lack of expense that made him choose *Godot* instead of the easier but more lavish *Eleutheria*. Beckett liked what Blin had done for the Strindberg, and the two men met in the summer of 1950, and immediately got on. Beckett went off to Dublin in mid-June, staying there until his mother died on 25 August, and waiting to make sure that his brother could deal with everything. He refused to take anything of his mother's away, and assumed when he left that he was leaving Ireland for the last time.

That November Jérôme Lindon, the owner of the Editions de Minuit, agreed to publish the trilogy of novels only because Beckett, who needed the money and the celebrity, but would have nothing to do with the negotiation, would not let him have the first two novels without the third. Lindon was certain only of *Molloy*. When Beckett did finally meet Lindon, he returned from the visit dispirited at the probability that he was causing the bankruptcy of an extraordinarily nice man. The news from Blin was good, and UNESCO was supplying more work. Then the trilogy was reviewed with something approaching enthusiasm. Lindon even offered to publish *Watt* in French translation, and bought up the rights to, and the unsold stock of *Murphy*, which Bordas had bought from Routledge. Lindon was now therefore Beckett's sole publisher, committed to "all future work." Beckett was flustered by all the commercial activity and able to write little, working only on the 13 *Textes pour rien* to appear in 1955. *Molloy* finally appeared in March 1951, selling 35,000 copies in the original edition, and 55,000 in the smaller pocket "10/18" series. None of the other novels sold more than 10,000 copies in France, although all the plays were to sell out in repeated editions. In 1952, however, even with a small arts grant, it was still impossible to find a theatre and actors for *Godot*, published by

Minuit on 17 November 1952. The first performance finally took place in January 1953, and the play was the subject of a cult before it ever opened at the Théâtre de Babylone, a former shop with 230 folding seats.

Watt was finally published in 1953 by the Olympic Press, which bought it from the literary quarterly *Merlin* without having it read, supposing it to be semi-pornographic and supplied under an agreement for the production of such material. Beckett was very tight-lipped. Apart from the *Textes pour rien*, he published no more prose fiction before *Comment c'est* of 1961. *Godot* was scheduled for simultaneous production in eight German cities, and there was to be a tour of the French provinces by the Blin production. The business side of success overwhelmed Beckett, although he still managed to translate *Godot* into English. The English production opened on 3 August 1955 to terrible notices and an empty auditorium. There had been great trouble in the Lord Chamberlain's office, but eventually the play transferred to a different theatre and started to attract full houses. The Grove Press, with which Beckett did consent to deal, had never known such an unworldly author, dedicated to nothing but the meticulous reproduction of his text. Beckett himself deliberately kept the circles in which he moved separate. What time he could he spent in the country at Ussy, in the small house which Suzanne and he had had built there.

In the summer of 1954 Beckett's brother was dying of lung cancer, and Beckett cared for him until the end, on 13 September. He could not write fiction any more, and he made at least two complete versions of *Fin de partie* before cutting it down to its final one-act form. The world premiere was given in French at the Royal Court Theatre in London in 1957. The correct translation of the title is "Endgame," as in chess, a game which Beckett found attractive partly because, in his view, each opponent necessarily weakened his own position from his very first move. By now he was writing to hold himself together whenever the pressures from the agents of the commercial world let up. He produced *Act Without Words I* and *II*. He still had no telephone, and only loyalty to friends kept him from being altogether unavailable to the outside world. *All That Fall* was finished in 1956, and the Pinget translation, *Tous ceux qui tombent*, appeared in France in *Les Lettres Nouvelles* in March 1957. On 1 February *Fin de partie* was published with *Acte sans paroles I*. Rehearsals for the London production became fraught with tension between Blin and Beckett, who wanted it to contain no possibility of humour, just stark hopelessness. The French press was annoyed at the fact that the French premiere had been held in London, and the Studio Champs Elysées agreed to stage the play from 27 April. Beckett toned down the staging, properties, and make-up to give it the power he wanted. He wrote to McGreevy about how weary translating himself into English, French, and German was making him.

In November 1957 the BBC broadcast *All That Fall*. Beckett had wanted to come to England for it, but he and Suzanne finally stayed at Ussy. They were now leading their own private lives as well as a joint one, and the arrangement apparently suited both of them, although Beckett was now relying more on whisky than before. It was a prop he needed only when he had to meet other people. He drank relatively little when alone. A brief liaison he had at this time resulted in *Play*, produced in German in 1963. Blin was pleased when *Fin de partie* finally ended in Paris after 97 performances, and Beckett disliked the German production. There was trouble again with the Lord Chamberlain's office over the language of the English translation when *Endgame*, too, was put on at the Royal Court on 28 October 1958. The authorities finally relented and allowed "that bastard" to be used of God.

Krapp's Last Tape of 1958 was written in English for Patrick Magee, who had performed in *All That Fall* as a better curtain piece than *Acte sans paroles I*. It is a carefully crafted, much-honed artefact, with every detail meticulously put in place, but it draws on all Beckett's most painful personal memories, hitherto no doubt unconsciously suppressed, and certainly the real reason for his choice of French as his language of literary creation. The recollection of intense personal pain in Beckett's creative work coincides with the reversion to English as the medium of creativity. The despair is now muted rather than savage, and the difficulty presented by ordinary social encounters is still extraordinary. Suzanne and Beckett did manage to slip away to have a holiday together in Yugoslavia, where *Molloy* and *Godot* had been accumulating non-convertible dinars. While in England to supervise every detail of *Endgame* and *Krapp*, Beckett, uncharacteristically, accepted an invitation to dinner from John Calder but, on finding other people present, he simply played the piano all evening, and had to be politely ignored. He broke with habit by staying on after the dress rehearsal to attend the first night, which he normally left to Suzanne, and this time he entertained while waiting for the reviews, which were hostile. He appears to have overestimated the importance of Kenneth Tynan's opinion. Tynan's later behaviour over the 120-word sketch "Breath," which Beckett gave him for the New York *Oh! Calcutta!*, so outraged the fastidiously courteous Beckett as to draw from him one of his rare public expressions of anger.

In late 1958 Beckett returned to Ireland to help his brother's widow and to see a dying friend. He spent Christmas alone in the country. In 1959 he felt compelled to accept a D. Litt. from Trinity College, although Suzanne was the only one to know until the news became public. *Les Lettres Nouvelles* published his French version of *Krapp*, entitled *La Dernière Bande*, in March, and Mihalovici turned it into an opera, *Das letzte Band*. The double bill of *Endgame* and *Krapp* flopped in Ireland. In his private life Beckett was now compromising with his growing activity in the theatre. In 1960 Suzanne and he finally moved into a larger apartment. At Ussy, where he had allowed a telephone to be installed, Beckett was chiselling out *Comment c'est,* to be published in 1961. He flew alone to Dublin for the degree, but Suzanne and a friend turned up unannounced for the ceremony, creating confusion by arriving in the midst of Frank's daughter's 21st birthday party, which they had not known was taking place, and from which Beckett had already fled. His radio play, *Embers*, nominated by the BBC, won the Prix Italia, and Suzanne persuaded Beckett to attend the presentation. Because of difficulties with taxis at Ussy, he bought a small car.

Comment c'est resisted all Beckett's efforts in spite of the balance he had established between the privacy of Ussy and the bustle of Paris. He wrote another play in English eventually to become *Happy Days*, attacking the Catholic Church and the English. He never knew whether he had finished or abandoned *Comment c'est*, but Lindon wanted it urgently. Beckett hoped he might sell 50 copies. Lindon sold at least 250 in the first week. The printer made difficulties, and Lindon was annoyed when bilingual and trilingual editions of the French poems appeared in England and Germany. Beckett had to limit Calder to the English poems and the French poems he had translated himself. On 25 March 1961 he married Suzanne in England, having successfully avoided public attention, in order to make her the undisputed legitimate heir to what was becoming a valuable inheritance. The Prix International des Editeurs was awarded jointly to Borges and Beckett that year and gave Beckett special pleasure, since he knew his international reputation, about which he was concerned, was suffering from his inability to make himself available for interviews.

In spite of the marriage, relations with Suzanne were declining into semi-hostility. She now wanted more public acknowledgement of her support, and Beckett's writing occasionally refers to a new sense of hopelessness and inescapability in his life. He refused to go to New York, but sent sheaves of minute directions for the staging of *Happy Days* as part of a triple bill with two Albee plays. Much of Beckett's time was now taken up with translating and supervising translations of his own work, but he did manage to write *Words and Music*. He wanted both to translate *Comment c'est (How It Is)* and to write an English version, then to put *Textes pour rien* into English and *Happy Days (Oh, les beaux jours)*, which was doing well in New York and Berlin, into French. He wrote *Cascando* for French radio and Mihalovici, refused to sign Sartre's petition, the "Manifeste du 121," protesting against France's policy in Algeria, and lent Lindon money to keep the Editions de Minuit afloat. He also allowed a partly biographical study of himself to be written, but could not face reading it, and in 1969 asked for biographical data to be removed from the manuscript. His life had become a perpetual rush in connection with performances, translations, and publications, but he still refused to accept help to deal with the crushing weight of his correspondence.

It was in Germany that Beckett most enjoyed working, because only in Germany was the direction of his plays left chiefly in his own hands. He never considered his plays as really important in the total context of his literary production. They did nevertheless claim most of his time and attention from 1950. He was sufficiently attracted by his notion of cinema as the frozen perfection of the author's intentions to face the long, loud cocktail party he thought New York would be. In the hot summer of 1964 he went to make *Film*, stoically suffering as much as his star, Buster Keaton, and returned to find he needed to have a tumour removed. Fortunately it turned out to be benign. He became dangerously renowned for his generosity, and increasingly distant from Suzanne, who resented his new-found ability to look after himself.

In 1965 Beckett finished *Eh Joe* and *Come and Go*, a translation of his *Va et vient*. *Film* won four awards, but was not taken for general distribution. Beckett himself translated *Eh Joe* and *Words and Music* into French and spent what time he could at Ussy, determined to write a prose work, but found his eyesight deteriorating. He became the centre of a coterie of Irish exiles although, unlike Joyce, it was he who insisted on doing the favours. He supervised radio productions and recordings of *End of Day* and *Imagination Dead Imagine*, and *Play* was filmed in French. Beckett went strongly on record against anyone's right to publish posthumously what an author had not published during his own life, knowing at the time that he had a drawerful of unpublished manuscripts. His own "first posthumous publication" was none the less issued in 1990, after his death, as *As the Story Was Told*.

Beckett allowed *Watt* to be translated into French, and on 21

August 1966 he was present at the death of his brother's widow from stomach cancer. That year he published two prose texts, *Assez* and *Ping*. His eyesight deteriorated so badly that in 1967 he fell into a mechanic's pit he had not seen while his car was being repaired. He refused Laurence Olivier and Joan Plowright permission to make a film of *All That Fall* and, on Blunden's retirement, refused to let Enid Starkie put him up for the Oxford chair of poetry. On 23 October 1969, in a Tunisian village, Beckett heard that he had been awarded the Nobel prize for literature. His name had first been put forward in 1957, and his was one of 103 names considered in 1969. He had known that the award was likely, since Lindon had told the Swedish Academy that he would not turn it down, as Sartre had done. He was delighted to have been undiscoverable when the world's press wanted to unearth him, and to find how little was publicly known about him. He agreed to be photographed, but the press respected their agreement not to ask any questions of him. Lindon accepted the award for him, and was rewarded with *Premier amour*, one of the stories written in 1946. The original model for the woman had now died. Beckett reluctantly produced an English translation in 1973.

He had two successful eye operations in the winter of 1970–71, and sporadically released very short items to clamouring publishers in several countries, including old translations, *The Lost One*, and various scraps and fragments. Only after 1972 could he produce new work: *Not I*, written in 12 days, and *That Time* (1974). *Lessness* had been published in 1970. Still to be published were *Footfalls, That Time, Ghost Trio, …but the clouds…, Ends and Odds, Six Residences, Company, Ill Seen Ill Said, Rockaby, Ohio Impromptu, Catastrophe*, and *Worstward Ho*. The genres blur as drama becomes dialogue, which merges indistinguishably into monologue and first-person narrative. Limited editions of very early works have appeared, and a *Journal of Beckett Studies* was founded during Beckett's lifetime. The complexities of his communicative codes have always drawn academic analysts to a study of his works, many of which are not easily accessible to the casual reader. *The Collected Shorter Plays* was published in 1984. Beckett died on 22 December 1989.

WORKS

Beckett's work has steadily moved towards the projection of a single consciousness focusing upon itself. It developed from an early delight in acrostic skills, a hybrid self-mocking vocabulary, and Joycean word conflations, through the great trilogy of novels written in French, to what are virtually dramatic monologues, in which the "action" is limited to a projection of voice or self. Beckett wanted his actors reduced to voices whose expression was enhanced by language, lighting, and atmosphere alone. He paid meticulous attention to the elimination of everything, such as acting, or idiosyncracies of emphasis, speech, or even vowel lengths, which was not wholly integrated into the machine-like effort to achieve the precise effect he had in mind. He had no choice but to take the immense pains for which he is famous. The temptation to allow an audience to titter at men in dustbins or other black humour on stage was almost irresistible to producers, but Beckett did not intend his characters to be funny, just bleak images of hopelessness and despair. The final effect of non-risible absurdity, of dignified resignation to ines-

capable incomprehensibility, was not to be achieved lightly.

Beckett was aware of the irony of combining the need to express with the futility of expressing. The memorable image in his only film is of a character in perpetual retreat from the camera and, of course, the cinema audience. Between the early work, culminating in *Murphy* and *Watt*, and the excessively minimalist, if rapier-sharp, later fragments of drama and fiction, lie the great masterpieces, the trilogy and the major plays, *En attendant Godot, Fin de partie, Krapp's Last Tape, Happy Days*, and *Play*, and perhaps *Comment c'est*, unclassifiable in its literary form, but nearer to prose than to verse, and nearer to narrative than to dialogue. The early work, like *Whoroscope*, is intensely clever and allusive. The title combines a typical linguistic conflation of "whore" and "horoscope" with an allusion to time. "Hora" in classical Greek means "age" or "period." This combination of conflation and allusion is made more dense by the derivation of the whole poem from the 17th-century life of Descartes. It records Descartes's fear of revealing his date of birth, from which his horoscope could foretell the date of his death. The poem contains clipped metres, faintly obscene puns, conflations like "prostisciutto," and fake anachronisms, like the straight-faced allusion to Descartes's breakfast egg, a double take because Descartes did in fact start the day with an omelette. Beckett never wholly lost his sense of irreverent fun or his delight at teasing anomalies and paradoxes out of his reader's or his audience's expectations.

But being clever with language was just the beginning. Beckett knew that characters, images, and language could well up in the creative artist from somewhere beyond the control of his conscious ego. Jung's lecture fitted this experience into a framework of psychological theory and, in answer to the question about children's "mythological" dreams, Jung had suggested the possibility of "improper birth," in which the "ego" never established its full function. An imperfectly developed consciousness, as revealed in the dreams, had to presage an early death. Beckett's ever more sharply focused view that language led an autonomous existence, and could therefore not be used communicatively, but only chase its own tail in an endlessly solipsistic circularity, is the key to his development, and to the horrifying vision of human experience as uncommunicable, and therefore pointless, which he explored with such remorseless concentration.

It is no doubt true that the attraction for Beckett of this explanation of experience derives from a psychologically disturbed relationship with his own mother, that Jung's theory came to provide an articulate framework within which Beckett could understand his own creative needs, and that ultimately Beckett's view, if taken to exclude other more normal functions of language, renders literature at first nugatory, and then impossible. Minimalism always derives from a tension between the effect striven for and the medium used, and Mallarmé's aesthetic had already made it pointless to write poetry. But, as Beckett's literary development shows, the intensifying exploration of the experience of a disturbed psyche which leads to totally purposeless language sheds, like the myth of Oedipus, an exceedingly powerful light on quite normal aspects of the human condition.

Beckett's personal trauma was essential to his development as a towering literary figure. It explains the stoic forbearance and careful courtesy which marked his personal dealings with others, the attempt to resolve his bewilderment imaginatively in a tongue which left his deepest wounds unopened, the refuge in literary minimalism to which he resorted, and the intensifying imaginative focus on the diminishing function he found for language. It also incidentally explains why the common attempts to relate Beckett's creative imagination to Kafka's do no justice to either author, and just how little Beckett's oeuvre owes to either the Irish origins which colour it, or the experiences, some of them disturbing enough, which he underwent in the opening years of World War II, and from which in due course he recovered. When Suzanne and he finally moved to their larger Paris apartment with separate entrances, Beckett was able to live with a window overlooking the prison courtyard where, after the war, they had hanged the infiltrator who had betrayed Péron's resistance network, "Gloria," to the Gestapo.

Finally, Beckett's developing exploration of the function of language and the meaninglessness of human experience, which followed from what he no doubt correctly found could be the case, and perhaps always to some extent necessarily was the case, explains why he has dragged in his wake such an enormous weight of academic interest in his work, an interest quite disproportionate to its popular appeal, even when boosted by avant-garde literary critics and up-market literary journalists. As Beckett said to a biographer, "The best possible play is one in which there are no actors, only the text. I'm trying to find a way to write one." He got as far as virtually eliminating the role of the director, and himself stipulating every last detail of lighting, movement, positioning, and voice inflection on the stage. In another half-revealing statement, Beckett seems to suggest that the mere chaos of uncontrolled, undirected, and uncommunicative utterance that he thought language might be creates a new problem of literary form: "the form itself becomes a preoccupation, because it exists as a problem separate from the material it accommodates. To find a form that accommodates the mess. That is the problem of the artist now." Beckett's late work must be seen as a valiant but unsuccessful attempt to perform that unperformable task.

Beckett's first published essay, "Dante...Bruno. Vico ...Joyce," published in transition for June 1929, does little more than demonstrate his skill at manipulating language. The story "Assumption" is important only for the fairly adolescent association of the religious and the sexual imagery, and Whoroscope is undoubtedly the product of a clever mind, although one not yet transcending in power that of the above-average chess and bridge player which Beckett was. He was later rightly to regard the small monograph on Proust as of no great account. It is intricate and careful, but it does not add very much to Proust criticism. The "Dream of Fair to Middling women" was never published. It would be important if it were, because it must show a Beckett who has not yet come to terms with himself, lashing out witheringly at anyone who has attempted to be kind to him.

It is an episodic, autobiographical novel, written by a "Mr Beckett," who is not named until halfway through the book, about Belacqua, Dante's lazy Florentine lutemaker, who goes from the ENS back to Trinity. Almost all the serious remarks are immediately undercut by the pretence that they are frivolous, so that the book already indicates stylistically a simultaneous need for, and fear of, self-revelation. Beckett's narrator, "Mr Beckett," then gives up trying to finish the story, although Beckett wrote two alternative endings. The book was too long for the little magazines, too blasphemous for Irish publication, and in the wrong language for Paris. It is only by chance that one of the three copies survived. As the need arose, Beckett salvaged what he could, for later use elsewhere.

The 10 stories of More Pricks than Kicks include "Dante and the Lobster," salvaged from, the "Dream" and already published in This Quarter for December 1932, the cruel treatment of Peggy Sinclair's letter, "The Smeraldina's Billet Doux," "A Wet Night" from the "Dream," caricaturing friends, and "Ding-Dong," which contains autobiographical accounts of Beckett's student days, plus six new ones about Belacqua. Beckett called them "bottled climates," and they show the beginning of his preoccupation with autonomously self-supporting fiction. Belacqua is the protagonist, but the stories, which are strung together like episodes in a picaresque novel, also vary in pace, form, and style. They contain fictionalized autobiography, and obscure bits of erudite information, often torpedoed by the narrator's sarcasm, which is sometimes at Belacqua's expense, and sometimes at his own. The 13 poems of Echo's Bones are personal, autobiographical, and derivative. They are also learned, when appropriate exactly mimicking medieval forms, without being pedantic.

Murphy is very carefully written, and was intended to illustrate philosophical principles. Beckett took three years to write it, and set it inside a disturbed mind in a mental hospital. The characters include a chess-playing patient, a Mr Endon, whose name may be a pun, or a double entendre, or both, and the half-educated Murphy, from an amorphous background of furnished apartments. In the general line of the Belacqua anti-heroes Murphy's peculiarity is to live without integrating body and soul. There are flashbacks, and time is specified with reference to the relative positions of astral bodies. The book ends with the game of chess, in which the ideal is not to move at all, since any move brings its perpetrator nearer to eventual disaster. The reader is confronted with the endless circularity of eternal orbit in the heavens, or chess, where the ideal situation in which all moves are reversible is unattainable and catastrophe therefore unavoidable.

Murphy is the narrator, and part of the action takes place only in his mind. The plot is complicated and, on the surface, as zanily amusing as Chaplin's films, whose inspiration is sometimes apparent in Beckett's early work. All normal practices are reversed, and all normal expectations are thwarted. The happy characters are the mad ones, and the glorious, lightly symbolic game of chess ends not in the defeat but in the self-annihilation of Murphy, who refuses to force from Mr Endon any acknowledgement of Murphy's existence. Mr Endon is like the circling sphere, needing nothing, achieving nothing, perfectly purposeless. The trouble with Murphy is that, being sane, he has desires that reach outside himself. Doomed to sanity, that is, conscious awareness and to some extent control of his activity, he cannot surrender, as Mr Endon does, to his inner self. When Murphy absent-mindedly blows himself up by igniting the gas, his desire that his body, mind, and soul should be flushed down the lavatory is ignored. Instead, they are flung around in a pub brawl and disposed of with the rest of the detritus. Murphy is a highly polished comic novel, containing an improbable number of incompatible morals, and displaying in its central character the real pathos of the clown. Its weakness, inevitably, is the lack of a satisfactory resolution.

Watt was written during the war in an effort by Beckett, cut off from all psychiatric help, to keep himself sane. Written in the open prison of a Provençal village, it is filled with dialogues and scenes from Beckett's own life, with stylistic exercises and consolatory conjurings of seasonal cycles. The most important things about the novel have little to do with literary excellence, but concern the shift away from Joyce, the carefully etched precision of expression, and Beckett's growing awareness that English was too native a medium for him to probe in it the important but painful corners of his own psyche. Watt is a servant in Mr Knott's house. He arrives, stays a while, then leaves, ending up in an asylum for the mentally ill, where he recounts his adventurs to Sam. The implications of the story, in which Watt goes mad by refusing irrationality any rights at all in his mind, are made clear in the "Addenda," in which Beckett tries to destroy all that has been revelatory of himself in Watt's fear of becoming mentally unbalanced. Beckett is telling the reader not to be afraid of "imperfect birth," while also saying that he himself is, and that the reader in fact should be. The structured lunacy of Mr Watt's household sounds like wartime Roussillon, but the novel is in English. To leave its analogies intact was more than Beckett could have borne.

Eleutheria, whose title means liberty, is an unpublished play in French, with three sets and 17 characters, about the efforts of Victor Krap to get away from the constraints of his middle-class background and upbringing. For two acts the stage is split between the family living room and Victor's hotel room. In the third, Victor's room fills the whole stage. The action takes place on three successive winter afternoons in Paris. The play is unsatisfactory because its central character is too inarticulate to be able to state why he needs to free himself, and, although he needed the money and Lindon wanted the play, Beckett never allowed it to be staged or published once Blin had preferred *Godot*. Much of it was subsequently used in later pieces, after Beckett had discovered how to make his drama impersonal as well as intimate, so avoiding such intrusive signs of self-consciousness as are indicated by his refusal to let reader or audience take seriously what clearly is serious, because it is also self-revelatory.

The trilogy of French novels starts with *Molloy*, written from September 1947 to January 1948, and considered by Beckett the first successful fictionalization of his experience. There are two parts, in which Molloy and Moran successively tell their stories. Molloy's is told from an unparagraphed mental haze, while Moran uses structured prose to narrate clear but bewildering events. Molloy is in his mother's room, where he is made to write his story, which ends when he is rescued from a ditch, taken to his mother's room, and made to write his story. His experience is therefore circular, autonomous, and meaningless. It does not change anything if the narrated events took place or did not take place. His story is about setting out on his bicycle, with his crutches fastened to his crossbar, to see his mother. After a series of apparently pointless incidents, during which he runs over a dog and is adopted by its owner as its replacement in her affections, he finds that his bicycle is missing, leaves on crutches, contemplates living in an alley, then suicide, and goes to the seaside to replace his 16 pebbles, each of which he sucks equally as he transfers them obsessively from pocket to pocket. He then feels an urgent need for his mother and crawls to the ditch, from which he is rescued.

The point is not so much the disentanglement of the Freudian regression symbolism as its successful use in the fictionalization of a psychotic state, and Beckett's breakthrough in allowing the mythological images to surface into conscious forms from the inarticulate depths of his psyche. The circularity of the plot,

which ends where it started and could go on for ever, indicates not only the impossibility but also the futility of communicating an experience which is uncontrolled, autonomous, and meaningless, apart from the therapeutic effect of writing it down, which is the implied "meaning" of the novel.

Moran has a first name, patterns of regular religious and gastronomic behaviour from whose interruption he suffers, and a function. He is a private investigator commissioned to report on Molloy. He tells us about himself, his household, his habits, and his patterns of behaviour. His narrative starts by announcing that it is midnight and raining. When he has written his report he tells us it is not midnight and not raining. In Moran's real world, therefore, structured events produce change. It is possible to break out of solipsistic circularity, but the cost is frightening. Moran's attempts to impose rationality on life result in a stiffening of the knee. Total paralysis is temporarily relieved only when he gratuitously batters someone to death with a stick which Molloy had seen a passer-by holding. Moran is ordered by his employer to return home. He becomes increasingly decrepit and finds everything in disorder. The vestigial control he exercises over the dark chaos of his mind results in an accommodation in which the highly structured but untenable mode of life is exchanged for a gentler proximity to nature and its seasons.

Beckett had intended to write two novels, not three, but *Malone meurt* was to require a successor. Malone is very old. He writes his stories, only stopping when he dies. His pencil and his consciousness give out together. Beckett's friends actually thought that Beckett might die when he reached the end of this novel, and Suzanne begged him to stop writing it. It has renewed recourse to a confusion of religious and erotic imagery, and Malone is obsessed above all by the need to understand what he is doing. What he is doing, of course, is undertaking the greatest of all epic journeys, leading to death, while undergoing a diminution of powers and possessions in a small space further confined by a decreasing ability to move.

Beckett's grotesque sense of comic parody takes on deeper levels of complexity as his writing simplifies and he writes about less and less. Malone, preparing to die, makes what amounts to an inventory of the pathetically little he has and can do. The minimalist form mimics the minimalism of content, of which it is a metaphor. Malone seeks to reach, and to know whether he can reach, an enduring or fictionalized self, as he attempts with his stick to reach real objects like his table and physically gather them to him, and as he physically diminishes in his progress towards the void. The casual, clear-headed style of the first-person narrator, with his descriptions and mutterings, is in terrifying counterpoint with the act of dying and the fight against encroaching extinction, portrayed as regressive annihilation: "Yes, an old foetus, that's what I am now." The soul, "denied in vain," is both a timeless self and a void: "I am being given birth to into death."

Malone meurt intersperses the first-person memories with scraps of third-person fiction, mostly concerned with questions about writing and heavily charged with archetypal symbols combining in non-logical patterns. Malone comments on the stories he tries to write. Beckett distinguishes the registers by using the present tense for Malone and the past for the narrators of Malone's stories. The text is sufficiently complex for the English publishers not to have inserted the gaps which indicate changes of narrative register, but the text reads in any case rather like a series of chess moves, with every name and every sentence giving rise to a whole new series of potential subsequent ones. The reader can guess that Beckett was a chess player, perpetually aware of the array of perspectives he was opening up.

At the same time Beckett reveals his limitations as a novelist. Malone, like his creator, cannot create any consciousness other than his own. He cannot tell stories without interrupting to talk about himself. Beckett forces the reader to identify with Malone identifying with the creatures of the narrators' stories, but in layered complexity, not with the sharpness of a hall of mirrors. Beckett vividly and harshly illuminates the psychic clash between atavism, fear, and need, but the beam, for all its intensity, is narrow. He is a magisterially clever, powerful, and disturbing writer, but always, whatever the genre, the archaeologist of his own psyche. His investigation achieves its power by revealing a great deal about the mental functions of all his readers and audiences, who, by definition, share his anthropolgical parameters, some of which are culturally conditioned.

Malone meurt reveals its own layered construction at the same time as it deconstructs itself when Malone denies his own authorial authority and suddenly transforms himself into Beckett, the writer of Beckett's books. In this passage, which is apparently conversational and relaxed in style, the narrator starts by being Malone, switches to being Beckett after the first comma, and remains Beckett until the last comma of the second sentence, when the voice is Malone's again:

> But let us leave these morbid matters and get on with that of my own demise, in two or three days if I remember rightly. Then it will be all over with the Murphys, Molloys, Morans, and Malones, unless it goes on beyond the grave.

Effectively, the reader is asked to assimilate the switch, so that "I," the subject of "remember," turns out to be Beckett. If he refuses, he has to accept the possibility that Malone is remembering that he is going to die in two or three days' time, or did die two or three days ago, and is conversationally recalling the fact like any other trivial event, a possibility which Beckett maliciously enjoys leaving open. It is as if he were playing chess with his reader and was rather pleased with the possibilities opened up by his move. Beckett also played bridge, and endplaying his opponent with a choice of two alternatives, either of which must lose him the hand, may be the better analogy here. He is at any rate winning a game against his reader.

In the third novel of the trilogy, and in the later plays, the narrative voices blend together, and there is only undifferentiated utterance, proceeding from nowhere, directed nowhere, and saying nothing that does not end with its own beginning, endlessly and purposelessly. The trouble with the later plays, first part of a double, then a triple bill, then mere fragments, is that they sin against an extra-literary cultural convention. They add up to a steel-tipped probe into the meaning of life, but not to an evening's entertainment.

L'Innommable, translated as *The Unnamable*, blends the narratorial voices into disembodied Voice. Voice is neither an allegory of anything nor related to any other human characteristic. Its owner has no name. He just sits in a jar with his hands on his knees. His head is just "a great smooth ball... featureless, but for the eyes, of which only the sockets remain." The unnamable has no sex and no nose as well as no name, and relates a series of stories, gradually abandoning all punctuation. He knows about

God, his mother, and his birthplace, but in his preamble is "afraid, as always, of going on." Rambling garrulously on? Or continuing to exist? "For to go on means going from here, means finding me, losing me, vanishing and beginning again..." At first the unnamable is Beckett:

> All these Murphys, Molloys, and Malones do not fool me. They have made me waste my time, suffer for nothing, speak of them when, in order to stop speaking, I should have spoken of me, and me alone.

Beckett deliberately gives the impression of gathering momentum before switching into controlled, psychotic caution, until the unending flow of words engulfs the speaker again, fitting in with Jung's view, expressed in that third Tavistock lecture, that unconscious contents could fascinate and grow stronger, "and conscious control vanishes in proportion until finally the patient sinks into the unconscious altogether and becomes completely victimized by it."

With *L'Innommable* Beckett goes beyond the limits of the readable. Fluency, register, length, and typography have become devices to be deciphered. What Beckett is writing here has reached the point of concentration at which it ceases to be literature and becomes merely raw material for critical or psychological analysis. *Malone meurt* had demonstrated what the problem was in a form still recognizable as literature. *L'Innommable* is no longer an exploration or an illumination. It is a demonstration that fiction, within the limits inside which Beckett could write it, was ultimately self-destructive. None of the fearsome assembly of techniques he could draw on could be deployed without polluting the purity of the product. Ambiguity of narrative voice taken to the absolute purity of anonymously voiced utterance is unattainable, because it defies the premise of all fiction that it is the product of consciousness.

What happened in the trilogy of French novels occurred again in the plays and dramatic fragments. The vividly theatrical image of Pozzo cracking his whip in *En attendant Godot* is pared away until, removed from space and time, *Play* relies simply on the physical effects of words and silences. Music emptied of sound becomes silence. Beckett empties theatre of action, character, movement, inflexion, and emphasis, leaving disembodied voice, a play of light, and too little sense of occasion. The result, after *Happy Days*, the last of the full-length plays, is not drama. In *En attendant Godot* Vladimir and Estragon converse while waiting for Godot to keep an appointment. There are two acts, in each of which Pozzo and his slave Lucky appear, and the principal characters are told that Godot will certainly come the next day. A tree that had been bare in the first act sprouts leaves in the second "to record the passage of time," as measured by change. The play is a long parable of the frustrations of expectation. The text was radically revised to make it dramatically more effective, and Beckett succeeded in creating an atmosphere of clowning underneath a layer of apparently normal conversation. The effect is created by the power with which the two levels parody one another.

The two tramps have physical problems, Estragon with his boot, Vladimir with his urination, and they are permanently bound to one another by their mutual contempt. They project metaphysical uncertainty by discussing time and purpose as comedian and stooge in dialogue that is clever, allusive, and witty, brilliantly exploiting a collision of styles with black humour, but also farce. Some of the jokes are sharpened by their New Testament origins. The action is a succession of let-downs. The fact that the four characters have names from four languages shows how Beckett's erudition is inclined to run away with him, but the play, in spite of its apparently loose construction, is still tautly theatrical in its calculated balances, and cleverly manipulates the audience.

By *Fin de partie* Beckett knew what theatrical effects he wanted, and began his pursuit of meticulous exactitude. Clove lives in the kitchen and cannot sit down. Hamm is blind and confined to a wheelchair. Beckett himself compared Hamm to the king on the losing side in a game of chess. All his actions are fruitless. Nagg and Nell are in dustbins, so that their entrances and their exits can be abrupt and unobtrusive. They are also immobilized, and can only pop up and down as required. Nell has no legs, no sight, and no hearing, and eventually dies, while Nagg is reduced to total silence. The play is a terrifying vision of doom and of the consequences of the willingness to embrace it, for which there is no real alternative. The four characters do interact in a grotesquely stylized way, and there is again mutual dependence between the characters in each pair, but the total effect, which is devastating, depends on the light-hearted confrontation with decrepitude and the parody of a tragic stance with which deprivation and annihilation are faced.

Krapp's Last Tape is a controlled monologue in which a single character acts out a dialogue with his younger self. Ancient disintegration confronts the hopes of youth and its memories, immutably fixed on the tape recorder, portable versions of which were still uncommon in 1958. An isolated old man, facing death, comments ironically on his previous experience. The 39-year-old Krapp had recorded himself 10 or 12 years earlier, when it would have been impossible to do so, so that the audience realizes that the register is fantasy, not realism, and that, for all the old man's ironic comments, Krapp has not changed in any essential way since he was young. He now appears as a clown, unable to cope with the reels of tape and clumsiness of the early tape recorders. The play is about his inability to escape from his never-changing self.

Happy Days centres on a woman, Winnie, whose optimistic chatter contrasts with her state of extreme and increasing deprivation. Her partner, Willie, scarcely appears, but Winnie futilely directs her unending monologue at him and, despite his grotesque inadequacy, continues to remain dependent on him. They are comic stereotypes superimposed on Winnie's disturbing inability to escape from herself into the real world. *Play* reduces the "characters" to three voices emerging from three isolated speakers in grey urns, speaking rhythmically, fast, and at first unintelligibly, responding to a spotlight as to a torturer. The talking automata do have human emotions, but the whole effect is now dominated not by what they say, but by the variations in rhythm, speed, and volume.

Beckett's world is always projected with pathos and irony. He urgently wanted public acclaim for his work, which he rightly considered important but difficult, although he made no concessions in the discomfort it so often engendered. The awkward, shambling, tramp-like figures of his novels became the vaudeville clowns of his plays, always linked in double acts, their invariably witty and often funny crosstalk opening up the terrifying inevitability of decrepitude, decay, and annihilation. Time erodes, murders, and destroys. The only possible view of life is to regard it as a chance to acquire the habit of disintegrating, one

that Beckett and his characters face with stoic fortitude. The characters' growing immobility mimics Beckett's view of life as a wearisome and occasionally entertaining journey to extinction. His clowns are generally reminiscent of Chaplin, unable to master the intricacies of modern life and its gadgets. Unlike Chaplin's, however, Beckett's characters are ultimately losers. The plays are not only uncomfortable, but also too short to slip easily into the social pattern of theatre-going. The radio scripts escape this dilemma, but have to sacrifice the visual reinforcement of the bleakness communicated by the words and the silences.

PUBLICATIONS

The first text mentioned indicates the language of the original version. Translations are by the author unless otherwise stated.

Plays and dramatic monologues

En attendant Godot (produced 1953), 1952; as *Waiting for Godot: Tragicomedy* (produced 1955), 1954

Fin de partie followed by *Acte sans paroles I*, with music by John Beckett (produced 1957), 1957; as *Endgame: A Play in One Act; Followed by Act Without Words: A Mime for One Player* (*Endgame* produced 1958; *Act Without Words* produced 1960), 1958

All That Fall, (broadcast 1957; produced 1965), 1957; as *Tous ceux qui tombent*, translated by Beckett and Robert Pinget, 1957

From an Abandoned Work, 1958; as *D'un ouvrage abandonné*, translated by Ludovic and Agnès Janvier in collaboration with the author, 1967

Krapp's Last Tape (produced 1958), with *Embers*, 1959; as *La Dernière Bande*, translated by Beckett and Pierre Leyris, 1960

Embers (broadcast 1959), with *Krapp's Last Tape*, 1959; as *Cendres*, translated by Beckett and Robert Pinget, 1960

Krapp's Last Tape and Other Dramatic Pieces (includes *All That Fall, Embers, Act Without Words I and II*), 1960

Happy Days (produced 1961), 1962; as *Oh, les beaux jours*, 1963; bilingual edition, edited by James Knowlson, 1978

Words and Music with music by John Beckett (broadcast 1962), in *Play and Two Short Pieces for Radio*, 1964; as *Paroles et Musique*, 1966

Play (as *Spiel*, produced 1963; as *Play*, produced 1964), in *Play and Two Short Pieces for Radio*, 1964; as *Comédie*, 1966

Play and Two Short Pieces for Radio, 1964

Acte sans paroles II, 1966; as *Act Without Words II* (produced 1960), in *Krapp's Last Tape and Other Dramatic Pieces*, 1960

Cascando with music by Marcel Mihalovici (broadcast 1963), 1966; as *Cascando: A Radio Piece for Music and Voice* (broadcast 1964; produced 1970), in *Play and Two short Pieces for Radio*, 1964

Film (screenplay, in English), 1967

Eh Joe (televised 1966), in *Eh Joe and Other Writings*, 1967; as *Dis Joe*, 1966; first televised in German, 1966

Eh Joe and Other Writings, (includes *Act Without Words II* and *Film*), 1967

Come and Go: Dramaticule (produced 1968), 1967; as *Va et*

for five years he failed to find a management to take it. In spite of support from well-known authors, seven theatres and 11 directors turned it down. The best plays by well-known authors like Verne and Dumas *père* were running for 400 or 500 performances, and both authors and managements naturally queued up for one another. There was little room for experiment or innovation. Becque therefore took to journalism, writing for *Le Peuple* for 15 months until June 1877, and later, for two months in 1881, for *Henri IV*, and then for *L'Union Républicaine*. He also turned back to light comedy, writing *La Navette*, produced at the Gymnase on 15 November 1878, and the one-act *Les Honnêtes Femmes*, produced at the Gymnase on 1 January 1880, before finally managing to get the Comédie-Française to accept *Les Corbeaux*, which had probably been written in 1872–73 but was not staged until 14 September 1882.

The first night was stormy, even though act one scene 12 was omitted because Vigneron's son makes fun at his father's expense just before the news of his father's death is announced. The play was regarded as offending against good taste and good stagecraft, and the last scene, in which, after the play's apparent resolution with the engagement of Teissier and Marie, Dupuis comes in as a creditor demanding money, also had to be dropped. There were several outbursts, and in act three scene 11 the actress playing Mme de Saint-Genis left the stage, but noisy first nights were by now firmly part of a Paris theatrical tradition which had been exploited by Victor Hugo and would carry on being exploited by Diaghilev. They were almost a rite in themselves. So, too, in a shorter time span, was the adverse review in *Le Temps* by Francisque Sarcey, no doubt less than pleased that 14 years earlier the director of the Vaudeville had preferred Sardou's judgement to his own before deciding to accept *L'Enfant prodigue*. The play, however, ran for only 18 performances.

Late in 1882 the Comédie-Française nevertheless commissioned *La Parisienne*, which was supposed to be ready in March 1883. Becque had still not completed the text early in 1885. He had been employed by *Le Matin* for several months in 1884, before moving on to the *Revue Illustrée* for three years. In both he attacked the new fashion for cremation: "You can have your father burnt for 15 francs." *La Parisienne* was finally played on 7 February 1885. It made Becque money, most of which went to pay off debts, and he found himself increasingly in demand as a journalist and speaker. He lectured in Brussels in 1885, on Molière in Paris in 1886, and wrote for *Le Gaulois*, which had published his poem "Le frisson" in 1884, wrote for *Le Figaro*, and on 29 December 1886 was made a member of the Légion d'Honneur. From 1889 he lived with his brother. Their sister, twice married, died on 14 November 1890, and her married daughter in April 1893. Then in March 1894 Charles died.

Becque was now writing for many of the leading newspapers and reviews, including the *Vie Parisienne, Le Journal*, and *Gil Blas*. In 1887 he started a new play, *Les Polichinelles*, which he never managed to finish to his own satisfaction. He failed several times to get elected to the Académie Française, travelled to Italy, began to frequent fashionable society, and published the two volumes of his *Théâtre complet* in 1890. There was to be a three-volume edition in 1898. Towards the end of his life Becque lived in some squalor and poverty. *Les Corbeaux* had finally brought him in 25,000 francs, including publishers' royalties, and *La Parisienne* 11,000 francs, but there were debts to pay off and Becque's income was never regular, nor was he ever careful about financial matters. He never married, had numerous brief

liaisons, was attached to his sister's daughter's two sons, and from 1894 was given a state pension, as well as an income from the Société des Auteurs and a normal old age pension. His income was nevertheless inadequate and he was heavily in debt when he died. From 1896 Becque's health deteriorated. In April 1899 he fell asleep in bed with a cigar in his mouth. He recovered from the effects of the resulting fire, was invited to the country, where he stayed for a few days, but returned to Paris to die on 12 May 1899 after four days in hospital.

WORKS

Of Becque's three performed and published plays that are not just routine comedies, the first, *Michel Pauper* of 1870, remains historically important for its introduction of a working-class hero. The play was staged barely weeks before the outbreak of the Franco-Prussian War, and the uprising which followed it, therefore at the twilight of the Second Empire. For obvious reasons the commercial formal theatre, whose function was still partly to provide entertainment for the relatively affluent, dealt more conservatively with social issues than did the novel, but even in the novel neither Balzac, whom Becque greatly admired, nor the mid-century realist (q.v.) school had introduced seriously tragic heroes from the working class. Zola's *Le Roman experimental* did not appear until 1880. Becque's play is not a tragedy, but it does inch forward in its social attitudes, even if its satire of Second Empire speculation, the quest for quick money, and the corrosive effects of luxury was becoming commonplace, even on the stage. There is a directness of tone in the study of the workman inventor who marries the spoilt and self-centred daughter of his rich backer which announces what is to come.

No doubt on account of what Becque knew to be its daring of tone and subject, *Les Corbeaux* is a meticulously written play, with all its effects, however unadventurous the theme may seem today, carefully calculated. That is why it took the best part of a year to write. It had to attract the theatre-going audience while presenting a true reflection of real life that was gripping without being witty, complicated, or just amusingly satirical. The play is about the Vigneron family, who are trying to save what they can from the collapse of their affairs with Vigneron's death, and the predations of the vultures of the title. Becque wants to hold the play together by atmosphere and tension, not by character or plot, so in the first act nothing at all happens. The scene is set by the introduction of the family, the whole group fulfilling the dramatic function given in a romantic (q.v.) play to a single figure. There are three Vigneron daughters: Marie, Blanche, and Judith. Marie's engagement is the penultimate note in the cadence which resolves the play's situation, while the romantic Blanche, whose engagement to Georges Saint-Genis has been broken off, may at the end be about to go mad, and Judith's situation is left in the air. The removal of the final scene completely altered the meaning of the play's resolution by removing the ironic comment on what was an unhappy ending. The role of all three daughters is subordinated to interest in the family group.

In order to prevent any of his characters becoming the focus of dramatic identification, Becque made his dialogue extremely economical. No character is allowed to say or do anything not strictly necessary to create a rounded presentation of the group. Mme Vigneron is a good, honest mother, out of her depth in the legal nastinesses of her situation. Her daughters are not strongly characterized, and the vultures are not exaggeratedly villainous. Only Vigneron, who dies in act one, is given obtrusive characteristics, and only in act one does the need for an exposition push Becque into departing from calculatedly realistic dialogue. His points have to be made without leaving the plane of the normal.

In the first act the table is being set for dinner. The family joke, tease, bicker, and make uncomplimentary remarks about the guests they expect, and who then arrive. In the meanwhile Vigneron has gone off to pay a brief visit to the factory, and the news of his death is announced. The rest of the play is about the plight of the family as the debts are revealed, projected marriages compromised as a result, and the vultures come to look for the pickings: first Mme de Saint-Genis, whose son Georges was to marry Blanche, then Teissier, Vigneron's former colleague, then Bourdon, the lawyer. Marie's marriage to Teissier is her self-sacrifice to the values of society for the sake of the group.

What makes this play so powerful is the refusal to allow the characters to depart from perfectly normal responses to an extraordinary and humiliating, once-in-a-lifetime situation. The resultant exploration of actual human psychology becomes painfully penetrating. Everything in the play, and particularly the intervals of time which are allowed to pass between the acts, is subordinated to unveiling the psychological motivation of the socially normative. The audience is very cleverly tricked out of its ordinary catharsis through the contrast of heroes and villains and given instead a much more deeply satisfying insight into how and why people behave as they do. The critics were not mistaken in catching a whiff of distaste from the play. Social behaviour is much more often distasteful than disgusting, and that is the point which Becque manages to get across so brilliantly. The extraordinary power of his play is apparent from the way in which it has proved independent of the actual social setting and bourgeois values which Becque had to assume in the France of the 1870s.

La Parisienne gives a biting account of a ménage à trois, and again strips away the haze of social hypocrisy through which we see how people behave and delude themselves. *Les Polichinelles* returned to the world of financial speculation, but since Becque was plainly dissatisfied with what he had written it would be unreasonable to comment on the text he never published in his own lifetime. The dialogue is already very polished, and the sense of overall distaste even more powerful than in *Les Corbeaux*. Becque's distrust of dramatization, in the sense of theatricality, is still sometimes criticized, but it is the foundation for the power of his plays.

PUBLICATIONS

Collections

Théâtre complet, 2 vols., 1890
Théâtre complet, 3 vols., 1898
Oeuvres complètes, 7 vols., 1924–26

Plays

L'Enfant prodigue, (produced 1868), 1868
Michel Pauper (produced 1871), 1870
L'Enlèvement (produced 1871), 1871

La Navette, (produced 1878); 1878; as *The Merry-Go-Round*, 1913
Les Honnêtes Femmes (produced 1880), 1880
Les Corbeaux (produced 1882), 1882; as *The Vultures*, 1950
La Parisienne (produced 1885), 1885; as *The Woman of Paris*, 1955

Other

Sardanapale (opera; produced 1867), 1867
Sonnets mélancoliques, 1887–88
Querelles littéraires, 1890
Souvenirs d'un auteur dramatique, 1895
Les Polichinelles, 1910

Biographical and critical studies

Arnaoutovitch, A. *Henri Becque*, 3 vols., 1927
Descotes, M., *Henry Becque et son théâtre*, 1962

BENDA, Julien, 1867–1956.

Essayist, novelist, political and social philosopher, and critic.

LIFE

Benda's outstanding literary importance depends neither on his fiction nor on his numerous volumes of criticism and political philosophy, but on his intellectual stance and his radical defence of rationality, and therefore of the role of the "intellectual," in a world of imaginations disorientated by two world wars and minds torn between competing political, religious, and social ideologies. He argued, notably against Bergsonianism, the need for a strictly rational interpretative evaluation of the phenomena of experience. He himself was clearly torn, however, between his passionate commitment to political pamphleteering and his conviction that it was the intellectual's duty to maintain a distance from all literary, intellectual, political, and social movements in order to establish a vantage point from which to deliver rational analysis and dispassionate comment. Not to maintain the necessary distance but to join the movements was what Benda termed "la trahison des clercs (the treason of the intellectuals)."

It has been argued against Benda that he himself did not avoid the sort of commitment which he deplored in others aspiring to the status of "intellectual." He did not himself see that commitment to social justice was incompatible, however, with the dispassionate appraisal of social values which he regarded as the intellectual's task. He was not at all the apostle of the ivory tower, and the most passionate of all his commitments was to disinterested intellectual appraisal.

Benda was born in Paris on 26 December 1867 and educated at Louis-le-Grand. Both his parents were Jewish, of bourgeois origin. At school, significantly for his later career, Benda was drawn towards both the classics and mathematics. The pattern was completed by his devotion to the piano. He started to study mathematics, preparing for entry to the Ecole Polytechnique at the Ecole Centrale, a period he did not enjoy. When that seemed like a false start, Benda moved to the Sorbonne to study history, obtaining his "licence" in 1894. He had formed a life-long attachment to the Graeco-Roman ideal of order and abstraction and a passionate commitment to rationality. He never ceased to enjoy music, never married, never regarded the world as tragic, and never thought of himself as its victim.

His chief activity was journalism. As a young man he became one of the extraordinarily talented team organized by Alexandre Natanson to write for the *Revue Blanche* (1891–1903). Léon Blum was the literary and drama critic, while Debussy covered music. Alongside Benda, the review published Mallarmé, Régnier, and Vielé-Griffin. It also introduced Ibsen and Tolstoy to French readers. Benda, who came to despise the sentimental and the mystical approach to life and literature, therefore started his literary career in the all-pervading cultural atmosphere of fashionable late symbolism (q.v.), although he later affirmed that he was never at home there, and graduated to write for the *Nouvelle Revue Française* (q.v.), the *Mercure de France, Divan*, and *Le Figaro*.

Benda's first volume publication was the *Dialogues à Byzance*, issued by the publishing house of the *Revue Blanche* in 1900, a series of philosophical reflections on the Dreyfus case first published in the review. Years later, in 1945, Benda was to return to the image of Byzantium in *La France byzantine; ou, Le Triomphe de la littérature pure: Mallarmé, Gide, Proust, Valéry, Alain, Giraudoux, Suarès, les surréalistes*, all of whom, with a dozen others, he condemned as guilty of romanticism (q.v.) or preciosity. Five years later still, in *De quelques constantes de l'esprit humain: critique du mobilisme contemporain*, Benda swept away Bergson, Bachelard, and Bruschvicg with the same brush. What shocks is not the vigour of his attack on the fashionable intellectual idols, but its lack of discrimination. Benda may have been broadly right, although not about Gide or Proust, to whom he in any case also deferred, but his intellectual discernment did not take into account the realities of cultural history, or the different needs felt by different authors at different dates to explore or expound different interpretations of actual or possible forms of personal and social experience. He almost arrogantly practised what he saw as "rationality" to the point of practically excluding himself from the cultural community in France, as if an isolation verging on intellectual ostracism was the best demonstration of right-mindedness. Benda's rationality was static, eternal, and Graeco-Roman, if not Platonic. He lacked any real sense of history or even temporality, a deficiency which prevented the possibility of any sympathy for Hegel, let alone Marx or Bergson.

The pro-Dreyfus articles collected in the *Dialogues* are especially important in the present context on two counts. Firstly, and perhaps surprisingly, they went against Benda's naturally fastidious and almost 18th-century sensual taste and his submergence in his adopted culture. His aesthetic preferences took him to the army's side, to the preservation of order in society, rather than towards the defence of Dreyfus and Péguy, whose close collaborator he became in the years leading up to World War I. Benda was bourgeois and authoritarian. He found any attachment to the mystiques of toil and soil distasteful. He was a Jew, but thoroughly Hellenized. He disliked Jewish assumptions of racial supremacy and Zionism, preferring the Judaism of his mother, "the little Jewess of the Paris Marais, scribbling and petulant," to that of his father, "a Jew of the Orient of antiquity, in love with eternity." The Jews disliked his distance from their religion, but during World War II, although he was not murdered, as he might have been, his books, files, and papers were destroyed by the Nazis and he was made to wear the Jewish yellow star.

Secondly, it was Benda who first ensured the survival of the term "intellectuel" as a French noun, with all the equivocal associations it acquired during the Dreyfus affair, when it was taken to mean someone who lived according to "intellectual" or rational norms, and was therefore on Dreyfus's side, and was used sneeringly of those who forgot the honour of France and the grandeur of its mystique in the name of what they argued was justice for some condemned Jew. As a noun the term was used by *L'Aurore* on 14 January 1898 at the head of a "Manifeste des intellectuels." Barrès and Brunetière immediately scoffed. The term was used derisively by Barrès in the title of the second chapter of the 1902 *Scènes et doctrines du nationalisme*, "Les intellectuels ou logiciens de l'absolu." Anatole France criticized the use of the word as bad French, and Barrès ridiculed it, but Dreyfus appropriated it, proud of the label. The word still has derogatory overtones in some French circles, as in the Anglo-Saxon world.

With the exception of the two attacks on Bergson, *Le Bergsonisme; ou, Une philosophie de la mobilité* and *Sur le succès du Bergsonisme*, published by the *Mercure de France*, the other books published by Benda prior to the outbreak of World War I were all issued by the publishing house associated with the *Cahiers de la Quinzaine: Mon premier testament, Dialogue d'Eleuthère, Une philosophie pathétique*, and the two-volume novel *L'Ordination*, which was set to obtain the Prix Goncourt until Léon Hennique placed an avowedly anti-semitic vote in favour of André Savignon's *Les Filles de la pluie*.

Immediately after the war Benda published one of his two most famous works, *Belphégor*, which can be grouped with the second, the famous *La Trahison des clercs* of 1927, by which Benda is usually remembered. The title of this second work made history, but the book did not sell. It took 17 years to clear the 500 copies of the 10th impression. Only since 1970 has Benda's manifesto begun to enjoy the prestige it undoubtedly deserves. The 11th impression of 2,795 copies was cleared in five years, and another 2,500 copies had to be printed. Although an English translation by Richard Aldington had appeared as early as 1928, a Penguin paperback in the UK, an Italian paperback of 1976, and the German translation of 1978 published by Ullstein testify to the relatively sudden increase in interest in Benda, now also available in Japanese, at the beginning of the last quarter of the century. The only possible reason for this interest is a growing feeling that he might have been right in pointing to a betrayal by the intellectuals of their independence of judgement in the interests of political commitment.

Benda himself came strongly to disapprove of the withdrawal from concern with political and social values of the cultural devotees of symbolism and other believers in the lofty elevation of artistic endeavour above the mundane considerations of social and political philosophy. He himself never felt that any of his passionate commitments had been wrong—not to Dreyfus, or to socialism, or to the Abyssians, or to the Spanish republicans. Where he differed from those he considered to have committed "treason" was that he never blinded himself to the terrible injustices being perpetrated in the name of the causes he considered most just. It has been pointed out that in Vienna in 1952, for instance, he did not pretend to agree that the Jewish doctors were plotting to murder Stalin in order not to offend the communists. If the world, perhaps feeling the need of a moral leadership it only diminishingly derives from religious leaderships, creates a serious role for a disinterested analysis of its values to be undertaken with rational objectivity by its "intellectuals," then Benda will turn out to have been one of its most important 20th-century prophets.

Works

Benda's fiction does not show to its fullest advantage his fierce talent as a pamphleteer crusading for objective intellectual independence. The personal and imaginative side of his literary creation finds a more adequate form in the anecdotal memoirs of his intellectual life from *Mon premier testament* onwards, including particularly *La Jeunesse d'un clerc*, *Un régulier dans le siècle*, and *Exercice d'un enterré vif*. The fictions all concern the temptations of the flesh which lead away from the life of the spirit. The most important novel, *L'Ordination*, concerns Félix, who starts a liaison with Madeleine, finds that her affection weighs him down, and breaks off with her. Ten years later, married to Clémence, he has a daughter, Suzanne. When Suzanne becomes ill, Félix falls prey to self-doubt and remorse. Has he been a bad husband? A bad father? Has he betrayed himself as an intellectual by his concern for Suzanne, "his moral race"?

In *Les Amorandes* the 26-year-old Etienne falls in love with a 43-year-old surgeon's widow, Irène Valentin, who becomes his mistress. His family is in despair, particularly his cousin and childhood companion, Geneviève, who is in love with him. Irène receives a letter from them persuading her to leave Etienne. He finally marries Geneviève, though he does not love her. They stay together, united by a child: Etienne has remained faithful to his race. The short stories of *La Croix de roses* also treat of similar plots, always with the same sort of sexual explicitness as contained in the novels. The critical reception of all three works of pure fiction was poor, and it looks as if Benda was achieving little more than an imaginative release for the suppressed affectivity of the dedicated intellectual.

His attacks on Bergson, although technically philosophical, are naturally connected with Bergson's hostility to Hegel, so implacably opposed to considering time as static. It is not the Bergsonian notion of duration which disturbs Benda, however, so much as the idea of intuition, the notion that it is possible to regard things as symbols or manifestations of ideas or ideals. Benda came therefore explicitly to reject the aesthetic of Mallarmé and Valéry, which, had it still been a force to be reckoned with, would have challenged his belief that rationality was the unique key to understanding and representing external reality. It is as if he had gone back beyond Hegel to Kant and the 18th century again. He did indeed take much from Kant, but he was also a French positivist, apt to refer approvingly to Comte, Renan, and Taine. He accepted Taine's notion of historical determinism.

The attack in *Belphégor* is directed at the artistic and intellectual degeneracy of French social life. For Benda both the authors and the readers of France around the time of World War I had lost their taste for intellectual pleasure. In his view, the real joy of the artist, the philosopher, and even the scientist should be the intellectual pleasure generated by their own activities themselves, and not even by their results. The political has its rights, even over life itself, but never over judgement. The betrayal of which Benda speaks in *La Trahison* is any deference of intellectual judgement to social or political pressure. The intellect must remain clear and the judgement analytical and independent. The intellectual is there to judge, evaluate, and if necessary condemn.

Truth and justice command loyalties beyond those of caste and country, and they should dictate conduct. What Benda denounces is the dependence of art and social life on sensation and emotion, on the irrational and half finished. He is of course right that it would have been a better world if rationality had been capable of calming sensibilities reeling from the impact of World War I. Benda lacks the imaginative vision to see why the world had turned away from his ideal. Whether that lack of sympathy disqualified him from leading it back to the ideal is not clear. His vision was clearly prophetic, probably utopian, and perhaps naive or even wrong-headed. He may have argued the 18th-century case too absolutely. None the less, a great deal of what he said needed saying, whatever forces were pulling his culture in the opposite direction to the one in which he wished to lead it. Intellectuals may commit themselves morally, even physically, but it is their duty to keep their minds free of the influence of passion. There are signs that Benda is a much greater imaginative thinker than has yet been acknowledged.

Publications

Political and social philosophy

Dialogues à Byzance, 1900
Mon premier testament, 1910 (dated 1908)
Le Bergsonisme; ou, Une philosophie de la mobilité, 1912
Sur le succès du Bergsonisme, 1914
Une philosophie pathétique, 1913
Les Sentiments de Critias, 1917
Belphégor: essai sur l'esthétique de la présente société français
    1918; as *Belphegor*, 1929
Le Bouquet de Glycère, 1918
Billets de Sirius, 1925
Lettres à Melisande pour son education philosophique, 1925
Pour les vieux garçons, 1926
La Trahison des clercs, 1927; as *The Treason of the Intellectuals*, 1928; as *The Great Betrayal*, 1928; as *The Betrayal of the Intellectuals*, 1955
Cléanthis; ou, Du beau et de l'actuel, 1928
Properce; ou, Les Amants de Tibur, 1928
La Fin de l'éternel, 1928
Supplément à De l'esprit du faction de Saint- Evremond, 1929
Appositions, 1930
Essai d'un discours cohérent sur les rapports de Dieu et du monde, 1931
Esquisse d'une histoire des Français dans leur volonté d'être une nation, 1932
Discours à la nation européenne, 1933
Délice d'Eleuthère, 1935
La Jeunesse d'un clerc, 1936
Un régulier dans le siècle, 1937

Précision (1930–1937), 1937
La Grande Epreuve des démocraties, 1942
Le Rapport d'Uriel, 1943
Un Antisémite sincère, 1944
La France byzantine; ou, Le Triomphe de la littérature pure: Mallarmé, Gide, Proust, Valéry, Alain, Giraudoux, Suarès, les surréalistes, 1945
Exercice d'un enterré vif, 1946
Non possumus, 1946
Du poétique, 1946
Tradition de l'existentialisme; ou, Les Philosophies de la vie, 1947
Du style d'idées, 1948
Trois idoles romantiques: le dynamisme, l'existentialisme, la dialectique matérialiste, 1948
Deux croisades pour la paix, juridique et sentimentale, 1948
Les Cahiers d'un clerc (1936–1949), 1949
Songe d'Eleuthère, 1949
De quelques constantes de l'esprit humain: critique du mobilisme contemporain, 1950
Mémoires d'infra-tombe, 1952

Novels and Short Stories

Dialogue d'Eleuthère, 1911
L'Ordination, 2 vols., 1911–12; as 1 vol., 1913; as *The Yoke of Pity*, 1913
Les Amorandes, 1922
La Croix des roses (short stories), 1923

Other

Entretien avec Julien Benda, with F. Lefevre, 1925

Critical studies

Niess, Robert J., *Julien Benda*, 1956
Nichols, Ray, *Treason, Tradition, and the Intellectual: Julien Benda and Political Discourse*, 1978

———

BERGSON, Henri (-Louis), 1859–1941.

Philosopher and essayist; winner of the Nobel prize for literature (1928).

LIFE

Henri Bergson's career was that of a normal academic philosopher, and he published nothing other than philosophy. However, his conception of what that discipline was, and of the way philosophizing should be conducted, determined his sometimes poetic style, which was full of metaphor and imagery and occasionally even rhapsodic. His philosophy, far from focusing on the technical analysis of thought, language, or mental processes, was devoted to the whole spectrum of human energy, from knowledge, thought, memory, perception, and feeling to religion, humour, morality, and the experience of duration. Bergson has therefore sometimes been regarded more as a poet or a mystic than as a philosopher, especially since the formal discipline of philosophy has tended since World War II to confine itself either to the technical analysis of language or to one or other of the developments of phenomenology (q.v.), leaving the broader field of the human sciences to the anthropologists, the philosophers of religion or history, the biologists, and a small handful of philosophers like Bergson himself. Bergson's theory of the imagination and his influence on imaginative writers make it not altogether surprising that he should have been awarded the Nobel prize for literature.

He was born in Paris on 12 October 1859, the son of a Jewish musician and an English mother. He was educated at the Lycée Condorcet, and, from 1878 to 1881, the Ecole Normale Supérieure (ENS). For the next 16 years he taught in various lycées, at Angers, Clermont-Ferrand, where he also lectured at the university, and Paris, where he taught at the Lycée Henri IV. He then taught for three years at the ENS before being appointed in 1900 to a chair at the Collège de France, which he kept until ill health forced him to resign it to Edouard Le Roy in 1924. Le Roy had in fact substituted for him since 1921. His doctorate was awarded for a thesis which Bergson published in 1889 as the *Essai sur les données immédiates de la conscience*. In 1891 he married Louise Neuberger, a cousin of Marcel Proust. His lectures were sufficiently non-technical to attract audiences from the non-academic and fashionable worlds of Paris. It was said at any rate that, to be sure of getting a seat for Bergson, you had to sit through the preceding lecture.

From 1901 Bergson was a member of the Académie des Sciences Morales et Politiques and he was sent on a number of cultural missions, notably to the US and to Spain before, during, and after World War I. In 1914 he became a member of the Académie Française and from 1922 to 1925 he was a member of the Commission Internationale de Coopération Intellectuelle. In the year of the Nobel prize he also received the Grand-Croix of the Légion d'Honneur. In the meanwhile he had published his most important works, *Matière et mémoire: essai sur la relation du corps avec l'esprit* in 1896, *Le Rire* in 1900, the "Introduction à la métaphysique" in 1903, and his most celebrated work, *L'Evolution créatrice* in 1907. His next really important work was to be *Les Deux sources de la morale et de la religion*, published 25 years later, in 1932. In the last year of his life Bergson said he would have become a Catholic, had it not been for his desire to avoid separating himself from his fellow Jews in this way. In fact he was on the list of eminent Frenchmen not to be molested by the occupying forces. He died in Paris on 3 January 1941.

WORKS

The central distinction on which Bergson's thought hinges is that between analysis, which is the reduction of the complex to simple constituents, and intuition, which is the direct awareness of a reality. Time, for instance, can be perceived spatially, broken up into moments for purposes of scientific measurement, or, as an inner experience of duration or continuity, it can be the object of intuition. The philosopher's point of departure is the intuitive or immediate awareness of the life of the spirit as it is lived and not, for example, as the psychologist can analyse it. In both method and subject matter philosophy therefore differs from science. Science is necessary for the understanding and manipulation of the real world, but the true nature of reality is revealed only by intuition. Bergson's whole philosophical work is a series of endeavours to deal with the problems connected with this view. Is there some stable reality underlying the flow of things which is the object of intuition and, if so, how do we know about it? Are individual things fictions created by intellection? How can an immediate awareness of a vital impetus in ourselves, the famous "élan vital," lead to objectively true statements about creative evolution, the "évolution créatrice"? These are some of the questions which Bergson tries, in a series of different ways, to answer.

Among the problems to which his way of philosophizing does provide a solution is that of freedom. If time is regarded as succession, then motives or feelings can precede actions and must seem to determine them by an assumption written into the premise about the nature of time. A motive is not a substantive thing which shoves from outside, although we talk as if it were. If, however, time is duration, and there is no succession but only simultaneity between motive and act, then acts can arise spontaneously from the flow of energy which is life without having preceding "motives." These acts are free: "We are free when our acts flow from our whole personality, when they express it, when they resemble it as an artist's work sometimes resembles him." Bergson has not exactly defined freedom here, since he saw perfectly well in the *Essai sur les données immédiates de la conscience* that any definition of freedom implied determinism. To define liberty of choice, for instance, the ego has to be conceived as capable of oscillation. The spatial analogy cannot be avoided. To define liberty of choice, it has to be analysed, and analysis transforms a process into a thing, duration into extension. In fact, we are rarely free, since most of our lives have to be lived under external constraints and therefore at the level of our superficial selves. Here Bergson is in fact engineering the philosophical mechanism which will liberate philosophy from Kantian categories and open the way for existentialism (q.v.).

After the *Essai* came *Matière et mémoire* and the problem of the mind–matter, soul–body dualism. Here Bergson needs to consider the nature of matter. Can mental processes be a product of cerebral organization? It might just be possible to describe the activities of the memory in that way, but Bergson distinguished between the memory of motor mechanisms and stimuli—by which we learn to recite a poem, for instance, a faculty we have in common with parrots—and spiritual memory, where images are stored and from which they can be recalled to consciousness, or can indeed thrust themselves upon it. Spiritual memory implies a level of mental activity which is infra-conscious. Bergson suggests that the function of the brain is to inhibit the invasion of consciousness by the pure memory and to exercise a selectivity in admitting to the consciousness that which is required by it. Pure memory, not linked to any specific part of the brain, is something humans do not share with parrots.

Perception and memory are different in kind, although in practice perception is invariably infected by memories. It is memory images contributed by the mind to concrete perception which give perception's object a coherent and meaningful form.

Pure perception, which never occurs, would be a material brain process. Pure memory is a spiritual activity of which the object is the material image. It is not clear that Bergson has in this way solved the problems raised by the interaction of mind and matter, and indeed he was conscious of having done little more than clear some of the obstacles out of the way. But his philosophy is the product of a new and powerful vision of man. This vision is taken much further forward in *L'Evolution créatrice*, in which Bergson introduces the notion of complexification which was so important, for instance, to Teilhard de Chardin. Although Bergson was fully won over to the idea of evolution, by 1907 Darwin's theory of natural selection was looking antiquatedly mechanistic. Chance cannot account for the development of the eye in both the mollusc and the mammal. Chance and teleological solutions to the direction of evolution seemed to Bergson equally inadequate. Evolution for Bergson is the product of an organizing central "élan," or vital impulse, proceeding onwards while producing differentiation at the periphery, where new species establish themselves prior to producing further differentiation, with each new species sharing in the "élan vital" of the continuum. The three levels of plant life, instinctive life, and intelligent life coexist in man as divergent, not successive, stages of life.

Here again, Bergson is conscious of having constructed no philosophical system. He has indicated a potentially fruitful approach to the solution of an important problem, just as he had done in *Le Rire*, which saw laughter as a social defence mechanism to enable us to readjust to abruptly changed circumstances, rules of behaviour, or events. Bergson's last main work, *Les Deux sources*, deals with man's moral and religious life. Bergson is at the other pole of moral philosophy from Kant's categorical imperative, but he does start with man's sense of obligation and the freedom which responsibility presupposes, "every obligation, taken separately, implies freedom." The source of obligation for Bergson is social. However isolated, each individual has or partly is his "social ego." Mostly we conform to social pressure without reflection or constraint. It is only when we rebel against social pressure that we become conscious of obligation.

By 1932 Bergson had started to write less rigorously. He was over 70, and his use of the term "obligation" is loose. The word has too many meanings. Is obligation a feeling? If so, it is caused by social pressure. But sometimes obligation is not the feeling, but the pressure itself, in which case it is non-moral. Bergson further confuses the issue by introducing the concept of "the totality of obligation," which is sometimes posterior to individual obligations, as being their sum or quintessence, and is sometimes seen as "the habit of contracting habits," in which case it would have to be a necessary precondition for the formation of the society which imposes obligations.

Bergson's literary power lies in the imaginative strength he deploys in his different efforts to tackle the perennial problems of philosophy, and in the new way in which he envisages human life and the development of the race itself. He is clearly right in much of what he sweeps away but, by contenting himself with converging efforts employing similar philosophical instruments, he conveys the immensity of the problems as well as the grandeur of the solutions it is necessary to envisage. He is one of the great innovators not in technical philosophy but in a philosophical approach to the understanding of the individual and social experience of human beings.

PUBLICATIONS

Collections

Oeuvres complètes, 3 vols., 1945–46
Oeuvres, Bibliothèque de la Pléiade, 1959

Philosophy

Quid Aristotle de loco senserit, 1889
Essai sur les données immédiates de la conscience, 1889; as
    *Time and Free Will: An Essay on the Immediate Data of Con-
    sciousness*, 1910
Matière et mémoire: essai sur la relation du corps avec l'esprit,
    1896; as *Matter and Memory*, 1910
Le Rire: essai sur la signification du comique, 1900; as *Laugh-
    ter: An Essay on the Meaning of the Comic*, 1911
"Le Rêve," in *Bulletin de l'Institut Général Psychologique*, 3,
    1901; as *Dreams*, 1914
"Introduction à la métaphysique," in *Revue de Métaphysique et
    de Morale*, 29, 1903; as *Introduction to Metaphysics*, 1912
L'Evolution créatrice, 1907; as *Creative Evolution*, 1911
La Perception du changement (lectures), 1911
Choix de textes, 1911
L'Intuition philosophique, 1911
Le Matérialsme actuel, with others, 1913
La Signification de la guerre, 1915; in *The Meaning of War, Life
    and Matter in Conflict*, 1915
The Meaning of War, Life and Matter in Conflict, 1915
L'Energie spirituelle: essais et conférences, 1919; as *Mind-
    Energy: Lectures and Essays*, 1920
Durée et simultanéitié: à propos de la théorie d'Einstein, 1922;
    as *Duration and Simultaneity*, 1965
Réflexions sur le temps, l'espace et la vie, 1929
Les Deux sources de la morale et de la religion, 1932; as *The
    Two Sources of Morality and Religion*, 1935
La Pensée et le mouvant: essais et conférences, 1934; as *The
    Creative Mind*, 1946
Le Bon Sens et les études classiques, 1947
Ecrits et paroles, edited by R.-M. Mossé-Bastide, 3 vols., 1957–59
Mélanges, 1972

Other

Translator and editor, *Extraits de Lucrèce: avec un commentaire
    des notes et une étude sur la poésie, la philosophie et la
    langue de Lucrèce* 1883; selections as *The Philosophy of
    Poetry: The Genius of Lucretius*, 1959

Bibliography

Gunter, P.A.Y., *Henri Bergson: A Bibliography*, 1974

Critical studies

Béguin, A., and P. Thévenaz (editors), *Henri Bergson: essais et
    temoignages*, 1942
Alexander, Ian W., *Bergson: Philosopher of Reflection*, 1957
Hanna, Thomas (editor), *The Bergsonian Heritage*, 1962
Pilkington, Anthony E., *Bergson and His Influence: A Reassess-
    ment*, 1976

BERNANOS, Georges, 1888–1948.

Novelist and essayist.

LIFE

Bernanos was the third child of Jean-François Bernanos, known
as Emile, an upholsterer from a partly Spanish family of artisans
who had come to Paris from Bouzonville during the Second
Empire. His mother, Hermance Moreau, was the daughter of a
farmer who came from a peasant family at Pellevoisin. One
child died in infancy, but Bernanos had an elder sister, Marie-
Thérèse, born on 17 December 1883. He himself was born in
Paris on 20 February 1888. The family moved within Paris, and
Bernanos spent his childhood and youth there, although he subsequently scarcely ever mentioned the city. Family holidays
were spent first at Pellevoisin and then, importantly for Bernanos's fiction, at Fressin in the Pas-de-Calais, where Bernanos's father acquired a large house in 1894. It became the
family's permanent residence from about 1904, and Bernanos
always remembered it fondly, claiming that he had spent the
happiest days of his youth there. He liked shooting, climbing
trees, and pretending to sing Mass.

From 1897 until 1900 Bernanos was educated by the Jesuits
in Rue de Vaugirard. He made his first Communion and wanted
to become a priest, but there is a year missing from the record
before we learn that he was at the junior seminary of Notre-
Dame-des-Champs as a boarder from 1901 to 1903. He very
much disliked the life there, and remained near the bottom of the
class, though he attracted attention for his French composition.
His parents finally moved him to the junior seminary at
Bourges, where Bernanos appears to have to come to life, and to
have done even better at French. However, in 1904 he twice
failed the oral part of his baccalauréat, and his parents finally
moved him again to board at Sainte-Marie d'Aire-sur-la-Lys,
where he once again passed the written and failed the oral examination of the first part of the baccalauréat, finally getting
through at the resit in November 1905. In 1906 he passed the
second part with ease. He continued to correspond with the
Abbé Lagrange, whom he had met at his last school, and who
was from Bourges. Lagrange clearly exercised a moderating
influence on his political and even religious enthusiasms, and
the major themes of his later fiction—childhood, death, and the
quest for sanctity—already began to appear in his letters. His
indifferent health had made him frightened of death from very
early in his life, although he went through a less intense period
before renewing his inner commitment to religion when he was
17.

At that age the fundamental structures of his spirituality were
already fixed. He knew that he did not wish to withdraw from
the world and become a priest, and he had a firm hierarchy of
spiritual values which differed from the categories of "mortal"
and "venial" sin which dominated the moral teaching of Catholic priests and schools at the turn of the century. He went to Mass
daily, was a daily communicant, said his rosary, and recited
daily at least a token part of the monastic office, compline, but
he was not merely an observant Catholic. He developed a profound sense of the power and presence of evil, and of the purificatory role of suffering. Bernanos's father was Catholic,
monarchist, and an adherent of the new nationalism. Like most
well-off artisans, he took the anti-semitic newspaper *La Libre*

Parole, founded by Edouard Drumont in 1892, partly in reaction to the misappropriation of funds by the Panama Canal Company uncovered in that year. Bernanos's father read from it aloud every day. Drumont's thick two-volume *La France juive*, 100,000 copies of which had been printed in 1886, had helped to capture the new middle class for the militarist right, inspiring them, as Bernanos was to point out, with "un sentiment héroïque (a heroic feeling)," which he took to be the true root of his values. It was through the eyes of Drumont that Bernanos discovered what he believed to be the injustices of society. *La France juive* also taught him not to over-value money or its pursuit.

Although Catholic research, particularly that of Monsignor d'Hulst, inspired Drumont, the specifically Catholic populism resulting from the Dreyfus affair found its expression in Marc Sangnier's *Le Sillon*, first established as a monthly in 1894, but reorganized in 1899 and condemned by the pope in 1910. The political counterpart to the organ was the Action Française movement, founded in 1899 but not producing a daily of that name until 21 March 1908. The anti-clerical Combes administration was formed in 1902, religious congregations were banned in 1903, and diplomatic relations with the Holy See broken in 1904. Church and state in France were separated in 1905, and Bernanos sympathized strongly with the opposition led by the Action Française, which was also against the "modernist" liberalization of Catholic dogma condemned by the pope in *Pascendi* in 1907. By 1906 Bernanos's intellectual position had shifted from the Action Française to Maurras's Catholic positivism to which he remained publicly faithful until 1932.

The other important influence on the young Bernanos was Balzac, in whom he also admired the Catholic and monarchist, the chronicler of the development of the society attacked by Drumont. Bernanos stole the key to his father's book cupboard to gain access to Balzac. From Balzac he moved on to Pascal and the now forgotten Catholic novelist Ernest Hello. In 1908, while studying law at the Institut Catholique, Bernanos joined the group of royalists, workers, and students who distributed *L'Action Française*. In 1913 he graduated in law and letters and, driven by Catholicism, nationalism, and monarchism, was ambitious to take part in political life. He had already got involved in street brawls in 1908 on the occasion of François Thalamas's anti-nationalist lectures on Joan of Arc. Twice in the early weeks of 1909 he was arrested, and in March he spent five days in prison. He wrote his first newspaper article on "Les effets du préjugé démocratique dans le monde des lettres." It was published in *Soyons Libres!* for 6 and 20 March.

It is important for an understanding of his later evolution to note Bernanos's experience of the alliance inspired by Maurras between militant socialist and Catholic royalist oppositions to the conservative, bourgeois, and democratic establishment. Although he enjoyed the group activity, Bernanos himself, was almost heretically liberal on social issues. Maurras attributed many of France's ills to Bernanos's revered Pascal, and admired both Anatole France and Renan, neither of whom could possibly appeal to the committedly idealistic Bernanos. He had more in common with the dashingly perverse Barbey d'Aurevilly, from whom, as a novelist, he was to take some of his characters.

It was through the Action Française that Bernanos, who had now obtained his "licence," was appointed editor of the weekly *L'Avant-Garde de Normandie*, an organ of "nationalisme intégral" with stongly right-wing and nationalistic overtones. In over 70 articles between October 1913 and August 1914 Bernanos defended the ideals and ideas of the Action Française against the republican weekly and the two Rouen dailies, one liberal republican and the other radical. Dreyfus's condemnation was just, the Revolution a disaster, a counter-revolution necessary, and the restoration of the monarchy was to be France's salvation. The great enemy was the republican, anti-clerical, and anti-militarist philosophy teacher Alain. The newspaper closed down with the outbreak of World War I.

Bernanos had been demobilized on health grounds in 1910 after four weeks of military service. He now managed to re-enlist, and served in the trenches until the end of the war, spending eight weeks attached to the air corps, and another two months recovering from a wound in 1918. In 1914 he had become engaged to Jeanne Talbert d'Arc, to whom he was finally married on 11 May 1917, with Drumont's strongly antisemitic collaborator, Léon Daudet, as his witness. Bernanos and his wife were to have six children, Chantal, Yves, Claude, Michel, Dominique, and Jean-Loup. He himself became a corporal, and was decorated for bravery. We have only a few letters, mostly to Jeanne, with which to follow Bernanos's intellectual evolution at this time, but it is clear from them that he became overwhelmed by the futility of the war, and lost his firm devotion to the principles defended by the Action Française, ending up more romantically royalist than nationalist. He also disliked the propaganda smoke screen, and began to write, trying to overcome the temptation to bolster his courage with hatred. He was later to fight shy of ex-service organizations.

By the end of the war Bernanos had found much to admire in Bloy, whose dislike of a society sullied by the mere pursuit of gain he was to echo, and whose attitudes to generosity, humility, and poverty he was to adopt. Above all, he derived from Bloy the elevating effects of the struggle between hope and despair, and the ideas of the communion of saints, vicarious sacrifice, and the sudden incursion of grace into ordinary life, which were to characterize his own spirituality.

Bernanos was demobilized in July 1919. His second child was born in August. The Action Française had decayed into just another parliamentary group instead of continuing to cherish counter-revolutionary dreams, and Bernanos resigned, although he did not make public the breach with Maurras until his "Réponse à Charles Maurras" published in *Le Figaro* on 21 May 1932. With the encouragement of his father-in-law, an executive of a large insurance company, Bernanos became an inspector for La Nationale with responsibility for the east of France. He lived in Paris until 1924, when he moved to Bar-le-Duc. He was disappointed that the post-war period failed to bring a spiritual renewal, wanted to write, felt the need to repudiate the society which was emerging from the turmoil, and finally wrote *Sous le soleil de Satan*, as he said in 1936, entirely for himself. Since he is known to have left unpublished other texts, now lost, it is perfectly possible that he did not originally write that novel for publication.

In 1919 Bernanos had met the Catholic writer Robert Vallery-Radot, editor of *L'Univers*, who passed on Bernanos's "Madame Dargent" to the *Revue Hebdomadaire*, which published it on 7 January 1922. He had begun *Sous le soleil de Satan* in 1919. The third part, "Le saint de Lumbres," was written first, finished by the summer of 1923, followed by the first, "L'histoire de Mouchette," and finally the second, "La tentation du désespoir," which was finished by April 1925. In June 1923 Bernanos had been recovering from an urgent operation for peritonitis, from which he had nearly died, but the book's lengthy gestation seems to have been due above all to a determination to create the novel which corresponded exactly to his imaginative needs. On 2 May 1925 he sent a typed copy of his manuscript to Vallery-Radot, who got it accepted by Massis at Plon in October, though not without some difficulty. Maritain was on the readers' committee, and Bernanos was published in the same collection as Maritain, Claudel, Ghéon, Ramuz, and Chesterton, "Le roseau d'or." Maritain insisted on toning down the power of Satan as originally depicted, and an extract appeared in the *Revue Hebdomadaire* for 13 March 1926. The novel was published at the end of the month. In a letter to a colleague announcing his resignation from La Nationale, Bernanos boasted in June 1926 of 58,000 copies sold in less than three months, five translations, and 215 reviews. Daniel Halévy meanwhile had forecast sales of 500.

For the rest of his life Bernanos was to be in financial difficulties. *Saint Dominique* was published in the *Revue Universelle* in November 1926. Begun that summer, *L'Imposture* was finished in March and published by Plon in November 1927. *La Joie* was begun in August 1927, finished in December 1928, and published by Plon in April 1929. In December it was awarded the Prix Femina. Bernanos's father had died of cancer of the liver on 2 January 1927, and his mother died on 8 March 1930. *La Grande Peur des bien-pensants* was published by Grasset in April 1931. In the meanwhile, late in 1926, Pius XI, looking for a rapprochement with republican France with its powerful left wing, had condemned the Action Française and put seven of Maurras's works on the index of prohibited books. He also banned the newspaper, in which Maurras's invective against the Jews, the left, the masons, and the Germans had gone as far as threatening murder. Bernanos rallied to Maurras's defence, but not to his excesses, and regretfully accepted the condemnation, deploring the failure of the Action Française to have renewed itself spiritually before the authorities intervened. He reaffirmed his monarchism and his dismay at what had happened in a whole series of articles and conferences between 1927 and 1930, after which he distanced himself increasingly from Maurras. In 1932, Maurras broke publicly with him, after which Bernanos also broke with *Le Figaro*, when it supported a policy of "national unity."

Bernanos and his family moved three times between 1926 and 1927. They lived at Clermont-de-l'Oise from 1927 until 1930, when Bernanos sold his house and rented a succession of villas on the Côte d'Azur until 1934. On 21 July 1933 he was knocked off his motorbike. He had to have several operations, and needed to use a stick to get about for the rest of his life. His sixth child was born on 30 September, and his financial situation was getting desperate. He started to turn his pen to detective novels, collaborating on *Un crime*. A new contract with Plon brought him further advances, but he decided to go and live in Majorca, where life was cheaper. His furniture, books, and some of his papers were auctioned by the owner of the villa near Hyères, where the family were living, on account of several months' arrears of rent. Although Bernanos wrote a succession of letters to say how cheap life was on Majorca, the family moved half a dozen times in their two and a half years in Palma, from October 1934 to March 1937.

Un crime was published in 1935, and Bernanos wrote *Un*

mauvais rêve, which was not published until 1950, the *Journal d'un curé de campagne*, which was finished in January and published in March 1936, and won the academy's Grand Prix du Roman, and the *Nouvelle Histoire de Mouchette*, finished in September 1936 and published in May 1937. Bernanos also kept a diary on political developments in Spain, publishing parts of it regularly in the Dominican review *Sept*. From 1934 Plon was paying him by the typescript page, 60 francs for each page of clean copy. Earlier original manuscripts had been virtually indecipherable with crossings out and insertions. The rhythm of production was weighing Bernanos down. "Pas de page, pas de pain (No page, no bread)," as he himself wrote. What broke him finally, however, was his spiritual reaction to the outbreak of the Civil War in Spain on 18 July 1936. Apart from the last chapter of *Monsieur Ouine* and the *Dialogue des Carmélites*, he was thereafter to write only essays and polemical pieces. To start with, he firmly supported Franco, and his son Yves volunteered to join the Falange. Later on he was revolted by Franco's repression and the attitude of the Spanish hierarchy, and after his return to France he wrote *Les Grands Cimetières sous la lune* between May 1937 and April 1938. The articles published in *Sept* can be seen in retrospect as a preliminary sketch for this last work.

The decision to leave Majorca was partly political, and had partly to do with the irregularity of the post and the flow of money from Plon. Bernanos's letters contain shrieks of urgency. For a time he considered going back to the world of insurance rather than see his wife worry herself to death. He knew that he would get interested in it again, and that that would be the end of the books. In January 1937 he asked a friend to see if his old company might give him an agency again. He left Majorca on 27 March and the on 31st was in Marseilles, where he stayed with friends, before moving to two successive villas near Toulon. *Les Grands Cimetières* was published on 22 April 1938. It fiercely attacked Franco's repression, and its first edition sold out in a fortnight.

The resultant easing of his financial plight revived Bernanos's old dream of going to Paraguay. Discouraged by the attitude of the Western Allies towards the threat of Hitler, he and his family embarked for Asunción on 20 July 1938. Three friends from his youth had settled in Paraguay 20 years earlier. The country was in the grip of a civil war, however, and Bernanos found the climate in August hard to tolerate, and the cost of living too high. He returned to Rio, arriving on 1 September, and spent the next seven years in Brazil, where he wrote his long series of important pamphlets. He cried with joy when he heard de Gaulle's stand on 18 June 1940, and could not understand how Maurras could have supported Vichy. Brazilian writers and friends rallied to his support, and after two preliminary attempts he was eventually found a farm he could hire which was big enough to keep him and his family. The farm failed, but Bernanos managed to buy another smaller property, where he stayed for five years. It suited him, he said, because the doors had no locks, the windows no panes, and the rooms no ceilings.

He wrote for the Brazilian press, for the BBC, for various Free French publications, and the *Lettres aux Anglais*, finally leaving Brazil with regret in June 1945. He needed the inspiration of the places where he had spent his youth if he was to write fiction again. De Gaulle had called him back, and his journalistic activity now became frenetic. Whereas in Majorca he had at least been able to keep the Spanish diary while writing for 60 francs a page, he now either had to produce articles or starve. *Le Chemin de la Croix-des-Ames* and *La France contre les robots* were written during the war in Brazil and published clandestinely. *Français, si vous saviez* collected some of the post-war articles written in France. Conscious of France's humiliation, Bernanos, along with others, like Raymond Aron, desired only to rebuild it. This was the theme of numerous articles, and of the lectures given in Belgium, Geneva, and Paris in 1946 and 1947 and published in 1953 as *La Liberté pour quoi faire?* Bernanos turned down the Légion d'Honneur, as also the possibility of election to the Académie Française. Mauriac had offered to propose him, and made his refusal the subject of a public polemic. Bernanos also quarrelled with Claudel, who had been too enthusiastic about the martyrs to Franco's cause for his taste.

Bernanos moved house another half-dozen times. The *Dialogue des Carmélites* was written as a favour for a priest friend who was making a film of a well-known short story by Gertrud von Le Fort, *Die Letzte am Schafott*. Later, of course, it became a play and a music drama. In January 1948 Bernanos fell ill with a liver complaint. He was brought back to Paris from Tunis and underwent operations in May and June. He died early on 5 July 1948 with his wife at his bedside. The only official representatives at his funeral were Spanish republicans and envoys from Latin American governments. Only André Malraux and Pierre Bourdan attended from the French literary world. Bernanos's literary monument was the Pléiade edition of his novels.

WORKS

Sous le soleil de Satan concerns the fate of man caught between God and the devil. It is a "Catholic" novel in the sense only that Bernanos, like other "Catholic" novelists, finds that he can understand his own experience and that of other people from within and not outside a Christian spirituality which fits more or less within the tight and supportive limits of Catholic dogmatic orthodoxy. It may be that the novelist finds that the exploration of his experience entails an imaginative identification with Jesus, the suffering, or prophetic, or even the glorious Jesus. The Catholicism of any Catholic novelist, because it depends for its power on the light it sheds on human experience, must nevertheless exploit the dogmas, and the story of Christ's life, as if they were myths, as indeed, in so far as they are embedded in, and widely understood by, a now largely secular culture, they are. This holds irrespective of whether or not novelist, character, or reader regards any aspect of the "myth" as literally true. Not only is the Catholic novelist not a teacher. He also invariably uses the myth to support a spirituality, which is something different from a theology, and even in the Western tradition of Latin Christianity has never been subject to the same constraints of orthodoxy.

Catholic imaginative writers, Greene, Waugh, Bloy, Claudel, Mauriac, Péguy, Huysmans, as well as Bernanos himself, have very often caused theological eyebrows to rise, but where they do, the theologians have missed the point. Any imaginative writer, Catholic or not, can be judged not by his orthodoxy, but only by the power of his exploration of experience, as judged by those for whom he writes, or who choose to read him. Bernanos's particular obsessions, the imaginative patterns within which he probes the significance of his world, isolate a particular set of values, which together constitute a particular Catholic

spirituality. It is not the same as Mauriac's, or Péguy's, or Claudel's.

Bernanos published his first fiction in 1907, but became famous only with *Sous le soleil de satan* in 1926. The first and most obvious characteristic of that novel is to give every ordinary human event a supernatural dimension, even those which do not require recourse to other than everyday experience for their explanation, as when Germaine Malorthy could have told from the change in colour of her lover's eyes what lay in store for her. Where a Barbey d'Aurevilly would merely have related the fact, Bernanos's psychology invites recourse to an awareness of supernatural forces behind quite ordinary phenomena, "Le regard du marquis hésita une seconde, puis se durcit… Le bleu pâle des prunelles verdit. A ce moment, Germaine eût pu y lire son destin (The marquis's gaze hesitated a second, then hardened…The pale blue of his pupils became green. At that moment Germaine could have read her destiny in them)."

The reader, prepared by these invitations to have to resort to supernatural explanations for reactions and events, is ultimately obliged by the narration to invoke them. In this gradual and plausible pressurizing of the reader to have recourse to explanations entailing the action of supernatural forces of whose presence he is constantly made aware that Bernanos's genius as a novelist lies. He gently guides the reader along a path which forces him to suspend disbelief in the constant miracles of sin and grace. They appear as the only possible explanations of common physical sensations, reactions, and events. It was Malraux who immediately saw how Bernanos did not analyse emotional crises, but first depicted the anguish of his character, then made the character react, and then allowed the character to surprise himself by having done something he was not consciously aware that he was doing.

The narrator of *Sous le soleil de Satan* makes all this explicit. The characters themselve perceive only the bewildering effects of divine, or diabolic, intervention on their behaviour. The first part of the book takes place around 1880. Five years after Mouchette's suicide Donissan is made parish priest of Lumbres, and Mouchette does not appear in the novel's second part. Yet, said Bernanos, Donissan does not appear by chance, "Mouchette's savage cry of despair made him indispensable." Without Mouchette's presence in the novel, Donissan would not have achieved sanctity by his terrifying expiation. Mouchette leaves the house at night and kills her second lover, not the the Marquis de Cadignac, by whom whom she was pregnant. It is on Christmas night that Donissan receives his vocation to redeem her action by overcoming the temptation to commit suicide out of self-contempt, after losing the way to Etaples and meeting the horse dealer. The reader becomes increasingly aware of the pervasive presence of Satan behind the joviality and in the oppressive circle inside which Donissan is hemmed. Bernanos is cleverly trading on the reader's awareness of biblical associations, Lucifer as the father of lies and the master of darkness, the bearer of false dawns, and Satan's domination during the night at Gethsemane.

In the last part of the novel Donissan meets Satan again at the bedside of little Havret, now dead. Donissan overcomes the classical temptation to spiritual pride, which is merely suggested by the narrator, using language that hints that what Donissan is feeling must come from Satan. It is the narrator here who counts on the reader to recognize from the language that the perfectly possible miracle of resurrecting the child is in fact a temptation.

Today the novel already requires detailed annotation, not only because of the subtlety of its biblical allusions, but also because of the whole history of the Curé d'Ars and his encounters with the devil, to which Donissan's in the novel are also an allusion. This would have been more readily understood by French Catholics in 1926 than it can be by Anglo-Saxon readers three quarters of a century later. The novel is about the achievement of sanctity through the acceptance of damnation as a means of saving others through love. This notion builds on a deep knowledge of a whole French mystical tradition and on the popular understanding of what happened to the Curé d'Ars. In Bernanos's case it probably derives from an interest in Sirmond and his 17th-century exorcisms at Loudun, which he may have known about through Bremond's delightful but unreliable *Histoire littéraire du sentiment religieux en France*.

L'Imposture of 1927 is about the renegade Abbé Cénabre, and is set in the darkness of Paris, while *La Joie* of 1929 is about the 17-year-old Chantal de Clergerie, who had first appeared in the fourth part of the earlier novel. She is a creature of brightness and hope, and the novel is set in the warm light of the Norman countryside in summer. The two novels together form a diptych, and Bernanos wrote that he would have liked to have fused them into a single whole. A second priest, Chevance, who dies in *L'Imposture*, links the novels, since he is present in Chantal's mind in *La Joie*. Both novels are about the redemption of Cénabre and draw heavily on the New Testament.

Cénable, a priest, finds that he has lost his faith. Metaphors of darkness predominate. The son of an alcoholic, poor, and ambitious, he chose the priesthood, not in response to a vocation but in pursuit of a career. He is probably also modelled on Henri Bremond, himself a priest with an inclination to modernism. Bremond wrote his history of mysticism in 17th-century France from a strictly literary point of view, with a detached irony which, while it makes the 11 volumes into a masterpiece, was not calculated to please Bernanos. Cénable is a tragic figure, an impostor who must start to live his lie over again every day until his dual personality reaches "son horrible maturité, connaît qu'il n'a plus de place pour lui sur la terre, et va se dissoudre dans la haine surnaturelle dont il est né (its horrible maturity, knows that there is nowhere left for it on earth, and dissolves in the supernatural hate in which it was born)." Once again the reader is led carefully into assuming the constant presence not only of supernatural force, but of the devil and his disguises.

The novel centres on the analysis not only of Cénabre's psychological but of his spiritual descent into the depths. The Latin for the depths to which Christ descended after death, the "inferi," usually translated as "hell," actually means something different. Bernanos plays on all the meanings of "depths," from the purely psychological, through the dark night of the soul as described by the classical mystics of the 16th and 17th centuries, to the actuality of eternal suffering. Cénabre can be redeemed only by the double sacrifice of the ignominious deaths of Chevance, whom Cénabre resents, and of Chantal: "Ce qui se formait en lui échappait à toute prise de l'intelligence, ne ressemblait à rien, restait distinct de sa vie, bien que sa vie en fût ébranlée à une profondeur inouïe. C'était comme la jubilation d'un autre être (What was forming inside him escaped any grasp of the intelligence, resembled nothing else, remained distinct from his life, although his life had been uprooted to an unheard-of depth. It was like the triumph of another being)."

As the devil takes possession of what used to be Cénabre's personality, which drowns in black despair, "from second to second the silence becomes denser, more motionless, around his despair." The night of Cénabre's despair is balanced by the night of Chevance's saintly and expiatory death. The description of the agony, with its multiple allusions and its dream quest for Cénabre, in which Chevance struggles with death, is one of the masterpieces of psychological description in French fiction. In his agonized dream Chevance begs Cénabre not to let him die and, meeting no response, takes a soft, inert hand from the darkness and presses it to his breast. The flame which brings light at the end of the dream is also the flame consuming Cénabre, or which might have consumed Cénabre in hell. Chantal, helping Chevance to die, offers him her own joy, implicitly accepting her own death. Bernanos expects the reader here to accept Chantal's self-identification with Theresa of Lisieux.

The saintly characters and the sinners in both novels, Cénabre, Chevance, and Chantal, contrast with the ordinary, worldly characters into whose lives the supernatural makes no obvious incursion, and who are the objects of Bernanos's satire. Chantal's father has no desire but to become a member of the academy. He lives surrounded by "Mama," who is ancient and half mad, the drugged chauffeur Fiodor, the psychiatrist La Pérouse, who is attempting what is really the priest's job, and Cénabre. The journalist Guérou's friends include a progressive monsignor, republican Catholics, religious journalists like Pernichon, who writes the religious chronicle for a radical paper, financed for socialist purposes by a conservative. Pernichon "exhausts the substance of shame with the patience and industry of an insect." Chantal is a pretty girl, innocent to the point of abnormality, who likes driving fast cars, cooks well, and feels like fooling around. The allusions again pile up as the earth she kisses at what she imagines to be the foot of the cross on which Judas hanged himself turns into the garden of olives, with its associations of betrayal. The reader is not spared Jesus's dying meditation on Judas. The sweat of blood arises from Jesus's despair at saving Judas, compassion for whom overwhelms him. It is after her prayer that Chantal's imagination stretches out to the dead Cénabre. What actually happens in the novel is told in metaphors and allusions rather than in narrative. Chantal is shot by Fiodor before he himself commits suicide, but the point is why she dies, not how, and what she accomplishes in dying.

The *Journal d'un curé de campagne* is Bernanos's best-known novel and is written in the first person, as its title implies. The diary form allows Bernanos to emphasize the importance of the mundane in a life of spiritual tension and to fix like a flash photograph the image of a fleeting moment. The Curé d'Ambricourt's character is instantly clear from the way in which he reflects about his ordinary preoccupations and his colleagues, referring to them formally as "M le curé de..." Bernanos allows the reader to perceive the obvious limits to the narrator's imagination and spiritual understanding. There are implicit allusions to John of the Cross and the dark night of the soul, but the curé's spirituality is the "little way" of Theresa of Lisieux.

The novel is in three sections, the major portion coming between two others of only a score of pages each. A final letter from the commercial traveller and ex-priest Louis Dufrety, with whom the curé had been staying, informs the Curé de Torcy of the Curé d'Ambricourt's final hours as he died of stomach cancer, the physical ailment used as a metaphor from the novel's first page. Bernanos fully exploits the potential of the diary form, with flashbacks, long reflections, pieces of narrative, short aphoristic phrases, notes to a possible reader, scratchings out, and second thoughts, in which only the reported direct speech and the longer pieces of narrative impose a strain on the reader's belief in the form's authenticity. The popularity of the novel derives, almost paradoxically, from the relaxation of mystical intensity relative to its predecessors. The social tensions in the château, the death of the perfunctorily practising but bitter and rebellious countess whom the curé wins over before she dies, the forwardness of her daughter, Chantal, aware of her father's adultery with her governess, and the cold insensitive correctness of the count are not only well depicted, but confront the reader with the social problems facing so many rural priests. Primarily there for their country parishioners, they are also obliged to demand deference from, although not to wield authority over the family at the local château.

What attracts the reader's attention is the psychology of the curé as it appears from his diary rather than the mystical doctrine against which Bernanos wants his readers to understand the curé's experience. *Monsieur Ouine* is more complex, and deals with reactions to the murder of a young servant. Bernanos removed such hints as he had originally included about the identity of the murderer, since he was not writing a detective novel. He had certainly envisaged pinning the blame on to M. Ouine, the language teacher who is always saying either "Oui" or "Non," and who is intended as a satire of Gide. The final text also leaves others open to suspicion, however, just as it leaves unresolved a number of other problems thrown up in the course of the narrative. The point is the spiritual event caused, or symbolized, in the village by the murder, and brought out by the reaction to the Curé de Fenouille's funeral sermon. The true events are the interior ones, not those out of which a conventional story might be woven, and which Bernanos goes out of his way to leave unresolved. There is a suggestion, little more, that Monsieur Ouine may be the force of evil incarnate, disguised, peaceful, apparently harmless, but the cause of death, or its analogues, such as emptiness.

La Grande Peur des bien-pensants and *Les Grands Cimetières sous la lune* are Bernanos's political testaments, the defence of Drumont expressing Bernanos's own monarchism, Catholicism, and disgust at the modern world, and then spiritual disillusionment with it, which destroyed the personal vision of sin and grace that lay behind his fiction. *La Grande Peur des bien-pensants* was thought out by 1928, written in the two following years, and published by Grasset in April 1931. With it belong the three short essays *Saint Dominique, Noël à la maison de France*, and *Jeanne, relapse et sainte*. There is a break between the preoccupations expressed in those works and those of *Les Grands Cimetières sous la lune*, which grew out of the diary Bernanos kept between May 1936 and January 1837. The Dominicans of *Sept* published seven of his articles, leaving an eighth to be published posthumously, but Bernanos was upset by the way in which the editors carefully abstained from committing themselves to his views. He lost his complete manuscript, and wrote a second version late in 1937, published by Plon in May 1938.

Bernanos continued to speak with a prophetic voice, no longer a great novelist, impossible to consider as belonging either to the right or to the left, but remaining true to his own fundamental values. These, too, developed, although less than his changes of political commitment might suggest, and seem to have been dominated to the end by values absorbed in childhood and youth. Bernanos disliked being called a polemicist, but his polemical writings are among the finest in French, just as his novels are among the most powerful to appear in France between the wars.

PUBLICATIONS

Collections

Oeuvres, 1947
Oeuvres romanesques, Bibliothèque de la Pléiade, 1974
Essais et écrits de combat, Bibliothèque de la Pléiade, 1971

Fiction

Sous le soleil de Satan, 1926; as *The Star of Satan*, 1940; as *Under the Sun of Satan*, 1949
L'Imposture, 1927
La Joie, 1929; as *Joy*, 1948
Un crime, 1935; as *The crime*, 1936
Journal d'un curé de campagne, 1936; as *The Diary of a Country Priest*, 1937
Nouvelle histoire de Mouchette, 1937; as *Mouchette* (in English), 1966
Monsieur Ouine, 1946 (1955 in completed form); as *The Open Mind*, 1945
Un mauvais rêve, 1950; as *Night is Darkest*, 1953
Dialogue des Carmélites, 1949; as *The Fearless Heart*, 1952; as *The Carmelites*, 1961; performed as a play 1952; opera with music by Francis Poulenc, 1960

Other

Saint Dominique, 1927
Noël à la maison de France, 1928
La Grande Peur des bien-pensants, 1931
Jeanne, relapse et sainte, 1934
Les Grands Cimetières sous la lune, 1938
Scandale de la vérité, 1939
Nous autres, Français, 1939
Lettres aux Anglais, 1942; with *Lettres aux Américains* and *Lettres aux Européens*, as *Plea for Liberty*, 1944
La France contre les robots, 1947 (Rio de Janeiro 1944)
Ecrits de combat, 1942–44
Le Chemin de la Croix-des-Ames, 1948
Les Enfants humiliés, 1949; as *The Tradition of Freedom*, 1950
La Liberté pour quoi faire?, 1953
Dialogue d'ombres (collected stories), 1955
Le Crépuscule des vieux, 1956
Français, si vous saviez, 1961
Last Essays, 1955
Combat pour la vérité (correspondence 1904–34), 1971
Combat pour la liberté (correspondence 1934–48), 1971

Critical and biographical studies

Blumenthal, Gerda, *The Poetic Image of Georges Bernanos*, 1965
Milner, Max, *Georges Bernanos*, 1967
Estève, Michel, *Georges Bernanos: un triple itinéraire*, 1981

See also the *Bulletin de la Société des Amis de G. Bernanos* and *Etudes bernanosiennes* (*Revue des Lettres Modernes*, 1961–).

————

BLOY, Léon (-Henri-Marie), 1846–1917.

Essayist, novelist, journalist, and author of religious polemic.

LIFE

Léon Bloy, who boasted about his working-class origins, actually came from a family of artisans, farmers, and soldiers. His father, Jean-Baptiste (born in 1814), became a civil servant. On 18 January 1844 he married Marie-Anne Careau, daughter of a comfortably off ex-soldier, by whom he had seven children, all boys. Bloy, born on 11 July 1846, was the second. The family lived near Périgueux, and Bloy was brought up fairly brutally. The atmosphere at home was republican and anti-clerical. Bloy's father was a free-mason, on the revolutionary side in 1848, and a believer in Rousseau. His wife was the less dominant influence on the children's education. She was Christian and pious, and was helped with her sons by her sister-in-law, who threatened Bloy that, if he wasn't good, the Jews would spit in his face.

At first Bloy had a conventionally Catholic education, but he was sent to the lycée at 12. He was rowdy and was expelled after a knife fight. His father took him to work with him to teach him geometry and industrial drawing, and at the same time Bloy rather unexpectedly started to read a good deal of poetry, and even began to write a verse tragedy, "Lucrèce." At the age of 18 he was sent to Paris with little more than a few addresses. He found a job as a draftsman in an architect's office at 100 francs a month, and shared an apartment with a friend, Victor Lalotte. In 1867, while trying to sell his 70-volume Voltaire because he was short of cash, Bloy presented himself to Barbey d'Aurevilly, who was passing the shop.

Barbey d'Aurevilly came to fascinate Bloy and rekindled his lost interest in religion. A letter of 15 February 1869 on faith and prayer shows Bloy's complete conviction of Catholicism's grandeur, but until 29 June 1869, like d'Aurevilly, he did not actually practise or communicate. There was already more than a hint of defiance in his reconversion, and it led to a break with his father. Barbey d'Aurevilly thought Bloy might become a Benedictine and Bloy considered a monastic vocation, but discovered that he did not have one. It was later to become clear that his Catholicism was overwhelmingly constructed on a sickly sensibility, responsive to beauty and suffering, but quick to violence, rebellious, and earthy. His piety was too sensual to lead to religious fulfilment, or, indeed, for him to remain orthodox.

Bloy had returned to Périgueux before the outbreak of the Franco-Prussian War on 19 July 1870. He joined the Garde Nationale, imagining himself to be fighting a "crusade" against "Protestant leprosy" and, looking at history's "vomitorium," convinced that the last day must surely be at hand. During his battalion's retreat to Brittany Bloy wrote an epic. In the contes

of *Sueur de sang* he was to write savagely about war scenes, some of which he imagined. On demobilization he nearly re-enlisted to fight the Commune in Paris. He had become rigidly conservative and authoritarian, but believed that prayer to Our Lady would resolve the world's political difficulties. Bloy seems to have given up literary ambitions after the war. He returned to Périgueux and worked in a lawyer's office, although he kept in touch with Barbey d'Aurevilly and with his friends Lalotte and Georges Landry. Relations with his father were tense, and Bloy complained about his own poverty, saying that only his religion saved him from suicide. In September 1872 he wrote a long meditation to Landry dwelling on the physical aspect of the crowning with thorns. They had communicated together at Périgueux on the feast of the Assumption on 15 August.

From 1871 to 1873 Bloy came under the influence of the Lyons Catholic philosopher Blanc de Saint-Bonnet, a believer in the divine right of kings, whose authoritarianism scarcely even pretended to a foundation in theological teaching. On Saint-Bonnet's advice Bloy turned down the offer of a teaching post at Périgueux and left definitively for Paris on 3 May 1873 to look for a post in Catholic journalism. He found a variety of brief jobs. For a short while he worked for Veuillot's *L'Univers*, then he spent a much longer period correcting Barbey d'Aurevilly's proofs. A daily communicant, Bloy was still looking for something to do in life, while his father, mother, and aunt were trying to make do at Périgueux on 800 francs a year. Bloy was making new friends, including the Catholic novelist Ernest Hello, Paul Bourget, and Arthur de Gobineau, and he remained close to Landry. In 1877 he found a new job with the railways, but was overwhelmed by a continuing sense of disgust. He was near a breakdown, knew himself to be psychologically weak, and found himself at once Catholic, royalist, and anti-clerical. Unlike Maurras, for instance, he recognized the intellectual impossibility of his position.

It seems to have been this situation which impelled Bloy to write. In 1876 he began work on the prose poem *La Chevalière de la mort*, and in 1877 he began a book on Barbey d'Aurevilly. That year his father died after a last-minute conversion, and Bloy became the lover of Anne-Marie Roulé. She had been abandoned by her unmarried mother and brought up by nuns, and was now a prostitute. She helped to keep Bloy, who could no longer communicate now that he was living in sin with her. Riddled with guilt, he was still concerned to convert others. He tried to give up Anne-Marie and to provide for her, went to confession, and vainly insisted on keeping his promise not to visit her at home. He decided to go on retreat to La Trappe, begging the loan he needed to go there. He wrote daily to Barbey d'Aurevilly, for whom he continued to work. In November 1877 he arrived at Périgueux to see his dying mother, but she was dead by the time he arrived.

He was still bound by his guilty attachment to Anne-Marie, which he tried again in vain to resolve by offering to marry her, and then pitching his financial needs too high for anyone to contemplate lending him the money. His next thought was to emigrate. He appears half to have foreseen the dominance of fascism and communism in Europe and to have been looking for a solution in the temporal supremacy of the papacy. By the end of the spring of 1878 he was in greater need than ever to flee Anne-Marie, his debts, and his job. He went back to the Trappist house at Soligny, determined to stay. The letters to Anne-Marie show a cooling of his continuing affection for her, but La Trappe this time revealed to him that he did love her. When he got back to Paris, they lived together again briefly, until Anne-Marie herself underwent a conversion which Bloy depicts as sudden, and which left him without a companion and without a job. The conversion may have been triggered by Anne-Marie's desire not to lose Bloy, whose sense of sin she probably knew to be too strong for their relationship to continue as it was.

At La Trappe Bloy had met a slightly mad old count, Roselly de Lorgues, who wanted to get Christopher Columbus canonized. Bloy undertook to write the four long articles which appeared in the *Revue du Monde Catholique* and formed the basis for his 1884 publication *Le Révélateur du globe: Christophe Colomb et sa béatification future*. His confessor, who was also Barbey d'Aurevilly's and Anne-Marie's, wanted Bloy to write about the appearance of the Virgin at La Salette in 1846, and took him on pilgrimage there in the late summer of 1878. Bloy was not moved, and the abbé fell ill. He was to die at La Salette three weeks after Bloy's return to Paris. Bloy did not have the training to write a critical account of the eschatological prophecies which were or were not made at La Salette but, partly kept by the Comtesse de Lorgues, did work on the subject of the apparitions.

Early in 1880 Anne-Marie met Ernest Hello, who was living in a state of mystical self-delusion. She rapidly began to think that the Holy Spirit had become incarnate in her, and Bloy, who was not given to mystical experiences of any sort and found even prayer arid, began to realize that she was mad. None the less, his own material and emotional circumstances had become so pitiful that he consciously began to move away from the Church by adopting a spirituality which he knew to be incompatible with Catholic orthodoxy. He began to look forward to the proximate reign of Christ on earth, the incarnation, suffering, and apotheosis of the Holy Spirit. Hello's wife refused to keep Anne-Marie at her house near Lorient in Brittany while Bloy went off again to La Salette, and Bloy and Hello, who had been very close, broke off relations. Bloy managed to borrow a considerable sum from the wife of a Jewish friend of Barbey d'Aurevilly, and took Anne-Marie to La Salette, from where he wrote further begging letters.

Little is known of his life in 1881. He worked as a clerk in the archives of the ministry of foreign affairs and made copies for the Bibliothèque Nationale. By early 1882 Anne-Marie had come to hate him, and at the end of June she was committed to an asylum. She was to spend the remaining 25 years of her life incarcerated. For his part, Bloy started to frequent Le Chat Noir, a literary cabaret in Montmartre, then still on the outskirts of Paris and with none of the associations the district was later to acquire. He became friendly there with Maurice Rollinat, with whom, thanks to another loan, he spent the summer of 1883. Bloy wrote about him for *Le Chat Noir*, in which he also defended Barbey d'Aurevilly against an attack on his *Une histoire sans nom*. That October Bloy went to the Grande Chartreuse to finish his book on Columbus. The monks helped him financially, and he lived by doing odd copying jobs and by begging from friends. He needed friends, but repulsed any offer of friendship, although he remained on close terms with one of the Carthusians. At the end of May 1884 he published his collected essays for *Le Chat Noir* as *Propos d'un entrepreneur de démolitions*, which is often violent in tone and generally directed at people. Although more discerning, the essays are more bitter and much less elegant than Barbey d'Aurevilly's attacks. Barbey

d'Aurevilly had himself written the preface to the book on Columbus, *Le Révélateur du globe*, which had appeared on 1 February.

On 14 June Bloy published a eulogy of Huysmans in *Le Chat Noir* and he and Landry became close friends of the novelist. Barbey d'Aurevilly was jealous. Bloy's letters of this date are full of vituperative insinuations, accusations, and libellously dismissive comments, as well as desperate pleas for money. The Carthusians sent him some more. By the end of 1884 he was working on *Le Désespéré*, complaining as ever about his perpetual state of mental and spiritual anguish. At the beginning of 1885 he began to publish *Le Pal*, for which the printer charged 300 francs per issue. The review appeared on 5, 10, and 25 March, its intention to release some of the bile festering inside Bloy, who scarcely managed to pay for the fourth and final issue of 2 April. In its four numbers Bloy really admired only Baudelaire and Barbey d'Aurevilly, and for the rest nourished his anger on originality, extraordinary vituperation, apocalyptic vision, and physical misery. Léon Daudet and Maurras were later to try unsuccessfully to turn Bloy's anger into a politically coherent doctrine. They are not generally thought to have succeeded in supplying an intellectual coherence, but what they lacked above all was the pain which inspired Bloy's bitterness.

By 5 March 1885 Bloy was living with Berthe Dumont and her mother, and was now friendly with Villiers de l'Isle-Adam. Bloy was looking despondently for money and for work. Berthe killed herself in May by using a dirty needle to inject herself with morphine. She died within four days and Bloy's distress was intense. Huysmans and Landry helped pay for the funeral, then Bloy and Landry stayed with Huysmans. However, Bloy owed money everywhere and was beginning to live as a tramp, breaking down and crying in the street. Late in 1885 he got some money from Rollinat and in October he was working again on *Le Désespéré*. Stock, the publisher, forced him to finish by having the book typeset while it was still being written, and obliged Bloy to make do with one set of proofs. In the end Bloy did finish, on 2 November 1886, but Stock refused to publish. Another publisher had to be found who would buy the sheets, or have the book printed again. Eventually, Soirat agreed to publish and had the type reset. The autobiographical novel, 2,000 copies of which were printed in its first edition, appeared on 15 January 1887. The critics were predictably venomous, and the novel ultimately caused a coolness between Bloy and Barbey d'Aurevilly, whom the novel had glorified, but who was under the influence of Bourget, whom it had attacked. It also gave rise to the eventual rupture with Huysmans. Only one or two reviews noticed the authentically prophetic nature of Bloy's denunciations underlying the sillinesses, the injustices, and the woolliness.

In 1887 Bloy was still seeing much of Huysmans and Villiers. *Le Désespéré* had failed commercially and Bloy spent the time miserably watching Barbey d'Aurevilly die and Villiers suffer. Huysmans was in despair at the encroaching madness of Anna Meunier, which made him break down and weep in front of Bloy. The only alleviation of this gloom was an offer to publish what became *Belluaires et porchers*. In 1888 a coolness developed between Bloy and Villiers, who had been working very hard and had neglected the friendship. On 4 July 1888 Bloy's mistress, a working woman, gave birth to his first child, Maurice Léon. The child died at the age of 12. At the end of 1888 Bloy finally found what looked like steady employment. Thanks to Huysmans, who had replaced Villiers on the newspaper, *Gil*

Blas hired Bloy. However, it dismissed him in February 1889, probably for his attack on the drama critic Francisque Sarcey (1827–1899) rather than for his dislike of the Eiffel Tower, which the whole of elegant Paris also deplored.

It was on his return from Villiers's funeral on 21 August 1889 that Bloy first met Johanne Charlotte Molbech, the daughter of a German professor of Scandinavian literature, and herself a former governess in England. At first she took pity on Bloy, then she fell in love with him, finally becoming a Catholic in order to marry him. They considered themselves engaged by the end of September 1889, and married on 27 May 1890. Bloy dedicated *Christophe Colomb devant les taureaux*, a collection of essays which he published that year, to his wife. A Belgian review published *La Chevalière de la mort*, and Bloy left with his wife for a lecture tour of Denmark. Their daughter Véronique was born on 16 June 1891. While Bloy was in Denmark he received a copy of Huysmans's *Là-bas* and recognized Henriette Maillat, his former mistress, in the guise of Hyacinthe Chantelouve, and thought Huysmans had poked fun at confidences he had made. His reaction, as prickly as could be expected, finalized the rupture that had been likely ever since the publication of *Le Désespéré*.

On Bloy's return he started a fresh life. He moved frequently, broke with many old friends, and wrote incessantly. *Le Salut par les Juifs*, an extraordinary prose poem in which Bloy identifies himself with Christ crucified by the Jews, and which ends with their conversion, appeared on 1 September 1892 in an edition of 2,000 copies. At the end of September he was taken back by *Gil Blas*. He attacked Bourget and Barrès, and published his first conte, "L'Abyssinien." Two more followed before the end of the year, and Bloy built up the two collections *Sueur de sang* and *Histoires désobligeantes*. On 1 February 1894 Bloy's wife gave birth to their son, André-Henry-Marie-Joseph. On 4 April Laurent Tailhade, who had defended an anarchist bomb in 1893, was himself wounded in a bomb attack. Some of the press applauded, led by an editor of the *Echo de Paris*, Edmond Lepelletier, whom Bloy then attacked in *Gil Blas*. He subsequently refused, in the most insulting terms he could think of, to fight a duel. The director of *Gil Blas* took his place, and the duel was stopped after a trivial wound, but Bloy was dismissed. Tailhade himself, interviewed about his friends, took care not to mention Bloy, who replied to the whole affair with *Léon Bloy devant les cochons*.

By the end of December 1894, Bloy was again destitute, with a wife and two children to support. A second son, Pierre-Ange-Lazare-Eugène-Marie-Joseph, was born on 24 September 1895. Bloy's wife had to go into a mental hospital for a time. His baby son was handed over to the Assistance Publique, but died on 10 December. As there was no baptism certificate, he was denied ecclesiastical burial. What saved Bloy was his new ability to work through everything. On 24 May 1897 he published *La Femme pauvre*. He had always kept a long daily journal, and now at last found that he was his own best subject, and best unadorned. At the end of April 1898 he published a section of the journal, *Le Mendiant ingrat*, to wide and discerning applause, but it was no more commercially successful than *La Femme pauvre*. The Dreyfus affair caused a break with Bloy's only remaining close friend, the painter Henri de Groux, who took Dreyfus's side. On 6 January 1899 Bloy left for Denmark, intending not to return to France. While there he wrote *Je m'accuse: notes sur Emile Zola*, and his book on Naundorff, *Le Fils de Louis XVI*.

He returned to Paris on 13 June 1900, staying with Henri de Groux and his wife. Within a week there was a serious estrangement, apparently the result of a mental aberration in de Groux, and the two friends did not see one another again for 17 years. Bloy moved to Lagny, 28 kilometres from Paris, where he stayed for four years. In 1901 he received the first letter from a rich patron, René Martineau. In the last period of his life Bloy reread much of his past material, with a view to publication or republication of some of it, finding it sad to dwell on the circumstances which had prompted *Le Désespéré*. He was no longer impressed by Maistre or by the letters of Barbey d'Aurevilly. Many former friends were dead. From late in 1900 he started to prepare the two-volume *L'Exégèse des lieux communs*. He retained many of his more irritating characteristics, such as a certain pig-headedness in his defence of the statues of Our Lady of La Salette.

In 1904 Bloy moved back to Montmartre, and then again, within what was still a village. In 1905 he got to know Jacques and Raïssa Maritain. At that date they had not been baptized and it was Bloy who converted them to Christianity. He moved again in 1906, remaining perpetually conscious of his failure on every level of his life. Even the title of *L'Invendable* suggests how haunted he was by inadequacy. Meanwhile, he had incurred the anger of the ecclesiastical authorities by publishing his 1908 book, *Celle qui pleure*, in which he revealed the message which Mélanie, one of the young persons concerned, said Our Lady had left with her at La Salette. Mélanie's own attempt to publish her account had, for good reason, been frustrated by ecclesiastical authority, since it was not only unorthodox, but dangerously unbalanced. In 1909 Bloy also wrote his great malediction of money, *Le Sang du pauvre*. A fifth volume of autobiography drawn from the diary, *Le Vieux de la montagne*, was published in 1911.

Bloy spent the winter of that year writing *L'Ame de Napoléon*, which appeared on 16 October 1912, and is generally considered to contain some of his best writing. Then came the sixth and seventh diary sections, covering the years 1910–12 and 1913–15, *Le Pèlerin de l'absolu* and *Au seuil de l'Apocalypse*. The war brought with it the inspiration for *Jeanne d'Arc et l'Allemagne*, published on 8 May 1915, again considered to be one of Bloy's best books, but still not commercially successful. That year he fell ill, but recovered sufficiently to work on *Les Méditations d'un solitaire* during the summer of 1916. His death came peacefully. Friends, including the Maritains, had watched over him for days. Martineau and the publisher Alfred Valette had called. Bloy told his wife he was curious about death. He died on Saturday, 3 November 1917.

WORKS

Although Bloy's best writing came from his mellow later years, he owes his genius to his tortured youth and early middle age. Had he been more educated his views would have been less wildly apocalyptic and, no doubt, more temperately expressed. The ferocious anger and bitterness engendered by the physical and mental tortures he undoubtedly courted later informed the great works of his maturity. Theological training, spiritual education, or psychological awareness would have dimmed the wick of his life and led to less violent resentments, fewer stiff-necked bouts of foolishness, a more coherent system of thought, but also less poetry, less strikingly prophetic a vision, and less burning a repudiation of injustice.

Bloy's possibly self-induced but acute feelings of inadequacy led him to almost paranoid bouts of insecurity. Something innate drove him to discover what depths of misery and humiliation he could drive himself to. By sending him gifts of money the Carthusians were helping him to survive a spiritual wound, a very deep personality disorder, the source of a spiritual experience which he and they valued. At almost any time Bloy could have traded it in for boredom and some sort of economic security, but he chose to live the life he led, or at least he chose the constraints which would determine it. The result was his imaginative need to project apocalyptic visions, like that of the incarnation of the Holy Spirit, the Holy Spirit's suffering, and the subsequent eschatological transformation of the world.

The images fit together according to the rules of what can only be a religious grammar, but which could not have been produced by a trained theologian. The meaning of the Greek and Latin terms for "nature" and "person" as applied to the theology of the Trinity and the incarnation of Christ in Western Christianity in the fourth and fifth centuries, and then defined by the rigorous theologians of the 13th, made the incarnation of the third person of the triune God literally unthinkable. It was a possibility the vocabulary was designed to exclude. Bloy's prophetic vision was spiritual rather than theological, and poetical rather than religious. Whatever he actually believed, and whatever the agonies he inflicted on himself by inhibiting his formidable sensual needs with guilt, his use of imagery taken from the life and death of Jesus, from Christian liturgy and devotion, was generally gruesome, always selective, and essentially poetic. Christianity's privileged position in French culture, and the exceptionally rich range of imagery it offers, has often led critics, not only of Bloy, to confuse theologies with spiritualities, and religion with imaginative vision.

Bloy returned to Paris from Périgueux after the Franco-Prussian War only in 1873, a Catholic again since 1869. His first important piece was the prose poem *La Chevalière de la mort*. The title, meaning "the horsewoman of death," alludes to the Apocalypse, the Catholic term for the Book of Revelation. The opening of the text immediately reveals how Bloy's imagination was working. Marie-Antoinette evokes associations of monarchism, of sacrifice, and of the desecration of the beautiful. She was born on All Souls' Day, 2 November, as was Barbey d'Aurevilly, although that link remains in Bloy's mind only. All Souls' Day, important in France for the custom of putting chrysanthemums on the graves of the dead, is heavily associated with everything in orthodox Catholic devotion which comes nearest to superstitition: praying for the dead in the first place, the practice of repeating the Mass three times, and the apocalyptic "sequence" hymn, the "Dies irae (Day of wrath)," repeated in each of the three liturgies. The word "lamentation" in this context necessarily recalls Jeremiah and the liturgy of the Passion in Holy Week. The text opens with three sentences, each longer than the one before, associating all these things in an evocation which is not at all religious, and has nothing to do with any theology or spirituality, but is mediated by the poetic juxtaposition of potent images:

Marie-Antoinette naquit le Jour des Morts. L'Eglise chantait la Colère et les assises épouvantables du juste Juge. Tous les sanctuaires catholiques retentissaient des lamentations des vivants priant pour les trépassés

(Marie-Antoinette was born on All Souls' Day. The Church was singing the wrath and the terrible judgement of the just Judge. All Catholic altars were resounding with the lamentations of the living praying for the departed)

The most striking feature of *Le Désespéré* is the horrifying way in which Bloy lashes himself with guilt over his liaison with Anne-Marie, which inspires the novel and which happened to coincide with the death of his father, whom he had never particularly loved. The central figure, a transposition of Bloy himself, regarded as a parricide like Cain in the Bible, is Caïn Marchenoir. The novel is shot through with incidents and people from Bloy's own life, but this does not make it an autobiography, or permit us to identify Bloy with Marchenoir. The novel celebrates the Catholic liturgy of the dead, monastic life, and the ugliness of domesticated piety and devotional literature. Bloy's description of the exhibition for sale of objects of piety is witheringly accurate.

The characters, although composite, are often intended to be recognized, but the tone oscillates rather uncertainly between something like authentic grandeur of inspiration and an almost demeaning literary pamphlet, hitting out at Mendès, Bourget, Brunetière, Daudet, and half a dozen others. Comfortable, established success, especially when it is without real imaginative vigour, arouses intense scorn, and a simple physical detail can turn a description instantly into a deft character assassination. Sometimes the insults heaped on the clergy seem there merely to display the muscle power of the dazzling vocabulary. They become detached from the deep indignation at the mediocritization implied in the substitution of the ordinary, the ugly, and the unheroic for the beautiful, the solemn, and the terrifying. The language startles by a grotesque vigour which skirts the merely silly, and sometimes falls in, often staggering under the weight of too many adjectives. Bloy is generally at his best when his language is at its simplest and his values are those merely of the Gospels.

On the whole he is better at the insults of *Le Désespéré* than at irony, as at the expense of a worldly priest in *Le Sang du pauvre*, or on the subject of a dogs' cemetery. Sometimes, as in the panegyric of poverty at the end of *Le Sang du pauvre*, lyrical intensity turns into moving prayer. The diaries are the most fascinating of all Bloy's writings, although imaginatively not his most powerful. The other major novel, *La Femme pauvre*, is less anguished than *Le Désespéré*. The heroine, Clotilde Maréchal, is based first on Berthe Dumont, and then on Bloy's wife, while the transposed figure of Bloy himself, Isidore Chapuis, is obviously based on an original too, as are virtually all the other characters. The novel's power still resides in dredging up hideous experiences from the past and crying out the values of poverty, humiliation, and suffering. Once again, however, it topples into a pamphlet, rather wildly directed against a random assortment of victims of Bloy's animosity.

Bloy was not a careful writer, but a wild prophetic figure calling out in the wilderness, pouring scorn on the comfortable bourgeois culture which he forced to reject him. A great figure, capable of moving, lyrical poetry, apocalyptic vision, and scorn, and of incredible strength of feeling, he genuinely believed in the value of the poverty which had caused him so much anguish. What stopped him from being truly great was not just his naivety, the inexpertise of his efforts at sustained imaginative endeavour, his brutality, credulousness, and incurable hostility to all established social structures, but the element of self-indulgence in the appalling circumstances of so great a part of his life. This was betrayed in his over-ready rebelliousness and the frequency with which he sank from the level of creative fiction he found it so difficult to sustain into what was over- written, maudlin, or at worst merely hurtful.

PUBLICATIONS

Collections

L'Oeuvre complète de Léon Bloy, 20 vols., 1947–49
Oeuvres de Léon Bloy, 15 vols., 1963–75

Fiction

Le Désespéré, 1887
Sueur de sang, 1893
Histoires désobligeantes, 1894
La Femme pauvre, 1897
Belluaires et porchers, 1905

Diary

Le Mendiant ingrat, 1898
Mon journal (1896–1900), 1904
Quatre ans de captivité à Cochons-sur- Marne, 1905
L'Invendable, 1909
Le Vieux de la montagne, 1911
Le Pèlerin de l'absolu (1910–1912), 1914
Au seuil de l'Apocalypse (1913–1915), 1916
La Porte des humbles, 1920

Other

Le Prince noir, 1877
Propos d'un entrepreneur de démolitions, 1884
Le Révélateur du globe: Christophe Colomb et sa béatification future, 1884
Brelan d'excommuniés, 1889
Christophe Colomb devant les taureaux, 1890
La Chevalière de la mort (prose poem), 1891
Les Funérailles du naturalisme, 1891
Le Salut par les Juifs (prose poem), 1892
Léon Bloy devant les cochons, 1894
Ici on assassine les grands hommes, 1895
Je m'accuse: notes sur Emile Zola, 1900
Le Fils de Louis XVI, 1900
L'Exégèse des lieux communs, 2 vols., 1902 and 1913
Les Dernières Colonnes de l'Eglise, 1903
L'Epopée byzantine, 1906
Celle qui pleure, 1908; as *She Who weeps*, 1956
Le Sang du pauvre, 1909
L'Ame de Napoléon, 1912
Jeanne d'Arc et l'Allemagne, 1915
Les Méditations d'un solitaire, 1916
Dans les ténèbres, 1918
Le Symbolisme de l'apparition, 1925
Lettres à sa fiancée, 1922
Lettres à Pierre Termier, 1927

Lettres à ses filleuls, 1928

Critical and biographical studies

Polimeni, E., *Léon Bloy: The Pauper Prophet*, 1947
Bollery, J., *Léon Bloy*, 3 vols., 1947–54
Béguin, A., *Léon Bloy*, 1948; translated by E. M. Riley, 1949
Heppenstall, R., *Léon Bloy* (in English), 1953
Fumet, Stanislas, *Léon Bloy, captif de l'absolu*, 1967
Steinmann, Jean, *Léon Bloy*, 1956

———

BONNEFOY, Yves (1923–

Poet, translator, critic of literature and art.

LIFE

Bonnefoy , born at Tours on 24 June 1923, was the son of an assembly worker and a teacher. As a child he spent his summers in his grandfather's large house at Toirac, near the River Lot. Bonnefoy attended the Lycée Descartes in Tours, then later studied mathematics at Poitiers and philosophy in Paris where he has lived since 1944. His poetry exploits certain numerical devices as a means of ensuring asymmetry in both syllables and lines. "One would have very little if one only had words," he writes. "What we need are the presences which words leave in dotted lines by their mysterious intervals, and which words in themselves cannot restore to life" (*Le Nuage rouge*). In order to reconcile formal perfection with flux, the poet must sometimes leave the forms incomplete and the reader's expectations unsatisfied. Poetry becomes an unending battle between form and formlessness (*L'Improbable*).

Bonnefoy also studied philosophy with Bachelard, Jean Wahl, and Hippolyte, but destroyed a thesis he wrote on Baudelaire and Kierkegaard. Affinities have been noted with Heidegger and Plotinus, but the poet with whom Bonnefoy seems to have most in common is Rilke, although his poetic theory certainly derives in part from Claudel's "Traité de la co-naissance au monde et de soi-même," in the *Art poétique*. The poet's function is to name the things on earth that are "most full of life" (*L'Improbable*), so giving them a sacral significance. It is for this reason that Bonnefoy is so engrossed by primitive myth and that he sees the poet's function as analogous to the painter's, with light conferring a transcendence on physical objects which the purely representational in painting, as in language, tends to destroy.

Bonnefoy married in 1968 and has one daughter. He has taught literature in many universities, including several in the US, and is co-founder of *L'Ephémère* (Paris, 1967). He received *L'Express* prize for essays in 1959. Other honours have included the Prix Critique (1971) and the Prix Fémina (1977). As well as collections of verse, he has published books and essays on art and art history. In 1981 Bonnefoy was made a professor at the

Collège de France, the first poet since Valéry to be given a chair there. He succeeded Roland Barthes. Bonnefoy's work has moved towards a greater simplicity, eliminating emblematic references, while the poet himself reflects increasingly on the value and function of language. Bonnefoy has been almost unanimously acclaimed as the most coherent, original, and brilliant poet living in France since World War II.

WORKS

Bonnefoy's collected poems, bringing together the four principal volumes—*Du mouvement et de l'immobilité de Douve*, a series of variations on the theme of the life and death of a loved woman, *Hier régnant désert, Pierre écrite*, and *Dans le leurre du seuil*—were published along with some short works in 1978, a year which therefore marks a convenient watershed in his continuing output. Important work, however, also includes *L'Improbable, Le Nuage rouge*, and *Entretiens sur la poésie*.

Bonnefoy, who has translated several Shakespeare plays and many Yeats poems, has also published on Bellini and Mantegna. He is aware of the differences between both the poetic and the critical traditions in Francophone and Anglophone countries. His own poetry derives from a particular Francophone tradition hostile to the use of verse as a vehicle for meaning, and finds its roots in the symbolist (q.v.) attitudes shared notably by Mallarmé, Valéry, and Rimbaud. It is erudite and sometimes philosophical, but relies for its effects on ambiguities of meaning and the juxtaposition of images.

Hier régnant désert is the title of a collection the effectiveness of which mimics the poetic technique of the collected poems themselves. Its appropriateness as a title derives from its multivalence. To give it one of several possible precise meanings by inserting a comma or by specifying to which of the grammatically possible parts of speech any one of its three component words belongs would be to subvert its function.

"Hier," meaning "yesterday" could be a noun or an adverb, for instance, and the three words together could mean "Yesterday reigning alone," or some as yet unspecified subject could yesterday have been reigning alone, or "yesterday" could be taken together with "alone" if something which used to reign alone does so no longer, and so on. In fact the phrase is the first half of a line used later in the collection,

Hier régnant désert, j'étais feuille sauvage
Et libre de mourir,
Mais le temps mûrissait, plainte noire des combes,
La blessure de l'eau dans les pierres du jour."

(Yesterday reigning alone, I was a leaf wild / and free to die, / but time, dark groan of the valleys, ripened / the wound of the water in the stones of the day)."

This is the end of a short poem, and it is characteristic of Bonnefoy, intimate, unpretentious, nostalgic, haunted by the fragility of experience, and given to exploiting the great natural images of water, light, dark, life, death, and fire.

However, if the emotional content is slight, the technique is strong. Bonnefoy keeps his reader waiting as the ambiguities reverberate before resolution. The meaning of the first three words is clear only when the subject "I" occurs, and their point only at the end of the second line, with its paradoxical notion of freedom to die. Is a wild leaf free to live? The adversive "but," suggests that whatever was the case in the first two lines is no longer the case in the last two. But "temps" can mean "weather" as well as "time," and both can affect the colour and life-span of a leaf, while "mûrir," "to ripen," can be transitive or intransitive in French as in English.

Does time or weather here ripen water's wound? Water itself is a magnificently ambiguous image, signifying the extremes of strength and weakness, concern and indifference, as the poet wills. It can after all be wounded at the flick of a pebble. Or does time just grow ripe, leaving the valleys to groan, water to bleed, day to prove unyielding? Or again, are the stones jewels? Only the way the images build up let us know that this is the end of a poem of helplessness. This is not symbolism, but the poetry of systematic multivalence, and in Bonnefoy's technically most successful poems, the ambiguities are not resolved. They go with the avoidance of highly charged emotions. Bonnefoy is a master of domestic verse, always sensitive, seldom intense, his feelings as fragile, mutable, and ambivalent as his images.

The 1963 *Anti-Platon* emphasizes the physically impenetrable qualities of material things and the mysterious forces to be uncovered poetically beneath them. The poem must therefore be considered and understood independently of the circumstances of its composition.

PUBLICATIONS

Bonnefoy has published a large number of articles. The works listed below are those which have appeared in book form.

Verse

Traité du pianiste, 1946
Anti-Platon, 1947
Du mouvement et de l'immobilité de Douve, 1953; as *On the Motion and Immobility of Douve*, translated by Galway Kinnell, 1968
Hier régnant désert, 1958; revised 1979
Dévotion, 1959
Anti-Platon, new version 1962
Pierre écrite, 1965; as *Words in Stone*, translated by Susanna Lang 1976
Selected Poems, translated by Anthony Rudolf, 1968
Dans le leurre du seuil, 1975
Poèmes, 1978

Other

Peintures murales de la France gothique: les fresques du XIIIe au XVe siècle, 1954
L'Improbable, 1959
La Seconde Simplicité, 1961
Rimbaud par lui-même, 1961
Miró, 1964; as Miró (in English), 1967
Un rêve fait à Mantoue, 1967
La Poésie française et le principe d'identité, 1967
Rome 1630: l'horizon du premier baroque, 1970
L'Arrière-pays, 1972
Garache, with Jacques Thuillier, 1975

L'Ordalie, illustrated by Claude Garache, 1975
Terre seconde, 1976
Rue traversière, 1977
Le Nuage rouge: essais sur la poétique, 1977
Trois remarques sur la couleur, 1977
Mantegna, 1978
Gilbert Lely, 1979
Entretiens sur la poésie, 1981
Présence et image, 1983

Translator, *Une chemise de nuit de flanelle*, 1951
Translator, Shakespeare: *Henry IV (première partie), Jules César, Hamlet, Le Conte d'hiver, Vénus et Adonis, Le Viol de Lucrèce*, 1957–60
Translator, Shakespeare: *Jules César, Hamlet, Le Roi Lear, Roméo et Juliette, Macbeth*, 1960–83

Bibliography

Prothin, Annie *Bulletin of Bibliography*, 1979.
Three collective volumes have been devoted to Bonnefoy's work: *L'Arc 66*, 1976, *World Literature Today*, vol. 53, 1979, *Colloque de Cerisy*, 1983 (Marseilles, 1985).
The *Collected Poems* (translated by John Galasi and Galway Kinnell) are forthcoming from Random House and *Selections of Prose* from the University of Chicago Press.

Critical studies

Jackson, John E., (in English), *Yves Bonnefoy*, 1976
Thélot, Jérôme, *La Poétique d'Yves Bonnefoy*, 1983
Caws, Mary Ann, *Bonnefoy* (in English), 1984
Naughton, John T., *The Poetics of Yves Bonnefoy* (in English), 1984
Leuwers, D., *Yves Bonnefoy*, 1988

BOREL, (Joseph-) Pétrus, 1809–1859.

Poet, novelist, and translator.

Very little is known of Borel's life. He was the son of a successful Lyons ironmonger, the 12th of 14 children, and was educated largely in Paris when his father retired there. A free place was obtained for him at a minor seminary. He appears to have qualified as an architect, to have been disastrously unsuccessful, and to have become passionately interested in romantic literature. He had written verse and attended the Sunday evening gatherings of Nodier's "cénacle" before leading a break-away group of his own, known as "le petit cénacle" and composing a dozen or so poets and artists, all exaggerated romantics whose anti-classical tastes led them to affect English or medieval names, eccentric dress, and outrageous manners. Nerval and Gautier were among them. They met from 1830, first at the studio of a young sculptor, Dusseigneur, then at Borel's. His literary prominence lasted scarcely a decade.

Hugo enlisted Borel to lead the claque for the famous first night of *Hernani*. Their notorious behaviour while locked in the darkening theatre was above all a protest against bourgeois society, the conflict between the "classical" and "romantic" (q.v.) literary styles being largely a spin-off from social, political, and economic unrest, enriched by ordinary student irreverence and the desire to draw attention to themselves. "Le petit cénacle" briefly became "Les Jeunes France" and then "Les Bousingos" (noise-makers), and set out to annoy the neighbours by making cacophonous noise sitting naked in the garden in summer. Borel was forced to move and his house-warming party featured custards served in skulls. In the end he and his attention-seeking friends were banned from recepions in Nodier's "cénacle." They finally achieved the notoriety they sought when *Le Figaro* started devoting satirical articles to them.

Borel was the leader of "Les Bousingos" and the most notorious among them. He claimed to be a lycanthrope, or wolf-man, and hailed tobacco and adultery as consolations for bad government. His 34 poems *Rhapsodies* appeared in December 1831 (dated 1832). The poems themselves, written before the 1830 revolution, are tamer than the truculence of the preface would suggest, and only three or four have been considered to have any merit at all. Yet they were clearly the work of a talented young man boisterously playing the clown and writing arrogantly perfunctory verse while knowing and showing that he could do better. There was only one review. In 1832 the group changed its name back to "Les Jeunes France" and Borel started a periodical, *La Liberté, Journal des Arts*, intended to attack all forms of classical art and all official institutions. It lasted six months.

Hugo was beginning to disappoint his young followers by joining, or at least taking money from, the establishment. Borel stepped for a moment into the limelight. He attended all the literary functions, but was obliged to write insipidly for money and contributed articles, rather incongruously, to *Keepsakes* and various fashion magazines. *Champavert, contes immoraux*, his most important work, came out in 1833. It was a collection of five macabre stories, relieved only by irony and grim gallows humour, and two autobiograhical sketches. The stories are not immoral, but only shocking, cynical, and fashionably cruel. The preface makes clear that Champavert is a fictionalized Borel, and some of the black humour is in fact very good, as in the satirical sketch in which the student Passereau tries to persuade the public executioner to guillotine him, saying that he required nothing extravagant: a back garden would do. The book was a financial failure and Borel lapsed into destitution, living from what he could get by writing for the women's magazines.

From about 1835 Borel's group began either to tire of him or simply to outgrow him. He had still to publish his translation of Robinson Crusoe and his bitter novel *Madame Putiphar*. He left Paris for a country village, lived like a tramp, and saved himself from starvation by growing his own vegetables. Unhappily his *Crusoe* coincided with another translation, by Madame Tastu, although in the end Borel's was thought superior. It appeared with five woodcuts by his old friends. He had to beg advances from his publisher for *Madame Putiphar*, which finally appeared in two volumes in 1839. It is long, rambling, full of horror, but with touches of compassion.

Borel returned to Paris and published only a few magazine pieces, almost none worthy of notice. His former companions had all achieved some degree of success. For six months in 1844 he edited a paper called *Le Satan*, and then an illustrated paper. He set up a publishing house with Nerval but, as a freelance critic and journalist, he was now a reproach to his friends. In 1846 Gautier finally found him a job in the colonial service in Algiers, but he was dismissed shortly before his death.

PUBLICATIONS

Verse

Rhapsodies, 1832

Other

Champavert, 1833
L'Obélisque de Louqsor, 1836
Madame Putiphar, 1839
Algérie. Colonisation. Des travaux exécutés à la Reghaia, province d'Alger, de septembre 1846 à avril 1847, 1847
Le Trésor de la Caverne d'Arcueil, 1927

Translator, *Robinson Crusoe* by Daniel Defoe, 1836

Critical and biographical study

Starkie, Enid, *Petrus Borel, the Lycanthrope*, 1954

BOURGET, Paul (Charles-Joseph-), 1852–1935.

Critic, novelist, and poet.

LIFE

Paul Bourget was born at Amiens, the eldest of seven children whose father was a professor of mathematics who became the director of the Collège Sainte-Barbe and then rector at the universities of Aix and Clermont. The family moved to Clermont-Ferrand in 1854 when Bourget's father was appointed to a chair there. In a "lettre autobiographique" later written for American readers, Bourget thought he had developed late, but that he had inherited not only the Latin lucidity of his father, but also the imagination of his mother, who was from Lorraine. A close disciple of Taine, since the end of World War I Bourget has attracted less attention with his novels than with his critical writings, although he is still remembered for *Le Disciple*. He was to publish three volumes of verse before he published anything else.

When the family returned to Paris, Bourget was sent to the Lycée Louis-le-Grand, which he attended from 1867 to 1871. He studied medicine and philosophy, but devoted increasing amounts of time to literature. He broke off his studies and for a time earned his living by tutoring, writing in the evenings. The *Revue des Deux Mondes* (*RDM* q.v.) began to publish his work in 1873. Bourget had read widely, but was always to be too influenced by more firmly committed writers, and in his early twenties had not formed any firm literary personality of his own. He had ceased to be a believing Christian and, while still a student, mixed in the circles of Parnassian (q.v.) poets, particularly Heredia. The publisher Lemerre, around whom the Parnassian poets congregated, published Bourget's three volumes of verse—*La Vie inquiète*, the long poem *Edel*, and *Les Aveux*—but the later works, which were all fiction, drama, or criticism, were to be published mostly by Plon. Bourget himself realized and was disappointed by his failure as a poet.

The two sets of biographical and critical essays, *Les Essais de psychologie contemporaine*, which examined Baudelaire, Stendhal, and Renan, and *Les Nouveaux Essais de psychologie contemporaine*, which studied Turgenev, Dumas *fils*, Leconte de Lisle, Amiel, and the Goncourts, are inspired by Taine's *De l'intelligence* (1870). They are an attempt by Bourget to establish what amounts to a series of charts, aids to navigation through the waters of literary composition, especially fiction, once the premises of Taine's determinism had been accepted. They examined, Bourget later said, the relationship between intelligence and the literary expression of a "sensibility." The resulting "moral portrait" of major French writers between 1850 and 1880 forced him to confront the phenomena of decadence (q.v.), cosmopolitanism, positivism, (q.v.) and dilettantism. He diagnosed a "moral sickness" in contemporary France and set about producing work which prompted reflection by touching the emotions, "faire du pathétique qui fait penser."

Bourget was to write fiction based on psychological analysis, but would emphasize, against Taine and Zola, the spiritual forces at work in man's development: "Le jour où un artiste apparaîtra qui ait une profonde entente des choses de l'âme, bien des ténèbres s'éclairciront (The day a writer appears who has a deep understanding of the things of the soul, a great deal of darkness will be lit up)." In fact, although in later life Bourget was to become increasingly identified with Catholic orthodoxy and monarchist policies, his attitudes were primarily based on what he saw as the need to support a crumbling social system. He never really challenged the validity of Taine's scientific method, but merely drew attention to the complexity of moral feelings and spiritual activities.

Bourget wrote chronicles for *Le Parlement* and the *Journal des Débats*, starting his career as a writer of fiction by publishing short stories and concerning himself exclusively with psychological analysis instead of the popular novels of manners. Before 1889 his subject was virtually always unhappy love. He published his first novel, *Cruelle énigme*, in 1885, following it with *Un crime d'amour* in 1886, and *André Cornélis* in 1887, serialized in the *Journal des Débats* from 21 October to 11 December 1886. Bourget's next novel, *Le Disciple*, appeared in the *Nouvelle Revue* during 1888 and 1889 before Lemerre's volume edition of June 1889. A provocative preface announced the need for a regeneration of France, the need to break away from both cynical materialism and dilettante epicureanism. Bourget pleads with his young reader to venerate France and to avoid becoming either "le positiviste brutal" (in this context, "the brutal sensualist") or "le sophiste dédaigneux (the mocking cynic)." He goes on, inspired by Spencer and Henry James, of whom he became a close friend, to proclaim the unknowability of what belonged beyond the realm of science. He had taken Brunetière's side in the long war against naturalism (q.v.), which Brunetière had been waging in the *RDM* since 1875. In 1889 Bourget, whose formal conversion to Catholicism dated from only two years later, none the less saw the novelist's role as that of secular moral guide. It was a view which encouraged him to weigh down his later fiction with ideology, and each of his subsequent novels deals with a moral problem, like heredity, the indissolubility of marriage, family responsibility, religion, or revolution.

Bourget seems to have sensed the swell of the anti-naturalist wave, and caught it just as Taine's scientific determinism was to be undermined by experimental psychology, the new philosophy of Bergson, and a movement of cultural reaction against scientific naturalism. Ranged against Brunetière, who naturally welcomed *Le Disciple*, was Anatole France in *Le Temps*. Taine complained that Bourget had distorted his position, which he had hoped was midway between France's defence of the primacy of science and the clear primacy Brunetière gave to moral teaching.

In 1890 Bourget married Minnie David, bringing back from his honeymoon in Italy the material for *Sensations d'Italie*. In 1891 he became a Catholic and on 5 August 1893, having visited the Holy Land, he took ship for New York. For six months in 1894 and 1895 he published an American chronicle simultaneously in the *New York Herald* and *Le Figaro*. On 13 June 1895 Bourget was elected to the Académie Française. He began to issue his *Oeuvres complètes* in 1899. His reply to Maurras's poll on the desirability of a return to the monarchy shows that Bourget had reached a right-wing position which was to strengthen even further after World War I, when he wanted "to see order restored" in France. His increasingly right-wing pessimism was already marginalizing him before the turn of the century, although *Le Démon de midi* of 1914 is sometimes thought to have been his best novel.

From 1908 onwards Bourget successfully adapted much of his fiction for the stage, either alone or in collaboration. *Le Disciple* undoubtedly marks the turning point in his work, which had previously been concerned with the psychology of love, and thereafter primarily focused on considerations of moral and social problems among the well-to-do. Bourget published 21 collections of short stories, which are less ideologically weighted and therefore generally considered imaginatively superior to the novels. In 1911–12 he published *Pages de critique et de doctrine*, and in 1922 *Nouvelles pages de critique et de doctrine*. When he died in 1935, he left much abandoned but unfinished material.

WORKS

Bourget was not a stylist but, in spite of the moral and social preoccupations which weighed down his later works, he was a good story teller. He is clearly linked to the anti-naturalist reaction in the very late 19th century but, if his later fiction is animated only by cardboard figures and moral didacticism, his criticism is considered to have retained its interest. The 10 years between 1873 and 1883 allowed Bourget to formulate precisely in his mind his attitude to the sensibility which produced the works we regard as realist (q.v.) and naturalist. His earlier fiction then led him to alter Taine's emphasis sufficiently for him still to regard Taine as the theoretician of at least some aspects of naturalism, and as the master with whom

he broke, although this is a matter in which hindsight helps. It was not so easy to detect a clear break in a sentence or two at the end *Le Disciple* and in its preface in 1889.

Le Disciple concerns a positivist philosopher, Adrien Sixte, who believes that human behaviour, being determined by the laws of instinct, cannot be called morally good or evil. His own life is remote, regular, and devoted to intellectual activity, while the disciple of the title, Robert Greslou, has become a tutor in the family of the Marquis de Jussat-Randon. At the start of the novel Greslou is in prison, about to be tried for the murder of the 19-year-old Charlotte de Jussat-Randon, who had died of poisoning a week before her fiancé, an officer in the same regiment as her brother, André, was due to arrive for the wedding. Everything points to Greslou as the murderer—a telegram calling him away that was never received, his relationship with the girl, a phial of poison found in his room, an eye-witness who had seen him leave the girl's room, the fact that nothing was taken from the room, and the prisoner's determined refusal to speak since his arrest. At first the reader knows only what happens as the trial is narrated.

In fact Greslou has sent Sixte a memorandum establishing his innocence, but prohibited him from using it. Greslou disliked Charlotte's elder brother and, to compensate for his own sense of social inferiority, he determined to seduce Charlotte. Oddly, Bourget is drawing on both Stendhal and Flaubert for his plot. Charlotte yielded after Greslou had threatened to commit suicide, but only on condition that after one night together they would kill themselves. Greslou decided not to, but Charlotte carried out her resolution, after warning Greslou that she had sent her brother a confession of the whole incident. Greslou's silence is the result of his determination that, in spite of his social status, his code of honour can equal that of Charlotte's officer brother, and of her fiancé. At every stage Sixte's philosophy had encouraged him to believe that his heredity, his upbringing, and his circumstances have determined him. Will Sixte now console him? At the last moment André reveals Greslou's innocence, procures his release, and shoots him: "On ne se bat pas avec les hommes comme vous, on les exécute (One does not fight with people like you. One executes them)."

Sixte watches Greslou's mother pray over her dead son's corpse and comes to doubt his own philosophy, which is depicted as having been that of Taine:

> …pour la première fois, sentant sa pensée impuissante à le soutenir, cet analyste presque inhumain à force de logique s'humiliait, s'inclinait, s'abîmait devant le mystère impénétrable de la destinée.

> (…for the first time, feeling his thought powerless to sustain him, this analyst, rendered almost inhuman by the rigour of his logic, humiliated himself, lowered his head, and bowed before the impenetrable mystery of destiny.)

The style is weak, the emotion sentimental, the moral lesson clear. The fiction is not so much a novel as a fable. It uses neither social nor moral perceptivity, does not really even attempt to probe or enlighten human experience, but simply illustrates a moral point—that there are regions of moral and spiritual life beyond the reaches of science—with a well-made plot. The literary skill reduces itself to leaving the reader with a sense of pleasure at the discomfiture of the blinkered philosopher.

The earlier *André Cornélis* is a similar novel built on a simple moral dilemma, but without the philosophical implications. André finds that his father was murdered by the man who is now his stepfather. He invites his stepfather to commit suicide and, when he will not, kills him with a knife. Before he dies, the step-father scribbles a note to André's mother saying that, finding that he is incurably ill, he has committed suicide. The dilemma is André's. Should he allow his mother to believe the lying sui-cide note? The dilemma in *L'Etape*, published in 1902, illus-trates only that no stability can be found outside the hierarchical structure of the Roman Church and its infallible moral stan-dards, and that it is impossible to move from the working class to the professoriate in one generation.

PUBLICATIONS

Collections

Oeuvres, 34 vols., 1885–1911
Oeuvres complètes (incomplete), 9 vols., 1899–1911

Fiction

L'Irréparable; Deuxième amour; Profils perdus, 1884
Cruelle énigme, 1885; as *Love's Cruel Enigma*, 1887; as *Land of Promise*, 1895
Un crime d'amour, 1886; as *A Love Life*, 1888
Mensonges, 1887; as *Lies*; as *A Living Lie*, 1896; as *Our Lady of Lies*, 1910
André Cornélis, 1887; as *André Cornélis*, 1889; as *The Son*, 1893; adapted as *The Story of André Cornélis*, 1909
Pastels, 1889; as *Pastels of Men*, 1891 and 1892
Le Disciple, 1889; as *The Disciple*, 1901
Un coeur de femme, 1890; as *A Woman's Heart*, 1890; as *Was It Love?*, 1891
Nouveaux pastels, 1891
La Terre promise, 1892
Un saint, 1893; with other contes, 1904
Un scrupule, 1893
Cosmopolis, 1894; as *Cosmopolis*, 1893
Steeple-Chase, 1894
Une idylle tragique, 1896; as *A Tragic Idyll*, 1896
Recommencements, 1897
Voyageuses, 1898; as *Some Portraits of Women*, 1898
Trois petites filles, 1899
Complications sentimentales, 1898
La Duchesse bleue, 1898; as *The Blue Duchess*, 1908
Drames de famille, 1900
L'Ecran, 1900; as *The Screen*, 1901
Un homme d'affaires, 1900
Le Fantôme, 1901
Monique, 1902
L'Etape, 1902
Un divorce, 1904
L'Eau profonde, 1904
Les deux soeurs, 1905; as *Two Sisters*, 1912
L'Emigré, 1907; as *The Weight of the Name*, 1908
Une nuit de Noël, 1907
Les Détours du cour, 1908
La Dame qui a perdu son peintre, 1910

L'Envers du décor, 1911
Le Démon de midi, 1914
Le Sens de la mort, 1915; as *The Night Cometh*, 1916
Lazarine, 1917
Némésis, 1918
Le Justicier, 1919
Laurence Albani, 1919
Anomalies, 1920
Un drame dans le monde, 1921
Le Testament, 1921
L'Ecuyère, 1921
La Geôle, 1923; as *The Gaol*, 1924
Coeur pensif ne sait où il va, 1924
Conflits intimes, 1925
Le Danseur mondain, 1926
Nos actes nous suivent, 1927
Deux nouvelles, 1928
Le Tapin, 1928
On ne voit pas les coeurs, 1929

Verse

La Vie inquiète, 1875
Edel, 1878
Les Aveux, 1882
Poésies (1872–1876), 1885
Poésies (1876–1882), 1887

Plays

La Barricade: chronique de 1910, 1920
Le Tribun, 1911; as *A Tribune of the People*

Other

Ernest Renan, 1883
Les Essais de psychologie contemporaine, 1883
Les Nouveaux Essais de psychologie contemporaine, 1886
Etudes et portraits, 2 vols., 1889
Sensations d'Italie, 1891; as *Impressions of Italy*, 1892; as *The Glamour of Italy*, 1923
Outre-mer, 2 vols., 1895
Pages de critique et de doctrine, 2 vols., 1911 and 1912
Nouvelles pages de critique et de doctrine, 2 vols., 1922
Hélène: dialogue lyrique, 1923
La Leçon de Barrès, 1924
Quelques témoignages, 1928
De profundis clamavi, 1928
Au service de l'ordre, 1929
Sur la Toscane, 1929

Critical and biographical studies

Austin, L.J., *Paul Bourget, sa vie et son oeuvre jusqu'en 1889*, 1940
Mansuy, M., *Paul Bourget*, 1961

———

BRASILLACH, Robert, 1909–1945

Novelist, critic, and political commentator

Brasillach, the elder of two children, came from an army family. His father was 27 and his mother 23 when he was born. His sister, Suzanne, was to marry Maurice Bardèche, a contemporary of Brasillach and Simone Weil at the Ecole Normale Supérieure who later worked with Brasillach on *L'Histoire du cinéma*. Brasillach was five when his father, a lieutenant, was killed by Moroccan rebels. In 1918 his mother remarried. The family moved from Perpignan to Sens. As a youth Brasillach was attracted to movements of anarchism and revolt, including Marxism and surrealism. Even as an adult he believed that the role of fascism was to protect the individual's right to self-affirmation which included, as he saw it, the freedom to scoff and jeer. Brasillach was an elitist, believing in the need to protect the creative individual, if necessary by force, against the unimaginative plebian masses. He despised what he regarded as their materilalistic aspirations and insensitive mediocrity. He was too much of an anarchist ever to have become a liberal.

From 1925 to 1928 Brasillach attended the the Lycée Louis-le-Grand. At 16 he had already had two articles published in a Perpignan weekly. His teachers included André Bellesort, who was later elected to the Académie Française. Bellesort contributed to the fascist newspaper *Je Suis Partout* which Brasillach was to edit and whose other contributors included Montherlant, Mauriac, Claudel, Ghéon, Anouilh, Thierry Maulnier, and Marcel Aymé. Brasillach published poems in mainly provincial reviews in 1926, and also articles on a broad range of subjects, including one a fortnight for *La Tribune de l'Yonne* in 1926 and 1927. He read widely, taking a special interest in obscure authors, wrote for publication without correction before he was 20, and went to the avant-garde theatre, where he was a fan particularly of the Pitoëffs.

While at the Ecole Normale Brasillach was befriended by Massis, the right-wing Catholic critic who formed a bridge between the Catholic business community and the political and patriotic Catholicism of Maurras's Action Française. Massis, who was famous for denouncing Gide for his corruption of traditional patriotic values, ghosted Pétain's moralizing panegyrics to French youth in favour of military pride, and deplored the opening up of higher education to "ambitious nonentities." Massis needed Brasillach's help in order to foster a new following at the Ecole. In return he succeeded in getting Brasillach's *Présence de Virgile* published in 1931. It was through the eyes of Massis that Brasillach saw Péguy on the left and Barrès on the right, both of course united by a patriotic devotion to France. Thanks to Massis Brasillach also received journalistic commissions and an introduction to the Action Française, took over the failing *Revue Française*, and met Bernanos, Supervielle, and Paulhan. He failed the agrégation in 1931 and 1932 and was forced to abandon the easy going Bohemianism of his student days. The right-wing *Candide* published a serialized report by Brasillach on "la fin de l'après-guerre (the end of the post-war)" period and at 22 he was made literary critic of the *Action Française*. Maurras wanted the literary page to appeal to a wider readership than the editorial contents, and Brasillach became perhaps the most widely read literary critic in Paris.

Maurras, however, was a French monarchist, while Brasillach was an internationalist whose attitude to French politics was dis-

dainful, and who was perfectly happy to be called a fascist. In Brasillach's view France had to move towards a reconciliation with Germany if another useless slaughter on the 1914 pattern was to be averted. It was clear to him that neither Britain nor the US would support France in enforcing the reparations agreed at Versailles in 1926. Maurras, meanwhile, tried to discredit the policy of reconciliation, attempting to force a wedge between government and its popular support. The new student poor of the 1920s made a perfect forcing ground for extreme right-wing protest movements since they saw what they regarded as their inheritance in jeopardy. Brasillach's own fascism grew out of his view that the West needed a new "myth" or value system to replace both exploitative capitalism and bureaucratic communism. He came to believe in the myth that Hitler and Mussolini had succeeded in imposing on their respective countries, not realizing that it was inexportable and incompatible with Maurras's fierce French nationalism. While diverging from Maurras in two essays of 1932 and 1934, Brasillach continued to eulogize him in increasingly effusive fashion.

Brasillach was slow among the fascists of *Je Suis Partout* to pay undiluted homage to Hitler, but he was impressed by Thierry Maulnier's 1933 *Nietzsche*, and he reported on the 1937 Nuremburg rally for Massis's *Revue Universelle*. *Cent heures chez Hitler*, was reprinted in his novel *Les Sept couleurs* of 1939 and with modifications, in *Notre avant-guerre* of 1941. Brasillach was impressed by the Nazi youth culture with its emphasis on health, strength, classlessness, and joy. He saw Nietzsche as forming the bridge between German and French fascism and from 1936, when the government of the Front Populaire took office, he affirmed his strong commitment to a Franco-German alliance in a series of articles for *Je Suis Partout*. From 1934 he was also associated with the Rive Gauche lectures, which, for all their apparent neutrality, fantasy, and sense of fun, became a forum for firm believers in Franco-German collaboration.

When *Je Suis Partout*, founded in 1931, was turned over to its staff in 1936, Brasillach became an enthusiastic member of the extremely distinguished editorial team. Circulation doubled in a year and went on climbing. Meanwhile Brasillach was currently also writing for the *Nouvelles Littéraires*, the *Revue Universelle*, *Combat*, *L'Assault*, *Candide*, *Gringoire*, the *Nouvelle Revue Française* (q.v.), and the *Revue de Paris*. His anti-semitism dated, he maintained, from the pro-Jewish excesses of the Front Populaire. He withdrew from *Combat* when, under Maulnier it shifted from its savage fascism to its wartime anti-collaborationist stance.

On the Spanish war Brasillach's position was Falangist, which allowed for a greater degree of anarchical sympathy than straight support for Franco's dictatorship. In 1939 Brasillach refused to see things as simply as Céline, whose *L'Ecole des cadavres*, which Brasillach reviewed for *Je Suis Partout*, took the view that, since France was lost in any case, German domination was preferable to Jewish. Over Poland *Je Suis Partout* had to face in two opposite directions at once, since France clearly had to honour its obligations to that country. Brasillach was mobilized as a lieutenant and sent to the Maginot line, where he wrote most of *Notre avant-guerre*. Summoned back to Paris for a police interrogation, he found that numerous letters and books had been confiscated from the flat he shared with his sister and brother-in-law. He returned to his post and almost voluntarily allowed himself to be taken prisoner.

On 1 April 1941 he was liberated at Vichy's request so that he could take charge of the cinema industry, on which his *L'Histoire du cinéma*, written in collaboration with his brother-in-law, was the standard work. *Je Suis Partout* had closed in 1940 but started up again in the occupied zone in 1941, and Brasillach now resumed its direction, totally persuaded of the need to collaborate with the Germans. He frequently used to spend nights more or less camping at the Centres de Jeunesse. The journal now attacked Maurras as well as the left, but Brasillach was disappointed that collaboration was not succeeding any more than the Action Française in promoting the emergence of a new elite, and his mood deepened into something like black despair. In his view there could be no salvation for France, except perhaps as a German satellite, though German defeat now began to look increasingly possible. Brasillach resigned at *Je Suis Partout* when the majority of his colleagues wanted to report more optimistically from the military fronts than was compatible with the truth.

Brasillach's life in occupied Paris had been pleasant enough. He spent June 1944 at Sens with his mother, stepfather, and the Bardèche's, corrected *Six heures à perdre*, already published serially, prepared a book on Giraudoux, and completed translations for his anthology of Greek verse. Life in Paris finally got very difficult as the Americans approached, with lengthy power cuts and infrequent public transport, but Brasillach spent the last days of the occupation there, securing false papers and a hiding place for himself. The Resistance had not troubled him during the war, but now arrested his mother in September as a reprisal for his disappearance, and he gave himself up. He was imprisoned at Fresnes, where he wrote some remarkable verse and his political testament, *Lettre à un soldat de la classe 60*. The trial on 19 January 1945 lasted five hours. Fifty-nine leading cultural figures, including Picasso and Aragon, signed a petition pleading for clemency. Sartre and Beauvoir were virtually alone in refusing to sign, but de Gaulle rejected the plea, although Mauriac had obtained a commitmenet from him that he would grant clemecy, and Brasillach was accordingly shot on 6 February.

PUBLICATIONS

Oeuvres complètes de Robert Brasillach, 12 vols., 1963–6

L'Enfant de la nuit, 1934
Portraits, 1935
L'Histoire du cinéma, with Maurice Bardèche, 1935
Léon Degrelle et l'avenir de Rex, 1936
Le Marchand d'oiseaux, 1936
Les Cadets de l'Alcazar, with Henri Massis, 1936
Comme le temps passe, 1937; as *Youth Goes Over*, 1938
Les Sept couleurs, 1939
Histoire de la guerre d'Espagne, 1939
Notre avant-guerre, 1941
La Conquérante, 1943
Les Quatre jeudis, 1944
Anthologie de la poésie grecque, 1950
Lettres écrites en prison, 1952
Six heures à perdre, 1953
Journal d'un homme occupé, 1955

Critical and biographical studies

Gibson, Wendy, *The Fascist Ego: a Political Biography of*

Robert Brasillach, 1975
Monferron, Parton, Marie-Luce, *Robert Brasillach maître de l'évasion*, 1988
Louvrier, Pascal, *Brasillach, l'illusion fasciste*, 1989

———

BRETON, André (-Robert) 1896–1966.

Poet and founder of the surrealist (q.v) movement.

LIFE

André Breton was born on 18 or, just possibly, 19 February 1896, the only child of parents of very modest means, a fact of which he was to feel increasingly aware in later life. Some of his later surrealist (q.v.) colleagues, like Pierre Naville and Philippe Soupault, came from backgrounds sufficiently well off for them not to share Breton's need to rebel against the tyranny of having to earn a living. Breton's father, Louis-Justin (born in 1867), came from Lorraine. He had two brothers, who both died young, and a sister, who stayed in farming. In 1893, as an ex-soldier, he married Marguerite-Marie-Eugénie Le Gouguès, a Breton and a dressmaker born in 1871.

Breton, their only child, was brought up until the age of four by his mother's father at Saint-Brieuc. He was born at Tinchebray in Normandy, where his father was a clerk at the police station until he resigned in 1898 and was a small businessman before he set up as a bookseller. In 1900 Louis-Justin was an accounts clerk at Pantin, near Paris, later becoming the junior director of a crystal-making company there. Breton had fond memories of his grandfather, and was on his guard against becoming too much his father's child. His mother seems to have been cold and straight-laced, to have placed much emphasis on respectability, and to have believed in inflicting physical punishment on her son.

The background of his extreme youth had an obvious effect on the rebellious Breton of later years, making him strangely restrained in his linguistic prudishness even when breaking sexual taboos. He was virile, but idealized radiant women to whom he was easily attracted, and was reproached by some of the other surrealists as priggish and puritanical. He nevertheless quickly broke with his mother's religious patterns of behaviour and her concern with the social proprieties, and was obviously at ease with his father's atheism. He was attached to the Lorraine he had never known. In 1900 he rejoined his parents and went to a kindergarten at Pantin run by nuns, made his first Communion, and from 1902 to 1907 attended the local primary school, where he appears to have been a model schoolboy. The family often spent their holidays at Lorient in Brittany, for which Breton acquired a lasting affection.

From 1907 to 1913 Breton went to the Collège Chaptal in Paris, travelling daily there and back by train. He appears not to have enjoyed school, but did reasonably well, except in mathematics, became enthusiastic about poetry, excelled in penmanship and recitation, read Huysmans, Baudelaire, and Mallarmé, and passed his baccalauréat in 1913. His school friends included René Hilsum, who was to run a publishing company which became a centre for dada (q.v.) activities, and Jean-Paul Samson, who became a convinced pacifist. By 1913 Breton was interested in anarchism, and that year he began pre-medical studies with his best friend, Théodore Fraenkel. Three of Breton's poems were published by Jean Royère in the post-symbolist (q.v.) *La Phalange* for 20 March 1914, and Breton began a long correspondence with Valéry. It is typical of him that, when Valéry showed his concern for the conventional system of literary honours by becoming a member of the Académie Française, Breton sold the autographs of Valéry's letters to him, but only after first copying them.

In 1915 he was called up and became a medical auxiliary with Fraenkel. Among the injured for whom he cared was Jacques Vaché, who systematically broke all literary norms and was dismissive of Breton's favourite authors, including Apollinaire. Suffering as much from the effects of drugs and alcohol as from his wounded leg, Vaché, who was only a year older than Breton, died in a hotel room of an overdose of opium on 6 January 1919 at the age of 23. Breton saw relatively little of him, but was fascinated by Vaché's striving for instantaneous behaviour of any sort, providing that it was gratuitous and eye-catching. He was perpetually dressing up, affecting to despise all art and artists, and boasting that he had never made love to the woman he lived with. At the first night of Apollinaire's *Les Mamelles de Tirésias* in 1917 he appeared waving a revolver in the aisle, making lunatic threats to shoot into the audience. His influence on Breton was considerable, and it has been observed, probably with some justification, that Vaché lived out the fantasies which Breton was too inhibited to realize in his own life. Like Aragon, Breton was to regard Vaché's death as deliberate, a view that has subsequently come widely to be doubted.

By 1916 Breton had written his first prose poems and undergone at least two emotional entanglements. He discovered Adrienne Monnier's bookshop, La Maison des Amis des Livres, whose owner left a memorable description of the timid young man with the determined chin. At around this time Breton called on Apollinaire, with whom he was to remain in contact until Apollinaire died. Breton's enthusiasm for Apollinaire diminished only after his death, and he was noticeably reserved about him by the date of an important lecture which Breton gave in 1922. At his own request Breton was attached to a psychiatric unit. There, for the first time, he heard about Freud, still virtually unknown in France. Breton's contact with mad patients had a profound affect on his attitude to uncontrolled mental activity, in which he was henceforward to become deeply interested. For a moment he feared that continued poetic activity would derange his own mind. He nevertheless spent 1917 largely preoccupied with poetry, after recovering from an operation for appendicitis with troublesome complications.

He had met Louis Aragon in the medical corps and Apollinaire had introduced him to Philippe Soupault at the Café Flore. With Aragon and Soupault, Breton became a regular visitor to Adrienne Monnier's bookshop. He also saw Royère and Valéry, and began to publish in Pierre Reverdy's new review, *Nord-Sud*, whose first number appeared in March 1917. Later in the year he and a number of his friends, together with some of the Montmartre painters who knew Apollinaire, were associated with various semi-comic or even wholly farcical poetry readings and art exhibitions. Breton was quite earnest in his admiration of Gide, however, and took real pleasure in Aragon's friendship, although in the end he was to become closer to Benjamin Péret than to any other of his surrealist associates. On 13 December 1917 his maternal grandfather died in Brittany.

The following year Aragon discovered Lautréamont, whose real name was Isidore Ducasse, in whose honour Breton and he started what amounted to a cult. Lautréamont's blasphemous and nightmarish *Poesies*, signed "Ducasse," expressing his hatred of mankind and God, were available only in the Bibliothèque Nationale, where Apollinaire must have discovered them, and Breton went to the trouble of copying them out. Lautréamont, as opposed to Ducasse was well known to the symbolists (q.v.). The Lautréamont *Les Chants de Maldoror* was on the shelves of Jarry and Gourmont. Breton himself was now experimenting with poetry which systematically broke all the recognizable conventions— syntax, line lengths, verses—and he started to send letters to his friends peppered with collages in the manner of Max Jacob. The decisive year in Breton's evolution towards what we know as surrealism was 1918. He overflowed with projects for books, articles, collections, and individual poems. He wrote a lot of letters to friends whose number now included Marie Laurencin, Rachilde, Pierre Albert-Birot, and Jean Paulhan, considered writing opera or drama, and discussed ideas for modern poetry. Apollinaire's death came as a shock since Breton had remained close to him despite Apollinaire's patriotic views and those on modern poetry which Breton, Aragon, and Soupault could not share. In March 1919 the three friends founded the review *Littérature*, using the term in Verlaine's contemptuous sense , "Tout le reste est littérature (All the rest is literature)." In July the review began to publish Vaché's letters, which Breton edited for Adrienne Monnier to publish in August.

As early as February 1919 Breton had been corresponding with Tzara, whose *Dada Manifesto 1918* (see dada) he had seen in January. Tzara almost immediately took Vaché's place in Breton's life. He also became friendly with Paul Eluard, whom he had first met at the opening of Apollinaire's *Les Mamelles*. In June Breton published his first volume of poetry, *Mont-de-Piété*, in a style reminiscent of Mallarmé, which Breton knew he had already outgrown. He had published Lautréamont's poetry in the second and third numbers of *Littérature* and, having discovered "automatic writing," produced most of *Les Champs magnétiques* in collaboration with Soupault. It was published by Adrienne Monnier in 1920, parts also appearing in the September number of the review. It is from the discovery of automatic writing in May and June 1919 that it has become customary to date the beginning of "surrealism."

Having passed his first medical examinations at the second attempt, Breton was officially appointed a medical auxiliary from 1 July 1919, pending demobilization on 19 September. He went home to Brittany for part of the summer, had a liaison with Georgina Dubreuil, and returned to Paris in the autumn, apparently intent on pursuing his medical studies. In fact he was already getting disillusioned with the review, which seemed to him not to be pursuing the "décomposition de l'homme contemporain (decomposition of contemporary man)," as he had intended, and he found a new enthusiasm in his friendship for Francis Picabia (see dada).

By January 1920 Picabia had got Tzara to come to Paris, and the Breton–Aragon–Soupault team, somewhat overawed by the revolutionary sophistication of Picabia and Tzara, organized a series of often noisy dada manifestations. *Littérature*, now printing 1,500 copies, published 23 dada manifestoes in May, after a strike had earlier interfered with publication. In March Breton had announced to his parents that he was giving up medicine for literature. Breton's mother was indignant and his parents cut off all financial help. His father wrote to Valéry asking him to use his influence to get Breton back to his studies. Breton broke off relations with home, and Valéry got him a post with the publishers Gallimard at 400 francs a month, together with 50 francs a session for reading his corrected proofs back to Proust.

Sometime during the first half of 1920 Georgina had unjustifiably become jealous and caused a storm at Breton's home, which was also the review's headquarters. She destroyed two Derains, three Marie Laurencins, and a Modigliani as well signed books, sketches, and letters. At the end of June, however, Breton met Simone Kahn, a young stuudent at the Sorbonne who did not like dada, and who was to become his first wife. He had got bored with dada himself, and become friendly with senior colleagues at Gallimard, including Jacques Rivière. He decided to break with both, left the publishing house, and declined to write a promised preface for Picabia's *Jésus-Christ Rastaquouère*. Simone's father, a banker, did not welcome their projected marriage, and Breton, now willing to resume his medical studies, found that his dada activities had ruined his chances of the 5,000-franc Blumenthal prize, although his nomination was supported by Gide, Proust, and Valéry. Gallimard printed an article by Breton, "Pour dada," in the August number of the *Nouvelle Revue Française* (q.v.), and in the autumn Breton supported himself by doing odd jobs in the literary and art worlds. Théodore Fraenkel married a close friend of Simone, who at this period wrote of Breton's penetrating intelligence as being characterized by "just the right amount of mental unbalance."

By 1921 Breton was clearly bored, although he continued to take part in dada activities and wrote a much-esteemed preface to an exhibition of collages by Max Ernst. He interrupted a lecture by the futurist painter Marinetti and inspired Barrès's mock "trial" for "crimes against the security of the mind," which caused Picabia to break with dada in an article published in *Comoedia* and prompted a general feeling in the press that dada had gone too far. Breton broke decisively with the movement by not taking part in its salon in June. Rivière got the couturier and collector Jacques Doucet to give Breton a job as his librarian and adviser at 20,000 francs a year, and Breton was able to marry Simone on 15 September, with Valéry as a witness. On his honeymoon in the Tyrol, he met Max Ernst and Tzara, discovered that he was far more optimistic than they were, and was confirmed in his conviction that they should follow different paths. He also called on Freud in Vienna, publishing the interview in *Littérature*. After *Littérature*'s 20th number, Soupault took Aragon and Breton's names off the cover. Meanwhile Breton was giving Doucet the perceptive advice which prompted him to acquire Picasso's *Les Demoiselles d'Avignon* and two now acknowledged masterpieces by Derain.

Breton and Simone set up house in Montmartre, where Breton was to live until 1949, when he moved downstairs. In February 1922 there was a serious split in the dada camp, and Breton later wrote about it in a piece in *Les Pas perdus* entitled "Après dada." *Littérature*, last published in August 1921, was relaunched on 1 March 1922, edited by Breton and Soupault, and with a new format. Doucet offered a subsidy, and Gallimard undertook the distribution, but Soupault departed as Picabia's role expanded, leaving Breton as sole editor. In the autumn and winter members of the group had themselves put to sleep by hypnosis, often with resulting emotional shock. Breton and Simone went to Barcelona with Picabia and his mistress, Germaine Everling, for an exhibition of Picabia's paintings.

By the winter the group surrounding Breton was splintering. Breton himself broke Pierre de Massot's arm with his stick in one incident in July 1923, and a brawl developed, during which Tzara called the police. In October Breton bought two Chirico paintings, for one of which he paid as much as 1,250 francs, and in November he published *Clair de terre*. In his advice to Doucet he was demonstrating extraordinary powers of discernment, picking out for luxury bindings, for instance, Reverdy's *Les Ardoises du toit* and Apollinaire's *Calligrammes*, and selecting for purchase paintings by Seurat, Matisse, Derain, Picasso, Chirico, Chagall, and Klee. He had also been proved right when he publicly contested the authenticity and unpublished nature of a sonnet attributed to Rimbaud by *Les Feuilles Libres*.

Early in 1924 Breton experimented again with automatic writing and thought of publishing the results with a theoretical introduction. Breton's group, who were characterized by their admiration for Reverdy and Picasso, and their dislike of Satie, decided to found a new review, *La Révolution Surréaliste*, the 13th and last number of *Littérature* having appeared in June. On 15 October Breton published the *Manifeste du surréalisme* together with the 32 texts of *Poisson soluble*, 31 of which were purely "automatic" in the sense of having been written as far as possible without the conscious control of the writer's imagination. Later in the year Breton became enthusiastic about the painting of a new friend, André Masson, and the first number of *La Révolution Surréaliste* appeared.

On 18 October, six days after the death of Anatole France, Breton and his group published a disconcertingly violent pamphlet against France entitled *Un cadavre*, provoking a confrontation with Doucet which eventually led to a break. They were attacked by Claudel in *Comoedia* for 24 June 1925, and in July produced a pamphlet printed on blood-red paper in reply. It was distributed at a banquet in honour of Saint-Pol-Roux (1861–1940), a symbolist poet admired by the surrealists. The banquet ended in a riot in which Michel Leiris was nearly lynched and Breton almost thrown out of a window. Various members of the group had also signed a letter to the communist newspaper *Humanité* denouncing the Moroccan war, provoking considerable public hostility to surrealism itself. Breton now took sole charge of *La Révolution Surréaliste*, starting with the fourth number in July, and publishing what was to appear in volume form in 1928 as *Le Surréalisme et la peinture*. His interests were becoming more political, however, and he found himself increasingly aligned with the communists on Poland, Russia, and Romania as well as on Morocco. With Aragon and Eluard he was to join the communist party in January 1927. In his celebrated article in *Les Temps Modernes* (q.v.), "Situation de l'écrivain en 1947," Sartre was later to use the surrealists as an example of how a revolutionary group that was politically uncommitted must necessarily disintegrate.

After a first exhibition of surrealist painting in November 1925, Breton was the chief organizer of the Paris Galerie Surréaliste in March 1926. For some time he had been obsessed by Lise Meyer, from whose coquettish domination he broke free in October 1927. In October of the previous year he had met Nadja and, although their close association lasted barely 10 days, it inspired the first of three remarkable works more, in fact, about personal liberation than about love—*Nadja, Les Vases communicants*, and *L'Amour fou*. It was in December 1926 that Breton published his *Légitime défense* in *La Révolution Surréaliste*, declaring himself opposed to any external constraint, "even Marxist," over "les expériences de la vie intérieure (the experiences of inner life)." The piece was to be reprinted in *Point du jour* of 1934. Breton was slowly defining himself in terms of a struggle for inner liberty, and it was this self-definition which came to dominate his attitude to Marx and Freud as well as to painting, literature, and life. His whirlwind affair with Emmanuel Berl's mistress, Suzanne Muzard, while he was in the middle of writing *Nadja* must be understood in this context. He and Suzanne spent three weeks touring the South of France late in 1927.

Joining and quarrelling and breaking away had become commonplace events within the group. They had left dada behind. Soupault, Artaud, and then Chirico either left or were excluded, or both, as were many other less well-known personalities. Desnos and Naville hovered on the perimeter of the inner circle. The overall impression is one of over-zealous commitment to revolutionizing social values, heady enthusiasm, and inevitable prickliness. Marxism and psychoanalytic theory were paths to freedom but also constraints upon it. Breton was to break with both. He had attacked the power exercised by psychiatrists over their patients in *Nadja*, although he was still clearly inspired by Freud in *Les Vases communicants* of 1932, and had already distanced himself from communism, at least inwardly. In May 1928 he was naively convinced that his irruption had not altered Suzanne's relationship with Berl, although by August she was demanding that Breton should divorce Simone, who agreed to the parting during a quarrel in October. On 1 December Suzanne married Berl. In December 1928 Breton came to blows with Soupault, the gallery had to close for lack of money, and there was not enough money to send the 12th number of *La Révolution Surréaliste* to the printers.

Breton's literary activity, *Nadja* apart, was mostly ephemeral—tracts, pamphlets, special numbers, editorial chores. On and off, between quarrels, he lived with the newly married Suzanne. He wrote the preface for the catalogue of Dali's first one-man exhibition in November 1929, published the 12th and last number of *La Révolution Surréaliste* in December 1929, and the *Second manifeste du surréalisme*, published as a volume in 1930, and attacked a host of ex-members of the group, including Vitrac, Artaud, Soupault, and Masson. They of course hit back, publishing a violent pamphlet in January 1930 signed by, among others, Leiris, Prévert, Queneau, Vitrac, and Desnos, who also published a third surrealist manifesto. Among those who refused to sign the anti-Breton pamphlet were Artaud, Soupault, Masson, and Naville. That year, with Char and Eluard, Breton compiled the collection of poetry entitled *Ralentir travaux*. He also effected a reconciliation with Tzara, founded a new review, *Le Surréalisme au Service de la Révolution*, which lasted until May 1933, and published *L'Immaculée Conception* with Eluard. In 1931 he wrote his most famous love poem, "L'union libre," on the erotic power of women, and had a liaison with Valentine Hugo. The following year he quarrelled with Aragon after coming to his defence, although only at the expense of criticizing the communist party.

By the early 1930s the heroic days of surrealism were over, and the movement whose leader Breton had striven hard to remain became semi-political. Breton met his second wife, Jacqueline Lamba, on 29 May 1934, marrying her on 14 August. She was to inspire *L'Amour fou*, and to bear him a daughter, Aube, on 20 December 1935. Surrealism had become international, and as a movement formally broke with the communist party in August 1935, after Breton and Ilya Ehrenburg had come to blows at a writers' congress in June. In 1938 Breton rallied to Freud, then in difficulties with the Nazis, and Saint-John Perse obtained a cultural mission for him to Mexico but, again for ideological reasons, he broke with Eluard. While in Mexico Breton had concocted a manifesto with Trotsky. Dali was excluded from the movement in 1939. Breton was mobilized as a military doctor and stationed at Poitiers. After the armistice in 1940 he took refuge with his wife and child in Marseilles, before embarking for Martinique in 1941 on the same boat as Lévi-Strauss. He got to know Aimé Césaire, but was moved on from Martinique and finally took refuge in the US, where he met up again with Ernst and Masson. He spent five years in New York, working for the French-speaking radio.

He founded a new review, *VVV* "*Triple V*," which had four numbers from 1942 to 1944. In 1943 his wife left him to marry the young painter and sculptor David Hare, and became a celebrated painter herself. Breton speedily remarried. His third wife, Elisa, was divorced and her 17-year-old daughter had recently drowned. Breton travelled with her to Canada, New Mexico, and then Haiti. In 1946 he returned to Paris, where he was now a senior literary figure, disavowing some of his less temperate youthful remarks in re-editions of the two surrealist manifestoes. He still attracted hostility, however, being attacked by Vailland and by Tzara again, as well as by Sartre. Breton interrupted a lecture by Tzara in the Sorbonne, and a brawl ensued. He joined Sartre, Camus, and Paulhan in the short-lived Rassemblement Démoctratique Révolutionnaire, and promoted further excommunications from the brotherhood.

Breton's political activity mostly took the form of public interventions on behalf of named individuals. In Prague Zavis Kalandra, whom he had briefly met before the war, was executed in spite of a telegram from Breton, Camus, Sartre, Beauvoir, Duhamel, Paulhan, Supervielle, and Vildrac. Breton's revolutionary gestures were no longer very threatening to the new order, since he was relegated to the revered status of left-wing revolutionary intellectual. He accepted this position with grace and dignity, making the gestures expected of him, but no longer a cultural force, his political and artistic attitudes now almost wholly predictable. He was in financial difficulties in the 1950s and published almost nothing during his last 10 years. In 1963 an attempt was made on his life. He had been suffering from asthma for some time, and died of respiratory failure on 28 September 1966.

WORKS

Breton's first major publication was written in conjunction with Philippe Soupault, and is the text normally considered to have inaugurated surrealism in literature, *Les Champs magnétiques*. Since it is an exercise in the "automatic writing" which is constitutive of literary surrealism, and which consists in writing in the absence of critical intervention, it is important that there exists a copy of the book showing which of the two authors wrote which portions of the text. That information, and much else concerning the genesis of the document, including the speed at which the various portions were written down, is most easily accessible in the first volume of the *Oeuvres* in the Pléiade edition (1988). The experiment of automatic writing results in a dense succession of images which, because conscious control is suppressed as far as possible, does not make logical sense, or display even the ascertainable connection between images to be found in the densest symbolist poetry. In order to eliminate critical judgement of what is being written down, speed in writing is essential. The images must succeed one another as nearly as possible as they simply come to mind, and therefore reflect unconscious memories and associations, like hallucinations, dreams, and the disturbed mental processes of the insane, of which Breton had experience during the war.

Automatic writing is intended to invite psychological analysis, and is a serious investigation into how the mind works, on the supposition that images, once acquired and associated with emotion, remain embedded and can occur spontaneously to the memory. The important theoretician of automatism was Pierre Janet (*L'Automatisme psychologique*, 1889), who gives as an example the involuntary recollection of the correct spelling of a word when conscious memory has forgotten it. For Janet, the intrusion of the involuntary into the consciousness of the mentally ill could reveal to the observer the patient's hopes and fears. In Breton it reveals a good deal about what impressed him in childhood.

> Nous touchons à la fin du carême. Notre squelette transparaît comme un arbre à travers les aurores successives de la chair où les désirs d'enfant dorment à poings fermés

> (We are reaching the end of Lent. Our skeleton shows through like a tree through the successive dawns of the flesh in which a child's desires sleep with closed fists)

It would not be difficult to elaborate a psychological commentary on these images, which undoubtedly reflect the authentic experience of childhood, but it is particularly to be noted that religious imagery, like "Lent" and "bells," recurs in Breton's automatic writing, although by 1919 he had long ceased to think in consciously religious terms.

Breton had a strong lyrical gift, more apparent in his prose poems than in his formal poetry, in which the dream associations between objects in the real world recall the workings of a child's mind. The 1924 *Manifeste du surréalisme* goes straight to the point:

> Tant va la croyance à la vie, à çe que la vie a de pluo précaire, la vie *réelle* s'entend, qu'à la fin cette croyance se perd. L'homme, ce rêveur définitif, de jour en jour plus mécontent de son sort, fait avec peine le tour des objets dont il a été amené à faire usage, et que lui a livrés sa nonchalance, ou son effort, son effort presque toujours, car il a consenti à travailler, tout au moins il n'a pas répugné à jouer sa chance (ce qu'il appelle sa chance!)

> (Belief goes out to life so often, to everything that is most fragile in life, *real* life, I mean, that in the end belief gets lost. Man, that essential dreamer, daily more unhappy with his fate, goes with difficulty round the objects he has come to make use of, and which his refusal to care has delivered to him, or his effort, actually almost always his effort

because he has consented to work, or at the very least he has not stood back from trying his luck [what he calls his luck!])

Here the suggestion of loose association is a teasingly surrealist way of masking a serious statement. Surrealism, at least on the general plane of cultural philosophy, starts with the proclamation of man as a dreamer, of work as a servility, and, in the allusion to a well-known proverb hidden in the first sentence, of commitment as something bound to be dissipated. In the first manifesto it is more a rallying call to personal liberty than any detailed prescription for its achievement.

The second manifesto of 1930 is more specific:

> Tout porte à croire qu'il existe un certain point d'où la vie et la mort, le réel et l'imaginaire, le passé et le futur, le communicable et l'incommunicable, le haut et le bas cessent d'être perçus contradictoirement. Or c'est en vain qu'on chercherait à l'activité surréaliste un autre mobile que l'espoir de déterminer ce point

> (Everything points to the belief that there is a certain point after which life and death, the real and the imaginary, the past and the future, the communicable and the incommunicable, the high and the low, cease to be perceived as contradictions of one another. You would be looking fruitlessly for any other motive for surrealist activity than the hope of pinning down that point)

Here the personal liberty which inspired the original idea is related more directly to the original notion of unconscious association and memory. It is not irrelevant that Breton had read Proust's proofs back to him. It was the revolutionary, rebellious element in Breton that made him identify so often with communist political alignment, although he was never an intellectually committed Marxist. Similarly, it was the interest in the mechanisms of repression and the phenomena of involuntary recollection that stimulated his interest in psychoanalysis, although in *Nadja* he forcefully and amusingly disapproved of the domination of the patient by the therapist: "I continue not to see why a human being should be deprived of liberty," and he quotes Sade, Nietzsche, and Baudelaire. Unlike some of his colleagues, Breton was not particularly concerned to describe surrealist activities in terms of participation in some universal, suprapersonal spirit, and was therefore less inclined than they were to use the terminology of the occult or of oriental spiritualities

Apart from the preparatory works, *Les Champs magnétiques* and *Poisson soluble*, Breton produced three major works loosely concerned with love and liberty, *Nadja*, *Les Vases communicants*, and *L'Amour fou*, and the final major work, *Arcane 17*. Since he aspired to a breakdown of all distinctions between literary genres, it is not really appropriate to refer to his work in terms of "prose," "poetry," or "prose poems," although these terms do have to be used for want of any others. *Nadja* starts with an interrogation, "Qui suis-je?" (Who am I?), and the whole work is a structurally incoherent presentation of the answer, which is none the less impressively moving. The text might best be described as a reflection on self-analysis, and it contains anecdote, literary allusions, references to people, places, books, paintings, and events, as well as considerations about the workings of the writer's mind. It is the dated diary of the writer's meetings with Nadja, and the power of the work lies in the delicate sensitivity with which the writer reveals himself as he reflects continuously on Nadja's experience, his own reactions, and the breakdown of the barrier between the rational and irrational activities of the mind.

Les Vases communicants portrays, or delivers, the writer's reaction to the disappearance from his life of X, whom he can not erase from his memory. His reaction to the phenomena of his conscious life is charged by desire and frustration, and the disconnected character of the sequentially narrated events emphasizes the fortuitous way in which real things take on unpredictable associations and significance. The importance of events is measured by their psychic force, not their economic or social, or even, in the ordinary sense, emotional impact on our lives. Duration, too, is measured psychically rather than in units of real time. Yet Breton does not present a retreat into a protected dream world. On the contrary, he is making a strident assertion of what was important in the writer's own life, and therefore suggesting what sort of thing is important in human life generally. He is noticeably dismissive, for instance, of the constraint to earn a living by which most people have to abide.

The places evoked poetically by the writer are illustrated by photographs, used as a device to draw attention to the contrast between what the eye sees and the impact of the visual reality on the poet. *L'Amour fou* alters the emphasis from dream organization and lack of mental control to the role of chance in its impact on life, and the arbitrariness of the associations with which people invest objects. There is a breathtakingly daring erotic metamorphosis of the Cinderella story in which the foot is receptive to the slipper of desire. Anything can become for the psyche the figuration of any of its drives or frustrations, and the loved object undergoes an immensely skilful sacralization. "L'amour fou" is both the adolescent term for the the state of being "madly in love," and the powerful erotic drive, seated in the irrational part of the mind, to transmute the loved one with the psychic energies liberated in lunacy.

Apart from the epic *Ode à Charles Fourier, Arcane 17* was Breton's last major work of the imagination. The title is hermetic and refers to the 17th card in the tarot pack of 22, coming after the works of the devil and depicting the beautiful woman who pours urns of fire and water on the earth. It celebrates the meeting with Elisa, Breton's third wife, and was written with her at Gaspé, on the Gulf of St Lawrence, with its dramatic climatic effects and its moving rainbow of birds. If the text has to do with basic ingredients of myth like war, love, and resurrection, it works by analogies, largely of darkness and light, woven round the legend of the sprite Melusina, doomed to hover ethereally as a warning to her family and their descendants because, in her human form, her husband had looked at her on the forbidden day of the week. She is dispossessed, like Breton in Canada, and, like Elisa, the bringer of supernatural support, closer than any human can get to both nature (since she is a water sprite) and supernature (since in her ethereal form she is quasi-divine). The geographical situation at Gaspé also presents Breton with a set of analogies objectivized in a progression of metaphors. The geological strata become metaphors of the layers of civilization laid down by passing ages, their deep rose colour cementing human cultures in blood, like wartime Europe, whose eventual dissolution is reflected in the erosion wreaked by storm and wind on the ultimately indestructible rock.

Breton's writing has progressed to something more than a density of kaleidoscopic imagery. Analogy and metaphor have become intensely powerful tools for the communication of a prophetic vision of the world and its values. Out of the bric-à-brac of youthful surrealism and adolescent rebellion, Breton achieved an imaginative power that depends on climaxes and cadences of metaphor and analogy to convey a wholly new way of envisaging the meaning of human life and the significance of human experience.

PUBLICATIONS

Collections

Oeuvres complètes, Bibliothèque de la Pléiade, 2 vols., 1988–

Verse

Mont-de-piété, 1919
Les Champs magnétiques, with Philippe Soupault, 1920
Clair de terre, 1923
Ralentir travaux, with René Char and Paul Eluard, 1930
L'Union libre, 1931
Le Révolver à cheveux blancs, 1932
L'Air de l'eau, 1934
Le Château étoilé, 1937
Fata morgana, 1941; as *Fata Morgana*, 1969
Les Etats-généraux, 1943
Pleine marge, 1943
Young Cherry Trees Secured Against Hares, translated by Edouard Roditi, 1946
Ode à Charles Fourier, 1947; as *Ode to Charles Fourier*, translated by Kenneth White, 1969
Martinique charmeuse de serpents, 1948
Au regard des divinités, 1949
Constellations, 1959
Le là, 1961
Selected Poems, translated by Kenneth White, 1969
Poems, translated by Jean-Pierre Cauvin and Mary Ann Caws, 1983

Other

Manifeste du surréalisme: Poisson soluble, 1924; augmented edition, 1929
Les Pas perdus, 1924
Légitime défense, 1926
Introduction au discours sur le peu de réalité, 1927
Le Surréalisme et la peinture, 1928; augmented edition, 1965; as *Surrealism and Painting*, 1972
Nadja, 1928; revised edition, 1963; as *Nadja*, 1960
Second manifeste du surréalisme, 1930
L'Immaculée Conception, with Paul Eluard, 1930
Misère de la poésie: "L'Affaire Aragon" devant l'opinion publique, 1932
Les Vases communicants, 1932
Point du jour, 1934; revised edition, 1970
Qu'est-ce que le surréalisme?, 1934; as *What Is Surrealism?*, 1936
Du temps que les surréalistes avaient raison, 1935
Position politique du surréalisme, 1935
Notes sur la poésie, with Paul Eluard, 1936

Au lavoir noir, 1936

L'Amour fou, 1937

Arcane 17, 1944; augmented edition, 1947

Situation du surréalisme entre les deux guerres, 1945

Yves Tanguy (bilingual edition), 1946

Les Manifestes du surréalisme, 1947; revised edition, 1955, 1962; complete edition, 1972; as *Manifestoes of Surrealism*, 1974

La Lampe dans l'horloge, 1948

Flagrant délit: Rimbaud devant la conjuration de l'imposture et du truquage, 1949

Entretiens 1913–1952, 1952; revised edition, 1973

La Clé des champs, 1953

Toyen, with Jindrich Heisler and Benjamin Péret, 1953

Adieu ne plaise, 1954

Farouche à quatre feuilles, with others, 1954

L'Art magique, with Gérard Legrand, 1957

Pierre Moliner: un film de Raymond Borde, 1964

Perspective cavalière, edited by Marguerite Bonnet, 1970

Editor, *Trajectoire du rêve*, 1938

Editor, with Paul Eluard, *Dictionnaire abrégé du surréalisme*, 1938

Editor, *Anthologie de l'humour noir*, 1940 (?); augmented edition, 1950

Bibliography

Sheringham, Michael, *Breton: A Bibliography*, 1972

Critical studies

Caws, Mary Ann, *Surrealism and the Literary Imagination: A Study of Breton and Bachelard*, 1966

Browder, Clifford, *Breton, Arbiter of Surrealism*, 1967

Caws, Mary Ann, *The Poetry of Dada and Surrealism*, 1970

Balakian, Anna E., *Breton, Magus of Surrealism*, 1971

Caws, Mary Ann, *Breton* (in English), 1971

Rosemont, Franklin, *Breton and the First Principles of Surrealism*, 1978

Béhar, Henri, *Breton*, 1990

BUTOR, Michel (-Marie-François), 1926–

Novelist, critic, and autobiographer.

LIFE

Michel Butor was the fourth of seven children, born on 14 September 1926 at Mons-en-Baroeul, where his father was a senior railway official, eventually to be promoted to senior inspector of commercial tarrifs. An eighth child died before birth, and Butor's mother became deaf on the birth of her final child. The family, which was devoutly Catholic, moved to Paris in 1929, where Butor attended the local Catholic school, as he did again when they moved within Paris in 1936. At the outbreak of war they moved to Evreux, where Butor attended the Jesuit school, before finishing at the Lycée Louis-le-Grand. Impressed above all by Shelley, he began to write verse. He also began to draw and to take an interest in surrealism (q.v.). His father sketched, the whole family was musical, and Butor tried without obvious success to learn the violin. Music and the visual arts, particularly surrealist painting and collages, were to affect him deeply, however, and much of his later imaginative work shows his desire to combine them with literature in some form of synthesis. Apparently unenthusiastic about academic work, Butor read widely, but did not take the examination for the Ecole Normale Supérieure, registering instead for a degree in classics at the Sorbonne. He failed his first-year examination and transferred to philosophy, in which he acquired his licence in 1946 and, under Bachelard's supervision, a diploma in 1947 for an essay on mathematics and the idea of necessity.

Asked for a contribution to the review *Vrille*, Butor published the poem "Hommage partiel à Max Ernst" in 1945. An article on Joyce was printed by the Dominican *Revue Intellectuelle* at a period when Butor was seriously interested in Catholic philosophy, while at the same time impressed by lectures given by Sartre and Leiris. He failed his agrégation a number of times, but worked for Jean Wahl at the Collège Philosophique until January 1950, when he became a replacement teacher at the Lycée de Sens. In the meanwhile he had met André Breton, the long-established leader of the surrealist movement, and spent three summers at international youth camps in Germany. In 1950 he began work on a doctoral thesis, again failed the agrégation, and accepted a post teaching French in Egypt. There, at Al Minya, 200 kilometres from Cairo, he began to write *Passage de Milan*.

From 1951 to 1953 Butor was employed by the French department of the University of Manchester. He visited North Africa and started his systematic tour of the major European galleries, then spent a year in Paris as a translator. Thanks to Georges Lambrichs at the Editions de Minuit, that house published *Passage de Milan* in 1954, but it was not commercially successful. Butor had come to the novel, "le laboratoire du récit (the laboratory of narrative)," he later declared, under the dual pressures of poetry and philosophy. It was a form he was later to abandon in favour of a more ambitious type of literature, "le livre futur…la partition d'une civilisation (the book of the future…the score of a civilization)." Meanwhile, in October 1954, he accepted a post to teach in the French lycée at Salonika. In 1955 he replaced Barthes as a course instructor for foreign French teachers at the Sorbonne, and in 1956 *L'Emploi du temps*, a novel in the form of a musical canon, was published. Written in Salonika, it was to win the Prix Fénéon. That autumn Lucien Goldmann got Butor a post at the international school in Geneva to teach French, philosophy, history, and geography. Less than two years later, in 1958, Butor married Marie-Josèphe Mas, one of his Geneva pupils, who was to bear him four daughters. Meanwhile, in 1957, he had finished and published his third novel, *La Modification*, and spent some time in Italy.

La Modification, published like the preceding novels by Lambrichs at the Editions de Minuit, was proposed for the Prix Goncourt, and was finally awarded the Prix Renaudot. Early in 1958 Butor, suddenly famous, went to Greece with "Marie-Jo," marrying her in August. At the Editions de Minuit Alain Robbe-Grillet had replaced Lambrichs, who had moved to Grasset, and it was that house which published Butor's *Le Génie du lieu* in May. From October Butor and his wife lived in Paris. He lectured in various European cities, and an agreement was concluded whereby Gallimard paid him a regular income in return

Les Compagnons de Pantagruel (lecture), 1976

Dotremont et ses écrivures: entretiens sur les logogrammes, with Michel Sicard, 1978

Matières et talismans (interview), with Michel Sicard, 1978

Editor, *Essais,* by Montaigne, 1964

Translator, with Lucien Goldmann, *Brève histoire de la littérature allemande,* by Georg Lukács, 1949

Translator, *La Théorie du champ de la conscience,* by Aaron Gurwitsch, 1957

Translator, *Tout est bien qui finit bien,* by Shakespeare, 1958

Bibliography

Mason, Barbara, *Butor: A Checklist,* 1979

Critical studies

Roudiez, Leon S., *Butor,* 1965

Sturrock, John, *The French New Novel: Claude Simon, Butor, Alain Robbe-Grillet,* 1969

Grant, Marion A., *Butor: L'Emploi du temps,* 1973

Spencer, Michael, *Butor* (in English), 1974

Waelti-Walters, Jennifer, *Butor* (in English), 1977

McWilliams, Dean, *The Narrative of Butor: The Writer as Janus,* 1978

Oppenheim, Lois, *Intentionality and Intersubjectivity: A Phenomenological Study of Butor's La Modification,* 1980

———

C

CAMUS, Albert, 1913–1960.

Novelist, dramatist, and essayist.

LIFE

Camus's work is dominated by images of childhood and, in the light of the cultural turmoil left throughout Europe by World War II and in France by the aftermath of the Algerian war, his life has been subject to a degree of mythologizing. Neither fact is extraordinary, but both are important in the context of any attempt to understand his personality and literary achievement.

Camus was born on Algeria's fertile interior plain. His father, of whom Camus knew only that he abhorred bloodshed and had vomited after once being forced to witness an execution by guillotine, was employed in the wine industry. Camus believed (wrongly, as it happened) that his family, having chosen to remain French after the Franco-Prussian War, had therefore moved from Alsace to Algeria. Both his French and his Algerian origins were to remain important to him.

Camus was the younger of two sons. His mother came from Minorca. His father was called up before he was one, was badly wounded on the Marne, and died in hospital. His mother took him to live with her own family in Belcourt, a working-class, racially mixed suburb of Algiers with a growing Arab population. Camus grew up street-wise and no doubt accustomed to look down on the non-French. His mother became a factory worker, then a charwoman. She was partially deaf, unable to read, and probably backward, and her brother Etienne treated her roughly. Camus himself undoubtedly suffered from emotional deprivation.

He did well at primary school and got a bursary to the lycée. He took to soccer and swimming and enjoyed the company of a hugely extrovert uncle, a butcher by trade. In 1930 he contracted tuberculosis and was looked after by his uncle, but he had to repeat a year at school, and eventually the disease spread to his other lung. One of his masters, Jean Grenier, was conscious of the suffering entailed by his double burden of poverty and ill health and was intelligent and sensitive enough to know how to help him. Camus lived henceforward with his uncle until his first marriage, although he returned to Belcourt frequently and often for lengthy periods, continuing to admire his mother for her dignity. He already believed strongly in values such as justice and freedom and sought to remain true to his class while rejecting all forms of political ideology. It was a combination of attitudes to which he held in later life and which was to cause him some anguish. He read Marx but was put off socialism by the party's inactive optimism. In company with friends he used to roam the seedier quarters of Algiers, frequenting cafés, and he began to reflect on protest as a necessary means to righting social injustices.

He read Dostoyevsky and Nietzsche, and he liked the *Nouvelle Revue Française* (*NRF*, q.v.), admiring Malraux especially, while also retaining an interest in Gide. Although inspired by Grenier, Camus was later to react against him, while Grenier took to denying that he had done anything special for Camus. In 1933 Camus, again supported by a scholarship, began to read philosophy at Algiers. Inspite of an apparent weakness in philosophical method, he was very self-assured. In 1934 he married Simone Hié, previously the girlfriend of his own close friend Max-Pol Fouchet and the daughter of a well-connected doctor whose first husband had left her. As an antidote to painful periods, Simone's mother prescribed morphine, and Simone soon became addicted. Her mother, whose second marriage also ended in disaster, was in favour of the match with Camus, although Camus's uncle was not. Camus was gambling by marrying out of his class, and his bride was gambling on Camus's strength to get her over her addiction. The gambles did not pay off.

Camus graduated in 1936, having finished his thesis for the Diplôme d'Etudes Supérieures and hoping to go on to the agrégation, but his marriage was by now running into difficulties. Simone went to a clinic for treatment and Camus moved in with her mother. He had joined the communist party in 1935. Disillusion soon set in there, too, and Camus left the party in 1937. Meanwhile, he had visited Austria and Czechoslovakia. His marriage finally disintegrated in 1936, when it became clear from a letter he opened that his wife was still taking drugs and paying for them with sex. Camus proceeded to give private tuition, worked for a time as a meteorologist, and did a variety of other casual jobs, including acting, while continuing to help organize a Maison de Culture for the party. It was designed to bring theatre and other cultural activities to the working classes and staged an important series of amateur theatrical productions, which Camus himself directed.

After breaking with the communists, Camus went to Savoy and Italy, but on his return his health prevented him from taking the agrégation which would have opened the way to a university career. He lived with friends in the autumn of 1937, had dozens of passing affairs, and two of a more serious nature, with Blanche Balain and Christiane Galindo. He continued to stage ever more ambitious productions for the Théâtre de l'Equipe and published his first collection of essays, *L'Envers et l'endroit*. He also wrote *La Mort heureuse*, a novel which he abandoned but which, when posthumously published in 1971, went to the top of the best-seller list. Despite recent adverse critical comment, Camus has remained Gallimard's best-selling author since his death.

In mid-1938 Camus began working for the *Alger-Républicain*, founded to express the views of the Front Populaire. Unfortunately, by the time the newspaper appeared the Front Populaire had virtually disintegrated. Camus became a factotum, deputy editor, chief reporter, special correspondent, and book reviewer, while hiring rooms by the week or the month and carrying on with his own non-journalistic writing. As war approached, he became conscious of the terrible compromises the situation in Europe entailed. Rearmament meant war and the strengthening of capitalism. Peace meant appeasement and the betrayal of Czechoslovakia.

When the newspaper's successor, *Le Soir-Républicain*, closed for lack of paper, Camus continued with his literary writing. Inspired at this time by a feeling for the harmony of life, he was to become increasingly preoccupied with a consciousness of mortality, and the consequent absurdity of the human condition. The youthful *La Mort heureuse* was abandoned, at least in part, because Camus could find no way of depicting a consciousness unaware of its own contradictions, but it reveals his starting point. The later work accepts the notion of a fractured consciousness and centres on the absurdity itself.

Camus was also falling seriously in love again, this time with Francine Faure, a well-educated middle-class girl from Oran who hoped to go to university and whom he was to marry in 1940. In 1938–39 she visited Algiers frequently and Camus went to Oran whenever he could. Francine abandoned her plans for higher study and settled for a teaching job in Oran. Camus then took a job setting pages on the conservative *Paris-Soir* (a paper he would never have agreed to work on editorially), the idea being that Francine would join him in Paris as soon as he was legally free to marry. He lived in one cheap hotel after another and disliked Paris, later moving with the paper first to Clermont and then to Lyons, where Francine finally joined him. They were married on 3 December 1940. Camus was laid off almost immediately and the couple returned to Oran, where both took up teaching posts, Camus in two private schools set up by the Oran Jews banned from the state system. Having finished *Caligula*, *Le Mythe de Sisyphe*, and *L'Etranger*, he began another sequence involving a novel, play, and book of essays: *La Peste*, *Le Malentendu*, and *L'Homme révolté*. This new cycle focuses on an acceptance of man's freedom rather than on the inhumanity which had preoccupied him in the first.

Camus suffered a renewed attack of tuberculosis and in 1942 Francine took him to stay with a cousin who ran a boarding house in the Massif Central, although she herself had to return to Oran when school reopened. The Allied invasion of North Africa cut Camus off, depriving him of both money and a job. Blanche Balain spent some time with him, but refused his invitation to stay on, and Gaston Gallimard paid him as a reader from 1942, something he often did to help writers in financial difficulties. Camus would have liked to join the Resistance, but his outlook was too coldly pessimistic, his attitude too cautious, and his health too precarious to make him an acceptable candidate. He did finally join late in 1943 or early in 1944, organizing a literary magazine for the "Combat" group, which had some 75,000 members. The magazine collapsed and Camus began working on the newspaper *Combat* itself. He spent some time in Paris, where he made several friends, including Gaston Gallimard's nephew Michel and the Dominican priest Father Bruckberger. He also got to know Malraux and Sartre, with whom he was on close terms from 1943 to 1945 in spite of his intense dislike of existentialism as Sartre understood it. Sartre was a witty companion, with a lively, boyish sense of humour, whose energy, drinking, and womanizing amused Camus. Gide, who had been cut off in North Africa and had got to know Camus's

friends there, installed Camus in the part of his Paris flat formerly tenanted by Marc Allégret. Camus now fell in love with the actress Maria Casarès, who starred in *Le Malentendu*, which was first performed, unsuccessfully, in 1944. The end of the war necessarily meant the end of their liaison, as of the defiant, drunken parties in the company of Sartre, Beauvoir, and others.

At the same time *Combat* ceased to be a clandestine publication. Sartre reported vividly on the German withdrawal and Camus's editorials aimed at the creation of a working-class democracy, combining moral fervour with a rhetoric that was at times vapid. The paper was also astringent, however, with regard to the "épuration" and rejected "the conformism of victory." Francine arrived from Algeria and soon became pregnant, though Camus continued to be unfaithful to her. If not rich, he was by now at least famous. He was reluctant to have anything to do with Sartre's *Les Temps Modernes* (q.v.), intended to replace the *NRF*. In 1945 he fell ill again and that same year returned to Algeria, where his mother was still living. While there he called on Gide, in whose flat he and Francine stayed temporarily. But Camus did not relish the formality of their otherwise cordial relations with Gide and later in 1945 he and his wife moved out. Francine gave birth to twins, a boy and a girl.

On 26 September *Caligula* had its first night. The critics were lukewarm. At Gallimard Camus now had his own series of publications to look after, called "L'Espoir", and for the *NRF* he took charge of the new writing of the liberation. He continued working for *Combat* and was also endeavouring to finish *La Peste*. *Combat* was attacked by the press as too libertarian, and itself attacked de Gaulle for his grandiose pretensions. By now it was losing its buoyant irreverence. In 1946 Camus undertook a successful lecture tour to the US and on his return met Koestler, whose anti-Stalinism led to a quarrel with Merleau-Ponty, Sartre's protégé, in which Camus took Koestler's side. The incident led to the famous quarrel between Sartre and Camus. Despairing of social transformation, Camus had fallen back politically on the simple rejection of violence, which was later to find expression in his campaign against the death penalty. *Combat* was in financial trouble now that it was faced with only two possible choices, either to represent an anti-communist, left-wing platform with no coherent policies, or to move to the right under the impact of views such as those expressed by Raymond Aron.

La Peste was published in 1947 and was an instant success. It sold 100,000 copies straight off and multiple translations were published. Camus became rich on the strength of it. He worked regularly, visited his mother annually, went on family holidays, and occasionally accepted invitations to lecture. There were sporadic reconciliations with Sartre, and a silly drunken brawl with Koestler. After a chance meeting in 1948 Camus resumed his affair with Maria Casarès and she played in his disastrous *L'Etat de siège* of that year, directed by Barrault. In 1949 Camus went to Latin America, which he disliked, returning to Paris in time for the triumph of *Les Justes*, in which Maria Casarès again starred. Francine and Camus moved several times, but Francine found it increasingly difficult to pin her husband down to any sort of domesticity and knew, of course, about Casarès and a host of other infidelities.

In 1951 Camus published *L'Homme révolté*, a large volume into which he had put a great deal of work, but which has been described as his worst book. Though well reviewed at the time, it had damaging consequences for Camus. It attacked Sartre in a manner that brought a quite devastating revenge, although Anglo-Saxon opinion was on Camus's side and the Jeanson–Sartre counter-attack, started in *Les Temps Modernes*, reads quite unconvincingly today. For a while Camus worked on *L'Express*. He visited Algeria, but found it impossible to contribute to a solution to the Algerian political problem, polarized into a conflict between terrorist insurrection and military repression. In May 1956 *La Chute* was published to a mixed reception. Camus agreed to move out of the family apartment, although he returned regularly to visit the twins. He published an immensely successful adaptation of Faulkner's *Requiem for a Nun*, also in 1956. In 1957 he was awarded the Nobel prize and borrowed a dinner jacket for the ceremony. In the ensuing publicity he found it difficult to avoid expressing both his left-wing views and his refusal to condemn outright the conduct of the French army in Algeria. He bought a house in Provence, and it was when Michel Gallimard was driving his own wife, his daughter, and Camus back from there to Paris that he crashed his car. Camus was killed instantaneously.

WORKS

Much of Camus's published work is journalism, partly collected together posthumously on account both of his high literary standing as a novelist and of his well-publicized controversy with Sartre. The sparse and factual reporting style developed in Algiers gave way in France to more floridly resounding expressions of moral outrage and an uncertainty of political stance. In the grand formal statement expected on such occasions, Camus devoted his speech of acceptance of the Nobel prize (*Discours de la Suède*) to the nature and limits of the writer's political commitment. Literary quality, he claimed, should neither be insulated from nor submerged beneath ideological conviction. His own best journalism is investigative, informed by strong moral feelings without actually enunciating them. The heavily ironic "Suetonius" pieces from *Combat*, considered by some as his best, are unfortunately not included in the Pléiade collected volume.

The first volume of five essays, devoted to Camus's childhood and his 1936 stays in Prague and Vicenza, *L'Envers et l'endroit*, has sometimes been preferred to all his other work. Although the subject is often hardship and poverty, the prose is at times lyrical and lush. Death appears as seductive, a force in harmony with life. *Noces* of 1939, another volume of essays, is a poem of ecstasy, almost pantheistic in inspiration, celebrating the sun and wind, the South of France, and the sea. In a sense it is anti-humanistic, denouncing the role of intelligence and artistry and exulting in the joys of physical, even barbaric, pleasures. *La Mort heureuse*, the abandoned first novel, first published in 1971, depicts some of Camus's favourite spots in Algeria. Its central figure, Patrice Mersault, commits a murder and a theft, thus liberating himself from his daily routine, has a love affair, goes to Prague, lives in identifiable parts of Algiers, and gradually sinks into lethargic indifference, both welcoming and abhorring the dissolution of his individual consciousness into the cosmic rhythm which requires his extinction. The novel, which was in any case too autobiographical for Camus to want to publish it, fails in its attempt to persuade the reader of Mersault's assent to a merging with the pantheistic harmony of the universe, and its lyricism occasionally seems strained.

Caligula, which grew out of Camus's work with the Théâtre de l'Equipe, is, for a number of technical reasons, a complicated dramatic failure, almost a pastiche of Greek drama without the elemental qualities. The question it poses, however, is clear. Does a nostalgia for innocence make it possible to sidestep the need for death as the punishment for guilt due to horrifying actions which, though inevitable, are sinful? The philosophical essay *Le Mythe de Sisyphe* concerns the acceptance of guilt rather than a striving for innocence. Man can never be at harmony with the world around him, but that is no reason for him to rebel and destroy himself. Lacking the potential for self-fulfilment, his situation becomes absurd. The God who alone could bring about man's fulfilment is "absent" but a source of values none the less, a situation thoroughly explored in the moral and theological literature of the Middle Ages and the early modern period, as well as in the 19th and 20th centuries. Camus draws too heavily here on his philosophical training instead of concentrating on imaginative parable, and the weakest part of the book is that demanding some acquaintance with Husserl, the founder of phenomenology (q.v.). Its strongest is its implied moral condemnation of violence under any circumstances and its defiant spirit of hope. There is a strong religious undertow.

L'Etranger is an imaginatively successful and technically innovative "récit." Its protagonist, Meursault, is alienated from the world because his experience is quite unrelated to the world's interpretation of it. In the first part of the book the first-person narrator uses a matter-of-fact style to give an account, generally in the perfect tense, of the various trivial details of his daily life, but includes, with no change of register to denote emotion, the fact that he attended his mother's funeral. Nothing is of any real importance to him, neither a proposed promotion and move to Paris, nor the question of whether he and girl-friend Marie should get married, nor of whether they actually love one another. Meursault ends up shooting an Arab on the beach in a momentary gesture whose motivation is quite deliberately left blurred. It is clear that he feels inebriated by the light, the heat, the sand, the sea, and the sun. His intentions are not aggressive, but the Arab, who was lying on his back, may reasonably have thought them to be. The Arab produced a knife. Meursault had taken a gun from a friend, Raymond, who had earlier wanted to shoot the Arab just for the sake of shooting him.

The second part of the novel opens with Meursault's arrest. The first part had ended:

"Je ne sentais plus que les cymbales du soleil sur mon front et, indistinctement, le glaive éclatant jailli du couteau toujours en face de moi. Cette épée brûlante rongeait mes cils et fouillait mes yeux doleureux. C'est alors que tout a vacillé. La mer a charrié un souffle épais et ardent. Il m'a semblé que le ciel s'ouvrait sur toute son étendue pour laisser pleuvoir du feu. Tout mon être s'est tendu et j'ai crispé ma main sur le revolver. La gâchette a cédé, j'ai touché le ventre poli de la crosse et c'est là, dans le bruit à la fois sec et assourdissant, que tout a commencé. J'ai secoué la sueur et le soleil. J'ai compris que j'avais détruit l'équilibre du jour, le silence exceptionnel d'une plage où j'avais été heureux. Alors j'ai tiré encore quatre fois sur un corps inerte où les balles s'enfonçaient sans qu'il y parût. Et c'était comme quatre coups brefs que je frappais sur la porte du malheur."

(I no longer felt anything except the sun's cymbals on my forehead and, indistinctly, the shining blade springing from the knife which was still in front of me. That burning sword gnawed at my eyelashes and searched my painful eyes. It is then that everything became unsteady. The sea drove forward a thick, burning puff of air. It seemed to me that the sky opened as far as it stretched to let fire rain down. My whole being became tense and I clasped my hand on the revolver. The trigger gave way, I touched the polished belly of the handle and it's then, in a noise both deafening and dry, that everything started. I shook off the sweat and the sun. I understood that I'd destroyed the harmony of the day, the extraordinary stillness of a beach where I'd been happy. Then I fired four more times on a motionless body into which the bullets sank without trace. And it was like four short knocks I struck on the gates of unhappiness).

In the second part of the book, it is only from the reaction of the courtroom that, completely bored by the whole game, Meursault finally recognizes his guilt, "j'ai senti alors quelque chose qui soulevait toute la salle et, pour la première fois, j'ai compris que j'étais coupable (Then I felt something which roused the whole room, and for the first time I understood that I was guilty)." The prose of L'Etranger is coolly precise and what Meursault undergoes, although taken here to its absolute and unbelievable limits, is actually part of everybody's everyday experience. Meursault fails to react emotionally on what society considers to be an appropriate level when his mother dies, as when he shoots the Arab. Camus shocks the reader by narrating Meursault's feeling that he had merely "destroyed the harmony of the day." What society feels ought to be his carefully nurtured mechanisms of inhibition suddenly break down when he is driven by a merely trivial impulse. What does that make him guilty of?

Technically the "récit" announced the "nouveau roman" in its psychology, its preoccupation with the trivial, its multiple viewpoints, and its ambiguities. The unreality of the trial in Meursault's consciousness is merely highlighted by the fact that the rules by which the court plays its games would also demand an acquittal on grounds of self-defence. The Arab had brandished a knife, and the firing of a few extra shots into a corpse does not constitute a murder. Meursault's ultimate defiance lies in his wish that crowds of people will attend his execution and welcome him with cries of hatred, so sinking themselves into the social stereotype demanded by the prosecutor.

The most effective of Camus's essays were also written at this period, but not published (in *Actuelles 1–3*) until 1950–58, although *Lettres à un ami allemand* appeared in 1945. *La Peste* was published in 1947 and was a runaway success. It is an allegory, written in the form of a diary in a dry, restrained style. Only at the end of the novel is the author of the diary identified as Doctor Rieux, one of a small group which tries to combat the plague and which includes Tarrou, a campaigner against the death penalty, the journalist Rambert, Paneloux the Jesuit, and Grand, the petty bureaucrat. The plague vanishes as abruptly as it had appeared. Paneloux and Tarrou have died. The diarist speculates, doubts, records opinions and direct speech, registers the news of each member of the group, but fails to come to any conclusions regarding the epidemic.

Quotes are taken from Tarrou's diary, where its author notes that the world, like the plague, does not make sense, although people have to go about their business as if it did. In the midst of the plague Tarrou describes trivia at length, if only because the "trivial" is no longer a meaningful category into which anything fits with certainty, a fact that Rieux cannot grasp. The trivial can in fact divert from the knowledge of impending death, which is both its usefulness and its danger. The allegory, which also applies to the Resistance, pinpoints the human values, courage and fraternity, which can continue to be upheld as a challenge to the suppression of sympathy. *La Peste* is not an encyclopedia of moral theory, or a practical guide to moral choice, but a slow grasping out towards such positive values as can be found in the face of disaster, together with a rejection of some of those Camus finds unacceptable including, the Christian ethic as caricaturized in the preachings of the Jesuit Paneloux, which involve acquiescing in the massacre of the innocent.

L'Homme révolté, which appeared in 1951, is generally regarded as a weak book, mainly because it fails to found a positive ethic on the notion of revolt and is in the end simply a sustained attack on any violence perpetrated in the name of an ideology. While attracting a great deal of sympathy, it lacked philosophical rigour. It did, however, reaffirm Camus's liberal reformist position, one which he would take up again during the Algerian war in his attempts to reconcile de Gaulle's ideas with those of the Front de la Libération Nationale.

The third great novel, *La Chute*, grew out of one of the short stories intended for *L'Exil et le royaume*, written while Camus was trying to mediate in the Algerian war. The narrator of *La Chute* is a self-righteous, womanizing lawyer, Jean-Baptiste Clamance. The multiple Christian resonance of the name is deliberate and the moral ambiguities of *La Chute* are more subtle than in earlier works. Camus continues the tradition of the classical French moralists who nourished him, and suggests here that good actions may have selfish motives, and evil actions partially good ones. The narrator shelters in his legal work for good causes, but is increasingly forced to repel admiration and parade his guilt as he assumes a growing diversity of roles. What holds the book together is largely the irony and the sardonic tone of Clamance's monologue, while there is some parody including self-parody, in the depiction of a professional moralist in the modern world. No flight into innocence is possible, in the novel as in the need to take sides in the Algerian war.

Camus's best works for the stage are his adaptations from Calderón, Pierre de Larivey, Buzzati, Faulkner, Lope de Vega, and Dostoyevsky. His greatness lies in his fictional wrestling with the fundamental moral problems of human life.

PUBLICATIONS

Collections

Théâtre, récits, nouvelles; Essais, Bibliothèque de la Pléiade, edited by Roger Quilliot, 2 vols., 1962–65
The Collected Plays of Albert Camus, 1965

Fiction

L'Etranger, 1942; as *The Stranger*, 1946; as *The Outsider*, 1946
La Peste, 1947; as *The Plague*, 1948
La Chute, 1956; as *The Fall*, 1957
L'Exil et le royaume, 1957; as *Exile and the Kingdom*, 1958
La Mort heureuse, 1971; as *A Happy Death*, 1973

Plays

Le Malentendu (produced 1944), with *Caligula*, 1944; as *Cross Purpose*, with *Caligula*, 1947
Caligula (produced 1945), with *Le Malentendu*, 1944; 1941 version (produced 1983), 1984; as *Caligula* (in English), with *Cross Purpose*, 1947
L'Etat de siège (produced 1948), 1948; as *State of Siege*, in *Caligula and Three Other Plays*, 1958
Les Justes (produced 1949), 1950; as *The Just Assassins*, in *Caligula and Three Other Plays*, 1958
La Dévotion à la croix, from the play by Calderón (produced 1953), 1953
Les Esprits, from the work by Pierre de Larivey (produced 1953), 1953
Un cas intéressant, from the work by Dino Buzzati (produced 1955), 1955
Requiem pour une nonne, from the work by William Faulkner (produced 1956), 1956
Le Chevalier d'Olmedo, from the play by Lope de Vega (produced 1957), 1957
Les Possédés, from the novel by Dostoyevsky (produced 1959), 1959; as *The Possessed*, 1960

Other

L'Envers et l'endroit, 1937
Noces, 1939
Le Mythe de Sisyphe, 1942; as *The Myth of Sisyphus and Other Essays*, 1955
Lettres à un ami allemand, 1945
L'Existence, 1945
Le Minotaure; ou, La Halte d'Oran, 1950
Actuelles 1–3: Chroniques 1944–1948, Chroniques 1948–1953, Chronique algérienne 1939–1958, 3 vols., 1950–58
L'Homme révolté, 1951; as *The Rebel: An Essay on Man in Revolt*, 1954
L'Eté, 1954
Réflexions sur la guillotine, in *Réflexions sur la peine capitale*, with Arthur Koestler, 1957; as *Reflections on the Guillotine*, 1960
Discours de la Suède, 1958; as *Speech of Acceptance upon the Award of the Nobel Prize for Literature*, 1958
Resistance, Rebellion, and Death (selection), 1961
Méditation sur le théâtre et la vie, 1961
Carnets: mai 1935-février 1942, 1962; as *Carnets 1935–1942* (in English), 1963; as *Notebooks 1935–1942*, 1963
Lettres à Bernanos, 1963
Carnets: janvier 1942-mars 1951, 1964; as *Notebooks 1942–1951*, 1970
Lyrical and Critical Essays, edited by Philip Thody, 1968
Le Combat d'Albert Camus, edited by Norman Stokle, 1970
Selected Essays and Notebooks, edited by Philip Thody, 1970
Le Premier Camus, 1973; as *Youthful Writings*, 1976
Journaux de voyage, edited by Roger Quilliot, 1978
Fragments d'un combat 1938–1940: Alger-Républicain, Le Soir-Républicain, edited by Jacqueline Lévi-Valensi and André Abbou, 1978
Correspondance 1932–1960, with Jean Grenier, edited by Marguerite Dobrenn, 1981

Translator, *La Dernière Fleur*, by James Thurber, 1952

Critical studies

Cruickshank, John, *Albert Camus and the Literature of Revolt*, 1959
Thody, Philip, *Albert Camus, 1913–1960* (in English), 1962
Brée, Germaine, *Camus*, 1964; revised edition (in English), 1972
Parker, Emmett, *Albert Camus: The Artist in the Arena*, 1965
O'Brien, Conor Cruise, *Camus* (in English), 1970
Maquet, Albert, *Camus: The Invincible Summer*, 1972
Lazere, Donald, *The Unique Creation of Albert Camus*, 1973
Lottman, Herbert R., *Camus: A Biography*, 1979
Rizzuto, Anthony, *Camus' Imperial Vision*, 1981
McCarthy, Patrick, *Camus: A Critical Study of His Life and Work*, 1982

CÉLINE, Louis-Ferdinand (pseudonym of Louis-Ferdinand Destouches), 1894–1961.

Novelist.

LIFE

"Céline," who took his pseudonym from one of his mother's Christian names, was born in a Paris suburb, the son of an insurance clerk and a shopkeeper specializing in lace. He was educated locally, and sent to England and Germany for short stays in the years 1907 to 1909, a fact which suggests that, given their background, his family had unusual educational ambitions for him. After school Céline took various jobs, working mostly as a clerk or an errand boy. He studied privately for the baccalauréat before the war and was to pass both parts in April and July 1919. In 1912, partly, perhaps, out of social ambition or a desire to escape from the dreary routine of his life, he volunteered to join a cavalry regiment, and when war broke out he was an NCO.

In November 1914 he was badly injured returning from a successful mission for which he had volunteered. He was invalided out of the army with 75 per cent disability and the Médaille Militaire, and in 1915 spent some months working in the passport office of the French consulate in London while waiting for his demobilization papers. He married a French dancer in London in January 1916, but abandoned her later that year to go to West Africa, where he became a trader. He was invalided home with dysentery and in 1919 began studying for a medical degree at the University of Rennes. He married the daughter of the faculty's director in August. His wife bore him a daughter in 1920. In 1924, at the age of 30, he qualified as a doctor. A few months later he left his wife and child and went to work for the League of Nations, which involved a good deal of travelling. His wife obtained a divorce in 1926.

In 1928 Céline established himself in private practice in a working-class suburb of Paris. From 1931 to 1938 he worked at the local municipal clinic. He travelled to Germany and the USSR and claimed that he had started writing in order to make money. His first novel, *Voyage au bout de la nuit*, published graphical travel narrative, starting with childhood, and moving through New York to Paris. Cendrars invents for himself seven improbable uncles, whom he later declared to have been real, and a history of family ruin involving the Panama financial scandal. The poem is laconic in its avoidance of emotional impact, written in the style of diary jottings, and filled with contemporary bric-à-brac, advertising slogans, references to trivial incidents, snatches of newspaper reports. Near the end the poet declares the birth of a new sort of poetry. In fact, this was virtually Cendrars's farewell to poetry. Whatever the skills it exhibits, *Kodak* (later entitled *Documentaires*) of 1924 is an elaborate tease, compiled from a popular science fiction book, Gustave Le Rouge's *Le Mystérieux Docteur Cornélius*, and another on elephant hunting by Maurice Calmeyn. The diminishing lyrical intensity of *Feuilles de route*, with its picture postcard style, consummates Cendrars's break with poetry.

Profond aujourd'hui and *J'ai tué* are short prose poems, although *J'ai tué* is very nearly a simple short story. *L'Eubage*, later dismissed by Cendrars as unimportant, was written for the patron and collector Jacques Doucet against monthly payments. "L'eubage" is a priest from ancient Gaul specializing in divination, and the text, which was to have been organized round the signs of the zodiac, is now split into 12 chapters, each with the name of a month. The first of the novels proper, *L'Or*, is about the Swiss fugitive who cheated his passage to New York with a forged letter of credit, and tricked his way across the continent, into the confidence of the governor of Monterey and of the Indians, until the discovery of gold brought about his spiritual and financial ruin. The text, in terse, swift prose, is in 74 numbered paragraphs split into 15 chapters, with the present tense conveying a cinematographic effect: "All this time John Augustus Sutter never once sets foot in the capital … For he must have money, money, and still more money."

The famous seventh chapter, in the English translation by Nina Rootes (1982), reads in its entirety:

Reverie. Calm. Repose.
It is Peace.
No. No. No. No. No. No. No. No: it is GOLD!
It is gold.
The gold rush.
The world is infected with gold fever.
The great gold rush of 1848, 1849, 1850, and 1851. It will last for fifteen years.
SAN FRANCISCO!

This is amiable pastiche of children's stories, newspaper reporting, and cinema technique, and it relies fashionably on elementary typographic effect. The prose clatters along like Chaplin's gait and the staccato movements of his mind in *The Gold Rush*, also of 1925. It explains why, for all the excitement of his life and the intensity of his imaginative experience, at best Cendrars, cannot be considered other than marginal as an author, and why the more thoughtful of his contemporaries, like the surrealists (q.v.), never took him very seriously.

Moravagine of 1926 does, however, share the surrealist preoccupation with dreams. The narrator, Raymond la Science, is an intern in a psychiatric establishment who helps the sad, withered old Moravagine to escape, and resigns his own post to observe him. Heir to the Hungarian throne and born prematurely on the day of his father's assassination, Moravagine went mad early on and had spent his whole life locked up. He becomes a visionary and, when freed, acts violently towards women, killing them wherever he goes. Arriving in Moscow in time for the 1905 uprising, he becomes the centre of terrorist activity. There follows a travelogue contrasting the New World with the Old, the primitive with the civilized. Imprisoned by Indians in Amazonia, Moravagine exploits his powers and, after a ritualistic massacre, is enabled to escape by the women he has magnetized. In a New World war he destroys the imperial seat in Vienna and is found by the narrator as a morphine addict who imagines himself on Mars. The dada (q.v.) author Soupault thought the book might be Cendrars's revenge against dada. It floats on plagiarism, fictionalized autobiography, and sado-masochistic fantasy. It does not create a myth, however, or function as a parable. It is not an adventure story, but a parody showing where surrealist theory might lead, what an irrational world could be, and how the parodied scientific narrator and the mad object of his observations need, reflect, and rely on one another.

The next novel, *Les Confessions de Dan Yack*, was published in 1929 in two parts, "Le plan de l'aiguille" and "Les confessions de Dan Yack." The form is that of the saga of a voyage to the Antarctic, where four men and a dog try to spend a year. Only Dan Yack, the flamboyant playboy from St Petersburg, survives. The composer drowns, the poet goes mad and dies in a fire, and the sculptor is crushed by the statue he has made of Dan Yack. Dan Yack becomes a successful whaler in a fairy-tale story who then sinks into melancholia. The second volume is presented as a series of dictaphone reels in which Dan Yack's memories alternate with the diaries of his dead wife, Mireille, for whom his feelings are portrayed as movingly tender and gentle, and whose diaries reveal the terrifying discovery of her own sexual ambiguity. The novel ends with Dan Yack's self-enclosure, his inability to communicate anything to anyone as he starts a new life. The novel has to be read as a parable of Cendrars's own experience of frustration with the novel form.

Rhum, l'aventure de Jean Galmot, published by Grasset in 1930, is the result of a take-over of Cendrars's reporting function trial by his imagination. Galmot had been poisoned in Guiana, where, after poor beginnings and later imprisonment for profiteering, he had built up a highly successful business. A native uprising in his favour had ensured his election as mayor against another candidate, who was a government agent. The style reverts here to that of *L'Or*. The final novel, *Emmène-moi au bout du monde*, of 1956, is an attack on the world of Jouvet and Giraudoux, who had dominated the world of the Parisian theatre in the decade before World War II. It is not serious satire. Raymone had after all been a member of Jouvet's company for 30 years. The novel is absurdly and light-heartedly disgusting in its prurience, too macabre to be funny, and grotesque in its insistence on erotic perversion. It reads as a final plea on the part of its author not to be taken too seriously.

PUBLICATIONS

Collections

Oeuvres complètes, 16 vols., 1968–71
Oeuvres complètes (Denoël), edition 1960–65
Poésies complètes, 1944
Du monde entier au coeur du monde (complete poems), 1957

Works

(Since Cendrars deliberately merges one genre with another, verse and prose poem, short stories and novels, all of which are both fictional and autobiographical, and since the autobiographical volumes are fictionalized for literary reasons, it has seemed better not to divide the works into categories.)

Les Pâques (later *Les Pâques à New York*), 1912

La Prose du Transsibérien et de la petite Jehanne de France, 1913; translated by John Dos Passos, 1931

Séquences, 1913

La Guerre au Luxembourg, 1916

Profond aujourd'hui, 1917; as *Profound Today*, 1922

Le Panama; ou, Les Aventures de mes sept oncles, 1918; translated by John Dos Passos, 1931

J'ai tué, 1918; as *I Have Killed*, 1919

Dix-neuf poèmes élastiques, 1919

La Fin du monde filmée par l'ange Notre- Dame, 1919

L'Anthologie nègre, 1921; as *African Saga*, 1927

Kodak (Documentaires), 1924; as *Complete Postcards from the Americas*, 1976

Feuilles de route, 1924, 1926, and 1927–28; in *Complete Postcards from the Americas*, 1976

L'Or, la merveillense histoire du général Johann August Sutter, 1925; as *The Days of 49*; as *Sutter's Gold*, 1936; as *Gold*, 1982

Moravagine, 1926; *Moravagine* (in English), 1968

L'ABC du cinéma, 1926

L'Eubage, 1926; as *At the Antipodes of Unity*, 1922

Eloge de la vie dangereuse, 1926

Petits contes nègres pour les enfants des Blancs, 1928; as *Little Black Stories for Little White Children*, 1919

Les Confessions de Dan Yack, 2 vols., 1929; part 1 as *Antarctic Fugue*, 1948

Une nuit dans la forêt, 1929

Rhum, l'aventure de Jean Galmot, 1930

Comment les Blancs sont d'anciens Noirs, 1930

Aujourd'hui, 1931

La Création du monde, 1931

Vol à voiles, 1932

Panorama de la pègre, 3 vols., 1935

Hollywood, la Mecque du cinéma, 1936

Histoires vraies, 1937

La Vie dangereuse, 1938

D'Oultremer à Indigo, 1940

Chez l'armée anglaise, 1940

L'Homme foudroyé, 1945; as *The Astonished Man*, 1970

La Main coupée, 1946; as *Lice*, 1973

Bourlinguer, 1948; as *Panus*, 1972

Le Lotissement du ciel, 1949

Blaise Cendrars vous parle (interviews with Michel Manoll), 1952

Noël aux quatre coins du monde, 1953

Emmène-moi au bout du monde, 1956; as *To the End of the World*, 1966

Trop, c'est trop, 1957

Films sans images, 1959

Critical and biographical studies

Miller, Henry, *Blaise Cendrars* (in English), 1951

Buhler, Jean, *Blaise Cendrars*, 1960

Flückiger, John Carlo, *Au coeur du texte: essai sur Blaise Cendrars*, 1977

Bochner, Jay, *Blaise Cendrars: Discovery and Re-Creation*, 1978

Chefdor, Monique, *Blaise Cendrars*, 1980

CÉSAIRE, Aimé, 1913–

Poet, dramatist, and politician.

LIFE

Aimé Césaire was born on 25 June 1931 in Basse-Pointe, Martinique, one of seven children of a minor civil servant. He went to the Lycée Schoelcher in Fort-de-France in 1924 and won a scholarship to Paris. He studied at the Lycée Louis-le-Grand from 1931 to 1935, and then at the Ecole Normale Supérieure from 1935 to 1939. He was an influential member of the group of black students who were promoting an awareness of black culture. In 1934 he, Léon Gontran Damas, and Léopold Senghor co-founded the review *L'Etudiant Noir*, in which the concept of "négritude," a word which Césaire coined, was first aired (See Senghor).

Césaire was more radical than his African friends in his views on negritude. He felt that Africa had at least been able to maintain a continuity of tradition under colonial rule, whereas the West Indies were not only economically exploited but had "ni langue véritable, ni religion, ni histoire (neither a language of their own, nor a religion, nor any history)."

After years of higher education in France, the return to underprivileged Martinique was a culture shock. Césaire's reactions were written down as the *Cahier d'un retour au pays natal*, first published in magazines in 1939. He taught at the Lycée Schoelcher from 1939 to 1945, edited *Tropiques*, and was elected mayor of Fort-de-France in 1945 and communist deputy for Martinique in 1946. He became the spokesman of the independence movement, his views on which are strongly expressed in the *Discours sur le colonialisme*. In 1956 he resigned from the French communist party, explaining his reasons in his *Lettre ouverte à Maurice Thorez*, and in 1958 he founded the Parti Progressiste Martiniquais. He also founded the Présence Africaine publishing company.

WORKS

Parts of the *Cahier d'un retour au pays natal* appeared in the review *Volontés* in August 1939, but the complete collection only came out in 1947, with an introduction by Césaire's friend André Breton. Its idiom is late surrealist (q.v.) and politically committed, influenced by the theory of negritude and the personal experience of cultural uprooting.

The poems in *Les Armes miraculeuses* are more mature and linguistically adventurous than Césaire's earlier work. They reflect the strong musical rhythms of the West Indies. *Soleil coupé*, whose title derives from the last line of Apollinaire's repudiated in the course of social evolution. The plot seems to be taken from the US cinema. Scott Fitzgerald, with whom Chamson had been friendly since 1928, had had the early novels translated in the US, and Chamson was working at the time on a film script for King Vidor, who wanted him to go to Hollywood. *L'Année des vanicus* is a highly thoughtful, imaginative treatment of a subject his strongest feelings on which Chamson kept for his polemical writings. The novel, which concerns the French reaction to the advent of Hitler's regime in Germany, has been criticized for lacking depth, for descending to the level of mere political protest. As a novel it cannot be said to reach the standard of the others, but it is none the less one more indication of the way in which cultivated French writers were being forced to confront the problems of the 1930s. *Quatre mois*, written before the defeat of France, is the most socialistically orientated of Chamson's books.

The post-war novels do not show any very fundamental changes in Chamson's attitudes. The subjects are predictable. How, asks *Le Dernier Village*, can the collapse of France in World War II have come about? The novel offers a series of intelligent and often penetrating comments. *Le Puits des miracles*, written in the first person, is more intense. The episodes are factual, the events mostly confined to a very narrow space, an inner courtyard. Some of the post-war novels concern the interplay of mysterious forces, symbolized in dense and often obscure ways. Some, like *Adeline Vénician*, display a carefully balanced symmetry of chapters. In that novel it is not clear whether the forces acting on Adeline do or do not send her mad, just as it is left deliberately unclear quite what force the spiral staircase symbolizes in *La Neige et la fleur*. These post-war novels are therefore less accessible than the *Suite cévenole*, although the mysterious forces at play here can in a sense be seen as related to those originally exercised by the mountains.

It was *La Neige et la fleur* which re-established Chamson's name with the post-war public. It appeared the same year as *La Petite Fille modèle* by his daughter Frédérique Hébrard, a budding actress of 24. With its sequel, *Le Rendez-vous des espérances*, it is the last of Chamson's fiction to survey contemporary society. The political themes are now abandoned with apparent relief, just as Chamson himself was relieved no longer to feel the urge to sign petitions or manifestoes. He does however, by implication, take issue with the existentialists (q.v.) and the literary practitioners of the absurd, writing an almost sentimental novel of hope, crammed with incident, in which things come right in the end. The sequel is a concentrated study in the heroine's failure to adjust to the world of *La Neige*, remarkable for its psychological penetration into the mind of a new generation, that of Chamson's daughter and her friends, and notable for a creeping disillusion. Parts of the dialogue read like a reported student conversation.

L'Homme qui marchait devant moi, written in the immediate aftermath of war, disappointed Chamson's readers, partly for its scorn of the post-war generation, and partly because of its lack of plot and excess of philosophizing. It has an anonymous central figure, and in some senses is not a novel at all, but a simple flow of consciousness. Like all the later novels, it suffers from an excess of implied moralizing and ponderous philosophical reflection about fate, destiny, time, and eternity, and perhaps from too rigid an architectural structure for proper imaginative investigation. The note of hope returns, however, in *La Superbe*, in which, for all its descriptions of harrowing physical pain, of

whippings, bastinadoes, and burnings alive, the spirit of the galley slaves, condemned for their part in religious revolution, still flickers with life.

PUBLICATIONS

Fiction

Roux le bandit, 1925; as *Roux the Bandit*, 1929; reprinted in *Suite cévenole*, 1968
Les Hommes de la route, 1927; as *The Road*, 1929; reprinted in *Suite cévenole*, 1968
Le Crime des justes, 1928; as *The Crime of the Just*, 1930; reprinted in *Suite cévenole*, 1968
Histoires de Tabusse, 1930; reprinted in *Suite cévenole*, 1968
Héritages, 1932
L'Auberge de l'abîme, 1933; as *The Mountain Tavern*, 1933; as *The Fugitive*, 1934
L'Année des vaincus, 1934
Les Quatre éléments, 1935; as *A Mountain Boyhood*, 1947
La Galère, 1939
Le Puits des miracles, 1945
Le Dernier Village, 1946
L'Homme qui marchait devant moi, 1948
La Neige et la fleur, 1951
Adeline Vénician, 1956
Nos ancêtres les Gaulois, 1958
Le Rendez-vous des espérances, 1961
Comme une pierre qui tombe, 1964
La Superbe, 1967

Other

L'Homme contre l'histoire, 1927
L'Aigoual, 1930; reprinted in *Les Quatre éléments*, 1935
La Révolution de dix-neuf, 1930
Affirmations sur Mistral, 1930

Critical study

Rolfe, Leonard H., *The Novels of André Chamson*, 1971

CHAR, René (-Émile), 1907–1988.

Poet, literary theoretician, dramatist and essayist.

René Char was born in Provence in L'Isle-sur-la-Sorgue, near Avignon, where he went to school before studying in Marseilles (1925) and doing his military service (1927–28) in Nîmes. He later owned a smallholding in Céreste, about 30 miles to the east of his birthplace. The poems in his first collection, *Les Cloches sur le coeur*, were written between 1922 and 1926. In 1929 he sent Eluard a copy of his privately printed *Arsenal*, received a visit from him, and went to Paris, where he was associated for a while with the surrealist (q.v.) group during its second period of activity. His publications dating from this time include the long prose poem *Artine*, *Ralentir travaux*, co-written with Breton and Eluard, and *Le Marteau sans maître* with its symbolist (q.v.) images from alchemy and from the architecture of castles. In 1933 Char married Georgette Goldstein and in 1935 he broke with the surrealists. His startling poetic images are already attenuated in *Dehors la nuit est governée* as a more personal, sober style emerges, clearly influenced by the Greek tragedians, Nietzsche, Baudelaire, and the symbolists.

Recognition came after the war, during which Char's activity as regional head of a Resistance group in the Maquis of the Vaucluse clearly modified his outlook, demolishing any residual traces of the literary poseur. Camus, who knew him well, thought Char the best poet since Rimbaud. The best of his work, often in prose poetry—such as that published in *Seuls demeurent* and *Feuillets d'Hypnos*, dedicated to Camus and included in *Fureur et mystère*—is inspired by his wartime experiences of violence, killing, and fear, which led him to reflect on enduring human values.

Char frequently refers to Heraclitus, whose doctrines of perpetual flux and the reconciliation of opposites underlie much of his poetry. He attempts to transform fleeting but traumatic experiences into what are virtually eternal perspectives, as moments from the flux of events are fixed and examined in the light of lasting human and social values. For Char poetic abstraction contains what is always changing as well as its lasting reality. Poetry in his often-quoted line is "the fulfilled love of desire remaining desire (Le poème est l'amour réalisé du désir demeuré désir)," the fixation of a momentary and fleeting aspiration in a permanent and polished poetic expression.

Char's poetry is both tender and strong, anecdotal and hermetic, a call to action which still breathes the rusticity of life in the Provençal countryside, full of references to its fruits, flowers, insects, soil, and light. The courage revealed in the war poetry becomes the force which elevates the humdrum to the plane of the eternal in an almost mystical movement, signifying man's eternal dissatisfaction, his awareness of the danger of meaningless destruction, and his quest for self-transcendence. The concentration achieved by Char's broken syntax, striking imagery, unusual vocabulary, and deliberate defiance of the rules of logical coherence ends up by making his poetry "difficult." Too often it merely reflects what is essentially enigmatic, instead of ordering and containing it, which is, according to Char, the true function of poetry. The poems, increasingly in prose, have become denser over time, and more aphoristic as they have striven to attain maximum compression.

The poems are always intensely felt, however, and Char pays minute attention to the interplay of sound, rhythm, and syntax so that, even when the poetry defeats its own theoretical aims, reflecting rather than resolving the enigmas of the external flux, it makes a meaningful protest against the confines within which language places it. At his clearest, the poet charges change with meaning, penetrates the secrets of the everyday, and combines concrete realities with their own inner significance, imposing order on the chaos with which it co-exists.

Char's poetry has long been regarded as almost indecipherable in spite of the flashes of obvious beauty, especially in the shorter pieces, and in those inspired by the Provencal landscape. Five years before his death Char gave an interview to a younger poet, Paul Veyne, and welcomed the chance to reveal himself, although some disclosures were made only after outbursts of fury. Of one poem Veyne was told, "You are forbidden to touch that poem. It's mine and mine alone." The poem was "L'Extravagant." It had been inspired by an order Char had given as a guerrilla commander to have two young men executed. Even Veyne's gentle probing has left the poetry its essential mystery, "You do not," said Char, "put a torch to the heart of the night."

Among Char's most highly regarded works are his plays, the *Lettera amorosa*, the *Recherche de la base et du sommet*, and the late *Aromates chasseurs*.

PUBLICATIONS

Collections

Oeuvres complètes, 1983–

Verse

Les Cloches sur le cœur, 1928
Arsenal, privately printed, 1929; as *De la main à la main*, 1930
Ralentir travaux, with André Breton and Paul Eluard, 1930
Le Tombeau des secrets, 1930
Artine, 1930; augmented edition, as *Artine et autres poèmes*, 1967
L'Action de la justice est éteinte, 1931
Le Marteau sans maître, 1934
Dépendance de l'adieu, 1936
Placard pour un chemin des écoliers, 1937
Dehors la nuit est gouvernée, 1938
Seuls demeurent, 1945
Le Poème pulvérisé, 1947
Fureur et mystère, 1948
Fête des arbres et du chasseur, 1948
Les Matinaux, 1950
Art bref, suivi de Premières alluvions, 1950
Quatre fascinants: la minutieuse, 1951
A une sérénité crispée, 1951
Poèmes, 1951
La Paroi et la prairie, 1952
Le Rempart de brindilles, 1952
Lettera amorosa, 1953
Choix de poèmes, 1953
A la santé du serpent, 1954
Le Deuil des nevons, 1954
Poèmes des deux années 1953–1954, 1955
Chanson des étages, 1955
La Bibliothèque est en feu, with etchings by Braque, 1956
Hypnos Waking, edited by Jackson Mathews, 1956
Pour nous, Rimbaud, 1956
En trente-trois morceaux, 1956
Jeanne qu'on brûla verte, 1956
Les Compagnons dans le jardin, 19:5
La Bibliothèque est en feu et autres poèmes, 1957
L'Une et l'autre, 1957
De moment en moment, with engravings by Miro, 1957
Poèmes et prose choisis, 1957
Elisabeth, petite fille, 1958
Sur la poésie, 1958
Cinq poésies en hommage à Georges Braque, 1958
L'Escalier de Flore, with engravings by Braque, 1958

La Faux relevée, 1959

Nous avons (prose poem), with engravings by Miro, 1959

Pourquoi la journée vole, 1960

Le Rebanque, 1960

Anthologie, 1960; revised edition, as *Anthologie 1934–1969*, 1970

Les Dentelles de Montmirail, 1960

L'Allégresse, 1960

Deux poèmes, with Paul Eluard, 1960

L'Inclémence lointaine, 1961

L'Issue, 1961

La Montée de la nuit, 1961

La Parole en archipel, 1962

Deux poèmes, 1963

Poèmes et prose choisis, 1963

Impressions anciennes, 1964

Commune présence, 1964; revised edition, 1978

L'An 1964, 1964

L'Age cassant, 1965

Flux de l'aimant, 1965

La Provence, point Omega, privately printed, 1965

Retour amont, 1966

Le Terme épars, 1966

Les Transparents, 1967

Dans la pluie giboyeuse, 1968

Le Chien de coeur, 1969

L'Effroi la joie, 1971

Le Nu perdu, 1971

La Nuit talismanique, 1972

Le Monde de l'art n'est pas le monde du pardon, 1975

Aromates chasseurs, 1975

Poems, edited by Mary Ann Caws and Jonathan Griffin, 1976

Chants de la Balandrame 1975–1977, 1977

Fenêtres dormantes et porte sur le toit, 1979

Plays

Trois coups sous les arbres: théâtre saisonnier (includes *Sur les hauteurs, L'Abominable Homme des neiges, Claire, Le Soleil des eaux, L'Homme qui marchait dans un rayon de soleil, La Conjuration*) 1967

Other

Moulin premier, 1936

Feuillets d'Hypnos (war journal), 1946; as *Leaves of Hypnos*, 1973

Arrière-histoire de "Poème pulvérisé," 1953

Recherche de la base et du sommet: pauvreté et privilège, 1955

Sur la poésie, 1958

La Postérité du soleil, with Camus, 1965

L'Endurance de la pensée, with Martin Heidegger, 1968

Sur la poésie 1936–1974, 1974

Translator, *Le Bleu de l'aile*, by Tiggie Ghika, 1948

Translator, with Tina Jolas, *La Planche de vivre: poésies*, 1981

Bibliography

Benoit, P. A., *Bibliographie des oeuvres de Char de 1928 à 1963*, 1964

Critical studies

La Charité, Virginia, *The Poetry and Poetics of Char*, 1968

Caws, Mary Ann, *The Presence of Char*, 1976

Caws, Mary Ann, *René Char* (in English), 1977

Lawler, James R., *Char: The Myth and the Poem*, 1978

Kline Piore, Nancy, *Lightning: The Poetry of Char*, 1981

Veyne, Paul, *René Char et ses Poèmes*, 1991

CHATEAUBRIAND, François-René (-Auguste), Vicomte de, 1768–1848.

Writer and diplomat.

LIFE

Chateaubriand was a dishevelled, melancholy, and bored figure, a grand poseur who affected to have no interest in his family history, although he was bred to be aware of his lineage. He could boast of the success of *Le Génie du christianisme* in reopening the churches, because he was an ardent Catholic. ("As a Frenchman one cannot be anything else.") He could boast that Jean-Baptiste, his elder brother guillotined in the Revolution, "was not the first Chateaubriand to lose his head on the scaffold," but only because he knew that Gilles, the founder of the youngest and humblest branch of the family, was the son of a Briand de Chateaubriand who, having fallen in love with his cousin, was beheaded for murdering her husband. That had been in 1570 but, although the founder of the senior branch had fought at Hastings in 1066, and his family's blood had mingled with that of the royal houses of France, England, Aragon, and Cyprus, the line founded by Gilles had decayed into a country squirearchy by the middle of the 18th century. The ancestry Chateaubriand affected to despise was in fact a decisive force in his upbringing. The first Brien's castle had given its name to the large town of Chateaubriant, between Nantes and Rennes, and signs of the family's former grandeur were to be found throughout Brittany.

Chateaubriand's father, René-Auguste (1718–1786), was the fifth of 12 children. When his father died in 1729, René-Auguste became the male heir, and when his elder brother François (1717–716) entered the priesthood, he became entitled to two thirds of his father's inadequate estate. It was decided that René-Auguste should join the navy, the only choice open to a penniless son of the Breton nobility, but the family had left the property undivided for the sake of the dynasty, and there was not enough money for him to attend the naval school at Brest. René-Auguste left home at 15, determined to make his fortune. He may have taken part in the attempt to relieve Danzig, where Stanislas Leczinsky, the father of the French queen, was being besieged after attempting to take due possession of the Polish throne. If so, he was lucky to return alive. He spent some years at Saint-Malo learning business and studying navigation, making three voyages to Newfoundland.

The boats would bring back cod, salt and dry it, sell it during the winter in Genoa or Marseilles, and return with olive oil and wine to Saint-Malo, when it was nearly time to sail again. Chateaubriand's father was shipwrecked and robbed, but became a ship's officer in 1740 and visited the West Indies. During the war of the Austrian succession (1741–48), like many Breton fishermen, he became a privateer. He was captured, spent seven weeks in a Plymouth jail, was released, took his captain's certificate, which enabled him to trade on his own behalf, and, after five voyages to the West Indies, returned in 1752 with 15,000 francs in sugar, a diamond, and a slave bought in San Domingo for 1,018 francs.

In 1753 he married the 27-year-old Apollinaire de Bédée, who brought to the marriage a small dowry of 4,000 livres. She came from a noble family, and was pious and well-educated. She bore her husband 10 children, of whom Chateaubriand was the last. René-Auguste had meanwhile been trading slaves between Dahomey and San Domingo for three years. Out of a cargo of 414 he prided himself on losing only 16 instead of the usual 80. He returned in 1757 with 30,000 livres. War with England had resumed in 1756. René-Auguste and his brother Pierre were lucky. By the time the war ended in 1762, René-Auguste had made 565,000 livres by legal piracy. He bought the château of Combourg and the title of count. It was the only time the château, founded in 1037, had ever been sold, and René-Auguste was its 32nd owner. Son of a rural squire, slave-trader and pirate, he was well on the way to achieving his aim in life, the re-establishment of the family fortune and social position.

Chateaubriand was born on 4 September 1868, and put in the care of his widowed maternal grandmother at Plancoët. He was weak as an infant, but returned home in good health in 1771, never having known his mother, who now left him to be tended chiefly by the housekeeper, La Villeneuve, as she was called. He became fiercely protective of his youngest, rather neglected, sister Lucile, and had his lessons with her. Chateaubriand, the unreliable principal historian of his own early emotions, acted as though he felt unloved, and developed rough habits, like those of his closest school friend Joseph Gesril. After one escapade in 1775, from which Chateaubriand emerged with a half-severed ear, the friends were separated, and Chateaubriand was exiled to Plancoët for the rest of that summer. His grandmother, who had been educated by Mme de Maintenon at Saint-Cyr, was 77, and still had 20 years to live. She lived with her 71-year-old sister, who died at the age of 90.

Chateaubriand's mother showed greater piety than affection where her children were concerned, and it was her hope that Chateaubriand might become a priest. She disliked Combourg, but the Saint-Malo apartment was destroyed by fire in 1776. The family escaped with only moments to spare, but no possessions were saved except the silver and some business papers. Still in occasional disgrace for prankish misbehaviour, Chateaubriand was destined by his father for the navy. Both fishing and slave-trading were now proving less remunerative, and ended when René-Auguste quarrelled with his brother, who was in charge of the boats. He had made very little money in the 15 years since acquiring Combourg, but stayed there each summer, proving himself an exceptionally mean landlord and indulging in countless petty lawsuits to establish his seigneurial authority. There had been a succession of poor harvests in the wake of the great storm of 1768, and epidemics of smallpox and dysentery were common. A 10th of the parish, 336 people, died in 1773. René-Auguste now bought a small house in Saint-Malo where his wife could spend the winters and where he could eat fresh fish in Lent, installing his family at Combourg in 1777. Chateaubriand

regarded the change of school and home as a punishment for bad behaviour.

Much later Chateaubriand had to break off his memoirs temporarily when he reached the moving moment of his arrival at Combourg. That can only be on account of what happened there later, since he was to spend only a fortnight at Combourg before setting off in tears for school at Dol, where he was one of less than a dozen boarders in a school of just over 100 boys. Boarding fees were 230 livres a year from October to July. Chateaubriand later recalled that he was popular, and had a good memory, and emphasizes in his memoirs his independence of spirit. At Combourg he mixed with the peasants, the children of other small landowners, and the gamekeeper, who died after being shot by a poacher. His father encouraged the peasants to play their role, reanimating medieval rites and pastimes, like wresting in the lake and the annual fair, and keeping open table for three days.

Chateaubriand's health deteriorated, and he had to be boarded near school with a writing master. He then caught measles, and was cared for by his old housekeeper, La Villeneuve, who, at 40, had recently married a widower. Chateaubriand's brother Jean-Baptiste (1759–1794), who had just been bought the post of parliamentary counsellor for 29,000 livres, took Chateaubriand to see Diderot's *Le Père de famille*, which disappointed him. France had joined in the War of American Independence against England, and there were soldiers billeted at Combourg, with 20 officers to dinner every day. At school Chateaubriand's brilliant memory enabled his achievement to appear prodigious. Two of his sisters were married, with handsome endowments, in a joint ceremony in the chapel at Combourg in 1780, both of them into the Breton aristocracy.

Chateaubriand read unexpurgated classics and got hold of a manual for confessors, which was exceedingly detailed in its classification of the guilt attaching to various sexual sins. He also successfully avoided the indignity of caning as a punishment for what had been flagrant disobedience in climbing a tree on a school outing. At home, as a future naval officer, he was refused the opportunity to learn to manage a horse properly, to his considerable future disadvantage. Despite republican inclinations, he also later felt infected by the family haughtiness. In 1781 his first Communion was the occasion for a religious crisis, no doubt due to the obligation to confess and the feelings of guilt prompted by the manual for confessors. That year he was confirmed on the steps of Combourg, adopting his new confirmation name rather stiffly, and henceforward calling himself in public François-Auguste. He moved to the more advanced Jesuit school at Rennes, where his conduct appears to have been wild. He left in December 1782, with good results in mathematics, Latin, and Greek, and early in 1783 was sent to the naval school at Brest, where his mother's cousin kept an eye on him. Without official admiralty authorization, which was unaccountably but not unusually delayed, he could not attend the official lessons, but was taught privately. He appears to have led a deliberately solitary life, and was bored. The American war was over. The official brevet had still not come. Without saying a word to anyone at Brest, Chateaubriand returned to Combourg in June.

Lucile, who was still unmarried, having proved the required eight generations of nobility on her father's side and three on her mother's, with something to spare, was now at 19 an honorary canoness, which also brought with it the title of countess. She was entitled to an apartment at the Lyons convent and a modest

tions of some of his younger contemporaries, to be side-tracked into self-indulgent melancholy. He broke an arm falling on to a ledge beside Niagara, but the incident merely served to prop up in Chateaubriand's mind the incredible conviction that nature inflicted only trivial damage.

However determined he was to demonstrate to himself the truth of his prejudices, Chateaubriand knew that the Indians could be cunning and cruel in their fight against the paleface tyrants. Somehow this fact had to be accommodated within the idyll, and what the Indians did to General St Clair's expedition, massacring 800 of their would-be chastizers, could at any rate not be compared with what the mob had done at the Bastille. Having journeyed virtually the length of the United States frontier, from the Great Lakes along the Ohio to its mouth, seen the Mississippi and the Louisiana shore, Chateaubriand returned from the lower Ohio to Philadelphia and the eastern seaboard. Money had not arrived from home, winter was coming, and the journey originally projected was clearly impossible. Since leaving Philadelphia Chateaubriand had travelled about 1,000 miles west, covering some 3,360 miles in less than 17 weeks, of which about three are estimated to have been spent in towns. He embarked at Philadelphia on 10 December 1791, and had to get home on credit.

He arrived at Le Havre on 2 January 1792, where his mother paid what he owed for his fare. In spite of his republican principles Chateaubriand was characteristically determined by his upbringing and wanted to emigrate and fight for the royalist cause. For that he needed money, and the obvious solution was to marry an heiress. Lucile had a suitable friend, the 18-year-old Céleste Buisson de la Vigne (1774–1847), her grandfather's ward. The marriage took place on 21 February, just seven weeks after Chateaubriand's return. It was challenged by revolutionary sympathizers from Céleste's mother's family eager to administer her estate, which, since her grandfather was 80, was quite likely to come to them if she remained unmarried. An arrangement was reached, although Céleste turned out to have only about 134,000 livres, a quarter of what had been expected, and that was invested in rapidly depreciating "assignats," already 30 per cent below par.

Chateaubriand contrived to meet Bernardin de Saint-Pierre, the author of Paul et Virginie and now director of the Jardin des Plantes, which was in fact the zoo. Chateaubriand was disappointed by him, and renewed his contact with Malesherbes. He and his wife had spent some weeks at Fougères and then Paris, but on 15 July Chateaubriand left Paris with his brother to join the royalist army in Belgium. Lucile had raised 10,000 francs for him, but the self-destructive urge took over again, and he immediately lost 8,500 francs gaming, apparently for the first and last time in his life. He left the remaining money in a cab, and was lucky that his wallet was found by a priest, the cabbie's third fare after Chateaubriand. He saw action alongside the Austrians at Thionville, where two bullets hit the haversack in which he was carrying the manuscript of Atala, and was wounded by a shell splinter. For some days he trudged on, hungry and in pain, having decided to try to get to Jersey, which his mother's family was making for. It was yet another unbelievable risk. He very nearly died in a ditch, but was found, and sought out by Jean-Baptiste.

Chateaubriand's wife of six months, Julie, and Lucile had all escaped the Paris massacre of 2 September 1792. Jean-Baptiste went back to France for his family's sake, and to avoid having his property confiscated as an émigré. Chateaubriand got to Jersey, where news of the king's execution on 21 January 1793 arrived some days later. On 17 May he disembarked at Southampton, making his way from there to London, where he led a life of destitution, real hunger, and illness. According to his own account he shared a loft with another Breton, who attempted suicide, lodged with a printer, and started his Essai historique, politique, et moral sur les révolutions. For five days he did not eat. In January 1794 a teaching post was found for him at Beccles in Suffolk, and in July 1795 he moved with the school to Bungay. He received the official émigré dole of a shilling a day and, until 1800, small sums from his family. In October 1793 Céleste and Julie were put under house arrest, where Lucile insisted on joining them. All three were then moved to Rennes. Chateaubriand's mother was arrested in February 1794, and released only in October, three months after the fall of Robespierre. Jean-Baptiste and his wife were guillotined on 22 April, the same day as Malesherbes, and in August the furniture of the pillaged Château de Cambourg was auctioned. Céleste, Julie, and Lucile were freed in November.

Chateaubriand's memoirs at this period are withering about all things English except the constitution, much as Voltaire's Lettres philosophiques had been. They are also impregnated with self-pity, as in his description of falling off a pony and being unable to move. He was befriended by a parson, and taught French and Italian to the daughter, Charlotte Ives, who was 16. Chateaubriand may have exaggerated the emotional relationship, but at the end of the academic year in 1796 he returned to London, where he went for solitary walks and did now indulge in long bouts of silent melancholy and self-pity. He later said that his suffering had been a full-time occupation. His physical disability, certified by a French and an English doctor, attracted financial support of 19 livres a year. In August 1796, just before her 32nd birthday, Lucile married the 69-year-old Jacques de Caud, the former commandant of Fougères, who was now living at Rennes. He was to die the following March, and the marriage was never consummated.

On 18 March 1797 the London printer Baylis, with whom Chateaubriand had lodged, brought out his Essai historique, politique, et moral sur les révolutions anciennes et modernes considérées dans leurs rapports avec la Révolution française. The book, seeming if not to justify, then at least to assign a reason for, the Revolution, caused offence, but it attracted attention in émigré circles, and Chateaubriand was now received by those who had lost power but not rank. Napoleon's star was rising, but after the coup d'état of 4 September 1797 the Directoire seemed to the émigrés like the rule of Robespierre without the guillotine. A 6,000-franc debt Chateaubriand had incurred in America was discharged by his elder sisters. In France 8,000 clergy were deported, and Fontanes, during a brief exile in London, admired Chateaubriand's work and strongly encouraged his literary ambitions. His mother died impoverished in 1798, and on 5 April 1799 Chateaubriand finished a first draft of Le Génie du christianisme, which was devoted to the relationship between Christianity and poetry. Christianity attracted him emotionally more than its doctrines convinced him intellectually, but he found in the social and cultural values of Christianity the link he was seeking between the old order and the new, and his new-found religious attachment may have been prompted or strengthened by his mother's death, or by the devout Julie, who had insisted in a letter how much pain the Essai had caused her. She was to die in July.

While he was in London Chateaubriand was given financial help to finish *Les Natchez* as a 24-canto epic in prose poetry. Bonaparte's coup d'état took place on 9 November 1799, and at Napoleon's invitation Fontanes had given a successful panegyric on George Washington on 9 February 1800. He now advised Chateaubriand to return. Chateaubriand accordingly disembarked at Calais on 6 May with a German passport and under an assumed name, which allowed him to return to Paris without going through the formality of being struck off the list of émigrés. He had with him such sheets of the first draft of *Le Génie* as Dulau had printed in London and the two extracts from *Les Natchez* now known as *Atala* and *René*. The rest of his papers were left in a trunk in London.

Chateaubriand left his wife living off her own modest fortune in Fougères and went to Paris, where he was met by Fontanes, who helped him both financially and in his quest for a publisher. Fontanes realized that Chateaubriand's cultural Christianity could be a useful tool in helping Napoleon to restore cultural continuity with the past in the newly egalitarian France. It also provided an apparently traditional moral anchor under Napoleon's control. Chateaubriand met Napoleon's sister, Elisa Bacciochi, and his brother Lucien, the new minister of the interior, who had appointed Fontanes as chief censor. He also started a liaison with Pauline de Beaumont, who was at the hub of slowly regrouping Paris society. *Atala*, although taken from *Les Natchez* and now destined for integration into *Le Génie*, was published on its own on 2 April 1801. It was immensely successful, provoking enthusiasm, parody, distaste, mockery, and imitation, and was discerningly welcomed by Joseph Joubert, generally regarded as France's most acute critic, who disliked the touches of Rousseau and Ossian and the references to Thames fog. Joubert, who was himself strongly attached to Pauline de Beaumont, having taken care of her while her family was in prison, wanted Chateaubriand to concentrate in *Le Génie* on the Cross, the savannah, and the ocean sunsets. Chateaubriand was to edit excerpts from Joubert's notebooks in 1838.

It was at a dinner given by Mme de Staël in May 1801 that Chateaubriand got to know Juliette Récamier, whose salon he had already attended. His relationship with her was to last until his death. That summer he stayed with Pauline de Beaumont at Savigny, where they were twice joined by Lucile, and finished *Le Génie*, with Joubert exercizing pressure through Pauline to cut back the quotations. On his return he took an apartment neighbouring Mme de Beaumont's. The book, entitled *Le Génie du christianisme; ou, Beautés de la religion chrétienne*, was published on 14 April 1802. It was praised by Fontanes in the *Mercure de France* the next day and three days after that, on Easter Sunday, Catholicism was re-established as the religion of France. Fontanes's article was reprinted underneath Napoleon's promulgation of the concordat in *Le Moniteur Universel*. In Chateaubriand's mind the power of the state was henceforward to need his support and guidance.

His aloofness, now accentuated by the periods of solitariness and depression, became tinged with the assumption of an almost mystical superiority which deceived him into supposing that he had intellectual and especially political gifts which in fact he lacked. He began to feel burdened by a responsibility conferred on him by his need to magnify to himself his own importance in the affairs of men. This touch of arrogance was nevertheless accompanied by great charm. Women fell readily for this fascinating, unattainable, melancholy, and famous poet. It did not

matter that he was married or that his mistress had helped him to finish a book with a section in praise of the monastic vows. His self-absorption made him easy female prey, and it seems not to have occurred to him that his seductive charms were casually ruining lives.

Chateaubriand scarcely hid his surprise that Napoleon was able to reorganize the administration of France without calling on his help. He went to see his wife, who was feeling neglected, and would have brought her back to Paris if he had had the fare. He needed her by his side for a successful political career. Then, in the summer of 1802, he began a liaison with Delphine de Custine, with whom General de Beauharnais had made love in prison just before being led to execution. In the autumn he travelled to the south, where he managed to get himself paid for a pirated edition of *Le Génie*. The following year, he was appointed secretary to the embassy at Rome, and left behind the two sorrowing mistresses, Pauline de Beaumont and Delphine de Custine, who shared most of his favours and whose extraordinarily colourful biographies are attributable in part to the traumatic experiences they underwent during the Revolution. In Rome Chateaubriand usurped ambassadorial authority and prerogative to such an extent that he was confined to the issue of passports.

Pauline joined him dramatically with the news that she had only weeks to live. Chateaubriand mourned her equally dramatically, erecting a marble monument for 9,000 francs he did not have. He also wrote a famous literary set piece in the form of a letter to Fontanes about the melancholy feelings which Rome's decay inspired in him. It was to be much admired and imitated, particularly by Germaine de Staël and by Corot, who strove to depict the same feelings in painting. Fontanes got Chateaubriand the post of chargé d'affaires at Sion in the Swiss canton of Valais, which Napoleon had recently made into a vassal state to secure the passes into Piedmont. Fontanes also got him an advance on his salary from the foreign minister, Talleyrand. Chateaubriand and his wife were living together again. On 19 March 1804 he attended a reception at the Tuileries given by a preoccupied Napoleon. On 21 March the Duc d'Enghien was shot at Vincennes after being kidnapped from Ettenheim as the result of mistaken information. Napoleon, who had narrowly escaped an assassination attempt on Christmas Eve 1800, needed in any case to make a firm gesture to show that no restoration of the Bourbon monarchy was possible. Chateaubriand had felt himself worthy of something more than Sion and immediately resigned, repaying the advance, although he had already spent it, and removing the dedication to Napoleon which *Le Génie* had carried since its third edition. From April he and his wife lived opposite Delphine de Custine.

He was right to suppose that turning his back on Napoleon would enhance his own prestige, although Fontanes feared he might be arrested, and even shot, in his turn. Delphine may have lent him money, although his contemporaries note his sporadic preference for dignified hardship and grand gestures to life on a budget of any size, a preference no doubt designed to draw attention to the neglect of his capabilities. He appears to have been bored, spent much time with Delphine, and met Natalie de Noailles, with whom he was to have a liaison from 1805. Her personal history was as colourfully distressing as that of Pauline and Delphine, and had left her, according to her contemporaries, unusually dependent on her power to attract men. She had suffered incurable psychological damage from the brutal destruction of her family and the degradation, physical deprivation, and mental dislocation to which she had been subjected in late adolescence and early womanhood. She later developed hypochondria, then persecution mania, and finally became insane.

The fascination Chateaubriand held for her, as for the other women in his life, was founded on the yearnings he aroused which no physical relationship could appease. What attracted Chateaubriand to women was not so much their physical beauty as the tumult of sentiments they provoked in him. It was in the literary release of such sentiments that he found his only refuge from boredom. In the idealized expression of his feelings he struck the chord which was to occasion vibrations in the sensibility of a whole new generation. At 34, he "supposed he had as long again to languish in this world." If he did not himself change the way in which people felt, he drew attention to a common change in the pattern of emotional response which, perhaps on account of the Revolution, seems to have occurred more sharply in France than elsewhere in western Europe.

On 10 November 1804 Lucile committed suicide. She had got engaged again after her husband's death, only to find that the prospective bridegroom, her brother's friend the poet Charles-Julien de Chênedollé, was already married. Her belongings were auctioned to pay for her funeral. Chateaubriand had been working since the end of 1803 on a book about Christian martyrs under Diocletian, and now felt the need to undertake a personal expedition to the Middle East. Through the mediation of Barbara Juliana von Vietinghoff, Baroness von Krüdener, a woman known for her vanity, literary pretensions, political ambitions, and influence at the Russian court, he raised 40,000 francs from the Tsarina, who fancied herself reflected in his works. He broke with Delphine de Custine in 1805 and in late summer travelled in the south-east with his wife, visiting Germaine de Staël. He and Mme de Staël were to remain close, Chateaubriand sympathizing with her implacable opposition to Napoleon, even when he could not help admiring him himself.

In July 1806 he left for his 11-month journey to the Middle East, Greece, Constantinople, Jerusalem, and Egypt, taking his wife as far as Venice, and carrying a letter of recommendation from Talleyrand. He returned via Spain and a rendezvous with Natalie now, after the death of her father-in-law, the Duchesse de Mouchy. The love story set in Granada, *Les Aventures du dernier Abencérage*, was written at about this time. It was read in Mme Récamier's salon in 1814, but not published until 1826. The travel sketches *Itinéraire de Paris à Jerusalem* were to appear in 1811. Chateaubriand arrived back in Paris on 5 June 1807 and bought the *Mercure de France* from Fontanes for 20,000 francs, money he may have raised from monarchist sources. The review was suppressed by Napoleon in 1811, was revived after his fall, and finally ceased publication in 1820. The title was to be revived in 1889 by Alfred Valette, whose review ran on until 1965, 30 years after his death. Napoleon forced Chateaubriand to resell the review within six weeks of purchasing it, when his attention was drawn to veiled attacks on him, but Napoleon's nominees allowed Chateaubriand a large profit. Chateaubriand, now presumably exiled from Paris, bought a house at La Vallée-aux-Loups near Sceaux. Like Fontanes and Mme de Staël, he simultaneously desired the victory of France, the defeat of Napoleon, the preservation of the new Napoleonic institutions, and vengeance for the way the old order had been destroyed.

Chateaubriand's friends now included a number of women of outstanding qualities of mind, the most important for him being the beautiful Claire Lechat de Kersaint, Duchesse de Duras, the author of the short novels *Ourika* (1824) and *Edouard* (1825). She was entirely devoted to Chateaubriand, but he remained no more than a brother to her in spite of her clear sexual advances. He was now writing more or less full time. *Les Martyrs* appeared in 1809, the year in which his cousin Armand was executed for espionage activities on behalf of émigré conspirators. Chateaubriand had tried and failed to save him, but arrived at the place of execution just in time to dip his handkerchief in his cousin's blood, a gesture which was interpreted as unnecessarily flamboyant. Napoleon needed to court Chateaubriand, France's most widely read author, but had a far greater respect for the richer, more dangerous, fundamentally more intelligent, and more politically acute Germaine de Staël. He tried, unsuccessfully, to get a prize awarded for *Le Génie*, but did get Chateaubriand elected to the Académie Française by the narrowest of voting majorities, 13 out of 25. Chateaubriand, however, was unable to pronounce the necessary eulogy of his predecessor, M.-J. Chénier, accused of support for Robespierre and even of complicity in the execution of his brother, the poet, André. Napoleon himself censored the projected speech, and Chateaubriand, who refused to change it, never took his seat, although he did accept Napoleon's invitation to Malmaison.

Towards the end of 1812, during which year he had a tiff with the censors, Chateaubriand became a focus for discontent with the emperor. When, in 1813, it first seemed that Napoleon might be defeated, Chateaubriand openly advocated the restoration of the monarchy in a pamphlet entitled *De Buonaparte et des Bourbons*. The spelling of the name indicates the tone of the piece. Chateaubriand exploits Napoleon's foreign origins but shows no great faith in the Bourbons, who are merely the legitimate monarchs, or the masses, of whom he continues to be scornful. He was now renting an apartment in the Rue de Rivoli, where the arcades were up, but not yet most of the buildings. It belonged to the brother of Natalie de Noailles, with whom he had broken early in 1813, and Chateaubriand hid his manuscript there, taking it in batches to the printer, Mame, who published it on 4 April 1814, four days after the fall of Paris to the Russian and Prussian armies, and two days before Napoleon's abdication.

Louis XVIII set about appeasing the remnants of Napoleon's administration. Talleyrand was reappointed, and Fontanes was made grand master of the university, but Chateaubriand was not called on. Claire de Duras got him one of two remaining ambassadorships, to Sweden, but he never went there. He continued to please the restored king by his political journalism, and in July reforged his friendship with Juliette Récamier, whom he had not seen since 1801. Convinced that he would be shot if Napoleon found him in Paris after landing in France in March 1815, Chateaubriand raised 12,000 francs through Mme Duras and followed the king to Belgium, reaching Lille in time to hear of Napoleon's entry into Paris. In Ghent the king offered him the ministry of the interior. On the king's return to Paris after Waterloo, Talleyrand was reappointed, but Chateaubriand was not. Joseph Fouché, who had voted for the king's brother to be executed and run Robespierre's Terror for him, was again minister of police. Chateaubriand became a minister of state, with no office but a salary of 24,000 francs, president of the Orléans electoral college, and a peer. He was still disappointed. He wanted political power, which he would willingly have exchanged for his literary prestige, and it is unlikely that loyalty to principles, institutions, or persons would have proved incompatible with its acceptance, from whatever quarter it might have been offered. He turned down the ministry of education in succession to Fontanes.

Chateaubriand's *Réflexions politiques* of November 1814 had been intended to please the king, as had his report on the state of France published on 12 May 1815 in the Ghent *Journal Universel*. On 16 September 1816, however, he published a pamphlet entitled *De la monarchie selon la Charte*, ostensibly arguing the case for a constitutional monarchy against the extreme legitimists, but in fact violently attacking the government in a postscript for dissolving the chamber. He lost his position as minister of state and, abandoning his own legitimist inclinations, joined the opposition. France was avenging itself on Napoleon's supporters. There were 70,000 arrests in three months. Ney was shot. Wellington imposed moderation internally and presided over a financial settlement with the allies over reparations. Reduced to his peer's salary, Chateaubriand had to sell first his books and then his house at La Vallée-aux-Loups. A public lottery failed, but a rescue was arranged partly through the good offices of Juliette Récamier. In 1818 Jean-Baptiste's second son also helped his uncle financially, but Chateaubriand and his wife now became itinerant guests. Chateaubriand himself continued to write important pieces of political journalism while working on his memoirs. His closeness to Juliette Récamier, who was to become the great love of his life, dates from a dinner alone with her in the room adjoining their ailing hostess, Germaine de Staël, on 28 May 1817.

There is no evidence that Juliette ever had a lover before Chateaubriand. It is possible that the 44-year-old banker she married at 15 may have been her father. She and her husband did not live together, and the marriage seems never to have been consummated. Before his ruin Récamier was in danger from the Terror, and the marriage secured the inheritance. Juliette grew into a person of enormous charm. Intellectually gifted and physically graceful, she is generally agreed to have been the most admired woman in France at this time and, neither wife nor mother, to have elevated coquetry to the status of an art form. She had had a romance with Prince August of Prussia, and Benjamin Constant adored her. She was certainly in love with Chateaubriand, and he was almost certainly her lover, however briefly. They exchanged daily letters and there were moments of great tenderness between them. While still wealthy, Juliette had taken a lease on Chateaubriand's house to help him out financially, but in 1818, when her husband was old and ruined, she left him, and in 1819 she took a small apartment at L'Abbaye-aux-Bois, a convent on the left bank of the Seine in the present Rue de Sèvres. She continued to receive here, although she now had to keep her husband and to economize herself. Chateaubriand called daily, and up until his death their relationship was virtually insitutionalized.

Chateaubriand now founded *Le Conservateur*, which was to become an important organ of the legitimist right. Its first number appeared on 8 October 1818. It was to be closed down on 30 March 1820 rather than submit to the new censorship laws which followed the assassination, on 13 February 1820, of the Duc de Berry, son of the future Charles X and the hope of the ultra-royalists. The liberalizing minister Elie Decazes, generally regarded as the architect of the restoration's success, and now president of the council, was blamed by the right for creating the atmosphere which made the assassination possible, threatened

with impeachment, dismissed, sent to London as ambassador, and made a duke. Chateaubriand was paid 100,000 francs to write the legitimist *Mémoires, lettres, et Pièces authentiques touchant la vie et la mort du duc de Berry*, and was able to buy the property in which, in 1819, his wife had established a retirement home for elderly priests and distinguished but impoverished ladies. She sold it to the archdiocese of Paris and relinquished its direction in 1838.

After a great deal of scheming, Chateaubriand emerged once more as a minister of state, and also as ambassador to Berlin, where he spent the earlier part of 1821. His non-literary annual income was now 80,000 francs as ambassador, 12,000 francs as a peer, and 24,000 francs as minister. Hoping for a government post in the 1821 reorganization, he resigned the ambassadorship in July 1821 but was outmanoeuvred in Paris. By their intrigues Juliette Récamier and Claire Duras got him appointed successor to Decazes as ambassador to London on 9 January 1822, at a salary of 300,000 francs a year. Characteristically, Chateaubriand kept a sumptuous household, entertained in lavish style, incidentally giving his name to what is now "diplomat's pudding" and to a way of serving steak, and worked when he could at his memoirs, his recollection sharpened by memories of his previous stay in London as a starving émigré.

Thanks to further intrigue Chateaubriand led the French delegation to the Congress of Verona in 1822. This brought him the credit for procuring, against the policy of Villèle, the new president of the council, the renewed glory of France when it intervened with force to shore up the tottering throne of Ferdinand VII of Spain. On his return from Verona Chateaubriand finally became France's foreign minister, taking up his post on 1 January 1823. Villèle may have thought that Chateaubriand would lose support for his Spanish policy more quickly than he did. In fact he strengthened English influence in Spain, and confirmed on the Spanish throne a mediocre autocrat with a taste for revenge, and no time for the constitutional government in which Chateaubriand himself believed. He also upset Juliette Récamier, who went to Italy for five months while he dallied with the uncomplicated, sensual 27-year-old Cordelia de Castellane, the daughter of a very rich banker who was married to an insignificant officer from an imposing lineage. Chateaubriand's dreams became ever more grandiose, and he himself more than ever convinced of his own capabilities, but while he should have been directing the destinies of France, his letters show that he was counting the hours until he could be with Mme de Castellane again.

It was this inability to take affairs seriously, because at bottom they bored him, that had hindered Chateaubriand's political career all along. It naturally attracted hostile comment and he was regarded as either arrogant, frivolous, or incurably self-absorbed. On 6 June 1824, Whit Sunday, he was called out of church to be handed the note informing him of his dismissal. The cause was primarily his known desire to increase the glory of France once more by regaining Rhineland territory, although the immediate occasion for it was his successful attack in the upper chamber on Villèle's attempt to lower the interest rate on state debt, now standing above par, from five to four per cent, in order to recompense the families of former émigrés with the resulting savings of 28,000,000 francs a year. The resultant lowering of bond values would also have advantaged the economy in other ways. Chateaubriand was supported by the royalist *Journal des Débats*.

That summer Louis XVIII died, and Chateaubriand tried to win the favour of his successor, Charles X, with *Le Roi est mort: vive le roi*. He was paid for writing it. Both of Jean-Baptiste's sons had fought in Spain. The younger had subsequently become a Jesuit and the elder, a colonel, was allowed to inherit Chateaubriand's peerage. He himself now lived with his wife in Paris, re-establishing his relationship with Mme Récamier in May 1825. The following year he signed an agreement for the publication of his complete works, which would grow from the 27 projected volumes to 32, for 550,000 francs, payable in instalments. In the end he reduced the amount to 350,000 francs when the publisher, Ladvocat, ran into difficulties. Chateaubriand also led the attack against the government's project to tighten the censorship laws, which provoked its fall in 1827. It was in fact his cloudy vision of what was taking place in the world, which he shared with Constant, for instance, and his sensitivity, in spite of what he had been trained to regard as his caste, to changing values rather than to the consequences of technological advance, which forced the government to abdicate and brought the Bourbon dynasty to an end. When the government fell Chateaubriand's power was such that he might have been invited to form an administration. He was not, and finally had to be satisfied with the ambassadorship in Rome, whence his wife accompanied him in September 1828.

In 1828 he withdrew his play *Moïse* from the Comédie-Française on the advice of friends, although he had been willing to subsidize its performance. Ladvocat went bankrupt, and sold his interest in Chateaubriand's works for 10,000 francs. Chateaubriand installed himself luxuriously in Rome, where he had 22 servants, was bored and subject to prolonged bouts of depression, and dealt with the business generated by a papal conclave. He started a liaison with Hortense Allart, who was later to be Sainte-Beuve's mistress. A quarrel about the new pope's choice of secretary of state resulted in a request for leave, and Chateaubriand resigned on receiving news that Polignac had formed an extreme right-wing government. Juliette successfully urged him to avoid compromising himself either by becoming involved with the Polignac administration or by imprudently opposing it. Talleyrand had already pledged support for the Orléans branch of the Bourbons, which was to come to power in 1830, but Chateaubriand remained unaligned. He arrived in Dieppe on 27 July 1830, but returned to Paris as soon as he heard of the terms of the king's ordinances to dissolve the chamber, suppress press freedom, alter the franchise, and set a new election date. He was torn between loyalty and liberalism, and wanted the king to abdicate in favour of his grandson, the posthumous son of the Duc de Berry, now Duc de Bordeaux, so keeping the legitimist continuity of the dynasty but destroying its political power.

With the inauguration of the July monarchy Chateaubriand's political career was at an end. He indulged in one more grand gesture when he sold his insignia for 700 francs, and then spent the rest of his life writing. He formed friendships with Lammenais and Béranger, and published new works, such as *Moïse* and the *Etudes ou discours historiques*, in the *Oeuvres complètes*. He was poor again, published a pamphlet in 1831 entitled *De la restauration de la monarchie élective*, supporting the legitimist position he had taken the year before, and another attacking the banishment of Charles X, but refused to take part in a conspiracy to overthrow Louis-Philippe, although he was imprisoned for a fortnight on suspicion when the plot was dis-

covered. He accepted loans of 20,000 francs from Charles X and from his nephew, but turned down the ex-king's offer to pay his emoluments as a peer.

Mme Récamier had moved to a larger apartment in the Abbaye-aux-Bois and was reunited with Chateaubriand in Switzerland in 1832. In spite of their ages, their emotional relationship was at its most intense. Chateaubriand returned to Paris to protest at the arrest of the Duchesse de Berry, published the pamphlet *Mémoires sur la captivité de Mme la duchesse de Berry*, which sold 30,000 copies in 10 days, was indicted for it, tried, acquitted, and congratulated by the legitimists. In 1833 he visited Charles X in Prague and met the freed duchess in Venice. Passages from his memoirs, which were not published in their entirety until after his death, were now circulating and being read in the salons, the breeding ground for loyalties and traditions which literacy had not yet quite emancipated from their tutelage. In 1834 *Moïse* was finally staged, and failed after five performances.

Chateaubriand sold his translation of *Paradise Lost* with an essay on English literature for 36,000 francs in 1835. Both were published the following year. He also concluded a deal for the *Mémoires* for 156,000 francs down and an annual 12,000 francs until the death of whoever survived the other, his wife or himself, to rise to 25,000 francs on delivery of the manuscript of the Spanish campaign. A batch of 18 bundles of *Mémoires* were left with a lawyer on 21 April 1836, although the last page was to be dated 16 November 1841. Chateaubriand finally accepted his peer's salary from Henri V in 1843. His literary income allowed him to travel a little, in particular to take his wife to Switzerland, although he found constant pretexts for returning to Juliette Récamier in Paris. Whenever he could, he wrote for 10 or 11 hours a day.

He had offended the Duchesse de Berry with a passage in his book on the Congress of Verona (1838), which had also been a commercial failure, and had difficulty putting matters right. His book about the 17th-century reformer of the Cistercian monastery of La Trappe, *La Vie de Rancé*, appeared in 1844, followed by a second edition within eight weeks, for which he received 5,000 francs. The rights to serialize *Les Mémoires d'outre-tombe* were sold on to Girardin at *La Presse*, where they duly appeared from 21 October 1848 to 5 July 1850 before the 12-volume edition of 1849–50. Chateaubriand revised them, and insisted that only the final revision should be published. On 8 February 1847 his wife died. A new will of 17 March 1847, made according to the written wishes of his wife, does not mention Mme Récamier, with whom, however, his relationship remained intact. The 18 bundles of *Mémoires* were replaced by 42 in 1847. Chateaubriand died on 4 July 1848, and Mme Récamier on 11 May 1849.

WORKS

Although Chateaubriand's actions, values, and behaviour were largely determined by the Revolution, his sensibility was formed before it. The hypersensitive outsider deprived of a place in the world had already appeared, if not in Rousseau's *Confessions*, written between 1764 and 1770, then in Goethe's literary objectivization of his unhappy love affair with Charlotte Buff in the 1774 *Die Leiden des jungen Werthers*. Chateaubriand's emotional withdrawal was the product of his upbringing and the lengthy periods of time spent alone with his sister Lucile, whose life ended in melancholia, persecution mania, and suicide. Home was a vast, dark, and empty castle, with a stern, snobbish, self-made father, and a bustling, pious, unloving mother, who had been through too many pregnancies and was already 42 when Chateaubriand was born.

At Brest in 1783, at the age of 15, Chateaubriand had already shown a preference for his own company which had not characterized his schooldays. From 1783 to 1786, when he spent only brief periods first at Dinan and then at Saint-Malo, he wandered in the woods at Combourg until he was approaching the point of mental disequilibrium. On three occasions he rapped the butt of an old gun on a rock to see if it would blow out his brains. When, shortly before his death, Chateaubriand's father tried to settle him in the army, he was almost 18, and the barriers within his personality were already almost fully erected. He kept his physical passions almost entirely separate from his emotional intimacies, and took refuge in the luxuriant beauty of his prose.

Although *Atala* was published on its own in 1801, in 1802 as part of *Le Génie du christianisme*, and in 1805 with *René* in the version which Chateaubriand considered definitive, the original version of 1791 has not survived. In the 1801 preface Chateaubriand relates how he had intended to write "l'épopée de l'homme de la nature (the epic of natural man)," and how *Atala*, by then part of *Le Génie du christianisme*, had originally been an episode of *Les Natchez*, into which the projected epic had developed. *Atala* was written "in the huts of the savages," and is "a sort of poem, half descriptive, half dramatic. Everything is in the depiction of the two lovers who walk in solitude; everything lies in the picture of love's anxieties in the middle of the calm of the deserts and of the calm of religion."

It must be presumed from Chateaubriand's correspondence that the original manuscript, shown to Malesherbes in 1792 and said by Chateaubriand to have deflected a bullet at Thionville, reworked in England, and in 1798 still destined to be one of the parts of *Les Natchez*, had by 1799 been rewritten to illustrate the moral and aesthetic values of Christianity. In spite of the lushness of the descriptive prose, an "extreme simplicity of content and style" is claimed as deliberate, and the models, we are told, were Homer and the Bible. Chateaubriand made some alterations to the third 1801 edition in response to his critics, and perhaps as a way of outmanoeuvring the pirated editions, but the book was published at a moment when France, having lost Canada, still had strong territorial ambitions in North America, and when the promise of the concordat with the Holy See was already a sign that France's new rulers were attempting to exploit the cultural and moral basis of Christianity. They needed to restabilize a society which, since the Revolution, had apparently lost all firm moral anchorage. Spain had ceded Louisiana to France on 1 October 1800; *Atala* was published on 2 April 1801; and the concordat with the Holy See was signed on 15 July 1801.

Atala consists of a prologue, four chapters of narrative, and an epilogue. The style is rotund, with elevated expression, elaborate periods, and lengthy rhetorical structures. The prose successfully strives for poetic effect, with sufficient proper nouns scattered through the luxuriant description to achieve local colour. Chactas, the old blind man, is well disposed towards the French who have ill-treated him, and has adopted a Frenchman called René and given him an Indian bride, Céluta. The body of the story is his account to René of his adventures, the civilized savage recounting his life history to the Frenchman who has become a "savage." Due to be burned at the stake, Chactas, was released by Atala, the daughter of the captors' chief, with whom he had instantly formed a bond of love at their first meeting. Chactas recounts the story of their flight, his passion, her firm but tender resolve to remain chaste, and their discovery by the missionary, Père Aubry, whose settlement is depicted as a Christian transformation of the earthly paradise. Atala finally explained that, to save her life, her Christian mother had vowed virginity on her behalf. Atala had accepted the vow, and learnt from Père Aubry too late that such vows could be annulled by religious dispensation: on the point of yielding to Chactas, she had to protect her virginity already taken the poison that would kill her.

The novel is given life not by its edifying messages about religion and the nobility of savage breasts, but by its infusion of real passion. It is an at times gratingly sanctimonious tragedy, but Chateaubriand's sympathy for the primitive ardours of love, courage, and loyalty, his sensitivity to the grandeurs of nature, even his blindness to nature's indifference and brutality, which he simply ignores, make *Atala* a powerful exploration of the nature, extent, and character of instinctive goodness, and of the sadness to which it can lead, and which echoes the melancholy of nature itself: "The moon rose in the middle of the night, like a white vestal come to weep at the tomb of a companion. Soon it spread through the woods the great secret melancholy which it liked to recount to the old oaks and to the antique shores of seas."

The much shorter *René*, in which Père Aubry's moral function is taken over by Père Souël, is the story of how René had come to want "to bury himself in Luisiana's deserts." We know from the *Mémoires* what is in any case evident from the text, that Chateaubriand's writing is more explicitly autobiographical than is the case with most writers. *René* is a reflection on the fictionalized account of his relationship with Lucile, the "Amélie" of the story, which overflows with nostalgia for calm and solitude: "the majestic mixture of the lakes and woods of that ancient abbey where I hoped to shelter my life from the fickleness of fate; I still wander at day's end in those echoing, solitary cloisters." Amélie takes the veil in a brilliantly dramatized ceremony during which she confesses to a "criminal passion" for her brother. Neither Byron nor Shelley had yet written about incest, and Chateaubriand was breaking new ground. René produces a letter from Amélie's superior narrating the story of her death. Père Souël's reaction is a tour de force. He is extremely severe on René for fleeing society in search of dreams. Solitude can be damaging: "On n'est point, monsieur, un homme supérieur parce qu'on aperçoit le monde sous un jour odieux (You are not, sir, a superior person because you see the world in an odious light)."

Les Natchez as we now have it is a prose epic in two parts, the first of which has 12 books. It contains the story of Chactas in France. Reminiscent in different ways of Voltaire, Rousseau, and Montesquieu, the book, much of it written in England between 1794 and 1799, was not published until 1826, when it no longer corresponded to public taste. The manuscript went through several different versions under different titles, and remained in London from 1800 until 1816. Chateaubriand was not displeased with the final patchwork, although what we now have is a series of fragments of poetically elevated prose scarcely ever reaching the degree of organization of *Atala*. *Le Génie du christianisme*, on the other hand, a work clearly linked to the religious revival, is a skilful exaltation of the fruits of Christianity in its social effects, as well as in the arts, and in literature. Chateaubriand himself provided detailed notes to the text, which, even if more notable for forensic skills than for real erudition, still draws on wide reading and immense lyrical energy.

The text is in four parts. "Dogmes et doctrines," which includes some not very convincing apologetic "proofs" with examples from nature, simply asserts that there can be no society without morality, and no morality without the immortality of the soul, although the existence of "atheist" societies had been proved by the late 17th century, and serious arguments about immortality, and the possibility of a moral order not based on a system of rewards and punishments after death, had preoccupied the "philosophes" throughout the 18th century. The second and third parts, entitled "Poétique du christianisme," are normally considered the most interesting. They subdivide into sections on poetry, fine art, and literature, but concentrate on poetry, taking up old aesthetic disputes about the literary treatment of supernatural forces. The arguments in favour of Christian epic and Christian drama, putting the Bible above Homer and Racine above Virgil, are ingenious and, although the book clearly misconstrues most of the great works it discusses, it presents a fascinatingly powerful integration of a cultivated literary sensibility with Christian piety. The whole Gothic revival is heralded in the sentence "On ne pouvait entrer dans une église gothique sans éprouver une sorte de frissonnement et un sentiment vague de la divinité (You could not enter a Gothic church without emotional excitement and an indistinct feeling of the divine)."

The weakness of analysis, psychology, and critical acumen need not destroy our appreciation of a tour de force exactly suited to its generation, not only on account of developments in Church–State relationships and in the colonization of the New World, but also in catering for its yearning for sweetly sad imaginative delights and, especially in France, for the stable social order, about which Byron and Goethe needed less to concern themselves. The fourth part of Le Génie, "Culte," is largely split between liturgy and good works, but devotes a whole book to the subject of tombs. The last chapter of all, showing how uncivilized the world would be without Christianity, sweeps the reader along in a torrential rhetoric of flawed arguments which it is difficult not to read with pleasure. Le Génie was enthusiastically received, but there were also attacks, especially in three articles by Guingené, and in 1803 Chateaubriand himself published a defence, Notes critiques, remarques et réflexions sur le "Génie du christianisme." Les Martyrs; ou, Le Triomphe de la religion chrétienne is a pendant to Le Génie, a prose epic in 24 books turning, as so often in Chateaubriand, on the conflict between Christian virtue and sexual passion.

The Itinéraire de Paris à Jérusalem et de Jérusalem à Paris inaugurated the vogue for a new sort of exotic travel writing which would be taken up by most of the major romantic (q.v.) authors. The first parts of Byron's Childe Harold were written and published only in 1812, a year after the Itinéraire. La Vie de Rancé, which is more of a personal view than a biography of the 17th-century Cistercian reformer and founder of the Trappist order, presents an idealized, almost lyricized, account of his life and work. It is a little masterpiece of pre-romantic (q.v.) biography, sharing with Chateaubriand's meditations on nature the suffused glow which illuminates the pen-portrait.

Chateaubriand's most important work is Les Mémoires d'outre-tombe, in which all his autobiographical, political, rhetorical, and social skills come together to give an account of a life which was impoverished only in a financial sense. With regard to his emotional life he is not so much reticent as inhibited, but in the exploitation of his temperamental ability to project into nature the echo of his own vision and his own feelings, in the narration of his literary and political successes, his career, his relationships with the powerful, the beautiful, and the brilliant, Chateaubriand could scarcely have wished for greater success, even at the cost of his cultivated melancholy, his endless yearning, and the clash between intelligence and feeling, intellectual conviction and instinctive, if acquired, loyalties.

Les Mémoires, although sold, and much rewritten, during his lifetime, were the subject of an embargo until after Chateaubriand's death. There are four sections—birth to 1800, 1800–14, 1814–30, and 1830 to old age—of which the first, heavily romanticized, section is certainly the finest, although memorable pen-portraits, passages of reflection, and descriptions are scattered throughout. Chateaubriand wanted to be, and to be regarded as, a man of political stature who could set in motion and control great events. He is primarily remembered for the brilliant vividness of his often limpid, sometimes fluid, and sometimes cadenced style, for the consolation he found not in solitude but in nature, and for the depths to which his emotions so easily moved him and still move his readers.

PUBLICATIONS

Collections

Oeuvres complètes, 31 vols., 1826–31, and later revised editions
Oeuvres romanesques et voyages, edited by Maurice Regard, 2 vols., 1969

Fiction

Atala; ou, Les Amours de deux sauvages dans le désert, 1801; edited by J.M. Gautier, 1973; as Atala (in English), 1802
René; ou, Les Effets des passions, 1802; edited by Armand Weil, 1947; edited by J.M. Gautier, 1970; as René: A Tale, 1813
Les Martyrs; ou, Le Triomphe de la religion chrétienne, 1809; original version edited by B. d'Andlau, 1951; as The Two Martyrs, 1819; as The Martyrs, 1859
Les Aventures du dernier Abencérage, in Oeuvres complètes, 1826; as The Last of the Abencérages, 1826
Les Natchez, 1826; edited by G. Chinard, 1932; as The Natchez, 1827

Other

Essai historique, politique, et moral sur les révolutions anciennes et modernes. Considérées dans leurs rapports avec la Révolution française, 1797; edited by Maurice Regard, 1978
Le Génie du christianisme; ou, Beautés de la religion chrétienne, 5 vols., 1802; edited by Maurice Regard, 1978; as The Beauties of Christianity, 3 vols., 1813; as The Genius of Christianity, 1856
Notes critiques, remarques et réflexions sur le Crénie du christianisme, 1803

Itinéraire de Paris à Jérusalem et de Jérusalem à Paris, 3 vols.,
1811; as *Travels in Greece, Palestine, Egypt, and Barbary*, 2
vols., 1812
De Buonaparte et des Bourbons, 1814
Réflexions politiques, 1814; as *Political Reflections*, 1814
Mélanges de politique, 2 vols., 1816
De la monarchie selon la Charte, 1816; as *The Monarchy
According to the Charter*, 1816
*Mémoires, lettres, et pièces authentiques touchant la vie et la
mort du duc de Berry*, 1820
*Maison de France; ou, Recueil de pièces relatives à la légitimité
et à la famille royale*, 2 vols., 1825
Voyage en Amerique, Voyage en Italie, 2 vols., 1827; as *Travels
in America and Italy*, 2 vols., 1828
Mélanges et poésies, 1828
*Etudes ou discours historiques sur la chute de l'empire romain,
la naissance et les progrès du christianisme, et l'invasion des
barbares*, 4 vols., 1831
Mémoires sur la captivité de Mme. la duchesse de Berry, 1833
La Vie de Rancé, 1844; edited by Fernand Letessier, 1955
Les Mémoires d'outre-tombe, 12 vols., 1849–50; edited by
Maurice Levaillant and Georges Moulinier, 2 vols., 1951; as
Memoirs, 3 vols., 1848; complete version, 1902; selections
edited by Robert Baldick, 1961
Souvenirs d'enfance et de jeunesse, 1874
Correspondance générale, edited by Louis Thomas, 5 vols.,
1912–24
Le Roman de l'occitanienne et de Chateaubriand (letters), 1925
Lettres à la comtesse de Castellane, 1927
Lettres à Mme. Récamier pendant son ambassade à Rome,
edited by Emm. Beau de Loménie, 1929
Lettres à Mme. Récamier, edited by Maurice Levaillant, 1951
Mémoires de ma vie: manuscript de 1826, edited by J.M.
Gautier, 1976
Correspondance générale, edited by Pierre Riberette, 1977–

Translator, *Le Paradis perdu*, by Milton, 2 vols., 1836

Critical and biographical studies

Maurois, André, *Chateaubriand, Poet, Statesman, and Lover*,
1938
Evans, Joan, *Chateaubriand: A Biography*, 1939
Sieburg, Friedrich, *Chateaubriand* (in English), 1961
Switzer, Richard, *Chateaubriand* (in English), 1971
Painter, George D., *Chateaubriand: A Biography*, vol. 1, 1977
Porter, Charles A., *Chateaubriand: Composition, Imagination,
and Poetry*, 1978

CLAUDEL, Paul (Louis Charles Marie), 1868–1955.

*Poet, dramatist, letter writer, autobiographer, and literary
theoretician.*

LIFE

Claudel regarded his work as dominated by a vocation which he
describes as "a great desire and a great movement towards
divine Joy and the attempt to attach the whole world to it...to
bring the whole Universe back to its previous state of Paradise."
For Claudel, therefore, the poet regains his old status as prophet,
as the link between man and God, in whose creative act the poet
participates.

He was born in the village of Villeneuve-sur-Fère in the Tar-
denois, where his maternal grandfather was the local doctor, an
uncle was parish priest, and his father a government official.
Claudel's parents, who were comfortably off, had married in
1862 and lost a child in 1863. In 1864 Claudel's sister Camille
was born. She was to play an important role in his life and had
to spend a protracted period at the end of her own in an asylum
under circumstances that have occasioned public discussion. A
second sister was born in 1866. In 1870 Claudel's father was
moved to Bar-le-Duc, in 1876 to Nogent-sur-Seine, and in 1879
to Wassy-sur-Blaise. Villeneuve remained the fixed point, however, in Claudel's life since, until his grandfather's death in
1881, the family continued to pay frequent and lengthy visits
there. The regional countryside made a permanent impression
on his imagination.

Claudel's education was conventionally Catholic but, after
his first Communion in 1880, he lost all interest in religious
practice. He was ill prepared for the disciplined rigours of the
Lycée Louis-le-Grand, which he entered in 1882. Camille was
working with Rodin, learning to be a sculptor in Paris, and the
family moved there, leaving Claudel's father to be transferred
from Wassy to Rambouillet in 1883. In that year Claudel failed
his baccalauréat, although he passed in 1884 and went on to pass
the second part in philosophy in 1885. His classmates included
Marcel Schwob, Léon Daudet, and Romain Rolland, with whom
Claudel took to concert-going. At this date Claudel shared the
dominant scientific materialism of his age with its emphasis on
monism and determinism. He pulled up short only before Kant's
ethical imperatives.

Claudel began studying for a law degree in 1885 and in 1886
read Rimbaud's *Illuminations*, published in *La Vogue* in May
and June, and the same author's *Une saison en enfer*, published
by the same review in September. The impact of this new and
daring poetry on Claudel's adolescent imagination was overpowering and broke the hold of mechanism, the idea of a world
endlessly moved according to rules which could be scientifically established: "I finally left behind this hideous world of
Taine, Renan, and the other Molochs of the 19th century, this
prison, this mechanism entirely governed by absolutely inflexible laws which, to cap its horrors, were knowable and teach
able...I possessed the revelation of the supernatural."

On Christmas Day of that year Claudel, who occasionally
attended High Mass because he enjoyed the sumptuous liturgy,
returned to Notre-Dame for Vespers. Behind a pillar during the
singing of the Magnificat "occurred the event which dominates
my whole life. In a moment my heart was touched, and I
believed." That faith, Claudel tells us, left no place for any sort of
doubt: "I had suddenly had the searing experience of Innocence,
of the eternal childhood of God...God is a being as personal as I
am. He loves me. He calls me." That experience certainly
changed Claudel's perception of the world and its inhabitants,
governed his subsequent beliefs and way of life, and penetrated
his poetic and dramatic works. It took him four years to return to
religious practice, but he began to read the Bible that same
evening. His whole literary output was to be shot through with

biblical allusions, imagery, literary forms, and poetic techniques.

In 1887 Claudel started to attend Mallarmé's Tuesday gatherings. He had already begun to write his first verse and his first play. In 1889 he continued his studies at the celebrated Institut des Sciences Politiques, coming first the following year in the "concours" for entry into the ministry of foreign affairs, which appointed him to its commercial section. In 1890 he published his first play, *Tête d'or*, and on Christmas Day confessed and received Communion for the second time in his life. During the next few years Claudel continued to move in literary circles and to write the early versions of his first dramas, including the first version of *La Jeune Fille Violaine*. *La Ville* was published in 1893, in which year Claudel was posted first to New York and then to Boston as consul. In 1894 he finished *L'Echange*, produced a second version of *Tête d'or*, translated Aeschylus' *Agamemnon*, probably started the second version of *La Jeune Fille Violaine*, received his posting to Shanghai, and began work on a second version of *La Ville*. In 1895, after three months leave spent in Paris and Villeneuve, he left for China, where he wrote his *Vers d'exil*, 11 poems which first appeared in collected form in 1950.

Claudel continued writing and rewriting during the tenure of his diplomatic posts in China, centred on Shanghai, to which he preferred Fou-Tchou, and later Tien-Tsin and Peking. This period, 1895–1908, was marked notably by the completion of the prose works *Connaissance de l'est* and *Art poétique*, with its important component treatises, including the *Traité de la connaissance au monde et de soi-même* and the *Connaissance du temps*. During this period Claudel also wrote *Cinq grandes odes*, *Le Repos du septième jour* and *Partage de midi*. In 1900 he published the play *L'Echange* in *L'Ermitage* and the first series of *Connaissance de l'est*, and in 1901 *L'Arbre* collected together five of the dramatic texts, including the second versions of *Tête d'or*, *La Ville*, and *La Jeune Fille Violaine*. In 1908 Claudel began *L'Otage*. Claudel's French public was still very small, but he remained known to the Parisian literary world. As he elaborated in China his view of poetic activity and, in spite of the scantiness of publication and therefore of critical reaction, he wrote his most famous verse and most stageable dramas. In 1898 Claudel visited Japan on leave, and late in 1899 returned to France for a year, travelling via Syria and Palestine and conveniently arriving at Bethlehem for Christmas Day. During the year, spent at Villeneuve and in Paris, Claudel met, among others, Gide, Jammes, and Suarès, and made a retreat at the Benedictine abbey of Solesmes, which is associated with the revival of plainchant. The first series of *Connaissance de l'est* was published before he left again for China.

A second year's leave, 1905–06, culminated in his marriage to Reine Sainte-Marie-Perrin in March 1906, three days before he set off again for China, where he was now first secretary in Peking. He had returned to Villeneuve, visited Jammes, stayed in the Pyrenees with his sister Camille, and made a pilgrimage to Lourdes. His daughter Marie was born in January 1907 and his son Pierre in July 1908. The marriage was to produce five children in all. Claudel travelled back to France on the Transsiberian railway in 1909 and took up a new posting in Prague before the end of the year. In 1911 he was posted to Frankfurt and heard Wagner's *Ring* cycle in Vienna. He also met his future collaborator, Denis Milhaud, and finished *L'Annonce faite à Marie*, the new adaptation of *La Jeune Fille Violaine*, which Lugné-Poe staged in Paris in 1912.

Claudel's father died the following year, and Camille was confined to a mental hospital from now on. Claudel himself attended performances of *L'Annonce* at Hellerau before being transferred to Hamburg. His dramatic work was beginning to be staged successfully. *L'Annonce* was staged in Prague and Lyons in 1914, and in Moscow in 1918; *L'Otage* at the London Scala in 1913 and by Lugné-Poe in Paris in 1914; *L'Echange* by Copeau at the Vieux-Colombier in Paris in 1914, and by Georges Pitoëff in Geneva in 1917. It was Claudel himself who refused permission for the staging of the intimate *Partage de midi*, whose first edition in 1906 was printed uniquely for friends and limited to 150 copies.

At the outbreak of war Claudel returned to France via Denmark, Norway, and England and was transferred to the ministry of war at Bordeaux. After several short journeys, in 1917 he left via Lisbon for Brazil, where he was to be French minister. His wife, who was pregnant, stayed behind with the children, and Claudel travelled with Milhaud as his secretary. In Rio de Janeiro he met Stravinsky. In 1919 he returned to Paris via New York and was appointed to Copenhagen, where he represented France on the commission overseeing the Schleswig-Holstein plebiscite. In 1921 he was given ambassadorial rank and sent to Tokyo, where his *La Femme et son ombre* was staged in 1923. The third part of *Le Soulier de satin*, regarded by Claudel as a grand and probably final treatment of all his major themes, was destroyed in an earthquake, but the drama was completed in 1924. The next year Claudel took leave in France, revisiting Solesmes, and gave lecture tours in Italy and Spain, then England, Belgium, and Switzerland. After another year in Tokyo he was posted to Washington. He arrived there in 1927, having bought the Château de Brangues in south-east France, about halfway between Lyons and Chambéry, during the summer.

By now Claudel was spending much of his time travelling, making use, as ever, of official journeys to widen his already enormous cultural knowledge. His mother died in 1929, but he did not return to France that year. In 1930 he was in Berlin for the staging of *Le Livre de Christophe Colomb* at the opera, and in Belgium and Switzerland for a lecture tour which he undertook before returning to the US. He returned to France in 1931 and 1932 and was increasingly occupied with high-level diplomatic negotiations. In 1933 he was posted to Brussels, where *L'Annonce* was staged in 1934, and in 1935 his retirement was announced. His bid for election to the Académie Française in 1935 failed, but he kept travelling and writing, although from 1936 he was seriously, intermittently ill. He represented France at the crowning of Pius XII and spent the war writing on religious themes, attending rehearsals and the 50th performance of *Le Soulier de satin* in Paris (1944) and further performances in Brussels in 1945. Camille had died in 1943, Jammes in 1938, Romain Rolland in 1945. Claudel was finally elected to the academy in 1946 and continued to give lectures and attend performances of his works. From 1946 he also had a Paris house. *Jeanne d'Arc au bûcher*, with music by Honegger, was staged at the Paris Opéra in 1950–01. Claudel continued to comment on biblical texts, to revise earlier works, and even to travel right up until his death. His last completed work was the *Conversation sur Jean Racine*.

WORKS

Claudel's work attracted much attention in the context of religious debates in French literary and intellectual circles, especially from the turn of the century until World War I. Since his career kept him away from France for such long periods, much of his contribution to debate on religious and cultural matters appears in his lengthy correspondence. The correspondence with Rivière, Gide, Suarès, Jammes, Gabriel Frizeau, Massignon, Milhaud, Barrault, Lugné-Poe, Pottecher, and Copeau has all been published, some in volume form and some in the *Cahiers Claudel* series. These letters are important not only for what they add to Claudel's autobiographical and theoretical works, but also for the light they shed on personalities from the world of the arts.

Of the three principal versions of *Tête d'or* (1890, 1901, 1919), the first has never been staged. The original, published anonymously in 1890 in an edition of 100 copies, reflects Claudel's own inner struggle and essentially treats the problem of self-creation, from which in the end the all-conquering, self-confident, self-affirming eponymous hero dies. The determination to conquer the world comes to its inevitably violent conclusion. The multivalent sun symbolism in the play is not too obtrusive, although Tête d'or, the colour of whose hair matches that of the setting sun, clasps that sun to his chest: "poitrine contre poitrine, tu te mêles à mon sang terrestre (chest against chest, you become fused with my earthly blood)." There is only a tentative solution as Tête d'or unnails the crucified princess from the tree. The perspectives are not really religious, but the poetic idiom, which is luxurious, exuberant, and rhetorical, already foreshadows the lyrical explosion which Claudel created the "verset claudélien" to accommodate. The "verset" is rhythmic prose, liturgically or biblically inspired, without rhyme or metre, mimicking the rhythms and cadences of the Vulgate Latin version of the Psalms and such anthems as the Magnificat.

Sketches and fragments for *La Ville* were written before and after Claudel's final conversion, in 1890 and 1891. The piece was largely rewritten in 1895, and again in 1898–99, always in the direction of greater simplification and a strengthening of the dramatic structure. The first edition of 225 copies was published anonymously in 1893, and the second in *L'Arbre* in 1901, together with *Tête d'or, L'Echange, La Jeune Fille Violaine,* and *Le Repos du septième jour,* which ends with the new emperor's Christian conversion. The first version of *La Ville* reflects Claudel's hesitations not so much about his conversion as about the need to reveal it to his family before the exile now certain to be imposed by the diplomatic career. Like *Tête d'or,* this first version contains vestiges of symbolism (q.v.) and even of anarchism. Long walks in Paris had nurtured in him an awareness of social problems. Claudel himself mentions the influence of Blake, Horace, and Virgil, but his final resolution of social problems is Christian. In Claudel's view God is as necessary for society as for the individual.

L'Echange, mostly written in 1894 while Claudel, in the US, was also translating *L'Agamemnon,* is the first of the dramatic pieces for which a staging is half envisaged. In fact it was not until 1914 that Jacques Copeau produced it at the Vieux-Colombier. Claudel, who had long thought that it alone of his early work did not need rewriting, entirely recast it for Jean-Louis Barrault in 1951. The earlier version, championed from 1917 to 1947 by the Pitoëffs, is generally regarded as superior. The play respects the unities and concerns the choice faced by a young exile drawn to independence, a life of free love, unre-

strained fantasy, and art, but also constrained by obligations to conscience, family, and religion. It was serialized in *L'Ermitage* in April, May, and June 1900.

Meanwhile Claudel was elaborating not only his poetic theory, but his whole vision of man and the world, in a series of works, *Connaissance de l'est, Art poétique,* and *Cinq grandes odes.* Claudel regarded *Connaissance de l'est* and the *Odes* as demonstrating the practical realization of the theories enunciated in his *Art poétique.* His whole poetic work is conceived as a celebration of God's creation, viewed as joyous and exhilarating in spite of the renunciation of lust called for by "l'évangélisation de la chair (the evangelization of the flesh)," which remains at the centre of the later dramatic works.

Connaissance de l'est explores the central view of the three treatises to be published as *Art poétique,* of which the *Odes* are the lyrical overflow. They deal with man's place in creation and the nature of poetry and are at the same time a lyrical exultation in the poet's quasi-divine status as a collaborator in the work of divine creation, and a definition of that status: "Ainsi quand tu parles ô poète.../Proférant de chaque chose le nom...selon que jadis/Tu participas à sa création, tu coopères à son existence. (So, poet, when you speak.../Uttering the name of each thing...– just as formerly/You took part in its creation, so now you cooperate in its existence)." This theory of the poet's function has a long history. The Hebrew view that naming things by their names could defile them and was the function of the prophet was notably important in 16th-century France. Claudel's theory is near that of Rilke in the *Duinesischer Elegien.*

From now on Claudel's most powerful work is dominated by the overwhelming strength of the desires of the flesh and the need to overcome them in the interests of spiritual transcendance. In *Partage de midi* the title refers both to sharing and to parting. The play was written in the wake of a passionate love affair and centres on the transformation of human into divine love. The most lyrical of Claudel's plays, it has been criticized for failing dramatically to resolve the dilemma on which it is based. Mesa is too suddenly struck by grace and too easily identifies his love for Ysé, who has abandoned him, with his love for Christ crucified and with Christ's for the human race. There is a spiritually enriching apotheosis without any true repudiation of romantic love. Only in *Le Soulier de satin* does the sacrifice lead with psychological plausibility to spiritual transcendence. In the interests of demonstrating the power of grace, *Partage* blackens Ysé almost beyond belief. She joins Mesa in inevitable death in the Chinese citadel which is blown up, after she has sent her husband to his death, abandoned her children and her lover, and murdered her child by him, all in the name of the love which brings her back to die with Mesa. Claudel would not allow the play to be staged until 1948, when Barrault had to struggle to keep much of the original text for his highly successful production. A final version (1949) was published after the last of the play's performances.

The first edition of *L'Annonce faite à Marie* under that title was published in the *Nouvelle Revue Française* (q.v.) in 1911–12 and produced in 1912 by Lugné-Poe at the Théâtre de Oeuvre. Jouvet and Copeau turned down offers to produce the play in 1937. Dullin accepted and persuaded Claudel to change the fourth act (1938 version). A further revision was made, following Jouvet's 1946 production, for Jacques Hébertot's in 1948. The text is a pseudo-medieval fable, more of a liturgy than a drama, and heavily dependent on a deliberate confusion of the

which characterized even his most private behaviour, and was certainly extended to the ways in which he presented himself publicly. At his weakest Cocteau was a not very amusing poseur, childish and amateur, although, at his strongest, he made a distinguished contribution to all sorts of aspects of French cultural life. He had an extraordinary gift for recognizing talent in others, and for drawing himself to the attention of the talented.

Cocteau was born on 5 July 1889 in the Paris suburb of Maisons-Laffitte. The suburban house was large, and the family, who were well-to-do, owned an apartment in central Paris as well. They were committed to the arts but, as Cocteau later complained, undiscriminating in their taste. His mother, who died in 1943, was a stockbroker's daughter, had apparently been unusually pretty when young, and had a brother in the diplomatic service. Cocteau had an older sister and brother, Marthe and Paul, who were 12 and eight, respectively, when he was born, and his closest childhood companion was a cousin, Marianne Lecomte. The circumstances surrounding the death of Cocteau's father, Georges (1842–1898) were not generally known until 1957. A former lawyer with no real career, who had dabbled in painting, he had found himself close to ruin and shot himself. Cocteau never spoke of the incident before the year of his own death, and up until the age of 12 frequently dreamt that his father had not died, but had become a parrot.

There has been persistent Paris gossip about Cocteau's possible illegitimacy, and his father may well have been homosexual. It is probable that Cocteau's own homosexuality has something to do with the way he was pampered by his mother after her husband's death. For a period during his adolescence, Cocteau became antagonistic towards her. There was a curious incident in which he made her buy a box of cigars for the family manservant, forced her to hide it beneath her skirt as they crossed a frontier, and then betrayed her to customs officials as they passed along the train. It is possible that, brought up by a mother and a German governess, and closely linked to a girl cousin, Cocteau had come to regard the manservant as a substitute father. The most intimate physical contact between a male and a female described in any of his works is that of himself curled up in the lap of his governess listening to the sounds of her digestion.

In 1928 Cocteau published *Le Livre blanc* anonymously. Narrated by a homosexual, it gives what must be a highly coloured account of his own schooling at the Lycée Condorcet, from which he was expelled. The book, which was intended to shock, depicts social autoerotic activities and suggests that Cocteau's imaginative fixation on strong masculine bully figures dates at least from early in his schooling. We know very little about his youth, since it has not been researched and his own accounts, which are the only ones we have, are clearly unreliable. We do know, however, that he liked the theatre, enjoyed everything theatrical, conceived a passion for Mistinguett, and twice failed his baccalauréat, in spite of private tutoring. He claims to have run away to Marseilles at 15 and to have gone into hiding there for a year. There are grounds for supposing that he did have some acquaintanceship with a milieu peopled with male and female prostitutes and opium smokers, but later works lay on the descriptions of this life with such lavish colouring that almost nothing can be pinpointed with real biographical accuracy.

Cocteau emerged from adolescence with a patina of experience and an aura of glamour, good-looking, charming, and passive, with clear homosexual leanings. He went to the trouble of laying a false trail to disguise his sexual orientation, although he first came to public attention as one of the 16-year-old companions of the flamboyant Romanian actor Edouard de Max. Max's lapses of taste sometimes led the young Cocteau into public embarrassments, but he organized and paid for a reading of Cocteau's poems by well-known theatrical personalities in the fashionable and intimate Théâtre Femina on 4 April 1908. It was Max, too, who invited the fashionable audience and introduced Cocteau to the theatrical and literary worlds. Cocteau's first book, *La Lampe d'Aladin*, contains poems dedicated to many well-known literary personalities. He was later to reject the work contained in this and his next two books of poems, *Le Prince frivole* and *La Danse de Sophocle*, which was virtually all he published before World War I.

In September 1908 he went to Venice, where he met Wilde's son Vyvyan Holland. One of his young male companions shot himself in the early hours of 25 September, leaving a letter for another, Langhorn Whistler. The number of Cocteau's friends who died prematurely has been remarked on, although Cocteau denied that any of these deaths were in any way connected with his own habits. There is no doubt that at around the age of 20 Cocteau was part of a smart cosmopolitan set of young homosexuals. A poem records a moment of police interest and maternal wrath, and we know that by this time Cocteau had rented from the government liquidator a cheap but architecturally distinguished bachelor room, which his mother did not know about, in the Hôtel Biron. Rodin, Rilke, Matisse, Max, and Isadora Duncan also had rooms in this splendid building at one time or another. Cocteau's guests at the Hôtel Biron included Catulle Mendès and Reynaldo Hahn. The building's tenants were finally evicted, apparently after a series of orgy-like parties.

Cocteau's chief source of income all his life seems to have been an allowance from his mother. He was comfortably off, occasionally flush, never rich, and occasionally keen to earn. In 1909 he co-founded the literary magazine *Shéhérezade* with François Bernouard, a former classmate, later famous as a publisher. They may have called the review after Rimsky-Korsakov's tone poem, which the composer had conducted in Paris during Diaghilev's first season in 1907. Beautifully produced, with a nude by Paul Iribe on the cover, it lasted until its fifth issue in March 1911, and published Dunoyer de Segonzac's sketches of Isadora Duncan, drawings by Bonnard and Marie Laurencin, Cocteau's first printed story, "Comment mourut M. de Trèves," and scores by Hahn and Massenet. Maurice Rostand, son of the dramatist Edmond Rostand, contributed the poem "Shéhérezade." Cocteau later claimed to have published a host of other famous names, just as he claimed a quite spurious friendship with Rilke, but the review was still a credit to its young editors, and seems to have been modelled on *The Yellow Book*, which had appeared from 1894 to 1897. It printed one poem by Apollinaire, "Stances," subsequently retitled "Signe," Cocteau's first connection with the world of Braque, Vlaminck, Matisse, Derain, and Vuillard.

Cocteau became inseparable from Maurice Rostand. By putting into his own poems the names of smart Paris establishments he was following the example of Montesquiou, who had mentioned the London shop Liberty's in a poem, and he became a Montesquiou sycophant. At this date it was clearly Cocteau's good looks, good connections, and effete charm that opened for him the doors of a highly precious section of the literary and social worlds. He met Lucien Daudet, Catulle Mendès, the critic

Jules Lemaître, a member of the Académie Française and crea-ture of Mme de Loynes, the Empress Eugénie, and in due course Proust. About 1911 Cocteau and his mother moved to the Rue d'Anjou, in the most elegant part of Paris, next door to Sacha Guitry, and Cocteau met the poetess Anna de Noailles, a friend of Proust and doyenne of the literary salons. It was she who took him in hand and taught him to avoid the exhibitionist behav-ioural excesses which threatened his admission to the really ele-gant sections of Parisian society, though he failed to escape Gide's mildly dismissive ridicule.

His other salvation came in the form of the Russian ballet. French ballet, as celebrated by Degas and Renoir, had degener-ated into operatic interludes. In St Petersburg, where Petipa's choreography still held sway, Isadora Duncan had revivified Russian ballet in 1905 with the fluidity of her style. The Rus-sians began to dance to Schumann and Chopin, and nurtured the talents of Fokine and Diaghilev. Benois and Bakst were in Paris. Diaghilev, the failed singer, composer, and theatre administra-tor, had turned impresario with the St Petersburg exhibition of Russian historical portraits in 1905, the Paris 1906 exhibition of Russian art, and the 1907 and 1908 seasons of Russian music in Paris, which brought Chaliapin to the Opéra. It was thanks to his association with Diaghilev's Ballets Russes that Cocteau first achieved any artistic importance.

From 1909 to 1929 Diaghilev presented 20 seasons of Rus-sian ballet. He started by teaming up with Gabriel Astruc, who had brought Wanda Landowska, Artur Rubinstein, the cake-walk, Caruso, and Toscanini to Paris. Astruc provided the fash-ionable cachet Diaghilev needed. His own initial contributions included Fokine, Nijinsky, and Pavlova, who missed the Bal-lets' opening night on 19 May 1909. Décor and costumes were by Benois, Bakst, and Roerich. Between them the two impresa-rios had assembled the whole of elegant Paris for the preview. Rodin, Ravel, and Montesquiou were present, and the front row of the balcony had been filled with the 52 prettiest actresses in Paris. Cocteau, who was not invited, instantly established an intimate association with the troupe, largely by charming his way into the affections of Diaghilev's closest associate, Misia Sert, ex-wife of Thadée Natanson, one of the three founders of the *Revue Blanche*, and friend of Debussy, Ravel, Jules Renard, Mallarmé, Tristan Bernard, Renoir, Toulouse-Lautrec, Vuillard, and Bonnard. She had gone on to marry Alfred Edwards, owner of the newspaper *Le Matin*, and later the painter José-Maria Sert. After meeting him at Prunier's, she had become friendly with Diaghilev, then Sert's most intimate collaborator, and was instrumental in helping him decide which of Astruc's "chers snobs" should be invited to what. She found Cocteau's conver-sation brilliant and his charm irresistible.

Since so much of Cocteau's reputation rests on his manners, charm, and wit, it can be said that he was largely the creation of Anna de Noailles and Misia Sert. For Diaghilev he became "Jeanchik." They shared an admiration for Beardsley, and Coc-teau, like Diaghilev, became obsessed with the heavily muscled and off-stage not at all graceful Nijinsky. In 1910, while trying very hard not to give Diaghilev cause for jealous petulance, he published in book form a six-line poem to Nijinsky, with an illustration by Iribe to accompany each line. *Vaslav Nijinsky, six vers de Jean Cocteau, six dessins de Paul Iribe* is a love letter. The form could scarcely be more precious.

The Ballets Russes turned Cocteau into a painter and draughtsman, and with Bakst's encouragement he began to play

an important part in the affairs of the company. He was commis-sioned to paint posters, to write publicity articles, and a libretto for *Le Dieu bleu* to an insipid score by Hahn which, as Stravin-sky said, was sure to galvanize salon support. Cocteau later dis-paraged the libretto, like the rest of his pre-war work. The ballet was dropped, but the season was saved thanks to the scandalous costume Bakst designed for Nijinsky in Debussy's *Prélude à l'après-midi d'un faune*. It made him look as if he was naked but for a bunch of grapes concealing his genital organs. Cocteau analysed Nijinsky's concept of the role in *L'Art décoratif de Léon Bakst* (1912) by Arsène Alexandre. In all he wrote about Nijinsky, Cocteau was never to refer to the dancer's unfortunate marriage, madness, or death. At the parties backstage or after performances he would sketch caricatures of the company, and it is at least arguable that, artistically, he was at his best doing witty cartoons. He enjoyed the "family" intrigues, rivalries, and jealousies that surrounded the portly, whimsical, vindictive, and despotic Diaghilev, whose extraordinary flair for talent-spotting led him to commission Stravinsky and Richard Strauss, Hahn and Debussy.

Stravinsky became famous overnight with the premiere of *L'Oiseau de feu* on 25 June 1910. Cocteau, who showed some courage in braving Diaghilev's jealous rivalry for Nijinsky's favours, did not write about Nijinsky until after the provocative first night of *Le Sacre du printemps* on 29 May 1913 at Astruc's new Théâtre des Champs-Elysées. He gives a vivid account of the evening, regarding it as a mistake to have pitted a strong, youthful work against an enervated public in unaccustomedly plush surroundings, and convincingly recounts the predictabil-ity of everything that happened. Stravinsky goes farther in sug-gesting that Diaghilev expected, and indeed planned for, the disturbance which took place. Cocteau also tells us, in tones which do not suggest any deep analysis of the problem, "It was when I knew Stravinsky, and later, when I knew Picasso, that I understood that rebellion is indispensable in art." Cocteau's own artistic life was to be dominated by Diaghilev's demand that he should astound him, and he was to suffer from the belief that the ability to astound was a sign of creative depth. He never achieved the artistic power that comes from the long, slow ges-tation of an artistic work.

The accounts which Cocteau has given of the birth of his close friendship with Stravinsky on the evening after the pre-miere of *Le Sacre* have been challenged by Stravinsky himself, who maintains moreover that Diaghilev did not like Cocteau, remarking that "Cocteau's story was only intended to make him-self feel important." In his own memoirs Nijinsky does not refer to Cocteau. It seems however to be a direct consequence of *Le Sacre*, and of the tensions which surfaced between Diaghilev, Nijinsky, Stravinsky, and Cocteau on the occasion of its famous first night—whichever of the disputed accounts is actually cor-rect—that Cocteau started to write *Le Potomak*, which he dedi-cated to Stravinsky and which was accepted by the *Mercure de France*, although the war prevented publication. At the same time Cocteau attempted to discuss with Stravinsky a new ballet that was to be called "David," though nothing came of it, and Cocteau's work became a first sketch for *Parade*. Having learnt of the project early on, probably through one of the indiscretions for which Cocteau became famous, Diaghilev was not pleased at what he regarded as an attempt by Cocteau to poach Stravin-sky. Stravinsky himself, suspicious about being visited in Swit-zerland by an over-insistent Cocteau, thought the dedication of

Le Potomak simply bait. It seems not unlikely that Cocteau did exaggerate his involvement with Stravinsky, as he may well have exaggerated his closeness to Proust. Diaghilev on the other hand seems genuinely to have liked him, however guardedly.

Cocteau's principal writings about World War I are not free from myth. He produced a novel, *Thomas l'imposteur*, and two long poems, *Le Cap de Bonne-Espérance* and the *Discours du grand sommeil*, which gave the titles to the collections in which they appeared. He had been exempted from military service in 1910 and, when war broke out, joined the Red Cross. Gide has left an account of meeting him on 20 August that year in which his distaste for Cocteau is unconcealed, although it is not difficult to see how shocking Cocteau's inability to be serious must have seemed at that date. In fact Cocteau did what he could during the war, working with Misia Sert for the wounded and editing with Iribe the ultra-patriotic *Le Mot* from 28 November 1914 to 1 July 1915, producing sketches for it of imagined German atrocities. Cocteau was also concerned with various theatre projects, and he met Satie, of whom he has left some skilful pen-portraits. He got himself introduced to Picasso in 1915, and in the following weeks managed to cheer the painter out of the depression into which he had been plunged by the death from tuberculosis of Marcelle Humbert, his mistress since 1912.

Cocteau now envisaged bringing together the cubist world of Picasso with the sumptuous exoticism of Diaghilev's company, but was called up for active service, then sent to the quartermaster corps and, late in 1915, back to the Red Cross. He worked with the well-known balletomane Etienne de Beaumont, who had collected an ambulance brigade of well-intentioned but often incurably frivolous authors. Finally, a desk job in Paris was found for him, as for a number of other figures connected with the arts. Cocteau never developed a very sure eye for painting, although he was interested in it, and was introduced by Picasso to Modigliani and Max Jacob. Apollinaire and Satie belonged to the world of his new "left-bank" painter friends, and *Parade* marked a serious attempt to achieve a cooperation between their world and the "right-bank" world of the ballet.

Diaghilev finally commissioned *Parade*, with music by Satie and sets by Picasso, and asked Massine to do the choreography. The first performance on 18 May 1917 was a matinée in aid of war charities at the Théâtre du Châtelet. The audience included many of Diaghilev's usual aristocratic patrons, but also Juan Gris, Poulenc, Auric, Firmin Gémier, Apollinaire, and e.e. cummings. The performance was met with rather ill-tempered bedlam, this time not calculated, and the reviews were poor. There were also exchanges of insults with critics, and both Satie and Cocteau ended up with fines. Satie was sentenced to a week in prison for sending an obscenely libellous postcard to Jean Poueigh, the critic of the *Carnet de la Semaine*, and it took months of appeals to get the sentence lightened, but there were also counter-manifestations amid the recriminations.

It is clear that Cocteau wanted to represent what had happened as analogous to the first night of *Le Sacre*, which it was not, but also that he was proud of the innovative modernity of *Parade's* idiom, which has generally been seen as little more than a cover for emptiness of serious imaginative content. It is not surprising to find Cocteau exaggerating his part in both the music and the choreography, virtually claiming to be responsible for both. In spite of Diaghilev's wariness, and the suppression of Cocteau's special effects, whose brittleness could only have drawn attention to a surface brilliance masking the imaginative void, *Parade* is often considered to have been the peak of Cocteau's artistic achievement.

Misia Sert observed that Cocteau's desire to bridge the divides between the two major artistic cliques was bound up with his need to be liked. He was anxious to ingratiate himself in too many places at once. When Satie encouraged his pupils Poulenc and Auric to cultivate Cocteau, it was because Satie rightly saw Cocteau chiefly as a gifted publicist. In 1918 Cocteau published his 74-page pamphlet on music, *Le Coq et l'arlequin*, dedicated to Auric, through a new publishing house which he founded with Blaise Cendrars. The cock, French, noisy, and the first syllable of Cocteau, is pitted against the masked and multicoloured harlequin, with suspiciously Russian or German origins. In spite of the manifest nonsense in the text, especially regarding the use of the harlequin figure, the pamphlet read as a manifesto for Satie's associates, and was clearly inspired by Satie's aphorisms, promoting the adoption of flippant titles, jazz rhythms, popular tunes, and the imitation of phonograph, hurdy-gurdy, ragtime, dance and march effects by the use of grating diatonic figures in different keys. Verlaine had prescribed for poetry "music above all, and preferably the uneven"; Cocteau prescribes "the even" for music, as "heavier and less soluble in air." On 12 July 1918 Cocteau, Max Jacob, and Apollinaire were witnesses at Picasso's wedding to Olga Koklova. Then on 9 November Apollinaire died and Cocteau was to exaggerate the closeness of the bond between them.

He was not proud of his part in the literary skirmishes which followed the war. His enemies were the serious poets surrounding Breton and the intellectuals of the *Nouvelle Revue Française* (*NRF*, q.v.). Cocteau was regarded as frivolous and snubbed by the four serious literary magazines, which also conducted bitter feuds with one another: Albert-Briot's *Sic*; Pierre Reverdy's "cubist" (q.v.) *Nord-Sud*, so-called after the Métro line linking the artists' districts of Montmartre and Montparnasse; *391*, the successor to New York's *291*, named after Stieglitz's Photo-Secession Gallery at 291, Fifth Avenue, whose editors, Francis Picabia and Tristan Tzara, tore up Cocteau's poems after he had corrected the proofs and stood them dinner at Prunier's; and the ironically named *Littérature*, the Breton–Aragon–Soupault review, founded in March 1919, whose title alluded to Verlaine's "The rest is literature" and which, at Satie's command and at the last moment, failed to publish *Le Coq et l'arlequin*. Cocteau did send Tzara poems for the *Anthologie dada* (1919), but his wit, social success, and elegance aroused the disdain of all embattled parties in the war of literary credos. Gide attacked him in the *NRF* for June 1919 in the continuing feud, which smouldered on until, after Gide's death, it was buried under its own ash.

What was at stake was ultimately the possibility, during and after the war, of restoring to art forms a high seriousness of purpose. Cocteau, with his painter and musician friends, offered merely unserious camouflage for life's emptiness in witty parodic skits, precise in detail, effervescent and evanescent in content, unpretentious in purpose, announcing the limitations of the forms they caricatured, and avoiding at all costs the expression of emotion. In the same way Cocteau's exquisite manners disguised a lack of real relationships, and it has been remarked that his instant readiness to use the intimate "tu" form of address was simply a theatrical substitute for intimacy.

Cocteau's flaunted frivolity might well have left him a fringe figure in Parisian artistic life, had it not been for *Parade*, which virtually launched Picasso and Satie as artistic figures of public importance, relaunched Diaghilev as a properly French impresario, and enabled Cocteau himself to become the cynosure of a wider public. His success in bringing together the artistic left of his painter and musician friends and the right of Diaghilev's ballet audience echoed the success of Adrienne Monnier's bookshop Aux Amis des Livres, which opened in 1915 and quickly became an arts club with organized poetry readings, dominated by Valéry and Gide, but ingeniously crashed by Cocteau, and of the Montparnasse studio at 6, Rue Huyghens, owned by the Swiss artist Emile Lejeune, who made it the focus of an art gallery and music club, which put concerts there on an inchoately organizational footing from 1915. The studio provided a forum for Debussy, Satie, Ravel, and Picasso, whose activities there culminated in a virtual festival from 19 November to 5 December 1916. There were paintings on display by Modigliani, Matisse, and Picasso, and readings by Cendrars and Cocteau, who brought Diaghilev and Ansermet to listen to Satie, and straight-facedly read the poems of his five-year-old niece. The remonstrations of Apollinaire and Reverdy left him unrepentent.

Among the musicians Cocteau's right-bank friends came to hear were a group who collected round Satie, including Georges Auric, Louis Durey, Germaine Tailleferre, and Arthur Honegger. The group, joined by Francis Poulenc and Darius Milhaud, were eventually to be referred to as "Les Six" by Henri Collet, the music critic of Comoedia, on the analogy of the Russian Five, Balakirev, Cui, Mussorgsky, Rimsky-Korsakov, and Borodin, although the Six had almost nothing in common, incompatible musical tastes, and personalities that clashed. Durey and Tailleferre very quickly dropped out. Cocteau referred to the Six as a group, and appointed himself their spokesman, agent, publicity manager, and impresario. Most of them set poems of his to music. For a moment, immediately after Parade, he appeared to be a more serious cultural figure than posterity has subsequently judged him to have been. Satie clearly felt in danger of being regarded by Cocteau as a private possession.

A translation of "Le Cap de Bonne-Espérance" appeared in the Brancusi number of The Little Review in the autumn of 1921. Meanwhile Cocteau had been invited to join the protest at the US customs seizure of issues of the review containing excerpts from Joyces's Ulysses, and in 1919 he had written a weekly column, of some 20 pieces in all, for Paris-Midi, collected as Carte blanche, a title which, as Cocteau reminded his readers in an effort to parade his avant-garde credentials, Reverdy had rejected for Littérature. The same year he also wrote a 15-minute pantomime scenario for Milhaud's suite Le Boeuf sur le toit featuring a Negro dwarf, a decapitated policeman searching for his head, a red-haired woman dancing round him on her hands, and a bar bill two yards long. The famous restaurant-cabaret Le Boeuf sur le Toit, immensely chic stronghold of all forms of camp, particularly homosexual, which owed its fortune to the left-bank artists the right-wing clientèle came to see, was named after Cocteau's farce. Owned by Louis Moysès, who moved there from the Bar Gaya he had originally founded, it opened on 10 January 1922, a fashionable and expensive but ostentatiously down-market quasi-club over which Cocteau more or less presided. Proust spent an uncomfortable evening there shortly before his death, and books by Maurice Sachs and Jacques Chastenet incorporated its name into their titles.

Cocteau publicized the revival of Parade in Comoedia on 21 December 1920, now associating it with dada (q.v.), which it had originally antedated, and so ensuring its success. Dada was actually disintegrating, but Picabia, who was about to dissociate himself from the movement, had staged a mock vernissage on 9 December at which Tzara had proclaimed 16 "songs" and Cocteau had performed on, among other things, an automobile horn, accompanied by Auric and Poulenc. In 1919 Cocteau had taken to dining regularly with friends on Saturdays. The dinners soon became ritualized and it was out of them that the broadsheet Le Coq developed. It ran from 6 March 1920 for a few months, its format modelled on Eluard's Proverbes, of which its content was a parody, with Eluard's linguistic experiments largely replaced by typographical jokes. It was a jeeringly belligerent series of aphoristic pronouncements by the musicians put together by Cocteau's new young friend Raymond Radiguet, who had been introduced to the circle by Max Jacob, to whom André Salmon at L'Intransigeant had passed him on. Cocteau quickly became infatuated with Radiguet. The relationship was to be a stormy one, and the clientèle of Le Boeuf took a lively interest in its development.

Cocteau's uneasy alliance with dada was based on shared dislikes, of Barrès, for example, whom both Cocteau and dada followers attacked in 1921, and did not last long. In the winter of 1920–21 the Swedish impresario and balletomane Rolf de Maré commissioned from five of the Six a new ballet to a libretto by Cocteau, Les mariés de la tour Eiffel, a pastiche of Greek tragedy and of vaudeville that was presented on 18 June 1921. Tzara and the dadaists willingly worked off a grudge against Jacques Hébertot, director of the Théâtre des Champs-Elysées, during the first night, although the manifestation increased public interest in Cocteau. He was writing two lectures on art, literature, and music, to be delivered in Geneva and Lausanne and published as Le Secret professionnel, and got Radiguet's novel Le Diable au corps accepted by Grasset. Radiguet's relationship with Cocteau was changing, however, and he began to liberate himself from his protector, going off to Corsica with Brancusi for a fortnight in 1922 and turning to female company at Le Boeuf. There was no danger of an affair between Radiguet and Brancusi, but in all his writing on art Cocteau never once mentioned Brancusi's name.

Parts of Cocteau's war poem the Discours du grand sommeil had appeared in Ecrits Nouveaux for November 1921, and the American critic Edmund Wilson began to take an interest in his work. Having seen Les Mariés, which he thought a masterpiece of nonsense, Wilson wrote an important article about it in Vanity Fair in 1922, "The aesthetic upheaval in France: the influence of jazz in Paris and the Americanization of French literature and art." Ezra Pound wrote about Cocteau in the same review and Wilson was rueful at the failure of Les Mariés in New York and Philadelphia in 1923, attributing it to American unfamiliarity with the Parisian vogue for getting married on the Eiffel Tower. In 1922 Cocteau published Plain-chant, which contains some of his best verse, the adaptation of Antigone, which opened on 20 December with music by Honegger, décor by Picasso, and costumes by Chanel, and the two short novels Le Grand Ecart and Thomas l'imposteur which both appeared in volume form in 1923.

Antigone marked the apogee of the Cocteau cult, attracting streams of young men to Dullin's Théâtre de l'Atelier at the top of Montmartre. As the years passed, Cocteau's memory characteristically doubled the number of performances from 100 to 200. Gide was waspish about a single performance at Copeau's Théâtre du Vieux-Colombier on 15 January 1923. The by now regular and generally organized disturbances were a feature which audiences had come to expect. In April 1923, to celebrate Radiguet's exemption from military service, Cocteau took him to England. That summer, after Cocteau's 3 May lecture at the Collège de France, there were parties almost every evening until Milhaud's house-warming on 5 July. On 25 July Cocteau, Radiguet, and Auric were at Arcachon. From here they went by launch to Le Piqueÿ, where sometime that summer Radiguet contracted typhoid from eating poisoned oysters. By December he was dead.

Cocteau had some part in creating the scenarios for Poulenc's *Les Biches* and Auric's *Les Fâcheux*, with décors by Marie Laurencin and Braque, at Monte Carlo in January 1924. Louis Laloy, friend of Debussy and secretary-general of the Paris Opéra, was hostile to Satie and the Six. He disliked Cocteau, but Cocteau, Poulenc, Auric, and he began smoking opium together. That caused a rift between Satie and his former friends, and for Cocteau, hitherto only an occasional opium smoker, it was the start of his lifelong addiction. He did however write the scenario for *Le Train bleu*, a ballet centred on the dancer Dolin, as Patrick Kay was now called. It was adopted by Diaghilev, who commissioned a score from Milhaud. Nijinsky's sister was now the Ballets Russes' choreographer, and Lifar had joined the company. Most of the Russians had been cut off from their homeland by the Revolution, and Massine's marriage had foundered. Diaghilev would not at first take him back, and Cocteau wrote an "adaptation" of *Romeo and Juliet* for a series of soirees put on to help him. The direction was inadequate and the rehearsals disintegrated, but about 10 performances were given in June 1924. Cocteau himself played Mercutio, but the richness of the production was almost entirely visual.

In 1924 the *NRF* printed a volume of Cocteau's poetry, and Cocteau published his *Dessins* (wrongly dated 1923) in an edition of 625 copies. It contained over 100 of his early line drawings and was his best-liked portfolio. He was smoking too much opium, no doubt in an effort to get over the shock of Radiguet's death, but in October 1924 sent the publisher Champion a new portfolio of 30 sketches of himself in different guises, threaded together with conversations between him and his different past or possible selves, *Le Mystère de Jean l'oiseleur, monologues*, which was published in a small facsimile edition. The title contains a double entendre, since "oiseleur," meaning "bird catcher," alludes to French slang usage in which "oiseau" or "bird" signifies "phallus."

Cocteau's return to the practice of his Catholicism under the tutelage of the art-loving, proselytizing, utopian scholastic philosopher and dreamer Jacques Maritain was partly due to a mixture of opium, grief at Radiguet's death, and the prodding of Max Jacob, who, together with Rouault, Chagall, and Claudel, regularly visited the Maritains. The shift back towards Catholicism had been gaining momentum thanks to Ghéon, Copeau, Reverdy, and Jacob, while Cocteau possibly needed both another substitute father and a camouflage for the less edifying side of his life, in which too many young men were still coming to grief. He was torn between the desire to supply them with opium and the desire to wean them from it. He himself underwent a cure in March 1926, at least partly to disengage himself from a young man, Jean Bourgoint, with whom he had slept,

smoked opium, and been on holiday at Villefranche in 1925. He convalesced with the Maritains. Bourgoint became a Trappist monk and his sister, also part of the fabric of Cocteau's social life, eventually married, contracted gonorrhoea from her husband, and finally committed suicide on the night of an ultra-fashionable ball. Since Radiguet's death Cocteau had abandoned Le Piqueÿ, and now spent the summers on the Riviera, mostly at the Hôtel Welcome at Villefranche, which had recently overtaken the Normandy resorts in fashionableness among the bohemian and aristocratic eccentrics left over from pre-war society or wrecked by the war and the Russian Revolution.

Cocteau's brother got married in the church where Radiguet's funeral had been held. In 1925 Cocteau wrote his *Lettre à Jacques Maritain*, with more than an element of posturing, the play *Orphée* (now less well known than the film he made in 1950), the text *Oedipus Rex* for the Stravinsky cantata, and the poem *L'Ange Heurtebise*, first published in *Les Feuilles-Libres* for May-June 1925, and began the poems of *Opéra*. The subject of Orpheus, like that of the angel, suggests Rilke, whose famous *Duino Elegies* and *Sonnets to Orpheus* date from 1923. The Pitoëffs took *Orphée* and produced it on 15 June 1926. Cocteau was still smoking an average of 10 pipes of opium a day, and was on the point of publishing his *NRF* essay "Le numéro Barbette" on the American impersonator and trapeze artist who inspired the portrayal of "Death" as a beautiful young woman in *Orphée*.

Cocteau says that it was on Christmas Day 1926 that he met Jean Desbordes, who was later tortured to death by the Gestapo and the French militia, but it must in fact have been earlier than that. He immediately fell in love with Desbordes, smoked with him, and helped him to write, took him to Chantilly, visited Gertrude Stein with him, and drove south with him in 1927. Maurice Sachs, now a seminarian, was still slowly extinguishing his individuality by identifying with Cocteau, whose mannerisms he had aped, whose signature he forged, and from whom he also stole. That September Isadora Duncan was strangled to death when her famous red scarf caught in the wheel of her car. It was the first year in which Cocteau recorded no artistic accomplishment. He had become very close to Gabrielle ("Coco") Chanel, who had provided the money for Radiguet's funeral, and invited Desbordes and Cocteau to stay, paid for some of his cures, gave Sachs money to put together a library for her, and very probably did call Cocteau, two of whose shows she had dressed, "a snobbish little pederast who did nothing all his life but steal from people." She was one of the first great couturiers.

During 1928 Cocteau wrote his anonymous *Le Livre blanc* and an essay on Chirico, *Le Mystère laïc*, while Desbordes was pouring out his affection in *J'adore*. Cocteau's enthusiasm regarding the literary value of this work has been seen as the first serious faltering of his aesthetic judgement. This cooperation with Stravinsky, whose shortness of melodic inspiration was showing through his gift for rhythm and orchestration, had run into difficulties, and it was indeed somewhat surprising that Stravinsky had turned to Cocteau to produce *Oedipus Rex*, which he knew would have to be translated into a Latin text for a large-scale dramatic work. Stravinsky made cuts that Cocteau later salvaged for *La Machine infernale* of 1934. Diaghilev was staging the work in spite of new imbroglios with Cocteau regarding young men and a growing preference for Prokofiev, who shared his pro-Bolshevik stances and his increasing dislike for French music. He refused to let Cocteau play the Narrator's role. Then Gabrielle Chanel urged Cocteau to take another cure for his addiction, and on 16 December 1928 he entered on a three-month one, during which he kept the notebook later published as *Opium*.

His first outing on 19 March 1929 was to read *La Voix humaine* to the reading committee of the Comédie-Française, which accepted it. Gabrielle Chanel, who was paying the bill, suggested that he might now leave the expensive clinic, but Cocteau was writing *Les Enfants terribles* and prolonged his stay by a few weeks. Subsequent recollections of how many pages a day he was writing vary from seven to 18. Gide called on him. Although their feud was to lose its intensity, Cocteau would always remain a hurtful, irreverent, and rebellious disciple of Gide's. Paul Eluard attempted a surrealist put-down of Cocteau at the preview of *La Voix humaine* on 15 February 1930, and hostilities were briefly reopened. Sometime that summer the Noailles family, with whom Auric and Cocteau were staying, offered them money to make a film. This was a new medium for both of them, and Cocteau later looked back with relish on the freedom he enjoyed in making *Le Sang d'un poète*, although the film was clearly inhibited by the allusions it makes to Buñuel's photography.

There was a hiatus in Cocteau's artistic life around the time of Diaghilev's death, which took place in Venice in 1929. His dramatic writing began speedily to disintegrate, although his greatest public success, *Les Parents terribles* of 1938, was still to come. In the 1930s he began producing streams of light journalism and in 1933 and 1936, following various police prosecutions, he underwent two more cures for opium addiction. His consumption had by then reached 30 pipes a day. There was an increasing tension between Cocteau's infatuation with luxury and his need for low-life pleasures as reflected in his music-hall skits and songs, the pieces he wrote for Piaf and Arletty. Social debasement titillated his refined erotic fantasies. In 1936 he was financed by *Paris-Soir* to emulate the feat narrated by Verne in *Le Tour du monde en quatre-vingts jours* to commemorate the 60th anniversary of the novel's publication, the trip to be paid for in articles. He took with him the replacement for Jean Desbordes, Marcel Khill, his permanent companion from late in 1931. The poetic production of a whole decade is contained meanwhile in the dozen poems of *Allégories*.

Cocteau made himself Al Brown's boxing manager and directed his detoxification and reconquest of the world bantamweight championship in 1938. Khill, like Desbordes, Radiguet, and Sachs had finally turned to female company. At the triumphant Al Brown fight Cocteau was accompanied by Radiguet's true successor, Jean Marais, the poor, beautiful, and versatile though untalented 24-year-old actor who had entered Cocteau's life in 1937. His own bills at the Hôtel Castille, where he had lived since the mid-1930s, were now being paid by Gabrielle Chanel, but he was able to indulge his addiction as he pleased, and when Marais, whom he had auditioned for a part in *Oedipe-roi*, fell ill, Cocteau took him to Le Piqueÿ. It was the first time since Radiguet's death that Cocteau had been back and he wrote *La Fin du Potomak* there while under the hallucinating influence of opium. Marais, who was the most hard-working, docile, and stateful of Cocteau's young friends, was mobilized in 1939.

By the outbreak of World War II Gide counted for much more than Cocteau in all the milieus in which Cocteau wished to excel. Their rivalry fascinated François Mauriac's son, Claude, then rebelling against the father in whose footsteps he was none the less so carefully treading, and in the June 1940 number of the *NRF* he published a devastating account of an interview with Cocteau, discovered with Marais at Versailles in a haze of opium smoke. Mauriac wrote Cocteau off as a mere exhibitionist, excepting only the poems to Radiguet from *Plain-chant*. Cocteau was now also taking cocaine and his personality was clearly suffering. He went to Perpignan briefly in 1939, but returned with Marais to Paris and an apartment in the Palais-Royal which he was to keep for the rest of his life. His collaboration with the occupying forces did not go significantly beyond the applications for licences to publish and produce made by the whole literary community, although he did publish one tactless article in *Comoedia* praising Hitler's favourite sculptor Arno Brecker, who had studied in Paris and now got many prominent Parisian artists taken on tours of Germany. Cocteau went no further than the naive assumption that he could extract publicity from the sometimes fashionable and at first well-behaved Germans, whose cultural sycophants publicized their distaste for his homosexuality, while remaining on ordinarily courteous terms with Jewish friends. He was not accused of collaborationist activities during the post-war reckoning known as the "épuration".

Cocteau's mother died in 1943. Marais had made him give up drugs in 1940, and Cocteau relied heavily on him during the unreality of life in wartime Paris. The Resistance would have nothing to do with Marais because of Cocteau's loose tongue, but Cocteau paid for Genet's defence when he was caught stealing from a bookshop, and was once beaten to the ground for failing to salute French volunteers marching off to join the German forces. Sachs, who had stolen from Cocteau and was now living with a German officer, wrote an attack on him. He was eventually killed, either shot by the Germans or lynched for one of the many betrayals which resulted in the deaths of others. Max Jacob died in a camp in 1944. Cocteau did what he could with Desbordes's posthumous works, undoubtedly improving some of them, after Desbordes had been tortured to death.

Cocteau wrote a liberation poem entitled "25 août 1944," which was published in the *Nouvelles littéraires*, and an article for *Vogue* on Diana Cooper during her husband's somewhat controversially forgiving tenure of the UK ambassadorship in Paris. After the war he was never really well, although he turned to film and proved a successful director as well as a writer of dialogue and scenarios. During the war he had written a long poem, *Léone*, which was admired by Ezra Pound, and a verse play, *Renaud et Arminde*. It was Marais's desire to be a film star that first brought Cocteau back to the cinema. He wrote the dialogue for the undistinguished *Le Baron fantôme*, then the scenario for *L'Eternel Retour*, which was both a critical and a popular success. He directed Marais in *La Belle et la bête* amid all sorts of post-war difficulties in addition to illness. Everything was in short supply, including unpatched sheets for the farmyard laundry scene. Auric wrote the music, and Cocteau published the diary of the film's making.

In Paris Cocteau produced *L'Aigle à deux têtes*, which he turned into a film the following year. Both versions had the advantage of starring Edwige Feuillère, and in the film Cocteau's last young man, Edouard Dermithe, who had replaced Marais in 1947, played a leading role. Cocteau also wrote the screenplay for *Ruy Blas* and made *Les Parents terribles* from his earlier play, followed two years later by *Les Enfants terribles*.

He went to the US in 1949, where he is said to have behaved with "ill grace and exquisite rudeness," and turned down the seven-month tenure of the chair of poetry at Harvard, returning to France to make *Orphée*. The film was universally admired for its exploitation of cinematic resources and won first prize at Venice. Even Claude Mauriac was won over.

Cocteau's showmanship had often acted as a blanket to blur the sharpness of his real talent. He was exhibitionist, self-absorbed, and given to posturing, but also curious, innovative, and possessed of a fragile but lively sense of fantasy. The early line drawings are brilliantly clever. Another blank 10 years followed *Orphée*, but in 1955 Cocteau became a member of the Académie Française. He died of a heart attack on 11 October 1963, just after being interviewed about Edith Piaf, who had died that morning. The last years of his life were marred by lapses of taste, failed artistic enterprises, and occasional acerbities with former colleagues.

WORKS

Summing up Cocteau's achievement, W. H. Auden wrote that he was the most striking example in his age of an artist who

> works in a number of media and whose productions in any one of them are so varied that it is very difficult to perceive any unity of pattern or development…Both the public and the critics feel aggrieved.

> His attitude is always professional, that is, his first concern is for the nature of the medium and its hidden possibilities: his drawings are drawings, and not uncoloured paintings, his theatre is theatre, not reading matter in dialogue form, his films are films, not photographed stage effects…

> Cocteau has never followed fashion, though he has sometimes made it. The lasting feeling that his work leaves is one of happiness; not, of course, in the sense that it excludes suffering, but because, in it, nothing is resented, rejected, or regretted.

The subject of *Le Potomak* is a formless aquatic monster that lives in a Paris aquarium on a diet including olive oil, gloves, spelling mistakes, a music box that plays Wagner, and a programme of the Ballets Russes. In the fiction the monster is visited by Cocteau and his friends, and by two clans, one cruel, called the Eugènes, and the other dull, the Mortimers. The text, developed from a series of drawings made for a small child, is scattered with epigrams. The sequence appears random, and is unified only by its projection of a spiritual quest involving the poet's search for his place in the world. The frivolity of the text, which contains pop, free verse, lullabies, and puns, is a clear sign of the author's vulnerability, his need to protect himself from the public gaze as well as to exhibit himself in peacock feathers.

Thomas l'imposteur is a novel about life among the Marines on the Flanders dunes and follows the fortunes of its poet hero. It is clearly a young man's book, studded with aphorisms and sometimes achieving a brilliance it rather obviously strives for. Full of fantasy and wit, the protagonist goes revealingly out of his way not to avert to the horrors of war, a social nobody who passes himself off as a general's nephew and who seeks death rather than reveal his homosexuality to the girl who loves him. The nonchalant narration of physical horror effectively communicates the mind's inability to comprehend and to adjust its response mechanisms to sudden, real menace, although it is doubtful if that was the author's articulate intention. Cocteau called the book a "nouvelle."

The title of *Le Grand Ecart* refers to what the gymnast or dancer terms "the splits." Here it also means, as Cocteau himself explained, the great divide between a woman of experience and a naive young man. The book is a serious portrait of an adolescent Parisian with a supporting cast of students riotously tumbling in and out of bed with girls, who occasionally end up in bed with one another. In the course of the book, which is sometimes thought to be the most accomplished of Cocteau's works of fiction, the hero gradually becomes aware of his own homosexual leanings.

Les Enfants terribles has also been considered a work of genius. It quickly established itself as a cult novel, revealing to the young the nature of their own adolescent impulses. The leading characters, Paul and Elisabeth, are a brother and sister who share a cluttered room and exclude the outside world as far as possible from their life, proud of their own superiority. Cocteau talked of their agoraphobia. The book includes residues liberated by opium from among Cocteau's deepest memories: "My unconscious self…dictated my book to me." It contains his famous bully figure, the erotically attractive Dargelos, and is a study of the destructive relationships in which its protagonists, starting with childish games and fetishes, later get caught up. Some of the incidents are related to those of *Le Sang d'un poète*.

Cocteau's poetry can be merely modish or playful, and is often full of fantasy. It self-consciously deploys purely verbal skills and virtuosity. *Le Cap de Bonne-Espérance* centres on the topic of flying, already used as a poetic metaphor and theme by Apollinaire, from whose *Calligrammes* the book partly derives. It is in part a tribute to the young aviator Roland Garros, who was eventually shot down, and spent much of World War I as a prisoner. The poet-aviator, transmuted into Jacob wrestling with the angel, reverses the result of that encounter and finds it difficult to be a man again. As in Apollinaire, effects are created with the help of typographical devices, but the poem's achievement is in fact slight in relation to its length.

Both the *Discours du grand sommeil* and *L'Ange Heurtebise* are in a sense concerned with inspiration. The poetic mission is conferred, however, by a de-celestialized angel who wakes up and stretches, evoking kaleidoscopic images of biblical visitations, Rilke's angel, and Mallarmé's fawn. In *Heurtebise* the angel is the object of brutal physical attraction. As in *Plain-chant*, it is the poems of intense physical desire which most impress, but even they do not disentangle the verse from verbal intricacies, trivial images, and mere witticisms. The protective patina is omnipresent, while there is nothing remotely solemn, or even unself-consciously serious here. The peacock's feathers are a display exhibited to disguise too vulnerable a reality. As with the sketches, so also with the poems: the wittiest may well be the best. Cocteau himself thought *Heurtebise* his most nearly perfect poetic work but, as in *Plain-chant*, where the model is Ronsard, the parade of derivativeness can be experienced as intrusive.

Cocteau's dramatic output also suffers from an over-reliance on surface skills. Its fantasy is intentionally too clever to allow for the communication of emotion. Even the primordial myths do not work in Cocteau's versions, although both Sartre and Giraudoux were able to extract from the Oedipus legend something of the psychological truth embedded in the myth. It is Auden who has analysed most convincingly the failure of *L'Eternel Retour*, which draws on the Tristan myth. Here the everyday matter-of-factness of the boy-loves-girl plot hinders the working of myth, which requires artificiality in the medium of communication. For this reason Auden thought opera the ideal medium for dramatic myth. For Cocteau, myth was an opaque sunshade for the apparent social satire of *La Machine infernale*, despite its clever fidelity to Sophocles and its borrowings from elsewhere. *Orphée*, the play, does contain a deeper meaning, although in the film Death plays a much more double-edged role, an object of love delivering from life as a midwife delivers a child from the womb. Underlying the film, there is the myth's implied defence of homosexuality, but on an insufficiently serious register. The myths are self-conscious shields against self-revelation. Cocteau does best when, as in the unmannered *Les Parents terribles*, he relinquishes the Greek trappings and lets his stagecraft, ear for speech, and sense of dramatic vitality take over.

Where Cocteau is undoubtedly successful is in *Le Boeuf sur le toit*, a hilarious mime with music by Milhaud, exactly the right composer for the jazz pastiche required. The adaptation of *Romeo and Juliet* is not generally considered to have been effective, but the return to satire with *Les Mariés de la tour Eiffel* was a witty achievement, an excellent example of its genre, complete with new-fangled gramophones and platitudinous dialogue. *La Voix humaine*, a slickly written one-woman telephone sketch with considerable human depth, is also undoubtedly successful. The woman knows that the man she is talking to is pretending to be alone in order to protect her. He knows she still loves him, and is in fact with his bride-to-be.

The deft assurance of technique, surface sheen, and inventive fantasy of his work point to the miniature genre of the line drawing or caricature or the largest genre of all, the cinema, as the ideal media for Cocteau's brilliance. All but the lighter forms of drama, fiction, and verse were outside the range of qualities he possessed. His literary criticism never confronted important issues, although the acuteness of their reflections should ensure that such volumes as *Le Rappel à l'ordre*, the *Essai de critique indirecte*, and above all *La Difficulté d'être* are not forgotten.

PUBLICATIONS

Collections

Oeuvres complètes, 11 vols., 1946–57
Théâtre complet, 2 vols., 1957

Plays

Les Mariés de la tour Eiffel (produced 1921), 1924; as *The Eiffel Tower Wedding Party*, in *The Infernal Machine and Other Plays*, 1963
Antigone (produced 1922; revised version, with music by Arthur Honegger, produced 1927), 1927; as *Antigone*, in *Four Plays*, 1962

Roméo et Juliette, from the play by Shakespeare (produced 1924), 1926
Orphée (produced 1926), 1927; as *Orpheus* (in English), 1933
Le Pauvre Matelot, with music by Milhaud (produced 1927), 1927
Oedipus Rex, with music by Stravinsky (produced 1927), 1949
Oedipe-roi (produced 1937), 1928
La Voix humaine (produced 1930), 1930; as *The Human Voice*, 1951
La Machine infernale (produced 1934), 1934; as *The Infernal Machine*, 1936
Les Chevaliers de la table ronde (produced 1937), 1937; as *The Knights of the Round Table*, 1963
Les Parents terribles (produced 1938), 1938; edited by R.K. Totton, 1972; as *Intimate Relations*, 1962
Les Monstres sacrés (produced 1940), 1940; as *The Holy Terrors*, 1962
La Machine à écrire (produced 1941), 1941; as *The Typewriter*, 1947
Renaud et Arminde (produced 1943), 1943
L'Aigle a deux têtes (produced 1946), 1946; as *The Eagle Has Two Heads*, 1948
Ruy Blas (screenplay), 1947
Le Sang d'un poète (screenplay), 1948; as *The Blood of a Poet*, 1949
Un tramway nommé désir, from the play by Tennessee Williams (produced 1949), 1949
Théâtre de poche (includes scenarios, sketches, and radio works), 1949
Orphée (screenplay), 1951; as *Orphée*, in *Three Screenplays*, 1972
Bacchus (produced 1951), 1952; as *Bacchus*, in *The Infernal Machine and Other Plays*, 1963
La Belle et la bête (screenplay), 1958; as *La Belle et la bête*, in *Three Screenplays*, 1972
Cher menteur, from the play by Jerome Kilty (produced 1960), 1960
Le Testament d'Orphée (screenplay), 1961; as *The Testament of Orpheus*, in *Two Screenplays*, 1968
L'Impromptu du Palais-Royal, 1962
L'Eternel Retour (screenplay), as *L'Eternel Retour*, in *Three Screenplays*, 1972

Screenplays: *Le Sang d'un poète*, 1930; *La Comédie du bonheur*, 1940; *Le Baron fantôme*, with Serge de Poligny, 1943; *L'Eternel Retour*, 1943; *Les Dames du Bois du Boulogne*, with Robert Bresson, 1945; *La Belle et la bête*, 1946; *Ruy Blas*, 1947; *L'Aigle a deux têtes*, 1947; *Les Parents terribles*, 1948; *Noces de sable*, 1949; *Les Enfants terribles*, 1950; *Orphée*, 1950; *La Villa Santo-Sospiro*, 1952; *La Corona negra*, 1952; *Le Testament d'Orphée*, 1960; *La Princesse de Clèves*, 1961; *Thomas l'imposteur*, 1965
Ballet scenarios: *Le Dieu bleu*, 1912; *Parade*, 1917; *Le Boeuf sur le toit*, 1920; *Le Train bleu*, 1924; *Le Jeune Homme et la mort*, 1946; *La Dame à la licorne*, 1953; *Le Poète et sa muse*, 1959

Fiction

Le Potomak, 1919; revised edition, 1934
Le Grand Ecart, 1923; as *The Grand Ecart*, 1925; as *The Miscreant*, 1958

Thomas l'imposteur, 1923; as *Thomas the Imposter*, 1925; as
    The Imposter, 1957
Les Enfants terribles, 1929; as *Enfants Terribles* (in English),
    1930; as *Children of the Game*, 1955; as *The Holy Terrors*,
    1957
Le Fantôme de Marseille, 1936
La Fin du Potomak, 1940
Deux travestis, 1947

Verse

La Lampe d'Aladin, 1909
Le Prince frivole, 1910
La Danse de Sophocle, 1912
Le Cap de Bonne-Espérance, 1919
Ode à Picasso, 1919
Discours du grand sommeil, 1924
Escales, with André Lhote, 1920
Poésies 1917–20, 1920
Vocabulaire, 1922
Plain-chant, 1923
La Rose de François, 1923
Poésie 1916–23, 1924
Cri écrit, 1925
Prière mutilée, 1925
L'Ange Heurtebise, 1926
Opéra: oeuvres poétiques 1925–1927, 1927
Morceaux choisis, 1932
Mythologie, 1934
Allégories, 1941
Les Poèmes allemands, 1944
Léone, 1945; as *Leoun* (in English), 1960
La Crucifixion, 1946
Poèmes, 1948
Le Chiffre, 1952
Appogiatures, 1953
Dentelle d'éternité, 1953
Clair-obscur, 1954
Poèmes 1916–1955, 1956
Gondole des morts, 1959
Cérémonial espagnol du phénix; La Partie d'échecs, 1961
Le Requiem, 1961
Faire-part, 1969

Other

Le Coq et l'arlequin: notes autour de la musique, 1918; as *Cock
    and Harlequin*, 1921
Dans le ciel de la patrie, 1918
Carte blanche, 1920
Visites à Maurice Barrès, 1921
Les Mariés de la tour Eiffel, 1921
Le Secret professionnel, 1922
Dessins, 1923
Picasso, 1923
Ferat, 1924
Le Mystère de Jean l'oiseleur, monologues, 1925
Lettre à Jacques Maritain, 1926
Le Rappel à l'ordre, 1926; as *A Call to Order*, 1926
Maison de santé: dessins, 1926
Le Mystère laïc, 1928

Le Livre blanc, 1928; as *The White Paper*, 1957
Une entrevue sur la critique avec Maurice Rouzaud, 1929
25 dessins d'un dormeur, 1929
Essai de critique indirecte, 1932
Opium, 1932; as *Opium* (in English), 1932
Portraits-souvenir 1900–1914, 1935; as *Paris Album 1900–
    1914*, 1956
60 dessins pour "Les Enfants terribles," 1935
Mon premier voyage: tour du monde en 80 jours, 1936; as
    Round the World Again in Eighty Days, 1937
Enigme, 1939
Dessins en marge du texte des "Chevaliers de la table ronde,"
    1941
Le Greco, 1943
Serge Lifar à l'opéra, 1944
Portrait de Mounet-Sully, 1945
La Belle et la bête: journal d'un film, 1946; as *Diary of a Film*,
    1950
Poésie critique, 1946
La Difficulté d'être, 1947 as *The Difficulty of Being*, 1966
Le Foyer des artistes, 1947
Art and Faith: Letters Between Jacques Maritain and Cocteau,
    1948
Drôle de ménage, 1948
Reines de France, 1948
Lettre aux américains, 1949
Maalesh: journal d'une tournée de théâtre, 1949; as *Maalesh:
    A Theatrical Tour in the Middle-East*, 1956
Dufy, 1949
Orson Welles, with André Bazin, 1950
Modigliani, 1950
Jean Marais, 1951
Entretiens autour de la cinématographie, edited by André
    Fraigneau, 1951; revised edition, edited by André Bernard
    and Claude Gauteur, 1973; as *On Film*, 1954
Journal d'un inconnu, 1952; as *The Hand of a Stranger*, 1956
Gide vivant, with Julien Green, 1952
La Nappe du Catalan, 1952
Aux confins de la Chine, 1955
Lettre sur la poésie, 1955
Le Dragon des mets, 1955
Journals, edited by Wallace Fowlie, 1956
Adieu à Mistinguett, 1956
L'Art est un sport, 1956
Impression: arts de la rue, 1956
Cocteau chez les sirènes, edited by Jean Dauven, 1956
Témoignage, 1956
Entretiens sur la musée de Dresde, with Louis Aragon, 1957; as
    Conversations in the Dresden Gallery, 1983
Erik Satie, 1957
La Chapelle Saint-Pierre, Villefranche-sur-Mer, 1957
La Corrida du premier mai, 1957
Comme un miel noir (in French and English), 1958
Paraprosodies, précédées de 7 dialogues, 1958
La Salle des mariages, Hôtel de Ville de Menton, 1958
La Canne blanche, 1959
Poésie critique: monologues, 1960
Notes sur "Le Testament d'Orphée," 1960
Le Cordon ombilical: souvenirs, 1962
Hommage, 1962
Anna de Noailles oui et non, 1963

Adieux d'Antonio Ordonez, 1963

La Mésangère, 1963

Entretien avec Roger Stéphane, 1964

Entretien avec André Fraigneau, 1965

Pégase, 1965

My Contemporaries, edited by Margaret Crosland, 1967

Entre Radiguet et Picasso, 1967

Professional Secrets: An Autobiography, edited by Robert Phelps, 1970

Lettres à André Gide, edited by Jean-Jacques Kihm, 1970

Cocteau's World (selections), edited by Margaret Crosland, 1972

Cocteau, poète graphique, edited by Pierre Chanel, 1975

Lettres à Milorad, edited by Milorad, 1975

Editor, *Almanach du théâtre et du cinéma*, 1949

Editor, *Choix de lettres de Max Jacob à Jean Cocteau 1919–1944*, 1949

Editor, *Amadeo Modigliani: quinze dessins*, 1960

Critical studies

Crosland, Margaret, *Cocteau* (in English), 1956

Oxenhandler, N., *Scandal and Parade: The Theatre of Cocteau*, 1957

Fowlie, Wallace, *Cocteau: The History of a Poet's Age*, 1966

Sprigge, Elizabeth, and Jean-Jacques Kihm, *Cocteau: The Man and the Mirror*, 1968

Brown, Frederick, *An Impersonation of Angels: A Biography of Jean Cocteau*, 1968

Steegmuller, Francis, *Cocteau: A Biography*, 1970

Crowson, Lydia, *The Esthetic of Cocteau*, 1978

COLETTE, Sidonie-Gabrielle, 1873–1954.

Novelist and dramatist.

LIFE

Colette was born and grew up in Burgundy, the daughter and last child of Jules Colette, an ex-soldier turned tax collector, and Sidonie Landoy. "Sido," as Colette's mother was known, was born in Paris, lost her mother when very young, and was brought up first by her father and then by her brothers. Her first husband, an alcoholic, was 21 years older than she was, and left her a widow at 29 with two children, Juliette and Achille, and a fortune in property. Sido remarried and had two further children, Léopold and Sidonie-Gabrielle, who signed herself after 1923 by her maiden name, "Colette." Colette's mother was to dominate her imagination throughout her life. Her half-sister Juliette became estranged from the family and married in 1885, later committing suicide, and Juliette's husband brought a lawsuit against them. Colette's father mismanaged Sido's inheritance. The contents of the family home were publicly auctioned in 1890, and the family moved in with Achille, who was practising as a doctor nearby. Colette fell in love with "Willy," Henry Gauthier-Villars, the son of a friend of her father, who had an illegitimate son he used to visit in the area. He was 33 when they married in 1893, an erudite member of the literary world, whose friends included Catulle Mendès and Marcel Schwob.

Willy was a womanizing, flamboyant self-publicist, a music and drama critic, and an advocate of Wagner. It was he who encouraged Colette to write once when they were experiencing one of their regular money shortages. He disliked and discarded the product of her efforts, then later rediscovered the jettisoned manuscript and, having added a seasoning of slang and lesbianism, got it published in 1900 as *Claudine à l'école*, signing it "Willy." It was a huge success and Willy got three more Claudine books out of Colette in quick succession. She also wrote a book from the point of view of animals witnessing the goings-on of their owners, *Dialogues de bêtes*, signed this time "Colette Willy." Willy's life was a succession of duels, lawsuits, and infidelities until, in 1906, he finally left Colette, who exorcized his memory by writing *La Retraite sentimentale*, again signed "Colette Willy," in which Claudine makes her final appearance as a principal character. Willy remarried. Colette began to make a living from dancing and mime and had an intense lesbian affair with the Marquise de Belbeuf, "Missy." Dressed as a man, Missy exchanged a long kiss with her on stage at the Moulin Rouge during *Rêve d'Egypte* in 1907. Her letters of this period tell us a great deal about her personality, although those to Sido, who died in 1912, have been destroyed.

In 1911 Colette fell in love with Henry de Jouvenel ("Sidi"), editor of *Le Matin*, for which she was writing at the time. Missy wanted her to mary Auguste Hériot, with whom she had travelled to Italy in 1910, but in 1912 Colette married Jouvenel, who fathered her only child, also called Colette, in 1913. Colette gave up dancing. She became literary editor of *Le Matin* in 1919 and continued to write weekly for the paper until 1924, when her pieces began to appear regularly elsewhere. In 1923 she and her husband separated. Much of her best writing was the product of the 1920s. In 1925 the play *L'Enfant et les sortilèges* with music by Ravel had its premiere in Monte Carlo.

Colette was also acting at this time, and doing translations, while continuing to be employed by various newspapers as a drama critic. In 1935 she married Maurice Goudeket, whom she had first met 10 years previously. They sailed to the US on the maiden voyage of the *Normandie*, and in 1938 flew to North Africa. During World War II Goudeket, who was a Jew, was arrested and detained for two months at Compiègne. *Gigi et autres nouvelles*, Colette's last work of fiction, appeared in 1944. It was Colette herself who discovered the ideal female lead for the Broadway musical version. She was the then unknown actress in Monte Carlo, Audrey Hepburn. Many of Colette's works were successfully adapted for the stage or the screen. She began to write obsessively now, producing six books of chronicles, journals, and reminiscences in 1948 alone. She wrote for money but though her work was prolific, she wrote suprisingly slowly and painstakingly, finding as much inspiration in the day-to-day and the trivial as in the glamorous elements of her life. She was elected to the Académie Goncourt and finally to its presidency (1949). Her *Oeuvres complètes* appeared between 1948 and 1950. Towards the end of her life Colette suffered from painful arthritis. On her death she was accorded a state funeral but, because of her two divorces, was refused a church burial.

WORKS

Colette's first four novels centre on the character of Claudine, starting with her schooldays, when she vies unsuccessfully with the headmistress for the affection of a new and attractive assistant mistress. The other three take her through loneliness, love, marriage, jealousy, and widowhood. They are entertaining and only slightly risqué, except perhaps on the subjects of male and female homosexuality (presumably deriving from Willy's contribution to the forgotten manuscript), amusingly exploiting Claudine's efforts to make sense of her experience by keeping a diary. The fourth book centres on the diary of Claudine's nymphomaniac friend Annie, and is the least satisfactory of the series. The third volume, *Claudine en ménage*, is the best.

In her writings from 1904 to 1922 Colette attempted to redefine those values which are in some fundamental sense compatible with innocence and purity, as in the two "Minne" novels, which Willy insisted on signing and which Colette worked into the single *L'Ingénue libertine* in 1909, the year in which Willy sold the rights to her novels. Colette is still curious here about the nature of sexual satisfaction and impatient with old age, ugliness, and infirmity. Later on she would write in the first person, as if to continue Claudine's diary under her own name. From 1904 she also started writing dialogues between household pets, the number of dialogues growing from edition to edition. The dialogues virtually turn the pets into human commentators on the domestic scenes of which they are witnesses, so that they, too, become replacements for Claudine, so many fictionalized Colettes commenting on their author's real life.

The major works of the second decade of the century include two novels, *La Vagabonde* and *Mitsou*, both in modified letter form, although the first section of *Mitsou* is also partly in the form of a dramatic dialogue and a third-person narrative. Both novels therefore still exploit the first-person and diary conventions, although now in more complex form, and both are set in a theatrical context. *L'Entrave* takes up one of the characters from *La Vagabonde*, Renée, and is also written in diary form. In *La Vagabonde* Renée, divorced and with unhappy memories of her first marriage, fights free of a second proposed marriage, so that her emotional and professional independence takes priority over her physical needs. In *L'Entrave* she has achieved financial security and, meeting her admirer again, now happy as a husband and father, begins writing a diary. She gives herself emotionally as well as physically to a conventional but extra-marital relationship with a friend's lover. Eventually he leaves her, but she wins him back by her total submissiveness—a quality she has come to regard as essential to female satisfaction in life. The novel, which could be seen as exploring just another possible solution to the problems of female sexuality, in fact goes against the whole thrust of Colette's imaginative quest, and she was defeated in her attempts to rewrite its conclusion.

Chéri is generally considered to be Colette's best novel, the first of a series extending to 1928—*Le Blé en herbe, La Fin de Chéri*, and *La Naissance du jour*—interrupted by *La Maison de Claudine* of 1922, with Claudine forced into the title by the publisher but not otherwise mentioned in the vignettes of which the book consists. At the start of *Chéri* the central character, Léa, is aged 49. She has kept a 25-year-old lover, Chéri, for six years, but he leaves her now to marry an 18-year-old. After six months of searching, Chéri finds Léa again and the couple are reunited, but in the morning he notices that her physical attractiveness has diminished and she sends him back to his new wife. In the sequel Léa has become a plump asexual 60-year-old with swollen legs, and Chéri, pining for Léa as a younger woman, shoots himself. Chéri is literally the creation of Léa's passion. She turns him from waif to lover and when her attractions have sufficiently diminished, his life has served its purpose.

La Maison de Claudine has been seen as a turning point in Colette's development. The title could mean either "Claudine's house" or "The house where Claudine lives," and the book mimics *Claudine à l'école*, completing and repudiating it by transforming the fictional fantasy of the earlier novel into a much more serious consideration of the situation, desires, needs, frustrations, and satisfactions of a mature woman. Although *Le Blé en herbe* has different central characters—a boy of 16, who is sexually initiated one summer by a 30-year-old, and a girl of 15 whom he in turn initiates—the novel is again about the transformation of adolescent sexuality into the acceptance of specific social roles. *La Naissance du jour* is a self-portrait which explores the renunciation of passion by a woman in her fifties. Colette, writing it at just that age, was in fact having a passionate love affair with the man who was about to become her third husband.

Of the last five novels, *La Seconde* concentrates on the clash between love and a friendship which is almost physical between a wife and her husband's mistress. In *La Chatte* a young bride attempts on impulse to kill the cat on which her husband dotes and husband and cat end up going home to his mother. If the symbolism in all the novels is clear cut, here it is downright obvious. Colette is not an intellectual. She writes as an intelligent, bewildered, sensitive, and reflective human being with animal impulses who is trying to come to terms not so much with the dominant role of sex in her life as with the nature of her sexuality and that of others. The palpably exploratory nature of her fictional and autobiographical writing gives her work an attractive quality of innocence. She is not trying to shock, even in the lesbian episodes, but to understand.

The problems may work themselves out according to the rules codified by Freud, but the reader can understand them without ever having heard of Freud, and it is difficult to suppose that Colette knew that her characters were acting in accordance with Freudian paradigms. It says much for the different susceptibilities of times and places that *Le Matin* abruptly suspended serialization of *Le Blé en herbe* when it discovered that the ending involved intercourse with a 15-year-old girl, whereas Wedekind's *Frühlingserwachen*, though potentially far more shocking, had been successfully staged 30 years earlier in Vienna, even before Freud had written his major works.

Duo and *Le Toutounier* are again full of highly charged symbols. In *Duo* Michel discovers his wife's physical but not emotional infidelity of the previous year and the novel follows the lives of the couple for a week before Michel finally drowns himself. Much use is made of colour, fire, and water. The second novel charts a day in the life of Michel's widow, Alice, three weeks later, as she returns to the intimacy of her life with two of her three sisters, an intimacy for which her relationship with Michel turns out to have been merely a surrogate. *Julie de Carneilhan*, the last full-length novel, is again about emotional intimacy, which takes precedence over the relationship the two female protagonists had both had with the same man. The initials "J de C," when reversed, stand for Colette de Jouvenel, but the novel also continues the fictionalized autobiography in more substantial ways. Colette's last major fictional work was *Gigi et autres nouvelles*, a collection of short pieces gathered together in 1944 but written during the bleakest days of the war. Groomed for success in life as a rich man's mistress, Gigi unthinkably succeeds in breaking strict family rules by becoming the man's wife.

Three books of more directly personal reflection, *Sido*, *Ces plaisirs* (later reprinted as *Le Pur et l'impur*), and *Mes apprentissages*, are interspersed with the later novels and deal with various initiations—into financial, sexual, and literary matters. The four major volumes of short stories, *Bella-Vista*, *Chambre d'hôtel*, *Le Képi*, and *Gigi*, were all written later and together comprise a new outlook on life for women, dissociating them on the whole from conventional dependence on men. The protagonists of these stories refuse either to be shaped by dominating male partners or to allow their sexuality to be confined by conventional relationships.

Colette's last two major works, *L'Etoile vesper* and *Le Fanal bleu*, examine with a knowledgeable and practical eye her own life and achievement. Never unsubtle or overstated, often relying on mere suggestion, her writing involved a mixture of passion, hauteur, and boredom. Colette is not a truly great writer. Her focus is too narrow for that. But her fiction kept at bay the clumsy relationships her life had to offer her, and she was quite unsentimental in her work as in her life. She wrote cheerfully and energetically, but her analysis of feeling, in the best French tradition, is too precise to allow her scope for great lyricism.

PUBLICATIONS

Collections

Oeuvres complètes, 15 vols., 1948–50
Oeuvres complètes, 16 vols., 1973–76
The Complete Claudine, 1976

Fiction

Claudine à l'école, with Willy, 1900; as *Claudine at School*, 1930
Claudine à Paris, with Willy, 1901; as *Claudine in Paris*, 1931; as *Young Lady of Paris*, 1931
Claudine en ménage, with Willy, 1902; as *The Indulgent Husband*, 1935; as *Claudine Married*, 1960
Claudine s'en va, with Willy, 1903; as *The Innocent Wife*, 1934; as *Claudine and Annie*, 1962
Minne; Les Egarements de Minne, 2 vols., 1903–05; revised version, as *L'Ingénue libertine*, 1909; as *The Gentle Libertine*, 1931; as *The Innocent Libertine*, 1978
Le Retraite sentimentale, 1907; as *Retreat from Love*, 1974
Les Vrilles de la vigne, 1908
La Vagabonde, 1911; as *The Vagrant*, 1912; as *Renée la vagabonde*, 1931; as *The Vagabond*, 1954
L'Entrave, 1913; as *Recaptured*, 1931; as *The Shackle*, 1963
Les Enfants dans les ruines, 1917
Dans la foule, 1918
Mitsou; ou, Comment l'esprit vient aux filles, 1918; as *Mitsou; or, How Girls Grow Wise*, 1930
La Chambre éclairée, 1920

Chéri, 1920; as *Chéri* (in English), 1929
Le Blé en herbe, 1923; as *The Ripening Corn*, 1931; as *Ripening Seed*, 1959
La Femme cachée, 1924
Quatre saisons, 1925
La Fin de Chéri, 1926; as *The Last of Chéri*, 1932
La Naissance du jour, 1928; as *A Lesson in Love*, 1932; as *Morning Glory*, 1932; as *Break of Day*, 1961
La Seconde, 1929; as *The Other One*, 1931; as *Fanny and Jane*, 1931
Paradis terrestres, 1932
La Chatte, 1933; as *The Cat*, 1936; as *Saha the Cat*, 1936; in *Seven by Colette*, 1955
Duo, 1934; translated as *Duo*, 1935; as *The Married Lover*, 1935
Bella-Vista, 1937; in *The Tender Shoot and Other Stories*, 1958
Le Toutounier, 1939; as *The Toutounier*, with *Duo*, 1976
Chambre d'hôtel, 1940; as *Chance Acquaintances*, 1952
Julie de Carneilhan, 1941; as *Julie de Carneilhan* (in English), 1952
Le Képi, 1943; in *The Tender Shoot and Other Stories*, 1958
Gigi et autres nouvelles, 1944; as *Gigi* (in English), 1953; in *The Tender Shoot and Other Stories*, 1958
Stories, 1958
Collected Stories, edited by Robert Phelps, 1983

Plays

En camerades (produced 1909), in *Oeuvres complètes 15*, 1950
Claudine, with music by Rodolphe Berger, from the novel by Colette (produced 1910), 1910
Chéri, with Léopold Marchand, from the novel by Colette (produced 1921), 1922; as *Chéri* (in English), 1959
La Vagabonde, with Léeopold Marchand, from the novel by Colette (produced 1923), 1923
L'Enfant et les sortilèges, with music by Maurice Ravel (produced 1925), 1925; as *The Boy and the Magic*, 1964
La Décapitée (ballet scenario), in *Mes cahiers*, 1941
Gigi, with Anita Loos, from the story by Colette (produced 1951), 1952
Screenplays: *La Vagabonde*, 1917; remake, 1931; *La Femme cachée*, 1919; *Jeunes filles en uniforme* (French dialogue for the 1931 German film *Mädchen in Uniform*), 1932; *Lac aux dames*, 1934; *Divine*, 1935

Other

Dialogues de bêtes, 1904; augmented edition, as *Sept dialogues de bêtes*, 1905; as *Douze dialogues de bêtes*, 1930; as *Barks and Purrs*, 1913; as *Greatest Conversations*, 1978
L'Envers du music-hall, 1913; as *Music-Hall Sidelights*, 1957
Prrou, Poucette, et quelques autres, 1913; revised edition, as *La Paix chez les bêtes*, 1916; translated in *Creatures Great and Small*, 1951
Les Heures longues 1914–1917, 1917
La Maison de Claudine, 1922; as *The Mother of Claudine*, 1937; as *My Mother's House*, 1953
Le Voyage égoïste, 1922
Rêverie du nouvel an, 1923
Aventures quotidiennes, 1924
Renée Vivien, 1928
Sido, 1929; as *Sido* (in English), 1953

Histoires pour Bel-Gazou, 1930

La Treille Muscate, 1932

Prisons et paradis, 1932

Ces plaisirs, 1932; as *Le Pur et l'impur*, 1941; as *These Pleasures*, 1934; as *The Pure and the Impure*, 1934

La Jumelle noire, 4 vols., 1934–38

Mes apprentissages. 1936; as *My Apprenticeships*, 1957

Chats, 1936

Splendeur des papillons, 1937

Mes cahiers, 1941

Journal à rebours, 1941; in *Looking Backwards*, 1975

De ma fenêtre, 1942; augmented edition, as *Paris de ma fenêtre*, 1944; in *Looking Backwards*, 1975

De la patte à l'aile, 1943

Flore et Pomone, 1943

Nudités, 1943

Broderie ancienne, 1944

Trois...six...neuf, 1944

Belles saisons, 1945; as *Belles Saisons: A Colette Scrapbook*, edited by Robert Phelps, 1978

Une amitié inattendue (correspondence with Francis Jammes), edited by Robert Mallet, 1945

L'Etoile vesper, 1946; as *The Evening Star: Recollections*, 1973

Pour un herbier, 1948; as *For a Flower Album*, 1959

Trait pour trait, 1949

Journal intermittent, 1949

Le Fanal bleu, 1949; as *The Blue Lantern*, 1963

La Fleur de l'âge, 1949

En pays connu, 1949

Chats de Colette, 1949

Creatures Great and Small, 1951

Paysages et portraits, 1958

Lettres à Hélène Picard, edited by Claude Pichois, 1958

Lettres à Marguerite Moréno, edited by Claude Pichois, 1959

Lettres de la vagabonde, edited by Claude Pichois and Roberte Forbin, 1961

Lettres au petit corsaire, edited by Claude Pichois and Roberte Forbin, 1963

Earthly Paradise: An Autobiography Drawn from Her Lifetime of Writing, edited by Robert Phelps, 1966

Places (miscellany; in English), 1970

Contes de mille et un matins, 1970; as *The Thousand and One Mornings*, 1973

Journey for Myself: Selfish Memoirs (selection), 1971

Lettres à ses pairs, edited by Claude Pichois and Roberte Forbin, 1973

Au cinéma, edited by Alain and Odette Virmaux, 1975

Lettres from Colette, edited by Robert Phelps, 1980

There is a series of *Cahiers de Colette*.

Critical and Biographical studies:

Crosland, Margaret, *Madame Colette: A Provincial in Paris*, 1952

Marks, Elaine, *Colette* (in English), 1961

Davies, Margaret, *Colette* (in English), 1961

Cottrell, R. D., *Colette* (in English), 1974

Mitchell, Yvonne, *Colette: A Taste for Life*, 1975

Sarde, Michèle, *Colette: Free and Fettered*, 1980

Stewart, Joan Hinde, *Colette* (in English), 1983

Lottman, Herbert, *Colette: A Life*, 1991

CONSTANT DE REBECQUE, Henri-Benjamin, 1767–1830.

Novelist and journalist.

LIFE

Henri Constant's father, Juste de Constant de Rebecque (1726–1812), an army officer who rose to the rank of general in 1796, married another officer's daughter, Henriette de Chandieu de Lisle (1742–1767) when she was 25 and he was over 40. Constant, the only child of the marriage, was born on 25 October 1767, and his mother died a fortnight later, on 10 November. The source of the family's inherited wealth is obscure, but at Constant's birth his father's family clearly belonged to the aristocracy of the canton of Vaud in Switzerland. They addressed one another as baron and owned several properties, to which feudal rights were attached, along the north side of Lake Geneva. Six of these properties belonged to Constant's father, whose principal residence was in Lausanne. That house, together with four of the others, later had to be sold. Constant himself inherited and later sold the sixth.

The boy's motherless upbringing naturally left its mark on him. His mother's name was never mentioned in his writings, or between him and his father, and as a result of her death Constant was to remain insecure and indecisive in later life. The first half of his career was marked by liaisons with older women, and the absence of tenderness in childhood led him to seek and even to imagine intense emotional experiences later in his life. He was brought up at the whim of his father's capricious eccentricities, with no one to moderate the precocious irony with which he sought to protect himself. His father was well read, an occasional poet, and a member of Voltaire's circle, and took part in dramatic performances at Ferney. Constant's fictionalized portrait of him in *Adolphe* depicted him as cold and inarticulate. He had an ironic turn of mind, was easily bored, and communicated with his son more easily in writing than in speech. Constant conjectures that his father was severely repressed and in need of affection, but his cold demeanour inhibited others from expressing it to him. Consequently, Constant himself was forced back on to the intelligent introversion which was to make him famous, and his critical faculties were developed at the expense of moral and social maturity.

He was entrusted to his paternal grandmother until the age of five, then for two years to the 20-year-old Jeanne Suzanne Magnin ("Marianne"), a girl whom his father had literally abducted from her family when she was nine in order to train her to become, in his own words, "the woman of his dreams." He eventually compensated the girl's family, had her educated, and, when she was 20, had her brought from Holland to Lausanne and put her in charge of Constant. Constant grew to dislike her with unusual intensity. His father may formally have married her, and certainly had two children by her, Charles (1784–1864) and Louise (1792–1850). Marianne tried to favour the interests of her own children at Constant's expense, although Constant seems not to have known of their existence until 1800, when he was 33.

Constant's letters to his grandmother showed such powers of observation and expression that Sainte-Beuve thought they had to be forgeries. His father had intended to turn him into a prodigy, forcing him to study Latin, Greek, counterpoint, and mathematics from the age of five under a German called Stroelin, who was dismissed after two years at Marianne's instigation. In 1774 Constant, now seven, was taken to the Low Countries by his father, who tried to educate him himself, but finally entrusted him to the regimental surgeon, who proved an unsuitably dissolute guardian. Constant then had a series of tutors. He was put into the house of a music teacher, where he read very widely but received no other education. His father was finally persuaded to confide his education to a dissipated charlatan called Gobert, who had had to flee Paris for Brussels, where he lived with several mistresses. The main source for these details is the diary *Le Cahier rouge*, covering the period to 1794, written in 1811, and first published in the *Revue des Deux Mondes* (*RDM*, q.v.) in 1907.

A fourth tutor was found in a 50-year-old ex-monk whom Constant liked. However, he came to an unfortunate end when he left. The sister of his next pupil flirted with him, and he fell so heavily in love with her that he shot himself. By now Constant was 12 and his father began to show him off. He could read Homer and translate Livy into Alexandrines, wrote poetry, and had begun a verse tragedy and a prose poem, *Les Chevaliers*, which his father had bound. He came to resent the suppression of sentiment in favour of irony which his education had encouraged, and to regard himself as having been "violent, quarrelsome, and sly." His father tried and failed to have him admitted to Oxford at 13, so employed instead an English tutor, taken on during the course of a 10-week trip, whose authority over Constant he undermined by sarcasm at his expense. Another tutor, this time French, was engaged and dismissed, and Constant was sent to Erlangen University, which at that time had 250 students, and from which he matriculated on 6 February 1782. During his 18 months in Erlangen he attended the court of his father's friend, the Margraf. To his father's amusement, he contracted gambling debts. He got himself talked about, and enjoyed the notoriety of appearing to have an affair that never took place. When a complaint was lodged, his father recalled him, taking him to Edinburgh, where they arrived on 8 July 1783. Constant was 15.

After an agreeable year studying with a professor of medicine, he then lodged with a family, studying history and Greek for 18 months, discussing social issues in a student society, and losing money by gaming. He left with his debts unpaid, spent three weeks in London, and was boarded out in Paris. He was now 17 and regarded his host, Jean Baptiste Suard, a member of the Académie Française, chief drama censor, and a distinguished man of letters, with sneering antagonism. Suard's wife, sister of the publisher Panckoucke, had a well-known salon. During the month before the Suards were ready to receive him, Constant was picked up by a young Englishman with whom he went to brothels and gaming houses. His father appointed an extra guardian called Baumier, recommended by the chaplain to the Dutch embassy. Although he abetted the profligate habits of his charge, Constant thought him "dull and insolent." Baumier was dismissed and Constant *père* took his son away from the Suards after four months, depositing him in Brussels, where he spent the next three.

In Brussels he had a brief liaison with a married Swiss woman, Marie Charlotte Johannot, who was living away from her husband. It lasted about four weeks. She later moved to Paris and committed suicide. Constant's father now came to Brussels and took his son back to Lausanne, where his family found him

amusing, disdainful, and flippant. Everything in his upbringing had driven him to superficial charm, emotional uncertainty, and personal insecurity. He remained at home from November 1785 to November 1786, distracting himself by working on a book about pagan mythology, which was eventually to turn into the five-volume *De la religion considérée dans sa source, ses formes et ses développements*, the final two volumes of which were published posthumously. The work was later completed by the two-volume *Du polythéisme romain considéré dans ses rapports avec la philosophie grecque et la religion chrétienne*, also published posthumously, in 1833. Constant had not, of course, had any professional experience, and by the time the works to which he had devoted so much time were published, they were out of date. In 1786 he laid the vast project aside, and tried to translate the first three volumes of Gibbon's *Decline and Fall*, but found the cadences too difficult. He settled instead far a translation of the recent *History of Greece* by John Gillies, which he did not finish.

It was during the summer of 1786 that he feigned a passion for, and almost succeeded in making himself fall in love with, the 35-year-old Harriot Trevor, who was renting a villa near Lausanne in order to escape the summer heat of Turin, where her husband was minister. She had an entourage of young men who gambled heavily in her house. Constant's passion was a game, but he felt he owed it to himself to pretend to be properly in love. He was always too tender, or affected, not to dress up passion, especially when it was real, as a grand and enduring emotion. We know from a cousin who accompanied him that Constant wept all the way to Paris when his father came to take him back there. We also know that he quickly forgot about Harriot Trevor and did not react at all when they met again. After a month with his father in a hotel Constant returned to the Suards, where he now enjoyed the salon and earned a reputation for his epigrams. He lost money gambling again, and had to borrow it from a elderly lady, who thought he was declaring a passion for her and was deeply upset when she found he was not.

In March 1787 he met Mme de Charrière, known as Belle de Zuylen, the author of two novels and two pieces of satirical fiction. She was then 47 and Constant was 20. Having an inadequate dowry, she had married her brother's arithmetic tutor, but was both livelier and more depressive than her rather dull husband. She was also given to flouting convention. The probability is that she and Constant became lovers soon after they met. They certainly enjoyed a close intellectual intimacy, but Constant had again incurred gambling debts and his attentions were being firmly directed towards the 16-year-old Jenny Pourrat, the daughter of an exceedingly prosperous banker. Although he was tongue-tied in her presence, Constant wrote passionate letters inviting her to elope. There was a scene when he was found alone with Jenny's mother by the mother's lover, and dramatically started to take opium rather than explain to a stranger that neither mother nor daughter loved him. He was prevented from swallowing more than a trace and took Jenny to the opera. He was, however, forbidden the house. After gaming he would spend the night drinking tea and taking opium with Mme de Charrière.

His father sent an officer to fetch him after the debacle with Jenny, but Constant had sold his carriage, so the two had to face the return journey in a cabriolet intended for one. While the officer spent the day in Paris, Constant borrowed 30 louis from Mme de Charrière and planned his escape. When the officer found the cabriolet too uncomfortable and decided to spend the night in Paris, Constant slipped off to a brothel and left for Calais with nothing but a shirt and the 30 louis. By the evening of 26 June he was in Dover. He wrote to Mme de Charrière and to his father, bought a monkey and two dogs, and set out for London. He exchanged the monkey for another dog, and then sold two of the dogs at a loss. He had enough money for four weeks, but remembered the address of his father's London banker and obtained £25. He met some friends from Edinburgh, accompanied them to Brighton, went to Newmarket, hoping to make money on the horses, found no races, hired a horse, bought a bitch, and rode via Kendal to Edinburgh, arriving at six p.m. on 12 August with just 10 shillings. He had enjoyed being alone. He met his old friends, found his gambling debts forgotten, enjoyed life for a fortnight, borrowed £10, rode south again via the Lakes, which reminded him of Switzerland and nearly drowned him, and returned the horse. In London he borrowed another £10 and arrived at Calais totally broke.

He pawned his watch and cadged his way to Holland and his father, whose only reference to the escapade was a passing remark about his son's torn coat. He was returned to Switzerland and went to stay with Mme de Charrière, who was at Colombier, four miles from Neuchâtel. He returned to Lausanne and heard that his father had found him a post in Brunswick, for which he set out in December 1787. He was delayed by the first of his many duels. A French officer's dogs had savaged Constant's and he had beaten them off with his riding whip. *Le Cahier rouge* ends with this incident on 8 January 1788. Constant had also picked up an infection in Lausanne, and spent some weeks convalescing with Mme de Charrière. His journey to Brunswick, where he arrived on 2 March, was punctuated by a new torrent of letters. As gentleman of the chamber to the duke, Constant was to be paid 66 louis a year. He stayed for five years, with his father contributing an allowance of 115 louis. He paid 10 louis for his lodgings, had a valet, a lot of free meals at court, and for several weeks kept a pledge to renounce gambling. He was in charge of protocol, and looked down on the officials and members of the court. They had clean shirts monthly and handkerchiefs fortnightly. Constant, half amused and half repulsed by their self-importance, made himself unpopular and spent a lot of time alone.

Mme de Charrière's letters became fussy and tart. Constant's father, who had not been getting on well with his army colleagues, was finally suspended from his command for six months and left his regiment. Constant left at once for Holland, thought his father must have committed suicide, found he had enormous debts, and determined to sell the Swiss properties. His father finally returned to his regiment, by which time the Berne government was involved, and was presented with a list of the 14 sentences pronounced against him. The ensuing legal proceedings lasted nine years and cost him all that remained of his fortune. In November 1788 Constant suddenly and astonishingly became engaged to a girl he had found in tears. His marriage to Wilhelmina von Cramm, who was nine years his senior, took place on 8 May 1789. Constant's father gave him a present and the duke increased his salary to 100 louis and gave him a free house. Mme de Charrière broke off relations, more probably because of his father's court case than because of the marriage, but the break lasted only three and a half months. Constant spent the winter of 1789 in the Low Countries, and visited Switzerland for three months in 1791.

Constant was a constitutional liberal, who at first welcomed the Revolution. He was soon to become disillusioned politically, as well as with his marriage. Mme de Charrière had fallen in love with someone else. Constant had a brief liaison with an actress and then, in January 1793, already seeking to end his marriage, he met Charlotte von Hardenberg. She was two years his junior and married to a much older man, Baron von Marenholtz, by whom she had a son. She instantly fell in love with Constant, and the couple lived openly together in Brunswick, Charlotte's husband having given her full liberty and a generous allowance. At first, Constant was not seriously in love, but he found Charlotte's submissiveness and her rapture refreshing after the asperities of his wife, from whom his separation became formal on 25 March, although not fully legal until 31 January 1794. Meanwhile, however, Charlotte's father had forced her to return home. Constant left Brunswick on formal leave of absence at the end of May 1793 and helped with his father's affairs, the lawsuits, and the sale of property. Some of the time he stayed with Mme de Charrière while waiting for his 4,000 books to arrive. He spent a final four months in Brunswick, where he was not made welcome by the friends of his ex-wife. His divorce became final on 18 November 1795. Wilhelmina died in 1823.

It was on 11 August 1793 that Mme de Staël, who had long admired Mme de Charrière's novel *Caliste*, visited her at Colombier. She came again on 24 September 1794, and on 28 September she met Constant, who had called on her at her house at Coppet. He later caught up with her on the road to offer his services in the delicate political situation which had resulted in Mme de Staël's mother's coffin being sealed in the mausoleum at Coppet. Constant's relationship with Mme de Charrière now dwindled to extinction. She was an invalid by 1802 and died in 1805. At Mézéry in 1794 Constant was introduced to really grand company for the first time in his life. It was close, elegant, and aristocratic without any of the comic pomposities of the court at Brunswick, although with less real power. What attracted Mme de Staël and Constant to each other was their shared relish in intellectual pyrotechnics, and perhaps their quite different backgrounds. He was fundamentally a bohemian. She delighted in great luxury and open display. She was totally dedicated to libertarian ideals, had an awesome personal energy, and an exceedingly clever mind. Constant worked himself up into a passionate frenzy, but Mme de Staël found his appearance repulsive. Although he staged a dramatic suicide scene, she did not yield easily. When she did, it was because she had decided to.

On 23 April 1795 Mme de Staël obtained her passport to return to Paris. She took Constant with her, determined to push him into politics and to have her father recalled from exile. She also hoped to get back the two million livres her father had lent the government. Constant did not distinguish himself in Paris. He was too insecure to be taken seriously and passed the time gambling. Mme de Staël overplayed her hand, and the pair returned to Coppet on 21 December 1795. The following year Constant wrote his pamphlet *De la force du gouvernement actuel et de la nécessité de s'y rallier* in favour of the Directoire, and published it in May. Mme de Staël was not allowed into France, but Constant returned to Paris briefly that year. He set about acquiring the French domicile and nationality which would allow him to become active in the country's politics. He borrowed money from Mme de Staël's father and bought a ruined abbey at Hérivaux, near Luzarches, for 50,000 francs, having sold his remaining property in Switzerland. He returned again to Paris to ensure a good press for Mme de Staël's book on the passions, and got permission for her to reside in France, although not in Paris. They went to Hérivaux at Christmas.

In 1797 Constant published two more political pamphlets and on 8 June his daughter, Albertine de Staël, was born in Paris. Mme de Staël was energetic that year in getting the foreign ministry for Talleyrand, hoping that he would obtain the secretary-generalship for Constant. Talleyrand tried, but Napoleon took no notice. Both Constant and Mme de Staël were put in a predicament by the left-wing coup of 4 September which overturned the counter-revolutionary election results of May. They both had to approve the upholding of republican sentiment, but were disgusted by the excessive barbarity of the deportations, almost reminiscent of the Terror. For what he later regarded as the mistake of defending the illegal coup, Constant was appointed president of the canton of Luzarches, but Mme de Staël was again exiled to Coppet in January 1798. Her household had naturally been infiltrated by a government spy. Bonaparte returned to Paris on 5 December 1797 and asked to be received by Talleyrand, who told Mme de Staël to be in the ante-room. Up to this point she had been Napoleon's fervent admirer, but she again overplayed her hand and made herself a nuisance to him.

Since France had annexed Vaud, Constant, now 30, was eligible to run for office, but failed on grounds of nationality to get himself elected in 1798. He published a pamphlet against any possible restoration on the English model of 1660. Bonaparte, having left the Egyptian campaign, arrived back in Paris in October 1799. Mme de Staël and Constant arrived on the evening of the coup d'état of 9 November. The Directoire had been dissolved and Bonaparte had effectively seized power, although he nearly lost it by a fumbling speech. Mme de Staël and Constant had just witnessed the end of representative institutions in France, as well as the end of a counter-revolutionary threat. They had cause for sorrow as well as joy. Constant immediately started job-hunting and was appointed to the Tribunat. The position conferred 15,000 francs a year and no power at all. By early 1800 hostilities had broken out between Bonaparte and Mme de Staël, while Constant needled him from the Tribunat. Prodded by Mme de Staël, Constant had spoken on 5 January against the time limit fixed arbitrarily on the Tribunat's powerless discussions. Virtually all Paris took the heavy hints and turned its back collectively on the couple.

Constant opposed the more outrageous of the laws the government intended to pass, and was retired from the Tribunat with the first group to be rotated. He left politics for 13 years. He had formed a friendly relationship with Julie Talma, who was 11 years older than he was and, from 1791 to 1801, married to the famous actor. It was in her salon that he met Anna Lindsay in 1800. She was five years his senior, had had three children, and had shown great courage during the Terror. He lost interest in their affair just as hers was aroused, and the satisfaction of his vanity, although it was not wanton, cost her great suffering. The relationship provides the background to Constant's only title to literary fame, *Adolphe*. Julie Talma pointed out that Constant's letters to Anna had the dual effect of making her despair and reviving her hopes. Anna and Constant both watched over Julie's final hours in 1805.

As Bonaparte consolidated his power, so both Mme de Staël and Constant were excluded from affairs. They spent more time at Coppet, but in spite of the thraldom in which she kept him,

Mme de Staël did not want to marry Constant. In 1803 she tried to gain entrance to Paris, but was forced to remove herself, and went to Germany. Constant, who had been working at the smaller property he had acquired to replace Hérivaux, known as Les Herbages, agreed to join her. In Weimar on 22 January he began to keep a diary. Goethe wrote a glowing tribute to him in his own. When Mme de Staël's father died on 9 April 1804, Constant had returned to Switzerland and immediately left to join Mme de Staël, whom he intercepted at Weimar on her way from Berlin. She had recruited August Wilhelm von Schlegel as tutor to her sons, but he and Constant disliked each another.

Constant was now caught up by his role in the entourage at Coppet. He had a brief escape when, early in 1805, he renewed his liaison with Charlotte von Hardenberg, now Mme du Tertre. She had divorced Marenholtz and remarried in 1798. Constant himself was restless and would have liked to break away from Mme de Staël, now sole mistress of Coppet. She of course knew this and strengthened her grip. Constant's diary explodes with resentment on 1 January 1807, and between 12 and 27 January he wrote the first draft of *Adolphe*. He also characteristically determined on the moral cowardice of a secret marriage to Charlotte, but on 31 August 1807 first offered again to marry Mme de Staël. When she turned him down and he withdrew his offer, she had a suicidal tantrum and he left the house at dawn next day. She went after him and took him back to Coppet.

Charlotte's husband agreed to a divorce on very reasonable terms while Constant was adapting Schiller's *Wallenstein* as *Wallstein*. Mme de Staël went off to Vienna, thus giving him a chance to be alone with a deeply distressed Charlotte. They married in secret, after Mme de Staël returned from Vienna, on 5 June 1808 at Dôle. Only Constant's father knew. Ironically, in view of the amount of pain he caused, Constant's inability to tell Mme de Staël about his marriage came from his unwillingness to inflict suffering. However, she began to suspect when she met Charlotte on a social occasion while Charlotte was staying nearby with her aunt. Escaping from the Staël household was always a problem. A visit to Constant's father was arranged by getting Marianne to write a letter saying that his father was ill. In May 1809 Constant persuaded Charlotte that she should herself announce the news to Mme de Staël, who duly called on her at her request, finding her with her feet in a mustard bath. The unpleasant interview lasted six hours. Constant was made to return to Coppet. Charlotte was told to go back to Germany. The "form of marriage," insisted Mme de Staël, must be kept a secret.

Constant seems genuinely, and perhaps not without reason, to have feared extreme reactions from Mme de Staël. Delaying his departure left Charlotte merely very distressed. In the early summer of 1809 he did leave to stay with Charlotte, only to be summoned to Lyons by Mme de Staël. He obeyed the summons when threatened by her son with a duel. Charlotte followed him to Lyons but in front of Mme de Staël, Constant begged her to go away. She wrote a suicide note and took poison, but the note was delivered in time to save her life. Far from being a play to gain attention, the suicide attempt was genuine and it took her months to recover. In the meanwhile, Mme de Staël herself was not far short of suicidal and needed Constant's presence even if she could no longer have his affection. She demanded that his father should deny the wedding, offered to provide for his children by Marianne, and asked Constant to return the loan from her father with which he had bought Hérivaux at the height of their passion. Constant promised to leave the money in his will and bought himself a little time in Paris. In the summer of 1810 however, he was, summoned to attend a glittering house party on the Loire hosted by Mme de Staël. She said she intended to make Constant suffer, and fancied herself in love with one of her guests, Prosper de Barante, but he, like Mme de Staël's son Auguste, was in love with Juliette Récamier, Mme de Staël's closest woman friend, who was being coquettish with Schlegel.

Mme de Staël was correcting the proofs of De l'Allemagne and enjoyed the summer. Napoleon tried to have the book destroyed and Mme de Staël was banished. Constant took up gambling, lost 20,000 francs in a single night, and had to sell Les Herbages and part of his library. Happily for everyone Mme de Staël, who, at 45, had bad skin, protruding teeth, and an ugly nose, now provoked a passion in Jean Rocca, a 23-year-old who had served in Spain. She married him and they had a child. In April 1811 Mme de Staël was still fond enough of Constant for Rocca to want to fight a duel with him. Constant said goodbye to her on 10 May and did not return to Switzerland for another 13 years. Charlotte and he went back to Germany, where Constant settled down to work in Göttingen, briefly visited his first wife, who was surrounded by 120 birds, 36 cats, eight dogs, and two squirrels, and heard of his father's death, which had occurred on 2 February 1812. Mme de Staël, who wanted Bernadotte, the Swedish crown prince, to succeed Napoleon, tried to get Constant to put himself at Bernadotte's disposal. They dined together and Bernadotte, whose hopes were fading with the allied victory at Leipzig, encouraged Constant to write an attack on military dictatorships. The result was De l'esprit de conquête et de l'usurpation. The strong position Constant had established for himself as a victim of Napoleon, however, was dissipated when the allies preferred a restoration of the Bourbons to Bernadotte, who retired hurriedly from Paris, frightened now of losing the Swedish throne too.

Constant knew that his impulsiveness, his Swiss Protestant origins, his admiration for the British constitution, and his private life all worked against the possibility of high office under a restored monarchy, although Talleyrand gave him an interview. He began to write his long series of political pamphlets, arguing the doctrine of the neutrality of the crown and the need for a constitutional monarchy, a hereditary peerage, unpaid representatives, trial by jury, religious toleration, and freedom of the press in Réflexions sur les constitutions, la distribution des pouvoirs et les garanties dans une monarchie constitutionnelle, which appeared in 1814. The censor's objections led to two further pamphlets on the need for freedom from censorship. The pamphlets pleased no party, but provoked wide discussion. Mme de Staël, having rallied to the Bourbons, arrived in Paris on 2 May 1814, but she had lost interest in Constant, although they resumed friendly relations.

A diary entry of 19 August suggests that Constant thought he was falling in love with Mme Récamier. She was 46 and he was 47, and he did indeed become infatuated, allowing his pen to be enlisted in the interests of her friend Murat's claim to the throne of Naples. The monarchists were not pleased, and neither was Mme de Staël, who stridently denounced Constant's new infatuation for her old friend. Further difficulties were caused by Mme de Staël's sudden need for money for Albertine's dowry. Most of her own was locked up in America and Italy, or still on loan to the French treasury. She threatened Constant with a lawsuit. He threatened to produce her letters in open court. She was furious. Six days later Napoleon was defeated and the again restored Louis XVIII repaid the two million francs.

During Napoleon's hundred days Mme de Staël had immediately fled Paris. Mme Récamier would not accompany Constant to Germany, so he stayed in Paris and wrote a famous article for the Journal des Débats, printed on 19 March. In it he openly and bravely attacked Napoleon, who was already being rapturously welcomed in Grenoble and Lyons, and defended liberal principles. By 20 March Louis XVIII had fled for Belgium and only hours later Napoleon had arrived in the Tuileries. Within weeks Constant was undertaking an exercise in damage limitation, helping Napoleon to draft a new constitution. He was to explain why in his Mémoires sur les cent jours, dated 1820. Constant had tried to flee from Paris on Napoleon's arrival, failed, and returned on 27 March to be enlisted by Napoleon in quest of a liberal image. In 1816 he wrote another pamphlet, De la doctrine politique qui peut réunir les partis en France, incidentally attacking Chateaubriand's La Monarchie sous la Charte. Mme de Staël, who had vacillated, enjoyed, as Talleyrand put it, rescuing the people she had drowned the night before. She had tried to help the Bonapartists under the first restoration, fled when Napoleon returned, but then tried to get Constant to use his influence with Napoleon on her behalf during the hundred days. When war became inevitable, she again became anti-Bonapartist.

On 19 April Constant had become a councillor of state, and on 24 April Le Moniteur Universal published his Acte additionnel aux constitutions de l'Empire guaranteeing religious liberty, freedom of the press, inviolability of the person, an elected house, an independent judiciary, and obligatory military service only with the consent of the chambers. The May elections returned a liberal majority. Only a military victory could now save Napoleon, and that was denied him at Waterloo on 18 June. He returned to Paris on the morning of the 21 June, considered trying to declare a military dictatorship, thought better of it, called for Constant at seven p.m., and talked to him for three hours in the garden. Napoleon was recognized from the street and could have let the mob loose on the defiant deputies in an effort to establish his dictatorship. He abdicated the next morning and the chambers asked Fouché to form a government. He had once been responsible for the Terror, had turned against Robespierre, may have betrayed Babeuf to Barras, had been ambassador in Milan and at the Hague, and was appointed minister of police in 1799 and again in 1815, having twice been dismissed by Napoleon, once to govern the Illyrian provinces. Louis XVIII would have re-employed him, but his vote for the execution of Louis XVI counted too strongly against him, and he retired to Trieste.

Constant saw Napoleon again on 24 June. Fouché removed him from Paris by appointing him to the commission to negotiate with Blücher, the real negotiations being conducted with Wellington by committed monarchists. When Louis XVIII returned on 8 July, the day after the allied armies had entered Paris, Constant wrote to the king, who deleted his name from the list of those to be exiled. His passion for Mme Récamier was desultorily rekindled, and he joined her at the seances of the Baroness von Krüdener.

Charlotte was writing appealingly. On 19 September Fouché was dismissed, and on 18 October the Constitution was suspended. Constant left Paris for Brussels, where Charlotte joined him. They went to London, with Constant aware that Mme

Récamier's hold on him had led him to ruin any future political career. *Adolphe* was published simultaneously in London and Paris in 1816 because Constant needed sterling.

Mme de Staël died in Paris on 14 July 1817. Constant had not been allowed to visit her to avoid distressing her. In July 1818 he irrevocably damaged his hip and had to use crutches for the rest of his life. His amorous adventures were over, but he still gambled. He was not elected in 1817, but was successful in 1819 and remained a deputy until the July revolution of 1830, with an intermission of two years from 1822 to 1824. He remained somewhere to the left of the liberals, fighting for the freedom of the individual wherever he could. His political pamphlets were widely influential. Constant was wrongly fined for association with General Berton's military conspiracy of 1822, and might have gone to prison if Mme Récamier had not used her influence with Chateaubriand, who rescinded the prison sentences, but increased the fines. In 1824 Constant had a slight stroke. He had fought his 20th recorded duel from an armchair on account of his crutches. He was not elected to the Académie Française, as it did not want him to sleep through its meetings after spending all night at the gaming tables, but in 1829 he published *Mélanges de littérature et de politique*. After the July revolution of 1830 he was made president of the legislative committee of the council of state and given 200,000 francs to pay off his personal debts. He died of general paralysis on 8 December 1830. Charlotte was to die from burns sustained in July 1845 after she had fallen asleep while reading in bed.

WORKS

The great bulk of Constant's published work is taken up with his political writings and his works on the history of religions. All religions, thinks Constant, are good in their time and their place. None is valid always and everywhere. He is virtually a deist, emptying Calvin's ferocious Protestantism of almost everything but Kant's moral imperatives. There are one or two critical articles, a substantial surviving correspondence, the autobiographical *Journaux intimes* and *Le Cahier rouge*, and the short novel *Adolphe*, on which for a long time Constant's literary reputation alone rested. Its setting is taken from his liaison with Anna Lindsay, but its content reflects the tensions in his relationship with Mme de Staël in 1807. Then, in 1948, *Cécile*, another short novel of fictionalized autobiography, was found. It was published in 1951 and seems to have been written in the last months of 1811. It also seems probable that Constant had destined it for eventual publication but never finished it.

Adolphe is a first-person novel whose eponymous narrator seduces a much older woman, Ellénore, who leaves her lover and two children to follow him. He soon finds her passion irksome and is obliged out of kindness to pretend to an emotion he does not feel. He dislikes being with her, yet is unhappy when away. He does not wish to hurt her and therefore cannot break with her. Eventually, Ellénore realizes what has happened and dies of grief. The narrator reflects that one day he will be sorry to have lost such faithful and absolute affection. The force of the novel, if it is not really only a conte, lies in its minute examination of sentiment and the narrator's lucid analysis of his vacillations. The genre is in fact instructive. *Adolphe* was written as an episode, presumably a chapter, in a novel from which it quickly became detached and which itself may not have been written.

Any of it that was, apart from *Adolphe*, has not survived.

In 1794, when he was 27, Constant had written to an aunt: "Puisque ce faste de dédain ne m'a pas rendu heureux, au diable la gloire d'être supérieur à ceux qui sentent; j'aime mieux la folie de l'enthousiasme (Since this display of contempt hasn't made me happy, to hell with the glory of being superior to people moved by their feelings. I'd rather have the madness of enthusiasm)." He goes on to say that, even if his motive is calculated selfishness, he would rather be calculating and selfish if that is the path to happiness. Which is he? Calculating and selfish, or sentimental and affectionate? The answer of course is neither, but the dilemma of being both at once is what is known as the "dédoublement constantien." The difficulty, as Constant's life repeatedly shows, arises from his childhood, his subsequent need for tenderness, instilled inability to allow full rein to his emotions, and consequent despair at either grasping his own happiness and success, whatever hardship that inflicts on others, or sacrificing and suppressing his gambler's calculating self-interest for the sake of the people he loves. The result is real vacillation, agony for himself and others, and a series of avoidable emotional entanglements which do his feelings more honour than his intelligence.

Adolphe is a trap, sufficiently well laid to make it reasonable to suppose that it was the high point of the work from which it became detached and which, if it was ever written, was subsequently as superfluous as scaffolding once the building is up. What postures as pitilessly lucid self-analysis is in fact a not unreasonable attempt at self-justification. The narration is simple. The work starts: "At 22 I had just finished my studies…" It is doubtful whether the opening could have been written except as an analysis of a real experience. Constant's first few pages give an arresting account of his caustic and inhibited father. The taste for "ironie" (nearer to sarcasm than to irony in English) that his own education was bound to drive him to was the product of exceptionally acute observation, even in an age in which the analysis of sentiment had already been of imaginative importance to the cultivated literate public for a generation.

Adolphe, by relating his own upbringing, has therefore justified the behaviour he is about to relate before launching into his story proper. We know before anything happens that the narrator's reactions will prove to have been determined by the constraints acting on him during youth, that he was accustomed "à renfermer en moi-même tout ce que j'éprouvais (to close within myself everything I experienced)," that he was thrown back on himself to make plans and execute projects, never talked about what was preoccupying him, and regarded the views, interests, assistance, and even presence of other people as an intrusion, "comme une gêne et comme un obstacle." Adolphe himself illustrates the trait he is describing by epigrammatically summing up; "Je n'avais point cependant la profondeur d'égoïsme qu'un tel caractère paraît annoncer: tout en ne m'intéressant qu'à moi, je m'intéressais faiblement à moi-même (Still, I didn't have the depths of egoism which such a character seems to suggest. While I was interested only in me, I was only weakly concerned about myself)."

In his self-presentation in five paragraphs before the narrative begins, Adolphe completes his preliminary appeal to the reader by icing the cake. He has a "besoin de sensibilité (a need for emotional sensitivity)," the death of an elderly woman had sent him at 17 into a "rêverie vague (an imprecise dreaminess)," he found that "aucun but ne valait la peine d'aucun effort (no goal

Ce fut un vrai poète: Il n'avait pas de chant.
Mort, il aimait le jour et dédaigna de geindre.
Peintre: il aimait son art—Il oublia de peindre...
Il voyait trop—Et voir est un aveuglement

(He was a true poet: he had no voice. / Dead, he loved the daylight and despised complaint. / Painter: he loved his art—He forgot to paint... / He saw too much, and seeing is a blindness).

Poem after poem expatiates on failure, hopelessness, and the inevitability of frustration, but never with self-pity. "Paria," one of the best poems, puts a brave face on the inadequacies for which solitude and freedom are small compensation:

Et ma moitié: c'est une femme...
Une femme que je n'ai pas.

(And my half: it's a woman... A woman I haven't got).

There are controlled clumsinesses, changes of mood, jokes, allusions, puns, verbal tricks, clever rhythms and rhymes, much mockery and self-mockery, a terror of taking himself seriously, a sensitivity, and a vibrancy which would indeed have pleased Des Esseintes.

PUBLICATIONS

Collections

Oeuvres complètes, Bibliothèque de la Pléiade, 1970

Verse

Les Amours jaunes, 1873
Selections from "Les Amours jaunes," translated, with introduction and notes, by C.F. MacIntyre, 1954

Critical studies

McElroy, Walter, *"Tristan Corbière: an essay with seven translations of his poems,"* Nimbus, vol. 3, no. 2, 1955
Sonnenfeld, Albert, *Corbière and the Moral Structure of "Les Amours jaunes"*, in "Dissertation Abstracts," Ann Arbor, XIX, 1958–59
Lindsay, Marshall, *The Poetry of Tristan Corbière*, in "Dissertation Abstracts," Ann Arbor, XX, 1959–60
Sonnenfeld, Albert, *L'Oeuvre poétique de Corbière*, 1960
Delpuech, Germain, *Corbière, poète maudit*, 1966

———

CROS, Charles (Hortensius-Émile-), 1842–1888.

Poet, inventor, author of comic dialogues.

LIFE

Cros was born at Fabrezan, between Carcassonne and Nar-

bonne, on 1 October 1842, the son of Simon-Charles-Henri Cros (1803–1876), himself the son of a mathematician, Greek scholar, and grammarian, and Joséphine Thore (born 1805), whom he married in 1832. The couple had three other children: Antoine (1833), Henriette (1838), and Henry (1840). Cros's father, a doctor of law, published a *Théorie de l'homme intellectuel et moral* in 1836, and from 1843 had a teaching appointment at Limoux and then, from late in 1844, in Paris. In 1849 he was teaching at Joigny, to the south-east of Paris, but was removed from his post on account of republican activities, and returned to Paris. Cros himself must have passed his baccalauréat, and by 1858 was studying mathematics and music. He knew some Hebrew and Sanskrit. In 1860 he obtained an assistant's post at the institution for the deaf and dumb. From 1861 his salary was 600 francs a year. His elder brother, Henry, who taught art in the same institution, made a bust of him. Cros began medical studies, but was to abandon them in 1865.

Cros had been Henry's second in a duel and the two brothers had been dismissed from their posts. Cros was allowed to return, but was again dismissed in 1863 for not taking his duties seriously enough. During the 1865 cholera epidemic he helped his brother Antoine, who was a doctor. He appears to have led a bohemian existence as a part-time inventor, experimenting with chemistry and physics. He invented a phonograph and a system of colour photography, but never brought any of his activities to a commercially successful conclusion. He also mixed with the bohemian literary world, knew Coppée and Verlaine, who was a friend of his brother Antoine and whose portrait Henry painted. Cros also frequented circles interested in spiritualism and the occult, and in September 1868 met Nina de Villard (also spelt Villars), who was then 25. In 1864, as Anne-Marie Gaillard, she had married the Comte de Callias, one of the editorial staff on *Le Figaro* and *L'Artiste*, but had separated from him in 1867 and taken her new name. She was rich, presided over one of the loudest and most brilliant of the late Empire salons, known as the "salon des ratés (the salon of failures)," and was the mistress of the revolutionary Edmond Bazire. It was for her that Cros wrote his first poems, and in her salon that he met the literary figures associated with symbolism and the Parnassians (qq.v.). He became particularly close to Charles de Sivry, Verlaine's brother-in-law, and to Villiers de l'Isle-Adam.

He was Anatole France's rival for Nina de Villard's affections, had become a sort of secretary and manager to her, and seems certain to have been her lover. One evening at a café he suddenly announced that he was going to throttle France, pinned him to the ground, and had to be prized off. France never reappeared at the salon, but effectively blocked any progress in Parnassian circles which Cros might otherwise have made. In 1869 Cros started to write "Chroniques" for *L'Artiste*, which also began publishing his poems. That year he also published poems in *La Parodie* and aroused controversy with a paper on colour photography which was published as an article in *Les Mondes*, and then as a plaquette. He also published a paper on interstellar communication in *Cosmos*. That, too, appeared as a plaquette. In 1870, during the Franco-Prussian War, Cros's parents' house was destroyed in a bombardment. They moved to the south, and his brothers moved in with him at the Verlaines. Around this time Cros apparently developed a process for creating precious stones synthetically. He joined the Garde Nationale and wrote *Le Coffret de santal*, the only collection of poems published during his lifetime.

In 1871 Cros accompanied Verlaine to meet Rimbaud at the station on his famous arrival in Paris, and later put him up for a fortnight in his studio. He took part in the meetings of the symbolist group known as the "Zutiques" at the end of the year, and contributed to the *Album Zutique*. At a café one evening in 1872 Rimbaud poured sulphuric acid into his glass. The same year Cros published prose poems in *La Renaissance* and sent the Académie des Sciences a paper on the mechanics of perception. When Verlaine left Paris with Rimbaud, Cros sided with Verlaine's wife, and broke with Verlaine. He negotiated with Lemerre, who was associated with the Parnassian group, to publish *Le Coffret*, and went by train to Switzerland and Italy, probably with Nina, with whom he may also have been in Baden in 1869. He appears to have had money problems, and certainly visited Milan, Genoa, and Nice, from where in January 1873 he sent Lemerre the poem "Morale" for *Le Tombeau de Théophile Gautier*, the collection published by Lemerre on 23 October 1873 to mark the first anniversary of Gautier's death, and for which 82 poets, including Mallarmé, Hugo, Banville, and Leconte de Lisle had been asked for contributions. He also offered Lemerre 200 francs to publish *Le Coffret*. In February he left the manuscript with a Nice printer, to whom he paid 250 francs. The volume appeared on 1 April in an edition of 500 copies at five francs.

By the end of April he was back in Paris, and later that year arranged to publish his *Revue du Monde Nouveau*, which had three numbers in 1874. In January 1875 the 200-line poem *Le Fleuve* appeared as a plaquette dated 1874 with eight etchings by Manet, to whom it was dedicated. It was taken into the 1879 edition of 1,000 copies of *Le Coffret* with 36 other new pieces at three and a half francs. Anatole France prevented Lemerre from accepting any Cros poems for the third issue of *Le Parnasse Contemporain* in 1875. Cros meanwhile worked at various forms of light entertainment for Nina's riotous salon, including the dramatic buffoonery "Le moine bleu," written with Germain Nouveau and Jean Richepin, which appeared in the *Feuillets Parisiens: Poésies* of Nina de Villars, edited by Edmond Bazire. The habitués had previously been entertained by Cros's "Machine à changer le caractère des femmes."

In 1876 an edition of 150 copies of the *Dizains réalistes* was published and reviewed by Mendès in *La République des Lettres*. For several successive summers Cros spent alternate Sundays with the publisher Stock and the actor Coquelin *aîné* (Constant-Benoît, 1841–1909) writing the comic monologues which, while not aspiring to literary merit, are in fact the principal reason for which he was at first remembered. In 1877 he continued to work on his "paléophone" or phonograph and on colour photography. Edison's application for a patent dates from 17 December 1877. Cros had talked of getting married, which provoked Nina to throw one of his manuscripts on the workings of the brain into the fire. Cros broke with her and on 14 May 1878 married a Mlle Hjardemaal. In October the "Hydropathes," another symbolist group was formed, with Cros as one of its members. His son Guy-Charles was born in February 1879.

Meanwhile Cros was involved in disputes about colour photography and won some recognition in the world of physics. He also contributed regularly to the fringe magazines of the literary world, *Les Hydropathes*, which became *L'Hydropathe* and then the *Tout Paris*, and *Molière*. Various monologues were published in different collections, and sometimes in plaquette form,

sometimes following textual revision by Coquelin, and from 1883 bearing a note that they were written for Coquelin *cadet* (Ernest-Alexandre-Honoré, 1848–1909). In 1880 Cros started to publish scabrous contes in *Gil Blas*. A second son was born in November 1880. He was to die in 1898.

The year 1881 saw the establishment of the Chat Noir cabaret and the newspaper *Le Chat Noir*, in which Cros published burlesque pieces. Most of Cros's poet, musician, and painter friends attended the cabaret on Fridays, and he became the monologuist of the house, his pieces appearing in a variety of collections published by Tresse or Ollendorff. Cros was now regularly receiving state grants and support for his physics research. They would turn into a pension for his widow. In 1883 he refounded the "Zutistes," as they were now called, but was by this time drinking heavily and his early mental instability was becoming apparent. Nina lost her reason from all sorts of excesses before dying in 1884, during which year Cros had a liaison with the dancer and singer "Thérésa." Huysmans wrote a stinging review of "La science de l'amour," a conte by Cros, now a well-known café alcoholic. His wife became an invalid and in September 1885 his books were sold publicly for non-payment of rent. He was now writing for money, selling 22 poems and three contes to *Le Chat Noir* and *Le Scapin* in 1886, and 11 more to *Le Chat Noir* in 1887. He died on 9 August 1888.

WORKS

Cros published only one collection of verse, *Le Coffret de santal*. It appeared in 1873 and was augmented for republication in 1879. His son, Guy-Charles Cros, edited his posthumous poems, *Le Collier de Griffes*, published by Stock in 1908. The importance of Cros's work lies not so much in its intrinsic value as in what it indicates about the changes taking place in literary culture after 1870, during the early years of the Third Republic.

As a poet Cros was never willing to commit himself to a high seriousness of purpose, just as in life he never pursued his experiments to the point at which serious exploitation of his ideas and discoveries became possible. Was there, as has been suggested, "a noble resignation worthily masking a deep distress" in Cros's life and work, or was there a fear of exploiting his clearly extraordinary gifts in situations or imaginative explorations which would call into question his life style or, more forbidding still, the fundamental values by which life can be lived? In his life, his scientific and his literary activity Cros combined great skill with devastating flippancy, and intelligence of execution with triviality of purpose.

Cros did, it is true, occasionally resent the reputation of being the resident clown at Nina's or at the Chat Noir, the author of monologue burlesques like "Pituite" or "Hareng saur," but it is not true that he was merely a dreamer, content to cast good scientific ideas to others better equipped to refine them, make them work, and exploit them commercially. Where possible, Cros always developed his applied scientific ideas to the point at which he could show that they worked. If, after that, he lost interest, it was not because his life style was independent of the profit potential he said he knew they contained. He left his inventions in the public domain so that "au plaisir de voir mon idée prendre forme et vie…s'ajoutera toute possibilité de récompenses diverses (to the pleasure of seeing my idea taking form…will be added every possibility of further remunerations)."

So also with his verse. "Morale" is a perfunctory sonnet for a ceremonial occasion. There has to have been a deep-rooted unwillingness in Cros to allow even the most serious poems to reach the emotional depths to which they could lead. *Le Fleuve* is a long metaphor which at times comes close to allegory, but it is imaginatively truncated. At its outset the river is pure, alive, torrential. The plains steady it. It yields gold, connives with the loggers, and the first dead fish appear, but the river still provides water for the cattle and nourishes the trees which bring it shade. Then comes the town, with factories, quays, rust, black water from the sewers, old shoes, dead cats. Then the smell of the sea

> Est là, terme implacable à la folle équipée
> De l'eau, qui vers le ciel chaud s'était échappée

> (Is there, implacable ending for the lunatic escapade / Of the water, escaping to the warm sky).

The sea, in a splendidly epic conclusion, demands everything from the river, but sorts and rejects the silt whose layers show the history of the human race. But nothing happens. Let your heart fall asleep to the sound of the river, The poet says. No moral is pointed, except perhaps that life is not something you should do anything about, but is best neglected, and the poem ends with no imaginative resolution. It is the work of a great poet who could never bring himself, even when he came as near to it as this, to write great poetry.

Rimbaud's drunken boat went beyond the limits of the knowable, as the poet set himself in the face of civilization. Cros's river is incurious, and when rid of the rejected debris simply dissipates its energy, just as Cros's life was a distraction and his scientific discoveries were left to find their concentration and exploitation in other people's minds. More important perhaps is the debris of the Second Empire which Cros's life and works reject, but do not replace. In retrospect we can see what paralleled the political revolution of 1870 in the music, the painting, and the literature of France. Cros was aware only of what had ended, what could no more be done, not of what would take its place.

PUBLICATIONS

Collections

Oeuvres complètes, Bibliothèque de la Pléiade, 1970

Verse

Le Coffret de santal, 1873; augmented edition, 1879
Le Fleuve, 1874
Le Collier de griffes, 1908

Others

La Vision du grand canal royal des deux mers, 1888

———

CUBISM.

See under **Apollinaire**

Cubism is essentially a movement in reaction to symbolism (q.v.) and is normally used exclusively of painting, but the term has, by extension, been applied to poetry, especially since some of the poets concerned were close associates of the principal cubist painters. The French poets usually mentioned in connection with cubism are Guillaume Apollinaire (1880–1918), Blaise Cendrars (1887–1961), Léon-Paul Fargue (1876–1947), Max Jacob (1876–1944), Pierre Reverdy (1889–1960), and André Salmon (1881–1969). They are said to share a common aim of describing several different aspects of the same object at the same time, and simultaneously to have combined a series of different images of a single object, like the cubist painters.

However, in poetic technique these similarities do not necessarily constitute a "school," and are not necessarily best, or even properly, described as "cubist." This was originally a term of derision, apparently employed casually by Matisse, and subsequently used of Braque by Louis Vauxcelles in *Gil Blas* for 14 November 1908. Apollinaire then accepted the designation "cubism" on behalf of a number of the Montmartre painters at that date, notably Picasso. The pictorial or emblematic typography sometimes used by Apollinaire himself is also often considered a manifestation of cubism, although the technique is virtually as old as printing itself, and was employed by Rabelais in the 16th century.

There are quite powerful reasons for avoiding the use of the term in a literary context at all, or at any rate, if it is used, for defining precisely what is meant by it, as there is no general agreement. In the visual arts cubism was one of the great innovative movements of the early 20th century. It reached its peak in the years between 1907 and 1914, and quite swiftly degenerated into mere decoration, but is held originally to have consisted of perspectives of superimposed, interlocking, and overlapping semi-transparent planes with a shallow picture space showing a minimum of recession. Used in this way, the term "cubist" clearly has reference only to the plastic values of two-dimensional painting which avoids creating the illusion of three-dimensional space. Objects are depicted as they are known, and not as they appear.

Cézanne had observed that everything in nature takes its form from the sphere, the cone, and the cylinder, a point of departure for cubism to which various sections of the movement returned, particularly the "Section d'Or" (Golden Section) painters of Puteaux, who took their name from the ratio between the length of a square's side and its diagonal. The first partly cubist painting is generally considered to have been Picasso's *Les Demoiselles d'Avignon* (1906–07), which owes its title to André Salmon. Its "cubist" characteristics are the dislocation of interlocking planes on the right of the picture, the superimposition of frontal and profile planes in the seated central figure, the obvious influence of Negro masks on the standing figure, and the non-optical but abstract logical perspectives of the still life in the lower centre. Cubism, however tentative the theoretical writings composed to support it, originally implied a new way of representing the world in two dimensions, the first major such innovation since the codification of the laws of perspective by Alberti (1404–1472). In the visual arts, as the poet and painter Max Jacob in particular insisted, cubism is a reaction against symbolism.

To transpose the technical innovations of cubism in painting into literary terms is obviously to risk emptying the word of any significant meaning. The simultaneous description of several aspects of the same object and the combination of different images of the same object are too non-specific to define a poetic technique. The term "cubism" used in a literary context risks being no more than vaguely analogous to something which took place in the visual arts, unless it is simply used pretentiously in the sense of a reaction to the definable techniques of symbolist verse, prose, or drama.

Braque rejected the term "cubism" outside the plastic arts, although he did allow that a poem printed in the shape of a guitar might be said to be using cubist typography without thereby becoming a cubist poem. Reverdy, who was himself often listed among the cubist poets, and whose expertise as a writer on painting Braque acknowledged, said: "La 'poésie cubiste'? Terme ridicule! (Cubist poetry? What nonsense!)." The poets of Montmartre certainly derived their techniques from the painters rather than the other way round and, if the term "cubist" is to be used of their work at all, it should be used in analogy with the painters' superimposition of different perspectives, and confined to the simultaneous use of multiple linguistic registers in the same passage to describe or express the same thing. There are examples in the prose poems of Jacob.

———

D

DADA

See under **Surrealism**; also Breton

Dada is a recognizable movement in literature and the fine arts founded in Zürich in 1916 by the Romanian Jew Tristan Tzara (1896–1963). Although almost entirely infantile in intention and content it was an important manifestation of the cultural dislocation and moral crisis caused in the civilized world by World War I. It is also of interest in the same way as are more serious artistic visions which have destroyed themselves in the end by minimalist reductions to absurdity, whether by removing sound from music, words from poetry, or actors from drama. Tzara claimed that he had hit on the word "dada," meaning hobbyhorse or pet subject, by opening a dictionary at random. The most socially and artistically disruptive manifestations of the movement crystallized in Paris. Some of its inspiration was drawn from the cubism (q.v.) of Picasso and Braque, itself involving a disruption of the accepted conventions of rendering three-dimensional objects on a two-dimensional surface.

Associated with cubism in painting through the "Section d'Or" painters of Puteaux, and through his friendship with several former members of the Montmartre group surrounding Picasso, was Francis Picabia (1879–1953), son of a wealthy Spanish industrialist, who became a diplomat in the Cuban embassy in Paris. Picabia was rich and debauched, spending freely and living whimsically, finding art, like life, tolerable only at the extremes. It was typical of him to take Apollinaire off for a spin in a new sports car an hour before Apollinaire had a public engagement and only to bring him back a week later. They had been to England. Similarly, it amused Picabia to employ the same midwife to deliver his wife and his mistress's babies within a matter of weeks of one another. From 1908 Picabia's painting quickly moved beyond cubism into geometrical abstraction and then into nonsensical designs, like that for an engine entitled *Portrait of Marie Laurencin*.

In 1910 he became friendly with Marcel Duchamp (1887–1968), who had a succès de scandale in 1913 when he exhibited the *Nude Descending a Staircase* (now in Philadelphia) at the Armory Show in New York, Chicago, and Boston. On a mission to Cuba in 1915, Picabia jumped ship in New York, Duchamp and he spearheaded a movement akin to Tzara's dada, but quite independent of it. Duchamp became the champion of the ready-made in art, exhibiting everyday objects, like his bicycle wheel mounted on a kitchen stool, as works of art. He occasionally said that any unregarded piece of bric-à-brac was a work of art when he declared it to be so, thereby denying the existence and utility of art, which, even if it did exist, would have no possible function. From 1915 to 1923 Duchamp produced a construct on glass called *The Bride Stripped Bare by Her Bachelors*, also now in Philadelphia, and went on to make useless mechanical gadgets.

He contributed to *391*, the avant-garde review which Picabia, Marie Laurencin, and her husband, Otto von Waëtjen, founded in Barcelona in 1916 and which published a poem by Tzara in 1917. The review continued to appear irregularly until 1924. Its alluted to Alfred Stieglitz's Photo-Secession Gallery at 291, Fifth Avenue, New York, which had presented the first one-man exhibition of the "Douanier" Rousseau in 1910 and specialized in works which were virtually anti-art. Picabia, like Duchamp, had produced large numbers of mechanical drawings, but finally turned to poetry when alcohol and opium made it impossible for him to continue painting. He returned to New York in 1917, and in 1918 committed himself to a psychiatric clinic in Switzerland, where he got to know Tzara, whose attention he had caught with his volume of verse, *Poèmes et dessins de la fille née sans mère*, published that year.

Picabia was back in Paris in 1919 and encouraged Tzara to join him. When Tzara arrived in January 1920, speaking only broken French, Breton, Aragon, and Soupault were there with Picabia to greet him. In March 1919 they had already founded the originally conservative literary review whose ironic title, *Littérature*, derived from Verlaine's contemptuous "The rest is literature…" But they had been interested by Tzara's reviews, *Dada* and *Dadaphone*, which had circulated widely in Paris avant-garde circles, and in January 1919 Breton had received a copy of *Dada Manifesto 1918*, to be followed in May 1919 by the *Anthologie Dada*.

The first dada manifestation in Paris took place in the Palais des Fêtes, a small hall between two cinemas, where Breton and Aragon used to go to watch their admired Fantômas, the film villain, and Chaplin, both of whom ridiculed society's ineptitudes in such a way as to become important sources of surrealist (q.v.) inspiration. The event was billed as a lecture by André Salmon with an ambiguous title intended to attract bankers, but in fact devoted to Apollinaire, and included music by Satie and "Les Six," readings by Cendrars and Drieu la Rochelle of verse by Max Jacob, Paul Reverdy, and Blaise Cendrars, and an appearance by Breton and Picabia carrying the letters LHOOQ (standing for the obscene "Elle a chaud au cul"), which it took the audience some time to decipher. Tzara finally appeared reading a right-wing speech drowned by bells rung by Aragon and Breton. Even André Salmon and Juan Gris complained that things had gone too far.

Dada's provocatively disruptive doctrine no doubt reflected the insecurity occasioned by war and affirmed the purposelessness of exploring the meaning of an experience so obviously devoid of meaning. From the dada point of view, human action is insignificant: "Il est inadmissible qu'un homme laisse une trace de son passage sur la terre (It is inadmissible that man should leave any trace of his passage on earth)." Beneath the apparently childish protests against logic, life, and meaning lies a childlike failure to achieve any personal or social identity. For

Souvenirs, 9 vols., 1939–40
Le Drame franco-allemand, 1940
Quand vivait mon père, 1940
Sauvetières et incendiaires, 1941

Critical and biographical studies

Joseph, R., *Les Combats de Léon Daudet, essai*, 1962
Dominique, P., *Léon Daudet*, 1964

————

DECADENCE.
See under **Symbolism**;
also Huysmans, Laforgue, and Verlaine.

————

**DESCHAMPS, Emile (-Anne-Louis-Frédéric de Saint-
    Amand), 1791–1871.**

Poet and translator.

LIFE

Emile Deschamps was born in Bourges on 20 February 1791,
the son of a tax official, Jacques Deschamps (1741–1826), who
was ruined in 1793, condemned to death, and saved only by the
fall of Robespierre. At the age of 49 he had married Marie de
Maussabré, a native of Bourges. She had a delicate constitution
and was to die in 1802, when her younger son, Antony (1800–
1869), was only two. Antony, whose name was spelled in the
English way according to French romantic (q.v.) custom,
although sometimes as "Antoni," was also to become a poet.
Both sons suffered from poor health and nervous illnesses, and
Antony lost his reason in 1834. Their father, who moved back to
Paris while Deschamps was still young, regularly received fig-
ures from the aristocratic, musical, and literary worlds, including many of those associated with the new romantic movement.
He admired the earliest work of Delphine Gay, a close associate
of the early romantic poets, and the future wife of Emile de
Girardin, editor of *La Presse*.

The two brothers were brought up by a devoted servant
known as "Bonne," whose fairy tales gave Deschamps an enduring taste for the fantastic. At eight he was sent to a boarding
school at Orléans, where he was unhappy. An extraordinary conviction one day that his mother had died, when she had in fact
fallen ill, suggests an unusual apprehensiveness. From the age of
15 Deschamps was educated by his father. He became a close
friend of Vigny and met other visitors to his father's salon,
including Victor Hugo and Henri de Latouche (1785–1851),
from 1825 editor of the *Mercure de France*. The salon became
an important nursery for the new school of poets. When
Deschamps's first published poem, "La paix conquise,"
appeared in 1812 in the *Journal de l'Empire*, Napoleon was
delighted and sent him a gold and diamond snuffbox.

His father arranged for Deschamps to be employed in the land
registry at Vincennes, where, as one of Napoleon's supporters,
he spent the sieges of 1814 and 1815 in the Garde Nationale
under General Daumesnil. In 1817 he married Aglaé Viénot,
about whom we know only that she was the daughter of a Vincennes lawyer and that she nursed Deschamps's father in old
age. The couple had no children. Deschamps himself was an
amiable dandy with literary pretensions, an admirer of Alexandre Soumet, the neoclassical dramatist and poet often regarded
as a precursor of Lamartine. He did in fact herald the arrival of
romantic drama, and co-founded *La Muse Française* with
Deschamps and others.

Deschamps's first successful works were for the theatre in
collaboration with Henri de Latouche. The three-act *Selmours
de Florian* and the one-act *Le Tour de Faveur*, both in verse,
were produced at the Théâtre Favart in June and November
1818, and were both well received. In 1823 Deschamps, Hugo,
and Vigny, founded *La Muse Française* with the help of Soumet,
Alexandre Guiraud, and others. The 60-page monthly review
lasted only from 18 July 1823 until June 1824, but it established
Deschamps as "le jeune moraliste."

In 1820 Hugo had revived Deschamps's translations of a
poem by Schiller and some odes of Horace in the *Conservateur
Littéraire*, and the reform of the theatre had started to preoccupy
the new romantic literary group. In 1820 the *Lycée Français*
reviewed *Il conte di carmagnola* by Manzoni, which was programmatically romantic in its disregard of the unities and its
exploitation of verse within a naturalistic idiom. The drama was
translated, with the same author's *Adelchi*, by M.-C. Fauriel in
1823. Manzoni's famous *Lettre sur les unités de temps et de lieu
dans les tragédies* of 1823 had already pointed to the importance
of fusing tragic and comic genres, a view towards which some
18th-century French dramatists had already been moving. However, it was not given canonical expression until Hugo's *Préface*
to *Cromwell* in 1827 proclaimed the need to unite the sublime
with the grotesque. By 1821 a young French group, including
Mérimée, was already defying the tradition that serious drama
should be in verse (see Dumas), and the interest of Deschamps
in foreign drama, English, French, Spanish, and Italian, his main
claim to importance in the literary history of France, had already
become clear.

The closure of *La Muse Française* was probably due to a split
in the young group associated with it, and in particular to a split
with Chateaubriand and Lamartine. The failure of the 1822
Shakespeare season in Paris owed as much to political agitation
and the inadequacy of the Ducis translation as to any lack of
interest in Shakespeare himself. The Covent Garden company's
1827–28 Shakespeare season in Paris was not only to be a spectacular success; it also captured verse as the medium for romantic tragedy, ensuring victory for the views of Hugo, already put
into practice with *Cromwell*.

In 1827 Deschamps co-translated *Romeo and Juliet* with
Vigny in a version which was never performed, but which
Deschamps rewrote for publication in 1844, along with his
translation of *Macbeth*, which was to be performed at the Odéon
in 1848. It was in November 1828 that he published the *Etudes
françaises et étrangères*, of which there were four editions in
two years, and whose preface became one of the principal manifestoes of French romanticism. The book itself included
Deschamps's own translations of Schiller, Goethe, and the
Poème de Rodrigue from a Spanish "romancero." It earned him

the Légion d'Honneur in 1829. Unlike many of the romantics and especially Sainte-Beuve, Deschamps enthusiastically welcomed Balzac's novels, eulogizing in particular *La Peau de chagrin* in the *Revue des Deux Mondes* (q.v.) in 1831. The reaction displeased the editor, Buloz, who subsequently turned down a poem submitted by Deschamps, "Retour à Paris." The episode clearly shows how early the Buloz team, including Sainte-Beuve and Planche, moved away from Vigny, Deschamps, and of course Balzac, to whom Sainte-Beuve was implacably hostile.

In 1841 Deschamps republished his own poems from the *Etudes* with those of his young brother, who had translated Dante in 1829. Deschamps became essentially a translator who worked extensively for the musical theatre, translating libretti for Mozart and Donizetti operas, writing the words for Berlioz's *Roméo et Juliette*, and collaborating on numerous projects with Meyerbeer and Niedermeyer. In 1847, two years after retiring to Versailles, he had a nervous breakdown but in 1854 he published the *Contes physiologiques* and the *Réalités fantastiques*. His wife died in 1855, and Deschamps, despite repeated operations for cataract, gradually went blind. Towards the end of his life he developed an interest in Russian and Polish literature, and until his death he remained in close contact with leading members of the literary world, especially those who were becoming prominent only in his old age.

WORKS

Deschamps's taste hovered between that of his neoclassical contemporaries and that of the romantics in the crucial years between 1820 and 1830, and most of his output consisted of translations, especially but not exclusively of Shakespeare, and of operatic libretti. He is better known today for his translations of such non-dramatic poetry as Schiller's "Das Lied von der Glocke" and Goethe's "Die Braut von Korinth." The translation of *Romeo and Juliet*, which is in fact an adaptation, shows both a concern for French classical norms and an inclination towards spectacle. The scene changes are prescribed in detail. The Capulets give a ball, with an orchestra on stage, but neoclassical scruples restrict the dancing to two quadrilles. At the end of the second, which Romeo dances with Juliet, sorbets are served.

The famous preface to the 1828 *Etudes françaises et étrangères* immediately links Deschamps with Germaine de Staël because of the importance he attached to foreign, particularly German, literature. The preface was written when Deschamps, still attuned to formal qualities in literature, was attempting to mediate between Vigny and Hugo. The probability is that the preface was the result of an animated discussion between Deschamps, Hugo, Vigny, and Lamartine in Hugo's salon on the evening of Saturday, 18 October 1828. Deschamps, who was working on the Spanish "romancero," had written to Vigny three days earlier and was clearly anxious to play down the novelty of the new school; "There is no such thing as romanticism, only a literature of the 19th century." The doctrine is essentially one of progress. Change is necessary in all the arts, as can be seen, says Deschamps, from Rossini, Berlioz, and Delacroix. The norms of art are not immutable, and Deschamps comes very near to saying that they depend on social change, although he himself could never quite have articulated so radical a declaration.

Insisting that France has already established superiority in the "épître," the "poème," and the "fable," Deschamps, taking his cue from Mme de Staël, encourages the new generation to turn towards the lyric, the elegy, and the epic, disagreeing with his mentor only about the superiority of philosophical literature, at which, of course, the Germans excelled. And if France had already made great strides forward with Chénier, there always remained the challenge of drama, which is where the romantics were finally to score most heavily. The attack is not on the innovatory Voltaire himself, but on his neoclassical imitators: "Le temps des imitations est passé: il faut créer ou traduire (The time for imitations has passed: we must create or translate)." The model is a refined Shakespeare, which has the life and variety of the original, and above all the mixture of comedy and tragedy, but without the coarseness. There has to be an "épuration" or sanitization of Elizabethan roughness. Deschamps agrees again with Mme de Staël that what should unite both sides in the dispute between supporters of the classical school and those of the modern is a common repudiation of what Mme de Staël was the first to refer to as "vulgarité."

PUBLICATIONS

Collections

Oeuvres complètes, 6 vols., 1872–74

Verse

La Paix conquise, 1812
Etudes françaises et étrangères, 1828
Retour à Paris, 1832
Poésies d'Emile et Antoni Deschamps, 1841
Aux Orphéonistes, 1847
Le Grand Frère à la crèche, 1852

Plays

Selmours de Florian, with Henri de Latouche (produced 1818), 1818
Le Tour de Faveur, with Henri de Latouche, (produced 1818), 1818
Roméo et Juliette (verse translation, co-translated with Vigny), with *Macbeth*, 1844
Macbeth (verse translation; produced 1848), with *Roméo et Juliette*, 1844

Fiction

Contes physiologiques, 1854
Réalités fantastiques, 1854

Other

Causeries littéraires et morales sur quelques femmes célèbres, 1837

Critical and biographical study

Girard, Henri, *Un bourgeois dilettante à l'époque romantique: Emile Deschamps*, 2 vols., 1921

DRIEU LA ROCHELLE, Pierre-Eugène, 1893–1945.

Poet, novelist, and essayist.

LIFE

Since the 1970s Drieu la Rochelle has been attracting increasing critical attention, although his career remains controversial on account of his fascist sympathies during World War II. Some of the experiences he underwent as a young man clearly disturbed him deeply.

An Anglophile of Norman origin, Drieu la Rochelle studied politics and law in Paris, but failed his politics examination in 1913. His best friend, André Jeames, to whose sister Colette he was unofficially engaged, was killed in 1914. He himself had what he subsequently described as a "mystical" experience while leading a bayonet charge in 1914, was wounded, and began to write. In 1916 Colette's father committed suicide. The couple married in 1917 but were divorced in 1920. Around this time Drieu la Rochelle formed a friendship with Louis Aragon, and in 1922–23 had an affair with a woman who was to die of cancer. In 1925, the year in which his mother died, a new mistress broke with him and returned to the US, and he himself broke with Aragon. He married again in 1927, but separated in 1929, the year in which Jacques Rigaut, a close friend, committed suicide. Drieu la Rochelle claimed that his most exhilarating experience had been bayonetting during the war, and he had had close experience of bereavement, twice as a result of suicide. None of the relationships with women—which he so clearly needed—had proved lasting.

Drieu la Rochelle had visited Greece and England and in 1931 his play *L'Eau fraîche* was successfully staged by Louis Jouvet. By now he was a man of letters, connected with the literary reviews *Les Derniers Jours* and *Sur*. In 1931 he refused the Légion d'Honneur, and the next year travelled and lectured in South America, where he got to know Borges, and in Germany, where he accompanied Bertrand de Jouvenel in 1934. He met Abetz, the future ambassador to France and, thinking that a political alliance of right and left might be possible, declared himself a fascist. He also went to Czechoslovakia, Hungary, and Italy, and put on an unsuccessful but critically esteemed play, *Le Chef*. In 1935 he began a 10-year liaison with Christiane Renault, attended the Nuremberg rally, and visited Moscow, joining the fascist Parti Populaire Français (1936), recently founded by an ex-communist. He wrote regularly for its review and visited Berlin, Italy, North Africa, and Franco's Spain. He was a close friend of Malraux. At this date a taste for action and violence could of course lead as easily to "left-wing" as to "right-wing" political affiliations. German fascism had flowed from Hitler's "national socialism."

In 1939 he resigned from the Parti Populaire and quarrelled with Jean Paulhan of the *Nouvelle Revue Française* (NRF, q.v.). His anti-semitism was growing. In 1940 a play, *Charlotte Corday*, was turned down in Paris and, on hearing rumours that his arrest was imminent, he fled to the Dordogne, offering his services to the Vichy government. Abetz called him to Paris and entrusted him with reviving the *NRF*. In 1941 visits to Weimer and Berlin left him disillusioned with Hitler, who was showing himself more nationalist than socialist. *Charlotte Corday* was played in Vichy, Lyons, and Clermont, and Drieu la Rochelle rejoined the Parti Populaire. In 1943 he got his first wife and two children released after their arrest by the Gestapo and published his last issue of the *NRF*, which was now drifting towards communism and an admiration for Stalin too forthright for the Germans. Drieu la Rochelle went to Switzerland, and for a year contributed regularly to the *Révolution Nationale*. In the summer of 1944 *Les Chiens de paille* and *Le Français d'Europe* were published, but immediately seized. His first attempt at suicide took place on 1 August. He tried again a few days later and was finally successful in March 1945.

WORKS

Drieu la Rochelle's first published work was a volume of lyrical and very personal war poems, *Interrogation*, written from 1915 to 1917 and exalting the virile qualities demanded by war. It was followed by *Fond de Cantine*, a less lyrical collection which included poems reacting to the post-war world. Other similar early writings, mostly poetic, followed in the 1927 *La Suite dans les idées*, and *Le Jeune Européen* of the same year, which contrasts the power of blood with that of ink, and deplores the way in which creative vitality has drained from the world. The four volumes were later grouped together as *Ecrits de jeunesse*. They come increasingly to reflect on the tensions between barbarity and civilization, between the ex-soldier who has known the physical and intellectual thrill of violence, and civil society trying to renew its old foundations. The obsessive theme of modern personal and social decadence prominent in Drieu la Rochelle's work derives from his attitude to this conflict. Woman dangerously deflects the male towards physically debilitating pleasure. Patriotic loyalty, physical strength, and strong leadership are all ideals superior to love.

The later fictions, in which Drieu la Rochelle develops the art of the short story, turn largely on the incompatibility between the violent needs of the self and the civilizing constraints and pleasures of society, so that his work constantly mixes confessional self-criticism with social satire. The first extended prose work is *L'Etat civil* of 1921, presented as an autobiography although in fact a first-person novel. It was followed by the social criticism of the four short stories *Plaintes contre inconnu* of 1924 and, in 1925, by the first novel to have as its hero Gille Gambier, *L'Homme couvert de femmes*, which rather hesitantly combines personal outbursts with satire of the relaxed sexual morals of Gille's circles. Like Drieu la Rochelle, Gille is a romantic idealist adrift in a cynical society to whose values he cannot adjust.

The literary qualities become clearer in what is almost a trilogy, starting with *Blèche*, which allies a slight plot and a tight formal structure to penetrating psychological analysis. The narrator is forced into a relationship with a world he has hitherto only written about. *Une femme à sa fenêtre* of 1929 is about the vigour and vitality of communism, seen as perhaps capable of annihilating the decadent West. Like its predecessor it tests an ideology in the crucible of sexual relationships. There are still insufficiently controlled lyrical outbursts, but Drieu la Rochelle has moved on from simple psychological analysis towards the style of his later "polyphonic" novels set against wider backgrounds. *Une femme* is set outside France and was immediately translated into English and Czech. Its successor, *Le Feu follet*, traces the last few hours of a drug addict before his suicide.

In *Drôle de voyage* Drieu la Rochelle returned to his protagonist Gille, still an idealist but one now trapped by the self and the society he despises. This novel was followed by six short stories, published in *La Comédie de Charleroi*, deploring the failure of modern push-button war to test qualities of manly strength and courage and to require effective personal leadership. Two other works appeared in the same year: a further collection of stories, *Journal d'un homme trompé*, satirizing the lack of male commitment in socio-sexual encounters, and the political essay *Socialisme fasciste*. The theme common to all three works was the individual's need for active personal involvement with his fellow men. This part of Drieu la Rochelle's output closes with *Beloukia*, which is notable for its exotic setting.

His series of "polyphonic" novels begins with *Rêveuse bourgeoisie* of 1937, which deals with three generations of a middle-class family and shows how the tensions which interest him had spread through the different strata of French society and had not been confined to the war and post-war generations. The plural title of *Gilles* hints at a desire to sum up. It is his most ambitious novel, and is generally considered his best. In it he continues to depict a whole society, this time including the period of the Spanish Civil War, but also touching on literary and political groupings in France. The wealthy Jewish family into which Gille marries represents the sterility of a mercantile society which has lost its creative vigour. Only a will to power, referred to in Nietzschean terms, can reconstruct society on the "harsh, cruel foundations of the possible." World War II is seen as inevitable, the Spanish Civil War as merely its prelude. The 1942 preface to the book contains valuable considerations on narratorial distortion and the author's relationship to the society in which he lives, which he tries to depict, and against which he reacts.

The three war-time novels, *L'Homme à cheval*, *Les Chiens de paille*, and *Mémoires de Dirk Raspe*, are devoted, respectively, to the nature of the imaginative process itself, the various political attitudes possible in France, and the importance of the artist. Dirk, modelled loosely on Van Gogh, was to have lived out Van Gogh's last months prior to his suicide. Instead Drieu la Rochelle lived them out himself, driven by the impossibility of imposing himself on a society he despised and by the pessimism which had led him to the fatal fascist embrace.

PUBLICATIONS

Fiction

L'Etat civil, 1921
Plaintes contre inconnu, 1924
L'Homme couvert de femmes, 1928
Blèche, 1928
Une femme à sa fenêtre, 1929; as *Hotel Acropolis*, 1931
Le Feu follet, 1931; as *The Fire Within*, 1965; as *Will o' the Wisp*, 1966
Drôle de voyage, 1933
Journal d'un homme trompé, 1934
La Comédie de Charleroi, 1934; as *The Comedy of Charleroi and Other Stories*, 1973
Beloukia, 1936
Rêveuse bourgeoisie, 1937
Gilles, 1939 (censored), 1942
L'Homme à cheval, 1943; as *The Man on Horseback*, 1979
Les Chiens de paille, 1944 (seized and destroyed), 1964
Plaintes contre inconnu, 1951 (withdrawn)

Histoires déplaisantes, 1963
Mémoires de Dirk Raspe, 1966

Early work, mostly verse

Interrogation, 1917
Fond de Cantine, 1920
La Suite dans les idées, 1927
Le Jeune Européen, 1927
Ecrits de jeunesse (the above four, including some non- verse), 1941

Other

Mesure de la France, 1922
Genève ou Moscou, 1928
L'Europe contre les patries, 1931
L'Eau fraîche (play), 1931
Socialisme fasciste, 1934
Doriot ou la vie d'un ouvrier français, 1936
Avec Doriot, 1937
Ne plus attendre, 1941
Notes pour comprendre ce siècle, 1941
Chronique politique 1934–1942, 1943
Charlotte Corday (play), 1944
Le Chef (play), 1944
Le Français d'Europe, 1944 (seized and destroyed)
Récit secret, 1951 (500 copies), 1961; as *Secret Journal and Other Writings*, 1973
Sur les écrivains, 1964

Critical studies

Andreu, Pierre, *Drieu la Rochelle, témoin et visionnaire*, 1952
Grover, Frederic, *Drieu la Rochelle and the Fiction of Testimony*, 1958
Soucy, Robert, *Fascist Intellectual: Drieu de la Rochelle*, 1979
Leal, Robert Barry, *Decadence in Love, Drieu la Rochelle*, 1973
Leal, Robert Barry, *Drieu la Rochelle* (in English), 1982

See also the following special numbers of reviews devoted to Drieu la Rochelle:

La Parisienne, October 1955
Défense de l'Occident, February-March 1958
Le Magazine Littéraire, December 1978

———

DU CAMP, Maxime, 1822–1894.

Novelist, archaeologist, travel writer, photographer, art critic, historian, and editor.

LIFE

Du Camp is best known for his close association with Flaubert. He left no single work of any great literary importance, but he was a significant imaginative writer who also played a prominent part in the literary life of 19th-century France. He was the well-to-do son of a surgeon urologist, lost his father when he was two, and his mother when he was 15, and was brought up by his grandmother. Du Camp gave the impression all his life of being an amateur and something of a dandy. There is no evidence at all that he was jealous of Flaubert, as has often been asserted, and very little that he deserves to be described, as he has been, as malicious, spiteful, unscrupulous, or incorrigibly egotistical.

He published the first book of photographs in France and refounded the *Revue de Paris* in 1851 with Louis de Cormenin and Théophile Gautier, to whose daughter Judith by Ernesta Grisi he was godfather. When the *Revue de Paris* was suppressed in 1859, he moved on first to the *Revue des Deux Mondes* (q.v.), and then in 1864 to the *Journal des Débats*, with which he stayed until his death. He was a successful social climber in artistic and literary circles, and was made an Officier of the Légion d'Honneur and, in 1880, successfully sought election to the Académie Française, of which he became director, but at which he had notoriously scoffed 25 years earlier. His fiction, travel writing, art criticism, and work as a social historian is colourless and unimaginative, if it was also accurate, facile, and successful. Flaubert, whom he helped considerably, and to whom he was also later patronizing, could not repress pangs of envy at Du Camp's career successes, although he rightly regarded Du Camp's conscientious reporting as intolerably flat in style. Du Camp was never knowingly other than genuinely helpful to Flaubert.

Du Camp's grandmother placed him, as was then the convention, in a boarding house, the Pension Goubaux, from which he attended the Lycée Louis-le-Grand. Then, after running away, he was sent to the Pension Favard and the Lycée Charlemagne. He is said to have fainted at the emotional impact of Marie Dorval's performance in Vigny's *Chatterton*, and at the age of 16 was deeply impressed by Hugo's *Les Orientales*. He became a passionate traveller and, after passing his baccalauréat in 1841, went to Rome and Algeria. It was in March 1843 that he first met Flaubert, who was two months older than he was, at the lodgings of a mutual friend, Ernest Le Marié. The two became close friends and, although much later in life they agreed to destroy one another's letters, some from 1844, written during Du Camp's first journey to the East, have survived, and show an intense, passionate affection, full of physical terms of endearment. They exchanged rings, and Le Poittevin, who had earlier been Flaubert's intimate friend and mentor, and remained close to him until he married in 1846, became jealous. Du Camp was similarly jealous of Le Poittevin when Flaubert turned back to his old friend during Du Camp's visit to the East from May 1844 to March 1845. Du Camp dedicated his first book to Flaubert, "Solus ad Solum (The Only One to the Only One)," and Flaubert looked up to the more sophisticated Du Camp as earlier he had looked up to Le Poittevin.

It was Du Camp who later said that Flaubert had been suffering from epilepsy, although it seems more probable that the illness which caused Flaubert's fainting fits on and after New Year's Day 1844 was venereal in origin, and that Du Camp was merely attempting to disguise the fact. As a result of his medical condition Flaubert's family rearranged their lives, and Du Camp had to obtain Flaubert's mother's permission to take him on their journey through Brittany. They left in May 1847 and returned to Rouen by way of the Loire châteaux on 7 August.

They wrote a book together, each contributing alternate chapters. Only two copies were made. Du Camp bequeathed his to the library of the Institut in Paris.

During the revolutionary disturbances of 23–26 June 1848 in Paris Du Camp served as an officer and was wounded in the leg. In 1876 he was to publish his *Souvenirs de l'année 1848: la révolution de février, le 15 mai, l'insurrection de juin*. In September 1849 he and Louis Bouilhet, another close friend of Flaubert whose poem *Melaenis* Du Camp had published in the *Revue de Paris* in 1853, attended Flaubert's private reading of his first *La Tentation de Saint Antoine*. They both recommended that he destroy it and, as a result of their advice, Flaubert abandoned florid romantic rhetoric for the austere stylistic precision of his great novels.

It was later that year that Du Camp took Flaubert to the Middle East. They set out from Paris on the coach on 29 October after an evening spent with Gautier, Bouilhet, and Louis de Cormenin. Although he was paying his own expenses, Du Camp wanted the protection afforded by official status and obtained a nomination to undertake an official "mission" whose object was archaeological research in Egypt, Syria, and Persia, on which he subsequently reported. He was able to quote in support of his application the publication of his *Souvenirs et paysages d'Orient* of 1848, the result of his 1844 journey. Flaubert and he left Marseilles on 4 November, calling at Malta and Alexandria before spending two months in Cairo, ascending the Nile, and crossing the desert on camel. They ran out of water, and Du Camp later reports his fury at Flaubert's lengthy evocations of the lemon ices at Tortoni's, the café famous in fashionable Paris. They moved on to Beirut and Jerusalem but, more to Du Camp's regret than to Flaubert's, had to abandon plans to cross the Syrian desert and pass through Baghdad on their way to the Caspian Sea. They had been shot at, and Flaubert's mother was anxious about the dangers attaching to their trip, although the change of plan was chiefly necessary because Flaubert had contracted syphilis on the way to Beirut.

The pair went on to Rhodes, Smyrna, Constantinople, Greece, and Naples. Du Camp then left Flaubert in Italy, where his mother had come to meet him, and was back in France by May 1851 to see to the publication of the first number of the new *Revue de Paris*, due out at the beginning of October, in which it vaunted its intentions to remain entirely free and politically independent. The review would have no opinions of its own, and would be willing to publish signed articles containing contradictory views. It might reject, but it would not censor. What the editors did not foresee was the coup d'état to come barely two months later, and the censorship which would lead to the extensive cuts Flaubert was obliged to make (some of them against his will) to the serialized *Madame Bovary* in 1856, and eventually, in 1859, to the suppression of the review by the authorities on account of a stance that was regarded as too liberal. From 1857 to 1859 Du Camp's relationship with Flaubert was to undergo a cooling off.

In the meanwhile the ministry of education sent Du Camp to Morocco on a brief mission later in 1851, and in 1852 he published 125 of the 200 "daguériennes" of the journey with Flaubert printed from waxed-paper negatives, the first book of photographs to appear in France, *Egypte, Nubie, Palestine et Syrie, dessins photographiques recueillis pendant les années 1849, 1850 et 1851, accompagnés d'un texte explicatif et précédés d'une introduction*. Du Camp had already been made

prolific literary production was to be dominated by two large-scale novel cycles: the five novels of the *Vie et aventures de Salavin*, published between 1920 and 1932, and the less successful 10 novels of the *Chronique des Pasquier*, which appeared from 1933 to 1941. On the death of Alfred Valette in 1935 Duhamel took over the *Mercure* for two years, and in 1936 he was elected to the Académie Française, of which he became provisional perpetual secretary in 1942. He had to resign in 1946 when the Alliance Française, of which he was president from 1937 until 1949, began to require too much of his attention. He was awarded the academy's Grand Prix de Littérature, and was an indefatigable ambassador for French culture, lecturing in dozens of countries throughout the world.

He was called up again in World War II, wrote *Mémorial de la guerre blanche* and *Positions françaises*, both of which were publicly burnt by the occupying forces after the defeat of France, and became a convinced pacifist. After his four volumes of reminiscences, *Lumières sur ma vie*, appeared in 1950, he went on publishing, but became sad that in old age he himself, as well as the humane values he had stood for, were gradually being forgotten. His most determined attempt after World War II to renew the inspiration of his "roman-fleuve" period, *Le Voyage de Patrice Périot*, is not normally regarded as successful. Duhamel died at Valmondois on 13 April 1966.

WORKS

Duhamel's ideas on the fellowship of men, the importance of submerging the individual in the community or group, and social responsibility were all formed during his student days. The two volumes of vivid sketches recalling his experiences as a soldier and surgeon in World War I contain detailed descriptions of hospital scenes, but are suffused with compassion and admiration for the qualities of heroic courage, fellowship, and resilience which Duhamel also witnessed. They contain a searing indictment of the stupidity of war and a satire on the incidental idiocies imposed by the hierarchy of rank. Physical sickness and the torture it inflicts are degrading, not ennobling. Suffering is humiliating, unjust, and, if inflicted by war, unnecessary. Bitterness creeps into the style as Duhamel reflects on the mutilations suffered by France's most handsome and bravest young men. What do the Negro stretcher bearers, recruited from parts of the world France has exploited, think of this lunatic slaughter of whites by whites? What is actually happening clashes with the technically perfected instruments of the surgeon's trade. It is important that Duhamel should have chosen to depict and reflect in a series of sketches on what he saw, not to conjecture beyond it into the realms of imaginative invention, and by writing a novel risk loss of power. He was to make the same choice after World War II in *Récits des temps d'affliction*.

Duhamel's output, although dominated by the novels, includes books for and about children, about gardens and literature, nature studies, poetry, plays, essays on his travels, on civilization and pacifism, and impressions of other forms of social organization, contemporary social topics, and many areas of public and private life. He always stresses the importance of individual freedom, moderation, and friendship, and is cynical about the advantages brought by technical progress in a world in which the pre-eminence of humane values is increasingly threatened.

After the books of war sketches, Duhamel's best work is generally considered to have been the *Salavin* series, whose eccentric, hypersensitive central character, Louis Salavin, sets out to become a saint. He is around 40, clumsy and shabby, well meaning, honest, thoughtful, and undistinguished. He is also diffident, inhibited, and indecisive. In the first volume, *Confession de minuit*, he loses his job as a clerk because he is overcome by an impulse to touch his employer's fat, red ear with his finger. The failure to which he is destined is deeper and more spiritual in *Deux hommes*, where he cannot find the generosity of spirit required to respond to genuine friendship. In *Le Journal de Salavin* of 1927, Salavin is eaten up with self-disgust and farcically takes steps to make himself into a saint. His determination to stamp out dishonesty results in his dismissal from a fraudulent dairy company for which he is working, and he again comes to grief when he seeks to live in chastity at home and find solace in religious observance. The novel, in diary form, accentuates the irony.

Salavin's failure to find any religious belief does not deter him from the pursuit of sanctity. The dictionary tells him what saints do, and he writes down his progress in his diary. He surprises both his mother and his wife, and is forced to lie to allay their fears for him. He tries to be helpful, but has to find old ladies to practise on, as helping the young can be misinterpreted, and there are not many lepers around. When the occasion arises he fails to achieve the heroism he has mentally rehearsed and is forced to recognize that he is a failure. A Protestant pastor thinks he is a crank. A Catholic priest suggests prayer as a solution. He ends up in hospital. The parable is bitingly ironic. Just as the pathetic Salavin has undertaken to humiliate himself fruitlessly and out of pride, so the builders of the brave new post-war world go round fruitlessly trying to heal those who do not regard themselves as ill and do not wish to be healed. They ought, like Salavin, to give up trying or, like him, they will end up wrecked by their own hubris in attempting to reform a world bent on its own perdition.

In *Le Club des Lyonnais* of 1929 Salavin just as fruitlessly seeks salvation in politics and becomes a communist, but this only intensifies his sense of spiritual failure. He is aware of the potential of the nobility of purpose which inspires him, and remains appealing, if ridiculous, because his intentions are so good. In the fifth volume, *Tel qu'en lui-même*, he decides to seek salvation outside Europe and goes to Tunis, where he runs a gramophone shop. He performs nauseating tasks at the local hospital which everyone else wants to avoid and undertakes to reform his sick Arab servant, who shoots him. His wife is sent for and takes him back to Paris, but he dies. The reader is left to decide how far he has got, and whether the mire of inadequacy in which he drowns is any reason for abandoning his heroic effort. Merely redirecting it is clearly not the answer.

The *Chronique des Pasquier* traces the development of a middle-class family between 1880 and 1920, and reflects many preoccupations of the period, like the clash between scientific advance and the civilized values being eroded. It is one of many saga novels about this period, including those of Thomas Mann and John Galsworthy and, like theirs, centres on a middle-class family and its reaction to social and political events. Laurent Pasquier becomes a doctor, but the early novels are dominated by his over-confident father Raymond, the archetypical entrepreneur, totally unrepentant for the messes in which he lands his family. We are then taken through the worlds of music, Duhamel's first love, the arts in *Le Désert de Bièvres*, and science. There is charm and skill in the writing, but Duhamel has sometimes been seen as the heir of Anatole France, too given to polished elegance. He has an acuteness of psychological observation which France lacked, but too much of his work is slight, and even the major novels are insufficiently relentless in their exploration of the consequences of what the characters do, might have done, or chose not to do.

PUBLICATIONS

Fiction

La Vie des martyrs, 1917; as *The New Book of Martyrs*, 1918
Civilisation 1914–1917, 1918; as *Civilisation*, 1918
Vie et aventures de Salavin:
  1. *Confession de minuit*, 1920
  2. *Deux hommes*, 1924
  3. *Le Journal de Salavin*, 1927
  4. *Le Club des Lyonnais*, 1929; vols. 1–4 as *Salavin*, 1936
  5. *Tel qu'en lui-même*, 1932
Chronique des Pasquier:
  1. *Le Notaire du Havre*, 1933
  2. *Le Jardin des bêtes sauvages*, 1934
  3. *Vue de la terre promise*, 1934; vols. 1–3 as *The Fortunes of the Pasquiers*, 1935
  4. *La Nuit de la Saint-Jean*, 1935
  5. *Le Désert de Bièvres*, 1937
  6. *Les Maîtres*, 1937
  7. *Cécile parmi nous*, 1938
  8. *Le Combat contre les ombres*, 1939
  9. *Suzanne et les jeunes hommes*, 1940
 10. *La Passion de Joseph Pasquier*, 1941
The Pasquier Chronicles:
  1. *News from Havre*, 1934 (also translated as *Papa Pasquier*, 1934)
  2. *Caged Beasts*, 1936 (also translated as *Young Pasquier*, 1936)
  3. *In Sight of the Promised Land*, 1935
  4. *St John's Eve*, 1935
  5. *The House in the Desert*, 1935
  6. *Pastors and Masters*, 1946
  7. *Cecile*, 1946
  8. *The Fight Against the Shadows*, 1946 (vols. 6–8 also translated as *Cecile among the Pasquiers*, 1940)
9–10 *Suzanne and Joseph Pasquier*, 1946
Inventaire de l'abîme; Biographie de mes fantômes, 1945; together as *Light on My Days*, 1948
Le Voyage de Patrice Periot, 1952

Plays

La Lumière (produced 1911), 1911
Dans l'ombre des statues (produced 1912), 1912
Le Combat (produced 1913), 1913
L'Oeuvre des athlètes, 1920
La Journée des aveux, 1924
Quand vous voudrez, 1924

Verse

Des légendes, des batailles, 1907

L'Homme en tête, 1909
Selon ma loi, 1910
Compagnons, 1912
Elégies, 1920
Voix du vieux monde, 1925

Prose

Propos critiques, 1912
Le Critique, 1913
Paul Claudel, 1913
La Possession du monde, 1919
Entretiens dans le tumulte, 1919
Les Livres du bonheur, 4 vols., 1922–48
Le Prince Jaffar, 1924
Deux hommes, 1924
Essai sur le roman, 1925
Lettre au Patagon, 1926
Le Voyage de Moscou, 1927
Entretien sur l'esprit européen, 1928
Les Sept dernières plaies, 1928
Scènes de la vie future, 1930
Pages de mon carnet, 1931
Géographie cordiale de l'Europe, 1931
Remarques sur les mémoires imaginaires, 1934
Fables de mon jardin, 1936
Le Dernier Voyage de Candide, 1938
Au chevet de la civilisation, 1938
Mémorial de la guerre blanche, 1939
Positions françaises, 1940
Les Confessions sans pénitence, 1941
Chronique des saisons amères, 1944
Paroles de médecin, 1944
Souvenirs de la vie du paradis, 1946
Tribulations de l'espérance, 1947
Le Temps de la recherche, 1947
Récits des temps d'affliction, 1948
La Pesée des armes, 1949
Lumières sur ma vie, 4 vols., 1950
Cri des profondeurs, 1951
Les Voyageurs de l'espérance, 1953
Les Espoirs et les épreuves, 1953
L'Archange de l'aventure, 1955
Les Compagnons de l'Apocalypse, 1956
Problèmes de l'heure, 1957
Le Complexe de Théophile, 1958
Nouvelles du sombre empire, 1959
Problèmes de la civilisation, 1962

Bibliography

Saurin, Marcel, *Bibliographie de Georges Duhamel*, 1951

Critical and biographical studies

Simon, Pierre Henri, *Georges Duhamel; ou, Le Bourgeois sauvé*, 1947
Falls, William, *Le Message humain de Duhamel*, 1948

DUMAS *père*, Alexandre, 1802–1870.

Novelist and dramatist.

LIFE

Everything about Dumas *père*'s background is colourful. His grandfather, Antoine-Alexandre Davy, Marquis de la Pailleterie (1714–86), could trace his ancestry back to the Renaissance. He and his younger brother Charles (1716–1773) both joined the army. Charles was sent as a subaltern to San Domingo, married well, became a rich planter, returned to France, but eventually over-extended himself and lost his money. Antoine-Alexandre, who was two years his senior, helped him to run the San Domingo estate for 10 years. In 1748 the brothers quarrelled and Antoine-Alexandre, who had much the weaker character of the two, took three of his brother's black slaves, of whom one was his concubine, into the interior with him. He sold them off, scraped a living in various ways, and bought another black woman slave, Marie-Cessette Dumas, by whom he had four children. The youngest, Thomas-Alexandre (1767–1806), was the novelist's father. Marie-Cessette died when Thomas-Alexandre was 10, and he alone of all the family was brought to France by the 60-year-old Antoine-Alexandre, but not before he had been sold to a ship's captain in Port-au-Prince and then redeemed again when Antoine-Alexandre, having established his identity, entered in 1775 into the family inheritance. Unaware that his elder brother was still alive, Charles had assumed the inheritance was his when his father died in 1758, but was now himself dead. Antoine-Alexandre's three other children by Marie-Cessette were left to fend for themselves.

Antoine-Alexandre spent a riotously dissipated life, first at Lisieux and then at Saint-Germain-en-Laye, before marrying his housekeeper, the 33-year-old Marie-Françoise-Elisabeth Retou, at the age of 70. Thomas-Alexandre, who, as a nobleman's bastard and slave-born son of mixed race, found himself excluded from Parisian society, refused to attend the wedding, which he regarded as a mésalliance. His father cut him off and he joined the army, refused to allow his father to buy him a commission, and apparently insisted on dropping the name de la Pailleterie, simply adopting that of his mother to become Thomas-Alexandre Dumas. His father died on 15 June, a fortnight after he had enlisted.

In August 1789 Thomas-Alexandre's squadron, a score of cavalry, was sent during the Revolution to Villers-Cotterêts, a staging-post of some 2,500 inhabitants about 40 miles to the north-east of Paris, where the Garde Nationale feared it could not defend the famous Renaissance château, which had notoriously been the scene of orgies during the regency of Philippe d'Orléans from 1715 to 1723. It was celebrated especially for the court supper parties known as the "Adam and Eve" nights, at which the guests undressed for mutual flagellation in the dark, to which even the gardners were sometimes invited, and of which we have passing accounts from the Duc de Richelieu, Saint-Simon, and Mme de Tencin. The court still used the town as a summer resort, and the inn-keeper who had summoned the military help, a former butler on the Regent's staff, billetted the good-looking mulatto Thomas-Alexandre in his own inn "A l'Enseigne de l'Ecu". His daughter, Marie-Louise-Elisabeth Labouret (1769–1838) married Thomas-Alexandre on 18 November 1972.

Military promotion during and after the Revolution was swift, and Thomas-Alexandre was to command a regiment from January 1793 and to become a brigadier six months later. He was a moderate republican, whose dislike of unnecessary executions imperilled his career. Reported to Paris for excessive leniency, he was saved only by his intrepidity in taking Mont Cenis and by Robespierre's fall. His wife bore him a daughter in September 1793, and in 1797 another who died in infancy. His relations with Napoleon were vicissitudinous, and ended badly, but his courage was undoubted, his physical strength prodigious, and he enjoyed moments of high favour. The break with Napoleon came after the suppression of the Cairo insurrection in 1799 when Thomas-Alexandre, in one of the fits of depression to which he was prone, applied to return to France. His ship took water, the cargo which might have made him rich had to be jettisoned, and he spent two years in captivity in Italy, from 17 March 1799 to 5 April 1801. He had incurred Napoleon's hostility, went uncompensated for his imprisonment, was taken off the active list, and lived in near-poverty at Villers-Cotterêts, where Dumas was born on 24 July 1802.

Dumas's mother and father were both relieved when he was born white. Only later in life did his appearance show strong traces of his African genes. At birth he already weighed nine pounds. His father had not succeeded in getting himself restored to favour and had only his retirement pension of 4,000 francs a year to live on, of which 1,200 francs went to pay the boarding school fees of Dumas's sister, Marie-Alexandrine-Aimée. He died on 26 February 1806. Their mother took Dumas and his sister, now three and 12, to live with her father, who had retired from his job as inn keeper. As a boy Dumas became keenly interested in animals, and virtually learnt to read from Buffon's *Histoire naturelle*. He flatly refused to go to the junior seminary where he could have had a bursary, and enough money was scraped together to send him to the school run by the local priest, where the only subject taught was Latin.

The Bourbon restoration of 1814 offered the chance of a reversion to noble status and perhaps therefore a lycée scholarship in Paris, but Dumas preferred to keep the name his father had chosen, although its association with Napoleon could not favour any future career. A sought-after licence to sell tobacco was obtained, however, for Dumas's mother from the state monopoly, enabling her to buy lessons for her son when the priest's school closed. He excelled, as it turned out, in calligraphy, taught to him on the side by his mathematics teacher, and poaching, taught by local professional practitioners. In a plot to which his mother was privy he also smuggled into prison some guns and money for two officers who had rallied to Napoleon during the hundred days.

When he was 14 Dumas was taken on as a clerk in a notary's office. There were sentimental episodes, with a first real girlfriend in Adèle Dalvin, who was an apprentice seamstress, continuous poaching, and an interest in dramatics kindled by strolling players and by two friends, Adolphe de Leuven and the older Amédée de la Ponce, a hussar from whom Dumas learnt Italian. He was excited by *Hamlet* as performed at Soissons in the Ducis "translation" of 1769, itself derived from those of Laplace and Letourneur. Ducis did not know English, and had in any case adapted Shakespeare's plots to suit 18th-century French taste. Dumas had learnt the role of Hamlet within three days of receiving the text from Paris.

From Leuven, Dumas heard about Antoine-Vincent Arnault,

whose *Germanicus* had provoked much discussion when it was staged in 1817; Casimir Delavigne, whose *Vêpres siciliennes* had been much admired in 1819; Schiller, whose *Maria Stuart* in French adaptation was the theatrical success of 1820; and Michel Pichat, whose *Léonidas* was to be banned in 1822 and have a memorable first night in 1825. From Leuven, Dumas also heard of the renewal of the melodrama, popularized by Pixérécourt at the Ambigu-Comique, with sets and stage machinery designed by Daguerre, and of Scribe's refurbished vaudevilles at the new Théâtre du Gymnase, which opened in 1820 and soon started to cater for the tastes of the new middle classes, many of whom could not read. It was not until Guizot's law of 1833 that the number of primary schools and pupils suddenly jumped by 50 per cent in 15 years, making illiteracy, at least among the middle classes, the exception.

From 1820 to 1821 Dumas and Leuven collaborated in writing plays, but their two vaudevilles and single melodrama were inevitably turned down by the Paris theatres. We know only the names. Dumas moved to another notary at Crépy, 70 miles from Paris, where he was given only board, lodgings, and pocket money. In November 1822 he contrived to visit Paris with the help of a friend who had a horse. They had 35 francs, and obtained lodgings in exchange for four hares, six brace of partridge, and two quails bagged by Dumas on the way. They saw a poster advertising the appearance of the famous actor Talma, who had inaugurated the vogue for historical realism by wearing a toga and sandals instead of a wig for classical Roman plays, and by suppressing the old rhetorical way of speaking verse. Dumas decided to call on him in the hope of getting free tickets. Talma, a former lover of Pauline Bonaparte, who had been a friend of Dumas's father, was washing and stripped to the waist when the two young men arrived, but he signed free admission slips for his performance that evening in *Sylla* by Jouy. Afterwards, backstage, Talma recognized Dumas by his height, and was delighted to flatter his ambitions. On his return to Crépy, Dumas gave up his job, settled his debts at Villers-Cotterêts, and went to seek his fortune in the world of the Parisian theatre.

It was thanks to his calligraphy that he was taken on at 1,200 francs a year by the Duc d'Orléans's secretariat. A fellow clerk, Lassagne, advised him to keep quiet at the office about his ambitions as a dramatist. He sensibly recommended him to read Aeschylus, Shakespeare, Molière, and Schiller, and forget about the currently successful spate of neoclassical plays, and that he reflect on Scott's success, and think about prose fiction. Dumas moved near to his work at the Palais-Royal, and the seamstress across the landing, Marie-Catherine-Laure Labay, became his mistress. On 27 July 1824 she gave birth to their son, Alexandre, who was always to refer to himself as "Dumas *fils*." Dumas's salary had risen to 1,500 francs. His mother, thinking he was doing well, decided to realize her assets at Villers-Cotterêts, and arrived in Paris with her life savings of 2,000 francs.

Dumas took an apartment with his mother at 350 francs a year, not daring to tell her about Catherine and the baby. The money soon ran out. Dumas and Leuven enlisted the help of a broken-down professional dramatist, who was dismissive of their work until he fastened on to Dumas's story-telling skill, and a poaching anecdote became the vaudeville *La Chasse et l'amour*. The Dumas–Leuven piece was turned down by the Théâtre du Gymnase, but successfully staged at the Ambigu-Comique on 22 September 1825. Dumas received six francs a performance, and 50 francs for his complimentary tickets, paid

by a professional tout who then advanced Dumas 300 francs to publish a small volume of contes in 1826, *Nouvelles contemporaines*. Only four of the 1,000 copies were sold.

Hugo had broken into the market in 1819 by establishing his own review, *the Conservateur Littéraire*, and after that had folded in 1821 he replaced it in 1823 with *La Muse Française*, so that his group had a forum which led to the salon of Emile Deschamps, the first "cénacle." Another "cénacle" centred on the art critic Etienne Délécluze, and the best-known circle of all round Nodier. Only such groups of more or less like-minded young men could hope to stimulate one another to literary success and achieve the critical mass necessary for the explosion which forced acceptance of new ways of writing. Despite tenuous acquaintanceships with Constant and Béranger, Dumas belonged to none of them, and was obliged to go on writing vaudevilles, the next being *La Noce et l'enterrement*, written in collaboration with Lassagne, to the disgust of their superiors in the Orléans office. The comedy was a success on 21 November 1826, and paid each of the authors eight francs an evening for a couple of score of performances—most of a year's rent.

Then in 1827 came the event that changed the course of the history of French drama and blew its conventions apart: the Odéon's Shakespeare season with the English Drury Lane company, including the tender and poetic Charles Kemble, known for the accuracy of his historical settings, and the wild, mean-spirited, and unheroic Edmund Kean, who had already dispensed with Shylock's red wig and beard in England. This season was decisive for the success of romantic (q. v.) drama in France. Delacroix, Vigny, and Hugo were enthusiastic. Berlioz, who knew no English, fell in love with Harriet Smithson, who played Ophelia, Juliet, and Desdemona. The first generation of actors and actresses to become famous after 1830, Marie Dorval, "Frédérick" (Antoine-Louis-Prosper) Lemaître, Pierre-François Tousez Bocage, and Mlle Anne-Françoise-Hippolyte Mars, were all influenced in their approach to acting by the English troupe. Dumas was deeply impressed, especially by *Hamlet*, which he saw on 11 September, followed by *Romeo and Juliet* on the 15th, and *Othello* on the 18th. The season was extended by six months, and Dumas probably saw *The Merchant of Venice*, *Richard III*, and *Macbeth* in the early months of 1828.

His verse play *Christine* was accepted by the Comédie-Française on 30 April 1828, although its staging had to be postponed, and it was eventually put on at the Odéon on 30 March 1830. In the meanwhile Dumas wrote *Henri III et sa cour* in eight weeks. There were three private readings in September 1828, at the third of which, arranged by Firmin of the Comédie-Française, five actors were present. The Comédie-Française accepted the play on 17 September 1828, and it was a sensational success on 10 February 1829, running for 37 performances. The Duc d'Orléans attended the first night, his party led the standing ovation, and the great soprano Maria Malibran had to hang on to one of the pillars of her box to stop herself falling out with excitement.

The duke's office had none the less forced Dumas to choose between his job and the theatre, and Dumas had made an enemy for life of Mlle Mars by insisting that one of Firmin's pupils should have the part of the page. What Mlle Mars disliked was the provocative romanticism of Dumas's plays, and his racial origins. The day after the first performance Dumas nevertheless sold the publication rights for 6,000 francs. The royalties from the first run would bring in another 15,000 francs, nearly a decade and a half's salary in all. *Henri III et sa cour* was the earliest of the great French romantic tragedies. Hugo had written *Cromwell* and what was to become *Marion Delorme*, but neither had been staged. The Vigny translation of *Othello* was not staged until October 1829, so that Dumas's tragedy was the first to be played. In the realm of literature, the inauguration of romantic tragedy would be his chief title to fame.

From 12 September 1827 Dumas had been the lover of the young and rather frigid Mme Mélanie Waldor, wife of an army captain and mother of a young daughter. He still saw Catherine Labay and their baby, and set her up with the profits from the play. He had put his mother into a flat near his new mistress's parents, with whom Mélanie lived, and had his own bachelor quarters in which he entertained the young romantics and people connected with the theatre. Devéria did a lithograph of him and, like Devéria, Dumas began to frequent Nodier's cénacle, the very proper Sunday receptions where the young romantics congregated. He met among others Sainte-Beuve, Mérimée, Vigny, Hugo, Musset, Nerval, Balzac, Delacroix, David d'Angers, Sophie Gay, and her daughter Delphine, later to become Emile de Girardin's wife. Dumas began to invite home the numerous women who found him attractive, and with many of whom he had affairs. He had meanwhile attended the private reading of Hugo's *Marion Delorme* in June 1829. The following year he began an affair with the provincial actress Belle Krelsamer, who had played the female lead opposite Firmin while *Henri III et sa cour* was on tour, and had been brought back to Paris by Firmin. She was to bear Dumas a daughter in March 1831.

In the summer of 1830 Dumas, who had been about to desert his new mistress for a visit to North Africa, felt that political events were making it more interesting to stay in Paris. During the July disturbances he roamed the streets with assorted bands of republicans, eagerly watching what was going on, especially at the theatres and newspaper offices, and taking sporadic part in the action. He got himself despatched to Soissons to requisition ammunition although, on his return to Paris, there remained no possibility of a republic being inaugurated. He had rightly guessed that the Duc d'Orléans would succeed to the throne, although the popular view was that there would in fact be a republic.

Although the director of the Comédie-Française company, Baron Taylor, to whom Nodier had provided Dumas with an introduction, liked *Christine* when he listened to it by appointment one morning at seven a.m. on emerging from his bath, the company had reservations, and Dumas had to make a number of important changes before the play was accepted on 30 April 1828. In the end Dumas withdrew it in favour of another play about Christina of Sweden, written by someone terminally ill and in a hurry to see his work staged. Dumas's play was not finally staged until 1830, and then at the Odéon, but it was a success, and in six weeks in the summer of 1830 he wrote *Antony*, irritatingly acclaimed by critics who have forgotten both Racine and Voltaire as the first French tragedy in a modern setting. Although not in that sense a "first," *Antony* was none the less remarkable for being a prose tragedy whose setting was remote in neither time nor place. The character is probably modelled, at least in part, on Emile de Girardin, the editor of *La Presse*, whose autobiographical novel about an illegitimate son, *Emile*, had been published anonymously in 1827. *Antony* was accepted by the Comédie-Française on 6 June 1830, but the text occa-

sioned quarrels. Dumas was requested to make cuts which would have turned the play, he said, into a vaudeville. Then, at the dress rehearsal, Mlle Mars asked if Dumas minded having the opening postponed until May 1831, by which time gas lighting would have been installed. (Drury Lane and Covent Garden had had it since 1817.) Firmin suggested that he should have his text revised by Scribe, the strongest of the opponents of the romantics. Dumas immediately retrieved his text and withdrew it.

The success of *Christine* at the Odéon had not been achieved without difficulty. Arnault had ceased to receive Dumas on account of his romanticism. Scribe was hostile. Soulié's *Christine* had failed at the Odéon, and he had given Dumas the rights to the debris, but Dumas was not an expert at verse, and there was a plot to bring down his play. Soulié packed Dumas's first night with the workmen from his sawmill. After the shouts and boos the play was declared a success, although at supper after the performance Hugo and Vigny sharpened some of Dumas's weaker lines for him. From the second night success was undoubted. Marie Dorval seduced Dumas, and he sold the book rights for 12,000 francs. The manager of the Odéon, Félix Harel, a professional administrator in the civil service, had taken over the closed theatre in 1829, largely because he was in love with the actress "Mlle George" (Marguerite-Joséphine Weimer), former mistress of Napoleon, Talleyrand, and Metternich. Both Harel and she were Bonapartists. He was intelligent, bumptious, witty, and always on the verge of bankruptcy. She was notorious for her plumpness, and as well as an actress an excellent hostess. They almost literally captured Dumas and made him write a play about Napoleon to follow on the success of *Christine*, forcing him to live in their flat. When he said he was worried about doing without Belle, Mlle George pointed out that there was no way out of his room except through hers. Dumas wrote *Napoléon Bonaparte* in a week. It was a work he regarded as having no literary merit although, with Lemaître in the lead, it played to large audiences for the rest of the winter after its first night on 10 January 1831.

On retrieving the text of *Antony*, Dumas took it straight to Marie Dorval. She disengaged herself from his embrace, having been taken under the protection of Vigny since their last meeting, but was instantly captivated by the idea of playing Adèle, the female lead, with Bocage as Antony and the cuts restored. The first night at the Porte-Saint-Martin on 31 May 1831 was as memorable as that of *Hernani*. All the young romantics were there, and they were deeply moved by the play, particularly by Dumas's famous curtain lines. His sense of theatre was acute enough for him to have trained the stage hands to change the scenery between the fourth and fifth acts fast enough not to allow the tension to dissipate. On the first night the applause lasted from the end of act four until the curtain went up again, and the skirt of Dumas's green coat was literally ripped from him as he left his box. The real risk had been the virtual on-stage rape at the end of act three. It had been followed by a long silence, then protracted applause.

In the summer of 1831 Belle got Dumas out of Paris and away from political demonstrations. There were no railways yet, so the couple travelled by stagecoach to Rouen, then by river boat to the mouth of the Seine. Dumas would work for four hours before breakfast, shoot snipe, work again, swim, dine, walk with Belle, and then work again. By 10 August he had finished the verse drama *Charles VII chez ses grands vassaux*. The piece, played at the Odéon with Mlle George in the lead, did not repeat the success of *Antony*, with its 30 performances in the first run, although it did as well as *Marion Delorme*, with Marie Dorval and Bocage, which Dumas considered far superior to his own play. He was so depressed that he returned his advance to Harel. Harel, misunderstanding the gesture, instantly offered to quintuple it. The next play, *Richard Darlington*, whose preview was on 10 December 1831, had been rewritten by Dumas from a draft he had been given. Although it owed much of its success to Lemaître, it nevertheless boosted Dumas's confidence again.

Early in 1832 Dumas had written up a scenario by Anicet Bourgeois to please Bocage and turned it into *Teresa*. Bocage then brought the rather surprising news that the Opéra-Comique had taken the play. He had great hopes of the actress Ida Ferrier, his protégée, who was to make her debut opposite him as Amélie Delaunay. The play opened on 6 February 1832 and turned into another great popular success. Ida, whose real name was Marguerite-Joséphine Ferrand, was well educated and decided to try for a stage career rather than take menial work. The going was hard, and the chance to star in a Dumas play the ultimate breakthrough for any aspiring actress. After the premiere she threw herself into Dumas's arms. They became lovers that night and, eight years later, husband and wife. The relationship was stormy, and temporarily broken off when Belle came back to Paris. *Angèle* was to be created in 1833 with parts for each, although by the end of that year Dumas and Ida were living together, and Belle had been definitively displaced.

Dumas had taken his son away from Catharine Labay, as a lapse in the registration of the birth allowed him to do, when Belle wanted to bring him up, but Belle found the eight-year-old too difficult to manage. Two years later, when Ida and Dumas were living together, Ida ironically took Belle's daughter by Dumas, Marie-Alexandrine, away from her. The situation was unsatisfactory. Alexandre remained attached to Catherine, but Marie became fonder of Ida than of her mother. Ida, however, disliked Marie. The Dumas–Ida ménage was socially improper. Among the socially acceptable, only Mlle Mars would dine with them, and her dislike of Dumas persisted.

The cholera epidemic reached its dreadful climax in mid-April 1932. The appalling hysteria redoubled the damage actually done by the disease, although that was bad enough. Frenzied panic ran through the population and gripped the authorities. The final result was that proper sanitation with piped water was installed in Paris. Dumas, who had been drinking tea with Boulanger and Liszt, may have had a mild dose of the disease. Intending to ward off the impending fever with sugar soaked in ether, he drank the ether, and nearly killed himself. Harel had not closed down during the epidemic, even though on one occasion he had a house of one, and the man hissed at the end of the performance. While Dumas was still convalescing he called on him with a manuscript, a revision by Janin of a play by Frédéric Gaillardet, which Dumas turned into *La Tour de Nesle*. It was probably his most popular play, and certainly a powerful contribution to the romantics' interest in the Middle Ages. He wrote it with Lemaître and Mlle George in mind, but Frédérick had fled Paris, and Bocage stepped in until Lemaître's return in September. The play was first given at the Porte-Saint-Martin on 29 May 1832. Later revivals included seasons in 1861, 1867, 1877, and 1882.

During the civil disturbances that summer Dumas broke into the theatre and distributed to a motley republican crowd the guns kept there for *Napoléon Bonaparte*. He was reported to have been arrested, and even executed, and Nodier asked him to dinner to tell him about the other world. It seemed prudent to lie low for a while, however, and Dumas went to Switzerland, publishing his impressions in the *Revue des Deux Mondes* (q. v.), and later as *Impressions de voyage: en Suisse*, his best-selling book prior to the novels. He was to write a whole series of travel books—on Russia, Spain, North Africa, the Rhine, and Italy—competing with Gautier, Stendhal, Chateaubriand, and scores of other writers in the romantic glorification of mountains and exotic localities. Dumas's travelogues were the most popularly successful of all such works, thanks no doubt to the immediacy of the excitement they communicated.

Dumas and Ida were married at a civil ceremony on 1 February 1840, followed by a church wedding four days later. The witnesses were Chateaubriand and the minister of education, Villemain. Four years later Ida was to leave Dumas, just as he was turning from drama to fiction. His most popular plays, the historical melodramas and domestic tragedies, were written before 1840, culminating in *Kean; ou, Désordre et génie*, written for Lemaître and at his suggestion, just three years after the English actor's death, and produced in 1836. The experimental comedy *Mademoiselle de Belle-Isle* was successfully produced in April 1839, with Mlle Mars, now 60, posturing as an 18-year-old, and serving as the butt of Gautier's sarcasm. Its success owed a good deal in fact to the expert acting, including that of Firmin and Lockroy.

From the moment he started to earn money, Dumas had been extraordinarily generous. He also entertained lavishly. In 1831 he held a memorable fancy-dress supper-dance for 400 in an empty apartment adjoining his own, with the rooms freshly decorated by the best-known painters in Paris. Apart from 300 bottles of claret, 300 of Burgundy, and 500 of champagne Dumas supplied his guests with a 30-pound salmon and a 50-pound sturgeon, swapped for three of the nine deer he had shot in the state forest, this time with permission. A fourth was exchanged for an immense galantine, and a couple of deer were roasted whole. The dancing overflowed on to the street at nine o'clock the next morning.

In 1837 Dumas had been awarded the Légion d'Honneur, and in that year the young critic Anténor Joly was given permission to open the Théâtre de la Renaissance, virtually a joint foundation of Hugo and Dumas. After Hugo's *Ruy Blas*, Dumas, who had already collaborated with Nerval on the comedy *Piquillo*, wrote *L'Alchimiste* and *Léo Burckart* with him for the new theatre. By 1838 Dumas's career as a writer of fiction had begun in earnest with the publication of *La Salle d'armes*, containing three nouvelles, and the serialization of the historical novel *La Comtesse de Salisbury* in Girardin's *La Presse*. Also in 1838, Armand Dutacq's *Le Siècle* published *Le Capitaine Paul*, from which Dumas made a five-act drama, *Paul Jones*, first performed on 12 October 1838. In fact the work was originally conceived as a drama, inspired by Fenimore Cooper's fictionalization of the hero of the War of American Independence in *The Pilot* (1823). Dumas wrote it in a week in 1835, on a chartered brig off the coast of Sicily, but Mlle George did not like it, so Harel turned it down. Dumas sent it to his agent, Porcher, and nothing happened until he was approached early in 1838 by *Le Siècle*, which was in need of a two-volume novel four weeks from then. Dumas for his part needed the money. His mother was to die on 1 August, but the strains on his resources had not yet diminished.

Le Séducteur et le mari, with Charles Lafont (produced 1842), 1842

Halifax, with Adolphe d'Ennery (produced 1842), 1842

Lorenzino (produced 1842), 1842

Les Demoiselles de Saint-Cyr (produced 1843), 1843; as *The Ladies of Saint-Cyr*, 1870

Le Laird de Dumbicky, with Adolphe de Leuven and Léon Lhérie (produced 1843), 1844

Louise Bernard, with Adolphe de Leuven and Léon Lhérie (produced 1843), 1843

Le Garde-forestier, with Adolphe de Leuven and Léon Lhérie (produced 1845), 1845

Un conte de fées, with Adolphe de Leuven and Léon Lhérie (produced 1845), 1845

Sylvandire, with Adolphe de Leuven and Léon Lhérie, from theb novel by Dumas and Maquet (produced 1845), 1845

Les Mousquetaires, with Auguste Maquet, from their novel *Vingt ans après* (produced 1845), 1845

Une fille du régent, from the novel by Dumas and Maquet (produced 1846), 1846

Echec et Mat, with Octave Feuillet and Paul Bocage (produced 1846), 1846

Intrigue et amour, from a play by Schiller (produced 1847), in *Théâtre complet*, 1864

Hamlet, with Paul Meurice, from the play by Shakespeare (produced 1847), 1848

La Reine Margot, with Auguste Maquet, from their novel (produced 1847), 1847

Le Chevalier de Maison-Rouge, with Auguste Maquet, from their novel (produced 1847), 1847; as *The Chevalier de Maison-Rouge*, 1859

Catalina, with Auguste Maquet (produced 1848), 1848

Monte-Cristo, parts 1–2, with Auguste Maquet, from their novel *Le Comte de Monte-Cristo* (produced 1848), 2 vols., 1848

Le Cachemire vert, with Eugène Nus (produced 1849), 1850

Le Comte Hermann (produced 1849), 1849

La Jeunesse des Mousquetaires, with Auguste Maquet, from their novel *Les Trois mousquetaires* (produced 1849), 1849; as *The Three Musketeers*, 1855; as *The Musketeers*, 1898

Le Chevalier d'Harmental, with Auguste Maquet, from their novel (produced 1849), 1849

La Guerre des femmes, with Auguste Maquet, from their novel (produced 1849), 1849

Le Connétable de Bourbon; ou, L'Italie au seizième siècle, with Eugène Grangé and Xavier de Montépin (produced 1849), 1849

Le Testament de César, with Jules Lacroix (produced 1849), 1849

Trois entr' actes pour L'Amour médecin (produced 1850), 1850

La Chasse au Chastre, from his own novel (produced 1850), 1850

Les Chevalier du Lansquenet, with Eugène Grangé and Xavier de Montépin (produced 1850), 1850

Urbain Grandier, with Auguste Maquet (produced 1850), 1850

Le Vingt-quatre février (produced 1850), 1850

La Barrière de Clichy (produced 1851), 1851

Le Vampire, with Auguste Maquet (produced 1851), 1851

Le Comte de Morcerf; Villefort, with Auguste Maquet, from their novel *Le Comte de Monte-Cristo* (produced 1851), 2 vols., 1851

La Jeunesse de Louis XIV (produced 1854), 1854; as *Young King Louis*, 1979

Le Marbrier, with Paul Bocage (produced 1854), 1854

Romulus (produced 1854), 1854; as *Romulus* (in English), 1969

La Conscience (produced 1854), 1854

L'Orestie (produced 1856), 1856

La Tour Saint-Jacques, with Xavier de Montépin (produced 1856), 1856

Le Verrou de la reine (produced 1856), in *Théâtre complet*, 1865

L'Invitation à la valse (produced 1857), 1857; as *Childhood's Dreams*, 1881

La Bacchante (Thais), with Adolphe de Leuven and A. de Beauplan, and music by Eugène Gautier (produced 1858)

L'Honneur est satisfait (produced 1858), 1858

Les Forestiers, from his novel *Catherine Blum* (produced 1858), in *Théâtre complet*, 1865

L'Envers d'une conspiration (produced 1860), 1860

Le Roman d'Elvire, with Adolphe de Leuven, and music by Ambroise Thomas (produced 1860), 1860

Le Gentilhomme de la montagne, from his novel *El Salteador* (produced 1860), 1860

La Dame de Monsoreau, with Auguste Maquet, from their novel (produced 1860), 1860

Le Prisonnier de la Bastille: fin des mousquetaires, with Auguste Maquet, from their novel *Le Vicomte de Bragelonne* (produced 1861), 1861

Les Mohicans de Paris, from the novel by Dumas and Bocage (produced 1864), 1864

Gabriel Lambert, with Amédée de Jallais, from the novel by Dumas (produced 1866); as *Gabriel le faussaire*, produced 1868), 1866

Madame de Chamblay, from his own novel (produced 1868), 1869

Les Blancs et les bleus, from his own novel (produced 1869), 1874

Ivanhoë; Fiesque de Lavagna, 1974

Other

La Vendée et Madame, 1833; as *The Duchess of Berri in La Vendée*, 1833

Gaule et France, 1833

Impressions de voyage: en Suisse, 5 vols., 1834–37; as *Adventures in Switzerland*, 1960

Quinze jours à Sinaï, 2 vols., 1839

Napoléon, 1840; as *Napoleon*, 1894

Le Capitaine Pamphile (juvenile), 1840; as *Captain Pamphile*, 1850

Les Stuarts, 2 vols., 1840

Excursions sur les bords du Rhin, 3 vols., 1841

Une année à Florence, 2 vols., 1841

Midi de la France, 3 vols., 1841

Le Speronare, 4 vols., 1842; as *The Speronara*, 1902

Le Capitaine Arena, 2 vols., 1842

Le Corricolo, 4 vols., 1843

La Villa Palmieri, 2 vols., 1843

Filles, lorettes, et courtisanes, 1843

Louis XIV et son siècle, 2 vols., 1844–45

Histoire d'un casse-noisette (juvenile), 2 vols., 1845; as *The Story of a Nutcracker*, 1846; as *The Nutcracker of Nuremberg*, 1930

La Bouillie de la comtesse Berthe (juvenile), 1845; as *Good
  Lady Bertha's Honey Broth*, 1846; as *The Honey Feast*, 1980
Italiens et flamands, 1845
Les Médicis, 2 vols., 1845
De Paris à Cadix, 5 vols., 1847–48; as *Adventures in Spain*,
  1959
Le Véloce; ou, Tanger, Alger, et Tunis, 4 vols., 1848–51; as
  Tales of Algeria, 1868; as *Adventures in Algeria*, 1959
Louis XV et sa cour, 4 vols., 1849
La Régence, 2 vols., 1849
Montevideo; ou, Une nouvelle Troie, 1850
Histoire de Louis XVI et la révolution, 3 vols., 1850–51
Mémoires de Talma, 3 vols., 1850
Le Drame de '93, 7 vols., 1851–52
Les Drames de la mer, 2 vols., 1852
Histoire de Louis-Philippe, 1852; as *The Last King; or, The New
  France*, 1915
Mes mémoires, 22 vols., 1852–54; annotated edition, 5 vols.,
  1954–68; selections as *Memoirs*, 2 vols., 1890; as *My Mem-
  oirs*, 6 vols., 1907–09
Une vie d'artiste, 2 vols., 1854; as *A Life's Ambition*, 1924
La Jeunesse de Pierrot (juvenile), 1854; as *When Pierrot Was
  Young*, 1975
La Dernière Année de Marie Dorval, 1855
Isabel Constant, 2 vols., 1855
*Les Grands Hommes en robe de chambre: Henri IV, Louis XIII,
  et Richelieu; César*, 12 vols., 1856–57
Causeries, 4 vols., 1857
L'Homme aux contes (juvenile), 1857
Le Lièvre de mon grand-père (juvenile), with de Cherville, 1857
Histoire de mes bêtes, 1858; as *My Pets*, 1909; as *Adventures
  with My Pets*, 1960
Marianna, 1859
Les Baleiniers, with Felix Meynard, 3 vols., 1860
Le Caucase, 1859; as *Adventures in Caucasia*, 1962
L'Art et les artistes contemporains au salon de 1859, 1859
Contes pour les grands et les petits enfants (juvenile), 2 vols.,
  1859
La Route de Varennes, 1860
Les Garibaldiens: révolution de Sicile et du Naples, 1861; as
  The Garibaldians in Sicily, 1861; complete version, as *On
  Board the "Emma": Adventures with Garibaldi's "Thou-
  sand" in Sicily*, edited by R.S. Garnett, 1929
Bric-à-brac, 2 vols., 1861
Les Morts vont vites, 2 vols., 1861
Le Pape devant les évangiles, 1861
I Borboni di Napoli, 10 vols., 1862–64
Impressions de voyage: en Russie, 4 vols., 1865; as *Voyage en
  Russie*, edited by Jacques Suffel, 1960; excerpts as *Cele-
  brated Crimes of the Russian Court*, 1906; as *Adventures in
  Czarist Russia*, 1960
Bouts-rimés, 1865
Etude sur "Hamlet" et sur William Shakespeare, 1867
Souvenirs dramatiques, 2 vols., 1868
Le Grand Dictionnaire de cuisine, with Anatole France, 1873;
  as *Dictionary of Cuisine*, 1958; selection as *Dumas on Food*,
  1978
Propos d'art et de cuisine, 1877
The Dumas Fairy Tale Book, edited by H.A. Spurr, 1924

Editor, *Un pays inconnu*, 1845

Editor, *Pierre précieuse*, by Saphir, 1854
Editor, *L'Arabie heureuse*, 1855
Editor, *Le Journal de Madame Giovanni*, 4 vols., 1856; as *The
  Journal of Madame Giovanni*, 1944
Editor, *Pèlerinage de Hadji-abd-el-Hamid-Bey (à la Mecque)*,
  6 vols., 1856–57

Translator, *Mémoires de Garibaldi*, 2 vols., 1860; revised edition, 5 vols., 1860–61; 3 vols., 1861; as *Garibaldi: An Autobiography*, 1860; revised edition, as *The Memoirs of
  Garibaldi*, 1931

Bibliography

Reed, F.W., *A Bibliography of Alexandre Dumas Père*, 1933
Munro, Douglas, *Dumas père: Works Published in French,
  Works Translated into English*, 2 vols., 1978–81

Critical studies

Bell, A. Craig, *Alexandre Dumas: A Biography and Study*, 1950
Maurois, André, *Three Musketeers: A Study of the Dumas
  Family*, 1957
Stowe, Richard S., *Alexandre Dumas Père* (in English), 1976
Hemmings, F.W.J., *The King of Romance: A Portrait of Alexan-
  dre Dumas*, 1979
Ross, Michael, *Alexandre Dumas* (in English), 1981

DUMAS *fils*, Alexandre, 1824–1895.

Novelist and dramatist.

WORKS

Dumas was the illegitimate son of Dumas *père* (see preceding
entry) and the seamstress Catherine Labay. His parents separated soon after his birth, and he was brought up by his mother,
although frequently visited by his father, until the age of nine,
when his father gave him into the custody of his new mistress,
Belle Krelsamer. He remained deeply attached to his mother, but
had an unhappy schooling at the Pension Goubaux, where he
was taunted about his illegitimacy and made acutely aware of his
father's growing notoriety. Eventually he was moved to a more
humane establishment, the Pension Saint-Victor, whose inmates
attended the Collège Bourbon. His relationship with his father,
whom he appears to have regarded with a mixture of admiration
for his achievements and contempt for his moral cowardice, was
inevitably chequered, although they mostly got on well until
quite late in Dumas *fils*'s life.

From 1843 Dumas lived with his father at Saint-Germain-en-
Laye, sharing his more or less disreputable pleasures and frivolities, and, apparently, his mistresses too. At this period they
greatly enjoyed one another's boisterous company and reciprocal teasing. It was at one of his father's plays that Dumas pre-

sented him to "La dame aux camélias," Alphonsine ("Marie") Duplessis, who was eager for a part in a Dumas play. Marie would wear a white camelia for 25 days in succession, and then a red one for three. She was of working-class stock, but swiftly made her way up the social scale, acquiring lovers and lady-like accomplishments, and by 1844 passed for one of the capital's most elegant women. She left Dumas for Liszt in 1845, and died on 3 February 1847.

In 1846–47 Dumas accompanied his father to Spain and Algeria, and thereafter continued to live off an allowance paid by his father while undertaking a certain amount of devilling on his behalf. When his father's financial crash came in 1851, Dumas went to live with his mother, who was then running a subscription library. While his father was in Brussels following his bankruptcy, Dumas helped to look after his affairs in Paris, where his *Benvenuto Cellini* was being staged. He had himself published a number of works which had failed, including the verse volume *Péchés de jeunesse* and a comic novel in six volumes, *Aventures de quatre femmes et d'un perroquet*. In 1848, the year after her death, Dumas fictionalized his affair with Marie Duplessis in his novel *La Dame aux camélias*. On turning it into a prospectively more remunerative play, he ran into difficulties with the censor, who refused to license it. Fortunately, the Duc de Morny was a friend, and after the coup d'état of 1 December 1851 became minister of the interior. He personally authorized the production, and the first performance took place at the Gymnase on 2 February 1852. Success was instantaneous and prodigious. Piave immediately turned the play into the libretto for Verdi's *La Traviata* (1853), and Dumas was set to become one of the Second Empire's most fashionable dramatists. His subsequent works have been largely forgotten, but on the proceeds of this first great success he was able to settle his mother in an apartment at Neuilly overlooking the Bois de Boulogne, where she could decline in comfort.

In 1850 Dumas had met Lydia Nesselrode, one of a number of rich, aristocratic Russian beauties in Paris with a taste for sexual indulgence. He fell in love with her, followed her to Belgium and Germany, but was not admitted to Russia, where she had to go to pick up her revenues. While waiting near the border, he uncovered the cache of autograph letters from George Sand known to have been left by Chopin, who had died in 1849. He returned them to their author, who burnt them. Dumas purged himself of the Nesselrode affair in *La Dame aux perles*, whose title clearly referred back to his earlier success, but which in fact marks his shift towards a somewhat sanctimonious moralizing. He had already drawn on his experience with Lydia in the suspense drama derived from his short story *Diane de Lys* and clearly intended as a pendant to his father's *Antony*, although the wronged husband now shoots his wantonly adulterous wife's lover. *Le Demi-monde* was sufficiently moral for the minister, Achille Fould, to want the play for the Comédie- Française. In his anxiety to remain faithful to the Gymnase under Montigny, Dumas deliberately introduced crudities of language, later removed, to ensure that the play would be rejected by the state theatre, for which the Gymnase was a serious rival for a time. Montigny's wife, Marie-Rose Cizos, known as Rose Chéri, conspired with Dumas behind her husband's back to reserve a handful of daring effects for the hugely successful first night.

From 1853 Dumas's mistress was the 26-year-old Nadejda Knorring, a friend of Lydia's. She was married to the elderly Prince Naryschkine, by whom she had a daughter, Olga, and who refused her a divorce. Nadejda's mother bought her daughter a house at Luchon in the south-west, where Dumas lived with her until, in 1859, they moved to a 44-bedroomed house near Cléry. He still venerated his father, and his relationship with him provided Dumas with material for his plays *Le Fils naturel* and *Un père prodigue*, although the contrast between the father's boisterous exuberance and the son's cool sense of responsibility became a commonplace remarked on by a number of their contemporaries. In 1859 Dumas and his mistress heard that Lydia Nesselrode had finally divorced and remarried. Her father, the governor of Moscow, was instantly dismissed by the tsar. Nadejda hoped that, by not divorcing and staying outside Russia, she could retain links with her homeland and financial base. Then in 1860 she conceived a child by Dumas. Marie-Alexandre-Henriette "Colette" was born on 22 November.

Dumas himself took refuge in hypochondria, turning for quasi-maternal help to George Sand, whose novel *Le Marquis de Villemer* he made into a play in 1861, and with whom he stayed for a month at Nohant. Nadejda, now known as "Nadine," found his hostess too intimidating to accompany him on this occasion, although she did go to Nohant with Dumas early in the autumn. Dumas's painter friend Charles Marchal stayed on after they left. Dumas gave George Sand the rights to the play, but derived the idea for his own controversial *L'Ami des femmes* from her. There were noisy interruptions to its performances and, when Dumas made a change insisted on by Montigny for a revival, Taine and, later, Bourget protested.

On 26 May 1864 Nadejda's husband died and she reverted to her maiden name, Knorring. As Dumas himself developed into a self-appointed custodian of public morality, he began to disapprove of his father's behaviour and was clearly tired of being regarded largely as the son of a famous man. He married Nadejda on 31 December 1864, the last occasion on which his parents ever met. Dumas now saw his father as infrequently as possible, although they met again at his mother's funeral. She had died on 22 October 1868. The strain in Dumas's relationship with his father dated from the previous year, when his father had had a final important affair with Adah Isaacs Menken. This extraordinary woman, who was probably born in 1833, had deserted her fourth husband, knew English, French, German, and Hebrew, wrote verse, had known Whitman, Twain, Bret Harte, Dickens and Charles Reade, had an affair with Swinburne, and recently astonished London in *Mazeppa*, her only role which she played stretched and bound, galloping her horse up a steep rise. Since 31 December 1866 she had been playing at the Gaîté in Paris, lashed to the back of her horse and dressed only in flesh-coloured tights. She had come to Paris to meet Dumas's father and early in 1867 Dumas had found the two of them embracing, with Adah practically naked at the time. Compromising photographs had been taken, and the photographer, who had caused a scandal by offering the prints for sale, went to jail for libel. Dumas had to step in to prevent his aging father from fighting a duel. Adah died in 1868.

In 1866, feeling too uneasy to write another play after the difficulties caused by what was regarded as the indelicacy of *L'Ami des femmes*, Dumas wrote the semi-autobiographical novel *L'Affaire Clemenceau*, which rapidly became a success. He then retired to the country in order to get back to writing for the theatre and produced *Les Idées de Madame Aubray*, again inspired by George Sand, to whom he read it. Edmond About confirmed her enthusiastic judgement, and Montigny accepted the play without hesitation. Its success was again remarkable. Following a miscarriage, Dumas's wife bore him another daughter, Jeannine, in April 1867. After his father's death in 1870 and the defeat of France in the same year, Dumas became convinced that France's decline was due to an erosion of moral vigour, and began to preach collective austerity. However, his high moral stance did not prevent him becoming obsessed with women younger than his wife, notably Aimée Desclée, who surprised Montigny by her success as an actress in a revival of *Diane de Lys*, and a successful new play in October 1871, *Une visite de noces*.

In 1870 Dumas started to write *La Femme de Claude*, which was to be a flop, but interrupted it to write another play, centring on an adulterous male, *La Princesse Georges*, which he completed in three weeks. The two female roles were written for Aimée Desclée and the Creole Blanche Pierson, whose beauty was the talk of Paris. The play succeeded, but the two actresses became bitter rivals. As a result of the reviews of *La Femme de Claude*, for whom no one ever had a good word, Dumas thought it necessary to defend himself, and issued a pamphlet of striking misogyny, *L'Homme-Femme*, defending the husband's right to murder a wanton wife which he had depicted on the stage. He hoped in vain to justify himself in *Monsieur Alphonse*, with Desclée in the title role, but she had been short of money after the failure of *Claude*, had been obliged to give 30 performances in London, and had returned terminally ill. She died of cancer on 8 March 1874. The play, with Blanche Pierson as Raymonde, had a happy ending and pleased the public. Dumas published it with a moralizing preface about the responsibilities of paternity.

Dumas was wealthy. He had a large and austere house, and regular habits. Politically, he was obsessed with the values of family life and with the protection of members of both sexes against exploitation by the other. He was elected to the Académie Française, and Edmond de Goncourt accompanied the Princesse Mathilde to the ceremony on 11 February 1875. Dumas's speech of acceptance was received with a clever reply from d'Haussonville, which was in fact a put-down. The Comédie-Française revived *Le Demi-monde*, and Dumas wrote *L'Etrangère* for it, defending divorce and infuriating the critics. If adulterers could be divorced and remarried, all parties, Dumas argued, would be spared humiliation and misery. Sarah Bernhardt played the lead to a full house, although Flaubert grumbled about filling the stage with ideas rather than people.

Dumas himself was not happy. His friend Charles Marchal, having become George Sand's lover and subsequently fallen out of favour, had committed suicide in 1877. Dumas had taken a mistress, Ottilie Flahault, who had a château near Châtillon-sur-Loing, where he frequently went to work. Nadine was consumed by jealousy and depressions, although Dumas and she remained on close terms. On Tuesdays, they entertained to dinner. Olga, Dumas's stepdaughter was unhappily married and had two little girls. His own elder daughter was to marry Maurice Lippmann (1847–1923) on 2 June 1880. When Dumas himself went out, it was without his wife. He ceased to publish personal prefaces to his plays, but wrote a series of open letters—on divorce to Alfred Naquet (1882), on the registration of paternity to Gustave Rivet (1883)—and returned to the stage with *La Princesse de Bagdad*, which had bad reviews and a stormy first night. It is universally regarded as a poor play.

Dumas now lived grandly, in Paris during the winter and in a borrowed country house during the summer. He bought pictures, collecting especially Meissonier, Marchal, and Tassaert, who had committed suicide in 1874, gave dinners for the distinguished, and behaved pompously, resolutely avoiding political affiliation. He became friendly with the wealthy collector Adèle Cassin, whom he met in 1880, and made yet another theatrical comeback, this time successful, with *Denise* at the Comédie-Française in 1885. During the first performance he sent Nadine 28 telegrams, describing the effect of each scene. The minister of the interior had given instructions to keep the Post Office open. A Dumas first night had become a national event. On 3 November 1883 Dumas was present at the unveiling of Doré's statue of his father in Place Malesherbes, and he was much moved by the death of his father's close companion, Adolphe de Leuven, who left him an estate at Marly. After the death of Emile Perrin, administrator-general of the Comédie-Française, his successor, Jules Claretie, extracted from Dumas the promise of another play. The lightweight result, *Francillon*, was highly applauded.

From 13 April 1887 Dumas had a new mistress, Henriette Regnier de la Brière, who divorced her architect husband in 1890. Nadine, now suffering from an incurable mental condition, left the Paris house in 1891 to live with Colette. Dumas started two more plays but finished neither. There were successful revivals, but he knew that his work was being displaced by the naturalist (q.v.) advanced guard, and sank into increasing despondency. On 2 April 1895 Nadine died, aged 68. She was buried with Catherine Labay and on 26 June Dumas married Henriette. Later that year he fell ill, spending whole days in a dazed state. He died on 28 November.

WORKS

La Dame aux camélias was written after Marie Duplessis, the model for its heroine, had died on 3 February 1847. Dumas had not been generous with her or sympathetic enough to her predicament. He had not been cruel, either, and she had had other liaisons which she constantly tried to conceal from him; but he clearly felt some guilt when he heard of her death. He had been in North Africa and received the news in Marseilles, where he was writing his picaresque novel, the *Aventures de quatre femmes et d'un perroquet*. On returning to Paris he had attended the auction of the contents of Marie's apartment and bought a gold chain, and in May he went to Saint-Germain, where he dreamt of the day when, after galloping with a friend, he had accompanied him to the Variétés and met Marie.

He took a room and wrote his novel, changing the heroine's name to Marguerite Gautier, and making the hero, Armand Duval, try to lead her to virtue by pure love. Marguerite, who is fond of camellias, lives quietly in the country with Armand. His father tries to make her give him up. She submits and returns to Paris, letting Armand think she has gone off with a rich architect. Already consumptive, she grows steadily weaker, and Armand learns the truth too late, arriving in time only for her to die in his arms. Marguerite is heroic in her atonement, selling her jewels and even her hair, so renouncing everything she holds most precious rather than hurt the man she loves. Alone and unsupported, she writes a series of heart-rending letters. Dumas no doubt assuaged his guilt by inventing the elements of the novel which most strongly call on the reader's emotional sympathy for its heroine, but the work struck a sentimental chord. In spite of its success, it might well have been forgotten were it not for the play and, of course, for Verdi's *La Traviata*.

The novel was published in 1848, after the failure of the early volume of verse. Dumas had been short of money and turned his novel into the play inside a week, but the political troubles of 1848 prevented its immediate staging. When it was performed, in February 1852, Dumas discovered that he could project emotion even more strongly from the stage than from the printed page. Eugénie Doche (Marie-Charlotte-Eugénie de Plunkett), playing Marguerite, had wept when the play was first read to her, and fainted in earnest. Charles Fechter as Armand tore 6,000 francs' worth of lace on the first night. Dumas's literary production was thereafter almost totally devoted to the drama. He joined Augier, Sardou, and Labiche as one of the favourite dramatists of the Second Empire. Later, his plays tended to preach, and were frequently directed against the lenient view which society took of male, but not female, marital infidelity. The emotion of *La Dame aux camélies* was no doubt facile, and its plot trite, but Dumas was a competent and frequently successful journeyman dramatist, who wrote about important social issues.

Alfred-Auguste Cuvillier-Fleury picked on *La Femme de Claude*'s obvious weak point in the *Journal des Débats*. In whose name does Dumas pretend to justify the murder of the woman guilty of marital infidelity? The women who had found a pretext for being maudlin about their emotions in *La Dame aux camélies* were now heavily against Dumas, whose hold on his public was in danger of slipping. Of the later plays Sarcey said that they were "théorèmes vivants et passionnés (living, passionate theorems)." They are indeed sermons, generally humanized, after *Claude*, by pity for the female victims of discrimination, but intended to serve a moral purpose and to achieve social change, whether in society's attitude to illegitimacy, to the repentant fallen woman, to the laws of commercial honesty, or to divorce, each the principal subject of one of the plays. Dumas is therefore superficially a realist (q.v.), reacting, after *Claude* had failed, against the romanticism (q.v.) of his father's early plays and the historical settings of Scribe.

Dumas's plays were predominantly set in middle-class drawing rooms with double doors at the back. The preface to *Un père prodigue* neatly defines the aim: "Le réel dans le fond, le possible dans le fait, l'ingénieux dans le moyen, voilà ce qu'on peut exiger de nous (What is real in the background, what is possible in the action, what is ingenious in the means, that is what can be expected from us)." "Ingenuity" is the technically important constituent of surprise and suspense, with the resolution of the plot pointing the moral lesson. Dumas seems to have started with the end of the play in his sights, and to have worked backwards, rather than to have followed the logic of a character or a situation from the outset to a perhaps morally inconclusive resolution. His theatre affirms without exploring, but it moves away from pitiless moral realism towards a more generous moral code after *Claude*, whose lesson Dumas seems to have learnt.

Diane de Lys concerns an unhappy aristocrat, Diane, who falls in love with an artist, Paul Aubry. The proposition to be demonstrated is that nothing can justify adultery, not even an arranged marriage, an unsympathetic husband, or the prohibition of divorce. Paul has to be punished for his adultery by Diane's husband, the Comte de Lys, who shoots him. The pistol shot alludes of course to the curtain of *Antony* by Dumas *père*, which it reverses. Dumas, who knew that the audience would sympathize with the lovers, hesitated a long time before choos-

ing, against Montigny's strong advice, to use the pistol shot. Even though he had warned Paul Aubry that he would shoot him if he persisted in the liaison with his wife, the husband's recourse to his arid legal right shocked and puzzled the audience, as Dumas had intended it to. The surprising thing is that the taste of the Gymnase's audiences in 1853 allowed the stage vindication of so conservative a set of moral values to be as successful as it was.

Le Demi-monde concerns a sharp defence of society against the machinations of a clever fallen woman and the world of compromised wives, inhabited by non-virginal brides who are not courtesans, but not quite respectable either. They need if not a husband, then at least a stable protector. "This society begins where the reign of the legal consort ends; it finishes where the venal consort begins. It is separated from that of honest women by public scandal; from that of the courtesan, by money," wrote Dumas in his preface. Olivier de Jalin wants to extricate his friend, Raymond de Nanjac, from the charms of the Baronne d'Ange, and Dumas is able to combine exemplary punishment of the Baronne with too lingering an interest in life in a gambling saloon, bringing together voyeurish titillation and moral rectitude in his first real comedy of manners. "Ce n'est pas moi qui empêche votre mariage," says Jalin to Nanjac, "c'est la raison…la justice…la loi sociale qui veut qu'un honnête homme n'épouse qu'une honnête femme (It isn't me who is preventing your marriage. It's reason, justice, the social order, which lays down that a well brought-up man marries only a well brought-up woman)."

The next play, *La Question d'argent*, was, like most of the others, concerned with social problems. *Le Fils naturel* and *Un père prodigue* are autobiographical in derivation. The later plays burn increasingly with reformatory social zeal. *L'Ami des femmes* caused controversy on account both of the heroine's description of the horrors of her wedding night and of the tedious M. de Ryons, who is beyond the reach of female charm. It was George Sand, in a moment of particular outspokenness, even for her, who had talked to Dumas about the horrors an inexperienced girl can undergo on her wedding night. Jane de Simerose is terrified by the memory of her own experience, and has left her clumsy and insensitive husband, whom she actually still loves. Ryons protects her from unwanted predation, acts as director of her conscience, and reconciles her to her husband. In the first version he is himself untouched by female affection, although Montigny insisted that he be married off for the revival, which caused the protests from Taine and then Bourget. Dumas, in his published preface, actually says that nature and society demand that women should be subservient to male domination.

Dumas's short autobiographical novel, *L'Affaire Clemenceau*, is again nourished by frustrated resentment against women. It is the confession of a murderer who has killed his wife, whose beauty appears to him simply as the outer disguise of a lying and deceitful nature. Pierre Clemenceau is the illegitimate sculptor son of a seamstress. He marries a Pole, Iza Dobronowska, who has much in common with Dumas's own first mistress. Writing the novel clearly operated an emotional release in Dumas and made it possible for him to write again for the stage. In *Les Idées de Madame Aubray*, the high-minded central character has either to repudiate her son or, against her principles and wishes, to allow him to marry Jeannine, whom he loves but who is now working to bring up a fatherless child. The decision to support her son is made the focus of a real dilemma for Mme Aubray.

In 1870 Dumas was thinking about a different play altogether when, in three weeks, he wrote *La Princesse Georges*. The princess, Séverine, a role written for Aimée Desclée, knows that her husband is having an affair with the Comtesse Sylvanie de Terremonde, to be played by Blanche Pierson. The princess knows, too, that the countess's husband is lying in wait for her lover. She could be avenged on her husband for his infidelity by doing nothing, allowing her husband to visit the countess, a seductive adventuress, and be killed by the count, but she prefers to save and forgive him. The play was a success, but the one that replaced and followed it, *La Femme de Claude*, was not. The protagonist, Claude Ruper, kills his wife, Césarine, who is guilty not only of infidelity but also, and improbably, of selling a state secret to a military enemy. The motive for the killing is thereby reinforced and removed from the domain of purely personal revenge. The public nevertheless found the private enforcement of so drastic a penalty on a female victim repugnant, however justly deserved. In addition the structure of the play was undoubtedly weak, not helped by a hazy symbolism in which Claude represented morality and conscience, and Césarine the Beast undermining, by adultery and treachery, the whole basis of French society. Dumas allowed himself to be drawn into a protracted controversy, and the anti-feminism of his pamphlet *L'Homme-Femme* caused a sensation.

Emile Perin had become general director of the Comédie-Française and, after a triumphant revival of *Le Demi-monde*, asked Dumas for a new play. The result was *L'Etrangère*, in which an American, Mrs Clarkson, seeks to arrange a wealthy marriage for her lover, the Duc de Septmonts. A suitable rich girl is found, but she is forced to accept the presence of Septmonts's mistress. He dies in a duel with Mrs Clarkson's husband, enabling the girl to marry the engineer she has always loved. In Dumas's eyes, social justice had been done by the removal of the duke, a social malignancy. The moral values exhibited in the play's resolution do not however withstand analysis. The play is simply a plea for easier divorce, which would have made the killing of Septmonts unnecessary, since his wife could have achieved happiness merely by divorcing him. The press was indignant, although the public enjoyed Bernhardt's acting.

Dumas's plays are important social history, telling us a good deal about French society, and they are sometimes acceptable entertainment, but they are generally thought to grow dramatically weaker as the portentous moral message is substituted for mid-century realism. The social problems are insufficiently dramatized.

PUBLICATIONS

Collections

Théâtre complet, 7 vols., 1882–93

Fiction

Aventures de quatre femmes et d'un perroquet, 6 vols., 1846–47
La Dame aux camélias, 2 vols., 1848; as *The Lady of the Camelias* n.d.
Césarine, 1848
Le Docteur Servans, 2 vols., 1848–49
Le Roman d'une femme, 4 vols., 1849

Antonine, 2 vols., 1849
La Vie à vingt ans, 2 vols., 1850
Tristan le roux, 3 vols., 1850; as *The Beggar of Nimes*, 1988
Trois hommes forts, 4 vols., 1850
Diane de Lys et Grangette, 3 vols., 1851
Le Régent Mustel, 2 vols., 1852 (originally published as *Les Revenants* as an offprint from *Le Pays*, 1852)
Contes et nouvelles, 1853
La Dame aux perles, 4 vols., 1853
Sophie Printems, 2 vols., 1854
Un cas de rupture, 1854

L'Affaire Clemenceau, 1866; as *The Clemenceau Case* n.d.

Plays

Atala, 1848
La Dame aux camélias (produced 1852), 1852; as *Camille*, 1934
Diane de Lys (produced 1853), 1853
Le Demi-monde (produced 1855), 1855; as *The Outer Edge of Society*, 1921
La Question d'argent (produced 1857), 1857; as *The Money Question*, 1915
Le Fils naturel (produced 1858), 1858; as *Le fils naturel* (in English), 1879
Un père prodigue (produced 1859), 1859
L'Ami des femmes (produced 1864), 1864; as *The Friend of Women* n.d.
Les Idées de Madame Aubray (produced 1867), 1867
Une visite de noces (produced 1871), 1872
La Princesse Georges (produced 1871), 1872; as *La Princesse Georges* (in English), 1881
La Femme de Claude (produced 1873), 1873; as *Claude's Wife*, n.d.
Monsieur Alphonse (produced 1873), 1874; as *M. Alphonse* (in English), 1886
L'Etrangère (produced 1876), 1877; as *The Foreigner*, 1881
La Princesse de Bagdad (produced 1881), 1881
Denise (produced 1885), 1885; as *Denise* (in English), 1885
Francillon (produced 1887), 1887

Verse

Péchés de jeunesse, 1847

Other

Histoire de la loterie, 1851
Histoire du "Supplice d'une femme," 1865
Les Madeleines repenties, 1869
Nouvelle lettre de Junius à son ami A.D., 1871
La Révolution plébéienne: lettres à Junius, 1871
Une lettre sur les choses du jour, 1871
Nouvelle lettre sur les choses du jour, 1871
L'Homme-Femme, 1872; as *Man-Woman*, 1873
Entr'actes, 3 vols., 1878–79
Les Femmes qui tuent et les femmes qui votent, 1880
La Question du divorce, 1880
Lettre à M. Naquet, 1882
La Recherche de la paternité, 1883
Nouveaux entr'actes, 1890

Critical and biographical study

Maurois, André, *Three Musketeers*: *A Study of the Dumas Family*, 1957

DURAS, Marguerite, (née Donnadieu), 1914–

Novelist, dramatist, script writer, film maker, journalist, and television presenter.

LIFE

Duras began her literary career as a novelist and short story writer but as she became increasingly aware of the difficulty of literary communication, she began to concentrate on drama, working as a script writer and film director. Her literary output came to act as springboard for creations in other media, with the same material often used several times. *La Musica*, for instance, was written as a television drama before being adapted for the theatre, turned into a novel, and then made into a film. Duras has also published much journalism, some of it in conjuction with her role as a TV presenter and some of it investigative in character.

Since the early 1970s her work has been chiefly directed towards cinema. Duras owes her success to a number of different factors. Her best work coincided with the peak of feminist interest in French cultural circles, and she was associated, on the whole wrongly, with the "new novel" and the "anti-novel" in the 1960s. Moreover, Alain Resnais invited her to write the script for *Hiroshima mon amour*. The first of his feature films, it displayed striking cinematographic innovations and won international acclaim. Finally, much of Duras's work centres on the crisis point in a relationship, avoiding if not the physical explicitness, at least the sexual boldness and interpretative difficulties of other female "new wave" writers. This makes her a popular choice as a college syllabus author representing new French writing, "feminist" in that her most strongly delineated characters are generally female.

Duras was born in what was formerly known as Indochina and is now Vietnam. Her father was a professor of mathematics and her mother a teacher. She went to school in Saigon and from 1931 studied in Paris for degrees in law and political science, graduating in both in 1935, when she started an administrative career in the French colonial office. She abandoned her job when the Germans occupied Paris and became a writer, publishing two unsuccessful works of fiction, *Les Impudents* and *La Vie tranquille*, in which however critics have retrospectively found evidence of developing talent. She was a communist for a time, but was expelled from the party for revisionism in 1950 and her early fiction is not politically committed. Her association with feminism in the 1970s was equally brief. Duras published three more novels in the early 1950s, *Un barrage contre le Pacifique*, *Le Marin de Gibraltar*, and *Les Petits Chevaux de Tarquinia*, of which the first furnished the material for a play and later a film

by René Clément (1958), and the second was made into a film by Tony Richardson (1966). In 1954 came a collection of short stories, *Des journées entières dans les arbres*, made into a play under the direction of Jean-Louis Barrault (1966) and a film (1976), and in 1955 *Le Square*, which was very popular in the US and was made into a successful play in 1960. It is the first of four novels, ending with *Le Vice-consul*, in which the impossibility of communication obtrudes into the writer's imagination. Plot is abandoned in these works, which attracted decreasing critical acclaim, as is traditional depth of characterization and stylistic effort.

In the meanwhile Duras published the novel *Moderato Cantabile*, later turning it, with Gérard Jarlot's help, into the script of the famous Peter Brook film. This was followed by a play, the script of *Hiroshima*, the novel *Dix heures et demie du soir en été* (turned into a film by Jules Dassin in 1966), and a further script in collaboration with Jarlot for Colpi's prize-winning *Une aussi longue absence*. The early 1960s saw the peak of Duras's journalistic activities, including her probe into the Ben Barka affair during the Algerian war. She wrote for a number of French and foreign periodicals, including various fashion magazines. She collaborated on two more film scripts in 1966 and turned the play *Les Viaducs de la Seine-et-Oise* (published in 1960) into a novel entitled *L'Amante anglaise*. Two volumes of *Théâtre* were followed by the 1969 *Détruire, dit-elle*, the first of Duras's novels whose film version she directed herself. The novel, which is about the interchange of identities within a group, provides a loose reference to the student uprising of 1968. Political points are also made in the film *Jaune le soleil* (1971) and the 1972 film of *Nathalie Granger*.

Although more conventional novels were to follow, mostly taking up old characters, locations, and themes, *L'Amour* of 1971 represents the self-extinction of the novel heralded by *Le Square*. A series of personal pronouns refers indifferently to generic prisons and beaches. *India Song* reproduces the action of *Le Vice-consul*, now reduced to mere images and memories. Duras devoted most of the 1970s to writing texts for the cinema and to making films, working in short, intense bursts. She once declared that writing was hopelessly constricting, whereas cinema made everything possible, increasing the means of communication a hundredfold, only to declare after her 1981 film *L'Homme atlantique* that the cinema is a snare, the written word the sole means of genuine communication. Since 1980, however, she has concentrated on writing slight pieces dealing with favourite themes such as the freedom of the individual. A special number of the *Cahiers du Cinéma* in June 1980 and a series of articles entitled *L'Eté* 80 present Duras's self-portrait.

WORKS

Duras's second novel, *La Vie tranquille*, is written in the first person and has virtually no plot. Its interest lies in the way understatement actually underlines the wistful longing of its youthful female narrator, although the work has been criticized for thinness and even banality. *Un barrage contre le Pacifique* confirms that Duras's real talent lies in the depiction of personal relationships, particularly through dialogue. The novel is indebted to Hemingway and Faulkner as well as Steinbeck and Caldwell, and Duras has clearly read Flaubert. However, there are too many digressions and almost violent authorial intrusions here regarding the social injustice suffered by the destitute colonial whites in Indochina. The last novel of clearly American inspiration is *Le Marin de Gibralter*, whose dominant theme is the horror and inevitability of solitude.

Les Petits Chevaux de Tarquinia reduces the narrative action even further to produce a discreet and subtle investigation into the difficulties of sincere communication. Though no more than a long short story, it succeeds in evoking a pervasive mood of desolation. *Des journées entières dans les arbres*, another long short story, reduces the plot still further, being a simple but successful exercise in the evocation of nostalgia for the innocence of childhood. *Le Square* is the turning point in Duras's fiction. Someone we suppose to be a maid, nameless and confused about her age, is in charge of a small boy and is joined on a park bench by an itinerant salesman. Both are world-weary and talk to one another in clichés. Although some sort of emotional intensity develops between these two people in the course of the narrative, it is doubtful whether the novel can in fact survive so much silence.

It is at this point that Duras's two paths diverge. On the one hand we have the immensely successful woman of the cinema, portraying sensitive relationships, compassionate and socially if not politically committed, the journalist writing for *Vogue* and the television presenter, making her novels into films and plays, and sometimes the other way round. Duras was still capable of writing novels unified by events as well as by moods and memories. On the other hand she now developed the techniques of *Le Square* through *L'Après-midi de Monsieur Andesmas* and *Le Ravissement de Lol V. Stein* to *Le Vice-consul*, in which the reader never finds out quite what happens. Critical comment and Duras appear to have felt that no renewal of fictional form could fruitfully continue in what had proved to be no more than a cul-de-sac. The pattern of generally impoverished middle-class characters winning temporary respites from spiritual voids by drinking too much, or rebelling, only to sink again into the oblivion of failure, was repeated with an ever sparser narrative and cinematic repertoire. It seemed that only total reticence could steer clear of tedious repetitiousness, and that no form of representative art, whether in literature or film, could adequately express Duras's vision, in spite of apparently inextinguishable flickerings of hope. However, in the brief *Emily L.* (1990), a woman and her lover sit in a bar overlooking the Seine estuary facing up to the end of their affair and watching an English couple whose story is an ironic commentary on their own relationship. To the uncomprehending characters destroying one another obsessively, the memories of violence and fear, and the unsentimental compassion is now added an elegiac sense. "Duras," one critic wrote, "has turned her attention to life's endings." Then in August 1991 Duras's new *L'Amant de la Chine du Nord* headed the best-seller list published by Elle.

PUBLICATIONS

Fiction

Les Impudents, 1943
La Vie tranquille, 1944
Un barrage contre le Pacifique, 1950; as *The Sea Wall*, 1952; as *A Sea of Troubles*, 1953
Le Marin de Gibraltar, 1952; as *The Sailor from Gibraltar*, 1966
Les Petits Chevaux de Tarquinia, 1953; as *The Little Horses of Tarquinia*, 1960
Des journées entières dans les arbres, 1954; as *Whole Days in the Trees*, 1981
Le Square, 1955; as *The Square*, 1959
Moderato Cantabile, 1958; as *Moderato Cantabile* (in English), 1960
Hiroshima mon amour, 1960; as *Hiroshima mon amour* (in English), 1961
Dix heures et demie du soir en été, 1960; as *10.30 on a Summer Night*, 1962
L'Après-midi de Monsieur Andesmas, 1962; as *The Afternoon of Mr Andesmas*, 1964
Le Ravissement de Lol V. Stein, 1964; as *The Ravishing of Lol Stein*, 1967; as *The Rapture of Lol V. Stein*, 1967
Le Vice-consul, 1965; as *The Vice-Consul*, 1968
L'Amante anglaise, 1967; as *L'Amante Anglaise* (in English), 1968
Détruire, dit-elle, 1969; as *Destroy, She Said*, 1970
Abahn Saban David, 1970
L'Amour, 1972
Ah! Ernesto, with Bernard Bonhomme, 1971
L'Amant, 1984; as *The Lover*, 1985
La Douleur, 1985; as *La Douleur* (in English), 1986
La Pute de la côte normande, 1986
Les Yeux bleus, cheveux noirs, 1986; as *Blue Eyes, Black Hair*, 1988
La Vie materielle, 1987
Emily L., 1987 as *Emily L* (in English), 1989
L'Amant de la Chine du Nord, 1991

Texts written or adapted for performance

Le Square, with Claude Martin, from the novel by Duras (produced, 1957; revised version, produced, 1965), included in *Théâtre 1*, 1965; as *The Square* (produced, 1961), in *Three Plays*, 1967
Hiroshima mon amour (screenplay), 1960; as *Hiroshima Mon Amour* (in English) 1961; with *Une Aussi Longue Absence*, 1966
Les Viaducs de la Seine-et-Oise, 1960; as *The Viaducts of Seine-et-Oise* (produced, as *The Viaduct*, 1967), in *Three Plays*, 1967
Une Aussi longue absence (screenplay), with Gérard Jarlot, 1961; as *Une Aussi Longue Absence*, with *Hiroshima Mon Amour*, 1966
Les Papiers d'Aspern, with Robert Antelme, adaptation of the play *The Aspern Papers* by Michael Redgrave based on the story by Henry James (produced, 1961)
Miracle en Alabama, with Gérard Jarlot, adaptation of the play *The Miracle Worker* by William Gibson (produced, 1961)
La Bête dans la jungle, with James Lord, adaptation of the story *The Beast in the Jungle* by Henry James (produced, 1962)
Théâtre 1 (includes *Les Eaux et fôrets*, *Le Square*, *La Musica*), 1965
Les Eaux et fôrets, in *Théâtre 1*, 1965; as *The Rivers and Forests* (produced, 1976), with *The Afternoon of Monsieur Andesmas*, 1964
La Musica, in *Théâtre 1*, 1965; as *The Music* (produced, 1966)
Des journées entières dans les arbres (produced, 1965), in *Théâtre 2*, 1968; as *Days in the Trees* (produced, 1966), in *Three Plays*, 1967

Three Plays, 1967

Théâtre 2 (includes *Suzanna Andler; Yes, peut-être; Le Shaga; Des journées entières dans les arbres; Un homme est venu me voir*), 1968

Le Shaga (also director; produced 1968), in *Théâtre 2*, 1968

Susanna Andler (produced, 1969), in *Théâtre 2*, 1968; as *Suzanna Andler* (produced, 1973), in *Suzanna Andler, La Musica, and L'Amante Anglaise*, 1975

L'Amante anglaise, from her own novel (produced, 1969), 1968; as *A Place Without Doors* (produced, 1970; as *The Lovers of Viorne*, produced, 1971); in *Suzanna Andler, La Musica, and L'Amante Anglaise*, 1975

Nathalie Granger; La Femme du Gange (screenplays), 1973

India Song (in French), 1973; as *India Song* (in English), 1976

Home (in French), from the play by David Storey, 1973

Suzanna Andler, La Musica, and L'Amante Anglaise, 1975

L'Eden cinéma (produced, 1977), 1977

Le Camion (screenplay), 1977

Le Navire Night, Césarée, Les Mains négatives, Aurélia Steiner, 1979

Vera Baxter; ou, Les Plages de l'Atlantique (screenplay), 1980

L'Homme assis dans le couloir, 1980

Agatha, 1981

L'Homme atlantique, 1982

Savannah Bay, 1983

La Maladie de la mort, 1983

Screenplays: *Hiroshima mon amour*, 1959; *Moderato Cant-*abile, with Gérard Jarlot and Peter Brook, 1960; *Une aussi longue absence (The Long Absence)*, with Gérard Jarlot, 1961; *10:30 P.M. Summer*, with Jules Dassin, 1966; *La Musica*, 1966; *Détruire, dit-elle (Destroy, She Said)*, 1969; *Les Rideaux blancs*, 1966; *Jaune le soleil*, 1971; *Nathalie Granger*, 1972; *La ragazza di Passaggio/La Femme du Gange*, 1973; *Ce que savait Morgan*, with others, 1974; *India Song*, 1975; *Des journées entières dans les arbres*, 1976; *Son nom de Venises dans Calcutta désert*, 1976; *Baxter—Vera Baxter*, 1977; *Le Camion*, 1977; *Le Navire Night*, 1978; *Césarée; Les Mains négatives; Aurélia Steiner*

Television play: *Sans merveille*, with Gérard Jarlot, 1964

Other

Territoires du féminin, with Marcelle Marini, 1977

L'Eté 80, 1980

Outside: papiers d'un jour, 1981

Critical studies

Cismaru, Alfred, *Marguerite Duras*, 1971

Murphy, Carol J., *Alienation and Absence in the Novels of Duras*, 1982

E

ÉLUARD, Paul (pseudonym of Eugène Grindel), 1895–1952.

Poet.

LIFE

Eluard was born the year before Breton, and two years before Aragon and Soupault; he was to form with them the core of the surrealist (q. v.) group of poets between 1924 and 1930. An only child, he was born in Paris into a family of modest means, who moved to Aulnay-sur-Bois, and then in 1908 back to Paris. Eluard's father was a book-keeper and his mother a dressmaker. The family spent weekends at Aulnay, and holidays in Switzerland or England.

Eluard had an uneventful secondary schooling, thanks to a scholarship, in the nearby Rue Clignancourt, and looked back on it with affection. Then, in 1912 he was sent for two years to a sanatorium in Davos. He read widely there, and met Hélène Dimitrovnie Diakonova, "Gala," who inspired his first love poetry, the genre at which he always excelled. Two or three hundred copies of his *Premiers poèmes* were printed at his own expense in 1913. In 1914 he returned to France and was mobilized in December. He had developed a precocious interest in old books and rare editions, and his early poetic style was noticeably eclectic as well as derivative. Eluard had clearly read Lamartine, Banville, Laforgue, and Verlaine. The *Revue des Oeuvres Nouvelles* pointed this out, while also publishing his prose "Dialogue des inutiles" in 1914. In 1916 Eluard signed for the first time with his pseudonym, the name of his maternal grandmother. The following year he married Gala, and in 1918 the couple had a daughter, Cécile. By the end of that year Eluard had published two more volumes of verse, *Le Devoir et l'inquiétude*, showing the influence of Whitman, and *Poèmes pour la paix*, which led to his friendship with Jean Paulhan.

In the years immediately after the war he met Breton, Aragon, Soupault, and Tristan Tzara, was attracted to the dada (q. v.) movement, and published *Les Nécessités de la vie et les conséquences des rêves*, which reflects an interest in Freud, and in Breton's "automatic writing." In 1922 he published *Répétitions*, before breaking with the dada movement in 1923. In 1924 he published *Mourir de ne pas mourir*, which showed a conflict between tradition and experiment. Eluard tried to resolve it with a voyage round the world. This was the year of Breton's first surrealist manifesto. Eluard also published works jointly with Max Ernst (*Les Malheurs des immortels*) and with Benjamin Péret (*152 proverbes mis au goût du jour*).

On his return, Eluard became friendly with Picasso, Chirico, Arp, Miró, Dali, and other surrealist or avant-garde artists. He also contributed to the surrealist reviews, *La Révolution Surréaliste*, *Le Surréalisme au Service de la Révolution*, and *Minotaure*. His *Capitale de la douleur* of 1926 is mostly surrealist in

tone and imagery, and Eluard became the principal poet of the movement. Among his surrealist collections are *L'Amour la poésie*, *La Vie immédiate*, *La Rose publique*, and *Donner à voir*, as well as the 1930 volume written jointly with Breton, *L'Immaculée Conception*. He also published a prose fantasy, *Les Dessous d'une vie ou la pyramide humaine*, in 1926, the year in which he joined the communist party.

In 1929 Eluard met Maria Benz, "Nusch," and the following year, during which Breton published his second surrealist manifesto, he separated from Gala. He was eventually to marry Nusch in 1934. From 1932 his poetry had abandoned dreams and fantasies to celebrate life in the real world. Breton was more interested in surrealism's intellectual and aesthetic roles, while Eluard had wanted the movement to develop on political lines towards a proletarian revolution. His interests were now liberal humanist idealism and the pursuit of human happiness. He left the communist party in 1933, and his new view of life appears in *La Vie immédiate*, *Les Yeux fertiles*, *Les Mains libres*, and *Cours naturel*. He renewed his affiliation to the communist party as the menace of fascism increased in 1938, and this led to a break with Breton.

Eluard was mobilized in 1939 and returned to Paris in 1940. From 1942 he worked for the Resistance, for which he wrote some of its best-known poetry, in particular "Liberté," published in *Poésie et vérité*, his own selection from his poems, and the pieces in the collection *Au rendez-vous allemand*. An international figure after the war, Eluard travelled to Italy, Yugoslavia, Greece, and Poland, which led to a volume summarizing his search for happiness and for a resolution of loneliness, *Poésie ininterrompue I*. In Switzerland at the time, he was devastated to learn of Nusch's death in 1946. In that year he also published *Le Dur Désir de durer*.

From now on Eluard's poetry, apart from *Poèmes politiques* of 1948, centres on the problems of unhappiness and the pain of loss, and on the difficulty of making any moral statement of belief in man and his destiny, as in *Pouvoir tout dire* and *Le Phénix*. In 1949 he had met Dominique Lemor in Mexico. She became his third wife in 1951, and his poetry shows renewed hope. Eluard remained a convinced communist until his death, and the underlying moral structure of human experience, the possibility of love as the basis for life, and a belief in human goodness are all apparent in the posthumous *Poésie ininterrompue II*. In 1952 he published *Les Sentiers et les routes de la poésie*, which is in dramatic form. In September of that year Eluard had a heart attack and on 18 November he died. He had made several selections from his own poems, including *Poésie et vérité*, *Choix de poèmes*, and *Le Livre ouvert*.

WORKS

Apart perhaps from the youthful and happy surrealist experi-

sity of initially adolescent emotion, with Flaubert's being the more passive role. He told Le Poittevin's sister, Laure de Maupassant, how jealous he felt in 1846 at her brother's marriage. It was Le Poittevin's Byronic romanticism, his disillusion with Christianity, his attraction to oriental mysticism, and his liking for Edgar Quinet's *Ahasvérus* (1833) which now informed Flaubert's imaginative development. During 1838 Flaubert wrote a number of short stories, and later that year, at not quite 17, his only autobiographical work, *Mémoires d'un fou*, dedicated to Le Poittevin. It was to be followed by *Smarh*, which he completed in April 1839.

In 1838 he had languished at Trouville among memories of Elisa, read Rousseau's *Confessions*, Goethe's *Die Leiden des jungen Werthers*, and Musset's recently published *La Confession d'un enfant du siècle*. He became a dayboy again, smoking his cigar at a café opposite the school while waiting for the bell to ring. *Mémoires d'un fou* is almost a pastiche of Byron and Goethe in romantic (q.v.) confessional style, written naively enough for the emotion aroused by the memory of Elisa to pierce through the unsophisticated text, and for the attitudinizing elsewhere to be clear. *Smarh* is also inspired by Byron and Goethe, although this time the Goethe of *Faust: erster Teil*, as translated by Nerval in 1829. Formally, however, it depends more on *Ahasvérus*, having a prologue, four "days," and an epilogue, and like that work it deals with the destiny of humanity. Grandiosely self-indulgent in its cynicism, prolix and lacking in artistic control, *Smarh* is of interest only in the context of Flaubert's development, and particularly of his movement towards the idea that art might perhaps offer a solution to the problems of life. Gautier's *Mademoiselle de Maupin*, with its famous preface, had appeared in 1836, and Flaubert drew heavily on its doctrine of "L'Art pour l'art" (q.v.) for a school essay in 1839.

It was Le Poittevin who elicited from Flaubert his two bacchic stories extolling drunkenness, written in 1838 and 1839. Both glorify death through drink and, while Flaubert's youthful cult of what he thought of as "Rabelaisian" need not be taken very seriously, the over-indulgence in adolescent world-weariness encouraged by his relationship with Le Poittevin was to cause him a great deal of trouble 10 years later. Many of the later letters between Flaubert and Le Poittevin were burnt. Some have been suppressed as too pornographic for publication. Those that have been destroyed must certainly have been obscene. Meanwhile, after the drinking story of August 1839, Flaubert gave up writing for three years.

In his last year at school Flaubert was one of several ringleaders who organized a protest against a master. He was expelled, and prepared alone for his baccalauréat in 1840 while, he said, learning Homer and Demosthenes by heart. He passed his baccalauréat and seems to have been drawn towards the cultivation of mystical experiences. Symptoms of a frustrated sexuality were relieved when later in 1840 his father sent him on a trip to the West of France and then to Corsica as a reward for success in the baccalauréat. Accompanied on his return only by a friend of his father, Flaubert stayed at a hotel in Marseilles kept by a Creole woman, Eulalie Foucaud de Langlade, who apparently enticed him into her room. They became lovers, and we have four passionate love letters which she later wrote to him. She was 35 and had a daughter while, by all accounts, Flaubert was a very handsome 18-year-old. He returned home, having apparently regained his self-confidence, reconciled now to studying law.

We do not know what sort of life he led during the year following his return. He registered as a student in the Paris law faculty in November 1841, intending to attend lectures from January 1842, when he duly made arrangements for the summer examinations before returning to Rouen two days later. He seems to have gone on reading Latin and Greek, but professed to Chevalier in January that he was simply idling. His attendance did not qualify him to take the August examination, so he went to Trouville, where he met the Collier family, four girls and a boy, whom the Flauberts got to know well. Le Poittevin was contemptuous about the reasons why he presumed Flaubert was unmoved by the experience of swimming with the girls. The Colliers, who were hard up, had an apartment in Paris where Flaubert used to visit them when he settled there in the autumn of 1842. In 1845 he became quite close to the second Collier girl, Henrietta. There had been a fire at Trouville in 1842 in which Flaubert had carried her to safety, and in 1845 her mother even wanted him to marry her, which was quite enough to frighten him off. In any case Flaubert had by now met Elisa Schlésinger again. Meanwhile, in 1842, he had written *Novembre*, a novel which he was subsequently pleased never to have published, although he showed it to Baudelaire as late as 1860, and to the Goncourts three years after that.

In November 1842 Flaubert took a small room in Paris, studied, and passed the examination he had not taken in August. It is difficult to disentangle the boasting from the facts, but he claimed in a letter to Louise Colet of 24 September 1846 that he had made love to a prostitute with a cigar in his mouth to demonstrate his contempt for the proceedings. He probably caught a venereal disease, from which he was recovering in 1844. He was certainly to catch syphilis in 1850. He spent some time with the Colliers. Le Poittevin thought he was considering marriage, which can only have been to Henrietta, but the Colliers moved out to Chaillot and Flaubert found it too far to go to visit them. He frequented the studio of the sculptor James Pradier, a former lover of Juliette Drouet, Victor Hugo's mistress, kept up with Pradier's wife Louise after she had left her husband, dined weekly with the Schlésingers, but came to dislike Paris. He failed his examinations in August 1843, but in March had met Maxime du Camp, with whom his friendship soon blossomed. It turned into warm affection, comparable to that which linked him to Le Poittevin, in which Flaubert's role was again submissive. Flaubert exchanged rings with Du Camp, who was a successful author and literary personality. In 1877, long after they had gone their different ways, they agreed to burn their letters to one another. The few that survive, because they were part of Du Camp's travel diary, contain strong expressions of physical affection. Du Camp had many female lovers and would have liked to add Louise Pradier to their number, but she was in love with Flaubert, who was not interested.

In 1843 Flaubert began the first version of *L'Education sentimentale*. Finished in 1845, it bears very little relation to the novel he was to publish under that name in 1869. He had to stop work on it while preparing for the examinations he failed, but then took it up again when he fell ill in January 1844, probably of a venereal complaint. He had had some form of seizure while driving with his brother from Rouen to Deauville, and had fallen to the ground while himself holding the reins. His brother bled him and took him back to Rouen, where his father took over. Flaubert returned to the novel, and finished it in January 1845, but was never completely well again. He tried to renew his registration as a student, but the nervous seizures became too frequent for him to carry on planning a professional career. His father sold the land at Deauville on which he had been planning to build, and bought a property at Croisset, a village a few miles downstream from Rouen, specifically on account of his invalid son. Flaubert was to live for the rest of his life in the small 18th-century château with an avenue of limes and a garden running alongside the river. He took up Greek again, read Shakespeare, swam, and rowed, but finally gave up boating since he disliked the need, imposed on him by his mother, of having a companion with him in case he should have a seizure.

Du Camp, who never understood Flaubert's meticulous perfectionism, left for the East in May 1844, and Flaubert renewed his friendship with Le Poittevin, who had felt hurt at the closeness of his association with Du Camp, and of whom Du Camp now felt jealous in turn. On 3 March 1845 Flaubert's sister Caroline married Emile Hamard, and from April to June the couple travelled in Italy with Flaubert and his parents. Flaubert was deeply affected at Genoa by Breughel's *Temptation of Saint Anthony*. The trip was not a great success. Flaubert's father's eyes were giving trouble, Caroline felt unwell, and in Rouen Achille was being overstretched, so the journey had to be cut short. The family spent the summer at Tréport. In November Flaubert's father fell ill. An operation by Achille failed to save him, and he died on 15 January 1846. On 21 January Caroline gave birth to her daughter, only to die herself on 20 March. Flaubert feared, as it turned out needlessly, for his mother's physical and mental health. In July that year Le Poittevin married a Maupassant, the sister-in-law of his sister, who was now Laure de Maupassant.

That month Flaubert went to Paris to commission a bust of his dead sister from Pradier. While there, on 29 July, he met Louise Colet, who was being kept by the father of her daughter, Victor Cousin, now minister of education. She was a mediocre poet but a very attractive woman who became highly skilled at the particular form of social climbing which involves exploiting the artistically and intellectually gifted, although Chateaubriand and Sainte-Beuve are known to have resisted her solicitations of patronage, and she was stingingly attacked by Alphonse Karr in his satirical paper *Les Guêpes*. On 4 August Flaubert and she became lovers. He left 120 letters to her. Those from the second period of their association, some of them very long, contain Flaubert's most important reflections on the nature of literature, and at times constitute almost a diary of the composition of *Madame Bovary*.

Even at its most passionate, the relationship was not an easy one. Louise could not understand that Flaubert needed an excuse to keep his mother happy every time he left home, and could not invite her to Croisset. She wanted more of his attention and energies than he could give her; she wanted to go away alone with him, and above all she wanted a child by him. He swore she was the only woman for whom he had ever made a journey, and finally agreed to meet her at Mantes, halfway between Rouen and Paris, for an afternoon. They ended up staying the night together, but meanwhile Flaubert's mother had been waiting for him at Rouen station and had spent a sleepless night. Next morning she was on the platform in a state of acute anxiety. Louise wrote a poem about it, and Flaubert could never bear to go to Mantes again. He was terrified when Louise appeared to be showing the usual early signs of pregnancy, but it was a false alarm. Louise continued to urge the overriding claims of love,

while Flaubert remained conscious of the demands of art. There were scoldings, reprimands, bitternesses, and jealousies, and a hint of fetichism has been noted in Flaubert's devotion to the slippers he took from Louise. The first phase of the relationship ended when, in 1848, Louise had a child by her husband, an only moderately successful musician.

Louis Bouilhet had been a pupil of Flaubert's father before abandoning medicine and opening a crammer in Paris. Flaubert and he became close friends on Le Poittevin's marriage, and Bouilhet, who spent weekends at Croisset, became Flaubert's literary guide. Flaubert thought highly of him as a poet and relied on him to such an extent that, without him, it is unlikely that he would have produced his great novels. They planned dramatic scenarios together. When Flaubert and Du Camp came to write the account of their 1847 journey together through Britanny and the Loire valley, Bouilhet appears to have advised Flaubert on the composition of his section of the travelogue, published posthumously as *Par les champs et par les grèves*. Du Camp had had difficulty getting Flaubert's mother to authorize the trip, and she met them at the towns where they stopped off. Flaubert was ill only once while he was away. In 1851 Louise Colet was to disapprove of the realistic detail he gave in his account of the journey.

At the end of February 1848 Flaubert was in Paris for the revolutionary fighting, which he was vividly to recall in *L'Education sentimentale*, but in April he was at Le Poittevin's deathbed, where he sat for two days and nights. Two months later, recalling the fair at Rouen, the Breughel in Genoa, and the influence of Le Poittevin during the years of their intimacy, Flaubert started to write the self-indulgently romantic, confessional *La Tentation de saint Antoine*, begun "on 24 May 1848 at three p.m." and finished "12 September 1849 at three-twenty p.m.," as he meticulously noted on the manuscript, adding the further gratuitous information that it was a sunny and windy Wednesday, and thereby revealing the habit of mind which prevented him from ever knowingly throwing away pieces of paper with writing on them, although he did in fact burn some. The text was an epic of mankind in the vein of Byron and Quinet, with metaphysics by Goethe, tinged with pseudo-mysticism. Like *Smarh*, it was in dramatic form. Writing it, Flaubert had regained his old fluency, and he was excited by his text.

Du Camp obtained permission from Flaubert's mother to take him on a trip to the East. Before going, Flaubert insisted first on finishing *La Tentation*, and then on reading it to Du Camp and Bouilhet. Du Camp's *Souvenirs littéraires* (1882–83) tells us that the reading took four days, with two four-hour sessions a day. Du Camp and Bouilhet agreed early on to make no comment at all until it was over. Before the last session they agreed that Flaubert was still allowing his talent to be dissolved in romantic fantasy, that his whole literary future was at stake, and that he had to be told the truth, although they were to differ on what Flaubert should do about it. Both of them knew that the flood tide of romanticism had long receded, but since we only know what happened from Du Camp's account, written over 30 years later, and since Du Camp may have been jealous of Flaubert, although he had not published anything at all since reaching adulthood, the legend must be treated with caution. Du Camp, who certainly wanted to be helpful, says he and Bouilhet agreed that "Il fallait l'arrêter sur cette voie où il perdrait ses qualités maîtresses (We had to stop him from following this path where he was going to lose all his greatest qualities)," and that after the reading Bouilhet said: "Nous pensons qu'il faut jeter cela au feu et n'en reparler jamais (We think you should throw that in the fire and never mention it again)."

That would have been uncharacteristic of Bouilhet but, whatever was actually said, it changed the course of Flaubert's life, and of the history of French literature. The three of them sat up all night discussing the text line by line until eight a.m. Flaubert was hurt, but recognized that his friends had operated on "the cancer of lyricism" just in time. Writing *La Tentation* had been "a deeply voluptuous pleasure." Thereafter he wrote only painstakingly, at immense cost in terms of care, effort, and control, sometimes screeching with pent-up emotion in a letter to Louise Colet after a night's work. A whole night's work could sometimes produce nothing. A page could take five days, or 20 pages a month of seven-hour days, or again 25 pages could take six weeks. To postpone the agony of composition, Flaubert was to spend weeks researching and documenting, for *Madame Bovary*, for instance, the symptoms of arsenic poisoning, the sorts of operation available for various types of club foot, and the eye complaint for which Homais treats the blind beggar. The result, however, included three of the world's greatest literary masterpieces, *Madame Bovary, L'Education sentimentale*, and *Trois contes*. Du Camp was the advocate of outward literary success based on skill, ambition, and industriously keeping up with the fashions (the recipe for his own success) rather than on any intensity of imaginative effort. It was Bouilhet, himself considerably helped by Du Camp to literary success, who, until his departure from Rouen in October 1853, came to check every line of *Madame Bovary* as Flaubert produced it.

Flaubert left Croisset on 22 October 1849, said an emotional farewell to his mother in Nogent, where she was to stay with relations, and, alone in the carriage on the way to Paris, simply wept, wanting to return home every time the train stopped. Du Camp found him sobbing on the floor of his apartment, "I'll never see my mother again." In the notebooks which he had left unfilled after his Corsican journey, but had not taken to Brittany, Flaubert kept detailed notes. Du Camp and he spent two months in Cairo, where they were summoned by the famous courtesan Kuschiuk Hanem. She danced for them the pornographic "danse de l'abeille," a description of which Flaubert was to use for Salomé's dance in "Hérodias," and Flaubert returned twice to spend the night with her. They then travelled up the Nile and across the desert by camel to Beirut. Flaubert caught syphilis and a letter from Du Camp provoked from Flaubert's mother a plea for his speedy return, so the rest of their journey, which would have been even more dangerous than that which they had just completed, had to be curtailed. They returned via Rhodes, Smyrna, and Constantinople, where they were entertained by Baudelaire's mother, anxious to know about her son's literary reputation, and her husband, the consul. A Murillo virgin in the Corsini gallery in Rome reminded Flaubert of Elisa and affected him deeply. The mercury treatment for his syphilis had deprived him of much of his hair, and his mother was horrified by her son's bloated and aged appearance when she met him in Rome 21 months after his departure. By July 1851 he was back at Croisset.

The East had completed Flaubert's disenchantment with the romantic aesthetic. He was fascinated by the "harmony of contrasts," "perfumes and nauseating smells," "gold-braided rags and vermin," "half-rotted skeletons and golden fruit." He had discovered something very close to Baudelaire's aesthetic. The

artist's function, as he saw it, was to create beauty out of the repulsive raw material of life. The portrayal of Emma's death in *Madame Bovary* was to elevate the harmony of contrasts to new aesthetic heights. Meanwhile the journey had put a strain on Flaubert's relations with Du Camp, of whom despite himself he was clearly sometimes envious. Du Camp did not linger in Italy but went off to Paris to refound the *Revue de Paris* with Louis de Cormenin and Gautier, taking over the name of Véron's successful 1829 review which had been killed off by the cheap press in 1845. Gautier had by now abandoned his "L'Art pour l'art" philosophy and is alleged by Arsène Houssaye to have come round to regarding literature, like handkerchiefs, as a commodity available in different qualities. The new review, which first appeared in October 1851, advertised that it was to be politically independent, and would alter and cut nothing it printed. It was to publish a quite heavily cut text of *Madame Bovary*.

Flaubert started work on *Madame Bovary* on 19 September 1851. He interrupted it to visit London with his mother to see the Great Exhibition, and to spend three weeks in Paris during the coup d'état that December. Otherwise he would deal with the post and the papers at 10 a.m., drink his first glass of water, and, smoke the first of his 20 pipes. His mother then sat with him until he got up. An enormous meal at 11 was followed by a walk, lessons with his niece, reading until seven, and dinner. Flaubert would again sit with his mother until she went to bed between nine and 10. He would then work most of the night. Bouilhet visited on Sundays. Isabel Hutton came as governess to Achille's children in November 1851, and was succeeded by Juliet Herbert, probably in 1854 and after a gap.

Within weeks of his return to Croisset, Flaubert was in contact again with Louise Colet. Juliette Récamier had died of cholera on 11 May 1849 and Louise had apparently forged a document which authorized her to publish Benjamin Constant's letters to Mme Récamier, which she arranged to do in *La Presse*, where they began to appear on 3 July 1849. The heirs stopped publication and sued Louise, who lost the case. Her husband had died in April 1851, and she was now in financial difficulties and eager to provoke Flaubert into marriage. Flaubert showed her *La Tentation* and the early *L'Education*, both of which she admired. He resumed their liaison, and she had a brief affair with Bouilhet, which both sides reported to Flaubert. It looks as if she even came to Croisset, and she certainly ferreted Flaubert out when he was staying in Paris in a hotel where he thought he would be safe from her. He saw her for the last time in 1854. She published a novel, *L'Histoire d'un soldat*, which included an unkind portrait of him, thinly disguised, had an affair with Champfleury, and, when Feydeau published *Fanny* in 1858, cashing in on the notoriety of *Madame Bovary*, made an approach to him. She was also unkind to Flaubert, as also to Vigny and Musset, depicted in the character of "Léonce" in *Lui* of 1859. Meanwhile Flaubert went on protecting his privacy, sometimes using his mother as an excuse. His imagination needed solitude rather than the external stimulation on which Du Camp relied. In a letter to Du Camp of 26 June 1852, Flaubert wrote: "May I die like a dog rather than hasten by one second a sentence of mine which is not ready."

Madame Bovary was finished in April 1856. Meanwhile, as if to steal Flaubert's thunder, in 1854 Champfleury had serialized his novel about provincial adultery, *Les Bourgeois de Molinchart* (1855), thereby becoming leader of the realist (q.v.) school. Flaubert went to live in Paris to correct his proofs, and

while there went to great lengths to ensure the success of Bouil-het's *Madame de Montarcy* at the Odéon on 6 November. Bouil-het was too nervous to sit through the performance, which was greeted enthusiastically by both public and critics. The *Revue de Paris*, which was to serialize *Madame Bovary*, was now run by Du Camp, Louis Ulbach, and Laurent Pichat, and there were serious difficulties with the censorship, which had become dra-conian since the coup d'état. The *Revue* was considered too lib-eral. The editors insisted on cuts, and Flaubert was finally obliged to consent to some. Others were made without his con-sent.

The novel appeared in six parts from 1 October to 15 Decem-ber 1856. The full text, with the cuts restored, was published in volume form by Michel Lévy at the end of April 1857, but not before a German edition had been pirated from the *Revue de Paris* text. The *Revue* paid 2,000 francs, the Germans naturally nothing, and Lévy 800 francs for all rights for five years. He did give Flaubert an extra 500 francs in August 1857, but the first printing amounted to 6,750 copies, and there were two further impressions by Lévy in 1857, one in 1858, and an emended edi-tion in 1862, together with a cheap one-volume edition. Further editions were to follow in 1869 and 1873. *Le Nouvelliste de Rouen* suspended simultaneous publication with the *Revue* when a dossier of things published in the *Revue* by other authors or in other numbers, compiled by an outraged Flaubert, came into the hands of a journalist who published it, thereby drawing the attention of the authorities to Flaubert's novel, and bringing down the famous prosecution of January 1857 on Flaubert him-self, Pichat the editor, and Pillet the printer. They were all found not guilty of outrage against public morality and religion, but were not awarded costs. Champfleury recoiled from some of Flaubert's realism, and Duranty wrote a highly critical review in *Le Réalisme*, taking to extremes his dislike of the unflinching details of appearance and behaviour which the novel contains. The review which gave Flaubert the most pleasure was Baude-laire's in *L'Artiste* for 18 October 1857.

In the meanwhile fragments of the second version of *La Ten-tation de saint Antoine* appeared in *L'Artiste* from December 1856 to February 1857. By 1 September 1857 Flaubert had started *Salammbô*, research for which was to include a six-week visit to North Africa in the spring of 1858. He now spent most of his winters in Paris, but wrote mostly at Croisset. His Paris apartment became celebrated in the literary world, notable members of which he received each Sunday. Among the habitués were Sainte-Beuve, Taine, Turgenev, Le Poittevin's nephew Guy de Maupassant, Gautier, Feydeau, and the Gon-court brothers. His mother rented an apartment one floor lower in the same building. From 1857 Bouilhet was the municipal librarian at Mantes. Flaubert now formed a close friendship with Jules Duplan, his letters to whom contain outspokenly porno-graphic passages, contrasting strongly with the works, in which the seduction scenes which so horrified censors, editors, and reviewers were in fact remarkable for their reticence and the use of controlled innuendo in place of explicit statement.

When Flaubert returned from North Africa on 5 June 1858, he realized he was going to have to scrap *Salammbô* and start again. As ever, other, easier projects tempted him, leaving traces in the "carnets" or notebooks. The *Revue de Paris* was suppressed in 1859. Du Camp went first to the *Revue des Deux Mondes* (*RDM*, q.v.) and then, in 1864, to the *Journal des Débats*. He and Flaub-ert reforged their friendship. The Goncourts were invited to a

reading of parts of *Salammbô* in May 1861, though the novel was completed only on 30 June 1862. Flaubert wanted 30,000 francs for it, but had to settle with Lévy for 10,000 francs, the deal to include a renewal of the rights to *Madame Bovary* and the first refusal of his next modern novel. Lévy also extracted permission to claim for publicity purposes that he had in fact paid 30,000 francs. Much larger sums were paid by the newspa-pers, which needed the "romans-feuilletons" to fill that part of the four pages for which they could not rely on getting daily news, but censorship of newspapers was much stricter than that of books. Hugo claimed that the famous 300,000-franc payment in advance for *Les Misérables* might have been virtually dou-bled had the novel been serialized. Flaubert went on to sell *L'Education sentimentale* to Lévy in 1869 for 16,000 francs, since the novel was in two volumes, but the 1862 agreement expired on 1 January 1873. Since Flaubert had quarrelled with Lévy in 1872, he went over on that date to Charpentier and Lemerre, more usually associated with the Parnassian (q.v.) poets.

Salammbô appeared on 24 November 1862 and was an instant success, bringing with it all the usual trappings, an opera, a stage parody, a new petit four, fashionable invitations of all sorts, entrée into the most exclusive salons, and the cross of the Légion d'Honneur. It also brought a number of new women friends, Mlle Leroyer de Chantpie, Amélie Bosquet, whose lover Flaub-ert wished in vain to become, and Mme Roger des Genettes, together with some well-known inhabitants of the demi-monde, Suzanne Lagier, Apollonie Sabatier, and Jane de Tourbey, who would be left a fortune by one of her lovers and acquire a title by marrying another. She became Mme la Comtesse de Loynes, a power in the Third Republic, and a close friend of Flaubert. It now seems certain that Flaubert had a series of short but pas-sionate interludes with Juliet Herbert in the 1870s.

In 1862 Flaubert was invited to join the famous dinners at the Restaurant Magny, which were also attended by Gautier, Renan, Sainte-Beuve, Taine, Turgenev, and the Goncourts. He got to know the Princesse Mathilde, forming a very close friendship with her, and George Sand, who was 17 years older than he was, and whom, up until her death in 1876, he came to regard almost as a second mother. With her he was able to have serious con-versations about literature. He went to visit her at Nohant, twice had her to stay at Croisset, and even invited her to the hitherto all-male Magny dinners. The Princesse Mathilde, Napoleon's cousin and the tsar's niece, was all-powerful in the Paris of the Second Empire, and probably its most famous hostess, receiving family and royalty on Sundays, ministers and ambassadors on Tuesdays, and artists, musicians, and literary Paris on Wednes-days, the salon for which she is now remembered. Her habitués included the ubiquitous Sainte-Beuve, Renan, Mérimée, Littré, Gautier, Coppée, Dumas *père* and *fils*, and Ary Scheffer. Flaub-ert stayed with her for weeks at a time, and it was for her that he wrote *L'Education sentimentale*. In spite of his failure to write successfully for the stage, the period from *Salammbô* to Bouil-het's death in 1869 was the happiest in Flaubert's life. He nev-ertheless made eight vain attempts to get his play *Le Château des coeurs* staged, and had to withdraw *Le Candidat* after three performances. The peak of his social success was the invitation, which he accepted, to attend the grand ball at the Tuileries on 10 June 1867 for all royal foreign guests to the International Exhi-bition.

Flaubert's niece Caroline married a timber merchant on 6

April 1864, when she was 18. Caroline, who was to live to the age of 85, dying in 1931, was obstinate, ambitious, snobbish, and inconsiderate. She had been brought up by Flaubert and his mother, and Flaubert was doubtful about the marriage, mostly on the grounds that Commanville's business was not sufficiently well established, and he wanted a rich husband for his niece, even if the alternative were to have been a genius without money. Commanville sometimes styled himself "de Commanville," but he had no right to the "de" or even to the Commanville name, being in fact illegitimate, and Flaubert found it disturbing to penetrate behind this wall of pretence. In his new fashionable life he himself had begun to slide into debt, sharing with Balzac and Sue a curious passion for gloves, for which he owed 500 francs, although he could no more have worked with Balzac's enormous financial pressures than Balzac could have without them. He borrowed from Duplan, and 5,000 francs from his publisher, but in 1865 his mother still had to sell a farm, giving half of the proceeds to each of her children, and Flaubert was in trouble again in 1866. In 1867 he put all his affairs into the hands of Commanville, and lost everything.

On 1 September 1864 Flaubert formally began *L'Education sentimentale*, although he had actually been working on it since 1862. It was "finished" on 16 May 1869. He had written to Elisa Schlésinger in 1856 to say he could not go to Baden for her daughter's wedding, and again in 1859 to commiserate on the death of her mother. In December 1862 he heard that Elisa had been in a mental home for 10 months. Du Camp, who went annually to Baden, wrote to Flaubert that he had seen her, and that she had been released. Notes for *L'Education* made in 1863, when the novel was going to be called "Madame Moreau" as a counter-title to *Madame Bovary*, make it clear that the novel was to be about Elisa and himself, and not yet the "portrait of the age" which it became. In July 1865 Flaubert went to Baden to see the model for his novel's proposed central character, and Elisa may have come to Paris in March 1867.

In 1867 Du Camp published *Les Forces perdues*, rather preempting Flaubert's subject during the long gestation of his novel, as Champfleury had done with *Les Bourgeois de Molinchart*. The Princesse Mathilde had had Bouilhet promoted to librarian at Rouen in 1868, when his health was already giving way. He died on 18 July 1869, and on 17 November Michel Lévy published *L'Education sentimentale* to a chorus of hostile reviews, the most vicious coming from Barbey d'Aurevilly. Banville alone was publicly favourable in *Le Constitutionnel*. An attack by Amélie Bosquet in *La Voix des Femmes* caused Flaubert particular pain, and ended their friendship. Flaubert spent Christmas 1869 with George Sand, and on his return immediately busied himself preparing an edition of Bouilhet's poems, trying to get his last play performed, and having a statue erected to him in Rouen. Sainte-Beuve had died in October 1869, and in March 1870 Flaubert's closest remaining friend, Jules Duplan, also died, followed in June by Jules de Goncourt. His mother died in April 1872 and George Sand in 1876. In 1875 Flaubert sold everything to save Commanville from bankruptcy, and had to live in penury for the rest of his life.

When war broke out in 1870, Flaubert enlisted as a lieutenant in the Garde Nationale, although he asked George Sand to note that he was defending a republic in which he did not believe. He hid the manuscript of the third version of *La Tentation de saint Antoine* in the grounds at Croisset, left for Rouen with his mother and the old servant Juliette, and resigned from the indis-

ciplined Garde Nationale. Caroline was busy learning German in London. After the war Elisa Schlésinger, whose husband had died in February 1871, came to Trouville and stayed at Croisset with Flaubert and his mother. She returned to Paris in 1872 for her son's wedding, the last time Flaubert was to see her. She was permanently in a mental hospital from 1875 until her death in 1888. When *La Tentation de saint Antoine* was finished on 1 July 1872, Flaubert decided to keep it until his contract with Lévy ran out, and to publish it at the same time as his next book, which was to be *Bouvard et Pécuchet*. In October 1872 Gautier died and, surrounded by such constant reminders of mortality, Flaubert now regretted having no children. He began to feel more cheerful in 1873, however, and went to stay with George Sand at Nohant in March. He made one last close male friend in Edouard Laporte and in 1872 managed to get Bouilhet's play *Aïssa* produced at the Odéon, where it had only 20 performances. He himself produced his own *Le Candidat* on 11 March 1874, though he had to withdraw it after the third performance. Antoine put it on again in 1910, but it was performed only once.

In March 1874 Flaubert agreed with Charpentier to publish *La Tentation de saint Antoine*, which appeared on 1 April. The first printing of 2,000 copies lasted only a week, and three other editions in 1875 and 1880 were sold out before Flaubert's death. The press was not enthusiastic and Barbey d'Aurevilly's now expectedly unpleasant review appeared in *Le Constitutionnel* on 20 April. In May 1875 Flaubert moved again within Paris, just a month before Commanville's threatened bankruptcy. He tried to borrow from the Princesse Mathilde, but her lawyer blocked the transaction. Croisset had been left to Caroline, but Flaubert had life tenure. Between them, Flaubert and Laporte found the money to stave off Commanville's disaster, which left Commanville, according to Flaubert, owing him a million francs which he had no hope of ever seeing. For the first time in his life, he tried to find a paid post. Caroline moved in with him, encouraged him to get a job, behaved with her accustomed selfishness, and eventually crowded Flaubert out of his own Paris flat.

Flaubert went to stay with a friend at Concarneau for two months in the autumn of 1875, but was unable to get on with Bouvard and wrote instead "La Légende de saint Julien l'Hospitalier," which was finished by the end of February 1876. The "legend" was an established genre. Liszt had published two famous ones for the piano in 1866, and it is vital for an understanding of Flaubert's conte that the genre is incorporated into the title. It emphasizes that Flaubert had no more intention than Liszt of writing history, and should instantly draw attention to the irony of the piece, a factor which keeps escaping modern biographers and critics. Between February and August 1876, Flaubert wrote "Un coeur simple" for George Sand. Unhappily she died before she could read it. He then wrote "Hérodias," finishing it on 1 February 1877. Turgenev had negotiated a Russian sale for the first two contes and Charpentier published the set of three as Trois contes on 24 April 1877. "Un coeur simple" also appeared in seven instalments in Le Moniteur Universel for 12–19 April, "La Légende" in Le Bien Public from 19 to 22 April, and "Hérodias" in Le Moniteur Universel from 21 to 27 April. Public reaction was favourable. Flaubert did not correct or revise any of the five authorized reprints published before he died.

Flaubert began to lead an active social life again, formed a firm friendship with Alfred le Poittevin's nephew, Guy de Maupassant, and in June 1877 returned to Croisset. He was invited to the dinner at Trapp's which marked the emergence of the naturalist (q.v.) movement, and was a guest of honour along with Zola and Edmond de Goncourt. The ardently republican Juliette Adam, who had founded the *Nouvelle Revue* in opposition to the *RDM*, asked Flaubert for something to publish. He promised *Bouvard et Pécuchet* and she published it in its unfinished state after his death, bowdlerized to an extent Flaubert himself would never have permitted.

In 1878 Commanville's financial difficulties were worse than ever. He had speculated with the money which Flaubert and Laporte had raised, and lost it. As usual, Flaubert was not kept informed. He found that bills were unpaid which he thought had been settled, and that he had guaranteed undertakings of which he had no knowledge. He had received none of the money due to him under the 1875 arrangement, and was borrowing from servants. Caroline was complaining about the amount of wood he was using to keep the damp out of Croisset. Laporte came to the rescue again, although his own factory had just gone bankrupt. His help was inadequate, however. Caroline's treatment of her uncle was well known, so that even Flaubert's friends were unwilling to help Commanville.

The Commanvilles moved their furniture into Flaubert's apartment and gave up their own. The saw mill, Commanville's last asset, was sold. Flaubert, who had fallen and broken his fibula, hoped that he might at last receive something, but he did not. His brother Achille willingly promised him an allowance, but he was now suffering from senile dementia, and Flaubert never received it. The general public got to know about the situation, and an article about Flaubert's financial difficulties appeared in *Le Figaro* for 17 February 1879. The librarianship of the Mazarine, a post which Sainte-Beuve had held, seemed to have been secured for him. The duties were not onerous, the salary was high, and a house with a view over the Seine came with the job, but Flaubert's supporters botched things. In the end they got him a state pension, which Maupassant persuaded him to accept. In 1879 he stayed for the last time with the Princesse Mathilde. Caroline, helped by Flaubert's connections, got a painting into the 1879 Salon.

Flaubert himself had visibly aged. He was bald, stout, lame, red-faced, and had practically no teeth. Commanville wanted a further guarantee from Laporte, who could not give it without pledging his one remaining asset, his house. Caroline insisted that Flaubert should break with him, which he did, and Laporte never got over it. Flaubert tried without great success to get Caroline to clear his Paris apartment of her furniture, and invited an all-male house party to Croisset for Easter Sunday, 28 March 1880. Daudet, Maupassant, Zola, Goncourt, and Charpentier all came. The conversation was of the bawdy sort that Flaubert enjoyed, and Goncourt left a glowing account of the visit. One more party was thrown in Flaubert's honour on 27 April, and he made final arrangements to leave for Paris on Sunday 9 May. He died the day before, after a hot bath, presumably of a stroke, and was buried on 11 May.

WORKS

During his life Flaubert published only five works of fiction, *Madame Bovary, Salammbô, L'Education sentimentale, La Tentation de saint Antoine*, and *Trois contes*. He himself thought the almost plotless *L'Education sentimentale* his greatest achievement. Only *Salammbô* and *Trois contes* were popular successes. Yet there is general agreement that Flaubert is one of the world's half-dozen greatest novelists, and that *Madame Bovary* and *L'Education sentimentale* both rank among the greatest dozen or so novels ever written. There is less agreement about exactly why, and about whether Flaubert was right to prefer *L'Education sentimentale*, which Henry James thought "elaborately and massively dreary," for other than the purely personal associations it continued to hold for him.

It is certain that, when Bouilhet and Du Camp made Flaubert scrap the first version of *La Tentation* in 1849, they constrained him to emancipate himself from the self-indulgent and confessional romantic lyricism from which the great masterpieces could never have emerged. The perfection of Flaubert's craftsmanship and the disillusion of his vision then came together to make him the most technically innovative and artistically accomplished creator of narrative fiction in 19th-century France, challenged only by Stendhal. At the core of Flaubert's mature achievement, the publications from 1856 to 1877, lies the superb control of sharply ironic comment, always with an implied moral content, on the lives, dreams, and experiences of characters with limited imaginations, philistine tastes, and lives empty of any ambition either worthwhile or achievable.

His prose is meticulously precise and his effects are exactly calculated. The feelings, illusions, and frustrations of his characters are more sharply conveyed because of the removal of any obviously interposed narrator. All the great works communicate a sense of the emptiness of life by drawing the reader in to share the characters' emotions, while making him or her perceive the inadequacy, banality, or vulgarity of the characters' reactions, though they are never directly described in those terms. The words chosen to express the characters' feelings are clearly Flaubert's, but an implied judgement about the moral quality of the emotion which the reader shares with the characters does not impair the immediacy with which that emotion is simultaneously communicated. That is the greatest of Flaubert's technical innovations, contrived by the systematic use of what is known as the "style indirect libre" (free indirect style), whereby we experience the world as the characters perceive it, but as they themselves could not express it.

The other purely technical innovation is the systematic incorporation into prose texts of effects more usually associated with the visual arts and with music. Flaubert paints with words, bringing scenes, surroundings, and settings visually alive with extraordinary vividness, often using simile and metaphor mingled with precisely delineated descriptions, as an artist will sharpen or blur the edges of a silhouette, sparingly adding from his palette touches of colour here and there. With a word, a phrase, or an image Flaubert can alter the colour tones of a whole passage and so create the precise visual effect for which he is striving.

His descriptions are often built up like pictures, from left to right or background to foreground, occasionally even moving through the senses, from sound and smell to touch and sight. Not only does Flaubert rely on the full power of words and their associations, using a whole panoply of sophisticated literary devices, but each phrase, sentence, paragraph, chapter, and work is architecturally moulded like a piece of music, down to the rhythmic cadences of each individual sentence. The rhythm reinforces the effect created by the meaning. It is sometimes forgotten how very widely read Flaubert was, especially in the Greek and Latin classics, how much they influenced his style, and how rich a variety of literary devices he called on. Almost never is it remarked on that, while producing his greatest works, Flaubert was under no particular financial constraint. He could afford the slow process by which his short masterpieces were reduced to such stylistic perfection from the enormously long drafts with which he started.

There are 84 sides of foolscap scenarios and 3,576 sides of minutely handwritten draft of *Madame Bovary* in the Rouen municipal library. The novel was reduced by Flaubert to 487 pages, subsequently to be scored over and cut still further. The professionally transcribed fair copy contains 489 pages and was subsequently much corrected. There are up to 11 versions of single passages. Even after restoring the cuts imposed by the *Revue de Paris* for the 1857 text, Flaubert continued to revise and correct the text for the editions of 1862, 1869, and 1873. Apart from the whole question of how adultery is treated in the novel, and the major disagreements between the author and the editors of the *Revue de Paris* on such matters as the excision of the famous cab ride from the end of the first chapter of the third part, the *Revue* correctly anticipated the public's reaction to all the small realistic details referring to bodily functions, like dribbling, snoring, sweating, and noises made during eating, references to which were removed. Yet they contribute something essential to the text.

Flaubert was given to gnomic utterances about his work. "Madame Bovary, c'est moi" means literally "Madame Bovary, that's me," but it has a deeper significance, more like "Mme Bovary is everybody," or even "There is something of the dreamer looking for escape from the real world in all of us." The writer must be true to his material, even while necessarily transforming it into a work of art. He must not seek therefore either just to prettify it, or merely to reproduce it. He needs on the one hand to be accurate and precise, even about things which during the era of romantic dreams and horrors had not normally been mentioned, like sordid bodily functions. This does not, Flaubert insists, make him a "realist", "On me croit épris du réel, tandis que je l'exècre; car c'est en haine du réalisme que j'ai entrepris le roman [*Madame Bovary*] (People think I'm in love with reality, when in fact I execrate it. It's out of hatred for realism that I undertook to write the novel [*Madame Bovary*])." On the other hand, art depends on beauty, "Le but de l'Art, c'est le Beau avant tout (The aim of Art is Beauty above everything)," and this transformation of life into art is a function of the artist's creative vision, not of its cosmeticization. Flaubert wrote in 1875, "Je me suis toujours efforcé d'aller dans l'âme des choses et de m'arrêter aux généralités les plus grandes, et je me suis détourné exprès de l'accidentel et du dramatique (I have always tried to get to the heart of things and to stay on the level of greatest universality. I have deliberately turned away from the fortuitous and the dramatic)."

This aesthetic, which must create objects of beauty but take account of deaths from arsenic poisoning, comes very near to Baudelaire's. "L'art n'est pas la réalité," wrote Flaubert to Huysmans in 1879, "quoi qu'on fasse, on est obligé de choisir dans les éléments qu'elle fournit (Art is not reality. Whatever you do, you have to choose between the things reality offers)." It is not difficult to supply a catena of quotations from Flaubert in support of different attitudes to the novelist's function, especially since Flaubert's theory evolved, and anyway did not either necessarily or in fact coincide with his practice. Even those letters which have come down to us offer so rich a discussion of literary problems that Gide could regard them as a new

Bible, but Flaubert can finally be properly judged only through an analysis of his works. The impersonality he affected was a psychological defence against the need to expose himself to a vulgar readership which he disdained and would have preferred to ignore. It is not an abdication of the moral vision, without which no literature can be great, since it does not refrain from laying bare systems of value.

Flaubert's stated aim was to write a novel without a plot, "un livre sur rien, un livre sans attache extérieure, qui se tiendrait de lui-même par la force interne de son style... qui n'aurait presque pas de sujet, ou du moins où le sujet serait presque invisible, si cela se peut (a book about nothing, a book without links to the outside, which would be held together on its own, by the internal strength of its style...which would scarcely have a subject, or at least whose subject would be almost invisible, if that were possible)." In *Madame Bovary* Flaubert did not quite succeed in abolishing plot. Indeed, he worked very carefully at the story, hesitating for a long time about whether to bring his heroine to Paris, where in the end she only dreams of going, or whether to let the first seduction of Emma by Rodolphe take place before or after the great central tableau of the "comices agricoles," the agricultural show. But the book none the less goes a long way in the direction of becoming a succession of tableaux, set pieces which stand on their own.

There are three parts. The novel starts with a straight-faced account, by an anonymous but not omniscient narratorial "Nous," of the ungainly Charles Bovary as he is introduced into the classroom. The narrator uses his first-person pronoun only once more, after which there is a very occasional "on" to indicate the narratorial voice. Flaubert has to make Charles stupid and unimaginative, but just adequately endowed to be a plausible husband for Emma, of whose imaginative and emotional needs he remains unaware throughout the novel. He comes over as a caricature of the lumpish peasant he remains, even after being educated to the level of a "medical officer," that is, not a full doctor. He alone of all the major characters emerges with moral credit, just one of the ironies deftly flicked by Flaubert on to a canvas seething with them. Flaubert uses a succession of poisoned adverbial phrases to tell us that "for reasons of economy" his parents had sent Charles to school as late as possible, and that "to avoid expense" they sent him a weekly piece of roast veal. That the character on whom Bovary was modelled was sent a veal casserole by his parents every week is a matter of recorded fact, but this is the first "realistic" detail which the editors of the *Revue* felt it necessary to cut. The next cut was made in a passage about the urgent night-time call on Bovary while he is asleep with his wife. The excised words were "Madame modestly stayed turned to the wall and showed her back." In the same chapter the editors removed "When he entered the yard his horse took fright and shied widely."

The farmer has a simple fracture, which even Bovary can set. He also has a pretty daughter, Emma. The second chapter ends with the death of Charles's wife. Charles goes home after the funeral and stays until evening lost in a sorrowful reverie. The last sentence reads: "After all, she had loved him." The savagery of that apparently innocent reflection, reported as Charles's thought, but in the words of the narrator, is characteristic of Flaubert's way of commenting with intense irony while appearing to narrate a simple, objective truth. In the second part, when we know all about Emma's romantic dreams, her adolescent sensual indulgence mistaken for mystical exaltation, her expectations of the experience of love, and after she has been at her convent, married, left home, stayed the night as a guest at La Vaubyessard, where the grand ball was held, become pregnant, and moved with Charles to Yonville l'Abbaye, the last paragraph of the second chapter begins: "C'était la quatrième fois qu'elle couchait dans un endroit inconnu (That was the fourth time that she had slept in an unknown place)," the other three being the convent, her first married home, and La Vaubyessard. A dozen words is enough to sum up what we were being told all along, how insignificant half a lifetime of Emma's experience had been.

The irony had sharpened as the wedding was arranged, with the breathtaking contrast between Emma's romantic dream of a candle-lit midnight wedding and the tableau of the hearty peasant feast. Emma's disillusion has begun by halfway through the first part of the novel, in the sixth chapter with its magisterial, bitterly ironic, and intensely compassionate flashback on Emma's convent education in which everything about her temperament is implied. The whole plot is now inevitable, and Flaubert has established his mechanism for retaining our sympathy for Emma, while making us realize how her limited imagination renders her suffering unavoidable as the attempts to realize her dream put her increasingly in tension with life. Eventually, fulfilled for a page and a half of bliss with Léon in the third chapter of part three, they lead to financial disaster and a cunningly executed suicide, disgusting in its physical details, but dignified in its conception. Flaubert's conception of his character was much too deep to allow her to kill herself as a result of financial insolvency or social disgrace. She commits suicide because her cynical first lover rejects her for the second time. She refuses to save herself by allowing her lawyer to make love to her: "Je suis à plaindre, mais pas à vendre (I am to be pitied, not to be bought)."

Visually, we are introduced to Yonville as if through a zoom lens as it approaches the town and focuses on the small hotel and the pharmacy where so much of the action takes place: "Il n'y a plus ensuite rien à voir dans Yonville (There is nothing else to see in Yonville)." The road leads into the town, as the chapter leads into the action. Some of the novel's irony is extremely daring as when, after Rodolphe has refused to carry her off, Emma prays to the Lord with "the same words of sweetness as she used to murmur to her lover in the outpourings of adultery," or when she implants on the crucifix with all her dying strength "the greatest love kiss she had ever given." Both the seduction scenes are wholly non-explicit, leaving everything to be inferred, but after Emma first gives in to Rodolphe while they are out riding, she still feels the blood "circulating in her flesh like a river of milk," while he lights a cigar and starts repairing a broken rein. Twice the adultery is held up: once when Rodolphe's conversation, which seems to be leading up to successful seduction, is presented between the rhetorical fatuities of the speeches and discussions at the agricultural show, and once when we are given a detailed tour of Rouen cathedral, where Léon is waiting for Emma.

Each of the characters is clearly inadequate: Emma, Charles, Léon the budding lawyer, Rodolphe the cynical bachelor, Homais the bombastic, self-satisfied, atheistic apothecary, and his standing opponent, Bournisien the country priest. Flaubert expertly communicates the inadequacies to the reader while leaving the characters too limited to be themselves aware of them. The novel continues after Emma's suicide, with Homais

and Bournisien arguing as usual, conveying its devastating vision of life through mostly ordinary and likeable characters and providing no flicker of real hope.

At the end of her endurance, Emma had suddenly thought of going to see Rodolphe again, "Il était si bon, si délicat, si généreux! (He was so good, so tactful, so generous!)." She would be able to persuade him. That was the culmination of all her romantic delusions. She recognized the trees, the bushes, as she approached the château. She recalled her earlier passion, went in, as previously, by the garden gate. The lime-trees swayed and whistled, and the dogs barked. Emotion had driven money, the purpose of her visit, out of her head. Rodolphe is not even particularly surprised to see her. Within minutes their earlier relationship seems re-established. The *Revue de Paris* suppressed a paragraph in which Rodolphe draws Emma on to his knees, strokes her hair, and kisses her eyelids with the tips of his lips. He asks why she has been crying. When she tells him, he changes. The formal "vous" replaces the intimate "tu." "Three thousand francs," and he addresses her "chère Madame," "I haven't got it."

The next paragraph is brilliantly ambiguous:

Il ne mentait point. Il les eût eus qu'il les aurait donnés, sans doute, bien qu'il soit généralement désagréable de faire de si belles actions; une demande pécuniaire, de toutes les bourrasques qui tombent sur l'armour, étant la plus froide et la plus déracinante

(He wasn't lying. Doubtless he'd given it had he had it, although such fine actions are generally unpleasant to make; of all the squalls which can fall on love, a monetary request is the coldest and most disconcerting).

Words, rhythm, tenses, moods, syntax, and punctuation have been quite exactly calculated. Is the narrator telling us that Rodolphe was not lying, or is that first sentence about not lying just what is going on in Rodolphe's head? Exactly what is the force of "doubtless?' Is that a statement of fact, or an abdication of narratorial omniscience, or a possibly second self-justificatory movement going on in Rodolphe's mind, as the antecedent convoluted subjunctive construction may be suggesting? Or is that construction just there to indicate that the passage deserves an almost ritualized literary style? The ordinary conditional would have been a more usual way of making a statement about what would have happened if he had had the money. The construction, butressed by the bewilderment into which Flaubert maliciously throws his reader with the "doubtless," does anything but leave the matter without doubt. Typically, gracefully, and ambiguously, Flaubert exits with an aphorism, taking us to the semicolon and expanded into a beautifully cadenced metaphor after it. What Flaubert is actually doing is simply using the known mechanics of Rodolphe's personality to propel the action towards its climax. We know that Rodolphe is not villainous, but that an impetuous impulse towards generosity, even if carried on a wave of sexual desire, will never be allowed to put him to more than trivial inconvenience.

Emma loses her calm, shouts and throws things. Rodolphe, now self-possessed, repeats "I haven't got it." The following four paragraphs repay very careful analysis. One consists of six words, "La nuit tombait, des corneilles volaient (night was falling, crows were flying)," but its effect derives totally from a context unusually dependent on rhythm, syntax, and variations of pace. Emma stumbles down the alley, looks back once, and hears only the deafening music of her beating heart. Recollections explode in her mind like fireworks, and the ground goes soft,

"car elle ne se rappelait point la cause de son horrible état, c'est-à-dire la question d'argent. Elle ne souffrait que de son amour, et sentait son âme l'abandonner par ce souvenir, comme les blessés, en agonisant, sentent l'existence qui s'en va par leur plaie qui saigne

(for she did not remember the cause of her terrible state, that is to say the question of money. She was suffering only from her love, and felt her soul abandon her through that remembrance, as the wounded, when they are dying, feel their existence ebb away through their bleeding wound)."

Globes of fire seem to break out in the air and melt in the snow, between the branches of the trees. "In the centre of each of them, the figure of Rodolphe appeared. They multiplied, and came nearer, penetrated her. Everything disappeared." Then, panting, "dans un transport d'héroïsme qui la rendait presque joyeuse (in a transport of heroism which made her almost joyful)," she ran down the hillside to the pharmacy to steal the arsenic.

There are more exquisitely subtle passages of psychological analysis, more daring contrasts between the elaborately constructed periods and the breathtaking statements they make, but few make it clearer what the novel is actually about, and with what terrifying inevitability Emma's romantic dreams drive her to a ghastly destruction, the process described clinically rather than tragically. Her death leaves scarcely a ripple on the surface of the boring life of a boring little provincial town.

Salammbô is quite different. The manuscript and four volumes of rough notes amount to 4,000 folio pages. The final fair copy of 340 pages has few corrections. The novel, based on Polybius' treatment of the Punic Wars, proceeds very largely in a series of tableaux of extreme violence, recounted in Ciceronian periods and a matter-of-fact tone so that even the most brutal scenes read inoffensively. There is a plot, but it is quite difficult to follow, and is clearly not the point of the book. Carthage is besieged by an army of mercenaries led by Mâtho, who is captured and flayed to death. The rivalry between the patroness of Carthage, the moon goddess Tanit, and Moloch, the god of fire, is reflected in the relationship between Tanit's virgin priestess, Salammbô, and Mâtho, the huge black warrior to whom she prostitutes herself as a means of retrieving Tanit's veil, which Mâtho had stolen. The male–female, sun–moon, strength–sensuality oppositions are erotically reinforced by various other symbolic devices, such as the breaking of the chain of virginity which attaches Salammbô's ankles, her death at seeing Mâtho's heart torn out, and her pet python. The reader can scarcely follow which army is winning, and the novel succeeds only as a series of brutally or exotically evocative tableaux quite loosely woven round a thin, erotically layered plot.

L'Education sentimentale is different again. The 4,710 folio pages of plans and dossiers for the novel became publicly available only in 1975, so that it is probable that further editions of the novel taking account of its genesis can still be expected. The fair copy contains 498 pages, and the novel's point is very nearly

that there is no plot, no hero, and no sentimental education. There is a central character, Frédéric Moreau, a dreamily romantic young man who has difficulty deciding whether he wants to be a poet, a painter, or a musician, and in whose life four women figure: Rosanette, a very limited but sexually attractive girl ready with her favours; Louise, a girl whom Frédéric might respectably have married; a social hostess, Mme Dambreuse; and an ideal loved one, Mme Arnoux, who finally offers herself to Frédéric when it is far too late. By then he has lost interest and she has white hair. At one point in the novel Frédéric contemplates suicide, but finds the bridge's parapet rather broad, and gives up "par lassitude (out of weariness)." He fights a duel, but his opponent falls and grazes his thumb. Blood has been shed, so honour is saved. The best of his memories turns out to be a visit he made while still at school, with his friend Des Lauriers, to a brothel, whose front parlour he never got past.

This is partly an anti-novel, therefore, with an anti-hero parodying the German Bildungsroman, or novel of initiation into emerging adulthood, in the tradition established by Goethe, Keller, and Stifter. It is also partly the history of the lost generation which experienced the revolution of 1848, naturally shown in the novel to have achieved nothing. One of Frédéric's revolutionary friends, Sénécal, changes sides, joins the police, and kills another of his friends, Dussardier, in a street battle. Flaubert took meticulous trouble with his historical accuracy. He rewrote a scene in which he brought Frédéric and the "cocotte" Rosanette back from Fontainebleau by train in 1845, because the railway had not yet been laid at that date. The whole set piece of the visit to Fontainebleau, with its historical associations and magnificent trees, is one of the book's great achievements, so difficult to do, wrote Flaubert to George Sand, that he ended up wanting to hang himself from one of the forest's trees.

"La diversité des arbes faisait un spectacle changeant. Les hêtres, à l'écorce blanche et lisse, entremêlaient leurs couronnes; des frênes courbaient mollement leurs glauques ramures; dans les cépées de charmes des houx pareils à du bronze se hérissaient; puis venait une file de minces bouleaux, inclinés dans des attitudes élégiaques; et les pins, symétriques comme des tuyaux d'orgue, en se balaçant continuellement, semblaient chanter. Il y avait des chênes rugueux, énormes, qui se convulsaient, s'étiraient du sol, s'étreignaient les uns les autres, et, fermes sur leurs troncs, pareils à des torses, se lançaient avec leurs bras nus des appels de désespoir, des menaces furibondes, comme un groupe de Titans immobilisés dans leur colère

(The diversity of the trees offered a changing spectacle. The beeches, with their white, smooth barks mingled their crowns; the ashes softly inclined their dark branches; in the coppices of hornbeam, holly bushes stood out like bronzes; then came a row of thin birches, bent in elegiac attitudes; and the pines, symmetrical as organ pipes swayed continually, seeming to sing. There were enormous, knotted oaks, convulsed, which were stretching themselves on the ground, embracing one another, and, steady on their trunks, like torsos, throwing out their bare arms in cries of despair, wild threats, like a group of Titans immobilized by their anger."

After the description, itself a tour de force, Frédéric and

Rosanette come across some rocks in a clearing which look as if they have been there since the beginning of the world and will last until it ends. When he says that, Rosanette turns away saying that that idea would "send her crazy," and goes off to pick heather, a breathtakingly inadequate reaction after the elaborately evocative description. In a sense the novel is a variation on the theme of life as a succession of vanities. Frédéric is by turns rich and poor, happy and miserable. The once wealthy Arnoux family goes bankrupt, and the reader is spared none of the multiple ironies when Frédéric and other principal characters attend the furniture sale. The magisterial evocation of "ennui (boredom)" on the first page runs right through to the last, the reader's attention riveted by the contrast between the all that might have happened and the nothing significant that does.

The penultimate chapter starts with a two-word paragraph, "Il voyagea (he travelled)." It is March 1867 and Mme Arnoux calls on Frédéric. She now declares her love. They go for a walk, discuss old times, and when they come back Frédéric sees her white hair. To hide his disappointment he goes on his knees and "se mit à lui dire des tendresses (began to make love-talk to her)." "Elle acceptait avec ravissement ces adorations pour la femme qu'elle n'était plus (she accepted with delight this worship of the woman she no longer was),"

"Frédéric soupçonna Mme Arnoux d'être venue pour s'offrir; et il était repris pur une convoitise plus forte que jamais, furieuse, enragée. Cependant, il sentait quelque chose d'inexprimable, une répulsion et comme l'effroi d'un inceste. Une autre crainte l'arrêta, celle d'en avoir dégoût plus tard... il tourna sur ses talons et se mit à faire une cigarette

(Frédéric suspected Mme Arnoux of having come to offer herself; and he was overwhelmed by a desire stronger than ever, furious, mad. However, he felt something inexpressible, a revulsion, something like the fear of incest. Another fear stopped him, of feeling disgust afterwards...He turned on his heels and began to make a cigarette)."

The final chapter rounds off the novel when Frédéric and Deslauriers come together and discuss what had happened to each of them, and to all their friends, successes, failures, drifters, and bourgeois, none with any right to feel they had fulfilled the romantic aspirations of their shared youth. The book ends with the agreement of Frédéric and Deslauriers that the most satisfying experience of each had been the failed visit to the brothel.

La Tentation de saint Antoine as we have it is the third work of that name. The first was scrapped on the advice of Bouilhet and Du Camp. Flaubert worked on the second in 1856 after he had finished *Madame Bovary*, but withdrew it for fear of another prosecution for offences against religion. It was a recognizable revision of the first version. The theme of the temptation of a saint in the desert by Satan is traditional, and Flaubert was clearly pleased to be able to concentrate in one historically careful book a vision of the plight of the whole of humanity. At the end of his life it was the book to which he himself attached most importance, although no modern critic thinks it his best. The series of temptations includes all the usual ones, banquets, riches, luxury, the physical rapture promised by the seductive queen of Sheba, before the more serious temptations of doubt and disbelief. The culminating temptation, like Adam's, is the offer of perfect knowledge.

Flaubert had clearly found difficulty in eliminating Christ from the end of the series of primitive and poetic gods, by implication as little the Son of God as they had been. There are seven copies of this episode in the notes, and it occurs in the fair copy. Flaubert changed the ending from an ecstasy with materialistic implications to a vision of Christ. Since the temptations of the flesh could well be the ordinary hallucinations of a starving anchorite, and since the subject was traditional, popular, and well known, the outcome of the "temptations" is never in doubt, but Flaubert does have the opportunity to weave a rich artistic tapestry out of man's metaphysical doubts and anxieties, which is the real point of the text. The work strikes most modern readers as too learned, although it does contain anachronisms. Flaubert had once more used the crutch of documented authenticity to sustain imaginative effort.

Trois contes is a masterpiece both as a whole and in each of its three parts. The contes are united in several ways. "Hérodias," like *Salammbô*, is set in antiquity. "La Légende" is set, like *La Tentation*, in the Middle Ages, and deals similarly with a non-variable outcome. "Un coeur simple" is modern, linked in technique and in subject matter to *Madame Bovary*. More important, not one character in any of the contes achieves anything at all by virtue of an act of will to which merit or guilt can be assigned, although one conte centres on a devoted, pious servant, one on a saint, and another on a coward and a tyrant notorious from Scripture. "Un coeur simple" was written to meet a challenge from George Sand to write something with a happy ending. Flaubert manages it, but only at the cost of turning down the wick of Félicité's expectations of life to the tiniest flicker.

The technique in "Un coeur simple" is magisterial. Flaubert writes with real compassion for the unimaginative, disdained, and increasingly deprived old servant, whose contentment contrasts audaciously with what actually happens to her as she is reduced to an elderly automaton, unable to distinguish the parrot she has had stuffed from a deathbed vision of the Holy Spirit. Flaubert begins with a favourite technique, slowly moving the focus of interest from the initial description of the past history and present habitation of Mme Aubain, up the staircase of her house, through a description of the rooms, to the attic that will be inhabited by Félicité, whose name, signifying happiness, is naturally ironic. Through desertion, departure, and death, she is successively deprived of everything she loves, until she dies as content as she had lived. Behind the simple story, simply told, is a viciously powerful comment on human life.

"La Légende de Saint Julien l'Hospitalier" is widely misunderstood by both biographers and critics. It is called a legend. The first sentence, which has a characteristically Flaubertian cadence, announces that it is a fairy story: "Le père et la mère de Julien habitaient un château, au milieu des bois, sur la pente d'une colline (Julian's father and mother lived in a castle in the middle of the woods on the side of a hill)." In case the reader has still not got the point at the end, the conte finishes: "Et voilà l'histoire de saint Julien l'Hospitalier, telle à peu près qu'on la trouve, sur un vitrail d'église, dans mon pays (And that is the story of Saint Julian the Hospitable, more or less as it is to be found on the stained glass of a church in my country)." In other words, this is a wholly incredible legend which does not purport to be true.

Not only is the story of the murderer of his parents, subsequently converted to heroic sanctity, not true, but, even if it were, it would not be due to any conscious act of will on the part of Julian. The blood lust leading to the jealous frenzy in which Julian kills his parents by mistake is psychologically beyond his control. The murder has been supernaturally predicted, and therefore by implication also determined. It takes place in a world in which stags speak, arrows stop in mid-air, and the miraculous is treated with exactly the same validity as the banal. The final act of heroism, the succouring of the leper, takes place in a world in which the physical laws governing the wind and the waves have already been suspended. There is no need to be surprised when the roof flies off and Julian is taken off to heaven by "Notre Seigneur Jésus." That, after all, is what is shown in the stained-glass window.

In "Hérodias" everything imaginable is done to mitigate Herod's moral responsibility for the beheading of John the Baptist, who is called by his old Essenian name to diminish the biblical associations. Herod is drunk, whipped up to erotic frenzy by Salomé's dance, under pressure from the Romans, from the Jews, from his own ambitions, and above all from Hérodias. Killings were commonplace enough. It had been prophesied that "un homme considérable" would die that night. If Jaokanann was really Elias, he would save himself. After the beheading, the head was shown round at the feast. The irony is in the reaction of those feasting on observing the severed head. It was rather heavy.

PUBLICATIONS

Collections

Oeuvres complètes (includes correspondence), 35 vols., 1926–54
Oeuvres, Bibliothèque de la Pléiade, edited by A. Thibaudet and R. Dumesnil, 2 vols., 1946–48
Complete Works, 10 vols., 1926

Fiction

Madame Bovary, 1857; as *Madame Bovary* (in English), 1881
Salammbô, 1862; as *Salammbô* (in English), 1886
L'Education sentimentale, 1869; as *Sentimental Education*, (in English) 1896
La Tentation de saint Antoine, 1874; as *The Temptation of Saint Anthony*, 1895
Trois contes, 1877; edited by S. de Sasy, 1973; as *Stories*, 1903
Bouvard et Pécuchet, 1881; edited by Alberto Cento, 1964; as *Bouvard and Pecuchet*, 1896; reprinted in part as *Dictionnaire des idées reçues*, edited by Lea Caminiti, 1966; as *The Dictionary of Accepted Ideas*, 1954
La Première Education sentimentale, 1963; as *The First Sentimental Education*, 1972
Le Second Volume de Bouvard et Pécuchet, edited by Geneviève Bollème, 1966

Plays

Le Candidat (produced 1874), 1874
Le Château des coeurs, with Louis Bouilhet and Charles d'Osmoy (produced 1874), in *Oeuvres complètes*, 1910

Other

Par les champs et par les grèves, 1886
Mémoires d'un fou, 1901
Souvenirs, notes, et pensées intimes, edited by L. Chevally-Sabatier, 1965; as *Intimate Notebook 1840–1841*, edited by Francis Steegmuller, 1967
November, edited by Francis Steegmuller, 1966
Flaubert in Egypt, edited by Francis Steegmuller, 1972
Correspondance, edited by Jean Bruneau, 2 vols., 1973–80
Letters, edited by Francis Steegmuller, 2 vols., 1980–82
Correspondance, with George Sand, edited by Alphonse Jacobs, 1981
Editor, *Dernières chansons*, by Louis Bouilhet, 1872

Bibliography

Demorest, D.L., and R. Dumesnil, *Bibliographie de Flaubert*, 1947

Critical studies

Steegmuller, Francis, *Flaubert and Madame Bovary*, 1947
Thorlby, Anthony, *Flaubert and the Art of Realism*, 1956
Tillett, Margaret G., *On Reading Flaubert*, 1961
Giraud, Raymond D. (editor), *Flaubert: A Collection of Critical Essays*, 1964
Buck, Stratton, *Flaubert* (in English), 1966
Bart, Benjamin F., *Flaubert* (in English), 1967
Starkie, Enid, *Flaubert* (in English), 2 vols., 1967–71
Nadeau, Maurice, *The Greatness of Flaubert*, 1972
Barnes, Hazel E., *Sartre and Flaubert*, 1981
Green, Anne, *Flaubert and the Historical Novel*, 1982

FORT, Paul, 1872–1960.

Poet, editor, and theatre director.

LIFE

Paul Fort was a long-lived and astonishingly prolific poet of nature whose reputation slowly faded during the course of his life and has not subsequently recovered. The neglect of his poetry, possibly on account of its superabundance, is clear from the dearth of critical and biographical interest in him, and from the absence of all but a ritual deference to his work in the pages of histories of literature. None the less, Fort's collected *Ballades françaises et chroniques de France* were published in 40 volumes from 1922 to 1951. Léon Dierx had succeeded Mallarmé as "Prince of Poets" in 1898 as the result of a poll conducted by *La Plume* and *Le Temps*. On his death a referendum was conducted by *Gil Blas*, and more than 400 of Fort's contemporaries elected him to the informal succession. By 1912, however, Fort was already moving well away from the mainstream of French poetic development.

He was born in Rheims on 1 February 1872, the son of a miller, and attended school in Paris. Gide, Verlaine, and Moréas introduced him to poetry, and he is usually associated with the second generation of symbolists (q.v.). Although he was sensitive to the poetic merits of Valéry, he was closer in fact to the older Parnassian (q.v.) ideal of Banville than to the work of Rimbaud or Mallarmé, whose "Tuesdays" he none the less attended. It is doubtful whether he was ever truly a symbolist although, as early as 1890, when he was 18, he founded the Théâtre de l'Art to promote symbolist drama. It seems probable that the intention to react against Antoine's naturalist (q.v.) Théâtre Libre (1887–1896) has been considerably overstated.

Théâtre de l'Art came under the directorship of Lugné-Poe in 1893, and became better known as the Théâtre de l'Oeuvre. Under Lugné-Poe, who had been a member of Antoine's naturalist company, Fort's theatre continued to put on symbolist drama, notably Maeterlinck, scenic adaptations by symbolist poets like Mallarmé, Rimbaud, and Laforgue, and later the plays of Claudel. However, it also specialized in presenting the work of foreign dramatists, including Strindberg and Hauptmann, who virtually created the German naturalist tradition. Such labels as "naturalist" and "symbolist" indicate no more than the general directions in which avant-garde dramatic activity was moving towards the turn of the century in France.

Fort's first work, the one-act prose comedy La Petite Bête, was put on by Théâtre de l'Art, and his early plaquettes of a dozen pages of verse were published by the Librairie de l'Art Indépendant. By 1894 he was collaborating with the Mercure de France and L'Ermitage, and in 1896 it was the Mercure that published Fort's first Ballades, subtitled "poèmes en prose." The collection was enthusiastically welcomed by Pierre Louÿs, who wrote a preface, and by François Coppée, who wrote an article in the Livre d'Art, which Fort had helped to found, and which was intended to follow the principles of the Théâtre de l'Art although, as Fort said, there was already "un retour vers la nature et une expression plus directe (a return towards nature and a more direct expression)," mixed in with "notre mystique de la poésie pure (our mystique of pure poetry)." Fort was in fact looking not for symbolism, but for simplicity and sincerity—a return to directness. Among those associated with him in founding the Livre d'Art were Alfred Jarry, Léon-Paul Fargue, Pierre Louÿs, Charles Guérin, Henri Bataille, and Francis Jammes. The illustrations were by Odilon Redon.

Fort published a long series of his Ballades with the Mercure's publishing house until, in 1905, he and André Salmon founded the review and publishing house Vers et Prose. Fort himself directed the review until 1914, and was the centre of a literary group which, until World War II, met at the Closerie des Lilas. At the age of 42 he was called up, but he spent World War I in an office job in Paris. He published several volumes of patriotic war verse, not generally considered to have suited his poetic style. Poèmes de France (1916), Que j'ai de plaisir d'être français! (1917), and L'Alouette (1917) bring the series of Ballades to 21 separately published volumes. Fort's devotion to France was also clear from the Chroniques de France, a series of historical plays or perhaps dramatic poems on medieval French themes which were published from 1922 to 1927. Fort also gave lectures, some of which he collected as A travers la librairie: dix causeries françaises. His Mémoires, which are historically important, were published in 1944.

Fort continued publishing verse until he was over 80. In 1926 he was awarded the Prix Lasserre and in 1936 the Grand Prix de Littérature of Paris. He died on his estate at Argenlieu, near Montlhéry, on 22 April 1960.

Works

It is presumably apocryphal that Alfred Valette paid the contributors to the Mercure de France only for their prose and not their verse. None the less, Fort's poems, which first appeared in the Mercure, were printed as prose, even though they often rhymed, in order to emphasize the superior importance of assonance, cadence, and rhythm. This also allowed Fort to write in a popular, familiar idiom, as fitted his subjects taken from nature, popular history, and folklore. The natural inspiration of his verse swept away the over-fastidious sensibilities of some of the symbolists, and laid foundations on which other poets, such as Desnos, Queneau, and Prévert, would build in order to write in popular language. Fort also drew inspiration from his own countryside in a way others were to imitate.

In the introduction to Louis XI, curieux homme, Fort explains his new poetic form: "I wanted to show the primacy of rhythm over versification (prosody)... I wanted a style which could follow the emotions from verse to prose and back: rhythmic prose provided the transition... Prose, rhythmic prose, and verse are only a single graduated instrument..." Fort himself poses as the last of the medieval ballad singers, the "trouvères," but deploys an astonishing richness of vocabulary and a luxuriant repertoire of images. Sometimes the inspiration flags, but very often it is carried along by the sheer poetic energy, the joy in nature, the writer's love of his native Champagne, the grandeur of France, and the boisterous if legendary image of its popular medieval culture:

ce jour mélodieux, couleur de tourterelle, où tous les gris roucoulent, entre ces nues d'argent, douces, nageant aux cieux et ces buées des champs qui filent leurs quenouilles

(this tuneful day, the colour of a dove, when all the greys are warbling, between those silver clouds, softly swimming in the skies, and those mists from the fields which weave their skeins)

Suis-je Bacchus ou Pan? Je m'enivre d'espace, et j'apaise ma fièvre à la fraîcheur des nuits. La bouche ouverte au ciel où grelottent les astres, que le ciel coule en moi! que je me fonde en lui!

(Am I Bacchus or Pan? I am drunk on air, and I lower my fever in the coolness of the nights. My mouth open to the sky where the stars shiver, let the sky flow through me, let me melt in it!)

The inspiration of nature in these extracts could be matched only by much longer ones to show respectively the dialect, folklore, and historical inspirations, but in the totality of Fort's copious production the popular medieval and historical veins, although chronologically later, are as strong as the poems about mountains, forests, nights, seas, and skies. Fort was an originator in introducing a familiar realism into his fresh and endearing response to nature. The danger of sentimentality is generally, although not always, warded off by the poet's ironic refusal to take himself completely seriously, especially when afflicted by touches of melancholy. The oeuvre is uneven and certainly needs pruning, but Fort's poetic achievement is greater than most critics have come to allow, and it is now to be expected that a positive revaluation will in due course take place.

PUBLICATIONS

Collection

Ballades françaises et chroniques de France, 40 vols., 1922–51

Verse

La Petite Bête, 1890
Premières lueurs sur la colline, 1893
Plusieurs choses, 1894
Il y a là des cris, 1895
Ballades françaises, 1894–1896, 1897; 3 vols., 1914
Ile de France, 1908
Coucy-le-Château, 1908
Saint-Jean-au-Bois, 1908
La Lanterne de Priollet; ou, L'Epopée de Luxembourg, 1918
Les Enchanteurs, 1919
Barbe-bleue, Jeanne d'Arc et mes amours, 1919
Chansons à la Gauloise, 1919
Poèmes au Danois, 1920
Pontoise; ou, La Folle Journée, 1920
Hélène en fleur et Charlemagne, 1921
Au pays des moulins, 1921
Louis XI, curieux homme: chronique de France, 1922
Les Compères du roi Louis: chronique de France, 1923
Ysabeau: chronique de France, 1924
Fantômes de chaque jour, 1925
Guillaume le bâtard, 1926
Le Camp de drap d'or, 1926
L'Or, Ruggieri: chroniques de France, 1927
La Conquête de l'Angleterre, 1933
L'Arlequin de plomb: nouvelles ballades, 1936
Joies désolées, 1937
Un jardinier du jardin de France, 1943
On loge à pied et à cheval, 1947
Mon grand pays, 1950
Empire de France, 1953

Other

Histoire de la poésie française depuis 1850, with Louis Mandin, 1926
Mémoires, 1944

Critical and biographical studies

Masson, G., *Paul Fort: son oeuvre*, 1924
Clauzel, R., *Paul Fort; ou, L'Arbre à poèmes*, 1925

FOUCAULT, Michel (-Paul), 1926–1984.

Philosopher, cultural historian, and essayist.

LIFE

The problems that occupied Michel Foucault concerned the relationship between social or political power, the institutionalized structures through which that power is exercized over individuals, and the concepts in any given society at any given time of both "truth" and "rationality." Is "truth" wholly or partly a socially determined orthodoxy, and is the boundary which is drawn in any given society between what is "rational" and what is "irrational" socially determined? If it is, how and under what social constraints did that situation come about historically in western European culture? In so far as Foucault probes the origins of modern forms of rationality, he is clearly both a philosopher and a historian. He defined what "rationality" was considered to be, and then asked how that definition came about. By what mechanisms does a society choose what forms of behaviour to exclude?

For the purposes of this volume Foucault is considered as a "writer" not because he wrote what were obviously works of literary imagination, as Sartre, Merleau-Ponty, Lévi-Strauss, Leiris, Teilhard de Chardin, and, before them, Bachelard, happen to have done, in addition to their technical works of philosophy, anthropology, ethnography, palaeontology, and psychology, and not just because Foucault played an immense role in the literary life of France during the 1960s and 1970s. A major role in literary life was also filled by a host of important and fascinating editors, publishers, historians, scholars, impresarios, and critics who, sometimes with outstanding success, led or catered for public taste and wielded immense literary power, but were not, in the sense in which this volume uses the word, major "writers."

Foucault is included because his writings, which do not really belong to any of the established university forms of historical or other discipline, brightly illuminate that "science de l'homme" (science of man) to which so many clearly imaginative writers are increasingly contributing, whether in purely imaginative works like those of Samuel Beckett, Claude Simon, Henri Michaux, or Benjamin Péret, or, as with those named in the last paragraph, in works belonging to recognizable scientific disciplines, philosophy, theology, or some form of social or cultural history. Both imaginative and academic writers now not only explore more frequently what society's values are and how they might or should be changed, but increasingly seek to discover any general rules about the process by which societies emerge and do change the values eventually incorporated into the working of social and political institutions, including legal and educational systems, health provision, and the regulation of financial and commercial activity.

Foucault's anthropology of what men have called "madness," or what he prefers to call "the archaeology of knowledge," is an imaginatively rather than scientifically powerful contribution to our understanding of man, his society, and his values, just as are the visions of Lévi-Strauss and Teilhard de Chardin. Like Foucault they, too, start off from an academic discipline but, like him, if more profoundly, go well beyond empirical findings into the realm of imaginative exploration. What Foucault referred to as the archaeology of knowledge might just as well be regarded as belonging to the anthropology of advanced societies. When he was finally given the chance to designate the subject of which he was to be professor at the Collège de France in 1970, he carefully decided on having himself named to the "Chaire de l'histoire des systèmes de pensée" (Chair of the history of systems of thought)," to distinguish his type of analysis of society's attitude to rationality from the simple "history of ideas," or even "history of culture."

Foucault was the son of a surgeon, born in Poitiers on 15 October 1926. He was educated in local schools until his father, unhappy with his progress, transferred him to a Catholic school, where he passed his baccalauréat with distinction. In 1945 he was a boarder at the Lycée Henri IV, where he was taught philosophy by Jean Hyppolite and from where he successfully gained admission to the Ecole Normale Supérieure, taking his "licence" in philosophy at the Sorbonne in 1948. Although Foucault was a communist party member out of political commitment for a while until 1951, Marxism as a philosophy had disillusioned him, as had the other modes of philosophical thinking descended from Hegel, notably existentialism and phenomenology (qq. v.), associated in Paris in the late 1940s with Sartre and Merleau-Ponty respectively. Foucault mixed chiefly with painters, poets, and musicians, and looked with dread on a future spent teaching the sort of philosophy he had learnt. The behavioural sciences interested him, and in 1950 he passed his "licence" in psychology, taking a diploma in psychopathology in 1952. He spent the next three years observing the practice of psychiatric therapy in mental hospitals.

Foucault also gave classes in psychopathology at the Ecole Normale, and in 1954 published *Maladie mentale et personnalité*. In its second part, Foucault, who was not a Marxist and no longer a communist, held the Soviet view that mental illness is environmentally conditioned. "Contradictions" in the environment lead to a disturbed mental balance between stimulating and inhibiting pressures. The implication is that sanity manifests itself in orthodoxy, and that insanity is a mental disturbance acting on a physiological model but activated emotionally by "alienation" from society's norms. Historical social alienation, as must no doubt have been experienced by the revolutionary proletariat for instance, should not be identified with mental alienation. Mental illness, on the other hand, is not just the result of physiological malfunction, but is connected with ideological non-conformity.

Foucault was to break with this view, and must have recognized its inadequacy early on. Unable to make progress with science any more than with philosophy, in what looks like a gesture of despair, he took a post in the French department at Uppsala in Sweden. There, too, he was disillusioned, but he stayed from 1954 to 1958, when he took the post of director of the French Institute in Warsaw, moving in the same capacity to Hamburg in 1959. He had become interested in the definition of madness or unreason, particularly in its historical manifestations as "folly," as found in Erasmus and Shakespeare, and had started to work on what was to become the *Histoire de la folie*. He took the finished manuscript to Hyppolite, who suggested that it should be presented for a doctorate, not in philosophy but in science. The degree was awarded, and Foucault took up the post of head of philosophy at the University of Clermont-Ferrand, where he stayed from 1960 to 1966. In 1962 he republished his first book, having changed the title to *Maladie mentale et psychologie* and totally rewritten its second part. Mental illness now appeared as

a socially conditioned category rather than as a state, and its form changed historically with changes in society's value systems. It had to be conceived without a physiological model.

However, Foucault went further. Unreason is the "mode of access to the natural truth of man." Psychology becomes "a thin skin on the surface of the ethical world." The primordial relation between reason and unreason examined by certain writers like Hölderlin, Nerval, Raymond Roussel, the poet regarded by the surrealists (q.v.) as a master in the meticulous examination of symbolic images from the dream world, and Antonin Artaud, is both pre-moral and pre-psychological. It is in that world that man discovers the truth about himself. This view abolishes the usefulness of psychology as a tool for discerning between reason and madness, and at any rate seems to lead to a view of mental health as requiring the breakdown of the barrier between what is regarded as rational and what, for social reasons, has been increasingly suppressed since the late 18th century. When the rewritten *Maladie mentale et psychologie* went out of print, Foucault, who had by then repudiated it, refused to authorize a reprint and successfully opposed the appearance of an English translation in the UK, although he was not successful in the US.

Foucault moved first to Tunis and then in 1968 to the new Paris faculty at Vincennes before being elected to his chair at the Collège de France in 1970. The doctorate thesis meanwhile underwent several transformations. It was turned down by two publishers and first, rather grudgingly, published as *Folie et déraison: histoire de la folie à l'âge classique* by Plon in 1961, then as a shortened paperback in the "10/18" series in 1963. It was this version, even with the addition of a chapter and other material only two fifths of the length of the 1961 version, that was translated as *Madness and Civilization* in the US in 1965 and in the UK in 1967. The Plon edition did not sell well, and even the cheap edition sold disappointingly. The reviews were uncomprehending, although Barthes in *Critique* was an exception. The *Nouvelle Revue Française* (q.v.) was uncomplimentary at first, but then Maurice Blanchot wrote a second much more enthusiastic piece on the book.

In 1972 Gallimard reprinted the original Plon 1961 version, now simply entitled *Histoire de la folie à l'âge classique*. Foucault insisted on suppressing the original preface and substituted a new one which did not refer to the book it prefaced, later relating the writing of the book to the political situation in the 1950s. Soviet behavioural science, whose principles were incorporated into Soviet penal institutions and psychiatric hospitals, was being discredited, and in 1977 Foucault said that it seemed to him important to examine the apparently tyrannical and possibly arbitrary relationship established by "reason" over "madness." The key subjects for examination, in addition to the four poets mentioned, seemed to him to be van Gogh and Nietzsche, and the first task, according to the 1961 preface, to examine the reasons for the exclusion of some forms of behaviour judged to be "mad."

Georges Canguilhem, who had taught Foucault and allowed himself to become titular supervisor for the already written doctoral thesis, commissioned Foucault's third book, *Naissance de la clinique*, which appeared in 1966. Sales were poor, and there were virtually no reviews. The English translation incorporates changes made by Foucault in the second (1972) edition, almost all of them in an attempt to distance himself from the vocabulary of Jakobson and Saussure, which was associating him with a "structuralism" (q.v.) whose partisans have always wanted to claim him for their side, but which he frequently protested was quite outside his field of interest. *Naissance de la clinique* points forward to Foucault's best-known and probably most accessible book, *Les Mots et les choses: une archéologie des sciences humaines* of 1966, which appeared after the short book on Roussel and a number of articles, including four important ones on Hölderlin, Georges Bataille, Maurice Blanchot, and Perre Klossowski, the first three of which are translated in *Language, Counter-Memory, Practice* of 1977. Gallimard's first edition of *Les Mots et les choses*, 3,000 copies, sold out within a week. A further 5,000 copies lasted only six weeks. In all, 50,000 copies of the French edition sold. When the English translation appeared in 1970, Foucault was asked to change the name, and said he preferred the one finally chosen, *The Order of Things*, to the original French title. He also gave a succinct account of his aims in a preface written for the English edition.

L'Archéologie du savoir of 1969 is a long postscript to its predecessor. It was written and published in the knowledge that it would be a best-seller, partly because the word had been passed round not only that Foucault was the high priest of structuralism, but that *Les Mots et les choses* was the best quick way in to the new intellectual fashion. Neither of course was the case, and Foucault wrote an austere book intended to deflate the ill-conceived expectations. From now on his work followed an almost predictable line. From madness he moved on to the philosophy of penology, punishment, and incarceration, based on the history of the French penal system over two centuries, and similarly on to sexuality, what was suppressed, when, and why. In 1971 he helped to found the Groupe d'Information sur les Prisons in the interests of penal reform. *Ceci n'est pas une pipe* of 1973 is a fascinating short study of the painter René Magritte (1898–1967), who had written twice to Foucault on the appearance of *Les Mots et les choses*.

Foucault died of Aids in Paris on 25 June 1984.

WORKS

Foucault's starting point was generally an observation, itself often based on an intuition. He then found that the hypothesis originally formed to account for observable phenomena was buttressed by a historical investigation. It was his great strength that he proceeded very slowly towards the identification of his real interest—social mechanisms for exclusion—and remained free of any of the great intellectual fashions of his age. His constant tendency to withdraw what he had said shows that he accepted the vulnerability of his viewpoint not so much from ideologues, with whom he did not greatly concern himself, but from the professional groups inside whose territory he needed to conduct investigations, the doctors, psychologists, penologists, and cultural historians. He maintained that he was interested only in "la discontinuité anonyme du savoir (the anonymous discontinuity of knowledge)," which ranged him firmly against the structuralists, and his work does in fact affirm, although its philosophical side cannot be said to depend on, two great discontinuities in French cultural history. The one, at the end of the 17th century, inaugurates the hegemony of the notion of representation as the key to understanding language and art, while the other occurs at the beginning of the 19th, when the concept of representation gives way to the study of man as himself mutable in his relationships and reactions.

Foucault himself pointed out that cultural historians had

recently been finding more and more discontinuites, whereas the most influential school of French historians, that associated with Lucien Febvre (1878–1956), Fernand Braudel (1902–1985), and Emmanuel Le Roy Ladurie (born in 1929), had recently been moving towards an assumption of stable structures. Debates in such global terms are necessarily unsatisfactory, and the conflicting needs for the periodization of the past by the present and assumptions of causality in the sequence of past events will never be avoided or satisfactorily negotiated. It is when he generalizes about discontinuities, and persists in finding historical confirmation for the existence of the ones on which he has chosen to concentrate, that Foucault's work is at its most vulnerable. Since, however, investigations into the past are for Foucault more strictly than for other historians tools for understanding the present, as they ironically had been for a whole generation of Hegelian historians in Germany, the interest of his analysis of the present is not vitiated by any legitimate reservations about the discontinuities.

Foucault's first book, *Maladie mentale*, was a false start. The immediate result was exile, science, and the slow elaboration of the *Histoire de la folie*. It is in the original 1961 preface to that work, later scrapped, that Foucault uses his key term "archaeology" for the first time. With reference to society's failure to heed "the mad" or its own necessary madness, he writes:

> The language of psychiatry, which is a monologue of reason about madness, could be established only on the basis of such a silence. I have not tried to write the history of that language, but rather the archaeology of that silence.

"Archaeology" is the word first chosen by Foucault to describe what he was doing. *Naissance de la clinique* was subtitled "une archéologie du regard médical," and *Les Mots et les choses*, "une archéologie des sciences humaines." The book that followed was entitled *L'Archéologie du savoir*. Something of the delicacy of Foucault's task is clear from the difficulty his translator had in distinguishing "madness" from "folly." The text of *King Lear* creates much confusion between what we would call madness, foolishness, and folly. In Foucault's view the distinction of meaning between these terms more or less disappears in the 17th century. Long before that, death, the threat from outside, is replaced by the madness which is a continuous experience threatening us from within, but which Foucault thought ceased to preoccupy imaginative writers from the 17th century.

Foucault's conclusions now follow the same lines as the focus of study changes. Only relatively marginal changes in methodology are required. Only in recent centuries has sexual constraint been imposed by society on the basis of a distinction between the "normal" and the "perverted," health and sickness. This occurred in order to protect the family as the basic social unit. At the extreme, sexual behaviour which threatened dynastic inheritance was regarded as "mad." Crime was a different form of unreason. Some of Foucault's analyses are very complex, and not all have proved convincing. Did clinical medicine emerge because old codes of knowledge were transgressed to make way for new ones in such a manner as to determine what it was that doctors saw? Was it because a new way of looking at the social status of the sick had developed? Did the creation of hospitals disturb "the laws that define the relationships between property and wealth, poverty and work"? It is questions of this sort which Foucault raises and seeks to resolve.

Les Mots et les choses examines whether the discontinuous periodization Foucault had found in society's attitude to the sick reveals a code of knowledge common to the ways in which three forms of discourse were conducted, those concerning human beings, language, and wealth. He finds the representational theory of knowledge common to the ways in which discussions were held about the three subjects over the "classical" period, up to the early 19th century, when the matrix of a static order is replaced by one emphasizing continuous development. Whether or not Foucault is right, his analysis of quite detailed phenomena like a Velazquez painting, or Borges's quotation from a Chinese encyclopedia's categorization of animals, forcefully jolts our minds into recognizing the vulnerability and the historical and social conditioning of our modes of thinking, and even of observing the reality outside us. It is the mental shock which Foucault seriously but provocatively administers, and the ingenuity with which he distils his identical codes from apparently quite disparate phenomena, which make him so powerful an imaginative author. He argued, for instance, knowing the scandalized horror with which his view would be received, what, now that he has said it, seems perfectly plain, that bourgeois mercantilist theory and Marxist economics were creations of exactly the same early 19th-century requirement of society to understand its own economic development. Marx's originality was to introduce discontinuities into history by refusing to regard the individual as the originator of development, ultimately determined outside the consciousness of the individual subject.

It is probable that, however weak his actual historical analyses and generalizations, Foucault will be regarded as a prophet. He allowed his generation to perceive the inevitability of the death of Marxism as a system of thought, and to recognize the blind alley into which literature moved as it dissociated itself from the discussion of values, ending with Mallarmé's "discovery of the word in its impotent power." Literature becomes "merely a manifestation of a language that has no other law than that of affirming…its own precipitous existence." Nietzsche heralded not so much the death of God as "the end of his murderer." Foucault's gloomy conclusion is "that man is in the process of disappearing." He meant that the possibility of codes of knowledge was rapidly being eroded, and that man, by which he clearly meant Western society, was realizing with increasing clarity that it was impossible to know anything.

PUBLICATIONS

Philosophy, psychology, and history

Maladie mentale et personnalité, 1954; revised edition, as *Maladie mentale et psychologie*, 1962; as *Mental Illness and Psychology*, 1976
Folie et déraison: histoire de la folie à l'âge classique, 1961; shortened edition, as *Histoire de la folie*, 1963; as *Madness and Civilization*, 1965
Naissance de la clinique: une Archéologie du regard médical, 1963; as *The Birth of the Clinic: An Archaeology of Medical Perception*, 1973
Raymond Roussel, 1963; as *Death and the Labyrinth: The World of Raymond Roussel*, 1986
Les Mots et les choses: une archéologie des sciences humaines, 1966; as *The Order of Things: An Archaeology of the Human Sciences*, 1970

L'Archéologie du savoir, 1969; as *The Archaeology of Knowledge*, 1972
Surveiller et punir, 1975; as *Discipline and Punish*, 1977
Les Machines à guérir (aux origines de l'hôpital moderne), with others, 1976
Histoire de la sexualité, vol. 1, *La Volonté de savoir*, 1976; as *The History of Sexuality*, 1979; vol. 2, *L'Usage des plaisirs*, 1984; as *The Use of Pleasure*, 1985
Language, Counter-Memory, Practice: Selected Essays and Interviews, edited by Donald F. Bouchard, 1977
Power/Knowledge: Selected Interviews and Other Writings 1972–1977, edited by Colin Gordon, 1980
The Foucault Reader, edited by Paul Rabinow, 1984

Other

Ceci n'est pas une pipe, 1973; as *This is Not a Pipe*, 1983
Editor, *Moi, Pierre Rivière, ayant égorgé ma mère, ma soeur et mon frère… Un cas de parricide au XIXe siècle*, with others, 1973; as *I, Pierre Riviere, having slaughtered my mother, my sister and my brother… A Case of Parricide in the 19th Century*, 1975
Translator, *Le Rêve et l'existence*, by Ludwig Binswanger, 1954
Translator, with others, *Etudes de style*, by Leo Spitzer, 1962
Translator, *Anthropologie du point de vue pragmatique*, by Kant, 1964

Bibliography

Clark, Michael: *Michel Foucault: An Annotated Bibliography: Tool Kit for a New Age*, 1983

Critical studies

Guédez, Annie, *Foucault*, 1972
Kremer-Marietti, Angèle, *Foucault*, 1974
Sheridan, Alan, *Michel Foucault: The Will to Truth*, 1980
Cooper, Barry, *Michel Foucault: An Introduction to the Study of His Thought*, 1981
Dreyfus, Hubert L., and Paul Rabinow, *Michel Foucault: Beyond Structuralism and Hermeneutics*, with an afterword by and an interview with Michel Foucault, 1982; second edition, 1983
Lemert, Charles E., and Garth Gillan, *Michel Foucault: Social Theory and Transgression*, 1982
Sedgwick, Peter, *Psycho Politics: Laing, Foucault, Goffman, Szasz, and the Future of Mass Psychiatry*, 1982
Major-Poetzl, Pamela, *Michel Foucault's Archeology of Western Culture: Toward a New Science of History*, 1983
Racevskis, Karlis, *Michel Foucault and the Subversion of Intellect*, 1983
Smart, Barry, *Foucault, Marxism and Critique*, 1983
Cousins, Mark, and Athar Hussain, *Michel Foucault* (in English), 1984
Poster, Mark, *Foucault, Marxism, and History: Mode of Production Versus Mode of Information*, 1984
Wuthnow, Robert, and others, *Cultural Analysis: The Work of Peter L. Berger, Mary Douglas, Michel Foucault, and Jürgen Habermas*, 1984
Megill, Allan, *Prophets of Extremism: Nietzsche, Heidegger, Foucault, Derrida*, 1985

L'Etui de nacre, 1892

La Rôtisserie de la reine Pédauque, 1893; as *At the Sign of the Reine Pédauque*, 1912

Les Opinions de M. Jérôme Coignard, 1893; as *The Opinions of Jérôme Coignard*, 1913

Le Lys rouge, 1894; as *The Red Lily*, 1908

Le Puits de sainte Claire, 1895

L'Orme du mail, 1897; as *The Elm-Tree on the Mall*, 1910

Le Mannequin d'osier, 1897; as *The Wicker-Work Woman*, 1910

La Leçon bien apprise, 1898

L'Anneau d'améthyste, 1899; as *The Amethyst Ring*, 1919

Pierre Nozière, 1899; as *Pierre Nozière* (in English), 1916

Clio, 1900

Monsieur Bergeret à Paris, 1901; as *Monsieur Bergeret in Paris*, 1921

L'Affaire Crainquebille, 1901

Histoire de Dona Maria d'Avals et de Don Fabricio, duc d'Andria, 1902

Historie comique, 1903

Sur la pierre blanche, 1905; as *The White Stone*, 1910

Les Contes de Jacques Tournebroche, 1908; as *The Merrie Tales of Jacques Tournebroche*, 1910

L'Ile des pingouins, 1908; as *Penguin Island*, 1909

Les Sept femmes de la Barbe-Bleue et autres contes merveilleux, n.d. (1909)

Les Dieux ont soif, 1912; as *The Gods are Athirst*, 1913

La Révolte des anges, 1914; as *The Revolt of the Angels*, 1914

Le Petit Pierre, 1918; as *Little Pierre*, 1920

Other

Alfred de Vigny, 1868

Les Poèmes dorés, 1873

Les Noces corinthiennes, (performed 1902), 1876

La Vie littéraire, 4 vols., 1888–92; as *On Lifted Letters*, 1911–24; vol.5, 1950

L'Elvire de Lamartine: notes sur M. et Mme Charles, 1893

La Société historique d'Auteuil et de Passy, 1894

Le Jardin d'Epicure, 1895; as *The Garden of Epicurus*, 1908

Au petit bonheur: comédie, 1898

Opinions sociales, 2 vols., 1902

L'Eglise et la république, 1904

Vers les temps meilleurs, 3 vols., 1906

Vie de Jeanne d'Arc, 2 vols., 1908

La Comédie de celui qui épousa une femme muette, 1912

Le Génie latin, 1913; as *The Latin Genius*, 1924

Sur la voie glorieuse, 1916

Ce que disent nos morts, 1916

La Vie en fleur, 1922

Promenades félibréennes, 1925

Trente ans de vie sociale, 3 vols., 1949–67

Critical and biographical studies

Chevalier H., *Anatole France: The Ironic Temper*, 1932

Tylden-Wright, David, *Anatole France* (in English), 1967

FROMENTIN, Eugène, 1820–1876.

Art critic, painter, and novelist.

LIFE

Fromentin was born on 24 October 1820, at La Rochelle, of well-to-do middle-class parents. His father, Toussaint (1786–1867), was a doctor and amateur painter and his mother, Jenny Billotte (1796–1879), was the daughter of a legal official. An elder son, Charles, born in 1818, became a doctor. The family had a house in the country at Saint-Maurice, where they lived from June to November. Fromentin was educated at La Rochelle, passed his baccalauréat in 1838 as top of his class, and stayed at home until November 1839, publishing some early poems in the local paper, *La Charente Inférieure*. In 1839 he began studying law in Paris, and translated the first five cantos of Dante's *Inferno*. During his law studies, he continued to write verse, made a synopsis of 19 books of the *Iliad*, and was connected with a Christian socialist group. In 1841, in response to his parents' wishes, he promised to break off a liaison with Jenny-Caroline-Léocadie Béraud (1817–1844), the wife of a family friend at La Rochelle. A series of poems was inspired by the separation and, early in 1842, a passing affair inspired Fromentin to write further poems.

Meanwhile he was running into debt, part of which was paid off by his mother through the mediation of a friend. By 1843, now a qualified lawyer, he had begun to paint, and published two accounts of the 1845 Paris Salon in a new review, the *Revue Organique des Départements de l'Ouest*, directed by a close friend from La Rochelle, Emile Beltrémieux, who was to die of tuberculosis in 1848. The review lasted for almost a full year. During 1845 it became quite clear to Fromentin that, in spite of his father's opposition, what he wanted to do was to paint. He knew the decision would entail poverty. At the beginning of the year he spent three months in the studio of L.-N. Cabat, with whom he had spent some time in 1844.

In 1846 Fromentin visited Algeria with the painter Charles Labbé, and showed three paintings in the 1847 Salon, one of which he sold for 350 francs. He now had a tiny studio and a group of painter friends in Paris, but spent from September 1847 to May 1848 in Algeria. Five canvases on Algerian subjects were accepted for the 1849 Salon, and one was awarded a prize. In 1851 Fromentin sold a painting for 1,000 francs, and in 1852 he married Marie Cavellet de Beaumont, the niece of a Paris friend, Armand Du Mesnil, who worked for the ministry of education.

The couple lived for a year in Algeria from November 1852, and then, until 1857, in Saint-Maurice. Their daughter Marguerite was born in 1854. (She was to die in 1938.) While at Saint-Maurice Fromentin painted, sending his canvases regularly to exhibitions and galleries. He also wrote the first of the two travel books for which he is remembered, and which are also painter's notebooks, *Un été dans le Sahara*, serialized in 1854 in seven instalments in the *Revue de Paris*. In 1855 and 1856 he worked for a period in the studio of Gustave Moreau. Fromentin's lack of money continued to cause him difficulties, but *Un été* was well reviewed by George Sand and by Gautier, and he had three paintings accepted by the 1857 Salon. Fragments of a draft of the second travel book, *Une année dans le Sahel*, were serialized in *L'Artiste* in 1857, when Fromentin moved to Paris with his wife and daughter. The annual rent was 325 francs. Ill health now exacerbated the painter's habitual poverty, but *Une année* was serialized in the *Revue des Deux Mondes* (*RDM*, q. v.) towards the end of 1858.

Gautier and Baudelaire both wrote favourable reviews of Fromentin's five pictures in the 1859 Salon, and he received the Légion d'Honneur. At Saint-Maurice that summer, he began work on *Dominique*. He had six paintings in the 1861 Salon, but found difficulty in finishing *Dominique*, promised to the *RDM* for November. It was finally rewritten in two months and serialized in the spring of 1862. Meanwhile Fromentin had gradually made his way into Paris society. He accepted an invitation from George Sand at Nohant to discuss *Dominique* during a five-day visit in 1862, before it was published in book form. A project for another book was dropped, but Fromentin sold a painting, now in the Louvre, to the state for 10,000 francs. *Dominique* enjoyed important acclaim, notably from Hetzel and Sainte-Beuve. Fromentin also started to write art criticism. It has been said that his essays on Dutch and Flemish painters, *Les Maîtres d'autrefois*, include some of the finest ever written in French. The volume contains an analysis of the effect of Flemish landscapes on French painters such as Claude and Théodore Rousseau. By 1865 Fromentin's own paintings were sought after and selling well. In 1867 he was a member of the Salon jury, but the following year his own entry was considered a failure. His father died suddenly in 1867.

Moving now in official circles, Fromentin became an Officier of the Légion d'Honneur, got himself invited to the opening of the Suez Canal, was put on a commission to examine state support for the visual arts, and was invited to report on painter candidates for the Légion d'Honneur. In 1870 he was in Venice when the Franco-Prussian War broke out. He was still painting but, as he said, mostly for money. His Venice paintings in the 1872 Salon were much admired for their handling of light but he had clearly lost his enthusiasm. In 1873 his daughter married an important official of the Bank of France. Soon afterwards Fromentin wrote a series of letters to Hortense Howland, whose salon he had frequented nearly 10 years previously. There are about 173 letters in all but his daughter prevented their publication in 1930. In 1875 he made the journey to Holland and Belgium of which *Les Maîtres d'autrefois* is the result. It was serialized in the *RDM* in 1876.

Fromentin's health had been weak since at least 1868, and he died in August 1876 in Saint-Maurice. He had failed in his efforts to become a member of the Académie des Beaux-Arts in 1867 and of the Académie Française in the year of his death. In 1877, 156 paintings and 900 drawings by Fromentin were sold for 433, 755 francs.

WORKS

Dominique is one of the rare novels of psychological analysis to appear before 1880. It is also a post-romantic novel, in which passion is sacrificed to dull respectability, success, and, in the end, contentment. It is partly autobiographical, a re-enactment 15 years later of Fromentin's love for Jenny-Caroline-Léocadie Chassé, as she then was. He had been not quite 14 and she 17 when she married in 1834, and it was in 1841 that Fromentin, just 21, promised not to see her again.

The story is simple. Dominique de Bray, the narrator, while still only an adolescent, had fallen in love with Madeleine d'Orsel. She discovered his devotion to her only after she had married. She was kind to him, and herself fell in love with him. She could not in the end conceal from him the fact that she was motivated by more than mere kindness towards him. On account of the moral distress the situation was causing her, Dominique agreed not to see her again. He left Paris, gave up a not very promising literary career, and retired to lead a useful life managing his estates in the country. Eventually he married. The book's minor characters have also all been identified as friends of the youthful Fromentin, Julie's passion for Dominique's friend Olivier balancing the main story.

Fromentin is relying on but de-romanticizing Senancour's *Oberman*, Constant's *Adolphe*, and Sainte-Beuve's *Volupté*, which he claimed to have read almost a score of times. He probably needed the long wait after the painful experience which yielded the 11 love poems of late 1841 in order to produce the literary achievement of *Dominique*, in which a clearly authentic and not merely invented passion is communicated the more intensely for being diffused by refraction through memory, and controlled in a way that only the passage of time could make possible. The tone is sober enough to be almost flat, and the simple story of love and renunciation is kept alive by Dominique's present detachment from the events which had once had so searing an effect on him. The style is also enhanced by Fromentin's sharp painterly eye for detail. The anti-romantic elements are the rigorous rejection of all posturing, self-pity, and sentimentality, and the satisfaction of a dull but well-ordered and contented existence. Something of a moral can be elicited from the story: that of being satisfied with one's own unheroic mediocrity and tailoring one's coat accordingly. The only concession to romantic writing is a tendency to endow natural phenomena with moral qualities, although landscapes "approve" and "disapprove" the novel's events in only the most dignified and restrained manner.

Now that the characters' connections with real people have been established beyond reasonable doubt, we can assess the degree and direction of the novel's fictionalization. The most interesting commentary on the text is probably that of George Sand, implied in her suggestions for changing it between serialization and the appearance of the book. Some of these suggestions were rejected by Fromentin, some accepted but, most interestingly of all, some were accepted and then rejected because they falsified what actually happened. There were essentially three versions of the novel during its period of gestation, including that finally printed by the *RDM* and written in two months almost without correction, and a comparison shows that, in spite of the fluency, Fromentin was as careful a craftsman with his pen as he was with his brush.

PUBLICATIONS

Collections

Oeuvres complètes, Bibliothèque de la Pléiade, 1984

Fiction

Dominique, 1863; as *Dominique* (in English), 2 vols., 1966 (best modern edition) reflective criticism into a series of volumes, some of which eventually grew into monographs, on Nerval, Balzac, and Baudelaire, and his travels were inspiring his verse, notably the 43 poems of *España* of 1845. The Spanish trip had yielded a harvest of newspaper articles, a travel book, a book of poems, a successful vaudeville, with 34 performances in 1843, and a crop of invitations to travel to and write about other places.

Between 1839 and 1850 Gautier wrote all or part of nine plays, of which the principal are *Une larme du diable, Le Tricorne enchanté, La Fausse Conversion*, and *Le Pierrot posthume*. He also wrote the libretti for several ballets at a stage when a prima ballerina's acting ability counted for as much as her technical dancing ability, and when plays were regularly adapted to ballet form. Gautier fell in love with the ballerinas Fanny Elssler and later Carlotta Grisi, for whom he wrote *Giselle* and who danced its premiere. Her sister Ernesta had become his mistress in 1844. Gautier was also writing numerous short stories at this period, some of which are important for their combination of ancient myth with modern psychological insights in a pre-Freudian age increasingly dominated by scientific positivism and social realism. *Une nuit de Cléopâtre* and *Le Roi Candaule* are both staging posts in this connection. Others are written in the "fantastic" style of so-called "vampire gothic." The most important of these is probably *Spirite*, written for Carlotta Grisi and set on her estate. In spite of his enduring relations with her sister and a passionate affair with Marie Mattéi (1849–1852), Gautier never really stopped loving her.

Gautier's single most important verse collection, *Emaux et camées*, was his final volume of poetry, containing only 18 octosyllabic poems in 1852, but ending up with 47 in 1872, although many poems written during these years and published elsewhere were not included. The novel *Le Capitaine Fracasse*, first announced in 1836, was finally published in the *Revue Nationale* from 1861 to 1863. All the indications are that it was sold several times before it had even been written, and the advance had to be repaid on at least one occasion. Serialization must have begun before the novel was anywhere near complete. The inspiration for it came largely from the exuberant baroque novels of the early 17th century.

The political events of 1870 seriously affected Gautier's health and when, in 1872, he died of a heart attack, more than 80 fellow poets wrote poems in his honour. "Le bon Théo," as he was known, had been one of the most popular literary figures of his age. The Goncourt journals give a good idea of his jovial personality. His six-volume *Histoire de l'art dramatique en France depuis vingt-cinq ans*, although incomplete, is still a pivotal and in some respects definitive work. Gautier also left unfinished a lively chronicle in the *Histoire du romantisme*. Gautier's life and works so often serve as a reference point in the history of 19th-century French literature, that the entries on "The Romantic Movement" and the other principal romantic authors should also be consulted, as should the index.

WORKS

Gautier's output includes works from the whole spectrum of sub-literary journalism and unsuccessful plays, poems, and fiction to the superbly executed poems of *Emaux et camées*, but his best work consists of literary transpositions of plastic art. In spite of his romanticism, he exemplified the French classical ideal of the poet who saw his task as the reproduction of nature: "ut pictura poesis" (poetry like painting). Addressing Titian, Gautier himself said: "Laisse-moi faire… / Changeant mon luth pour ta palette / Une transposition d'art" (Exchanging my lute for your palette, / Let me transpose my art). His painter's training led him to concentrate on perfection of form. His work consequently heralded the impersonal formal ideals of Leconte de Lisle and the Parnassians (q.v.), even before he himself had totally abandoned the more ghoulish forms of romantic fiction (which he was also ready to parody). Gautier came to believe increasingly in the rigorous discipline of an exacting technique. Books had nourished the imagination of the romantic painters. Their sense of form—the sensuous calligraphy of the thoroughly romantic Ingres rather than Géricault's vortices of colour—was now to prove his model.

Mademoiselle de Maupin centres on the characters of Albert and his mistress, Rosette, both of whom are in love with Madelaine de Maupin disguised as a young man. Her true sex is revealed, and she makes love to both of the others in one night before disappearing for ever, the symbol of the ideal beauty which, if not quite unattainable, is nevertheless destroyed by physical contact. It seems possible that the first five chapters, in letter form, were fictionalized autobiography, dusted down rather than adapted for use in the novel. Albert is an exaggerated romantic, reaching out longingly for the unachievable and lamenting his frustrated desires. Rosette fulfils the role of his physically satisfying mistress who claims the other half of his personality. Apart from her single concession to physical realities, Madelaine represents the true beauty which is only to be found in art. She promises, as she leaves Albert for ever, that she will never sleep with another man.

In the field of art criticism, romanticism was merely a passing phase for Gautier. He was attracted to the notion of universality of form—part of the classical ideal—although in theory (and, with Delacroix, in practice) he admitted the principle of selection and arrangement according to an inner personal principle or "prism." What was useful, such as domestic sanitary arrangements, for instance, was also ugly. In his more reflective pieces on literary figures Gautier, along with the rest of his generation, misunderstood the norms of French classicism, although he was shrewd enough to see why Chapelain's *La Pucelle* was a failure. In 1868 he published *Les Progrès de la poésie française depuis 1830*. Its judgements are often obscure, although its dry wit (like that of the *Histoire de l'art dramatique*) is attractive.

La Comédie de la mort of 1838 comprises three poems on death prefacing 56 shorter poems on a variety of themes, including the aspiration to an impossible ideal. The poems are of mixed interest. The lack of intellectual and imaginative depth which was to lead to Gautier's concern with technical mastery and form for beauty's sake was becoming more apparent as he approached 30 years of age. Most of the short stories of this period—*Fortunio, Le Roi Candaule, Une nuit de Cléopâtre, Le Roman de la momie*, and *Le Pied de momie*—deal with the quest for distant ideals, while the weird and unimaginable occurs in all the "fantastic" stories—mostly early and not very serious essays on the macabre, such as *La Cafetière*, and *Onuphale. La Morte amoureuse* creates a pre-Freudian myth about split identities that is carried on in *Le Chevalier double* and the more ambiguous *Arria Marcella*. In *Avatar* a mystic exchange of identities occurs between two people while they are both in an unconscious state.

Emaux et camées deliberately sets out to treat small subjects in a restricted manner. The collection is partly remembered for its advocacy and exemplification of the "L'Art pour l'Art" doctrine. The famous poem "L'art" suggests that painstaking craftsmanship, using hard and resistant materials, can create an art to outlive society. Some of the poems are personal, even autobiographical. All strive for, and generally attain, formal perfection in at times intricately difficult metrical patterns. The collection has been criticized, however, for its failure to grapple with important themes.

Le Capitaine Fracasse is regarded by some as Gautier's prose masterpiece. A pessimistic historical adventure story set in the early 17th century, it owes something to Scarron and uses irony to skilful effect. The original was too pessimistic for the publisher's taste and had to be changed to accommodate the present fairy-tale happy ending, which is seriously flawed in terms of motivation. In a way this creates a final irony at the expense of the reader, who only discovers at the end that what he has been reading is not the gruesomely realistic adventure story he had imagined it to be, but in fact a fairy story. Written in a great hurry, it is a work which can scarcely be accorded any very high literary status.

PUBLICATIONS

(Volumes of articles collected and published posthumously have not been listed).

Collections

Poésies complètes, 3 vols., 1948
The Gentle Enchanter, Thirty-Four Poems, 1960

Fiction

Les Jeunes-France: romans goguenards, 1833
L'Eldorado, 1837
Mademoiselle de Maupin, 2 vols., 1835; as *Mademoiselle de Maupin* (in English), 1836
Nouvelles, 1845
Militona, 1847
Les Roués innocents, 1847
Les deux étoiles, 2 vols., 1848
Jean et Jeannette, 2 vols., 1850
La Peau de Tigre, 3 vols., 1852
Le Roman de la momie, 1858
Romans et contes, 1863
Le Capitaine Fracasse, 2 vols., 1863
Spirite, 1866
The Romances of Théophile Gautier, 10 vols., 1903

Plays and ballets

La Comédie de la mort, 1838
Une larme du diable, 1839
Giselle, 1841
La Péri, 1843
Un voyage en Espagne, 1843

La Juive de Constantine, 1846
Le Selam, 1850
Pâquerette, 1851
Gemma, 1854
Sacountala, 1858
Théâtre de poche, 1855
Théâtre (including *Une larme du diable, Le Tricorne enchanté, La Fausse Conversion, Le Pierrot posthume*), 1872

Criticism and travel

Les Grotesques, 2 vols., 1844
Tra los montes, 2 vols., 1843; as *The Romantic in Spain*, 1926
Les Fêtes du Madrid, 1847
Salon de 1847, 1847
Caprices et zigzags, 1852
Italia, 1852
Constantinople, 1853
Les Beaux-Arts en Europe, 2 vols., 1855–6
L'Art moderne, 1856
Histoire de l'art dramatique en France depuis vingt-cinq ans, 6 vols., 1858–59
Honoré de Balzac, 1858
Abécédair du Salon de 1861, 1861
Quand on voyage, 1865
Loin de Paris, 1865
Ménagerie intime, 1869
La Nature chez elle, 1870
Tableau de siège Paris 1870–71, 1871
Voyage en Russie, 2 vols., 1867; extracts in *Russia by Théophile Gautier and Other French Travellers of Note*, 1970
Les Progrès de la poésie française depuis 1830, 1868
Tableau de siège, 1871
Henri Regnault, 1872
Histoire du romantisme, 1872

Verse

Poésies, 1830
Albertus ou l'Ame et le péché, 1832
La Comédie de la mort, 1838
España, 1845

Emaux et camées, 1852; definitive edition, 1872

Critical studies

Dillingham, Louise, *The Creative Imagination of Théophile Gautier*, 1927
Richardson, Joanna, *Théophile Gautier: His Life and Times*, 1959
Smith, Albert B., *Ideal and Reality in the Fictional Narratives of Théophile Gautier*, 1969
Spencer, Michael Clifford, *The Art Criticism of Théophile Gautier*, 1969
Grant, Richard B., *Théophile Gautier* (in English), 1975

GENET, Jean, 1910–1986.

Novelist, poet, and dramatist.

LIFE

Genet, whose paternity is unknown, was abandoned by his mother at birth, brought up by the Assistance Publique and placed with peasant foster parents at Le Morvan, to the northeast of the Massif Central, at the age of seven. His extraordinary career and output have been exploited as source material for so many psychoanalytical, sociological, pedagogical, criminological, and political theses that it is now difficult to provide uncontaminated biographical facts. For instance, acting under the different pressures exerted by publication in *Les Temps Modernes* (q. v.) in July 1946, in his own *Journal du voleur*, in the London *Evening Standard* in 1957, and in *Playboy* (US version, April 1964), Genet first gave one explanation of why he stole at 10 from his foster parents, then tacitly withdrew that explanation, and finally replaced it with an incompatible one. According to Sartre's famous analyses in *Saint Genet, comédien et martyr*, published in 1952, parts of which were serialized in *Les Temps Modernes* in 1950, Genet needed to own things in order to constitute himself a real person, and had to steal in order to own. Sartre also held that Genet felt the need to constitute himself by becoming as evil and sordid in his actions as he was made to feel. Not the least of the difficulties, as Genet complained to *Playboy*, is that Sartre's analyses themselves altered his understanding of himself, and so had a devastating effect on his behaviour.

From 1926 to 1929 Genet was sent to the reformatory Colonie Agricole at Mettray, an event for which he has again provided two incompatible alternative explanations. He may have gouged out another boy's eye. After 1929 the biographical data are uncertain for 15 years. Genet may have joined the Légion Etrangère and deserted. He may have been a prostitute and was certainly a homosexual. He lived in Germany, Holland, Yugoslavia, and Spain, begging, stealing, smuggling, and drug trafficking, and appears to have been a relatively successful robber, acting in partnership with a safe-breaker. Critics often refer to his "transvaluation of all values," or quest for absolute evil, and Genet certainly spent some time in prisons around Europe. In Fresnes prison he wrote a poem, "Le condamné à mort," in memory of a 20-year-old murderer executed at Saint-Brieux on 2 February 1939. The poem is in formally regular Alexandrines, romanticizing its theme with extreme obscenity.

Notre-Dame-des-Fleurs, a novel displaying considerable knowledge of art and literature, was written at La Santé prison, where Genet was being confined for what is said to have been a seventh offence, and published in an edition of 350 privately printed copies. We do not know by whom, where, or at whose expense, but the date was probably 1942. Cocteau may have had a hand in the publication, which was probably by Barbezat, who published a second edition in 1948, and an unexpurgated edition in 1966. It is the story of a country boy who becomes a homosexual prostitute in Paris. A scene was printed in Barbezat's *L'Arbalète* next to the first edition of Sartre's *Huis clos* in the spring of 1944, the year in which Sartre and Genet got to know one another. In 1945 Genet's poem "La galère" appeared in the third number of *La Table Ronde*, and in March 1946 his second novel, *Miracle de la rose*, also written in prison, was published by *L'Arbalète* in a luxurious first edition of 475 copies for subscribers only. Extracts from the third novel, *Pompes funèbres*, were published in *Les Temps Modernes* in 1945, followed by extracts from the *Journal du voleur* in July 1946. Genet had been taken up immediately after the war by that section at least of Parisian literary society dominated by Sartre.

In 1946 Genet's ballet '*Adame Miroir* had been staged to Milhaud's music, and in April 1947 Jouvet produced *Les Bonnes* to mixed critical reception. The full text of *Pompes funèbres* contained too detailed a description of homosexual activity, and a suggestion of pro-Nazi sympathies. It was therefore turned down by Gallimard and published privately "in Bikini." The play *Haute surveillance* was then published in *La Nef* for March and April 1947. It was performed in Paris in February 1949, precipitating a violent attack on Genet by Mauriac in *Le Figaro Littéraire*. Genet's views and literary activities were becoming the object of public controversy. *Notre-Dame-des-Fleurs* must have been openly on sale at the Théâtre des Mathurins when *Haute surveillance* was staged, although officially available only in the second edition (Barbezat, Lyons 1948), which was still supposed to be reserved for subscribers. In 1949 the *Journal du Voleur* appeared in a commercial edition by Gallimard as well as in a private printing of 400 copies, and Frechtman's English translation of *Our Lady of the Flowers* was issued in a limited edition of 300 copies in Paris. In December 1947 Genet's fourth novel, *Querelle de Brest*, was privately printed, with a limited German edition of 850 copies.

Cocteau, who was probably also associated with the translation of *Our Lady of the Flowers*, and Sartre obtained a pardon for Genet in 1948, when he faced life imprisonment for assuming responsibility for a crime committed by Jean Decarnin, a friend who had been killed during the Paris street fighting at the liberation. From 1951 to 1953 Gallimard published three volumes of the *Oeuvres complètes*, toned down and including Sartre's 1952 study of Genet. The first two plays, the *Journal du Voleur* and the banned radio talk *L'Enfant criminel*, which was to have followed a series of interviews in which all the proposed participants refused to take part, were all omitted. Only one review appeared. Genet did not write a major non-dramatic prose work after 1949. It is difficult to believe that either he or Gallimard would have consented to an *Oeuvres complètes* without pressure from Sartre, or that Genet would have become as widely known as he is without Sartre's initial study of him. Sartre certainly believed that Genet's life and works illustrated a psychological theory he already held.

Les Bonnes had a second series of performances in Paris in 1954. *Le Balcon* had its world premiere in London in 1957, but was not played in France until 1960. Genet did not like the London production, which was not a great success. Real triumph as a dramatist came with Roger Blin's production of *Les Nègres* in October 1959 at the Théâtre de Lutèce, where the play's reception led to a three-year off-Broadway run from 1961 to 1964. This success led to the French production of *Le Balcon*. In May 1966 *Les Paravents*, a play about the Algerian war, which had been staged in Berlin in 1961, was given 20 performances by Blin, directed by Jean-Louis Barrault; it was revived in September. The play was seen as a direct attack on the French army, but received the Palmarès de la Critique for the best play of the season. In 1957 the *Oeuvres* were impounded by the British customs but *Le Balcon* was made into a film, and various translations of Genet began to appear more widely in the 1960's, when the British ban was also rescinded.

WORKS

What has shocked the Western world about Genet's work is its unrepentant and shame-free celebration of evil. Readers and audiences have been provoked to such a degree that the critical reaction has largely either followed Sartre's lead in using Genet's career and output as an illustration of some psychological theory, or at least focused on the validity, if not the psychological origins, of Genet's aesthetic aims. Reaction has ranged from serious literary acclaim to punch-drunk disgust. After the initial announcement in *Notre-Dame-des-Fleurs* that the book is written to "celebrate" the crimes of Weidman, a mass murderer, of Pilorge, a soldier who killed his lover for a trifling sum, and of a young officer who committed treason for its own sake, it is difficult calmly to discuss the novel's literary qualities. Genet's works apparently seek to explore the possibility that moral evil for its own sake, however dull and unoriginal, might be a desirable goal, without reference to pleasure or to higher or different moral norms from those commonly observed.

In fact, of course, and whether he knows it or not, Genet forces his public to ask whether evil and good are mere illusions, or at any rate conventions, and this is what explains his close understanding with Sartre, at least between 1944 and 1952. If the merely disgusting is no more than the result of conditioning, can it be presented poetically? Critical opinion agrees on the whole that Genet did not succeed in his extreme attempt to suggest that evil may be just an illusion. The tension with a necessary and not only a conventional morality is too great for any poetization of the values in which Genet is interested to work. Genet can be said to have tested for and found a legitimate moral basis for aesthetic revulsion, and little support for the view that what is deliberately depicted as stupidly and self-defeatingly wicked might also be presented as attractive.

Of the four novels, *Notre-Dame-des-Fleurs* concerns the various affairs of a country boy, Louis Culafroy, as a homosexual prostitute in Paris, some of which last for relatively protracted periods. One lover deserts him, another is guillotined, and he himself dies of tuberculosis. The narrative begins with his funeral and is intertwined with meditative reflections by the narrator, who is in prison awaiting trial, and contains a psychological analysis of the narrator's homosexuality. No one knows where or how Genet acquired his literary culture and his mastery of language, but some of the effects he achieves are strikingly paradoxical, and at times genuinely poetical. *Notre-Dame-des-Fleurs*, with its ironical title, is probably Genet's best novel. It is certainly his most unified fiction, presented as a dream creation with an element of ironic detachment not found elsewhere in his work.

Miracle de la rose, like *L'Enfant criminel* of 1949, suggests that wrongdoers should be brutally punished so that their power to rebel is retained and reinforced. Even if he did not intend to be ironic, Genet comes very close to properly constructive social criticism in proposing that only society's brutality can prove that the wrongdoers were right in the first place to reject its norms. In *Miracle* Harcamone, a former inmate of Mettray, betrayed to the police by another, deliberately kills a warder in order to get himself executed, so avoiding having to serve a life sentence. As if aware that he has been taken off his guard by

being constructively critical, Genet turns the end of *Miracle* into a positive association between what is beautiful and what is both intellectually null and morally perverse. A haunting effect is certainly achieved, but in the end few critics uncommitted to a philosophical system would agree that the achievement endows the work with real literary merit. The narrator's inconsistent value system, too, undermines any power the novel might otherwise have possessed.

Pompes funèbres is probably more explicit about homosexuality than the other novels, but it also trails a cloak which has been interpreted as pro-Nazi, although this may be not more than mischievous. The events of the novel, like those of *Notre-Dame-des-Fleurs*, but unlike those of the other two novels, are presented as taking place partly in the imagination. A German boy soldier, "Riton," has a homosexual relationship with Erik, the German lover of the mother of Genet's friend Decarnin. Riton eventually kills Erik after he has stood by while other soldiers treated him brutally. To allow honour among thieves would be to disturb evil with positive moral values. *Pompes* is the least ironic of the novels, and therefore probably the weakest. There is no tension between the repugnant horrors narrated and an awareness that the transvaluation inspiring them may itself be a romantic illusion.

Querelle de Brest has a relatively coherent plot. A sailor, Georges, kills a friend and successfully frames a young stonemason called Gil, himself a murderer. Georges, also a successful drug-runner and thief, goes free. Psychologically, there is a new element of subtlety here, but the text gives the feeling that Genet, having thought his own personality through, and at times even aspired to an almost mystical poetic elevation, has now written himself out.

The Journal du voleur is the last and shortest of the major prose works, and was the first to be published openly in France. Genet says it is about "theft, treason, and homosexuality," and it combines a sketchy autobiography with a good deal of reflection. We are not told much about what, how, or when Genet burgled, and the book is more forthcoming on the subjects of begging, homosexuality, and personal humiliation. There are now signs that Genet is being influenced by Sartre's view of him. The book has a social and political dimension and is dedicated to Sartre and Simone de Beauvoir.

The earliest of the plays to be written, *Haute surveillance*, derives in part from Sartre's *Huis clos* and has been made into a film, although not generally released. Genet himself directed the Paris production, but the play has never been commercially staged in London or New York. It concerns three criminals, Yeux-Verts, Maurice, and Lefranc, locked up in the same cell, and "unfolds as in a dream" as the stage direction says. It turns in the end on responsibility. Did all or any of the three deliberately embrace criminality, and is there a hierarchy of grandeur in evil which is quite gratuitous?

Les Bonnes is also a short play. Two sisters, Claire and Solange Lemercier, are maids who take turns at being Madame, while the other takes her sister's place, so that when Solange is Madame, Claire is Solange. Claire tries to poison her mistress, but Madame goes off to visit her lover without drinking the poisoned tea. Claire takes the role of Madame and forces Solange to make her drink the poisoned tea. Claire dies, and Solange will naturally be executed. The play clearly has a moral, social, and political significance. Its success derives more probably, however, from the fact that it is good theatre, which leaves the audience with intelligible questions to ask about their reactions.

The action of *Le Balcon* takes place in a brothel and offers much scope for the discussion of perversions, mostly centred on playing power roles and using sex for the pursuit of power. The plot contains a good deal of irony about where political authority really lies. The chief of police is disappointed that none of the clients chooses his role as the important key to exercising power. Eventually the leader of the revolution admits defeat to the chief of police by castrating himself, and the seat of real power in the community is acknowledged. Genet was annoyed with Peter Zadek's production because he thought the play had been turned into a satire on the British monarchy. Zadek was working from an earlier version of the play, and even when Peter Brook finally put on his Paris production, cuts were made in the political second half.

One of the Negroes in *Les Nègres*, which deliberately exploits the connotations of "The Niggers" rather than "The Blacks" of the toned-down English title, plays at being a white woman who is murdered by another Negro. Genet wanted the Negroes on stage to behave as badly as they had ever been accused of behaving by their white oppressors. In the play the white judges who condemn the Negroes for murder turn out to be black after all. There is a subplot to reinforce the incitement to freedom through violence. The ideas that the whites are supposed to want to have of the blacks are corroded by satire, and the play is about the assumption of power by the blacks.

Genet's last play, *Les Paravents*, is extremely long and contains 104 characters in 17 tableaux. Barrault cut it back for the 1966 production. The title, "Screens," refers to the movable screens on the stage, shifted around to change the tableaux. The French army is depicted as a bunch of bumbling homosexuals, and the French presence in Algeria as 130 years of useless colonialization, while the Algerian rebels are no more competent than their oppressors. Saïd, a young Algerian dropout, is used by the Algerian extremists as the symbol of a revolution which he in fact repudiates in pursuit of gratuitous evil. The play concludes nothing except the isolation of the individual, and was Genet's greatest dramatic success.

PUBLICATIONS

Collections

Oeuvres complètes, 4 vols., 1951–68

Fiction

Notre Dame des Fleurs, 1942 revised edition, in *Oeuvres complètes 2*, 1951; as *Our Lady of the Flowers*, 1949; as *Gutter in the Sky*, 1956; as *Our Lady of the Flowers*, 1963
Miracle de la rose, 1946; revised edition, in *Oeuvres complètes 2*, 1951; as *Miracle of the Rose*, 1965
Pompes funèbres, 1947; revised edition, in *Oeuvres complètes 3*, 1953; as *Funeral Rites*, 1969
Querelle de Brest, privately printed, 1947; revised edition, in *Oeuvres complètes 3*, 1953; as *Querelle of Brest*, 1966

Plays

Les Bonnes (produced, 1946; revised version, produced, 1954), 1954; as *The Maids*, with *Deathwatch*, 1954

'Adame Miroir (ballet scenario), with music by Milhaud, 1948
Haute surveillance (produced, 1949), 1949; as *Deathwatch*, with *The Maids*, 1954; definitive edition, 1965
Le Balcon (produced, 1960), 1956; revised versions, 1956, 1960; as *The Balcony*, 1957
Les Nègres (produced, 1959), 1958; as *The Blacks*, 1960
Les Paravents (produced, 1961), 1961; as *The Screens*, 1962
Screenplays: *Un chant d'amour*, 1950; *Goubbiah*, 1955; *Mademoiselle*, 1966

Verse

Chants secrets, 1947
La Galère, 1947
Poèmes, 1948; revised edition, 1966
Poems, 1980
Treasures of the Night: Collected Poems, translated by Steven Finch, 1981

Other

Journal du voleur, 1949; as *The Thief's Journal*, 1954
L'Enfant criminel, 'Adame Miroir, 1949
Lettres à Roger Blin, 1966; as *Letters to Roger Blin: Reflections on the Theatre*, 1969
May Day Speech, 1970
Reflections on the Theatre and Other Writings, 1972

Bibliography

Webb, Richard C., *Genet and His Critics: An Annotated Bibliography 1943–1980*, 1982

Critical studies

Sartre, Jean-Paul, *Saint-Genet, Actor and Martyr*, 1963
McMahon, Joseph H., *The Imagination of Jean Genet*, 1963
Driver, Tom F., *Jean Genet* (in English), 1966
Knapp, Bettina, *Jean Genet* (in English), 1968
Thody, Philip, *Jean Genet: A Study of His Novels and Plays*, 1968
Coe, Richard N., *The Visions of Genet*, 1968
Savona, Jeanette, *Genet* (in English), 1983

GIDE, André, 1869–1951.

Novelist, essayist, dramatist, diarist, and winner of the Nobel prize for literature (1947).

LIFE

Gide was an only child. Born into a Provençal family with a strongly Huguenot background, his father, who had come first in his year's national examination for the agrégation, became an eminent professor of Roman law in Paris. His mother, whose absorbing love and puritanically strict principles marked Gide for life, was a rich Calvinist heiress from Normandy. Gide's upbringing was constrained by his mother's determination to conceal from him the family's wealth, though holidays were spent in rotation on the large family estates, surrounded by cousins from all over France. It was one of these cousins Madeleine—two years older than himself—whom Gide was eventually to marry.

At school Gide learnt what it meant to be a Protestant. Bullying by his school-fellows provoked in him reactions of extreme nervous tension and neurotic behaviour that were only half histrionic. In 1877 he was suspended from school, apparently for masturbating, and at the age of 12 found Madeleine, now 14, in tears at the discovery of her mother's adultery. Gide developed a strongly puritan ethic and a quasi-mystical dedication to the alleviation of his cousin's distress. He devised for himself a rigorously ascetic routine, while she developed a repugnance for all relationships involving physical contact.

Gide, still obsessed by Madeleine, now read very widely. He spent five hours most days at the piano, considered becoming a concert pianist, but in 1887 rejoined his class at the Ecole Alsacienne. It was at this excellent Parisian lycée that he became the friend and rival of Pierre Louÿs, with whom he founded the symbolist (q.v.) adolescent *Potache-Revue*. At 15 he had begun to write his *Journal*. In 1889 he passed his baccalauréat only on the resit, and early the next year went to Switzerland to escape the practical jokes in which Louÿs indulged at his expense, and to work up the sustained lyrical intensity necessary to write *Les Cahiers d'André Walter*. Madeleine had turned him down in 1889 and he hoped this work would win both her, and his family, over to the idea of marriage.

The novel, published anonymously in 1891 in a de luxe edition of 200 copies, failed in its purpose, although it was rather astonishingly welcomed by Parisian literary society, including Huysmans, Maeterlinck, Barrès, Bourget, Schwob, Régnier, Maurras, and Gourmont, most of whom Gide had met either at Mallarmé's symbolist Tuesdays or at Heredia's Parnassian (q.v.) salon, which was held on Saturdays. Through Louÿs, Gide also met Valéry, later his close friend, for and with whom he wrote *Le Traité du Narcisse*. Subtitled "Theory of the Symbol," it already contained the anti-symbolist view that symbols were penetrable and related to underlying truths or ideas.

Gide, now influenced by Oscar Wilde, whom he had met in Paris in 1891, began to move away from symbolism and towards a more pronounced interest in the literature of moral values, publishing *Le Voyage d'Urien* and *La Tentative amoureuse* in 1893. That year he set out for North Africa with Paul-Albert Laurens, the painter's son. At Susa Gide fell ill and whilst recuperating that winter at Biskra he attempted to normalize his sexuality with a young Arab prostitute named Meriem. This experience taught him that his sexual inclinations were in fact irreversibly, although he had still to discover how deeply, pederastic.

Gide's mother, alarmed by reports about his health, went to fetch him home. They travelled together via Rome and Florence to Geneva, where a doctor friend correctly diagnosed a weakness in Gide's nervous system. Gide wintered in the mountains, where he was joined by Louÿs, who later went off to find Meriem for himself. Louÿs's witty but wounding practical jokes and Gide's outraged recognition of the moral triviality of sym-

bolism nearly drove him to suicide. He spent the autumn of 1894 in Switzerland, where he wrote *Paludes*. In 1895, he returned to North Africa and met Wilde, with whom he went in exhilarating and successful search of adventures with young Arab boys. He wrote *Les Nourritures terrestres* before his mother's health recalled him to Paris. She died in May. In June Gide and Madeleine became engaged, and on 8 October 1895 they were married. The marriage appears never to have been consummated, although a deep moral and spiritual dependence developed between the two cousins. Gide betrayed Madeleine not by his passing sexual encounters with adolescents, but by his emotional dependence on the 15-year-old Marc Allégret, which began in 1917. Madeleine reacted by destroying the enduring symbol of their love and what Gide no doubt rightly regarded as his best work, his letters to her.

The honeymoon journey reversed the previous return route from Africa, included photographic sessions of nude boys by Gide, and ended in May 1896. On his return Gide was elected mayor of La Roque in Normandy, where he had inherited a 600-acre estate from his mother. He took the job seriously and did his best to right social wrongs. Meanwhile he finished *Les Nourritures terrestres*, which sold only 500 copies in 10 years. He spent the next few years travelling in Italy, Switzerland, and North Africa. *Saül, Le Prométhée mal enchaîné*, and the dramatic texts *Philoctète, Le Retour, de l'enfant Prodigue*, and *Le Roi Candaule* date from this period. Gide also dedicated himself to caring for his wife's delicate health. *L'Immoraliste*, published in a formal first edition of 300 copies in 1902, marks the end of an era in his literary development. He was still virtually unknown outside a narrow literary circle, and for the next 10 years he neither wrote nor travelled very much, publishing only *Amyntas, Le Retour de l'enfant prodigue, La Porte étroite*, and *Isabelle*, although he sat for a while on the editorial board of *L'Ermitage* and in 1909 was active with Jean Schlumberger, Jacques Copeau, André Ruyters, Marcel Drouin, and Henri Ghéon in the foundation of the important avant-garde *Nouvelle Revue Française* (*NRF*, q.v.).

Gide had sold La Roque in 1900 and spent much time gardening at Cuverville, the estate inherited by his wife. He also built himself a large and expensive house at Auteuil, which proved something of a white elephant. From 1908 he began regularly to visit Italy again. It was during this decade, too, that Gide tussled with Claudel and Jammes in an attempt to resolve the tensions within himself between opposing ethical and religious attitudes: hedonism and asceticism, atheism and some, most likely Protestant, form of Christianity. He withstood the temptation to embrace a polarized position through his implicit rejection of an ascetic ideal in *La Porte étroite*, just as in *L'Immoraliste* he had already rejected the hedonist seduction. That left him able to pose as the supreme ironist, a position which he assumed with obvious relish in *Les Caves du Vatican* of 1914. *La Porte étroite*, of which the Catholic faction mistakenly approved, sold out its 1,000-copy edition in two months. In 1911 Gallimard founded what was the *NRF* in-house publishing firm, to which Gide moved.

During the war Gide worked for the Red Cross until he retired, in exasperation, to garden at Cuverville in 1916. There he underwent a spiritual crisis, which was to be recorded in *Numquid et tu…?*. This was partly occasioned by his wife's discovery of a letter from Ghéon, recently converted to Catholicism, alluding to their shared interest in adolescent Arabs. At

work, a fastidiously precise and penetrating self-analysis informed by remorse and the increasingly intense need to assess the balance achieved between duty, commitment, and love on the one hand, and the desire for sensual indulgence on the other.

Corydon, an ironic and witty defence of homosexuality, is partly based on satirical overstatement and ends the series of self-revelatory works. The pamphlets, travel diaries, political and social tracts scarcely call for comment, although *Voyage au Congo* and *Le Retour du Tchad* are such precise, carefully structured, and charming evocations that they offer greater literary interest than much travel literature with serious literary pretentions. *L'Ecole des femmes*, ostensibly the story of a marriage gone stale, is another beautifully controlled, apparently simple novel which yields profound ambivalences with regard to motives, inadequacies, and guilt in its central human relationship. *Robert* is a pendant in the form of a complaint to Gide by the husband, hustling up much sympathy for this amusing but seriously limited Catholic conformist of goodwill.

Oedipe is a serious family comedy set in contemporary society but following the course of the old myth, while *Perséphone* is the verse libretto for a choral ballet, for which Stravinsky wrote the music, with strongly socialist tendencies. *Les Nouvelles Nourritures* is a reaffirmation of joy in the face of life's difficulties and social injustices. Happiness is sought in the acceptance of duty, and is necessarily shared. *Thésée*, Gide's last novel, is a clever adaptation of the myths of Oedipus, Theseus, Daedalus, and Icarus which centres on the last of Gide's free individuals, who, having founded Athens, looks forward to a contented old age. The book is scattered with reminiscences of old friends and enemies, now presented in mythological guise.

Jean-Louis Barrault was still to produce Gide's prose translation of *Hamlet*. Gide also wrote dramatic adaptations of Kafka's *The Trial* and of *Les Caves*. The 1949 *Anthologie de la poésie française* is introduced by an important essay on the nature of poetry, but has been heavily criticized for lapses of taste. In fact it is a work of sly propaganda in support of Gide's literary principles. His correspondence, notably with Claudel, Jammes, and Valéry, which ranges in tone from banter and anecdote to the serious discussion of fundamental issues, is of importance to a much wider readership than historians of culture. *Ainsi soit-it; ou, Les Jeux sont faits*, written shortly before his death, is still full of vitality and fun. Self-mocking to the end, Gide produced a title which combines the church congregation's endorsement of a prayer with the croupier's call twisted to mean "You've made your choice." The farewell is less artless than it seems in its selective recall and reaffirmation of all that Gide's life stood for.

PUBLICATIONS

Collections

Oeuvres complètes (works to 1929), edited by Louis Martin-Chauffier, 15 vols., 1932–39; *Index*, 1954

Romans, récits et soties; Oeuvres lyriques, Bibliothèque de la Pléiade, 1958

Théâtre complet, 8 vols., 1947–9

Journal 1889–1939 with *Journal 1939–1949; Souvenirs*, 2 vols., Bibliothèque de la Pléiade, 1951–4

Fiction

Les Cahiers d'André Walter, 1891; as *The White Notebook*, 1965; as *The Notebook of Andre Walter* 1968

La Tentative amoureuse, 1893; as *The Attempt at Love*, in *The Return of the Prodigal*, 1953

Le Voyage d'Urien, 1893; as *Urien's Voyage*, 1964

Paludes, 1895; as *Marshlands*, 1953

Les Nourritures terrestres, 1897; as *Fruits of the Earth*, 1949

Le Prométhée mal enchaîné, 1899; as *Prometheus Illbound*, 1919; as *Prometheus Misbound*, with *Marshlands*, 1953

L'Immoraliste, 1902; as *The Immoralist*, 1930

Le Retour de l'enfant prodigue, 1907; as *The Return of the Prodigal*, 1953

La Porte étroite, 1909; as *Strait Is the Gate*, 1924

Isabelle, 1911; as *Isabelle*, in *Two Symphonies*, 1931

Les Caves du Vatican, 1914; as *The Vatican Swindle*, 1925; as *Lafcadio's Adventures*, 1927; as *The Vatican Cellars*, 1952

La Symphonie pastorale, 1919; as *The Pastoral Symphony*, in *Two Symphonies*, 1931

Les Faux-Monnayeurs, 1926; as *The Counterfeiters*, 1927; as *The Coiners*, 1950

L'Ecole des femmes, 1929; with *Robert* and *Geneviève*, 1947; as *The School for Wives*, with the other two, 1950

Deux récits, 1938

Thésée, 1946, as *Theseus*, in *Two Legends*, 1950

Plays

Philoctète (produced 1919), 1899; as *Philoctetes*, in *The Return of the Prodigal*, 1953; also in Jackson Mathews, *My Theatre*, 1951

Le Roi Candaule (produced 1901), 1901; as *King Candaules*, in Jackson Mathews, *My Theatre*, 1951

Saül (produced 1922), 1903; as *Saul*, in *The Return of the Prodigal*, 1953; also in Jackson Mathews, *My Theatre*, 1951

Le Retour de l'enfant prodigue (produced 1928), 1909

Bethsabé, 1912; as *Bathsheba*, in Jackson Mathews, *My Theatre*, 1951

Antoine et Cléopatre, from the play by Shakespeare (produced 1920), in *Théâtre complet*, 1949

Amal; ou, La Lettre du roi, from the play by Tagore (produced 1928), 1922

Robert: supplément a l'école des femmes (produced 1946), 1930; as *Robert; ou, L'Intérêt général*, 1949

Oedipe (produced 1931), 1931; as *Oedipus*, in *Two Legends*, 1950

Les Caves du Vatican, from his own novel (produced 1933), 1950

Perséphone, with music by Igor Stravinsky (produced 1934), 1934; edited by Patrick Pollard, 1977; as *Persephone*, 1949, and in Jackson Mathews, *My Theatre*, 1951

Geneviève, 1936; as *Geneviève*, in *The School for Wives*, 1950

Le Treizième Arbre (produced 1939), in *Théâtre complet*, 1942

Hamlet, from the play by Shakespeare (produced 1946), in *Théâtre complet*, 1949

Le Procès, with Jean-Louis Barrault, from the novel by Kafka (produced 1947), 1947; as *The Trial*, 1950

Verse

Les Poésies d'André Walter, 1892

Other

Le Traité du Narcisse, 1891; as *The Treatise of the Narcissus*, in *The Return of the Prodigal*, 1953

Réflexions sur quelques points de littérature et de morale, 1897

Feuilles de route 1895–1896, 1899

Philoctète, suivi de Le Traité du Narcisse, La Tentative amoureuse, El Hadj, 1899

De l'influence en littérature, 1900

Lettres à Angèle (1898–1899), 1900

Les Limites de l'art, 1901

De l'importance du public, 1903

Prétextes, 1903; as *Pretexts*, 1959

Amyntas, 1906; as *Amyntas* (in English), 1958

Dostoïevsky d'après sa correspondance, 1908

Oscar Wilde, 1910; as *Oscar Wilde* (in English), 1951

Charles-Louis Philippe, 1911

CRDN, 1911

Nouveaux prétextes, 1911; as *New Pretexts*, in *Pretexts*, 1959

Souvenirs de la cour d'assises, 1914; as *Recollections of the Assize Court*, 1941

Corydon, 1920; as *Corydon* (in English), 1950

Si le grain ne meurt, 2 vols., 1920–21; as *If It Die…*, 1935

Numquid et tu…? 1922; translated in *Journal*, 1952

Dostoïevsky, 1923; as *Dostoevsky* (in English), 1925

Incidences, 1924; as *Angles of Incidence*, 1959

Caractères, 1925

Le Journal des faux-monnayeurs, 1926; as *The Logbook of the Coiners*, 1952

Dindiki, 1927

Emile Verhaeren, 1927

Joseph Conrad, 1927

Voyage au Congo, 1927; as *Travels in the Congo*, 1929

Le Retour du Tchad, suivi du Voyage au Congo, Carnets de route, 1928; as *Travels in the Congo*, 1930

Essai sur Montaigne, 1929; as *Montaigne* (in English), 1929

Un esprit non prévenu, 1929

Lettres, 1930

L'Affaire Redureau, suivie de Faits divers, 1930

La Sequestrée de Poitiers, 1930

Jacques Rivière, 1931

Divers, 1931

Les Nouvelles Nourritures, 1935; as *Later Fruits of the Earth*, in *Fruits of the Earth*, 1949

Retour de l'URSS, 1936; as *Return from the USSR*, 1937

Retouches à mon Retour de l'URSS, 1937; as *Afterthoughts on the USSR*, 1937

Journal 1889–1939, 1939; *1939–1942*, 1946; *1942–1949*, 1950; as *Journal 1889–1949* (in English), 1952

Découvrons Henri Michaux, 1941

Attendu que, 1943

Interviews imaginaires, 1943; as *Imaginary Interviews*, 1944

Jeunesse, 1945

Lettres à Christian Beck, 1946

Souvenirs littéraires problèmes actuels, 1946

Et nunc manet in te, 1947; as *The Secret Drama of My Life*, 1951; as *Madeleine*, 1952; as *Et nunc manet in te* (in English), 1953

Paul Valéry, 1947

Poétique, 1947

Correspondance 1893–1938, with Francis Jammes, edited by Robert Mallet, 1948

Notes sur Chopin, 1948; as *Notes on Chopin*, 1949

Préfaces, 1948

Rencontres, 1948

Correspondance 1899–1926, with Paul Claudel, edited by Robert Mallet, 1949; as *The Correspondence between Paul Claudel and André Gide*, 1952 *Correspondence*, 1952

Feuillets d'automne, 1949; as *Autumn Leaves*, 1950

Lettres, with Charles du Bos, 1950

Littérature engagée, edited by Yvonne Davet, 1950

Egypte 1939, 1951

Ainsi soit-il; ou, Les Jeux sont faits, 1952; as *So Be It; or, The Chips Are Down*, 1960

Correspondance 1909–1926, with Rainer Maria Rilke, edited by Renée Lang, 1952

Lettres à un sculpteur (Simone Marye), 1952

Correspondance 1890–1942, with Paul Valéry, edited by Robert Mallet, 1955; as *Self-Portraits: The Gide–Valéry Letters*, 1966

Lettres au Docteur Willy Schuermans (1920–1928), 1955

Correspondance inédite, with Rilke and Verhaeren, edited by C. Bronne, 1955; as *Self-Portraits: The Gide- Valéry Letters*, 1966

Correspondance, with Marcel Jouhandeau, 1958

Correspondance 1905–1912, with Charles Péguy, edited by Alfred Saffrey, 1958

Correspondence 1904–1928, with Edmund Gosse, edited by Linette F. Brugmans, 1960

Correspondance 1908–1920, with André Suarès, edited by Sidney D. Braun, 1963

Correspondance 1911–1931, with Arnold Bennett, edited by Linette F. Brugmans, 1964

Correspondance 1909–1951, with André Rouveyre, edited by Claude Martin, 1967

Correspondance 1913–1951, with Roger Martin du Gard, edited by Jean Delay, 2 vols., 1968

Lettres, with Jean Cocteau, edited by Jean-Jacques Kihm, 1970

Correspondance 1912–1950, with François Mauriac, edited by Jacqueline Morton, 1971

Correspondance, with Charles Brunard, 1974

Correspondance, with Jules Romains, edited by Claude Martin, 1976

Correspondance 1897–1944, with Henri Ghéon, edited by Jean Tipy, 2 vols., 1976

Correspondance 1892–1939, with Jacques-Emile Blanche, edited by Georges-Paul Collet, 1979

Correspondance, with Dorothy Bussy, edited by Jean Lambert, 2 vols., 1979–81; as *Selected Letters*, edited by Richard Tedeschi, 1983

Editor, *The Living Thoughts of Montaigne*, 1939

Editor, *Anthologie de la poésie française*, 1949

Translator, *Typhon*, by Conrad, 1918

Translator, with J. Schiffrin, *Nouvelles; Récits*, by Pushkin, 2 vols., 1929-35

Translator, *Arden of Faversham*, in *Le Théâtre élizabethain*, 1933

Translator, *Prométhée*, by Goethe, 1951

Bibliography

Naville, Arnold, *Bibliographie des écrits de Gide*, 1949, supplement, 1953

Critical studies

Hytier, Jean, *André Gide* (in English), 1938
Archambault, Paul, *Humanité d'André Gide*, 1946
Painter, George D., *André Gide* (in English), 1951
O'Brien, Justin, *Portrait of André Gide* (in English), 1953
Starkie, Enid, *André Gide* (in English), 1953
Brée, Germaine, *Gide* (in English), 1963
Ireland, G.W., *Gide* (in English), 1963
Fowlie, Wallace, *Gide: His Life and Work*, 1965
Guérard, Albert J., *André Gide*, 1963; revised edition, 1969
Painter, George D., *Gide: A Critical Biography*, 1968

GIONO, Jean, 1895–1970.

Novelist.

LIFE

The values explored by Giono in his novels are not essentially either conservative, pastoral, romantic, or regional, although they were also all of these things. Nor, in spite of the impracticality of realizing his pacifist ideals and recipes for rural living, was he fundamentally a visionary or an idealist, although he was both. These forces are all tangential to the huge tidal thrust of his imagination. He was warning his generation, especially in the early 1930s, with shrilly prophetic gravity of the need to find serenity somewhere between the sophisticated corrosive power of modern industrial society and nature's fearful power to wreak disaster.

Giono was a moralist, not a sage, a seer and not a planner, and his imagination probed with something like terror the possibility of finding a grip on life which could link man to happiness. The path lay between a whole variety of opposing dangers, destitution and opulence, erudition and ignorance, withdrawn self-sufficiency and political commitment, civilized urban society and primitive natural exposure. Like most great imaginative authors, he found it much easier to identify what was wrong in the human quest for fulfilment than to specify precisely how to put it right. His mind retained the canny peasant ability to move round and round in concentric circles of distrust, first in pursuit of survival, and then towards what might prove to be merely the elusive mirage of contentment. He himself spoke the last word about the path he had discovered for himself. For a barely educated adolescent it does not seem a modest one. In fact, given the simplicity of the life Giono had led, it was a perfectly natural ambition. Intoxicated by translations of the Greek classics which he had been able to buy in the cheap Garnier editions, Giono proclaimed in an interview of 13 March 1937 that he had set out from the beginning "to renew the great Greek tragedies." It seemed to him that the characters lived on around him in the people he knew.

Giono's family was partly Italian and wholly peasant. His great grandfather had been a smelter. His grandfather (born in 1795) was a small Italian market gardener turned revolutionary, a refugee from a death sentence in Italy, who served with the French in Algeria in 1835, was a labourer on the new railway from Avignon to Marseilles in 1840, and finally a concierge at Saint-Chamas, where he married an Italian. He died at Aix-en-Provence in 1854, when Giono's father Jean Antoine (1845–1920), was nearly nine. Before settling at Manosque, Jean-Antoine had been an itinerant shoe repairer. In 1892 he married Pauline Pourcin (1857–1946), who was from Boulogne, and had a small workshop in Manosque where she took in ironing. Giono was born in Manosque on 30 March 1895, and brought up in a very large building with no modern conveniences at all. He has left fictionalized reminiscences of his childhood in *Jean le bleu*.

From 1902 to 1911 Giono attended the local school, spending at least two holidays on nearby sheep farms. His reading has been variously described, but it certainly included, in those cheap editions, Aeschylus, Sophocles, rather surprisingly Aristophanes, and above all Homer, as well as Shakespeare, Spinoza, and then Stendhal, Dostoyevsky, Melville, and Whitman. He was to become very friendly with Gide, whom he had not read, liked Virgil, inevitably preferred the *Odyssey* to the *Iliad*, and developed a liking for Mozart and Bach. His father had often read the Bible to him aloud, and Giono himself gradually built up a collection of around 100 books. Although he had obtained a scholarship which would have allowed him to take his baccalauréat in sciences and languages, Giono chose to leave school to help with the family income, and in 1911 became an office boy with the local branch of a small bank at 10 francs a month. It was to reading Kipling on a bank errand to Marseilles by train that Giono traced his desire to write.

In spite of his pacifism, in 1915 Giono was called up for service in the Alpine infantry. In May he was at Grenoble and, although at Verdun, and one of only 11 members of his company to escape alive, in *Refus d'obéissance* he later proudly announced that he was quite sure he had killed no one. He was at the Somme and had his eyebrows blistered by gas. His harsh war experiences were unalleviated by any ideological commitment and were strongly to reinforce his pacifist principles. Demobilized in October 1919, he was at Manosque in time for his father's death on 26 April 1920. On 20 June he married Elise Maurin (born in 1897), the hairdresser's daughter from the shop opposite. He was promoted at the bank, and was sent to Marseilles, where he got to know the painter Lucien Jacques, who became a life-long friend. Bernard Buffet was to become another close painter friend. Jacques wrote for a small local magazine, *La Criée*, which appeared from 1920 to 1925, and which printed Giono's first poems, and Jacques paid for the publication of a 300-copy edition of Giono's first prose poems, *Accompagné de la flûte*, only 10 copies of which were sold. One of them was bought by the publisher Adrienne Monnier.

By 1923 Giono had become an undermanager at the bank. His writing continued to be a spare-time occupation until *Colline*, the first of the "Pan" trilogy, was published in 1928 in the Parisian review *Commerce*, where it attracted Gide's interest and admiration. Grasset published it in the *Cahiers Verts* collection, edited by Daniel Halévy at the Editions de Minuit in 1929, the year of Giono's first visit to Paris. Its success with the critics was immediate, and the novel was awarded the 1,000-dollar Prix Brentano. A note in Giono's own chronological account of his life tells us that the dollar was then worth 15 francs. When he was appointed manager of the Antibes branch of the bank Giono preferred to resign. Several texts had remained unpublished: "Les larmes de Byblis," "En plus du pain," "Le voyageur immobile," and a novel, "Angélique," of 1923. Grasset, who had turned down *La Naissance de l'Odyssée* a year after it had been written, in 1927, rushed to get the other two panels of the "Pan" triptych, *Un de Baumugnes* and *Regain*, into print. *La Naissance de l'Odyssée* came out in 1930, and the collection of short stories *Solitude de la pitié* in 1932. This includes Giono's first strong reaction against urban civilization, "Destruction de Paris," and introduces other themes important for his later work: the joys of rural life in "Prélude de Pan," and the aspiration to supreme harmony for the world in "Le chant du monde." In 1930 Giono also published the 80-page *Présentation de Pan*, a series of poetic texts chiefly drawing on the inspiration of the foothills of the Alps.

Giono's daughters Aline and Sylvie were born on 25 October 1926 and 11 August 1934, respectively. Giono and his family moved to Le Parais, a house just outside Manosque, and honours came with the rapid succession of publications, starting with the Légion d'Honneur on 9 July 1932. Although Giono never cared much for travel, at this period he did give talks in Germany (1931) and Switzerland (1932). In 1935 a group of about 50, including Giono, bought a house with a little land at Contadour in an attempt to promote a life as close as possible to nature in occasional camping sessions, during which poetry and pacifism would be discussed. Giono was later to regard the whole episode as an embarrassingly naive undertaking, but he and Lucien Jacques kept it going for six years, founding the *Cahiers du Cantadour*, which published nine numbers from 1936 to February 1939.

From 1935 Giono wrote for the communist paper *L'Humanité* and the left-wing weekly *Vendredi*, breaking with this last in 1937 when ideological visions hardened into political commitments with the approach of war. The integral pacifism of the 1937 *Refus d'obéissance*, the subsequently played-down naivety of the Contadour inspiration, the 1938 *Lettre aux paysans sur la pauvreté et la paix*, recommending the limitation of agricultural production strictly to household needs in case of war, the signing of the telegram congratulating Chamberlain and Daladier, and the famous remark of 14 October 1938, "Je n'ai honte d'aucune paix; j'ai honte de toutes les guerres (I'm not ashamed of any peace; I am ashamed of every war)," all suggest that the prophet was turning himself into a sage. In fact it may well be that the real power of Giono's creative imagination started running down as early as 1935, the year of publication of what is probably his greatest novel, *Que ma joie demeure*, leaving his really important literary production compressed into scarcely more than half a decade, 1929 to 1935. *Batailles dans la montagne* of 1937, an ambitious attempt at an epic, already overburdens the characters, who are no longer capable of carrying the myth and are crushed by it into symbols. The language begins to show signs of lack of imaginative control.

From the mid-1930s the ideological obsessions took over from the literary imagination. They were to create difficulties for Giono both when he tore up his call-up papers for World War II and after the war, when he was called to account for the publication of an article perfectly consistent with his fundamental pacifism, but which was not unreasonably taken to have been an act of collaboration with the occupiers. Then came the post-war change of direction, the reversion to well-confected but now escapist story telling, removed from the proximate perils facing Giono's society, and remote from the difficult reconstruction of the civilized world which was being undertaken around him. The post-war fiction is devoid of the sweeping myths and sumptuous language of the early 1930s, and with it came participation in the cinema industry, increased travel, the assumption of the mantle of the man of letters, membership of the Goncourt jury, presidency of the Cannes festival jury in 1961, and the polished professionalism of the eight-hour-a-day author with regular holidays in the once-hated Mediterranean.

Giono's creative activity during the four years leading to World War II was paralysed by the waste he foresaw, the unnecessary suffering which he predicted, and the great fissures that would be rent in civilized living which obsessed his imagination and terrified him personally. He thought the peasants should starve the parliaments and the military into submission. They should refuse the martyrdom which Giono had seen imposed on them in World War I, and of which he had himself so nearly been a victim. Arrested in September 1939 for the destruction of his call-up papers, Giono was a problem for the authorities. Asked if he would write pacifist tracts for dropping on Germany, he replied that he would, but only if they were also dropped on Britain and France. He had to be locked up until, as these things are arranged in France, the right people said the right things in the right places, at which point Giono was released and demobilized. He was at home again in November, translated *Moby Dick*, and wrote a highly fictionalized "biography" of Melville.

Giono's pre-war advocacy of the simple life nourished by the land fitted in admirably with Pétain's view of what Vichy society should be, but Giono tried to avoid political involvement. After the war he was nevertheless imprisoned on account of his wartime contribution of "Deux cavaliers de l'orage" to the pro-Nazi *La Gerbe*, edited by Alphonse de Chateaubriant, and for publishing, in 1941, *Le Triomphe de la vie*, which, though scarcely subversive, was popular with the occupying forces. Charges against him were dropped, and he was subsequently left unmolested in the reprisals of the "épuration."

Giono's literary career was generally thought to have ended with the war, on account both of the rejected ideology and the declining quality of his production, but there followed a spate of post-war works which are often wrongly regarded as similar in inspiration to those of Stendhal. The likeness is superficial. Giono's post-war production was none the less commercially successful, and filled a real need for a generation battered with explanations of human experience in terms merely of its absurdity. He travelled to the UK in 1952 and to Italy in 1953, then to Switzerland, Austria, and Italy again in 1958.

His daughter Sylvie had married in 1959, and in 1961 Lucien Jacques died. From 1954 Giono had to attend the December lunch of the Goncourt committee in Paris. It was after the 1969 lunch that he had his first sign of impending incapacity, although he had suffered a slight thrombosis two years earlier. He died on the night of 8–9 October 1970. His work was immediately monumentalized in the five Pléiade volumes of his fiction which appeared from 1970 to 1980. Pagnol had made films based on the novels, and Giono had founded his own film company, and written his own scripts, from 1958. His wartime plays and post-war films are not, however, generally regarded as successful.

Giono's early published work is direct and moving, unsentimental in its emotional vigour, and often rhapsodic with joy, although the exuberance of spirit and luxuriance of language were still to come. The first work is dry, more exactly evoking the arid landscape of Provence in which it was rooted. *Colline* is instantly remarkable for its avoidance of any literary artifice and the extreme simplicity of its central peasant character, Gagou. Life moves in a natural rhythm, in harmony with the ungenerous land, which begrudges even its parsimonious yield. The story deals with peasant witchcraft and superstition, and Giono, mimicking peasant speech in the narratorial style as well as in the patches of conversation, exploits his inexperience as a writer, as well as the lessons he has learnt from his Greek classics, in extremely brief sentences, not infrequently reduced to an essential three words, and often enough with an exclamation mark: "Une porte bat; des vitres dégringolent. Au fond du vacarme, des cris des femmes (A door bangs. Windows creak. Beneath the noise, women's shouts)." The omission of the main verb, imitating actual utterance, particularly among the uneducated, becomes an almost intrusive mannerism.

Colline has a narrator who does not pretend not to be there, but sometimes comments on the story he is telling. *Un de Baumugnes* is recounted in the first person by a farm labourer. In a café he meets Albin, an ungainly, kind-hearted expert on the mouth organ. Albin had been much taken by a farm girl, Angèle. Another man had lured her away from home, and she had returned with a fatherless baby, afraid to face her family, and reduced to prostitution. When she did return home, her parents hid her, locking her up out of shame. The narrator gets himself hired on the farm, discovers the girl, calls Albin, who reveals himself to Angèle by playing the harmonica and, taking the baby, elopes with her.

Giono's achievement is to have written a conte of innocence and joy, ending in happiness ever after, with Angèle's father playing the wicked fairy role, without allowing the myth to collapse into a fairy story, and without resorting to the contrived devices which Alain-Fournier, for instance, had to use to achieve the same end. By the time he wrote *Regain* the stylistic tricks were contrived, down to the smattering of argot. The text has a narrator who adopts a conversational tone with the reader from the beginning, spends half a dozen pages rather obviously evoking atmosphere before we know what or who the story is about, and scarcely avoids the fairy story with its moral. By now the very short sentences have become monotonous. There are two parts, and the text is headed "roman," although it is scarcely more than a conte, labouring the seasonal cycle, and ending with the joyous optimism of spring, rich earth, and the promise of further plentiful harvests to come.

The tryptich is short enough, surprising enough in its joy, and evocative enough in the authenticity of its atmosphere, for the trilogy considered as a whole to constitute a major work. None of Giono's books is a sustained masterpiece, although many have magnificent scenes or episodes. Of the war books *Le Grand Troupeau* of 1931 is neither sentimental nor shocking in its depiction of gruesome war scenes. The effect is better achieved for its controlled dryness, and this is one of the occasions when Giono's striving for epic effect succeeds in creating a myth to support a message without even importing a story. What makes the book is the series of horrifying sketches of the front line presented in counterpoint with the rhythm of life in the villages to the rear, and the sheer imaginative strength with which Giono, glossing over nothing, again sustains a vision of hope.

Jean le bleu was published in 1932 and is largely made up of autobiographical evocations of childhood. Giono was moved to his lushest writing here, relishing in language that is now much more confident as well as more luxuriant, and in the sounds, sights, and smells of youthful reminiscence. The book, like the rest of what Giono wrote, cannot reasonably be regarded as pantheistic or pagan. Its preoccupations are neither theological nor religious, but concerned with the primitive thoughts, feelings, and reactions of a peasant community for which sophistication is a snare, nature a menace, and a living hard to make, requiring pacts with the seasons and the soil, as well as with hard-pressed neighbours. As he feels death drawing near, the reflective shoemaker regards life, death, suffering, and God not as objects of awe, but in their direct relationship to the experience of all those engaged in the battle to survive.

God is not the term of a religious aspiration, a philosophical enquiry, or a divine revelation, but simply plays in human affairs a role whose proper nature is open to discussion. Peasant shoemakers have a shrewd idea what it should be. Again Giono's strength is to make the triumph of man over nature seem possible, providing the scale of the combat is kept small enough, and even though man is doomed to death. The secret is to realize that the triumph of happiness comes through relationships and not through technology. Even though that piece of wisdom is part of the shoemaker's legacy to Jean, it does not weigh the book down. The possibility of triumph is evoked by an indulgence in the sensuous joys of life, communicated here by ripeness of language.

The next three books constitute what could be described as a crescendo in Giono's literary production. *Le Serpent d'étoiles* is notable for the closely felt relationship with the high alpine summer pastures which it depicts. The shepherds improvise a wide-ranging drama in which Giono said he had preserved the integrity of primitive epic. The natural setting is described in magnificent images, and Giono gives the work the authenticity of the secular folk story which produced antiquity's greatest epics. In 1934 he followed it with *Le Chant du monde*, which only apparently conforms to the ordinary patterns of the novel. Here Giono creates a myth which he recounts as a parable. The passions of nature combine with those of men to cause destruction as well as giving rise to serenity. There is a primitive healer, Toussaint, a recurring character in Giono's epics, who stands above the story and combines in himself the force and wisdom of nature.

Antonio, a fisherman, sets off with the older Matelot in search of Matelot's son, the twin of one who had been killed in a brawl. They arrive at a city halfway up a mountain ruled by a tyrant called Maudru. Here they find a wise and affluent old hunchback, who was long ago disappointed in love and now spends his time caring for the sick and the vagrant. He had taken in Matelot's son, who had fallen in love with Gina, a member of Maudru's family, and eloped with her after killing Maudru's nephew. The couple remain in hiding, waiting for the thaw to unfreeze their raft, and Matelot is ambushed and killed by Maudru's men. Antonio helps Matelot's son set fire to the stables, and the bulls which are released overpower Maudru's cowherd vassals. Antonio and Matelot's son launch their raft, freed in the spectacular spring thaw, taking with them Gina and the blind Clara, whom Antonio had befriended in the woods while she was giving birth. As they sail down the river, Clara learns to use her remaining senses to decipher the secrets of nature, which trees they pass, which stars are shining. The novel brings together violence and tenderness, joy and pain, combining its rhythms to carry along the parable of the vulnerability of the weak without the protection of the strong, who none the less rely on the weak for the intuitive skills they are able to develop.

Que ma joie demeure of 1935 is the peak of Giono's achievement. The title is taken from a Bach chorale addressed to Jesus, whose name Giono has removed. His reference is not religious and Christian, but natural and cosmic. The point of the novel is not its meandering plot but its magnificent set pieces, all converging in the aspiration to intense, emotional joy. The narrative is interrupted with ostentatiously interpolated descriptions. "Voilà ce qu'on voyait (This is what you saw)" says the narrator, and the brilliance of the description which follows is breathtaking. The eye's focus moves farther away, fixing on objects, then colours, then the sky, which is given first physical characteristics, "infinie viduité (infinite emptiness)," and then moral ones: "cruauté effrayante et sans borne (frightening and limitless cruelty)," "A partir de là, ça n'était pas grand'chose, si vous voulez, mais c'était la joie et l'amour (From there on there wasn't much, if you like, but there was joy and love)." There follows a series of striking images and metaphors. Man is not, as we thought, made of cells and blood. He is in fact like foliage, not a block, but scattered images through which the wind has to blow so that it can sing. Giono now elaborates the difference between what happens when a stone is dropped into water and when a branch is dropped on to it. The stone makes a hole, but the water is not wounded, makes the necessary repairs, and wins back its original form as the residual ripples fade away. The branch on the other hand floats, its gaze turned to the sun; it germinates, and new shoots appear in the sand.

The language which, if taken to include imagery, is the point of the novel, can now get very complex indeed. "The wind was speaking," and like everything else it was "creamy," "full of forms, full of images, of glimmers, of lights, of flames which didn't light up a centimetre of ground, but all the inside of a body." What the wind said is a torrent of words: "mountain, ice, fir tree sap, the Ouvèze valley, with water, reeds, wallows of birds ready for love…" The simple vocabulary of natural vigour is now mixed in with a recondite selection of words and coinages. What follows the colon telling us what the wind said is only punctuated like a sentence, with four dashes and half a dozen semi-colons, but has an apparently quite disordered variety of subjects, tenses, pronouns, indicatives, imperatives, and registers of language, from the most colloquial to the formally descriptive, with lists and repetitions, comprising 25 perfectly coherent and quite unconfusing lines of darting thoughts, ideas, and mental flashes.

The novel's main characters are the forces of nature, such as wind and frost, thunder, lightning, night, and growth, but there is a central prophetic idiot figure, Bobi, who tells a worried farmer, risen to plough in the middle of the night, to look at the stars and leave some of his field to daffodils, hawthorn, and daisies. If he does this he will be happy, says Bobi. The peasants stop distrusting one another, and their new cooperation is forged at a great feast. They catch hinds for Bobi's stag. Tragedy breaks into the sweetness and light when Aurore commits suicide, having secretly fallen in love with Bobi, who realizes he has tried to create utopia in too much of a hurry, ignoring nature's laws of slow growth. He is killed by lightning as he leaves: "Thunder planted a golden tree between his shoulders."

Giono's work quite swiftly falls away after his imagination has exhausted itself in this great romantic parable, in which no one should look for depth of characterization or psychological analysis. Giono calls it a novel, but it is in fact a parable, not even a myth. The post-war production represents a flight from the sempiternal as well as from the present. In the five volumes of *Chroniques* the exuberance has now given way to humour and, although the narrators have often taken part in the action, they relate it in such a way that the reader is not drawn into personal involvement with what happens. The narratives are swift, the sketched vignettes skilful, and the language still earthy, but the stories are short, merely entertaining. They do not attempt to create myths, and there is nothing epic about their conception.

The most highly regarded of the post-war novels is *Le Hussard sur le toit* of 1952. The hero is a young colonel who returns to his native city to find it in the grip of a cholera epidemic. He escapes over the rooftops and flees with a woman of aristocratic birth, escaping the plague and the hostility of the citizens who are afraid of the cholera. It is a long adventure novel in which the couple exhibit chivalrous humour and restraint, with all too few of the soaring images which make Giono one of the masters of French prose writing.

PUBLICATIONS

Fiction

Colline, 1929; as *Hill of Destiny*, 1929
Un de Baumugnes, 1929; as *Lovers Are Never Losers*, 1931
Regain, 1930; as *Harvest*, 1939
Présentation de Pan, 1930
La Naissance de l'Odyssée, 1930
Manosque des plateaux, 1930
Le Grand Troupeau, 1931
Eglogues, 1931
Jean le bleu, 1932; as *Blue Boy*, 1946
Solitude de la pitié, 1932
Le Serpent d'étoiles, 1933
Le Chant du monde, 1934; as *The Song of the World*, 1937
Que ma joie demeure, 1935; as *Joy of Man's Desiring*, 1940
Batailles dans la montagne, 1937
Triomphe de la vie, 1942
Faust du village, 1944
L'Eau vive, 1944
Noé, 1947
Un roi sans divertissement, 1947
Les Ames fortes, 1949
Mort d'un personnage, 1949
Les Grands Chemins, 1951
Le Hussard sur le toit, 1952; as *The Horseman on the Roof*, 1954
Le Moulin de Pologne, 1952; as *The Malediction*, 1955
Voyage en Italie, 1954
Le Bonheur fou, 1957
Angelo, 1958; as *The Straw Man*, 1959
Deux cavaliers de l'orage, 1966
Ennemonde, 1968
L'Iris de Suse, 1970

Les Récits de la demi-brigade, 1972
La Terrasse de l'île d'Elbe, 1973
Le Déserteur et autres récits, 1973

Plays

*Le Bout de la route, Le Lanceur de graines, La Femme du bou-
    langer*, 1943
Le Voyage en calèche, 1947
Domitien, Joseph à Dothan, 1959

Other

Accompagné de la flûte, 1924
Les Vraies Richesses, 1937
Refus d'obéissance, 1937
Le Poids du ciel, 1938
Lettre aux paysans sur la pauvreté et la paix, 1938
Précisions, 1939
Pour saluer Melville (with *Moby Dick*), 1941
Le Voyage en Italie, 1953
Recherches de la pureté, 1953
Notes sur l'affaire Dominici, 1955
Oppède (album), 1960
Arcadie, with woodcuts by Lucien Jacques, 1960
Camargue (album), 1960
Images de Provence, 1961
Le Désastre de Pavie, 23 février 1525, 1963

Critical and biographical studies

Boisdeffre, Pierre de, *Giono*, 1965
Redfern, W. *The Private World of Jean Giono*, 1967
Goodrich, N., *Giono, Master of Fictional Modes*, 1973
Citron, P., *Giono* (in English), 1990

———

GIRAUDOUX, Jean (-Hippolyte), 1882–1944.

Diplomat, dramatist, novelist, critic, and essayist.

LIFE

Admirers of Giraudoux's work, especially of the plays which
dominated the French theatre in the 1930s, will not be surprised
to learn how much Giraudoux cherished his privacy. As a diplomat, discretion and confidentiality became instinctive, but so
little trace of his biography remains that it is to be assumed that
he himself ensured a posthumous protection of privacy by
having his papers destroyed. Not even the official ones have
been traced. Giraudoux clearly preferred to keep his diplomatic
career separate from both his political commitment and his literary activity, as might well be guessed from the purposeful trivialization and amused, ironic distance with which, in his novels
and on the stage, he treated even the most searing of private
events, such as love, lunacy, and death, and even the most cata-

clysmic of public phenomena, such as war and the state of the
economy. The surprising absence of so much documentation
and the peculiar circumstances of Giraudoux's death suggest,
however, that it was the activities of his last years which led him
to erase his tracks.

He was born in Bellac on 29 October, the second son of a
minor civil servant, then aged 32. His father was attached first
to transport administration and subsequently to a tax office in
the heart of rural France, first at Pellevoisin and then at Cérilly.
His mother, Anne Lacoste, was 29 when he was born. Giraudoux, who was to leave only fictionalized recollections of his
childhood in *Simon le pathétique*, was closer to her than he
depicted in the novel. In Cérilly the family lived next door to
Charles-Louis Philippe, the cobbler's son whom Barrès had
taken up and whose novel *Bubu de Montparnasse* was successfully published in 1901. At school the young Giraudoux was
laughed at for boasting that he knew Philippe. He never forgot
that experience. In an essay on Philippe he was to publish in the
October 1937 issue of the *Nouvelle Revue Française* (q.v.), subsequently reprinted in *Littérature*, Giraudoux reflected on the
monopoly of literary expression possessed by the educated
middle class to which he belonged, and for whom he himself
necessarily, as he saw it, had to write.

From the beginning of his schooldays Giraudoux showed outstanding intellectual brilliance. After attending the local primary
school at Pellevoisin, he won a scholarship to join his elder
brother in 1893 as a boarder at the Châteauroux lycée. After two
further years (1900–02) of preparation at the Lycée Lakanal at
Sceaux, in Paris, where Giraudoux came first in the national
Greek prose examination and distinguished himself for his
sporting abilities, he was called up for military service, and in
1903 he entered the Ecole Normale Supérieure with the intention of taking the agrégation in German. He was taught by
Charles Andler, at that date a militant socialist and Pan-Germanist, but spent a good deal of time at the Café Vachette and began
to write. In December 1904 Giraudoux's first short story "Le
dernier rêve d'Edmond About," was published in *Marseille-étu-
diant*.

Early in 1905 he left the Ecole after coming first in his year,
with his "licence", and with a travelling scholarship and a teaching post in Germany. He spent most of the next 18 months in
Munich, where he became friendly with Paul Morand. He travelled widely in central Europe and, having finished his diploma
of higher German studies, lived a leisurely life in Paris, wrote
many of what were to become the short sketches of rural life, the
Provinciales, but failed his agrégation, and through influential
friends obtained a post as French-language assistant at Harvard
for a year. In 1907 he returned to Paris, where he became secretary to the director of *Le Matin* and editor of its literary page. He
wrote for it under the pseudonym of J. E. Manière, but was dismissed for printing two contes of which the readership disapproved, one by a friend from the Café Vachette and the other by
Charles-Louis Philippe.

Giraudoux now gave up hopes of the agrégation and, with
Paul Morand, took the competitive foreign office entry examination, failing at the higher grade, but coming first at the lower
level. From 1910 he worked as a civil servant at the foreign
press office in Paris, and in 1911 was sent briefly to Russia. Gide
had welcomed the *Provinciales*, and Giraudoux now published
L'Ecole des indifférents. He spent the summer of 1911 with
Morand, writing a first draft of what was still called "Simon."

On the outbreak of war Giraudoux returned to his former regiment as a sergeant and an interpreter. On 16 September 1914 he was wounded on the Marne in the leg and the groin and, after an operation had gone wrong, was sent to Bordeaux to recover. He returned to his regiment at Roanne but during 1915 was able to spend much free time in Paris. He met his future wife, Suzanne Boland, and saw something of Henri de Jouvenel, Edmond Jaloux, and the Princesse de Polignac, at whose house he met Bergson. After volunteering for the eastern front, Giraudoux was sent as a sublieutenant to the Dardanelles, wounded in the hip, and sent home again, where he became the first writer to be awarded the Légion d'Honneur for war services. He was to write about his experiences in *Lectures pour une ombre* and in the novel *Adorable Clio* of 1920.

Philippe Berthelot, who was to quarrel with Poincaré in 1922 and to figure in Giraudoux's *Bella* in 1926, then sent Giraudoux as a military instructor to Portugal during the summer of 1916. On his return Giraudoux was sent to the US, where he arrived in the spring of 1917, returning to Paris in August, ready to write *Amica America*. He ended the war as liaison officer with the US army in Paris, and in 1918 published *Simon le pathétique* (first version) and married. In 1919 his only son, Jean-Pierre, was born, and he published *Elpénor*. By 1921 Giraudoux, now an established literary figure, was also progressing in his diplomatic career. With the rank of secretary, he was director of French cultural services abroad until that post was abolished in 1924, and he was sent to Berlin. In the same year he became chief government press officer.

The foreign service career entailed a good deal of travel all over the world, and progressed sideways to membership of the committee on war damage in Turkey in 1926. The diplomatic career was beginning to look rather like one of those traditional and enlightened French arrangements, whereby members of the academic and cultural communities are selectively supported in undemanding posts, in this case offering the perquisite of travel, while they develop their real talents, particularly if these might redound to the cultural glory of France. Giraudoux's increasingly public concern about urban planning and other social matters may have led to his virtual sidetracking into the inspectorship of consulates in 1934. Although he was a minister plenipotentiary from 1933, the posts he was offered were not important, and his warnings about the likely outbreak of war in the 1935 stage success *La Guerre de Troie n'aura pas lieu* cannot have been welcomed in official circles. In 1939 the lectures published as *Pleins pouvoirs* sketched a plan for France's economic recovery, which was an indictment of the authorities, but in August 1939 Giraudoux was finally appointed by Daladier to the post of director general of information services, which he had long wanted.

This last appointment proved disastrous when the department was attached to the ministry of war and Giraudoux became president of the committee on propaganda. Reynaud had succeeded Daladier, but when he in turn gave way to Pétain on 16 June 1940, Giraudoux retired from Bordeaux, where his ministry had moved, to live with his brother at Cusset. He had failed to join his son with the Free French forces in Portugal and turned down the Vichy government's offer of the Athens embassy. Five somewhat inept radio speeches and his subsequent resignation had left him compromised in the eyes both of Pétain's supporters and of those who were to fight for the liberation, although it gradually became clear that Giraudoux was strongly opposed to

the occupying forces. Aragon reports Giraudoux's dismay in Bordeaux at discovering that he was expected to administer a censorship which he may himself have eventually succeeded in outwitting, although it seems unlikely that the German censor's office in Paris was as uncomprehending of the plays it allowed to be staged as is generally supposed (see Sartre), and probable that it had intelligent reasons for the licensing of manifestations of dissidence. Giraudoux's reflections on this period are contained in *Ecrits dans l'ombre*, published posthumously in 1944.

Giraudoux's liking for German romanticism (q.v.) had gone hand in hand with a firm dislike of the Nazi regime and a commitment to France which was both political and social. On 27 December 1943, a month before his death, he published in *Le Figaro* the manifesto of the Urban and Rural League which he had founded. At the beginning of January 1944 he was staying at the Hôtel de Castille in Paris, continuing some form of "research," perhaps into war crimes, but relevant in any case to the reconstruction that would follow the war. It is known that he had worked clandestinely in the interests of the liberation forces, and also that he remained in contact with Aragon. He died mysteriously and unexpectedly, after much pain, on the morning of 31 January. He was 61. His mother had died a year previously. His estranged wife was present.

Sodome et Gomorrhe was first played at the Hébertot on 11 October 1943 with Edwige Feuillère in the lead, but begun in 1941 in strong reaction to Pétain's speeches and finished by May 1942. It is apparently a play about marital discord set against the backdrop of the end of the world, but is in fact strongly anti-Nazi, shot through with resentment at Pétain's capitulation and role in France's self-abasement. It may be that the censor had missed those implications, but the official Nazi reaction to Giraudoux's death, as enunciated on 4 February 1944 in the collaborationist *Je Suis Partout*, and confirmed in a letter to the paper from Céline printed on 11 February, mentioned with vituperation both the play and the theatre, which had already been in trouble for staging Cocteau. A total of 214 performances were given before the play closed at the end of May.

Giraudoux's son, also a writer, had fought in the Free French navy and in 1945 was aide-de-camp to de Gaulle, who attended the first night of Giraudoux's *La Folle de Chaillot* on 19 December 1945, directed by Jouvet, much more having been made of the occasion than might ordinarily have been expected even for a Giraudoux first night. All the evidence suggests that, however discreetly manifested, Giraudoux's political commitment during the war to an independent France was intense. It is not unlikely that it had something to do with his death.

Since the end of World War I, Giraudoux's literary career had followed three parallel tracks: fiction, drama, and the works of personal, social, and political reflection and commitment. Latterly he also worked for the cinema. By 1921 Giraudoux had already established his reputation as one of France's more brilliant young writers. The novel *Suzanne et le Pacifique* of that year was much discussed, but shows little sign of an imagination disrupted by war. That came with the still reticent, first-person *Siegfried et le Limousin* of 1922, a novel about the political situation in post-war Germany, which was criticized because of the favourable way in which some of the German characters were depicted. Then in 1924 came *Juliette au pays des hommes*, reverting to the complex and subtle interior monologue of *Suzanne*, to be followed in 1926 by *Bella*, the new version of *Simon le pathétique*, and in 1927 by *Eglantine*.

It was at this point, when Giraudoux was also raised to a higher grade in the Légion d'Honneur, that the Morands suggested that he should write for the theatre. Louis Jouvet, who had worked with Copeau as actor and stage manager from 1913, had left him in 1922 to establish his own theatre and, now settled at the Théâtre des Champs- Elysées, was looking for new dramatists. *Siegfried*, adapted from Giraudoux's novel, was the result of a close cooperation with Jouvet, who staged it on 3 May 1928, inaugurating one of the great 20th-century theatrical partnerships in France. The play was a success, in spite of parading German uniforms on the stage, and Jouvet played the leading role 302 times. In 1929, with Jouvet again in the leading role, there followed *Amphitryon 38*, so-called because Giraudoux said he knew of 37 previous dramatic treatments of the Greek legend, but less critically acclaimed because it was too esoterically precious. It ran for 254 performances. The 1937 Theatre Guild's adaptation, with Alfred Lunt and his wife, Lynn Fontanne, in the leading roles, was a notable success, however, in both London and New York.

Giraudoux's next important book was the novel *Les Aventures de Jérôme Bardini*, published in 1930. There were to be two more: *Combat avec l'ange* of 1934 and *Choix des élues* of 1938. The biblical tragedy *Judith*, played at the Pigalle on 4 November 1931, was a relative failure, but in 1932 Giraudoux published a successful collection of contes reusing the characters from *Bella*, and on 1 March 1933 he returned to Jouvet and the Champs-Elysées with the highly successful *Intermezzo*, played in London by the Renaud-Barrault company in 1956. Following an adaptation of *The Constant Nymph* in 1934, with Jouvet in the lead, in 1935 Giraudoux presented the resoundingly successful *La Guerre de Troie n'aura pas lieu*. Jouvet played the lead 255 times, but the play was equally successful when the war Giraudoux was really warning about had actually taken place, and Michael Redgrave played the lead in Christopher Fry's translation in London and New York in 1955. The *Supplément au voyage de Cook*, like *L'Impromptu de Paris*, was a curtain-raiser, followed on 13 May 1937 by *Electre*, one of Giraudoux's weaker and less successful plays, and one lacking dramatic unity.

Giraudoux had turned down the post of director of the Comédie-Française in 1936, but it was there that the slight one-act *Cantique des cantiques* was given in 1938. Giraudoux returned to Jouvet with *Ondine* on 27 April 1939. It is often thought to be his best play and was later given successfully in London, in French in 1953 and by the Royal Shakespeare Company, with Leslie Caron in the lead, in 1961. Jouvet had spent the war years in neutral countries partly, he says, because he was forbidden to present Giraudoux's work in Paris. He gave Giraudoux's variously named and lightweight *L'Apollon de Bellac* in Rio de Janeiro in 1942. He returned to Paris in time for the posthumously staged *La Folle de Chaillot*, of which he gave 397 performances. Martita Hunt was an instant success in the lead in New York in 1948, but her London performance in 1951, although much praised, had only a short run. The posthumous *Pour Lucrèce* was given by Barrault at the Marigny in 1953 with Edwige Feuillère in the lead. Giraudoux also made two films: from Balzac's *La Duchesse de Langeais* in 1942, and *Les Anges du péché* of 1943.

Giraudoux's views on the theatre are presented most clearly in the essays collected in *Littérature* of 1941, but also in *L'Impromptu de Paris*. He was interested in the promotion of sport as a means to better health, the quest for which also lay behind his interest in urban planning and his advocacy of green spaces. He felt, not unreasonably, that in the matter of urban planning Paris lagged behind some, perhaps most, of the other major cities of the Western world. He published his views on sport in 1928, and on urban planning in *Pleins pouvoirs* of 1939. Its counterpart, *Sans pouvoirs*, appeared only posthumously in 1946. The brilliance of his dramatic writing, particularly the fruitful collaboration with Jouvet, has eclipsed interest in his other work to the unfortunate detriment of his reputation, and even of an understanding of the real purport of the plays.

WORKS

The autobiographical writings, the social and political pamphlets, and the novels written in Giraudoux's thirties and forties hold the key to the underlying themes of his drama. Giraudoux fully accepted the need to provide audiences with a night out, and deliberately injected a dose of escapism into his theatre. None the less, he intends the enchantment to carry the audience into a higher, more enriched and intense plane of experience than that offered by everyday life. Almost all the plays use some dramatic device or other to insist on the difference of level between the imaginative concentration of what is presented and the humdrum diffuseness of the audience's day-to-day awareness of the values by which it lives. For Giraudoux the theatre is "la seule forme d'éducation morale ou artistique d'une nation (a nation's only form of moral and artistic education)," and the audience must be made to realize the true purpose of the experience it is paying to undergo. There is much more to Giraudoux than the civilized, witty, ironic, and elegant entertainer for which he has sometimes been taken.

Behind the esoteric and rather precious novels, the amused ironic treatment of myth in the plays, and the apparently insubstantial plots about women, nymphs, and marital relationships, there is a deep personal and political seriousness which it is easy to miss, and to which the other works sometimes open access. Even taken by themselves the plays are clearly not about their superficial subjects, which are often merely frivolous. When, in *La Guerre de Troie*, a serious debate gives way to a drunken dispute which sets off the war, Giraudoux is delivering a serious lesson which Europe as a whole would have done well to heed. The play is not about what might not have happened at Troy, but about mankind, its disputes, and how important it is to settle them rationally; not about the fickleness of Hélène, the lecherousness of Troy's old men, Pâris's jokes or Demokos' touchiness, but about the serious issues discussed between Hector and Ulysse. The combination of planes is essential to Giraudoux's theatrical purposes. The weakest plays are those in which it is least clear.

It is his attempt to make the ideal appear attainable, without merely lecturing an audience that wants to be entertained, which forces Giraudoux to depict the ideal as something towards which his attractive, sometimes empty-headed young heroines stretch out. The language is poetically elevated to the outer edge of easy comprehensibility, as when Alcmène concludes: "Il est plus facile de revêtir l'uniforme de la guerre que celui de l'absence (The uniform of war is easier to put on than that of absence)," or Electre tells us that waiting is the only form of happiness she has experienced. But this aphoristic concentration is the code by which the transfer of level is communicated.

When he uses precious plots or periphrastic language, Giraudoux is telling us, through his register of discourse, that what he is saying has a significance beyond the platitudinous.

This is clear from the beginning. The *Provinciales*, rustic scenes viewed apparently with the eyes of a child, are written in a cultivated, even mannered style, with enormously long periods, punctuated with a whole series of colons and semi-colons, interspersed with short, rapid sentences consisting simply of subject and verb. They are ornately chiselled sculptures of the banal. Gide noted in *L'Ermitage*, in a piece he subsequently republished in *Nouveaux Prétextes*, Giraudoux's "poetic animation, which is tender, sensitive, loving, and delicately rhythmic." Berthelot, then a minister, sent for Giraudoux and told him he had seen one of the ambassadors laughing at a passage in the *Mercure de France*, had asked him what it was, and been told it was the following passage from the *Provinciales*: "Un cheval passa. Les poules suivirent, remplies d'espoir (A horse passed. The hens followed, full of hope)." The detail is accurate, trivial, and amusing but, since hens are not actually capable of hope as humans know it, it endows the most banal of rustic sights with almost symbolic significance. The effect depends on the conjunction of brevity and incongruity, and that conjunction is the linguistic means used later in the plays to indicate that the often trivial and amusingly lightweight surface relationships are intended to lead the audience's imagination to something of deeper significance.

In general the novels are not as successful as the plays because they flinch from allowing a fundamental seriousness to come to the surface, preferring to elaborate beautiful myths about life which offer a means of escaping from it. The structure is generally episodic, the nostalgia escapist, and the refinement too often simply affectation. Elements of narcissicism intrude. The mood of cultivated distraction is first broken in *Siegfried et le Limousin*, which is more than a fantasy, although its plot gets lost in witty anecdotes and diverting reminiscences. Jean, the narrator, purports to be writing in January 1922. Fascinated by a series of articles in the *Frankfurter Zeitung*, he discovers that they are by a Frenchman, picked up for dead and trained as a German political philosopher, and now a prominent statesman called Siegfried von Kleist. He is told about Kleist by Zelten, whom he once knew in Munich, and who is now a revolutionary. Zelten contrives his own downfall as well as that of Siegfried, in this way representing the disintegration of the two forces striving for control of post-war Germany, self-interested statecraft and revolution. Siegfried, in symbolic repudiation of both, is returned to his French homeland.

The novel is hasty and too episodic, and the nature of its genesis is too apparent. Giraudoux says he flung it together in 27 days, starting without a plot or characters, and as a literary work it is still embryonic, whimsically sketching a contrast between French and German attitudes. In January 1922 Jean could not have known the public events to which he refers, and which led to the treaty of Rapallo, in which Germany and Russia renounced their mutual indebtedness. Rathenau, the German foreign minister who signed the treaty, was assassinated on 24 June 1922. The clumsy inclusion of events subsequent to January, and the kaleidoscope of allusions to political, economic, and industrial matters, point particularly to Giraudoux's concern about the German–Bolshevik rapprochement and the worsening of Franco-German relations.

The novel was made into a play largely because Giraudoux wanted to present to a wider public the concerns he had developed partly as a result of Andler's teaching. Whereas Andler had come to think Marxism obsolete, Giraudoux had paradoxically delighted in showing ways in which German Marxism might well have been working in the interests of France. Giraudoux's problem was to achieve unity of action for the stage. The adaptation of the novel underwent several metamorphoses before becoming the *Siegfried* staged by Jouvet. The intermediate stage of the text, "Siegfried von Kleist," is Giraudoux's clearest exposition of his views on Franco-German relations. Zelten continues to combat Pan-Germanist militarism, but he is not quite a Bolshevik on economic issues. He proposes a programme, but no special form of government. Siegfried is a constitutionalist without a specific programme. Snippets discarded from versions of *Siegfried* were to appear in the *Nouvelle Revue Française* for July 1928, and in *Fugues sur Siegfried* of 1930, but the message of the interim version is clear. Both Pan-German militarism and the constitutional republic fail, and the confidence of the Allies in the new Germany was misplaced.

In an interview for *L'Intransigeant* of 9 August 1928 Giraudoux complained that the critics had not taken the political content of *Siegfried* seriously. In fact he had generalized it to a level at which it was no longer specific enough to call for comment. The play as we have it merely shows general goodwill towards a Franco-German entente, represented in the relationships between Siegfried and Geneviève, who wants him to come back to France, and Eva, who wants him to stay in Germany. In the end, at the frontier in a scene of banter with comic customs officials, Geneviève decides she loves the new German Siegfried and, instead of taking him off to France and allowing the play's message to collapse altogether, decides to stay with him in Germany. The play's message is now so subtle that it had to be put in the programme notes, quoting from the 1924 *Visite chez le prince*, and the allusions in the text require elaborate exegesis. They are not intended to be accessible to the theatre audience. Jouvet had made the expensive mistake of shocking public taste with his production of Crommelynck's *Tripes d'or* in 1925, and may well have demanded the modification of Giraudoux's original minatory curtain fall.

Amphitryon 38 and *La Guerre de Troie n'aura pas lieu* are not myths or legends, but fables or morality plays. *Amphitryon 38* is a witty comedy in which Alcmène demonstrates that human friendship can be strong enough to conquer all, even Jupiter's desire. The previous adaptation of the story which Giraudoux chiefly has in mind is Molière's, but Giraudoux introduces the new and serious idea that Jupiter's passion, on which Mercure pours irony, is too pure to admit of the necessary compromise represented by friendship. Giraudoux exploits his sense of paradox by demonstrating the superiority of the human over the divine world but, in this like Molière, he is clear about human limitations. Jupiter does, after all, triumph over Alcmène, and Hercules is going to be born. The moral is quite subtle, but it is ultimately reducible to the wisdom of knowing that some things are unavoidable, purity is unattainable, and compromise in the pursuit of absolutes always necessary. The reduction of the divine to merely human dimensions is a traditional comic defence mechanism, often more crudely displayed than in the boisterous and witty fun of Molière, who was also writing court satire, and of Giraudoux, who is also raising the question of marital fidelity.

The title of *La Guerre de Troie n'aura pas lieu* is of course

L'Ecole des indifférents, 1911
Simon le pathétique, 1918
Elpénor, 1919
Adorable Clio, 1920
Suzanne et le Pacifique, 1921; as *Suzanne and the Pacific*, 1923
Siegfried et le Limousin, 1922
Juliette au pays des hommes, 1924
Bella, 1926; as *Bella* (in English), 1927
Eglantine, 1927
Les Aventures de Jérôme Bardini, 1930
La France sentimentale, 1932
Combat avec l'ange, 1934
Choix des élues, 1938
Les Contes d'un matin, 1952
La Menteuse, 1958; as *Lying Woman*, 1972

Other

Retour d'Alsace, août 1914, 1916
Lectures pour une ombre, 1917
Amica America, 1919
Visite chez le prince, 1924
Le Sport, 1928
Racine, 1930; as *Racine* (in English), 1938
Fugues sur Siegfried, 1930
Fontrages au Niagara, 1932
De pleins pouvoirs à sans pouvoirs, 1935
Les Cinq tentations de La Fontaine, 1938
Le Futur Armistice, 1939
Pleins pouvoirs, 1939
Littérature, 1941
Ecrits dans l'ombre, 1944
Armistice à Bordeaux, 1945
Sans pouvoirs, 1946
Pour une politique urbaine, 1947
La Française et la France, 1951
Visitations, 1952
Portugal, suivi de Combat avec l'image, 1958
Or dans la nuit: chroniques et préfaces littéraires 1910–1943, 1969
Carnets des Dardanelles, edited by Jacques Body, 1969
Souvenir de deux existences, 1975

Critical studies

Inskip, Donald, *Giraudoux* (in English), 1958
LeSage, Laurence, *Giraudoux: His Life and Works*, 1959
Raymond, Agnes G., *Jean Giraudoux: The Theatre of Victory and Defeat*, 1966
Cohen, Robert, *Giraudoux: Three Faces of Destiny*, 1968
Lewis, Roy A., *Giraudoux: La Guerre de Troie n'aura pas lieu* (in English), 1971
Mankin, Paul A., *Precious Irony: The Theatre of Giraudoux*, 1971
Marker, Chris, *Giraudoux* (in English), 1978

GOBINEAU, Joseph-Arthur, Comte de, 1816–1882.

Novelist, political philosopher, historian, and diplomat.

LIFE

Joseph Gobineau, who has come to be associated with a theory of Aryan racial supremacy wrested from his *Essai sur l'inégalité des races humaines*, by no means taught "le Gobinisme" in the doctrinal form in which it underlay the ideology of Rosenberg, the views of 20th-century Pan-Germanists, and in particular the political philosophy of Hitler's National Socialism. He was a conservatively pessimistic political philosopher, whose debate with his more forward-looking friend and protector Tocqueville was at the time a matter of serious intellectual interest. As a writer, his distinctive tone and manner are reminiscent of Stendhal's, and Gobineau was indeed one of the very few to acknowledge Stendhal's literary stature from the start. He was also a successful diplomat and an important orientalist.

Gobineau spent much time compiling a dossier about his ancestry. He was born into a family of fading gentry, on his father's side formerly merchants and landowners from the Bordeaux area, who never quite succeeded in establishing themselves as "noblesse de robe" in the 18th century. His mother's father may have been an illegitimate son of Louis XV and was the king's last tax farmer for the Bordeaux region. Her mother was of Creole origin. Gobineau's paternal grandfather had two children, the irascible and dissolute Pierre "Thibaut-Joseph" (1775–1855), Gobineau's uncle, who was to leave him a fortune in 1855, and Louis, his father, born in 1784. On 9 September 1810 Louis married Anne-Louise-Madeleine de Gercy, born in 1791. Gobineau's younger sister Caroline was born on 6 October 1820, although there were rumours that her real father might have been her godfather, the archaeologist Frédéric de Clarac. In 1822 Gobineau's mother had a third child, Suzanne, by her children's tutor, Charles Sottin la Coindière. Suzanne was to marry her music teacher in July 1840, after which nothing more is known about her.

In 1807 Gobineau's uncle and his father sold the house which his paternal grandfather had had built in Bordeaux in 1786. Gobineau's parents were strongly royalist, and, on the evidence of her highly fictionalized memoirs, *Une vie de femme* (1835), published under her maiden name, his mother appears to have worked in Bordeaux for the Bourbon cause. In 1812, after she had tired of life so far from Paris, the Gobineaus moved back to the capital, where Louis was imprisoned from 1813 to 1814 for his part in a royalist conspiracy. On 25 March 1815 Louis XVIII rewarded him for his loyalty by attaching him to the staff of the future Charles X and elevating his military rank. Gobineau himself was born on 14 July 1816, a fortnight before his future wife.

Gobineau's father served in Spain from 1823 until 1828. After prolonged sick leave he was posted to Rennes, while his wife settled with la Coindière at Evreux, taking the children with her. When charged with fraud, she fled to Basel in September 1830. In her absence she was condemned to 10 years in prison, and France applied for her extradition. She moved to the state of Baden, then to Biel in the canton of Bern in Switzerland, where Gobineau attended the high school. His father, hostile to the republican revolution of 1830, was meanwhile placed on the retired list and lived at Redon, then at Lorient. Gobineau's mother appears to have lived comfortably and frequented bourgeois society at Biel, where de la Coindière was appointed a teacher in 1833.

Gobineau's father now demanded the return of the children and Gobineau, whose academic record at Biel had been good, attended the Collège de Lorient, from which he was expelled for persistent insubordination in December 1834. He then prepared for the competitive entry examination for the military academy at Saint-Cyr, which he failed in 1835, the year in which his mother published *Une vie de femme liée aux événements de l'époque*. Gobineau wanted to marry a girl from Lorient, Amélie Laigneau, but her family was opposed to the marriage. For solace he decided to seek a literary career and went to Paris in October 1835, gave lessons, and found a job in a gas lighting company. It took until March 1836 for Gobineau to discover that he was not to be paid, and he sought help from a banker to whose wife his mother had now become a companion.

Help was slow in coming. Gobineau translated from German, wrote poetry of which he did not think very highly, was forbidden to speak to Amélie Laigneau of marriage, and quarrelled with both la Coindière and his mother. However, in 1837 he succeeded in getting *La Mode* to publish part of his poem "Dilfiza," and *L'Echo de la Jeune France* published his piece on Mlle de Feauveu (1803–1860), a royalist sculptor living in Florence. At this time too he pleaded to be excused from military service on grounds of health. In 1837 he had begun to meet potential sources of patronage in royalist circles in Paris. He had also begun to take a real interest in the culture of the East, and succeeded in having an article on Persian poetry accepted by the *Gazette de France*, which then began sporadically to publish his work, including fiction. Three pieces on intellectual currents in the East were taken by *France et Europe*.

From early in 1839, thanks to the patronage of Mme de Serre, the wife of Louis XVIII's minister who had died in 1824, Gobineau was found a linguist's job in the postal service, working between 11 a.m. and four p.m. for 100 francs a month. He had begun to learn Italian, and in 1840 started Spanish lessons. His great hope lay in receiving a legacy from his uncle, whose dissolute way of life Gobineau helped him to conceal from the family. He himself was making little headway in the world of journalism, but with Hercule de Serre, the nephew of his patron, Maxime du Camp, and one or two others he founded a little group whose aim was to foster one another's interests. He wrote a play which has been lost, but in 1840 *La France* published his first short story, "Le mariage d'un prince." In an attempt to educate his sister's taste, Gobineau wrote to her that art, far from being an attempt to imitate nature, was "an aspiration towards the manifestations of the ideal world." Their correspondence in 1840 reveals that Gobineau had become religiously sceptical. Meanwhile, he was associated with a project to publish a review about Christianity in the East which came to nothing. On 15 April 1841, after a long delay, the *Revue des Deux Mondes* (*RDM*, q.v.) published an acclaimed article by Gobineau attacking Greece's Russian policy.

Gobineau's mother was imprisoned from 8 July 1841 until 17 February 1848, and he himself, still finding difficulty in getting material published in spite of some success in Greek newspapers, became associated with the new illustrated weekly *L'Unité* "as one of its four chief editors." It lasted only from February to June 1843. He published "Scaramouche" in it early in 1843, and defended Germany against Quinet's attacks in the *RDM*. He also left the postal service and was presented to Rocqueville, who offered him 2,000 francs a year to undertake research for him. From 1843 to 1847 Gobineau wrote regularly on foreign affairs for the legitimist *La Quotidienne* at 2,000 francs a year, although Laurentie, the editor, distrusted both his youth and his judgement. In 1843 he also rewrote a dramatic poem, "Don Juan," whose first volume, his first book, was published at his own expense as *Les Adieux de Don Juan* in February 1844. That summer he was seriously ill with internal bleeding, for which he was prescribed sea bathing. His health improved after some weeks at Fécamp, where the dips in the sea were cautiously limited to five or six minutes each. That winter Gobineau published articles on Musset, Balzac, and Stendhal, and wrote regularly for the *Revue Nouvelle*.

Imaginative writing now took its place beside political journalism, especially concerning foreign affairs, but with particular attention to Germany. Alongside general articles on literary topics, in 1845 Gobineau worked at a two-volume novel and at the poem "Jean Chouan." *Les Aventures de Jean de la Tour-Miracle, surnommé le prisonnier chanceux* appeared in *La Quotidienne* from 31 March until the end of May 1846. On 10 April Gobineau published *La Chronique rimée de Jean Chouan*, this time trying hard, but in vain, to make the book a commercial success. *La Presse* asked him for a serial, "Carlo Gozzi," of which no more has been heard, but Gobineau somehow received a 300-franc state subsidy for literature. Not until 22 August did he tell his family of his intention to marry Clémence Monnerot, described as a merchant's daughter. The wedding took place on 10 September. Later in the year *La Quotidienne* published a series of Gobineau's articles on contemporary literary critics, including Jules Janin, Gustave Planche, Sainte-Beuve, Saint-Marc Girardin, and Charles Magnin, the best of which were published in a collected edition in 1926.

From 29 January to 20 February 1847 *Le National* published *Mademoiselle Irnois*, but Gobineau lost his position on *La Quotidienne*. From 4 June *L'Union Monarchique* serialized his *Nicolas Belavoir*, and in the same month the *Journal des Débats* agreed to take the novel which would become *Ternove*. It was duly published from 22 October to 23 December 1847, and Armand Bertin, the editor, paid the relatively high price of 1,500 francs. Further novels, of which no more has been heard, were projected for *La Mode* and *Le National*, to be simultaneously published in the new review *Le Conservateur*, which also agreed to take *L'Abbé de Typhaines* for serialization later in the year. It was finally to appear in *L'Union Monarchique* from 24 August until 10 November 1849, and in the royalist Brest *l'Océan* from 27 June to 8 October 1850. In August 1847 the *Revue Nouvelle* ceased publication. Later in the year "Les conseils de Rabelais" was published in the *Courrier Français* and "L'aventure de jeunesse" in the *Gazette de Metz*.

Gobineau had become very friendly with his wife's elder brother Jules, and their friendship was to outlast the eventual breakdown of Gobineau's marriage. The revolution of 1848 had left him with democratic but not republican sympathies. Elected workers seemed to him greatly preferable to left-wing bourgeois. His wife gave birth to their daughter Diane on 13 September 1848, two days before the appearance of the first number of the *Revue Provinciale*, which Gobineau co-founded with Louis de Kergorlay. The review appeared monthly until August 1849 in Redon, where Gobineau had moved. There was a single paying subscriber, and by April 1849 Gobineau was financially hard pressed. Tocqueville had him appointed a secretary at the ministry of foreign affairs, and thus began his diplomatic career at a salary of 7,000 francs. On 9 November he was made first secretary of the Bern legation, in which capacity he prepared a series of important reports on Swiss political and economic affairs for Tocqueville. In 1850 his mother was again condemned in her absence to 10 years in prison and a fine of 3,000 francs.

Apparently at his own request, Gobineau was made a member of the Légion d'Honneur in 1851. He declined a post in Constantinople, preferring not to be so far from France, and filled in at Hanover before returning to Berne, which he increasingly disliked, and where his wife found that the climate did not suit her. In December 1852 he paid the publisher Firmin-Didot 1,500 francs on account for 500 copies of the *Essai sur l'inégalité des races humaines*, for which the final bill was 3,415 francs. The king of Hanover accepted the dedication. Gobineau adopted the title of count, to which he had no right, and the first two volumes of the *Essai* were published in September 1853. Gobineau's sister was afraid that he was attacking the biblical chronology of the development of humanity. In the *Journal des Débats* Jean Alloury found the *Essai* too absolute and too materialistic, and doubts were cast on the anthropological and deterministic assumptions underlying the work. In 1854 Gobineau was moved to Frankfurt. The final two volumes of the *Essai* were rewritten three or four times, then completely corrected several times more before they went to the printer, but Gobineau was sent to Persia in 1855 before he could see the proofs of the final volume. The first two volumes were by then already being translated in the US in the interests of defending a theory of white racial supremacy.

Gobineau left Paris with his wife and daughter on 10 February 1855, disembarked at Alexandria, and arrived by caravan at Tehran on 2 July. In the meantime, Gobineau's uncle Thibaut had died, leaving him 294,142 francs. After paying off debts, he was to buy the Château de Trye, owned by Conti in the 18th century. Meanwhile, in Persia he toyed with various academic projects. Disillusion with life there set in during 1856, and late that year Gobineau accompanied his wife and daughter as far as the Russian frontier, leaving them on 1 November to go back to France while he returned to Tehran. His second daughter, Christine, was born on 23 March 1857 in Paris. He was to take charge of the interests of British subjects in Iran during the Anglo-Iranian hostilities of 1856–57. He returned to Paris in the spring of 1858, wrote *Trois ans en Asie*, to be published by Hachette in September 1859, published *La Lecture des textes cunéiformes*, and worked on the *Histoire des Perses*. In the summer of 1859 he was sent on a mission to Newfoundland. He was to publish an account of his journey late in 1860, although the *Voyage à Terre-Neuve*, published by Hachette in the "Bibliothèque des Chemins de Fer" series, was dated 1861. Late that year he returned on a mission to Tehran which lasted until the autumn of 1863. The following year he was posted to Greece, where he worked not only at his orientalist works, but also at his family genealogy, which was eventually to become the fiction *Histoire d'Ottar Jarl*.

On 8 April 1866 Gobineau's elder daughter married Ove de Guldencrone in Athens. His first grandson was born on 30 November 1867. Early in 1868 his sister became a Benedictine nun at Solesmes, where Gobineau visited her shortly before her clothing on 10 February 1869 and his own departure for Brazil, where, against his preferences, he had been posted. He

had taken up sculpture, and was back in France on sick leave before the outbreak of the Franco-Prussian War. After the defeat of France at Sedan, Gobineau refused to be associated with anti-Prussian resistance at Trye, of which he had become mayor, and became friendly with German officers living in his château. Its upkeep had been too costly for him, and he was reduced to a state of financial distress. After the peace in 1871 he successfully negotiated compensation with the Germans. He was to show disgust at the joy with which Paris had greeted the reprisals against those who had fought for the Commune in May. He worked at a "big novel" and had to be dissuaded from seeking election to the Académie Française. In 1872 he was made head of a mission to Norway and Sweden, and in Stockholm that summer he began a liaison with Mme de la Tour, the wife of the Italian minister. In July three short stories, *Souvenirs de voyage*, were published.

Gobineau was joined in Stockholm by his wife and Christine for the winter of 1872–73, after which the family broke up. His elder daughter wrote asking her father to take her mother away from Athens, where Diane was living, while Gobineau himself was infuriated that his wife had promised their second daughter a dowry he could not afford. He found difficulty in getting a publisher to take the "big novel," *Les Pléiades*, but it was finally published by Plon on 9 April 1874. It took 25 years to sell 500 copies. In 1876 the first part of Gobineau's poem *Amadis* appeared, and he accompanied the emperor of Brazil to Russia. During his absence further short stories were published as *Nouvelles asiatiques*, but his prolonged absence from his post had displeased Paris and, although he returned to Stockholm, he was made to ask for retirement. None the less, Gobineau was gratified at the success of three of his busts, and in 1876 was awarded a medal at Philadelphia. Recognizing how he had contributed to the abbreviation of Gobineau's career, the emperor of Brazil bought a statue from him for 15,000 francs, the only commercial advantage Gobineau's sculpting activities ever brought him.

La Renaissance, originally called "La fleur d'or," was finally published on 1 June 1877. The Académie Française gave Gobineau a 1,000-franc prize for it the following year. In September he decided to settle in Rome with Mme de la Tour and try to make a living from his sculpture. He had come increasingly to dislike living in France. In 1878 the château and its furnishings were sold for 70,000 francs. The *Histoire d'Ottar Jarl* was published on 5 November 1879. Gobineau sold some books in 1881, apparently finding himself again in financial need, although it is difficult to see how that could have come about. Mme de la Tour bought the furnishings of his study for 3,000 francs, while allowing Gobineau to continue to use them, and suggested a less costly residence. He had become friendly with Liszt and his daughter Cosima, and stayed occasionally with her and her second husband, Wagner. Gobineau's health had been declining for several years, and in the winter of 1882, after staying in the château which Mme de la Tour had inherited 18 months earlier, he left for Rome, where it was less cold than in Auvergne. He arrived in Turin on 12 October, dictated a last note to the hotel secretary for Mme de la Tour, and died there on 13 October. The son of his wife's half-brother was the only family mourner at the funeral.

Some works appeared posthumously, notably the second part of *Amadis*, the tragedy *Alexandre le Macédonien*, and the *Etudes critiques*.

WORKS

The happenstance of documentary survival has left us very large amounts of correspondence by and concerning Gobineau, so that his not uninteresting life is known, and often related, in more detail than the works themselves might warrant. The admiration for Gobineau in Germany generally, but especially in the Wagner entourage, and in certain circles in France, and his exploitation both by the partisans of white supremacy in the US and by the advocates of Aryan supremacy, especially in National Socialist Germany, have given the *Essai sur l'inégalité des races humaines* a literary importance not intrinsic to its contents and attracted an attention to the works of scholarship and fiction which they might not have acquired by their literary interest alone. It is the *Essai* which accounts for Gobineau's literary survival, in spite of the excellent early articles on literature and critics, and of the later short stories, however important the works of scholarship and fascinating the travel books.

The *Essai sur l'inégalité des races humaines* is essentially a poetic vision of history, not a work of scientific anthropology or of political, social, or anti-semitic propaganda. When he wrote it, Gobineau had never been further from Paris than Berne. He was a would-be poet and novelist scraping a living from translations and journalism, but also a potential scholar and a philosopher, an almost exact contemporary of Darwin, less than a decade older than Renan and Taine, seeking in a generalized, poetic vision of mankind some understanding of himself. By culture he was a visionary and a royalist. He was obsessed by his ancestry and yearned to discover that he had an honourable lineage, but internally he settled for nobility of character rather than blood. The world in which he was brought up made him an unbeliever and a positivist (q.v.), and gave him a powerful impulsion towards determinism. It was a republican, post-romantic (q.v.) world of social and political revolution.

Gobineau's background might have made him much more schizoid than he was. Descended on both sides from families of modestly successful social climbers under the ancien régime, son of a romantically legitimist soldier with no discernible gifts other than military ones and a mother who spent 10 years in prison for fraud, brother to a devout Catholic sister who became a nun and defended the biblical line concerning the development of the human race, regarded as academically promising by his first school, and as irretrievably recalcitrant at his second, poetic by temperament and more than half-scholarly by inclination, clearly gifted imaginatively, it is not surprising that Gobineau should have wished to enquire into his origins with more visionary enthusiasm than mature scholarship.

The success of the *Essai* in 19th-century right-wing circles is due to its pessimistic criticism of the social philosophy of the Enlightenment and its anti-republicanism. The implied assertion that government, morality, and institutions have little to do with human destiny, which is otherwise determined, could not have recommended the book to 19th-century Catholic monarchists. That assertion, however, was generally overlooked, except by Tocqueville. In the middle of the 19th century in France, a certain Anglophobia paid no more than decent deference to Waterloo. A pro-German stance was not provocative even to the left before 1870, and Guizot, Michelet, and Tocqueville were all less cautious than Gobineau about the contribution of the Aryan races to the peaks of culture and government. Gobineau's difficulty was the mode of transmission of his ideas, one that was ensured by the closeness of the relationship between his mistress, the Comtesse de la Tour, and Richard Wagner, the second husband of Liszt's second daughter.

Gobineau supposes that the physio-biological elements in man determine his intellectual and moral powers, and therefore the forms of religion and the institutions of government characteristic of the homogeneous groupings of men we call races. The cause of the decay of civilizations is to be sought not in moral corruption, divine vengeance, or bad government, but in the mixing of races—what Gobineau refers to as the "moral geology" of society. Hegelian, determinist, profoundly pessimistic, he does not believe in the superiority of any of the three primitive races, white, black, and yellow, and devotes only four chapters of book six to the German peoples. The posthumous notoriety of the *Essai* is the result of a wilful misreading of cultural history and a failure to analyse what the text actually contains. The most shocking thing was that degree of determinism in 1850.

A great deal of Gobineau's fictional output appears to have been lost. It was immediately after his marriage that, no doubt spurred by the need to earn, he became successful in selling his fiction. The lightweight "Scaramouche" had appeared in the short-lived *L'Unité*, but after his marriage in 1846 Gobineau quickly published in serial form *Les Aventures de Jean de la Tour-Miracle, Nicolas Belavoir, Mademoiselle Irnois*, and *Ternove*. The most accomplished of the short novels is normally thought to be *L'Abbaye de Typhaines*, but all of them are derivative, ultimately from Scott, and without real literary pretensions or interest, although as in Stendhal, a well-conceived psychological theory underlies the feelings and motivations of the characters, whose dominant traits are sharpened by instinctive energy.

More important are the three short stories of *Souvenirs de voyage*—"Le mouchoir rouge," "Akrivie Phrangopoulo," and "La chasse au caribou"—taken together with *Adélaïde*, originally destined for the same collection, and the six stories of the *Nouvelles asiatiques*—"La danseuse de Shamakha," "L'illustre magicien," "Histoire de Gambèr-Aly," "La guerre des Turcomans," "Les amants de Kandahar," and "La vie de voyage." Gobineau does not free himself from models and is, for instance, notably less broad and less penetrating in his depiction of Eastern culture than were *The Arabian Nights*, of which he naturally had a copy in translation and from which he derives. His stated effort, "J'ai agi de mon mieux pour saisir et garder ce qui m'était apparu de plus saillant, de mieux marqué, de plus étranger à nous (I tried my best to catch and to keep what seemed to me most striking, most characteristic, and most foreign to us)," gives these nouvelles a great freshness. Like all Gobineau's work, they are characterized by the highly intelligent quality of the author's reflection on the experiences he depicts, and the personal psychology, if not the cultural phenomena, is now the subject of revealing analysis. The underlying psychological theory may not compel agreement, any more than does Stendhal's, but it unifies the text, and is used subtly and skilfully. The irony, too, is deployed with delicacy and tact. A passionately idealized view of human love underlies all Gobineau's fiction.

The major work of fiction is *Les Pléiades* of 1874, to which may be added the five dialogues of *La Renaissance* ("Savonarole," "César Borgia," "Jules II," "Léon X," and "Michel-Ange"). *Les Pléiades* was Gobineau's imaginative pendant to the *Essai*, exploring the possibility of a moral and intellectual elite even in a decaying culture. The plot is conventional and the characters scarcely come to life, but the imaginative vision is strong and well focused, even if it be found unacceptable or repugnant. A Frenchman, Louis de Laudon, the Englishman Wilfrid Nore, and the German Conrad Lanze go through their sentimental entanglements uncaptivatingly, but they have selected one another from the crowd because of the aristocratic temperament and character they have recognized in each other. Gobineau always denied that *Les Pléiades* was a novel. It was intended to irritate its readers into Gobineau's own "sphère de passion (level of passion)," as he wrote to Mme de la Tour. The key note is Gobineau's authoritarian ideology, his notion of an aristocracy of character which has nothing to do with birth, his distrust of technical progress, and his disbelief in moral or social perfectibility.

At the outset Lanze talks of "des êtres lumineux, entrecroisant leurs pas dans des courbes célestes (luminous beings crossing one another's paths in heavenly movements)," while for Nore to be a king's son has nothing to do with caste: "cela signifie: 'je suis d'un tempérament hardi et généreux…l'indépendance de mon esprit, la liberté la plus absolue dans mes opinions sont des privilèges inébranlables de ma noble origine' (that means: 'I have a bold and generous character…independence of mind and the most absolute freedom of opinion are the unshakeable privilege of my noble origin')." What the text is intended to explore is the social, moral, and personal superiority of an elite capable of recognizing this superiority in others with whom a natural alliance is formed against the depressing tide of cultural decay and ambient mediocrity.

PUBLICATIONS

Collections

Oeuvres, Bibliothèque de la Pléiade, 3 vols., 1983–87
Nouvelles, 2 vols., 1956

Fiction

Le Prisonnier chanceux, 3 vols., 1847; as *The Lucky Prisoner*, 1926
Nicolas Belavoir, 3 vols., 1847
Ternove, 3 vols., 1848
L'Abbaye de Typhaines, 1867
Souvenirs de voyage, 1872; as *The Crimson Handkerchief and Other Stories*, 1927
Les Pléiades, 1874; as *The Pleiads*, 1928
Nouvelles asiatiques, 1876; as *Tales of Asia*, 1947
La Renaissance, 1877; *The Renaissance*, 1913
Histoire d'Ottar Jarl, pirate norvégien, conquérant du pays de Bray, en Normandie, et de sa descendance, 1879
Le Mouchoir rouge et autres nouvelles, 1968

Verse

Les Adieux de Don Juan, 1844
La Chronique rimée de Jean Chouan et de ses compagnons, 1846
L'Aphroessa, 1869
Amadis, 1876; part 2, 1887
Poemi inediti di Arthur de Gobineau, 1965

Other

Essai sur l'inégalité des races humaines, 4 vols., 1853–55; as *The Inequality of Human Races*, 1915
La Lecture des textes cunéiformes, 1858
Trois ans en Asie, 1859
Voyage à Terre-Neuve, 1861
Traité des écritures cunéiformes, 2 vols., 1864
Les Religions et les philosophies dans l'Asie centrale, 1865
Histoire des Perses, 2 vols., 1869
Alexandre le Macédonien (tragedy), 1902
La Troisième République française et ce qu'elle vaut, 1907
Etudes critiques, 1927
Mémoire sur diverses manifestations de la vie individuelle, edited by A. B. Duff, 1935
Ce qui est arrivé en France en 1870, edited by A. B. Duff, 1970
Several of the correspondences have also been posthumously published, some only in periodicals. Of particular interest are those with Tocqueville (edited by M. Degros, 1959) and with Gobineau's sister Caroline, Mère Bénédicte (edited by A. B. Duff, 2 vols., 1958).

Critical and biographical studies

Lange, M., *Le Comte de Gobineau: étude biographique et critique*, 1924
Rowbothan, A., *The Literary Works of the Comte de Gobineau*, 1929
Spring, G., *The Vitalism of Count de Gobineau*, 1932
Buenzod, J., *La Formation de la pensée de Gobineau*, 1967
Gaulmier, J., *Gobineau et sa fortune littéraire*, 1971
Rey, Pierre-Louis, *L'Univers romanesque de Gobineau* (includes bibliography), 1981

GONCOURT, Edmond (-Louis-Antoine Huot) de, 1822–1896, and Jules (-Alfred) de, 1830–1870.

Novelists, diarists, historians, and dramatists, connoisseurs, collectors, and joint authors of all works until 1870.

LIVES

The brothers Goncourt ("Les Frères Goncourt") were the only sons of Marc-Pierre Huot de Goncourt (1787–1834), a lawyer's son who ran away from home to become an army officer, distinguished himself in Napoleon's campaigns, became a member of the Légion d'Honneur, and married in 1815. After the death of his first wife, on 10 July 1821 he married Annette-Cécile Guérin (1798–1848). He and she both came from minor aristocratic stock, and were at first well enough off, but not rich. Marc-Pierre, whose maternal grandfather had owned nearly a dozen farms, brought two farms to the marriage, and Annette-Cécile a total of 44,000 francs. One of their daughters died in infancy. The other died in the 1832 cholera epidemic.

Marc-Pierre's father and mother, who died in 1829 and 1832,

respectively, had lived at the Château de Somerécourt, near the tiny village of Goncourt, and at Neufchâteau, where both they and Marc-Pierre's elder brother, Pierre-Antoine-Victor (1783–1857), were to die. Marc-Pierre and his wife lived at Bourmont, not far from Neufchâteau, and then at Nancy. Marc-Pierre himself had been put on half-pay in 1818, but tried in vain to get back into active service in 1823, 1824, and 1825, alleging the difficulties he had in supporting his family. However, he had not rallied to the king after Waterloo, and in 1828 he was retired altogether. Like his brother, whose army record was also distinguished, he had republican leanings. One of the farms was sold for 26,000 francs, and in 1826 Marc-Pierre bought a house at Breuvannes for 12,500 francs. He returned to favour with the abdication of Charles X and the accession of Louis-Philippe in 1830. In 1833 he was granted a pension of 2,960 francs a year on top of the 1,000 francs he received as an Officier of the Légion d'Honneur.

The brothers were to be touchy about the fragile nobility of their birth, and disliked being thought richer than they were. Edmond was born at Nancy on 26 May 1822. Eighteen months later the family, with its cook and its maid, moved to Paris, where Jules was born on 19 December 1830. He was not quite four when Marc-Pierre died, leaving Annette-Cécile with 500 francs a year. To save money, she moved in with a brother and then, in 1838, with a friend, who left her 2,000 francs in 1842. Edmond was sent to the Pension Goubaux. His tutors included Alphonse Karr and Michel de Bourges, and Dumas *fils* was in the class below. Edmond was not a good pupil, and left to attend the Lycée Henri IV for two years, before finishing his studies at the Collège Bourbon. Thanks to the complicity of one the servants, Rose Malingre, who would open the door to him at dawn, he used to attend the notorious dances at the old Opéra. His mother, her sister, Nephtalie de Courmont, and her sister's sister-in-law would take him to second-hand shops on Sundays, giving him the experience and the taste which later turned him into a collector and a bibliophile.

Jules, whose health was always delicate, was a dayboy at the Collège Bourbon, now the Lycée Condorcet. He was good-looking and spoiled, and disliked by the other boys. First his mother, then the school, worked him hard, and he distinguished himself in Latin and Greek. Edmond started to study law in 1841, and began to frequent sale rooms, acquiring sketches, engravings, small objets d'art, and his first Watteau. He disliked the sordid aspects of life revealed by his study of law, contemplated suicide, and moved to the city finance department at a salary of 1,200 francs. He was to stay there for two years. Jules, though not assiduous at his books, was clearly gifted and passed his baccalauréat with ease.

Before their mother died in September 1848, she had been selling off her silver. Her estate was valued at 4,500 francs. Edmond, who was given to bemoaning and disapproving, later on complained of the dreadful life he had to lead, his artistic and literary sensibility swamped in the vulgarity of his associates and his surroundings. Their mother's death had left the brothers in short-term financial trouble, but otherwise modestly independent. Jules had begun to toy with writing verse. Edmond had dreamt of attending the Ecole des Chartes, the archivist school, and undertaken to write a history of France's medieval châteaux. Jules was determined to do nothing. Both began to paint, and together they headed south, hiking and sketching, but avoiding the Italian peninsula, which they regarded as too dangerous

to visit on account of the political situation. They started to note down their day's impressions, beginning their famous diary, which Edmond carried on after his brother's death, and which records in vivid and often spiteful detail the social and artistic life of literary Paris during the second half of the 19th century.

Instead of Italy they went to Algeria. Some of the notes they made on the journey were published in 1852 in *L'Eclair*, a review of literature, theatres, and the arts founded on 12 January 1852 by their cousin, Pierre-Charles de Villedeuil. It was that trip, Edmond was later to say, that turned them from painters into writers. Their notes became increasingly full of impressions and descriptions, until they were quite overwhelmed by Algeria. They were away from July until 17 December 1849, when they took a dark ground-floor flat and properly began their life in common. Other apartments, according to the *Journal*, were occupied by a prostitute, who paid 1,200 francs rent and had to borrow money if rain stopped her from working, and by a woman who sent her maid armed with night clothes to the lodgings of whichever man she was to spend the night with. There was a different colour for each of her lovers, one of whom seems to have been Jules. Other occupants of the block included a notorious actress, and during the time the brothers lived there the building was very nearly the scene of a murder. The apartments were cheap, because in the next-door factory they were inventing the saxophone. The brothers moved upstairs, but stayed in the building for 20 years.

Edmond had so for engaged only in minor flirtations. Neither brother ever had a prolonged emotional relationship. It has been said that, as in literature, so also in love they were realists. They had passing liaisons from their late teens, including one between Jules and a girl suffering from tuberculosis whose first lover had been Edmond. It is a subject on which Edmond was more discreet than Jules, whose seductive powers were certainly the greater. The brothers took refuge in art from what they regarded as the only possible political stance, which was socialist, conscious that they were still living by 18th-century values. Edmond was inclined to be malicious, reserved, and morose. Jules was more full of fun, imagination, and daring.

The brothers went to Switzerland and Belgium in the spring of 1850, and to Normandy in the autumn of the same year. Sometime that summer Jules caught the syphilis which was to kill him. The brothers had begun to write. Edmond contributed a portrait of a cook to a book of self-portraits of French people, and one scene of a play entitled "Hégésippe Moreau" was printed. The brothers worked on opposite sides of a table they had had made for them at Goncourt, and decided to write a vaudeville for Sainville, who was popular for his impersonations of unimaginative bourgeois. Sainville did not take it, although he stole a scene from it, and it was burnt, like its successor. The brothers' first three stage entertainments failed to find takers.

In 1851 they went to Switzerland, returning via Neufchâteau and their cousin's wedding, which lasted six hours a day from 28 August to 6 September. That summer they wrote their first novel, *En 18...*, printed at their own expense, and for which they had already taken the trouble to get themselves sent the precise menu of an enormous meal they had actually eaten. The novel derives from Heine, whom they would later defend against Sainte-Beuve, and Poe. Unhappily the publication date was 2 December 1851, the morning of the coup d'état. The book appeared three days later, but with allusions that had become

ing against was Flaubert's personal lack of decorum, the vulgarity of the inclinations he so carefully reined back in the great novels.

The Goncourts took their 18th-century view sufficiently far to think Bernardin de Saint-Pierre's literary achievement greater than Flaubert's. Edmond even claimed to be shocked when Flaubert allowed Lévy, who had paid 10,000 francs for *Salammbô*, to give out for publicity purposes that the sum was 30,000 francs. The Magny dinners did not make the Goncourts any more indulgent towards their provincial friend, whom they nevertheless visited at Croisset in 1863, minutely describing the interior, which they disliked, and the hospitality, which they found ungenerous, although they had enjoyed it often enough on Sundays when Flaubert was in Paris. With Flaubert, as with Sainte-Beuve, they seemed to feel that it was a sign of superiority to be caustic in private about the vulgarity of those with whom they were on public terms of affability. The *Journal* is self-consciously spiteful.

The Goncourts were to become the chroniclers of the Princesse Mathilde's important salon although when, on 16 August 1862, they first dined with the princess, Gavarni, Chennevières, Nieuwerkerke, and two other guests at Saint-Gratien, their impressions were again patronizing. The princess was then 42. They found her more appealing at their second dinner, in the Rue de Courcelles in early December. At the third, on 31 December, Sainte-Beuve and Paul de Musset were also present. Invitations from the princess then poured on the brothers, and their elevation to the ranks of her closest circle gave them an enviable literary dignity. They found in her strength of mind and intelligence, but not subtlety, coquettishness, or tenderness. The company was never especially entertaining, and quickly became sycophantic. The princess could be cruel as well as capricious. Her literary function, apart from bestowing patronage, was to ensure discreet communication between officialdom and the bolder, if already established, members of the Magny group.

Renée Mauperin was serialized in *L'Opinion Nationale* in December 1863 and the early weeks of 1864, and the critical reception was encouraging. Meanwhile the brothers had been documenting the other side of Rose Malingre's life for *Germinie Lacerteux*. The publisher Charpentier finally prevailed on them, if not to replace "louse" with "vermin," then to omit the account of the Caesarian operation on a dwarf. "What sort of a mistress is this public? What right has it to make a novel lie to it the whole time and shield it for ever from life's ugliness?" were the brothers' reaction. *Germinie Lacerteux* finally appeared on 16 January 1865, presented as a true study of lower-class life, unlike what the brothers regarded as the prettified versions of Hugo and Sue. For *La Fille Elisa* they went to visit the women's prison at Clermont the following September, later causing trouble with their view that solitary confinement led to insanity.

Germinie ran into a predictably virtuosic battery of denigration, with only Zola, in the Lyons *Salut Public*, and Jules Claretie in the *Nouvelle Revue de Paris* finding something favourable to say in public. In private Flaubert was ambiguous and Hugo pompous. The Princesse Mathilde felt repugnance at the idea that Rose and she made love in the same way. The Goncourts wrote: "Only aristocrats could have written *Germinie Lacerteux*," no doubt meaning that you could only describe what was destroying a culture, and therefore what was enduring and important, if you were above it. It was the first fully naturalistic novel to be written in French. By May 1865 the *Journal* could

say the only real interest left in the brothers' lives was "l'émotion de l'étude sur le vrai (the emotion of the study of the true)." They were no longer interested in history, whose truth they felt they had penetrated, but only in living truth, the social history of their own society.

The Goncourts had finished their play *Henriette Maréchal* in December 1863. It was turned down by the Vaudeville and forgotten. When someone asked about it, they had lost it. It was eventually found, and read in the princess's salon on 7 April 1865. After difficulties discussed in the press and involving administrative decisions at the highest government levels, the play was finally staged on 5 December 1865 and was the occasion for anti-government riots which lasted until it was taken off after six performances. There were no arrests, but considerable public emotion, particularly among the republican students, who thought the play had been put on out of favouritism. One newspaper article nearly caused a duel. *L'Evénement* published the full text, paying the brothers 3,000 francs. When the second edition came out in volume form in 1866, it was prefaced by a history of what had happened. Among those thanked by the brothers were Janin, Gautier, Feydeau, Vallès, and Claretie. In fact their superciliousness had by now alienated support for the brothers from all but Princesse Mathilde's circle.

At this date the brothers had between them not quite 12,000 francs a year, a fourth-floor apartment, and a maid, as they declared in the preface to the published play, written on 12 December. The preface, alleging victimization by a cabal, killed the play, although it was received enthusiastically on its first evening. The brothers were threatened, as was the princess. Official pressure was brought to bear, and the play was taken off, virtually by order of the empress. Box-office sales had been good, around 4,000 francs a performance after the first night. Sainte-Beuve was so frightened by the disturbance that he had the police on call for the Magny dinner of 18 December. Flaubert was kind, but the brothers were badly shaken for at least six months by the whole affair and went to Le Havre to recuperate. The play itself was well received in Marseilles, as also when played to a working-class Paris audience in Montparnasse.

The brothers did write another play that was nearly put on in 1868, but was finally published only in 1873, *La Patrie en danger*. In 1866 they published extracts from the *Journal*, *Idées et sensations*, dedicated to Flaubert. Though commercially unsuccessful, it drew an important article from Sainte-Beuve, reprinted from *Le Constitutionnel* in the *Nouveaux Lundis*. In 1866 the brothers finished *Manette Salomon*, which was serialized in *Le Temps* early in 1867, and as a volume in the autumn. It was dedicated to the Magny group, and predictably annoyed the artistic community. In April 1867 the Goncourts left for a month in Rome, and spent part of the summer in Vichy. Their next novel, *Madame Gervaisais*, was not finished until 22 December 1868. Zola, who had come to lunch, printed three chapters in *Le Gaulois* early in 1869, but the novel, like its predecessor, excited comparatively little attention. It sold very badly.

In 1867 the brothers acquired a neighbouring apartment to accommodate their books and antiques, but the noise was beginning to be intolerable for the increasingly sensitive Jules. In 1868 they bought their dream house in Auteuil for 83,000 francs. It was quiet, and rural, but, thanks to the railway, convenient for the centre of Paris. Neither of them believed in an afterlife, in progress, or in politics, although they did not formally repudiate their view that the private lives of the great rather than the physical combats of nations would become the main material of historians. They regarded universal education as dangerously disruptive of family life, enabling a younger generation to vault socially over its elders, and as leading to an undesirable undermining of the social order. On the other hand, they believed in civilization, and an aristocracy open to high intelligence of whatever social class. It is clear from the *Journal* that they were unaware of the paradoxes and contradictions of their various positions.

They shared a feeling of moral superiority over their fellows, regarded their taste as more refined, were never venal or even very concerned about money, were almost never irritated by one another, and, after their early work, it is almost impossible to guess what each brother contributed to the texts on which they worked together. The probability is that, when they stopped working together at the same table, they decided how a particular part of a particular chapter had to be tackled, worked separately for an hour or two, and then met to fuse their efforts. The secret of their relationship is largely hidden in the total dedication of each to the communal task, daily redefined as it developed, of artistic creation. Auteuil did not quite offer the quiet that Jules needed. He was disturbed by noise from a nearby horse, and by crying children. His disease progressed distressingly as he gradually lost control of his social behaviour, then of his mental and physical capacities. He died at Auteuil on 20 June 1870.

By August Edmond, who was himself suffering from a liver complaint, which afflicted him sporadically for the rest of his life, had begun to resume a normal life. Zola came to lunch on the 27th. When the siege of Paris began on 18 September, Edmond continued to take long walks. It was a difficult year for everyone, and his personal grief may have been dulled by the need to survive the siege and the Commune. By July 1871, when the trouble was over, he had begun *La Fille Elisa*. On 1 July he called on the Princesse Mathilde. Her circumstances had been reduced, but she started to receive again. Goncourt wrote in the *Journal* that he now frequently had sexual intercourse, but only out of boredom, for an hour or two of release. In 1872 he saw something of Hugo, returned from exile, and spent some time with Gautier during his last months. In 1873 his *Gavarni* appeared, still over the names of both brothers, with a preface dated January 1870, although altered in some details at the request of Nadar, who had read the serialization in *Le Bien Public*.

Goncourt now revised and republished many of the works of 18th-century social history, and allowed Lemerre to reprint the earlier novels. Behind *La Fille Elisa* lies a considerable body of documentation, taken from Maria, the midwife and mistress, and her prostitute daughter, from letters, anecdotes, impressions, and a fistful of books on prostitutes and prisons. Work was interrupted when a debtor to whom he had lent 80,000 francs was unable to make payments, but the matter seems to have been quickly put in order. Settlement was arranged, and the book finished on 30 December 1876. One fragment appeared in *La République des Lettres* three days before the book was published on 21 March 1877. Goncourt had been deeply worried at the prospect of a possible prosecution on account of his subject and had excised anything which could have given offence even to the most prudish. The bookshops rushed to get hold of the book in case it was seized. Charpentier sold 10,000 copies in a few days. Five editions were sold out. There was no prosecution, although some of the critics were concerned to keep their hands clean of all praise.

The next novel, first mentioned in 1876, and ostensibly about two clowns, *Les Frères Zemganno*, is part of the final stage of the process by which Goncourt overcame his grief at his brother's death by fictionalizing their relationship. The collaboration between two acrobats, like that of two writers, has to be extremely close and coordinated. The novel is not mentioned again until 1878, when Goncourt was going to the circus to study his subject. It was finished on 10 March 1879. Daudet, Zola, Turgenev, and Charpentier were present at the reading, but Flaubert had broken his leg and could not come. The company was enthusiastic and the book appeared on 30 April 1879, dedicated to Daudet's wife. Goncourt's preface irritated Barbey d'Aurevilly and, for different reasons, Zola. The book was followed by *La Faustin*. Sometimes Goncourt was totally preoccupied by it; sometimes he left it untouched as he sat and smoked, answered letters, and corrected proofs until evening, when he could generally work again. In so far as there is a model for the actress, it is Rachel. The novel was bought by *Le Voltaire*, which wanted to use it for large-scale publicity purposes. A total of 120,000 copies of the paper were given away. *Gil Blas* sought permission to offer advance copies. Paul Bourget in *Le Parlement*, Daudet in *Le Réveil*, his wife in *Le Temps*, Maupassant in *Le Gaulois*, Zola in *Le Bien Public*, and Céard in *L'Evénement* supported the novel against the inevitable attack by Barbey d'Aurevilly. Just as inevitably, Brunetière used the book to attack naturalism.

The preface to *La Faustin* had asked for help from female readers. Goncourt wanted to write about the life of a young girl during the Second Empire. The result was *Chérie*, which aimed at excising all but the banalities of an everyday life. It appeared in *Gil Blas* in March 1884, and a volume edition of 8,000 copies was published in April. *La Maison d'un artiste* had appeared in two volumes in 1881, describing the decoration of the Auteuil house room by room and the layout of the garden. Goncourt was one at any rate of the pioneers among collectors and connaisseurs of Japanese art, and the volumes are valuable because they give a good idea of the state in 1881 of the library and the collection whose sale fetched the 1,350,000 francs which, with the rest of the estate, including the literary income, established the fund for the Prix Goncourt. In 1889 Goncourt admitted to an income of 9,000 livres, having bought objets d'art for 200,000 during the preceding 10 years. By 1892 he was spending between 15,000 and 30,000 francs a year on his collections. It is not at all clear where the money came from that enabled him to overspend his apparent income so comfortably.

During the last decade of his life Goncourt was to write about further 18th-century women and about Japanese art. From 1874 he became very close to Alphonse Daudet. They kept the same company, attended the same social occasions, and knew one another's friends. Goncourt was charged with transmitting a last message to Daudet's wife if he were to be killed in a duel in May 1883, in which, in the event, his opponent, Albert Delpit, was slightly wounded. Like his brother, Goncourt had always been anti-semitic. It was no doubt part of his affectation of aristocracy. As he grew older the anti-semitism united him more closely with Daudet, who acted as one of the witnesses of Edouard Drumont, author of the 1886 *La France juive*, in his famous duel with Arthur Meyer. Goncourt took to dining with

Zola, Flaubert, Daudet, and Turgenev after Flaubert's Sunday afternoon receptions. All these authors claimed to share the distinction of having had their work hissed off the stage. They formed a small group, more intimate than the Magny circle.

Goncourt was embarrassed by the protest against Zola's *La Terre* on 18 August 1887, published in *Le Figaro* by five former followers of Zola (Paul Bonnetain, Joseph-Henri Rosny, Gustave Guiches, Lucien Descaves, and Paul Margueritte). Zola always thought that Goncourt and Daudet were behind the protest, and had been told so by a number of leading figures in the world of journalism. Four of the five were indeed regular visitors to Goncourt's "grenier," the second floor of the Auteuil house, where, from 1885, Goncourt regularly received young writers and artists on Sunday mornings, deliberately taking over from Flaubert, who had died in 1880. The fifth (Guiches) was soon to join them. In fact, neither Daudet nor Goncourt approved of the precise way the manifesto was drawn up and, although they did agree with most of what it said, they had not actually written or deliberately occasioned it. In the end the quarrel was patched up, at least in public, although relations between Zola and the other two existed henceforth only on a diminished and contrived level.

Almost all the Goncourt novels were turned into plays, although with little acclaim apart from *Soeur Philomène* in 1887 and *La Fille Elisa* in 1890. At first the plays were mostly staged at the Odéon, but then Antoine took several at the Théâtre Libre and, in spite of the plays' comparative lack of success, the theatre revenue came to contribute substantially to Goncourt's income. During the last two decades of his life Goncourt also became much closer to the Princesse Mathilde, although their friendship cooled some years before his death. The idea of founding an academy dates from about 1867, and was discussed between the brothers during Jules's lifetime. Essentially, Goncourt came to want to provide for the perpetuation of his own and his brother's name. He disliked the official Académie Française and all it stood for, and wanted to provide for the material support of a group of young writers, drawing his inspiration partly from the Magny dinners, and partly from Flaubert's Sundays, continued in his own "grenier," whose decoration for the purpose had plunged him into debt, and where the Sunday receptions were regarded as rather wearisome occasions.

The *Journal*, modelled on Bachaumont's *Mémoires secrets*, was intended for publication, but only part of it during the lifetime of whichever brother was to survive. Some fragments had already appeared in the 1866 *Idées et sensations*, and a further series, published by *Le Figaro* in 1886, attracted little interest. The Princesse Mathilde was annoyed by parts of what was published, particularly those appearing to slight Gautier, but Goncourt published a volume in 1887 and then, later in the same year, a second. A third appeared in the spring of 1888. The first volume of a second series was serialized in *L'Echo de Paris* from March to July 1890, and appeared as a book on 6 October, selling 3,500 in its first month. Daudet's *Souvenirs de jeunesse* had been printed in an edition of 30,000 copies, and both Barrès and Renard imitated Goncourt by starting their own diaries for publication. Goncourt published a fifth volume in February 1891, replying to criticisms by Renan of remarks he had made about him in the preceding volume, and a sixth volume appeared in February 1892. A new series started to appear in *L'Echo* on 25 April 1894, and old friends began to take offence. The seventh volume appeared in June 1894 and the eighth on 8 May 1895. The ninth and last volume appeared on 26 May 1896.

Goncourt spent his final years in a leisurely fashion. He was invited out most days, once a week to the Princesse Mathilde's and twice to the Daudets. From 1893 his health started to fail. In 1896 an anti-semitic stage version of *Manette* was boycotted. Seats were paid for, but left empty, and the play had to be taken off. Goncourt died quite suddenly while staying with the Daudets on 16 July 1896. His will founded the academy which bears his name and that of his brother, and which awards the annual literary prize. His heirs attacked the will, since the academy did not juridically exist at the moment of his death, but it was defended by Poincaré, and the Académie Goncourt met for the first time on 7 April 1900. Its members appointed by the will were Alphonse Daudet, S.-J. Rosny, J.-K. Huysmans, Léon Hennique, Octave Mirbeau, Paul Margueritte, J.-H. Rosny, and Gustave Geffroy. Zola had been dropped because he had stood for election to the Académie Française. On 7 April 1900 the academy elected Léon Daudet to succeed his by then deceased father, along with Elémir Bourges and Lucien Descaves. Goncourt stipulated in considerable detail how the academy should conduct its affairs. It was charged with the publication of the *Journal* and, at one of its monthly lunches in December, with the bestowal of the annual prize on a young author of talent.

WORKS

The literary importance of the 22 volumes of the Goncourt brothers' *Journal* derives partly from what it tells us about the literary life of Paris during the second half of the 19th century, or at any rate from about 1860 until soon after 1890, partly from its own character as a work of the imagination, and partly from what it reveals about the nature of the brothers' cooperation and the genesis of their works. It also provides important information about their non-literary activities, such as collecting, and their desire to found an "academy."

As a source for the history of the literary life of Paris, the *Journal*, to which may be added the correspondence, gives a valuable insight not only into the day-to-day sayings and doings of a whole series of often major authors, publishers, editors, and patrons, but also into the social arrangements of the literary world. From the accounts of the dinners at Magny's, the Sunday receptions given by Flaubert, and then at the Auteuil "grenier," the intimate "dîners à cinq," and the social activities centred on the Princesse Mathilde, it is possible to see how the processes of literary self-selection operated, how pecking orders were established, and what they were.

Not only did authors have to sell material, and editors, publishers, and impresarios have to buy it, but they all had to get to know one another in the first place. Ultimately, of course, it was the public who decided what was published, printed, or staged, and the publishers, who needed to second-guess public taste as well as to discover, promote, and evaluate literary talent financially, who took the biggest risks and stood to gain the greatest rewards. None the less, the smooth operation of the system of interlocking interests and coteries depended on such things as private invitations, the semi-private "elections" to the Magny group, and the reactions of authors to the published opinions of their colleagues about their own work, and in this respect the *Journal* provides valuable information.

There are surprises. The Dreyfus affair (see Zola) would have anyway split wide open the naturalist camp, still unaware in the late 1880s that its fissures would open along pro- and anti-semitic faults, with something more fundamental separating Zola and his admirers from Edmond de Goncourt and Daudet than any excesses in Zola's *La Terre*. The precise way in which, in spite of her weak political position, the Princesse Mathilde was allowed to exercise power both with the censorship and in obtaining sinecures and subventions for indigent authors also becomes clearer from the *Journal*. Above all, however, once the brothers' pathological reactions have been discounted, the *Journal* tells us who was taken seriously by whom, and often why. The dependability with which Barbey d'Aurevilly's critical judgements, for instance, were always wrong underlines the extent to which apparently literary values could be, and were, used to cover ideological positions. The *Journal* is no objective guide to who was who, but it does provide reasonably dependable information about a large number of people important in the history of late 19th-century French literature, very often in their most unbuttoned moods, as they reacted to one another.

As a work of the imagination, the *Journal* is a remarkable feat of self-analysis, in the sense that the brothers consciously reflect on their own collaboration, its conditions, and limitations. There was obviously an extraordinary harmony between them. The first part of the manuscript is almost all in the hand of Jules, which grows erratic, with an increasing amount of crossing out, until it suddenly becomes controlled again. As his illness progressed, Jules must have started to make a draft before writing a fair copy. Then Edmond takes over. Neither could stand the absence of the other, and if one went out the other would worry until he returned, leaving doors open to catch the sound of footsteps and the assurance that nothing untoward had happened: "Ce journal est notre confession de chaque soir: la confession de deux vies inséparées dans le plaisir, le labeur, la peine, de deux pensées jumelles, de deux esprits recevant du contact des hommes et des choses des impressions si semblables, si identiques, si homogènes, que cette confession peut être considérée comme l'expansion d'un seul *moi* et d'un seul *je* (This diary is the confession we make every evening, the confession of two lives unseparated in pleasure, in work, in toil, of two twin ways of thinking, of two minds receiving from their contact with men and with things impressions so alike, so identical, so similar, that this confession can be considered as the expansion of a single *me*, a single *I*)."

The analysis of this double self is sometimes almost disturbingly penetrating. The brothers are not driven to the subterfuges which ordinary relationships with the opposite sex entail: "love takes five hours a week, from 10 to 11, without a thought before or after." "Another of our strengths, and a fairly rare one, is the spirit of observation, judging people, a knowledge and an intuition of moral profiles which makes us undress people in front of our eyes." The brothers' judgements of other people were untiring, harsh, and identical. Nightly they wrote down the results of their discussion of the day's feelings, impressions, and desires. They both preferred plump women, they had sympathetic illnesses, and identical tastes in trivial matters, yet, as they recognized, their temperaments were fundamentally different, and in *En 18...* it is possible to discern which brother wrote what. Their reactions to other people lacked finesse, but their analyses of character are forceful, based on real traits, even when supercilious or downright hostile. The *Journal* is a pene-

tratingly reflective piece of self-analysis in its own right.

Its main literary interest, however, has to do with the history not only of late 19th-century narrative fiction, but also of a broader phenomenon in the history of literature, and indeed of all artistic creation. The Goncourt brothers never went to a university. Edmond trained to be a lawyer for a couple of years, and then worked in the treasurer's office. The accidents of death and inheritance allowed both of them to go off to the south to see landscapes and works of art in 1848. When they came home, although they continued to paint, if never in oils, they were ready to start trying to write. By 1850 virtually all French school leavers could read, but fewer than half of their parents, and the stage presented the most obviously lucrative form of literary outlet. After their almost ritual attempts to write for the stage had failed, the Goncourt brothers took to writing history. It is essential to an understanding of their work and of its importance to realize that, being untrained, they made up their own rules as they went along. The trained historians, like the writers who earned their living from teaching or as civil servants, knew what to do. The Goncourt brothers did not. Wars and politics did not interest them personally, and they did not experience the pressure, to which a proper training would have exposed them, to regard them as of any overwhelming historical importance.

Later on, when they saw an Académie Française without Flaubert and Gautier, and which had done without Diderot, conferring wealth and prestige on its members, they quite deliberately set out to emend the process of self-selection which, in the official academy, had anyway become corrupted. The Académie Goncourt was founded to promote those with talent but without achievement, and to protect them from the need to earn a living by becoming either teachers or functionaries. The Goncourts' money worries, although serious, were never really pressing, and they were attempting to procure their own succession outside the framework of established pressures. Given the nature of the social institutions of civilized societies, theirs was perhaps a dream that could never be realized, or at any rate not for very long, but they nevertheless dreamt it.

As incipient historians the brothers did not even know the rules for writing social history. All they had to go on was their youthful inclinations, and the taste to which Edmond had been trained by his aunt Nephtalie de Courmont, and by her 18th-century house at Ménilmontant. Sensitivity about the nobility of their lineage, youthfulness, masculinity, relative financial ease, and familiarity with the pre-Revolutionary delicacies of 18th-century taste constituted the precise formula calculated to prompt them to write about the aristocratic mistresses of important 18th-century gentlemen. Edmond was already interested in books, manuscripts, and autograph letters, and so their particular brand of social history was invented, the almost exactly predictable product of their previous experiences and current situation.

So much emerges quite clearly from the *Journal*, although not all of it is openly stated. Jules in particular might have been hypersensitive, but the brothers knew that they were fighting against established values: "Il est comme une entente pour nous empêcher de prendre possession, de notre vivant, de notre petit morceau de gloire...cela nous est amer de sentir que, pendant toute notre vie, rien ou presque rien ne nous sera payé pour tout ce que nous avons apporté de neuf, d'humain, d'artiste (It is like a conspiracy to stop us from taking possession of our little piece of glory during our lifetime...it is painful for us to feel that for the whole of our lives nothing, or nearly nothing, will be credited to us for everything new, human, artistic we have contributed)."

After the history came the fiction. The obsessive documentation of the sordid to which the brothers felt compelled is given the same half-perceived justification, although the subjects of their study, the surroundings of prostitutes, the behaviour of Rose's lover, the female prison at Clermont, the hospital where Soeur Philomène worked, all appeared to them as disgusting as they seemed important. They did not quite realize what instinct was driving them on, only half articulating their view that what was important was happening now, at the lowest social level, that it was already destroying the present order, would determine the future, and needed to be described exactly as it was, however repugnant its aspect.

The *Journal* shows the abilities and the drive necessary to invent naturalism, but not the analytic powers to describe and justify it. The academic training which would have allowed the brothers to say precisely what they felt it necessary to do, and why it was not a threat to public morals to do it, would have inhibited their creative impulsion to undertake the task. They could inaugurate naturalism in literature only by deluding themselves about the future of strife and the statistical basis necessary for proper social history. They were proved wrong about solitary confinement. There was no evidence available in France in 1865 that it led to insanity. It was sad for the Goncourts personally that literary naturalism, as distinct from determinism, never found its adequate critical exponent. The very paradoxes and even contradictions in the principles enunciated in the *Journal*, or implied in the brothers' remarks about Sainte-Beuve and Flaubert, offer the key to what naturalism actually was. They rightly saw the importance of drawing attention to what society considered it indecent to refer to, and they had in the process unjustly, disdainfully to look down on those who failed to feel the same impulse, particularly if they were as successful as Sue or as conceited as Hugo, or if, like the bourgeois bohemians, they merely affected destitution to give the impression of genius. Precisely by failing to reduce "naturalism" to a set of coherent principles, the *Journal* succeeds in presenting its nature and necessity.

Les Hommes de lettres, subsequently entitled *Charles Demailly*, is an early novel with identifiable characters drawn from life. The work is confused, introverted, and in fact too heavily dependent on the *Journal*. It is intended to be a counterpart to Balzac's *Illusions perdues* and concerns the life of a journalist, Charles Demailly, driven mad by a former mistress. Gruesome without being realistic, the novel is now chiefly of historical interest, showing the Goncourts' early misogyny and expounding the theory that artistic dedication requires the devotion of the celibate. *Soeur Philomène* is the first important novel, and deals with the subject of a nursing nun's love for a young hospital doctor who commits suicide. The technique is generally considered still to be immature. The novel is too long, with laborious conversations and inept descriptions. From a literary point of view, it is not well enough written, although historically it points in the direction in which the Goncourts were to travel. *Renée Mauperin*, which is still weak on characterization, is the story of an unsophisticated young girl, based on a real model, in love with horses, and apt to faint at the sight of blood. It is charming, unpretentious, but still lacks real power. The family of the girl, though not the girl herself, upon whom Renée was modelled took offence.

It was the death of their beloved Rose Malingre and the subsequent discovery of her real character that shocked the brothers into writing powerfully. They were determined to reconstitute in exact detail this woman they thought they had known so well. The *Journal* had already been dismissive about Hugo's *Les Misérables* on the grounds that it was sentimental and did not really penetrate properly into the realities of what it purported to describe. *Germinie Lacerteux* has been criticized on the grounds that Germinie's mistress could not have been as blind to her behaviour as she is portrayed as having been, and it is this blindness which leads to the surprise essential to the denouement. But the Goncourts had themselves been as blind as is Mlle de Varandeuil in the novel. It is also true that the language is too contrived, so that the effect of dull ordinariness striven for is not in fact achieved: "In the burning days of August the keepers won't let people go there: there are flies carrying the poisons of charnel houses, anthrax-carrying flies that kill!" On the other hand, the narrative now moves briskly and the concierge's speech and manner are perfectly reproduced. *Germinie Lacerteux* is not quite a great nouvelle, and the genre of the long conte had not yet attained the perfection it was to achieve with Maupassant 20 years later, but it ends on just the right note of pathos and is a minor masterpiece in its own right. Its place in literary history is, of course, outstandingly important: "J'ai donné la formule complète du naturalisme dans *Germinie Lacerteux*, et les livres qui sont venus après ont été faits absolument d'après la méthode enseignée par ce livre (I gave the complete formula of naturalism in *Germinie Lacerteux*, and the books that came afterwards were made exactly in accordance with the method taught in that book)."

The last two novels of the brothers' partnership taking up the new formula caused them trouble. *Manette Salomon* revealed too much about untalented painting, and the means of achieving success in Paris as a painter. It is an attack on a Jewish woman, Manette, and the influence she has over an artist, whose hopes she flatters. She succeeds in abasing him into painting simply for honours and financial success. Whereas Charles Demailly, victim of his former mistress, had died insane, Coriolis, Manette's victim, sinks into subhuman torpor. The misogyny had already become the focal point of an imaginative pattern, reflecting what we know from the *Journal* as well. The anti-semitism was to increase. Edmond de Goncourt gave permission for the offensive staging of the play drawn from the novel only on condition that Manette remained a Jewess. The interesting features of the novel have mostly to do with painting, in particular the age-old battle between the protagonists of line and those of colour. Defenders of anti-academic art, in spite of their strong dislike of Manet and of impressionism, the Goncourts use as the background of the novel the atmosphere from which the "salon des refusés" emerged in 1863. The refusal to create a character with whom the reader can identify is deliberate. What the brothers have succeeded in writing is a documentary. It is not great literature, but a fascinating literary experiment.

Documented in Rome, *Madame Gervaisais* is a novel based on Nepthalie de Courmont, who died there, and a study of religious mania. Like the other novels, it is a series of tableaux in the manner of Flaubert rather than a story. The best scenes are those which take place outside, on the street. Like the other novels, too, it is short and impressionistic, relying on mannered effects. Sainte-Beuve lectured the brothers on having gone too far, stressing that the effects were those of music or painting, not of literature. The book can scarcely have been intended to be read by more than a small public curious about literary innovation. Sainte-Beuve was of course right. The book was not intended to attract a large readership. The Goncourts had invented the naturalistic novel, and could now only exaggerate it.

PUBLICATIONS

Fiction

En 18…, 1851
La Lorette, 1853; as *Love in the Eighteenth Century*, 1905
Les Hommes de lettres (later editions as *Charles Demailly*), 1860
Soeur Philomène, 1861; as *Sister Philomene*, 1890
Renée Mauperin, 1864; as *Renée Mauperin* (in English), 1902
Germinie Lacerteux, 1864; as *Germinie Lacerteux* (in English), 1891; same title, 1984
Manette Salomon, 1867
Madame Gervaisais, 1869
La Fille Elisa, 1877
Les Frères Zemganno, 1879
La Faustin, 1882; translated 1906
Chérie, 1884

Plays

La Nuit de la Saint-Sylvestre, 1852
Henriette Maréchal, 1866
La Patrie en danger, 1873

Other

Salon de 1852, 1852
Mystères des théâtres 1852, 1853
La Révolution dans les moeurs, 1854
Histoire de la société française pendant la Révolution, 1854
Histoire de la société française pendant le Directoire, 1855
La Peinture à l'exposition de 1855, 1855
Une voiture de masques, 1856
Les Actrices, 1856
Sophie Arnould, d'après sa correspondance et ses mémoires inédits, 1857
Portraits intimes du dix-huitième siècle, 2 vols., 1857–58
Histoire de Marie-Antoinette, 1858
L'Art du dix-huitième siècle, 1859–70, as *French 18th-Century Painters*, 1948
Les Maîtresses de Louis XV, 2 vols., 1860; as *The Confidantes of a King*, 1907
La Femme au dix-huitième siècle, 1862; as *Women in the 18th Century*, 1927
Idées et sensations, 1866
Gavarni, l'homme et l'oeuvre, 1873
L'Amour au dix-huitième siècle, 1875; as *Love in the 18th Century*, 1905
La Du Barry, 1878; as *Madame du Barry*, 1914
Madame de Pompadour, 1878
La Duchesse de Châteauroux et ses soeurs, 1879
Pages retrouvées, 1886
Journal des Goncourt: mémoires de la vie littéraire, 9 vols.,

1887–96; 9 vols., 1935–36; 22 vols., 1956–59; extracts translated Julius West, n.d.; 1851–70 *Journal* edited in English by Lewis Galantière, 1937
Préfaces et manifestes littéraires, 1888
L'Italie d'hier, 1894

Non-fiction by Edmond de Goncourt

La Maison d'un artiste, 2 vols., 1881
Madame Saint-Huberty, 1882
Mademoiselle Clairon, 1890
Outamro, le peintre des maisons vertes, 1891
A bas le progrès!, 1893
Le Guimard, 1893
Hokousai, 1896

Critical and biographical studies

Ricatte, Robert, *Création Romanesque chez les Goncourt*, 1953
Billy, André, *La Vie des Frères Goncourt*, 3 vols., 1956
Caramaschi, Enzo, *Réalisme et impressionisme dans l'oeuvre des Frères Goncourt*, 1971

———

GOURMONT, Remy (-Marie-Charles) de, 1858–1915.

Critic, novelist, journalist, and essayist.

LIFE

Remy de Gourmont came from an ancient line of Norman aristocracy. He was born on 4 April 1858, the eldest son of Auguste-Marie, Comte de Gourmont (1829–1913), who could trace his ancestry back to the Middle Ages or earlier, and Mathilde de Montfort, who could trace hers back to at least the 17th century. He lived in the château where he was born until the age of 10, when the family moved to Mesnil-Villeman, near Coutances. It is there that his brother Joseph (1877–1928), known as "Jean," was born. Jean became a novelist, like Remy, and, like him, was to be closely associated with the *Mercure de France*. He was to publish two books about his elder brother, a bibliography in 1922 and *Souvenirs sur Remy* in 1924. We know more about Gourmont's ancestry than about his parents, but we do know that his upbringing was pious. His brother Henri said that Remy and his parents had a perfect relationship except in matters of religion. Gourmont became, and then remained, a religious sceptic, but the break with Catholicism was not definitive until he wrote the prologue to *D'un pays lointain* in 1898, and he believed in a sort of mysticism which regarded institutional religion as a necessity.

He boarded at the Coutances lycée from 1868 to 1876, later maintaining that he had been unhappy there. He withdrew into himself and, from 1874 to 1880, kept a diary in which he recorded a fairly commonplace adolescent crisis. He describes love and memories as nothing but ashes, and mentions a girl, but already, and significantly, writes about real life as if he were relating dreams, to the point where it becomes impossible to distinguish what actually happened from what did not. Gourmont was later to develop the view already implicit in the diary that the only world that matters is the world of experience, whether the experience originates outside the self or not. In 1876 he began to study law at Caen. By 1878 he was recording his intention to become a poet. He did not attend lectures, but spent most of his time reading in the municipal library. Barbey d'Aurevilly was one of his favourite authors. He started to write verse, and to send poems to magazines.

In 1877 Gourmont was in Paris, although we do not how he kept himself. He appears to have graduated at Caen in 1879, and it is likely that his first printed material was a series of critical articles published in 1882 in the *Vie Parisienne* and *Le Monde*. On 7 November 1881 he had joined the staff of the Bibliothèque Nationale. His job application claims that he knew English, Italian, and Spanish, and had some experience of bibliography. No doubt in order to supplement his salary, he began his long career of popularizing journalism, publishing nine books of no serious interest between 1882 and 1893 (*Un volcan en éruption; Une ville ressuscitée; Tempêtes et naufrages; Bertrand du Guesclin; En ballon; Les Derniers Jours de Pompéi; Les Français au Canada et en Acadie; Chez les lapons; Les Canadiens en France*). During these years he wrote literary journalism for a large number of reviews, and by the end of his life he had contributed to over 30. Gourmont lacked, however, both a strong personal reaction to literature and a defined point of view, which might have enabled him to sum up, or even define, the symbolist (q.v.) achievement in *Le Livre des masques* of 1896 and 1898.

Gourmont believed in nurturing his taste in the classics, even though his personal preference in youth had been for romantic (q.v.) literature. By 1909 he could say that he felt at home before Boileau and after Baudelaire. For a period his model as a critic was Sainte-Beuve, but he developed that critic's views in the direction of symbolism: "Le beau est l'idéal, la beauté en est la représentation imparfaite (The beautiful is the ideal; beauty is its imperfect representation)." Gourmont turned increasingly against romanticism and naturalism (q.v.), and in the end against all contemporary literature, but, since he wrote in heavy paradoxes, it is necessary to be cautious of selective quotation: "Idealism is an immoral and despairing doctrine, anti-social and anti-humane; for that reason it is much to be recommended at a time when it is more important to destroy than to conserve." He finally reverted to the taste that had been inculcated in him at the lycée.

His first personal book was the novel of 1886, *Merlette*, but by this time he had also written other more serious work, like the poems to be collected as *Divertissements* in 1912. A second novel, "Patrice," was never published. At this period Gourmont, who had been a good gymnast at school, is said to have been good-looking, full of physical energy, and to have preferred a non-literary social life. He met Berthe de Courrière, who interested him in black magic, occultism, and Eastern religions, and formed a liaison with her. The relationship is reflected in the 1890 novel *Sixtine: roman de la vie cérébrale*. Gourmont's naive, passionate, and sometimes eloquent letters to Mme de Courrière in 1887 were published in 1921 as *Lettres à Sixtine*. It was with her that, through Villiers de l'Isle Adam, he met Huysmans. His friendship with Mme de Courrière did not however last more than three years.

Gourmont's interest in symbolism was awakened by chance when he flicked through the pages of the first number of *Vogue*

in 1886. He says that first encounter changed his whole literary outlook. Three years later, in 1889, he published his symbolist play *Théodat* in the *Revue Indépendante*. It was written in late 1888, played unsuccessfully at the Théâtre Moderne on 11 December 1891, and published as a volume in 1893. Between 1886 and 1890 Gourmont began to take a real interest in symbolism and started to frequent advanced literary society. Although never assiduous in his attendance at Mallarmé's famous Tuesdays, he began to meet the other symbolist writers.

When the *Mercure de France* was founded after a café discussion on 13 November 1889, most of the money came from Jules Renard, but others—Albert Samain, Louis Dumur, Albert Aurier, Edouard Dubus, Julien Leclercq, Louis Denise, Jean Court, Ernest Raynaud, and Goncourt—put up capital according to their means. In the first number, published in January 1890, the editor, Alfred Valette, announced that the review's intention was not to represent any particular aesthetic point of view, but that its contributors were to be independent of one another in their literary outlook and values. As an admirer of Mallarmé and Villiers, Gourmont, who was introduced to the group by a colleague at the Bibliothèque Nationale, found much sympathetic interest in his symbolist experiments. His first piece, one of the *Proses moroses*, appeared in February 1890, and his first critical article was on Villiers's *Axel*. Although he contributed to virtually every number until he died, Gourmont's interests widened after 1896, and the *Mercure* itself, although intended to replace the avowedly symbolist *La Pléiade*, did honour its promise to publish material written from all points of view and by authors of different nationalities.

The total freedom Gourmont enjoyed is illustrated by his edition of *Le Latin mystique*, an anthology of the poetry of a medieval Latin antiphonary, published in 1892. The 220 copies were printed on seven different sorts of paper. In the *Mercure* for April 1891 he had published "Le joujou patriotisme," arguing against the still strong anti-German feeling in France that France and Germany had complementary qualities, and that their fruitful cooperation was prevented chiefly by a perverted patriotism. The piece was written in Gourmont's most provocatively paradoxical style. He would not give a little finger for the forgotten territories, he said. "We are not patriots." Offence was immediately taken, notably by Henri Fouquier, "Nestor," in *L'Echo de Paris* for 26 March 1891, and on 28 April 1891 Gourmont was dismissed from the Bibliothèque Nationale. *L'Echo* refused to print a reply to Nestor by Octave Mirbeau or a letter by Gourmont, and a considerable controversy ensued, during which Gourmont's explanations and tone concealed what was in effect a climbing down. He was left without a job, however, while the large-circulation, remunerative papers and magazines were now closed to him.

In the same year Gourmont was afflicted by a tubercular ulceration of the skin, caught apparently from an old book, which had to be cauterized, leaving permanent and serious facial disfigurement, with distortion of the lower lip as well as a hideous skin wound. For some months he went out only at night and was cared for by Mme de Courrière. Eventually he found the courage to return to the offices of the *Mercure*. The deformity was such that Gourmont's father did not at first recognize him, and the *Times Literary Supplement* later noted that it had "falsified his whole imaginative work." Gourmont's early intellectual disdain had been balanced by confident physical energy in his approach to life, and might well have disappeared in middle age.

In fact, after the onset of permanent disfigurement, he withdrew much more acutely into himself. In 1890, while *Sixtine* was being written, the disease had not yet fully established itself, but the work was significantly entitled a "cerebral novel." Gourmont's sensuality was subsequently to inflame only his imagination, and his symbolism allowed him to take refuge in the view that reality lay only in the brain.

Sixtine is dedicated to Villiers, whom Gourmont had met in January 1888 and whose unpublished works he had published after Villiers's death. Later on, in the second series of *Promenades littéraires*, Gourmont wondered if his enthusiasm for Villiers had gone too far in 1889, when he was frankly imitating him, but at that date he had also been much impressed by Huysmans, with whom he broke in 1893. The literary incompatibility had come to a head with Huysmans's conversion. By the beginning of 1892, just after the staging of *Théodat*, Gourmont was publishing *Le Fantôme* in the *Mercure*. It had been written before *Lilith*, which had appeared a year earlier. Gourmont had written about Huysmans's *A rebours* in March 1890, and it is from the famous pages consecrated to the reading of the novel's hero Des Esseintes that Gourmont felt inspired to undertake *Le Latin mystique*. His interest in the Middle Ages, in Mme de Courrières and her satanism, his friendship with Huysmans, and his even shorter association with Léon Bloy, combined with his attraction towards symbolism in literature, all show how, in the immediate aftermath of his disfigurement, Gourmont lived in a semi-rational, semi-mystical, half-religious and half-occult world. He had not surprisingly undergone a crisis of self-definition.

His first collection of verse was the edition in 25 copies of *Hiéroglyphes* in 1894. Two years earlier the prose poems *Litanies de la rose* had been published in an edition of 84 copies, with a further collection, *Fleurs de jadis*, published in an edition of 47 copies in 1893. All three volumes show a concern for the musical values of words, a subject on which Gourmont wrote in "L'ivresse verbale," published in *L'Ermitage* for February 1892. He was later to renounce what he called the poetry of verbal effects, characteristic of his work at the beginning of what was to prove his most productive decade of non-critical works. A great deal appeared in small magazines, some signed with a pseudonym—N. le Danois, J. Drexelius, later on M. Coffe, and "L'Ymagier," the name Gourmont shared with G. A. Aurier, whose miscellaneous papers he was to edit for the *Mercure* after Aurier's death in 1892. The principal critical piece of this period is *L'Idéalisme*, first published in 170 copies in 1893, but reprinted in the 1902 *Le Chemin de velours*. Articles were appearing, not only in the 30 or so reviews to which Gourmont contributed, but also in Chicago, London, Buenos Aires, Brussels, Madrid, and Lausanne.

Up to 1895 Gourmont had been in charge of English and Italian literature at the *Mercure*. About this time he ceased his experiments in symbolism, although he continued to contribute his "Epilogues" to the *Mercure* until his death. Symbolism became for him more of a philosophy than an artistic phenomenon or an aesthetic. After 1896 he produced only two more verse collections and one more play. Of the three novels, *Les Chevaux de Diomède* and *Le Songe d'une femme* are both still philosophical in content, but the third, *Un coeur virginal*, reverts to the classic conception of a novel dominated by its narrative. From 1896 Gourmont was chiefly engaged in applying what had become a philosophy to literary criticism, notably in the *Promenades littéraires* of 1904, 1906, 1909, 1912, and 1913.

After 1908 his health began to decline. In 1910 he formed a sentimental friendship with Natalie Clifford-Barney (born in 1876), which brought a new warmth into his work. Mauriac maliciously referred to the couple as "the pope of letters and the queen of Lesbos." During the last period of his life Gourmont and his friends took to exchanging letters. Despite a regular income from his journalism, Gourmont continued to work under considerable financial pressures. He died of a cerebral haemorrhage on 27 September 1915. Almost all the obituaries concentrated on his work during the symbolist period before 1896, with virtually no mention of the poetry and the novels, and very little reference to the literary criticism of the years of hardship and enforced journalism after Gourmont's dismissal from the Bibliothèque Nationale.

WORKS

The first of Gourmont's works normally regarded as having any literary interest is *Merlette*, which moulds its characters round the thin plot. Hilaire de Montlouvel is in love with Elisabeth Davray. She does not love him, but is jealous of the miller's daughter, Merlette, whose mother was Hilaire's wet nurse. When Hilaire and Elisabeth marry, it is Merlette who dies of disappointment and despair. The characters are insubstantial, and the novel is distinguished chiefly for its descriptions of the Norman countryside.

With *Sixtine: roman de la vie cérébrale* of 1890, we enter into the phase of Gourmont's publications which is ordinarily considered the most interesting, although it is possible that the literary criticism of the last decade of his life is generally underestimated. The infection was beginning to spread in Gourmont's cheek, and the novel affirms the supreme importance of "la vie cérébrale (the life of the mind)," independent of the realities of physical existence. It transposes Gourmont's relationship with Mme de Courrières on to the plane of intellectual experience. The intelligent and well-educated Hubert d'Entragues is in love with the mysterious Sixtine, but they are kept apart by their perpetual aloofness, and by d'Entragues's need to analyse his every thought and feeling. He cannot bring himself to declare his love, and the Russian Sabas Moscowitch, who is weakly delineated as a man of action, rushes in and carries off Sixtine, leaving d'Entragues to wonder what has happened, and to write his novel about it.

There is historical interest in the pre-Raphaelite mixture of romanticism and decadence, and the posturing, affected attitude of Sixtine, who is described as "fairly 14th century, a prisoner in her abbatial chair." Dressed in red, her fingers covered with jewels, she seems more like a piece of stained glass than "carved woodwork resembling a pale flower." Gourmont's characters, like Villiers's, regard living as a degrading substitute for talking, and the novel can stir only the literary historian in search of the recipe for symbolism and eager to observe the confluence of idealism, anti-naturalism, romanticism, decadence, and a pre-Raphaelite sensibility during the half-decade following *A rebours*. The novel was well received by the literary public, who particularly appreciated the way it intensified experience by etherealizing it.

Théodat was written in the same half-decade, but before *Sixtine* and the incipient disfigurement. It concerns the sixth-century bishop of Clermont, who repudiated his wife Maximienne in favour of consecration to his episcopal see. Although he instructs young neophytes in the cultivation of celibacy, the bishop still feels the desires of the flesh. His wife comes disguised into his palace, and Théodat's sexuality overcomes his ambitions and high-minded new responsibilities. The play centres on physical desire and calls for a sumptuous physical décor, even stipulating the exotic carpet design of red lions with the inchoate symbols of a gold cross and gold stars against a blue background. Underlying the action is the symbolism of the seductress holding the male back from his pursuit of the absolute, and the notion that existence is conferred on the female only by male love.

Le Fantôme moves the symbolist action to the forefront. Damase picks Hyacinthe out from her sisters and takes her off to teach her how to transpose her experience on to a purely spiritual plane. She is a fantom, having had no existence until Damase loved her: "Je ne suis ni chair ni esprit, je suis femme et fantôme: je deviendrai—ce que tu me feras (I am neither flesh nor spirit, I am woman and phantom: I shall become—whatever you make of me)." Physical love teaches Hyacinthe that her body is disgusting. Damase ensures that the point is made clear in a little lecture on the importance of pure thought, the plane of serious existence, in which relations with the physically real are reduced to the indispensable minimum necessary for the upkeep of the "material substratum." Hyacinthe subverts Damase's strategy, dragged down by her nature, which is "heavier than spiritual air." The action has no geographical location, and the lovers walk on the dead leaves of autumn, but the unity is fractured by the author's inability to forego some delectation in the scenes of deflowering and flagellation.

Gourmont is inevitably impelled to move towards a view of the superiority of the artist, the priest of etherealized experience from which all sensation has been excised, and he slips into bandying about terms like "purity," "vulgar," and "profane," defending himself with paradox. The intensification of the cult of the self leads to spiritual independence and quasi-divine power in the conte "Le château singulier" of 1894, a full decade on from *A rebours*. Symbolism has collapsed into the cult of freedom, the cult of the self: "Admettons donc que le symbolisme, c'est, même excessive, même intempestive, même prétentieuse, l'expression de l'individualisme dans l'art (Let us admit that symbolism, even when excessive, when untimely, when pretentious, is the expression of individualism in art)." It has been correctly remarked that in this formulation from the 1896 *Le Livre des masques*, "the principle of the ideality of the world," which is symbolism, is defined in a way more appropriate to romanticism.

It is not surprising that Gourmont's later criticism is still strongly anti-naturalist. There are remarkable insights jumbled up with provocative pronouncements, and it may well be that, mixed in with the chaff and the paradoxes, there lurks a remarkable perceptivity. None the less, Gourmont is unlikely ever to emerge as the great critic he might actually have been because in his critical writings there is plainly too much ill-considered judgement, too much haste, too much pleasure in shocking. There is no easily discernible unifying attitude, and no obvious skill, taste, or sensitivity running through all the literary journalism. It is quite possible that he would long have been forgotten if his painful disfigurement had not driven him to distil a pure essence of symbolism, and take it to the point at which it dissolved again into a vaporous form of decadent romanticism.

PUBLICATIONS

Fiction, poetry, and drama

Un volcan en éruption, 1882
Une ville ressuscitée, 1882
Bertrand du Guesclin, 1883
Tempêtes et naufrages, 1883
Les Derniers Jours de Pompéï, 1884
En ballon, 1884
Merlette, 1886
Les Français au Canada et en Acadie, 1888
Sixtine: roman de la vie cérébrale, 1890; as *Very Woman: A Cerebral Novel*, 1922
Chez les lapons, 1890
Lilith, 1892
Litanies de la rose (prose poems), 1892
Théodat (produced 1891), 1893
Le Fantôme, 1893
Fleurs de jadis (prose poems), 1893
Les Canadiens de France, 1893
Histoires magiques, 1894
Le Château singulier, 1894
Proses moroses, 1894
Hiéroglyphes (poems), 1894
L'Ymagier, 1894–96
Histoire tragique de la princesse Phénissa, 1894
Phocas, 1894
Le Pèlerin du silence, 1896
Le Vieux Roi, 1897
Les Chevaux de Diomède, 1897
Almanach de l'Ymagier, 1897
D'un pays lointain, 1898
Les Saintes du paradis, 1899
Le Songe d'une femme, 1899
Oraisons mauvaises, 1900
Simone: poème champêtre, 1901
Une nuit au Luxembourg, 1906; as *A Night in the Luxembourg*, translated by Arthur Ransome, 1912
Un coeur Virginal, 1907; as *A Virgin Heart*, translated by Aldous Huxley, 1921
Couleurs, 1908; as *Colours*, 1929; same title, *1931*
Divertissements (poems), 1912

Essays, autobiography, and letters

Le Latin mystique, 1892
L'Idéalisme, 1893
La Poésie populaire, 1896
Le Livre des masques, 2 vols., 1896 and 1898
Esthétique de la langue française, 1899
La Culture des idées, 1900
Le Chemin de velours, 1902
Le Problème du style, 1902
Epilogues: réflexions sur la vie, 6 vols., 1903, 1904, 1905, 1907, 1910, 1913
Promenades littéraires, 7 vols., 1904, 1906, 1909, 1912, 1913, 1926, 1927
Promenades philosophiques, 3 vols., 1905, 1908, 1909
Chronique stendhalienne (as M. Coffe), n.d.

Dante, Béatrice et la poésie amoureuse, n.d.
Le Chat de misère, n.d.
Lettres d'un satyre, 1913
La Petite Ville: paysages, 1913
Lettres à l'Amazone, 1914; as *Letters to the Amazon*, 1931
La Belgique littéraire, 1915
Pendant l'orage, 1915
Dans la tourmente, 1916
Pendant la guerre: lettres pour l'Argentine, 1916
Les Idées du jour, 1918
Monsieur Croquant, 1918
Les Pas sur le sable: pensées, 1919; as *Epigrams*, 1923
Pensées inédites, 1920
Lettres à Sixtine, 1921
Petits crayons, 1921
Le Puits de la vérité, 1922
Le Vase magique, 1923
Journal intime, 1923
Dernières pensées inédites, 1924
Nouvelles dissociations, 1925
Les Femmes et le language, 1925
La Fin de l'art, 1925
Deux poètes de la nature: Bryant et Emerson, 1925
Lettres intimes à l'Amazone, 1926
Le Joujou et trois autres essais, 1926

Other English translations and selections

Decadence and other Essays, 1921
Mr Antiphilos, Satyr, 1922
Stories in green, zinzinolin, rose, purple, mauve, blue and orange, 1924
Stories in yellow, black, white, blue, violet and red,
The Natural Philosophy of Love, translated by Ezra Pound, 1926
The Dream of a Woman, 1927
Selections, translated by Richard Aldington, 1928
Dust for Sparrows, translated by Ezra Pound in *The Dial*, 1920–21
Gourmont's editions of mostly medieval texts are not listed.

Bibliography

Gourmont, Jean de, *Bibliographie des Oeuvres de Remy de Gourmont*, 1922

Critical and biographical studies

Escoube, Paul, *Remy de Gourmont et son oeuvre*, 1921
Escoube, Paul, *La Femme et le sentiment de l'amour chez Remy de Gourmont*, 1923
Gourmont, Jean de, *Souvenirs sur Remy*, 1924
Crawford, W. R., *The Freeman's Morals: A Critique of the Philosophy of Remy de Gourmont*, 1926
Barney, Natalie Clifford, *Aventures de l'esprit*, 1929
Bencze, Eugène, *La Doctrine esthétique de Remy de Gourmont*, 1929
Jacob, P.-E., *Remy de Gourmont*, 1931
Rees, Garnet, *Remy de Gourmont: essai de biographie intellectuelle*, 1940

GRACQ, Julien (pseudonym of Louis Poirier), 1910–

Novelist and critic.

LIFE

Louis Poirier was born on 27 July 1910 in the house at Saint-Florent-le-Vieil which his grandfather Emmanuel (1839–1926) shared with the families of his son and daughter, each of the three households also having its resident maid. Gracq, as he was later to be known, was the second child of Emmanuel Poirier junior (1868–1941) and Alice Belliard (1875–1971). The couple's only other child, Suzanne, was born on 2 February 1901. Both their families had lived close to one another in the Loire valley for centuries, and both were descended from long lines of artisans. The republican and anti-clerical Emmanuel senior had become a baker and done well, buying houses, gardens, and vineyards along the Loire. His wife was pious. Gracq's father and his brother-in-law founded a wholesale drapery business together. It was while travelling on its behalf that Emmanuel met Gracq's mother. Although unusually well educated, she helped her mother in a small shop they owned. Gracq's father himself liked drawing and played the violin.

Gracq was happy at nursery and primary schools, in spite of the background of World War I. At 46 and as the father of two children, Gracq's father was not called up. In 1920 the family moved across the road to a house which Gracq and his sister kept until after their mother's death. The only time that the smooth progress of Gracq's life was broken before the outbreak of World War II was when he entered the Lycée Clemenceau at Nantes, to continue boarding thereafter at the Lycée Henri IV in Paris and then, until 1935, at the Ecole Normale Supérieure. He disliked all three experiences, finding Nantes boring and over disciplined, the food poor and the education, even in French, severely classical. Only a few details have been recorded from this time in his life: a fondness for Stendhal, the launching of the *Ile-de-France*, and his first opera, which was *Tosca*. Gracq did well at school, coming mostly top of his class. He enjoyed rugby, but not music.

By the time he got to Henri IV in 1928 he was wearing a monocle and a white cravat. He was much impressed by Alain as a teacher, although he did not later remember having learnt anything from him. He immediately felt his provincialism, and became excited by exposure to Paris, cinema, painting, Gide, Valéry, Claudel, Cocteau, Giraudoux, and Bernanos. Sundays were split between football and the cinema. Early in 1929 Gracq was deeply impressed by *Parsifal* and that summer spent two months lodging in London to learn English. He watched a lot of cricket and in 1930 came sixth in the entry examination for the Ecole, where, under the influence of Jules Verne, he opted for geography. As usual Alain's pupils from Henri IV formed a closed circle at the Ecole, where Gracq's fellow pupils included more than a handful whose names would later be known worldwide: Georges Pompidou, Jacques Soustelle, Robert Brasillach, Thierry Maulnier, and René Etiemble among others. Gracq began to take an interest in Breton and Max Ernst, then in Aragon and Eluard, travelled on an exchange to Budapest, stopping in Vienna and Venice, and seeing the Alps for the first time. His studies ended brilliantly with his geography diploma in 1933 and two articles which were published in 1934 and 1935 and won a prize which he spent on a trip to Cornwall. He also

turns out to have discovered from archives the architect's plan of the castle, and he and Albert find the secret passage leading from the salon to the beautiful Heide's room.

The plot lies in the atmosphere and in the dream sequences revealing the unconscious desires, feelings, and fears of the three main characters. The smallest incidents are heavily pregnant with all sorts of significance. There are mysterious, unexplained happenings, and dream sequences and enacted forebodings are narrated as if they were events. Herminien nearly dies in a riding accident; Heide finally kills herself, and Herminien leaves. The real focus of interest of the "récit," however, is the metaphysical experiment undertaken in the spook-laden experimental chamber, the castle in the woods, which transmits a high-voltage shock to the three subjects, revealing to each their place in the universe. This is not a fable or a fairy story, but a powerful myth, an updating of Novalis or Wagner for 1939.

Un beau ténébreux does without a formal narrator, although Gérard's diary entries contain long passages, sometimes of conversation, that scarcely depend on the adoption of Gérard's point of view. The novel is more skilfully written than its predecessor, although atmosphere is still more important than motivation. However, the statement that "Une sorte de vacuité indécise règne dans ces lieux mornes (A sort of vague emptiness reigns in these mournful places)" is more acceptable as a subjectively noted diary entry than it would be if it came from an omniscient outside narrator. The diary lasts from 29 June to 24 August, after which a narrator takes over. There is an ominous masked fancy-dress ball, the climax of the novel, on 1 September, and the text is dizzy with implicit literary allusions—to Vigny, Kleist, and Bourget for the suicide pact alone. The cast is now much bigger, and the plot ends with the execution of the suicide pact. The emotional electricity is again strong as, under its impact, the six characters congregated in the Hôtel des Vagues reveal themselves both to themselves and to one another.

Le Roi pêcheur is a Wagnerian retelling of the Grail legend, while *La Littérature à l'estomac*, the Breton volume, and *Préférences* contain Gracq's penetrating views on literature as well as on the effect of the publishing industry on writers. *Le Rivage aux Syrtes* is the first of the novels to have a historical setting, although it is not at all a novel about the past. Written in the first person, it is linked to the others by the implicit quest for self-knowledge and by its reliance on a here storm-laden atmosphere. The universality of the social and political realities, however, tie the novel more closely to the real world than its two predecessors. The characters now have backgrounds, families, pasts, and even public offices. The novel represents the furthest Gracq could go. Its successor was abandoned in favour of *Un balcon en forêt*, a "récit" in which he drew on his war experiences of 1940. The subject is the development of the hero's inner life, naturally revealed more by the reality of dreams than by the rationalizations which seek to suppress them.

Le Rivage des Syrtes is the only novel not to have been translated into English. Two chapters had been published in *La Table Ronde* before the volume publication of 7,000 copies in September 1951. The notoriety resulting from Gracq's refusal of the Goncourt prize and the subsequent controversy called for a second edition of 127,000 copies in December 1951. Gracq was trapped: he had made more money and created a bigger commercial impact by turning the prize down than he would have done by accepting it. He could always have torn up the cheque, as he threatened he would if it were sent to him. The committee pompously issued statements saying that since there were no candidates for the prize, there was no way of refusing it. They would simply bestow it in accordance with the terms of the will—something most people, including Gracq, thought they had often conspicuously failed to do. A third edition for bibliophiles (2,000 copies) was published in July 1952. All the critics remarked on the difficulty and literary polish of the novel's meticulously careful language.

PUBLICATIONS

Collections

Oeuvres complètes, Bibliothèque de la Pléiade, 2 vols., 1989

Fiction

Au château d'Argol, 1938; as *The Castle of Argol*, 1951
Un beau ténébreux, 1945; as *A Dark Stranger*, 1951 ·
Le Rivage des Syrtes, 1951
Un balcon en forêt, 1958; as *Balcony in the Forest*, 1959
La Presqu'île (stories), 1970

Play

Le Roi pêcheur (produced *1949*), 1948

Other

Liberté grande (prose poems), 1946; augmented edition, with
    La Terre habitable, 1958; further augmented edition, 1969
André Breton: quelques aspects de l'écrivain, 1948
La Littérature à l'estomac, Paris, Corti, 1950
La Terre habitable, with six erchings by Jacques Herold, 1951
Prose pour l'étrangère, 1952
Farouche à quatre feuilles, with others, 1954
Préférences, 1961
Lettrines, 2 vols., 1967 and 1974
Les Eaux étroites, 1976
En lisant, en écrivant, 1981

Translator, *Penthésilée*, by Kleist, 1954
Autour des sept collines, 1988

Bibliography

Hoy, Peter C., *Gracq: essai de bibliographie 1938–1972*, 1973

Critical studies

Leutrat, J.-L., *Gracq*, 1966
Dobbs, A.-C., *Dramaturgie et liturgie dans l'oeuvre de Gracq*, 1972
Hetzer, Friedrich, *Les Débuts narratifs de Gracq (1938–1945)*, 1980
Grossman, Simone, *Gracq et le surréalisme*, 1980

GREEN, Julien (Hartridge), 1900–

Novelist and diarist.

LIFE

Julien Green is a convert to Roman Catholicism who believes human lives follow an impenetrable pattern set by God: "Nous sommes des personnages de roman qui ne comprennent pas toujours ce que veut notre auteur (We are characters in a novel who do not always understand what our author wants)." His novels convey deeply felt emotional experience without being intrusively Catholic.

Green was born in Paris on 6 September 1900 of American parents from the southern US. His father Edward (1853–1927) was a Virginian who inherited cotton plantations and an export business in Savannah, Georgia, where he met and married Mary Hartridge (1857–1914). Mary's father, Julian Hartridge, was a judge and Congressman who supported the Confederates in the Civil War of 1861–65. Both families were profoundly influenced by the war and their resulting sense of a vanished homeland.

The first four of the Greens' seven children were born in the US: Eleonor in 1880, Mary in 1883, Charles in 1885, and Anne in 1891. In 1883, after losing all their money, the family moved to France. They stayed first in Le Havre, before moving to Paris in 1897, where Edward Green was secretary to the American chamber of commerce. Retta was born in 1894, Lucy in 1895, and Julien in 1900. He was educated at the Cours Sainte-Cécile with Retta and Lucy, and from 1908 to 1917 at the Lycée Janson-de-Sailly.

Julien Green had a happy childhood in a household full of sisters—his only brother Charles went back to the US for good in 1904. Mary Green doted on her youngest son, but it was she who instilled in him a horror of carnal impurity before he even understood what it meant. In the summers of 1909, 1910, and 1911 the Greens rented holiday houses in Andrésy on the Seine. Julien was so scared of the 1910 house, at 5 Grande-Rue, that he could not go up to bed by himself, but used to wait on the stairs until his parents' bedtime. His early melodramatic novels, *Adrienne Mesurat*, *Léviathan*, and *Minuit*, are stories of passive victims trapped in nightmarish country houses or châteaux from which there is no escape but death or madness.

The happy childhood came to an abrupt end in 1914 when Julien's mother died. He was deeply upset: "En moi il n'y avait que du silence et cette inexprimable solitude que je n'oublierai jamais (There was nothing but silence inside me, and an inexpressible loneliness that I will never forget)." He decided to become a Catholic after reading the works of Cardinal Gibbons, and was accepted into the Church in 1916, a few months after his father's conversion. Green served as an ambulance driver with the American Field Service in Italy in 1917–18, then joined the French army, and went to the Ecole d'Artillerie at Fontainebleau. He had considered joining the Benedictine monastery of Quarr on the Isle of Wight, but changed his mind in 1919 and went instead to the University of Virginia, Charlottesville. He regarded this as cultural exile—"J'allais vivre trois ans chez les Barbares (I was going to spend three years living among the Barbarians)"—but he was glad to be able to visit his family's old estates. Although he never felt completely at ease with the other students, there was one young man who had a profound effect

on his life and his writing. In describing his first sight of Mark, in early 1920, he said: "Je demeurai immobile quelques minutes… Assurément, je n'avais jamais rien éprouvé de semblable. Tout à coup, la liberté m'était enlevée (I couldn't move for a few minutes… I had definitely never felt anything like this before. All of a sudden my freedom had been taken away)."

Back in France in July 1922, Green began training as an artist at La Grande Chaumière, but gave up after a few months and in 1923 started writing seriously. Mark came to France in the summer of 1923, and it was during a walk with him beside the Seine that Green experienced a crippling inability to make a declaration of love. The "aveu manqué (failed declaration)" was to become a leitmotiv of his novels. In the words of the narrator of *L'Autre Sommeil*:

> J'étais partagé entre la terreur qu'il eût quelque intuition de mon amour et le désir violent de le lui confesser…"C'est fini," pensai-je. "Je ne parlerai pas." Je savais pourtant que jusqu'à ma mort, je porterais comme un fardeau le poids de cette minute.

> (I was torn between terror that he might have some inkling of my love, and the violent longing to confess it to him…"It's over," I thought. "I won't tell him." Yet I knew that, until the day I died, I would carry the weight of this moment with me like a heavy burden.)

Mark inspired the figure of "l'homme qui vient d'ailleurs (the man from somewhere else)" who appears in many of Green's novels as a disruptive influence, unleashing hidden emotions in the other characters.

The themes of sex and death, and revulsion for sensual experience, which recur in Green's fiction were transposed from his personal life. His concern that religious conviction was incompatible with sensual gratification came to a head on a trip to Holland and Germany in 1929, from which he dates his break with the Church:

> Avec la bouleversante invasion du plaisir, le monde parut se transformer à mes yeux. Une liberté m'était offerte dont il était grisant d'abuser.

> (I was bowled over by the invasion of pleasure into my life, and the world seemed to be transformed before my eyes. I was being offered a form of freedom, and it was intoxicating to abuse it.)

During the 1930s he developed an interest in Buddhism, which is reflected in *Minuit* and *Varouna*. From 1928 onwards he regularly kept a diary—he had previously written diaries, but destroyed them—and continued it throughout his life apart from a break in 1939–40, when the upheavals in Europe made him feel that "le bonheur n'était plus possible (happiness was no longer possible)." He spent the 1930s based in Paris but travelling frequently in Europe, setting the working pattern for most of his life. He returned to the Church in 1939 after "une pénible crise religieuse (a painful religious crisis)" brought on by reading the *Traité du Purgatoire* of St Catherine of Genoa. When Grasset suggested he should publish his journal, Green was initially hesitant about exposing his private thoughts in public, but the hesitation was brief, and he realized he could cut out any sections he felt were unsuitable. The first two volumes came out in 1938 and 1939. *Varouna*, published by Plon in 1940, was his last book to appear in French until after the war.

In May 1940, after the Nazis had taken Paris, Green moved to Pau. Then, in July, he went to the US, where he remained for the duration of the war. He lectured at Goucher College, Baltimore, in 1941, was called up for a few months in 1942, and taught at Camp Ritchie, then spent 1943 in an undemanding position at the office of war information. He wrote *Memories of Happy Days* from 1940 to 1942, and published translations from Péguy, entitled *Basic Verities*, in 1943. He was painfully homesick for Paris.

In September 1945 Green returned to Paris and entered a new phase in his writing career. He was not only reintegrated into the Church but also had a religious experience in April 1948 which he later (1970) described in his journal as "une nuit singulière. Tout ce que je peux en dire aujourd'hui est que je vis du souvenir de la splendeur de Dieu!" (a strange night. All I can say about it today is that I am living on the memory of the splendour of God!). *Si j'étais vous…* was published in 1947 and his masterpiece, *Moïra*, in 1950. In 1951 Green was elected to the Belgian royal academy. He wrote three plays which were performed and published in the 1950s: *Sud* in 1953, *L'Ennemi* in 1954, and *L'Ombre* in 1956. He was now less tormented by the dichotomy between the spiritual life and sexual orientation. In the introduction to *Le Malfaiteur* he comments that the Bible says nothing about non-heterosexual love:

> Le problème de la chair y est traité, si je peux dire, en bloc, et il ne semble pas que des distinctions soient faites entre l'une et l'autre forme d'un même péché…On ne saurait rien conclure d'un silence. On peut, en tout cas, l'imiter— et suspendre son jugement.

> (The problem of the flesh is dealt with there as a single entity, so to speak, and it seems as if no distinctions are made between one and the other form of the same sin…You can't draw any conclusions from a silence. What you can do, though, is imitate it—and suspend judgment.)

In 1960 Green published *Chaque homme dans sa nuit*, whose title comes from a line of Victor Hugo, "Chaque homme dans sa nuit s'en va vers sa lumière (Each of us in his darkness is moving towards the light)." Although the novel still deals with Green's familiar refrain of the conflict between the flesh and the spirit, it ends on a newly optimistic note of forgiveness. After finishing *Chaque homme dans sa nuit*, Green felt sufficiently liberated from his past to embark on his autobiography, publication of which began in 1963. He simultaneously published volumes of his journal.

Green was awarded the Grand Prix National des Lettres in 1966 and the Grand Prix du Roman of the Académie Française in 1970. He was elected to the academy in 1971, to the seat left vacant by François Mauriac.

WORKS

Green's early novels are in the tradition of the "gothic" novels of the 19th century. Themes of violence, death, madness, and erot-

icism are played out against a background of claustrophobic terror. In *Adrienne Mesurat* the heroine is trapped in her family house. She kills her father by pushing him downstairs, and finally goes mad. *Léviathan* is set in a provincial restaurant and a big country house and deals with Guéret's obsessive desire for a prostitute called Angèle, whom he attacks and disfigures. In *Minuit* Elisabeth is trapped in a tiny room in her aunt's house, and later in the frightening Château de Fontfroide. Her mother commits suicide after an unhappy love affair with the owner of the château, and Elisabeth and her lover Serge finally throw themselves out of a window. The exaggerated implausibility of the settings stresses the dreamlike inescapability of the victims' situation.

Epaves is set in Passy, the district of Paris where Green grew up. It is "un roman immobile" in contrast to the violence and disorder of the earlier ones, but the themes of mental suffering and fear of death are still present. The events of the novel blow up and subside again within a few weeks, and the Seine flows through it, indifferent to human torments. Green's break from the Church and interest in Buddhism coincided with the writing of *Le Visionnaire* and *Varouna* which have a dimension of mysticism and fantasy resulting from the author's own spiritual development. After his return to the Church, Green was able to embody his intense religious awareness in the character of Joseph Day in *Moïra*, but he makes Joseph a Protestant. "J'ai mis en scène un protestant comme on prend un pseudonyme (I have produced a Protestant character, rather like using a pseudonym)," he remarked in his journal in 1948. The story is set in the University of Virginia in the 1920s. Joseph Day arrives from the country, aged 18, with a fierce puritanical belief in good and evil and a feeling that he should try to "save" others. He believes sin lies in carnal impurity and is obsessed with thoughts of fornication. His apparent pursuit of purity is paralleled by an unacknowledged homosexual attraction towards another student, Bruce Praileau. The attraction he does acknowledge is for Moïra, the local siren, whose reputation is far from pure. Having betrayed his principles by making love to Moïra, Joseph murders her, but at the end of the novel he chooses not to take the escape route offered by Praileau. Several critics commented on Green's lack of moral judgement of his hero's action, and considered it a defect of the book.

In 1987 Green published his very long *Les Pays lointains*, which sold 650,000 copies in France in its first three years. It is the story of an adolescent English girl landed penniless in the crumbling aristocratic world of the southern states of the US on the eve of the Civil War. Elizabeth moves between grandiose mansions and stuffy relations trying to find her a husband. She falls in love with the one really wicked young man she meets, but they both marry someone else. Elizabeth's husband turns out to be unpleasant, and she arranges an assignation with her rakish lover. Her husband and her lover kill one another in a duel, and she is left with the baby fathered by her lover. The novel contains no real psychological interest, merely various sorts of emotional crisis, some deference to contemporary politics, pleasant descriptions of Savannah, visits to a cotton plantation and a tobacco factory, a haunted house, and some black magic. It is really an idyll with a sad ending, sprinkled throughout with threats of lurking and future evils, and was not, on its appearance, considered to be of serious literary interest.

PUBLICATIONS

Collections

Oeuvres complètes, 10 vols., 1954–65
Oeuvres complètes, Bibliothèque de la Pléiade, 5 vols., 1973–77

Fiction

Mont-Cinère, 1926; revised edition, 1928, 1984; as *Avarice House*, 1927
Le Voyageur sur la terre (short story), 1927; as *The Pilgrim on the Earth*, 1929
Adrienne Mesurat, 1927; as *The Closed Garden*, 1928
Christine, 1927; in *Christine and Other Stories*, 1930
La Traversée inutile, 1927
Les Clefs de la mort, 1928
Léviathan, 1929; as *The Dark Journey*, 1929
Le Voyageur sur la terre (collection), 1930; as *Christine and Other Stories*, 1930
L'Autre Sommeil, 1931
Epaves, 1932; revised edition, 1978; as *The Strange River*, 1932
Le Visionnaire, 1934; as *The Dreamer*, 1934
Minuit, 1936; as *Midnight*, 1936
Varouna, 1940; revised edition, 1979; as *Then Shall the Dust Return*, 1941
Si j'étais vous…, 1947; revised edition, 1970; as *If I Were You*, 1949
Moïra, 1950; as *Moïra* (in English), 1951
Le Malfaiteur, 1955; revised edition, 1974; as *The Transgressor*, 1957
Chaque homme dans sa nuit, 1960; as *Each in His Darkness*, 1961
L'Autre, 1971; as *The Other One*, 1973
L'Apprenti psychiâtre (translation into French by Eric Jourdan of *The Apprentice Psychiatrist* 1920), 1976
Le Mauvais Lieu, 1977
Histoires de vertige, 1984
Les Pays lointains, 1987; as *The Distant Lands*, 1990
Les Etoiles du sud (sequel to *Les Pays lointains*), 1989

Plays

Sud (produced 1953; opera version, with music by Kenton Coe, produced 1973), 1953; as *South* (produced 1955), in *Plays of the Year 12*, 1955
L'Ennemi (produced 1954), 1954
Je est un autre (broadcast 1954), included in *Oeuvres complètes*, 1973–77
L'Ombre (produced 1956), 1956
Léviathan (screenplay), in *Les Cahiers du cinéma*, 1962
Inigo; La Dame de Pique; La Mort d'Ivan Ilytch (screenplays), in *Oeuvres complètes*, 1973–77.
Demain n'existe pas, with *L'Automate*, 1985
Screenplays: *Inigo*, 1947; *Léviathan*, 1962; *La Dame de Pique*, 1965; *La Mort d'Ivan Ilytch*, 1965
Radio play: *Je est un autre*, 1954

Other

Pamphlet contre les Catholiques de France (as Théophile Delaporte), 1924

Suite anglaise, 1927; revised edition, 1972
Un puritain homme de lettres: Nathaniel Hawthorne, 1928
Journal:
  1. *Les Années faciles 1928–1934*, 1938; revised edition, as *Les Années faciles 1926–1934*, 1970
  2. *Derniers beaux jours 1935–1939*, 1939; vols. 1 and 2 as *Personal Record 1928–1939*, 1939
  3. *Devant la porte sombre 1940–1943*, 1946
  4. *L'Oeil de l'ouragan 1943–1945*, 1949
  5. *Le Revenant 1946–1950*, 1951
  6. *Le Miroir intérieur 1950–1954*, 1955
  7. *Le Bel Aujourd'hui 1955–1958*, 1958; vols, 1–7 as *Journal: 1928–1958*, 1961; abridged translation as *Diary 1928–1957*, edited by Kurt Wolff, 1964
  8. *Vers l'invisible 1958–1967*, 1967; vols. 1–8 as *Journal 1928–1966*, 2 vols., 1969
  9. *Ce qui reste de jour 1966–1972*, 1972
  10. *La Bouteille à la mer 1972–1976*, 1976
  11. *La Terre est si belle 1976–1978*, 1982
  12. *La Lumière du monde 1978–1981*, 1983
  13. *L'Arc-en-ciel 1981–1984*, 1988
  14. *L'Expatrié 1984–1990*, 1990
Memories of Happy Days, 1942
Gide vivant, with Jean Cocteau, 1952
Autobiographie:
Partir avant le jour, 1963; revised edition, 1984; as *To Leave Before Dawn*, 1967
Mille chemins ouverts, 1964; revised edition, 1984
Terre lointaine, 1966; revised edition, 1984
Jeunesse, 1974; revised edition, 1984 *Jeunes années*, 2 vols., 1984
Qui sommes-nous? (acceptance speech to the Académie Française), 1972
Liberté, 1974
La Nuit des fantômes (juvenile), 1976
Memories of Evil Days, edited by Jean-Pierre Piriou, 1976
Ce qu'il faut d'amour à l'homme, 1978
Dans la gueule du temps (journal 1925–1976), 1978
Une grande amitié: correspondance 1926–1972, with Jacques Maritain, edited by Henry Bars and Eric Jourdan, 1979; as *The Story of Two Souls*, 1988
Frère François, 1983; as *God's Fool: The Life and Times of Francis of Assisi*, 1986
Paris, 1983; as *Paris* (in English), 1991
Florence avec Julien Green, 1986
Le Langage et son double, 1987
Liberté chérie, new, augmented edition, 1989

Translations

Péguy, Charles, *Basic Verities: Prose and Poetry*, with Anne Green, 1943
Péguy, Charles, *Men and Saints*, with Anne Green, 1944
Péguy, Charles, *God Speaks: Religious Poetry*, 1945
Péguy, Charles, *The Mystery of the Charity of Joan of Arc*, 1943

Bibliography

Hoy, Peter C., *Green: Essai de bibliographie des études en langue française consacrées à Green 1923–1967*, 1970

Critical studies

Green, Anne, *With Much Love*, 1948
Stokes, Samuel, *Green and the Thorn of Puritanism*, 1955
Cooke, M.G., *Hallucination and Death as Motifs of Escape in the Novels by Green*, 1960
Burne, Glenn S., *Green* (in English), 1972
Dunaway, John M., *The Metamorphosis of the Self: The Mystic, the Sensualist, and the Artist in the Works of Green*, 1978

―――――

GUÉRIN, (Georges-Pierre-) Maurice de (1810–39).

Poet.

LIFE

Maurice de Guérin was born on 4 August 1810 in the small, isolated château at Cayla, near Albi, about 40 kilometres north-east of Toulouse. In the 1980s the nearest village, Cahuzac-sur-Vère, eight kilometres away, had a bus service which even then went only once a week to the local town of Gaillac, 17 kilometres away. Guérin was the weak fourth child of a sickly mother, formerly Gertrude Fontanilles (1776–1819), who died of tuberculosis when he was nine. He was brought up largely by his elder sister Eugénie (1805–1848), considered by Sainte-Beuve, on account of her letters and diary, to be Guérin's literary equal, if not his superior. The oldest child, a boy called Erembert, was born in 1803. The younger girl, Marie or "Mimi," was born in 1806. Asthmatic and prematurely aged, Guérin's father, Joseph (1778–1848) busied himself with his small property.

The rhythm of life was slow. It generally took an hour or so to walk to Mass on Sunday, visits to neighbours took weeks to arrange, and Eugénie had travelled no further than Toulouse before Guérin's marriage in 1838. The family's small farm produced mostly corn and wine, and perhaps six or eight staff were employed for house and farm together. With poultry, a few sheep, and bread baked every three weeks, the unit was virtually self-sufficient, and bought in little more than cheap clothing from the local market, fish in Lent, sugar, and sometimes coffee. The budget just about balanced, with enough to keep the boys boarding in Toulouse or Montpellier, and then Paris. There is a fascinating set of meticulously kept account books, from which every detail of material existence in its impoverished gentility can be reconstructed. In addition we have Eugénie's remarkable diary, kept for Guérin from 1834, continued after his death until 1842, and published in 1862.

In 1822 Guérin was sent to the minor seminary at Toulouse, and from 1824 to the Collège Stanislas in Paris, where in 1827 he became friendly with Jules Barbey d'Aurevilly, but also decided not to carry on studying for the priesthood. This caused consternation to his father, who regarded it as insubordination, and to Eugénie, whose sisterly love drove her to wish to exclude other possible outlets for her young brother's affections. From absences and alterations in the documentation left to posterity, it

seems certain that Eugénie, who had no dowry and whose seasons in society in 1829–30 and at the beginning of 1833 had left her with no other hopes of marriage, was thrown into emotional disarray by a letter from Guérin in February 1836. The supposition must be that one of them suspected the other of semi-erotic feelings. This view is supported by the diary kept by Guérin from 1832 to 1835, known as *Le Cahier vert*, and the probability that both Eugénie and Maurice were conversant with Chateaubriand's relationship with his sister Amélie.

In 1827, however, Guérin's decision not to become a priest immediately raised all the traditional problems associated with the careers of younger sons of impoverished nobility. The first of these was the obligation to undertake military service, or to pay for a substitute career. The obvious alternatives—law, medicine, teaching, and journalism—did not appeal to Guérin. The only thing that interested him was poetry, another link with Eugénie, although her work was to be rejected for the third time at the Jeux Floraux of Toulouse in 1828. Guérin returned to Cayla in 1829, and that summer, while he was out shooting, his gun went off by accident and nearly killed Eugénie. The incident sparked off strong expressions of affection between brother and sister. Guérin was later urgently recalled from Paris again because of the 1830 revolution and the cholera epidemic of 1832.

That same year Guérin's father asked on his behalf for the hand in marriage of Louise de Bayne, a close friend of Eugénie, but was turned down. Guérin began to show the first signs of tuberculosis, and in 1833 came under the influence of Lamennais in Paris. He went to stay at Lamennais's country establishment at La Chênaie, where he had an exalted and close romantic friendship with François de Breil du Marzan, who was just a little younger than he was. François became jealous when Guérin formed the same sort of close friendship with Hippolyte de la Morvonnais, a young Breton noble to whom François had introduced him, and who had just returned to religious practice under the influence of Lamennais. It has been suggested that Hippolyte's wife, who died suddenly in the middle of a conversation during January 1835, not long after Guérin's departure from the Morvonnais home, may have been perturbed by Guérin's relationship with her husband, or that she herself had not been unmoved by his presence.

It was probably in 1835 that Guérin wrote his prose poem *Le Centaure*, to be published posthumously in the *Revue des Deux Mondes* (*RDM*, q.v.) with an introduction by George Sand. He probably also wrote *La Bacchante*, his other prose poem, late in 1835. When the community at La Chênaie was dissolved, Guérin returned to Paris and struggled to live by writing and teaching. He now made clear to his father that he no longer felt the necessity of justifying his actions to him, stating his intentions in a letter of 27 July 1835. In fact, he left the house where his cousin, Auguste Raynaud, took in pupils and started living with his school friend and now close companion, Barbey d'Aurevilly, first in the rue de Lille, and then, until Guérin's marriage on 15 November 1838, in the Hôtel de Neustrie in the Rue de Port-Mahon.

Barbey d'Aurevilly tells us that he left a portrait of Guérin as Somegod in the prose poem *Amaïdée*, with himself as Altaï. Sainte-Beuve had the text among his papers, from where its author recovered it, presumably on Sainte-Beuve's death in 1869, and it was eventually published by Paul Bourget in 1890 after Barbey d'Aurevilly's death in 1889. Barbey d'Aurevilly had also produced a day-by-day account of his life, inspired by Byron, in the *Memoranda* written for Guérin. Later on, in a long letter to Guillaume-Stanislas Trebutien, who was to publish Guérin's *Reliquiae*, Barbey d'Aurevilly, perhaps projecting his own fantasies on to Guérin, is explicit about Guérin's relationship with women. He claimed that Guérin indulged himself by dreaming about them, but had never had a physical relationship with one, not even his wife. Eugénie and Guérin took to exchanging their intimate correspondence through Eugénie's confessor, the Abbé de Bories, parish priest of Cahuzac since 1829.

In 1836 Guérin shared Barbey d'Aurevilly's life as a Paris dandy, associating him with Byron, of whose incestuous relationship with his own sister, by whom he had a child, Guérin must have been aware. This is the point at which Guérin wrote the long letter to Eugénie which has since disappeared. It is not improbable that his relationship with his sister was dominating his imagination when he wrote his prose poems. In 1836, however, while Barbey d'Aurevilly had hot water sent round for his morning bath, and they both daily ate their ices at Tortoni's, Guérin gave lessons to the young Charles de Gervain, a rich orphan from a family which traded in indigo, who had a 17-year-old sister called Caroline. Barbey d'Aurevilly tried to arrange a marriage, but Guérin's lack of means resulted in rejection by Caroline's aunt and guardian.

By 1837 Guérin's health had deteriorated. Barbey d'Aurevilly took him to stay with Henriette-Marie de Maistre, the sister of a school friend, who had already shown a passing interest in Guérin, and who now reciprocated his attentions. It is not impossible that the prospect of a serious liaison worsened his tuberculosis. He started coughing up blood, and had to go back to Cayla, where he arrived with a fever on 13 August 1837, having had to travel by river, the longest way, but also the least exhausting possible.Caroline, her brother Charles, the aunt, and their dog came to visit him, and Guérin and Caroline were allowed to become engaged. Almost immediately the poet realized he had made a mistake. He was much happier in the company of Barbey d'Aurevilly in Paris, and spent 1838 living with him as a dandy, his pocket money somewhat grudgingly provided by Caroline's aunt. Guérin was behaving almost frenetically, and meditated writing a "Hermaphrodite." Eugénie came to Paris for the wedding, having travelled by diligence for 60 francs. It took seven days from Toulouse, but cost a lot less than the 200 francs fare for the post chaise. Eugénie had a presentiment of Guérin's coming death. So, apparently, did he.

Eugénie quarrelled with the Gervains, so on her visits in December 1838 and the late spring of 1839 she stayed with Marie de Maistre, whose close friend she was to become. A letter from Barbey d'Aurevilly to Trebutien suggests that Guérin felt humiliated after his marriage by his total impotence. His health quickly declined. By early July 1839 he, his wife, and Eugénie had returned to Cayla, where Guérin died on 19 July. Eugénie spent much time in the company of Barbey d'Aurevilly, for whom she now wrote her diary. She herself died of tuberculosis at Cayla on 31 May 1848.

WORKS

Guérin published nothing during his lifetime, and it was only Eugénie's persistence that got his prose poems published after his death. Barbey d'Aurevilly had promised to see to their publication, but it was finally undertaken by his friend Trebutien. However, it was George Sand who prefaced *Le Centaure* with a memoir and published it with some extracts from the letters in the *RDM* for 15 May 1840, calling Guérin "Georges." Her attention had been drawn to him by a certain C.-A. Chopin, regarded by Barbey d'Aurevilly as a clown, but who clearly saw Guérin as a victim of society and sought to use his texts to distract Sand from her preoccupation with a weaver whose poetry she had recently taken up. In fact, immediately after Guérin's death his manuscripts were being widely copied and his prose poems became a salon cult. Parisian hostesses vied to get manuscripts from Eugénie, but the 1840 social success was merely a flash in the pan. What continued was a tiny literary cult, which was to astonish Sainte-Beuve, who wrote the preface to Trebutien's two-volume edition of the *Reliquiae* in 1861. *La Bacchante* was included only in the 1862 edition.

Only from 1853, when he sent the first notebook, did Barbey d'Aurevilly begin to send material constantly to Trebutien at Caen. A coolness had developed between him and Eugénie, who was anxious to suppress the works of her brother which were least compatible with orthodox Catholicism. On Eugénie's death, Guérin's other sister, Marie, who lived until 1862, took over the relationship with Barbey d'Aurevilly with less bitterness, but without at first any more success.

In *Le Centaure* the young mortal, Mélampe, seeks out the old centaur Macarée, half horse and half man, born of a cloud, signifying illusion, by the violent Ixion, and listens to the story of his youth. The centaur's ancestry endows him with a thirst for blood and the power of dreams. The text is a prose poem in praise of nature. The centaur feels his ancestry stirring. When his mother returns:

> ces retours qu'elle faisait sans m'instruire jamais des vallons ni des fleuves, mais suivie de leurs émanations, inquiétaient mes esprits, et je rôdais tout agité dans mes ombres…je m'inquiétais de mes forces, j'y reconnaissais une puissance qui ne pouvait demeurer solitaire, et me prenait soit à secouer mes bras, soit à multiplier mon galop dans les ombres spacieuses de la caverne, je m'efforçais de découvrir dans les coups que je frappais au vide, et par l'emportement des pas que j'y faisais, vers quoi mes bras devaient s'étendre et mes pieds m'emporter

> (the way she used to come back without ever telling me about the valleys and rivers, although she brought with her their emanations, disquieted my spirits, and I wandered around nervously in the dark… I was anxious about my vigour, recognizing a power which could not remain alone, and which made me shake my arms or speed up my gallop in the lofty darkness of the cave. In the blows I struck in the emptiness, and in the way I was carried off by the steps I took, I tried to find out what my arms should stretch towards and my feet should carry me to).

The message is much the same as that carried by Mallarmé's awakening fawn. Both are clearly anchored to within a year or two in their dates of origin. Here the symbolism is cruder, the text in prose and still obviously based on Latin rhythms, and the lasciviousness is more nearly stated than suggested, but the meaning is close. The passage is clearly about the uneasy, disquieting stirrings of adolescent desire, and it controls everything

ter of the architect of the Quebec parliament buildings. An older cousin with whom Hébert spent much of her childhood, Hector de Saint-Denys Garneau (1912–1943), became a painter and a well-known poet, and was part of the group which founded *La Relève* in the late 1930s. The review was intended to serve as a focus for the effort to renew the intellectual, spiritual, and artistic life of French Canada. Hector exerted a powerful influence on Hébert. He underwent a religious crisis, and had a weak heart, and died very young as a result of a heart attack one evening, after canoeing to an island where he was building a cabin. A year previously Hébert had published her first book of verse. *Les Songes en équilibre.* She had watched closely Hector's growing sense of alienation from society, and final retreat into an obsessively puritan spirituality.

Hébert was born on 1 August 1916 at Sainte-Catherine-de-Portneuf, about 25 miles north-west of Quebec city, where her cousin's family lived, and where the Héberts always spent the summer. In four successive summers she produced plays in the local parish hall, before her brother took over from her. As a child she had read widely, listened to her father's radio programmes, and acquired an impressive informal education, although her health precluded regular attendance at her schools in Quebec, Notre-Dame-de-Bellevue, and Mérici. Her father was slow to take her writing seriously, but from 1939 she was regularly publishing poems and short stories in reviews, several a year for 15 years.

Hébert later came virtually to disown the 1942 collection of verse as childish and derivative. It does in fact give a melancholy account of Hébert's world, although it shows a delicate and unaffected sensibility at work. It also comes to grips with physical realities in a way not considered orthodox by the literary hierarchy of the province, still largely attuned to religious, rural ways of thinking. Hébert's most famous short story "Le Torrent," which gave its name to a volume of six contes in 1950, is a revised version of a conte originally published in 1947 as "Au bord du torrent." It is virtually an allegory of the experience of growing up in the stifling artistic and intellectual atmosphere of Quebec, which the young talent of *La Relève* had not yet succeeded in opening up.

A radio play of Hébert's was broadcast on 20 July 1952. Exactly a week later her sister Marie died suddenly, though previously in good health. From 1950 Hébert had been working for the Canadian Broadcasting Corporation, which she left in January 1953 for the National Film Board. A second volume of verse, *Le Tombeau des rois*, was published in 1953 and is obsessed with guilt, despair, and thoughts of death. It marks the apex in the curve of Hébert's inner anguish and the nadir in her morale. She worked for the Film Board until 1960, at first in Ottawa and then in Montreal, mostly writing scripts for pedagogical films, but in 1954 obtained a grant which enabled her to travel to Paris. Then in 1958 came her first novel, *Les Chambres de bois*, published in Paris. Although Hébert was awarded two Quebec prizes, and then Canada Council grants in 1960 and 1961, it was only with the appearance of *Poèmes*, published in Paris in 1960, that she began to be well known to the French reading public. The volume reprinted *Le Tombeau des rois*, but included the *Mystère de la parole*, a hymn of almost ecstatic joy indicating a complete change of mood.

The plays were written for radio or television, or as screenplays for the cinema. After 1960 Hébert first divided her time between Canada and Paris, and then settled in Paris, and her literary production became exclusively fictional. Her most important novel is generally considered to have been *Kamouraska*, which was published in Paris in 1970, and in 1971 won the Prix des Libraires, now considered by literary France to be the most reliable of all the guides to literary excellence. It sold 100, 000 copies in less than a year, was translated into English, Finnish, Spanish, Czech, Italian, German, Japanese, Chinese, and Portugese, and was speedily made into a film. *Kamouraska* was followed by *Les Enfants du sabbat*, *Héloïse*, and *Les Fous de Bassan*, which won the Prix Femina. In spite of the changes of mood between the two volumes of mature verse, the fiction establishes clear imaginative patterns. Hébert creates powerful myths, but they all have to do with the progressive liberation of a stifled talent, often by violent rebellion against stultifying or repressive force. These myths derive their power from strong and meticulously recorded roots in actual historical situations, and from building on permanent associations in her readers' minds between the characters and incidents she creates and well-known figures from other myths in folklore and/or fairy tale.

WORKS

Hébert celebrates her own liberation from the depressive gloom in which she lived, from the death of her cousin until after the death of her sister, in the splendidly baroque poem of reintegration into the human race, the *Mystère de la parole*, published in the 1960 *Poèmes:*

Les trois coups de la création du monde sonnèrent à nos oreilles, rendus pareils aux battements de notre sang

En un seul éblouissement l'instant fut. Son éclair nous passa sur la face et nous reçumes mission du feu et de la brûlure

The three knocks of the creation of the world rang in our ears, made like the beating of our blood/ In a single flash the world existed. Its lightning passed over our face and we received the mission of fire and burning

The violent and repugnant images of *Le Tombeau des rois* are now repudiated in favour of the heady intoxication of nature. The seasons, river, elms, and heather take over from the blind bird, its eyes gouged out, turning towards the dawn sun.

The change comes more gradually in the fiction. *Le Torrent* is a first-person narrative which ends, not quite successfully, in blurring the limits of the physically real with those of the imaginary and phantasmagoric. François Perrault escapes the dominating tyranny of his mother, Claudine, who cuffed his ears so hard with a bunch of keys when he refused to become a priest that he went deaf. He seeks to release the young horse his mother cannot tame, takes a female companion to spite his mother, knows he will never be free, and merges himself in a hallucinatory vision with the on-flowing river, whose power over him, like that of this mother, is irresistible.

Les Chambres de bois is more a prose poem than a simple narrative conte. Its protagonists, Catherine and Michel, are similarly trapped by the dream world which encloses them. It is only with the 1970 *Kamouraska*, which explores the interior night of its heroine, Elisabeth, that we emerge, however, into the full panoply of Hébert's fictional world. The novel is set in the great plains and winters of early 19th-century Canada, and contains the characteristic conflict between the pressure towards stifling social conformity and the need of passion to free itself. The heroine, Elisabeth d'Aulnières, is about 40, and had married her second husband, Jérôme Rolland, 18 years previously. As he lies dying, Elisabeth relives her past, including the murder of her first husband, Antoine Tassy, by her lover, the doctor George Nelson. She remembers the disasters of the first marriage, contracted when she was 16, the infidelities, the moments of drunkenness, the night of the murder, the prosecution, George's flight to the US, and the abandonment of all proceedings against her. At the end of the novel we are returned to the bedside of Jérôme Rolland, who has just received extreme unction. The narrator is Elisabeth.

Kamouraska is a historic village about 150 kilometres downriver from Quebec, where, on 26 January 1839, George Holmes killed Achille Taché, the husband of his mistress, Joséphine d'Estimauville, before fleeing to Vermont. The incident had already been recounted by Georges-Isidore Barthe in the 1894 *Drames de la vie réelle*. Taché was Hébert's mother's family name and Hébert had also heard the story from her mother. She keeps to the exact historical details, partly to ensure that the fiction retains its air of authenticity, with imagination nowhere allowed to slip into mere fantasy. The rebellion of 1837–38, and the menace from regrouping government forces, form the background to the story. The adulterous passion, which was naturally regarded from a Jansenist point of view in 1839, is still regarded as irredeemably wicked in the 1970 novel, as a situation that leads not surprisingly to murder, and Elisabeth feels the penetrating anguish of guilt more on account of the passion than on account of the murder. In the guise of a historical novel Hébert has written not only something of an account of her own spiritual anguish, but also an attack on the puritan provincialism of what still existed of old Quebec.

There are other elements pushing Elisabeth towards suicide, such as her meditation in front of the fire, whose flames are those simultaneously of her former passion and of hell. Much play is made of fire and water, black and white, snow and blood, life and death, to lift the novel from the plane of a story to that of an elemental myth in which the whole parade of hostile characters who once peopled Elisabeth's world and now fill her nightmares signify the guilt which she is made to feel by the world and all it contains. Catherine's black and white patterned floor tiling in the kitchen in *Les Chambres de bois* returns in *Kamouraska*, a mirroring device frequently used by Hébert to link her oeuvre together. At crucial moments the style starts to pant, with very short sentences, or even mental flashes that are not sentences, separated off by full stops. Some of the technical devices, like those involving Elisabeth's mirrors and glass panes, may lack literary sophistication, but the novel gains its impact from its bitter range of symbols commenting on a present predicament under the guise of a recollection of a past event, Jérôme's death, which recalls an even more distant past event, the murder. It constitutes a powerful and penetrating imaginative vision of a world which overflows French-speaking Canada.

Les Enfants du sabbat opposes the mountain forest where Soeur Julie de la Trinité was born and the Quebec convent of the Ladies of the Precious Blood where she is now a novice. She comes from a line of witches and was brought up in a mountain hut where her parents made illicit liquor, celebrated orgies and Black Masses, and undertook abortions, and where her father abused her sexually. Again there is the conflict in one person of wild, untamed passion, leading to a virtual epitome of all that is regarded as wicked, and all that is both socially acceptable and religiously austere. Revolted by all that went on in the cabin, and by his mother's desire to have sexual relations with him, Julie's brother, Joseph, enlisted for war. His mother, Philomène, has died, burned to death in the cabin, and Julie has taken the habit to sacrifice her life for Joseph's. All of this is revealed in retrospective flashes, like the events leading to Elisabeth's nightmare of guilt in *Kamouraska*.

Pandemonium breaks out in the convent, with hysteria, dubious supernatural manifestations, exorcisms, apparitions, sexually ambiguous phenenomena, lunacy, and simple sexual complications. Those well read in the history of religious hysteria will pick up associations here with the witches of Salem, Saint-Médard, Grandier, and the devils of Loudun. The doctor, two chaplains, and the mother superior are all sucked under. Then Julie learns of what she regards as Joseph's treason, since he has married an Englishwoman, who is expecting his child, and whose death Julie magically encompasses. Joseph is killed. Julie herself gives birth to a monster, conceived by the evil spirit, and the chaplain smothers it under the snow in front of the superior.

Julie's morbid fantasies have become real. The narration is in the third person, broken by interior monologues, and a bibliography on diabolic manifestations in Quebec is appended. Again an occasional lack of technical sophisticiation obtrudes, but the picturesque extravagance of the narrative denotes the same sort of reasserted inner joy as the *Poèmes* of the same year. The satire switches to burlesque, and the baroque of the *Mystère de la parole* to the frankly rococo. Julie appears as a fox, dancing the foxtrot. The absolute distinctions between life and death, like those between good and evil, fantasy and reality, the symbolic and the actual, are simply abolished.

PUBLICATIONS

Fiction

Le Torrent, 1950; as *Le Torrent suivi de deux nouvelles inédites*, 1963; as *The Torrent: Novellas and Short Stories*, 1973
Les Chambres de bois, 1958; as *The Silent Rooms*, 1974
Kamouraska, 1970; as *Kamouraska* (in English), 1973
Les Enfants du sabbat, 1975; as *Children of the Black Sabbath*, 1977
Héloïse, 1980
Les Fous de Bassan, 1982

Plays

Le Temps sauvage, La Mercière assassinée, Les Invités au procès: Théâtre, 1967
Screenplays and commentaries: *Les Indes parmi nous*, 1954; *Drôle de mic-mac*, 1954; *Le Médecin du nord*, 1954; *La Canne à pêche*, 1959; *Saint-Denys-Garneau*, 1960; *Le Déficient mental*, 1960
Radio Play: *Les Invités au procès*.
Television Plays: *Le Temps sauvage*; *La Mercière assassinée*.

Verse

Les Songes en équilibre, 1942
Le Tombeau des rois, 1953; as *The Tomb of the Kings*, 1967
Poèmes (includes *Le Tombeau des rois* and *Mystère de la parole*), 1960; as *Poems*, 1975
Saint-Denys-Garneau and Hébert (selected poetry), translated by F.R. Scott, 1962; revised edition, 1978

Other

Dialogue sur la traduction, with F R Scott, edited by Jeanne Lapointe, 1970

Critical studies

Lacôte, René, *Hébert*, 1969
Pagé, Pierre, *Hébert*, 1971
Major, Jean Louis, *Hébert et le miracle de la parole*, 1976
Lemieux, Pierre-Hervé, *Entre songe et parole: structure du Tombeau des rois de Hébert*, 1978
Thériault, Serge A., *La Quête de l'équilibre dans l'œuvre romanesque de Hébert*, 1980

HEREDIA, José-Maria de, 1842–1905.

Poet.

LIFE

Heredia's father was a Spanish immigrant to Cuba, a coffee planter, who had had a daughter and three sons by a previous marriage when he married Heredia's mother, Louise Girard. They had three daughters and a son, the youngest child, who was born on 22 November 1842. Heredia's maternal grandfather was from Normandy and had also become a coffee planter in Cuba. Heredia's father had a business associate at Senlis, Nicolas Fauvelle, who had become a close family friend, and who undertook to bring up the new male child in France, if the family had not by then retired there. Several Heredia children were educated in France and, after the revolution of 1848, an elder daughter was brought back to Cuba where slave emancipation was naturally unpopular among the French planters. Heredia's father had a breakdown and, on the way back to recuperate in France, died at sea on 15 April 1849. His mother considered having Heredia educated in Spain, where his half-brother, Manuel, was doing well. He died as governor of the Philippines. However, Fauvelle's wife died in 1850, and Fauvelle came to spend the following summer in Cuba. In October 1851 he took Heredia back to France with him, and sent him to the Catholic school run by the diocesan priests of Beauvais, the Institution de Saint-Vincent.

In 1852 an earthquake destroyed the family house in Cuba and was followed by a cholera epidemic, but the family escaped both unscathed. Heredia did well at school, where he was trained essentially in classics, jumped a class, and won an assortment of prizes. He also enjoyed sports. His name was Gallicized to Joseph-Marie, but to the various cousins with whom he lived in France he appeared unsophisticatedly colonial. He passed his baccalauréat in November 1858 and was summoned home by his mother, and told to bring a good saddle with him. He arrived in June 1859 and started to learn Spanish, following courses in philosophy and literature at Havana. He was not allowed to matriculate, however, as he had not registered his baccalauréat with the Spanish embassy in Paris.

Heredia's first known efforts to write verse date from 1859 in Cuba, and are a clear transposition into Cuban terms of Leconte de Lisle's African poems. (Heredia had bought a copy in Paris on the day of his baccalauréat, because he liked the cover.) He even borrowed the rhymes. On 15 April 1861 he left Cuba again with his mother and a half-brother's son to return to France. His mother took a house in Paris, and in November Heredia started to study law. Nicolas Fauvelle married again, but died in 1865. His wife, who had known the Heredias before her marriage, died in 1870. While continuing to study law, Heredia entered the Ecole des Chartes, the training school for archivists. He stayed near the top of his year, but never completed his thesis. He was well enough off not to need a job, and by the mid-1860s had turned to poetry, but was sufficiently conscientious to retake a law examination he had failed. In the end he did well at law, though he never completed the final series of examinations.

On his arrival in Paris in 1861 Heredia became a prominent member of a student literary society, which had had half a dozen future members of the Académie Française among its 45 founding members in 1857. The 18-year-old Catulle Mendès had also just arrived in Paris, and was in the process of founding the *Revue Fantaisiste*, with the encouragement of Hugo, Baudelaire, Gautier, and Banville. Early contributors to the review included Champfleury, Gozlan, Bouilhet, Sully Prudhomme, Villiers de l'Isle-Adam, and Wagner. It was the avant-garde publication round which the Parnassians (q.v.) rallied. Mendès was fined 500 francs and sent to prison for a month for a 500-line piece of his own which he printed in it. By the end of 1861 the review had folded and been succeeded by the *Revue Française*. Founded in December, this was less wholly favourable to the "L'Art pour l'art" (q.v.) school, and more inclined to naturalism (q.v.). Heredia published four sonnets in its 1 May and one in its 1 November 1863 number. He had sent three pieces, only one of which was unpublished, to the *Revue de Paris* while it was still controlled by Maxime du Camp, and found himself published after it had been taken over from Du Camp and Laurent Pichat by Henry de la Madelène in 1864.

By 1863 Mendès and his friends were meeting at the Hôtel du Dragon Bleu. Two of the group, Albert Mérat and Léon Valade, were just publishing a volume of sonnets. That winter they were joined by François Coppée, and started to meet at the Café Procope. Léon Gambetta, who had just graduated as a lawyer, came to recite his work, and Louis-Xavier de Ricard devoted a legacy to founding the monthly *Revue du Progrès*, which published early work by Verlaine, and was consistently hostile to Monsignor Dupanloup, the noted preacher and educationalist with overtly clerical views. The editor went to prison for three months and the owner for one in spite of Gambetta's defence. After the hearing Ricard took the group to his mother's at 10, Boulevard de Batignolles. Chabrier came and played the piano, and it was here at no.10, and in the salon of Mme Virginie Ance-lot, wife of the playwright Jacques-Arsène, that the Parnassian group was founded.

Mendès, Ricard, and his mother frequented one another's salons, and the group came to cohere round Leconte de Lisle, whom Mendès, recommended by Houssaye and Banville, met at Louis Ménard's house, along with Coppée and Villiers. Sully Prudhomme was another frequent visitor at Leconte de Lisle's, while Léon Cladel and Léon Dierx also belonged to the group. Mendès received on Wednesdays and the Marquise de Ricard on Fridays. It was at her home that the group are, surprisingly, recorded to have acted Hugo's strongly romantic (q.v.) *Marion de Lorme*. By 1866 the group, who were to be found most Sun-days at the Pasedeloup concerts, were also associated with Gounod and Saint-Saëns, and with picnics and evening gather-ings in the Luxembourg gardens, which they would leave at closing time by the gate nearest to the Café Bobino. One of the memorable occasions for which they assembled was the first night of the Goncourt brothers' *Henriette Maréchal* on 5 December 1865.

Verlaine knew an amateur violinist, Ernest Boutier, who wrote poetry but published nothing, and whose friends included the young bookseller Alphonse Lemerre. Lemerre's customers mostly bought prayer books. It was Verlaine who suggested taking Ricard to see him. Lemerre was thinking of publishing the 16th-century Pléiade poets, but said he would take on the unknown young poets of the group, lending his name and shop to the enterprise if they would pay for the printing. They ended up coming daily to the shop between four and seven. Lemerre also took over the publication of another review edited by Ricard, *L'Art*, although he was not a little perturbed by the noise and hairstyles of his new friends, which so frightened his old customers that he found the poets a back room reached via a spiral staircase that led up from a back entrance. Lemerre pub-lished Ricard's *Ciel, rue et foyer* (1865). The poets joked about his probable bankruptcy, but Leconte de Lisle, Gautier, and the ageing Antoni Deschamps all came to the back room.

Lemerre did not go bankrupt. Many of the poets became members of the academy, and Heredia had found the milieu he needed, one that centred increasingly on Saturday tea time at Leconte de Lisle's. The high period of the Parnassian group, at first about 40 poets, lasted from the early 1860s until the Franco-Prussian War of 1870. One of their number remarked on its decline as cigarette-smoking women joined the pipe-smoking men. Meanwhile, however, *L'Art* became the group's review, publishing Leconte de Lisle, Sully Prudhomme, and Catulle Mendès. It did go broke, and Mendès suggested that Ricard should change over to a luxury series of fascicules devoted exclusively to poetry. The title *Le Parnasse Contemporain* alluded to the 17th-century *Parnasse satirique* by Théophile de Viau, recently republished in 1861.

It looks as if the title, whose paternity is contested, was thought up by Mendès, although its author may have been Charles Marty-Laveaux, the founder of the Bibliothèque de la Pléiade, then being published by Lemerre. It was Ricard and Mendès at any rate who designed and marketed the fascicules. Heredia approached potential contributors. Sainte-Beuve would not help, and Hugo merely gave the enterprise his blessing. The first number, 16 pages published on Saturday 3 March 1866, contained five pieces by Gautier, Banville's "L'exil des dieux," and five sonnets by Heredia. The second fascicule was entirely

devoted to Leconte de Lisle, but exhausted Ricard's resources. Lemerre took over the publication, and the 18th and last fasci-cule of the first series appeared in June 1866, before the bound volume of 284 pages went on sale at eight or 16 francs, accord-ing to the paper used.

There were 37 contributors, and the enterprise would have collapsed had not Barbey d'Aurevilly produced the atrocious attack which ought to have been foreseen, but was not. For Barbey d'Aurevilly so grand a chance to be wrong again was not to be missed. The Académie Française had 40 seats and Barbey d'Aurevilly's *40 Médallions de l'Académie Française* had first appeared in *Le Nain Jaune* in 1864. He now published his *37 Médaillonets* in the same review demonstrating the inadequacy of his reactions in the dreadful prose style of his invective, lit-tered with rows of dots, exclamation marks, and italics.

By the end of 1866 a parody of the collection had appeared, the *Parnassiculet Contemporain*, wrongly dated 1867, and Mendès very nearly fought a duel with Paul Arène, the leader of authors of the lampoon. At least two reviews sprang up to pub-lish the work of the Parnassian group, *La Gazette Rimée*, which ran for six numbers, and *La Parodie*, which ran for a few months in 1869 but changed its address three times and its printer six. All the Parnassians disliked the repressiveness and the bour-geois ascendancy of the Second Empire, although not all were politically minded.

Two more collections of fascicules of *Le Parnasse Contem-porain* were published, that of 1869, postponed by the war until 1871, and that of 1876. Heredia was on both editorial commit-tees, and published 25 "sonnets héroïques" in the 1876 volume, while a prologue, "Les Conquérants de l'or," to a long poem which he never completed had appeared in that of 1869. Other poems by Heredia were contained in further anthologies pub-lished by Lemerre in 1868, 1874, 1875, and 1893, and in the four volumes of the *Anthologie des poètes français du XIXe siècle* (1887–88). Arsène Houssaye had published six of Heredia's sonnets in *L'Artiste* during 1868, but it was not until 1885 that he finally breached the citadel when he had his triptych "Persée et Andromède" accepted by the *Revue des Deux Mondes* (q.v.).

The first properly Parnassian review, edited by Villiers de l'Isle-Adam, was the *Revue des Lettres et des Arts*, which appeared on 13 October 1867, quickly to be replaced by *La Renaissance Littéraire et Artistique*, in which Heredia published three sonnets. In 1874 he published his Egyptian cycle, "La terre de Khèmi," in the *Revue du Monde Nouveau*, edited by Charles Cros, and in 1875 and 1876 a piece in each of two numbers of *Le Siècle Littéraire*. Late in 1875 Catulle Mendès established yet another review, this time with more success. *La République des Lettres* lasted three years and published Hennique, Maupas-sant, Huysmans, Alexis, and three of Heredia's sonnets. Three more reviews sympathetic to the Parnassian poets were founded when *La République* ceased publication, in each of which Here-dia published: *Le Monde Poétique*, Anatole France's *Les Lettres et les Arts*, and Charpentier's weekly *La Vie Moderne*, which also published impressionist painting, Degas, Forain, Manet, Meissonier, Puvis de Chavanne, Renoir, and others. Reviews were founded with "Parnasse" in the title. The avant-garde had become established, and were to be dislodged only by the sym-bolists (q.v.).

In March 1867 Heredia had married Louise Despaigne, who was from a Nantes family but had been born in Cuba. Heredia had already visited Italy in 1864, and the couple now went to

Milan, Venice, Florence, and Rome for their honeymoon. In Paris they lived with Heredia's mother, regularly entertaining Leconte de Lisle, Coppée, Sully Prudhomme, Bourget, and Anatole France on Thursday evenings. Later in 1867 Heredia's mother left again for Cuba, where she was ruined in the uprising of 1868. She returned to France, where she died on 22 January 1877. Heredia himself had frequented Marie d'Agoult's salon, was close to Banville and Gautier, and later became friendly with Victor Hugo and Flaubert. His closest associate in the literary world, however, remained Leconte de Lisle, whose weekly receptions he later continued himself. Later on he came to know Edmond de Goncourt and Daudet, as well as Zola and his young friends. He became an avuncular, literary figure, more respected than loved, and more tolerated than admired by his juniors. Hélène, the eldest of his three daughters, married Maurice Maindron in 1899 and then, widowed, René Doumic in 1912. The second daughter married Henri de Régnier in October 1895 and wrote under a pseudonym inspired by her grandmother's name, Gérard d'Houville. The third daughter married Pierre Louÿs in May 1900, divorced him in July 1913, and married Gilbert de Voisins in June 1915.

Heredia's literary activity was not restricted to the scant poetic output for which he is now remembered, essentially the 118 sonnets of *Les Trophées*, published in volume form by Lemerre on 16 February 1893, the year before Heredia's election to the Académie Française. He also wrote a large amount of prose, editions, translations, and reviews, as well as prefaces and works of travel. He translated the four volumes of a 16th-century history of the conquest of "New Spain," published in 1877, 1879, 1881, and 1887. *Les Trophées* was nevertheless his major success. Heredia had been able to afford to cultivate his reputation, and by 1893 it was an elegant accomplishment to know his latest sonnet by heart. The volume sold 5,000 copies in a few days, and Heredia was awarded a prize of 6,000 francs by the academy the same year. His material circumstances had now straitened, however, and he was obliged to earn a living. He was offered the literary direction of *Le Journal* by its founder, Fernand Xau, but was not happy with the paper's commercial atmosphere. In the late 1880s he began to write for the *Journal des Débats*, and in 1901 became the Paris correspondent for the Buenos Aires newspaper *El País*. On 2 February the desirable sinecure librarianship of the Arsenal was procured for him. He was never prolific, even as a translator and then as a journalist, but his output now dwindled still further, and his new position allowed him to become a bibliophile.

Towards the end of his life Heredia spent more time in the country. He had rented a small villa, but often stayed with friends, spending the last months of his life with his friend Georges Itasse at the Château de Bourdonné at Condé- sur-Vesgres, where he finished his edition of Chénier's *Bucoliques*. He was afflicted with enormous debts, went deaf, and developed cancer of the stomach. He died on 2 October 1905, and was buried with his mother at Rouen.

WORKS

Heredia's single important collection of verse, *Les Trophées*, is divided into five sections, "La Grèce et la Sicile," "Rome et les barbares," "Le moyen âge et la renaissance," "L'orient et les tropiques," and "La nature et le rêve." The sonnets are normally taken as the supreme expression of the Parnassian ideal, and are striking for their carefully delineated visual imagery, mirrored in the quasi-sculpted perfection of the poems' obvious craftmanship, and the evocative power of the last lines. The subjects might be texts or book bindings, coral reefs, antique buildings, works of art, or anything else that caught Heredia's fancy and might be used as the basis for a work of imagination.

Between their first publication in reviews and their appearance in the 1893 volume, the sonnets were often improved. None of them concedes anything at all to the simple outpouring of emotion, although emotional and aesthetic responses do naturally inform them. The derivation of inspiration and aesthetic from Leconte de Lisle remains plain, and there is a similar striving for the exotic, although without the supporting framework of Leconte de Lisle's ambitious plan to reconstruct the basic myths of the races. Heredia's scale is altogether smaller, but he is an accomplished miniaturist, avoiding the cumulative imagery of successive lines starting with "And." Most of the images are contained within a single line:

Sous un grand hêtre au tronc musculeux comme un torse

(Under a big beech, its trunk as muscular as a torso)

L'aube d'un jour sinistre a blanchi les hauteurs

(The dawn of a sinister day has whitened the heights)

There is a pattern. Many of the sonnets begin with a reference to the sky, or the time of day, so setting the scene. Among the usual words like "flamme" (flame) and "ombre" (shade/shadow) signifying merely that the diction is formally poetic, there is a striking preoccupation with colour. There are changes of pace and rhythm in narration, rudimentary dramatic effects, and changes of mood and tense:

Le four rougit; la plaque est prête. Prends ta lampe

(The furnace is becoming red. The plate is ready. Take your blowlamp)

Occasionally the sonnets take on an almost ferocious intensity, as in "La messe noire."

It would be possible to trace Heredia's techniques, sources, or influence. It seems more appropriate to append a single sonnet as an example of how his sensibility differs from that of the romantics, and how his imagery provoked the symbolists to rebellion. The passion is intensely felt, but its expression is controlled, fitted into Alexandrines, but observing stricter poetic conventions than had the romantics. The concrete realities which so shocked the symbolists are still relished here. The rhyme scheme could have been more rigorous at the end, and not all the lines are perfect, but the effect is achieved partly by containing the fierceness of passion within strict rules for its expression, and partly by mixing direct address, desires expressed as subjunctive wishes, hesitation, and defiance.

Enlace-moi plus fort! Que mon désir soit tel
Qu'il prête à nos baisers une ivresse sublime!
Que ton sein soit le gouffre où le remords s'abîme;
Prends, et brûle mon coeur sur le bûcher charnel.

Parjure du serment que je crus éternel,
Mon amour s'est pour toi grandi de tout mon crime
Et, sacrificateur aussi bien que victime,
J'ai de ton flanc divin fait mon suprême autel.

Que m'importent la mort, l'éternité future,
Dieu l'ineffable espoir, l'indicible torture?
Rien ne peut de tes bras me distraire un instant;

Car en ta chair ardente où se dissout mon âme,
J'ai savouré, caresse ou brûlure de flamme,
Et le Ciel que je brave et l'Enfer qui m'attend!

(Bind yourself more tightly to me! May my desire be one that gives our kisses a sublime intoxication! May your breast be the gulf in which remorse is extinguished. Take and burn my heart on this carnal stake.

Unfaithful to the oath which I believed to be everlasting, my love for you has increased by my whole crime and, author as well as victim of the sacrifice, I have made my highest altar of your divine flesh.

What does death matter to me, a future eternity, God the inexpressible hope, the unspeakable torture? Nothing can distract me an instant from your arms.

For in your burning flesh in which my soul dissolves I have tasted, in a caress or the scorch of a flame, both the Heaven which I defy and the Hell which awaits me!)

PUBLICATIONS

Collection

Poésies complètes, 1924

Works

Les Trophées, 1893; as *Sonnets of José-Maria de Heredia*, translated by Edward Robeson Taylor, 1897; as *The Trophies*, translated by Frank Sewall, n.d.

Other

Translator, *Véridique histoire de la conquête de la nouvelle Espagne*, by Bernal Diaz del Castillo, 4 vols., 1877–87
Translator, *La Nonne Alferez*, 1894

Biographical and critical studies

Ibrovac, Miodrag, *José-Maria de Heredia: sa vie, son oeuvre*, 1923
Chatelain, U.V., *José-Maria de Heredia, sa vie et son milieu*, 1930

HUGO, Victor (Marie), 1802–1885.

Poet, novelist, dramatist, and theoretician of the romantic (q.v.) movement.

LIFE

Hugo, once considered France's greatest poet, was born in Besançon, the youngest of three brothers. His mother was a royalist. His father was made a general and a count under the new Spanish monarchy established by Joseph Bonaparte, Napoleon's elder brother, but switched his allegiance to Louis XVIII in 1815. Hugo's boyhood was spent mostly in Corsica, Italy, and Spain. His parents had been living apart since 1808 and, from 1809 until his arrest in her house in 1810, Hugo's mother had an affair with an anti-Napoleonic conspirator. The family was briefly reunited in Spain in 1811, but Hugo's parents separated for good in 1812, and Hugo went to live with his mother and brothers in Paris.

He decided early on that he wanted to become a writer, and poems of his came to the notice of the Académie Française. They won two prizes at the Jeux Floraux of Toulouse in 1819, while Hugo was still at Cordier and Decotte's school in Paris. That same year, at the age of 17, he co-founded *Le Conservateur Littéraire* with his brother Abel, aged 20. The review ran until 1821 and became one of the principal organs of the romantics, with Hugo as spokesman for the incipient literary movement. Although the word *romantisme* dates from 1822, the literary movement, whose theory derived from some of Mme de Staël's writings, was already erupting in France with Lamartine's *Méditations* of 1820, followed by Vigny's 1822 *Poèmes*, and Hugo's own *Odes et poésies diverses* of the same year. From 1823 a group of like-minded young writers began to attend regular meetings, the "cénacles" from which the new movement emerged, the first being centred round Charles Nodier at the Arsénal library, then at Hugo's own house, and finally at Sainte-Beuve's.

The *Odes et poésies diverses*, published in June, gained Hugo a pension of 1,000 francs from Louis XVIII, who awarded him a second pension of the same amount for the 1823 novel *Han d'Islande*. The *Nouvelles odes* of 1824 and the *Odes et ballades* of 1826 were then followed between 1829 and 1840 by a torrent of novels, essays, travel literature, the famous romantic manifesto in the preface to *Cromwell*, a drama not really destined for the stage, no less than five volumes of verse, and most of Hugo's dramatic output. Only after 1826, following the stir caused by his novel *Bug-Jargal* of that year, did Hugo openly attack the "classicism" to which the new type of literature was opposed.

Hugo's mother had died in 1821 and Hugo, who had been secretly engaged for three years to Adèle Foucher, married her in October 1822 on the strength of the first pension granted that summer. He was 20 at the time. His wife bore him three sons and two daughters, but Hugo's domestic happiness was shattered in 1831 by Adèle's well-publicized love affair with Sainte-Beuve, whom Hugo had met in 1827. She died in 1868 and Hugo moved in with Juliette Drouet, his mistress since 1833, continuing to live with her until her death in 1883. Hugo's brother Eugène had gone mad at Hugo's wedding and it seems that there may have been a strain of mental weakness in the family.

Hugo had been invited to the coronation of Charles X and in 1825 had travelled with Nodier in the Alps and Switzerland. His father died in 1828. The year 1830 saw the riotous scenes at the first night of *Hernani* and in 1832 the Hugos moved to the fashionable Place Royale, now Place des Vosges. Hugo travelled a little, in 1837 to Belgium with Juliette Drouet, in 1839 to Germany and Switzerland, and in 1840 again to Germany. In 1841 he was elected to the Académie Française.

Of his children his elder daughter Léopoldine, born in 1824, was to affect his life and his poetry most deeply. She died with her husband in a boating accident at the mouth of the Seine on 4 September 1843. The couple had been married only the previous February. For 10 years Hugo, who was in Spain with Juliette at the time of the accident, published almost nothing, his depression deepened still further by the failure of *Les Burgraves*. By then the tide had in any case turned against the romantic movement.

From 1844 Hugo had a second mistress, and in 1845 he was created a peer as a reward for his support for Louis-Philippe. His never very fervent Catholicism had collapsed in the 1830s. The romantics generally had turned their backs on royalism, Catholicism, and nostalgia for the Middle Ages, favouring instead an alliance with the liberalism that was being crushed by the July monarchy. In the face of the economic depression, the failed harvest, and the potato blight of 1847, industrial action inevitably led to intense political pressures. In 1847, Hugo spoke for the recall of the Bonapartes, although in 1848, while speaking against the death penalty, he also did his best to save the July monarchy. He founded a paper, *L'Evénement*, later *L'Evénement du Peuple*, and was elected to the legislative assembly in 1849. He was clearly looking for a political role.

In 1849 he broke with the political right, spoke on the papacy and poverty, making speeches the following year in favour of lay control of education, against deportation, and in favour of universal suffrage and freedom of the press. The social situation had made him a republican in 1848 and did much to assist Louis-Napoleon's accession to power, but Hugo turned against him when he received no offer of high political office. The 1851 coup d'état whereby Louis-Napoleon finally consolidated his position and established the Second Empire, and against which Hugo had helped to organize futile resistance, turned disgruntlement into fury, and Hugo went into exile, leaving Paris disguised as a workman. He went to Belgium and then to Jersey (1853), settling finally in Guernsey when he was expelled from Jersey in 1855.

From now on he lived a largely solitary life with his family and Juliette, concentrating on his writing and producing his best work. From 1853 to 1855 he held "spiritualist" seances, largely moved by a desire to communicate with his beloved Léopoldine, but the seances were discontinued when one of the participants went mad. Hugo bitterly attacked Louis-Napoleon while retaining his respect for the first emperor and, refusing to return to France with the amnesties of 1859 and 1869, he began once more to make pronouncements on matters of international importance, speaking in 1860 in favour of Garibaldi. From 1865 he remained in Guernsey with Juliette while his wife and sons moved between Brussels and Paris. His daughter Adèle, born in 1830, had by now become insane.

In 1870, the day after the Third Republic was proclaimed, Hugo returned to France and was immediately elected to the Assemblée Nationale from which, however, he resigned in 1871 on account of its rightist tendencies, but also because his republican idealism had become seriously out of touch with the polit-

ical realities. He was eventually to be made a senator of the Third Republic in 1876, but exerted no political influence. Though he returned briefly to Guernsey, he was living mostly in Paris at this time. In 1877 he published *Histoire d'un crime* in an endeavour to ward off an anticipated right-wing coup, but in 1878 had a stroke and wrote virtually nothing more. Although works by Hugo continued to appear, the public was unaware that they had been written long before. His body lay in state under the Arc de Triomphe before being borne across Paris on a pauper's hearse, in accordance with Hugo's own wishes, and buried in the Panthéon.

WORKS

Hugo led the romantic revolution in the three genres to which he chiefly contributed: poetry, drama, and fiction. Then, after his quieter middle years, when the peak of the romantic movement had passed and the Parnassian and symbolist (qq.v.) vogues were already being established in poetry by the avant-garde, and realism had given way to naturalism (q.v.) in the novel, Hugo produced the finest examples of lyric poetry ever to be written in the high romantic style. The early odes had reflected the solemnly encomiastic tone associated with the genre in classical times. Hugo's subject matter was elevated (as in the odes of the French Renaissance) and his style "sublime," although he falls well short of Ronsard in showing what can be done with Pindar's classical form. The "ballades" of the third collection tended to be a pastiche of the medieval moralizing fable, while the early novels were little more than lurid gothic melodramas in fictional form. For Hugo's dramatic works in particular, see the entries "The Romatic Movement" and those on the other major romantic authors. On particular aspects of Hugo's life and works, the index should be consulted

In 1827 the preface to the six-hour historical drama *Cromwell* sketches the history of literature from the primitive and lyrical ode through the epic of classical antiquity to Christian drama, which mixes evil with good, and ugliness with beauty. Hugo lays down the norms for modern drama, drawing on the practice as he understood it of Shakespeare and Schiller in their historical dramas, Stendhal, and the aesthetic theories of Mme de Staël and Schlegel. He proposed the mixed genre of tragedy and comedy, combining the sublime and the grotesque, but not mingling both ingredients in the manner of Diderot. Hugo liked coups de théâtre but did not believe in the unities or the constraints of classical verse forms, maintaining that the stage should concentrate on real life, even down to the use of local colour.

This is in fact an atrocious misreading of dramatic history and a recipe for melodrama with comic interludes. But it does provide a means—after the social engineering and simpering bourgeois dramas of the 18th century in France—of exploring the possibility that, to be true to him or herself or to some higher mission, the dramatic protagonist may have to behave in a way that exceeds society's norms. This was to be Hugo's most successful formula, as also that of Dumas, Vigny, and Musset, before being adopted by the librettists of the bel canto operas, Donizetti, Bellini, and even Verdi, who found in Hugo's plays such attractive subjects for grand opera. It is because of Cromwell's unheroic magnanimity, a pale reflection of that of Corneille's *Cinna*, that *Cromwell* lacks the sustained drama necessary for stage performance. The hastily written preface is not seriously related to the play, but was rapturously welcomed by the new generation of dramatists and poets.

Marion de Lorme, written in 1829, was banned by the censor for its disrespectful treatment of Louis XIII. The motivation of the characters and the mechanics of the contrived plot (in which two lovers fight a forbidden duel over a prostitute, are tried, and executed in front of a satisfied Louis XIII) are both particularly weak elements in a poor play. It was not staged until 1831— after *Hernani*, in other words, whose first night on 25 February 1930 was attended by a crowd of young supporters including Gautier and Sainte-Beuve. They were loudly dressed and riotously disposed, and the manager of the Comédie was silly enough to let them into the theatre early in the afternoon. By the time the doors were opened for the first-night audience the interior of the theatre was a mess and the aisles reeked of urine. The play's first line, in conversational rather than stylized French, flaunts the accepted laws of versification thanks to its enjambement. A masked man enters through a hidden door, and there follows a mixture of caricature, fantasy, melodrama, contemporary political allusion, unmotivated acts, and conspiratorial effects no longer associated with the tragic stage. Many of the devices are basically comic. *Hernani* was followed by *Le Roi s'amuse*, the basis for *Rigoletto*, then *Lucrèce Borgia*, the first prose drama, *Marie Tudor*, and *Angelo, Tyran de Padoue*, both also in prose and dramatically weak, *La Esméralda*, *Ruy Blas* (in verse), and the final failure, *Les Burgraves* of 1843. Hugo was to write one more verse drama, *Torquemada*, in 1882. A posthumous collection of short plays, his *Théâtre en liberté*, was published in 1886.

In 1829 Hugo published *Le Dernier Jour d'un condamné*, the diary of a convict's last six weeks, and in 1834 *Claude Gueux*, a more weighty short story of slightly sentimental social concern attacking the death penalty. By 1830 Hugo could define romanticism in the preface to *Hernani* as having a political content, "le libéralisme en l'art" (liberalism in art), a view with which some of his younger followers, such as Gautier, were to disagree, and which differed from his own in the almost contemporaneous preface to *Les Orientales*, which had preached art for art's sake, "L'art pour l'art" (q.v.).

In 1831 Hugo published the very carefully written early novel *Notre-Dame de Paris*. Both plot and characters lack depth and real interest, but the social picture of 15th-century Paris gives the work an artistic interest as well as affording the reader an idea of how the romantics glamourized medieval life. The novel is held together by the minatory presence of its overpowering Gothic cathedral, seen in all its moods and awesome strength. Hugo recognized that the building, though not pretty, had a certain beauty, embodying as it did the faith and ideals of the teeming mob who had erected it, but frightening onlookers into blasphemous and alchemical beliefs.

In 1829 Hugo also began to publish his remarkable series of five volumes of verse. *Les Orientales* of that year still carries the verbal exuberance and extraneous exoticism (mostly half remembered from Spain) of the young romantic movement, but breaks new ground in visual inspiration, in verse forms, and metrical patterns, announcing the developments of the Parnassians and the symbolists. Precise images give way to clouds of metaphor, much as sharpness of outline can give way to swirls of colour in painting. In the other four volumes, *Les Feuilles d'automne*, *Les Chants du crépuscule*, *Les Voix intérieures* and *Les Rayons et les ombres*, political themes obtrude more obvi-

ously. Alexandrines split here into three sets of four syllables rather than two of six, and assonance and enjambement are systematically employed.

Hugo's direct lyricism replaced the periphrasis of traditional high-style poetry, notable even in Chénier, and his reflections on nature developed into a whole philosophical vision. The later volumes, unlike the earlier ones (including *Les Orientales*), are diverse in content, ranging from the solemn, quasi-official, to the domestic and almost trivial. Much of the inspiration is religious, some of it social, and some patriotic, but the religious, however vague its object, offers the richest poetic vein. Hugo draws on classical poets, notably Virgil, but never for mere extrinsic decoration, and he relies on verse "paragraphs" of various lengths, as well as variations of style and register to achieve his effects, though not always without some unevenness of tone. The verse is fluent, drawing on the widest range of rhetorical devices, as well as the whole repertoire of romantic poetic techniques and vocabulary, but the ease and variety of versification should not disguise the complicated and deep emotions which Hugo expresses and evokes more deeply, powerfully, diversely, and directly than any earlier French poet.

Hugo's next volume of verse, *Les Châtiments*, was not published until 1853, following the 10-year break in his literary output. Satirical and invective verse attacking Louis-Napoleon, written in all registers, it shows superb mastery of the linguistic resources of the French language. It was followed by Hugo's greatest single volume of verse, *Les Contemplations* of 1856, which includes in its fourth book ("A Villequier") the elegy for Léopoldine and demonstrates the mature, confident lyricism of a poet sure now of his mission. The volume is virtually a spiritual autobiography, although Hugo practised a deliberate deception about dates of composition. It draws its inspiration not only from Léopoldine's death and Juliette's affection, but also from a sense, engendered in Hugo by the table-rapping sessions, that death is merely part of some universal cosmic experience. The poetry achieves as a result a mysterious grandeur that swamps the purely personal inspiration. At its best, however, Hugo's lyric poetry is sharp, domestic, moving and simple.

La Légende des siècles, published in 1859, with a complementary series, of which some was written much earlier, added in 1877 and 1883, is a series of small epics strung together in the loose and unserious form of a history of the human race, giving Hugo plenty of scope for indulging his biblical and medieval enthusiasms in a variety of styles. The volume includes visionary material relating to God and the universe, together with Hugo's ideas on man's place in the universal scheme and the forms of organization of the human race. There are lyrical as well as narrative poems here, and an immense variation of mood, metre, and rhythm, but, most importantly, the volume proclaims Hugo's vision of human progress in which evil is finally swallowed up by good.

The final important novel, *Les Misérables*, was published in 1862, though Hugo had begun planning it as early as the 1840s. Flaubert and Baudelaire both disliked it. Although Hugo was failing by now to keep up with public taste, the novel was a great success and brought him financial security. It contains a complex plot and numerous digressions, some of which are quite irrelevant to the story but contribute nevertheless to a realistic tapestry, more densely woven than that even of *Notre-Dame de Paris*. The plot concerns social redemption, and the characters are largely allegorical, personifications of moral qualities, death and expiation.

Hugo's stature, bound up initially with his position as leader of the romantic movement, came to rest on his magnificently all-embracing vision, imaginatively projected in poetry of frequent technical brilliance. His plays, novels, pamphlets, and political activity all take second place. In the end it was his unshakeable confidence in his prophetic status and in the quasi-religion he evolved which made him the great figure whose stature has somehow transcended the series of well-founded criticisms of his individual works.

PUBLICATIONS

Collections

Oeuvres complètes, edited by Jean Massin, 18 vols., 1967–70
Oeuvres poétiques, Bibliothèque de la Pléiade, 3 vols., 1964–74

Fiction

Han d'Islande, 1823; as *Han of Iceland*, 1825; as *The Demon Dwarf*, 1847; as *The Outlaw of Iceland*, 1885
Bug-Jargal, 1826; as *The Slave King*, 1833; as *The Noble Rival*, 1845; as *Jargal*, 1866
Le Dernier Jour d'un condamné, 1829; as *The Last Day of a Condemned*, 1840
Notre-Dame de Paris, 1831; edited by Jacques Seebacher and Yves Gohin, 1975; as *The Hunchback of Notre-Dame*, 1833; as *La Esmeralda*, 1844
Claude Gueux, 1834
Les Misérables, 1862; as *Les Misérables* (in English), 1862
Les Travailleurs de la mer, 1866; edited by Jacques Seebacher and Yves Gohin, 1975; as *Toilers of the Sea*, 1866
L'Homme qui rit, 1869; as *By Order of the King*, 1870; as *The Laughing Man*, 1887
Quatre-vingt-treize, 1874; as *Ninety-Three*, 1874
Novels, 28 vols., 1895
Romans, edited by Henri Guillemin, 3 vols., 1963

Plays

Amy Robsart, from *Kenilworth* by Scott (produced 1827)
Cromwell, 1827; edited by Annie Ubersfeld, 1968
Marion de Lorme (produced 1831), 1829; as *The King's Edict*, 1872
Hernani (produced 1830), 1830; as *Hernani* (in English), 1830
Le Roi s'amuse (produced 1832), 1832; as *Le Roi s'Amuse* (in English), 1843
Lucrèce Borgia (produced 1833), 1833; as *Lucretia Borgia*, 1847
Marie Tudor (produced 1833), 1833
Angelo, Tyran de Padoue (produced 1835), 1835; as *Angelo* (in English), 1855
La Esméralda, with music by Louise Bertin, from *Notre-Dame de Paris* by Hugo (produced 1836), 1836
Ruy Blas (produced 1838), 1838; edited by Annie Ubersfeld, 2 vols., 1971–72; as *Ruy Blas* (in English), 1860
Les Burgraves (produced 1843), 1843
Torquemada, 1882
Théâtre en liberté, 1886
Théâtre complet, edited by Roland Purnal, 2 vols., 1963–64

Verse

Odes et poésies diverses, 1822
Nouvelles odes, 1824
Odes et ballades, 1826; edited by Pierre Albouy, 1980
Les Orientales, 1829; edited by Pierre Albouy, 1981
Les Feuilles d'automne, 1831; edited by Pierre Albouy, 1981
Les Chants du crépuscule, 1835; as *Songs of Twilight*, 1836
Les Voix intérieures, 1837
Les Rayons et les ombres, 1840
Le Rhin, 1842; as *Excursions along the Banks of the Rhine*, 1843
Les Châtiments, 1853; edited by P.J. Yarrow, 1975, and René Journet, 1977
Les Contemplations, 1856; edited by Pierre Albouy, 1973
La Légende des siècles, 3 vols., 1859–83; edited by André Dumas, 1974
Les Chansons des rues et des bois, 1865
L'Année terrible, 1872
L'Art d'être grand-père, 1877
Le Pape, 1878
La Pitié suprême, 1879
Religions et religion, 1880
L'Ane, 1880; edited by Pierre Albouy, 1966
Les Quatre vents de l'esprit, 1881
La Fin de Satan, 1886
Toute la lyre, 2 vols., 1888–93
Dieu, 1891; edited by René Journet and Guy Robert, 3 vols., 1969
Poésies, edited by Bernard Leuilliot, 3 vols., 1972
The Distance, The Shadows: Selected Poems, translated by Harry Guest, 1981

Other

Littérature et philosophie mêlées, 1834; edited by Anthony R.W. James, 1976
Lettres sur le Rhin, 1846
Napoléon le petit, 1852; as *Napoleon the Little*, 1852
Dessins de Hugo (art), 1862; edited by J. Sergent, 1955
L'Archipel de la Manche, 1863
Hugo raconté par un témoin de sa vie, 1863
William Shakespeare., 1864; as *William Shakespeare* (in English), 1864
Actes et paroles, 3 vols., 1875–76
Choses vues, 2 vols., 1887–1900; edited by Hubert Juin, 4 vols., 1972; translated in part as *Things Seen*, 1887; revised edition, edited by David Kimber, 1964
Alpes et Pyrénées, 1890; as *The Alps and Pyrenees*, 1896
France et Belgique, 1892; edited by Claude Gély, 1974
Les Années funestes, 1896
Mémoires, 1899
Post-scriptum de ma vie, 1901; edited by Henri Guillemin, 1961; as *Hugo's Intellectual Biography*, 1907
Dernière gerbe, 1902
Océan, tas de pierres, 1942
Correspondance, 4 vols., 1947–52
Pierres: vers et prose, edited by Henri Guillemin, 1951
Carnets intimes, edited by Henri Guillemin, 1953
Journal 1830–1848, edited by Henri Guillemin, 1954
Hugo dessinateur, edited by Roger Cornaille and Georges Herscher, 1963

Lettres à Juliette Drouet 1833–1883, edited by Jean Gaudon, 1964

Correspondance, with Pierre-Jules Hetzel, edited by Sheila Gaudon, 1979–

Bibliography

Lestha Doyle, Ruth, *Hugo's Drama: An Annotated Bibliography 1900–1980*, 1981

Critical studies

Grant, Elliott M., *The Career of Hugo*, 1945

Grant, Richard B., *The Perilous Quest: Image, Myth, and Prophecy in the Narratives of Hugo*, 1968

Maurois, André, *Hugo*, (in English) 1956

Maurois, André, *Hugo and His World*, 1966

Affron, Charles, *A Stage for Poets: Studies in the Theatre of Hugo and Musset*, 1971

Porter Houston, John (in English), *Hugo*, 1974

Edwards, Samuel, *Hugo: A Biography*, 1975

Ward, Patricia A., *The Medievalism of Hugo*, 1975

Richardson, Joanna, *Hugo* (in English), 1976

Nash, Suzanne, *"Les Contemplations" of Hugo: An Allegory of the Creative Process*, 1977

Peyre, Henri, *Hugo: Philosophy and Poetry*, 1980

Brombert, Victor, *Victor Hugo and the Visionary Novel*, 1984

HUYSMANS, Joris-Karl, 1848–1907.

Novelist and art critic.

LIFE

Huysmans was born in Paris on 5 February 1848. His father came from a long line of artists in Breda, where he was born in 1815. He came to Paris as a lithographer and miniaturist, set up in business with a printer called Janson, and in 1845 married the teacher Elisabeth Malvina Badin, born in 1826 of a family of administrators. Huysmans's father took out naturalization papers, and Huysmans was baptized Charles-Marie-Georges, but later deliberately adopted what he took to be the Dutch form of his name, Joris-Karl. The family were Catholic and led a well-regulated life. They employed a maid, and Huysmans was taken to play in the Luxembourg gardens every afternoon by his mother. In summer the family would visit his father's brother at Tilburg, or his grandparents near Brussels. Huysmans's father died in 1856. In later life he never mentioned his parents, though he treasured three of his father's oil paintings.

His mother took Huysmans to live with her parents and got a job in a department store. In 1857 she married a 34-year-old Protestant called Og, by whom she had two daughters, Juliette and Blanche. The profound effect of her remarriage on Huys-

mans is clear from the absence in his novels, which are often fictionalized autobiography or autobiographical fantasy, of mothers who survive the first chapter. The only exception is the dropsical monstrosity in *Les Soeurs Vatard*. M. Og is not present at all. The tenderness of Huysmans's later devotion to the Mother of Jesus may also have resulted from boyhood emotional trauma, the most likely cause of his later fear of women. Huysmans's stepfather had a little money, which he invested in a book-bindery. It prospered in a small way, and from 1856 Huysmans was a weekly boarder in a pension, which he hated. In 1862 he was awarded a bursary to the Lycée Saint-Louis, where he was bullied and where his relative poverty was obvious. In 1865 he refused to go back, and was so determined that one of the masters was hired to give him private tuition. He obtained his baccalauréat in March 1866.

He became a "fonctionnaire" on a salary of 1,500 francs in April 1866, when he was just 18, and in the autumn enrolled as a law student, pursuing both careers concurrently, although he was more interested in literature than in law. He had been sexually initiated by a kindly prostitute he had approached at 16 while still at school, but did not enjoy the experience or repeat it for some months. In 1867, acting out the role from Murger's *Scènes de la Bohème* in which he had cast himself, he took a soubrette as his mistress. He had managed to get an article on landscape painters accepted by the short-lived *Revue Mensuelle*, which published it on 25 November 1867, and also to get himself commissioned to write a review of a light entertainment, *Cocher, à Bobino*, for whose principal singer he had fallen at first sight. The review was actually published in the last number of the magazine, dated 25 December 1867. Although Huysmans never received any money for the article, being paid finally in sample bottles of liqueur given to the proprietor by an advertiser, the commission to write the piece had got him the access he required, and he successfully conquered his soubrette. He was no longer living at home, and in August 1867 had passed his first law examinations. In December his stepfather died.

Huysmans spent the money for his second-year studies on his mistress. The attraction of brothels had paled, and his sexual tastes were leading him to demand blue eye shadow, rouge, black silk corsets, and flounced skirts. Unhappily the theatre, like the magazine, folded, joint income diminished, and Huysmans's soubrette turned out to be pregnant by someone else. When the baby came, Huysmans had to hold it all night and vomited, conceiving a lasting hatred of babies. We do not know exactly how the liaison broke up. In 1870, when we next catch up with him, Huysmans was called up, just after the outbreak of war.

Huysmans was in hospital at Châlons with dysentery when the Prussians advanced. After an adventurous journey he ended up in Evreux, where he was cared for in hospital by a nun who much impressed him. With the help of some improbable coincidences he was sent back to Paris, supped with his mother, and returned to his lodgings. It was 8 September, just days before the siege. In November he was posted to the war ministry, returning after the capitulation in February to his own ministry of the interior, now at Versailles, thereby missing the carnage of the Commune, its burnt-out buildings, and its 20,000 dead. In late summer he moved back to Paris and took to dropping in on churches to listen to choirs and on galleries to look at pictures. He started work on a range of literary projects from his war memoirs to a verse drama to be called "La comédie humaine."

ously to Brussels and the Exposition Universelle in Paris commemorated the centenary of the Revolution of 1789. Huysmans was contemptuously amused by both Boulanger and the Exposition, as well as by M. Eiffel's tower. He and Mallarmé were instrumental in getting Villiers to marry his old maid and mistress to legitimize their son, without actually telling Villiers he was dying of cancer. Villiers was finally persuaded by Father Sylvestre, the Franciscan chaplain of the hospice, who had comforted Barbey d'Aurevilly on his deathbed.

Huysmans had already been interested in the occult when he wrote *A rebours*, and even more so when he came to *En rade*. In 1889 Remy de Gourmont, who wanted to dedicate his story "Stratagèmes" to Huysmans, introduced him to his mistress, Berthe Courrière, a supposed expert in the occult. Huysmans also met Henriette Maillat, another self-proclaimed expert, with whom he had a brief affair. His interest in witchcraft, werewolves, and satanism was an important staging post on his road to Catholicism. It attracted him as another escape from the squalor of daily life, a possible door to the spiritual fulfilment with which love and literature had failed to provide him. He began to take an interest in Rosicrucianism, met the novelist Paul Adam, a member of the Supreme Council, and read up on hermeticism. He planned a political novel full of other pretenders, cranks, and eccentrics, and was mesmerized by the spiritualist manifestations he witnessed at Berthe Courrière's flat. What he actually produced was *Là-bas*, an attempt to ally the documentation of naturalism, in spite of its materialism, with some supernatural dimension. The fusion of dream and reality in *En rade* had pointed the way and, like Paul Adam, Huysmans had become fascinated with the 15th-century Gilles de Rais.

Huysmans's disgust with the everyday Paris of tourists and gigolos, "people with a damp, canine odour," as he wrote to Odilon Redon, spilled over into *Certains*, a collection of articles on art and architecture, complaining at municipal tree planting, urban planning, and the Eiffel Tower, and rejoicing in Degas's humiliating treatment of the women who, in all Huysmans's novels, wielded maleficent spells and inflicted so much misery on men. Huysmans's may well have attended the Black Mass of *Là-bas*, and certainly did become mixed up in the whole community of depraved and deranged poets and religious figures in whose minds the sources of disgust and the objects of their veneration had fused. The mystico-erotic jargon they produced generally cloaked perverted sexual practices, and they were drawn to fantasizing about intercourse with the crucified Christ, mingling the spiritual, the sexual, and the crudely repugnant in manifestations of a recognizable psychological disorder. Their attention tended to focus on exorcism and satanism, and it occasionally involved ritual human sacrifice. Huysmans took to using strange devices and practices to ward off evil spirits. *Là-bas* was serialized in 1891 by the *Echo de Paris* and, although it provoked some outrage, in general it was favourably received, being banned only by the railway bookstall monopoly, which was almost a laughing stock.

By 1890 Huysmans's relationship with Bloy had frozen over without any dramatic break, but well before Bloy's marriage to Johanne Molbech. In that year Huysmans's *La Bièvre* appeared, issued in volume form by Genonceaux. Huysmans had already written about La Bièvre, Paris's second river, in an 1877 article for *La République des Lettres*, subsequently reproduced in *L'Artiste*, and in *Croquis parisiens*. By 1886, when *La Bièvre* appeared in the Amsterdam *De Nieuwe Gids*, the river had

become for Huysmans a symbol of feminine degradation, an innocent country girl flowing through the city which corrupted her. The idea may have derived from a poem by Corbière, who appears, rather astonishingly, on Des Esseintes's list of preferred reading.

By the winter of 1890 Huysmans had returned to his old habit of attending church on Sunday evenings to listen to the choirs. He had been touched by the ceremony of the clothing of a Carmelite nun to which he had been taken, and by the simple ceremony of Benediction. His conversion, prompted by a yearning which Christian devotion and art alone could satisfy, was under way. He was to describe its undramatic occurrence in *En route*. Deferred at first by what he considered the incredibility of Catholic dogma, he was later daunted by the need for sexual abstinence or marriage. After the onset of Anna Meunier's illness, tired of Henriette Maillat's spiritual pretentiousness, Huysmans had again taken to visiting brothels, in spite of the self-disgust with which they inspired him.

Berthe Courrière found him a spiritual director, Arthur Mugnier, whom he met on 28 May 1891. He was still taking advice from a black magician, the defrocked Joseph-Antoine Boullan, known as Dr Johannès, on how to defend himself against Rosicrucian attack. It was with Boullan that he went to La Salette, where the Virgin Mary was alleged to have appeared and left an apocalyptic message in 1846. Huysmans was still more easily impressed at this time by Boullan's Sacrifice of Glory of Melchizedek than by La Salette or the Grande Chartreuse, but in 1892 he went to a Trappist monastery at Igny to make a retreat, confessed and communicated, underwent a variety of unexpected sensations, and dramatized to himself everything that had happened to him. After his retreat he returned to Boullan at Lyons. Boullan had been convicted of practising medicine illegally and Huysmans apparently paid his 2,000-franc fine. On his return to Paris he started a novel, intended to be a mystical work, but dropped it. His experience with the Trappists finally purged him of all interest in the manifestations of satanism, and his later novels were to be both autobiographical and didactic.

Boullan died at the beginning of 1893 and Huysmans, suspected of blaming the Rosicrucians, nearly got involved in a duel. Two of the principal Rosicrucians later died of drug overdoses, and Huysmans bought a grant on a grave in a Lyons cemetery for Boullan's remains. Anna Meunier had to be sent to an asylum, where Huysmans visited her regularly until her death on 22 February 1895. He was beginning to be interested in spiritualities involving vicarious suffering, mystical substitution, expiation, and reparation, and in 1893 he returned to Igny, still dramatizing his spiritual experiences. That September he was made a Chevalier of the Légion d'Honneur for his 27 years of faithful service to the administration, and in 1894 he went to the Benedictine monastery of Saint-Wandrille, to which he briefly transferred his ecclesiastical loyalty. In February 1895 Stock published *En route*, the fictionalized account, under the name of Durtal, of Huysmans's conversion, an event which was greeted with universal scepticism. The book was talked about, and sold very well, attracting for Huysmans a vast correspondence from would-be spiritual children.

The next novel, *La Cathédrale*, based on Chartres, was intended to show the pervasive effect of medieval art and architecture on Durtal. Art had been a significant stepping stone for Huysmans on the way to the intellectual, religious, and spiritual position he now occupied. On a visit to a ruined Benedictine abbey at Fiancey, he attended all the monastic offices, and seemed to be looking for a small monastery to which to retire. In the autumn of 1896 he visited Solesmes, revisiting Chartres on his way back. The *Echo de Paris* published 14 lengthy extracts from *La Cathédrale*, beginning on 27 October 1897, all of them of purely artistic rather than religious interest. The ministry, where the predominant tendency was strongly secularist, invited Huysmans to take his retirement, and when the novel did appear it was attacked not only by the secularists, but also by the diocesan clergy, at whose expense Huysmans had made clear his higher esteem for the regulars, whose intellectual training and spiritual formation he regarded as invariably superior. Huysmans muttered in response about priestly philistinism.

Huysmans retired as a civil servant in February 1898 and thought seriously of entering a monastery as an oblate, or associate member of the community. He visited Solesmes in July, in spite of the ecclesiastical warfare going on in the order, then the abbey of Saint-Maur, before returning to Paris. After a change of mind about where to spend the summer, Huysmans accepted an invitation to visit Gustave Boucher, an old friend with whom he had roamed Paris and visited its churches, now editor of *Le Pays Poitevin* and a museum curator. He accordingly went to Ligugé, near Poitiers, where there was a small Benedictine monastery. He was persuaded to buy a plot of land near the monastery and the station, and a great deal of negotiation took place about the possibility of founding a small lay community, loosely attached to the monastery.

Plans by assorted ill-wishers to have *La Cathédrale* put on the Roman index of forbidden books, and by the Countesse de Galoez, who had become obsessed with Huysmans through his books, to seduce him, were foiled, and in 1899 Huysmans settled in on one floor of the new house he had had built at Ligugé. He shared the project with an unlikely middle-class couple, the Leclaires, with whom he had become extremely friendly. They were protégés of the Abbé Ferret, Huysmans's confessor and close friend. The husband, Léon, born in 1862, had been a manager of family quarries before becoming a shopkeeper. Huysmans began to acquire a taste for nature, and in November he allowed Mugnier to extract from his works a series of *Pages catholiques*, described by their author as "herbal infusions for colds in the head." In January Huysmans prepared for his clothing as an oblate novice.

He then needed and obtained the prior's permission to travel to Paris, where the formation of the Académie Goncourt had been the subject of litigation. One of the eight people named in Edmond's will had died, so that to make the full complement of 10 it was now necessary to elect three others. The final list was Huysmans, Mirbeau, Hennique, Joseph Rosny, Justin Rosny, Margueritte, Geoffroy, Bourges, Descaves, and Léon Daudet, whose father, now dead, had been among the eight chosen by Goncourt. During 1900 Huysmans worked on *Sainte Lydwine de Schiedam*, which he completed on 6 November. He had contracted with a new publisher to bring out a series of old articles, *De tout*, but the publisher went bankrupt, and the vigilant Stock brought it out in November 1901, although he dated it 1902. *La Bièvre; les Gobelins; Saint-Séverin* had also appeared in 1901, the year the monks had to leave Ligugé with the expulsion of religious communities from France. Huysmans himself returned to Paris in October, pleased that his social life was now restricted by his religious obligations, which included being

home by nine p.m. On 5 December he started the last novel of his Catholic trilogy, *L'Oblat*, interrupting his work to write the *Esquisse biographique sur Don Bosco*. The dental troubles he was having must have been the early symptoms of the cancer which was to kill him.

The oblates from Ligugé dispersed. The Leclaires went to Lourdes, where Huysmans went to visit them in 1903 and was excited to vituperation by the tastelessness of everything. That year he also travelled to Strasburg, Colmar, and Basel, then Freiburg, Mainz, and Frankfurt, Cologne, Brussels, and Antwerp. The result of this journey was *Trois primitifs*. In 1904 Huysmans moved house for the last time, and that September he went to Lourdes again, having decided to write a book on it, impelled by the need to counteract Zola's 1894 publication. Early in 1905 he wrote two articles, "St-Germain l'Auxerrois" and "La symbolique de Notre Dame," for *Le Tour de France*, later to be included in the posthumous *Trois églises et trois primitifs*. He was reading the dozens of novels entered for the Prix Goncourt and fended off two more women who were in love with him and wanted something other than the spiritual support they professed to need. "Les deux faces de Lourdes" left him unenthusiastic, although he was enchanted to discover that each time the Virgin had spoken to Bernadette there had been some connection between her words and the liturgy of the day.

In 1906, after an almost sightless winter, he recovered sufficiently to finish his book, now entitled *Les Foules de Lourdes*, and finally published in October. It sold 17,000 copies in the first month, but Huysmans, as his friend and literary executor Descaves observed, had now written himself out, and reached the end of all the avenues he could explore. In November he made a will, leaving his royalties to his half- sisters. In January he was given the Croix of the Légion d'Honneur for his work as a writer and, after a series of painful operations, including the extraction of all his remaining teeth, he died on 12 May 1907.

WORKS

Banville described *Le Drageoir aux épices* as a "skilfully cut jewel from the hand of a master goldsmith." All Huysmans's books, the art criticism as well as the novels, were written in a self-conscious, elaborately crafted style, with mannered syntax and a very careful use of words. In the early prose poems of *Le Drageoir*, Huysmans's stylistic talents were as yet underdeveloped, as if he was still looking for the subject matter which would bring them to fruition. His writing already had a certain preciosity, which later shone through the naturalistic, decadent, art historical, and religious contexts. The prose poems themselves included the first sketch of the poor Bièvre district in Paris, a piece in praise of Villon, some verbal evocations of paintings, a popular dance, a village fête, an address to a prostitute, and a contrastingly idealistic "extase" deploring the carnal aspects of love. The language throughout is polished and evocative.

Marthe, histoire d'une fille is not at all pornographic, even though Huysmans felt obliged to publish it in Belgium, and Mugnier left it out of his list of Huysmans's works in his introduction to *Pages catholiques*. It is the fictionalized narrative of Huysmans's first serious liaison, when he was living out the Mimi-esque fantasies of his student life. There is only one short description of a brothel, and most of the book is devoted to the unhappy love affair between Léo, the young journalist, and the unintelligent Marthe, who, far from stimulating her lover's imagination, gets in the way of his talent by making demands on his energies, emotions, time, and purse. The book is characteristically misogynous. It is also episodic, and written in a nervous style of cultivated garishness which lifts it above the prostitute novels of Zola and Edmond de Goncourt.

Les Soeurs Vatard is about two unhappy love affairs. Céline's lover Cyprien Tibaille, is a well-to-do artist, who soon tires of her vulgarity and working-class habits. She leaves him for a man who beats her but loves her. Her younger sister, Désirée, loves the equally naive Auguste, but there is no excitement in the relationship to keep it from sagging into mutual independence. The gradual falling away of the uniting bond is portrayed with delicacy. The stylist in Huysmans is asserting himself, and must clearly share some of the miniaturist perfectionism which Huysmans had come to admire in what he knew of his father's work. The two women are slightingly depicted, as is the very ordinary Auguste. Cyprien on the other hand can be recognized as a quick sketch for Des Esseintes. The book sold well, and there was a reprint even before Zola's review. Ulbach's objection was rationalized into the assertion that the novel attacked the Parisian working class, which it clearly did not. Others, like Wolff in *Le Figaro*, sighed over the raw, bleak, and sordid picture of life which the novel did nothing to alleviate.

The realistic *Croquis parisiens*, superbly evocative of the tawdry gilt-ornamented debris of Second Empire society, smelling unrelievedly of stale cigars and inadequate hygiene, naturally raised a chorus of disgust, but some of the sketches are none the less brilliant. The piece on the Folies-Bergère in 1879 evokes exactly the same vacuous disillusioned boredom as the barmaid's smile in Manet's 1882 *Un bar aux Folies-Bergère*. The street scenes could be those which Daumier set out to illustrate. The shift of emphasis in Daumier from pure description to psychological analysis is clear in Huysmans, too.

En ménage contains at least two analyses of Huysmans himself in André Jayant and Cyprien Tibaille, but it is important above all for the perceptiveness of its character studies and its ability to recount the inconsistent experiences of the characters' interior lives. The disillusion of Flaubert blankets all excitement. Adultery is just as boring as marriage. In his belief in progress, Huysmans's Désableau is as platitudinous as Flaubert's Homais. Like Flaubert's *L'Education sentimentale*, the novel ends with a melancholy summing-up of wasted opportunities by the main protagonist and a boyhood companion. The characters are recognizably modelled on real people, Cyprien on Huysmans himself, and Jeanne on Anna Meunier. This was no longer a low-life work, but the critics disliked it, fastening on to the thin plot and pessimistic philosophy. Cézanne, however, was enthusiastic, and so was Pissarro, to whom Cézanne lent his copy. The novel's pessimism was further developed in *A vau-l'eau*, "the Missal of Minor Misfortunes," as Huysmans later called it. Its hero, Folantin, is another lost young man. The critics thought its subjects too trivial, but the material distress of the hero clerk is not the point: behind the search for a small share in life's material gratifications lies the quest for happiness and spiritual satisfaction in the face of life's harshness.

A rebours has a central figure rich enough to indulge every whim and realize every fantasy. What he is not rich enough to do is to find spiritual satisfaction, so he substitutes for it the cult of refined sensation, of exquisite luxury, and exotic pampering. The character of Des Esseintes is compounded of those of other wealthy fantasizers like Ludwig II in the fairy-tale castle of Neuschwanstein, coming alive only to Wagner's music, or Edmond de Goncourt, who catalogued every single detail of his house in Auteuil, or Barbey d'Aurevilly, Beau Brummel's admirer and biographer, the youthfully dandified Baudelaire, and, of course, Robert de Montesquiou-Fezensac, the calculatedly eccentric friend and enemy of Proust, whose house contained one room furnished like a yacht cabin, another like a monastery cell, a third like a church. Pierre Loti was doing something similar to another house at much the same time, and it could have been a rich man's craze. Above all, however, Des Esseintes is the repository of Huysmans's own secret tastes and untold dream: "In their sickly sensibility, their yearning for solitude, their abhorrence of human mediocrity, and their thirst for new and complex sensations, author and character were one."

The abhorrence of squalor, or even ordinariness, which entails the break with the naturalistically orthodox approach to fiction, leads Des Esseintes to seek complexities of experience, unnatural loves, and perverse pleasures not available in the everyday world, which is too disgustingly monotonous for temperaments as refined as his own. Ultimately Rousseau was wrong about the interest of nature's threatening peaks and torrents. They are no less boringly banal than the sea and the countryside. Beauty for Des Esseintes, whose principal real model must be Baudelaire, is the fruit of sickness of soul as well as its palliative. The novel expanded as it was written, in the end including gardens, perfumes, jewels, tailoring, and shoe-making among the objects and pursuits making up the encyclopedia of exotic pleasure. Quite apart from the aesthetic philosophy expressed by Des Esseintes, Huysmans uses the philosophizing itself to aesthetic effect, writing with a refinement of style to mirror the tastes of the central character. Although he cannot say so, Huysmans might have added his own name to the list of authors whose work constituted the preferred reading of Des Esseintes.

To draw attention to a canon of authors capable of mediating a new sort of frisson was almost the starting point of *A rebours*, and it is really to Huysmans that we owe the first grouping of Verlaine, Valéry, Corbière, and Mallarmé, more often perceived as connected with Baudelaire and with one another than with other members of the symbolist (q.v.) group. Huysmans later wrote that Des Esseintes would have added Rimbaud and Laforgue to his list of preferred authors if they had published anything in time. In the novel, Huysmans writes for his hero an exasperated diatribe against industrialized society. Not even Schopenhauer can console him, only the impossible belief in a future life. The seeds of Huysmans's later spiritual development need never have germinated, but this novel shows that they had been planted.

Un dilemme of 1884 is a short conte written as if intended to be set off against the literary extravagance of *A rebours*. It concerns the sordidness of bourgeois life. A businessman and his lawyer deprive his son's mistress of her inheritance on the son's death. Written in 1884, it was published by the *Revue Indépendante* in September and October, but failed as a book in 1887. *En rade* was a failure because the dream sequences, whatever they betokened for Huysmans's future development, do not readily integrate with the vestigial naturalism of the rest of the novel, which includes a brutal description of mating cattle. Huysmans himself agreed with Zola's criticism that the novel lacks unity of tone.

Là-bas was controversial. It introduced Huysmans's alter ego, Durtal, meditating on the possibility of a non-naturalistic novel, and contained an attack on the "cheapjack magicians" of satanism and Rosicrucianism which involved Huysmans in an entanglement with the horrific ex-abbé Boullan, an attempt to blackmail him for using Henriette Maillat and her letters as a model, and magical practices, blood-stained hosts, incantations, and an exorcistic paste which he took to using. The novel exceeded Huysmans's own expectations. It was serialized in the *Echo de Paris*, one of the least sensational newspapers in Paris, was well reviewed, and well received by the public. The trouble, stirred up by Boullan, was Huysmans's fear of some sort of demonic revenge for his attack on satanism. Even in this novel, however, an attempt is made to use the religious and even crudely irreligious thematic material for aesthetic purposes, and to exploit terror for its curiosity value and literary effect rather than its emotional impact.

En route aroused interest primarily on account of the disputes about the authenticity of the conversion experience which it relates. In fact the religious sentiment was anything but pure, although the conversion narrated is genuine enough. Durtal lives through Huysmans's own struggle with his dilettantism, recounted in Huysmans's habitually mannered and variegated style, as when he is taken to Igny and seriously faces the petty inconveniences of conversion: "Et si je me décide…ah! non, par exemple…car alors il faudra s'astreindre à un tas d'observances, se plier à des séries d'exercices, suivre la messe le dimanche, faire maigre le vendredi; il faudra vivre en cagot, ressembler à un imbécile" (And if I decide to…no, for goodness' sake…I should have to force myself to observe a heap of rules, perform a whole set of exercises, go to Mass on Sundays, abstain on Fridays. I'd have to live like a hypocrite, look like a fool). The real difficulty with this novel is the impossibility of adequately exploring the religious experiences it seeks to illuminate on the basis of purely external documentation without ending up, as in the passage quoted, by trivializing them. Huysmans himself saw the difficulty, but few of his commentators have appreciated it.

La Cathédrale, based on Chartres, again confronts the technical problem of relating religious experience to its external manifestations, and the proposed solution is not entirely successful. Art, architecture, and religious symbols are the product of authentic religious experience, and can no doubt mediate it to others, but Huysmans has too many lists, and does not always avoid giving the impression of a guided tour. It is true that the cathedral represents a religious reduction of the macrocosm, including its moral qualities, but the reader is not always made aware of the full force of this structural device. The novel does however contain fascinating autobiographical instalments and Huysmans's famous lyrical description of the cathedral at dawn.

Sainte Lydwine de Schiedam, for whose projected translation into Dutch Huysmans refused permission because the proposed translator was a Jew, is primarily devoted to the mystery of suffering, and especially the spirituality of vicarious suffering. The spiritualities of reparation, expiation, and mystical substitution had intensified during the 19th century, and with them correspondingly dubious theologies of the redemption, which were foreign at least to the spiritualities which informed the normative Church councils of the first five centuries. French Catholicism in particular was thoroughly permeated with them. Boullan was obsessed by them, took them to the point certainly of psychological abnormality, and probably of heresy, and profoundly

impressed Huysmans with them, in whose temperament the novels reveal clear if largely suppressed tendencies to sadism. The life of Saint Lydwine is held up as an example of the spirituality to which Huysmans was attracted, whereas his life of Don Bosco was a simple, unpretentious pamphlet intended to help the Salesians founded by Don Bosco. It was an orphanage run by the Salesians which provided the choirboys for the church at which Huysmans's worshipped.

L'Oblat is the third of the Durtal autobiographical trilogy, written when Huysmans was already ill. Its central theme is again the mystery of suffering. Huysmans goes into detail about the Virgin Mary's concern that the physical suffering of her son should be increased. Durtal accepts the onus of suffering in the interests of atonement. The novel has ceased to be fiction and has become an illustration of, and virtually an invitation to share in, Huysmans's by no mean unique but none the less dangerous spirituality. The encyclopedic aspect of *La Cathédrale* here bursts its seams, and Huysmans allows his preference for surface effects over structure to sweep away literary form altogether.

PUBLICATIONS

Collections

Oeuvres complètes, 18 vols., 1928–34

Fiction

Marthe, histoire d'une fille, 1876; in *Down Stream* and *Other Works*, 1927; as *Martha, the Story of a Woman*, 1948
Les Soeurs Vatard, 1879; as *The Vatard Sisters*, 1983
Sac au dos, in *Les Soirées de Médan*, 1880
En ménage, 1881
A vau-l'eau, 1882; as *Down Stream*, in *Down Stream and Other Works*, 1927; same title, 1952
A rebours, 1884; as *Against the Grain*, 1922; as *Against Nature*, 1959
En rade, 1887
Un dilemme, 1887
La Bièvre, 1890
Là-bas, 1891; as *Down There*, 1924; same title, 1930
En route, 1895; as *En Route* (in English), 1896
La Cathédrale, 1898; as *The Cathedral*, edited by C. Kegan Paul, 1898
Pages catholiques, 1899
L'Oblat, 1903; as *The Oblate*, 1924

Other

Le Drageoir aux épices (prose poems), 1874; as *A Dish of Spices*, in *Down Stream and Other Works*, translated by Samuel Putnam, 1927
Croquis parisiens, 1880
L'Art moderne, 1883; translated in *Down Stream and Other Works*, 1927
Certains, 1889; translated in *Down Stream and Other Works*, 1927
La Bièvre, 1890
La Magie en Poitou: Gilles de Rais, 1899
La Bièvre; les Gobelins; Saint-Séverin, 1901

Sainte Lydwine de Schiedam, 1901
De tout, 1902
Esquisse biographique sur Don Bosco, 1902
Trois primitifs, 1905
Le Quartier Notre-Dame, 1905
Les Foules de Lourdes, 1906; as *The Crowds of Lourdes*, 1925
Trois églises et trois primitifs, 1908
Pierrot sceptique, with Léon Hennique, 1881

Critical and biographical studies

Baldick, Robert, *The Life of J.-K. Huysmans*, 1955
Griffiths, Richard, *The Reactionary Revolution: The Catholic Revival in French Literature 1870–1914*, 1966
Laver, James, *The First Decadent*, 1954

I

IONESCO, Eugène, 1912–

Dramatist.

Eugène Ionesco was born on 26 November 1912 in Slatina, Romania, the first child of Eugen Ionescu, a Romanian lawyer, and his French wife Thérèse Icard. In 1913 they moved to Paris, where Ionesco's sister and brother were born. His brother, Mircea, died of meningitis at 18 months. The family frequently moved house, and at one stage Ionesco's father moved into a hotel by himself to get peace and quiet to study for his doctorate in law.

Ionesco's parents had a stormy marriage. One row, which Ionesco witnessed when he was four, culminated when his mother poured a bottle of iodine into his silver christening mug and threatened to poison herself. His father stopped her, as she probably intended him to, but Ionesco regards the incident as crucial to his attitudes:

Cette scène s'est gravée en moi et la frayeur qu'elle m'a causée à l'époque n'a jamais pu être soulagée par la raison...J'ai l'impression que c'est à cause de cela que je hais l'autorité, là est la source de mon antimilitarisme, c'est à dire de tout ce qui est, de tout ce que représente le monde martial, de tout ce qui est société fondée sur la primauté de l'homme par rapport à la femme.

(This scene is engraved in my memory, and reason has never been able to calm the terror it caused me at the time...I have a feeling that it is because of this incident that I hate authority, that this is the source of my anti-militarism, meaning everything the military world is and everything it represents, everything society is when it is founded on man's primacy over woman.)

In 1916 Ionesco's father went back to Romania to fight in World War I. Postal links between France and Romania were suspended during hostilities, and Ionesco's mother lost touch with her husband. She took a series of jobs in Parisian factories to support the two children, who both spent some time in children's homes. Ionesco remembers several months in an institution outside Paris when he was five. His mother could only visit him every other weekend. Miserable without her, he hated the prison-like atmosphere and lack of privacy. He also remembers going with his mother and aunts to visit his sister, then aged about three, in a children's home founded by Zola in Médan, but does not know why she was there.

Ionesco started school at the Ecole Communale in the Rue Dupleix, but after the war he was very anaemic and he and his sister were sent to live in the country. They were among several children staying in a mill in La Chapelle-Anthenaise, near Laval, looked after by an elderly peasant couple known as Père Baptiste and Mère Jeannette and a middle-aged spinster called Marie. Ionesco missed his mother but loved being a country child. He went to the village school and became an avid reader. He remembers a winter when American soldiers were billeted in the village on their way home from the war. The one who stayed in the mill was a dancing teacher and he and his musician friends used to entertain the household in the evenings. They also shared leftover puddings from their canteen with the villagers. Ionesco's years in La Chapelle-Anthenaise were the happiest in his life.

A year before he would have gone to secondary school in Laval's his mother took him back to Paris, where they lived with his grandparents in the Rue de l'Avre. The family assumed Ionesco's father had died in the war, and his mother did not attempt to trace him until 1925. She then found out that he was still alive, had become chief of police in Bucharest, and had divorced her on the alleged grounds that she had abandoned the matrimonial home by going abroad. As the plaintiff in the divorce case, Ionesco's father won custody of the children. At the age of 13, Ionesco had therefore to adjust to a new country, a new language, and a hostile stepmother, who took a particular dislike to his sister: "A month after we arrived in Bucharest, Lola threw my sister out, and she went off in tears with her bundle of belongings to stay with my mother. I stayed behind. That was the only concession Lola made to her husband."

Ionesco's mother tried to contest the divorce settlement, which her husband had obtained by forging signatures, but he was now practising as a lawyer again and had invincible power in legal circles.

Tous les avocats avec qui ma mère prenait contact se dégonflaient les uns après les autres après les visites que mon père allait leur rendre. "Non, non, ils ne pouvaient pas faire ça à un confrère, ils ne pouvaient pas mettre un confrère en prison."

(All the lawyers my mother contacted would deflate one after another following the visits my father paid them. "Oh, no, they couldn't do that to a colleague; they couldn't send a colleague to prison.")

Until the age of 17 Ionesco lived with his father and Lola, in the same house as his father's brothers- and sisters-in-law. He loathed them all. His father's second marriage was as turbulent as the first, with the addition of physical violence. Whenever they had a row, Lola would get her brothers to beat up her husband, and would set a price on reconciliation:

Lola acceptait de revenir non sans avoir obtenu des concessions importantes: ne plus jamais faire revenir ma soeur

Very soon language takes over the play and the characters start *thinking* in the stereotypes demanded by the language-learning record and textbook. Words are invented, used or made up alliteratively or onomatopoeically, and the characters' minds work according to the demands of tenses and pronouns, and the need to memorize by repetition. Reduced to monosyllabic stammering, they appear to revert to infancy. The clock virtually becomes a character, and there are short snatches of naturalistic conversation to make clear that most people's language is stereotyped most of the time.

In *La Leçon* language takes over completely. The knife the professor uses to kill the girl pupil who wants to take her "doctorat total (doctorate of everything)" is symbolic of a relationship which is at once male tyranny, sexual desire, and mental dominance. The knife can be real or imaginary "selon le goût du metteur en scène (as the producer likes)." In the end the imaginary and the real become indistinguishable. The pupil is the professor's 40th victim but, absurdly, it becomes important that she should be moved out without being hurt. The maid gives him an armband with a sign, "perhaps the Nazi swastika," tying it on for him with the remark: "C'est politique"—meaning either that it is prudent, or that is political.

Jacques; ou, La Soumission, a "comédie naturaliste (naturalistic comedy)," was followed by *Les Chaises*, a "tragic farce." The cast of *Les Chaises* consists of a man of 95, a woman of 94, an orator, and "lots of other characters," all of whom are invisible, but for whom more and more chairs are brought on stage. Dementia overtakes the two elderly characters, who had appeared sane to begin with, but end up throwing themselves out of windows. Ionesco talked about "an ontological vacuum, a sort of whirlwind of emptiness." Whether a single joke could be protracted to sustain the interest of an audience for an entire play was a risk he was prepared to take. *Les Chaises* is silly enough to keep an audience amused for most at any rate of its length. Its play on what reality, madness, unreality, or incapacity to communicate may reveal or conceal can actually keep an audience thinking for a good deal longer than the piece takes to stage.

There are three plays linked by the character of Bérenger, the possessor of the only relatively undisturbed mind in a world of lunatics who spend their time regulating traffic, going to offices, having their hair cut, getting promoted, and telling the truth. In *Tueur sans gages* Bérenger goes after the murderer of the title. The characters are types. Dany the typist is "a conventional pin-up," while the uncaring architect is "as old as a bureaucrat." Bérenger ends the play with an immense monologue in which he persuades himself that the assassin was right after all, but his plea to the assassin to let people, even the police, live stupidly reduces the play's impact. Ionesco's stage directions become necessarily more explicit as the meaning of the action becomes more difficult for the audience to grasp. Here, for instance, the producer is told that Bérenger has to find in himself, in spite of himself, against himself, arguments in favour of the assassin. He is to "deflate like a balloon."

The order in which the characters of *Rhinocéros* undergo their transformation into rhinoceroses is important and depends on the degree of conformism of their initial attitudes. As usual in a Ionesco play, nothing very serious seems amiss to start with, but the action escalates to make the significance of the opening situation increasingly clear. Has a rhinoceros escaped from the zoo? People begin to develop incipient signs of scales, those who are promptest at work and best organized, with the tidiest

desks, first. Daisy, Bérenger's girlfriend, is the last to undergo the metamorphosis. Is that because she almost escapes, but not quite, because she is almost in love with Bérenger, but not quite? When the curtain comes down we know that Bérenger is the last human being left. What we do not know is how long he will hold out. How much did he love Daisy? Is that what it might depend on? Ionesco prompts the questions, but does not provide the answers.

The later plays become heavier and more symbolic. The fear of death permeates the third Bérenger play, *Le Roi se meurt*, when, as King Bérenger I, he undergoes the ceremony of dying. *La Soif et la faim* is a serious parable about the importance of loving enough actually to trust one's partner. Jean's failure to love Marie-Madeleine, to whom his bondage in the monastery now prevents him from returning, is not absolved by his either embracing or abandoning religion. The difficulty Ionesco clearly feels in the three episodes, staged by the Comédie-Française in 1966, is that of creating a form strong enough to carry the myth after the lightweight structures, largely verbal humour, and generally much lighter, more fantastic content of the earlier plays.

PUBLICATIONS

Collections

Oeuvres complètes, Bibliothèque de la Pléiade, 1991

Plays

La Cantatrice chauve (produced 1950), included in *Théâtre I*, 1954; as *The Bald Soprano* (produced 1956), in *Plays I*, 1958
La Leçon (produced 1951), included in *Théâtre I*, 1954; as *The Lesson* (produced 1958), in *Plays I*, 1958
Les Chaises (produced 1952), included in *Théâtre I, 1954*; as *The Chairs* (produced 1957), in *Plays I*, 1958
Sept petits sketches (*Les Grandes Chaleurs, Le connaissez-vous?, Le Rhume onirique, La Jeune Fille à marier, Le Maître, Le Nièce-épouse, Le Salon de l'automobile*; produced 1953). *La Jeune Fille à marier* included in *Théâtre II*, 1958, as *Maid to Marry*; in *Plays III*, 1960; *Le Maître* included in *Théâtre II*, 1958; as *The Leader*, in *Plays IV*, 1960; *La Nièce-épouse* as *The Niece-Wife*, in *Ionesco* by Richard N. Coe, 1971; *Le Salon de l'automobile* included in *Théâtre IV*, 1966; as *The Motor Show*, in *Plays V*, 1963
Victimes du devoir (produced 1953), included in *Théâtre I*, 1954; as *Victims of Duty* (produced 1960), in *Plays II*, 1958
Théâtre I (*La Cantatrice chauve; La Leçon; Jacques, ou, Comment s'en débarrasser*), 1954
Amédée; ou, Comment s'en débarrasser (produced 1954), included in *Théâtre I*, 1954; as *Amedee* (produced 1955), in *Plays II*, 1958
Jacques; ou, La Soumission (produced 1955), included in *Théâtre I*, 1954; as *Jack* (produced 1958), in *Plays I*, 1958
Le Nouveau Locataire (produced 1955), included in *Théâtre II*, 1958; as *The New Tenant* (produced 1956), in *Plays II*, 1958
Le Tableau (produced 1955), included in *Théâtre III*, 1963; as *The Picture* (produced 1969), in *Plays VII*, 1968
L'Impromptu de l'Alma; ou, Le Caméléon du berger (produced 1956), included in *Théâtre II*, 1958; as *Improvisation; or, The*

Shepherd's Chameleon (produced 1960), in *Plays III*, 1960

L'Avenir est dans les oeufs; ou, Il faut tout pour faire un monde (produced 1957), included in *Théâtre II*, 1958; as *The Future Is in Eggs; or, It Takes All Sorts to Make a World*, in *Plays IV*, 1960

Impromptu pour la Duchesse de Windsor (produced 1957)

Plays I (*The Chairs; The Bald Soprano; The Lesson; Jack, or,* Obedience), 1958; as *Four Plays*, 1958

Théâtre II (*L'Impromptu de l'Alma; ou, Le Caméléon du berger; Tueur sans gages; Le Nouveau Locataire; L'Avenir est dans les oeufs; ou, Il faut tout pour faire un monde; Le Maître; La Jeune Fille à marier*), 1958

Tueur sans gages (produced 1959), included in *Théâtre II*, 1958; as *The Killer* (produced 1960), in *Plays III*, 1960

Plays II (*Amedee; or, How to Get Rid of It; The New Tenant; Victims of Duty*), 1958

Rhinocéros (produced 1959), included in *Théâtre III*, 1963; as *Rhinoceros* (produced 1960), in *Plays IV*, 1960

Scène à quatre (produced 1959), included in *Théâtre III*, 1963; as *Foursome* (produced 1970), in *Plays V*, 1963

Apprendre à marcher (ballet scenario; produced 1960), included in *Théâtre IV*, 1966; as *Learning to Walk*, in *Plays IX*, 1973

Plays III (*The Killer; Improvisation; or, The Shepherd's Chameleon; Maid to Marry*), 1960

Plays IV (*Rhinoceros; The Leader; The Future Is in Eggs; or, It Takes All Sorts to Make a World*), 1960

Délire à deux (produced 1962), included in *Théâtre III*, 1963; as *Frenzy for Two*, in *Plays VI*, 1965

Le Roi se meurt (produced 1962), 1963; as *Exit the King* (produced 1963), 1963; in *Plays V*, 1963

Le Piéton de l'air (produced 1962), included in *Théâtre III*, 1963; as *A Stroll in the Air* (produced 1964), in *Plays VI*, 1965

Théâtre III (*Rhinocéros; Le Piéton de l'air; Délire à deux; Le Tableau; Scène à quatre; Les Salutations; La Colère*), 1963

Plays V (*Exit the King; The Motor Show; Foursome*), 1963

Les Salutations (produced 1970), included in *Théâtre III*, 1963; as *Salutations*, in *Plays VII*, 1968

La Soif et la faim (produced 1964), included in *Théâtre IV*, 1966; as *Hunger and Thirst* (produced 1969), in *Plays VII*, 1968

La Lacune (produced 1965), included in *Théâtre IV*, 1966

Plays VI (*A Stroll in the Air; Frenzy for Two*), 1965

Pour préparer un oeuf dur (produced 1966), included in *Théâtre IV*, 1966

Théâtre IV (*Le Roi se meurt; La Soif et la faim; La Lacune; Le Salon de l'automobile; L'Oeuf dur; Pour préparer un oeuf dur; Le Jeune Homme à marier; Apprendre à marcher*), 1966

Plays VII (*Hunger and Thirst; The Picture; Anger; Salutations*), 1968

Jeux de massacre (produced 1970), 1970; as *Killing Game* (as *Wipe-Out Game*, 1971), 1974

Plays VIII (*Here Comes a Chopper; The Oversight; The Foot of the Wall*), 1971

Macbett (produced 1972), 1972; as *Macbett* (in English), in *Plays IX*, 1973

Plays IX (*Macbett; The Mire; Learning to Walk*), 1973

Ce formidable bordel (produced 1973), 1973

Théâtre V (*Jeux de massacre; Macbett; La Vase; Exercices de conversation et de diction françaises pour étudiants américains*), 1974

L'Homme aux valises (produced 1975), 1975; as *Man with Bags* (produced 1977), 1977; as *The Man with the Luggage*, in *Plays XI*, 1979

A Hell of a Mess, 1975

Plays X (*Oh What a Bloody Circus; The Hard-Boiled Egg*), 1976

Plays XI (*The Man with the Luggage; The Duel; Double Act*), 1979

Théâtre VII (*Voyages chez les morts: thèmes et variations*), 1981; as *Plays XII* (*Journey among the Dead*), 1983

Screenplays: "La colère" episode in *Les Sept péchés capitaux*, 1962; *Monsieur Tête* (animated film), 1970

Ballet scenarios for television, with Fleming Flindt: *La Leçon*, 1963; *Le Jeune Homme à marier*, 1965; *The Triumph of Death*, 1971

Fiction

La Photo du Colonel, 1962; as *The Colonel's Photograph*, 1967

Le Solitaire, 1973; as *The Hermit*, 1974

Other

Elegii pentru fiinti mici, 1931

Nu!, 1934

Notes et contre-notes, 1962; revised edition, 1966; as *Notes and Counter-Notes*, 1964

Entretiens avec Claude Bonnefoy, 1966; as *Conversations with Ionesco*, 1970

Journal en miettes, 1967; as *Fragments of a Journal*, 1968

Présent passé, passé présent, 1968; as *Present Past, Past Present*, 1971

Conte pour enfants, 4 vols., 1969–75; as *Story for Children*, 1968–75

Découvertes, with illustrations by the author, 1969

Mise en train: première année de français, with Michael Benamou, 1969

Monsieur Tête (animated film text), 1970

Discours de réception à l'Académie franaise..., 1971

Entre la vie et le rêve: entretiens avec Claude Bonnefoy, 1977

Antidotes, 1977

Un homme en question, 1979

Le Noir et le blanc, 1980

Hugoliade, 1982

Bibliography

Hughes, Griffith R., and Ruth Bury, *Ionesco: A Bibliography*, 1974

Leiner, Wolfgang, *Bibliographie et index thématique des études sur Ionesco*, 1980

Critical studies

Coe, Richard N., *Ionesco* (in English), 1961; revised edition, 1971

Pronko, Leonard C., *Ionesco* (in English), 1965

Jacobsen, Josephine, and William Randolph Mueller, *Ionesco and Genet*, 1968

Wulbern, J. H., *Brecht and Ionesco: Commitment in Context*, 1971

Hayman, Ronald, *Ionesco* (in English), 1972

Lewis, Allan, *Ionesco* (in English), 1972

Lamont, Rose C. (editor), *Ionesco: A Collection of Critical Essays*, 1973

Lamont, Rose C., and M. J. Friedman (editors), *The Two Faces of Ionesco*, 1978

ISTRATI, Panaït, 1884–1935.

Novelist and travel writer.

Istrati was a Romanian who wrote a total of 18 books in French during the last decade of his life. He was born at Braïla in Romania on 11 August 1884. His father was a professional smuggler, and his mother a washerwoman. Partly on that account, and also because he was self-taught and had had little formal education, Istrati has been regarded as a "proletarian" novelist, although it might be more correct to refer to him as an adventurer than as a "worker." He differs from many of the authors with whom his name has been associated in the extent, at least, of his travels.

He earned his living by doing odd jobs, having been at various times a painter, a sandwich man, a pub waiter, a pastry cook, a labourer, a garage mechanic, and a photographer. After 12 years of rootless wandering, primarily in France, Istrati tried to commit suicide by slitting his throat on the Promenade des Anglais at Nice in 1921. Shortly afterwards he met and was taken up by Romain Rolland, who had his short story "Kyra Kyralina" published in *Europe* in 1923.

In 1927 Istrati went to live in the USSR, hoping to find, or to help build, a communist utopia. He became disillusioned with what he discovered there, and returned to France in 1929, describing his Russian experience in *Vers l'autre flamme. Après seize mois dans l'URSS*. He became one of the group of writers of "modern popular expression" promoted by Henri Poulaille, the "école prolétarienne" founded in reaction to the populist school of middle-class authors writing for a working- class readership. Poulaille was the author of a history and manifesto of the movement, the *Nouvel âge littéraire* of 1930, and the editor of a succession of reviews devoted to proletarian writing as he understood it. Literary editor of *Le Peuple* from 1926, and an author in his own right, he founded the "Prix sans nom" for Istrati's *Oncle Anghel*, and edited *Nouvel Age* (11 numbers in 1931), *Prolétariat* (12 numbers in 1933), and *Maintenant* (10 numbers from 1945 to 1948).

Romain Rolland regarded Istrati as "the Gorky of the Balkans." His novels are grouped into three cycles, forming the life story of their central character, Adrien Zograffi. They are all set in Rumania and evoke the social problems of that country, as well as its scenery and history. Istrati also wrote works of autobiography and travel. He returned to Bucharest, where he died on 16 April 1935.

PUBLICATIONS

Fiction

Les Récits d'Adrien Zograffi, 1924–26:
  Kyra Kyralina, 1924; as *Kyra, My Sister*, 1930
  Oncle Anghel, 1924; as *Uncle Anghel*, 1927; as *Balkan Tavern*, 1931
  Présentation des Haïdoucs (Les Haïdoucs, I), 1925; translated jointly with *Domnitza de Snagov* as *The Bandits*, 1929
  Domnitza de Snagov (Les Haïdoucs, II), 1926; translated jointly with *Présentation des Haïdoucs* as *The Bandits*, 1929
Jeunesse d'Adrien Zograffi, 1926–30:
  Codine (Enfance d'Adrien Zograffi), 1926
  Mikhail (Adolescence d'Adrien Zograffi), 1927
  Les Chardons du Baragan, 1928
  Pour avoir aimé la terre, 1930
Vie d'Adrien Zograffi, 1933–35:
  La Maison Thüringer, 1933
  Le Bureau de placement, 1933
  Méditerranée: lever du soleil, 1934
  Méditerranée: coucher du soleil, 1935

Other

Trecut si Viitor (autobiography), 1925
La Famille Perlmutter with Josué Jéhouda, 1927
Mes départs, 1928
Vers l'autre flamme. Après seize mois dans l'URSS, 1929
La Russie nue; as *Russia Unveiled*, 1931
Le Pêcheur d'éponges, 1930
En Egypte, 1931
Ma croisade ou notre croisade, translated from the Romanian by Ion Capatana, 1941
Le Pèlerin du coeur, 1984

J

JACCOTTET, Philippe, 1925–

Poet and translator.

LIFE

Better known as a translator than for his verse or prose, Jaccottet is the author of four major verse collections, *L'Effraie et autres poésies, L'Ignorant: poèmes 1952–1956, Airs: Poèmes 1961–1964*, and *Leçons*, of which he himself regards *A la lumière d'hiver* as a continuation. He has been poetry editor for the *Nouvelle Revue Française* (q.v.), and also published reflective and poetic prose, sometimes in notebook form, and critical studies. Apart from Homer and Plato, Jaccottet has translated Hölderlin and Rilke, Mann and Musil, Leopardi and Ungaretti.

Jaccottet was born at Moudon in the canton of Vaud in Switzerland on 30 June 1925, although he has lived for a long time in the country in the South of France. He was brought up in Lausanne, where he attended the university, and graduated in arts in 1946. On graduation he travelled in Italy and became friendly with the Italian poet and translator Giuseppe Ungaretti. Jaccottet settled in Paris, but started to work straight away as a professional translator for the Lausanne publishing house Mermod. He stopped in 1953, the year of his marriage to Anne-Marie Haesler, when he moved to Grignan, to the east of the Rhône, just south of Montélimar. Jaccottet, who has a son and a daughter, has won a number of Swiss and German literary prizes, prizes for translation, and, in 1978, he was awarded the Larbaud prize.

Jaccottet's first verse collection, *Requiem*, was published by Mermod in the year after his graduation. Much attention has been paid to the subsequent evolution of his prosody, which has moved from regular Alexandrines and rhymed couplets in sonnet form to a very loose rhythm based on an octosyllabic line, which is frequently speeded up by the inclusion of lines of seven or five syllables. At the same time he shifted from the lyrical first person to the plural, until that also disappeared. The *Odyssey*, which appeared in 1955, is translated in rhythms similar to those used in the earliest of the major collections, a mixture of 12 and 14 syllables to the line. Jaccottet's own poetry has always been dark in tone, filled with anxious forebodings and images of darkness and winter, though *Leçons* announces a fresh departure.

The imagery and rhythms have become broken, as if to announce a new intensity in the sense of life's precariousness. Where once the brightness of the Provençal sun illuminated the dark shadow cast by the mountains, now the hope seems more fragile, the awaited voice less confidently expected. Jaccottet's religious hopes, in the broadest sense of the term, have receded. *Leçons* can be seen as a doomed attempt to regain hope and, nourished by a sense of paradox and doubts about the utility of poetry, is virtually a lament, centred on the themes of humility and quest, mourning more for the future than the past.

WORKS

Apart from their rigidly formal structure, the characteristic of Jaccottet's early poems chiefly remarked on has been the way in which the poet tends to withdraw from any affirmation he has made. To talk of a "poétique du retrait (poetics of withdrawal)" may be pretentious, but Jaccottet has been seen as avoiding the use of symbols and favouring what has just as pretentiously been called "the rhetoric of allegory." This is essential in order to reintroduce into his verse, in place of static symbolism (q.v.), the dimension of chronological sequentiality, represented in its new critical usage by "allegory," which allows the characteristic retracing of steps and withdrawal of what seems just to have been stated or suggested.

The order of the first six poems in *L'Effraie* seems deliberate. The sixth is a conclusion, mixing the three themes of poetry, love, and death in such a way as to suggest an affirmation of the intensity of loving, and even the necessity of its poetization, in the constant awareness of a death to come. God, the poet suggests, alone knows when or how, but it will come. It is a poem of extraordinary effectiveness, especially if situated precisely in its date and context. They determine the nuances achieved by Jaccottet's not in themselves unusual technical devices. In particular he achieves a tension by slightly daring rhyme schemes in a poem whose form is strictly classical, except in the way its sense is not contained by its classical structure. The deliberately literal translation has to distinguish between the French singular and plural usages of "you," and cannot hope to reproduce the effects of reiterated consonants, the ambiguities in the correlatives of pronouns, the effect of sentences overflowing from one line to another, or the resonance of other well-known French poems by earlier authors. The second time it comes "même quand (even when)" is spelt in a deliberately archaic, stylized way.

The opening of the poem is more complex than it seems. The "Sois tranquille (Hush)" is addressed to the reader, and partly has the sense of "Don't worry" or even "Just you wait." It also deliberately alludes to Baudelaire's poem "Recueillement," which employs childlike language to great effect and starts with the admonition adults use to children: "Sois sage (Be a good boy/girl)." Finally "Sois tranquille, cela viendra! Tu te rapproches,/tu brûles!" is the language associated with the children's game of "Hunt the thimble," and should be translated more or less as "Hush...You're getting close/you're warm." The tense of "venir" (to come) will change as the indifferent "it" comes to refer to death.

Sois tranquille, cela viendra! Tu te rapproches,
tu brûles! Car le mot qui sera à la fin
du poème, plus que le premier sera proche
de ta mort, qui ne s'arrête pas en chemin.

Ne crois pas qu'elle aille s'endormir sous des branches
ou reprendre souffle pendant que tu écris.
Même quand tu bois à la bouche qui étanche
la pire soif, la douce bouche avec des cris

doux, même quant tu serres avec force le noeud
de vos quatre bras pour être bien immobiles
dans la brûlante obscurité de vos cheveux,

elle vient, Dieu sait par quels détours, vers vous deux,
de très loin ou déjà tout près, mais sois tranquille,
elle vient: d'un à l'autre mot tu es plus vieux.

(Hush, it'll come! You (singular) are getting close! You're
warm! For the word which will come at the end of the poem
will be, more than the first one, near your death, which does
not stop on the way.

Don't imagine it will go away and sleep under the branches
or stop to get its breath back while you're writing. Even
when you drink from the mouth which quenches the worst
thirst, the soft mouth with its cries

(which are) soft, even when you clasp forcefully the knot
of your (plural) four arms to be quite motionless in the
burning darkness of your (plural) hair

it is coming, by God knows what twists and turns, towards
you two from far off or already quite near, but hush, it's
coming: from one word to the next you're (singular) older).

The prose works, *La Promenade sous les arbres*, whose title
deliberately recalls Rousseau, *Eléments d'un songe*, *Paysages
avec figures absentes*, and *A travers un verger*, are reflective,
poetic meditations on the countryside. In "L'approche des
montagnes," for instance, we are told from the beginning that
the distant range of mountains presents itself as a puzzle,
camped on the horizon, an invitation not so much to resolve as
to linger over the feeling of puzzlement. Words, anyway,
cannot solve the puzzle: "les mots traînent après eux des
représentations machinales qu'il me faut d'abord écarter
(words drag after them mechanical representations which I
first have to get rid of)." Geographically, the puzzle can be
unravelled. The slopes, bends, and fields indicate the presence
of a river that cannot be seen, but which must be there. There
is a merciful limit to the intellectual bewilderment, "Il a ya des
gens qui ne respirent à leur aise qu'au seuil de l'illimité; j'aime
plutôt cet espace que les montagnes définissent mais n'empris-
onnent pas (There are people who can breathe at their ease
only on the threshold of the limitless. I prefer the space which
the mountains define but do not imprison)." The view is
blocked, as by a garden wall. The occupant is protected, but
there is always a way out, a pass, a passage.

In prose as well as in verse Jaccottet is the poet of passionately intense feeling, immensely sensitive, fanciful, easily
moved, but in complete control of the half-tones, the shades,

the waves of feeling breaking at cross-purposes in his work, as
tentative in his imagination as his feelings are deep, and their
expression well defined. It has often been remarked on that
Jaccottet reveals his Swiss origins or, at any rate, the mixture
within him of German and French, northern and Mediterranean, cultures, depth of feeling and delicate clarity of imagination. Much of the poetry has been effectively translated into
English as *Breathings*. The notebooks, too, are filled with
rural, agricultural themes for meditation. Jaccottet has always
felt a special affinity for the Swiss poet and translator Gustave
Roud.

PUBLICATIONS

Verse

Requiem, 1947
L'Effraie et autres poésies, 1953
L'Ignorant: poèmes 1952–1956, 1958
Airs: poèmes 1961–1964, 1967
Leçons, 1969
Poésie 1946–1967, 1971
Chants d'en bas, 1974
Breathings, translated by Cid Corman, 1974

Fiction

L'Obscurité: récit, 1961

Other

La Promenade sous les arbres: proses, 1957
Eléments d'un songe: proses, 1961
La Semaison: carnets 1954–1962, 1963; revised edition, as *La
    Semaison: carnets 1954–1967*, 1971; as *Seedtime*, 1977
Paysages de Grignan, 1964
Autriche, 1966
L'Entretien des muses: chroniques de poésie, 1968
Paysages avec figures absentes: proses, 1970
Rilke par lui-même, 1971
A travers un verger, 1975; as *Through an Orchard*, 1978
Adieu à Gustave Roud, with Maurice Chappaz and Jacques
    Chessex, 1977
Beauregard, 1981

Editor, *Elégies et autres vers*, by Francis Jammes, 1946
Editor, *Gustave Roud*, 1968

Translator

La Mort à Venise, by Mann, 1946
L'Odyssée, by Homer, 1955
L'Homme sans qualités, by Musil, 1957
Les Désarrois de l'élève Törless, by Musil, 1967
Le Vaisseau des morts, by B. Traven, 1967
Oeuvres complètes, by Hölderlin, 1967
Correspondance, by Rilke, 1976
Le Banquet, by Plato, 1979
Also translator of novels by Carlo Cassola and others.

became closer. He visited Versailles, but avoided Paris on the way back, and in February 1899 he and Duparc were witnesses at Bordeu's marriage. Later that year, feeling depressed, he wrote a series of elegies. Finally, in what he later called a "folie de pureté (mad quest for purity)," Jammes wrote a novel, *Clara d'Ellébeuse; ou, L'Histoire d'une ancienne jeune fille*, which he dedicated to its heroine, whose name he had used several times before. Hellebore ("ellébore") is supposed to cure madness, and Clara in the novel is clearly unbalanced. The novel appeared in June 1899, published by the *Mercure* after appearing in the review. The reception was favourable, especially warm from Rachilde, Valette's wife, but also from Colette, Claudel, and Remy de Gourmont. In July 1957 the novel was classed among the best dozen to have appeared between 1875 and World War II, and its quest for purity also inspired Jammes's poem *La Jeune Fille nue*, published in *L'Ermitage* for July 1899, then in plaquette form, and then incorporated into *Le Deuil des primevères*. That summer Jammes accompanied his mother on a holiday visit to the foothills of the Alps, where she had spent her youth. On his return, he wrote another long poem, *Le Poète et l'oiseau*, dated October 1899, which apeared in *L'Ermitage* for January 1900, in plaquette, and then in *Le Deuil des primevères*.

The old enemy of demoralization snapped at his heels on his return. Accepting an invitation to lecture in Belgium in early 1900, he returned by way of Paris. On the way home late in March, he stayed with Gide, and the two visited Claudel, with whom they discussed religion. The next day Jammes and Schwob, who knew he was dying, lunched with Claudel at Lapérouse, at that date one of the best restaurants in the world. Jammes was unimpressed by Claudel's religious certainty. On his return to Orthez in April, newly depressed by hostile press comment, especially by Catulle Mendès, Jammes began to write his second, very short, novel, *Almaïde d'Etremont; ou, L'Histoire d'une jeune fille passionnée*, to be published in June 1901 by the *Mercure*. Samain died in the summer of 1900, and Jammes wrote a verse comedy, *Existences*, published in *Le Triomphe de la vie* of March 1902, but which he later repudiated. Still depressed, he spent the winter quietly in country pursuits. The collected poems 1898–1900 appeared as *Le Deuil des primevères* in March 1901 and in the summer, on holiday with Charles Guérin, Jammes conceived his long poem "Jean de Noarrieu," also to appear in *Le Triomphe de la vie*. The *Revue Blanche* published four elegies in December. What lifted the depression was a nascent relationship early in 1902 about which we know almost nothing, so discreet are the later reminiscences. However, nothing came of it except the "novel" *Le Roman du lièvre*, in fact a prose poem, published by the *Mercure* in 1903.

Early in 1902 Jammes's relationship with Gide began to cool. Jammes had published *Existences* and Gide *L'Immoraliste*, and the clash between their systems of value had come out into the open. A trivial incident now inspired Jammes to write another short novel, *Pomme d'Anis; ou, L'Histoire d'une jeune fille infirme*, printed in *La Renaissance Latine* for 15 February 1904 before appearing with the *Mercure* in May. A prospective marriage foundered when the girl's parents refused permission over the question of Jammes's income. His conversion to committed Catholicism was triggered by that experience and by the cunning proselytization of Claudel from China. Jammes's "Méditation sur la foi" appeared in *Le Gaulois* for 9 October 1904, dedicated to the girl who had turned him down and who was then thinking of becoming a nun. In the spring of 1905 Claudel

returned to France on leave from China and in July had long conversations with Jammes, with whom he stayed at Orthez. They went together to see a Benedictine friend of the family of Jammes's lost fiancée. He heard their confessions and they communicated at his Mass on 7 July. In 1906 Jammes published a collection of poems, *L'Eglise habillée de feuilles*, having completed *Pensée des jardins*, also published by the *Mercure*, but begun before his conversion. In October 1906 the *Mercure* published as *Clairières dans le ciel* the poems written since the compilation of *Le Deuil*.

Jammes married on 8 October 1907. Earlier in the year his close friend Charles Guérin had died and Jammes had visited the family at Lunéville. On his return he found a letter awaiting him from a 24-year-old admirer, Ginette Goedorp, who lived with her sister and mother, the widow of a military commandant from Saint-Cyr. Her father's family were officers, her mother's magistrates. The correspondence flourished. Jammes took it all as a sign from God, and they were practically engaged, due enquiries in the French manner having been made by Ginette's mother about Jammes's moral standing, when they met, during the Goedorps' annual Lourdes pilgrimage, at Pau on 18 August, under the auspices of Jammes's surviving great-aunt. The couple had seen only photographs of each other, but became formally engaged next day in front of the grotto at Lourdes. Ginette and her mother returned to Orthez, and in September Jammes stayed with them. Gide attended the wedding. On 1 December Jammes, his wife, and his mother moved into a larger house and, on 4 December, went to spend Christmas with Ginette's family, lunching on the return journey with Gide, who liked Jammes's new poems.

Jammes was now happily domesticated. His daughter Bernadette was born on 19 August 1908 and a second daughter, Emmanuèle, was to be born on Christmas Day 1909. Relations with Gide were still good, and Jammes visited him at his new Auteuil residence. Ruyters asked Jammes for a contribution to the newly established *Nouvelle Revue Française* (*NRF*, q. v.), and immediately received the "Poème à Paul Claudel." Gide reviewed Jammes's eclogues *Rayons de miel* favourably on 1 May 1909, and on 1 December the review published a fragment of Jammes's *Ma fille Bernadette*, but the cooling of his relationship with Gide caused Jammes to stop contributing after that date. From 1906 Jammes and Gide had agreed not to discuss religion. They broke their rule at a lunch after the appearance of Gide's *La Porte étroite* on 13 May 1909, about which Jammes also wrote favourably in *L'Occident* in July. However, he had clearly failed to penetrate the irony which Gide had made quite obvious in the passages from Alissa's diary at the end of his novel.

By this date Jammes was no longer short of admirers and imitators. Many young authors, particularly Catholic, including François Mauriac, André Lafon, and Valery Larbaud looked on him as their leader, but the final break with Gide had come. Gide had turned down an article by Jammes for the number of the *NRF* devoted to Charles-Louis Philippe, who had died of typhoid on 23 December 1909, and the number finally appeared without anything at all by Jammes. Thereafter Gide and Jammes scarcely exchanged letters, and never intimate ones. Jammes went on to write *Les Géorgiques chrétiennes* but, in spite of his evident success, he remained troubled by refusals of public acknowledgement of his talents. He did get a minor academy award of 3,000 francs for *Les Géorgiques* on 20 June 1912, which allowed him to take his wife on a cure to Vichy. When Dierx died in 1912 and Gil Blas organized an election among prominent literary personalities to find a successor, Paul Fort won easily, with three times as many votes as the runner-up. After him came, in order, Ponchon, Rostand, Richepin, Verhaeren, and Mistral. Jammes was disappointed.

In 1913 Lugné-Poe, who had staged Claudel's *L'Annonce faite à Marie* since the withdrawal of *Un jour*, was looking for another Catholic play, and chose Jammes's *La Brebis égarée*, published by the *Revue Hebdomadaire* in 1910, and incorporated into *Feuilles dans le vent* of 1913. Jammes went to Paris for the dress rehearsal. The play was to have 100 performances. His fourth child was born on 6 June and called Paul after Claudel, his godfather. Yet Jammes was again depressed to learn that he had been refused the Légion d'Honneur, and his third child, Marie, developed anaemia. It was this sadness which provoked Jammes to publish his uncollected "méditations" as *Feuilles dans le vent*, a volume which demarcates the end of a whole creative period in his life.

At the outbreak of World War I his age and his four children exempted Jammes from mobilization, but he became the administrator of the local ambulance service at Orthez. In 1916 he published *Cinq prières pour le temps de la guerre*, which was followed by the two novels *Le Rosaire au soleil* and *Monsieur le Curé d'Ozeron*. By this time Jammes had seven children, and the rented house was to be sold. Happily, the Benedictine friend who had received him back to the sacraments had virtually nominated him as the beneficiary of the will of a 75-year-old with no family who wanted to leave her possessions to a large and deserving Catholic family. Unfortunately, the bequest involved moving to Hasparren in the Basque country, where his benefactress's property was located. Jammes was passed over a second time in an attempt to be elected to the Académie Française, and now, although offered the Légion d'Honneur, turned it down. The offer had come too late, and Jammes must have realized that his combative attitudes, especially the Catholic ones, had made him enemies.

He wrote four volumes of memoirs, published in the early 1920s, but seldom left home. In the four books of *Quatrains* that followed, and which were much admired by Claudel and Mauriac, Jammes tried to express concentrated meditative experience along the lines of the Japanese *Haï Kaï*. Ghéon had become a Catholic, and called on him. Darius Milhaud had made an opera out of *La Brebis égarée*, but it was not a success. By 1927 Bernadette alone of Jammes's children was at home, acting as his secretary. The two boys were boarding with the Jesuits at Sarlat. Anne, Marie, and Françoise were boarding with the sisters of Saint-Maur at Fontarabie, and Emmanuèle had left for Paris. The seven or eight volumes Jammes had still to publish contain nothing of great literary originality. The spiritual maturity which he is sometimes thought to have attained in his late verse reflects the lack of spiritual tension in his domestic circumstances, as his family grew up and he was for a period comparatively affluent.

Jammes did go to Loyola, and made occasional visits to Bayonne and Biarritz. In 1934, at the age of 93, his mother died. Jammes visited Orthez for the last time to bury her next to his father. His literary revenue was decreasing and financial worries were beginning again. He reacted quite bitterly against those cultural tendencies, like surrealism (q. v.), of which he disapproved and which he was incapable of understanding. The attack in effigy on Gide in *L'Antigyde* of 1932 was at best inept, and Jammes was bitter, too, at what he took to be the hostility provoked in press and public by his religion. His last few years were spent as a recluse and unhappily showed the disintegration of a once vigorous imagination. He received what seemed to him an insulting consolation prize of 10,000 francs from the academy, which was as humiliating as it was useful, but he kept writing, especially when Jean Paulhan invited him to contribute a monthly column entitled "Airs du mois" to the *NRF* from 1937.

That same year Jammes scored a great success at the Paris International Exhibition when the press dropped its defences against the elderly writer's embittered attacks and applauded him. Early in 1938 he fell ill. His daughter Anne married. Françoise entered a convent. Jammes lingered on for six months, slowly dying of cancer. The end came on the evening of 1 November 1938.

WORKS

It seems at first strange that Jammes should have desired and been chosen to be the leading figure of a literary movement, so resolutely did he refuse to participate in the activities and outlook of a literary mainstream, which nevertheless hurt him by refusing to look up to him, honour him, and follow his lead. His initial closeness to Gide is more surprising than the inevitable later clash, and it is on the whole surprising that the resolutely simple, regional, rustic Catholic, who only rarely strayed far from the Pyrenees, and wrote with a determined and not wholly unaffected naivety about country joys and spiritual bliss, should have attracted as much attention as he did. The early association with the *Mercure de France*, Gide, and the *NRF*, and then the aggressive Catholicism undisturbed by the sense of sin to be found in Bloy and Bernanos, Claudel, and Mauriac, helped to make him known, but his real affinities were with other friends and admirers, like Loti, Alain-Fournier, Valery Larbaud, and Lafon, not necessarily Catholic at all.

It is axiomatic that literature can never lose its way, if only because what we choose to call literature is, by definition, that which has not explored totally blind alleys. But it is arguable that the literary quest for new modes of expression in which to explore alternative systems of value in the last decade of the 19th century became sufficiently heterogeneous and self-consciously original to have eased the burden of later critics and literary historians by fashionably issuing manifestoes, thereby creating "-isms" and pigeonholes. The great adventure of symbolism had ceased to promise the creation of literature. Its prophet and martyr, Mallarmé, had taken by the end of his life to talking and writing about it rather than producing it. Then, as always, it was necessary to look for new paths forward. What had got out of hand, as Jammes rightly saw, was the labelling process. When he referred to his own preferred literary procedures as "Jammisme" in the *Mercure de France* for March 1897, he was being understandably sarcastic at the expense of Kahn's "vers-librisme," Ghil's "instrumentisme," Moréas's "romanisme," Saint-Pol-Roux's "magnificisme," Péladan's "magisme," Darzens's "socialisme," Tailhade's "anarchisme," Verhaeren's "paroxysme," "ésotérisme," "naturisme," and "scientisme," all terms used within the preceding 10 years. As many labels again were to be created in the next 10.

The pigeonholes, always prone to sub-compartmentalization, sometimes provided personal experimentation with the crutch of collective identity and sufficient corporate enthusiasm to create the essential forum of one or more reviews. The publication of Jammes's manifesto by the *Mercure* must be seen in the context of Valette's attempt to unite in one title all that was best in new writing. Neither Jammes nor Valette realized that homogenous literary impulses needed discrete forums, with the result that the *Mercure's* factitiously eclectic experiment in literary publishing has led to a blurring in the critical understanding of Jammes's aims, and to an over-personalized account of his differences with Gide, which were about matters of social and moral principle rather than simply style and temperament. What Jammes stood for in moral terms was a spiritual purity, however attained, which would lead to joy and a harmony between man and nature. Less aware of nature's potential hostility than Giono, he was more of a poet and less of a visionary, although, like Giono for most of his life, Jammes shunned Paris, publicity, and the literary life. With just a touch of arrogance, Jammes expected his fellow authors to wish to make the pilgrimage to the Pyrenees. It is a tribute to his stature that so many of them did.

The seven paragraphs of Jammes's manifesto laid down the unique literary procedure, which was the depiction of the truth, by which he meant, rather like Claudel, the proclamation of the major truths of creation and the praise of God; "Toutes choses sont bonnes à décrire lorsqu'elles sont naturelles, aussi bien un thyrse qu'une paire de bas (Everything is suitable material for description if it is natural, a staff as well as a pair of stockings)." In *Un jour* Jammes had already used the example of a pair of stockings eaten by a cow. On the manifesto's publication he was instantly looked to as the leader of a movement of Christian simplicity, reincarnating the values associated with Francis of Assisi. In fact, Jammes's literary paradigm included elements of rusticity, of exoticism, of chastely sensual hedonism from which all sense of guilt had been exorcized, and microscopic realism in the veneration for all natural objects. He moved progressively further towards the spiritual climate of the Song of Songs in his later work.

The key is firmly announced with *Un jour*, in which nothing very much happens: life is not a series of crises, and real drama needs no climax. One day, like any other, is capable of giving and yielding the whole of life's essential demands. The characters are a 26-year-old poet, the same age as Jammes, his soul, in the form of a girl in white heard only by himself, his parents, his fiancée, the maid, and the dog. The setting is rustic, domestic, and contented. In the first scene the poet's soul welcomes him home from his shooting, and the poet tells of his day, empties the game bag, and relates how the cow ate the stockings put out to dry on a hedge. His father comes in wearing a straw hat and holding a watering can. The table is laid, and only the conversation is too full of moral lessons not to be contrived.

In the second scene the poet and his fiancée are in the garden. She is cheerful, he morose. They exchange vows. The third scene is in the kitchen after supper. The poet appears anxious, smokes his pipe, and is soothed by his mother. "Who told you to talk to me like this? God." In the last scene, at night, cowbells are heard, and only two words are spoken, "Des cloches (The bells)," and the poet, having stared into the darkness, his elbows on the sill, shuts his window, puts down his pipe, and kneels to say his prayers. At the next window the silhouette of his fiancée is seen, also kneeling and praying. This is very nearly symbolist

drama, even using the silhouette in a way spectacularly to be developed by Claudel, and it is about the perennial aspiration to a sensual and physical fulfilment which is also pure and spiritually satisfying. What comes across is not any pre-Raphaelite sentimentality, into which the piece could so easily have degenerated, but the primeval, if culturally conditioned, longing in Western man to integrate his spiritual, emotional, and physical needs. There is Claudel's view of the poet's function, too:

Les poètes pèsent au ventre des femmes plus que les autres parce que les poètes qui vont naître portent le monde

(Poets weigh more heavily in the wombs of women than do others because poets about to be born carry in themselves the world)

La Naissance du poète takes the symbolist technique and the theme of the poet's function even further. The first part takes place in heaven. It is snowing on earth, where the poet is to be born in the countryside. The characters include a choir, angels, God, and spirits, and a dying soul ascending meets the soul descending into the poet to be born. The universe rejoices at the birth of the poet, whose function is to glorify it. The second part takes place on earth and the third at sea, while the fourth unites heaven, earth, and sea. The work was modestly successful. Régnier, Samain, Mallarmé, Paul Fort, and Gide all liked it. Less surprisingly, it brought a letter from Claudel. *La Mort du poète* presents again the family from *Un jour*. The poet dies on the feast of Corpus Christi, offering his death to God. The poem is important in the context of Jammes's oeuvre because he intervenes in the narration himself, indicating that the poem, while closing the triptych, also reflects a personal mood.

De l'Angelus de l'aube à l'Angelus du soir, part of which is dedicated to Mallarmé, is a dense collection in which all Jammes's major poetic concerns are represented. The almost perfunctory philosophical attitudes are not intended to be important, but the celebration of creation now takes into account death, suffering, and incomprehension. The versification is loose and the syntax, although declamatory, is deliberately that of the simple prose statement. The atmosphere is rustic, and the world which is celebrated is that of the countryside and of rustic living, sharply observed and movingly depicted. The effects are cumulative, often deriving from parallels and antitheses of syntax, and there are very few isolated striking lines. It is a mark of Jammes's powerful imagination that the Guadeloupe for which he feels nostalgia, but has never seen, is so authentically portrayed. (He had discovered his grandfather's letters in the house.) The idealized female figure is often taken from the past, voluptuously but not unchastely desired, and the poetry is created, in the absence of cadence, metre, rhyme, and rhythm, purely by sound values, syntactical simplicity, lexical variety, and the overpowering strength of the imagery, helped occasionally by the deliberate flouting of classical norms while continuing to use classical forms.

The novels, too, are innovative. *Clara d'Ellébeuse; ou, L'Histoire d'une ancienne jeune fille* is dedicated to its heroine and is a prose poem. Clara is 17 and morbidly hypersensitive, oppressed by feelings of guilt and inadequacy. She is intrigued by a gravestone naming a "Laura Lopez" who seems to have some connection with an Uncle Joachim who died on Guadeloupe. Two letters from Uncle Joachim which she finds disentangle the mystery: Laura, made pregnant by her uncle, was sent back to France, where she committed suicide. Clara falls in love and finds herself alone with her handsome poet, Roger Fauchereuse, in the house where Laura had lived, now a ruin. Clara leans against Roger, who strokes her neck, which is enough to make her feel the same guilt as she projects into Laura. Condemning herself to expiate a sin she has not committed, and in spite of efforts to help her, she poisons herself with laudanum on Laura's grave. The essential Jammes is all here. The desirable, untouchable girl, the country setting, the exoticism of Guadeloupe, a castle, a country churchyard, a sense of family, descriptions of nature, highly coloured images, and swift narrative prose rhythms. There is one sentence about Clara's death: "It was on a clear March morning that Clara d'Ellébeuse killed herself." There follows a magnificently figured description of the sky, the trees, the birds, and the flowers, the sights, colours, and sounds of the countryside, and in the background the Pyrenees, "trembling in the distance, like blocks of ice on which floated blue and snow." The descriptive writing is vivid, precise, startling, and unremittingly exact.

The heroine of *Almaïde d'Etremont* is a 25-year-old orphan who lives with a sick and elderly uncle who acts as her tutor. All her friends are getting married and, desperate to give and receive affection herself, she plays at lovemaking with a 16-year-old local boy, Guilhem. He is also a local guide and falls on the mountain, killing himself. Almaïde finds that she is pregnant with his child. Her uncle dies, and she is looked after by M. d'Astin, a neighbour, to whom she confides her secret. He confesses to her a love affair he once had on a boat with a Chinese girl who had died without leaving him a child. Almaïde has her child on a beautiful autumn day. M. d'Astin dies, leaving his wealth to the child. This is another prose poem, its psychology as sensitive as its descriptions are vivid, in which physical, emotional, and spiritual fulfilment come together in an almost believable world, so idealized is the plane on which the narrative moves. Technically it is a brilliant piece of writing, resorting almost exclusively to register of language, established through the meticulously precise use of highly coloured description and penetrating analysis, to communicate its poetic vision of a fully integrated human life.

Le Roman du lièvre is another poem, this time in the guise of a fable rather than a novel, in spite of its title. The work starts with a minute description of the hare's activities, its excitements, anxieties, cunning, catnaps, meals, and mating. One day Francis of Assisi passes by, followed by a wolf, a bitch, a lamb, some hawks, and some doves. Hare is invited to join the troop, whose killer instincts have, where appropriate, been overcome, but famine arrives and all except hare die. Francis tells hare to lead his dead companions to the animals' paradise, where, at rest, they leave him to wander around. Hare cannot be happy with nothing to worry about and pines for the agonies of terrestrial existence. Francis allows him back to earth, where he is immediately shot. Unalloyed, insulated satisfactions are impossible. A surfeit of spiritual satisfactions awakens earthly needs. Again, what makes the poem is the astonishing effectiveness of its exquisitely figured language, reduced to the simplest of syntactical levels.

The central features of Jammes's verse and prose do not change after 1903, except to diminish in spiritual tension. The images simplify and the psychology becomes less urgently probing. It has been suggested that some of the later work is rather thin. Towards the end, as Jammes attacks values other than those he celebrates, the imaginative vigour diminishes. His real strength lies in his poetic craftsmanship and the extraordinary power of his descriptive prose poetry.

PUBLICATIONS

Verse

Six sonnets, 1891
Vers, 1892
Un jour, 1895
La Naissance du poète, 1897
Quatorze prières, 1898
De l'Angelus de l'aube à l'Angelus du soir, 1888–1897, 1898
Le Poète et l'oiseau, 1899
La Jeune Fille nue, 1899
Le Deuil des primevères, 1888–1900, 1901
Le Triomphe de la vie, 1900–1901, 1902
Clairières dans le ciel, 1902–1906, 1906
L'Eglise habillée de feuilles, 1906
Poèmes mesurés, 1908
Rayons de miel, 1908
Les Géorgiques chrétiennes, 3 vols., 1911–12
Feuilles dans le vent, 1913
Cinq prières pour le temps de la guerre, 1916
La Vierge et les sonnets, 1919
Epitaphes, 1921
Le Tombeau de Jean de la Fontaine, 1921
La Brebis égarée, 1923
Les Quatrains, 4 vols., 1923–25
Brindilles pour rallumer la foi, 1925
Ma France poétique, 1926
Diane, 1928
L'Arc-en-ciel des amours, 1931
De tout temps à jamais, 1935
Sources, 1936
Elégies et poésies diverses, 1943
La Grâce, 1946

Prose

Clara d'Ellébeuse; ou, L'Histoire d'une ancienne jeune fille, 1899
Almaïde d'Etremont; ou, L'Histoire d'une jeune fille passionnée, 1901
Le Roman du lièvre, 1903
Pomme d'Anis; ou, L'Histoire d'une jeune fille infirme, 1904
Pensée des jardins, 1906
Ma fille Bernadette, 1910
Le Rosaire au soleil, 1916
Monsieur le Curé d'Ozeron, 1918
Une vierge, 1919
Le Noël de mes enfants, 1919
La Rose à Marie, 1919
Le Poète rustique, 1920
Le Bon Dieu chez les enfants, 1921
Mémoires, 3 vols.:
    De l'âge divin à l'âge ingrat, 1921
    L'Amour, les muses et la chasse, 1922

L

LABICHE, Eugène (Marin), 1815–1888.

Dramatist.

LIFE

Eugène Labiche was born in Paris on 6 May 1815 into a comfortably off, bourgeois family. His father owned factories in Paris that made syrup and starch, and he was descended from a long line of lawyer-landowners in the Beauce region. After attending the Collège Bourbon, Labiche went on a grand tour of Italy and Switzerland in 1834. His family expected him to be a lawyer, and he studied for a law degree, but gravitated towards the theatre. He wrote drama criticism for the *Revue du Théâtre* until his first success as a playwright in 1838 with *Monsieur de Coyllin; ou, L'Homme infiniment poli* at the new Palais-Royal theatre, which opened under Dormeuil in 1831.

His earliest play, *La Cuvette d'eau* (1837), has been lost. From 1838 to 1877 he was constantly busy writing comedies, apart from an interruption in 1842 when he married a rich heiress, Adèle Hubert. Since it was considered slightly disreputable to write plays for a living, Labiche had to promise Adèle's family that he would give it up, but after a year, he was so obviously miserable that Adèle herself encouraged him to start writing again.

The accepted method of creating comedy and vaudeville in the mid-19th century was to use at least one collaborator, and Labiche had help with almost all his plays. The team approach ensured speed of production, which was essential, as Labiche sometimes had up to six plays in performance at a time. Altogether he wrote over 170 in his lifetime. The only occasion when a collaborator's contribution was greater than Labiche's was when Ernest Legouvé worked with him on *La Cigale chez les fourmis*. In all his other co-productions it was Labiche who did most of the work.

Labiche not only had a gift for the standard action-packed vaudeville, but was also an acute observer of society. He was himself from the background he portrayed on stage, the second-generation bourgeoisie whose inherited wealth freed them from the necessity of getting their hands dirty by earning a living. He entertained his middle-class audiences with exaggerated portraits of their own pretensions and obsessions, and they laughed without taking offence. His plays have preserved the leisure class of the Second Empire, dominated by money, manipulating advantageous marriages for their offspring, speaking an affected language which they hoped would sound refined, and dabbling in adultery.

Although he ridiculed bourgeois attitudes on the stage, Labiche was a political conservative in real life. He stood as a candidate for the legislative assembly in 1848, opposing republican and socialist reforms, and advocating freedom for employers rather than workers. He was not elected. After the first performance of *Rue de l'Homme-armé, numéro 8 bis* at the Variétés theatre on 24 September 1848, Labiche and his co-writer Eugène Nyon were condemned to death by a revolutionary club from the Faubourg Poissonnière.

Most of Labiche's comedies were performed in the boulevard theatres, the Gymnase under Monsigny, the Palais-Royal, and the Vaudeville, reopened under that name only in 1868, but occasionally he aimed higher. *Moi* was first performed at the Théâtre-Français on 21 March 1864. It was less successful than Labiche's usual type of play. He liked to cast particular actors in particular parts: Grassot and Hyacinthe were regularly "bouffons," and Geoffroy so often played Labiche's bourgeois father figure that the critic Francisque Sarcey declared: "Geoffroy, c'était le Bourgeois." Sarah Bernhardt played Douchinka in *Un mari qui lance sa femme* in 1864, when she was 20.

In 1853 Labiche bought a château and estate in Sologne and became a part-time gentleman farmer, while continuing to write plays at a phenomenal rate. He divided his time between Sologne and Paris, and served as mayor of Souvigny. He wisely stayed on his estate during the Franco-Prussian War of 1870. After the failure of *La Clé* at the Palais-Royal in 1877, Labiche realized that public taste was changing and decided to stop writing for the stage. He then concentrated on preparing his *Théâtre complet* for publication, but included only 57 plays, a third of his total output. These comedies in published form were a revelation to people who had enjoyed them in performance but classified them as typically superficial vaudevilles; Labiche now emerged as a worthwhile social commentator in the tradition of Molière. When he was elected to the Académie Française in 1880, he dazzled his contemporaries with his reception speech. He spent the rest of his life farming his estate in Sologne, and died of heart disease in Paris on 23 January 1888.

WORKS

The central character of Labiche's comedies is the wealthy bourgeois whose self-confidence is based on material success. He becomes laughable when he is exposed to situations he cannot cope with, often because he has stepped out of his familiar surroundings. This may be the result of a physical journey, as in *Le Voyage de Monsieur Perrichon*, or because he is moving in a different social circle, at a lower level than his own, in *Edgard et sa bonne*, or a higher one, as in *Un mari qui lance sa femme*, or *Le Point de mire*. Labiche was aware that a social class defines itself by its use of language, and he captured the tone of the newly affluent bourgeoisie. In some cases this theme was so important that it provided the title of the play—*Les Precieux, La Grammaire, Un gros mot*. The inability of the bourgeois to adapt to unexpected events is reflected in his inability to express himself without the support of clichés and pomposity.

Labiche's achievement was in raising vaudeville from its rather disparaged position as light entertainment for the illiterate classes to the level of memorable character comedy. One of his best, and best-known, plays is *Un chapeau de paille d'Italie*, which Zola described as having created a genre, to be known in the UK as "Palais-Royal" farce. It was obviously going to be different even before it opened. Dormeuil, the manager of the Montansier theatre, thought it so absurd that it was bound to flop; indeed, he left town rather than sit through the first performance on 14 August 1851. But the public was delighted and *Un chapeau de paille* broke box-office records by running for 300 performances.

Labiche exploits the traditional abundant movement of vaudeville, making it the theme of the play, which consists of a hectic chase around Paris in pursuit of a straw hat. The central character, Fadinard, goes for a drive in the park on the morning of his wedding day and his horse eats a straw hat hanging on a tree. The hat belongs to a married woman, Anaïs, who is temporarily in the bushes with a soldier. She and the soldier, Emile, follow Fadinard home and insist that he replace the hat because it was a present from Anaïs's husband. They refuse to leave until Fadinard cooperates, and Emile starts destroying the furniture. Fadinard promises to do his best, but his wedding guests arrive and whisk him off to get married.

Throughout the play, the wedding party assumes that every event that takes place is part of the wedding, though the audience knows better. On the way to the ceremony, Fadinard stops at a milliner's, where he is embarrassed to meet a former lover, and the wedding guests think they have arrived at City Hall. Having learnt that a baroness has just bought the kind of hat he needs, Fadinard sets off for her house, managing to fit in the marriage service on the way. The baroness thinks he is an Italian tenor who has come to sing to her dinner guests; the wedding party thinks it is in a restaurant and eats the baroness's dinner. The baroness has given the hat to her goddaughter, so Fadinard hurries to the goddaughter's house and finds a gentleman trying to recover from a headache. The wedding guests think they are in Fadinard's house and settle in for the night. Fadinard explains his predicament to the owner of the house, who happens to be Anaïs's husband, and they rush off together to Fadinard's house. The situation is saved by Fadinard's deaf uncle, Vézinet, who has brought the bride a wedding present of an Italian straw hat identical to the missing one. The characters convince Anaïs's husband that she never lost her hat in the first place and has not behaved improperly. The bride's father, Nonancourt, had been having grave doubts about Fadinard's suitability as a son-in-law, but is enchanted when the story is explained to him: "C'est beau, c'est chevaleresque, c'est français! (It's splendid! It's chivalrous! It's French!)," which was exactly what the public thought, too.

The events that assail Fadinard in *Un chapeau de paille* may appear to be arbitrary, but he actually sets them in motion himself through being mercenary. His horse was given the opportunity to eat the hat because Fadinard dropped his silver-handled whip and stopped to pick it up—not because he particularly needed it, but because it was expensive. His marriage to Nonancourt's daughter has been arranged for financial reasons, and many of Labiche's plays show bourgeois parents disposing of their daughters to the highest bidder: "Nous nous sommes dit:

Célimare n'est pas jeune, Célimare n'est pas beau; mais la jeunesse, la beauté, ça passe, tandis que quarante mille livres de rente, quand on a de l'ordre, ça reste! (We said to ourselves: Célimare isn't young and he isn't handsome; but youth and good looks fade away, whereas an income of forty thousand pounds, if you're well organized, will go on and on!)" (*Célimare le bien-aimé*).

In *Le Voyage de Monsieur Perrichon* the central character is literally "dépaysé (in another country)" because he takes his family to Switzerland. Monsieur Perrichon made his fortune in the carriage-building business and celebrates his retirement with a trip to Chamonix. His daughter Henriette has two suitors, who both follow her to Switzerland in the hope of impressing her father; she herself has no say in deciding whom she is to marry. M. Perrichon falls down a crevasse in the Great Glacier and is rescued by Henriette's suitor Armand. He is initially grateful, but is soon distracted by the more cynical suitor, Daniel, who deliberately "falls" into the glacier so that M. Perrichon can have the satisfaction of rescuing him.

M. Perrichon has a disagreement with a fellow guest in the hotel, Major Mathieu, who corrected a spelling mistake of Perrichon's in the hotel visitors' book and is insulted by Perrichon's response. When they get back to Paris, the major challenges M. Perrichon to a duel. Since duelling is illegal, M. Perrichon is confident that the police will prevent it, and writes a letter to the prefect of police to let him know what is happening. He then pretends to be brave about accepting the challenge, not knowing that his wife and Daniel have also written letters on the subject, and Armand has arranged for the major to be imprisoned for debt, so as to save M. Perrichon from having to fight. But the major escapes from prison and M. Perrichon is humiliated by having to apologize. He is ungrateful to Armand and inclined to let Daniel marry his daughter, until he overhears Daniel explaining his strategy to Armand: "Les hommes ne s'attachent point à nous en raison des services que nous leur rendons, mais en raison de ceux qu'ils nous rendent (People aren't fond of us because of the things we do for them, but because of the things they do for us)." M. Perrichon is furious with Daniel for exploiting him, and chooses Armand as his son-in-law, the right decision, for the wrong reasons, but both acceptable to the audience with which Labiche connives.

Collections

Oeuvres complètes, 1967–
Théâtre complet de Eugène Labiche (about a third of the plays, with a preface by Emile Augier), 10 vols., 1878–79
Théâtre choisi (includes *La Grammaire, L'Affaire de la rue de Lourcine, La Poudre aux yeux, La Cigale chez les fourmis, Les Deux timides, Embrassons-nous Folleville!*), 1895
Eugène Labiche, Théâtre, 5 vols., 1949–50

Fiction

Etudes de moeurs: la clef des champs, 1839

Plays

Monsieur de Coyllin; ou, L'Homme infiniment poli, with Marc-Michel and Lefranc, 1838

L'Avocat Loubet, with Marc-Michel, 1838

L'Article 960; ou, La Donation, by Ancelot and "Paul Dandré" (Labiche, Lefranc, and Marc-Michel), 1839

Le Fin Mot, by "Paul Dandré" (Labiche, Lefranc, and Marc-Michel), 1840

Bocquet, père et fils; ou, Le Chemin le plus long, with Laurencin and Marc-Michel, 1840

Le Lierre et l'ormeau, with Lefranc and Monnier, 1841

Les Circonstances atténuantes, with Mélesville and Lefranc, 1842

L'Homme de paille, with Lefranc, 1843

Le Major Cravachon, with Lefranc and Jessé, 1844

Deux papas très bien; ou, La Grammaire de Chicard, with Lefranc, 1845

Le Roi des Frontins, with Lefranc, 1845

L'Ecole buissonnière, with Lefranc, 1845

L'Enfant de la maison, with Varin and Nyon, 1845

Frisette, with Lefranc, 1846; as *John and Jeannette*, adapted by L. MacHale and others, 1884

Mademoiselle ma femme, with Lefranc, 1846

Rocambole le bateleur, with Lefranc, 1846

L'Inventeur de la poudre, with Lefranc and Nyon, 1846

L'Avocat-pédicure, with Lefranc, 1847

La Chasse aux jobards, with Lefranc, 1847

Un homme sanguin, with Lefranc, 1847

L'Art de ne pas donner d'étrennes, with Lefranc, 1847

Un jeune homme pressé, 1848

Le Club champenois, with Lefranc, 1848

Oscar XXVIII, with Decourcelle and Barbier, 1848

Une chaîne anglaise, with Saint-Yves, 1848

Histoire de rire, with Saint-Yves, 1848

Agénor le dangereux, with Decourcelle and Karl, 1848

A bas la famille; ou, Les Banquets, with Lefranc, 1848

Madame Veuve Larifla, with Choler, 1849

Les Manchettes d'un vilain, with Lefranc and Saint-Yves, 1849

Une dent sous Louis XV (monologue), with Lefranc, 1849

Trompe-la-balle, with Lefranc, 1849

Exposition des produits de la République, with Dumanoir and Clairville, 1849

Rue de L'Homme-armé, numéro 8 bis, with Nyon, 1849

Traversin et couverture (parody of "Toussaint-Louverture"), with Varin, 1850

Le Sopha, with Mélesville and Desnoyer, 1850

Un bal en robe de chambre, with Marc-Michel, 1850

Les Petits Moyens, with Lemoine and Decourcelle, 1850

Les Prétendus de Gimblette, by "Paul Dandré" (Labiche) and "Senneif" (Matharel and Fiennes), 1850

Embrassons-nous Folleville!, with Lefranc, 1850

Un garçon de chez Véry, 1850

La Fille bien gardée, with Marc-Michel, 1850

Une clarinette qui passe, with Marc-Michel, 1851

La Femme qui perd ses jarretières, with Marc-Michel, 1851

On demande des culottières, with Marc- Michel, 1851

Mamz'elle fait ses dents, with Marc-Michel, 1851

En manches de chemise, with Lefranc and Nyon, 1851; as an operetta, with music by Villebichot, 1869

Un chapeau de paille d'Italie, with Marc-Michel, 1851; as *Horse Eats Hat* (produced 1936); as *An Italian Straw Hat*, 1955

Maman Sabouleux, with Marc-Michel, 1852

Un monsieur qui prend la mouche, with Marc-Michel, 1852

Les Suites d'un premier lit, with Marc-Michel, 1852

Le Misanthrope et l'Auvergnat, with Lubize and Siraudin, 1852

Edgard et sa bonne, with Marc-Michel, 1852

Soufflez-moi dans l'oeil, with Marc-Michel, 1852

Canadar père et fils, by "Laurencin" (Labiche) and Marc-Michel, 1852

Deux gouttes d'eau, with Bourgeois, 1852

Piccolet, with Lefranc and Montjoie, 1852

La Chasse aux corbeaux, with Marc-Michel, 1853

Le Chevalier des dames, with Marc-Michel, 1853

Mon Isménie, with Marc-Michel, 1853

Une charge de cavalerie, with Moreau and Delacour, 1853

Un ami acharné, with Jolly, 1853

On dira des bêtises, with Delacour and Deslandes, 1853

Un notaire à marier, with Marc-Michel and Beauplan, 1853

Un ut de poitrine, with Lefranc, 1853

Un feu de cheminée, with Beauplan, 1853

Deux profonds scélérats, with Varin, 1854; as *Two Gay Deceivers; or, Black, White and Grey*, n.d.

Un mari qui prend du ventre, with Marc-Michel, 1854

Espagnolas et boyardinos, with Marc-Michel, 1854

Otez votre fille s'il vous plaît, with Marc-Michel, 1854

Les Marquises de la fourchette, with Choler, 1854

La Perle de la Canebière, with Marc-Michel, 1855

Monsieur votre fille, with Marc-Michel, 1855

Les Précieux, with Marc-Michel and Lefranc, 1855

Si jamais je te pince!…, with Marc-Michel, 1856

Un monsieur qui a brûlé une dame, with Bourgeois, 1856

Les Cheveux de ma femme, with Battu, 1856

En pension chez son groom, with Marc-Michel, 1856

Monsieur de Saint-Cadenas, with Marc-Michel, 1856

La Fiancée du bon coin, with Marc-Michel, 1856

Mesdames de Montenfriche, with Marc-Michel, 1856

L'Affaire de la rue de Lourcine, with Monnier and Martin, 1857

Les Noces de Bouchencoeur, with Monnier and Martin, 1857

Le Bras d'Ernest, with Leroux, 1857

La Dame aux jambes d'azur, with Marc-Michel, 1857

Le Secrétaire de Madame, with Marc-Michel, 1857

Le Clou aux maris, with Moreau and Mme Réal, 1858

L'Avare en gants jaunes, with Bourgeois, 1858

Un gendre en surveillance, with Marc-Michel, 1858

Je croque ma tante, with Marc-Michel, 1858

Madame est aux eaux, with Vilmar, 1858

Le Calife de la rue Saint-Bon, with Marc-Michel, 1858

Le Baron de Fourchevif, with Jolly, 1859

Les Petites Mains, with Martin, 1859

En avant les Chinois, with Delacour, 1859

L'Avocat d'un Grec, with Lefranc, 1859

L'Amour, un fort volume: prix: 3 fr 50, with Martin, 1859

L'Ecole des Arthur, with Bourgeois, 1859

L'Omelette à la Follembuche (comic opera), with Marc-Michel, with music by Delibes, 1859

Le Rouge-gorge, with Choler, 1859

J'invite le colonel, with Marc-Michel, 1860

La Sensitive, with Delacour, 1860

Les Deux timides, with Marc-Michel, 1860; as *The Two Cowards*, 1915

Le Voyage de Monsieur Perrichon, with Martin, 1860; as *The Journey of M. Perrichon*, 1924

Un gros mot, with Dumoustier, 1860

Le Voyage autour de ma marmite, with Delacour, 1860

La Famille de l'horloger, with Deslandes, 1860

J'ai compromis ma femme, with Delacour, 1861
Les Vivacités du capitaine Tic, with Martin, 1861
La Poudre aux yeux, with Martin, 1861; as *Throwing Dust in People's Eyes*, 1930
L'Amour en sabots, with Delacour, 1861
Le Mystère de la rue Rousselet, with Marc- Michel, 1861
La Station Champbaudet, with Marc-Michel, 1862
Les Petits Oiseaux, with Delacour, 1862; as *A Pair of Spectacles*, adapted by S. Grundy, 1899
Le Premier Pas, with Delacour, 1862
Les 37 sous de Monsieur Montaudoin, with Martin, 1863
Célimare le bien-aimé, with Delacour, 1863
La Dame au petit chien, with Demoustier, 1863
Permettez, madame!, with Delacour, 1863
Le Point de mire, with Delacour, 1864
La Commode de Victorine, with Martin, 1864
La Cagnotte, with Delacour, 1864
Moi, with Martin, 1864
Un mari qui lance sa femme, with Deslandes, 1864
Premier prix de piano, with Delacour, 1865
L'Homme qui manque le coche, with Delacour, 1865
La Bergère de la rue Monthabor, with Delacour, 1865
Le Voyage en Chine (comic opera), with Delacour, with music by Bazin, 1865
Un pied dans le crime, with Choler, 1866
La Grammaire, with Jolly, 1867; as *Grammar*, 1915
La Main leste, with Martin, 1867
Le Fils du brigadier (comic opera), with Delacour, with music by Massé, 1867
Le Chemin de fer, with Delacour and Choler, 1867
Le Petit Voyage, 1868
Le Corricolo (comic opera), with Delacour, with music by Poise, 1868
Le Papa du prix d'honneur, with Barrière, 1868
Le Choix d'un gendre, with Delacour, 1869
Le Dossier de Rosafol, with Delacour, 1869
Le Plus heureux des trois, with Gondinet, 1870
Le Cachemire X.-B.-T., with Nus, 1870
Le Livre bleu, with Blum, 1871
L'Ennemie, with Delacour, 1871
Il est de la police, with Leroy, 1872
La Mémoire d'Hortense, with Delacour, 1872
Doit-on le dire?, with Duru, 1873
29 degrès à l'ombre, 1873
Garantie dix ans, with Gille, 1874
La Pièce de Chambertin, with Dufrenois, 1874
Madame est trop belle, with Duru, 1874
Brûlons Voltaire!, with Leroy, 1874
Les Trente millions de Gladiator, with Gille, 1875
Les Samedis de Madame, with Duru, 1875
Un mouton à l'entresol, with Segond, 1875
Le Prix Martin, with Augier, 1876
La Cigale chez les fourmis, with Legouvé, 1876
La Clé, with Duru, 1877; as *Artful Cards*, 1877
La Lettre chargée, 1877
L'Amour de l'art, 1877
Un coup de rasoir, 1878

Critical studies

Zola, Emile, *Nos auteurs dramatiques*, 1881

Soupault, Philippe, *Labiche, sa vie, son oeuvre*, 1945; revised edition, 1964
Autrusseau, J., *Labiche et son théâtre*, 1971
Pronko, L., *Eugène Labiche and Georges Feydeau*, 1982

LACRETELLE, Jacques de, 1888–1985

Novelist.

Lacretelle was born in the Château de Cormatin near Mâcon, into a recently ennobled family of liberal barristers. He was brought up partly in the Middle East, suffered from poor health, and was educated by an English governess and a series of private tutors. After his father's death in 1898 his mother took her two children to Paris, where the family lived at the outer edges of artistic Parisian circles, coming into contact with Daudet, Hugo, Cortot, Hahn, leavening the dough of failed writers. Lacretelle was unsuccessful at school, failing the baccalauréat twice. He then went into banking, a career at which he proved inept. After a period of active service during the war, he travelled widely in Europe.

La Vie inquiète de Jean Hermelin emerged out of the anonymity of a series of provincial hotel rooms. After three rejections Grasset offered to publish it, partly at Lacretelle's own expense. The book is clearly derivative from Proust, who liked Lacretelle. Critical reception of it was mixed. Lacretelle's brother was a literary journalist and Lacretelle himself now began writing articles, reviews, and short stories. Proust got the *Nouvelle Revue Française* (q.v.) to provide financial backing and Lacretelle began the novel for which he is now alone remembered, *Silbermann*. Largely inspired by Gide, it concerns the difficulties experienced by a precocious young Jew in fitting into French society. Ultimately he gives up and focuses simply on making money. Severely classical in style the book missed the prix Goncourt but was awarded the Prix Fémina.

There followed a four-volume "roman-fleuve" called *Les Hauts Ponts*, which cemented Lacretelle's reputation. It is a long, poetically sensitive story of provincial life centring on an attachment to property. *La Bonifas* of 1925 is now virtually forgotten, although it was translated into English, and *Amour nuptial* of 1929 obtained the Grand Prix du Roman of the Académie Française. Lacretelle was elected to the Académie Française in 1936. His other works include a novelette, *Deux coeurs simples*, and autobiographical volumes.

PUBLICATIONS

Fiction

La Vie inquiète de Jean Hermelin, 1920
Silbermann, 1922; as *Silbermann* (in English), 1923
La Bonifas, 1925; as *Marie Bonifas*, (in English) 1927
Amour nuptial, 1929; as *A Man's Life*, 1931

Le Retour de Silbermann, 1929
Les Hauts Ponts: Sabine; Les Fiançailles; Années d'espérance;
    La Monnaie de plomb, 1932–35
Le Pour et le contre, 2 vols., 1946
Deux coeurs simples, 1953

Play

Une visite en été, 1953

Critical study

Alden, Douglas, *Jacques de Lacretelle: An Intellectual Itiner-
    ary*, 1958

————

LAFORGUE, Jules, 1860–1887.

Poet.

Laforgue was born in Montevideo, where his father was a
teacher. At the age of six he was brought back to France by his
mother, and went to school in Tarbes, where he and his brother
Emile lived with cousins. His father came back briefly in 1867,
and in 1869 Laforgue entered the Tarbes lycée. His parents
returned for good only in 1875, and the following year the family moved to Paris, where Laforgue attended the Lycée Fontanes
(now Condorcet). His mother died in 1877. In 1879 his father
moved house in Paris and himself returned to Tarbes, leaving
Laforgue and his sister Marie in the Paris flat. That same year
Laforgue, who had clearly been deprived of parental affection as
a child, began to publish verse in the Toulouse reviews *L'Enfer*
and *La Guêpe*. At 20 he was still living with his sister, poor, ill-
dressed, and saddened, he later tells us, by the joyousness of the
surrounding neighbourhood.

He got to know Gustave Kahn and Paul Bourget, and must
have met Maupassant, and probably Moréas and Coppée, at the
"Hydropathes" (see Symbolism), but led a life that was essentially solitary, spending his time reading for five hours a day in
the big national libraries and living, he says, off "two eggs and
a glass of water" a day. He kept a diary and wondered, on
rereading it two years later, how he had survived. His Catholicism had disintegrated and all that was left to him was the vague
and pessimistic legacy of Schopenhauer, in so many ways the
philosopher of romanticism (q. v.). That led in 1880 to a crisis
in which he produced a volume of verse in five parts, significantly entitled "Lama Sabactani," "Angoisses," "Les poèmes de
la mort," "Les poèmes du Spleen," and "Résignations." The volume, called *Le Sanglot de la terre*, was never published. By the
end of 1882 Hartmann's philosophy had led Laforgue to reject
his own early poems, fragments of which were published only
posthumously in the third volume of the 1901 *Oeuvres complètes*, "Mélanges posthumes." Laforgue also sketched an autobiographical novel, *Le Raté*, in which *Le Sanglot* is referred to
as a "danse macabre du XIXe siècle." Elsewhere he speaks of

"l'épopée de l'humanité, la danse macabre des derniers temps
de la planète (the epic of humanity, the death dance of the last
days of the planet)," suggesting an apocalyptic epic of vast
romantic scope that would outdo Hugo's *Légende des siècles*,
Vigny's *Les Destinées*, and Leconte de Lisle's oriental poems.

In 1881 the crisis was over. Laforgue became secretary to the
director of *La Gazette des Beaux-Arts*, Charles Ephrussi, then
writing his great study of Dürer, and wrote a novel entitled
Stéphane Vassiliew. His sister returned to Tarbes to nurse their
father, who died of tuberculosis in November 1881, and
Laforgue took furnished rooms. Literary friends obtained for
him the post of reader to Empress Augusta, grandmother of Wilhelm II and he left on 29 November to spend five years in Germany. While based in Berlin, he also visited Baden, Hamburg,
and Koblenz. By December 1882 his intellectual evolution was
virtually complete, and he had a flash of insight: his aesthetic
would be dominated by Hartmann's theory of the determining
role of the unconscious, combined with Darwinian transformism and the psychological theories of Helmholz on the harmon-
ics of vowel sounds. This eclectic synthesis must have done
more to resolve a psychological crisis with a moment of exaltation than to have laid the foundation of any rigorous aesthetic,
but during 1883 Laforgue would write most of his first great collection, *Les Complaintes de Jules Laforgue*. His aesthetic of
progress, influenced also by Hegel and Taine, is refracted
through Hartmann's ideas on the subconscious, and necessarily
becomes an aesthetic of the individual and the transitory. The
Complaintes appeared in 1885, as did *L'Imitation de Notre-
Dame la Lune*.

Life at court was dull but comfortable, full of distracting
social obligations. Laforgue nevertheless continued to publish:
Le Concile féerique in 1886, his translation of Walt Whitman's
The Leaves of Grass, and the six prose *Moralités légendaires*,
parodying well-known stories and published posthumously in
1887. In 1886 he also wrote the 12 poems posthumously collected as *Derniers vers* and *Des fleurs de bonne volonté*. He
started English lessons with a Miss Leah Lee, whom he married
in London on 31 December 1886. The couple returned to Paris,
but Laforgue died of tuberculosis on 20 August 1887. Leah died
of the same disease a year later.

WORKS

Laforgue's importance as a poet is at least partly historical,
although much injustice has been done to his verse by critical
concentration on its influence rather than its achievement. His
aesthetic explored what was to be an important avenue out of
late romanticism towards symbolism. Although he scrapped his
early verse, not all that has been posthumously published as *Le
Sanglot de la terre* can originally have been intended for that
volume, and Laforgue incorporated into *Derniers vers* what he
wanted to retain of *Des fleurs de bonne volonté*. The 12 poems
themselves of *Derniers vers* have known an extraordinary
growth of critical acclaim since September 1936, when Martin
Turnell, writing in *Scrutiny*, called them "the most important
single poem published in Europe since the seventeenth century."
Between the first collection, which he suppressed, and the last,
published posthumously, Laforgue undertook a remarkable
range of formal experiment, striving towards a verse form which
would show "the mind simultaneously possessed by diverse and

even conflicting feelings" (Turnell). Until recently, the only French critic to write perceptively about Laforgue was Léautaud, although in England he was admired by Symons as early as *The Symbolist Movement in Literature* (1899), and later by the young T.S. Eliot and Ezra Pound.

The rejected *Le Sanglot de la terre* was conceived as an "Oeuvre de prophète des temps nouveaux (a work of prophecy of the new era)." It would have been a compendium of despair, carrying on in the vein of Lamartine, Vigny, and Hugo's philosophical lyricism, but owing much to *Le Spleen de Paris* by Baudelaire, with whom Laforgue shared the desire to find a style to express the disharmony of post-industrialized man. We know that by December 1880 some 900 lines existed, and that one of the book's proposed parts was complete in 25 sonnets. The collection, centring on the lonely seer pondering the future and the nature of civilization, would have been too rhetorical, full of exclamation marks and unanswered questions, broken rhythms, prayers, and vogue words for "abyss." "J'en suis dégoûté," wrote Laforgue, "à cette époque je voulais être éloquent (They disgust me. At that time I wanted to be eloquent)." He had by now abandoned what he referred to as his "ambitions littéraires."

He was clear about the need for a new aesthetic. E. von Hartmann's *Philosophie des Unbewußten* was published in French in 1877, and Laforgue's art criticism shows an impatience with purely intellectual norms devised to eternalize pictorial moments in favour of seizing the ephemeral, and treating it as such. His abandonment of the notion of absolute beauty is underwritten by the psychological and historical determinism of Taine, whose lectures Laforgue had attended. For Taine, "Each man is like a piano on which the outside world plays in a certain way, according to his moment in time, his racial and social milieu, and his stage of personal development. My piano is always changing, and there is none identical to mine. All pianos are legitimate." But whereas Taine sought an aesthetic norm based on universality, permanence, and moral uplift, Laforgue seeks the particular, the evanescent, and the real, even if it degrades. His basis for poetic inspiration is Hartmann's unconscious, a moving spirit within, related to Hegel's "Spirit" or Schopenhauer's "will" rather than to the repressed subconscious of Freud or the collective unconscious of Jung. It is Hartmann's unconscious which, for Laforgue, links the mutable and determining external forces of race, milieu, and moment to a reality which, dependent on Darwin's natural selection, is none the less universal and transcendent. Laforgue's new aesthetic is based on an ideal in perpetual evolution which, developed by natural selection, underlies the changing world of contingent phenomena. For an understanding of his poetic achievement, it is more important to consider his own utilization of this aesthetic than its manifest philosophical weaknesses. It gives an apparently respectable philosophical basis for formal experimentation, modernity of subject, and fundamental pessimism.

Les Complaintes de Jules Laforgue of 1885 uses material from the abandoned *Le Sanglot* and includes a "Complainte propitiatoire à l'Inconscient." In spite of the great care taken with the verse, the volume is deliberately disordered. These "little poems of fantasy having only one purpose, to be original at any cost" are in fact full of daring, if ultimately dandified, plays with sounds and meanings, like the verb "vivoter," compounded of "vivre" (to live) and "radoter" (to ramble on in a senile way), "éternullité," composed of "éternité" (eternity) and "nullité" (uselessness, incompetence), or "spleenuosités" from "spleen"

(in the poetic sense, self-loathing or self-disgust) and "sinuosité" (winding or curve). This cloak of triviality extends to syntactical enormities, the importation of slang, and the pastiche of philosophical language. The mute "e" is dropped, and rhyme schemes progress towards "vers libres", metres become arbitrary, and structures unclear. Images reinforce, or contrast with, one another to make a central poetic point, but apparently result from a simple dislocation of ordinary speech patterns, with the poet unseriously playing a whole variety of roles throughout the collection.

L'Imitation de Notre-Dame la Lune is a slim volume, much more unified and less provocative than its predecessor. Pierrot is the high priest of the moon, travestying the Catholic cult of the Virgin Mary, but too frivolous to approach real blasphemy. Actual publication of the book was in November 1885, and the cult of sterility associated in Laforgue with the moon had already been given prominence by the hyperaesthetic Des Esseintes in Huysmans's *A Rebours* of 1884. Much of the force of the poems depends on the bathos of a still adolescent sense of humour, mostly put into the mouths of pierrots whose semi-serious sadness underlies simple buffoonery. The verbal tricks are perhaps subtler, the hymn "Ave maris stella" applied to the Virgin Mary becomes "Ave Paris stella," which is not Latin at all, and more play is made on sound values. The first five lines of "Stérilités" contain only 15 words and do not mean very much, but hard "g"s are heaped on hard "c"s, "f" sounds are piled on "l"s, and the whole relies on a long "i" sound: "Cautérise et coagule/En virgules/Ses lagunes des cerises/Des félines Ophélies/Orphelines en folie (Cauterize and coagulate / In commas / Its lagoons of cherries, / Cat-like Ophelias, / Mad orphans)." Were the first word to be printed on a separate line, there would be a rhyme scheme of the type "abbacc", deliberately based on sound patterns rather than the visual ones which do not permit singulars to rhyme with plurals. As it is, Laforgue has simply thrown in an extra internal rhyme, félines / (Or)phelines.

The title *Des fleurs de bonne volonté* might contain an implied reference to the Mass hymn "Gloria in excelsis Deo" with its "peace to men of goodwill," and certainly parodies Baudelaire's title *Les Fleurs du mal*, which itself contains a double meaning. Some of the contents of this collection, which was scrapped, are used for *Le Concile féerique*, and some of it was rewritten for *Derniers vers*, whose 12 poems were published separately in *La Vogue* or the *Revue Indépendante* between August and December 1886. It is not unlikely that they were, or would have been, forged into a single poem. The poems are unified by a central Hamlet-like figure and are about love. They range in tone from the light-hearted and amusingly ironic to the meditative and frustrated as the lover ponders the compatibility between the idealization of love and its physical satisfaction.

Laforgue has created a complex series of poetic forms, often using direct speech, although not always in dialogue, in which conflicting desires are effectively expressed simultaneously. He often draws on bewildering dislocations of poetic register, but also on bathos, antithesis, the mutual reinforcing or cancellation of images, rapid changes of pace as well as of rhythm, metre, and stanza patterns, and a considerable number of rhetorical devices, including repetitions, clauses in parallel syntax, exclamation marks, quotation marks, and sets of dots to indicate incomplete expression. The "vers libres" for which he is celebrated are used tentatively, the rhyming support they withdraw replaced by assonance and internal rhyme.

PUBLICATIONS

Collections

Poésies complètes, 1894
Oeuvres complètes, 3 vols., 1901–03
Les Complaintes de Jules Laforgue, 1885
L'Imitation de Notre-Dame la Lune, 1886
Le Concile féerique, 1886
Moralités légendaires, 1887
Derniers vers, 1890

Critical studies

Ramsey W., *Laforgue and the Ironic Inheritance*, 1953
Collie M., *Laforgue* (in English), 1963

————

LAMARTINE, Alphonse (-Marie-Louis) de Prat de, 1790–1869.

Poet, diplomat, statesman, historian, and journalist.

LIFE

Lamartine's family were artisans in the 17th century and rose slowly to the ranks of the minor aristocracy in the 18th, acquiring scattered rural holdings and patents of nobility, but retaining uncertain orthography for the family name. As late as 1825 the poet signed himself "de la Martine" and "Delamartine." Known today as a poet, he himself regarded his political career as more important. His literary fame, founded on the immensely successful *Méditations poétiques* of 1820, was due to the conjunction of anti-Napoleonic political sentiment in the years immediately following the Bourbon restoration of 1815 and the poetic sensibility developed by Chateaubriand which cultivated the emotional vulnerability of the individual in reaction to the political and social preoccupations of the revolutionary and Napoleonic eras. Both the political sentiment and the new artistic sensibility which it allowed to flourish peaked simultaneously towards the end of the second decade of the 19th century. Lamartine's political career slowly led him to embrace the political values which underlay and gave rise to the 1848 revolution. For a few months he could easily have become a new dictator, and for a year his power was immense. From 1849 it quickly subsided, and Lamartine spent his final 20 years in some financial hardship, doing the work of a literary hack.

Lamartine's father, Pierre (1752–1840), had served in the army from the age of 16 and appears to have been politically inclined to liberalism, although he was imprisoned under the Terror and released only on the fall of Robespierre. Pierre's eldest brother was an invalid and the next brother became a priest, so that a good marriage was sought for him, while his sister was relegated to a worldly convent catering for young ladies of high birth but small dowries, with one of whom he fell in love. Pierre Lamartine married Alix Des Roys (1770–1829), both of whose parents had been in the service of the Duc d'Orléans, on 7 January 1790, and on 21 October of that year Lamartine was born at Mâcon. He was to have five sisters, but no brothers. After Pierre's release from imprisonment, the Lamartines lived a modest existence at Milly, near Mâcon. The house was to come into Lamartine's possession around 1830, and in 1861 he sold it to raise money.

Lamartine's father was emotionally distant, so that his early family attachments were necessarily to his mother and sisters, a circumstance which was to have a clear effect on his sensibility as he came to maturity. He was the male heir to the family name and, no doubt on that account, his family was supported by his uncles. Lamartine read widely at home and spent a year at the school in the neighbouring village of Bussières under the Abbé Dumont, later the model for Jocelyn, whose passions included hunting and reading the 18th-century "philosophes." The companionship of local children was balanced by the feminine influence at home until, in March 1801, Lamartine was sent to school at the then celebrated Institut Puppier in Lyons. There were conventional holidays, but school life was rough and Lamartine, together with two other boys, eventually ran away in December 1802. He was kept at the school, however, until his mother managed to obtain permission from her husband's family for his transfer to the former Jesuit school at Belley, where he spent the period from 1803 to 1807. There he underwent an adolescent crisis of religiosity, and acquired the Catholic, royalist attitude tinged with rationalism and a liking for the aesthetic splendours of Catholic religious practice characteristic of such institutions. By the time he had left school, he had begun to write verse. His health was less than robust, and may have been the reason for his withdrawal from school.

The 80-odd letters to former school friends provide a better guide to the years from 1807 to 1811 than the unreliable *Les Confidences* and *Les Nouvelles Confidences*, but they tell us little except that Lamartine read a great deal, took much exercise, and easily fancied himself in love. He was being trained as a country gentleman, was given an allowance, and permitted to spend part of the winter in Lyons. He seems to have had an idyllic relationship late in 1809, and again spent several months in Lyons. His senior uncle was resolutely opposed to his marrying a girl, Henriette Pommier, from the local magistracy, to whom Lamartine had become attached late in 1810, and in July 1811 he was sent to Italy. He left on the 15th in the company of a young honeymoon couple, and visited Florence, Rome, and Naples, where he had a liaison with "Antoniella," the prototype of the "Grazie" in the 1852 conte of that name. There is no reason to suppose more than a commonplace adventure, although it may have helped to delay Lamartine's departure from Naples until 18 April. He returned via Lausanne to a frosty welcome, and in 1816 was to hear of Antoniella's death.

Lamartine was made mayor of Milly in May 1812 to avoid conscription, and on 1 March 1813 Nina de Pierreclau gave birth to his son Léon. Outwardly Lamartine's life remained uneventful, with visits to Paris in 1812 and 1813, when he took to gaming, neglecting work on his poem "Saül." His eldest sister, Cécile, had married in March 1813, and his mother and second sister, Eugénie, came to rescue him from Paris. Lamartine wrote a "Médée" and started a "Zoraïde," but was interrupted in 1814 when the Austrian army was threatening Milly, and French officers were billeted in the house. After Napoleon's abdication on 4 April 1814, news of which reached Milly only on 10 April, Lamartine enlisted in Louis XVIII's Garde-du-Corps. He served in Paris and at Beauvais, which he disliked, and where he acted as a riding instructor.

After three months he returned home on a leave which lasted until Napoleon's return in March 1815. He was part of the cortège which fled Paris for Belgium in the wake of Louis XVIII, but led the officers' movement which preferred to surrender to the Bonapartist army at Béthune rather than follow the king into exile. After various adventures, some of which put him in real danger, Lamartine returned home, but found it prudent to take refuge in Switzerland in May. Short of money, he contemplated a tutorship in England or Russia, and began another liaison. His money held out until the arrival of the news of Napoleon's defeat at Waterloo on 18 June and of his second abdication on 22 June, and by 22 July Lamartine was certainly in Paris. He spent a few weeks in the reformed Garde-du-Corps at Beauvais before definitively resigning his commission.

He was already interested in a public career, and already found the illiberal views of his ultra-monarchical friends distasteful. By 1816 he was in Paris, a constitutional monarchist looking for a diplomatic post and writing political journalism. He became unwell, went to Aix-les-Bains on 30 September for a cure, and in his pension met Julie Charles (1784–1817), the young consumptive wife of the balloonist and physicist J. A. Charles, with Lamartine's wife and Antoniella the inspiration for "Elvire." In an episode later fictionalized in *Raphaël* Lamartine saved Julie from drowning on the lake. She had married her much older husband in 1804, and her love letters to Lamartine make it clear that they did in fact have a liaison, if not at Aix, then later in Paris, where Lamartine's uncle had given him money to go, ostensibly to resume his quest for a diplomatic post. He left home on 4 January, arriving four days later. His family were in the throes of a financial crisis, and Lamartine had either to earn money or to return and share in the retrenchment. He tried to publish his verse but was turned down, sold a diamond given to him by his mother, prolonged his stay in Paris by a few weeks, but eventually returned to Milly in May. In late September he waited for Julie in Aix, but she was too ill to travel and died on 18 December 1817. Lamartine received the news on Christmas Day.

On 16 April he finished *Saül*, a verse tragedy programmatically based on Shakespeare and Racine, a combination of sources made significant by Voltaire, and which was to remain important for the high romantic (q.v.) generation. Lamartine now contemplated seeking out a wife, was urgently summoned to Paris, and sold his horse to get there, but no appointment came of his visit. The immensely influential and innovatory French actor Talma, who had recently returned with Mlle George (see Dumas *père*) from Kemble's farewell performance at Covent Garden, turned *Saül* down in October, recommending modifications to bring it into closer conformity with current neoclassical convention.

At the marriage of his sister Césarine on 15 February 1819 to the elder brother of his close friend Vignet, Lamartine met his sister's English Protestant friend Maria Anna ("Marianne") Eliza Birch (1790–1863), whom he was later to marry. During 1819 he read some of his verses in Parisian and provincial salons, had a liaison with Léna de Larche in the spring, and in the autumn asked for Marianne's hand. There were delays and difficulties, partly due to their different religions, but Lamartine's family paid off his debts and he was promised a diplomatic appointment. He also underwent a religious crisis which coincided with, and may have resulted from, a dangerous bout of pneumonia. He married on 6 June 1820, more deeply committed to Catholicism than hitherto. Marianne abjured Protestantism, but there was an "English" as well as a "French" marriage ceremony to appease her mother. The settlement produced about 212,000 francs from the bridegroom, who was to receive 3,500 francs a year from the income, and 250,000 francs from the bride, who was to be allowed 1,500 francs spending money a year. Lamartine also received the Château de Saint-Point near Mâcon, although about half its value of 100,000 francs was entailed. The couple, accompanied by the bride's mother, departed immediately for Naples, where Lamartine had been appointed to the embassy as an attaché, and on 15 February 1821 his wife bore him a son, Alphonse, who was to die late in 1822.

The first edition of the *Méditations poétiques*, 500 copies of an octavo of 113 pages, unsigned and comprising 24 odes and elegies, had been published by Nicolle on 11 March 1820. A second edition of 1,500 copies with two more poems, this time signed, appeared in April. Lamartine was paid an advance of 1,200 francs for the second edition and given a pension by the king. Five further editions had followed by February 1821. Gosselin published an eighth edition in January 1822. A ninth edition, dated 1823 but published the preceding 28 December, added four new poems. Finally 11 more poems were added to the "Premières méditations" in 1849. Excluding pirated editions, there were seven Nicolle and 19 Gosselin editions by 1831. Sales are estimated at 35,000 to 40,000 during that period, and Hachette sold 22,625 copies in the dozen years following Lamartine's death in 1869. By 1914 the figure had reached 81,226. There were translations into most European languages. The work's plaintive and majestic cultivation of personal melancholy, and its new openness to grief and nature, had revived lyric poetry. Its contents were compatible with orthodox Catholic spirituality, with a new but still genuinely religious sensibility, and, in spite of the implied cult of the isolated, reflective, and emotionally vulnerable individual, with conservative political and social attitudes. Its immediate and prodigious success clearly swept away all obstacles to the diplomatic appointment and to the marriage.

The journey to Naples was complicated by the troubled political situation there after the uprising of July 1820, and Lamartine soon began to feel short of money. All the French legations in Italy were under direct control from Rome, where the reactionary ambassador, Blacas, followed a policy dictated by the king and at variance with that of Pasquier, the foreign minister. Lamartine spent the early months of 1821 in Rome, where his son was born, and returned on leave to France in March, spending most of the next four years there until his appointment as secretary to the embassy in Florence in 1825. His disappointment in his first diplomatic posting may have been partly due to indifferent health as well as to his lack of sympathy for the unconstitutional and repressive attitudes supported by Blacas towards the Naples uprising. His wife gave birth to their daughter Julia in 1822, and Lamartine spent three months that summer in England, where the ambassador was Chateaubriand, whom Lamartine admired, but who treated him with some disdain. On his return to Paris after the death of his infant son, Lamartine sold the still unfinished second volume of verse, *Nouvelles méditations poétiques*, for 14,000 francs. He was invariably optimistic about the fundamental soundness of his financial position and, in spite of lavish expenditure, was for the moment reasonably provided for. He obtained 6,000 francs for his philosophical poem *La Mort de Socrate*.

The *Nouvelles méditations*, published on 27 September 1823, was received more coolly than its predecessor had been, and in 1824 Lamartine failed to get elected to the Académie Française. His sister Césarine, Marianne's close friend, had died in February 1824, and Byron died in April of that year. Lamartine's *Le Dernier Chant du pèlerinage d'Harold*, an ending to Byron's *Childe Harold*, was published on 14 May 1825. Exactly a fortnight later he published the *Chant du sacre* in honour of the coronation of Charles X the next day. Like Hugo, who had also written a congratulatory ode, Lamartine had been made a Chevalier of the Légion d'Honneur a few days earlier, but the Duc d'Orléans took quite reasonable exception to a tactless reference to his father in a line of Lamartine's, and its correction, enforced by the king, was calculated not to improve matters much. The scandal may even have helped Canel to sell 20,000 copies in a few days.

In July Lamartine was appointed to Florence, where he arrived on 2 October, having in the meanwhile entertained Hugo and Nodier at Saint-Point on their way to Switzerland with their families. On 24 September he published the *Epîtres*. Although he had been invited to align himself with *La Muse Française* and what was to be known as the romantic movement, Lamartine preferred to remain aloof from the quarrels about classicism and romanticism around 1830. It is in any case easier to see him as united by his sensibility with the earlier "pre-romantic" (q.v.) group, with which the names of Chateaubriand, Constant, and Mme de Staël are associated, leaving the term "romantic" for the group which formed round Nodier and Hugo, and came to prominence with the tragedies of Dumas, Vigny, and Hugo, partly inspired by the 1827 Shakespeare season in Paris. Lamartine's lyric poetry may nevertheless have contributed much to the styles of his younger contemporaries. His *Pèlerinage*, in continuing Byron's exaltation of the Greek fight for independence, had inevitably annoyed the Italians, and Lamartine eventually had to fight a not very serious duel over a quarrel picked by an over-sensitive Italian. The duel was fought with swords, since no one wanted the serious damage which a pistol might cause. Lamartine was slightly wounded, and relations with the Italians were thereby healed.

In May 1826 Lamartine inherited the estate of Montculot, near Dijon, from an uncle. He returned to Florence, promoted to chargé d'affaires, and in 1827 came into the family inheritance from his senior uncle. His expenditure, chiefly on houses, horses, and hospitality, had by now become ostentatiously lavish. He kept a stud, and frequently had 50 people at his table. He left Florence in 1828 to await a new posting and, in the 1829 atmosphere of growing republicanism in Paris, took the opportunity to assess the possibilities of a political career. It seemed not unlikely that he would be appointed to Athens, and Sainte-Beuve, who would have accompanied him, wrote three articles on him for *Le Globe*. On 5 November 1829 he was elected to the academy a few days before his mother died of shock after a serious scalding, and in the following year Lamartine published a collection of his verse from 1826 to 1830 under the title *Harmonies poétiques et religieuses*. The seventh edition of the *Nouvelles méditations* of July 1830 contains three fragments of the abandoned "Les visions."

By the time the July monarchy was inaugurated in 1830 Lamartine was a liberal, although a constitutional monarchist still hankering after his former "legitimist" position. Nevertheless, he could not fail to feel satisfaction at the outcome of the political crisis. He looked forward to the prospect of constitutional rule under the Duc d'Orléans, now Louis-Philippe, even though it meant the abandonment of belief in sovereignty by right of birth alone, without reference to consent. Lamartine's retrograde legitimist nostalgia led him, however, to abandon his diplomatic career. His wife's mother died in 1831 and business called Lamartine to England. He failed to be elected to the chamber of deputies for Bergues, Toulon, and Mâcon in turn, and fell under the influence of the "humanitarian" Jean-Marie Dargaud, a utopian radical seeking the rationalist regeneration of an egalitarian humanity. Lamartine embodied his own political philosophy, an idealistic intellectual dream, in *De la politique rationnelle*, from which the whole of his later political philosophy can be seen to have developed. The pamphlet, which was too long for publication as originally intended in the *Revue Européenne*, presents a loosened allegiance to Catholicism and a shift towards pantheistic idealism. It also takes up a halfway position in Lamartine's move towards fervent republicanism. The change in his thinking entailed an abhorrence of the crasser forms of materialist ambition, an increased dislike of the death penalty, against which he had published an ode in 1830, support for universal suffrage, and the separation of Church and State, with each supreme in its own sphere.

Late in 1831 Lamartine started the narrative poem *Jocelyn* and finally began to make arrangements for the visit to the Middle East which he had been hoping to make since 1826, although his purpose was now religious and political, concerned with the nature of Christianity rather than with any quest for renewed poetic inspiration. He sailed from Marseilles on 11 July 1832 in a chartered boat with his wife, daughter, three guests, and six servants. The *Voyage en orient* was eventually banned as too rationalistic by Rome, but its most striking feature is the exaltation of natural beauty at the expense of the monuments to dead beauty which Lamartine discovered in Greece. His thought never clarified sufficiently for him to produce a coherent philosophy, but remained in a spiritual haze of religious convictions and philosophical speculations which did not go far enough for Dargaud, under whose supervision the final version of the *Voyage* was written. During the journey Lamartine's daughter, Julia, died. Her poor health had held up the original departure, and Lamartine was stoically resigned when she died on 6 December 1832. His wife, however, became physically ill at the loss. Lamartine nursed her back to health, made the visits abroad for which he had contracted with his publishers, and returned home much disturbed by the pope's condemnation of Lammenais in the encyclical *Mirari vos* of 15 August 1832, of which he heard only in November in Beirut. On 7 January 1833 Lamartine's sister had procured his election as deputy for Bergues. He took his seat in December, having arrived back the previous month from Marseilles, where he had gone to fetch Julia's body.

His optimistic calculations showed a considerable profit on his journey. He had travelled in state, brought back carpets, horses, and other valuables worth a total of 40,000 francs, and calculated total expenses of 120,000 francs, against two years' income of 80,000 francs a year and 80,000 francs from Gosselin. In fact the journey was the beginning of Lamartine's financial ruin. A first period of his life was now over, about to give way to the political career which took him from 1833 until the coup d'état of 1–2 December 1851. These years also saw the peak of his prolific literary output in quantity and quality, if not celebrity. He spent a final period of retirement from political life in the vain attempt to pay off 5,000,000 francs' worth of debts, and to re-establish his position, and in earning money from his prodigious literary output, including the 28 volumes of the *Cours familier de littérature*, issued in monthly instalments from 1856 to 1869, the histories of Turkey and Russia, and the immensely popular *Histoire des Girondins*, a work of extreme liberal enthusiasm romanticizing the Revolution, which appeared in volume form in 1847.

Still affected by Julia's death, Lamartine resisted an invitation to join Thiers's administration, preferring to proclaim his political independence. His early speeches in the chamber on Turkey, Russia, and Egypt betrayed legitimist sympathies and did not go down well. He later regretted them. He and his wife were living in a large furnished apartment, rented for 6,000 francs a year. The annual housekeeping bill was about 40,000 francs, and they kept four horses. Lamartine received the official and literary worlds on Saturdays, but there were always a few guests at table, and occasionally larger gatherings for dinner. Known maliciously as "le pleurard (crybaby)," Lamartine was not highly regarded by the younger generation of romantics, although Sophie Gay and her daughter Delphine, the former toast of the romantics, who married Emile de Girardin and whose political sympathies had evolved in much the same way as Lamartine's, continued to frequent his salon. Other habitués from the literary and stage worlds included Deschamps, co-editor with Hugo of *La Muse Française*, Jules-Gabriel Janin, theatre critic of the *Journal des Débats*, and François Ponsard, who was to lead the reaction against romantic drama with his neoclassical verse tragedy *Lucrèce* (1843). Janin's discovery, Elisa Félix Rachel, who had been coached by Talma's famous pupil, Joseph-Isidore Samson, had played the lead in *Lucrèce* shortly after Hugo's *Les Burgraves*. Most members of the academy also called.

Politically, Lamartine was now advocating a liberal social policy, with clemency and toleration whenever the occasion presented itself. The 1834 elections had greatly strengthened the independents in the chamber, but Lamartine devoted a high proportion of his energy to writing, no doubt rightly suspecting that it would be prudent to ensure the possibility of living by his pen. He probably also realized that the sensibility first articulated by Chateaubriand, and which was responsible for the success of the 1820 volume, had already been overtaken, perhaps partly due to the effect on general public taste of the increase in literacy. Lamartine's *Oeuvres complètes* were now appearing. He had distanced himself from the Lammenais of the 1834 *Paroles d'un croyant*, and followed the 1835 *Voyage en orient* with *Jocelyn* in February 1836. Both works were to be proscribed by Rome just after *Jocelyn*'s third edition in September.

After *Graziella*, *Jocelyn* was Lamartine's most popular book. It sold 24,000 copies in 27 days, during which 14 pirated editions are known to have originated in Germany and Belgium. The poem *La Chute d'un ange*, its heterodoxy restrained by Lamartine's now ultra-orthodox wife, appeared in May 1838 and was banned in August. In that year Lamartine changed his constituency to Mâcon. He had spoken uninformedly, although with good sense, against protectionist legislation, and favoured only gradual abolition of the slavery on which the French economy still depended, with 40,000 nationals controlling 250,000 slaves in the overseas territories. At Monceau Lamartine regularly received Edmond Texier, the translator in 1854 of *Uncle Tom's Cabin* (1852), which did so much to favour the French anti-slavery movement, but he also attempted, without attracting damaging legitimist support, to defend Molé and Louis-Philippe against attacks on the royal usurpation of power led by Guizot, Thiers, and the left. Lamartine's move towards real political influence was gathering momentum. Talleyrand, who died in 1838, had noticed it before anyone else and had for some years been taking Lamartine into his confidence.

In 1839 Lamartine published the *Recueillements poétiques*, and with it virtually ended his career as a poet. In 1840 his father died and on 26 July 1841 he was present at the deathbed of his illegitimate son by Léna de Larche. By this time Lamartine was in serious financial trouble, urgently seeking 200,000 francs and considering the abandonment of his political career just as his support in the chamber was approaching that of the government itself. Girardin, now married to Delphine Gay, was willing to throw the political influence of *La Presse*, now one of the three large-circulation newspapers, behind Lamartine, although in 1848 he resigned as a deputy before the revolution and would have preferred a regency to Lamartine's republic. By 1842 Lamartine had clearly gone into opposition over the government's refusal to countenance an extension of the suffrage, although he still kept his independence.

During the next few years his financial worries were to increase and to keep him from giving political matters as much attention as he wanted to, although he did speak on railways, getting what was to become the Marseilles line extended from Châlons to Mâcon, and on prisons, regarding deportation as more humane than solitary confinement. Impatience with the cumbersome procedures of government and the need to pay bills threatened none the less to turn to boredom. In 1844 an Italian holiday with his sisters and nieces refreshed him, and in the following two years he defended his independent position vigorously, pointing out the disastrous political errors and betrayals of principle by both governments and oppositions since 1830. In August 1846 he was re-elected by 321 votes out of 330.

When the *Histoire des Girondins* appeared in March 1847, sales for 500,000 francs were recorded in two months. Lamartine had sold the copyright for 250,000 francs, but his publishers now added another 150,000, and Lamartine signed a contract to write a further six-volume work on the Revolution itself. It was never written. Since political gatherings were prohibited, Mâcon put on a "banquet" lunch on 18 July 1847 for 3,000 guests to honour their "author." About 6,000 people attended, and listened to Lamartine in drenching rain. By 1847 he was quite clear about how he wanted society organized, with sovereignty of the people, universal suffrage, an independent, salaried executive, freedom of religion and freedom from censorship, universal instruction, free trade, and the abolition of slavery. But he would have preferred to see his policies implemented without a revolution. He nearly emerged as the strong leader who could successfully have negotiated their acceptance without one.

He did not appear in the chamber from June 1846 until the end of January 1848. The banquet formula caught on, and at one point Lamartine had 48 invitations to speak at such gatherings. About 70 were held in republican interests throughout France in the second half of 1847. Lamartine was regularly expounding his policies in *Le Bien Public*, refusing invitations to banquets and offers of political support from the radical left, whose success, he was sure, would compromise stability. His long-held view that Guizot's reactionary politics and Calvinist moral principles would lead to his overthrow was visibly being proved correct. He needed to do nothing except wait for opportunity. Raindrops were beginning to form in the vast cloud of political development, but the intensity and exact location of the coming storm were not yet precisely predictable. In the end, on 19 February, Lamartine made the decisive speech, which he later regretted, inciting attendance on 20 February at a monster "banquet" in a comparatively isolated part of Paris, which the government had been panicked into threatening to break up by force. The British ambassador thought the government's folly "inconceivable." It would lose in the courts even if it did not provoke a revolution. Lamartine has been accused of succumbing in the excitement to a desire to present himself as the messianic leader of France. An accommodation was in fact reached about the banquet, to be held on 22 February, but the opposition press had already publicized the meeting on the 21st.

The government thereupon made the demonstration illegal, although the press called on members of the Garde Nationale to attend in their uniforms. The deputies decided not to take part, so making it easier for the government to use force. The organizers abandoned the demonstration, and on the 22nd groups drifted around reading copies of the ban posted on walls before moving aimlessly towards Place de la Concorde. The deputies assembled across the river, and the impeachment of the government was moved. There were only 53 signatures, and Lamartine did not sign. The debate was fixed for 24 February. On the 22nd only minor insurrectionary incidents occurred. On the 23rd it rained. There were sporadic riots and a few barricades, but the military appeared not to sympathize with the government. Louis-Philippe asked Molé to form a new cabinet, which he might just have succeeded in doing, and public rejoicing was beginning when the officer commanding a batallion on Boulevard des Capucines refused to allow a throng to pass. Someone fired a shot and the soldiers responded with a volley. There were about 50 deaths.

At midnight the king heard that Molé could not form a government and summoned Thiers, who arrived at 2.30 a.m., an hour after General Bugeaud had been given command of the 30,000 troops in Paris. Thiers offered to form a government on his own terms, which were accepted. Bugeaud, who probably wanted a place in it, forbade the troops to shoot, but on the morning of the 24th, 1,500 barricades were put up by republicans. Things had gone too far. No government was acceptable, and neither was Bugeaud. Thiers advised the king to call for the leader of the radical left, Odilon Barrot, but it was too late. A year later, in his *Histoire de la révolution de 1848*, Lamartine says that at this point only his own name was acceptable to the mob.

By midday an abdication was being demanded, with the dissolution of the parliament and a general amnesty. The king, persuaded by Girardin and others, abdicated in favour of his grandson, under the regency of the Duchesse d'Orléans, and escaped to England via Saint-Cloud. It seems clear that Lamartine, who had stayed indoors since the evening of the 21st, had accepted the first position in the republic to be formed. At 10.30 a.m. on the 24th, still in bed, he was summoned by a friend to go to the chamber, which the crowd was about to invade. At 1 p.m. the crowd invaded the Tuileries, from which the king had left an hour before. By 1.0 p.m. the session in the chamber had been opened. Thiers announced that he thought it too late to save the regency, and left. The provisional government was the result of bargaining between *Le National* and *La Réforme*, with a circulation between them of only 6,000. Both aligned behind Lamartine at a meeting in the early afternoon of the 24th. Lamartine chose a republic rather than the regency.

The Duchesse d'Orléans and her son came to the chamber. Lamartine demanded her withdrawal, as pandemonium had broken out when she had forced her way in. The duchess stayed and Lamartine had to fight his way to the rostrum. He spoke calmly in front of the duchess against a regency before being interrupted by the mob, led by Dunoyer, who was pointing a gun at him. Lamartine read out a proposed list of members of a provisional government, but the confusion made acceptance impossible, and he led the crowd to the Hôtel de Ville. The Duchesse d'Orléans left with her children for Germany. By the evening Lamartine headed a de facto government, not knowing what had happened to the king or the duchess, or whether to expect a counter-revolution and, if so, whether on behalf of the abdicated king or of the regency. Reaching the Hôtel de Ville alive had been a near-miracle. The mob was naturally divided, open to threats, exploitations, and inducements from any demagogue with enough determination and sufficient rhetoric.

Seven members of the projected provisional government did eventually get access to an empty room in the Hôtel de Ville in which to compose a manifesto proclaiming a republic and its own legitimacy. Two new "secretaries" of the government, Blanc and Albert, forced their names on to the list. The president, Dupont de l'Eure, was 70, and Lamartine was made vice-president as well as foreign minister. The original manifesto was amended in proof to read that the government "desired" rather than "proclaimed" the republic and, despite bitter internal dissensions, some sort of administrative framework was in place. France was in fact being governed for the moment by a coalition of two low-circulation newspapers under the independent presidency of Lamartine. Seven times that evening Lamartine had to calm a suspicious, determined, and ruthless mob pointing guns and bayonets at him, with some of its members calling for his death.

He was hot and filthy, and his clothes were torn, but he was calm enough to be witty in bantering the crowd into inaction. It was an extraordinary feat of moral courage and physical endurance although, as ever, Lamartine was less effective in formulating actual policies. His refusal to accept the red flag in place of the tricolour on 25 February was the symbolic occasion of his most difficult confrontation with the hysterical and largely drunken crowd, who carried many of the 12,000 muskets looted from Vincennes, and had brought corpses from around Paris to the steps of the Hôtel de Ville. Lamartine was not alone in attempting to control the mass but, in the unanimous judgement of his contemporaries and of subsequent historians, his was the courage which won the day for the republic.

Lamartine did not leave the Hôtel de Ville for six days, after which he moved to his ministry and had mattresses installed. His later writings reflect calmly on the laws enacted during the republic's first few hours, and in particular on the near-bankruptcy of France caused by the guarantee of state employment at a wage fixed by commissioners. The situation in Paris remained critical for weeks, with the serious risk of a successful take-over from the left and a new Terror, but also with some threat of a regrouping on the right, and a counter-revolution. Lamartine had indefatigably to draft, write, cajole, and act. He now saw quite clearly that he would either win his political battle, or perish in it, but he has been accused of being too much to too many, of wanting too much to project an image of lofty generosity, and of betraying the right to toady to the left. He kept an army of 26,000 men near Lille on whom he felt he could rely if Paris fell to anarchists, as it might have done on 16 April. A planned mass insurrection in which Lamartine quite expected to be killed finally came to nothing.

He later said that the reason why he did not assume the dictatorial powers which could have been his in both March and May was that he would have needed two scaffolds, one on his right and the other on his left. In the meanwhile he had to refuse support for foreign insurrectionary leaders looking for help in Paris. By 28 April Lamartine, standing as usual for humaneness and moderation, headed all candidates at the polls in a vast vote of confidence, but it represented the peak of his power. Lamartine was perhaps less personally ambitious, less vain, and more righteously determined than has been supposed, but he almost wilfully disdained the cultivation of his populist power base.

On 15 May another act of great courage was called for when the assembly's proceedings were interrupted by a mob while revolutionary leaders attempted to proclaim a government at the Hôtel de Ville. Lamartine called for a horse and led the Garde Nationale at considerable personal danger to arrest the leaders, once more winning the mob round to his side. On 23 June he again exposed himself recklessly at the head of a military force, 400 of whom died or were wounded in the attempt to quell the "insurrection of hunger," a spontaneous demonstration, exploited by the Bonapartists, on the part of those, often starving, who had been thrown out of work by the closing of the state workshops, which were draining the country's economic resources.

On 24 June the executive commission handed over military and civil power to General Cavaignac. Lamartine immediately became an object of calumny, partly because of his earlier, apparently arrogant independence preceding his virtuoso political performance during the crisis. Among the accusations those of profiteering were among the most unfair. Lamartine had in fact torn up a contract selling his literary works for 540,000 francs because the political situation was causing his publishers so much difficulty. He continued to speak in the chamber, but his actions became the subject of a public enquiry. He emerged exonerated but dejected. In the presidential ballot of 10 December, Lamartine came only fifth, with less than 20,000 votes, against 5,434,226 in favour of Louis-Napoléon. Cavaignac came second, with 1,500,000.

In January 1849 Lamartine's *Les Confidences* began to appear in *La Presse*, and *Raphaël* was published. He still spoke occasionally in the chamber, and reached an agreeable relationship with Louis-Napoléon, but resigned after the coup d'état. He spent his last 20 years writing to pay off debts. All his estates were sold, and only at the very end of his life was he given a state pension of 25,000 francs. His enormous literary output was inadequate to satisfy his debts, which were chiefly attributable to his attachment to owning land. Too often Lamartine bought out his co-inheritors at inflated prices, and then failed properly to manage the estates. From April 1849 to December 1851 he edited the *Conseiller du Peuple* for 2,000 francs a month. The *Histoire de la révolution de 1848* and the first volume of the subscription edition of the *Oeuvres* appeared late in 1849. Lamartine's play *Toussaint Louverture* opened at the Porte-Saint-Martin on 6 April 1850, after the actor Frédérick Lemaître had come to Saint-Point with the publisher Michel Lévy to settle the details. The despondent ode *Au comte d'Orsay* was published in October 1850 after Lamartine had visited Turkey at the invitation of Sultan Abdul Medjid, to whom his policy had always been friendly. He had to raise funds for the journey, but failed to find in London or Paris the 500,000 francs of working capital he would have needed to exploit the vast estate on which he had been offered a 25-year concession, and was forced to commute the concession into an annual pension of 25,000 francs.

The betrayal of the 1848 revolution by the 1851 coup d'état left Lamartine again embittered against Louis-Napoléon. He realized that it was the price France had to pay for his surrender of too much ground to the left. In 1851 *Les Nouvelles Confidences* had appeared, and from 1852 to 1854 Lamartine edited *Civilisateur*, a non-political review. In July 1851 the eight-volume *Histoire de la restauration* began to appear, and the *Nouveau voyage en orient* was published in *Les Foyers du Peuple*. In March 1852 Lamartine also began to write for *Le Siècle*. A conte, *Graziella*, was published in 1852 and was to be Lamartine's most widely read work.

Various expedients were contemplated for paying off the debts, which the emperor himself twice offered to discharge. In 1857 Lamartine managed to pay off over 1,000,000 francs, but his accounts were still hopelessly optimistic. A lottery to buy his estates was proposed and, when that was found too difficult, a subscription was organized. Nothing succeeded, particularly not the high-cost promotion of the multi-volume works, like the 40-volume *Oeuvres*, or the *Cours familier de littérature*, which is really a collection of scattered souvenirs. Refusing to be bought politically by the regime, Lamartine had to sell all his estates except the heavily entailed Saint-Point. After his death the company owning his copyright sold nearly 600,000 volumes in 25 years, but Lamartine's rehabilitation as a saleable author did not set in before 1869, and the last 10 years of his life contained long unproductive periods of rheumatism and failing powers. *Fior d'Aliza* was finally staged at the Opéra-Comique on 5 February 1866.

Lamartine's wife, who had done much work as his literary secretary after 1848, died in 1863. A cottage had been made available by the municipality of Paris in 1860, so there had no longer been any need to retain the small apartment Lamartine had kept in Paris after his resignation, although at times there had been no ready money for fares between Paris and Saint-Point. Yet the six volumes of the *Histoire de la Turquie* were sold in advance for 150,000 francs. It was only during his last months that Lamartine's powers really failed him. He spent his last summer at Saint-Point, and after his return to Paris had a second comparatively slight stroke. He died in his sleep during the night of 27 February 1869 clutching to his chest the crucifix that Julie Charles had kissed as she died.

WORKS

The first anonymous edition of the *Méditations poétiques* of 11 March 1820 contained 24 poems. Lamartine added to the second edition early in April "La retraite" of 1819 and "Le génie" of 1817, both of which emphasize in their titles the grandeur of the solitary individual. The four new poems added to the ninth edition officially dated 1823 were "A Elvire," "Ode," "La naissance du duc de Bordeaux," and "Philosophie." Of the four, only the last two were written after the publication of the first edition, at the end of 1820 and in the late summer of 1821, respectively. Finally Lamartine added 11 poems for the Edition des Souscripteurs of 1849.

The *Méditations* is one of the half-dozen best-known collections of verse published in French. Culturally, the revolutionary and Napoleonic eras represent an interruption in development rather than a real discontinuity in French history. With the restoration of what looked like a modified ancien régime and the resumption of obviously continuous cultural evolution, a new sensibility had emerged which turned away from projects for social engineering, the Industrial Revolution, which came later and bit harder in France than it did in England, and the coarser pursuit of material advantage. It nourished formless longings and tender yearnings in the self-absorbed cultivation of melancholy, and was nurtured on nature's boundlessness and benignity, the lurking menace of its lakes and mountains effectively ignored in favour of its majesty and stillness. A vaguely grandiose Christianity, reconciled with the rationalist religion of at least some of the "philosophes," was expanded beyond a religious cult to feelings of goodwill towards a humanity whose instincts were themselves virtuous.

Lamartine catered exactly for the emotional needs of his own generation. What is powerful and original in the *Méditations* could have been conceived and expressed as it was, and with the collection's concentration of effect, only in France, and only within a couple of years of 1820. The lyricism of the 29-year-old Lamartine could scarcely have been better tailored to fit the imaginative requirements of the 25 per cent of 20-year-olds who were literate and therefore capable of absorbing an imaginative experience which could not be mediated by stage drama, the only form of imaginative literary experience, apart from recitation and readings, which did not depend on literacy.

Born of Rousseau and nurtured by Goethe, Chateaubriand, and Byron, heralded by Constant, Senancour, and Mme de Staël, a generation reached maturity just as French society was settling back into normality, and the threat of sordid materialist limits to its ambitions began to make itself felt. It needed to examine the implications of its regained security, and could afford to explore the vulnerabilities, sensitivities, and higher aspirations of the individual. It was a generation which later gave birth to romanticism but needed first to establish a harmony with itself, a sensibility attuned to its ideology, and to test the depths of its spiritual, or at any rate emotional, potential. It wanted to nestle in nature's immensity, the eternity of God, and the infinity of its own need for spiritual fulfilment, to feel sure that nature had a design and the individual a purpose, and to cultivate its tenderest longings in a form which appealed directly to the feelings and did not require too demanding an intellectual effort. In this at least Lamartine was its messiah.

The fluidity of Lamartine's verse and its nonchalant approach to the techniques of polished versifying are the necessary conditions for what he achieved, and not, as has sometimes been supposed, its core. Lamartine refused to correct, improve, or modify what he had written, and did not make much use of the rhetorical devices on which his romantic successors so often drew, but his verse is not careless. His repetition of words with a vast range of reference and an imprecision of definition is deliberate. It was correctly calculated to create the impression of dignity, loftiness, and a nobility of spirit which eschewed attention to petty and vulgar detail. He intentionally strove for vagueness. The stanza quoted below, from "L'automne," was probably written in December 1819. It describes nothing very much, any walk on any clear autumn evening, by anyone, in any wood, anywhere. What makes it "poetic" is the writer's response to a trivial but pleasing experience, the musicality of the verse, and the elevation of a moment's sensation to a plane of open-ended and universalized significance with all sorts of semi-mystical overtones. The awareness of light has implications regarding the dependence of the individual's harmony with himself on the harmony bred of communion with nature.

Je suis d'un pas rêveur le sentier solitaire,
J'aime à revoir encor, pour la dernière fois,
Ce Soleil pâlissant, dont la faible lumière
Perce à peine à mes pieds l'obscurité des bois!

(I follow with a dreamy footstep the lonely path. / I enjoy seeing again for the last time / This Sun becoming paler, whose weak light / Scarcely pierces to my feet through the darkness of the woods).

The deliberately prosaic translation shows that the poetry is not in the meaning of the text. The only objects mentioned are the path, the sun, the woods, and the walker's feet, but even these are not real objects. "Path" is merely what is implied by any movement; "sun" and "woods" represent, respectively, the source and the absence of light; "feet" are not here physical objects, but part of a phrase indicating what is on the ground. And even if any of the nouns were to prove concrete enough to curb the poet's yearnings with a reference to physical reality, his footstep follows a path to dreams, the very image of what is illimitable. "For the last time" simply underlines the poignancy of the feeling which is carried by the sound values. If sound has to be disturbed by meaning, then it is to be in elevated, infinite, and imprecise indications of feeling. The stanza is in Alexandrines, the rhyme scheme almost perfunctory, the syntax conversational, and the rhythms prosaic. Only the spelling of "encor" looks odd, the mute "e" syllable omitted before the comma, as was traditionally permitted, to help with the metre.

The first line contains a maximum of long vowels, languishing in the three pronounced "r" sounds, with three sibilant "s" sounds to give rhythmic accentuation; and there is an intensification of the repeated "r" sounds and long vowels in the second line. The third line varies the sound, mixing five pronounced "l" sounds with the lingering long vowels, and returning to two sibilants near the beginning of the line, echoed by the triple "p" and double "b" of the final line, which still relies on long vowels. Taken together, the sound patterns are arresting, although not apparently contrived. The effect, however, is certainly conscious. That the stanza is intended to evoke feeling is clear from the rhetoric of its punctuation, the final exclamation mark in particular, picking up on five exclamation marks in the poem's first stanza, with one at the end of each of the next three. The poet's feelings are then resolved with the help of question marks in stanzas six and seven, a series of dots suggesting an infinity of the inexpressible, and a single-sentence final stanza with three semi-colons, a form of punctuation not previously used in the poem.

The means used to achieve the poem's resolution in the last stanza include a facile inversion in the second line, with no less than six "m" sounds in the penultimate line and the "x"s, "m," and "l" sounds caught up in and caressed by the long vowels in the last line. The consonantal sounds have an effect only in repetition and conjunction, like musical notes, although notes in music depend on interval and harmony as well. In poetry consonantal and vowel sounds individually or in random order have no special significance, any more than a musical note.

La fleur tombe en livrant ses parfums au zéphire;
A la vie, au soleil, ce sont là ses adieux;
Moi, je meurs; et mon âme, au moment qu'elle expire,
S'exhale comme un son triste et mélodieux.

(The flower falls, delivering its scents to the breeze. / To life, to the sun, these are its goodbyes. / Me, I am dying; and my soul, at the moment it expires, / Breathes out as it were a sad, melodious sound).

The subject of the poem is scent, sound, autumnal melancholy, departure, and death, spent leaves and fading summer, without the exhilaration of autumn's frosts and fruits, but limitlessly evoked in a whole series of images of expiry, exhalation, evening, diminution, and sadness.

The other subjects of the poems, which are often more complex in metre or rhyme scheme than "L'automne," can be grouped as sacred or secular more by title than by content. The secular titles exactly correspond to the sensibility at which "L'automne" is directed: "L'isolement," "L'homme," "A Elvire," "Le soir," "L'immortalité," "Le vallon," "Le désespoir," "Le lac," "Le génie," "Philosophie." There are also poems on Christian death, God, sacred poetry, Holy Week, Saul, prayer, and faith, and there is an ode on the birth of the posthumous son of the Duc de Berry, who was assassinated in 1820.

La Mort de Socrate was originally intended to be the principal piece of the new 1823 "Méditations," but was finally sold to the publisher Ladvocat for 6,000 francs and published on its own. There were three editions in four weeks. Within a narrative framework, the poem contains the conversation between Socrates and his friends immediately before his death. It loosely elaborates Plato's account in the *Phaedo*, and shows a familiarity with Greek culture as it was known in 1823. The verse is fluent, the tone grandiose, and the content lofty. Death comes to Socrates as a slow, radiant transfiguration, free from pain.

Canel paid 14,000 francs for the unwritten *Nouvelles méditations poétiques*, a less unified collection than its predecessor, containing more pieces reminiscent of Ronsard and the 16th-century "hymnes," which are the prototypes of the *Harmonies*. The quality, too, is more varied, but the nature of the poetry has scarcely developed. The task of compilation simply bears more signs of haste, and the verse is a little less careful. There is also more direct description of physical objects and events, like Julie's death, and there are one or two hints of political liberalism which were felt to be disturbing.

The *Harmonies poétiques et religieuses*, published by Gosselin in 1830, with three editions in as many weeks, reposes on the 16th-century assumption that it is the poet's function to celebrate God's creation, and to bring man into union with God, thereby elevating the status of the poet to that of prophet and priest. This is Lamartine's most carefully polished collection, containing an invocation, hymns to night and morning, a poem on the symbolism of the sanctuary lamp indicating the presence of the Blessed Sacrament, various poems of consolation, the evocation of landscapes, and the commemoration of events. The landscape poems are non-specific, relating not to particular places, but only to feelings in the poet. The technique has developed, and there is now more conscious reliance on rhetorical devices and such poetic innovations as a syntax permitting the sense of a phrase to overflow a line ending. The sentiment remains stylized, however, and large sections of most poems could still be grafted on to other poems with similar metres. We are at Lamartine's most "sublime." Stars are poetic "astres," not prosaic "étoiles," and water, more often "flot" or "onde" than the everyday "eau," is clearly poetically useful because it is part of nature, flat, out of doors, often apparently endless, reflects light, is the stuff of tears, and can suggest either transience in its movement or permanence in its stillness. Lamartine has a whole repertoire of images which he develops into signs, if not symbols. "Azur" is blue/sky/infinity, and the outside world in its harmonious organization reflects what is going on in the poet's soul. Baudelaire was to use the same reflection of inner reality in external objects and events.

Lamartine published no further lyrical collection before the 1839 *Recueillements*. *Jocelyn*, published in February 1836, had a "fifth" edition in December, which may only have been a fourth, and contains a dedication, a prologue, nine "époques (eras)," and an epilogue. It is a poem of self-sacrifice. Its central figure becomes a priest, so ensuring that his sister will have an adequate dowry. He is driven away from his seminary by the Revolution, falls in love, but has to take priestly orders, with their accompanying vow of chastity, in order to hear the confession of the bishop who ordains him before he is executed. The poem is written in diary form, with dates and places as if the poet were writing purely for himself, but with the occasional variation of metre, and the insertion of a letter or a piece of dialogue. The sentiments are high-minded, dissolving now and then into prayer, and the images are stylized. But the fluency and the musicality remain, and the lofty idealism, no longer born primarily of grief, still appealed to the public which had been attracted to the first collection.

It became increasingly apparent however, that the easy fluency of melodious verse, well enough suited to the early lyrics, could not be extended into epic. The relentless uplift, sustained too long, lacks the suspense and the changes of mood then being offered by romantic drama. Lamartine scarcely, and never successfully, wrote for the stage, just as Balzac and Dumas never wrote good lyric poetry. His five-act verse tragedy, *Saül*, written in 1818 in response to his grief at the death of Julie Charles, was not performed, nor published in Lamartine's lifetime. It is an essential characteristic of his verse that, at its best, it was restricted to the length of a lyric poem, just long enough to develop a mood, to set a scene, to expose a yearning, and to contrive a fitting, often prayerful resolution.

La Chute d'un ange is another attempt at a narrative poem, but is weakened by its unevenness, due no doubt to the excessive haste with which it was composed. The poem, which was written in two spurts in 1836 and 1837, is about an angel who becomes human out of love for a woman, and consists of a "récit," 15 "visions," and a brief epilogue, with interpolations. The 12,000 lines are now fluent to the point of being facile, even puerile. Only the final "La vigne et la maison," inspired by a visit to Milly in 1857, catches again the quality of the early verse. Both Michelet and Sainte-Beuve compare it to the contents of the 1820 *Méditations*. The feeling in the poem is naturally nostalgia, and the form is that of a dialogue between the self and the soul in five brief sections. It harks back to happier times in the youthful form which caught the imagination of a whole generation.

Lamartine's most widely read work was the conte *Graziella*, published separately in 1852. It recounts the story, clearly derived from Lamartine's own life, of a Frenchman who travels in Italy and lives for a period with a fisherman from Naples whose daughter falls in love with him. She dies when he has to return to France. The episode had already figured in *Les Confidences*, just as the death of Julie Charles had been fictionalized in *Raphaël*, published separately in 1849, in which the main character retains the name Julie.

PUBLICATIONS

Collections

Oeuvres complètes, 13 vols., 1834–43
Oeuvres (Edition des Souscripteurs), 14 vols., 1849–50
Oeuvres complètes de Lamartine publiées et inédites, 41 vols., 1860–66
Oeuvres, 22 vols., 1900–07
Oeuvres poétiques complètes, 1963

Verse

Méditations poétiques, 1820; as *Poetical Reveries*, translated by Henry Christmas, 1839
La Mort de Socrate, 1823; as *The Death of Socrates, a Poem*, translated by Harriet Cope, 1829
Nouvelles méditations poétiques, 1823
Le Dernier Chant du pèlerinage d'Harold, 1825; as *The Last Canto of Childe Harold's Pilgrimage*, 1827
Epîtres, 1825
Chant du sacre, 1825
Harmonies poétiques et religieuses, 2 vols., 1830
Contre la peine de mort, 1830
A Némesis, 1831
Jocelyn, 2 vols., 1836; as *Jocelyn: An Episode*, translated by F.H. Jobert, 1837; *Jocelyn: A Romance in Verse*, translated by Hazel Patterson Stewart, 1954
La Chute d'un ange, 2 vols., 1838
Recueillements poétiques, 1839
Poésies inédites, 1873

Travel, history, and political writings

De la politique rationelle, 1831
Souvenirs, impressions, pensées et paysages pendant un voyage en orient (1832–1833), ou notes d'un voyageur, 4 vols., 1835; as *A Pilgrimage to the Holy Land*, 1835; facsimile reprint, 1978

Histoire des Girondins, 8 vols., 1847; as *History of the Girondists*, 3 vols., 1847–48
Histoire de la restauration, 8 vols., 1851–52; as *The History of the Restoration of Monarchy in France* (in part written in English by Lamartine himself, the remainder translated from the French), 4 vols., 1851–53
Histoire de la révolution de 1848, 2 vols., 1849; as *History of the French Revolution of 1848*, n.d.
Nouveau voyage en orient, 1851
Histoire des Constituants, 2 vols., 1854; as *History of the Constituent Assembly*, 4 vols., 1858
Histoire de la Turquie, 5 vols., 1854; 8 vols., 1855; as *History of Turkey*, 2 vols., 1855–57
Histoire de la Russie, 1855
Cours familier de littérature, 26 vols., 1856–68
Jeanne d'Arc, 1863; as *Joan of Arc*, 1867
Homère et Socrate, 1863
Nelson, 1864
Cromwell, 1864; as *Life of Oliver Cromwell*, n.d.
Vie d'Alexandre le Grand, 2 vols., 1859
La France parlementaire (1834–1851), oeuvres oratoires et écrits politiques, 6 vols., 1864–65
Vie de César, 1865

Plays

Toussaint Louverture, 1850
Fior d'Aliza, 1863

Fiction

Raphaël, 1849; as *Raphaël* (in English), 1849
Les Confidences, 1849; as *Confidential Disclosures*, 1849; as *Memoirs of My Youth*, 1849
Les Nouvelles Confidences, 1851; as *The Wanderer and His Home*, 1851
Le Tailleur de pierres de Saint-Point, récit villageois, 1851; as *The Stonecutter of St-Point*, 1851; as *The Stonemason of St-Point*, 1851
Geneviève, 1851; as *Genevieve; or, The History of a Servant Girl*, 1850; as *Genevieve: A Tale of Peasant Life*, 1851
Graziella, 1852; as *Graziella; or, My First Sorrow, and Other Poems…*, translated by W.C. Urquhart, 1871

Other

Mémoires inédites, 1870
Manuscrit de ma mère, 1871
Correspondance, 4 vols., 1873–74

Critical and biographical studies

Whitehouse, H. Remsen, *The Life of Lamartine*, 2 vols., 1918
Fréjaville, G., *Les Méditations de Lamartine*, 1931
Guillemin, H., *Lamartine, l'homme et l'oeuvre*, 1940

LAMENNAIS (or LA MENNAIS), Hugues-Félicité Robert de (known as "Féli"), 1782–1854.

Writer on religious and social matters; founder and editor of 'L'Avenir.'

LIFE

Lamennais, as he came in deference to his democratic convictions to spell his name, dropping the "de," was born on 19 June 1782 at Saint-Malo. He was the fourth of five sons and one daughter of Pierre-Louis Robert (1743–1828), a partner with his brother Denys-François Robert des Saudrais (1744–1829) in the family ship-owning business. Lamennais was delicate and diminutive as an infant. He had an elder brother, a priest by the name of Jean-Marie (1780–1860), who was to play a considerable role in his life. Their mother, who was cultured and devout, died in 1787, when Lamennais was five. He does not seem to have learnt much from the series of nursemaids and tutors who looked after him, and it was his uncle des Saudrais who took his education in hand by letting him loose among his books and giving him some sense of direction. Des Saudrais appears to have been an enthusiast for Rousseau's ideas on education, although he may also have retreated from them later. He translated 20 odes from Horace.

The boy's reading was unusually wide and he picked up English, Spanish, German, Italian, Latin, and Greek, and later acquired some Hebrew. The fact that his reading had been wide and spasmodic rather than profound and directed, leaving him without any formal erudition, was to become clear in his later polemic, which was impassioned, moving, and immensely skilful, but never based on any sound grip of the principles involved. In due course he was apprenticed to the family business and began to spend long periods at La Chênaie, the small country house near Dinan which Lamennais and Jean inherited from their maternal grandfather in 1799, and which was later to become famous as the home of Lamennais's religious movement.

Brittany's role in fostering the Revolution (see Chateaubriand) was unique. The bourgeoisie there played a larger part than anywhere else in France in the movement to administrative reform, were on the whole more liberal and more anxious to have the privileges of the Church and the nobility curtailed, and were ready to welcome any move towards provincial independence. In 1782, two months after Lamennais's birth, his father was appointed the Saint Malo sub-delegate of the Intendant, the king's representative in Brittany, who was known for his benevolent paternalism. Lamennais *père* had strong humanitarian principles and was less inclined than his superior to rely on direct government interference in times of stress. Although devout Catholicism was a stronger force in Brittany than in most of France, he was interested in religion chiefly as a bastion of morality. Louis XVI ennobled him, but not without some resistance from an aristocracy keen to keep out the third estate. He objected to paying for the registration of his title on the grounds that he already contributed vast sums to the public welfare. The matter was not settled before the Revolution, and at the height of the Jacobin ascendancy Pierre-Louis was happy to prove that he had not been registered as an aristocrat.

The sub-delegacy stopped at the Revolution, but des Saudrais became a town councillor, supported the monks who took advantage of the decrees liberating them from the cloister, and guardedly welcomed the Revolution's civil constitution for the clergy, reorganization of diocesan administration, and expropriation of ecclesiastical property, estimated at between a fifth and a half of France's land and buildings. He accepted the proclamation of the Republic in September 1792, but ceased to be a councillor at the end of that year. Lamennais was 10. His father and uncle were regarded as being heavily on the side of the Revolution, although their enthusiasm waned with the coming of the Terror, and they both changed their minds about the Church. Saint-Malo, threatened by the English from across the Channel, as well as by the royalist forces in the Vendée, was governed on behalf of Paris from mid-December 1973 until the fall of Robespierre on 27 July 1894 by Jean-Baptiste le Carpentier, who instituted a particularly savage purge of aristocrats, freemasons, and non-juring priests. The Lamennais family weathered the storm, but only at the cost of vast extortions and semi-ruin. By 1799 they were ready to welcome the consulate and in 1802 the restoration of the Church.

Lamennais's sub-aristocratic but privileged liberal bourgeois upbringing, with his second decade spent under the Terror, the Directory, and the beginnings of the Consulate, left him fundamentally liberal in outlook. Anecdotes suggest a touch of priggishness. He was a sensitive, introspective, and rather sickly child, who early on developed a morbid view of life which was to dominate his thinking during his last two decades. He was clearly headstrong, but plainly in need of the maternal affection of which he had been deprived early in life. The death of his des Saudrais aunt during the Terror had removed all close feminine influence over him, while his uncle had treated him from boyhood as an equal.

Both uncle and nephew were much impressed by the conversion of the outspoken atheist La Harpe to Catholicism in 1797, but Lamennais was not yet ready to practise Catholicism himself. In 1800 he thought of emigrating, but did not. In April 1802 Napoleon pretended to restore Catholicism as France's state religion because he needed the internal cohesion which that would entail, but the "organic articles" he promulgated with the concordat implied that he intended the Gallican Church to be even more subservient to the civil power than it had been under Louis XIV in the 17th century. Napoleon achieved his aim of interior pacification, visibly symbolized by the pope's visit to Paris to crown him in December 1804. In May that year, when Jean had become a priest, Lamennais started to practise his religion and began privately to study theology and look forward to a Catholic renaissance in France.

The joint work of Lamennais and Jean resulted in the *Réflexions sur l'état de l'église en France pendant le XVIIIe siècle, et sur sa situation actuelle*, which Lamennais included in both editions of his *Oeuvres complètes* and of which he was probably the principal author, and the *Tradition de l'eglise sur l'institution des évêques*, which may have been chiefly by Jean. The *Réflexions* was finished by 18 February 1809, shown to the superior of Saint-Sulpice, M. Emery, modified slightly, and published in late June. The date "1808" carried by the first edition is wrong, but may have been a precaution since, by June 1809, the rupture between Napoleon and Pius VII had become irreparable.

The Papal States had been occupied in 1808. On 17 May 1809 they were "reunited" with the French empire by Napoleon's decree. The tricolour went up in Rome on 10 June, and on 11 June the pope excommunicated the emperor, although not by name, to avoid the embarrassment of the obligation it would have imposed on all Catholics not to do business with him. The French invaded the Quirinal on 5–6 July, arrested the pope, and kept him at Savona until 1812. Since the *Réflexions* contained a bitter account of the imprisonment of Pius VI by the Directory, it had become virtually seditious while it was being printed. It was in fact seized and pulped, but apparently not before Jean had salvaged enough sheets for the second edition, which appeared in 1814, mostly using the sheets of the first, but with some pointedly ultramontane additions, and passages about Napoleon omitted.

In 1809 Lamennais was sufficiently outraged by Napoleon to take the first steps towards ordination, the tonsure on 16 March and minor orders on 23 December, in both cases after making a retreat at Rennes. In 1809 he also translated Blois's *Guide spirituel*. The squabble between Napoleon and the pope now hinged on Rome's right to refuse to appoint governmental nominees to vacant episcopal sees. Napoleon had appointed Cardinal Maury to the archbishopric of Paris, but did not want a schism, and it was Pius VII's refusal to give way on this vital point that converted Lamennais to ultramontanism. Catholicism could be kept together, it seemed to Lamennais, only by the reservation in the last resort of jurisdiction in the matter of appointment to the Church's spiritual hierarchy to the holy see.

The three-volume *Tradition* was an investigation, supported by M. Emery, into the history of the institution of bishops. When it was finished, Lamennais thought it totally vindicated the ultramontane position, reserving jurisdiction in appointments to hierarchical posts to the see of Rome by divine right, and not only in virtue of ecclesiastical law promulgated in support of medieval disciplinary arrangements. He found no grounds, however, for supposing that the pope had authority in secular matters, which were the domain of sovereigns. The grounds for the strenuous later defence of the separation of powers had been laid. The probability is that Lamennais became a priest in 1816 because, in the end, he believed that the regeneration of European society depended on the integrity and liberty of the Church, to which henceforward he wished to devote himself.

In the immediate circumstances of the Bourbon restoration in 1814 no one was very interested in the ultramontanism of the *Tradition*, published early in August. Lamennais's father and uncle were now bankrupt and had to be supported by Lammenais, Jean, and a brother-in-law. Jean became chaplain to the bishop of Saint-Brieuc. Lamennais considered journalism and was already thinking of setting up an ultramontane newspaper. He published a violent pamphlet against the centralization of secondary and higher education, contributed to *L'Ami de la Religion et du Roi*, and was disillusioned at the refusal of the restoration governments to rescind Napoleon's administrative reorganization of France. When Napoleon returned during the hundred days of 1815, Lamennais left for Guernsey and London, probably to make it look as if he alone was responsible for the *Tradition*, whose author Napoleon would be unlikely to forgive. This allowed Jean to continue unmolested at Saint-Brieuc, where he was now vicar capitular. A teaching post was found for Lamennais in a London school by a Breton priest, Guy Carron, who became his spiritual director. After a long retreat in 1815 Lamennais decided to become a priest and stayed on in London in order to be with Carron, with whom he returned to France in November 1815. He was ordained at Vannes on 9 March 1816.

The first volume of the *l'Essai sur l'indifférence en matière de religion* was published in 1817, the second in 1820, and volumes three and four were published in 1823. A fifth volume was projected but not completed, and in 1821, between volumes two and three, Lamennais published his *Défense de l'Essai sur l'indifférence en matière de religion*. He was still living with Carron when the first volume appeared anonymously. It was an astounding success for a work of apologetics, going through four editions in its first year, during which it sold 13,000 copies. It was also widely misunderstood, so that the second volume, published on 7 July 1820, came as a shock. Lamennais had made enemies between 1817 and 1820 with the biting hostility of his journalism to anything which seemed to threaten the liberty of the Church. The royalists thought him a natural ally, which he was not, and the liberals disliked him for his attacks on the university system, and for collaboration with the royalist press. When the second volume appeared and the apologetic argument was finally seen to rest on the establishment of general or universal consent as the infallible criterion of truth, the Catholic reaction was much more guarded. Lamennais had overstated his case, had made enemies, and had seemed to come near to demolishing his own argument when arguing the extreme weakness of individual reason, although technically he does avoid contradicting himself.

The truth of Catholicism rested, according to Lamennais, on its unity, universality, perpetuity, and holiness. The unwritten fifth volume of the *Essai* would have developed the argument that the pope was the infallible organ of the testimony of the human race to the one true religion, a view which was in fact clearly to be set out in *De la religion considérée dans ses rapports avec l'ordre politique et civil*. The Jesuits, in spite of their own allegiance to the pope, were unhappy with the second volume and extracted seven propositions not to be taught in their colleges, thereby incurring Lamennais's lasting hostility. Those attracted to his doctrine, as also later to his spirituality, were the young Catholics aware of the need for a new theology and a new apologetics based on a head-on confrontation with scepticism. Against the deists Lamennais counter-attacked by attempting to show the need for authoritarian teaching even in science and philosophy. There were initial victories. His opponents failed to get the imprimatur for the Italian translation of the *Essai* withheld. He was himself alternately elated and depressed, but felt a growing sense of mission. There is a half truth buried in the assertion that he was becoming "chaplain to the romantic movement (q.v.)."

Lamennais translated and added notes to *The Imitation of Christ*, his most reliable source of income until the end of his life. In 1824 he went to Rome, apparently for recreational purposes, although he stayed three months and was warmly welcomed by Leo XII, who would have liked to attach him to the papal curia, and may conceivably have made him a cardinal "in petto" (in secret) at the consistory of 2 October 1826. The French government wrongly suspected that Lamennais was in Rome as an emissary of the "ultra" party. Lamennais, who himself regarded the *Essai* as only a beginning, was already contemplating the later *Esquisse d'une philosophie*, at this date still to be entitled "Essai d'un système de philosophie catholique," which, as he wrote to Victor Cousin on 30 June 1825, would not stifle but "stimulate reason and make it fertile." Lamennais's health had already broken down once, and in 1827 he suffered another serious illness. He recovered, convinced that providence had a mission to confide to him.

The social regeneration of France and, indeed, Europe through the renaissance of Catholicism, the goal which dominated Lamennais's life, needed more than just a foundation in apologetics and philosophy. His vision between leaving Rome and the foundation of *L'Avenir* in 1830 centred on the relationship to be envisaged between Church and state. He also abandoned his hopes of the royalists and began to elaborate the alliance between liberalism and Catholicism, so important at the apex of the romantic movement in France. A small presage of royalist hostility greeted him on his return from Rome when the aristocratic prelate, the Prince de Croÿ, grand almoner and later a cardinal, let it be known that Lamennais was unwelcome in the apartment of which, as his chaplain until very recently, Lamennais's brother still had the use.

Louis XVIII had died on 16 September 1824, France had been militarily successful in Spain, and the army rallied to the new king, Charles X, who was intent as far as possible on restoring the pre-1789 status quo, and so fanatically devout as to have been the principal cause of the anti-clerical aspect taken by the 1830 revolution. In *De la religion considérée dans ses rapports avec l'ordre politique et civil*, the first part of which was published in May 1825 and the second in February 1826, Lamennais was not only unconcerned about the plight of the returned émigrés or the struggle for political power, but he ridiculed the idea of a return to the pre-Revolutionary state of France and attacked Gallican ecclesiastical liberties. His solution in 1826 was to restore to the Church, and in particular the papacy, an authority at once wider and more absolute. Both spiritual and temporal powers were, in his view, divine in origin, but it was for the Church to decide what was the law of God and what pertained to the purely temporal realm. At the back of Lammenais's mind was the desire to impede civil tyranny in the name of political autonomy. The second part of his work was published in an atmosphere of near-hysteria induced by accusations of a huge Jesuit and ultramontane conspiracy to overthrow both Church and state. The accusations were launched in an extremely popular *Mémoire*, published on 1 March 1826 by Comte Montlosier, and called by the *Journal des Débats* "Le flambeau de la France (the torch of France)." Lamennais was charged with having attacked the rights of the king and inciting civil disobedience. He was fined a mere 30 francs, on the second charge only, but his book was suppressed.

Meanwhile, Belgian Catholic leaders, feeling oppressed as a result of the incorporation of Belgium into the joint Netherlands kingdom in 1815, made contact with Lamennais. He was impressed by the union in Belgium between Catholics and liberals achieved in the autumn of 1828, just before he finished the text of *Des progrès de la révolution et de la guerre contre l'église*. Published in February 1829, it was inspired by the idea of a possible similar alliance in France, where Charles X was driving the liberal opposition into a stance firmly hostile to the Church. Debate now centred on the private secondary schools which had been allowed to open, although, strictly speaking, only seminaries were permitted. On 21 April 1828 the control even of primary schools was transferred to the public sector. Lamennais was in Turin when, on 16 June, ordinances were signed suppressing secondary schools run by religious orders and controlling the other Catholic schools in the private sector. Rome, still anxious about the situation in France, told the French hierarchy to withdraw its objections, and in *Des progrès* Lamennais changed his own view, asking now only for Catholics to be

accorded liberty of conscience, of the press, and of education, but no longer for the state to submit to papal authority in the name of the law of God. He was preparing for the liberal Catholic position he would adopt after the July revolution of 1830, which he foresaw in his preface.

Lamennais's abandonment of his previous position caused shock waves, and 6,000 copies of *Des progrès* were sold in a fortnight. He was denounced for liberalism in pastoral letters issued by various bishops on the death of Leo XII on 10 February 1829. He replied with two open letters to the archbishop of Paris, Monsignor de Quélen, of March and April 1829, full of lofty disdain and whipping irony. It is said that the government tried to get its minister in Rome, Chateaubriand, to have *Des progrès* put on the index of forbidden books, but no archival support for this contention has been found. In the meantime, Lamennais had founded a powerful movement of spiritual renewal based at La Chênaie, which, from 1828 to 1833, was a sort of retreat house where gifted young Catholics stayed for periods of varying length. Lamennais's brother, who had founded the teaching order the Frères de l'Instruction Chrétienne in 1819, also founded the Congrégation de Saint-Pierre in 1828 to create some sort of community life for the diocesan clergy. A seminary was also established. Lamartine was strongly attracted to the movement, and Lamennais was Hugo's intellectual guide as well as his confessor for a number of years, at least one of the sources of his political liberalism. Lamartine, Hugo, and Sainte-Beuve all abandoned Catholicism on the condemnation of Lamennais. Others to come under his strong influence at different times and for different periods included Auguste Comte, Vigny, and Balzac.

The archbishop of Paris, whose palace was sacked during the July revolution of 1830, had been a provocatively open sycophant of the monarchy and had to go into hiding. It is difficult to see how the republican administration could be anything but anti-clerical in posture, but Pius VIII recognized Louis-Philippe in the traditional way and the 1801 concordat was allowed by both sides to continue in force, that of 1817 never having been ratified in France. Lamennais was now the ardent advocate of the separation of Church and state. "On tremble devant le libéralisme: eh bien, catholicisez-le, et la Société renaîtra (We shudder at liberalism. Well, Catholicize it, and society will be reborn)." The prospectus for *L'Avenir* distinguished between old 18th-century anti-Christian liberalism and the young liberalism, content with the separation of Church and state.

In October 1830, after one of his periodic financial crises, Lamennais settled at Juilly, which the Abbé de Salinis had reopened as a college for those who might otherwise have gone to a Jesuit school. *L'Avenir* was published as a four-page daily newspaper from 16 October 1830 to 15 November 1831, when it closed for lack of subscribers. To some extent it inherited the "young" liberal tradition from *Le Globe*, which had been founded by P.F. Dubois in 1824 and had become Saint-Simonian in 1830, and it also replaced the monthly *Le Mémorial Catholique*, founded by Philippe-Olympe Gerbet and Salinis. *L'Avenir* claimed to be the first European daily published as a Catholic paper and reached a peak circulation of about 1,500. It promptly rallied to the new regime, but the alliance between liberalism and Catholicism was too novel. A memorial service for the Duc de Berry, the son of Charles X assassinated on 13 February 1820, was held on 14 February 1831. The clearly unfair denunciation of the royalist demonstrators by *L'Avenir* led to the sacking of the church of Saint-Germain-l'Auxerrois by a hostile crowd and was too much for the large numbers of "legitimist" Catholics who were loyal to the Bourbons.

In its last issue *L'Avenir* announced that Lamennais, Lacordaire, later to become the brilliant Dominican preacher, and the Comte de Montalembert were going to Rome to seek support. The decision had been sudden. Lamennais had to stay in Rome from December 1831 until July 1832 because various financial transactions had rendered him liable to imprisonment in France. The pope's position was difficult on account of the need he felt to protect the Papal States, which meant invoking the help of the tsar and, on 9 June 1832, condemning the Polish insurrection of 1830–31 against him. Lamennais had no idea of the impending catastrophe when, at Munich on 30 August, he received news of the brief condemning *L'Avenir, Mirari vos,* dated 15 August 1832. The encyclical was in fact mild, but Lamennais immediately thought that *L'Avenir,* like the Poles, had been sacrificed to political expediency. He did, however, draw up and sign a public act of submission in Paris in September, before going back to La Chênaie, where he worked on his philosophical essay.

His view that the Church's teaching authority was concentrated in the pope had to be modified. It is not always easy to distinguish when the pope was speaking personally from the occasions when he was speaking in the name of the Church. Lamennais's tone became increasingly apocalyptic in the correspondence of the first half of 1833. In May and June he wrote most of the *Paroles d'un croyant,* although it was not published until 1834. He wrote the book as a prophet, feeling impelled to impart God's message to the poor and the suffering. The regeneration of society now seemed as though it would have to be undertaken independently of the Church. In May 1833 the French translation of *Le Livre des pèlerins polonais* by Adam Mickiewicz was published, defending the Polish uprising. Lamennais had contributed an epilogue. Rome was naturally displeased at the dissemination of the book in French. A private letter from the pope to the archbishop of Toulouse was published. Lamennais's submission to *Mirari vos* was called into question, and in the diocese of Rennes he was temporarily suspended from his priestly functions. The *Paroles d'un croyant,* seen through the press by Sainte-Beuve, was published on 30 April 1834. It caused a sensation, was read aloud in public, immediately translated, and reprinted, and instantly became, on account of its grave prognostications and denunciations, one of the century's really important books.

None the less, Lamennais was taken by surprise when, on 15 July 1834, he heard of the condemnation of the book in the encyclical *Singulari nos,* rightly suspecting the intervention of Metternich. Lamennais had, however, now openly repudiated the fullest form of the submission to the earlier encyclical exacted from him, thereby rendering some doctrinal reprisal inevitable. Even after his article "De l'absolutisme et de la liberté," which appeared in the *Revue des Deux Mondes* (q.v.) for 1 August 1834 and attacked the untrammelled authority of the temporal power in matters concerning civil liberties, Lamennais had no intention of leaving the Church. One by one, all his close colleagues accepted the condemnation, submitted, and remained Catholic. Lamennais himself, never excommunicated, simply drifted out of the Church, which he had definitively left by 1836, essentially because he felt that it had allied itself with the doctrine of absolute civil power against the forces of liberalism and

democracy. He continued to live at La Chênaie until May 1836. By 1841 he no longer believed in a supernatural order, and had rejected the notion of revelation, miracles, traditional Christology, and the theologically normative theories of the redemption as expiation, leaving himself only with a deep compassion for the suffering and outcasts.

Lamennais spent his last years in relative obscurity, although George Sand was inspired by him. After *Les Affaires de Rome, les maux de l'église et de la société* Lamennais published collected articles as *Le Livre du peuple, De l'esclavage moderne,* and *Politique à l'usage du peuple. Le Pays et le gouvernement* resulted in a prison sentence. He was ill, in difficult financial circumstances, and lost friends, although faithful to his belief in the sovereignty of the people and president of the Société de la Solidarité Républicaine, which attracted half a million members in a fortnight. The four volumes of the *Esquisse d'une philosophie* appeared from 1840 to 1846, and in 1840 Lamennais also published *Une voix de prison.* After the 1848 revolution, in which he started two newspapers which failed, he was elected to the Assemblée Constituente but, disheartened by the 1851 coup d'état, retired to private life, spending his last years on a translation of Dante. Lamennais died in Paris on 27 February 1854. At his own request he was given a pauper's burial.

WORKS

In writing about Lamennais it has obviously been necessary to consider the changes of view which affected his career in the context of his life. From a literary point of view, however, and whatever the merits of Lamennais's skilled polemical writing and its withering irony, the most important works are the later, more lyrical ones. The central points at issue in the earlier controversial works have already been identified, but it is perhaps Sainte-Beuve who best seized on the fundamental unity of Lamennais's work up to the *Paroles d'un croyant.* When discussing that work he pointed out that Lamennais's aim had always been the same.

On entering into his maturity, Lamennais had found a society depraved and exhausted by the Revolutionary and Napoleonic periods. It required a regeneration which, at first, he felt could come only from above: "L'autorité peut tout, soit pour le bien, soit pour le mal;…on n'agit sur les peuples que par l'autorité (Authority can do everything, either for good or for evil…only through authority can you act on the people)." It was no doubt Carron and Lamennais's brother who between them persuaded him that the regeneration required a supranational authority, which meant in effect the Catholic religion, of whose truth Lamennais was already persuaded, and of which he thought he could easily persuade others, acting through its identifiable and infallible head, the pope.

Governments were the channel for the regenerative impulses originally envisaged by Lamennais, but the French governments of the restoration were clearly unwilling to remove the obstacles Napoleon had put in the way of the Church's action on society. Lamennais went over to the attack. The state is really atheist, he declared. It finances the Church as it finances the arts and the stud farms. Its yoke, and that of the monarchy, must be thrown off. The state organization of secondary education was to stay in place, even when the papal right to appoint to the episcopacy had been conceded. Lamennais therefore invoked the holy see over the heads of governments. This was the era when he argued most strongly for the separation of Church and state.

When the holy see, partly responding to political constraints, failed to exert the authority with which Lamennais believed it to be invested, he turned again directly to the people, bypassing hierarchical authority in his attempt to forge a union between Catholicism and liberalism. By 5 April 1836 he could write, "On se récriera tant qu'on voudra; je soutiens, moi, que le peuple, le pauvre peuple, travaillant chaque jour, est partout ce qu'il y a de meilleur, et qu'en lui seul sont les éléments avec lesquels on peut refaire la société (People will say what they like. I myself hold that the people, the poor people, working daily, is the best everywhere there is to be found, and that in it alone are the elements with which society can be rebuilt)."

Sainte-Beuve was doubtless correct in identifying Lamennais's principal aim from the beginning. By 1834 it was not yet clear how closely Lamennais was to identify himself with the figure of the people's saviour, the prophet who would transmit the regenerative vigour needed to lead them to the Promised Land. It is also possible that Sainte-Beuve, at that date pardonably, had missed some of the apocalyptic visions that were beginning to haunt a mind which Metternich, at least, thought deranged. It is also clear that the relative superficiality of Lamennais's grasp of the basic principles of political philosophy, his tendency to overstate, to be carried away by his sense of outrage and swept on by his own magnificent rhetoric did untold damage to the causes to which he devoted himself. He did not, until it was much too late, identify the difficulty of distinguishing the areas of competence of spiritual and temporal authority, and he was therefore continually obliged to shift his position. He similarly failed to think through the question of the foundation for papal infallibility or the difficulty of distinguishing the occasions on which it was being exercised from those when it was not. The result was not politically effective activity, but sometimes immense popular appeal, superb rhetoric, great invective skills, and some very fine lyrical prose.

Lamennais's arguments, and the circumstances in which they were forged, have summarily been indicated. The 23rd chapter of the *Paroles d'un croyant* consists principally of a litany. The rhythm is not, as has been thought, Hebrew, but Latin. A whole series of single-line metaphors for suffering humanity is followed by the line "We cry to you, Lord,"

> Lord, we cry to you from the depths of our misery.
> Like animals who lack pasture with which to feed their
>   young,
>   We cry to you, Lord.
> Like the lamb whose ewe is taken from it,
>   We cry to you, Lord...

Lamennais's taste was based on the magnificent rhythms, cadences, and syntactical devices of the poetry he knew best, which came from the early medieval Latin poetry of the Roman breviary, at some remove from the lingering inspiration of Hebrew psalmody. The chapter ends in a prayer comparing the suffering people to the suffering Christ, not at all a pastiche, but itself a liturgy.

> O Père! vous n'avez point délaissé votre Fils, votre Christ,
>   si ce n'est qu'en apparence et pour un moment; vous ne
>   délaisserez point non plus à jamais les frères du Christ. Son

divin sang, qui les a rachetés de l'esclavage du Prince de ce monde, les rachètera aussi de l'esclavage des ministres du Prince de ce monde. Voyez leurs pieds et leurs mains percés, leur côté ouvert, leur tête couverte de plaies sanglantes… Encore trois jours, et le sceau sacrilège sera brisé, et la pierre sera brisée, et ceux qui dorment se réveilleront, et le règne du Christ, qui est justice et charité et paix et joie dans l'Esprit saint, commencera. Ainsi soit-il.

(O Father! You did not desert your Son, your Christ, except apparently and momentarily; neither will you for ever desert the brothers of Christ. His divine blood, which redeemed them from the slavery of the Prince of this world, will also redeem them from the slavery of the ministers of the Prince of this world. See their feet and hands pierced, their opened side, their head covered with bleeding wounds… Three more days and the sacrilegious seal will be broken, and the stone will be broken, and those who sleep will awake, and the reign of Christ, which is justice and charity and peace and joy in the Holy Ghost, will begin. Amen.)

PUBLICATIONS

Collections

Oeuvres complètes, 12 vols., 1836–37
Oeuvres complètes, 10 vols., 1844
Oeuvres posthumes, 1855–58
Oeuvres inédites, 2 vols., 1866

Works

*Réflexions sur l'état de l'église en France pendant le XVIIIe
    siècle, et sur sa situation actuelle*, 1809 (wrongly dated 1808)
Tradition de l'église sur l'institution des évêques, 3 vols., 1814
Essai sur l'indifférence en matière de religion, 4 vols., 1817–23;
    as *Essay on Indifference in Matters of Religion*, 1895
Du droit du gouvernement sur l'éducation, 1817
Recherches philosophiques, 1818
Défense de l'Essai sur l'indifférence en matière de religion,
    1821
De la religion considérée dans ses rapports avec l'ordre politique et civil, 2 vols., 1825–26
Mélanges, 3 vols., 1826
Des progrès de la révolution et de la guerre contre l'église, 1829
Lettre à Mgr l'Archevêque de Paris, 1829
Paroles d'un croyant, 1834; in *The People's Prophecy*, 1943; as
    Words of a Believer, 1834
Les Affaires de Rome, les maux de l'église et de la société, 1836
Le Livre du peuple, 1837; as *The People's Own Book*, 1839
Politique à l'usage du peuple, 2 vols., 1838
De l'esclavage moderne, 1840
Esquisse d'une philosophie, 4 vols., 1840–46
Le Pays et le gouvernement, 1840
Une voix de prison, 1840; in *The People's Prophecy*, 1943
De la religion, 1841
Du passé et de l'avenir du peuple, 1841;
Amschaspands et Darvands, 1843
Le Deuil de la Pologne, 1846

De la société première et de ses lois; ou, De la religion, 1848
Correspondance générale, 9 vols., 1971–81

Translator *Le Guide spirituel*, by Louis de Blois, 1809
    L'Imitation de Jésus-Christ, by Thomas à Kempis,
        1824
    Les Confessions, by St Augustine, 1844
    Les Evangiles, 1846
    Le Nouveau Testament, 1851
    La Divine Comédie, by Dante, 1855

Biographical and critical studies

Boutard, Charles, *Lamennais, sa vie et ses doctrines*, 3 vols.,
    1905–13
Sparrow Simpson, W.J., *French Catholics in the 19th Century*,
    1918
Vidler, Alec R., *Prophecy and Papacy: A Study of Lamennais,
    the Church, and Revolution*, 1954

———

LARBAUD, Valery (-Nicolas), 1881–1957.

Novelist, translator.

LIFE

It is arguable that Valery Larbaud contributed more to French
literary culture by his life than by his writings, and by his translations more than by the works of his imagination. Lucky
enough to be born wealthy, he travelled often, but not very far
and not for very long at a time. He did, however, assimilate himself into the cultures in which he lived and brought the fruits of
his rare experiences back to France. Often compared with travellers like Cendrars, Larbaud was in fact quite different. He mastered English, Spanish, and Italian well enough to write in them
for publication, spoke German and Portuguese, knew and was
interested in Romanian and half a dozen dialect forms of his
major languages, and was thoroughly grounded in Latin and
Greek. He never stayed in hotels if he could rent an apartment or
a room.

He liked to make friends locally, ate the local cuisine,
believed firmly in the real possibility of a European federation,
although he was not interested in its political organization, and
read the literatures written in the languages of the countries he
visited. Few have any inkling of what this sort of experience
entails. While maintaining that there was a country called
Europe and dismissive of mere differences of nationality, Larbaud in fact became something like the comparative anthropologist of advanced European cultures, especially the literary
aspects of those cultures. He has always been better known outside France than within it. Culturally, the most important figure
in his life was probably Walt Whitman, not a European at all.

In 1935 Larbaud suffered from a severe cerebral haemorrhage
which left him voiceless and completely incapacitated for the
rest of his life. He was the only son of a chemist at Lyons, who
owned the mineral water spring at Saint-Yorre, and of Isabelle
Bureau des Etivaux, whose republican father had been forced
into exile, first at Annecy in Savoy, when it still belonged to Sardinia, and then in Geneva. Larbaud's mother had been brought
up in Geneva in a rich and thoroughly cosmopolitan atmosphere, and often took her son there while he was a small child.
He was later to recall with amusement all the business of travel
involving passports and registration at consulates. From very
early on he was interested in other countries, collected flags,
coloured in maps, noted where his friends came from, and read
books about explorers.

Larbaud's health was always fragile and he spent long periods
away from school, friends, and the normal activities of childhood. The family was Protestant. Larbaud's father died when he
was eight. His dominating, strict, uncomprehending mother
reinforced Larbaud's tendency, already a consequence of his
health, to turn inwards on himself and live a life of the imagination. Larbaud later recalled how unpleasant he found his childhood years at Vichy as he was just approaching double figures.
On account of his health he was sporadically taught by private
tutors, but in 1891, when he was 10, he was sent to board at the
expensive school of Sainte-Barbe-des-Champs in Fontenay-
aux-Roses, just south of Paris.

Larbaud enjoyed his three years at Sainte-Barbe, filled with
the cosmopolitan aristocracy of all races and colours, and had
his first emotional relationship with a little girl. His letters to his
aunt, which are much freer in style than those to his mother,
convey his enthusiasm for the school. By the time he left, at 13,
he was reading the symbolists and the Parnassians (qq.v.), Turgenev, Tolstoy, and the 19th-century French novelists. He had
also come into contact with the Catholicism which he was to
convert to in February or March 1910, when he was 28. He had
kept diaries to help his memory from quite an early age, destroying portions as he later drew on them, and, when he started to
write his own adolescent verse, it was free verse deriving from
the minor symbolists. Early on he made a habit of consciously
looking for unknown authors he enjoyed. The family library, a
special building in the park, contained 20,000 volumes, their
bindings colour-coded to indicate the language they were written in. Reviews arrived from all over the world. The third of the
10 volumes of the 1950–55 *Oeuvres complètes* is devoted to the
"unpunished vice of reading," and shows how well Larbaud
used the privileged opportunities at his disposal. From 1895 he
had attended the Lycée Henri IV in Paris, already probably the
best school in France, then in 1896 moved to the Lycée Bainville
de Moulins.

Holiday travel, at first in Italy and Spain, started when Larbaud was 15. Later, after his baccalauréat, he travelled widely,
often accompanied by the manager of the family estates. The
itineraries appear formidable: 1897, Spain; 1898, Spain and
North Africa (16 towns), then Russia (five towns), Bulgaria,
Yugoslavia, Austria; 1899, Italy (five towns); 1900, Italy (11
towns); 1901, Belgium, Holland, Germany; 1902, Germany,
England, German sanatorium; 1903, Czechoslovakia, Italy,
Yugoslavia, Belgium; 1904, Greece, Italy; 1905, North Africa
(grand tour), Germany, Denmark, Sweden, Spain; 1907,
England; 1908, Spain; 1909, Italy, England; 1911, north-west
England; 1912, Italy; 1913, Scotland, Ireland, Iceland; 1914 and
1915, England; 1916–19, Spain; 1919, England; 1920, Spain;

1921, Switzerland, England; 1922, Italy; 1923, Spain; 1924, Italy (nine towns), Belgium; 1925, Italy; 1926, Portugal, Italy; 1927, Luxembourg, Belgium, Holland; 1928, 1929, 1931, Italy; 1932, Italy, Greece; 1933, Switzerland; 1934, England, Switzerland, Belgium; 1935, Albania, Italy.

In all Larbaud spent over 30 months in England before his illness, and there were two long stays in Spain, 10 in Italy. Some of the travel was to escape from his mother in Vichy, and from literary life in Paris, which prevented him from working. His dedication to a unified Europe was total and Larbaud became expert at identifying the moments in European history when it might have been achieved. His thesis was simple: the capital of a united Europe ought to be Paris, with other large towns as autonomous as small states. The European would behave as a Parisian in Paris, as a Londoner in London, as a Roman in Rome, and as an Argentinian in Buenos Aires.

Larbaud acquired his languages slowly. We know that he worked hard at Italian during the winter of 1900–01, by the end of which he had a good reading knowledge and had made his first translations of English prose by Poe, Hawthorne, and de Quincey, and English poetry by Milton, Swinburne, and Rossetti. In 1901 his translation of Coleridge's *The Ancient Mariner* (1798) was published. By 1907 he had completed his "licence" in English, although he had only once visited England, and begun the doctoral thesis on Walter Savage Landor which he was never to finish. By 1917 Larbaud was noting in his diary that, while Spanish was the first foreign language he ever spoke fluently, he never thought in Spanish and could never have translated a Spanish literary work. Spanish was the language for conversation with school friends at Sainte-Barbe, while Italian and English became literary languages. Larbaud wrote letters from Paris for *The New Weekly* for 14 weeks in 1914, and from 1920 to 1935 he was associated with Fargue, Valéry, and the Italian Marguerite Caetani in the publication of *Commerce*. He married an Italian and his command of the language was to become virtually perfect, but in 1912 he noted in a diary he kept in English that he was still speaking with a noticeably French accent.

He was to become better known in literary circles abroad than in Paris. In England he knew Alice Meynell, and through her became acquainted with the work of Coventry Patmore, who had become a Catholic in 1864. He also used to stay with Arnold Bennett, whose *Five Towns* he translated and about whom he wrote, and there is an unpublished correspondence with James Joyce, of whom Larbaud was an early advocate in France. He was to translate five novels by Samuel Butler, and numbered among his Anglo-Saxon friends Eliot, Symons, Conrad, Chesterton, Edith Sitwell, H.G. Wells, and Logan Pearsall Smith. Several of Larbaud's "enfantines" and short stories have English settings, or were written in English.

From the fictionalized autobiographical passages of the novels, taken together with the travel diaries, we know that Larbaud had a long liaison with a young woman with whom he visited Italy in 1903, at which date he was still travelling quite often with his mother. In 1908 he published 100 copies of a book called *Poèmes d'un riche amateur*, published anonymously and containing the biography of Archibaldo Olson Barnabooth, attributed to X.-M. Tournier de Zamble, Barnabooth's poems, and the story "Le pauvre chemisier." Barnabooth, who is modelled in part on Max Lebaudy, was born, we are told, on 23 August 1883 at Campamento, a province of Arequipa, whose ownership at the time was disputed by Bolivia, Chile, and Peru. Barnabooth was to have himself naturalized a citizen of the US, where his father lived, a one-time farmer, gold miner, and saloon-keeper who had made a fortune in Peru. Barnabooth's mother was an Australian dancer, and he himself had been sent to Europe when he was six, accompanied by his father's secretary. Larbaud's cosmopolitan fantasy, Barnabooth, is already being blended into his own autobiography. Barnabooth and his father's secretary go to Russia. His parents die when he is nine, and he is sent to board in New York, escapes, and goes to live with a Russian friend of his father, a grand duke. Certain details about Barnabooth's existence, especially his reading, provide a reasonably sure guide to Larbaud's own activities.

Larbaud published Barnabooth's *Journal intime* in 1913. He had originally intended to call the book "Journal d'un homme libre." The 1908 volume was included, and in 1913 the whole volume became the *Oeuvres complètes* of A.O. Barnabooth, by Larbaud. Meanwhile, Larbaud had published his first novel, *Fermina Marquez* of 1911. By now he was also writing his "enfantines," to be published as a volume of that title in 1918. Much of his fiction was published in the three collected volumes: *Jaune Bleu Blanc, Amants, heureux amants...*, and *Ce vice impuni, la lecture*, where the title comes from Logan Pearsall Smith's description of reading as "this polite and unpunished vice" in *Trivia*, 1918–23). There were also essays, travel notes in *Jaune Bleu Blanc* and *Allen: aux couleurs de Rome*, and a vast corpus of critical writing and translation, never reprinted. Many pieces of high literary quality, to judge by the generally reliable opinions of some of those who have read them, have never been published at all. Larbaud also published a penetrating study of translation, *Sous l'invocation de saint Jérôme*. In the end, however, his masterpiece may well turn out to have been his two volumes of the *Journal inédit*, published a few years before his death.

WORKS

Larbaud is probably of greater literary interest than is generally acknowledged, although much of his creative energy went into translations, unpublished criticism, travel sketches, fragments of various sorts in several languages, and diaries. As an imaginative author he clearly lacked power.

Fermina Marquez is a novel about a 16-year-old from Peru, and the impact she and her sister have on an exclusive boys' boarding school attended by their brother. She is attracted towards two of the boys, one eloquent and expansive, the other silent, mysterious, and physically attractive. The novel, although delicate and perceptive, is generally thought, like so much of Larbaud's fiction, to lack the sustained power of penetrating imaginative vision.

Larbaud's most memorable creation is Barnabooth. All the texts are presented in *A.O. Barnabooth: ses oeuvres complètes*. The travels of this restless and insatiably curious figure are portrayed partly as fictionalized autobiography, partly as travelogue, and partly as meditative poetry. These writings also make serious points about internationalism and the need to travel in order to understand one's own background and roots. In the end Barnabooth returns to his native Spanish, abandoning his adopted language, French, marries a girl from his native Peru, and settles down at home again, although he had considered himself "an honorary American... fundamentally European-ized," and his poems had regarded Europe as a single town. The three adopted fatherlands are "Italy, Paris, and Germany," and Barnabooth's poems recall the famous *Cartes postales* of Henry-Jean-Marie Levet, published by Larbaud in 1921. Barnabooth himself needs not so much the thrill of the exotic, the ruins of ancient civilizations, the museums and galleries, as the appeasement of his own restlessness, and is unlike Larbaud in his preoccupation with the bustle of travel:

> ...je sens qu'il faut à ce coeur de vagabond
> La trépidation des trains et des navires,
> Et une angoisse sans bonheur sans cesse alimentée.

> (...I feel that what this wandering heart needs is/The anxiousness of trains and boats,/And an agony without happiness which is continually rekindled.)

The published *Enfantines* is a series of short sketches of adolescents or younger children whose sentimentality has not yet crystallized into mature love. There is grace and psychological delicacy here, but again no real power. Much the same is true of the short stories like "Beauté, mon beau souci," published in *Amants, heureux amants...*, written in Spain, in French, and about London. The conte is bathed in peaceful calm and begins with the description of an apartment in London, which is the one in which Larbaud had lived in 1909 and whose fictional inhabitant, Marc Fournier, employs a 38-year-old house-keeper, Edith Crossland. Her character, and that of other Englishwomen, like her 14-year-old daughter Queenie, or Queenie's aunt, Mrs Longhurst, is sketched with subtlety and deftness, although the impression it makes is not strong enough to stamp itself firmly on the mind. English incompetence at anything except love is too insubstantial a theme to support a major imaginative work, or even an important conte, unless it is somehow universalized.

Larbaud clearly had a weakness for Englishwomen, whom he normally treats with indulgence. "Disque," published in *Jaune Bleu Blanc*, is about an Englishwoman married to an Italian and is written in the form of an interior monologue, like much else of Larbaud's, whose temperament, largely formed by his upbringing, the form exactly suited. "Sulpicia" is a letter written by an Englishwoman. "Vaisseau de Thésée," written in 1931 and published in *Allen: aux couleurs de Rome*, evokes Liverpool as seen by the cosmopolitan hotelier Charles-Marie Bonsignor, and "Tan Callando," from the same collection, is set in Birmingham and the industrialized Midlands. The swift depiction of the boys in the street, the girls who lift up their skirts for them, the alarm they give to anyone selling alcohol without a licence when a policeman comes in sight, and the smoky spring drizzle in the warm air matches the best descriptive writing to have been produced in France between the wars, although it lacks the powerful vision that would make it truly significant.

The real interest of Larbaud lies not in the distraction of Barnabooth, nor the subsequent short stories, but in the meditative reflections and the travel sketches themselves, the cosmopolitanism of his outlook, the often acutely perceptive but uncollected criticism, the diaries which reveal the over-sensitive, withdrawn personality, and, apparently, in the unpublished correspondence.

PUBLICATIONS

Collections

Oeuvres complètes, 10 vols., 1950–55
Oeuvres, Bibliothèque de la Pléiade, 1957

Fiction

Poèmes d'un riche amateur, 1908
Fermina Marquez, 1911
A.O. Barnabooth: ses oeuvres complètes, c'est- à-dire un conte, ses poésies, et son journal intime, 1913; as *A.O. Barnbooth: His Diary*, 1924
Enfantines, 1918
Amants, heureux amants..., 1920
Jaune Bleu Blanc, 1927

Other

Ce vice impuni, la lecture, 1925
Allen: aux couleurs de Rome, 1938
Sous l'invocation de saint Jérôme, 1946
Journal inédit, 2 vols., 1954 and 1955

Bibliography

Famerie, Jacqueline, *Valery Larbaud: Essai de bibliographie*, 1958

Biographical and critical studies

Contreras, Francisco, *Valery Larbaud, son oeuvre*, 1930
Aubry, Georges Jean, *Valery Larbaud, sa vie et son oeuvre: la jeunesse (1881–1920)*, 1949
Weissman, Frida, *L'Exotisme de Valery Larbaud*, 1966

LAUTRÉAMONT, Comte de (Pseudonym of Isidore-Lucien DUCASSE), 1846–1870.

Author of lyrical prose fragments.

LIFE

Very little is known of Lautréamont's life. He was born in Montevideo on 4 April 1846, the only child of a French schoolmaster turned civil servant and his wife, who probably took her own life in December 1847. In 1859 Ducasse sent his son back to Tarbes, where he had formerly taught, to board at the lycée. Lautréamont spent his holidays nearby with his Uncle Marc, and lost a year while making up a class from 1862 to 1863. His final two lycée years were spent in Pau. Nothing is known of his life from 1865 to 1867, although it appears from his passport that he visited Montevideo. From 1867 until his death in November

1870 he lived in small Paris hotels. There is some evidence that he intended to study mathematics.

Les Chants de Maldoror was published in 1868 (canto i) and 1869 (cantos i-vi). The first canto, a pamphlet of 32 pages, printed by Balitout at Lautréamont's expense, also appeared in a collection of texts entitled "Parfums de l'âme," which was published in Bordeaux in January 1869. Both editions were anonymous. Lautréamont appears to have taken his pseudonym for the edition of all six cantos from the name of a 17th-century adventurer which figured as the title of a book by Eugène Sue. Lautréamont subsidized this publication, too, and the publisher, Lacroix, passed the book over to his Belgian associate Verboeckhoven for fear of prosecution and sold the rights to a French bookseller, Rozez, living in Brussels. The 1869 edition was never put on sale, though it appeared with a new cover in 1874. A further edition appeared in 1890.

In April 1870 Poésies I, a 16-page brochure printed by Balitout and signed Ducasse, was submitted to the ministry of the interior. Poésies II was submitted in June and the two-part work was advertised in July, the month in which the Franco- Prussian War broke out. Lautréamont's death certificate was signed on 24 November 1870 by a hotel manager and an employee. He was buried the next day, but his body was removed for burial elsewhere in January 1871. Lautréamont's father came to Paris in 1873, presumably to sort out his son's affairs. He died in Montevideo in 1889.

WORKS

Les Chants de Maldoror is a series of prose poems written in a hyperbolic style and centring on a hero of super-Byronic arrogance, given to sadism. It contains vampires, corpses, and a great deal about the sea, a large number of details pillaged from books on medicine, travel, and natural history, and sexual fantasies, some macabre, recounted with at times sardonic humour, at times ironic savagery. Maldoror copulates with a female shark which he has just watched tearing sailors to pieces. The experiences of God in a brothel are recounted, and a young girl is raped by a dog. The lucidity of these nightmarish images, their careful organization, and the author's clear awareness of what he is attempting, mean that they cannot be written off as the ravings of a madman. Parts of the text are written in the straightforward, non-hallucinatory style of a suspense narrative even while recounting the impossible, and consequently attracted the attention of the surrealists.

Poésies I and II are again in prose. They take an ironic stance with regard to the earlier work and announce the abandonment of nightmares in favour of a work of optimism, of which the Poésies may be either the preface or the realization. The epigraph states that melancholy is to be replaced by courage, doubt by certainty, desire by hope, and evil by God. Critics have regarded the Poésies as both a repudiation of the Chants and a continuation of them. In the depths of his psyché Lautréamont had found new sources for the cries of hatred and anguish with which he disrupts the rational world in which he now intends to seek reintegration. He turns his back on his romantic predecessors, comparing Musset to absinth, praising the academic and the rationalistic, though in ironic terms, and viewing literature as the path to the good life.

Critical interest in Lautréamont increased sharply around 1920, and new editions of both the Chants and the Poésies appeared. Breton, Aragon, Soupault, Malraux, and Gide all drew attention to his work. A whole number of Le Disque Vert was devoted to him in 1925—with articles by Supervielle, Ungaretti, Maeterlinck, Cocteau, and Paulhan—as have been whole numbers of Cahiers du Sud (1946), L'Arc (1967), and Entretiens (1971). Bachelard published his famous study of Lautréamont in 1939, enlarging it in 1963.

PUBLICATIONS

Collections

Oeuvres complètes, edited by Philippe Soupault, 1927
Oeuvres complètes, edited by M. Saillet, 1963
Oeuvres complètes, 1970
Les Chants de Maldoror, 1868–9, 1874, 1890, and 1920; English translation, 1944
Isidore Ducasse, Poésies I and II, 1870 (not put on sale)
Poésies d'Isidore Ducasse, 1960

Biographical and Critical studies

Nesselroth, P., Lautréamont's Imagery: A Stylistic Approach, 1969
Caradec, François, Isidore Ducasse, comte de Lautréamont, 1970
Peyrouzet, E., Vie de Lautréamont, 1970

LÉAUTAUD, Paul (-Firmin), 1872–1956.

Essayist, critic, and diarist.

Léautaud's works were never intended to be other than ephemeral, even if many have subsequently been collected into volumes, and his literary importance now depends chiefly on his diary.

Léautaud was the illegitimate child of a prompter at the Comédie-Française and was deserted by his mother a few days after his birth. His father, Firmin, treated him on the whole harshly, and the young Léautaud lived in fear of beatings, while the family's cramped accommodation, meant that he was forced to share a bed with his father and his father's mistresses. As a young man he met his mother again. She was still attractive, and Léautaud developed an ambiguous and only semi-repressed passion for her. All his liaisons with other women were purely physical. His true affections he kept for his collection of pets, mostly cats and dogs, but occasionally more exotic animals, including a monkey, a goose, and a donkey.

Writing was to become Léautaud's whole life, but he had a humble post on the Mercure de France, which helped to keep him from 1908 until 1941, and was for a time its uncompromising drama critic, writing under the name of "Marcel Boissard." From adolescence to old age he lived in shabby lodgings, dressed in shabby clothes, and ate shabbily, often nibbling from stale crusts he kept in his pockets. His greatest contribution to literature was his *Journal littéraire*, which is also an invaluable document on Parisian literary life, written nightly by candlelight using a quill pen. Léautaud gained a certain notoriety in later life as an eccentric.

Firmin had started out in an uncle's jeweller's shop before being accepted by the Conservatoire, where he won a number of prizes, but his native brogue limited his range as an actor, and he became a well-known character in Paris's theatrical life as well as a prompter and a womanizer. Léataud's mother, Jeanne Forestier, succeeded her elder sister as Firmin's mistress after sharing their bed for a night. She was an ambitious budding actress who had already had a child by Firmin that died in infancy. Léautaud, whose godparents were also actors in the Comédie-Française troupe, was sent out to nurse, then looked after at home by an elderly former prostitute, Marie Pezé, with maternal instincts to indulge. When her legs failed, Léautaud was taken to school and fetched by one of Firmin's dogs, "Tabac," who apparently fulfilled his duties in exemplary fashion and allowed no loitering. Marie Pezé took Léautaud home at night, and he slept in her bed, Firmin's flat being in her view no place to bring up a small boy. She bought him clothes and treats. He was occasionally visited by his mother, aunt, and grandmother.

When Paul was 15 Marie Pezé was dismissed for upbraiding Firmin, who, at 48, had made a 15-year-old girl a permanent member of the household. Tabac was given away. Although sometimes treated brutally at home, Léautaud was taken to the prompt box and the green room several times a week. When he was 10, a visit to his mother, who was lying in bed with very little on and then proceeded to dress in front of him, impressed itself firmly on his imagination. He made friends with the son of a local businessman, Adolphe van Bever, who was also maltreated at home. A "stepmother," who disliked Léautaud, tried to seduce him when he was 12. When she had a child, and a maid was hired, Léautaud slept in the maid's bed and she, too, tried to seduce him. Firmin not infrequently had two women with him at once.

Léautaud left school at 15, having proved his ability at essay writing, and worked in a variety of offices, dressed in cast-offs from the theatre wardrobe, which provoked derision from his workmates. A friend's sister fell in love with him, and he moved in with her family, and then to lodgings of his own, which a destitute van Bever came to share until he went to work for the theatrical director Lugné-Poe. Léautaud started to write and the girl left him, but remained a close friend. Jobless, he volunteered early for his military service. He came near to committing suicide, then fell ill, and was finally invalided out of the army. His first poem appeared in the *Courrier Français* on 16 July 1893, and it was probably through van Bever and Lugné-Poe that he got to know Alfred Valette, editor of the new *Mercure de France*. While accepting a poem from him, Valette shrewdly suggested that Léautaud should try prose. In 1900 Léautaud and van Bever issued an anthology of symbolist poetry, *Poètes d'aujourd'hui 1880-1900*.

Valette only rarely read the articles and books he published, but he liked authors and was a shrewd publisher. He had married Rachilde (1860-1953), who dressed in male clothes and was the author of about 60 salacious novels as well as of an autobiographical book containing an interesting account of the symbolist (q. v.) milieu, *Quand j'étais jeune* (1948). From 1896

Léautaud spent Sunday afternoons with the Valettes and their friends. The most important of them was Remy de Gourmont (1858-1915), who shared a squalid flat with his brother Jean and in 1891, aged 33, had been hideously disfigured down the right side of his face. His was the mind behind the *Mercure*, and he was especially fond of the young Léautaud.

Léautaud also got to know Marcel Schwob and Valéry well, started his *Journal* in earnest, and had another encounter with his mother, which revived his barely repressed incestuous leanings and gave him the impulse he needed to finish his novel. His mother was now respectably married and living in Geneva. Léautaud's correspondence with her became so intimate that she had to forbid him to send her postcards and eventually the correspondence, which she had initially encouraged, so embarrassed her that she coldly broke it off. Jeanne's new family apparently disliked her, and something of Léautaud's relationship with her appears in *Le Petit Ami*, serialized by the *Mercure* in 1902 and published in 1903, selling only 295 copies in two years. In 1903 Firmin died, and this time Valette read the autobiographical volume Léautaud devoted to his relationship with his father, *In Memoriam*, declaring it "even better" than its predecessor. He serialized it in 1905. Had it been longer there is every chance that it would have won the Prix Goncourt. Léautaud now set to work on a third autobiographical novel, *Amours*. Serialized in 1906, it was again too short to be submitted for the Goncourt, in spite of insistent invitation.

Léautaud had been working for 12 years as a solicitor's clerk, having spent last four with a liquidator of bankruptcies. He now started office work for the *Mercure*, and from 1908 until 1941 he was a salaried employee of the paper. His salary was small, starting at 150 francs a month, but his duties were scarcely onerous. He had been living with a variety of women, and was to stay with one of them, Blanche Blanc, on and off from 1897 to 1914. He began to collect his cats and dogs. As his collection grew, so did his general misanthropy, coupled with a generosity towards the destitute which he could ill afford. He had a little money from his share in a liquidation, and in 1911 bought a house from Blanche.

In 1907 Valette, knowing Léautaud's theatrical background and sensing that his gifts were critical rather than creative, had made him the *Mercure*'s theatre critic for a year. He was to fill the post again from 1911 until 1920, by which time his intransigence had aggravated both Valette and his subscribers. The reviews, often in a mocking style, spoke too plainly and did indeed offend too many people, although they were at first good for circulation. Léautaud was more concerned about authors than actors. He supported Firmin Gémier, Lugné-Poe, Antoine, and Copeau. He welcomed Jouvet's debut, looking for actors to make of each part a unique creation rather than just playing themselves, just as his criterion of a book's readability was that no one but its author could have written it. In 1920 he was given a "Gazette" to write, for which he was not obliged to keep to deadlines.

The *Mercure* did not try to make him sacrifice his precious, if sometimes acerbically expressed independence. At the *Mercure* he got to know André Billy, who became a life-long friend. He rescued Apollinaire's *La Chanson du mal-aimé* from a pile of "pending" manuscripts, where it had been mouldering for months, and got Valette to publish it. Apollinaire was subsequently given a regular column and Léautaud sent him money during the war when the *Mercure* had shut down and they were both penniless. He also got to know Gide, who frequently relaxed in the decaying disorder of Léautaud's office. Both were shattered by Valéry's apparently brilliant paradoxes and met to recover. Gide tried to recruit Léautaud for the *Nouvelle Revue Française* (*NRF*, q. v.), succeeding only when he ceased to be theatre critic for the *Mercure*, where Gide found the influence of Gourmont, whom he disliked, far too powerful. He realized that Léautaud was not just the "ridiculous" and "lubricious" "embittered misanthropist" which some recent critics have thought him to be.

From 1914 Léautaud had a passionate affair with a Mme Cayssac, whom he had met in 1908. She was jealous, possessive, and incapable of true affection. Her temperament can only be described as vicious. Her husband was complacent until his death in 1914, but the affair was unhappy in all but its purely physical manifestations, which were as intense as its emotional aspects were disastrous. Mme Cayssac was three years older than Léautaud, and the affair carried on into her sixties. In 1916 Léautaud's mother died following an attack by a servant she had dismissed.

In 1917 an incident occurred which, while important in itself, also illustrates the spikiness which Léautaud was ready to employ to defend the integrity of his judgement. He gave Valéry's *La Jeune Parque* a not unfavourable review which, however, referred to Valéry as a disciple of Mallarmé, whom Léautaud disliked. Valéry was deeply hurt. The two were friends, but Léautaud regarded Valéry's verse as mannered rubbish, and the honours he now so clearly enjoyed as so much buffoonery. Valéry needed the money, but Léautaud had naturally observed how far out of his depth the anti-Dreyfusard was prepared to go to get it, lecturing for instance on Goethe, of whom he had never read a word, and enslaving himself to literary deals. Léautaud, himself hard pressed financially, sold 70 letters he had received from Valéry, together with presentation copies of his books, for 22,500 francs. Valéry knew of the traffic in his intimate letters and, although he never mentioned Léautaud's transaction, they met henceforward only in Léautaud's office, with an amical relationship not fully restored until the 1930s, by which time Valéry was lecturing on Pushkin, whom he had also never read. Like many others, he was afraid of Léautaud's *Journal*.

The diary was the literary form which best suited Léautaud. He was sufficiently egotistical to think a record of his views and the events of his day worth preserving. *Le Petit Ami* had shown him that he could write autobiographical material and, as Valette saw, he was a brilliant critic, even if tact made a diary the best repository for his views. The diary records a less lavish Parisian literary life than did the Goncourts, and is devoted to a host of often minor literary characters, but it tells us a great deal about publishing economics and the wildly inflated claims put about regarding sales, print runs, and advances for purposes of public relations, all of them pure invention. The days of the really big sellers, Zola and Daudet, were now over. The hypocrisies and maliciousness of literary life revealed by Léautaud make surprising as well as entertaining reading. He could not understand how writers of talent could stoop to the scheming, back-biting, and back-scratching of the writing and publishing trades.

When in 1921 the *NRF* recruited Léautaud through Gide's good offices, its editor, Rivière, was delighted, and Gallimard, its owner, wanted to publish the *Mercure* criticism in two vol-

umes. Characteristically, Léautaud, who had hesitated before accepting the post, took until 1926 to deliver the text of the first volume, and until 1943 to deliver the second (*Le Théâtre de Maurice Boissard 1907–1923*, vol. 1, 1926, and vol. 2, 1943). But the inevitable had occurred. Léautaud wrote a witheringly sarcastic attack on Jules Romains, one of the *NRF*'s principal authors. Gide said it was the best piece of dramatic criticism Léautaud had written, but Rivière would not publish it. Léautaud walked out, to be taken on two days later by Maurice Martin du Gard's *Les Nouvelles Littéraires*, on the condition that it printed the Romains piece. Three months later he walked out from his new post, too, over a quip about militarism the review would not print, although he continued to write ocasionally for it, as for his "Gazette" column in the *Mercure*.

In 1927 van Bever died from a form of consumption. Léautaud established a firm friendship with Marie Dormoy, the principal beneficiary of Jacques Doucet's legendary patronage, which had extended to Louÿs, Régnier, Valéry, Suarès, Cendrars, Reverdy, and the surrealists (q. v.). When Doucet died in 1929, Marie was his librarian, and she remained in charge of his collection when it was handed over to the state. She tried in vain to get the library to buy Léautaud's *Journal* and failed, too, to get a publisher to put out an illustrated, limited edition of *Le Petit Ami*. Though he was offered 25,000 francs for doing virtually nothing, Léautaud turned this scheme down. Marie Dormoy felt compassion and tenderness for him, but no more. She typed for him, tidied his garden, and commissioned Vuillard to draw him for an edition of one of his essays. In return Léautaud was ungracious and ungrateful. Marie knew the value of the *Journal*, but so did Valette, who got Léautaud to put together from it a memoir of Remy de Gourmont. Marie offered to type it and, against strict instructions, made a surreptitious copy. She then transcribed the complete journal, except for what Léautaud had lost or Mme Cayssac had destroyed. It ran to 12,000 pages and took 18 years of spare-time typing. Valette signed a contract, but he began to have serious arguments with Léautaud, who continued to upset subscribers. Léautaud, meanwhile, reserved his anger for the *Journal*.

Had it not been home for him, Léautaud would have left the *Mercure*, but he got free stationery, postage, a superb chance to observe literary life, and mint copies of books for review which he could sell. Valette railed at his eccentric time-keeping. Léautaud, although he despised honours, did what was necessary to get Valette made an Officier of the Légion d'Honneur. He was with him when he died in 1935. His successor, the novelist Duhamel, had been a doctor and a poet and was now what Léautaud once described as "un écrivain pour familles nombreuses" (a writer who catered for large families). He installed typewriters, telephones, and electric wiring and inaugurated film reviews, but found that he had taken on too much and handed over the direction of the *Mercure* to Jacques Bernard. Léautaud, who had finally broken with Mme Cayssac, felt unsettled by these changes.

Jean Paulhan again asked him to write for the *NRF*, and his theatre criticism appeared once more from 1 January 1939. But history repeated itself. Readers protested, and Léautaud gave up his contract, while continuing to write occasional pieces. Bernard offered to serialize the *Journal* to compensate for the cut in his salary. In the end, however, Léautaud was sacked by the *Mercure*. Life under Bernard had become intolerable. He was an admirer of Hitler, an enthusiastic collaborator with the occupying powers, and had been responsible for a number of deportations. He had neither Valette's business sense nor Duhamel's literary taste.

Léautaud paused only to take down the Marie Laurencin painting of himself and the Rouveyre drawing and to gather up his papers and quill pens. In the unoccupied zone rumours of his death began circulating, and he read his own obituaries. They showed unanimous goodwill comparing him with Chamfort, La Bruyère, and La Rochefoucauld, and some were very moving. Léautaud had always lived very simply, and now, at 69, he had no work to go to and only his animals for company. Marie Dormoy's copy of Léautaud's life work had been evacuated from Paris with the Doucet archive. Friends, editors, and the literary world generally helped him to survive the war. Editors rushed to commission pieces from him. The ministry of education gave him a small pension. Valéry and Duhamel got the Institut to make him a grant, and Florence Gould was extremely kind to him, though he showed her little gratitude.

Although at first hostile to the Allies, Léautaud began to read more English. The liberation, when it came, sickened him for its acts of private vengeance and opportunism. Denunciations out of jealousy or revenge were all too common. Léautaud, for his part, refused to give evidence against Bernard. Rouveyre insisted on publishing a Léautaud anthology and the *Choix de pages* came out in 1946, but Rouveyre had included a letter from Léautaud critical of Gide's hypocrisy and weakness for compliments. Léautaud was furious, Gide determined not to be upset, and both broke with Rouveyre. There was another upset when Marie Dormoy got Matisse to do a sketch of Léautaud as a favour, and Léautaud then borrowed the sketch and sold it to Rouveyre, who promptly told Matisse.

The *Mercure* reopened and invited Léautaud to rejoin the staff, but he preferred to keep his independence. He did, however, allow extracts from the *Journal* to appear in its pages, partly about Mme Cayssac, who seems to have mellowed with time. Léautaud saw her again when she was 77 and in hospital, after a boy on skates had knocked her over. She died at home in 1950. In a fit of melancholy Léautaud burnt a huge and no doubt invaluable collection of letters, notes, and manuscripts, including a new version of *In Memoriam*. Eventually he was persuaded to be interviewed on radio, but only after a struggle, his resistance increasing at the mention of much-needed money. He finally agreed to give 10 interviews. Dinner parties were cancelled and engagements postponed in order to hear the 80-year-old showering his wit on the nation. In the end he gave 43 interviews in all, becoming a national celebrity in spite of what he said about his mother, his father, women in general, and patriotism. The *Entretiens avec Robert Mallet* (1951) was a publishing success and Léautaud's books were reprinted. The first volume of the *Journal littéraire*, covering the years 1893 to 1906 and published by the *Mercure*, sold out in five weeks. On the strength of these successes Léautaud bought six pairs of shoes, six hats, two overcoats, and an electric coffee grinder.

Of all his acquaintances, Léautaud admired Gide the most. When Gide died he had a long talk with an interviewer at Gide's graveside, during which he declared: "I like solitude, an ordered life, and meditation." He nearly went blind and relied increasingly on Marie Dormoy for help. The animal collection was run down, but Léautaud continued to live in squalor and to write by candlelight. Early in 1956 he left home for hospital with a handful of quill pens, a pocket handkerchief, some woollen hats, and

Diderot's *Le Neveu de Rameau*. He died on 22 February, just 84.

It is too early to expect a serious literary evaluation of Léautaud's work, although it is clear that he was independent to the point of needless belligerence and adhered uncompromisingly to his own intellectual and aesthetic judgements. He exhibited eccentricity, but no element of posturing. He had to pay for his independence by the squalid conditions in which he lived, deprived of the appurtenances of the good life, but he retained an aura of fastidiousness as well as honesty. He could peel filthy potatoes for his animals during a train journey home, but icily ask a woman who had used "réaliser" in the anglo-Saxon sense of "to understand" rather than the French one of "to make real" if she would mind speaking French, please. His aesthetic left not only no room for cant, hypocrisy, or pretentiousness (which he saw all around him), but also none for the stylistically imprecise, the vague, or the mysterious. Léautaud has certainly been underestimated as a writer, but his major work has been available only since the 1960s. He may turn out to belong to the great classical tradition of French moralists, his ruthless honesty and trenchant wit ranking him among the most savagely perceptive writers of 20th-century France.

PUBLICATIONS

Apart from the 19-volume *Journal littéraire* (1956–1966) and *Le Petit Ami* (1903), virtually all Léautaud's publications are articles, reviews, collections of ephemera, or other anthologies, short memoirs, extracts, interviews, or parts of correspondence, many of which feature in different volumes. Sections of the diary have been published in English as *Journal of a Man of Letters 1898–1907*, 1960.

A complete list of Léautaud's contributions to newspapers and magazines has been compiled by Marie Dormoy (*Léautaud*, 1958). This volume also gives details of all editions and printings of Léautaud's works. Léautaud is mentioned in many French and some English volumes of criticism. The only full-scale study available in English is:

Harding, James, *Lost Illusions: Paul Léautaud and His World*, 1974

LE CLÉZIO, Jean (-Marie-Gustave), 1940–

Novelist and essayist.

LIFE

Jean Le Clézio's father was an English medical officer in Nigeria who retired to Nice, where Le Clézio was born on 13 April 1940. His mother was French. The family moved about France during World War II and Le Clézio spent three years from 1947 to 1950 in Africa before returning to his home base at Nice, where he attended the lycée, graduating at the age of 18. In 1958 he taught for a year at Bath Grammar School in England, while attending Bristol University. From 1960 to 1961 he was a student at London University, and in 1961 he married Rosalie Piquemal, "Marina," who was to bear him one daughter. From 1959 he had been registered at what is now the University of Nice, graduating with his "licence" in 1963 and writing an essay on the theme of solitude in Henri Michaux for his diplôme from the University of Aix-en-Provence, awarded in 1964. For a time Le Clézio wanted to write a thesis on Lautréamont and dreamt of becoming a painter.

In the meanwhile, in 1963 Gallimard had published *Le Procès-verbal*, which just missed the Prix Goncourt, but won the more important Prix Renaudot, awarded by literary critics. The title, referring to judicial proceedings, means "statement," or it can refer to a set of minutes. The English title, *The Interrogation*, is simply a mistranslation, although a "procès-verbal" can, among other things, be the minutes of an interrogation. In 1965 Le Clézio published the nine short stories of *La Fièvre*, following it in 1966 with *Le Déluge*. Called up for military service, he chose the options which allowed him to teach abroad, and went to Thailand to teach at the Buddhist University of Bangkok, moving from there to the University of Mexico in 1967. After he had finished his military service there, Le Clézio stayed on to spend four years in the forest of Panama with the Embera Indians. He returned to France in 1973, but has subsequently made other protracted visits to Central America. He withdrew a book on the Indians because he felt it betrayed what he had been taught by them, but both Thai Buddhist and Mayan influences have been prominent in his subsequent work. Since 1973 Le Clézio has been based in Nice. He won the Prix Larbaud in 1972 and the Prix Académie Morand in 1980. In 1991 he returned to the best-seller list with *Onitsha*.

WORKS

Le Clézio's works include the translation of ancient Mayan texts. His exploration of Thai Buddhist and Mayan spiritualities, of the forest life of the Panamanian Indians, and of the world of psychiatric disorder and dreams constitutes a powerful examination of urban Western living and implies an indictment of its most prominent features. Le Clézio's imagination constantly returns to man's relationship with his body, with his sensations, with the objects which surround him, and with the elemental forces of nature and those immutable, immeasurable, and virtually spiritual forces which control human life, like the sun, the sky, and water, generally in the form of sea. The key to this relationship is constantly sought in language, which is not only the unique means of access to consciousness, but also the arena in which man confronts society, assents to it and its injustices, disharmonies, and competitiveness. To rebel against society as we know it, the first step has therefore to be the dislocation of language, which appears in Le Clézio's work ambiguously as a weapon, a shield, and an instrument. For him language is "not a harmony, but an explosion." Each person, particularly each writer, by constructing his own language, affirms himself and his attitude to the rules which govern not only the grammar of his language, but also the values of his society.

Although Le Clézio's study of Michaux, *Vers les icebergs*, was not published until 1978, it grew out of the thesis which Le Clézio wrote for the University of Aix in 1964, "The theme of solitude in the works of Henri Michaux," and is therefore contemporaneous with *Le Procès-verbal*. The unpublished 1964 essay starts by pointing to man's recently increasing isolation in his double alienation from nature and his fellow men, and his attempt both to profit from it and to heal it in his systems of verbal communication as well as in his commercial activity. Le Clézio sees in Michaux this double movement, which attempts to relate to the external world before it attempts a self-annihilating withdrawal from it. The relationship to the outside world can take the form of love, rage, or hatred on the level of feeling, or humour, irony, or cynicism on the level of language.

It seems certain that Le Clézio was reading something of his understanding of himself into his understanding of Michaux as he wrote *Le Procès-verbal*. Michaux, it must be remembered, had to some extent found his way out of solipsistic isolation in India, as Le Clézio was himself to seek the help of Thailand, Mexico, and Panama in his own search for spiritual peace. Le Clézio sees in Michaux's recourse to imaginative introversion and hallucinogenic drugs both a withdrawal from the outside world and an active recreation of it within himself. It is by no means clear that Le Clézio has read Michaux accurately, but his 1964 essay sheds much light on his own *Le Procès-verbal*.

Although *Le Procès-verbal* can in retrospect be seen to contain embryonically many of Le Clézio's later themes and techniques, it enabled nobody to predict them. The central theme was to become the abatement of hostility to society and the flight from objects and sensations towards an inner self of peaceful simplicity, from which a new relationship with man and nature could proceed. However, that is not totally apparent from the beginning. In 1963 Le Clézio had, it is true, spent three formative years in Nigeria, but he had not yet been to Thailand, Mexico, or Panama. Published when its author was 23 and immediately successful enough to win the Renaudot, having narrowly missed the Goncourt, *Le Procès-verbal* is still clearly a first novel in which the author's personal style and vision are not yet fully developed. It is still shaped by a reading of Sartre, Camus, and Robbe-Grillet, although it is also inspired by Michaux and, at least on the surface, by Lautréamont.

There is no plot to speak of. The central character, whose name deliberately alludes to two human prototypes, Adam and Apollo, is the 29-year-old Adam Pollo. He is a refugee from society, but does not know whether he deserted from the army or escaped from an asylum, their association immediately making them representatives respectively of society's socio-political and its connected logico-linguistic and mental disciplines. He uses of himself both "I" and "He," and intersperses his monologue with bits of a diary and letters to Michèle, which he writes in a notebook. He has thrown his motorbike into the sea, so everyone except Michèle thinks he is dead. He includes bits of broken dialogue, snippets of all sorts, and in the end an account of questioning in a psychiatric hospital.

He wanders around Nice, watches animals, pretends to be a dog, meets Michèle, and goes for a walk with her, during which they have intercourse by the sea. Acutely aware of all the sensations in his body, he settles in an abandoned house near the beach and tries to work out a way of living undisturbed by society. To eat, he occasionally goes out, and sometimes steals. He is quarrelsome and cruel. He sadistically but reflectively kills a white rat with billiard balls, identifying with what he destroys, pretends to want to buy records that do not exist for the pleasure of watching the shopgirl look for them, talks about drowning with a man who has just been saved from the water, and gives us glimpses of the lives of various couples. He spends a whole night looking for Michèle. Finally he goes out for food, finds Michèle with an American, borrows money from her, gets drunk, and picks a quarrel with the American.

The police come to pick him up, but he escapes, finds a letter from his mother at the post office begging him to come home, makes a speech, exposes himself, is arrested, gets taken to the mental hospital, outwits the psychiatry students, and withdraws into his own inner vision. The psychiatrists assume the role of some praetorian guard, protecting the mental order with grammar and logic, as the police protect the social order, which is linked to it. There is a tension in the novel summed up in Adam's alternate attempts to relate with the real world, even to the extent of metamorphosing himself into the animals within it, and his withdrawal from it, on the one hand in aggressive hostility and on the other in protective flight.

Le Clézio's dislike of society, his aggressive reaction to it, and the imaginative quest for an inner serenity lurking somewhere within the least logical and most primitive regions of the psyche did not, however, lead him further to explore the possibility of refuge in madness, dream, or hallucination. On the contrary, Adam can sometimes be seen to be in pursuit of a real order and a real language proceeding from an inner peace, withdrawn from a hostile world in which language and actions are used only as weapons of offence. For Le Clézio, Michaux in his withdrawal was looking on at the annihilation of his own personality and "was watching the substance of his existence dissolve and fade away." Le Clézio's problem was to share Michaux's hostility to society without undergoing the same annihilatory deprivation that he believed Michaux had experienced in withdrawing from the world.

The nine stories of *La Fièvre* conclusively established the patterns of Le Clézio's creative imagination. In the title story Roche Estève's fever, which abates, leads him to the double movement familiar from *Le Procès-verbal*. The sight of a couple copulating in a public garden brings out in Estève a strongly aggressive reaction. He fights the man and throws a brick through the window of the travel agency where he himself works. Yet he hallucinates about his wife, Elizabeth, to the point at which he believes he is a woman. In his fever, sexual stimulation produces reactions both of aggressive hostility and empathetic identification. In the second story, "Le jour," Beaumont's toothache turns into an animal attacking his brain. Alcohol allows serenity to return, and at the end of the story Beaumont is sitting calmly but uncomfortably inside his own tooth, the threat from the outside world represented by toothache successfully repelled. All the stories, except "Martin," deal with some sort of hostile reaction or intrusion and the restoration of inner serenity. In "Martin" the movement is reversed: inner serenity is abandoned for a movement of mental hostility when the hydrocephalic genius allows himself to be regarded as a prophet, and the world instantly retaliates.

Le Déluge is a somewhat mannered parable of flight from the world. François Bresson has a vision of a young girl swallowed by the sound of a siren. He receives a tape from a friend explaining her own possible suicide. For the next 13 days he gradually withdraws from the world, from people, from his fiancée Josette, food, cigarettes, and his own past, and causes his own blindness by burning out his eyes in the sun. He listens to the tape on which Anna Passeron has explained her suicide. The novel is carefully and obviously structured with clear allusions to the Oedipus myth.

Le Clézio's oeuvre now begins to look for solutions to the problems which his characters have been fleeing. *L'Extase matérielle* of 1967 is a series of meditations suggesting how man may be part of material nature rather than a creature alien to it, and may be led to inner and outer harmony by self-study. Le Clézio had by now become acquainted with Buddhism at Bangkok. *Terra amata* returns to fiction loosely woven around the life of a man called Chancelade, and opens with a powerful evocation of earth without man. Chancelade's relationship with his wife Mina and other women is less tense and aggressive than those of the earlier male characters, and Le Clézio needs all his descriptive brilliance to sustain his reader's interest here. There is a famous passage incorporating both attraction for and repulsion from a townscape of endlessly reflecting glass:

La rue était parfaitement droite, encaissée entre les immenses panneaux de verre des immeubles, et on n'en voyait pas la fin. A gauche, à droite, il y avait une infinité d'autres rues toutes pareilles, longs couloirs de sol glacé qui entraient les uns dans les autres, se mélangeaient désespérément. Les vitrines étincelaient de lumière, les vitres luisaient férocement, les centaines de vitres similaires, mais on ne voyait rien à travers elles...

(The street was absolutely straight, boxed in between the immense glass panels of the buildings, and you couldn't see its end. To its left and right was an infinity of other similar streets, long corridors of iced earth leading into one another, desperately coming together. The windows sparkled with light, the panes shone fiercely, hundreds of identical panes, but you couldn't see anything through them...)

This reflecting back and forth of echoing emptiness is an image of urban life, the opposite of what Le Clézio was to experience in Panama. It no doubt explains the fascination with forest life which he was to develop, the first literary result of which was *Haï* of 1971, where what is outside man does not finally resolve itself into a cosmic void, leaving him alone, attached to nothing beyond himself. Meanwhile, in *Terra amata* Chancelade grows up from being a child who killed insects to full maturity and then old age. To the story of his life Le Clézio attaches discussions of life, birth, death, truth, lies, and communication, the communication problem always running in parallel with the psychological and moral difficulties. He describes sexual contact as something with which to occupy the time when there is nothing else left. Birth is a painful experience, and in the woman's womb lies the source of power because it is the source of life. Chancelade is no longer afraid of women, as Adam Pollo and François Bresson had been. He "gave in and became a woman, the same invincible woman who possessed the earth from the dazzling centre of her body."

Le Clézio admits to having needed to keep himself entertained while he wrote, and it is to be supposed that he partly achieved his aim by reflecting in his writing on the problems of what he was doing. At the end of *Terra amata* we are told: "There is no Chancelade, there never was any Chancelade. All there ever was, was me writing these words." In other words, Le Clézio is making fun of his own seriousness. He also breaks up the text typographically, with lists, poems, quotations, and the use of different typefaces, to break the monotony for the reader.

In *Le Livre des fuites* Jeune Homme Hogan tours the world

looking for somewhere acceptable to stay. Le Clézio was to say in an interview that Young Man Hogan was a mask for himself, but then Le Clézio was also a mask for himself; "To deceive others is to get to know oneself." The spiritual problems of personal identity are always identified with problems of communication, the key to, if not the ultimate essence of, man's relationship with himself, with nature, and with other men. The book is split into 44 sections, some in the third person, describing Young Man Hogan's journey, some meditations in the first person, some reflections by the author about the act of writing, and a smaller group of single pages which break up the text with strings of insults, quotations, and references.

Language, by which we belong to humanity and therefore exist, is necessarily a mask, and must create a fiction, on the nature of which *Le Livre des fuites* is partly a reflection. The author is caught up in language, and therefore in a culture. He appears to be reluctant to explore the abandonment of culture in simple withdrawal, like Adam Pollo, sensing that self- annihilation lies along that path. There remains the possibility of fleeing from the reverberating emptiness of *Terra amata* which we know to have been the avenue explored personally by Le Clézio, and fictionally by Hogan. Chancelade could not escape: "He had never seen anything so beautiful, and so *terrible*. He went down the alleys of the glass labyrinth, but never arrived anywhere. It was always the same street endlessly renewing itself." The other possibility came to the same thing. Other things were absolutely alien and not possible objects to which to relate.

This is what NajaNaja felt looking at the passing ships from her window in *Voyages de l'autre côté*, as remote from her innermost personality as the signs of writing on a page. Hogan in his perpetual flight can only hope to become conscious of his problem, virtually symbolized by the choice between the cities, which must be repudiated aggressively because they are destructive, corrosive, and alien, and the villages, the lotus lands which beckon alluringly towards the dangers lurking within them, leper colonies, the island that paralyses with nostalgia, the island that blinds. Formally the allusion is to the *Odyssey*, with Hogan's Laure left at home like Penelope. Hogan is torn between the cities, which are dangerous like women, and the tranquil, self-contained, dignified life of squalor and suffering outside the developed world, and finds his pilgrimage to religious ecstasy reduced to waiting blindly for death in the dust.

The imperfect consistency and clarity of Le Clézio's imagination, and its occasional trivialization of important themes, may prevent his work from emerging as great literature. His imagination lacks, for instance, the sharpness of Beckett's. He has, however, raised with power and energy what he sees as the chief problems of the advanced urban industrialized cultures of the West in the second half of the 20th century. Essentially they are the spiritual problems of the individual. Avenues of solution are tentatively probed, but mostly, like aggressive hostility, withdrawal, and flight, left imaginatively unendorsed. They are always, perhaps sometimes factitiously, linked to Le Clézio's own problems as a writer and, indeed, in view of his own flight to the forest, to spiritual problems which may be common, but which he has himself experienced. It is unclear whether he regards the problems of communication as symptomatic or constitutive of spiritual malaise, and Le Clézio's work has been criticized as often unsatisfactorily ambiguous in its resolution.

In *La Guerre* the central characters, symbolically Bea B. and Mr X, study city life and watch a plane take off above them while they lie on the runway. Bea B. goes to an apartment store, a crossroads, and a dance hall. She is picked up by a carload of people who go on a manhunt and kill a pedestrian. We are told virtually nothing about either of the characters, nor about their evidently shifting relationship. Perhaps they do not retain single identities throughout the text, but put on and change masks from time to time. They are at war with the city and at times seem to win. Bea B. is Le Clézio's first female protagonist, but she is subordinated to the anonymous Mr X, gets raped by a car, and is a weapon exploited by the advertising industry. Woman, herself the epitome of the consumer, none the less cooperates in turning people into identical objects. As in *Le Livre des fuites* there is not total imaginative control or consistency. The novel does not succeed in achieving what it appears to attempt, but it again presents a powerful vision of the modern city.

In *Les Géants* the preoccupation with giant stores is continued. Bogo the Mute watches two girls walk along the beach and go rowing. He will see them again at the end. Meanwhile, he sits in the car park of the Hyperpolis hypermarket. Depersonalized crowds are hypnotized by the sounds, colours, and visual displays. Tranquilité goes to meet her friend at the information desk, trying to keep her individuality alive. Later on the letters and words which she sees while driving with her friend become blurred. The two of them, who may be the girls Bogo saw, are friendly with Machines, who pushes trolleys in Hyperpolis and whose favourite place is a petrol station. There, away from cars roaring past on the road, he is at peace. Bogo has left home and is dodging the police. Machines and Tranquilité write notes to one another on a bed for fear of being overheard if they speak. They are frightened of the mirror, and Machines says he will burn down Hyperpolis if Tranquilité does not run away with him.

When they break the mirror, they find that it is indeed a two-way mirror and there are three men behind it. Le Clézio describes the police system with its five colours of uniform. Those in red pretending to do road works have slit eyes to watch with. Some look behind them at what is reflected in the cinema windows, in front of which they light cigarettes. Tranquilité is attached to a lie detector by Hague, of Hague System Inc., and questioned. A mirror lights up and five observers give orders. The security men want to know who intends to burn Hyperpolis and turn up the piped music which runs through the hypermarket. Underneath it Tranquilité hears "Hyperpolis must be burnt." Machines had absorbed the subliminal message. His rebellion had in fact been organized by the Masters themselves as an experiment. On the beach Bogo, representing the author as an observer of what happens, watches two girls row out and commit suicide. At the end of the novel the destructive power of language is unleashed in Bogo. He destroys the Master by saying in English: "EGGS."

The text also contains disquisitions on language and thought control, fake advertising copy, pages of Algol 60 computer print-out, and learned quotations. When the reader, who will have skipped the advertising copy, turns back to it, he finds in tiny print at the bottom right-hand corner of each page "Hyperpolis must be burnt." The sections of the book which have a first-person narrator could almost be reprinted in a different order. The corruption of the mind starts with the dislocation of language in a war whose strategy is directed by the Masters of language. For each desire they invent, there is a corresponding hatred. The Masters of thought, masquerading as Varium

Broadcasting Properties, make men dream, make them put themselves to sleep and devour themselves. When men defend themselves in the fortress of consciousness, the Masters spy on them and film what goes on in their citadel. The narrator incites the reader to free his words and use them for himself. For the first time, Le Clézio has resorted to a plot of sorts. The plot, however, is a distraction.

The register is defensively comic, but the threat both more dreadful and more realistic than that in *1984*, published exactly a quarter of a century earlier, which must have inspired *Les Géants*. In the intervening quarter-century it had become possible to engineer human responses by surgical intervention as well as sophisticated techniques of psychological reaction control. Man can be made to order, "ready to give himself totally to the building up of a great industrial future." Le Clézio scatters his text with Chinese signs for birth and death, and with high voltage electricity warning signs which turn into swastikas. The initial advertisement for a self- cleaning oven is so worded as to put the reader in mind of the gas chambers of Belsen. Suicide is escape, but there is defence in culture: "When the words are inside, the Masters of language suddenly become small and their ruses ridiculous." Literature is the weapon by which men regain control, but it is not at all clear at the end whether literature can or will win.

Voyages de l'autre côté starts when the earth is under water and ends when it is all stone. Naja means cobra, and in the meanwhile we follow the travels of NajaNaja, Gin Fizz, Syrsum Corda, Alligator Barks, Yamaha and Louise and Léon, who even share one another's dreams, into objects and experiences like olive trees and the setting sun. NajaNaja tells stories and finally disappears. She is the formless universal spirit, snake, and earth goddess also capable of gestating department stores. She undergoes endless metamorphoses. The book, in the form of a series of daydreams, situates objects and events in the context of astral forces. "The other side" of the title refers to the realm beyond fear, which means the interior realm beyond dreams. NajaNaja leads the reader past the sleeping giant into the dive into infinity, where, however, there are still dangers, including another giant, the irresistibly attractive Bételgeuse. Le Clézio's magnificent gift for evocative descriptive writing is here at its best, but the novel retains all the old ambiguities, while probing the possibility of escape. It again gives the impression that Le Clézio has identified the problems more certainly than the avenues of resolution. Although the negative attack in his work is much firmer and more surely directed than the explorations of possible ways in which man might rehumanize himself, unlike the major satirists, he is not content, however, simply to pour scorn on what is wrong.

NajaNaja feels a peculiar hypnotic sleep come over her as Algol, the demon of the white star, paralyses her will. She jumps into the river of the Milky Way and is carried off to stars with primeval names like Scorpio and Hydra. None the less, the book is not an allegory. It is a projected literary fantasy about the unity of the cosmos, deliberately written in a variety of styles and meaningful on a number of different registers, deliberately neither scientific nor psychologically analytical, but an ambitious imaginative experiment. It sums up Le Clézio's achievement as far as early middle age. Both in ambition and achievement, by virtue of the problems raised in his fiction and the scale on which they are envisaged, and in spite of the uncertainty of his vision and even of his aim, Le Clézio is clearly one of the more important authors to write in French since Camus and Beckett. Perhaps it is a coincidence, but he is also one of the only authors of fiction of his generation to have remained almost totally outside the orbit of late surrealism (q.v.) and the "nouveau roman."

PUBLICATIONS

Fiction

Le Procès-verbal, 1963; as *The Interrogation*, 1964
Le Jour où, Beaumont fit connaissance avec sa douleur, 1964
La Fièvre, 1965; as *Fever*, 1966
Le Déluge, 1966; as *The Flood*, 1968
Terra amata, 1968; as *Terra Amata*, (in English), 1969
Le Livre des fuites, 1969; as *The Book of Flights*, 1971
La Guerre, 1970; as *War*, 1973
Les Géants, 1973; as *The Giants*, 1975
Mydriase, 1973
Voyages de l'autre côté, 1975
Voyage aux pays des arbres, 1978
Mondo et autres histoires, 1978
Désert, 1980
Trois villes saintes, 1980
La Ronde et autres faits divers, 1982
Le Chercheur d'or, 1985
Journal du chercheur d'or, 1986
Onitsha, 1991

Other

L'Extase matérielle, 1967
Haï, 1971
L'Inconnu sur la terre, 1978
Vers les icebergs, 1978
Lullaby, 1980
Le Rêve mexicain, 1982
Voyage à Rodrigues, 1986
Printemps et autres saisons nouvelles, 1989

Translator, *Les Prophéties du chilam Balam*, 1976

Critical studies

Lhoste, P., *Conversations avec Le Clézio*, 1971
Waelti-Walters, Jennifer, *Le Clézio* (in English), 1977

———

LECONTE DE LISLE, Charles (-Marie-René), 1818–1894.

Poet.

LIFE

Leconte de Lisle's work dominated the poetic activity of the third quarter of the 19th century in France. It is itself a product of that era's interest in science, historic scholarship, evolutionary theory, and comparative religion. The "L'Art pour l'art" (q.v.) movement associated with Gautier, had distilled from romanticism (q.v.) the cult of objective beauty and turned its back on the subservience of art to any other purpose, in particular on the use of poetry directly to express personal emotion. The Parnassian (q.v.) movement founded, or at any rate spearheaded, by Leconte de Lisle, goes further. To the suppression of any direct expression of personal emotion it adds a devotion to plasticity and technical perfection of form, and a commitment to 19th-century scientific positivism as an indispensable basis for poetry, especially in so far as positivism hinges on determinist and evolutionary theories of human physical and cultural development, whether biological, social, or religious.

Leconte de Lisle was to make this clear in prefaces to two of the three major collections of verse published during his lifetime—the *Poèmes antiques* of 1852, and the *Poèmes et poésies* of 1855—as also in the avant-propos of 3 August to *Les Poètes contemporains*, a series of articles published in *Le Nain Jaune* during 1864. It is true that he rejects Du Camp's alliance of poetry and science and Comte's didactic view of art, and that he rather sententiously postures as poetry's saviour from all sorts of romantic degeneracy, but for all his ponderousness, and even his infidelities to his stated intentions, Leconte de Lisle directly reveals in his poetry almost nothing about his personal life, treating it as far as he could as if it were suspended in a vacuum from which all personal experience had been removed. The assumption that his verse can be considered in complete isolation from any personal experience he may have undergone is part of his poetic theory. As an approach to literature that assumption still has devotees, but in the 19th century it was intended to be a full-scale repudiation of what Leconte de Lisle regarded as romantic self-indulgence, and it was linked to the discussion of sweeping theories about the development of cultures.

Leconte de Lisle's father was a Breton from Dinan and an army surgeon who, after Waterloo, had emigrated to Bourbon (now Réunion), off the east coast of Africa, to become a sugar planter. There he married into an aristocratic French family descended from the Marquis François de Riscourt de Lanux, which had settled on the island in 1720. Leconte de Lisle, the couple's eldest child, was born in Saint Paul on 22 October 1818. At the age of three he was sent to relations in Brittany, where he remained until he was 10. From 1828 until 1837, when, aged 18, he returned to France, Leconte de Lisle was brought up in Réunion, his imagination by then indelibly marked by the childhood decade of craggy coasts, stormy seas, and Druidic legends from a culture nurtured by peasants and sea farers used to regarding nature as hostile, an obstacle to be overcome in the struggle to survive. The adolescent years of langorous warmth, luxuriant vegetation, superb scenery, colonial comfort, and social superiority impregnated Leconte de Lisle's imagination with a contrasting stratum of experience. However little he tells us about the love life which in fact inspired his early versifying and much of his later poetry, his imagination was formed by early adulthood, and was bound to reveal its constitutive layers when drawn on for subsequent creative activity.

He had an early infatuation with a Riscourt de Lanux cousin on Réunion, the chief inspiration, together with the gorgeous vegetation and splendid sky, of the portfolio of verse which Leconte de Lisle took back to Europe with him when he set sail on 11 March 1837. The cousin, object of "cet éternel premier

amour, fait de désirs vagues et de timidités délicieuses (that everlasting first love, made up of vague desires and delicious hesitancies)," died prematurely, and the 18-year-old Leconte de Lisle returned to Brittany to study law at Rennes, his exercise book pompously headed "Essais poétiques de Ch. Leconte de Lisle," its contents testifying to the impact of Hugo's celebrated 1829 volume, *Les Orientales*. Leconte de Lisle spent six years in Rennes without getting his degree. His correspondence does not suggest that he took the prospect of a legal career seriously. He did, however, attend arts faculty lectures and acquired the classical grounding which was to enable him later to make distinguished translations of Homer, Euripides, Sophocles, and Aeschylus. With his close friend Julien Rouffet he produced a volume of verse which neither Lamartine's publisher, Gosselin, nor any other would take.

Leconte de Lisle did succeed in publishing occasional short, anonymous pieces and, already convinced of the existence of a spiritual realm superior to that of everyday reality, in 1840 he took part in the launching of the Christian *La Variété*. He eventually became its editor, although its Catholicism was more than tinged with a commitment to Lammenais, whose somewhat anti-clericalist spiritualism, completely divorcing Church and state, had resulted in his condemnation in the 1832 encyclical *Mirari vos*, and again in 1834, after the appearance of the *Paroles d'un croyant*. *La Variété* lasted from May 1840 until April 1841. There was another attempt to found a review, *Le Scorpion*, said to have been intended as a declaration of war against bourgeois society in Rennes, but the printer refused to set the copy.

In January 1845 Leconte de Lisle wrote to a friend that he had been offered 1,800 francs a year and publication of a volume of his verse to work for the Fourierist daily *La Démocratie Pacifique* and the associated quarterly *La Phalange*, which published a number of pieces on classical subjets, of which the first was "Hélène," based on Goethe's *Faust*, in July 1845. By this date it is possible to speak of Leconte de Lisle's "philosophy," which was largely inspired by Victor Considerant's *La Destinée sociale* of 1834. He believed in a spiritual realm, conceived with poetic rather than theological pantheism, that is metaphorically, in an intelligence directing the world, and in the necessity of suffering. He deeply admired George Sand, whose Fourierist political and religious views he shared. By 1845 Leconte de Lisle was himself a convinced Fourierist on social matters, believing in the possibility of happiness, in social and agronomic reform, the emancipation of women, life in small cooperatives called "phalanstères" close to the land, free love, and shared goods.

The differences between Leconte de Lisle and Fourier were metaphysical and psychological. Leconte de Lisle's God was nearer to the world soul commonly associated with Spinoza than to the transcendent divinity of Fourier. The difference is obviously important in the context of an aesthetic, since for Leconte de Lisle the external world is a manifestation of the universal soul, and the poet assumes a sacerdotal mantle in leading the public, by contemplation, to the vision of the ideal beyond external realities. Moral failure becomes an obstacle to poetic initiation. Secondly, for Fourier the free flight of passion leads to fulfilment, whereas Leconte de Lisle, although ambiguous, inclines to think that passion requires restraint, causing a suffering which is itself the path to moral elevation. The probability is that in 1845 Leconte de Lisle was ready to publish a volume of poetry entitled "Odes à la France," generally Fourierist in some sense more specific than that merely entailing a vague belief in the moral brotherhood of men or in social progress through industrial and scientific advance, as advocated by Saint-Simon. Leconte de Lisle was at this date aligned with the vulgarized, practical Fourierism of *La Démocratie Pacifique* and *La Phalange*.

In the spring of 1845 Leconte de Lisle returned briefly to Réunion, and on the way back he destroyed a good deal of what he had written. The three accounts of how many lines vary from 1,000 to 6,000. He disembarked at Nantes on 21 June 1845. His ideas were changing rapidly. The projected volume was never published and, as delay followed delay, he replaced earlier poems with newer ones. He was moving away from Fourierism and at the same time beginning to insist on more rigorous standards of scholarly accuracy. In 1846 Thalès Bernard had published his translation of Jacobi's *Dictionnaire mythologique universel*, a much more precise work than Creuzer's influential work on myth of 1812, *Symbolik und Mythologie der alten Völker*, and Leconte de Lisle began to replace the names of antique gods in his poems with their authentic Greek forms. When writing on Byron in September 1846, he also distinguished carefully between transcendent dogmas taking different mythological forms, but denoting an identical human aspiration to spiritual fulfilment, and the historically changing aspirations specific to given cultures at definite times in which he himself believed. A society is identified and politically unified by its religion.

Leconte de Lisle was not the only major author to pass through a Fourierist phase. Banville, Nerval, George Sand, and Dumas were all attracted by its idealism. Leconte de Lisle's break came in June 1847, partly in a puritan reaction to Fourier's liberal views on sexual morality, but, more importantly, because poetry, requiring the free play of the imagination in its aspiration to the ideal, was necessarily hostile to dogmatism. The product of art was a quest and not, as Fourier thought, a fruit. As Victor Cousin had announced in the 1836 *Cours de philosophie*, to be republished as *Du vrai, du beau et du bien* in 1853, art always required increasing freedom in religious thought. In more down-to-earth ways Leconte de Lisle's tyrannical rule as self-styled literary editor was also being challenged as the ideological divergence became more apparent. Fourierism had attracted him when he first needed to move from personal lyric to more perfectly crafted verse forms, but by 1847, now that he was far down the path to the 1852 *Poèmes antiques*, his need had outgrown its compatibility with the Fourierist press.

Between 7 November 1847, the date of the last piece published by Leconte de Lisle in *La Démocratie Pacifique*, and 9 February 1852, the date of the appearance of his poem "Midi" and of Sainte-Beauve's article "De la poésie et des poètes en 1852" in *Le Constitutionnel*, Leconte de Lisle collaborated with Lammenais, but published nothing of his own. The *Poèmes antiques* was published on 4 December 1852 by Marc Ducloux, who may well, as the tradition has it, have offered to publish the collection in compensation for losing the manuscript of the translation of Homer that Leconte de Lisle had submitted to him.

In 1848 Leconte de Lisle had taken part in the revolution, spending 48 hours in prison. In spite of pleas from his father, who had come to Paris in 1847, and the remonstrances of a brother, he had signed a petition for the abolition of slavery in the French colonies. Slavery was in fact abolished, but that meant the threat of ruin for sugar planters in Réunion, and

Leconte de Lisle's father, who was both furious and frightened, cut off his allowance, which had never been very large. Leconte de Lisle failed to make a living from translations and journalism, so he gave lessons in Latin and Greek. When his father died on 28 July 1856, his ruined mother and two sisters came to Paris, where Leconte de Lisle, as eldest son, had to care for them.

The preface to the 1852 volume testifies to the crisis occasioned by the break with Fourierism. Leconte de Lisle wrestles with the problem of the nature of poetry. The poet's function was surely to contemplate the rediscovered glories of an unalterable past in a world of industrial activity, political disappointment, and moral decay, and to accept the discipline imposed by historical authenticity, repudiating any element of personal effusion. Leconte de Lisle takes up where Proudhon had left off in his castigation of poets for all they have contributed to the relaxation of moral standards, to contempt for work, and to disdain for duty. Comte had made the same reproaches in more measured terms.

Jouffroy, in his *Comment les dogmes finissent* of 1825, had proclaimed that the true religious, moral, and political values, which would come again to govern the world, would find their repository for the time being only among those who chose to lead stoic lives of isolation and privacy. Leconte de Lisle was joining the stream of positivist, scientific reaction in the wake of the defeat of literary romanticism in the 1830s, and then of its associated political movement, culminating in the revolution of 1848. The romantic poets had been committed to the reform of a society in which they sought recognition as prophets. Leconte de Lisle accepts the defeat of attempts at political reform, and the withdrawal from society of the poet as moralist: "Si la poésie est souvent une expiation, le supplice est toujours sacré (If poetry is often an expiation, suffering is always sacred)."

The 1852 volume contains 31 poems, of which 11 had appeared in *La Phalange* and "Midi" in Sainte-Beuve's article in *Le Constitutionnel*. It included the four important "Poèmes," "Hélène," "Niobé," "Khirôn," and "Bhagavat," and made its author's reputation, especially on account of the combative preface. The next volume, *Poèmes et poésies*, published by Dentu in June 1855, is prefaced by a reply to criticisms of the 1852 preface. Leconte de Lisle again regards modern industrial society with distaste and as lacking any place for poets, writing instead a panegyric of the Greek epic cycles, of the great Greek myths as expressing as magnificently as possible the whole range of emotions of which the human soul is capable, and of the Hindu "Itihaças," although these lack Greek order and clarity. The poet's function is to take man back to the values and sensibility of their first bloom of strength and beauty, not to produce flat photographs of contemporary events and behaviour. Louise Colet, whom Leconte de Lisle had met early in 1853, had introduced him to the *Revue de Paris*, which had published "Le Runoïa" on 15 August 1854. The poem concerned the introduction of Christianity into Finland and implied a view about the way in which cultures erode from within as, it is hinted, Christianity would in its turn crumble in Finland and was already crumbling in Second Empire France. Three occasional poems had appeared in *Modes Parisiennes Illustrées*, and five pieces had appeared together in the *Revue des Deux Mondes* (q.v.) on 15 February 1855.

It is clear that the new collection begins to reflect Leconte de Lisle's aspiration to put into verse not only the great cycles of Nordic epics, but the whole series of epic or religious cycles which, taken together, would be the history of the cultures of the human race. He took himself as seriously as a philosopher as he did as a poet and as a historian of the development of primitive religions and societies. In the second half of the 19th century, with its great encyclopedic compilations and its interest in cultural as well as biological evolution, the undertaking envisaged by Leconte de Lisle did not appear absurd. However, as it in fact appeared, *Poèmes et poésies* is full of poems inspired by the personal emotion almost entirely excluded from the *Poèmes antiques*.

Of the 28 poems, 14 were dedicated to individuals, although the dedications were later dropped. Seven of the poems are dedicated, although not openly, to Mme de Jobbé-Duval, and the cycle reflects the end of a liaison of which it can be deduced from the poems that Leconte de Lisle had tired. As usual, autobiographical references are fictionalized, transposed, amalgamated, and disguised. But we know that Leconte de Lisle was reduced by poverty to living with Mme de Jobbé-Duval and her husband, and he may have been reproaching her in these poems with not wishing to join him in a suicide pact. There is external evidence that he was talking a good deal about killing himself. There is also an almost masochistic obsession with violence in poems unconnected with the liaison, which testifies to a recurring imaginative pattern of depression of almost suicidal intensity in Leconte de Lisle. That imaginative pattern certainly found expression in his preoccupation with the spiritual self-annihilation of oriental mysticism, and therefore also in his total religious philosophy. In the background of Leconte de Lisle's poetry, as of *Madame Bovary*, lurk the climbing official suicide statistics in France, moving inexorably upwards from 1,739 in 1836 to 4,946 in 1865. It is not difficult to read too much biographical fact into the workings of a poet's imagination, but it looks likely that further poems in the collection constitute a cycle of guilty love for Henriette Colet, born in 1840 and still only 14 in 1854, when Leconte de Lisle was 36, reflecting an attachment later than that which inspired the Jobbé-Duval cycle.

In 1861 Leconte de Lisle published a prose translation of Anacreon with the *Idylls* of Theocritus. He was publishing six or eight major poems a year in reviews, notably the *Revue Contemporaine* and then the *Revue Européenne*, but the collections of 1857, 1858, and 1862 added no new poems to the earlier volumes. He appears to have abandoned a play and to have undergone a severe emotional crisis in 1856, when he was no longer calling on Louise Colet. After the death of his father, and an apparent reconciliation with the rest of his family, Leconte de Lisle was again contemplating suicide. On 12 September 1857 he married. We know very little about the marriage, except that its emotional intensity cannot have lasted very long. In 1861 there is every sign from the poetry that Leconte de Lisle formed both a firm but purely emotional attachment, and a passionately physical one. There is evidence of a feeling of hurt at being rejected, but it is clear that there is a considerable gulf between the emotional life of Leconte de Lisle's imagination and what took place in reality. He may well have had an infatuation for the wife of Hippolyte Foucque, who may well have rejected his advances, but the biographical details are speculative and disputed.

From 1864 Leconte de Lisle accepted a pension of 3,600 francs a year from the emperor's privy purse, but lost it in 1870 after the proclamation of the republic. In 1868 he had already lost a small pension from Réunion. In August 1870 he was to turn down the Légion d'Honneur, but from 1868 the need to earn money was imperative, and Leconte de Lisle embarked on a whole series of commitments with Lemerre, the publisher of the three volumes of *Le Parnasse Contemporain*, to enable him to keep himself and his wife, and to help his mother and two sisters. The *Catéchisme populaire républicain*, the *Histoire populaire du christianisme*, the *Histoire populaire de la révolution française*, and the *Histoire du moyen-âge* were all written as quickly as Leconte de Lisle could manage, and there were other uncompleted, unwritten, or subsequently amalgamated works of popular compilation projected in the interests of making money quickly. Eventually the emperor's pension was restored and in 1872 Leconte de Lisle was given a sinecure assistant librarianship at the Senate, allowing him to live in reasonable comfort until his death at Louveciennes, near Versailles, in July 1894.

From 1862, with the publication of the *Poésies barbares*, as the collection was called until 1872, Leconte de Lisle was the acknowledged leader of the young Paris poets whom Lemerre specialized in publishing. Leconte de Lisle held a weekly salon for them in his fifth-floor apartment on the Boulevard des Invalides, where their works were read and discussed, together with new aesthetic norms. He had in fact virtually accomplished what he thought of as his life work—the versification of the principal accounts in myth and legend of the creation and religious and cultural development of the human race—and a deeper study in verse of the myths of Greek antiquity. In spite of a momentary indulgence in sympathy with the republicanism of 1870, expressed in his poems "Qaïn" and "Le sacre de Paris," Leconte de Lisle was regarded essentially as a member of the quasi-academic establishment. He understood the choice open to him, and decided to remain a poet, using only his formal family name and not the "Charles" to emphasize his status, when he might have stood outside the society he affected to despise but which, in the end, for temperamental as well as economic reasons, he joined. He ended his life playing the part of learned sage in which, for overtly commercial reasons, Lemerre had cast him.

The translation of the *Iliad* was published in 1867, with that of the *Odyssey* the following year, and those of Hesiod, Aeschylus, Horace, Sophocles, and Euripides between the years 1869 and 1884. The *Poèmes tragiques* appeared in 1884, and two years later Leconte de Lisle was elected to the Académie Française, succeeding to the seat of Victor Hugo. The poems from *Poèmes et poésies* were redistributed between augmented re-editions of the *Poèmes antiques* and the *Poèmes barbares*, and in 1895 Leconte de Lisle's family posthumously published his *Derniers poèmes*.

WORKS

Leconte de Lisle adumbrated the symbolist (q.v.) aesthetic, towards which the Parnassians were beating a path, when he wrote that poetic vision depends on the true poet because he "voit du premier coup d'oeil plus loin, plus haut, plus profondément que tous, parce qu'il contemple l'idéal à travers la beauté visible (sees at first glance further, higher, and deeper than any, because he contemplates the ideal through visible beauty)." This statement implies that aspiration to ideal beauty depends on the perception of visible beauty. Its expression cannot take place in an imaginative void. In fact Leconte de Lisle's *Poèmes barbares* sometimes draw on the different strata of his imagination separately, while sometimes his poetry fuses them. It would be a mistake to interpret his advocacy of impersonality in poetry in favour of pursuing an ideal beauty as implying any abnegation of imagery, however sensual or emotionally charged, prompted by the poet's imagination, although the word "barbare" is to be taken not in its normal sense of "ferocious" or "barbaric," but merely as referring to that which, generally Nordic, is outside the Greek and Indian epic traditions.

Much of Leconte de Lisle's work was didactic. His epics carry morals and teach what has proved to be an unscientific and vulnerable view of the meaning and development of myth. He ceased to believe in the possibility of happiness and came to dislike Christianity. He was not a philosopher, but took on the task of stating in definitive poetic form the great truths of human culture as shown in the religious history of the race. Not only did he come to celebrate the Greek myths for their exploration of the whole range of possible human experience, but he also accepted and poetically celebrated the view that each race had at different periods solved its cultural and religious problems in conformity with its temperament, its climate, and its stage of development.

The full thrust of Leconte de Lisle's poetic effort is contained in his verse epics of the myths and legends of humanity, as uncovered by what he must have known was not really scientific historical investigation. In fact he came to rely heavily on such works, in addition to those mentioned, as Eugène Burnouf's *Introduction à l'histoire du Bouddhisme* of 1845, Maury's *Histoire des religions de la Grèce antique* of 1857, and Louis Ménard's *Polythéisme hellénique* of 1863. As stated in his speech of reception at the Académie Française, Leconte de Lisle wished to "accorder une part égale aux diverses conceptions religieuses dont l'humanité a vécu, et qui toutes ont été vraies à leur heure, puisqu'elles étaient les formes idéales de ses rêves et de ses espérances (grant equal validity to each of the different religious visions by which humanity has lived, and which were each true in their time, since they were the idealized forms of humanity's dreams and hopes)."

The *Poèmes antiques* is dominated by Leconte de Lisle's desire to merge the art of poetry with the depiction of the history of the human race as 19th-century theory had materialistically reconstructed it. The most important pieces are the four entitled "Poèmes." Although Leconte de Lisle does demonstrate epic qualities, moving for instance in "Hélène" from the vague menace of the gods to the specific prophecy of catastrophe, there is still an element of the conventional, even the perfunctory, in the evocation of Greek antiquity. The poem comes to life when, under the guise of Sparta, Leconte de Lisle celebrates Réunion:

Et les nappes d'azur de tes cieux étoilés,
Et le Féerique éclat de tes soirs enflammés,
Et tes larges récifs, où la lame, dans l'ombre,
Jette, aux échos des monts, son accent long et sombre.

(And the layers of blue in your skies scattered with stars ,/
The Magic brightness of your evenings in flames, / Your broad reefs where, in the shade, the wave, / Echoing the mountains, gives out its long, dark sound.)

Leconte de Lisle's strength as a poet lay not in the fulfilment of his inflated philosophical or vatic ambitions, but in his ability to rekindle in his imagination memories of Réunion and Brittany, the tensile vigour of tamed nature becoming an image of defeat and deep pessimism. His best imagery is vivid and violent, often visual, occasionally static and sculpted, derived from exotic locations, jungle life, or antique architecture. Invariably it is inspired by an unstated personal emotion, like the attachment he felt to his home and his mother in "Hélène." Indeed, Leconte de Lisle's poems almost always have a contemporary social, political, or personal relevance, whatever their ostensible subject. "Hypatie et Cyrille" and "Les paraboles de Dom Guy" are actually full of anti-Christian polemic, while "Nurmahal," "Djihan-Arâ," and "Le conseil du Fahkir" celebrate the fierce independence of the Indians and are set in opposition to English colonial mercantilism. In "Qaïn" the main character is not disguised as a spokesman for Leconte de Lisle. In "Nurmahal," where the moral is not obvious from the story, it is explicitly added. It is clear that Leconte de Lisle is attempting to distil the essence of a culture from the narration of its epics. One of his more brilliant successes is "L'épée d'Angantyr." Angantyr's daughter, Hervor, asks her dead father for his sword in order to avenge him, weeping like a woman for the privilege of taking on the virile role of a man. The hidden theme of castration lies behind the narration of Angantyr's surrender.

Angantyr, soulevant le tertre de sa tombe,
Tel qu'un spectre, les yeux ouverts et sans regard,
Se dresse, et lentement ouvre ses bras blafards
D'où l'épée au pommeau de fer s'échappe et tombe.
Et le héros aux dents blanches dit: Prends et pars!

(Angantyr, lifting the mound from his grave, / Like a spectre, with his eyes open and unseeing, / Rises and slowly opens his pale arms, / From which the sword with the iron pommel escapes and falls./And the hero with white teeth says: "Take and go!")

The imaginative patterns remain the same beneath the diversity of the myths. There is female treachery seen from the point of view of the lover in "Nurmahal" and the husband in "Le conseil du Fahkir." In the Breton legend "Le jugement de Komor," the situation is much the same, but resolved now by the history of the old husband. Husbands expiate by death the intensity of their love. The poet admires the virility of the lovers and the strength of the women passionate enough to kill. The silent allusions to his own love life are clear, but the poems also contain religious, caring women, and frequently the brooding philosophical figure still romantically at odds with the society around him or her, the fresh vigour of the dawn of the world, the subsequent corruption of transient beliefs which change as the values which they embody corrode. A foreboding is built up before a single catastrophic, violent action, or event.

It has been pointed out that the ballad form best suits Leconte de Lisle's long poems, and that a less pretentious aesthetic would have served him better than that which led him to long lists of unfamiliar oriental or Nordic names. "Ekhidna" of 1862, stripped of its Greek trappings, is a finely evocative love poem, while, in spite of the bric-à-brac of snows and crows, blood and battles, death and dying, the Nordic colour, and the ballad form, "Le cœur de Hialmar" of 1864 is a touching poem in which a woman appears in the imagination of the dying hero. The opening sets a swift rhythm:

Une nuit claire, un vent glacé. La neige est rouge.
Mille braves sont là qui dorment sans tombeaux,
L'épée au poing, les yeux hagards. Pas un ne bouge.
Au-dessus tourne et crie un vol de noirs corbeaux.

(A clear night, a freezing wind. The snow is red. / A thousand braves are there, asleep without tombs, / sword in hand, with haggard eyes. Not a single one moves. / Above, a flight of black crows turns and cries.)

At the end there is a cadence not so much in the rhythm as in the imagery, as Hialmar dies:

Je vais m'asseoir parmi les Dieux, dans le soleil.
(I am going to sit among the Gods, in the sun.)

Leconte de Lisle's poems work best when the pretentious use of sonorous and exotic names, the morals, and the long sentences of complex narrative are removed and we are left, as in "Midi," with the evocation of a plain scorched bare by the sun, or in "Les éléphants" with a composite image drawing on several of the senses, marvellously conjuring up the physical sensations of jungle life. The poet's subsequent reflection is almost an anti-climax after one of his bests stanzas:

L'oreille en éventail, la trompe entre les dents,
Ils cheminent, l'oeil clos. Leur ventre bat et fume,
Et leur sueur dans l'air embrasé monte en brume;
Et bourdonnent autour mille insectes ardentes.

(With ears fanned out, trunks between teeth, / They make their way, with closed eyes. Their bellies heave and smoke, / Their sweat rises into the burning air like a mist, / And a thousand bustling insects buzz round.)

PUBLICATIONS

Collections

Poésies complètes, 4 vols., 1927–28

Verse

Poèmes antiques, 1852
Poèmes et poésies, 1855
Le Chemin de la Croix, 1856
Poésies complètes, 1858
Poésies barbares, 1862
Le Soir d'une bataille, 1871
Le Sacre de Paris, 1871
Poèmes barbares, 1872
Poèmes antiques, 1874
Poèmes tragiques, 1884
Derniers poèmes, 1895
Premières poésies et lettres intimes, 1902

Other

Catéchisme populaire républicain, 1870
Histoire populaire de la révolution française, 1871

Histoire populaire du christianisme, 1871
Les Erinnyes (verse tragedy in two acts), 1873
Histoire du moyen-âge, 1876
L'Apollonide, 1888
Translator Theocritus, *Idylles,* 1861
        Odes anacréontiques, 1861
        L'Iliade, by Homer, 1867
        L'Odyssée, by Homer, 1868
        Hymnes orphiques, by Hesiod, 1869
        Aeschylus, *Oeuvres*, 1872
        Horace, *Oeuvres,*1873
        Sophocles, *Oeuvres*, 1877
        Euripides, *Oeuvres*, 2 vols., 1874

Biographical and critical studies

Fairlie, Alison, *Leconte de Lisle's Poems on the Barbarian Races*, 1947
Putter, I., *Leconte de Lisle and His Contemporaries*, 1951
Brown, Irving, *Leconte de Lisle: A Study of the Man and his Poetry*, 1966
Pich, Edgard, *Leconte de Lisle et sa création poétique*, 1975

––––––––

LEDUC, Violette, 1907–1972.

Autobiographer and novelist.

Leduc was the illegitimate daughter of the son of a prosperous family and a woman who worked for them. She was disowned by her father and brought up by her grandmother. Painfully aware that she was an expense and an embarrassment, that she was ugly and that men, as she perceived them, were dangerous, Leduc was further embittered by her mother's subsequent marriage and the birth of a legitimate son. She had a series of lesbian relationships, for one of which she was expelled from boarding school, made a disastrous and short-lived marriage, took on a succession of ill-paid jobs, and entered into what turned out to be a satisfying friendship with the homosexual Maurice Sachs. The colourful Sachs could be an engaging and at times generous companion, but he was ultimately a pitiable trickster who made money during the war by helping fellow Jews to escape the Germans, selling their possessions for them at considerable profit to himself, and then informing on them. He was finally either shot by the Germans or lynched by those on whom he had informed, leaving a brilliantly cynical autobiography and some cruel portraits of figures from Paris society between the wars. It was he who encouraged Leduc to write.

Yearning for artistic fulfilment, Leduc worked on the fringes of the glamour world and idolized its stars, taking jobs with a publisher and a film director and writing assorted articles for women's magazines. During the war she agreed to provide cover for Sachs by living next door to him in the country. He initiated her into black-market profiteering, the only job that ever earned her respectability. Immediately after the war Simone de Beauvoir, whom she has been considered to outstrip as a writer, took Leduc under her wing.

Beauvoir ensured publication of parts of Leduc's first manuscript in the second number of *Les Temps Modernes* (q.v.) in 1945 and got Gallimard to publish the complete text, *L'Asphyxie*. This was followed by *L'Affamé* and *Ravages*, from which Gallimard excised the lesbian episodes, which it was later forced to publish separately. Beauvoir was a powerful, sensitive, and devoted protector, who provided discreet financial support and had Leduc treated in a clinic when her hallucinations degenerated into acute paranoia. She was also a stern task-mistress who imposed exacting literary standards on the incoherent and delirious fantasies that permeated Leduc's early works.

In 1958 Leduc published two short stories. Beauvoir suggested a proper autobiography and the result, *La Bâtarde*, brought the breakthrough. It is undoubtedly too prolix, if in this respect still an improvement on the work of Leduc's mentor. Subsuming all the earlier work, it is both uninhibitedly self-revelatory and clearly fictionalized, direct, open, and poetic. The book sold 165,000 copies in two years, but its literary status remains uncertain.

Some of the comparisons made on the book's appearance were undoubtedly extravagant. It was successful partly because it was connected with the smart left-wing chic of *Les Temps Modernes*, partly because it provided grist to the feminist and homosexual mills, and partly because Leduc, betraying a perhaps understandable short-sightedness, allowed herself to be lionized by fashionable Paris, whose hostesses, starlets, and couturiers found their purposes well served by the unabashed exploitation of naive eccentricity.

Leduc bought an old house in Provence, where she spent increasingly longer periods, wrote a novella, a dialogue, and two further volumes of autobiography. She died of cancer in 1972.

PUBLICATIONS

Novels and autobiography

L'Asphyxie, 1946
L'Affamée, 1948
Ravages, 1955; as *Ravages* (includes *Thérèse and Isabelle*), 1966
La Vieille Fille et le mort (includes *Les Boutons dorés*), 1958
Trésors à prendre, 1960
La Bâtarde, 1964; as *La Bâtarde* (in English), 1965
La Femme au petit renard, 1965; as *The Woman with the Little Fox Fur: Three Novellas* (includes *The Old Maid and the Dead Man, The Golden Buttons, The Woman with the Little Fox Fur*), 1966; as *The Lady and the Little Fox Fur*, 1967
Thérèse et Isabelle, 1966
La Folie en tête, 1971; as *Mad in Pursuit*, 1971
Le Taxi, 1971; as *The Taxi*, 1972
La Chasse à l'amour, 1973

Additional translations

The Golden Buttons, 1961
In the Prison of Her Skin, 1970
Thérèse and Isabelle, 1967; also included in *Ravages*, 1966

Short stories

"Le dézingage," *Les Temps Modernes*, December 1945

"Train noir," *Les Temps Modernes*, March 1946
"Les mains sales," *Les Temps Modernes*, December 1946
"Au village," *Les Temps Modernes*, March 1951
"Désirée Hélée," *Les Temps Modernes*, June 1952
"Brigitte Bardot," *Adam*, June 1966

Critical study

Courtivron, Isabelle de, *Violette Leduc*, 1985

LEIRIS, Michel, 1901–1990.

Poet, novelist, anthropologist, and critic.

LIFE

Michel Leiris's works are often grouped roughly into those regarded as "imaginative" and those pertaining to ethnology, and his life is generally considered to have been discontinuous, completely changing as a result of a mental breakdown. This was followed by a prolonged psychoanalysis with Adrien Borel from 1929 to 1935, and his consequent transformation from the surrealist (q.v.) poet, who powdered his face white and painted landscapes on his already bare scalp, into the serious anthropologist, curator of the Musée de l'Homme, and director of research at the Centre National de Recherche Scientifique. The reason why this view of Leiris is untenable derives primarily from the fact that wordplay, communication, and the nature of linguistic signs preoccupied him both as a poet and as an anthropologist, linking both sides of his activities and all periods of his life. Language provides a key to the understanding of his life as well as of his works. That Leiris as a youth worked his way to a condition that could be called mentally disturbed seems certain, but his break with surrealism and his later divergence from Sartre towards Freudian determinism in fact argue that the development of his personal view of the world underwent no serious change of direction at all.

Leiris was born in Paris on 20 April 1901, the son of a stockbroker's agent. His influence on French intellectual life was to be enormous, but his academic beginnings did not promise well. He claims several times to have been expelled from the Lycée Janson-de-Sailly, mostly for encouraging his fellow students to get drunk in "bars frequented by aviators." After his baccalauréat he took his "licence" in literature at the Sorbonne, and followed it with a diploma from the Ecole des Hautes Etudes Scientifiques et Religieuses. His rebellion against the multiple constraints imposed on him by his environment culminated in an almost dada (q.v.) desire to shock, and he was in severe trouble in 1925 for shouting "Long live Germany!"

Leiris's chemistry studies coincided with his literary beginnings. He had met and become friendly with André Masson, who, having studied in Brussels, was advised by Verhaeren to come to Paris, where the gallery owner Daniel Kahnweiler made it possible for him to devote himself entirely to painting. He joined forces with the surrealists, to whom he introduced Leiris in 1924. Leiris, who now lived in the same street, the Rue Blomet, as Masson, Joan Miró, and Antonin Artaud, had meanwhile met the Marxist sociologist Georges Bataille and was writing his first poems under the inspiration of Max Jacob. Leiris was deeply involved with Breton in the production of the first surrealist manifesto of October 1924, and Masson produced the lithographs for Leiris's first book of poems, *Simulacre*. Some 40 years later, in *Fibrilles*, the third part of *La Règle du jeu*, Leiris was to explain the attraction of surrealism, "que je n'ai jamais renié (on which I have never turned my back)," as its promise of "un système total: sous une forme propre à nourrir l'imagination, le beau, le bien, le vrai, rebrassés dans l'irrespect des idées reçues et décoiffés des majuscules qui les posent en grands principes figés (a total system: in a form calculated to feed the imagination, the beautiful, the good, the true, mixed with disrespect for received ideas and stripped of the capital letters which make them into big unalterable principles)." What Leiris says in 1966 he has rejected from surrealism is the automatism and the naive grasp of the marvellous.

In 1926 he married and went to Egypt. He published *Le Point cardinal* the following year, but then nothing in volume form until *L'Afrique fantôme* of 1934. However, by the late 1920s Leiris was working on *Aurora*, a gothic, surrealist novel written mostly in 1927 but not published until 1946, *Grande fuite de neige*, written in 1927 but published only in 1964, the poems to be collected as *Haut mal* in 1943, and the celebrated *Glossaire, j'y serre mes gloses*, first published with Masson's lithographs in 1940, a book containing a list of words defined in brief wordplays. A prefatory note of 1925 indicates that dictionaries give only information based on customary usage, the lowest criterion of signification, and etymology, which is perfectly useless. By defining words in accordance with the personal meaning they have for us we can arrive at our whole personal system of associations "to guide us through the Babel of our minds." To make his point, Leiris put a triple pun into the title.

The whole book consists of fun made with assonance, near-anagrams, and repeated syllables which permute into clever but mildly funny definitions. "Génie," which means "genius," is "defined" with relative simplicity, "naît de la neige, son nid (born of snow, its nest)." The "definition" takes the word's first vowel sound and puts it after its second consonant in two different words, each totally unconnected with "génie" and with one another, then takes the second syllable, spells it differently, and ends up with the absurd "nest of snow," the word for snow being an anagram of "génie." As usual with the more serious surrealists, the intense concentration on a simple object or, as here, sound, creates a superficially startling incongruity which draws attention to the arbitrary and different ways in which we personally and collectively assign meaning to, and create a grammar and a syntax for, noises and pronounceable combinations of letters. It is not impossible to see how surrealist nonsenses can lead to serious ethnographic considerations.

The then still unpublished *Aurora* reveals the author's mind as crushed by anxieties, sexually perverted both sadistically and masochistically, and unable to face life. Leiris had in fact made an attempt at suicide, which he would recount in *Fibrilles* and which was apparently a solution he seems to have considered more than once. His personality was eroded by self-loathing. He was impotent and able to achieve nothing by the time the analy-

sis started, although he had been publishing material in Georges Bataille's *Documents*, mostly republished in *Brisées* of 1966. From about 1930 Leiris worked on his classic *L'Age d'homme*, to be published in 1939 and again in 1963, with the famous preface "De la littérature considérée comme une tauro machie (Literature considered as a bullfight)." From 1931 to 1933 he was with the Dakar–Djibouti expedition under Marcel Griaule, which inspired *L'Afrique fantôme*, published the year after his return, when he joined the staff at the Musée de l'Homme.

In 1939 Leiris was mobilized and sent to the Sahara, then demobilized in France. He ran a Resistance cell at the Musée de l'Homme and, with his wife Zette, harboured Jews in his apartment. At this period he became friendly with Sartre and Beauvoir, as well as with Raymond Queneau, taking part with them in the apparently enjoyable parties at which there was little either to eat or drink. Leiris was a founding member of the board of *Les Temps Modernes* (q.v.), of which he was also literary editor. He was not formally to take part in the dispute about anthropology which later broke out between Sartre and Lévi-Strauss. In quest of the unwritable existential ethic, Sartre, however, was veering away from the Freudian determinism to which Leiris was by now much more sympathetic. Sartre was not very interested in the literary side of the review, but continued to like and respect Leiris, and the two never disagreed in their attitude to colonialism, both actual and metaphorical, in the sense in which the term can be used of what happens to the therapist–patient relationship in the course of an analysis.

From 1947 Leiris began his series of ethnographic journeys to Africa, the West Indies, and, most importantly of all, China. He attended the congress of intellectuals in Cuba in 1968, and from 1969 was on the editorial board of *L'Ephémère*. The four volumes of *La Régle du jeu* (*Biffures; Fourbis; Fibrilles;* and *Frêle bruit*) constitute a difficult but brilliant extension of autobiographical writing into what is virtually a new dimension. They are a Freudian reconstruction of Leiris's life drawing on the analysis, naturally, but also having recourse to the old surrealist preoccupation with the contents of the subconscious. The complications of the genre are hinted at in the titles. "Biffures" means "crossings-out," but is closely associated with the word for crossroads. Leiris also wrote a long series of essays and articles on painters and poets which were never published in volume form and so do not occur in the appended list of publications. Among the essays worthy of note are those on Masson, Cranach, Roussel, Picasso, Butor, Miró, Jacob, Bacon, and Proust. Leiris died in Paris on 30 September 1990.

WORKS

The intellectual life of France just after World War II was in a narrow sense dominated by an anthropological debate about the significance of ritual gift-giving among primitive peoples. Lévi-Strauss had written a gloss on Mauss's primordially important *Essai sur le don*, which developed the author's theory in such a way as to make Lévi-Strauss's structural anthropology incompatible with Sartre's Marxism (see Sartre, Lévi-Strauss), and Lévi-Strauss's final view is contained in his celebrated but technical *Les Structures élémentaires de la parenté*. Leiris had published *Biffures* before Lévi-Strauss had written his new preface to Mauss's essay, and before the first publication of *Les Struc-*

tures élémentaires. Extracts from *Biffures* appeared in *Les Temps Modernes* for February and March 1946. They explain how Leiris's anthropological perspectives are clearly linked to his linguistic preoccupations, as Lévi-Strauss's anthropological matrix had by this date been derived from Roman Jakobson's linguistics. However, they also explain how Leiris's exploitation of Mauss offered Sartre a model which, if it did not stop him from quarrelling with Lévi-Strauss, at least established in *Les Temps Modernes*, Sartre's own review, a means of relating literature to the anthropological model of gift-giving. This reined in Sartre from the extremes to which he was later prepared to go to defend political commitment on ideological grounds.

Leiris envisages literature as gifts in primitive cultures are regarded by Mauss—the communicated concretizations of the creative endeavours of the imagination communicated in the manner of a gift.

Toute la question est là: faire passer dans la tête ou dans le coeur d'autrui les concrétions—jusqu'à là valables seulement pour lui—déposées, par le présent ou le passé de sa vie, au fond de sa propre tête ou de son propre coeur: communiquer, pour valoriser; faire circuler, pour que la chose ainsi lancée aux autres vous revienne un peu plus prestigieuse, tels ces boucliers des Indiens du Nord-Oeuest américain qui se trouvent doués d'une valeur d'autant plus grande qu'ils ont fait l'objet de plus nombreux échanges cérémoniels.

(The whole question is there: to pass into the head or the heart of someone else the concretizations, hitherto valid for oneself alone, left by the past or the present of one's life at the bottom of one's own head or heart; to communicate, in order to bestow value; to circulate so that what is thrown out to others comes back to oneself that much more prestigious, like those shields of the north-west American Indians which increase in value according to the number of ceremonial exchanges of which they have been the object.)

The powerful theory of literature as gift, to be received, accepted, and returned enhanced with understanding, which Leiris has developed here, quite simply opens the way to a synthesis of the major strands in modern critical theory and practice. This was no doubt firstly due to its publication at a date and in a place which links Mauss's theory, independently of Lévi-Strauss's gloss on it, to the later irreconcilable dispute between scientific anthropology and Marxism, which dominated French intellectual life for nearly three decades, and, secondly, due to its justification of linking life and works in an effort to understand Leiris's thinking and the creative works of his imagination. It makes apparent the common roots of structuralist (q.v.) anthropology and the structuralist criticism of literature, giving meaning to both. It comes quite near to providing a foundation on which to build a whole science of man, and makes it probable that Leiris will come to figure much more prominently in histories of 20th-century thought, as time allows the ephemeral disputes with their abrasive attitudes to be seen as secondary in the development of the "science de l'homme," to which all the humane disciplines are clearly moving, but for which we do not yet have even a name in Anglo-Saxon.

Leiris's prose writings are more often the object of critical attention than his cleverly self-conscious verse, most of which

is collected in *Haut mal*. Of the prose writings, *Aurora* is interesting primarily for its revelation of the workings of a sick mind. Its interest is more biographical than literary and it was, of course, not published until after a cure had been effected for the mental condition it reveals. That condition is described with powerful restraint in the deliberately cruel self-revelation of *L'Age d'homme*, in which Leiris informs us of his weaknesses, his fears, and even his sexual inadequacies. The book, published as World War II broke out, attracted little attention, although it has now been reprinted and has appeared in English.

La Règle du jeu, the second part of which won the Prix des Critiques, is also a heavily self-conscious undertaking, fascinatingly full of complex reflections of all that its author has achieved, and about what that achievement means, from the initial integration into the community, as Leiris acquired the means of communication, to the establishment of firmer relationships with the outside world. He recounts how he discovered that words gave reality a new dimension, by limiting memory, for instance, to the chronologically sequential presentation of things. In fact, childhood events are later important not for their chronology but for the emotional charge they carried. *La Règle du jeu* therefore becomes an autobiography which attempts to replace the sequential narration of events with some account of their associations and personal significance. It contains a great deal more reflection than narrative, about World War II, the Algerian war, and the student revolution of May 1968, for instance, and the complicated wordplay is still there, but the reflection is of a very high order of intelligence, of breadth of cultural concern, and of courageous introspection.

Leiris asks how the truth can ever be as clear as an autobiography must make it seem. How can the mind unravel the truth about its past from the fictions it has spun to disguise what it once could not confront, and how far can or dare it now go in confronting what it once hid? The subject of the autobiography is depicted as escaping the pen's attempt to pin it down, turning the work into more of a collage than a narrative. While always wrestling to find the story, the mind cannot help commenting on what it is doing, relating the present in which the writing takes place to the past, which is its ostensible object. The need to tell the whole truth brings incessant modifications, touchings up, and these turn inevitably into falsifications because the mind safeguards its present by distorting its past. The purpose of writing an autobiography is to establish a relationship with the death to come. The "Jeu" of the title is a pun on the subject of the book "Je" (I) and the magic of the "Jeu" (Game) of palmistry. The four volumes ask all sorts of questions about the activity of autobiography, and they also raise the standards of autobiographical writing in several ways—by their intelligence, by their shrewdness of introspective insight, by their ironic but unflinching honesty, and by the width of their interest in all cultural phenomena, social, political, literary, belonging to other arts and sciences, or concerning the writing of autobiography.

PUBLICATIONS

Verse

Simulacre, 1925
Le Point cardinal, 1927
Haut mal, 1943

Bagatelles végétales, 1956
Vivantes cendres, innommées, 1961
Marrons sculptés pour Miró, 1962
Autres lancers, 1969

Prose other than ethnography

L'Afrique fantôme, 1934
Tauromachies, 1937
Miroir de la tauromachie, 1938; as *The Autobiographer as Toreo*, 1968
L'Age d'homme, 1939; as *Manhood*, 1963
Glossaire, j'y serre mes gloses, 1940
Nuits sans nuit et quelques jours sans jour, 1945
Aurora, 1946
André Masson et son univers, with Georges Limbour, 1947; as *André Masson and His Universe*, 1947
La Règle du jeu I: Biffures, 1948
Toro, 1951
La Règle du jeu II: Fourbis, 1955
Balzacs en bas de casse et Picassos sans majuscules, 1957
Grande fuite de neige, 1964
Brisées, 1966
La Règle du jeu III: Fibrilles, 1966
Mots sans mémoire, 1970
Fissures, 1970
Wilfredo Lam, 1970; *Wilfredo Lam* (in English), 1970
André Masson: massacres et autres dessins, 1971
Francis Bacon, 1974
La Règle du jeu IV: Frêle bruit, 1976
Le Ruban au cou d'Olympia, 1982
Langage, tangage, ou ce que les mots disent, 1985
Roussel l'ingénu, 1987
Ondes, 1988
A cor et à cri, 1989

Ethnography

La Langue secrète des Dogons de Sanga, 1948
Contacts de civilisations en Martinique et en Guadeloupe, 1955
La Possession et ses aspects théâtraux chez les Ethiopiens de Gondar, 1958
Cinq études d'ethnologie, 1969
L'Afrique noire, with Jacqueline Delange, 1967; as *African Art*, 1968

Published as volumes only in English

Prints of Joan Miró, 1947
Picasso and Human Comedy, 1954
Race and Civilization (later *Race and Culture*), 1951

Biographical and critical studies

Bréchon, Robert, *"L'Age d'homme" de Michel Leiris*, 1973
Chappuis, Pierre, *Michel Leiris*, 1973

LÉVI-STRAUSS, Claude, 1908–

Social anthropologist, philosopher, and essayist.

LIFE

In so far as Lévi-Strauss must find his place in a compendium of literary authors, it is not only on account of the celebrated meditative essay *Tristes tropiques* and the poetic quality of so much of his writing. Both by themselves would make his inclusion necessary, but it is also on account of the derivation of his thought from the linguistic model of Ferdinand Saussure, the resulting close connection between his anthropological work and structuralism (q.v.) as a literary phenomenon, and his long and close, if turbulent, association with *Les Temps Modernes* (q.v.) from World War II until at any rate 1963, while it was still considered to be the leading literary review in France. From its inception in 1945 until its contents became first half, and then overwhelmingly, political in 1963 and 1971, it devoted as much or more space to literature as it did to "sciences humaines," including Lévi-Strauss's own discipline of social anthropology.

Lévi-Strauss, grandson of a rabbi and son of an artist, was born in Brussels on 28 November 1908. The family moved to Versailles in 1914. As a child Lévi-Strauss was fascinated by geology and the relationships between rock formations, soils, and fauna. He liked to go on walking expeditions and collected outdoor objects such as pebbles and plants, out of which he made designs. To that activity he later attributed a role in the elaboration of his anthropological theories. He abandoned the Ecole Normale Supérieure (ENS) to study law in Paris, but disliked both his fellow students and his prospective clients, took his "licence" in philosophy, and in 1932, at his first attempt and as the youngest member of his year, passed the agrégation in philosophy. He chose the subject largely because, he says, he found philosophy less tedious than the other subjects he had tried, but both the courses and the subject disillusioned him. He found that they mostly concerned a reflection on the history of solving intellectual problems, rather than the discovery of the truth.

None the less, he discovered Marx, through whom he made the further discoveries of Kant and Hegel, and who taught him the basic method of the social sciences. This, he says, consists in constructing laboratory models, experimenting with them, and then testing them against empirical events. After Marx, Lévi-Strauss discovered Freud, who seemed to have resolved the contradictions between the rational and the irrational he took to have been left by Bergson. Lévi-Strauss tells us how he found in ethnography the bridge between, on the one hand, the social sciences of Marx, concerned with society, and Freud, concerned with the individual, and, on the other, the physical science of geology. He became interested in primitive sociology largely because, after a telephone call from the director of the ENS at nine o'clock one Sunday morning in the autumn of 1933, he had until midday to accept a chair of sociology at São Paulo. He left Marseilles in February 1934, did not find the promised Indian tribes in the suburbs of São Paulo, and was at that time in full reaction against Durkheim's sociology, which he was expected to teach. His position on Durkheim subsequently softened.

Lévi-Strauss had married Dina Dreyfus in 1932 and become dismayed at the prospect of the philosophy teaching career which he had started in 1932, first at the Lycée Mont-de-Marsan and then at Laon. Trips into the Brazilian interior gave him the chance to become acquainted with primitive tribes, although he disliked fieldwork and in the view of traditional anthropologists did little of it. The whole of his subsequent work explains that, because what he finally sought to study was the anthropology of culture generally, particularly modern Western culture, he did not think it necessary to learn the indigenous languages or to immerse himself in tribal life in the traditional way in order to learn how, even in advanced civilizations, communication was coded in the symbolic relationships of myth and behaviour, as well as in language, of which words were only a part.

In 1939 he returned to France to join up, but left after its fall to the Germans to teach in the New School for Social Research in New York, where he formed a friendship with Roman Jakobson and became interested in structural linguistics. He was not given tenure and returned to Paris, but was back in the US as cultural attaché at the Washington embassy from 1946 to 1947. For the next two years he was associate curator of the Musée de l'Homme in Paris and then, from 1950, director of studies at the Ecole Pratique des Hautes Etudes. From 1959 to 1983 he was professor of social anthropology, and after 1983 an honorary professor at the Collège de France. His first marriage ended in divorce, and in 1946 he married Rosemarie Ullmo, by whom he had a son. In 1954 he married Monique Roman. He became a member of the Académie Française in 1973, and acquired 10 honorary doctorates and a large number of other distinctions. In 1976 he was made a Commandeur of the Légion d'Honneur.

Lévi-Strauss published nothing until 1948. After the first, largely technical works on kinship and totemism came *Tristes tropiques*, written and published in 1955. This is partly an autobiographical account of his mental itinerary and of his work in Brazil, and partly a reflection about the need for civilized Western man to study his own culture, particularly in terms of the myths, codes, and conventions which distort society. The two volumes of the *Anthropologie structurale* were published in 1958 and 1973. The views expounded in the first volume reflected Lévi-Strauss's growing divergence from Sartre, who appears at first not to have understood the moral and political implications of structuralism. These were pointed out when, in an article entitled "L'échange et la lutte des hommes" in *Les Temps Modernes* for February 1951, Claude Lefort criticized a passage from Lévi-Strauss's introduction to the 1950 re-edition of Marcel Mauss's *Sociologie et anthropologie*.

Lévi-Strauss had used a linguistic model, actually Jakobson's "zero phoneme," to describe the exchange of gifts, whose nature he thought Mauss had misunderstood, and which he thought should have been described as a phenomenon of the unconscious. For Lefort, Lévi-Strauss's insistence on the unconscious made him even less easy to reconcile with the new Marxism being developed by *Les Temps Modernes* than Mauss himself had been. For Lefort the roots of exchanging gifts are economic and not grounded in an unconscious cultural code. For Lévi-Strauss the individual is responding to unconscious social structures, while for Sartre social behaviour is the result of individual economic determinants. Behind what might look like a dispute regarding the anthropological description of a point of social behaviour, the exchanging of gifts, lies an important ideological clash. Lévi-Strauss's structural anthropology, with its reliance on models derived from structural linguistics and its dependence on the unconscious, was incompatible with Sartre's refurbished Marxism.

The dispute rumbled on, with Lefort writing in the *Cahiers Internationaux de Sociologie* in 1952 and coming close to agreement with Lévi-Strauss's pamphlet of the same year, *Race et histoire*, later summarized in an article, "Diogène couché," published in *Les Temps Modernes* for March 1955. By 1954 Lévi-Strauss was giving his anthropology a Sartrean gloss, but there were now personal tensions to be contended with between the protagonists, allies, enemies, and would-be mediators; Sartre, Lévi-Strauss, Maurice Merleau-Ponty, Roger Caillois, Claude Lefort, Jean Pouillan, and Michel Leiris. The attempted rapprochement of 1954 was simply terminological.

Sartre and Lévi-Strauss had partly supported one another in the disputes of each with others, like Caillois and Lefort, and had been brought together by personal and political sympathies, but finally Lévi-Strauss's structuralism, founded on symbolic relationships anchored in the unconscious, and Sartre's economically based Marxism were bound to prove incompatible. As he recounted in *Tristes tropiques*, Lévi-Strauss could not accept the phenomenological (q.v.) contention that there was a continuity between experience and reality, where structuralism postulated only a symbolic relationship. Experience for Lévi- Strauss came in again only at the final point of "objective synthesis," that is, when the laboratory model was empirically tested. He also thought that existentialism (q.v.) was moving in the wrong direction by locking itself into the "subjectivity" of "personal preoccupations." Malevolently describing existentialism in 1955 as "metaphysics for shopgirls," Lévi-Strauss disliked both phenomenology and existentialism because, instead of abolishing metaphyics, they "introduced two ways of finding alibis for it."

In 1957 Sartre renewed his fight for a synthetic but non-structuralist anthropology, which he called an "anthropologie structurelle," because Lévi-Strauss was to use the "-ale" ending for the title of his 1958 volume. Sartre's 1957 articles were incorporated into the 1960 *Critique de la raison dialectique as Questions de méthode*. Lévi-Strauss's *La Pensée sauvage* of 1962 contains an attack on Sartre and another on Lucien Lévy-Bruhl (1857–1939), each of whom is accused of denying full human status to primitive tribes. From 1964 to 1971 he published the four volumes of his great work *Mythologiques*, opening out the perspective already hinted at in the ironically titled *La Pensée sauvage*. The work is ostensibly about Brazilian myths, but in fact about the nature of myth itself and therefore of the processes by which we understand the world. It takes off from close argument to move with sweeping, almost lyrical intellectual brilliance towards a vision of the nature of man and the ultimate destiny of humanity, dazzling in its scope, but finally heedless of the restrictions imposed by scientific method and logical argument.

On 14 July 1991 Lévi-Strauss was awarded the Grand-Croix of the Légion d'Honneur, the highest of its five classes.

WORKS

Lévi-Strauss's habit of writing "poetically" not surprisingly disconcerts readers trying to pin down his concepts and arguments, but the mingling of facts with ideas, fancies, and hypotheses gives his books literary merit and imaginative importance, even if it is possible that such books ought not to have them. He claimed that geology, psychoanalysis, and Marxism, his "three mistresses," using the term to mean teacher as well as lover, had taught him the discontinuity between the order of superficial experience and that of true reality. It has been pointed out that he could well have added music to the three "maîtresses." *Mythologiques*, especially in its first volume, *Le Cru et le cuit*, depends quite heavily on a musical model in which chromaticism functions as a "mediator" between harmony and mere noise. In so far as Lévi-Strauss is the father of "structuralism," it is because the fundamental structures of language and behaviour are unconscious and concern not independent entities but created, symbolic relationships, like notes in music. The word "unconscious" is used where the French might employ "inconscient" because, of the two alternative renderings, "subconscious" has connotations in English that are too specifically Freudian, and "pre-conscious" has unfortunate chronological associations.

The method applied by Lévi-Strauss in his treatment of myth is strikingly analogous to that employed by Barthes in his analysis of language. Myths are separated into versions and broken down into constituent units which acquire significance only in relation to one another. Lévi-Strauss extends his method well beyond the analysis of unconscious mythological structures, and some of his arguments leap unconvincingly over unconsidered objections. It does not require anthropological expertise to see that they become generalized much too quickly. Single instances of what occurs when "nature" is transformed into "culture" become foundations on which grandiose hypotheses are sometimes constructed.

In some of Lévi-Strauss's writing on myths, the musical analogy is extended to give to the chapters the titles of musical forms like "sonata" and "fugue," and the chapter organization is like that of a complete musical work, with fast and slow movements in contrasting keys. At the same time the language idiosyncratically exploits abstract metaphors, using for instance "the contained" for "beverage" in a cup. There is virtual unanimity that, whatever his qualities as a writer, Lévi-Strauss abused figurative language in the processes of argument, often smuggling in assumptions that should have been made clear, but would no doubt have upset the rigour of the argument if they had been. Occasionally the argument seems unduly influenced by some illogical impulse, like that of pursuing the reaction against Bergson, developed when the young Lévi-Strauss discovered Marx and Freud, by looking for what he calls a "supra-rationalism," which would integrate that which was experienced into that which was understood.

None the less, Lévi-Strauss can be an author of lyrical intensity and powerfully moving vision, whatever the scientific credentials of the original investigation. His mixture of exact but vivid description and highly cultivated reflection makes *Tristes tropiques* an unrivalled classic in the travel writing genre. He may be compared to Pierre Teilhard de Chardin, although Teilhard's vision is more sweepingly poetic and all-embracing than Lévi-Strauss's, although the basis of scientific fact in palaeontology, from which he starts is perhaps necessarily less solid.

If it is the mixture of speculation, autobiographical narrative, scientific reflection, and unsual descriptive powers which makes *Tristes tropiques* an important imaginative work, the book is also important because of the insight it offers generally into the relationship between imagination and science, and into the thought and method in particular of one of the most powerful thinkers of the 20th century. This is apparent whether he is amusingly noting details of the sanitary arrangements on the deck of the ship taking him to Brazil, or describing with magnificent precision every detail of a sunset, starting with the exact time it began and using descriptive metaphors that Chateaubriand would have envied. The description of the sunset, from chapter seven of part two, is a set piece, printed in italic, but it builds up with a breathtaking poetic skill and imaginative invention, based on absolute accuracy in the vivid account of visual effects, and interspersed with generalized, if often implied, personal reflections about the analogies between sunsets and the working of the mind.

PUBLICATIONS

Anthropology

La Vie familiale et sociale des Indiens Nambikwara, 1948
Les Structures élémentaires de la parenté, 1949; as *The Elementary Structures of Kinship*, 1969
Race et histoire, 1952
Tristes tropiques, partial translation as *A World on the Wane*, 1961; as *Tristes Tropiques*, 1961; complete translation, 1979
Anthropologie structurale, 2 vols., 1958–73; as *Structural Anthropology*, 2 vols., 1963–76
Le Totemisme aujourd'hui, 1962; as *Totemism*, 1963
La Pensée sauvage, 1962; as *The Savage Mind*, 1966
Mythologiques: vol. 1, *Le Cru et le cuit*; vol. 2, *Du miel aux cendres*; vol. 3, *L'Origine des manières de table*; vol. 4, *L'Homme nu*, 1964–71; as *Introduction to the Science of Mythology*: vol. 1, *The Raw and the Cooked*; vol. 2, *From Honey to Ashes*; vol. 3, *The Origin of Table Manners*; vol.4, *The Naked Man*, 1969–81; vols. 3 and 4 published separately, 1973–81
The Scope of Anthropology (address), 1968
La Voie des masques, 2 vols., 1975; as *The Way of the Masks*, 1982
Myth and Meaning: Five Talks for Radio, 1978
Le Regard éloigné, 1983; as *The View from Afar*, 1985
Histoire de lynx, 1991

Other

Entretiens avec Claude Lévi-Strauss, edited by Georges Charbonnier, 1961; as *Conversations with Claude Lévi-Strauss*, 1969
Discours de reception à l'Académie française, 1974

Bibliography

LaPointe, François Y., and Claire C. LaPointe, *Claude Lévi-Strauss and His Critics: An International Bibliography of Criticism (1950–1976) Followed by a Bibliography of the Writings of Claude Lévi-Strauss*, 1977

Critical studies

Leach, Edmund, *Claude Lévi-Strauss*, 1970; revised edition, 1976
Paz, Octavio, *Claude Lévi-Strauss: An Introduction*, translated by J.S. Bernstein and Maxine Bernstein, 1970

Maranda, Elli Kongas, and Pierre Maranda, *Structural Models in Folklore and Transformational Essays*, 1971

Boon, James A., *From Symbolism to Structuralism: Lévi-Strauss in a Literary Tradition*, 1972

Gardner, Howard, *The Quest for the Mind: Piaget, Lévi-Strauss, and the Structuralist Movement*, 1973

Clarke, Simon, *The Foundations of Structuralism: A Critique of Lévi-Strauss and the Structuralist Movement*, 1981

LOTI, Pierre (Pseudonym of Louis-Marie-Julien Viaud), 1850–1923.

Novelist, dramatist, essayist, political writer, and diarist.

LIFE

Loti is now chiefly known from the works prescribed for school syllabuses, but once drew a wide reading public. He was born at Rochefort of a Catholic father who converted to Protestantism, a local administrative official of modest means with an interest in the arts, and a Huguenot mother. His parents married in 1830 and, when Loti was born, both were over 40. They already had a daughter, Marie, of 19, and a son, Gustave, aged 12. The family also included Loti's mother's mother, sister, and aunt and his father's mother. Not surprisingly Loti was spoilt. In his works he exaggerated the melancholy of his childhood, as probably also the importance of family prayers. In 1865 Gustave, who was a ship's surgeon, died of anaemia, aged 27, and the next year his father lost his job and spent a few days in prison on suspicion of embezzlement. By the time he was vindicated, he was seriously in debt, and the family had to tighten their belts. Lodgers were taken in, domestic staff reduced, and Loti was not only left with the unpleasant memory of poverty and public disgrace, but had to leave the Ecole Polytechnique. In 1866 he was allowed to join the navy, as he had wished.

Loti was sent to Paris to the Lycée Henri IV, where he was lonely and began the diary which eventually ran to 200 notebooks. From 1867 he became a cadet at Brest. Despite periods in hospital due to sore throats and mumps, he graduated as a midshipman in 1869. The Franco-Prussian War of 1870 meant that he very soon saw action, blockading the Prussian navy. In 1870, too, Loti's father died, aged 66, and Loti himself had to help to support the family. In 1871 he sailed for South America and the Pacific. He was appalled by the slaughter of monkeys and birds in the Brazilian jungle, and was clearly more gifted as an observant traveller than as a naval officer. His interest in sketching was aroused, particularly by Tahiti, and from San Francisco he sent back sketches and diary excerpts from exotic Pacific locations, which Marie had published in *L'Illustration* in August 1872 and September–October 1873. His first three novels were to be exotic diary extracts woven round a simple story, and relying for their effect on sentimental and sensuous impressionistic writing. Their style was simple, direct, and musical, and the novels were generally written in a period of relative inactivity some time after the long voyages that inspired them.

A friend, Lucien Jousselin (1851–1932), put Loti in touch with the publisher Michel Lévy, and in March 1878 Loti signed a six-year contract with the publishing house Calmann-Lévy, which published *Aziyadé*, claimed by him to be "his memoirs of his stay in Turkey," in January 1879. In the winter of 1878 to 1879 he wrote *Rarahu ou le mariage de Loti*, which was serialized anonymously in Juliette Adam's newly founded *Nouvelle Revue* in January and February 1880. It had almost been turned down. Dedicated to Sarah Bernhardt, whom Loti had probably met through Juliette Adam, the novel is partly based on his brother Gustave's relationship with a Tahitian girl called Tarahu by whom he had had two children. Marie had already based an idyllic novel on Gustave's experiences.

Early in 1874 Loti had had an affair in Dakar with a Creole girl, Coumba Felicia, which he made the subject of his third novel, *Le Roman d'un spahi*, also serialized anonymously in the *Nouvelle Revue* from March to May 1881 before being published by Calmann-Lévy as a book, signed "Pierre Loti," in September of that year. Loti had spent seven months on a physical training course in 1875, possibly to compensate for an apparent recent lack of success in attracting women. His Protestantism had by now crumbled. The sheer brutality in *Le Roman d'un spahi* and the brothel scenes, borrowed from the experiences of his friend Pierre Le Cor in Uruguay, suggest feelings of defiance and revolt against the domestic atmosphere imposed by his mother, although Loti's exotic and sometimes violent realism was also to become a vehicle for oblique moral commentary on French society.

From his return to Turkey in 1877 to his departure for Indochina in May 1883, Loti never sailed far from home. By 1880 he had cleared the family debts, and the family house was free of lodgers by October 1884. Loti became a friend of Daudet and began to rely emotionally on Juliette Adam, to whom in 1882 he wrote of his "melancholy pantheism." In February 1883 he wrote of having recourse to prostitutes before committing suicide, a threat he had already made in 1879. The writing up of his memories of voyages in fictionalized form was a personal catharsis as well as a way of paying off debt, but Loti was personally caught up in conflicting desires for a simple life in France, like that of "my simple friends from Brittany," and the exotic romanticism of "the sun and the solitude of the forests." His next novel, *Fleurs d'ennui*, takes the form of a dialogue between Loti and his friend Plumkett and was thought a failure by Juliette Adam, who nevertheless published it, after considerable cutting, in May and June 1882. Like the short story "Suleïma," published in the same volume, it expresses Loti's nostalgia for the unsophisticated innocence of his early faith and for a pre-industrial natural society free from the ills which civilization had brought.

It is partly to this mood that Loti owes the inspiration which produced the novels of life in Breton fishing communities for which he is still remembered. In 1878 his Breton friend Pierre Le Cor got married. He drank too much and provided the model for *Mon frère Yves*, finished in 1883 and published in the *Revue des Deux Mondes* (*RDM*, q. v.) in August and September. That same year Loti sailed for Indochina, where the province of Annam had transferred its allegiance to China, and the French, determined to teach the mandarins a lesson, perpetrated atrocities in taking it back which caused much dismay in France. Loti wrote three articles, the first two of which were anonymous, for *Le Figaro* (28 September, 13 and 17 October 1883). The government recalled him on 28 November and put him first on half-pay and then on the supernumerary list for the next year. Further impressions of the expedition and his return from it are the subject of *Propos d'exil*, published in 1884 and 1885 in the *RDM*. Thanks to Juliette Adam's intercession, Loti was sent back to the East in 1885. Early that year he had started the short story "Au large," which grew into *Pêcheur d'islande*, his most famous novel, which won the Prix Vitet and was published in the *Nouvelle Revue* from March to June 1886. There were 200 editions by 1900. The book was finished in the East, where Loti lived for a few weeks with a Japanese girl, a formally arranged affair, registered at the police station, which was the basis for *Madame Chrysanthème*, published in December 1887.

The 1885 voyage involved a short visit to Indochina before a return to Japan, which Loti then explored, publishing his impressions in the *Nouvelle Revue*, the *Grande Revue*, and the *RDM* in 1888. They were gathered together as *Japoneries d'automne* in 1889. Loti returned to Europe in February 1886. He had been turned down by a Breton girl engaged elsewhere, and now asked his mother and Juliette Adam to seek him out a suitable wife. He married Jeanne Blanche Franc de Ferrière on 20 October 1886. She was from a wealthy Protestant Bordeaux family, and Loti had met her brother in the navy in Indochina. Loti was given a posting in naval administration at Rochefort, and his own command there in 1888. His wife had a miscarriage in May 1887 and gave birth to a son in 1889.

Loti was depressed by his marriage however, as he indicated in a letter to Juliette Adam. He looked after his mother, and appeared in public with young sailors, using make-up and increasing his height by using shoe-pads. He gave and attended fancy-dress parties, including a 15th-century party in April 1888 at which he was partnered by Juliette Adam. The old parts of the Rochefort house were kept as they had been in his childhood, but Loti decorated some rooms in a variety of styles, Turkish, Oriental, Breton, or medieval, and the lavish frivolity of the parties he gave there understandably raised a few eyebrows. He spent his first wedding anniversary searching in Turkey for the original of Aziyadé. He discovered that she had died seven years after he had left her, partly as a result of being abandoned by him, and wrote about his pilgrimage in the *Nouvelle Revue* from December 1891 to February 1892. His wife spent increasingly long periods with her own family, and essentially lived a quiet life of her own, visiting Loti and her son only occasionally. She died in 1940, at the age of 86.

In September 1887 the queen of Romania, who had translated *Pêcheur* using the pen name "Carmen Silva," invited Loti to stay. He was to write about her in *L'Exilée*, and it was at her request that he wrote his most famous autobiographical novel, *Le Roman d'un enfant*, published in the *Nouvelle Revue* from January to April 1890. Loti visited Bucharest briefly again in April 1890, and then in August 1891 saw the morbidly religious queen in Venice, now a virtual exile thanks to her encouragement of the young heir to the throne in his romance with her secretary. Loti had been elected to the Académie Française on 21 May 1891 at the sixth ballot on his second attempt, and his life now developed a pattern of "literary" visits to Paris, where he frequented various aesthetes and literary dilettantes, and stayed mostly in a small hotel. He attended rehearsals of dramatizations of some of his works, but Lafcadio Hearn said of him that, from being a poet, he had become "a little, morbid, modern, affected Frenchman." His writing became less fluent and technically less expert, with authorial intervention more and more frequent. The style started to betray a sense of strain. He continued to report on his travels for the better literary reviews, developing a taste for the more sensuously indulgent aspects of Islamic culture, whose criminal code disturbed him. His naval career alternated between administrative and command postings.

In 1893 *Matelot* appeared, dedicated to the queen of Spain and picking up the autobiographical thread of *Le Roman d'un enfant*, although increasing the degree of fictionalization. In his quest for his Christian origins, Loti trekked across the Arabian desert in 1894, publishing his account as *Le Désert* from September to December 1894 in the *Nouvelle Revue*, which also printed his account of his subsequent pilgrimage to the Holy Land, published as *Jérusalem* and *Galilée*. They record Loti's disillusion at finding the culture associated with the Christianity of his childhood eroded by Western values. On his return, near to despair, he began *Ramuntcho*, a novel set in the Basque country, which was published in the *Revue de Paris* from 15 December 1896 to 15 February 1897. Loti had been moved by the independence and remoteness from modern life of Basque culture and admired its virile as well as its sensuous elements. The novel draws heavily on the diary entries of some years previously. Loti's best biographer alleges that he had three illegitimate Basque children and a Basque mistress, Crucita Gainza, which suggests that his Basque novel, like his earliest books, is very largely autobiographical, adapted from the diary.

Loti's mother died at Rochefort on 12 November 1896, and Loti spent much of his time thereafter at Hendaye. In 1898 he was retired prematurely from the navy but on protesting, was reinstated. He needed his travels in order to continue to write. He was sent to India for the ministry of foreign affairs. *L'Inde sans les anglais* was published in 1902 and 1903 numbers of the *RDM*. From Bombay he went with a sailor companion to Persia. *Vers Ispahan* was published by the *RDM* from 15 December 1903 to 15 February 1904. After a month in France Loti was sent to help suppress the Boxer Rebellion in China. His travels involved journeys by train and by junk, and yielded the inevitable crop of publications nostalgic for the mysterious charms of lost civilizations. He also visited Angkor for the first time and the sites of the 12th-century city of Khmer. He arrived back in 1902, wrote up his travels, translated *King Lear* (successfully produced in 1904) with Emile Vedel, and used materials bought for 15,000 francs in Damascus, and some stolen in China, to create a mosque and a Chinese room at Rochefort. He gave more frivolous and expensive parties to keep his melancholy at bay, and undertook another tour of duty as a naval attaché in Istanbul. *Les Désenchantées* of 1906 was the result of a spoof by a French journalist and two Turkish sisters. Loti's measure had been taken, but some critics instantly saw that he had fallen into a trap and allowed himself to be used for feminist propaganda purposes, as he was to be again when he toured Egypt with Mustapha Kemel in 1907.

In 1906 Loti was promoted capitain and in 1909 he paid a brief visit to London, where his dislike for the English mellowed a little. He retired definitively from the navy in 1910. A little less than half his time had been spent at sea. There was still a sentimental and self-pitying account of a further visit to Turkey to come (*Suprêmes visions d'orient*), but Loti also published an impassioned and biased defence of Turkish political interests in the first Balkan war (*Turquie agonisante*), a collection of press articles mostly written after a fleeting visit to New York in 1912 which accused the Bulgar–Serb–Greek alliance, whose side France was taking, of every sort of atrocity in an attempt to destroy Islamic culture. During World War I Loti was given various commissions in connection with the war and wrote only propagandist works, crammed with racial hatred and patriotic intransigence.

After the war Loti attacked the terms of the Turkish settlement together with the Greeks, the Armenians, and the British. He was now ill most of the time and his son helped him to write more autobiography, which became increasingly nostalgic in tone. The results were *Prime jeunesse* of 1919 and the slightly revised diary extracts *Un jeune officier pauvre* of 1923. On 12 May 1920 Loti attended his son's wedding and in December he received the Grand Croix of the Légion d'Honneur. In 1922 a stroke deprived him of movement and speech, but he could still write to Juliette Adam, now aged 87. She visited him on 28 April 1923. He was moved to Hendaye, and could still walk in the garden, but fell ill on 8 June and died the following day. He was given a state funeral.

Works

Loti's relationship to his public has been compared with that of Kipling. Like his friend Daudet, he is disappearing from the works of reference and literary history. Yet by 1905 his five top-selling novels had between them already gone into some 550 editions, of which 261 (in only 20 years) were for *Pêcheur d'islande* alone. It is already clear, however, that even the best two novels are of little more than marginal interest in literary historical terms, while there is little further call for Loti's brand of nostalgic exoticism in a world in which travel has become so much easier. In a world of homogenized urban cultures, Loti's privileged nationalistic reaction against creeping industrialized uniformity seems based on an unpleasant realism which is no longer perceived as daring, an esoteric experience which has lost its flavour, and a sentimentality which pretends that the real world of human experience never existed. From the collection of novels, travelogues, essays, political tracts, and autobiographical writings only two works of more than specialized interest remain, *Mon frère Yves* and *Pêcheur d'islande*.

Of the three early novels, *Aziyadé*, is largely taken from the actual correspondence of a serving officer, which concerns a love affair in Salonica, with the names changed, the nationality thinly disguised, and an obvious narcissistic falsification in the denouement. The novel's interest was thought to lie in its exoticism and in its menacing political challenge to the power of the colonial authority. Loti's touch was not yet assured, and the work is scattered with reminiscences of Musset and Hugo, while Turkish words and allusions to Persian poetry are added for the sake of verisimilitude. Loti was also clearly sensitive to the lush sensuousness of the Pacific islands which were to appear so attractive to Gauguin a few years later. Sophisticated sensual delights seemed to combine there with primitiveness and simplicity to constitute an idyll, and *Le Mariage de Loti* is worked up from the diary notes of Loti's stay on Tahiti, its fictional element derived largely from his brother's experiences. Even the letters in Tahitian are real ones sent to a naval surgeon. *Le Roman d'un spahi* is set in Senegal and concerns a white officer

surrounded by Africans endowed with primitive, animal instincts and agile strength. The death of the central figure, Peyral, signifies that he has become part of the natural processes of the African wild, but the novel makes too obvious its basis in Loti's desire to disguise from himself his own childish inadequacies, and owes more to fantasy than to imagination.

After the unsatisfactory *Fleurs d'ennui* came *Mon frère Yves*, which is partly derived from Loti's experience in Brittany, to which he was introduced by his friend Le Cor. The novel is primarily the story of the relationship between the two friends, the athletic, virile, and simple Breton and the sentimental writer with his artistic sensibility. Its interest lies in the realistic depiction of the life of a Breton fisherman at sea for half the year, and driven by the experience to drink. The harsh simplicity of life is romanticized in the heroism called for in men engaged in a struggle against the gigantic forces of nature. Their failures are realistically described, and their experiences reflected in the equal harshness, heroism, and ineluctability of the natural forces to which the women and children left behind are prey. Loti's descriptive writing here is sufficiently brilliant for the Goncourt brothers to have remarked that the novel would have been better without its characters.

Pêcheur d'islande, founded on Loti's own experience of rejection by an Icelandic girl, clearly illustrates his dependence on what he observed with his own eyes. The famous North Atlantic storm was one he actually witnessed in the South Pacific, where most of the novel was written. The physical toughness of the sailors inevitably masks tender feelings and naive personalities, and a relationship is maintained between the sailors' lives at sea and the shore life of their women and children. Yann refuses the young and beautiful Gand because of the superior wealth and culture which she tries to dissimulate, since it represents a way of living and a social status which he cannot accept. Yann's young friend Sylvestre leaves for the Far East, where he dies bravely in action, so that Loti can mix in with the bravery and stoicism he portrays passages of great tenderness, creating the blend which sold the work so well. In the end Gand, left penniless, and Mme Moan, who has lost virtually the last of her family, console one another, and Yann and Gand do at last come together now that Gand is poor. The richness of the description, the harshness of the life, the toughness of the characters, and the sentimentality of the wedding scene, set against the background of the premonitory storm, which presages Yann's death, created the perfect formula for a Loti novel, in which the stronger elemental forces always win through against the puny strength of human heroism.

The other novels and travelogues contain passages of very fine writing, while the correspondence and the autobiographical material touchingly reveal and articulate the writer's inner insecurity with its manifestations of exoticism, fetishism, masochism, sentimentality, and the quest for unachievable, simple, physical perfection, and hierarchically organized, undisturbed, and uncorrupted societies. The reason why their interest has faded is not just a change of fashion, or even of common experience, but the relative banality of the quest for unattainable innocence insufficiently elevated by poetry or psychological insight. Loti's political writings are stereotyped and of historical interest only. There is a series of *Cahiers Pierre Loti*, started in 1952, which took over from the "Bulletins trimestriels de l'Association internationale des Amis de Pierre Loti," published from 1933 to 1951.

PUBLICATIONS

Collections

Oeuvres (to 1905), 11 vols., 1893–1911

Fiction

Aziyadé, 1879; as *Aziyadé* (in English), 1927
Le Mariage de Loti, 1880; as *The Marriage of Loti*, 1925
Le Roman d'un spahi, 1881; as *The Romance of a Spahi*, 1890
Fleurs d'ennui, 1883
Mon frère Yves, 1883; as *My Brother Yves*, 1887
Les Trois Dames de la Kasbah, 1884
Pêcheur d'islande 1886; as *An Iceland Fisherman*, 1887
Propos d'exil (contes), 1887; as *From Lands of Exile*, 1888
Madame Chrysanthème, 1888; as *Madame Chrysanthenum*, 1888
Le Roman d'un enfant, 1890; as *A Child's Romance*, 1891
Livre de la pitié et de la mort, 1891; as *The Book of Pity and of Death*, 1892
Fantôme d'orient, 1891; as *A Phantom from the East*, 1892
Matelot, 1893; as *Sailor*, 1893
Ramuntcho, 1897; as *Ramuntcho* (in English), 1897
La Troisième Jeunesse de Madame Prune, 1905; as *Madame Prune* (in English), 1919
Les Désenchantées, 1906; as *The Disenchanted*, 1906
Prime jeunesse, 1919

Travel

Japoneries d'automne, 1889
Au Maroc, 1889; as *Into Morocco*, 1889
L'Exilée, 1893
Le Désert, 1895
Jérusalem, 1895; as *Jerusalem*, 1915
La Galilée, 1896
Figures et choses qui passaient, 1898
Reflets sur la sombre route, 1899
Les Derniers Jours de Pékin, 1901; as *The Last Days of Pekin*, 1902
L'Inde sans les anglais, 1903; as *India*, 1906
Vers Ispahan, 1904
La Mort de Philae, 1908
Le Château de la belle au bois dormant, 1910
Un pèlerin d'Angkor, 1912

Plays

Pêcheur d'islande, 1893
Judith Renaudin, 1898
Ramuntcho, 1908
La Fille du ciel, 1911 (with Judith Gautier)

Other

Turquie agonisante, 1913
La Grande Barbarie, 1915
La Hyène enragée, 1916
Quelques aspects du vertige mondial, 1917
L'Horreur allemande, 1918
Les Massacres d'Arménit, 1918

Les Alliés qu'il nous faudrait, 1919
La Mort de notre cher France en orient, 1920
Suprêmes visions d'orient, 1921
Lettres à Mme J. Adam, 1880–1922, 1924
Correspondance inédite, 1865–1904, 1929
Un jeune officier pauvre (diary extracts), 1923
Journal 1878–1881, 1925
Journal 1882–1885, 1929

Critical studies

Auvergne, E.B. d', *Pierre Loti: The Romance of a Great Writer*, 1926
Lerner, Michael G., *Pierre Loti*, 1974

LOUŸS, Pierre, 1870–1925.

Poet and novelist.

LIFE

A scrupulous stylist, Louÿs spent his life in poor physical and financial health, but flamboyantly provoked the upholders of contemporary social proprieties. His literary output, concentrated into the decade 1890–1901, is of slighter interest than the role he played as a catalyst in French literary life. He was highly intelligent, but a series of affectations, including his transformation by stages of the common family name "Louis" (he thought eventually of doing away with the "u" and then perhaps the "o" as well), suggest confusion about his personal and subsequently his literary identity. Louÿs was apparently a fourth child, but in fact probably the son of his half-brother, Georges (the second child of his mother's first marriage), to whom he remained unusually close. When Georges died in 1917, his widow Paz wanted Pierre to marry her.

In *Si le grain ne meurt* Gide describes the close friendship that developed from 1887 between him and Louÿs, who so easily outstripped him at school. Their literary views gradually diverged as Louÿs's voluptuous decadence clashed increasingly with Gide's cool restraint. Gide also came to rebel against Louÿs's personal ascendancy over him, and he finally broke with him in 1895.

From 1890 Louÿs had begun to frequent Mallarmé's Tuesday receptions. He had met Verlaine and was to form close friendships with Régnier, Heredia, and Valéry, who found in Louÿs's views a reflection of his own quasi-mystical attitude to art. Among Louÿs's other idols were Hugo, Wagner, and the painters Gustave Moreau, Monet, and Albert Besnard.

In 1891 Louÿs went to Bayreuth, where he attended four performances of *Parsifal*. In 1892, on receipt of his patrimony, he had *Astarté* privately printed in a luxury edition of 100 numbered copies. That same year he visited London, where he entertained beyond his means, met up almost daily with Oscar Wilde and was introduced by him to Sarah Bernhardt, for whom he wrote what was intended as a play but which turned into the novel *Aphrodite*. He was to break with Wilde in 1893, the year in which he accepted the dedication of *Salomé*, forcing Wilde to choose between friendship with him and his homosexual relationship with Lord Alfred Douglas. Louÿs's flaunting of the conventions did not go that far.

On his return to Paris he failed his "licence," went again to Bayreuth, attended further performances of *Parsifal* and, in Paris once more, playfully boasted to a disgusted Gide about the dissipated life he claimed to be leading. He probably attended the successful first night of Maeterlinck's *Pélleas et Mélisande* in the company of Mallarmé, Whistler, Régnier, Clemenceau, Barrès, and Debussy, with whom he subsequently became close friends and whom he took to Ghent to get Maeterlinck's permission to turn his play into an opera. He also became inseparable from two aspiring but now largely forgotten authors, André Lebey and Jean le Barbier de Tinan.

In 1894, on his way to Bayreuth, Louÿs made a detour to see Gide, who had just returned from Biskra, was regularly swimming in ice-cold water on medical advice, and was full of the sensual delights of his recent experiences with the young Arab girl Meriem ben Atala, whom Louÿs now went to meet, abandoning the projected visit to Bayreuth. He composed the *Chansons de Bilitis* with her in mind. Published in 1894 at his own expense, this purported, more as a prank than a hoax, to have been written by a contemporary of the Greek poetess Sappho.

On his return to Paris, Louÿs suffered intermittently from bouts of illness and intense hardship. He did not declare his in fact requited passion for Heredia's daughter, Marie, who accepted Régnier's proposal of marriage instead. The wedding took place in 1895. In 1896, following the spectacular success of *Aphrodite*, Louÿs could again afford to travel. Sales of 50,000 copies in the year of publication were helped by a remarkable review by François Coppée, whose "sentimental populism" Louÿs had long disdained. This time he went to Algiers, boasting in a letter to Georges of his chronic promiscuity there.

He became ill and, against advice, brought back to France a Moorish girl, Zohra ben Brahim, with whom he lived from March to December 1897, while also having an affair with Marie de Régnier, as she now was. He broke off that relationship in May 1898 after returning from a winter with Georges in Egypt. He had probably learnt that Marie had become Tinan's mistress in the interim. In September she bore a son, claiming that Louÿs was the father and they resumed their liaison, although Louÿs was seriously considering marrying a friend's sister, Germaine Dethomas. Meanwhile Marie's younger sister Louise, whom he did eventually marry, was falling seriously in love with him.

Gilbert de Voisins, whom Louÿs had met in Algiers and with whom he had struck up a close friendship, wrote a flattering article about him in the *Saturday Review*. Voisins, among the many to lend money to Louÿs, was to marry Louise after she had divorced Louÿs in 1913. Louÿs's wedding in 1899 meanwhile was attended by many prominent literary figures, including Brunetière, Sully-Prudhomme, Catulle Mendès, and François Coppée acting as Louÿs's witness, a gesture not only of gratitude, but of right-wing, anti-semitic, anti-Dreyfus political alignment.

The liaison with Marie continued and, in 1900, Louÿs, who smoked 60 cigarettes a day, developed asthma. From 1901 until his death he was never out of debt, in spite of innumerable re-editions, adaptations, and translations of his works. From 1915 to 1919 he had a liaison with a young dancer, Claudine Rolland,

whose half-sister, Aline, later displaced her, bearing Louÿs three children (in 1920, 1923, and 1925, three days after his death). They had married in October 1923, and in 1927 Aline married Louÿs's last secretary, Georges Serrières.

After the death of his half-brother Georges Louÿs developed a drug and an even more serious alcohol dependency and almost went blind due to syphilis. A great deal of what money he had went on building up his collection of antique books and fine bindings. Before he was forced to sell it in 1918, the collection was regarded as the best in Paris, and Louÿs became a very knowledgeable literary historian, publishing a series of frequently controversial articles on literary historical matters, notably arguing that Corneille was the real author of substantial portions of some of Molière's plays. For periods he lived the life of a semi-recluse, spending some time in hospital, and suffering from serious poverty. He remained a bohemian, a decadent cultivating the experience of the senses, and an accomplished stylist even when what he wrote was pastiche.

WORKS

Louÿs often rewrote, abandoned, or only half completed projects, adapted and republished what he had written, and incorporated what had been individual pieces into larger works. His bibliography is therefore complicated. After the adolescent *Potache-Revue*, founded with Gide, which ran to three issues in 1889, Louÿs was associated with Gide, Régnier, and Valéry in the foundation, in 1891, of *La Conque*, whose 11 issues published poems by Leconte de Lisle, Mallarmé, Verlaine, Heredia, Swinburne, Blum, Moréas, Maeterlinck, and Louÿs himself, and, in 1896, of *Le Centaure*, whose two issues included material by Gide, Valéry, and Louÿs. The poems for *La Conque*, some of which were pseudonymous, were republished in *Astarté*, many of them revised and retitled.

Louÿs's main works also include *Les Poésies de Méléagre*, a translation of the erotic epigrams from the first century BC which form the basis for the *Greek Anthology*; *Lêda*, the first of seven projected stories on antique subjects and, like the *Poésies*, widely acclaimed; and *Chansons de Bilitis*.

In 1896 came the triumphantly successful novel *Aphrodite*, which explores the author's personal difficulties regarding the relationship between sensuality and art. Inspired by Massenet's oratorio *Maria Magdalene*, it was itself the basis for operas by Arturo Berutti, by Camille Erlanger, whose *Aphrodite*, as first played at the Opéra-Comique in 1906, ultimately failed to create the desired illusion of a naked Chrysis visiting her lover's studio, and by Max Oberleithner, whose heroine at the Vienna Opera (Mitzi Jeritza) did in fact appear naked, and by Arturo Luzzati. Debussy kept exclusive rights for two years, but lost interest, and Puccini toyed with the subject, but preferred *Madame Butterfly*. In 1898 *La Femme et le pantin* appeared. Eulogized by Edmund Gosse in *The Contemporary Review*, this also narrowly missed forming the subject of an opera by Puccini, who withdrew his interest when the eroticism of Richard Strauss's *Salome* caused a scandal in New York.

Les Aventures du roi Pausole contains a skit on Gide's puritanical Protestantism. Later adapted as an operetta by Honegger, it was staged in 1930 with Edwige Feuillère, one of the century's greatest actresses, in a walk-on part. In 1901 the story *L'Homme de pourpre* was serialized and published in volume form, and

1903 saw the publication of *Sanguines*, a collection of short stories, which sold 4,200 copies on the first day. Louÿs left his novel *Psyché* unfinished, probably destroying the final part as being too intimately autobiographical. He offered the title to Valéry, who would have preferred it for his *La Jeune Parque* but Valéry regarded the offer as overly generous and turned in down. The novel finally appeared in 1927 with a summary of the concluding chapters as recollected by Louÿs's devoted friend Claude Farrère. The *Journal intime 1882–1891* provides four glimpses into Louÿs's life and dreams as an adolescent.

Virtually all Louÿs's works were erotic and exotic, although often erudite and always very carefully written and rewritten in the quest for formal, impersonal, but none the less sensual beauty, qualities associated with the "Parnassians" (q.v.), whose emphasis on the importance of rhyme, however, Louÿs totally rejected. "I want to write essentially musical poetry, that is *rhythm*, not rhyme," he wrote. He regarded poetry as easier to write than prose and "vers libres" as the most perfect form of poetry.

PUBLICATIONS

Collections

Oeuvres complètes, 13 vols., 1929–31
Les Poëmes de Pierre Louÿs 1887–1924, edited by Yves-Gérard Le Dantec, 2 vols., 1945
The Collected Works of Pierre Louÿs, containing "Aphrodite," "Woman and puppet," "The songs of Bilitis," "The adventures of King Pausole," "The twilight of the nymphs" (the five completed stories of the *Lêda* cycle), "Sanguines," and "Psyche," 1932

Works

Astarté, 1891
Lêda ou la louange des bienheureuses ténèbres, 1893
Les Poésies de Méléagre, 1893
Les Chansons de Bilitis, 1894; revised edition, 1898
Aphrodite: moeurs antiques, 1896
La Femme et le pantin: roman espagnol, 1898
Les Aventures du roi Pausole, 1900
L'Homme de pourpre, 1901
Sanguines, 1903
Le Crépuscule des nymphes, 1925
Psyché, 1927
Journal intime 1882–1891, 1929

Critical study

Clive, H. P., *Pierre Louÿs 1870–1925: A Biography*, 1978

A series of commemorative volumes appeared in 1925. An "Association des Amis de Pierre Louÿs" was founded in 1977 for the purpose of publishing a quarterly *Bulletin* and an annual *Cahier*.

M

MAETERLINCK, Maurice (Mauritius Polydorus Maria Bernardus), 1862–1949.

Poet, dramatist, and essayist; winner of the Nobel prize for literature (1911).

LIFE

Maeterlinck is more important for his influence than for his achievement as a writer. His major work was concentrated into the period between 1890 and 1911, the year in which he was awarded the Nobel prize. After that date he wrote nothing to equal his earlier verse and drama. His creative career splits roughly into two periods: 1890 to 1895, during which time he was a leading figure in the French and Belgian symbolist (q.v.) movements, and 1895 to 1911, which saw a thinner stream of rather more optimistic works. Less than a dozen of Maeterlinck's total output of almost 60 "major" works are remembered today.

Maeterlinck's father, a lukewarm Catholic, was a lawyer who retired early and lived off investment income. His mother was the daughter of another wealthy but rather tight-fisted lawyer. They belonged to the rich, professedly Catholic, French-speaking bourgeoisie of Ghent and owned both a town house and a summer residence. Maeterlinck was one of four children. He grew up a rather dreamy, melancholic, and morbid child who was nevertheless an adept gymnast. At six he was sent to a girls' school run by nuns, which took only very junior boys. From there he was sent to a private establishment before going on to the Jesuit college. Governesses were also hired to teach the children English and German at home. None of them lasted long, Maeterlinck's father apparently having a roving eye and his mother a sharp nose. At school Materlinck was good at French and also enjoyed acting. Out of 16 pupils in his class, seven were to become priests and three poets: Maeterlinck, Van Lerberghe, and Le Roy. The three future poets became friends. Maeterlinck, meanwhile, became the first lover of a milliner's errand girl.

In 1881 he began studying law. He was also deeply interested at this time in the Belgian literary renaissance. Part symbolist, part Parnassian (q.v.), it centred on three reviews: *La Jeune Belgique*, *La Wallonie*, and *L'Art Moderne*. When the official quinqennial literary prize was not awarded by the Belgian Academy, *La Jeune Belgique* organized a dinner in honour of Camille Lemonnier, one of the writers who had been passed over. Maeterlinck was one of the 212 guests present at the dinner. The Middle Ages and the English pre-Raphaelites began increasingly to attract his interest. *La Jeune Belgique* published his first poem in 1883. In 1885 Maeterlinck graduated in law and took the barrister's oath, persuading his father to let him go to Paris to apply for the Paris Bar. His real intention, however, was to indulge his literary ambitions. He ended up in Paris that winter

along with Van Lerberghe and Le Roy. In Paris he was befriended by Villiers de l'Isle-Adam, a poet whose work he came to venerate. At around this time a new review, *La Pléiade*, sprang up under the patronage of Banville. The review, which published pieces of prose and verse by Maeterlinck, had only 18 subscribers and folded after publication of the sixth issue.

In 1886, the year he met Verlaine, Maeterlinck returned to Belgium, where he practised rather sporadically as a barrister. He began to publish further prose and verse and printed a collection of poems, *Serres chaudes*, using money borrowed from his family. One hundred and fifty-five copies were printed, but very few sold. Maeterlinck's translation of a number of Ruysbroek's poems appeared, however, in the *Revue Générale* in 1889 and did occasion favourable notice. By the end of the year his first play, *La Princesse Maleine*, was being published in *La Société Nouvelle*. Maeterlinck again borrowed from his family in order to print an edition. In Ghent in 1890 Mallarmé gave a speech about Villiers, who had just died. Maeterlinck had had a further 150 copies of *La Princesse Maleine* printed and, although only some 15 were sold, Mallarmé was enthusiastic about the copy he received. As a consequence Mirbeau published an absurdly adulatory review in *Le Figaro* for 24 August 1890. The ensuing furore was considerable and involved much adverse criticism. The play itself was never in fact staged. Maeterlinck read Villiers, Mallarmé, and Huysmans, suffered from fits of depression, and discovered that his health was being undermined by over-eating.

In May 1891 his youngest brother died after a skating accident and Maeterlinck wrote "Les avertis," which was to be included in *Le Trésor des humbles*. His one-act play, *L'Intruse*, included in a benefit programme for Verlaine and Gauguin in 1891, was well received. Maeterlinck now went out of his way to quarrel with the Belgian cultural authorities, refusing to be considered for a literary prize and vociferously explaining his reasons why. That same year he published *Les Sept princesses*, and in Paris Lugné-Poe persuaded Paul Fort to stage *Les Aveugles*, which was performed on 11 December 1891. The three plays constitute Maeterlinck's so-called "trilogy of death."

By 1892 Maeterlinck had completed *Pelléas et Mélisande* and developed a close friendship with Lugné-Poe. He became interested in telepathy, and he joined the committee of a new literary review, *Le Réveil*. The famous premiere of *Pelléas* took place in Paris on 17 May 1893. The play was given a hostile reception in Belgium, where it was performed twice in June, but was welcomed in Holland. By August Maeterlinck had given permission for Debussy to work on the score. In 1896 some Rosetti-like pieces were published as *Album de douze chansons*. The first period of Maeterlinck's drama closed with a marionette trilogy of 1894 which, together with *L'Etoile*, an essay published by *Le Figaro* in the same year, marked the low point of despair for its author.

In January 1895 Maeterlinck met Georgette Leblanc, a singer

with whom he was to share his life until 1918. The relationship was slow to develop but it lifted Maeterlinck out of his gloom. Lugné-Poe continued to promote him in Paris. *Pelléas* toured successfully in Holland again, although the English tour was a failure. Maeterlinck wanted to marry Georgette, but she was already bound by a previous token marriage to a Spaniard, and in Spain no divorce laws as yet existed. While on holiday with Georgette in 1896 Maeterlinck finished *Aglavaine et Sélysette*, a farewell to symbolism, and the surrender to a reactionary movement of hope. Maeterlinck and Georgette were separated for months at a time by Georgette's professional career, and Maeterlinck was certainly unfaithful. She craved recognition in his writing, and *La Sagesse et la destinée* came out in 1898 with a fulsome dedication to her, suppressed in the 1926 edition following the break-up of the relationship. In 1897 Maeterlinck and Georgette had moved to Paris as a means of furthering her career.

Georgette was finally supplanted by Renée Dahon, who was to become Maeterlinck's wife in 1919. Meanwhile Maeterlinck and Georgette entertained Mirbeau, Barrès, Gide, Jules Renard, Paul Fort, Rodin, Jules Gaulthier, Anatole France, and Colette. By 1898 Maeterlinck's international reputation was established. His books were published in London, New York, and Berlin before either Paris or Brussels. Translation of his works into English and German had become almost automatic by now, but the London success of *Pelléas* that year was short-lived. Maeterlinck was to travel a great deal; he still had *Ariane et Barbe-Bleue* to finish, which Dukas was to set to music, and he would go on to write *Monna Vanna* and the fairy play *L'Oiseau bleu*, as well as his books of essays, but his real importance as the leading symbolist dramatist was already finished. *Monna Vanna* had a mixed reception, *Joyzelle* a disastrous one; and over *Pelléas* Maeterlinck had a noisy clash with Debussy, who refused to let Georgette sing the role of Mélisande. Gide was by now becoming increasingly disillusioned with Maeterlinck. *Aglavaine et Sélysette*, for which Gide had expressed qualified approval, was staged in Paris in 1896, and then not again until 1904 in Naples, where the reception was as lukewarm as that given to *Monna Vanna*.

The last play written for Georgette Leblanc, *Marie-Magdaleine, 1913*, was begun in 1908, but did nothing to hoist Maeterlinck's waning reputation in France. *L'Oiseau bleu* was premiered by Stanislavsky in Moscow in 1908, played in London in 1909, but not in Paris until 1911, when Renée Dahon was a member of the cast. Maeterlinck did not go to Stockholm to receive the Nobel prize, nor to Boston for *Pelléas*, with Georgette as Mélisande. The production was a failure. Maeterlinck's works, including the volumes of popular science, the dozen or so collections of essays and the 10 or so plays still to be written, still further damaged his reputation. He now became especially interested in psychic phenomena and animal intelligence.

In the company of his wife Maeterlinck made a rather unsuccessful trip to the US. He shattered many of his former idols, shocking the socialists by his adherence to the Action Française, decrying his early verse, calling the *Nouvelle Revue Française* (q. v.) a clique of snobs, and writing off Proust. He finished three entomological trilogies, journeyed a good deal, and wrote much pseudo-science. In 1932 he was made a count. He was attracted to fascism and gained a reputation for petulantly ill-mannered behaviour and increasing foolishness.

Maeterlinck spent the early years of the war in Portugal,

before finally fleeing to the US. In 1947 he returned to France. He died peacefully, attended by his wife.

WORKS

The works which made Maeterlinck's name were the vague, romantic, and allegorical plays. To add to the work's mysterious, ethereal effect a thin gauze curtain separated the stage from the auditorium for the premiere of *Pelléas*. Much in the early plays came from Shakespeare, injudiciously mixed with pre-Raphaelite influences, and a cult of renunciation leading to death. *La Princesse Maleine*, in which love succumbs to the forces of destiny and death, owes much to Grimm and is largely pastiche, drawing also on Poe and on Shakespeare. The play, which was in strong reaction to the naturalistic tradition, employed the traditional tools of symbolist drama: ambiguity and suggestion. *L'Intruse*, with its Flemish setting and ambiance, focuses suggestively on the of death and the terror which precedes it: man is condemned to live out his life blindly groping in the shadows, with only occasional perceptions of the truth. The "trilogy of death" is completed by *Les Sept princesses*, a tableau rather than a play, with a princely lover returning to find his beloved dead—love pursuing an ideal of unattainable purity. Here Maeterlinck is much nearer the English pre-Raphaelites than to such continental symbolists as Villiers.

In *Pelléas* love actually challenges death but still loses in the end. The symbolist element of the play lies in Maeterlinck's attempt to probe the possible alleviation of life's horror through the advent of love. The play as we have it may reflect Maeterlinck's unusual psychological make-up. Why, for instance, does Mélisande need to be killed? In *Les Aveugles*, too, death isolates its victim before consummating its victory. Why? It must be to generate a foreboding which makes forearming plausible. In the meanwhile the atmosphere is heavy with presentiment.

Aglavaine et Sélysette continues to rely on silence and enigma, on a self-parodying simplicity of dialogue. When Méléande falls in love with Aglavaine, his wife Sélysette chooses a course of renunciation and commits suicide in such a way as to make her death look like an accident. This play, like the others, has been criticized for its sleepwalking characters making unconvincingly symbolic gestures.

Monna Vanna turns its back on symbolism. Maeterlinck wrote that the time had come to confront a truth no longer shrouded in symbols. In spite of Lugné-Poe's dislike of having Georgette Leblanc foisted on him, the play was a success at its Parisian premiere on 7 May 1902; it was to be an even greater success in Berlin. Death here has at last yielded some of its power to love, wisdom, and happiness. Vanna, wife of Colonna, the Pisan commander, consents to give herself for one night to Prinzivalle, the general of the Florentine forces besieging Pisa. In the event, however, Prinzivalle does not violate her because he recognizes in her someone he has loved since childhood. Vanna returns to Pisa with Prinzivalle in the morning, but her husband refuses to believe that their night together has been innocent, and Vanna decides to flee with Prinzivalle to happiness. The moral theme of the play is clear: sexual fidelity may rightfully be sacrificed on occasion to greater issues like the salvation of thousands of lives. Further more Vanna is presented as justified in breaking her marital vows in the name of her love for Prinzivalle. In Vanna Maeterlinck had finally provided Georgette with the Sarah Bernhardt role she had been badgering him to create as a vehicle for her charms. Both Sarah Bernhardt and Mrs Patrick Campbell had played Mélisande.

L'Oiseau bleu goes deeper than Peter Pan, but the children never find the bird, which signifies not only happiness, but also the secrets of the universe. Maeterlinck's essays comparing bees and flowers to men are of little literary or intellectual interest. In 1935 the play *La Princesse Isabelle*, written for his wife, was produced in Paris, and between 1934 and 1942 Maeterlinck published a series of six books of reflections on life. Both the influences on him and the geographical areas of his success make it important to remember that his artistic sensibility was recognizably Flemish as much as, or more than, it was French.

PUBLICATIONS

Plays

La Princesse Maleine, 1889; as *The Princess Maleine*, 1890
Les Aveugles, L'Intruse (produced 1891), 1890; as *The Blind, The Intruder*, 1891
Les Sept princesses, 1890; as *The Seven Princesses*, in *Plays*, 1895
Pelléas et Mélisande (produced 1893), 1892; as *Pelleas and Melisande*, 1894
Trois petits drames pour marionnettes (includes *Alladine et Palomides, Intérieur, La Mort de Tintagiles*), 1894; as *Alladine and Palomides, Interior, and The Death of Tintagiles*, 1895
Intérieur (produced 1895), in *Trois petits drames*, 1894
Alladine et Palomides (produced 1896), in *Trois petits drames*, 1894
La Mort de Tintagiles (produced 1905), in *Trois petits drames*, 1894
Annabella: 'Tis Pity She's a Whore, from the play by John Ford (produced 1894), 1895
Aglavaine et Sélysette (produced 1896), 1896; as *Aglavaine and Selysette*, 1897
Ariane et Barbe-Bleue, music by Paul Dukas (produced 1907), in *Théâtre 2*, 1901; as *Ariane and Barbe-Bleue*, 1901
Soeur Béatrice, in *Théâtre 2*, 1901; as *Sister Beatrice*, 1901
Théâtre, 3 vols., 1901–02
Monna Vanna (produced 1902), 1901; as *Monna Vanna* (in English), 1903
Joyzelle (produced 1903), 1903; as *Joyzelle* (in English), 1906
Le Miracle de Saint-Antoine (produced 1903), 1919; as *The Miracle of Saint Anthony*, 1918
L'Oiseau bleu (produced 1908), 1909; as *The Blue Bird*, 1909
Macbeth, from the play by Shakespeare (produced 1909), 1910
Marie-Magdeleine (produced 1910), 1913; as *Mary Magdalene*, 1910
Le Malheur passe (produced 1916?), 1925; as *The Cloud That Lifted*, 1923
Le Bourgmestre de Stilmonde, suivi de Le Sel de la vie. 1919; as *The Burgomaster of Stilmonde*, 1918
Les Fiançailles (produced 1918), 1918; as *The Betrothal; or, The Blue Bird Chooses*, 1919
Berniquel (produced 1923), 1929
La Puissance des morts, 1926; as *The Power of the Dead*, 1923
Marie-Victoire, 1927
Juda de Kérioth, 1929

La Princesse Isabelle (produced 1935), 1935
L'Abbé Sétubal (produced 1941), in *Théâtre inédit*, 1959
Jeanne d'Arc, 1948
Théâtre inédit (includes *L'Abbé Sétubal, Les Trois justiciers, Le Jugement dernier*), 1959

Fiction

Deux contes: Le Massacre des innocents, Onirologie, 1918

Verse

Serres chaudes: poèmes, 1889; as *Poems*, 1915
Album de douze chansons, 1896; as *XII Songs*, 1912
Serres chaudes, suivi de quinze chansons, 1900
Serres chaudes, quinze chansons, vers de fin, 1947

Other

Le Trésor des humbles, 1896; as *The Treasure of the Humble*, 1897; excerpt as *The Inner Beauty*, 1910
La Sagesse et la destinée, 1898; as *Wisdom and Destiny*, 1898
La Vie des abeilles, 1901; as *The Life of the Bee*, 1901; excerpt as *The Swarm*, 1906
Le Temple enseveli, 1902; as *The Buried Temple*, 1902
Le Double Jardin, 1904; as *The Double Garden*, 1904; as *Old-Fashioned Flowers and Other Out-of-Door Studies*, 1905; excerpt as *Our Friend the Dog*, 1904; as *My Dog*, 1906
L'Intelligence des fleurs, 1907; as *Life and Flowers*, 1907; as *Intelligence of the Flowers*, 1907; excerpt as *Measure of the Hours*, 1907
La Mort, 1913; as *Death*, 1911; revised edition, as *Our Eternity*, 1913
Hours of Gladness, 1912; as *News of Spring and Other Nature Studies*, 1913
L'Hôte inconnu, 1917; as *The Unknown Guest*, 1914
Les Débris de la guerre, 1916; as *The Wrack of the Storm*, 1916
Les Sentiers dans la montagne, 1919; as *Mountain Paths*, 1919
Le Grand Secret, 1921; as *The Great Secret*, 1922
En Egypte: notes de voyage, 1928; as *Ancient Egypt*, 1925
En Sicile et en Calabre, 1927
La Vie des termites, 1927; as *The Life of the White Ant*, 1927
La Vie de l'espace, 1928; as *The Life of Space*, 1928
La Grande Féerie: immensité de l'univers, notre terre, influences sidérales. 1929; as *The Magic of the Stars*, 1930
La Vie des fourmis, 1930; as *The Life of the Ant*, 1930
L'Araignée de verre, 1932; excerpt as *Pigeons and Spiders (The Water Spider)*, 1934
La Grande Loi, 1933; as *The Supreme Law*, 1934
Avant le grand silence, 1934; as *Before the Great Silence*, 1935
Le Sablier, 1936; as *The Hour-Glass*, 1936
L'Ombre des ailes, 1936
Devant Dieu, 1937
La Grande Porte, 1939
L'Autre Monde: ou, Le Cadran stellaire, 1942
Bulles bleues: souvenirs heureux, 1948
Le "Cahier bleu," edited by Joanne Wieland-Burston, 1977
Translator, *L'Ornement des noces spirituelles*, by Jan van Ruysbroeck, 1891; as *Ruysbroeck and the Mystics*, 1894
Translator, *Les Disciples à Saïs*, by Novalis, 1895

Bibliography

Lecat, Maurice, *Bibliographie de Maeterlinck: littérature, science, philosophie*, 1939

Critical studies

Mahoney, P., *The Magic of Maeterlinck*, 1951
Halls, W. D., *Maeterlinck: A Study of His Life and Thought*, 1960
Andrieu, J.M., *Maurice Maeterlinck*, 1962 Knapp, Bettina, *Maeterlinck*, 1975

MAISTRE, Joseph, Comte de, 1753–1821.

Moralist and political philosopher.

LIFE

When Joseph de Maistre was born there on 1 April 1753, Chambéry was the capital of Savoy, which was the French-speaking portion of the Italian kingdom of Sardinia. His father, a member of the Savoy senate, had married a judge's daughter, Christine Desmotz, when he was 44 and she was 27. She bore him 15 children, five of whom died young. Joseph was the third. He was brought up by Jesuit tutors, went to the Collège Royal at Chambéry, studied law in Turin from 1769, graduated in 1772, began to practise, and in 1773 became a freemason. When his mother died in 1774, Maistre was established as a magistrate in Savoy. Masonry had not yet been condemned by the Church, and was in fact tending to split into rationalist anti-monarchist groups and Catholic royalist ones. Maistre, still under the spiritual direction of the Jesuits, and given to good works under their guidance, naturally belonged to the fashionable "ultra" wing of masonry, actually regarded by its adherents as a somewhat superior sort of Catholicism because of the higher realms of mystical rites and doctrines to which it was considered to give access.

It was in connection with masonry that in the early 1780s Maistre travelled to Lyons, where he got to know about theosophy and the illuminist doctrines of Saint-Martin, by whose religiosity Maistre was taken in, and in whose mystical fervour he never ceased to believe. Saint-Martin was to call on Maistre at Chambéry in 1787. His obscure illuminism, as put forward in his *Des erreurs et de la vérité* (1775) and interpreted by the Portuguese Jew Martines de Pasqually, was seen as something of a bastion against rationalism by the "ultra" monarchist masons. In 1778, after four years in his lodge, Maistre and some friends founded a new lodge, and four years later Maistre wrote a memoir to the Lutheran Duke of Brunswick, masonic grand master, about the future of masonry in Europe. The memoir, which was not published until 1925, held that masons should concern themselves only with the religious enlightenment of mankind and was vigorously anti-rationalist, calling for a root-and-branch rethinking of the activities and organization of free-

masonry. United in the name of religion and humanity, masons should not renew but create their movement again along ecclesiastical and, indeed, papal lines. The memoir implicitly alluded to German anti-Catholic illuminism, which was opposed to the whole sacramental system, and was presented to the duke at a meeting convened in an attempt to bring together the order's two wings.

The Catholic Church, it claimed, was the sole repository of the fullness of divine truth, and the esoteric doctrines of the order should be regulated by its teachings. In the meanwhile, however, the masonic movement should strive for the reunion of all the Christian churches, promoting both patriotism and piety, and paying particular attention to the figurative sense of Scripture. Maistre, who warns against the "excès de déraison (excesses of madness)" which can be entailed by the "fureur de chercher et d'expliquer des mystères (madness in chasing after .... explaining mysteries)," later felt that occultism had won only a ... rrhic victory at the Wilhelmsbad council, since the full inspiration of the Holy Spirit had not been heeded. During the Revolution Maistre's lodge was suspected of sedition and meetings were voluntarily suspended.

In 1786 Maistre married Françoise-Marguerite de Moraud, by whom he was to have three children: Adèle in 1787, Rodolphe in 1789, and Constance in 1793. When, in 1789, his father died, Maistre became head of the family, inherited the title of count, and undertook the administration of the family estate. However, in 1792 the French conquered Savoy. Maistre had left his estate in September, returned briefly to Chambéry in November, found the anti-clericalism of the Revolutionary administration intolerable, and decided that he could not live under the new regime. He fled to Lausanne, where he lived from 1793 to 1797 and took charge of Sardinian diplomatic affairs in Switzerland, organizing an espionage network, though forced to live in modest financial circumstances. Maistre continued to regard himself as French in all but political affiliation. It was while he was in Lausanne that he began to emerge as a leading pre-romantic (q. v.) writer.

In 1793 he published his *Lettres d'un royaliste savoisien à ses compatriotes* anonymously and began a number of essays. He became known with his first signed book, the 1796 *Considérations sur la France*, in which he treated the Revolution as a divine purification and predicted a glorious future for a restored aristocracy. The book was unsurprisingly popular in émigré circles, and there were three editions in two years. Maistre was then made regent of the island of Sardinia, before being sent as minister plenipotentiary to St Petersburg, where he took up residence in 1803. His son joined him in 1805, but for financial reasons his wife and daughters could not come until 1815. Knowing of the tsar's disapproval, Maistre did not accept the invitation extended to him to join a masonic lodge. He lived penuriously and his task was made more difficult as not only adequate finance but also official support were withheld. His post demanded that he keep a footman and carriage, but he breakfasted on bread and water. Maistre was respected at the Russian court, however, and was on good terms with the tsar, from whom he obtained appointments for Rodolphe and for his brother Xavier, the writer and author of the *Voyage autour de ma chambre* (1794), who rose to become a general in the Russian army.

Maistre was befriended by the high-born Mme Anne-Sophie Swetchine (1782–1857), whose spiritual guide he became, and whom he eventually converted to Catholicism in 1815. In 1816 she left St Petersburg for Paris, where her salon was to attract Lacordaire, Montalembert, and Alexis de Tocqueville. Meanwhile, Maistre missed his family, but enjoyed the diplomatic life of the Russian court. It was his Jesuit sympathies which forced him to leave on 27 May 1817. On the way to Sardinia he took his family to Paris, met the newly restored Louis XVIII, cool towards Maistre on account of his opinions about the constitution, and, having failed to obtain from Rome the patronage he solicited, was repulsed by Chateaubriand, whom he disliked, in his request for aid in finding a publisher for the intransigent *Du pape*. Maistre strongly disapproved of Mme de Staël's intellectual pretensions, while clearly enjoying her company. He settled in Turin, and eventually returned to Chambéry. His nephew married Lamartine's sister, and Maistre himself was present as a formal witness at Lamartine's own marriage. His letters are the principal source for his biography, but in spite of Rodolphe's edition of his father's correspondence in 1851 and the six volumes in the Vitte edition (1884–87), some political letters remain unpublished. Although he felt that he belonged to France, Maistre was loyal to Sardinia and deplored the Russo-French pact of 1808, which was a de facto recognition of the French conquest of Sardinia. He died at Chambéry on 26 February 1821.

Between 1808 and 1809 he wrote the *Essai sur le principe générateur des constitutions politiques*. Essentially devoted to the relationship he envisaged between Church and state, it was published in 1810. The first of the other works written in St Petersburg was *Du pape*, which had to be considerably toned down before a publisher could be found, and even then occasioned much hostility, a lukewarm reception in Rome, and real enthusiasm only from Lamennais and his supporters. It was eventually published by Rusland at Lyons in December 1819. Maistre wrote the preface to the second edition of 1821 at Chambéry, signing it 1 July 1820 and now including *De l'Eglise gallicane dans son rapport avec le Saint-Siège*, originally intended as an integral part of *Du pape*. The other work written at St Petersburg was the *Soirées de Saint-Pétersbourg; ou, Entretiens sur le gouvernement temporel de la Providence*, a witty series of 11 "entretiens" or conversations between "the Count," a Russian senator, and a young French aristocrat, summarizing Maistre's personal philosophy. The count is taken from Maistre himself, the senator from the Russian ex-ambassador to Constantinople, and the impulsive young French aristocrat is probably an amalgam, but chiefly based on the Bavarian ambassador to the Russian court. The *Soirées* were published in July 1821, six months after Maistre's death, and appear to have been mostly written in 1809.

WORKS

The *Considérations sur la France* of 1796 starts with an allusion to the opening sentence of Rousseau's *Du Contrat social*. Rousseau says that man was born free, but is everywhere in irons. Maistre counters: "Nous sommes attachés au trône de l'être suprême par une chaîne souple qui nous retient sans nous asservir (We are attached to the throne of the supreme being by a flexible chain which restrains without constraining us)." War and violence are terrible normalities. He chiefly but not exclusively blames Robespierre for what happened in France. The clergy also let the country down. The conflict of blood mirrors that between Christianity and the "philosophes." The Revolution is God's punishment. There will be a counter-revolution, a return to the monarchy, and France will show the world an example again. Maistre's analysis of the French situation and its likely resolution is clearly inspired by religious paradigms, whether of man's dependence on the ultimate monarch, or of the cycle of death and resurrection.

The earlier but unpublished *Fragments sur la France* had insisted on France's cultural primacy in Europe. Maistre could admire English institutions with reservation, but France's axiomatic cultural hegemony to the exclusion of Germanic inspiration, while compatible with a pre-romantic reaction against the "philosophes," none the less shows how far his thought diverges from that of Mme de Staël, no doubt less lucid a stylist than Maistre, but fundamentally more sensitive to cultural change. In the *Essai sur le principe générateur des constitutions politiques et des autres institutions humaines* Maistre, like Metternich, is clearly inspired by Edmund Burke's *Reflections on the Revolution in France* of 1790, defending the hereditary right to govern. Maistre denied the right of a people to create a constitution by which it agreed to be ruled. Ironically, Maistre's instruction to his publisher had been to issue the book anonymously, but it appeared in 1814, just after the restored Louis XVIII had granted a constitutional charter to France following Napoleon's defeat by the allies. The *Essai*, by turns witty, aphoristic, and ironic, is a rather rambling attack on all aspects of the Enlightenment, a handbook to Maistre's views in philosophy and political theory. Its interest lies in its being so clearly a product of the best of Enlightenment writing used against the fundamental tenets of Enlightenment thought. The unpublished "Etude sur la souveraineté" derides the idea of the sovereignty of the people despite its by then venerable antiquity in post-Renaissance Europe. There is in this work a deference to the idea that the "European character" was born among "the forests and glaciers of the north," although there is in Maistre no suggestion that primitive man was noble, or nature beneficent.

Du pape brings Maistre to the analogue for his monarchist political theory, the hierarchical government of the Church. It unambiguously asserts papal infallibility and argues from it, reminding the reader how much Maistre was a lawyer and how little a theologian. He hopes that a stable political order based on divine law will return to Europe. France would play a key role in leading the world back to Catholicism. It accords well with the general tenor of his thought that he should grant women only a subordinate role in society. They owe their status to Christianity. In a sense Maistre was writing an answer to Chateaubriand's *Génie du christianisme*, basing the claims of Christianity not on the artistic sensibilities it has nourished and drawn on, but strictly on a system of laws, rights, and obligations. The highest artistic authority is the product, not the justification for Christianity. The interest of *De l'Eglise gallicane* is largely centred on its attack on Jansenism.

Maistre's *Soirées*, undoubtedly his literary masterpiece, exploits a well-known literary convention in order digressively to discuss a universally important concern, the nature of providence and the existence of evil in a universe created by a benevolent God. Since physical evil can have entered the world only by the fault of free creatures, it had to be present as a remedy or an expiation, and cannot have had God as direct author. The conversations are witty, sometimes fanciful and light, as the genre demands, frequently relaxed, and generally optimistic. What, Maistre asks, is the relation between sickness and sin? The mosquitoes interrupt a discussion of Voltaire's thoughts on the problem of evil. Other subjects are war, Locke, prayer, Fénelon, Bacon, sacrifice, the nature of science, and Saint-Martin.

PUBLICATIONS

Collections

Oeuvres complètes, 14 vols., 1884–93

Works

Lettres d'un royaliste savoisien à ses compatriotes (published anonymously), 1793
Considérations sur la France, 1796
Essai sur le principe générateur des constitutions politiques et des autres institutions humaines, 1814; as *Essay on the Generative Principle of Political Constitutions*, 1847; as *On God and Society: Essay on the Generative Principle of Political Constitutions and of Other Human Institutions*, n.d.
Du pape, 1819
De l'Eglise gallicane dans son rapport avec le Saint-Siège, 1821
Soirées de Saint-Pétersbourg; ou, Entretiens sur le gouvernement temporel de la Providence, 1821
Eclaircissement sur les sacrifices, 1821
Mémoires politiques et correspondance diplomatique, edited by Albert Blanc, 1858
Correspondance diplomatique, 1811–1817, 2 vols., edited by Albert Blanc, 1860

Biographical and critical studies

Le Brun, Richard A., *Throne and Altar*, 1965
Lombard, Charles M., *Joseph de Maistre* (in English), 1976

————

MALLARMÉ, Stéphane, 1842–1898.

Poet.

LIFE

Mallarmé's parents came from families of government officials. His father and his mother's father both worked for the land registry. Mallarmé himself was born in Paris in March 1842. His mother died in 1847, leaving Mallarmé and a younger sister to be looked after by his maternal grandmother in Passy. His father remarried in 1852, and Mallarmé was sent to a religious boarding school in Passy, switching to one considered socially superior in 1854. In 1856 he was sent as a boarder to the lycée in Sens

to be near his father. A pupil of average ability, he toyed with writing verse. His sister died in 1857. Mallarmé passed his baccalauréat at the second attempt in 1860, started work as an accountant, and came under the influence of des Essarts, a teacher whose father was a writer in Paris.

In 1862 des Essarts published a volume of verse, which was enthusiastically reviewed by the young Mallarmé in *Le Papillon* and, two months later, in *Le Sénonais*. Mallarmé had meanwhile published his own first poems, "Placet futile" in *Le Papillon*, and "Le guignon" and "Le sonneur" in *L'Artiste*. All three were subsequently to be revised more than once. The influence of Baudelaire, whom Mallarmé had discovered in 1861, is apparent in the vocabulary, technique, and poetic inspiration of these early poems, although it later paled beside that of Poe. It was Baudelaire himself who first discovered Poe, whose literary aesthetic he enthusiastically embraced, while Mallarmé translated some of Poe's poems in 1863. In his quest for the ideal, for an inner absolute—which was necessarily inexpressible—Mallarmé was to take Poe's aesthetic to its ultimate conclusion: poetic self-extinction. Such an ideal could only be approached through the creation of symbols whereby words and objects from the real world hinted at the existence of that which transcended reality.

Outwardly Mallarmé's life was uneventful. Between 1862 and 1866 he published 17 short poems in literary magazines, and he began to make a name for himself in literary circles. In the summer of 1862 he got to know Henri Cazalis, Henri Regnault, Nina Gaillard, and Eugène Lefébure, and fell in love with Marie Gebhard, who taught German privately to a local family. At the age of 20 he went to England to learn the language, accompanied by Marie and armed with a number of introductions to various priests and prelates supplied by his devout grandmother. Marie returned to France in January, unable to put up with the English weather and their impecunious style of living, but after repeated meetings, partings, and hesitations, she and Mallarmé were married in London on 10 August 1863. Mallarmé's father had died in April of that year, Marie's mother in 1861. In September 1863 Mallarmé obtained his English teaching certificate and was immediately given a post as English teacher in Tournon. He would continue to teach English until his early retirement, neither enjoying nor excelling at it, but protected by the inspectorate on account of his literary reputation.

His teaching, interrupted only in 1870 and 1871, involved posts at Besançon (1866–67) and Avignon (1867–70), followed by three posts in Paris, at the Lycée Fontanes (1871–84), the Lycée Janson de Sailly (1884–85), and as professor at the Collège Rollin. Mallarmé continued in this last post until his retirement early in 1894, when he went to live at Valvins, near Fontainebleau. In 1883, while at Fontanes, he was made a member of the Académie Française. Marie gave birth to a daughter, Geneviève, on 19 November 1864, and on 16 July 1871 to a son, Anatole, who died at the age of eight. In 1883 or 1884 Mallarmé became the lover of Méry Laurent, who enjoyed the friendship of several poets and painters, in particular Manet and Coppée. From 1880, when he began to receive at his famous Tuesday gatherings, Mallarmé gradually found himself the centre of an esoteric literary circle. His ideal world had crystallized into an intellectual abstraction, reflected by the solitary heroine of *Hérodiade* and the satyr of *L'Après-midi d'un faune*, and even Mallarmé's most intimate relationships and letters display a curious lack of passion, except perhaps for developing the poetics which would allow him to compose "L'Oeuvre," as he called it, the great poetic masterpiece of which he dreamed.

In 1863 Mallarmé had acquired Gautier's new volume of *Poésies nouvelles*. He hoped to start writing again himself, but "L'azur," written in Tournon and still stylistically influenced by Baudelaire, laments the impossibility of escape from the everyday into the infinite. One of his friends commented on the poem's impenetrability, a characteristic which Mallarmé would later consider an indispensable condition for a successful poem. The massive correspondence (generally on literary matters) which began at around this time shows that the exchange of letters was currently one of Mallarmé's primary preoccupations. He established a pattern of visiting and being visited by other poets of his circle, which included the Parnassian (q. v.) group, seldom travelling with his wife. In 1864 two of his prose poems were published in the *Semaine de Vichy*, and in October of that year, finding his teaching a more and more intolerable burden, Mallarmé began work on *Hérodiade*. Although he was still only 22, he was perfectly aware that he was inventing a new poetics of allusion and suggestion: "peindre, non la chose mais l'effet qu'elle produit (to paint not the thing, but the effect which it produces)." Baudelaire had gone this far, but Mallarmé was to go still further by creating symbols which took their meaning exclusively from their own immediate context (see Symbolism). What are called "symbols" in Baudelaire are often no more than universal signs, like "azur" or "ennui," transferable from one poem to another and constituting a private poetic language which merely requires decoding.

Mallarmé, whose only real pleasure lay in writing poetry, kept breaking off his work on *Hérodiade* to write more sonnets in his Baudelairean style. He began a piece entitled *Le Faune*, which Banville had led him to believe might be performed at the Théâtre-Français. Called first "L'improvisation...," and then "Le monologue d'un faune," the poem was not considered sufficiently dramatic, however, and Mallarmé left it untouched until the following spring, continuing to work on *Hérodiade* instead. *L'Après-midi d'un faune* may have been finished by the summer of 1866, but it was not in fact published until 1876. The edition of 200 copies was printed on three sorts of paper, with illustrations by Manet, and was bound in white felt with gold leaf edging and silk ties. Debussy, who was not the first composer to set the poem to music, began work on his "Prélude" in 1892 and finished it in 1894. Mallarmé attended its first performance.

Meanwhile Mallarmé was making himself physically ill in his attempt to get every word of *Hérodiade* exactly right. On the night of 2 March 1866 he appears to have made a sudden breakthrough and he wrote to Aubanel, a poet friend, next day: "I am going to try to finish 'l'Oeuvre' tonight." His friends and correspondents were now beginning to understand his ambition to distil the absolute from all ordinary experience and to encapsulate it in one "Grand Oeuvre." The aim was self-defeating, since it threatened to lead to a wordless poem, and the effort almost cost Mallarmé a nervous breakdown and could have destroyed his sanity.

The 18 fascicules of the first series of *Le Parnasse Contemporain*, which made a loss of 2,000 francs, appeared from March to June of 1866, and in May 10 of Mallarmé's poems appeared in it, although the promised payment never arrived. Mallarmé's teaching stint at Tournon had not proved professionally successful, but it was during his time at Besançon, where he found his

pupils less refractory, that his mental state reached its critical point. He was now torturing himself with the notion of an "Oeuvre" in five volumes which it would take him 20 years to produce. His problem is elucidated in the three finely crafted but frustrated sonnets "Tout orgueil fume-t-il du soir," "Surgi de la croupe et du bond," and "Une dentelle s'abolit," published in the *Revue Indépendante* in January 1867 and written following a reading of Hegel. The sonnets define the ideal in terms of the absence of everything except suggestions and hints; anything concrete acts as a barrier to the ideal. Mallarmé's health had been unusually poor even for him, and he wondered if he would have the 10 years necessary to finish even a version of the Oeuvre limited to three verse and four prose poems on the spiritual notion of annihilation "of a purity unattained, and perhaps unattainable."

Lefébure warned him that he had "severed his flowers from their earth-bound roots." Since nothing could follow the creation of absolute purity and quintessential beauty, such notions must necessarily remain unattainable. Mallarmé himself later described his poetic dream at this time as a cul-de-sac. Two important sonnets, infinitely reworked, consider the function of the poet as expressing the mysterious void of distilled essences which exists beyond the real: "Ses purs ongles" and "Quand l'ombre menaça." Mallarmé was being driven towards a language and imagery of such intensity and concentration as to be virtually hermetic, and he was indeed tempted to regard his poetics as the pursuit of a mystical consummation, with initiatory and purificatory rites.

In 1867 Mallarmé was posted to Avignon, where he fell seriously ill with congestion of the lung. In 1869 he sent the fragments of his unfinished *Hérodiade* to Catulle Mendès for the second series of *Le Parnasse Contemporain*, but publication was delayed until 1871 by the Franco-Prussian War. By this time Mallarmé was attempting to explain in the prose work *Igitur* how absolute purity could be identified with nothingness and coexist with eternal beauty. Like the Salomé of *Hérodiade* Mallarmé wanted to do away with the external manifestations of the pure and the absolute, putting increasingly difficult burdens on poet and reader alike. It was becoming clear to him that ever denser and more concentrated imagery lead via obscurity to ultimate silence, and that he must consequently change his poetic aesthetic: the poet's aim can only be to raise up and transform the world from the merely physical. For 15 years, while this realization sank in, Mallarmé was to publish almost nothing.

The 1873 "Toast funèbre" for *Le Tombeau de Théophile Gautier*, the 1876 *Le Tombeau d'Edgar Allan Poe*, and the 1877 sonnet "Sur les bois" are slender punctuations of this silence. After six further years of silence Mallarmé began publishing again, but almost only elegant and refined verses of circumstance. Only *Un coup de dés n'abolira jamais le hasard* takes up again the theme of *Igitur*. It was never finished, and Mallarmé instructed his family to burn it. The pseudo-scientific Orphic cult, its occult overtones, its experiments in the replacement of syntactical by typographical effects (as in *Un coup de dés*), the more than faintly ridiculous idea of a 20-volume "Grand Oeuvre" to be perused first without cutting the pages, thus revealing only two pages in eight, and the masonic brotherhood atmosphere of the "Mardis" are so many concessions to the failure of a grandiose project, which—by posing fundamental questions about its nature—nevertheless changed the whole evolution of modern poetry. Baudelaire's influence over a century of poets, artists, and musicians was to be more obvious, Mallarmé's more radical.

Mallarmé's health had prompted a successful request for leave early in 1870. His close friend Henri Regnault was killed in the January fighting of 1871. Mallarmé was actively looking for a new career, hoping for a post as a librarian or archivist—supplemented perhaps by some journalistic work—or possibly as a private English tutor. There was also the possibility that he might obtain work with the publishers Hachette, of which Regnault's fiancée's father was a director. In the end he went to Paris without a job. His son was born in Sens in July, and Mallarmé obtained a commission to go to England, where he wrote three pseudonymous articles on the Exhibition, but was forced by his circumstances to take the teaching post at the Lycée Fontanes offered him by the ministry. He became increasingly involved in Parisian literary life, which provided him with the distractions necessary to divert him from his failure to produce his "Grand Oeuvre." In spite of the miniscule amount which he had published by the age of 29, he was able to live off the reputation he had thus far acquired.

In 1872 he republished five prose poems, and in 1873 *Le Tombeau de Théophile Gautier* appeared. *Le Faune* was turned down in 1874, and for four months Mallarmé edited *La Dernière Mode*. In 1877 the last of his translations of Poe's poems were published. Despite this slender list of publications, by the time Mallarmé's "Mardis" started in 1880 he was known, talked about, and generally cultivated in several like-minded literary circles.

Mallarmé met Rimbaud and became friendly with Manet, who painted his portrait and introduced him to Zola. Montesquiou and Laforgue were among his correspondents, and he enjoyed acting as patron to younger writers such as Gide, Valéry, and Claudel, all of whom wrote to him. In 1897, just before his 55th birthday, he was presented with an album of poems by younger contemporaries, including Vielé-Griffin, Régnier, Louÿs, Claudel, Dujardin, Verhaeren, and Valéry. He took up work again on *Hérodiade*, but was to die the following year.

WORKS

Mallarmé's *Poésies*, including some hitherto unpublished pieces, were published in 1899. Some had been endlessly reworked, some were probably as near as he could get them to what he wanted, while others no doubt, had he lived longer, would have been subject to further endless revision. The volume, which is liberally strewn with empty spaces, is very slender. It includes 15 poems, often subsequently revised, from 1862 to 1865, or what has been called Mallarmé's first period. They were written originally in Sens, London, or Tournon and are heavily dependent on Baudelaire. In general they are poems of aspiration in which hope is often frustrated:

—Le Ciel est mort.—Vers toi, j'accours! donne, ô matière,
L'oubli de l'Idéal cruel et du Péché
A ce martyr qui vient partager la litière
Où le bétail heureux des hommes est couché.

(The Sky/Heaven is dead. I run to you [Boredom]! Give, oh matter, / Forgetfulness of the cruel Ideal and of Sin / To this martyr who comes to share the litter / On which lies the happy herd of man.)

The poem, of nine four-line stanzas, is called "L'azur" and uses Baudelaire's devices of poetic self-dramatization, assonance, the rhetorical form of address, and enjambement, in which the sense and the syntax are carried over the line ending. It also uses Baudelaire's "signs" of infinite aspiration, "azur" (blue sky) and frustration, "remords" (remorse). The fog both blankets the aspiration with its euphonious "cendres monotones" (dreary ashes) and hints at the existence of the unknown as it forms a "plafond silencieux" (silent ceiling). The poem ends with the frustrated cry "I am obsessed":

Je suis hanté L'Azur! l'Azur! l'Azur! l'Azur!

Hérodiade focuses essentially on the rejection by a proud and solitary princess of her nurse's temptations to impurity signified by the sensuality of the kiss, the perfume, the arrangement of her hair, and the touch. Beauty and death are both gateways to the achievement of the ideal and its betrayal by the senses: "un baiser me tûrait / Si la beauté n'était la mort... (a kiss would kill me / If beauty were not death...)." The notion of poetic consummation in the poet's sensual self-extinction—a long way from the romantic idea of the consummation of love in death—is at the heart of the Besançon aesthetic's self-contradiction, the clash between the nothingness of absolute purity and the ecstasy of absolute beauty.

The density of expression and complexity of imagery together with the euphony and musicality of the verse in *Hérodiade* are used to support the poetic message of the Besançon period. The princess looks in the mirror for her quintessence, her "ombre lointaine" (far-off shadow). The mass of associated images and striking metaphors builds up to communicate the princess's determination to strip herself of everything sensuous, human, physical, leaving her only with her spiritual world of ethereal dreams. Similarly, in the "Toast funèbre" from *Le Tombeau de Théophile Gautier*, the poet delicately distinguishes the eternal significance of Gautier's life from his physical remains, with the absence of shadow indicating immateriality:

Le splendide génie éternel n'a pas d'ombre.
(The splendid eternal genius has no shadow.)

L'Après-midi d'un faune again relies on so intense a build-up of images as to warrant a line-by-line, if not word-by-word, commentary, but its essential theme is the same as that of *Hérodiade*. The fawn, the epitome of all that is sensual, rejects the sensual world which the poem successfully evokes. The technique has advanced in so far as Mallarmé, in the interests of making his imagery denser, has begun to suppress his syntax and rely on the simple juxtaposition of words to create symbols. The *Prose pour des Esseintes*, which is in verse, is a deliberately hermetic statement of Mallarmé's poetics, the invariable subject of the best of the poetry itself, and bristles with allusions. The "Prose" of the title is not merely ironic but adds the meaning "liturgy" to the word's usual associations, which themselves include "prosody" and, ironically, "prosaicism." The poem starts by rhetorically addressing the unattainable poetic ideal "Hyperbole," demanding that it encapsulate the poet's ideal self-realization in words for, as the second stanza develops, all the poet can do is produce the untransfigured material, culled from a selection of bookish sources, atlases, herbals, and rituals, all of which deal with objects and events in the real world but avoid narrative forms. The poet treats the poem as if it were itself the woman into whom the poet is transformed, leaving words, not syntactically contrived meaning, to evoke by their reverberating associations the reaction which leads the reader to the goal: the poet has "eliminated himself."

Mallarmé pays much attention to the sound and even, occasionally, to the visual appearance of a line. He was mystified that Debussy wanted to set *Le Faune* to music, since he thought the work was already musical enough, and he was capable of explaining at some length to Swinburne why he preferred the line "Pour y cueillir rien qu'un souffle d'amour" (to pick up there merely a breath of love) to "Pour recueillir rien qu'un souffle d'amour" (to pick up again merely a breath of love). A comparison of the 1868 version of the very important sonnet "Ses purs ongles" with its revised version of 1887 further demonstrates Mallarmé's preoccupation with sonority and visual effects. In the original version Mallarmé had set himself a rhyme scheme involving six rhymes in i/yx(e) of almost acrostic difficulty, since he also reverses masculine and feminine rhymes for the last six lines. Anxious to use the word "ptyx," he eventually discovered some justification for its existence: it could perhaps be regarded as a French transcription of a Greek word meaning seashell, and since, in the context of the poem, it merely needs to signify an ornamental object that might be found on a table, it is perhaps acceptable. In an empty room, which is a figure of the poet's soul, the ornaments have been removed: "nul ptyx / Aboli bibelot" (there is no ptyx,/The knick-knack has gone). The ascenders in the syntactically doubtful phrase "Aboli bibelot," added in 1887, contribute *visually* to the poem's impact, adumbrating the later typographical effects, in addition to the contribution made by the alliterations and assonances, with "b" occurring three times, "l," "i," and "o" twice each in six syllables. The 1868 version makes the poem perfectly intelligible syntactically. In 1887 the syntax is clearly strained to accommodate the increasingly dense and sonorous imagery.

The extraordinary concentration for which Mallarmé continued to strive in his verse has tended to relegate the often remarkable prose poems to comparative neglect. They show the same quest for the achievement of an absolute which is beyond the power of language to express, but towards which Mallarmé hoped language could be made to lead. Here, too, however, Mallarmé is so preoccupied by what he feels to be the poet's task, that he returns to poetry and to the difficulty of writing it as his subject, "Tout écrit, extérieurement à son trésor, doit, par égard envers ceux dont il emprunte, après tout, pour un objet autre, le langage, présenter, avec les mots, un sens même indifférent (Every piece of writing, outside its own treasure, must, out of considerateness for those from whom it is after all borrowing language for a different purpose, present a meaning, however unimportant, with words)." The syntax in French is complicated to the point almost of caricature. The difficulty is the same as in the verse. Poetry had for Mallarmé to achieve what words could not alone accomplish, however much suggestiveness could be bestowed on them by their removal from ordinary syntax, and however much continual revision and endless pondering over a word or a sound increased the stimulations of assonance and musicality to force reader or listener to look beyond semantic meaning.

Mallarmé's relationship with the Parnassian (q.v.) group of poets continued to deteriorate on his installation in Paris in 1871, and it is probably to the 1867 poems that we should turn for an example of Mallarmé's poetry before he had at any rate prepared himself interiorly for the ultimate abandon of his self-defeating poetic ambition, exchanging it for the Tuesday discourses in the Rue de Rome. They lasted from 9.0 p.m. to about midnight, were attended by about a dozen of the young poets undergoing what seemed like initiation, and were devoted to the presentation of the poetic task as a virtually sacred function. By 1880, however, Mallarmé had himself clearly abandoned any real hope of performing the achievement of which he had dreamed. His ambition has been regarded as so overwhelmingly important in the history of French literature that it is not inapposite to quote one of the 1867 sonnets:

Une dentelle s'abolit
Dans le doute du Jeu suprême
A n'entr' ouvrir comme un blasphème
Qu'absence éternelle de lit.

Cet unanime blanc conflit
D'une guirlande avec la même,
Enfui contre la vitre blême
Flotte plus qu'il n'ensevelit.

Mais chez qui du rêve se dore
Tristement dort une mandore
Au creux néant musicien

Telle que vers quelque fenêtre
Selon nul ventre que le sien,
Filial on aurait pu naître.

"(A Lace vanishes /in the doubt of the supreme Game/Risk, / only half-opening like a blasphemy / an everlasting absence of bed. // This unanimous white conflict / of a garland with the same, / fled against the pale window-pane / floats more than it buries. // But in him who gilds himself with dream / a mandola sadly sleeps / musician to the hollow nothingness // as towards some window / for no other belly than his own / childlike could have been born)."

The poem is generally agreed to be obscure. It deliberately retains only the appearance of syntax, and seeks to use language musically and evocatively, not to communicate sense, but to convey something which is not perceivable, hinting at that which is beyond experience. So the lace dissolves. Its whole point is the point of the poetic Task, to leave doubt, to hint. The poem evokes the image of lace round a four-poster bed which disintegrates to reveal only the bed's eternal absence. The fourth line of the second quatrain uses the two verbs "float" and "bury," intentionally leaving us in doubt as to whether or not they are transitive. The lace, white, a garland, vanishes against the window. The gender of "fled" tells us that it must refer syntactically to "conflict." We do not know with any certainty to whom the "in him" of the first line of the first tercet refers, but the tercets clearly repeat the revelation of unexpected emptiness. The sleeping mandola's shape may have been suggested by that of the womb whose potentiality is unrealised, but there is no music and no child.

Enfance, ton regard, 1966

La Maison de papier, 1970; as *The Paper House*, 1971

Le Roi qui aimait trop les fleurs (juvenile), 1971

Les Feuilles mortes d'un bel été (juvenile), 1973

J'aurais voulu jouer de l'accordéon, 1975

Juliette Greco, with Michel Grisolia, 1975

Jeanne Guyon, 1978

Editor, *Nouvelles*, Paris, 1957

Editor, *Le Rendez-vous donné par Mallet-Joris à quelques jeunes écrivains*, 1962

Editor, *Lettres*, by Madame de Sevigné, 1969

Critical study

Frackman Becker, Lucille, *Françoise Mallet-Joris* (in English), 1985

MALRAUX, (Georges-) André, 1901–1976.

Novelist, philosopher of art, and successively left-wing political activist and minister under de Gaulle.

LIFE

Malraux's biography is still obscured by the myths about himself which he deliberately generated and which go hand in hand with his constant role-playing. Latterly, if he answered questions about himself at all, he would answer differently to different people, so that much that is assumed about him remains pure surmise. Since, in addition, some of the sources available to us, like the autobiographical volumes of his divorced wife Clara, are spiked to prick the myth's balloon, they, too, are less than totally reliable. Comic and pretentious episodes during his career as minister of culture from 1958, together with his later publications on the philosophy of art, did nothing to add to his public status.

We know little about Malraux's youth. His parents had broken up and he left school without a baccalauréat. He was brought up by his mother and a grandmother, and received financial help from both sides of the family. He made a living by buying rare books from the stalls along the Seine and reselling them to dealers. At 19, now married to Clara Goldschmidt, he was shot at one day, and apparently himself drew a gun which, one assumes, he must regularly have carried. He had already published some dilettante reviews and some dadaist and surrealist (qq.v.) items in little magazines. He moved into publishing, putting out erotica and what he fraudulently claimed to be unpublished work by Laforgue. He seems to have modelled himself on T.E. Lawrence, and at any rate based his attitudes on an overt belief in the power and rights of the individual will, both during his strongly pro-communist period and as de Gaulle's lieutenant from 1945. His Marxism derived from the attraction which revolutionary activism held for him rather from any argued political conviction. It is noteworthy that women are never more than a shadowy presence in his novels.

According to Clara, the 1923–24 trip to Cambodia was intended as a means of recouping her fortune—which they had lost—by finding, stealing, and selling Khmer statuary. Malraux was caught, tried, and apparently released on a technicality with a suspended jail sentence. The 1925–26 journey to Saigon was hardly more successful. It involved unsavoury journalism and was politically ineffective. What Malraux brought back was an authentically exotic setting and an experience out of which to build his early novels. He worked for the *Nouvelle Revue Française* (NRF, q.v.) and then for the parent house, Gallimard. Although he published 16 reviews in the *NRF* from 1927 to 1932, we do not know where he was or what he was doing at this time. His three most successful novels were published between 1928 and 1933. In 1934 he accompanied Gide to Berlin to help the defenders in the Reichstag Fire trial and, financed by a newspaper, explored the Arabian desert by air. He wrongly claimed to have found the lost city of the Queen of Sheba. In 1936 he visited Moscow in connection with a grandiose project for a Marxist encyclopedia, but nothing came of it.

From 1936 to 1937 Malraux worked actively with the Republican air force in Spain, buying planes and raising money, partly in the US. He was now famous, and a central figure at the Madrid Writers' Congress. He had published *L'Espoir* in 1937 and subsequently made a film of the novel in Spain. However, his communist sympathies do not seem to have withstood the Nazi–Soviet pact of 1939. In 1941 he wrote the strictly non-political *Les Noyers de l'Altenburg*, having joined a tank regiment during the early stages of the war. He was taken prisoner, escaped, and after the fall of France joined the Resistance. He was captured, rescued, and became a full colonel in the Maquis, retaining that position in the reconstituted post-war French army. He first met de Gaulle in 1944 and became his minister of information in 1945, resigning with him in 1946 and returning with him to power in 1958.

Malraux had had one daughter by Clara and two daughters by Josette Clotis, whom he is rumoured to have married and who died in a rail crash. He did marry his brother's widow in 1948, with the result that his nephew became his stepson. In 1933 he had been awarded the Prix Goncourt and during his last years he accepted several honorary doctorates and, in 1974, the Nehru peace prize. He continued to publish occasional books, some pseudo-autobiographical, like the *Anti-mémoires*, some devoted to the philosophy of art, and some collections of political papers and speeches.

WORKS

Malraux's first substantial work, *La Tentation de l'occident*, a series of letters between a young Frenchman in China and a young Chinese in Europe, is chiefly of interest for its attempt to dissect Western culture, based, it is suggested, on the quest of individualism with the consequent alienation of the individual from his environment. Love in the West subordinates simple pleasure to a mental superstructure, to the dynamic myth of history, and to the metaphysical solace of art. Malraux's analysis here cannot be regarded as properly thought through, whatever its nascent power. The 1927 *D'une jeunesse européenne* drops the fictional form and foresees the intensification of individualist values.

La Voie royale, which is generally taken to be the first of his three best-known novels to have been written, was excluded by Malraux himself from the 1947 collected Pléiade edition. It concerns an "archaeologist," Claude Vannec, who sets out to plunder the Khmer temples along the former Royal Road, and a Danish adventurer, Perken, who joins him. The adventure succeeds but, at the climax of the book, after Perken has successfully negotiated a safe passage in the company of a group of exceedingly dangerous natives, he steps on a poisoned dart. Strength of will is all there is to cultivate but it, too, leads to defeat. Malraux seems to have taken up the book again only in order to complete his contract with the publishing house Grasset.

Les Conquérants was serialized by the *NRF* before being published by Grasset in 1928. The violent action, in an exotic location, Canton in 1925, is now linked to a political commitment, and the individualism takes on a social significance. The style is vivid, with a first-person, present-tense narrator commenting on the action and, in the second of the three parts, joining the central character, Garine, a commissar working as Soviet adviser to the Canton nationalists. Although Malraux adjusted the balance of the action, the novel nevertheless starts slowly. The third part concerns Garine's motivation and his relationship with his communist superiors, contrasting his personal failure with his political success. Political commitment can thus be a pretext for self-destructive action. Malraux lingers here over gratuitous cruelty, unnecessary to the plot, and over-exploits the resonances of such words as "will" and "absurdity."

La Condition humaine is generally considered Malraux's most important novel. It was published by Gallimard after serialization in the *NRF*. The title derives from Montaigne. Set in the midst of violent left-wing revolutionary activity, the novel focuses on the personal attitudes of a whole spectrum of characters, not all of whom are communists, as each seeks a different way of coming to terms with "the human condition" and its inevitable failure. The bourgeois revolutionary, Kyo, who refuses to save his own life by betraying his colleagues and seeks a solution in the preservation of human dignity, is contrasted with Tchen, a former pupil of Kyo's opium-smoking father Gisors, a professor of sociology dismissed for left-wing views. Tchen seeks a solution in terrorist violence for its own sake. In the end Kyo kills himself, so that even his death is an act of will. He has also been wounded by his wife's infidelity, in an episode which has nothing at all to do with the plot, because his dignity demands a relationship which is more than simply erotic. Katow's sense of brotherly communion in action, however, is superior to love. In the fates of Hemmelrich and Tchen life's absurdity is heavily laboured and, of course, religious solutions are too passive to hold out attractions for any of Malraux's characters. Opium, perhaps; God, no. The story telling in *La Condition humaine* is often threatened, but never entirely destroyed, by the characters' awareness of the metaphysical implications of their attitudes.

Le Temps du mépris is by universal consent Malraux's weakest novel, omitted by him from the Pléiade volume. There is no psychological difference between the communist heroes and the fascist villains, as Malraux tries unsuccessfully to put imaginative flesh on three of his personal preoccupations at this period: anti-fascism, desert flying, and the different sorts of love and loyalty.

L'Espoir, twice the length of *La Condition humaine*, is a panoramic depiction of the first nine months of the Spanish Civil War. Isolated incidents, like the two plane crashes, may not have happened exactly as narrated, but the reconstruction is authentic. This is little more than a novel about strategic efficiency, though Malraux does briefly explore the compatibility of Catholicism and Republicanism. "Christ is an anarchist who succeeded," he remarks. "The only one." It is this sort of shallow, and incorrect, rhetorical boutade—characteristic of Malraux's style as a whole—together with his abstract probing into the implications of actions that are intended to illustrate attitudes rather than to advance the plot which keeps Malraux's work on a level of relative literary superficiality—for all the attractiveness to the 1930s of his clipped, American-style narration.

Les Noyers de l'Altenburg is narrated by a prisoner of the Germans at Chartres in 1940, reflecting on his own experience, and on that of his father during World War I, before returning to his own recent history. The three central sections on the narrator's father, Vincent Berger, are flanked by two in italics. The narrator's family lives in Alsace, so that the father (in 1914) was German but the son (in 1939) is French. The conditions of life and its ethical problems do not depend on nationality, however, and the central episode of the novel, "le colloque de l'Altenburg," is devoted to their discussion. This was Malraux's last novel, and the signs of imaginative exhaustion are clear. No longer able to work up political enthusiasm, he has written what is virtually no more than a series of dialogues.

From 1945 Malraux's writing was predominantly concerned with the philosophy of art. The three-volume *La Psychologie de l'art* was published in Geneva in 1947–49, and then reissued in a revised form in Paris as *Les Voix du silence* in 1951, with part of the argument further developed in *La Métamorphose des dieux*. Malraux seeks to broaden the idea of art beyond the limits of Western humanism, and views it as a substitute for religion in the process of human self-affirmation. The general tenor of Malraux's philosophy of art is Nietzschean, but the concept on which it is based, at heart neo-romantic, has its roots in the German idealist tradition and is little more than an amalgam of unassimilated and unreconciled ideas. These are volumes of grandiose ambition which have been regarded as making serious progress towards a viable philosophy of art for the 20th century, but they have also been heavily criticized for their lack of rigour and expert knowledge of either the history or the psychology of art.

PUBLICATIONS

Fiction

Lunes en papier, 1921

La Tentation de l'occident, 1926; as *The Temptation of the West*, 1961

Les Conquérants, 1928; as *The Conquerors*, 1929

Royaume farfelu, 1928

La Voie royale, 1930; as *The Royal Way*, 1935

La Condition humaine, 1933; as *Man's Fate*, 1934; as *Storm in Shanghai*, 1934; as *Man's Estate*, 1948

Le Temps du mépris, 1935; as *Days of Wrath*, 1936; as *Days of Contempt*, 1936

L'Espoir, 1937; as *Man's Hope*, 1938; as *Days of Hope*, 1938

Les Noyers de l'Altenburg, 1943; as *The Walnut Trees of Altenburg*, 1952
Et sur la terre… (unpublished chapter of *L'Espoir*), 1977

Other

Le Démon de l'absolu, 1946
Esquisse d'une psychologie du cinéma, 1946; translated in *Reflections on Art*, edited by Susanne Langer, 1958
La Psychologie de l'art: Le Musée imaginaire, La Création artistique. La Monnaie de l'absolu, 3 vols., 1947–49; as *The Psychology of Art: Museum Without Walls, The Creative Act, The Twilight of the Absolute*, 3 vols., 1949–51; revised edition, as *Les Voix du silence*, 4 vols., 1951; as *The Voices of Silence*, 4 vols., 1953
The Case for De Gaulle, with James Burnham, 1949
Saturne: essai sur Goya, 1949; as *Saturn: An Essay on Goya*, 1957
Le Musée imaginaire de la sculpture mondiale: Le Statuaire, Des bas-reliefs aux grottes sacrées, Le Monde chrétien, 3 vols., 1952-54
La Métamorphose des dieux:
  L'Inaccessible, 1957; revised edition, as *Le Surnaturel*, 1977; as *The Metamorphosis of the Gods*, 1960 *L'Irréel*, 1974
  L'Irréel, 1974
  L'Intemporel, 1975
Brasilia, la capitale de l'espoir (multilingual edition), 1959
Discours 1958–1965, 1966
Le Miroir des limbes:
  Anti-mémoires, 1967; revised edition 1972; as *Anti-Memoirs*, 1968
La Corde et les souris:
  Les Hôtes de passage, 1976
  Les Chênes qu'on abat, 1971; as *Fallen Oaks*, 1972; as *Felled Oaks*, 1972
  La Tête d'obsidienne, 1974; as *Picasso's Mask*, 1976
  Lazare, 1974; as *Lazarus*, 1976
Le Triangle noir, 1970
Oraisons funèbres, 1971
Paroles et écrits politiques 1947–1972, 1973
L'Homme précaire et la littérature, 1977

Critical studies

Frohock, W.M., *Malraux and the Tragic Imagination*, 1952; revised edition, 1967
Hartman, Geoffrey H., *Malraux*, 1960
Blend, Charles D., *Malraux, Tragic Humanist*, 1963
Blumenthal, Gerda, *Malraux: The Conquest of Dread*, 1963
Lewis, R.W.B. (editor) *Malraux: A Collection of Critical Essays*, 1964
Righter, W., *The Rhetorical Hero*, 1964
Boak, Denis, *Malraux*, 1968
Lacouture, Jean, *Malraux*, 1975
de Courcel Martine, (editor), *Malraux: Life and Work*, 1976
Madsen, Axel, *Malraux: A Biography*, 1977
Tarica, Ralph, *Imagery in the Novels of Malraux*, 1980

MARTIN DU GARD, Roger, 1881–1958.

Novelist, winner of the Nobel prize for literature (1937).

LIFE

Martin du Gard was born into a wealthy Parisian family. His religious upbringing was marked by his spiritual director, Marcel Hébert, who encouraged him to read Tolstoy and who later lost his faith and gave up the priesthood. For his last two years at school Martin du Gard boarded with a private tutor and began to read Zola, while reacting against the family milieu. Having failed his examinations at the Sorbonne, he studied on his own initiative for the archivist and librarian diploma at the Ecole des Chartes and wrote a thesis on the Norman abbey of Jumièges. His novels reflect an occasionally exaggerated reliance on card index documentation.

In February 1906, the month of his graduation, he married. He was no longer a believing Catholic. His wife, known for her piety, bore him a daughter in 1907. Martin du Gard had known that he wanted to be a writer ever since he had read Tolstoy at the age of 17. He became a close friend of Gide, but we have very little information on his private or social concerns. He travelled, began a dialogue novel, which he destroyed after completing the equivalent of two volumes, took courses in psychiatry, and then, in a matter of a few weeks, wrote *Devenir!* printed at his own expense in 1908. He started another novel, *Marise*, the complete picture of a woman's life, but destroyed the draft, salvaging only a fragment, *L'Une de nous*, which he had published by Grasset at his own expense, but which he later recalled.

From 1910 to 1913 Martin du Gard installed himself at Verger d'Augy in order to write *Jean Barois*. Grasset, who had undertaken to publish it, found it unwieldy and insisted that it would be a failure. Martin du Gard considered destroying the manuscript, but met up with Gaston Gallimard, an old school friend, then engaged with Gide, Schlumberger, and Copeau in founding the *Nouvelle Revue Française* ("*NRF*," q. v.), and Gide encouraged Gallimard to publish it. The book was a literary success and attracted favourable attention from Remy de Gourmont, Péguy, Suarès, and Alain. Martin du Gard became friendly with the *NRF* team, also connected with the newly founded Théâtre du Vieux-Colombier, which staged his first play, *Le Testament du père Leleu* in February 1914.

Martin du Gard kept a diary from the beginning of the war, when he was mobilized, but, like the rest of his papers, it was deposited at the Bibliothèque Nationale on his death, subject to the normal 30 year embargo. It is likely that the next decade or so will see an increase in critical interest in his works. On demobilization Martin du Gard concentrated on reopening the Vieux-Colombier, retiring again to Verger in 1920 to plan *Les Thibault*, on which he worked at first in a solitary retreat an hour's drive away from Paris. His reading consisted mostly of wide, panoramic works.

The first parts of *Les Thibault* were published in 1922 and 1923. In 1924 Martin du Gard finished a play, *La Gonfle*, and in 1926 settled into a new property known as Le Tertre. He published three further parts of *Les Thibault* in 1928 and 1929, the year of his daughter's marriage. Then in 1931 he and his wife were injured in a bad car accident. In hospital he revised his plan for *Les Thibault* and during his convalescence wrote a play, *Un taciturne*, which was produced by Jouvet in October

1931. He also destroyed most of what he had written for the seventh part of his novel. In 1932 he wrote the naturalistic *Vieille France* and in 1933 revised the plan and documentation for *Les Thibault*. The seventh part in three volumes appeared in 1936, and the final part in 1940. Martin du Gard travelled increasingly in Italy and the South of France, also visiting Martinique and the US (1939). He spent the war years in Nice. His wife died in 1949 and he was present when Gide died in 1951. *Notes sur André Gide* was Martin du Gard's only published work after *Les Thibault*, although he was working on his autobiographical *Souvenirs de Colonel de Maumort*. He felt increasingly that the world he understood had disappeared and that despite the Nobel prize and Gide's encouragement, nothing he could do would improve on what he had already done. The multiple volume, multi-generation depiction of a social order in which he believed was now beyond his powers and beyond recall.

WORKS

Jean Barois and *Les Thibault* (I "Le cahier gris," 1922; II "Le pénitencier," 1922; III "La belle saison," 1923; IV "La Consultation," 1928; V "La sorellina," 1928; VI "La mort du père," 1929; VII "Eté 1914," 1936; VIII "Epilogue," 1940) are the works by which Martin du Gard is remembered. *La Confidence africaine* is a first-person fiction by a narrator passing on to an editor a "true" story. The story was probably told to Martin du Gard and may well in fact be true. It flatly recounts a love affair between a brother and a sister who bears him a sickly child which dies. *Vieille France* is a series of village scenes riddled with a sarcasm and bitterness displayed as much by the narrator as by the character themselves. Of the three plays, *Le Testament du père Lelieu* is a peasant farce, using dialect, of tables turned, while *La Gonfle*, which has never been staged, is both cruder and more complex. *Un taciturne*, which deals with a businessman's homosexual love, is naturalistic in the tradition of dark psychological studies where every relationship ends in tragedy.

Jean Barois followed the fashion for dialogue novels and, using the Dreyfus affair as its focal point, depicts a whole society torn by the force of individual reactions to the events as they unfolded. At the centre is the conflict between liberal attitudes, whether in religious or in social matters, and the conservative Catholicism of the old order. The book sustains its tension in spite of giving greater weight to the characters' emotional confrontations—as the young protagonist moves from faith to scientific positivism and back again—than to its narrative structure. The novel depends on meticulous research into the public events, is sceptical about the alliance of political liberalism, which it favours, and free thought, about which it is more equivocal. Brilliantly summing up the whole spectrum of social values and attitudes prevalent in French middle-class society shortly before World War I, it is regarded as its author's greatest achievement.

Martin du Gard lost his faith in liberal humanism as the tool with which to forge an ideal social order. As late as 1936 he wrote that anything at all was preferable to war—"*Tout*: Hitler plutôt que la guerre" (Anything at all: Hitler rather than war)—and *Les Thibault* displays his awareness of man's inherently flawed nature. The novel is a story of disillusion with the ideal of peaceful social revolution, and revolves round the two Thibault brothers, Antoine and Jacques. Antoine is the exemplary doctor who loses his Catholic faith but retains his sense of duty and his belief in the virtues of patriotism and sacrifice. He dies in 1918, having been gassed in the war. Jacques will not submit to parental discipline, becomes a writer, is involved in socialist politics, and has a child by the sister of a Protestant school friend with a liberal father and an austerely religious mother. Jacques dies when he is shot down on a mission dropping pacifist leaflets.

The literary technique is realist, even naturalist (qq. v.), in its pitiless description of the clinically aseptic details of physical decline, although the repercussions of events are delineated *before* the events themselves are narrated. The skill lies in the author's tight control, his avoidance of all temptation to self-indulgence, so that developments are never allowed to become lurid, traits of character to be exaggerated, situations to go beyond the merest suggestion of the sordid, or ideological confrontations to become over-symmetrical. The action is allowed to unroll smoothly according to the demands placed on it by the characters, with the result that it is almost impossible to detect with whom the narrator's sympathies really lie.

Martin du Gard's model, as he made clear in his Nobel prize acceptance speech, is Tolstoy, but he lacks Tolstoy's depth of passion. His chosen genre, the saga novel, reveals a hardening of attitude, an increasing disconsolateness, as the author impassively portrays his characters' defeats. In Martin du Gard's work there is no sin and no redemption, no reward or punishment, only inadequacy and its consequences.

PUBLICATIONS

Collections

Oeuvres complètes, 2 vols., 1955. (Préface by Albert Camus)

Works not contained in the *Oeuvres complètes*

L'Une de nous, 1910
Noizemont-les-Vierges, 1928
Dialogue, 1930
Notes sur André Gide (1913–1951), 1951
Correspondance, with André Gide, 1967

Fiction

L'Abbaye de Jumièges, 1909
Devenir!, 1909
Jean Barois, 1913
Les Thibault
  i)   *Le Cahier gris*, 1922
  ii) *Le Pénitencier*, 1922
  iii) *La Belle saison*, 2 vols, 1923
  iv) *La Consultation*, 1928
  v) *La Sorellina*, 1928
  vi) *La Mort du père*, 1929
  vii) *Eté 1914, 1936*
  viii) *Epilogue*, 1940
La Confidence africaine, 1931
Vieille France, 1933

Drama

Le Testament du Père Leleu, 1921 (produced 1914)
La Gonfle, 1928
Un taciturne, 1932

Translations

The Thibaults, 1939
Summer 1914, 1941
Jean Barois, 1949
Recollections of André Gide, 1953
The Postman, 1955

Critical studies

Rice, Howard C., *Roger Martin du Gard and the World of the Thibaults*, 1941
Figaro Littéraire, "Hommage à l'écrivain des *Thibault*," 30 August 1958
Gibson, Robert, *Roger Martin du Gard* (in English), 1961
Boak, Denis, *Roger Martin du Gard* (in English), 1963
Robidoux, Réjean, *Roger Martin du Gard et la religion*, 1964
Schalk, D. L., *Roger Martin du Gard: The Novelist and History*, 1967
Savage, Catherine, *Roger Martin du Gard*, 1968
Alluin, Bernard, *Martin du Gard, romancier*, 1989

MAUPASSANT, (Henri-René-Albert-) Guy de, 1850–1893.

Writer of short stories, poet, novelist, and dramatist.

LIFE

Whether Maupassant was born in the large and impressive 18th-century country house near Dieppe resembling a Louis XIII château and known as Miromesnil, or at his grandmother's small, ugly summer apartment at Fécamp, some 30 miles away on the coast, was a matter of some importance for the social pretensions of his parents. They rented Miromesnil apparently so that their first child should be born there, but he may have arrived prematurely. Maupassant's parents later split up, but both were concerned with their public respectability. Each of their two sons became insane before dying of syphilis, but neither parent attended either funeral, and both went out of their way to enhance what they wrongly took to be their elder son's untarnished public image and to avoid any suspicion of the taint of inherited morbidity. The cover-up insisted that Maupassant's "breakdown" was due to overwork and that his brother Hervé (1856–1889) had died of sunstroke. Maupassant's mother was later to feel attacked not by insinuations of her husband's philandering, but by the accusation that she had sent Maupassant out to be wet-nursed. Indeed, her boast that she weaned him only

at 20 months may be an indication that the over-mothering, to which the patterns of his imagination later testify, began very early.

Gustave de Maupassant had his right to use the particule "de" officially confirmed a few months before his marriage in 1846. He was a somewhat dandified amateur painter, living comfortably off an allowance made by his father, a local director of the national tobacco monopoly and a gentleman farmer. He was born in 1821, the same year as his more cultivated wife, Laure née Le Poittevin (1821–1904). Her parents owned cotton mills and ships. The Le Poittevin family, who lived in Rouen, were on very intimate terms with the Flauberts. Laure's elder brother Alfred, who married her husband's sister, Louise, was a close friend of the novelist, who dedicated *La Tentation de Saint-Antoine* to him. Laure also knew Flaubert well, and exploited his friendship for her brother, at whose deathbed in 1848 Flaubert had spent two days, in the justified hope that he might help her son. The two couples, composed of the Maupassant and Le Poittevin siblings met while honeymooning in Italy. Laure could read Shakespeare in English, was from youth inclined to independence and eccentricity, had grandiose ambitions, smoked, rode, affected short skirts and felt hats before their day, and kept religious observance to a perfunctory minimum. She was a dedicated and domineering mother.

The family left Miromesnil shortly after Maupassant's birth, moved about Normandy, and in 1854 rented a more modest château near Etretat, where Hervé was born. Maupassant's father began to experience financial difficulties and the family settled in Paris, where Maupassant first went to school in 1859 at the Lycée Napoléon (now Henri IV) and his father found a post in a bank. The marriage however was disintegrating, conjectured contributory causes being Gustave's casino losses and extramarital affairs, and in 1860 Maupassant went to live with his mother and Hervé at the tiny but fashionable Normandy coastal resort of Etretat. By a notaried agreement of 1863 Gustave was to pay Laure 1,600 francs a year, with the parents assuming joint responsibility for bringing up their sons. When Gustave visited his wife and family, he was accorded the status of guest, sitting at his wife's right while his son sat in the host's place.

Maupassant lived near his grandmother and his mother's younger sister, a few hundred yards from the sea. It was here that he acquired his fascination for boats and swimming and, more importantly, the friendship of the local fishing families whose patois he learnt to speak. He was taught by his mother, although the local village priest was hired as a tutor to supplement her lessons. From 1863 to 1868 Maupassant boarded at the local "petit séminaire" at Yvetot, which was religious but whose intake was not confined to prospective priests. Maupassant strongly disliked the discipline to which he was now subjected, and for a while in 1866 he was withdrawn from school. His mother saw that he was adequately fed and allowed him to walk and to go out with the local fishermen. On one occasion he played some part in rescuing Swinburne, who had a cottage at Etretat and had got into difficulties while swimming. By 1868 Maupassant had clearly outgrown Yvetot, although "expulsion" is probably too dramatic a term to describe what happened to him at the seminary, on account no doubt of cumulative impertinence.

In 1866, when Laure's mother died, Flaubert, who had sent Laure a copy of *Salammbô* when it appeared in 1862, wrote her a letter of condolence. She replied in histrionically courageous terms about her ordeal, her hopes, and her sons. She had clearly conceived literary ambitions for Maupassant, but may not have realized when she welcomed him back from Yvetot that too much contact with her own dramatic personality could be damaging to a son who was clearly sensitive, however physically robust. Maupassant's later uncontrollable promiscuity may well be at any rate partly explained by his relationship with his mother, who was proud of his first sexual conquests at 16. For the moment she merely moved to Rouen so that he could complete his education. There Maupassant became a close friend of Louis Bouilhet, who had replaced Alfred Le Poittevin as Flaubert's closest companion, and who helped Maupassant with his verse. He was to die in July 1869, at the age of 46. Maupassant duly passed his baccalauréat in that month and, after the summer at Etretat, began to study law in Paris, living in the same building as his father, of whom he saw a good deal.

The threat of war forced him to interrupt his studies and enlist, and his father managed to pull enough strings to see that his army career was smoothed, although the Franco-Prussian War was to furnish the background for some of the more memorable later short stories or "contes," which were critical of both the Prussian invaders and the military swaggering of France's new army of shopkeepers turned generals. Maupassant wrote patriotic letters to his mother, and he seems from his later journalism to have been critical of both sides in the Commune uprising in Paris which followed the armistice, although he did not witness it at first hand. He passed the aptitude tests for the supply corps, was based at Rouen, and was once nearly taken prisoner while on a mission to the front. He was posted to Le Havre, and left Paris before the siege. With his father's help he managed to find a paid replacement and thereby achieve demobilization before the end of 1871.

His father, who appears to have had another financial crisis in 1872, got Maupassant into the admiralty. He worked his way through various posts until, with Flaubert's help, he was appointed to the ministry of education in 1878, at which date his father was still paying him a small allowance. His initial salary had been 125 francs a month with an annual bonus of 150 francs. As a Parisian bureaucrat he largely completed the repertoire of backgrounds he was to draw on for the contes, and which included Norman peasants, the Franco-Prussian War, Paris clerks, soldiers, and the Parisian working classes enjoying their rumbustious pleasures on the banks of the Seine below Paris.

Maupassant had just about enough money to live carefully in Paris. Bored by the lack of a social life and the philistinism of his colleagues, under Flaubert's tutelage he began to take his writing more seriously. From 1876 Flaubert lived mostly at Croisset, visiting Paris only occasionally, but by then he had started to take Maupassant in hand. He wrote flatteringly to Laure in 1873 about Maupassant's verse, "as good as anything published by the Parnassian school of poets (q.v.)," encouraged his young protégé to write "some broader and longer work," invited him to his Sunday afternoon gatherings in the Rue Murillo, and effected introductions to Parisian literary society, to patrons like Mme Brainne and Princesse Mathilde, editors and publishers like Charpentier, Mendès, and Raoul-Duval, actresses like Suzanne Lagier and Apollonie Sabatier, and authors like Turgenev, Taine, Zola, Daudet, Heredia, Huysmans, Céard, Gautier, Renan, Mérimée, and Edmond de Goncourt.

Meanwhile, however, Maupassant also spent much time swimming, boating, and roistering with congenial friends, girls,

and drinking companions at Argenteuil and further down the Seine, frequenting the floating cabaret at La Grenouillère, painted by Renoir and Monet, the Restaurant Fournaise at Chatou, where Renoir painted *Le Déjeuner des canotiers*, and generally indulging in the idling with which in a letter of 15 August 1878 Flaubert reproached him: "Far too many women, much too much rowing." Outings on the river provided the Paris clerks and their girls with exuberant and cheap weekend recreation, noisily and colourfully releasing the pent-up energies accumulated during weekdays spent in dark offices and gloomy apartments.

At different moments Maupassant owned various boats and took rooms which he shared with friends, spending evenings and nights as well as weekends on the river, rowing and swimming before getting the train back to Paris, and acquiring real prowess with boat, gun, and sword. He was a considerable athlete, with the build of a boxer, and took his manly sports, like his writing, seriously. His whole group gave one another nicknames. It was doubtless in their midst that Maupassant contracted syphilis in 1874. The disease was endemic, often undiagnosed, and incurable. The nature of Maupassant's illness was not at first obvious, and he was to undergo a number of cures for nervous, glandular, and rheumatic conditions. He may well in fact have inherited a glandular complaint from his mother. She suffered from hyperthyroidism and his early physical symptoms, like his later eye troubles, resembled hers. But in spite of losing some hair, which eventually grew back, he continued to look robust and tanned.

Maupassant attended wild parties in Paris, too, although they were often more literary in nature. He was good at making up dirty jokes and collaborated with Robert Pinchon in writing one particularly pornographic sketch, *A la Feuille de rose, maison turque*, of which he boasted to his mother. It was about a young couple going to a brothel by mistake, with the female roles played by men. Reactions to the piece varied. Flaubert laughed, Turgenev and the not exactly prudish Suzanne Lagier were shocked, and Edmond de Goncourt was bored. Vulgar to the core, the sketch, published in a limited edition in 1945, depends on a sophisticated knowledge of sexual techniques.

Flaubert, who knew the importance of realism (q.v.), the nature of Maupassant's talent, his financial circumstances, and the size of the new newspaper market for the conte, recently exploited by Daudet and Zola, began referring publicly to Maupassant as his pupil. Léon Fontaine, a friend from his Rouen days who also worked in Paris and with whom Maupassant shared the house at Argenteuil, asked him for a short story for his cousin's newspaper, and Maupassant's first published conte, a horror story called "La main d'écorché," appeared under the riverside pseudonym of Joseph Prunier in *L'Almanach Lorrain de Pont-à-Musson* in 1875. He had by now turned to the conte without totally abandoning poetry, and was increasing the size of his portfolio. A one-act verse comedy of 300 lines written late in 1875 called "Une répétition" seems never to have been performed, and although at Flaubert's request Raoul-Duval published two critical pieces by Maupassant in *La Nation* in 1876 and 1877, his regular critic protested, and no more were accepted. Negotiations for journalistic work took place, and in 1876 a poem and a second short story were published. Maupassant began work on a historical drama. Zola sent him one of his new novels and Maupassant started to attend Mallarmé's Tuesdays. In the literary world he was still making very little real progress, perhaps because he was still uncertain of the direction he should take.

From 1877 Maupassant's salary improved, but the nature of his infection was now suspected and the hair loss embarrassed him. His association with naturalism (q.v.) increased and he regularly attended the dinners of the group, starting with the famous one at Trapp's given for Zola, Flaubert, and Edmond de Goncourt in 1877. He obtained leave to go to Switzerland for a cure, pseudonymously published another short story, and began *Une vie*, but his literary success remained slight, with a short story published here or there, once or twice a year. In 1879 a play of his, *Histoire du vieux temps*, was produced through the mediation of Pinchon at one of Ballande's matinées, but only on condition that no expenses or fees were involved. Both critics and public liked it. In March 1876 Mendès had published an erotic poem by Maupassant in *La République des Lettres*. Retitled "La fille," it was republished pseudonymously on 1 November 1879 in the *Revue Moderne et Naturaliste*. In 1880 the authorities, who wanted the review suppressed, indicted Maupassant and the review, which defiantly published another poem, "Le mur," and the prosecution, having been discredited, was dropped. Maupassant was now beginning to attract serious attention in naturalist circles.

In May 1880, on Flaubert's intercession, Zola's publisher, Charpentier, published Maupassant's poems, *Des vers*. The volume was well received, and Zola published an article about it. Maupassant now began to contribute regularly to *Le Gaulois*, which had taken his poem "Vénus rustique" when Juliette Adam, to whom Flaubert had forwarded it for the *Nouvelle Revue*, had turned it down on moral grounds. The *Nouvelle Revue*, now referred to by Maupassant as Mme Adam's "boring magazine," did, however, publish his conte "En famille" alongside the final instalment of Flaubert's *Bouvard et Pécuchet* on 1 March 1881. In fact Maupassant, who was never really a naturalist, had merely been exploiting the vogue for naturalist literature by making his erotic poems more explicit. His eye for the market was developing shrewdly, and he became more careful after the reaction provoked by the publication of Zola's *Nana* in 1880. He was to write for *Le Gaulois*, to which Zola had introduced him and which was to be the main vehicle for his journalism until 1888, but with its publication of his poem and the beginnings of his long association with it, the publication of *Des vers*, and the appearance in the 1880 *Les Soirées de Médan* (see Zola) of "Boule de Suif," Maupassant was, at nearly 30, on the threshold of success.

Flaubert had been in financial difficulties since 1876, alleviated in 1879 by a state pension which Maupassant had helped him to obtain. He died in May 1880. Laure, who had been having trouble with her eyesight, had a nervous breakdown, precipitated partly by Flaubert's death and partly by the behaviour of Hervé, who had turned into a profligate, run away, and was deeply in debt. She went to live in Corsica, and Maupassant, whose own eyes had begun to give him trouble, went on a leave which he protracted until his resignation, hoping now to be able to live from his journalism. "Boule de Suif" had been easily the most successful conte in the collective *Les Soirées de Médan*, published on 16 April, a month before *Des vers*. The volume went through eight reprints in a fortnight, and Maupassant eagerly approached Charpentier to find out what his share of the proceeds would be. On 17 April Maupassant had published an account in *Le Gaulois* of how the six authors came to collaborate on the volume.

In 1880 Maupassant's journalism was building up to substantial levels and Tolstoy was beginning to take an interest in his work. "En famille" was about to be published. It was the comic story of the pathetic Caravan, relegated by paternal neglect to a miserable post, conspicuously like Maupassant's own, in the admiralty. This major piece barely disguised the scarcely reasonable resentment Maupassant felt towards his own father, a resentment that was no doubt caused by the intensity of his relationship with his mother. It was Louis Bouilhet who had told Maupassant to "find a subject in harmony with all the tendencies of his mind," and the rejection of a father as worthless is a feature of several powerful contes, such as "Le papa de Simon," written in 1877 and first published in 1879, and the celebrated "Histoire d'une fille de ferme," published three weeks after "En famille" in the *Revue Bleue*. The imaginative patterns confirm a later softening in Maupassant's attitude towards his father, for which there is also historical evidence. Above all, however, Havard was about to publish, in May 1881, Maupassant's first volume of fiction, *La Maison Tellier*, a success with the public but not with the critics. The principal volumes now followed rapidly, the weight being gradually transferred from contes to novels in the course of the 22 volumes of fiction published between 1881 and 1890. Maupassant continued to need money and demanded increasing sums for his work, carefully avoiding contracts which would tie him to any particular publisher.

He had already been to Corsica to see his mother and in June visited North Africa with Harry Alis, proprietor of the *Revue Moderne et Naturaliste*, possibly at the instigation of Arthur Meyer, editor of *Le Gaulois*, which, with the *Revue Bleue*, printed the reports Maupassant wrote and later published as *Au soleil*. Further more or less pornographic poems were published in *Le Nouveau Parnasse Satyrique* of 1881, printed in Belgium to avoid the French censorship, and Maupassant started a long association with the paper *Gil Blas*. He also began to see a good deal of Vallès, who had returned to Paris after the pardon granted to the Communards. In January 1882 Maupassant accidentally shot himself in the hand with a pistol, and in May *Mademoiselle Fifi* appeared. By 1883 there were outward signs in his life of the prosperity brought by literary success, such as his new yacht, the Louisette. In February, the month in which serialization of Maupassant's first novel, *Une vie*, began in *Gil Blas*, Joséphine Litzelmann gave birth to a son, Lucien, whose father is often thought to have been Maupassant, although there is no hard evidence to support the fact. Havard published *Une vie* as a book in April, and the booksellers Hachette were sufficiently frightened by its contents to withdraw it from all French station bookstalls, of which they had the monopoly. Maupassant forced them to rescind and put the book back on sale.

In 1884 Maupassant began to have his house, La Guillette, built at Etretat and hired François Tassart (1866–1949), the valet who refused to wear livery and who made his views about Maupassant's acquaintances quite clear, but wrote so vividly and respectfully about Maupassant himself in the *Revue des Deux Mondes* for 1 March 1911. By now Maupassant was publishing something every week and making a name for himself in Russia, where Tolstoy, sceptical about the moral tone of *La Maison Tellier*, had been won over by *Une vie*. Again the evidence is not hard, but Maupassant seems almost certainly to have been the father of a child born to Hermine Lecomte du Noüy in December 1883, a year in which he published some 70 contes or "Chroniques." He also published a study of Zola in the *Revue Bleue*, stressing the distance between Zola's theory and his practice.

By 1885 his second novel, *Bel-Ami*, was finished and was being serialized in St Petersburg. Maupassant's mother was now wintering near Grasse and Maupassant spent much of the winter at Cannes, where he kept the Louisette. His eyes were giving him increasing trouble, and he cancelled a visit to the Near East, going no further than Italy, which he toured from April to June. He had to write an article defending *Bel-Ami*, which had been serialized in *Gil Blas* during April and May. By 7 July 13,000 copies had been sold, and there were 37 printings in four months. Brunetière, the dedicated opponent of naturalism, thought it the least offensive of the naturalist writings. Maupassant was now leading a more leisured life. He frequented Princesse Mathilde's salon, went to Cannes in winter, to Normandy in the autumn for the shooting, and in the summer to Châtelguyon, a spa in central France virtually owned by a doctor called Potain where Maupassant sometimes took his father. Hervé got engaged and Maupassant helped him to start a farm near a house he had bought for his mother at Cannes. The tally of contes and "Chroniques" in the dailies was diminishing, however, following the 1883 peak. There were about 60 in 1884 and 30 in 1885. Maupassant boasted that they took him no more than a day each to write.

Hervé was married in January 1886, in which year Maupassant dashed off five articles on the annual Salon. He came close to fighting a duel after an attack on him, but continued his social life in literary circles, now meeting, among others, Mirbeau, Alexis, Bourget, and Barrès. He also continued to womanize. He visited England at the invitation of the Rothschilds, going first to their home in Piccadilly, and then to Waddesdon. He saw little of London except Mme Tussaud's, the Savoy Theatre, and the Café Royal. Selections of his stories and second editions were now beginning to appear. In the space of five years he had become a literary celebrity. *Mademoiselle Fifi* was turned into a play but never staged, and Maupassant joined in the protest against Eiffel's projected tower, due to be finished in 1889. During the summer of 1887 at Etretat he canoed, read the first pages of *Pierre et Jean* to Hermine Lecomte du Noüy, and oversaw the building of his house. The number of contes and "Chroniques" continued to diminish, to 24 in 1886 and 20 in 1887.

In July 1887 Maupassant flew from Paris to Belgium in a balloon amid considerable publicity, sending a telegram to Hermine to announce his safe arrival. Joséphine Litzelmann's second child had been born in 1884 and a third was born in July 1887. Maupassant's paternity of all three is likely. He was gaining a reputation for pricing his work too highly, but was driven by the desire not only to enjoy a luxurious life style, but also to provide for his mother, brother, and father, and pay his own medical expenses. By the autumn of 1887 Hervé showed the first signs of being mentally unbalanced. Maupassant went to Normandy as usual for the shooting, and spent some of the winter in North Africa, negotiating further and increasingly lucrative contracts for journalistic and literary work. In 1888 Marpon and Flammarion published a personal book of Maupassant's, *Sur l'eau*, to which he attached great importance. His mother, whose health had now broken down completely, was living on the Côte d'Azur. Maupassant spent some time in Normandy selling one of her farms for her. Towards the end of the year the decline in Hervé's health accelerated and Maupassant says that his own headaches prevented him from working for two months. There seems to have been a remission in his illness,

however, and Maupassant went cruising in the Mediterranean on his new 40-foot Bel-Ami II, swimming daily, appearing to be in good health, and entertaining a horde of distinguished guests from the social as well as the literary world. He was accorded what was beginning to look like the ultimate literary accolade when Nadar took his photograph, but by 1888 the number of contes and "Chroniques" in the dailies was down to eight. His *La Paix du ménage*, a two-act comedy was accepted in 1888, although not staged until 1893.

Maupassant's mother was asking 30,000 francs for the farm, and on Maupassant's side money was now flowing in from rights to his works. He received 100 francs for the German rights to "M Perle," 400 francs for the German rights to "Le champ d'oliviers," 1,000 francs for the rights to the novel *Fort comme la mort* in Spain and another 500 for Latin America. The serialization of *Une vie* had brought 8,000 francs and the royalties were 40 centimes a copy on the first 2,000 copies of each book and one franc a copy thereafter. Contracts were for six years only and reserved the rights to de luxe editions, for which Maupassant charged 2,000 francs for 500 copies. The Russian translation of *Une vie* brought in 2,000 francs. Newspaper articles brought in between 500 and 1,500 francs each. Maupassant's sales were exceeding those of Loti, Bourget, and Anatole France, but he was working and necessarily socializing too much for his health. His income had risen from 40,000 francs in 1885 to 120,000 francs, but he found a use for all the money his work could bring him. He had homes in Paris, Etretat, and Antibes, yachts and staff to maintain, while his particular extravagance was luxurious travel, taking for instance 44 pieces of luggage to Algeria in 1890. He continued to be generous, too, not only with his family but in subscribing, for instance, to Mallarmé's fund for Villiers de l'Isle-Adam.

Maupassant also hired a villa at Triel, near Vaux, where he entertained, one of his more frequent guests being the beautiful young Countess Potocka, famous for her perverted whims and orgiastic dinners. He exchanged intimate letters with her, and she appears to have been the first woman to dominate him since his mother, the partners in his other documented relationships being clearly submissive. From 1888 Maupassant also had as his mistress a dancer called "Yvonne," for whom he wanted to hire a house at Aix. She died at the end of 1891, two years after Hervé, and Tassart opposed a last visit by Maupassant to the hospital of Saint-Lazare. In June 1889 Mirbeau had already remarked on Maupassant's own haunting fear of death as the cause of his incessant movement. His continued gaucheness and the coarseness of his private humour did not stop him from frequenting the grander salons, such as those of Marie Kann, the former mistress of Paul Bourget, and Génevieve Straus, with each of whom he had an affair. He abandoned Triel, where the succession of visitors was preventing him from working, for Etretat, and during 1889 his relationship with Emmanuela Potocka intensified. He went for a long cruise on the Bel-Ami, visited Tunis, was ill in Florence and, on Hervé's death on 13 November, went to stay with his mother, destroying his notes on his journey through Italy. In 1889 he published about 10 contes and "Chroniques" in the dailies.

From 1890 Maupassant's health declined erratically, although he was scarcely ever free of pain. He still moved about a great deal, and still managed to work, although his eyes were causing increasing trouble. His travel book *La Vie errante* was published in 1890 and Maupassant had a copy printed on special paper for Marie Kann. In the summer he experienced a period of intellectual hyperactivity characteristic of his disease, and renewed his friendship with Henry Cazalis, the doctor and, under the name of "Jean Lahor," poet who would watch over his last months. He scarcely worked again, attended with difficulty to business affairs, allowed Nadar to sell the proofs of his portrait photographs, consulted well over half a dozen medical authorities, and continued to travel. When he did work, it was on his unfinished novels. The diagnosis of syphilis had been mentioned only once since the mid-1870s as a possible explanation in 1883 for his eye trouble, and before that references in his correspondence had been merely jocular. Towards the end of 1891, however, Maupassant knew what he was dying of. He had become irascible, litigious, and high-handed, and was by now lucidly aware of the progress of the disease. On the night of 1 January 1892 he tried to shoot himself, but Tassart had removed the bullets from his pistol. Maupassant then tried to pierce his throat with a paper knife and subsequently to throw himself out of the window. On 7 January he was taken to hospital in Paris in a straitjacket, accompanied by Tassart and a nurse. He died there 18 months later, six months after his sanity had finally given way, on 6 July 1893.

WORKS

Compared only with his mentors, Flaubert and Zola successively, Maupassant remains a minor author with a limited range of subject matter. The contes are admittedly small in scale and mainly limited to sketches of peasant and working-class life. They do not have the depth to support the architecture or sustain the characterization required of a full-scale novel, and it has been argued that his six published novels are not among Maupassant's best work. On the other hand a panel of distinguished writers consisting of Gide, Giraudoux, Jaloux, Mauriac, and Maurois put *Une vie* on the list of France's 10 greatest novels, and most critics would put *Pierre et Jean* above it. As a writer of contes, Maupassant towers above those contemporaries who approached him in popularity, Daudet and Loti. The literary qualities of the work of both are now commonly thought to have been overvalued, while the value of Maupassant's work, although it does not always avoid the opposing perils of coarseness and sentimentality, may still for that reason have been underestimated. It is of much more than period charm and merely historical interest.

Of the four genres in which Maupassant published, poetry, journalism, the short story, and the novel, the short story is the one in which he succeeded most unfailingly and in which his world-class mastery is undisputed. The poetry, on which Flaubert commented favourably, appealed to that part of Flaubert's imagination which did not inspire his own best work, and too often merely exploits a vogue for naturalism in a way which degrades both love and its female object. This is obviously true of the poems published under the naturalist umbrella of the *Revue Moderne et Naturaliste* ("La fille" and "Le mur"), and of those which appeared in *Le Nouveau Parnasse Satyrique* ("Ma source," "Salut, grosse Putain," and "La femme à barbe"), but even elsewhere the poems do not express or explore any personal emotion in a particularly interesting light. They are at best worthy examples of a literary trend, but in Maupassant's productive life they came first, and they straightaway raise the difficult question of his allegedly degrading treatment of women.

All Maupassant's biographers agree on the domineering and selfish nature of his mother's relationship with him. Over-ambitious for his literary success, she was almost certainly to blame for his later inability to form a stable emotional bond with any other woman, and therefore for his blatant tendency both personally and in his literary work to regard women from the exclusive point of view of their sexual appeal. Maupassant's treatment of fathers in the contes confirms that some important patterns of later imaginative investigation derive from the experiences of his early youth. His prostitutes may therefore be courageous, generous, sympathetically sketched, and amusingly anomalous characters, but the short story form protects Maupassant from the need to plumb the full depths of their human potential.

There are ways in which Maupassant's achievement resembles Daumier's. Like the caricaturist he can isolate and satirize a single vividly striking characteristic or attitude. The reasons he chose to concentrate on the short story form, at least until the balance shifted towards the novels in his late thirties, cannot have been exclusively bound up with space or payment, since serialization of novels removed any limitations on length, and on the whole produced a larger financial return than the placing of short stories, the alternative form of the fiction which comprised virtually the entire printed content of many of the "newspapers." Maupassant may of course have felt, particularly during the early years of his productive decade that the short story, with its lesser imaginative demand on the emotions, was more time-effective in the generation of income, even if less lucrative word for word.

Maupassant's journalism makes no serious pretensions to literary merit, although it sometimes raises important considerations with regard to literature or the visual arts. We have lost sight of most of his articles for *Le Gaulois* and *Gil Blas*. What is important is the way in which the "Chroniques" tended more and more to include anecdote. The journalist was preparing the ground for the short story writer, as perhaps the short story writer for the novelist, even when the three types of literary activity were virtually simultaneous. When in the later 1880s Maupassant, now well off but still short of money, reduced the number of articles and short stories in favour of the more ambitious novels, it may well have been a genuine desire to deepen and broaden his literary range that was at stake. He was after all not yet 43 when he died.

It is clear from his biography that Maupassant used the publicity and shock generated by association with Zola and his followers to attract attention and sales, but that he was uncommitted to any form of naturalistic dogma. He stressed Zola's own divergence in practice from the norms he professed in theory and he withdrew from too close an association with the *Revue Moderne et Naturaliste* when the threatened prosecution endangered his post at the ministry of education, to which, until 1882, he retained the right to return. In a letter to Flaubert of 24 April 1879 Maupassant criticizes Zola for a touch of arrogance in wanting to make himself the leading literary scientist of his age, ridiculing Zola's claim to reveal the ultimate truth about man and his environment. Nothing remains of any school, Maupassant says, but a few individual treatments of great men. When, encouraged by Daudet and Goncourt, five of Zola's younger colleagues attacked *La Terre* in *Le Figaro* in 1887, Maupassant sat on the fence, simply declaring his preference for the text as it appeared in the book over the serialized extracts. The preface to *Pierre et Jean*, a short treatise on the contemporary novel added because the text was too short, is not really naturalistic, but merely restates Flaubert's views on what the author adds to his subject matter by choosing, ordering, and presenting it. Flaubert had been expressing his hostility to all schools and manifestos, but was in fact thinking of Zola's naturalism. Maupassant's preface, published by *Le Figaro* on 7 January 1888, is the most concise expression of his literary credo, but caused disproportionate attention because the subediting so mutilated Maupassant's text as to make it in parts unintelligible. He even threatened legal action.

The early short stories include some which lean towards the gothic terrors of the supernatural and the macabre, reflecting the tastes of the romantics (q.v.) and the influence of Poe. The protagonists of "Le docteur Héraclius Gloss" (unpublished until 1921) and "La main d'écorché" both go mad. Other early contes, including the sketches "Les dimanches d'un bourgeois de Paris," uncollected in Maupassant's lifetime, draw realistically on contemporary life, its bourgeois attitudes and the values of the Second Empire, peasants' superstitions and tragedies, and the recreational life of the working classes. Maupassant excellently fabricates the instant suspense which he later preferred to avoid, and is an intriguing narrator, capable of generating real terror.

Beneath the surface of most of his fiction, there is a disillusioned idealism which juxtaposes dreams with the dehumanized and the macabre, an imaginative pattern which reflects the author's own insecure psychological make-up, ultimately no doubt the result of an overprotected upbringing. Comparatively few of the contes end in the ironic twists which, when they occur, are so memorable, but underlying most of them is pessimism at the futility of human effort. Just as in *Des vers* love's idealism is shattered on its harshly sensual reality, love in the contes is generally ephemeral, destined to die, unsatisfied, its ecstasy perpetually thwarted and incapable of resuscitation. The best that can be hoped for is crude physical satisfaction. The romantic obsession with the medieval motif of death and the maiden, in which sexual satisfaction is linked with death, as it so often is in Zola, is never far away. In Maupassant the object of love is quite likely to turn out to be a prostitute or to die in the lover's arms. The implied moral is clear. The only way to protect oneself from disillusion is to indulge in the promiscuity which promises nothing. Stable, satisfying, and mutually supportive relationships do not exist at the centre of Maupassant contes.

Like the contes of the other five writers (Zola, Huysmans, Hennique, Céard, and Alexis) who had contributed to *Les Soirées de Médan*, "Boule de Suif" had to have a connection with the Franco-Prussian War. Huysmans had apparently been dismissive of Mérimée, quipping that a short story writer was someone "who, not knowing how to write, expressed himself pretentiously on insignificant things." The idea behind the collective volume, about whose title there was some dispute, was to be not anti-patriotic but unchauvinistic and devoid of hyped enthusiasm, giving "une note juste sur la guerre (an accurate flavour of the war)", cynical perhaps, but not satirical. The generals after all were not supermen, but ordinary people, not particularly endowed, who got people killed not from ill will but from simple stupidity. To say that would exasperate the bourgeois a good deal more than a direct attack on the military. The

accounts would not be unpatriotic, simply true to the reality. In fact the preface to the volume was inevitably interpreted as a provocatively naturalistic manifesto. Flaubert, who was enthusiastic about "Boule de Suif," counselled the cautious removal of two gratuitous touches capable of appearing provocative.

"Boule de Suif" is about a French prostitute obliged by her fellow-passengers to sleep with a Prussian officer. She had shared with the others the food she had brought, but the tearful woman is subsequently snubbed by those travelling with her in the coach. The story was modelled on life. The Rouen prostitute, Adrienne Legay, was an acquaintance of Maupassant's uncle, called Cornudet in the conte. It did Maupassant no harm that his story, which contained a strong denunciation of bourgeois hypocrisy, was clearly the best of the six. The contrasts of peoples, situations, and standards make it a short masterpiece, shot through with irony and parody, amusing and at the same time both trenchant and compassionate. The subject is low-life, but the sentiments are not. Henry James much admired the paring back of physical description and psychological analysis in order to allow the story to make its own vivid point as succinctly as possible, very often in direct speech. In a sense the conte is anti-naturalistic, so clearly does it indicate the author's attitude towards his characters.

"La Maison Tellier" uses a more sentimental and directly humorous irony. The prostitutes of a Rouen brothel attend the first Communion of the proprietor's niece and have to close the brothel for the day. The matter-of-fact way in which the men go to the brothel as they might go to the tobacconist's or the paper shop, and the business-like efficiency of Mme Tellier in running her house, contrast with the reticence hypocritically observed among the bourgeois but not the working class about such things. The prostitutes themselves are honest, hard-working girls, presented as almost innocently satisfying the perfectly natural needs of the men. In church the girls are touched to tears. Madame takes her niece, nervous before the ceremony, into her own bed. There is no biting satire here, except perhaps of those who wish to pretend that brothels do not exist, or that their employees are not ordinary, sentimental girls, anxious to please and prepared to be moved. The satire could only hit those who regard as wicked what is normal, natural, and therefore in a profound sense innocent. At most Maupassant laughs at the frustration of the men who find the brothel incongruously closed for a first Communion.

The third famous conte involving prostitution is "Mademoiselle Fifi." A band of Prussian officers try to kill their boredom by destroying the works of art in the château in which they are billeted and then call for a group of prostitutes for the evening. One officer, sardonically nicknamed "Mademoiselle Fifi" because of his contempt for the French, proposes a toast to the Prussian conquest of all the women of France, and is stabbed to death by Rachel, the Jewish prostitute he has on his knee. She escapes and ironically rings the church bell at the Prussian's funeral. The savagery of the irony here lies in the fact that the patriot is working-class, a prostitute, and a Jew. She marries a wealthy husband and is then, by inference, worthier of bourgeois privilege than those whose caste she joins.

Maupassant's characters, the Norman peasants, the Paris clerks, bureaucrats, soldiers and sailors, misfits and outcasts, are sometimes treated farcically, as in "Toine," occasionally with nearly undiluted tragedy, as in "Monsieur Parent," but mostly with the pathos which is a mixture of both. Idylls, when they happen, occur in the memory. They are recalled, not real. Dramas, when they take place, are frequently defused by the interposition of a narrator who, since he knows the outcome, removes much of the suspense. Women can gain control of their lives only by defiance. The narrators sympathize with the deceivers rather than with the comically deceived husbands. There is almost always implied moral comment, and invariably artistry in the deft selection of telling detail, in the narrator's refusal to succumb to the temptation to dazzle or shock, whatever the content of the story, and in the compassionate depiction of the ordinary, the despised, and the unregarded.

Although many of the characters do come from a bougeois environment, Maupassant is at his least constrained when satirizing the system of values they have erected to buttress the crude wealth which supports their elevated status. In the *Mademoiselle Fifi* volume, there is an amusing conte entitled "Un réveillon" (the term used for Christmas night when Mass is said at midnight) in which a Norman peasant couple remove the grandfather's corpse from his deathbed and stick it in a box under the table where they are eating, since they want the bed. They speak in patois, and this conte is in fact a satire of grim peasant realism, with the narrator taking the side of the bourgeois who, not having to sleep on the floor, can afford to show more respect for the dead.

Mademoiselle Fifi also contains contes which show women in a much less favourable light than did the title story of the volume. In "Marroca" a woman is depicted as willing to murder her husband with an axe in order to get from the narrator the sexual satisfaction that she needs: "Et voilà...comment on comprend ici les devoirs conjugaux, l'amour et l'hospitalité (And that is...how they understand marital duties, love, and hospitality here)." Not only is sex portrayed as brutal and unfulfilling at any but the physical level, but the conte, in spite of its tabloid quality, is aimed straight at the educated readers of *Gil Blas*, a "newspaper" founded in 1879 by Auguste Dumont to exploit the public taste for indelicacy, and consisting almost entirely of articles, stories, and gossip. Its speciality was the Pygmalion-like creation of real-life pseudo-aristocratic courtesans with false titles whose doings then became the matter of its gossip columns. The rest of the Paris press organized in vain what amounted to an invitation to the authorities to prosecute, only managing thereby to increase the paper's circulation. In writing for it Maupassant used the pseudonym "Maufrigneuse," although his real identity was revealed almost immediately by the publication of the *Mademoiselle Fifi* volume by Kistemaeckers.

In "La bûche," another of the stories from *Mademoiselle Fifi* originally published in *Gil Blas* by "Maufrigneuse," the narrator makes clear his lowly view of women. Explaining why he never married, he recounts how, but for having had to get up to put a burning log back into the fire, he would have been caught making love to a woman by her husband, his former inseparable companion, who had returned home unexpectedly early. The narrator explains:

> When a friend gets married, it's over, all over. A woman's jealous love, a brooding love, anxious and carnal, can't abide the strong open union of minds and hearts, the trust that exists between two men. You see, whatever the love that joins them, a man and a woman are always strangers to one another's minds and souls. They stay hostile. They

come from different races. One is always the tamer, the other the tamed...They are never equal.

The difficulty is to know how far this view, which could reasonably be regarded as sexist, is Maupassant's own. It is put into the mouth of a narrator of a piece of fiction, and could be as lame an excuse for not marrying as the need to use a bed was for removing a corpse. It was published in a newspaper which was increasing its circulation by going down-market in taste by an author not yet well off, whose first concern was to sell his material.

That there was a complacency in Maupassant's mind when he wrote stories featuring physical sex is clear from the style as well as from his biography, and the recurrence of the imaginative patterns suggests that they had deep roots in his experience. We cannot however merely assume that Maupassant shared the view of the narrator of "La bûche," or even that the recourse to titillation in the famous *Gil Blas* pieces excuses any neglect of their often consummate literary artistry. A careful reading of "Une aventure parisienne" from the same newspaper, also collected in *Mademoiselle Fifi*, about the wife of a provincial lawyer who goes to Paris, sees a famous writer in a bookshop, follows him, sleeps with him, and is disillusioned by the experience, reveals reticence where sexual explicitness would have been possible, a deadly use of adverbs ("dully virtuous"), and the recurrent bursting of the bubble of romantic dreams which is Maupassant's strength, as it was Flaubert's: "She was simple, as only the legitimate wife of a country lawyer could be, and he more demanding than a lord with three tails." Maupassant or his narrators judge the characters more directly than Flaubert ever did, but what makes these vignettes into masterful literary sketches is the irony of disillusion, the ruthlessness with which hypocrisy is exposed, and the sardonic realism with which the characters are depicted. There is also a dazzling virtuosity in the selection of detail and an appositeness of metaphor and image.

In *Le Gaulois* of 20 and 28 July 1882, a few weeks after the appearance of the *Mademoiselle Fifi* volume, Maupassant defended his protest against the idealistic and poetic view of life still hypocritically affected by the opponents of naturalism. The concentration on low-life social levels redresses a balance, as he sees it. Here, basing himself on Schopenhauer's view of women, as recently translated by his friend Jean Bourdeau, and speaking in his own name, he does attack the idealization of women, for which he blames Christianity, but his concern is not to degrade, merely to burst again the romantic bubble thanks to which, under the Second Empire, the minds of the upper middle classes continued to be dominated by essentially hypocritical values. It followed of course that literature must shock those for whom it was written by jolting them into an understanding of the hypocritical or otherwise objectionable character of the values to which they adhered. Literature, if it was to fulfil its function, had to disturb those to whom it had to be sold, even in newspaper form. The public, as Maupassant knew, and as every newspaper editor very well knows, has to be pleased while it is being shocked and enlightened, or it will cease to buy, but authors, publishers, and editors who refrain from shocking at all simply in order to please do not produce "literature." Maupassant was stung by Vallès into admitting in *Le Gaulois* for 11 December 1883 that "we do not write for ordinary people...Art is only for the intellectual aristocracy."

Of the six novels, *Une vie* (1883) *Bel-Ami* (1885) *Mont-Oriol* (1887) *Pierre et Jean* (1888) *Fort comme la mort* (1889) and

Notre coeur (1890), *Pierre et Jean* was considered the best both by Zola and by Henry James. The protagonists are the doctor and lawyer sons of a retired Parisian jeweller living in Le Havre. Both love the same woman, the young widow Mme Rosémilly. Jean Roland inherits a fortune from an old family friend and frequent visitor to the house, M. Maréchal. Pierre assumes he must have been Jean's real father. Mme Rosémilly has always seemed to prefer Jean and agrees to marry him. Pierre persecutes his mother in an attempt to discover the truth, and his mother knows what he suspects. Pierre, jealous on account both of the money and of Mme Rosémilly, blurts out his suspicions to Jean and, in a dramatic and moving confrontation, Jean learns from his mother that Pierre is of course right. Jean rids the family of Pierre's embarrassing presence by getting him on to a transatlantic liner as the ship's doctor, and the novel ends with Pierre's departure.

Pierre's harrowing disillusion as his envy turns to jealous fury makes the novel too cruel, as Maupassant later came to realize, to have sold as well as he would have wished. Pierre's pessimism, misogyny, and disillusion, though here treated corrosively, are attitudes common to characters in the contes. In the high-life setting of this almost full-length novel, the idealism of love remains alive thanks to the relationship between Jean and his mother, and despite Pierre's disillusion, Jean's bereavement, and his father's continued ignorance of Jean's parentage. Maupassant avoids here the destruction of a deceitful front by gossip and scandalemongering which the reader half expects. Hermine Lecomte du Noüy tells us that Maupassant went to Le Havre to research the background for the novel, further linking himself to the tradition inaugurated by Flaubert and carried to such lengths by Zola.

Bel-Ami is the story of a social climber who also uses the political ladder as he moves from the prostitutes of the Folies Bergères to a sumptuous wedding in the Madeleine with the promise of ennoblement and the hope of political power. It is probably the most widely read of Maupassant's novels today and, like all the novels except the first, it has a high-life setting. *Une vie* had included the gratuitous ill-treatment of a mother by her son, which it is temptingly easy to tie in with Maupassant's own need to exorcize his emotional disturbances at the level of imaginative exposition, particularly since the pattern is repeated, if less stridently, in *Pierre et Jean*, where it is also counterbalanced by the relationship to his mother of her second son. *Bel-Ami*, the secoWnd novel, still treats women at best summarily, since the steps of Georges Duroy's ladders are a series of seductions which result in the humiliation of the four women principally involved. The episodic action is appropriate to newspaper serialization, and the selection of reticent detail is as deft as Maupassant readers would, in 1885, have come to expect, but nothing yet alleviates the underlying sense of the futility of the protagonist's climb, and nowhere yet does idealism survive the cynical moral observation that only the strong endure.

The low-life conte *Yvette*, which immediately preceded *Bel-Ami*, relates with compassion the story of a courtesan's naively innocent daughter who, at 18, discovers that she is, and will remain, an outcast. Her mother, now known as the Marquise Obardie, is a former cook, and the longish conte contains a marvellous, economical, and evocative description of the famous floating cabaret La Grenouillère. The story concludes with Yvette, having attempted suicide, about to accept Jean de Servigny as her lover, although he is too well born to contemplate marrying her. Tolstoy rightly found the ending too hurtful.

The scathing moral comment on Servigny's self-satisfied egotism is too piano and betrays Maupassant's continuing low valuation of female integrity, although he seems to be struggling to overcome it here. In the full-length high-life novel which immediately followed the conte he does little to conceal his contempt for the narcissistic unpleasantness of the central male figure, of whose ultimate downfall the reader remains confident.

Pierre et Jean confirms Maupassant's ability to sustain the novel form, and combines that form and a high-life background with at least one idealized relationship between man and mother. Unhappily, though, Maupassant's powers of concentration were diminishing as he became increasingly interested in the full-length novel and the depiction of bourgeois characters. The patterns of his imagination were changing, and while he was just as keen as ever to earn money, his technique was by now sufficiently developed for him no longer to have to rely on such relatively facile devices as patois and interposed story tellers to make his moral comment on society. His technique was better than Zola's, and there are signs that he might have been developing into a more powerful novelist. Stendhal was 44 when he published his first fiction, 50 when he wrote his first great novel. Maupassant finally became insane at the age of 42.

Publications

Collections

Oeuvres complètes, 29 vols., 1907–10
Contes et nouvelles, edited by Albert-Marie Schmidt, 2 vols., 1964–67
Oeuvres complètes, 20 vols., 1969–73
Contes et nouvelles, Bibliothèque de la Pléiade, 2 vols., 1974–79
Romans, Bibliothèque de la Pléiade, 2 vols., 1987
Complete Works, 9 vols., 1910
Works, 10 vols., 1923–29
Complete Short Stories, 3 vols., 1970

Fiction

La Maison Tellier, 1881
Mademoiselle Fifi, 1882
Une vie, 1883
Contes de la Bécasse, 1883
Miss Harriet, 1883
Clair de lune, 1884
Les Soeurs Rondoli, 1884
Yvette, 1885
Bel-Ami, 1885; as *Bel-Ami* (in English), 1891
Contes et nouvelles, 1885
Contes du jour et de la nuit, 1885
Monsieur Parent, 1885
Toine, 1886
La Petite Roque, 1886
Mont-Oriol, 1887; as *Mont-Oriol* (in English), 1891
Le Horla, 1887
Pierre et Jean, 1888; as *Pierre and Jean*, 1890
Le Rosier de Madame Husson, 1888
La Main gauche, 1889
Fort comme la mort, 1889; as *Strong as Death*, 1899; as *The Master Passion*, 1958

L'Inutile Beauté, 1890
Notre coeur, 1890; as *Notre Coeur (The Human Heart)*, 1890
Les Dimanches d'un bourgeois de Paris, 1901
88 Short Stories, 1928

Plays

Une répétition, 1879
Histoire du vieux temps (produced 1879), in *Des vers*, 1880
Musotte, with Jacques Normand, from a story by Maupassant
    (produced 1891), in *Oeuvres complètes illustrées*, 1904
La Paix du ménage, from a story by Maupassant (produced
    1893)
A la femille de rose, maison turque (privately performed, 1875),
    1945

Verse

Des vers, 1880

Other

Au soleil, 1884
Sur l'eau, 1888
La Vie errante, 1890

Bibliography

Artinian, Artine, *Maupassant Criticism in France 1880–1940*,
    1941
Artinian, Robert Willard, *Maupassant Criticism: A Centennial
    Bibliography 1880–1979*, 1982

Critical studies

Bond, Ernest, *Maupassant: A Biographical Study*, 1928
Steegmuller, Francis, *Maupassant: A Lion in the Path*, 1949
Sullivan, Edward D., *Maupassant the Novelist*, 1954
Kirkbridge, R. de L., *The Private Life of Guy de Maupassant*,
    1961
Sullivan, Edward D., *Maupassant: The Short Stories*, 1962
Ignotus, Pál, *The Paradox of Maupassant*, 1967
Dugan, John R., *Illusion and Reality: A Study of the Descriptive
    Techniques in the Works of Maupassant*, 1973
Wallace, Albert H., *Maupassant (in English)*, 1973
Lerner, Michael G., *Maupassant (in English)*, 1975

MAURIAC, Claude, 1914–

Writer and journalist.

LIFE

Claude Mauriac was born in Paris on 25 April 1914, the son of
the novelist and journalist François Mauriac and of his wife,
Jeanne Lafon. The family was affluent, owning houses in and
estates near Bordeaux, and Mauriac's father, once a firm supporter of de Gaulle, was internationally known. Claude was
educated in Paris, at the Lycée Janson-de-Sailly, and brought
up in constant contact with writers, editors, journalists, and
political figures of renown. His younger brother, Jean, born in
1924, was also to become well known as a writer and journalist. Mauriac studied at the Sorbonne, where he graduated in
arts before taking his doctorate in law. He had already published his first book of essays, the *Introduction à une mystique
de l'enfer*, at the age of 24, in 1938, in which year he visited
Czechoslovakia.

Mobilized at the outbreak of war, Mauriac spent the winter of
1939–40 at Saint-Cyr. After the defeat of France he escaped to
join the Free French forces and finished the war as de Gaulle's
private secretary, which he remained from 1944 to 1949. In
1949 he founded the review *Liberté de l'Esprit*, remaining a
director until 1953. As a journalist after the war, he worked
chiefly for *Le Figaro* (1946–77), where he had also worked
briefly from 1938 to 1939, and from 1947 to 1972 he was film
critic for *Le Figaro Littéraire*. In 1977 he became film critic for
Vendredi, Samedi, Dimanche. A convinced Gaullist during and
immediately after the war, Mauriac moved slowly towards the
left. In 1978 he moved to *Le Monde* and in 1986 to *Le Matin*. On
11 July 1951 he married Marie-Claude Mante, who was to bear
him three children, Gérard, Nathalie, and Gilles.

Shortly after the war Mauriac published *Malraux; ou, Le Mal
du héros*, virtually a formal welcome to Malraux into the
Gaullist fold. The following year he published his much-
admired *André Breton*, which won the Prix Sainte-Beuve, but
thereafter nothing in volume form until his first novels—*Toutes
les femmes sont fatales* and *Le Dîner en ville*—with the exception of the first diary snippet, *Conversations avec André Gide* of
1951, the year Gide died. Although Mauriac was awarded the
Prix Médicis for his second novel, critical reception had been
mixed, and Mauriac was straining to free himself from his
father's literary image, which, as we know from his diary, he
found overwhelming. He continued, however, to publish novels.
They share with those of many of his contemporaries a preoccupation with the nature of time and the problems of writing
novels. They are ingenious, technically interesting, umbilically
attached to themselves, but happily less pretentious than some
of the critical writing that has been devoted to them.

It has been suggested that Mauriac is more gifted as an
essayist, theoretician, and diarist than as a novelist. He
describes himself as a "writer and journalist" and, although the
classification into genres is uncertain, claimed by the age of 60
to have written nine novels, including *L'Agrandissement* of
1963, which is really a reflection in the form of a novel on how
the three novels which preceded it came to get written. It is a
conventionally punctuated but unparagraphed interior monologue of perhaps 75,000 words. Since early youth Mauriac has
kept a diary, five volumes of extracts from which have been
published. He has also compiled the small book on his father,
François Mauriac, sa vie et son oeuvre. However, since 1974
Mauriac has been publishing what will no doubt turn out to
have been his greatest achievement, a series of diary extracts
arranged according not to chronological sequence, but to
mental associations, so that the reader is asked to leap years
between relatively short extracts, and then perhaps halfway
back again, before going on, or back, a bit more. Significantly

the work has the overall title of its first volume, *Le Temps immobile*. The 10th volume, *L'Oncle Marcel* of 1988, was awarded the Prix Marcel Proust.

Works

It is possible that the essential inspiration of *Le Temps immobile* comes from the cinema, with its ability to manipulate chronology by using flashbacks, visions of the future, dream sequences, and other ways round ordinary sequential narrative by which, until World War II, the conventional novel was generally felt to be constricted. The trouble about *Le Temps immobile* is that Mauriac is not no one and did not start from nowhere. The struggle to free himself from the tutelage of a father to whom he was, incidentally, deeply attached, is quite clear throughout. None the less, Mauriac could not simply shrug off his inheritance. Writing in French for a literate French public, he could not both publish an honest diary and not mention the household names whom he meets, eats or drinks with, writes to or hears from daily. *Le Temps immobile* starts with the disadvantage that the reader expects, and wants, a straight narrative account of what it was like to live as Mauriac did, with his father and the rest of his family, in the milieu in which he was brought up, and then in the inevitably half-literary and half-political environment into which fate had simply decreed that he should be projected.

Le Temps immobile consists solely of dated diary extracts which quite frequently refer back or forwards to other extracts, perhaps in other volumes, and quite often artificially include short qutotations from letters received or books read. As in his novels, only here with more literary justification, Mauriac openly reflects in his diary about the composition of the work into which he is inserting extracts from it, sometimes as he writes them. No index is provided, so that the reader cannot use the diary as he can, for instance, Gide's diary to follow autobiographical threads, notably by following the chronological development of particular relationships.

For the reasons given, it is doubtful whether the text works exactly as it was intended to. The "motionless time" of the title is not brought about by juggling with the arrangement of the extracts and adding an overlay of reflection about the process while it is going on. Mauriac tried to create the fictional illusion that time stands still, but it does not. The diary, like so many other literary diaries, was in its original form clearly written for publication, but as a diary, not as part of an experiment in the writing of fiction. The text is too self-conscious, the events it records are too minutely observed for posterity, the reflections too calculated, the names dropped too imposing, for the diary to be absorbed into the lengthy experiment of which Mauriac has made it the subject.

Publications

Fiction

Le Dialogue intérieur: Toutes les femmes sont fatales, 1951; as *All Women Are Fatal*, 1964; as *Femmes fatales*, 1966
Le Dîner en ville, 1959; as *The Dinner Party*, 1960; as *Dinner in Town*, 1963

Le Marquise sortit à cinq heures, 1961; as *The Marquise Went Out at Five*, 1962
L'Agrandissement, 1963
L'Oubli, 1966
Le Bouddha s'est mis à trembler, 1979
Un coeur tout neuf, 1980
Radio nuit, 1982

Plays

La Conversation (produced Paris 1966), 1964
Les Parisiens du dimanche (produced Montreal, 1967), in *Théâtre*, 1968
Théâtre (includes *La Conversation; Ici, maintenant; Le Cirque; Les Parisiens du dimanche; Le Hun*), 1968
Screenplays: *Les Sept péchés capitaux* (*The Seven Deadly Sins*), with others, 1962; *Thérèse*, with François Mauriac and Georges Franju, 1963

Other

Introduction à une mystique de l'enfer, 1938
La Corporation dans l'état, 1941
Aimer Balzac, 1945
Jean Cocteau; ou, La Vérité du mensonge, 1945
Malraux; ou, Le Mal du héros, 1946
André Breton: essai, 1949
Conversations avec André Gide: extraits d'un journal, 1951; as *Conversations with André Gide*, 1965
Hommes et idées d'aujourd'hui, 1953
L'Amour du cinéma, 1954
Petite littérature du cinéma, 1957
L'Alittérature contemporaine, 1958; revised edition, 1969; as *The New Literature*, 1959
De la littérature à l'alittérature, 1969
Le Temps immobile:
    1. *Une amitié contrariée*, 1970
    2. *Les Espaces imaginaires*, 1975
    3. *Et comme l'espérance est violente*, 1976
    4. *La Terrasse de Malagar*, 1977
    5. *Aimer de Gaulle*, 1978
    6. *L'Eternité parfois*, 1978
    7. *Le Rire des pères dans les yeux des enfants*, 1981
Un autre de Gaulle: journal 1944–1954, 1971; as *Aimer de Gaulle*, 1978; as *The Other de Gaulle: Diaries 1944–1954*, 1973
Une certaine rage, 1977
Laurent Terzieff, 1980
François Mauriac, sa vie et son œuvre, 1985
Editor, *Proust*, 1953

Critical Studies

Johnston, S., "Structure in the novels of Mauriac," *French Review 38*, February 1965

MAURIAC, François (Charles), 1885–1970.

Novelist, journalist, essayist, biographer, dramatist, and poet, winner of Nobel prize for literature (1952).

LIFE

Mauriac is generally regarded as a strongly guilt-obsessed Catholic novelist in the French "moraliste" tradition, who seeks to depict and understand, rather than lay down norms for, human behaviour. He was also a strictly regional author, unable to set his novels, he said, anywhere except in Bordeaux and its surroundings, the "Landes" of the Atlantic coast. His father made his fortune from textiles, although the family also owned a number of vineyards. In 1860 Mauriac's grandfather built a château, fictionalized in *Genitrix*, at Langon to the south-east of Bordeaux, on the banks of the Garonne. His marriage had brought him a pine forest, from whose cultivation the family lived. His elder son, Mauriac's father, had literary leanings, but was withdrawn from school before his baccalauréat and eventually went into banking. Mauriac was the youngest of his five children. Mauriac's bourgeois Bordeaux background made him focus more keenly in his novels on feelings of spiritual unrest than on economic constraints.

Mauriac's father was an atheist. He died at the age of 35, before Mauriac was two. The family then moved a few streets away to occupy a floor in the house belonging to Mauriac's maternal grandmother, a woman whose ostentatious piety was tinged with an obsession with death. She died in 1888, shortly followed by her husband, apparently just after he had entered a church for the first time in years. Mauriac's mother built a chalet in the forest, where even during the summer holidays Mauriac was to receive private tuition. His guardian was a free-thinking uncle. The chalet "Jouanhaut," became the "Argelouse" of *Thérèse Desqueyroux*.

The Bordeaux quarters were cramped, but Mauriac was nevertheless brought up among a cohort of nannies and servants. Holidays during his early childhood were spent on any of a number of nearby family estates. After nursery school Mauriac spent two unhappy years at a school run by the Marian Fathers. In 1894 the family moved again within the fashionable centre of town. Mauriac made his first Communion and the rigorously ritualistic Catholic education, often wrongly referred to as Jansenist, even by Mauriac himself, continued. When in 1898 the Mauriacs moved again, Mauriac went to another Marian school, where he was again unhappy, although there is no evidence to suggest that he objected either to the sniggering prurience of which he later wrote or to the anti-semitism that was rife there. He started writing letters, keeping a diary, and eventually writing verse. He also read widely, mostly authors who touched his emotions. The Mauriacs moved again. Mauriac's mother was clearly more attached to the strictness of his Catholicism than to the excellence of his education. When Mauriac spoke of it as "Jansenist," he was referring to its obsessively puritanical spirituality, not to its theology.

Mauriac only finished the first part of his baccalauréat, moved to the lycée, and in 1904 started to study for his degree. As part of an adolescent rebellion he developed a distaste for the strict propriety which was a sign of the alliance between the Church and the monied classes, and his sympathies shifted from the right-wing *Action Française* to the Christian democracy of *Le Sillon*. He was intellectually attracted by the Catholic "modernist" movement, which reduced as far as possible the supernatural content of religion, and by the adaptation of German idealism elaborated by Blondel. Barrès remained his hero, however, and he read Bourget, Lemaître, Anatole France, Dostoyevsky, and Balzac, and got to like the works of Cézanne and Ravel. While boarding at a house belonging to the Marian Fathers in Paris, he tried for entry to the Ecole des Chartes, the training school for the top echelon of archivists. At his second attempt he succeeded, but decided after six months at the school that he wanted to write instead. He had met an old school friend who offered to publish his verse if Mauriac would put up the money. *Les Mains jointes* was published in 1909 and drew an effusive welcome from Barrès.

In Paris Mauriac got to know Gide, Cocteau, Radiguet, and Drieu la Rochelle. He moved to a four-room apartment in the Rue Vaneau, visited Italy in 1910, and in 1912 published his first novel, *L'Enfant chargé de chaînes*, which Mauriac later virtually disowned, first appeared in the *Mercure de France*. It was reissued by Grasset in 1913. A second volume of verse, *L'Adieu à l'adolescence*, had also been published in 1911, in which year Mauriac had a frustrating love affair. In 1912 he married Jeanne Lafon, a banker's daughter. They set up home in Paris, and in 1914 the first of their four children, Claude, was born, and Mauriac's second novel, *La Robe prétexte*, was published by Grasset.

Mauriac's earlier pleurisy made him unfit for military service and he joined the Red Cross, serving as an orderly in Salonika, from where he was invalided home with malaria in 1917. The Mauriacs went out a great deal together and increasingly frequented the literary salons, though there are hints at this time that Mauriac was strongly tempted to be unfaithful. He still believed in the alliance between Church and bourgeoisie, and derived from Barrès, of whom such Catholics as Claudel and Jammes were becoming increasingly wary, the dangerous view that what France lacked was an elite and a great leader. He was still attracted to Maurras's views, and did not get on with the future Cardinal Gerlier, later famous for his more liberal social views. On his return to Paris after recuperating from influenza, in 1919, Mauriac found that his new novel, *La Chair et le sang*, was being serialized. Published in 1920, it shows a new sensitivity to social class and alludes to a number of contemporary religious issues such as modernism and the Catholic conversions of a number of prominent writers such as Jammes, Du Bos, Rivière, Ghéon, Copeau, and even, briefly, Cocteau.

By this time Mauriac had developed a close relationship with Gide, whom he defended against Henri de Massis, the ultra-Catholic critic of the extreme right. Mauriac wrote one of the few favourable reviews of Gide's *Saül* and was never shocked by Gide's homosexuality. For Mauriac the question was one of resistance or submission to any importunities of the flesh, irrespective of sexual orientation. In 1921 he published *Préséances*, which satirizes the sons of the rich commercial aristocracy of Bordeaux. He was later to disavow this novel, too, but it attracted favourable attention from Proust, with whom Mauriac dined in his bedroom shortly before his death. The next novel, *Le Fleuve de feu*, was accepted by that arbiter of literary excellence, the *Nouvelle Revue Française* (*NRF*, q.v.), which serialized it in 1922–23. It was later published in full by Grasset. The real breakthrough however, came, later the same year with *Le Baiser au lépreux*, which broke the 3,000 sales peak of the earlier novels by selling 18,000 copies. Written before all but draft sketches for *Le Fleuve de feu*, *Le Baiser* was the first of Mauriac's novels to be translated into English and Mauriac celebrated by taking his family on holiday to the Côte d'Azur.

From 1923 until the war Mauriac's fame increased with each novel. *Genitrix*, *Le Désert de l'amour*, published serially in the *Revue de Paris* and awarded the Grand Prix du Roman, *Thérèse Desqueyroux*, which, unusually for Mauriac, had been radically rewritten before publication, *Le Noeud de vipères*, *Le Mystère Frontenac*, and *La Pharisienne* are among the best-known from this period. In 1928 Mauriac appears to have experienced a crisis over the relationship between his Catholicism and his vocation as a novelist. This was brought to a head by an *NRF* invitation to write about Bossuet's *Traité de la concupiscence*. How could a Catholic bound, as Mauriac thought, to an implacable hostility towards the sins of the flesh also be a convincing novelist, sympathetically portraying sinners as well as the just? Gide viewed Mauriac's dilemma as perhaps only Gide could. He published his letter to Mauriac on the subject in the *NRF*.

Mauriac worked out his crisis in a series of essays on Molière, Rousseau, and Flaubert (1930), on "Le roman," and the life of Racine, in a reply to Gide's letter, *Dieu et Mammon*, and in *Blaise Pascal et sa soeur Jacqueline*. The crisis, evidence of which can already be found in the third volume of poems, *Orages*, of 1925, was resolved partly with the help of a priest, Jean-Pierre Altermann, Mauriac's confessor, who had been responsible for converting Du Bos. They went together to the monastery of Solesmes, home of the 20th-century rebirth of plainchant, and to Lourdes, Mauriac's impressions of which are recorded in *Pèlerins*. The abbé appears to have been a little shocked at Mauriac's choice to travel first-class and patronize the best hotels and the most expensive restaurants, feeling that some gesture towards asceticism should have been made.

The Mauriacs moved house in 1930. In 1932, hoarse on the eve of a lecture, Mauriac was told that he had cancer. Immediate surgery followed, but left his voice permanently impaired. In 1933 he was elected to the Académie Française and the stream of essays began to dwindle. The 1935 novel *La Fin de la nuit*, with a preface which Mauriac later suppressed, revolved once more round the character of Thérèse. Mauriac unfortunately opened himself up to an undoubtedly well-argued, if malevolent and tiresome, gadfly attack by the as yet unknown Sartre, published in 1939 by the *NRF* in 20 pages of close reasoning. Thérèse did not of course conform to what was going to become Sartre's stereotype of true freedom. Mauriac had published a score of novels and was a member of the academy. Sartre's first publication had appeared the year before and his adolescent desire to make mischief did not yet even seem out of place, but Mauriac was clearly nettled, and the flow of fiction stopped. He had in any case already shifted his attention to the theatre, for which he had written *Asmodée*.

Mauriac had begun to travel a little, to Salzburg in search of music, but also elsewhere in the interests of political journalism. He had been to Madrid and become politically active against Franco, and in 1935 *Le Figaro* sent him to Rome. Gide came to stay in 1939 following his disappointing Russian visit. When war broke out, one of Mauriac's daughters became engaged to Alain le Roy, who was to become leader of the Grenoble Resistance after escaping from Colditz. Mauriac cast about for a political leader to support, rejecting first Reynaud and then Pétain, to whom Claudel published an ode. De Gaulle and Maurice Schu-

mann, on the other hand, attracted his approval. Of France's literary establishment, only Bernanos had openly attacked the Vichy government, but he was in Brazil. Mauriac's opposition became more courageous, especially in the extracts from his diary published in *Le Cahier noir* under the pseudonym of Forez. In 1943 he confided to his son Claude that he had written himself out as a novelist: "I am the prisoner," he said, "of an outmoded formula." *La Pharisienne*, regarded by Julien Green as his best novel, had been written in haste during the first weeks of the Occupation, as if Mauriac already sensed that his energy for creating fiction was failing. The Mauriacs spent the first winters of the war at their house, Malagar, bought by Mauriac's grandfather in 1843, on the property above the Garonne, now partly occupied by German troops.

From the mid-1930s, Mauriac regularly wrote political journalism whose volume did not diminish until near his death. His opposition to Franco and to Mussolini's invasion of Ethiopia were catalytic turning points for liberal Catholic opinion in France. He may have been under-estimated as a political figure.

At the invitation of Flammarion, who had published the less than successful *Vie de Jésus* in 1936, Mauriac now turned to hagiography. Saint Margaret of Cortona, whose vocation had followed the accidental death of her lover, by whom she had conceived a child, was, according to Flammarion, "just the person" for Mauriac. He wrote further essays and, in some danger due to *Le Cahier noir*, frequently changed his address in the Paris suburbs. On the day Paris was liberated an article about de Gaulle written by Mauriac for *Le Figaro* was read out on the radio and the next day he lunched with de Gaulle himself. He denounced the purge which followed the liberation and tried to intervene for Maurras, who was sentenced to life imprisonment, and for Brasillach, who was shot, despite the promise made to Mauriac by de Gaulle that he would not be. Mauriac appears to have achieved pardons for others during the "épuration" trials for collaboration under the German occupation, and became a public political figure, writing three times a week for *Le Figaro* and organizing the soiree at the Comédie Française for the poets of the Resistance.

After the war Mauriac also enjoyed success in the theatre. Oxford awarded him an honorary doctorate in 1947. His journalism was aimed largely at the Soviet-dominated French communist party and he became head of the editorial committee of *La Table Ronde*, intended to replace the old *NRF*. In 1952 he was awarded the Nobel prize. He joined some left-wing students in opposing French policy in Morocco, creating for himself enemies so powerful that neither *La Table Ronde* nor *Le Figaro* dared to go on employing him. Consequently he took his "Blocnotes" to *L'Express*, then edited by Jacques Servan-Schreiber, and began to support Mendès-France. He rallied again to de Gaulle, but ended up being trusted politically by very few. He wrote another novel, *Un adolescent d'autrefois*, and signed a contract for a further three at the age of 84. His health was deteriorating, however, and he died at home on the morning of 1 September 1970.

WORKS

In a well-known passage from his *Journal 1932–1939* Mauriac writes: "J'essaie de rendre sensible, tangible, odorant, l'univers catholique du mal. Ce pécheur dont les théologiens nous don-nent une idée abstraite, je l'incarne (I try to make the Catholic universe of evil something that can be experienced, felt, tasted. I make this sinner, of whom the theologians give us an abstract idea, into real flesh)." When, as usual, Mauriac succeeds in this aim, he always avoids didacticism, presenting his characters as struggling between good and evil, drawn particularly to sins of the flesh or against the family, but sins that are always redeemable. The theological scaffolding of temptation, grace, divine intervention, and salvation or damnation is generally, though not always, absent from his work. In common with other Catholic novelists, Mauriac can confront the heights and depths of human experience without trivializing it by substituting for the arbitrary and inexplicable some determinist or totally rational explanation.

The first novel to interest the *NRF* was *Le Fleuve de feu*, which was heavily influenced by Jacques Rivière. The novel is in two parts. In the claustrophobic atmosphere of a Pyrenean hotel a young man, Daniel, casts around for some distraction. A girl called Giselle arrives, and they get on well together. A day or two later a middle-aged woman, Mme de Villeron, arrives with a child, which is clearly Giselle's. Giselle spends the night with Daniel, and Mme de Villeron is waiting in the corridor when she leaves his room. In the second part, Mme de Villeron turns out to have adopted the child, born of a brief affair between Giselle and a soldier, now dead. Giselle tells Mme de Villeron that it was her intolerable supervision which threw her into the arms of Daniel. Daniel comes to find her. She is playing the organ, and when she stays on after Mass to pray, he quietly withdraws. The ending is weak and the psychology implausible, leaving the repressed Mme de Villeron the most interesting of the three characters.

Le Baiser au lépreux of the same year was Mauriac's first great popular success. It is a regional novel, set in the pine-clad Landes, about a plump, pious girl who is manoeuvred into a loveless marriage with the physically repulsive son of a local landowner. She is faithful, but finds no joy in marriage, and is attracted to a young doctor. While she blossoms, her husband, knowing that she will never love him, leaves her to seek some consolation in Paris. On his return he dies of tuberculosis, but a clause in his will forbids his widow to remarry, so that her reciprocated love for the doctor remains frustrated. The title of the novel refers to the kiss she gave her husband, which resembles those "which the lips of saints would give to lepers."

Genitrix concerns Félicité Cazenave's tenacious relationship with her 50-year-old son Fernand. She is the widow of the husband's brother in *Le Baiser au lépreux*. Fernand has his ladies in Bordeaux but the atheist Félicité does not mind. When Fernand marries despite her, he leaves his wife seriously ill as the result of a miscarriage, to sleep alone. As predicted, and fervently desired by Félicité, the wife dies, but Fernand reveres her memory too much for his mother's liking. When she in turn dies, Fernand continues to be enslaved by the elderly servant who takes her place.

Le Désert de l'amour brings in the character of Maria Cross. It is the story of Doctor Courrèges, his son Raymond, and Maria, a former schoolmistress, now, at the age of 27, secretary, hostess, and mistress to a wealthy businessman whose wife is dying of cancer. The doctor falls in love with her, and she falls half in love with Raymond. She shows him pictures of her child, who has recently died, and Raymond tries to take her by force. He feels badly hurt by her rejection, while Maria in turn is bored by

his father. She meets Raymond 17 years later in a Paris bar, where the novel begins. She has now married her lover and become attached to his son and feels nothing for Raymond, nor for his father, who happens to be in Paris and is called in professionally when her husband collapses. The novel ends with universal loneliness as Raymond sees his father off on the train. The brilliance of these novels of renunciation lies not in any drama in the plot, but in its handling and organization, a favourite device being that used here, where a situation is depicted before the reader learns how it has come about.

Thérèse Desqueyroux originated in an actual court case. Thérèse does not love her husband Bernard, although she recognizes that her marriage makes good business sense. Just as *Le Désert de l'amour* begins and ends with the Paris scene and relies on flashbacks, so *Thérèse Desqueyroux* begins cinematographically on the steps of the Palais de Justice at Bazas in the Landes, after Thérèse's release following a charge for the attempted murder of her husband. For the sake of the family name, Bernard had given false evidence, but instead of receiving the forgiveness she had hoped for from her family, Thérèse is isolated in a rarely used family house, where she is looked after by two maids and does little other than chain-smoke. Eventually even her cigarettes are taken away from her. Her only public appearances are in the company of her husband for Sunday Mass. When she is finally allowed is go to Paris she returns only for those social occasions at which her presence is considered indispensable.

The novel is a superb psychological study and an attack on scandal-mongering bourgeois Bordeaux society. Thérèse is morally superior to Bernard and his family, so that the novel, like the last three discussed, shocked the "bien-pensants" it ridiculed. As Mauriac once wrote, his heroes and heroines at least know their own depths and are not afflicted by "la seule chose que je haïsse au monde…et qui est la complaisance et la satisfaction (the only thing in the world which I hate…complacency and self-satisfaction)." *Destins* is another regional novel with passages of heavy social satire, again written on cinematographic principles. *Ce qui était perdu*, written after the 1928 crisis, tries too hard to edify and to avoid scandal.

Well before the attack by Sartre, critics had remarked that, prior to 1929 or thereabouts, Mauriac's novels had been supported by the tension between an impossible desire for purity and a leaning towards what had at all costs to be avoided, sin. After 1929, they saw the theologian attempting to edify at the expense of the artist. *Le Mystère Frontenac* of 1933 draws on Mauriac's own family life as a child and a young man, and has been both criticized for and defended against slackness and sentimentality. Sartre was right, if unnecessarily abrasive, in his judgement of *La Fin de la nuit*.

Le Noeud de Vipères, along with *Thérèse* one of Mauriac's most popular novels, successfully calls on all his greatest gifts, in particular linking physical atmosphere with spiritual drama. In a letter to his wife Isa, who has pre-deceased him, Louis recounts his life and conversion from his partly political and partly social anti-religious attitude. His son Hubert finds the unfinished letter and comments unfavourably on it. Louis's self-hatred is the fundamental cause of the dislike he provokes in others. He is clever but ill-favoured, becomes rich, and marries the consumptive daughter of a family socially superior to his own. He is shocked to learn that, although she has been faithful to him, her heart belonged elsewhere, is hostile to her punctilious devotions, and is himself assiduously unfaithful, mostly with prostitutes. He has a son, Robert, by a previous mistress, with whom he conspires to defraud his family of their inheritance. Robert gives the plot away to the family in return for the promise from them of an adequate income for life. Louis's conversion derives from the discovery of the goodness in himself, demonstrated in his attitude towards his children. He turns out to be the only non-hypocrite in the book, and until his conversion has never had a confrontation with authentic Christianity.

In spite of Julien Green's praise and Mauriac's own high opinion of it, *La Pharisienne* is weakened by a lack of psychological motivation in the denouement. The first-person narrative provides a compassionate study of a totally loveless Christianity, gradually stripped of all its hypocrisy until it can in the end become authentic. This novel brings to a close the series of major imaginative works.

Mauriac continued to write compulsively, political and autobiographical works, essays and biographies, letters to Gide, and above all journalism. He will doubtless be remembered for the economy and vigour of his evocation of physical atmosphere and for his psychological penetration. The label "Catholic novelist" is in a sense misleading, since his best novels tend to be those which see human behaviour least in terms of theological categories.

PUBLICATIONS

Collections

Oeuvres complètes, 12 vols., 1950–56
Oeuvres romanesques et théâtrales complètes, edited by Jacques Petit, 3 vols., 1978–81

Fiction

L'Enfant chargé de chaînes, 1913; as *Young Man in Chains*, 1963
La Robe prétexte, 1914; as *The Stuff of Youth*, 1960
La Chair et le sang, 1920; as *Flesh and Blood*, 1954
Préséances, 1921; as *Questions of Precedence*, 1958
Le Baiser au lépreux, 1922; as *The Kiss to the Leper*, 1923
Le Fleuve de feu, 1923: as *The River of Fire*, 1954
Genitrix, 1923; as *Genetrix, in The Family*, 1930
Le Désert de l'amour, 1925; as *The Desert of Love*, 1929
Fabien, 1926
Thérèse Desqueyroux, 1927; as *Thérèse* (in English), 1928
Le Démon de la connaissance, 1928
Destins (includes *Coups de couteau* and *Un homme de lettres*), 1928; as *Destinies*, 1929; as *Lines of Life*, 1957
La Nuit du bourreau de soi-même, 1929
Trois récits, 1929
Ce qui était perdu, 1930; as *Suspicion*, 1931; as *That Which Was Lost*, with *Dark Angels*, 1951
Le Noeud de vipères, 1932; as *Vipers' Tangle*, 1933; as *Knot of Vipers*, 1951
Le Mystère Frontenac, 1933; as *The Frontenac Mystery*, 1952
La Fin de la nuit, 1935; as *The End of the Night*, in *Therese: A Portrait in Four Parts*, 1947
La Mal, 1935; as *The Enemy*, with *The Desert of Love*, 1949
Les Anges noirs, 1936; as *The Dark Angels*, with *That Which Was Lost*, 1951; as *The Mask of Innocence*, 1953

Plongées, 1938
Les Chemins de la mer, 1939; as *The Unknown Sea*, 1948
La Pharisienne, 1941; as *A Woman of the Pharisees*, 1946
Therese: A Portrait in Four Parts, 1947
Le Sagouin, 1951; as *The Little Misery*, 1952
Galigaï, 1952; as *The Loved and the Unloved*, 1952
L'Agneau, 1954; as *The Lamb*, 1955
A Mauriac Reader, edited by Wallace Fowlie, 1968
Un adolescent d'autrefois, 1969; as *Maltaverne*, 1970

Plays

Asmodée (produced 1937), 1938; as *Asmodee: or, The Intruder*, 1939
Les Mal-aimés (produced 1945), 1945
Passage du malin (produced 1947), 1948
Le Feu sur la terre (produced 1950), 1951
Le Pain vivant, 1955
Screenplay: *Thérèse*, with Claude Mauriac and Georges Franju, 1963

Verse

Les Mains jointes, 1909
L'Adieu à l'adolescence, 1911
Orages, 1925, revised edition, 1949
Le Sang d'Atys, 1940

Other

De quelques cœurs inquiets: petits essais de psychologie religieuse, 1920
La Vie et la mort d'un poète (on André Lafon), 1924
Le Jeune Homme, 1926
Le Tourment de Jacques Rivière, 1926
Les Beaux Esprits de ce temps, 1926
Proust, 1926
La Province, 1926
Bordeaux, 1926
La Rencontre avec Pascal, 1926
Conscience, instinct divin, 1927
Dramaturges, 1928
Supplément au Traité de la concupiscence de Bossuet, 1928
Divagations sur Saint-Sulpice, 1928
La Vie de Jean Racine, 1928
Le Roman, 1928
Voltaire contre Pascal, 1929
Dieu et Mammon, 1929; as *God and Mammon*, 1936
Mes plus lointains souvenirs, 1929
Paroles en Espagne, 1930
Trois grands hommes devant Dieu, 1930
L'Affaire Favre-Bulle, 1931
Blaise Pascal et sa soeur Jacqueline, 1931
Le Jeudi saint, 1931; as *Maundy Thursday*, 1932; as *The Eucharist: The Mystery of Holy Thursday*, 1944
Souffrances et bonheur du chrétien, 1931; as *Anguish and Joy of the Christian Life*, 1964
René Bazin, 1931
Pèlerins, 1932; as *Pèlerins de Lourdes*, 1933
Commencements d'une vie, 1932
Le Drôle (juvenile), 1933; as *The Holy Terror*, 1964

Le Romancier et ses personnages, 1933; reprinted in part as
    L'Education des filles, 1936
Journal, 5 vols., 1934–53
Vie de Jésus, 1936; as *Life of Jesus*, 1937
Les Maisons fugitives, 1939
Le Cahier noir, 1943; as *The Black Note-Book*, 1944
La Nation française a une âme, 1943
Ne pas se renier…, 1944
Sainte Marguerite de Cortone, 1945; as *Saint Margaret of Cortona*, 1948
La Rencontre avec Barrès, 1945
Le Bâillon dénoué, après quatre ans de silence, 1945
Du côté de chez Proust, 1947; as *Proust's Way*, 1950
Mes grands hommes, 1949; as *Men I Hold Great*, 1951; as *Great Men*, 1952
Terres franciscaines, 1950
La Pierre d'achoppement, 1951; as *The Stumbling Block*, 1952
La Mort d'André Gide, 1952
Lettres ouvertes, 1952; as *Letters on Art and Life*, 1953
Ecrits intimes, 1953
Paroles catholiques, 1954; as *Words of Faith*, 1955
Bloc-notes 1952–1967, 5 vols., 1958–71
Trois écrivains devant Lourdes, with others, 1958
Le Fils de l'homme, 1958; as *The Son of Man*, 1958
Mémoires intérieures, 1959; as *Mémoires Intérieures* (in English), 1960
Rapport sur les prix de vertu, 1960
Second Thoughts: Reflections on Literature and Life, 1961
Cain, Where Is Your Brother?, 1962
Ce que je crois, 1962; as *What I Believe*, 1963
De Gaulle, 1964; as *De Gaulle* (in English), 1966
Nouveaux mémoires intérieures, 1965; as *The Inner Presence: Recollections of My Spiritual Life*, 1968
D'autres et moi, 1966
Mémoires politiques, 1967
Correspondance 1912–1950, with André Gide, edited by Jacqueline Morton, 1971
Lacordaire, edited by Keith Goesch, 1976
Correspondance 1916–1942, with Jacques-Emile Blanche, edited by Georges-Paul Collet, 1976
Mauriac avant Mauriac (early writings), edited by Jean Touzot, 1977
Chroniques du Journal de Clichy, with Paul Claudel (includes Claudel-Fontaine correspondence), edited by François Morlot and Jean Touzot, 1978
Lettres d'une vie (1904–1969), edited by Caroline Mauriac, 1981
Editor, *Les Pages immortelles de Pascal*, 1940; as *Living Thoughts of Pascal*, 1940
Editor, with Louise de Vilmorin, *Almanach des Lettres 1949*, 1949

Bibliography

Goesch, Keith, *Mauriac: Essai de bibliographie chronologique 1908–1960*, 1965

Critical studies

Pell, Elsie, *Mauriac* (in English), 1947
Jarret-Kerr, Martin, *Mauriac* (in English), 1954
Jenkins, Cecil, *Mauriac* (in English), 1965
Flower, John, *Intention and Achievement: An Essay on the Novels of Mauriac*, 1969
Speaight, Robert, *Mauriac: A Study of the Writer and the Man*, 1976
Scott, Malcolm, *The Politics of a Novelist*, 1980

MAURRAS, Charles (-Marie-Photius), 1868–1952.

Poet, essayist, political philosopher, and journalist.

LIFE

Charles Maurras was born at Martigues, in Provence, on 20 April 1868. His father died in 1874, and from 1876 to 1885 Maurras was at school in Aix. In 1882 he fell ill and, although a recovery at first seemed possible, he lost his hearing, a disaster which reinforced an early adolescent crisis from which his personality, already wounded by the death of his father and his exile at school, was never to recover. In December 1885, having failed the second part of his baccalauréat, Maurras moved with his brother and mother to Paris, and registered as a history student at the Sorbonne. He read widely, worked unnaturally hard, and carried on an intimate correspondence with a priest, the Abbé Penon, who had taught him at Aix and who later helped him direct his life spiritually, emotionally, and intellectually, allying in some way the roles of real and spiritual fathers. We know that in 1887 this mentor was preaching the "triumphant return of Christ" into French schools and French laws, and the importance of devotion to "God, Church, and Fatherland," whose interests "are indissolubly bound up with those of the Catholic Church." Although Maurras later repudiated everything he had written before 1893, the structure of his religious and political thinking, within its internal inconsistencies, was already fixed by that date. Only its form and its aesthetic basis were to change.

It is also clear that at this time Maurras was highly sensitive to injustice in all its forms. He read *La Jeune France*, and we have the letters reporting to the Abbé Penon on his reading from about 1883. Much later, in 1944, when he thought he was facing execution, Maurras reflected in writing on his youth, and we know how much importance he attributed to a personal experience which he made the subject of one of the contes published in the *Oeuvres capitales*, the third "Nuit" of *Les Quatre nuits*. It seems certain that Maurras underwent an intense adolescent experience in which he felt he had gone through the process of discovering his true self.

In Paris Maurras quickly began to find journalistic work. Clerical connections helped. The Abbé Guieu, director of the *Annales de Philosophie Chrétienne*, accepted a review from Maurras, and invited him to contribute regularly, if pseudonymously, to the *Instruction Publique* from the autumn of 1886. That winter Maurras was ill, still reading voraciously and writing pretentiously about philosophy, literature, and religion to the

Abbé Penon, but confined indoors. He began to spend time with the Abbé Huvelin, to whom the Abbé Penon had passed him on. In the spring of 1887 his mood was despondent and bitter, and early in 1888 he signed his letters to Penon with a pseudonym meaning "bitter." By that date he was working on the subject of his first book, the Provençal poet Théodore Aubanel (1829–1886), was in contact with Mistral, the leading Provençal poet, and was becoming known in the Paris circle interested in "félibre" or Provençal literature, on which he was later to publish a number of works.

Barrès had noticed one of Maurras's columns and introduced him to the *Revue Indépendante*, and Maurras also began to write for *L'Observateur*. Early in 1890 he was again ill, struggling unsuccessfully against the idea of the world's absurdity, and seeking an anchorage in right-wing social views. He met Anatole France, began to be accepted by Parisian literary circles, and was invited to write for the *Gazette de France*. A number of autobiographical fragments incorporated into later works make it possible to trace Maurras's intellectual evolution in his early twenties. After the short book on Aubanel came one on Moréas. Maurras was now also working for the monarchist *Le Soleil* and for Larousse's encyclopedia, but publishing his best material in the *Gazette de France*, which sent him to Athens in 1896 to cover the first of the new Olympic Games. This experience was to lay the foundations of his strong Hellenism, although from about 1891 he had already been associated with Moréas and others in the establishment of an anti-symbolist (q. v.) group of poets, which sought to revive Latin as well as Greek aesthetic norms, and was called by Maurras the "Ecole Romane."

His Greek experience may well have much to do with Maurras's intransigently anti-Dreyfus, anti-semitic position. Israel appeared to him to embody the temptations of the Orient, against which Greece had had to protect its classical heritage. The anti-semitism became mostly political rather than racist, but aesthetic norms, spilling over into elevated ideas about moral quality, were where it started, and they certainly did nothing to diminish it later. The *Revue Grise*, founded in 1899, and from which the *Action Française* emerged, was initially the organ of a republican but anti-Dreyfus group. On 29 July 1900 the *Gazette de France* had started to publish the results of Maurras's enquiry about the popularity of returning a monarchy to France, on the basis of which Maurras started his new movement. *Anthinéa*, a travel book of personal reminiscences, had been published, although not yet in volume form, and Maurras published his "L'invocation à Minerve" anonymously in the first number of the review *Minerve* on 1 March 1902. The Roman name of the Greek goddess was used intentionally.

It was January 1913 before Albert Thibaudet published his article on Maurras's three traditions—classicism, Catholicism and monarchism—in the *Nouvelle Revue Française* (*NRF*, q.v.). The *NRF* discontinued "L'esthétique des trois traditions" on Protestant objections from Jean Schlumberger, but Thibaudet later turned it into a book. Maurras had not been particularly preoccupied by the Dreyfus affair in its early stages. He had published *Trois idées politiques* in 1898, after a year spent travelling, mostly in Italy and Corsica, and certainly took the view that Dreyfus's interests should not prevail over those of the army, but it was only during the later stages of the Dreyfus case, about 1899, that Maurras became a monarchist. The constellation of his attitudes suggests that the commitment to right-wing, authoritarian political structures, anti-bureaucratic as well as

anti-democratic, came both chronologically and hierarchically before monarchism, Catholicism, anti-Protestantism, anti-romanticism, and anti-semitism. The anti-semitism, grounded in aesthetic classicism, hardened into the projection of a conspiracy of powerful interests constituting a state within a state, in spite of Maurras's initial scepticism, when Drumont, in the two-volume *La France juive* of 1886, first put forward the idea that French institutions were being corroded from within by an informal conspiracy of Jewish interests. Had the Jews not seemed to constitute a community with a non-assimilated identity, it is doubtful whether Maurras would have been hostile to them on grounds of race or religion alone.

After his public participation in the later stages of the Dreyfus dispute Maurras became closely associated with Léon Daudet in the Action Française, and with the associated newspaper, a fortnightly pamphlet until 1908, when it became a daily. The paper lasted until 1944, having supported Vichy and Pétain during World War II. Maurras sometimes used the pseudonym "Criton" when writing for it, and the movement, which did not avoid becoming a rallying point for right-wing hooliganism, was repudiated by royalist circles and condemned by the Vatican on account of its attempt to give Catholicism a clear political colouring.

Both the newspaper and five of Maurras's books were placed on the Roman index of forbidden books in 1926, and in 1936 Maurras was sent to prison for threatening a member of parliament who supported sanctions against Mussolini. He also threatened with death members of the 1936 Front Populaire coalition. He had to condemn the rise of German and Italian fascism in the name of French nationalism and security, but he also had to condemn anti-fascism because it was democratic, just as his principles drove him to campaign at the same time for rearmament and peace. The contrast in Maurras between the discriminating taste of his criticism and the embittered fanaticism of his political and journalistic activities suggests that his complete deafness and the early loss of his father may fundamentally have affected his personality.

In 1938 he became a member of the Académie Française. After World War II he was arrested and condemned to life imprisonment for his strident support of Pétain, in whom alone he saw hope for France's future, and of Vichy. He was released on grounds of ill health a few months before his death on 16 November 1952. His final task was to revise the *Oeuvres capitales*, which he believed would finally vindicate him.

WORKS

Maurras's claim to literary fame is slender. His poetry is no more than finely drawn, and he overestimated the importance of his small literary coterie of anti-symbolists, the "Ecole Romane." His critical writings show taste and discernment, although not more than might be expected from any gifted literary critic. There are no discoveries or new approaches. Maurras is not even in any real sense a political philosopher, since his commitments, contempts, and aversions contain too many knee-jerk reactions incompatible with one another. The political thought coheres in neither content nor method.

In so far as Maurras is an important author, it is for his place in rallying anti-democratic national opinion for almost half a century. He was an expert polemicist, master of the innuendo, the snide implication, the presentation of partisan opinions of extreme simplicity and single-mindedness, and well skilled in the use of emotive language. The strength of his polemic lies in its directness: "the government of the King of France will, at the commencement of its dictatorship, inevitably be obliged to take repressive and retributive measures in order to make possible subsequent acts designed to restore order and justice." It is difficult not to associate so brutal a statement of the intention to suppress political opposition with the worst excesses of 20th-century government, but few even of the most viciously repressive governments of a century which has seen so many have been so open about what they intended to do as Maurras would have had the king be. The only surprise in the declaration is that Maurras should have bothered to justify the means "to take repressive and retributive measures" by referring to the end, the specious "order and justice" which is to be restored. Whose?

The vigour of Maurras's coolly paranoid prose is capable even today of startling the reader by its mixture of naivety, self-deception, ignorance, and fear—one of the not unusual, but exceedingly potent emotional cocktails on which Maurras was so frequently high: "National industry and national labour will be protected not only against the inroads of foreign industry and foreign labour, but also against international speculators based in our midst." Even after allowance is made for the date of the text (1899), it is difficult not to see in it a crude exploitation of the fear of all things foreign or, worse, international. Unfortunately, the text exactly reveals the mechanism by which self-doubt inhibits simple intelligence in its projection of a bogeyman. Its most obvious quality is mindlessness. The prose increases in emotional intensity, cascading through inverted commas, italicized words like *earth, soil, land,* and *country,* and exclamation marks. The rhetoric of bombast can seldom have rung out more loudly and emptily.

The political thought cannot be isolated from the literary criticism. Both derive from the same hierarchy of order, and since the order is classical, but the Greeks were known advocates of democratic systems, the order at the base of Maurras's world view must primarily be aesthetic, "Romanticism and revolution," he wrote, "resemble nothing so much as two stems, which, though they look different, grow from the same root… Morality, politics, poetry, history, philosophy, religion. We never fail to discover in this profuse, entangled undergrowth of the complexity of man and events the unity of the human spirit." The text is from *Romantisme et révolution* of 1922 in the context of Taine's attempt to reconcile the spirit of revolution and the classical tradition. It would be difficult to take speciousness much further than the following example, betrayed by its broken syntax, consisting of a whole sentence: "Democratic deviation—undergone by the classical spirit, not perpetrated by it." All that can be wondered at is Maurras's single-minded determination to wrest the conclusion from the evidence by juggling with verbs denoting activity, like "perpetrate," and verbs denoting passivity, like "undergo." There is polemical skill here, technical mastery of the medium of partisan presentation, but nothing that can be regarded as literary quality.

Maurras was an important figure in the literary life of France, prepared to make statements which repelled people or made them rally to his call. Much that he left is simple journalism. He showed sensitivity to landscape, to regional roots in Provence, loyalty to his idealized France, and occasional delicacy of feel-

ing. He has a place in literary history, even as a writer. But he can scarcely be regarded as a writer of imaginative interest or power.

PUBLICATIONS

Collections

Oeuvres capitales, 4 vols., 1954

Political philosophy

Le Chemin de Paradis, 1895
Trois idées politiques, 1898
Décentralisation, 1898
Enquête sur la monarchie, 1901
Anthinéa, d'Athènes à Florence, 1901
L'Avenir de l'intelligence, 1905
Un débat nouveau sur la République et la décentralisation, 1905
Libéralisme et liberté, démocratie, et peuple, 1905
Le Dilemme de Marc Sangnier, 1906
Si la coupe de force est possible, 1910
Idées royalistes, 1910
Kiel et Tanger, 1910
Une campagne royaliste au "Figaro," 1911
La Politique religieuse, 1912
Athènes antique, 1913
L'Action Française et la religion catholique; Les Eléments d'une imposture; Agressions libérales, démocratiques, sillonistes; Les Maîtres de "L'Action Française"; L'Action Française et la morale, 1913
Quand les Français ne s'aimaient pas, 1913
Les Conditions de la victoire, 4 vols., 1916–18
Le Pape, la guerre, et la paix, 1917
Aux républicains de Russie, 1917
La Part du combattant, 1917
La Paix de sang, 1918
Les Chefs socialistes pendant la guerre, 1918
Les Trois aspects du Président Wilson, 1920
Romantisme et révolution, 1922
L'Allée des philosophes, 1923
Les Nuits d'épreuve et la mémoire de l'état, 1924
La Violence et la mesure, 1924
Pour en sortir, 1925
Le Mauvais Traité, 1926
Réflexions sur l'ordre en France, 1927
Le Tombeau du prince, 1927
La Politique 1926–1927, 1927
Petit manuel de l'"Enquête sur la monarchie," 1928
Les Princes des nuées, 1928
Corps glorieux; ou, Vertu de la perfection, 1928
Napoléon avec ou contre la France, 1929
Le "Bibliophile" Barthou, 1929
Lettre à Schramek, 1929
De Demos à César, 1930
Méditation sur la politique de Jeanne d'Arc, 1931
Pour la défense nationale, 1931
Casier judiciaire d'A. Briand, 1931
Le Quadrilatère, 1931
Au Signe de Flore (selections), 1931

Nos raisons, 1933
Dictionnaire politique et critique, 5 vols., 1934
Louis XIV et la France, 1936
L'Amitié de Platon, 1937
Les Vergers sur la mer, 1937
Mes idées politiques, 1937
Devant l'Allemagne éternelle, 1937
Jeanne d'Arc, Louis XIV, Napoléon, 1937
La Dentelle du rempart, 1937
Louis XIV ou l'homme-roi, 1939
Pages africaines, 1940
La Seule France, 1941
Sans la muraille des cyprès, 1941
De la colère à la justice, 1942
Avenir de l'intelligence française, 1943
Vers l'Espagne de Franco, 1943
Pour un réveil français, 1943
L'Allemagne et nous, 1945
Réponse à Paul Claudel, 1945
Quelques pensées de Charles Maurras, 1945
Procès de Charles Maurras et de Maurice Pujo devant la Cour de Justice du Rhône, 1945
Le Patriotisme ne doit pas tuer la patrie, 1946
Les Deux justices; ou, Notre "J'accuse," 1947
Le Parapluie de Marianne, 1948
L'Ordre et le désordre, 1948
Réflexions sur la révolution de 1789, 1948
Inscriptions sur nos ruines, 1949
Au grand juge de France, with Maurice Pujo, 1949
Pour réveiller le grand juge, 1951
Les Mensonges de l' "Expert" Verdenal au procès de Lyon, 1951
Jarres de Biot, 1951
Le Guignon français, 1952
Votre bel aujourd'hui, 1953
Le Bienheureux Pie X, sauveur de France, 1953
The French Right (from De Maistre to Maurras), edited by J.S. McClelland, 1970
Selections, edited by Jacques Vier, 1978

Verse

Pour Psyché, 1911
Inscriptions, 1921; revised edition, 1931
Le Mystère d'Ulysse, 1923
La Bataille de la Marne: ode historique, 1923
La Musique intérieure, 1925
Quatre poèmes de Eurydice, 1937
Où suis-je?, 1945
Au-devant de la nuit (as Léon Rameau), 1946
Le Cintre de Riom, 1946
Music Within Me, 1946
Prière à deux voix; Le Lai d'Arioste, 1950
Pour l'honneur d'un fleuve "apostat," 1950
A mes vieux oliviers, 1951
Ni peste ni colère, 1951
La Balance intérieure, 1952
Dear Garment, 1965

Other

Théodore Aubanel, 1889

Jean Moréas, 1891
Les Amants de Venise, George Sand et Musset, 1902
L'Etang de Berre, 1915
Le Conseil du Dante, 1920
Tombeaux, 1921
Poètes, 1923
Ironie et poésie, 1923
Anatole France, politique et poète, 1924
Barbarie et poésie, 1926
Gaulois, Germains, et Latins, 1926
Lorsque Hugo eut les cent ans, 1926
Un débat sur le romantisme avec Raymond de la Tailhède, 1928
Mar e Lono, 1930
Mistralismes, 1930
Quatres nuits de Provence, 1931
Tryptique de Paul Bourget, 1931
Paysages et cités de Provence, 1932
Prologue d'un essai sur la critique, 1932
Le Long du Rhône et de la mer, 1934
Dans Arles au temps des fées, 1937
Jacques Bainville et Paul Bourget, 1937
La Montagne provençale, 1938
Discours de réception a l'Académie, 1939
Aux mânes d'un maître, 1941
Mistral, 1941
La Contre-révolution spontanée, 1943
Paysages mistraliens, 1944
Poésie et vérité, 1944
Marseille en Provence, 1946
Une promotion de Judas, 1948
Maurice Barrès, 1948
Pour un jeune français, 1949
Mon jardin qui s'est souvenu, 1949
Tragi-comédie de ma surdité, 1951
Le Beau Jeu des reviviscences, 1952
Pascal puni: conte infernal, 1953
Lettres de prison, 1958
Maurice Barrès, Charles Maurras: la république ou le roi: correspondence inédite 1888–1923, edited by Helène and Nicole Maurras, 1970

Critical studies

Rodiez, Léon S., *Maurras jusqu'à l'Action Française*, 1957
Curtis, Michael, *Three Against the Third Republic: Sorel, Barrès, and Maurras*, 1959
Massis, H., *Maurras et notre temps*, 2 vols., 1961
Weber, Eugen, *Action Française: Royalism and Reaction in Twentieth Century France*, 1962
Vandromme, Pol, *Maurras: l'Eglise et l'ordre*, 1965
McCearney, James, *Maurras et son temps*, 1977
Vatré, Eric, *Charles Maurras: un itinéraire spirituel*, 1978
Sutton, Michael, *Nationalism, Positivism, and Catholicism: The Politics of Charles Maurras and French Catholics, 1890–1914*, 1982
Boutang, Pierre, *Maurras: la destinée et l'oeuvre*, 1984

MÉRIMÉE, Prosper, 1803–1870.

Novelist, archaeologist, translator, and dramatist.

LIFE

Mérimée's father, Léonor (1757–1836), was a painter and teacher and, like his mother, Anne-Louise (née Moreau, 1775–1852), solidly middle-class. They met at the school in Passy kept by Anne's mother, where Léonor taught drawing, and married in 1802. Prosper, who was to be greatly embarrassed by his first name, was born on 28 September 1803, by which time his father had virtually given up painting to run the Ecole des Beaux-Arts, of which he became secretary in 1807. Neither of his parents were believers, and Mérimée was probably not baptized. Léonor was active in promoting French industrial development, as he was in the manufacture of oil paint, and in 1820, after reporting on English industry, was made a Chevalier of the Légion d'Honneur. His friends included Ingres, the actor Talma, Ampère, and Hazlitt. Although at first republican, he shifted to a more cynical view of government "by the multitude." He was also pleased to see the waning of the romantic (q.v.) school of painting before his death. Mérimée's mother had been brought up in England, and both parents were Anglophiles.

Mérimée was taught English at home, did reasonably well at the renamed Lycée Napoléon (Henri IV), winning occasional prizes in Latin and Greek, was taught Italian by his father, who had spent five years in Rome, passed his baccalauréat in 1819, and graduated in law in 1823. At the age of seven he had been infatuated with a Mlle Dubost, who boarded at his mother's school and married a doctor, Régnier, in 1910. Another boarder, Fanny Lagden (1797–1879), the elder of two sisters, was probably Mérimée's first mistress. She became a lifelong friend. At school Mérimée formed a firm friendship with Jean-Jacques Ampère, who was three years older than he was and full of enthusiasm for the romantics. They translated Ossian (q.v.) together. Other friends included Charles Lenormant, who was to become a numismatist and archaeologist, Albert Stapfer, the first French translator of *Faust*, and the botanist Adrien Jussieu.

Unlike most of his generation, Mérimée was not swept up in the enthusiasm for Shakespeare, Ossian, Byron, and Scott, although he was impressed by all these authors until he reacted against Scott, certainly as early as 1832. He was more at home with the political liberalism of Constant and Béranger than with the poetic romanticism of Chateaubriand and Lamartine. The law degree was expected to lead to a profession or an administrative career, but Mérimée was in no hurry. He met Stendhal at a private party, stayed with the Régniers, and wrote a lost prose tragedy, "Cromwell," as far as we know independently of Balzac and Hugo, both of whom wrote dramas on the same subject within a few years. The interest of Cromwell for the first generation of French romantics is no doubt illustrated as well as explained by the publication of his apocryphal memoirs in a French translation by Charles Malo in 1816, as well as by Villemain's *Histoire de Cromwell* of 1819.

Mérimée was exempted from military service, and began to attend the politically liberal salons, which were opposed to the influence of the aristocracy and the Church, although not fully republican. The political stance he took was to bring Mérimée rapid promotion in government service in the inspectorate of historical buildings after the inauguration of the July monarchy in 1830, but Stendhal, Sainte-Beuve, and Renan all felt that salon decorum inhibited Mérimée's artistic potential. He was received by both Emmanuel Viollet-le-Duc, father of Eugène with whom he was later to work closely on the restoration and refurbishment of historical buildings, and Viollet-le-Duc's brother-in-law, Etienne Delécluze. The literary atmosphere at Delécluze's gatherings was more aggressive, concerned with historical realism but opposed to the romantic revival of a religious sensibility, as also to strictly classical literary principles.

In 1824 Mérimée wrote four articles on the present state and historical traditions of Spanish drama, published unsigned in November by the newly founded *Le Globe*. He had also started a novel, now lost, met Stendhal, of whom he was to become an inseparable friend, and begun to frequent the salon of Virginie Ancelot, an amiable specialist in academic intrigue. In April 1824 Mérimée wrote "La Bataille," his first attempt at the long short story, "conte" or "nouvelle" rather than "roman," for which he has become famous. He was also planning his first literary spoof, a series of six short plays attributed to a fictitious Spanish actress to be known as the *Théâtre de Clara Gazul*. The book was published by Mérimée's friend Sautelet, who committed suicide the following year, with a portrait by Delécluze of the author, Mérimée, in a mantilla, necklace, and frilly dress. It was enthusiastically reviewed, translated into English, and admired by Goethe.

Mérimée's literary ambitions now crystallized. He wrote a preface for a new translation of *Don Quixote* and took great care over a second hoax, *La Guzla*, a collection of fake translations of national songs from Illyria, the states of the eastern Adriatic which had been occupied by France from 1805 until 1815. Floated on the romantic vogue for folk material and good enough to take in Pushkin, the poems again attracted favourable reviews, were translated into German, and some of them into English, Russian, and Polish. Mérimée himself saw to it that the hoax was rumbled late in 1827, thereby also ensuring that he got the credit for it. His literary future was assured. In 1825 and 1826 he visited England.

He was a fashionable young man of letters and leisure, belonging by the late 1820s to a dandified group with a high-life style of living and low-life tastes, which also included Delacroix, Stendhal, and Musset. Mérimée appears to have thought of marriage, an institution for which he later developed an aversion. In 1827 he became the lover of Emilie Lacoste (born 1798), the mother of Joseph Bonaparte's son, whom he had met at the salon of Mme Davillier. To her own annoyance and that of Joseph Bonaparte, she had returned to France from America in the spring of 1827 when her husband's business there failed. The husband, Félix, discovered one of Mérimée's letters, and Mérimée had to fight a duel with him. He was wounded in the left arm while chivalrously refraining from firing himself. Félix then returned to America. Mérimée's liaison carried on until about 1832, when he was replaced by Louis-Edmond Anthoine, to whom Mme Lacoste bore a son, later known as Duranty, the realist (q.v.) novelist. In 1828 Mérimée had himself become momentarily infatuated with Mary Woolstonecraft Shelley, the poet's widow, who had been detained by smallpox in Paris. She wrote a flattering article about him in *The Westminster Gazette* for January 1829.

In 1828 Mérimée published *La Jaquerie, scènes féodales*, a sequence of historical dialogues, a genre with which Ludovic Vitet had had some success in Delécluze's salon, together with the scabrous *La Famille du Carvajal*. Both works were added to the third edition of the Clara Gazul series. The second edition, published in 1830, had already added two of the short stories published by Mérimée in the *Revue de Paris* in 1829. *La Jaquerie*, openly copying Scott, Shakespeare, and Goethe, was a stepping stone to the historical novel the *Chronique du règne de Charles IX*, published in 1829, the year of Balzac's *Les Chouans*, but after Vigny's *Cinq-Mars* (1826), and before Hugo's *Notre-Dame de Paris* (1831). The *Chronique* was almost immediately translated into German and Mérimée was warmly congratulated by Hugo, with whom he became more closely associated. He assisted at the reading of *Marion Delorme* in Hugo's drawing room in 1829, and was a member of the claque for *Hernani* in 1830. He also attended the private reading of Musset's *Contes d'Espagne et d'Italie*, and encouraged Musset when, at a later reading, his work was given only a very cool reception. Mérimée was finding it difficult to retain his ties with Stendhal while being sucked into Hugos' entourage, where only deferential behaviour was acceptable. Sainte-Beuve, who was still very close to Hugo at this time, has left an amusing account of Hugo's hostility to Stendhal at a dinner at Mérimée's parents' house to which Mérimée invited them both.

During 1829 and the early part of 1830 Mérimée had published a dozen pieces, mostly contes, in the *Revue de Paris*, whose first number had appeared on 5 April. This was his principal forum, although he also began to write for the new *Revue Française* and *Le National*. He had prudently turned down a diplomatic post under Charles X, a decision which stood him in good stead when, in 1830, Charles was replaced by Louis-Philippe. Several prospective marriage projects failed to crystallize, and Mérimée spent from late June until early December 1830 in Spain. His parents had financed the trip, whose purpose was to investigate the museums, partly to help him get over the disappointing realization that he could never aspire to the hand of Mélanie Double (1812–1865). She was to marry successively a lawyer and the mathematician Guillaume Libri-Carucci (1803–1869), who became inspector general of libraries.

Mérimée sent back a series of letters for publication in the *Revue de Paris* and became intoxicated on the local colour—bullfights, a hanging, brigands, and prostitutes, including a guaranteed virgin of 15 at only 42 francs—but came back uncured of his melancholy, affecting a sardonic contempt for the females so capable of hurting him. He was called up on his return in December and served in the Garde Nationale with Dumas and Alexandre Bixio, a co-founder of the *Revue des Deux Mondes* (*RDM*, q.v.). Early in 1831 Mérimée was acting as secretary to the minister for the navy, looking for a diplomatic post under the new regime. He followed his minister, d'Argout, through different posts, which involved turning down more immediately lucrative offers elsewhere. He was clearly an excellent administrator, and in 1832 was given responsibility for containing the dreaded cholera epidemic which ravaged Paris and eventually led to the installation of proper sewers. In May 1831 he was made a Chevalier of the Légion d'Honneur, and in December 1832 he became Maître des Requêtes. Thiers had earlier offered him the same title, his own carriage, the powers of the ministry's secretary-general, and a salary of 10,000 francs to become his private secretary.

The leisured life lent itself to a profligate round of coarse letters, expensive dinners, opera girls, outings on the river, and a borrowed flat when occasion demanded. In 1833 the famous fiasco occurred when George Sand surrendered to Mérimée without either succeeding in arousing the other. They probably did become lovers briefly, until Mérimée became exasperated by Sand's indiscretions to Marie Dorval, who repeated them to Dumas, who with huge delight leaked them round Paris. In 1832 Mérimée had met an admirer, "Jenny" Dacquin (1811–1895), whose life came to revolve around her friendship for him, and who may have become his mistress. Early in the 1830s he set out to conquer Valentine Delessert wife of the much older Benjamin Delessert, Protestant banker who became chief of police under Louis-Philippe. Mme Delessert, whose salon rated quite high on the social scale, was a staunch supporter of a constitutional monarchy. She became Mérimée's mistress in 1836, sharing her favours between him and Charles de Rémusat until both were usurped by Maxime du Camp in 1852. In 1854 she returned Mérimée's letters to signify a complete break.

Mérimée had not produced much since his visit to Spain, but in 1833 he published the collection of short pieces *Mosaïque*, most of which had already appeared in the *Revue de Paris* and which are largely responsible for his literary reputation. The collection was pirated twice in Belgium in the year of publication. Like Stendhal, Mérimée had become more and more critical of romantic historical extravagance and social involvement, and increasingly imposed his own classical instincts for sobriety and control on material which remained colourful, but not visionary. His relationship with Hugo cooled to near-hostility, and his political radicalism had evaporated into disillusion with the July monarchy. He exchanged bawdy letters with Stendhal in Italy, and was clearly feeling bored, hurt, and cynical, attempting to distract himself with a debauchery from which part of him always stood aloof, and which he does not appear to have enjoyed.

In April 1834 Mérimée's patron d'Argout was dismissed from the government, and Mérimée accepted an offer from Thiers to become inspector general of historic monuments. The salary was less than Thiers had offered in 1832 to entice him away from d'Argout, but still 8,000 francs, and the post, which had been created only in 1830, not only offered travel but was one of many, including some consular posts and state and local librarianships, intended to support France's authors. In many instances they provided accommodation, while imposing some rarely invoked limits on freedom of expression in return for at most not very onerous duties. Bouilhet, Sainte-Beuve, Sandeau, Flaubert, Philarète Chasles, and Stendhal all enjoyed such benefits of the patronage system. Appointments were largely on the personal recommendations of influential friends, often salon hostesses. Mérimée's predecessor and friend Ludovic Vitet, who had pioneered the historical dramatic sketch, had set up the department and defined his own duties. Mérimée himself, although he spent decreasing periods travelling round France, was conscientiously to visit, list, and supervise the restoration of important ruins. His annual tours at first took three months but were later reduced to less than four weeks.

Mérimée took his duties seriously none the less. He managed to have his department's budget raised in steps from 120,000 francs in 1836 to 800,000 in 1848. In just over 20 years it spent over nine million francs. Mérimée became a skilled fighter for his conservationist corner, both against the central bureaucracy anxious to retain control of expenditure, and against often incompetent local authorities wishing to preserve a treasured autonomy, or modernizers who, as at Avignon, found that old bridges were getting in the way of new railways, and priests who found that rood screens were getting in the way of processions. The architect Mérimée came chiefly to rely on was Eugène Viollet-le-Duc, who at 26 took on the redoubtable task of saving the cathedral at Vézelay from collapse, and then in 1842 undertook the restoration of the fabric of Notre-Dame in Paris. Later on he became increasingly inclined to substitute innovation for restoration. Mérimée himself preferred romanesque and early Gothic to later Gothic and the architecture of the Grand Siècle, and under his regime the papal palace at Avignon, the Roman theatres at Arles and Orange, the cathedrals of Laon and Strasbourg, and the châteaux at Blois and Chinon were saved. He appears to have relished both the respect and the respectability his position conferred.

During the 1830s and 1840s Mérimée published extensively on history and archaeology. In 1835 Céline Cayot (born 1812), the actress and singer whose lover he had been since 1832, was still his regular mistress. Fanny Lagden came back into his life in about 1836, and his epistolary flirtation with Jenny Dacquin continued. When in 1836 Mérimée became Valentine Delessert's lover, he was close to her husband and her two children and she became the emotional centre of his life. In that year Mérimée's father died, and he lived with his mother until, in 1852, she too died. At first they lived in the same building as Buloz, the editor of the *RDM*, who was anxious to publish any contes which Mérimée could provide. In the meanwhile Mérimée visited England again, then Spain and the Rhine, in addition to touring France. In 1839 he went to Corsica and Italy, where Stendhal, who had recently seen much of him while on extended leave in Paris, decided that he had become pompous. In 1841 he travelled to Greece and Asia Minor on a sponsored archaeological visit. He thought that Stendhal's "Happy Few" owed to Greece their taste for beauty.

The 1833 *Mosaïque* had contained everything that Mérimée had not previously published in volume form. In 1833 he had published two further contes in the *Revue de Paris*, "La double méprise" (extracts and plan), published in volume form the same year, and "Les sorcières espagnoles," which appeared in volume form only in the *Dernières Nouvelles*. Mérimée continued to publish a series of travel notes, but the rare contes now appeared in the *RDM*: "Las âmes du purgatoire" in 1834, "La Vénus d'Ille" in 1837, "Colomba" in 1840, and "Carmen" in 1845. The first three were published as a volume, entitled *Colomba*, in 1841, although there had been a pirated Belgian volume edition in 1840, often accepted as the first edition, which, in all except a bibliographical sense, it was. *Carmen* appeared as a volume in 1847, although it carries the date 1846 on the title page. The volume included "Arsène Guillot," published by the *RDM* in 1844, and "L'abbé Aubain," published anonymously in *Le Constitutionnel* in 1846. In 1842 Mérimée signed a contract for the publication of his *Oeuvres* with Charpentier, to whom he gave a receipt for 800 francs. The *Dernières nouvelles*, including "Lokis," "Il viccolo di Madama Lucrezia," "La chambre bleue," "Djoûmane," Pushkin's "Le coup de pistolet," published in 1856 in *Le Moniteur Universel*, and "Les sorcières espagnoles," were published posthumously in 1873.

In 1843 Mérimée acquired the professional status he desired by being elected to the Académie des Inscriptions. The following year he was to be elected, with Sainte-Beuve, to the Académie Française. The appearance of "Arsène Guillot" on 15 March 1844, the day after the election, caused considerable annoyance. It was obviously calculated to be either an emphatic reaffirmation of freedom in the face of election, or a countersnub should he not have been elected. From about 1841 Mérimée became largely immersed in academic interests, especially Roman history and gypsy dialects, and less caught up in his social life although, like Flaubert and George Sand, he was taken by the new passion for billiards.

During the 1848 troubles Mérimée rejoined the Garde Nationale, having now cast aside all traces of earlier republican leanings. He was offered asylum abroad but decided to stay in France, and was fortunate enough to keep his post under the new republican administration. Vitet and Delessert both lost theirs. Mérimée's writing now took the form of history rather than fiction. He was to write no more fiction for 20 years, although he continued to publish other pieces occasionally. He began to learn Russian and even published a translation of Pushkin's *The Queen of Spades* (1834) in the *RDM* in 1849. He visited England in 1850, and again for the Great Exhibition of 1851. In 1850 Arsène Houssaye staged *Le Carrosse du Saint-Sacrement*, but it failed. Then in 1852 the ever-chivalrous Mérimée published a strong defence in the *RDM* of Mélanie Double's second husband, who had been accused of stealing antique books. Buloz was fined and, in addition to receiving a 1,000-franc fine for insulting the officers of the court, Mérimée was sent to prison for a fortnight. It all turned into rather a joke, with Libri-Carucci offering to pay Mérimée's fine, and Mérimée that of Buloz. The sentence was served at Mérimée's convenience with a friend who also had to put in a few days in jail that summer.

In June 1853 he became a senator and gave up the salary and duties but not the title of his inspectorship, which he retained until 1860. In January Louis-Napoléon had married Eugénie, the daughter of a close friend of Mérimée, the half-Scottish Countess of Montijo, whom he had met on his first visit to Spain. Mérimée had taught French to Eugénie when she was nine. Since January 1852 he had been an Officier of the Légion d'Honneur and an apparent friend of the new regime. From his mother's death in April that year Fanny Lagden and her widowed sister Emma kept his house, and at the end of the year he had published his *Episode de l'histoire de Russie, les faux Démétrius*. It was an immediate success, translated into English and German and pirated in Belgium within the year. In late 1851 he had already published a piece on Gogol in the *RDM* and in 1853 he published a translation of Gogol's *The Inspector General*. That year Mérimée also reviewed the Salon for *Le Moniteur Universel*. He disliked the new vogue for realism, although his letters still at times came near to the pornographic. Russia, its history, and its literature were now the focus of his interests, and he was certainly instrumental in introducing Pushkin to a French public. In 1857 he was to become friendly with Turgenev.

The last 15 years of Mérimée's life were filled with court functions. He helped Louis-Napoléon with his work on Roman history and found a new inseparable companion in Anthony Panizzi. He made plans for reorganizing the Imperial Library into the Bibliothèque Nationale, doing what Panizzi had done for the British Museum. He would spend the winter at Cannes, the spring in Paris, and a month or so in London each summer. At Cannes he met and again became friendly with the aging Victor Cousin, who died in 1867, and saw something there of Juliette Adam, as of Augier in Paris. He disliked Hugo's *Les Misérables*, detested Flaubert's *Salammbô* and, after the famous

Paris concert of 1861, thought Tannhäuser cacophonous. He remained the empress's favourite confidant during all her husband's notorious infidelities, although this necessarily made Princesse Mathilde, who disliked her sister-in-law, more cautious about allowing Mérimée into her salon. Towards the end of his life Mérimée produced three stories, "La chambre bleue" in September 1866, "Lokis" in 1868, and "Djoûmane" in 1870. None was intended for publication, although Buloz persuaded Mérimée to allow him to publish "Lokis" in the *RDM* in 1869. From about 1864 Mérimée had been intermittently ill with asthma and emphysema. He had admired Bismarck, and the outbreak of war in 1870 profoundly depressed him. He went back to Cannes to burn letters and to die. He was miserable and exhausted in the few days before he died, peacefully, on 23 September.

WORKS

While the early hoaxes, the Théâtre de Clara Gazul and *La Guzla*, are not themselves of great literary interest, they alert the reader to features of Mérimée's dry, sardonic style that are later just as potent, but not so obvious. The four articles in *Le Globe* had been a vehicle for advocating a non-classical dramatic aesthetic. They commend naturalistic, non-elevated speech, historical subjects, and lifelike dialogue. In the *Gazul* collection, for instance, the playlets end with what is not at all the conventional plea to the audience from the company's leader to excuse the faults of the production, but what amount to self-mocking authorial declarations that the plays, with all their violence, murder, and systematic subversion of classical norms, are not to be taken seriously.

The prologue had attacked the classical unities of time, place, and action, and the subsequent plays contain frequent scene changes, a time scale for the action of weeks or even months, unrestrained language, thickly layered local colour, prose rather than verse, violence and deaths on the stage, and a mixture of genres, tragic, comic, sublime, and grotesque. The plays' attribution to a liberal Spanish actress driven into exile by the monarchists was intended to be a provocatively liberal political act, while the laconically melodramatic presentation of the plots naturally betrays the pastiche for what it is before the endings, which are always parodic, do the same. The spoof was not very serious because the attack on classical norms was so exaggerated, like that on the Church, whose representatives are instantly recognizable as caricatures, not characters. Patriotic feelings and the aristocracy are ridiculed to the point of farce. The volume was a manifesto, but it successfully made the point that outrageously "romantic" dramatic norms were acceptable to a French reading public, provided that their provenance was Spanish. The settings of the plays added later to the collection were not Spanish, but South American.

The two plays later added to the *Théâtre* for the 1830 edition, *Le Carrosse du Saint-Sacrement* and *L'Occasion*, were both actually produced, and *Le Carrosse*, after failing in 1850, now has a place in the repertoire of the Comédie-Française and inspired the 1953 Renoir film *Carrosse d'or*. *L'Occasion* is a more tender, less ironic play, which attempts psychological depth. Maria, a boarder at a convent, falls in love with a priest, only to find that he is in love with another pupil. She resolves to give them enough money to flee together, and then to commit

suicide, but at the last moment gives her rival the poisoned lemonade she had intended to drink herself. The third play, *La Famille Carvajal*, added in the 1842 and subsequent (1850, 1857, 1860, 1862, 1865, 1870) editions printed in the author's lifetime, is presented as another deliberate exaggeration, not intended to be taken at face value, however serious the underlying point, and however real the fantasy. Don José conceives an incestuous passion for his daughter Catalina. He murders his wife before attempting to rape his daughter, who stabs him and disappears into the jungle.

La Jaquerie, scènes féodales must be accounted a failed attempt to exploit the vogue for the picturesque evocation of historical situations. Like much that was written in dramatic form in the late 18th and early 19th centuries, it was not intended for the stage but, as with the pieces by Delécluze Mérimée had heard read, or Dittmer and Cavé's *Les Soirées de Neuilly*, the form was intended simply to give greater immediacy to the 36 scenes of vivid action, including battles and beheadings. There is no central character or plot, merely a confusion of local colour in the depiction of the 14th-century peasants' revolt. The characters include a peasant monk, a coward, a drunkard, the monk who leads the revolt, a local lord, a haughty lady, a languishing lover, soldiers, and outlaws. *La Jaquerie* is most usefully seen as an exercise in the technique, which Mérimée later used successfully, of embodying in characters the characteristics of an age in such a way as to make them its true representatives rather than near-allegorical figures. Unlike Vigny, but like Scott, Mérimée would in future prefer to people historical events with invented figures.

The *1572 Chronique du règne de Charles IX* is another imaginative reconstitution of history exploiting the vogue for Scott, with rich, earthy dialogue, and vivid use of local colour, but the interpolated eighth chapter is a dialogue between the reader and the author, imitating a clumsy device used by Diderot, Sterne, and Scott himself. It breaks the narrative to attack Scott and to draw attention to Mérimée's own literary techniques in an even shriller way than the *Gazul* collection had done. The choice of subject, the St Bartholomew's Day Massacre of 1572, is characteristic of Mérimée's anti-clericalism and emphasizes the dangers of religious fanaticism, although Mérimée's concerns were in fact wider. He was clearly uneasy at the violence of the era, its resolute political activity, and its strong emotions. The preface argues that the massacre was the unpredictable result of a series of coincidences, although the novel itself makes it a consequence of deliberate choice. The historical picture is obviously intended to be authentic, but is in fact a free fictionalization, and the moral thrust is against factional commitment of any sort, Protestant or Catholic, as represented by George de Mergy, whose religion is only nominal.

The aesthetic is made clear, and it governs all Mérimée's historical works: "Je n'aime dans l'histoire que les anecdotes, et parmi les anecdotes je préfère celles où j'imagine trouver une peinture vraie des moeurs et des caractères à une époque donnée (In history I like only anecdotes, and among anecdotes I prefer those which seem to me to present a true picture of the customs and characteristics of a given period)." This conception gives rise to the short story techniques of the nouvelles and contes for which Mérimée was to become known: swiftness of narrative, vividness of local colour, period authenticity, and accurate psychology. Longer works with broader canvases cannot be merely anecdotal and sustain interest, while shorter ones do not give the author the chance to develop historical verisimilitude.

Mérimée goes on to record his preference for memoirs which are "causeries familières (intimate conversations)" between author and reader, so that the historical canvas provides a vivid background to the narrated or expressed reactions of the characters. The result in the *Chronique* is the subsidiary importance of plot and the focus of interest on background. The "novel" is simply a series of episodes. What holds it together is the detached narration of such horrific events as the massacre itself and the ensuing siege of La Rochelle. Mérimée again refuses to allow his reader to take his fiction at its face value, not only by interpolating the eighth chapter, but through his self-conscious inability to write a fictional conclusion. He ends: "Mergy se consola-t-il? Diane prit-elle un autre amant? Je le laisse à décider au lecteur, qui, de la sorte, terminera toujours le roman à son gré (Did Mergy manage to console himself? Did Diane take another lover? I leave the decision to the reader, who, that way, will be able to finish the novel as he likes)."

The nouvelles of *Mosaïque* exploit Mérimée's preference for presenting sudden action untrammelled by too much psychological analysis. He writes in clipped sentences to give his text a sense of urgency. The immediacy much improves on the lumbering prolixity of earlier practitioners of the short story genre such as Nodier. Mérimée has at last found real literary proficiency, incidentally inventing the form which Maupassant was brilliantly to develop, shortening it to the conte and lengthening it to a novel at will.

"Mateo Falcone" adapts a well-known Corsican story. A peasant hides a bandit, whom his son betrays, and the peasant shoots his son for his treachery. This is a conte almost worthy of Maupassant, although it wastes more words, particularly in its introductory fifth. The laconic narration of the ending is almost realist. The old peasant, having allowed his son to say his prayers, refused to listen to his plea for mercy, and shot him dead, goes off to look for a spade with which to bury him. "La vision de Charles XI" is shorter and swifter, but still concentrates on the background. The narration leads up to the vision and the terrible prophecy, finishing with the dozen lines which explain to the reader how the prophecy was fulfilled. "L'enlèvement de la redoute" is shorter still, interesting not on account of the urgency with which the taking of the fortress is narrated, but primarily for its evocation of atmosphere. Mérimée's romanticism, which is more restrained in practice than in theory, seems in these nouvelles to be a halt on the route from the neoclassicism of the 18th century, which has already lost the classical concentration on psychological profundity, to the realism of Flaubert.

"Tamango" runs to a score of pages. Verbs are heaped on top of one another to hurry the action along, and narrative expectancy is sustained by concision of style as the horrified narrator is coolly informed of the skilful arrangments made by Ledoux, captain of the ironically named slave ship *L'Espérance*, to transport black slaves. The unspeakably callous Tamango, a slave merchant, is himself taken captive by Ledoux, three of whose cargo have died. Tamango frees himself, and kills Ledoux by biting his throat and running him though with his own sabre. Mérimée then throws away the ending: "Why should I tire the reader with the disgusting description of the tortures of hunger?" We are told that Tamango alone survived, rather as if what Mérimée had just related had been a fairy story for which a happy ending was obligatory. The strength of these brilliant vignettes is in the contrast between the vivid portrayal of the often horrifyingly cruel atmosphere and the sardonic cynicism of the swift narration, heightened by its irony. Ledoux finds that he can cram in ten slaves more than any one else into a similarly sized boat, even more if necessary, but one has to be humane: "blacks after all are men, just as much as whites."

Mérimée was not happy with "Federigo," was unsure whether to include it in the *Mosaïque* collection, and dropped it from the 1842 reprint. It is a story about the supernatural in which the protagonist, Federigo, collects a bag full of souls from Pluton. Jesus Christ knocks on the door, is well received by Federigo, and grants him three favours. The point of the story is the laconic narration of an absurd caricature of the miraculous. "Le vase étrusque" is more delicate in its portrayal of the sensitive Saint-Clair, although the story is still recounted with ironic detachment: "J'oubliais un point important… (I forgot an important point…)," the narrator admits on one occasion. The plot meanders, and almost contains a moral. Less happens than in the previous contes, but the story is now in the emotions, and the psychological interest is greater. The quixotic death in a duel is deprived of any excitement by the manner of its narration over ices at Tortoni's, the fashionable Paris café. The fact that later writers used many of Mérimée's techniques to much greater literary effect does not detract from his innovatory achievement in undermining the romantic taste for melodrama while building on its rejection of what had become stultifying constraints.

The contes of Mérimée's middle period develop the techniques used in the earlier ones. "La double méprise" is about the inability of Julie and her lover Darcy to understand one another's motives. Julie, long faithful to a husband who treats her badly, commits adultery almost on impulse and dies of the subsequent remorse. Mérimée's narrator, like those of Stendhal, is here obtrusive in his direct address of the reader—"Qu'on se représente la pauvre Julie étendue sur son lit (Just think of poor Julie stretched out on her bed)"—and there is a clear moral about social convention—"these two hearts which failed to understand one another were perhaps made for each other"—but again it is the innovatory technique rather than any imaginative power that gives this nouvelle its literary interest, although it has been picked out as one of the best novels written in French in the 19th century.

"Arsène Guillot" was written in reaction to a wave of religious feeling which had swept over France, and contrasts the superstitious and simple Arsène, who takes a lover in order to be able to keep her sick mother, and tries to kill herself when she is abandoned, with the arid and conventional piety of Mme de Piennes. Again the emotional potential of the situation is scarcely explored and, given the circumstances of its publication, it is not surprising to find a restrained striving after surface effect in the conte. Mérimée's own favourite was "La Vénus d'Ille," in which a statue of Venus may be responsible for the death of a bridegroom on his wedding night. This conte is not so much just another ghost story as the recreation of a myth. The object of love is beguiling but also destructive. Stendhal thought the style too arid.

Of the two best-known nouvelles, the quite lengthy "Colomba" returns to the background of a society in which strength of feeling is not constrained by convention. Orso della Rebbia returns from the French army to Corsica, where his sister Colomba urges him to avenge their father's murder in a vendetta with the Barricini family, while Lydia Nevil, the English woman with whom he has fallen in love, forbids him to behave so barbarously. The passionate Colomba carries the reader's sympathy, but the point of the story is Orso's need to choose between the two cultures, that of England and metropolitan France, and that of Corsica. In the end Orso is fired on by the Barricini brothers, and kills both with his return shots. In this way he is allowed to evade the choice.

"Carmen," on the other hand, takes passion to its tragic conclusion, although Mérimée rewrote the ending in 1847. The narrator meets Don José, who tells him the story while awaiting execution for Carmen's murder. Don José had twice murdered out of jealousy, then killed Carmen because she could never have remained faithful. In this way Mérimée removes some of the immediacy from the story and imposes a starting point of conversational normality by interposing a listener between the real narrator and the reader. The removal of immediacy is the price Mérimée pays for drawing attention to the plausibility of the extraordinary happenings recounted, while retaining in the reader an awareness of their tragic significance. Any deflating or moralizing comment from a conventional third-person narrator would be out of place. The archaeologist, a scholar devoted to the truth, narrates simply what he hears, so that Mérimée achieves both confessional vividness and an awareness in the reader of the tragic nature of the story. The metaphors are those of the passionate Spanish lover, not the sophisticated French author.

"Lokis" was roughed out in 1868 and, though not originally intended for publication, was in fact published by the *RDM* in 1869 under the title imposed by Buloz, "Le manuscrit du Professeur Wittenbach." It started as an attempt to out-do by parody the literature of the fantastic, which was the favoured reading matter at Fontainebleau. It is about a Lithuanian count, Michel Szémioth, whose mother was raped by a bear, and who, a half-bear in temperament, kills his bride on his wedding night. The story is again the revivification of a myth, and Mérimée shows some imaginative skill in getting the local colour right and the touch of the fantastic not to ring false. The actual fact of rape is toned down so that it is just possible that the mother's fright or a hallucination might have been responsible, but the bride's corpse, on the other hand, has teeth marks on its throat. Again there is a narrator, a doctor whom the count consults. The story concerns a latent atavism supposedly present in every one of us, and Mérimée said he found the mixture of humanity and bestiality "poetic." Psychologically the imaginative pattern restates the fear of the strength of unleashed erotic frenzy which runs through so many of the stories. It no doubt explains too the cool cynicism, irony, laconic style, and sardonic attitude whereby Mérimée the author, often using an interposed rather than a simple third-person narrator, distances himself from the disturbing violence which animates his literary production.

The text of "Djoûmane" was given to Paul Dalloz, the editor of *Le Moniteur Universel*, but Mérimée never sanctioned its publication, and it should not therefore be considered as part of his œuvre. It was published only posthumously in January 1873, is largely devoted to the dream of a French officer about a snake, a little girl who dies, a little girl who is bitten by a snake, and a ravishing girl in a cave. It is a nicely written-up sexual fantasy, less heavily disguised than those that lie behind so many greater literary masterpieces, but too little fictionalized to be seriously interesting as literature. "La chambre bleue" was found in the

imperial papers in the Tuileries after the fall of the Empire in 1870. We know from a letter to Turgenev that Mérimée regarded it as part of a bad joke which was the continuation of a family party game.

PUBLICATIONS

Collections

Oeuvres complètes, 1927–
Théâtre, romans, nouvelles, Bibliothèque de la Pléiade, contains an excellent bibliographical guide to the early editions and works of history, archaeology, and criticism, 1978
Correspondance générale, 17 vols., 1941–64
Romans et nouvelles, 2 vols., 1967
The Writings, 1905

Plays

Théâtre de Clara Gazul, 1825; revised editions, 1830, 1842
La Jaquerie, scènes féodales, 1828
Le Carrosse du Saint Sacrement, 1850
Les Deux héritages, 1867

Other

La Guzza (verse), 1827
Chronique du règne de Charles IX, 1829; revised edition, with "1572" prefixed, 1832
Mosaïque, 1833; as *Mosaica*, 1903
La Double Méprise, 1833
Colomba, 1841
Carmen, 1847; (in English), 1878
Nouvelles, 1852
Dernières nouvelles, 1873
Translator, *The Inspector General* by Gogol 1853

MERLEAU-PONTY, Maurice, 1908–1961

Philosopher and journalist.

Merleau-Ponty was born on 14 March 1908 in Rochefort-sur-Mer and educated at the Lycée Janson-de-Sailly and then the Lycée Louis-le-Grand. He studied at the Ecole Normale Supérieure, where he took his agrégation in philosophy in 1930. He taught at lycées in Beauvais, Chartres and Paris before becoming professor of philosophy at Lyons (1945–48) and then of child psychology in Paris (1949–52). During the war he had been an infantry officer (1939–40).

In 1952 he reached the peak of his profession when he was given the chair of philosophy at the Collège de France, his sole duty being to give an annual series of lectures, which were to be very well attended. For a period Merleau-Ponty was a protégé and drinking companion of Sartre, from whom he later came to diverge in philosophy, no doubt since they never really shared the same starting point. Merleau-Ponty's literary and general cultural as distinct from his professionally philosophical importance derives from his debates with representatives of structuralist (q.v.), psychoanalytic, and anthropological approaches to philosophical and literary analysis. Such debates frequently appeared in the pages of *Les Temps Modernes* (q. v.), of whose editorial board Merleau-Ponty was a founding member in 1945. It was Sartre who had advised Merleau-Ponty to turn from Scheler and Marcel to Husserl.

Merleau-Ponty was a phenomenologist (q.v.), ultimately deriving from Husserl his whole approach to the subject of philosophy. He went on from Husserl's positions openly to attack body–soul dualism on the one hand and materialist behaviourism on the other. While Sartre never intended *Les Temps Modernes* to be merely a forum for his own views, he was its founder, and Merleau-Ponty was led eventually to attack Sartre's sharp Cartesian distinction between consciousness and its object. For Merleau-Ponty the concept of the "body-subject" bypasses the need for a body–spirit dualism by making the human body at once material and spiritual, avoiding the reduction of mind to body or the identification of man with an incorporeal spirit. Not surprisingly, his chosen philosophical field was perception, understood as the pre-conscious mode of the body-subject, presupposed by consciousness. For Merleau-Ponty the phenomenological method could take the form not of an analysis of the content of consciousness, but only of an investigation into the foundation of conscious, rational activity, and the nature of the pre-conscious activity by which meaning is conferred on an environment, thereby constituting it as such.

For Merleau-Ponty phenomenology is therefore quite near psychology, in that a living dialectical relationship between the body-subject and the world precedes the epistemological distinction between the perceiving subject and the perceived object. The child has a true reflective perception of its mother as its mother before it ever infers the nature of the bond. The objective body has only a conceptual existence, useful for a variety of purposes, but the phenomenal body exists at various levels of organization, one of which is "soul." The non-dualistic conception of spirit and matter does away with any distinction between thought, representing the subjectivity of the body-subject, and language, representing its corporeality. Thought and language constitute a single reality and cannot come into existence separately.

Merleau-Ponty also necessarily came to challenge Sartre's voluntaristic view of freedom as the foundation of the human condition. He held that all our actions are in some sense predetermined by a pre-existing situation, and indeed later came to state that man constitutes his own world, in that he makes its structures appear. The role of the artist gives him direct access to the pre-reflective area of consciousness which science cannot reach. Being is simply the field of all possible structures.

Merleau-Ponty was strongly drawn to Marxism, although he came to admit that the Marxist view of history led inevitably to Stalin's repressive dictatorship. During the late 1940s he was the legally responsible director of *Les Temps Modernes*, but after giving up that position in 1949 he slipped gradually into the background as Sartre repoliticized the review. He eventually left it in 1953. While the anthropologists and psychoanalysts continued the intellectual struggle with Sartre's Marxist existential-ism, Merleau-Ponty moved closer to the position of his friend Lévi-Strauss. By 1952 he was directly pointing out how far Sartre was limited by his subject–object dualism, by his reduction of human relationships to conflict, and of all historical human activity to a voluntarism deriving from a dialectic of human and material factors which cannot be understood. His criticism goes further in relation to the origin of consciousness and assumes an almost moral dimension. Merleau-Ponty was political editor of *Les Temps Modernes*, however, and had to struggle with a political view he could not personally embrace, although he might well have continued comfortably enough in a non-political position, even given the review's increasingly structuralist orientation after 1951. At the end of his life, Merleau-Ponty was clearly moving away from Husserl's transcendental idealism towards a renewed preoccupation with Hegel and Heidegger, as can be seen from his last completed work *L' Oeil et l' esprit* (1964).

Merleau-Ponty's philosophy is a form of humanism, demanding a respect for freedom and a recognition of others such as to entail a commitment to the cause of social justice. His phenomenological enquiries, never completed nor intended to be definitive, indicate one of the sharpest minds to emerge in 20th-century France, philosophically superior to that of any of his contemporaries.

PUBLICATIONS

Works

La Structure du comportement, 1942; as *The Structure of Behaviour*, 1963
La Phénoménologie de la perception, 1945; as *The Phenomenology of Perception*, 1962
Humanisme et terreur, essai sur le problème communiste, 1947; as *Humanism and Terror*, 1969
Sens et non-sens, 1948; as *Sense and Nonsense*, 1964
L'Eloge de la philosophie (inaugural lecture at the Collège de France), 1953; as *In Praise of Philosophy*, 1963
Les Aventures de la dialectique (attack on Sartre), 1955; as *Adventures of the Dialectic*, 1973
Signes, 1960; as *Signs*, 1964
Le Visible et l'invisible (unfinished), 1964
The Primacy of Perception and Other Essays (collected essays), 1964
L'Oeil et l'esprit, 1964

Critical studies

Kwant, R.C., *The Phenomenological Philosophy of Merleau-Ponty*, 1963
Kwant, R.C., *From Phenomenology to Metaphysics: An Inquiry into the Last Period of Merleau-Ponty's Philosophical Life*, 1966
Langan, T. *Merleau-Ponty's Critique of Reason*, 1966
Rabil, Jr, A. *Merleau-Ponty: Existentialist of the Social World*, 1967 (contains useful bibliographical material)
Bannon J.F. *The Philosophy of Merleau-Ponty*, 1967
Langan T. *Speaking and Semiology: Maurice Merleau-Ponty's Phenomenological Theory of Existential Communication*, 1972
Mallin S.B. *Merleau-Ponty's Philosophy*, 1979
Archard D. *Sartre and Merleau-Ponty*, 1980

Kruks S. *The Political Philosophy of Merleau-Ponty*, 1981

Froman W.J. *Merleau-Ponty: Language and The Act of Speech*, 1982

Bibliography

LaPointe F.H. *Maurice Merleau-Ponty and His Critics: An International Bibliography (1942–1976), Preceded by a Bibliography of Merleau-Ponty's Writings*, 1976

MICHAUX, Henri, 1899–1984.

Poet.

LIFE

It has been said of Henri Michaux that he did not inhabit his own life. In his late forties he was still writing poetry in which the poet refuses any particular identity, "Je crache sur ma vie. Je m'en désolidarise (I spit on my life. I dissociate myself from it)." This feeling of alienation from his own identity is a constant theme in Michaux's poetry: "Quand vous me verrez,/Allez,/Ce n'est pas moi (When you see me, go away. It isn't me);" "Tu t'en vas sans moi, ma vie (My life, you are going away without me)." It is this feeling of never being totally committed to any of the actions, values, ways of reacting, and attitudes which are constitutive of a personality that Michaux found painful. Where possible, he also eluded all publicity and even well-disposed interest in his affairs.

Rather like Beckett, Michaux was conscious that he was to an unusual degree experiencing a psychological problem which, while it might be the source of a creative activity which could appease the agonies of others as well as his own, he could not bear to expose to public analysis. He therefore fled the world of photographers and journalists and when, on 1 December 1965, he was awarded the Grand Prix National des Lettres, he turned it down on account of the public exposure it entailed. He did, however, give a skeleton chronology of his life to Robert Bréchon in 1958, but he spoke of himself in the third person, tossing away one of many masks to keep the inquisitive happy, and filled his revelations with irony to show how he felt about making them.

Michaux was born in Namur, Belgium, on 24 May 1899. He tells us that his family was bourgeois and French-speaking, although one grandparent was of German origin, and that he had a brother three years older than himself. He claims to have been difficult, unwilling to adapt, or enjoy himself, or return affection, and to have been uninterested in eating or being amused, preferring to sulk, to dream, not to budge, and above all to avoid the need to show gratitude. There is corroborative evidence that, at least until early adolescence, Michaux was turned in on himself, closed to the outside world, secretive, and unwilling to enter into any relationship. He says he was sent "to the country," and from 1906 to 1910 he certainly attended boarding school at

Putte-Grasheide in northern Belgium. There is an element of social contempt in his note that the teaching was in Flemish and that his fellow pupils were lower-class "peasants." By his own account he refused to eat, threw food away, and was overwhelmed by a sense of shame at himself and his surroundings.

After this joyless, defensive childhood Michaux says he rejoiced at the return to Brussels in 1911. The skeleton chronology suggests that he began to take an interest in what was going on around him and in books. He was sent to school with the Jesuits, gently directed by them towards literature, and was taught Latin by his father. He began to be interested in music and to read religious works, Tolstoy, and Dostoyevsky. The university was closed on account of the German occupation, so Michaux had two years after his baccalauréat to spend reading. In 1919 he studied for entry into medical school, but did not take the examination. He then thought of becoming a Benedictine, but his father refused permission, so in 1920 he went to sea, at first in a five-mast schooner. He enjoyed the travel and the camaraderie, and visited North and South America. When the crew walked out in protest at the food, Michaux rather unwillingly left the ship with them, so avoiding its shipwreck three weeks later. In 1921, with the return of peacetime conditions, it became impossible to find a ship and Michaux notes his disgust and despair at being obliged to return to town life and a variety of odd jobs.

He began to write under the stimulus of reading Lautréamont, and found some encouragement from Jean Paulhan. Franz Hellens published his first prose texts in the Belgian *Le Disque Vert* in 1922, but left Michaux feeling that communication in a literary medium did not fulfil his needs. Michaux did however publish in Belgium his first two prose plaquettes, *Les Rêves et la jambe* and *Fables des origines*. By 1924 he had left Brussels for good and moved to Paris, although he was still publishing articles on Freud, Chaplin, Lautréamont, and surrealism (q. v.) in *Le Disque Vert*. He wrote, he says, without finding a personality which "embraced him himself, his tendencies, and his potentialities," and was still devoured by a burning sense of shame. Paris is merely "a great brothel where they speak French." He was poor, insomniac, and suffered from incipient heart disease, but did manage to publish in the *Nouvelle Revue Française* (*NRF*, q. v.) *Revue Européenne, Cahiers du Sud*, and *Commerce*. For a while he worked for a publisher, then as secretary to Jules Supervielle, who encouraged and befriended him, and to whom Michaux could look up as a true poet. Jean Paulhan of the *NRF* helped him to publish his first collection of verse, *Qui je fus*, in 1927. Although he sympathized with the imaginative experiences which gave rise to surrealism and dada (q. v.), Michaux did not feel the need to adhere to any group. He discovered painting as a medium of expression in the work of Klee, Ernst, and Chirico.

In 1827 he set off for Ecuador, Quito, and the Amazon with the Ecuadorean poet Alfredo Gangotena and another companion, André de Monlezun. Michaux left Amsterdam on 28 December 1927 and disembarked again at Le Havre on 15 January 1929. *Ecuador*, his first major work, published in 1929, is the account of his stay on the Equator and is renowned for the brilliance of its non-lyrical descriptive writing. The journey had not, however, relieved Michaux's malaise. His parents died in January 1929 within 10 days of one another, and Michaux set off again for Turkey, Italy, and North Africa. "He travels *against*," says the chronology, to cleanse himself of any feeling of belonging and of anything attaching to Greek, or Roman, or Belgian, or German culture, but the skeleton chronology also indicates a glimmering of desire for assimilation. What he finally discovered, in 1930, was India, and later Indonesia and China. At this point the skeleton chronology almost gives up, but outside evidence for the biography becomes available. Michaux had by now published the prose poem *Mes propriétés* and the first of his books featuring the character Plume, *Un certain Plume*. *Un barbare en Asie* was to be the first fruit of his Asian travels.

Michaux himself notes his journey to Lisbon in 1932, to Buenos Aires and Montevideo in 1935, his first graphic exhibition, the two years 1938 and 1939 spent editing the review of mysticism *Hermès*, the journey to Brazil in 1939, his marriage, the German occupation, his brother's death in 1944, his wife's tuberculosis from 1945, the cure, and the journey of convalescence to Egypt in 1946, her death from burns in February 1948, his shift from literature to painting, French naturalization in 1955, the first experiments with mescalin in 1956, and then the exhibitions in the US, Rome, and London, and the loss of use of his right hand in 1957. His sketch naturally does little justice to the emotional and spiritual realities of his life, even to the limited depth in which they were probed by his verse, and it says little about his success as a painter. He exhibited canvases in three Paris galleries, in Seattle (1954), New York and Rome (1956), London (1957), Venice and Stockholm (1960) before the retrospective in Paris at the Musée d'Art Moderne in 1965. From 1956 Michaux was experimenting with hallucinogenic drugs. In 1973 he broke his right arm, probably due to a calcium deficiency from which he said he had suffered.

The South American journey of 1935 left Michaux depressed and provoked from him "La ralentie," one of his most tragic poems, as well as his first journey to an imaginary country, the *Voyage en Grande Garabagne*. During the next relatively stable years Michaux wrote the poems to be collected in *Lointain intérieur*, preceding *Plume* of 1938. From 1936, however, he devoted his time increasingly to painting. His first exhibition was in 1937, the second in 1938. He was in Brazil when war broke out. He returned to Paris in 1940 and then lived for three years painting on the Côte d'Azur. In 1941 he married Louise Ferdière and published his second imaginary journey, *Au pays de la magie*. It was through Gide's interest in his work, and a conference Gide prepared but was in the end unable to give, that Michaux began to be more widely known. By the end of the war his reputation as both a poet and a painter had been established. He returned to Paris in 1943 and in 1945 published his poems written during the war, *Epreuves, exorcismes, 1940–1944*, and an anthology of previously published work, *L'Espace du dedans*. From 1946 René Bertelé's *Henri Michaux* in the series "Poètes d'aujourd'hui" ensured that Michaux became a well-known figure to the reading public in France.

In 1948 the short *Nous deux encore* commemorates Michaux's dead wife. His poetic style developed, with the creator of myth emerging alongside the humorous and fantastic poet. The poems of this period were mostly collected in *La Vie dans les plis, Passages 1937–1950*, and *Face aux verrous*. None the less, Michaux was devoting more and more time to painting. He published *Peintures et dessins* in 1946, held exhibitions in Paris again in 1948 and 1949, and in painting, too, discovered a new style in 1950, abandoning figurative painting for the splashed colour published in *Mouvements*. After 1956 the period of experimenting with drugs, including LSD, had begun and

most of the later work can be regarded as a commentary on the resulting experiences, particularly the four big works *Misérable miracle, L'Infini turbulent, Connaissance par les gouffres*, and *Les Grandes Épreuves de l'esprit*, to which must be added the two poems *Paix dans les brisements* and *Vers la complétude*. Michaux died on 17 October 1984.

WORKS

The most helpful way to approach Michaux's literary oeuvre is through the problem, which he so often talked about, of finding a unified poetic identity. His poetic self never discovered "Qui je fus (Who I was)," the title of his first collection, because the conquest of an identity was for him never more than a momentary achievement. What prevented its permanent attainment was the refractory tension impeding the integration of the primitive, sensation-thirsty, myth-building with the intelligent, critical, intellectually aloof functions of his mind. The concrete phantoms and images of random experience produce moments of intensity in Michaux's work, which escape the dominating central organizing will of the logical, conceptual, abstract force within the poet's mind. The whole of his work either exemplifies or discusses this inner struggle, and its power derives if not uniquely, then at least essentially, from the strength of the organizing power and the ferocious unruliness of the images imposed by peripheral experience. The justification for using terms like "central" and "peripheral" as they are employed here lies within the province not of the critic but of the psychologist. Most critics would accept their usefulness in any attempt to understand the focuses of Michaux's imagination, and to evaluate his literary strengths and limitations. Exactly the same tussle between the crude emotive power of disorganized impulsive reactions and the imposition of coolly abstract figuration is, as a matter of fact, characteristic of Michaux's painting.

Qui je fus is a book of short fragments, aphorisms, narratives, and poems in three parts. The first is devoted principally to themes centring on the non-integration of the poet's personality, the second, "Partages de l'homme," to the forms of anxiety which derive from non-integration—"Je suis un creux fermé (I am a closed hollow)"—and the third, "Poèmes," to the frustrations of trying to find an integrated linguistic system, as if the problems of integrated identity lay in linguistic structures rather than psychological combats. *Ecuador* succeeds primarily not as a diary or for descriptive brilliance, but as an account of the psychological reactions provoked by the traveller's experiences. Michaux's outlook is pessimistic. Only the imagination assuages. Experience provokes turbulence.

Un barbare en Asie is not the same sort of personal reflection, but a series of travel narratives describing cultures and spiritualities rather than local colours and sights. The tension between emotional shock and critical reflection is quite clear, but the book is good-humoured, cheerful, almost relaxed. *La Nuit remue*, as it has existed from 1935 and not as it was originally published, consists of prose and verse poems to which have been added the previously published *Mes propriétés*. "Mon roi" is a parable of the impossibility of imposing centralizing authority. The king is heroic and astute, but also childish and shabby. His subject kicks him around, but the king has the animals brought before him properly subjugated, and the symbiotic relationship between the king and the subject moves from mutual dependence to complete identity. "Mes propriétés," the text, is a prose poem, only apparently about a land owner whose properties cause him much trouble. They are marshy and recalcitrant, and gradually turn into products of the poet's imagination. The text is an extended metaphor of a psychic struggle in which everything that is concrete escapes control. Time and space dissolve with the concrete things they used to contain and define. The "Sciences naturelles" in the volume announce the imaginary countries to come.

Plume is in fact six works, some previously published in volume form. *Lointain intérieur* contains such important prose poems as "La ralentie," also partly set in the landscape of the imagination, and is followed by verse poems in "Poèmes," and by *Difficultés*. *Un certain Plume* appears here with four new chapters. Plume is a tragi-comic, Chaplinesque character defeated by the outside world whose mechanisms he fails to understand and therefore to control. Michaux's verbal humour reaches its peak. Plume's experience is the opposite of the abstract, possessed, absorbed, and concentrated experience of the mystics to whom the pages of *Hermès* were devoted. The last two sections are dramatic pieces. In "Chaînes" revolt against the constrictions of heredity and education is the indispensable precondition of maturity, and "Le drame des constructeurs" is another one-act play, in which two madmen construct their own lunatic world. The "Postface" regards the "I" as an equilibrium between balancing forces, whose stability is therefore always threatened.

Epreuves, exorcismes brings together several works, of which three had previously been published separately. The volume effectively unites the dark poetry written during World War II. After an anthology of his verse, and an album of paintings and drawings preceded by an essay to be reprinted in *Passages*, Michaux published *Ailleurs*, containing three imaginary journeys: "Voyage en Grande Garabagne," "Au pays de la magie," and "Ici, Poddema." Although the countries visited show cultures which reflect by selection, exaggeration, or contradiction those of the real world, it is not unlikely that the paradigm Michaux chiefly had in mind was that of the primitive tribe, in which hierarchical order was regarded as fragile. All reflect the mind's need to control the activity of the imagination, and in *Ailleurs* Michaux replaced the original introduction of "Voyage en Grande Garabagne" with a shorter text which did not lead the reader to expect a naturalistic conte. The fourth imaginary culture, that of the Meidosems, is included in the next volume, *La Vie dans les plis*, which is in five parts, mostly prose.

Passages is a volume of essays, some of which end as poems, mostly about the experiences of engaging in painting or musical activities. Many are occasional pieces, written over a period for special occasions, although together they give an idea of what is a portion only of Michaux's poetics, and his ideas on the arts and the imagination. There is an interesting attempt in the prose text to represent the fluidity and confusion of memory in the destabilization of meaning and the melting incomprehensibility of the syntax. The reader cannot reasonably be expected to understand the longer sentences at first reading.

The later works try to express the sensations induced by hallucinogenic drugs, or to discuss and analyse them. They include verse, prose poems, and analytical essays on the nature of hallucination, and therefore also of normality. The central theme is again the control exercised by the mind over mental and physical sensations and images.

PUBLICATIONS

Verse

Qui je fus, 1927
Mes propriétés (includes prose), 1929
Un certain Plume, 1930
La Nuit remue, 1935; revised edition, 1967
Plume, précédé de Lointain intérieur, 1938; revised edition, 1967
Au pays de la magie (includes prose poems), 1941; edited by Peter Broome, 1977
Epreuves, exorcismes 1940–44, 1945
Liberté d'action, 1945
Apparitions, with illustrations by the author, 1946
Ici Poddema, 1946
Ailleurs (includes prose), 1948; revised edition, 1967
La Vie dans les plis, 1949
Poésie pour pouvoir, 1949
Passages 1937–1950, 1950; revised edition, 1963
Mouvements, with illustrations by the author, 1952
Face aux verrous, 1954; revised edition, 1967
Paix dans les brisements, with illustrations by the author, 1959
Vers la complétude (Saisie et dessaisies), 1967
Selections translated by Teo Savory, 1967
Moments: traversées du temps, 1973
Choix de poèmes, 1976

Plays

Quand tombent les toits, 1973
Screenplay: *Images du monde visionnaire*, with Eric Duvivier, 1963

Fiction

Voyage en Grande Garabagne, 1936

Other

Fables des origines, 1923
Les Rêves et la jambe, 1923
Ecuador: journal de voyage, 1929; revised edition, 1968; as *Ecuador: A Travel Journal*, 1968
Un barbare en Asie, 1933; revised edition, 1967; as *A Barbarian in Asia*, 1949
Entre centre et absence, with illustrations by the author, 1936
Sifflets dans le temple, 1936
Peintures, 1939
Arbres des tropiques, with illustrations by the author, 1941
Exorcismes, with illustrations by the author, 1943
Tu vas être père (published anonymously), 1943
Labyrinthes, with illustrations by the author, 1944
Le Lobe des monstres, with illustrations by the author, 1944
L'Espace du dedans, 1944; revised edition, 1966; as *Selected Writings: The Space Within*, 1951
Peintures et dessins, 1946
Arriver à se réveiller, 1947
Nous deux encore, 1948
Meidosems, with illustrations by the author, 1948
Lecture, 1950

Tranches de savoir, 1950

Veille, 1951

Nouvelles de l'étranger, 1952

Quatre cents hommes en croix, with illustrations by the author, 1956

Misérable miracle, with illustrations by the author, 1956; revised edition, 1972; as *Miserable Miracle: Mescaline*, 1963

L'Infini turbulent, by the author, 1957; revised edition, 1964; as *Infinite Turbulence*, 1975

Vigies sur cible, 1959

Connaissance par les gouffres, 1961; as *Light Through Darkness: Explorations Through Drugs*, 1963

Vents et poussières 1955–1962, with illustrations by the author, 1962

Les Grandes Epreuves de l'esprit et les innombrables petites (autobiography), 1966; as *The Major Ordeals of the Mind and the Countless Minor Ones*, 1974

Parcours, edited by René Bertelé, 1967

Façons d'endormi, façons d'éveillé, 1969

Poteaux d'angle, 1971; revised edition, 1981

Emergences-Résurgences, with illustrations by the author, 1972

En rêvant à partir de peintures énigmatiques, 1972

Bras cassé, 1973

Par la voie des rythmes, 1974

Moriturus, 1974

Idéogrammes en Chine, 1975

Coups d'arrêt, 1975

Face à ce qui se dérobe, 1975

Les Ravagés, 1976

Jours de silence, 1978

Saisir, 1979

Une voie pour l'insubordination, 1980

Comme un ensablement, 1981

Affrontements, 1981

Chemins cherchés, Chemins perdus, Transgressions, 1981

Les Commencements, 1983

Par surprise, 1983

Par des traits, 1984

Déplacements dégagements, 1985

Critical studies

Bertelé, René, *Michaux*, 1946; revised edition, 1980

Bréchon, Robert, *Michaux*, 1959

Bellour, Raymond, *Michaux; ou, Une mesure de l'être*, 1965

Leonhard, Kurt, *Michaux* (in English), 1967

Bowie, Malcolm, *Michaux: A Study of His Literary Works*, 1973

Broome, Peter, *Michaux* (in English), 1977

La Charité, Virginia, *Michaux* (in English), 1977

Shepler, Frederic, *Creatures Within*, 1977

MICHELET, Jules, 1798–1874.

Historian and essayist.

LIFE

Although it is impossible to describe Michelet other than as a historian, his literary importance derives not from any work of scientific history, but from his supremely creative vision of the French past to accord with the sense of national identity, political commitment, and social values of the romantic movement (q.v.) in France. The relationship between his reading of France's past and his interpretation of its present was symbiotic. Each was the product of a powerful creative imagination. In the light of modern scholarly techniques, especially quantitative ones, Michelet can naturally be faulted as a historian, but it is not simply as a historian that he should be considered. History as taught by Michelet could be, and indeed was, subversive. The government sent spies into his lectures. His historical writing was coloured by, and itself coloured his writing about every aspect of mid-19th century French society.

On Michelet's death in 1874, thousands of pages of unpublished notes, correspondence, and diaries passed into the hands of his widow, his second wife Athenaïs, who died in 1899. Among the volumes she published were two to which she appended Michelet's name, *Ma jeunesse* of 1884 and *Mon journal* of 1888, both purporting to be extracts from parts of Michelet's autobiography. The volumes in fact contain much that is not by Michelet, but by his widow, who has also been accused of suppressions and distortions in the love letters and in Michelet's biography of her. The accusations are true, although circumstances make almost all the widow's actions understandable.

On her death the personal papers passed to Gabriel Monod, who was not allowed by the terms of the bequest to publish Michelet's personal documents, and who himself died before he could complete his biography. The historical notes went to the Bibliothèque Historique de la Ville de Paris, but there was a mix-up, and the personal papers up to 1828 also went to the library by mistake. In accordance with Mme Michelet's wishes, the *Journal*, which contains intimate revelations about Michelet's unusual sex life, was deposited at the Bibliothèque de l'Institut, where it remained sealed until 1950. Part of the *Journal*, particularly for the important year 1841, was either never written or subsequently destroyed. Although the extant papers have now been published in their entirety, it has only been possible to make an overall assessment of the biographical information since the last two volumes of the *Journal* were published in 1976, just over a century after Michelet's death.

Michelet was born on 21 August 1798, the only child of Jean-François Furcy Michelet, a struggling artisan who had come to Paris from Laon in October 1792 and worked as a printer, and the former Angélique Constance Millet, who came from a family of peasant smallholders. They had married on 27 March 1795, when he was 25 and she was 34. Michelet later exaggerated the poverty of his antecedents. His mother's mother had left her children 99,473 francs, and the three unmarried sisters helped the struggling Michelets in Paris. His father's parents, married in 1769, had wanted Furcy to become a priest. As a printer he eventually opened his own unsuccessful press, lucky to have escaped with his life when it was discovered that he had been working on material which displeased Robespierre. He continued to work dangerously on his own account, printing material which could have caused him more serious trouble than it did, until one of Napoleon's decrees limiting the number of presses finally closed down his printing shop in 1811. The family had moved five times in his first 14 years, mostly to escape creditors. Furcy, who was clearly naive as well as warm-hearted, was imprisoned for debt for nearly a year in 1808. Michelet himself never relented in his hatred of Napoleon and most of what happened under his rule.

In *Le Peuple* of 1845 Michelet devoted 10 pages to his childhood, projecting back his later preoccupation with class problems and religious controversy, but sketching a picture of family harmony. The autobiographical *Mémorial*, written during five months in 1820 and a short period in the spring of 1822, and available only since 1959, gives a more powerful, less harmonized view of the young Michelet's life, as seen from the ages of 21 and 23. Michelet paints a youth of virtual destitution, sustained only by money from the aunts, a youth that was emotionally sad, physically cold, friendless, and without entertainment other than solitary walks. His mother died on 9 February 1815, but his father survived until 1846, helping Michelet with his research when his son was already famous.

Michelet went to school only when he was 12, although he was by then able to read. When his mother died he was virtually adopted by Mme Fourcy, the housekeeper of the sanatorium run by a Dr Duchemin where, from October 1815, Michelet's father did odd jobs. When the sanatorium closed in 1818, Mme Fourcy opened a lodging house which Michelet's father managed. Under her influence Michelet had himself baptized in 1816 and, when he heard of her daughter's suicide after an unhappy love affair, he cut off a budding relationship of his own with a 15-year-old girl, Thérèse Tarlet. Although his father had Jacobin sympathies and the educational establishment was on the whole liberal, in late adolescence and early manhood Michelet was at ease in royalist, Catholic surroundings, allowing his admiration for Christianity's defence against temptations of the flesh to reinforce the ascetic devotion to work which he had learnt from his mother.

Mme Fourcy died in 1823, and it was her former assistant at the nursing home and subsequent tenant in the lodging house, the aristocratic but illegitimate Pauline Rousseau, whom Michelet married in 1824. By then they had been lovers for six years. His mother had been older than his father and his wife was six years older than he was. He himself later thought that he was partly seeking a substitute for his mother. His wife was not handsome, and Michelet notes grudgingly that he loved her "even physically." He wrote to his aunts giving a series of eminently practical reasons why he should marry Pauline, neglecting to add that she was pregnant by him. They had two children: Adèle in August 1824, and Charles four years later. Pauline died on 24 July 1839.

Meanwhile, his father had realized as a printer the power wielded by those who could write, and Michelet's parents became determined to have him educated, although it meant turning down a promising apprenticeship. In 1810 he was sent to learn Latin from a former bookseller and entered the Lycée Charlemagne. He had to repeat the first year, but soon became the star pupil of François Villemain, the future minister of education. Mockery from other boys, together probably with the weak paternal model, drove Michelet inward. He focused on his

school work, and his academic career swiftly became brilliant. He finished his schooling at the Sorbonne in September 1821, coming third in his year nationally at the agrégation. He attributed the bullying attitude at school to his social awkwardness in the fresher *Mémorial*, to his poverty in the class-obsessed *Le Peuple*.

He did, however, make two close friends. These were Paul Poinsot, who became a pharmacist but died of consumption in 1821, and Hector Poret, who was to help Michelet get a teaching job at the royalist stronghold of Sainte-Barbe in September 1822, and then in 1824 introduced him to Victor Cousin, considered by the government to be dangerously liberal. Cousin was imprisoned for six months in Germany at the instigation of the French government in case he made contact with revolutionaries. Hegel had to agitate for his release. Michelet's profile was sufficiently low and his sympathies insufficiently formed for him to have a foot in both camps. He had even refused to leave Paris for a lucrative post in Toulouse, but had managed to get a job at his old school for a year after graduating in 1821. He was more concerned not to leave Paris than firmly to align his political sympathies.

From June 1818 until April 1829 Michelet kept a diary of his reading, and from 1821 until 1829 a diary of his ideas. It was Cousin who encouraged him to translate the *Scienza nuova* of Giambiattista Vico on the universal principles underlying the history of nations. It was Michelet's translation, finished in 1825 and published in 1827, that brought Vico's work to the attention of a wider public. Michelet himself had seen it referred to only in the appendix to Dugald Stewart's newly translated history of modern philosophy (3 vols., 1820–23). Between 1824 and 1827 Michelet also wrote three introductory textbooks on history. Speaking on 17 August 1825 at the annual prize-giving at Sainte-Barbe, Michelet declared the unity of all knowledge, regarding all ages and all branches of knowledge as unified by the Hegelian collectivity "humanity." Integration into the collectivity was by way of studying history, the method of discovering the meaning of the present, a view which explains both Michelet's devotion to history and his use of history as a tool for the forging of contemporary political and social attitudes.

Michelet's interests, still heavily encouraged by Cousin, were clearly veering towards the philosophy of history rather than to history itself. Cousin was the most distinguished figure at the Ecole Normale Supérieure, refounded by Napoleon in 1808. He had replaced Condillac's sensualism with the teaching of Hegel and the German idealists, but relied on Condillac's notion of social perfectibility. His liberalism ensured that he was among the first to be purged after the assassination of the Duc de Berry in 1820. He was dismissed from the Sorbonne, and his election to the Collège de France was annulled. In September 1822 the Ecole Normale was closed. A few months after it reopened at the end of 1826, Michelet was appointed on 3 February 1827 to lecture on history and philosophy. He remained there until 1838, but the authorities split the two disciplines of philosophy and history in August 1829 and would not allow Michelet to choose philosophy as, in spite of his introductory textbooks to history, he had wished. In a sense that made him a historian.

Adopting the Hegelian concept of "humanity" as the basic social unit, Cousin wanted to synthesize all forms of scientific enquiry and had replaced Hegel's dialectical reading of the development of human thought with a more deterministic notion of linear progress. Michelet began to rival Cousin and finally, while keeping Cousin's concept of "humanity" as the collectivist agent of human progress, came out in 1831 against the determinist element in Cousin's thought. Meanwhile, the still apolitical Michelet was sufficiently well regarded by the monarchists to have been appointed tutor in September 1828 to the nine-year-old granddaughter of Charles X. Just two months after the revolution of 1830 he was appointed tutor to Louis-Philippe's daughter, Clémentine, and although he failed at his first effort to get elected to the Collège de France, his publications during the 1830s brought him public acclaim, especially from liberals. From 21 October 1830 Michelet had also been appointed head archivist of the historical section of the national Archives, a post he treasured and retained for 22 years, working almost daily at the administration of his section and at the organization of what he was determined to make into France's national archives.

The *Histoire de la république romaine* was published in 1831 and the first two volumes of the *Histoire de France* appeared in 1833. The following year Michelet was made the substitute at the Sorbonne for Guizot, now minister of education, and in 1838 he was finally elected to the Collège de France. It was only in retrospect that he came to attach great importance to the 1830 revolution, although in the 1831 *Introduction à l'histoire universelle* he had proclaimed it the first revolution without heroes to emanate from a whole society as such. In 1869 Michelet was to say that the revolution of July 1830 crystallized his vision of France and inspired him to write its history. His diaries show that he had begun gestating the idea four years earlier. It was, however, in the years between 1830 and 1833 that Michelet dropped Cousin's idea of a cosmopolitan synthesis, and came to identify "humanity" with France.

In 1839, after years of heavy drinking, Pauline died of tuberculosis, and in 1840 Michelet began a close relationship with the mother of one of his students. Françoise-Adèle Dumesnil was the first woman he had met with whom he could share his spiritual and intellectual lives. She was the same age as him and at 17 had married a wealthy Rouen banker 19 years her senior. Mme Dumesnil was to die on 31 May 1842. In 1841, already knowing she had cancer, she moved in with Michelet for the last year of her life, during which time Michelet's interpretation of history reflected a new energy, given expression particularly in the famous pages he wrote on the Renaissance. The Renaissance volume of his history, the seventh, did not appear until 1855. Its draft introduction, written in May 1841, was entitled "Renaissance, fécundité, maternité." The Middle Ages, associated with images of the Virgin and Joan of Arc, gave way to the iconography of the Mother of Christ. For the first time Michelet saw the Renaissance, the very concept of which has subsequently been regarded by historians as vulnerable, as a general European phenomenon.

After the death of Mme Dumesnil, Michelet took a brief holiday with her husband and then took her son Alfred, secretly engaged to his own daughter, Adèle, with Adèle and his son, Charles, to Germany. Alfred and Adèle were to marry on 3 August 1843. Michelet's appointment to the Collège de France in 1838 had put him in a position of public prominence, and he was largely to suspend his serious historical writing for a decade in favour of polemical pamphlets on educational matters, attacking the Church's right to establish its own schools, and conducting a public campaign against the Jesuits in particular. It was these works which were read in the 1840s, especially *Des Jésuites* of 15 July 1843, which sold 15,000 copies that year, and *Du prêtre, de la femme et de la famille*, and *Le Peuple* of 1846. It is difficult to know how much Michelet's personal circumstances prompted his repudiation of Catholicism and the Middle Ages, and generally inspired this activist phase in his career, but his jealousy of her confessor's ascendancy over Mme Dumesnil in her last months was certainly not without its bearing on the realignment of Michelet's priorities.

Migne's *L'Univers* had started publication in 1833 in the spirit of Lamennais's *L'Avenir*, but Louis Veuillot took it over from 1842 and immediately attacked the university educational monopoly, vilifying 18 Paris professors by name, among them Michelet. His circulation rose from 1,700 to 7,000 in five years. The Lyons Jesuits had instantly joined in with their *Monopole universitaire* of April 1843. The educational system was naturally regarded by those who ran it as a powerful force for a united nationhood, and the defence was spearheaded by the three professors at the Collège de France, Michelet, his close friend Quinet, and Adam Mickiewicz. Mickiewicz, born in the same year as Michelet, was the author of the Polish national epic *Pan Tadeusz*. His tenure of the chair of Slavic languages and literature, created for him at the Collège de France on 22 December 1840, was brief and stormy. He fell under the enchantment of the Lithuanian mystic Towiansky, who had cured Mickiewicz's mentally disturbed wife. Mickiewicz was given a leave of absence on 28 May 1844 which was in fact a dismissal. By the middle of the decade the government, originally not unfavourable to keeping Church control over education to the primary level, was seeking reconciliation with the militant clerics. *Du prêtre* was put on the index of forbidden books by Rome.

Michelet's defence of the state educational monopoly was now followed by an attack on the class differences which in his view also corroded the united nationhood to which he was committed. In the five years leading up to 1852, when he was dismissed from the Collège de France and the national archives, Michelet not only cultivated a wide audience in his lectures, delivered in a room capable of seating 1,000, but also published each of them separately. He had become unashamedly populist, and politically committed. The presence of anti-monarchists as well as police spies in his audience did not deter him. He was now lecturing in any case on contemporary France, the press, the literacy rates, and the need for non-literate forms of communication. A student mocked a recent speech by Louis-Philippe before Michelet's third lecture. Republican songs were sung, and the government had an excuse for suspending the lecture course. There was a student protest at the suspension on 7 January 1848, and Michelet published the seven lectures he was not allowed to deliver. He could have had a place in Lamartine's cabinet after the proclamation of the republic on 24 February, but he preferred to avoid open political involvement.

On 6 March Michelet resumed his lectures, but they continued to be the occasion for public disturbances. Concocted versions of lectures attributed to him were circulated by government agents. In an administratively unusual move, Michelet was suspended on 13 March 1851. The decree of expulsion was delayed until 12 April 1852. On 4 June, at the Archives, where the government had also been making trouble for him, Michelet refused to take the oath of loyalty to the new government, thereby dismissing himself. He went into semi-retirement at Nantes, unrepentantly publishing *Le Banquet*, the last of his pamphlets on contemporary social history, in 1854.

Between 1846 and 1854 he had written his greatest historical work, the seven-volume *Histoire de la révolution française*.

Between 1843 and 1848 Michelet had had at least three mistresses: Mme Aupèpin, then his housekeeper Marie, who became an embarrassment and was dismissed in 1844, and finally his new housekeeper, Victoire. On the afternoon of 8 November 1848 Michelet met and instantly became infatuated with the woman who was to become his second wife. Athenaïs Mialaret, a respectable 21-year-old governess from Vienna, was born on 17 October 1826 near Montauban, the fourth of six children. Having first written to him on 23 October 1847, she had come to Paris to see him. She had lost her father when she was 14, did not wish to become a nun, was disillusioned with the Church, had read *Du prêtre*, and was under her mother's instructions either to find a position or to enter a Catholic institution. She wanted to know if Michelet could help her find a position. It took only weeks for Michelet's daughter and son-in-law to find Athenaïs's presence intolerable and for Michelet to seek to move out. After 12 years he left his house on 11 March 1849, and the following day he married Athenaïs, his "spiritual daughter," seeking one of the "individual attachments" he had renounced in favour first of humanity and then of France. The witnesses were Béranger and Mickiewicz for the bride, Quinet and Poret for Michelet. The register was also signed by Lamennais.

Lamartine's 1847 *Histoire des Girondins* easily outsold Michelet's *Histoire de la révolution française*, whose publication he had himself financed. Not many more than 1,500 copies can have been sold and Planche's review was particularly cutting. Subsequent volumes, with an average printing of 2,500 copies, sold about 1,000 copies each. Only after 1868 did the work become popular, with nine editions between 1868 and 1900. In spite of its deficiencies, Michelet's work has the advantage of having trawled sets of archives destroyed during the Commune of 1871, and which are now obviously irrecoverable. The last volume, published in 1853, was Michelet's 27th book in 29 years. In the 20 years which remained to him from 1854 he published 26 more volumes, including the 11 final volumes of the *Histoire de France* and the three of the *Histoire du XIXe siècle*. There were four volumes on nature, and parts of *L'Amour* and *La Femme* were directed to the moral reform of society. His works on women, love, and nature were read more widely even than the pamphlets of the 1840s.

Michelet's final years were not happy. Athenaïs absorbed and monopolized him. In 1850 she gave birth to a son, Lazare, who lived only 11 days. Michelet was distressed that Athenaïs insisted on having him baptized before his death. She resented Alfred Dumesnil, and he her. Michelet and his son-in-law never got back on to intimate terms, even after Adèle's death in 1855. In the autumn of 1853 Michelet suffered from intestinal trouble and went to Italy, where he stayed eight months, but was unable to write serious history. Quinet went into an 18-year exile against the emperor in 1852. Michelet quarrelled with him in 1868, probably on account of what he felt about Quinet's work on the Revolution. In 1853 Michelet had been ill and it was then that Athenaïs inspired him to write his works of natural history; *L'Oiseau* of 1856, *L'Insecte* of 1857, *La Mer* of 1861, and *La Montagne* of 1868. Success was overwhelming, each book selling around 30,000 copies in a few years. Nature, in the form of geography, climate, and race, from being an obstacle to human unity in the 1830s, had become a place of refuge, just as at the same time the works on women and love had hinted at another source of comfort in Michelet's life. In 1862 *La Sorcière* attacked the medieval attitude to women propagated by the Church, while the 1864 *Bible de l'humanité* placed the source of the harmony of woman and nature in India.

On the outbreak of the Franco–Prussian War in July 1870 Michelet signed the petition for a cessation of hostilities, as did his enemy Louis Blanc and two authors he did not know called Karl Marx and Friedrich Engels. Michelet and Athenaïs left Paris on 2 September to avoid involvement, as Michelet had done in 1830 and 1848, and in October they arrived in Florence, where Michelet wrote a short patriotic tract, *La France devant l'Europe*. In May 1871, during the government's siege of Paris, he had a stroke. He recovered and thereafter spent his winters at Hyères. The preface to the third volume of the *Histoire du XIXe siècle* was signed in January 1874. A month later, on 9 February 1874, Michelet died following a heart attack.

Works

Neither the polemical tracts of the 1840s nor the works about nature, love, and women of the 1850s are great works of the imagination, whatever their biographical importance in the context of Michelet's career and its development. The historical works on the other hand are. They contain a powerful, if changing, vision of the origins, the nature, and to some extent even the destiny of the human race. They focus quite quickly on France, uncovered from what, for all the wide reading and archival research, are in the end simply meditations about, as much as narrative of, the history of France. They reflect its contemporary political and social situations, and also the changing personal circumstances of Michelet himself.

The vision is at its most powerful, not necessarily on account of the subject matter, when in 1841 Michelet was writing the first draft of the introduction to the Renaissance volume. His views both of the Middle Ages and, perhaps even more, of the Renaissance have become totally untenable as straightforward history, although that is something they were never really intended to be. Michelet would scarcely have claimed to be going further than wàs required to illustrate the application of a particular philosophy of history to actual historical writing, incidentally thereby showing up the inadequacy of other philosophies of history, like those first of Hegel and then of Cousin, which is not at all the same thing as writing history.

For similar reasons of different personal circumstance, like the experience of the 1848 revolution, the anti-clerical polemic, the commitment to united nationhood and the university monopoly of the educational system, the loss of both his major posts in 1852, and his personal loneliness at that time, much of Michelet's work on revolutionary France is imbued with a passion which allows it to transcend the inadequacy of the statistics available to him. The power with which the Paris of 1789 and 1790 is evoked in portions of the work makes parts of the great history, and even more of the *Histoire de la révolution française*, an important imaginative achievement as a re-creation of the period, for all its lapses in accuracy.

Quinet published his translation into French and abridgement of T.O. Churchill's 1800–03 English translation of Herder's *Ideen zur Philosophie der Geschichte der Menscheit* in 1827, the year of Michelet's translation of Vico. After Vico, Herder was the philosopher of history who most attracted Michelet, and Quinet was his closest intellectual companion until their final break in 1868. What emerged in Michelet's mind, which had also absorbed something of Hegel's teaching through Cousin, was the central concept of "humanity" as the subject of history and the object of its study:

> L'humanité est son oeuvre à elle-même. Dieu agit sur elle, mais par elle… Les grands hommes qui dominent la foule ne sont pas d'une autre espèce; l'humanité peut se reconnaître dans toute son histoire, une et identique à elle-même.

> (Humanity is its own entity. God acts on it, but through it… The great men who tower over the crowds do not belong to a different species. Humanity can recognize itself throughout its whole history, unified and identical with itself.)

The historian's task is to bring the whole continuum to life again, nothing less than "une résurrection intégrale du passé (an integral resurrection of the past)." In fact, Michelet's use of great figures—Joan of Arc, Louis XI, Danton, and Robespierre—produces some of his best writing, but he set out with the view that history was the story of the mass of human beings. History, like the 1830 revolution as seen by Michelet in 1831, has no heroes.

The first six volumes of the 17-volume *Histoire de France* appeared between 1833 and 1844. Like the *Introduction à l'histoire universelle* of 1831, they oppose nature and liberty. The second volume contains the evocation of France in the Middle Ages, and the fifth the study of Joan of Arc, but more important than either is the celebrated "tableau" of France province by province. The first volume had dealt with the racial mixture that fused into France: "France has fused herself out of these elements, while any other union might have been produced… there remains the mixture of a special and peculiar nature to be accounted for." What accounted for the specific Frenchness of France was not any historical fusion of races, but the geographical constraints. The physical characteristics of the country—rivers, mountains, and valleys—very nearly account for its history, and Michelet starts on his detailed analysis of the concordance between geographical features and political organization: "Mere geography becomes history."

Michelet appears to have stumbled on this discovery, arguably his most important contribution to the writing of history. Not only has the geographical basis of history made a strong comeback in the late 20th century against historians relying on quantitative and statistical analyses, but it allows Michelet to produce his most lyrical prose. He first states his conclusion, "The true starting point of our history is a political division of France, founded on its natural and physical division. At first, history is altogether geography." He then goes on to describe the individual characteristics of the provinces: "Let us ascend one of the highest summits of the Vosges, or, if you choose, let us seat ourselves on the Jura…" The vividness of the portrait is astonishing, although the geographical diversity is for Michelet merely the starting point from which France itself forged its own unity, and nowhere, naturally, was that task better fulfilled than in Paris: "Paris alone had both received and given the national character; it is not a country, but the epitome of the country." As history, this is a questionable view and it may even be a wrongheaded plea for further centralization in a country already too

administratively unified by Napoleon. However, it is a splendid vision of humanity concentrating its history in France, and France concentrating its history, conceived as forward advance, in Paris.

Michelet's history has to be read as the panegyric of France's steady move towards unification. The Renaissance, when it came, cannot have been an Italian import. It must have been a French invention. If the Reformation had undeniably German origins, Calvin, at least, was French. In 1831 the July revolution of 1830 was the culmination of French history. By 1842, when personal tragedy had overtaken Michelet, history was no longer a struggle between nature and liberty. It had become a struggle to break down the barriers erected by distinctions of class and religion, philosophies and ideologies.

Michelet's anti-Jesuit polemic shows him at his weakest—paranoid about conspiracies, chauvinistic about foreign influences, intemperate even in the eyes of a liberal, anti-clerical government. The sociological analysis of France's class structure in *Le Peuple* is neither particularly well informed nor particularly convincing. Its defence of the right to own property against Proudhon reveals little insight into French social structures, and the pamphlet's importance is almost entirely biographical, not only on account of the stage it marks in Michelet's personal affairs, but because of the way it contrasts with what we now know him to have written earlier about his own youth.

The *Histoire de la révolution française*, which comes between the two big sections of the *Histoire de France*, is important for the use it makes of the concept of "the people," and for the way in which the whole of the post-Renaissance is seen as leading up to this one great event. It is significant for its use of "oral tradition," unverifiable, but authentic as mythologized family legend, if not reliable as historical fact. Michelet's father had, after all, been in Paris since 1792 and had suffered the Terror and at least the Napoleonic aftermath of the Revolution itself. But the volumes on the Revolution contain no more of the rhapsodic prose which marks Michelet's peak as a purely literary author in 1841 and the years leading up to it.

The later volumes of the *Histoire de France*, those published from 1855 to 1867, are marred by obvious intrusions of bitterness against kings, emperors, prelates, religion, and the monarchy. There are still vivid pen-portraits, and the narrative is admirably swift and evocative, but the moments of imaginative power are not those in which Michelet lets his bêtes noires obsess his mind. He does not write ironically and his invective is not strong. As a result, the smooth flow of the early volumes, which communicate Michelet's excitement at his great discovery about the geographically determined base line from which "history" starts around AD 1000, gives way to a jerky, half-resentful, half-disillusioned account of what happened from the Renaissance onwards, the fruit of the tree having, so to speak, already been plucked in the volumes on the history of the Revolution. The genre of history demands at least the apparent observance of rules of impartiality, which Michelet in the end too freely breaks.

PUBLICATIONS

Oeuvres complètes, 40 vols., 1893–98
Oeuvres complètes, 46 vols., 1898–1903
Oeuvres complètes, 20 vols., 1971–

History

Tableau chronologique de l'histoire moderne, 1825
Tableaux synchroniques de l'histoire moderne, 1836
Précis de l'histoire moderne, 1827
Histoire de la république romaine, 1831
Introduction à l'histoire universelle, 1831
Précis de l'histoire de France jusqu'à la révolution française, 1833
Tableau de la France, 1833
Histoire de France, 2 vols., 1833; as *The History of France*, 2 vols., 1845 and 1848
Histoire de France, 17 vols., 1833–67
Histoire de la révolution française, 7 vols., 1847–53; as *History of the French Revolution*, 1967
Les Femmes de la révolution, 1854; as *Women of the French Revolution*, 1855
Histoire du XIXe siècle, 3 vols., 1875–76

Other

Origines du droit français, 1837
Des Jésuites, 1843
Du prêtre, de la femme et de la famille, 1845
Le Peuple, 1846; as *The People*, 1973
L'Oiseau, 1856; as *The Bird*, 1869
L'Insecte, 1858
L'Amour, 1858; as *Love*, 1859
La Femme, 1860; as *The Woman*, 1860
La Mer, 1861; as *The Sea*, 1864
La Sorcière, 1862; as *Satanism and Witchcraft*, 1939
Bible de l'humanité, 1864
La Montagne, 1868; as *The Mountain*, 1872
Nos fils, 1870
La France devant l'Europe, 1871; as *France Before Europe*, 1871
Le Banquet, 1879
Ecrits de jeunesse, 1959
Journal, 4 vols., 1959–76

Critical and biographical studies

Kippur, Stephen A., *Jules Michelet: A Study of Mind and Sensibility*, 1981
Mitzman, Arthur, *Michelet, Historian*, 1990

MIRBEAU, Octave, 1848–1917.

Novelist, playwright, journalist, and critic.

LIFE

Octave Mirbeau was born into a family of lawyers at Trévières in Normandy on 16 February 1848, although his father (1815–1900) was an "officier de santé"—licensed to practise medicine, but not fully qualified as a doctor. He was also deputy mayor, a local councillor, a Catholic, and a monarchist. In 1844 he married Eugénie Augustine Dubosq (1825–1870), a lawyer's daughter. Mirbeau had an elder sister, Marie, born in 1846, and a younger one, Berthe-Marie, born in 1850. His childhood was happy, although his later bitter disillusion suggests that his early idealism was the product of hypersensitivity. He no doubt suffered from the sudden restriction of freedom when he was sent to school with the Jesuits at Vannes from 1859 to 1863. Here he thought he was made to feel commoner among the sons of the Breton nobility, but an analysis of his school year shows that there was no social distinction to speak of between Mirbeau and his colleagues. Forty years later he was still writing resentfully about the philistinism and superstitiousness of his education. His marks were poor, and he was either sent or taken away before his schooling was finished. In the fictionalized autobiography *Sébastien Roch* Mirbeau explains how a certain aristocracy of temperament can lead to apparent laziness and a failure to assimilate what is being insensitively taught. He must at any rate have had a deep-rooted personality problem as early as 1859.

In *Sébastien Roch* Mirbeau regards school as a microcosm of society, with the same power structures, tyranny, injustices, peer groups, and proletarians. He uses Roch to justify the monarchist and Catholic attitudes he had himself adopted in a series of articles published in *Les Grimaces* in 1883. Mirbeau appears to have studied at home from 1863 until 1866, when he took his baccalauréat at Caen. In 1866, when his father forced him to choose between medicine and law, Mirbeau registered as a law student. He last appeared in the college register in January 1868 and told Edmond de Goncourt that he had been eating virtually nothing and smoking up to 180 pipes of opium a day. In 1870 the Franco-Prussian War broke out, Mirbeau's mother died, and Mirbeau, whose military service had been undertaken by a paid deputy, joined the Garde Nationale, becoming a lieutenant on 27 September 1870. In December he was wounded. He wrote about the atrocious suffering he saw in *Le Calvaire* of 1887, and conceived a passionate loathing for the absurdity of war. He regarded heroes as, for the most part, "blind and bloody beasts." In 1899 he wrote: "L'humanité meurt d'avoir des héros; elle se vivifie d'avoir des hommes (Humanity dies of having heroes; it is brought to life by having men)." Roch sees the point in fighting and killing to live, to eat, and to think, but not between nations. War is the least efficient way of controlling the world's population.

In 1871 Mirbeau was accused of desertion, but he was acquitted in 1872. The papers show that he was acting under medical instructions, but the incident contributed considerably to his later bitterness. On his return to Paris after the war, he took up journalism, writing for *L'Illustration* (1872–73). He was made art critic of the Bonapartist *L'Ordre*, owned by a family friend, but so unrestrainedly praised Monet, with whom he was to sustain a close friendship, and Cézanne, to the disparagement of the artistic establishment, that he was moved to drama, which he covered until 1875. From 1876 to 1877 he wrote unsigned political articles for the Bonapartist *L'Ariègeois*. For some months in 1877 he became head of the prefect's office at Ariège, but he was quickly disillusioned with politics and returned to Paris. During his time there he had several liaisons. For a while he managed to earn 12,000 francs a month on the stock exchange until, broken by his mistress's infidelities, he returned to Brittany, where he bought a boat for 7,000 francs and fished for 18 months. He was later to say, and his fiction confirms, that women were always an unfathomable mystery for him.

From 1880 to 1882 Mirbeau worked again in Paris as a journalist, writing for the monarchist *Le Gaulois*, and publishing a conte in *Le Figaro* on 21 August 1882. He was dismissed from *Le Gaulois* as his opinions grew too radical, but he wrote for it again in 1884 and 1885, as well as for the radical *La France* and *Paris-Journal*. A stinging attack on actors, which he published in *Le Figaro*, caused dismissal, public controversy, and a later retraction. Mirbeau had to offer to fight a duel. Subsequently, he and three others founded a satirical weekly called *Les Grimaces*. It was strongly patriotic and ran from July 1883 to January 1884. In it Mirbeau indulged his tendency to paradox, extremism, and overstatement. At least four of his 12 known duels were fought on account of articles he published in *Les Grimaces*, and his opponents included Paul Bonnetain and Catulle Mendès. Mirbeau was later to regard duelling as imbecile. It has been pointed out that, although he was by turns Bonapartist, monarchist, republican, and anarchist, Mirbeau never deviated from the programme announced in *Les Grimaces*—"to cauterize wounds, unmask scoundrels, trounce evil-doing, and exalt virtue" as he saw them. His initial targets were Jews, foreigners, financiers, the government, and mindless theatre.

By 1885, writing on the need for reform of the penal code in *La France*, he clearly exhibited left-wing sympathies. He began to combine his polemical vigour with his narrative gift, and to produce the short stories with a social or moral significance for which he was to become famous. The *Lettres de ma chaumière*, published individually in *La France* and then as a volume in January 1886, was the first collection and originally contained 21 contes. In May 1887, after a long liaison, Mirbeau married Alice Regnault, a widowed young actress with a son born in 1866. That year she published an unsuccessful novel, which was to be followed by another two years later. Mirbeau began to write his own, finishing *Le Calvaire* in November 1886. It was published in 1887, followed a year later by *L'Abbé Jules*. About 1888 Mirbeau grew closer to Edmond de Goncourt, to whom *Sébastien Roch* would be dedicated. Like Goncourt, Mirbeau loved flowers, and their friendship was partly based on a common interest in gardening. Later Mirbeau was to be a founder member and assiduous supporter of the Académie Goncourt. Like Goncourt himself, he was to move away from Zola, whom Goncourt had taken off the list of his foundation's trustees in 1885 for seeking election to the Académie Française.

Meanwhile, however, Mirbeau's left-wing sympathies were becoming clearer as he attacked the politically inspired ban on Zola's stage version of *Germinal* in October 1885. His leanings were no doubt also helped by his friendship with Gustave Geffroy, another founder member of the Académie Goncourt, an art critic, and the biographer of Louis-Auguste Blanqui. That year had also seen the publication of Tolstoy's *Ma religion* in French, and Kropotkin's anarchical *Paroles d'un révolté* with a preface by the geographer Elisée Reclus, both of which Mirbeau read. Bakunin had died in 1876, and Kropotkin was in jail, but Paris was now the liberal capital of the West. Kropotkin's *Le Révolté* transferred there from Geneva in 1885, and the influence of Vallès, the Russians, and anarchism were coming together to offer one of many alternative ideologies, but one to which Mirbeau found it possible to commit himself. None the less, it was

the increasingly right-wing Paul Bourget, a former close associate of Mirbeau's in the milieu which included both Zola and Barbey d'Aurevilly, and shortly to become a target for attack in the Dreyfus affair, who procured the publication of *Le Calvaire*. Bourget had introduced Mirbeau to Juliette Adam and the *Nouvelle Revue*, which serialized the novel from September to November 1886, insisting, however, on the omission of the "unpatriotic" second chapter. This was later reinstated by Ollendorff for volume publication in December.

In the history of late 19th- and early 20th-century French literature it is obviously important not to overlook the connection between writers and painters. The mutual support of Mirbeau and the group centred on Monet, Rodin, and Gauguin must not be underestimated in any realistic evaluation of what inspired the work of any of them. Fortunately, for Mirbeau we also have the catalogue of his library, and can trace the effect on him not only of his recorded friendships and enmities, but of his reading, which included Spencer, Darwin, Büchner, and Jean-Marie Guyau, whose *L'Irréligion de l'avenir* was published in 1887. We also know of his growing friendship with Mallarmé, whose Tuesday gatherings he attended, although he was interested neither in symbolism (q.v.) nor in poetry. However, it was at one of the gatherings that Mirbeau met and became friendly with Félix Fénéon, art critic, anonymous contributor to anarchist reviews, and for a while co-editor of the briefly symbolist *Revue Indépendante* of Edouard Dujardin.

Mirbeau wrote two articles of support during Fénéon's 1894 trial on suspicion of anarchism. His first open contact with the anarchist movement must have been when his stinging attack on the French electoral system somehow appeared in *Le Figaro* on 28 November 1888. Jean Grave must have asked Mirbeau's permission to reprint the piece on the front page of *La Révolte* on 19 December 1888. Grave had had the idea of using literary material to further the anarchist cause, although both Kropotkin and Reclus had been doubtful. Mirbeau was to become his close associate, especially after Grave published *La Société mourante et l'anarchie* in 1891, for which Mirbeau wrote an important preface in dialogue form, setting out in embryo the whole of his later position.

Late in 1888 Mirbeau went to Menton to counter the neurasthenic pains which were troubling him, and to start work on *Sébastien Roch*. He returned to Paris in May 1889 with only 100 pages written, but then established himself first at Pont-de-l'Arche and then at Carrières-sous-Poissy in the north-western suburbs of Paris on the banks of the Seine. From now on his fiction was increasingly concerned with the criminal ignorance in the rich of how they were crushing the poor, stifling the signs of revolution before they could become visible. The worst of all their crimes was to destroy the dignity of the poor, so promoting their physical and moral degradation to slave or animal status. The power of the wealthy classes depended on the servitude of the poor. Neither Mirbeau nor the anarchist leaders would have anything to do with terrorist violence. When there was an outbreak of terrorism in the years 1892–94, Kropotkin and Grave were especially denunciatory. Mirbeau was the stylish iconoclast of the anarchist movement, not one of its terrorist supporters. The four best-known terrorists—Ravachol, Vaillant, Henry, and Caserio—were in fact all slightly mad. Mirbeau was particularly careful to confine his remarks about Ravachol's bombs to general issues about society and the death penalty. His views were both influential and quite widely shared. Claudel, whose

Tête d'or Mirbeau read in proof, was at this time a sympathizer.

Mirbeau's next novel, *Le Jardin des supplices*, did not appear until 1899. For almost a decade before that, he devoted himself to polemic and to the journalism by which he earned a living, although by 1897 he had turned to the theatre. *Les Mauvais Bergers* was played at the Théâtre de la Renaissance on 14 December 1897, and the one-act *L'Epidémie* at the Théâtre Antoine on 29 April 1898. Catulle Mendès was among those who admired *Les Mauvais Bergers*, although its general reception had been lukewarm. The first May Day demonstrations had taken place in 1890, and Mirbeau had made his sympathies clear by the following year. Grave served a six-month prison sentence for "incitement to rebellion" for printing a piece in which soldiers were exhorted not to fire on workers. There were difficulties in correspondence, and indications that Mirbeau's mail was tampered with, possibly by the police, but also possibly by his wife or the maid. Eventually Camille Pissarro, who was a frequent caller and who shared the views of both Mirbeau and Grave, brought a message from Grave. In 1893 Mirbeau's wife put an end to Pissarro's regular visits.

At this time Mirbeau became close to Anatole France, whose articles were frequently printed alongside his own in Grave's literary supplement. Grave went to prison again in 1894, and 130 writers published a strong letter of protest in *L'Echo de Paris*. Mirbeau, seeing Grave for the first time in court, gave evidence for the defence with Paul Adam and Bernard Lazare. Mirbeau's wife firmly supported him in his strongly pro-Dreyfus stance during the famous affair, which brought about a rapprochement with Zola, who had quarrelled with Grave on behalf of the Société des Gens de Lettres about royalties for material Grave had reprinted in the literary supplement to *La Révolte*. Mirbeau wrote comparatively little about the affair, a few columns in *L'Aurore* and some pages in the fictional form he was subsequently to abandon, *Le Journal d'une femme de chambre* and *Les Vingt et un jours d'un neurasthénique*. He was none the less active in organizing the pro-Dreyfus movement.

Mirbeau had stopped writing for *Le Figaro* after October 1892, but he continued to publish in *L'Echo de Paris*. An operation on his knee in April 1893 and a move to Poissy revived him from a depression. Between 1897 and 1908 he wrote nine plays, of which the best known, and undoubtedly the best, was *Les Affaires sont les affaires*, a development of one of the contes from the story collection reissued in 1894 as the *Contes de la chaumière*. It was staged at the Comédie-Française on 20 April 1902 to critical acclaim, but Jules Claretie, administrator of the theatre, turned down its successor, *Le Foyer*, written with Thadée Natanson, who was co-director of the *Revue Blanche* with his brothers. It was eventually staged on 7 December 1908, but only after several sets of changes and a court case which cost the company 300,000 francs in damages. That made the play a success, but the critics were no doubt rightly disappointed.

La 628-E-8, named after a railway engine, is a series of personal jottings more or less dressed up as a travel book. Mirbeau by now had an automobile, a C-G-V, in which he travelled round France and abroad, and the form of *La 628-E-8* makes it clear how undisciplined his imagination had become and why he abandoned fiction. He simply reflects about whatever takes his fancy, almost as in a series of unconnected newspaper columns. His last "novel," *Dingo*, is the story of a dog, and gives much the same free rein to his imagination.

From about 1905 Mirbeau's health began to decline. He had always kept an apartment in Paris while owning or renting houses in the country. Eventually he and his wife had a house built according to their own plans at Cheverchemont, a few miles north-west of Paris on the Seine, where they lived when doctors recommended a move from Paris. The property had a very large garden, of which Edmond de Goncourt left a detailed description. From 1913, partly demoralized by the war, Mirbeau wrote little. He returned to Paris to live opposite his doctor, who saw him several times a day. He died early on the morning of 16 February 1917, his 69th birthday. His wife left the country house to the Société des Gens de Lettres, with which Mirbeau had quarrelled a quarter of a century before, but there was not enough capital for its upkeep, so it had to be sold. His collections, books, manuscripts, letters, and paintings were sold after his death for 600,000 francs. His wife and his publisher, Flammarion, posthumously issued a great deal of unpublished or newly collected material. His wife outlived Mirbeau by 14 years and left everything to the Académie des Sciences.

WORKS

Mirbeau's first three novels draw directly and extensively on what we know to have been the author's own experience. However, they are presented as novels rather than autobiography, and the degree of fictionalization makes it dangerous to rely on them for direct evidence of Mirbeau's experiences or opinions.

Le Calvaire is a novel in two parts. In the first Jean-François-Marie Mintié narrates the story of his life up to the end of his experiences as a soldier in the Franco-Prussian War, and in the second he recounts his liaison with Juliette Roux, which brings him near to despair and weighs down his talents. Mintié's father is a lawyer, the mayor of a small Norman town. His mother is fascinated by death. Mintié's parents and schoolmasters fail to understand him, and out of ignorance or indifference destroy all that is noble in him. He studies law in Paris, joins up when war breaks out, and observes the absurdity and horror of the ensuing massacre. There is an outspoken passage, which caused much offence, questioning the right of the fatherland to demand so much of its sons. Love of one's fellow men is regarded as more noble than love of one's country, and Mintié embraces the corpse of a Prussian he has just killed.

After the war Mintié finds that his father has died. He goes to Paris and writes a novel, meets a painter called Lirat, whose view of love does not conceal the suffering it inflicts, and in his studio gets to know Juliette Roux. They become lovers and Mintié is made to suffer grievously. Mirbeau returns to recurrent themes, from the hatred of war to the fear of women on account of the pain they can cause, and the need to inflict humiliation on them in self-defence. There is a connection in Mintié's mind between sexual passion, killing, and death. To pay for Juliette's extravagances he sells his father's house, sacks his loyal retainers, and finally submits to the humiliation of being kept by her in a furnished room. She is unfaithful. He flees to Brittany and the sea, goes back to Paris, kills Juliette's dog, and finds that Lirat and she are having a liaison. Mintié chooses to expiate his sins in the public confession comprised by his present narration. The novel was enthusiastically received.

Mirbeau's gift for narrative scarcely extended to the composition of novels, and *L'Abbé Jules* is already episodic to the point of disintegration. Mirbeau continues to attack society, seen as repressing the instinctive desires which point the only route to happiness. The first part of the novel narrates the lonely childhood of Albert Dervelle, a doctor's son, with a flashback to the childhood of the later abbé Jules, Albert's uncle, whose decision to become a priest is a mystery, but who does well and becomes the bishop's secretary. His imagination is morbid, which is both the book's strength and its weakness. Mirbeau had intended the abbé to be the victim of sexual repression imposed by society on its priests, but in fact it is Jules's perverted mind, as seen through Albert's eyes, which gives the novel its interest. At his first Mass he accuses himself of all sorts of sins, wreaks havoc in the diocese, and is portrayed as the clear victim of sexual repression. He nearly commits suicide, but a half-superstitious remnant of belief stops him. He finds the body of a monk, Père Pamphile, long dead in the pursuit of an unattainable ideal to rebuild a ruined chapel and reconstitute an obsolete religious order, a symbol of himself, or perhaps of Mirbeau.

In the second part the Dervelles, hoping for a legacy, ask Jules to take care of Albert's education. Albert is the narrator. The educational philosophy is simple: society is evil, and nature is good, but only if not complicated by mental activity. Catholicism traps men with its superficial attractions, its mysticism, its incense, and its praying. Jules dies, bequeathing his estate to the first priest in the diocese to leave the priesthood. An old trunk he had asked to be burnt turns out to be full of pornographic pictures. The novel was not written to be a popular success, but the symbolists liked it, and some modern critics have praised it. It prompted congratulations from Edmond de Goncourt.

Sébastien Roch completes the set of three novels written in close succession and called "the novels of revenge." Sébastien is 11 when the story starts in 1862. His father, the widower Joseph-Hippolyte-Elphège Roch, like all Mirbeau's bourgeois characters, is physically repulsive as well as morally corroded. In *L'Abbé Jules* the Dervelles' neighbours, the Robins, were even gratuitously given a retarded child. In *Sébastien Roch* the eponymous hero is snatched away from a peaceful, happy childhood in the country and sent to Jesuit college for what is described as "un viol de sa virginité intellectuelle (a rape of his intellectual virginity)," the prelude to his physical rape by a priest. Sébastien's schoolfellows are noble and contemptuous. Only on his solitary walks and at High Mass does he feel at peace. He is not at ease with the Jesuit God of moral rigour, creating laws for the suppression of instinctive desires for beauty and simplicity. After three years the priest who raped him gets rid of him, accusing him of a "particular friendship" with a boy called Bolorec.

Sébastien spends three years at home, keeps a diary, and is precociously lucid about what has happened to him. He sees his own village as the microcosm of society and discovers how the lowest orders are kept from rebelling by "the lie of charity." He falls in love with a girl called Marguerite and discovers perverted and sadistic desires. These are fed by an incestuous feeling for his mother, which is transferred to Marguerite's mother. When the Franco-Prussian War breaks out, Sébastien has to fight. He meets Bolorec again at the front, and is killed. It is in this novel that Mirbeau uses the expression "la sublime beauté du laid (the sublime beauty of the ugly)," which has been regarded as linking him with naturalism (q.v.).

The final novel, *Le Jardin des supplices*, draws on Taine's theory of the environment, particularly that chosen by priests to encourage the intellectual impoverishment and moral subjection of their flocks, when the setting of the pilgrimage to Ste-Anne

d'Auray is described. The "novel," centred on the monstrous Clara, is almost as anecdotal as the fictions which followed it, *Le Journal d'une femme de chambre* and *Les Vingt et un jours d'un neurasthénique*. Mirbeau moves from political to social circles, unmasking hypocrisies and perverted designs everywhere. The narrator accepts a mission to go to China, and meets Clara on the boat. He breaks loose from her, but returns to her in the second part, which deals with the agony in the garden of the title. For Clara murder and lovemaking are both instinctive and connected needs. The object of the aggression is the lawmaker in all his forms.

The play with which Mirbeau is chiefly associated, *Les Affaires sont les affaires*, has as its central character Isidore Lechat, who is described by his daughter Germaine before we see him. His wife and an employee, Germaine's lover, the young chemist Lucien Garraud, also fill in the portrait. Lechat lives only for his business, but he too has an absurd ideal—the abolition of colonies, and hence of war, by making everyone self-sufficient. Germaine wants to run away with her lover. Lechat has promised her to a neighbour with whom he is doing a business deal. He is overcome with grief at the death of his thankless son, but recovers sufficiently not to allow business advantage to be taken of his distress.

In his theatre and sustained fiction, all Mirbeau's characters are in some ways victims of society, and therefore not explored for heroic stature. On the other hand, nature and instinct are examined for the happiness and fulfilment to which they might lead, if not perverted by education, reflection, or social repression. The danger in all Mirbeau's works is that any serious imaginative examination of the interaction between society and individual may be swamped by powerful surges of rage and prejudice, as well perhaps as an over-simplification of the forces exerted. His work lacks power, but not passion. What makes it interesting is its outstanding honesty of purpose, whatever the political colouring of his thought at any given moment.

PUBLICATIONS

Collections

Théâtre, 3 vols., 1921–22
Oeuvres, 1934ff.
Contes cruels, 2 vols., 1990
Combats politiques, 1990

Fiction

Lettres de ma chaumière, 1886; reissued, reduced in size, but with new material, as *Contes de la chaumière*, 1894
Le Calvaire, 1887
L'Abbé Jules, 1888
Sébastien Roch, 1890
Le Jardin des supplices, 1899; as *Torture Garden*, 1931
Le Journal d'une femme de chambre, 1900; as *The Diary of a Chambermaid*, 1900
Les Vingt et un jours d'un neurasthénique, 1902
La 628-E-8, 1907
Dingo, 1913
Dans le ciel (novel), 1989

Plays

Les Mauvais Bergers (produced 1897), 1898
L'Epidémie (produced 1898), 1898; as *The Epidemic*, 1952
Vieux ménage, 1901
Le Portefeuille, 1902
Farces et moralités, 1902
Les Affaires sont les affaires (produced 1902), 1903
Le Foyer, with Thadée Natanson (produced 1908), 1913

Other

Le Comédien, 1882
Le Salon de 1885, 1885
Le Pour et le contre, 1887
Claude Monet, Auguste Rodin, 1889
La Grève des électeurs et Prélude, 1902
La Vie tachetée, 1918
La Pipe de cidre, 1919
Chez l'illustre écrivain, 1919
Un gentilhomme, 1920
Des artistes, 1885–1896, 1922
Des artistes, 1897–1912, 1924
Gens de théâtre, 1924
Les Ecrivains, 1884–1894, 1925
Les Ecrivains, 1895–1910, 1926
La Mort de Balzac, 1989

Critical and biographical studies

Schwarz, Martin, *Octave Mirbeau: vie et oeuvre*, 1966
Carr, Reg, *Anarchism in France*, 1977
Michel, Pierre, and J.-F. Nivet, *Octave Mirbeau: l'imprécateur au coeur fidèle*, 1990

———

MISTRAL, Frédéric (-Joseph-Etienne), 1830–1914.

Poet.

LIFE

Mistral is chiefly known as the leader of the "Félibrige," a movement whose members, the "Félibres," sought to restore Provençal as a living language in the mid-19th century. At an annual meeting in 1854 a group of seven Provençal poets decided to attempt to revive interest in Provençal customs and history, to restore the Provençal language, to have it taught in schools, and themselves to write in Provençal. The term "félibres" comes from an old Provençal tale in which Jesus was found disputing in the temple with "li sét felibre de la léi," which Mistral took to mean "the seven doctors of the law." In 1855 a popular annual almanac, *L'Armana prouvençau*, was founded to give information about Provence and its literature. Associated with Mistral were Joseph Roumanille, Théodore Aubanel, Jean

Brunet, Paul Giéra, Remy Marcellin, and Anselme Mathieu. The group was soon joined by an eighth member, Alphonse Tavan.

Mistral was born at Maillane on 8 September 1830, the only son of a prosperous farmer and a simple, pious woman who taught him to love the country songs and legends of the region. Mistral recounts his early life with charm and directness in the autobiographical sketch prefixed to *Lis Isclo d'or* (The Golden Islands). After attending the local school at Saint-Michel-de-Frigolet until the age of eight, he was sent to school at Avignon while living at the Pension Dupuy. Here he greatly resented the curtailment of his freedom to roam the countryside at will, but he came to enjoy Homer and Virgil, whose first eclogue he translated. He also made friends with Mathieu, a fellow pupil, and Roumanille, an assistant teacher, whose dialect poems deeply impressed him. Mistral left school in 1847, returned to Maillane for a year, and sketched a dialect pastoral poem in four cantos, "Li meissoun" (The harvest), as well as writing French verse partly inspired by the 1848 revolution. He then went on to study law at Aix, where he graduated in 1851. He returned home to spend the following years at the family house, Le Mas du Juge, until his father's death, when he moved to another house in Maillane. In 1852 he contributed his first published poems to Roumanille's *Li Prouvençalo*, having first published them in Roumanille's *La Commune*. He devoted the rest of his life to the renaissance of Provençal language, literature, and culture.

The group of Provençal poets met at Arles in 1852 and Aix in 1853 before the decisive 1854 meeting at the Château de Font-Ségugne, near Avignon. In 1859 Mistral published his tragic verse romance of rural life in epic form, *Mirèio* (Mireille), with a facing translation into French. Gounod made it into an opera. Adolphe Dumas, a Provençal from Paris who admired the poem, presented Mistral to Lamartine, who devoted his 40th *Entretien de la littérature* to it, hailing Mistral as a new Virgil and proclaiming that "un pays est devenu un livre (a country has become a book)." The "Félibrige" was organized and adopted its first constitution in 1862, becoming widely accepted from the Alps to the Pyrenees and beyond. Mistral also became associated with the renaissance of Catalan, inspired by the example of his own movement, and was enthusiastically welcomed in Barcelona. From 1863, genuinely interested in linguistic phenomena, he began compiling his two-volume *Lou Tresor dóu Felibrige*, a Provençal–French dictionary and thesaurus, having in the meanwhile published in 1867 the allegorical poem *Calendau*, again with a facing translation into French.

In 1876 Mistral married Marie Rivière from Dijon, publishing in that year the collection of short poems *Lis Isclo d'or* with facing translation. The poems, written since 1848, included two which caused considerable controversy on their first appearance: "La coupe," which, inspired by a gift from the Catalans, became the rallying hymn of the "Félibrige," and "La princesse." Mistral was accused of trying to promote discord between north and south in France. The nouvelle *Nerto* appeared in 1884, still with a translation, and the panoramic spectacle *La Rèino Jano*, a verse tragedy in five acts, was published in a bilingual edition in 1890. Mistral's other major works were the Rhône epic in 12 cantos of blank verse, *Lou Pouème dóu rose*, published in a bilingual edition in 1897 by Lemerre; the memoirs *Moun espelido, memòri e raconte* (*Mes origines, mémoires et récits*), published in 1906 by Plon in separate Provençal and French editions; and *Lis Oulivado*, songs of the olive harvest published in 1912 by Lemerre with a French translation. In 1904 Mistral shared the Nobel prize for literature with the Spanish dramatist José Echegaray.

In addition to being a poet and a scholar, Mistral was also a journalist and a publicist. He tirelessly wrote letters and prefaces, and made speeches, some of which were collected in the 1906 *Discours e dicho*. He attempted to found a linguistic union of Latin-based languages, paying particular attention to Romania, presided over the Latin poetic and philological congresses at Montpellier, founded his own newspaper, *L'Aîòli*, and in 1899 established the Museon Arlaten, the Arles museum of Provençal life and culture to which he gave most of the Nobel prize money. Mistral continued to be active into old age, publishing a translation of Genesis into Provençal in 1910 to show what the language was capable of. He died suddenly on 25 March 1914. Much of his correspondence is still unpublished. He is important for his federalist, Pan-Latin, but regionalist and anti-centralist ideology, as well as for his literary output.

WORKS

Lamartine's enthusiasm for Mistral was partly rooted in his own populist views in and immediately after 1848. Mistral was a poet of the people before he was a regional, an epic, or a lyric poet, and before he was a publicist and journalist. He resented the downgrading of Provençal into a mere patois, was enough of a scholar to be interested in its linguistic roots, and enough of a historian to realize the immense value of the troubadour inheritance. He also recognized the need to standardize Provençal orthography and grammar. Mistral's commitment to spiritual values, to regional economic independence and political autonomy, and his dislike of the suffocation of regional France by a centralized bureaucracy take second place to his commitment to the people of French Mediterranean culture. The culture union of Latin-based linguistic regions which he strove for might have resulted in a federalist structure, but it was imperative to Mistral that the individuality of each country and region should be respected. It is possible that the populist and even revolutionary nature of his inspiration has been underestimated. At school what he had initially wanted to do with Roumanille had been "to restore the language according to national traditions and characteristics."

Mirèio, which was an instant success, is the story of a rich girl kept by her parents from a poor lover. She wanders across country to the church of the three Marys of the Gospel story in the hope that they might help her, but is overwhelmed by the effort and dies exhausted in the presence of her grieving parents and frenzied lover. Mistral has woven into the poem accounts of Provençal life, scenery, customs, and legends, so that it becomes a rustic epic peopled by simple, unassuming characters. The absence of serious psychological analysis allows them to play out their simple epic roles in a way which adds force to the poem.

Calendau of 1867 relates the story of a beautiful princess, Esterello, held captive by a brigand and rescued by a youthful fisherman. Mistral was particularly fond of this work, but it is generally considered a less successful poem than *Mirèio*, in spite of the primeval structure of the story and the descriptions of Provençal scenery. Some of the folk background has been thought artificial, and the allegorical form, in which the princess represents Provence, the brigand France, and the youthful hero the "Félibrige," is too laboured to be entirely convincing.

Lis Isclo d'or exploits old Provençal legends, fables, and "sirventes," or poems with a moral point, and contains some of Mistral's best and most populist lyrics. *Nerto* is described as a nouvelle but is in fact a tragic narrative poem or lyrical drama in four acts. A girl from medieval Avignon, whose dissipated father has sold her soul to the devil, charms her lover into idealizing his passion for her, and the story recalls stylized medieval depictions of love. Mistral's next work, *La Rèino Jano*, was intended to be a tragedy. It was in fact his only failure, presumably because it consists more of a series of tableaux without dramatic action or depth of character than of a tragic action. *Lou Pouèmo dóu rose*, an epic poem narrating the history of the Rhône since Roman times, depicts the barge life of the river, interweaving it with legends adhering to its banks and with a charming love idyll. Mistral uses blank verse for the first time, and with a mastery which has been much admired, although the ancient Provençal lore is, from a literary point of view, undoubtedly intrusive.

Lou Tresor dóu Felibrige is a scholarly dictionary of dialect words, with usages and meanings, illustrations, quotations, etymologies, comparative notes on dialect differences, technical and popular expressions, place names and family names, notes on customs, proverbs and biographical, bibliographical, and historical sketches. Finished in 1886, it is a work of devotion and erudition. Publication was in fascicules, bound into two volumes.

PUBLICATIONS

Collections

Oeuvres, 6 vols., 1886–1921
Oeuvres poétiques complètes, 2 vols., 1966–68
Proso d'Armana, 3 vols., 1926, 1927, 1930

Verse

Mirèio, 1859; translated by C. Grant, 1867, and (in verse) H. Crjchton, 1868, and Harriet W. Preston, 1872
Calendau, 1867
Lis Isclo d'or, 1876
Nerto, 1884
La Rèino Jano, 1890
Lou Pouèmo dóu rose, 1897; as *Anglora: The Song of the Rhone*, translated by Maro Beath Jones, 1937
Lis Oulivado, 1912

Other

Thèse, 1851
Lou Tresor dóu Felibrige; ou, Dictionnaire provençal–français, 2 vols., 1879–87
Les Secrets des bêtes (translated from *L'Aîòli*), 1896
Discours e dicho, 1906
Moun espelido, memòri e raconte, 1906; translated, 1907, 1928
Correspondance de Frédéric Mistral et Adolphe Dumas, 1856–1861, 1959

Biographical and critical studies

Lasserre, P., *Frédéric Mistral, poète, moraliste, citoyen*, 1918

André, M., *La Vie harmonieuse de Mistral*, 1928

Thibaudet, A., *Mistral; ou, La République du soleil*, 1930

Girdlestone, C. M., *Dreamer and Striver: The Poetry of Frédéric Mistral*, 1937

Devoluy, P., *Mistral et la rédemption d'une langue*, 1941

Decremps, M., *Mage de l'occident*, 1954

Lafont, R., *Mistral; ou, L'Illusion*, 1954

Peyre, S.-A., *Frédéric Mistral*, 1959

MONTHERLANT, Henry (Millon) de, 1896–1972

Novelist, essayist, and dramatist.

LIFE

Montherlant was born into an aristocratic family on 21 April 1896 in one of Paris's wealthier quarters, the seventh arrondissement. His father, who has been described as "a connoisseur of art and horses," came from Picardy and was of distant Spanish ancestry. His mother, Marguerite Camusat de Riancey, came from a family in the papal service, exercised a possessive affection over her son, and suffered when its demands were not met by an equal devotion. She herself had been brought up by a devout mother haunted by the prospect of death, whose room was full of pictures of mourning and sketches of friends on their deathbeds.

The family moved, and in 1905, at the age of eight, Montherlant was sent to the Lycée Janson-de-Sailly. Then, for a year, he was tutored privately. The family moved again to Neuilly, where Montherlant attended the Institution Saint-Pierre from 1907 to 1910. From January 1911 he attended the Ecole Sainte-Croix, where he was very happy, but from which he was dismissed in March 1912, apparently due to his high spirits and emotional intensity. He passed his baccalauréat, none the less, and began to study law at the Institut Catholique, though not through need or any sense of vocation. He also took dancing lessons and began to paint, having already written a play and been deeply impressed by the novel *Quo vadis?* (1896) by the Nobel prize winner Henryk Sienkiewicz. In 1913 Montherlant failed his law examinations. Already enthusiastic about bullfighting after holidaying in Spain and fighting his first bulls in 1911, he was to develop serious interests in athletic pursuits, especially football, and in the history of Roman civilization, particularly in Iberia.

After the death of his father in March 1914, Montherlant wanted to enlist, but was restrained by his mother. She herself died on 15 August 1915, after pleading with her son not to become a writer. Montherlant admired Barrès and d'Annunzio and, in spite of non-conformist inclinations apparently clear in his behaviour, read widely, wrote but did not publish, remained pious, and devoted himself to good works. Among the pieces he wrote in 1914 was a remarkable play, *L'Exil*, to be published only in 1929. Before enlisting in 1916 he left with a publisher the manuscript of *La Relève du matin*, a volume of essays to be published at his own expense in 1920. He was wounded in 1918, and in 1919 became an interpreter with the US forces.

Montherlant's literary reputation rests on his achievements as a dramatist, although his first play was performed and published only in 1942. Until World War II he was known exclusively as a novelist and essayist and, although his reputation as both has moved sharply downwards, he was much acclaimed by the interwar generation, including Barrès, Mauriac, Romain Rolland, Maurois, and Gide, with the culminating accolade from Bernanos, who, in 1939, called him "Le plus grand peut-être de nos écrivains vivants (Perhaps the greatest of our living writers)."

Although *La Relève du matin* is still an adolescent text, full of timid hypersensitivity and spiritual enthusiasms, the novel *Le Songe*, published in 1922, was not so well received at first. In spite of its luxuriant language and lyrical tone, it remains dominated by memories of the war. During the decade following World War I Montherlant published further largely autobiographical lyrical novels which were almost prose poems: the two-volume *Les Olympiques*, a mixture of prose, poetry, and dramatic fragments written between 1920 and 1924 in time for the Paris Olympic Games of that year and glorifying sport; *Les Bestiaires*, which elaborates the mystique of bullfighting; and *La Petite Infante de Castille*, which is partly a diary of Montherlant's wanderings in Europe and Africa and may originally have been intended as the beginning of a conventional novel.

It belongs with *Aux fontaines du désir*, the 1927 volume which contains the key essay "Syncrétisme et alternance," as a testimony to Montherlant's long quest to establish his own identity and values. Like the hero of *Les Bestiaires*, Alban de Bricoule, he had freed himself from the environment of his upbringing. He had also long shed the Catholic beliefs of his family, although not yet the spirituality of his youth. The essays explore the possibilities of reducing happiness to physical well-being and of abolishing obligation to other people, rather like the Ménalque of Gide's *L'Immoraliste*. Montherlant, too, had been ill in North Africa, and the "Syncrétisme" essay, which is the key to his later imaginative investigations, suggests the possibility of life without transcendent values or the veneer of civilization. Is man merely a human animal? If his humanity lifts man above animality, how has it failed him? The grandiose and sonorous tirades of the plays clothe a man who, for Montherlant, is still being probed for primitive, unelevated passions.

Man, for Montherlant, is not likely to be found *Au-dessus de la mêlée*, as he is for Romain Rolland. His warrior nature may bring out his finest qualities, patriotism, sacrifice, and the killer instinct to protect the herd. The idea is repugnant, but this is the possibility which Montherlant examines, and he has been accused of lacking the necessary distaste for what he finds. He is insufficiently aghast, it has been urged, at man's horrific capacity for destroying his like, and comes near to finding in animal nature the basis for a human ethic, glorying in physical strength and readiness for combat. Even some of his greatest admirers have been inclined to find more sympathy in Montherlant for man's brutal drives than for cultivated moral codes and cultural values, which are tested for what they may contain in terms of posture and attitudinizing. Moral codes are apt to break down because they are not really natural to the human animal, or such at least is the possibility which Montherlant examines—with too little fastidiousness, according to his critics. For him, hatred, greed, the striving for power, and the desire to possess all have their not unadmirable place in the values which man's nature has established.

> Je suis poète, je ne suis même que cela, et j'ai besoin d'aimer et de vivre toute la diversité du monde et tous sès prétendus contraires, parce qu'ils sont la matière de ma poésie, qui mourrait d'inanition dans un univers où ne régneraient que le vrai et le juste… Etre à la fois, ou plutôt faire alterner en soi, la Bête et l'Ange, la vie corporelle et charnelle et la vie intellectuelle et morale, que l'homme le veuille ou non, la nature l'y forcera.

> (I am a poet, I am even only that, and I need to love and to live the whole of the world's diversities and all its supposed opposites because they are the material of my poetry, which would die of starvation in a universe where only the just and the true reigned… To be at the same time, or rather to allow to alternate in oneself, the beast and the angel, the life of the body and the flesh and intellectual and moral life, whether man wants it or not, nature will force him to it.)

The essay *Chant funèbre pour les morts de Verdun* had appeared in 1924, and at Tunis in 1928. Montherlant had begun a play entitled "Les Crétois," of which he published only a fragment as a dramatic poem, *Pasiphaé*, in 1936. "Les Crétois" was to have been a symbolic drama based on the myths surrounding the house of Minos, but Montherlant found it impossible to combine the full richness of the myths, which he did not want to sacrifice, with the dramatic unity essential for a successful play. However, he did attempt two other dramatic works in 1929; "Don Fadrique," a three-page extract of which was published in 1935, and a play called "La ville dont le prince est un enfant," which may have been the basis for the play of that name which Montherlant did publish in 1951 and which is often considered to have been one of his best. *Mors et vita*, a collection of essays, was published in 1932, and *Encore un instant de bonheur*, Montherlant's major collection of verse, in 1934. He had resigned himself to mortality, extinction at death, praising those who interred hopes of immortality, but was shaken by reading Sainte-Beuve's *Port-Royal*. He spent Holy Week at the Benedictine abbey of Solesmes, made a religious retreat at the monastery of Montserrat, an age-old place of pilgrimage, and went to Rome, becoming not so much a Christian as a rigid puritan.

In 1934 Montherlant published his first major novel, *Les Célibataires*, which is about three bachelors belonging to the fading caste of the Breton nobility, although only two of them are strictly essential to the story of the dissolution of the once-proud family. The novel, originally published in the *Revue des Deux Mondes* (q. v.), won an English literary prize, the Northcliffe, as well as the Grand Prix de Littérature of the Académie Française. It was also translated immediately into Russian and Spanish. The earlier conventional novel *La Rose de sable*, written between 1932 and 1934, had not been published. A fragment, *L'Histoire d'amour de "La Rose de sable,"* described as a "novelette," did appear in 1954, and Montherlant said that publication of the original text at the date it was written was awkward because the novel was an exposé of French colonial policy in North Africa. It was plausibly suggested that the real reason for suppressing the book was that it exaltated passionate, combative, warrior-like qualities which Montherlant wished to softpedal after his Easter at Solesmes and his retreat at Montserrat. A full version appeared in 1968.

After this came the tetralogy examining the relationship of four different women to the same writer, largely seen through their correspondence with him. The whole was called by the title of the first novel, *Les Jeunes Filles*. The other three were *Pitié pour les femmes, Le Démon du bien*, and *Les Lépreuses*. It is largely on the tetralogy that Montherlant's reputation as a misogynist is based. He came to regret the generalized assumptions which could be drawn from his treatment of what he did not make sufficiently clear was a special class of women. He returned to the novel, after his successful theatrical career, with the brief and pessimistic *Le Chaos et la nuit* of 1963. It is often considered to be his finest work, ending with the identification of the anarchist Celestino, a political failure who is also personally defeated, with a dying bull in the ring—part of a ritual whose mystique has now been commercialized and degraded.

Montherlant has produced further volumes of essays: *Service inutile* in 1935, *L'Equinoxe de septembre* in 1938, and *Le Solstice de juin* in 1941. *Un voyageur solitaire est un diable* was to follow in 1945, and then *Textes sous une occupation* in 1953. Apart from his notebooks, he published nothing else in volume form outside drama, and it was in drama that he was to find the discipline he needed to achieve true literary excellence. The plays are not Catholic plays, although they are often about religious problems in Catholic contexts and settings, and they have very little external action, concentrating on the psychological problems of the characters. Unusually for a living dramatist, Montherlant's plays were often first staged by the Comédie-Française. The order of their performance and publication is not the same as that of their composition.

A scene from *L'Exil* was performed in 1934, and *Pasiphaé* was produced in 1938, but it was only with the success of *La Reine morte* in 1942 that Montherlant became known as a dramatist. The plot takes up an Iberian legend, on several of whose forms Montherlant appears to have drawn. The king of Portugal's passions triumph over his duty. He wants his son to marry the Infanta of Navarre, finds him already secretly married to Inès, who is pregnant by him, and, for reasons of thwarted domination rather than political expediency, has her killed. When the play was published Montherlant surrounded the text with long explanations, failing to understand that, once a play had been staged, he could no longer change anything by saying what it was meant to mean.

La Reine morte was published with a prefatory account of the sources of the legend, and a brief letter to Jean-Louis Vaudoyer of the Comédie-Française, explaining what Montherlant wanted to portray, was followed by no fewer than five articles and essays going as far as 1954 by way of explanation. As a matter of biographical fact, Montherlant attached much importance not only to justifying but also to changing the imaginative patterns he had established in the light of the public reaction they had occasioned. As a matter of historical and critical principle, as well as of biographical fact, he inaugurated a discussion with his critics, which has sometimes been fierce, by attempting to gloss his own texts. The argument hinges on the view that an author may deplore or withdraw what he has published, but cannot change the imaginative patterns in a published text, even if he subsequently suppresses it, or exercises his right to change them in a new version of the text. The murder of Inès in the 1942 text of *La Reine morte* clearly remains the result of a man's thwarted desire to impose his will on a weaker woman.

Fils de personne and *Un incompris* were written to balance one another on the same programme in 1943, but production is said to have been precluded by the curfew. Both were published in 1944, but a new second play, *Demain il fera jour*, was written in 1948, to be published and performed only in 1949. *Malatesta*, a tragedy set in Renaissance Rimini and Rome, was begun in 1943, published in 1946, but not produced until 1950. *Le Maître de Santiago* of 1947 again has a historical setting, this time Spanish. Donald Wolfit produced both this play and its predecessor at the Lyric Theatre in Hammersmith in 1957, while *La Reine morte*, as *Queen after Death*, was staged in Dundee in 1952 and revived in 1961. Montherlant's plays have nevertheless had little success in the UK.

At the end of World War II Montherlant was put on the list of banned writers for a period, although there were no serious accusations against him of collaboration with the occupying forces. In 1949 he wrote *Celles qu'on prend dans ses bras*, which was performed in 1950, and in 1951 he published *La Ville dont le prince est un enfant*, together with a large dossier of notes, correspondence, and explanation which shows a real hesitation about allowing the play to be produced for fear of shocking Catholic opinion. The play recalls Montherlant's expulsion from the Ecole Sainte-Croix in 1912. It was followed by what he himself regarded as the culmination of his dramatic career, *Port-Royal*. This celebrated not so much the religion, and still less the theology, of the nuns of Port-Royal, the home of Jansenism in 17th-century France, as the firmness of their spiritual commitment to a cause in which they believed. The first performance was on 8 December 1954.

The last four plays, which together with the *Carnets* complete Montherlant's literary output, were *Brocéliande, Don Juan, Le Cardinal d'Espagne* and *La Guerre civile*. As a result of sunstroke in 1959 Montherlant started to go blind. In 1968 he lost all sight in his left eye. At four p.m. on Thursday, 21 September 1972 he committed suicide, declaring: "Je deviens aveugle, je me tue (I am going blind. I am killing myself)." His ashes were scattered over the forum in Rome in April 1973.

WORKS

Although *Le Songe* is overshadowed by the war in which Stanislas Prinet, the hero's close friend, dies, the novel chiefly concerns its central character, Alban de Bricoule, and his search for independence, action, and domination. He goes to the front because he needs to develop and demonstrate his virility and strength, and must dominate Prinet, who is already there and whose dog Bricoule sadistically insists on killing. He treats his undemanding mistress, Douce, as if she existed only to give him pleasure, and views the acceptance or return of love, or any form of emotional dependence, as weakness. Bricoule could have found companionship more easily with the athletic and boyish young Dominique Soubrier, but he rejects her because of her need for him. She follows him to the front as a nurse, but arouses him only when he humiliates her. He achieves identity only by destroying those dependent on him. The war, like Dominique and Prinet, is an instrument which Bricoule exploits in an attempt to find himself, although what he finds is a personality

ruled by the need to be cruel. In fact Bricoule is presented as a defeated character, with no meaning and no purpose because he is totally enclosed in himself, capable of self-definition only in destruction. The character of Bricoule was developed in Costals, the writer who is the link between the four women in *Les Jeunes Filles*.

The two volumes of *Les Olympiques*, "Le paradis à l'ombre des épées" and "Les onze devant la porte dorée," have virtually no structure except that upheld by their central figure, Jacques Peyrony. The lyrical interludes are devoted to the cultivation of health and vigour, to which Montherlant adds intelligence and poetry, which of course increase the power of domination. Sport fosters understanding, camaraderie, and order in an atmosphere very close to the primitive pitting of rival physical strengths. The emotions are downgraded in this ambiance. They belong to the bourgeois world of Peyrony's parents, not to the defiant independence of the athlete hero, but to the social entanglements of the world of chaos. Rather like the youth culture Hitler was to foster in Germany, Montherlant's world of elevated values has a strongly homosexual undertow. The most desirable of his fictional women are semi-male, and few readers of Montherlant's lyrical works, written in his twenties, would be surprised to know that their author was never to marry.

Alban de Bricoule returns as the hero of *Les Bestiaires*, delighted to be able to cast off the social restrictions of Paris as he leaves for Spain. There are incantatory passages to Mithra as bullfighting is elevated to the status of a cult. Montherlant elaborates the well-known mystique associated with blood sports, in which primeval violence is formally ritualized and made subject to complex codes. The bull is the enemy, symbol of huge strength and destructive power, to be overcome, but only within the limits of the ritualization of the killing whereby respect for the sacrificial victim is expressed. For Bricoule the struggle of man against bull is somewhat improbably widened to include that of Christianity against the cult of Mithra, and the blood of the bull to encompass that of the lamb. The bullfight is seen almost blasphemously as an analogy of the Christian Mass, in which the sacrificial victim is not conquered, but adored. The boy in the abattoir who helps carve up the carcass of the dead bull is called Jesus, and as the fight approaches Bricoule gradually puts Soledad, the sensually distracting daughter of his host, out of his mind. Tourists, onlookers, sightseers, and the public are not deemed worthy to partake of the mystery.

The importance of these early works lies in the key they offer to the imaginative patterns which are woven into the later works with more conscious literary sophistication. *Les Célibataires* is a novel about the crumbling dignity of a family of Breton grandees reduced to a state of social, moral, and financial disintegration. Baron Elie de Coëtquidan is 64 and shares an apartment with his nephew, comte Léon de Coantré, who is 53. Coantré's mother, who is Coëtquidan's sister, has just died, and the house must be sold to settle the estate. The two bachelors are unable to communicate properly and helpless against the financial blow life has inflicted. Their caste does not allow them the escape route open to others—for Coëtquidan to live in a home, for Coantré to work—so they become anxious and embittered, and Coantré slowly declines, increasingly unable to grasp the dimensions of major crises and therefore euphoric about them. He eats more in order to sleep more, and finally fades away into death. He has dominated his surroundings to the end, but only in the empty name of pride. The novel, after a hesitant start, concentrates on Coantré, but there is a third bachelor, a social climber and successful banker called Octave, who ultimately helps to destroy Léon, whom he despises. It is in the passages of psychological depiction which show the workings of Coantré's mind gradually silting up that the novel's power really resides.

The four volumes of *Les Jeunes Filles* are linked by the character of the writer Costals, who fascinates and destroys three different women in turn. Costals works out a set of values for himself which, as we have by now come to expect, centre on independence of emotional constraints. Rather lower down the ethical scale than Bricoule, Costals deliberately exploits the women by subjecting them to what are virtually laboratory experiments in the hope that they will furnish him with material for his fiction. The correspondence is initiated through their fan letters to him. Thérèse Pantvin looks on Costals as an object of religious devotion, a role he naturally feels unable to fill. Thérèse is provincial, unimaginative, and slightly mad, out of her depth in the male province of religious spiritualities. In the second novel she does in fact go mad. Andrée Hacquebaut, on the other hand, is looking for a cautiously sentimental relationship, which Costals again finds it impossible to reciprocate. At 30, Andrée already finds her life hopeless and empty. She is doomed from the beginning to die of boredom, and her ingratiating pursuit of literary interests only makes her slightly threatening to Costals, whose province she is invading.

The way in which Costals fails to do more than play at the fatherhood of his illegitimate son (whom he none the less quite likes as long as ties of kinship are not urged) reinforces his central role. It is not only the destruction of weak women he needs to nourish his masculinity. The occasional weak male is needed, not so much to vary the diet as to concentrate the interest on the real central character, who is none of the young women of the title. The novel is built up of letters, documentation, and notes, with some long passages of narration. Solange Dandillot, who does attract Costals, is predictably boyish, attractive, Parisian, and emerges from the world of sport. She is companionable, has taste, and likes the bourgeois formalities of proper arrangements, with booked tickets and tables. So long as she does not jeopardize his independence, Costals allows her to make demands. Like the others, however, she furnishes him with yet more good reasons for looking down on women. She consents to witness the terrifying humiliation which Costals inflicts on Andrée, daring her to hurt him, when he knows she wants more than anything else to be hurt by him herself. The morality is appalling, but the psychology daring and accurate. Andrée accuses Costals of homosexuality. In her mind, of course, his request to her to bully him had demonstrated it.

Solange falls in love with Costals, and in her anxiety to marry him agrees to his absurdly chauvinistic demands, even to having an abortion should she become pregnant after marriage. In the end Costals thinks he has caught leprosy from the only non-threatening woman in the novel, a mere casual gratification, but it turns out that he has not. He loses interest in Solange, who marries an engineer. Andrée is the woman who has come nearest to understanding him, and the tetralogy ends with a series of aphorisms on the ignobility of women.

The last of the novels, *Le Chaos et la nuit*, is divided into two parts. In the first Celestino lives the life of an exiled anarchist in Paris, with his daughter Pascualita and a small income. In the second part they return to Spain, where Celestino finds himself an alien without inner resources to help him to start out again.

Pascualita integrates into the new Spain, leaving her father not to erode, like Coantré in *Les Célibataires*, but positively to destroy himself by casting off residual friendships and putting himself in situations which he knows he will not be able to withstand.

La Ville dont le prince est un enfant is a play about an emotional attachment between the 16-year-old André Sevrais and the 14-year-old Serge Soubrier. Sevrais is expelled from school because one of the teachers, the Abbé de Pradts, is himself emotionally attracted to Soubrier, and the headmaster gets rid of Soubrier because he represents a danger. *L'Exil* is still concerned with the values of *Le Songe* and those of Montherlant's youth. Geneviève de Presles prevents her son Philippe from going off to war, but Sénac, Philippe's close friend, comes back from the front with a new maturity and is unable to renew his relationship with Philippe. This incapacity is revealed in various dramatically effective ways, as when Sénac brings friends from a less sophisticated social background into the Presles drawing room. Sénac returns to the front, but war has lost all attraction for Philippe, who was in search not of fighting but of Sénac. He enlists, nevertheless, and goes to the front, in search now of masculinity.

Montherlant's three most important plays start with *La Reine morte*. The difficulties of Ferrante's position emerge only gradually. He genuinely likes both the Infanta of Navarre, to whom he wanted to marry his weak son Pedro, and Inès de Castro, who is expecting Pedro's child and is already secretly married to him. Had she left the court and accepted the rejected Infanta's invitation to accompany her back to Navarre, she would have escaped death. But she wants to be near Pedro, and Ferrante has her killed. Montherlant appears to have considered that Inès's sentimental weakness in deciding to stay on at the court of the king whose plans she has thwarted makes her ultimate execution acceptable to the audience. The massive documentation wrapped round the play, as published during Montherlant's lifetime in the Pléiade edition, shows him backtracking about the motive for the execution. This was Montherlant's first major play, and his dramatic technique had not yet attained the pitch of accomplishment it was to reach a decade later. It seems likely that his imagination trapped him into showing a more dismissive view of sentimental weakness than, on reflection, he wished to reveal.

Malatesta, too, in the play *Malatesta* finds obstacles in his way, but his death at the end of the tragedy is not portrayed as a defeat. He is murdered because Porcellio, a man of letters attached to his court, and whose life he had once saved, had refused to help with Malatesta's plan to have the pope assassinated and betrayed him to the pope. A long last act tries to make clear the characters' motivations, but in the end Malatesta stands out as bent on self-destruction, much like Coantré in *Les Célibataires* and Celestino in the forthcoming *Le Chaos et la nuit*. Ferrante had imposed his will and Malatesta had chosen the alternative, submitting to the urge to allow himself to be destroyed, since there was no reason why he should ever have come to Rome. He dies by poisoning.

With *Le Maître de Santiago* we are still only in 1947, seven years before the last of the great plays, and 16 before the final novel. Don Alvaro Dabo is the head of a missionary order who sees that the Church in 16th-century Spain is being cast in the role of propping up the economic exploitation of the Americas. Don Alvaro decides not to help the American Indians, who are being brutally treated by the conquerors, but instead to withdraw from the world. Like Ferrante, he controls great affairs while inwardly withdrawing from them, and he sends a young man whom he despises to help the Indians. Montherlant's later heroes dominate by maturity of wisdom, not by force of masculinity. Don Alvaro's daughter, Mariana, who wants to marry Jacinto, now stands in the way of her father's spiritual quest, as the marriage would preclude his renunciation of all worldly constraints. Mariana gradually comes to agree with her father, to renounce the prospect first of having children, then of marriage itself, and finally to need to sacrifice herself. The play ends with father and daughter covered together by the order's symbolic cloak in an apotheosis of self-destructive transcendence. Montherlant sees Don Alvaro as a misunderstood Christian, virtually pleading for the acceptance of his own still-pagan values as authentically Christian in some proud, independent way. The play's power lies in the psychology of Don Alvaro's conflict, not in the ideology his daughter comes, without clear dramatic motivation, to share with him.

Port-Royal deals with a single day in the amply documented history of the Jansenist movement. Montherlant invents a principal character, but is otherwise outwardly faithful to the events of 21 and 26 August 1664, here compressed into one day, one act, and, naturally, one room. The celebrated Mère Angélique, whom the French theatre-going public would have known from the legend of her intransigence, moves towards inner doubt as the play progresses, while the invented Soeur Françoise moves from doubt towards commitment and serenity. Montherlant allows a strong element of human attachment between the two nuns to be understood by the audience. The archbishop arrives to deal with the indiscipline of the nuns, which arises from their commitment to a spirituality based on a theology they do not pretend to understand. The plot concerns the demand that the nuns should sign a formulary, or doctrinal declaration, which the archbishop tells them is a necessary dogmatic commitment to the doctrine of free will. The document implies an acknowledgement that five condemned propositions are in Jansen's *Augustinus*. The nuns take the view that it is a crime to make them sign a document on an obscure point of theology. In the play no one is allowed to be quite right or quite wrong, but the nuns are expelled from the monastery in the end because they defy the will of the archbishop.

Everything hinges on the nuns' obedience; "Obéissez, et l'on ne vous demandera plus rien (Obey, and no one will ask anything else of you)." But, however reasonable the archbishop thinks he is, and may in fact actually be, the conflict is between that of a superior male and weaker females.

Voilà le plus grand orgueil de fille que j'aie jamais connu… De là cette rigueur qui enfle la présomption, nourrit le dédain, entretient un chagrin superbe et un esprit de fastueuse singularité…

(That is the greatest piece of female pride I have ever heard… From it comes that severity which inflates presumption, feeds contempt, maintains a haughty disapproval and a spirit of fastidious individualism…)

The psychological confrontations and hesitations are brilliantly dramatized, with the spiritual and theological issues naturally popularized in confrontational terms which enlist the audience's sympathies for the oppressed, simple, but proud nuns, while not totally alienating them from the archbishop with his worldy, temporizing stance and desire for apparently reasonable behaviour. Montherlant did go on to write more plays, but *Port-Royal* stands as his masterpiece. It brings to their climax all the principal Montherlant themes and conflicts—fear, the mutability of human nature in changing circumstances, psychological uncertainty, the relationship between young and old, male and female, but above all the importance of a quality of commitment which either imposes domination or ends in self-destruction.

PUBLICATIONS

Montherlant published a number of works in limited editions which have not been included below

Collections

Théâtre, Bibliothèque de la Pléiade, 1958
Romans, Bibliothèque de la Pléiade, vol. 1, 1959; vol. 2, 1982
Essais, Bibliothèque de la Pléiade, 1963

Plays

L'Exil (one scene produced 1934), 1929
Pasiphaé (produced 1938), 1936
La Reine morte, 1942; as *Queen after Death* (produced 1952), 1951
Fils de personne, 1944; as *No Man's Son*, 1951
Un incompris, 1944
Malatesta (produced 1950), 1946; as *Malatesta* (in English; produced 1957), 1951
Le Maître de Santiago, 1947; as *The Master of Santiago* (produced 1957), 1951
Demain il fera jour (produced 1949), 1949; as *Tomorrow the Dawn*, 1951
Celles qu'on prend dans ses bras (produced 1950), 1950
La Ville dont le prince est un enfant, 1951
Port-Royal (produced 1954), 1954; edited by Richard Griffiths, 1976
Brocéliande, 1956
Don Juan, 1958
Le Cardinal d'Espagne, 1960
La Guerre civile, 1965

Fiction

Le Songe, 1922; as *The Dream*, 1963
Les Olympiques, 2 vols., 1924; portions in *Selected Essays*, 1960
Les Bestiaires, 1926; as *The Matador*, 1957
La Petite Infante de Castille, 1929
Les Célibataires, 1934; as *Lament for the Death of an Upper Class*, 1935; as *Perish in Their Pride*, 1936; as *The Bachelors*, 1960
Les Jeunes Filles, 4 vols.:
  Les Jeunes Filles, 1936; as *Young Girls*, 1937
  Pitié pour les femmes, 1936; as *Pity for Women*, 1937
  Le Démon du bien, 1937; as *Demon of Good*, 1940

Les Lépreuses, 1939; as *The Lepers*, 1940
L'Histoire d'amour de "La Rose de sable," 1954; as *Desert Love*, 1957
Le Chaos et la nuit, 1963; as *Chaos and Night*, 1964
La Rose de sable, 1968
Les Garçons, 1969
Un assassin est mon maître, 1971

Other

Portions of many of the volumes of essays have been translated in *Selected Essays* (1960)
La Relève du matin, 1920
Chant funèbre pour les morts de Verdun, 1924
Aux fontaines du désir, 1927
Mors et vita, 1932
Encore un instant de bonheur (poems), 1934
Service inutile, 1935
L'Equinoxe de septembre, 1938
Le Solstice de juin, 1941
Un voyageur solitaire est un diable, 1945
Textes sous une occupation, 1953
Carnets 1930–1944, 1947–56
Va jouer avec cette poussière (Carnets 1958–1964), 1966
La Tragédie sans masque: notes de théâtre, 1972
La Marée du soir (Carnets 1968–1971), 1972

Critical and biographical studies

Batchelor, J., *Existence and Imagination: The Theatre of Henry de Montherlant*, 1967
Cruickshank, J., *Montherlant* (in English), 1964
Johnson, Robert B., *Henry de Montherlant* (in English), 1968
Becker, Lucille, *Henry de Montherlant: A Critical Biography*, 1970

————

MORÉAS, Jean (pseudonym of Iannis Pappadiamantopoulos), 1856–1910.

Poet.

LIFE

Moréas is best known for his use of the word "symbolism" (q.v.) in the preface to his collection of poems *Les Cantilènes* in 1886, and his subsequent definition of the new "symbolist" aesthetic, as distinguished from "decadence," in *Le Figaro Littéraire* of 18 September 1886. Moréas was born in Athens of Greek parents on 15 April 1856, but had a French governess and spent some time as a child in Marseilles. His father was a prominent lawyer, born in 1815, who had studied in Germany and lived to be 92. Moréas is said to have decided to become a French poet at the age of 10, and when he came to Paris he left a library of 2,000 French classics in Athens. After studying at the Athens lycée, he

was sent to study law in Germany, stopping off on the way at Bologna and Florence, more for the social life than the museums. His journey took him to Prague, Munich, Heidelberg, and down the Rhine. He visited Bonn, Cologne, then also Stuttgart, Vienna, Zurich, Geneva, and Marseilles, having discovered symbolism in Germany.

In 1872 he spent six weeks in Paris and returned in 1879, remaining there until his death. He returned only twice to Greece in that time. He came to dislike travel and, apart from a journey to Brussels and one to Algeria, and one or two visits to the Black Forest or the Midi for health reasons, he stayed in Paris, frequently changing his address, but generally to be found in one café or another, mostly Le Napolitain or La Vachette. The first artistic movement which can be said to have been totally the product of café society was impressionism. By the end of the century café life had become a ritual. "I arrived around one in the afternoon," wrote Moréas, "stayed until seven, and then went to dine. About eight we came back, and didn't leave until one in the morning." Draughts and dominoes were frequent café pastimes.

Moréas would meet Verlaine at the François Ier, frequented the Voltaire on Mondays and the Steinbach after midnight. The "Ecole Romane", which broke away from symbolism, was founded at the Avenir, and the poet Paul Fort, associated in particularly with symbolist drama, was to be found at the Closerie des Lilas. Personal addresses mattered less in the establishment of those literary movements not associated more grandly with salon society than the cafés which were frequented by the different groups. Moréas himself hated to be alone. In his cafés, he could be surrounded by his disciples. Sometimes he would stay all night, taking the first omnibus home at five am. The quality of his verse alone would not account for his literary significance if he had not dominated the appropriate café coteries at the moment when symbolism became an acknowledged literary movement. Elegantly dressed, with white gloves, monocle, and buttonhole, he behaved in lordly fashion and was correspondingly intolerant, while being supported in part by the revenue from a small estate he owned in Patras, and partly by money supplied secretly by his mother. Eventually he was unable to keep up the dandified appearance. On several occasions he also proved himself a skilled duellist.

Moréas had already published an anthology of contemporary poetry in Greece, as well as some of his own criticism in 1874. He had also translated from French into Greek and edited in Greece an ephemeral French literary review. Proclaiming from the beginning his admiration for the authors of the French Renaissance, in France Moréas published his early poems in the *Chat Noir*, the review of the "Hydropathes" (see Symbolism). His first volume of verse, however, *Les Syrtes*, first appeared in the "Zutiste" (see Symbolism) *La Nouvelle Rive Gauche*, for which Moréas also reviewed. In 1884, when invited with other poets to define poetry, he replied with 12 question marks. He was the editor of *Le Symboliste* for its four issues in October 1886, and also contributed to other short-lived periodicals published by and for the audacious youth of the literary world, *La Cravache, Sagittaire, La Conque* (edited by Louÿs), *La Vogue* (edited by G. Kahn), *L'Art Indépendant*, and *La Plume* (founded on 15 April 1889 and edited by Léon Deschamps), which gave special prominence to Moréas and his group, to which the number of 1 January 1891 was devoted. Contributors met on Saturday evenings at the Café Fleurus, and then at the Soleil d'Or.

Moréas earned some money from journalism, especially for *Paris-Journal* and *La Gazette de France*. His tastes were modest, his relationships with women never lengthy.

Les Cantilènes, a second collection of sonnets and lyrics, with a title denoting short medieval songs, appeared in 1886, followed in 1891 by *Le Pèlerin passionné*, the occasion for a banquet (on 2 February) for 200 artists and writers which marked the apotheosis of symbolism as a literary movement. The banquet, which was Moréas's own idea, was organized, for the sake of decorum, by Régnier and Barrès, and presided over by Mallarmé. It turned into a boisterous, rather juvenile rag in celebration not so much of Moréas as of the "jeunesse aurorale (the youth whose dawn it was)," toasted by Mallarmé. As so often at this period, a serious literary movement was thus distilled out of a great deal of adolescent effervescence. Equally significant is the way in which like-minded young artists came together and recognized one another, often grouping themselves round esoteric figures like Mallarmé or flamboyant ones like Moréas. The banquet was something more ambitious. It brought together all sorts of creators and critics, and incidentally marked the destruction of any very precise meaning of the term "symbolist." It made the general public aware that here was a new artistic movement to be taken notice of, rather than merely a hundred or so little magazines and a few score of miniscule and predominantly immature avant-garde groups.

Moréas himself, with Charles Maurras and Ernest Raynaud, had by this time moved on to found a new "Ecole Romane," one which was much more classical in its taste. They cultivated what they regarded as the Greco-Roman origins of French culture, and deliberately imported classical archaisms into their work. Moréas ceased to use "vers libres" , for instance, in the later poems of his 1907 collection *Poèmes et sylves, 1886–1896*. His finest poems are generally considered to be those which are most classically sober in form and style, published in *Les Stances*. He resented his disappearance from the limelight, became poorer, more disillusioned, and bitter, and in 1891 denounced his symbolist origins. Many of his old followers turned against him when he deserted the symbolist cause, while Maurras's fervent personal admiration came to give Moréas's work moral and political overtones it was never intended to have. His *Iphigénie*, written between 1895 and 1900, was a success in 1904, and went with the company playing it to Greece and Algeria. Moréas had been made a Chevalier of the Légion d'Honneur in 1906. In 1909 he became a naturalized Frenchman. He died of a stroke aggravated by kidney failure on 30 March 1910.

WORKS

Moréas could have had a literary career in Greece. In 1874 he published his *Parnassus*, an anthology of contemporary poets, and he wrote reviews for the *Attic Monitor*, translating Arsène Houssaye's *Le Nid de corbeaux* and the work of other French authors. He began to translate Goethe's *Werther*, and founded a short-lived French-language review, *Papillon*. For a while he edited another review, *Parthenon*, and published his own verse anonymously. He co-edited *Les Hirondelles*, in which he published more of his own verse and a translation of Goethe's *Hermann und Dorothea*. He also published a Greek translation of Lamartine on Balzac and further material of his own. His *Tourterelles et vipères* of 1878 contains a collection of Greek and

French poems already showing considerable skill in the handling of language and a neoclassical inspiration with leanings towards pessimism. When Moréas arrived in Paris in 1879, his taste was classically formed, but he was clearly stimulated both by romanticism (q.v.) and the classical reactions to it.

Les Syrtes borrows obviously but only superficially from Baudelaire and Verlaine, and is permeated by world-weary late romantic disillusion, dependent on the images of twilight and autumn. What heralds the symbolism to come is the medieval and gothic German imagery which creeps in, the flowers with magic properties, and the exploitation of the ethereal and the mysterious. A hundred and twenty-four copies were printed, and the volume was published anonymously. *Les Cantilènes* of 1886 is an illustration of the symbolist manifesto published the same year in *Le Figaro Littéraire*. There is now more hauteur, and disdain for everyday events and objects, but too programmatic an exploitation of an accomplished technique experimenting with forms. The collection lacks both real poetry and depth of feeling. Just as the poems inspired by Baudelaire mimicked the techniques and the vocabulary without being informed by the same inner tensions.

Le Pèlerin passionné announces the desire to bypass romanticism, linking the Middle Ages and the Renaissance with a modern post-romantic sensibility, and evincing nothing but contempt for naturalism "déjà caduc (already trivial)." Composed over four years from 1886, the volume is less unified than its predecessors. The preface, which still leant towards symbolism, was dropped, together with 21 poems, in 1893, although the volume's success was due to the symbolist movement, and its appearance became the pretext for celebrating that movement with the banquet at the Hôtel des Sociétés Savantes. The medieval legends on which the poems were based contributed powerfully to the nostalgic effects sought by the symbolists, and several new poems were added. Moréas, whose symbolism was limited to the exterior trappings of the poetry associated with the movement (notably archaisms and neologisms), had already moved on, however, and the famous symbolist manifesto in *Le Figaro Littéraire* of 1886 was followed on 14 September 1891 by a declaration of adherence to the "principe gréco-latin." Romanticism had altered this principle, "frustrant ainsi les Muses françaises de leur héritage légitime (so depriving the French Muses of their legitimate inheritance)."

The "Ecole Romane Française" was to link up once more the chain "broken by Romanticism, and its Parnassian, naturalist, and symbolist offspring." Symbolism, "which I more or less invented," as Moréas said, was only a transitional phenomenon, and it was now dead. His associates in the new school were Maurice du Plessys, Raymond de la Tailhède, Ernest Raynaud, and Charles Maurras. In fact the two aesthetics, symbolist and "Roman," coalesce, sometimes in the same poems, in *Le Pèlerin passionné*. The use of "vers libres," far from being abandoned, reaches a virtuoso level here, but Moréas insists on clarity, discipline, and intelligibility.

Moréas's best work is undoubtedly *Les Stances*, in which despair met with stoic fortitude gives way to renunciation and sacrifice. The themes are still among those dear to the romantics—death, solitude, the solace of nature—but the emotion is now strongly felt, lacking self-pity and expressed with syntactical and lexical discipline. Barrès even identified a moral improvement behind the maturing aesthetic. The final poems have been said to be symbolist still, but without the foggy sense

titute. When the *Bohème* vignettes came to an end the following year, he asked Hugo to help him find a job, and was in fact saved by Barrière's offer to assist him in turning *Bohème* into a play. Barrière was a young clerk, author of successful vaudevilles, but not yet known. He proved himself a skilful writer for the stage, sketching the skeleton plot to be fleshed out with Murger's episodes. The arbitration over whether Mimi was to die was itself farcical, although successful. The Paris cholera of 1849 did not help to attract an audience but the first night was nevertheless attended by Louis-Napoleon as well as the model for Musette, Marie-Christine Roux, Champfleury's mistress and probably the first nude subject, Nadar's, in the history of photography. Among the critics were Gautier, Houssaye, and Banville.

Murger now moved to the Right Bank and adopted a tactless tone in the preface and epilogue to the novel with reference to his former life in Bohemia. Some of his old friends felt for a moment that he had turned his back on them. The aristocratic Goncourts, on the other hand, were frankly jealous. They had taste, money, and education, but their first novel sold only 60 copies and no one would take their plays. Michel Lévy published another book of Murger's short stories, *Scènes de la vie de jeunesse*, in the same year as the book of *Bohème*. Houssaye, now director of the Théâtre-Français, got Murger, with the help of a new collaborator to turn one of his new stories into a play, *Le Bonhomme Jadis*, which was successfully produced in 1852. Gautier wrote a particularly enthusiastic review. More importantly, Buloz at the *Revue des deux Mondes* (RDM, q. v.), was in search of new talent and after some hesitation, offered Murger a contract for three or four volumes of fiction a year at 200 francs for the first and 150 for each succeeding instalment. The function of the artist in society was being taken seriously, even in the more staid reviews, an attitude which, it is important to note, also improved circulation.

Murger began to frequent the forest of Fontainebleau, took rather ineptly to shooting, and found a mistress with whom he was to live for the rest of his life. There was always more than a touch of timidity in his approaches to women, and even perhaps of masochism, but Anaïs and he became lovers in the summer of 1852, and thereafter were, if occasionally unfaithful to one another, married in all but name. They spent eight months of the year at Marlotte, and their separations were as short as Murger could make them. The *RDM* tried to wean him from themes relating to Bohemia. The result, *Le Dernier Rendez-vous*, was not enthusiastically received. Murger had gone back to Bohemia for *Les Buveurs d'eau*, which neither he nor the public considered a success. Dissatisfied with his efforts, he produced nothing, further for a while and was again hard up. His father, who had not approved of *Bohème*, died in December 1855, but left him nothing, so Murger moved to a cheaper flat.

Les Vacances de Camille, whose heroine was clearly modelled on Anaïs, was a considerable success. Murger's background was now the country, about which he wanted to write realistically, and he turned down an invitation to write a gossip column, having peopled *Scènes de campagne: Adeline Protat* with the citizens of Marlotte. Champfleury had just published his manifesto in *Le Réalisme*, and in their different ways Champfleury, Flaubert, Nadar—who was publishing unflattering photographs and taking the first aerial pictures of Paris—and Courbet—rejected by the Salon of 1855 and dedicated to painting what was vulgar and modern—were adopting realist approaches to their art forms, while Buloz was still exerting a

conservative preference for the romanticism of George Sand, Musset, Mérimée, and Vigny. Murger took Balzac's *La Cousine Bette* as his model for the last novel he published *Le Sabot rouge*, but set it in the forest of Fontainebleau. The result was a highly skilled novel which was well received, but brought him little money. Debts were pressing. Buloz at the *RDM* made Murger a handsome advance of 1,500 francs and even allowed him to write for rival reviews, like *Le Moniteur*. Attempting to shake off the image of Bohemia and to pay some of his debts, Murger was now clearly living beyond his means.

He received the Légion d'Honneur in 1858. *Le Figaro* contracted with him for a humorous column. He started a new novel, *Les Roueries de l'ingénue*, (never published) began making an anthology of his poems, and started a play and a melodrama. He also made arrangements to have *Les Vacances de Camille* adapted for the stage and wrote a boulevard comedy with a collaborator. His last play, *Le Serment d'Horace*, opened on 28 November 1860 and was greeted with enthusiasm. Early in 1861 Murger moved house in Paris, but was soon taken ill. Michel Lévy gave him 100 francs, and the government arranged for an official visitor to slip 300 francs under his pillow. Murger died, in some pain, of an obstructed artery in his left leg. Lévy had sent a copy of his book of poems, *Les Nuits d'hiver*, to all the periodicals, so ensuring that the obituaries turned into reviews. The Goncourts were as vindictive as ever in response to the glowing acclaim Murger now received. *Le Figaro* for 3 February 1861 had inaugurated the practice of listing the prominent mourners at a funeral and it appears that there were over 1,500 people at Murger's graveside, including half the writers and journalists in Paris and all the surviving water-drinkers and models for *Bohème*.

WORKS

It is difficult to assess the significance of Murger's work without appreciating the aesthetic and social or political relationships that existed between the romantic and realist movements in France; it is in this context that his importance and achievement as a writer lie. Murger's poems are of no real literary interest. Apart from the early poems and a few occasional pieces, his first success was a whimsical prose fantasy commissioned by Houssaye for *L'Artiste*. "Les amours d'un grillon et d'une étincelle" is about a cricket who falls in love with a star. One Christmas night the cricket serenades a series of sparks coming from a log burning in the hearth; one spark lodges in the corner of the fireplace, but fades to ash as the hopeful cricket approaches it. Houssaye and Murger were both pleased with the piece, but Champfleury and Courbet seem to have persuaded Murger jointly, now that he was at last writing prose, to switch from fantasy to realism. Murger's first contributions to *Le Corsaire* were written in what he referred to as "the language of the theatre," "a menagerie of neologisms in a realistic idiom."

His first more ambitious piece, the first of the "Scènes," was "*Un envoyé de la providence*," the story of a painter who, lacking the jacket required for a society dinner he wishes to attend, gets a rich sitter to slip his off and pose in the informality of a smoking jacket. A friend, Schaunard, keeps the sitter immobilized until the dinner is over. The story earned Murger 15 francs and is a brilliant miniature of the fiction of ironic suspense. Murger had decided to utilize comically the grim reality of the lives of the artists and writers by whom he was surrounded and of whom at least a substantial number considered what they were doing more important than earning a secure and comfortable living in a conventional job. Murger was at first uncertain about exploring this new vein and, although the editor of *Le Corsaire*, who liked to be known as Le Poitevin de Saint-Alme, pressed for more, Murger dallied, dictating the next season's fashions for *Le Moniteur*, writing his caustic art and drama criticisms and his gossip column. When it came, the second "Scène" concerned Rodolphe/Murger's week-long affair with a girl named Louise, probably Lucile Louvet, picked up at the Bal du Prado. Lucile was certainly the model for Mimi in the third "Scène" (July 1846), and Mimi's life with Rodolphe features regularly thereafter. From the very different impressions of Lucile that have been left by other members of Murger's group, we may infer that Murger's portrait idealized her to a now unascertainable extent, but that he was comically ironic (at his own expense) about Rodolphe, and even about his own tendency to idealize.

Many of Murger's characters have been portrayed by Champfleury and also by Schaunard/Schanne, whose memoirs, *Les Souvenirs de Schaunard* (1887), scarcely raise the incidents related above their original banality. Murger, who felt vulnerable to the accusation of romanticizing Bohemia, does not avoid sickness, suffering, destitution, and death in spite of his preferred fate for Mimi in the play. His achievement lies in making his characters, like the subjects on whom they were modelled, touchingly display their need to defend themselves against present pain and future prospects by refusing to treat such matters tragically. Schanne's "mimetic symphony" entitled "The Influence of Blue upon the Arts," which featured on the invitation to one of Nadar's parties, at which all persons wishing to read or to recite poetry were to be expelled, was a real, not an imaginary joke. When Lucile finally left Murger, he characteristically turned the upset into a "Scène," The "Epilogue des amours de Rodolphe et Mademoiselle Mimi," and equally characteristically omitted the last stanza of Rodolphe's lament from the book as too indelicate, since Lucile, the model for Mimi, had died during the interval.

Murger had to have been using a model, however obliquely reflected, and something of the style of realistic humour covering the depressing grimness of life may easily have come from the commedia dell'arte tradition. It was impossible, in the middle of the 19th century, to invent a chapter heading "Comment fut institué le cénacle de la Bohème" outside reference to a literary culture which included Voltaire, and probably Rabelais. Rodolphe's laconic acceptance of Mimi's death is simply a realistic expression of the attitudes towards transient love affairs, and serious disasters involving their participants, in Murger's Bohemia. The play, when it came, was primarily acclaimed for its wit and its pathos. Gautier remarked on the closeness of its laughter to tears. It contains whimsy, but everything is observed, felt, and suffered beneath the endless stream of witticisms. The work was clearly lived before it was written. In the famous deglamorization of Bohemia in the published book, Murger wrote that Bohemia was the probationary period of artistic life, the preface to the academy, the Hôtel-Dieu (hospital), or the morgue. Some of its inhabitants did nothing but praise one another as disciples of Art for Art's sake and wait for the pedestals to be placed beneath their feet. Others, the amateurs, had no need to lead the life of destitution.

The real citizens of Bohemia knew what they wanted to say and regarded the drawbacks of their life style as a hindrance to be endured. They wanted to be known, listened to, and taken seriously. The epilogue refuses to indulge the nostalgia of the successful for Bohemia and includes Murger's best poem, the "Chanson de Musette."

"Le souper des funerailles" in the *Scènes de la vie de jeunesse*, also of 1851, contains unequivocally unsentimental ideas about the egalitarianism and socialism with which the Goncourts had reproached Murger, who states that cunning and hypocrisy, common to all, are deployed more brutally and cynically in the lower reaches of society. In this "Scène," as in two others in the collection, one girl is deliberately assimilated in the mind of her lover with another who has either died or left him, as if drawing on some personal attempt to recreate Marie Fonblanc in the other girls he also later called "Mimi," including the prototype of the Bohemia Mimi. The new "Scènes" are more cynical than the earlier ones and their irony is more biting. The realism is also more gruesome, as in the scene where a group of medical students gossip over the sound of the saw and the patient's howls during an amputation. Despite another attack on poverty posturing as fidelity to an artistic calling, there is also nostalgia and sentimentality to relieve the realism in *Le Bonhomme Jadis*. Buloz's assistant at the *RDM*, Armand de Pontmartin, told Murger frankly that his invitation to contribute was an attempt by the review to move away from the outdated romanticism still favoured by Buloz, and an admission that the romantic attempt to react against the "pagan, ironic school of the 18th century" was mistaken in supposing that "revolutionary art" could in any way further the great spiritual and Christian traditions of French idealism. It was bound in the end to be dominated by literary demagoguery and physical and moral ugliness. Murger was being hired to help restore literature to its "lofty spheres."

Le Pays latin, originally entitled *Claude et Marianne*, lacks the vitality and humorous sparkle of the original "Scène" from *Bohème*, partly no doubt because Murger was writing too slowly, conscientiously trying to adapt his style to what he supposed the readers of the *RDM* wanted. Furthermore, the characters are no longer real, but imagined, and therefore lifeless. Murger needed his real models if he was to avoid drifting back into fantasy. While *Le Pays latin* was being published, Buloz tried to get Murger to change his subject matter altogether, but *Le Dernier Rendez-vous*, although drawing on Murger's own experience again, reads too much like a rehash of "Les amours d'Olivier" from the *Scènes de la vie de jeunesse*. Its successor, *Les Buveurs d'eau*, was a failure because it transformed Murger's former companions into arrogant layabouts, with no sparkle or wit, only artistic priggishness.

When, after his creative hiatus, Murger returned to the life he was actually living in *Les Vacances de Camille* of 1857, the result was one of his most successful novels. With Théodore and Camille, modelled on Murger and Anaïs, the sparkle and sense of fun return, but without the student humour and vulgarity. There are naturally scenes from country life, as there are in *Scènes de campagne: Adeline Protat*. Drawing on the people and events in Murger's daily life and dedicated to Buloz, this last is a sentimental story about a painter who educates a cobbler's apprentice to make him into a better suitor for Adeline, only to fall in love with her himself. It was popular, but Murger found it insufficiently realistic.

The last novel Murger published during his lifetime, *Le Sabot rouge*, mixed psychological analyses with a strongly dramatic plot and realistic description. It is about a farmer who murders his son's mistress before the son shoots the father by mistake and then dies in agony after falling into the ditch where his father's body is lying. The characters have acquired depth and the view of human nature is bleak. Not all Murger's readers were pleased, but some critics thought it turned Murger at last into a serious novelist. (Edmond About wrote Murger a very enthusiastic letter in response to it.) Murger gave it to *Le Moniteur* and as a book to Lévy, who pointed out that the advances already covered the payment due for the novel. With some advances dropping as low as 10 francs, Lévy had paid Murger a total of 1,633 francs 60 centimes between 1855 and 1859, and gave him another 100 francs on his death-bed, thinking he had treated him generously. He is estimated to have made 25,000 francs out of the original *Scènes de la Bohème*, for which he had paid 500 francs over dinner after the play's first night.

PUBLICATIONS

Fiction

Scènes de la Bohème, 1851; first translated, 1887; as *Vie de Bohème* (in English), 1949
Le Pays latin, 1851
Scènes de la vie de jeunesse, 1851
Propos de ville et propos de théâtre, 1853
Les Buveurs d'eau, 1853
Scènes de campagne: Adeline Protat, 1853
Le Roman de toutes les femmes, 1854
Le Dernier Rendez-vous, 1856
Les Vacances de Camille, 1857
Madame Olympe, 1859
Le Sabot rouge, 1860
Le Roman du Capucin, 1869

Plays

La Vie de Bohème, with Théodore Barrière, 1853
Le Bonhomme Jadis, with Michel Carré, 1852
Le Serment d'Horace, with Lambert Thiboust, 1861

Verse

Les Nuits d'hiver, 1861; as *Winter Nights* 1923

Biographical and critical studies

Moss, Arthur, and Evalyn Marve, *The Legend of the Latin Quarter*, 1947
Baldick, R., *The First Bohemian: The Life of Henry Murger*, 1961

MUSSET, (Louis-Charles-) Alfred de, 1810–1857.

Poet, dramatist, and writer of fiction.

LIFE

Musset was born in Paris. The family owned a manor house in the Vendôme, though Musset appears to have spent only a few days there, in 1822, with his elder brother and later biographer, Paul. His father was a government official, scholar, and author who had the boys educated first by a private tutor in a borrowed country house and then, when Musset was eight, at the Collège (later Lycée) Henri IV. The family lived two doors down from Musset's paternal grandfather, and the children had a garden to play in—even then a rarity in Paris.

Musset was an intellectually precocious, spoilt, good-looking child who underwent a good deal of bullying as a result. At 16 he left school with inter-collegiate prizes in Latin (second), philosophy (first), and French (second), and the ambition to be a writer. For a while he drifted rather aimlessly, rapidly becoming bored with law and disgusted with the dissections involved in medicine, before going on to study art. Then Paul Foucher took him to Nodier's "cénacle" and he began to write verse (inspired initially by Chénier), though he destroyed what he wrote. In 1828 he published a loose translation of de Quincey's *Opium Eater*, and his poem "Un rêve," inspired by Hugo, was published in the Dijon paper *Le Provincial*.

Musset's poems—later to be published in *Les Contes d'Espagne et d'Italie*—found an admiring audience at Nodier's gatherings. Dumas remarked on the personal note which distinguished Musset from Lamartine, Hugo, Vigny, and others. In fact Musset was too aristocratic and too moderate by temperament for the "cénacle" He disliked Hugo's equation of romanticism with social dogmas, and he was reluctant to set the new romanticism (which he took at first to new peaks of frenzy and violence) against the classical ideal of beauty of form.

At the approach of his 18th birthday Musset fell in love with a Mme Grosellier, a young married woman suffering from consumption, who used his infatuation to screen her affections for someone else. Thereafter Musset never completely trusted any of the women with whom he became involved. Mme Grosellier left him in 1830, and he later dramatized his role as decoy lover in the character of Fortunio in *Le Chandelier*. By 1829 Musset was attending the "cénacle" meetings less and less and devoting more and more time to socializing in the Paris described in *Les Deux Maîtresses* and *Les Caprices de Marianne*, gambling, leading a generally swashbuckling life of luxury and fashion for which, as his brother pointed out, he could ill afford even the tailoring bills.

At this point his father found him a clerical job with some military heating contractors. The job was sufficiently unrewarding and time-consuming to sting Musset into action and he got his *Contes* published as a prelude to living by his pen. The publisher Canel asked for a further 500 lines and, following a three-week summer holiday on an uncle's estate, Musset obliged him. Mérimée and Vigny were invited to a preliminary reading of the *Contes* at the Musset family home on Christmas Eve 1929. Approximately half the reviews were favourable, although reviewers at that date were divided according to their own bias towards or against the new romantic (q. v.) movement. Musset's ironic comments on Hugo's *Les Orientales*, published in 1829, were to become famous.

In 1830 Musset was already moving away from romanticism, adopting a more independent attitude, and incorporating into his work a moderation, irony, and sense of the ridiculous. For two years he wrote little. The July revolution of 1830 had prevented the performance of his play *La Quittance du diable* at the Théâtre des Nouveautés, but Musset was now invited to write a play, which he called *La Nuit vénitienne*, for L'Odéon. With his father's agreement he had given up his job. *La Nuit vénitienne* was greeted by uproar and had to be withdrawn after two performances. It was poetic rather than melodramatic romanticism, but it led the editor of *Le Temps*, the only paper to publish a review upbraiding the audience for its behaviour, to offer Musset a column, for which, from February to June 1831, he wrote the "Revues fantasques." Musset never again wrote for live performance on stage, adopting what was already a respectable French tradition, employed notably by Diderot, of writing dramatic pieces only to be read.

Musset's father contracted cholera and died in 1832. The family's financial prospects looked gloomy and Musset decided that, if he could not make a living from his writing, he would join a fashionable regiment. What saved him from such a fate was a long-term connection with the *Revue des Deux Mondes* (*RDM*, q. v.). The private reading of his *Un spectacle dans un fauteuil* late in 1832 met with a lukewarm response, only Mérimée showing any enthusiasm for it. Lamartine was referred to as a "pleurard" (crybaby) and the press too was generally unfavourable. It was Sainte-Beuve's favourable reaction to the work in the *RDM*, however, that procured an invitation for Musset to write for the review, in which he now published *André del Sarto* (1 April 1833) and *Les Caprices de Marianne* (15 May).

In the spring of 1833 the review gave a dinner for its contributors at which Musset found himself sitting next to George Sand. Sand, was 28 and the author of two novels; she had separated from her husband and was living in Paris with her two children. Musset was 22. Although she was at first hesitant about this witty, elegant womanizer, and he uncertain about his ability to trust another woman, the two must have been lovers by August, when they stayed at Fontainebleau. Sand was at first reluctant to allow Musset to accompany her to Venice in the autumn, but he persuaded her and she herself then persuaded Musset's mother. The couple travelled via Genoa—where Sand fell ill and Musset, bored, took to amusing himself with other companions—and Florence, arriving in Venice on 19 January 1834. They had already quarrelled and a fortnight after their arrival in Venice Musset fell ill with malarial fever, from which his heart was to be permanently damaged. Their affair was probably over by now, but Sand nursed him devotedly, undoubtedly saving his life. She was strongly attracted to Musset's doctor, Pagello, who may have become her lover while still tending her patient. Musset certainly thought so. He had bouts of delirium and violence, and seems to have felt completely destroyed by Sand's assertion that he was to blame for everything that had happened, and that he might be losing his mind, a view she repeated in a letter to him which she later published.

Musset returned to Paris alone on 29 March. Sand and Pagello arrived in Paris on 14 August, and Musset left for Baden on 22 August in an endeavour to distract himself at the gaming tables. Pagello returned to Venice in September, and Musset resumed his turbulent relationship with Sand in October. Frequent quarrels and separations led up to the final break, on 7 March 1835, when Sand went back to her country house at Nohant. Both she and Musset seem to have suffered from their liaison with quite unusual intensity. She was to record her impressions of their relationship in *Lettres d'un voyageur* (1834–36) and *Elle et lui* (1859), while Musset fictionalized his in *La Confession d'un enfant du siècle*.

Musset had meanwhile published *On ne badine pas avec l'amour* in the *RDM* in July and *Lorenzaccio*, written in Venice, in August 1834. After the break with Sand, Musset had a brief affair with a Mme Jaubert and during 1835 wrote "La nuit de mai" and "La nuit de décembre," followed in 1836 by "La nuit d'août" and "La nuit d'octobre," in which he reflected on and attempted to relieve the pain of his experience. The idea of a series of "Nuits" may well have been inspired by Edward Young's *Night Thoughts* (1742–45), reflections on the death of his wife and of his daughter-in-law. Translated in 1769, the book made a powerful impression in France and Germany. The *RDM* published *La Quenouille de Barberine* on 1 August, part of *La Confession* in September, and *Le Chandelier* on 1 November 1835. Musset's social life also began to revive, interrupted principally by bouts of writing in an attempt to raise funds. The financial pressure was to ease in February 1838 with his appointment as librarian to the ministry of the interior.

There had been other liaisons, in 1836 with Louise Lebrun and in 1837 with Aimée d'Alton, years during which Musset's literary production reached its most prolific with the publication of *La Confession d'un enfant du siècle* in two volumes and, in the *RDM*, of *Il ne faut jurer de rien* (1 July 1836), the *Lettres de Dupuis et Cotonet* (September 1836 to May 1837), *Un caprice, Emmeline,* and *Les Deux maîtresses* (15 June, 1 August, and 1 November 1837). In 1838 Musset published, also in the *RDM*, the three short stories *Frédéric et Bernerette, Le Fils du Titien,* and *Margot* (15 January, 1 May, and 1 October). In 1839 he had an affair with the Racinian actress Rachel, who strengthened his already independent position in the classicism versus anti-classicism battle, and published *Croisilles* (*RDM*, 15 February). Ten years later Mme Allan-Despréaux performed, to great acclaim, in *Un caprice* in St Petersburg. She then brought the play successfully to Paris and persuaded Musset to rewrite the small plays, by then known as *Comédies et proverbes*, for the Paris stage, where they enjoyed a considerable vogue during the following years.

The first editions of *Comédies et proverbes* and of the *Poésies nouvelles* were published in 1840. That September Musset went to stay with a friend, Berryer, near Malesherbes, and the route took him through the forest of Fontainebleau, where he recognized many of the places he had visited with George Sand seven years previously. On 15 February 1841 he accidentally met her in the lobby of the Théâtre des Italiens and that night wrote the poem "Souvenir." He had been seriously ill with pleurisy in 1840, putting further strain on his heart. He was nursed by, and received spiritual consolation from, a nun, Sister Marcelline. Musset needed to resort to excessive drinking and womanizing, however, to ward off suicidal depression and soon engaged in a slow downward spiral, undermining first his powers of concentration, although not his creative ability, and finally his physical condition. He was never ostentatiously dissolute, his habits remaining regular and dignified to the end. He had never worked long hours at a desk, and during his last 17 years he continued to write as before, if more slowly. Still witty and capable of great charm, he came to depend increasingly on the eternal round of prostitutes, working girls, society women, and actresses, as he depended on the absinth and beer he drank every evening at the Café de la Régence from eight till midnight, generally alone.

In 1843 Musset was reconciled with Hugo and Nodier. He lost his librarianship abruptly in 1848, but was elected to the Académie Française on his third attempt, in 1852. He had become the lover meanwhile of Mme Allan-Despréaux, who had been responsible for the stage success of his *Comédies et proverbes*. He also had an affair with Louise Colet for six months in 1852, the year of the definitive edition of his *Poésies nouvelles*. He was given a new librarianship at the ministry of education in 1853. From 1846, when his sister married and his mother went to join her in Angers, Musset had been taken care of by a housekeeper chosen for him by his mother. He would regularly dismiss her in a tantrum, only to take her back again after she had packed, left by the front door, and slipped in again by the back. He began to suffer from hallucinations and furious rages, interspersed with bouts of illness, yet he could still write with a graceful lightness of tone and an unsurpassable elegance.

By the winter of 1856 his heart was further weakened, and excursions into Paris society exhausted him. After a dinner given by Prince Napoleon at the Palais-Royal, at which he displayed his glittering conversational powers, Musset returned home, never again to leave his bed. He seemed to be in no imminent danger when, talking to his brother, he suffered the sudden heart attack which killed him.

WORKS

Musset needed to be in exactly the right mood to write and much preferred the multiple resonances and musicality of verse to prose. Despite this, however, the light-hearted and graceful *Comédies et proverbes* have come to be regarded as a greater achievement than either Musset's lyric poetry or his prose fiction. *L'Anglais mangeur d'opium* of 1828 was more a set of variations on de Quincey's text than a translation. Important material is omitted, and the melodramatic incidents—ball and duel—are added. *Les Contes d'Espagne et d'Italie* of 1830 contains examples of passionate frenzy, improbable incidents, excessive daubs of local colour, and disdain of poetic craftsmanship, wrapped in the romantic trappings of love, woods, lakes, masks, and moonlight. The volume lays strong emphasis on the pain of love, with its cherished wounds, skirting both sentimentality and self-pity. What adumbrates the later Musset with the fastidiously ironic wit is a certain inability to take his own romanticism seriously, except in so far as it dwells on the pain of love. The flippancy of the later author of the dramatic sketches redeems some of the passionate ardour, the vivid sensuousness of the imagery, and the glamorous clichés. The early drama is equally stereotyped. *La Nuit vénitienne* opens at night, in Venice, and the setting includes a balcony and a gondola, while *La Quittance du diable*, not published until 1896, boasts a ruined chapel, a storm, and a cemetery, in imitation of Walter Scott.

Un spectacle dans un fauteuil—containing *La Coupe et les lèvres*, *A quoi rêvent les jeunes filles*, and *Namouna*—is dated 1833, although it was published in fact at the end of 1832. This collection of verse and plays deploys non-romantic themes and avoids some of the more facile clichés of the *Contes* along with the romantic prescription of rich rhymes (that is, rhymes involving three rather than two rhyming elements). Italy is now lik-

ened to a worn-out prostitute, still a romantic image, though a world-weary one savouring of late romantic disillusion. But the mountains of the Tyrol are still the hackneyed haunts of independence, and there is still an element of the macabre here, mixed in with the Byronic. Only occasional hints of revolt can be detected, such as the refusal to specify settings and attire in *A quoi rêvent les jeunes filles*. Very little distinguishes Musset's early work, in fact, from the frenetic exaggerations of romantic melodrama, except when fantasy is taken to the point of absurdity and opens the door to satire.

Even in 1833 *André del Sarto* still opens with a cloaked man climbing from his mistress's window and lungeing at a servant with a dagger, while *Les Caprices de Marianne* is permeated with premonitions and forebodings. An element of comic irony and the timid encroachment of realism do not yet signal the end of romanticism. Of the plays published in 1834, *Fantasio* is an interestingly introspective study of the bored and melancholy dreamer transformed by love into a creative artist, while *On ne badine pas avec l'amour*, based on a woman's grief at discovering that her lover's feelings for her were merely feigned, retains the makings of a tragic melodrama despite the introduction of determinedly comic elements. *Lorenzaccio*, on the other hand, with its young hero sacrificing himself in order to free the people of Florence from imperial tyranny, is sufficiently complex to avoid being classed as a stereotyped romantic tragedy.

Musset must have taken the idea of dramatizing this episode of Florentine history from George Sand, and have written most of his piece late in 1833. He sticks quite closely to a different version of Varchi's historical account of the assassination of Alessandro from the one used by Sand, but his handling of the political theme is not adroit, the crowd scenes are too programmatically comic in their combination of the grotesque and the sublime, and the narrative is still littered with dreams, faintings, and premonitions. What is new is the demonstrated futility of the heroic act: here Musset gives a perverse twist to the assertion of personal independence and fidelity to an inner mission which is the principal thread of romantic drama, and of the bel canto opera to which it is so closely related. Lorenzo adheres to his inner mission—like the painter Tebaldeo, his function is "réealiser ses rêves (to make his dreams into realities)"—but the debauchery he has to assume as a mask almost saps his personality to the core. His mission accomplished, all Lorenzo can do is surrender to fate and abandon Florence once more to the tyrant.

The romantic themes employed in *Lorenzaccio* foreshadow future symbolist devices. Death is viewed as a consummation, while different characters stand for Church and State, republicanism and tyranny, and much play is made on the analogy with Brutus, the rising and setting of the sun, and the function of the artist in transfiguring what is intrinsically ugly. *Lorenzaccio* was performed in 1896 with Sarah Berhardt in the title role. She also played it in London, where it was given in French and English, and revived in 1933 as *Night's Candles*.

The *Comédies et proverbes* no doubt owe their success to their light and graceful touch. *Un caprice*, *Il faut qu'une porte soit ouverte ou fermée*, and *Il ne faut jurer de rien* brought back to the French stage a poetry and a fantasy which had once been its strength but which, by the mid-19th century, were in danger of disappearing. Modern critics, however, have tended to prefer Musset's dramatized partial self-portraits playing out emotional conflicts to the lighter plays. Such works—probably on account of the way in which they generate atmosphere, thanks to their freedom from the constrictions of 19th-century staging, and their strong delineation of female characters—have attracted the attention of directors such as Baty, Copeau, Vilar, and Krejca.

Until recently at least it was for his lyric poetry, particularly that written in the aftermath of his liaison with George Sand, that Musset was chiefly remembered. By 1833 he had already put behind him the more overtly Byronic posturings of the French romantics, and was being deliberately ironic at the expense of his own early verse with its exotic paraphernalia and range of moods from the satanic to the picaresque. He had made minor declarations of independence in the 1831 *Les Secrètes Pensées de Raphaël, gentilhomme français* and the 1833 dedication of *La Coupe et les lèvres*, but his fullest satirical attack on romantic convention is contained in the *Lettres de Dupuis et Cotonet*, which purports to reduce to simple terms the antagonistic aesthetics of the "classical" and the "romantic"—ultimately no more than "adjectives run wild."

After about 1830 Musset's verse becomes more personal and serious beneath the exoticism and the light-hearted cynicism, deepening rather than sloughing off the romanticism of which the poems written after the break with George Sand have long been regarded as the supreme expression in French verse. In "La nuit de mai" the muse invites the unconsolable poet to use rather than distract himself from his grief, ending with the almost unbearably vivid image of the pelican destroying itself to feed its young. "La nuit de décembre" recalls a real hallucination and, like the earlier poem, gains strength from the formal poetic expression of intense grief. The list of places where the poet sought consolation is not intended as an authentic account of Musset's own travels. Its weakness lies not in the fictionalization but in the merely conventional characteristics given to each of the places mentioned.

The "Lettre à Lamartine," written in February 1836, begins rhetorically and rather weakly, the homage to Lamartine also sounding rather perfunctory alongside the reference to Musset's feelings for George Sand, whose betrayal is blended here with that of Mme Grosellier. The poem ends on a note of hope and in a sense leads into "La nuit d'août," which attempts to take an earthier, more lusty view of love. Here the poet has tried to distract himself with other women, but the spectre of the one he truly loves returns to haunt him, as it does in "La nuit d'octobre," in which the poet regards his passion as definitively overcome, only to be overwhelmed once more by feelings of bitterness and reproach. Only in "Souvenir" is the anguish finally stilled. The poetic craftsmanship of these six poems is open to criticism, and the verse sometimes sinks to the level of mere rhetoric, while Musset's taste is too uncertain, or his emotion too unrestrained, for him to avoid occasional bathos. But it is from their very lack of restraint that the poems draw their impact and succeed in providing a rare expression of the depths of unhappiness that can be occasioned by love.

La Confession d'un enfant du siècle is also a formally rather weak and overwrought fictionalized account of Musset's affair with George Sand, sustained simply by its intensity of feeling. The central character, Octave, looks back over his affair with Brigitte and analyses the debauchery and cynicism which prevented him from believing in her love. Sand returned Musset's letters to help him write the novel, and through Octave Musset blamed himself by implication, as Sand had wanted him to, for all that had gone wrong in their relationship. It remains difficult

to believe that Musset actually did consider himself totally to blame.

Musset continued to publish short stories and occasional pieces in dramatic form after 1840, now more often in reviews other than the *RDM*. None of his later works, published after the *Poésies complètes*, served to enhance his reputation, however, except for those "comédies et proverbes" of which the last were added to the original 1840 edition for the two-volume edition of 1853.

PUBLICATIONS

Collections

Oeuvres complètes, edited by Paul de Musset, 10 vols., 1865–66
Oeuvres complètes, 8 vols., 1907–09
Oeuvres complètes illustrées, 10 vols., 1927–29
Oeuvres complètes en prose; Théâtre complet; Poésies complètes, Bibliothèque de la Pléiade, 3 vols., 1951–58
Oeuvres complètes, Bibliothèque de la Pléiade, 1963
Complete Writings, 10 vols., 1905

Plays

La Nuit vénitienne (produced 1830), in *Un spectacle dans un fauteuil*, 1834
André del Sarto (produced 1848), in *Un spectacle dans un fauteuil*, 1834; revised version (produced 1848), 1851
Les Caprices de Marianne (produced 1851), in *Un spectacle dans un fauteuil*, 1834; revised version (produced 1851), 1851; edited by P.-G. Castex, 1979; as *A Good Little Wife*, n.d. (1847?)
On ne badine pas avec l'amour (produced 1861), in *Un spectacle dans un fauteuil*, 1834; edited by P.-G. Castex, 1979; as *No Trifling with Love*, in *Comedies*, 1890
Fantasio (produced 1866), in *Un spectacle dans un fauteuil*, 1834; as *Fantasio*, in *Comedies*, 1890
Lorenzaccio (produced 1896), in *Un spectacle dans un fauteuil*, 1834; edited by Paul Dimoff, in *La Genèse de Lorenzaccio*, revised edition, 1964
Comédies et proverbes, 1840; augmented and revised edition, 2 vols., 1853; edited by Pierre and Françoise Gastinel, 4 vols., 1934, 1952–57
Le Chandelier, in *Comédies et proverbes*, 1840; revised version (produced 1848), 1848
Il ne faut jurer de rien (produced 1848), in *Comédies et proverbes*, 1840
Un caprice (produced 1847), in *Comédies et proverbes*, 1840
La Quenouille de Barberine, in *Comédies et proverbes*, 1840; revised version, as *Barberine* (produced 1882), in *Comédies et proverbes*, 1853; as *Barberine*, in *Comedies*, 1890
Il faut qu'une porte soit ouverte ou fermée (produced 1848), 1848; as *A Door Must Be Either Open or Shut*, in *Comedies*, 1890
L'Habit vert, with Emile Augier (produced 1849), 1849; as *The Green Coat*, 1914
Louison (produced 1849), 1849
On ne saurait penser à tout (produced 1849), in *Comédies et proverbes*, 1853
Bettine (produced 1851), 1851

Carmosine (produced 1865), in *Comédies et proverbes*, 1853; as *Carmosine* (in English), n.d. (1865?)
L'Ane et le ruisseau (produced 1876), in *Oeuvres posthumes*, 1860; as *All Is Fair in Love and War*, 1868
La Quittance du diable (produced 1938), 1896

Fiction

La Confession d'un enfant du siècle, 2 vols., 1836; as *The Confession of a Child of the Century*, 1892
Nouvelles, 1848; as *Tales from Musset*, 1888; as *The Two Mistresses, etc*, 1900
Contes, 1854

Verse

Les Contes d'Espagne et d'Italie, 1830; edited by Margaret A. Rees, 1973
Poésies complètes, 1840
Premières poésies, Poésies nouvelles, 2 vols., 1852
Poésies complètes, 2 vols., 1854

Other

Un spectacle dans un fauteuil (verse and plays), 1833; second series, 2 vols., 1834
Mélanges de littérature et de critique (essays and criticism), 1867
Oeuvres, Correspondance, edited by Léon Séché, 1907
Lettres d'amour à Aimée d'Alton, edited by Léon Séché, 1910
Oeuvres complémentaires, edited by Maurice Allem, 1911
George Sand et Musset: correspondance..., edited by Louis Evrard, 1956
Translator, *L'Anglais mangeur d'opium*, by de Quincey, 1828

Bibliography

Siegel, Patricia Joan, *Musset: A Reference Guide*, 1982

Critical studies

Haldane, Charlotte, *Alfred: The Passionate Life of Musset*, 1960

Gochberg, Herbert S., *Stage of Dreams: The Dramatic Art of Musset*, 1967
Rees, Margaret A., *Musset* (in English), 1971
Affron, Charles, *A Stage for Poets: Studies in the Theatre of Hugo and Musset*, 1971
Sices, David, *Theatre of Solitude: The Drama of Musset*, 1974

MUSSET, Paul de, 1804–1880.

Biographer and writer of children's books.

Paul de Musset wrote a defensive biography of his younger brother Alfred, the *Biographie d'Alfred de Musset: sa vie et ses oeuvres*, in which he understandably whitewashed his brother's debauchery, but also provided the definitive account of his childhood and schooldays. When George Sand published her account of her affair with Alfred de Musset, *Elle et lui*, in 1859, Paul de Musset riposted the same year with *Lui et elle*, a thinly disguised narrative of the journey to Italy undertaken by Alfred and George Sand in 1833–34, together with an account of their ruptures, separations, and reconciliations before the final breakup in March 1835. It is a strong attack on his brother's mistress.

Musset also wrote a classic children's book, *Monsieur le Vent et Madame la Pluie* (1860).

PUBLICATIONS

Lui et elle, 1859
Monsieur le Vent et Madame la Pluie, 1860
Biographie d'Alfred de Musset: sa vie et ses oeuvres, 1877

N

NADAR (Pseudonym of Gaspard-Félix TOURNACHON), 1820–1910.

Photographer, balloonist, essayist, and journalist.

If Nadar was not quite the first to have brought photography to the level of an art form, he was the first to combine art photography with the roles of a gifted satirist, a businessman, and a passionate aeronaut. He played an active role in literary and artistic circles in the middle and later parts of the 19th century and was, for instance, a patron of the Café Momus along with Murger, Champfleury, and the original cast of the *Scènes de la Bohème*. He was also a friend of Daumier, who published a famous cartoon of Nadar taking a photograph from a balloon entitled "Nadar élevant la photographie à la hauteur de l'art (Nadar raising photography to the heights of art)." Nadar invented aerial photography, took the first aerial photographs of Paris in 1858, and left celebrated portrait photographs of, among others, François Guizot, Victor Cousin, George Sand, Gautier, Dumas *père*, Proudhon, Pasteur, Zola, Sarah Bernhardt, Clemenceau, Jaurès, and Jules Verne.

He was born in Paris on 6 April 1820, studied medicine, worked in a bookshop, and wrote essays and bitingly satirical commentaries for a number of newspapers and small magazines. He also worked in the theatre and founded his own magazine, *Le Livre d'Or*, joining *Le Commerce* in 1842 and signing a five-year contract with *Le Charivari* in 1848. He also founded the *Revue Comique* and published caricatures in *Le Journal pour Rire*. He issued a 38-page brochure of comic sketches on the 1853 Salon, and in 1854 achieved fame with his huge lithograph "Le panthéon Nadar." In that year, while still active as a journalist and publisher, he began to study photography with Camille d'Arnaud, and opened his own studio, which quickly became a centre for literary and artistic society.

In 1856 Nadar founded *Le Petit Journal pour Rire*, a weekly which survived for six years, edited *L'Image pour Tous*, and published *Quand j'étais étudiant*. By the following year he was experimenting with electric lighting and he later opened a salon of electric photography. He travelled throughout Europe taking photographs from his balloon, Le Géant, from 1866. His business prospered and he opened several branch studios in Paris and Marseilles. In 1861 he photographed the sewers and catacombs of Paris, in 1863 he became editor of *L'Aéronaute*, and in 1870 he organized a system for sending microphotographs by carrier pigeon to carry news from the besieged city. His son Paul took over the business in 1886.

Nadar published small brochures as well as complete books, some comic and some devoted to photography or ballooning, and in 1900 his autobiography, *Quand j'étais photographe*. He left an intimate memoir of Baudelaire, which was published posthumously in 1911.

PUBLICATIONS

Works

Nadar (vol. 1 "Photographies"; vol. 2 "Dessins et écrits"), with prefaces and commentaries by J.-F. Bory, P. Néagu, and J.-J. Poulet-Allamagny, 1979
Nadar jury au Salon de 1853, album comique de 60 à 80 dessins coloriés; compte rendu d'environ 6 à 800 tableaux, sculptures etc, 1853
Quand j'étais étudiant, 1856
Nadar jury au Salon de 1857, 1857
Le Miroir aux alouettes, 1859
Album du plaisir, almanach charivarique, drôlatique, comique, hippique et cynégétique pour 1862, 1862
La Robe de Déjanire, 1862
Mémoires du "Géant", 1864
Le Droit au vol, 1865
Simple lettre d'un petit de sixième à l'élève de seconde Cavaignac, 1868
Les Ballons en 1870, ce qu'on aurait pu faire, ce qu'on a fait, 1870
La Grande Symphonie héroïque des punaises, with Charles Bataille, 1877
Histoires buissonnières, 1877
L'Hôtellerie des Coquecigrues (Notes au crayon), 1880
Les Dicts et faits du chier cyre Gambette le Hutin en sa court, 1882
Le Général Fricassier, 1882
Sous l'incendie, 1882
La Passion illustrée, sinon illustre, de N.-S. Gambetta, selon l'Evangile de St (Charles) Laurent…, 1882
Le Cas des cloches…, 1883
Le Monde où on patauge, 1883
Quand j'étais photographe, 1900
Charles Baudelaire intime, 1911

————

NATURALISM

See also Becque, Bourget, Goncourt, Huysmans, Maupassant, Zola, and realism.

Historians of literature are not spared, any more than other historians, from the law which puts the nature of a current or a movement into a reciprocal relationship with the dates assigned to it. What naturalism is depends on whether it is dated, as it plausibly has been, from as early as 1862, with the inauguration of the dinners at Magny's (see Goncourt), or as late as 1880, the date of the appearance of *Les Soirées de Médan*, the six stories connected with the Franco-Prussian War written by a group of writers closely associated at the time with Zola, whom they regularly visited at his newly acquired house near the river at Médan. Zola himself contributed "L'attaque au moulin" to the volume, and the other five contes were "Boule-de-suif" by Maupassant, "Sac au dos" by Huysmans, "La saignée" by Henri Céard, "L'affaire du grand 7" by Léon Hennique, and "Après la bataille" by Paul Alexis. As a literary movement the inauguration of naturalism is sometimes dated to the celebratory dinner at Trapp's attended by Zola, Flaubert, the Goncourt brothers, and the future Médan group on 16 April 1877, soon after the appearance of Zola's *L'Assommoir.*

Like other historical phenomena, too, naturalism tends to disintegrate under microscopic examination. Stendhal's Fabrice del Dongo in *La Chartreuse de Parme* wondered whether all that noise and smoke was "the battle of Waterloo." Trying to pin down a literary movement like naturalism could be compared to looking for a battle in acres of skirmishes or for the ultimate constituent of matter inside an atom. Their true nature cannot be defined except in terms of their total effect. Flaubert encouraged the young Maupassant, who was hard up, to exploit the vogue for realism (q.v.) in the short story. He disliked the theoretical basis for naturalism—"Ce matérialisme m'indigne…(I'm outraged by this materialism)"—but liked Zola's work. There are signs that Zola, who often used the word "poème" of his novels, regarded the theoretical principles of heredity on which he said they were based partly as a way of gaining publicity for them rather than providing them with a serious scientific background. Naturalism is not so much a theory or a doctrine as a tendency which cannot be precisely defined, and about whose description and dating there is only rough critical agreement.

The word "naturalism" is not itself new. Zola used it of his own work, and it had long been used as meaning simply the imitation of nature. Baudelaire referred to Ingres as belonging to the naturalist school in drawing, while Littré (see realism) thought the term referred to a philosophical doctrine which derived everything from nature, not God. The difficulty lies in disentangling the aesthetic movement we call "naturalist" from the social and political attitudes with which it is interwoven, but with which it can of course not be identified. Just as with Delacroix romantic painting had made a liberal political gesture by replacing the luminous glazes and contrasting tone values of neoclassical painting with loud colours and unconcealed brushwork, so Courbet's realism after 1855 reflects a lessened commitment to socialist political policies with lighter colours and a return to landscape, seascape, and female subjects.

The aesthetic interest in subjects formerly thought intrinsically ugly, and the novelists' increasing preoccupation with the life of the poor, is clearly connected with the rise of the new social and political values which they explore, or even seek to promote, although the relationship between literary style, subject matter, focus of interest, and social reality is not as simple as that between cause and effect. Hugo's "romantic" (q.v.) novel *Les Misérables* of 1862, like the novels of Sue, clearly examines the possibility that crime is often the effect of poverty. What distinguishes it from Zola's novels is not the social and political attitudes involved, which are similar in both. As the century pro-

gressed an increasingly systematic interest in investigating the impossibility of individual heroism became apparent. Although Hugo's novel was published after Flaubert's quite systematic exploration of the possibility that heroism cannot exist, his protagonist, Jean Valjean, is still recognizably a romantic hero. Zola's flaunted theories of heredity, even if publicity-conscious, at least ensured the absence of any real hero in any of the Rougon-Macquart novels. Indeed, it is the absence of any heroic figure that eventually forces Zola into sentimentality as a means of resolving his plots. Simple tragedy too easily leads to the romanticization of the central figure.

Jules de Goncourt himself situated the break with the past in the first novel he wrote with his elder brother Edmond, *Germinie Lacerteux* of 1864:

> Il faudra bien reconnaître un jour… que *Germinie Lacerteux* est le livre type qui a servi de modèle à tout ce qui a été fabriqué depuis nous, sous le titre de réalisme, naturalisme etc.

> (One day it will have to be acknowledged… that *Germinie Lacerteux* is the prototype book which has served as a model for everything done since in the name of realism, naturalism, etc.)

What distinguished the Goncourt brothers and Zola from their predecessors, or such roughly contemporaneous writers as Flaubert and Maupassant, was their way of writing rather than the final product and, in the case of Zola, Taine's theory of social determinism as well as that of Claude Bernard on heredity, as laid out in the *Introduction à l'étude de la médicine expérimentale* of 1865.

The Goncourts' and Zola's meticulous documentation of the environments and types of people they wrote about says more about their own social situations and mental processes than about the literary power of their work. Apart from Huysmans for a period, they are the only really powerful naturalist authors of fiction to have written in France. Maupassant was never really a naturalist in the same sense. Applied to him, the word has more to do with realistic description and the use of dialect conversation. It is the date at which he wrote, his association with naturalistically inclined painters, and the settings he chose for his contes, which have led critics to pigeonhole him conveniently as a naturalist. No doubt reacting against his earlier taste for the romantic and the grotesque, Flaubert went out of his way in *Madame Bovary*, though not in his other works, to give details of such bodily functions as sweating, dribbling, and spitting. That was the nearest he got to naturalism, unless naturalism is taken, as no doubt it should be, but is not, for the systematic elimination of the heroic. In each of his major works Flaubert deliberately raises expectations of heroic or tragic status, and in each case he shows the activity concerned to be neither heroic, nor wicked, nor saintly, nor tragic.

Taine's determinism and the theory of heredity, originally deriving from Prosper Lucas's *Traité philosophique et physiologique de l'hérédité naturelle* (1847–1850), are in fact epiphenomena of Zola's naturalism. It is difficult to take literally Zola's assertion in the 1880 *Le Roman expérimental* with regard to Claude Bernard's book which Céard had lent him, "Le plus souvent il me suffira de remplacer le mot *médecin* par le mot *romancier* (More often than not it will be enough for me to replace the word "doctor" by the word "novelist")." Edmond de Goncourt was to distance himself from the Médan group, which was strongly attacked by Barbey d'Aurevilly and Brunetière (see the *Revue des Deux Mondes*) as well as by Francisque Sarcey, the celebrated drama critic of *Le Temps*. One notable associate of the group was Octave Mirbeau, author of *Le Calvaire* of 1886 and three novels, *Le Jardin des supplices* (1898), *Le Journal d'une femme de chambre* (1900), and *Les Vingt-et-un jours d'un neurasthénique* (1901), and a bitter satire on a financier, *Les Affaires sont les affaires* (1903). Other former associates included Lucien Descaves, Gustave Guiches, Paul Bonnetain, Paul Margueritte, and Joseph-Henri Rosny, who issued the anti-Zola manifesto in 1887 (on which, see Goncourt). The attack, occasioned by Zola's *La Terre*, had not involved Edmond de Goncourt or Alphonse Daudet, although Zola had thought that they had inspired it, and they no doubt agreed with its content.

Transposed to the sphere of drama, Zola's naturalism effectively used a stage cluttered with props, reducing the plots to a succession of grand scenes that were melodramatic in their impact. At the Théâtre Libre (1887–1894), the actors of André Antoine spoke in flat tones without emphasis. The company presented Ibsen's *Ghosts* and the plays of Strindberg and Hauptmann, and gained an international reputation. It failed in 1894, although Antoine was himself to re-emerge at the Odéon, working with the young Jacques Copeau (see the *Nouvelle Revue Française*). Zola had written *Le Naturalisme au théâtre* in 1881, but there were no great naturalist dramatists writing in French, since neither Becque nor Mirbeau wrote in an idiom that was in any sense truly naturalist. Zola himself was to abandon the austerities of naturalistic determinism for his later lyrical socialism, already apparent in *Germinal*. Céard regretted that he had lent Zola Bernard's book.

NERVAL, Gérard de (Pseudonym of Gérard Labrunie) 1808–1855.

Poet, journalist, author of fiction, and travel writer.

LIFE

Gérard de Nerval, born Gérard Labrunie on 22 May 1808, was the son of an upholsterer from a working-class family in the south of France. Etienne Labrunie, who survived his son, joined the revolutionary army at the age of 16, was wounded, and, in order to get back into the army, studied medicine and became a doctor. On 1 or 2 July 1807 he married Marie-Antoinette-Marguerite Laurent, the second of three children of a linen merchant, of whose family Nerval gives a fictionalized account in *Promenades et Souvenirs*. His godfather was his father's uncle, a Paris pharmacist, and his godmother was his maternal grandmother. His father was almost immediately made an army doctor and his mother went with him to the Rhine in December, leaving Nerval with a nurse. Initially his father was put in charge of hospitals in Hanover, but then moved to Glogau in Poland. Here, his mother

crossed a bridge piled with corpses and caught a fever, from which she died on 29 November 1810 at the age of 25. Her sister, who was 14 years younger, was to die at the same age. Nerval may have inherited some weakness of physical make-up from his mother's family.

Etienne Labrunie took part in the Russian campaign, was wounded in the foot, and taken prisoner. He returned to Paris in 1814 and retired the following year, continuing to practise as a doctor in civilian life. Nerval, who had been brought up in the country at Mortefontaine by his great-uncle since the age of two, rejoined his father on his return when Nerval was nearly seven. He continued to spend holidays at Mortefontaine until his great-uncle's death in 1820. From that year Nerval attended the Lycée Charlemagne, where Gautier was a fellow-pupil. The absence of his mother virtually from birth, coupled with the absence of his father, his attachment to his great-uncle as a substitute, and his inherited physical fragility, may explain much about Nerval's later physical and mental illnesses and the mental patterns, as of dream castles, which recur in his imagination. Traces of Nerval's great-uncle appear in the contes, and the parts played in his imagination by Germany, Faust, the Rhine, the Lorelei, and by his feelings of guilt probably all have roots in the experiences of his earliest years.

His later relationship with his father was a complex one which never progressed beyond that to be expected from an emotionally deprived child. It included affection, awe, and an aggressive need for self-assertion, as shown by his refusal to use his family name in the world of letters, which his father tried to prevent him from joining, and in which he was to meet financial ruin. The complexity of the relationship with his father was important for Nerval's later biography, as was also the Rhine which lured him, but which also guarded the country from which he was beckoned by the mother he never knew, and which in his imagination he also fused with the East. Germany, however, was always the subject of a quest as well as a source of guilt because it was associated with his mother's death. The confusion of geographical with parental imagery in Nerval's mind explains much about his psychological make-up and his physical travels.

In Paris his father's younger brother lived with them. At school Nerval had begun to write verse in exercise books which still exist. He knew of the new romantic (q.v.) literary movement and his work could already be classified as either lyrical or alternatively satirical. In 1826, while still at school, he published his first "plaquettes" or brochures of poems, together with the pro-Napoleonic *Napoléon et la France guerrière: élégies nationales* and the satirical dialogue in verse *L'Académie; ou, Les Membres introuvables*, an act of revenge for not having been awarded that year's academy prize. By the time Nerval left school, he had published half a dozen plaquettes, and he immediately started placing his prose and verse pieces in reviews. By the end of 1826 he had begun his translation of *Faust*. His verse translation of the last scene was published in *Le Mercure de France au XIXe siècle* in 1827, and the whole of Goethe's *Faust (Der Tragödie erster Teil*, "Part One," 1808) in verse and prose translation in November 1827, though dated 1828. The probability is that Nerval had relied on Stapfer's 1823 version, but in 1830 Goethe himself was to tell Eckermann that he liked Nerval's version, and it also inspired Berlioz. What had fascinated Nerval had been Faust's unquenchable thirst for knowledge and his interest in the occult as a way of assuaging it.

The *Faust* translation immediately made Nerval's reputation

the way home. The journey must have been partly official, as Nerval had some government privileges, but seems to have been financed primarily by a publisher's advance. The *Voyage en orient* is only a fictionalized account of what happened. Nerval thought he had come back cured, but instantly threw himself into a tornado of activity, in the middle of which he went to Belgium and Holland with Houssaye in 1844, and again took over from Gautier at *La Presse* in 1845. He became friendly with Baudelaire, who shared his and Hugo's fascination with the imagery of Watteau's famous 1717 painting *L'Embarquement pour l'Ile de Cythère*.

From the beginning of 1844 to the revolution of 1848 Nerval's life was that of a working journalist with a specialist sideline in impressionistic travel literature. In 1845 he spent a week in London, and in 1846 began the promenades in the environs of Paris for which he quickly became famous, and which are the basis for *Promenades et souvenirs*, as well as for "Angélique." The latter typically appeared as part of a feuilleton in *Le National* late in 1850, was taken up into *Les Illuminés* of 1852, with fragments used in *La Bohème galante* in *L'Artiste* and in *Lorely* the same year, before the whole story of Angélique was adopted as the first story of *Les Filles du feu*. In 1847 Nerval went only as far as Le Havre, although the project may well have been to go farther, and he signed a contract for a book, abandoned when the revolution broke out, on the coast and islands of the Mediterranean. He constantly contributed drama criticism to *L'Artiste* and *La Presse*, but the most important event at this period of his life was probably the close friendship he gradually formed with Heinrich Heine, who had been living in Paris since 1831, and some of whose poems Nerval had translated. With Heine, on whom he called daily, he revised his translations of Heine's poems to appear in the *RDM* in July and September 1848, and in that year, in the wake of the February revolution, he worked with Nadar on Karr's *Journal*, which appeared from 28 July to 31 October.

Among the writings of this period are tardy examples of the "physiologies" associated with the early Balzac, as well as contes turning on the occult, the macabre, and the death of Christ. A corner of Nerval's imagination was particularly obsessed by Jean-Paul's "Rede des toten Christus (Discourse of the dead Christ)," affixed to the 1796–97 *Siebenkäs* which had so affected Nodier, Vigny, Musset, and Hugo. Much of his work was ephemeral, like the defence of Houssaye, some was travel journalism, but some of the more alarmingly obsessive themes, particularly the hostile beloved which was to culminate in *Aurélia*, begin to recur at this time. The *RDM* paid well for the reminiscences of Egypt and Syria from 1 May 1846 to 15 October 1847 and Nerval sold the volume rights to Sartorius for the book, *Les Femmes du Caire*, but publication was delayed until the eve of the revolution, February 1848, and the book was a commercial failure. Sartorius did not take the second volume on Syria and Lebanon. From January 1849 to January 1850 Nerval published further reminiscences in *La Silhouette*.

The travel articles had reused much already published material, joining and dividing it in different ways, and inventing whatever was necessary to move geographically from one reminiscence to another. On 31 March 1849, more than a year after its first version had been submitted to the censorship, *Les Monténégrins* opened at the Opéra-Comique. It is clearly inspired by Nodier and Goethe, and owed its success largely to the politically liberal mood of the public. In April Nerval was in

hospital again briefly with mental trouble, and in May and early June he was in London, but he returned to Paris in time for the insurrection of 13 June. He had got to know Delaage, a fellow mason, but also a devotee of the occult, and had contributed "Le diable rouge" to *L'Almanach cabalistique pour 1850*, which proved to be a first sketch for parts of *Les Illuminés*.

Nerval's theatrical ventures continued to disappoint him. Many remained unfinished, or were sold as ideas only. There were troubles with the censorship, and about infringements of the Opéra's monopoly of music. The verse drama *Le Chariot d'enfant*, on which Méry collaborated, ran for only 17 performances. Each setback in the theatre brought on a bout of depression, and Nerval needed treatment again in June 1850. The correspondence between failure in theatrical ventures, whether or not they ever got as far as being staged, and spates of depression amounting to clinical illness is not exact. It is clear, however, that Nerval pinned too many of his hopes on the theatre, potentially very lucrative, but not his real gift, and that there is some correspondence between disappointment in undertakings to do with the theatre and relapses into mental illness. By 1850 the introversion was becoming more acute, and it was to Germany that Nerval went when his symptoms subsided in August and September.

During that time the *RDM* published "Les confidences de Nicolas" and from October to December *Le National* published "Les Faux-Saulniers," both pieces essential to an understanding of Nerval's mental biography. His self-identification with Restif de la Bretonne in the *RDM* is important not only for the indication it gives of how Nerval saw himself, but also for its literary consequences. He had started to use Restif as a model. The picaresque adventures of the Abbé de Bucquoy in *Le National*, on the other hand, which were later to be used in *Les Illuminés*, *Les Filles du Feu*, *La Bohème galante*, and *Lorely*, allowed Nerval to return to his own country childhood at Mortefontaine. The character of Adrienne from *Sylvie* began to emerge, while Restif was taking Nerval towards the definitive versions of Sylvie and Aurélie. Nerval had got himself sent to Germany as a journalist to report on the special celebrations at Weimar in honour of Herder and Goethe, arriving late, though he was present at the premiere of *Lohengrin* on 28 August. Liszt helped him to write about Wagner, who was very pleased by the article in *La Presse*. When he got back to Paris Nerval found that his lodgings were to be demolished and that *Le Corsaire* had attacked him for accepting government missions under the July monarchy while pretending to be a liberal.

In January 1851 the contract for the *Voyage en orient* was signed, and the final text shows the clear intention of turning the journalist's articles into a work of literary standing. Houssaye, now director of the Comédie-Française, commissioned a translation of Kotzebue, and Nerval was negotiating with Lecour to publish a volume of *Les Illuminés*. He was also writing "Quintus Aucler" for Du Camp at the newly revived *Revue de Paris*, while Marc Fournier at the Porte-Saint-Martin at last gave Nerval the opportunity he had wanted for years to put on a dramatized "Faust." The final product, *L'Imagier de Harlem*, was performed on 27 December, after Nerval had injured himself in a fall, perhaps occurring during a depression but following which he had another bout of mental illness. Unhappily, Fournier was not covering his costs and took *L'Imagier* off after 27 performances, although the public had at first liked it. The critics had been more reserved. Fournier asked Méry and

Nerval for an "Alcibiade," but Nerval was too devastated to carry on.

He was ill again at the beginning of 1852, cared for partly by Nadar until he had to go to hospital for three weeks. By May he could travel again and saw Dumas in Belgium, with accounts of Dutch May festivals appearing in the *RDM* as early as June. That same month the contract was signed for *Lorely: souvenirs d'Allemagne* and an assortment of old articles, together with some very recent ones. *Léo Burckart* was published in August. *Les Illuminés*, another collection of previously published bits and pieces, appeared in November. A month later came another collection of odds and ends, *Contes et facéties*. By the end of the year, however, Nerval was again in financial distress and asked for more government help. In October *Les Nuits d'octobre*, drawing on his experiences of walking around Paris, appeared in *L'Illustration*, and the contract for the *Petits châteaux de Bohème* was signed on 14 December. The volume appeared on 1 January 1853, dedicated to Nodier. During 1852 Nerval had been shamelessly recycling very old material in *L'Artiste*, of which Houssaye had given him the freedom. He made extensive use of it, mostly reminiscing about the Impasse du Doyenné under the new and—in the wake of Murger's now famous novel, published in volume form the preceding year—fashionable title of *La Bohème galante*.

Nerval suffered another bout of illness early in 1853 and received government help. He was now writing his masterpiece, *Sylvie*, which was to appear in the *RDM* on 15 August. Ten days later he was again ill. He received a further state subvention, but his furniture was now moved into the clinic. In August and September *Le Pays* had published "La reine de Saba" from the *Voyage en orient* in a dozen instalments and, although there has been some confusion about dates, it seems certain that *Pandora* was finished in 1853. At the end of that year Dumas published Nerval's "El desdichado." *Les Filles du feu* was put together around "Corilla," pressed into service again, together with "Isis" and "Octavie," published as it now exists for the first time on 17 December 1853 in *Le Mousquetaire*. There is considerable cross-contamination in the works published from late 1853, the date at which, under medical orders, Nerval started to note down his dreams, giving us *Aurélia*. The psychiatric attention he received seems to have been remarkably perceptive, kind, and efficient.

In 1854 an official mission to the East was arranged with medical encouragement, but had to be cancelled on account of Nerval's health. Houssaye was officially authorized to advance Nerval 1,500 francs for what proved to be his last visit to Germany in 1854. He may have visited his mother's grave. He certainly had a serious relapse. After a return to the clinic he was released and spent the winter without any fixed dwelling. On 20 January 1855 he was at the *Revue de Paris* and on 23 January handed a list of his complete works to a bibliophile he had known since his literary beginnings. He spent the evening of the 24th with two friends and an actress, ending up at a police station after being arrested in a round-up. Nerval emerged in the morning to borrow the seven sous he needed for the public library. That evening he called on Houssaye, who was out. He seems to have eaten near Les Halles. It was exceedingly cold. The next morning he was found hanged from a railing in the street. Nerval's letters from these days seem to have been written in a delirium of excitement, and it has been plausibly suggested that in hanging himself Nerval may have been acting out some fantasy and had not actually intended to kill himself. He was accorded an ecclesiastical funeral at Notre Dame on the grounds that, if he had committed suicide, it was while mentally deranged.

WORKS

Driven by the ferocious need to make money after the financial disaster of 1836, Nerval became a journeyman journalist, publishing what he could, mostly dramatic criticism, contes, and travel sketches, wherever and whenever possible. Apart from his writing for the stage, he did not write "works," but combined, adapted, reused, and resold material. It is scarcely possible to talk of patterns of imaginative interest, since these emerged not from the need to probe the meaning of experience so much as from the urgency of recycling what was saleable. Since the repackaging was often hurried and undertaken in conditions of extreme stress, it is not even possible to point with any sureness to a development in Nerval's literary output except, perhaps, to note the moments at which he draws inspiration from different outside sources—Nodier, Goethe, and Restif, for instance, or Germany and the Middle East.

What makes Nerval a great author is the imaginative vigour with which he was driven by his illness to explore those seething depths of a morbid mind from which there are occasional eruptions in even the least mentally sick. Phantoms, fears, obsessions, hallucinations, and dreams surfaced from those depths in Nerval, repressed only by equally dangerous euphoric illusions. Thus, in the conscious, articulate imagination from which his writing issued, there are grotesque and warped fantasies, as well as visions of rarely recounted splendour. There are focuses, too, which awake universal resonance—attractive but hostile women, castles, exotically beautiful but dangerous places like Germany or Cythera, idyllic country pursuits, the murderously compelling forces of madness appearing as darkness, Satan, death, and the power of the occult.

Nerval is quite conscious of what he is doing. Jules Janin had written about him on 1 March in the *Journal des Débats* when the mental disequilibrium first demanded treatment. Nerval replied over 10 years later in the preface to *Lorely* in 1852. On 1 December 1853 Dumas, presenting "El desdichado (The disinherited)" to the readers of *Le Mousquetaire*, wrote of Nerval that sometimes his reason deserted him and left him deluded into thinking he was King Solomon, that he had found the seal by which he could conjure spirits, or that he was waiting for the Queen of Sheba. Nerval replied in the letter to Dumas prefacing *Les Filles du feu* of 1854, largely taking up a text of 1844;

> … on arrive pour ainsi dire à s'incarner dans le héros de son imagination, si bien que sa vie devienne la vôtre et qu'on brûle des flammes factices de ses ambitions et de ses amours! … Inventer, au fond c'est se ressouvenir… ne pouvant trouver les preuves de l'existence matérielle de mon héros, j'ai cru tout à coup à la transmigration des âmes… il ne m'en coûtait pas plus d'avoir été prince, roi, mage, génie et même Dieu… Ce serait le Songe de Scipion, la Vision du Tasse ou la *Divine Comédie* du Dante, si j'étais parvenu à concentrer mes souvenirs en un chef-d'oeuvre.

> (… you come to incarnate yourself in your imaginary hero, so that his life becomes yours, and you burn with the

artifical flames of his ambitions and his loves!…Inventing in the end is only remembering…unable to find the proofs of my hero's material existence, I suddenly believed in the transmigration of souls…it cost me no more to have been prince, king, magus, genius, or even God…If I had succeeded in concentrating my memories into a masterpiece it would have been the Dream of Scipio, the Vision of Tasso, Dante's *Divine Comedy*.)

The borderline between imagination and delusion has become too fragile, but the imagination in the end can draw only on memory and "chaque homme devient ainsi un miroir où chacun peut s'étudier (each man becomes in this way a mirror in which everyone can study himself)." Literary creation can only probe personal experience, and each person's individual experience is in some ways that of others too. By dipping into his own mental morbidity and extracting communicable images, combining literary craftsmanship with poetic vertigo, Nerval is holding an intensifying mirror to common experience, much in fact as the Greek myths did. Whether or not Nerval's view should be called an aesthetic, it is a description of how he thinks his writing works and an excellent description of the general nature of literary communication.

The *Voyage en orient* purports to start in Germany and Austria, suggesting that everything evoked in Nerval's mind by both was somehow fused. He writes entertainingly, evoking sights and colours as popular taste demands, and filling his quota of descriptive set pieces, although without the flair of a Chateaubriand or a Flaubert. Nerval is more interested in the spiritual heritage which goes back to the origins of humanity, in tracing in his travels something like the history or at least the manifestations of the human spirit. It is because his journeys were always a quest for a spiritual home, a search for the secrets of life and death, that he can interpolate into the *Voyage* everything that he believed had been brought together in the illuminism of Swedenborg. This is best illustrated in the *Voyage*'s "Histoire du Calife Hakem" and the "Histoire de la reine du matin et de Soliman prince de Génies," a fable of masonic origins about the inner descent to self-awareness, personified as a beautiful and destructive woman, a manifestation of the archetype of which the sirens were another. The fable however is also about the fall from holiness, suggesting Lucifer, the tree of knowledge, paradise, the fall, and "the saint of the abyss." Nerval is looking for a means of communicating the depths of his own experience. His narrative is simple and direct, alternating between amusing effects and tragic ones, but with the exaltation of the visionary and the perpetual exploitations of the mythical reverberations of archetypes.

The archetypes cannot be reduced to symbols. That is the point of using them. They are exploited in order to create myths. Balkis, the Queen of Sheba, is a real character who emerges from the legend narrated by the "conteur" or "rhapsode" to whom the "Je" of the *Voyage* listens in a café. In 1832 *Les Annales Romantiques* published the poem "Fantaisie," printed at least five other times with three different titles ("Souvenirs d'une autre vie" in the *Journal des Gens du Monde* of 1834, "Vision" in *La Sylphide* for 1842, and "Odelette" in *L'Artiste* of the same year). This drew on another archetype, the castle with a woman at its casement window, at once beckoning and forbidding, but remembered from 200 years ago and therefore perennial, actually a prototype of Adrienne from *Sylvie*. Whatever the woman may have to do with memories of Jenny and the castle with recollections of Mortefontaine, the combination is not a symbol, but a sign indicating attractiveness and unattainability.

In the poem there is a brick château with cornerstones, rose-tinted windows, great parks, and a river. The woman is "Blonde, aux yeux noirs (Blonde, with dark eyes)," and therefore already a contradiction, whom the "I" of the poem associates with a tune which takes him back 200 years, and

Que, dans une autre existence peut-être,
J'ai déjà vue…et dont je me souviens!

(Whom, perhaps in another existence/I have already seen…and whom I remember!)

The figure is clearly legendary. In "Adrienne," the second chapter of *Sylvie*, the narrator is obliged by the rules of a dance to kiss Adrienne. He cannot prevent himself from pressing her hand. The dance then demands that Adrienne shall sing. When she has finished, the narrator rushes out into garden, breaks two branches off some potted laurels, ties a ribbon round them, and puts the crown on Adrienne's head. The narrative is deliberately on a fairy-tale register.

Quand je revins près de Sylvie, je m'aperçus qu'elle pleurait. La couronne donnée par mes mains à la belle chanteuse était le sujet de ses larmes.

(When I returned to Sylvie, I noticed that she was crying. The crown given by my hands to the beautiful singer was the subject of her tears.)

Next year he hears that Adrienne has become a nun.

What Nerval has created is not a metaphysical parable, but an affective myth, a story whose surface simplicity masks and indicates a deep psychological response. In a sense the myth is well worn, and the fusion in Nerval's mind between Sophie Dawes, Mortefontaine, and Jenny Colon, and then the fusion between the dead Jenny and Nerval's dead mother in *Aurélia*, is simply irrelevant, although Nerval's clinical narration of his dreams in *Aurélia* undoubtedly increases the power of the fable to move us. The first chapter of the first part of *Aurélia* links Jenny to Adrienne through the figure of Béatrix, and Sylvie, the village sweetheart, is a partial projection of Adrienne, the idealized object of dream love. The point, however, is the way in which, even without *Aurélia*, which merely confirms what is anyway obvious from literary analysis, Nerval's imaginative power derives from the probing of his own most intimate and disturbing experiences. In Nerval's work the communication of his paradigmatic reactions in the simplicity of generalized or universalized myth is always forceful in proportion to the simplicity of its narration. Nerval's experience with Jenny, everyone's experience of what is attractive but unattainable, achieves almost aphoristic power of expression in the third chapter of *Sylvie*: "Aimer une religieuse sous la forme d'une actrice! (Loving a nun in the form of an actress!)." *Les Filles du feu* is not itself a unified book. It contains two contes of personal reminiscence, *Sylvie* and *Octavie*, a romantic historical conte, *Angélique*, and a folklore conte, *Chansons et légendes du Valois*, the reflections of *Isis*, and a dramatic sketch, *Corilla*. The volume is nevertheless unified by a glowing tenderness which suffuses the whole collection.

The high point of Nerval's achievement is often thought to be the collection of a dozen poems now known as *Les Chimères*, although they were not written as a group. They do not always impose the logical connections of rational thought on their contents, so that the individual words, or images, have a significance totally dependent on the semi-conscious dream life of the poet. It is possible to work out the probable connections and allusions which might "explain" the poems in terms of a rational exposition of the poet's experience to which they refer. To do that, however, is to deny their autonomy as a jumble of concepts whose relationships with one another only the poet can grasp. Whatever their interest for students of surrealism (q.v.) or psychology, the poems set out merely to show how inarticulate levels of personal experience give rise to an assembly of still raw concepts or images which merely mimic logical organization and cannot be used for the purposes of rational communication as they stand. They exist first as products of the unorganized experience which is madness, to be desired as well as feared by rational man because, while it extinguishes properly human levels of response, it also removes the need for mental and emotional effort.

Even the most easily accessible of the poems, which do communicate rationally and with controlled syntax, the five sonnets of "Le Christ aux oliviers," first published in 1844, evoke the frightening experience of Christ's discovery after death that there is no God. Inevitably, there are clever word games and proliferations of meaning. In "Artémis" the opening line, "La Treizième revient... C'est encore la première (The Thirteenth returns... It is still/again the first)," offers a choice of meanings, but refers in fact to the 24-hour clock, on which 13 hours is one p.m., while the third line offers not a choice but a multiplicity of meanings: "Car es-tu reine, ô toi! la première ou la dernière? (Are you queen, you, the first or the last?/You, the first or the last, are you queen?)." The second line, "Et c'est toujours la seule—ou c'est le seul moment (And it is always the only one, or it is the only moment/the moment alone)," twice uses the word "seul(e)" (only/alone), and the fourth is in counterpoint with the third, whose syntax it echoes: "Es-tu roi, toi le seul ou le dernier amant?... (Are you king, you who are the first/only or the last lover? / Are you, oh king, you, the first lover or the last?...)." Since each alternative meaning can go with each other alternative offered elsewhere, the stanza is simply untranslatable, although any possible translation would have to be concerned with the relationships between identity, succession, and gender.

PUBLICATIONS

Collections

Oeuvres complètes, 6 vols., 1867–77
Oeuvres complètes, 6 vols., 1926–32
Oeuvres (Garnier edition), 2 vols., 1958
Oeuvres, Bibliothèque de la Pléiade, 2 vols., 1952–56

Verse

Napoléon et la France guerrière: élégies nationales, 1826
La Mort de Talma: élégie nationale, 1826
Les Hauts Faits des Jésuites: dialogue en vers, 1826
Monsieur Deutscourt; ou, Le Cuisinier d'un grand homme,
1826; reprinted in the 1827 edition of the *Elégies*
Les Chimères, in *Les Filles du feu*, 1854; edited by Norma Rinsler, 1973; as *The Chimeras*, translated by Andrew Hoyem, 1966, and Derek Mahon, 1982
Fortune's Fool: Thirty-Five Poems, translated by Brian Hill, 1959

Plays

L'Académie; ou, Les Membres introuvables: comédie satirique en vers, 1826
Piquillo, with Dumas *père* (produced 1837), 1837
Léo Burckart, with Dumas *père* (produced 1839), 1839
L'Alchimiste, with Dumas *père* (produced 1839), 1839
Les Monténégrins, with E. Alboize (produced 1849), 1849
Le Chariot d'enfant, with Joseph Méry (produced 1850), 1850
L'Imagier de Harlem, with Joseph Méry and Bernard Lopez (produced 1851), 1852
Nicolas Flamel (English translation by Seumas O'Sullivan), 1924

Fiction

Scènes de la vie orientale: Les Femmes du Caire, 1824; *Les Femmes du Liban*, 1850
Les Faux Saulniers, 1850
Les Illuminés, 1852
Contes et facéties, 1853; *Sylvie* (in English), 1887; translated, including *Aurelia*, 1930; as *Dreams and Life*, 1933
Les Filles du feu, 1854; as *The Daughters of Fire*, 1922

Other

Etudes sur les poètes allemands (as Gérard), 1830
Nos adieux à la Chambre des Députés de l'an 1830 (as le Père Gérard), 1831
Voyage en orient, 1851; as *The Women of Cairo. Scenes of Life in the Orient*, 1929
Lorely: souvenirs d'Allemagne, 1852
Petits châteaux de Bohême: prose et poésie, 1853
La Correspondance de Gérard de Nerval (1830–1855), 1911

Editor, *Choix de poésies de Ronsard, du Bellay, Baïf, Belleau, du Bartas, Chassignet, Desportes, Régnier* (as Gérard), 1830
Editor, J. Cazotte, *Le Diable amoureux*, 1845

Translator, *Faust* (as Gérard), by Goethe, 1828
Translator, *Poésies allemandes* (as Gérard), 1830
Translator, *La Damnation de Faust:* légende, 1846

Bibliography

Senelier, Jean, *Nerval: essai de bibliographie*, 1959; supplement, 1968, 1982
Villas, James, *Nerval: A Critical Bibliography 1900–1967*, 1968

Critical studies

Cellier, Léon, *Nerval: l'homme et l'oeuvre*, 1956
Dubreck, Alfred, *Nerval and the German Heritage*, 1965

Rinsler, Norma, *Nerval* (in English), 1973
Sowerby, Benn, *The Disinherited: The Life of Nerval*, 1973
Beauchamp, William, *The Style of Nerval's Aurelia*, 1976

NIZAN, Paul, 1905–1940.

Novelist, essayist, and journalist.

LIFE

Paul Nizan was born in Tours, the son of a railway engineer. He attended the lycée in Périgueux, and in 1916 moved to the Lycée Henri IV in Paris as a dayboy. It was there that he met Jean-Paul Sartre, whose remarkable 1960 preface to the re-edition of Nizan's *Aden-Arabie* was to relaunch Nizan as a major literary figure. Sartre and Nizan's close friendship dated from their time together at Henri IV, and continued at Louis-le-Grand from 1922 and the Ecole Normale Supérieure from 1924. In 1929 Nizan passed his agrégation in philosophy at the Ecole. Sartre, who shared a room with him there, remembers that Nizan never shouted, but could go white with rage. He stammered and had a squint, but his behaviour carried with it a touch of superiority and Sartre looked up to him as his intellectual superior. He carried off prizes with apparent ease, spoke ironically about his parents, used a cane, wore a monocle, and was generally fashion-conscious. Occasionally he would disappear for a few days and be found drunk.

Nizan read very widely, worked hard, but was recurrently depressed. He spent the period from October 1926 to May 1927 in Aden as tutor to a leading commercial figure, Antonin Besse, who was later to endow the new St Anthony's College at Oxford. Nizan sailed from Greenock, and while in Aden must have written most of *Aden-Arabie*, which clearly mingles homesickness with a repudiation of his own background and upbringing. On returning home, he joined the communist party and mixed with a number of self-consciously left-wing groups, some much more rigorous and committed than others, and some allied with the surrealists (q.v.). He also fulfilled his intention of marrying Henriette Alphen, and Sartre and Raymond Aron were his witnesses. His children were born in 1928 and 1930. After graduation in 1929, Nizan became editorial secretary of the luxury avant-garde periodical *Bifur*, which was publishing Chirico, Giono, Joyce, Buster Keaton, Eisenstein, and Heidegger. It also published Sartre's "Légende de la vérité" and extracts from Nizan's second pamphlet, *Les Chiens de garde*. Although he tried hard to push *Bifur* politically to the left, Nizan failed, and later wrote for the communist review *Europe*. His wife's parents had provided them with a modern house, and they appeared to be much better off than they in fact were. They were both passionate film-goers and had a lively sense of fun.

From 1931 to 1932 Nizan taught philosophy at Bourg. Although he kept his political militancy out of the classroom, the municipality applied for his removal. In 1932 he stood for election as a communist, but was heavily defeated by the candi-date of the orthodox radical left. Three years later he was to write a series of articles on the educational system. In the meanwhile, he published both *Aden-Arabie* and his pamphlet attacking the current state of philosophy, *Les Chiens de garde*. His next book, *Antoine Bloyé*, an ideologically but not yet politically committed novel about a railway worker, was published in 1933. Nizan had returned to Paris in 1932, worked for the communist daily *L'Humanité*, and lectured on Soviet literature and the history of materialism at the "Workers' University." In addition to his activities as a popular journalist and as an informed commentator, Nizan was also to run courses at the party's headquarters, and he and his wife ran the communist bookshop in Paris. Among the opponents for whom he showed an element of respect was Julien Benda.

Nizan spent a year in the USSR with his family from 1934 to 1935, travelling as a Soviet guest, but also supported by royalties from Russian translations of his books while he worked mostly at the Marx-Lenin Institute. His Russian was adequate, and for Leninist purposes he adapted Aristophanes' *The Acharnians* for the Moscow Jewish theatre. He also visited Soviet Asia. On his return to France he immersed himself in cultural political activities of all sorts, attending meetings, working parties, and liaison groups, tirelessly writing and lecturing. His political novel, *Le Cheval de Troie*, originally entitled "Le jour de la colère" and partly written in the USSR, was published in 1935. Two large sections had been excised from it and published earlier as "Présentation d'une ville." It was Nizan who recommended that Gallimard should publish Sartre's *La Nausée*, although his review in *Ce Soir* for 15 May 1938 was harsh regarding Sartre's failure to achieve any serious grasp of ethical problems.

By 1937–38 Nizan had freed himself from much of the foot-slogging hack work he had undertaken for the party, and was writing for the more relaxed party evening paper *Ce Soir* rather than *L'Humanité*. In 1936 he had published a selection from the materialistic philosophers of antiquity, *Les Matérialistes de l'antiquité*, and in 1938 came his final novel, *La Conspiration*, which won the Prix Interallié. He had made several trips to Spain for *La Correspondance Internationale* before the Civil War and had projected another novel, "La soirée à Somosierra." Throughout 1938 he followed the party line. He visited Poland, Romania, Czechoslovakia, and Yugoslavia, criticized the appeasement, and published a book on the Munich crisis, *Chronique de septembre*, in 1939. That year he broke with the party over the Nazi–Soviet pact, although he still regarded himself as a communist. His resignation statement was brief and dry. He was called up, excused from combat duty because of his defective eyesight, and given the task of writing a record of military operations. In March 1940 Nizan got himself transferred to a British regiment as interpreter and liaison agent. While with that regiment in May 1940 he was shot in the head and killed by a stray bullet. The communist party, prompted by Aragon, were at some pains to discredit Nizan on account of his break with them.

WORKS

The two essays or pamphlets and the three novels were all republished in the 1960s, *Aden-Arabie* with the famous, if wrong-headed, introduction in which Sartre explained away Nizan's attitudes where they differed from his own at the time.

Sartre's interpretation of *La Conspiration* and of Nizan's final break with the party has been contested.

Aden-Arabie is chiefly interesting as the reaction of a brilliant left-wing French intellectual of Nizan's generation on coming into contact with the real world of slums, rich businessmen, and commercial projects. Indeed, had he been right- rather than left-wing, Nizan would no doubt have excelled in the business world. He is clearly steeling himself against ordinary human reactions in the interests of the abstract categories he feels he has to impose on experience. He is caustic about his employer, but was obviously quite attracted by the idea of working permanently in his organization. *Les Chiens de garde* is chiefly an attack on philosophical thinking which will not support Nizan's own social and political attitudes. He picks off some easy targets, like Léon Brunschvicg, but wrestles uncertainly with more difficult ones, like Benda. The book is more about ideologies than philosophies.

Antoine Bloyé is intended to be a novel about the alienation of a workman, with whose death it starts and ends. The funeral at the beginning, as observed by Antoine's son, Pierre, allows Nizan scope for sarcasm at the mimes of mourning and the class distinctions fixed in the cemetery by the size of the gravestones. The novel fleshes out Antoine's life as a railway worker, destined to live and die at the bottom of the social pyramid, and allows Nizan to comment on everything from primary education, through engineering school and life as an off-duty engine driver, shoddily mimicking the dissolute behaviour of the rich and parasitic, to forming what amounts to a personal relationship with the engine he works. Antoine marries, has children, grows older, is imprisoned by his lack of imagination, moves house, sees death coming, and finally dies. There are comparatively few events and little serious analysis of the nature of Antoine's experience, which is unvaried throughout his life, but the novel's point about the alienation of his existence is clear enough.

Le Cheval de Troie, set in the small, inbred "Villefranche," brings political struggle down to the level of street fighting and contains an incidental attack on the repressive social constraints exercised by the Church. Bloyé, the schoolteacher, acts as the link between the various groups he observes at their habitual self-deceptions. Lange, a colleague from the Ecole Normale Supérieure, still lives in the world of philosophical abstractions rather than social realities. A group of militants includes Paul, an unemployed political refugee, and Philippe, with whom Bloyé sets up a news sheet for the cable factory, where the workforce is not yet politically organized. It is printed by Albert and Catherine, who needs an abortion because they cannot afford the child with which she is pregnant. As the town becomes politicized, the bosses group together, which arouses the curiosity of the uncommitted Lange, a local commander, an ex-mayor, and an industrialist. There are fascist louts for whom politics is "un jeu violent comme un sport (a violent game, like a sport)," and a popular front forms. Death comes to Catherine like a form of asphyxiation. Lange, viewing the battle from the fascist side, is caught up in their rout. The riot police then reverse the situation, but make the mistake of carrying the fighting into the back streets. Paul dies. Bloyé and the young Marie-Louise go for a walk, conscious that death has to be risked to make life worth living. The character of Lange adds balance to the plot and allows Nizan to comment from an apparently disinterested viewpoint.

In *La Conspiration* Rosenthal, Laforgue, Bloyé, and Pluvinage are philosophy students who decide to found an organ of rebellion against official philosophy teaching. They call it *La Guerre Civile*. Nizan is dryly ironic; "Comme ils n'étaient pas pressés par la nécessité déprimante de gagner leur pain sur le champ, ils se disaient qu'il fallait changer le monde (Since they weren't hurried by the depressing need to earn their bread straightaway, they told themselves that the world had to be changed)." The debate is between the ideological, philosophical dispute and political engagement, advocated by Laforgue. Rosenthal gets Simon, an old school friend undergoing national service, to steal some army contingency plans. He is caught, but gets out of trouble by saying he was looking for material for a science fiction novel. His superiors refuse to believe that he could be a rebel because he is the son of a wealthy business family. Laforgue criticizes Rosenthal for his intellectual approach to subversion by cloak and dagger. Rosenthal seduces his brother's wife Catherine so that the civil war of the periodical's title breaks out within the Rosenthal family. The family finds out, but the matter is passed over quietly. Rosenthal, however, is determined to make himself into a tragic figure. He gets drunk, and kills himself with poison. Pluvinage never really belonged to the group, is eventually excluded from it, and betrays it. Laforgue falls ill, but survives, transformed into an adult capable of leading a properly responsible life.

The novels pretend to investigate life, but the situations are designed to yield ideologically acceptable conclusions. The books are well written and Nizan's ingenuity is considerable, as was the influence of his work on the student generation of the 1960s when it was relaunched with the strong boost of Sartre's introduction to *Aden-Arabie*.

PUBLICATIONS

Fiction

Antoine Bloyé, 1933
Le Cheval de Troie, 1935; as *Trojan Horse*, 1937
La Conspiration, 1938

Other

Aden-Arabie, 1931; as *Aden-Arabie* (in English), 1968
Les Chiens de garde, 1932
Chronique de septembre, 1939
Pour une nouvelle culture, 1971

Critical and biographical studies

Leiner, Jacqueline, *Le Destin littéraire de Paul Nizan*, 1970
Redfern, W.D., *Paul Nizan: Committed Literature in a Conspiratorial World*, 1972

NODIER, Charles, 1780–1844.

Novelist and essayist.

LIFE

Most of what is known about Charles Nodier's early upbringing comes from his own unreliable *Souvenirs*, but among the
few certain facts are his date of birth (29 April 1780), the professional advancement of his lawyer father, who presided over
the Besançon criminal court and became mayor of the town,
and Nodier's very early interest in natural history. The family
had clearly swum with the tide, and at the age of 11, on 22
December 1791, Nodier was already giving a patriotic speech
to the Besançon Société des Amis de la Constitution. He was
later to become a committed monarchist. Within two years he
was being trained in natural history, mostly botany and entomology, by an old friend of the family, M. Girod de Chantrans.
He also spent a few weeks in Strasbourg, staying with the
public prosecutor, Euloge Schneider, who was later guillotined.

In 1796, as a schoolboy at the Ecole Centrale of the region,
Nodier was associated with a secret society of adolescent
friends, who called themselves the "Philadelphians" and had
vaguely subversive literary and political ambitions. His reading
during adolescence included Shakespeare, *The Imitation of
Christ*, and Bonneville's *Théâtre allemand*. His closest friend,
Charles Weiss, later wrote to Mérimée, who was looking for
information about Nodier for his "Discours de réception" at the
Académie Française, that he was particularly obsessed by Goethe's *Die Leiden des jungen Werthers*. Nodier is said to have
stabbed himself at the age of 16. He was certainly violently emotional, suffered easily from Weltschmerz, and took his emotional entanglements very seriously. He wrote to a friend in
1797: "J'ai senti que le bonheur n'était pas fait pour moi (I felt
that happiness was not made for me)," and three years later
claimed to have exhausted the dregs of unhappiness.

By 1798 Nodier had published his first entomological paper,
on the use of antennae in insects. On 31 October, at the age of
18, he was appointed assistant librarian at the Ecole. The following year, already a monarchist, he took part in a play satirizing
the Besançon Revolutionary club known as the Société Populaire, and was suspended from his librarianship. Charles Weiss
was arrested. Nodier was reinstated in the spring of 1801, having
spent three or four of the winter months in Paris, where he also
spent the academic year 1801–02 looking for an opportunity to
establish a career.

In 1802 he published his first novel, the strongly emotional
Stella; ou, Les Proscrits, first sketched in 1797, but he repudiated it as "détestable" immediately after publication. That same
year he also wrote an anonymous anti-Napoleonic ode, *La
Napoléone*. In Paris he had fallen in with "Les Méditateurs,"
who fostered a partly biblical and partly hermetic cult, sat round
carpets and smoked oriental tobacco, and ate oranges and dried
figs. They wore their hair long and dressed in white tunics.
Nodier brought all his youthful zeal to the admiration of their
leader, Maurice Quaï, in whom he found united the genius of
"Ossian, Job, and Homer." Among his fellow initiates were two
young painters, Joseph Franque and his wife Lucile. Nodier
seems to have been in love with Lucile, but in 1808 he was to
marry her half-sister, Désirée-Liberté Charve, the daughter of a

judge who was a friend of his father.

Both Lucile and Maurice Quaï died in 1803, and Nodier was
sufficiently upset to write voluntarily to Napoleon admitting his
authorship of the ode, which he had circulated as a pamphlet. He
was sent to prison for 36 days on 23 December 1803. On his
return to Besançon in 1804 he published an affective tribute to
his two dead friends in his *Essais d'un jeune barde*. Lucile was
also to become the inspiration for the Amélie of *Souvenirs de
jeunesse*, as well as for several of Nodier's heroines. These
included Eulalie sitting on a tomb in "Le peintre de Saltzbourg:
journal des émotions d'un coeur souffrant," inspired in 1803 by
Werther, the Lucile of "Les jardins d'Oberheim," and the
Eléonore of "Le tombeau des grèves du lac" from the 1806 *Les
Tristes; ou, Mélanges tirés des tablettes d'un suicide.*

Nodier was not to write any more contes for 15 years, but he
did not give up his political sympathies, and in 1805 fled for a
period to wander in the countryside. For some time he had been
protected by the region's prefect, with whose support he started
a course in philosophy, literature, and natural history at Dôle on
4 July 1808. On 31 August he married Lucile's half-sister and
on 10 October his father died. It was in the following year, 1809,
that Nodier became research assistant to the learned British
eccentric Sir Herbert Croft and Lady Mary Hamilton at Amiens.
After apparently fulfilling a two-year contract, Nodier and his
wife lived in a house at Quintigny belonging to her family. Their
daughter Marie was born there on 26 April 1811. Thanks to his
future brother-in-law, on 6 January 1813 Nodier became librarian at Laibach in Illyria, then under French occupation. He also
became editor of the tetraglot *Télégraphe Illyrien* and secretary
to Joseph Fouché, the notorious police chief and minister of the
interior, temporarily out of office since 1810. These posts lasted
only until September when, after a return to Quintigny, Nodier
and his family moved to Paris.

Still in 1813 Nodier began to work for the *Journal de l'Empire*, soon to become the *Journal des Débats*. On the Bourbon
restoration, he was decorated with the Ordre du Lys, and he had
to take refuge during the hundred days in 1815. During this time
he published his *Histoire des sociétés secrètes de l'armée* anonymously. A son, born in 1814, was to die in 1816, and a second
son was to be born and die in 1821. Nodier tried to go to Odessa
in 1818, but nothing came of the project and he returned to Quintigny. That year he published his novel *Jean Sbogar* and in 1819,
when he went back to Paris, *Thérèse Aubert*, on which Sainte-
Beuve nourished his youthful melancholy. This was followed in
1820 by *Adèle*, and a staging of the melodrama *Le Vampire*,
which Nodier co-authored. He also began a collaboration on the
Voyages pittoresques et romantiques dans l'ancienne France.
The following year he went to Scotland, published *Promenade
de Dieppe aux montagnes d'Ecosse* (see Ossian) and *Smarra;
ou, Les Démons de la nuit*, and staged his melodrama *Bertram*.
Probably his best-known conte, *Trilby; ou, Le Lutin d'Argail*,
was published in 1822.

Nodier was a prolific writer, and is best known for his
contes. His literary importance, however, derives largely from
his role in foreshadowing and then encouraging the young
school of romantic (q.v.) writers. This arose partly through his
co-founding of *La Muse Française* (1823–24) with Hugo and
Deschamps, and partly through the role he played in assembling the first romantic "cénacle," a group loosely formed
during his elegant receptions at the Bibliothèque de l'Arsenal.
This library, called after the old munitions factory whose site

it occupied, had been confiscated by the state during the Revolution, opened to the public in 1797, and subsequently restored to its original owner, the Comte d'Artois, later to become Charles X. He made Nodier his librarian on 3 January 1824. That year and in 1825 Nodier went to Savoy and Switzerland, the second time accompanied by Victor Hugo, with whom he visited Lamartine.

Nodier's *Poésies* appeared in 1827, and in 1829 he started a long association with the newly founded *Revue de Paris*. He was much affected by his daughter's marriage in 1830, which plunged his emotional life into a real crisis. The early, cultivated melancholy of adolescence and young manhood had given way to a fascination with the grotesque around 1820. When Nodier was 50 he began to turn away from the positivism of the restoration and seek refuge in cultivated dreams of madness. His contes can be split chronologically into half a dozen different cycles without doing too much violence to his imaginative development, and the history of his imagination presents certain similarities with that of Nerval. Nodier also produced works of criticism, lexicography, and entomology, however, many of them obviously the product of a cultivated dilettante mind. Some, like the account of the Scottish journey and the essay *Du fantastique en littérature* of 1830, are of particular importance, chiefly by virtue of their subject and date.

Much of his work is whimsical, but his semi-scientific study of sleep, "De quelques phénomènes du sommeil," is important for the view that dreams do not merely surge up from an unconscious void, but constitute a plane of awareness that is not entirely unconscious at all. The contes may rely on the standard stage properties of medieval gothic, the fantastic, and the grotesque, but Nodier's exploration of the worlds of madness and sleep opened up new literary paths, most of which the romantics themselves chose not to follow. His development confirms the view that "romanticism" is a term better kept for the literary movement which started in the theatre in the wake of the Drury Lane Shakespeare season in Paris from 1827 to 1828. Romanticism almost marks a discontinuity in Nodier's preoccupation with the irrational world and the manifestations of a cultivated, religious melancholy to be found in Mme de Staël, Constant, Chateaubriand, Lamartine, Senancour, Deschamps, and other authors prior to 1828, whether deist or Catholic, and irrespective of the often vaguely liberal political views to which they sometimes subscribed.

Nodier's handsome rooms in the library allowed him to play host to the inevitably self-selected group consisting of virtually all the adventurous young literary personalities active around 1830. They sought one another out and were presented to Nodier, who was usually to be found playing cards, or telling stories, or narrating often fabricated history. His daughter Marie was a centre of attraction, as was Delphine Gay. There were dances in the drawing room, often in fancy dress, and on Saturdays the ornate salon was filled, the principal amusements being dancing and cards. Here Lamartine recited "Le lac," and Hugo wrote "Le cor" in Marie's album. Sainte-Beuve was often present, as were Hugo and all his associates—Musset, Balzac, Liszt, Janin, Planche. Among the painters and sculptors who attended were the Dévéria brothers, Boulanger, the Johannot brothers, Delacroix, and David d'Angers. It was the first romantic "cénacle," and the intensity of its existence in the librarian's quarters at the Arsenal did not diminish until after 1830, when Nodier's literary production correspondingly increased.

Nodier was, however, living beyond his means. Apart from his literary revenue, which must have been considerable, he was receiving 4,000 francs a year as librarian and a literary pension of 2,400 francs. None the less, he borrowed heavily and in 1827 had to sell part of his library. He is reticent about how he came to lose 9,000 francs in 1829 in "business affairs." In 1830 his literary pension was reduced to 1,500 francs and he had to sell a lot more books to help Marie during the first years of her marriage. Efforts to increase his literary income were successful, but his health began to fail from about 1830. That year an accident to his leg kept him in bed for three months. He wrote to Weiss that he was now bored by what amused other people. In his work he began to look for escape into a world of fantasy. In 1832 he escaped the cholera by going to Metz to stay with Marie's parents-in-law. His literary production continued in spate, and the 13 volumes of the original *Oeuvres complètes* began to appear. In 1833 Nodier was elected to the Académie Française and he continued to produce increasingly whimsical fiction until about 1840. He died on 27 January 1844.

WORKS

The first cycle of contes, *Les Tristes; ou, Mélanges tirés des tablettes d'un suicide*, contains the piece heavy with cultivated sadness whose subtitle announces its derivation, "La filleule du seigneur; ou, la nouvelle werthérie." In the second conte, "Une heure ou la vision," the narrator meets the central character, who already wonders whether madness may not be an elevated rather than a degrading state, "le symptôme d'une sensibilité plus énergique, d'une organisation plus complète (the symptom of a more energized sensibility, of a tighter organization)," an idea taken further in *Stella*.

Nodier's second inspiration comes from the macabre "The vampire," attributed to Byron in the *New Monthly Magazine*, translated by Faber in 1819, and reviewed by Nodier in the *Journal des Débats* for 1 July 1819. It is in that review that Nodier uses the word "smarra" for the first time, explaining it as the Dalmatian for nightmare. He then went on to write *Smarra; ou, Les Démons de la nuit*, whose inspiration carries on from that of the novel *Jean Sbogar* of 1818, which had also been Byronic. *Smarra* concerns a brigand, rebelling for the most noble reasons against the tyranny of society, the eternal "corsair" figure so often borrowed in France from Byron, who in *Sbogar* assumes the name Lothario and wins the love of the ethereal Antonia. His love, like the vampire's, brings with it death, and he is himself finally captured and shot by the French. Apart from one or two clearly authentic descriptions, the novel is simply an assemblage of conventional trappings in plot, characters, and décor, a stage in the development of the full-blooded romantic hero. *Sbogar* refers to ghosts, giants, reptiles, and monsters. Other youthful writings refer to flesh hanging off bones, discoloration, triple rows of fangs, and strange limbs.

It seems certain that Nodier's obsession with the macabre in *Sbogar* and *Smarra* at this date still goes back to his youthful reminiscences of the destruction of statues and the memory of the guillotine in Besançon and Strasbourg. In *Smarra* he writes: "ma tête était tombée…elle avait roulé, rebondi sur le hideux parvis de l'échafaud… Un homme venait de mourir devant le peuple (my head had fallen…it had rolled, rebounded on to the hideous square in front of the scaffold… A man had just died in front of the people)." There is another public execution in "La fée aux miettes," and there are similar incidents betraying the same obsessions elsewhere. The blood-sucking demon Smarra is almost realistically described, but Nodier is still far too restrained to allow the frightening visions of his imagination their liberty. *Smarra* is recounted as a dream inspired by the opening chapter of Apuleius' *The Golden Ass*, and the frightening potential power of the conte is defused. In the 1832 preface Nodier downgrades his own terror. His conte is "worth at most a composition prize at school."

The third inspiration, Scottish, produced only one full conte, *Trilby; ou, Le Lutin d'Argail*, said by Nodier to be derived from Scott. It concerns the two lovers Jeannie and Trilby, who are separated and become tragic symbols. Nodier's skill lies in endowing a bad dream with mythological significance. His style is now less grandiloquent and periphrastic than in his youth, and it is clear that he has felt his way into the mechanics of the conte as a literary form, but the interest of *Trilby* remains largely confined to its use of dream, its creation of myth, and its place in the history of the development of the conte.

Trilby was first published in 1822. Money worries, the librarianship, and the receptions took their toll of Nodier's time, and his literary production slackened. When it resumed in 1830, he had passed the crises of Marie's marriage, his own financial difficulties, and a bout of bad health which was quite distinct from the accident to his leg, but his imagination took refuge in a whimsy which is reflected in most of the later contes. "La fée aux miettes" contains a protest against the treatment of the insane in a Glasgow sanatorium which Nodier had read about in the *Revue de Paris*, dated May 1829. The style of the story makes it clear that he must have read Hoffmann; it also borrows from Balzac and Hugo. However, unlike many other of the contes, it does have a happy ending. Michel le Charpentier finds, if not actual happiness, at least stability. The world without logic or rationality, the world of dreams, of unreason, of the mad, takes the place of the grotesque, the macabre, and the terrors of the earlier contes as, following Marie's marriage, Nodier himself becomes prematurely aged.

He is an important figure, not only because of the "cénacle" and his role in the development of the conte, but also because of his reined-in exploration of the hidden regions where the mind keeps the terrors, fantasies, and dreams which it needs to control.

PUBLICATIONS

Collections

Oeuvres complètes, 13 vols., 1832–37
Oeuvres, 7 vols., 1850ff.
Contes, edited by Castex, 1961

Fiction

Many of the contes were published first in reviews, and then only in one of the collected editions.
Stella; ou, Les Proscrits, 1802
Le Peintre de Saltzbourg: journal des émotions d'un coeur souffrant, 1803
Les Tristes; ou, Mélanges tirés des tablettes d'un suicide, 1806

Jean Sbogar, 1818
Thérèse Aubert, 1819
Smarra; ou, Les Démons de la nuit, 1821
Infernaliana, 1822
Trilby; ou, Le Lutin d'Argail: nouvelle écossaise, 1822; as *Trilby*, 1895
Histoire du roi de Bohème et de ses sept châteaux, 1830
Paris; ou, Le Livre des cent-et-un, 1831
Mademoiselle de Marsan, 1832
Les Cent-et-une nouvelles des cent-et-un, 1832

Other

La Napoléone, 1802
Essais d'un jeune barde, 1804
Questions de littérature légale, 1812
Histoire des sociétés secrètes de L'armée, 1815
Mélanges de littérature et de critique, 1820
Le Vampire (melodrama), 1820
Voyages pittoresques et romantiques dans l'ancienne France, with others 1820
Bertram (melodrama), 1821
Promenade de Dieppe aux montagnes d'Ecosse, 1822; as *Promenade from Dieppe to the Mountains of Scotland*, 1822
Poésies, 1827
Souvenirs de jeunesse, 1832
Rêveries, 1832

NOUVELLE REVUE FRANÇAISE, (LA)

See index for writers whose work was published by the review.

The guiding spirit of the *Nouvelle Revue Française* (*NRF*) was always André Gide (born on 22 November 1869), as from its inception in 1909 the review's critics said it would be. In 1902 Gide had been hurt by the unenthusiastic reception accorded to his *L'Immoraliste*, which he had hoped would become his first literary success. He had contributed to the symbolist (q.v.) review *L'Ermitage*, (1890–95 and 1896–1906), with a circulation of between 200 and 400, and had published sporadically in the Natanson brothers' *Revue Blanche* (1891–1903), which had a much larger circulation, printing 2,500 copies from the outset, and from 1896 was edited by Félix Fénéon. For six months before he lost interest, Gide succeeded Léon Blum as the *Revue Blanche's* literary editor. Along with the entire avant-garde, however, Gide was turning against symbolism. He was already looking for a public and for a forum which could only turn out to be a review of his own.

Gide had introduced his brother-in-law, Marcel Drouin, to both *L'Ermitage* and the *Revue Blanche*, and had got to know his Belgian admirer André Ruyters, and Henri Vangeon, now universally known as Ghéon, so that by 1897 the founding group of the *NRF* already existed. Relations with Ghéon were to be complicated on account of a young male tennis partner whom

Gide passed on to Ghéon in 1904, after Gide's wife had already written to Ghéon about the need to keep Gide from getting overexcited. Later on, after his conversion to Catholicism, Ghéon was to write Gide an explicit exhortation about their common misbehaviour which, much to her distress, Gide's wife opened by mistake. The small group of four were very closely linked. Jean Schlumberger and Jacques Copeau were still to be recruited, but they would form an outer circle, with whom Gide did not use the intimate "tu" pronoun until World War I.

The group had practically colonized the Belgian monthly periodical *Antée* (January 1905–January 1908) when at the beginning of 1908, Gide had a disaster with *Le Roi Candaule* in German translation in Berlin. There was only one performance. The whole group attended a dinner given by Jean Royère at the symbolist *La Phalange*, incidentally also attended by Apollinaire, on 25 January. During part of February and March, while Gide was away, *Antée* and *La Phalange* were proposing a merger, and the five who now regarded themselves as Gide's team started making serious plans for a new review. The *NRF*, its title fitting in with a whole pattern of other recently founded reviews like the new daily version of *L'Action Française* and *La Patrie Française*, invited caricature as an unwieldy coalition of the rich and the literate. It aspired in its pre-publication announcement to fill the role once held by the *Mercure de France* and the *Revue Blanche*. It was to be the review of the generation "qui a suivi immédiatement le symbolisme (immediately following symbolism)." The first number would appear on 1 November, all copy to be in by 15 October. It was 15 days late, and Gide objected to two of the articles, and to the way his own "notes" had been treated. He wanted the review to reflect a corporate view, others wanted free debate and were willing to risk giving offence. It took only a few days for the editorial committee to break up with plentiful recriminations over that central issue.

Gide, Schlumberger, and Copeau met on Sunday 7 December 1908. On 16 December they announced a second number of the *NRF* for February 1909. It was to become known as the first issue, giving one no. 1 in November 1908, then a series nos. 1–68 from 1 February 1909 to 1 August 1914. A new series was then to be started with no. 69 on 1 June 1919. A distributor was found, and the important decision taken to fix the price so that the review could be big enough to accommodate the long texts that later helped to make its name. Both *L'Ermitage* and *Antée* had suffered from a paucity of texts of sufficient quality that were also short enough. Gide was not easy to work with. He was extremely fussy, particularly about printing and the meticulous correction of proofs, and often late with copy. However, the *NRF*'s first three numbers in February, March, and April 1909 carried the three parts of his *La Porte étroite*. The first number also contained "Considérations" by Schlumberger, which tried to gloss over the earlier break, while making the intention not to adopt the viewpoint of a coterie sound plausibly compatible with having the "forte unité d'un groupe (strong unity of a group)." The impression is given that whatever the review printed was going to be properly done, and the texts it announced its intention to print were indeed impressive, with a stiffening of material on Nietzsche and Goethe.

The review has been described as ostentatiously impartial. Its team of writers leant slightly left of centre, were pro-Dreyfus but loudly patriotic, and preferred to keep politics out of literature. There is a clear and cleverly drawn distinction between acceptable works born of Catholic conviction and those of conventionally pious sentiment, and the first numbers conscientiously tried to insulate aesthetic from moral values. The note of liberal, civilized comment on all cultural phenomena, especially literary ones, is struck from the beginning. The *NRF* has been criticized for not noticing a great deal of what was going on, particularly in painting, but outside literature the review was not especially interested in encouraging the young, and certainly not the rebellious. It took no formal notice of the anti-symbolist reaction in both painting and poetry that was taking place in Montmartre, and very little of the Ballets Russes, and it was left to *Le Figaro* to publish the futurist manifesto.

Like most successful reviews, the *NRF* wanted to publish its own offprints and its material in volume form. The review was a success. The issues had reached 185 pages and it needed to start its own publishing house. A search was started for someone who was rich, enlightened, competent, and docile, known to the group and trusted by them. There was only one suitable candidate, the son of the owner of the Théâtre des Variétés. His name was Gaston Gallimard. Only his provenance, from the Variétés by way of *Le Figaro*, raised doubts. They were overcome, and the *NRF* publishing venture, with the famous *NRF* imprint, became the Editions Gallimard, started in 1911 as a sort of workers' cooperative, but which would eventually swallow its parent when the *NRF* committee found that they could not run their own publishing business and sold out to their publishing manager. Gaston's nephew, Michel, was killed in a car crash with Camus in 1960 and his son, Claude, took over as managing director. The business was valued at 1.8 billion francs for a well-publicized court case in 1990. Claude Gallimard bought the *Mercure de France* publishing house for his wife, Simone, from whom he was later divorced, and handed over the Editions Gallimard not to his first but to his second son, Antoine, in 1988.

The *NRF* had already sponsored the "décades" or 10-day workshops, the "Entretiens d'été," at the home of Paul Desjardins at Pontigny, and was to help establish Copeau in his spectacular theatrical career from 1913 at the Vieux-Colombier, where he took on, and trained, two of the great Parisian producer-actors of the inter-war period, Louis Jouvet and Charles Dullin. After World War I, with Gide still very much the guiding presence, the review was restarted under Jacques Rivière. Its writers now included Louis Aragon and André Breton as well as Marcel Jouhandeau, François Mauriac, Paul Morand, and finally, but briefly, Proust, once turned down by Gide. From 1935 the director was Jean Paulhan. The review had continued to attract, and to find, much of the best literary talent available, but had become more openly political in the 1930s. Its supremacy was partly based on the excellence of its cultural chronicles. In June 1940 it ceased publication, but was then started up again under Drieu la Rochelle in December 1940, continuing as a "collaborationist" journal until June 1943. Fewer of the top authors were now willing to contribute.

After World War II the review was authorized to appear only from 1953 as the *Nouvelle NRF*, under the joint editorship of Jean Paulhan and Marcel Arland. In 1987 Jacques Réda was appointed director.

O

OSSIAN (Oisin)

Legendary third-century Gaelic warrior and bard.

James Macpherson (1736–1796) attributed to this legendary warrior the originals of a series of "poetic translations" in rhythmic prose which he said he had made, and which he published as *Fragments of Ancient Poetry Collected in the Highlands of Scotland, and Translated from the Gaelic or Erse Language* (1760), *Fingal*, produced in six books with the assistance of "several gentlemen in the Highlands" (1762), and *Temora*, in eight books (1763). Their authenticity was impugned by Dr Johnson, but was widely accepted.

According to legend Oisin was the son of Finn or Fionn (from whom "Fingal" derives), the principal hero of the southern or later cycle of Irish legends, who may have been a historical personage. Whether real or mythical, Finn Mac Coul was the son of Cumal or Comhal and a contemporary of King Cormac, who chose him, on account not of his physical strength but of his qualities of wisdom and generosity, to lead the Fenians or "Fianna," who mutinously killed him in 283 AD. Macpherson calls him Fingal, makes him a Scot, and regards him as contemporaneous with Cuthullin, Macpherson's form of Cuchulain, the miraculously born first-century hero of the Ulster cycle of Irish mythology. In *Fingal* and *Temora*, Fingal goes to Ireland and helps Cuthullin against Scandinavian invaders, and in the Ossianic poems he generally figures as a righter of wrongs and defender of the oppressed. Walter Scott describes his celebrated cave in the fourth canto of "The Lord of the Isles."

Macpherson was the lettered son of a farmer from Kingussie and was educated at the universities of Aberdeen and Edinburgh. When called on to produce the originals from which he claimed to have translated Ossian, he was forced to fabricate them. After his death a committee discovered that he had in fact liberally edited traditional Gaelic poems and inserted passages of his own. He went on to write a history of Great Britain from the Restoration to the Accession of George I and became MP for Camelford from 1780 until 1786. He was buried in Westminster Abbey.

The three Ossianic works were enormously important in European literature. In *De la littérature considérée dans ses rapports avec les institutions sociales* of 1800 Mme de Staël held that the whole of northern literature derived from them, as southern literature did from Homer. They were translated into German hexameters by J.N.C.M. Denis in 1768–69 and the translation was revised after the appearance of Macpherson's own revised edition. Herder wrote an enthusiastic essay on the poems, which he included in the 1773 *Von deutscher Art und Kunst*, and Goethe translated passages into German for incorporation into *Die Leiden des jungen Werthers* of 1774. German translations continued to appear until 1847, with one as late as 1924.

The first French translation of any of the Ossianic poems appeared in London in 1762 as *Carthon*, anonymously translated by the Duchesse d'Aiguillon. The fragments appeared in the *Journal Etranger* for September 1769. Letourneur translated the poems into French in 1777, and they were translated into verse by Louis Fontanes and translated again in 1810 by Pierre Baour-Lormian, one of the early contributors to *La Muse Française* (see Deschamps), with a preface by Pierre-Louis Ginguené. Both because they were foreign and because of their wild spirit, they were much admired and imitated by the pre-romantic (q.v.) generation in France. They much impressed the Chateaubriand of the *Essai sur les révolutions*, and fragments or imitations of Ossian appeared virtually every year from 1780 to 1825 in the annual *L'Almanach des Muses*, the most important of the literary forums. The most enthusiastic reception of Ossian in France however, was Nodier's in the 1821 *Promenades de Dieppe aux montagnes d'Ecosse*. His journey had convinced him of the authenticity of Macpherson's originals, even if the Scot had "enriched" the translations.

One or two students of popular culture, like Augustin Thierry and the journalist François-Adolphe Loève-Veimars, who wrote for the *Revue de Paris*, the *Revue des Deux Mondes* (q.v.), and then *La Presse* and published the *Ballades et légendes d'Angleterre et d'Ecosse* in 1825, took a more serious interest in Ossian. Otherwise, Ossian's role in French literature, together with that of Byron, Shakespeare, and Scott, was to provide a vast and powerful inspiration with which to nourish the newly emerging sensibility of the pre-romantic generation.

P

PAGNOL, Marcel, 1895–1974.

Dramatist, essayist, and film producer.

LIFE

It is arguable both that Marcel Pagnol's most important work was for the cinema, and that, no doubt partly on account of his business activities in cinema, publishing, and photography, his general importance in the history of cultural life in France has consistently been underestimated. Two of the most prominent film makers associated with "neorealist" cinema immediately after World War II, Vittorio de Sica and Roberto Rossellini, regarded that movement as having been inaugurated by Pagnol, notably in *Angèle*, the 1934 film he made from Giono's novel *Un de Baumugnes*.

Pagnol was born at Aubagne, just east of Marseilles, on 28 February 1895. His father, Joseph, was a teacher and his mother, Augustine Lansot (1873–1910), a dressmaker. They had married in 1889. Pagnol was the eldest of four children: Paul (born in 1898), Germaine (born in 1902), and René, (born in 1909). His mother died in 1910, when René was still an infant. From 1903 family holidays were spent in the nearby hills above La Treille, a countryside to which Pagnol's imagination kept returning in later life. In 1904 his father was moved to Marseilles, where Pagnol completed his secondary education at the Lycée Thiers before taking his degree in English at Montpellier. As early as 1913 he and some friends founded a literary review, *Fortunio*. Publication was interrupted by World War I, but the review was re-established at the end of the war by Jean Ballard, one of the early pre-war team, and in 1925 became the famous *Cahiers du Sud*.

From 1915 until 1922 Pagnol had a variety of teaching posts at Tarascon, Pamiers, Aix, and finally Marseilles. In 1923 he was posted to the Lycée Condorcet in Paris. He had translated Virgil's *Bucolics* and Shakespeare's *Hamlet*, and written his first novel, *Pirouettes*, although it was not published until 1932. On his arrival in Paris, with nothing yet published, he began to write for the theatre, starting with a piece written in collaboration with Paul Nivoix, *Les Marchands de gloire*. This satirical comedy of no more than ordinary interest was staged in 1926 and published the following year. It was followed by a second rather lightweight satirical play, *Jazz*, successfully staged in Monte Carlo and at the Théâtre des Arts in Paris, and published in 1927.

It was at this point that Pagnol's spectacular talent burst out. *Topaze* began its still legendary Paris run at the Variétés in 1928, and within a matter of weeks Pagnol's reputation was made. That success enabled him to get the backing he needed for *Marius*, which was remarkable for a quite new theatrical realism, and whose even greater success began in 1929. Its successor, *Fanny*, was staged in 1931. *Marius* inaugurated the partnership between Pagnol and his friend and favourite actor, Jules Muraire (1883–1946). "Raimu," as he was known, also came from Marseilles and was one of France's most popular actors in the 1930s. Although he appeared in only two stage roles, he played in 34 films and, after starring in the stage version of *Marius*, he appeared in the film version, followed by *Fanny* and *César*, both written by Pagnol specifically for the screen. He then gave perhaps his best cinema performance in *La Femme du boulanger*, a Pagnol film adapted from *Jean le bleu* by Giono, an old Provençal friend. *Topaze* and *Marius* were published in 1931, *Fanny* in 1932.

The big stage successes were filmed with the help of professional producers: Alexander Korda for *Marius* and Marc Allégret for *Fanny*. Korda was engaged by Paramount to make the film at their Joinville studios, but Pagnol retained considerable control, as he did during the filming of *Fanny* by Allégret. Pierre Fresnay and Fernand Charpin played alongside Raimu in both films, and the success enabled Pagnol to build his own studios, where he made *César* in 1936. The text of *César* was published in 1937, prefaced by a statement from Pagnol about his views on cinema. The play was performed in Paris only in 1945. As films, *Marius*, *Fanny*, and *César* are known as Pagnol's "Marseilles trilogy." Several foreign versions were made, and in 1960 the rights for a remake of the whole trilogy were sold to Joshua Logan. Louis Gasnier filmed *Topaze* in 1933, and Pagnol himself refilmed it in 1951.

The introduction of sound into cinema with the inauguration of the "talkies" is normally dated to 1929, which is about the time when Pagnol was adapting his stage successes for cinema. In fact, he was much criticized for making "théâtre filmé (canned theatre)," in other words for merely photographing stage performances. Controversy was sharp, and Pagnol's defenders have conceded that his first two films may be open to that criticism. However he has been strongly defended for his later film-making career. What drew Pagnol inexorably to the cinema, apart from the new commercial viability of cinema with synchronized sound, was that his work was perfectly suited to the new medium. While his gift for dramatic dialogue was wonderfully suited to the stage, his narrative gift required a medium which permitted flashbacks, foreshortening of timescales, and a general independence in the utilization of time and space, not bounded by the duration of theatrical time or the need to change sets. In Pagnol both gifts needed if possible to be combined in a single outlet, and the "talkies" came along to provide it.

Between 1931 and 1954 Pagnol is said to have made 21 films. He very soon set up his own film studios, and then ran other more or less related commercial activities, including publishing, alongside them. He also made his own films, not only from his own original material, but often from Giono and, memorably, from Daudet, another fellow Provençal, with the 1954 *Lettres de mon moulin*.

Pagnol avoided political comment in his writings and films. During the German occupation of France in World War II he made only one film, *La Fille du puisatier* of 1940. After the war a background broadcast by de Gaulle was discreetly substituted for one by Pétain. In 1945 Pagnol married Jacqueline Bouvier, who played in his *Manon des sources*. The following year he was elected to the Académie Française. He returned to stage work with *Judas* at the Théâtre de Paris in 1955 and *Fabien* at the Bouffes-Parisiens in 1956, although neither play was a notable success. Then, in 1957, came the immensely successful first volume of the *Souvenirs d'enfance*, entitled *La Gloire de mon père*. Two more volumes, *Le Château de ma mère* and *Le Temps des secrets*, were published during Pagnol's lifetime. *Le Temps des amours*, containing memories of adolescence, appeared posthumously in 1977. Very successful films have more recently been made based on some of Pagnol's autobiographical writings. His own films have also inspired subsequent reworkings. Pagnol died in Paris on 18 April 1974 and was buried at La Treille.

WORKS

Pagnol's oeuvre poses in an unusually acute form a literary problem to which attention must from time to time be drawn. A dramatic text is not a play until it is staged, and a film script is not a fully realized work of the imagination until the film has been made. There are analogies in all the performing arts, but it is impossible to assess or even describe Pagnol's literary production in isolation from its actual realization and from the associated activity of film direction. There are two reasons for this: firstly, he wrote virtually nothing, apart from his memoirs, except as a script for performance and, secondly, part of his creative talent was channelled into directing as well as scripting films.

Topaze concerns a 30-year-old teacher at a small and rather seedy private school who is imposed on by everybody. His unshakeable honesty allows him to be exploited and he is eventually dismissed, although he has done wonders for the school, because he does not lend himself determinedly enough to the principal's crooked determination to extract money from his establishment. Through a pupil, Topaze is in contact with a dishonest local politician and businessman, Régis Castel-Bénac, just as intent on making money as his former employer, but more successful at it and an altogether grander sort of crook. Topaze is employed, soon sees what his role in the furtherance of a shady scheme is supposed to be, and turns it to his own profit and Castel-Bénac's discomfiture. The text is scarcely biting in its satire and the moral is obvious, but the dialogue is brilliantly written and it would be difficult not to make a stage presentation amusing. It is easy to see why it made an untaxing evening's entertainment with just the right touches of social comment about forms of seediness, dishonesty, and society's caste system.

Marius is the story of a man torn between the security of a home and the need for adventure. Marius, the son of a café owner, wants to go to sea. His childhood girlfriend, Fanny, knowing that Marius will not be happy if he simply marries her, pretends not to care in order to give him the courage to break free from her. All the minor characters, including César, Marius's father, and Honorine, Fanny's mother, are strongly drawn, and some of the scenes not necessary for the furthering of the action are given over entirely to creating the atmosphere of the Marseilles café, mostly through the brilliantly written dialogue. Again, more than staging, the text invites filming. To make it a work of more than passing interest, in spite of the power of its myth, it required Alexander Korda and the acting team of Raimu, Pierre Fresnay, and Fernand Charpin, but it also needed Pagnol as director. Raimu's César is particularly unforgettable, and only Pagnol, Charpin, and he knew what a Marseilles café was really like. Fresnay did not come from the Midi, and Korda was a Hungarian.

In *Fanny* the eponymous heroine is married to Panisse, while in *César* Panisse dies and Fanny is reunited with Marius. Pagnol's work always has charm, tenderness, and a touch of the bittersweet. It has been called sentimental, which it may occasionally be, and vulgar, which it is not. Indeed, historically, it was noteworthy for its realism, with which vulgarity is incompatible. Pagnol's greatness is essentially as a writer-director. When he writes the dialogue, decides how to use space and time, and assembles a cast from which he draws memorable performances, as in the Marseilles trilogy, the result is an impressively harmonious work of the imagination, gently floating on a swell of self-parody.

PUBLICATIONS

Collections

Théâtre complet, 1949
Oeuvres complètes, 1970

Plays

Les Marchands de gloire (produced 1926), 1927
Jazz (produced 1927), 1927
Topaze (produced 1928), 1931
Marius (produced 1929), 1931
Fanny (produced 1931), 1932
Cigalon, 1936
César (produced 1945), 1937
Judas (produced 1955), 1955
Fabien (produced 1956), 1956

Screenplays: *Marius*, 1931; *Fanny*, 1932; *Angèle*, 1934; *Merlusse*, 1935; *César*, 1936; *Regain* (from the novel by Giono), 1937; *La Femme du boulanger* (from the novel by Giono), 1938; *Le Schpountz*, 1938; *La Fille du puisatier*, 1940; *La Belle Meunière*, 1948, *Topaze*, 1951; *Manon des sources*, 1952; *Trois lettres de mon moulin* (from the novel by Daudet), 1954

Other

Pirouettes, 1932
Le Premier Amour, 1946
Notes sur le rire, 1947
Critique des critiques, 1949
Souvenirs d'enfance:
   1. *La Gloire de mon père*, 1957
   2. *Le Château de ma mère*, 1957
   3. *Le Temps des secrets* 1960; as *The Time of Secrets*, 1962

4. *Le Temps des amours*, 1977; as *The Time of Love*, 1979
L'Eau des collines, 1962
Le Masque de fer, 1964
Le Secret du masque de fer, 1973

Translator, *Hamlet*, by Shakespeare
Translator, *Les Bucoliques*, by Virgil, 1958
Translator, *Le Songe d'une nuit d'été*, by Shakespeare, 1970

PARNASSE, (LE)

See also Gautier, Heredia, Leconte de Lisle, Mallarmé,
Rimbaud, Sully Prudhomme, Verlaine, naturalism and
symbolism.

"Le Parnasse" came to be the name given to a group of poets
who in the 1860s surrounded as their chief source of inspiration
the poet Charles-Marie-René Leconte de Lisle. They met in his
house, after having earlier come together as a group centred on
Catulle Mendès (1841–1909), the husband from 1866 to 1874 of
Judith Gautier (1845–1917). The poets derived their aesthetic
largely from the belief of Théophile Gautier (1811–72), Judith's
father, in "L'Art pour l'art" (q.v.). The phrase was first used by
Victor Cousin, and Leconte de Lisle made a ringing declaration
on behalf of the principle as late as 1864 in his foreword to *Les
Poètes contemporains*, a series of articles he had published that
year in *Le Nain Jaune*. Although Leconte de Lisle in particular
can be shown to have been nourished by romantic (q.v.) attitudes, he came to lead the group of poets surrounding him into
a reaction against any romantic expression of emotion or
attempt to write directly moving verse.

Leconte de Lisle's reaction against romanticism was to have
the effect, however, of encouraging the "pathetic fallacy" bred
by the romantics. This was the name given to the assumption
that nature is itself a veil for larger, hidden forces behind it with
which we are, or can become, in harmony, and which reflect
human needs, aspirations, and even moods. The Leconte de
Lisle group, by turning from the expression of feelings to the
depiction of animals or things, accentuated this romantic tendency by viewing objects and living beings as obstacles block-
ing, or gates opening access to a higher and grander reality
beyond them. They were thereby led towards symbolism (q.v.),
and in fact by the time the third collection of *Le Parnasse contemporain* appeared in 1876, the aims of the poets contributing
to the anthology had become dispersed. Verlaine, Mallarmé and
then Rimbaud developed what we can now see to have been
symbolist tendencies out of the Parnassian aesthetic.

Judith Gautier, whose first two books were to be published by
Lemerre, was brought up among household literary names. Her
father had been a friend of the exiled Hugo. Maxime du Camp
was her godfather, while Flaubert and Baudelaire both called at
her father's house, as indeed did most of literary Paris. She herself became an ardent advocate of Wagner, and in 1864 published her first review in Arsène Houssaye's *L'Artiste*, for which
she then continued to write. She also learnt Chinese. It was prob-

ably at one of the Pasdeloup concerts, which had started in 1861,
that she met Mendès, also a Wagner fan. He had travelled widely
round Europe in extreme youth, was then brought up in Toulouse, and came to Paris in 1860. Shortly thereafter he began to
receive an allowance from his family, bankers now resigned to
their son's literary career, and started to receive literary friends.
It was in his small apartment in the Rue de Douai, where the
group met on Wednesdays, and at the home of the mother of his
friend Louis-Xavier de Ricard (1843-1911), where it met on Fridays, that "Le Parnasse" first came together. Members of the
group included Albert Glatigny (1839-1873), Léon Dierx
(1838-1912), Heredia, and Villiers de l'Isle-Adam.

In February 1861 Mendès had founded the *Revue Fantaisiste*,
notable for its support of Wagner, who had three successful Paris
concerts in 1860. His *Tannhäuser* was given at the Opéra on 13
March 1861 by order of the emperor, but had to be withdrawn
after three performances, partly no doubt on account of the hostility its imperial backing had aroused. Mendès enlisted the support of Baudelaire and Gautier, and threw the nascent review
behind Wagner. He also published his own verse drama "Le
roman d'une nuit," for which he was sentenced to a month's
imprisonment and fined 500 francs. The review collapsed in
November, and Mendès lived for a while as a student in Heidelberg. He was back in Paris by 1863 and, as soon as she reached
her majority, Judith Gautier married him, against her father's
advice. Her father had been right, and the marriage was to prove
a humiliating failure for her. Meanwhile, however, in March
1863, Ricard had founded the *Revue du Progrès Moral, Littéraire, Scientifique*, clearly intending to ally literature with
social and technological progress in accordance with Leconte de
Lisle's ambitions. The review lasted a year, and was replaced by
another review founded by Ricard, *L'Art*, which ran only from
November 1865 to January 1866.

By 1866 Verlaine had put the group centred on Mendès and
Ricard in touch with the young bookseller Alphonse Lemerre,
who became quasi-official publisher to the movement (see Heredia). *Le Parnasse Contemporain, Recueil de Vers Nouveaux* was
to be a magazine of verse, selected by an editorial committee,
intended to replace Ricard's bankrupt *L'Art*. The first volume
consisted of 18 fascicules, with verse by some 40 poets, including Baudelaire, Mallarmé and Verlaine. It lost money. The criteria of the selectors had included craftmanship and avoidance of
sentimentality, and although the work of Banville, Leconte de
Lisle, and Gautier continued to be much admired, the main
inspiration came from Heredia. Mendès and his wife assiduously attended Leconte de Lisle's Saturday afternoon receptions
and the group began to gestate not only symbolism, but also naturalism (q.v.). It enthusiastically welcomed the stage production
of the Goncourt brothers' *Henriette Maréchal* in 1865 and took
part in the anti-government demonstrations it occasioned.

Although Leconte de Lisle, who moved house in 1873, continued to receive, the original Parnassian group, in so far as it
had remained a collectivity, was split up during the Franco-Prussian War of 1870-71. Because of the war publication of the
second volume of *Le Parnasse Contemporain*, now little more
than an anthology of verse by poets no longer clearly united in a
common aim, was delayed until 1871. The monthly dinners
resumed that year, and Verlaine brought Rimbaud to the first.
The diffusion of aim was even clearer in the third and last collection of 1876, selected by Banville, Anatole France, and
François Coppée (1842-1908), and now in three volumes. By

that date Lemerre, well established now that his risky venture with the poets had paid off, was using Leconte de Lisle, who was hard up, for a variety of publishing ventures, of which *Le Parnasse Contemporain* had become merely one.

Along with the now well-known names and the authors of grand scientific or exotic pieces, a small group of minor poets were connected with "Le Parnasse." These included Coppée whose muse with leaden wings and moralizing voice was a source of amusement among the habitués of Leconte de Lisle's tea parties, Albert Mérat (1840-1909), author of half a dozen collections of verse, Léon Valade (1840-1883), André Lemoyne (1822–1907), and Eugène Manuel (1823-1901). Ricard himself became increasingly left-wing and spent much of his later life writing political journalism and living in the south. Others associated with the group (apart from those, like Sully Prudhomme and Anatole France, who have entries under their own names) included the scholar and philosopher Louis Ménard (1822-1901), Henri Cazalis (1840-1909), who published under the name of Jean Lahor and was interested in orientalism and occultism, Henri Céard (1851-1924), part of the original naturalist group, and Léon Dierx (1838-1912), Mallarmé's successor as "Prince des poètes."

PÉGUY, Charles, 1873–1914.

Poet and essayist.

LIFE

Péguy was born in Orléans and was almost aggressively proud of his working-class background. His father, a carpenter, died before he was one. His grandmother could neither read nor write, and his mother left school at 10. She kept the family by re-weaving straw seats on chairs. Péguy was proud to be at school, where he learnt Latin, Greek, and philosophy, although he was also well aware of the tension that existed between the Church and the academic world. Carried by examination successes and grants, in 1885 he went to the lycée in Orléans and in 1891 to the famous Lycée Lakanal in Paris to prepare for entry to the Ecole Normale Supérieure, where the elite of France's teachers was trained. He failed the difficult entrance examination in 1892, did his military service, sat and failed the exam again, and moved to the Collège de Sainte-Barbe, where he met his great friend Marcel Baudouin. He was finally accepted for the Ecole Normale Supérieure in 1894. It was in Paris for the first time that he met not just poverty, of which he had had first-hand experience, but unemployment and desperate economic need, which led him, under the influence of Jaurès, to proselytize on behalf of the socialists at the Ecole.

Péguy had already formed a dismissive view of a social hierarchy built on examination successes rather than labour. In his study, known to his fellow students as "Utopia," he set about planning an ideal society. He had already rejected the bourgeois values of the Church and now turned increasingly from the his-

torical positivism of Taine. What he wanted from philosophy was a rule of life, not a history of ideas. Much of his later prose writing was directed against the philosophical implications of the rigidly "academic" educational system. This fact explains the inordinate enthusiasm with which he welcomed Bergson's philosophy.

In 1895 Péguy was given leave of absence from the Ecole to work on Joan of Arc, his aim being to uncover the personality and motivation of the historical figure rather than to analyse the known facts. He was to write two trilogies on Joan, published in 1897 and 1910. He returned to the Ecole in 1896 and was well briefed by the Ecole's librarian on the Dreyfus affair before the publication of Zola's famous *J'accuse* of January 1898. Péguy called on Zola, who complained about the hesitations of the socialists, which Péguy put right, although at the cost of excluding the Marxist group from the battle. His socialist bookshop, opened in 1898, rapidly became the Dreyfusard headquarters of the Latin Quarter, while Péguy himself published a long series of articles on the affair in the *Revue Blanche*.

Marcel Baudouin had died suddenly in 1896. Péguy, who left the Ecole in 1897, gave Latin lessons to Baudouin's sister Charlotte, whom he later married. Mme Péguy opposed the marriage, which brought with it a dowry of 30,000 francs, and the Baudouin family insisted on a civil ceremony only. Any children were not to be baptized. The young couple lived with Charlotte's mother. In 1898 Péguy published *Marcel, le premier dialogue de la cité harmonieuse*. He had 1,000 copies printed, 200 of which he gave away. Having failed his philosophy agrégation, Péguy now abandoned all formal study, although he attended Bergson's lectures at the Ecole and at the Collège de France. In spite of his comments on the educational system, he had at least been supported by bursaries at the Orléans lycée, Lakanal, Sainte-Barbe, and the Ecole. A further subsidy was, unusually, also offered to him as a married man running a business.

Péguy continued to hero-worship Jaurès, and socialism, for him, continued to signify a bloodless moral revolution. In 1900 he founded *Les Cahiers de la Quinzaine*, largely as a medium for attacking the hypocrisy of according a pardon to Dreyfus for a crime he had not committed. The *Cahiers* contain a valuable collection of reports, articles, and speeches, nowhere else available verbatim, as well as Péguy's observations on current events and his personal reflections. One of the greatest difficulties in reading them is Péguy's refusal to refrain from chasing all the hares he starts, so that while he returns to an original subject much enriched by consideration of related matters, his train of thought can be difficult to follow, especially since the relationship of ancillary material to the main theme is seldom made sufficiently explicit. He spent the whole of his life as a writer exploring ever more deeply the same themes, history, education, the Dreyfus affair, Christianity, Bergson, and patriotism, but themes which were chiefly related only in his own mind. The *Cahiers* as movement gradually took precedence over the *Cahiers* as review. At the end of the first year, there were 263 subscribers and 300 non-paying readers, with piles of unsold copies serving as seats at the bookshop's Thursday gatherings.

The Péguys were obliged to move home several times. The rent on the bookshop was 3,250 francs and its finances were precarious. Albert Baudouin, Péguy's brother-in-law, invested, and lost, his fortune in the business. Bits of the office were let off, though the underground meetings must have been well attended since, in addition to using the piles of unsold reviews, Péguy had to buy a further 46 chairs to accommodate members. In order to sidestep bankruptcy and form a new company, the Société Nouvelle de Librairies et d'Editions, 50,000 francs were raised, of which 20,000 came from Léon Blum. Péguy was employed by the company at 250 francs a month, rather less than the starting wage of a schoolmaster. He had lost 15,000 francs out of the 40,000 he had invested and was given 250 shares of 100 francs in the new enterprise.

Péguy soon quarrelled with the new board, which tended to support class warfare and hard-line Marxism, and found a new office from which to launch the *Cahiers*. Under the influence of Sorel, he began to diverge from Jaurès's more optimistic views. He also began to sympathize seriously with the Church after Combes, the president of the Council (1902–05), had suppressed religious education and most of the religious congregations, and he was to become more and more critical of the socialist party machine. In 1901 he found a set of permanent, if tiny, premises, at 1,500 francs a year. Parts of the accommodation continued to be let out and right up until the *Cahiers'* final disappearance, at the outbreak of war, subscriptions very rarely rose above 1,000. Bernard Lazare, the prominent Jewish friend of whom Péguy wrote in *Notre jeunesse*, came to his help financialy whenever the position was desperate.

Péguy was gradually feeling his way back towards a Christian synthesis of attitudes which would ally the defence of social justice with that of civilization and the anti-materialism of Bergson. He was particularly incensed at the purges being carried out against university teachers on religious grounds. The works of 1904 to 1908 attack the purely naturalistic and materialistic scientism of "academic method" as understood by the followers of Renan and Taine. Some of Péguy's works from this period— *Esprit de système, Un poète l'a dit, Deuxième élégie…*, and *Le Thème*—were published posthumously, but he deals with the same anti-rationalist themes in the "Situations" *Cahiers* of 1906 to 1907. The 1904 *Zangwill* attacks the textual criticism which was the legacy of Taine and which broke the hold his Christian faith had exerted on Renan. Its presuppositions are disturbing. The mysterious, the poetic, the religious, all were the subject of rigorous but, according to Péguy, misplaced scientific enquiry. Péguy regarded science, which knows neither justice nor love, as an idol, not a god.

Notre patrie of 1905, though full of digressions, shows a developing sense of patriotism, a sense of belonging to the French nation, only superficially at odds with the discredit of the army following the Dreyfus affair. It posits the discovery of a "racial memory" and expresses alarm at the vulnerability of undefended civilizations. Together with *Par ce demi-clair matin* and *Les Suppliants parallèles*, also of 1905, *Notre patrie* explains Péguy's readiness to fight for France in the conflict he foresaw. The next *Cahier*, "Louis de Gonzague" of December 1905, looked to the Jews for lessons in racial survival and to Christianity for a belief in eternal life. Where Péguy at this date differs most from Barrès is in his unwillingness to temporize politically.

Even democracy incurred Péguy's increasing suspicion as its alliance with declericalization and aggressive scientism became stronger. Literature was now seen to begin with the Enlightenment and what was taken for anti-Christian liberalism, and attempts were even made to remove 17th-century literary texts from university syllabuses. Meanwhile, in 1908 Péguy moved

perceptibly nearer to Catholicism, although his wife remained a strong non-believer and his children were not brought up as Catholics. The *Cahiers* again brought serious financial worries and 1909 passed for Péguy in a mood not far from despair. *A nos amis, à nos abonnés* of 1909 and *Notre jeunesse* of 1910, both relating to the Dreyfus case, show a heightened appreciation of France and of French culture, but in a quite apolitical way. The Church, according to Péguy, should have capitalized on, not opposed, the spiritual yearning of the Dreyfusards, which he regarded as akin to Bergson's pure spiritual energy, and the great danger he foresaw was the tragedy that did in fact occur. A mystique, an ideal, became a political stance, an ideology.

From 1910 to 1912 Péguy published his "Mystères": *Le Mystère de la charité de Jeanne d'Arc, La Porche du mystère de la deuxième vertu*, and *Le Mystère des Saints-Innocents*, written in irregular "vers libres". These are fully Christian investigations into the major mysteries of sacrifice, suffering, and salvation with a contemporary, and clearly patriotic, resonance. The prose polemics continued through the writing and publication of the "Mystères" and then, in December 1913, came the 8,000 unbroken Alexandrines of *Eve*, a new Christian epic whose hero is Christ. In 1914 Péguy published the two *Notes*, ostensibly devoted to Bergson and Descartes respectively. He was mobilized in August and killed a month later while leading his company at Villeroy, where he took an almost wilful risk, during the first battle of the Marne.

WORKS

If it is broadly true that the Dreyfus case united the free-thinking, republican, socialist, internationalizing, and academic communities against the haute bourgeoisie, the military, the aristocracy, the mystics of French patriotism, and the higher clergy, the polarization was nevertheless incomplete, and on each side some attitudes could be held while others were rejected. It was piecemeal that Péguy drew away from his fellow Dreyfusards, and he never parted company with them on all counts. From about 1905, after the affair itself had degenerated into a sordid political affray, his sense of justice led him from the need to be active on behalf of Dreyfus to the need to defend France against renewed aggression. In spite of everything that separated him from Maurras, Péguy's patriotism and love of France necessarily took the *Cahiers* into an increasingly close alliance with the Action Française as the inevitability of war became apparent.

By 1910 Péguy was maintaining that what chiefly distinguished the French was their developed sense of the heroic. His generation, he writes, needed military heroism, sacrifice, martyrdom, and sanctity. In the *Prière pour nous autres charnels* of the same year Péguy evinced the same exultant spirit as those who were to march enthusiastically to the battlefields in 1914. His particular constellation of attitudes can only be understood in the light of his peasant and artisan background, his love of Catholic, rural, and provincial French life, the sheer ordinariness of his experience, and his acuteness as an undisciplined and self-taught thinker in search of spirituality. For Péguy the natural and supernatural orders were in harmony: "Et l'arbre de la grâce et l'arbre de la nature/Ont lié leurs deux troncs de noeuds si solennels (Both the tree of grace and the tree of nature have bound their trunks with such solemn knots)." Bergson acknowledged that Péguy understood his thought better than he did himself, and it is certainly true that Péguy foresaw more clearly than Bergson the direction which this thought would later take.

Almost all Péguy's work was published first in the *Cahiers*, where the tone in the non-lyrical pieces was common-sense and the style matter-of-fact. Péguy could be repetitive and over-insistent, and its lack of academic polish often makes his thought difficult to follow. In spite of the constant changes of viewpoint, however, his output is inspired by an overall integrity that gives his work the characteristically disconcerting flavour of originality that only deep intellectual honesty can impart, by refusing to link together altitudes which are only conventionally and not intrinsically associated. The *Cahiers*, he argued, united those who did not cheat. The danger was that an intuition, rather than retaining its purity of incarnation, would crystallize into an ideology: "Tout commence en mystique et finit en politique (Everything starts in intuitive awareness and ends in ideology)" runs Péguy's most famous aphorism. Hence his personal combination of the "mystiques" of Judaism, Catholicism, socialism, and patriotism without regard to the clash of their associated ideologies.

The Joan of Arc trilogy opens with *Domrémy*, in which Jeanne, inspired by a simple, Christ-like vision, rebels against hell, hunger, and war. By offering to suffer in their place, can she save from eternal damnation those driven by war to murder and theft? Jeanne's rejection of hell, her feeling for the poor, and her revolt against injustice make it difficult for her to submit unquestioningly to the will of God. In this first play we encounter, almost surprisingly, echoes of Hugo, Ronsard, and Schiller. The second play, *Les Batailles*, is devoted to a discussion of Jeanne by ordinary people and centres on the success at Orléans, the failure to free Paris, and the retreat to the Loire. Jeanne is a lonely, doubting human figure, bereft of the traditional voices. Her purity exasperates the soldiers who are forbidden to plunder. The third play, *Rouen*, centres on the historical trial. Jeanne, a prey to self-doubt, breaks down. Is she, she wonders, damned for all eternity?

With the appearance of the first *Cahier* on 5 January 1900, Péguy had created the ideal forum for his long, digressive essays. *De la grippe*, *Encore de la grippe*, and *Toujours de la grippe* are, for instance, reflections on life, death, and Pascal, offered in conjunction with a selection of documents on the socialist congress. The parallels are disconcerting. In *Les Suppliants parallèles* Péguy talks about Greek antiquity in the context of the Russian revolution of 1905. In *Par ce demi-clair matin* he describes an academic oral examination in a discussion of the mortality of civilizations. There were 15 series and 229 issues of the *Cahiers*, which published plays, novels, short stories and poetry, dreams of world peace and Jewish poetry, considerations about the inevitability of war, Greek myths, extracts from Bergson and Benda's attack on Bergson, revolutionary diaries, translations of Shakespeare, and articles on Michelangelo and Beethoven. Péguy never left France, but the *Cahiers* reported on Poland, Finland, Romanian anti-Jewish pogroms, the Turkish massacre of Armenian Christians, and conditions in the French and Belgian Congos. Péguy boasted that the *Cahiers*, as a movement, were a "perfectly free association of men who all believe in something."

Notre patrie, which emphasizes the "racial memory" of the French, is a consideration of France in 1905 presented as a set of vignettes. Apparently casual, these vignettes already fore-

shadow the move towards war which, from this date, became almost an obsession with Péguy. Only Hugo escapes a light-hearted treatment here, on account of his pacifism. The three "Mystères" published from 1910 to 1912 united what had become symbols for two opposing ideologies: Joan of Arc and Dreyfus. *Notre jeunesse* was to be Péguy's answer to those who welcomed what they took to be his change of heart over the Dreyfus affair. The work includes a moving portrait of Bernard Lazare and a sensitive depiction of the state of Jewry under the Diaspora. *The Jewish State* by Herzl, the founder of political Zionism, was a direct outcome of Dreyfus's degradation.

In 1912 Péguy, whose second son's life had been at serious risk, made a pilgrimage to Chartres and wrote *La Tapisserie de Ste Geneviève et de Jeanne d'Arc*, to be followed in 1913 by *La Tapisserie de Notre Dame de Chartres*: two attempts to weave together religious symbols and everyday virtues, in which the national feeling is as strong as the religious. Both "Tapisseries" lead up to *Eve*, an invocation by Jesus, speaking after the Nativity in the second person plural, which develops panoramically into an account of Christianity in the over-commercialized modern world. In spite of the repetitiousness of the litany-like sentence and stanza structures, the thought here is dense. The poem is composed of scenes, or "climates," not necessarily linked chronologically, and moves from Paradise, inhabited by farmers and artisans, to the second climate, where Eve is the eternal housewife. This leads in turn to the Fall, although the Genesis story, with Adam, serpent, and apple, is omitted entirely. The poem constantly mixes the supernatural with identifiable geographical landmarks. It attacks the commerce which pays current value for future security, and insists on the union of the carnal with the spiritual.

The poem contains burlesque, self-parody, and a sweeping account of world history, conceived not as converging on Christ, but as an inheritance which Christ simply accepts. After an immense passage on the modern world, the poem ends with Saint Geneviève and Joan of Arc, patrons respectively of Péguy's two cities of Paris and Orléans. In spite of its castigation of the modern world *Eve* is a poem of hope. It is not a Catholic poem, either religiously or theologically; nor does it degenerate into myth. The radical vision it expresses, that striving for the incarnation of pure, intuitive thought, may be summed up in the often-quoted line "Heureux ceux qui sont morts pour la terre charnelle (Blessed are those who have died for carnal earth)."

PUBLICATIONS

Collections

Les Cahiers de la Quinzaine, 1900–1914
Oeuvres complètes, 20 vols., 1916–55
Oeuvres poétiques complètes, Bibliothèque de la Pléiade, 1957
Oeuvres en prose, 2 vols., Bibliothèque de la Pléiade, 1987–88

Marcel, 1896
Jeanne d'Arc, 1897
Notre patrie, 1905
De la situation faite à l'histoire et à la sociologie dans les temps modernes, 1906
Les Suppliants parallèles, 1906

Le Mystère de la charité de Jeanne d'Arc, 1910
Notre jeunesse, 1910
Le Porche du mystère de la deuxième vertu, 1911
Victor-Marie, Comte Hugo, 1911
La Mystère des Saints Innocents, 1912
L'Argent, 1913
La Tapisserie de Sainte Geneviève et de Jeanne d'Arc, 1913
Eve, 1914
Note sur Bergson et la philosophie bergsonienne, 1914
Notre patrie, *(1873-1914)*, 1918

Translations (mostly selections)

Basic Verities, 1943
God Speaks, 1945
Men and Saints, 1947
The Mystery of the Charity of Joan of Arc, 1950
The Holy Innocents and Other Poems, 1956
Temporal and Eternal, 1958

Bibliography

Delaporte, J., *Connaissance de Péguy*, 2 vols., 1944
Cattaui, G., *Péguy, témoin du temporel chrétien*, 1964

Critical studies

Rolland, Romain, *Péguy*, 2 vols., 1944
Servais, Y., *Charles Péguy* (in English), 1953
Dru, A., *Péguy* (in English), 1956
Villiers, M. *Charles Péguy: A Study in Integrity*, 1965
Jussem-Wilson, N., *Charles Péguy* (in English), 1965

———

PEREC, Georges, 1936–1982.

Novelist, dramatist, and essayist.

LIFE

Georges Perec's importance as a novelist was initially underestimated in the Anglo-Saxon world. His first novel *Les Choses: une histoire des années 60*, published in 1965, won the Prix Renaudot, was translated into most European languages other than English, was widely read in eastern Europe for what Perec regarded as the wrong reasons, appeared on university syllabuses all over the world within two or three years of its publication, was published in student editions in Moscow and New York, and speedily became a set text in French secondary education. In the UK a translation made by Helen R. Lane in 1968 was not issued at all by the publishing house which had commissioned it, although it appeared in the US, where, however, critical reaction showed it not generally to have been understood. The book eventually appeared in the UK in 1990 as *Things*, translated by David Bellos.

Perec was born in Paris on 7 March 1936 of Jewish–Polish

parents. Icek Perec, a metal worker, and Cyrla Szulewicz had emigrated a decade earlier. Icek was killed at the front in June 1940, when his son was just four, and his wife was deported as a Jew in 1943. She died in a concentration camp, probably Drancy. Perec was adopted by his father's sister and brought up at first in the foothills of the Alps, in two small towns just southwest of Grenoble, Villard-de-Lans and Lans-en-Vercors. Recollections of that period are contained in *W; ou, Le Souvenir d'enfance*. Perec's aunt brought him back to Paris in 1945 at the end of the war, and he was educated at the Collège d'Etampes, a state boarding school, then the Lycée Claude-Bernard, and finally at the Lycée Henri IV.

When he left school in 1954, Perec registered at the Sorbonne for an arts degree, but worked only desultorily at a course in history and sociology for two years, knowing before he was 20 that he wanted to be a writer. His whole oeuvre shows his need to create a world which made sense and whose constituent elements did not simply fall into structureless piles around him. He was a Pole, a Jew, an orphan, an exile and a refugee. His father had been killed and his mother had died in transit to extermination, not an inheritance it was easy for a child to carry into adolescence in the shattered Paris of 1945. He described one of his books as "built like a house whose parts fitted together like the pieces of a puzzle." For Perec the activity of writing was "essayer méticuleusement de retenir quelque chose, de faire survivre quelque chose (to try meticulously to hold on to something, to make something survive)." It was also a sacred duty to his parents: "j'écris parce qu'ils ont laissé en moi leur marque indélébile et que la trace en est l'écriture…l'écriture est le souvenir de leur mort et l'affirmation de ma vie (I write because they have left their indelible mark on me, and its traces are to be found by writing…writing is the memory of their death and the affirmation of my life)."

Finally, however, in a text published in 1979, Perec made what was perhaps, for its understanding, the most important of all his statements about his oeuvre. He knew that it would need to be taken together and that its constituent elements would not be comprehensible if taken only individually:

Chacun de mes livres est pour moi l'élément d'un ensemble; je ne peux pas définir l'ensemble, parce qu'il est par définition projet inachevable…je sais seulement qu'il s'incrit lui-même dans un ensemble beaucoup plus vaste qui serait l'ensemble des livres dont la lecture a déclenché et nourri mon désir d'écrire.

(Each of my books forms for me part of a whole; I can't define the whole because it is by definition incomplete…I know only that this project is part of a much vaster whole, which would comprise all the books whose reading has unleashed and nourished my desire to write.)

It does not seem to be necessary to have read everything to which Perec refers in order to understand his work, but it is clear that his own works are themselves parts of a literary totality which he knew he was constructing.

The result was that Perec avoided obvious literary affiliations with such contemporaries as Robbe-Grillet and those associated with him as "new novelists," and entered the quite different league to which Kafka and Beckett had belonged. The bitingly sharp exploration of experience to be found in Kafka and Beckett is also present in Perec. If in him it is less concentrated, and *Les Choses* is less instantly overwhelming than Kafka's *Die Verwandlung*, that is only on account of Perec's diffidently witty indulgence in self-parody, and a vulnerability which made him at least affect to regard literature as a purely gratuitous activity, and authors as more or less highly skilled technicians, who ought not to set up as purveyors of culture, myth, or ideologies which were often patently evil and always opened their vulnerable originators to unbearable repudiation or mockery.

The difficulty connected with his writing and its reception in the Anglo-Saxon world has to do with the way a desperate search for structures is combined with the clown's mocking compulsion to self-parody. Perec is too diffident to demand that his seriousness of purpose be taken seriously in case it is not. Like the clowns of Picasso's rose period, Perec needs to make fun of his own seriousness. In his work he shows a tendency to avoid committing himself to the structures he needs, and to take refuge in showing them as only a hollow sham. By clever manipulation he demonstrates that literary writing can be reduced to the observance of a set of quite arbitrary formal rules. Perec rewrote Mallarmé's famous poem "Brise marine," keeping everything but the letter "e." The entire text of the novel *La Disparition*, written in 1969, avoids the vowel "e." which is the only vowel used in the whole of *Les Revenentes*, published in 1972.

As early as 1955 Perec was writing book reviews and essays on literature and the cinema for the *Nouvelle Revue Française* (*NRF*, q.v.) and for *Les Lettres Nouvelles*. After two years at the Sorbonne he went through a period of extreme depression, remembered in *Un homme qui dort*, and did his military service from 1958 to 1959, being exempted from active service in Algeria. On demobilization he drifted into market research, and on 28 October 1960 married Paulette Petras. For over a year he resumed his studies in Tunis and lived at Sfax. On his return to Paris in 1962, Perec became an archivist for the Centre National de Recherche Scientifique in its neuro-physiological laboratories, a post which he retained until 1979, when the success of *La Vie mode d'emploi*, for which he was awarded the Prix Médicis, allowed him to devote himself to full-time writing.

From 1960 Perec was writing articles about literature, mostly for *Partisans*. He wrote *Les Choses*, as he said in a lecture at the University of Warwick, which had instantly put it on its new French studies syllabus, to fill a gap between four works which were important to him: Barthes's *Mythologies*, Flaubert's *L'Education sentimentale*, Nizan's *La Conspiration*, and Antelme's *L'Espèce humaine*. It is not difficult to see how its aim is related to that of these four works, or to see how *Un homme qui dort* of 1967 is related to the six progenitory models Perec claimed for it: Kafka, Melville, Lowry, Le Clézio, Joyce, and Proust, to whom the title alludes. To claim descent from six such models, however, does suggest that, in 1967 at least, Perec still had more ambitious pretensions towards literary endeavour than the exhibition of pointless technical virtuosity which he half trapped the critics into expecting of him, however reactionary his serious interest in literary craftsmanship actually was.

In his second novel, *Quel petit vélo à guidon chromé au fond de la cour?* which appeared in 1966, Perec is less ambitious. He continues to use the obsessional techniques of accumulation used in the first novel, but adds a whole catalogue of rhetorical forms inspired by a lecture given by Barthes, and perhaps also by a passage from Joyce's *Ulysses*. He develops the systematic use of repetition which he was to employ to such effect in *Un*

homme qui dort.

Perec underwent psychotherapy three times. In 1949, when he was 13, he was treated by Françoise Dolto and in 1956 he began an analysis with Michel de M'Uzan. His four-year analysis with J-B. Pontalis lasted from May 1971 until June 1975.

He had started writing in 1953 when he was 17, but he said at Warwick that he was grateful that the novel he then began, and which he finished in 1958, was never published. All his early projects were either autobiographical or fiction heavily based on autobiography until he finally resorted to writing according to immensely complex mathematical formulae. The 1976 *Alphabets*, for instance, is a collection of 176 poems of eleven lines, each with eleven letters. Each poem uses each of the ten most frequent letters of the alphabet and one each of the remaining 16 letters. Eleven poems use each of the remaining letters to give 11 × 16 = 176 poems. In a manner analagous to that in which serial music uses notes, no letter may be re-used until each of the other ten has been used. The rules for displaying each poem on the page are of comparably complex symmetry.

"J'avance masqué," was a novel in which the narrator recounted his life story, fictionalizing it differently three times. When it was written in 1961, an early autobiographical text already existed, and soon after this a project for a series of nine "auto-portraits" was drawn up. In 1965 Perec wrote "Les Lieux d'une fugue," finally published in 1975 in *Présence et Regards*, which he turned the following year into a short film. In 1966 he began "Les Lieux de la trentaine," about life at the age of 30, and later thought of introducing into it one of the intricate structures in which he was to specialize. Perec changed its title before abandoning it, turning in 1967 to a novel about his paternal and maternal families, itself to be integrated into *W; ou, Le Souvenir d'enfance*. He worked on a series of projects with "Lieux" in the title, finally publishing half a dozen from 1977 to 1980, none of them autobiographical, and in 1969 was still considering "a vast autobiographical compendium" centred on four books which he thought would take 12 years to write. Part of an early section was in fact serialized as *W* in *La Quinzaine Littéraire* from October 1969 to August 1970, but its character changed as it preceeded, and Perec announced *W; ou, Le Souvenir d'enfance* to appear in 1971. Its complex structure was to be modified before it finally did appear in 1975.

Perec continued to compile dossiers of subjects and objects to write about. He listed his dreams and from 1974 kept a meticulously precise diary with very few intimate facts, and started, but did not finish, an attempt to write the chronology of his youth and young manhood from 1945 to 1958. In 1972, after the beginning of the analysis with Pontalis, Perec could write in an "Autoportrait" that he thought he was beginning to understand why he felt the need to write, and the personal inadequacies which the fascination with writing revealed in himself:

L'écriture me protège. J'avance sous le rempart de mes mots, de mes phrases, de mes paragraphes habilement enchaînés, de mes chapitres astucieusement programmés. Je ne manque pas d'ingéniosité.

Ai-je encore besoin d'être protégé? Et si le bouclier devenait un carcan?

(Writing protects me. I move forward underneath the ramparts of my words, my phrases, my skilfully joined paragraphs, my cleverly calculated chapters. I'm not short of ingenuity.

Do I still need to be protected? And if the shield threatened to garotte me?)

The autobiographical fragments were, however, by the end of the analysis becoming less and less personal.

By 1967 Perec was already experimenting with the "e"-less text of the novel to become *La Disparition*, when he became associated with the Ouvroir de Littérature Potentielle (OULIPO), a small and not wholly serious working group of highly gifted wordsmiths founded in 1961 by François le Lionnais and Raymond Queneau, and dedicated to the rediscovery of "contraintes littéraires (literary constraints)," that is, literary forms, however arbitrary, which demand the development of extraordinary linguistic skills. It was Perec's search for increasingly demanding formal constrictions which eventually led him to write *La Vie mode d'emploi*. By that time he had been crossword puzzle editor for two years at the weekly *Le Point* and, like Barthes's best writing, his literary efforts tended to demonstrate how the ordinary language we use conceals an ideology. Barthes analyses it, starting from something apparently innocuous, like an advertising slogan. Perec uses ridicule to satirize it mercilessly.

From *Les Choses* to *La Vie mode d'emploi*, he ruthlessly strips objects of any significance outside themselves. They are objects whose end function is to feature on a list, not to denote status, wealth, or satisfaction, to stimulate appetites, indulge dreams, or crowd out disappointments. The title of *La Vie mode d'emploi (Life: A User's Manual)* implies that life is at best a piece of complicated machinery, like a vacuum cleaner, a TV, or a car engine. It takes a mechanic to make it work and maintain it so that it functions satisfactorily. The collector in the novel collects unique objects like the boxing gloves used by prizefighter Jack Dempsey to knock out Georges Carpentier on 21 July 1921, the gloves Rita Hayworth wore in *Gilda*, and the first milligram of radium isolated by the Curies in 1898. But by being assembled unique objects lose their associations, their unicity, and go back to being what they always were, just things. The structure has dissolved.

Perec carried on his essentially demythologizing activity, executing his elegant and funny verbal arabesques so as deliberately to remove from formal structures the myths and messages clinging to language. The words we choose, let alone the syntax, choice of tense, mood, tone, or register, give even the written language all sorts of significances. We can use, choose, and arrange words in ways which threaten, blandish, try neutrally to inform, emphasize or diminish differences of class or status, be deferential or rude, or both at once. Doing something as superficially absurd as writing a novel without using the letter "e" is a pointed demonstration that language can be stripped of the associations as well as the forms we normally give it:

La suppression de la lettre, du signe typographique, du support élémentaire, est une opération plus neutre, plus nette, plus décisive, quelque chose comme le degré zéro de la contrainte, à partir duquel tout devient possible.

(The suppression of the letter, the typographical sign, the basic support, is more neutral, more clear-cut, more decisive, something like the freezing point of constraint, from where everything becomes possible.)

The reference to freezing alludes to Barthes's "freezing point of writing/style" and shows what Perec was semi-humorously trying to achieve—the freedom, at its freezing point without an "e," of the French language from all emotional or other messages, implications, and innuendoes not strictly linguistic in character. He was frightened of the ridicule to which he might be exposed if he allowed his structures to carry any cultural message with which he might endow them, and disliked the coded cultural significance from which language could be liberated only by "freezing."

From 1964 Perec was literary adviser to *Les Temps Modernes* (q.v.). He came to put less emphasis on narrative fiction in the context of his literary activities and to turn more to the stage, the cinema, poetry, and the essay. The plays started with *L'Augmentation* of 1970, followed by *La Poche parmentier* of 1974. The three principal verse collections are *Alphabets: cent soixante-seize onzains héterogrammatiques* of 1976, very much a fruit of the OULIPO collaboration, *La Clôture, et autres poèmes* of 1980, and *Ulcérations*, which appeared in 1986. With the essays *Espèces d'espaces* of 1974 and the collaborative work *Créations, re-créations, récréations* of 1973 can be grouped three works which are partly autobiographical in formal structure, *La Boutique obscure, W; ou, Le Souvenir d'enfance*, and *Je me souviens*. Perec wrote several works in collaboration, and his participation in cinema included scriptwriting and directing. The film of *Un homme qui dort*, made with Bernard Queysanne, was awarded the Prix Jean Vigo in 1974.

Perec had just begun work on another novel, *53 jours*, when he fell ill with lung cancer. He died a few months later, on 3 March 1982.

WORKS

Perec was adept at making what he wrote read quite innocuously. One careless critic was trapped into writing of *Les Choses* that it resembled "a laborious and tedious sociological survey of the daily life, worries, and joys of a middle-class couple…a caricature of Robbe-Grillet's technique." The book, about the young Parisian couple Jérôme and Sylvie, has two parts, which are uneven in length, and an epilogue. There are untitled and unnumbered divisions into what have to be called chapters. The first is written entirely in the conditional tense and contains the minutely detailed description of a luxury apartment and how the good life would be lived in it:

Ils décachetteraient leur courrier, ils ouvriraient les journaux. Ils allumeraient une première cigarette. Ils sortiraient.

(They would open their mail; they would unfold the papers. They would light a first cigarette. They would go out.)

We do not know who "they" are, but the tense tells us that they are dreaming, and the plural subject that it is a shared daydream.

The second chapter starts off still in the conditional, but the clipped sentences warn the reader of a change. This is no longer a dream:

Ils auraient aimé être riches. Ils croyaient qu'ils auraient su l'être. Ils auraient su s'habiller, regarder, sourire comme des gens riches.

(They would have liked to be rich. They thought they would have known how to be. They would have known how to dress, how to look at things, how to smile like rich people.)

The switch of tense comes in the second paragraph:

Ces choses-là ne sont pas faciles, au contraire. Pour ce jeune couple, qui n'était pas riche, mais qui désirait l'être, simplement parce qu'il n'était pas pauvre, il n'existait pas de situation plus inconfortable.

(These things aren't easy. On the contrary. For this young couple, who were not rich, but who wanted to be, simply because they weren't poor, there was no more uncomfortable situation.)

Their flat was too small, their meals were too ordinary, their holidays too cheap. The trouble is that, while this was what their social and financial status warranted, the surrounding streets were full of the

offres fallacieuses, et si chaleureuses pourtant, des antiquaires, des épiciers, des papetiers… Paris entier était une perpétuelle tentation. Ils brûlaient d'y succomber, avec ivresse, tout de suite et à jamais. Mais l'horizon de leurs désirs était impitoyablement bouché

(illusory offers, but so welcoming, from antique dealers, delicatessens, stationers… The whole of Paris was a perpetual temptation. They wanted passionately to give in, intoxicated, immediately, and for ever. But the horizon of their desires was pitilessly blocked.)

There follows a description of where they actually do live. Three or four pages later we learn their names, and at the beginning of the following chapter that they are 24 and 22. They have drifted into market research and are among the principal victims of the consumerism they have created. They are hooked on cinema, the same restaurants, the same people, the same parties; they are vaguely left wing and too proud, lazy, and sophisticated to submit to the discipline of mind and life style that would earn them serious money.

Ils s'étaient installés dans le provisoire. Ils travaillaient comme d'autres font leurs études; ils choisissaient leurs horaires. Ils flânaient comme seuls les étudiants savent flâner.

(They had set themselves up in what was temporary. They worked the way other people go about their studies, choosing their timetable. They wasted time as only students know how to waste time.)

The things they want, the cinemas where they meet their friends, the places they go to, the phrases they use, the gestures they make, the questions they ask, are mercilessly listed and

there is not a word of conversation in the whole gripping novelload of catalogues. Seek not to know whose attitudes are being sent up. The satire is total, unsparing, remorseless, and vicious. Only the tone is indulgent, and the irony seems discreet only until it is scrutinized.

The couple's group disintegrates. Friends give in, get proper jobs. Jérôme and Sylvie go to Tunis to teach and could stay there, with a car, a villa, and a garden. "Mais il ne leur sera pas si facile d'échapper à leur histoire (But it won't be so easy for them to escape their past)." They will go back to Paris and write CVs. Friends will find them a job. They will leave Paris again one morning in early September to open an advertising agency in Bordeaux. This is the epilogue, written as they decide to opt in again, and it is all in the future tense.

Eastern Europeans read *Les Choses* as an attack on the consumer society. In the US it was greeted as a belated attempt at a "nouveau roman." In the UK it was not read at all, except by students and professors. Even when it was widely reviewed on its UK appearance in 1990, the pointed starkness of the questions it examines was missed. How tawdry are the rewards offered by the daily commuting, and how possible, or even desirable, is it to avoid them?

The narrative is sympathetic to the couple, but the analysis of their situation quite merciless: "Ainsi rêvaient-ils, les imbéciles heureux (That was their dream, the happy fools)." Among the lists of magazines they read, films they see, and questions they ask, the dreadful stereotype of their lives is gently but sharply etched. Even the moral is obvious, and Perec makes clear that it is the third-person narrator who speaks:

Les gens qui choisissent de gagner d'abord de l'argent… n'ont pas forcément tort. Ceux qui ne veulent que vivre, et qui appellent vie la liberté la plus grande, la seule poursuite du bonheur, l'exclusif assouvissement de leurs désirs ou de leurs instincts, l'usage immédiate des richesses illimitées du monde—Jérôme et Sylvie avaient fait leur ce vaste programme—ceux-là seront toujours malheureux.

(People who choose to make money first… aren't necessarily wrong. Those who only want to live, who call life the greatest freedom possible, the pursuit of happiness alone, the exclusive appeasement of their desires and instincts, immediate access to the world's limitless riches—Jérôme and Sylvie had made that immense programme their own—such people are always going to be unhappy.)

Un homme qui dort, written in the second-person singular, has no strong narrative thread and explores the option of dropping out. It ends in the Place Clichy with the student addressed by the narrator waiting for the rain to stop. In the film Perec made the text is used as a voice-over against images of a young man performing routines of self-effacement. A female voice is used to make clear that the text is neither a dream nor an interior monologue. A young man studying for his sociology exam fails to get up for the exam, ignores notes poked under his door, forms pictures in his mind with the cracks in the ceiling. The room is miniscule. The student's attention focuses on how his nose and eyebrows vanish from his field of vision. You get up, you walk round Paris, you play a lot of pinball, you go to the cinema without knowing what is on, you play patience, read old newspapers, and soak your socks in a bowl, accuses the narrator. Perec gives us the lists of newspapers and prospectuses "you" reads. "You" is suffering from paralysis of the will, permanent, self-induced, and self-indulged semi-somnolence. At the end the central character accepts that he has to live like everyone else. The conclusion, or implied moral, is that it is no use dropping out, even if it could be done.

Perec's first play, *L'Augmentation*, is about asking for a pay rise and how to set about giving yourself the best chance of succeeding. What might have been a psychological struggle is reduced to the movement of pieces on a board, as in chess. The drama has gone. Only its structure remains. The six characters are called after the rhetorical figures they use: the Proposition, the Alternative, the positive Hypothesis, the negative Hypothesis, the Choice, and the Conclusion. *La Boutique obscure* is the transcription of three years of dreams, listing their objects, while *Un cabinet d'amateur* enumerates the pictures in the imaginary collection of Heinrich Kürz to be assembled into one huge canvas and buried, the absolute achieved, and immediately cancelled in its own self-destruction. *W; ou, Le Souvenir d'enfance* is a mixture of fiction and autobiography, at first apparently unrelated, and whose convergence remains implied. It is a mystery story which works its way towards a vision of horror as the author's reconstituted and sometimes painful childhood and adolescence come to meet a vision based on the idealism of the Olympic Games, but which turns into the concentration camp which is the lunatic apotheosis of Olympic capitalism.

Perec's most important work is generally taken to have been the very long *La Vie mode d'emploi*, conceived nine years before it was published. His guiding image, described in *Espèces d'espaces*, is an apartment bulding with its facade taken off so that everything going on inside its different apartments is simultaneously visible. We are given multiple biographies, quite harshly ironic lists of all the people who are, or ever were, in the building, and all the objects it contains, from its cellars to its attics. All the people and all the objects are in the end merely things, and imagined ones at that. *La Vie mode d'emploi* is therefore a collection of mini-novels in which the novel being written destroys itself underneath the accumulated weight of the novels which bury it. The lists pile on allusions, pseudo-references, and invented "facts," and it is true that there is an obsessiveness in the spatial description which can be related to the Robbe-Grillet of *La Jalousie*, although any borrowing is trivial and technical. Perec's stylistic master is quite recognizably Flaubert, and he has read Voltaire too, but much more modern writers also haunt his imagination. None of them, however, goes quite as far as Perec himself in *La Vie mode d'emploi*.

To start with he caricatures himself by giving a list of his dozens of characters and scores of anecdotes in an appendix. He later revealed that each chapter's contents were determined by a formula which permuted "21 times two series of 10 elements." He tells us that he first thought of a novel based on a number square 10 x 10 in 1967. Then came the idea of a building with its facade taken off and, in 1969, the idea of borrowing Bartlebooth from Valery Larbaud and Melville. The building would have 10 stories and each storey 10 street-facing rooms. The contents of each chapter would be determined by the structure of the building, each chapter having a different combination of furniture, location, literary allusions, quotations, people, décors, and so on. There are 42 "themes" to each chapter, and it is part of the game that chapter 23 has to have quotations from Verne and Joyce, from whom Perec took for it Bloom's dream of a doll's

house. The book had a series of different titles—*La Vie; La Vie (mode d'emploi); La Vie: mode d'emploi; La Vie, mode d'emploi*—before the definitive *La Vie mode d'emploi*. The succession of chapters follows a chess solution adapted from one of the many in which a knight moves on to all 64 squares of the board without stopping on any square more than once.

The central figure, Percival Bartlebooth, is a rich eccentric whose sole ambition has been to travel the world in order to paint 500 watercolours. The idea came to him when he was 20. He decided to organize his whole life around the execution of a single project sufficiently arbitrary to have no end other than itself. The project had to be difficult, but not impossible, neither heroic nor spectacular; identical events had to take place at times and places fixed for them to happen, and it had to be useless:

> Inutile, sa gratuité étant l'unique garantie de sa rigueur, le projet se détruirait lui-même au fur et à mesure qu'il s'accomplirait; sa perfection serait circulaire: une succession d'événements qui, en s'enchaînant, s'annuleraient

> (useless, since its gratuitousness was the only guarantee of its rigour, the project would destroy itself as it was completed; its perfection would be circular: a succession of events which, by being linked together, would cancel one another out)

Bartlebooth would spend 10 years from 1925 to 1935 learning to paint watercolours, then from 1935 to 1955 he would travel the world painting a watercolour of a sea port every fortnight. Each watercolour, stuck to a thin piece of wood, was then to be sent to Gaspard Winckler, now dead, to be turned into a 750-piece jigsaw puzzle. From 1955 to 1975 Bartlebooth would solve the jigsaw puzzles, obviously at the rate of one a fortnight. On reassembly, each puzzle would be taken back to where its picture was painted, exactly 20 years previously. The watercolour, removed from its support, would be dipped into a detergent which would wipe the paper clean.

> Aucune trace, ainsi, ne resterait de cette opération qui aurait, pendant cinquante ans, entièrement mobilisé son auteur.

> (So no trace would remain of the operation, which would have completely occupied its author for 50 years.)

At the end of the novel Bartlebooth dies 20 years later attempting to solve the 439th puzzle, his perfectly arbitrary task arbitrarily cancelled as his watercolours revert to blank paper, the only way to stop them conveying the oppressive cultural message of which Perec himself, not Bartlebooth, is frightened. Serge Valène, a painter friend of Bartlebooth and Winckler, wants to paint his apartment block without its facade, showing what is happening in every room. He, too, dies before he finishes and his canvas goes blank. We have therefore allegorical master, servant, and artist-outsider figures. All die. The only one to finish his work is the one whose work is wholly destructive. The unfinished achievements of the other two self-destruct into entirely arbitrary structures with no meaning whatsoever.

The novel takes to its culmination Perec's quest for formal constraints, devoid of the insistent patterns of significance with which culture has invested both language and literature, as the key to the possibility of living. The quest for formal constriction, already obvious in *Les Choses*, clearly lay behind the apparently frivolous verbal virtuosity *La Disparition*. Everywhere Perec needs to find or create the structures he never had as a child, but, whenever he writes about them in his fiction, they crumble. As in the case of Beckett and Kafka, Perec's own acute psychological need allowed him to create a myth of immense power because it examined in great depth a serious psychological pressure which, in its sub-acute "normal" forms, is as universal in our culture, and perhaps even beyond it, as is a son's erotic relationship with his mother. However, he also constantly makes the point that the structures are impossibly fragile, capable of destruction by the PR-enflamed desires of Jérôme and Sylvie in *Les Choses*, by the dream refuge offered to *Un homme qui dort*, by the erotic intrusions into *Les Revenentes*, and by the covert scenes revealed behind the facade in *La Vie mode d'emploi*. Perec did not dare seriously to try to recreate on an imaginative level the structures absent from life, however strongly he felt the urge to do so. Instead, he hid behind his clown's mask and used all his circus performer's agility to accomplish ever more difficult tasks, to compile ever more penetrating catalogues, mockingly aware of the futility of doing anything else, and of the wounding consequences of failing if you tried.

In *La Vie mode d'emploi* no structure is completed, neither Bartlebooth's nor Valène's. All that is left is the valiant but unsuccessful effort to undo Winckler's deconstruction. Bartlebooth has nevertheless escaped the clash between programmed conformity and programmed non-conformity. The power struggle of human society can be escaped only if, as by writing novels without the letter "e" or else with no vowel other than "e", you undertake something which may be difficult enough to keep you going, but which is perfectly and pointlessly futile. You escape even more certainly if, unlike Perec but like Bartlebooth, you do not succeed. In *Un cabinet d'amateur* Perec wickedly shows the reader the trap he has guided him into, just as he guided his readers up the garden path in *Les Choses*. *Un cabinet* concludes:

> Des vérifications entreprises avec diligence ne tardèrent pas à démontrer qu'en effet la plupart des tableaux de la collection…étaient faux, comme sont faux la plupart des détails de ce récit fictif, conçu pour le seul plaisir, et le seul frisson de faire-semblant.

> (Investigations undertaken with care did not long delay in showing that in fact most of the paintings in the collection…were counterfeit, as most of the details of this narrative fiction are counterfeit. It was conceived simply for the pleasure and the thrill of making believe.)

Make-believe, inside tightly structured constraints, is the best substitute we can achieve for living, itself an unattainable goal. Perec did not actually believe that, but his literary importance derives from his revealing, in his fiction more than his non-fiction, what it was that made him afraid of leaving the shelter afforded by that absurd proposition. Life is not a machine for which you can write a user's manual, any more than literature is reducible to verbal games which do not involve subjecting real human experience to glaring light. Perec's really valuable contribution to literature is to have revealed why it is sometimes necessary to pretend otherwise. Life is a high-voltage electric pylon, far too dangerous to go near. Life, like the sun, will burn out your eyes if you try to look at it.

PUBLICATIONS

Works

Les Choses: une histoire des années 60, 1965; as *Les Choses: A Story of the Sixties*, 1968; as *Things*, 1990
Quel petit vélo à guidon chromé au fond de la cour?, 1966
Un homme qui dort, 1967; as *A Man Asleep*, 1990
La Disparition, 1969
Petit traité invitant à l'art subtil du go, with Pierre Lusson and Jacques Roubaud, 1969
L'Augmentation (play), 1970
Les Revenentes, 1972
La Boutique obscure, 1973
Créations, re-créations, récréations, with OULIPO, 1973
La Poche parmentier (play), 1974
Espèces d'espaces (essay), 1974
W; ou, Le Souvenir d'enfance, 1975
Alphabets: cent soixante-seize onzains héterogrammatiques (poems), 1976
Je me souviens, 1978
Les Choses communes, 1978
La vie mode d'emploi, 1978; as *Life: A User's Manual*, 1990
Les Mots croisés, 1979
Un cabinet d'amateur, 1979
La Clôture, et autres poèmes, 1980
Récits d'Ellis Island: histoires d'errance et d'espoir, with Robert Bober, 1980
L'Oeil ébloui, with White Cuchi, 1981
Théâtre I, 1981
Tentative d'épuisement d'un lieu parisien, 1982
Sur les pas fauves de vivre, 1983
Penser-classer, 1985
Ulcérations (poems), 1986
53 jours, 1989
Georges Perec: entretien avec Gabriel Simony, 1989
Voeux, 1989
L'Infra-ordinaire, 1989
Presbytère et prolétaires: le dossier PALF, with Marcel Benabou, 1989

PÉRET, Benjamin, 1899–1959.

Poet.

LIFE

Benjamin Péret was in many ways the most faithful adherent of the surrealist (q.v.) movement in literature, although he exercised considerable intellectual control over verse whose "surrealist" effects were sometimes frivolous or contrived, and often very funny. Just as Breton was the spokesman for the intellectual, experimental side of the movement he led, Péret was its leading spokesman for its social, revolutionary aspects. Like Breton, whose close associate he remained throughout the furious internal dissensions within the group, Péret was as uncompromising a poet as he was a revolutionary. Similarly, Péret broke with Aragon over his acceptance of Stalinism, having never been other than an uneasy communist, unable to commit himself to the repressive form the proletarian revolution had taken in the USSR.

Péret has been criticized for his fidelity to Breton, but the evidence points strongly against his being a mere disciple. His reputation, even more than Breton's, suffered from what amounts to a campaign of disparagement by those committed communist intellectuals in France after World War II who had decided in the end to support Stalinism. However, both writers seem likely still to rise in critical esteem. Péret did in fact join the communist party in 1926, but he disliked what he took to be its betrayal of the proletarian revolution and rallied to the Trotskyist fourth Internationale. He never lacked courage, forthrightness, or brutal intellectual integrity, and he was seldom out of high spirits.

Péret was born at Rezé, near Nantes, on 4 July 1899. In 1917, when he and a friend were caught one night painting a town statue, the authorities offered him the choice of joining the army or going to prison. His mother, whom he never forgave, came down firmly on the side of the army, so Péret was sent to the Balkans. He was repatriated to Lorraine in 1919, and in 1920, an admirer of Mallarmé, went to Paris, where he hoped to join in the capital's literary life. He later claimed to have been influenced by Apollinaire on account of a poem in *Sic* picked up on a station bench, but he quickly came into contact with Breton, Eluard, and Aragon at a reception at the ironically named review *Littérature*, founded in March 1919 by Breton, Aragon, and Philippe Soupault. Péret's earliest published text was long thought to be that which appeared in *Littérature*'s 15th number for July–August 1920, but it now seems likely that a number of early poems were published in 1919 in obscure reviews like *Les Tablettes Littéraires et Artistiques*, of which no complete run appears to have survived. The issues were neither numbered nor dated, and their appearance was probably irregular. Max Jacob, who presented Péret to Picabia, may well have introduced him to *Les Tablettes*. In *Littérature*'s second series, Péret appeared nine times in 12 issues.

Dada (q.v.) was nearly finished, and the first public manifestation in which Péret participated was the notoriously provocative mock "trial" of Barrès on 13 May 1921. At this event, organized by Breton and Aragon, he took the part of the unknown soldier, dressed in a gas mask and marching with a goose step. The "trial" was intended to be a publicly offensive, strident manifestation, but a rag none the less. However, all those who participated in such manifestations were deeply committed to promoting changes in social and political structures which would prevent conflicts like World War I from ever happening again. From the literary point of view the revolutionary forms of imaginative creativity explored by the surrealists must be understood as being rooted in the same horrified bewilderment that produced their commitment to revolutionary programmes, but their motives were also utopian, social, and political.

In 1921 Péret published *Le Passager du transatlantique* with four engravings by Hans Arp. Arp was associated with the German "Blaue Reiter" group, named after Kandinsky's *Le Cavalier bleu* and formed when one of Kandinsky's pictures was rejected by his own "Neue Künstlervereinigung" in 1911 and exhibited in a rival exhibition at Munich's Gallery Thannhauser. He was later associated with Robert Delaunay, then with dada, and finally with the Paris surrealists (see Apollinaire). At this date Péret was at his most amusing, known for his happy, relaxed attitude to life. He was in fact adept at playing the fool, an important part of his serious poetic repertoire. In 1923 he published *Au 125 du boulevard Saint Germain*, with an engraving by Max Ernst, followed in 1924 by *Immortelle maladie*. That same year he also became a director of the new review *La Révolution Surréaliste* with Pierre Naville, continuing his collaboration when, after the second number, he no longer directed it. His preface to the catalogue of the Joan Miró exhibition in June 1925 at the Galerie Pierre was greeted with the same derision as the paintings, to which it was compared. Less prominent in the surrealist movement than Breton, Aragon, Eluard, Soupault, or even Naville, Desnos, and Leiris, Péret was nevertheless always at its centre.

In 1925 he published *Il était une boulangère* and, with Eluard, *152 proverbes mis au goût du jour*. In 1927 he married the singer Elsie Houston and became the brother-in-law of a leading Brazilian Trotskyite, Mario Pedrosa. That year he published *Dormir, dormir dans les pierres*, illustrated by Yves Tanguy, followed the next year by his best-known collection, *Le Grand Jeu*, as well as *…et les seins mouraient…* In 1929 he published *1929* in collaboration with Aragon and for the next two years he was in Brazil, where his political activities got him sent to prison and finally expelled. He returned in the middle of the quarrel between Aragon and Breton, refused to declare surrealism counter-revolutionary, and sought a non-communist, democratic form of left-wing political opposition. He earned his living as a printer's proofreader and was an official in the powerful printers' union, which was later to make sure Péret found work, even when he denounced its Stalinist political alignment. He was particularly assiduous in promoting the political commitment of surrealism to a democratic left wing, and was briefly associated with Georges Bataille in opposing Breton for his attempt to destroy bourgeois culture without rooting out bourgeois political ideologies. In 1934 Péret published *De derrière les fagots* with an etching by Picasso.

After organizing an international surrealist exhibition in the Canaries with Breton in 1935–36, Péret fought in the Spanish Civil War. His letters to Breton tell us of his disillusion with the Stalinist "counter-revolutionary" manoeuvres on the Spanish left, and he returned to Paris in 1937. In 1936 he published *Je ne mange pas de ce pain-là* in an edition of 200 copies, and *Je sublime*, illustrated by Max Ernst. The following year his *Trois cerises et une sardine* appeared, and in 1938 the "divertissement" *Au paradis des fantômes*. Péret then went to Mexico, where he met Trotsky, and when World War II broke out, he was called up. His job was to draw up lists of suspects, so he gleefully took off all the communists, substituting the names of parish priests. Not for the first or last time, his naivety caused him trouble, and in May 1940 he was sent to prison by the Germans for subversive activities. He worked again as a proofreader in Paris, but was constantly denounced, so he took refuge in Marseilles, from where he went to Mexico again in October

1941. He was accompanied by Remedios Varo, whom he would marry in 1943, having been refused a US visa on account of his political activity. He found life difficult in Mexico, writing a little, especially for the Trotskyite press, and giving French lessons. The Mexican Trotskyites had been encouraged by Trotsky before his assassination fundamentally to rethink his whole position—virtually a mandate to rethink anti-totalitarian forms of Marxism—and Péret spent some time assisting in that task. At the end of 1947 a sale was organized in France to pay his fare back to Europe.

During the war Péret had published *Les Malheurs d'un dollar* and *La Parole est à Péret*. In 1945 came *Le Déshonneur des poètes*, an aggressive attack on the subservience of poetry to ideology, as it was evident in the communist poets of the Resistance. Breton's inclination was to keep out of the party political struggle. He was a more profound thinker than Péret, who was always more inclined to aggressive political activity, as the satirical style of *Je ne mange pas de ce pain-là* had shown. The reactions to *Le Déshonneur* were none the less to reverberate for a score of years and may well explain the way in which Péret's contribution to surrealism seems to have been marginalized. It may also show why the distance between him and Breton has come to be presented as one of substance rather than style. He published three more books—*Dernier malheur, dernière chance, Main forte*, and *Feu central*—before returning to Paris, where he again became a proofreader. He was to return to Brazil for six months in 1955 to live with the Amazon Indians. He died of a thrombosis on 18 September 1959.

WORKS

Given the strength of his social feelings, the most remarkable characteristic of Péret's verse is its absolute integrity. Nowhere does he compromise with his poetic expression for social or political reasons, as even Breton was prepared to. If "le poète lutte contre toute oppression (the poet fights against all oppression)," poetry is never a political tool. Its job is "continually to pronounce the sacrilegious and the blasphematory," which means little more than to attack whatever is, or seems to the poet, to be wrong with society's values which "put a tariff on the sun and sea." The poet has to be a revolutionary or he can no longer be a poet. Ironically Péret, as surrealist and revolutionary, adheres to the long-established bourgeois identification of the poet with the figure of the prophet and the priest, the visionary and not the propagandist. More than most western European countries, France has always been aware of the need to nourish the critics of the values enshrined in its own social institutions.

Only after the destruction of unjust and inhuman values can the poet, according to Péret, hope for the mass audience for which collective myths can be created. He himself was of course fascinated by the primitive societies in which the poet-priest did fulfil this role, and where the scale did not make his own naivety about social organization seem out of place. The poetry and magic of primitive societies were for him the flesh and blood of poetry. What surrealism in his own society did for Péret the poet was very largely to open his eyes to the absurdities and marvels of everyday life. He had an acute eye for both, and specialized in the poetization of commonplace objects and in cascades of brilliant, sparkling images, their vivid, sensual impression creating charges of primitive delight in the reader. He wrote without

correcting, collected his poems in limited editions to be illustrated by painter friends, published, and forgot about them. It became a game to quote his own poems back at him and laugh at his inability to identify their author, but a game which points to their freshness and total sincerity. There is very little complicity with the reader, except when Péret is being satirical or simply witty. Mostly the sheer poetic energy simply takes over, resulting in effects which are sometimes merely trivial.

In the early days of surrealism, with the serious practice of automatic writing, Péret was always one of the easiest to put to sleep and to get to externalize his unconscious. He had an uncanny ability to metamorphose himself mentally into almost any material object or animal, which confirms that he had unusually easy access to a store of interior images and experiences, and we know that he required very little in the way of external poetic stimulus. When in exotic places, he preferred to shut out the experiences of the picturesque. This mental peculiarity, which entailed the consignment of what he had written to speedy oblivion, explains the nature of much of his poetry and his engaging delight in exploiting what appeared to be mental acrobatics to produce sometimes hilarious surprise effects depending on devices like unexpected juxtapositions and sudden, illogical transformations. He would use nouns in swarms, avoid adverbs, and disrupt syntax, while retaining an atmosphere of serenity in his poetry:

La vieille valise la chaussette l'endive
se sont donné rendez-vous entre deux brins d'herbe

(The old suitcase, the sock, the chicory / agreed to meet between two blades of grass)

Sometimes the effect depends simply on incantation, or on echoing words or constructions, sometimes on amusing trivialities, as in the poem "26 points à préciser." This gives 26 details about the poet in the form of mathematical expressions, each adding a letter of the alphabet to the last until you get, printed mathematically, an expression containing all 26 letters. If read out in English, it would begin: "The whole of m over n times the g root of de over cb minus a times f, plus kl and o, all over the t root of s times pq plus r…" All 26 letters are used for the date of birth, but only one, at the beginning, for the date of death. Sexual activity requires 20 letters, but it takes 21 to give the length of the poet's hair. One poem is entitled "$x = \infty -\pi$" Then the frivolity unexpectedly develops a cutting edge. The "Mystère de ma naissance" starts:"…he replied to me 19, 22 if you have time to be rich," and ends:

Pour le reste je suis pâle et hypnotique mais occupez-vous de vos pavés cher docteur et laissez à l'eau claire le soin de devenir de l'eau sale

(For the rest I am pale and hypnotic, / but you, my dear doctor, look after your paving slabs, / and leave to fresh water the task of turning into dirty water).

The wit is not the essence of the poetry, but it explains its nature: heaped detail, or untypical object selected in isolation, instead of a more general, less closely focused vision. Péret is different from Dali, but pays the same meticulous attention to the depiction of objects, however distorted, improbable, or out of place. *Le Grand Jeu* became unobtainable as a book and the object of a cult; "I have a hair on my head…there is a fly in my nose…" Unfortunately, the serious assumptions underlying the attention-catching spontaneity can only emerge on reading through a collection. The naive attitude to the magic of the physical world plucked without apparent effort, if in distorted form or shocking association, from the inner store contains a powerful comment on man's relationship with his environment and implies a social comment about values which it is never poetry's business to state. The light-heartedness is not out of place and, indeed, goes some way towards finding the popular register which Péret only ever half attained, but it also conveys a satirical comment which is none the less forceful for not weighing the poetry down.

Péret was also a theoretician of surrealism, not only in his defence of the independence of poetry from political alignment, but also in the important studies of poetry and myth which were the result, or even perhaps the cause, of his Mexican and Amazonian adventures. The clearest expression of his view dates not from the posthumous 1960 anthology of myths, legends, and popular stories of America, but from a text of 1942 sent to the painter E. F. Granell and translated from Spanish. Poetry firstly contained in symbolic form all human knowledge expressed as myth in defined social and cultural conditions. The collective poetry expressed in myth gives way to individual poetry still, however, based on myth. The first rejection of the collective and mythical origin of poetry was what we call romanticism (q.v.), which discovered the inner universe of man, and from romanticism Baudelaire, Lautréamont, Rimbaud, and Jarry led the way to surrealism, now in search of a new myth.

Péret's hasty history of human culture may be vulnerable and his aesthetic may simply be a rationalization of what his colleagues and he were being impelled to do for some other reason, but his views on the relationship between the primitive and the modern may yet prove to have been an early effort to restore a relationship increasingly sought by the more visionary figures of modern literature.

PUBLICATIONS

Collections

Oeuvres complètes, 5 vols., 1969–89

Verse

Le Passager du transatlantique, with engravings by Arp, 1921
Immortelle maladie, 1924
152 proverbes mis au goût du jour, with Eluard 1925
Dormir, dormir dans les pierres, with illustrations by Tanguy, 1927
Le Grand Jeu, 1928
1929, with Aragon, 1929
De derrière les fagots, with an etching by Picasso, 1934
Je ne mange pas de ce pain-là, 1936
Je sublime, with illustrations by Ernst, 1936
Trois cerises et une sardine, 1937
Au paradis des fantômes, 1938
Les Malheurs d'un dollar, 1942
Dernier malheur, dernière chance, 1946

Feu central, 1947
Mort aux vaches et au champ d'honneur, 1953
Les Rouilles encagées, 1954

Other

Au 125 du boulevard Saint-Germain, 1923
Il était une boulangère, 1925
…et les seins mouraient…, 1927
La Parole est à Péret, 1943
Le Déshonneur des poètes, 1945
Le Manifeste des exegètes (as Perlata), 1946
Main forte, 1946
La Brebis galante, 1949
Air mexicain, 1952
Toyen, 1953
Les Rouilles encagées (as Satyremont), 1954
Livre de Chilam Balam de Chumayel, 1955
Anthologie de l'amour sublime, 1956
Le Gigot, sa vie et son oeuvre, 1957
Anthologie des mythes, légendes et contes populaires d'Amérique, 1960

Biographical and critical studies

Bédouin, Jean-Louis, *Benjamin Péret*, 1961
Courtot, Claude, *Introduction à la lecture de Benjamin Péret*, 1965
Goutier, Jean-Michel, *Benjamin Péret*, 1982

———

PHENOMENOLOGY

See also Merleau-Ponty, Sartre, existentialism, and structuralism.

Phenomenology as a philosophical system or method is important in France outside the context of technical philosophical discussion chiefly for its exploitation by Sartre and Merleau-Ponty, its use in the elaboration of Sartre's existentialist (q.v.) ontology, and as a point of reference in the great structuralist (q.v.) debate which split Sartre from Lévi-Strauss during the 1950s.

The word was first used in the *Neues Organon* (1764) of the German mathematician and philosopher J.H. Lambert (1728–1777), where it referred to possibly misleading appearance as distinct from essence, "Schein" rather than "Sein." The word's first memorable occurrence is in the title of Hegel's *Die Phänomenologie des Geistes: Wissenschaft der Erfahrung des Bewußtseins* (The Phenomenology of Mind: The Science of the Experience of Consciousness) of 1807. Hegel wanted to show that the mind can develop itself so as to reach absolute knowledge, and needed to explain how this would happen at a particular moment. Part of absolute knowledge, and the justification for regarding it as such, would have to be knowledge of the process by which absolute knowledge was to be attained.

prix de la Nouvelle. *La Motocyclette* is based on a crude erotic fantasy in which a woman rides a fast motorbike which becomes a primeval force, her "black bull," and contains scenes of sadistic sexual excess. *Porte dévergondée* consists of four contes whose sexual content derives from a professed desire to shock, and *La Marge*, which scales up the now usual themes, is set in the realistically described red-light district of Barcelona. It was awarded the Prix Goncourt.

Pieyre de Mandiargues still travelled widely, spending much time in Italy, but also visiting other European countries, Mexico for six months in 1958, and Cuba for a writers' congress in 1968 in support of Fidel Castro. The author strongly sympathized with the communist parties in France and Italy for their "struggle against social injustice," and also regarded as "morally exemplary" the regimes of Mao in China, Boumedienne in Algeria, and Castro in Cuba. The US he pronounced "the champion of criminality in the world today." In the context of literary biography these views are important not simply for what they may contain of truth or falsehood, but because they argue an ability to suppress evidence in order to insulate prejudice from the corrosion of fact. They also point to what may be regarded as a flight from creative imagination into personal fantasy which can only result in the trivialization of the literary product. It is not surprising that Pieyre de Mandiargues's political sympathies in World War II embraced Italian fascism and turned anti-communist again in the 1970s. It is also not irrelevant that he was proud of never having voted. He signed the "Manifeste des 121" against French Algerian policy as a moral rather than political protest, and his attitude always assumed that the moral and political orders could be kept insulated from one another. He refused the Légion d'Honneur and never sought election to the Académie Française.

He continued to publish fiction throughout the 1970s and early 1980s. *Mascarets* of 1971 was a collection of eight heavily erotic short stories, which include episodes of bestiality, oral sex, and a suggestion of necrophilia. The title alludes to the pattern of river currents flowing into the sea as the tide changes, but is also French slang for ejaculation. The six pieces of *Sous la lame* that followed in 1976 come up to the expectations of sadism, lust, and blood conveyed by the title. One is dedicated to the shades of Mishima, whose cruelty and sadism fascinated Pieyre de Mandiargues and whose *Madame de Sade* he translated into French. In 1979 he reissued under his own name the series of sadistic incidents inspired by Sade which had led to suffering, torture, and death, sometimes pleasurably undergone for the enjoyment of the two main characters. This book, *L'Anglais décrit dans le château fermé*, was originally published under the pseudonym of Paul Morion in 1953.

Pieyre de Mandiargues continued to publish poetry, winning the Grand Prix de la Poésie for *L'Ivre Oeil* in 1978. Only his first play, *Isabella Morra* of 1973, was performed. Jean-Louis Barrault played the lead, but it was not a success. Pieyre de Mandiargues also established a reputation as a critic of avant-garde painting and published a great deal of literary criticism.

Works

The literary status of Pieyre de Mandiargues's work must depend squarely on its author's ability to create myths which reveal or explore important truths about the human mind. The critical journalism is only of ephemeral and marginal interest, even when it concerns his avant-garde contemporaries among the painters; and the lyricism of his major poetic collections, *Astyanax*, *L'Age de craie*, and *Le Point où j'en suis*, is nostalgic and self-consciously literary:

C'est le cri des mouettes et des hirondelles de mer devant les hautes falaises de craie, percées de nids, qui ont muré les meilleurs jours de mon enfance

(It is the cry of the gulls and the sea swallows in front of the high chalk cliffs pierced with nests which enclosed the best days of my childhood.)

There are clearly elements of myth in the story of Rebecca travelling to her lover on her motorbike in *La Motocyclette*, of Sigismond Pons wandering round Barcelona in *La Marge*, and of Vanina meeting her lover in the dark wood of *Le Lis de mer*, although it may still be asked how powerful they are, or whether Pieyre de Mandiargues poeticizes such high points sufficiently to endow them with some deep significance. But there are also the morbid fantasies—the white girl raped by the black shepherd amid milling sheep in a hut smelling of animal excrement in "Le sang de l'agneau" from *Le Musée noir*, the bound woman whipped with roses and brutally raped in *La Motocyclette*, the girl bound, beaten, and killed by her brothers in *Isabella Morra*, and a great deal that is even more extreme. The sadism in *L'Anglais décrit dans le château fermé* may be said to explore potential extremes of human reaction to sexually stimulating experiences, but, on a literary register, it rises no higher than the indulgence or exorcism of fantasy. It is not a work of imagination and suggests nothing about the workings of the human personality.

It is undoubtedly true that Pieyre de Mandiargues is a writer of wide erudition and cultivated writing skills. He creatively examines the possibility of experiencing the marvellous in daily life, and his fiction is exceedingly well crafted. It is not, however, on a par with Maupassant's, whose humanity it also lacks, and it is centuries too late to have the imaginative vigour of Sade, Poe, or even Nerval, dealing with similar sexual and dream horror fantasies. Among the contemporaries with whom he is often compared, Pieyre de Mandiargues lacks the intelligence of Breton, the serious imaginative purpose of his surrealist contemporaries, the moral integrity of Camus, and the political consciousness of Sartre. It is arguable that even Cocteau was a more fundamentally serious, if less technically skilled, writer. What makes Pieyre de Mandiargues historically interesting is his attempt to combine the purely fantasy element of surrealism with a classically polished literary style rather than his attempt to present as unsullying, because religiously ritualized, the horrific enactment of violent erotic fantasies.

Le Lis de mer moves briskly in a sensuous Mediterranean atmosphere. Vanina and her friend Juliette are on holiday in Sardinia. On the beach after a swim Vanina passes a local youth who has been watching her. She is attracted to him and goes to meet him. Although still a virgin, she has a ready sexual imagination and is aware of taking part in some initiatory ritual she cannot control. She makes the youth come to her room, but he is overawed by the ritualism of the scene, Vanina naked on the bed, carefully made up, with candles at her side and lilies at her feet. On another occasion she insists that he should come to a clearing in the woods perfumed by flowers, seize her, bind her hands, and reverently deflower her. To increase the sense of quasi-religious sacrificial offering, Vanina undertakes what is virtually a fast, washes herself in preparation, dresses as simply as she can, ritually cleanses her feet in a stream, and surrenders to the joy of being weak, seized, bound, and thrown to the ground, envying the Polynesian girls who swim out to sailors, give themselves to them, and find pleasure in being thrown back into the sea afterwards.

The question of whether or not Pieyre de Mandiargues succeeds in creating myth by the religious ritualization of generally cruel sexual encounters, pleasurably undergone by women who willingly submit to brutal male virility, is even more acutely raised by *La Motocyclette*. The heroine, born Rebecca Res and married to a nice, prosaic lycée teacher called Nul, is awakened by a dream and leaves her husband sleeping early one morning in a French border town. She sets out on her motorbike to meet her athletic, skilled lover, Daniel, who lives in Germany. The places she passes through evoke memories of past journeys, as if Pieyre de Mandiargues were trying to achieve, with some originality, the sort of complicated confusion of chronological planes which had been more or less commonplace since Proust.

We are given detailed accounts of how the motorbike works and of the route taken. Rebecca remembers the occasion, deliberately evoking associations with the scourging of Jesus and his crowning with thorns, when, having gained access to a private room at the heart of a Turkish bath, she had been tied naked to a pipe and whipped with rose thorns before her bleeding body was untied and seized with a hitherto unknown brutality. Rebecca's body is referred to as a cross, and on another occasion her arms are stretched out by Daniel so that her body assumes the shape of a cross against a tree trunk. Rebecca lies as if dead and Daniel "helped the dead girl to rise up," a phrase intended to put the reader in mind of the gospel narratives about Jesus's resurrection.

Erotic stimulation derived from contemplative obsession with the sufferings of Jesus is a widely known symptom of a psychological abnormality found more often in women than in men. Such thoughts have often been regarded as blasphemous, but the desacralization of Christ's Passion by its transposition into ritualized erotic fantasy has seldom on a serious literary register been taken further than it is here. On other occasions, too, Rebecca is compared to a sacrificial victim, while she often compares Daniel to a priestly figure, a preacher or a saint. He arrives in the room at the Turkish bath dressed in a white robe. The religious associations are almost over-emphatic, intended no doubt to help preserve the sense of purity which Pieyre de Mandiargues strives to keep alive in Vanina, Rebecca, and all the others.

The characters come to regard themselves as dissociated from the fantasies they ceremonially act out. Their purity is depicted as deriving from their merely ceremonial role. Both Vanina and Rebecca behave in ways they do not themselves understand. Each has a fundamentally erotic relationship with nature and its primeval manifestations, like sun, sand, sea, light, and darkness, and Rebecca's change of name on marriage even indicates her move from being something, "Res," to being a non-thing, "Nul." The difficulty in Pieyre de Mandiargues's fiction lies in its lack of psychological analysis. There is no serious exploration of whether purity of mind could coexist with the infliction or endurance of such cruelty in pursuit of

sexual gratification, because the participants are depicted as ritualized automata participating in an elaborate pre-ordained ceremonial.

The crux of the problem is to be found in the novel that won the Prix Goncourt, *La Marge*. Sigismond Pons, replacing his sick cousin for a few days, goes to Barcelona on a business trip. While there he receives a letter from his old governess telling him that his wife, Sergine, has committed suicide. Unable to read the rest of the letter or to absorb this shocking news, he puts it away, wanders round the Barcelona bars, and picks up a prostitute. Three days later he reads the rest of the letter, learns that his son has accidently drowned, goes in his car to the outskirts of the city, and shoots himself. Clearly the lost three days were an effort to shut out the information about his wife's suicide which he could not take in. Is it plausible that a human mind can totally refuse to acknowledge the reception of information, but none the less require three days' debauchery before being forced to allow it access to consciousness?

Pieyre de Mandiargues does not bother with the plausibility but, unlike the surrealists, writes in such a way that his refusal to concern himself with psychology causes all real power to drain away from his work. The symbols are too crudely sexual and not manipulated with sufficient skill to throw light on the meaning or meaninglessness of Sigismond's reactions to the letter. Pieyre de Mandiargues merely depicts as a fiction one man's experience of time, sex, and death, replacing psychological analysis with a system of symbolic references—to the Columbus monument dominating Barcelona, which, according to *Le Désordre de la mémoire*, appears to Sigismond as a huge phallus; to what he takes to be the techniques of Robbe-Grillet and Butor; and to minutely realistic descriptions of streets, bars, prostitutes, brothels, and Barcelona's low life. Pieyre de Mandiargues is intensely concerned in his fiction not only with what are generally regarded as sexual aberrations, but also with man's relationship with nature and its primeval forces. Whether or not this relationship and its laws is examined in such a way as to throw meaningful light on human experience is a question that does not appear to have been answered.

PUBLICATIONS

Fiction

Le Musée noir, 1946
L'Etudiante, 1946
Soleil des loups, 1951
Marbre, 1953
L'Anglais décrit dans le château fermé (as Paul Morion), 1953; revised edition (as André Pieyre de Mandiargues), 1979
Le Lis de mer, 1956; as *The Girl Beneath the Lion*, 1958
Feu de braise, 1959; as *Blaze of Embers*, 1971
Sabine, 1963
La Motocyclette, 1963; as *The Motorcycle*, 1965; as *The Girl on the Motorcycle*, 1966
Porte dévergondée, 1965
La Marge, 1967; as *The Margin*, 1969
Le Marronnier, 1968
La Nuit de mil neuf cent quatorze: ou, Le Style liberty, 1970
Mascarets, 1971
Sous la lame, 1976

Crachefeu, 1980
Des cobras à Paris, 1982
Le Deuil des roses, 1983

Plays

Isabella Morra (produced 1973), 1973
La Nuit séculaire, 1979
Arsène et Cléopâtre, 1981

Verse

Dans les années sordides, 1943
Hedera; ou, La Persistance de l'amour pendant une rêverie,
    1945
Astyanax, 1956
Cartolines et dédicaces, 1960
L'Age de craie, suivi de Hedera 1960
La Nuit d'amour, 1962
*Le Point où j'en suis, suivi de Dalila exaltée et de La Nuit
    d'amour*, 1964
Jacinthes, 1967; as *Hyacinthes*, 1967
Ruisseau des solitudes, suivi de Jacinthes et de Chapeaugaga,
    1968
Croiseur noir, 1972
Parapapilloneries, 1976
*L'Ivre Oeil, suivi de Croiseur noir et de Passage de l'Egypti-
    enne*, 1979

Other

Les Incongruités monumentales, 1946
Les Sept périls spectraux, 1950
Les Masques de Léonor Fini, 1951
Les Monstres de Bomarzo, 1958
Le Cadran lunaire, 1958
Le Belvédère, 1958; *Deuxième Belvédère*, 1962; *Troisième
    Belvédère*, 1971
Sugaï, 1960
Beylamour, 1965
Les Corps illuminés, 1965
Larmes de généraux, 1965
Critiquettes, 1967
Le Lièvre de la lune, 1970
Eros solaire, 1970
Bona: l'amour et la peinture, 1971
Terre érotique, 1974
Chagall, 1975
Le Désordre de la mémoire: entretiens avec Francine Mallet,
    1975
Arcimboldo le merveilleux, 1977; as *Arcimboldo the Marvelous*,
    1978
Le Trésor cruel de Hans Bellmer, 1979
Un Saturne gai, 1982
Sept jardins fantastiques, 1983

Translations

Tommaso Landolfi, *La Femme de Gogol*, 1969
Octavio Paz, *La Fille de Rappuccini*,1972
W. B. Yeats, *Le Vent parmi les roseaux*, 1972

F. de Pisis, *Le Petit Bassaride*, 1972
F. de Pisis, *Onze plus un*, 1975
Mishima Yukio, *Madame de Sade*, 1976

Critical studies

"Pieyre de Mandiargues issue," *Cahiers Renaud-Barrault 86*,
    1974
Stétié, Salah, *Pieyre de Mandiargues*, 1978
Bond, David J., *The Fiction of Pieyre de Mandiargues*, 1982

————

PINGET, Robert, 1919–

Novelist and dramatist.

LIFE

Pinget was born in Geneva, studied and practised law there,
moving in 1946 to Paris, where he studied painting at the Ecole
des Beaux-Arts. For some years he worked as a painter, exhibited, and was well regarded by the critics. He also tried his hand
at journalism and interior decoration, visiting Yugoslavia and
Israel. He taught at a secondary school near London, where he
learnt English. Since 1951 he has lived as a freelance writer in
Paris, receiving a Ford Foundation grant (1960), the Prix de Critique (1963), and the Prix Fémina (1965). He has been included
among the practitioners of the "nouveau roman," grouped
together as a school by the review *Esprit* in July-August 1958.
In fact he is far more ruthlessly destructive of the conventions
and presuppositions of the popular novel, and more esoteric in
the demands he makes on his readers, than any of those with
whom he has been associated. His "novels" are little more than
experiments in technique. They dispose of plot, progression, and
characterization, and are of interest to few who do not share
Pinget's intellectual curiosity about the possibility of radically
eliminating all established literary conventions.

Pinget sent his first collection of stories, *Entre Fantoine et
Agapa*, to a provincial publisher and agreed to finance the publication costs. The book was accepted on these grounds and duly
published in 1951. Camus read the second book for Gallimard
and was enthusiastic (though it was ultimately taken on by Laf-
font), but Pinget had difficulty in finding a publisher for his third
book. It was finally accepted, on the recommendation of Robbe-
Grillet, by Gallimard. Les Editions de Minuit, with whom
Pinget has subsequently stayed, later reissued revised versions
of all three. For some time Pinget was more popular in the UK
than in France, where the elaborately tedious atmosphere of a
practical joke held back public esteem for his work. His popularity has subsequently spread to Germany and the US. Between
them his novels have been translated into at least 11 languages.

WORKS

Pinget's characters have been said "perpetually and aimlessly to
wander in the labyrinth of their identity crisis." "His dislocated

narrative forms" and "feathery moonstruck verbal fantasies" play games with language, so that "both content and form express the kaleidoscopic mental world of the times." The reader is constantly teased as assertions in the text are contradicted, questioned, or changed. Pinget trades on the reader's expectations, only to frustrate them, creating tensions which he refuses to resolve, but his work as a clever technician does succeed in making exactly the demands on the reader which he wants, and thereby elicits the desired intellectual reaction.

His work has been divided into three stages. The first, from *Entre Fantoine et Agapa* to *Le Renard et la boussole*, Pinget's third book, concentrates on simple verbal acrobatics. During the second period, from *Graal Flibuste* of 1956 to *Quelqu'un* of 1965, Pinget parodies the conventions of different forms of popular fiction. Finally, from *Le Libéra* of 1968 at least as far as *Cette voix* of 1975, Pinget experiments with clichés, themes, and words while grotesquely parodying the cyclical novel of country life in all its aspects, from the role of the narrator to the words, symbols, and phrases used to describe non-events in non- chronological order. The text is intended to work by setting up a series of associative reverberations through the use of repeated phrases. It is still open to question whether the calculated risk of frustrating the reader's narrative expectations with displays of verbal acrobatics, irrelevant anecdote, and the skilful dangling before him of a plot which never emerges actually works, but a great deal of intelligent thought and humour has been put into the experiment. Most critics would agree that its success has yet to be determined.

PUBLICATIONS

Fiction

Entre Fantoine et Agapa (stories), 1951; as *Between Fantoine and Agapa*, 1982
Mahu; ou, Le Matériau, 1952; as *Mahu; or, The Material*, 1966
Le Renard et la boussole, 1953
Graal Flibuste, 1956; revised edition, 1966
Baga, 1958; as *Baga* (in English), 1967
Le Fiston, 1959; as *No Answer*, 1961; as *Monsieur Levert* (in English), 1961
Clope au dossier, 1961
L'Inquisitoire, 1962; as *The Inquisitory*, 1966
Quelqu'un, 1965; as *Someone*, 1984
Le Libéra, 1968; as *The Libera Me Domine*, 1972
Passacaille, 1969; as *Recurrent Melody*, 1975; as *Passacaglia*, 1978
Fable, 1971; as *Fable* (in English), 1980
Cette voix, 1975; as *That Voice*, 1982
L'Apocryphe, 1980
Monsieur Songe, 1982

Plays

Lettre morte, from his novel *Le Fiston* (produced, 1960), 1959; as *Dead Letter* (produced, 1961), in *Plays 1*, 1963
La Manivelle/The Old Tune (radio play; bilingual edition), 1960; *The Old Tune* (produced, 1964), in *Plays 1*, 1963
Ici ou ailleurs, suivi de Architruc et de L'Hypothèse, 1961
Ici ou ailleurs, from his novel *Clope au dossier*, in *Ici ou ailleurs*

(collection), 1961; as *Clope* (produced, 1954), in *Plays 1*, 1963
Architruc, in *Ici ou ailleurs* (collection), 1961; as *Architruc* (produced, 1967), in *Plays 2*, 1967
L'Hypothèse, in *Ici ou ailleurs* (collection), 1961; as *The Hypothesis* (produced, 1967), in *Plays 2*, 1967
Plays 1, 1963; as *Three Plays*, 1966
Autour de Mortin (radio play), 1965; as *About Mortin*, in *Plays 2*, 1967
Plays 2, 1967; as *Three Plays*, 1966
Identité, suivi de Abel et Bela, 1971
Paralchimie, suivi de Architruc, L'Hypothèse, Nuit, 1973
Lubie (radio play), in *Présence Francophone 22*, spring 1981

Critical study

Henkels, Robert M., Jr, *Pinget: The Novel as Quest*, 1979

————

PIXÉRÉCOURT, René (Charles Guilbert) de, 1773–1844.

Dramatist.

LIFE

René Pixérécourt, "the king of the boulevards," was born in Nancy on 22 January 1733 into a family of Lorraine aristocrats, who spelt their name with only one accent. Subsequent usage has established the second one. When the Revolution broke out, Pixérécourt was studying law and in 1791 had to escape to Koblenz with his father. He returned secretly to Paris, married, had a child, and went to ground for 18 months. During this time he painted fans for a living and started to write seriously for the theatre. His life was in danger during the Terror, but he was saved by Lazare Carnot (1753–1823) and employed at the war office. Some of his early plays had been accepted but not yet staged when, in 1797, his 17th, the one-act comedy *Les Petits Auvergnats*, was produced at the Théâtre Ambigu-Comique. The following year *Victor; ou, L'Enfant de la forêt* was a triumph at the Théâtre Favart. Based on a true story, *Victor* was the writer's first melodrama and inaugurated the success of that genre in the French theatre. For the rest of his life Pixérécourt's melodramas dominated the boulevard theatres. On their appearance they were immediately translated into English, German, and Dutch.

Pixérécourt's creative energy was enormous. Only after 1830 did he use collaborators to help him with his apparently endless stream of melodramas, all written to much the same formulas, interspersed with vaudevilles, comic operas, and pantomimes. No one knows the exact number of stage entertainments he produced, but estimates have been as high as 120 for melodramas alone, with an average of three or four new productions a year. His most successful single play was *Coelina; ou, L'Enfant du mystère* of 1800, but his most prolific year was 1801, when he had nine productions in Paris. His subjects were often taken from ancient and modern history, and also from novels. The literacy rate did not begin its sharp upward climb until 1825, so the boulevard theatres filled a role for a still sub-literate public that was subsequently played by the less imaginatively demanding forms of serialized fiction during the era of cheap newspapers. Pixérécourt could boast of filling a real social need when he said: "J'écris pour ceux qui ne savent pas lire (I write for those who can't read)." There are estimated to have been some 30,000 performances of his stage pieces during his lifetime, and Pixérécourt acknowledged that they brought him an annual 25,000 francs.

Unfortunately, he lost most of it when the Gaîté theatre burnt down in 1835. He had been a director from 1825 and his best plays had been staged there, although he was also a director of the Opéra-Comique. In addition, to provide himself with a comfortable retirement, he also kept his civil service job, now as Directeur des Domaines, so he was hardly destitute. In 1835, after the fire, he retired to Nancy, having already been seriously ill. In spite of the mixture of violence and tenderness in his melodramas, Pixérécourt's personal taste was almost classical. He formed a large library and wept when it was dispersed. He led an oddly unhappy life, writing quickly, but spending much time on the scenery and production of his melodramas. His death was lingering and painful.

WORKS

The similarities between Pixérécourt's melodramas and high romantic (q.v.) drama may be explained by the fact that different social layers of the same society had much the same imaginative needs. If there was a difference in refinement of sensibility, there was much less difference in the general need to come to terms with the values which emerged throughout French society in the wake of the Revolution, the Napoleonic wars, and the restoration. Pixérécourt was in fact much admired by Gautier and Hugo, who plundered his plots and elevated his material. Hugo and Dumas were doing in the theatre at a sophisticated cultural level exactly what Pixérécourt was doing for an unlettered public. Both Pixérécourt and Hugo needed to replace the old codes and conventions with new social and imaginative norms that were very similar. The differences in the form of their productions can be accounted for chiefly by society's division into those who could read and might attend the established theatres, and those who could not and were more likely to look for entertainment and imaginative satisfaction on the boulevards.

It was Pixérécourt, with his melodrama, who came earlier and was more conservative; "J'ai respecté dans les drames les trois unités autant qu'il m'a été possible (As far as possible I have respected the three unities in my plays)." Later on, he found the more daring norms of romantic drama morally dangerous as well as aesthetically shocking: "Depuis dix ans, on a donc produit un très grand nombre de pièces romantiques, c'est-à-dire mauvaises, dangereuses, immorales, dépourvues d'intérêt (For the past 10 years people have been producing a large number of romantic plays, that is to say, plays that are bad, dangerous, immoral, and without interest [Dernières réflexions sur le mélodrame])." None the less, he exploited the stage's full potential for spectacle rather than mere declamation. His scripts contained detailed descriptions of scenery and often called for special effects to depict storms, floods, and volcanic eruptions, for which Pixérécourt himself invented the necessary machinery. Battle scenes were not narrated afterwards, but took place on stage.

He took his new genre very seriously indeed and was quite as conscious of its social and imaginative functions as of its entertainment value:

Le mélodrame…quand la saine morale est sa boussole, surtout quand rien ne s'y passe qui ne soit à la portée de l'intelligence de la classe ouvrière et manufacturière, ne peut qu'être utile, politique même, et contribuer de plus à maintenir cette même classe dans le bon chemin des qualités morales, si nécessaires au repos de chaque famille et de la société entière.

(When a healthy morality is melodrama's compass, especially when nothing happens in it beyond the grasp of the intelligence of the working and manufacturing classes, it can only be useful and, indeed, politically expedient, contributing further to keeping that same class on the right road towards those moral qualities which are so necessary to the wellbeing of every family and of society as a whole.)

Pixérécourt wrote two treatises on melodrama in 1832 and 1843. Melodramas had to conform to a fixed pattern, usually depending on a cruelly treated beautiful young heroine rescued from her plight by a dashing hero, usually only after many and dangerous adventures, and preferably only in the nick of time. There had to be stereotyped characters—an innocent heroine, a cowardly villain (later the wicked pantomime uncle to be hissed at), a wise "fool" in the Shakespearean sense, and a courageous hero. There had to be suspense, even though everyone knew that the heroine would be saved and that the hero would survive the array of knives, poisons, and treachery which lay in wait for him. There had to be a distribution of just deserts, violent and highly coloured action, changes of fortune, and complex plots. The English versions lay behind the Penny Plain and Twopence Coloured drawings of the Toy Theatre.

Coelina; ou, L'Enfant du mystère was one of Pixérécourt's early and enduring successes and provides an example of his black and white portrayal of morality. It is set in Savoy, largely in the house where the "good" characters live: the elderly M. Dufour, his son Stephany, his niece Coelina, his servants Tienette and Faribole, and the mysterious Francisque, whom Dufour once rescued from the brink of death and restored to health. The forces of evil are represented by Dufour's brother-in-law Truguelin and his son Germain. Truguelin wants Germain to marry Coelina because she has a large dowry. When they go to the house to ask for Coelina's hand, Truguelin recognizes Francisque from the past and he and Germain try to kill him. Fortunately, Coelina has overheard them plotting and prevents the murder. Truguelin is ordered out of the house, but tells Dufour that Coelina is not really his niece but Francisque's daughter. The mystery is clarified by Dufour's doctor: Coelina's mother was secretly married to Francisque but Truguelin forced her to marry Dufour's brother. Truguelin had then tried to murder Francisque, at which point he was saved by Dufour. Everyone gets their just deserts: Truguelin is punished, and Coelina and Stephany marry, having been in love with each other all along.

PUBLICATIONS

Collections

Bibliothèque de M. Guilbert de Pixérécourt, 1838
Théâtre choisi de Guilbert de Pixérécourt, 4 vols., 1841–43

Plays

Sélico, 1793
Claudine, 1793
Le Jacobin en mission, 1794
Les Petits Auvergnats, 1797
La Forêt de Sicilie, 1798
Victor; ou, L'Enfant de la forêt, 1798
Le Château des Apennins; ou, Les Mystères d'Udolphe, 1799
Le Petit Page; ou, La Prison d'état, 1800
Rosa; ou, L'Hermitage du torrent, 1800
Coelina; ou, L'Enfant du mystère, 1800; as *Caelina; or , A Tale of Mystery*, 1802
La Soirée des Champs-Elysées, 1800
Zozo; ou, Le Mal-avisé, 1800
L'Homme à trois visages; ou, Le Proscrit, 1801; adapted as *The Venetian Outlaw, His Country's Friend*, 1805
Flaminius à Corinthe (opera in one act), with L.T. Lambert, 1801
La Peau de l'ours, with L.T. Lambert, 1802
Le Pèlerin blanc, 1802; adapted as *The Wandering Boys; or, The Castle of Olival*, 1850
Pizarre; ou, La Conquête du Pérou, 1802
La Femme à deux maris, 1802; as *The Wife of Two Husbands*, 1803; as *The Wife with Two Husbands*, 1803
Raymond de Toulouse; ou, Le Retour de la Terre-Sainte, 1802
Les Deux valets, 1803
Les Mines de Pologne, 1803
Téléki; ou, Le Siège de Montgatz, 1804
Les Maures d'Espagne; ou, Le Pouvoir de l'enfance, 1804
Avis aux femmes; ou, Le Mari en colère, 1804
Robinson Crusoé, 1805
La Forteresse du Danube, 1805
Le Solitaire de la Roche-Noire, 1806
Koulouf; ou, Les Chinois, 1807
L'Ange tutélaire; ou, Le Démon femelle, 1808
La Citerne, 1809
La Rose blanche et la rose rouge, 1809
Marguerite d'Anjou, 1810
Les Trois moulins, with J.B. Dubois, 1810
Les Ruines de Babylone, 1810
Le Berceau: divertissement en un acte, à l'occasion de la naissance du Roi de Rome, 1811
Le Précipice; ou, Les Froges de Norwège, 1811
Le Fanal de Messine, 1812
Le Petit Carillonneur; ou, La Tour ténébreuse, 1812
Charles le Téméraire; ou, Le Siège de Nancy, 1814
Le Chien de Montargis; ou, La Forêt de Bondy, 1814; as *The Forest of Bondy; or, The Dog of Montargis*, 1820
L'Ennemi des modes; ou, La Maison de Choisy, 1814
Christophe Colombe; ou, La Découverte du Nouveau Monde, 1815
La Chapelle des bois; ou, Le Témoin invisible, 1818
La Fille de l'exilé, 1819
Le Belvédère; ou, La Vallée de l'Etna, 1819
Les Chefs Ecossais, 1819
Bouton de Rose; ou, Le Pêcheur de Bassora, 1819
Valentin; ou, La Séduction, 1821
Le Mont sauvage; ou, Le Solitaire, 1821
Ali-Baba; ou, Les Quarante voleurs, 1822
Le Château de Loch-Leven, 1822

Le Pavillon des fleurs; ou, Les Pêcheurs de Grenade, 1822
La Place du palais, 1824
La Peste de Marseille, 1828
La Tête de mort; ou, Les Ruines de Pompeia, 1828
Polter; ou, Le Bourreau d'Amsterdam, with V.H.J.B. Ducange, 1828
L'Aigle des Pyrénées, with Mélesville (Anne Honoré Joseph Duveyrier), 1829
Ondine; ou, La Nymphe des eaux, 1830
Le Petit Homme rouge, with Brazier and Carmouche, 1832
L'Abbaye aux bois; ou, La Femme de chambre, with B.L.H. Martin, 1832
L'Allée des Veuves; ou, La Justice en 1773, 1833
Les Quatre éléments, with Brazier and Durmersan, 1833
Valentine; ou, Le Château et la Ferme, with Francis Cornu, 1834
Latude; ou, Trente-cinq ans de captivité, with A.A. Bourgeois, 1834

Other

Observations sur les théâtres et la Révolution, 1795
Vie de Dalayrac…contenant la liste complète des ouvrages de ce compositeur célèbre, 1810
Guerre au mélodrame, 1818
Le Mélodrame, 1832
Dernières réflexions sur le mélodrame, 1843

———

PONGE, Francis (-Jean-Gaston-Alfred), 1899–1988.

Poet and essayist.

LIFE

Francis Ponge was born at Montpellier of middle-class Protestant parents on 27 March 1899. His childhood was comfortable. He loved, respected, and admired his parents, and as a small boy attended the local Protestant school on the days when the state school was closed. That experience left him with a familiarity with the Bible and a moral awareness which he retained even when, in later years, he developed into an Epicurean and a materialist. The family was liberal in outlook and Ponge inherited from them, as well as from his primary school Protestantism, a streak of individualism, of pertinacity verging on obstinacy, which was later to characterize his life, as well as his devotion to poetry.

In 1909 Ponge's father was appointed manager of his bank's branch at Caen, and the family moved to Normandy, although Ponge later attributed to his Provençal childhood something of his sense of stable order in a world of surface flux. For the next seven years he attended the Lycée Malherbe at Caen, where he distinguished himself with an essay on the art of thinking for oneself, learnt Latin, and became aware of the development of the French language. The family spent their holidays abroad, and after erratic beginnings Ponge developed an excellent academic record, culminating in the baccalauréat in 1916. In that year he was sent to the Lycée Louis-le-Grand in Paris to prepare for university, and from 1917 he studied philosophy at the Sorbonne and law at the Ecole de Droit. He was already beginning to write poetry and to find both modern literature, the symbolists (q.v.) and the early Gide, and modern philosophy, through the works of Bergson and Renouvier, flabby and wordy in comparison with the classical texts on which he had been trained at school.

Ponge found Paris repellently cynical and turned for intellectual support to Schopenhauer, Locke, and Spinoza, although he enjoyed Lalande's logic classes. World War I quickly made him aware of social and political problems, and he enthusiastically supported the Bolsheviks in the October Revolution, although his urge to see revolution abroad did not prevent ardent patriotism at home. Then, in 1918, Ponge failed the oral component of his degree examination, and in 1919 the oral component of his examination for entry into the Ecole Normale Supérieure. He was petrified by the need to expound his material orally, and it is to this inhibition that he later attributed his persistence with the written word. Much of his later preoccupation with language shows how sharply conscious he remained of the difference between written and oral forms of communication. He spent the period from April 1918 until September 1919 in the army, where he was horrified by the coarseness, stupidity, and injustice of everything that went on, especially the lying, intimidation, and standardization. He reacted strongly against military intolerance of individualism.

In 1919 Ponge left home, joined the socialist party, went to live on the Left Bank in Paris, and started to write the predominantly satirical short texts which were to constitute *Douze petits écrits* of 1926. Feeling restless, after a few months he left his job as an assistant editor with Gallimard. He wanted to write, but found himself out of sympathy with avant-garde as well as more established trends, sensing a displeasing self-importance and self-indulgence even in those about to become surrealists (q.v.). Ponge himself started writing short pieces investigating problems of language, some of which were to appear much later in *Proêmes*, a title confected out of "Prose" and "Poème" and designed to indicate the recourse to poetic devices such as rhythm and assonance in pieces about things, like morality and aesthetics, more usually discussed in discursive prose.

In 1923 Ponge was deeply distressed by the death of his father and went to live with his mother. A small inheritance in 1927 allowed him to devote himself to literary work. By 1930 he was moved to join Breton, Aragon, and Eluard's group, partly in disgust at the elation in the bourgeois press which the break-up of the surrealist group had caused, and partly because he was aware that theirs was the only plausible aesthetic protest against the economic depression and the threatening rise of fascism. He signed the manifesto announcing the review *Le Surréalisme au Service de la Révolution*, in whose first number he published a text, but left the group in 1931 in order to marry Odette Chabanel, whose family would have nothing to do with his surrealism. His wife was to bear him one child. He sold his de luxe surrealist editions and took a job with Hachette, where the conditions, to be described in "R.C. Seine No" from *Le Parti pris des choses*, were bad enough to drive him to direct political and union activity. The title alludes to the form in which his firm was entered on the company register. He became a union official in 1936 at the time of the June strikes, ostensibly for increased

wages but in fact more for union recognition, and in 1937 joined the communist party. It was his need at this period to dictate letters and give speeches which obliged him more or less to overcome his inhibition at oral expression. He continued to write verse and, in 1937, after the collapse of the Blum government, Hachette found an excuse to dismiss him. From 1937 until 1939 he sold insurance.

Ponge was demobilized after the fall of France in 1940, worked again in insurance, and then for the newspaper *Le Progrès de Lyon* at Bourg-en-Bresse until it closed. He then began serious work for the Resistance. In 1942 Gallimard had published *Le Parti pris des choses*, accepted before the war, and Ponge's first published volume since the early *Douze petits écrits*, of which 13 copies had been sold. Sartre's long essay "L'homme et les choses," published in *Poésie 44*, had brought Ponge's name before the public, and after the war Ponge was just able to make a living as literary editor of the communist weekly *L'Action*. However, he quickly came to dislike the postwar party dogmatism, left his post in 1946, and resigned from the party itself in 1947. He worked briefly for a publisher, but was very hard up between 1948 and 1952, when the Alliance Française offered him a teaching job in Paris. He held it until retirement in 1964.

Since 1947 Ponge had been accepting invitations to lecture all over Europe and preferred not to use a written text. This was not because he had now totally overcome his inhibitions in communicating orally, but because interaction with the audience allowed him to make the point about language as communication, requiring a receiver as well as an originator, which lay at the heart of his poetic message. The lecture fees and royalties from de luxe editions of the works of painters could not keep Ponge and his family, so books had to be sold, possessions pawned, and at least one visit from the bailiffs endured. Ponge none the less continued his determined struggle with the problems of expression. After 1952 his steady income enabled him to publish the stream of works which have subsequently made his reputation. Literary success was acknowledged by a special number of the *Nouvelle Revue Française* (q.v.) devoted to a "Hommage" in 1956, a poetry prize and the Légion d'Honneur in 1959, and then a US lecture tour in 1965, and a visiting professorship at Columbia in 1966–67. Ponge became a corresponding member of the Bavarian academy in 1969, lectured again in the US in 1970 and in Britain in 1971, and in 1975 attained the accolade of a colloquium on his work at Cerisy in 1975. He was by now slightly frightened of becoming co-opted into the literary establishment and no longer regarded as subversive. He died in Paris at the age of 89.

WORKS

"My critical texts, my texts on painters for example, are just as difficult to write as those texts considered poetic, and often more difficult. I make no distinction. My audacities and my scruples are the same, whatever genre you assign to the text." Ponge's refusal in 1974 to acknowledge the bibliographer's pigeonholes merely acknowledges a truth felt by many of his contemporaries as well, of course, as by younger writers, but it underlines the central thrust of his creative endeavour. Literary communication can be distinguished not according to genre, but only according to register. It is more important to know that the texts in *Douze petits écrits* were mostly satirical than to know whether they were in prose or verse. In fact, when, acting on behalf of Gallimard, Jean Paulhan asked Ponge to omit seven pieces, including all those in verse, from the manuscript of *Le Parti pris des choses*, he did not demur, although he did save them up for later use and eventually published all of them.

What *Le Parti pris des choses* clearly shows however, is, a move away from satire, which obviously did not suit Ponge's gleefully iconoclastic temperament, as he himself admitted in 1970. It was also alien to his delight in the physicality of the material objects which, he not infrequently said, turned to the poet in supplication to give them voice. The striking dozen lines of "Les plaisirs de la porte" give a brilliantly sensuous account of the pleasure to be had from embracing a door and opening it. Almost all the 32 miniatures in this volume concern objects and most have single-word titles. The mock heroic "Escargots," with 115 lines one of the longer pieces, gives a meticulously honed comment on human behaviour by describing the look and habits of snails as they might appear to a small child, pleased with his discoveries that snails only come out of their shells to move, and that they like damp, not wet, earth. The language itself slithers, mimicking the movement of the snail it describes, and Ponge turns the protracted metaphor into a fable. He saves it from weakness by making its moral self-mockingly perverse, arguing from the natural perfection of the snail's slimy movements to the human need to reflect in perfection of language the highest of moral achievements.

Snails, like shellfish, have a lesson to teach men about the nature of sanctity. Not only do they act in an unpretentious way perfectly consistent with their nature, their very diminutiveness makes it clear that moral perfection derives from fulfilling and not constraining nature: "Perfectionne-toi moralement et tu feras de beaux vers (If you perfect yourself morally you will write good poetry)." Ponge now alludes, without saying so, to the famous humanist principle of the Renaissance, proclaiming the intimate relationship between language and morality, or eloquence and philosophy as they were called. But if snails are saints because they obey their nature, what about self-knowledge as a precondition of sanctity? Snails do not have it, so it cannot be necessary, Ponge implies. What is required is self-acceptance, proportionality even in vice. Ponge returns to the medieval logician's concept of a logical "proprium." The standard example was man's ability to laugh, notoriously made fun of by Rabelais in the well-known poem prefacing *Gargantua*. "Mais quelle est la notion propre de l'homme: la parole et la morale. L'humanisme (What is the concept which defines the "proprium" of man: language and morality. Humanism)."

The short, dense, rounded-off presentations of objects in *Le Parti pris des choses* and *Pièces*, written between 1924 and 1957, but published only in *Le Grand Recueil* of 1961, are written in prose but are in fact poems by virtue of the density and complexity of their language. They are not even prose poems, which seek to produce in prose effects normally achieved only through a "poetic" elevation in the register of language. Ponge wrote alongside his poems texts best referred to as non-poems because their effect is not rounded off. They belong to "une espèce de journal de mon appréhension textuelle de quelque objet ou de quelque notion (a sort of diary of my textual assimilation of some object or idea)." They may contain poetry, stop rather than finish, are generally longer than the poems, and mostly consist of jottings, sometimes including even the most trivial of notes made in the course of preparing a text, and published with it. The effect is sometimes to publish reflections on the nature of language and poetry intermingled with finished texts themselves.

Together with his rounded-off poems and the self-interrogating diary type of text with notes or reflections or both commenting on the nature of verse, there are the *Proêmes* from the interwar years, originally published in 1948 and mostly critical reflections produced while composing the texts of *Le Parti pris des choses*. Somewhat similar to these are the pieces produced for special occasions. Ponge was invited to contribute a text at the opening of the Beaubourg centre, and was commissioned to write a text for architects by the French electricity board, and another on the Seine by a book club publishing a volume of photographs of the river. Virtually his whole oeuvre is about language.

A piece of 15 lines on fried fish, "Plat de poissons frits," written in 1949, turns out to be a reflection partly on the distinction between written and spoken language, trivial sensory experiences, and their effect on the imagination. The second part of the poem stridently draws the reader's attention to the manipulation of language by the poet in the first part, in which the unalerted reader, on whom Ponge enjoys playing tricks, is unlikely to have noticed the apparently ordinary but in fact precisely controlled effect achieved. It even requires a degree of alertness for the reader to take in the stridency of the second part of the poem, which lies in the clash of images, sounds, puns, and implied references to the first half, since the tone of the language, as controlled by its syntax, is quite unremarkable. Superficially, the whole poem reads like a brief attempt to record a sensation, perhaps for future use, or as a simple exercise. This is a poem whose point is largely to reflect on the language of poetry, and it ends in a cadence of imagery when, after three lines on heavy seas in the harbour outside the window, the lighthouse is transformed back into the carafe of wine awaiting the fried fish and within easy reach.

Among the texts on painters are seven on Ponge's friend Braque written between 1946 and 1970. They not only illustrate Ponge's capacity for saying the same essential things about man, art, and society in a variety of ways for a variety of audiences, and point to certain similarities in the aesthetic aims of the two men, but they give him the chance to extend his awareness of his own aims and procedures by addressing himself to those of Braque, although he ends up by being more informative about himself than about the painter. The final text, "Braque ou un méditatif à l'oeuvre," is also a meditation on the literal, associative, and metaphorical registers of the language he is using.

PUBLICATIONS

Verse

Douze petits écrits, 1926
Le Parti pris des choses, 1942; revised edition, 1949; edited by
   Ian Higgins, 1979; as *The Voice of Things*, 1972
L'Oeillet, La Guêpe, Le Mimosa, 1946
Le Carnet du bois de pins, 1947
Liasse: vingt-et-un textes suivis d'une bibliographie, 1948
Le Peintre à l'étude, 1948
Proêmes, 1948

La Crevette dans tous ses états, 1948

La Seine, 1950

L'Araignée, 1952

La Rage de l'expression, 1952

Des cristaux naturels, 1952

Ponge (selection), edited by Philippe Sollers, 1963

Tome premier, 1965

Nouveau recueil, 1967

Ponge (selection), edited by Jean Thibaudeau, 1967

Two Prose Poems, translated by Peter Hoy, 1968

Rain: A Prose Poem, translated by Peter Hoy, 1969

Ici haute, 1971

Things, translated by Cid Corman, 1971

Ponge: inventeur et classique, 1977

The Sun Placed in the Abyss and Other Texts, translated by Serge Gavronsky, 1977

The Power of Language: Texts and Translations, edited and translated by Serge Gavronsky, 1979

Other

Le Grand Recueil: Lyres, Méthodes, Pièces, 3 vols., 1961; revised edition, 1976–78

De La nature morte et de Chardin, 1964(?)

Pour un Malherbe, 1965; revised edition, 1977

Le Savon, 1967; as *Soap*, 1969

Entretiens de Ponge avec Philippe Sollers, edited by Sollers, 1970

La Fabrique du "pré," 1971; as *The Making of the "Pré,"* 1979

Méthodes, 1971

Georges Braque, de Draeger, with Pierre Descargues and André Malraux, 1971; as *Georges Braque* (in English), 1971

Picasso de Draeger, with Pierre Descargues and Edward Quinn, 1974

L'Atelier contemporain, 1977

Comment une figue de paroles et pourquoi, 1977

L'Ecrit Beaubourg, 1977

Nioque de l'avant-printemps, 1983

Critical studies

"Ponge issue," *Nouvelle Revue Française*, 1956

Willard, Nancy, *Testimony of the Invisible Man: William Carlos Williams, Ponge, Rainer Maria Rilke, Pablo Neruda*, 1970

Higgins, Ian, *Ponge*, 1979

Sorrell, Martin, *Ponge*, 1981

POSITIVISM

See Renan and Taine.

Positivism is principally but not exclusively associated in France with the names of Auguste Comte (1798–1857) and Emile Littré (1801–1881). The movement emerged in European thought from the confluence of three already intertwined strands of cultural development: the immense confidence in science generated by late 18th- and early 19th-century discoveries; the technological innovations based on them; and a growing sense of history as a continuing process of which the present is merely a part. From science came the exclusive reliance on empirically observable and quantifiable facts; from technology railways, steamboats, and factories; and from the 18th-century doctrine of human perfectibility, and the growing hostility to revelation as a source of truth, the sense that humanity was undergoing not only a physical but also a spiritual evolution. Western civilization had progressed from a mythological to a rational understanding of experience. Comte's "loi des trois états (law of the three states)" was to characterize the three periods he distinguished in human cultural development as "theological" (characterized by the attribution of natural phenomena to the will of an arbitrary divinity and ending with the Reformation), "metaphysical" (attributing natural phenomena to invariable forces and ending with the Revolution), and "positivist."

The idea of progress was not new in France, and much that Comte systematized, coordinated, and codified can already be found in Turgot and Condorcet, but Comte enabled the historical study of the evolution of society itself to become the subject of proper scientific investigation, thereby establishing the theoretical basis for regarding sociology as an autonomous discipline as well as the necessary foundation for a proper political science. Social phenomena had naturally been studied earlier than this. Montesquieu is a notable 18th-century pioneer. But Emile Durkheim (1858–1917), who did not accept either Comte's law of the three stages or his approach to sociology, none the less recognized him as its founder. The whole of Comte's vast enterprise was directed towards coordinating and assembling the sciences, from the simplest, most abstract, and most developed, like mathematics, to the most complex and least developed, like sociology, in order to make possible a science of the structure of human behaviour and of the structures underlying the evolution of society.

Comte was born in Montpellier and brought up a Catholic and a royalist, both affiliations he repudiated in adolescence, with his resultant expulsion in 1816 from the Ecole Polytechnique, strongly royalist under the Bourbon restoration. He became secretary to Saint-Simon (1760–1825) in 1817 and absorbed from him a realization of the need for a true science of human behaviour on which to found a restructured society, although Comte, unlike Saint-Simon, believed that each science should develop its own method as it evolved. Saint-Simon had thought that there was a universal scientific method which became increasingly abstract in accordance with a mathematical model as it evolved. Comte broke with Saint-Simon in 1824, when he rightly suspected that Saint-Simon was about to publish some of Comte's work as his own. He made an unhappy marriage, broke down, and tried to commit suicide. In 1829, however, he resumed the course of private lectures he had started in 1826 and which were to become the *Cours de philosophie positive* (6 vols., 1830–42). The Saint-Simonian basis for his early thought is clear from the title of the 1822 *Plan des travaux scientifiques nécessaires pour réorganiser la société*, which was not published until 1883. He was himself an authoritarian, perfectly prepared to settle for a world in which order was imposed by a properly advised monarch.

In 1844 Comte conceived a passion for Clothilde de Vaux,

whose husband had disappeared to avoid prosecution for embezzlement, and who inspired the religious dimension in Comte's thought. In the *Discours sur l'esprit positif* of 1844 and the *Discours sur l'ensemble du positivisme* of 1848 he sketched his idea of the religion of humanity. By this time, except for the *Imitation of Christ* and some poetry, Comte had altogether given up reading. He wrote his books entirely in his head before putting them on paper, and then never corrected what he had written, or wanted to see more than one set of proofs. He supported himself by private teaching and a part-time post at the Polytechnique, from which, however, he was dismissed in 1842 for arrogant and intolerant behaviour, and then from funds provided by his own followers. He attempted to bring together his scientific and religious thinking in the four-volume *Système de politique positive, instituant la religion de l'humanité* (1851–54) and the *Catéchisme positiviste* (1852), but never completed the great synthesis of which only the first volume was published in his lifetime, the *Synthèse subjective ou système universel des conceptions propres à l'état normal de l'humanité* of 1856.

The essence of Comte's positivism is in fact a rejection of revelation founded on a determinist theory of social evolution, but his importance derives from the way in which he turned over the notions fundamental to a science of man as a social and historical individual with a capacity for communication. Knowledge of man depended on a mixture of physiology and "la physique sociale (social physics)." Like so many of his generation, Comte was inspired by the desire to lay the foundations for a stable society, organized along the lines indicated by observable facts about human behaviour. But in order to design a functioning society, he was forced to rely, like so many of his predecessors, on some principle in man, the religious dimension, which transcended the merely selfish. Comte coined the word altruism to describe it, and it disappointed him that the revolution of 1848 failed to bring a utopia. Disillusion led him to regard with favour the institution of the Second Empire.

Comte's literary importance is entirely historical. He gave philosophical form to an enquiry already being imaginatively conducted by Balzac and suggested the concrete form which the study of the structures and evolution of society should take. The 19th century undertook many of the great works of synthesis of which the 18th century had dreamt. It was to become the true age of the encyclopedia as well as that of the great editions, as of all the Latin and Greek Fathers of the Church by the Abbé Jacques-Paul Migne (1800–1875). Comte's intellectual achievement is considerable. His imaginative power, however, is almost incidental to it. It must surely reside in the way in which, by demanding a structural analysis of society which would also reveal the laws of its evolution, he laid the foundation of a true science of man.

Comte's most important disciple in France was Emile Littré, who spoke of Comte's "immense mental revolution," although he rejected the whole religious edifice which Comte had erected on top of his epistemology. Littré studied medicine for a time, but devoted his life to assembling the four volumes of his great *Dictionnaire de la langue française* (1863–72). While the dictionary is an impressive work of erudition, Littré's importance in a literary context derives from what came to be regarded as his extreme hostility to the Church. When he was finally elected to the Académie Française in 1871, the year in which he also became a deputy, the noted preacher and educationalist Monseigneur Félix Dupanloup (1802–1878) resigned in protest.

While he was preparing the dictionary, Littré, who also became a senator for life, analysed and popularized Comte's positivism in a number of works published from 1845 to 1852, the year in which he broke with Comte. Littré both criticized Comte for making morals, in the sense of social psychology, into a seventh science alongside mathematics, astronomy, physics, chemistry, physiology, and biology, and also believed in the need for a descriptive study of human moral behaviour. He leaves us in doubt as to whether he thinks that society's evolution is the source of moral obligation or not, and was not clear in his own mind. His concern with human behaviour is of obvious importance, however, in the background of 19th-century literary development towards the sorts of imaginative explorations conducted in their different ways by Taine and Zola.

————

PRE-ROMANTIC

See also Chateaubriand, Constant, Fromentin, Lamartine, Maistre, Senancour, Staël, and the romantic movement.

The term "pre-romantic" risks being misleading. It was obviously first employed as a critical category later than "romantic" (q.v.). It is often used as if the sensibility it indicated, and about which there is general agreement, were a halfway house between 18th-century rationality and the sensibility of romanticism itself, sometimes defined in terms of its direct appeal to the emotions, but sometimes also otherwise. It is safer to assume nothing about the relationship of pre-romanticism to romanticism except one of chronological priority, especially since the body of reactions and attitudes constitutive of pre-romanticism only slowly asserts itself in what remains, until the appearance of Hugo's first radically new collection of verse, an era in which educated taste is still predominantly neoclassical.

It is then possible to discern in those authors generally considered pre-romantic, and who wrote mostly after the Revolution but before the late 1820s, a common attitude to nature and sentiment which might merely have preceded, but perhaps also have been incorporated into, the work of the romantic authors of imaginative literature, as distinct from those who were simply calling for often merely formal change in the pages, for instance, of *La Muse Française* from January 1824 until its suppression (see: the romantic movement). The periodization is fragile because literary historical convention demands that the inception of the romantic lyric should be dated from Lamartine's 1820 *Méditations poétiques*, whereas in terms of sensibility it could be argued that Lamartine's volume, its expanded version of 1823, and Hugo's collections not only of 1824, but also of 1826 and 1828, were still pre-romantic. That Hugo was achieving the break with the past announced in the *Préface* to *Cromwell* of 1827 became quite clear only with his 1829 collection *Les Orientales*.

Much that is associated with the pre-romantic sensibility can already be discerned in the works of Rousseau, possibly the first major European author clearly, consistently, and powerfully to explore the beauty of natural phenomena, such as mountains, glaciers, lakes, waterfalls, and storms, hitherto considered men-

Poetically, Prévert's real hostility is towards the poetic mystifiers who regard their craft as the initiation into an esoteric experience, and towards those who reject the ordinary events of daily life as insignificant or meaningless. It is noteworthy that Prévert never wrote a word of literary criticism and never needed to pontificate about his poetics. Unusually for so successful a modern writer he never even explained what he was trying to do.

PUBLICATIONS

Verse

Paroles, 1946
Histoires, with André Verdet, 1946
C'est à Saint-Paul-de-Vence...,, 1949
Spectacle, 1951
La Pluie et le beau temps, 1955
Poèmes, edited by J.H. Douglas and D.J. Girard, 1961

Other

Quai des brumes, 1938
Enfants, 1945
Le Rendez-vous (ballet), 1945
Miró, 1956
Portraits de Picasso, 1959
Fatras, 1966
Imaginaires, 1970
Hebdromadaires, with André Pozner, 1972
Choses et autres, 1972
Arbres, 1976

Critical studies

Baker, William E., *Jacques Prévert* (in English), 1967
Greet, Anne Hyde, *Jacques Prévert's Word Games*, 1968

———

PROUST, (Valentin-Louis-Georges-Eugène-) Marcel, 1871–1922.

Novelist, essayist, and journalist.

LIFE

Proust was the eldest son of an eminent doctor and professor of public health, who advised governments on cholera epidemics, and a well-educated, wealthy mother from a Jewish stockbroking family. She was musical, fluent in German and English, and could read some Latin and Greek. They married in 1870 and survived the siege of Paris, although the barricades were scarcely down when Proust's mother went to her uncle's home in Auteuil for her confinement. Proust, born on 10 July, was a delicate baby whose health gave his parents cause for concern. As a child it remained delicate. He was effeminate and continued to have a very close relationship with his mother. Family holidays were spent at Auteuil or Illiers, to the south-west of Chartres, where Proust's paternal aunt lived and where his ancestors had been family officials of the local nobility.

At nine Proust developed severe asthma and also suffered intermittently from indigestion. He was already intellectually precocious and socially rather priggish. From 1882 to 1889 he attended the Lycée Condorcet, although he missed much schooling through ill health. He was not popular with his peers and began to cultivate the company of older women, seeking invitations from them and paying special attention to the highest ranking courtesans. He had a brief affair with a girl in the summer of 1888, spent at Auteuil. His letters were affected and histrionic, but his artistry with words was already remarkable and already remarked upon by others. He read a great deal and by the end of his final year at the Lycée had helped edit the usual precious schoolboy literary magazine and achieved the top French essay prize. Proust was by now determined to become a "writer."

He completed his military service (1889–90) and spent what time he could, dressed in his ill-fitting uniform, in fairly smart, although middle-class, Paris salons. In 1890, to satisfy his parents, Proust registered for degrees in law and political science. He already had remarkable powers of observation and a habit of analysing apparently trivial objects and experiences with passionate intensity. He also met and talked endlessly with other young men of literary ambition, very few of whom later achieved eminence, and appears to have been a fascinating conversationalist.

Proust was also a kind person, friendly and interested in other people, if a little affected, and was generally dependent on some particular close friend, preferring either effeminate, sensitive men or masculine women. He was an almost scandalous flirt, particularly with elder, middle-class women with some position in society. He co-founded a literary review, *Le Banquet*, with various friends, openly using it, to the fury of his collaborators, as a means to social climbing.

Proust's social ambitions interfered with his examination preparations and in 1892 he appears to have failed in law. He also suffered from bouts of depression. He met Bergson at a dinner given by his parents and the poet Robert de Montesquiou-Fezensac at one of the Lemaires' soirees, where the true aristocracy occasionally mingled with actresses, painters, and musicians such as Massenet and Saint-Saëns. The arrogant and precious Montesquiou maintained a pose of aesthetic sensitivity and drew Proust into virtual discipleship, providing him with socially elevating introductions and invitations in exchange for his flattery.

In 1893, somewhat to his dismay, Proust qualified as a lawyer and immediately set about finding an excuse for undertaking further study so as not to disrupt his social life. Negotiations with the family led to a degree in philosophy, but to no further mention of professional activity. Proust, who was writing now for the *Revue Blanche*, relapsed into distracting himself socially, observing and analysing, preparing himself, without knowing it, to become the social historian of his generation and the greatest French novelist of his century. He was also progressing socially and had met Comte Boni de Castellan, who planned to build a replica of the Grand Trianon on Avenue du Bois, as well as Raynaldo Hahn, the salon musician par excellence, who shared Proust's admiration for Saint-Saëns. Proust would often ask him to play the "little phrase" from the piano transcription of the violin sonata in D Minor.

Proust graduated in philosophy and, although his mother kept him very short of "pocket money," he did take an unpaid and undemanding administrative job, from which he got leave of absence on being transferred to the ministry of public instruction, which did not in fact want him. In 1895 he went to Kreuznach with his mother and to Normandy with Hahn. *Les Plaisirs et les jours*, a collection of short stories, sketches, and poems, was finally published at outrageous cost the following year. Anatole France signed the preface, although it was in fact written by his mistress. The volume dealt mostly with love marred by guilt, jealousy, or mere disillusion. The only critic to praise the work was Maurras.

The first reference to work on a long novel came in 1896. This was to become *Jean Santeuil* and then, ultimately, *A la recherche du temps perdu*. Proust's health was deteriorating by now. The medicines which enabled him to sleep also encouraged his bouts of depression, and his daily letters to his mother detailed the times of day when he took his hypnotics and his stimulants, together with the precise dosages of each. In the notebooks he had begun to keep he frequently wrote up real episodes which he would later draw on for his novel. He fought a duel, in which no one was hurt, over an attack on *Les Plaisirs et les jours* and, although his old friends from *Le Banquet* were publicly laughing at him, he scored notable social successes in the season of 1897. His notebooks were filling fast when the Dreyfus affair broke. Proust came out unequivocally for Dreyfus, although he did nothing else to alienate his middle-class hostesses, on principle much less likely to be anti-Dreyfus than the aristocracy.

By 1899 the notebooks contained the best part of the 1,000 pages of autobiographical fragments published comparatively recently as *Jean Santeuil*. The casual method employed here pays no attention to continuity, only to a vaguely chronological structure, so that the work can be understood only as a sketch, neither an autobiography nor a novel. Proust had 70 full notebooks, which he left for six or eight years before he took them up and tried to form them into a structured novel. In the interim he turned to his study of Ruskin and the Gothic style, retracing Ruskin's steps first to Amiens, then to Venice and Padua, the most ambitious journey Proust was ever to make. He translated two of Ruskin's books, but most of the material published as articles found its way via the notebooks into *A la recherche*.

In 1900 the family moved and Proust was to became more of a recluse, struggling with his asthma and his insomnia. His mother nursed him during his periods of illness, fitting the household routine round his guests and his asthma attacks. He wrote her long notes, almost letters, and generally received friends in the dining room during the afternoons and evenings. To avoid feelings of claustrophobia he also had to go out, at whatever cost to his health. He grew bored with Montesquiou's ill-tempered posing now that he no longer needed his patronage and wrote a number of articles on the Paris salons, but was too distracted socially to work very much. He attended his younger brother Robert's wedding, but quarrelled increasingly with his mother, whom he was beginning to exasperate.

Proust's father died in November 1903. Proust returned later and later from his evening jaunts, went out late at night, and slept during the day. He still led a smart social life in 1904, both giving and attending dinner parties, but he was taking his illness more seriously, if also using it as a convenient excuse to avoid doing what he did not want to do. Then in 1905 his mother died. At his friends' request Proust now consented to go into a nursing home, but could not decide which; then, just as suddenly, he moved to Boulevard Haussmann, where he lived in the midst of noise, alterations, repairs, and restorations, managing to write sporadically for *Le Figaro*. By 1907 he felt strong enough to take a holiday in Normandy. On his return he began to work in earnest on *A la recherche*, while contributing more than previously to *Le Figaro*.

Proust's original intention for *A la recherche* was that the experience of its hero, even as a child, should always be presented as a totality, including simultaneously and from the beginning art, architecture, love, society, nature, and travel. The comic and serious would blend, with the hero understanding his experience better as the cycles unfolded. But the novel still lacked a central theme. Then Proust alighted on the notion of memory: the involuntary recollection of the past would be the only happiness that life offers. Such a theme would at least justify this fictionalized autobiography in its status as a novel.

For a while, however, Proust set his novel aside and worked on *Contre Sainte-Beuve*, which was not to be published in his own lifetime. When he was too ill to write, he dictated to his valet. Economically, he was better off than before, although he continued to feel short of money. He had had frequent disputes about money with his mother, who had continued to keep a tight hold on his spending during her lifetime. He complained a lot about the unaffordability of hotels in Normandy, but he still had his room in Paris, its walls lined with unsightly cork and its windows always kept tightly closed in an attempt to muffle the street noise. Proust's favourite taxi driver turned valet, Alfred Agostinelli, and his wife now lived with him, Agostinelli's main ostensible duty being to type the novel. Proust also gambled heavily on the stock market, losing 40,000 francs on one transaction in 1912.

He almost convinced himself that he was too poor to spend the summer in Cabourg, but on 7 August he ordered his valet to pack for the afternoon train and took five adjoining rooms on the top floor of the Grand Hotel. By the autumn of 1912 Proust had more than three chapters of his novel ready and could set out to find a publisher. In fact he laid siege to about half a dozen. Gide rejected the book on behalf of the *Nouvelle Revue Française* (*NRF*, q. v.), and Fasquelle, on whom Proust had pinned his highest hopes, followed with a second rejection. Ollendorff also refused it. Grasset accepted, however (though without enthusiasm), since Proust had offered to pay for the printing. Remembering the trouble caused by the price of *Les Plaisirs*, Proust lowered Grasset's recommended price and royalty, but immense difficulties still arose over format, publicity, title, number of volumes, and proof corrections.

Du côté de chez Swann finally appeared in 1913 to prearranged rockets of praise from Cocteau, Daudet, and Maurice Rostand and benign disdain from most other critics. Public reaction was not unfavourable. Gide apologized handsomely for his earlier rejection and the *NRF* offered to take over the rest of the novel, publishing at its own expense, but for the moment Proust preferred to stay with Grasset. Agostinelli left him to attend a flying school on the Riviera and was killed in an accident, so that Proust had to look now for a new typist. He also busied himself placing articles in important journals defending his first volume. War was coming and his investments dwindled. His financial transactions were disastrous, and for the first time he was forced to envisage earning a living with his pen.

Proust kept only one servant in Paris, Céleste, who became as much his confidante as his maid. He himself spent the early months of the war in Cabourg, where he had first known Agostinelli. By mid-1915 he had returned to his novel, which he referred to simply as "Swann." Turned down for military service on health grounds, he was none the less saddened by the news of various friends' deaths. More and more of his recent experiences were written up and pasted by Céleste into the notebooks. Proust now decided to switch to Gallimard and enlisted the help of Léon Blum to disengage him from Grasset, currently recovering from typhoid in Switzerland, without appearing ungrateful. Grasset was not pleased, but the two remained on friendly terms. With the *NRF*, on the other hand, relations became predictably stormy.

Proust's health now improved and he began to give smart dinner parties again in spite of his heavy capital losses. He developed a fondness for mildly anti-semitic jokes which entertained the aristocracy without betraying his mother outright and, thanks to his wit and frivolity, became once more the cynosure of amused attention. For purely practical reasons he began almost exclusively to frequent the Ritz, where he gave his infrequent but elegant dinners. Away from home his life style became extravagant, and he considered selling some furniture to recoup his losses. He did in the end sell half a dozen pieces for 14,000 francs.

Towards the end of the war Proust's health deteriorated once more. He put together *Pastiches et mélanges*, received news of a serious accident his brother had had, became short of money again and arranged to sell more furniture. The house in the Boulevard Haussmann had just been sold and Proust had to move twice, ending up in the Rue Hamelin, which he referred to as his "rat hole." In spite of enormous rent arrears he made a little money from the compensation paid by the Boulevard Haussmann developers. He became fastidious about chilly drawing rooms, where coffee was normally served after dinner, and their anticipated temperature dictated whether he accepted or declined invitations. In the course of such dinners he met more and more statesmen and politicians, ambassadors and minor monarchs.

A l'ombre des jeunes filles en fleurs appeared in June 1919 just as Proust was moving. The placed press accolades were unsurprisingly flattering, and even the other reviews were generally favourable. After some hesitation Proust was awarded the Prix Goncourt although there was a vociferously hostile backlash to the decision. He refused to receive the press and was not at all pleased with the way Gallimard was handling distribution and sales of his books, having already had trouble over the extent of his rewriting in proof. He did, however, develop a friendship with Rivière, his strongest *NRF* admirer, to whom he lent money and recommended a doctor, whose fee he then paid.

Proust was given the Légion d'Honneur but never became a member of the Académie Française. He became slovenly about both his appearance and his housekeeping. He frequently went out unshaven and wearing dirty cuffs and his bed linen was often unchanged when he received at home. Too ill to get up, he received from his bed and even entertained a disconcerted Mauriac to dinner from it. He enjoyed bouts of better health and went on day-time excursions—to exhibitions, for example—which entailed not going to bed the night before, and even in the winter of 1921–22 he attended two balls, went to the famous avant-

garde nightclub Le Bœuf sur le Toit, and took hostile critics out to dinner. From the middle of 1921, however, Proust's health went into terminal decline, in spite of visits, excursions, a soiree, and a dinner given in the summer of 1922.

The theme of homosexuality, which comes into increasing prominence in his novel, kept both Proust and the *NRF* on edge. He sold extracts from the novel, to the displeasure of the *NRF*, whose sales promotion still seemed to Proust inadequate, refused to sell the manuscript and corrected proofs of one volume, but sold more extracts, and vigorously objected to the *NRF* deal for an English translation, correctly pointing out that "Remembrance of Things Past" was a simple mistranslation of "A la recherche du temps perdu." Proust was now living largely off beer and ice from the Ritz, occasionally sending round for an apricot or a peach. He appears to have corrected what he dictated after speaking to his brother on 17 November. He died late in the afternoon of the following day.

WORKS

"A la recherche du temps perdu" could be rendered "In pursuit of past time," which instantly places the work in the context of a particular view of memory's function. It is scarcely possible to talk of a plot, or even of a series of plots. The novel is "about" time and memory, but is also a social satire and a series of exquisitely delineated vignettes, whether of salon conversation or, as one publisher put it, "of turning over in bed." The novel as we know it falls roughly into three blocks: the "Swann cycle," the "Guermantes cycle," and the final "Albertine cycle." There is a first-person narrator, twice referred to as Marcel, and such structures as inform the novel concern the apparently arbitrary workings of involuntary memory, by which seemingly unconnected elements of the narrator's past experience come unbidden into his consciousness, at the stimulus perhaps of a sensation or a dream, and evoke multiple associations. Importantly, in the light of many other contemporary artistic experiments involving the unconscious, Proust is dealing with the intellectual processing of the raw data of consciousness.

The account of the narrator's career progresses, therefore, in all sorts of directions at once and, as the book advances, most of the characters make an appearance in most of the chapters, so that the "action" appears to be going on everywhere, all the time. Yet in a way the work is also a Bildungsroman, an unstructured account of the narrator's development, often by disconcerting jumps, from childhood to maturity through episodes relating to snobbery, sadism, homosexuality, passion, and disillusion. The 1954 Pléiade three-volume edition prints a "résumé" of each volume, showing much more clearly the order of vignettes than that of events.

The first volume, whose title would scarcely be mistranslated as "About Swann," contains the almost arbitrary insertion of an episode concerning the unconscious operation of memory. This appears as a practically factitious structural device in the first chapter, "Combray." On 1 January 1909 or thereabouts, Proust had come home through the snow to the Boulevard Haussmann. He proceeded to read in his room, shivering from the cold, and Céline brought him up a cup not of his usual coffee, but of tea. He dipped a finger of dry toast in it, put it in his mouth, and was instantly overwhelmed by the scent of orange blossoms and a sensation of light and joy. Suddenly he recalled his great-uncle's garden at Auteuil and the flavour of the rusks soaked in tea his grandfather used to give him in the 1880s.

He realized instantly how the association revealed the nature of artistic creation, a pure and universal sensation combining the feeling of the artistic creator with that of the everyday self, with its habits and vices, which it is the job of the artistic vision to penetrate. That had been the conclusion about the relationship between inner genius and everyday existence as constitutive of the nature of artistic experience in *Contre Sainte-Beuve*, itself a stage in the gestation of *A la recherche*. What Proust did not realize until the following July was that the relationship of which he thought Sainte-Beuve took no account could provide the unifying thread for his novel. Involuntary memory, possibly stimulated by association, could provide the everyday author with access to the unpolluted spring of creative genius. Proust now wrote the preface to the new version of *Contre Sainte-Beuve*, containing in a few pages the key that unlocks the meaning of the whole vast panorama of *A la recherche*, casting aside intellect as an artistic tool and quoting four instances of the artistic operation of involuntary memory.

Just as in 1899 Proust had abandoned *Jean Santeuil* for Ruskin, so in early July, probably between the fourth and the sixth, 1909, he abandoned *Contre Sainte-Beuve* for what was to become *A la recherche*. He had discovered that the joy of vision need not be dissipated by the disillusion of experience. At the end of the first chapter Proust therefore introduced the story of the "madeleine" cake. The narrator remembers that one Sunday morning when he went to say good morning to his Aunt Léonie in bed, she gave him a piece of her "madeleine" dipped in lime blossom tea. Seeing the cake meant nothing to him. He muses on the reasons for this in explicit detail, and in sentences of enormous length. The *taste* of the cake, on the other hand, suddenly unleashed his involuntary memory: "et tout Combray et ses environs, tout cela qui prend forme et solidité, est sorti, ville et jardins, de ma tasse de thé (and all Combray and its surroundings, everything which had form and solidity, town and gardens, came out of my cup of tea)." The chapter ends there, with the next describing Combray again, not as distorted by subsequent experience, but as the narrator actually experienced it. His childhood life is recreated. The novel is the result of his resolve to recapture his past as it actually was, and to crystallize it in art. Hence its title, "In Pursuit of Lost Time."

In fact involuntary memory does not explain the threading together of the novel's lush but precise and sometimes cruel vignettes, and Proust's "discovery," while it may have given his novel its direction, does not really explain its mechanics. At times the intrusion of involuntary memory into a loose structure held together by style and a refusal to compartmentalize the world of experience comes almost as a distraction. The novel's important quality is the meticulous brilliance of its descriptive writing, the sardonic depth, ruthlessness, and variety of its psychological analyses. There is too much didacticism, and towards the end Proust cannot be absolved from harping on the themes of homosexuality, sadism, and literary theory, all of which concerned him deeply. But the richness of the comic description of aristocratic Parisian society in decay, in spite of the incidental snobbery, is also subtle, penetrating, and surprisingly economical. There are not many superfluous words. Even such obvious weaknesses as the novel's relatively superficial treatment of most of the female characters cannot obscure its remarkable penetration, beyond the ordinary, the everyday, and the trivial, to the ultimate sources of life and energy.

Almost all the characters are composite. Not even Charlus is quite Montesquiou, although the depiction was intended to wound. The work expanded and split several times as it was written and, had Proust lived, further proof corrections would no doubt have been made. As published by the *NRF*, it comprised:

Du côté de chez Swann (1917; reissued in 2 vols., 1919)

A l'ombre des jeunes filles en fleurs (1918; later reissued in 2 and then 3 vols)

Le Côté de Guermantes, part 1 (1920)

Le Côté de Guermantes, part 2 (1921; published in 1 vol. with *Sodome et Gomorrhe*, part 1, 1921)

Sodome et Gomorrhe, part 2 (3 vols., 1922)

La Prisonnière (Sodome et Gomorrhe, part 3) (2 vols., 1923)

Albertine disparue (La Fugitive) (2 vols., 1925)

Le Temps retrouvé, parts 1 and 2 (2 vols., 1927)

PUBLICATIONS

Fiction

A la recherche du temps perdu, 1913–27; as *Remembrance of Things Past*, 1922–31; revised translation, 1981
  Du côté de chez Swann, 1913; as *Swann's Way*, 1922
  A l'ombre des jeunes filles en fleurs, 1919; as *Within a Budding Grove*, 1924
  Le Côté de Guermantes, 1920–21; as *The Guermantes Way*, 1925
  Sodome et Gomorrhe, 1921–22; as *Cities of the Plain*, 1927
  La Prisonnière, 1923; as *The Captive*, 1929
  Albertine disparue, 1925; as *The Sweet Cheat Gone*, 1930
  Le Temps retrouvé, 1927; as *Time Regained*, 1931; as *The Past Recaptured*, 1932
Jean Santeuil, 1952; as *Jean Santeuil* (in English), 1955

Other

Les Plaisirs et les jours, 1896; as *Pleasures and Regrets*, 1948
Pastiches et mélanges, 1919
Chroniques, 1927
Correspondance générale, 6 vols., 1930–36; selection, as *Letters*, edited by Mina Curtiss, 1950
A Selection, edited by Gerald Hopkins, 1948
Contre Sainte-Beuve, 1954; as *On Art and Literature 1896–1919*, 1958; as *By Way of Sainte-Beuve*, 1958
Letters to His Mother, edited by George D. Painter, 1957
Textes retrouvés, edited by Philip Kolb and Larkin B. Price, 1968
Correspondance, edited by Philip Kolb, 1970–
Le Carnet de 1908, edited by Philip Kolb, 1976
Selected Letters 1880–1903, edited by Philip Kolb, 1983
Translator, *La Bible d'Amiens*, by Ruskin, 1904
Translator, *Sésame et le lys*, by Ruskin, 1906; Proust's preface, as *On Reading*, edited by Jean Autret and William Burford, 1972

Bibliography

Graham, Victor E., *Bibliographie des études sur Proust et son Oeuvre*, 1976

Biographical and critical studies

Painter, George D., *Proust: A Biography* (in English), 2 vols., 1959–65
Shattuck, Roger, *Proust's Binoculars* (in English), 1965
Brady, Patrick, *Proust* (in English), 1977
Cocking, J. M., *Proust* (in English), 1982

Ellison, David R., *The Reading of Proust*, 1984
Thody, Philip, *Marcel Proust* (in English), 1987
Hayman, Ronald, *Proust* (in English), 1990

———

Q

QUENEAU, Raymond, 1903–1976.

Poet, comic novelist, writer of short stories.

LIFE

Born and educated in Le Havre, in 1920 Queneau moved with his family to Paris, where he studied philosophy and met members of the surrealist (q. v.) group. He published in their review, *La Révolution Surréaliste*, before finally rejecting their ideas. His serious interests included psychoanalysis, mathematics, Hegel, and the phenomena of madness. From 1933 he underwent six years or so of analysis himself and edited the lectures he had attended on the then unfashionable Hegel given by Alexandre Kojève. His reading included Joyce, Husserl, Heidegger, Marx, and Engels. He suffered from asthma from 1923. His interests were wide, although references to them in the works are generally smothered in frivolousness or absurdity. He was in earlier years at least, a satirical polemicist who wrote for *La Critique Sociale* and was interested in poetics, the theory of knowledge, and left-wing politics. In 1928 he married André Breton's sister-in-law.

Queneau's first novel, *Le Chiendent*, which bubbles over with parody, was published by Gallimard in 1933. *La Gueule de pierre* was published the following year, during which Queneau's son was born, but his *Encyclopédie des sciences inexactes* was twice rejected. His life was relatively uneventful: he published a novel most years and was engaged as English reader at Gallimard from 1938. His first collection of verse, *Les Ziaux*, was published in 1943, followed by *L'Instant fatal* in 1946 and *Bucoliques* in 1947, although in 1937 Queneau had published a long "novel in verse," *Chêne et chien*. He was elected to the Académie Goncourt in 1951 and became a jury member at the Cannes Film Festival in 1955. In 1956 he wrote a screen play for Buñuel, but his first best-seller, *Zazie dans le métro*, which was itself to be made into a film, was not published until 1959. Novels and verse were interspersed with non-literary works, notably on mathematics, philosophy, and history. Selections of Queneau's essays and reviews were also published in collected editions.

Exercices de style, which takes a set of trivial components and uses 99 different styles in order to make different narratives of them, had proved popular before *Zazie*, and Queneau came to be well known and liked in different cultural circles. Following his brush with the surrealists he became associated with Jacques Prévert and Michel Leiris, then Georges Bataille. He also knew the anti-Stalinist socialist Boris Souveraine, and later befriended Sartre, Beauvoir, and Boris Vian. Queneau was interested in oriental literature as well as in the world of popular song, film, and radio. He was also seriously sceptical, believing that science could not offer real knowledge, but only the mathematical formalization of relationships. His irresistible urge to parody and his sense of the absurd kept him in the public eye, and his sense of mischief led him to poke fun at matters he nevertheless considered quite serious. He was badly affected by the death of his wife in 1972.

WORKS

Beneath the word games and the puns the early poems—some of which had been written by 1920—are pessimistic to the point of nihilism. In them man's desire for happiness is consistently thwarted, and Queneau connives at man's secret taste for unhappiness. The wordplays are undoubtedly clever, skilfully exploiting the most unexpected associations, and the allusions are sufficiently erudite and obscure to elude even the most highly educated reader. Queneau scarcely expected them to be subjected to the detailed exegesis which they have received, but which nevertheless misses their point. The comedy in these poems can be grotesque, but the underlying imaginative patterns invariably repeat the hopelessness of man's situation.

The later poetic texts include the *Petite cosmogonie portative*, a sceptical scientific poem in the 16th-century manner wryly parodying Lucretius, *Sonnets* and *Le Chien à la mandoline*, and the trilogy *Courir les rues*, *Battre la campagne*, and *Fendre les flots*. In *Cosmogonie*, the associations are wildly at odds with one another and are intended to confuse. Mercury, for instance, also known as Hermes, is a god, a metal, a messenger, and a poet. The last volume of the trilogy explores whole webs of interrelated metaphors associated with the sea. The final collection of verse, *Morale élémentaire*, is stylistically related to the *Cosmogonie* and bafflingly hermetic, defying causal logic in its description of the development of the cosmos. No critical consensus has been reached as to either its meaning or its value as a poem. In writing it Queneau may have had Chinese verse forms in mind.

The novels are often parodies of books, movements, states of mind, and literary or other theories. *Le Chiendent* degenerates into the absurd, and the characters get tired of the narrator. The narrative modes are jumbled, and there is obvious reference to *Ulysses*, if also to Parmenides, Descartes, Proust, and a host of problems about the nature of knowledge. *Les Derniers Jours* is really an anti-modernist novel, in which events all jostle for simultaneity. *Odile*'s characters include recognizable caricatures of real people. This novel, which has a first-person narrator and a nearly classical form, ends in an anti-romantic acceptance of banality as the best that can be hoped for. *Les Enfants du Limon* is a novel about related characters from different social classes, all seeking salvation, redemption, or happiness in a world which does not afford such luxuries. Here Queneau uses the results of some of his own research into madness, and one of his characters compiles his own unpublished encyclopedia of lunatic facts and theories.

Un rude hiver is a political novel ostensibly relating to the events of 1916, but which in fact makes constant reference to the choice confronting the French in 1939. *Pierrot mon ami* invites the reader to create his own novel out of the whimsically ill-assorted episodes which are set before him. Like its predecessors, it draws on the comic elements of popular culture, mocking the novel form itself. *Loin de Rueil*, which follows it, is essentially about the psychology of cinema.

Queneau's first post-war novel was *Saint Glinglin*, which incorporates already published material and is concerned with an imaginary society. Narrative registers and style change from section to section, and there is an obvious but oblique reference to Rabelais in the novel's many absurdities with their uncomfortable undertones of real life. Like Rabelais, Queneau shows off his riotous inventiveness at the expense of any potential contribution to social anthropology. The next two novels were published under the name of "Sally Mara" and appear to have been written in response to a hack commission for some quick-selling sex and violence. Their fantasy is scattered with obscene allusions. *Le Dimanche de la vie* centres round the carnival figure of Valentin, whose attitudes and activities mock the seriousnes and tragedy of life, while *Zazie dans le métro* continues the joyous travesty of ordered reality, satirized through the obscene mind of an ingenuous young girl. The novel's tone is set by its famous and brilliant opening: a jumble of letters transliterating vulgar Parisian argot.

Les Fleurs bleues is another experimental text of Chinese and Joycean ancestry which exploits dream states and again undermines historical chronology. Queneau's last novel, *Le Vol d'Icare*, exploits the ambiguity inherent in its title, since "Vol" can mean both flight and theft. One of the characters in a novel by a Queneau character has been either blown away or stolen, and the novel is the story of his pursuit, with liberal blocks of satire, as of psychoanalysis, thrown in. Queneau is ironically aware here, as throughout his work, that language—even the spoken language to which he accords preference—is as much a construct as fiction, and that neither of them has any right to pretend to be anything else.

PUBLICATIONS

Fiction

Le Chiendent, 1933; as *The Bark Tree*, 1968
La Gueule de pierre, 1934
Les Derniers Jours, 1936
Odile, 1937
Les Enfants du Limon, 1938
Un rude hiver, 1939; as *A Hard Winter*, 1948
Les Temps mêlés, 1941
Pierrot mon ami, 1942; as *Pierrot*, 1950

Loin de Rueil, 1944; as *The Skin of Dreams*, 1948
Exercices de style, 1947; as *Exercises in Style*, 1958
Sally Mara, *On est toujours trop bon avec les femmes*, 1947; as *We Always Treat Women too Well*, 1981
Saint Glinglin, 1948
Sally Mara, *Journal intime*, 1950
Le Dimanche de la vie, 1952; as *The Sunday of Life*, 1976
Zazie dans le métro, 1959; as *Zazie in the Metro*, 1960
Les Fleurs bleues, 1965; as *Between Blue and Blue*, 1967; as *The Blue Flowers*, 1967
Le Vol d'Icare, 1968; as *The Flight of Icarus*, 1973
Contes et propos, 1981 (collection of Queneau's short fiction)

Verse

Chêne et chien, 1937
Les Ziaux, 1943
L'Instant fatal, 1946
Bucoliques, 1947
Petite cosmogonie portative, 1950
Si tu t'imagines, 1951 (mostly work previously published)
Sonnets, 1958
Le Chien à la mandoline, 1958
Cent mille milliards de poèmes, 1961; as *One Hundred Million Million Poems*, 1983
Courir les rues, 1967
Battre la campagne, 1968
Fendre les flots, 1969
Morale élémentaire, 1975

Other

Bâtons, chiffres et lettres, 1950
Le Voyage en Grèce, 1973

Bibliography

Hillen, Wolfgang, *Bibliographie des études sur l'homme et son oeuvre*, 1981
Two reviews are devoted exclusively to Queneau: "Les Amis de Valentin Brû" (see no. 23, 1983, for a further bibliography), and "Temps mêlés—Documents Queneau."

Critical studies

Queval, Jean, *Essai sur Raymond Queneau*, 1960
Bens, Jacques, *Queneau*, 1962
Bergens, André, *Raymond Queneau*, 1963
Guicharnaud, Jacques, *Raymond Queneau* (in English), 1965
Thiher, Allen, *Raymond Queneau* (in English), 1985
Shorley, Christopher, *Queneau's Fiction*, 1985

R

RADIGUET, Raymond, 1903–1923.

Novelist and poet.

LIFE

Radiguet was the eldest of seven children, the son of a cartoonist said to have been descended from Mme de Pompadour, and of Jeanne-Louise-Marie Tournier, His mother, who was 18 years younger than his father, was descended from Josephine Tascher, whose second husband was Napoleon. The family lived on the Marne just outside Paris, and were not well off. Once he was in a position to, Radiguet later sent money home to help out. Radiguet often absented himself from school before finally leaving at 15, and his father tried, ineffectually, to teach him Latin and Greek. He did read widely, however, especially in the French classics, borrowing books from his father's library.

Radiguet effectively left home in 1918, missing the last train more and more frequently after delivering his father's two weekly cartoons to *L'Intransigeant*. He had decided to be a writer and was already marked by two incidents he had witnessed, both of which he was to use in his first novel. In one instance a maid had committed suicide by throwing herself off the roof of a neighbour's house; in the other a young girl, sharing a park swing with her fiancé, had fallen off as the swing reached the near-vertical and been killed. Radiguet's autobiographical writing, which represents his childhood as a happy one, barely mentions the house the family lived in, his brothers and sisters, or his mother.

André Salmon, the editor of *L'Intransigeant*, was impressed by the young ill-clothed Radiguet and anxious to help him for his father's sake. Assisted by Salmon, Radiguet, (who signed himself Rajky) placed work in avant-garde magazines and got to know Apollinaire, Picasso, Tzara, Breton, Stravinsky, Satie, and "Les Six" (Milhand, Auric, Poulenc, Honegger, Durey, and Tailleferre), some of the major figures, in other words, of the Parisian avant-garde. The list of acquaintances and friends soon included names like Brancusi, Gris, Modigliani, Derain, Marie Laurencin, Aragon, Reverdy, Valéry, and Max Jacob, who was to exert a strong influence on Radiguet, and with whom he may have had a homosexual affair. He had already had an affair with an older woman when he was just 15, and used to spend the nights after missing the last train home in run-down hotels in the neighbourhood of Jacob's house. He certainly had an affair with his later patron, Cocteau, who aspired to be the artistic darling of Parisian avant-garde cultural circles. Cocteau's least superficial work was written, in fact, under Radiguet's influence. They quickly became inseparable and were associated in various madcap ventures, including the publication of *Le Coq*, a broadsheet which lasted only four issues.

Radiguet wrote most of *Le Diable au corps*, whose title refers not so much to lust as to the desire to grow up, while spending the summer of 1921 with Cocteau on the Atlantic coast. In 1922 the couple spent the summer on the Mediterranean, where Radiguet wrote most of *Le Bal du comte d'Orgel*. Grasset, whose flair for publicity verged on both bad taste and overkill, was to ensure the success of *Le Diable au corps* in 1923. Meanwhile Cocteau and Radiguet took to visiting Le Bœuf sur le Toit, a nightclub, much frequented by writers, where opium smoking and homosexuality were, if anything, the norm. Radiguet had the occasional affair with other men, and a few women. He was for a time close to Brancusi. Cocteau, who instituted a new literary prize and saw that it was awarded to Radiguet, took his protégé to England and seems to have become increasingly possessive.

Radiguet rented a flat, which he shared with Bronya Perlmutter (later to marry René Clair), and began drinking heavily. He went back to the Atlantic with Cocteau in the summer of 1923, but they were pestered by a stream of friends. Radiguet was 20 that June and therefore eligible for military service, but Grasset obtained a deferment for him so that he could correct the proofs of *Le Bal*. In the autumn Radiguet fell ill with typhoid, probably contracted from eating infected oysters at Le Piqueÿ. He died in hospital, alone and apparently in agony, early in the morning of 12 December. Bills were either paid or cancelled. Cocteau did not attend the funeral, the arrangements for which were made by Gabrielle "Coco" Chanel.

WORKS

Le Diable au corps concerns the love affair between the anonymous narrator and his mistress, Marthe (three years his senior), who marries Jacques, a soldier in world War I. The events span the years 1914 when the narrator is 12, until the spring of 1919. With the end of the war comes Marthe's death and the end of the liaison, together with the birth of her son by the narrator, assumed by Jacques to be his own. The text gives no details of people or appearances, but is quite specific about times and places, so that the reader's attention is focused on the narrator's precocious psychological development from adolescence to maturity during the course of the war.

In this war novel the war is seen, therefore, not as the horror it was, but as a liberation from normal constraints. The narrator grows distant from his family and closest friend as his sentimental education quickens its pace. Childish gaucheness and complex carelessness in deception—the result of astute observation and self-analysis—are depicted with impressive sensitivity and the balance of the novel is maintained through the judicious use of letters, from Jacques and the narrator to Marthe, and from Marthe—tender replies dictated by the narrator—to Jacques.

Le Bal du comte d'Orgel is written in the third person. The young noble, François de Séryeuse and Mahaut, Comtesse d'Orgel, fall in love. Each eventually learns that their love is reciprocated but social order is maintained and the count still invites François to the ball of the title. The action, which takes place in 1920, contains medieval overtones of courtly love, but was almost certainly inspired by *La Princesse de Clèves*. Letters again play an important part in the action. Radiguet does not in fact appear to have corrected the proofs himself, and his text seems to have been improved by Cocteau with the connivance of Grasset and his reader, the novelist Joseph Kessell, after Radiguet's death. Gide and Rivière both admired the novel's psychological delicacy, and Gide put it above Alain-Fournier's *Le Grand Meaulnes*. Its effect is enhanced by the inclusion of even less physical detail than its predecessor contained.

Radiguet also published a number of volumes of verse. Notable for its careful craftsmanship, each poem often turns on a single visual image. These volumes created some thing of a stir in avant-garde circles of the time largely on account of their typogrophical experimentation. *Vers libres* is licentious.

PUBLICATIONS

Collections

Oeuvres complètes, 1952
Oeuvres complètes de Raymond Radiguet, 2 vols., 1959 (much more complete)
Gli inediti, 1967

Fiction

Le Diable au corps, 1923; as *Devil in the Flesh*, 1932; as *The Devil in the Flesh*, 1971
Le Bal du comte d'Orgel, 1924; as *Ball at Count d'Orgel's*, 1929; as *Count d'Orgel Opens the Ball*, 1952

Verse

Les Joues en feu, I, 1920
Devoirs de vacances, 1921
Les Joues en feu (expanded version), II, 1925; as *Cheeks on Fire: Collected Poems*, 1976
Vers libres, 1925
Jeux innocents, 1926

Critical and biographical studies

Goesch, Keith, *Raymond Radiguet: étude biographique*, 1955
Boillat, Gabriel, *Un maître de 17 ans, Raymond Radiguet* (commercial and publishing history of the novels), 1973
Cahiers Jean Cocteau 4, 1973: an important special issue on Radiguet
McNab, James P., *Radiguet*, 1984

REALISM

See also Barbey d'Aurevilly, Champfleury, Feydeau, Flaubert, the Goncourts, Murger, and naturalism.

As applied to literature, the categories "realist" and "naturalist" (q.v.) have come to denote neither clearly distinct literary doctrines, nor clearly distinct periods. The distinction is largely conventional. The term "realist" is generally reserved for a movement common to literature and painting which reacted against the "romanticism" (q.v.) that had preceded it. Realism is associated primarily with the period between about 1850 and 1870, or a little later. "Naturalism" is normally regarded as a later extension of realism after 1870, developed along the same lines but more extreme in its practice, its attention more exclusively concentrated on the sordid and squalid aspects of human existence, and relying on the more precisely formulated philosophical background provided by positivism (q.v.) and Taine. In the fine arts the transition is that between the generation of Gustave Courbet (1819–1877) and the caricaturists Honoré Daumier (1810–1879), Henri Monnier (1799–1877), and Gavarni (1804–1866), and that of Paul Cézanne (1839–1906), Edouard Manet (1832–1883), and impressionists like Claude Monet (1840–1926) and Auguste Renoir (1841–1919). Realism in French literature can have a satirical cutting edge, but avoids the sentimentality into which naturalism sometimes lapses.

The romantics had explored the heroism of the individual, and had concentrated on exotic and colourful aspects of the world. Theirs had been a literature, and in Eugène Delacroix (1798–1863) a painting, of exalted feelings and wild emotions, of sometimes self-indulgent melancholy and often egalitarian dreams. The mechanism by which the imaginative needs of succeeding generations change with social and political circumstances includes a capacity for collective reaction, always finally reflected in the producer–consumer relationship, even in imaginative literature and the fine arts. The time had to come when individuals, often clustering at first in little groups, sometimes encouraged by a publisher, an editor, or a producer, realized that romantic drama, having served its necessary and once exciting purposes, had become "stereotyped," that is, adrift from the concerns of its public. It was no longer exploring the real values its public lived by, or desirable ways of changing them and the society which they nourished.

In the case of realism, particularly since the written word was on the whole more easily censored than the illustration, the caricaturists came first, pointing out the solemn fatuities, self-aggrandizement, grubbiness, and greed of the socially and financially ambitious, and exposing the real values by which society lived. As early as 1830, at the moment when romantic drama was touching its short-lived peak, Henri Monnier, the constant contributor to the subversive but generally tolerated *Le Charivari*, founded in 1832, was steering his stolidly platitudinous, fat-bellied bourgeois caricature, Joseph Prudhomme, in his *Scènes dessinées à la plume*, on to a wave which would build up until it broke over the last retreating waters of romanticism with the *Mémoires de M. Joseph Prudhomme* of 1857. The same year saw the volume publication of Flaubert's *Madame Bovary*. Flaubert detested being called a realist because of his distaste for the real world, but his whole oeuvre, as he published it, none the less constitutes a protracted examination of the non-sustainability of a romantic vision of life, starting with the remorseless account of how her romantic illusions ground Emma Bovary into her final unromantically depicted self-destruction.

Realism is perhaps best defined as a wave of imaginative activity which can be seen building up from as early as the peak of public response to romantic literature, drama, and painting. It was the imaginative investigation required by and produced for the idealists of the generation attaining its majority in the 1850s, disillusioned by the failure of the 1848 revolution and the subsequent coup d'état of December 1851. The imaginative requirements of the new decade included an exploration of the real world, in which something was felt, by the educated if not the money-making classes, to have gone wrong. The romantics had catered for the public whose imagination was leading it towards what turned out to be the failed revolution. The realists needed to investigate lives lived lower on the social scale than those to which the romantics had, in their examination of the heroic, naturally turned. When the realists came themselves to define their aims, their spokesmen, like Champfleury, or the novelist Louis-Emile-Edmond Duranty (1833–1880), founder of Le Réalisme (1856), took their cue from Courbet, who in 1848 had announced his intention of painting only the modern and the vulgar. In fact this stated aim has perpetuated a literary confusion. The outstandingly powerful imaginative author of the realist generation, Flaubert, repudiated both the title chosen by authors whose aims he shared and exclusive reliance on the means they enumerated for satisfying the needs of the educated public of the Second Empire.

Dissatisfied with his allocation of space at the 1855 exhibition, Courbet organized a pavilion of his own, in which he exhibited 40 canvases, including L'Atelier du peintre, subtitled "The allegory of realism" (and much disliked by Huysmans). After 1855 Courbet's works no longer avoided landscapes, and his attitude to his painting became somewhat less doctrinaire. He remained, however, almost as resolutely anti-sentimental and unemotional as Flaubert. Gavarni (see also Goncourt), like Monnier a contributor to Le Charivari, in which he first published his series Fourberies de femme en matière de sentiment and Les Lorettes, was also a sharp satirist of bourgeois life, whose work, like Courbet's, had strong political overtones. These were particularly apparent in Les Propos de Thomas Vireloque (1851–53). It was to distract Gavarni, a close friend of the Goncourt brothers, that the Magny dinners were founded (see Goncourt). Towards the end of his life Gavarni's depictions of London low life became politically bitter in tone.

Daumier, a third contributor to Le Charivari, is more important as a caricaturist than either Monnier or Gavarni. He mastered the art of lithography while it was still new, contributed to Charles Philipon's weekly Caricature, and was sent to prison for six months for a cartoon of Louis Philippe swallowing bags of gold extorted from the people. Although his political work was done at the height of the realist period, Daumier's early fraudulent but amusing villain, Robert Macaire, lifted from an 1823 melodrama, became a comic hero memorably played by the great romantic actor "Frédérick" Lemaître (1800–1876) as early as 1834. Daumier's early work was in fact still clearly romantic in inspiration.

After writing three realist novels, Le Malheur d'Henriette Gérard (1860), La Cause du beau Guillaume (1862), and La Canne de Mme Desrieux, époque de 1822 (1862), Duranty himself went on to write a famous puppet show before collaborating with Paul Alexis on work which belongs to the naturalist move-

ment. As a critical category "realism" is normally reserved in literature exclusively for prose fiction, although the development of Parnassian (q.v.) poetry away from romanticism towards symbolism (q.v.) is in some ways analogous. Among the minor realist authors not mentioned in the headnotes to this entry, the sententiously moralizing novelist and playwright Octave Feuillet (1821–1890) is an author of insufficient imaginative depth to be important, in spite of the great popularity of his Roman d'un jeune homme pauvre of 1858. Much the same might be said of the less pretentious and more amusing Edmond About (1825–1885), a journalist with a witty mind and a taste for the fantastic, whose novel about thoroughly modern Greek bandits, Le Roi des montagnes (1857), is totally unsentimental, but who otherwise has a tendency to moralize.

Ernest Feydeau (1821–1873), a stockbroker and archaeologist, and father of the famous writer of vaudevilles, published a novel entitled Fanny in 1858. It was immensely successful and, primarily on that account, Feydeau deserves a mention in the context of realism, although nothing else he wrote is now considered worthy of attention. Finally, mention should also be made of a pair of successful collaborators who eventually quarrelled and split up, Emile Erckmann (1822–1899) and Alexandre Chatrian (1826–1890). Both came from Alsace, and their best fiction contains handed-down narrative memories of the collapse of Napoleon's retreating forces. Although published between 1862 and 1868, their half-dozen novels—Le Fou Yégof (1862), Madame Thérèse (1863), L'Ami Fritz (1864), Histoire d'un conscrit de 1813 (1864), Waterloo (1865), and Histoire d'un paysan (1868)—still show traces of a romantic sensibility amid the strongly realist emphasis on rotting corpses and general fidelity to unpleasant physical detail. The category is now too firmly entrenched to change the accepted usage which puts into the pigeonhole "realist" any prose fiction which contains such detail or concerns the poor and the deprived. Flaubert will therefore continue, against his will, to be enlisted in the realist ranks. The essence of the movement, however, lies not just in dwelling on what is physically unpleasant, and the realistic details are there because they are demanded in the context of the exploration, following the coup d'état, of the reasons for the destruction of the romantic dream. What needed to be understood after 1851 was the mundane, the disillusion felt at the victory of the unheroic.

RENAN, (Joseph-) Ernest, 1823–1892.

Historian, Semitic scholar, archaeologist, and theologian.

LIFE

Renan was born on 28 February at Tréguier, an old cathedral town on the Breton coast. About a third of the town's population had been reduced to begging for a living by 1823. Renan was the third child of a fisherman, Philibert, and of his wife Magdeleine Féger, who kept a small grocer's shop which the family had inherited from Philibert's father, an ardent republican. Renan's mother's family were strongly royalist. His brother was 14 and his sister 12 when he was born, sufficiently prematurely for his survival to be in doubt. His father died at sea when he was five. The small business was liquidated and the family moved to Renan's maternal grandmother's home in Lannion. Two years later his mother's creditors allowed her to return to her shop. Renan himself was seriously ill in 1831.

His sister, Henriette, appears to have taken over as the moral and financial head of the family. She opened a school, which had to close, and, in 1835, went to teach in Paris. In 1832 Renan entered the mixed Collège Ecclésiastique, where he did well enough for his sister to show his results to someone in Paris, who mentioned them to the Abbé Dupanloup. Dupanloup immediately gave Renan a place at his school for bright seminarists and young aristocrats—an educationally successful and politically important mixture for both categories under the July monarchy—in the hope that Renan might go on to study for the priesthood.

After three years, in 1841, Renan proceeded to the seminary proper at Issy to learn philosophy. Henriette, who had by now lost her faith, took up a position as a private tutor in Poland with a view to improving her means of supporting the family, and remained there until 1850. Renan had begun to feel uneasy about the idea of joining the priesthood, and Henriette tried in her letters to wean him from it, suggesting that he should travel for a year. It was before the revival of Thomism in Catholic seminaries, and Renan's mind was being unsettled by Kant and German idealist philosophy. He postponed taking the tonsure, although it implied little more than a perfunctory commitment to go on with his ecclesiastical studies, but was suspected of being too much of a rationalist to be readily able to accept the degree of intellectual conformity to dogmatic pronouncements expected of priests. He nevertheless went on to study theology in 1843, now at the seminary of Saint-Sulpice itself, which he liked. He mastered Hebrew so well that he was given a class to take, for which he wrote his own textbook.

Renan duly accepted the tonsure, but by May 1845 his doubts were reaching crisis point. He realized that the two parts of Isaiah matched one another neither in style nor in date, that the Book of Daniel was apocryphal, and that Moses could not have written the Pentateuch, as had actually been recognized outside orthodox Catholic circles for well over a century. He did not accept the subdiaconate, considered on account of its implied vow of chastity the first serious commitment to the priesthood, but returned after the summer with the intention of reviewing his situation with his superiors. He found himself prematurely confronted with the need to make a decision, however, on being sent to the new institute of biblical studies. The divinity of Christ and the divine inspiration of the Bible seem to have been the breaking points. Renan's superiors found him a teaching job in a nearby Catholic college, but he refused to wear ecclesiastical dress, and ended up as a pupil-teacher in a lay school until 1848, free during school hours but on duty in the evenings.

Unwilling merely to exchange one orthodoxy for another by going to the Ecole Normale Supérieure, Renan studied privately for his "licence" and then his agrégation, which he passed in 1848. In 1847 he had won the Volney Hebrew prize awarded by the Académie des Inscriptions. The revolution of 1848 took him by surprise but stimulated in him a belief in human progress within the context of which the events of 1848 could be understood. He became liberal, republican, and anti-clerical and contributed to La Liberté de Penser. By 1849 he was envisaging in its pages a utopia in which noble, dedicated souls in pursuit of the true and the beautiful would create a new law for mankind, although the new era would, as he saw it, be preceded by a social cataclysm of some sort.

Renan's inchoate thirst for persecution was tempered with prudence, since he also wrote for the official Journal de l'Instruction Publique. He was dissuaded from publishing his L'Avenir de la science (eventually to appear in 1890) and contented himself for the moment with publishing two articles on Strauss and the German rationalist historians of Christianity, which appeared in March and April 1849, signed only with Renan's initials. Pieces of L'Avenir appeared in the review and revealed a Hegelian reading of the three ages of man's history, the creation of myth, the age of science and historical analysis, and the synthesis of imaginative insight and historical understanding, of religion and science. Human progress, in Renan's view, is the acting out of a grand providential drama that neglects the individual.

In spite of his association with La Liberté de Penser, in 1849 Renan was sent by the minister of education to classify the manuscripts of some of the major Italian libraries previously open only to the country's German and Austrian occupiers. Renan's romanticism was stimulated by simple Italian Catholicism, and he found his peculiar sexuality was aroused more by the veiled than by the nakedly voluptuous statuary. He was attracted by women modestly at prayer. Naples, where he thought religion had degenerated into superstition, disappointed him, but he was enchanted by the rational, liberal attitudes at Monte Cassino, where biblical exegesis was as advanced as in Germany.

In the meanwhile Henriette had begun to assume for him the role of idealized womanhood. On his return to Paris in 1850 after touring northern Italy, Renan found that she was ill. He went to see her in Berlin, and only her diminished physical attractiveness seems to have saved him from an equivocal spiritual intimacy with her. From April 1851 they lived together in Paris, where Renan became completely absorbed in his work for the manuscript section of the Bibliothèque Nationale. His doctoral thesis, Averroës et l'averroïsme, appeared in 1852, but he was meanwhile also writing middlebrow pieces for the Revue des Deux Mondes (q.v.) and the Journal des Débats. La Liberté de Penser had come to an end with the 1851 coup d'état.

In 1856 Renan was elected to the Académie des Inscriptions and decided to marry Cornélie Scheffer, the painter's niece, which threw Henriette into tantrums of jealousy. Renan had twice previously dissuaded Henriette herself from marrying and now told Cornélie that he could not see her again if it was going to break Henriette's heart. He also told Henriette that he would renounce Cornélie for her. At this her resistance broke down, she called on Cornélie, and there followed a tearful encounter between the two women. Renan and Cornélie were married in 1856, though not before Renan himself had suffered a fit of jealousy on account of Cornélie's former fiancé, in two separate services, a Protestant and a Catholic one, and Henriette moved in with the couple, who were financially dependent on her. Renan's brother had failed in business and his mother proposed to end her days in a convent, but was eventually persuaded to live with her family in Paris, which she did from 1857 until her death in 1868.

Renan now published two volumes of collected essays, previously published in the *Revue des Deux Mondes* and the *Journal des Débats*, the *Etudes d'histoire religieuse* and the *Essais de morale et de critique*. He believed in Brittany as the home of dreamers marked by sadness and delicacy of sentiment and thought that reverence towards legend and man's need for faith was to be preferred to old-fashioned aggressive rationalism. He still found a sublimity and a poetry in Christianity to which he was attached, while also accepting its moral code. His translations of Job and of the Song of Songs were intended to retain their poetry and so release them from the hold of rationalist scepticism as well as of Christian dogmatism.

In 1860 Renan led an archaeological expedition to Byblos, taking the devoted Henriette as the expedition's accountant and his secretary. Cornélie joined the party at the end of the year, leaving their child (born deformed) behind. Members of the party noted the rivalry between the two women in their attentions to Renan. In 1861 he visited the Holy Land with them both. Cornélie then returned to France and Renan's later account in *Ma soeur Henriette* rhapsodizes about the encouragement and support Henriette gave him while he worked on his *Vie de Jésus*. Both fell ill of malaria on 19 September 1861, and medical help came too late to save Henriette, who died on the 24th. Renan, who himself narrowly escaped death, was deeply upset and returned to Paris, where he was elected to the chair of Hebrew at the Collège de France. It was a position he sought partly because of his family responsibilities, partly because he wanted to engineer the revival of semitic studies in France, and partly because he thought himself distinguished enough to have a right to a privileged status in French society. His inaugural lecture was intended to be inoffensive, and was in fact both tasteful and tactful, but there had been scuffles before the lecture began between the liberals and the Catholics, who protested at the content of the lecture. Renan's course was suspended, although he in fact continued to teach it in his own house, and neither his title nor his salary was affected.

He began to frequent the liberal salon of Princesse Mathilde, where he met Sainte-Beuve, Flaubert, Taine, Mérimée, and the Goncourt brothers. From March 1963 he became a guest at the Magny dinners. Although advised to await the revision of Strauss's *Life of Jesus*, Renan, who wanted revenge for the disruption of his inaugural lecture, published his *Vie de Jésus* in 1863, before he had properly planned the *Histoire des origines du christianisme*, of which it was the first volume. By the end of the year the *Vie de Jésus* had gone through 10 editions of 5,000 copies and been translated into most European languages. A revised edition appeared in 1864, the year which also saw the publication of Renan's account of the archaeological expedition. In June his appointment to the Collège de France was cancelled and he was given a post in the Bibliothèque Impériale, as the Bibliothèque Nationale was again known under the Second Empire, which he refused. In November, in the company of his wife, he explored Egypt and the Upper Nile as far as Aswan. The couple visited Henriette's grave and Renan visited the major sites associated with Saint Paul, ending up more fascinated by Greek than by scriptural antiquity. From 1865, while continuing to work with his customary intensity, he thirsted for political activity.

Renan continued to publish and to frequent liberal circles, including those of Prince Jérôme Napoléon, with whom he shared the misconception that the Prussian intellectual elite would put truth and civilization before national advantage. He had failed as liberal candidate for Meaux in 1869. During the war he sent his family to Brittany and in November 1870 was restored to his chair at the Collège de France. By now he had become a democrat, although he could still write in the *Journal des Débats*: "What is needed at the moment is an intellectual and spiritual elite." He was conciliatory when the Francophobe Mommsen wanted to restore communication between Berlin and French academies. His reflections on the political events of 1870 to 1871 led to the writings collected as *Dialogues et fragments philosophiques*, unpublished until 1876, and *La Réforme intellectuelle et morale*, finished by March 1871 and published in November of that year. Renan was disillusioned by both Bismarck and David Strauss.

From 1875 Renan suffered acutely from rheumatism and spent his summers in Italy, gradually despairing of France's political future, menaced, as he saw it to be, by the lack of a responsible conservative class. He wrote a series of philosophical dialogues which continue the oligarchical fantasies of the *Dialogues*, was elected to the Académie Française, and gave the Hibbert lectures in London in 1870. By now he was publishing his autobiographical *Souvenirs d'enfance et de jeunesse* and still travelling, though after 1880 no longer to Ischia. In 1881 he finished his translation of Ecclesiastes and, although his position as director of the Académie allowed him to make some important speeches, he largely devoted the remaining years of his life to the *Histoire du peuple d'Israël* and to playing the ironic, detached, and witty sage, paradoxical and brilliant, if at times superficial. He remained appreciative of the "aroma of old ecclesiastical manners," as he put it. In 1884 he brought out a new collection of religious studies, the *Nouvelles études d'histoire religieuse*, and from 1885 began to spend his summers in Brittany. As late as 1892, in the *Feuilles détachées*, although a republican, Renan regarded the army and the Church as two of the remaining bulwarks against decadence. Barrès called on him, but failed to penetrate the ironic mask and afterwards wrote an impertinent pamphlet recounting the visit, entitled *Huit jours chez M. Renan*.

Renan's last piece of speculative writing was the *Examen de conscience philosophique* of 1888, published in the following year. In 1889 he gave a speech at the Académie in which his denunciation of the past and pessimistic outlook on the future were only apparently ironic. It reminded Romain Rolland of Nero. Renan's rheumatism got worse, but he continued to lecture and to carry out his administrative duties at the Collège de France, of which he had been director since 1883. Standing for nearly an hour at an official Elysée ceremony on 1 January 1892 left him exhausted, and he knew he had not much longer to live.

In the summer he was back in Brittany, but returned to Paris unwell in September. His wife, wondering what she would do without him, was told that her task would be to uphold his reputation and to continue his life vicariously. On his deathbed he still refused to believe that death could be the absolute end, but was not drawn back towards Catholicism in spite of his artistic sensibility and profound commitment to a Christian morality. He died on 2 October.

WORKS

Renan's fame depended on the magically seductive power of his prose and his enigmatic wit. Most of his works, apart from some purely technical pieces on archaeological matters or semitic studies, aspire to literary significance. This is even true of his absorbingly interesting correspondence, edited by his grand-daughter Henriette Psichari. His first full-length work, *L'Avenir de la science*, was written by 1849 in an attempt to change public opinion, although it was not published until 1890. It was a defence of intellectual liberty, which seemed to Renan to be threatened even by a liberal government. The consolidation of scientific progress and revolutionary achievement seemed to require a charismatic leader of quasi-messianic authority. Given France's political history over the preceding 60 years it was not surprising that Renan thought a period of military tyranny not unlikely. It was his rationalistic hostility to ecclesiastical dogma rather than any firm commitment to democracy that made him an ally of liberalism.

L'Avenir itself might be diffuse and repetitive, the imaginative and unpractical response of a young idealist, but it would be a mistake to think of this committed semitic scholar as impervious to the social and economic crisis which caused the revolutionary wave to break in 1848. Of the 900,000 adult inhabitants of Paris only a third earned their living in identifiable ways, including begging and prostitution. Of the 15,000 registered prostitutes, nearly 2,000 were under 12. About half the babies born live failed to live a year. The radical idealism of thinkers like Fourier, Proudhon, Lammenais, and Leroux was inevitable. "Wherever you go," wrote Musset, "you tread on a messiah." What must be faulted in *L'Avenir* is not the moral response, the imperfect analysis, and the clumsy solutions, so much as the faint paranoia detectable in the proposal of historical research, Renan's new life commitment, as the panacea for social ills because it permitted a scientifically based insight into the nature of societies.

The collections of previously published articles, the *Etudes d'histoire religieuse* and the *Essais de morale et de critique*, define Renan's values in the mid-1850s, calling for the defence of traditional morality together with learning, scepticism, reverence, and austerity against the threats from materialism, the uniformity which tyranny would impose, and plebeian vulgarity of mind. What was required, in Renan's view, was informed imaginative insights into the nature of social, religious, and political systems.

The *Vie de Jésus* is of greater historical importance than literary merit. It drew its appeal from the emotional and aesthetic impact of Christianity and provoked an unexpectedly strong response. The way had been prepared by the romantic Christianity of Mme de Staël and Chateaubriand, although Renan's religious sensibilities are more refined, and his scholarship immeasurably superior to theirs. Renan, however, tries to harmonize the Gospels, leans in the first edition too heavily on the factual historicity of John, and makes Jesus into a figure of remote benignity. It was not only literary critics and historians who found traces of an idealized self-portrait in Renan's depiction.

His conjectures about the origins of Christianity do not pin Renan down to trying to reconstitute the historical Jesus, since he regards the Gospels as not factual but historical accounts of what happened. The miraculous interpretation of an event by a crowd or a person is thus itself part of the historical record. While the *Vie* holds to the existence of the historical Jesus, it does suggest that some of the miracles must have been deliberate deceptions, a view which naturally caused immediate and strong offence. Renan's Jesus was a religious leader trying to bring about a moral revolution. It is here that we see how entangled Renan's political aspirations and publications are with all that he wrote about the religious history of Israel and Christianity. The Crucifixion was the culmination of pressure from a frustrated people, brought up on the prophetic books, for a God-like messiah who wills his own death. It was the people who assigned him his place at the right hand of God, and the kingdom he founded was one of spiritual perfection. Renan, normally more cautious, does not draw back from speaking of Jesus's "transcendental disdain," and he does not mention the religion of love. In his view Christianity simply manifested what was divine in human nature, and was the creation of the popular Jewish mind. Jesus was the charismatic creation and victim of a collective myth.

The other volumes of the *Histoire des origines* take their note from the *Vie*. *Les Apôtres* presents the disciples as creators of their own illusions. It consoled Renan that Jesus should live on in the minds and imaginations of his followers, to whom he remained sympathetic. He momentarily goes back on the quietist implications of his view of Christianity, that society is to be purified rather than changed, but is too prudent to want to risk the apocalyptic explosion of social and religious ideas in France, which he thought had created Christianity in Palestine after Augustus had put an end to the public disorders. Renan's descriptions of Antioch and of the pagan world generally at the end of the first century were reverberations of his reflections on contemporary France.

The *Questions contemporaines* of 1868 is another collection of previously published essays, partly autobiographical, partly on higher education in France, partly a defence of constitutional monarchy. Renan now attacks the Revolution for its emphasis on individual rights, and comes to prefer German political and military solutions to French social ones. *Saint Paul*, the third volume of the *Origines*, covers the years 45 to 61 AD and carries on the social analysis of the Roman Empire, noting that, like contemporary socialism, Christianity was born out of the corruption of great cities. The blindness of the intellectual elite to what was happening in the Roman Empire was bound to be punished, Renan argues. When philosophy abdicates, religion stifles it. Renan's view of the Greek ideal, which derives from Chateaubriand, moved him so much that in 1876, after being confronted with the remnants of Greek civilization in Athens, he composed a *Prière sur l'Acropole* to Athena, although in it he rejected her absolute rule. In *Saint Paul* Greek religion is contrasted unfavourably with Celtic Christianity. Athena was the goddess of another orthodoxy and one which, unlike Christianity, repudiated the dialectical flux unveiled by historical scholarship.

La Réforme intellectuelle et morale would be merely a political pamphlet of largely ephemeral significance if it did not mark a turning point for Renan, in which his national pride, in the wake of the Franco-Prussian War, asserted its priority over his idealism. The political ideal is still authoritarian, however, and the old admiration for the Prussian virtues lingers on. The next volume of the *Origines, L'Antéchrist* of 1873, cannot refrain from implying a comparison of the siege of Jerusalem by Titus in 70 AD with that of Paris in 1871, first by the Prussians and then by Thiers. Here inevitably Renan turns against Prussia, setting out quite forcefully the historical parallels. The future may belong to the masses in France, amongst whom ideas were fermenting, as it did to the messianic and revolutionary movements which were to ruin the social structures of the Jews, but which were also their vocation and their lasting contribution to civilization. Renan seems to be aware that he is persuading the reader into fantasy with his seductively overstretched identification of Nero with Antichrist and the Beast of Revelation.

The philosophical dramas, *Caliban, L'Eau de Jouvence, Le Prêtre de Nemi*, and *L'Abbesse de Jouarre*, are of scant literary importance, but they do illustrate Renan's changing political views as he comes to accept the democratic side of liberalism despite the old aristocracy of temperament. They are also characteristic of his less academic manner of writing. Being so accessible, they did much to promote Renan's misleading image as a subversive.

The *Histoire du peuple d'Israël* is a much slighter work than the *Origines*, and it contains fewer descriptive interpolations. It sits lightly in relation to its sources and Renan even considered using different-coloured inks to indicate the relative probabilities of his conjectures. The work is in its way serious, but also imaginative and entertaining, even if its basic hypothesis about Judaic monotheism was already practically untenable when Renan took it up. In some respects subsequent discoveries, with regard to the Essenes for example, have proved Renan correct, and the *Histoire* is still interesting for its analysis of the literary expression of Jewish religious consciousness, although sometimes Renan's grating modernisms now sound out of place.

The autobiographical works, notably the *Souvenirs d'enfance et de jeunesse* and *Ma soeur Henriette*, intended only for Henriette's close friends, are not great literature, although they are well written and imaginatively stimulating. Part straight account, part anecdotal reminiscence, and part philosophical reflection, they inevitably put a gloss on the factual truth. The volumes of *Souvenirs* do not cohere into a unified autobiography, although all are autobiographical, and Renan cannot entirely be trusted when recalling his childhood, his seminary days, and later more philosophical attitudes. His writing, however, exudes his usual seductive charm and, in his own sense of the word history, his account is faithfully historical.

PUBLICATIONS

Collections

Oeuvres complètes, edited by Henriette Psichari, 10 vols., 1947–61

Works

Averroës et l'averroïsme, 1852
Etudes d'histoire religieuse, 1857
Le Livre de Job, traduit de l'hébreu…, 1858
Essais de morale et de critique, 1859
Le Cantique des Cantiques, traduit de l'hébreu…, 1860
Histoire des origines du christianisme:
    1. *Vie de Jésus*, 1863
    2. *Les Apôtres*, 1866
    3. *Saint Paul*, 1869
    4. *L'Antéchrist*, 1873
    5. *Les Evangiles*, 1877
    6. *L'Eglise chrétienne*, 1879

    7. *Marc-Aurèle*, 1882
Mission de Phénicie, 1864–74
Questions contemporaines, 1868
La Réforme intellectuelle et morale, 1871
Dialogues et fragments philosophiques, 1876
Mélanges historiques et de voyages, 1878
L'Ecclésiaste, traduit de l'hébreu…, 1882
Souvenirs d'enfance et de jeunesse, 1883
    1. *Le Broyeur de lin*, 1876
    2. *Prière sur l'Acropole*, 1876
    3. *Le Petit Séminaire Saint-Nicolas du Chardonnet*, 1880
    4. *Le Séminaire d'Issy*, 1881
    5. *Le Séminaire Saint-Sulpice*, 1882
    6. *Premiers pas hors de Saint-Sulpice*, 1882
Nouvelles études d'histoire religieuse, 1884
Histoire du peuple d'Israël, 1887–93
Discours et conférences, 1887
Drames philosophiques, 1888
L'Avenir de la science, pensées de 1848, 1890
Feuilles détachées, 1892
Ma soeur Henriette, 1895
Lettres intimes, 1896
Cahiers de jeunesse, 1906
Nouveaux cahiers de jeunesse, 1907
Fragments intimes et romanesques, 1914
Essai psychologique sur Jésus-Christ, 1921
Nouvelles lettres intimes, 1923

Bibliography

Girard, H., and H. Moncel, *Bibliographie des oeuvres de Ernest Renan*, 1923

Critical studies

Mott, L. F., *Ernest Renan*, 1921
Chadbourne, Richard M., *Ernest Renan as an Essayist*, 1957
Charlton, D.G., *Positivist Thought in France During the Second Empire, 1852–70*, 1959
Millepierres, F., *La Vie d'Ernest Renan*, 1961
Psichari, Henriette, *Renan, d'après lui-même*, 1927
Psichari, Henriette, *Renan et la guerre de '70*, 1947
Psichari, Henriette, *La Prière sur l'Acropole et ses mystères*, 1956
Wardman, H.W., *Ernest Renan: A Critical Biography*, 1964

RENARD, Jules (-Pierre), 1864–1910.

Novelist.

LIFE

Jules Renard was the fourth and last child of François Renard, a railway engineer and keen freemason, and his wife, Anne-Rosa Colin. The couple had married in October 1854, when they were 29 and 17. Their eldest daughter died when she was two; the second daughter, Amélie, the model for Ernestine in *Poil de carotte*, was born in 1859; and the third child, Maurice, the model for Félix, was born in 1862. Renard himself was born on 22 February at Châlons-sur Marne. His father was supervising the laying of the railway line from Laval to Caen.

Renard's correspondence and diaries kept from 1887 allow an exceptional insight into the relationship between his experiences in life, both before and after marriage, and his later fiction. While it is virtually impossible to determine whether or not the process of fictionalization, with its attendant distortions, was in some way extraordinary, Renard's documentation of the relationship between his youth and his fiction, especially his best-known novel, *Poil de carotte*, certainly is unusual. Renard himself was known in his family as "Poil de carotte (Redhead)," and he refers in his diary to his parents as M. and Mme "Lepic," the name of the parents in *Poil de carotte*. Both name and character had changed from those of the parents in *Les Cloportes*, which was also about family life.

In *Poil de carotte* the effects on the hero of incidents drawn from Renard's own childhood are exaggerated. The miseries of an unhappy childhood are only obliquely inspired by autobiographical reminiscences. Members of the family, especially Mme Lepic, are depicted more harshly than their real counterparts warranted, although from the correspondence we know that Renard's mother was mean and unpleasant to his young wife early in 1889, when "Marinette," then aged 18, was giving birth to her first baby, "Fantec," at the Renard family home at Chitry-les-Mines. Renard's mother used apparently to "forget" to lay a place for her daughter-in-law at table, to give her a dirty fork, or to leave a pile of collected crumbs there, as Renard noted in his diary for 12 March 1889. When he reread that passage in January 1906, he added in the margin that it was that attitude in his mother which impelled him to write *Poil de carotte*. It was certainly early in 1889 that Renard first adopted the focus on family life to be found in *Poil de carotte*, in which, he later said, he wished to avenge himself for his mother's spitefulness.

In considering the focuses of Renard's imaginative interest, it is important to refer to his explicit account of early incestuous feelings towards his mother, and their repression, as he recalls them in the diary on 18 October 1896, two years after the novel's publication and while his mother was still alive. After talking in the diary about the use of the tongue in kissing, Renard goes on to recall how his mother lifted up her arms and neck to tie ribbons round her throat, how she revealed her thighs, yawned, or put her head in her hands:

Ma mère, dont je ne parle qu'avec terreur, me mettait en feu. Et ce feu est resté dans mes veines. Le jour, il dort, mais la nuit, il s'éveille, et j'ai des rêves effroyables

(My mother, about whom I only speak with fear, set me on fire. And that fire has remained in my veins. During the day, it sleeps, but at night it wakes up and I have horrible dreams.)

The content of the recurrent dream is narrated in the present tense. M. Lepic reads his paper.

Je prends ma mère qui s'offre et je rentre dans ce sein d'où je suis sorti. Ma tête disparaît dans sa bouche... Aussitôt après nous redevenons ennemis... De ces bras dont je l'en-laçais passionnément, je la jette à terre, l'écrase; je la piétine, et je lui broie la figure sur les carreaux de la cuisine

(I take my mother, who offers herself to me, and I return to this womb I came out of. My head disappears into her mouth... Immediately afterwards we become enemies again... With these arms with which I had passionately embraced her I throw her to the ground and crush her. I trample on her and grind her face into the kitchen tiles.)

When Renard was two, the family had returned to Chitry-les-Mines, near Nevers, and Renard's father became mayor of the commune. Renard and his elder brother were boarded at a pension, whose pupils attended the lycée at Nevers. Renard was a pupil there from 1875 until he failed the first part of his baccalauréat in 1881. Academically his record had been good and his family wanted him to try for the Ecole Normale Supérieure. He was sent to Paris, successfully resat the failed examination, was sent to the Lycée Charlemagne, but early in 1883 abandoned any ambition of a teaching career, although he passed the second part of the baccalauréat.

Supported by a small family income, he had begun to write, sending articles to provincial reviews, and thought seriously about a political career. He began to frequent literary and journalistic circles, and his name became linked with that of the actress Danièle Davyle, who recited his poems, especially *Les Roses*, at public performances and was to become the model for Blanche in *Le Plaisir de rompre*. While in principle studying law, Renard began to read widely and write fiction. He successfully strove for publicity, and articles about him appeared in *Gil Blas* and on 27 October 1884 in *La Presse*, and Rachilde wrote about him in *Zig-Zag* in 1885. Renard wrote to his sister that he owed everything to women. Having hoped to stay in Paris, he had to go to Bourges for his military service, which he started in November 1885.

Les Roses appeared at Renard's own expense in 1886 and was reviewed by Camille Delaville in the *Revue Verte* for 25 July. Renard was beginning to publish occasional journalism, but in 1885 had been let down by Monnier, who had agreed to publish the eight contes of *Crime de village*, but eventually had to return them. Military service bored Renard, who was determined not to go back to Chitry. In 1886 he passed the examinations for a job with the eastern railway company at 125 francs a month whenever one became available. That winter he tried for a whole variety of jobs, finally taking a journalist's post in March 1887 at 100 francs a month. It lasted only until June. In March the conte "Une passionnette" had been published by Léo d'Orfer's *Revue de Paris*. This was about to change its name to the *Revue de Paris et de Saint-Petersbourg* from April, when it turned out that Arsène Houssaye had re-registered the more famous title 24 hours earlier.

From the summer of 1887 Renard became tutor to the novelist Augustin Lion's three sons, receiving 175 francs a month for working three hours a day. In August he undertook a small literary commission in Barfleur about the nature of which he is vague. There was trouble with the Lion family and Renard was dismissed as tutor, although he continued to do occasional literary work for the novelist. It was probably at Barfleur that he met the 17-year-old Marie Morneau, who had a potential dowry of 300,000 francs. Renard married her on 28 April 1888. His relationship with his mother-in-law, who lived in the same building, quickly became tense. He was now reasonably well off, could send d'Orfer 50 francs towards what he was collecting for Verlaine, and had his wife's portrait painted for 650 francs. Orfer offered him an editorial position on the *Revue de Paris*, and in 1889 he took the largest shareholding (six shares out of 25) among the co-founders of the *Mercure de France*, which was to be edited and managed by Alfred Valette. Renard spent from January to late summer at Chitry, where Fantec was born on 2 February, where he began to keep his diary, and where his attitude towards his mother began to inspire the invention of "Mme Lepic."

The first number of the *Mercure*, dated 1 January 1890, had appeared on the preceding Christmas Day with a conte by Renard, the first of many which the review was to publish, although Renard also published elsewhere. From 1890, however, he was a prominent member of the literary world, associated largely through the review with Valette, his wife Gabrielle, known as "Rachilde", Coppée, Huysmans, Daudet, and Descaves. He became an early member of the committee of the Académie Goncourt (see Goncourt), was close to Marcel Schwob, and got to know Maeterlinck and Claudel. His first novel, *Les Cloportes*, published posthumously in 1919, had been turned down, although we do not know by whom, and Renard met Lemerre, who published the collection of contes from the *Mercure* under the title *Sourires pincés*, in October. Renard publicly announced his intention of giving up the verse which he had been sporadically publishing in magazines over the preceding eight years and succeeded in establishing himself as a leading literary journalist. In 1891 he began his association with *Gil Blas*, with Théâtre de l'Art of Paul Fort, founded to encourage symbolist (q.v.) drama, and with André Antoine's naturalistic Théâtre Libre, founded in 1887.

In January 1892 Ollendorff published 6,500 copies of Renard's *L'Ecornifleur*, to be serialized in *L'Echo de Paris*, from which Renard was now earning 200 francs a month. In addition to this and his other sources of literary and journalistic income, now including *Gil Blas* and *Le Figaro*, as well as the *Mercure*, Renard was receiving 200 francs a month from *Le Journal* for 80–100 lines a week. In fact, he augmented his income by considerably increasing the amount of copy he was contracted to write, publishing wherever possible in reviews before allowing his work to appear in volume form, and even serializing after volume publication. In the midst of his growing success, Renard's daughter "Baïe" (Julie-Marie) was born on 22 March 1892. Ollendorff now bought the unsold sheets of *Sourires pincés* from Lemerre, relaunched the book, and in February 1893 published *Coquecigrues*, to be followed in June by *La Lanterne sourde*. Ollendorff, however, sold *Sourires pincés* to Flammarion, the company who in 1894 published *Poil de carotte* at as much as three and a half francs. The original 43 episodes, which became 48 in the second edition, had never been serialized, but included five chapters rescued from *Les Cloportes* and the first part of *Sourires pincés*. It was the third edition of *Poil de carotte* in Calmann-Lévy's 95-centime "Nouvelle collection illustrée" in 1907 that established the work's popular success. Some 80,000 copies were sold within a year. Renard meanwhile energetically pursued his hobby of bicycling, while increasingly important literary names were dropped into his diary. The short notes and maxims written for the *Mercure, Le Vigneron dans sa vigne*, were published by the paper and the 1900 edition became famous for its introduction of Renard's

gardener Philippe.

Despite his success, Renard remained depressed. He knew that *Poil de carotte* merely stopped, but did not end, and that it could have been shorter or longer, with more or fewer episodes. He was disillusioned with journalism. He wrote in the diary for 29 November 1894: "I haven't succeeded anywhere. I've turned my back on *Gil Blas, L'Echo de Paris, Le Journal, Le Figaro*, the *Revue Hebdomadaire*, the *Revue de Paris*, etc. None of my books has had a second edition. I'm earning on average 25 francs a month… I quickly have enough of my friends… My imaginatic is an empty bottle, the dregs of a jar." In fact, Renard continued to publish in most of the newspapers and reviews he mentions and wrote increasingly for the *Revue Blanche*. He attached much importance to his standing in the literary world and turned to the theatre. His one-act play *La Demande*, written in collaboration with Georges Docquois but adapted from one of his own short stories, opened in Boulogne in January 1895, then at the Odéon in Paris on 9 November. Renard began to go to the theatre more often, met Rostand, found that Sarah Bernhardt admired his work, and went to the opera for the first time. In March 1897 his one-act play *Le Plaisir de rompre* established him as a playwright. His father, who was incurably ill, shot himself on 19 June, an action his son much admired.

In 1898 Renard came out strongly against the condemnation of Zola, thereby siding with Dreyfus in the dispute. He was too shocked by his father's death to want to work, and increasingly preferred to socialize and spend time with his friends from the world of theatre. Shooting had been his father's favourite pastime. Renard took it up after his father's suicide, but was to give it up from 1904 to 1906. He continued to produce a continuous stream of journalism and short imaginative pieces. The *Histoires naturelles* of 1896 indicate a new direction in his work, hingeing on detailed but poetically resonant descriptions of plant and animal life, but Renard also continued to publish short stories, articles, reviews, and plays. The stage version of *Poil de carotte* was successfully launched in March 1900 and published later the same year.

Literary success brought public honours and Renard became a councillor and a member of the Légion d'Honneur. In May 1904 he became major of Chitry, as his father had been, but experienced the first signs of heart trouble after his campaign. Ollendorff published a volume of his plays, including *Le Plaisir de rompre, Le Pain de ménage, Poil de carotte*, and *Monsieur Vernet*, the stage adaptation of *L'Ecornifleur*. His journalistic activity became increasingly restricted to dramatic criticism. The election to the Académie Goncourt came in 1907. A review of *Ragotte* by Rachilde led to a break with the *Mercure*, and Renard sold his shareholding to Maurice Pottecher in 1909. In August of that year his mother drowned in the well at Chitry. It is not clear whether her death was an accident or suicide. Renard himself died in May 1910.

WORKS

Only critical slovenliness in search of categories has affiliated Renard with one of two movements with which he has virtually nothing in common. The first is symbolism (q.v.), on account of his association with the *Mercure* and Paul Fort's Théâtre de l'Art. The second is naturalism (q.v.) because of his use of dialect, his one-act plays of cynical, if not bitter disillusion about country life, of the amount of bile sharpening his vision of human nature at its meanest and sourest, and of the 45 *Histoires naturelles* of the first Flammarion edition, five of which Ravel and two of which Rollo Myers set to music. They are extremely sharp vignettes, described with quasi-scientific rigour, but often by metaphor, and were powerfully helped by the later Floury edition of 22 texts limited to 100 copies, published in 1899 with 22 lithographs by Toulouse-Lautrec. Flammarion's 1904 edition contained 70 texts, to which the 1909 Fayard edition added a further 13. The number grew to 85.

The eight short fictions of *Crime de village* were selected from 15 written in five weeks in 1885 and, although Monnier had accepted them, it was not until Renard's marriage in 1888 that he could afford to pay the 250 or 200 francs to get d'Orfer to print them. Their only interest is to show an over-excitable and easily irritated sensibility. *Les Cloportes* was half written at the beginning of 1888, abandoned at the time of the marriage, and probably not taken up again until the stay at Chitry for Fantec's birth, when Renard's inspiration was already becoming sharper, more hostile, and bitter as the episodes for *Poil de carotte* formed in his imagination. He did not find a publisher for *Les Cloportes* and quite quickly became dissatisfied with the episode where its heroine, Françoise, commits self-immolation. Renard was always prompt with self-criticism, but he was right about the inadequacy of his first novel.

The most interesting aspect of Renard's work is how he drew on events, judgements, and incidents narrated in his *Journal* and letters and combined them with his modest fictional and dramatic talents to point out life's meannesses. There is imaginative power in the way *Poil de carotte* ruthlessly strips away all psychological indulgence in its character depiction, but much interest in watching how the experiences of youth, and the stay at Chitry in 1889, transformed the Lérin family of *Les Cloportes* into the unpleasant and occasionally brutal Lepic family of the 1894 novel. There is a similar fascination in seeing the superficially and only moderately entertaining pieces of *Sourires pincés* emerge from the attempt to establish norms appropriate to the new *Mercure*, for which they were almost all first written. Its foundation, according to the diary entry for 14 November 1889, took place at a meeting whose tone was more light-hearted than formal, however serious the business may in fact have been.

L'Ecornifleur was written in 1890 and concerns a scrounging writer who shamelessly exploits the vanity and self-deceptive prowess of a bourgeois couple, M. and Mme Vernet. M. Henri seduces first the wife and then the niece, analysing himself as he goes along. The novel is written partly in dialogue form and printed like a play, with the name of each speaker preceding his or her words. Renard thought this device was original, but later discovered it had been used much earlier. This made it easier for him to take up the challenge he was now repeatedly encountering, that he could write nothing expect the shortest vignettes. Autobiographical details are cynically distorted to Renard's own disadvantage. Self-criticism is taken almost to the point of self-torment, so that an unflinching irony sometimes outbalances the sympathy and the poetry of the work. It is the novel's harsh intensity which reveals its origins in diffident self-assessment, and for a long time Renard could not decide whether to make *L'Ecornifleur* an episode in Poil de carotte's life, thus giving it a more formally autobiographical anchorage. Almost all the critics saw the irony and bitterness as the reaction of too delicate a sensibility, and enjoyed the detailed accumulations of petty van-ities, prejudices, and false assumptions whose interaction is the novel's strength.

Coquecigrues consists of texts published from 1890 to 1892, and *La Lanterne sourde* of texts mostly published in the winter of 1892–93. The subjects are reduced to almost nothing—waiting for a storm, making a snowball, the smallest surprise, or the tiniest of life's ironies. The texts themselves are too short to make more than a single point, but they do it unhurriedly and with a fine ironic sense. *Poil de carotte* is not in any ordinary sense a novel. It is a series of very loosely connected scenes of country life in a family where the boy, Poil de carotte, is miserable, dreamy, and sensitive, occasionally bullied and neglected, and occasionally loved. The now polished irony prevents any emotional sympathies from bonding the reader too closely to even the central character, who is also dirty, dishonest, cowardly, and cruel, but who nevertheless provokes feelings of protectiveness and empathy. The power of the novel lies in the inflexibility of its psychological realism. No ripple of emotional complacency, self-deception, or self- indulgence in any of his characters escapes the narrator's unblinking but not malevolent eye. Mme Lepic may be cruel, but the narrator is not. He surprises the reader by revealing the motivation behind the simplest as well as the most complex of actions or reactions. Outward appearances—"Grand frère Félix," "Soeur Ernestine," "Mme Lepic"—are respected, even when the inward realities reveal a betrayal of the outward social, domestic roles. The result shows the perverse charm which often underlies the hypocrisies and hesitancies of social behaviour. Remorseless analysis of the psychological vulnerabilities which determine responses to trivial events, particularly on the level of personal relationships, makes some of the vignettes very powerful indeed, however insubstantial their apparent topic—going out into the dark to lock up the hens, debating how to greet parents returning from holiday, or the reception at home of a school report.

PUBLICATIONS

Collections

Oeuvres complètes, 17 vols., 1925–27
Correspondance complète, 1953
Théâtre complet, 1957
Oeuvres, Bibliothèque de la Pléiade, 1970ff.

Fiction, vignettes, prose poems

Crime de village, 1888
Sourires pincés, 1890
L'Ecornifleur, 1892; as *The Sponger*, 1957
Coquecigrues, 1893
La Lanterne sourde, 1893
Le Vigneron dans sa vigne, 1894
Poil de carotte, 1894; as "*Carrots*," 1946
Bucoliques, 1898
Les Philippe, Patrie, 1907
Nos frères farouches. Ragotte, 1908
Les Cloportes, 1919

Plays

La Demande, with Georges Docquois, 1896

Le Plaisir de rompre (produced 1897), 1898
Le Pain de ménage, 1899
Poil de carotte (produced 1900), 1900; as "*Carrots*," 1904; same
    title, 1946
Comédies, 1904
La Bigote, 1909
Huit jours à la campagne, 1912

Verse

Les Roses, 1886

Other

Histoires naturelles, 1896; as *Hunting with the Fox*, 1948
Mots d'écrit, 1908
Causeries, 1910
L'Oeil clair, 1913
Correspondance, 1928
Lettres inédites 1883–1910, 1957
Journal 1887–1910, 1960

Critical and biographical studies

Coulter, H.B., *The Prose Work and Technique of Jules Renard*,
    1935
Schneider, P., *Jules Renard par lui-même*, 1956
Guichard, L., *Renard*, 1961

————

REVERDY, Pierre, 1889–1960.

Poet, critic, writer of fiction, and editor.

LIFE

Reverdy was born in Narbonne on 13 September 1889. He spent a happy childhood, largely in the country near Carcassone, and received his early education locally before going as a boarder to the lycée at Toulouse, where he proved a poor scholar. His father had continued the family trade by becoming a carver, and his death is a recurring memory in Reverdy's imagination. In 1910 Reverdy went to Paris, and settled in Montmartre, attracted by the city's literary glitter but, as he says, scarcely knowing how to read, and unable to write at all. He was employed by a printer as a proof reader, and later as a secretary by J.-J. Brisson, editor of the *Annales*, but quickly got to know Picasso, Braque, Gris, and Apollinaire, without whom, he later said, he "would have amounted to nothing." He also knew Matisse, Gleizes, Jacob, and the whole circle of poets and painters whom he joined in Montmartre just before the group split up. By 1924 Breton, Soupault, and Aragon said they regarded him as "the greatest living poet." Even if the claim made on his behalf that he was a principal founder of modern poetry goes too far, Reverdy was certainly one of modern poetry's most articulate theorists.

He quickly gained a reputation for his knowledgeable writing about painters, and as early as 1912 he is to be found as editor of the single-number *Bulletin* of the "Section d'Or" cubist (q.v.) painters. The *Bulletin* appeared on 9 October, the day of the preview of their first exhibition at the Galerie La Boétie, with contributions by, among others, André Salmon, Apollinaire, and Jacob. Reverdy helped Apollinaire choose the title *Alcools* for his famous 1913 collection of verse, and himself published 100 copies of his *Poèmes en prose* in October 1915. Most were townscapes in the manner of Rimbaud, but with nothing about them to indicate either Reverdy's later connection with surrealism (q.v.), his rebellion against conventional values and social norms, or his later mystical devotion. Forty of the 50 *Poèmes en prose* were to be reprinted in *Epaves du ciel*, an anthology of pieces from his nine earlier volumes, and all 50 in *La Plupart du temps: poèmes 1915–1922*. The early volumes were published at Reverdy's own expense, no doubt with Brisson's help, and often with drawings or etchings by Matisse, Picasso, Derain, or Gris.

After the 12-page *Quelques poèmes* and the slim *La Lucarne ovale* of 1916, Reverdy, who had been declared unfit for the military service for which he had volunteered, started the short-lived literary review *Nord-Sud*. The name derived from the north–south underground line between Montmartre, which had been the artists' headquarters, and Montparnasse, south of the river, to which Picasso, Jacob, Apollinaire, and Salmon had now moved. The first issue of 15 March 1917 is a tribute to Apollinaire. Reverdy, Picasso, Jacob, Gris, Cendrars, and Dermée had organized the famous lunch given for Apollinaire on 31 December 1916 and attended by the whole of literary Paris. Apollinaire naturally contributed to the review, which appeared monthly until May 1918, and then only once more, that October.

Reverdy was extremely reticent about his travels and the business affairs which appear to have occupied him. We know only of his literary life and, after World War I, little enough about that, except for what is revealed in the succession of books of verse, the contes, the novels that were really prose poems, and the books of aphorisms and notes. Under Jacob's influence he became a Catholic, being baptized in 1921, and from 1926 retired to a life of solitude close to the monastery of Solesmes. Apart from occasional journeys, he remained there in austere solitude until his death, without however taking any committed part in the monastery's life. Religion, he says in the 1927 "notes" *Le Gant de crin*, was a "circle of fire and ice," a light strong enough to have "burnt his eyes." He complained that, having left his literary life to look for God, what he found was a religion. Further autobiographical notes appeared as *Le Livre de mon bord* of 1948 and *En vrac* of 1956.

WORKS

Reverdy is often described as a "cubist" poet, although, like Braque, who regarded him as the only perceptive art critic among the writers associating with the cubist painters, Reverdy himself thought the idea of cubist poetry "absurd." After the semi-humorous poetic novel about Montmartre, *Le Voleur de Talan*, he did, however, contribute to the *Anthologie Dada* of 1919, although his texts, unlike most of the contents, appeared only in the French and not the bilingual version of the volume. The anthology text "199—Cs" is a cryptic attack on Picabia (see

dominating position in French culture which it had enjoyed during the 19th century.

――――――

RIMBAUD, (Jean-Nicolas-) Arthur, 1854–1891.

Poet.

LIFE

Rimbaud's father was born in 1814 into a family of artisans and, after joining the army at 18, worked his way up through the ranks to become a captain, held for a while a post in the military administration of Morocco, and retired in 1864. Some of his reports have been published, and he left a number of manuscript volumes. His style was concise, factual, and clear. In 1853 he married Vitalie Cuif, who was almost 28 at the time. Her outlook was severely religious, very narrow, and highly moral. As well as compulsively devout, she seems to have been socially ambitious, and quarrelsome, and Rimbaud's life as a poet was in part a devastatingly explosive revolt against his mother's tenacious grip. His parents lived with Rimbaud's maternal grandfather, and a first child, Frédéric, was born at the end of 1853. Rimbaud himself was born in October 1854. Both babies were sent out to be nursed. A first daughter, born in 1857, died in infancy, but two more daughters, Vitalie and Isabelle, were born in 1858 and 1860, the year in which Rimbaud's parents separated. One of his mother's brothers had died young. The other, after having practically ruined the family farm, became a drunkard. The family lived at Charleville, about 10 miles from the Belgian border, quite near Sedan, and about 40 miles from Charleroi in Belgium, which is on the main Paris–Brussels line.

Rimbaud was a brilliant pupil at Charleville's famous school, the Institution Rossat, which he attended from 1861 to 1865, when he was transferred to the more traditional and religiously orientated Collège de Charleville. From 1 November 1869, when the second set started to appear, he bought the monthly issues of Lemerre's *Le Parnasse Contemporain* and, modelling himself on Hugo and Marceline Desbordes-Valmore, whose poems appeared in the *Revue Pour Tous*, himself got a poem, "Les étrennes des orphelins," published in that review on 2 January 1870. Rimbaud used to submit supplementary exercises to the master in charge of his class, often French or Latin verses. His mother objected strongly to the fact that Georges Izambard, the 22-year-old class master during Rimbaud's final year, loaned her son his private books, such as Hugo's *Les Misérables*. The class itself was divided into ordinary pupils and prospective priests, who wore clerical dress, and was the forum in which Rimbaud's anti-religious views were forged, even if they were developed chiefly in reaction to his mother. By 1869 his tastes and attitudes had homogenized. He inclined towards Parnassian (q.v.) anti-Christian poetry, taking Banville and Leconte de Lisle as his idols, and towards left-wing republicanism in politics, and a materialist and atheistic outlook in religion. Emotionally and psychologically his upbringing had

exerted a powerful effect on him, and his intellectual positions did not prevent serious emotional conflicts.

At the end of the school year in 1870 Rimbaud carried off a portfolio of prizes. In May he wrote to Banville, enclosing three poems which he hoped might appear in *Le Parnasse Contemporain*. Izambard had left Charleville in July. The Franco-Prussian War was about to break out. Rimbaud, who had had another poem published in August, sold some books for 20 francs and tried to run away to Paris. The war had cut the train services, but he reached Paris via Belgium, and was arrested for fare evasion. Izambard was alerted, had Rimbaud sent to Douai, where he lived, and informed his mother before returning him to Charleville. Rimbaud ran away again, but failed to get a job in Belgium and fled to Dieppe, having in various ways persistently abused Izambard's friendship. He was returned home once more and did not meet his former teacher again, although Izambard did send Mme Rimbaud a bill for his out-of-pocket expenses.

The college had not reopened in the autumn, and on 1 January 1871 Charleville was itself occupied by the Germans. Rimbaud, whose relations with his mother were by now extremely tense, sold his watch and ran away a third time, just possibly with a girl, hoping to mix in the literary Bohemia he had dream about. He returned a fortnight later, broke. The college reopened, but Rimbaud got a job with *Le Progrès des Ardennes*, a paper that was suppressed within days. Although the war came to an end with the armistice of 29 January, the revolutionary movement in France was now struggling for power and Rimbaud returned to Paris in the latter part of April to join it. The insurrection, known as the Commune, lasted from mid-March until 28 May, by which date the government had re-established control of Paris. Distaste had forced Rimbaud to withdraw from the mob of volunteer revolutionaries, and he returned to Charleville in time to write the two important letters on his aesthetic ideas, dated Charleville 13 and 15 May 1871, addressed respectively to Izambard and to Paul Demeny, a young poet to whom Izambard had introduced him, and to whom he had sent his entire portfolio of 22 poems in October 1870. Early in May, probably while still in Paris, Rimbaud had written three poems, "Chant de guerre parisien," "Les mains de Jeanne-Marie," and "Paris se repeuple," and in June he asked Demeny to destroy the poems sent the previous October and sent him three new ones, "Les poètes de sept ans," "Les pauvres à l'église," and "Le coeur du pitre."

During the summer of 1871 Rimbaud continued to read voraciously and experienced a spiritual crisis that was profoundly anti-Christian. He went on writing poetry and began to express a sometimes violent dislike of the female sex, not altogether surprisingly in view of his mother's imperious moral stance and domination of the fatherless household, but apparently provoked by the rejection of timid advances he had made to a girl in the spring. Rimbaud was now entering what was to become an extreme phase of adolescent rebellion. He started by growing his hair very long, in the Parnassian style, and by unleashing his resentment on representatives of authority of all sorts, including God, Napoleon, his mother, librarians, and Belgian frontier officials. He took to stealing, borrowing, and buying books on credit. From Izambard he extorted 35 francs to pay a debt of which notice had been served on his mother. On 15 August he sent an offensive letter and an even more offensive poem to Banville, who had not responded to the poems Rimbaud had sent in 1870. In August he also sent some poems to Verlaine through the mediation of a friend of Izambard, Charles

Bretagne, who had known Verlaine at Fampoux in 1869. He wrote again two days later. Verlaine, who was 27, and had been married just over a year, and whose wife was expecting their first child, responded sympathetically to the "whiff of lycanthropy" in Rimbaud's letter, and a little later sent him some money that had been collected among the Parnassians, inviting Rimbaud to come to Paris. When he left for Paris on about 10 September, Rimbaud had with him the manuscript of his best-known poem, "Le bateau ivre."

Rimbaud's total poetic output was produced between 1870, when he was 15, and 1875, when he was not quite 21. In spite of its extraordinary richness and power, particularly in its mastery of strident imagery, in retrospect it appears to have been almost a by-product of his adolescence. He had written more than half his surviving verse poems by the time he arrived in Paris. Verlaine and Charles Cros, a poet friend, went to meet Rimbaud's train, missed him, and returned home to find him waiting, sullenly monosyllabic, in the company of Verlaine's wife and her mother, Mme Mauté, with whom the Verlaines lived and who was to put Rimbaud up for the time being. He was surprised at the middle-class household, and behaved so appallingly that he had to be moved out before M. Mauté returned from the south. He was lodged in a succession of spare rooms and on studio floors, intent on taking out his resentment on everyone and, while alienating everyone he met, trying to enlist their support for the protest against social order and controls which had underlain the aesthetic outlined in his May letters to Izambard and Demeny. He wanted poetry accorded what he saw as its rightful place in leading the movement to destroy the bourgeois social order.

Verlaine, who believed equally strongly in the reformatory power of emotion and music, was half won over. Rimbaud was seated at Verlaine's right for the Parnassians' monthly September dinner, the first since the outbreak of war a year previously. He recited "Le bateau ivre" to general acclaim, but his curt and sulky behaviour and defiance of all conceivable social rules, even such as existed in radical and bohemian circles, left the Parnassians unimpressed. Whatever his poetic potential, Rimbaud appeared to them little more than a tedious adolescent. Coppée, Mendès, and Heredia were left cold by the brilliant but infantile newcomer, and the enthusiasm of that first dinner was extinguished as swiftly as it had flared, never having spread outside the little Parnassian group of the Latin Quarter. Rimbaud met Banville, to whom he was again insolent, but neither Gautier nor Leconte de Lise. He was photographed, but took absolutely no care of personal cleanliness or appearance.

Rimbaud detested his dependence on others, particularly on the idolized poets who turned out to be as middle-class as anyone he had known at Charleville. Banville gave him houseroom and blankets, and he cynically exploited all offers of financial aid in cash or kind, taking pleasure in whatever discomfort he could cause, and doing whatever he could to make a bad impression. Paris had disillusioned him. The group that had crystallized round *Le Parnasse Contemporain* seemed to consist of so many office clerks, and Verlaine was clearly distracted by the birth of his infant son on 30 October. His wife, Mathilde, began to reproach him with his obsession for the good-looking, ill-kempt, sulky, and aggressive Rimbaud, who subsequently disappeared for a few days. A search was instituted, and Rimbaud was found living rough with a group of tramps, covered with lice, and eating out of dustbins He was clearly seeking a way to

sacrifice himself to his poetic vocation. The Banvilles, in particular, took it upon themselves to help him, and he was found a job, with free lodging, in the Parnassian bar of the short-lived "Club Zutique" (q.v.), established that October. The poems he wrote in Paris at this time include the famous sonnet "Voyelles." When the club closed Verlaine's friends paid for a room for Rimbaud, and Verlaine, who was drinking too much, spent more and more time with him, to the bitter reproaches of his wife, with whom he was now seriously quarrelling. Her counter-offensive included getting Parnassian friends to allude openly in the papers to Verlaine's close liaison with Rimbaud.

Mathilde took the baby to Périgueux and refused to return unless Rimbaud left Paris. By now his behaviour was violent as well as loutish and arrogant, and Verlaine's marriage was already effectively lost. Rimbaud did go back to Charleville and Mathilde did return, but Rimbaud was back in Paris by May 1872, perhaps because Verlaine had ceased to send him any money. He was writing poetry throughout, and the Charleville poems show a renewed concern for poetic form, while their tone is less full of adolescent anger. From May, however, the relationship with Verlaine ceased to be merely emotional, no doubt on Verlaine's insistence, although Rimbaud's desire to flout conventional morality combined with the circumstances of his youth may well have left him homosexual inclinations.

In Paris he found that, his captivation of Verlaine apart, he was not wanted. He had published nothing to speak of, and he decided to leave in search of a warmer climate, somewhere beyond society's reach. His last poem was dated 27 June 1872. Verlaine had had a job since April. Rimbaud went to deliver a note to Verlaine telling him he was going to Belgium, unexpectedly met him, and told him his plans in person. After a day spent drinking and talking to Rimbaud, Verlaine decided to accompany him. Verlaine's mother and Mathilde followed him to Belgium in an attempt to get him back, but failed. In September Verlaine and Rimbaud went to England, where Rimbaud noted down the fragmented pieces that would later become *Les Illuminations*. He was unhappy in England, particularly disliking London's damp, wintry fog, and returned to Charleville in December, but went back to London with Verlaine's mother, who paid his fare, when Verlaine fell ill in January 1873. He stayed with Verlaine, who was now regularly getting drunk, until April, when he went to the family's farm at Roche.

At Roche he wrote sketches for *Une saison en enfer*, intending the title to refer to the period of his relationship with Verlaine, which he had once regarded as a season in heaven rather than hell. He returned to London and Verlaine in May. Although they both gave French lessons and continued to receive financial support from Verlaine's mother, the poverty and the quarrels became intolerable. Rimbaud was now writing the final version of *Une saison en enfer*. He and Verlaine had taken to wrestling with one another, sometimes with the points showing from cloth-covered knives, and in July Verlaine left for Brussels, followed by his mother. He intended to commit suicide if Mathilde refused to return to him but, after a highly charged and emotional exchange of messages, Rimbaud came from London to meet him.

Verlaine was close to absolute despair and, as usual, had been drinking when, on 10 July, he brandished a pistol he had bought that morning, intending to kill either Rimbaud or himself. He wounded Rimbaud with the first shot he fired, aimed apparently at the floor, and then, overcome with remorse and in an alcoholic haze, gave Rimbaud the pistol and asked him to shoot him in the temple. Verlaine and his mother took Rimbaud to a hospital, where the wound was dressed. Rimbaud persisted, however with his intention to leave and on his way to the station, accompanied by Verlaine and his mother, was again threatened by Verlaine with his pistol. Verlaine had walked a few paces ahead. It was at this point that Rimbaud had him arrested. He was sentenced to two years in prison and in despair Rimbaud returned to Roche, where he finished *Une saison en enfer*. His mother paid a deposit and he had 500 copies printed, sending some to friends in October. He could not afford to pay for the printing, however, and left the bulk of the copies on the printer's hands, losing all interest in them.

In March 1874 Rimbaud went back to London with Germain Nouveau (1852–1920), a poet whom Rimbaud must have met in Paris and who would later be greatly influenced by the converted Verlaine of *Sagesse*. In England both taught French, and Rimbaud's mother spent July with him. Rimbaud, himself already under police surveillance prior to the shooting incident, seems to have returned to Charleville before going to Stuttgart in 1875. On his release from prison Verlaine visited him there and took charge of the manuscript of *Les Illuminations*. Verlaine's last letter to Rimbaud was sent from London, dated 12 December 1875. Much of Rimbaud's remaining life is now conjecture. He certainly crossed the Alps on foot, visited Milan, where he fell ill, and contemplated going to Spain, probably to enlist in the Carlist army. He went to Paris instead, returned to Charleville, and learnt to play the piano on an instrument hired by his mother, while continuing to study his languages.

In 1876 he was refused admission to Austria, crossed southern Germany on foot, and arrived in Brussels, where he joined the Dutch foreign legion. He deserted three weeks after reaching Indonesia, joined a Scottish boat as a sailor, and returned to Charleville in December 1876. In 1877 he may have worked as an interpreter for a French circus in Germany, Sweden, and Denmark. After trying to join the US navy from Bremen, and certainly being in Stockholm in June, he continued to wander through Europe, leaving traces of his visits at Marseilles, Civitavecchia, and Rome. He was in Charleville and Paris, intermittently, helped with the 1878 harvest at Roche, crossed the Vosges on foot later that year, and got to Switzerland, Genoa, and Alexandria. In October he was in Cyprus.

Rimbaud had abandoned all interest in literature and could not tolerate cold climates. He caught typhoid in 1879, worked on the farm at Roche, returned to Cyprus in 1880, and got a job on a construction site in charge of 50 building workers. He left for the Red Sea and found a job in Aden, from where he was sent to Harar, in what was not yet Abyssinia, where he spent 1881, partly exploring and looking for ivory. He spent the next few years between Aden and Harar, touchy about the climate and about his conditions of service. From 1885 his principal occupation was gunrunning, at which he was commercially unsuccessful. In 1887 he was writing articles from Cairo for the French press, amusing himself with false reports as time went on. The following year he set up a commercial agency in Harar, unaware that Verlaine had written an essay on him in his *Les Poètes maudits* of 1884, and had published *Les Illuminations* in *La Vogue* in 1886.

By February 1891 Rimbaud had what turned out to be cancer of the right knee, rheumatic in origin but aggravated by syphilis. He had himself transported back to Aden, then to France. Rimbaud's mother was called to Marseilles, where the leg was amputated in the paying part of the hospital on 27 May 1891. Rimbaud returned to Roche, tried to leave once more for the East, but was hospitalized again in Marseilles. He confessed and received the last sacraments before dying on 10 November 1891 at the age of 37.

WORKS

Rimbaud's immense poetic ambitions as an adolescent and his later complete indifference to literature were matched step for step, firstly by the exaggerated rebelliousness of his cult of indiscipline and the high tensions of his relationship with Verlaine, and secondly by the adventurous but not disordered life of an East African trader into which they subsided. His letters home from East Africa were laconic, factual, but not unaffectionate. The legacy of his literary activity and social behaviour during the period of its production left its mark none the less on the history of European literature. Rimbaud's poetic activity, although extraordinary in content, was neither as original nor as rich as has sometimes been supposed. At its high point it continued to be subjected to an element of formal discipline. The aesthetic expounded in the letters to Izambard and Demeny in May 1871, *Les Illuminations*, and the increasing disillusion of the central section of *Une saison en enfer* may well have charted the path for 20th-century developments in which artistic creation was freed from formal constraints, or contributed to agreements that such constraints needed to be rethought.

It is probable that 20th-century developments would have taken place as they did even without the stimulus provided by Rimbaud, but as a matter of historical fact Rimbaud's work, linked to the reputation left by his behaviour, did give a powerful boost to, and come to symbolize, those subsequent artistic developments which depended on the loosening or abandonment of rational control by the artist. It is possible that Rimbaud's personal history of hope and disillusion has had greater importance for the history of literature than his aesthetic theories, and his aesthetic theories than his verse, which, however unsustainably intense and vivid at its peak, has suffered from attempts to bulk out its volume with schoolboy exercises and later business correspondence.

The first published poem, "Les étrennes des orphelins," combines reminiscences of a Latin poem with lines derived from the recollection of Coppée, Hugo, and Baudelaire. It was written, when Rimbaud was 15, with a potential church-going, middle-class, sentimental readership in mind, and is naturally pastiche. The poem that followed, "Soleil et chair," was sent to Banville in May 1870, together with "Sensation" and "Ophélie," which was inspired by Banville's own "L'exil des dieux" from the first number of the second series of *Le Parnasse Contemporain*, published on 1 November 1869. Rimbaud later changed the title of "Soleil et chair" to "Credo in unam," significantly altering the opening of the Nicene Creed. It begins the attack on Christianity for its middle-class values and its suppression of the sensual side of man which was to be continued in "Les premières communions" and to culminate in the poems of 1871.

All the early poems of 1870 and 1871, even those which most potently express feelings of religious, social, political, or merely domestic rebellion, are largely conventional in form. They contain neologisms, popular, scientific, and even quasi-dialect terms and deliberately shocking vulgarities, but apart from their provocative forthrightness and occasional strong sarcasm their only extraordinary feature is merciless realism. Even if the content seethes with rebellious sentiments, most are written in Alexandrines and a third of them are sonnets. All of them alternate masculine and feminine rhymes. Even after declaring his aesthetic in the letters of May 1871, Rimbaud stuck to familiar patterns of rhyme and rhythm, thereby forcing himself to disregard his own new poetic principles in favour of traditional, consciously organized poetic composition.

On 13 May 1871 Rimbaud wrote a letter to Izambard which its recipient described as a "profession de foi littératuricide (profession of faith of literature's executioner)," concerning what Rimbaud calls "encrapulement," the systematic degradation and repudiation of the whole social system, but especially, given the context, its academic side. Izambard's poetry will never be other than "fadasse" (wretchedly pale), Rimbaud says. He himself is on strike. His tone is intensely sarcastic, but still teasing: "Maintenant, je m'encrapule le plus possible. Pourquoi? Je veux être poète, et je travaille à me rendre *voyant*: vous ne comprendrez pas du tout (Now I'm becoming as dissolute as I can. Why? I want to be a poet and I'm working at becoming a *seer*: you won't understand)." The idea of the poet as endowed with superior vision or supernaturally inspired knowledge is antique, taken up in the Renaissance and the 18th century, and frequently by the romantics (q.v.) and the early Parnassians. The means of attaining the unknown is for Rimbaud "le dérèglement de *tous les sens* (the disorientation of *all the senses*)." The young Rimbaud postures about the enormous burden of suffering his appointed task lays on him: "Je me suis reconnu poète. Ce n'est pas du tout ma faute (I have recognized that I'm a poet. It isn't my fault);" "JE est un autre ("I" is someone else);" "It's tough on the wood that finds itself a violin."

Two days later Rimbaud wrote his famous "Lettre du voyant" to Demeny. It starts pretentiously, sweeping away poetry's past, from the Greeks to the romantics, as no more than rhymed prose: "Car JE est un autre." "If brass wakes up as a bugle, it is not its own fault…I am simply present at the flowering of my thought. I look at it, listen to it…" What Rimbaud does not tell us is who plays the violin or blows the bugle. If the poet is simply an instrument, then who or what plays it? If the implied answer were to be the subconscious rather than any external or metaphorical agency, we would not be far away from surrealism (q.v.). Music and rhyme, writes Rimbaud, are the stuff of games: "Le Poète se fait *voyant* par un long, immense et raisonné *dérèglement* de *tous les sens*. Toutes les formes d'amour, de souffrance, et de folie (The Poet makes himself a *seer* by a long, immense, and logical *disorientation* of *all his senses*. All the forms of love, of suffering, of madness)." The poet distils the very essence from every poison: "unspeakable torture: to arrive at the unknown the poet must become an outcast." He has only seen his visions when he has ceased to understand them. The poet steals the fire from the gods, he takes charge of humanity, of all creation, bringing his discoveries into the world with form if they have it, or without if they do not. There will be a universal language, because words represent ideas, and that language will be soul for the soul, synthesizing everything, scents, sounds, colours.

Rimbaud's language is already highly metaphorical, the product more of buzzing images than of clear ideas, and his coherence diminishes as the letter continues, but the essential is clear,

not unrelated to what the romantics, especially Vigny, felt about the poet, although nearer in spirit to Baudelaire and in articulate theory to Mallarmé, Maeterlinck, and Valéry. Rimbaud's staccato affirmations also take in their stride number, harmony, and the liberation of women, who will become poets' and enrich our understanding. The poetic outcome of all this theory was "Le bateau ivre," written some three months later.

The poet identifies himself with the drunken boat which drifts, out of control, in the uncaring waters, although he sometimes appears to be in charge of it. The first stanzas depict in strict poetic form the poet's progressive liberation. He is alone, insulated from society's economic and social constraints, both going where he wishes and directed by the uncontrolled boat. There are no fixed points. Even the landmarks are mobile. The imagery is not entirely consistent, and the points are uncertainly made, but Rimbaud was only just 17 when he wrote "Le bateau ivre." The poet is purged of what is merely human, and begins in the sixth stanza to discover the universe, "le Poème/De la Mer" (the Poem/Of the Sea). The eighth stanza starts to describe the new knowledge in a vertiginous rhapsody of images of light, colour, sound, opacity, rainbows, gulfs, and cataracts. Then in the 16th and 17th stanzas the world of fantasy gives way nostalgically to the real world, before the poet's identification of himself with the boat is reasserted and he becomes self-conscious, uncertain: "Je regrette l'Europe aux anciens parapets (I miss Europe and its ancient parapets)." The poem ends on a note of disillusion and timidity—"Toute lune est atroce, et tout soleil amer (Every moon strikes dread and every sun bitterness)"—but also of impatience with the world how that the vision is lost. The poet does not dare to endure the liberation he has glimpsed, or perhaps dreamt. Rimbaud's message to his elders in Paris was that he was frightened of the poetic mantle he felt he could neither dare to don nor bear to reject.

The contact with Verlaine brought about an immediate change in his style. The famous "Voyelles," by assigning colour to sounds, takes up a technique, common enough in 19th-century France, of emphasizing the parallels which exist between painting, poetry, and music, but with the exception of the last, the sonnet's rhymes are all feminine, a metrical scheme never hitherto used by Rimbaud, though favoured by Verlaine. After Rimbaud's arrival in Paris in 1871, he wrote only three poems in Alexandrines. Several have odd numbers of syllables to the line, as advocated by Verlaine's "Art poétique," which was written about this time, though first published only in 1884. Rimbaud was soon to out-distance Verlaine in poetic innovation, however, using assonance and alliteration as a substitute for rhyme, and sometimes abandoning rhythm. He was moving swiftly towards the prose poems of *Les Illuminations*, most of which must date from 1872 and early 1873.

The transition, even if swift in time, was gradual in degree. Unhappily we do not know the order, or even with certainty the date, of *Les Illuminations*, although the title would change in meaning according to date of composition, referring to "visions" if written early or, more likely, "printed engravings" or "colour plates" if the title dates from later than 1873, which is what Verlaine said, although the evidence suggests that he is here mistaken. *Les Illuminations* is not a series of deft sketches like Baudelaire's prose poems, and the individual pieces continue to contain elements of versification, especially assonance, alliteration, and rhythmic effects, even when printed as prose, but they work by accumulating images, almost in lists, as to some extent

"Le bateau ivre" had done, though they pile them on more densely and without resorting to that poem's complex syntax. The anger expressed in *Les Illuminations* is fiercer and broader in target than in the 1871 poems, and the desire for escape more compelling. The attack on Christianity is sharpened. *Les Illuminations*, as we have the work, including what may be the 1875 postscripts of "Guerre," "Jeunesse I," and "Solde," and the Scandinavian "Dévotion" and "Démocratie," is generally acknowledged to contain the best of what Rimbaud wrote.

It is a work of frustrated hopes rather than disillusion. There is doubt even in "Matinée d'ivresse," which refers to Rimbaud's relationship with Verlaine, and the hoped-for conquest of the categories of good and evil in the God, Satan dichotomy. "A une raison" had been a paean to the new harmony and the new love which that conquest would make possible. It is "Matinée d'ivresse" which celebrates it, but the "promesse surhumaine faite à notre corps et à notre âme créés (superhuman promise made to our body and our soul)" will not easily be fulfilled. The interment of the tree of good and evil, the removal of the tyranny of good behaviour to make way for our all-pure love, will end in a release of perfumes, but we must wait, "ne pouvant nous saisir sur-le-champ de cette éternité (unable to take immediate possession of this eternity)." In "Royauté" the ecstasy lasts only one morning, although in "Vies" nothing disturbs the "stupeur" of the promised land. In perhaps most of the pieces disillusion creeps in, as in the beginning of "Vagabonds" and the endings of "Ouvriers" and "Les ponts." The high points are the descriptive rather than the meditative pieces, but the work overwhelmingly conveys the impression (much stronger still in *Une saison en enfer*) of a failed attempt to create a new poetic harmony in a universe beyond good and evil.

Une saison en enfer admits that the idyll has turned into an inferno. The values of society and their Christian core have in the end enslaved the poet. The heart of the "livre païen" or the "livre nègre," as it was going to be called, lies in the two parts of "Délires," beginning "Ecoutons la confession d'un compagnon d'enfer (Let's listen to the confession of a companion in hell)." There is a connection between these two parts. The first admits to disillusion with the prospect of a social revolution, and the second with the proposed poetic revolution which would have brought about the social one. A great sense of guilt wells up in an intense lyrical lament, and staccato sentences add to the effect of short, breathless utterance, as in "Je suis esclave de l'époux infernal (I'm the slave of the satanic spouse)." Verlaine's wife speaks of her husband's union with Rimbaud, and the emotive force is very strong. The first "Délire" ends "Drôle de ménage! (Some marriage!)."

The second "Délire" is autobiography, half of it printed as verse, dealing with Rimbaud's childhood and the "voyance," now regarded as a simple delusion, "hallucination simple": "Je finis par trouver sacré le désordre de mon esprit (I ended up finding my mental disorder sacred)." In "L'impossible" the glimpse of the ideal reduces the poet to silence. The allusions from the literature of alchemy make some of the prose poems difficult, but they are seldom as hermetically unintelligible as, for instance, some symbolist texts. The disillusion is now more bitter. Pride in "Adieu" has fallen. To do without a moral order is impossible. It is to live a lie.

Since Rimbaud abandoned his work, and since virtually none of what has subsequently been considered of importance was published by him during his lifetime, he must be regarded as having written off his whole adolescent literary endeavour and social protest. He no doubt wished to see it forgotten. Indeed his brother-in-law, Paterne Berrichon, who first published the *Oeuvres* in 1898, tells us that this was in fact the case. However, while he was in Africa Verlaine was publishing the poems of "the late" Arthur Rimbaud in Paris and alone profiting from them. Subsequent generations have retrospectively adopted Rimbaud as an influence, for which purpose they have had to rely on Verlaine's 1886 magazine publication of *Les Illuminations* and the few copies of *Une saison en enfer* which Rimbaud himself had disseminated. Yet, however forthright, Rimbaud was a child and a poet of the very early 1870s. His first published poem was written the year Gide was born.

In Paris Rimbaud may have been arrogant and boorish but, as Gide rightly insisted in opposition to Claudel, his achievement was precisely due to his adolescent fierceness, uncomplicated by culture in any but the technical sense of reading and skill in Latin and French versification. Neither Mallarmé nor Lautréamont can ever have read him. Only the surrealists can really claim his inheritance, since only they took up his attempt to fix in writing the promptings of the subconscious. As he himself said, "J'écrivais des silences, des nuits, je notais l'inexprimable. Je fixais des vertiges (I wrote of silences, of nights; I noted the inexpressible. I fixed the moments of vertigo)." Whatever the rights and wrongs of publication and claims of "influence," it is certain that Rimbaud has in fact enriched the body of lyrical writing in French.

PUBLICATIONS

Collections

Poésies complètes, edited by Paul Verlaine, 1895
Oeuvres de J.-A. Rimbaud, edited by Paterne Berrichon, 1898
Oeuvres complètes, edited by Antoine Adam, 1972
Oeuvres, edited by Suzanne Bernard and André Guyaux, 1981
Complete Works, Selected Letters, edited by Wallace Fowlie, 1966

Verse and Prose

Une saison en enfer. 1873; as *A Season in Hell*, translated by Delmore Schwartz, 1939, Louise Varese, 1945, Norman Cameron, 1950, and Enid Rhodes Peschel, 1973
Les Illuminations, edited by Paul Verlaine, 1886; edited by A. Py, 1967, and Nick Osmond, 1976; as *Les Illuminations*, translated by Enid Rhodes Peschel, 1973
Le Reliquaire, edited by L. Genonceaux, 1891
Les Stupra, 1923
Selected Verse Poems, translated by Norman Cameron, 1942
Selected Verse, translated by O. Bernard, 1962

Critical studies

Fowlie, Wallace, *Rimbaud* (in English), 1946; revised edition, 1965
Miller, Henry V., *The Time of the Assassins*: *A Study of Rimbaud*, 1956
Hackett, C.A., *Rimbaud* (in English), 1957
Starkie, Enid, *Rimbaud* (in English), 1961
Frohock, W.M., *Rimbaud's Poetic Practice*, 1963

Houston, J.P., *The Design of Rimbaud's Poetry*, 1963
Cohn, Robert Greer, *The Poetry of Rimbaud*, 1973
Saint Aubyn, Frederic C., *Rimbaud* (in English), 1975
Chadwick, C., *Rimbaud* (in English), 1979
Hackett, C.A., *Rimbaud: A Critical Introduction*, 1981
Ahearn, Edward J., *Rimbaud: Visions and Hesitations*, 1984

ROBBE-GRILLET, Alain, 1922–

Novelist and film maker.

LIFE

Robbe-Grillet's theoretical writings are not a blueprint for his fiction, but an attempted justification of it. His family, whose interests lay mostly in engineering and science, lived in Paris, where Robbe-Grillet took the mathematics baccalauréat before successfully studying for the agrégation in agronomy. In 1942 he was deported with his whole class to work in a factory in Nuremberg, but was sent home ill after a year and graduated in 1945. For two years he worked for the national statistical institute before joining his sister's laboratory, doing ill-paid, part-time work on hormones in order to write a novel. He then took a regular government post, for which, in 1949, he had to go to the West Indies to oversee banana plantations. The background to his life there did service for *La Jalousie*. Robbe-Grillet fell ill, went to hospital, and was repatriated, finishing *Les Gommes* on the way home in 1952.

His first novel, *Un régicide*, had been left with the publisher Gallimard, who had sent it on to Editions de Minuit. Robbe-Grillet suggested that they publish *Les Gommes* instead. It was not particularly well received, but did attract favourable reviews in literary magazines and in 1954 was the subject of an important article published by Barthes in *Critique*. It also won the Prix Fénéon. Robbe-Grillet was still an agronomist, just surviving financially, when, in 1955, he was offered a permanent position as literary consultant with responsibility for the fiction list at Editions de Minuit. That same year *Le Voyeur* appeared and, amid much controversy, was awarded the Prix des Critiques, a prize that had gone to Françoise Sagan the year before. *Le Voyeur* gave rise to considerable offence, but the publicity helped it commercially and it sold 10,000 copies in its first year.

Robbe-Grillet now started to write his assertive and simplistic pieces on literary theory in the popular *L'Express*. Further theoretical writings appeared, notably in 1956 and 1958, and a revised selection as *Pour un nouveau roman* in 1963. Meanwhile, in 1957 Robbe-Grillet published *La Jalousie* and married Catherine Rstakian. She acted minor roles in some of his films, took the stills on set, and may well have written the pornographic novel *L'Image* (1956). *Dans le labyrinthe* was published in 1959. From that year Robbe-Grillet devoted much of his time to the cinema, directing and publishing "ciné-romans," as well as publishing full-length novels. He has lectured and taught in the US and taken part in symposia devoted to the "nouveau roman" (1971) and to his own work (1975) at Cerisy. He has collaborated on a number of works and written several screenplays and occasional pieces. The film with which he is chiefly associated, Alain Resnais's *L'Année dernière à Marienbad*, won prizes in Venice and in France. In 1960 Robbe-Grillet signed the anti-colonialist political "Manifeste des 121."

WORKS

For Robbe-Grillet the 19th-century novel communicated in representational form to its readers some truth of which the author, linked to the rising bourgeoisie, was in possession. In his view only the novel, not painting or music, continued to reflect 19th-century values after World War II. Encouraged by Barthes, Robbe-Grillet increasingly abolished the story line in his novels in favour of long, intricate descriptions of shapes, forms, and textures, transferring the interest from character and plot to the world as perceived, throwing light only on the ways in which we perceive external realities in reaction to certain stimuli. However, even Barthes was taken aback by *La Jalousie*, which tracked the distorting effects of jealousy on perception. The title refers both to the emotion and to the slotted window blinds through which the narrator perceives the world. It sold only 600 copies in its first year, provoked numerous essays on literary theory, but within a decade or so was widely used as a literary textbook both inside and outside France.

The theoretical writings are aggressively polemical, de facto reflections on the nature of the novel rather than facets of a carefully thought-out literary theory. Robbe-Grillet regularly changes his mind or adjusts his emphasis, for ever challenging his own "theory" for fear that, once expressed, it might become stratified. The constant is that writing does not state what is known, possessed, or preconceived. It is a search for statement, so that the form is in fact the content. Robbe-Grillet provided inspiration for the avant-garde group which founded the review *Tel Quel* in 1960, but the group dissociated itself from him when he began to appear on (and clearly enjoy) the writers' circuit, visiting Tokyo, Athens, Belgrade, California, and Leningrad. His novels have been translated into 25 languages and had sold half a million copies in France by the mid-1980s.

Les Gommes could be read as a perversely written detective story with an ironic twist at the end and met with a shocked reaction. Its real purpose is veiled. This was to show the reader that objects, events, and people cannot be made to yield meanings that exist only with reference to an intellectual grid which imposes such categories as causation and consequence from outside the text. The reader is teased for repeatedly falling into the trap of looking for clues to explain the attempted murder. Time, place, and communication all appear subject to some Einsteinian warp in which announcements are incomprehensible, messages indecipherable, and memory's functions erased. The title signifies "The Erasers." The sleuth is forced on to the defensive by his refusal to let go of his external references in time and space, and so becomes ridiculous, ending up by committing the murder he is investigating.

The protagonist of *Le Voyeur* is a sexually obsessed psychotic who may or may not have committed a rape. It is never made clear whether the rape actually took place or was merely an unenacted fantasy. It does not matter, any more than it matters in *La Jalousie* whether A… and Franck do or do not have sexual intercourse, or whether the owner of the narrative voice is or is not A…'s husband. In each case what is at stake is the effect a mental event has on physical perception and emotional reaction. In *Le Voyeur* times and places fuse. One part of the work invites the reader to construe Mathias as guilty and the rest, after a blank page, invites him to view Mathias's guilt as the result of pure fantasy. In *La Jalousie*, on the other hand, everything depends on the tension between the reader's emotional identification with or repudiation of the reaction of the anonymous narrating presence.

The subject of *Dans le labyrinthe* is a delirious soldier who is experiencing hallucinations. The novel takes the dissolution of real events to their ultimate extreme, starting with the weather, which is whatever the narrator says it is or wants it to be, and continuing with the elaborate ambivalence between references to the painting on the wall and the world outside. The narration shifts from the soldier to one or more other poles of perception as the novel continues. Whatever the final judgement on Robbe-Grillet's literary stature, there is already virtual unanimity that *La Jalousie*, *Le Voyeur*, and *Dans le labyrinthe* represent the peak of his achievement.

For the next six years Robbe-Grillet concentrated on making films. By the time he began writing novels again his style had changed. The later novels, starting with *La Maison de rendez-vous*, no longer concentrate on the description of objects as perceived, but on the associations they generate. Anecdote reappears in the form of irrepressible self-parody with complicated reference to other parts of the text and to Robbe-Grillet himself. Trivial objects grow in stature as they are subjected to increasingly minute description. The reader is invited to read erotic significance into what is described, suggested, but never stated, as Robbe-Grillet manipulates the erotic fantasies of the popular and sometimes degrading culture which he evokes.

Projet pour une révolution à New York takes the complex self-parodies of *La Maison* even further, as the narratives run in disharmonious counterpoint to one another, defying the reader's normally inexhaustible capacity to create meaning. *Topologie d'une cité fantôme* allows the written text to disintegrate into a collage of previously written fragments. This work, like *Souvenirs du triangle d'or*, is intended to be playful, but Robbe-Grillet's taste has become increasingly questionable, and he appears here to have abandoned any attempt to refine and distil the early critical insights, perhaps in the later self-parodies even doubting their value.

PUBLICATIONS

Fiction

Les Gommes, 1953; as *The Erasers*, 1964
Le Voyeur, 1955; as *The Voyeur*, 1958
La Jalousie, 1957; as *Jealousy*, 1959
Dans le labyrinthe, 1959; as *In the Labyrinth*, 1960
L'Année dernière à Marienbad, 1961; as *Last Year at Marienbad*, 1962
Instantanés, 1962; as *Snapshots*, with *Towards a New Novel*, 1965
L'Immortelle, 1963; as *The Immortal One*, 1971
La Maison de rendez-vous, 1965; as *La Maison de Rendez-Vous* (in English), 1966; as *The House of Assignation*, 1970
Projet pour une révolution à New York, 1970; as *Project for a Revolution in New York*, 1972
Glissements progressifs du plaisir, 1974
Topologie d'une cité fantôme, 1976 as *Topology of a Phantom City*, 1977
Souvenirs du triangle d'or, 1978; as *Memories of the Golden Triangle*, 1984
Un régicide, 1978
Djinn, 1981; as *Djinn* (in English), 1982

Plays

Screenplays: *L'Année dernière à Marienbad* (*Last Year at Marienbad*), 1961; *L'Immortelle*, 1963; *Trans-Europ-Express*, 1967; *L'Homme qui ment* (*The Man Who Lies*), 1968; *L'Eden et après*, 1970; *Glissements progressifs du plaisir*, 1974; *Le Jeu avec le feu*, 1975; *La Belle Captive*, 1983

Other

Pour un nouveau roman, 1963; revised edition, 1970; as *Towards a New Novel*, with *Snapshots*, 1965; as *For a New Novel: Essays on Fiction*, 1966
Rêves de jeunes filles, with photographs by David Hamilton, 1971; as *Dreams of a Young Girl*, 1971; as *Dreams of Young Girls*, 1971
Les Demoiselles d'Hamilton, with photographs by David Hamilton, 1972; as *Sisters*, 1973
La Belle Captive, with René Magritte, 1976
Temple aux miroirs, with Irina Ionesco, 1977

Critical studies

Alter, Jean, *La Vision du monde d'Alain Robbe-Grillet: structures et significations*, 1966
Watson Fraizer, Dale, *Alain Robbe-Grillet: An Annotated Bibliography of Critical Studies, 1953–1972*, 1973
Morrissette, Bruce, *The Novels of Robbe-Grillet*, 1975
van Wert, William, *The Film Career of Alain Robbe-Grillet*, 1977
Fletcher, John, *Alain Robbe-Grillet* (in English), 1983
Leki, Ilona, *Alain Robbe-Grillet* (in English), 1983

ROLLAND, Romain (-Edmé-Paul-Emile), 1866–1944.

Novelist, dramatist, essayist, historian, and critic of music and painting and winner of the Nobel prize for literature (1915).

LIFE

Romain Rolland was born on 29 January 1866 into an old French bourgeois family at Clamecy, an ancient and beautiful small town in Burgundy about 60 miles west of Dijon. His father, Emile, was a lawyer from a republican family; his mother, Marie Courot, was a retiring woman of great piety who was exceedingly fond of music. It was she who fostered Rolland's musical interests, taught him to play the piano, and familiarized him with Beethoven, whose life he was later to write and whose music was to fulfil him until his death. Rolland himself left souvenirs of his peaceful, introverted, and somewhat intense childhood in *Souvenir d'enfance*, written in 1910 but not published until 1930. Music was the most important influence in his life, and the fact that much of what he heard and played was German, and was associated with a peaceful and relatively contented childhood, accounts for something of his later internationalism. The other important early influence was Shakespeare.

A sister, Madeleine, born in 1868, died in 1871, and when in 1872 another daughter was born, she too was given the name Madeleine. Rolland's schooling at Clamecy made it clear that he was academically gifted, so his parents decided to sell the legal practice, give up life in the country, and move to Paris, where Rolland could undertake the preparatory lycée studies necessary to enter the Ecole Normale Supérieure. It was a considerable sacrifice, but Rolland's father found a post in a Paris bank, and Rolland duly entered the Lycée Louis-le-Grand in 1882. He began to keep a diary and attended the Sunday Pasdeloup concerts until they stopped in 1884, sharing an enthusiasm for Wagner with his school-fellow Paul Claudel. He also read widely, especially Spinoza, and then Tolstoy and Hugo, but twice failed the entrance examination for the Ecole Normale.

He passed in 1886, coming fourth, and lost sight of Claudel, who failed. In his second year Rolland, rather unusually, deserted philosophy and literature for history and geography, a decision which again affected his future outlook. Had the choice been left to him, Rolland would almost certainly have studied music, but parental ambition left him no choice, and he took the agrégation in history in 1889, coming ninth out of 14 successful candidates. In 1887 he had been badly shaken when his idol, Tolstoy, issued *Que devons-nous faire?* attacking a great deal he believed in, including his idolized Beethoven and Shakespeare. He exchanged letters with Tolstoy, accepting the Russian's view that manual work had a higher moral significance than the aestheticism and intellectualism he found in Paris. The other influence which had impinged on him a few months before his first letter to Tolstoy was Renan, who had allowed Rolland to visit him on 26 December 1886. Rolland had broken with Catholicism four or five years earlier, and was impressed by Renan's vision that day of a future in which mankind would know the truth not through religion, but through science.

In the year of his agrégation Rolland was awarded the annual scholarship for the best history student graduating from the Ecole Normale, which allowed him to spend two years studying history at the French School in Rome. Two fellow students had turned it down, and he himself was not enthusiastic until he arrived and was overwhelmed by the Renaissance rather than the antique splendours of the city. He then neglected his thesis to write several unpublished historical dramas inspired by Shakespeare. He also met the woman he was to call his second mother, Malwida von Mysenbug, whom he had already met in fact at Versailles, and on whom he now called daily. Malwida had been a close friend of Mazzini, Nietzsche, and Wagner. She was a German socialist refugee living in Italy, former guardian of Olga

Herzen, the daughter of the Russian anarchist who had married the French historian Gabriel Monod. Rolland played to her and she virtually formed him to her European-wide taste in literature.

The idea of a world literature which would transcend national boundaries was not new. Goethe had spoken of it to Eckermann in 1827, but when Rolland wrote about it in the *Mercure de France* in 1903, it was under the influence of Malwida von Mysenbug:

> Nous ne sommes ni latins, ni germaniques…Notre nation est le plus riche mélange de l'Europe, et c'est là sa grandeur… Plus nous serons Européens, plus nous serons nous-mêmes.

> (We are neither Latin nor Germanic… Our nation is the richest mixture in Europe, and that is its strength… The more European we are, the truer we shall be to ourselves.)

Perhaps just as importantly, Malwida von Mysenbug had restored to Rolland the concept of artistic and intellectual heroism which Tolstoy had undermined. In 1891 he visited Bayreuth with her.

In Paris again from 1891, Rolland finished his thesis on the history of opera before Lulli and Scarlatti, obtaining his doctorate on 19 June 1895. Shortly after his return, on 11 April 1892, he had met Clotilde Bréal, whom he married on 31 October the same year. They spent some months in Rome from November 1892, while Rolland completed his research, and from his return in 1893 he taught first at the Lycée Henri IV, and then at Louis-le-Grand. His plays were neither published nor, in spite of all his efforts, performed. In 1895 he started to teach the history of art at the Ecole Normale. He was later to move to the Sorbonne, where he taught music. A student brought him a copy of Péguy's *Jeanne d'Arc* and at his own request Rolland met Péguy, for whose *Cahiers* he wrote before they became the *Cahiers de la Quinzaine*, which Rolland himself helped to found. During the last years of the century he travelled to Belgium and Holland, to Germany, and then again to Italy.

In 1895 Rolland became attracted to socialism and also published his theses. The minor one, still in the then obligatory Latin, concerned the decline of painting in 16th-century Italy. He also published an early article in the 1892 *Mélanges d'Archéologie*, the in-house review of the French School in Rome, followed in 1897 by the tragedy *Saint Louis* in the *Revue de Paris*. The next year Rolland began to write for the *Revue d'Art Dramatique*, which published *Aërt*, a verse tragedy performed that year on 3 May by the Théâtre de l'Oeuvre. *Les Loups*, one of his three dramas about the Revolution, which had an implicit reference to the Dreyfus affair, was also staged at the Théâtre de l'Oeuvre under the title *Morituri* and over the pseudonym "Saint-Just." On 21 June 1899 *Le Triomphe de la raison* was performed by the same troupe and, like the later *Danton*, was published in the *Revue d'Art Dramatique*. There were two trilogies: *Les Tragédies de la foi*, comprising *Saint Louis, Aërt*, and *Le Triomphe de la raison*; and *Le Théâtre de la Révolution*, comprising *Les Loups, Danton*, and *Le 14 juillet*.

Rolland's first biographical study was of Millet, which was published only in English translation in 1902. Then followed the three lyrical biographies in the series "Vies des hommes illustres." The *Cahiers de la Quinzaine* published the *Vie de*

Beethoven in January 1903, the *Vie de Michel-Ange* on 1 July and 21 October 1906, while *Tolstoï* was published by the *Revue de Paris* in February and April 1911. All three were popular successes. The volume on Beethoven grew partly out of Rolland's friendship with Malwida von Meysenbug, who was enthusiastic about the composer, and partly out of a journey to Mainz in 1901, after Rolland's marriage had failed, to hear Weingartner conduct the symphonies. The enthusiastic account of that experience, which Rolland published in May 1901 in the *Revue de Paris*, was the nucleus of the *Vie*, and Beethoven was the first of the figures whom Rolland could portray in the style of the artist hero he was looking for.

In the preface to the 16th edition Rolland stated that the biography was not written as historical research "pour la science," but that it was "un chant de l'âme blessée (the song of a wounded soul)." The *Vie de Michel-Ange* was inspired more by compassion than by hero-worship, and grew out of the secondary thesis in Latin, some elements of which had been rewritten for the *Revue de Paris* of 1 January 1896. In an article, "Les Salons de 1901," published in the *Revue de Paris*, Rolland had already generally denounced contemporary art, excepting Rodin, whose position among his contemporaries he compared to that of Michelangelo. The *Vie de Tolstoï* was the result of a direct invitation in 1911 from the *Revue de Paris*, one of whose directors, Ernest Lavisse, then also director of the Ecole Normale, had been one of Rolland's teachers. When Rolland received the invitation, he was still in bed recovering from an automobile accident on 27 October 1910. Of the three biographical subjects, Tolstoy was the one with whom he could most closely identify, although he continued to reject Tolstoy's Christianity. It was in 1908 that Rolland published his *Musiciens d'autrefois* and *Musiciens d'aujourd'hui*.

Rolland's relationship with Péguy later cooled, but it was in the *Cahiers de la Quinzaine* that the impressionistic, 10-volume "roman-fleuve" *Jean-Christophe* first began to appear. This follows from birth to death the career of Jean-Christophe Krafft, a German musical genius who makes France his second country. Although still close to Péguy and convinced of the innocence of Dreyfus, Rolland kept out of the public controversy surrounding the affair. There are, nevertheless, allusions to it in the life of Beethoven, as there had been in the earlier *Les Loups*. During the first decade of the 20th century Rolland was mainly busy with the plays, then with the biographies and *Jean-Christophe*, but he continued to teach the history of music at the Sorbonne from 1904 to 1912. He wrote mostly in Switzerland, where he was staying at the outbreak of World War I. In 1901 he and his wife had been divorced. Rolland returned to live with his parents, and he also founded the *Revue d'Histoire et de Critique Musicale*, later the *Revue Musicale*. *Jean-Christophe* was to reflect the mental journey that Rolland himself had undertaken—from initial stoicism to a more relaxed view of the world, as can be traced in the biographies.

Rolland spent the war years in Geneva, where he wrote a famous series of articles for the *Journal de Genève*. Later collected as *Au-dessus de la mêlée* and published in November 1915, the articles advocated mutual understanding between the warring nations. The book occasioned much resentment in France, where Rolland had been awarded the Grand Prix Littéraire of the Académie Française in 1913. For nine months from October 1914 he worked with prisoners of war. A liaison with Helena van Brugh de Kay ("Thalia") ended when she

returned to the US in 1915, the year in which Rolland was awarded the Nobel prize for literature. He gave the money to charity. In January 1916 he helped to found the review *Demain*, remaining with it until it ceased publication in October 1918. The following year he returned to France, where his mother died on 19 May.

Rolland's international reputation for pacifism was now established. He became seriously interested in Buddhism and communism, and his intellectual itinerary can be followed not only in the diaries and the correspondence, but also in a series of collected essays: *Les Précurseurs*; the *Essai sur la mystique et l'action de l'Inde vivante; Par la Révolution, la paix; Quinze ans de combat: 1919–1934*; and *Le Voyage intérieur*, concerning the years 1926 to 1942. Rolland also turned again to fiction and drama, publishing the sketches of Burgundian peasant life *Colas Breugnon* in 1919, although it had been written six years earlier, and *Pierre et Luce* in 1920, as well as the second "roman-fleuve," the four-part, seven-volume *L'Ame enchantée*. His dramatic output included *Liluli* of 1919 and *Le Jeu de l'amour et de la mort* of 1925. In 1923 Rolland helped to found the review *Europe*. At this time he also undertook his much more elaborate, although still episodic and in part dithyrambic work on Beethoven, the seven-volume *Beethoven: les grandes époques créatrices*. In 1934 he married Maria Koudacheva, with whom he had corresponded since 1923, and whom he had known since 1929, when she came to Villeneuve to prepare a Russian edition of his works.

Much of the period between the wars was taken up with political activity, with Rolland taking a serious interest in Indian non-violence and in Soviet socialism. He was friendly not only with Gorky, but also with Stefan Zweig, Panaït Istrati, Hermann Hesse, Sigmund Freud, Jawaharlal Nehru, Rabindranath Tagore, Jan Masaryk, Henri Barbusse, and Louis Aragon. A series of articles on Mahatma Gandhi of 1923 became a biography in 1924, to be followed by the *Ramakrishna* of 1929, and the two-volume *Vivekananda* of 1930. Resolutely anti-fascist, Rolland denounced Mussolini as early as 1924, sided with the republicans in the Spanish Civil War, and broke with the USSR on the signing of the Soviet--German pact in 1939. At first opposed to Barbusse's advocacy of violence in the cause of revolution, Rolland had gradually come to accept its inevitability, and his enthusiasm for Indian and Asian mysticism waned. He had become very close to Gorky before his death in 1936. He was still to write the two-volume biography of Péguy in 1944, but the later works, like *Le Périple* of 1946, show a highly individual and almost idiosyncratic mixture of Marxist ideology and Buddhist spirituality. Rolland also wrote an early work on dramatic theory, explaining his enthusiasm at the turn of the century for popular theatre in *Le Théâtre du peuple* of 1903, and a half-fictional account of his own struggles of conscience, *Clérambault: histoire d'une conscience libre pendant la guerre*.

From 1922 Rolland lived at Villeneuve, moving to Vézelay only in 1938. He was sporadically ill from early 1943 and his old friend Claudel came to stay. Rolland turned again to Christianity, reading the Gospels and meditating on them, but without apparently returning to Catholic belief or practice. He died on 30 December 1944 and was given a religious funeral. Since his death numerous volumes of correspondence and diary extracts have appeared. A number of critics have expressed the view that this still largely unpublished material will prove of more interest to later generations than the novels, theatre, biographies, journalism, criticism, and autobiographical reflections which Rolland published during his lifetime. A great deal has been published in the *Cahiers Romain Rolland*.

WORKS

Rolland divided *Jean-Christophe's* 10 volumes into three sections: volumes one to four as "Jean-Christophe," five to seven as "Jean-Christophe à Paris," and eight to ten as "La fin du voyage." Jean-Christophe Krafft is a young German musical prodigy, very like Beethoven, born in a small town on the Rhine. His family background is one of poverty and drunkenness. By temperament highly emotional, he becomes a young virtuoso at a German court and is intellectually formed by Mme de Kerich, whose daughter, Minna, is his pupil. Minna and he love each other, but there are social obstacles to their union. Jean-Christophe undergoes an adolescent crisis, but has a religious soul, recovers, and finds in himself, in music, and in nature the universal presence of the divine spirit. Life reveals to him the growing discrepancy between the inner joy of the creative artist, the instrument of a transcendent divinity whose art allows him to see the true value of things, and the vulgarity and baseness of the world around him.

At his widowed mother's request he returns to the family home, where he spends his time furiously composing. The stifling narrowness of German art and life leads to a fracas which makes him liable to arrest, so Jean-Christophe flees to Paris, where he becomes friendly with Olivier Jeannin, later to be killed in the course of an uprising. The young Jean-Christophe commits himself to fight in the cause of social justice. Rolland gives a stark impression of factitious and corrupt artistic life in Paris. Its fashionable musical world rejects Jean-Christophe, who nearly starves. He finally discovers the "real" France through a new friend, Olivier, whose sister, Antoinette, now dead, Jean-Christophe had already met in Germany. Antoinette recounts the story of her and Olivier's upbringing until her death.

The two young men set up house together, and Olivier teaches Jean-Christophe to sympathize with the uncultivated masses, while also introducing him to the heights of French culture. Olivier marries unhappily and Jean-Christophe crosses paths once more with an Italian woman, Grazia. She is married, but forms a lofty friendship with the German musician. Olivier dies in a May day uprising. Jean-Christophe, who has killed a policeman, flees to Switzerland and is looked after by an old friend, a doctor in a small Swiss town, with whose wife he has a liaison. There is a marvellous flowering of creative energy as the "burning bush" of smouldering creativity springs into productive flame. In the last volume Jean-Christophe returns to Paris, where he is honoured and liked, but also finds new griefs. He dies serenely, purified by suffering.

It is not difficult to trace through the novel the different forms it came to take in its author's mind while he was writing it. It became more and more of a tract, turning from a panorama to the tragedy of a generation. The term "roman-fleuve (river-like novel)" comes from Rolland's later preface:

Jean-Christophe m'est apparu comme un fleuve... il est, dans le cours des fleuves, des zones où ils s'étendent, semblent dormir... ils n'en continuent pas moins de couler et changer...

(Jean-Christophe seemed to me to be like a river... there are, in the course of rivers, lengths where they stretch out, seem to sleep... but they none the less continue to flow and to change...)

In a sense the action of the whole 10-volume work has as its axis the River Rhine.

Rolland had also intended the work to be a musical novel, using the effects normally achieved by music, but this aspect of the project was quickly abandoned as unrealisable. The bundle of sketches woven together to make the novel do, however, appeal directly to the emotions of the reader, almost to some assumed artistic and religious nobility of heart. The reader is expected to feel the emotions which are expressed, but not analysed or explained. The most remarkable characteristic of the novel, underlying the clear changes of its plan in the author's mind, is its sense of impending doom, as if Rolland sensed the coming catastrophe of 1914 well before most of his contemporaries. Death allows the human spirit to be passed on as each takes the place of others—Olivier of Antoinette, Jean-Christophe of Olivier. The third entity, of which the river is the analogue, is humanity itself.

Au-dessus de la mêlée was immediately translated into all the principal western European languages except German. The articles, published between 2 September 1914 and 1 August 1915, are lofty in tone, invoking justice and peace, idealistic almost to the point of fantasy, although quite incapable of inspiring the sort of sentiment that would have put an earlier end to the slaughter. It is incomprehensible that their author should not have foreseen the furore their publication would cause in France. As so often with Rolland, we are left with the impression that he was an eclectic pursuer of chimeric ideals, as unrooted in time as he wished to be supranational in outlook. He wrote prolifically and was once quite widely known to a readership that was itself somewhat remote from the real world. Not even in Rolland's reluctant conversion to militant Stalinism does he seem to have comprehended the issues, or the nature of politically effective activity, and not even then did he exert any real personal influence. If his works have so rapidly slipped out of date, it must be mainly on account of their lack of real roots in any actual society.

In spite of some technical originality in combining impressionistic sketches into a 10-volume extension of what remains essentially a Bildungsroman, even if it takes its artistic hero up to death, *Jean-Christophe* is not particularly well written. What it really lacks is imaginative power. The substitution of flabby idealism, however morally admirable, does not turn the novel into great literature. In fact, nothing that Rolland wrote is today considered to be a great work of the imagination. Even the later *Beethoven*, with its detailed biography and skilled musical analysis, self-indulgently picks and chooses too much to be more than a tribute. Indeed, it is more significant for what it tells us about Rolland than for what he says about Beethoven.

None the less, parts of Rolland's work are undoubtedly moving. He is adept at communicating emotion and admiration, which is conveyed not through his excess of rather naive sociological and moral analysis, but through the intensification of the personal involvement he feels: "J'appelle héros, seuls, ceux qui furent grands par le coeur (I call those heroes, only, who showed greatness of heart)." In the end, however, none of the biographies is a serious work even of scholarly reverence. They are expressions of enthusiasm, especially perhaps those of Beethoven, Tolstoy, and Péguy, in which the author's sense of identification with his subject is strongest.

Colas Breugnon is a historical novel in the form of a diary kept from Candlemas (2 February) 1616 to the Epiphany (6 January) 1617 by a carpenter from Clamecy, the small town in Burgundy where Rolland was born. It is the portrait of a serene artisan who learns in the course of a year that he is master of his own universe only because he can vanquish unhappiness by lucidity of mind. The book is short, full of life, energy, and charm.

The second "roman-fleuve," *L'Ame enchantée*, concerns two sisters, Annette and Sylvie. As in *Jean-Christophe*, the action finishes at the point in history at which the author finished the novel. The fiction becomes part of contemporary history. Annette Rivière is the more important of the sisters. She gives birth to a son, Marc, after having broken with his father, Roger Brissot. She struggles, and years later takes a French lover, Germain, who makes friends with the Austrian prisoner, Franz, thus overcoming the atmosphere of 1914. In the second part, after a gap of three years in the composition of the novel, Rolland allows Marc to sacrifice himself in the struggle against capitalism so that a new world can be born. After his death, his mother takes up the struggle for the revolution and against fascism. The voluntary sacrifice of a generation has given birth to a new era, as a mother gives birth to a child.

PUBLICATIONS

The *Oeuvres complètes*, published during Rolland's lifetime, was abandoned after publication of *Colas Breugnon* (1930), *Jean-Christophe* (1931–33), and *L'Ame enchantée* (1934). A 26-volume series of *Chefs-d'Oeuvres* (1971–72) contains many of the most important works.

Fiction

Jean-Christophe, 10 vols., 1904–12; as *Jean-Christophe* (in English), 1910
Colas Breugnon, 1919
Clérambault: histoire d'une conscience libre pendant la guerre, 1920
L'Ame enchantée, 7 vols., 1922–34; as *The Soul Enchanted*, 1927–35

Plays

Aërt (produced 1898), 1897
Les Loups (produced 1898) 1898
Le Triomphe de la raison (produced 1899), 1899
Danton (produced 1901), 1901
Le 14 juillet (produced 1902), 1902
Le Temps viendra, 1903
La Montespan, 1904
Le Théâtre de la Révolution, 1909
Les Tragédies de la foi, 1913
Liluli: farce lyrique, 1919

Le Jeu de l'amour et de la mort, 1925
Pâques fleuries, 1926
Les Léonides, 1928
Robespierre, 1939

Essays and biography

Les Origines du théâtre lyrique moderne, 1895
Cur ars picturae apud Italos XVI saeculi deciderit, 1895
Vie de Beethoven, 1903
Le Théâtre du peuple, 1903
Vie de Michel-Ange, 1905
Musiciens d'autrefois, 1908
Musiciens d'aujourd'hui, 1908
Handel, 1910
Vie de Tolstoï, 1911
Handel et la Messie, 1912
Au-dessus de la mêlée, 1915; as *Above the Battlefield*, 1916
Aux peuples assassinés, 1917
Salut à la Révolution russe, 1917
Empédocle d'Agrigente, 1918
Les Précurseurs, 1919
Voyage musical aux pays du passé, 1919
Mahatma Gandhi, 1923
Beethoven: les grandes époques créatrices, 7 vols., 1928–45; translated in part, 1925ff.
Essai sur la mystique et l'action de l'Inde vivante, 2 vols., 1929–30
Souvenir d'enfance, 1930
Goethe et Beethoven, 1931
Par la Révolution, la paix, 1935
Quinze ans de combat: 1919–1934, 1935
Compagnons de route, 1936
Le Voyage intérieur, 1943
Péguy, 2 vols., 1944
Souvenirs sur Richard Strauss, 1948

The *Cahiers de Romain Rolland*, appearing since 1948, contain much previously unpublished autobiographical material and correspondence.

Bibliographies

Starr, W.T., *A Critical Bibliography of the Published Writings of Romain Rolland*, 1950
Vaksmakher M.N., and others, *Romain Rolland: index bio-bibliographique*, 1959

Critical and biographical studies

Robichez, Jacques, *Romain Rolland*, 1961
Sipriot, Pierre, *Romain Rolland*, 1968
Starr, William T., *Romain Rolland, One Against All*, 1971

ROMAINS, Jules (Pseudonym of Louis Farigoule), 1885–1972.

Poet, dramatist, essayist, and novelist.

LIFE

Jules Romains, the legally adopted pseudonym of Louis Farigoule, is chiefly known for his 27-volume cyclical novel *Les Hommes de bonne volonté*, to which a 28th volume was added in 1956. But perhaps even more importantly, he is also known for his association with the Abbaye group at Créteil (see Duhamel), and for the doctrine of "Unanimisme," founded on the notion of universal brotherhood and on psychological theories of group emotion. It owed allegiance to Whitman's social lyricism, and took its name from Romains's *La Vie unanime*, printed on the Abbaye's press in 1908. Essentially it was one of a number of poetic, and in this case also social, movements of reaction against the mystic individualism to which the symbolist (q.v.) movement had led.

Louis Farigoule was born on 26 August 1885 at Saint-Julien-Chapteuil in the Cévennes, but brought up from infancy in Paris, where his father was a schoolmaster. From the Lycée Condorcet he obtained entry to the Ecole Normale Supérieure in 1905, and passed his agrégation in philosophy in 1909. He then taught until 1919, while simultaneously pursuing alternative careers in the literary world, to which he thereafter devoted himself full time. The Abbaye, an old house at Créteil, was leased by a group of young writers and artists—René Arcos, Georges Duhamel, Albert Gleizes, Henri Martin-Barzun, and Charles Vildrac. They proposed to live as a community from the cultivation and sale of garden produce, and the printing of books at the press they installed, to which each devoted an agreed number of hours a week. Duhamel wrote about the venture in *Le Désert de Bièvres* (1937), and Jules Romains was one of a number of weekend visitors during the 14 months it lasted.

Romains later maintained that the doctrine of unanimism came to him suddenly in 1903 and inspired his first poems. In a Paris street he had "l'intuition d'un être vaste et élémentaire, dont la rue, les voitures et les passants formaient le corps, et dont le rhythme emportait ou recouvrait les rhythmes des consciences individuelles (the intuition of a vast and elemental being, of which the street, the carriages, and the passers-by formed the body, and whose rhythm carried with it or covered over the rhythms of the individual consciousnesses)." First attracted to verse, Romains published the collection *L'Ame des hommes* in 1904, followed by the conte *Le Bourg régénéré: conte de la vie unanime* in 1906. *La Vie unanime* is a collection of philosophical poems asserting that men cannot always be regarded as individuals independent of groups into which their personal identity may merge.

The views expressed in this collection led later to the development of unanimist views in prosody, enunciated in the 1923 *Petit traité de versification* written by Romains and G. Chennevière. The unanimist inspiration was to last throughout Romains's career, not only in verse and drama, but also in fiction. It was connected with a certain Pan-Europeanism of outlook. Further volumes of verse were published sporadically throughout Romains's career: *Un être en marche, Odes et prières* (including a first book of *Prières* already published), *Europe, L'Ode génoise*, and *L'Homme blanc. Choix de poèmes* of 1948 offers a good selection from those volumes, and was followed by *Pierres levées* and *Maisons*.

Alongside the verse Romains published a good deal of fiction, both before and after his major success as a dramatist in the 1920s. The novels and the plays, while continuing to convey the unanimist message, were characterized by their irony, intellectual brilliance, and sense of burlesque. On the stage real success came only when Romains abandoned the philosophical seriousness of the verse plays, *L'Armée dans la ville*, performed at the Paris Odéon in 1911, and *Cromedeyre-le-vieil*, produced at the Vieux-Colombier by Copeau's company. In 1919, when he gave up teaching, Romains worked for a while at the Vieux-Colombier, but it was Jouvet, who left Copeau in 1922 to establish his own company, who produced and acted in Romains's most successful three plays, satirical farces written partly under the influence of Copeau and Cocteau, with both of whom Romains had become friendly. He enjoyed three major successes with the farces *Knock; ou, Le Triomphe de la médecine* of 1923, translated by Harley Granville-Barker and successfully produced in London in 1926 and New York in 1928, *M. le Trouhadec saisi par la débauche*, also of 1923, but revived with great success in 1956, and *Le Mariage de M. le Trouhadec* of 1925.

Jean le Maufranc, published in 1926, was initially unsuccessful, but rewritten as *Musse; ou, L'Ecole de l'hypocrisie*, it was turned into a success by Charles Dullin in 1926. Dullin was a pupil of Firmin Gémier, who, like Copeau, had carried on the tradition of Antoine. He too had worked with Copeau, but, on returning from the US after World War I, had left him to found his own company, a venture that finally became the Théâtre de l'Atelier. As a teacher Gémier emphasized the importance of improvisation and imported Stanislavsky's influence to the French stage. The technique was enthusiastically taken up by Dullin, whose acting was so important in making Romains's plays a success. The author's other plays, produced before the virtual ending of his theatrical career, included *Le Dictateur*, which was more successful outside France than in Paris; an adaptation of *Volpone* of 1928, successfully revived by Barrault at the Marigny in 1955; *Boën; ou, La Possession des biens*, in which Gémier made one of his last appearances; and *Donogoo*, an adaptation of Romains's own 1920 novel successfully revived by the Comédie-Française in 1951. After 1930, *L'An mil*, produced by Dullin in 1947, was Romains's only other full-length piece for the stage, although the one-act *Amédée; ou, Les Messieurs en rang* was a success in 1956.

Romains's fiction continued after 1906 with *Les Puissances de Paris* and *Mort de quelqu'un*, both of 1911, and *Les Copains* of 1913. Only the last two have generally been remembered, together with *Le Vin blanc de la Villette* of 1914, *Donogoo-Tonka* of 1920, the amorous *Psyché* trilogy consisting of *Lucienne, Le Dieu des corps*, and *Quand le navire...*, and the enormous "roman-cycle," *Les Hommes de bonne volonté*. Romains travelled widely and spent World War II in New York, where he finished the novel, returning to France by way of Mexico. He was elected to the Académie Française in 1946.

WORKS

The unanimist doctrine which underlay the whole of Romains's oeuvre is itself only the modern anti-symbolist reassertion of the very old view, current in Europe since the early Middle Ages, that individual human personalities are in some sense manifestations of a common spirit. The idea had lingered on from Averroës into the Renaissance, Spinoza, and then Hegel. In Romains's incarnation it has a specifically social, anti-individualistic tinge inherited from Whitman:

> Comment savoir si j'ai un coeur qui a aimé
> Quand la foule remue et que je suis en elle?

> (How can I know if I have a heart that has loved / When the crowd stirs and I am part of it?)

The group's feelings cannot be fully present in any single individual, and the poet's task is to show how the individual's personality becomes merged with and emanates from the collectivity of any group to which the individual belongs, whether nation, church, workforce, or regiment; "Je cesse d'exister tellement je suis tout (I cease to exist, so much do I become all)." In the early conte, *Le Bourg régénéré*, an incidental discovery brings an entire village to a sense of corporate identity and collective purpose.

Unanimism was intended to be a substitute for orthodox religion, correcting the individualism fostered by scientific positivism in the late 19th century, which regarded the individual as the unit, even when it bred awareness of social problems. Romains explained his aim in *Les Hommes de bonne volonté* as:

> saisir d'abord la vie et le mouvement de la société en elle-même, des groupes dont elle se compose, les courants psychiques qui la traversent et la modifient

> (first to grasp the life and the movement of society itself, of the groups which it comprises, the psychic currents which move through it and change it)

Romains's aim differs from that of Balzac, whose *La Comédie humaine* merely reproduces and points up the nature of individuals reacting to one another, and that of Zola, who depicts the individual as determined by but also as reacting against society. For Romains the individual's fulfilment is measured according to his success in merging with the one, supreme, eternal human spirit. Not even two world wars could shake Romains in his fundamentally humanistic belief.

His robust humour began to assert itself only after the novel *Mort de quelqu'un*, which is about the bond created between people only remotely connected to one another through the death and burial of an obscure railway official. The broad farce of *Les Copains* shows the existence of imagination and fantasy even in the group. The most important and deservedly the most successful of the plays is *Knock*, in which the burlesque doctor amusingly exploits the collective personality of the inhabitants of Saint-Maurice, the small town where he arrives to take over the practice of Dr Parpalaid. He finds everyone too healthy or too ignorant to call on his services, so he organizes a system of making them all feel ill. He publicizes his practice by offering free consultations and soon common superstition has the whole population clamouring to be treated for their newly developed, non-existent ailments.

Les Hommes de bonne volonté carefully avoids having a hero or a plot, as neither fits into the unanimist vision of the world. The 28 novels are not even joined together as a series of linked tableaux; they illustrate no theory, and their unity is entirely panoramic. The novel is a depiction of the economic, social, and political life of the years 1903 to 1933. It is centred on two friends, Jallez and Jerphanion, and is written with a sophisticated and slightly ironic humour, as well as careful documentation. Individuals are neither submerged by nor allowed to dominate the collectivity and are linked not by the sharper, more tragic emotions of envy and jealousy so much as by friendship and camaraderie. To retain the reader's interest Romains happily has very considerable narrative skills at his disposal, having a large repertoire of registers and an ease of style which help hold the novel together.

The individuals are responsible, moral characters, whose acts flow positively from decisions and demonstrate the "bonne volonté" (goodwill) of the title. The novels contain meditations on history and occasional hymns to humanity, and transport the reader between different groups, countries, and areas of activity. There is high as well as low life, city and country, Church and state. Characters and groups appear and disappear, perhaps to reappear again, and perhaps not. The novel comes near to mingling the panoramic with the epic as the forces of goodwill gently surge forward against inertia and moral squalor. It is not entirely clear that there is a diminution of confidence in the goodwill of men, as some critics have discerned towards the end, and which, by the middle of World War I, one might have expected.

The novel opens in October 1908 as Parisians go to work, unaware of the turmoil that is slowly creeping up on Europe. A few of the leading characters from the cast of over a thousand are introduced. By the second volume we are in the underworld. The bookbinder who takes up murder in volume two occurs again in volumes 17, 18, 24, and 27. (He actually dies in volume 24.) Pierre Jallez and Jean Jerphanion enter the Ecole Normale Supérieure together and make friends. The sophisticated Parisian Jallez will become a man of letters, while the raw mountain youth, Jerphanion, will become a politician. Four volumes are devoted to Paris in the last three months of 1908. Then come two volumes introducing the English journalist Bartlett as he views the high and low lives of Paris, from its shady businessmen with their seedy ethics downwards. By the end of volume 10 we have surveyed the industrial, ecclesiastical, political, and diplomatic activities of the capital. Jallez and Jerphanion graduate. There are two volumes on literature and art, and two more to take us through international politics in Rome to the eve of World War I. Volumes 15 and 16 show France fighting for survival at Verdun.

After the war, we witness the low life of the intellectual Jallez, and by volume 19 we have been introduced to the problem of the USSR in the Europe of 1922. Both Jallez and Jerphanion go there. There is an election which Jerphanion wins, and a crime puzzle that never gets solved in volume 21. In volume 22 the profiteer Haverkamp shows his good side, before crashing in volume 25 and living happily in Yugoslavia in volume 26. Much of the action is devoted to people taking stock of their lives. Jallez falls in love and talks a lot. The novel ends as it had begun—with Jallez and Jerphanion. It is 1933. The stock market has crashed, the slump has wreaked havoc, and World War II is looming. Extraordinarily, the novel is a tour de force, the work of an extremely gifted writer whose philosophical position, impeding the deployment of the ordinary means of moving a novel along, has forced him into a straitjacket which literary brilliance of an exceptional sort has turned to advantage.

PUBLICATIONS

Collections

Théâtre de Jules Romains, 7 vols., 1924–35

Verse

L'Ame des hommes, 1904
La Vie unanime, 1908
Un être en marche, 1910
Odes et prières, 1913
Europe, 1916
Le Voyage des amants, 1920
L'Ode génoise, 1925
L'Homme blanc, 1937
Choix de poèmes, 1948
Pierres levées, 1948
Maisons, 1954

Plays

L'Armée dans la ville (produced 1911), 1911
Cromedeyre-le-vieil (produced 1920), 1920
Knock; ou, Le Triomphe de la médecine (produced 1923), 1923;
    as *Knock* (produced 1926), 1935
M. le Trouhadec saisi par la débauche (produced 1923), 1923
Amédée; ou, Les Messieurs en rang (produced 1956), 1923
Le Mariage de M. le Trouhadec (produced 1925), 1925
Le Déjeuner marocain, 1926
Démétrios, 1926
Jean le Maufranc, 1926
Le Dictateur (produced 1926), 1926
Chants des dix années (produced 1978), 1928
Donogoo (produced 1930), 1930
Musse; ou, L'Ecole de l'hypocrisie (produced 1926), 1930
Boën; ou, La Possession des biens (produced 1930), 1930
Grâce encore pour la terre, 1937
L'An mil (produced 1947), 1947

Fiction

Le Bourg régénéré: conte de la vie unanime, 1906
Mort de quelqu'un, 1911
Les Puissances de Paris, 1911
Les Copains, 1913
Le Vin blanc de la Villette, 1914
Donogoo-Tonka, 1920
Psyché:
    1. *Lucienne*, 1922
    2. *Le Dieu des corps*, 1928
    3. *Quand le navire...*, 1929
Les Hommes de bonne volonté, 28 vols., 1932–1956; as *Men of
    Good Will*, 1933
Bertrand de Ganges, 1947
Le Moulin et l'hospice, 1949
Salsette découvre l'Amérique, 1950

Violation de frontières, 1951
Une femme singulière, 1957
Le Besoin de voir clair, 1958
Mémoires de Madame Chauverel, 1959
Un grand honnête homme, 1961
Portraits d'inconnus, 1962

Essays

Manuel de déification, 1910
Petit traité de versification, with G. Chennevière, 1923
La Vérité en bouteilles, 1927
Problèmes d'aujourd'hui, 1931
Problèmes européens, 1933
Le Couple France–Allemagne, 1934
Visite aux Américains, 1936
Pour l'esprit et la liberté, 1937
Cela dépend de vous, 1938
Sept mystères du destin de l'Europe, 1940
Messages aux Français, 1941
Une vue des choses, 1941
Retrouver la foi, 1945
Le Problème numéro un, 1947
Saints de notre calendrier, 1952
J.W. Hicks: interviews avec Dieu, 1952
Confidences d'un auteur dramatique, 1953
Examen de conscience des Français, 1954
Passagers de cette planète, où allons- nous?, 1955
Situation de la terre, 1958
Souvenirs et confidences d'un écrivain, 1958
Hommes, médecins, machines, 1959
Les Hauts et les bas de la liberté, 1960
Pour raison garder, 1961
Ai-je fait ce que j'ai voulu?, 1964

Critical and biographical studies

Cuisenier, A., *Jules Romains et l'unanimisme*, 1935
Cuisenier, A., *L'Art de Jules Romains*, 1949
Figueras, A., *Jules Romains*, 1952
Berry, M., *Jules Romains, sa vie, son oeuvre*, 1953
Cuisenier, A., *Jules Romains et les hommes de bonne volonté*,
    1954
Norrish, P.J., *The Drama of the Group: A Study of Unanimism in
    the Plays of Jules Romains*, 1958
Berry, M., *Jules Romains*, 1959

————

ROMANTIC MOVEMENT

*See also Deschamps, Dumas père, Gautier, Hugo, Lamartine,
    Michelet, Musset, Nerval, Nodier, Ossian, Sainte-Beuve,
    Vigny, and pre-romantic.*

The "romantic movement" has, of course, no precise beginning or end, but it has two different meanings, as a historical category

ing and by participation in dangerous undertakings as a member of a comradely team of equals. Saint-Exupéry found it necessary to live with that particular form of intensity in order to experience and resolve the moral, social, and metaphysical problems which obsessed him intellectually and lie beneath the surface of his books, none of which was ever published until their author was in a position to draw the moral consequences from the physical and social experiences narrated.

Saint-Exupéry's literary output is slim and no longer nourished by the faith of his childhood, for which it sometimes appears to seek a substitute. There are four short works of fiction, a fairy tale, some essays, posthumous reflections, letters, and an unfinished novel. He strove for brevity so that the poetry and the seriousness of the underlying intention would become more apparent. *Courrier-sud* is not yet technically proficient but, like the film based on it, was moderately successful and already showed Saint-Exupéry's considerable gifts as a stylist. It is the partly first-person narrative of a pilot, Bernis, a friend of the book's formal narrator, interwoven with weather and flight reports. Its real subject is the need to restrain dreams and regrets, and to submit to the discipline of the group task, here partly conditioned by the weather reports, of relaying the mail on which other people, too, depend. This is the only "récit" in which there is a female character. Bernis meets an old friend who has left a selfish husband. An affair seems too sordid, and marriage is impossible. She needs comfort and security, he the pilot's challenge, danger, discomfort, and insecurity, and their love cannot bridge the gap. Bernis returns to his mail run, a world of wind, water, stars, sun, and sand, and is killed flying.

Saint-Exupéry is beginning here to develop his philosophy of life, almost a humanist transposition of the ascetic ideal of Christian monasticism, in which the ordinary comforts are necessarily excluded in pursuit of higher satisfactions attainable only as a member of a group. The ideal is adapted to a new era and refracted through Saint-Exupéry's own sensibility as conditioned by his upbringing, a sensibility that is in some ways touchingly tender, but linked also to the thrill of flying, and of scientific advance, and to life lived at the edge of the technologically possible. Bernis hears a sermon at Notre Dame which fails as dismally as nightclub distractions to satisfy his spiritual needs.

In *Vol de nuit* the moral reflections are more skilfully woven into the narrative. Gide, who had himself explored this avenue, instantly saw the importance of investigating the possibility that happiness was to be achieved not through unbridled licence, but through the acceptance of duty. *Vol de nuit* is the story of a mail flight in South America. A morning call wakes the pilot and takes him away from his bride of a few weeks. In a dramatic sequence of events he is caught in a hurricane, loses the fight to conserve enough fuel to land, and is killed. The moral conflict is not that of the pilot, Fabien, but of Rivière, who is responsible for ordering the pilots to take the risks. His harshness calls up unsuspected reserves of courage and determination in his pilots, but he is left privately to question the spiritual values which justify the sacrifice of ordinary human consolations and of the lives of young men.

Terre des hommes abandons all pretence of being formally a "novel." It is a set of stylistically linked miniatures, tersely but not laconically written, carefully studding sparse and factual narrative with vividly striking images. Seen from the air, the earth is inhospitable, our comfortable life on it only a beckoning memory, and the whole ensemble of wind, stars, darkness, light, water, rocks,

ice, and sand a mystery which leads man, in the same way as suffering and deprivation do, to a greater awareness of what his race is and is not. Comradeship is the supremely unifying value, a reflection which dominates Saint-Exupéry's attitude to war. His pacifism was no doubt limited by a hatred of Nazi fascism, but it may not be pure chance that his wartime flying was restricted to reconnaissance missions which provided danger without calling for aggression. War is too expensive a way of creating comradeship in danger, and there is an underlying community of purpose between peoples in *Terre des hommes* which reveals its uselessness. The incidents in the book are predictable, the preparation for the first night flight, camping in the desert, rescuing Guillaumet in the Andes, with further chapters on the aeroplane, the aeroplane and the planet, the oasis, all offering opportunities for the communication of a philosophy which some critics of *Vol de nuit* had thought too reminiscent of Nietzsche.

The final major prose work, again not really fiction at all, *Pilote de guerre*, has been called "the finest prose work that World War II seems to have produced." The book contains a note of impatience at the ease with which France's humiliation has been accepted but is ostensibly an understated, objective account of one incident, narrated with the maximum economy of means in order to communicate Saint-Exupéry's values. The odds against surviving the mission described here are enormous, and the mission is designed in any case to bring back only unusable information, but the charade of fighting the war as if it were winnable has to go on. Events are packed into the few hours of flight in which luck more than skill saves Saint-Exupéry half a dozen times from death, but it is all food for meditative reflection, contrasting reminiscences, and ever-deepening self-knowledge. From the air every sort of misery is evident among the refugees. What is it that justifies the illogicality of the war and the acceptance of defeat? For what is it that Saint-Exupéry knows he will die?

The spirituality of comradeship and shared responsibility comes too near perhaps to the doctrine which, turned on its head, yields the notion of corporate guilt, but that is not in Saint-Exupéry's mind. He is thinking, rather, of a humanized version of the Christian adage that in the blood of martyrs lie the seeds of faith, that the seed must die for the tree to be born (the basis of Gide's *Si le grain ne meurt*). In defeat, carnage, and humiliation corporately accepted by the national community must, for Saint-Exupéry, lie the roots of national regeneration. In New York he was to confront bleak pessimism, but *Pilote de guerre* offers irrepressible, if apparently unrealistic hope that the national community will rise again strengthened, its differences fused and its oppositions merged. Saint-Exupéry was not a philosopher, and his views are not bred of liberal humanism; they are the product of an intense vision, poetically conveyed with great literary artistry.

Saint-Exupéry published two other works. The first was the slim *Lettre à un otage*, first published in New York in 1943 and ostensibly addressed to an old Jewish friend, Léon Werth, who had remained in France, but in fact to all the inhabitants of occupied France. It consists of six sections and culminates in a denunciation of totalitarianism and a proclamation of the kinship of man, more concerned about civilized values than about political systems. *Le petit prince* is a charming satire for children on the pomposities, toings and froings of the adult world, which preserves a child's sense of wonder and awe at deserts and planets. The terse simplicity and imaginative sympathy with a child's mind make it an excellent fairy story as well as a utopian allegory of a world without selfishness or warfare. Of the posthumous works *Un sens à la vie* contains some pessimistic views about the materialism of the world. The pessimism which has so often been commented on comes from an unsent letter published in this volume. It is interesting to know that Saint-Exupéry once penned it, but all it tells us about his view that the world may be moving towards its darkest days is that he never sent the letter containing it. *Citadelle* is an almost incomprehensible set of jottings, allegories, aphorisms and parables, some of which might have been utilised in the context of composing a book that was never written.

PUBLICATIONS

Collection

Oeuvres, 1959

Fiction

Courrier-sud, 1929; as *Southern Mail*, 1933
Vol de nuit, 1931; as *Night Flight*, 1933
Terre des hommes, 1939; as *Wind, Sand, and Stars*, 1939
Pilote de guerre, 1942; as *Flight to Arras*, 1942
Lettre à un otage, 1943; as *Letter to a Hostage*, 1948
Le petit prince, 1946; as *The Little Prince*, 1943
Citadelle, 1948; as *The Wisdom of the Sands*, 1949

Other

Lettres de jeunesse, 1953
Carnets, 1953
Lettres à sa mère, 1953
Un sens à la vie, 1956

Critical and biographical studies

Rumbold, Richard, and Margaret Stewart, *The Winged Life*, 1954
Smith, Maxwell A., *Knight of the Air*, 1956
Migéo, Marcel, *Saint-Exupéry*, 1958
Cate, Curtis, *Antoine de Saint-Exupéry: His Life and Times*, 1970
Robinson, Joy D. Marie, *Antoine de Saint-Exupéry*, 1984

SAINT-JOHN PERSE (Pseudonym of Marie-René Alexis Saint-Léger Léger), 1887–1975.

Poet, diplomat, and winner of the Nobel prize for literature (1960).

LIFE

Saint-John Perse is the poetic pseudonym of the diplomat Alexis Leger, as he came to spell his name. He kept his two careers rig-

orously separate, and not until after 1940 was it known that the two names belonged to the same person, and not until the Pléiade volume of *Oeuvres* (1972) were texts signed by both names united in one publication.

Born in Guadeloupe, where his parents owned two plantations, Leger was the only boy in a family of five. In 1899 economic circumstances dictated a move back to France, and the family settled at Pau. Leger studied law at Bordeaux (1904–10), where he mixed with Jammes and Claudel, who attempted to convert him to Catholicism, and Jacques Frizeau's circle, which included Jacques Rivière and Alain-Fournier as well as some painters of note. Following his military service (1905–06) and the death of his father (1907), Leger was faced with the task of supporting his family financially. He followed Claudel's advice and example in choosing a diplomatic career.

Though strongly drawn to music, Leger concentrated on writing, producing *Images à Crusoé* when he was 17. In 1908 he succeeded in publishing "Des villes sur trois modes," a 73-line poem dated 1906. In 1907–08 he began the poems of *Eloges*, wrote "Pour fêter une enfance" and, while still studying law, contributed half a dozen articles on music and painting to the Pau *Gazette*. The *Eloges* poems were printed in the new *Nouvelle Revue Française* (*NRF*, q.v.) in 1909. Valery Larbaud sought out the young author and Gide had the 1911 volume printed in order to eradicate the original printing errors. It was signed Saint-Léger Léger.

Leger spent the years 1911–14 preparing for the entry examinations to the French diplomatic corps. He travelled in Spain and England, where he came to know Conrad, Belloc, Chesterton, Bennett, and Tagore, studied in Germany, where he met Dehmel, and in Paris in 1914 became friendly with Satie and Stravinsky. Without fortune or connections, his hopes of passing the diplomatic examinations, which he could not resit, were slight, and he nearly withdrew after the written papers. He did do well in the oral, however, and within 20 years, having served in China (1916–21), he was permanent head of the French diplomatic service.

Much that he wrote was lost in 1940, but *Anabase*, written in a disused Taoist temple, received immediate critical acclaim on publication, and some occasional poems were now published anonymously or under the new pseudonym, notably "Amitiés du prince," written on the way back from China, the "Poème pour Valery Larbaud: jadis Londres," the "Chanson du présomptif," and the adaptation of Eliot's "The hollow men," "Aumône aux hommes de peu de poids." The prose "Lettre sur Jacques Rivière" published in the testimonial volume of the *NRF* (1925) is signed A. Saint-Léger Léger and disclaims any literary acquaintanceship with the honorand in order to preserve the distinction of identities. From 1925, on promotion by the foreign minister, Leger withdrew from all literary activity in France, allowing only translations of his work to appear abroad.

A confirmed anti-Nazi, he was dismissed overnight by Reynaud on 18 May 1940. On 16 June he left for England and, a few weeks later, for New York. The Nazis ransacked his flat, no doubt looking for official documents. They removed five cycles of poems, a play, and a philosophical essay. Leger spent the war working for the Library of Congress, careful to avoid being in the pay of any particular government. He also wrote "Exil," "Poème à l'étrangère," "Pluies," and "Neiges," to be published as the tetralogy *Quatre poèmes 1941–1944* in 1945, the year in which he wrote *Vents*. Leger stayed in the US, was allowed permanent residence in a special bill, and in 1950 became the first foreigner ever to receive the quinquennial prize of the American Academy.

In the post-war years Leger also wrote a number of prose essays celebrating dead or living friends: Gide, Schéhadé, Claudel, Larbaud, Mounier, Ungaretti, Tagore, John Kennedy, Jackie Kennedy, Char, and Braque. In 1957 he published *Amers* and returned for the first time since 1940 to France, where American admirers had bought him a house on the Mediterranean. In 1958, at the age of 70, he married. He was to spend part of each year until 1967 in the US.

In 1959 he published *Chroniques* and in 1960 he was awarded the Nobel prize. His speech of acceptance, *Poésie*, is his only published writing on poetic theory. In 1962 he published *L'Ordre des oiseaux*, with etchings by Braque; and several short poems have appeared subsequently: the collections *Chanté par celle qui fut là...*, *Chant pour un équinoxe*, and "Nocturne." Leger also assembled many unpublished pieces for the Pléiade *Oeuvres*. The honours bestowed on him include an honorary doctorate from Yale, the Grand Prix National des Lettres, and the Grand Prix International de Poésie.

WORKS

Like that of his friend and mentor Claudel, Saint-John Perse's poetry is celebratory rather than elegiac. It makes room for the nostalgia of rootlessness, but explores man in his relationship to nature, to his history and his future, reconciling, guiding, and pointing the way. The poet rejoices in the burning of sands, the violence of winds, the features of approaching land which guide sailors, the sky, the sea, the earth, and the rain. His purpose is to consecrate the alliance between man and the physical world.

Nostalgia, first experienced for France the unknown homeland, and then for Guadeloupe the lost paradise of childhood, dominates the early poems and returns in a different form during the American exile of World War II. Perse changed the order of his poems, so that we now have them arranged as he wished them to be, irrespective of the dates at which individual poems or passages were written. *Eloges* now opens with a preliminary poem in "vers libres", "Ecrit sur la porte," which accurately and economically presents a well-ordered colonial hierarchical society opening up to the prospect of its coming dissolution. "Pour fêter une enfance," "Eloges," and "Images à Crusoé" develop the beckoning of a distant infinity with a non-symbolist simplicity, but in a series of very complex metres, verse rhythms, and cross-references. Traces of symbolist (q.v.) techniques in the arbitrary lengths of lines, richness of elliptical imagery, and esotericism would later disappear from Perse's verse, but *Anabase*, for instance, still omits any logic which would link the images into a coherent whole. In fact, the connecting link is often visual. It can be texture, viscosity, form, or almost anything admitting similarity and contrast.

The hierarchy of the island idyll gives way to the social oppression of the industrialized city, Guadeloupe to Bordeaux, dignity of formality to the distinction between masters and slaves. The images derive overwhelmingly from real memories and historical events. The skill is in the recreation of the child's innocent, unified vision of the world, not distorted by the imposition of adult categories like time, colour of skin, or social rank. There is a moral, too. The desires of the self must be reconciled with the real limitations imposed by the world, and these, too, have their important coordinating function, as shown by the unattainable sexual attractions of the tribal queen in "Récitation à l'éloge d'une reine," drawing the warriors into harmony with the cosmic cycle of life and death.

T.S. Eliot's 1930 translation of *Anabase* has made it Perse's most important poem for the English-speaking world, not least because of its influence on Eliot himself and on Auden, although the translation actually travesties the diction, intention, and meaning of Perse's original. The title means "expedition to the interior," both geographical and spiritual, as well as simply "getting into the saddle," as Perse wrote to Eliot. The poem itself, 10 cantos enclosed between two "chansons," expresses the onward march of humanity, dissolving what is created as the cycle of rebirth continues. The individual retains inner peace only by standing aloof from the society he creates. It is "le poème de la solitude dans l'action," the poem of solitude in action, whether action in relation is oneself or to others, physical or mental. Because it is a poem, however, it must work through physical imagery: "c'est le poème le plus chargé de concret," Perse declares. The poem is lyrical rather than epic and has weaknesses. It is too complex and inaccessible, and its lack of geographical, chronological, or even cultural asymptotes wrongly suggests an allegory of unsatisfied but vague yearning, repressed by images of the unyielding and the bitter which contrast with the need to create and to act. Not surprisingly it gained for its author the reputation of aloofness. In fact it is a poem of fulfilment achieved while leaving open the path to future progress.

Exil, also written in cantos, although the versification is more regular, turns the beach on which it was written into the representation of its subject, exile. The beach leads from the security of the hut to the openness of the sea, and the poem moves between formlessness and self-creation as the poet reasserts his positive values. The incantatory verse, as Perse himself points out, sometimes recreates the sound of lapping waves. A similar technique is used in the build-up of irregular staccato rhythms to indicate the downpour in canto seven of "Pluies" before the rains subside and the three-line verses take over again. Rain, like the beach, stands for the poet's relapse into the silence of exile. It drenches, drowns, and destroys, but also purifies, cleanses, and makes fertile. Protection from rain means stagnation, decay, and shelter from the sources of vivification so that, whatever its dangers may be, without its benefits poetry is impossible.

Technically the brilliance of the images displays even more virtuosity than the prosody, but again the connection between images often calls for considerable effort from the reader. Snow in "Nuages" is as ambivalent as rain. It signifies the poet's geographical position, and with it his past and his future, the temperature, and his purest relationships, which are with his mother and with poetry. The reality of snow, like poetry, transforms other realities into magic. It also obliterates the past and throws the present into relief. The fourth poem of the tetralogy, although written second, re-establishes the exiled poet's links with society.

The poems of *Exil* are static. After the war *Vents* takes up again from *Anabase* the spirit of hope in humanity. Both poems open and close with the image of a tree, relating them as pieces of music are related by a key signature. *Vents* explores the sweeping away of the past into the future as the winds tear over the American continent, but the poem is like a tree in which the wind whispers only the neat patterns of known fact, the "quin-conces" Perse will have remembered from the square in Bor-deaux. This tree is regenerated at the end of the poem as the sap rises, producing new maxims in place of the withered leaves, the old proverbs which passed for wisdom at the poem's opening.

The winds blow away the poem's lines, as it were introducing images of dynamism, a sense of urgency, sensations of fresh air and speed, but, like rains, winds are the dangerous, if also the necessary, condition for blowing away cobwebs and destroying the temple of dusty books. The ambiguity of wind is typically caught up in the intoxication it induces, an intoxication that must remain clear-headed, an "ivresse" which avoids the over-reach-ing and blinding pride of "hubris" from the same Greek root. The winds sweep through America's geographical areas and historical eras, inspiring the ultimate achievements. The final sections of the cycle recall France, evoking the sediment pro-tected by the self-indulgent south wind that still needs to be blown away. In conception *Vents* is almost baroque.

In *Amers* Perse returns to the archetypical poetic image of flux, potentiality, and movement: the sea. He interpreted man's attraction to the sea as the high point of human dissatisfaction, but also of human need, spiritual, intellectual, individual, and social. The sea's power and its autonomy represent the absolute towards which men must strive. The verbal associations of *Amers* bestow on the whole poem an extremely dense pattern of meanings and sounds, so that the text becomes even less possi-ble to take in at a single reading than *Vents*. The meanings and associations are clear, but almost too densely interwoven, invit-ing intellectual dissection rather than provoking more than superficial imaginative stimulation.

PUBLICATIONS

Collections

Oeuvre poétique, 2 vols., 1953; revised edition, 1960; 3 vols., 1967–70
Collected Poems, 1971
Oeuvres, Bibliothèque de la Pléiade, 1972
Selected Poems, edited and translated by Mary Ann Caws, 1982

Verse

Eloges (as Saint-Léger Léger), 1911; as *Eloges and Other Poems* (bilingual edition), 1944; revised edition, 1956
Anabase, 1924; translated by T.S. Eliot as *Anabasis*, 1930; revised editions, 1938, 1949, 1959
Exil, 1942; edited by Roger Little, 1973
Pluies, 1944
Quatre poèmes 1941–1944, 1944; as *Exil, suivi de Poème à l'étrangère, Pluies, Neiges*, 1945; revised edition, 1946; as *Exile and Other Poems*, translated by Denis Devlin, 1949
Vents, 1946; as *Winds*, translated by Hugh Chisholm, 1953
Etroits sont les vaisseaux, 1956
Amers, 1957; as *Seamarks*, translated by Wallace Fowlie, 1958
Chroniques, 1959; as *Chroniques* translated by Robert Fitzger-ald, 1961
L'Ordre des oiseaux, 1962; as *Oiseaux*, 1963; as *Birds*, trans-lated by Robert Fitzgerald, 1966
Eloges, suivi de La Gloire de rois, Anabase, Exil, 1967

Chanté par celle qui fut la…(bilingual edition), 1970
Chant pour un équinoxe, 1971; as *Song for an Equinox*, trans-lated by Richard Howard, 1977
Amitiés du prince, edited by Albert Henry, 1979

Other

La Publication française pendant la guerre: bibliographie restreinte 1940–1945, 4 vols., n. d.
On Poetry (Nobel prize acceptance speech; bilingual), 1961
Letters, edited by Arthur J. Knodel, 1979

Bibliography

Little, Roger, *Saint-John Perse: A Bibliography for Students of His Poetry*, 1971; revised edition, 1982

Critical studies

Knodel, Arthur, *Saint-John Perse: A Study of His Poetry*, 1966
Horry, Ruth N., *Paul Claudel and Saint-John Perse*, 1971
Galand, René M., *Saint-John Perse*, 1972
Little, Roger, *Saint-John Perse* (in English), 1973
Jackson, Elizabeth R., *Worlds Apart: Structural Parallels in the Poetry of Paul Valéry, Saint-John Perse, Benjamin Péret, and René Char*, 1976
In 1965 Gallimard issued a volume, *Honneur à Saint-John Perse*, with nearly 150 articles, notes, and tributes to the poet.

SAINTE-BEUVE, Charles-Augustin, 1804–1869.

Critic, historian, novelist, and poet.

LIFE

Sainte-Beuve was born on 23 December 1804 at Boulogne, then fast expanding and already France's busiest fishing port. His father, Charles-François (1752–1804), who had literary inclina-tions, had made his career as a customs inspector and was at one time responsible for checking the strength of imports of Dutch gin. He had the right to use before his name the aristocratic "de," dropped by Sainte-Beuve and his mother, and owed to his reformist views his reappointment after the Revolution as a tax inspector. He was a town councillor, achieved modest profes-sional promotion, decided to marry, and chose the sister of one of his assistants, Augustine Coilliot, the daughter of a sea cap-tain. She was 40 when they married in March 1804. That Octo-ber, two months before his birth, Sainte-Beuve's father died suddenly of an abscess of the throat. His mother, who had a little money of her own, was granted small pensions by the state and the town. She also inherited the 24-room house in which she lived. A licence to sell playing cards was obtained for her, and a widowed sister-in-law came to join her. In 1809 the big house was sold and the family moved to a smaller one.

Sainte-Beuve was called "Sainte-Beuve" by his mother from infancy, and was brought up strictly, in fairly comfortable surroundings. He was given no pocket money and not allowed to play with his schoolfellows. He went to the best school in Boulogne, where the curriculum did not however extend to languages or literature, mastered the Latin classics, and won all the class prizes. He was clearly gifted, and in 1818, apparently at his own request, was sent to Paris, where he could learn Greek properly, boarding in one of the many pensions which sent its pupils to the Lycée Charlemagne. The first major work of the romantic (q.v.) movement, Lamartine's *Méditations poétiques* (1820), was about to appear, but Paris still had a population of only 700,000, and as yet no proper sanitation. In 1818 the first property speculators began moving in, omnibus services started up, and there were experiments with gas street lighting, finally installed in the Place Vendôme in 1828. A new liberal atmosphere prevailed, and the censorship laws were being eased. Sainte-Beuve began to keep a diary, from which we know that he read widely and that at 15 it was already his firm intention to be a "writer." He was at first homesick, became infatuated with a girl during his first summer holidays, and continued to win prizes for Latin, Greek, and French composition.

In 1821 Sainte-Beuve's pension moved, probably on account of a purge of liberal teachers that year, and he was enrolled at what is now the Lycée Condorcet. At his mother's request he was also taken in hand by Pierre Daunou, the "idéologue" who took him to the evening lectures at the Athénée on physiology, history, botany, philosophy, chemistry, geology, and even literature, frequented by Lamarck, Cuvier, Constant, and others. The heady intellectual diet gave Sainte-Beuve a taste for materialism in philosophy, and swept away his carefully nurtured religious belief. He read Locke, Bacon, Cabanis, Condillac, Destutt de Tracy, whom he came to know personally, Hobbes, and the Swiss mystic and naturalist Charles Bonnet. He met, and was not impressed by, Stendhal, whose Grenoble school had benefited much earlier than Sainte-Beuve's from the educational reform of 1794, and who in 1796 had been taught drawing, mathematics, grammar, logic, languages, and literature. Yet Sainte-Beuve's development was running on lines very similar to those of Stendhal and Balzac a few years earlier. In 1823 he finished school with a string of prizes for Latin and French essays and mathematics.

Medicine seemed to be the obvious profession, and Sainte-Beuve's mother came with her sister-in-law to make a new home for him in Paris. In Paris she rented, and in Boulogne she let. Sainte-Beuve passed his science baccalauréat in 1824, at the end of his first year of medicine. He heard that one of his former masters, Paul-François Dubois (1793–1874), forced out of Charlemagne during the purge of liberal teachers, was about to start a new literary magazine. Dubois persuaded Sainte-Beuve to carry on with his medical studies, but allowed him to contribute occasional pieces to *Le Globe*, which appeared thrice weekly from September 1824 and became a daily from the later 1820s.

Dubois recruited a remarkable team of contributors, including Thiers, the liberal politician and historian who founded *Le National* in 1830, the brilliant politician and social historian A.-F. Villemain, J.-J. Ampère, professor of literature, archaeologist, and close friend of Sainte-Beuve and later of Tocqueville, the politician and dramatist Charles de Rémusat, Charles Magnin, the liberal scholar who also wrote for the *Revue des Deux Mondes* (*RDM*, q.v.), Louis Vitet, archaeologist and pre-

decessor of Mérimée as inspector of historical monuments, the historian Augustin Thierry, and the mystical revolutionary Pierre Leroux. The other strong influence on Sainte-Beuve at this time was Théodore Jouffroy, who also wrote for *Le Globe*. A pupil of Victor Cousin and professor at the Ecole Normale Supérieure (ENS) until its suppression in 1821 (for the second time in 10 years), Jouffroy was a sceptic, liberal, and philhellene interested in the new non-materialistic branch of philosophy called aesthetics, which refused to reduce sympathy to sensation.

What Sainte-Beuve chiefly inherited from his time with *Le Globe*, to which he contributed some 30 pieces in six years, was the critical dilemma, which neither he nor others of his generation ever solved, of reconciling absolute standards of taste and literary achievement with a proper appreciation of a work's relevance to the historical circumstances which give rise to it. The full force of that dilemma was to be particularly obvious in Sainte-Beuve's early work on the French Renaissance. *Le Globe*, while welcoming innovations on principle, was suspicious of the politically royalist but aesthetically anarchic romanticism of Hugo, Vigny, and Nodier. It was Daunou, with his strictly classical principles in literature, who headed Sainte-Beuve back to the Renaissance to compete in a prize competition for an essay offered by the Académie Française, thereby forcing him gradually to realize that Boileau's 17th-century criteria could not be applied to 16th-century poetry and drama.

In 1825 Sainte-Beuve moved nearer the hospital where for a year he was to continue his medical studies. He had fallen in love again, and found his medical studies "revolting." For literary political reasons Dubois wanted a more favourable review of Hugo's *Odes et ballades* (1826) than he was likely to get from his more senior colleagues. He gave the task to Sainte-Beuve, having already prepared his readers for a judicious mixture of praise for the work's innovatory boldness and blame for its lapses of taste. Sainte-Beuve took the hint and did what was required. Goethe noted that, now he had *Le Globe* on his side, Hugo's success was assured, and the 25-year-old Hugo called on Sainte-Beuve, who was a close neighbour of his. Sainte-Beuve returned the visit, was invited to literary readings, and became a devotee of the self-confident young poet with an already noticeable streak of arrogance. Hugo and his wife moved to the new residential area of Notre-Dame-des-Champs. Sainte-Beuve, whose aunt had now died, and his mother followed the Hugos and became close neighbours again. Hugo and Sainte-Beuve saw one another daily and Sainte-Beuve's latent enthusiasm for poetry was now released from the constrictions imposed by his environment and his seniors at both *Le Globe* and the Athénée.

Hugo's son Charles-Victor, born on 2 November 1826, was called partly after Sainte-Beuve, who now met Dumas, Vigny, the sculptor David d'Angers, and a dozen other young poets, who christened themselves "le cénacle" in 1828. In a sense Sainte-Beuve himself remained an outsider, not interested in Shakespeare, drama, or the Middle Ages, but he did go to Nodier's elegant drawing room at the Arsenal on Saturday evenings, where cards, dancing, book-collectors' gossip and conversation were to be had. Liszt, Balzac, Lamartine, Planche, and Delacroix also attended these evenings, as did a number of well-known and well-behaved pretty young women, including Nodier's daughter and Pauline Magnin, Charles's sister. Sainte-Beuve began to write verse. He gave up his medical career, and in 1827 *Le Globe* published 11 chapters of his prize essay, the *Tableau historique et critique de la poésie française et du théâtre français au XVI siècle*, which was still wrapped in the constraints of Boileau's dismissive vision. The tone of the work changed in mid-serialization, however, and the text was rewritten for volume publication in July 1828, as again for the 1843 revision, to show Ronsard and his companions as Hugo's glorious predecessors. Meanwhile *Le Globe* had had enough of the dashing young Hugo, and turned down two pieces by Sainte-Beuve on his play *Cromwell*. By the end of the *Tableau* the classical principles of Malherbe himself have accompanied to the scrap heap the mechanistic theories of perception of the "idéologues," and the last section, written in April 1828, is a romantic manifesto to compare with Hugo's preface to the 1827 *Cromwell* and the author's preface to the poems in the *Etudes françaises et étrangères* (1828) of Emile Deschamps. Sainte-Beuve's new models became Schiller, Goethe, Byron, Chateaubriand, and Mme de Staël.

In the summer of 1828 Sainte-Beuve went to England, and on his return hawked a volume of verse round the publishers, collecting rejections from Ladvocat, Sautelet, and Urbain Canel, and gratefully accepting from Nodier's friend Delangle 400 francs for one year's rights on an edition of 1,000 copies. Hugo had already received 3,600 francs for the *Orientales*. Sainte-Beuve's *Vie, poésies et pensées de Joseph Delorme* was published on 4 April 1829. The book sold because it was talked about, but the reviews, with the exception of Magnin's in *Le Globe*, were hostile, and occasionally virulent. They attacked the angularity, religious subversiveness, and crudeness of Delorme's poetry, which was prefaced by heavily ornamented autobiographical scraps, presented as fragments posthumously put together by Delorme's editor. Sainte-Beuve fell out with Dubois, who hedged his editorial support, but Gautier, Baudelaire, and Verlaine all liked the collection, and Sainte-Beuve came back to *Le Globe* in August 1829 with a major piece on Corneille.

Although Vigny thought that Sainte-Beuve was dominating Hugo's literary, political, and social outlooks, by 1829 Sainte-Beuve's extravagant loyalty to Hugo had spread to pieces for the *Journal des Débats*, the *Mercure de France*, the London *Foreign Quarterly*, and the *Revue de Paris*. At the same time the strong religious feelings of Hugo's wife, Adèle, probably account for Sainte-Beuve's returning respect for Christian sentiment, if not for ecclesiastical orthodoxy. Since Sainte-Beuve's relationship with *Le Globe*, which closed down in April 1832, was now uncertain, he welcomed the invitation of the wealthy ex-pharmacist, doctor, and bon viveur Louis Véron, known for his yellow calèche and lavish entertaining, to collaborate at 200 francs a sheet on his new *Revue de Paris*. In 1849, exactly 20 years later, Sainte-Beuve was to start writing the *Causeries du lundi* for another paper which Véron bought, *Le Constitutionnel*, but it was for the *Revue de Paris* that he virtually invented the literary portrait as a genre.

Sainte-Beuve spent the autumn of 1829 visiting the Rhine, Strasbourg, Mainz, Frankfurt, Cologne, and Worms. He returned to Paris on 9 November to find relations between Hugo and Vigny strained, with Hugo having tried and failed to push his *Hernani* in front of Vigny's translation of *Othello*, which had won the race but, partly due to a hostile claque, had nearly failed on the stage. Determined to avoid the same fate, Hugo spent much of the winter so noisily organizing his own claque in sup-

port of his play that his landlord gave him notice to quit. Readings and rowdy receptions were given in his famous drawing room, which could be made to hold 60 at a pinch and where the play, like *Marion Delorme* on the preceding 10 July, had been given its first private reading on 30 September 1829 to invited friends. Sainte-Beuve found Hugo's truculent behaviour distasteful, and disillusion began to set in, although he was present at the first night on 25 February and remained at Hugo's side throughout the tumult. He did not go into the theatre with the queue of supporters at two p.m., but he was in Hugo's box on that and subsequent evenings. He refused to write a review and, when Hugo wanted to know why, he replied in a convoluted letter in which, in passing, he regretted the disappearance of Vigny from the entourage and the replacement of "old and noble friends" by "fools and madmen," by whom he meant Gautier and Nerval. There was a vigorous debate at *Le Globe*, but the review, signed by Magnin, was in the end favourable.

The froideur in Sainte-Beuve's relationship with Hugo thawed out, but he was beginning to feel restless, uncertain about his future as a writer and unwilling to settle for the position of Hugo's chief acolyte. He quarrelled a second time with Véron, made peace with *Le Globe*, which published three important pieces on Lamartine, and published the volume of poetry *Les Consolations* on 17 March 1830. The reviews in general were good, that in *Le Globe* fulsome, but Stendhal wrote an astute letter reproaching Sainte-Beuve with vestigial romantic posturing. For some weeks that spring Sainte-Beuve stayed at Honfleur with Ulric Guttinguer. He was a poet and widower friend of Hugo and an habitué of Nodier's salon who, having recovered during a tour of Provence from desertion by his mistress, bought a property and set up house with her more subservient successor, Alexandrine Bouquet, who was also his housekeeper. She was illiterate. Guttinguer was counting on Sainte-Beuve's help to write *Arthur* (two volumes published in reverse order, 1836 and 1834), intended to be the definitive novel of the broken heart. In watching as well as helping Guttinguer, Sainte-Beuve was also developing his later style of biographical criticism.

Some time between the end of May and the beginning of August 1830 the great passion of Sainte-Beuve's life, his love for Adèle Hugo (née Foucher), broke into the articulate awareness of each of them. She had married at 17, was almost a year older than Sainte-Beuve and two years younger than her husband, to whose fifth child she gave birth on 28 July. Hugo, who had moved house earlier in the year, came round to the offices of *Le Globe* to ask Sainte-Beuve to be godfather. He was not yet jealous, and the break with Sainte-Beuve, partly occasioned by literary touchiness, did not occur until 1834. Over six years Adèle wrote 334 letters to Sainte-Beuve, most of them in 1834 and 1835. They were burnt in 1885.

When the political disturbances broke out in July 1830 Sainte-Beuve had returned to Honfleur. With the establishment of the new regime many members of the staffs of *Le Globe* and *Le National* moved into official posts. A quarrel at an editorial meeting led to a farcical duel between Dubois and Sainte-Beuve on 20 September, followed by a picnic breakfast for all. Dubois resigned as editor, became a deputy and was rewarded with the directorship of the ENS. Three other members of the team at *Le Globe* immediately became deputies, one achieving ministerial rank. Jouffroy did not become a deputy until 1841, while Villemain, Cousin, and Guizot simply annexed ministerial duties to their academic chairs. The staff at *Le National* did better still, and even Stendhal was given a consulship. The recently founded *RDM* printed "La curée," a vitriolic verse satire by Auguste Barbier on the place seekers, and Tocqueville described the middle-class take-over of power with lofty sarcasm. Sainte-Beuve could hope for nothing, on account of the duel and his association with Hugo, but accepted a salary of 200 francs a month and an increased editorial role at *Le Globe*, which Leroux tried to make into a vehicle for social reform. His backers soon withdrew, however, and the review was sold to the Saint-Simon group, for whom he continued to edit it. Armand Carrel at *Le National* stayed republican, and Lamennais denounced the bourgeois constitutional monarchy in the short-lived *L'Avenir*.

Writing in his weekly column that autumn, Sainte-Beuve attacked Jouffroy and pointed French romanticism along the new path of social reform. On 30 October, on the occasion of a reissue of *Joseph Delorme*, he published an anonymous article renouncing the artistic sterility of the "cénacle," which after all was only a salon, and looking forward to a new fusion of romanticism with a deeper social purpose. The amalgamation of romanticism in the arts and socialism in politics had been inaugurated. The implementation of the programme for fusing romanticism with social reform, articulated in the tentative form of a reflection about his own character's successes and failures by Sainte-Beuve, was spearheaded by George Sand, Vigny, and Lamartine, then also by the Hugo of *Les Misérables*.

After a visit to Brussels with Leroux in April 1831, however, Sainte-Beuve felt he could no longer continue to tread the path of mystical utopian socialism with him and left *Le Globe*. He produced no more "humanitarian" writing of the sort inspired by Saint-Simon, Enfantin, and Bazard. He had told Hugo about his feelings for Adèle, but Hugo remained for the moment unperturbed and invited Sainte-Beuve to continue to call. Sainte-Beuve for his part was trying to keep out of the way, and preferably to find a post abroad. Through Hugo he met Buloz, the editor of the *RDM*, who suggested that he might like to write about Hugo's forthcoming *Notre-Dame de Paris*. Sainte-Beuve replied that he regarded Hugo as the greatest living writer, but that he no longer regarded him as part of his life.

It seems likely that Sainte-Beuve was suffering from an undeveloped urethra, rendering him incapable of normal sexual activity but not of strong sexual desire. This condition, of which his medical studies had made him aware, may well explain the violence and frustrations of his love affairs, his epicene appearance, baldness, obesity, and the relief he sought in chance and other encounters with prostitutes. It would also explain his fastidious self-loathing. The situation smouldered on. The Hugos had moved again, this time to the fashionable Champs-Elysées, and there is a gap in the correspondence with Sainte-Beuve, who had been to stay with Lamennais's group at Juilly in May 1831. It was probably in September 1831 that Sainte-Beuve and Adèle Hugo first became lovers, and not until October 1832 that the Hugos moved again this time to what had become the Place des Vosges. Sainte-Beuve took a room in a nearby hotel, and the liaison, together with the breakdown of Hugo's marriage, may be assumed to have become more or less public knowledge at about this time. Hugo's own first known infidelity was with Juliette Drouet, whom he met in February 1833. Thereafter, in spite of daily lovemaking with a multitude of partners, he regarded Juliette as his unofficial spouse.

Apart from poetry and letters, Sainte-Beuve quite often sent

Adèle coded messages in his public articles, many of which she may not have read. He broke with her finally in 1837, and she died in her husband's arms in 1868. The estrangement between Hugo and Sainte-Beuve became permanent in February 1834 when Sainte-Beuve, still reacting against the romantic cult of the hero and the idea of men as instruments of destiny, touched a raw nerve in Hugo's self-esteem. In an article written for Buloz he had at least implied criticism of Hugo's critical study printed at the end of Mirabeau's recently published *Mémoires*. When in November 1835 Sainte-Beuve, reviewing Hugo's *Les Chants du crépuscule* for the *RDM*, unpardonably drew public attention to Hugo's equally unpardonable inclusion of a tribute to his wife in a volume intended for his mistress, it was clear that he regarded the breach as irreparable.

In 1843 Sainte-Beuve had his poems to Adèle printed privately, with her approval, in 204 copies, intended for posthumous distribution. He kept the 203 sewn copies, the unsewn copy, and all the proofs known to him locked up, and mentioned them in his wills of 1843 and 1858. Unhappily for him, the compositor leaked a proof copy to Alphonse Karr, editor of the satirical *Les Guêpes*, who broke the scandal in April 1845, after which Sainte-Beuve allowed one or two friends, including Arsène Houssaye and Hortense Allart, to see the book. The intention was presumably to elevate the liaison on to the poetic level occupied by such other famous lovers as Petrarch or Ronsard, although the collection does not contain Sainte-Beuve's best verse. The timing of Karr's disclosure was unfortunate, as Hugo had just been caught with another friend's wife. He contented himself with a vicious sonnet to be published, like Sainte-Beuve's book, only posthumously.

In 1831 Sainte-Beuve took up again his first sketch for the novel *Arthur*, which was eventually published by Guttinguer, and reworked it into *Volupté*, to be published in 1834. Buloz carefully vetted all Sainte-Beuve's material for suitability for the public he was aiming at, and relied on him to recruit contributors for the *RDM*. Sainte-Beuve brought him Cousin, Michelet, and Lamennais. Later on Sainte-Beuve had to formulate major policy statements for the review, aimed against "industrial literature," a term of opprobrium used to describe Balzac's novels. His generally hostile attitude to Balzac was certainly influenced by Balzac's quarrel with Buloz. Sainte-Beuve also started to write for *Le National* and its "conservative republican" editor, Armand Carrel, who was eventually killed in 1836 in a duel with Emile de Girardin over an apparently political dispute. Carrel, who was poor, was also prickly. He fought several duels, drew police harassment down on *Le National*, went to prison several times, and even found some difficulty in presenting himself at a moment convenient to all parties on his return from abroad to serve a prison sentence of some weeks in 1834 for "press offences." In 1830 he had turned down a prefecture from Guizot, who had stipulated that he should not bring his mistress with him. The paper was more sharply political than the *RDM*, and its collaborators included Désiré Nisard, who was especially hostile to the romantics. Sainte-Beuve was much impressed by Carrel, and later wrote three major articles about him.

Sainte-Beuve successfully evaded his turn of duty for the Garde Nationale, and moved away from his mother, changing his address to one he did not readily disclose. He was breaking with both literary romanticism and his political past as the regime closed ranks round a monarchy protected by censorship as well as patronage, and hostile to most of the social and political change that many of the 1830 republicans had stood for. Satire, like political change, was already getting harsher and more dangerous. Following the terrifying cholera epidemic of April 1832, Sainte-Beuve turned down an offer from Hugo to get him employment on the *Journal des Débats*, although it paid well and he was desperate for money. He still preferred independence from Hugo, from old associations, and from all literary movements. He cut himself off from the younger generation—Nerval, Gautier, Borel, Murger—and filled the pages of the *RDM* for Buloz with older names—George Sand, Lamartine, Senancour, Béranger, Marceline Desbordes-Valmore, Heine, and even Jouffroy. At the same time Sainte-Beuve was slowly perfecting the art of the literary portrait. At first he mixed more general critical reflections with commentary on specific works and the biographical details supplied by the "sitters," as he called them. The portraits of Béranger, Hugo, George Sand, Marceline Desbordes-Valmore, and Musset belong to this group. Only in the treatment of Lamartine does the pen-portrait as we know it begin to emerge.

Sainte-Beuve's desire for independence in 1833 was extreme and expensive. In his eagerness to preserve it and to stay free of literary alignments, he turned down posts, including chairs offered to him in spite of his lack of a university degree. He was gradually to be tempted out of his lair, by "Juliette" Récamier in particular, whose friend Ballanche he already saw regularly, and in whose salon in the rented flat at the old Cistercian convent the Abbaye-aux-Bois the whole of literary Paris congregated. Way had been made for writers and academics now that Mme Récamier's last and greatest admirer, Chateaubriand, had retired from active political life, and ambassadors no longer flocked to pay their respects. Sponsored by J.-J. Ampère, who had succeeded to the chair at the Collège de France which he himself had refused, Sainte-Beuve was presented to Mme Récamier, who was anxious to meet him, sometime in the autumn of 1833. Only Michelet and George Sand held out against the rigid formalities with which Sainte-Beuve, who attended her salon perhaps three times a week, never felt ill at ease. He also began to attend Mme de Rauzan's Saturday evenings, and at least three other salons, of which the most important was that of Henriette de Castries, who had written to him in 1834 after the publication of *Volupté*. In 1831 she had similarly introduced herself to Balzac. His replacement by Sainte-Beuve did nothing towards smoothing over the hostilities between the two writers.

Henriette de Castries was 38, and had long since left her husband. Her lover, Metternich's son Victor, had died in 1829, leaving her with a son. Though crippled in a riding accident, she was still vivacious and good-looking, with a presence Sainte-Beuve describes as "incomparably graceful." Balzac had vainly hoped to become her lover. Her friendship for Sainte-Beuve was one of tender affection. He attended her Thursdays sporadically and occasionally dined with her in select company, and she gave him the silver crucifix which Victor Metternich had given her on his deathbed. The secret of the considerable salon success of so confirmed a recluse as Sainte-Beuve was his waspish intelligence and his readiness to listen and to discuss. As a critic he was already influential on account of his ability to mould his response to his material in such a way as to show it off to the best possible effect. He did not deliver monologues, and his conversation was witty, amusing, spiked with malice, but always entertaining.

By 1834 Sainte-Beuve had also become preoccupied with Port-Royal, the monastery which in the 17th century had been the focus of Jansenist spirituality. *Volupté* had appeared to a mixed reception in the summer of 1834. Sainte-Beuve was still being partly supported by his mother, and in September a trivial complaint to the *RDM* about his use of the word "sectarian" had given rise to a challenge to duel. He withdrew to the country, hurt at the lack of support from Buloz, Carrel, and Leroux, wrote poetry, meditated on the personalities of the principal Jansenists, and made a further perceptible break with the past. He was becoming less intransigently independent, and at the same time more scholarly. The summer poems of 1834 were incorporated into a new edition of *Les Consolations* that December, although they reverted into the "Pensées d'août" of the *Poésies* of 1861–62, the unsold sheets of which were sold on by Poulet-Malassis to Michel Lévy, who published them as *Poésies complètes* in 1863.

Late in 1834 Sainte-Beuve accepted an appointment at 3,000 francs a year as secretary to the ministerial commission for historical documents, a virtual sinecure. The other members of the commission were Cousin, Mérimée, Vitet, Lenormant, and Hugo. Since Sainte-Beuve had given the royalties from the new edition of *Les Consolations* to his goddaughter, Adèle Hugo, as a Christmas present, it was possible for Hugo to shake hands in temporary reconciliation when the commission met on 18 January 1835. Sainte-Beuve was still seeing Adèle, but otherwise his life was quiet. He was working on *Port-Royal*, which started out as the "academic" book which Guizot required from him for preferment to the highest honours in the academic world. He had little inclination and no money for travel, would lunch or dine with his mother, pick up a book in a library or along the "quais," dining out and going to the theatre perhaps once a week. When the final break with Hugo came, the two ostentatiously avoided one another, although in April 1837 there was a grotesque moment when, at the funeral of Gabrielle Dorval, daughter of the actress Marie Dorval and mistress of Antoine Fontaney, they had to share a cab with Bonnaire, a backer of the *RDM*, whom Hugo was also cutting. Sainte-Beuve wryly remarked that they only needed Vigny to complete the party. Hugo was not speaking to him either.

A month earlier, in March, Sainte-Beuve had, unusually, published in the *RDM* a conte entitled "Madame de Pontivy," clearly intended to signal to Adèle by its plot that he wanted to continue a stable relationship with her. She however, once so passionate, was now content with nostalgic dreams. She may never have read "Madame de Pontivy"; even if she had, she did not reply, and it was clear that the liaison had ebbed away. Sainte-Beuve borrowed a little money in advances from Renduel, his publisher, was able to pay some back to his mother and Charles Magnin, and hired a reader to avoid straining his eyes. He failed to produce either the study of medieval poetry or the study of the knowledge of the Middle Ages in modern literature that the ministry had asked for, voluntarily and unnecessarily gave up his salary and, in December 1836, turned down the Légion d'Honneur. Many of his friends offered help, and Buloz offered regular monthly advances to be paid off with articles when possible, but in the wake of the break with Adèle in 1837 Sainte-Beuve had lost the will to work. In the summer of 1837 he took the coach for Geneva.

The lake was a literary pilgrimage to the places associated with Rousseau, Voltaire, Mme de Staël, Byron, and Gibbon. After long hesitation Sainte-Beuve accepted a visiting chair at

Lausanne for 1837–38 to lecture three times a week on any subject he liked for 3,000 French francs. He chose to lecture on Port-Royal and its connection with the whole of French classical literature. Before he left Renduel put the *Pensées d'août* on sale anonymously. Sainte-Beuve was puzzled by the coolness of the reviews, and angered by the attack in the *RDM* by Gustave Planche, the occasion for a brief quarrel with the not easily perturbable Buloz. The Lausanne lectures, of which there were 81, baffled the audience at first, but then provoked enthusiasm. They cost Sainte-Beuve an immense amount of solitary concentration and constitute what is often thought to be the finest work of criticism in the French language. The six books of lectures were published slowly from 1840 to 1859, starting after Sainte-Beuve had returned to Switzerland and gone on to Italy in 1839.

From his return to Paris that year dates his close friendship with the intellectually pretentious, prudish, and ambitious Marie d'Agoult, whose affair with Liszt had just ended. Sainte-Beuve had met them both in Rome, and the countess's salon soon filled up when she returned to Paris in October. Delacroix, Sue, Didier, Vigny, Ampère, Ingres, and Girardin all called, and Lamennais and Balzac accepted formal invitations. Sainte-Beuve resigned himself to being no more than the countess's literary lion. She played with him, teased him, flirted with him and, to Liszt's mild horror, then campaigned for Vigny against him as a candidate for the Académie Française. A more straightforward but short-lived relationship with Hortense Allart may have produced in her a half-formed hope of marriage, but Sainte-Beuve turned to another bluestocking, Sophie d'Arbouville. Like Marie, she also led him a dance. This sentimental drifting was no doubt the result of his break-up with Adèle, but it also points to the tentative way in which Sainte-Beuve was discovering his real vocation. The next step was his acceptance of the quasi-sinecure of a librarianship at the Mazarine, with lodgings overlooking the river, at a salary of 4,000 francs a year, and the task of supervising the reading room from ten to three on Wednesdays and Saturdays. The post was a reward for getting Karr to back off Victor Cousin in *Les Guêpes*. Cousin, minister of public instruction, was trying to carry his budget through the Chamber when Karr discovered that Louise Colet, early in her career in pursuit of great men, was carrying Cousin's child. Louise had tried to stab Karr with a kitchen knife when *Les Guêpes* alluded to the pregnancy.

Surprisingly, Sainte-Beuve now entertained thoughts of marriage. He had accepted his librarianship on 8 August 1840 and proposed to the 20-year-old Frédérique Pelletier on the 29th. Frédérique turned him down, but had no objection to his publishing the poems he had written for her. They appeared as "Un dernier rêve" at the end of the *Poésies complètes* of 1862. In 1839 Sainte-Beuve, still in pursuit of self-definition, had called down on himself an undignified journalistic dispute, which began with what was virtually an attack on Balzac in "De la littérature industrielle," published in the *RDM* in September. Literature, according to Sainte-Beuve, had deserted the moral high ground and become an industrial enterprise whose products were priced by the line. The attack was aimed at newspapers floated by advertising revenue, like Girardin's *La Presse*, selling at 40 francs a year for half the normal price and dispensing literature in serial form; at vulgarity, banner headlines selling news, the crude loss of literary standards and moral values; and at press notices of future events. No matter that Buloz paid by the line or that Balzac had already led the attack in the second

part of *Illusions perdues*. Sainte-Beuve drew down on Buloz as well as on himself the anger of Girardin and Balzac, and Buloz would not publish his final and most virulent piece. Sainte-Beuve had been foolhardy, and not wholly right, and his opponents had been allowed to draw blood, insinuating that his literary judgements were distorted by malice. He was nevertheless elected to the Académie Française in 1844. It fell to Hugo to pronounce the speech of welcome, which he did graciously, not yet knowing about the *Livre d'amour*, containing the poems to Adèle.

In spite of his election, his salaries from the librarianship and the academy's dictionary committee, his free lodgings, lack of dependents or expensive tastes, and the income from his articles, Sainte-Beuve continued to be short of money. He asked Charles Magnin for a loan of 100 francs as late as 1846. It seems likely that he spent a good deal in brothels and on casual prostitutes. We know that Sainte-Beuve, always overcome with a sense of failure, found it difficult to accept his unattractiveness to women, and in 1875 one of his secretaries, A.-J. Pons, published a book about the casual relationships on which he apparently relied, *Sainte-Beuve et ses inconnues*. Such a reliance would explain the high expenditure and fit in with his unusual inability to summon up adequate reserves of self-confidence at so many crucial points in his life.

He continued to make perfectly honourable mistakes in misunderstanding the reactions of women and was eventually to lose the very close friends and admirers, Juste and Caroline Olivier, who had invited him to Lausanne and treated him royally while he was there. It is difficult to suppose that a more confident awareness of what was happening would not have saved him in 1847 from having his smoking stove rectified after the appropriate ministerial works budget had been exhausted, thereby leading to suspicions of peculation. The authorization of a special payment from secret funds made him look like a spy, and he resigned his librarianship in 1848. Happily he was invited to lecture in Liège, and left for Belgium in 1848, later elaborating his course into *Chateaubriand et son groupe littéraire sous l'Empire*. Here, too, although it was reasonable for Sainte-Beuve to seek to see the romantic decades in perspective, he should have known that it was too soon to begin to demythologize Chateaubriand, who had died only earlier in 1848, especially in view of his own connection with Juliette Récamier, who was still alive.

On his return to Paris in 1849 Sainte-Beuve rented three rooms owned by a friend, but he still needed a steady income. In 1846 he had put up 2,000 francs to help enable the *RDM* to become a company, and asked for repayment according to the terms of the agreement. Buloz did repay, but in instalments, and the old, easy relationship could not be re-established. Sainte-Beuve therefore applied to the *Journal des Débats*, but found the response unenthusiastic. Then Véron wrote from *Le Constitutionnel* inviting him to contribute every Monday on a literary or historical topic of his choice at 100 francs a time, later increased to 125. Véron, unlike Buloz, had never paid by the line, and so put no premium on the prolixity of his authors. Astonishingly it was Véron, not noted for his finesse in such matters, who first observed that Sainte-Beuve was really a historian rather than a critic.

The first "lundi" appeared on 1 October 1849. The series ran for 20 years, interrupted only when Sainte-Beuve had to prepare his lectures as professor of Latin at the Collège de France

(1855–56), published in 1857 as the *Etude sur Virgile*, and while he was teaching at the ENS (1858–61). In 1852, when Véron sold *Le Constitutionnel* to the banker Mirès, Sainte-Beuve moved his "lundis" to the official government *Le Moniteur Universel*. Only gradually did he become disillusioned with the Second Empire and in 1861 he restarted the "lundis," in return for much greater financial rewards, in *Le Constutionnel*, the organ of the upper middle-class conservative Bonapartists, who were wary of social reform. When he finally moved to the opposition paper, *Le Temps*, at the very end of his life, he was irrevocably associated in the public mind with the regime of Louis-Philippe and the salon of Princesse Mathilde.

On 17 November 1850 Sainte-Beuve's mother had died, and Sainte-Beuve moved into her house. The last serious prospect of marriage he entertained came to nothing in 1852, but he was nearly forced to marry Mme Vazquez, his domineering, greedy, and bad-tempered housekeeper and mistress. She died in 1854, the year Sainte-Beuve was elected to the chair of Latin Poetry at the Collège de France. The sparse audience for the first lecture, on 9 March 1855, was hostile to the slightly ridiculous figure who did not attempt to rise until the derision had died down, and then opened his lecture with an ill-judged series of remarks so sycophantic to the regime that, for the second lecture a fortnight later, the hall was packed with angry students and the police had to be called. Sainte-Beuve tried to resign, and the course was continued by substitutes.

By now Sainte-Beuve's eyesight was deteriorating, and he was finding it physically difficult to write, but in 1857 he accepted the post of lecturer in French literature at the ENS, intended to be a seven-year appointment at 6,000 francs a year, and gave his first lecture on the interpretation of literary tradition on 12 April 1858. This was the position from which Véron poached him in 1861, recompensing him for the future loss of salary, to continue his "lundis." The lectures were not a great success, partly because lecturing was something Sainte-Beuve had neither the presence nor the imagination to do well, and partly because his anti-romanticism, his panegyrics of lucidity and order, and his political allegiance caused his predominantly young audience to regard him as a turncoat. His meticulous research and scholarship were better suited to written pieces than to oral presentation.

He was a methodical worker and a frugal eater, who liked his house kept properly. On the death of Mme Vazquez he engaged a housekeeper and two maids, but was as indifferent to furniture, painting, and decoration as he was to the countryside. The Goncourts concurred with the general view that, when he went out, "he always gave the impression of a professional haberdasher in his Sunday best." On Mondays he would dine with Véron, and often at first with Véron's mistress, Rachel, the tragic actress discovered by Jules Janin of the *Journal des Débats*, who was to make the great classical tragic roles of Corneille and especially of Racine come to life again on the Paris stage. Janin himself, a friend of Sainte-Beuve, was to succeed to his chair at the academy. At these Monday dinners Sainte-Beuve and Véron would discuss the next week's topic. Sainte-Beuve would then block out his article, and work away at it, adding layers of information and scholarship rather as if he were building up a portrait in oils. His secretary of the moment would read the article back to him on the Friday, before taking it to the printers on Saturday morning. On Sunday afternoon Sainte-Beuve would himself take the corrected proof back to the printer, dine at Pinson's and go to the

theatre or the circus. He would borrow up to 25 books for an article and publish 25 articles to a volume. There are 28 volumes of *Lundis* and *Nouveaux lundis*.

Sainte-Beuve's manner was unattractively submissive and he almost never inspired affection. In 1865 he was made a member of the Senate at a salary of 30,000 francs a year, at Princesse Mathilde's second attempt on his behalf, and he became the princess's devoted servant. Along with Flaubert, Gautier, Renan, Taine, the Goncourts, and Turgenev he attended the Magny dinners, founded by the lithographer and caricaturist Gavarni in 1862. In spite of the pigeonholing which dogged him, Sainte-Beuve was never really aligned politically. He had avoided being a fully paid-up romantic republican, and he did not now become an orthodox Bonapartist. His two or three speeches in the Senate advocated liberalism. He defended Renan, attacked the citizens of Saint-Etienne who wanted to ban Voltaire, Rousseau, Renan, Balzac, and George Sand from their municipal library, and mildly criticized a bill stiffening newspaper censorship. In 1868 he had invited Flaubert, About, Taine, Renan, and Prince Napoléon to dinner. When he discovered it was Good Friday, he suggested a postponement, but the prince said no, and the matter caused a scandal that was exploited by the political right. It was when *Le Moniteur Universel* turned down an attack on the Bishop of Montpellier that Sainte-Beuve switched to *Le Temps*, where his first article appeared on 4 January 1849. Princesse Mathilde was furious and called round to say so. They never met again, although they did write to one another on friendly terms.

For some years Sainte-Beuve had been suffering from an obstruction of the bladder. In January 1866 and twice again in 1867 he had undergone operations. There were remissions in the progress of the disease, and on 29 April 1869 he was well enough to go out and have a haircut, take a bath, lunch at the Véfour, and return via the academy, where he voted for Gautier. On 7 September his last article appeared, devoted to Marceline Desbordes-Valmore. A further operation was attempted on 12 October, and he died the next day. At his own request, he was buried next to his mother.

WORKS

Sainte-Beuve had a remarkable memory and wrote extensive notes on everything he read, and on letters he sent, naturally keeping those he received. He scribbled in books, kept a commonplace book, and meticulously ordered the 30 years' accretion of notes without which he could never have written the volumes of literary portraits and literary history. He turned only slowly from aspiring to be a poet and a novelist to being a critic and a historian. As a critic he missed the importance of Stendhal, Musset, Balzac, Gautier, and Baudelaire. Proust objected to his subtleties of style, innuendoes, and self-interested toadying, his overvaluation of intelligence and manners, feline preference for the salon hostesses, and desire for social acceptability. Sainte-Beuve was also, he said for good measure, given to double adjectives, to directly apostrophizing the reader, and to pretentious literary allusions. Anatole France found in him a lack of courage and an unwillingness to penetrate to the moral core of an author and to judge it. Sainte-Beuve's preferred authors were therefore the witty, glittering, brightly superficial ones. Sainte-Beuve himself found Stendhal Italianate, brilliant at skirmishes but useless in a campaign, Flaubert congested with "inexorable detail," Balzac's grammar imprecise, his adjectives platitudinous, his humour smutty, his imagination obsessed by female age and physical development, and his ability to discover a drama behind every curtain ridiculous.

Although Baudelaire admired Sainte-Beuve's poetry, especially the 1827 "Les rayons jaunes," published in *Poésies*, it has found few other defenders. The poems of the *Livre d'amour*, printed in 1843 but published only in 1904, return to the manner of those in the *Vie, Poésies et pensées de Joseph Delorme*, but the best poetry is generally thought to be that of *Les Consolations* of 1830. Sainte-Beuve himself regarded the *Pensées d'août* as inferior, and subsequent critics have found them an intellectual and arid distillation of moral fervour with no real poetic input, so that the most pretentious poems, "A M. Villemain" and "Monsieur Jean," are the weakest. Amédée Pichot had published his *Voyage historique et littéraire en Angleterre et en Ecosse* in 1825, the year in which he founded the *Revue Britannique* with Philarète Chasles, and Sainte-Beuve, who wrote three articles about the book in *Le Globe* that year, thought of himself as an anglophile follower of what he insisted on describing as the "Lake School," Wordsworth, Crabbe, and Cowper. Sainte-Beuve had his own followers among the continental admirers of English nature verse, especially his Swiss friend, admirer, host, and one-time literary executor Juste Olivier, but nature did not really inspire him, and even his best verse is rhetorical, moralizing, and insipid.

Unlike most of his romantic contemporaries Sainte-Beuve never wrote for the stage. The *Tableau historique et critique de la poésie française et du théâtre français au XVIe siècle* of 1828 was useful in its day, but created a myth about French Renaissance literature based on little real historical insight into its problems and, even after the change of perspective which occurred during the serialization of his text, presented the Pléiade as "interrupting" a natural development from the Middle Ages to Boileau. The single novel, *Volupté* of 1834, is a vastly ambitious work which seeks to explore how an inner uncertainty, leading only to self-indulgent dreams, permeates and paralyses the whole personality of its priest protagonist, Amaury, who relates the story. The novel attempts far too much self-revelation and drains into the sand as it dissipates all suspense in exhaustively tracing the subtle path of Amaury's progress. The structure dissolves into episodes without balance, and what is intended to be edifying introspection is both unctuous and attitudinizing. Like Sainte-Beuve's historical criticism at its worst, the novel glitters with intelligent surface comments supported only by inadequate fictionalization.

Even if the reader does not know the writer's circumstances, the intimacy of tone suggests autobiography. A studious, dreamy orphan has his sensuality titillated by classical authors, goes through a moment of calf love and, attached to a local aristocratic household, becomes obsessed by the lady of the house, Lucy de Couaën. Amaury accompanies the family to Paris, learns of political plots which misfire, wastes his time, gets caught up in royalist conspiracies, flirts with a salon beauty, and is eventually left with her in Paris. He breaks with her, turns to religion, and finally, after much analysis of examples and discussion of spiritualities, becomes a priest. His adolescent sweetheart, Amélie, is now married, but he feels the need to return to his Breton home. He officiates at the funeral of the marquise, for whom his love is now entirely spiritualized and whose request

that he should be called to give her the last sacraments he fulfils. He writes his novel in America for the edification of a young friend. Nothing in the plot is inevitable, and what it contains is at most the occasion rather than the cause of the narrator's emotions. As an attempt to portray the whole panorama of possible manifestations of a particular sensibility, partially through thematic symbols like lakes and rocks, the novel still comes across as a magnificent failure, its exhaustive display of the various aspects of Amaury's sensibility unequalled by anything before Proust. It appealed to George Sand, Chateaubriand, and Nisard, and stimulated Flaubert to produce *L'Education sentimentale*.

What Sainte-Beuve excelled at was neither poetry nor the novel, nor even literary criticism, but the literary art of historical portraiture, even if the subjects were still living. From 1843 to 1845 he contributed an anonymous series of *Chroniques parisiennes* to his friend Olivier's *Revue Suisse*. Rather heavy-handed gossip, it was a good deal more frank than the signed pieces written for the French press. But of all his works, it is the series of literary portraits of women, authors, historical figures, and contemporaries which constitutes in its totality a masterpiece of astounding breadth and considerable depth. Literary texts written by his subject were Sainte-Beuve's most fruitful starting point, especially if there was development through successive editions or publications, but then any historical detail, whether of biography, or of gossip, or of the environment chosen or the social situation inherited by the subject, would be voraciously tracked down and used to build up the portrait.

Port-Royal, for instance, is a series of very carefully constructed portraits. The six volumes are not institutional history, or even the properly related history of Jansenist spirituality. They almost fail to find a central character on which to focus. Instead, Sainte-Beuve comes across some unexpected figures he finds interesting and turns them into fascinating portraits. Layer by layer he reconstructs motivations, inspirations, aims, and achievements, although what he succeeds in best is the surface shine, the portrayal of outward demeanour and external appearance. He is not a psychologist, and he never really understood the spirituality whose manifestations he writes about. He is not a theologian, and does not even attempt to sketch the theology elaborated by the Jansenists in support of their spiritual attitudes. He was probably an atheist, and certainly had no feeling for the deeply religious impulses of the characters connected with Port-Royal. But he has written brilliant portraits of the movement's principal figures and a painstakingly detailed reconstruction of its outward appearance.

The psychology of the portraits, whether in the *Lundis*, the *Portraits des femmes*, or *Port-Royal*, although never deep, is sometimes shrewd, and there are brilliant miniatures within the masterpiece of cumulative portrayal, but also the elements of a salon game aiming at wittily malicious epigrams. Some of the criticisms of Balzac's coarseness are perceptive and amusing, but there is also an element of playful provocation in which Sainte-Beuve caricatures himself as the effete and fastidious critic analysing the vulgar but imaginatively energetic peasant. It is difficult to suppose that either was unaware of the wry amusement afforded to their literate contemporaries by their occasionally factitious disputes, with each successful in a domain in which the other vainly aspired to succeed. Balzac was well aware of Sainte-Beuve's salon popularity, and Sainte-Beuve of Balzac's attractiveness to women.

For an example of a successful early portrait, in which the

strongly personal style bursts through the sophistication of polite rhetoric, Sainte-Beuve's piece on the translation by Montalembert of Mickiewicz's *Le Livre des pèlerins polonais* (Polish edition, 1832), published in *Le National* for 8 July 1833 might be examined. The original was to be immensely influential in Poland. Mickiewicz had been exiled from Lithuania to Russia and had travelled in Europe before settling in Paris. He embodied and did much to create a romantic awareness of Polish national identity, and had a distinguished career in France. He was in fact to die at Constantinople trying to help the Poles in the Crimean War. He made a politically sensitive subject in 1838. Sainte-Beuve starts off with a sage-like reflection of sufficient generality to disarm any reader, establishing the genre of causerie with an "à ma connaissance (as far as I know)," and "J'ai lu quelque part (Somewhere or other I read...)." We are a third of the way through the piece before Sainte-Beuve tells us what he is writing about. Then comes one trenchant paragraph. The lesson of this book lies, he says, in the combination of ancient Catholicism and modern liberalism. Unlike the rationalist republicanism of France, the Irish and the Polish national identities have been bound up with a religious culture involving "une armée qui s'agenouille au nom de Marie (an army which genuflects at the name of Mary)."

The Poles, like the Jews, are for the moment martyrs, a captive people, but "le seul vivant entre les tribus idolâtres, le seul par qui la cause de Dieu vaincra (the only people alive among the idolatrous tribes, the only one through whom God's cause will be victorious)." The style is mannered, and Sainte-Beuve goes on to introduce a catena of quotations with learned allusions served up in excessively figured but stereotyped language. There is a word of reproach for Mickiewicz's strictures on all that is not Polish, a clear indication that he goes too far, a conventional compliment to Montalembert, and the job is done. The causerie form is scarcely even camouflage. It is a mere courtesy, an envelope for a quite sharp political message, beautifully pointed in an almost succinct final paragraph. The future of France depends on the alliance of Catholicism and republicanism.

Sainte-Beuve the critic fares a lot less well than Sainte-Beuve the portraitist. The carefully informed erudition of *Port-Royal* breaks out in the last book into a eulogy of Racine, again a personal causerie, full of the first-person singular. The rector of Lausanne University, where the lecture was delivered, regarded it as the culmination of the course. In fact it gives a lamentably stereotyped account of Racine which shows no hint of understanding what the great tragedies were about. Their principal beauty is in "the perfection, unity, and harmony of the ensemble." Sainte-Beuve has discovered the surface skill of the verse writing, but overlooked the ferocity of female passion at the centre of all Racine's great plays. He does not, for instance, see why Racine so far departed from tradition as to invent the character of Aricie for *Phèdre*, although it is her introduction alone which allows Phèdre herself to be jealous, and to become morally guilty of the death of the person she loves.

Given the generally upper middle-class conservative opinions of most of literate France, the readership on whom his editors counted, it is not surprising that Sainte-Beuve wrote in a form of polite rhetoric that strikes today's readers almost as a code. In the *RDM* for 18 June 1842 he published a scintillatingly stylized portrait of Mme de Rémusat. The style is again conventionally stereotyped, its informality only apparent: "A few quotations from Horace which she dropped even show me that she knew Latin...she learnt it thanks to the help of her husband at the cradle of her son." In other words, she was married at 16 to someone twice her age, had a son at 17, and was taught by her husband how to present herself socially. To do her justice, says Sainte-Beuve, we need "the history of conversation in France, unhappily almost impossible to write." Her charms, in other words, were all on the bright social surface. "Let us get back to our subject...I will talk a little only about her novels. She has written several. I have read two of them..." All through we are kept aware of the privileged intimacy with his subject to which Sainte-Beuve has been admitted, although she had died 21 years previously. He knows all the details of her existence, but is uninterested in a psychological study, quite content to focus on his subject's persona, what we might, without being derogatory, call her performance.

This is a fascinatingly well-executed miniature, cleverly contrived and carefully built up. Perhaps on account of the slightness of his subject, it demonstrates Sainte-Beuve's technique more clearly than usual. His breadth, from the classics of Greece and Rome to the whole of the literatures of the 17th and 18th centuries in France, has long been legendary. The "portrait littéraire," generally presented as a causerie, is his own creation, no doubt facilitated, or even required, by the development of the press and the foundation of the major literary reviews. The scholarly appetite for recondite or intimate detail adds weight to the portraits, and Sainte-Beuve's connections with all the major literary figures of the mid-19th century, as well as his direct access to all the important literary salons, make his personal career of obvious interest for literary, and indeed social, historians. But his series of portraits, including those in *Port-Royal*, built up volume by volume, constitute an important contribution to literature itself, even more than to its history. They make an impressive, informative, and artistically executed achievement of great technical brilliance. There is no rival to *Port-Royal* as a gallery of historical portraits in the whole of French literature, and the sum total of the literary portraits constitutes a brightly lit masterpiece, as impressive in its breadth of subject as it is fascinatingly brilliant in its execution.

PUBLICATIONS

Collections

Port-Royal, Bibliothèque de la Pléiade, 3 vols., 1952–55
Oeuvres, Bibliothèque de la Pléiade, 2 vols., 1956–60

Verse

Vie, poésies et pensées de Joseph Delorme, 1829
Les Consolations, 1830
Livre d'amour (printed, 1843), 1904
Poésies complètes, 2 vols., 1861–62 (the word "complètes" was added by Michel Lévy for his 1863 edition of the unsold sheets left over from the Poulet-Malassis 1861–62 edition: the edition is not in fact complete)

Critical and historical works

Tableau historique et critique de la poésie française et du théâtre français au XVIe siècle, 1828

Critiques et portraits littéraires, 5 vols., 1836–39
Port-Royal, 6 vols., 1840–59
Portraits de femmes, 1844
Portraits contemporains, 3 vols., 1846
Causeries du lundi, 15 vols., 1851–62
Derniers portraits littéraires, 1852
Etude sur Virgile, 1857
Chateaubriand et son groupe littéraire, 1861
Nouveaux lundis, 13 vols., 1863–70
Chroniques parisiennes, 1876

Other

Volupté, 1834
Lettres à la Princesse, 1873
Les Cahiers de Sainte-Beuve, 1876
Correspondance, 2 vols., 1878
Le Clou d'or, La Pendule, 1880
Nouvelle correspondance, 1880
Arthur (draft in *Sainte-Beuve inconnu*), edited by Spoelberch de
     Lovenjoul, 1901
Voyage en Italie, 1922
Mes poisons, 1926
Notes inédites, 1931
Correspondance générale, 13 vols., 1934–
Lettres à deux amies (1854–1857), 1948

Bibliography

Bonnerot, J., *Bibliographie générale*, 3 vols., 1937–52 (lists
     critical works only)

Critical and biographical studies

Nicolson, Harold, *Sainte-Beuve*, 1957
Lehmann, A. G., *Sainte-Beuve: A Portrait of the Critic
     1804–1842*, 1962

———

SALACROU, Armand (-Camille), 1899–1989.

Dramatist.

LIFE

In addition to the two volumes of autobiography (*Dans la salle des pas perdus*: I, *C'était écrit*; II, *Les Amours*) which Armand Salacrou published out of his originally projected three, the 30 or so plays of the eight-volume *Théâtre* are interspersed with autobiographical notes and comments. He himself perceived both his life and his theatrical activity on the one hand, and his personal and his dramatic writing on the other, as unities. It is as if, on the level of literary production, autobiography took off into drama, which Salacrou then felt the need to explain in terms of autobiography. The autobiography may naturally, like the drama, be partly or wholly a product of fantasy.

The key to an understanding of Salacrou's apparently kaleidoscopic range of dramatic styles lies in the fact that he regarded his life, which moved from a humble home and communist convictions to an affluent mode of living and a set of aggressive business attitudes, as symbiotically related to his persona as a dramatist. He went out of his way to prevent his life and works being insulated from each other, and we can therefore see that the imaginative force of his oeuvre depends on Salacrou's personal need to reconcile moral absolutes in a world without God with the absurdity of the bourgeois world as he sees it. It would certainly be more difficult to establish the sense of his dramatic oeuvre taken as a whole if Salacrou had not sprinkled its published texts with autobiographical annotation.

He was born in 1899, the son of modest, petit bourgeois parents who kept a herbalist shop in Rouen. When Salacrou was two the family moved to Le Havre, where his father, Camille, one of 11 children from a family of poor agricultural workers, became a radical socialist municipal councillor from 1908 to 1940, by which date he was exceedingly affluent. Salacrou's mother was left to run the shop, while he himself was condemned to a lonely, introspective childhood. He was not allowed to join in the other children's street games, and as an adolescent was to feel a strong need to make up for his frustrated childhood desire to be accepted by the group. However, the aloofness imposed on him did eventually let up as his parents' economic standing improved and he was able to attend the local lycée. It was replaced by a sense of underprivilege, another feature of the later drama to which Salacrou drew attention in his autobiographical writings. In later life he realized the degree to which he was driven to overcompensate for the mediocrity of his parents and his childhood surroundings. Meanwhile, his continuing sense of isolation led him towards a state of metaphysical anxiety, and his imagination became preoccupied with thoughts of death.

His state of mind deteriorated when, in 1910, a young trade-unionist, Jules Durand, was condemned to death for murder, driven mad in the death cell, and subsequently found to have been the innocent victim of a political conspiracy set up by his employers. In 1961 Salacrou was to put on a play, *Boulevard Durand*, about the affair, and it is partly thanks to his lingering recollection of the Durand incident that the themes of death, injustice, and solidarity are so prominent in his later drama: "The experience I had of the goodness and evil of men continued almost unconsciously to serve me as a yardstick to measure all the events I was to witness during the rest of my life." He learnt that, in the end, man is always alone and that, if the social harmony which appeared to exist in the society of his childhood was an impertinent sham, the only escape for the individual lay in being sustained by the convictions of a more fundamental human group than the Le Havre bourgeoisie.

His conformism led him to accept ordinary, left-wing, republican, anti-Catholic attitudes and a positivistic, atheistic philosophy. He became politically committed in a way that was hostile to the attitudes of the employers' sons at the lycée, convinced that the absurd economic system, which they upheld in the name of French patriotism, was in fact preventing the creation of the universal brotherhood of man. According to an essay later printed in *Les Idées de la nuit*, he believed the capitalist system to be the "fraternity of the doomed." In 1916 Salacrou had set up a socialist youth group in Le Havre. He also had a picture of the murdered socialist leader Jaurès on his bedroom wall, and was a communist in all but name. He was to join the French party on its foundation after the Tours congress of December 1920.

The alternative to socialism as an escape from solitude was art. On 6 August 1916 Salacrou had also published, in *L'Humanité* of course, his first short story, "L'éternelle chanson des gueux," which is about an Algerian immigrant arriving in Le Havre. At 20 he said: "je croyais écrire poussé par ce seul besoin de chercher et de trouver des amis (I believed I was writing driven simply by the need to look for and to find friends)." He wanted to "write to be loved, to flee an isolation. To forget myself," and he explicitly stated that he was substituting a literary vocation for a religious one. A visit to Florence in 1920 confirmed Salacrou in the view that his solitude had been necessary to generate in him the simultaneous enthusiasm for Dante, Leopardi, and Gobineau, but that after the initiation he belonged to the group of those who announce to men "an eternally still dawn" in which "the sun never rises but is felt always to be just beneath the horizon." The after-effects of World War I were slowly to erode this adolescent outlook. Salacrou later noted that the war had so fragmented civilized value systems as to make the reconstitution of theatre impossible. All his early plays, before *Atlas-Hôtel*, directed by Charles Dullin in 1931, reflected the demoralization, and were to be disastrous failures.

Salacrou studied philosophy, medicine, and law at the Sorbonne and wrote extensively for the communist press in 1921 and 1922. His first signed article appeared in *L'Humanité* on 6 March 1921, and he then wrote for *L'Internationale* until July 1922, organizing a circulation-boosting competition to find the worst employer in Paris. The readers nominated Louis Renault. His studies revealed to him that the sense of participation in a mechanistically determined universe was not enough to provide an intellectual and emotional anchorage: "Alors, je compris la nécessité de Dieu, sans pouvoir croire à Dieu (Then I recognized the need for God without being able to believe in God)." Salacrou had refused to make his first Communion, and his experience of war had been limited to helping after lessons with the wounded received into the school, which also served as a hospital. But the socialist sense of fraternity which might have replaced Christian fellowship could not withstand the impact of the war's butchery, of the armless and legless wounded with whom the adolescent Salacrou came into contact. In the 1936 *Un homme comme les autres* God becomes a binding, communicative force: "si Dieu existait, il serait ce langage qui permettrait de nous comprendre (if God existed he would be the language which allowed us to understand one another)."

After two years as a leading communist journalist, Salacrou left the movement in 1922, unable to accept subordination to Moscow's party line, and also because he was unable to believe in communism as wholeheartedly as its propagandists should. Education and class had now put him outside the working-class movement except in conviction and sympathy. He was closer to surrealism and dada (qq.v.), movements on whose fringes he loitered, and which influenced his early work for the theatre. In 1922 he married Jeanne Jeandet, by whom he was to have two daughters, and it was about this time that Salacrou began to write pieces in dramatic form, the "pièces à lire" (plays to be read), not intended for performance. Salacrou later said that dozens of them had been lost. What attracted him to write for the theatre was no doubt partly the recollection of Gounod's *Faust* at Le Havre, which he had been taken to see when he was eight,

and whose melodramatic elements—love, death, and the devil—had impressed him less than the completeness of the illusion, the "mysterious possibility of beginning life all over again." Later, Salacrou wrote for the theatre because it gave physical form to the creations of his imagination in words and movements. He was conscious of creating the reflection of his own personality, his own world, and his own concerns.

He knew, and could not help being inspired by, Tzara, Max Jacob, Robert Desnos and, among the painters, Juan Gris, but mere iconoclasm was never more than a temptation for him, any more than it had been for them. He could not rejoice in the disordered world he had not wished to discover, although he was prepared to take automatism (see Breton) and the exploration of the subconscious seriously. The early texts succeed in exteriorizing images without rational ordering from the world of dream and hallucination. It is not surprising that Salacrou believed that Artaud, whom he knew well, had plundered his material. Salacrou, however, developed beyond the chaotic texts of this early period. Before becoming a successful dramatist he was profoundly influenced by Pirandello's *Sei personaggi in cerca d'autore*, published in 1921, but drastically revised in 1925, and translated into English as *Six Characters in Search of an Author*. Pirandello's play was put on in Paris by the Pitoëffs in April 1923 and his emphasis on theatre as created drama by making the production of a play the theme of his own play provoked Salacrou to write plays too. The first was *Le Casseur d'assiettes*, completed in 1923, published in 1924, performed as a radio play in 1941, and finally staged in Leiden in 1954. The impact of Pirandello is clear, as it also is in *Le Pont de l'Europe*, published in 1932, having been performed in 1927, and *Patchouli*, completed in 1927, then directed by Charles Dullin and published by Gallimard in 1930.

From about 1925 Salacrou had turned to a commercial career, at first in two film companies, and then in a company he set up in 1929 to retail his father's pharmaceutical products. He bought space in major newspapers, disguised advertising copy as news, pushed sales up, promoted further patents, and by 1938 did well enough to increase the company's annual marketing budget to about 13 million francs—more than the amount spent by Citroën. In 1929 he had completed *Atlas-Hôtel*, and he at last ceased to create dramatic exteriorizations of his own internal conflicts. Instead, he offered audiences the sort of theatrical experience they were prepared to pay for on a night out. This was in stark contrast to the view he had expressed in 1925, when he declared that the theatre had died with the introduction of obligatory primary education—a view articulated by the protagonist of *Le Casseur d'assiettes*, who is contemptuous of the audience and mocks the stupidity of its members.

Even before the failure of *Patchouli* on 22 January 1930, Salacrou had come to learn that the constraints imposed by the public contribute to the creation of a play from the moment the dramatist first conceives its idea: "Il y a des publics ratés et des publics de génie (There are audiences which are failures, and audiences of genius)." The audience is "*literally* the author of the plays of its period." Taken to its extreme, this view suggests that the dramatist should merely pander to an audience's desire to be amused or entertained, which would empty dramatic enterprise of imaginative vigour. Salacrou had always thought that the dramatist should lead his audience to realise what had not been clear to it before and, particularly when writing about *La Dame aux camélias* in 1930, makes it clear that the dramatist needs to find ways of creating, or recreating, myths—a lesson that Ionesco, Giraudoux, Sartre, and Anouilh were all shortly to learn.

After 1930 Salacrou's theatre contains sharp social comment and his plays generally feature a provincial bourgeois figure in a state of moral and emotional bankruptcy. It is clear from *Dans la salle des pas perdus* that Salacrou himself felt moral discomfiture at commercial success, both inside the theatre, and outside, where he now belonged to the wealthy class of employers. He had adulterous affairs, felt that he had betrayed his own principles at every level of personal, social, economic, artistic, and political life, and half disliked his own frenetic and luxurious life style, thus generating internal conflicts he was willing to discuss in his autobiographical writings and still externalize in his dramatic creations. In May 1937 he wrote: "Je ne suis même pas heureux, ces jours-là, dans ces heures de cohues froufroutantes où je me sens si étranger (I'm not even happy on those days, in the moments of bustling crowds in which I feel so alien)." In December he felt too tired even to find an empty space where he could start again. *Un homme comme les autres* of 1936 and *La Terre est ronde*, published by Gallimard and directed by Dullin in 1938, reflect these feelings, together with the disgust Salacrou experienced at the rise of fascism. He denied that his plays had a contemporary political relevance, but the diary entries suggest that, at the very least, he was externalizing his own strong political and social feelings. In *La Terre est ronde* the depiction of Savonarola savagely indicts the bourgeois Florentine society which called him forth to make him its tyrant. There is a new change of direction in Salacrou's dramatic writing between 1936 and 1937.

He was called up in 1940 and requested a transfer from the auxiliary to the armed service of the air force. Refusing to obey the order to await capture, he made his way south in 1941 and, when the armistice was signed, settled in Lyons. He joined the left-wing Front National, participated in the underground press, returned to Paris in 1943, and generally tightened his commitment to the political left, although he also wrote for *Le Figaro* and had reservations about the communist position, expressed in "Certitudes" from the sixth volume of the *Théâtre* (1954). Not surprisingly the liberation of France marked a final turning point in the direction of Salacrou's drama. He became much more interested in the relationship between theatre and society, struck by the contrast between the contemporary relevance of the novels he read as a member of the Goncourt committee and the escapism of the post-war theatre in Paris. Together with his political commitment, this contrast led him closer to the idea of a popular theatre.

The effeteness of theatrical life in Paris seemed to Salacrou to derive from its dependence on a demoralized bourgeois audience lacking moral cohesion. He probably took from Sartre the idea of a theatre which was not only relevant to contemporary society, but committed to political activity within it. Such new ideas about the nature of drama's relationship to society are reflected in *Les Nuits de la colère*, put on by Jean-Louis Barrault in 1946, and *Boulevard Durand* (performed in 1961), and themselves led Salacrou towards the documentary. Much of his post-war drama is an attempt to fuse bourgeois theatre with plays clearly relevant to contemporary social and political problems. It has been said that he failed to opt either for popular drama or his earlier bourgeois style, and that the result was confusion in the texts. Some uncertainty of purpose is in fact clear. Although

scrupulously faithful as a documentary, *Boulevard Durand* came too close to commenting on the Algerian war for Malraux, then minister of culture, who banned its performance by the Barrault company in a state theatre. Even Jean Vilar, a former close associate of Dullin and in 1962 about to resign in protest against inadequate government support, refused to touch it at the Théâtre National Populaire.

At the end of his career Salacrou generalized his view of the political and social function of drama and saw the playwright's role as a heightening of the audience's awareness of the possibility and implications of choice. In 1953 he said that he wrote plays not only to externalize his own anguish and malaise, but also to force audiences to face the truth, by which he meant forcing them to reflect about their assumptions and values. His whole work, he says: "n'est qu'un cri pour éveiller les assoupis, pour les déranger (is only a cry to awake the complacent, to disturb them)." To some extent this meant striving for the same sort of effect as Brecht wanted. Since 1923 Salacrou had wanted the audience to remain aware of theatre as created drama rather than simply to surrender themselves to it as an illusion. In *L'Inconnue d'Arras* of 1935, *Les Nuits de la colère* of 1946, *Une femme trop honnête* and *Le Miroir*, written in 1953 and 1954 but both produced in 1956 Salacrou allows the characters to shatter the dramatic illusion by addressing the audience directly. This is the first step towards Brechtian alienation, and in the context of Salacrou's oeuvre is clearly working up to the effects achieved in *Boulevard Durand*, his first play written after Brecht's company, the Berliner Ensemble, had performed in Paris in 1955. *Boulevard Durand* was the peak of Salacrou's dramatic achievement. "For the first time I feel I have written exactly what I wanted to write," he declared.

The next two plays returned to bourgeois themes, and Salacrou left Paris to live in Le Havre again, surrendering to what he called "cette terrible attirance d'entrer, les yeux ouverts, dans le pays de la Mort (the terrible attraction of entering with open eyes the country of Death)." His last dramatic problem, that of integrating a fully committed hero into an acceptable satire of bourgeois society, was still unresolved, and perhaps as incapable of resolution as that of recreating a truly popular theatre. Salacrou left the theatre with a sense of failure. He has never found a large public outside France, although in the winter of 1946–47 three of his plays were running simultaneously in Paris, and a number have been translated into Italian. It is impossible not to recognize in Nathalie, the commercially rather than militantly tyrannical heroine of *La Rue noire*, a projection of Salacrou's personal condemnation of what he saw as his own betrayal of what he had once stood for.

WORKS

Precisely because Salacrou was too content for too long to regard his theatre and his life as continuous, the one reflecting, externalizing, and exorcizing the tensions of the other, he too easily felt that his literary work as a dramatist was over when he delivered his text. In this he was at the exact opposite of Beckett, who was minutely concerned with the staging of his plays, so the limits to Salacrou's reputation may well stem partly from his refusal to go beyond committing his script to paper. Are the works of a dramatist scripts or plays? Should the dramatist be regarded as a mere composer, whose work may require half a regiment of hierarchically organized interpreters for its realization, or is he responsible for the totality of a theatrical experience, which includes coaxing the right creative input from the audience? In giving an account of Salacrou's works it is important to remember that, although he would have said that he felt responsible for the dramatic experience, he could in fact abandon his finished scripts, once their externalization of inner tensions was completed on paper, to theatrical realizations that have sometimes betrayed his dramatic intentions.

As his own harshest judge, Salacrou draws attention to what he regards as his failure in this respect, regretting in *Dans la salle des pas perdus* his neglect of the staging of his plays. The dreamlike structure of *Histoire de rire* lent itself to realization as boulevard entertainment. Billed ironically as a "farce dramatique," it was finished in 1939 and first performed at the Théâtre de la Madeleine on 22 December 1939. It was produced by Alice Cocéa, who played Adé opposite two boulevard stars, André Luguet and Fernand Gravey, was dressed by Schiaparelli, and was a huge commercial success in the first Paris winter of World War II, generally regarded as a lightweight escape for bourgeois theatre patrons from their more pressing day-to-day concerns. It had been intended as a withering indictment of their moral failure as a social group. In *Le Soldat et la sorcière*, completed in 1943 but not staged until Dullin's production in December 1945 at the Théâtre Sarah Bernhardt, the script itself is at fault. The play was billed as a "divertissement" and its historical elements obscure instead of underlining the intrinsic indictment of fascism.

Atlas-Hôtel of 1931, directed like the failed *Patchouli* of the previous year by Charles Dullin at the Théâtre de l'Atelier, was Salacrou's first success and marks his shift towards the satire of bourgeois values and his own guilt at adopting them. Albany was once a poet, but prostituted himself to write mindless novels, and acquired wealth, power, and a taste for business. He arrives at Auguste's hilarious hotel to find his former wife, Augustine, now married to Auguste. Albany had abandoned her at the time he lost his integrity as an artist. Meeting her again shocks him into nostalgia for the pure idealist he once was. "I have robbed myself," he says. "Moi-même je suis mort, puisque j'ai fait de moi une image qui ne me ressemble pas! (I myself am dead since I've made myself into an image which isn't like me!)."

L'Inconnue d'Arras, directed by Lugné-Poe at the Comédie des Champs-Elysées in 1935, is chiefly famed for its flashback. The play covers the whole of Ulysse's life as it passes before him in the moment before he pulls the trigger of a revolver he is holding to his temple. He has discovered that his wife is having an affair with his closest friend. Salacrou starts the play with the revolver's bang and then breaks the naturalistic convention of theatrical illusion. The audience eavesdrops when the manservant abuses his employer's wife and speaks directly to it, drawing attention to the fact that he is an actor in a play, not part of a real event. The suicide finally picks himself up, although dead, and speaks quite normally. The effect is to add a metaphysical dimension to a drawing room play; a perfectly ordinary life is observed both as it occurs and from the point of death, with occasional deliberate blurrings about which perspective is being used, that of the suicide or that of the observer before the suicide takes place. Sometimes phantoms from the memory of the dying Ulysse remain on stage when he is no longer there, as if their existence were independent of him. From time to time Salacrou

reminds his audience sharply of the double perspective, which works rather like a cubist (q.v.) painting, as when Maxime, the lover, reminds Ulysse's wife Yolande that she is only a phantom.

Salacrou's plays continued to depend on temporal dislocation sometimes exploited for comic incongruity. This is especially true in *Sens interdit*, written in 1952 and first performed in 1953, when real time clashes with the illusory time of the octogenarians regressing to a pre-natal state in search of a period of happiness free from deception. It is a recurring theme in the plays that man is a prisoner of his past. "Our past does not die. Our past is our eternity... We are condemned to be the person we have been," says a character in *Le Miroir*, completed in 1954 and first staged in 1956. Our past is even called our hell.

Together with the dislocation of time, Salacrou depends frequently on the use of symmetrical patterns within his plots. In *Histoire de rire* the lighthearted eternal triangle becomes the vehicle for serious comment when it is mirrored by a second triangle. Adé, the frivolous wife, is about to leave Gérard, her husband, for her young lover Achille. The more mature Hélène is about to leave her husband, Donaldo, for her lover, Jean-Louis. The link in the plot is the life-long friendship between Gérard and Jean-Louis, the first husband and the second lover. The darker tones are established when Adé realizes that she will be unable to return to Gérard until Hélène returns to Donaldo, to whom Adé therefore reveals Hélène's whereabouts. Although Hélène is genuinely in love with Jean-Louis, she has to return to Donaldo, and in an ironic comment the most meaningful relationship in the play is sacrificed to the restoration of trivial social order.

In *Le Miroir* Lucien is involved in both triangles. His wife Maryse has been unfaithful with his best friend Antignac. Lucien then seduces the naive young Cécile, married to the Catholic Laurent, reducing her to the status of a substitute for Maryse. Cécile rebels against this tyranny: "I want to become Cécile." But she cannot confess to Laurent without destroying him and hurting Lucien, whom she loves. The darker side of the imbroglio is Cécile's dilemma about reconciling her integrity with her responsibility to Laurent and Lucien. She commits suicide, a solution which Salacrou tries to represent as an assertion of freedom.

In *La Terre est ronde* it is the morally bankrupt bourgeoisie which is condemned as responsible for the arrival of the tyrant Savonarola. The plot is schematic, with Renaissance science and optimism represented by the rich, middle-aged pharmacist Manente, whom Luciana, pregnant by the wealthy young Silvio, is persuaded to marry. Luciana is the daughter of Minutello, the wool merchant who represents the old, bourgeois Florence, its moral cohesion eroded by a respect for money alone. Minutello sides for purely pragmatic reasons with Savonarola, who imposes tyrannical order by having books burnt, citizens spied on, and Jews burnt or flogged. In a parody of Rousseau Savonarola is ready to force people to be free: "la liberté que je vous offre, si vous la refusez, je vous contraindrai à la subir (if you refuse the liberty I offer you, I will force you to undergo it)." Savonarola's regime is destroyed and he has achieved his own apotheosis as a saint only by destroying the corrupt society whose moral disintegration created the void which provoked the need for his dictatorship in the first place.

Silvio, originally attracted by Luciana's ascetic purity, becomes one of Savonarola's fiercest acolytes when Luciana deserts him. He meets Luciana again, attempts to persuade her to renounce earthly happiness, fails because of the pressure exercised on her by her sister Faustina, materialist mistress of a Roman cardinal, and content to pick up on earth whatever pleasures she can, and is faced with the dilemma of compromising his heavenly aspirations or renouncing earthly pleasures altogether. The dilemma is again unresolved by Silvio's martyrdom. He had implied the nature of his choice between compromise and the sacrifice of everything for the unattainable in his words to Faustina:

Tu es heureuse, toi? Non. Car tu méprises ta joie, tu méprises tes rires. Tu t'y résignes, c'est tout! "Il n'y a pas mieux, et je ramasse ce que je trouve." Moi, c'est ce qu'il y a de méprisable en moi que je méprise. Et quand je suis heureux, au moins, je peux aimer mon bonheur.

(Are you happy? Yourself? No, because you despise your joy, you despise your laughter. You resign yourself to it, that's all! "There's nothing better, and I take what I find." It's what's despicable in myself that *I* despise. And when I'm happy, at least I can love my happiness.)

Boulevard Durand has been described as rather obvious in its social realism. It is a series of episodic sequences arranged in epic form, clearly inspired in part by the theatrical techniques and preoccupations of Brecht. There is a narrator, called simply "L'Homme," and the tone is deeply pessimistic. Durand's death has already occurred, and can have achieved something to relieve the cruelty in the world only by having been re-enacted in front of subsequent generations. When Durand asks if his suffering has been in vain, L'Homme replies that a street now carries his name and that that name is honoured even as others are being taken to their deaths. The analogy between the society which destroyed Durand and that of Salacrou's own day can escape no one. For Salacrou, remembering the soldier on duty in 1822 at a performance of *Othello* in Baltimore who shot the actor playing Othello just as he was about to kill Desdemona, theatrical stylization can intensify the audience's emotion rather than assuage it.

The characters from the original Durand affair are summoned back from death to re-enact their roles on the stage with a fatalistic ritualism which is dramatically effective and, partly on account of the stylization, emotionally powerful. Salacrou is now concerned with staging. Not only is a newspaper headline projected on to the stage, but the trial scene effectively uses spotlighting and blackout. Since the trial is merely a ritual, the characters speak in clipped, sharp, inhuman voices, incantatory in the delivery of rehearsed evidence. A drum roll effectively intensifies parts of the drama. It can be argued that this is Salacrou's best play because it forces the audience to reconsider the values by which it is actually living, if only by making it aware of them. We are not left with another unsatisfactory attempt to resolve a clearly perceived dilemma which, as so often in real life, is incapable of dramatic resolution.

Les Nuits de la colère is the Salacrou play which probably had the sharpest impact, especially as staged at the Marigny by the Barrault company in 1946, and incidentally by the same company in London five years later. The theme of the play is partly responsibility, although it is also a celebration of Resistance heroism. Partly, too, the play is a documentary of the occupation years, using for instance "Rivoire" as the name of one of the Resistance movement's leaders. This had been the name actually used by the communist Resistance leader René Blech. The hero of the piece, Cordeau, regards Bazire as a collaborator simply because he does nothing, thereby accepting the occupation. Later on Bazire does in fact become a traitor and is responsible for Cordeau's death.

Cordeau himself is rescued from inertia by a situation in which he is forced to assume responsibility. Before the war the absurdity of the world had made him unable to find any justification for action. Now the war allows him to take responsibility for an entirely predestined role. He can say, like the drop of water in a waterfall, that he has chosen to go down rather than up. The concept of freedom used by Salacrou is not logically defensible, as he admitted, but it was dramatically effective. Cordeau felt an inner compulsion to join the Resistance, partly because of his need to belong to the group, but he did at least have the freedom to assent to the inner compulsion. He analyses his feelings as he waits with his companions to blow up a train. Morality has been inverted. Dédé points out that in the present situation they would be criminals if they had not turned assassins.

PUBLICATIONS

Collections

Théâtre, 8 vols., 1943–66; revised edition, 1977–

Plays

Le Casseur d'assiettes (produced 1954), 1924
Tour à terre (produced 1925), with *Le Pont de l'Europe*, 1929
Le Pont de l'Europe (produced 1927), with *Tour à terre*, 1929; separately 1932
Patchouli (produced 1930), 1930
Atlas-Hôtel (produced 1931), 1931
La Vie en rose (produced 1931), 1936
Les Frénétiques (produced 1934), 1935
Une femme libre (produced 1934), with *Atlas-Hôtel*, 1934
L'Inconnue d'Arras (produced 1935), 1936; as *The Unknown Woman of Arras* (produced 1948)
Un homme comme les autres (produced 1936), 1937
La Terre est ronde (produced 1938), with *Un homme comme les autres*, 1938; as *The World Is Round*, in *Three Plays*, 1967
Histoire de rire (produced 1939), 1940; as *No Laughing Matter* (produced 1957); as *When the Music Stops* (produced 1957), in *Three Plays*, 1967
La Marguerite (produced 1944), with *Histoire de rire* and *Le Casseur d'assiettes*, 1941; as *Marguerite* (produced 1951), 1967; in *Three Plays*, 1967
Les Fiancés du Havre (produced 1944), 1944
Le Soldat et la sorcière (produced 1945), 1946
Les Nuits de la colère (produced 1946), 1946; as *Men of Darkness* (produced 1948)
L'Archipel Lenoir (produced 1947), 1948; as *Never Say Die* (produced 1966)
Pourquoi pas moi? (produced 1948), with *Poof*, 1948
Poof (produced 1950), with *Pourquoi pas moi?*, 1948
Dieu le savait (produced 1951), with *Pourquoi pas moi?*, 1951
Sens interdit (produced 1953), 1953

Les Invités du Bon Dieu (produced 1953), 1953
Le Miroir (produced 1956), in *L'Avant-Scène 139*, 1956
Une femme trop honnête (produced 1956), 1956
La Boule de verre, 1958
La Beauté du diable (screenplay), with René Clair, in *Comédies*,
    by Clair, 1959
Boulevard Durand (produced 1961), 1960; edited by Colin Rad-
    ford, 1975; as *Boulevard Durand* (in English; produced 1963)
Comme les chardons, 1964
La Rue noire, 1967
Three Plays (includes *Marguerite, The World Is Round, When
    the Music Stops*), 1967
Screenplays: *Histoire de rire*, with Georges Neveux, 1941; *La
    Beauté du diable*, with René Clair, 1950

Other

Les Idées de la nuit, 1960
Impromptu délibéré: entretiens avec Paul-Louis Mignon, 1966
Dans la salle des pas perdus, 2 vols., 1974–76

Critical studies

Mignon, Paul-Louis, *Salacrou*, 1960
Guicharnand, Jacques, *Modern French Theatre*, 1961
Knowles, Dorothy, *French Drama of the Inter-War Years*, 1967

SALMON, André, 1881–1969.

Poet, art critic, and novelist.

LIFE

Virtually nothing is known about André Salmon's early life
except what he himself has told us in *Souvenirs sans fin*, the
three volumes covering, respectively, the periods 1903–08,
1908–20, and 1920–24, published by Gallimard in 1955, 1956,
and 1961. He was born in Paris on 4 October 1881, the son of a
sculptor turned engraver, descended, he claims, from a Champagne family of boat builders. In 1897 he left with his family for
St Petersburg, where, by 1900, he had a room on Gagarinskaïa
Street and was employed as a clerk in the French consulate. He
returned to France to undergo his military service, which began
on 16 November 1902. He later dated his "birth to poetry" from
1903, when he began to frequent the literary circles of *La Plume*,
where he was welcomed by Karl Boes, and of the *Mercure de
France*, where Adrien van Bever had his early poems accepted
for publication. At *La Plume* he got to know the later symbolists
(q.v.), Francis Vielé-Griffin, Stuart Merrill, and Jean Moréas, as
well as Alfred Jarry, Guillaume Apollinaire, and Charles-Louis
Philippe. He became a close friend of Paul Fort, with whom he
was to found the review *Vers et Prose* and its associated publishing house in 1905, and greatly influenced Apollinaire, of whom
Max Jacob used frequently to say that Salmon was the true
teacher.

From 1903 to 1909 when it began to disintegrate, Salmon was
a member of the highly talented group surrounding Picasso, to
whom he had been introduced by the sculptor Manolo at the
Bateau Lavoir in the Rue Ravignan (see Apollinaire). Then,
from 1908 until his marriage in July 1909, he was to share a floor
of the next-door house, no.7, with Juan Gris. His stature as a
poet has been partially eclipsed by the immense talent of some
of the friends who surrounded him, but he was part of the group
which built up into its critical mass the forces which exploded as
cubism (q.v.) into Western European culture. His specific contribution was the crucial change in the treatment of the pierrot
figure, transposing the acrobatic saltimbanque into the insecure
clown of Picasso's rose period, as taken over by Cocteau and
Stravinsky and echoed in the poems of Jacob and Apollinaire,
and the paintings of Marie Laurencin. It was Salmon who, in
1907, named Picasso's famous painting *Les Demoiselles d'Avignon*. Following a chance meeting at Picasso's studio, Salmon
and Max Jacob became inseparable friends as well as neighbours in the Rue Ravignan.

Paul Fort was the senior partner at *Vers et Prose*, where the
whole capital of 200 francs is said immediately to have been
spent on 10-centime stamps for mailing prospective subscribers.
It was here, however, that Salmon published his first collection
of verse, the 1905 *Poèmes*, having already published in the
short-lived *Revue Immoraliste* that April the first pages of what
would become *Le Manuscrit trouvé dans un chapeau* (with 60
drawings by Picasso). In 1907 *Vers et Prose* published Salmon's
second collection, *Les Féeries*. About his marriage on 13 July
1909 to Jeanne Blazy-Escarpette, Salmon said that it had been a
good date because the state, preparing for the national holiday
the next day, paid for the street lighting, the dancing, and the
flags. Like Stravinsky, Picasso, Jacob, and Braque, Salmon was
keen on popular culture, and he not infrequently incorporated
bits of, or allusions to, popular tunes and lyrics in his work. He
recalls, perhaps apocryphally, the roundabout with Apollinaire
on the elephant, Marie Laurencin on the giraffe, René Dalize on
the lion with the poodle's head, Cremnitz on the rabbit, and
Julien Callé on a pink pig. At Salmon's wedding party Apollinaire, the groom's witness, read the famous poem printed in his
Alcools.

From the winter of 1909 Salmon was the art critic of *L'Intransigeant*, where he defended cubism. When he left for *Paris-
Journal* the following year, he proposed Apollinaire as his
replacement. In 1910 Salmon published his third collection of
verse, *Le Calumet*, to be republished in 1920 with engravings by
Derain. All three collections were republished in 1926 under the
title *Créances (1905–1910)*. Since his marriage Salmon had
turned to journalism to earn a stable income, writing also for *Gil
Blas, Le Soleil, L'Homme Libre*, and *Le Matin*, where Colette
had taken him on. From 1910 he wrote on whatever was of
public interest, but from 1928 specialized in reporting court
cases for *Le Petit Parisien*. However, he also covered the Tour de
France for 1932, 1933, and 1934. Salmon's journalistic career
entailed a good deal of travelling, and inspired his "Romancero
du voyageur," a poem printed in the *Mercure* for 1 December
1924 and republished in the 1927 *Tout l'or du monde*. His only
other volume publications before World War I were the collection of art criticism *La Jeune Peinture française*, republished in
1919, and the contes collected from *Paris-Journal* and reworked
into the 1913 novel *Tendres canailles*, to be republished in 1921.

Salmon spent World War I in the infantry, and burst into

she calculated to be about half her debt to Buloz. As Musset's health improved, his jealousy, tantrums, and drinking increased. Sand threatened him with an asylum and in the end sent him home. Much later she was to give her account of what happened in *Elle et lui*, while Musset wrote about it in the *Confession d'un enfant du siècle*.

Pagello, who lived a totally bohemian existence, was also short of money, and Sand and he had to abandon projected trips to the Tyrol and Constantinople. She worked as furiously as she could, sending Musset her *Lettres d'un voyageur*, which he passed on to Buloz, who was enthusiastic. Two excerpts were published in the *RDM* in May, but Buloz only paid 300 francs for each. Sand finished *André* and a second *Lettre*. A third was sent when a missing payment of 1,100 francs, which the post had mislaid, finally turned up and Sand was solvent again. Her final word on Venice was saved for *L'Histoire de ma vie*. During the six months she was in Venice, Sand had written two novels, *André* and *Jacques*, the long short story *Leone Leoni*, and two of the three *Lettres d'un voyageur*, an output which she valued at 14,000 francs. Pagello agreed to accompany her to Paris, and they left on 24 July, arriving on 14 August. The first part of *Leone* had been enthusiastically received when published in the *RDM*. Sand saw Musset again on 17 August. He left for Baden and she for Nohant on 24 August. She pretended to have sold four Zuccarelli landscapes which Pagello had brought for sale, and sent him 1,500 francs. Musset, who had sworn to keep their friendship on a purely spiritual level, was nevertheless writing passionately demanding letters, while Sand's affection for Pagello was simply disintegrating. No doubt exhausted, she was also in despair at her increasingly obvious inadequacies where intimate personal relationships were concerned.

Feeling unwanted in Paris, Pagello returned to Venice in late October, 12 days after Musset's return. The winter saw a series of temporary and partial reconciliations between Sand and Musset, some of them stormy and passionate, and during this time Sand also met Heine and the 23-year-old Liszt, already the foremost piano virtuoso of his day. The final break with Musset came on 6 March 1835. Sand had returned his letters to help him write the *Confession*. She now cut off her hair and, in a final histrionic gesture, sent it, together with Musset's last letter, in a skull, and once more contemplated suicide.

On 5 December 1834 Buloz, who had commissioned Sand's portrait from Delacroix, had signed a contract with her for 40,000 francs, 10,000 to be paid in monthly instalments of 500 francs for the right to publish her complete works, and 30,000 in annual sums of 1,000 for the memoirs she intended to write. Sand had to finish *Engelwald* for him by May 1835, as her contract contained a penalty clause deducting 250 francs for each month's delay. In fact she never did finish it, partly because it may have contained seditious innuendoes, but after finishing the "Poème de Myrza" and "Mattéa" wrote the short story "Mauprat." She then demanded it back and turned it into a full-length novel with a social focus quite new for her. Most of Sand's friends from Berry were republican sympathizers, and in April, while still in the country, she met a firebrand republican lawyer, the stooped and balding Michel de Bourges, as he was called. He wrote her an impassioned plea to interest herself in social matters, and she spent the rest of April composing a sixth *Lettre d'un voyageur* dedicated to him. They met again in Paris, where he was defending the 121 ringleaders of the Lyons disturbances following the silk workers' strike of January 1834 in the "procès

monstre." His father had been a woodcutter and was murdered by royalists, and he foresaw the emergence of a society without property after an apocalyptic revolution. In July they became lovers.

Sand worked on *Simon*, a novel whose central figure combined something of Michel with something of Liszt, for whom Marie d'Agoult had abandoned her aristocratic count and their children, thereby causing a public scandal. Sand thought Liszt was taking his revenge for not being allowed to marry Caroline de Saint-Cricq, the daughter of a cabinet minister. Early in 1835 she and her husband had agreed on a legal separation. Sand was to keep Nohant and Solange, he to retain Maurice and the income from the Paris property. Shortly before he was due to hand over Nohant in November, he became violent, however, and a new settlement was imposed by the court whereby Sand kept both children. That month, too, Buloz accepted her request for a revision of the December 1834 contract and came to Nohant. The new agreement was much more favourable. Her complete works would be published in 16 volumes, with Sand to receive one and a half francs per volume sold. Buloz was to have until November 1841 to complete the publishing. The final three volumes would contain *Simon*, and the two-volume *Engelwald*, which was now overdue. This was to be delivered on 1 January 1836 although there was still a volume to write, but the penalty clause remained.

In Paris Sand was now at the centre of a coterie which included Etienne Arago, the lawyer who had collaborated on potboiling vaudevilles with Balzac and Sandeau, Guéroult, a journalist who worked for *Le Globe*, and the Swiss poet Charles Didier. They were all younger than she was. Although Michel was jealous of him, it is on the whole unlikely that Sand's relationship with Didier was more than maternal, except possibly during the summer at Nohant. However, Michel's wife was jealous of Sand, and Sand scarcely saw Michel again after June 1837. Despite passionate reunions earlier that year, Sand's attitude seems again to have veered towards the possessively maternal. Meanwhile Casimir had decided to appeal against the court settlement. Sand won, defended by Michel, and Casimir went on to appeal to the royal court at Bourges. Michel again represented Sand, and Casimir capitulated when, in July 1836, the judges split five–five. He received the income from the Paris property on condition that he pay Maurice's boarding school expenses and guarantee him an annual income of 2,400 francs when he reached the age of 19. Sand got access to Maurice, sole custody of Solange, and Nohant.

The airing of Sand's extra-marital relationships had naturally embarrassed her. She was in any case wrongly taken to be an advocate of free love, an apologist for divorce, and a believer in the abolition of marriage. In fact she believed in marital fidelity, condoning infidelity only as a last-resort escape from marital enslavement. She regarded neither child-bearing nor "feminine" pursuits, including housekeeping, as demeaning. But the reform of marriage required the prior reform of society. Michel de Bourges had weaned her from her apolitical stance, and Sand, too, now earnestly desired social reform, but she felt that, while women's education should be improved, there was an unalterable difference between the male and the female character. Until society and the education of women were reformed, it was useless to look to women to fill the highest offices of government or justice. Her views had changed none the less. The personal and somewhat stoical pessimism of the early novels had given way to the social "humanitarianism" of the revised *Mauprat*.

She was offered a platform for her views when Désiré Nisard attacked her in the *Revue de Paris* in May 1836 for what he took to be her elegant and eloquent defence of adultery. A fortnight later she defended herself, pointing out that different standards of moral behaviour were, but should not be, applied to men and to women, on whom society was infamously stricter. The formal exposition of Sand's views on women and society is to be found in the six "Lettres à Marcie" written in 1836–37 for Lamennais as editor of *Le Monde*, but so badly cut by him that Sand discontinued writing for the newspaper. The "Lettres" were not published in volume form. In August, the case with Casimir settled, Sand took the children to Switzerland, hoping to find in Geneva Liszt and Marie d'Agoult, who had now given birth to the first of her three children by Liszt, and finally catching up with them in Chamonix. One of the children was to become Cosima Wagner. Returning to Paris via Nohant, Sand stayed with Maurice and Solange at the Hôtel de France in Paris, one floor below Liszt and Marie. It was that November that Chopin allowed Liszt to bring Marie and Sand to see him. Liszt played and then Chopin parodied Meyerbeer's *Les Huguenots*. Sand did not see him again until she was invited by him to meet Sue and Custine on 13 December.

Liszt and Mme d'Agoult came twice to stay at Nohant for several weeks in the first months of 1837. Maurice's tutor fell in love with Sand and had to be replaced by another, Félicien Mallefille, with whom she did in fact have a brief affair. Otherwise Nohant offered its usual mixture of hard work and practical jokes, especially when Liszt and Marie were there. That summer, Sand had another brief affair, with a Parisian actor, Pierre Bocage, who wanted her to write a play for him. Then Sand's mother died. She and her half-sister Caroline nursed her at the end, and Sand insisted that the annual pension of 2,500 from the Dupin de Francueil estate should now go to Caroline to help pay for her son's education. Casimir's stepmother had also died, and Casimir had wanted to borrow 30,000 francs to free the estate he had inherited in Nérac from debt, and so double its revenues. Sand's refusal provoked Casimir's brief kidnapping of Solange and a great deal of drama before order was once more restored. *Mauprat*, finished in mid-May, had been followed by *Les Maîtres mosaïstes*. Buloz was pressing for another novel Sand owed. She wrote *La Dernière Aldini* in six weeks during the summer. It was again about love across class barriers, and she regarded it as the merest potboiler, referring to it as trash.

During the winter of 1837 Sand suffered badly from rheumatism. She wrote one of the many derivatives of Byron's "Corsair," *L'Uscocque*, and dictated some of *Spiridion*, for which she adopted a new philosophical style. Buloz expanded the project for the complete works to 20 volumes and made her a further advance of 6,000 francs. Balzac came to Nohant early in 1838 and stayed for a week, writing perceptively of Sand: "She is boyish, an artist, she is great-hearted, generous, devout, and *chaste*." It was when she had to go to Paris in April to settle the compensation for Casimir on retaking possession of the Paris property that Sand got to know Chopin better. She met him again at a dinner for Marie Dorval when he improvised at the piano, and then on 8 May at a formal concert-dinner given by Adolphe de Custine, who was to provide Proust with inspiration, attended by Hugo, Nodier, Sophie Gay, and the Duchesse d'Abrantès.

Chopin was not really a romantic. His formal perfectionism

and delicacy of taste prevented him from indulging in the almost vulgar rhetorical flourishes of a Liszt or a Berlioz, and his output was always more carefully polished than that of the slapdash Musset. What he needed was the intensity of intimate feeling which the shy, almost tongue-tied Sand, masculine in manner and gushing only with her pen, was desperate to lavish on handsome and vulnerable young men. Chopin was the younger of the two by five and a half years. Their liaison started in June. Sand first thought of it, characteristically, as an entirely spiritual surrender. In the course of a long letter to Chopin's close friend Albert Grzymala, she recognized that her infidelity to Mallefille was the worse for that. The headstrong Mallefille was exceedingly angry when he learnt that he had been supplanted, and appears to have fought a duel with Alexandre Rey, a protégé of Liszt and another of Maurice's tutors, who took him to task for his violent behaviour.

A new agreement allowed Casimir to have the children for four weeks each year, and a new contract with Buloz guaranteed Sand 5,000 francs for each volume she published in return for a virtual monopoly on serial rights until the end of 1840. *Spiridion* was now put aside for *Les Sept cordes de la lyre*, a five-act play which Buloz found full of pseudo-philosophy and inflated rhetoric. He sent Sand 500 francs instead of the 2,000 she expected after repaying a 6,000-franc advance made in October 1838 and taking reprints into account, reminding her that she owed him 4,500 francs by reason of the *Engelwald* penalty clause. The 6,000 francs had been borrowed so that Sand, Chopin, and the two children could spend the winter of 1838–39 in a warm climate, thought to be more cheaply available in Mallorca than elsewhere. Pleyel was to have a piano shipped out and would pay 2,000 francs for 24 preludes, one in each of the major and the minor keys, of which 500 francs would be paid in advance. A banker friend lent Chopin 1,000 francs. Sand left Paris on 18 October 1838, travelling as much as possible by boat. Chopin joined her at Perpignan.

Mallorca was a nightmare. Sand had no idea how to manage, and the epic catastrophes, although predictable, were a real endurance test. Both of them worked through every discomfort. Chopin, racked by illness, came back coughing blood, but he had produced the preludes, the F major ballade, the C sharp minor scherzo, a mazurka, and two polonaises. The party spent 14 weeks in Mallorca and 10 in Marseilles recuperating. They arrived at Nohant on 1 June 1839. Sand's affection for Chopin, who now weighed a mere 95 pounds and could be reduced by the slightest exertion to paroxysms of coughing, grew firmly and exclusively maternal. She was afraid, as she had been in the case of both Sandeau and Musset, that his physical involvement with her was driving him to the point of dangerous exhaustion. Still, by early summer Chopin had completed the B flat minor sonata, a new scherzo, and a dozen smaller pieces. He was enchanting everyone by his musical wit and gift for parody.

Sand's financial affairs were now in real disorder. She owed 80,000 francs, although she had 10 years in which to pay it. Nohant was yielding only 7,000 francs a year. Hippolyte, who had sided with Casimir in the long dispute, now lent her 14,000 francs. She exchanged barbed letters with Buloz, now a royal commissioner to the Comédie-Française, who had displeased her by publishing a piece on Goethe by his brother-in-law when she had one ready for him, and threatened to break off relations. Buloz came with his wife to Nohant, took two plays, *Gabriel*, which retreated from the pantheistic humanism Sand had taken from Leroux's Christian messianism, and *Cosima*, named after Liszt's second daughter, and peace was made, although the actors at the Comédie had *Cosima* forced upon them only with the greatest difficulty. Sand would willingly have withdrawn the play, knowing the reception being prepared for it, but Buloz was determined to impose his authority on the company. *Lélia* had made Sand powerful enemies, and they seized their chance to pack the theatre. Even Marie Dorval's acting was affected by the reception. The play was staged in April 1840 and was taken off after seven performances.

From 1839 Chopin and Sand had separate Paris apartments but would meet for dinner at five and spend the evening together. Sand found living in Paris and educating the children expensive. *Cosima* had taken 10 months of her time and brought in only 5,000 francs in volume form. Chopin was earning 400–500 francs a week giving piano lessons. Since composing at Nohant brought in less than half that, the couple stayed in Paris. Maurice meanwhile joined Delacroix's studio. Buloz now turned down two novels in succession, *Le Compagnon du tour de France* on account of its utopian socialism, and *Horace*, which supported a revolutionary struggle to do away with private property. Sand had abandoned the thinking of Lamennais for that of Pierre Leroux, and was now purveying his belief in natural goodness, progress, reincarnation, and the abolition of private property. The new lofty, idealistic descriptions of proletarian existence and Sand's break with Buloz occasioned a great deal of comment in literary Paris. Sand, now internationally considered France's leading social prophet, moved her publishing to Aristide Perrotin.

Sand's relationship with Marie d'Agoult, although not with Liszt, had been difficult as early as February 1838, when Balzac had stayed at Nohant. It became irrevocably soured when Balzac contrasted the two women under transparent disguises and to Sand's flagrant advantage in *Béatrix*, serialized in the spring of 1839. Balzac deliberately made matters worse in the preface to the volume edition of the same year. An unkind anonymous review of Sand's *Le Compagnon* by Marie early in 1841 was countered by a portrait of Marie as the Vicomtesse de Chailly in *Horace*. In 1841, by an unhappy coincidence, Liszt gave a concert in Paris on 25 April and Chopin made his first public appearance for eight years on the 26th. Both were brilliantly successful, and Liszt was hyperbolic about Chopin in the *Revue et Gazette Musicale*, but Marie, who felt her hold on Liszt slipping, resented they way in which Sand was pushing Chopin into the limelight once occupied by Liszt.

Sand's next novel, *Consuelo*, was about rivalries between musical performers and rival philosophies of musical performance, ornamental ostentation and pyrotechnics of the Liszt/Paganini sort or Chopin's subtlety and purity of melodic invention. It was inspired by the career of the singer Pauline García, the younger sister of the singer who had inspired Sand's earliest fiction. Her voice had an exceptional range and purity, and she spoke five languages. Clara Schumann thought her the greatest female genius she had met, Berlioz found her remarkable, Chopin was overwhelmed by her, and Musset wrote two highly eulogistic articles about her for the *RDM*. Sand warned her against a possible marriage to Musset, and may have promoted the suit of the art critic Louis Viardot, who was 21 years older than García. She married him at the age of 18 in April 1840, and Viardot gave up the management of the Théâtre des Italiens to promote his wife's career. In 1841 Sand was solvent again

thanks to a 7,500-franc advance from Perrotin and a rash 5,000-franc advance from Buloz and could spend the summer at Nohant with Chopin, whose concert had also brought in 6,000 francs. The Viardots came to stay.

Even before the break, Sand had wanted to be free of Buloz, but serialization in the *RDM* meant both money and publicity. Perrotin could offer only half of her accustomed receipts per volume. The answer seemed to lie in establishing a new review. The *Revue Indépendante*, deliberately suggesting by its name the sycophancy of the *RDM*, was consequently launched on 5 November 1841 by Sand, Viardot, and Pierre Leroux, who was charged with finding the necessary 50,000 francs of working capital. Sand gave *Horace* and *Consuelo* to the new review and wrote almost a third of the first issue herself, and almost as much of the second, since Leroux's evangelical messianism met mostly with hostility or indifference. Various retrenchments were made at Nohant and in Paris, the plan being that Chopin would move into the apartment hitherto occupied by Maurice, who would move upstairs.

Meanwhile Pauline, of whom Sand was intensely fond, found her career halted, not only because she had a baby in December 1841, but also because jealousy, particularly that of Giulia Grisi at the Italiens and Rosine Stoltz at the Opéra, and the malice of Buloz at the *RDM* and the *Revue de Paris*, controlled by his associate Florestan Bonnaire, effectively kept her off the Parisian stage, leaving her to triumph in Spain, Austria, London, St Petersburg, and Berlin. When she was finally allowed on stage at the Italiens in the winter of 1842, Buloz's brother-in-law wrote a terrible review, throwing in a sneer at Chopin. Grisi, Stoltz, Agoult, and Musset had all been pilloried in *Consuelo*, and Leroux kept asking for more. Sand eventually stretched it to 105 chapters, changing its focus from purity in music to purity in religion, before she started its continuation, *La Comtesse de Rudolstadt*. Pauline had meanwhile been invited to sing for the emperor at the Hofburg in Vienna. She even succeeded in impressing Metternich's haughty wife.

In 1842 Sand welcomed overtures from Louis Véron to assume control of the *Revue Indépendante*. Formerly editor of the *Revue de Paris*, he was now editing the daily *Le Constitutionnel*, which, with 20,000 subscribers and no speedy means of news transmission, could offer double Buloz's rates for serialized fiction. Sand signed a contract for *Jeanne*, published by the newspaper from 25 April to 2 June 1845, and a novel about contemporary French society. The paper followed *Jeanne* with Eugène Sue's *Le Juif errant*. Sue ran out of inspiration and asked for a respite, and Sand was promised an enticing figure if she would bring forward the completion of her second novel. When she delivered *Le Meunier d'Angibault*, a work permeated with Proudhon's view that all riches are the result of theft, exploitation, or expropriation, Véron refused to publish it, eventually paying Sand an indemnity.

Sand's social commitment was central to her concerns. In 1844 she had published four articles on "La politique et le socialisme" in the regional *L'Eclaireur de l'Indre et du Cher*, which Leroux had taken over. Only gradually did she come to realize that he was a fraud, on the scrounge for himself, his nine children, his brothers, and, since they rejected bourgeois marriage, their concubines. She had let him help himself to 6,000 francs, and written a preface for a "new" version of *Die Leiden des jungen Werthers* which he had stolen from a dead translator, but by 1845 even her goodwill had been overstretched. Meanwhile *Le Meunier* was sold to *La Réforme*, one of whose editors was the social historian Louis Blanc, with whom Sand had had a brief affair, but the editors serialized her work without regard to its internal divisions and were slow to pay, so Sand ceased her association with them.

In 1845 Sand had dashed off the lightweight novelette *Teverino* in order to get together enough money to go to Nohant in mid-June with Chopin and Pauline, with whom, to his mother's dismay, Maurice had now fallen in love. She no longer worked all night, but from noon to six pm, and that summer finished *Le Péché de Monsieur Antoine*, the last of her ideological novels. Tediously full of revolutionary rhetoric, it had surprisingly been pre-sold to the conservative *L'Epoque*. Following a four-day outing with Chopin, the last they were to take together, Sand wrote *La Mare au diable*, the first of her new pastoral idylls, in just four days. She let Chopin return to Paris without her. They had been drifting apart for some time, and Sand wanted to go to Chenonceaux to renew her acquaintance with the favourite cousin who should have been her guardian, René de Villeneuve. Her reputation as a radical was bad enough, but she knew she could not take her famous lover. She was also embarrassed because of the social unacceptability of her smoking habits.

In early May 1846 Sand signed a 12,000-franc contract for a new novel, *Lucrezia Floriani*. When she read parts of it at Nohant one evening later that summer, Delacroix could not believe that Chopin, who had genuinely liked what he had heard, had not recognized a cruel lampoon of his own jealousy in what was a fictionalization of his relationship with Sand. The new fad at Nohant that summer was theatricals, replacing the billiards which had been all the rage during Chopin's reign. Floods kept the large house party together, and marriage between Solange and Fernand de Preaulx, an impecunious aristocrat, seemed possible. The strong-willed and impetuous Solange rejected him but almost immediately accepted Auguste Clésinger, an ex-soldier turned sculptor. He was unstable, dissolute, spendthrift and had a reputation for beating his mistresses. They were married on 19 May and left for Paris on the 23rd.

Sand followed on 31 May only to meet up with a tearful Solange. Clésinger had patently married her for her money, was heavily in debt, and spending lavishly. Her dowry, the Paris property, already seemed threatened. The debts were 24,000 francs but, as Solange was a minor, she could neither sell nor mortgage the Paris house. When the Clésingers came to Nohant to ask for help, there were unpleasant and complicated quarrels. Clésinger's behaviour was predictably boorish and bullying, but Solange herself behaved in a variety of disgraceful ways, particularly towards her mother and Maurice. Chopin was not there, but he had gradually been transferring his affection to Solange for some years, and from a distance now took her side. In despair Solange finally appealed to Casimir, who allowed her to stay, but refrained from helping Clésinger. It was Chopin who, at a chance encounter with Sand, told her that she was a grandmother. The infant survived only a few days.

Late in 1847 Victor Borie, a friend of Leroux, had become Sand's lover. She had written *Calio Floriani* in April 1847, and now finished another idyll, *François le champi*, but could not get it serialized. The value of her undelivered work had fallen to zero during the Leroux years and Hetzel, the publisher of whom Chopin had been needlessly jealous, advised Sand to write the history of her extraordinary life. He came to Nohant three times and arranged a contract for five volumes, each at 26,000 francs,

copy to be delivered at eight-week intervals with 1,000-franc penalties for a fortnight's delay. Sand was as unprepared as the rest of Europe for the events which led to Louis-Philippe's abdication in 1848. In Paris she issued two lyrically republican manifestos, then she returned to Nohant. She wrote further "Letters to the people" and helped to found a new weekly, *La Cause du Peuple*, which lasted only three issues. Her chief concern was for the education of women and the affirmation of women's legal rights within marriage. She became disillusioned with the "pedants and theocrats" of republicanism, and finally turned her back on politics.

Her next idyll, *La Petite Fadette*, had to be sold for a mere 2,000 francs. There were pressing debts to pay off. Solange and Clésinger refused to retrench, and the Paris house and furniture were sold. Solange had numerous lovers, but in 1854 was caught by her husband, who was thereby able to have a separation imposed on his own terms. Hippolyte died of drink in 1848, and in 1849 both Chopin and a destitute Marie Dorval also died. From 1849 the theatre became the new focus of Sand's activity, and with help from Pierre Bocage, now director of the Odéon, seven plays of hers were staged between 1851 and 1856. She had several new lovers, including from 1850 the 32-year-old Alexandre Manceau, who also helped with Sand's work for the theatre, although he was essentially another young man to educate. In 1852 Sand was able to obtain clemency for a number of condemned republicans. In 1854 *L'Histoire de ma vie* was serialized in *La Presse*. Solange's second child, of whom Sand had become very fond, died of scarlet fever in 1855. Sand, Solange, Manceau, and Maurice all went to Italy to recover. By this time there was a railway linking Marseilles and Paris.

The anti-papalist *La Daniella* caused a predictable furore when it was serialized in *La Presse*. Even old republican antipapalist friends were shocked, and some of the more lurid passages had to be cut. In 1856 three hastily written plays flopped. Sand was now spending money on the families of political prisoners and as usual was financially hard pressed. In 1857 she and Manceau discovered the small village of Gargilesse, south-east of La Châtre and not far from Nohant, and for 1,100 francs, including the cost of installing plumbing, Manceau bought a small cottage there. Sand was to write part of 13 novels at Gargilesse, and it was there that in 1858, she finished *Elle et lui*, the account of her liaison with Musset. Buloz, with whom she was now reconciled, was as embarrassed by it as the rest of salon society, but after months of hesitation he serialized it in the *RDM*. It provoked Paul Musset's *Lui et elle* and the intervention of Louise Colet, whose pursuit of famous men had led her to have an affair with Flaubert and subsequently with Musset, and who now published *Lui*. Her theatrical interlude now over, Sand was writing popular novels again. *Le Marquis de Villemer* is considered one of her more successful. It was followed by *Valvèdre*, which was particularly admired by Matthew Arnold, who had stayed at Nohant. Sand was now using Hetzel as her literary adviser, as once she had used Sainte-Beuve before the Leroux influence changed the nature of her output.

Sand's last known lover, Charles Marchal, was brought to Nohant in 1861 by Dumas *fils*. He was a year younger than Maurice, and was one of those young men who stirred Sand's maternal instincts until they ended up taking over altogether from her sexual needs. Maurice himself married the following year. He was 38 and his wife, "Lina," the daughter of one of Sand's oldest friends, was 19. His son died just after his first birthday, but

Maurice's wife bore him further children in 1866 and 1868. From 1862 Sand lived largely at Manceau's flat in Paris, and they dined daily at Magny's. Manceau was to die in 1865. In September 1862 Pierre Bocage died. He had lost his post at the Odéon under the new regime and fallen on hard times. Hearing that Sand, helped by Paul Meurice, was planning another play, *Les Beaux Messieurs de Bois-Doré*, he asked to be allowed to play the elderly Sylvain. He had to lock himself up alone all day to keep enough voice to see the play through its 100 performances. He died shortly after the last performance. That summer Sand received Fromentin at Nohant to discuss the volume version of *Dominique*. She also finished two more plays and a further anti-clerical novel, *Mademoiselle la Quintinie*, serialized by Buloz in the *RDM* to the enthusiasm of Paris's younger literary society. Sand's production during the late 1850s and early 1860s was prodigious, and ever more eminent literary guests were received at Nohant. Gautier has left a fascinating account of one such visit.

In 1865 Sand entered into her last great literary friendship, with Flaubert, who got her invited to the Magny dinners, from which even Princesse Mathilde had been excluded. She did not think much of what she got for her 10 francs, but she enjoyed the compliment and the relaxed atmosphere of literary gossip. She stayed twice with Flaubert, and he came to Nohant. She also became intimate with Juliette Lamber, later Juliette Adam, a close friend of Marie d'Agoult, whose hostility to Sand had not relaxed since her break with Liszt. Sand took Juliette to a Magny dinner in 1867 and spent the winter with her and her husband at Cannes. They were together again at Nohant in 1868.

The following year Sainte-Beuve died. Sand and he had re-established their friendship, and Sand's hostility to the Second Empire began to abate. Juliette's husband weaned Sand from her pro-Prussian stance and she watched the events of 1870 and 1871 with consternation. Pauline Viardot came to Nohant again, followed by Turgenev and then Flaubert again. Casimir died. Both children were established financially, although Sand had probably made their lives too easy for them to work as fruitfully as she herself had had to. She worked until almost the very end. In 1876, after a short but painful stomach illness, she died, with her children and grandchildren in attendance.

WORKS

Even if we discount the attraction her remarkably colourful career has had for biographers, and allow that her status as a 19th-century novelist may once have been estimated too highly, George Sand remains an important woman of letters who exercised in correspondence and conversation a significant power over authors of no doubt greater imaginative discipline than her own. Sand wrote very fast, frequently producing potboilers for money, and always under a financial constraint, which her biography suggests she may probably not, like Balzac, have needed in order to produce the immense output of not all of which she was proud. She also wrote for a discriminating public which could distinguish literature from entertainment, and craftsmanship from shoddiness, a public as wide open to radical ideas and forms of behaviour as is actually to be expected from a predominantly metropolitan literary culture in an age not yet unified by mass media and instant global communication. It was sufficiently cohesive for clusters of opinion to form and sides to be

taken, but still sufficiently dispersed to prevent the domination of glib cultural orthodoxies.

Sand's serious philosophical, social, and political attitudes remained at the level of possibly unattainable ideals and were seldom on this practical level thought through, and she was acutely aware of the need to assuage the psychological tensions which give her life and her imaginative works their characteristic patterns, and which were disruptive of the distinctions imposed by class and rigidity of etiquette. The alert that her work should be regarded with a seriousness not usually now devoted to it comes not only from the avidity of her contemporaries' interest in her writings, but also because Elizabeth Barrett, not yet Robert Browning's wife, regarded her as the greatest woman genius to date, Sainte-Beuve as the finest and most original of French prose writers, better than Balzac, with whom he had admittedly quarrelled, and Heine as a great prose poet whose achievement he ranked higher than Victor Hugo's. Béranger thought of her as the "queen of the new literary generation," and in Moscow and St Petersburg, still culturally more sophisticated than London, she was commonly ranked higher than Dickens.

Sand produced enormous quantities of what we call "copy," much of it ill-considered or intemperate, and in view of its quantity and speed of composition, necessarily uneven in quality. All of it was the product of a shy personality's fluent pen, generally working at white heat, often at no great imaginative depth. While she was working all night and sleeping from dawn to noon, the working pattern of much of her life, she could finish one novel halfway through the night and then start on the next. It is difficult, in view of the known biographical facts, to resist the impression that the situation in which she lived and worked was forced on her by psychological necessity, one, that is, that she knew she was choosing, even to the detriment of her earning power and literary, not to mention social, standing. The number of her lovers and the types of her relationship with them were, like her work, clearly the result of a personal need rooted in some psychological mechanism which operated in her from early youth. Sand's biography makes the reasons at least probable.

The production of uneven work in enormous quantities and under unbelievable pressures is not accounted for by the shortage of money. That was unwillingly endured. Sand never considered raising money against her considerable property assets, but piled on herself humanitarian, charitable, and maternal obligations. She was the antithesis of the well-off Flaubert, a meticulously careful worker who spent a lifetime producing two or three of the world's great literary masterpieces. Flaubert was unamused by the card games and practical jokes of the Nohant way of life, as Sand was unamused by the malice and coarseness of Flaubert's mind. In contrast to Flaubert, Sand did not at all care if every word she produced did not contribute to an unblemished literary masterpiece. But the lack of adequate imaginative quality control, coupled with a naive social philosophy and an inability to rein in a lyrical rhetoric deployed for didactic purposes, while they may have been self-indulgent, do not detract from her real achievements.

In the mid-1830s, when Sand was at the peak of the Parisian literary pyramid, the more pretentious novels, the plays, and the simple country tales were still to come, but so were the undoubtedly important discussions of literary matters to be contained in her correspondence. The judgement of her contemporaries, admirers and critics alike, was far more discriminating than that of modern critics has been, especially those who have seen in her nothing but the precursor of feminism and the liberation of women, which she simply was not. The spiteful and tight-fisted Buloz, the fastidious Latouche, the trenchant Planche, the financially astute Lévy, and the culturally populist Véron all knew that Sand could be infuriating, slapdash, naive, silly, and unrealistic, but they nevertheless depended for their living on an understanding of literary intelligence and French society. They make a quintet of severe but sympathetic critics who are unlikely to have been collectively wrong about the imaginative power that lay behind Sand's fluency.

The most consistent patterns in Sand's work concern emotional relationships which cross class barriers, and forms of behaviour which disrupt codes of etiquette. A preoccupation with personal dilemmas led naturally to a more general consideration of the social questions involved. While Sand was undoubtedly an advocate of the utopian reform of social organization and, under the influence of Michel de Bourges, felt fiercely the injustices of the French social system after the Industrial Revolution, her imagination explored socialist idealism rather than republican ideology. Her commitment was social, not political, and her disillusion with the republican political programme explains how she could combine the wildest of utopian dreams, however naively and provocatively she expressed them, with an almost conservative political stance.

Fourier, Leroux, Saint-Simon, and Proudhon may have inflamed her vision, but what Sand wanted was a reform of social life in which women would be accorded a legal status reflecting both their equality with and difference from men. Legally women were chattels, yet the social system had long acknowledged that they were not. The law needed reforming. There was nothing more demeaning in child-bearing or undertaking domestic chores than there was in digging and fighting. For the moment, and until social reform led to a proper education for women, women remained more artistic than men, and men made better legislators and judges than women. Even with their didactic and rhetorical communism, however ill-judged, the middle-period novels remained works of the imagination. At her worst Sand merely slipped below any acceptable degree of imaginative fictionalization, allowing her characters to remain mere representatives of or vehicles for ideas.

Indiana already deals tragically, like so many of the later novels, with the problems of love across the class divide. Much obviously comes from Sand's own recent experience. A young nobleman, Raymon de Ramière, breaks into the property of the 19-year-old Indiana, who is married to the much older Colonel Delmare, in pursuit of an affair with her maid Noun. There have been thefts, for which, of course, Ramière was not to blame, but he is shot as an intruder by Delmare. However, he turns out to have "noble features" and a properly tailored jacket, and Indiana bandages his hand. What brings the novel forward into the 19th century is the observation that Noun's courage in offering herself to the nocturnal visitor, while it would have been heroism in an aristocrat, is effrontery in a maid. Raymon comes to his social senses, falls in love with Indiana, and repudiates Noun, who drowns herself. He soon gets bored with Indiana, who, in the first draft, commits suicide too, but not before she ringingly denounces the system which makes her Delmare's chattel. Society gives him the right to shackle her, but her will to bestow her love where she wants remains her own. What is specifically

romantic about the novel, and dates it to within a few years, is the individual's affirmation of his or her own rights against arbitrary norms imposed by society in a situation sufficiently serious to make resolution by suicide acceptable.

A socially impossible passion is again the theme of *Valentine*. The heiress Valentine de Raimbault has artistic ambitions but is going to marry a diplomat. At a country fair she meets Bénédict, who comes from a family of tenant farmers. His inner nobility of spirit is indicated by his learning and his voice. They play a duet together before Bénédict, in despair, shoots himself and is nursed back to life by Valentine. Here it is the suicide attempt and the role of music as well as increasing exasperation at the class barrier which allow the novel to be almost exactly dated to the early days of the July monarchy. Precisely this novel could not have been written in precisely this way in France more than five years earlier or later than 1832. An earlier dating would make the social vibrations anachronistic and at a later one the style would have been a recognizable pastiche of something produced by a sensibility which had changed.

Lélia, written in 1833, was rewritten in 1839. Parts of the novel are again obviously autobiographical, and parts suggest that by 1833 Sand was afraid that she was too masculine in some aspects of her sexual make-up. It is her most intimate novel, although the fictionalization is weak at times, with the characters too nearly mere symbols of their attitudes. Sténio, a young poet, is in despair that Lélia no longer loves him, and takes to a life of dissipation as advocated by Lélia's sister, Pulchérie, into whose arms he is pushed. The remedy is worse than the frustrated love it was supposed to cure, and Sténio, having become a disillusioned cynic, commits suicide, implying the authorial repudiation of Pulchérie's doctrine of sexual profligacy. Stoic endurance of unrequited love is to be preferred to any solution involving infidelity to it. Beyond that there is no clear moral or message. Lélia is as full of maternal solicitude of Sténio as she is of doubt about her own capacity to love in a physically satisfying way. Magnus, the Irish monk who represses his instincts, remains frustrated to the point of desperation, while Trenmor has arrived at philosophical detachment after suffering for his earlier gambling follies, so possibly offering a solution to life's problems which steers between Leibnitzian optimism and Nodier's pessimism. In 1833 Sand intended Lélia's problem, in which soaring dream proves incompatible with sordid reality, to express the anguish of a particular generation. The 1839 version was a little less candid in its personal revelations.

Jacques, which is written in letter form, relates the efforts of an unhappy wife to find happiness with a dandified lover. It was damned by the critics' faint praise, granted because they were already unwilling to find any novel from Sand's pen uninteresting, and owes much of what success it enjoyed to gossip about Sand's relationship with Musset, and to *Lélia*. *Mauprat* is a tight novel which signposts a change of direction. It is said to have no literary pretensions and to be merely a dramatic story well told, but it foreshadows both the idyllic rustic characters who populate the later novels and the messianic socialism of Sand's middle period: "Aimez le peuple; détestez ceux qui le détestent—faites-vous l'ami du peuple (Love the people; hate those who are against them...make yourself a friend of the people)," says old Patience, the solitary peasant, to Bernard de Mauprat, the narrator. In fact *Mauprat* is more than just the workmanlike story of espionage for which it might be taken. Edmée successfully tries to civilize her brutish husband, so not only raising the question of the power of love to ennoble its object, but refusing to despair at the doctrine of the sanctity of marriage.

Le Compagnon du tour de France is a didactic "humanitarian" novel whose hero, the carpenter Pierre Huguenin, is modelled on a real-life carpenter who strove to unite the factions of the French working-class movements. Huguenin is loved by Iseut de Villepreux, the daughter of a count, himself in sympathy with liberal ideas until they impinge on his own household. Love now conquers class barriers, but the function of the love interest here is merely to carry the social message. Chopin found Huguenin too idealized a moral exemplar, and Buloz found him didactically exploited to convey a whole spectrum of radical ideas. The entire brew of pseudo-medieval guild egalitarianism was worse, in Buloz's view, than the pseudo-mysticism derived from Ballanche of the immediately preceding *Spiridion* and the play *Les Sept cordes de la lyre*. For Sand wealth and social status have become corruptive of honest working-class artisans. When the *RDM* refused to publish the novel and it appeared as a volume it created an uproar. Sand's riposte was *Horace*, the story of a clever but lazy student, Horace Dumontet, who gives up serious study for literature, spends his way through his parents' hard-earned savings, and abandons his working-class mistress for an aristocrat. He contrasts with the hard-working jeweller Paul Arsène, and the book comes near to justifying the mob destruction of the archbishopric of Paris in 1831. This was the book which caused the long rupture with Buloz after eight years. Nor did Lamennais like it. It veered further towards Proudhon than Leroux's mystical farrago had done, and for Mazzini, Herzen, and Bakunin, it turned Sand into France's leading radical propagandist.

It was followed by the best known of the middle-period works, *Consuelo*, a long, formless work said by Sand herself to contain enough material for three or four novels, and *La Comtesse de Rudolstadt*, its sequel. Consuelo is a young Spaniard of gypsy blood, a singer of sweet innocence who comes unscathed through the adventures of the 105 chapters until she marries Comte Albert de Rudolstadt only moments before his death. She dresses in male peasant dress and goes to Vienna with Joseph Haydn. Her musical life starts in Venice and moves through Austria, Bohemia, and the courts of Frederick the Great and Maria Theresa. The novel is an extraordinary achievement in terms of the way in which narrative interest is sustained through the maze of personal vendettas, friendships, freemasonry, mysticism, the transmigration of souls, messianism, republicanism, the fantastic, the grotesque, and the slavery of marriage. Fascinating, if not at first apparently relevant to the story line, is Sand's attack on the virtuosic liberties of Paganini and Liszt, and her defence both of Pauline García's refusal to sustain high notes for the sake of applause, and of Chopin's delicacy, subtlety, and power of melodic invention against the ostentatious ornamentation of Liszt. Understandably, the tranposition of the vindictive spite of the Parisian musical world to 18th-century Venice made compulsive reading.

Albert de Rudolstadt's disappearance into the subterranean passages of his castle in order to be mystically reunited with his Hussite ancestors is a painful literary device, but the linking of musical purity with purity in religion enables Sand's condemnation of the elaborate display of Catholic ceremony to be transformed into a panegyric of Hus's revolt against an unjust feudal society. Albert de Rudolstadt is therefore a mixture of Chopin's musical brilliance, Mickiewicz's mystical patriotism, and Ler-

oux's socialist Christianity. Once Albert is dead, Consuelo can make her way through a morass of Rosicrucians, illuminists, and Swedenborgian mystics. The utopian projection of universal harmony in religion, international relations, and social institutions under a Christian umbrella seemed a not totally lunatic dream to many alert minds in pre-Marxian Europe.

Sand's humanitarian optimism continued in the 1845 *Le Meunier d'Angibault*, where, once again, love conquers class barriers. A rich farmer allows his daughter to marry a poor miller, while a young proletarian agrees to marry an aristocratic but penniless widow. A small profit-sharing, hard-working community is founded. Véron refused to publish the novel, which was too obviously dominated by Proudhon's ideas. But by late in 1845 no trace of revolutionary fervour was left in *La Mare au diable*, the first of several nostalgic pastoral idylls Sand was now to write, virtually creating what has come to be known as the "regional novel." The whole group, including *La Petite Fadette, François le champi*, and *Les Maîtres sonneurs*, shows a more conscious literary effort than her earlier work as she tries to blend narrative with reminiscences of rustic life. All the novels in the group resolve initially distant or difficult relationships into sadness or joy and succeed because the characters, their background, and their speech, are once again credible to the point of realism.

It is possible to regret that Sand published much that is of little interest, either because its composition was uninspired and perfunctory, or because the propagation of a didactic creed was dressed up as fiction, but it is not possible to deny the power of the often imperfectly communicated vision towards which her work continued to grope. Sand was not a great dramatist, but she was a splendid letter writer, and some of the vignettes in *L'Histoire de ma vie* are magisterial. Her contemporaries discriminated with what, as is now apparent, was a certainty of touch between her better books and the others, so that neither the evangelical preaching of secular socialism nor the apparent excesses of her private life can explain the strength of Sand's reputation. She was admired by too many of her peers for it not to be certain that her work as a whole, in spite of its patchiness, has come to be undervalued.

PUBLICATIONS

Colletions

Oeuvres, 27 vols., 1837–42 (and later editions)
Oeuvres autobiographiques, Bibliothèque de la Pléiade, 2 vols., 1970

Fiction

Rose et Blanche, with Jules Sandeau, 1831
Indiana, 1832; as *Indiana* (in English), 1850
Valentine, 1832; as *Valentine*, in *Masterpieces*, 1900–02
Lélia, 1833; revised edition, 1839; as *Lélia* (in Enlgish), 1978
Le Secrétaire intime (includes *Métella, La Marquise, Lavinia*), 1834; *Lavinia* translated as *Lady Blake's Love-Letters*, 1884
Jacques, 1834; as *Jacques* (in English), 1847
Leone Leoni, 1835; as *Leone Leoni*, in *Masterpieces*, 1900–02
André, 1835; as *André* (in English), 1847
Simon, 1836

Mauprat, 1837; as *Mauprat* (in English), 1847

Les Maîtres mosaïstes, 1838; as *The Mosaic Workers*, 1844; as *The Mosaic Masters*, 1847; as *The Master Mosaic Workers*, 1895

La Dernière Aldini, 1838; as *The Last Aldini*, 1847

L'Uscoque, 1838; as *The Uscoque*, 1850

Spiridion, 1839; as *Spiridion* (in English), 1842

Pauline, 1840

Le Compagnon du tour de France, 1840; as *The Companion of the Tour of France*, 1847; as *The Journeyman Joiner*, 1847

Horace, 1842

Consuelo, 1842–43; as *Consuelo* (in English), 1846

La Comtesse de Rudolstadt, 1843–44; as *The Countess of Rudolstadt*, 1847

Jeanne, 1844; edited by Simone Viernne, 1978

Le Meunier d'Angibault, 1845; as *The Miller of Angibault*, 1847

Isidora, 1845

Teverino, 1845; as *Teverino* (in English), 1855; as *Jealousy; or, Teverino*, 1855

Le Péché de Monsieur Antoine, 1846; as *The Sin of M. Antoine* in *Masterpieces*, 1900–02

La Mare au diable, 1846; as *The Haunted Marsh*, 1848; as *The Enchanted Lake*, 1850; as *The Devil's Pool*, 1861; as *Germaine's Marriage*, 1892

Lucrezia Floriani, 1846

Fanchette (in English), 1847

Le Piccinino, 1847; as *The Piccinino*, 1900

François le champi, 1848; as *Francis the Waif*, 1889; as *The Country Waif*, 1930

La Petite Fadette, 1849; as *Little Fadette*, 1850; as *Fadette*, 1851; as *Fanchon the Cricket*, 1863

Le Château des Désertes, 1851; as *The Castle in the Wilderness*, 1856

Mont-Revêche, 1853

La Filleule, 1853

Les Maîtres sonneurs, 1853; as *The Bagpipers*, 1890

Le Diable aux champs, 1856

Evenor et Leucippe, 1856; as *Les Amours de l'âge d'or*, in *Oeuvres*, 1871

La Daniella, 1857

Les Dames vertes, 1857

Les Beaux Messieurs de Bois-Doré, 1858; as *The Gallant Lords of Bois-Doré*, 1890

L'Homme de neige, 1858; as *The Snow Man*, 1871

Narcisse, 1859

Elle et lui, 1859; as *He and She*, in *Masterpieces*, 1900–02; as *She and He*, 1902

Flavie, 1859

Jean de la Roche, 1860

Constance Verrier, 1860

La Ville noire, 1860; edited by Jean Courrier, 1978

Le Marquis de Villemer, 1860–61; as *The Marquis of Villemer*, 1871

Valvèdre, 1861

La Famille de Germandre, 1861; as *The Germandre Family*, in *Masterpieces*, 1900–02

Tamaris, 1862

Antonia, 1863; as *Antonia* (in English), 1870

Mademoiselle la Quintinie, 1863

Laura, 1864

La Confession d'une jeune fille, 1864

Monsieur Sylvestre, 1865; as *M. Sylvestre* (in English), 1870

Le Dernier Amour, 1867

Cadio, 1868

Mademoiselle Merquem, 1868; edited by Raymond Rheault, 1981; as *Mademoiselle Merquem* (in English), 1868

Pierre qui roule; *Le Beau Laurence*, 1870; as *A Rolling Stone*, 1871, and *Handsome Laurence*, 1871

Malgrétout, 1870

Césarine Dietrich, 1871; as *Césarine Dietrich* (in English), 1871

Francia, 1872

Nanon, 1872; as *Nanon* (in English), 1890

Ma soeur Jeanne, 1874; as *My Sister Jeannie*, 1874

Flamarande; *Les Deux frères*, 1875

La Tour de Percemont; Marianne, 1876; as *The Tower of Percemont*, 1877, and *Marianne*, 1880

Plays

Gabriel, 1839

Les Sept cordes de la lyre, 1839

Cosima (produced 1840), 1840

François le champi, from her own novel (produced 1849), 1856

Claudie (produced 1851), 1851

Le Mariage de Victorine (produced 1851), 1851

Molière (produced 1851), 1851

Le Démon du foyer (produced 1852), 1852

Mauprat, from her own novel (produced 1853), 1854

Maitre Favilla (produced 1855), 1855; as *La Baronnie de Muhldorf*, n.d.

Lucie (produced 1856), 1856

Les Beaux Messieurs de Bois-Doré, with Paul Meurice, from the novel by Sand, 1862

Le Marquis de Villemer, with Dumas *fils*, from the novel by Sand (produced 1864), 1864

Le Drac, with Paul Meurice (produced 1864), 1865

Cadio, with Paul Meurice (produced 1868), 1868

Théâtre complet, 3 vols., 1879

Other

Lettres d'un voyageur, 1837; as *Letters of a Traveller*, 1847

Un hiver à Majorque, 1842; as *Winter in Majorca*, 1956

Histoire de France écrite sous la dictée de Blaise Bonnin, 1848

Adriani, 1853

L'Histoire de ma vie, 20 vols., 1854–55

La Guerre, 1859

Journal d'un voyageur pendant la guerre, 1871

Impressions et souvenirs, 1873; as *Recollections*, 1874; as *Impressions and Reminiscences*, 1876

Contes d'une grand'mère (juvenile), 2 vols., 1873–76; as *Tales of a Grandmother*, 1930

Questions d'art et de littérature, 1878

Questions politiques et sociales, 1879

Journal intime, edited by Aurore Sand, 1926; as *Intimate Journal*, edited by Marie Howe Jenney, 1929

Letters, edited by Veronica Lucas, 1930

Correspondance inédit, with Marie Dorval, edited by Simone André-Maurois, 1953

Sand et Alfred de Musset: correspondance…, edited by Louis Evrard, 1956

Lettres inédites de Sand et de Pauline Viardot 1839–1849, edited by Thérèse Marix-Spire, 1959
Lettres à Sainte-Beuve, edited by Sten Södergård, 1964
Correspondance, edited by Georges Lubin, 24 vols., 1964–90
Correspondance, with Flaubert, edited by Alphonse Jacobs, 1981

Bibliography

Colin, Georges, *Bibliographie des premières publications des romans de Sand*, 1965

Critical studies

Maurois, André, *Lélia: The Life of Sand*, 1953
Edwards, Samuel, *George Sand* (in English), 1972
Cate, Curtis, *Sand: A Biography*, 1975
Jordan, Ruth, *Sand: A Biography*, 1976
Thomson, Patricia, *Sand and the Victorians*, 1977
Winegarten, Renée, *The Double Life of Sand: Woman and Writer*, 1978
Blount, Paul G., *Sand and the Victorian World*, 1979
Waddington, Patrick, *Turgenev and Sand*, 1981

SARDOU, Victorien, 1831–1908.

Dramatist.

Victorien Sardou was born in Paris on 7 September 1831. His father, Léandre, a school headmaster and a scholar of the Niçard language, wrote *Vida de Saint-Honorat* and *Lou martire de Santo*, and edited the *Gramatico de l'idiomo niçard*, making it a branch of Provençal.

As a 19th-century dramatist, Victorien Sardou was unusual because he seldom used a collaborator. He was a great admirer of Scribe, and trained himself as a playwright by reading the first act of Scribe's plays, then setting out to complete them by following the pattern of clues presented in the exposition. In his own plays he plotted the action as skilfully as Scribe and made maximum use of stage sets and visual effects. He was an entertainer rather than an innovator, and made his way in the theatrical world partly through judicious contacts. He was a protégé of Déjazet, and married an actress, Mlle de Brécourt. His taste was conspicuously commonplace and his view of life vulgar.

The political and social climate of the times is reflected in Sardou's career. He found favour with the imperial regime of Napoleon III by attacking the older generation in *Les Ganaches*, and at the beginning of the Third Republic he satirized the new political generation of ambitious rabble-rousers in *Rabagas*. He was elected to the Académie Française in 1877.

During the 1880s Sardou depicted the fashionable preoccupations of fin-de-siècle life without committing himself to judgements or solutions. *Divorçons!* treats the theme of marital breakdown in a light-hearted and cheerful manner; *Odette* concerns an adulterous wife who loses the chance of bringing up her daughter; and *Georgette* is about a courtesan.

Sardou's most popular plays were spectacular historical dramas, and he created roles for Sarah Bernhardt that were among her greatest successes: *Fédora* in 1882, *Théodora* in 1884, *Tosca* in 1887, and *Cléopatre* in 1890. Puccini's opera *La Tosca* achieved more lasting fame for Sardou than any of his other works. *Patrie!*, published in 1869, was a serious historical melodrama combining the theme of patriotic resistance to foreign occupation with an insoluble love triangle. It was made into an opera by Paladilhe in 1886.

In 1891 *Thermidor* upset the republicans by depicting their Revolutionary heroes Saint-Just and Robespierre in an unfavourable light, and it was banned. The publicity probably did Sardou no harm, but he avoided further political embarrassment. His triumph, *Madame Sans-Gêne*, produced in 1893, was an uncontentious historical vaudeville.

As a talented opportunist and careful craftsman, Sardou achieved his intention of entertaining his own generation. Zola described him as one of those "qui sont de leur temps, qui travaillent suivant leur force à une formule qu'ils n'ont pas eu le génie d'apporter tout entière (who are of their time, who work as hard as they can to a formula they didn't have the talent to invent all on their own.)"

PUBLICATIONS

Collections

Théâtre complet, 1934.

Plays

La Taverne des étudiants, 1854
Les Gens nerveux, with T. Barrière, 1859
Candide, 1860
Monsieur Garat, 1860
Les Pattes de mouche, 1860; as *A Scrap of Paper*, adapted by J. P. Simpson, n.d.
Les Premières Armes de Figaro, 1860
L'Ecureuil, 1861
Les Femmes fortes, 1861
Piccolino, 1861
Les Ganaches, 1862; as *Progress*, adapted by T. W. Robertson, 1893
Nos intimes, 1862; as *Friends or Foes?*, adapted by H. Wigan, n.d.; as *Our Friends*, 1879
La Papillonne, 1862
La Perle noire, 1862; as *The Black Pearl*, 1915
Les Prés Saint-Gervais, 1862; as *The Meadows of St. Gervais*, 1871
Bataille d'amour, 1863
Le Dégel, 1864
Les Diables noirs, 1864
Don Quichotte, 1864
Les Pommes du voisin, 1864
La Famille Benoîton, 1865
Les Vieux Garçons, 1865
Nos bons villageois, 1866

Maison neuve, 1867

Patrie!, with Gallet, 1869; as *Patrie!: An Historical Drama*, 1815

Fernande, 1870; *Fernande* (in English), adapted by J. Schönberg, 1883

Rabagas, 1872

Le Roi Carotte, 1872

Les Merveilleuses, 1873; as *The Women Dandies*, adapted by Basil Hood, with lyrics by Adrian Ross, 1906

Le Magot, 1873

Ferréol, 1873; as *Ferreol*, 1876

Andréa, 1875

La Haine, 1875

L'Oncle Sam, 1875

Dora, 1877; *Dora* (in English), 1877

L'Heure du spectacle, 1878

Les Bourgeois de Pont-Arcy, 1878; as *The Inhabitants of Pontarcy*, 1878

Séraphine, 1879

Daniel Rochat, 1880

Divorçons!, with Emile de Najac, 1880; as *Let Us Be Divorced!*, 1881

Odette, 1881

Fédora, 1882, as *Fedora*, 1883; as *Foedora: A Romance*, adapted by H. L. Williams, 1883

Théodora, 1884; *Theodora* 1885

Georgette, 1885; *Georgette* (in English), 1886

Le Crocodile, 1886

La Tosca, 1887; as *La Tosca* (opera), with L. Illica and G. Giacosa, and music by Puccini; as *Tosca* (opera), English version by W. Beatty-Kingston, 1900

Marquise, 1889

Belle-Maman, 1889

Cléopatre, 1890

Thermidor, 1891

La Maison de Robespierre, 1895; as *Robespierre: The Story of M. V. Sardou's Play, Adapted and Novelised under His Authority*, by Ange Galdemar, 1899

Spiritisme, 1898

Les Barbares, with Pierre Gheusi, 1901

Par instinct, 1904

La Sorcière, 1904

Tel chante le vieux coq!, 1904

Fiorella, with Pierre Gheusi, 1905

La Piste, 1906

Madame Sans-Gêne (produced 1893) with Emile Moreau, 1907

L'Affaire des poisons, 1908

Other

Mes plagiats, 1883

Notes et croquis, 1885

Carlin (novel), 1932

Les Papiers de Victorien Sardou; notes et souvenirs, collected and edited by Georges Mouly, 1934

SARRAUTE, Nathalie, 1900–

Novelist.

LIFE

Sarraute's Russian Jewish parents studied in Geneva and married on their return to Russia, where her father opened a dye factory in Ivanovo. Sarraute was born in Tcherniak. Her parents divorced in 1902, and Sarraute's childhood was spent mostly in Paris with her mother, who remarried and returned to St Petersburg, where she worked for a literary review and published her own prose fiction. Sarraute's father also remarried and moved to Paris, where Sarraute later settled with him. Russia was seeking the extradition from Sweden of his brother, a member of a revolutionary group later found asphyxiated on a boat for Antwerp. From the age of eight Sarraute was brought up by her stepmother's family, surrounded by Russian émigrés, learnt to play the piano and to speak German and English. She read widely in the French and Russian classics. She specialized in physics at school, took a degree in English at the Sorbonne, abandoned history studies at Oxford in order to study sociology in Berlin, and then read law in Paris, where she was a member of the Bar from 1925 to 1941. She married a fellow law student and had three daughters.

Her first book collects together vignettes of commonplace situations and feelings, generally of a rather insipid or platitudinous nature, some of which were written as early as 1932–33. Turned down by two publishers, *Tropismes* was eventually published in 1939, its title, used now for fleeting patterns of instinctive reaction, no doubt taken from Gide's parody of a scientific technical term to describe the subject studied by a particularly inane zoologist. Sarraute was 38, and the book attracted only a single review.

She spent the war in hiding, but finished her first novel in 1946. *Portrait d'un inconnu* was published in 1948 but sold only 400 copies. In a preface to the 1956 edition Sartre referred to it as an "anti-novel." Meanwhile Sarraute had begun to publish theoretical works, collected in the 1956 *L'Ere du soupçon*, justifying her approach to fiction. *Martereau* had appeared in 1953, followed by *Le Planétarium* in 1959 and *Les Fruits d'or* in 1963, for which Sarraute was awarded the Prix International de la Littérature.

The radio plays *Le Silence* and *Le Mensonge* were chosen by Barrault as a double bill to celebrate the 20th anniversary of the foundation of his troupe and were published with a third play, *Isma*, in 1970. In 1968 Sarraute published the novel *Entre la vie et la mort*, and a further novel, *Vous les entendez?*, appeared in 1972. The play *C'est beau* was produced in 1973, the year of its publication, and Sarraute's latest novel, *"disent les imbéciles"*, appeared in 1976. *Elle est là* was produced in 1978, when it was published with Sarraute's collected plays. Sarraute has travelled widely in Europe and in the US. Her books have been translated into a total of 23 languages, with all the novels appearing in both German and English.

WORKS

The first edition of *Tropismes* consisted of 19 unrelated vignettes. One was later deleted and six were added. The book established what was to be the key note of the "anti-novel": the banality of what is stated or evoked, in contrast to what might be analysed or narrated in a conventional novel according to the perception of an author or of one or more of the novel's characters. The highly focused and sometimes ironic depiction of fugitive patterns of insignificant behaviour in *Tropismes* constitutes the substance of the later novels. The theoretical writings justifying this innovatory technique are the product of a mind which is ingenious rather than incisive, and deploy arguments apparently too weighty for the slightness of the literary achievement they support, in spite of its undoubted technical skill. Sarraute is in fact probably best known, and most important, as the leading theoretician of a number of writers who have allowed themselves to be regarded as a group and whose work has corporately become known as the "nouveau roman" (see Robbe-Grillet, Duras, Butor, Simon).

Sarraute's belief that new literary techniques are constantly required to express a vision which is for ever changing derives from the view that the novel's function is to dissipate the mystery of experience in so far as this can be done through the medium of fiction. It must at least be asked, however, how much the techniques of the "nouveau roman" owe to cinematographic techniques and to the contemporaneous emergence of film as a serious art form, in which apparently harmless poses or trivial gestures can suggest underlying attitudes of doubt, attraction, or fear. Sarraute's insistence that the reader must supply words or thoughts that have been left unstated merely underlines what has always been true about the experience of reading, but which has been given more obvious prominence through the analysis of film.

Sarraute uses conversation, partly inspired by Ivy Compton-Burnett, in an effort to abstract from external chronological time and to endow seeming trivia with meaning in a permanent present of which the reader is always a part. Her technique works best in the varied, casual, and ironic triteness of *Tropismes*. In the novels it can appear over-extended, making them feats of technical virtuosity lacking significant events, characters, or tension, except perhaps in the mind of the narrator, who gives the reader little guidance in endowing with meaning what is stated other than through the occasional hint of satirical purpose.

PUBLICATIONS

Fiction

Tropismes, 1939; revised edition, 1957; as *Tropisms*, with *The Age of Suspicion*, 1963
Portrait d'un inconnu, 1948; as *Portrait of a Man Unknown*, 1958
Martereau, 1953; as *Martereau* (in English), 1959
Le Planétarium, 1959; as *The Planetarium*, 1960
Les Fruits d'or, 1963; as *The Golden Fruits*, 1964
Entre la vie et la mort, 1968; as *Between Life and Death*, 1969
Vous les entendez? 1972; as *Do You Hear Them?*, 1973
"disent les imbéciles," 1976; as *"fools say,"* 1977
L'Usage de la parole, 1980; as *The Use of Speech*, 1980

Drama

Le Silence, suivi de Le Mensonge (produced Paris, 1967), 1967; as *Silence, and The Lie* (produced London, 1972), 1969

Isma (produced Paris, 1973), with *Le Silence* and *Le Mensonge*, 1970; as *Izzuma*, in *Collected Plays*, 1980
C'est beau (produced Paris, 1975), in *Théâtre*, 1978; as *It's Beautiful*, in *Collected Plays,* 1980
Elle est là (produced Paris, 1978), in *Théâtre*, 1978; as *It Is There*, in *Collected Plays*, 1980
Théâtre (includes *Elle est là, C'est beau, Isma, Le Mensonge, Le Silence*), 1978
Collected Plays (includes *It Is There, It's Beautiful, Izzuma, The Lie, Silence*), 1980

Other

L'Ere du soupçon, 1956; as *The Age of Suspicion*, 1963; with *Tropisms*, 1963
Enfance (autobiography), 1983; as *Childhood*, 1984

Critical studies

Temple, Ruth Z., *Sarraute* (in English), 1968
Rous Besser, Gretchen, *Sarraute*, 1979
Allemand, André, *L'Oeuvre romanesque de Nathalie Sarraute*, 1980
Minogue, Valerie, *Sarraute and the War of the Words: A Study of Five Novels*, 1981
Watson-Williams, Helen, *The Novels of Sarraute: Towards an Aesthetic*, 1981

———

SARTRE, Jean-Paul (-Charles-Aymard), 1905–1980.

Novelist, dramatist, philosopher, journalist, and essayist.

LIFE

Sartre deliberately mythologized his childhood in his autobiographical *Les Mots* in order to cultivate as far as possible the impression that he sprang fully gifted but otherwise unformed into adolescence. The depiction of his childhood is scant, gloomy, and falsified. His father, Jean-Baptiste (1874–1906), son of a doctor, was a naval officer who had distinguished himself at the Ecole Polytechnique, from which he graduated in 1897. On 3 May 1904 he married Sartre's mother, Anne-Marie Schweitzer (1882–1969), the youngest of the four children of a successful teacher of German from Alsace, and cousin of the pastor, musicologist, and doctor Albert Schweitzer (1875–1965). Sartre's parents met at Cherbourg, where his mother's brother was a marine engineer. When they married on 3 May 1904, Sartre's father seemed to have recovered from the enterocolitis which was to kill him when Sartre was 15 months old. Sartre was born in Paris on 21 June 1905, in a building in which his mother's parents also lived. From 1906 to 1911 the family lived with Sartre's maternal grandparents at Meudon, totally dependent on them until Sartre's mother could convince the authorities that her husband had died from a disease contracted on active service. The family returned to Paris in 1911 on her father's retirement.

Sartre's mother was treated as an adolescent by her parents, and his grandparents' authority at home was paramount. His grandfather's appearance and behaviour were patriarchal and autocratic. He was fiercely anti-Prussian and Protestant, although his wife's family was Catholic. At 65 he took a former pupil as his mistress. Sartre's grandmother retreated into migraines and took to her bed. His mother had no choice but to submit to her father's domineering manner. Sartre's psychological conditioning by his grandfather's authoritarian grip on the household was compounded by his mother's emphasis on the feminine side of his nature, an influence that lay no doubt at the root of his later compulsively defensive sexual promiscuity. A severe cold in 1909 led to a 90 per cent loss of sight in Sartre's right eye, and a lasting squint. He was brought up a not very committed Catholic, and at home religion was the main field of battle.

Sartre's grandfather, who now started a language institute in Paris, was very fond of the boy, taking Sartre's side against his mother whenever need arose. Sartre's recollection of childhood was of doing well exactly what was expected of him. His grandfather, descended from generations of teachers, took charge of his elementary education. Sartre was probably only seven when he could reply in verse to a letter in verse from his grandfather. He began to rewrite some of La Fontaine's fables in Alexandrines and also started early on to write adventure stories. *Les Mots* regards literature as escapist, and blames Sartre's grandfather for the psychological damage he suffered, although the work is a reflection by the mature Sartre rather than a real attempt to reconstitute the young one. None the less it was clearly under his grandfather's influence that Sartre began to read the French classics, an activity subverted by his mother, who diverted him to comics and addicted him to the silent cinema.

In 1913 he was entered at the Lycée Montaigne, where, because his grandfather described him as advanced, he was put in a class two years above his age group. He was demoted again by two years as the result of his first dictation. His grandfather took him away, and he was given private lessons until he attended primary school while the family was staying at Arcachon. Sartre was not allowed to play with the other children. In 1914 there followed a semester at the advanced Poupon Institute, where the mothers attended the classes, before a further succession of private tutors. Sartre, conscious of his diminutive stature, made no friends and was not allowed to display high spirits, although the psychological interpretation the 58-year-old put on his boyhood experiences is unreliable, especially when they are blamed for the choices of the man. He was in fact given an exceptionally privileged but lonely education until 1915, when he was sent to the Lycée Henri IV, probably the best school in France, where he was taught by Alain, undoubtedly the most highly reputed schoolmaster in the country. It took Sartre a year or two to adapt to the competition. In 1916 Paul Nizan, who was four months his senior, joined his class at school, and as his grandfather grew older and less formidable, Sartre's relationship with the other "child" at home, his mother, became closer. In 1917 she married Joseph Mancy, another graduate of the Ecole Polytechnique whom she had known in Cherbourg. The son of a railway worker, he had felt that marriage to Mlle Schweitzer was out of the question, but he had subsequently done well, and now

felt he could replace Sartre's father in helping to bring up the boy.

Sartre was moved to La Rochelle, where his stepfather had been appointed manager of a shipyard. His mother thought her arts-educated son impertinent to his engineer stepfather and once slapped his face on that account, to the annoyance of Mancy. Sartre walked out of the room, but there may be some exaggeration in later accounts of his supposed rejection by his mother, the only person to whom he felt close. Mancy's attitudes as a manager seemed to him prejudiced and intolerant, Sartre tells us. Although he did well at school he was apparently unhappy, felt socially inadequate, and stole from his mother in order to treat his friends. He also lost interest in religion, stopped writing, but continued to read widely. Since the chief source for all the non-verifiable information in this account is Sartre himself, it is difficult to penetrate the mythologization, although the incidents reported did themselves undoubtedly occur. Sartre learnt to play the piano. He was slapped when he was 14 because, when his mother bought him a hat which he had coveted for a fortnight, he then threw it under a tram.

In 1920 he was sent back to the Lycée Henri IV as a boarder. He became a close friend of Nizan, who was better read and the dominant partner in the relationship. After passing both parts of his baccalauréat in 1921 and 1922 Sartre transferred with Nizan to the Lycée Louis-le-Grand, reputed to be better at preparing pupils for the Ecole Normale Supérieure (ENS). Sartre was now writing again sporadically and living at home. The La Rochelle shipyard had gone bankrupt and his mother and stepfather had returned to Paris. In 1923 Sartre fell out for some considerable time with Nizan, to whom he had become emotionally closer than he was ever to be to anyone again, and published in the *Revue sans Titre* the short story "L'ange du morbide" and, pseudonymously, some chapters of "Jésus la chouette." He told Simone de Beauvoir that he had made love for the first time at 17, apparently without enthusiasm, to a doctor's wife of 30 who had asked for an assignation in a friend's flat. Another casual sexual encounter was to follow. In his final year before the ENS Sartre chose to specialize in philosophy, partly because of its relationship to the psychology necessary for the writer he hoped to become, and partly so that he could earn a living teaching the history of thought. He often absented himself from the school, but did well enough to come seventh in the entry examination for the ENS. Nizan had dropped the idea of becoming a priest, and Sartre was beginning to be interested in the phenomena of contingency.

Sartre admits to having been happy at the ENS from 1924 to 1929. He shared a room with Nizan, was one of a group of Alain's ex-pupils noted for aggressively bad manners, bullying, and taunting, and one of only five philosophy students in his year. He cut the Sorbonne courses he was supposed to attend, attended classes in pathology and psychology, worked from nine to one and five to nine each day, and could not afford the boxing classes he would have liked to have had. His virtuosic fluency on the basis of half-digested ideas and an inadequate foundation in factual knowledge was allowed to develop without the inhibitions which rigorous research or criticism would have imposed, but at least Sartre was surrounded for the moment by his intellectual peers, a situation he would not willingly allow to recur in later life, unless his peers were also his juniors. At the ENS he gave piano lessons and took on a philosophy pupil with whose mother he was very friendly, earning enough to enable him to escape the notorious catering. He contemplated becoming a jazz singer, successfully impersonated the ENS principal, Gustave Lanson, in an end-of-year concert sketch, and came much nearer to being an anarchist than to taking any active part in politics.

His mother and stepfather left Paris for Saint-Etienne, where Mancy had been appointed a factory manager, but the business failed, and Mancy returned to Paris to work as a manager for the Electricité de France. It is quite clear that Sartre was conscious at this time of his lack of stature and his ugliness and determined to make himself physically stronger and, more importantly, freer. Many of his attitudes and activities were dominated by a certain self-disgust coupled with a tenderness which could not find an outlet. At a funeral at Thiviers in September 1925 he met a cousin, Simone-Camille Sans, who was two years older than him, and for four days they became inseparable companions. He called her "Toulouse" and had a very close although largely epistolary relationship with her. She was sexually quite experienced and Sartre pretended to her that there were already two women in his life. They regarded themselves as engaged, and Sartre, who wrote to her that he was trying to create a stronger character for himself, contemplated writing a novel for her, which was to be called "Une défaite" and based on Nietzsche's ideas about willpower. It was turned down by Gallimard. When Sartre raised the money to visit "Toulouse" at Easter 1926, she told him she was "not free." He was furious, and she relented. After a visit to the cinema they spent the night together. The correspondence continued, revealing much about Sartre's intellectual evolution as he worked on the nature of images and tried to elaborate an aesthetic.

"Toulouse" came to the ENS ball in December, but was unimpressed by the way in which she was entertained by Sartre, who had borrowed money for the purpose. It was only in April 1927 that Sartre began to address her as "tu." The following month he was implicated in an elaborate hoax which involved the impersonation of Lindbergh at the ENS, and which led to Lanson's resignation. Nizan spent the winter of 1926–27 in Aden, and later joined the communist party, while Sartre remained simply an anti-establishment student. His close friends now included Pierre Guille and René Maheu. His fellow student Raymond Aron alerted him to the importance of Husserl, the father of phenomenology (q.v.) as a philosophical school, and of the philosophy of history. Aron and Sartre were Nizan's witnesses at his marriage in 1927 to Henriette Alphen. Sartre himself had got unofficially engaged to a grocer's daughter that summer, but was rejected when the girl's parents were approached. Like Nizan, he was bitterly opposed to the voluntary training as an army reserve officer offered by the ENS. In 1928, when Aron came top, Sartre failed his agrégation.

Early in 1929 Sartre renewed his relationship with "Toulouse," now the mistress of Charles Dullin, whose Théâtre de l'Atelier rivalled the Vieux-Colombier as a centre for experimental theatre. That summer he met Simone de Beauvoir, who soon joined in outings and discussions with the small group centred on the Nizans and himself. That year he came top in the agrégation and Beauvoir came second. By August they were lovers and expected to be partners for life. Sartre followed her into the country, putting up in a hotel near the château where she was staying, and she would bring him stolen lunchtime picnics. Her father asked him to leave the area and when he did, a week later, he and Beauvoir exchanged daily letters, meeting again daily in Paris while Sartre was awaiting call-up for military ser-

vice, after which he proposed to teach French in Japan. They agreed to a very close relationship which would permit interludes apart and infidelities, and promised never to lie to one another. Emotionally Sartre seems to have been looking for a replacement for what he lost when his mother remarried. He saw something of his mother, less of his stepfather, became a closer friend of Raymond Aron, now a socialist, and made home movies with Nizan.

When he was called up in 1929, Aron was Sartre's instructor in meteorology at Saint-Cyr before he was transferred to Saint-Symphorien, near Tours. His grandmother died the following year at the age of 84, leaving him 80,000 francs, which he got through in two or three years, detesting bank accounts, investments, and thrift. He continued to write poetry and sketch novels but Nizan, who had tried at least twice before on Sartre's behalf, could not get a publisher interested. Sartre was stimulated by the cinema and enjoyed luxuries like taxis and restaurants, while despising comforts such as easy chairs. At weekends Beauvoir and he would generally meet at Tours or in Paris. Sartre failed to get the job in Japan. The agrégation entitled them both to teaching jobs, but his was in Le Havre and hers in Marseilles. He offered to marry her, which would have entitled them to a joint appointment. She thought Sartre would feel his freedom diminished by marriage, but they agreed not to have a prolonged separation until they were in their thirties. Meanwhile, in January 1931, Nizan had published *Aden-Arabie*, and that summer Sartre and Beauvoir went to Madrid, where Sartre was much impressed by the paintings in the Prado. It was the first time either of them had left France.

Beauvoir would argue with Sartre and criticize whatever he wrote, but never challenge his intellectual supremacy, which made her the ideal companion for him. It is ironic that the prophet of an important phase in women's emancipation should herself have spent her life in virtually total intellectual and spiritual thraldom to a man. She organized his work and ran his chaotic business affairs, while he set her off on her writing career. They stimulated one another to write endlessly about themselves. Sartre was constantly buoyed up by the way Beauvoir moulded her opinions, attitudes, and life style, even her changes of mind, to his own. They were one another's preferred travelling companions throughout their lives, and were to carry on seeing one another daily. Sartre cast her partly in the role of mother, and for years she was to look after him.

At Le Havre Sartre had to come to terms with the situation he had long been dreading. He was involved in an organization with a hierarchy and rules to be obeyed and enforced. He could no longer dream student dreams of what he would one day become. He was a provincial schoolmaster. It was this that made him take his writing seriously. He was relaxed with his pupils and went on picnics with them, establishing the pattern of the rest of his life by surrounding himself with a circle of intimates junior to himself, aware that they were not allowed to challenge his intellectual authority. He appears to have got drunk with them, and on one occasion visited a brothel with a party of them. He also boxed with them in a local gym. He spent a lot of time in Paris, and finished his "La légende de la vérité," a philosophical tale modelled on Nietzsche, of which Nizan got an extract published in the June issue of the monthly *Bifur*.

Sartre had only about 16 teaching hours a week and, when the publishers Rieder turned down *La Légende*, now a volume of essays, in October he began his "factum on contingency" that would, thanks to Beauvoir's insistence on fictionalization, turn into *La Nausée*. Beauvoir came to Paris at every opportunity, occasionally feigning illness in order to get time off. At Easter 1932 they went to Brittany together, and in the summer to Morocco and Spain, where Sartre returned to look at the Murillos in Cadiz. Politically Sartre was moving to the left and, although he did not vote in the 1932 elections, he was becoming conscious of the bourgeois or clerical origins of most of the great works in the history of art. A sympathetic bureaucracy posted Beauvoir to Rouen for the next academic year. Sartre and she now saw one another quite frequently on weekdays as well as at weekends.

Aron was studying phenomenology with Husserl in Berlin, and it was now that it occurred to Sartre that phenomenology, by blending, as he imagined, philosophical reflection with direct experience, could give him the key to his novel. He had been reading Dos Passos and come to regard him as "the greatest writer of our time," but still needed to find a means of transition between the isolated contingent events which Dos Passos described and the philosophical notion of contingency which they represented. Meanwhile he spent the Easter holidays of 1933 in London and the summer holidays in Italy. Sartre's reactions seemed unified by some only imperfectly formulated system. He liked Canterbury cathedral, but refused to enter the Oxford colleges, generally preferring slums to acknowledged sights. From autumn 1933 he succeeded Aron as a scholar at the French Institute in Berlin, working on Husserl, but also writing his novel, other pieces, and returning as usual for Christmas to Paris, where Beauvoir and he stayed together in a small hotel. In Berlin he became involved for a while with the wife of a fellow member of the French Institute.

During 1934 Sartre rewrote his novel and wrote *La Transcendance de l'Ego*. His habit of covering his intellectual tracks, dropping names, and mythologizing his past makes it difficult to detect the exact dates and extent of the influence of Husserl and Heidegger on his thought, but he must have read Kafka before he finished *La Nausée*. The novel itself, while reflecting the preoccupations of the two philosophers, does not show a full understanding of either. Beauvoir joined him in Berlin in February 1934, was taken to the famous Alexanderplatz nightspots, and met his mistress. At the end of Beauvoir's term, Sartre met her in Hamburg. They cancelled a projected trip to Vienna on news of Dollfuss's assassination, but went to Prague, Nuremberg, Munich, and Oberammergau for the Passion Play.

Sartre returned to his post at Le Havre, where Aron had been filling in for him. He postponed the necessary pruning back of his novel when the publishers Alcan commissioned him to rewrite his ENS thesis on images from his new phenomenological point of view. Increasingly, he was having recourse to stimulants and sedatives. He was not fond of open-air pursuits, but bravely made an attempt to ski with Beauvoir above Chamonix. He began to have fits of depression. Nizan was publishing successfully, but Sartre had not found a publisher for *La Transcendance de l'Ego*. In February 1935, in pursuit of his study of images, he had himself injected in hospital with mescalin. It took him six months to get over the hallucinations it produced. Sartre's grandfather died in March 1935. That summer, following a cruise to Norway with his mother, with whom Beauvoir got on well, and Mancy, whom she was never to meet, Sartre went hiking with Beauvoir in central France. Additional complications had come into his life when he conceived a passion for one

of Beauvoir's pupils, Olga Kosakiewicz, who lived entirely for the intensity of present experience. She would stay awake with Sartre for up to 40 hours on end, and sometimes dance until she passed out with exhaustion. Beauvoir allowed her to become integrated into their lives to the point that they formed a ménage à trois, and Olga remained very close to Sartre, even when she later married one of his pupils, Jacques-Laurent Bost.

Alcan now decided to publish only the first, less original part of the reworked thesis, which appeared as *L'Imagination* in 1936. After further revision, the second part was finally published in 1940 as *L'Imaginaire* by Gallimard, who had rejected *La Nausée* in 1936. Sartre was hurt: "In turning it down, it's me they were rejecting, my experience that was being shut out." He naturally tried to make the situation he had reached at the age of 30 less intolerable by finding a philosophy to explain it, while continuing during 1936 to write short stories. At Easter Beauvoir and he were to see twice through Chaplin's *Modern Times*, from which the name of the post-war review *Les Temps Modernes* (q.v.) was to be taken. The film released in 1936, is important because Chaplin caricatured the style he had made famous before synchronized sound created the "talkies" in 1930. Chaplin refused to use synchronized sound, so the title of the film, and later of the review, was ironic. *Modern Times* was a parody of the out-of-date, not what Satre at all intended *Les Temps Modernes* to be.

In the summer of 1936 Satre and Beauvoir went to Italy, where the close juxtaposition of squalor and elegance dismayed them. Sartre did not vote in the elections of 1936, but supported the Front Populaire in an article which was rejected by *Vendredi*. Although he was offered a higher post in Lyons, he preferred to take one at Laon, much nearer Paris, while Beauvoir was transferred from Rouen to the Lycée Molière in Paris. Sartre looked after her when she was ill that winter, and continued to invent student-type escapades with Bost.

In 1937 things began to look up. *La Transcendance de l'Ego* appeared in Jean Wahl's series of *Recherches philosophiques*, and Gaston Gallimard was finally persuaded by Dullin and Pierre Bost, the novelist and father of Olga's future husband, to publish *La Nausée*, while the *Nouvelle Revue Française* (*NRF*, q.v.), hitherto despised by Sartre, published the short story "Le mur," which caused a furore. In the summer Sartre, Beauvoir, and Bost went to Greece, and Sartre returned to a post in Paris. He reported all his experiences, reflections, and brief affairs in explicit and intimate detail to Beauvoir. The beginnings of success were now forcing him to stabilize his life at the outer edge of the bourgeois world, although he boasted that the only objects he had owned for 10 years were a pen and a pipe. In 1938 he began a new work on psychology, but abandoned it, although a fragment was published in 1939 as the *Esquisse d'une théorie des émotions*, a first step towards denying the imagination any power to create. The emotions are seen here as forms of consciousness which can also be forces of delusion.

Sartre also published three short stories, "La chambre," "Intimité," and "Nourritures." The first two, with "Erostrate" of 1936, and "L'enfance d'un chef," were to be published with "Le mur" in a volume of that title by Gallimard in February 1939. *La Nausée* was well reviewed when it appeared in March 1938, although the literary prize for which it was being considered went to Nizan, the author of one of Sartre's most enthusiastic reviews. In 1938 the *NRF* also published articles by Sartre on Faulkner and Dos Passos, to be followed in 1939 by half a dozen

Oreste does return the people to freedom, but it weighs heavily on them. He refuses the throne and symbolically takes responsibility for the people's freedom by removing the plague of flies from their city, which the flies leave in order to follow him. Sartre makes allusions to the German occupation, which the censors must have noted, and he exploits the myth form, which, like the fairy tale, has a non-variable ending. Even if not known to the audience, the ending can at least be revealed in a programme note destined for reading before the performance.

Huis clos uses the techniques of simultaneity to be found in the *Les Chemins de la liberté* novels. In Sartre's screenplay the characters have no terrestrial location, and the Paris of the dead coincides with the Paris of the living. The living characters cannot see the dead ones, although the audience can, and the dead find it difficult to stay out of the dialogue. The scene is the metaphorical hell of a Second Empire salon, and the play deals ironically with the bad faith of the three characters, a coward about to be shot as a deserter, a lesbian, and an infanticidal mother. Each of them is in some way the torturer of the others. Hell depends not on other peoples' behaviour, but on their very existence, and therefore on limits to individuality: "L'enfer, c'est les autres (Hell is other people)." In *Morts sans sépulture* the Vichy militia are trying to find out from Resistance fighters the whereabouts of their leader, Jean. He turns up, but his captors do not know who he is. His lover, Lucie, is the sister of the 15-year-old François, to whose murder she consents because he is so likely to crack under torture. One of the older men, Sorbier, throws himself out of the window because he does not trust himself either. Lucie is raped, and the others are tortured, and Sartre goes quite deeply here into the psychology of torture.

La Putain respectueuse was written speedily and is set in the Deep South, based on a real case. A prostitute gives false evidence against a black in order to protect a middle-class white who had shot a black man while drunk. The young white's uncle, who is a senator, convinces Lizzie, the prostitute, that his nephew's life matters more to America than does the black's. The prostitute sleeps with the senator's son, Fred, who tries to bully her into saving his cousin's life and who has himself shot another innocent black. Lizzie, unable to shoot Fred as she had intended, is set up as his mistress, and Sartre deliberately deprives the audience of the moral resolution the situation demands, thereby trapping it into desiring violence.

In *Les Mains sales* Hugo, the young middle-class intellectual, wants to commit himself to action, but finds commitment to the party incompatible with honesty. The working-class Hoederer is a born leader moved by real compassion. After ordering Hugo to kill Hoederer, the party then ironically changes its policy to that which Hoederer has been advocating. Hugo does kill Hoederer, but only out of jealousy, since his wife has slept with him. The moral dilemma remains unresolved, but the play was treated as anti-communist. Marguerite Duras wrote a hostile review in *Action, Humanité* attacked Sartre, and in *Les Lettres Françaises* Ilya Ehrenberg later regarded him as a traitor to left-wing causes. The play was a huge success, however, and is now generally regarded as one of Sartre's better-written plays, on account of the way in which Hugo's relationship with Hoederer progressively coarsens.

Le Diable et le bon Dieu reflects Sartre's new preoccupation in 1951 with the possibility of transcending the opposition between good and evil. The play is loaded down with rhetorical tirades, abstract discussions, and aphorisms. The historical char-

acter Goetz cheats in order to lose a game in which his forfeit is to live altruistically. The two women have only slight roles in the drama, while the two men, Heinrich and Nasty, too obviously "represent," respectively, the denial that man is free, and the attitudes of the communist party. Unlike *Nekrassov, Les Séquestrés d'Altona* enjoyed a public success when it was staged, yet neither is now generally regarded as an artistically satisfactory play. *Nekrassov*, a farce, tries too openly to undermine anti-Soviet propaganda. A confidence trickster impersonates a Soviet minister, making it seem that he has defected, to the joy of the Western press. *Les Séquestrés*, its title borrowing from Sartre's 1957 essay on Tintoretto, fails in its attempt to encompass the outlooks of Marx and Freud. Frantz von Gerlach is the son of a powerful German shipbuilder who has kept on good terms with Hitler's Reich. When Frantz, who is psychologically ill, helps a Polish rabbi, his father can save him, but not the rabbi, who is beaten to death. There are biographical reasons for these failures, connected with Sartre's intellectual evolution and personal relationships, but the works themselves are not of great dramatic merit.

None of the three biographies is a straightforward account of the life concerned. Each argues a specific position taken during Sartre's personal intellectual journey, and is not of great interest in terms of what it purports to be. Such importance as these works have they share with *Les Mots*. They attempt to impose on personal or vicarious experience an interpretation which is of interest primarily for what it reveals about Sartre's reasons for wanting to interpret the raw materials of his experience, and that of Baudelaire, Genet, and Flaubert, in the ways in which he does. *L'Etre et le néant*, a technical philosophic meditation, is similarly important for the light it sheds on what Sartre was attempting to do. Sartre later implicitly repudiated the work's content, but it retains its interest thanks to the definition of freedom which is central to it, but which created ethical problems Sartre was never able to resolve, or even to write about other than imaginatively.

L'Existentialisme est un humanisme is a first attempt at the ethic. The individual is forced to choose for the whole of humanity. It is tempting here to see Kant's categorical imperative passed to Sartre through the Protestant Schweitzer inheritance, but Sartre never completely elaborates his view, which is clearly in tension with the determinisms imposed by history and childhood in which he also believed. There remains a segment of choice defined by an angle too small for freedom to mean much more than responsibility for actions which are not willingly chosen from a variety of equally available alternative options. *Réflexions sur la question juive* is, as Sartre admitted, a superficial book, well meaning but not thought through. The book uses the word "Aryan," with its implied racialism, five times with inverted commas and 12 times without. Sartre has half assimilated a racialist attitude without remotely intending to.

Questions de méthode makes an about-turn. Sartre here accepts Marx's view that there can be no freedom until there is no need for oppression and violence, although he had previously always started his ethical speculations from the premise that man was free, whatever that turned out to mean. He now chooses the dilemma's other horn, but his Marxism is not reconciled with his existentialism. His final effort to make the synthesis, and what should have been his greatest book, the *Critique de la raison dialectique*, was abandoned. The task was impossible. Sartre's German may not have been quite as good as is often supposed, and was probably not good enough to penetrate Heidegger's dense thought. Heidegger certainly repudiated Sartre's interpretation of his philosophy. But Sartre never quite understood Husserl's phenomenology either, although its most important statement, the *Méditations cartésiennes*, was published in French before it appeared in German.

In the *Critique* Sartre turns to Hegel for help, although he condemns him, in arguing that both individuals and collectives are part of a "totalization," from which they derive and which goes beyond them. In the second part of the *Critique*, history comes to ignore individual consciousnesses. As with the attempted synthesis of Marx and Freud, Sartre was arguing himself into a head-on collision with a brick wall. He will be remembered not so much as a philosopher who failed, but as a perceptive, patchily brilliant, sometimes tender, and always clever master of French prose, as revealed particularly in *La Nausée*, some of the short stories, and parts of *Les Chemins de la liberté*.

PUBLICATIONS

Fiction

La Nausée, 1938; as *The Diary of Antoine Roquentin*, 1949; as *Nausea*, 1949

Le Mur, 1939; as *The Wall and Other Stories*, 1949; as *Intimacy and Other Stories*, 1949

Les Chemins de la liberté (Paths of Freedom):
L'Age de raison, 1945; as *The Age of Reason*, 1947
Le Sursis, 1945; as *The Reprieve*, 1947
La Mort dans l'âme, 1949; as *Iron in the Soul*, 1950; as *Troubled Sleep*, 1951

Oeuvres romanesques, edited by Michel Contat and Michel Rybalka, 1981

Plays

Bariona; ou, Le Fils du tonnerre (produced 1940), 1962; as *Bariona; or, The Son of Thunder*, in *The Writings 2*, 1974

Les Mouches (produced 1943), 1943; as *The Flies*, in *The Flies and In Camera*, 1946

Huis clos (produced 1944), 1945; as *In Camera*, in *The Flies and In Camera*, 1946; as *No Exit*, in *No Exit and The Flies*, 1947

The Flies and In Camera, 1946

Morts sans sépulture (produced 1946), 1946; as *Men Without Shadows*, in *Three Plays* (UK), 1949; as *The Victors*, in *Three Plays* (USA), 1949

No Exit and The Flies, 1947

Les Jeux sont faits (screenplay), 1947; as *The Chips Are Down*, 1948

Les Mains sales (produced 1948), 1948; as *Crime Passionnel*, in *Three Plays* (UK), 1949; as *Dirty Hands*, in *Three Plays* (USA), 1949

L'Engrenage (screenplay), 1948; as *In the Mesh*, 1954

Three Plays (UK; includes *Men Without Shadows, The Respectable Prostitute, Crime Passionnel*), 1949

Three Plays (USA; includes *The Victors, The Respectable Prostitute, Dirty Hands*), 1949

Le Diable et le bon Dieu (produced 1951), 1951; as *Lucifer and the Lord*, 1953; as *The Devil and the Good Lord*, in *The Devil and the Good Lord and Two Other Plays*, 1960

Kean, from the play by Dumas *père* (produced 1953), 1954; as *Kean* (in English), 1954

Nekrassov (produced 1955), 1956; as *Nekrassov* (in English), 1956

Les Séquestrés d'Altona (produced 1959), 1960; as *Loser Wins*, 1960; as *The Condemned of Altona*, 1961

The Devil and the Good Lord and Two Other Plays (includes *Kean* and *Nekrassov*), 1960

Les Troyennes, from a play by Euripides (produced 1965), 1965; as *The Trojan Women*, 1967

Screenplays: *Les Jeux sont faits* (*The Chips Are Down*), 1947; *L'Engrenage*, 1948; *Les Sorcières de Salem* (*Witches of Salem*), 1957

Other

L'Imagination, 1936; as *Imagination: A Psychological Critique*, 1962

La Transcendance de L'Ego, 1937; as *The Transcendence of the Ego: An Existentialist Theory of Consciousness*, 1957

Esquisse d'une théorie des émotions, 1939; as *The Emotions: Outline of a Theory*, 1948; as *Sketch for a Theory of the Emotions*, 1962

L'Imaginaire: psychologie phénoménologique de l'imagination, 1940; as *Psychology of the Imagination*, 1948

L'Être et le néant: essai d'ontologie phénoménologique, 1943; as *Being and Nothingness*, 1956

L'Existentialisme est un humanisme, 1946; as *Existentialism*, 1947; as *Existentialism and Humanism*, 1948

Explication de "L'Etranger," 1946

Réflexions sur la question juive, 1947; as *Anti-Semite and Jew*, 1948; as *Portrait of an Anti-Semite*, 1948

Baudelaire, 1947; as *Baudelaire* (in English), 1949

Situations 1–10, 10 vols., 1947–76; selections as *What Is Literature?*, 1949; *Literary and Philosophical Essays*, 1955; *Situations*, 1965; *The Communists and Peace*, 1965; *The Ghost of Stalin*, 1968 (as *The Spectre of Stalin*, 1969); *Between Existentialism and Marxism*, 1974; *Life/Situations*, 1977; *Sartre in the Seventies*, 1978

Entretiens sur la politique, with others, 1949

Saint Genet, comédien et martyr, 1952; as *Saint Genet, Actor and Martyr*, 1963

L'Affaire Henri Martin, with others, 1953

Critique de la raison dialectique: théorie des ensembles pratiques (includes *Questions de méthode*), 1960; as *Critique of Dialectical Reason: Theory of Practical Ensembles*, 1976

On Cuba, 1961

Search for a Method, 1963

Les Mots (autobiography), 1964; as *Words*, 1964; as *The Words*, 1964

Essays in Aesthetics, edited by Wade Baskin, 1963

Que peut la littérature?, with others, 1965

The Philosophy of Sartre, edited by Robert Denoon Cumming, 1966

Of Human Freedom, edited by Wade Baskin, 1967

Essays in Existentialism, edited by Wade Baskin, 1967

On Genocide, 1968

Les Communistes ont peur de la révolution, 1969

L'Idiot de la famille: Gustave Flaubert de 1821 à 1857, 3 vols., 1971–72; as *The Family Idiot: Gustave Flaubert 1821–1857*, 1981–82

War Crimes in Vietnam, with others, 1971
Un Théâtre de situations, edited by Michel Contat and Michel
    Rybalka, 1973; as *On Theatre*, 1976
Politics and Literature, 1973
The Writings 2: Selected Prose, edited by Michel Contat and
    Michel Rybalka, 1974
On a raison de se révolter, with others, 1974

Bibliography

Contat, Michel, and Michel Rybalka, *The Writings I: A Biblio-
    graphical Life*, 1974
Wilcocks, Robert, *Sartre: A Bibliography of International Crit-
    icism*, 1975
Lapointe, François and Claire, *Sartre and His Critics: An Inter-
    national Bibliography 1938–1980*, 1981

Critical studies

Murdoch, Iris, *Sartre, Romantic Rationalist*, 1953
Thody, Philip, *Sartre: A Literary and Political Study*, 1960
Thody, Philip, *Sartre: A Biographical Introduction*, 1971
Warnock, Mary (editor), *Sartre: A Collection of Critical Essays*,
    1971
Rahv, Betty T., *From Sartre to the New Novel*, 1974
Halpern, Joseph, *Critical Fictions: The Literary Criticism of
    Sartre*, 1976
Caws, Peter, *Sartre* (in English), 1979
Perrin, Marius, *Sartre and Surrealism*, 1980
Collins, Douglas, *Sartre as Biographer*, 1980
Barnes, Hazel E., *Sartre and Flaubert*, 1981
Schilpp, Paul Arthur (editor), *The Philosophy of Sartre*, 1981
Hayman, Ronald, *Writing Against: A Biography of Sartre*, 1986

———

SCHWOB, Marcel (Mayer-André-), 1867–1905.

Essayist, critic, and novelist.

LIFE

Marcel Schwob, a scholar of wide culture, is of literary interest
primarily on account of his association with symbolism (q.v.)
and the early days of the *Mercure de France*, founded in 1890
(see Renard). Jarry and Valéry dedicated works to him. Alfred
Valette, the *Mercure's* editor, and his wife, Rachilde, knew of
Schwob, and he was an almost exact contemporary of Remy de
Gourmont on the review. Schwob's father was descended from
a line of rabbis and doctors. He had known Flaubert and
belonged to the literary circle which included Gautier and Banville. He had collaborated with Baudelaire on *Le Corsaire-Satan*
and cooperated with Jules Verne on a play which flopped.
Attracted by the theories of Fourier, he wrote for *La Démocratie
Pacifique*. He subsequently abandoned literature, became an
insurance inspector, and, for the sake of his health, spent 10

years in Egypt in charge of the ministry of foreign affairs.
Schwob's mother, née Cahun, had a distinguished Jewish ances-
try, although her father had arrived in Paris as a poor immigrant.
He prospered and sent his daughters to an English boarding
school, and passed on to them a refined and cosmopolitan
Jewish culture.

Schwob was born in Paris on 23 August 1867, soon after his
father's return from Egypt. The family moved to Tours, where
Schwob's father founded a republican, anti-Prussian newspaper
in 1870, during the Franco-Prussian War. He was a councillor
and a republican, and a friend of Gambetta. In 1876 he moved to
Nantes, having bought from Evariste Mangin the only major liberal newspaper in western France, *Le Phare de la Loire*, which
numbered Littré, Hugo, Michelet, and George Sand among its
contributors. Schwob was brought up trilingual, speaking
English and German as well as French. He adored his father, but
was intimidated by his mother. At home culture meant everything, and in the hierarchy of expenditure English governesses
and German tutors headed the list. Schwob's school career was
predictably brilliant. He took a pride in his race, and was grateful to his parents for his education, but in later life was reluctant
to talk about his family or to talk about Nantes.

In 1882 Schwob went to live in Paris with his uncle, librarian
of the Mazarine library and author of *La Vie juive*. He was sent
to board at Sainte-Barbe while attending Louis-le-Grand, where
his fellow pupils included Claudel and Léon Daudet. In spite of
further academic distinctions, Schwob failed his baccalauréat on
his first attempt. On his second try he received a congratulatory
pass. Encouraged by his uncle, he developed a precocious interest in textual work on Greek manuscripts, and translated Catullus into 16th-century French when he was 16 in the astounding
and inaccurate belief that Latin in the time of Catullus had
reached the stage of development of French under Henri IV.
Schwob says he got the idea from Littré. Whatever can be said
about his education, it is clear that his fascination for the history
and development of languages began at an early age.

A notebook of juvenilia has survived, faithfully reflecting the
first signs of adolescent disillusion, an early infatuation, the first
poetic attempts, and an embarrassing admiration for Hugo,
whose portrait Schwob had in his bedroom. In his late teens he
was reading Schopenhauer, working on a "Faust," and wondering whether to learn Sanskrit. He found contemporary literature
"sad." Change, he thought at 16, was happening too fast. He finished sententiously with an adaptation of a tag from Horace. He
was already writing short stories and later destroyed thousands
of lines of adolescent verse.

From 1885 to 1886 Schwob did his military service at Vannes
before returning to Louis-le-Grand to prepare for the Ecole Normale Supérieure. His verse had become firmer, striving for the
Parnassian (q.v.) ideals of Heredia and Leconte de Lisle. He did
not get into the Ecole Normale, but in 1888 came first in his year
at his "licence". Schwob then apparently began to study for his
agrégation, although he spent most of his time on philology
rather than philosophy. He began to take an interest in dialect as
well as Greek palaeography, and to attend Saussure's classes on
phonetics. He also contemplated writing various sorts of fiction
in the manner of his models, Verne, Twain, Poe, and Whitman.
In fact, in 1886 Schwob sent his verse drama on Prometheus to
Georges Guieysse, a fellow student, with whom he was later to
exchange letters in Greek and to write his first learned work, a
study of French slang. With Guieysse, who was to die very

young in 1889, Schwob wrote his study on French argot, published that year. By 1890 he had proved in an important article that Villon's slang poems were not written in a fantasy language, as had been supposed, but in a real one used by a particular group of law-breakers to which Villon belonged.

Schwob, who had no intention of returning to Nantes, sent short pieces to his father's paper from time to time, but otherwise scraped a living in Paris as a journalist. He wrote carefully, changing nothing when his pieces were later published in volume form, and made his real debut in *L'Evénement*, for which he worked from November 1890 to April 1891. The management did not pay him willingly, disliking his insufficiently gossip-like approach to journalism. He had written about Anatole France and Brunetière. In the second half of 1890 he was writing for *L'Echo de Paris*, effectively run by Catulle Mendès. The team of writers included Mirbeau, Maupassant, Margueritte, Courteline, Maurras, Remy de Gourmont, Paul Arène, Jules Renard, Anatole France, Paul Bourget, and Maurice Barrès. Mendès invited Schwob to join him in editing a literary supplement, and Schwob produced for the paper the contes to be republished in *Coeur double, Le Roi au masque d'or*, and the Greek stories of *Mimes*. Schwob's father became increasingly concerned about the amount of popular journalism flowing from his son's pen and rightly supposed that it was taking precedence over preparation for the agrégation. Schwob duly failed in July 1891.

The family were none the less impressed by the first signs of literary attention being paid to Schwob, although they would have liked him to earn more money. In 1894, two years after his father died, he published *Le Livre de Monelle*, and was now friendly with Alphonse and Léon Daudet, with Edmond de Goncourt, Claudel, Courteline, Barbusse, and above all Jules Renard. Claudel later became a particular friend, and Schwob formed a close relationship with Jammes and especially Colette. *Le Livre de Monelle* is his personal manifesto. Almost nihilistic and certainly obscure, it is his bridge to a symbolist aesthetic. It was inspired by a woman named Louise, whom Schwob had met after a series of short liaisons sometime before 1891. She was to die of tuberculosis, aggravated by the trappings of poverty, aged about 25, on 7 December 1893.

It was in January 1895 that Schwob met the actress Marguerite Moreno, to whom he immediately became devoted. Indeed, his love for her helped him survive a severe illness during 1895–96, although the five operations he endured left him dependent on self-injected morphine. The nature of the illness is not clear, but it is known that the operations involved cauterization. The experience changed Schwob's whole personality and he was henceforward to be an invalid, unable to walk properly, unwilling to conceal his incapacity and his physical pain, and increasingly irritable. His literary work became primarily devoted to historical studies and translations from English. His translation of *Moll Flanders* was published in the *Revue Hebdomadaire* in September 1894, and appeared as a volume in 1895. That year the *Mercure* published the "récits" which were to be collected as *La Croisade des enfants* and published as a volume in 1896. *Les Vies imaginaires* was also serialized before volume publication, as were the critical studies of Villon, Stevenson, and Meredith, whom Schwob had visited in 1894, and other critical pieces collected in *Spicilège*.

In 1892 Fernand Xau had founded *Le Journal*. He had started off with Schwob's father in Nantes on *Le Phare*, and enabled Schwob to publish in *L'Echo* (owned by the Simonds), before starting up *Le Journal* (owned by the Letelliers) in rivalry. Paul Hervieu urged Schwob to move to *Le Journal*, which would guarantee to publish his contes regularly and to pay more for them. After 1894 Schwob's contributions to *Le Journal* became intermittent, but it was there that he first published most of the contes collected in *Les Vies imaginaires* and *La Croisade des enfants*. In 1896 and again in 1898 Schwob moved house, still with Marguerite Moreno, seeming to seek refuge from his own ill health. He dreamt of writing for the theatre, translated *Hamlet* in a version in which Sarah Bernhardt was to play Ophelia in 1900, and went on working in the Bibliothèque Nationale or at the archives. In 1900 Schwob needed a respite and spent a month in England. Marguerite joined him and they were married in London in mid-September on the day after her arrival.

In Paris, where he had a constant male nurse and a Chinese servant, Schwob went on working at the library and the archives. He planned a work on Villon, but had to leave Paris for some sea air, and in April 1901 went to Jersey, which he so much disliked that he counted the days before leaving in August. His mind had become more and more concentrated on the desirability of a long sea voyage, so, accompanied by his Chinese servant, he took a six-month cruise on *La Ville de la Ciotat* from Naples to Australia, New Zealand, and the Pacific islands. There were money worries while Schwob was away and his health was sometimes dangerously poor. On his return he was unable to work seriously, but began his *Les Moeurs des diurnales*, extracts from which were published by the *Mercure* early in 1903.

That year Schwob moved to the Ile Saint-Louis in Paris. His journalism had become harshly satirical, and the focus of attack was now the Comédie-Française, which his wife was soon to leave, and which had turned down material he had proposed. *La Lampe de Psyché* was a new title for previously published contes. Schwob began to receive literary friends, especially English ones, regularly in his new apartment. He made one more journey, to Portugal, returning via Barcelona, Naples, and San Agnello, where he stayed with Marion Crawford, returning to Paris in October 1904. That winter he lectured at the Sorbonne on Villon. He published his last literary pieces in *Vers et Prose*, recently founded by Paul Fort and André Salmon. In the end death took him by surprise. He went down with flu on 19 February 1905, was well enough to write a normal letter to his wife, who was on tour, but died a week later.

WORKS

Leaving aside Schwob's works of erudition, his translations, and his literary journalism and connections, his importance as a writer derives from his short stories and from his fictional reconstitution of historical scenes and figures. His abandonment of an academic career, even if it dated from soon after his graduation in 1888, left only seven years before the onset of permanent disability, and 17 years of life, during which time he had to support himself with journalism. His relatively unadventurous life, scholarly habits, and need for a regular income left him without much scope to develop his imaginative writing as he well might have done, had he not become ill. On the other hand, his wide reading, cultured background, and linguistic skills allowed him to broaden the scope of the French short story both historically and by adopting literary techniques drawn from non-Francophone and especially antique literatures.

Schwob was particularly given to writing in a dream style, turning away from the Parnassian ideal, and combining a childlike pseudo-naivety with a historically important imaginative complexity. He would read his stories to small groups of friends, who, by all accounts, were magnetized. They were also much admired by his fellow writers, and during his short, active life Schwob became the focus of a cult which we should now regard as late symbolist decadence.

The early *Coeur double* is not at all symbolist, but based on Schwob's military experiences. It was compiled, he said, to show the path between the need for self-preservation and the need for sacrifice: "il y a une route à faire pour arriver à la pitié, et ce livre vient en marquer les étapes (there is a path to be indicated to arrive at pity, and this book attempts to mark its stages)." He foresees the need to get away from naturalism (q.v.), from "pseudo-scientific" descriptions, in order to concentrate on personal and social crises. The contes are classified according to the different sorts of terror which they evoke. Schwob's mind works mathematically, but his fantasy still derives from Poe, de Quincey, Rosetti, and Petronius. The book was successful, with two editions in its first year, and drew significant praise from Renard in particular.

Le Roi au masque d'or, officially dated 1893, appeared in November 1892. Before Ollendorff took it, it had been turned down by one publisher, who did not anticipate that it would cover the costs of its first edition. It went on to have three editions in two years. Another collection of previously published contes, the volume is linked together by its preface, rather factitiously insisting on the diversity of masks worn by its characters. Schwob, however, has moved perceptibly nearer late symbolism here. On the strength of *Coeur double*, Anatole France had called him "prince de la pitié, duc de la terreur, roi des épouvantements (prince of pity, duke of terror, king of horrors)," and it is to the decadent poets of antiquity, as well as to Villon and the Elizabethans, that Schwob increasingly turned for inspiration. The contes are undoubtedly precious and pander to the over-refined taste which derived from the worn-out palate of Des Esseintes in Huysmans's *A rebours* of 1884. They are less solidly anchored in ethnic robustness than the work of Maeterlinck, who admired Schwob, but are not unlike the work of Pierre Louÿs. Their chief characteristics are the precision with which they analyse dream and nightmare, their use of associations to get away from direct descriptions, and their play on sound and colour. Objects themselves become mysterious and suggest realms of mystery and excitement. It is not surprising that the conte which gives the collection its name should be the story of Buddha. The often erudite sources of the stories in the contes have been catalogued. Their point lies in the originality of the treatment.

Le Livre de Monelle offers little clue to the love of Louise which inspired it. The decadence of taste is quite clear, however, the style quite deliberately biblical pastiche:

Et Monelle dit encore: je te parlerai des moments. Regarde toutes choses sous l'aspect du moment. Laisse aller ton moi au gré du moment. Toute pensée qui dure est contradiction… Tout amour qui dure est haine… Toute justice qui dure est injustice… Tout bonheur qui dure est malheur. Aie du respect pour tous les moments, et ne fais point de liaisons entre les choses… Vois: tout moment est un berceau et un cercueil. Sois semblable aux roses: offre tes feuilles à l'arrachement des voluptés; aux piétinements des douleurs… Que toute extase soit mourante en toi, que toute volupté désire mourir… N'attends pas la mort: elle est en toi.

(And Monelle went on to say: I will speak to you of moments. Look at all things under the aspect of the moment. Let your "me" go where the moment takes it. All thought which lasts is a contradiction… All love which lasts is hate… All justice which lasts is injustice… All happiness which lasts is unhappiness… Have respect for all moments and do not make links between things… See, each moment is a cradle and a coffin. Be like the roses. Offer your petals to be taken by pleasures, to be stamped on by pain… Let every ecstasy in you be expiring, let every pleasure seek to die… Do not wait for death. It is within you.)

The sensibility, with its extreme craving for any stimulus that will still work, is quite explicitly attached to the first half of the 1890s in France, after Des Esseintes, but before Dreyfus. The passage quoted could not have been written at any other time or in any other place. The false naivety of the pseudo-biblical language makes it specific to Schwob.

Mimes of 1893 is an incantatory evocation of decadent antiquity, given over to the cult of the exquisite in full scholarly awareness of the social realities. *La Croisade des enfants* is a connected set of short stories recounting the adventures of a group of pilgrims. They die, and Pope Gregory forgives the sea:

Here is the sea which devours, which looks blue and innocent. Its folds are gentle, and it is bordered with white like the dress of a god. It is liquid sky, and its stars are alive… O Mediterranean sea! I pardon you and absolve you. I give you most holy absolution. Go and sin no more. Like you I am guilty of faults of which I know nothing. You ceaselessly confess on the beach with your thousand groaning lips, and I confess to you, great sacred sea, with my withered lips.

Schwob's most important book was *Les Vies imaginaires* with its almost visionary reconstructed existences. The style is again highly coloured, on a register of pseudo-naive simplicity, with a highly complex vocabulary. In its way the book is a tour de force of condensed evocative power, its restraint making it possible for Schwob to take decadent symbolist imaginative exploration virtually as far as it would go. The reaction was about to set in with such literary events as the founding of Paul Fort's *Vers et Prose*, to which Schwob himself contributed his own last pieces, and the work of the Montmartre poets, Max Jacob, André Salmon, and Guillaume Apollinaire, during the first decade of the new century.

Publications

Collections

Oeuvres complètes, 10 vols., 1927–30

Fiction

Coeur double, 1891
Le Roi au masque d'or, 1893
Mimes, 1893
Le Livre de Monelle, 1894
La Croisade des enfants, 1896
Spicilège, 1896
Les Vies imaginaires, 1896

Other

Etude sur l'argot français, with others, 1889
La Porte des rêves, 1899
Les Moeurs des diurnales, 1903
La Guerre commerciale, 1904
Parnasse satyrique du XVe siècle, 1905
Le Petit et le Grant Testament de Villon, 1905

Translator, *Moll Flanders*, by Daniel Defoe 1895
Translator, *Hamlet* (produced 1890), by Shakespeare, 1899
Translator, *Francesca de Rimini*, by F.M. Crawford 1902

Critical and biographical studies

Champion, P., *Marcel Schwob et son temps*, 1927
Trembley, G., *Marcel Schwob, faussaire de la nature*, 1969

SCRIBE, (Augustin) Eugène, 1791–1861.

Dramatist.

Eugène Scribe was born in Paris on 24 December 1791 into a family of bourgeois businessmen. His father, a silk merchant, died when Scribe was very young, and the boy subsequently became a boarder at the Collège Sainte-Barbe. From there he went to the Lycée Napoléon, where he won a prize in his final exams. On leaving, he was accepted for training in a law practice, but he soon gave up law in favour of the theatre.

His first play was the anti-romantic *Le Prétendu sans le savoir; ou, L'Occasion fait le larron*, produced at the Variétés in 1810. It flopped, as did his other early vaudevilles. Scribe's perseverance was rewarded in 1815, however, when he produced *Encore une nuit de la garde nationale* in collaboration with Delestre-Poirson. From then until 1850 Scribe was the "King of the Boulevard," writing more than 300 scripts, alone or in collaboration, and amassing a large fortune. Apart from Vaudevilles, he wrote comedies of manners, both light and serious, and historical plays. However, some of his most lucrative contracts were for opera libretti, and he worked with the most prominent composers of the day: Boieldieu, Auber, Gounod, Rossini, Donizetti, and Meyerbeer.

L'Ours et le pacha was Scribe's first major vaudeville triumph, and as his popularity became established, he was awarded a contract to write for the Gymnase. He wrote more than 100 plays for this company, practically all of them public successes, but he also wrote for other boulevard theatres, particularly the Vaudeville, and increasingly for the Comédie-Française. It was the official company which put on *Bertrand et Raton* in 1833, *La Camaraderie; ou, La Courte Echelle* in 1837, *Le Verre d'eau; ou, Les Effets et les causes* in 1840, and *Adrienne Lecouvreur* in 1849, with Rachel in the title role, to be succeeded by Sarah Bernhardt.

Scribe is famous as the great exponent of the "pièce bien faite (well-made play)." Taking the traditional components of vaudeville—action, suspense, surprise, and an inevitable denouement—he evolved his own formula, adding topical satire, gradually eliminating the conventional songs and couplets, and incorporating the colloquial language of his bourgeois audience and the Voltairean philosophy of "petites causes," where an apparently minor cause can lead to a huge and unforeseen effect.

In a Scribe play the exposition typically absorbs the first act and meticulously sets the plot in motion. Plot is far more important than character, and the action moves at high speed through extremes of luck and complication towards the "scène à faire," in which a secret (never of an adulterous nature) is revealed in an unexpected manner. This is followed by a reversal of events that leads to a final denouement, and the audience is kept in delightful suspense throughout the entertainment. Scribe was perfectly in tune with public taste, and his life-long popularity was due to superb theatrical craftsmanship rather than any intrinsic literary merit. His contribution to the development of French theatre is best seen in the influence he had on the technique of other writers and in the fun he made of romantic pretentiousness.

Despite his enormous success and wealth, Scribe remained a kind and approachable person, with a reputation for generosity towards his collaborators. He was elected to the Académie Française in 1834. He died suddenly, in a cab in Paris, on 20 February 1861. He may have written or collaborated in as many as 400 stage pieces. Legouvé, Scribe's collaborator, wrote his biography in 1874.

PUBLICATIONS

Collections

Théâtre, 10 vols., 1828–32
Théâtre complet de M. Eugène Scribe, 24 vols., 1834–42
Oeuvres complètes, 5 vols., 1840–47
Oeuvres illustrées, 12 vols., 1853–55
Oeuvres complètes, 76 vols., 1874–85
Théâtre choisi de Scribe, with a biographical and literary notice by M. Charlot, 1911

Plays

Les Dervis, with Delavigne, 1811
L'Auberge; ou, Les Brigands sans le savoir, with Delestre-Poirson, 1812
Thibault, comte de Champagne, with Delavigne, 1813
Koulikan; ou, Les Tartares, with Dupin, 1813
La Chambre à coucher; ou, Une demi-heure de Richelieu, 1813
Encore une nuit de la garde nationale, with Delestre-Poirson, 1815

Le Bachelier de Salamanque, with Dupin and Delavigne, 1815
La Mort et le bûcheron, with Dupin, 1815
La Pompe funèbre, with Dupin, 1815
La Jarretière de la mariée, with Dupin, 1816
Gusman d'Alfarache, with Dupin, 1816
Farinelli; ou, La Pièce de circonstance, with Dupin and Eugène, 1816
Le Valet de son rival, with Delavigne, 1816
Flore et Zéphire, with Delestre-Poirson, 1816
Les Montagnes russes; ou, Le Temple de la mode, with Delestre-Poirson, Merle, and Dupin, 1816
Encore un Pourceaugnac, with Delestre-Poirson, 1817
La Barrière de Mont-Parnasse, with Delestre-Poirson and Désaugiers, 1817
Tous les vaudevilles; ou, Chacun chez soi, with Delestre-Poirson and Désaugiers, 1817
La Princesse de Tarare; ou, Les Contes de ma mère, with Delestre-Poirson and Dupin, 1817
Le Petit Dragon, with Delestre-Poirson and Mélesville, 1817
Les Deux précepteurs; ou, Asinus asinam fricat, with Mélesville, 1817
Le Combat des montagnes; ou, La Folie Beaujon, with Dupin, 1817
Le Café des variétés, with Dupin, 1817
Le Solliciteur; ou, L'Art d'obtenir des places, with Dupin, 1817
Les Comices d'Athènes; ou, Les Femmes orateurs, with Varner, 1817
Le Nouveau Nicaise, with Dupin, 1818
L'Hôtel des Quatre-Nations, with Dupin and Brazier, 1818
L'Ecole de village; ou, L'Enseignement mutuel, with Dupin and Brazier, 1818
La Fête du mari, with Mélesville, 1818
La Volière du Père Philippe, with Mélesville and Delestre-Poirson, 1818
Les Dehors trompeurs, with Mélesville and Delestre-Poirson, 1818
Les Frères invisibles, with Mélesville, 1819
Les Deux maris, with Varner, 1819
Le Fou de Péronne, with Dupin, 1819
L'Homme noir, with Dupin, 1820
Marie Jobin, with Dupin and Carmouche, 1820
Le Vampire, with Mélesville, 1820
Le Témoin, with Mélesville and Saintine, 1820
L'Ours et le pacha, with Saintine, 1820
Le Spleen, with Delestre-Poirson, 1820
Le Mystificateur, with Delestre-Poirson and Cerfberr, 1820
L'Ennui; ou, Le Comte Derfort, with Mélesville and Dupin, 1820
Le Parrain, with Mélesville and Delestre-Poirson, 1821
Le Boulevard Bonne-Nouvelle, with Mélesville and Moreau, 1821
Scène ajoutée au Boulevard Bonne-Nouvelle, pour l'anniversaire de la naissance de Molière, with Mélesville and Moreau, 1821
L'Amant bossu, with Mélesville and Vandière, 1821
Frontin mari-garçon, with Mélesville, 1821
L'Amour platonique, with Mélesville, 1821
Le Secrétaire et le cuisinier, with Mélesville, 1821
La Meunière, with Mélesville, 1821
La Petite Soeur, with Mélesville, 1821
Le Beau Narcisse, with Saintine and de Courcy, 1821

Le Gastronome sans argent, with Brulay, 1821; as *A Race for Dinner*, adapted by J.T.G. Rodwell, 1829
La Somnambule, with Delavigne, 1821; as *The Somnambulist*, 1850
Le Mariage enfantin, with Delavigne, 1821
Le Colonel, with Delavigne, 1821
L'Intérieur de l'étude; ou, Le Procureur et l'avoué, with Dupin, 1821
Le Ménage de garçon, with Dupin, 1821
Michel et Christine, with Dupin, 1821; as *Love in Humble Life*, adapted by J.H. Payne, 1850
La Nouvelle Clary; ou, Louise et Georgette, with Dupin, 1822
La Demoiselle et la dame; ou, Avant et après, with Dupin and Delestre-Poirson, 1822
Le Prince charmant; ou, Les Contes de fées, with Dupin and Delestre-Poirson, 1822
Le Vieux Garçon et la petite fille, with Delavigne, 1822; as *The Popular Farce Called Old and Young*, 1822
Philibert marié, with Moreau, 1822
La Veuve du Malabar, with Saint-Amand, 1822
Les Eaux du Mont-d'Or, with de Courcy and Saintine, 1822
La Petite Lampe merveilleuse, with Mélesville, 1822
Le Paradis de Mahomet; ou, La Pluralité des femmes, with Mélesville, 1822
La Petite Folle, with Mélesville, 1822
Mémoires d'un colonel des hussards, with Mélesville, 1822
Le Bon Papa; ou, La Proposition de mariage, with Mélesville, 1822
L'Ecarté; ou, Un coin du salon, with Mélesville and Saint-George, 1822
La Rosière de Rosny, 1823
Une heure à Porte Sainte-Marie, 1823
La Maîtresse du logis, 1823
Partie et revanche, with Francis and Brazier, 1823
Trilby; ou, Le Lutin d'Argail, with Carmouche, 1823
L'Intérieur d'un bureau; ou, La Chanson, with Ymbert and Varner, 1823
Un dernier jour de fortune, with Dupaty, 1823
Rossini à Paris; ou, Le Grand Dîner, with Mazères, 1823
La Vérité dans le vin, with Mazères, 1823
La Loge du portier, with Mazères, 1823
La Neige; ou, Le Nouvel Eginard, with Delavigne, 1823
L'Avare en goguette, with Delavigne, 1823
La Pension bourgeoise, with Dupin and Dumersan, 1823
Le Marchand d'amour, with Dupin and Carmouche, 1823
Le Retour; ou, La Suite de Michel et Christine, with Dupin, 1823
Les Grisettes, with Dupin, 1823
Le Plan de campagne, with Dupin and Mélesville, 1823
Le Menteur véridique, with Mélesville, 1823; as *He "Lies like Truth,"* 1850
Rodolphe; ou, Frère et soeur, with Mélesville, 1823
Le Valet de chambre, with Mélesville, 1823
Valérie, with Mélesville, 1823
Leicester; ou, Le Château de Kenilworth, with Mélesville, 1823
Monsieur Tardif, with Mélesville, 1824
Le Dîner sur l'herbe, with Mélesville, 1824
Le Parlementaire, with Mélesville, 1824
Les Adieux au comptoir, with Mélesville, 1824
Léocadie, with Mélesville, 1824; as *Leocadia*, adapted by Cavillini, 1835
Coraly; ou, La Soeur et le frère, with Mélesville, 1824

Le Concert à la cour; ou, La Débutante, with Mélesville, 1824

La Mansarde des artistes, with Dupin and Varner, 1824

Le Bal champêtre; ou, Les Grisettes à la campagne, with Dupin, 1824

Les Trois gendres, with Pichat and Dupaty, 1824

Le Coiffeur et le perruquier, with Mazères and Saint-Laurent, 1824

Le Fondé de pouvoirs, with Carmouche, 1824

Le Leycester du faubourg; ou, L'Amour et l'ambition, with Carmouche, Henry, and Saintine, 1824

L'Héritière, with Delavigne, 1824

La Haine d'une femme; ou, Le Jeune Homme à marier, 1824

La Dame blanche (comic opera with music by Boieldieu), 1825

Les Premiers Amours; ou, Les Souvenirs d'enfance, 1825

Le Maçon, with Delavigne, 1825

Le Plus Beau Jour de la vie, with Varner, 1825

La Charge à payer; ou, La Mère intrigante, with Varner, 1825

Les Empiriques d'autrefois, with Alexandre, 1825

Le Mauvais Sujet, with Pillet, 1825

L'Artiste, with Perlet, 1825

Caroline, with Menissier, 1825

Le Charlatanisme, with Mazères, 1825

Vatel; ou, Le Petit-fils d'un grand homme, with Mazères, 1825

La Quarantaine, with Mazères, 1825

Les Inséparables, with Dupin, 1825

Les Manteaux, with Dupin and Varner, 1826

Fiorella, 1826

Le Mariage de raison, with Varner, 1826

La Belle-mère, with Bayard, 1826

L'Oncle d'Amérique, with Mazères, 1826

La Vieille, with Delavigne, 1826

Une visite à Bedlam, with Delestre-Poirson, 1826

Simple histoire, with de Courcy, 1826

Le Timide; ou, Le Nouveau Séducteur, with Saintine, 1826

La Lune de miel, with Mélesville and Carmouche, 1826

La Demoiselle à marier; ou, La Première Entrevue, with Mélesville, 1826

Le Confidant, with Mélesville, 1826

Le Médecin des dames, with Mélesville, 1826

L'Ambassadeur, with Mélesville, 1826

La Chatte métamorphosée en femme, with Mélesville, 1827; adapted as *The Woman That Was a Cat*, 1840

Les Elèves du conservatoire, with Saintine, 1827

Le Diplomate, with Delavigne, 1827

La Marraine, with Lockroy and Chabot, 1827

Le Loup-garou, with Mazères, 1827

Le Comte Ory (opera), with Delestre-Poirson, and music by Rossini, 1828; as *Il Conte Ory; The Count Ory*, 1829

Malvina; ou, Un mariage d'inclination, 1828

Le Mariage d'argent, 1828

La Muette de Portici (opera), with Delavigne, and music by Auber 1828; as *Mansaniello; or, The Dumb Girl of Portici*, 1850

Les Moralistes, with Varner, 1828

Le Château de la Poularde, with Varner and Dupin, 1828

Le Baron de Trenck, with Delavigne, 1828

Le Baiser au porteur, with de Courcy and Gensoul, 1828

La Manie des places; ou, La Folie du siècle, with Bayard, 1828

Yelva; ou, L'Orpheline russe, with Villeneuve and Desvergers, 1828

Avant, pendant et après: esquisses historiques, with Rougemont, 1828

Le Mal du pays; ou, La Batelière de Brienz, with Mélesville, 1828

Le Vieux Mari, with Mélesville, 1828

La Famille du baron, with Mélesville, 1829

La Bohémienne; ou, L'Amérique en 1775, with Mélesville, 1829

Louise; ou, La Réparation, with Mélesville and Bayard, 1829

Les Héritiers de Crac, with Dupin, 1829

Aventures et voyages du petit Jonas, with Dupin, 1829

Les Actionnaires, with Bayard, 1829

La Belle au bois dormant, with Aumer, 1829

Les Deux nuits, with Bouilly, 1829

Théobald; ou, Le Retour de la Russie, with Varner, 1829

Mme de Saint-Agnès, with Varner, 1829

La Fiancée (comic opera), with music by Auber, 1829

Chansons de Scribe, tirées de ses meilleures pièces, 1829

Manon Lescaut (ballet-pantomime), 1830; (opéra comique), 1856

Le Dieu et la Bayadère (opera-ballet), with music by Auber, 1830; *Programme of, and Songs …in the Maid of Cashmere…*, 1833

Les Inconsolables, 1830

La Cour d'assises, with Varner, 1830

Les Nouveaux Jeux de l'amour et du hasard, with Delavigne, 1830

Zoé; ou, L'Amant prêté, with Mélesville, 1830

Une faute, with Mélesville and Bayard, 1830

Philippe, with Mélesville and Bayard, 1830

Jeune et vieille; ou, Le Premier et le Dernier Chapitre, with Mélesville and Bayard, 1830

Le Foyer du Gymnase, with Mélesville and Bayard, 1830

La Seconde Année; ou, A qui la faute?, with Mélesville, 1830

Le Soprano, with Mélesville, 1831

Le Luthier de Lisbonne, with Bayard, 1831

Le Budget d'un jeune ménage with Bayard, 1831

Le Comte de Saint-Ronan; ou, L'Ecole et le château, with Dupin, 1831

L'Orgie, with Corali, 1831

Robert-le-Diable (opera), with Delavigne, and music by Meyerbeer, 1831; *Robert-le-Diable* (in English), 1832

La Marquise de Brinvilliers, with Castil-Blaze, 1831

Le Quaker et la danseuse, with Duport, 1831

Les Trois maîtresses, with Bayard, 1831

Le Suisse de l'hôtel, with Rougement, 1831

Le Philtre (opera), with music by Auber, 1831; as *Songs…* in the New Comic Opera, Called the Love Charm; or, The Village Coquette, 1831

La Famille Riquebourg; ou, Le Mariage mal assorti, 1831

La Favorite, with Royer and Vaëz, and music by Donizetti, 1831

Schahababam II; ou, Les Caprices d'un autocrate, with Saintine, 1832

L'Apollon du réverbère; ou, Les Conjectures de carrefour, with Saintine and Mélesville, 1832

Le Serment, with Mélesville, 1832

Le Moulin de Javelle, with Mélesville, 1832; as *The Regent*, 1834

La Médecine sans médecin, with Bayard, 1832

Dix ans de la vie d'une femme; ou, Les Mauvais Conseils, with Terrier, 1832

Le Savant, with Monvel, 1832

La Vengeance italienne; ou, Les Français à Florence, with Delestre-Poirson and Desnoyer, 1832

Une monomanie, with Duport, 1832

Le Chaperon, with Duport, 1832

Toujours; ou, L'Avenir d'un fils, with Varner, 1832

La Grande Aventure, with Varner, 1832

La Prison d'Edimbourg, with Planard, 1833

Dugazon; ou, Le Choix d'une maîtresse, with Duport, 1833

Un trait de Paul I; ou, Le Czar et la vivandière, with Duport, 1833

Camilla; ou, La Soeur et le frère, with Bayard, 1833

Le Gardien, with Bayard, 1833

Les Malheurs d'un amant heureux; ou, Le Nouvel Homme à bonnes fortunes, 1833

Gustave III; ou, Le Bal masqué (opera), with music by Auber, 1833; as *Gustavus the Third; or, The Masked Ball*, adapted by J.R. Planché and arranged for the English stage by T. Cooke, 1833

Bertrand et Raton; ou, L'Art de conspirer, 1833; as *The School for Politicians; or, Non-Committal*, 1840

Les Vieux Péchés, with Mélesville and Dumanoir, 1833

Ali-Baba; ou, Les Quarante voleurs, with Mélesville, 1833

Le Chalet (comic opera), with Mélesville, and music by A. Adam, 1834; as *Betly: An Opera*, 1838

Salvoisy; ou, L'Amoureux de la reine, with Rougemont and Comberousse, 1834; as *The Queen's Champion*, 1886

La Chanoinesse, with Cornu, 1834

La Frontière de Savoie, with Bayard, 1834; as *A Peculiar Position*, adapted by J.R. Planché, 1837

L'Ambitieux, 1834

La Passion secrète, 1834

Le Fils du prince, 1834

Lestocq; ou, L'Intrigue de l'amour, 1834

Estelle; ou, Le Père et la fille, 1834

La Juive (opera), with music by Halévy, 1835; as *The Jewess*, adapted by J.R. Planché, 1835; as *The Jewess*... Libretto, by Henri Drayton, 1854

Le Cheval de bronze, 1835; as *Songs, Duets, Trios, Choruses etc*... in the... Opera of The Bronze Horse, adapted by A. Bunn, 1836

Le Portefaix, 1835

Une chaumière et son coeur, with Chavannes, 1835

Etre aimé, ou mourir, with Dumanoir, 1835

La Pensionnaire mariée, with Varner, 1835

Le Fils d'un agent de change, with Dupin, 1836

Sir Hugues de Guilfort, with Bayard, 1836

Le Mauvais Oeil, with Lemoine, 1836

Marie Seymour; ou, Le Dévouement filial, with Mélesville, 1836

Valentine, with Mélesville, 1836

Les Huguenots (opera), with music by Meyerbeer, 1836; as *The Huguenots*, n.d.

Actéon, 1836

Les Chaperons blancs, 1836

Fra Diavolo; ou, L'Hôtellerie de Terracine (comic opera), with music by Auber, 1836; as *Fra Diavolo: A Comic Opera*, 1854

Chut!, 1836

La Camaraderie; ou, La Courte Echelle, 1837

Le Remplaçant, 1837

Le Domino noir (comic opera), with music by Auber, 1837; as *The Black Domino; or, A Night's Adventure*, 1837

L'Ambassadrice, with Saint-Georges, 1837

Les Dames patronesses; ou, A quelque chose malheur est bon, with Arvers, 1837

Avis aux coquettes; ou, L'Amant singulier, with Comberousse, 1837

César; ou, Le Chien du château, with Varner, 1837; as *Caesar: The Watchdog of the Castle*, 1886

L'Etudiant et la grande dame, with Mélesville, 1837

Clermont; ou, Une femme d'artiste, with Vanderburgh, 1838

Guido et Ginevra; ou, La Peste de Florence, 1838

La Figurante; ou, L'Amour et la danse, with Dupin, 1838

Le Fidèle Berger, with Saint-Georges, 1838

Les Indépendants, 1838

Marguerite, 1838

Les Treize, with Duport, 1839

Région; ou, Deux nuits, 1839

La Reine d'un jour, with Saint-Georges, 1839; as *Songs, Duets*... Choruses etc in the ...Opera of A Queen for a Day, adapted and arranged for the English stage by J.T. Haines, 1841

Le Sherif, 1839

La Xacarilla, 1839

Le Lac des fées (opera), with Mélesville, and music by Auber, 1839

La Calomnie, 1840

Carlo Broschi, 1840

Le Drapier, 1840

La Grand-mère; ou, Les Trois amours, 1840

Les Martyres, 1840; as *I Martiri, The Martyrs*, 1852

Le Verre d'eau; ou, Les Effets et les causes, 1840; as *A Glass of Water*, adapted by W.E. Suter, 1850

L'Opéra à la cour, with Saint-Georges, 1840

Zanette; ou, Jouer avec le feu, with Saint-Georges, 1840

Japhet; ou, La Recherche d'un père, with Vanderburgh, 1840

Les Diamants de la couronne (comic opera), with Saint-Georges, and music by Auber, 1841; as *The Crown Diamonds*, 1844

La Main de fer; ou, Un mariage secret, with de Leuven, 1841

Carmagnola, 1841

Une chaîne, 1841; as *In Honour Bound*, 1885

Cecily; ou, Le Lion amoureux, 1841

Le Veau d'or, with Dupin, 1841

Le Guiterrero, 1841

Le Duc d'Olonne, with Saintine, 1842

Oscar; ou, Le Mari qui trompe sa femme, with Duveyrier, 1842

Le Code noir, 1842

Le Diable à l'école, 1842

Le Fils de Cromwell; ou, Une restauration, 1842

Don Sébastien, roi de Portugal, 1843; as *Don Sebastiano: A Tragic Opera*, 1860

La Part du diable, 1843; as *Asmodeus, the Little Demon; or, The -----'s Share*, adapted by T. Archer, 1850

Lambert Simnel, with Mélesville, 1843

Le Puits d'amour, with de Leuven, 1843

Cagliostro, with Saint-Georges, 1844

La Tutrice; ou, L'Emploi des riches, with Duport, 1844

Babiole et Jablot, with Saintine, 1844

Les Surprises, 1844

La Sirène (comic opera), with music by Auber, 1844; as *The Syren*, adapted by G.S. Soane, 1849

Rebecca, 1845

La Barcarolle; ou, L'Amour et la musique, 1845

L'Image, with Sauvage, 1845

La Charbonnière, with Mélesville, 1846

La Loi salique, 1846

Geneviève; ou, La Jalousie paternelle, 1846

La Protégée sans le savoir, 1847

Daranda; ou, Les Grandes Passions, 1847

Une femme qui se jette par la fenêtre, with Lemoine, 1847

Irène; ou, Le Magnétisme, with Lockroy, 1847

Maître Jean; ou, La Comédie à la cour, with Dupin, 1847

Ne touchez pas à la reine, with Vaëz, 1847

Jeanne et Jeanneton, with Varner, 1848

O amitié!; ou, Les Trois époques, with Varner, 1848

Haydée; ou, Le Secret (comic opera), with music by Auber, 1848; as *Haydee; or, The Secret*, translated and adapted by G. Soane, 1848

Jeanne la folle, 1848

Le Prophète (opera), with music by Meyerbeer, 1849; as *The Opera of "The Prophet,"* 1850

Les Filles du docteur; ou, Le Dévouement, with Masson, 1849

La Fée aux roses, with Saint-Georges, 1849

Adrienne Lecouvreur, with Legouvé, 1849; as *Adrienne Lecouvreur*, adapted by H. Herman, 1883

Les Contes de la reine de Navarre; ou, La Revanche de Pavie, with Legouvé, 1850

Héloïse et Abailard; ou, A quelque chose malheur est bon, with Masson, 1850

La Chanteuse voilée, with de Leuven, 1850

L'Enfant prodigue, 1850; as *Il Prodigo, The Prodigal*, 1851

Giralda; ou, La Nouvelle Psyché, 1850; as *Giralda; or, Which Is My Husband?*, adapted by Mrs Davidson, 1850; as *Giralda; or, The Invisible Husband*, adapted by H. Welstead, 1850

La Dame de pique, 1851; as *The Queen of Spades*, adapted by Dion Boucicault, n.d.

Mosquita la sorcière, with Vaëz, 1851

Bataille des dames; ou, Un duel d'amour, with Legouvé, 1851; as *The Ladies' Battle*, 1850

Zerline; ou, La Corbeille d'oranges, 1851; as *Zerlina*, 1851

Les Mystères d'Udolphe, with Delavigne, 1852

Le Juif errant, with Saint-Georges, 1852

Le Nabab, with Saint-Georges, 1853

Marco Spada, 1853; as *Marco Spada*, adapted by J.P. Simpson, 1850

L'Etoile du nord, with music by Meyerbeer, 1854; as *The Star of the North*, 1855

Mon étoile (prose comedy), 1854

La Fiancée du diable, with Romand, 1854

La Nonne sanglante (opera), with Delavigne, and music by Gounod, 1854

Les Vêpres siciliennes, with Duveyrier, 1855

Jenny Bell, 1855

La Czarine, 1855

Manon Lescaut, 1856

Broskovano, with Boisseaux, 1858

Les Doigts de fée, with Legouvé, 1858; as *The World of Fashion*, 1860

Feu Lionel; ou, Qui vivra verra, with Potron, 1858

Les Trois Maupin; ou, La Veille de la régence, with Boisseaux, 1858

Les Trois Nicolas, with Lopez and de Lurien, 1859

Rêves d'amour, with Biéville, 1859

Yvonne, 1860

La Fille de trente ans, with Najac, 1860

La Frileuse, 1861

La Circassienne, 1861

La Fiancée du roi de Garbe, with Saint- Georges, 1864

L'Africaine, 1865; as *L'Africaine* (in English), 1866

Other

La Maîtresse anonyme (novel), 1840

Proverbes et nouvelles, 1840

Maurice (novel), 1845

Piquillo Alliaga; ou, Les Maures sous Philippe III (novel), II vols., 1847; as *The Victim of the Jesuits; or, Piquillo Alliaga: A Romance*, 3 vols., 1848

Nouvelles, 1856

Historiettes et Proverbes, 1856

Le Filleul d'Amadis; ou, Les Amours d'une fée, 3 vols., 1858

Les Yeux de ma tante (novel), 6 vols., 1859

Fleurette la bouquetière, 6 vols., 1861; as *Fleurette, after the French of E. Scribe*, 1886

Noélie, 4 vols., 1862

Critical study

Cole Arvin, N., *Eugène Scribe and the French theatre (1815–1860)*, 1924

————

SEMIOLOGY, SEMIOTICS

See under Structuralism.

————

————

SENANCOUR, Etienne Pivert de, 1770–1846.

Novelist.

LIFE

Etienne Senancour's literary reputation once came very near to eclipse, and is still uncertain. At its 19th-century peak it rested on the two famous "lundi" articles which Sainte-Beuve devoted to *Oberman* in 1832 and 1833, and on Sainte-Beuve's introduction to a second edition of the novel in 1833, which he had some difficulty in getting the author's permission to publish. Only in the second edition was the spelling "Obermann" adopted. Matthew Arnold was relying on Sainte-Beuve when he aroused British enthusiasm in his poems "Obermann" and "Obermann once more" of 1852 and 1867, and in his essay "Obermann," first printed in *The Academy* for 9 October 1869. None the less, by the middle of the 20th century, Senancour's name was being dropped from the canon of great French writers, omitted altogether from histories of French literature, or considered of interest only because of a common enough "rationalist-sentimental duality of temper." Senancour's *Oberman* "inevitably suffered from a comparison" with Chateaubriand's *René*.

However, many important critics have written appreciatively of the best-remembered work which featured the eccentric, destitute, and elderly recluse of the Rue de la Cérisaie with his pet monkey. These included Sainte-Beuve, Ballanche, and George Sand, who published an important article on Senancour in the *Revue des Deux Mondes* (*RDM*, q.v.) of 1833, and wrote a preface to her 1840 edition of its text. Other admirers included authors and critics as different as Senancour's close friend Nodier, Barbey d'Aurevilly, who underwent a momentary fascination, Vigny, of whose imaginative nourishment he was the chief source, Maurice de Guérin, Nerval, and Michelet, to say nothing of such non-authors as Delacroix and Liszt. Miguel de Unamuno thought Senancour "the most tragic of all thinkers, not excepting Pascal." Two very early works were discovered and published in the 1960s and at least three important critical studies have appeared since then. However, it was already clear that, whatever he may have shared with Chateaubriand, Constant, Fromentin, and the pre-romantic (q.v.) generation, Senancour was also acutely aware of the reasons for the imaginative interest in the world of dreams, and therefore at least partially the originator of an important current of imaginative literature which has been flowing ever since.

Brought up as an only child in a comfortable and fervently religious Paris household and educated at the Collège de la Marche, Senancour was expected to enter the Church. The family had aristocratic origins and was to be ruined by the Revolution, although Senancour was already in Switzerland. As an adolescent he fell in love with a school friend's sister, Félicité Marcotte, but ran away on 14 August 1789 rather than spend two years in a seminary, as his father had intended. His mother appears to have been fussy, and his father dour. In his teens Senancour was already a wide reader, forced by life at home to lose himself in dreams and to nourish him his imagination on Rousseau, Bernardin de Saint-Pierre, and the early Goethe. His flight to Switzerland, where he avoided the French-speaking towns of Geneva and Lausanne, culminated in what has been seen as a self-imposed initiation rite. After arriving at Saint-Maurice and losing his watch, perhaps remembering that Rousseau had notoriously thrown his away, Senancour dismissed his guide and climbed the Dents du Midi alone. He then tried to reach the Great St Bernard hospice (at 8,000 feet) and climb his way through to Italy. According to a narrative written by 1834 and inserted into the *Oberman* of 1840, Senancour flung himself into the glacial waters of the River Drance, knowing that it would either take him down to the village of Bourg-Saint-Pierre or kill him. A short-lived fever, long-term rheumatism, ultimate impotence, and a winter of nervous ailments at Saint-Maurice were the result of that escapade.

In Fribourg in September 1790 he married Marie-Françoise Daguet. Senancour wanted to live at Etroubles in the Aosta valley, apparently a "retraite profonde (far-away hiding place)," but in fact with good communications. His wife appears to have found it too isolated, so the couple returned to be near her family at Fribourg. They had two sons, one of whom died in infancy, and a daughter, Virginie, who later lived with Senancour in the Rue de la Cérisaie. The marriage was not a success. Senancour was poor, his in-laws were unfriendly, and his wife was unfaithful. In 1795 he inherited some money from his parents, which did not last him long, but he returned to Paris, where he met Félicité again, now Baroness Walckenaer. He lived with his son and daughter, and for a period he also looked after his wife's illegitimate child. Twice in September 1797 and once again in February 1798 Senancour wrote to the Directoire for support to lead a life as a solitary thinker. He outlined his broken marriage, his ruined nervous system, and his financial disasters, but got no response. In Paris he drifted, bored and disillusioned, suffering from spiritual depression and physical lassitude. He took drugs and for two years acted as tutor to the grandson of the Mme d'Houdetot with whom Rousseau had fallen in love.

Senancour lived mostly as a literary hack, writing articles for encyclopedias, undertaking critical and political journalism, and compiling popular history. He moved among a small circle of friends, including Nodier, but shunned fame, preferring solitary meditation and harmony with nature to human company. He suppressed his early works and tried to suppress *Oberman* too, refusing to publish its sequel and scattering reworked sections of the first part through *De l'amour*. The only creative work for which he showed real concern around 1830 was the *Rêveries sur la nature primitive de l'homme*, its title alluding to Rousseau, first published in 1799, but on which he was still working 30 years later. The book to which he finally paid most attention was the *Libres méditations d'un solitaire inconnu* of 1819, the reworked text of 1834 being Senancour's final testament. From 1833 until his death he was given a state pension.

Senancour's first two books, *Les Premiers âges: incertitudes humaines* and *Sur les générations actuelles: absurdités humaines*, were written in Switzerland in 1792 and 1793 respectively. They were signed "Rêveur des Alpes" and justify their pessimism by reference to a mythical primitive state of nature, although the language shows a fusion in Senancour's mind between the world's lost youth and the lack of any "véritable enfance (true childhood)" of his own. *Aldomen* of 1795, subtitled "le bonheur dans l'obscurité (happiness in obscurity)," now appears to be a first sketch for *Oberman*, and was followed by the 1799 version of the *Rêveries sur la nature primitive de l'homme*, augmented and rewritten in 1809, and again, simply as *Rêveries*, in 1833. There are four different versions of *De l'amour considéré dans les lois réelles et dans les formes sociales de l'union des deux sexes*: the first edition of 1806, and the three reworked versions of 1808, 1829, and 1834. The *Libres méditations d'un solitaire inconnu sur le détachement du monde et sur d'autres objets de la morale religieuse* was published in 1819, and in a reworked form in 1834.

The *Libres méditations* are more conciliatory towards Christianity than the earlier versions of the *Rêveries*, which look for guiding principles in man's own nature and in nature itself rather than in organized religion. There was a second epistolary novel, *Isabelle* of 1833. A manuscript of a work to be entitled "De la religion éternelle" was lost, but it is reasonable to suppose that his failed marriage, dreary Paris existence, and a certain lack of intellectual vigour, coupled with a quite early physical decline, diminished Senancour's enthusiasm for the imaginative exploration of man's harmony with a nature which was threatening as well as majestic, and that his imaginative daring subsided soon after *Oberman* and *De l'amour*.

WORKS

The first two books, signed by the "Rêveur des Alpes," start with the great metaphysical questions about the meaning of life, and go straight to the heart of the matter. If life has a meaning, is there a moral order? "J'ai la puissance d'agir, que dois-je faire? (I have the power to act. What ought I to do?)" The questions, at that date and in that form, come from Rousseau, but the answers do not. Like Rousseau, however, Senancour's reflection moves immediately to the nature of the constraints imposed by society on the individual's liberty. If nature can destroy, although when given the chance in the Alps, it did not, then society can enslave. In its full vigour Senancour's intellectual life was spent looking for ways to balance nature's menace against the therapeutic effects it exercised on the sensibility, and to weigh society's protection against its pressures to conform and its moral constraints. If only society could protect without constraining, there would be "un seul besoin social, un ami (only one social need, a friend)." Unfortunately, Senancour resigned himself to bafflement and the shoulder-shrugging despair it brought with it, and which Vigny would turn into the moral grandeur of stoicism. But in an appendix to the 1792 text Senancour speculates on the annihilation of the social order, "le néant de l'ordre social," and by 1804 he is quite clear, if by then unoriginal, about the primacy of feeling over reason.

In his *Rêveries* of 1799 Senancour is clearly inclined to believe that political tyranny and religious moral sanctions derive from the same source. In the first *Rêverie*, printed in capitals, is "TOUT EST NÉCESSAIRE (everything is necessary)." Birth, growth, maturity, and death are universal phenomena and man undergoes them, as do blades of grass. Senancour is very close to the hypothesis of an impersonal, eternal presence. He is reacting against the Christianity Chateaubriand was rediscovering in London, and only veers away from virtual atheism about 1810, after primeval necessity has yielded in his mind to the possibility of a cosmic harmony which postulates a designer. The *Rêveries* of 1799 are a series of speculations, tentative explorations of paths which turn into blind alleys. They do not represent a firm, coherent, or consistent philosophy, but merely a series of meditations about the non-viability of all the answers to all the important questions.

Senancour's views come from the late 18th-century deists or materialists, Helvétius, Diderot, and d'Holbach, and attribute to Spinoza and Locke philosophical doctrines which, at most, they merely toyed with. Senancour, however, trusts neither nature nor reason. Rousseau was the first to use the term "perfectibilité," which he italicized in the discourse on inequality, whereas by 1793 Senancour had already openly doubted the dogma of progress, envisaging "la dégénération de l'espèce (the degeneration of the species)." By 1833 the text of the *Rêveries* embraces the possibility that the natural sentiment leading us towards good "s'est formé dans l'enfance comme il semble survenir dans les songes (was formed in childhood and persists, it seems, in dreams)." This text is important both for the idea that we have suppressed natural aspirations to goodness, and for the consequent literary need to examine the world of dreams.

Oberman is a novel of fictionalized intellectual quest rather than of emotional self-discovery. It consists of 91 letters, frequently reflects on its hero's inner contradictions, suggesting, for instance, that Senancour himself respected the parents against whom he had rebelled. Of all the early 19th-century novels of introspection, it has been regarded as "the most impressive human document." The hero is fraught with awareness of all the questions and the absence of convincing answers to any of them: "Je ne vois pas du tout pourquoi partir, comme je ne vois pas bien pourquoi rester... La vie m'ennuie et m'amuse (I don't at all see why I should go, just as I don't see why I should stay... Life bores me and amuses me)." Oberman's bewilderment fascinates him, is the source of his desire for self-disclosure, and is the only thing impelling him onwards in his quest to discover truth. His aim is to discover what he is: "Je déterminerai ce que je suis (I shall find out what I am)." He is the object of his own observation, and in his pursuit of self-knowledge he examines his reactions to a whole variety of phenomena from the worlds of society and nature—capital punishment, suicide, the role of women, marriage, religion, the absence of religion, loneliness, fear, and others. Among the things Oberman reveals to himself is his capacity for self-deception.

Many of the letters are written among the mountain tops in "la paisible harmonie des choses (the peaceful harmony of everything)," in grandiose settings remote from other humans. None the less, Oberman remains aware of his dependence on people. The need for isolation in which to carry out his self-analysis undisturbed by the "sentiment indéfinissable de nos pertes (indefinable feeling of our losses)" led Senancour to claim that *Oberman* is not a novel. It has no dramatic movement, no events, and no denouement. In fact, the book is in a way unfinished. There is a Mme Del**, who is based on Félicité Marcotte, and her brother appears as Fonsalbe. The 1833 edition adds a new letter. In place of the earlier ending, "Elle que j'ai perdue... (She whom I have lost...)," Mme Del ** now comes back, leaving the ending again unresolved, with a reference to the secular flow of the eternal torrent, real and figurative: "Le torrent subsistait dans sa force, s'écoulant, mais s'écoulant toujours, à la manière des siècles (The torrent continued in its vigour, flowing, always flowing on, like the centuries)." The work does, of course, stand up without such formal structures as beginning, end, or defined plot. Its shapelessness gives the impression of uninhibited directness which Senancour wanted, and which he never achieved again to the same degree. Matthew Arnold was right to see in him "the least attitudinizing" of writers.

The greatness of *Oberman* derives from the way it turns a philosophical quest into a voyage of intimate self-discovery. It is a remarkably direct and moving account, admittedly based on a pre-romantic sensibility, of emotional involvement in a philosophical investigation undertaken in the light of emotional reactions to experiences, including those of nature at its grandest and most threatening, as well as abstract intellectual reflection. What Senancour added later, when his positions were modified, perhaps to remove the urgency from a quest he no longer felt able to sustain, was the need to examine the dream world which might point the way to a solution of some of the problems.

Senancour was to be almost necessarily preoccupied by the problem of love, the most intimate of personal feelings while also at the root of social bonds. *De l'amour* lyrically describes the awakening of love, the soul's expectation of pleasures of which as yet it knows nothing. But if love is "le mobile, l'erreur, la consolation de nos jours (the motive, the error, and the consolation of our days)," it is also "un voile sur le néant" (a veil drawn over nothingness). Almost as inevitably as he once wrote about love, Senancour turned in the end to Eastern mysticism as a solace if not a solution in his intellectual and emotional quest.

This seems to explain the importance he finally accorded to the *Libres méditations*. The final acceptance of an esoteric and intellectually impenetrable mystery without truths, myths, or allegories to which he appears to have been moving is at best a compensation for intellectual defeat, an attempt to keep some tenuous link with emotional vibrancy together with a rational anchor.

PUBLICATIONS

Works

Aldomen; ou, Le Bonheur dans l'obscurité, 1795
Rêveries sur la nature primitive de l'homme, 1799; revised edition, 1809, 1833
Oberman, 1804; revised edition, 1833, 1840; as *Oberman* (in English) 1903
De l'amour considéré dans les lois réelles et dans les formes sociales de l'union des deux sexes, 1806; revised edition, 1808, 1829, 1834
Observations critiques sur l'ouvrage intitulé "Génie du christianisme," 1816
Libres méditations d'un solitaire inconnu sur le détachement du monde et sur d'autres objets de la morale religieuse, 1819; revised edition, 1834
Résumé de l'histoire de la Chine, 1824
Résumé de l'histoire des traditions morales et religieuses, 1825
Petit vocabulaire de simple vérité, 1833
Isabelle, 1833
Sur les générations actuelles: absurdités humaines, 1963
Les Premiers âges: incertitudes humaines, 1968

Critical and biographical studies

Merlant, Jacques, *Senancour, sa vie, son oeuvre, son influence*, 1907
Raymond, Marcel, *Senancour: sensations et révélations*, 1965
Le Gall, B., *L'Imaginaire chez Senancour*, 1966
Senelier, Jean, *Hommage à Senancour: textes et lettres inédits; bibliographie des oeuvres*, 1971

———

SENGHOR, Léopold Sédar, 1906–

Poet and politician; president of Senegal, 1960–80.

LIFE

Léopold Sédar Senghor was born on 9 October 1906 in Joal, a town established by the Portuguese on the coast of Senegal, south of Dakar. His father, Basile Dyogoye (meaning "Lion"), was a member of the Serer tribe, the second-largest ethnic group in Senegal. He was a rich landowner and exported groundnuts to Bordeaux.

Although nominally a Catholic, Basile Dyogoye Senghor was polygamous, and Léopold Sédar was one of 24 children. The family lived in an elegant Portuguese-style house with separate wings for the father's wives. Léopold's mother, Nyilane Bakhoum, was an animist from a Fulani family, and until the age of seven Léopold was brought up in the animist tradition. He had a close relationship with his mother's brother Waly, who used to take him to pour libations on the graves of their ancestors.

In 1913 Senghor started school with Père Dubois at the Catholic mission in Joal. From 1914 to 1923 he went to the mission school in N'Gazobil run by the Pères du Saint-Esprit, where he learnt French and Woloff, the majority language of Senegal. His father hoped he would become a priest and sent him to Dakar in 1923, where the Pères du Saint-Esprit had a seminary, the Collège Liebermann.

At the seminary Senghor came up against the widespread Western assumption that Africa had no culture, and that civilization was a gift bestowed by colonialism. He objected so strongly to this view that Père Lalouse told him he was unsuited to the priesthood and should aim for a teaching career. Senghor duly transferred to the non-denominational school in Dakar to take the baccalauréat in Greek and Latin. He later wrote that Père Lalouse had crystallized his awareness of cultural identity: "Je lui dois non pas le mot de *négritude*... mais son idée: au sens des valeurs de civilisation du monde noir (What I owe to him is not exactly the word *negritude*... but the idea of it, in the sense of appreciating the value of black civilization)."

In 1928 Senghor was awarded a scholarship to study classics in Paris. The authorities normally supported students of science or technology and were only prepared to give a half-grant to an arts student. Senghor started studying for entrance to the Ecole Normale Supérieure at the Lycée Louis-le-Grand, where he became a close friend of Georges Pompidou: "C'est lui qui m'a converti au socialisme, qui m'a fait aimer Barrès, Proust, Gide, Baudelaire, Rimbaud, qui m'a donné le goût du théâtre et des musées. Et aussi le goût de Paris (He was the person who converted me to socialism, made me love Barrès, Proust, Gide, Baudelaire, Rimbaud, and appreciate the theatre and museums. And also appreciate Paris)."

Having failed to obtain a place at the Ecole, Senghor moved to a room in the Cité Universitaire and continued his classical studies at the Sorbonne, where he obtained his "licence" in 1931. He joined the Etudiants Socialistes and became a focal point, with Césaire and Damas, of a group of African and West Indian students who were determined to promote an understanding of black culture. They were encouraged by the example of black Americans in Paris who were asserting their distinctive culture at a time when most Francophone blacks still aspired to assimilation. The concept of negritude evolved in 1933–35 as a protest against political frustration:

L'horizon était bouché. Nulle réforme en perspective, et les colonisateurs légitimaient notre dépendance politique et économique par la théorie de *la table rase*. Nous n'avions, estimaient-ils, rien inventé, rien créé, rien écrit, ni sculpté, ni peint, ni chanté. Des danseurs! et encore... Pour asseoir une révolution efficace, *notre* révolution, il nous fallait d'abord nous débarasser de nos vêtements d'emprunt— ceux de l'assimilation—et affirmer notre être, c'est-à-dire notre *négritude*. Cependant, la Négritude, même définie comme "l'ensemble des valeurs culturelles de l'Afrique noire," ne pouvait nous offrir que le début de la solution de notre problème, non la solution elle-même.

(The horizon was blocked. There was no prospect of any reform, and the colonialists justified our political and economic dependence by the theory of the *tabula rasa*. According to them, we had invented nothing, created nothing, never written or sculpted or painted or sung anything. Dancers! for goodness' sake... To establish an effective revolution, our *own* revolution, we first had to cast off our borrowed clothes—the clothes of assimilation—and assert our being, which meant asserting our *negritude*. Yet negritude, even when defined as "all the cultural values of black Africa," could only provide us with the beginnings of a solution to our problem, not the solution itself.)

In 1934 Senghor co-founded *Etudiant Noir* with Aimé Césaire and Léon Gontran Damas.

In order to be eligible for the agrégation exam, Senghor had to become a naturalized French citizen in 1933. He was then liable for French military service and spent a year from October 1934 to October 1935 in the colonial infantry. In 1935 he became the first African ever to pass the Agrégation de Grammaire, and he was appointed to the Lycée Descartes in Tours, where he tought a "sixième" class from 1936 to 1938 and was active in the trade union movement, giving French lessons to union members. He studied African languages at the Institut d'Ethnologie in Paris and was beginning to publish poems in reviews.

In October 1938 Senghor was transferred to the Lycée Marcelin-Berthelot in Saint-Maur-des-Fossés, but he was called up in September 1939. After a break to recover from eye trouble he rejoined the colonial infantry in February 1940 and was taken prisoner in June at La Charité-sur-Loire. He spent the next 18 months in German prison camps. In 1941 the manuscript of his war poems, *Hosties noires*, was smuggled out of the camp and delivered to Georges Pompidou by an Austrian friend. The Germans released Senghor for health reasons in January 1942, and he was demobilized by the French authorities and able to resume his teaching post in Saint-Maur.

In November 1944 Senghor was appointed to the chair of black African languages and civilization at the Ecole Nationale de la France d'Outre-Mer. His first collection of poetry, *Chants d'ombre*, was published in 1945. His political career began in March 1945 when General de Gaulle appointed him to a committee studying the representation of the colonies in the future constituent assembly. That same year Senghor received a six-month scholarship to research the oral poetry of the Serer and Woloff languages with a view to writing a doctoral thesis. He returned to Senegal in August, and in November was elected to the constituent assembly as a socialist member for Senegal with Lamine Gueye. He served on the committee on the constitution and the committee for the overseas territories. A major achievement of the assembly was the Loi Lamine Gueye of 7 May 1946 giving French citizenship to all inhabitants of the colonies.

Senghor married for the first time in September 1946. He felt he had a moral duty to marry either an African or a West Indian, and his wife, Ginette Eboué, was the daughter of black Guyanese politicians, although she was born and educated in France. The Senghors had two sons, Francis and Guy, born in 1947 and 1948 respectively, but were divorced in 1955.

Hosties noires was published in 1948 and confirmed Senghor's reputation as a poet. That same year he founded the journal *Condition Humaine*, resigned from the Section Française de

l'Internationale Ouvrière, and founded the Bloc Démocratique Sénégalais, which amalgamated into the Bloc Populaire Sénégalais in 1956. He was regularly re-elected as deputy for Senegal and served in Edgar Faure's cabinet in 1955–56. Senghor married a white Frenchwoman, Colette Hubert, in 1957. Their son Philippe was born in 1958.

General de Gaulle announced a referendum in 1958 in which the Francophone African colonies had to decide between secession and federation. Senghor's newly formed Union Progressiste Sénégalaise ensured a "yes" vote in favour of federation for Senegal. The country was declared independent in August 1960, and Senghor was elected president on 5 September.

Having put down an attempted coup d'état by his prime minister, Mamadou Dia, in December 1962, Senghor was re-elected president in 1963, 1968, 1973, and 1978. He continued to publish poetry and political essays, and won numerous international awards, including the Médaille d'Or de la Langue Française in 1963, the Grand Prix International de la Poésie in 1970, and the Haile Selassie Prize in 1973. He organized the Festival des Arts Nègres in Dakar in 1966, and was involved in the OAU's Pan-African Festival in Algiers in 1969. He was elected a foreign associate member of the Académie des Sciences Morales et Politiques in 1969.

Senghor resigned voluntarily from the presidency on 31 December 1979, and was automatically succeeded by the prime minister, Abdou Diouf, on 1 January 1980. In 1983 he was the first black African ever elected to the Académie Française.

WORKS

Senghor's bi-cultural experience is fundamental to his poetry and his critical writing. The control and balance of his style reflects his classical education, but the themes and subjects of the poems come from his childhood in rural Africa. His first published collection, *Chants d'ombre*, contrasts the loneliness of a black expatriate's life in white European cities with the communal involvement of black African society. The poems in *Hosties noires*, written while Senghor was a prisoner of war, express his sorrow for the African soldiers he saw being sacrificed to the requirements of European policy. The influences of Claudel and Perse are clearly discernible in his lyric poetry.

The central figure in *Ethiopiques* is the legendary Chaka, who represents heroism, love, and the tragedy of Africa. This collection shows a tendency to incorporate linguistic devices from West African poetry into French, such as omitting connecting words and stringing together a series of nouns. In his postscript to *Ethiopiques* Senghor refers to the influence on his work of listening to the poetess Marône and translating traditional African poems into French.

In his prose writing Senghor was concerned with presenting the African way of life and the principle of negritude to French readers, and identifying a genuinely black African style in the works of contemporary writers. In *Négritude et humanisme* he defines black African culture as a system where religion, social structure, and art all result from a relationship between man and the universe. "La Négritude c'est, essentiellement, cette chaleur humaine, qui est *présence à la vie*: au monde. C'est un existentialisme... enraciné dans la Terre-Mère, épanoui au soleil de la Foi (Negritude is essentially that human warmth which means *presence in life*, in the world. It is a form of

her readers. A son, Johnny, was born to Denise in September 1949. In 1952 Simenon triumphantly returned to Le Havre on board the *Ile-de-France*, and travelled in Belgium and Italy. On 23 February 1953 his daughter Marie-Georges was born. Simenon received congratulatory letters from Henry Miller, T.S. Eliot, Martin du Gard, Jean-Louis Barrault, Marcel Pagnol, and Cocteau. In 1957 he moved to Switzerland, where his son Pierre was born on 5 May 1959. Further letters arrived from Daniel-Rops, Paul Morand, and Jean Anouilh, and friendships developed with Miller, Fellini, Bernard Buffet, Yves Montand, and Simone Signoret. By this time, however, Simenon's wife.had become an alcoholic.

The Georges Simenon library was opened at Liège in 1961, the year the author became a grandfather. Térésa, who was to become his companion, now entered his service. His marriage, which had begun to show signs of strain in 1955, was clearly in trouble by late 1962, but early in 1963 Denise underwent a cure. The family took a holiday in 1965, the year in which Simenon fell in his bathroom and broke several ribs. In 1967 the 72 volumes of the *Oeuvres complètes* began publication, and Simenon undertook a lecture tour of Italy. The following year he published his 200th novel since *Pietr-le-Letton*. His mother died in 1971, and in 1972 Simenon decided to give up writing. He was awarded an honorary degree by the University of Pavia and announced that he was selling his vast house, his furniture, and his paintings to found a Simenon archive at the Leningrad public library. In 1973 he broke his femur, but kept on writing, and in 1976 he established a Simenon archive at the University of Liège. His daughter committed suicide on 16 May 1978. A book written by his wife caused him annoyance, and she in turn had some passages suppressed in his *Mémoires intimes* of 1980. It was his last book. The first biography of Simenon appeared in 1983, in English by Fenton Bresler. The Association of Friends of Georges Simenon was founded in 1987. He died in 1989.

WORKS

It has proved possible to establish a central matrix to Simenon's novels, which he adapted by adding certain variables to individualize the plots. Leading on from this, it is possible to classify his novels into three categories, very roughly coinciding with chronological periods. It is clear that no one can write at Simenon's speed without consciously or unconsciously drawing on a repertoire of themes, relationships, motives, and plot mechanisms combined in different permutations. However, even at the level of pure entertainment, there is a difference between Simenon's novels and the best Anglo-Saxon examples of the genre. His detective stories do not fascinate the reader in the same way. They are not crosswords or parlour games which involve the reader in solving puzzles with the clues provided. Maigret works by intuition. He empathizes with his criminals, and first discovers not who or how, but why.

It need scarcely be said that the novels are skilfully narrated, but the psychological insights they provide are more important. The entertainment novels keep to fairly strict rules. They do not refer to contemporary or recent historical events, or discuss religion or metaphysics, and they exclude politics and war. In that sense alone they strive for timelessness. Simenon does not want to be externally anchored to a date or a controversy, although he is interested in individuals who, even if he does not refer to it,

must be affected by the events, arguments, and beliefs of the real world. The novels are narrated in chronological order of events, and they have stories or plots. They can be tragic or melodramatic, but they are never comic.

Simenon generally starts at or near the moment of crisis and then uses flashbacks to inform the reader how the situation arose. The situations in the detective novels are those indigenous to the genre—murders resulting from disputes about money, sibling rivalry, jealousy, and maintaining face in front of the world. The recurring Maigret, linking each book to the others in which he appears, increases the reader's pleasure. Part of the popularity of the Maigret novels derives from the way in which Simenon makes his hero connive with the reader's sympathies. The character is built up only slowly, even in physical appearance, and only slowly acquires a background and a past. We learn of his mother's death at his birth only in the 36th volume of *Les Mémoires de Maigret* of 1950.

Since Simenon's prodigious output, his life style, and his social sympathies have attracted attention, there have naturally been attempts to find psychological patterns in his work, and to analyse his work as a sociological phenomenon. From a literary point of view what is most important is probably the evocation of Paris during the first half of the century, although this is never the focus of interest. It is also possible to point to the vividness of character portrayal. Only Maigret of all the folk heroes came alive principally from the printed page. He initially existed without the aid of the visual material, unlike the films of Fantômas and the comic strips of Tintin and Astérix which relied on it.

The most important work for an understanding of the rest of the oeuvre, and especially of its cast of characters, is *Pedigree*, which concerns the Mamelin and Peters families. Elise Peters's father, a rich merchant, becomes an alcoholic and commits suicide. She herself, the last of 13 children, moves to Liège with her mother and works as a shop assistant until she marries Désiré Mamelin, who works for an insurance company. Désiré is educated, psychologically balanced, devout, and almost cultured. Simenon often uses musical metaphors to describe him. His family rejects Elise, who is clearly a fictionalized version of Simenon's mother, a petite bourgeoise, insecure socially and personally, dependent on the opinion of others, conformist, reactionary, and given to compensating by tyrannical behaviour towards her husband and son. She lacks self-confidence, and dislikes the rich, but is impressed by respectability and houses with servants. Simenon puts lots of silent replies into her mouth to make his point.

Elise scrapes to save money and becomes an habitual cheat, while Désiré has a heart condition and can do nothing to alleviate the family's economic situation. Their son Roger rebels against his mother's domination, and their relationship is changed by her strictness regarding his nascent desires for physical sex. Roger is sent to the Jesuits to catch up on his education, but finds himself surrounded by boys from better-off backgrounds who treat him with disdain. The affluent boys can talk to the Father Superior in the corridor while Roger, urged by his mother, undergoes punishment for a misdemeanour for which he feels no responsibility. He grows up affecting a bourgeois style which is recognizably faked, overcompensating in dress and extravagance, by indulgence in both low life and high life. He imports his sex life into the house, condemned to despise the petite bourgeoisie but to be looked down on by the rich. His father tries to help him, plays billiards with him, and offers him cigarettes, reproaching him only gently for his late hours and neglect of school work. He is the opposite of Elise's brother Léopold, Simenon's archetype of an anarchist. Eventually, when his father becomes ill and dies, Roger resolves matters by assuming the paternal role, completely toning down his formerly flamboyant and rebellious nature, and treating his mother almost as a daughter:

Roger est ému de la sentir frémissante à son bras, si petite fille en somme, si désarmée qu'il en devient un homme

(Roger was moved to feel her quivering on his arms, such a little girl, really, so helpless that it made him feel a grown man)

The importance of *Pedigree* lies in the link it provides between Simenon's own youthful experiences and the fictional world he later created. It is halfway between an autobiography and a novel, and shows the stems emerging which will eventually carry the whole spread of characters in his fiction. Almost all the serious non-detective novels have characters rooted in those of *Pedigree*. Simenon is extremely class-conscious and plays on the tiniest gradations of class which are so precisely defined within French society. Although critics have spoken of a vulgarized existentialism (q.v.) in Simenon, his characters normally lack lucidity. They do not recognize the forces which carry, elevate, or destroy them, and they seldom understand themselves. As a result, the social category of crime is emptied of the moral quality of guilt. Simenon's murderers do not choose evil, any more than Zola's, but their actions are more convincing because Simenon, unlike Zola, has no structured and explicit psychological theory of how behaviour is determined. His characters are not moved by striking ambitions or passions, but simply by instinct. Maigret, the father figure, is there to help the reader understand that.

Au bout du rouleau, published in 1947, has been seen as a paradigm novel. As a procurer Marcel Viau can belong neither to the underworld nor to the respectable well-to-do. He drifts into a small provincial town and tries one last time to adopt the behaviour patterns that will give him a social standing which he does not himself despise, and which others will respect. He ends up committing suicide.

In *L'Homme qui regardait passer les trains* Kees Popinga, a chess-playing accountant with a tranquil home life, meets his employer, Julius de Coster, in a sleazy bar. Partly out of condescension, Coster reveals that he himself is to be the subject of a fraud investigation the next day. Coster fakes his own suicide and goes off. Popinga feels suddenly more confident and, when he gets up next day, takes the sort of train he could never afford. In Amsterdam he strangles his employer's former mistress, Pamela, who had rejected his advances. Jeanne Rozier, a prostitute, helps him to hide in Paris, but Popinga suspects a trap, wounds Jeanne, who had also rejected him, and flees along a nearby railway line. The newspapers turn him into a monster, so he writes to them in an effort to show people that he is not as the media have depicted. The effort is unsuccessful. In the end, depressed by the police search, and having had his purse stolen, he decides to commit suicide, but in such a way as to render his corpse unrecognizable. A letter to the press suggests that, under another name, Kees Popinga has reached the summit of success. He ends up in a psychiatric hospital, unable to communicate any

longer across the artificial social chasm created by the press between ordered society and himself. Simenon is again playing on the theme of assumed and acceptable identities.

In *Les Pitard* Lannec Pitard and his wife Mathilde travel from Rouen to Reykjavik on the *Tonnerre de Dieu* to supervise the cargo which Lannec has been able to purchase only by borrowing from his rich mother-in-law. Mathilde irritates the crew, who bring some prostitutes on deck during a stopover. In protest Mathilde locks herself in her cabin, despite the discomforts of the voyage. She also reproaches her husband for exploiting her family so that he can join his mistress in the US. There is a storm and Lannec goes to the help of a boat in distress. Mathilde jumps into the water. Lannec the sailor, the male, and the worker triumphs over Mathilde, who is at home only on land, female, and bourgeoise. She has been unable either to break loose from her mother and her family, or to join Lannec's. Perhaps, if the journey had lasted a few more days, "Mathilde would have been capable of becoming a Lannec." Meanwhile, Lannec himself is torn between satisfaction at having saved the drowning sailors and sorrow at the loss of his wife.

The 1947 *Lettre à mon juge* is generally regarded as one of Simenon's masterpieces. On the death of his father, an alcoholic, womanizing farmer, Charles Alavoine, a doctor, has settled with his mother in the village of Ormois. His widowed mother quickly finds him a wife. He fishes, shoots, and has an occasional liaison with a patient. His wife dies giving birth to their second child. Two years later he goes to La Roche-sur-Yon, meets the wealthy widow Armande, and marries her. She comes to dominate the household. On a journey to Caen, Alavoine meets Martine Englebert, a young Belgian in trouble, whose lover he becomes and whom he introduces into his household. His wife surprises them together and, after a confrontation, Alavoine leaves with Martine for Issy-les-Moulineaux. His passion increases, and with it his jealousy. He cannot bear the thought of Martine's past, beats her as if to expiate it, and finally, imagining that she is encouraging him, strangles her. After his sentencing, Alavoine writes all this to the judge, Ernest Coméliau, in an attempt to make him understand. Comélian receives Alavoine's account on the day that his suicide is reported in the papers.

Society, as represented by the court, did not understand Alavoine, who had felt the need to communicate across a gulf of language and understanding which could not be bridged. Where *Lettre à mon juge* differs from the other novels is in Alavoine's consciousness that it is not possible to communicate successfully across two sets of social values. Simenon has created a social myth for 20th-century France. Alavoine is as dedicated a doctor as he would have been a priest, but his caste allows certain deviant patterns of behaviour, his liaisons, provided he does not move outside the limits of the social code which tolerates such minor infringements. Aware of her son's liaisons, his mother reacts according to the caste rules by hiring a maid. Alavoine perfectly understands why: "c'est à ma seule intention qu'elle s'est décidée un beau jour à prendre une bonne (it was purely for me that she decided one fine day to hire a maid)."

The myth has to do with the caste system. Here it not only probes the operations of a matriarchy within it, it also beautifully analyses the dominance of the second wife. She loves with an "indulgent severity." She, too, then, is part matriarch: "I've never been her husband, let alone her lover. I was someone she took charge of, was responsible for, and over whom she felt she had rights." Rather obviously perhaps, everything fits in. They now live not in a village or a metropolis but in the sort of small town to which Armande naturally belongs. She has travelled. Her social role is in complete harmony with her personality, with just enough touch of class to break the strict rules governing middle-class behaviour.

Alavoine suddenly feels ashamed of the furniture. Armande sees it as her first duty to make him lose weight. She behaves exactly like a doctor's wife, careful of his comfort, health, and reputation. She takes charge of the household finances, the social relationships, the care of the house, "our" patients: "Pendant dix minutes, elle me parla de la dipthérie comme j'aurais été incapable de le faire (For ten minutes she spoke to me about diptheria in a way I could not have done myself)." Simenon is conscious of his readership. He instinctively makes his myth clear enough for its power to be felt by those who have not read Freud, to whom he himself had come rather late. It is clearly unlikely that Armande accorded sexual favours to compensate Alavoine for the new matriarchy.

Alavoine tries desperately to observe the caste rules. He keeps up appearances, visits his patients, puts Martine under the supervision of his mother and Armande, and is torn between his two roles of master in league with Armande and his mother, and of lover rebelling against their domination. When he leaves, everything is accomplished according to the rules. He leaves the car to his family, and enough money, keeping enough for himself to open a practice near, but not within, Paris. If he cannot reconcile his two lives, his two sets of values, he blames Martine:

> J'ai tout vomi, tout ce que j'avais sur le coeur, toutes mes humiliations, mes lâchetés, mes désirs rentrés, j'en ai rajouté, et tout cela, je te l'ai jeté sur le dos, à toi seule, comme si tu étais seule à devoir en porter désormais la responsabilité

> (I've brought everything up, everything I had on my mind, all my humiliations, my cowardices, my frustrated desires, and more still, and I've thrown all that on your back, as if you alone had to carry the responsibility for it in future)

Martine is conditioned by her social background and her misfortunes to accept the blame and expiate it. The caste system of bourgeois provincial life has no place for her, and her self-confidence is finally annihilated when it spews her out.

Obviously Simenon is not writing for the readers of Camus's L'Etranger, who can assimilate a more powerful, because more subtly expressed, myth, and cope with its ambiguities. But Simenon's mythologization of the caste structure of middle-class French society is perceptive, powerful, and quite unambiguous. The mythical tentacles extend much further and in all sorts of directions, particularly in attitudes to death and in the father–son relationship, and its effect on the sexual attitudes of the son. The novels of literary power, which are those in which the mythologization is firmest, are generally thought to include La Neige était sale and Les Anneaux de Bicêtre, where the action links perennially recurring psychological situations to specifically French local colour and social stratification. The reason for taking a serious interest in Simenon as a literary figure, which his skill as a writer of entertainment fiction has come near to denying him, is the potency of the mythological structure he gives to the French caste system, encoding it in such a way as to make its psychological coordinates clear. The main structure of

the normally concealed myth is brought into the open by the male attempt to conquer the maturity which Lannec and Alavoine conspicuously fail to achieve.

PUBLICATIONS

Collections

Oeuvres complètes, edited by Gilbert Sigaux, 72 vols., 1967–75

Fiction

Etoile de cinéma (as Georges d'Isly), 1925
Voluptueuses étreintes (as Plick et Plock), 1925
Le Chéri de Tantine (as Plick et Plock), 1925
Bobette et ses satyres (as Bobette), 1928
Un petit poison (as Kim), 1928
Hélas! Je t'aime… (as Germain d'Antibes), 1929
Des deux maîtresses (as Jean Dossage), 1929
Trop belle pour elle! (as G. Violis), 1929
Pietr-le-Letton, 1931; as *The Strange Case of Peter the Lett*, 1933; as *The Case of Peter the Lett*, in *Inspector Maigret Investigates*, 1934
Au rendez-vous des Terre-Neuves, 1931; as *The Sailor's Rendezvous*, in *Maigret Keeps a Rendezvous*, 1940
Le Charretier de "La Providence," 1931; as *The Crime at Lock 14*, with *The Shadow on the Courtyard*, 1934; in *The Triumph of Inspector Maigret*, 1934; as *Maigret Meets a Milord*, 1963
Le Chien jaune, 1931; as *A Face for a Clue*, in *The Patience of Maigret*, 1939
La Danseuse du Gai-Moulin, 1931; as *At the Gai-Moulin*, in *Maigret Abroad*, 1940; with *A Battle of Nerves*, 1951
M. Gallet décédé, 1931; as *The Death of Monsieur Gallet*, 1932; in *Introducing Inspector Maigret*, 1933; as *Maigret Stonewalled*, 1963
La Nuit du carrefour, 1931; as *The Crossroad Murders*, in *Inspector Maigret Investigates*, 1934; as *Maigret at the Crossroads*, 1963
Le Pendu de Saint-Pholien, 1931; as *The Crime of Inspector Maigret*, 1933; in *Introducing Inspector Maigret*, 1933; as *Maigret and the Hundred Gibbets*, 1963
Un crime en Hollande, 1931; as *A Crime in Holland*, in *Maigret Abroad*, 1940; with *A Face for a Clue*, 1952
La Tête d'un homme, 1931; as *L'Homme de la Tour Eiffel*, 1950; as *A Battle of Nerves*, in *The Patience of Maigret*, 1939
Le Relais d'Alsace, 1931; as *The Man from Everywhere*, in *Maigret and M. L'Abbé*, 1941
L'Affaire Saint-Fiacre, 1932; as *The Saint-Fiacre Affair*, in *Maigret Keeps a Rendezvous*, 1940; as *Maigret Goes Home*, 1967
Chez les Flamands, 1932; as *The Flemish Shop*, in *Maigret to the Rescue*, 1940
Le Fou de Bergerac, 1932; as *The Madman of Bergerac*, in *Maigret Travels South*, 1940
La Guinguette à deux sous, 1932; as *Guinguette by the Seine*, in *Maigret to the Rescue*, 1940
Liberty Bar, 1932; as *Liberty Bar*, in *Maigret Travels South*, 1940
L'Ombre chinoise, 1932; as *The Shadow in the Courtyard*, with *The Crime at Lock 14*, 1934; in *The Triumph of Inspector Maigret*, 1934; as *Maigret Mystified*, 1965

Le Port des brumes, 1932; as *Death of a Harbor Master*, in *Maigret and M. L'Abbé*, 1941

Le Passageur du "Polarlys," 1932; as *The Mystery of the Polarlys*, in *In Two Latitudes*, 1942; as *Danger at Sea*, in *On Land and Sea*, 1954

Les Treize mystères, 1932

Les Treize enigmes, 1932

Les Treize coupables, 1932

L'Ecluse no. 1, 1933; as *The Lock at Charenton*, in *Maigret Sits It Out*, 1941

L'Ane rouge, 1933; as *The Night-Club*, 1979

Le Coup de lune, 1933; as *Tropic Moon*, in *In Two Latitudes*, 1942

Les Fiançailles de Mr. Hire, 1933; as *Mr. Hire's Engagement*, in *The Sacrifice*, 1958

Les Gens d'en face, 1933; as *The Window over the Way*, with *The Gendarme's Report*, 1951; as *Danger Ashore*, in *On Land and Sea*, 1954

Le Haut Mal, 1933; as *The Woman in the Grey House*, in *Affairs of Destiny*, 1942

La Maison du canal, 1933; as *The House by the Canal*, with *The Ostenders*, 1952

L'Homme de Londres, 1934; as *Newhaven-Dieppe*, in *Affairs of Destiny*, 1942

Maigret, 1934; as *Maigret Returns*, in *Maigret Sits It Out*, 1941

Les Suicidés, 1934; as *One Way Out*, in *Escape in Vain*, 1943

Le Locataire, 1934; as *The Lodger*, in *Escape in Vain*, 1943

Les Clients d'Avrenos, 1935

Les Pitard, 1935; as *A Wife at Sea*, with *The Murderer*, 1949

Quartier nègre, 1935

Les Demoiselles de Concarneau, 1936; as *The Breton Sisters*, in *Havoc by Accident*, 1943

L'Evadé, 1936; as *The Disintegration of J.P.G.*, 1937

Long cours, 1936; as *The Long Exile*, 1982

45° à l'ombre, 1936

L'Assassin, 1937; as *The Murderer*, with *A Wife at Sea*, 1949

Le Blanc à lunettes, 1937; as *Tatala*, in *Havoc by Accident*, 1943

Faubourg, 1937; as *Home Town*, in *On the Danger Line*, 1944

Le Testament Donadieu, 1937; as *The Shadow Falls*, 1945

Les Sept Minutes, 1938

Ceux de la soif, 1938

Chemin sans issue, 1938; as *Blind Alley*, 1946; in *Lost Moorings*, 1946

Le Cheval blanc, 1938

L'Homme qui regardait passer les trains, 1938; as *The Man Who Watched the Trains Go By*, 1942

La Marie du port, 1938; as *A Chit of a Girl*, with *Justice*, 1949; as *The Girl in Waiting*, with *Justice*, 1957

Monsieur La Souris, 1938; as *Monsieur La Souris*, with *Poisoned Relations*, 1950; as *The Mouse*, 1966

Les Rescapés du Télémaque, 1938; as *The Survivors*, with *Black Rain*, 1949

Les Soeurs Lacroix, 1938; as *Poisoned Relations*, with *Monsieur La Souris*, 1950

Le Suspect, 1938; as *The Green Thermos*, in *On the Danger Line*, 1944

Touriste de bananes, 1938; as *Banana Tourist*, in *Lost Moorings*, 1946

Le Bourgmestre de Furnes, 1939; as *The Bourgomaster of Furnes*, 1952

Chez Krull, 1939; as *Chez Krull*, in *A Sense of Guilt*, 1955

Les Inconnus dans la maison, 1940; as *Stranger in the House*, 1951

Malempin, 1940; as *The Family Lie*, 1978

Bergelon, 1941

Cour d'assises, 1941; as *Justice*, with *A Chit of a Girl*, 1949

Il pleut bergère, 1941; as *Black Rain*, 1947; with *The Survivors*, 1949

La Maison des sept jeunes filles, 1941

L'Outlaw, 1941

Le Voyageur de la Toussaint, 1941; as *Strange Inheritance*, 1950

Le Fils Cardinaud, 1942; as *Young Cardinaud*, in *The Sacrifice*, 1956

Oncle Charles s'est enfermé, 1942

La Vérité sur Bébé Donge, 1942; as *The Trial of Bébé Donge*, 1952; as *I Take This Woman*, in *Satan's Children*, 1953

La Veuve Couderc, 1942; as *Ticket of Leave*, 1954; as *The Widow*, with *Magician*, 1955

Maigret revient, 1942; translated in part as *Maigret and the Spinster*, 1977; as *Maigret and the Hotel Majestic*, 1977

Le Petit Docteur, 1943; as *The Little Doctor*, 1978

Les Nouvelles Enquêtes de Maigret, 1944

Le Rapport du gendarme, 1944; as *The Gendarme's Report*, with *The Window over the Way*, 1951

Signe Picpus, 1944; as *To Any Lengths*, 1958

Les Dossiers de l'Agence O, 1945

L'Aîné des Ferchaux, 1945; as *Magnet of Doom*, 1948; as *The First Born*, 1949

La Fenêtre des Rouet, 1945; as *Across the Street*, 1954

La Fuite de M. Monde, 1945; as *Monsieur Monde Vanishes*, 1967

Le Cercle des Mahé, 1946

Les Noces de Poitiers, 1946

Lettre à mon juge, 1946; as *Act of Passion*, 1952

Trois chambres à Manhattan, 1947; as *Three Beds in Manhattan*, 1964

Au bout du rouleau, 1947

Le Clan des Ostendais, 1947; as *The Ostenders*, with *The House by the Canal*, 1952

Le Passager clandestin, 1947; as *The Stowaway*, 1957

Maigret et l'inspecteur malchanceux, 1947

Maigret à New York, 1947; as *Maigret in New York's Underworld*, 1956

Maigret se fâche, suivi de La Pipe de Maigret, 1948

Maigret et son mort, 1948; as *Maigret's Dead Man*, 1964; as *Maigret's Special Murder*, 1964

Les Vacances de Maigret, 1948; as *Maigret on Holiday*, 1950; as *No Vacation for Maigret*, 1953

Le Bilan Maletras, 1948

Le Destin des Malou, 1948; as *The Fate of the Malous*, 1948

La Jument perdue, 1948

La Neige était sale, 1948; as *The Snow Was Black*, 1950; as *The Stain on the Snow*, 1953

Pedigree, 1948; as *Pedigree*, 1962

Maigret chez le coroner, 1949; as *Maigret and the Coroner*, 1980

Maigret et la vieille dame, 1949; as *Maigret and the Old Lady*, 1958; in *Maigret Cinq*, 1965

Mon ami Maigret, 1949; as *My Friend Maigret*, in *The Methods of Maigret*, 1957

La Première Enquête de Maigret, 1913, 1949; as *Maigret's First Case*, 1965; in *Maigret Cinq*, 1965

Les Fantômes du chapelier, 1949; as *The Hatter's Ghost*, in *The Judge and the Hatter*, 1956; as *The Hatter's Phantom*, 1976

Le Fond de la bouteille, 1949; as *The Bottom of the Bottle*, in *Tidal Wave*, 1954

Les Quatre jours du pauvre homme, 1949; as *Four Days in a Lifetime*, in *Satan's Children*, 1953

L'Amie de Mme. Maigret, 1950; as *Madame Maigret's Own Case*, 1959; as *Madame Maigret's Friend*, 1960

Les Petits Cochons sans queues, 1950

L'Enterrement de Monsieur Bouvet, 1950; as *The Burial of Monsieur Bouvet*, in *Destinations*, 1955; as *Inquest on Bouvet*, 1958

Les Volets verts, 1950; as *The Heart of a Man*, 1951; in *A Sense of Guilt*, 1955

Un nouveau dans la ville, 1951

Tante Jeanne, 1951; as *Aunt Jeanne*, 1953

Le Temps d'Anaïs, 1951; as *The Girl in His Past*, 1952

Une vie comme neuve, 1951; as *A New Lease on Life*, 1963

Un Noël de Maigret, 1951; as *Maigret's Christmas*, 1976

Maigret au Picratt's, 1951; as *Maigret in Montmartre*, in *Maigret Right and Wrong*, 1954; as *Inspector Maigret and the Strangled Stripper*, 1956

Maigret en meuble, 1951; as *Maigret Takes a Room*, 1960; as *Maigret Rents a Room*, 1961

Maigret et la grande perche, 1951; as *Maigret and the Burglar's Wife*, 1955

Les Mémoires de Maigret, 1951; as *Maigret's Memories*, 1963

Maigret, Lognon, et les gangsters, 1952; as *Maigret and the Killers*, 1954; as *Maigret and the Gangsters*, 1974

Le Revolver de Maigret, 1952; as *Maigret's Revolver*, 1956

Marie qui louche, 1952; as *The Girl with a Squint*, 1978

Les Frères Rico, 1952; as *The Brothers Rico*, in *Tidal Wave*, 1954; in *Violent Ends*, 1954

La Mort de Belle, 1952; as *Belle*, in *Tidal Wave*, 1954; in *Violent Ends*, 1954

Antoine et Julie, 1953; as *Magician*, with *The Widow*, 1955; as *The Magician*, 1974

L'Escalier de fer, 1953; as *The Iron Staircase*, 1963

Feux rouges, 1953; as *The Hitchhiker*, in *Destinations*, 1955; as *Red Lights*, in *Danger Ahead*, 1955

Maigret et l'homme du banc, 1953; as *Maigret and the Man on the Bench*, 1975; as *Maigret and the Man on the Boulevard*, 1975

Maigret a peur, 1953; as *Maigret Afraid*, 1961

Maigret se trompe, 1953; as *Maigret's Mistake*, in *Maigret Right and Wrong*, 1957; in *Five Times Maigret*, 1964

Le Bateau d'Emile, 1954

Maigret à l'école, 1954; as *Maigret Goes to School*, Hamilton, 1957; in *Five Times Maigret*, 1964

Maigret et la jeune morte, 1954; as *Maigret and the Young Girl*, 1955; as *Inspector Maigret and the Dead Girl*, 1955

Crime impuni, 1954; as *Fugitive*, 1955; as *Account Unsettled*, 1962

Le Grand Bob, 1954; as *Big Bob*, 1969

L'Horloger d'Everton, 1954; as *The Watchmaker of Everton*, in *Danger Ahead*, 1955; with *Witnesses*, 1956

Les Témoins, 1955; as *Witnesses*, with *The Watchmaker of Everton*, 1956; in *The Judge and the Hatter*, 1956

La Boule noire, 1955

Maigret tend un piège, 1955; as *Maigret Sets a Trap*, 1965

Maigret chez le ministre, 1955; as *Maigret and the Calame Report*, 1969; as *Maigret and the Minister*, 1969

Maigret et le corps sans tête, 1955; as *Maigret and the Headless Corpse*, 1967

Les Complices, 1956; as *The Accomplices*, with *The Blue Room*, 1964

En case de malheur, 1956; as *In Case of Emergency*, 1958

Le Petit Homme d'Arkhangelsk, 1956; as *The Little Man from Arkangel*, 1957; with *Sunday*, 1966

Un échec de Maigret, 1957; as *Maigret's Failure*, 1962

Maigret s'amuse, 1957; as *Maigret's Little Joke*, 1957; as *None of Maigret's Business*, 1958

Maigret voyage, 1957; as *Maigret and the Millionairess*, 1974

Le Fils, 1957; as *The Son*, 1958

Le Nègre, 1957; as *The Negro*, 1959

Le Passage de la ligne, 1958

Le Président, 1958; as *The Premier*, 1961; with *The Train*, 1966

Strip-Tease, 1958; as *Striptease*, 1959

Dimanche, 1958; as *Sunday*, 1960; with *The Little Man from Arkangel*, 1966

Les Scruples de Maigret, 1958; as *Maigret Has Scruples*, 1959; with *Versus Inspector Maigret*, 1960

La Vieille, 1959

Une confidence de Maigret, 1959; as *Maigret Has Doubts*, 1968

Maigret et les témoins recalcitrants, 1959; as *Maigret and the Reluctant Witness*, 1959; in *Versus Inspector Maigret*, 1960

The Short Cases of Inspector Maigret, 1959

L'Ours en peluche, 1960; as *Teddy Bear*, 1971

Le Veuf, 1960; as *The Widower*, 1961

Maigret aux assises, 1960; as *Maigret in Court*, 1961

Maigret et les vieillards, 1960; as *Maigret in Society*, 1962

Betty, 1961; as *Betty* (in English), 1975

Le Train, 1961; as *The Train*, 1964; with *The Premier*, 1966

Maigret et le voleur paresseux, 1961; as *Maigret and the Lazy Burglar*, 1963; in *A Maigret Trio*, 1973

Maigret et les braves gens, 1962; as *Maigret and the Black Sheep*, 1976

Maigret et le client du samedi, 1962; as *Maigret and the Saturday Caller*, 1964

Les Autres, 1962; as *The House on Quai Notre Dame*, 1975; as *The Others*, 1975

La Porte, 1962; as *The Door*, 1964

Maigret et le clochard, 1962; as *Maigret and the Bum*, 1973; as *Maigret and the Dosser*, 1973

La Rue aux trois poussins, 1963

Les Anneaux de Bicêtre, 1963; as *The Patient*, 1963; as *The Bells of Bicetre*, 1964

La Colère de Maigret, 1963; as *Maigret Loses His Temper*, 1965

La Chambre bleue, 1964; as *The Blue Room*, with *The Accomplices*, 1964

L'Homme au petit chien, 1964; as *The Man with the Little Dog*, 1965

Maigret et le fantôme, 1964; as *Maigret and the Ghost*, 1976; as *Maigret and the Apparition*, 1976

Maigret se défend, 1964; as *Maigret on the Defensive*, 1966

La Patience de Maigret, 1965; as *The Patience of Maigret*, 1966

Le Petit Saint, 1965; as *The Little Saint*, 1965

Le Train de Venise, 1965; as *The Venice Train*, 1974

Les Enquêtes du Commissaire Maigret, 2 vols., 1966–67

Le Confessionnal, 1966; as *The Confessional*, 1967

La Mort d'Auguste, 1966; as *The Old Man Dies*, 1967

Maigret et l'affaire Nahour, 1966; as *Maigret and the Nahour Case*, 1967

Le Voleur de Maigret, 1967; as *Maigret's Pickpocket*, 1968

Le Chat, 1967; as *The Cat*, 1967

Le Déménagement, 1967; as *The Neighbours*, 1968; as *The Move*, 1968

La Main, 1968; as *The Man on the Bench in the Barn*, 1970

La Prison, 1968; as *The Prison*, 1969

L'Ami d'enfance de Maigret, 1968; as *Maigret's Boyhood Friend*, 1970

Maigret à Vichy, 1968; as *Maigret Takes the Waters*, 1969; as *Maigret in Vichy*, 1969

Maigret hésite, 1968; as *Maigret Hesitates*, 1970

Il y a encore des noisetiers, 1969

Novembre, 1969; as *November*, 1970

Maigret et le tueur, 1969; as *Maigret and the Killer*, 1971

Le Riche Homme, 1970; as *The Rich Man*, 1971

La Folle de Maigret, 1970; as *Maigret and the Madwoman*, 1972

Maigret et le marchand de vin, 1970; as *Maigret and the Wine Merchant*, 1971

La Cage de verre, 1971; as *The Glass Cage*, 1973

La Disparition d'Odile, 1971; as *The Disappearance of Odile*, 1972

Maigret et l'homme tout seul, 1971; as *Maigret and the Loner*, 1975

Maigret et l'indicateur, 1971; as *Maigret and the Informer*, 1972; as *Maigret and the Flea*, 1972

Les Innocents, 1972; as *The Innocents*, 1973

Maigret et Monsieur Charles, 1972; as *Maigret and Monsieur Charles*, 1973

Complete Maigret Short Stories, 2 vols., 1976

Fiction as Georges Sim

Au pont des arches, 1921

Les Ridicules, 1921

Les Larmes avant le bonheur, 1925

Le Feu s'éteint, 1927

Les Voleurs de navires, 1927

Défense d'aimer, 1927

Le Cercle de la soif, 1927

Paris-Leste, 1927

Un monsieur libidineux, 1927

Les Coeurs perdus, 1928

Le Secret des Lamas, 1928

Les Maudits du Pacifique, 1928

Le Monstre blanc de la terre de feu, 1928; as *L'Ile de la désolation* (as Christian Brulls), 1933

Miss Baby, 1928

Le Semeur de larmes, 1928

Le Roi des glaces, 1928

Le Sous-marin dans la forêt, 1928

La Maison sans soleil, 1928

Aimer l'amour, 1928

Songes d'été, 1928

Les Nains des cataractes, 1928

Le Lac d'angoisse, 1928; as *Le Lac des esclaves* (as Christian Brulls), 1933

Le Sang des gitanes, 1928

Chair de beauté, 1928

Les Mémoires d'un prostitué, 1929

En robe de mariée, 1929

La Panthère borgne, 1929

La Fiancée aux mains de glace, 1929

Les Bandits de Chicago, 1929

L'Ile des hommes roux, 1929

Le Roi du Pacifique, 1929; as *Le Bateau d'or*, 1935

Le Gorille-roi, 1929

Les Contrebandiers de l'alcool, 1929

La Femme qui tue, 1929

Destinées, 1929

L'Ile des maudits, 1929; as *Naufrage du "Pelican,"* 1933

La Femme en deuil, 1929

L'Oeil de l'Utah, 1930

L'Homme qui tremble, 1930

Nez d'argent, 1930; as *Le Paria des bois sauvages*, 1933

Mademoiselle Million, 1930; as *Les Ruses de l'amour*, 1954

Le Pêcheur de bouées, 1930

Le Chinois de San-Francisco, 1930

La Femme 47, 1930

Katia, acrobate, 1931

L'Homme à la cigarette, 1931

L'Homme de proie, 1931

Les Errants, 1931

La Maison de l'inquiétude, 1932

L'Epave, 1932

Matricule 12, 1932

La Fiancée du diable, 1932

La Femme rousse, 1933

Le Château des sables rouges, 1933

Deuxième bureau, 1933

Fiction as Jean du Perry

Le Roman d'une dactylo, 1924

Amour d'exilée, 1925

L'Oiseau blessé, 1925

L'Heureuse Fin, 1925

La Fiancée fugitive, 1925

Entre deux haines, 1925

Pour le sauver, 1925

Ceux qu'on avait oubliés…, 1925

Pour qu'il soit heureux, 1925

Amour d'Afrique, 1925

A l'assaut d'un coeur, 1925

L'Orgueil d'aimer, 1926

Celle qui est aimée, 1926

Les Yeux qui ordonnent, 1926

Que ma mère l'ignore!, 1926

De la rue au bonheur, 1926

Un péché de jeunesse, 1926

Lili Tristesse, 1927

Un tout petit coeur, 1927

Le Fou d'amour, 1928

Coeur exalté, 1928

Trois coeurs dans la tempête, 1928

Les Amants de la mansarde, 1928

Un jour de soleil, 1928

La Fille de l'autre, 1929

L'Amour et l'argent, 1929

Coeur de poupée, 1929

Une femme a tué, 1929

Deux coeurs de femme, 1929
L'Epave d'amour, 1929
Le Mirage de Paris, 1929
Celle qui passe, 1930
Petite exilée, 1930
Les Amants du malheur, 1930
La Femme ardente, 1930
La Porte close, 1930
La Poupée brisée, 1930
Pauvre Amante!, 1931
Le Rêve qui meurt, 1931
Marie-Mystère, 1931

Fiction as Georges-Martin Georges

L'Orgueil qui meurt, 1925
Un soir de vertige, 1928
Brin d'amour, 1928
Les Coeurs vides, 1928
Cabotine..., 1928
Aimer, mourir, 1928
Voleuse d'amour, 1929
Une ombre dans la nuit, 1929
Nuit de Paris, 1929
La Victime, 1929
Un nid d'amour, 1930
Bobette, mannequin, 1930
La Puissance du souvenir, 1930
Le Bonheur de Lili, 1930
La Double Vie, 1931

Fiction as Christian Brulls

La Prêtresse des Vaudoux, 1925
Nox l'insaissable, 1926
Se Ma Tsien, le sacrificateur, 1926
Le Désert du froid qui tue, 1928; re-edited as *Le Yacht fantôme* (as Georges Sim), 1933
Mademoiselle X, 1928
Annie, danseuse, 1928
Dolorosa, 1928
Les Adolescents passionnés, 1929
L'Amant sans nom, 1929
Un drame au Pôle Sud, 1929
Les Pirates du Texas, 1929; re-edited as *La Chasse au whiskey*, 1934
Captain, S.O.S., 1929
Jacques d'Antifer, roi des Iles du Vent, 1930; re-edited as *L'Héritier du corsaire*, 1934
L'Inconnue, 1930
Train de nuit, 1930
Pour venger son père, 1931
La Maison de la haine, 1931
La Maison des disparus, 1931
Les Forçats de Paris, 1932
La Figurante, 1932
Fièvre, 1932
L'Evasion, 1934
L'Ile empoisonnée, 1937
Seul parmi les gorilles, 1937

Fiction as Gom Gut

Un viol aux Quat'z'arts, 1925
Perversités frivoles, 1925
Au grand 13, 1925
Plaisirs charnels, 1925
Aux vingt-huit négresses, 1925
La Noce à Montmartre, 1925
Liquettes au vent, 1926
Une petite très sensuelle, 1926
Orgies bourgeoises, 1926
L'Homme aux douze étreintes, 1927
Etreintes passionnées, 1927
Une môme dessalée, 1927
L'Amant fantôme, 1928
L'Amour à Montparnasse, 1928
Les Distractions d'Hélène, 1928

Fiction as Luc Dorsan

Histoire d'un pantalon, 1926
Nine violée, 1926
Nichonnette, 1926
Mémoires d'un vieux suiveur, 1926
Nuit de noces; Doubles noces; Les noces ardentes, 1926
La Pucelle de Benouville, 1927
Une petite dessalée, 1928
Un drôle de coco, 1929

Fiction as Jean Dorsage

L'Amour méconnu, 1928
Celle qui revient, 1929
Coeur de jeune fille, 1930
Soeurette, 1930
Les Chercheurs de bonheur, 1930

Fiction as Gaston Vialis

Un petit corps blessé, 1928
Haïr à force d'aimer, 1928
Le Parfum du passé, 1929
Lili-Sourire, 1930
Folie d'un soir, 1930
Ame de jeune fille, 1931

Fiction as Jacques Dersonne

Un seul baiser..., 1928
La Merveilleuse Aventure, 1929
Les Etapes du mensonge, 1930
Baisers mortels, 1930
Victime de son fils, 1931

Plays

Quartier nègre (also director; produced 1936)
La Neige était sale, with Frédéric Dard, from the novel by Simenon (produced 1950), in *Oeuvres Libres 57*, 1951
Ballet scenario: *La Chambre*, with music by Georges Auric, 1955

Other

Les Trois crimes de mes amis, 1938
La Mauvaise Etoile, 1938
Je me souviens…, 1945
Long cours sur les rivières et canaux, 1952
Le Roman de l'homme, 1960; as *The Novel of Man*, 1964
La Femme en France, 1960
Entretiens avec Roger Stéphane, 1963
Ma conviction profonde, 1963
Le Paris de Simenon, 1969; as *Simenon's Paris*, 1970
Quand j'étais vieux, 1970; as *When I Was Old*, 1971
Lettre à ma mère, 1974; as *Letter to My Mother*, 1976
Un homme comme un autre, 1975
Des traces de pas, 1975
Vent du nord, vent du sud, 1976
Les Petits Hommes, 1976
Mes apprentissages: A la decouverte de la France, A la recherche de l'homme nu, edited by Francis Lacassin and Gilbert Sigaux, 2 vols., 1976
De la cave au grenier, 1977
A l'abri de notre arbre, 1977
Un banc au soleil, 1977
Tant que je suis vivant, 1978
Vacances obligatoires, 1978
La Main dans la main, 1978
Au-delà de ma porte-fenêtre, 1978
Point-virgule, 1979
A quoi bon jurer?, 1979
Je suis resté un enfant de choeur, 1979
Le Prix d'un homme, 1980
On dit que j'ai soixante-quinze ans, 1980
Quand vient le froid, 1980
Mémoires intimes, 1980
Les Libertés qu'il nous reste, 1981
La Femme endormie, 1981
Jour et nuit, 1981
Destinées, 1981

Bibliography

Fallois, Bernard de, *Simenon*, 1961; revised edition, 1971
Young, Trudee, *Simenon: A Checklist of His "Maigret" and Other Mystery Novels and Short Stories in French and English Translations*, 1976

Critical studies

Narcejac, Thomas, *The Art of Simenon*, 1952
Raymond, John, *Simenon in Court*, 1968
Frank, Frederick, *Simenon's Paris*, 1970
Frackman Becker, Lucille, *Simenon* (in English), 1977
Bresler, Fenton, *The Mystery of Simenon: A Biography*, 1983
Piron, Maurice, *L'Univers de Simenon* (includes bibliography), 1983
Bertrand, Alain, *Georges Simenon*, 1988

_____

SIMON, Claude (-Eugène-Henri), 1913–1984.

Novelist, dramatist, and winner of the Nobel prize for literature (1985).

LIFE

It is no accident that comparatively little is known about Claude Simon's life. He repeatedly stated his desire that his works should stand on their own, without reference to his private life or, we may add, to any literary theories he may have had. His novels do have plots, but they are essentially an organization of simultaneously existing images, communicated almost as if the writer were a painter, and it is indeed as a painter that Simon started his career. The resulting complexity of his novels is such that Simon had to devise a system of colour-coding for himself in order to keep track of the characters and themes he proposed to project simultaneously in *La Route des Flandres*. His sentences can straggle over several pages, abandoning all punctuation, and, if Simon's account of his method of composition had been universally true, the manuscripts would look like colourist paintings. In fact, the coloured pencils were employed to elaborate a structural plan, and there are some brilliant sketches in the manuscript margins, with indications that the text itself is built up from almost innumerable individual elements, words or sentences, which existed in isolation before they were assembled.

Born on 10 October 1913 in Tananarive, Madagascar, Simon lost his father, a cavalry officer, at the outset of World War I, when he was only a few months old. He was brought up in Perpignan, where he was later to grow vines. Although in later life he took to living in Paris, he still spent part of every year at Salses in the eastern Pyrenees. Just before his mother died in 1924 he went to school at the Collège Stanislas in Paris, and then studied painting with André Lhote. He served for a year with the French cavalry (1934–35) and in 1936 he made a brief visit to Barcelona in republican Spain, taking a pro-republican but anti-communist stance, not unlike Orwell's. There then followed a period of travel through other European countries. Unlike many of his contemporaries, Simon did not at first travel widely, although his work, as he proclaims, is partly inspired by Faulkner, as also by Conrad, Joyce, and Dostoyevsky. Called up in 1939, Simon was taken prisoner in May 1940. He escaped from his prisoner-of-war camp at Muhlberg on the Elbe in October and finished the novel *Le Tricheur*, which he had begun before the war, but which would not be published until 1945. For the rest of the war he worked with the Resistance movement at Perpignan. In 1951 he married Yuonne Ducaing. The marriage was dissolved and in 1978 Simon married Rea Karavas.

Simon published the autobiographical fragment *La Corde raide* in 1947, *Gulliver* in 1952, and *Le Sacre du printemps* in 1954, following two years of serious illness, but it was only with *Le Vent: tentative de restitution d'un retable baroque*, published in 1957, that he became widely known. He got to know Robbe-Grillet, Butor, and Pinget, and so became associated with other practitioners of what has been labelled the "new novel." However, he was not widely read either in France, where his texts were felt to be simply too demanding, or in translation, where they too closely recalled Faulkner. During the Algerian war Simon signed the "Manifeste des 121" (see Sartre) protesting at France's Algerian policy. In 1958 he published *L'Herbe* and in 1960 *La Route des Flandres*, which was awarded the Prix de

L'Express. After two more works, *Le Palace* of 1962 and *Femmes: sur vingt-trois peintures de Jòan Miró* of 1966, the Prix Médicis was awarded to *Histoire*, which was published in 1967. In 1973 Simon received his first honorary doctorate from the University of East Anglia. It was in 1985, four years after producing the monumental *Les Géorgiques*, his 13th novel, that he was awarded the Nobel prize. In the remaining years of his life he travelled widely in Europe, the USSR, the US, Japan, South America, and India.

WORKS

In a rare series of interviews Simon remained true to his basic contention that the writer creates primarily for himself, or for the sake of what is created, not in order to communicate any particular vision to a reading public. In fact he must, of course, communicate a vision or at least a series of attitudes and preoccupations. It is clear, however, that he did not think it the writer's responsibility to analyse either the object or the process of literary creation. He merely points out, for instance, that his own fiction is based on thick renderings of metaphor, not on plot or character, and that it does without description and conversation: "Toute mon oeuvre est construite sur la nature métaphorique de la langue (All my work is built on the metaphorical nature of language)." What overwhelmed Simon, triggering the creative process, was generally an image, though not so trivial a one as has sometimes been suggested. For instance, the basic image of *La Route des Flandres*, from which the whole novel derives, is that of his colonel killed in 1940 by a German parachutist waiting behind a hedge. That was what Simon called the "mother image," to which all the others came to adhere.

Le Vent sets out to disturb the reader's perception of time and generally disorientate his senses. The narrator announces the impossibility of organizing what is remembered into a coherent pattern; "to reconstitute what happened is a little like trying to stick together the scattered, incomplete debris of a broken mirror…" The prose is rich and sensuous, and strives through metaphor for poetic effect. The sailor Montès has come back to the windswept city. He is trying to recover a vineyard which belonged to his dead father, whom he had never known, but it is not clear what happens among the lawsuits, the emotional entanglements, and the criss-cross of relationships. The wind sweeps away the order that man imposes on the fragments which constitute life. Montès is a Dostoyevsky-like "idiot" or innocent, as Simon himself said. He has a semi-paternal relationship with two little girls whose servant mother had had an affair with a flamboyant gypsy thief. He exercises a disastrous charm on a rich member of his family, as on the servant mother, whose gypsy kills her when he discovers that she has entrusted to Montès some jewellery he had stolen. The police kill the gypsy and the young girls end up in an orphanage. A letter written by the infatuated rich relation is stolen and used in an attempt to blackmail her. She then gives herself to her former fiancé before sending him away. Montès loses his case and departs, leaving nothing to mark his passage.

Le Vent would not be a particularly daring experiment in narrative fiction if the narrator himself were not trying vainly to piece together what had happened. The reader never really finds out what that was because it is blurred first by Montès's recollection, and then by the narrator's incomplete recollection of what Montès had told him but about things to which Montès had not been paying full attention. For good measure, as the narrator points out, "any account of events after the fact is bound to be false." Memory invests even the most insignificant events with importance. The novel is really about the impossibility of discovering the plot that dangles tantalizingly before the reader. To make the point clear, the narrator keeps intruding comments on the unreliability of his own recollection. Where Simon has progressed beyond such predecessors as Gide is in making the narrator's faulty recollection the subject itself of the novel.

The central protagonist of *L'Herbe* is Marie, a peasant's daughter turned village schoolmistress who, with her dead sister Eugénie, devoted herself to the education of her younger brother, Pierre. Pierre became a university professor. Marie has sacrificed her whole life and now all she has left is her book of accounts. Driven out of her home by the war, she has come to die in her brother's house. Pampered and ungrateful, he is now ill himself. He has a snobbish alcoholic wife, and a daughter-in-law, Louise, who is on the point of leaving her gambling husband Georges for a lover. Louise, the narrator, and her lover meditate during Aunt Marie's last 10 days on how she has spent her time. The syntax is systematically disrupted by parentheses, and the sentences seem endless. It is 1940, the time for death, decay, and corruption among nature's insolent beauties. The book is about sacrifice and the inexorability of time, which erases the heroism and futility of human endeavour. Life is reduced to an account book and a few possessions. Louise's present time is experienced by her as a reality, although the experience is warped by gazing at the distorting mirror of what time has done with Aunt Marie—it has simply ignored her.

The subject of *La Route des Flandres* is again the order which consciousness imposes on events, in spite of the futility of memory and the indifference of time. The disruption of the conscious order imposed by the mind is mimicked in the disruption of the syntax. There is no punctuation, and the sentences dissolve into seemingly endless successions of present participles. The language, in counterpoint, is luxuriant. To the image of the dying colonel are added other Flanders images, evoking World War I, and other images of death. Simon was haunted, he said, by two things: "by discontinuity, the fragmentary aspect of the emotions we experience and which are unrelated to one another, and yet by their contiguous place in our consciousness." The narrator, Georges, remembers his relative and company commander, Captain de Reixach, who rides into an ambush wanting to die. His wife had been unfaithful with his jockey Iglésia. Georges ends up in a prisoner-of-war camp with Iglésia and Blum, the argumentative Jewish companion Georges may have invented. Georges fantasizes about Reixach's wife, Corinne, and in his mind confuses, or conflates, Reixach, whose death may have been a form of suicide, with an ancestor whose death after a defeat in war may also have been suicide. Characters and themes become confused. The communication of the disorder of defeat is immediate, instantaneous, and artistically effective, but it involves the bypassing of fiction. It is quite possible that Simon's immense imaginative power derives from a form of communication which is not fictional.

Les Géorgiques takes off from the papers of one of Simon's ancestors, General Lacombe Saint Michel, and also comments explicitly on Orwell's *Homage to Catalonia* of 1938, translated into French as *La Catalogne libre* in 1955. Simon deliberately leaves the reader vague about whether he is following Orwell or not, or even talking about a war different from that fought in

Spain. He is also ambiguous in his admiration and suspicion of the political position of the writer he calls "O." In this instance Simon is simultaneously writing a meditation on his own earlier work, *Le Palace* of 1962. (The palace of the title was based on the communist headquarters at the Hotel Colón in Barcelona.)

The work is a protracted reflection about time and the ordering of events into "history." Parts of it are autobiographical, and others, apart from those concerning Lacombe Saint Michel, the revolutionary general, are written as if they were straight historical narrative, the objective authenticity underlined by the fact that he is referred to throughout as "L.S.M." The straight narration of history is subverted openly and obviously. When, for example, the cavalrymen realize that they are going to be killed in an ambush, the narrator suddenly intrudes with a remark about the impossibility of the reader understanding the experience he is talking about. The point only needs making once, and the whole idea of a historical novel as traditionally conceived collapses. Simon is communicating, but not fictionally, that to write about an experience is not the same thing as undergoing it, and that it can only have its intended effect if the reader is aware that he is not experiencing what is being evoked. Without that awareness, Simon is suggesting, there can be no literature.

Put bluntly, a literary experience depends on the reader's awareness that he is not undergoing the experience he is reading about. Simon demonstrates this because in 1981 it still needed demonstrating as well as stating. Given the amount of critical analysis and literary theorizing to which his work has been subjected, it not altogether surprising that he tended to be reticent in discussing what his work had already communicated clearly enough about the nature of narrative.

PUBLICATIONS

Works

Le Tricheur, 1945
La Corde raide, 1947
Gulliver, 1952
Le Sacre du printemps, 1954
Le Vent: tentative de restitution d'un retable baroque, 1957; as *Wind*, 1959
L'Herbe, 1958; as *The Grass*, 1961
La Route des Flandres, 1960; as *The Flanders Road*, 1962
Le Palace, 1962; as *The Palace*, 1964
Femmes: sur vingt-trois peintures de Jòan Miró, with 23 colour plates by Miró, 1966
Histoire, 1967; as *History*, 1969
La Bataille de Pharsale, 1969; *Death of Pharsalus*, 1971
Orion aveugle, 1970
Les Corps conducteurs, 1971; as *Conducting Bodies*, 1975
Triptyque, 1973; as *Triptych*, 1973
Leçon de choses, 1976; as "The world about us," in the *Ontario Review*, 1983
Les Géorgiques, 1981; as *Georgics*, 1981
L'Invitation, 1988
Album d'un amateur, 1988
L'Acacia, 1988

Critical and biographical studies

Loubère, J.A.E., *The Novels of Claude Simon*, 1975

Sykes, S.W., *Les Romans de Claude Simon*, 1979
Duncan, Alastair B. (editor), *Claude Simon: New Directions*, 1985
Dällenbach, L., *Claude Simon*, 1988
Fletcher, John, *Claude Simon and Fiction Now*, 1975

SOUPAULT, Philippe, 1897–1990.

Poet, editor, and writer of fiction.

LIFE

Philippe Soupault was born on 2 August 1897 at Chaville, between Paris and Versailles, into a well-off suburban family. It was a milieu against which he quickly came to rebel, despising the regard for money which he thought was the sole value it really respected. Things were not so much right or wrong as "done" or "not done." It was not done to kill, steal, or be without means. In 1927, at the age of 30, Soupault recounted the story of his youthful rebellion in an 80-page memoir, *Histoire d'un blanc*.

His father was a doctor and probably the least conventional member of the family, being cheerful, carefree, and open, but he died of diabetes when Soupault was seven. He had written a book on stomach ailments. His mother's sister had married the eldest son of a cloth merchant, who made a chair which set off a musical box when Soupault sat in it, and in 1898 had invented and patented a gear system used in all the new automobiles. His name was Louis Renault. Later he became rich, powerful, and legendary for the harshness of the regime imposed on his workforce. He was once voted the worst employer in Paris, and his company adopted the practice of regularly dismissing workers in order to hire others at lower wages. He was to be the model for Gavard in Soupault's novel *Le Grand Homme* of 1929 and, according to the preface in the 1947 edition, had to be sternly dissuaded by his lawyers from resorting in response to the book to actions other than those permitted by law. Soupault expressed resentment of his uncle's greed and hypocrisy, but reserved particular anger in his 1947 preface for his uncle's role as a Nazi collaborator during World War II.

Soupault later compared his religious school, the Collège Fénelon, to a prison, but appears to have got on better at the Lycée Condorcet, especially after being sent to the Rhineland in the summer of 1912. He read widely, was impressed by Gide and Rimbaud, spent the summer holidays of 1913 in Cabourg, where he first became aware of girls, and found the Grand Hôtel dominated by the presence of Proust. The novelist apparently hated sunlight even more than he hated noise, and Soupault later vividly remembered his reputed effect on the hotel, where he had taken five rooms in order to keep two quiet on either side of him. In 1914 Soupault went to London, where the sight of barges on the Thames filled his imagination with poetic images. He said he became a poet on the banks of the Thames that July,

Manning, yet another dissatisfied soul who has been in prison in the US, achieved success in Paris, and with the military in Portugal, and who how seeks solitude in the heart of Africa.

Les Dernières Nuits de Paris was translated into English by William Carlos Williams. It is a simple narrative about the things that arouse interest or curiosity during a night-time stroll around Paris. Soupault has a poet's curiosity about the people his narrator sees, suspecting that their business may be what is normally and not necessarily wrongly considered criminal, immoral, or merely reprehensible. A group of students from the Ecole Normale Supérieure who wrote a regular Paris chronicle for a provincial paper simply sent a chapter from this novel one week when they found themselves short of copy. *Le Grand Homme* is little more than a portrait of Soupault's uncle, Louis Renault, under the name of Gavard. The portrait was intended to be recognized and the 1947 preface deliberately made it even more hurtful. *Les Moribonds*, set in pre-Nazi Berlin, is another quasi-autobiographical novel about an affluent young man who tries to shake off his background. He is taught how to do it by a young woman. The secret is just to do an ordinary job.

Unfortunately, a 1940 novel was destroyed by the Vichy police. Soupault wrote "Les moissonneurs," as it was to have been called, on his dismissal from Radio Tunis. He had been meditating on it for years, and it concerned neither love nor friendship, but camaraderie among five unemployed young people who form a closed squatters' group. Each chapter was written differently: one of narrative, one of each of the diaries kept by the five, one in the form of a newspaper article. Gide had read the novel and wanted Soupault to rewrite it. However, it was seized by the police when Soupault was arrested and is believed to have been burnt in 1942. By that time, however, Soupault had come to prefer other forms of narrative prose, mostly the extended report.

Astonishingly, parts of his text for *Les Champs magnétiques* read like polished prose poetry rather than the jumble of erotic and aggressive images one would expect to tumble out from any attempt to shed the subconscious of its uncoordinated contents instantaneously:

Ce soir, nous sommes deux devant ce fleuve qui déborde de notre désespoir. Nous ne pouvons même plus penser. Les paroles s'échappent de nos bouches tordues et, lorsque nous rions, les passants se retournent, effrayés, et rentrent chez eux précipitamment. On ne sait pas nous mépriser.

Nous pensons aux lueurs des bars, aux bals grotesques dans ces maisons en ruines où nous laissions le jour. Mais rien n'est plus désolant que cette lumière qui coule doucement sur les toits à cinq heures du matin. Les rues s'écartent silencieusement et les boulevards s'animent: un promeneur attardé sourit près de nous. Il n'a pas vu nos yeux pleins de vertiges et il passe doucement. Ce sont les bruits des voitures de laitiers qui font s'envoler notre torpeur et les oiseaux montent au ciel chercher une divine nourriture.

(This evening we're both in front of this river which is overflowing with our despair. We can't even think any longer. Words escape from our twisted mouths and, when we laugh, passers-by turn round, frightened, and go hurrying home. They don't know how to despise us.

We think of the glimmering lights in bars, the grotesque dances in those ruined houses where we left the day. But nothing is more depressing than that light flowing softly over the roofs at five in the morning. The roads open up silently and the boulevards come to life. A late stroller nearby smiles. He hasn't seen that our eyes are full of dizziness and he goes past quietly. It's the noise of milkmen's vans which wake us from our torpor, and the birds climb into the sky to look for divine nourishment.)

Soupault's poetry has always been too delicate to create its effect with a single line or image, or even a simple juxtaposition from beneath the level of rationality, grammar, and syntax. Even in his surrealist days he avoided Aragon's rhetoric, Eluard's erudition, and Breton's luxuriant verbiage, looking for simplicity, almost fragility, and coming nearer to Reverdy than to anyone else. His rhythms often allude to popular songs, and his poems contain the same repetitive structures, insistent assonances, and variations on vowel sounds. At its best Soupault's poetry moves into arabesque, but some of the published material scarcely rises above the trivial or the facile. The strongest inspiration comes from Lautréamont, but even in the more serious poems, like the moving "Ode à Londres," there is a non-poetic striving for effects which are merely striking. The opening is impressive, at least as a declaration of serious poetic intent, in spite of its overdependence on pure sound:

Cette nuit Londres est bombardée pour la centième fois
nuit noire nuit d'assassinat et de colère

(Tonight London is being bombed for the hundredth time / night dark night of assassination and rage)

The rendering is difficult because "dark night" has spiritual connotations in English, but not in French, for which the equivalent is "nuit obscure." On the other hand, the sense cannot be reproduced through an English concatenation of "n" sounds. Yet Soupault had used them before the 1943 ode in a "chanson" that scarcely deserved inclusion in anyone's *Poésies complètes*:

Monsieur Miroir marchand d'habits
est mort hier soir à Paris
Il fait nuit
Il fait noir
Il fait nuit noire à Paris

(Monsieur Miroir the tailor / died in Paris yesterday / It is night / It is dark / It is dark night in Paris)

Soupault's real strength is lyrical prose, the sort of reporting to be found in the relatively early *Carte postale*, as well as in many of the novels and most of the essays:

To get as far as the port you go along a street where the flags of all the nations are flapping. Every self-respecting building does in fact contain a credit establishment. Typewriters sing out in scales the credits and debits. There are innumerable customers round the cash desks. These establishments are as numerous as wine shops in Paris. After five people drink in the stock exchange prices, take a sip of Royal Dutch or de Beers…

PUBLICATIONS

Collections

Poésies complètes, 1917–1937, 1937
Poèmes et poésie, 1917–1973, 1973
Odes, 1930–1980, 1980

Verse

Aquarium, 1917
Les Champs magnétiques, with André Breton, 1920
Rose des vents, 1920
Westwego, 1922
Georgia, 1926
Bulles Billes Boules, 1930
Etapes de l'enfer, 1934
Il y a un océan, 1936
Sang Joie Tempête, 1937
Ode à Londres bombardée, in *Odes*, 1946; as *Ode to Bombed London*, translated by Norman Cameron, 1944
L'Arme secrète, 1946
Message de l'île déserte, 1947
Chansons du jour et de la nuit, 1949
Chansons, 1949
Sans phrases, 1953

Fiction

Le Bon Apôtre, 1923
A la dérive, 1923
Les Frères Durandeau, 1924
Le Voyage d'Horace Pirouelle, 1925
Le Bar de l'amour, 1925
En joue!, 1925
Corps perdu, 1926
Le Coeur d'or, 1927
Le Nègre, 1927
Les Dernières Nuits de Paris, 1928; as *Last Nights of Paris*, translated by William Carlos Williams, 1929
Le Roi de la vie: contes, 1928
Le Grand Homme, 1929
Les Moribonds, 1934

Essays and studies

Carte postale, 1926
Henri Rousseau, le Douanier, 1927
Guillaume Apollinaire, 1927
Histoire d'un blanc, 1927
Lautréamont, 1927
William Blake, 1928; as *William Blake* (in English) 1928
Terpsichore, 1928
Jean Lurçat, 1928
Paolo Uccello, 1929
The American Influence in France, 1930
Charlot, 1931
Baudelaire, 1931
Souvenirs de James Joyce, 1943
Le Temps des assassins, 1945; as *Age of Assassins*, 1946
Eugène Labiche, 1945

Lautréamont, 1946
Essai sur la poésie, 1950
Alfred de Musset, 1957

Other

Tous ensemble au bout du monde (play), 1943
Ecrits de cinéma, 1918–1931, 1979
Ecrits sur la peinture, 1980
Mémoires de l'oubli, 1914–1923

Critical and biographical study

Dupuy, Henry-Jacques, *Philippe Soupault*, 1957

SPIRE, André, 1868–1966.

Poet.

Spire was a prolific Jewish poet from Nancy who came to Paris to study law and political science and was seriously interested in social questions. He was involved with Daniel Halévy and Maxime Leroy in the attempt in 1898–99 to set up a people's university, to be called "L'Enseignement Mutuel." His poetry was partly polemical, formulating "de belles petites malédictions" (nice little curses) against the enemies of the human race and of Jewish blood. *Versets* was much admired by Apollinaire and, after reading *Fournisseurs*, Valery Larbaud thought that Spire was France's only true satirical writer. *Samaël* was set to music by Milhaud.

Spire's verse has been held to be remarkable for its supple vocal intensity and ability to affect the emotions. In the tradition of Descartes, Spire assumed that physiological states underlay affective states, so that conscious or even imperceptible physiological movements accompanied feelings of pleasure, pain, awkwardness, disgust, and so on. What corresponded to these feelings was not the play of vocal sounds, depending on assonance, rhyme, rhythm, metre, and other purely literary qualities of the written or spoken word, but the disposition of the whole physiological apparatus—larynx, lungs, palate, lips, and tongue—used in the spoken word, even if it was written down. It was therefore through physiological movements that true emotion was communicated, and the art of poetry consisted in the exploitation of the physiological movements associated with certain feelings, supported by mime or gesticulation. Poetry could thus aspire to communicate emotion which was not yet articulate (*Plaisir poétique et plaisir musculaire*).

Spire was influenced by Whitman and was a friend of Péguy. He died on 29 July 1966.

PUBLICATIONS

Verse

La Cité présente, 1903
Et vous riez!, edited by Charles Péguy, 1905

Versets, 1908
Vers les routes absurdes, 1911
Et j'ai voulu la paix, 1916
Le Secret, 1919
Poèmes juifs, 1919; revised edition, 1959
Tentations, 1920
Samaël, 1921
Fournisseurs, 1923
Poèmes de Loire, 1929
Poèmes d'ici et de là-bas, 1944
Poèmes d'hier et d'aujourd'hui, 1953
Souvenirs à bâtons rompus, 1961

Other

Plaisir poétique et plaisir musculaire, 1949

STAËL, Germaine de (born: Anne-Louise-Germaine Necker), 1766–1817.

*Novelist, moralist, literary theoretician, and political
pamphleteer.*

LIFE

Staël, as she came to be called, was the only child of a rich Swiss Protestant banker, director-general of finance in France for four years from 1777 and again from 1788 until July 1789. He returned to France after the fall of the Bastille. Her mother, also Swiss, had been attracted to the historian Edward Gibbon, who broke with her on his father's orders. She became a governess and companion and married Jacques Necker, five years her junior, in 1764. She was a strict Calvinist who scrupulously repressed a naturally passionate disposition. Charitable works brought her into contact with the sick and she became obsessed with the idea of premature burial, on which she wrote a treatise. She and her husband were preserved in a private mausoleum in a marble bath filled with alcohol. Staël was instilled with strong feelings of guilt from infancy, was encouraged to read seriously, and taught English and Latin by her mother, who made no secret of trying to mould her daughter's mind.

In 1776 the family went to England, where Staël's mother was reconciled with Gibbon. Staël met Horace Walpole and was taken to see Garrick act. In Paris a companion was selected for her to play with, and eminent men spoke to her at dinner as if she were an adult. From 1785 she kept a diary, which reveals her sensitivity to her plainness of feature. In 1778, at the age of 12, she was taken by her mother to visit Voltaire, and that same year the 29-year-old Swedish attaché sought her hand in marriage. She was sent to live at Saint-Ouen, near Paris, with a governess and a maid. In 1786 she was to marry the Swedish attaché, who had connections and expectations but no money, although he was at least a Protestant. By this time her father had bought the Château de Coppet near Geneva and Staël herself had written her first short stories. She felt deprived of parental affection,

once writing to her mother during a brief absence to say how unhappy she felt without her. The reply was a reprimand for the style of the letter and for the lack of taste betrayed by such expression of emotion. As an adolescent Staël formed a strong attachment to her father.

Negotiations for her hand took about five years. Gustave III of Sweden was dismayed by Necker's situation: the Neckers had no lineage and were not even French. The matter may well have been settled by Marie-Antoinette, whose lover was also interested in Mlle Necker's richly endowed hand. In any case Louis XVI, Marie-Antoinette, and the princes of the blood signed the contract. Catherine II of Russia thought Staël was marrying beneath herself in choosing someone of less than her father's distinction. Staël's diary shows she had no illusions, although she did not know how much she would come to loathe the institution of marriage. She was commonly regarded as far too self-assured, opinionated, and ill-favoured, and inevitably known as "the Genevan upstart."

Staël had begun to write, first a play, then a series of letters on Jean-Jacques Rousseau. She wrote an entertaining series of newsletters to Gustave III, a second play, and in 1787 had her first baby, Gustavine, who died before she was two. The king and queen of Sweden were the child's godparents. Staël started her own salon, mostly for the liberal-minded aristocracy, had a brief affair with Talleyrand and in 1778, through him, met Narbonne, who was eleven years her senior, and by whom she was to have two children (1790 and 1792). He was married, a well-known womanizer, and may chiefly have been interested in Staël's money, but she clearly staked her happiness on him for the six years their liaison lasted.

Like her father, Staël believed in a constitutional monarchy. Much of the new constitution of 1791 was formulated in her salon, and she herself anonymously published moderate political material. Her father, having failed to persuade the king to follow his advice, resigned in 1780, leaving the treasury 2,000,000 francs against the king's bond. Staël's parents spent most of the remainder of their lives at Coppet. Her relationship with them became strained and her husband openly took a mistress. Staël succeeded in getting Narbonne made minister of war, but he lasted only three months in that position. She invented a new escape route for the royal family, but Marie-Antoinette turned it down. By the late summer of 1792 the constitutional monarchists had been forced into hiding. Staël saved the lives of many of her friends, made one serious miscalculation with Robespierre by sweeping out of Paris in the Swedish embassy coach, but was given a passport for Coppet. She had also got Narbonne to England, where she joined him after the birth of their second child.

In May 1793 Staël returned to Coppet, leaving Narbonne exhausted by her openly declared passion, by the scandal that surrounded their liaison, and by his propulsion into and ejection out of high office. At Coppet Staël wrote him emotional letters, worked on her book on the passions, and maintained an icy silence with her mother. When Narbonne did finally come, the relationship was at an end and Staël had found a new partner in Count Ribbing, who had been exiled for his part in the conspiracy to murder Gustave III. By 1794 Staël was writing her shorter literary and political works. Her mother had died in May, after increasing Staël's sense of guilt by blaming her illness on the grief her daughter's public liaison had caused her. Robespierre fell in July and in September Benjamin Constant, who was only months her senior, called on her. By the beginning of 1795 he was living at Coppet as her lover, an unfaithful one, but at least her intellectual equal. In May she returned to Paris with him, where she reopened her salon. She was under attack from both Jacobins and royalists and was about to become a leading opponent of Bonaparte, who exiled her from 1795 until late in 1796.

Having obtained Constant's release from jail, Staël spent some time with him at Coppet writing. For the first half of 1797 she stayed at Hérivaux, Constant's newly acquired estate, and helped him with his political works. She returned to Paris in May and in June 1797 gave birth to a daughter, presumably Constant's. She approved of the Directoire's coup d'état on 4 September, but not of the subsequent purge, from which she saved at least one friend. For a while she was on good terms with Bonaparte, though she did not succeed in retrieving her father's 2,000,000 francs. She was exiled by the Directoire in July 1799, but returned when Bonaparte overthrew it in November.

Staël's serious literary reputation depended initially, in part, on her opposition to an increasingly dictatorial Bonaparte. When Constant addressed the Tribunal on 5 January 1800 in favour of a more radical view of liberty than Bonaparte's, Staël's salon emptied. It was even suggested that the 2,000,000 francs might be returned in exchange for her support. That spring she published *De la littérature considérée dans ses rapports avec les institutions sociales*, her first major work. It attacked Bonaparte by implication, but her salon began nevertheless to fill up again. In December 1800 she officially separated from her husband, who went on to declare himself bankrupt. He died in 1802 while she was taking him back to Coppet to care for him. In the summer of 1802 Staël's father published his final views on politics and finance, calling for a republican government. Bonaparte, who had just made himself consul, wrongly suspected Staël's hand in her father's work.

In September she published *Delphine*. Its treatment of political themes exasperated Bonaparte, who exiled her from Paris. After trying to elude the ban, she left for Metz with Constant on 28 October 1803, travelled widely in Germany, engaged A.W. Schlegel as tutor to her children, met Wieland, Schiller, and ultimately Goethe, and took lessons in German philosophy. Constant returned to Switzerland from Leipzig after Staël and he had exchanged written promises to marry. She heard of her father's illness and prepared to return to Switzerland herself, but Constant met her at Weimar with news of his death. Staël now busied herself at Coppet with publishing her father's papers and her own tribute to him. In December she left for Italy, returning to Coppet in the summer after the now traditional tour of grand people and places, and started work on *Corinne*, which was to be an immense success on its publication in May 1807. She embarked on a new liaison with the future historian Prosper de Barante. Constant was still staying with her north of Paris when he renewed his own liaison with Mme de Tertre. Bonaparte tried to enforce the exile to the 40 leagues outside Paris he had imposed, and Staël enjoyed slipping in and out of the forbidden territory.

In the summer of 1807 Staël was in Vienna talking to friends about Metternich, and Bonaparte began to view her as serious opposition. She finished *De l'Allemagne* between 1808 and 1810, but the new minister of police, Ravigo, suppressed it, ordering Staël to leave France again and confiscating all her manuscripts and proofs. The book was by implication sharply critical of Bonaparte, but Schlegel managed to get a set of proofs

to Vienna, and in 1813 the volume was finally published in London from a second set secreted by Staël herself, flamboyantly prefaced by Ravigo's letter of suppression. In October 1810, however, Staël retired to Coppet, leaving her book to be pulped.

She had had a brief affair in Vienna in 1808, the year in which Constant married Mme de Tertre, although Staël persuaded them not to make the marriage public. Constant continued in her entourage until the advent of John Rocca, who was 23 years her junior and suffered from consumption. Staël promised to marry Rocca and in 1812 bore him a son. She was harrassed at Coppet, and friends such as Mme Récamier were themselves sent into exile for visiting her. In 1813, on the pretext of taking an afternoon drive, she escaped to Vienna, now allied to France, and from there travelled via Kiev and Moscow to St Petersburg and Stockholm, where she devoted her energies to setting up Count Bernadotte as a liberal hero. She left him Schlegel as his secretary while she spent nearly a year in England, the last place Bonaparte would have wished to see her, where she was welcomed as an anti-Napoleonic hero and laughed at for her tactlessness and disdain for English social convention.

Staël's second son by Narbonne was killed in a duel in 1813. When she returned to Paris on Napoleon's downfall in 1814, she could do nothing for Bernadotte and found herself supporting the Bourbon restoration. Her salon was fuller than ever, and the abolition of slavery added to her list of liberal causes. She had let Bonaparte know of a plot against his life when he was on Elba, and political overtures were made to her after his escape. Staël did not approve of the reactionary regime in Paris which followed Bonaparte's final defeat at Waterloo, but she got her 2,000,000 francs back. She spent the winter of 1815–16 in Italy, married her daughter Albertine to the leading liberal, Victor de Broglie, and returned to Coppet, which overflowed now with distinguished literary and political visitors. She married Rocca in the autumn. On 21 February 1817 she suffered a stroke. Wellington, Chateaubriand, and Mme Récamier all called, but a visit from Constant was not thought desirable. She died on 14 July.

WORKS

The *Lettres sur Jean-Jacques Rousseau*, published in a limited edition in 1788, records Rousseau's overwhelming impact on Staël, and particularly that of *La Nouvelle Héloïse* and attempts to defend the moral values exhibited in it. Staël's own style is prolix and over-enthusiastic. She is not a subtle thinker, but she glimpses and half-defines great panoramic vistas of unfocused truth and is inspired by a vigorous, almost imperious intelligence. In defence of moral and mental impetuosity she declares: "tout ce qui arrive par degrés est irrémédiable!" (everything that happens by degrees is irremediable). She differs from Rousseau only where she rightly assumes that he has deviated from Montesquieu's defence of individual political liberties.

In 1790 came the limited edition of *Sophie*, a play in rather inexpert verse obliquely reflecting the intimacy of Staël's relationship with her father, and its companion piece, *Jane Grey*. Like the short stories *Mirza* and the *Histoire de Pauline*, *Jane Grey*, with its ill-fated heroine, reflected Staël's own sense of desolation at the outset of her marriage and before her meeting with Talleyrand. The 1793 *Réflexions sur le procès de la Reine* suggests an almost naive surprise that the liberalism she supported could have turned into the Terror she loathed, a feeling which also permeates her posthumously published *Considéra-tions sur les principaux événements de la Révolution française.* The 1794 *Réflexions sur la paix*, published in Switzerland, attacked Pitt's alliance with the reactionary émigrés rather than the moderates, and again decried Robespierre and the Terror. Charles James Fox borrowed from this work in his famous anti-war speech to Parliament on 24 May 1795, the year in which Staël reaffirmed her support for the republic and an alliance of moderates in the *Réflexions sur la paix.*

More important are the moral works which followed, *L'Essai sur les fictions* of 1796 on the moral guidance to be sought from writers, and *De l'influence des passions sur le bonheur des indi-vidus et des nations* of the same year, an occasionally lyrical essay pointing to the political dangers of "l'esprit de parti" (party zeal). According to this work the romantic soul, exceptional and sensi-tive, was alone susceptible to passion, but the individual quest for happiness, like the national quest for freedom, was doomed to frustration. Staël was reflecting here on her liaison with Narbonne and her experience of the Revolution. In spite of the disillusion which marks all her works from now on, she could still believe with Condorcet that scientific and material progress brought soci-ety, itself perfectible, to an ever higher moral level. This is the underlying thesis of the 1800 *De la littérature considérée dans ses rapports avec les institutions sociales*, in which she intended to enquire into the reciprocal influence of literature and society, with its religion, moral values, and laws.

Staël's judgements in *De la littérature* are breathtakingly bold and one-sided. The Greeks are dismissed and Spanish and Italian literatures relegated in favour of the Romans, Ossian (q.v.), and French literature of the 17th and 18th centuries. Two great groups of literatures are identified, anchored respectively in the climate, geography, and societies of the North and the South. The ideas expressed here are powerful, unrefined, prejudiced, and ill-assorted, admitting of no synthesis and distorted by Staël's own classical taste. By introducing a consideration of the relationship between literature and the society in which it is produced, how-ever, they provided a fertile breeding ground for the sociology of literature as well as for much modern critical theory. Staël also emphasizes the importance of Christianity for the Middle Ages, again laying foundations for the romanticism (q.v.) to come.

Staël now turned her attention to the novel, partly driven, no doubt, by the need to unload the contents of an overburdened heart. The eponymous heroine of *Delphine*, a novel in letter form, is a flattering self-portrait. The novel brims over with prejudice and special pleading: against Catholicism, for divorce, and the redemptive quality of love. Parisian society manners are satirized; and the political overtones of the work were to annoy Bonaparte. The rare women of refined sensibility are doomed here to frustra-tion since they are unlikely to find love in marriage, an ideal of the supreme good which had been alternately praised and derided in French literature since the late 17th century. *Corinne* concerns a half-Italian, half-British poet, actress, and musician who dies of unrequited passion. It is a novel of ideas and feeling, probing what were later to emerge as romantic values. The characters are inter-estingly aristocratic, since even on the eve of the romantic move-ment elevation of sentiment was clearly still more credible when it was the consequence of refinement of breeding. Much of the book is about Italy, its monuments, and their effects on those sen-sitive enough to react to them, and Staël fulfils a fantasy when she has Corinne crowned on the Capitol. The work was an immense success and had gone into its 40th edition by 1872.

Napoleon correctly discerned the book's hostility to his Ital-ian policy, so the censor's permission for *De l'Allemagne* was suddenly revoked, although in the end it was printed from a smuggled set of proofs in London in 1813. Its sin was to mediate a better knowledge of German culture to the French. The picture it conveys is commonplace, often crass, even an implausible caricature, but infused with much sympathy and goodwill. There are romantic emphases, on liberty and nationalism for instance, and a priority of feeling over form, although Staël ignores the beginnings of German romantic literature, concen-trating her attention on Goethe and Schiller, and preferring Kant to Fichte and Schelling. For the first time she uses the categories "classicism" and "romanticism," in the sense derived from Schlegel, of dreamy melancholy, anxious to oppose some spe-cifically German cultural characteristic to classic French literary norms. Goethe liked the book, and it does contain some sharp observation to underpin its almost crushing enthusiasm.

Staël's real inspiration was by now exhausted. Apart from the fascinating account of her travels, *Dix années d'exil*, published posthumously in 1821, her remaining works were mostly political pamphlets. Originally intended to justify her father's policies, they turn into sharply anti-Napoleonic tirades, frequently idealiz-ing English liberalism in the 18th-century French tradition.

PUBLICATIONS

Collections

Oeuvres complètes, 17 vols., 1820–21
Oeuvres inédites, 3 vols., 1830–36
L'Oeuvre imprimée de Mme Germaine de Staël, edited by F.-C. Lonchamp, 1949

Works

Lettres sur Jean-Jacques Rousseau, 1788
Sophie (1786) and *Jane Grey*, 1790
Réflexions sur le procès de la reine, 1793
Réflexions sur la paix, 1795 (ed. Cordié, 1945)
Mirza (short stories), 1795
L'Essai sur les fictions, 1796 (ed. Tournier, 1979)
De l'influence des passions sur le bonheur, 1796 (ed. Tournier, 1979)
De la littérature considérée dans ses rapports avec les institu-tions sociales, 2 vols., 1800 (ed. van Tieghem, 1959)
Delphine, 4 vols., 1802
Du caractère de M. Necker et de sa vie privée, 1804
Corinne, 3 vols., 1807
De l'Allemagne, (pulped edition 1810), 3 vols., 1813
Réflexions sur le suicide, 1813
Zulma (short stories), 1813
Considérations sur la Révolution française, 3 vols., 1818
Dix années d'exil, 1821 (republished 1966)
Essais dramatiques, 1821

Correspondence

Correspondence générale, edited by B. Jasinski, 1962ff.
Lettres de Mme de Staël à Benjamin Constant, edited by Mme de Nolde, 1928

Lettres de Mme de Staël à Juliette Récamier, edited by E. Beau de Loménie, 1952

Lettres de Mme de Staël à Narbonne, edited by G. Solovieff, 1960

Lettres de Mme de Staël à Ribbing, edited by S. Balayé, 1960

Lettres de Mme de Staël à Pedro de Souza, edited by B. d'Andlau, 1979

Bibliography

Cordié, C., in *Cultura e Scuola*, 17, January–March 1966

Cordié, C., in *Annali della Scuola Normale sup. di Pisa*, 1964, 1967, and 1969

Critical studies

Herold, J.C. *Mistress to an Age: A Life of Mme de Staël*, 1958

Gutwirth, M., *Mme de Staël, Novelist*, 1978

Balayé, S., *Mme de Staël: Lumières et Liberté*, 1979

Diesbach, G. de, *Mme de Staël*, 1983

Winegarten, Renée, *Mme de Staël* (in English), 1985

STENDHAL (Pseudonym of Marie-Henri Beyle), 1783–1842.

Novelist, journalist, and critic

LIFE

Marie-Henri Beyle was born in Grenoble on 23 January 1783, the first surviving child of a prosperous lawyer, Chérubin-Joseph Beyle, who remained loyal to the aristocracy and the Church during the Revolution, and of Henriette-Adélaïde-Charlotte Gagnon, a doctor's daughter, reported by a family servant, as Stendhal somewhat gleefully relates, to have been physically repelled by her husband. This fact takes on possible significance in the light of other information included by Stendhal in his *Vie de Henry Brulard*, the somewhat cynical account of his youth written in 1835 and 1836, where he recounts, for instance, that he desired to cover his mother with kisses, "and I wanted there not to be any clothing." He resented being interrupted by his father when kissing or being kissed by his mother, and severely criticizes his father both for his blinkered concern with prosperity and for losing what would have been his patrimony by speculating in grandiose agricultural schemes.

Both biographers and critics have often considered Stendhal's overtly Oedipal relationship with his parents important for his life, as for the patterns of his literary imagination. The difficulty is that we know of Stendhal's feelings towards his parents only through "Henry Brulard," one of many personalities assumed from time to time by the writer now universally known as "Stendhal," but for whom that itself was only one of a couple of hundred pseudonyms he used in the course of his life. Stendhal, like the major characters in his novels, was perpetually seeking to discover, and anxious to disguise, his own private identity. His autobiographical works, apart perhaps from the very personal *Journal*, which was not intended for publication, are apt to distort and exaggerate. For all his ostensible meticulousness, he quite offhandedly falsifies his age, for instance, in the *Vie de Henry Brulard*.

Before dying in childbirth in 1790, his mother gave birth to two daughters, Pauline (born 1786), with whom Stendhal's relationship became virtually one of tutelage, and Zénaïde-Caroline (born 1788), whom he disliked. After his mother's death Stendhal remained very close to his maternal grandfather, but slept in his father's room. The room in which his mother had died was kept locked for 10 years. He tells us of his father's disgust and his own delight at the execution of Louis XVI in 1793. Recurring imaginative patterns in the novels, interweaving domestic and political attitudes, show frequently disguised traces of Stendhal's formative emotional experiences. He seeks in particular to justify his strong youthful feelings of rebellion against the adult world, and seems to have been unable when young to believe that his father, or any other adult after his mother's death, was genuinely fond of him. He may at least partly have projected on to his mother's sister, Séraphie, the dislike of himself which he attributed to her, and he must have clamped his emotional responses at an early age. He could not cry normally at his mother's death, or at the death from concussion in 1793 of Lambert, his childhood friend and his grandfather's valet, and it was not until he was ill that he found himself unable to hold back tears.

The Revolution brought one or more periods of brief imprisonment for Stendhal's conservative father in 1789, but in 1794 the anti-clerical patriotic, and republican youth movement attracted the young Stendhal. It cannot be ruled out, therefore, that the roots of his later republican political stance were more psychological than intellectual. Stendhal may also have exaggerated the Italian origins of the Gagnons on account of the warmth he felt for his grandfather, an admirer of Voltaire and a carry-over from Enlightenment taste and literacy, whose southern candour could be made to stand for all the sensitivity, passion, and Spanish energy of will which contrasted with the peasant cunning of the northern Beyles. Room had to be found in this mythology for the exception of his mother's sister Aunt Séraphie, the domestic ally of Stendhal's father until her death in 1797. Some of the posturing fell at the first jump when Stendhal's aristocratic distaste for the coarseness of republican manners diminished his political commitment to the republican cause. By his own admission he repeatedly failed to carry through the rebellious roles in which he had cast himself. Even when, at the age of 14, he fought a duel with another boy who had pulled his chair from under him in drawing class, it is unlikely that the seconds loaded the pistols, neither of which went off.

Stendhal developed an early love of music and of the visual arts, although his interests were mostly literary, and in adolescence centred largely on Shakespeare, who overwhelmed him, and on erotic 18th-century novels. He was particularly sensitive to the emotional force of Rousseau's *La Nouvelle Héloïse*. As he grew older, he got to know his mother's young brother better, a lawyer, dandy, and womanizer, who acquired a young wife and an estate in Savoy, which represented for the young Stendhal a foretaste of Italy. From 1797 he had been allowed to go to the theatre by himself, and his first recorded infatuation is for a 19-year-old actress, Virginie Kubly, whom he watched night after night, but never spoke to. His shy adoration, which prevented him from approaching her when he passed her in the street, became an imaginative mechanism for dramatizing his sexual encounters in his own mind and in his books.

anonymously in 1825. Stendhal knew him and wrote a eulogistic review, attributing the book to the duchess. He then tried to write his own version, which turned into *Armance* in the wake of his liaison with "Menti" Curial. Stendhal always avoided sexual explicitness in his novels, and Octave never actually confesses the nature of the impediment to his love for Armance, although Stendhal had in fact considered the sexual mechanics of a honeymoon which would still leave Armance blissful. The novel was considered bizarre by a readership which did not know that Stendhal's Octave had to be identified with Latouche's Olivier, but its fundamental weakness lies in the transfer to Octave of Stendhal's own recent gloom, which is not convincingly grafted on to Octave's personal plight. While Stendhal fantasized about committing suicide at around this time, Octave actually does so.

In *Armance* Stendhal had done away with the cumbersome descriptions of Balzac and with Scott's rich accumulation of copious detail to create the illusion of authenticity. His incidents were too abrupt, however, and above all insufficiently motivated by the interaction of the characters. He had not achieved what he was striving for, the classic psychological perfection of Mme de Lafayette's *La Princesse de Clèves*. That novel was set a century earlier than it was written. *Le Rouge et le noir*, which does have the psychological subtlety Stendhal sought, is subtitled "Chronique de 1830." It was set in the year it was published, not only in a France in which materialism, hypocrisy, self-serving, and caste consciousness were, as ever, rife, but at a precise moment of explosive tension in the relationships between the aristocracy, the bourgeoisie, the working people, the monarchy, and the clergy. It is not the story of the 1830 revolution, but a chronicle from the society, provincial and Parisian, in which it took place.

The narrative skeleton is relatively simple and conflates the account of a crime committed in 1827 with the Paris gossip of 1830 about Marie de Neuville, a fiery aristocratic girl who defied all conventions of class by running away to London with a lover. Stendhal discovered, probably in 1829, the account of a crime committed by one Antoine Berthet, the 23-year-old son of an artisan who had been taken on as a tutor by a local family and become the lover of his pupil's mother, 12 years his senior. He was dismissed, spent some time in a seminary, again obtained a position as tutor, became involved with the daughter of the house, was again dismissed, and fired a gun at his first mistress, whom he found in church. He was guillotined.

The real interest of Stendhal's novel does not of course reside in the story, but Stendhal went to the trouble of markedly changing the second love affair. It is Mathilde de la Mole who makes the advances to Julien Sorel, who responds but is emphatically not a social climber. Mathilde's father, to avoid scandal, arranges for Julien to be ennobled and commissioned in the army, but makes enquiries of Mme de Rênal, the mistress of the first household whom Julien had seduced and still loved. Mathilde shows him Mme de Rênal's reply to her father, accusing Julien of using seduction as a means of procuring social advancement. Julien, almost without reflection, goes to her church and shoots her during Sunday Mass. After Julien's execution Mathilde takes his head, kisses it, and gives it a magnificent burial. Mme de Rênal, recovering from a wound that turned out to be slight, dies of grief.

Significant details in the novel are drawn from Stendhal's own experience, and much is made of the pride, arrogance,

energy, and daring that he admired, as well as of the timidity and hesitancy he also shared and which wins Mme de Rênal for Julien. The novel also contains an originality of psychological analysis and narrative technique. Stendhal concentrates on the characters' consciousness not so much of what is happening as of what impression they are making and how events, people, and situations appear to them personally, revealing as much about themselves as about what they are observing. The narrator now clearly has two roles, as the apparently objective recorder of events and as the author who makes the events happen. Because Stendhal's narrator can record the impressions of one character at a time, and combine what seems to a character to be happening with a narrator's comment about that character's powers of perception, Stendhal also breaks the dichotomy which had hitherto obtained between a first-person narrator, confined to one point of view, and a third-person narrator who pretends merely to record what happens, drawing on his own omniscience about what people are thinking, what is happening elsewhere, or what would have happened in circumstances that are never realized. By breaking this dichotomy, Stendhal's narrative technique opens the way to Flaubert, Tolstoy, and the modern novel generally.

Stendhal no longer needs detailed physical descriptions or the formal presentation of characters, while the apparently casual narrative technique allows the lightest possible touches of irony. No one had written with quite this grace, delicacy, and lightness of ironic touch before. The mayor, M. de Rênal, is anxious to buttress his local importance. Having been prompted by his wife to employ young Sorel as a tutor, he finds that Sorel's father, the timber worker, has gone back on his offer and now wants more money for his son's services:

> At these words the mayor's face was thunderstruck. He recovered, however, and after a learned conversation of two whole hours, in which not a single word was not calculated, the peasant's cunning beat that of the rich man, who did not depend on it for a living.

The narrator is here commenting quite openly on the events he is narrating, but with an unusual delicacy until the twist of the knife in the final clause, itself worthy of Voltaire. The reader learns a great deal about the formalities and realities of class relationships in provincial France as well as about what is happening in the story. The earlier author most nearly capable of writing like this was Jane Austen, whom Stendhal appears not to have read.

Even the episodes of sexual intimacy, whose primary purpose is to impel the narrative along, are clearly analysed in terms of psychological relationships. Julien feels a duty to himself to seduce Mme de Rênal, or at least to hold her hand in the garden in her husband's presence as they all converse in the dark one evening. Of the gestures of love between Mathilde and Julien, the narrator tells us that they were "un peu voulus (rather forced)" before, switching into Mathilde's mind, he adds:

> Mlle de la Mole thought she was fulfilling a duty towards herself and towards her lover. The poor boy, she said to herself, has behaved with perfect gallantry. He must be happy, or perhaps it is I who am short of strength of character. But she would have paid the price of an eternity of unhappiness to avoid the cruel necessity she was in. In spite of the terrible violence she was doing to herself, she was in perfect command of her speech.

The absence of quotation and interrogation marks is a feature of the style. Stendhal does not want to make the narrator's changes of role too obvious here; and the transition from speaking from within the mind of Mathilde to apparently objective narration is achieved gradually over the final three sentences. The psychology is also mercilessly true to Stendhal's own experience of life. It perfectly matches external steadfastness of demeanour with the inner diffidence which that steadfastness belies, and blends lucidity of introspection with the projection of fantasy, but it required the suppleness of Stendhal's mature narrative techniques to communicate the psychological subtleties so swiftly to the reader.

The Waterloo narrative of *La Chartreuse de Parme* seems to have been written previously but, by delaying the action until three centuries after the date of the original short piece on the origins of the Farnese family, Stendhal could bring in Napoleon's downfall, satisfy his desire to chronicle his own age, and avoid the political embarrassment of writing, as French consul in Civitavecchia, about the scandalous behaviour of a historical pope. Alexander Farnese, who had abducted an aristocratic lady, was imprisoned, but escaped with the help of a Borgia cardinal in love with his beautiful aunt, who had Alexander made a cardinal at 24. He lived with another aristocratic woman called Cleria and became Pope Paul III in 1534, at the age of 67. In the novel Alexander became Fabrice, Cleria became Clélia, the jailer's daughter, while the aunt and her Borgia lover became Gina, Countess Piatranera, later Duchess of Sanséverina, and Count Mosca. The novel was written at breakneck speed, dictated for 10 or more hours a day between 4 November and 26 December 1838, as if it had been welling up in its author's mind for years and suddenly gushed out, like water from a bursting dam.

La Chartreuse, with its peaks of ecstasy and lyrical interludes, is poised between nostalgia for revived youth and consciousness of encroaching age, between Fabrice and Mosca, and between different feelings within Gina. As in *Le Rouge et le noir* solitude is the final condition for self-fulfilment, and sexuality is wielded for the power it confers. The incidents from Stendhal's own life still crowd in, most obviously in the relationship between Fabrice and his aunt, but Fabrice, in contrast to Julien, is really in love only with the younger of the two women in his life, so that Stendhal's imagination is at any rate not confined to Oedipal patterns.

The plot of *La Chartreuse* is even less important than that of *Le Rouge et le noir*. After Waterloo, Fabrice returns to Parma, where his aunt is the mistress of Count Mosca, the chief minister. She arranges an ecclesiastical career for Fabrice, whom she loves, and the count's enemies try to get rid of all three. The plot succeeds. Fabrice is imprisoned but escapes from the tower, helped by the count, the duchess, and the traditional jailer's daughter, Clélia Conti. The duchess arranges for the Prince of Parma to be poisoned, and a pardon is obtained for Fabrice from his successor. Fabrice's ecclesiastical career advances and he becomes the lover of Clélia, now married. He kidnaps the son he has had by her, but the son dies, as does Clélia herself. Fabrice retires to the Charterhouse, the "Chartreuse" of the title, and dies a year later, followed soon after by his aunt.

Stendhal richly exploits the ambiguous roles of his narrator, who is allowed to laugh with ironic lucidity at the emotional fantasies acted out by the characters. The pre-existing but rewritten Waterloo scene is an especially brilliant set piece. "Waterloo" for Fabrice is a matter of charging about, mostly lost, trying to connect what is going on with what he knows, from his reading, a battle should be like. Large sections of the narrative seem simply to be left out, although the reader knows what has happened. Stendhal uses his narrator not only to change the point of view from character to character more frequently than in *Le Rouge et le noir*, but also to comment more openly on the characters and on his own role in a way now reminiscent of Diderot. The narrator also comments on the differences between Italy and France to the detriment of both. Stendhal, having established complete mastery over his material, can now afford a richer seam of ironic comedy. Superior to *Le Rouge et le noir* in technical mastery, *La Chartreuse* may go too far in ironically putting its central characters beyond the reach of the reader's powers of identification. The publisher demanded the somewhat peremptory ending out of considerations of cost.

Lucien Leuwen is too far from complete for any comment to be made about its qualities other than that the text we have contains some brilliant pieces of writing, notably in the analysis of political life. Lucien is the son of a rich banker. His youthful and enthusiastic republicanism gets him expelled from the Ecole Polytechnique, and he resigns himself to a military career. Unfortunately we have no idea how Stendhal would have ended up shaping his material, what tones, registers, or techniques he would have used, or even at what stage he decided that he either could not or would not turn it into a finished novel. For lovers of Stendhal and connoisseurs of literature it remains merely a fascinating mine of technically brilliant writing.

PUBLICATIONS

Collections

Oeuvres complètes (incomplete), 34 vols., 1914–40
Oeuvres complètes, 79 vols., 1927–37
Oeuvres complètes, edited by Victor del Litto and Ernest Abravanel, 18 vols., 1960–62
Romans et nouvelles, Bibliothèque de la Pléiade, 2 vols., 1966 and 1968

Fiction

Armance; ou, Quelques scènes d'un salon de Paris en 1827, 1827; as *Armance* (in English), 1928; translated with *L'Abbesse de Castro* and other stories, 1946; as *Armance* (in English), 1961
Le Rouge et le noir: chronique du XIXe siècle, 1830; as *Red and Black*, 1900; as *The Red and the Black*, 1914; as *Scarlet and Black*, 1938; as *The Red and the Black*, 1953
La Chartreuse de Parme, 1839; as *La Chartreuse de Parme* (in English), 1895; as *The Charterhouse of Parma*, 1925; new translations, 1956, 1960
L'Abbesse de Castro (includes *Vittoria Accoramboni* and *Les Cenci*), 1839
Chroniques italiennes, 1855
Lucien Leuwen, in *Nouvelles inédites*, 1855; published separately, 1894; as *The Green Huntsman* and *The Telegraph*, 1950; as *Lucien Leuwen* (in English), 1951
Lamiel, edited by Casimir Stryiensky, 1889; edited by Victor del Litto, 1971; as *Lamiel* (in English), 1952
Feder; or, The Moneyed Husband, 1960

Other

Lettres écrites de Vienne…sur…Haydn,…Mozart et… Métastase, 1814; as *Vies de Haydn, de Mozart, et de Métastase*, 1817; as *Haydn, Mozart, Métastase* (in English), 1817

Histoire de la peinture en Italie, 1817

Rome, Naples, et Florence en 1817, 1817; revised edition, 1826; as *Rome, Naples, and Florence*, 1818; same title, 1959

De l'amour, 1822; edited by Victor del Litto, 1980; as *On Love*, 1928; as *Love*, 1957

Racine et Shakespeare, 2 vols., 1823–25; as *Racine and Shakespeare*, 1962

La Vie de Rossini, 1823; as *The Memoirs of Rossini*, 1824; as *Life of Rossini*, 1970

Promenades dans Rome, 1829; as *A Roman Journal*, edited by Haakon Chevalier, 1959

Mémoires d'un touriste, 1838

Vie de Napoléon, in *Oeuvres complètes.*, 1876; as *A Life of Napoleon*, 1956

Vie de Henry Brulard, edited by Casimir Stryiensky, 1890; revised edition, edited by Henry Debraye, 2 vols., 1913; edited by Beatrice Didier, 1978; as *The Life of Henry Brulard*, 1925; same title, 1958

Souvenirs d'égotisme, edited by Casimir Stryiensky, 1892; edited by Henri Martineau, 1927; as *Memoirs of an Egotist*, 1949

Journal, edited by Henry Debraye and Louis Royer, 5 vols., 1923–34; edited by Henri Martineau, 5 vols., 1937; selection, as *Private Diaries*, edited by Robert Sage, 1955

To the Happy Few (selected letters), edited by Norman Cameron, 1952

En marge des manuscrits de Stendhal, edited by Victor del Litto, 1955

Feuillets inédits (journal of 1837–38), edited by Marcel A. Ruff, 1957

Selected Journalism from the English Reviews, edited by Geoffrey Strickland, 1959

Correspondance, Bibliothèque de la Pléiade, 3 vols., 1962–68

Stendhal and the Arts, edited by David Wakefield, 1973

Voyages en Italie, Bibliothèque de la Pléiade, 1973

Oeuvres intimes, Bibliothèque de la Pléiade, 2 vols., 1981–82

Bibliography

del Litto, Victor, *Bibliographie stendhalienne 1938–1946*, 1948 (and supplements)

Critical studies

Adams, Robert Martin, *Stendhal: Notes on a Novelist*, 1959

Brombert, Victor (editor), *Stendhal: A Collection of Critical Essays*, 1962

Hemmings, F.W.J., *Stendhal: A Study of His Novels*, 1964

Brombert, Victor, *Stendhal: Fiction and the Themes of Freedom*, 1968

Morris, Herbert, *The Masked Citadel: The Significance of the Title of Stendhal's Chartreuse de Parme*, 1968

Gutwirth, Marcel M., *Stendhal*, 1971

Tillett, Margaret G., *Stendhal: The Background of the Novels*, 1971

Wood, Michael, *Stendhal* (in English), 1971

Chaitin, Gilbert D., *The Unhappy Few: A Psychological Study of the Novels of Stendhal*, 1972

Mitchell, John, *Stendhal: Le Rouge et le Noir* (in English), 1973

Strickland, Geoffrey, *The Education of a Novelist*, 1974

May, Gita, *Stendhal and the Age of Napoleon*, 1977

Morris, Herbert, *The Romantic Prison*, 1978

Alter, Robert, *Stendhal: A Biography*, 1979

Finch, Alison, *Stendhal: La Chartreuse de Parme* (in English), 1983

STRUCTURALISM

See also Barthes, Foucault, Lévi-Strauss, and Sartre

In the context of French intellectual discussion since World War II the words "semiology," "semiotic(s)," and their cognates, and "structural(ism)" are all flagship terms in the sense that advocates of different ideologies have sought to capture them for their exclusive use, and to use them to denote ideological positions rather than to convey a precise semantic content. Since the ideological differences always latent in the respective outlooks of Sartre and Lévi-Strauss came out into the open, the spelling itself, "structural(e)" or "structurel(le)," has come to indicate an ideological position, although the two spellings convey no obvious distinctions of meaning. It is difficult to write about the meaning or usage of any of these terms without being caught up in the ideological alignments their use presupposes, but it is generally admitted that "structuralism" emerged separately as a phenomenon in linguistics, in which it was associated with the development by Roman Jakobson of the linguistic ideas of Saussure, and as a phenomenon in ethnology and sociology, where it was associated with views developed by Lévi-Strauss in reaction to Marcel Mauss.

It is important, therefore, to bear in mind that, like "existentialism" (q.v.), structuralism is not capable of precise definition, since it has commonly been used to denote friendliness or hostility to groups of persons or reviews, as well as to a variety of positions which may or may not have been closely related to one another in ethnology, linguistics, and politics. The success of Michel Foucault's *Les Mots et les choses* (1966) was at least partly due to his reputation as a "structuralist," although he frequently repudiated the term and, indeed, wrote his next book, *L'Archéologie du savoir* (1969), partly to dissociate himself from his structuralist reputation. Yet Foucault is treated as one of eight major French "structuralists" in what might well prove to be the definitive history of the movement, Edith Kurzweil's *The Age of Structuralism* (1980). The other seven authors to whom individual chapters are devoted are Claude Lévi-Strauss, Louis Althusser, Henri Lefebvre, Paul Ricoeur, Alain Touraine, Jacques Lacan, and Roland Barthes, although the introduction points out that Lefebvre, Ricoeur, and Touraine represent "the main intellectual movements contending with structuralism." Other historians of French intellectual debate would no doubt have chosen different dates and different thinkers to define the structuralist movement.

Since *The Age of Structuralism* treats "the structuralist debate" as concerned with "the most important trends in French social theory since the decline of existentialism," no chapter is devoted to Sartre, although the period covered is from "about 1955 to the early 1970s" and Sartre was still bidding for the use of the term, spelt "structurel," in 1960. The debate about the distinction of meaning, if any, implied by the two ways of spelling the adjective was in fact carried on into the special number of *Les Temps Modernes* (q.v.) devoted to structuralism edited in November 1966 by Jean Pouillon. The fundamental divergence between Lévi-Strauss and Sartre became clear when, at the invitation of Georges Gurvitch, Lévi-Strauss contributed an introduction to a new edition of Mauss's work *Sociologie et anthropologie* (1950), which was in fact a reaction against Mauss's theory of the ritual exchange of gifts in primitive tribes, using the linguistic model which Lévi-Strauss had taken from Roman Jakobson.

Mauss attributed the exchange of gifts to a system of social obligations. Lévi-Strauss holds in his introduction that Mauss should have concentrated not on the different discrete actions, which he regards as constituting "un donné purement phénoménologique, sur lequel l'analyse scientifique n'a pas de prise" (a purely phenomenological occurrence which cannot be the object of scientific analysis), but on the underlying "nécessité inconsciente" (unconscious necessity) of the social system of gift-giving itself. This view implies an incompatibility between structural anthropology and phenomenology as Lévi-Strauss understood them, and would in fact have meant treating the exchange of gifts in the same way as that in which Jakobson was explaining the latent organization of language as a system of opposing phonemes. In each case it was the underlying system of organization which was the appropriate subject of study, not the neutral exchange of words, which could link subjects and objects without actually meaning anything (called by Jakobson "zero phonemes"), or of gifts, which, for Lévi-Strauss, did not, necessarily imply any relationship between giver and recipient at all. For Sartre, the exchange of gifts had to have an economic and a social significance, like that of oppression and submission, while the Lévi-Strauss view promoted the unconscious to a prominence incompatible with Sartre's views about freedom.

Noam Chomsky (born in 1928) was notoriously to develop certain of Jakobson's views when he held that we share a common corpus of structures of thought: "our systems of belief are those that the mind, as a biological structure, is designed to construct." Chomsky does not of course belong to the mainstream of French structuralism, although he did become associated with the political activities of the editorial team of *Les Temps Modernes*. His development of Jakobson's thought nevertheless parallels that of Lévi-Strauss, a close associate of Jakobson in New York during World War II. Jakobson himself had been a founder of the Russian formalist school (see *Tel Quel*) and continued in later life to emphasize the importance of structural relationships in literature and languages.

The 1950 split between Sartre and Lévi-Strauss hinged partly on Lévi-Strauss's lack of commitment to Sartre's anti-colonialism as the basic premise rather than the conclusion of all anthropological discussion, but also on Lévi-Strauss's promotion of the structural, proceeding in anthropology and linguistics alike from the unconscious, over the phenomenological. Sartre, on the other hand, was increasingly obliged to ignore the unconscious

in order to keep to the phenomenological level, where he could find the social relationships which he needed for his projected reconstitution of Marxism, for which he wanted to capture anthropology, and even the word "structurel." It has become more usual to refer to Sartre's anthropology as "synthetic," keeping the term "structural" for Lévi-Strauss. For Sartre social structures were the expression of the interaction of individual purposes, while, for Lévi-Strauss, it was the other way round. The whole of French intellectual life was caught up in the debate about structuralism, which in fact involves the viability and relevance of such mainstream intellectual figures and concerns as Freud, Marx, phenomenology, and linguistics, not to speak of the nature of anthropology and sociology. What was at stake in the debates about structuralism was the whole of the "science de l'homme (science of man)," the nature of man and his relationship to his environment.

The narrower dispute, between Sartre and Lévi-Strauss, moved away from the debate about the autonomy of the individual. For ideological reasons Sartre held that the individual could bestow meaning on the constraints of his or her situation. The structuralists thought on the other hand that meaning was constrained by society as a pre-consciously conditioned cultural system. As time went on, the dispute moved to the question of the structuralists' downgrading of history as an agent in social change in favour of explanation in more static "structuralist" terms, such as those, for instance, involving immigration as the catalyst or cause of change. Part of the difficulty of defining structuralism lies in the ebbing and flowing of political and personal sympathies and alignments which resulted in the sort of despairing attempt at compromise being carried in *Les Temps Modernes* by Jean Pouillon as late as November 1966. Structure becomes "the syntax of change" and structural constraints limit the possible forms of historical change. "'Structural' renvoie à la structure comme syntaxe, 'structurel' renvoie à la structure comme réalité ('Structural' refers to structure as a syntax, 'structurel' to structure as [historical] reality)." Pouillon's own intellectual acrobatics show that, however much paper was put over the cracks, by 1966 structuralism had definitively parted company with Marxism in France.

The debate moved from the arena of the philosophers and the anthropologists into that of the linguists and the historians. Jakobson had introduced a preoccupation with structures into phonology and literature, and Chomsky into general linguistics, where deep pre-conscious structures provided the rules of generative grammar, by which we make up new sentences. It was A.-J. Greimas who introduced structuralist methods into semantics, and Roland Barthes whose reintroduction of structuralist method into literary criticism gave rise to semiology, the name Barthes popularized for Saussure's general science of linguistic signs. The theoretical distinction between structure and history applied to literary texts was to be eroded, not least by Greimas. The sequences of events and utterances in narrative are not perceived differently by the reader according to whether they are history or fiction. History has to be integrated into the present in order to be narrated, and it is therefore governed by the same structures as those that govern imaginative literature. Semiology, as understood in practice by Barthes in the 1964 *Eléments de sémiologie*, is therefore structuralism applied to literary theory and criticism.

In the early 1960s Barthes became fascinated by Lévi-Strauss's forlorn attempt to find the universal mental structures underlying the common origin of all myth and all thought by breaking myths down into their smallest constituent pieces. Saussure had introduced the distinction between linguistic systems and actual language. Lévi-Strauss had absorbed this distinction from Jakobson and differentiated between the language system, "langue," and individual speech, "parole." Barthes explored the possibility that structures might provide the link between the abstract but possible level of language and its actual but necessarily limited realization. His own practice had dramatically changed from *Mythologies* through his famous analysis of *Phèdre* in *Sur Racine* of 1963, and it would change again in *S/Z* of 1970, but the 1964 essay shows that Barthes specifically used semiology in his title to denote structuralism, applied to the theory of linguistic creativity but stripped of the ideological overlay which the word "structuralism" had acquired by 1964.

Semiotics is both a wider and a more sharply defined field of enquiry than semiology. It has acquired its own ideological baggage and is, for instance, opposed to conventional forms of literary criticism, favouring more exact, scientific models for its techniques, and relying less on sensitivities and other forms of reaction that are at least partly conditioned by culture, social situation, age, personality, and other personal factors. It embraces the "theoretical possibility and the social function" of a unified approach to all possible phenomena of communicating or signifying. In *A Theory of Semiotics* (1976) Umberto Eco defines the term as covering a general theory "considering codes, sign production, the common use of languages, the evolution of codes, aesthetic communication, all types of interactional communicative behaviour and use of signs." Although Eco mentions the evolution of codes, the emphasis of those who write about semiotics or are active in the field is almost entirely analytical. There is no longer a reliance upon structuralism in the full Lévi-Strauss sense of promoting a unified "science de l'homme" by linking the disparate phenomena of communication—whether in the ritual gestures of primitive tribes or the sophisticated techniques of literary communication in advanced societies—through structures generated by a pre-conscious controlling faculty. The term structuralism is coming to be used more and more of increasingly technical analyses of systems or instances of signs or communication of a linguistic or literary nature.

SUE, Marie-Joseph, known as Eugène, 1804–1857.

Novelist.

LIFE

Sue came from a family of surgeons, many of them distinguished, as were both his grandfather, Jean-Joseph Sue I (1710–1792), and his father, Jean-Joseph Sue II (1760–1830). On 28 September 1794 Sue's father, then 34, married the 19-year-old Adélaïde-Elisabeth-Rosalie ("Adèle") Sauvan. Her father, a wealthy supporter of the Duc d'Orléans, had been due to be guillotined on 26 July that year, but his execution was post-

poned by one day, and he was saved by the fall of Robespierre on 27 July. Adèle would no doubt have married the Girondin Pierre Victurnien Vergniaud (1753–1793) had he not been guillotined. The couple had two children, one of whom died in infancy, but divorced by mutual consent on 22 June 1800. On 30 October that year Sue's father was made chief surgeon to the Imperial Guard at a salary of 4,800 francs, which was paid only erratically, however, and two years later he married Marie-Sophie Derilly ("Tison de Rilly"), the mother of Eugène and of his sister Victorine, born in 1810.

Jean-Joseph's lectures on botany and other scientific subjects became fashionable, and he is remembered for his repeatedly expressed view that, far from being as painless a form of death as had been believed when it was reserved for the aristocracy, instantaneous decapitation allowed thought and sensation to continue for a period after the severance of the head. The new scientifically designed machine we know as the guillotine, first used on 25 April 1792, had been intended to democratize painless execution. Sue's father's, although less successful than some of his colleagues, made a comfortable living from his profession. Patients notoriously failed to pay, but were charged up to 20 francs a visit, and a professorial salary of 2,400 francs came on top of the military stipend, making 7,200 francs a year plus whatever came in from private practice. In 1812 he took part in Napoleon's Russian campaign.

Sue was educated from 1816 at what is now the Lycée Condorcet. In 1820 his mother died and, on 6 December, his father married Marie-Edmée-Françoise Rosella de Milhau, by whom he was soon to have a son. Sue's half-sister Flore, Adèle's daughter, had married in 1820. Sue himself strongly resisted the family pressure to study medicine. In 1821, the year after Sainte-Beuve arrived there, he was taken away from what was certainly one of the best schools in France. His escapades were making him virtually uncontrollable at home and, after his father discovered him using some of his best wines to give a particularly drunken party, Sue was sent with a medical team to serve at the Spanish border, eventually becoming a medical orderly.

He may have been wounded during France's successful intervention on behalf of the Spanish king, organized by Chateaubriand in 1823. In 1825 Sue returned to Paris and, rejoining old companions, quickly fell into appalling debt, enjoying the credit allowed to him on account of his father's name to lead an elegant life of spendthrift luxury. When his father discovered the extent of his debts, Sue was immediately sent back to his medical post at Toulon. There he was attracted by the theatre, resigned his post from 29 October 1825, and after seven months returned to Paris. Among his friends was a cousin who had just founded a newspaper, *La Nouveauté*, whose first number, two pages of two columns each, had appeared on 1 September 1825. Although, following another family tradition, Sue now wanted to be a painter, he helped with the paper, and it printed the first piece of writing that can be attributed to him with certainty, the anonymous "Première lettre de l'homme-mouche à M. le Préfet de Police," which appeared on 23 January 1826, already part of a serial. Further "Lettres" appeared on 25, 29, and 31 January, but the dates Sue gives for the earlier contes to be reprinted in *La Coucaratcha*—1824 for "L'idiot" and 1825 for "L'embuscade" and "Récifs de Saint-Mandry"—are almost certainly wrong, so that an exact chronology of his literary beginnings is now virtually impossible.

Sue belonged to an irreverent, anti-establishment group of elegant young men that was snobbish but liberal. His invention of lively underworld characters, showing off his exuberant dramatic sense, partly derives no doubt from a deliberately disdainful attitude to the solid bourgeois virtues for which his family stood. On Shrove Tuesday 1826, at the climax of the pre-Lenten carnival, Sue and his friends nevertheless went too far. They slaughtered, roasted, and ate one of his father's sheep, which turned out to be a valuable Merino. Sue was immediately sent to sea as a medical auxiliary, third class, serving from 21 February 1826. He was promoted, visited the East, saw action against the Turks on 20 October 1827 and, although later reproached with cowardice, appears to have managed to perform amputations under fire. His powers of observation were sharp, and his experiences as a dandy, as well as those at sea and in the East, were all to nourish his future fiction as richly as his animosity towards his father's bourgeois values. On 12 December 1827 he requested permission to leave his vessel before the expiration of the normal quarantine period and arrived in Paris with a portfolio of sketches. He began working at the studio of the maritime painter Théodore Gudin, who had exhibited with Delacroix in the Salon of 1822 and gone on to win prizes in 1824 and 1828. It was at Gudin's studio that Sue met Henri-Bonaventure Monnier, the cartoonist who invented the personage of "Joseph Prudhomme" as a vehicle for ridiculing the new middle classes, all of whose limitations he systematically exaggerated.

Sue's fun-loving group of dandies continued to make minor public nuisances of themselves in sometimes amusing ways. *La Nouveauté* had closed in January 1827, to reopen in June 1830 as a fashion magazine, but on 5 April 1828 Sue's illegitimate duel-prone cousin, who posed as his brother and was later to achieve power and fame as editor of *La Presse* after winning a court battle which allowed him to call himself Emile de Girardin, founded the weekly gazette *Le Voleur*. True to its name, it stole from elsewhere everything printed in its first number. The group also included another figure who was to be of immense importance in the cultural life of 19th-century Paris, the pharmacist Louis Véron, whom Sue had met while attending medical classes. He was to run the *Revue de Paris* before becoming director of the Opéra. The group's favourite haunts were Tortoni's and the Café de Paris, and they were the fashionable men about town of their generation, solidly middle class but inclined to liberalism in politics and apt to poke fun at the dull conservatism of their professionally or commercially successful families.

Only its social historical background makes Sue's success and his importance intelligible. When Haussmann destroyed the Paris of little villages with his broad boulevards and town planning, he also destroyed most of the dark, dirty, and rat-infested slums of a Paris whose population in 1815 is estimated to have been some 630,000. Modernization had already begun before the cholera epidemic swept through the city for two months from February until April 1832, but it was the cholera, leaving 20,000 dead in its wake, that finally forced the provision of piped water and proper sewers. Gas had begun to replace oil street lighting in 1828, the year of the first omnibus line, and brighter lighting was already leading to a cleaner city. Literacy, if not the sort of education that could lead to a professional career, was soon to become universal. The new romantic (q. v.) movement was exploring the social as well as the artistic values of the generation which precipitated the revolution of 1830. It is against this background that the press, which was to be the

source of Sue's success, was revolutionized when, after the widely read *Journal des Connaissances Utiles* had adopted a new format in 1836, Girardin and Armand Dutacq founded, respectively, *La Presse* and *Le Siècle*. The new newspapers were to be supported by advertising revenue and sold at an annual subscription of 40 francs, half the usual newspaper price.

In 1829 Girardin had started another weekly, *La Silhouette*, still necessarily relying on the best cartoonists available. He was condemned to six months in prison and a fine of 1,000 francs for publishing a cartoon of Charles X as a Jesuit. Not at all discouraged, he founded *La Mode* in October of the same year. Sautelet of *Le National*, who was to commit suicide on 13 May 1830, and Dubois of *Le Globe* were sent to prison for three and four months respectively for articles which appeared in February 1830. "Gavarni" (Sulpice-Guillaume Chevalier), the lithographer and caricaturist whose life was written by the Goncourt brothers in 1873 and for whom the Magny dinners were first organized, was soon to begin publishing his increasingly bitter sketches of Parisian low life. In November 1830 Charles Philipon founded the satirical weekly *La Caricature*, which was suppressed in 1835 after 251 issues, and in 1832 the daily *Le Charivari*, which lasted for more than 30 years and printed Gavarni's most famous series, "Fourberies de femme en matière de sentiment" and "Les Lorettes."

In 1831 *La Caricature* was confiscated 19 times and Philipon went to prison for six months. Money to pay his fine was raised by the sale of lithographs by his constant contributor, Honoré Daumier, who spent six months in prison himself for depicting Louis-Philippe swallowing bags of money extorted from the people. Sue reached the age of majority, still 25, in 1829, in this milieu of often satirical gazettes and newspapers. After the renewed suppression of political satire in 1835, the newspapers turned increasingly to lithographs of ordinary life and to the "feuilleton," which generally filled the bottom third of the front page, and was devoted to the traditional "gazette" of events in the worlds of society, the arts, and politics, shifting slowly to fiction, much of it written for those levels of society newly but rapidly acquiring elementary levels of literacy. Feelings of frustration and rage at the establishment were assuaged or stimulated first by cartoons with pithy captions, and then by the only partially escapist adventure novels which made fortunes for Sue, Soulié, and Dumas, and a lot of money for Balzac and George Sand. Demand for serialized novels peaked in the early 1840s, but diminished when newspapers carrying fiction had to pay a special stamp tax.

Sue's first Paris theatrical venture was the vaudeville *Monsieur le Marquis*, the result of a collaboration with Philippe-Auguste Deforges, a colleague over whose initials *La Nouveauté* had printed Sue's work as well as his own. It was presented on 17 March 1829 at what would become the Gymnase. Sue's first signed piece of journalism was a review of an exhibition for *La Mode* in the last quarter of 1829. He wrote several pieces in *La Psyché*, reprinted in *La Coucaratcha*, but continued to regard himself largely as a painter, somehow transcending by the hauteur of his attitudes and the arrivisme of his bourgeois aspirations the great gulf between the starving poor he so sharply observed and the dandified rich with whom he consorted.

At this date a labourer could not earn enough to keep a wife and two children in food alone, however hard he worked. Nineteenth-century literature, romantic, realist, or naturalist (qq. v), and the parallel developments in all the other arts in 19th-century France, can really only be understood when the statistics are kept in mind. By the 1840s, when Paris had some 900,000 adult inhabitants, the records show one in three births as illegitimate, 15,000 registered prostitutes, of whom one in eight was under 12, one child in four abandoned at birth, and a perinatal death rate of 50 per cent. Only a third of the adult population was earning a living in identifiable ways, including begging and prostitution. The newspapers resorted to bitter caricatures, the authorities to firm repression, the major authors to liberal inclinations, if not utopian visions, and social and political frustrations regularly erupted into violence, notably in the revolutions of 1830, 1848, and 1870–71.

Sue's sexual encounters seem to have been frequent and casual. On inheriting 80,000 francs from his maternal grandfather early in 1830, just before his father's death on 21 April, he could have mixed in whatever society he pleased. His stepmother, who continued to look after his 20-year-old sister Victorine, and had borne Sue's father a son, Joseph-Dieudonné, in 1823, was to remarry and to bear her second husband twins, the Rose and Blanche who appear in *Le Juif errant*. Eugène's father left each of his three unmarried children 700,000 francs. Sue now gave up all thoughts of medicine and abandoned his hitherto sporadically active naval career, which had spanned seven years. Accounts written by others after the spectacular successes of *Les Mystères de Paris* and *Le Juif errant* are all clearly distorted by the accretion of legend, such as Sue's alleged cowardice, born of envy.

By 1830, aged 26, and now rich, Sue had acquired real experience of the East, of life at sea, and of conducting gruesome medical procedures. He had received the best education France had to offer, had lived the life of a Paris dandy, observed the poor, been carried by the romantic reaction against bourgeois conservatism and insensitivity, mixed in theatrical, journalistic, and artistic circles, and hovered on the fringes of high society. He had also enjoyed the facile cynicism of Béranger's dithyrambs to purity of heart, and read Byron and Scott, although he was to show signs of having been more impressed by Fenimore Cooper than by either. Energetic, cheerful, and sentimental, he was about to become one of the most popular novelists ever to write in French.

He furnished an apartment luxuriously and took an expensive mistress with extravagant tastes, the well-known Olympe Pelissier, daughter of an obscure actress known as "la Descuillier." She had been hostess to numerous journalists, painters, sculptors, musicians, and minor aristocrats, including the best of each, and was to leave Sue for Rossini in 1834. Sue had got to know them all, had become friendly with the still unknown Balzac, and begun to publish, or to republish, short pieces in *La Mode* and *Les Annales Romantiques*. There are clear signs that he did not take himself quite seriously as a writer. He was too young and too rich to want to belong to any literary group and if, when he needed to earn money by his pen, he later settled for popular acclaim, the loser was posterity. Sue could never have achieved the imaginative penetration of a Flaubert, a Zola, or a Balzac, but he is a more interesting writer of fiction than Dumas, and could well have been as important an author as George Sand.

Sue already had a lively social conscience, was intentionally conservative on some issues while also anti-establishment, showing a characteristically impertinent hauteur which pre-

vented any real alliance with the romantics or their realist successors. He published *Plik et Plok*, a conflation of two short stories to make a maritime novel, which ran to three editions in 1831 and attracted excellent reviews. Although he still regarded himself more as a gentleman than as a writer, Sue continued with "Le combat de Navarin" for *La Mode*, "Le bonnet de Maître La Joie" for the *Revue des Deux Mondes* (*RDM*, q. v.), and *Atar-Gull*, on whose carelessnesses the reviewers seized. There followed a series of short pieces, of trivial dramatic collaborations, and unambitious jostling with the professionals at the offices of the *RDM*, Gozlan, Gautier, Sainte-Beuve, Planche, and Musset, who more or less constituted a team, which Sue had no wish either to join or to rival.

Sue's elegance opened the doors of the society salons, although he also frequented the literary ones. He may have had affairs with the Duchesse de Rauzan and Marie d'Agoult. He entertained with great distinction, offering the best in food, table linen, silver, china, and crystal, and eschewing vulgarities like foie gras, oysters, or wine at lunch. Tailor, bootmaker, glover, reserved table at Tortoni's for lunch: fashion in Paris dictated with absolute precision the which, where, and what of smartness. The political upheavals of 1830 and 1831 changed all this much less than the cholera of 1832. Sue was to remember the epidemic well and draw carefully on his observation. Early in 1832 he had published *La Salamandre*, which, as usual with successful fiction at that date, was immediately adapted for the stage, although not by Sue himself. It was played at the Gymnase on 24 July 1834 as *Le Capitaine de vaisseau*. On 1 May 1832 the *RDM* published one of his stories, and during the summer, while staying with his now married sister, Sue wrote the preface to the collection of contes *La Coucaratcha*, announcing that his future novels would be historical. He was moving away from Cooper and towards Scott.

His first long novel was the four-volume *La Vigie de Koat-Ven*. On its appearance Sue, who was also to become an earnest, if dilettante, historian, was invited to undertake a history of the navy. The first fascicules appeared in 1835 and the 10 volumes, finished in 1837, were shocking, even at that date, for their lack of professionalism. Sue had been admitted to the immensely exclusive jockey club from its founding in 1833, and in 1836 had landed in prison briefly for some trivial escapade. He could afford to live outside the conventional social and political categories and seems to have enjoyed predominantly right-wing, royalist company without sharing either its views or its respectability. By 1837 he was being sought after by the new newspapers. Events had moved fast since Girardin's *La Presse* and Dutacq's *Le Siècle* had appeared on 1 July 1836. The *Journal des Débats* eventually came down on the side of the newcomers, adopting their style. Attacks on Girardin led in 1836 to the duel with Armand Carrel of *Le National* in which Carrel, representing the newspapers of old-fashioned opinion, was killed by a bullet in the stomach. Girardin, representing the "industrial journalism" bitterly attacked by Sainte-Beuve and less bitterly caricatured by Balzac, was wounded in the thigh and insisted on speaking at Carrel's funeral, which he attended on crutches.

In 1837 Sue published *Latréaumont*, which was cut to pieces by Planche in the *RDM* for 1 January 1838 on account of its pretentiousness. Its anti-monarchical scepticism was regarded as shocking, especially in the light of Sue's personal life style. Girardin knew that the *Journal des Débats* was publishing part of Soulié's *Mémoires du diable*, that Balzac was lined up to follow, and that Buloz was on the look out for authors for the *RDM*, and was himself anxious to publish Sue. Not only was he an old friend, but his extravagant habits had suddenly bankrupted him. Dumas estimated Sue's assets at 15,000 francs against debts of 130,000. Sue had agreed to write a new novel for Gosselin at 3,000 francs a volume, and two episodes of a feuilleton *Journal d'un inconnu* appeared in *La Presse* for 5 December 1837, a possible beginning to any sort of novel. Sue could not continue it, went to stay with friends while facing financial ruin, and managed to turn the novel begun in *La Presse* into *Arthur*. It was published by Gosselin, and also serialized by Girardin in *La Presse*, ending on 28 June 1839.

Meanwhile Sue's life in Paris remained comfortable, although much reduced in extravagance. He saw a great deal of a few close friends, including Marie d'Agoult after her break with Liszt, sold two further pieces to *La Presse* and one to the *Journal des Débats*. Demand from the press continued to increase. Even the respectable if popular *Le Constitutionnel* had yielded. It was publishing Scribe and Balzac, with George Sand to come. *Le Siècle* had Dumas, whose *Le Capitaine Paul* increased the circulation by 5,000 in three months and who had signed up for 100,000 lines a year at one and a half francs a line. Sainte-Beuve's attack on industrial literature on 1 September 1839 had fallen flat, and Buloz would not even publish his third piece on the subject. Sue drew on his racing expertise for "Godolphin Arabian," which ran in *La Presse* from 29 September to 9 October 1838, published "L'art de plaire" in the *Journal des Débats* from 11 to 31 October 1838, and "Kardiki" in *La Presse* from 25 February to 5 March 1839. Gosselin published the first of these three as *Le Marquis de Létorière* and the other two as *Deleytar*. Authors were for hire, and editors poached. In spite of what Planche had done to Sue in the *RDM*, the redoubtable Buloz bought Sue's *Un juge* for his second string, the *Revue de Paris*, which he also edited, and where he tended to off-load the material that he did not think quite up to *RDM* standards. In 1839 Sue also published the three-volume *Correspondance de Henri Escoubleau de Sourdis*, on the French navy from 1636 to 1642, "L'archiprêtre des Cévennes" in the *Revue de Paris*, and a mysterious text which he refers to as "Les flibustiers" but which was never published under that title. It could be *Le Morne-au-Diable* of 1842.

Sue was now facing another financial crisis. His friends, led by Camille Pleyel, rallied to run his affairs, ration the supply of straw-coloured gloves, and reschedule the payment of debts alongside a monthly living allowance. Sumptuousness, now an unaffordable expense, was redirected into Sue's fictional salons and the living standards of his characters. From 1838 until 1840 Sue wrote at speed, modelling himself on Dumas. The second part of "L'archiprêtre des Cévennes" appeared in the *Revue de Paris* in January 1840 as "La belle Isabeau." Gosselin published both parts as *Jean Cavalier*, and another two feuilletons as *Deux histoires, 1778–1810*. These were first published in *La Presse* from 26 April to 22 May of that year ("Aventures de Hercule Hardi" or "La Guyenne en 1772") and *Le Constitutionnel*, now owned by Véron, from 29 June until 30 July ("Le colonel de Surville, histoire du temps de l'Empire"). The stage version of *Latréaumont* failed at the Comédie-Française in 1840 after 14 performances. Sue's history of the navy had got him the Légion d'Honneur in 1839, and on 15 September 1840 Sainte-Beuve wrote about him in the *RDM*, drawing complimentary comparisons with Balzac, no doubt in pursuit of his vendetta against that

author. In a return to the novel of manners, Sue published *Mathilde, mémoires d'une jeune femme* in *La Presse* from 22 December 1840 to 26 September 1841. It was put out by Gosselin in six volumes the same year, and Dostoyevsky wanted to translate it into Russian.

Sue was still able to frequent the fashionable establishments, above all Tortoni's and the Café de Paris, although he had ceased to associate closely with many of his rich jockey club friends. It was on 26 May 1841 that the dramatist Félix Pyat, whom Sue had met at the publisher Ladvocat's, took him and Véron to dine with an engraver, Fugères, to be killed on the barricades in 1848, to show them how the workers lived and what they were capable of thinking. Sue's early cynical political indifference, like his conservative values, had slowly been thawing in reaction to the ascendancy of the middle classes chronicled by Balzac. Sue had observed it with understanding, on account of his origins, but from on high, on account of his wealth. After 26 May 1841 he was virtually a socialist, his view less visionary than that of George Sand, less aloof than Balzac's, and no doubt less morally intense than Zola's, but still productive of a serious literary and later political commitment.

Sue was writing under enormous pressure, contributing to *La France maritime* (1842) while also fully occupied with novels and plays. *Mathilde* had already been concerned with social problems, particularly those of women, and the dramatic adaptation by Pyat and Sue, given at the Porte-Saint-Martin on 24 September 1842, was enthusiastically applauded by Gautier, who talked of 200,000 readers and 200,000-strong audiences. That year Sue had also published three shorter novels, *Le Morne-au-diable*, *Paula Monti*, and *Thérèse Dunoyer*, showing a change of direction towards sentimental idealization and towards a new relationship between happiness, hope, fear, and catastrophe. From 19 June 1842 until 15 October 1843 the *Journal des Débats* serialized *Les Mystères de Paris*. Its success was scarcely to be imagined.

The newspaper's circulation doubled from 5,000 to 10,000, a much greater percentage increase than that achieved by Dumas for *Le Siècle*. Véron was to save *Le Constitutionnel* by buying *Le Juif errant* from Sue for a famous 100,000-franc fee, serializing it from June 1844 to July 1845, and boosting the paper's circulation from its low point of, according to Véron, 3,600 in 1844 to a certified figure of nearly 25,000 in 1846. Although the cheaper and less solidly bourgeois *Le Constutionnel*, for which George Sand, Dumas, and later Sainte-Beuve also wrote, was down-market from the *Journal des Débats*, with less than half its circulation (9,300 in 1846), the advertising revenues were about the same, at 350,000 francs. It was Véron, a shareholder in *Le Constitutionnel* from 1838 and its managing director from 1844, who invented the formula of cliff-hanging suspense at the end of each episode, to be so successfully exploited by Sue and Dumas.

Gosselin had brought Sue an illustrated book depicting the "mysteries" of London. What tempted Sue to write *Les Mystères de Paris* was the reproach of his literary mentors, Goubaux, Pyat, and Legouvé, themselves members of the stage and newspaper worlds, that, unlike Balzac or Sand, he had limited his observation to one layer of society. His interest in the poorer sections of the population was deepening, and his sympathies for them had already begun to develop. He diffidently sent drafts of the new work to Goubaux and Legouvé, both of whom were enthusiastic. Gosselin accepted the drafts and proposed a two-

La Bonne Aventure, 1851
La Marquise d'Alfi, 1853
L'Amiral Levacher (short stories), 2 vols., 1852
Jeanne et Louise, 1853
Fernand Duplessis, 1853
La Famille Jouffroy, 1854
Gilbert et Gilberte, 1855
Le Diable médecin, 7 vols., (originally including *Adèle Verneuil* and *La Duchesse douairière de Sénancour*), 1855–57
Adèle Verneuil, with *Le Diable médecin*, 1855–57
La Lorette, with *Le Diable médecin*, 1855–57
Les Sept péchés, 6 vols., 1851–54
Les Fils de famille, 9 vols., 1857
Les Mystères du peuple, 12 vols., 1857; as *The Mysteries of the People*, 1867; 21 vols., 1904–16
Les Mystères du monde, 1859

Plays

Monsieur le Marquis, 1829
Le Fils de l'homme, 1831
Le Secret d'état, 1831
Atar-Gull, 1832
Rita l'Espagnole, 1837
Latréaumont, 1837
La Prétendante, 1841
Les Pontons, 1841
Mathilde, 1842
Pierre le noir, 1842
Les Mystères de Paris, 1844
Martin et Bambouche on les amis d'enfance, 1847
Le Trésor des pauvres, 1847
Le Morne-au-diable, 1848
Le Juif errant, 1849

Other works

Histoire de la marine française, 10 vols., 1835–37
Correspondance de Henri Escoubleau de Sourdis, 3 vols., 1839
Histoire de la marine militaire, 1841
Le Républicain des campagnes, 1848–51
Le Berger de Kravan ou entretiens socialistes et démocratiques, 1848–49
De quoi vous plaignez-vous?, 1849
Aux électeurs, 1850
Lettre sur la question religieuse en 1856, 1857
Une page de l'histoire de mes livres, 1857
La France sous l'Empire, 1857
Ce qu'est le protestantisme, 1858

Critical and biographical studies

Atkinson, Nora, *Eugène Sue et le roman feuilleton*, 1929
Moody, John, *Les Idées sociales d'Eugène Sue*, 1938
Bory, Jean-Louis, *Eugène Sue: dandy mais socialiste*, 1962

SULLY PRUDHOMME, René-François-Armand, 1839–1907.

Poet, philosopher, and winner of the Nobel prize for literature (1901).

LIFE

Armand Prudhomme adopted the name "Sully Prudhomme," spelled more correctly without a hyphen, in order to avoid a humiliating association with the pompous imaginary bourgeois, Joseph Prudhomme, the well-known figure of fun originating in the caricatures of Henri Monnier in his celebrated *Scènes populaires* of 1830. "Sully" had been the nickname of his father, a businessman who died when Sully Prudhomme was two. His mother, said to have been withdrawn and dreamy, allowed his uncle to direct his material affairs, and Sully Prudhomme was sent to various boarding establishments. He finished his schooling at the Lycée Bonaparte, now the Lycée Condorcet, specialized in mathematics, passed his science baccalauréat in 1857, but developed ophthalmia, and was prevented from continuing to the military preparatory school, the Ecole Polytechnique. He passed his arts baccalauréat in 1858.

The key to Sully Prudhomme's personality has been seen as a combination of his scientific cosmological curiosity, melancholy introspection, and moral isolation. Edmund Gosse, writing in 1910, when Sully Prudhomme's poetic achievement was much more highly esteemed than it now is, defined the originality of his personality in terms of the combination of "a soul aspiring to what lies above and beyond science, and a conscience perpetually in agitation." During a religious crisis in late adolescence, Sully Prudhomme's Catholicism had briefly intensified under the influence of his mother's family at Lyons. His first religious doubts are to be found in the sonnets of *Les Epreuves*, written after his return to Paris, and after he had published his first volume of poetry, *Stances et poèmes*, with Faure. Gaston Paris had brought this volume to the attention of Sainte-Beuve, who had given it an enthusiastic review in *Le Constitutionnel* for 26 June 1865.

For 18 months after his return to Paris Sully Prudhomme had worked in the offices of the Schneider factory at Creusot. He began his translation of Lucretius' *De rerum natura*, to be published in 1869, which showed in the preface the strong influence of German idealism. In later life Sully Prudhomme was to abandon poetry in favour of philosophy, and from the beginning of his literary career he devoted himself to the combination of poetry and cosmology in "la poésie scientifique (scientific poetry)." He would have liked his philosophy to have been taken as seriously as his poetry was. After abandoning all ambition for a business career, Sully Prudhomme decided to read law, and in 1861 entered a notary's office in Paris. Like Heredia, he belonged to the student literary society, the Conférence La Bruyère, and he inherited a sum large enough to ensure his future financial independence.

With Heredia he met Alphonse Lemerre, whose shop in the Passage Choiseul was the focal point for a group of young poets, including Catulle Mendès and Xavier de Ricard, who were then forming what was to be called the Parnassian (q.v.) movement. In 1866 Sully Prudhomme contributed a number of pieces to Lemerre's first set of the three volumes of fascicules to be known as *Le Parnasse Contemporain* (1866, 1871, 1976) and, since Faure had gone bankrupt, Lemerre republished Sully Prudhomme's *Stances et poèmes* as well as publishing his *Les Epreuves* in 1866. In fact, Lemerre was to publish all Sully Prudhomme's remaining verse, starting with *Les Solitudes* in 1869 and finishing with *Le Nymphe des bois de Versailles* in 1896, although very little new poetry was produced after 1888. Collected volumes containing important new material, including *Le Zénith*, appeared in 1872, 1879, 1880 and 1882, and 1888, and all this verse was collected and republished as *Poésies*, occupying four of the eight volumes of the *Oeuvres*. A few poems were later published in reviews, but there is little posthumously published verse. Sully Prudhomme also published two volumes of prose criticism, *L'Expression dans les beaux-arts* and *Réflexions sur l'art des vers*.

In January 1870 a series of family bereavements left Sully Prudhomme with only one close relative, his sister. When the Franco-Prussian War came, he enlisted in the Garde Nationale. The experience destroyed his health and brought on a serious paralytic illness. Both *La Justice* and *Le Zénith* contain echoes of the war. The philosophical works came only later, mostly after he was elected to the Académie Française on 8 December 1881, and were the work of late middle age. Sully Prudhomme produced a number of philosophical articles, mostly in reviews, but some were published in volume form by Lemerre: *Que sais-je?: examen de conscience* and *Sur l'origine de la vie terrestre* appeared in 1895, and *Le Testament poétique* in 1901. Thereafter the philosophical works were published by Alcan: *Le Problème des causes finales*, written in collaboration with Charles Richet, appeared in 1902; *La Vraie Religion selon Pascal*, which grew out of three essays published by the *Revue des Deux Mondes* (q.v.) in 1890 and the *Revue de Paris*, appeared in 1905; and *La Psychologie du libre arbitre*, which had originally appeared in the *Revue de Métaphysique et de Morale* during the preceding year, appeared in 1907.

Alfred Nobel, whose will established the celebrated five annual prizes, had died in 1896, and when Sully Prudhomme was awarded the prize for literature on 8 December 1901 the will's stipulation that the work should show an "idealist" tendency was interpreted more literally than it has subsequently been. Sully Prudhomme gave most of the money to found a prize for poetry to be awarded by the Société des Gens de Lettres. He strongly championed Dreyfus in the famous dispute, but after the turn of the century lived in isolation and suffered ill health. His paralysis got worse before his sudden death on 6 September 1907. He left *Le Lien social*, a revised introduction to Michelet's *La Bible de l'humanité*.

WORKS

Sully Prudhomme's philosophy has not proved of particular interest to subsequent ages, no doubt because it was too enduringly positivistic for a generation ready for Bergson and Blondel. His scientific poetry, although a clear reaction against romanticism (q.v.) attempts to turn philosophical systems into epic verse, and gives the continuing impression of trying to fit a sublime vision into a vessel technically inadequate to contain it. It is not that scientific poetry is itself an inferior genre, as Lucretius had made clear and such French Renaissance poets as Ronsard amply demonstrated, but that Sully Prudhomme was attempting something which he, at any rate, is considered not to have achieved.

Where his verse is remembered today, it is for its gently sentimental lyricism. "Le vase brisé" has become a well-known anthology piece. In Sully Prudhomme's own time critics generally considered the grandiosity of the versified philosophical vision, as he poetically expressed it, very nearly to have succeeded, and at any rate to constitute the greatness of his poetic achievement. Jules Lemaître (1853–1915), the critic of the *Journal des Débats*, thought that Sully Prudhomme "could very well be" the greatest living poet. The Nobel committee, still mindful of the terms of the will, mentioned his "elevated idealism." It also admired the artistic perfection, which later generations have found missing, and the union of intelligence and feeling in his work. It is certainly true that Sully Prudhomme can successfully draw poetic inspiration from scientific images. Light from distant stars already on its way to us for thousands of years but destined to be seen only by future generations ("L'idéal" from *Stances et poèmes*) is a powerful image of the immensity of the cosmos.

Sully Prudhomme's other commonly admired quality, introspective melancholy, is expressed in an anti-romantic manner by exploiting subtleties of expression and a carefully polished diction which is precise, concrete, and evades the vague, the evocative, and anything redolent of self-pity. Even so, Leconte de Lisle remarked of Sully Prudhomme that in spite of his talent: "il n'est pas de la maison (he is not one of us)." He himself regarded his activity as above all philosophical:

> Je dois à mon éducation scientifique et à ma passion pour la philosophie un ardent désir de faire entrer dans le domaine de la poésie les merveilleuses conquêtes de la science et les hautes synthèses de la spéculation moderne... Par le progrès des connaissances humaines, une infinité d'objets qui n'auraient pas encore ébranlé le sens esthétique de l'homme, et qui, par suite, n'étaient pas matière à la poésie, le sont devenus.

> (I owe to my scientific education and my passion for philosophy a burning desire to bring into the realm of poetry the marvellous conquests of science and the elevated syntheses of modern speculation... Through the advance in human knowledge an infinite number of things have become material for poetry which would not have been because they would not yet have impinged on man's aesthetic awareness.) (*Le Testament poétique*)

Sully Prudhomme defined himself as a poet against the model of Lamartine. He regarded him as the epitome of all that was poetic, but rebellious against numbers, statistics, and the "tyranny of algebra," given over to vague dreams and accounts of semi-mystical states. His own poem "La métaphysique," by contrast, contains firstly a strophe of introduction about man's curiosity. The second stanza strives for poetic effect through elevated language and contrived metaphor, in which "radieuse Aurore (radiant Dawn)" seems to offer to the world the white first fruits of day in a huge rose, and ends with man's discovery of beauty. The following three stanzas are devoted, respectively, to man's discovery of the infinite, the absolute, and substance, and a brief epilogue deals with the discovery of the God of science. Each stanza after the first ends with the summing up of the discovery recounted and an exclamation mark. The last stanza runs:

Heureux d'un ferme appui, fort d'une foi sensée,
De ses grossiers autels il négligea le feu,
Et, fier de n'obéir qu'aux lois de la pensée,
Il sut alors qui nommer Dieu!

(Happy with a firm support and strong with a rationally
based faith, / He ignored the flame of his crass altars / And,
proud to obey the laws only of thought, / He knew then who
to call God!)

Whatever Sully Prudhomme may have succeeded in achieving
or failed to achieve, it is important to remember that the poetici-
zation of modern science did once respond to a real imaginative
need in western European culture. Sully Prudhomme's aim was
clear. Any critical assessment of his achievement must come to
grips with the underlying strengths and weaknesses of his poetic
technique.

PUBLICATIONS

Collections

Oeuvres, 8 vols., 1883–1908

Verse

Stances et poèmes, 1865
Les Epreuves, 1866
Les Solitudes, 1869
Les Destins, 1872
Poésies, 1872
La Révolte des fleurs, 1874
La France, 1874
Les Vaines Tendresses, 1875
La Justice, 1878
Poésies, 1879
Poésies, 1880
Poésies, 1882
Le Prisme, 1886
Le Bonheur, 1888
L'Institut, 1895
Le Nymphe des bois de Versailles, 1896

Philosophy and criticism

L'Expression dans les beaux-arts, 1883
Réflexions sur l'art des vers, 1892
*Que sais-je?: examen de conscience; Sur l'origine de la vie ter-
   restre*, 1895
Le Testament poétique, 1901
Le Problème des causes finales, with Charles Richet, 1902
La Vraie Religion selon Pascal, 1905
La Psychologie du libre arbitre, 1907 *Le Lien social*, 1909
Journal intime; Lettres, 1923

Critical and biographical studies

Hémon, C., *La Philosophie de Sully Prudhomme*, 1907
Zyromski, E., *Sully Prudhomme*, 1907
Morice, H., *La Poésie et l'esthétique de Sully Prudhomme*, 2
   vols., 1920

Estève, E., *Sully Prudhomme, poète sentimental et poète philos-
   ophe*, 1925

SUPERVIELLE, Jules, 1884–1960.

Poet, novelist, and dramatist.

LIFE

Jules Supervielle tragically lost both his parents when he was
less than a year old. His father's family came from the Pyrenees,
where his great-grandfather had settled and become a lawyer's
clerk. His grandfather had wound up Oloron's town clocks on
Tuesdays, Thursdays, and Saturdays. Supervielle's father was a
third son. The eldest, Bernard, rebelled against being sent to
school in a knitted cloak and had gone to sea at 14, done well,
and set up as a banker in Montevideo. The second son had gone
to look for him, but died of yellow fever in Rio de Janeiro.
Supervielle's father, Jules, was sent for by Bernard and joined
him as a banking partner in Montevideo. The two brothers and
partners married two sisters of Basque origin, Marie-Anne and
Maria Munyo. When Supervielle was born on 16 January 1884,
Bernard and Marie-Anne already had two children. Both families returned together to France for a reunion with the Supervielle parents, landing at Marseilles in September 1884. The
Munyo sisters' mother, who had remarried, came to Oloron for
the reunion, and there was a joint excursion to the village of
Saint-Christau the day before she was due to return to her husband.

   While on the outing, Supervielle's parents drank water from a
rusty tap in the street, but Bernard and his family were more cautious. Both Supervielle's parents died, presumably of cholera,
his mother on the same day, his father within a week. Bernard
and his wife immediately adopted Supervielle, but Marie-Anne
was too upset to take the boy straightaway, so he spent two years
with his maternal grandmother and an Argentinian nanny. He
then returned to Montevideo, was brought up by his uncle and
aunt as if he were a brother to their own children, and did not
learn the truth until he was nine, when he overheard a visitor's
chance remark. He had to be shown photographs to establish his
true identity for himself. It was a comfortable childhood and
although Supervielle later wrote about the loneliness of infancy,
it is difficult to suppose that the tragic circumstances of his first
three years can have had a great effect on him at the time, whatever his poetic imagination later projected back into his own
past. He did, however, always partly belong to a Latin American
literary tradition, and his regular trips between Uruguay and
Europe no doubt made him feel that he belonged to two conti-
nents. He was brought up trilingual, attending an English
school, speaking French at home, and playing with Spanish
school friends.

   At 10 he was sent back to France to board at the Lycée Janson-
de-Sailly in Paris, returning annually to Montevideo for holi-

days from 1901 to 1903. At 16 he had a pamphlet of 23 poems called *Brumes du passé* privately printed. In these he made some reference to social problems and current affairs, prostitution, liberty, hunger, and the Boer War. After his baccalauréat in 1902, he completed his military service, which he found an unpleasant constraint on his liberty. Then, in 1906, he finished his "licence", or first degree, in arts, specializing in Spanish. On one of his holiday visits home Supervielle had met a Spanish girl, Pilar Saavedra, whom he married on 18 May 1907 in Uruguay. Here, his wife bore him the first of their six children. His first published volume of verse, *Comme des voiliers*, appeared in 1910 and is dedicated to Pilar. After its publication the family returned to Paris, where Supervielle was conscripted during World War I. During his period of service he contracted the heart condition which was to trouble him intermittently for the rest of his life.

In the years following the war Supervielle made Uruguay his permanent home, although he frequently returned to Europe and travelled extensively in South America, particularly into the Brazilian hinterland. In 1919 he had published first *Les Poèmes de l'humour triste*, including a section of "Mélancolies manutentionnaires," a title he later changed to "Militaires mélancolies," and then a volume of *Poèmes*, which included *Les Poèmes de l'humour triste*. Over the next nine years he was to publish four more volumes of verse: *Débarcadères* of 1922, *Gravitations* of 1925, *Oloron-Sainte-Marie* of 1927, and *Saisir* of 1928, the last two to be incorporated into *Le Forçat innocent* of 1930. He also published a trilogy of novels between 1923 and 1928: *L'Homme de la pampa, Le Voleur d'enfants*, and *Le Survivant*. In the third novel Supervielle salvages the hero of the second, Colonel Philémon Bigua, who had thrown himself into the ocean to commit suicide at the end of *Le Voleur d'enfants*.

Supervielle spent the 10 years before World War II mostly in Passy, a suburb of Paris. His poems had been noticed by Gide and Valéry, and Jacques Rivière was publishing him in the *Nouvelle Revue Française* (*NRF*, q.v.). He had formed a friendship with Jean Paulhan, and was mixing in Parisian literary circles. In 1927 Supervielle had published a short story, *La Piste et la mare*, which was republished in 1931 in the collection entitled *L'Enfant de la haute mer. Trois mythes* had appeared in 1929. The connection between these works is complicated, since the short stories are often fables, often grow out of already published poems, and often appear in different collections. For instance, "L'enfant de la haute mer," the story from which the 1931 collection takes its name, is essentially a fable. It grew out of a poem entitled "Village sur les flots" from *Gravitations*, and was the first of the *Trois Mythes*.

From fables Supervielle moved to drama. In 1932 he wrote *La Belle au bois*, first produced in South America by the Pitoëffs, then in Paris by Louis Jouvet. In 1935 he adapted Shakespeare's *As You Like It* into French and a year later he wrote the historical drama *Bolivar*, performed in 1936 by the Comédie-Française. It was printed with the one-act farce *La Première Famille*, which was performed by the Pitoëff company. A volume of memoirs, *Boire à la source*, appeared in 1933, and a further volume of short stories, *L'Arche de Noé*, in 1938. Two volumes of verse subsequent to *Le Forçat innocent* (*Les Amis inconnus* of 1934 and *La Fable du monde* of 1938) complete Supervielle's catalogue of volume publications during the 1930s.

He was in Montevideo for the marriage of one of his children when war broke out in 1939, so he spent the war years in Uruguay, much troubled both by the situation in France and by his own health. The Paris winter of 1938 had left him with a tubercular condition in the left lung, and his scant production during this time reflects both his unhappiness for France and his more personal anxieties. In 1941 he published *Poèmes de la France malheureuse*, which was republished in an augmented edition in 1945 and again in the *1939–1945 Poèmes*. In 1952 the augmented *Boire à la source* contained extracts from the diary he kept from 1939 to 1946, the *Journal d'une double angoisse*. During the war Supervielle published the short stories of *Le Petit Bois*, to be republished in the collection *Premiers pas de l'univers* in 1950. With the coming of peace his literary output began to increase.

When the Montevideo bank failed, Supervielle and his family returned to France, settling again in Passy in 1946. That year he produced a new set of short stories, *Orphée*, and the following year his only long poem, *A la nuit*. There then came three plays, *Robinson* of 1948, followed by *Schéhérazade* and a dramatic adaptation of *Le Voleur d'enfants* in 1949. The poems of *Oublieuse mémoire* and another volume of short stories, *Les B.B.V.*, also appeared in 1949. In 1950 Milhaud set to music a new version of *Bolivar*, which was produced at the Opéra on 12 May of that year. Further new poems followed in *Naissances* of 1951. *Boire à la source* appeared in its augmented form in 1952, and in that year the short story *Le Jeune Homme du dimanche* was republished from the *NRF*. An adaptation of *A Midsummer Night's Dream* remained unpublished.

Le Jeune Homme du dimanche was expanded into a novel by adding material already published in the *NRF* in 1955, and there were two new volumes of verse. The first, which included material already published, was *L'Escalier* of 1956; the second was *Le Corps tragique* of 1959. In 1955 Supervielle was awarded the Grand Prix de Littérature.

WORKS

Although he had several different veins of inspiration, moving between animal fable, parable, fantasy, humour, and myth, and in poetry using free verse as well as traditional verse patterns, Supervielle's work always has a classical construction. The verse is easily accessible and usually built up according to traditional models: "Je suis d'une famille d'horlogers, je tiens à ce que mes poèmes soient bien agencés (I come from a family of clockmakers. I like my poems to have properly balanced mechanisms)." It takes from South America much of its powerful simplicity and striking use of metaphor, the attraction of the exotic, and a desire to merge with the inescapable endlessness of such natural phenomena as Supervielle's beloved pampas.

The short stories treat the bizarre as if it were the everyday, but almost always work as fables, more rarely as parables, myths, legends, or simple fantasies. The humour, fantasy, and freshness of vision go together with the poet's constant awareness of the proximity of death, but Supervielle's poetry cannot be called pessimistic. It is more often playful, but even when it approaches the great cosmic themes, it insists on finding structure and meaning in the universe, and it is very often delicate, even fragile.

The whole corpus of imaginative works is permeated by a restlessness which reflects Supervielle's constant travelling. The imaginative patterns are especially obvious in the novels because Supervielle attributes to Guanamiru, the hero of the first one, the authorship of some of his own poems in *Gravitations*. This is surely requesting the reader to make at least a partial identification between Supervielle the author and Guanamiru the hero. The first novel, *L'Homme de la pampa* of 1923, is a fantasy. Its hero dies from an eruption of megalomania which scatters his habits and ideas around the world by explosion. In order to make his fellow Uruguayans happy, Guanamiru decides to enliven the monotony of the pampas by erecting a volcano to give free public eruptions on national holidays. The prohibitive price of lava is constricting, but on Thursdays there is a special eruption for schoolchildren, producing useful recipes, pumice stone, and games of patience. Occasionally Guanamiru arranges for his volcano to produce surprise eruptions, spewing out medicines, books of ethics, and agricultural implements, lambs, piglets, and mechanical sheep shearers. In spite of strong press criticism of his project, Guanamiru's volcano does more good in a matter of days than the rest of the world's volcanoes had done in centuries, but he is upset, plans to take his volcano to Paris, where it will be properly appreciated, gets obsessed by it, and explodes himself.

Life is everywhere and infinitely varied—in the pampas, under the sea, and in Paris—but its reality always turns out to be the product of fantasy, like the mermaid under the sea or the girl in Paris, Line-du-Petit-Jour, who disintegrates when Guanamiru tries to make love to her. The fantasy works according to strictly logical models, rather like that of *Alice in Wonderland* or the novels of Jules Verne. The sky is above the earth to make navigation possible, but with better technology and more advanced systems of navigation, the sea could be above the sky. The law of such fantasy is that it must admit the logic of the real world while suspending the known operations of physical forces. Physical forces are actually suspended as the mechanical agencies through which they should work malfunction. Taps, clocks, a leaking pen, the way portraits peer cross-eyed at him, cupboards empty, safes change their combinations, pictures change places, and his cigars don't draw appear to conspire against Guanamiru as the megalomania gains hold. Inanimate objects take on human characteristics, as when he asks for a "male whiskey." *L'Homme de la pampa* is a form of entertaining escapism without the power, for instance, of the much less entertaining contemporary experiments of surrealism (q.v.).

Supervielle uses childish fantasy and the genres appropriate to it as a retreat from life's horrors, particularly in the short stories. In *Le Voleur d'enfants*, however, horror intrudes into the fantasy. Colonel Philémon Bigua abducts children because his own marriage is sterile, but he begins to doubt his own justification for his actions. He found Joseph dying of typhoid in squalor in Paris, but was he really abandoned? Antoine's mother may have been more interested in her lovers than in her son, but she died of grief on losing him. Marcelle might have been at the mercy of a drunken father and a prostitute mother, but she is now exposed to seduction by Joseph. Bigua, now also in love with Marcelle, turns Joseph out, returns with the abducted family to Uruguay, discovers that Marcelle loves Joseph and intends to marry him, and throws himself into the ocean.

In *Le Survivant* Bigua turns out to have been saved by a life belt and to have got back to Uruguay, but his mother casts out Marcelle, and Bigua cannot stand living with his wife, his mother, and his sisters. Taking the three remaining children with him, he wanders off to look for Marcelle, becomes penniless, does odd jobs, finds Marcelle with her lover, lets them go, and

sends for his wife to come and settle down with him again. Thus, he narrowly and improbably escapes the self-destruction with which his obsessive fantasy was threatening him. The reader is implicitly invited to join Bigua in escaping from the menace of his own dreams just, no doubt, as the author was fantasizing about escaping from his own terror.

The central character of Supervielle's only other novel, *Le Jeune Homme du dimanche et des autres jours*, as it emerged in 1955, escapes like Bigua from the horrors in which the author's fantasy has trapped him. Philippe-Charles Apestègue, a South American poet studying in Paris, falls in love with Obligacion, the beautiful wife of another South American in whose house he is entertained every Sunday. Apestègue falls asleep one day over a book on metempsychosis and dreams that he has become a fly. The hero's fantasy now becomes the author's, since Apestègue does in fact become a fly. His human form disappears and he is left to fulfil his desire to be near Obligacion as a common housefly. That is unsatisfactory, since he remains unrecognized and his form is repellent. After a brief spell in his old form, the poet's spirit then inhabits Obligacion's cat.

When Obligacion's husband commits suicide and she returns to South America, Apestègue's spirit inhabits Obligacion's own bodily form, but even that leaves him unsatisfied, so in the second part of the novel he migrates into the body of the dwarf Gutierrez, himself also in love with Obligacion. However, Apestègue's desires now conflict with those of his unwitting host, and his spirit is released by the doctor's attempted suicide. It returns to the poet's own body, which is now nearly dead from neglect and refuses to acknowledge the identity of its native spirit until Apestègue gives it the password. Then, like Bigua, he resumes normal life with all its frustrations, having narrowly avoided permanent disembodiment. In none of the four novels does the central fantasy afford escape from life's frustrations. In the first it makes them worse, as it would also have done in the second if Supervielle had not reversed its ending by writing the third. The novels are therefore fantasies, certainly, but also parables of vain efforts to take refuge in fantasy. The short stories, too, whether fables or fantasies, are also parables of the same type.

The poems are naturally much more direct, but they show the same imaginative patterns. Their relative brevity means that some are devoted entirely to the poetic expression of a single desire, a whimsy, or an imaginative flight, and that the ordinary lyric themes of aspiration, frustration, and desire are everywhere present. The single most striking characteristic of the poetic emotion expressed is its focus on flight. The collection *Oloron-Sainte-Marie*, published in 1927, was taken up again in *Le Forçat innocent* of 1930. The first poem, dedicated to Rilke and called "Oloron-Sainte-Marie," has 86 lines of varying length and uncertain rhyme scheme. It ends in half a dozen four-line stanzas and a final five-line stanza. Essentially the poet is conversing in the Pyrenees with his ancestors, who have exhausted their experience, but are not adequately forthcoming in passing on its lessons. The poet offers to recreate their living environment. His ancestors assure him of their union with him.

The second poem "Whisper in agony," has 13 lines of six syllables, followed by 12 Alexandrines and a last line of six syllables, and moves from a mood of wistfulness—conveyed through images of stone, ice, bareness, and emptiness—to the timid expression of desire. In a dark room, a trembling pillow is like a sailing boat feeling the approach of the tide. "Am I part of the crew, or the arm waving goodbye?", asks the poet. "Supplique" asks the dead if they have not yet learnt to die. It is a parable of dying, a plea to the dead to leave the living to get on with their lives, and again presents a series of strikingly fresh images that are concise, not too dense, and classic in their simplicity. "La chambre voisine" is a 28-line poem about a man dying or dead in the next room.

The following poem, in which the poet exhorts himself to overcome his guilt, presumably refers to a precise event because it mentions the afternoon of 10 February. In "Sans Dieu," a slightly shorter poem than the first, the poet is lost in the world, achieving nothing, going nowhere, prey to every passing weapon, with even his friends "Sentant que je suis seul égaré dans l'espace (Feeling that I am alone, wandering in space)." As a last resort the poet buries himself in an indifferent sky. The last four poems, too, concern loneliness, isolation, and the attempt to flee from pain and assuage grief. As in the novels, so in the poems Supervielle explores the vain desire to flee and finds there is no escape.

PUBLICATIONS

Verse

Brumes du passé (privately printed), 1901
Comme des voiliers, 1910
Les Poèmes de l'humour triste, 1919
Poèmes, (includes previous item), 1919
Débarcadères, 1922
Gravitations, 1925
Oloron-Sainte-Marie, 1927
Saisir, 1928
Le Forçat innocent, (contains most of previous two items), 1930
Les Amis inconnus, 1934
La Fable du monde, 1938
Poèmes de la France malheureuse, 1941; augmented edition, 1945
1939–1945 Poèmes, 1946
18 Poèmes, 1946
A la nuit, 1947
Oublieuse mémoire, 1949
Naissances, 1951
L'Escalier, 1956
Le Corps tragique, 1959
The Shell and the Ear (twelve poems), translated by Marjorie Boulton

Fiction

L'Homme de la pampa, 1923
Le Voleur d'enfants, 1926; as *The Colonel's Children*, 1950
La Piste et la mare (short story), 1927; in *L'Enfant de la haute mer*, 1931
Le Survivant, 1928; as *The Survivors*
Trois mythes, 1929
L'Enfant de la haute mer (short stories), 1931; as *Souls of the Soulless*, 1933
L'Arche de Noé (short stories), 1938
Le Petit Bois et autres contes, 1942
Orphée et autres contes, 1946; as *Orpheus*

Les B.B.V. (short stories), 1949
Premiers pas de l'univers (short stories), 1950
Le Jeune Homme du dimanche et des autres jours, 1955

Plays

La Belle au bois, 1932
Bolivar; La Première Famille, 1936
Robinson, 1948
Schéhérazade, 1949
Le Voleur d'enfants, 1949
Les Suites d'une course; L'Etoile de Séville, 1959

Other

Boire à la source, 1933; augmented edition, 1952
Comme il vous plaira, 1935
En songeant à un art poétique, 1951

Critical and biographical studies

Roy, Claude, *Jules Supervielle* (in English), 1949
Blair, Dorothy S., *Jules Supervielle: A Modern Fabulist*, 1960
Greene, Titania W., *Jules Supervielle*, 1958
Hiddlestone, J., *L'Univers de Jules Supervielle*, 1965

SURREALISM

See also Aragon, Breton, Char, Cocteau, dada, Eluard, Gracq, Leiris, Péret, Soupault, and the index.

Surrealism was primarily a literary movement led by André Breton, the clearly imaginative exploration of the total disorientation of values brought about in the wake of World War I, and of the efforts, as the surrealists thought, to reconstitute western European society as if nothing had happened. The movement emerged from the even shriller cultural and social protests of dada (q.v.), found a serious basis in the exploitation of possible means of creative access to pre-conscious levels of mental activity by experimenting with automatic writing, and was organized by Breton into a fairly tight group with shifting membership, which poets and other creative writers joined, broke with or were expelled from, all with a certain degree of formality. The movement's relationship with organized revolutionary political groupings, notably the communist party, caused many of the internal schisms and lesser dissensions, which Sartre later pointed to in a famous article in *Les Temps Modernes* (q.v.) entitled "Situation de l'écrivain en 1947" as evidence that no radical reappraisal of social values could command the adhesion of a literary group unless there was a prior political commitment. Associated with the literary movement was, of course, the movement in painting.

The word "surrealism" itself has changed its meaning. Apollinaire coined it to describe his *Les Mamelles de Tirésias*, "drame surréaliste," performed on 24 June 1917, but its first published usage was in his programme note for *Parade*, the joint work of Satie, Picasso, Massine, and Cocteau. The programme note was published in *Excelsior* on 18 May 1917. Apollinaire was looking for a word to signify "above and beyond nature," but could not use "surnaturel," which the theologians had pre-empted to mean "supernatural." In the end the word "surréal-iste" came of course to mean something like "unreal," or hallu-cinatory, but that was only after it had been picked up by the graphic arts. Breton himself used the term "surréalisme" to mean absolute or "super"-reality, and talked of "resolving the previously contradictory conditions of dream and reality into an absolute reality, a super-reality." Freud himself was interested in the Breton–Soupault experiments in automatic writing, the first of which, dating from May and June 1919, were published as *Les Champs magnétiques* in 1920. It is customary to date "surrealism" from the beginning of those experiments, just after the foundation by Breton, Aragon, and Soupault of *Littérature* in March 1919. There were to be 20 numbers in the first series, ending in 1921 with an account of the mock "trial" of Barrès. Gide, Valéry, and Fargue appeared alongside Vaché's letters, Lautréamont, extracts from *Les Champs magnétiques*, and the dada texts, including "23 Manifestes du mouvement dada."

The experiments with hypnotic sleep described by Aragon in *Une vague de rêves* (1924) took place in the autumn and winter of 1922, and on 15 October 1924 Breton published the first *Manifeste du surréalisme* together with the "automatic" texts of *Poisson soluble*, produced earlier that year. Early in 1922 dada had virtually broken up, *Littérature* had been relaunched in a second series, which ran for 13 numbers, although without Aragon, and the surrealist group under the leadership of Breton was a recognizable force in avant-garde circles. On 1 December 1924 the review *La Révolution Sur-réaliste*, edited at first by Pierre Naville and Benjamin Péret, joined by Breton for the fourth number, replaced the now defunct *Littérature*. It was to run for 12 numbers, issued between 1924 and 1929. The first number called for a new dec-laration of the rights of man, adding an explicit social, if not political, dimension to the group's declared aims, while the first *Manifeste* defined surrealism as:

Automatisme psychique pur par lequel on se propose d'exprimer… le fonctionnement de la pensée. Dictée de la pensée en l'absence de tout contrôle exercé par la raison, en dehors de toute préoccupation esthétique ou morale. Le surréalisme repose sur la croyance à la réalité supérieure de certaines formes d'association négligées jusqu'à lui, à la toute-puissance du rêve, au jeu désintéressé de la pensée. Il tend à ruiner définitivement tous les autres mécanismes psychiques et à se substituer à eux dans la résolution des principaux problèmes de la vie.

(Pure psychic automatism by which it is proposed to express… the functioning of thought. Thought dictated without any control imposed by reason, outside any aes-thetic or moral concern. Surrealism rests on the belief in the higher reality of certain hitherto neglected forms of associ-ation, in the omnipotence of the dream, and in the disinter-ested play of thought. It aims at definitively destroying all other psychic mechanisms and at substituting itself for them in the resolution of the principal problems of life.)

The first sign that surrealism might promise a more optimistic cultural response to the artistic life of post-war France than dada had done was probably the survey conducted in 1919 by *Littéra-ture* on the subject "Why do you write?" The answers were all wittily dismissive of literary activity, but not as destructively so as the dada vogue might have suggested. Gide said the review would be able to classify the writers according to whether their replies started "in order to," "out of," or "because." Valéry said "out of weakness," Rachilde "because I like silence," and Jacob "in order to write better." It has been pointed out that 50 years earlier the answers would have been incomparably more pomp-ous. Creative artists, concerned with exploring the values by which their society lived, did not have to be surrealists to find it impossible in 1919 to look what they found straight in the face. The defensive humour of the established figures covered the apocalyptic social and aesthetic revolutionary rumblings of sur-realism.

Much later, in response to a Yugoslavian survey of 1932 and in *Qu'est-ce que le surréalisme?* of 1934, Breton was to hold that "C'est par ses désirs et ses exigences les plus directes que tend à s'exercer chez l'homme la faculté de connaissance (It is through his desires and deepest requirements that man's faculty of knowledge is exercised)." There was a serious philosophical quest looking for an understanding of man through the sort of exploration of his instinctive, irrational, pre-conscious life undertaken, for instance, in the collaborative Breton–Eluard *L'Immaculée Conception* of 1930. Breton's wartime experi-ences, and his fascination with Jacques Vaché, had led him towards a serious interest in forms of mental aberration, and the history of surrealism in the late 1920s shows a sustained interest in the phenomena of psychological disturbance, starting with the *Lettre aux médecins-chefs des asiles des fous* of 1925. Breton had called on Freud in 1921, but their aims were of course fun-damentally different. Freud the therapist was interested in the sublimation of the instinctive drives, whose manifestations Breton wished merely to explore, or even to liberate. Freud's interest in the group cooled, and in *Nadja* of 1928. Breton attacked the tyranny of the analyst over his patient, although his work continued to show Freudian inspiration, at least up to *Les Vases communicants* of 1932.

The interest in automatism, pre-conscious, hallucinatory, and hypnotic states goes together with the promotion of desire over rational thought as a source of information about the workings of the human mind, especially, but not only, about its artistic creativity. At the time of his cooperation with Luis Buñuel on the first surrealist films, *Un chien andalou* (1928) and *L'Age d'or* (1930), Salvador Dali had introduced in painting what he called "paranoiac-critical activity," a technique he described as a "spontaneous method of irrational understanding based on the interpretative critical association of delirious phenomena." The alliance between literature and painting was sealed when the surrealist gallery in Paris was opened in 1926. There had already been a big exhibition in November 1925, and there would be fur-ther important exhibitions in London in 1936 and in Paris in 1947. However, the gallery had to close for lack of money at the end of 1928, the year in which Breton published *Le Surréalisme et la peinture*.

It was inevitable that the attempt to liberate the manifestations of instinctive energy, the promotion of desire over rational con-trol, and the radical reassessment of private and social values being undertaken by the surrealist group should raise the ques-

1945 he was head of drama, then, from 1945 to 1960, head of the "Club d'Essai" or experimental drama studios. In 1954 he had also become programme director, from which post he retired to become a council member from 1964 to 1974.

Although Tardieu continued to publish verse during and after the war, and was awarded the Grand Prix for poetry by the Académie Française in 1972 and the Prix Critique in 1976, his reputation rests chiefly on his own experimental drama, and especially on his exploitation of the new possibilities, particularly for drama written for broadcasting using sound montages, opened up by the invention and refinement of sound recording on magnetic tape. The new technology of sound recording and reproduction led Tardieu to an interest in language which he has always used in a particularly rigorous manner. He was made a member of the Légion d'Honneur in 1976.

The shorter dramas, which reflect not only on the real world, but also on drama, and language itself, include *Un mot pour un autre* and *Conversation-sinfonietta*. They have been collected as *Théâtre de chambre* and become avant-garde classics. Although mostly written for radio, some of the dramas of this period have also been successfully staged. The division of Tardieu's work into drama and verse is necessarily arbitrary, but from about 1951 his style in both genres changed to one that was classical but more intimate and amusing. *Monsieur Monsieur, Une voix sans personne*, and *Histoires obscures* mostly consisted of monologues or recordings about apparently ordinary, routine matters, showing considerable distrust of anything which might be regarded as specifically poetic language and cynicism about social conventions. Tardieu's drama relies much less on words than on geometrically devised scenery, noises, and lighting, and is the product of careful technical research. Verse remained his favourite medium for using words.

Tardieu has also published reflections and studies, *Pages d'écriture*, and a series of what are clearly or virtually prose poems about painting, starting with the 1944 *Figures* and including prefaces and commentaries on illustrated editions. He has also edited the medieval rondeaux of Charles d'Orléans and translated Goethe and Hölderlin.

WORKS

Tardieu's later works are characterized by a sardonic turn of mind which ridicules social conventions by demonstrating their logical conclusions. He has a wit which can make a source of great amusement out of his complete and devastating inability to take seriously any convention or social, linguistic, or dramatic norm. He notices that the norms and conventions are there, but keeps pointedly prodding his readers or audience into asking themselves why they are there, and whether they ought to be, at least in the way that they are. Words are arranged so as not to convey meaning, which makes the use of language itself the subject of satire. In half a dozen of the plays words are mere sounds. In *La Sonate et les trois messieurs*, for instance, they are used as if they were musical notes, capable of arrangement in classical sonata form. Three actors simply sit on stools rhythmically and dreamily uttering words which do not "make sense," that is, do not convey semantic meaning.

Among the plays which make their point by taking attitudes and modes of behaviour to an apparently logical but in fact grotesque, absurd, or macabre conclusion are *Le Meuble, Le Guichet*, and *La Serrure*, in which a voyeur goes to a brothel in order to see a girl undress. A girl and a huge keyhole are accordingly provided, and the voyeur's life reaches its high point as he watches the girl strip naked. When she goes on to take off her eyes, lips, and skin, peeling everything off her skeleton, he drops dead. It is an amusing, lightweight, witty, shocking way of asking what is actually an important question about the nature of sexual stimulation and its role in life. In *Un geste pour un autre* social conventions are shown up for the harmless but quite arbitrary gestures which they actually are. In the Nameless Archipelago a guest arrives at a party, puts on his hat, takes off his shoes and socks, and kisses his hostess's foot. The guests politely cough, spit, and insult one another. Among the serious points to which Tardieu returns are man's helplessness in the face of nameless authority and his enslavement to conformity by social pressure. Social institutions, erected to protect us, have come to weigh us down, need to be questioned, and can probably often do as much harm as good.

Some of the poems make explicit the points implicit in the others. In *Une voix sans personne* the poet of "Les mots égarés" meets disembodied voices in the storm, more persistent than a horde of jackals, more suffocating than the snow's anger, "whispering, whispering," "souffles semés par des lèvres absentes (breaths strewn by absent lips)," muttering words like "How," "here," "it's me," and "I told you so." The verse is totally free, but the sense falls naturally into its lines. The syntax is conversational, but the imagery is intense. The effect is to show up the ordinary as actually not ordinary at all, but bizarre, extraordinary, conventional, and marvellous. The frightening consequence of the words' behaviour is drawn by the poet as if it were a moral at the end of a fable. The storm has made debris of dialogue. The wind has whisked the words all over the place, and they land randomly, unattached to the cries which produced them and not arriving at their intended destinations, like waves "toutes ainsi l'une à l'autre/inconnues mais à se joindre condamnées/dans l'intimité de la mer (like that, unknown to one another/but condemned to be joined together/in the intimacy of the sea)." Words have ceased to fulfil their function. Men have lost the power to communicate.

"La masque" from *Histoires obscures* makes a similar point. A heavy, hollow mask of bronze rises slowly and alone from the "désert sonore (resonant desert)," climbing to the green star, a surface that has been silent for 10,000 years. The poet takes wing and knocks with closed finger on the mask's hard forehead and puffed-out eyelashes. Frightened by the noise, he does not dare to violate the secret, to find out the answer to the cosmic riddle, to force the face behind the mask to break its silence:

Cependant tout autour la splendeur c'est le vide,
brillants cristaux nocturnes de l'été.

(However, all round the splendour, there is emptiness ,/
brilliant crystals of the summer night.)

PUBLICATIONS

Plays

Qui est là (produced 1949), included in *Théâtre de chambre*, 1966; as *Who Goes There?*, in *The Underground Lovers*, 1968

La Politesse inutile (produced 1950), included in *Théâtre de chambre*, 1966; as *Courtesy Doesn't Pay*, in *The Underground Lovers*, 1968

Un mot pour un autre (produced 1950), included in *Théâtre de chambre*, 1966

Faust et Yorick (as *Mi-figure, mi-raisin*, produced 1951), included in *Théâtre de chambre*, 1966; as *Faust and Yorick*, in *The Underground Lovers*, 1968

Oswald et Zénaïde (produced 1951), included in *Théâtre de chambre*, 1966

Ce que parler veut dire (produced 1951), included in *Théâtre de chambre*, 1966

Il y avait foule au manoir (produced 1951), included in *Théâtre de chambre*, 1966; as *The Crowd up at the Manor*, in *The Underground Lovers*, 1968

Un geste pour un autre (produced 1951), included in *Théâtre de chambre*, 1966

Conversation-sinfonietta (produced 1951), included in *Théâtre de chambre*, 1966; as *Conversation-Sinfonietta*, in *The Underground Lovers*, 1968

Eux seuls le savent (produced 1952), included in *Théâtre de chambre*, 1966; as *They Alone Knew*, in *The Underground Lovers*, 1968

Les Amants du métro (produced 1952), included in *Poèmes à jouer*, 1969; as *The Underground Lovers* (as *The Lovers in the Metro*, produced 1962; as *The Underground Lovers*, produced 1969), in *The Underground Lovers* (collection), 1968

Le Meuble (produced 1954), included in *Théâtre de chambre*, 1966; as *The Contraption* (produced 1980), in *The Underground Lovers*, 1968

La Serrure (produced 1955), included in *Théâtre de chambre*, 1966; as *The Keyhole* (produced 1962)

Le Guichet (produced 1955), included in *Théâtre de chambre*, 1966; as *The Enquiry Office* (as *The Information Bureau*, produced 1962), in *The Underground Lovers*, 1968

La Société Apollon (produced 1955), included in *Théâtre de chambre*, 1966; as *The Apollo Society*, in *The Underground Lovers*, 1968

Théâtre de chambre, 1955; augmented edition (includes *Qui est là?*, *La Politesse inutile*, *Le Sacre de la nuit*, *Le Meuble*, *La Serrure*, *Le Guichet*, *Monsieur Moi*, *Faust et Yorick*, *La Sonate et les trois messieurs*, *La Société Apollon*, *Oswald et Zénaïde*, *Ce que parler veut dire*, *Il y avait foule au manoir*, *Eux seuls le savent*, *Un mot pour un autre*, *Un geste pour un autre*, *Conversation-sinfonietta*), 1966

Une voix sans personne (produced 1956), included in *Poèmes à jouer*, 1969

Les Temps du verbe (produced 1956), included in *Poèmes à jouer*, 1969

Rythme à trois temps (produced 1959), included in *Poèmes à jouer*, 1969

Poèmes à jouer, 1960; augmented edition (includes *L'A.B.C. de notre vie*, *Rythme à trois temps*, *Une voix sans personne*, *Les Temps du verbe*, *Les Amants du métro*, *Tonnerre sans orage*, *Des arbres et des hommes*, *Trois personnes entrées dans des tableaux*, *Malédictions d'une Furie*), 1969

Monsieur Moi, in *Théâtre de chambre*, 1966; as *Mr. Me* (produced 1972), in *The Underground Lovers*, 1968

La Sonate et les trois messieurs, in *Théâtre de chambre*, 1966; as *The Sonata and the Three Gentlemen* (produced 1972), in *The Underground Lovers*, 1968

The Underground Lovers and Other Experimental Plays (includes *Who Goes There?*, *Courtesy Doesn't Pay*, *The Contraption*, *The Enquiry Office*, *Mr. Me*, *Faust and Yorick*, *The Sonata and the Three Gentlemen*, *The Apollo Society*, *The Crowd up at the Manor*, *They Alone Knew*, *Conversation-Sinfonietta*), 1968

Une soirée en Provence (includes *Une soirée en Provence*; *Un clavier un autre*, with music by Claude Arrieu; *Joyeux retour*; *Souper*, with music by Marius Constant; *Le Club Archimède*), 1975

Le Professeur Froeppel, 1978

Verse

Le Fleuve caché, 1933
Accents, 1939
Le Témoin invisible, 1943
Poèmes, 1944
Figures, 1944
Les Dieux étouffés, 1946
Le Démon de l'irréalité, 1946
Jours pétrifiés, 1947
Monsieur Monsieur, 1951
Une voix sans personne (includes prose), 1954
L'Espace et la flûte, with illustrations by Picasso, 1958
Histoires obscures, 1961
Choix de poèmes 1924–1954, 1961
Le Fleuve caché: poésies 1938–1961, 1968
Formeries, 1976; as *Formeries* (in English), 1982
Comme ceci, comme cela, 1979

Other

Bazaine, Estève, Lapicque, with André Frénaud and Jean Lescure, 1945
Il était une fois, deux fois, trois fois, 1947
Un mot pour un autre, 1951
La Première Personne du singulier, 1952
Farouche à quatre feuilles, with others, 1954
De la peinture abstraite, 1960
Hans Hartung, 1962
Hollande, 1963
Pages d'écriture, 1967
Les Portes de toiles, 1969
Grandeurs et faiblesses de la radio, 1969
La Part de l'ombre, 1972
Obscurité du jour, 1974
Bazaine, with Jean-Claude Schneider and Viveca Bosson, 1975

Critical studies

Esslin, Martin, *The Theatre of the Absurd*, 1961; revised edition, 1968

Wellwarth, George E., *The Theater of Protest and Paradox*, 1964

Nowlet, E., *Tardieu*, 1964; revised edition, 1978

Vernois, Paul, *La Dramaturgie poétique de Tardieu*, 1981

TEILHARD DE CHARDIN, Pierre, 1881–1955.

Jesuit philosopher and palaeontologist.

LIFE

Pierre Teilhard de Chardin's life and posthumous reputation can only be understood in the context of his determined devotion to the Jesuit order to which he belonged, and to the intellectual disputes both within the Catholic Church and between it and the mainstream of scientific evolutionary thought. Theologically, the doctrines concerning the transmission of original sin, the redemption of the human race, and the immortality of the individual human soul had seemed to demand monogenesis, that is the descent of the whole human race from a single set of parents, and a direct act of God by which an immortal soul was created at precise but disputed stages in the development of the human embryo. The doctrine of monogenesis was strongly reaffirmed in the papal encyclical *Humani generis* of 1950. In the preceding century the Church had felt its teaching threatened not only by the assertions of contemporary science, but also by the general movement towards a wholly rational explanation of the truths of faith known as "modernism."

The first Vatican Council of 1869–70 had defined that "not all the dogmas of faith can be understood and demonstrated from natural principles," and the battle against modernism was continued in the decree *Lamentabili* of 3 July and the encyclical *Pascendi* of 7 September 1907. Teilhard de Chardin therefore spent his life totally committed both to his palaeontological studies of the origins and development of the human race and to the dogmatic definitions of his Church, with which his ecclesiastical superiors seemed to think his scientific conclusions possibly incompatible. As was normal in the Jesuit order in such situations, Teilhard de Chardin was allowed, enabled, and encouraged to pursue his scientific investigations, but permitted to publish only scientific papers and not the works designed for a wider public on which his reputation now largely rests, and which attempted a visionary synthesis of man's biological past and future with his religious destiny. The accuracy of Teilhard de Chardin's vision is naturally disputed, but its scientific basis, religious orthodoxy, poetic nature, and imaginative power are now generally admitted.

Teilhard de Chardin had been encouraged by friends to entrust the manuscripts of his major non-technical works to literary executors who would organize their publication after his death, since publication during his lifetime would have been regarded as an act of defiance. His Jesuit superiors, perhaps understandably, wished to preserve the homogeneity of religious teaching within the order and, especially in view of the order's history, could not willingly risk open condemnation of the teaching of one of its members. However, permission was given by the order for legal steps to be taken which would ensure the posthumous publication of Teilhard de Chardin's writings. Any danger of the formal censure of a living member of the order by ecclesiastical authority was thereby avoided. As a result seven major works, including the two most important, *Le Phénomène humain* and *Le Milieu divin: essai de vie intérieure*, appeared within four years of his death, selling over 300,000 copies in their first five years. Like Lévi-Strauss, Teilhard de Chardin has used a scientific base, palaeontology as against Lévi-Strauss's anthropology, to construct a powerful vision of the meaning of human experience and of the destiny of the human race.

Teilhard de Chardin was born into a middle-class family of devout Catholics on 1 May 1881 at Sarcenat, just west of Clermont-Ferrand, the fourth of 11 children. His father owned farms, was interested in natural history, and lived to be 86. With Teilhard de Chardin's mother, who died in 1936, he was a daily communicant. One sister, Françoise, became a Little Sister of the Poor, was elected superior of her convent, and died in 1911, nursing in Shanghai. Before joining her order, she had read Plato in Greek, written long essays on Descartes, Pascal, and Malebranche, and was contemplating a study of the German philosophers in German. Teilhard de Chardin was brought up in a household in which learning and piety were integrated with one another as a matter of course. In 1892 he was sent to the Jesuit college of Mongré in Villefranche, and in 1899 he entered the Jesuit order following, after an initial period of ill-health, the normal pattern of training, which started with a two-year noviciate involving a minimal amount of formal study.

In 1902 the political situation in France under the Combes administration forced the Jesuits, who trained their own members in colleges of philosophy and theology, to move their training centres outside France. After his two years at Aix, Teilhard de Chardin accordingly studied philosophy for three years at the Jesuit house now established in Jersey, where he spent his spare time collecting and writing about prehistoric animals and plants. For the usual interim period of "regency" he was sent to Cairo, so that he could easily pursue his scientific interests while living at a French Jesuit school. Here he taught chemistry and physics and had charge of a museum. Thereafter, in the normal way, he went on to do four years of theology in a house opened for the exiled French students near Hastings. Although not yet an expert in palaeontology, he discovered near the theology house the tooth of a new species of small mammal. As leisure permitted, he helped with digs and looked on as experts argued about evidence, some of which turned out to have been fraudulently planted. Jesuit students are ordained priests after their third year of theology, which for Teilhard de Chardin meant in 1911. It also meant taking the anti-modernist oath imposed on all ordinands.

It was during his time at Hastings that Teilhard de Chardin read Bergson's *L'Evolution créatrice* of 1907. It was through his reflection on Bergson that he produced his key concepts of the divergent evolutionary movements of complexification and convergence. From the observable evolutionary phenomenon of convergence, Teilhard was to elaborate his more religious and visionary concepts of "unanimization" in the "noosphere," or realm of self-consciousness, a concept developed in 1925, and of the "Omega point," "amorization," and "Christification." From 1913 he had been studying for his doctorate at the Institut Catholique and then the Museum d'Histoire Naturelle in Paris, where he came into contact with Edouard Le Roy. They were to become close associates in China, but Bergson, the subject of Roman condemnation in 1914, was to be the starting point of their important discussions. Le Roy's four most important works were put on the index of forbidden books on 14 June 1931.

Together with Bergson, the other important philosophical influence on the formation of Teilhard de Chardin's thought during the second and third decades of the century was Le Roy's personal friend Maurice Blondel, who had defended the orthodox position against modernism, although with more help from the German idealist philosophers than was realized at the time. The first of the three versions of Blondel's *L'Action*, the original thesis, is dated 1893, before the height of the modernist crisis, which came with the condemnation of Alfred Loisy in 1903, but Blondel had replied in his *Histoire et dogme* of 1904 to Loisy's *L'Evangile et l'eglise*, which had precipitated the crisis in 1903. Teilhard de Chardin met Blondel, who was also a close friend of Auguste Valensin, a Jesuit contemporary, and submitted his early papers to him for comment. Blondel no doubt inspired Teilhard de Chardin to keep Christ at the culminating point in which he saw humanity's consummation, and to avoid a sympathy with modernism which he might otherwise easily have developed. Teilhard de Chardin certainly regarded his theory of the evolutionary capacity of biological energy as affiliated to Blondel's concept of action.

His spiritual training as a Jesuit ended at Canterbury before the outbreak of World War I, which he spent as a stretcher bearer. For outstanding courage he was awarded the Croix de Guerre in 1915, the Médaille Militaire in 1917, and the Légion d'Honneur in 1920. He had turned down a commission, and now spent three years as professor of geology at the Institut Catholique in Paris. Although witty, indiscreet, and protected by a developed sense of humour, Teilhard de Chardin's letters, taken with the reminiscences of numerous friends, testify to the strain he felt himself under on account of his dual commitment as a priest and a scientist, although that strain was to be the spring which forced him to develop his full spiritual and scientific vision of man's development and destiny. Further evidence of the tension and how he dealt with it can be found in *Le Prêtre*, written in 1918 at the time of his final vows, but not published until 1965.

In 1923 Teilhard de Chardin was sent to teach at the Jesuit college of higher education in Tientsin, to which he remained nominally attached until 1946. *La Messe sur le monde*, published in 1962, was written in 1923 on the journey between Peking and Ordos, and the religious meditation *Le Milieu divin*, published in 1960, was written in 1926–27. A paper on evolutionary transformism delivered in 1921 and printed in *La Vision du passé*, had led to Teilhard de Chardin's exclusion from the Institut Catholique and virtual banishment to China. For his doctorate, awarded on 22 March 1922, he had expanded his work on carnivorous mammals at Quercy in the centre of France into a thesis on mammals in the Lower Eocene by field work near Reims. He had undergone the philosophical influence of Blondel, Bergson, and Le Roy, been trained as a scientist chiefly by Marcellin Boule of the Museum d'Histoire Naturelle, and had worked there with the charming Henri Breuil. He was now, in 1929, to publish his first paper on the finding of *Sinanthropus*. By 1930 he had mentally reconciled his palaeontological work on human origins with his theological concept of the cosmic Christ as the consummation of the cosmic process. He was ready to write *Le Phénomène humain*: "Evolutionism can give to the universe the grandeur, profundity, and unity which are the natural atmosphere of the Christian faith."

Teilhard de Chardin returned to France in November 1924 and was to travel extensively in the East and to Africa, but remained notionally based in China, where he was kept under Japanese control during the whole of World War II. He had spent nine months on the Yellow River in 1931 and 1932, toured Shansi by cart in 1933, travelled up the Yangtze almost to Tibet in the spring of 1934, and continued to travel almost incessantly on scientific expeditions. He was in France again for a year from 1927 to 1928 and returned to China via Somaliland. He made at least five visits to the US, and was in France again in 1938, when he was allowed to accept a post at the Institut de la Paléontologie Humaine. The first version of *Le Phénomène humain*, entitled "L'esprit de la terre," was ready in 1931. The final text was to be written between 1938 and 1940. Teilhard de Chardin returned to Paris in 1946, planning what would have been his second visit to South Africa, but in 1947 he had a severe heart attack. He recovered at his brother's house in the Auvergne and did in fact make the postponed visit in 1951, after which he went on to South America. He then went to New York, where he took up a post with the Wenner-Gren foundation, and soon afterwards was offered a chair at the Collège de France.

His superiors sent him to Rome with a copy of *Le Phénomène Humain*, but he was not allowed to accept the chair or to publish either *Le Phénomène humain* or *Le Milieu divin*. On his return to Paris he wrote of feeling the need to devote the rest of his life to an analysis of the human community as the fulfilment and the Christification of mankind. His interest in palaeontology had receded in favour of studying rock formations, and in 1953 he returned again to South Africa, crossing directly from New York. His New York appointment carried no very definite duties, but specified as its discipline "palaeo-anthropology," which allowed Teilhard de Chardin to devote himself to the relationship of scientific progress to religious experience. Most of his final projects for conferences devoted to the discussion of mankind's future development bore little or no fruit. His last and most intimate apologia, *Le Coeur de la matière*, is dated from his brother's house in the Auvergne on 15 August 1950. He died in New York on Easter Sunday, 10 April 1955.

WORKS

Teilhard de Chardin's life ended in apparent failure. He had made no really major scientific discoveries, and his interest in palaeontology had in any case waned. No parts of the great imaginative synthesis of scientific evolutionary theory and Pauline spirituality had been published, and the grandiose projects for world conferences on the convergence of mankind's biological and spiritual destinies had evaporated. The publication of his major works was greeted with some scepticism, notably by scientists who failed to understand the literary register of the texts with which they were confronted, and could therefore think, as one of them wrote, that Teilhard de Chardin had practised "an intellectually unexacting sort of science" in which he "had achieved a moderate proficiency," that he catered to the market for "philosophy-fiction," writing "tipsy, euphoric prose poetry," and that "he can be excused of dishonesty only on the grounds that before deceiving others he has taken great pains to deceive himself."

Such a misreading of Teilhard de Chardin's texts diverged sharply from the public perception of their significance. However, there were other dangers. His works attracted liberalizing theologians with whose spiritualities their author would have been sharply at odds. The Vatican was still warning about his "ambiguities" and even his "serious errors" as late as 1962, just before the Second Vatican Council incorporated some elements of his thought into its official documents. Teilhard de Chardin's interests developed firmly towards their concentration in his spiritual vision. What he finally wanted to communicate most

TOCQUEVILLE, Alexis (-Henri-Charles-Maurice Clérel, Comte de), 1805–1859.

Historian, memorialist, and politician.

LIFE

Alexis Tocqueville was born in Paris on 29 July 1805. His mother was descended from ancient Norman nobility and was the granddaughter of the liberal 18th-century director of censorship Malesherbes (1721–1794). His father, Hervé de Tocqueville, was prefect of Metz, and later of Amiens and then Versailles. He ended his career prematurely when he could not give his allegiance to the July monarchy inaugurated after the 1830 revolution. The peerage bestowed by Charles X was revoked. Both parents had been arrested under the Terror, and saved only by the fall of Robespierre in July 1794, when other members of the family had already been executed.

The source of Tocqueville's later influence was largely to derive from the aristocracy of his lineage allied to his acceptance of egalitarian democracy. It seemed to him, even during his student days from 1825 to 1827, and before his visit to America, that democracy offered hope against tyranny of the sort France had known before, during, and after the Revolution. The American journey would confirm this view. There, without judging, he would observe it "chez le peuple où elle a atteint le développement le plus complet et le plus paisible, afin d'en discerner clairement les conséquences naturelles et d'apercevoir s'il se peut, les moyens de la rendre profitable aux hommes (in the nation in which it has achieved its most complete and peaceful development, so as to see clearly its natural consequences and, if possible, to recognize the ways of making it profitable to men)." To him it seemed to have conformed to the whole pattern of historical development, "le mouvement le plus continu, le plus ancien et le plus permanent qu'on connaisse dans l'histoire (the most continuous, oldest, and most permanent movement known to history)."

The author and his brothers were tutored by the family chaplain, the abbé Lesueur, until at 15 Tocqueville began his formal studies at the Collège de Metz. From 1823 until 1827 he studied law in Paris. He then travelled in Italy and Sicily, returning to take up the position of "judge auditeur (assistant magistrate)" at Versailles, which his father obtained for him. He was to retain this post until 1835. Tocqueville was a person of extraordinary energy, driven by a striving for perfection which he thought he inherited from his father, but also liable to moments of acute depression and elation. A letter to Louis de Kergorlay, written in 1827 when he was privately circulating his "Voyage en Sicile," is riddled with doubts about his ability to apply in practice the legal principles with which, in theory, he was perfectly familiar. He was frightened, he said, of narrowing his vision.

A subsequent letter to the same friend in 1828 showed him alert to the political and social temper of France in the months leading up to the 1830 revolution. In order to understand the workings of constitutional monarchy he read deeply in English history, mastering not its detail but its broad sweep, and particularly the development of power relationships between crown and feudal nobility. By the end of 1828 we know from Tocqueville's informal correspondence that he had identified equality of power as the goal towards which history was moving. He concluded that equality is man's natural state, since nations were arriving at it from such different starting points and along such different routes. In 1830 he took the required oath of loyalty to the new administration.

Different explanations have been put forward concerning the degree of Tocqueville's self-interest in taking the oath. His father remained true to his aristocratic caste in refusing it. Tocqueville was considered suspect by the new regime, which kept him waiting five months before giving him leave to undertake the American mission it had accorded him. He saw democracy as inevitable, but perceived its dangers and viewed it with some distaste. The decision to take the oath, and to have himself nominated for the American mission so that he could see democracy in action and collect the evidence he needed, and the career decisions which depended on the outcome, must have been taken more or less together.

Early in 1831 Tocqueville, together with his life-long friend and fellow magistrate Gustave-Auguste de Beaumont de la Bonninière (1802–1866), obtained the mission to examine the US penal system. This allowed him to travel widely in the US, where he arrived on 18 May 1831. Within a week he had written back for copies of the lectures on Rome and the Middle Ages by Guizot (1787–1874), which he and Beaumont needed in order "to help us to analyse American society." Guizot had been a professor of history at the Sorbonne, where his liberal views caused his lectures to be technically suspended from 1822 to 1828. This was before he began a political career under the July monarchy, which ended with the revolution of 1848. Tocqueville's journey to the US lasted until February 1832. On returning to France, he and Beaumont wrote their official report, *Du système pénitentiaire aux Etats-Unis et de son application en France*, published in 1833. Tocqueville also began to note down his impressions of political life and power in the US, the famous *De la démocratie en Amérique*. The two volumes of the first part, analysing in detail American democracy, were published in 1835, and the second part, discussing democracy in general, "l'influence qu'exercent les idées et les sentiments démocratiques sur la société politique (the influence exercised by democratic ideas and feelings on the political body)," appeared in 1840.

The book was immediately and immensely successful. It was also highly influential both in the US and in England, which Tocqueville had already visited in 1833, and where he went again in 1835. In 1836 he married Mary Mottley from Stonehouse in Devonshire. There were no children of the union. On 6 January 1838 Tocqueville was elected a member of the Académie des Sciences Morales et Politiques, and in 1841, at the age of only 36, he was elected to the Académie Française. That year he also went on an official mission to Algeria. From 1835 he had lived at Tocqueville on his private means, more or less aping the way of life of the English gentry. He stood unsuccessfully for the chamber of deputies, but turned down the offer of a government post from Molé (1781–1855), against whom Guizot had joined Thiers in opposition. On standing again, he was elected deputy for Valognes in 1839, and made his maiden speech on 2 July. After the 1848 revolution, Tocqueville retained his seat, becoming vice president in 1849 and minister for foreign affairs from 2 June to 31 October. He had been a member of the Assemblée Nationale from 1848, and in that year was also a member of the Committee for the Constitution. He spent the winter of 1850–51 at Sorrento writing his memoirs of the Second Republic. Among the liberal deputies arrested following Louis-Napoleon's coup d'état in 1851, Tocqueville retired from public life and devoted himself to writing, visiting Germany in 1854.

In 1856 he published the first part of *L'Ancien Régime et la Révolution*, based on painstaking research into official archives and municipal records. The book, almost as great a success as its predecessor, was intended to be the first of three volumes, of which the other two would have dealt with the Revolution itself and the Napoleonic era. *L'Ancien Régime* studies the social and political framework of pre-Revolutionary France, the ways in which 18th-century French society gestated the Revolution which appeared to destroy it, and the reasons why the monarchy's collapse was so sudden and so total. In 1857 Tocqueville paid a triumphant visit to England. The following year he burst a blood vessel and was advised to live in the south. He moved to Cannes, where he died on 16 April 1859. Apart from his two great works, he had published only minor pieces during his lifetime, but Michel Lévy published a volume of *Oeuvres et correspondance* in 1861, before publishing Tocqueville's *Oeuvres complètes*, including much of the correspondence, edited by Beaumont in nine volumes from 1860 to 1865. *Les Souvenirs* was published only in 1893, and the correspondence with Gobineau in 1908. Publication of a definitive edition of the complete works started in 1951.

WORKS

Like Montesquieu, whose works he knew well and whom in many ways he resembled, Tocqueville was primarily a political "moraliste" in the French sense of the term, an observer rather than a preacher. In *Les Souvenirs* he chronicled events. His account of the 1848 revolution, with the situations which led up to it and followed from it, is still an indispensable source of information about the social and political history of the July monarchy. *L'Ancien Régime* is a serious work of documented historical scholarship. Tocqueville's greatest work, however, is certainly his first, the product of his youthful excitement at Guizot's liberal bourgeois history lectures and the occasion of his own visit to the US. He had known not only that the US consisted of small communities scattered over huge areas, but that it thereby resisted centralization. Consequently, equality could flourish there without sacrificing liberty. The point being made was that France was smaller, that it had created equality, but that liberty had been sacrificed in the centralizing process which the Revolution and the Napoleonic era had actually accelerated.

Democracy is inevitable. That much, Tocqueville holds in his introduction, is clear from its universality, its durability, and its independence of attempts to interrupt its progress: "Fait providentiel, il en a les principaux caractères, il est universel, il est durable, il échappe chaque jour à la puissance humaine; tous les événements comme tous les hommes servent à son développement (A work of fate, it has all the characteristics of such. It is universal. It is lasting. It daily escapes human control. All events and all men contribute to its development)." No single generation can halt it. It destroyed feudalism and monarchies. It will not be checked by the rich or the middle class. All we can do is see how to profit by it if we can. Guizot had not perceived the force of democracy quite as clearly. He wanted to encourage, direct, and control it, ultimately keeping it in the middle classes, to whom his reforms still effectively restricted education. Tocqueville, like Machiavelli, did not like what he observed, but thought he ought to analyse how it worked. What was confirmed in America was the importance of the small, relatively self-contained community, which allowed equality to develop without tyranny, which depended on centralized, bureaucratic control.

The US experience taught Tocqueville that democracy, in the right conditions, could respect rights of property and opinion, and promote lesser inequality of wealth. It was certainly not without risks, and depended on a certain enlightened outlook and a private code of integrity. He seems in many ways to have observed in action the sort of society Rousseau had envisaged in theory in *Du contrat social*. The question, as Tocqueville put it in a famous letter to Eugène Stoffels of 21 February 1835, is to know whether the democratic onslaught can be contained within a system of public order and private morality, or whether it has to overflow into disruptive and depraved passions which impose "a heavier yoke than any which has weighed on men since the fall of the Roman Empire." Tocqueville's view of the possible political structures which democracy could lead to is the result of an accurate sociological analysis made on the basis of acute observation, together with his constant preoccupation with grand lines of development rather than with individuals and particular events.

Men seek liberty, runs Tocqueville's analysis, to escape the inequities which create dependence. But no sooner have they overthrown one tyranny than they willingly submit to another. The overthrow of political despotism leads to democratization and moral equality, but not to political liberty. The key observation in Tocqueville's analysis is that the othertthrow of political despotism leads to the desire of individuals to safeguard equality by surrendering its custody to the collectivity. They end up exchanging the tyranny of the despot for that of the collectivity. Centralization is encouraged because of the hope individuals place in it as the protector of equality. Tocqueville's particularly fine analysis of this phenomenon is in chapter six, at the end of the fourth book. The remedy is to reinforce the demand for liberty in the face of the growing exigencies of equality, and the only way of preventing the gestation of absolute power in the name of protecting equality is by creating small communities or at least by breaking down centralization.

Tocqueville confirmed in America what Rousseau had assumed but never really made explicit: a citizen's democracy could only ever work if it were composed of small units. Tocqueville's American experience specifically emphasized for him the importance of local association, the freedom of the press, and the respect for religion. These were all necessary for the cultivation of a moral sense in each individual (already insistently required by both Montesquieu and Rousseau), on which the political liberties of the whole political body depended. Expressed simply, democracy without healthy grass roots would degenerate into tyranny. The danger lay in that "multitude représentée par quelques hommes. Ceux-ci parlent seuls au nom d'une foule absente ou inattentive; seuls ils agissent au milieu de l'immobilité universelle (multitude represented by a few, who speak alone in the name of an absent or unheeding crowd. They act alone in the middle of universal inactivity)." Pessimistically, Tocqueville seemed to suppose that envy would lead to stronger demands for equality, achievable only at the cost of liberty, and that a mediocre wellbeing would lead to the willing sacrifice of personal liberty.

L'Ancien Régime argues that the increasing demand for equality actually accelerated the growth of centralization during the Revolution. The decadence of the aristocracy was the result of the centralization of power. The archival research was undertaken especially at Tours, but Tocqueville, always apt to be dismissive of other men's faults, was appalled by the vulgarity of Louis-Napoleon, as well as by his ambition to destroy the personal and political liberties which Tocqueville had stood for during his political career. The documents he now studied confirmed his fears that tyranny could be kept alive, indeed made necessary, by war between the classes. Class war put a higher price on liberty. It could be held in check by tyranny, or it could lead to a revolution and a worse tyranny, but during the ancien régime the class war had been an instrument of government until it inevitably gestated revolution and, with it, the Terror. Some chapters of this short book took Tocqueville "more than a year's labour," but the work does hold a glimmer of hope for France, in spite of the depressing evidence that men would rather be subservient to tyrants than make the effort required to preserve personal liberties. Tocqueville has long been acknowledged as one of the greatest political "moralistes" to have written in French.

PUBLICATIONS

Collections

Oeuvres et correspondance inédites, 2 vols., 1861
Oeuvres complètes, 9 vols., 1864–66.
Oeuvres complètes, 27 vols., 1952–.

Works

Note sur le système pénitentiaire et sur la mission confiée par le Ministre de l'Intérieur à de Beaumont et de Tocqueville, 1831
Du système pénitentiaire aux Etats-Unis et de son application en France, with Gustave-Auguste de Beaumont de la Bonninière, 1833
Mémoire sur le paupérisme, 1833
Etat social et politique de la France, 1834
De la démocratie en Amérique, part 1 (2 books) 1835, part 2 (4 books), 1840; as *Democracy in America*, 2 vols., 1945
Histoire philosophique de la règne de Louis XV, 1846
Des enfants trouvés et des orphelins pauvres, 1850
L'Ancien Régime et la Révolution, 1856; as *The Old Regime and the Revolution*, 1856; as *The Old Regime and the French Revolution*, 1955
Correspondence and Conversations of Alexis de Tocqueville with Nassau William Senior from 1834 to 1859, 2 vols., 1872
Les Souvenirs d'Alexis de Tocqueville, 1893; as *The Recollections of Alexis de Tocqueville*, 1959
Journey to England and Ireland, 1958
"The European Revolution" and Correspondence with Gobineau, 1959
Journey to America, 1960

Critical and biographical studies

Gargan, Edward T., *Alexis de Tocqueville: The Critical Years, 1848–1851*, 1955
Meyer, J.-P., *Alexis de Tocqueville: A Biographical Study in Political Science, with a New Essay*, 1960
Herr, Richard, *Tocqueville and the Old Regime*, 1962
Lively, Jack, *The Social and Political Thought of Alexis de Tocqueville*, 1962
Gargan, Edward T., *De Tocqueville*, 1965

TOURNIER, Michel (Édouard), 1924–

Novelist.

LIFE

Michel Tournier was born on 19 December 1924 in Paris, "la ville la plus inhospitalière du monde, en particulier à l'égard des jeunes (the most inhospitable city in the world, especially towards the young)." He maintains that Paris is populated by provincials, like his own father and mother, who came, respectively, from the Douai region of northern France and from Bligny-sur-Ouche, Burgundy. He rejects the idea of himself as a Parisian: "Etant né à Paris, je me considère comme n'étant né nulle part, tombé du ciel, météore (Having been born in Paris, I regard myself as having been born nowhere, dropped from the sky, a meteor)." Tournier now lives in Choisel, a village in the Chevreuse valley, and is an enthusiastic and extensive traveller, with a predilection for Germany and North Africa.

The connection with Germany was hereditary. Tournier's great-uncle, Gustave Fournier, was a priest and teacher of German in Dijon. In 1910 he took his niece Marie-Madeleine Fournier to Freiburg-im-Breisgau, where they stayed in a Catholic students' hostel run by nuns. She did her "licence" in German at the Sorbonne and met Alphonse Tournier, who was preparing for the agrégation in German. He should have taken the exam in August 1914 but was called up instead. He was disfigured by wounds during the war and lost interest in becoming a German teacher, but after their marriage Mme Tournier continued her annual holiday visits to the nuns in Freiburg, and when the children were old enough she took them with her.

Alphonse Tournier was the founder and managing director of the Bureau International des Editions Musico-Mécaniques (BIEM), which controlled contracts and copyright on recorded music exported to European countries. The foreign subsidiaries of the BIEM sent a stream of interesting visitors through the Tournier household, and there was a plentiful supply of free records. Michel's favourite toy was a phonograph, even at the age of three, when he was too small to wind it up himself.

As a child Tournier used to spend holidays in Brittany, at Saint-Jacut-de-la-Mer, and with his mother's family in Bligny-sur-Ouche. His grandfather, Edouard Fournier, was a pharmacist who mixed all his own prescriptions. By watching him in his dispensary, and reading medical books in the attic, Michel absorbed enough information to be able to treat his own ailments in later life and to avoid doctors.

Tournier's dread of doctors began when he had his tonsils out at the age of four, without prior warning and without anaesthetic. He describes this event in *Le Vent Paraclet* as "l'Aggression, l'Attentat, un crime qui a ensanglanté mon enfance et dont je n'ai pas encore surmonté l'horreur (the Aggression, the Outrage, a crime that bloodied my childhood; I still have not got over the horror of it)." Tournier sees tonsillectomy as a vestige of a primitive initiation rite, significantly inflicted on boys far more often than girls. Initiation is a major theme in his novels and in his theories of childhood:

L'initiation d'un enfant se fait par un double mouvement: entrée dans la société—principalement des hommes—, éloignement du giron maternel. En somme, passage d'un état biologique à un statut social.

(The initiation of a child is effected in a double process: entry into society—mainly a society of men—and moving away from the mother's lap. Basically, the passing from a biological state to a social status.)

Tournier experienced the second half of this process when he was six. As he was chronically unhealthy in Paris, he was sent to a boarding school for sickly children in Gstaad, in the Bernese Oberland. He marvelled at the snow and the waterfalls, suffered from constant thirst, and was bullied by his older room-mate, who was supposed to be looking after him.

Gstaad fut mon premier voyage, mon premier exil, une expérience au total assez dure, mais enrichissante, à laquelle ma grande soif et les sévices de Niño donnèrent ce qu'il faut de profondeur et de pesanteur.

(Gstaad was my first journey, my first exile, on the whole a fairly tough but enriching experience, to which my great thirst and Niño's tortures lent the necessary depth and weightiness.)

Tournier learnt to read relatively late, a fact he attributes to immaturity, "qui continue je crois à faire le fond de ma nature (which I believe is still a basic part of my nature)." The first book that really captured his imagination was a translation of *Nils Holgersson's Marvellous Journey Across Sweden* by Selma Lagerlöf, "un livre superbe de découverte et de libération, un traité d'initiation (a wonderful book of discovery and liberation, a treatise on initiation)." His other favourite was Hans Andersen's *The Snow Queen*:

Il n'y a pas d'oeuvre dont je regrette autant de n'être pas l'auteur. Je n'en connais pas qui marie aussi heureusement la familiarité la plus quotidienne et le fantastique le plus grandiose.

(There is no other book that I am so sorry not to have written myself. No other book that I know achieves such a happy marriage of everyday familiarity with the most grandiose fantasy.)

Tournier had a chaotic and disrupted school career. His talent was for working alone, not absorbing information from a teacher, and he had a mental block about mathematics. At school the only subjects he did well in were theology and German. He spent four years at Catholic schools: three as a dayboy at the Collège Saint-Erembert in Saint-Germain-en-Laye and one as a boarder at the Collège Saint-François d'Alençon. He then attended the Lycée Pasteur in Paris. He regards the Catholic religion as a vital counterbalance to an education based on mathematics and science. He loved the imagery of the Church and later rediscovered it in metaphysics.

The first teacher Tournier appreciated as a human being was M. Letréguilly, his form master in the "sixième" at the Collège Saint-Erembert. If Tournier had been able to fulfil his ambition of becoming a teacher, he would have liked to teach the "sixième" age group (eleven-year-olds):

C'est l'âge adulte de l'enfance, celui où l'enfant a atteint le plein épanouissement de son être sans avoir été encore abîmé par la puberté.

(This is the adult age of childhood, when the child has reached the full flowering of his being without yet being ruined by puberty.)

His other memorable teacher was Laurent de Gouvion Saint-Cyr, in the "quatrième" at the same school, who was only 10 years older than his pupils. He was brilliant at riding and fencing, but taught himself Latin and Greek as he went along, keeping just a step ahead of his class. He had no time for the traditional French literature syllabus and concentrated on modern authors—Cocteau, Giono, and Giraudoux. Tournier thoroughly approves of this approach, and believes that literature taught to children should be as contemporary as possible.

Before World War II Tournier used to go to Freiburg with his mother and brothers and sister. As well as going on excursions into the Black Forest, they witnessed the growth of Nazism: "In the streets, there was a permanent political and military rally." By the time the war came the Tourniers were more aware than most French people of what was in store. Michel was perversely relieved by the occupation: "J'étais dévoré par la soif de désordre et de catastrophe qui tourmente certains adolescents (I was consumed by the thirst for disorder and catastrophe that torments some adolescents.)"

The Tourniers' house in Saint-Germain-en-Laye was taken over as a transit billet for the German army, and the family were left with only the ground floor to themselves. By the spring of 1941 the Tourniers had ceased to believe that the war would soon be over and moved to a rented apartment in Neuilly. Michel hated living in Paris and used to cycle 200 kilometres in a day to get to their holiday villa in Villers-sur-Mer, on the coast of Normandy. It also had been commandeered, and the beach was inaccessible through the barbed wire. Michel sometimes had meals with the soldiers and earnestly impressed upon them that the misty coastline in the distance around Le Havre was really England, and that they would soon be be invaded.

Life in occupied Paris became steadily harder and colder. Mme Tournier realized that food and fuel would be easier to come by in the country and managed to rent the disused presbytery in Lusigny, a tiny village near her native Bligny. She moved there with her two younger sons, Jean-Loup and Gérard, while Alphonse Tournier and their daughter Janine stayed in Neuilly, and Michel gravitated between the two. He was studying philosophy at the Sorbonne but had to work on the land in the summer with a family called Fournier in Lusigny. On 30 March 1944 Lusigny was raided by a Wehrmacht detachment in reprisal for Resistance activity, and 14 villagers were taken to Buchenwald, including M. Fournier and his two eldest daughters. Those that came back were casualties of the war as much as those who died in captivity: "Ils vegétérent et se laissèrent mourir (They vegetated and allowed themselves to die)."

In 1944 Tournier was called before an examining board for the Service du Travail Obligatoire. He was declared fit for labour camp, but was saved by the liberation. He watched the Germans retreating through Lusigny for three days and nights, dumping their weapons in ditches and taking every bicycle they could find, including his.

Tournier and his friends had discovered Sartre in 1943 when *L'Etre et le néant* was published, but were bitterly disappointed by his lecture in October 1945, when Sartre, in an attempt to appease anxieties, announced that existentialism was "un humanisme." They decided he had turned into his own creation, the Autodidacte of *La Nausée*. Tournier's special subject was Plato, and he presented his thesis in June 1946. He was more eager to get back to Germany than to take the agrégation straightaway and found an opportunity in July 1946. The University of Tübingen was in the French occupation zone, and the officer in charge invited a group of French students of German to spend three weeks there. Tournier pulled strings and ended up joining them. Tübingen was undamaged by the war and was a revelation of what peacetime student life could be like: "If I ever knew the intoxication of being young, it was certainly that summer of 46, on the banks of the Neckar."

When the three weeks were up, the French students were offered the chance to stay longer. The only one who applied was Tournier, and he stayed in Tübingen on and off until 1950. He lived as part of a growing nucleus of French students, but also had German friends, went riding with the French military governor, and continued to study philosophy and to follow Lévi-Strauss's ethnography courses in Paris. He was in Germany for the birth of the economic miracle on the night of 19–20 June 1948, when the Reichsmark was withdrawn and replaced with a strictly rationed quantity of Deutsche Marks, providing an essential spur to production. Tournier met a Swabian peasant who claimed to be a former French prisoner of war and had taken German nationality rather than return home. He began to think about a novel of wartime Germany involving a French prisoner, but was not to complete the project until *Le Roi des Aulnes* came out in 1970.

In July 1949 Tournier went back to Paris to take his long-postponed "agrégation de philosophie," which he failed. His pride was dented and, refusing to contemplate the option of teaching with any lesser qualification, he gave up his aspirations to a teaching career. He gradually moved towards fiction writing, as did his contemporary Michel Butor, for the same reason.

Initially Tournier earned a living by translating copious quantities of German for the Plon publishing company. He discovered by experience that it was excellent training for a creative writer: "By doing translations, the apprentice writer not only acquires a mastery of his own language, he also learns patience, and the thankless effort conscientiously carried out, without hope of money or glory. It's a school of literary virtue."

He also worked as a scriptwriter and broadcaster for Radio-Télévision Française until 1955. Reading listeners' letters made him aware of a vast and vociferous public he had never met as a student. In late 1954 he was one of the broadcasters poached from French state radio by Charles Michelson for his new commercial station, Europe No.1, based in the independent state of the Saar. Tournier was hesitant about joining such an overtly money-conscious organization, but was overwhelmed by Michelson's charm and the force of his personality.

Commercial radio was an uncomfortable but formative experience for Tournier. The programme "Vous êtes formidables" was an example of how the relationship between presenter and listener can be manipulated, not only to sell more of the sponsor's product, but also to involve the listener in community action. In *Le Vent Paraclet* Tournier describes two of the programme's campaigns in 1956. One involved the paralysed daughter of a railway crossing keeper, whose only moment of interest in the day was when an unknown train driver tooted his whistle to cheer her up. "Vous êtes formidables" told its listeners to go out and buy presents for Andrée Jammet and take them to main-line stations for the driver, Robert Ferret, to collect. He then stopped his special train at Andrée's door and delivered thousands of presents to her. The other campaign was prompted by the Soviet invasion of Hungary. "Vous êtes formidables" chartered an aeroplane and told its listeners to bring donations of medicine to Orly airport for the suffering people of Budapest. Some volunteers drove all night from the farthest parts of France. Tournier was impressed, but also repelled, by the power of the media over ordinary people.

He was convinced that somewhere between the solitary perfectionism of translating and the cynical manipulation of advertising he could find his own way of communicating with the public. He was determined not just to write fiction, but to incorporate his own philosophical background into his work. His first novel was not published until 1967. In the meantime, from 1958 to 1968, Tournier worked as senior literary editor for Plon. He divides writers into sprinters and marathon runners, regarding himself as a marathon runner: "Un manuscrit mûrit dans ma tête et sur ma table quatre ou cinq années (A manuscript matures in my head and on my desk for four or five years)." This is an understatement in the case of *Le Roi des Aulnes*, which started life in Tübingen in the late 1940s. It won the Prix Goncourt in 1970, while *Vendredi; ou, Les Limbes du Pacifique* won the Grand Prix du Roman de l'Académie Française when it was published in 1967.

Tournier became a member of the Académie Goncourt in 1972. He has been a full-time writer since 1970, but has continued his hobby of photography, an interest he traces back to his Fournier grandfather, who photographed all the special occasions in Bligny-sur-Ouche. He has published joint collections of prose and photographs with Edouard Boubat and Arthur Tress: *Des clefs et des Serrures* and *Vues de dos*.

WORKS

Tournier's novels recreate familiar myths in unusual ways. *Vendredi; ou, Les Limbes du Pacifique* is based on the same story as Daniel Defoe's *Robinson Crusoe*, but approached from a different direction. Studying anthropology under Claude Lévi-Strauss convinced Tournier that so-called primitive societies have an equal cultural value to the self-styled developed nations. Defoe's Man Friday was an ignorant savage, turned into a faithful servant by Robinson Crusoe. Tournier's Vendredi acts as a saviour and tutor to Robinson, whose personality changes through years of solitude, and whose relationship with his desert island is influenced by a person much better adapted to Pacific circumstances.

The repackaging of myths is Tournier's way of introducing metaphysics into the novel. "Je suis contrebandier," he explained in a BBC2 interview in February 1991. "Je fais semblant de transporter des bananes, mais en fait je transporte des explosives (I am a smuggler. I pretend I'm transporting bananas, but in fact I'm transporting explosives)." The form of his novels is strictly conventional. The explosions take place in the content: the reader is invited to accept descriptions of gluttony, garbage, excrement, and execution, and characters who are homosexual, paedophile, incestuous, or multiply perverted. In his own obituary (in *Des clefs et des Serrures*) Tournier suggests labelling himself as a "naturaliste mystique" (mystical naturalist): "C'est qu'à ses yeux tout est beau, même la laideur;

tout est sacré, même la boue (This is because everything in his eyes is beautiful, even ugliness; everything is sacred, even muck)."

In European fairy tales the ogre is a menacing figure who kidnaps and eats children. Tournier translated the title of *Le Roi des Aulnes* from Goethe's famous poem *Erlkönig*, in which the Ogre, invisible to adults, tries to persuade a little boy to come with him to his kingdom and finally steals his soul by force. Tournier's Abel Tiffauges has many of the traditional characteristics of an ogre: abnormal size, vast appetite (for raw food, in particular), poor eyesight, love of animals and children. Yet the main theme of the novel is Tiffauges's vocation of "phoria," a word Tournier coined from the Greek for "carry," which makes him St Christopher, the bearer of Christ, as well as the Erl-king who carries off children. As a prisoner of war in East Prussia, Tiffauges feels at home in Germany, and Tournier identifies Nazi Germany, with its obsessive youth cult and ultimate destructiveness, as an archetypal ogre. Superficial critics have interpreted *Le Roi des Aulnes* as a novel of homosexuality, but Tiffauges's interest in children is that of an immature ogre, not an adult, and his fantasy erotic impulses do not differentiate between boys and girls.

Alexandre in *Les Météores* is definitely homosexual. He is, however, so colourful and dominant a character that many readers see him as the hero, and are consequently disturbed when he dies before the end of the book. He and his friend Thomas Koussek are one couple in the novel, but Tournier's central concern is with Alexandre's twin nephews, Jean and Paul. Through them he examines the nature of twinship as the basis for a self-sufficient unit, including the sexuality of the automatic couple, and follows the effect on the unit when one twin breaks away and experiments with life as a single person.

Tournier considers *Les Météores* the most ambitious of his novels and had originally planned to give it a stronger religious and cosmological dimension, with the twins as intercessors between heaven and earth. When the novel developed differently, he reassigned its working title, *Le Vent Paraclet*, to a collection of autobiographical essays published in 1977. In these he describes his personal development as a writer and the evolution of his major novels. He has also written about his views on writing and his special relationship with German literature in *Le Vol du Vampire*.

Tournier has used and amplified the journey of the Magi in *Gaspard, Melchior et Balthazar*, adding a fourth wise man, Tasor, who appears in oral tradition but not in manuscripts. *Gilles et Jeanne* is the story of Joan of Arc, with Gilles de Rais as her demonic "twin," the evil side of a split conscience. Tournier's concern for the underprivileged of the Third World is expressed in *La Goutte d'or*, in which Idriss, an immigrant worker from North Africa, brings a talisman to France. It is made of gold, in the shape of a drop of water, the most precious commodity in the desert.

Tournier's reverence for childhood has led to relatively few books specifically for children. *Vendredi; ou, La Vie sauvage* is a young person's version of the earlier *Vendredi; ou, Les Limbes du Pacifique*, as *Les Rois mages* is reworked from *Gaspard, Melchior et Balthazar*. *Pierrot; ou, Les Secrets de la nuit* is a children's book. *Amandine; ou, Les Deux jardins* was published as a children's story in 1977 but also figures in the adult collection *Le Coq de Bruyère* and deals with Tournier's recurrent theme of initiation into adulthood. Tournier seems happiest when analysing childhood with the benefit of hindsight:

L'enfance nous est donné comme un chaos brûlant, et nous n'avons pas trop de tout le reste de notre vie pour tenter de le mettre en ordre et de nous l'expliquer.

(Childhood is given to us as a burning chaos, and the whole of the rest of our life is hardly long enough to try to sort it out and understand it.)

To understand Tournier's novels, it is important to start, as he does, with the underlying myth. It is the key to their meaning: "C'est le mécanisme mythologique et symbolique qui est si contraignant, qu'il détermine entièrement l'action des personnages (It is the mechanism of the myth and the symbol which so imposes constraints that it totally determines the action of the characters)." Tournier sees himself primarily as the author of metaphysical novels, rather on the model of Thomas Mann and, one suspects, Heimito von Doderer or Robert Edler von Musil, while more overtly adapting a well-known myth to create a new one, and so imposing on himself the constraint which his imagination found necessary for the development of its maximum power. Style for Tournier is not so much a means of expression as part of the finishing process, a way to "rendre claires et agréables les choses subtiles et difficiles que j'ai à dire (make clear and pleasant to read the subtle and difficult things I have to say)." Tournier's great German predecessors could have said the same, but none of his French ones.

PUBLICATIONS

Fiction

Vendredi; ou, Les Limbes du Pacifique, 1967; (revised edition, 1978); as *Friday; or, The Other Island*, 1969

Le Roi des Aulnes, 1970; as *The Erl-King*, 1972; as The Ogre 1972

Vendredi; ou, La Vie sauvage (juvenile), 1971; as *Friday and Robinson: Life on Esperanza Island*, 1972

Les Météores, 1975; as *Gemini*, 1981

Amandine; ou, Les Deux jardins (juvenile), 1977

Le Coq de bruyère, 1978; as *The Fetishist and Other Tales*, 1983

La Fugue du petit Poucet (juvenile), 1979

Pierrot; ou, Les Secrets de la nuit (juvenile), 1979

Gaspard, Melchior et Balthazar, 1980; as *The Four Wise Men*, 1982

Barbedor (juvenile), 1980

L'Aire du Muguet (juvenile), 1982

Gilles et Jeanne, 1983; as *Gilles and Jeanne* (in English), 1987

Les Rois Mages racontés par Michel Tournier d'après "Gaspard, Melchior et Balthazar (juvenile), 1983

Sept Contes (*Pierrot; ou, Les Secrets de la nuit*; *Amandine; ou, Les Deux jardins*; *La Fugue du petit Poucet*; *La Fin de Robinson Crusoë*; *Barbedor*; *La Mère Noël*; *Que ma joie demeure*) (juvenile), 1984

La Goutte d'or, 1985; as *The Golden Droplet*, 1987

Le Médianoche amoureux, 1989; as *The Midnight Love Feast*, 1991

Les Contes du médianoche (juvenile), 1989

Essays

Le Vent Paraclet, 1977; as *The Wind Spirit*, 1989
Le Vol du Vampire, 1981
Petites Proses, 1986
Le Tabor et le Sinaï: écrits sur l'art, 1988

Illustrated non-fiction

Mythologies, with original engravings by Pierre Yves Trémois, 1970
Miroirs: autoportraits, with photographs by Edouard Boubat, 1973
Journal de voyage au Canada, with photographs by Edouard Boubat, 1977
Des clefs et des serrures, 1979
Rêves, with photographs by Arthur Tress, 1979
Vues de dos, with photographs by Edouard Boubat, 1981
Morts et résurrections de Dieter Appelt, 1981
François Mitterand: pouvoir de l'image et images du pouvoir, with photographs by Konrad R. Müller, 1983
Le Vagabond immobile, with drawings by Jean-Max Toubeau, 1984
Angus, with illustrations by Pierre Joubert, 1988

Critical and biographical studies

Bonfomié, Arlette, *Michel Tournier: le roman mythologique*, 1988
Davis Colin *Michel Tournier . Philosophy and Fiction*, 1988

TROYAT, Henri (Pseudonym of Lev Tarassoff), 1911–

Novelist, biographer, and dramatist.

LIFE

Troyat was born in Moscow, the youngest of three children of a well-to-do merchant and a doctor's daughter who was herself a capable business woman. The family owned what was in effect a nation-wide conglomerate, and Troyat spent his childhood in a way commensurate with his family's position. His Swiss governess had taught him French before the Revolution, when the family fled with its retinue first to Kharkov, and then to their estate in the Caucasus, taking the last boat out of the Crimea for Constantinople. They reached Venice and in 1920, after a short spell in Paris followed by a period in Mainz, they settled in Paris, where Troyat attended the Lycée Pasteur from 1920 to 1929, the year he passed his baccalauréat. He studied law in Paris, graduating in 1933, and took out naturalization papers in order to enter government service.

He was appointed to the finance office of the prefecture of the Seine, and from 1933 to 1935 completed his military service in Metz. His family meanwhile had lapsed into genteel poverty. The lycée bills had only been paid with difficulty, and his mother now took to making hats. Troyat's later fiction was to be affected by this increasing hardship, which ended with the seizure of the family furniture, as it was by their concrete memories of a lost grandeur in Russia, and his own cultural integration into the French professional classes. For Troyat exile was part of the family folklore rather than a real experience, but economic pressure was real enough, and as a student he had worked as a film extra and as a salesman for carbon paper.

Troyat's literary interests date from his last years at school. He co-founded a magazine entitled *Fouillis*, which ran to six numbers, and became interested in the philosophy of Bergson and in psychoanalysis, the subject of his first short story, *La Clef de voûte*, whose composition antedated *Faux jour*. While still at school he helped adapt into French a series of Russian sketches devised and compered by his uncle Nikita Balieff (1877–1936) and performed by the Chauve-Souris cabaret troupe, which enjoyed a successful run in London and New York. Troyat showed the text of *La Clef de voûte* to Maurois's daughter, Michelle, with whom he was friendly, and Maurois suggested going straight to the top by submitting the piece to Jean Paulhan at the *Nouvelle Revue Française* (q. v.) who turned it down, or to Robert de Saint-Jean at the *Revue Hebdomadaire*, who took it. On Saint-Jean's advice, Troyat sent *Faux jour* to Plon, who published it in 1935, insisting only that it should be signed with a French name to distinguish it from the flood of Russian émigré publications. Troyat changed his name from Tarassoff, and simply adopted "Henri." The novel was awarded the Prix Populiste.

Its successor, written largely in the regimental radio workshop at Metz, attracted reviews which were more mixed. Troyat began to make a name for himself and to gravitate towards the group who composed the jury of the Prix Populiste, Jules Romains, Georges Duhamel, Gabriel Marcel, Robert Kemp, André Thérive, and Frédéric Lefèvre, and to those who had reviewed him favourably and their friends. His administrative duties allowed him plenty of time to write, and his long stream of publications had begun to flow. In 1938 *L'Araigne* won the Prix Goncourt, and in 1959 Troyat was elected to the Académie Française.

Early in 1939 he married and started his biography of Dostoyevsky, which led him towards the historical novel, a genre which he was to exploit in a series of novel cycles. Troyat was mobilized in 1940 and released at the armistice. Although he was able to return to his post, he was insensed at the anti-semitic law which forbade government employment to anyone not French by birth. In 1942 he resigned in order to devote himself to writing. His wife bore him a son in 1943, but they divorced in 1944. During the war Troyat published little, partly on account of paper rationing, but mostly because he was concentrating on his first "roman fleuve," *Tant que la terre durera*. In 1948 he remarried, and his second wife, a widow whose husband had died in the war, became his literary collaborator. Troyat wroked briefly as a theatre critic and in 1946 founded with Maurice Druon the weekly *Cavalcade*, of which he was literary editor until the review was wound up in 1948. The first job of the theatre critic he appointed was to review Troyat's own *Les Vivants*, which he disliked. Although Troyat tried again with a comedy, *Sébastien*, he did not find drama a suitable outlet for his creative energies.

Troyat had visited the US in 1947 and tried his pen at documentary writing (*La Case de l'Oncle Sam*), which did not suit him either, although he was to make a further attempt after a journey to Central and South America in 1954 (*De gratte-ciel en cocottier: à travers l'Amérique indienne*) and with an account of car manufacture (*Naissance d'une Dauphine*). As a writer of extraordinary fluency Troyat concentrated in the end on fiction, mostly novels and novel cycles, and on biographies. His six cycles contain 22 novels in all. He wrote 17 other novels, short stories, and short novels, and half a dozen full biographies. He received much critical recognition and a number of prizes, and his books regularly sold 100,000 copies a piece. He stayed away from politics, worked regular hours, and kept his professional and private lives as separate as possible. He always wanted to be considered a working writer, which is what he was, and in consequence he did not write articles, give lectures, or keep a diary.

WORKS

Troyat's gift is that of a story teller and a biographer. The volume and popularity of his output, the consideration lavished on him by his French compatriots, and the official recognition bestowed on him, make his contribution to 20th-century French literature worthy of notice, although his literary gifts scarcely exceeded those of a number of his contemporaries. His books have been criticized for lacking psychological depth and passionate intensity, for being too long and, where the historical romances are concerned, for their conventionality. They read smoothly, are written with talent, but scarcely involve the emotions of the reader, offering well-constructed escapism and charm without probing the more fundamental values by which life has to be lived. Outside France, Troyat's works have not been widely read.

In the shorter pieces Troyat's themes are predominantly claustrophobia, domination, and the contrast between the real and the imaginary, while in the historical cycles he turned to general reflections on history and its futility, and on the phenomena of exile. Troyat considered the short stories a "relaxation." They offer a release from realism into fantasy and have been considered the most interesting of his writings, partly because they have required of him a heightened consciousness in the use of language.

The earlier novels are all quite short, with a small number of characters acting emotionally upon one another. *Faux jour* is about the use of a dream world to escape from real life. The story is related by the protagonist's son, Jean, who recounts how his father tries in vain to pursue his dreams in a world which increasingly enforces its laws through the economic pressures it exerts. Father and son end up drifting through life and the story's ending, on the death of the father, does not avoid sentimentality. The title is a pun, referring to false light as well as false hope, and the novel itself is more complex in conception than most of its successors. It is generally recognized that *Le Vivier*, of the same year, loses rather than gains momentum.

It is only with the fourth novel, *L'Araigne*, which was awarded the Prix Goncourt, that Troyat, no doubt on that account, acquired a wide readership. The novel is not generally thought to be well constructed, but the story of Gérard. who believes that his intellectual superiority gives him the right to dominate his three sisters when their mother dies, does at least raise universal questions relating to behaviour and values. Troyat says he found it the most difficult of his novels to write. He had to balance the male brought up in a female environment against the interest more easily aroused by his three sisters.

Gérard ends up his own victim, trapped by a superficially convincing Oedipal neurosis, but the novel's power is unacceptably weakened by his failure as an intellectual, so that his philosophy, which Troyat rightly supposes the reader will find contemptible, is never even put to the test. The conclusion is almost provocatively fatalistic, and memories of Chekov's *The Three Sisters* and Gide's *L'Immoraliste*, which are bound to occur to the reader, can only show up the weakness of *L'Araigne*. The title, meaning "spider," takes its 16th-century spelling from the quotation from Marguerite de Navarre which prefaces the book.

La Neige en deuil, which became well known to English-speaking audiences through the Dmytryk film version, *The Mountain*, concerns a physically and mentally wrecked Alpine guide who recovers his physical and moral strength when his younger brother uses moral blackmail against him to go and loot a crashed plane. He finds an Indian woman alive in the wreckage, and carries her to safety. His brother dies on the mountain, and he finds that the woman has died in his arms during the descent. Troyat maintained that the novel's interest lay in its psychology, not in the story of the climb. The moral—that neither cupidity nor heroism achieves very much—is bleak, but the unmotivated relapse of the guide at the end of the story does not so much resolve as avoid the dilemma which is the novel's point.

There are six cycles of novels, *Tant que la terre durera*, *Les Semailles et les moissons*, *La Lumière des justes*, *Les Eygletière*, *Les Héritiers de l'avenir*, and *Le Moscovite*. The first cycle took nearly 10 years to write, and goes from childhood in tsarist Russia through the Russo-Japanese War, the riots, and the Revolution and ends with the outbreak of World War II. The other cycles to do with Russia go back further into the 19th century to trace the more deeply rooted causes of the collapse of the tsarist regime. It was writing Dostoyevsky's biography that prepared Troyat for the first cycle, but the models are Tolstoy and, perhaps, Gogol.

Les Eygletière concerns the collapse of a Parisian family from the haute bourgeoisie of lawyers. The head of the family loses interest in his young and beautiful second wife, who falls in love with his son. The daughter attempts suicide. In the second novel another son makes a hopeless teenage marriage with his pregnant girlfriend, and the family tragedy is completed in the third volume. There is a smooth inevitability about the plot, with the characters merely acting out their assigned and virtually predictable roles. The time scale of two years is too rapid for Troyat to achieve even the sort of depth to be found, for instance, in Galsworthy. The last three cycles are less broad and less ambitious than their predecessors. *Les Héritiers de l'avenir*, in particular, contains historical insights into the mutual dependence of nobles and serfs, the fragmentation of whose relationship is presented as the root cause of the instability that led to the Revolution.

The short stories differ from the fiction of the novel cycles mostly in that they are free of the heavy determinism of historical inevitability and psychological predictability. They open the way to forces of superhuman origin and malignancy. Not all are serious. Some are obviously derivative, from Wells and Verne as well as Gogol. Some are merely entertaining mystery stories, ghost stories, and science fiction. Overall they also contain complex levels of narration, and sometimes a real humanity.

It is quite possible that Troyat will be remembered not for his verse at school, and may have thought of becoming a priest or a small-holder. In fact he married a local girl of poor parents in 1829, and lived in Le Puy, where he taught at a school for the deaf and dumb from 1830 to 1832. He then went to a college where, apparently, his conduct was found to be unsatisfactory and, in spite of annual applications from 1835, it was not until 1839 that he could get another school post. Between 1829 and 1838 the couple moved seven times and had seven children, of whom five died at birth or in infancy. In the remarkable autobiographical trilogy for which he his famous, *Jacques Vingtras*, comprising *L'Enfant, Le Bachelier*, and *L'Insurgé*, Vallès gives us precise information about his early childhood, the irritable home atmosphere, the hair-pulling, the ear-twisting, and the beatings. His upbringing as a small child was exceptionally severe and deprived of ordinary childhood pleasures.

Vallès was born at Le Puy. From the age of five for he attended a private infants' school two years, and in 1839 he moved to the Collège Royal, which was attended by about 200 pupils, and to which his father had been appointed. The headmaster had been sent there on demotion. Vallès got the second prize in his first year, but was dressed in ridiculous garb by his mother, and made to stay on with his father after school hours, giving him a 12-hour school day. His father, like Vallès himself, was derided at school. The root cause of Vallès's miseries was acute poverty, and he naturally came to hate school as he hated home. He could relax only with relatives, on the streets, or in the fields. His mother fell ill and his father, who wanted to study for his agrégation, could not accept promotion until December 1840, when he began a five-year teaching spell at Saint-Etienne. Continuously seeking promotion, he failed the oral part of the agrégation in 1845, but did well enough to be promoted to Nantes from January 1846.

Vallès distinguished himself in classical languages, although he was always in trouble at school. In 1845 his mother discovered that his father was having an affair, and life at home became even more intolerable. She was intensely ambitious for Vallès, who had by now come top in his class, but the discipline she tried to impose simply deepened his bitterness, festering in an imagination already intoxicated with adventure stories. Vallès began to withdraw into himself. At Nantes his father passed his agrégation. The school inspectors thought him too ready to punish, so that discipline actually suffered. The mistake he was making with Vallès at home was being more moderately repeated at school, where, in order to keep himself out of trouble, his son was doing very well indeed academically. The resentment continued to grow, however, and his mother's harshness irked more especially because it was given the sanction of religious authority.

During the revolution of 1848 Vallès became inflamed with the popular enthusiasm and, although he did not realize what was at stake, he soon became extremist and intransigent, joining a no doubt self-consciously excited group of adolescents to propose the abolition of the baccalauréat and all other examinations in the name of equality, together with "the absolute liberty of childhood." Feeling at Nantes was heavily on the side of Bonaparte, and Vallès, still understanding very little, was instinctively anxious to be active in what he saw as the people's uprising, in fact suppressed on 26 June. His social and political consciousness aroused, Vallès was to take his inspiration from Blanqui and Proudhon. Too close an association with the mother of a co-pupil suggested to his parents that he should be sent to

Paris, where he could prepare for the Ecole Normale Supérieure, but his interests had become so strongly political that he not only failed to carry off the expected prizes in 1849 but, in spite of apparently brilliant essays, failed his baccalauréat at Rennes in 1850 after another year at Nantes. He was to fail twice again before passing in 1852, having in the meanwhile fought a duel with a youth who had insulted his father.

After selling a few possessions, including books, Vallès set himself up in Paris on 40 francs a month. He mixed with poets, with what was left of the bohemian world of Murger and Champfleury, and attended Michelet's famous lectures at the Collège de France. When Michelet was suspended, Vallès helped to organize the student protest, living in the midst of a tumult that was half political rage and half high-spirited exuberance, until the coup d'état in December turned the irreverent youths into a serious political force. Vallès, who by this time had a mistress, was summoned home by his father. The ruin of his bourgeois and academic ambitions for his son so dismayed him that he had Vallès locked up in an asylum until the fear of scandal forced him to get the doctors to change their mind about his son's mental condition. Vallès now mysteriously inherited 13,000 francs, which guaranteed his monthly rent, and returned to Paris, where he lost no time in compromising himself politically, and spent six weeks in prison for his part in one of the rather absurd plots to assassinate Napoleon III. Vallès's younger sister Louise was now in a mental hospital, and his father, perhaps on account of a marital quarrel following an affair, obtained a posting to Rouen, where he was again criticized by the inspectorate for excessive severity.

Vallès agreed to study law, but idled, ran into debt, became something of a dandy, and generally revenged himself on his upbringing and his parents. He took ill-paid jobs writing dictionary entries and turned to journalism, writing first commercial advertisements, and then articles for trade papers and women's magazines. He fought another duel with an old friend with whom he shared an attic. In 1857 his father died. For a while Vallès even worked as a financial journalist, publishing a pamphlet on financial speculation and five articles, said to be technically incompetent, in *Le Figaro*. These were followed by a series of "Chroniques" in *Le Présent*, soon to be renamed the *Revue Européenne*, which passed convincingly for a gossip column and were not lacking in pure effrontery. Vallès had become a close ally of Gustave Planche, whose obituary by Vallès was admired, but his boldness was too much for the review, and Vallès moved to the *Chronique Parisienne*.

In the meanwhile, the family's financial situation had become desperate and Vallès took the examination which opened up an administrative career in Paris, for which he worked from 1860 to 1862 and 1863 to 1865, climbing from 1,200 to 1,600 francs a month. In 1860 he published in *Le Temps, Illustrateur Universel* two highly considered articles on the Latin Quarter as it had been in 1840 and as it was in 1860, explaining the difference in terms of Hausmann and Napoleon III. On 1 November 1860 *Le Figaro* published Vallès's "Dimanche d'un jeune homme pauvre," to be followed by "Les réfractaires" on 14 July 1861, "Les morts" on 3 November, and "Les victimes du livre" on 9 October 1862. His only other article appears to have been a poetic fantasy, "L'habit vert," published in *Le Boulevard*. He had taken a job as an assistant master (1862–63) at Caen, where he also attended the university.

Vallès resumed his journalistic activity on his return to Paris with an article on Maurice and Eugénie de Guérin in *Le Moniteur du Calvados* (8 July 1863) and book reviews in *Le Progrès de Lyon* in 1864 and early 1865. He also gave an important lecture on Balzac on 15 January 1865. The circumstances were politically sensitive and the authorities, but not the public, reacted with hostility. Vallès lost his job with the city administration at the instigation of the minister Duruy himself, but had started again to write for *Le Figaro*, and in a public contest won the editorship of the newspaper for one day. His issue, in spite of its subversiveness, was a sensation, and Vallès was now known as a successful writer. He wrote "Chroniques" for Ernest Feydeau's *L'Epoque*, and spent the autumn of 1865 in England, writing two long articles on Dickens for the *Courrier du Dimanche*. He wrote *Jean Delbenne* for *L'Epoque* and then for a large salary joined the staff of the new *L'Evénement*. He attacked Hugo, praised Daumier, and defended the Goncourts. Editors feared the aggressiveness of his style and his often intemperately expressed opinions, but enough doors were now open for Vallès to make a good living, at least until he attacked the recently deceased General Yusuf in the *Courrier de la Semaine*. Then the doors closed at *L'Evénement, Le Figaro,* and the other periodicals.

Vallès now collected together selected pieces of journalism in *Les Réfractaires* and *La Rue*. The first, conceived at Murger's funeral, was to correct the impression of Bohemia Murger was thought to have left, and to replace it with one peopled by the despairing and the threatening. *Le Courrier Français* changed hands, and accepted Vallès's "Chroniques" again, fighting for freedom in art, literature, and politics from May to September 1866. In 1867 Vallès founded his own weekly newspaper, *La Rue*. It was naturally to be an organ of radical opinion, and subscriptions were plentiful, but the paper ran into trouble and, after harrassment, was suppressed in just over six months. The daily *Le Globe* was founded, and Vallès wrote a piece for which he was sent to prison for a month. His attacks on establishment figures, even republicans, had become intemperate in tone and unpredictable in target, governed only sometimes by social principles, but rarely by discernible critical or aesthetic norms. Even the pieces defending Musset and the Goncourts were driven by a desire for paradox. Vallès, who had attacked the academies and salon juries as mechanisms to ensure the continuation of mediocrity, was sent to prison again for two months at the end of 1868 for exciting hatred and contempt of the government, despite public protests at such a flagrant abuse of power. Of 137 new periodicals founded in Paris in 1868, 110 failed to survive the year. Survival in the face of official hostility was virtually impossible.

None the less, on his release from prison in 1869 Vallès founded a political daily paper, *Le Peuple*. It lasted from 4 to 18 February, killed partly by a government-backed paper of the same name which started publication on 2 February. Vallès sold more than 10,000 copies. His *Le Peuple* was replaced by *Le Réfractaire* on 10 May. That, too, was killed. That year Vallès stood in vain for parliament as a revolutionary socialist. He was working on several novels, one of which, *Un gentilhomme*, was published in September and October 1869. His mind was strewn with unfinished projects, many of which had been publicly announced. He wanted to write the *Histoire de vingt ans (1848–1868)* in four or five volumes. Eventually, after changes of title and dates, these became the last two volumes of *Vingtras*. An autobiographical novel, *Pierre Moras*, published in *Paris*

from November 1869 to January 1870, was only rediscovered half a century later. Meanwhile Vallès was devoting more and more of his energies to political activity.

He followed up his work as a propagandist and journalist with a complex and active part in the insurrection of 1871. From 26 March he was a member of the Commune, and one of the last defenders of the barricades against the government of Thiers left alive. Thinking he would be caught and executed, he went into hiding, escaping in disguise by train to Belgium, from where he sailed for England. His extradition was demanded and refused. He had managed to save a little money, and 52,000 francs was left to him by an unknown admirer. In 1872 his mother died. He was condemned to death in his absence, travelled to Switzerland for three months, and returned to England, where he became friendly with Gounod and attempted in vain to restart his career as a journalist. In 1879 he moved to Brussels and in July 1880 he was amnestied.

On his return to Paris, Vallès rebuilt his journalistic career. Politically he was more restrained, although his social commitment was as intense as ever. He renewed his attack on fashions in literature and drama, including naturalism (q.v.). His admiration for Michelet and Clemenceau increased, and his interest turned to social history, in which Marx and Proudhon had shown the way. More gently, but steadily, he poured out satire on the fashions of his youth, as well as on contemporary French institutions. He also began to publish longer works: *Le Bachelier* in 1881, and the first version of *L'Insurgé* in the *Nouvelle Revue* of 1884. He engaged in a number of campaigns: anti-militarist, anti-colonialist, for legal and educational reform, for the liberty of the individual and the decentralization of government, and for policies promoting full employment. He wrote for two big dailies, *Le Cri du Peuple* and *Le Matin*. He had become diabetic and was intermittently ill from 1883. In August 1884 he fell seriously ill. In January 1885, as the result of a mishandled campaign, he was forced to resign as editor of *Le Matin*. It was the fatal blow and Vallès died on 14 February.

WORKS

Interest in Vallès has recently been increasing, largely no doubt on account of his career in social and political journalism, but also because the three-volume *Jacques Vingtras*, originally intended to be an impersonal work of history, before it became first a novel and then a virtually unfictionalized autobiography, has begun to emerge as a powerful work of imaginative literature, not only for the rich seam of social history which it mines.

Unhappily, what is still the best account of Vallès, by Gaston Gille, was published before the eight-volume *Oeuvres* and the more recent two-volume *Oeuvres* in the Pléiade collection, so that we have only a rough idea of the changes of form *Vingtras* underwent in Vallès's mind as, alone in London, he struggled with his material. Early on he toyed with a lightweight frivolity, to be called *Les Farceurs de Paris*, then added substance to it through serious research, considering by March 1876 that it should be "un bouquin intime, d'émotion naïve, de passion jeune" (an intimate book, of naive feeling and young passion), probably called *Jacques Vingtras* after a doctor in London. However, the book's name continued to change. It was not easy to arrange publication, but *Jacques Vingtras* was finally serialized pseudonymously in *Le Siècle* from June to August 1878.

was in part responsible for Verlaine's conversion back to Catholicism and resulted in the volume of largely religious verse, *Sagesse*, published in 1880.

For a year after his early release from jail in January 1875 Verlaine taught quietly in Lincolnshire, then in Bournemouth, and finally for two years at a Catholic seminary at Rethel in north-east France. While still hoping for a reconciliation with Mathilde, he became deeply attached to one of his pupils, Lucien Létinois. He had also taken to drinking heavily again. When his post failed to be renewed, Verlaine took Létinois to England. Both taught for three months before Verlaine bought a farm near Rethel and settled there with Létinois and the latter's parents in 1880. Financially, the farm was a disaster, and in 1882 it had to be sold at a considerable loss. Verlaine returned to Paris in search of a job, and in 1883 Létinois died of typhoid. Verlaine was well past the peak of his creative abilities, but his literary reputation was still growing, helped by the famous 1882 poem "Art poétique" and a series of essays, some of which were published in the 1884 *Les Poètes maudits*, which appeared from 1883 to 1886 in *Lutèce* and *La Vogue*.

In 1883 Verlaine bought their farm from Létinois's parents and went to live there with his ever-doting mother. He led a life of legendary drunkenness and treated his mother with brutality. In the spring of 1885 he was condemned to a month's imprisonment for assaulting her, and to a fine of 500 francs, which he paid out of the proceeds of the sale of the farm. His mother had made it over to him, but he received back only about half what had been paid. From 1885, the year he returned to Paris, he was virtually destitute. His mother came to live with him, but died in January 1886. What money she had left was claimed by the Mauté family for the upkeep of Verlaine's son. In 1894 15 friends, including Barrès and Montesquiou, offered Verlaine regular financial support, which was supplemented by various government grants.

Verlaine's health finally gave out. When he was not in hospital he spent his time in cafés, down-market hotels, and rented rooms with one of either two women, Eugénie Krantz or Philomène Boudin. Yet from 1885 to 1893 he still managed to contribute some 30 articles to the periodical *Les Hommes d'Aujourd'hui*. He also gave lecture tours in Holland, Belgium, and England, and defeated Mallarmé and Heredia in winning for himself the title "Prince of Poets." Some of the pieces contained in *Jadis et naguère* (mostly written well before publication of the volume in 1884) are regarded as Verlaine's last poems of any merit. Much of his later work was autobiographical, some of it high in moral tone. Two volumes, of which one is posthumous, are obscene. On Verlaine's connection with the Parnassing group and his association with Rimbaud, see the entries on "Le Parnasse" and on Rimbaud.

WORKS

Poèmes saturniens, a reflection of Parnassian (q. v.) aesthetics, concentrates on the beauty which is the product not of inspiration but of industry. Other sources of inspiration, such as Baudelaire and Hugo, are here detectable, along with intimations of a powerful originality. Melancholy and other emotions are conveyed indirectly, through blurred, non-Parnassian images, hesitant rhythms, fragile rhymes, and above all repeated or contrasted internal sound values. The clarity of line, colour, and

sensation associated with the so-called Parnassians is already dissolving in this early work.

Fêtes galantes is clearly inspired by the great 18th-century pastoral artists and successfully reproduces the hidden wistfulness of their Arcadia. It contains more experimental verse forms than the earlier collection, fewer Alexandrines, and no sonnets. A number of poems have eight or fewer syllables to the line, and some are in the difficult "vers impairs," with lines containing odd rather than even numbers of syllables.

La Bonne Chanson is full of enthusiastic compliments to Verlaine's young bride, and of poems basking in sunshine and hope. The verse is less experimental with many more Alexandrines and fewer instances of enjambement, where the sense runs over from one line to the next. *Romances sans paroles* of 1874, reflecting the opposing attractions of Rimbaud and Mathilde, is an uneven volume, moving from the quasi-tragic to the merely querulous. The blurred images reappear, along with unusual rhyme schemes and a reliance on alliteration, sound values, and assonance.

Sagesse contains poems which could have appeared in the preceding volume. Verlaine's religious conversion removes from this collection the note of anxiety that characterizes, and indeed breathes life into, so much of the earlier poetry, replacing it with a simplicity and directness of tone. Some of the political poems, however, are poor artefacts, and the absence of taut emotional content renders other poems merely laborious. The patterns of rhyme and rhythm are often traditional again, and the tone is light, indicating the poet's momentary stability. *Jadis et naguère*, on the other hand, uses a certain relaxed syntax to convey emotions of violence and rage. As a collection the volume is rather a ragbag, but it does contain some of Verlaine's last great poems. What is important in Verlaine's work is not his use of the awkward and uneven metres of the "vers impairs" but the blurred images whereby emotion is conveyed in carefully graduated intensity, and the musical qualities praised in the "Art poétique." His best verse is rhythmic, fluid, and unconstrained.

Verlaine has too often been seen as a theoretician rather than as an erratic but at his best a superb practitioner of his art. In particular, the "Art poétique," published in the 1884 collection *Jadis et naguère*, although written earlier, has been read as a quasi-Parnassian plea for the difficult and rigidly formal structure of "l'impair," the line with an uneven number of syllables. In fact the opening line is the more important one as the complete opening stanza, with its nine-syllable lines, makes clear,

> "De la musique avant toute chose,
>   Et pour cela préfère l'Impair
>   Plus vague et plus soluble dans l'air,
> Sans rien en lui qui pèse ou qui pose

> (Music above everything else, / and for that prefer uneven [numbers of syllables] / vaguer and more soluble in air, without anything that weighs down or sets down)."

This is a movement away from the sculptured form and solid content of Leconte de Lisle's poetry and the directness of approach in his verse to well-defined objects and rhythms. Verlaine is looking, although in a different way from Mallarmé, for an escape from the immediacy of actual experience into the world of intangible beauties beyond it, evoked by sounds and rhythms rather than by the semantic communication of meaning,

Les sanglots longs
Des violons
De l'automne
Blessent mon coeur
D'une langueur
Monotone.

(The long sobbings / of violins / of autumn / wound my heart / with a / monotonous languor)."

Verlaine brilliantly evokes moods. Unlike the pre-romantic Lamartine, he mentions concrete objects but, like him, he does not define the mood which he communicates. He takes from Baudelaire the equivalence of an external object with an internal, emotional event, so that he can talk about each while referring to the other, and the musicality by no means excludes properly structured organization of the poem, not infrequently by the employment of such rhetorical devices as repeated lines or unanswered questions. The sonnet "Crépuscule du soir mystique," clearly derived from Baudelaire, conveys the struggle between memory, loosely connected with dusk, and hope, associated with the bright colours of sunset, and the evocation of struggle intensifies throughout the single sentence of the poem's 14 lines.

Some of the poems are deliberately obscure, while lulling the reader by the simple music of vowels and consonants, and many of the technically most accomplished poems appear in *Romances et paroles*, written at the height of Verlaine's association with Rimbaud, from whose work Verlaine was later to profit, both by the essay on Rimbaud included in his *Les poètes maudits* of 1884, and by publishing *Les Illuminations* in *Vogue* in 1886. The poems of *Sagesse*, although uneven in quality, do include some, however, which show, if not a further technical advance, at least a greater poetic intensity even than the best in *Romances et paroles*, particularly when Verlaine writes of the conflict between erotic impulses, his inclination to alcoholic bohemianism, and respectable new-found Catholic piety.

PUBLICATIONS

Collections

Oeuvres complètes, edited by H. de Bouillane de Lacoste and Jacques Borel, 2 vols., 1959–60
Oeuvres poétiques complètes, Oeuvres en prose complètes, Bibliothèque de la Pleiade, 2 vols., 1962–72

Verse

Poèmes saturniens, 1866
Les Amies, 1868
Fêtes galantes, 1869; as *Gallant Parties*, 1912
La Bonne Chanson, 1870
Romances sans paroles, 1874; edited by D. Hillery, 1976; as *Romances Without Words*, 1921
Sagesse, 1880; revised edition, 1889; edited by C. Chadwick, 1973
Jadis et naguère, 1884
Amour, 1888
Parallèlement, 1889
Dédicaces, 1890; revised edition, 1894
Femmes, 1890

Bonheur, 1891
Chansons pour elle, 1891; as *Chansons pour elle* (in English), 1926
Choix de poésies, 1891
Liturgies intimes, 1892
Elégies, 1893
Odes en son honneur, 1893
Dans les limbes, 1894
Epigrammes, 1894
Poems, translated by Gertrude Hall, 1895
Invectives, 1896
Chair, 1896
Hombres, 1903 or 1904; edited by Huber Juin, 1977
Biblio-sonnets, 1913
Hashish and Incense, translated by François Pirou, 1925
Selected Poems, translated by C.F. MacIntyre, 1948
The Sky above the Roof: Fifty-Six Poems, translated by Brian Hill, 1957
Selected Poems, translated by Joanna Richardson, 1974
Femmes/Hombres, edited and translated by William Packard and John D. Mitchell, 1977; also translated as *Women, Men* by Alistair Elliot, 1979

Other

Les Poètes maudits, 1884; revised edition, 1888
Mémoires d'un veuf, 1886
Louise Leclercq (short stories and play, *Madame Aubin*), 1886
Mes hôpitaux, 1891
Mes prisons, 1893
Confessions, 1895; as *Confessions of a Poet*, 1950
Oeuvres posthumes, 1903
Correspondance, edited by A. van Bever, 3 vols., 1922–29
Oeuvres oubliées, 2 vols., 1926–29
Lettres inédites à Cazals, edited by Georges Zayed, 1957
Lettres inédites à Charles Morice, edited by Georges Zayed, 1964
Lettres inédites à divers correspondants, edited by Georges Zayed, 1976
Editor, *Illuminations*, by Rimbaud, 1886
Editor, *Poésies complètes*, by Rimbaud, 1895

Biographical and critical study

Adam A., *The Art of Paul Verlaine*, 1963
Chadwich, C., *Verlaine*, 1973
Stephan, Phillip, *Verlaine and the Decadence, 1882–1890*, 1974

————

VERNE, Jules (-Gabriel), 1828–1905.

Novelist

LIFE

Verne was the second son of a lawyer from Nantes. His father, Pierre, was called to the Bar in 1825. He was 27 when he met the 26-year-old Sophie Allotte de la Fuye a year later. They were serious cultural statement made in an unusually oblique way. The 1946 novel *J'irai cracher sur vos tombes* ("I'll go and spit on your graves") was signed by Vernon Sullivan and published in French with a preface by Vian, who purported to have translated it from the manuscript of a black American author unable to find a publisher in the US. It was immediately, and correctly, suspected that he was himself the real author, amusing himself with the brilliant, if scandalous, pastiche of a tough American novel, a serious statement, provided it was recognized as pastiche, launched in the form of a not impenetrable hoax. Vian wrote three other novels over the name of Sullivan, and five over his own name.

He was born on 10 March 1920 at Ville-d'Avray. His father came from the South of France and his mother was a Parisian. Vian was the second of four children. His brothers Lélio and Alain were, respectively, 16 months older and a year younger, and his sister, Ninon, was five years younger than Vian. His father had had a defective heart from the age of 16 and Vian himself developed one at the age of 12 as the result of a fever. The family spent the summers in a small house in the countryside near Cherbourg. They were well off until, as a result of the depression, investments fell in value and they were forced to move to a smaller house. Vian appears to have had a happy childhood and to have done well at the Versailles lycée from 1933 to 1936, although he was often absent from the Lycée Condorcet in the year 1936–37. His mother prided herself on having instilled in him a contempt for money and a taste for freedom, which, she admitted, he took rather far at times. He passed his baccalauréat and at 19, when the war was just breaking out, began to study engineering at the Ecole Centrale des Arts et Manufactures. The school was moved to Angoulême for the year 1939–40 and the family evacuated to Cap Breton. Here Vian got to know Michelle Léglise, whom he married in July 1941. Their first child, Patrick, was born in 1942. Vian obtained his diploma that year and joined the professional association, which made his work an "essential public service," a conception of his activities from which he later derived some amusement, although he continued them until 1947.

It was in 1938 that he began learning the trumpet. Vian later spoke of three jazz concerts—by Duke Ellington, Dizzy Gillespie, and Ella Fitzgerald—as the "three great moments of my life." Ellington and Armstrong were his life-long heroes. He never went to the US. What he learnt about racial prejudice there he learnt from US musicians in Paris. In 1941 he met the clarinettist Claude Abadie and played in his band. The 1946 novel, and the circumstances of its publication, show how diffident Vian was about publicly exposing his clearly vulnerable personality. When, that same year, he had to jot down brief biographical details for Gallimard's publication of *L'Ecume des jours*, he made a joke of it. In 1943 he had started to write a novel "simply to amuse my mates." He later noted, with an equal lack of solemnity, that the novel, *Vercoquin et le plancton*, obtained Queneau's approval "with reservations," and was taken by Gallimard. Accepted in 1945, it was not in fact published until 1946. In the meanwhile, Vian had written the first stories to appear as *Les Fourmis* in 1949. The first, "Les fourmis," was published in *Les Temps Modernes* (q.v.) in June 1946. It was Vian's first publication, and the same number of the review printed the first of his "Chroniques du menteur," which were to appear over the course of the next five years.

In October 1946 *Les Temps Modernes* published fragments of *L'Ecume des jours*. Earlier that year Vian had written the play *L'Equarrissage pour tous*, and between September and November he wrote *L'Automne à Pékin*. He had also begun to write for *Jazz-Hot* and *Combat*. Jean d'Haluin of the Editions Scorpion was apparently jealous of Gallimard's success with the French version of J.H. Chase's *No Orchids for Miss Blandish* and was looking for an American thriller to have translated. Vian is said to have responded: "Why look for an American? Give me a fortnight." The result was *J'irai cracher sur vos tombes*. Vian's first wife, who had suggested the title, thought the book must have come out in August 1946. The press rumbled the hoax immediately, and mostly saw through the pastiche too. "It must be said that it treats no serious problem, not even by allusion," wrote Robert Kanters in *Le Spectateur*. Vian later remarked that it was a good piece of engineering, but a very bad novel, not worth wasting time over. He was right. What is serious about it is the gesture which composition and publication make about the life in Paris in 1946 of an engineer who would rather have been a jazz trumpeter. There was an attempt, led by a Daniel Parker, to have it banned for pornography. Dan Parker is the name given to the black sex maniac and assassin hero of Vernon Sullivan's second novel, *Les Morts ont tous la même peau*.

In the end *J'irai cracher* did get Vian into trouble. It was reprinted after the amnesty which allowed it to escape the first time, sold 100,000 copies, and cost 100,000 francs in fines, against the likely 2,000,000 francs in profit. Vian says he did not use a lawyer because lawyers did not have the imagination to lie convincingly enough, and was indignant to have sold about twice as many copies as an average winner of the Prix Goncourt, while the critics let more serious writing, including, he no doubt meant, his own, languish for lack of public attention. The novel was made into a play, which, in spite of the assistance of a ban on posters in the Métro, a distinction also accorded to Sartre's *La Putain Respectueuse*, failed after less than three months. The play has not been published. Vian, who knew Sartre well, pokes gentle fun at the cult surrounding a certain Jean-Sol Partre in *L'Ecume des jours*. He kept teasing the press for not understanding when he was joking, and not understanding that those who wrote, as he did, for *Les Temps Modernes* had the freedom not to be existentialists (q.v.), as he wrote in the "Postface" to *Les Morts*.

In 1947 Vian gave up being an engineer, having invented a rubber wheel in 1943. He wanted to write, to play jazz, and to listen to it. He spent much of his time in two bars cultivated successively by those who knew where to go and would not be seen near Le Flore with its visitors in search of Sartrean associations. *Barnum's Digest* of 1948 is a joke, published by "the Two Liars," but Vian also started translating in earnest—two Raymond Chandlers and Dorothy Baker's *Young Man with a Horn*. He continued to write for *Combat* and worked very hard without pay for *Jazz-Hot*. His daughter, Carolle, was born in 1948. He translated Cheyney and enjoyed writing about jazz, particularly since his heart was preventing him from playing the trumpet as much as he would have liked. His jazz writing was diligent, very well researched, well informed, and much appreciated by his readers. One evening in the summer of 1949 Vian met Ursula Kübler at one of Gaston Gallimard's cocktail parties.

L'Equarrissage was finally played in 1950. Vian was touchy about the reviews and published sometimes vengeful replies to them. That year his novel *L'Herbe rouge* failed, selling only 1,000 copies. Vian also published 200 copies of a book of verse entitled *Cantilènes en gelée*. He appears to have lost the manuscript and proofs of another book set in type by the publishers of the failed novel. He translated, became music director of a record company, and wrote hundreds of songs, but began to find it difficult to make a living. In September 1952 Michelle and he divorced, and on 8 February 1954 he married Ursula. Michelle was for a while very close to Sartre, with whom she had a protracted liaison. In 1953 Vian published his last novel, *L'Arrache-coeur*, which was eventually remaindered. *L'Automne à Pékin* was reissued in 1956, and at the time of his death Vian had three plays, one of which existed in two versions, that had not been staged. The translations were undertaken for a living, and on demand. At least one, the memoirs of the American general Omar N. Bradley, was at first suspected of being another fake. Vian also collaborated on two operas, one of which, *Fiesta* was set to music by Milhaud.

From 1956 he was increasingly unwell. There was talk of an operation, but success seemed unlikely, and Vian was not able to take life calmly enough. He had decided to give up the record company he had just moved to, and to make his living by song writing. On 23 June 1959 he went to see the film of *J'irai cracher* to decide whether or not to let his name appear among the credits. He had forgotten to take his pills and died in the cinema.

WORKS

Vian quite quickly became a cult figure and his reputation has continued to grow, no doubt boosted by an excellent short monograph, the product of a New York Ph.D. thesis by David Noakes.

His first novel, *Vercoquin et le plancton*, is universally regarded as a witty but adolescent book. The outlook on life which it presents is overwhelmingly that of the male adolescent. Vian starts on his trail of demonstrations that most human activities are absurd, especially the serious ones. The principal under-engineer Léon-Charles Miqueut and his colleagues at the National Consortium of Unification are employed in the regulation of all forms of human activity, entered into mouse-grey folders. The book is largely about what the French call "surprise parties," and it looks as if Gallimard wanted the bureaucratic part strengthened to give the novel balance. The characters are real. Both types of environment, that of the office routine and that of the gay young things, are sent up. Vian's chief source of inspiration must have been Jarry.

Vian regarded the book as a private joke and said that the surprise parties actually happened, that all the characters were real, although only one retained his real name, Major. The other names were said to have been taken from the equivalent of *The Civil Service Handbook*, *L'Annuaire des fonctionnaires*, but they are far too hilarious to have come from any such work, even if it existed. The book was written for the people who would recognize the characters. The ludicrous, the impossible, and the absurd are recounted as perfectly normal, and much fun is made of idiotic lists, as of things to eat—pyramids of cakes, cylinders of gramophones, cubes of ice, triangles of freemasons, magic squares, high political spheres, cones… Vian portrays a world of sexual athletics in which women are treated good-humouredly, but with adolescent male contempt. The Major, whose party it is, fails to win the hand of Zizanie. Women are expected to be vertical only in order to dance. If they have minds of their own, then

it is no use pursuing them: they will already be married.

L'Ecume des jours, parts of which were published in *Les Temps Modernes*, is Vian's most personal book, a caricature of the high priest Sartre. Michelle Vian, with whom Sartre tended to sympathize over the divorce, said that Sartre was delighted with Vian's Jean-Sol, Partre. Simone de Beauvoir enjoyed her role as Alise, the publication of whose encyclopedia the great man agrees to defer for at least 10 years. When Alise murders Jean-Sol, Beauvoir agreed that "it would happen like that." Language is again ripped out of its normal context. A bell unhooks itself and shoes are watered with wax to allow the leather to grow again. The environment is hostile. Corners of rooms become rounded. Doors become narrower. As Chloé dies, the ceiling and the floor come together, just giving the grey mouse time to escape. A water lily implants itself in Chloé's chest and drives out all life. Mice dance to the sound of sun rays on kitchen taps.

The suspension of the whole natural order is a not unusual poetic device, and it has been exploited in all sorts of different ways, linked or not linked to systematic syntactical dislocation by the surrealists (q.v.), by Joyce, Beckett, Jarry, and others. Walls can clearly close in to signify the increasingly anxious mental state of the occupant of a room, and the totally absurd in drama or fiction is now no longer extraordinary. Vian is using such devices in a quite personal way, however, not striving for the effects which a Ionesco or a Kafka might have sought. For Vian nature, its laws in suspense, acts in harmony with human feeling, growing limp, flaccid, angry, or quiet. The violence is itself almost gentle in its operation. Refusing to say why Chloé had to die, Jesus adjusts the crown of thorns on his head and looks for a more comfortable position on his nails. Saying with a yawn that Chloé's death has nothing to do with religion, he goes to sleep. The street changes when Colin and Chloé have gone and night forms round them in concentric layers. The theme of the novel is the elusiveness of happiness. What holds it together is not its plot, but its poetry.

L'Automne à Pékin is difficult to follow since the focus is dispersed, involving four different groups from the very beginning. Three "movements," each with chapters, are set between "passages," which allow the narrator to comment on the action and the characters. One of them, Amadis Dudu, is "untrustworthy, haughty, insolent, and pretentious. Homosexual, too." He had better be got rid of. Everyone is heading for Exopotamie, but they only start getting the railway built at the end. The plot is entirely open-ended, largely on account of the qualities of the sun in Exopotamie, and the nature of the soil. Besides, there is already an archaeologist there with his assistants, a hermit, a black woman, and the Abbé Petitjean, inspector of hermits. It is impossible to tell what will happen to them all because anything could. The book is studded with portentous quotations. "People who have not studied the question might be led into error…," Vian says, giving a precise page reference to a book, date, author, and publisher. At whatever level of universality or, within the novel, particularity, that sentence can refer to almost anything, or absolutely nothing. Is Vian simply asking not, for goodness's sake, to be taken seriously? Probably, but he would not like the reader altogether to decline the invitation, and we know he did not like bad reviews.

He is being serious too—about the nature of love and the requirements imposed by its structures on its realization. Why does Angel love Rochelle, and why does he kill her? Why must he love the vulgar woman who comes to terms too quickly with the death of his male friend, Anne? The book is about why people fall in love with the people they do, and not with the ones they "ought" to. *L'Automne* has a good sprinkling of private allusions, including some malicious ones aimed at Gallimard, with which house Vian had by now broken. It has been suggested that he had given up serious writing for a wide public, paid off with the Vernon Sullivan novels, and was becoming almost hermetic in his more intimate work.

L'Herbe rouge comes back to two couples: Wolf and Lil, Saphir Lazuli and Folavril. The women are passive, pretend to be ignorant, and survive. The men do not. As soon as sentimental complications arise in his sexual relationships, Lazuli becomes impotent. He kills himself, and Vian, having told us nothing about his infancy, virtually warns us to stay away from Freud:

—Je crois qu'il a honte de moi, dit Folavril.
—Non, dit Lil, il doit avoir honte d'être amoureux.
—Je n'ai pourtant jamais dit de mal de sa mère, protesta
 Folavril.

("I think he must be ashamed of me," said Folavril. "No," said Lil, "he must be ashamed of being in love." "But I've never said anything bad about his mother," protested Folavril.)

The trouble with Wolf is that there is nothing he wants. He has made a time machine for someone and uses it to try to wipe his memory blank since, if you do not want anything any more, there is no point in remembering what makes you what you are. Knowing about his past is a burden for Wolf. Getting rid of the knowledge is progress towards death. Wolf is not Vian, but some of his past sounds suspiciously like Vian's. Is *L'Herbe rouge* Vian's time machine? The account of an overprotected childhood, religious disillusions, adolescent rebellion? The trouble here is that intimate confidence and novel are not really integrated.

In *L'Arrache-coeur* Jacquemort is a psychiatrist, whose job it is to "psychiatrize." This requires total identification with the passions his ideal patient does not even know he has. Jacquemort tries "psychiatrizing" a cat and starts behaving in ways which make him, but not the villagers he is imitating, feel ashamed. The novel is also about Clémentine's overprotective mothering of Joël, Noël, and Citroën, and about the guilt felt by a father too concerned with his own freedom. The guilt is not strong, however: Angel is not blamed for leaving. The book's anti-clericalism is mild, and the work as a whole remains enigmatic. Vian used a number of pseudonyms between 1948 and 1954. Anyone who wants to force an understanding of his work must begin by remembering that Vian instinctively knew when to use his own name.

PUBLICATIONS

Fiction

Vercoquin et le plancton, 1946
J'irai cracher sur vos tombes (as Vernon Sullivan), 1946
L'Ecume des jours, 1947

L'Automne à Pékin, 1947
Les Morts ont tous la même peau (as Vernon Sullivan), 1947
Elles se rendent pas compte (as Vernon Sullivan), 1948
Et on tuera tous les affreux (as Vernon Sullivan), 1948
Les Fourmis (short stories), 1949
L'Herbe rouge, 1950
L'Arrache-coeur, 1953

Other

Barnum's Digest, 1948
Cantilènes en gelée (poetry), 1950
L'Equarrissage pour tous (produced 1950), with *Le Dernier des métiers*, 1950
Fiesta (opera), in collaboration, with music by Milhaud, 1958
En avant la Zizique ... et par ici les gros sous, 1958
Les Bâtisseurs d'Empire, 1959
Le Goûter des généraux, 1962
Je voudrais pas crever, 1962

Bibliography

Caradec, François, *Dossiers du Collège 'Pataphysique*, nos. 12 and 18–19 (23 June 1960 and 29 March 1962)

Critical and biographical study

Noakes, David, *Boris Vian* (in French), 1964

VIGNY, Alfred (-Victor) (Comte) de, 1797–1863.

Poet, novelist, and dramatist.

LIFE

It was the source both of Vigny's poetic stature and of his personal unhappiness that he was born of a lineage which on both sides was ancient and had been ennobled. His family was excessively conscious of caste, and he was its surviving heir. Although rightly considered a leading romantic (q.v.) poet, Vigny had little enough in common with Victor Hugo, from whom he diverged politically, with Lamartine, from whose poetic sensibility his own was quite different, and with Musset, of whose lyrical outpourings he was totally incapable.

His father, the Chevalier Léon de Vigny (1737–1816), one of a family of nine boys and three girls, had served in the Seven Years' War as an infantry captain and been injured in 1758. Vigny's mother, Jeanne-Marie de Baraudin, was the daughter of a senior naval officer and 20 years younger than his father. Both families had suffered much in the Revolution, and Vigny's parents married late. Their first three sons did not survive infancy. When Vigny was born on the 8 Germinal of the year V (27 March 1797), his father was 60 and his mother 40. Partly no doubt on account of his parents' ages, and the disparity between them, and partly because he knew himself to be the repository of so many family hopes, Vigny spent an unhappy childhood. Both sides of the family were ultra-royalist in commitment and both convinced him of his superiority by right of birth and looked to him to continue the line.

As an infant he was sent out to nurse, and his mother then took charge of his education herself until he was 10. In matters of religion, she adopted a strict moral view, although tolerating a broader spectrum of dogmatic belief. In view of his elevated status Vigny was not allowed to play with boys of his own age, however, and was encouraged to look on them with a sense of superiority. He was instilled therefore with a notion of the innate privilege conferred by his aristocratic breeding, and not helped by being brought up to cultivate a certain effeminate fastidiousness. When he finally went to school, to the Lycée Bonaparte (now Condorcet), he was a good-looking, over-sensitive child, cleverer than most of the rest of his class, and was not surprisingly bullied. His feelings of superiority were only reinforced by his consequent sense of isolation, and he had to finish his schooling at home. His tutor made him translate the *Iliad* into English, and he took lessons in painting and music. He toyed with the idea of going to the school for officers, the Ecole Polytechnique.

In 1814, when he was 17, he was commissioned into the upper-class household cavalry, where his colleagues, although his social equals, did not share his refined and distinctly poetic tastes. He broke a leg in 1815, left Paris in the wake of Louis XVIII's flight to Belgium, and spent Napoleon's 100-day campaign at Amiens. The household troops were reorganized, and Vigny was eventually relegated to a less socially desirable line regiment, making slow progress to the rank of captain in 1823. His dreams of glory on active service were never realized, and he was to leave the army disappointed, but apparently no longer in need of a salary, in 1827.

Vigny's father died in 1816, and his mother moved house. In or soon after that year Vigny wrote his first verse, and probably two tragedies, which he would have destroyed with the rest of his juvenilia in 1832. Translations of Byron began to appear in France in 1819, and in 1820 Vigny, who could of course read him in English, published the first part of an article on Byron and a poem in the *Conservateur Littéraire*, founded a year previously by the Hugo brothers. This activity had an immediately adverse effect on his military prospects. From 1821 Vigny had his own Paris flat and increased his literary output, publishing in 1822 the 10 poems of *Poèmes*, which contains some poems written no later than 1819. From 1822 frequent leaves of absence were accorded to him for family or health reasons, sometimes on half-salary or without salary.

In October 1822 Vigny published the poem "Le trappiste", with two further editions in December 1822 and March 1823, and in 1822 he also wrote "Moïse," which was his own favourite among his poems and would be placed at the head of his collection when it grew into the 1826 edition entitled *Poèmes antiques et modernes*. Vigny remained very close to Victor Hugo and was one of the witnesses at his marriage in October 1822. At this period, too, he formed a close relationship with Delphine Gay, who was certainly in love with him and whose mother wanted them to marry. She was an innocent, brilliant, and beautiful girl with whom many of the romantic poets are said to have been in love. Mme de Vigny opposed the marriage, partly for social reasons, but mostly because of Delphine's relative poverty, and the couple had to give up the relationship.

"La neige" was published in the January *Tablettes Romantiques* of 1823, during which year Vigny, disappointed at not seeing active service in Spain, wrote most of his poem "Eloa," the second of the *Poèmes antiques*, taking up and dropping many other projects, but publishing "Dolorida" in October in Hugo's new review, *La Muse Française* (1823–24), for which he then wrote regularly. In 1824 he might have married Liszt's friend Marie de Flavigny, later the Comtesse d'Agoult, but this time it was her social status which was too high. Vigny also had a close relationship with the literary hostess Virginie Ancelot and attended the meetings of Nodier's romantic "cénacle." In June 1824 he sketched the plan for *Cinq-Mars* and began to keep a note of his literary plans and projets, many of which had already been shelved. Garrisoned at Pau that autumn, he met Lydia-Alice Bunbury, born in 1796 into a rich colonial family from St Vincent. Her mother had died when she was five, and in 1822, at the age of 61, her father married again. He was touring Europe with his daughter and very young wife when Lydia met Vigny at a ball and fell in love with him. In Vigny's mother's eyes, her apparent wealth compensated for her lack of French, her religion, and her nationality, and the couple were married in 1825, the Protestant ceremony, not attended by Vigny's mother, being held at Pau on 8 February, and the Catholic ceremony in Paris at the Madeleine on 15 March. Vigny's marriage was to bring him 6,500 francs a year, which was paid regularly until his father-in-law's death in November 1838.

The marriage was an unhappy one. After a series of miscarriages Lydia developed an internal complaint which made her a life-long invalid, unable to bear children. She forgot her English without ever learning French and was unable to give Vigny any intellectual companionship. She lost her beauty, became obese and half blind, and had difficulty in moving. Vigny, however, was devoted to caring for her mental and physical welfare. Her inheritance involved a series of lawsuits with her step-brothers, as her father's new wife bore him further children, but for the next 30 years Vigny was her nurse, companion, and secretary, sometimes not daring to leave her side for a whole day at a time. *Poèmes antiques et modernes* appeared in 1826. In the same year the novel *Cinq-Mars* appeared to wide critical acclaim. Through his wife's uncle, Vigny met his model, Walter Scott, in Paris. The novel's fourth edition was preceded by *Réflexions sur la vérité dans l'art*. Vigny took Lydia to Dieppe in 1827, had a brief affair with a 16-year-old bride, Tryphina Holmes, and at the end of the year translated *Romeo and Juliet* for the Théâtre-Français, although it was not staged. He followed it with *Othello*, played on 24 October 1829 as *Le More de Venise*, and with *The Merchant of Venice*, for which difficulties were made however and which, being in verse, could not legally be played outside the Théâtre-Français and the Odéon. *Le More de Venise* was published in January 1830 with a prefatory "Lettre à Lord*** sur la soirée du 24 octobre et sur un système dramatique." In the meanwhile Vigny's relations with Hugo had cooled, partly on account of Hugo's liberalism, and partly because Vigny's *Le More de Venise* had beaten Hugo's *Hernani* to its grand romantic premiere.

In 1830 Vigny was still faithful to the Bourbons, although convinced that their cause was lost. During the revolution of 1830 he nevertheless engaged as a sublieutenant in the Garde Nationale at its restoration, but fulfilled much more important commands, and also finished his play *La Maréchale d'Ancre*, dedicated to the actress Marie Dorval, to whom he presented passionate verses on

31 December. The following year, the 258-line "Paris" was published separately and a "Lettre parisienne," signed with a simple "Y," was published in *L'Avenir*. A long association with the *Revue des Deux Mondes (RDM*, q.v.), founded only in July 1929, began with the publication of what was intended to be the first four chapters of *L'Almeh*, "Scènes du désert," begun in 1828, but which never got any further. After *L'Avenir* turned it down, the *RDM* published a "Lettre sur le théâtre à propos d'"*Antony*" being the play by Dumas, signed with the simple "Y." Marie Dorval had played the lead at the Porte-Saint-Martin, and Vigny had read *La Maréchale d'Ancre* at least twice to groups in her salon. Rehearsals were continuously postponed, however, and Marie Dorval played the lead in Hugo's *Marion Delorme* instead. The theatre took Hugo's play on 14 May and the premiere was on 11 August. Vigny took his play to the Odéon, presumably after 14 May, where had its premiere on 25 June.

Marie Dorval had been reserved with Vigny, but their seven-year liaison began in the summer of 1831, and "Y" signed a review of a book by her husband in the September *RDM*. The *RDM*, which appeared fortnightly only from October 1831, published the first two of the three stories in Vigny's *Stello* on 15 October and 1 December 1831, followed by the 118-line poem "Les amants de Montmorency" on 1 January and the third episode of *Stello* on 1 April 1832. The volume appeared as a book later in the year. Both Vigny and Lydia caught cholera in the 1832 epidemic, which killed 20,000 Parisians, and during it Vigny destroyed those youthful works he did not wish to survive. His work began to contain ominous references to suicide. On 1 March 1833 the *RDM* published the first episode of *Servitude et grandeur militaires*. His mother had a stroke in the same month and henceforward became part of his household. Vigny himself was made a Chevalier of the Légion d'Honneur for his services to the Garde Nationale. *Quitte pour la peur*, with Marie Dorval in the lead, was played at a benefit for her on 30 May and printed on 1 June by the *RDM*, which published the other episodes of *Servitude* during 1834 and 1835.

In May 1834 invited by Berlioz, Vigny met Liszt and Chopin. He also finished *Chatterton*, taken from the second story in *Stello*, to create a part for Marie Dorval, who had now moved to the Comédie-Française, where she had so far had parts only in poor plays or repeats. The play was turned down, but then accepted on account of royal intervention, although Vigny still had to struggle to get the lead for Marie Dorval. The premiere on 12 February 1835 had a mixed reception from the critics, although the audiences liked it. The play was published in April. From 28 February Hugo had a rival play, *Angelo*, sharing the stage at the Théâtre-Français. In the *RDM* for 1 September Vigny had to defend himself against the accusation that his play advocated suicide. The last episode from *Servitude* was published in the *RDM* on 1 October, when the book came out to mixed reviews. *Chatterton* was revived in January 1836.

By that year the relationship between Vigny and Marie Dorval was waning. Vigny and Lydia spent a holiday in England, where Bunbury's still young wife was expecting her seventh child. It looks likely that Vigny had a brief affair in Paris with a singer, Pauline Duchambge, who was about 60 and for the moment without a lover. In 1837 he toyed with a project for a new novel and with a first episode, "Daphné," and decided to publish his complete works in seven volumes (1837–39). The death of his mother in December 1837 brought Vigny to a clear but short-lived religious crisis. In the following year he broke

definitively with Marie Dorval, who had taken a new lover, while Vigny himself started a liaison with Julia Dupré, a 20-year-old American. He never wrote again for the stage. On his father-in-law's death he took Lydia to London, where his stepmother was expecting her eighth child and where they stayed with Lydia's grandmother. Her father had disinherited her with the other child of his first marriage, and endless lawsuits now followed. From 1838 Vigny worked sporadically on the philosophical poems to be published posthumously as *Les Destinées*.

His plays were revived, and Vigny took Julia to Le Havre, from where she left for home and, a year later, marriage. He got involved in fighting for a law, eventually passed in 1845, governing authors' rights to their work as well as freedom to publish or stage the works of deceased authors. The *RDM* published the philosophical poems as and when Vigny released them from 1843, and he appears to have had an affair with Alexandra Kossakowska, the original of Wanda in the poem of that name, who was married to a Polish count. Vigny was elected to the Académie Française at his sixth attempt in 1845, and turned down a peerage offered him in exchange for a royalist acceptance speech. His acceptance speech to the academy, on the poet as philosopher, caused some friction with the president, by whom Vigny refused to be presented to the king, as custom demanded.

By 1848 he was on the side of moderate republicanism, but failed twice in local elections. For three months in 1849 he was director of the academy. In the years that followed he took up and dropped various projects, including the *Mémoires de famille* and *Mémoires politiques*. He met and had an affair, which seems to have lasted three years, with Flaubert's ex-mistress Louise Colet in 1854, considered another project for his complete works (1856–59), was made an Officier of the Légion d'Honneur, entered into a lengthy correspondence with the 20-year-old Elisa le Breton, which her father asked him to stop, and seems to have acted as a political informer about inhabitants of the Bordeaux region. He became interested in Buddhism, and one other young girl, Augusta Froustey, a 20-year-old teacher, played a serious role in his life. In 1861 he began to suffer from what was almost certainly the cancer of the stomach from which he was to die. Lydia died quite suddenly in December 1862. Vigny spent his remaining months tidying his affairs and died on 17 September 1863. It is more than possible that the child born in October 1863 "of unknown father and mother," but later recognized as her own by Augusta, was also Vigny's. Outside his two main heirs and their parents, his only bequest was 20,000 francs to Augusta.

From 1835 Vigny had led an increasingly retired and uneventful life, seeing only intimate friends and often living as a country recluse for months or even years on end. He felt that his literary career had not brought him the recognition he merited. His military career had been a failure. Politically, all he represented for most of his life was out of date, and his marriage had been unhappy and had not restored his fortune. He published very little, and during the last years of his life only 11 poems, but his *Journal* shows that his powers of perception and sympathy remained intact. Towards the end of his life his pessimistic stoicism seemed to moderate.

WORKS

Vigny wrote slowly and with difficulty. He left less than three

endeavours to regain the family's pre-revolutionary riches. His mother's family also claimed medieval lineage. She was brought up by a well-off maiden aunt who insisted that her niece and her husband, Villiers's mother and father, should come to live with her. "Mathias," as he was known, had an unstable background, moving frequently, attending and being expelled from half a dozen schools, and finishing his haphazard education with a number of prizes but no formal qualification. As an adult his Paris address changed at least 30 times, on average once a year.

Villiers took early in life to music and writing. His artistic fantasies were further nurtured at 17, when the girl with whom he was in love died. His family, presumably discerning no other talent, encouraged him to write, and Villiers lived in Paris for some months in 1855, returning to live in various houses in Brittany when his father was imprisoned for debt. He returned to Paris in 1857, his head full of the metaphysical melodramas he was planning. In 1858 *Deux essais de poésie* appeared, to be followed in 1859 by a magnificent edition of the unsuccessful *Premières poésies*, both works printed at Villiers's own expense. He did begin to meet a number of literary figures, however, attending the literary and philosophical salon of Pontavice de Heussey, who tried to foster in him more practical political and social attitudes. Baudelaire, of whom Villiers was at first in awe, introduced him to the occult, and a close friendship developed between the two men.

Villiers lived either with his mother's aunt or, when he could afford it, on his own. He formed friendships with Catulle Mendès and Jean Marras, a patron who helped him financially. In 1862 he published, at his own expense, the first part of an extravagantly romantic historical novel. *Prolégomènes* appeared in an edition of 100 copies, of which only 23 were sold over the next 25 years. The heroine of the novel, endowed with occult powers, loses her invulnerability by falling in love; but no other part of *Wilhelm de Strally*, later retitled *Isis*, ever appeared. After a suitable number of amorous, political, and religious adventures Villiers became a familiar figure in Parisian literary circles. In 1863 he met Mallarmé, who was deeply influenced by him and with whom he formed a close friendship. He frequented the salon of Leconte de Lisle, was thought a genius by Banville, was welcomed by Gautier, and was on calling terms with Flaubert and Dumas *fils*. He was, incredibly, at the centre of the self-selected group which made up advanced Parisian literary society.

In 1865 Villiers had a play, *Elën*, privately printed. Though never offered for sale it was praised extravagantly by his friends. In 1866 20 copies of *Morgane*, a drama of conspiracy, love, jealousy, betrayal, murder, disguise, poison, and death, were printed "for the use of its actors." In fact, totally rewritten as *Le Prétendant*, the play narrowly missed being staged in 1875. Meanwhile Villiers moved between Paris and Brittany, where he assisted his bankrupt father's schemes to achieve wealth. He contributed three poems to *Le Parnasse Contemporain* and was associated with Mendès, Leconte de Lisle, Gautier, Heredia, Banville, Sully Prudhomme, and Dierx, a group with whose aesthetic ideals Mallarmé, Verlaine, and Villiers were to break in what amounted to another literary revolution. With the help of a backer Villiers produced 25 weekly issues (October 1867–March 1868) of a new literary review, the *Revue des Lettres et des Arts*, notable for its well-known contributors and its championship of Wagner. He published a number of short stories and now skirted the edges of high society, even trying his hand at a much-despised society drama of the Second Empire, a collection of fragments published in 1956 as *La Tentation*. In 1869 Villiers, Catulle Mendès, and Judith Gautier, who was to have a passionate love affair with Wagner, succeeded in getting themselves invited to Triebschen to visit the composer, of whose operas only *Tannhäuser* and *Rienzi* had been performed in Paris (See Le Parnasse). They returned, less successfully, the following year with Camille Saint-Saëns and Henri Duparc just as the Franco-Prussian War was about to break out, but Villiers attended half a dozen of the operas in all, met Nietzsche, and got on to cordial terms with the Wagners. Villiers's unbounded admiration for Wagner, his Parnassian dislike of commercialism, and his preference for esoteric language compromised the success of his one-act *La Révolte* when it was performed in 1870. Its open contempt for the bourgeois values depicted by Augier and Dumas *fils* was applauded only by his literary friends and the piece was taken off after five performances. Villiers wrote a preface thanking his defenders, Wagner, Banville, Gautier, Leconte de Lisle, Liszt, Mendès, and even Dumas *fils* and Anatole France. Of the critics hostile to the work, only Barbey d'Aurevilly was to become an important literary figure. For the remainder of his life, Villiers cherished the dramatic project which was to become *Axël*.

The first part of *Axël* was published in 1872 in *La Renaissance Littéraire et Artistique*. It was intended to preface a drama of renunciation in which the protagonists seek death since the gratification of desire can never equal the aspiration towards an impossible ideal. The text as we have it, much expanded and rewritten although still incomplete, carries the same message: "Vivre? Les serviteurs feront cela pour nous (Live? The servants can do that for us)."

With the death of his mother's aunt in 1871 her annuities ceased, and for the rest of his life Villiers lived in generally degrading poverty, apparently sleeping wherever he could, using his "addresses" merely to pick up mail, and accepting "loans" from friends. He did publish more short pieces of prose fiction and he won an important prize in a competition for a play to celebrate the centenary of the declaration of independence in 1876. Dozens of efforts to stage *Le Nouveau-Monde* came to nothing however, until 1883, when it was a relative failure. Villiers's further efforts to publish prose fiction also foundered. At one time he seems to have scraped a living by giving boxing lessons: taking macabre jobs to demonstrate to society to what extremities a writer of genius could be reduced. He had at least one child, stood as a royalist candidate for the municipal council, lost most of his former literary associates, though his friendship with Mallarmé deepened, and in 1882 managed finally to publish his *Contes cruels* and a second instalment of *Axël*.

The 28 *Contes cruels*, including one cycle of love poems, had originally been published over the preceding 15 years and the volume, like *Le Nouveau-Monde* when it was staged, had a benevolent reception, although the play degenerated into a series of quarrels between author, cast, backers, and management and lasted only 17 performances. Villiers, however, was well known by now and began contributing regularly to the right-wing *Le Figaro*. Huysmans became a critical admirer, and Léon Bloy a friend. The short stories had shown a development in Villiers's literary imagination, which now centred on the macabre, above all the guillotine, and the occult, although they were still capable of dropping realism and irony in order to depict idealized love or skilfully evoke an exotic atmosphere. Villiers's prose fiction became increasingly sought after and *L'Eve future*, rewritten to lessen its glorification of a revolt against God, was serialized, with breaks for continual revision, in *La Vie Moderne* from 1885 to 1886.

Axël was revised in a way which made the suicide pact—a variation on the romantically commonplace consummation of physically ungratified love in death—morally more ambiguous and less anti-Christian. Villiers, whose admirers included Remy de Gourmont, Mallarmé, and Verlaine now shared an aesthetic in which poetry was the means of expressing an ideal world only shadowed in the material one, an aesthetic which was to influence Verhaeren and Maeterlinck.

In 1887, after many delays and revisions—which aimed at downgrading the Hegelianism and upgrading the Christian content—Villiers incorporated the earlier conte *Claire Lenoir* as the centrepiece of *Tribulat Bonhomet*, a collection of tales about a naively stupid and overly enthusiastic doctor (the antithesis of Villiers himself). The volume *L'Amour suprême* had appeared in 1886, followed in 1888 by the more bitingly satirical *Histoires insolites* and the *Nouveaux contes cruels*. Villiers's friends rallied round him in the end and ensured his deathbed marriage to his charwoman Marie, the mother of his beloved and finally legitimized son Totor.

In spite of its appearance in *La Jeune France* of 1885, *Axël* was never finished. The posthumous 1890 edition was accompanied by a note signed by Mallarmé and Huysmans explaining that the third part was only half revised and the fourth part untouched. They pointed to the significance of the Christianizing sketches Villiers had left. It is difficult to see how the work could ever have been completed in a Christian or in any other dramatically satisfying sense, since its essence was the repudiation of everything which this world or the next had to offer.

Axël, as it was published in 1885, was not written for the stage. The first two parts had appeared in 1872, with further fragments in 1882 and 1884. As a volume, the text appeared in 1890, six months after Villier's death. Mallarmé, close to Villiers since their meeting in 1864 at Catulle Mendès's house at Choisy-le-Roi, had written of *Elën* that the stage would be too "banal" for its "divine beauté (divine beauty)." Nothing tangible and no sensual stimulus should come between the imagination and the distillation of pure beauty which the imagination strove to grasp.

Axël's text derives closely from the *Dogme et rituel de haute magie* (2 vols., 1862) of Eliphas Lévi, the pseudonym of Alphonse-Louis Constant, 1810–85, which advocates that adherence to "supreme reason" which renders our intelligence invulnerable to whatever happens, and consequently makes it immortal, even after the change which is death. For Lévi this adherence to reason demands independence of the forces which bring about life and death, demanding an ethic of suffering, renunciation, abstention, and death. Villier's text contains many verbal reminiscences of Lévi, and the presumption is that Villiers wished to spread Lévi's doctrine. The final double suicide in the text is not an end. but the opening of a transfiguration in the unwritten last part, which was to have been entitled "Le Monde astral," and might be expected to have shown the world of actual experience as no more than a base shadow of the ultimate ideal reality.

"Le Monde religieux," with which the present text opens, concerns the refusal of Eva Sara Emmanuèle de Maupers to accept the ritual religious initiation involving the renunciation of every earthly joy, and even life itself. The name is heavily symbolic of woman before the period of the Law, during the covenant, and in the Christian era, and the atmosphere is clearly intended to intensify that of a religious profession, with a choir, a white robe, the symbolic scissors, candles, the trappings of monasticism, and pseudo-liturgical Latin incantations. Birth, death, and marriage coalesce. Sara however repudiates "The Light, the Hope, and the Life." The archdeacon locks her in an underground vault to repent and find peace, but Sara escapes. In "Le Monde tragique," there are further take-offs of the Catholic liturgy. Axël in his castle, keeper of the great secret, fights a duel and kills his relative, the Commandeur, whose views about the pursuit of power and wealth are merely worldly, relying in human forces, strength, and cunning. After his death Maître Janus comes in.

In "Le Monde occulte," Maître Janus turns out to be the possessor of wisdom. He predicts the coming together of Axël and Sara to conquer the symbols of gold and love which humanity must be taught to overcome. Like Sara, Axël refuses to accept Light, Hope, and Life, as proffered this time by Janus. Sara's arrival is announced, and Janus foresees the accomplishment of the Work. In "Le Monde passionnel", the castle's treasure cave opens to magic incantatory command, and the beautiful Sara offers herself to Axël's knife. They kiss, and in pursuit of life, death, and sexual union take poison together, "L'homme n'emporte dans la mort que ce qu'il renonça de posséder dans la vie (Man only carries in to death the things whose possession was renounced in life)."

The personal sympathy between Mallarmé and Villiers is reflected in their shared artistic ideal. That which is ordinary, the world of experience, however, ecstatic, intense, and beautiful, is also a sordid degradation of the Ultimate, the Infinite, and the Ideal. Truth, like poetry and fulfilment, can only be hinted at through the fleshly squalors of language and experience. The late 19th century needed to escape form the scientism, the social climbing, and the greed generated by the industrial revolution. The imaginations of a whole generation of symbolists, like those of the authors of the Catholic renewal, concentrated between about 1880 and perhaps as late as 1905 on investigating possible, and sometimes more obviously impossible, avenues of escape from the mundane vulgarities of direct experience.

PUBLICATIONS

Collections

Oeuvres complètes, 11 vols., ed. Marcel Longuet 1914–31
Oeuvres, ed J.-H. Bornecque, 1957
Oeuvres complètes, Bibliothèque de la Pléiade, 2 vols., 1986

Printed volumes (some unpublished)

Deux essais de poésie, 1858
Premières poésies, 1859
Isis, 1862
Elën, 1865
Morgane, 1866
La Révolte, 1870
Le Nouveau-Monde, 1880

Maison Gambade Père et Fils Successeurs, 1882
Contes cruels, 1883 (tr. H. Miles, *Sardonic Tales*, 1927; tr. R. Baldick, *Cruel Tales*, 1963)
L'Ève future, 1886
L'Amour suprême, 1886
Akëdysséril, 1886
Tribulat Bonhomet, 1887
Histoires insolites, 1888
Nouveaux Contes cruels, 1888
Chez les passants, 1890
Axël, 1890 (tr. H.P.R. Finberg, 1925; tr. Marilyn Gaddis Rose, 1970)
L'Évasion, 1891
Nouveaux contes cruels et Propos d'au-delà, 1893
Trois Portraits de femmes, 1929
Reliques, 1954
Le Prétendant, 1965
Nouvelles Reliques, 1968

Additional translations

The Revolt and the Escape, 1901

Claire Lenoir, 1925
Queen Ysabeau, 1925

Correspondence

Correspondance générale, 1962

Biographical and Critical studies

Bollery, J., *Biblio-iconographie de Villiers de l'Isle- Adam*, 1939
Bürgisser, P., *La Double Illusion de 'or et de l'amour chez Villiers de l'Isle-Adam*, 1969
Bornecque, J.-H., *Villiers de l'Isle-Adam créateur et visionnaire*, 1974
Conroy, Jr, W.T., *Villiers de l'Isle-Adam* (in English), 1978
Raitt, A.W., *The Life of Villiers de l'Isle-Adam*, 1981

W

WEIL, Simone, 1909–1943.

*Religious thinker, diarist, and essayist on religious,
philosophical, social, and political topics.*

LIFE

Weil's works, many of them simply letters or aphoristic jottings
in a notebook or diary, are never more than essay length. Their
importance lies in their radical intelligence, their articulateness,
and the record they provide of the moral choices which directed
Weil's life, and the consequences of those choices. Weil has
been called the greatest spiritual thinker of the West in the 20th
century, although the interest of her ill-integrated spiritual
thought primarily derives from the way it resists synthesis and
articulates her own very individual spiritual needs as they developed, and her dissatisfaction will all religious and social orthodoxy.

Weil was the second child of a cultured and assertive Jewish
mother who encouraged her to ignore her gender, and a mild,
considerate, radical Jewish doctor, who had reacted against his
strictly orthodox Jewish upbringing by becoming an atheist.
Simone was sickly as a small child and learnt early on in life to
avoid all physical contact with others. As a young girl she was
almost truculently egalitarian. Her schooling was repeatedly
interrupted during the war. From 1919 she intermittently
attended the highly reputed Lycée Fénelon in Paris, while still
receiving some instruction at home. She was particularly
attracted to Pascal and Dostoyevsky. At the Lycée Victor-
Duruy, to which she later transferred, she was taught philosophy
by René Le Senne.

She left school after her baccalauréat in 1925, already fiercely
identifying with the social under-dog. Her moral attitudes were
instinctive, intense, and uncompromising. She was a pacifist,
staunchly left-wing and, outwardly at least, something of a prig.
At the Lycée Henri IV, to which she now transferred in order to
prepare for the Ecole Normale Supérieure, she was taught by
Alain. In 1931 she graduated seventh in the agrégation examination. One hundred and seven students sat the exam, and 96 of
them failed. Lévi-Strauss came third.

Intellectually, in spite of her strong views, Weil's political
thought was always muddled, and her academic progress was
inhibited by a lack of interest in history. Her gifts were intellectual clarity—which she tended to wield to destructive effect—
and an unremitting quest for what she called "purity," the attainment of which she felt must necessarily entail personal suffering
and deprivation. She became obsessively, even morbidly, preoccupied with an unrealizable ideal of absolute spiritual integrity.

For most of her life Weil suffered intermittently from violent
headaches. She wanted to become a manual worker, but in the
end applied for the government teaching post to which her agré-

gation entitled her. She was posted to Le Puy, a small, staunchly
Catholic town in the heart of the Massif Central, where she lived
in disarray in a room she refused to heat, on the grounds that the
unemployed could not afford heating. She lived at the level of
social security, giving the rest of her income to strike funds. As
a teacher she was a maverick, generous and helpful, but uninterested in syllabuses and set books, and most of her pupils failed.
As a token of her involvement with the plight of the unemployed
Weil devoted some of her spare time to breaking stones for a pit-
tance near the school entrance—to the predictable dismay of her
pupils' families and of the school authorities. She also gave
evening classes to manual workers.

Weil had an unexplained personal need to share the experience of exploited members of society, though reflection would
have shown her the impossibility of becoming integrated into
their communities: for a start she was separated from them by
having enjoyed the best education obtainable in France. She
nevertheless spent six weeks in the summer of 1932 getting to
know working-class Berlin. She thought Germany held the key
to future changes in social and economic forces, a subject on
which she now began to write a series of essays. In the autumn
she was posted to Auxerre and then, after spending the summer
of 1933 in Spain with her family, to Roanne. Her pupils continued to fail their exams, and she found that her search for a non-
communist revolutionary left jarred with the pro-Soviet attitudes of the French communists. In Spain she had discovered an
ideal form of workers' organization at Valencia, and in August
1933 published her first major essay, *Allons-nous vers la révolution prolétarienne?* Weil was a great admirer of Trotsky, who,
disapproved however, of her individualistic views. A year later
she broke with revolutionary syndicalism in *Oppression et liberté*, rejecting the view that modes of production were the key
determinant, and preferring an explanation in terms of the opposition between buyers and sellers of labour. Against Marx she
held that work was always inherently servile, and pointed to
what she saw as the contradiction in Marx between social analysis and revolutionary politics.

In the autumn of 1934 Weil obtained a year's leave of absence
in order to work in a factory and write a thesis on the relationship between French social organization and French culture. In
her factory work she was clumsy, ill-coordinated, and slow, and
she was dismissed from two successive jobs. Her notes comment on the dangerous unpleasantness of the factory worker's
life and on the spirit of submission it bred. In 1935 she went on
holiday to Spain and Portugal before returning to teach at
Bourges, where she studied mathematics and began to shed her
pacifist views. In August 1936 she enrolled in a commando
group of foreigners in Spain, but had to return home as the result
of a serious burn on her foot. She was still a non-interventionist,
but her attitudes were changing. She recognized the similarities
between communism and fascism and began to probe the mean-

ing of euphemisms such as "the national interest," summing up her position in 1937 in "Ne recommençons pas la guerre de Troie."

Free from the demands of teaching, Weil spent some time in a Swiss clinic for her headaches and visited Italy, where she went to the opera and studied selectively but at length the paintings in Milan, Bologna, Ferrara, Ravenna, Florence, and Rome. She also developed a taste for plainchant and attended the Maggio Musicale in Florence. Her aesthetic taste shifted from Beethoven to Monteverdi, and from Michelangelo to Giotto. She wrote verse and made intelligent observations on quantum theory and Heisenberg's indeterminacy principle without, however, really understanding either. She started teaching again—Greek as well as philosophy—at Saint-Quentin. "Society," she declared, "is founded only on relations of force." By early 1938 she was again on sick leave, and never returned to teaching. She had twice contemplated suicide. She spent Easter at Solesmes, the abbey of plainchant's rebirth, attending the Holy Week offices. Her aesthetic pleasure was intermixed with the intense pain of her headaches and both became associated in Weil's mind with the sufferings of Christ, on which the liturgy cast an ethereal gloss. In November she had what is sometimes described as a mystical experience, but which was in fact an elevated state of intense calm which she expressed in terms of "possession by Christ" and "the presence of a love." The experience, and the terms used to describe it, are in fact classic, but Weil was poorly acquainted with mystical theology.

On leaving Solesmes, Weil revisited Italy, joining her parents at Venice. She smoked cigarettes, bought books, and went to the opera. She still held to some extent to her pacifist principles, but these were finally to crumble with the establishment of the Vichy government. In May 1939 she contracted pleurisy and lived for a while in the South of France, returning to Paris when war broke out. She spent the first months of the war reading ancient history, in spite of her aversion for Caesar's mass murders and her distaste for the Roman conviction of racial superiority. Since the French right wing saw themselves as the cultural heirs of Rome, so the left naturally gravitated towards an admiration for Greek democracy. Weil, however, powerfully indicted the *Iliad*, too, for its glorification of force. The Gospels are the last expression of Greek genius, but Weil recoiled from the Hebrew ethics of the Old Testament. She was attracted, on the other hand, to the Albigensian religion of medieval Provence, which held that the body was an obstacle to spiritual perfection.

During the war, Weil looked for a combative role, but in the end caught the last train south with her parents, ending up in Vichy. As a Jew she was forbidden to teach. She started to write a play, which she never finished. When the family moved to Marseilles, in an attempt to join Weil's brother André in New York, she began an active collaboration with the *Cahiers du Sud*, the most influential French review still in existence at the time.

The *Cahiers* published Weil's essays on the Albigenses and on the *Iliad*, and she began organizing her notebooks, which were to be published posthumously. Following an abortive attempt to get to England, she became a close friend of the Dominican Joseph-Marie Perrin, who introduced her to Gustave Thibon, an amateur philosopher on whose farm Weil was given work. She clearly enjoyed uncommitted intellectual jousting with intelligent Catholic priests, who, on the whole, attached for greater importance than she did to belief and less to spiritual experience. One priest commented that, however sharp her insights and dialectical skills, her intelligence displayed "rigidity and crudeness." Weil never in fact got very near to a global acceptance of Catholic belief, but she started reading the mystics, including John of the Cross in Spanish, and to pray, an activity she had hitherto avoided on account of the danger of auto-suggestion. Her moments of intense peace increased.

By the end of 1941 Weil could find no more agricultural work and returned to Marseilles. Her time there was taken up with writing a second article on the Albigensians, collaborating with the incipient Resistance movement, assuming responsibility for the distribution of a new Catholic review, *Témoignange Chrétien*, and reading Greek and Buddhist texts. In May 1942 she went to New York with her parents, leaving behind important valedictory letters to Thibon, Perrin, and Joë Bousquet, one of the *Cahiers* group with whom she had struck up a close intellectual friendship, although he found her too intransigent in her thinking. Subsequent critical interest has centred on her writings during the Marseilles period.

Weil insisted on travelling fourth class to New York, worked on Pythagoras and Plato during the trip, and struck her fellow passengers as standoffish. From New York she tried to return to London to work for the Free French, her aim being to organize a mobile nursing commando. She went to daily Mass, found more priests to argue with and, in *Lettre à un religieux*, expounded the reasons which held her back from conversion. Only in ancient Greece had there been a real union between the sacred and the profane, she declared. Jesuit attempts to integrate the explicit truths of oriental religions attacked by Pascal had been right. Faith was not an intellectual assent, and defined dogma merely obliged respect. The prospect of a return to Europe had encouraged Weil to start work again on the Notebooks, the background to the *Lettre*, which develop the ideas that creation marks a voluntary abdication of God's power and that faith is the acknowledgement that desire for the absolute good cannot be frustrated. The Gospels, in her view, contained not a theology, but a conception of human life. On 10 November Weil left New York for London having, as on leaving Marseilles, sent a number of testamentary letters setting out her thought.

In England Weil sought work with the Free French, endeavouring to involve herself in hardship and danger. She refused to eat properly because, as she said, the French were dying of starvation. She contracted tuberculosis and a bad cough, but refused to heat her room. She was given political documents from the Resistance to analyse and papers to write relating to the eventual production of a new French constitution. Her ideas tended towards utopianism and some were quite unrealistically radical. The major works of this period include "Cette guerre est une guerre de religions," *L'Enracinement: prélude à une déclaration des devoirs envers l'être humain*, which sums up Weil's political thought, and an essay entitled "Human personality." An essential component of her current thinking was that obligations were absolute, but that rights were not. Her hopes were pinned on a spiritual rather than an economic revolution.

Weil went to the theatre periodically and taught her landlady's children, but from March 1943 her health and spirits began to disintegrate. She went to daily Mass, practically begged to be sent to France on what would have amounted to a suicide mission, wrote about the sacraments, and made a final restatement of her religious position in *La Connaissance surnaturelle*. By this time she was sleeping only three hours a night. She was found unconscious on the floor of her room on 15 April, diagnosed as tubercular in both lungs, and though she recovered a little in hospital, she continued to eat too little. Her digestive system was probably by now so damaged that she had no chance of survival. A friend appears to have baptized her a Catholic with her consent. Weil resigned from the Free French in July, disillusioned by the political manoeuvering. She was moved to a sanatorium, where she died on 24 August. The coroner's verdict of suicide by self-imposed starvation was almost certainly wrong.

Weil's important work was published only posthumously, at first in collections compiled by her Catholic friends Perrin and Thibon, while Camus edited some of her early political writings. In order to be able to love, Weil also felt an extreme need to suffer; and yet she was not a masochist. The best description of her is that given by her biographer David McLellan, who defined her as a "utopian pessimist."

PUBLICATIONS

Collections

Oeuvres complètes, 3 vols., 1987

Works

La Pesanteur et la grâce (Thibon's selection from the Marseilles Notebooks), 1947; as *Gravity and Grace*, 1952

L''Enracinement: prélude à une déclaration des devoirs envers l'être humain, 1949; as *The Need for Roots*, 1952

Attente de Dieu (letters to and articles for Perrin), 1950; as *Waiting for God*, 1951

La Connaissance surnaturelle (New York Notebooks), 1950

Cahiers (the Marseilles Notebooks), 3 vols., 1951, 1953, 1956; augmented edition, 1970ff.; as *The Notebooks of Simone Weil*, 1956

Intuitions préchrétiennes (writings on Greek philosophy), 1951; as *Intimations of Christianity among the Ancient Greeks* (with most of *La Source grècque*), 1957

La Condition ouvrière (factory journal and articles), 1951

Lettre à un religieux (New York letter to Couturier), 1951; as *Letter to a Priest*, 1954

La Source grècque (essays on the *Iliad*, Greek tragedy, and Plato), 1953

Oppression et liberté (contains shorter essays as well as the principal one), 1955; as *Oppression and Liberty*, 1958

Ecrits de Londres et dernières lettres (writings of the last six months of her life), 1957

Leçons de philosophie de Simone Weil (notes of a pupil on the Roanne classes) edited by A. Reynaud 1959; as *Lectures on Philosophy*, 1978

Ecrits historiques et politiques (short articles), 1960

Pensées sans ordre concernant l'amour de Dieu (articles from the Marseilles period), 1962

Sur la science (letters to her brother, articles, student thesis on Descartes), 1966

Poèmes, suivis de "Venise sauvée" (poetry and unfinished play), 1968

Further translations

Selected Essays, 1934–43, (mostly, but not entirely, early political essays), 1962

Seventy Letters, 1965

On Science, Necessity and the Love of God, 1968

First and Last Notebooks (pre-war Notebooks and *La Connaissance surnaturelle*), 1970

Gateway to God, 1974

The Simone Weil Reader, 1977

Simone Weil: An Anthology, 1986

Formative Writings, 1929–41, 1987

Bibliography

Cabaud, J., *Simone Weil: A Fellowship in Love*, 1964, pp.364–85 Little, J.P., *Simone Weil: A Bibliography*, 1973; supplement, 1979. See also McLellan, D., *Simone Weil: Utopian Pessimist*, 1989.

Biographical and critical studies

Perrin, J.-M., and G. Thibon, *Simone Weil as We Knew Her*, 1953

Cabaud, Jacques, *Simone Weil: A Fellowship in Love*, 1965

Pétrement, Simone, *Simone Weil: A Life*, 1976

Anderson, David, *Simone Weil* (in English), 1977

Dunaway, John, *Simone Weil* (in English), 1984

Coles, Robert, *A Modern Pilgrimage*, 1987

Dietz, Mary, *Between the Human and the Divine: The Social and Political Thought of Simone Weil*, 1989

Fiori, Gabrielli, *Simone Weil: An Intellectual Biography*, 1989

Winch, Peter, *Simone Weil: The Just Balance*, 1989

McLellan, David, *Simone Weil: Utopian Pessimist*, 1989

Z

ZOLA, Émile (-Édouard-Charles-Antoine), 1840–1902.

Novelist, journalist, pamphleteer, and author of short stories.

LIFE

Zola was born in Paris of a French mother, Emilie-Aurélie (née Aubert), and an exuberant and ambitious Italian father, a 45-year-old engineer whose family came from Dalmatia and whose mother had been Greek. He sold a water system of three dams and a seven-kilometre canal to Aix-en-Provence, caught a cold while working on one of the dams, failed to shake it off before a business trip to Marseilles, and died there of pneumonia in 1847. Although Zola's mother had shares in the canal company and a claim on the Aix municipality, she quickly fell into financial difficulties. At his first school, which was pleasant but undemanding, Zola met the future sculptor Philippe Solari and Marius Roux, the future novelist and editor of *Le Petit Journal*. He was in fact a year or two behind his age group when in 1852 he went on to the Collège Bourbon at Aix, although by his final year, 1856–57, he had succeeded in carrying off most of the prizes. While at school he was befriended by the painter, Paul Cézanne, who was a year older than he was, Baptistin Baille, later a professor at the Ecole Polytechnique. The trio became inseparable companions who shared a passionate interest in art and literature. Zola's particular enthusiasm was Musset.

In the autumn of 1857 Zola's maternal grandmother died, and his mother left for Paris in search of financial help. In February 1858 she told Zola to sell whatever was left at Aix and use the money to buy tickets for his grandfather and himself. A scholarship had been found for him at the Lycée Saint-Louis, which he entered on 1 March 1858. Somehow his mother got together the money to finance a holiday for Zola in Aix that summer, but he fell ill and failed the oral part of the baccalauréat in August 1859. After another break in Aix he failed the written part of the examination at the November resit. At Aix he had started to write, apparently some poems and a verse comedy, while a fairy story of his seems to have been accepted for publication. The family's financial situation became desperate. A job of mind-crushing boredom and derisory wages was found for Zola at the Paris docks in 1860, but he gave it up, exchanging letters meanwhile with Cézanne about realism (q. v.) and with Baille about literature. At this date Zola believed in God, in the moral teaching of Christianity, in the attractiveness of virtue, and in the utility of art. He finished a poetic trilogy, planned another one, started a verse play, and wrote short stories, at least one of which, "Le carnet de danse," was later to be published. There was no money to go to Aix that summer, and mother and son were forced to move into different rooms in the same street. We may probably infer that Zola's mother was using hers to earn a living. Zola was in a top-floor room once inhabited by Bernardin de Saint-Pierre, but had to move to an even cheaper one, while frequently living on a sub-subsistence diet. Sometime in the winter of 1860–61 he had a love affair, from which he emerged disillusioned.

In April 1861 Cézanne arrived in Paris. He had a reasonable allowance, but was uncertain about his painting. Zola, though destitute, was the more confident of the two. He was growing away from romanticism (q. v.) and wrote an essay on progress in science and poetry which was published in the *Journal Populaire de Lille* in April 1864. In February 1862, following a bitterly hard winter, Zola obtained a job in the shipping department of the publisher Hachette at 100 francs a month. He used his weekends for writing. Baille was now in Paris, but Cézanne had returned to Aix. Zola composed short stories, wrote verse, and suggested to Hachette the creation of a series for new authors, an idea which Louis Hachette turned down, but which earned Zola promotion to the advertising department, where he met Michelet, Taine, About, and Littré. It was apparently Louis Hachette who persuaded him to abandon verse. He became a naturalized French citizen, but was not called for military service by the lottery system then in force. Cézanne returned to Paris and seems to have introduced Zola to Gabrielle-Alexandrine Meley, who was a year older than him. She became his mistress and, in 1870, his wife. Her mother was dead and she rarely saw her father.

Zola was already a literary advocate of realism. He had been reading Stendhal, Taine, and probably Darwin, and had certainly taken part in the discussions centred on the Salon des Refusés of 1863 and on Manet's *Déjeuner sur l'herbe*, which created the scandal leading to the closure of the exhibition. Cézanne was to cut back the impressionist palette of 20 colours to only six, and omit black altogether. Zola was already arguing that art, like a transparent screen, distorted nature, making absolute realism impossible, but he advocated that the distortion so prominent in classical and romantic art should be minimized. He was already quite near his famous definition in *Le Salut Public* of 1865, "Une oeuvre est un coin de la nature vu à travers un tempérament" (a work of art is a corner of nature seen through a sensibility), coined in the course of a piece on Proudhon and Courbet. His first volume of short stories, *Contes à Ninon*, containing mostly early romantic work such as "Le carnet de danse," "La fée amoureuse," "Simplice," and "Le sang," was now ready for publication. The longest story, "Aventures du grand Sidoine et du petit Médéric," is reminiscent of Voltaire.

Zola now began to write "Chroniques" for *Le Petit Journal* and the *Courrier du Monde*, with literary criticism fortnightly for *Le Salut Public* of Lyons, including a strong defence of the Goncourts' *Germinie Lacerteux*, then much derided for the moral depravity of its characters. Zola's first, and partly autobiographical, novel, *La Confession de Claude*, appeared late in 1865 and attributes to his central character Zola's own experience of pawning coat and trousers. One critic noted the incursion of a poetry Zola was unable to keep out of the text, but the reviews were generally poor, and there was some possibility of a prosecution. In 1866 Zola wrote a short story and two plays, one of which, *Madeleine*, became a novel (*Madeleine Férat*) and was also staged as a play in 1889. Louis Hachette, however, had died in 1864, and after the quasi-failure of *Claude* Zola decided to leave Hachette and to live by his pen.

He resigned on 31 January 1866. The next day his first literary "Chronique" appeared in *L'Evénement*, a daily linked to the still weekly *Le Figaro*, which had appointed Zola literary chronicler and critic. He also wrote for the *Revue Contemporaine* and addressed the Congrès Scientifique de France, moving slowly towards a full commitment to realism. He expressed reserves about Taine's determinism and an increasing enthusiasm for Balzac on account of his factual studies of the influence of the environment on individuals. Financial need pressed him to write potboilers for serialization in addition to the considerable quantity of journalism in which he was engaged, and he began to frequent the Friday meetings at the Café Guerbois of a group of artists which included Manet, Pissarro, and Monet, while he himself received on Thursdays. He wrote a number of pieces on the 1866 Salon for *L'Evénement*, attacking the jury system for selecting the paintings for exhibition and lauding Manet for truthfully painting reality as he saw it, repeating the formula about art as a "corner of nature." His articles were sufficiently forceful for the editor to feel the need to have them counterbalanced by a series defending a more conservative point of view. Zola spent part of the summer on the long study of Manet printed on 1 January 1867 in the *Revue du XIXe Siècle*.

He spent much of 1867 working on *Thérèse Raquin*, published in December of that year. The reviews of the novel, which derives partly from Flaubert's *Madame Bovary*, were strikingly bad, although in a letter to Zola Sainte-Beuve mixed encouragement with harsh criticism. Zola defended the novel in the preface of the April 1868 edition: "I tried to study sensibilities, not characters... I chose people governed by their nerves and their blood, devoid of free will, led into every act of their lives by the determinism of their flesh. I was performing on living bodies what surgeons do to corpses." For the second edition he used as an epigraph the famous formula "Vice and virtue are products like vitriol and sugar," so shielding himself with Taine's determinism.

Madeleine Férat, developed from the 1866 play, was serialized in *L'Evénement Illustré* under the title *La Honte* before publication in book form in December of the following year. It is an attempt to apply science to fiction and depends too much on coincidences to be a good novel. Madeleine's child by Guillaume looks like Jacques, with whom she had an emotional bond. The influence of the imagination on the physical appearance of offspring is biblical and has a long history in European literature, while variations on the theme of a similarity of appearance between a child and the true object of its mother's affection figure in Claudel and Gide, and appear to derive from Goethe's *Die Wahlverwandtschaften*. Zola's use of the device is usually attributed to Michelet (*L'Amour—La Femme*), who himself attributes the underlying theory to Prosper Lucas's 1847 *Traité philosophique et physiologique de l'hérédité...*, a book which Zola certainly knew a little later but where, however, the theory is a good deal more tentative than in Michelet. Zola's novel occasioned further protests, and a further threat of prosecution, and in *La Tribune* of 29 November 1868 he defended

himself against accusations of immorality, refusing to make the cuts in the book suggested by its publisher, Lacroix.

Zola's journalistic career virtually came to an end when, in November 1866, the daily *L'Evénement* was absorbed into *Le Figaro* and in December, he was dropped from *Le Salut Public*. The following year was economically difficult as a result. Zola borrowed money from friends and placed pieces in half a dozen reviews. *Les Mystères de Marseilles* was serialized in the *Messager de Provence* at two centimes a line, and staged unsuccessfully as a play later in the year. Censorship was being relaxed and *Le Globe*, which lasted only from January to February 1868, took several articles from Zola, including a review of Letourneau's *La Physiologie des passions*, a book of some importance for Zola's novels. The following year was a better one for him. From June *La Tribune* published a weekly article, and for *L'Evénement Illustré* Zola wrote not only a series of weekly "Chroniques," but also a series of articles on the Salon of that year, published from 2 May until 16 June, including one devoted wholly to Manet. Cézanne, whose paintings had been turned down but defended by Zola the year before, was not referred to, although he had been turned down again by a more liberal jury in 1868. Pissarro, Monet, Corot, the Morisot sisters, Courbet, and Degas, on the other hand, were all praised.

It was Balzac's *Comédie humaine* which gave Zola the idea for "Les Rougon-Macquart, histoire naturelle et sociale d'une famille sous le Second Empire." Zola admired Flaubert, and had even referred to Stendhal as "France's greatest novelist." In spite of the reservations expressed earlier, he readily admitted Taine's influence. He read lengthily in what was then the Bibliothèque Impériale (the present Bibliothèque Nationale) and, largely spurred on by his reading of Lucas, decided to make his panorama the history of a single family. We have three sets of Zola's notes on the subject, showing the gradual emergence of heredity as the chief force, modified by the environment, making the saga the scientific study of a family and the effect on it of the contemporary organization of society. He intended to create characters made exceptional by their environment and wanted to shock the public into remembering his books, without however giving it nightmares.

Zola's "family" was to descend from the hysterical Adelaïde Fouque, who marries Rougon the gardener, by whom she has a son. On being widowed she takes a lover, the smuggler Macquart, and dies insane in 1873. The Macquart heredity is tainted. Zola used Lucas's *Traité* to classify a score of Adelaïde's descendants, and began to adopt the term "naturalism" (q. v.), "which widened the field of observation." A few years later he allied to it "experimentation" from Claude Bernard's *Introduction à la médicine expérimentale* (1865), creating what amounts to a slogan for the series: "Observation and experimentation." "Experimentation" was the placing of a character in different, testing situations and the depicting of his or her reactions. Both heredity, by its manipulation of genetic transmission through suitable marriages, and environment, which daily affects the individual, were to be used by the naturalistic novelist, who was both an experimental literary artist and a practical sociologist hoping to modify the organization of society. Happily Zola did not let himself be bound by his own theory, and avoided the arid application of strictly scientific procedures to literary composition, as set out in his *Le Roman expérimental* of 1880. He was to use them almost more for purposes of commercial promotion than for fictional creation.

Zola proposed to write two novels a year for five years, starting with the 1851 coup d'état in a provincial town, and continuing with novels on gilded youth, financial speculations, politics, religion, the Italian war, the proletariat and the drink problem in working-class Paris, the demi-monde, the world of art, and the courts' attitude to hereditary criminality. This original project, dating from the winter of 1868–69, was to be modified and expanded. By 1871 Zola had added seven more books, one of which he never wrote. In the end there were 20 novels in the cycle, published from 1871 to 1893. Lacroix agreed to advance Zola 500 francs a month for a trial period of two years. Normally Zola would begin with a character and a general theme together with its social implications, then elaborate a "sketch" with theme, atmosphere, characters, plot, and some of the incidents. There followed the documentation phase, and for future use detailed notes were kept of towns, battlefields, farms, racetracks, markets, strikes, and whatever else might provide an appropriate setting. Notes were made establishing the age, appearance, character, health record, and heredity of each "personnage," the French word for a character in a play. Then came the chapter plans.

Zola worked regular hours, in the mornings on the novels and in the afternoons on journalism and his correspondence. Then came exercise, usually a walk; and finally dinner, reading, or visits to or from friends filled the evening. The journalism, mostly for opposition papers and mostly on literary topics, together with his Salon articles, earned Zola his living. Alongside the uncontroversial "Chroniques," he was publishing trenchant and sometimes satirical social, literary, and even political comment. His political and social liberalism had become firmer, and journalism was teaching him the writer's craft. Until the Dreyfus case Zola's life remained relatively uneventful. He married in 1870, removed his wife and his mother from the path of the Prussian advance to the safety of the south, and in September 1870 founded a short-lived but strongly republican newspaper, *La Marseillaise*, which lasted from 27 September to 16 December, but no copies of which have survived. He gradually broadened the base and diminished the amount of his journalism, acquired wealth and property, and increased his interest in the theatre, and in 1888 he took a mistress, Jeanne-Sophie Adèle Rozerot, by whom he had a daughter in 1889 and a son in 1891. The 20th novel of his saga, *Le Docteur Pascal*, appeared in 1893, the year before the condemnation of Dreyfus.

Le Siècle had offered to serialize the first Rougon novel, *La Fortune des Rougon*, but the first instalment appeared eight months late, on 28 June 1870, and publication was interrupted for seven months from 10 August on account of the Franco-Prussian War. The last instalments, from 18 March to 21 March 1871, coincided with the Paris insurrection. On 5 August 1870 Zola, who had been criticizing the government with increasing stridency, denounced the war in *La Cloche* and was indicted for civil disobedience. He was saved from trial by the overthrow of the government. Foreseeing the collapse of *La Marseillaise*, Zola obtained an administrative post in Bordeaux and when the armistice was signed he arranged to report on the proceedings of parliament, which had temporarily moved there, for *La Cloche*, in which he published some 200 articles before its suppression in 1872, and for *Le Sémaphore de Marseille*, for which he wrote until 1877. He returned to Paris on 14 March 1871, just in time to report on the Commune. When *La Cloche* was suppressed Zola wrote briefly for *Le Corsaire*, but published an attack of

such virulence on some members of parliament for their indifference to the plight of the unemployed that that paper, too, was suppressed for a period. Zola's article, "Le lendemain de la crise," subsequently became a short story, "Le chômage."

The serialization in *La Cloche* of the second Rougon novel, *La Curée*, was suspended at Zola's request after the authorities had intervened, although the unexpurgated text was published in book form in 1872. What upset the public was primarily the incest scenes. The critics, with the exception of Huysmans and Maupassant, were severe with regard to the third novel, *Le Ventre de Paris*, published in 1873 by Charpentier, who had taken over the contract after Lacroix's bankruptcy. Zola's own dramatization of *Thérèse Raquin* ran for only a brief period. Real success was still eluding him, although he was making a name for himself in literary circles. He had become friendly with Flaubert, and in 1874 he took to dining most months with Flaubert, Edmond de Goncourt, Turgenev, and Daudet. All of them claimed to have had plays hissed at. Zola also got to know Alexis, Céard, Huysmans, and Maupassant. However, in 1874 *La Conquête de Plassans* was greeted with virtual silence, although Flaubert liked it, both Brunetière and Anatole France praised parts of it, and Turgenev had it serialized in Russia. In the same year Zola published the 11 often autobiographical *Nouveaux contes à Ninon*, increasing the number to 14 in 1885. All had already been published in periodicals.

The next novel, *La Faute de l'abbé Mouret*, was serialized in February and March 1875 in the St Petersburg *European Messenger*, for which Zola began to write a monthly column in March 1875. In Paris, where it was published in the same year, it broke the critics' silence. It included a hymn of joy, almost an ode, to nature, to its vital, reproductive forces and its fecundity. It outraged Barbey d'Aurevilly. The *Revue de France* and the *Revue Bleue* disliked it, and Brunetière was unfavourable in the *Revue des Deux Mondes* (q. v.). Only Maupassant expressed unreserved admiration, and that was in a private letter. None the less the reaction was enough to create a small-scale succès de scandale, and there were four printings of the novel in 1875. *Son Excellence Eugène Rougon* was serialized in *Le Siècle* from January to March 1876 and published by Charpentier a few days later, but it failed to sustain the momentum of its predecessor.

The storm really broke that summer. Guyot's *Le Bien Public* suspended publication of *L'Assommoir* in June after chapter six, not for immorality but because of Zola's unflattering depiction of the working classes. Catulle Mendès then took it for *La République des Lettres*, publishing chapters seven to 13 from July 1876 to January 1877, although a violent attack by Albert Millaud had appeared in *Le Figaro* in September. Zola replied, but Millaud attacked again, and this time Zola was not allowed a reply. *Le Gaulois* printed a particularly harsh criticism by Fourcauld, who commented: "The novelist does not spare us a single drunkard's vomiting." Zola felt he was attacking social evil "with a red-hot iron" and, when the book was published in January 1877, he re-established bits of the text cut by Guyot and Mendès, omitting other passages he now considered unnecessary. All the major critics, including Houssaye, were denunciatory, but there was also praise for the work, even in *Le Figaro*. Georges Brunet, Anatole France, Bourget, Maupassant, Huysmans, and Mallarmé were impressed by the vigour and the realism of Zola's creation. Above all, the public bought the book. There were 38 printings in 1877, 12 more in 1878, and 91 in all by the end of 1881. Charpentier was generous enough to tear up the old contract and pay Zola royalties. *L'Assommoir* was the first French novel to give a truly realistic picture of working-class life in France. During the 18th century characters successively lower in the social scale had become vehicles for tragedy. Only in Zola do we gain genuine working-class heroes and heroines. *L'Assommoir* was Zola's first masterpiece, and it made him rich.

The next novel, *Une page d'amour*, was less successful, and its accompanying play a failure, but Zola was now able to move his Paris quarters, to buy his house at Médan, and to take a holiday. For some years he had been active in dramatizing his novels and the stage version of *L'Assommoir* lasted 350 performances. Zola also published critical articles and other non-fiction, often propagating the dogmas of naturalism, collecting journalistic pieces into volumes, and writing prefaces. *Le Figaro* now commissioned him to write on any subject he chose. The resulting pieces would be published as *Une campagne*. Naturalism became a movement with Zola as its leader, a jealous Edmond de Goncourt and a slightly hostile Flaubert on the periphery, and Huysmans, Céard, Alexis, Mirbeau, and Maupassant among its members. *Les Soirées de Médan* (1880) contained six "naturalist" short stories connected with the Francoprussian War, one by each of a group who had dined together and met afterwards at Zola's house, officially launching naturalism as a school. There had also been a ceremonial dinner at Trapp's on 16 April 1877, soon after the appearance of *L'Assommoir*. Naturalism was assuming a conscious literary identity, confirmed in 1880 by the publication of Zola's next novel, *Nana*, which caused as much of a stir as *L'Assommoir* had done, and sold even better.

The next novel, *Pot-bouille*, elaborates one of the articles Zola wrote for *Le Figaro* in 1881 on adultery among the bourgeoisie, and centres on the idea that "If in the working class, environment and upbringing push girls into prostitution, in the middle class they lead them to adultery." Mothers give their daughters "a veritable course in decent prostitution." *Au bonheur des dames* and *La Joie de vivre* both concern the fear of death, with which Zola became almost morbidly preoccupied. On the brink of his greatest achievements he had revealed his preoccupation in a short story published in Russia in 1879, "La mort d'Olivier Bécaille," and then in 1880 he had lost successively Edmond Duranty, who had introduced him to Manet, Flaubert, and, worst of all, his mother.

When the miners' strike broke out at Anzin on 21 February 1884 Zola had already started a sketch for the book which he decided would be about just such a strike. He immediately left for the scene, with the recent split between moderates and revolutionaries in the French socialist movement fresh in his mind. Various stratagems enabled him to attend meetings to which he would not ordinarily have been admitted, and he frequented the miners' shops and cafés. He carefully interviewed leaders on both sides, and managed to get down a pit. On returning to Paris he severely pruned back melodrama in favour of observed authenticity, and the product of his research, *Germinal*, was to be one of the most heavily documented novels of the cycle. It was Zola's greatest literary triumph and remains the most famous of his novels, probably his best book.

The next novel, *L'Oeuvre* of 1886, is about an unsuccessful painter's struggle with nature. Claude Lantier, the chief protagonist, contains much of Zola ("I shall relate my own intimate life as a creative artist"), but he is also "a Manet, a dramatized Cézanne, nearer to Cézanne." Lantier is therefore an amalgam,

with something of Monet in him, too, but after publication of the novel Cézanne broke definitively with Zola, his old friend. One of the other characters is partially modelled on Baptistin Baille. A stage adaptation of *Germinal*, written in collaboration with William Busnach, who had already helped with the dramatization of *Pot-bouille*, was delayed by government censors on account of its socialist tendencies, although it was finally played in April 1888. It has never been published. In the meanwhile the dramatized version of *Le Ventre de Paris* had opened on 18 February 1887, with Zola and Busnach again experimenting with an exaggeratedly melodramatic stage version. *La Terre* of 1887 parallels *L'Assommoir* in being the first extended realistic description of non-idealized peasant life in French literature. It is again extensively documented, and it produced an even greater furore. While it was still appearing serially in *Gil Blas*, *Le Figaro* published a "manifesto" signed by five critics attacking it. Anatole France and Brunetière also criticized it, but a few critics praised it, and it sold well. In its treatment of the peasant's struggle with the land and of the life-cycle themes of growth and fertility it was obviously intended to be an achievement to parallel *L'Assommoir* and *Germinal*. In his sketch for the novel Zola refers to "the living poem of the land" which he wanted to write.

In 1887 and 1888 Zola dieted, lost a quarter of his weight, and Jeanne Rozerot became his mistress. In 1888 he set her up in a Paris flat, where she had his two children. His wife was anonymously informed and extremely jealous, although she eventually acquiesced in the situation, and even allowed Jeanne's children legally to bear their father's name. Three more novels were published for the Rougon cycle, *Le Rêve* in 1888, *La Bête humaine* in 1890, and *L'Argent* in 1891, the first to mention the anti-semitism about which Zola would have known from Drumont's now infamous *La France juive* of 1886. Two more novels remained to be written for the saga, *La Débâcle* and *Le Docteur Pascal*. *La Débâcle* was to compress a great deal: a military narrative, the fall of Napoleon, the Commune, and the overthrow of the government. The political situation also favoured a reminder of the dangers of renewed military rule. The book outsold all previous volumes in the series. Unhappily *Le Docteur Pascal*, which winds up the series in no more than an intellectually satisfying way, is one of the poorest of the 20 novels. On 21 January 1893, to celebrate the cycle's completion, Charpentier and Fasquelle gave a magnificent luncheon for all the literary personalities of Paris, headed by Poincaré himself, the minister of education.

Zola now conceived the trilogy of novels *Lourdes*, *Rome*, and *Paris*, which are not generally considered to have been successful. They are too polemically anti-clerical, too loosely linked by a central figure who fails to carry emotional conviction, and everything that happens in them is too symbolic. During publication the Dreyfus case broke out, splitting conservatives from liberals, monarchists from republicans, Catholics from atheists, the aristocracy from the people, the Church from the state, and the advocates of nationalism from the defenders of justice. Only extremists and bigots found themselves without divided loyalties. Zola had denounced anti-semitism as "a monstrosity" in *Le Figaro* in 1896. He first wrote about Dreyfus in the same newspaper on 25 November 1897, almost three years after the condemnation, following up his first article with two others on 1 and 5 December. *Le Figaro* then refused to print more, so Zola published two pamphlets, "Lettres à la jeunesse" on 14 December and "Lettre à la France" on 6 January 1898. Then on 11 January the army cover-up acquitted the real betrayer of the secrets to the Germans, Major Walsin-Esterhazy. On 13 January Zola published a furious letter to the president of France in *L'Aurore*. The editor, Clemenceau, put it on the front page and called it "J'accuse." The letter named various high officers, charging them with outright lies and lesser offences. Zola was sued, sent to prison for a year, and fined 3,000 francs, with the jury ranged seven to five against him. An appeal was granted, and Zola left for England, pending a reopening of the case against Dreyfus. He was away 11 months. Esterhazy confessed and fled. Colonel Henry, who had been instrumental in the cover-up, committed suicide. Dreyfus was found guilty again at the retrial, but pardoned, and was not completely exonerated until 1906.

When the retrial was ordered, Zola returned to France, publishing three of his four anti-clerical novels written in England, *Fécondité, Travail*, and *Vérité*. In September 1902 the Zolas returned to Paris from Médan and a fire was lit in their bedroom. The chimney was blocked, and Zola was found dead from asphyxiation next morning. His wife was discovered just in time to save her life. At the funeral Anatole France gave the principal oration. On 4 June 1908 Zola's remains were removed to the Panthéon. Rejected 31 times, Zola was never elected to the Académie Française. Because he had put his name forward, Edmond de Goncourt had removed him from the list of trustees named in his will as founder members of his own academy.

WORKS

Zola's sketches show that his writings were overwhelmingly intended to be demonstrations of scientific and ecological truths, even if their concern with individuals and the theories of hereditary and environmental determinism was paraded more to attract attention to the literary endeavour than to explain it. The novels, with their unrelenting depiction of sex, violence, squalor, cant, and the more sordid aspects of human behaviour, were often considered shocking, subversive of the social and moral bourgeois values which Zola regarded as hypocritical. Their survival, however, is due less to the momentary succès de scandale of some among them than to the way in which they confer the poetry of tragedy on representatives of the most economically and socially deprived sections of society. It is because the novels concern recognizable individuals that some of them at least are literary masterpieces. By general consent, the greatest achievements are considered to be *L'Assommoir* and *Germinal*.

Zola's social concerns, not yet given structure by scientific hypothesis, grew clearly from their embryonic state in the *Contes à Ninon*, where they remained adjacent to the romantic themes rather than blended in to them, and were generally expressed satirically rather than lyrically, as in some of the saga novels. *La Confession de Claude*, while drawing heavily on Zola's emotional experiences as well as on his economic circumstances, broaches the subject of feminism, already developed by Michelet. Zola was beginning now to blend poetry into his realism rather than simply set the two alongside one another, but *Thérèse Raquin*, two years later, was almost programmatically realistic. It is based on an earlier novel which Zola had read when it was published serially in *Le Figaro* and which was itself based on a real crime. Zola first wrote a short story, "Un mariage d'amour," published in *Le Figaro* on 24 December 1866, before writing the novel itself. Arsène Houssaye accepted it for *L'Artiste*, where it appeared in three instalments in 1867 before final

publication in book form that December. Like *Claude, Thérèse Raquin* takes sex as its major theme, and it may be that Zola's experience of sexual abuse when he was five by a 12-year-old Arab servant boy played its part in determining his adult imaginative patterns. Sex in Zola's novels is seldom portrayed as emotionally satisfying.

The family tree of the score of descendants of Adélaïde Fouque projected for the Rougon-Macquart cycle, and drawn up according to Lucas's categories, was first published only on 5 January 1878 in *Le Bien Public*. Throughout the cycle Zola wanted his chapters to follow on smoothly as a logically ordered series of tableaux. He felt that the novelist's job was to produce and direct the phenomena whose mechanism is merely demonstrated. The novelist does not therefore, like the scientist, operate on facts which exist prior to his invention. Zola is not solely concerned with heredity, however, as Lucas was, and his view of the novel appears less idiosyncratically programmatic when we learn that the environmental component of the determinist mechanism includes the desires and appetites which affect all social classes. He wanted to portray the Second Empire panoramically, "from the ambush of the coup d'état to the betrayal of Sedan." *La Fortune des Rougon* starts therefore with the coup d'état of December 1851 establishing the Second Empire and the reign of Napoleon III, and the defeat of republican resistance in and around Plassans, for which we can read Aix. The family of Pierre Rougon plays an important part in establishing the conservative triumph and thereby lays the foundation of its fortune.

The reader is introduced to Adélaïde Fouque, whose marriage to Rougon is placed in 1786. She gives birth to Pierre in 1787, and Rougon dies unexpectedly in 1788. Adélaïde gives birth to two more children by Macquart, Antoine in 1789 and Ursule in 1791. Zola provides an aridly conscientious account of the genealogy, but the book gains pace with the depiction of the class struggle at Plassans. There is a strongly comic but biting undercurrent of satire at the expense of the bourgeois Bonapartists who are in the political fray for what they can get out of it. The idyllic love of Silvère and Miette is from the beginning closely associated with their deaths, setting up in the connection between love and death what was to be a recurring pattern in Zola's imagination, part of nature's unstoppable cycle of fertility, birth, growth, death, and even rebirth. There is a charmingly poetic flashback portraying the innocence of their young love, now successfully interwoven with the theme of their republican militancy rather than a mere lyrical intrusion into what had just been advertised as the first novel of a naturalistic cycle, clearly dependent on close documentation as well as on scientific hypothesis.

The first six novels show Zola at less than his full maturity. They still display ungainly features of style, such as top-heavy enumeration, and the excessive use of favourite verbs, adjectives, and adverbs, while the comic, epic, and poetic qualities of the literary vision are neither fully developed nor yet fully integrated. What does emerge is the author's growing preoccupation with unlikeable temperaments and with self-interest as the dominant motivation of all but a few idealistic characters. The materialism of the majority is at best alleviated by the idealism of the few.

In the sketch for *L'Assommoir* Zola felt that he could only save himself from platitude by the "enormity and truth" of his depiction of the working class. The title denotes a cheap bar where people knock themselves out ("assommer") with alcohol. In the novel the bar is owned by Colomb, and contains its own still, a machine which is given almost human characteristics and moral qualities. The 22-year-old Gervaise Macquart has had two illegitimate children, Claude and Etienne, by Lantier, who makes hats and who abandons her at the end of the first chapter. Gervaise's life is physically as well as socially determined by the working-class environment in which she lives although, after marrying Coupeau, a roofer, she goes up in the world and acquires her own shop. Coupeau falls, breaks a leg, and starts drinking too much. Their lives begin to fall apart. Gervaise spends too much, grows fat, and Zola uses a series of set-piece tableaux—a birthday party, a wedding, an uncomprehending visit to the Louvre—to impel the plot along.

He admits that he cheated with Goujet, the ironsmith respectfully in love with Gervaise, to whom he gave feelings "that do not belong to his environment." Machines are described in a way which anthropomorphizes their power to render Goujet unemployed, and the story of Gervaise's downfall is narrated partly in terms of where in the big tenement she actually lives. She moves upwards to the attic as she loses her shop; then as her fortunes plunge downwards she moves to a location beneath the stairs. Coupeau has become an alcoholic and dies of drink in a manner carefully documented by Zola. He had earlier invited Lantier back to share a room with Gervaise and himself, and Lantier now lives off Gervaise, abandoning her again when she becomes destitute. Gervaise is not able to achieve the modest security she aspires to, and dies at 41, very slowly and nastily. The novel shocked its readers by its use of a working-class vocabulary outside direct speech, and Zola makes no distinction of style between the dialogue and the narrative voice. The date of the action is not intrinsically linked to the novel's place in the cycle, of which it is generally judged independently, as a free-standing masterpiece only fortuitously taking its place in a cycle at all. What makes it an outstanding achievement is its exploitation of compassion as a spur to social action.

Nana is the story of a prostitute, an actress who ensnares and devours important members of Second Empire society, "a force of nature" that is both destructive and corruptive. She has no acting ability, but appears virtually naked on stage, epitomizing the object of lust. She is set up as a banker's mistress, gives herself out of the goodness of her heart to a young man, seduces Comte Muffat, and then takes up with an actor who treats her brutally. She has a lesbian affair and then renews her relationship with Muffat, who keeps her in luxury while she treats him with degrading contempt. Zola was quite unacquainted with the world he describes and, although he tried to provide himself with adequate factual documentation, he takes Muffat's degradation too far to be credible. His description of Nana's corpse at the end of the novel is intentionally disgusting.

In *Germinal*, the other great masterpiece of the cycle, Zola succeeds in tackling unsentimentally and with great dramatic skill one of the most severe and intractable problems of the 19th century. Virtually all the characters, but especially the miners and their families, are predestined to defeat though, oddly and illogically, this novel, like the cycle as a whole, ends on a note of unmotivated hope. There are three principal middle-class characters: a shareholder in the mine where the miners are on strike, at whose expense Zola permits himself no more than light irony; the owner of a small neighbouring mine who is ruined; and the local manager of the Montsou mine, who grinds no personal axe. Lantier's character moderated considerably in the passage from sketch to novel, and the attitudes of Rasseneur, his

rival for the leadership of the miners, point up the differences between their political groupings in the spectrum from hardline militant revolutionaries to moderate reformists.

The action centres round a miner's family, the Maheus, one of whose daughters, Catherine, develops a fondness for Lantier and dies in his arms, another of those moments in which love and death are united. Two other members of the family die during the action, one of starvation and the other from a bullet wound, while the shareholder's daughter is strangled by a third Maheu. The action is largely symbolic. The fate of the individuals is touching, but there is a sense in which they are acting out mythical roles governed by forces which dwarf considerations of individual characters and temperaments. Again the novel, which has 40 chapters and seven parts, proceeds in a series of tableaux that move the action forward. Violence alternates with repose, and individuals act in unpredictable ways. In the final part Souvarine sabotages the mine to create an epic ending of death, heroism, and dissolution.

The two other major novels deal respectively with peasant workers on the land, and with war. While undertaking the usual documentation for *La Terre* (in this case a visit to La Beauce, France's principal arable area), Zola was conscious that he wanted to write the poetic myth of the implacable natural cycle of generation, birth, growth, death, and rebirth. Here the recurrent primeval forces are the seasons, the weather, fertility, growth, and death. The novel was generally found shocking, but there is nothing provocative in the description of a bull inseminating a cow or of a cow giving birth to a calf while Buteau's wife is giving birth to a baby a few feet away. Buteau, Hyacinthe, and Fanny Delhomme, the children of the old peasant Fouan, take over their father's land in return for an annuity which they fail to pay. Buteau's marriage to Lise, by whom he already has an illegitimate child, brings him Lise's land, and he tries to stop Lise's sister Françoise from marrying Jean Macquart, so that he can keep her land, too. Buteau rapes Françoise, who is more attracted to him than to the worthy Macquart, whom she does in fact marry. The novel has many lyrical passages, but ends in catastrophe as Fouan starves to death, Lise murders Françoise after assisting at the rape, and the buildings of a bigger farmer burn down and the farmer himself dies. The Franco-Prussian War is looming and agricultural prices force widespread bankruptcies. "La terre est épuisée" (the land is exhausted), exclaims the bigger proprietor, but the novel ends on a defiantly hopeful note. Zola adds a magnificent final three paragraphs, ending: "Des morts, des semences et le pain poussaient de la terre" (The dead, seeds, and bread grew out of the earth).

La Débâcle consists of three parts, each of eight chapters, and is documented with Zola's usual care. Historical characters mingle with fictitious ones, and the interest centres on the fate of Jean Macquart's six-man platoon. As in *La Terre*, the action proceeds in tableaux, like the set piece of the defence of Bazeilles. The war scenes render battle as meaningless an experience as it had been for Fabrice in Stendhal's *La Chartreuse de Parme*, but it is now far more brutal. There is no real story here; there are only episodes linking characters and events from Sedan to the Commune. Zola's political sympathies are at best subdued, and the novel again ends with the defiant phoenix of hope rising out of a great catastrophe, the burning of Paris, death, and rebirth. Again the novel's final paragraphs contain a magnificently written set piece, its only weakness the overt sentimentality of unmotivated hope in the last four lines.

Agatha (p Duras), 1981
Agathe (v Valéry), 1956
Age cassant (v Char), 1965
Age de craie (v Pieyre de Mandiargues), 1960
Age de l'humanité (v Salmon), 1921
Age de raison (f Sartre), 1945
Age d'homme (Leiris), 1939
Age d'or (p Feydeau),1905
Age of Reason (f Sartre), 1947
Age of Suspicion (Sarraute), 1963
Agence Thompson (f Verne), 1907
Agenor de Mauleon (f Dumas père), 1897
Agénor le dangereux (p Labiche), 1848
Aglavaine and Selysette (p Maeterlinck), 1897
Aglavaine et Sélysette (p Maeterlinck), 1896
Agneau (f F. Mauriac), 1954
Agrandissement (f C. Mauriac), 1963
Ah! Ernesto (f Duras), 1971
A-Hunting We Will Go (p Feydeau), 1976
Aigle a deux têtes (p Cocteau), 1946
Aigle des Pyrénées (p Pixérécourt), 1829
Ailes du diable (f Troyat), 1966
Ailes rouges de la guerre (v Verhaeren), 1916
Ailleurs (v Michaux), 1948
Aimer l'amour (f Simenon), 1928
Aimer, mourir (f Simenon), 1928
Aimez-vous Brahms? (f Sagan), 1959
Aîné des Ferchaux (f Simenon), 1945
Ainsi soit-il (Gide), 1952
Air de l'eau (v Breton), 1934
Air et les songes (Bachelard), 1943
Aire du Muguet (f Tournier), 1982
Airs (v Jaccottet), 1967
Akëdysséril (Villiers de l'Isle Adam), 1886
Albert Savarus (f Balzac), 1842
Albertine disparue (f Proust), 1925
Albertus (v Gautier), 1832
Albine (f Dumas père), 1843
Album de douze chansons (v Maeterlinck), 1896
Album de vers anciens (v Valéry), 1920
Album d'un amateur (Simon), 1988
Alchemist (f Balzac), 1861
Alchimiste (p Dumas père, Nerval), 1839
Alcools (v Apollinaire), 1913
Aldomen (Senancour), 1795
Alexis (f Yourcenar), 1929
Ali-Baba (p Pixérécourt), 1822
Ali-Baba (p Scribe), 1833
All Is Fair in Love and War (p A. Musset), 1868
All Men Are Mortal (f Beauvoir), 1956
All Said and Done (Beauvoir), 1974
All Strange Away (p Beckett), 1979
All That Fall (p Beckett), 1957
All Women Are Fatal (f C. Mauriac), 1964
Alladine and Palomides (p Maeterlinck), 1895
Alladine et Palomides (p Maeterlinck), 1894
Allée des Veuves (p Pixérécourt), 1833
Allégories (v Cocteau), 1941
Allegra (f Mallet-Joris), 1976
Allégresse (v Char), 1960
Aller retour (f Aymé), 1927

Alliés sont en Arménie (Jacob), 1916
Almaïde d'Etremont (Jammes), 1901
Almanach de l'Ymagier (Gourmont), 1897
Alms of Alcippe (v Yourcenar), 1982
Alouette (p Anouilh), 1953
Alphabets (Perec), 1976
Amadis (v Gobineau), 1876
Amaïdée (f Barbey D'Aurevilly), 1889
Amal (p Gide), 1922
Amandine (f Tournier), 1977
Amant (f Duras), 1984
Amant bossu (p Scribe), 1821
Amant complaisant (p Anouilh), 1962
Amant de la Chine du Nord (f Duras), 1991
Amant des Amazones (f Salmon), 1921
Amant fantôme (f Simenon), 1928
Amant sans nom (f Simenon), 1929
Amante anglaise (f Duras), 1967
Amante anglaise (p Duras), 1968
Amants de la mansarde (f Simenon), 1928
Amants du malheur (f Simenon), 1930
Amants du métro (p Tardieu), 1952
Amants, heureux amants (f Larbaud), 1920
Amaury (f Dumas père), 1844
Ambassadeur (p Scribe), 1826
Ambassadrice (p Scribe), 1837
Ambitieux (p Scribe), 1834
Âme à naître (f Dumas père), 1844
Ame de jeune fille (f Simenon), 1931
Ame des hommes (v Romains), 1904
Ame enchantée (f Rolland), 1922–34
Ame et la danse (Valéry), 1923
Amédée (p Ionesco), 1954
Amédée (p Romains), 1923
Amelia in Love (f Troyat), 1956
Amélie (f Troyat), 1955
Amélie and Pierre (f Troyat), 1957
Amers (v Saint-John Perse), 1957
Ames fortes (f Giono), 1949
Ames mortes (p Adamov), 1960
Amethyst Ring (f France), 1919
Améthystes (v Banville), 1861
Ami acharné (p Labiche), 1853
Ami des femmes (p Dumas fils), 1864
Amies (v Verlaine), 1868
Amiral Levacher (f Sue), 1852
Amis inconnus (v Supervielle), 1934
Amitiés du prince (v Saint-John Perse), 1979
Ammalet Beg (f Dumas père), 1859
Amorandes (f Benda), 1922
Amoreux de Sainte-Périne (f Champfleury), 1859
Amour (f Duras), 1972
Amour (v Verlaine), 1888
Amour à Montparnasse (f Simenon), 1928
Amour absolu (f Jarry), 1899
Amour d'Afrique (f Simenon), 1925
Amour d'exilée (f Simenon), 1925
Amour en sabots (p Labiche), 1861
Amour en visites (f Jarry), 1898
Amour et l'argent (f Simenon), 1929

Amour et piano (p Feydeau), 1887

Amour fou (Breton), 1937

Amour impossible (f Barbey D'Aurevilly), 1841

Amour la poésie (Éluard), 1929

Amour, les muses et la chasse (Jammes), 1922

Amour méconnu (f Simenon), 1928

Amour nuptial (f Lacretelle), 1929

Amour platonique (p Scribe), 1821

Amour suprême (Villiers de l'Isle Adam), 1886

Amour, un fort volume prix 3 fr 50 (p Labiche), 1859

Amoureuses (v A. Daudet), 1858

Amours de l'âge d'or (f Sand), 1871

Amours jaunes (v Corbière), 1873

Amphion (p Valéry), 1931

Amphitryon 38 (p Giraudoux), 1929

Amschaspands et Darvands (Lamennais), 1843

Amy Robsart (p Hugo), 1827

An mil (p Romains), 1947

An 1964 (v Char), 1964

Anabase (v Saint-John Perse), 1924

Anabasis (v Saint-John Perse), 1930

Anatomy of Dandyism with Some Observations on Beau Brummel (f Barbey D'Aurevilly), 1928

Ancien Régime et la Révolution (Tocqueville), 1856

André (f Sand), 1835

André Cornélis (f Bourget), 1887

André del Sarto (p A. Musset), 1834

Andréa (p Sardou), 1875

Ane (v Hugo), 1880

Ane et le ruisseau (p A. Musset), 1860

Ane rouge (f Simenon), 1933

Ange (v Valéry), 1946

Ange Heurtebise (v Cocteau), 1926

Ange Pitou (f Dumas père), 1851

Ange tutélaire (p Pixérécourt), 1808

Angèle (p Dumas père), 1833

Angelo (f Giono), 1959

Angelo, Tyran de Padoue (p Hugo), 1835

Anges noirs (f F. Mauriac), 1936

Anglais décrit dans le château fermé (f Pieyre de Mandiargues),
  1953

Anglora (v Mistral), 1937

Anicet (Aragon), 1921

Annabella (p Maeterlinck), 1894

Anne Prédaille (f Troyat), 1973

Anneau d'améthyste (f France), 1899

Anneaux de Bicêtre (f Simenon), 1963

Année dernière à Marienbad (f Robbe-Grillet), 1961

Année des vaincus (f Chamson), 1934

Année terrible (v Hugo), 1872

Années d'espérance (f Lacretelle), 1932

Annette et le criminel (f Balzac), 1824

Annie, danseuse (f Simenon), 1928

Annonce faite à Marie (p Claudel), 1912

Anomalies (f Bourget), 1920

Anomalous Phenomena (f Verne), 1878

Antarctic Fugue (Cendrars), 1948

Antarctic Mystery (f Verne), 1898

Anthologie (v Char), 1960

Anthologie nègre (Cendrars), 1921

Anthropologie structurale (Lévi-Strauss), 1958–73

Antigone (p Anouilh), 1944

Antigone (p Cocteau), 1922

Antigyde (Jammes), 1932

Anti-Platon (v Bonnefoy), 1947

Anti-Semite and Jew (Sartre), 1948

Antisémite sincère (Benda), 1944

Antoine Bloyé (f Nizan), 1933

Antoine et Cléopatre (p Gide), 1920

Antoine et Julie (f Simenon), 1953

Antonia (f Sand), 1863

Antonine (f Dumas fils), 1849

Antony (p Dumas père), 1831

Aphrodite (Louÿs), 1896

Aphroessa (v Gobineau), 1869

Apocryphe (f Pinget), 1980

Apollo Society (p Tardieu), 1968

Apollon de Bellac (p Giraudoux), 1959

Apollon de Marsac (p Giraudoux), 1942

Apollon du réverbère (p Scribe), 1832

Apologie du luxe (Aragon), 1946

Apparition de l'homme (Teilhard de Chardin), 1956

Apparitions (v Michaux), 1946

Apparus dans mes chemins (v Verhaeren), 1891

Appearance of Man (Teilhard de Chardin), 1965

Appel aux nations chrétiennes en faveur des Grecs (Constant de
  Rebecque), 1825

Appogiatures (v Cocteau), 1953

Appositions (Benda), 1930

Apprendre à marcher (p Ionesco), 1960

Apprenti psychiâtre (f Green), 1976

Après-midi de Monsieur Andesmas (f Duras), 1962

Après-midi d'un faune (v Mallarmé), 1876

Aquarium (v Soupault), 1917

Araigne (f Troyat), 1938

Araignée (v Ponge), 1952

Arbres et des hommes (p Tardieu), 1969

Arcane 17 (Breton), 1944

Arc-en-ciel des amours (v Jammes), 1931

Archaeology of Knowledge (Foucault), 1972

Arche de Noé (f Supervielle), 1938

Archéologie du savoir (Foucault), 1969

Archipel en feu (f Verne), 1884

Archipel Lenoir (p Salacrou), 1947

Archipelago on Fire (f Verne), 1886

Archiprêtre des Cévennes (f Sue), 1840

Architruc (p Pinget), 1961

Archives du club des onze (f Salmon), 1923

Arcimboldo le merveilleux (Pieyre de Mandiargues), 1977

Arcimboldo the Marvelous (Pieyre de Mandiargues), 1978

Ardèle (p Anouilh), 1948

Ardoises du toit (v Reverdy), 1918

Argent (f Zola), 1891

Argent (Péguy), 1913

Argent, Rentiers, agioteurs, millionnaires (Vallès), 1857

Ariane and Barbe-Bleue (p Maeterlinck), 1901

Ariane et Barbe-Bleue (p Maeterlinck), 1901

Arlequin de plomb (v Fort), 1936

Arlésienne (p A. Daudet), 1872

Armance (f Stendhal), 1827

Arme secrète (v Soupault), 1946

Armée dans la ville (p Romains), 1911

Armes miraculeuses (v Césaire), 1946
Aromates chasseurs (v Char), 1975
Around the World in Eighty Days (f Verne), 1874
Arrache-coeur (f Vian), 1953
Arrest (p Anouilh), 1978
Arrestation (p Anouilh), 1975
Arsenal (v Char), 1929
Arsène et Cléopâtre (p Pieyre de Mandiargues), 1981
Art bref (v Char), 1950
Art de ne pas donner d'étrennes (p Labiche), 1847
Art de plaire (f Sue), 1839
Art d'être grand-père (v Hugo), 1877
Art poétique (Claudel), 1907
Art poétique (Jacob), 1922
Art romantique (Baudelaire), 1868
Artful Cards (p Labiche), 1877
Arthur (f Sue), 1838
Article 960 (p Labiche), 1839
Artine (v Char), 1930
Artiste (p Scribe), 1825
Artists' Wives (f A. Daudet), 1890
As We Were (p Adamov), 1957
Ascanio (f Dumas père), 1843–44
Asmodée (p F. Mauriac), 1937
Asmodeus, the Little Demon (p Scribe), 1850
Asphyxie (f Leduc), 1946
Assassin (f Simenon), 1937
Assassin est mon maître (f Montherlant), 1971
Assassinated Poet (f Apollinaire), 1923
Assez (f Beckett), 1966
Assommoir (f Zola), 1877
Astarté (Louÿs), 1891
Astonished Man (Cendrars), 1970
Astyanax (v Pieyre de Mandiargues), 1956
At the Antipodes of Unity (Cendrars), 1922
At the Gai-Moulin (f Simenon), 1940
At the Sign of the Reine Pédauque (f France), 1912
Atala (f Chateaubriand), 1801
Atala (p Dumas fils), 1848
Atar-Gull (f Sue), 1831
Atar-Gull (p Sue), 1832
Atlas-Hôtel (p Salacrou), 1931
Attack on the Mill (f Zola), 1892
Attempt at Love (f Gide), 1953
Attente de Dieu (Weil), 1950
Au bonheur des dames (f Zola), 1883
Au bord de la route (v Verhaeren), 1891
Au bout du rouleau (f Simenon), 1947
Au grand 13 (f Simenon), 1925
Au regard des divinités (v Breton), 1949
Au rendez-vous allemand (Éluard), 1944
Au rendez-vous des Terre-Neuves (f Simenon), 1931
Au temps de Judas (f L. Daudet), 1920
Auberge (p Scribe), 1812
Auberge de l'abîme (f Chamson), 1933
Auberge des Ardennes (p Verne), 1860
Aubes (p Verhaeren), 1898
Au-dessus de la mêlée (Rolland), 1915
Au-devant de la nuit (v Maurras), 1946
Augmentation (Perec), 1970
Aujourd'hui (Cendrars), 1931

Aunt Jeanne (f Simenon), 1953
Aurelia (f Nerval), 1930
Aurélia Steiner (p Duras), 1979
Aurélien (Aragon), 1944
Aurora (Leiris), 1946
Aussi longue absence (p Duras), 1961
Autobiographer as Toreo (Leiris), 1968
Automate (p Green), 1985
Automne à Pékin (f Vian), 1947
Autour de la lune (f Verne), 1870
Autour de Mortin (p Pinget), 1965
Autre (f Green), 1971
Autre étude de femme (f Balzac), 1842
Autre Sommeil (f Green), 1931
Autres (f Simenon), 1962
Autres lancers (v Leiris), 1969
Autres poèmes durant la guerre (v Claudel), 1916
Aux antipodes (p Feydeau), 1883
Aux Orphéonistes (v Deschamps), 1847
Aux vingt-huit négresses (f Simenon), 1925
Avant, pendant et après (p Scribe), 1828
Avare en gants jaunes (p Labiche), 1858
Avare en goguette (p Scribe), 1823
Avarice House (f Green), 1927
Avec mon meilleur souvenir (f Sagan), 1984
Avenir de la science (Renan), 1890
Avenir de l'homme (Teilhard de Chardin), 1959
Avenir est dans les oeufs (p Ionesco), 1957
Aventure d'amour (f Dumas père), 1860
Aventures de Hercule Hardi (f Sue), 1840
Aventures de Jérôme Bardini (f Giraudoux), 1930
Aventures de John Davys (f Dumas père), 1840
Aventures de la dialectique (Merleau-Ponty), 1955
Aventures de Lyderic (f Dumas père), 1842
Aventures de Mademoiselle Mariette (f Champfleury), 1853
Aventures de quatre femmes et d'un perroquet (f Dumas fils), 1846–47
Aventures de Télémaque (Aragon), 1922
Aventures de trois russes et de trois anglais (f Verne), 1872
Aventures du Capitaine Hatteras (f Verne), 1864
Aventures du dernier Abencérage (f Chateaubriand), 1826
Aventures du roi Pausole (Louÿs), 1900
Aventures et voyages du petit Jonas (p Scribe), 1829
Aventures prodigieuses de Tartarin de Tarascon (f A. Daudet), 1872
Aventurière (p Augier), 1848
Aveugles (p Maeterlinck), 1890
Aveux (v Bourget), 1882
Avez-vous lu Victor Hugo? (Aragon), 1952
Avis aux coquettes (p Scribe), 1837
Avis aux femmes (p Pixérécourt), 1804
Avocat d'un Grec (p Labiche), 1859
Avocat Loubet (p Labiche), 1838
Avocat-pédicure (p Labiche), 1847
Avvroës et l'averroïsme (Renan), 1852
Axël (Villiers de l'Isle Adam), 1890
Aziyadé (f Loti), 1879

Babiole et Jablot (p Scribe), 1844
Bacchante (Guérin), 1862
Bacchante (Thais) (p Dumas père), 1858

Bacchantes (f L. Daudet), 1932
Bacchus (p Cocteau), 1951
Bachelier (Vallès), 1881
Bachelier de Salamanque (p Scribe), 1815
Bachelors (f Montherlant), 1960
Bachelor's Establishment (f Balzac)
Baga (f Pinget), 1958
Bagatelles végétales (v Leiris), 1956
Bagpipers (f Sand), 1890
Bague d'Annibal (f Barbey D'Aurevilly), 1843
Bain de ménage (p Feydeau), 1889
Baiser (p Banville), 1888
Baiser au lépreux (f F. Mauriac), 1922
Baiser au porteur (p Scribe), 1828
Baisers mortels (f Simenon), 1930
Baker, The Baker's Wife, and the Baker's Boy (p Anouilh), 1972
Bal champêtre (p Scribe), 1824
Bal des voleurs (p Anouilh), 1938
Bal du comte d'Orgel (f Radiguet), 1924
Bal en robe de chambre (p Labiche), 1850
Bal masqué (Jacob), 1932
Balance intérieure (v Maurras), 1952
Balcon (p Genet), 1956
Balcon en forêt (f Gracq), 1958
Balcony (p Genet), 1957
Balcony in the Forest (f Gracq), 1959
Bald Soprano (p Ionesco), 1956
Balkan Tavern (f Istrati), 1931
Ball at Count d'Orgel's (f Radiguet), 1929
Ball of Snow (f Dumas père), 1895
Ballades (Jacob), 1938
Ballades françaises (v Fort), 1897
Balle au bond (v Reverdy), 1927
Ballets, sans musique, sans personne, sans rien (p Céline), 1959
Balthasar (f France), 1889
Balthazar (f Balzac), 1859
Balzacs en bas de casse et Picassos sans majuscules (Leiris), 1957
Banana Tourist (f Simenon), 1946
Bandits (f Istrati), 1929
Bandits de Chicago (f Simenon), 1929
Bankrupt (f Balzac), 1959
Banlieue de l'aube à l'aurore (v Butor), 1968
Bar de l'amour (f Soupault), 1925
Barbare en Asie (Michaux), 1933
Barbares (p Sardou), 1901
Barbarian in Asia (Michaux), 1949
Barbe-bleue, Jeanne d'Arc et mes amours (v Fort), 1919
Barbedor (f Tournier), 1980
Barberine (p A. Musset), 1853
Barcarolle (p Scribe), 1845
Bariona (p Sartre), 1940
Bark Tree (f Queneau), 1968
Baron de Fourchevif (p Labiche), 1859
Baron de Trenck (p Scribe), 1828
Baroness (f Troyat), 1961
Baronnie de Muhldorf (p Sand)
Barrage contre le Pacifique (f Duras), 1950
Barricade (p Bourget), 1920
Barrière de Clichy (p Dumas père), 1851
Barrière de Mont-Parnasse (p Scribe), 1817

Barynia (f Troyat), 1959
Basic Verities (Péguy), 1943
Basses-Pyrénées (Jammes), 1926
Bastard of Mauleon (f Dumas père), 1849
Bataille d'amour (p Sardou), 1863
Bataille de la Marne (v Maurras), 1923
Bataille de Pharsale (Simon), 1969
Bataille des dames (p Scribe), 1851
Batailles dans la montagne (f Giono), 1937
Bâtard de Mauléon (f Dumas père), 1846
Bâtarde (f Leduc), 1964
Bateau d'Emile (f Simenon), 1954
Bateau d'or (f Simenon), 1935
Bathilde (p Dumas père), 1839
Bathsheba (p Gide), 1951
Battle of Love (p A. Daudet), 1892
Battle of Nerves (f Simenon), 1939
Battre la campagne (v Queneau), 1968
B.B.V. (f Supervielle), 1949
Beast in Man (f Zola), 1958
Beatrix (f Balzac), 1839
Beau Laurence (f Sand), 1870
Beau Léandre (p Banville), 1856
Beau mariage (p Augier), 1859
Beau Narcisse (p Scribe), 1821
Beau Tancred (f Dumas père), 1861
Beau ténébreux (f Gracq), 1945
Beau Voyage (v Bataille), 1905
Beauté du diable (p Salacrou), 1959
Beauties of Christianity (Chateaubriand), 1813
Beaux Messieurs de Bois-Doré (f Sand), 1858
Beaux Messieurs de Bois-Doré (p Sand), 1862
Beaux Quartiers (Aragon), 1936
Becket (p Anouilh), 1959
Before We Were So Rudely Interrupted (p Feydeau), 1973
Beggar of Nimes (f Dumas fils), 1888
Begum's Fortune (f Verne), 1880
Behind a Mask (f A. Daudet), 1890
Being and Nothingness (Sartre), 1956
Bel-Ami (f Maupassant), 1885
Bella (f Giraudoux), 1926
Bella-Vista (f Colette), 1937
Belle (f Simenon), 1954
Belle au bois (p Supervielle), 1932
Belle au bois dormant (p Scribe), 1829
Belle et la bête (p Cocteau), 1958
Belle Image (f Aymé), 1941
Belle Isabeau (f Sue), 1840
Belle Lisa (f Zola), 1882
Belle Nivernaise (f A. Daudet), 1886
Belle saison (f Martin du Gard), 1923
Belle Vie (p Anouilh), 1980
Belle-Maman (p Sardou), 1889
Belle-mère (p Scribe), 1826
Belles Images (f Beauvoir), 1966
Bells of Basel (Aragon), 1936
Bells of Bicetre (f Simenon), 1964
Belluaires et porchers (f Bloy), 1905
Beloukia (f Drieu la Rochelle), 1936
Belphégor (Benda), 1918

Belvédère (p Pixérécourt), 1819
Belvedere (Pieyre de Mandiargues), 1958
Berceau (p Pixérécourt), 1811
Berceuse (p Beckett), 1982
Bergelon (f Simenon), 1941
Bergère de la rue Monthabor (p Labiche), 1865
Bergsonisme (Benda), 1912
Berniquel (p Maeterlinck), 1923
Bertrand de Ganges (f Romains), 1947
Bertrand du Guesclin (Gourmont), 1883
Bertrand et Raton (p Scribe), 1833
Besoin de voir clair (f Romains), 1958
Bestiaire (v Apollinaire), 1911
Bestiaires (f Montherlant), 1926
Bête dans la jungle (p Duras), 1962
Bête humaine (f Zola), 1890
Bethsabé (p Gide), 1912
Betly (p Scribe), 1838
Betrayal of the Intellectuals (Benda), 1955
Betrothal (p Maeterlinck), 1919
Better Late (p Feydeau), 1976
Bettine (p A. Musset), 1851
Betty (f Simenon), 1961
Between Blue and Blue (f Queneau), 1967
Between Fantoine and Agapa (f Pinget), 1982
Between Life and Death (f Sarraute), 1969
Bewitched (f Barbey D'Aurevilly), 1928
Biblio-sonnets (v Verlaine), 1913
Bibliothèque est en feu (v Char), 1956
Bièvre (f Huysmans), 1890
Big Bob (f Simenon), 1969
Bigote (p Renard), 1909
Bilan Maletras (f Simenon), 1948
Billet de loterie (f Verne), 1886
Billet de mille (p Feydeau), 1885
Billets de Sirius (Benda), 1925
Bing (f Beckett), 1966
Biographie de mes fantômes (f Duhamel), 1945
Bird of Fate (f Dumas père), 1906
Birds (v Saint-John Perse), 1966
Birth of the Clinic (Foucault), 1973
Black (f Dumas père), 1858
Black Domino (p Scribe), 1837
Black Pearl (p Sardou), 1915
Black Rain (f Simenon), 1947
Black Sheep (f Balzac), 1970
Blacks (p Genet), 1960
Blanc à lunettes (f Simenon), 1937
Blanche (Aragon), 1967
Blancs et les bleus (f Dumas père), 1867–68
Blancs et les bleus (p Dumas père), 1869
Blaze of Embers (f Pieyre de Mandiargues), 1971
Blé en herbe (f Colette), 1923
Blèche (f Drieu la Rochelle), 1928
Blés mouvants (v Verhaeren), 1912
Blind (p Maeterlinck), 1891
Blind Alley (f Simenon), 1946
Blood of a Poet (p Cocteau), 1949
Blood of Others (f Beauvoir), 1948
Blue Bird (p Maeterlinck), 1909
Blue Boy (f Giono), 1946

Blue Duchess (f Bourget), 1908
Blue Eyes, Black Hair (f Duras), 1988
Blue Flowers (f Queneau), 1967
Blue Lantern (Colette), 1963
Blue Room (f Simenon), 1964
Bobette et ses satyres (f Simenon), 1928
Bobette, mannequin (f Simenon), 1930
Bocquet, père et fils (p Labiche), 1840
Boën (p Romains), 1930
Boeuf clandestin (f Aymé), 1939
Bohémienne (p Scribe), 1829
Bolivar (p Supervielle), 1936
Bon Apôtre (f Soupault), 1923
Bon Dieu chez les enfants (Jammes), 1921
Bon Papa (p Scribe), 1822
Bon Sens et les études classiques (Bergson), 1947
Bonheur (v Sully Prudhomme), 1888
Bonheur (v Verlaine), 1891
Bonheur de Lili (f Simenon), 1930
Bonheur fou (f Giono), 1957
Bonheur impair et passe (p Sagan), 1964
Bonhomme Jadis (p Murger), 1852
Bonifas (f Lacretelle), 1925
Bonjour, Tristesse (f Sagan), 1954
Bonne Aventure (f Sue), 1851
Bonne Chanson (v Verlaine), 1870
Bonnes (p Genet), 1946
Book of Christopher Columbus (p Claudel), 1930
Book of Flights (f Le Clézio), 1971
Book of Pity and of Death (f Loti), 1892
Boor Hug (p Feydeau), 1982
Bottom of the Bottle (f Simenon), 1954
Bouches inutiles (p Beauvoir), 1945
Bouddha s'est mis à trembler (f C. Mauriac), 1979
Boulanger, la boulangère, et le petit mitron (p Anouilh), 1968
Boule de neige (f Dumas père), 1859
Boule de verre (p Salacrou), 1958
Boule noire (f Simenon), 1955
Boulevard Bonne-Nouvelle (p Scribe), 1821
Boulevard Durand (p Salacrou), 1960
Bouquet de Glycère (Benda), 1918
Bourg régénéré (f Romains), 1906
Bourgeois de Molinchart (f Champfleury), 1855
Bourgeois de Pont-Arcy (p Sardou), 1878
Bourgeon (p Feydeau), 1907
Bourgmestre de Furnes (f Simenon), 1939
Bourgmestre de Stilmonde (p Maeterlinck), 1919
Bourgomaster of Furnes (f Simenon), 1952
Bourlinguer (Cendrars), 1948
Bourses de voyage (f Verne), 1903
Bout de la route (p Giono), 1943
Boutique obscure (Perec), 1973
Bouton de Rose (p Pixérécourt), 1819
Bouton de Rose (p Zola), 1878
Boutons dorés (f Leduc), 1958
Bouvard and Pecuchet (f Flaubert), 1896
Bouvard et Pécuchet (f Flaubert), 1881
Boy and the Magic (p Colette), 1964
Bras d'Ernest (p Labiche), 1857
Break of Day (f Colette), 1961
Break of Noon (p Claudel), 1960

Breath (p Beckett), 1969
Breathings (v Jaccottet), 1974
Brebis égarée (v Jammes), 1923
Breton Sisters (f Simenon), 1943
Brigand (f Dumas père), 1897
Brin d'amour (f Simenon), 1928
Brindilles pour rallumer la foi (v Jammes), 1925
Brisées (Leiris), 1966
Brocéliande (Aragon), 1942
Brocéliande (p Montherlant), 1956
Bronze Horse (p Scribe), 1836
Broskovano (p Scribe), 1858
Brotherhood of the Red Poppy (f Troyat), 1961
Brothers Rico (f Simenon), 1954
Broyeur de lin (Renan), 1876
Bruissement de la langue (Barthes), 1984
Brûlebois (f Aymé), 1926
Brûlons Voltaire! (p Labiche), 1874
Brumes du passé (v Supervielle), 1901
Bucoliques (f Renard), 1898
Bucoliques (v Queneau), 1947
Budding Lovers (p Feydeau), 1969
Budget d'un jeune ménage (p Scribe), 1831
Bug-Jargal (f Hugo), 1826
Building the Earth (Teilhard de Chardin), 1965
Bulles Billes Boules (v Soupault), 1930
Burbank the Northerner (f Verne), 1888
Bureau de placement (f Istrati), 1933
Bureaucracy (f Balzac), 1889
Burgomaster of Stilmonde (p Maeterlinck), 1918
Burgraves (p Hugo), 1843
Burial of Monsieur Bouvet (f Simenon), 1955
…but the clouds… (p Beckett), 1977
Buveurs de cendres (f Du Camp), 1866
Buveurs d'eau (f Murger), 1853
By Order of the King (f Hugo), 1870
By Way of Sainte-Beuve (Proust), 1958

Cabinet d'amateur (Perec), 1979
Cabinet des antiques (f Balzac), 1839
Cabinet noir (Jacob), 1922
Cabotine… (f Simenon), 1928
Cachemire vert (p Dumas père), 1849
Cachemire X.-B.-T. (p Labiche), 1870
Cachet d'onyx (f Barbey D'Aurevilly), 1919
Cadastre (v Césaire), 1961
Cadets de l'Alcazar (Brasillach), 1936
Cadio (f Sand), 1868
Cadio (p Sand), 1868
Caelina (p Pixérécourt), 1802
Caesar (p Scribe), 1886
Caesar-Antichrist (p Jarry), 1971
Café Céleste (f Mallet-Joris), 1959
Café des variétés (p Scribe), 1817
Cage de verre (f Simenon), 1971
Caged Beasts (f Duhamel), 1936
Cagliostro (p Scribe), 1844
Cagnotte (p Labiche), 1864
Cahier (f Troyat), 1968
Cahier d'un retour au pays natal (v Césaire), 1947
Cahier gris (f Martin du Gard), 1922

Cahier rouge (Constant de Rebecque), 1907
Cahiers d'André Walter (f Gide), 1891
Cahiers d'un clerc (Benda), 1949
Calendau (v Mistral), 1867
Calife de la rue Saint-Bon (p Labiche), 1858
Caligula (p Camus), 1944
Caligula (p Dumas père), 1837
Call Me Maestro (p Feydeau), 1973
Call to Order (Cocteau), 1926
Calligrammes (v Apollinaire), 1918
Calomnie (p Scribe), 1840
Calumet (v Salmon), 1910
Calvaire (f Mirbeau), 1887
Camaraderie (p Scribe), 1837
Camera Lucida (Barthes), 1981
Camilla (p Scribe), 1833
Camille (p Dumas fils), 1934
Camion (p Duras), 1977
Camp de drap d'or (v Fort), 1926
Campagnes hallucinées (v Verhaeren), 1893
Canadar père et fils (p Labiche), 1852
Canadiens de France (Gourmont), 1893
Candidat (p Flaubert), 1874
Candide (p Sardou), 1860
Cantate à trois voix (v Claudel), 1931
Cantatrice chauve (p Ionesco), 1950
Cantilènes (v Moréas), 1886
Cantique à Elsa (Aragon), 1941
Cantique des cantiques (p Giraudoux), 1938
Cap de Bonne-Espérance (v Cocteau), 1919
Capitaine Burle (f Zola), 1882
Capitaine de quinze ans (f Verne), 1878
Capitaine Fracasse (f Gautier), 1863
Capitaine Paul (f Dumas père), 1838
Capitaine Richard (f Dumas père), 1858
Capitale de la douleur (Éluard), 1926
Caprice (p A. Musset), 1840
Caprices de Marianne (p A. Musset), 1834
Caprices du poète (Jammes), 1923
Captain Antifer (f Verne), 1895
Captain of the Guidara (f Verne), 1884
Captain Paul (f Dumas père), 1848
Captain, S.O.S. (f Simenon), 1929
Captive (f Proust), 1929
Cardinal d'Espagne (p Montherlant), 1960
Cariatides (v Banville), 1842
Carlin (Sardou), 1932
Carlo Broschi (p Scribe), 1840
Carmagnola (p Scribe), 1841
Carmelites (f Bernanos), 1961
Carmen (Mérimée), 1847
Carmosine (p A. Musset), 1853
Carnet du bois de pins (v Ponge), 1947
Carnets de voyage (Taine), 1896
Caroline (p Scribe), 1825
Carrosse du Saint Sacrement (p Mérimée), 1850
Carrots (f Renard), 1946
Carrots (p Renard), 1904
Carte postale (Soupault), 1926
Cartolines et dédicaces (v Pieyre de Mandiargues), 1960
Cas de rupture (f Dumas fils), 1854

Chien jaune (f Simenon), 1931
Chien-Caillou (f Champfleury), 1847
Chiendent (f Queneau), 1933
Chiens de paille (f Drieu la Rochelle), 1944
Chiffre (v Cocteau), 1952
Child of the Cavern (f Verne), 1877
Childhood's Dreams (p Dumas père), 1881
Children of the Black Sabbath (f Hébert), 1977
Children of the Game (f Cocteau), 1955
Child's Romance (f Loti), 1891
Chimeras (v Nerval), 1966
Chimères (v Nerval),1854
Chinois de San-Francisco (f Simenon), 1930
Chips Are Down (p Sartre), 1948
Chit of a Girl (f Simenon), 1949
Choéphores (p Claudel), 1920
Choix des élues (f Giraudoux), 1938
Choix d'un gendre (p Labiche), 1869
Choses (Perec), 1965
Choses communes (Perec), 1978
Chouan (f Balzac), 1838
Chouans (f Balzac), 1834
Christ évoluteur (Teilhard de Chardin), 1965
Christianisme (Constant de Rebecque), 1825
Christianity and Evolution (Teilhard de Chardin), 1971
Christine (f Green), 1927
Christine (p Dumas père), 1830
Christophe Colombe (p Pixérécourt), 1815
Chronique (v Saint-John Perse), 1960
Chronique de la Grande Guerre (Barrès), 1931–39
Chronique des Pasquier (f Duhamel), from 1933
Chronique du règne de Charles IX (Mérimée), 1829
Chronique rimée de Jean Chouan et de ses compagnons (v
    Gobineau), 1846
Chroniques (v Saint-John Perse), 1959
Chroniques de l'homme masqué (Vallès), 1882
Chroniques du bel canto (Aragon), 1947
Chroniques italiennes (f Stendhal), 1855
Chut! (p Scribe), 1836
Chute (f Camus), 1956
Chute d'un ange (v Lamartine), 1838
Cigale chez les fourmis (p Labiche), 1876
Cigalon (p Pagnol), 1936
Ci-gît (v Artaud), 1947
Cigognes (f A. Daudet), 1883
Ciguë (p Augier), 1844
Cinématoma (Jacob), 1925
Cinq cents millions de la Bégum (f Verne), 1878
Cinq grandes odes (v Claudel), 1910
Cinq poésies en hommage à Georges Braque (v Char), 1958
Cinq prières pour le temps de la guerre (v Jammes), 1916
Cinq semaines en ballon (f Verne), 1863
Cinq-Mars (f Vigny), 1825
53 jours (Perec), 1989
Cintre de Riom (v Maurras), 1946
Circassienne (p Scribe), 1861
Circonstances atténuantes (p Labiche), 1842
Circuit (p Feydeau), 1909
Cirque (p C. Mauriac), 1968
Citadelle (f Saint-Exupéry), 1948
Cité présente (v Spire), 1903

Citerne (p Pixérécourt), 1809
Cities of the Plain (f Proust), 1927
City (p Claudel),1920
City in the Sahara (f Verne), 1965
Civilisation (f Duhamel), 1918
Civilisation 1914–1917 (f Duhamel), 1918
Claim on Forty Mile Creek (f Verne), 1963
Clair de lune (f Maupassant), 1884
Clair de terre (v Breton), 1923
Claire (p Char), 1967
Claire Lenoir (Villiers de l'Isle Adam), 1925
Clairières dans le ciel (v Jammes), 1906
Clair-obscur (v Cocteau), 1954
Clan des Ostendais (f Simenon), 1947
Clara d'Ellébeuse (Jammes), 1899
Clarinette qui passe (p Labiche), 1851
Claude Gueux (f Hugo), 1834
Claude's Confession (f Zola), 1888
Claudie (p Sand), 1851
Claudine series (f Colette), from 1900
Claudine (p Colette), 1910
Claudine (p Pixérécourt), 1793
Claudius Bombarnac (f Verne), 1892
Clavier un autre (p Tardieu), 1975
Clé (p Labiche), 1877
Cléanthis (Benda), 1928
Clef de voûte (f Troyat), 1937
Clefs de la mort (f Green), 1928
Clefs et des serrures (Tournier), 1979
Clemenceau (Halévy), 1930
Clemenceau Case (f Dumas fils)
Cléopatre (p Sardou), 1890
Clérambard (p Aymé), 1950
Clérambault (f Rolland), 1920
Clermont (p Scribe), 1838
Clients d'Avrenos (f Simenon), 1935
Clin d'œtl de l'ange (f Mallet-Joris), 1983
Clio (f France), 1900
Clipper of the Clouds (f Verne), 1887
Cloches de Bâle (Aragon), 1934
Cloches pour deux mariages (Jammes), 1923
Cloches sur le cœur (v Char), 1928
Cloître (p Verhaeren), 1900
Clope (p Pinget), 1954
Clope au dossier (f Pinget), 1961
Cloportes (f Renard), 1919
Clorinda (f Zola), 1880
Close Shave (p Feydeau), 1974
Closed Garden (f Green), 1928
Clotilde de Lusignan (f Balzac), 1822
Clôture (Perec), 1980
Clou aux maris (p Labiche), 1858
Cloud That Lifted (p Maeterlinck), 1923
Clovis Dardentor (f Verne), 1896
Club Archimède (p Tardieu), 1975
Club champenois (p Labiche), 1848
Club des Lyonnais (f Duhamel), 1929
Code noir (p Scribe), 1842
Codine (f Istrati), 1926
Coelina (p Pixérécourt), 1800
Coeur de chêne (v Reverdy), 1921

Coeur de femme (f Bourget), 1890
Coeur de jeune fille (f Simenon), 1930
Coeur de la matière (Teilhard de Chardin), 1976
Coeur de poupée (f Simenon), 1929
Coeur d'or (f Soupault), 1927
Coeur double (f Schwob), 1891
Coeur exalté (f Simenon), 1928
Coeur pensif ne sait où il va (f Bourget), 1924
Coeur tout neuf (f C. Mauriac), 1980
Coeur Virginal (Gourmont), 1907
Coeurs perdus (f Simenon), 1928
Coeurs vides (f Simenon), 1928
Coffret de santal (v Cros), 1873
Coiffeur et le perruquier (p Scribe), 1824
Coin in Nine Hands (f Yourcenar), 1982
Coiners (f Gide), 1950
Colas Breugnon (f Rolland), 1919
Colère (p Ionesco), 1963
Colin Maillard (p Verne), 1853
Colis (p Feydeau), 1885
Collages (Aragon), 1965
Collier de griffes (v Cros), 1908
Collier de la reine (f Dumas père), 1849–50
Colline (f Giono), 1929
Colomba (Mérimée), 1841
Colombe (p Anouilh), 1951
Colombe (f Dumas père), 1851
Colombe Blanchet (f Alain-Fournier), 1922
Colonel (p Scribe), 1821
Colonel Chabert (f Balzac), 1844
Colonel de Surville (f Sue), 1840
Colonel's Children (f Supervielle), 1950
Colonel's Photograph (f Ionesco), 1967
Colours (Gourmont), 1929
Combat (p Duhamel), 1913
Combat avec l'ange (f Giraudoux), 1934
Combat contre les ombres (f Duhamel), 1939
Combat des montagnes (p Scribe), 1817
Come and Go (p Beckett), 1967
Comédie (p Beckett), 1966
Comédie académique (f Champfleury), 1867
Comédie de Charleroi (f Drieu la Rochelle), 1934
Comédie de la mort (p Gautier), 1838
Comédie de l'apôtre (f Champfleury) 1886
Comédie humaine (f Balzac), 1842–53
Comédiens sans le savoir (f Balzac), 1846
Comédies et proverbes (p A. Musset), 1840
Comédies sociales et scènes dialogues (f Sue), 1846
Comedy of Charleroi (f Drieu la Rochelle), 1973
Comices d'Athènes (p Scribe), 1817
Coming of Age (Beauvoir), 1972
Comme ceci, comme cela (v Tardieu), 1979
Comme des voiliers (v Supervielle), 1910
Comme le temps passe (Brasillach), 1937
Comme l'eau qui coule (f Yourcenar), 1982
Comme les chardons (p Salacrou), 1964
Comme nous avons été (p Adamov), 1953
Comme Shirley (v Butor), 1966
Comme un homme (f Salmon), 1931
Comme une pierre qui tombe (f Chamson), 1964
Comment c'est (f Beckett), 1961

Comment j'Ai Ecrit Certains de mes Livres (Roussel), 1935
Comment je crois (Teilhard de Chardin), 1969
Comment les Blancs sont d'anciens Noirs (Cendrars), 1930
Commode de Victorine (p Labiche), 1864
Commune présence (v Char), 1964
Communistes (Aragon), from 1949
Communistes ont peur de la révolution (Sartre), 1969
Compagnie (p Beckett), 1980
Compagnon du tour de France (f Sand), 1840
Compagnons (v Duhamel), 1912
Compagnons dans le jardin (v Char), 1956
Compagnons de Coquelicot (f Troyat), 1959
Compagnons de Jéhu (f Dumas père), 1857
Compagnons de la Marjolaine (p Verne), 1855
Companion of the Tour of France (f Sand), 1847
Company (p Beckett), 1980
Company of Jehu (f Dumas père), 1894
Compères du roi Louis (v Fort), 1923
Complainte du pauvr' propriétaire (p Feydeau), 1915
Complaintes (Laforgue), 1885
Complete Postcards from the Americas (Cendrars), 1976
Complications sentimentales (f Bourget), 1898
Complices (f Simenon), 1956
Comte de Monte-Cristo (f Dumas père), 1846
Comte de Morcerf (p Dumas père), 1851
Comte de Moret (f Dumas père), 1866
Comte de Saint-Ronan (p Scribe), 1831
Comte Hermann (p Dumas père), 1849
Comte Ory (p Scribe), 1828
Comtesse à deux maris (f Balzac), 1835
Comtesse de Charny (f Dumas père), 1852–55
Comtesse de Rudolstadt (f Sand), 1843–44
Comtesse de Salisbury (f Dumas père), 1839
Concert à la cour (p Scribe),1824
Concile féerique (Laforgue), 1886
Condemned of Altona (p Sartre), 1961
Condition humaine (f Malraux), 1933
Condition ouvrière (Weil), 1951
Condor et le morpion (v Apollinaire), 1931
Conducting Bodies (Simon), 1975
Confession de Claude (f Zola), 1865
Confession de minuit (f Duhamel), 1920
Confession d'un enfant du siècle (f A. Musset), 1836
Confession d'une jeune fille (f Sand), 1864
Confession of a Child of the Century (f A. Musset), 1892
Confessional (f Simenon), 1967
Confessionnal (f Simenon), 1966
Confessions de Dan Yack (Cendrars), 1929
Confidant (p Scribe), 1826
Confidence africaine (f Martin du Gard), 1931
Confidences (f Lamartine), 1849
Confidential Disclosures (f Lamartine), 1849
Conflits intimes (f Bourget), 1925
Conjuration (p Char), 1967
Connaissance de l'est (Claudel), 1900
Connaissance surnaturelle (Weil), 1950
Connaissez-vous? (p Ionesco), 1953
Connétable de Bourbon (p Dumas père), 1849
Conquérante (Brasillach), 1943
Conquérants (f Malraux), 1928
Conquerors (f Malraux), 1929

Conquest of Plassans (f Zola), 1887
Conquête de l'Angleterre (v Fort), 1933
Conquête de Plassans (f Zola), 1874
Conscience (f Dumas père), 1905
Conscience (p Dumas père), 1854
Conscience l'innocent (f Dumas père), 1852
Conscript (f Dumas père)
Conseils à une jeune poète, conseils à une jeune étudiant
    (Jacob), 1945
Considérations sur la France (Maistre), 1796
Considérations sur la Révolution française (Staël), 1818
Consolations (v Sainte-Beuve), 1830
Consommation (p Aymé), 1967
Conspiration (f Nizan), 1938
Conspirators (f Dumas père), 1910
Conspirators (f Vigny), 1877
Constance Verrier (f Sand), 1860
Constellations (v Breton), 1959
Construire la terre (Teilhard de Chardin), 1958
Consuelo (f Sand), 1842–43
Consultation (f Martin du Gard), 1928
Contacts de civilisations en Martinique et en Guadeloupe
    (Leiris) 1955
Contagion (p Augier), 1866
Conte de fées (p Dumas père), 1845
Conte Ory (p Scribe), 1829
Contemplations (v Hugo), 1856
Contes à Ninon (f Zola), 1864
Contes bruns (f Balzac), 1832
Contes cruels (Villiers de l'Isle Adam), 1883
Contes de Jacques Tournebroche (f France), 1908
Contes de la Bécasse (f Maupassant), 1883
Contes de la chaumière (f Mirbeau), 1894
Contes de la reine de Navarre (p Scribe), 1850
Contes d'Espagne et d'Italie (v A. Musset), 1830
Contes domestiques (f Champfleury), 1852
Contes drolatiques (f Balzac), from 1832
Contes du chat perché (f Aymé), 1939
Contes du jour et de la nuit (f Maupassant), 1885
Contes du lundi (f A. Daudet), 1873
Contes du médianoche (f Tournier), 1989
Contes d'un matin (f Giraudoux), 1952
Contes d'une grand'mère (Sand), 1873–76
Contes et facéties (f Nerval), 1853
Contes et propos (f Queneau), 1981
Contes physiologiques (f Deschamps), 1854
Contraption (p Tardieu), 1968
Contre la peine de mort (v Lamartine), 1830
Contre Sainte-Beuve (Proust), 1954
Contrebandiers de l'alcool (f Simenon), 1929
Convention Belzébir (p Aymé), 1967
Conversation (p C. Mauriac), 1964
Conversation-sinfonietta (p Tardieu), 1951
Convict's Son (f Dumas père), 1905
Copains (f Romains), 1913
Coq de bruyère (f Tournier), 1978
Coquecigrues (f Renard), 1893
Coraly (p Scribe), 1824
Corbeaux (p Becque), 1882
Corde raide (Simon), 1947
Cordélia (f Mallet-Joris), 1956

Corinne (Staël), 1807
Cornet à dés (Jacob), 1917
Corona benignitatis anni dei (v Claudel), 1915
Coronal (v Claudel), 1943
Corps conducteurs (Simon), 1971
Corps perdu (f Soupault), 1926
Corps perdu (v Césaire), 1950
Corps tragique (v Supervielle), 1959
Correspondances (v Salmon), 1929
Corricolo (p Labiche), 1868
Corsican Brothers (f Dumas père), 1880
Cortège priapique (v Apollinaire), 1925
Corydon (Gide), 1920
Cosima (p Sand), 1840
Cosmopolis (f Bourget), 1894
Côte (Jacob), 1911
Côté de Guermantes (f Proust), 1920–21
Coucaratcha (f Sue), 1832
Coucy-le-Château (v Fort), 1908
Couleur du temps (p Apollinaire), 1918
Couleurs (Gourmont), 1908
Count d'Orgel Opens the Ball (f Radiguet), 1952
Count of Monte Cristo (f Dumas père), 1846
Count of Moret (f Dumas père), 1868
Count Ory (p Scribe), 1829
Counterfeiters (f Gide), 1927
Countess of Charny (f Dumas père), 1858
Countess of Rudolstadt (f Sand), 1847
Country Parson (f Balzac)
Country Waif (f Sand), 1930
Coup de couteau (f F. Mauriac), 1928
Coup de dés jamais n'abolira le hasard (v Mallarmé), 1914
Coup de grâce (f Yourcenar), 1939
Coup de lune (f Simenon), 1933
Coup de rasoir (p Labiche), 1878
Coup de tête (p Feydeau), 1882
Coup d'oeil sur la tendance générale des esprits dans le dix-neu-
    vième siècle (Constant de Rebecque), 1825
Cour d'assises (p Scribe), 1830
Cour d'assises (f Simenon), 1941
Courir les rues (v Queneau), 1967
Couronne de Vulcain (Jacob), 1923
Courrier de Paris (Halévy), 1932
Courrier-sud (f Saint-Exupéry), 1929
Cours naturel (Éluard), 1938
Courtesy Doesn't Pay (p Tardieu), 1968
Cousin Betty (f Balzac), 1888
Cousin du roi (p Banville), 1857
Cousin Pons (f Balzac), 1847
Cousine Bette (f Balzac), 1847
Crachefeu (f Pieyre de Mandiargues), 1980
Cravates de chancre (v Reverdy), 1922
Création du monde (Cendrars), 1931
Création et rédemption (f Dumas père), 1872
Créations, re-créations, récréations (Perec), 1973
Creative Evolution (Bergson), 1911
Creative Mind (Bergson), 1946
Crépuscule des nymphes (Louÿs), 1925
Crève-coeur (Aragon), 1941
Crevette dans tous ses états (v Ponge), 1948
Cri écrit (v Cocteau), 1925

Crime (f Bernanos), 1935

Crime at Lock 14 (f Simenon), 1934

Crime d'amour (f Bourget), 1886

Crime de Sylvestre Bonnard (f France), 1881

Crime de village (f Renard), 1888

Crime des justes (f Chamson), 1928

Crime en Hollande (f Simenon), 1931

Crime impuni (f Simenon), 1954

Crime in Holland (f Simenon), 1940

Crime of the Just (f Chamson), 1930

Crime Passionnel (p Sartre), 1949

Crimes célèbres (f Dumas père), 1839–40

Crimson Handkerchief (f Gobineau), 1927

Cristaux naturels (v Ponge), 1952(?)

Critical Essays (Barthes), 1972

Critique de la raison dialectique (Sartre), 1960

Critique et vérité (Barthes), 1966

Critique of Dialectical Reason (Sartre), 1976

Crocodile (p Sardou), 1885

Croisade des enfants (f Schwob), 1896

Croiseur noir (v Pieyre de Mandiargues), 1972

Croix des roses (f Benda), 1923

Cromedeyre-le-vieil (p Romains), 1920

Cromwell (p Hugo), 1827

Cromwell and Mazarin (f Dumas père), 1847

Cromwell et Charles Ier (p Dumas père), 1835

Crop-Ear Jacquot (f Dumas père), 1903

Croquis parisiens (Huysmans), 1880

Cross Purpose (p Camus), 1947

Crossroad Murders (f Simenon), 1934

Crowd up at the Manor (p Tardieu), 1968

Crown Diamonds (p Scribe), 1844

Cru et le cuit (Lévi-Strauss)

Crucifix du poète (Jammes), 1934

Crucifixion (v Cocteau), 1946

Cruel Tales (Villiers de l'Isle Adam), 1963

Cruelle énigme (f Bourget), 1885

Crusts (p Claudel), 1945

Cry of the Peacock (p Anouilh), 1950

Cryptogram (f Verne), 1881

Cubist Painters (Apollinaire), 1949

Culotte (p Anouilh), 1978

Culture et les hommes (Aragon), 1947

Curé de village (f Balzac), 1841

Curée (f Zola), 1872

Curiosités esthétiques (Baudelaire), 1868

Cycle sur neuf gouaches d'Alexandre Calder (v Butor), 1962

Czarine (p Scribe), 1855

Dalila exaltée (v Pieyre de Mandiargues), 1964

Dame au petit chien (p Labiche), 1863

Dame aux camélias (f Dumas fils), 1848

Dame aux camélias (p Dumas fils), 1852

Dame aux jambes d'azur (p Labiche), 1857

Dame aux perles (f Dumas fils), 1853

Dame blanche (p Scribe), 1825

Dame de chez Maxim (p Feydeau), 1899

Dame de Monsoreau (f Dumas père), 1846

Dame de Monsoreau (p Dumas père), 1860

Dame de Pique (p Green), 1965

Dame de pique (p Scribe), 1851

Dame qui a perdu son peintre (f Bourget), 1910

Dames de Sibérie (f Troyat), 1962

Dames patronesses (p Scribe),1837

Dames vertes (f Sand), 1857

Dance and the Soul (Valéry), 1951

Danger Ahead (f Simenon), 1955

Danger Ashore (f Simenon), 1954

Danger at Sea (f Simenon), 1954

Daniel Rochat (p Sardou), 1880

Daniella (f Sand), 1857

Dans la foule (f Colette), 1918

Dans la fournaise (v Banville), 1891

Dans la pluie giboyeuse (v Char), 1968

Dans le ciel (f Mirbeau), 1989

Dans le cylindre (f Beckett), 1967

Dans le labyrinthe (f Robbe-Grillet), 1959

Dans le leurre du seuil (v Bonnefoy), 1975

Dans les années sordides (v Pieyre de Mandiargues), 1943

Dans les limbes (v Verlaine), 1894

Dans l'ombre des statues (p Duhamel), 1912

Dans un mois, dans un an (f Sagan), 1957

Danse de Sophocle (v Cocteau), 1912

Danseur mondain (f Bourget), 1926

Danseuse de Gai-Moulin (f Simenon), 1931

Danton (p Rolland), 1901

Danube Pilot (f Verne), 1967

Daphné (f Vigny), 1912

Daranda (p Scribe), 1847

Dark Angels (f F. Mauriac), 1951

Dark Journey (f Green), 1929

Dark Stranger (f Gracq), 1951

Daughter of Eve (f Balzac)

Daughters of Fire (f Nerval), 1922

Days in the Trees (p Duras), 1966

Days of Contempt (f Malraux), 1936

Days of 49 (Cendrars)

Days of Hope (f Malraux), 1938

Days of Wrath (f Malraux), 1936

De derrière les fagots (v Péret), 1934

De guerre lasse (f Sagan), 1985

De la démocratie en Amérique (Tocqueville), 1835–40

De la Littérature (Staël), 1800

De la main à la main (v Char), 1930

De la religion (Lamennais), 1841

De la religion considérée dans sa source, ses formes et ses développements (Constant de Rebecque), 1824–31

De la religion considérée dans ses rapports avec l'ordre politique
et civil (Lamennais), 1825–26

De la rue au bonheur (f Simenon), 1926

De la situation faite à l'histoire et à la sociologie dans les temps
modernes (Péguy), 1906

De la société première et des ses lois (Lamennais), 1848

De la terre à la lune (f Verne), 1865

De l'âge divin à l'âge ingrat (Jammes), 1921

De l'Allemagne (Staël), 1810

De l'amour considéré dans les lois réelles et dans les formes
sociales de l'union des deux sexes (Senancour), 1806

De l'Angelus de l'aube à l'Angelus du soir (v Jammes), 1898

De l'Eglise gallicane dans son rapport avec le Saint-Siège
(Maistre), 1821

De l'esclavage moderne (Lamennais), 1840

De l'idéal dans l'art (Taine), 1867
De l'influence des passions sur le bonheur (Staël), 1796
De l'intelligence (Taine), 1870
De moment en moment (v Char), 1957
De personis platonicis (Taine), 1853
De quelques constantes de l'espirit humain (Benda), 1950
De tout temps à jamais (v Jammes), 1935
Dead Letter (p Pinget), 1961
Dead Woman's Wish (f Zola), 1902
Dear Antoine (p Anouilh), 1971
Dear Garment (v Maurras), 1965
Death and the Labyrinth (Foucault), 1986
Death of a Harbor Master (f Simenon), 1941
Death of Monsieur Gallet (f Simenon), 1932
Death of Pharsalus (Simon), 1971
Death of Socrates (v Lamartine), 1829
Death of Tintagiles (p Maeterlinck), 1895
Death on the Installment Plan (f Céline), 1938
Deathwatch (p Genet), 1954
Débâcle (f Zola), 1892
Débâcles (v Verhaeren), 1888
Débarcadères (v Supervielle), 1922
Debauched Hospodar (f Apollinaire), 1958
Début dans la vie (f Balzac), 1844
Décadence de la liberté (Halévy), 1931
Décapitée (p Colette), 1941
Dédicaces (v Verlaine), 1890
Défense d'aimer (f Simenon), 1927
Défense de Tarascon (f A. Daudet), 1886
Défense de Tartufe (Jacob), 1919
Dégel (p Sardou), 1864
Degré zéro de l'écriture (Barthes), 1953
Degrees (f Butor), 1961
Degrés (f Butor), 1960
Dehors la nuit est gouvernée (v Char), 1938
Dehors trompeurs (p Scribe), 1818
Deïdamia (p Banville), 1876
Déjeuner marocain (p Romains), 1926
Deleytar (f Sue), 1839
Délice d'Eleuthère (Benda), 1935
Délire à deux (Ionesco),1962
Delphine (Staël), 1802
Déluge (f Le Clézio), 1966
Demain il fera jour (p Montherlant), 1949
Demande (p Renard), 1896
Déménagement (f Simenon), 1967
Démétrios (p Romains), 1926
Demi-monde (p Dumas fils), 1855
Democracy in America (Tocqueville), 1945
Demoiselle à marier (p Scribe), 1826
Demoiselle et la dame (p Scribe), 1822
Demoiselles de Concarneau (f Simenon), 1936
Demoiselles de Saint-Cyr (p Dumas père), 1843
Demoiselles Tourangeau (f Champfleury), 1864
Démon de la connaissance (f F. Mauriac), 1928
Démon de l'irréalité (v Tardieu), 1946
Démon de midi (f Bourget), 1914
Démon du bien (f Montherlant), 1937
Démon du foyer (p Sand), 1852
Demon Dwarf (f Hugo), 1847
Demon of Cawnpore (f Verne), 1881

Demon of Good (f Montherlant), 1940
Denier du rêve (f Yourcenar), 1934
Denise (p Dumas fils), 1885
Dent sous Louis XV (p Labiche), 1849
Dentelle d'éternité (v Cocteau), 1953
Dentelles de Montmirail (v Char), 1960
Dépendance de l'adieu (v Char), 1936
Dépeupleur (p Beckett), 1971
Député d'Arcis (f Balzac), 1854
Deputy of Arcis (f Balzac), 1896
Dernier Amour (f Sand), 1867
Dernier Chant du pèlerinage d'Harold (v Lamartine), 1825
Dernier Chouan (f Balzac), 1829
Dernier des métiers (Vian), 1950
Dernier jour de fortune (p Scribe), 1823
Dernier Jour d'un condamné (f Hugo), 1829
Dernier malheur, dernière chance (v Péret), 1946
Dernier Rendez-vous (f Murger), 1856
Dernier Village (f Chamson), 1946
Dernière Aldini (f Sand), 1838
Dernière Bande (p Beckett), 1960
Dernière Fée (f Balzac), 1823
Dernière Idole (p A. Daudet), 1862
Dernière Incarnation de Vautrin (f Balzac), 1848
Dernières Nuits de Paris (f Soupault), 1928
Derniers Jours (f Queneau), 1936
Derniers Jours de Pompéï (Gourmont), 1884
Derrière chez Martin (f Aymé), 1938
Dervis (p Scribe), 1811
Des bleus à l'âme (f Sagan), 1972
Des cobras à Paris (f Pieyre de Mandiargues), 1982
Des journées entières dans les arbres (f Duras), 1954
Des légendes, des batailles (v Duhamel), 1907
Des progrès de la révolution et de la guerre contre l'église (Lamennais), 1829
Désenchantées (f Loti), 1906
Désert (f Le Clézio), 1980
Désert de Bièvres (f Duhamel), 1937
Désert de l'amour (f F. Mauriac), 1925
Désert du froid qui tue (f Simenon), 1928
Desert Love (f Montherlant), 1957
Desert of Love (f F. Mauriac), 1929
Déserteur et autres récits (f Giono), 1973
Désespéré (f Bloy), 1887
Désirs de Jean Servien (f France), 1882
Désordres secrets (f Troyat), 1975
Dessous d'une vie ou la pyramide humaine (Éluard), 1926
Destin des Malou (f Simenon), 1948
Destinations (f Simenon), 1955
Destinées (f Simenon), 1929
Destinées (v Vigny), 1864
Destinies (f F. Mauriac), 1929
Destins (f F. Mauriac), 1928
Destins (v Sully Prudhomme), 1872
Destroy, She Said (f Duras), 1970
Détours du cour (f Bourget), 1908
Détruire, dit-elle (f Duras), 1969
Deuil de la Pologne (Lamennais), 1846
Deuil des nevons (v Char), 1954
Deuil des primevères (v Jammes), 1901
Deuil des roses (f Pieyre de Mandiargues), 1983

Deux ans de vacances (f Verne), 1888

Deux cavaliers de l'orage (f Giono), 1966

Deux coeurs de femme (f Simenon), 1929

Deux cœurs simples (f Lacretelle), 1953

Deux croisade spour la paix, juridique et sentimentale (Benda), 1948

Deux essais de poésie (Villiers de l'Isle Adam), 1858

Deux étoiles (f Gautier), 1848

Deux étreintes (f L. Daudet), 1900

Deux frères (f Balzac), 1842

Deux frères (f Sand), 1875

Deux gouttes d'eau (p Labiche), 1852

Deux héritages (p Mérimée), 1867

Deux hommes (f Duhamel), 1924

Deux jardiniers (p Banville), 1877

Deux maîtresses (f Simenon), 1929

Deux maris (p Scribe), 1819

Deux nuits (p Scribe), 1829

Deux papas très bien (p Labiche), 1845

Deux poètes (f Balzac), 1837

Deux précepteurs (p Scribe), 1817

Deux profonds scélérats (p Labiche), 1854

Deux soeurs (f Bourget), 1905

Deux sources de la morale et de la religion (Bergson), 1932

Deux timides (p Labiche), 1860

Deux travestis (f Cocteau), 1947

Deux valets (p Pixérécourt), 1803

Deuxième amour (f Bourget), 1884

Deuxième bureau (f Simenon), 1933

Deuxième Sexe (Beauvoir), 1949

Devant la douleur (f L. Daudet), 1915

Dévenir! (f Martin du Gard), 1909

Devil and the Good Lord (p Sartre), 1960

Devil in the Flesh (f Radiguet), 1932

Devil's Pool (f Sand), 1861

Devoir et l'inquiétude (Éluard), 1917

Devoirs de vacances (v Radiguet), 1921

Dévotion (v Bonnefoy), 1959

Dévotion à la croix (p Camus), 1953

Diable à l'école (p Scribe), 1842

Diable au corps (f Radiguet), 1923

Diable aux champs (f Sand), 1856

Diable et le bon Dieu (p Sartre), 1951

Diable médecin (f Sue), 1855–57

Diables noirs (p Sardou), 1864

Diaboliques (f Barbey D'Aurevilly), 1874

Dialectique de la durée (Bachelard), 1936

Dialogue (Martin du Gard), 1930

Dialogue d'Eleuthère (f Benda), 1911

Dialogue des Carmélites (f Bernanos), 1949

Dialogue intérieur (f C. Mauriac), 1951

Dialogues à Byzance (Benda), 1900

Dialogues et fragments philosophiques (Renan), 1876

Diamants de la couronne (p Scribe), 1841

Diane (p Augier), 1852

Diane (f Dumas père), 1901

Diane (v Jammes), 1928

Diane au bois (p Banville), 1863

Diane de Lys (p Dumas fils), 1853

Diane de Lys et Grangette (f Dumas fils), 1851

Diane française (Aragon), 1945

Diary of a Chambermaid (f Mirbeau), 1900

Diary of a Country Priest (f Bernanos), 1937

Diary of Antoine Roquentin (f Sartre), 1949

Dick Sands (f Verne), 1879

Dickie-Rol (f Mallet-Joris), 1979

Dictateur (p Romains), 1926

Dictionary of Accepted Ideas (f Flaubert), 1954

Dictionnaire des idées reçues (f Flaubert), 1966

Dieu (v Hugo), 1891

Dieu des corps (f Romains), 1928

Dieu dispose (f Dumas père), 1851–52

Dieu et la Bayadère (p Scribe), 1830

Dieu le savait (p Salacrou), 1951

Dieux étouffés (v Tardieu), 1946

Dieux ne sont pas morts (v Yourcenar), 1922

Dieux ont soif (f France), 1912

Difficulté d'être (Cocteau), 1947

Difficulty of Being (Cocteau), 1966

Dilemme (f Huysmans), 1887

Dimanche (f Simenon), 1958

Dimanche de la vie (f Queneau), 1952

Dimanches d'un bourgeois de Paris (f Maupassant), 1901

Dindon (p Feydeau), 1896

Dîner en ville (f C. Mauriac), 1959

Dîner sur l'herbe (p Scribe), 1824

Dingo (f Mirbeau), 1913

Dinner in Town (f C. Mauriac), 1963

Dinner Party (f C. Mauriac), 1960

Dinner with the Family (p Anouilh), 1957

Diplomate (p Scribe), 1827

Directeur de l'Opéra (p Anouilh), 1972

Directions de l'avenir (Teilhard de Chardin), 1973

Director of the Opera (p Anouilh), 1973

Dirty Hands (p Sartre), 1949

Dis Joe (p Beckett), 1966

Disappearance of Odile (f Simenon), 1972

Disciple (f Bourget), 1889

Discipline and Punish (Foucault), 1977

Discours à la nation européenne (Benda), 1933

Discours du grand sommeil (v Cocteau), 1924

Discours sur le colonialisme (Césaire), 1950

Discourse on Colonialism (Césaire), 1972

Disenchanted (f Loti), 1906

Disent les imbéciles (f Sarraute), 1976

Dish of Spices (Huysmans), 1927

Disintegration of J.P.G. (f Simenon), 1937

Disjecta (Beckett), 1983

Disparition (Perec), 1969

Disparition d'Odile (f Simenon), 1971

Disputed Inheritance (f Dumas père), 1847

Distance, The Shadows (v Hugo), 1981

Distant Lands (f Green), 1990

Distractions d'Hélène (f Simenon), 1928

Divertissements (Gourmont), 1912

Divine Douleur (Jammes), 1928

Divine Milieu (Teilhard de Chardin), 1960

Divine Tragédie (v Bataille), 1916

Divorce (f Bourget), 1904

Divorçons! (p Sardou), 1880

Dix années d'exil (Staël), 1821

Dix ans de la vie d'une femme (p Scribe), 1832
Dix heures et demie du soir en été (f Duras), 1960
Djinn (f Robbe-Grillet), 1981
XDo You Hear Them? (f Sarraute), 1973
Docteur mystérieux (f Dumas père), 1872
Docteur Pascal (f Zola), 1893
Docteur Servans (f Dumas fils), 1848–49
Doctor Basilius (f Dumas père), 1860
Dr. Ox's Experiment (f Verne), 1874
Doctor Pascal (f Zola), 1893
Doigts de fée (p Scribe), 1858
Doit-on le dire? (p Labiche), 1873
Dolorosa (f Simenon), 1928
Dominique (f Fromentin), 1863
Domino noir (p Scribe), 1837
Domitien (p Giono), 1959
Domnitza de Snagov (f Istrati), 1926
Don Juan (p Montherlant), 1958
Don Juan de Marana (p Dumas père), 1836
Don Quichotte (p Sardou), 1864
Don Sebastiano (p Scribe), 1860
Don Sébastien, roi de Portugal (p Scribe), 1843
Donat vainqueur (f Salmon), 1928
Donner à voir (Éluard), 1939
Donogoo (p Romains), 1930
Donogoo-Tonka (f Romains), 1920
Door (f Simenon), 1964
Door Must Be Either Open or Shut (p A. Musset), 1890
Dora (p Sardou), 1877
Dormez, je le veux! (p Feydeau), 1897
Dormir, dormir dans les pierres (v Péret), 1927
Dos d'arlequin (Jacob), 1921
Dossier de Rosafol (p Labiche), 1869
Dossiers de l'Agence O (f Simenon), 1945
Double Act (p Ionesco), 1979
Double Conversion (v A. Daudet), 1861
Double Méprise (Mérimée), 1833
Double noces (f Simenon), 1926
Double Vie (f Simenon), 1931
Doublure (Roussel), 1897
Douleur (f Duras), 1985
Douze petits écrits (v Ponge), 1926
Dove (f Dumas père), 1906
Down Stream (f Huysmans), 1927
Down the Amazon (f Verne), 1881
Down There (f Huysmans), 1924
Downfall (f Zola), 1892
Drac (p Sand), 1864
Drageoir aux épices (Huysmans), 1874
Dragonne (f Jarry), 1943
Drama in Livonia (f Verne)
Drame au bord de la mer (f Balzac), 1835
Drame au Pôle Sud (f Simenon), 1929
Drame dans le monde (f Bourget), 1921
Drame dans les airs (f Verne), 1874
Drame dans les prisons (f Balzac), 1847
Drame en Livonie (f Verne), 1904
Drames de famille (f Bourget), 1900
Drames galants (f Dumas père), 1860
Drames philosophiques (Renan), 1888
Dram-Shop (f Zola), 1897

Drapeau noir (f Salmon), 1927
Drapier (p Scribe), 1840
Dream (f Montherlant), 1963
Dream (f Zola), 1893
Dreamer (f Green), 1934
Dreams (Bergson), 1914
Dreams and Life (f Nerval), 1933
Drink (f Zola), 1903
Droit de rêver (Bachelard), 1970
Drôle de coco (f Simenon), 1929
Drôle de voyage (f Drieu la Rochelle), 1933
Du caractère de M. Necker et de sa vie privée (Staël), 1804
Du côté de chez Swann (f Proust), 1913
Du Dandyisme et de George Brummel (f Barbey D'Aurevilly), 1845
Du droit du gouvernement sur l'éducation (Lamennais), 1817
Du miel aux cendres (Lévi-Strauss)
Du mouvement et de l'immobilité de Douve (v Bonnefoy), 1953
Du pape (Maistre), 1819
Du passé et de l'avenir du peuple (Lamennais), 1841
Du philanthrope à la rouquine (f Troyat), 1945
Du poétique (Benda), 1946
Du polythéisme romain considéré dans ses rapports avec la philosophie grecque et la religion chrétienne (Constant de Rebecque), 1833
Du style d'idées (Benda), 1948
Du système pénitentiare aux Etats-Unis et de son application en France (Tocqueville), 1833
Duc d'Olonne (p Scribe), 1842
Duchess of Langeais (f Balzac), 1946
Duchesse bleue (f Bourget), 1898
Duchesse de Senancourt (f Sue)
Duchesse des Folies-Bergères (p Feydeau), 1902
Duchesse douairière de Sénancour (f Sue), 1855–57
Duel (p Ionesco), 1979
Duel of Angels (p Giraudoux), 1958
Dugazon (p Scribe), 1833
D'un château à l'autre (f Céline), 1957
D'un ouvrage abandonné (p Beckett), 1967
D'un pays lointain (Gourmont), 1898
Duo (f Colette), 1934
Dur Désir de durer (Éluard), 1946
Duration and Simultaneity (Bergson), 1965
Durée et simultanéitié (Bergson), 1922

Each in His Darkness (f Green), 1961
Eagle Has Two Heads (p Cocteau), 1948
Earth (f Zola), 1954
East I Know (Claudel), 1914
Eau et les rêves (Bachelard), 1942
Eau fraiche (Drieu la Rochelle), 1931
Eau profonde (f Bourget), 1904
Eau vive (f Giono), 1944
Eaux du Mont-d'Or (p Scribe), 1822
Eaux seuls le savent (Tardieu), 1952
Ecarté (p Scribe), 1822
Echange (p Claudel), 1901
Echarde (p Sagan), 1966
Echec et Mat (p Dumas père), 1846
Echo's Bones and Other Precipitates (v Beckett), 1932
Eclaircissement sur les sacrifices (Maistre), 1821

Ecluse no. 1 (f Simenon), 1933
Ecole buissonière (p Labiche), 1845
Ecole de village (p Scribe), 1818
Ecole des Arthur (p Labiche), 1859
Ecole des femmes (f Gide), 1929
Ecole des indifférents (f Giraudoux), 1911
Ecole des ménages (p Balzac), 1907
Ecole des Robinsons (f Verne), 1882
Ecornifleur (f Renard), 1892
Ecoute, ma fille (v Claudel), 1934
Ecran (f Bourget), 1900
Ecrits de Londres (Weil), 1957
Ecrits historiques et politiques (Weil), 1960
Ecume des jours (f Vian), 1947
Ecumes de la mer (v Reverdy), 1926
Ecureuil (p Sardou), 1861
Ecuyère (f Bourget), 1921
Edel (v Bourget), 1878
Eden cinéma (p Duras), 1977
Edgard et sa bonne (p Labiche), 1852
Edmund Kean (p Dumas père), 1847
Education sentimentale (f Flaubert), 1869
Effraie (v Jaccottet), 1953
Effroi la joie (v Char), 1971
Effrontés (p Augier), 1861
Egarements de Minne (f Colette), 1905
Eglantine (f Giraudoux), 1927
Église (p Céline), 1933
Eglise habillée de feuilles (v Jammes), 1906
Eglogues (f Giono), 1931
Eh Joe (p Beckett), 1966
Eiffel Tower and Other Mythologies (Barthes), 1979
Eiffel Tower Wedding Party (p Cocteau), 1963
El Hadj (Gide), 1899
El Salteador (f Dumas père), 1854
Eldorado (f Gautier), 1837
Electra (p Giraudoux), 1957
Electre (p Giraudoux), 1937
Electre (p Yourcenar), 1954
Elégie à Pablo Neruda (Aragon), 1966
Elégie pour Alizés (v Senghor), 1969
Elégies (v Duhamel), 1920
Elégies (v Jammes), 1943
Elégies (v Verlaine), 1893
Elementary Structures of Kinship (Lévi-Strauss), 1969
Eléments de sémiologie (Barthes), 1964
Eléments d'un songe (Jaccottet), 1961
Elements of Semiology (Barthes), 1968
Elën (Villiers de l'Isle Adam), 1865
Eléphant blanc (f Troyat), 1970
Elèves du conservatoire (p Scribe), 1827
Elisabeth, petite fille (v Char), 1958
Elizabeth (f Troyat), 1959
Elle est là (p Sarraute), 1978
Elle et lui (f Sand), 1859
Elles se rendent pas compte (f Vian), 1948
Elm-Tree on the Mall (f France), 1910
Eloa (v Vigny), 1824
Eloge de la philosophie (Merleau-Ponty), 1953
Eloge de la vie dangereuse (Cendrars), 1926
Eloge de Sir Samuel Romilly (Constant de Rebecque), 1819

Eloges (v Saint-John Perse), 1911
Elpénor (f Giraudoux), 1919
Elsa (Aragon), 1959
Elseneur (p Butor), 1979
Emaux et camées (v Gautier), 1852
Embers (p Beckett), 1959
Embrassons-nous Folleville! (p Labiche), 1850
Emigré (f Bourget), 1907
Emily L. (f Duras), 1987
Emma Lyonna (f Dumas père), 1864
Emmanuel Philibert (f Dumas père), 1852–54
Emmène-moi au bout du monde (Cendrars), 1956
Emotions (Sartre), 1948
Empire Céleste (f Mallet-Joris), 1958
Empire de France (v Fort), 1953
Empire des signes (Barthes), 1970
Empire of Signs (Barthes), 1982
Empiriques d'autrefois (p Scribe), 1825
Emploi du temps (f Butor), 1956
Employés (f Balzac), 1865
En arrière (f Aymé), 1950
En attendant Godot (p Beckett), 1952
En avant les chinois (p Labiche), 1859
En ballon (Gourmont), 1884
En camerades (p Colette), 1909
En case de malheur (f Simenon), 1956
En 18 (f Goncourt), 1851
En fiacre (p Adamov), 1959
En français dans le texte (Aragon), 1943
En joue! (f Soupault), 1925
En manches de chemise (p Labiche), 1851
En ménage (f Huysmans), 1881
En pension chez son groom (p Labiche), 1856
En rade (f Huysmans), 1887
En robe de mariée (f Simenon), 1929
En route (f Huysmans), 1895
En trente-trois morceaux (v Char), 1956
Enchanted (p Giraudoux), 1950
Enchanted Lake (f Sand), 1850
Enchanteur pourrissant (f Apollinaire), 1909
Enchanteurs (v Fort), 1919
Encore un instant de bonheur (Montherlant), 1934
Encore un Pourceaugnac (p Scribe), 1817
Encore une nuit de la garde nationale (p Scribe), 1815
Encounter (f Troyat), 1962
End of the Journey (f Verne)
End of the Night (f F. Mauriac), 1947
Endgame (p Beckett), 1958
Endormie (p Claudel), 1947
Ends and Odds (p Beckett), 1976
Enemy (f F. Mauriac), 1949
Energie humaine (Teilhard de Chardin), 1962
Energie spirituelle (Bergson), 1919
Enfant (Vallès), 1879
Enfant chargé de chaînes (f F. Mauriac), 1913
Enfant de la haute mer (f Supervielle), 1931
Enfant de la maison (p Labiche), 1845
Enfant de la nuit (Brasillach), 1934
Enfant et les sortilèges (p Colette), 1925
Enfant maudit (f Balzac), 1837
Enfant prodigue (p Becque), 1868

Enfant prodigue (p Scribe), 1850
Enfantines (f Larbaud), 1918
Enfant-roi (p Zola), 1905
Enfants (p Feydeau), 1887
Enfants dans les ruines (f Colette), 1917
Enfants du Capitaine Grant (f Verne), 1867–68
Enfants du Capitaine Grant (p Verne), 1878
Enfants du Limon (f Queneau), 1938
Enfants du peuple (Vallès), 1879
Enfants du sabbat (f Hébert), 1975
Enfants terribles (f Cocteau), 1929
Enfants trouvés et des orphelins pauvres (Tocqueville), 1850
Engagement rationaliste (Bachelard), 1972
Engagements of the Heart (f Sagan), 1987
English at the North Pole (f Verne), 1874
Engrenage (p Sartre), 1948
Enjambées (f Aymé), 1967
Enlèvement (p Becque), 1871
Ennemi (p Green), 1954
Ennemi des modes (p Pixérécourt), 1814
Ennemie (p Labiche), 1871
Ennemonde (f Giono), 1968
Ennui (p Scribe), 1820
Enone au clair visage (v Moréas), 1893
Enough (f Beckett), 1967
Enquiry Office (p Tardieu), 1968
Enracinement (Weil), 1949
Enseigne de Gerseint (Aragon), 1946
Enslaved (p Jarry), 1953
Ensorcelée (f Barbey D'Aurevilly), 1854
Enterrement de Monsieur Bouvet (f Simenon), 1950
Enterrement d'une étoile (f A. Daudet), 1896
Entrave (f Colette), 1913
Entre deux haines (f Simenon), 1925
Entre Fantoine et Agapa (f Pinget), 1951
Entre la vie et la mort (f Sarraute), 1968
Entre-deux guerres (f L. Daudet), 1915
Entrepreneur d'illuminations (f Salmon), 1921
Entretiens avec Francis Crémieux (Aragon), 1964
Entretiens sur le musée de Dresde (Aragon), 1959
Envers de l'histoire contemporaine (f Balzac), 1846
Envers du décor (f Bourget), 1911
Envers d'une conspiration (p Dumas père), 1860
Envois (v Butor), 1980
Epave (f Simenon), 1932
Epave d'amour (f Simenon), 1929
Epave du Cynthia (f Verne), 1885
Epaves (v Baudelaire), 1866
Epaves (f Green), 1932
Epaves du ciel (v Reverdy), 1924
Epidemic (p Mirbeau), 1952
Epidémie (p Mirbeau), 1898
Epigrammes (v Verlaine), 1894
Epilogue (f Martin du Gard), 1940
Epingles (f Apollinaire), 1928
Episode de la vie d'un auteur (p Anouilh), 1948
Episode sous la terreur (f Balzac), 1846
Epitaphes (v Jammes), 1921
Epîtres (v Lamartine), 1825
Epreuves (v Michaux), 1945
Epreuves (v Sully Prudhomme), 1866

Equarrissage pour tous (Vian), 1950
Erasers (f Robbe-Grillet), 1964
Ere du soupçon (Sarraute), 1956
Erinnyes (Leconte de Lisle), 1873
Eriphyle (p Moréas), 1894
Erl-King (f Tournier), 1972
Ermine (p Anouilh), 1955
Errants (f Simenon), 1931
Escales (v Cocteau), 1920
Escalier (v Supervielle), 1956
Escalier de fer (f Simenon), 1953
Escalier de Flore (v Char), 1958
Escape in Vain (f Simenon), 1943
Esmeralda (f Hugo), 1844
Esméralda (p Hugo), 1836
Esope (p Banville), 1881
Espace du dedans (Michaux), 1944
Espace et la flûte (v Tardieu), 1958
Espagnolas et boyardinos (p Labiche), 1854
España (v Gautier), 1845
Espèces d'espaces (Perec), 1974
Espoir (f Malraux), 1937
Esprit de conquête (Constant de Rebecque), 1813
Esprits (p Camus), 1953
Esquisse d'homme d'affaires (f Balzac), 1846
Esquisse d'une histoire des Français dans leur volonté d'être une nation (Benda), 1932
Esquisse d'une philosophie (Lamennais), 1840–46
Esquisse d'une théorie des émotions (Sartre), 1939
Essai de critique indirecte (Cocteau), 1932
Essai d'un discours cohérent sur les rapports de Dieu et du monde (Benda), 1931
Essai psychologique sur Jésus-Christ (Renan), 1921
Essai sur la connaissance approchée (Bachelard), 1928
Essai sur l'accélération de l'histoire (Halévy), 1918–61
Essai sur le mouvement ouvrier en France (Halévy), 1901
Essai sur le principe générateur des constitutions politiques et des autres institutions humaines (Maistre), 1814
Essai sur les données immédiates de la conscience (Bergson), 1889
Essai sur les fables de La Fontaine (Taine), 1853
Essai sur les fictions (Staël), 1796
Essai sur l'indifférence en matière de religion (Lamennais), 1817–23
Essai sur l'inégalité des races humaines (Gobineau), 1853–55
Essai sur Tite-Live (Taine), 1856
Essais critiques (Barthes), 1964
Essais de critique et d'histoire (Taine), 1858
Essais de morale et de critique (Renan), 1859
Essais dramatiques (Staël), 1821
Essay on Indifference in Matters of Religion (Lamennais), 1895
Essay on the Generative Principle of Political Constitutions (Maistre), 1847
Essays in Existentialism (Sartre), 1967
Estelle (p Scribe), 1834
Esther (f Balzac), 1845
Et j'ai voulu la paix (v Spire), 1916
Et les chiens se taisaient (p Césaire), 1956
Et on tuera tous les affreux (f Vian), 1948
Et sur la terre… (f Malraux), 1977
Et vous riez! (v Spire), 1905

Etape (f Bourget), 1902

Etapes de l'enfer (v Soupault), 1934

Etapes du mensonge (f Simenon), 1930

Etat civil (f Drieu la Rochelle), 1921

Etat de siège (p Camus), 1948

Etat social et politique de la France (Tocqueville), 1834

Etats-généraux (v Breton), 1943

Été 1914 (f Martin du Gard), 1936

Eternel Retour (p Cocteau), 1943

Ethics of Ambiguity (Beauvoir), 1948

Ethiopiques (v Senghor), 1956

Etoile au front (Roussel), 1924

Etoile de cinéma (f Simenon), 1925

Etoile de Séville (p Supervielle), 1959

Etoile du nord (p Scribe), 1854

Etoile du sud (f Verne), 1884

Etoile vesper (Colette), 1946

Etoiles dans l'encrier (v Salmon), 1952

Etoiles du sud (f Green), 1989

Etoiles peintes (v Reverdy), 1921

Etonnante Aventure de la mission Barsac (f Verne), 1919

Etranger (f Camus), 1942

Etrangère (p Dumas fils), 1876

Etrangers sur la terre (f Troyat), 1950

Etre aimé, ou mourir (p Scribe), 1835

Être en marche (v Romains), 1910

Être et le néant (Sartre), 1943

Etreintes passionnées (f Simenon), 1927

Etroits sont les vaisseaux (v Saint-John Perse), 1956

Etudes de moeurs (f Labiche) 1839

Etudes de moeurs au XIXe siècle (f Balzac), from 1833

Etudes d'histoire religieuse (Renan), 1857

Etudes françaises et étrangères (v Deschamps), 1828

Etudes philosophiques (f Balzac), 1835–40

Etudiant et la grande dame (p Scribe), 1837

Etudiante (f Pieyre de Mandiargues), 1946

Etui de nacre (f France), 1892

Eubage (Cendrars), 1926

Eugénie Grandet (f Balzac), 1833

Euménides (p Claudel), 1920

Eupalinos (Valéry), 1923

Europe (v Romains), 1916

European Revolution (Tocqueville), 1959

Eurydice (p Anouilh), 1942

Eux et fôrets (p Duras), 1965

Evadé (f Simenon), 1936

Evangelist (f A. Daudet), 1899

Evangéliste (f A. Daudet), 1883

Evasion (f Simenon), 1934

Evasion (Villiers de l'Isle Adam), 1891

Eve (Péguy), 1914

Eve future (Villiers de l'Isle Adam), 1886

Evening Star (Colette), 1973

Evening with Mr. Teste (Valéry), 1925

Evenor et Leucippe (f Sand), 1856

Eventail (v Salmon), 1922

Evolution créatrice (Bergson), 1907

Excommuniée (f Balzac), 1837

Excursions along the Banks of the Rhine (v Hugo), 1843

Exemple de Courbet (Aragon), 1952

Exercice d'un enterré vif (Benda), 1946

Exercices de conversation et de diction françaises pour étudiants américains (p Ionesco), 1974

Exercices de style (f Queneau), 1947

Exercises in Style (f Queneau), 1958

Exil (p Montherlant), 1929

Exil (v Saint-John Perse), 1942

Exil et le royaume (f Camus), 1957

Exile (v Saint-John Perse), 1949

Exile and the Kingdom (f Camus), 1958

Exilés (v Banville), 1867

Existentialism (Sartre), 1947

Existentialism and Humanism (Sartre), 1948

Existentialisme est un humanisme (Sartre), 1946

Exit the King (p Ionesco), 1963

Expérience de l'espace dans la physique contemporaine (Bachelard), 1937

Expérience vécue (Beauvoir), 1949

Experimental Novel (Zola), 1893

Exploits d'un jeune Don Juan (f Apollinaire), 1907

Exposition des produits de la République (p Labiche), 1849

Extase matérielle (Le Clézio), 1967

Extrême amitié (f Troyat), 1963

Eygletière (f Troyat), 1965

Fabien (f F. Mauriac), 1926

Fabien (p Pagnol), 1956

Fable (f Pinget), 1971

Fable du monde (v Supervielle), 1938

Fable sans moralité (Jacob), 1931

Face au drapeau (f Verne), 1896

Face aux verrous (v Michaux), 1954

Face for a Clue (f Simenon), 1939

Faces of Brass (p Augier), 1888

Facino cane (f Balzac), 1837

Fadette (f Sand), 1851

Fading Mansions (p Anouilh), 1949

Faim des lionceaux (f Troyat), 1966

Faire-part (v Cocteau), 1969

Faiseur (p Balzac), 1849

Faits et les mythes (Beauvoir), 1949

Fall (f Camus), 1957

False Step (p Augier), 1879

Famille Benoîton (p Sardou), 1865

Famille de Germandre (f Sand), 1861

Famille de l'horloger (p Labiche), 1860

Famille du baron (p Scribe), 1829

Famille Jouffroy (f Sue), 1854

Famille Riquebourg (p Scribe), 1831

Famille sans nom (f Verne), 1889

Family Idiot (Sartre), 1981–82

Family Lie (f Simenon), 1978

Family Without a Name (f Verne), 1890

Fanal bleu (Colette), 1949

Fanal de Messine (p Pixérécourt), 1812

Fanchette (f Sand), 1847

Fanchon the Cricket (f Sand), 1863

Fanfarlo (Baudelaire), 1868

Fanny (p Pagnol), 1931

Fanny and Jane (f Colette), 1931

Fanny Minoret (f Champfleury), 1882

Fantaisie du Docteur Ox (f Verne), 1872

Forgeron (p Banville), 1887

Formation de l'esprit scientifique (Bachelard), 1938

Formeries (v Tardieu), 1976

Fort comme la mort (f Maupassant), 1889

Forteresse du Danube (p Pixérécourt), 1805

Fortune des Rougon (f Zola), 1871

Fortune of the Rougons (f Zola), 1886

Fortune's Fool (v Nerval), 1959

Fortunes of the Pasquiers (f Duhamel), 1935

Forty-Five Guardsmen (f Dumas père), 1847

Fosse commune (f Troyat), 1939

Fou d'Amour (f Simenon), 1928

Fou de Bergerac (f Simenon), 1932

Fou de Péronne (p Scribe), 1819

Fou d'Elsa (Aragon), 1963

Foundling Mick (f Verne), 1892

Four Days in a Lifetime (f Simenon), 1953

Four Wise Men (f Tournier), 1982

Fourberies de Nérine (p Banville), 1864

Fourchambault (p Augier), 1878

Fourmis (f Vian), 1949

Fournisseurs (v Spire), 1923

Foursome (p Ionesco), 1970

Fous de Bassan (f Hébert), 1982

Foyer (p Mirbeau), 1908

Foyer du Gymnase (p Scribe), 1830

Fra Diavolo (p Scribe), 1836

Fragment de Théâtre (p Beckett), 1974

Fragments d'un discours amoureux (Barthes), 1977

Fragments intimes et romanesques (Renan), 1914

Français au Canada et en Acadie (Gourmont), 1888

France (v Sully Prudhomme), 1874

France byzantine (Benda), 1945

France sentimentale (f Giraudoux), 1932

Francia (f Sand), 1872

Francillon (p Dumas fils), 1887

Francis I (f Dumas père), 1849

Francis the Waif (f Sand), 1889

François le champi (f Sand), 1848

François le champi (p Sand), 1849

Frénétiques (p Salacrou), 1934

Frenzy for Two (p Ionesco), 1965

Frère aîné (p A. Daudet), 1864

Frères corses (f Dumas père), 1844

Frères Durandeau (f Soupault), 1924

Frères invisibles (p Scribe), 1819

Frères Kip (f Verne), 1902

Frères Rico (f Simenon), 1952

Frères Zemganno (f Goncourt), 1879

Friday (f Tournier), 1969

Friday and Robinson (f Tournier), 1972

Friends or Foes? (p Sardou)

Frileuse (p Scribe), 1861

Frisette (p Labiche), 1846

From an Abandoned Work (p Beckett), 1958

From Honey to Ashes (Lévi-Strauss)

From Lands of Exile (f Loti), 1888

From the Earth to the Moon (f Verne), 1873

Fromont jeune et Risler aîné (f A. Daudet), 1874

Fromont jeune et Risler aîné (p A. Daudet), 1886

Fromont jr and Risler sr (f A. Daudet), 1894

Front dans les nuages (f Troyat), 1977

Frontenac Mystery (f F. Mauriac), 1952

Frontière de Savoie (p Scribe), 1834

Frontin mari-garçon (p Scribe), 1821

Fruitfulness (f Zola), 1900

Fruits d'or (f Sarraute), 1963

Fruits of the Earth (f Gide), 1949

Fugitive (f Chamson), 1934

Fugitive (Proust), 1925

Fugitive (f Simenon), 1955

Fugue du petit Poucet (f Tournier), 1979

Fuite de M. Monde (f Simenon), 1945

Funérailles du naturalisme (Bloy), 1891

Funeral Rites (f Genet), 1969

Fur Country (f Verne), 1873

Fureur et mystère (v Char), 1948

Future Is in Eggs (p Ionesco), 1960

Future of Man (Teilhard de Chardin), 1964

Gabriel (p Sand), 1839

Gabriel Lambert (f Dumas père), 1844

Gabriel Lambert (p Dumas père), 1866

Gabriel le faussaire (p Dumas père), 1866

Gabrielle (p Augier), 1850

Galère (f Chamson), 1939

Galère (v Genet), 1947

Galigaï (f F. Mauriac), 1952

Gallant Lords of Bois-Doré (f Sand), 1890

Gallant Parties (v Verlaine), 1912

Galley Slave (f Dumas père), 1849

Gamara (f Balzac), 1839

Ganaches (p Sardou), 1862

Gaol (f Bourget), 1924

Garantie dix ans (p Labiche), 1874

Garçon de chez Véry (p Labiche), 1850

Garçons (f Montherlant), 1969

Garde du coeur (f Sagan), 1968

Garde-forestier (p Dumas père), 1845

Garden of Priapus (f Jarry), 1936

Gardien (p Scribe), 1833

Gaspard, Melchior et Balthazar (f Tournier), 1980

Gastronome sans argent (p Scribe), 1821

Gateway to God (Weil), 1974

Gaudissart II (f Balzac), 1846

Géant du soleil (Jacob), 1904

Géants (f Le Clézio), 1973

Gemini (f Tournier), 1981

Gemma (p Gautier), 1854

Gendarme's Report (f Simenon), 1951 33,

Gendre de M. Poirier (p Augier), 1854

Gendre en surveillance (p Labiche), 1858

Geneviève (p Gide), 1936

Geneviève (f Lamartine), 1851

Geneviève (p Scribe), 1846

Genie du christianisme (Chateaubriand), 1802

Génie du lieu (Butor), from 1958

Genitrix (f F. Mauriac), 1923

Genius of Christianity (Chateaubriand), 1856

Gens d'en face (f Simenon), 1933

Gens nerveux (p Sardou), 1859

Gentilhomme de la montagne (p Dumas père), 1860

Gentle Libertine (f Colette), 1931
Geôle (f Bourget), 1923
George (f Dumas père), 1846
Georges (f Dumas père), 1843
Georgette (p Sardou), 1885
Georgia (v Soupault), 1926
Georgics (Simon), 1981
Géorgiques (Simon), 1981
Géorgiques chrétiennes (v Jammes), 1911–12
Germaine's Marriage (f Sand), 1892
Germandre Family (f Sand), 1900–02
Germinal (f Zola), 1885
Germinal (p Zola), 1888
Germinie Lacerteux (f Goncourt), 1864
Gervaise (f Zola), 1879
Geste d'Eve (f Troyat), 1964
Geste pour un autre (p Tardieu), 1951
Gestes et opinions du docteur Faustroll, pataphysicien (f Jarry), 1911
Get Out of My Hair! (p Feydeau), 1973
Ghost Trio (p Beckett), 1976
Giant Raft (f Verne), 1881
Giants (f Le Clézio), 1975
Gibier de potence (p Feydeau), 1885
Gigi (f Colette), 1944
Gigi (p Colette), 1951
Gil Blas in California (f Dumas père), 1933
Gilbert et Gilberte (f Sue), 1855
Gil-Blas en Californie (f Dumas père), 1852
Gilles (f Drieu la Rochelle), 1939
Gilles et Jeanne (f Tournier), 1983
Gillette (f Balzac), 1847
Gin Palace (f Zola), 1952
Giralda (p Scribe), 1850
Girl Beneath the Lion (f Pieyre de Mandiargues), 1958
Girl in His Past (f Simenon), 1952
Girl in Waiting (f Simenon), 1957
Girl on the Motorcycle (f Pieyre de Mandiargues), 1966
Girl with a Squint (f Simenon), 1978
Girl with the Golden Eyes (f Balzac), 1928
Giselle (p Gautier), 1841
Glass Cage (f Simenon), 1973
Glass of Water (p Scribe), 1850
Glissements progressifs du plaisir (f Robbe-Grillet), 1974
Gloire de rois (v Saint-John Perse), 1967
Gloire des vaincus (f Troyat), 1961
Glossaire, j'y serre mes gloses (Leiris), 1940
God Speaks (Péguy), 1945
Godfrey Morgan (f Verne), 1883
Godolphin Arabian (f Sue), 1845
Gods are Athirst (f France), 1913
God's Will Be Done (f Dumas père), 1909
Going to Pot (p Feydeau), 1970
Gold (Cendrars), 1982
Golden Buttons (f Leduc), 1966
Golden Droplet (f Tournier), 1987
Golden Fruits (f Sarraute), 1964
Golden Volcano (f Verne), 1963
Gommes (f Robbe-Grillet), 1953
Gondole des morts (v Cocteau), 1959

Gondreville Mystery (f Balzac), 1898
Gonfle (p Martin du Gard), 1928
Good for Evil (p Augier), 1860
Good Little Wife (p A. Musset), 1847
Good Night's Sleep (p Feydeau), 1973
Gorille-roi (f Simenon), 1929
Gout de miel (p Mallet-Joris), 1960
Goutte d'or (f Tournier), 1985
Gown for His Mistress (p Feydeau), 1969
Graal Flibuste (f Pinget), 1956
Grâce (v Jammes), 1946
Grâce encore pour la terre (p Romains), 1937
Gracques (p Giraudoux), 1958
Grain de la voix (Barthes), 1981
Grain of the Voice (Barthes), 1985
Grammaire (p Labiche), 1867
Grammar (p Labiche), 1915
Grand Bob (f Simenon), 1954
Grand Ecart (f Cocteau), 1923
Grand Frère à la crèche (v Deschamps), 1852
Grand Homme (f Soupault), 1929
Grand homme de province à Paris (f Balzac), 1839
Grand honnête homme (f Romains), 1961
Grand Jeu (v Péret), 1928
Grand Meaulnes (f Alain-Fournier), 1913
Grand Troupeau (f Giono), 1931
Grande Aventure (p Scribe), 1832
Grande Epreuve des démocraties (Benda), 1942
Grande et la Petite Manœuvre (p Adamov), 1950
Grande fuite de neige (Leiris), 1964
Grande Gaieté (Aragon), 1929
Grande nature (v Reverdy), 1925
Grande Peur des bien-pensants (Bernanos), 1931
Grandes Chaleurs (p Ionesco), 1953
Grandeur et décadence d'une serinette (f Champfleury), 1857
Grandeur nature (f Troyat), 1936
Grand-mère (p Scribe), 1840
Grands Chemins (f Giono), 1951
Grands Cimetières sous la lune (Bernanos), 1938
Grass (Simon), 1961
Gravitations (v Supervielle), 1925
Gravity and Grace (Weil), 1952
Graziella (f Lamartine), 1852
Great Betrayal (Benda), 1928
Great Lover (p Dumas père), 1979
Great Man of the Provinces in Paris (f Balzac), 1893
Green Coat (p Augier), 1914
Green Huntsman (f Stendhal), 1950
Green Ray (f Verne), 1883
Green Thermos (f Simenon), 1944
Grenadière (f Balzac), 1833
Grimbosq (f Troyat), 1976
Gringoire (p Banville), 1866
Grisettes (p Scribe), 1823
Grive (f Troyat), 1956
Gros mot (p Labiche), 1860
Grotte (p Anouilh), 1961
Grotte (p Anouilh), 1970
Guelfes et Gibelins (f Dumas père), 1836
Guelphs and Ghibellines (f Dumas père), 1905
Guermantes Way (f Proust), 1925

Guerre (f Le Clézio), 1970
Guerre au Luxembourg (Cendrars), 1916
Guerre civile (p Montherlant), 1965
Guerre de Troie n'aura pas lieu (p Giraudoux), 1935
Guerre des femmes (f Dumas père), 1845–46
Guerre des femmes (p Dumas père), 1849
Guetteur mélancolique (v Apollinaire), 1952
Gueule de pierre (f Queneau), 1934
Guichet (p Tardieu), 1955
Guido et Ginevra (p Scribe), 1838
Guignol's Band (f Céline), 1944
Guillaume le bâtard (v Fort), 1926
Guinguette à deux sous (f Simenon), 1932
Guinguette by the Seine (f Simenon), 1940
Guirlande des dunes (v Verhaeren), 1907
Guitare endormie (v Reverdy), 1919
Guiterrero (p Scribe), 1841
Gulliver (Simon), 1952
Gusman d'Alfarache (p Scribe), 1816
Gustalin (f Aymé), 1937
Gustave III (p Scribe), 1833
Gustavus the Third (p Scribe), 1833
Gutter in the Sky (f Genet), 1956
Guzla (v Mérimée), 1827

Habit vert (p Augier, A. Musset), 1849
Haï (Le Clézio), 1971
Haine (p Sardou), 1875
Haine d'une femme (p Scribe), 1824
Haïr à force d'aimer (f Simenon), 1928
Half Brothers (f Dumas père), 1858
Halifax (p Dumas père), 1842
Hamlet (p Dumas père), 1847
Hamlet (p Gide), 1946
Han d'Islande (f Hugo), 1823
Han of Iceland (f Hugo), 1825
Handsome Laurence (f Sand), 1871
Happy Days (p Beckett), 1961
Happy Death (f Camus), 1973
Happy Hunter (p Feydeau), 1973
Hard Winter (f Queneau), 1948
Hard-Boiled Egg (p Ionesco), 1976
Harlot High and Low (f Balzac), 1970
Harlot's Progress (f Balzac)
Harmonies poétiques et religieuses (v Lamartine), 1830
Harvest (f Giono), 1939
Hashish and Incense (v Verlaine), 1925
Hatter's Ghost (f Simenon), 1956
Hatter's Phantom (f Simenon), 1976
Haunted Marsh (f Sand), 1848
Haut Mal (f Simenon), 1933
Haut mal (v Leiris), 1943
Haute surveillance (p Genet), 1949
Hauts Faits des Jésuites (v Nerval), 1826
Hauts Ponts (f Lacretelle), 1932-35
Havoc by Accident (f Simenon), 1943
Haydée (p Scribe), 1848
He and She (f Sand), 1900–02
He "Lies like Truth," (p Scribe), 1850
Head in the Clouds (f Troyat), 1979
Heart of a Man (f Simenon), 1951

Heart of the Matter (Teilhard de Chardin), 1978
Heart-Keeper (f Sagan), 1968
Hector Servadac (f Verne), 1877
Hedera (v Pieyre de Mandiargues), 1945
Heirs of Rabourdin (p Zola), 1893
Hélas! Je t'aime (f Simenon), 1929
Hélène (f Zola), 1878
Hélène de Sparte (p Verhaeren), 1908
Hélène en fleur et Charlemagne (v Fort), 1921
Héliogabale (Artaud), 1934
Hell of a Mess (p Ionesco), 1975
Héloïse (f Hébert), 1980
Héloïse et Abailard (p Scribe), 1850
Henri III et sa cour (p Dumas père), 1829
Henriette Maréchal (p Goncourt), 1866
Her Last Stake (p Augier), 1882
Herbe (Simon), 1958
Herbe rouge (f Vian), 1950
Here Comes a Chopper (p Ionesco), 1971
Heresiarch and Company (f Apollinaire), 1965
Hérésiarque et Cie (f Apollinaire), 1910
Héritage de Birague (f Balzac), 1822
Héritages (f Chamson), 1932
Héritier du corsaire (f Simenon), 1934
Héritière (p Scribe), 1824
Héritiers de Crac (p Scribe), 1829
Héritiers de l'avenir (f Troyat), from 1968
Héritiers Rabourdin (p Zola), 1874
Hermine (p Anouilh), 1932
Herminie (f Dumas père), 1858
Hermit (f Ionesco), 1974
Hernani (p Hugo), 1830
Héros (v Verhaeren), 1908
Heure à Porte Sainte-Marie (p Scribe), 1823
Heure du spectacle (p Sardou), 1878
Heures claires (v Verhaeren), 1896
Heures d'après-midi (v Verhaeren), 1905
Heures du soir (v Verhaeren), 1911
Heureuse Fin (f Simenon), 1925
Hier et demain (f Verne), 1910
Hier régnant désert (v Bonnefoy), 1958
Hiéroglyphes (Gourmont), 1894
Hill of Destiny (f Giono), 1929
Hiroshima mon amour (f Duras), 1960
Hiroshima mon amour (p Duras), 1960
His Excellency (f Zola), 1958
His Excellency Eugène Rougon (f Zola), 1886
His Masterpiece (f Zola), 1886
Histoire (Simon), 1967
Histoire d'amour (f Du Camp), 1888
Histoire d'amour de "La Rose de sable," (f Montherlant), 1954
Histoire de Dona Maria d'Avals et de Don Fabricio, duc d'Andria (f France), 1902
Histoire de France (Michelet), 1833
Histoire de la folie (Foucault), 1963
Histoire de la grandeur et de la décadence de César Birotteau (f Balzac), 1838
Histoire de la guerre d'Espagne (Brasillach), 1939
Histoire de la littérature anglaise (Taine), 1863–64
Histoire de la révolution française (Michelet), 1847–53
Histoire de la sexualité (Foucault), from 1976

Histoire de lynx (Levi-Strauss), 1991
Histoire de Napoléon (f Balzac), 1833
Histoire de rire (p Labiche), 1848
Histoire de rire (p Salacrou), 1939
Histoire de Tobie et de Sara (p Claudel), 1947
Histoire des origines du christianisme (Renan), from 1863
Histoire des treize (f Balzac), 1834–35
Histoire d'Ottar Jarl (f Gobineau), 1879
Histoire du cinéma (Brasillach), 1935
Histoire du peuple d'Israël 1887–93
Histoire du roi de Bohème et de ses sept châteaux (f Nodier), 1830
Histoire du roi Kaboul Ier et du marmiton Gauwain (Jacob), 1904
Histoire du vieux temps (p Maupassant), 1879
Histoire d'un cabanon et d'un chalet (f Dumas père), 1859
Histoire d'un pantalon (f Simenon), 1926
Histoire d'une histoire (Halévy), 1939
Histoire parallèle (URSS-USA) (Aragon), 1962
Histoire philosophique de la règne de Louis XV (Tocqueville), 1846
Histoire sans nom (f Barbey D'Aurevilly), 1882
Histoire tragique de la princesse Phénissa (Gourmont), 1894
Histoires (v Prévert), 1946
Histoires de Boches (f Salmon), 1917
Histoires de Tabusse (f Chamson), 1930
Histoires de vertige (f Green), 1984
Histoires déplaisantes (f Drieu la Rochelle), 1963
Histoires désobligeantes (f Bloy), 1894
Histoires insolites (Villiers de l'Isle Adam), 1888
Histoires magiques (Gourmont), 1894
Histoires naturelles (Renard), 1896
Histoires obscures (v Tardieu), 1961
Histoires vraies (Cendrars), 1937
Historie comique (f France), 1903
History (Simon), 1969
History of English Literature (Taine), 1871
History of France (Michelet), 1845–48
History of Sex (Beauvoir), 1961
History of Sexuality (Foucault), 1979
History of the French Revolution (Michelet), 1967
History of the Grandeur and Downfall of Cesar Birotteau (f Balzac), 1860
History of the Thirteen (f Balzac), 1974
History of the USSR from Lenin to Kruschev (Aragon, Cocteau), 1964
Hitchhiker (f Simenon), 1955
Hiver à Majorque (Sand), 1842
Hollywood (Cendrars), 1936
Holy Innocents (Péguy), 1956
Holy Terrors (f Cocteau), 1957
Holy Terrors (p Cocteau), 1962
Holy Week (Aragon), 1962
Hombres (v Verlaine), 1903
Home (p Augier), 1893
Home (p Duras), 1973
Home Town (f Simenon), 1944
Home Truths (p Augier), 1860
Homeward Bound (f Verne), 1878
Homme à cheval (f Drieu la Rochelle), 1943
Homme à la cigarette (f Simenon), 1931

Homme à trois visages (p Pixérécourt), 1801
Homme assis dans le couloir (p Duras), 1980
Homme atlantique (p Duras), 1982
Homme au bracelet d'or (f Du Camp), 1861
Homme au petit chien (f Simenon), 1964
Homme aux douze étreintes (f Simenon), 1927
Homme aux valises (p Ionesco), 1975
Homme blanc (v Romains), 1937
Homme comme les autres (p Salacrou), 1936
Homme communiste (Aragon), 1946
Homme couvert de femmes (f Drieu la Rochelle), 1928
Homme d'affaires (f Bourget), 1900
Homme de bien (p Augier), 1845
Homme de chair et l'homme reflet (Jacob), 1924
Homme de la pampa (f Supervielle), 1923
Homme de la Tour Eiffel (f Simenon), 1950
Homme de lettres (f F. Mauriac), 1928
Homme de Londres (f Simenon), 1934
Homme de neige (f Sand), 1858
Homme de paille (p Labiche), 1843
Homme de pourpre (Louÿs), 1901
Homme de proie (f Simenon), 1931
Homme économe (p Feydeau), 1885
Homme en tête (v Duhamel), 1909
Homme est venu me voir (p Duras), 1968
Homme et son désir (p Claudel), 1921
Homme foudroyé (Cendrars), 1945
Homme intègre (p Feydeau), 1886
Homme noir (p Scribe), 1820
Homme nu (Lévi-Strauss)
Homme qui dort (Perec), 1967
Homme qui manque le coche (p Labiche), 1865
Homme qui marchait dans un rayon de soleil (p Char), 1967
Homme qui marchait devant moi (f Chamson), 1948
Homme qui regardait passer les trains (f Simenon), 1938
Homme qui rit (f Hugo), 1869
Homme qui tremble (f Simenon), 1930
Homme révolté (Camus), 1951
Homme sanguin (p Labiche), 1847
Hommes de bonne volonté (f Romains), 1932–56
Hommes de fer (f Dumas père), 1867
Hommes de la route (f Chamson), 1927
Hommes de lettres (f Goncourt), 1860
Honnêtes Femmes (p Becque), 1880
Honneur est satisfait (p Dumas père), 1858
Honorine (f Balzac), 1845
Horace (f Sand), 1842
Horla (f Maupassant), 1887
Horloger d'Everton (f Simenon), 1954
Horoscope (f Dumas père), 1858
Horse Eats Hat (p Labiche), 1936
Horseman on the Roof (f Giono), 1954
Hortense a dit "Je m'en fous!" (p Feydeau),1916
Hostage (p Claudel), 1917
Hosties noires (v Senghor), 1948
Hotel Acropolis (f Drieu la Rochelle), 1931
Hôtel des Quatre-Nations (p Scribe), 1818
Hôtel du Libre-Echange (p Feydeau), 1928
Hotel Paradiso (p Feydeau), 1957
Hourra l'Oural (Aragon), 1934
House by the Canal (f Simenon), 1952

House in the Desert (f Duhamel), 1935
House of Assignation (f Robbe-Grillet), 1970
House of Fourchambault (p Augier), 1915
House of Lies (f Mallet-Joris), 1957
House on Quai Notre Dame (f Simenon), 1975
How It Is (f Beckett), 1964
How Jolly Life Is! (f Zola), 1886
Hugo, poète réaliste (Aragon), 1952
Huguenots (p Scribe), 1836
Huis clos (p Sartre), 1944
Huit jours à la campagne (p Renard), 1912
Human Beast (f Zola), 1891
Human Comedy (f Balzac)
Human Energy (Teilhard de Chardin), 1969
Human Heart (f Maupassant), 1890
Human Voice (p Cocteau), 1951
Humanism and Terror (Merleau-Ponty), 1969
Humanisme et terreur (Merleau-Ponty), 1947
Humiliation of the Father (p Claudel), 1945
Humulus le muet (p Anouilh), 1958
Humulus the Great (p Anouilh), 1976
Hun (p C. Mauriac), 1968
Hunchback of Notre-Dame (f Hugo), 1833
Hunger and Thirst (p Ionesco), 1968
Hunting with the Fox (Renard), 1948
Hurluberlu (p Anouilh), 1959
Hussard sur le toit (f Giono), 1952
Hyacinthes (v Pieyre de Mandiargues), 1967
Hymn of the Universe (Teilhard de Chardin), 1965
Hymne de l'univers (Teilhard de Chardin), 1962
Hymnis (p Banville), 1879
Hypnos Waking (v Char), 1956
Hypothèse (p Pinget), 1961
Hypothesis (p Pinget), 1967

I Have Killed (Cendrars), 1919
I Take This Woman (f Simenon), 1953
Iceland Fisherman (f Loti), 1887
Ici haute (v Ponge), 1971
Ici, maintenant (p C. Mauriac), 1968
Ici ou ailleurs (p Pinget), 1961
Ici Poddema (v Michaux), 1946
Ideal in Art (Taine), 1868
Idéalisme anglais (Taine), 1864
Idées de Madame Aubray (p Dumas fils), 1867
Identité (p Pinget), 1971
Idiot de la famille (Sartre), 1971–72
Idylle tragique (f Bourget), 1896
Idylles prussiennes (v Banville), 1871
If I Were You (f Green), 1949
If It Die… (Gide), 1935
Ignorant (v Jaccottet), 1958
Il est de la police (p Labiche), 1872
Il est important d'être aimé (p Anouilh), 1964
Il fait beau jour et nuit (p Sagan), 1978
Il faut qu'une porte soit ouverte ou fermée (p A. Musset), 1848
Il ne faut jurer de rien (p A. Musset), 1840
Il ne m'est Paris que d'Elsa (Aragon), 1964
Il y a encore des noisetiers (f Simenon), 1969
Il y a là des cris (v Fort), 1895
Il y a un océan (v Soupault), 1936

Il y avait foule au manoir (p Tardieu), 1951
Ile à hélice (f Verne), 1895
Ile de feu (f Dumas père), 1870
Ile de France (v Fort), 1908
Ile de la désolation (f Simenon), 1933
Ile des hommes roux (f Simenon), 1929
Ile des maudits (f Simenon), 1929
Ile des pingouins (f France), 1908
Ile empoisonnée (f Simenon), 1937
Ile mystérieuse (f Verne), 1874–75
Ill Seen, Ill Said (f Beckett), 1981
Illuminations (v Rimbaud), 1886
Illuminés (f Nerval), 1851
Illusionist (f Mallet-Joris), 1952
Illusions perdues (f Balzac)
Illustrations 1–4 (v Butor), 1964–76
Illustre Gaudissart (f Balzac), 1833
Image (p Scribe), 1845
Image, Music, Text (Barthes), 1977
Images japonaises (v Verhaeren), 1906
Imagier de Harlem (p Nerval), 1851
Imaginaire (Sartre), 1940
Imagination (Sartre), 1936
Imagination Dead Imagine (f Beckett), 1966
Imagination morte imaginez (f Beckett), 1965
Imitation de Notre-Dame la Lune (Laforgue), 1886
Immaculée Conception (Breton, Éluard), 1930
Immoralist (f Gide), 1930
Immoraliste (f Gide), 1902
Immortal (f A. Daudet), 1889
Immortal One (f Robbe-Grillet), 1971
Immortel (f A. Daudet), 1888
Immortelle (f Robbe-Grillet), 1963
Immortelle maladie (v Péret), 1924
Imposter (f Cocteau), 1957
Imposture (f Bernanos), 1927
Impressions anciennes (v Char), 1964
Impressions d'Afrique (Roussel), 1910
Impressions of Africa (Roussel), 1966
Impromptu de l'Alma (p Ionesco), 1956
Impromptu de Paris (p Giraudoux), 1937
Impromptu d'Ohio (p Beckett), 1982
Impromptu du Palais-Royal (p Cocteau), 1962
Impromptu pour la Duchesse de Windsor (p Ionesco), 1957
Improvisation (p Ionesco), 1960
Impudents (f Duras), 1943
In Camera (p Sartre), 1946
In Case of Emergency (f Simenon), 1958
In Honour Bound (p Scribe), 1885
In Praise of Philosophy (Merleau-Ponty), 1963
In Sight of the Promised Land (f Duhamel), 1935
In the Labyrinth (f Robbe-Grillet), 1960
In the Mesh (p Sartre), 1954
In the Prison of Her Skin (Leduc), 1970
In Two Latitudes (f Simenon), 1942
Incidental Music (f Sagan), 1983
Inclémence lointaine (v Char), 1961
Incompris (p Montherlant), 1944
Inconnue (f Simenon), 1930
Inconnue d'Adolphe (Constant de Rebecque), 1933
Inconnue d'Arras (p Salacrou), 1935

Inconnus dans la maison (f Simenon), 1940
Inconsolables (p Scribe), 1830
Indépendants (p Scribe), 1838
Indes noires (f Verne), 1877
India Song (p Duras), 1973
Indiana (f Sand), 1832
Indulgent Husband (f Colette), 1935
Inequality of Human Races (Gobineau), 1915
Infernal Machine (p Cocteau), 1936
Infernaliana (f Nodier), 1822
Information Bureau (p Tardieu), 1962
Infra-ordinaire (Perec), 1989
Ingénue (f Dumas père), 1854
Ingénue libertine (f Colette), 1909
Inhabitants of Pontarcy (p Sardou), 1878
Inigo (p Green), 1947
Innocent Libertine (f Colette), 1978
Innocent Wife (f Colette), 1934
Innocents (f Simenon), 1972
Innommable (f Beckett), 1953
Inquest on Bouvet (f Simenon), 1958
Inquisitoire (f Pinget), 1962
Inquisitory (f Pinget), 1966
Inscriptions (v Maurras), 1921
Inséparables (p Scribe), 1825
Instant fatal (v Queneau), 1946
Instantanés (f Robbe-Grillet), 1962
Institut (v Sully Prudhomme), 1895
Insurgé (Vallès), 1886
Interdiction (f Balzac), 1836
Intérieur (p Maeterlinck), 1894
Intérieur d'un bureau (p Scribe), 1823
Intérieur de l'étude (p Scribe), 1821
Interior (p Maeterlinck), 1895
Intermezzo (p Giraudoux), 1933
Interrogation (v Drieu la Rochelle) 1917
Interrogation (f Le Clézio), 1964
Intervalle (f Butor), 1973
Intimacy (f Sartre), 1949
Intimate Relations (p Cocteau), 1962
Intimations of Christianity among the Ancient Greeks (Weil),
     1957
Into the Abyss (f Verne), 1890
Into the Labyrinth (f Mallet-Joris), 1953
Into the Niger Bend (f Verne), 1965
Intrigue et amour (p Dumas père), 1847
Introduction to Metaphysics (Bergson), 1912
Introduction to the Science of Mythology (Lévi-Strauss), from
     1969
Intruder (p Maeterlinck), 1891
Intruse (p Maeterlinck), 1890
Intuition de l'instant (Bachelard), 1932
Intuition philosophique (Bergson), 1911
Intuitions atomistiques (Bachelard), 1933
Intuitions préchrétiennes (Weil), 1951
Inutile Beauté (f Maupassant), 1890
Invasion (p Adamov), 1950
Invasion de la mer (f Verne), 1905
Invectives (v Verlaine), 1896
Inventaire de l'abîme (f Duhamel), 1945
Inventeur de la poudre (p Labiche), 1846

Invitation (Simon), 1988
Invitation à la valse (p Dumas père), 1857
Invitation au château (p Anouilh), 1947
Invitée (f Beauvoir), 1943
Invités au procès (p Hébert), 1967
Invités du Bon Dieu (p Salacrou), 1953
Invraisemblance (f Dumas père), 1844
Iphigénie (p Moréas), 1904
Irène (p Scribe), 1847
Iris de Suse (f Giono), 1970
Iron in the Soul (f Sartre), 1950
Iron Staircase (f Simenon), 1963
Irréparable (f Bourget), 1884
Isaac Laquedem (f Dumas père), 1852–53
Isabel of Bavaria (f Dumas père), 1846
Isabella Morra (p Pieyre de Mandiargues), 1973
Isabelle (f Gide), 1911
Isabelle (Senancour), 1833
Isabelle de Bavière (f Dumas père), 1836
Isidora (f Sand), 1845
Isis (Villiers de l'Isle Adam), 1862
Isma (p Sarraute), 1970
Issue (f Beckett), 1968
Issue (v Char), 1961
It Is There (p Sarraute), 1980
Italian Straw Hat (p Labiche), 1955
It's Beautiful (p Sarraute), 1980
It's Later Than You Think (p Anouilh), 1970
Ivanhoë (p), 1974
Ivre Oeil (v Pieyre de Mandiargues), 1979
Izzuma (p Sarraute), 1980

J'abats mon jeu (Aragon), 1959
Jacinthes (v Pieyre de Mandiargues), 1967
Jack (f A. Daudet), 1876
Jack (p A. Daudet), 1882
Jack (p Ionesco), 1958
Jacobin en mission (p Pixérécourt), 1794
Jacques (p Ionesco), p 1954
Jacques (f Sand), 1834
Jacques d'Antifer, roi des Iles du Vent (f Simenon), 1930
Jacques Vingtras (Vallès), from 1879
Jacquot sans oreilles (f Dumas père), 1860
Jadis et naguère (v Verlaine), 1884
J'ai compromis ma femme (p Labiche), 1861
J'ai mal aux dents (p Feydeau), 1883
J'ai tué (Cendrars), 1918
Jalousie (f Robbe-Grillet), 1957
Jane (f Dumas père), 1859
Jane Grey (Staël), 1790
Jane la pâle (f Balzac), 1836
Jangada (f Verne), 1881
Janot-poète (Jammes), 1928
Japhet (p Scribe), 1840
Jaqueire (p Mérimée), 1828
Jardin des bêtes sauvages (f Duhamel), 1934
Jardin des chimères (v Yourcenar), 1921
Jardin des supplices (f Mirbeau), 1899
Jardinier du jardin de France (v Fort), 1943
Jargal (f Hugo), 1866
Jarretière de la mariée (p Scribe), 1816

Jarvis l'honnête homme (p Dumas père), 1840
Jaune Bleu Blanc (f Larbaud), 1927
Jazz (p Pagnol), 1927
Je croque ma tante (p Labiche), 1858
Je est un autre (p Green), 1954
Je…ils… (f Adamov), 1969
Je me souviens (Perec), 1978
Je m'explique (Teilhard de Chardin), 1966
Je ne mange pas de ce pain-là (v Péret), 1936
Je ne trompe pas mon mari (p Feydeau), 1914
Je sublime (v Péret), 1936
Jealousies of a Country Town (f Balzac)
Jealousy (f Robbe-Grillet), 1959
Jealousy (f Sand), 1855
Jean Barois (f Martin du Gard), 1913
Jean Cavalier (f Sue), 1840
Jean de la Roche (f Sand), 1860
Jean de Thommeray (p Augier), 1874
Jean et Jeannette (f Gautier), 1850
Jean le bleu (f Giono), 1932
Jean le Maufranc (p Romains), 1926
Jean Santeuil (f Proust), 1952
Jean Sbogar (f Nodier), 1818
Jean-Christophe (f Rolland), 1904–12
Jean-Louis (f Balzac), 1822
Jeanne (f Sand), 1844
Jeanne d'Arc (p Maeterlinck), 1948
Jeanne d'Arc (Péguy), 1897
Jeanne d'Arc au bûcher (p Claudel), 1938
Jeanne et Jeanneton (p Scribe), 1848
Jeanne et Louise (f Sue), 1853
Jeanne la folle (p Scribe), 1848
Jeanne la Pucelle (f Dumas père), 1842
Jeanne qu'on brûla verte (v Char), 1956
Jeannic le breton (p Dumas père), 1841
Jenny Bell (p Scribe), 1855
Jeu de l'amour et de la mort (p Rolland), 1925
Jeu du souterrain (f Mallet-Joris), 1973
Jeune Enchanteur (Baudelaire), 1868
Jeune et vieille (p Scribe), 1830
Jeune Européen (v Drieu la Rochelle) 1927
Jeune Fille à marier (p Ionesco), 1953
Jeune Fille nue (v Jammes), 1899
Jeune Fille Violaine (p Claudel), 1901
Jeune Homme du dimanche (f Supervielle), 1955
Jeune homme pressé (p Labiche), 1848
Jeune Parque (v Valéry), 1917
Jeunes Filles (f Montherlant), 1936
Jeunes-France (f Gautier), 1833
Jeunesse (p Augier), 1858
Jeunesse d'Adrien Zograffi (f Istrati), 1926–30
Jeunesse d'un clerc (Benda), 1936
Jeunesse de Louis XIV (p Dumas père), 1854
Jeunesse de Proudhon (Halévy), 1913
Jeunesse des Mousquetaires (p Dumas père), 1849
Jeux de massacre (p Ionesco), 1970
Jeux innocents (v Radiguet), 1926
Jeux sont faits (p Sartre), 1947
Jewess (p Scribe), 1835
Jézabel (p Anouilh), 1946
J'invite le colonel (p Labiche), 1860

J'irai cracher sur vos tombes (f Vian), 1946
Joan the Heroic Maiden (f Dumas père), 1847
Jocaste et le Chat maigre (f France), 1879
Jocelyn (v Lamartine), 1836
Jockeys camouflés (v Reverdy), 1918
John and Jeannette (p Labiche), 1884
Joie (f Bernanos), 1929
Joie de vivre (f Zola), 1884
Joies désolées (v Fort), 1937
Joseph à Dothan (p Giono), 1959
Joues en feu (v Radiguet), 1920
Joueur de flûte (p Augier), 1897
Jour (v Jammes), 1895
Jour (f Le Clézio), 1964
Jour de soleil (f Simenon), 1928
Jour et la nuit (v Salmon), 1937
Journal de Salavin (f Duhamel), 1927
Journal du chercheur d'or (f Le Clézio), 1986
Journal du voleur (Genet), 1949
Journal d'un curé de campagne (f Bernanos), 1936
Journal d'un homme occupé (Brasillach), 1955
Journal d'un homme trompé (f Drieu la Rochelle), 1934
Journal d'une femme de chambre (f Mirbeau), 1900
Journal d'une poésie nationale (Aragon), 1954
Journal intime (f Queneau), 1950
Journée des aveux (p Duhamel), 1924
Journées entières dans les arbres (p Duras), 1965
Journey among the Dead (p Ionesco), 1983
Journey of M. Perrichon (p Labiche), 1924
Journey Through France (Taine), 1897
Journey to America (Tocqueville), 1960
Journey to England and Ireland (Tocqueville), 1958
Journey to the Centre of the Earth (f Verne), 1872
Journey to the End of the Night (f Céline), 1934
Journeyman Joiner (f Sand), 1847
Jours et les nuits (f Jarry), 1897
Jours pétrifiés (v Tardieu), 1947
Joy (f Bernanos), 1948
Joy of Life (f Zola), 1901
Joy of Man's Desiring (f Giono), 1940
Joyeux retour (p Tardieu), 1975
Joyzelle (p Maeterlinck), 1903
Juda de Kérioth (p Maeterlinck), 1929
Judas (p Pagnol), 1955
Judge and the Hatter (f Simenon), 1956
Judith (p Giraudoux), 1931
Judith Madrier (f Troyat), 1940
Judith Renaudin (p Loti), 1898
Jugement de Dieu (f Troyat), 1941
Jugement dernier (p Maeterlinck), 1959
Juif errant (p Scribe), 1852
Juif errant (f Sue), 1845
Juif errant (p Sue), 1849
Juive (p Scribe), 1835
Juive de Constantine (p Gautier), 1846
Jules Michelet (Halévy), 1928
Julie (v Apollinaire), 1927
Julie de Carneilhan (f Colette), 1941
Juliette au pays des hommes (f Giraudoux), 1924
Jumeaux du diable (f Aymé), 1928
Jument perdue (f Simenon), 1948

Jument verte (f Aymé), 1934
Juré (p Feydeau), 1898
Just Assassins (p Camus), 1958
Justes (p Camus), 1949
Justice (f Simenon), 1949
Justice (v Sully Prudhomme), 1878
Justicier (f Bourget), 1919

Kamouraska (f Hébert), 1970
Kardiki (f Sue), 1839
Katia, acrobate (f Simenon), 1931
Kean (p Dumas père), 1836
Kean (p Sartre), 1953
Keep an Eye on Amélie (p Feydeau), 1958
Képi (f Colette), 1943
Kéraban le tétu (f Verne), 1883
Kéraban le tétu (p Verne), 1883
Keraban the Inflexible (f Verne), 1884
Keyhole (p Tardieu), 1962
Kill (f Zola), 1895
Killer (p Ionesco), 1960
Killing Game (p Ionesco), 1974
King Candaules (p Gide), 1951
King's Edict (p Hugo), 1872
King's Favorite (f Dumas père), 1906
Kings in Exile (f A. Daudet), 1879
Kiss to the Leper (f F. Mauriac), 1923
Knights of the Round Table (p Cocteau), 1963
Knock (p Romains), 1923
Knot of Vipers (f F. Mauriac), 1951
Kodak (Cendrars), 1924
Kommen und Gehen (p Beckett), 1966
Koulikan (p Scribe), 1813
Koulouf (p Pixérécourt), 1807
Krapp's Last Tape (p Beckett), 1958
Kyra Kyralina (f Istrati), 1924
Kyra, My Sister (f Istrati), 1930

La Fontaine et ses fables (Taine), 1861
Là-bas (f Huysmans), 1891
Labor (f Zola), 1901
Laboratoire central (Jacob), 1921
Lac d'angoisse (f Simenon), 1928
Lac des esclaves (f Simenon), 1933
Lac des fées (p Scribe), 1839
Lacune (p Ionesco), 1965
Ladies of Saint-Cyr (p Dumas père), 1870
Ladies' Battle (p Scribe), 1850
Ladies' Delight (f Zola), 1957
Ladies' Man (p Feydeau), 1982
Ladies' Paradise (f Zola), 1883
Lady and the Little Fox Fur (f Leduc), 1967
Lady Blake's Love-Letters (f Sand), 1884
Lady from Maxim's (p Feydeau), 1971
Lady of Belle Isle (p Dumas père), 1872
Lady of the Camelias (f Dumas fils)
Lafcadio's Adventures (f Gide), 1927
Lai d'Arioste (v Maurras), 1950
Laird de Dumbicky (p Dumas père), 1843
Lamb (f F. Mauriac), 1955
Lambert Simnel (p Scribe), 1843

Lament for the Death of an Upper Class (f Montherlant), 1935
Lamiel (f Stendhal), 1889
Lampe d'Aladin (v Cocteau), 1909
Lanceur de graines (p Giono), 1943
Land of Promise (f Bourget), 1895
Landru (p Sagan), 1963
Language, Counter-Memory, Practice (Foucault), 1977
Language, tangage, ou ce que les mots disent (Leiris), 1985
Langue secrète des Dogons de Sanga (Leiris) 1948
Lanterne de Priollet (v Fort), 1918
Lanterne sourde (f Renard), 1893
Lark (p Anouilh), 1955
Larme du diable (p Gautier), 1839
Larmes avant le bonheur (f Simenon), 1925
Last Aldini (f Sand), 1847
Last Canto of Childe Harold's Pilgrimage (v Lamartine), 1827
Last Day of a Condemned (f Hugo), 1840
Last Nights of Paris (f Soupault), 1929
Last of Chéri (f Colette), 1932
Last of the Abencérages (f Chateaubriand), 1826
Last Vendee (f Dumas père), 1894
Last Year at Marienbad (f Robbe-Grillet), 1962
Latréaumont (f Sue), 1837
Latréaumont (p Sue), 1831
Latude (p Pixérécourt), 1834
Laughing Man (f Hugo), 1887
Laughter (Bergson), 1911
Laura (f Sand), 1864
Laurence Albani (f Bourget), 1919
Lavigerie (Jammes), 1927
Lavinia (f Sand),1834
Lazare (p Zola), 1921
Lazarine (f Bourget), 1917
Le là (v Breton), 1961
Léa (f Barbey d'Aurevilly), 1919
Leader (p Ionesco), 1960
Leader of the Resistance (f Verne), 1890
Learning to Walk (p Ionesco), 1973
Leaves of Hypnos (Char), 1973
Leçon (p Ionesco),1951
Leçon bien apprise (f France), 1898
Leçon de choses (Simon), 1976
Leçon inaugurale (Barthes), 1977
Leçons (v Jaccottet), 1969
Leçons de philosophie (Weil), 1959
Leçons poétiques (Jammes), 1930
Lectures on Art (Taine), 1871 and 1875
Lectures on Philosophy (Weil), 1978
Lêda (Louÿs), 1893
Legend of Lovers (p Anouilh), 1951
Légende de l'aile (Jammes), 1938
Légende de Prakriti (v Claudel), 1934
Légende des siècles (v Hugo), 1859–83
Leicester (p Scribe), 1823
Lélia (f Sand), 1833
Léo Burckart (p Dumas père, Nerval), 1839
Léocadia (p Anouilh), 1940
Leocadia (p Scribe), 1835
Léocadie (p Scribe), 1824
Léon Degrelle et l'avenir de Rex (Brasillach), 1936
Léone (v Cocteau), 1945

Leone Leoni (f Sand), 1835

Léonides (p Rolland), 1928

Léonie est en avance (p Feydeau), 1911

Leoun (v Cocteau), 1960

Lepers (f Montherlant), 1940

Lépreuses (f Montherlant), 1939

Lesser Bourgeoisie (f Balzac), 1896

Lessness (f Beckett), 1970

Lesson (p Ionesco), 1958

Lesson in Love (f Colette), 1932

Lesson in Love (f Zola), 1953

Lestocq (p Scribe), 1834

Let Me Explain (Teilhard de Chardin), 1970

Let Us Be Divorced! (p Sardou), 1881

Letter to a Hostage (f Saint-Exupéry), 1948

Letter to a Priest (Weil), 1954

Lettera amorosa (v Char), 1953

Letters from a Mill (f A. Daudet), 1893

Lettre à mon juge (f Simenon), 1946

Lettre à un otage (f Saint-Exupéry), 1943

Lettre à un religieux (Weil), 1951

Lettre chargée (p Labiche), 1877

Lettre morte (p Pinget), 1959

Lettres à Melisande pour son education philosophique (Benda), 1925

Lettres à un absent (f A. Daudet), 1871

Lettres de ma chaumière (f Mirbeau), 1886

Lettres de mon moulin (f A. Daudet), 1868

Lettres d'hivernage (v Senghor), 1973

Lettres d'un royaliste savoisien à ses compatriotes (Maistre), 1793

Lettres écrites en prison (Brasillach), 1952

Lettres sur Jean-Jacques Rousseau (Staël), 1788

Léviathan (f Green), 1929

Léviathan (p Green), 1962

Leycester du faubourg (p Scribe), 1824

Liasse (v Ponge), 1948

Libéra (f Pinget), 1968

Libera Me Domine (f Pinget), 1972

Liberté (Senghor), from 1964

Liberté d'action (v Michaux), 1945

Liberté des mers, sable mouvant (v Reverdy), 1960

Libertinage (Aragon), 1924

Liberty Bar (f Simenon), 1932

Libres méditations d'un solitaire inconnu sur le détachement du monde et sur d'autres objets de la morale religieuse (Senancour), 1819

Lice (Cendrars), 1973

Lie (p Sarraute), 1969

Lierre et l'ormeau (p Labiche), 1841

Lies (f Bourget)

Life: A User's Manual (Perec), 1990

Life and Matter in Conflict (Bergson), 1915

Life and Work of Semmelweis (Céline), 1937

Life of Friedrich Nietzsche (Halévy), 1911

Life of the Bee (Maeterlinck), 1901

Light on My Days (f Duhamel), 1948

Lighthouse at the End of the World (f Verne), 1923

Lili Tristesse (f Simenon), 1927

Lili-Sourire (f Simenon), 1930

Lilith (Gourmont), 1892

Liluli (p Rolland), 1919

Lily of the Valley (f Balzac), 1891

Lines of Life (f F. Mauriac), 1957

Lionnes pauvres (p Augier), 1858

Lions et renards (p Augier), 1870

Liquettes au vent (f Simenon), 1926

Lis de mer (f Pieyre de Mandiargues), 1956

Lis Isclo d'or (v Mistral), 1876

Lis Oulivado (v Mistral), 1912

Lise Tavernier (p A. Daudet), 1872

Lit défait (f Sagan), 1977

Lit la table (Éluard), 1944

Litanie d'eau (v Butor), 1964

Litanies de la rose (Gourmont), 1892

Littératures soviétiques (Aragon), 1955

Little Bit to Fall Back on (p Feydeau), 1973

Little Black Stories for Little White Children (Cendrars), 1929

Little Doctor (f Simenon), 1978

Little Fadette (f Sand), 1850

Little Good-for-Nothing (f A. Daudet), 1878

Little Horses of Tarquinia (f Duras), 1960

Little Man from Arkangel (f Simenon), 1957

Little Misery (f F. Mauriac), 1952

Little Parish Church (f A. Daudet), 1899

Little Pierre (f France), 1920

Little Prince (f Saint-Exupéry), 1943

Little Saint (f Simenon), 1965

Liturgies intimes (v Verlaine), 1892

Living Lie (f Bourget), 1896

Livre bleu (p Labiche), 1871

Livre d'amour (v Sainte-Beuve), 1843

Livre de Christophe Colomb (p Claudel), 1929

Livre de la pitié et de la mort (f Loti), 1891

Livre de mon ami (f France), 1885

Livre de Monelle (f Schwob), 1894

Livre de saint Joseph (Jammes), 1921

Livre des fuites (f Le Clézio), 1969

Livre du peuple (Lamennais), 1837

Livre et la bouteille (v Salmon), 1920

Livre mystique (f Balzac), 1835

Livre ouvert (Éluard), 1940

Livre posthume (f Du Camp), 1853

Locataire (f Simenon), 1934

Lock at Charenton (f Simenon), 1941

Locus Solus (Roussel), 1914

Lodger (f Simenon), 1943

Loge du portier (p Scribe), 1823

Loi salique (p Scribe), 1846

Loin de Rueil (f Queneau), 1944

Lointain intérieur (v Michaux), 1938

Long cours (f Simenon), 1936

Long Exile (f Simenon), 1982

Long March (Beauvoir), 1958

Longue Marche (Beauvoir), 1957

Look after Lulu (p Feydeau), 1959

Lorenzaccio (p A. Musset), 1834

Lorenzino (p Dumas père), 1842

Lorette (f Goncourt), 1853

Lorette (f Sue), 1855–57

Loser Wins (p Sartre), 1960

Lost Illusions (f Balzac), 1893

Lost Moorings (f Simenon), 1946
Lost Ones (p Beckett), 1972
Lost Profile (f Sagan), 1974
Lotissement du ciel (Cendrars), 1949
Lottery Ticket (f Verne)
Lou Pouèmo dóu rose (v Mistral), 1897
Louis Lambert (f Balzac), 1835
Louis XI, curieux homme (v Fort), 1922
Louise (p Scribe), 1829
Louise Bernard (p Dumas père), 1843
Louise Leclercq (Verlaine), 1886
Louisiane (p Aymé), 1961
Louison (p A. Musset), 1849
Loup (p Anouilh), 1953
Loup-garou (p Scribe), 1827
Loups (p Rolland), 1898
Lourdes (f Zola), 1894
Louves de Machecoul (f Dumas père), 1859
Love (f Balzac), 1893
Love Affair (f Zola), 1957
Love and Liberty (f Dumas père), 1916
Love Charm (p Scribe), 1831
Love in Humble Life (p Scribe), 1850
Love in the Eighteenth Century (f Goncourt), 1905
Love Life (f Bourget), 1888
Love of Hyppolita (p Augier), 1881
Loved and the Unloved (f F. Mauriac), 1952
Lovely Lady Hamilton (f Dumas père), 1903
Lover (f Duras), 1985
Lovers Are Never Losers (f Giono), 1931
Lover's Discourse (Barthes), 1978
Lovers in the Metro (p Tardieu), 1962
Lovers of Viorne (p Duras) 1971
Love's Cruel Enigma (f Bourget), 1887
Lubie (p Pinget), 1981
Lucarne ovale (v Reverdy), 1916
Lucie (p Sand), 1856
Lucien Leuwen (f Stendhal), 1855
Lucienne et le boucher (p Aymé), 1947
Lucienne 1922 (f Romains), 1922
Lucifer and the Lord (p Sartre), 1953
Lucky Prisoner (f Gobineau), 1926
Lucrèce Borgia (p Hugo), 1833
Lucretia Borgia (p Hugo), 1847
Lucrezia Floriani (f Sand), 1846
Lui et elle (P. Musset), 1859
Lullaby (Le Clézio), 1980
Lumière (p Duhamel), 1911
Lumière de Stendhal (Aragon), 1954
Lumière des justes (f Troyat), from 1959
Lundi series (Sainte-Beuve), from 1851
Lune de miel (f Balzac), 1845
Lune de miel (p Scribe), 1826
Lunes en papier (f Malraux), 1921
Luthier de Lisbonne (p Scribe), 1831
Lutte pour la vie (p A. Daudet), 1889
Luttes et problèmes (Halévy), 1911
Lycéenne (p Feydeau), 1887
Lyderic, Count of Flanders (f Dumas père), 1903
Lying Woman (f Giraudoux), 1972
Lys dans la vallée (f Balzac), 1836

Lys rouge (f France), 1894

Ma fille Bernadette (Jammes), 1910
Ma France poétique (v Jammes), 1926
Ma soeur Henriette (Renan), 1895
Ma soeur Jeanne (f Sand), 1874
Ma Tante Péronne (f Champfleury), 1867
Macbeth (p Deschamps), 1844
Macbeth (p Maeterlinck), 1909
Macbett (p Ionesco), 1972
Machine à écrire (p Cocteau), 1941
Machine infernale (p Cocteau), 1934
Machines à guérir (Foucault), 1976
Maçon (p Scribe), 1825
Mad in Pursuit (f Leduc), 1971
Madame Aubin (Verlaine), 1886
Madame Bovary (f Flaubert), 1857
Madame Caverlet (p Augier), 1876
Madame Chrysanthème (f Loti), 1888
Madame Chrysanthemum (f Loti), 1888
Madame d'Aigrizelles (f Champfleury), 1854
Madame de… (p Anouilh), 1959
Madame de Chamblay (f Dumas père), 1859
Madame de Chamblay (p Dumas père), 1868
Mme de Saint-Agnès (p Scribe), 1829
Madame est aux eaux (p Labiche), 1858
Madame est trop belle (p Labiche), 1874
Madame Eugenio (f Champfleury), 1874
Madame Gervaisais (f Goncourt), 1869
Madame Olympe (f Murger), 1859
Madame Prune (f Loti), 1919
Madame Sans-Gêne (p Sardou), 1907
Madame Sourdis (f Zola), 1929
Madame Veuve Larifla (p Labiche), 1849
Madeleine (p Zola), 1889
Madeleine Férat (f Zola), 1868
Mademoiselle de Belle-Isle (p Dumas père), 1839
Mademoiselle de Marsan (f Nodier), 1832
Mademoiselle de Maupin (f Gautier), 1835–36
Mademoiselle du Vissard (f Balzac), 1950
Mademoiselle Fifi (f Maupassant), 1882
Mademoiselle la Quintinie (f Sand), 1863
Mademoiselle ma femme (p Labiche), 1846
Mademoiselle Merquem (f Sand), 1868
Mademoiselle Million (f Simenon), 1930
Mademoiselle X (f Simenon), 1928
Madman of Bergerac (f Simenon), 1940
Madness and Civilization (Foucault), 1965
Madrigaux (v Mallarmé), 1920
Madwoman of Chaillot (p Giraudoux), 1949
Magic Skin (f Balzac), 1888
Magician (f Simenon), 1955 34,
Magnet of Doom (f Simenon), 1948
Magot (p Sardou), 1873
Mahu (f Pinget), 1952
Maid of Cashmere (p Scribe), 1833
Maid to Marry (p Ionesco), 1960
Maids (p Genet), 1954
Maigret, Inspector Jules series (f Simenon), from 1931
Main (f Simenon), 1968
Main coupée (Cendrars), 1946

Mémoires d'Hadrien (f Yourcenar), 1951
Mémoires d'infra-tombe (Benda), 1952
Mémoires d'outre-tombe (Chateaubriand), 1849–50
Mémoires du "Géant" (Nadar), 1864
Mémoires d'un colonel des hussards (p Scribe), 1822
Mémoires d'un maître d'armes (f Dumas père), 1840–41
Mémoires d'un médecin (f Dumas père), 1846–48
Mémoires d'un prostitué (f Simenon), 1929
Mémoires d'un valet de chambre (f Sue), 1846
Mémoires d'un vieux suiveur (f Simenon), 1926
Mémoires d'une jeune fille rangée (Beauvoir), 1958
Mémoires pour servir à l'histoire de la révolution française (f Balzac), 1829
Memoirs of a Dutiful Daughter (Beauvoir), 1959
Memoirs of a Physician (f Dumas père), 1847
Memoirs of a Valet-de-Chambre (f Sue), 1847
Memoirs of Hadrian (f Yourcenar), 1954
Memoirs of My Youth (f Lamartine), 1849
Memoirs of Two Young Married Women (f Balzac), 1894
Memorandum on My Martinique (v Césaire), 1947
Memories of the Golden Triangle (f Robbe-Grillet), 1984
Men (v Verlaine), 1979
Men and Saints (Péguy), 1947
Men of Darkness (p Salacrou), 1948
Men of Good Will (f Romains), 1933
Men Without Shadows (p Sartre), 1949
Ménage de garçon (p Scribe), 1821
Ménage de garçon en province (f Balzac), 1843
Meneur de loups (f Dumas père), 1857
Mensonge (p Sarraute), 1967
Mensonges (f Bourget), 1887
Mensonges (f Mallet-Joris), 1956
Mental Illness and Psychology (Foucault), 1976
Menteur véridique (p Scribe), 1823
Menteuse (p A. Daudet), 1892
Menteuse (f Giraudoux), 1958
Méprises de l'amour (p Augier), 1852
Mercadet (p Balzac), 1901
Mercier and Camier (f Beckett), 1970
Mercière assassinée (p Hébert),1967
Mère Noël (f Tournier), 1984
Meridiana (f Verne), 1873
Merlette (Gourmont), 1886
Merrie Tales of Jacques Tournebroche (f France), 1910
Merry-Go-Round (p Becque), 1913
Merveilleuse Aventure (f Simenon), 1929
Merveilleuses (p Sardou), 1873
Merveilleux Nuages (f Sagan), 1961
Mes apprentissages (Colette), 1936
Mes caravanes et autres poèmes (Aragon), 1954
Mes hôpitaux (Verlaine), 1891
Mes prisons (Verlaine), 1893
Mes propriétés (v Michaux), 1929
Mesdames de Montenfriche (p Labiche), 1856
Message de l'île déserte (v Soupault), 1947
Messager (p Banville), 1880
Messaline (f Jarry), 1900
Messe de l'athée (f Balzac), 1837
Messe là-bas (v Claudel), 1919
Messe sur la monde (Teilhard de Chardin), 1962
Messidor (p Zola), 1897

Métamorphoses de la harpe et de la harpiste (v Salmon), 1926
Métella (f Sand), 1834
Météores (f Tournier), 1975
Meuble (p Tardieu), 1954
Meunier d'Angibault (f Sand), 1845
Meunière (p Scribe), 1821
Michel et Christine (p Scribe), 1821
Michel Pauper (p Becque), 1870
Michel Strogoff (f Verne), 1876
Michel Strogoff (p Verne), 1880
Michelet par lui-même (Barthes), 1954
Middle Classes (f Balzac), 1898
Midnight (f Green), 1936
Midnight Love Feast (f Tournier), 1991
Mi-figure, mi-raisin (p Tardieu), 1951
Mikhail (f Istrati), 1927
1938: Une année d'histoire (Halévy), 1938
1929 (v Péret), 1929
Milieu divin (Teilhard de Chardin), 1957
Military Necessity (f Vigny), 1953
Military Servitude and Grandeur (f Vigny), 1919
Militona (f Gautier), 1847
Mille et un fantômes (f Dumas père), 1848–51
Miller of Angibault (f Sand), 1847
Mimes (f Schwob), 1893
Mind-Energy (Bergson), 1920
Mines de Pologne (p Pixérécourt), 1803
Minne (f Colette), 1903
Minotaure (p Aymé), 1967
Minuit (f Green), 1936
Miracle de la rose (f Genet), 1946
Miracle de Saint-Antoine (p Maeterlinck), 1919
Miracle en Alabama (p Duras), 1961
Miracle of Saint Anthony (p Maeterlinck), 1918
Miracle of the Rose (f Genet), 1965
Mirage de Paris (f Simenon), 1929
Mire (p Ionesco), 1973
Mirèio (v Mistral), 1859
Mirlitonnades (v Beckett), 1978
Miroir (p Salacrou), 1956
Miroir de la tauromachie (Leiris), 1938
Mirror-Wardrobe one Fine Evening (Aragon), 1964
Mirza (Staël), 1795
Misanthrope et l'Auvergnat (p Labiche), 1852
Miscreant (f Cocteau), 1958
Mise à mort (Aragon), 1965
Misérables (f Hugo), 1862
Miss Baby (f Simenon), 1928
Miss Harriet (f Maupassant), 1883
Mission de Phénicie (Renan), 1864–74
Mr. Hire's Engagement (f Simenon), 1958
Mr. Me (p Tardieu), 1968
Mistress Branican (f Verne), 1881
Mitsou (f Colette), 1918
Mixed Doubles (p Feydeau), 1982
Moderato Cantabile (f Duras), 1958
Modification (f Butor), 1957
Moeurs de la famille Poivre (f Salmon), 1919
Mohicans de Paris (f Dumas père), 1854–59
Mohicans de Paris (p Dumas père), 1864
Mohicans of Paris (f Dumas père), 1875

Moi (p Labiche), 1864
Moi, laminaire (v Césaire), 1982
Moines (v Verhaeren), 1886
Moïra (f Green), 1950
Molière (p Sand), 1851
Molloy (f Beckett), 1951
Môme dessalée (f Simenon), 1927
Moments (v Michaux), 1973
Mon étoile (p Scribe), 1854
Mon frère Yves (f Loti), 1883
Mon grand pays (v Fort), 1950
Mon Isménie (p Labiche), 1853
Mon premier testament (Benda), 1910
Mon univers (Teilhard de Chardin), 1965
Monday Tales (f A. Daudet), 1901
Monde de l'art n'est pas le monde du pardon (v Char), 1975
Mondo et autres histoires (f Le Clézio), 1978
Money (f Zola), 1894
Monique (f Bourget), 1902
Monna Vanna (p Maeterlinck), 1901
Monnaie de plomb (f Lacretelle), 1932–35
Monocle à deux coups (f Salmon), 1968
Monomaniac (f Zola), 1901
Monomanie (p Scribe), 1832
Monseigneur Gaston Phoebus (f Dumas père), 1839
Monsieur Alphonse (p Dumas fils), 1873
Monsieur Bergeret à Paris (f France), 1901
Monsieur Bergeret in Paris (f France), 1921
Monsieur chasse (p Feydeau), 1896
Monsieur Coumbes (f Dumas père), 1860
Monsieur Crinet (f Sue), 1846
Monsieur de Boisdhyver (f Champfleury), 1857
M. de Chimpanzé (p Verne), 1858
Monsieur de Coyllin (p Labiche), 1838
Monsieur de Saint-Cadenas (p Labiche), 1856
Monsieur Deutscourt (v Nerval), 1826
M. Gallet décédé (f Simenon), 1931
Monsieur Garat (p Sardou), 1860
Monsieur La Souris (f Simenon), 1938
Monsieur le Curé d'Ozeron (Jammes), 1918
Monsieur le Marquis (p Sue), 1829
M. Le Modéré (p Adamov), 1968
M. le Trouhadec saisi par la débauche (p Romains), 1923
Monsieur le Vent et Madame la Pluie (P. Musset), 1860
Monsieur Levert (f Pinget), 1961
Monsieur libidineux (f Simenon), 1927
Monsieur Moi (p Tardieu), 1966
Monsieur Monde Vanishes (f Simenon), 1967
Monsieur Monsieur (v Tardieu), 1951
Monsieur Ouine (f Bernanos), 1946
Monsieur Parent (f Maupassant), 1885
Monsieur Poirier's Son-in-Law (p Augier), 1915
Monsieur qui a brûle une dame (p Labiche), 1856
Monsieur qui est condamné à mort (p Feydeau), 1899
Monsieur qui n'aime pas les monologues (p Feydeau), 1882
Monsieur qui prend la mouche (p Labiche), 1852
Monsieur Songe (f Pinget), 1982
Monsieur Sylvestre (f Sand), 1865
Monsieur Tardif (p Scribe), 1824
Monsieur Teste (Valéry), 1946
Monsieur Tringle (f Champfleury), 1866

Monsieur Vincent (p Anouilh), 1951
Monsieur votre fille (p Labiche), 1855
Monstre blanc de la terre de feu (f Simenon), 1928
Monstres choisis (f Salmon), 1918
Monstres sacrés (p Cocteau), 1940
Mont sauvage (p Pixérécourt), 1821
Montagnes russes (p Scribe), 1816
Mont-Cinère (f Green), 1926
Mont-de-piété (v Breton), 1919
Monte-Cristo (p Dumas père), 1848
Montée de la nuit (v Char), 1961
Monténégrins (p Nerval), 1849
Montespan (p Rolland), 1904
Mont-Oriol (f Maupassant), 1887
Mont-Revêche (f Sand), 1853
Morale élémentaire (v Queneau), 1975
Moralistes (p Scribe), 1828
Moralités légendaires (Laforgue), 1887
Moravagine (Cendrars), 1926
More de Venise (p Vigny), 1829
More Pricks than Kicks (f Beckett), 1934
Morgane (Villiers de l'Isle Adam), 1866
Moribonds (f Soupault), 1934
Morne-au-diable (f Sue), 1842
Morne-au-diable (p Sue), 1848
Morning Glory (f Colette), 1932
Mort à crédit (f Céline), 1936
Mort aux vaches et au champ d'honneur (v Péret), 1953
Mort conduit l'attelage (f Yourcenar), 1934
Mort d'Auguste (f Simenon), 1966
Mort dans l'âme (f Sartre), 1949
Mort de Belle (f Simenon), 1952
Mort de quelqu'un (f Romains), 1911
Mort de Socrate (v Lamartine), 1823
Mort de Talma (v Nerval), 1826
Mort de Tintagiles (p Maeterlinck), 1894
Mort d'Ivan Ilytch (p Green), 1965
Mort du père (f Martin du Gard), 1929
Mort d'un personnage (f Giono), 1949
Mort et le bûcheron (p Scribe), 1815
Mort heureuse (f Camus), 1971
Mort saisit le vif (f Troyat), 1942
Mort très douce (Beauvoir), 1964
Morticoles (f L. Daudet), 1894
Morts ont tous la même peau (f Vian), 1947
Morts sans sépulture (p Sartre), 1946
Mosaic Masters (f Sand), 1847
Mosaic Workers (f Sand), 1844
Mosaica (Mérimée), 1903
Mosaïque (Mérimée), 1833
Moscovite (f Troyat), 1974
Mosquita la sorcière (p Scribe), 1851
Mot pour un autre (p Tardieu), 1950
Mother of Claudine (Colette), 1937
Motocyclette (f Pieyre de Mandiargues), 1963
Motor Show (p Ionesco), 1963
Motorcycle (f Pieyre de Mandiargues), 1965
Mots (Sartre), 1964
Mots croisés (Perec), 1979
Mots et les choses (Foucault), 1966
Mots sans mémoire (Leiris), 1970

Nuit au Luxembourg (Gourmont), 1906
Nuit d'amour (v Pieyre de Mandiargues), 1962
Nuit dans la forêt (Cendrars), 1929
Nuit de carrefour (f Simenon), 1931
Nuit de la Saint-Jean (f Duhamel), 1935
Nuit de la Saint-Sylvestre (p Goncourt), 1852
Nuit de l'Iguane (p Aymé), 1962
Nuit de mil neuf cent quatorze (f Pieyre de Mandiargues), 1970
Nuit de noces (f Simenon), 1926
Nuit de Noël (f Bourget), 1907
Nuit de Noël 1914 (p Claudel), 1915
Nuit de Paris (f Simenon), 1929
Nuit des rois (p Anouilh), 1952
Nuit du bourreau de soi-même (f F. Mauriac), 1929
Nuit remue (v Michaux), 1935
Nuit séculaire (p Pieyre de Mandiargues), 1979
Nuit talismanique (v Char), 1972
Nuit vénitienne (p A. Musset), 1830
Nuits de la colère (p Salacrou), 1946
Nuits d'hiver (v Murger), 1861
Nuits que me chantent (Jammes), 1928
Nuits sans nuit et quelques jours sans jour (Leiris), 1945
Numa Roumestan (f A. Daudet), 1880
Numa Roumestan (p A. Daudet), 1890
Nymphe des bois de Versailles (v Sully Prudhomme), 1896

O amitié! (p Scribe), 1848
Oberman (Senancour), 1804
Objet aimé (p Jarry), 1953
Oblat (f Huysmans), 1903
Oblate (f Huysmans), 1924
Obscurité (f Jaccottet), 1961
Observations critiques sur l'ouvrage intitulé "Génie du christianisme" (Senancour), 1816
Obstacle (p A. Daudet), 1890
Obvie et l'obtuse (Barthes), 1982
Occidentales (v Banville), 1875
Occupe-toi d'Amélie (p Feydeau), 1908
Ode à Charles Fourier (v Breton), 1947
Ode à Londres bombardée (v Soupault), 1946
Ode à Picasso (v Cocteau), 1919
Ode génoise (v Romains), 1925
Ode to Bombed London (v Soupault), 1944
Odelettes (v Banville), 1856
Odes en son honneur (v Verlaine), 1893
Odes et ballades (v Hugo), 1826
Odes et poésies diverses (v Hugo), 1822
Odes et prières (v Romains), 1913
Odes funambulesques (v Banville), 1857
Odette (p Sardou), 1881
Odeur de poésie (v Salmon), 1944
Odile (f Queneau), 1937
Oedipe (p Anouilh) , 1986
Oedipe (p Gide), 1931
Oedipe-roi (p Cocteau), 1928
Oedipus (p Gide), 1950
Oedipus Rex (p Cocteau), 1927
Oeil de l'Utah (f Simenon), 1930
Oeil ébloui (Perec), 1981
Oeil et l'esprit (Merleau-Ponty), 1964
Oeillet blanc (p A. Daudet), 1863

Oeillet, La Guêpe, Le Mimosa (v Ponge), 1946
Oeuf dur (p Ionesco), 1966
Oeuvre (f Zola), 1886
Oeuvre au noir (f Yourcenar), 1968
Oeuvre des athlètes (p Duhamel), 1920
Oeuvres burlesques et mystiques de Frère Matorel, mort au couvent (Jacob), 1912
Oeuvres et les hommes (Barbey d'Aurevilly), from 1860
Of Human Freedom (Sartre), 1967
Off Limits (p Adamov), 1969
Ogre (f Tournier), 1972
Oh, les beaux jours (p Beckett), 1963
Oh What a Bloody Circus (p Ionesco), 1976
Ohio Impromptu (p Beckett), 1981
Oies de Noël (f Champfleury), 1853
Oiseau blessé (f Simenon), 1925
Oiseau bleu (p Maeterlinck), 1908
Oiseaux (v Saint-John Perse), 1963
Oiseaux de lune (p Aymé), 1956
Old Age (Beauvoir), 1972
Old and Young (p Scribe), 1822
Old Maid and the Dead Man (f Leduc), 1966
Old Man Dies (f Simenon), 1967
Old Regime and the French Revolution (Tocqueville), 1955
Old Regime and the Revolution (Tocqueville), 1856
Old Tune (p Pinget), 1960
Oloron-Sainte-Marie (v Supervielle), 1927
Olympe de Clèves (f Dumas père), 1852
Olympiques (f Montherlant), 1924
Ombre (p Green), 1956
Ombre chinoise (f Simenon), 1932
Ombre dans la nuit (f Simenon), 1929
Ombre de mon amour (v Apollinaire), 1947
Omelette à la Follembuche (p Labiche), 1859
On a raison de se révolter (Sartre), 1974
On a String (p Feydeau), 1975
On African Socialism (Senghor), 1964
On Art and Literature (Proust), 1958
On demande des cullottières (p Labiche), 1851
On dira des bêtises (p Labiche), 1853
On est toujours trop bon avec les femmes (f Queneau), 1947
On Genocide (Sartre), 1968
On God and Society (Maistre)
On Happiness (Teilhard de Chardin), 1973
On Intelligence (Taine), 1871
On Land and Sea (f Simenon), 1954
On loge à pied et à cheval (v Fort), 1947
On Love (Teilhard de Chardin), 1972
On Love and Happiness (Teilhard de Chardin), 1984
On ne badine pas avec l'amour (p A. Musset), 1834
On ne saurait penser à tout (p A. Musset), 1849
On ne voit pas les coeurs (f Bourget), 1929
On purge bébé (p Feydeau), 1910
On Racine (Barthes), 1964
On Science, Necessity and the Love of God (Weil), 1968
On Suffering (Teilhard de Chardin), 1975
On the Danger Line (f Simenon), 1944
On the Marry-Go-Wrong (p Feydeau), 1970
On the Motion and Immobility of Douve (v Bonnefoy), 1968
On Theatre (Sartre), 1976
Oncle Anghel (f Istrati), 1924

Oncle Charles s'est enfermé (f Simenon), 1942
Oncle d'Amérique (p Scribe), 1826
Oncle Sam (p Sardou), 1875
Ondes (Leiris), 1988
Ondine (p Giraudoux), 1939
Ondine (p Pixérécourt), 1830
One Hundred Million Million Poems (v Queneau), 1983
One Minus Two (f Troyat), 1938
One Way Out (f Simenon), 1943
Onirologie (f Maeterlinck), 1918
Onze jours de siège (p Verne), 1861
Onze mille verges (f Apollinaire), 1907
Open Mind (f Bernanos), 1945
Opéra (v Cocteau), 1927
Opéra à la cour (p Scribe), 1840
Opinions de M. Jérôme Coignard (f France), 1893
Opinions of Jérôme Coignard (f France), 1913
Oppression and Liberty (Weil), 1958
Oppression et liberté (Weil), 1955
Or (Cendrars), 1925
Or (v Fort), 1927
Orage immobile (f Sagan), 1983
Orages (v F. Mauriac), 1925
Oraisons mauvaises (Gourmont), 1900
Orange Plume (f Dumas père), 1860
Orchestra (p Anouilh), 1967
Orchestre (p Anouilh), 1962
Ordalie (p Anouilh), 1966
Order of Things (Foucault), 1970
Ordination (f Benda), 1911–12
Ordre des oiseaux (v Saint-John Perse), 1962
Orestie (p Dumas père), 1856
Orgie (p Scribe), 1831
Orgie à Saint-Pétersbourg (f Salmon), 1925
Orgies bourgeoises (f Simenon), 1926
Orgueil d'aimer (f Simenon), 1926
Orgueil qui meurt (f Simenon), 1925
Orientales (v Hugo), 1829
Origin of Table Manners (Lévi-Strauss)
Origine des manières de table (Lévi-Strauss)
Origines de la France contemporaine (Taine), 1875–93
Origins of Contemporary France (Taine), 1888–1931
Orion aveugle (Simon), 1970
Orme du mail (f France), 1897
Ornifle (p Anouilh), 1955
Orphée (p Cocteau), 1926
Orphée (f Supervielle), 1946
Orpheus (f Supervielle)
Orpheus (p Cocteau), 1933
Oscar (p Scribe), 1842
Oscar XXVIII (p Labiche), 1848
Ostenders (f Simenon), 1952
Oswald et Zénaïde (p Tardieu), 1951
Otage (p Claudel), 1911
Otez votre fille s'il vour plaît (p Labiche), 1854
Other One (f Colette), 1931
Other One (f Green), 1973
Others (f Simenon), 1975
Otho the Archer (f Dumas père), 1860
Othon l'archer (f Dumas père), 1840
Où suis-je? (v Maurras), 1945

Oubli (f C. Mauriac), 1966
Oublieuse mémoire (v Supervielle), 1949
Oultremer à Indigo (Cendrars), 1940
Our Friends (p Sardou), 1879
Our Lady of Lies (f Bourget), 1910
Our Lady of the Flowers (f Genet), 1949
Ouragan (p Zola), 1901
Ours en peluche (f Simenon), 1960
Ours et la lune (p Claudel), 1919
Ours et le pacha (p Scribe), 1820
Outer Edge of Society (p Dumas fils), 1921
Outlaw (f Simenon), 1941
Outlaw of Iceland (f Hugo), 1885
Outsider (f Camus), 1946
Oversight (p Ionesco), 1971

Package Holiday (f Verne)
Page d'amour (f Zola), 1878
Page d'histoire (f Barbey D'Aurevilly), 1886
Page du duc de Savoie (f Dumas père), 1855
Page of Love (f Zola), 1897
Page of the Duke of Savoy (f Dumas père), 1861
Pages catholiques (f Huysmans), 1899
Pages choisies (Roussel), 1918
Pailles rompues (p Verne), 1850
Pain de l'étranger (f Troyat), 1981
Pain de ménage (p Renard), 1899
Pain dur (p Claudel), 1918
Pain vivant (p F. Mauriac), 1955
Painted Lady (f Sagan), 1983
Painting in Blood (f Sagan), 1987
Pair of Spectacles (p Labiche), 1899
Paix conquise (v Deschamps), 1812
Paix dans les brisements (v Michaux), 1959
Paix du ménage (p Maupassant), 1893
Palace (Simon), 1962
Paludes (f Gide), 1895
Paméla Giraud (p Balzac), 1843
Panama (Cendrars), 1918
Panorama de la pègre (Cendrars), 1935
Pantagruel (p Jarry), 1911
Panthère borgne (f Simenon), 1929
Panus (Cendrars), 1972
Paolo Paoli (p Adamov), 1957
Papa du prix d'honneur (p Labiche), 1868
Papa Pasquier (f Duhamel), 1934
Pape (v Hugo), 1878
Papesse Jeanne (p Jarry), 1981
Papiers d'Aspern (p Duras), 1961
Papillonne (p Sardou), 1862
Pâquerette (p Gautier), 1851
Pâques (Cendrars), 1912
Pâques à New York (Cendrars), 1912
Pâques fleuries (p Rolland), 1926
Par instinct (p Sardou), 1904
Par la fenêtre (p Feydeau), 1881
Paraboles (v Valéry), 1935
Paradis artificiels (Baudelaire), 1860
Paradis de Mahomet (p Scribe), 1822
Paradis des fantômes (v Péret), 1938
Paradis terrestres (f Colette), 1932

Paralchimie (p Pinget), 1973
Parallèlement (v Verlaine), 1889
Parapapilloneries (v Pieyre de Mandiargues), 1976
Paravents (p Genet), 1961
Parents pauvres (f Balzac), 1847–48
Parents terribles (p Cocteau), 1938
Parfum du passé (f Simenon), 1929
Paria des bois sauvages (f Simenon), 1933
Pariétaires (v Augier), 1855
Paris (f Nodier), 1831
Paris (f Zola), 1898
Paris Spleen (v Baudelaire), 1869
Parisienne (p Becque), 1885
Parisiens du dimanche (p C. Mauriac), 1967
Parisiens et provinciaux (f Dumas père), 1868
Paris-Leste (f Simenon), 1927
Parlementaire (p Scribe), 1824
Parnasse contemporain (v Baudelaire), 1866
Parodie (p Adamov), 1950
Paroi et la prairie (v Char), 1952
Parole en archipel (v Char), 1962
Paroles (v Prévert), 1946
Paroles d'un croyant (Lamennais), 1834
Paroles et Musique (p Beckett), 1966
Parrain (p Scribe), 1821
Part du diable (p Scribe), 1843
Partage de midi (p Claudel), 1906
Parti pris des choses (v Ponge), 1942
Partie d'checs (v Cocteau), 1961
Partie et revanche (p Scribe), 1823
Pas (p Beckett), 1977
Pas moi (p Beckett), 1975
Pascal Bruno (f Dumas père), 1837
Pasiphaé (p Montherlant), 1936
Pasquette (f Champfleury), 1876
Pasquier Chronicles (f Duhamel), from 1934 11,
Passacaglia (f Pinget), 1978
Passacaille (f Pinget), 1969
Passage de l'Egyptienne (v Pieyre de Mandiargues), 1979
Passage de la ligne (f Simenon), 1958
Passage de Milan (f Butor), 1954
Passage du malin (p F. Mauriac), 1947
Passager clandestin (f Simenon), 1947
Passager du transatlantique (v Péret), 1921
Passages (v Michaux), 1950
Passageur du "Polarlys" (f Simenon), 1932
Passe-muraille (f Aymé), 1943
Passing Time (f Butor), 1960
Passion dans le désert (f Balzac), 1837
Passion de Joseph Pasquier (f Duhamel), 1941
Passion secrète (p Scribe), 1834
Past Recaptured (f Proust), 1932
Pastels (f Bourget), 1889
Pastels of Men (f Bourget), 1891
Pasteur d'Ashbourne (f Dumas père), 1853
Pastoral Symphony (f Gide), 1931
Pastors and Masters (f Duhamel), 1946
Patchouli (p Salacrou), 1930
Paths of Freedom (f Sartre), from 1947
Patient (f Simenon), 1963
Patrie! (p Sardou), 1869

Patrie en danger (p Goncourt), 1873
Patte-en-l'air (p Feydeau), 1883
Pattes de mouche (p Sardou), 1860
Paul Forrester (p Augier), 1868
Paul Jones (f Dumas père), 1889
Paul Jones (p Dumas père), 1838
Paula Monti (f Sue), 1842
Pauline (f Dumas père), 1838
Pauline (f Sand), 1840
Pauvre Amante! (f Simenon), 1931
Pauvre Bitos (p Anouilh), 1956
Pauvre Matelot (p Cocteau), 1927
Pavés de l'ours (p Feydeau), 1896
Pavillon des fleurs (p Pixérécourt), 1822
Paying the Piper (p Feydeau), 1975
Pays de la magie (v Michaux), 1941
Pays des fourrures (f Verne), 1873
Pays des moulins (v Fort), 1921
Pays et le gouvernement (Lamennais), 1840
Pays latin (f Murger), 1851
Pays lointains (f Green), 1987
Pays parisiens (Halévy), 1929
Paysages avec figures absentes (Jaccottet), 1970
Paysan de Paris (Aragon), 1926
Paysans (f Balzac), 1855
Peasantry (f Balzac)
Peau de chagrin (f Balzac), 1831
Peau de l'ours (p Pixérécourt), 1802
Peau de Tigre (f Gautier), 1852
Pêche aux filets (f Dumas père), 1864
Péché de jeunesse (f Simenon), 1926
Péché de Monsieur Antoine (f Sand), 1846
Péchés de jeunesse (v Dumas fils), 1847
Pêcheur de bouées (f Simenon), 1930
Pêcheur d'islande (f Loti), 1886
Pêcheur d'islande (p Loti), 1893
Peculiar Position (p Scribe), 1837
Pedigree (f Simenon), 1948
Peindre (v Salmon), 1921
Peintre à l'étude (v Ponge), 1948
Peintre de la vie moderne (Baudelaire), 1863 51,
Peintre de Saltzbourg (f Nodier), 1803
Peintres cubistes (Apollinaire), 1913
Peinture au défi (Aragon), 1930
Pèlerin blanc (p Pixérécourt), 1802
Pèlerin de Lourdes (Jammes), 1936
Pèlerin du silence (Gourmont), 1896
Pèlerin passionné (v Moréas), 1891
Pelleas and Melisande (p Maeterlinck), 1894
Pelléas et Mélisande (p Maeterlinck), 1892
Pendu de Saint-Pholien (f Simenon), 1931
Penguin Island (f France), 1909
Pénitencier (f Martin du Gard), 1922
Pénitents en maillots roses (Jacob), 1925
Pensée des jardins (Jammes), 1906
Pensée et le mouvant (Bergson), 1934
Pensée sauvage (Lévi-Strauss), 1962
Pensées sans ordre concernant l'amour de Dieu (Weil), 1962
Penser-classer (Perec), 1985
Pension bourgeoise (p Scribe), 1823
Pensionnaire mariée (p Scribe), 1835

People (Michelet), 1973
People's Own Book (Lamennais), 1839
People's Prophecy (Lamennais), 1943
Perception du changement (Bergson), 1911
Père Goriot (f Balzac), 1835
Père humilié (p Claudel), 1920
Père la Ruine (f Dumas père), 1860
Père prodigue (p Dumas fils), 1859
Péri (p Gautier), 1843
Perish in Their Pride (f Montherlant), 1936
Perle (p Banville), 1879
Perle de la Canebière (p Labiche), 1855
Perle noire (p Sardou), 1862
Permettez, madame! (p Labiche), 1863
Persécuté persécuteur (Aragon), 1931
Perséphone (p Gide), 1934
Personnages (f Mallet-Joris), 1961
Perversités frivoles (f Simenon), 1925
Pesanteur et la grâce (Weil), 1947
Peste (f Camus), 1947
Peste de Marseille (p Pixérécourt), 1828
Petit Ami (Léautaud), 1903
Petit Bois (f Supervielle), 1942
Petit Carillonneur (p Pixérécourt), 1812
Petit Chose (f A. Daudet), 1868
Petit corps blessé (f Simenon), 1928
Petit Docteur (f Simenon), 1943
Petit Dragon (p Scribe), 1817
Petit Homme d'Arkhangelsk (f Simenon), 1956
Petit Homme rouge (p Pixérécourt), 1832
Petit Ménage (p Feydeau), 1883
Petit Page (p Pixérécourt), 1800
Petit Pierre (f France), 1918
Petit poison (f Simenon), 1928
Petit prince (f Saint-Exupéry), 1946
Petit Saint (f Simenon), 1965
Petit Séminaire Saint-Nicolas du Chardonnet (Renan), 1880
Petit traité invitant à l'art subtil du go (Perec), 1969
Petit vocabulaire de simple vérité (Senancour), 1833
Petit Voyage (p Labiche), 1868
Petite Bête (v Fort), 1890
Petite cosmogonie portative (v Queneau), 1950
Petite dessalée (f Simenon), 1928
Petite exilée (f Simenon), 1930
Petite Fadette (f Sand), 1849
Petite Folle (p Scribe), 1822
Petite Infante de Castille (f Montherlant), 1929
Petite Lampe merveilleuse (p Scribe), 1822
Petite Molière (p Anouilh), 1959
Petite Paroisse (f A. Daudet), 1895
Petite Révoltée (p Feydeau), 1880
Petite Roque (f Maupassant), 1886
Petite Soeur (p Scribe), 1821
Petite très sensuelle (f Simenon), 1926
Petites légendes (v Verhaeren), 1900
Petites Mains (p Labiche), 1859
Petites misères de la vie conjugale (f Balzac), 1845–46
Petits Auvergnats (p Pixérécourt), 1797
Petits Bourgeois (f Balzac), 1856
Petits Chevaux de Tarquinia (f Duras), 1953
Petits Cochons sans queues (f Simenon), 1950

Petits contes nègres pour les enfants des Blancs (Cendrars), 1928
Petits Moyens (p Labiche), 1850
Petits Oiseaux (p Labiche), 1862
Petits poèmes en prose (v Baudelaire), 1869
Petits Robinsons des caves (f A. Daudet), 1872
Petits Vieux (v Verhaeren), 1901
Petty Annoyances of Married Life (f Balzac), 1861
Peu de soleil dans l'eau froide (f Sagan), 1969
Peuple (Michelet), 1846
Phanérogame (Jacob), 1918
Phantom from the East (f Loti), 1892
Phare du bout du monde (f Verne), 1905
Pharisienne (f F. Mauriac), 1941
Phénix (Éluard), 1951
Phénomène humain (Teilhard de Chardin), 1955
Phénoménologie de la perception (Merleau-Ponty), 1945
Phenomenology of Perception (Merleau-Ponty), 1962
Phenomenon of Man (Teilhard de Chardin), 1959
Philibert marié (p Scribe), 1822
Philiberte (p Augier), 1853
Philippe (p Scribe), 1830
Philippe II (p Verhaeren), 1900
Philippe, Patrie (f Renard), 1907
Philoctète (p Gide), 1899
Philoctetes (p Gide), 1953
Philosophes français au XIXe siècle (Taine), 1857
Philosophie de l'art (Taine), 1865
Philosophie de l'art dans les Pays-Bas (Taine), 1868
Philosophie de l'art en Grèce (Taine), 1869
Philosophie de l'art en Italie (Taine), 1866
Philosophie du non (Bachelard), 1940
Philosophie pathétique (Benda), 1913
Philosophy of No (Bachelard), 1969
Philtre (p Scribe), 1831
Phocas (Gourmont), 1894
Photo du Colonel (f Ionesco), 1962
Physiologie de l'employé (f Balzac), 1841
Physiologie du mariage (f Balzac), 1829
Physiologie du rentier de Paris et de province (f Balzac), 1841
Physiology of Marriage (f Balzac), 1904
Piano dans l'herbe (p Sagan), 1970
Piccinino (f Sand), 1847
Piccolet (p Labiche), 1852
Piccolino (p Sardou), 1861
Picture (p Ionesco), 1969
Pièce de Chambertin (p Labiche), 1874
Piece of Monologue (p Beckett), 1982
Pièces baroques (p Anouilh), 1974
Pièces brillantes (p Anouilh), 1951
Pièces costumées (p Anouilh), 1960
Pièces grinçantes (p Anouilh), 1956
Pièces noires (p Anouilh), 1942
Pièces roses (p Anouilh), 1942
Pièces secrètes (p Anouilh), 1977
Pied dans le crime (p Labiche), 1866
Pierre and Jean (f Maupassant), 1890
Pierre de touche (p Augier), 1854
Pierre écrite (v Bonnefoy), 1965
Pierre et Jean (f Maupassant), 1888
Pierre, la feuille et les ciseaux (f Troyat), 1972

Pierre le noir (p Sue), 1842
Pierre Nozière (f France), 1899
Pierre qui roule (f Sand), 1870
Pierres blanches (v Reverdy), 1930
Pierres levées (v Romains), 1948
Pierrette (f Balzac), 1840
Pierrot (f Queneau), 1950
Pierrot (f Tournier), 1979
Pierrot mon ami (f Queneau), 1942
Piéton de l'air (p Ionesco), 1962
Pietr-le-Letton (f Simenon), 1931
Pilgrim on the Earth (f Green), 1929
Pilote de guerre (f Saint-Exupéry), 1942
Pilote du Danube (f Verne), 1908
Ping (f Beckett), 1967
Ping Pong (p Adamov), 1959
Ping-pong (p Adamov), 1955
Piping Hot! (f Zola), 1885
Piquillo (p Dumas père, Nerval), 1837
Piquillo Alliaga (Scribe), 1847
Pirates du Texas (f Simenon), 1929
Piste (p Sardou), 1906
Piste et la mare (f Supervielle), 1927
Pitard (f Simenon), 1935
Pitié pour les femmes (f Montherlant), 1936
Pitié suprême (v Hugo), 1879
Pity for Women (f Montherlant), 1937
Pizarre (p Pixérécourt), 1802
Placard pour un chemin des écoliers (v Char), 1937
Place du palais (p Pixérécourt), 1824
Place Without Doors (p Duras) 1970
Plague (f Camus), 1948
Plain-chant (v Cocteau), 1923
Plaines (v Verhaeren), 1911
Plaintes contre inconnu (f Drieu la Rochelle), 1924
Plaisir de rompre (p Renard), 1897
Plaisir du texte (Barthes) 1972
Plaisirs charnels (f Simenon), 1925
Plaisirs de la capitale (Aragon), 1923
Plan de campagne (p Scribe), 1823
Planétarium (f Sarraute), 1959
Play (p Beckett), 1964
Pleasure of the Text (Barthes), 1975
Pléiades (f Gobineau), 1874
Pleiads (f Gobineau), 1928
Plein verre (v Reverdy), 1940
Pleine marge (v Breton), 1943
Pleut bergère (f Simenon), 1941
Plik et Plok (f Sue), 1831
Plongées (f F. Mauriac), 1938
Pluie et le beau temps (v Prévert), 1955
Pluies (v Saint-John Perse), 1944
Plume (v Michaux), 1938
Plupart du temps (v Reverdy), 1945
Pluralisme cohérent de la chimie moderne (Bachelard), 1932
Plus Beau Jour de la vie (p Scribe), 1825
Plus heureux des trois (p Labiche), 1870
Plusieurs choses (v Fort), 1894
Poche parmentier (Perec), 1974
Poème à l'étrangère (v Saint-John Perse), 1945
Poème pulvérisé (v Char), 1947

Poèmes à jouer (p Tardieu), 1960
Poèmes à Lou (v Apollinaire), 1955
Poèmes allemands (v Cocteau), 1944
Poèmes antiques (v Leconte de Lisle), 1852
Poèmes antiques et modernes (v Vigny), 1826
Poèmes au Danois (v Fort), 1920
Poèmes barbares (v Leconte de Lisle), 1872
Poèmes de guerre (v Claudel), 1922
Poèmes de la France malheureuse (v Supervielle), 1941
Poèmes de l'humour triste (v Supervielle), 1919
Poèmes de Loire (v Spire), 1929
Poèmes d'hier et d'aujourd'hui (v Spire), 1953
Poèmes d'ici et de là-bas (v Spire), 1944
Poèmes du dimanche (v Mallet-Joris), 1947
Poèmes d'un riche amateur (f Larbaud), 1908
Poèmes élastiques (Cendrars), 1919
Poèmes en prose (v Reverdy), 1915
Poèmes et paroles durant la guerre (v Claudel), 1916
Poèmes et paroles durant la guerre de trente ans (v Claudel),
    1945
Poèmes et sylves (v Moréas), 1907
Poèmes juifs (v Spire), 1919
Poèmes légendaires de Flandre et de Brabant (v Verhaeren),
    1916
Poèmes mesurés (v Jammes), 1908
Poèmes politiques (Éluard), 1948
Poèmes pour la paix (Éluard), 1918
Poèmes saturniens (v Verlaine), 1866
Poèmes tragiques (v Leconte de Lisle), 1884
Poems of a Black Orpheus (v Senghor), 1981
Poésie et vérité (Éluard), 1942
Poésie ininterrompue (Éluard), 1946
Poésie pour pouvoir (v Michaux), 1949
Poésies barbares (v Leconte de Lisle), 1862
Poésies d'André Walter (v Gide), 1892
Poésies de Méléagre (Louÿs), 1893
Poète assassiné (f Apollinaire), 1916
Poète et l'inspiration (Jammes), 1922
Poète et l'oiseau (v Jammes), 1899
Poète rustique (Jammes), 1920
Poètes (Aragon), 1960
Poètes maudits (Verlaine), 1884
Poetic Art (Claudel), 1948
Poetical Reveries (v Lamartine), 1839
Poetics of Reverie (Bachelard), 1969
Poetics of Space (Bachelard), 1964
Poétique de la rêverie (Bachelard), 1960
Poétique de l'espace (Bachelard), 1957
Poil de carotte (f Renard), 1894
Poil de carotte (p Renard), 1900
Point cardinal (v Leiris), 1927
Point de mire (p Labiche), 1864
Point of Departure (p Anouilh), 1951
Point où j'en suis (v Pieyre de Mandiargues), 1964
Poisoned Relations (f Simenon), 1950
Poisson soluble (Breton), 1924
Poissons rouges (p Anouilh), 1970
Polish Spy (f Dumas père), 1869
Politesse inutile (p Tardieu), 1950
Politique à l'usage du peuple (Lamennais), 1838
Politique des restes (p Adamov), 1963

Polter (p Pixérécourt), 1828
Pomme (p Banville), 1865
Pomme d'Anis (Jammes), 1904
Pommes du voisin (p Sardou), 1864
Pompe funèbre (p Scribe), 1815
Pompes funèbres (f Genet), 1947
Pont de l'Europe (p Salacrou), 1927
Pont de Londres (f Céline), 1963
Pont des arches (f Simenon), 1921
Pontoise (v Fort), 1920
Pontons (p Sue), 1841
Poof (p Salacrou), 1948
Poor Bitos (p Anouilh), 1963
Poor Relations (f Balzac), 1880
Porche du mystère de la deuxième vertu (Péguy), 1911
Port des brumes (f Simenon), 1932
Porte (f Simenon), 1962
Porte close (f Simenon), 1930
Porte dévergondée (f Pieyre de Mandiargues), 1965
Porte étroite (f Gide), 1909
Portefaix (p Scribe), 1835
Portefeuille (p Mirbeau), 1902
Portrait de l'artiste en jeune singe (f Butor), 1967
Portrait d'un inconnu (f Sarraute), 1948
Portrait of a Man Unknown (f Sarraute), 1958
Portrait of an Anti-Semite (Sartre), 1948
Portraits (Brasillach), 1935
Portraits contemporains (Sainte-Beuve), 1846
Portraits des femmes (Sainte-Beuve), 1844
Portraits d'inconnus (f Romains), 1962
Port-Royal (p Montherlant), 1954
Port-Royal (Sainte-Beuve), 1840–59
Port-Tarascon (f A. Daudet), 1890
Positivisme anglais (Taine), 1864
Possédés (p Camus), 1959
Possessed (p Camus), 1960
Possession et ses aspects théâtraux chez les Ethiopiens de
    Gondar (Leiris) 1958
Postman (Martin du Gard), 1955
Post-scriptum (p Augier), 1869
Potache (p Feydeau), 1883
Pot-bouille (f Zola), 1882
Pot-bouille (p Zola), 1883
Potomak (f Cocteau), 1919
Poudre aux yeux (p Labiche), 1861
Poupée brisée (f Simenon), 1930
Pour avoir aimé la terre (f Istrati), 1930
Pour en finir avec le jugement de Dieu (p Artaud), 1948
Pour et le contre (f Lacretelle), 1946
Pour finir encore et autres foirades (f Beckett), 1976
Pour le sauver (f Simenon), 1925
Pour les vieux garçons (Benda), 1926
Pour l'honneur d'un fleuve "apostat," (v Maurras), 1950
Pour Lucrèce (p Giraudoux), 1953
Pour nous, Rimbaud (v Char), 1956
Pour préparer un oeuf dur (p Ionesco), 1966
Pour Psyché (v Maurras), 1911
Pour qu'il soit heureux (f Simenon), 1925
Pour un nouveau roman (Robbe-Grillet), 1963
Pour un réalisme socialiste (Aragon), 1935
Pour une morale de 1'ambiguïté (Beauvoir), 1947

Pour venger son père (f Simenon), 1931
Pourquoi la journée vole (v Char), 1960
Pourquoi pas moi? (p Salacrou), 1948
Poussière de soleils (Roussel), 1926
Pouvoir tout dire (Éluard), 1951
Power/Knowledge (Foucault), 1980
Power of Language (v Ponge), 1979
Power of the Dead (p Maeterlinck), 1923
Praxède (f Dumas père), 1841
Précieux (p Labiche), 1855
Précipice (p Pixérécourt), 1811
Précision (Benda), 1937
Premier (f Simenon), 1961
Premier amour (f Beckett), 1970
Premier Pas (p Labiche), 1862
Premier prix de piano (p Labiche), 1865
Première famille (p Supervielle), 1936
Premières alluvions (v Char), 1950
Premières Armes de Figaro (p Sardou), 1860
Premières lueurs sur la colline (v Fort), 1893
Premières poésies (Villiers de l'Isle Adam), 1859
Premiers âges (Senancour), 1968
Premiers Amours (p Scribe), 1825
Premiers pas de l'univers (f Supervielle), 1950
Premiers pas hors de Saint-Sulpice (Renan), 1882
Prés Saint-Gervais (p Sardou), 1862
Presbytère et prolétaires (Perec), 1989
Préséances (f F. Mauriac), 1921
Présentation de Pan (f Giono), 1930
Présentation des Haïdoucs (f Istrati), 1925
Président (f Simenon), 1958
Presqu'île (f Gracq), 1970
Prétendant (Villiers de l'Isle Adam), 1965
Prétendante (p Sue), 1841
Prétendus de Gimblette (p Labiche), 1850
Prêtre (Teilhard de Chardin), 1965
Prêtre marié (f Barbey D'Aurevilly), 1865
Prêtresse des Vaudoux (f Simenon), 1925
Prière à deux voix (v Maurras), 1950
Prière mutilée (v Cocteau), 1925
Prière sur l'Acropole (Renan), 1876
Priest in the House (f Zola), 1957
Prikaz (v Salmon), 1919
Primacy of Perception (Merleau-Ponty), 1964
Primaires (f L. Daudet), 1906
Prime jeunesse (f Loti), 1919
Prime of Life (Beauvoir), 1962
Prince charmant (p Scribe), 1822
Prince de la Bohème (f Balzac), 1845
Prince frivole (v Cocteau), 1910
Princess Maleine (p Maeterlinck), 1890
Princesse de Bagdad (p Dumas fils), 1881
Princesse de Tarare (p Scribe), 1817
Princesse Flora (f Dumas père), 1859
Princesse Georges (p Dumas fils), 1871
Princesse Isabelle (p Maeterlinck), 1935
Princesse Maleine (p Maeterlinck), 1889
Princesses (v Banville), 1874
Printemps (Le Clézio), 1989
Printemps 71 (p Adamov), 1961
Prisme (v Sully Prudhomme), 1886

(Senancour), 1825

Retour (p Scribe), 1823

Retour à Paris (v Deschamps), 1832

Retour amont (v Char), 1966

Retour de l'enfant prodigue (f Gide), 1907

Retour de l'enfant prodigue (p Gide), 1909

Retour de Silbermann (f Lacretelle), 1929

Retraite sentimentale (f Colette), 1907

Retreat from Love (f Colette), 1974

Retrouvailles (p Adamov), 1955

Return of the Prodigal (f Gide), 1953

Return to My Native Land (v Césaire), 1968

Revanche de la nuit (v Jarry), 1949

Rêve (f Zola), 1888

Rêve d'Irénée (f Butor), 1979

Rêve qui meurt (f Simenon), 1931

Revenants (f Dumas fils), 1852

Revenentes (Perec), 1972

Rêveries sur la nature primitive de l'homme (Senancour), 1799

Rêves d'amour (p Scribe), 1859

Rêveuse bourgeoisie (f Drieu la Rochelle), 1937

Revolt and the Escape (Villiers de l'Isle Adam), 1901

Revolt of the Angels (f France), 1914

Révolte (Villiers de l'Isle Adam), 1870

Révolte des anges (f France), 1914

Révolte des fleurs (v Sully Prudhomme), 1874

Révoltés de la Bounty (f Verne), 1879

Révolver à cheveux blancs (v Breton), 1932

Rhapsodies (v Borel), 1832

Rhin (v Hugo), 1842

Rhinocéros (p Ionesco), 1959

Rhum (Cendrars), 1930

Rhume onirique (p Ionesco), 1953

Rich Man (f Simenon), 1971

Richard Darlington (p Dumas père), 1831

Richard III (p Anouilh), 1964

Riche Homme (f Simenon), 1970

Ridicules (f Simenon), 1921

Rigadon (f Céline), 1969

Rigadoon (f Céline), 1974

Right to Dream (Bachelard), 1971

Rimes dorées (v Banville), 1869

Ring round the Moon (p Anouilh), 1950

Ripening Corn (f Colette), 1931

Ripening Seed (f Colette), 1959

Riquet à la houppe (p Banville), 1884

Rire (Bergson), 1900

Rire de Laura (f Mallet-Joris), 1985

Rita l'Espagnole (p Sue), 1837

Rivage des Syrtes (f Gracq), 1951

Rivages (Jacob), 1934

Rivalités en province (f Balzac), 1838

River of Fire (f F. Mauriac), 1954

Rivers and Forests (p Duras), 1964

Road (f Chamson), 1929

Robe de noces (f Dumas père), 1844

Robe mauve de Valentine (p Sagan), 1963

Robe prétexte (f F. Mauriac), 1914

Robert (p Gide), 1930

Robert Helmont (f A. Daudet), 1874

Robert-le-Diable (p Scribe), 1831

Robespierre (p Rolland), 1939

Robespierre (p Sardou), 1899

Robinson (p Supervielle), 1948

Robinson Crusoé (p Pixérécourt), 1805

Robinsons basques (Jammes), 1925

Robur le conquérant (f Verne), 1886

Rocambole le bateleur (p Labiche), 1846

Rockaby (p Beckett), 1981

Rodolphe (p Scribe),1823

Roi au masque d'or (f Schwob), 1893

Roi Candaule (p Gide), 1901

Roi Carotte (p Sardou), 1872

Roi de Boétie (Jacob), 1922

Roi de la vie (f Soupault), 1928

Roi des Aulnes (f Tournier), 1970

Roi des Frontins (p Labiche), 1845

Roi des glaces (f Simenon), 1928

Roi du Pacifique (f Simenon), 1929

Roi pêcheur (p Gracq), 1948

Roi s'amuse (p Hugo), 1832

Roi sans divertissement (f Giono), 1947

Roi se meurt (p Ionesco), 1962

Rois en exil (f A. Daudet), 1879

Rois en exil (p A. Daudet), 1884

Rois Mages (f Tournier), 1983

Roland of Montreval (f Dumas père), 1860

Rolling Stone (f Sand), 1871

Roman de la momie (f Gautier), 1858

Roman de toutes les femmes (f Murger), 1854

Roman d'Elvire (p Dumas père), 1860

Roman du Capucin (f Murger), 1869

Roman du Chaperon-Rouge (f A. Daudet), 1862

Roman du lièvre (Jammes), 1903

Roman d'un enfant (f Loti), 1890

Roman d'un spahi (f Loti), 1881

Roman d'une dactylo (f Simenon), 1924

Roman d'une femme (f Dumas fils), 1849

Roman expérimental (Zola), 1880

Roman inachevé (Aragon), 1956

Romance in A Flat (p Feydeau), 1982

Romance of a Spahi (f Loti), 1890

Romances sans paroles (v Verlaine), 1874

Romances Without Words (v Verlaine), 1921

Romans et contes philosophiques (f Balzac), 1831

Rome (f Zola), 1896

Roméo et Jeannette (p Anouilh), 1946

Roméo et Juliette (p Cocteau), 1924

Roméo et Juliette (p Deschamps), 1844

Romulus (p Dumas père), 1854

Ronde et autres faits divers (f Le Clézio), 1982

Rosa (f Dumas père), 1854

Rosa (p Pixérécourt),1800

Rosaire au soleil (Jammes), 1916

Rose à Marie (Jammes), 1919

Rose and Ninette (f A. Daudet), 1892

Rose blanche et la rose rouge (p Pixérécourt), 1809

Rose de François (v Cocteau), 1923

Rose de sable (f Montherlant), 1968

Rose des vents (v Soupault), 1920

Rose et Blanche (f Sand), 1831

Rose et Ninette (f A. Daudet), 1892

Rose publique (Éluard), 1934
Roses (v Renard), 1886
Roses de Noël (v Banville), 1878
Rosier de Madame Husson (f Maupassant), 1888
Rosière de Rosny (p Scribe), 1823
Rossini à Paris (p Scribe), 1823
Rôtisserie de la reine Pédauque (f France), 1893
Roués innocents (f Gautier), 1847
Rouge et le noir (f Stendhal), 1830
Rouge-gorge (p Labiche), 1859
Rough for Theatre I and II (p Beckett), 1976
Rougon-Macquart (f Zola), from 1871
Rouilles encagées (v Péret), 1954
Roussel l'ingénu (Leiris), 1987
Route des Flandres (Simon), 1960
Roux le bandit (f Chamson), 1925
Roux the Bandit (f Chamson), 1929
Royal Way (f Malraux), 1935
Royaume farfelu (f Malraux), 1928
Ruban (p Feydeau), 1894
Ruban au cou d'Olympia (Leiris), 1982
Rude hiver (f Queneau), 1939
Rue (Vallès), 1866
Rue à Londres (Vallès), 1883
Rue aux trois poussins (f Simenon), 1963
Rue de L'Homme-armé, numéro 8 bis (p Labiche), 1849
Rue noire (p Salacrou), 1967
Rue sans nom (f Aymé), 1930
Ruggieri (v Fort), 1927
Ruines de Babylone (p Pixérécourt), 1810
Ruisseau des solitudes (v Pieyre de Mandiargues), 1968
Ruses de l'amour (f Simenon), 1954
Rush for the Spoil (f Zola), 1886
Russian Gipsy (f Dumas père), 1860
Rustle of Language (Barthes), 1986
Ruy Blas (p Cocteau), 1947
Ruy Blas (p Hugo), 1838
Rythme à trois temps (p Tardieu), 1959
Rythmes souverains (v Verhaeren), 1910

S/Z (Barthes), 1970
Sabine (f Lacretelle), 1932–35
Sabine (f Pieyre de Mandiargues), 1963
Sabot rouge (f Murger), 1860
Sac au dos (f Huysmans), 1880
Sac et la cendre (f Troyat), 1948
Sackcloth and Ashes (f Troyat), 1956
Sacountala (p Gautier), 1858
Sacre de la nuit (p Tardieu), 1966
Sacre de Paris (v Leconte de Lisle), 1871
Sacre du printemps (Simon), 1954
Sacrifice (p A. Daudet), 1869
Sacrifice (f Simenon), 1958
Sacrifice impérial (Jacob), 1929
Sade, Fourier, Loyola (Barthes), 1971
Sagesse (p Claudel), 1939
Sagesse (v Verlaine), 1880
Sagouin (f F. Mauriac), 1951
Saha the Cat (f Colette), 1936
Sailor (f Loti), 1893
Sailor from Gibraltar (f Duras), 1966

Sailor's Rendezvous (f Simenon), 1940
Saint (f Bourget), 1893
Saint Genet (Sartre), 1952
Saint Glinglin (f Queneau), 1948
St. John's Eve (f Duhamel), 1935
Saint Louis (Jammes), 1941
Saint Matorel (Jacob), 1911
Saint-André (v Salmon), 1936
Sainte Agnès (v Claudel), 1963
Sainte Europe (p Adamov), 1966
Saintes du paradis (Gourmont), 1899
Saint-Fiacre Affair (f Simenon), 1940
Saint-Jean-au-Bois (v Fort), 1908
Saints de glace (v Salmon), 1930
Saisir (v Supervielle), 1928
Saison au Congo (p Césaire), 1966
Saison en enfer (v Rimbaud), 1873
Salamandre (f Sue), 1832
Salammbô (f Flaubert), 1862
Salavin (f Duhamel), 1936
Salle d'armes (f Dumas père), 1838
Salmigondis (f Balzac), 1832
Salon de l'automobile (p Ionesco), 1953
Salons et journaux (f L. Daudet), 1917
Salsette découvre l'Amérique (f Romains), 1950
Salteador (f Dumas père), 1854
Salut par les Juifs (Bloy), 1892
Salutations (p Ionesco), 1963
Salvage of the Cynthia (f Verne)
Salvator le commissionnaire (f Dumas père), 1854–59
Salvoisy (p Scribe), 1834
Samaël (v Spire), 1921
Samedis de Madame (p Labiche), 1875
San-Felice (f Dumas père), 1864–65
Sang d'aquarelle (f Sagan), 1987
Sang d'Atys (v F. Mauriac), 1940
Sang de la coupe (v Banville), 1857
Sang des autres (f Beauvoir), 1945
Sang des gitanes (f Simenon), 1928
Sang du pauvre (Bloy), 1909
Sang d'un poète (p Cocteau), 1948
Sang Joie Tempête (v Soupault), 1937
Sanguines (Louÿs), 1903
Sans (f Beckett), 1969
Sans phrases (v Soupault), 1953
Sapho (p Augier), 1851
Sapho (f A. Daudet), 1884
Sapho (p A. Daudet), 1892
Sardonic Tales (Villiers de l'Isle Adam), 1927
Satan's Children (f Simenon), 1953 34,
Satin Slipper (p Claudel)
Sauce for the Goose (p Feydeau), 1974
Saül (p Gide), 1903
Sauvage (p Anouilh), 1938
Savage Mind (Lévi-Strauss), 1966
Savage Paris (f Zola), 1955
Savannah Bay (p Duras), 1983
Savant (p Scribe), 1832
Savon (Ponge), 1967
Scarlet and Black (f Stendhal), 1938
Scarpante the Spy (f Verne), 1884

Scars on the Soul (f Sagan), 1974
Scénario (p Anouilh), 1974
Scène à quatre (p Ionesco), 1959
Scène ajoutée au Boulevard Bonne-Nouvelle, pour l'anniver-
saire de la naissance de Molière (p Scribe), 1821
Scènes de campagne (f Murger), 1853
Scènes de la Bohème (f Murger), 1851
Scènes de la vie de jeunesse (f Murger), 1851
Scènes de la vie orientale (f Nerval), 1824
Scènes de la vie privée (f Balzac), 1830
Scènes de la vie privée et publique des animaux (f Balzac), 1842
Schahababam II (p Scribe), 1832
Schéhérazade (p Supervielle), 1949
School for Politicians (p Scribe), 1840
School for Wives (f Gide), 1950
Science and Christ (Teilhard de Chardin), 1968
Science et Christ (Teilhard de Chardin), 1955
Scope of Anthropology (Lévi-Strauss), 1968
Scrap of Paper (p Sardou)
Screen (f Bourget), 1901
Screens (p Genet), 1962
Scrupule (f Bourget), 1893
Se Ma Tsien, le sacrificateur (f Simenon), 1926
Sea of Troubles (f Duras), 1953
Sea Serpent (f Verne), 1967
Sea Wall (f Duras), 1952
Seamarks (v Saint-John Perse), 1958
Séance de nuit (p Feydeau), 1897
Search for a Method (Sartre), 1963
Season in Hell (v Rimbaud), 1939
Season in the Congo (p Césaire), 1969
Sébastien (p Troyat), 1949
Sébastien Roch (f Mirbeau), 1890
Second Sex (Beauvoir), 1953
Second sous-sol (f Butor), 1976
Second Thoughts (f Butor), 1958
Second Year Ashore (f Verne), 1889
Seconde (f Colette), 1929
Seconde Année (p Scribe), 1830
Seconde patrie (f Verne), 1900
Secret (v Spire), 1919
Secret de M. Ladureau (f Champfleury), 1875
Secret de Wilhelm Storitz (f Verne), 1910
Secret des Lamas (f Simenon), 1928
Secret des Ruggieri (f Balzac), 1837
Secret d'état (p Sue), 1831
Secret of Wilhelm Storitz (f Verne), 1965
Secrétaire de Madame (p Labiche), 1857
Secrétaire et le cuisinier (p Scribe), 1821
Secrétaire intime (f Sand), 1834
Séducteur et le mari (p Dumas père), 1842
Seeds (p Zola), 1966
Seedtime (Jaccottet), 1977
Seine (v Ponge), 1950
Sel de la vie (p Maeterlinck), 1919
Selam (p Gautier), 1850
Sélico (p Pixérécourt), 1793
Selmours de Florian (p Deschamps), 1818
Selon ma loi (v Duhamel), 1910
Semailles et les moissons (f Troyat), 1953
Semaine sainte (Aragon), 1958

Semaison (Jaccottet), 1963
Semeur de larmes (f Simenon), 1928
Séminaire d'Issy (Renan), 1881
Séminaire Saint-Sulpice (Renan), 1882
Sémiramis (p Valéry), 1934
Sens de la marche (p Adamov), 1953
Sens de la mort (f Bourget), 1915
Sens dessus dessous (f Verne), 1889
Sens et non-sens (Merleau-Ponty), 1948
Sens interdit (p Salacrou), 1953
Sense and Nonsense (Merleau-Ponty), 1964
Sense of Guilt (f Simenon), 1955
Sensitive (p Labiche), 1860
Sentiers et les routes de la poésie (Éluard), 1952
Sentimental Education (f Flaubert), 1896
Sentiments de Critias (Benda), 1917
Sept cordes de la lyre (p Sand), 1839
Sept couleurs (Brasillach), 1939
Sept femmes de la Barbe-Bleue (f France), 1909
Sept Minutes (f Simenon), 1938
Sept péchés (f Sue), 1851–54
Sept péchés capitaux (f Salmon), 1926
Sept princesses (p Maeterlinck), 1890
Séquences (Cendrars), 1913
Séquestrés d'Altona (p Sartre), 1959
Séraphine (p Sardou), 1879
Séraphîta (f Balzac), 1835
Serment (p Scribe), 1832
Serment d'Horace (p Murger), 1861
Serpent de mer (f Verne), 1901
Serpent d'étoiles (f Giono), 1933
Serres chaudes (v Maeterlinck), 1889
Serrure (p Tardieu), 1955
Servitude et grandeur des Français (Aragon), 1945
Servitude et grandeur militaires (f Vigny), 1835
Seul baiser… (f Simenon), 1928
Seul parmi les gorilles (f Simenon), 1937
Seuls demeurent (v Char), 1945
Seven Princesses (p Maeterlinck), 1895
Shackle (f Colette), 1963
Shadow Falls (f Simenon), 1945
Shadow in the Courtyard (f Simenon), 1934
Shadow on the Courtyard (f Simenon), 1934
Shaga (p Duras), 1968
Shame (f Zola), 1954
She and He (f Sand), 1902
She Came to Stay (f Beauvoir), 1949
She Wolves of Machecoul (f Dumas père), 1895
Shell and the Ear (v Supervielle)
Sherif (p Scribe), 1839
Shop Girls of Paris (f Zola), 1883
Show on Ice (f Verne), 1891
Shylock (p Vigny), 1905
Si jamais je te pince!… (p Labiche), 1856
Si j'étais vous… (f Green), 1947
Si le grain ne meurt (Gide), 1920–21
Si l'été revenait (p Adamov), 1970
Si tu t'imagines (v Queneau), 1951
Sicilian Bandit (f Dumas père), 1859
Siège de Jérusalem (Jacob), 1914
Siegfried (p Giraudoux), 1928

Siegfried et le Limousin (f Giraudoux), 1922
Signe du taureau (f Troyat), 1945
Signe Picpus (f Simenon), 1944
Signes (Merleau-Ponty), 1960
Signes et les prodiges (f Mallet-Joris), 1966
Signification de la guerre (Bergson), 1915
Signs (Merleau-Ponty), 1964
Signs and Wonders (f Mallet-Joris), 1966
Silbermann (f Lacretelle), 1922
Silence (p Sarraute), 1967
Silènes (p Jarry), 1926
Silent Rooms (f Hébert), 1974
Silken Eyes (f Sagan), 1975
Simon (f Sand), 1836
Simon le pathétique (f Giraudoux), 1918
Simone (Gourmont), 1901
Simple histoire (p Scribe), 1826
Simulacre (v Leiris), 1925
Sin of M. Antoine (f Sand), 1900–02
Sin of the Abbé Mouret (f Zola), 1904
Sir Hugues de Guilfort (p Scribe), 1836
Sirène (p Scribe), 1844
Sister Beatrice (p Maeterlinck), 1901
Sister Philomene (f Goncourt), 1890
Situations (Sartre), 1947–76
Six aventures (f Du Camp), 1857
628-E-8 (f Mirbeau), 1907
Six heures à perdre (Brasillach), 1953
6 810 000 litres d'eau par seconde (p Butor), 1965
Sixtine (Gourmont), 1890
Sketch for a Theory of the Emotions (Sartre), 1962
Skin of Dreams (f Queneau), 1948
Sky above the Roof (v Verlaine), 1957
Slave King (f Hugo), 1833
Smarra (f Nodier), 1821
Snapshots (f Robbe-Grillet), 1965
Snow Man (f Sand), 1871
Snow Was Black (f Simenon), 1950
So Be It (Gide), 1960
Soap (Ponge), 1969
Société Apollon (p Tardieu), 1955
Socrate et sa femme (p Banville), 1885
Socrates and His Wife (p Banville), 1889
Sodome et Gomorrhe (p Giraudoux), 1943
Sodome et Gomorrhe (f Proust), 1921–22
Soeur Béatrice (p Maeterlinck), 1901
Soeur Philomène (f Goncourt), 1861
Soeurette (f Simenon), 1930
Soeurs Lacroix (f Simenon), 1938
Soeurs Rondoli (f Maupassant), 1884
Soeurs Vatard (f Huysmans), 1879
Soif et la faim (p Ionesco), 1964
Soil (f Zola), 1888
Soir d'une bataille (v Leconte de Lisle), 1871
Soir de vertige (f Simenon), 1928
Soirée avec Monsieur Teste (Valéry), 1919
Soirée des Champs-Elysées (p Pixérécourt), 1800
Soirée en Provence (p Tardieu), 1975
Soirées de Saint-Pétersbourg (Maistre), 1821
Soirs (v Verhaeren), 1887
Soldat et la sorcière (p Salacrou), 1945

Soldier's Honour (f Zola), 1888
Soleil cou-coupé (v Césaire), 1948
Soleil des loups (f Pieyre de Mandiargues), 1951
Soleil du plafond (v Reverdy), 1955
Solitaire (f Ionesco), 1973
Solitaire de la Roche-Noire (p Pixérécourt), 1806
Solitude de la pitié (f Giono), 1932
Solitudes (v Sully Prudhomme), 1869
Solliciteur (p Scribe), 1817
Solo (p Beckett), 1982
Some Portraits of Women (f Bourget), 1898
Someone (f Pinget), 1984
Somnambule (p Scribe), 1821
Somnambulist (p Scribe), 1850
Son (f Bourget), 1893
Son (f Simenon), 1958
Son Excellence Eugène Rougon (f Zola), 1876
Sonata and the Three Gentlemen (p Tardieu), 1968
Sonate et les trois messieurs (p Tardieu), 1966
Song for an Equinox (v Saint-John Perse), 1977
Song of the World (f Giono), 1937
Songe (f Montherlant), 1922
Songe d'Eleuthère (Benda), 1949
Songe du critique (p Anouilh), 1959
Songe d'une femme (Gourmont), 1899
Songes d'été (f Simenon), 1928
Songes en équilibre (v Hébert), 1942
Songs of Twilight (v Hugo), 1836 18,
Sonnailles et clochettes (v Banville), 1890
Sonnets (v Queneau), 1958
Sons of the Soil (f Balzac), 1890
Sopha (p Labiche), 1850
Sophie (f Troyat), 1963
Sophie (Staël), 1786
Sophie Printems (f Dumas fils), 1854
Soprano (p Scribe), 1831
Sorcier (f Balzac), 1837
Sorcière (p Sardou), 1904
Sorcières de Salem (p Aymé), 1955
Sorellina (f Martin du Gard), 1928
Soufflex-moi dans l'oeil (p Labiche), 1852
Souffrances du Professeur Delteil (f Champfleury), 1853
Soul Enchanted (f Rolland), 1927–35
Soulier de satin (p Claudel), 1929
Souls of the Soulless (f Supervielle), 1933
Souper (p Tardieu), 1975
Source grècque (Weil), 1953
Sources (v Jammes), 1936
Sources du vent (v Reverdy), 1929
Sourires pincés (f Renard), 1890
Sous la lame (f Pieyre de Mandiargues), 1976
Sous le rempart d'Athènes (p Claudel), 1927
Sous le soleil de Satan (f Bernanos), 1926
Sous-marin dans la forêt (f Simenon), 1928
Sous-préfet aux champs (p A. Daudet), 1898
South (p Green), 1955
Southern Mail (f Saint-Exupéry), 1933
Soutien de famille (f A. Daudet), 1898
Souvenirs à bâtons rompus (v Spire), 1961
Souvenirs d'Antony (f Dumas père), 1835
Souvenirs de voyage (f Gobineau), 1872

Souvenirs d'enfance et de jeunesse (Renan), 1883
Souvenirs des funambules (f Champfleury), 1859
Souvenirs du triangle d'or (f Robbe-Grillet), 1978
Souvenirs d'une favorite (f Dumas père), 1865
Space Within (Michaux), 1951
Spectacle (v Prévert), 1951
Spectacle dans un fauteuil (A. Musset), 1833
Spectre Mother (f Dumas père), 1864
Sphinx des glaces (f Verne), 1897
Spicilège (f Schwob), 1896
Spider and the Fly (f Vigny), 1925
Spiel (p Beckett), 1963
Spiridion (f Sand), 1839
Spirite (f Gautier), 1866
Spiritisme (p Sardou), 1898
Spleen (p Scribe), 1820
Splendeurs et misères des courtisanes (f Balzac), 1845
Sponger (f Renard), 1957
Square (f Duras), 1955
Square (p Duras) 1957
Stain on the Snow (f Simenon), 1953
Stalactites (v Banville), 1846
Stances (v Moréas), 1899
Stances et poèmes (v Sully Prudhomme), 1865
Star of Satan (f Bernanos), 1940
Star of the North (p Scribe), 1855
State of Siege (p Camus), 1958
State of the Union (v Césaire), 1966
Station Champbaudet (p Labiche), 1862
Steam House (f Verne), 1881
Steeple-Chase (f Bourget), 1894
Stella (f Nodier), 1802
Stello (f Vigny), 1832
Sténie (f Balzac), 1936
Stepmother (p Balzac), 1901
Still Storm (f Sagan), 1984
Stonecutter of St-Point (f Lamartine), 1851
Stonemason of St-Point (f Lamartine), 1851
Stories and Texts for Nothing (f Beckett), 1967
Stories for Ninon (f Zola), 1895
Storm in Shanghai (f Malraux), 1934
Story of André Cornélis (f Bourget), 1909
Story Without a Name (f Barbey D'Aurevilly), 1891
Stowaway (f Simenon), 1957
Strait Is the Gate (f Gide), 1924
Strange Case of Peter the Lett (f Simenon), 1933
Strange Inheritance (f Simenon), 1950
Strange River (f Green), 1932
Stranger (f Camus), 1946
Stranger in the House (f Simenon), 1951
Strangers in the Land (f Troyat), 1956
Stratagème (f France), 1880
Straw Man (f Giono), 1959
Strip-Tease (f Simenon), 1958
Striptease (f Simenon), 1959
Stroll in the Air (Ionesco), 1964
Strong as Death (f Maupassant), 1899
Structural Anthropology (Lévi-Strauss), 1963–76
Structure du comportement (Merleau-Ponty), 1942
Structure of Behaviour (Merleau-Ponty), 1963
Structures élémentaires de la parenté (Lévi-Strauss), 1949

Stuff of Youth (f F. Mauriac), 1960
Stupra (v Rimbaud), 1923
Succession le Camus (f Champfleury), 1857
Sud (p Green), 1953
Sueur de sang (f Bloy), 1893
Suicidés (f Simenon), 1934
Suisse de l'hôtel (p Scribe), 1831
Suite cévenole (f Chamson), 1968
Suite dans les idées (v Drieu la Rochelle) 1927
Suites d'un premier lit (p Labiche), 1852
Suites d'une course (p Supervielle), 1959
Sultanetta (f Dumas père), 1895
Summer 1914 (f Martin du Gard), 1941
Sun in Eclipse (f Verne), 1873
Sun Placed in the Abyss (v Ponge), 1977
Sunday (f Simenon), 1960
Sunday of Life (f Queneau), 1976
Sunlight on Cold Water (f Sagan), 1971
Superbe (f Chamson), 1967
Superbe Orénoque (f Verne), 1898
Supermale (f Jarry), 1968
Supplément au voyage de Cook (p Giraudoux), 1937
Suppliants parallèles (Péguy), 1906
Sur la pierre blanche (f France), 1905
Sur la poésie (v Char), 1958
Sur la science (Weil), 1966
Sur la souffrance (Teilhard de Chardin), 1974
Sur l'amour (Teilhard de Chardin), 1967
Sur le bonheur (Teilhard de Chardin), 1966
Sur le succès du Bergsonisme (Benda), 1914
Sur les générations actuelles (Senancour), 1963
Sur les hauteurs (p Char), 1967
Sur les pas fauves de vivre (Perec), 1983
Sur Racine (Barthes), 1963
Surmâle (f Jarry), 1902
Surprises (p Scribe), 1844
Surrealism and Painting (Breton), 1972
Surréalisme et la peinture (Breton), 1928
Sursis (f Sartre), 1945
Surveiller et punir (Foucault), 1975
Survivant (f Supervielle), 1928
Survivors (f Simenon), 1949
Survivors (f Supervielle)
Survivors of the Chancelor (f Verne), 1875
Survivors of the Jonathan (f Verne)
Susanna Andler (p Duras), 1968
Suspect (f Simenon), 1938
Suspicion (f F. Mauriac), 1931
Sutter's Gold (Cendrars), 1936
Suzanna Andler (p Duras) 1973
Suzanne (f L. Daudet), 1896
Suzanne and Joseph Pasquier (f Duhamel), 1946
Suzanne and the Pacific (f Giraudoux), 1923
Suzanne et le Pacifique (f Giraudoux), 1921
Suzanne et les jeunes hommes (f Duhamel), 1940
Swann's Way (f Proust), 1922
Swarm (Maeterlinck), 1906
Sweet Cheat Gone (f Proust), 1930
Sylvandire (f Dumas père), 1844
Sylvandire (p Dumas père), 1845
Sylvanire (p Zola), 1921

Sylvère (f Salmon), 1956
Sylvie (f Nerval), 1887
Symphonie pastorale (f Gide), 1919
Syren (p Scribe), 1849
Syrtes (v Moréas), 1884
Système de la mode (Barthes), 1967
Systéme Ribadier (p Feydeau),1892

Table aux crevés (f Aymé), 1929
Tableau (p Ionesco), 1955
Tableau de la bourgeoisie (Jacob), 1929
Taciturne (p Martin du Gard), 1932
Tailleur de pierres de Saint-Point (f Lamartine), 1851
Tailleur pour dames (p Feydeau), 1886
Taking the Bastille (f Dumas père)
Tales of a Grandmother (Sand), 1930
Tales of Asia (f Gobineau), 1947
Tamaris (f Sand), 1862
Tant que la terre durera (f Troyat), 1947
Tante Jeanne (f Simenon), 1951
Tapin (f Bourget), 1928
Tapisserie de Sainte Geneviève et de Jeanne d'Arc (Péguy),
    1913
Tartarin on the Alps (f A. Daudet), 1886
Tartarin sur les Alpes (f A. Daudet), 1885
Tartarin sur les Alpes (p A. Daudet), 1888
Tartuffe (p Anouilh), 1960
Tatala (f Simenon), 1943
Tauromachies (Leiris), 1937
Taverne des étudiants (p Sardou), 1854
Taxi (f Leduc), 1971
Teddy Bear (f Simenon), 1971
Tel chante le vieux coq! (p Sardou), 1904
Tel qu'en lui-même (f Duhamel), 1932
Telegraph (f Stendhal), 1950
Téléki (p Pixérécourt),1804
Témoin (p Scribe), 1820
Témoin invisible (v Tardieu), 1943
Témoins (f Simenon), 1955
Température (p Apollinaire), 1975
Tempête (p Césaire), 1969
Tempêtes et naufrages (Gourmont), 1883
Temporal and Eternal (Péguy), 1958
Temps d'Anaïs (f Simenon), 1951
Temps du mépris (f Malraux), 1935
Temps du verbe (p Tardieu), 1956
Temps immobile (C. Mauriac), from 1970
Temps mêlés (f Queneau), 1941
Temps retrouvé (f Proust), 1927
Temps sauvage (p Hébert), 1967
Temps viendra (p Rolland), 1903
Temptation (f Sue), 1845
Temptation of Saint Anthony (f Flaubert), 1895
Temptation of the West (f Malraux), 1961
Tender and Violent Elizabeth (f Troyat), 1961
Tender Shoot (f Colette), 1958
Tendre comme le souvenir (v Apollinaire), 1952
Tendre et violente Elizabeth (f Troyat)
Tendres canailles (f Salmon), 1913
Tendresses premières (v Verhaeren), 1904
Ténébreuse affaire (f Balzac), 1842

Tentation de l'occident (f Malraux), 1926
Tentation de saint Antoine (f Flaubert), 1874
Tentations (v Spire), 1920
Tentative amoureuse (f Gide), 1893
Tentative d'épuisement d'un lieu parisien (Perec), 1982
10.30 on a Summer Night (f Duras), 1962
Terme épars (v Char), 1966
Ternove (f Gobineau), 1848
Terra amata (f Le Clézio), 1968
Terrain Bouchaballe (Jacob), 1923
Terrasse de l'ile d'Elbe (f Giono), 1973
Terre (f Zola), 1887
Terre des hommes (f Saint-Exupéry), 1939
Terre est ronde (p Salacrou), 1938
Terre et les rêveries de la volonté (Bachelard), 1948
Terre et les rêveries du repos (Bachelard), 1948
Terre promise (f Bourget), 1892
Terreur prussienne (f Dumas père), 1867
Tessa (p Giraudoux), 1934
Testament (f Bourget), 1921
Testament de César (p Dumas père), 1849
Testament Donadieu (f Simenon), 1937
Testament d'Orphée (p Cocteau), 1961
Testament du Père Leleu (p Martin du Gard), 1914
Testament d'un excentrique (f Verne), 1898
Testament of Orpheus (p Cocteau), 1968
Tête de mort (p Pixérécourt), 1828
Tête des autres (p Aymé), 1952
Tête d'or (p Claudel), 1890
Tête d'un homme (f Simenon), 1931
Tête sur les épaules (f Troyat), 1951
Tetesa (p Dumas père), 1832
Teverino (f Sand), 1845
Texar the Southerner (f Verne), 1888
Thaïs (f France), 1891
That Time (p Beckett), 1976
That Which Was Lost (f F. Mauriac), 1951
Théâtre (p Anouilh), 1970
Theatre and Its Double (Artaud), 1958
Théâtre de chambre (p Tardieu), 1955
Théâtre de Clara Gazul (p Mérimée), 1825
Théâtre de la cruanté (Artaud), 1933
Théâtre de la Révolution (p Rolland), 1909
Théâtre de poche (p Cocteau), 1949
Théâtre de poche (p Gautier), 1855
Théâtre de situations (Sartre), 1973
Théâtre en liberté (p Hugo), 1886
Théâtre et son double (Artaud), 1938
Their Island Home (f Verne), 1923
Then Shall the Dust Return (f Green), 1941
Théobald (p Scribe), 1829
Théodat (Gourmont), 1893
Théodora (p Sardou), 1884
There is One in Every Marriage (p Feydeau), 1970
Theresa (f Zola), 1952
Thérèse (f F. Mauriac), 1928
Therese (f F. Mauriac), 1947
Thérèse and Isabelle (f Leduc), 1966
Thérèse Aubert (f Nodier), 1819
Thérèse Desqueyroux (f F. Mauriac), 1927
Thérèse Dunoyer (f Sue), 1842

Usage des plaisirs (Foucault), 1984
Uscoque (f Sand), 1838
Use of Pleasure (Foucault), 1985
Use of Speech (f Sarraute), 1980

Va et Vient (p Beckett), 1966
Vacances de Camille (f Murger), 1857
Vagabond (f Colette), 1954
Vagabonde (f Colette), 1911
Vagabonde (p Colette), 1923
Vagrant (f Colette), 1912
Vague de rêves (Aragon), 1924
Vaines Tendresses (v Sully Prudhomme), 1875
Valentin (p Pixérécourt), 1821
Valentine (p Pixérécourt), 1834
Valentine (f Sand), 1832
Valentine (p Scribe), 1836
Valérie (p Scribe), 1823
Valet de chambre (p Scribe), 1823
Valet de son rival (p Scribe), 1816
Valeur inductive de la relativité (Bachelard), 1929
Valse des toréadors (p Anouilh), 1952
Valvèdre (f Sand), 1861
Vampire (p Dumas père), 1851
Vampire (Nodier), 1820
Vampire (p Scribe), 1820
Vanished Diamond (f Verne), 1885
Vanité (f Butor), 1980
Variété (Valéry), 1924–44
Variety (Valéry), 1927–28
Varouna (f Green), 1940
Vase (p Ionesco), 1974
Vases communicants (Breton), 1932
Vatard Sisters (f Huysmans), 1983
Vatel (p Scribe), 1825
Vatican Cellars (f Gide), 1952
Vatican Swindle (f Gide), 1925
Vauban (Halévy), 1923
Vaurien (f Aymé), 1931
Vautrin (p Balzac), 1840
Veau d'or (p Scribe), 1841
Veillées du "Lapin agile," (f Salmon), 1919
Vendredi (f Tournier), 1967
Venetian Outlaw, His Country's Friend (p Pixérécourt), 1805
Vengeance italienne (p Scribe), 1832
Venice Train (f Simenon), 1974
Venise sauvée (Weil), 1968
Vénitienne (p Dumas père), 1834
Vent (Simon), 1957
Ventes d'amour (v Salmon), 1921
Ventre de Paris (f Zola), 1873
Ventre de Paris (p Zola), 1887
Vents (v Saint-John Perse), 1946
Vénus dans la balance (v Salmon), 1926
Vêpres siciliennes (p Scribe), 1855
Vera Baxter (p Duras), 1980
Vercoquin et le plancton (f Vian), 1946
Verdugo (f Balzac), 1847
Vérité (f Zola), 1903
Vérité dans le vin (p Scribe), 1823
Vérité sur Bébé Donge (f Simenon), 1942

Verre d'eau (p Scribe), 1840
Verrou de la reine (p Dumas père), 1856
Vers de circonstance (v Mallarmé), 1920
Vers d'exil (v Claudel), 1895
Vers le roi (f L. Daudet), 1921
Vers les routes absurdes (v Spire), 1911
Vers libres (v Radiguet), 1925
Vers retrouvés (v Baudelaire), 1929
Versets (v Spire), 1908
Very Easy Death (Beauvoir), 1966
Very Woman (Gourmont), 1922
Veuf (f Simenon), 1960
Veuve Couderc (f Simenon), 1942
Veuve du Malabar (p Scribe), 1822
Viaducs de la Seine-et-Oise (p Duras), 1960
Viaduct (p Duras), 1967
Viaducts of Seine-et-Oise (p Duras), 1967
Vicaire des Ardennes (f Balzac), 1822
Vice-consul (f Duras), 1965
Vice-Consul (f Duras), 1968
Vicomte de Bragelonne (f Dumas père), 1848–50
Victim of the Jesuits (Scribe), 1848
Victime (f Simenon), 1929
Victime de son fils (f Simenon), 1931
Victimes du devoir (p Ionesco),1953
Victims of Duty (p Ionesco), 1958
Victor (p Anouilh), 1962
Victor (p Pixérécourt), 1798
Victor-Marie, Comte Hugo (Péguy), 1911
Victors (p Sartre), 1949
Vie (f Maupassant), 1883
Vie à vingt ans (f Dumas fils), 1850
Vie comme neuve (f Simenon), 1951
Vie d'Adrien Zograffi (f Istrati), 1933–35
Vie dangereuse (Cendrars), 1938
Vie dans les plis (v Michaux), 1949
Vie de Bohème (f Murger), 1949
Vie de Bohème (p Murger), 1853
Vie de Nietzsche (Halévy), 1909
Vie de Proudhon (Halévy), 1948
Vie des abeilles (Maeterlinck), 1901
Vie des martyrs (f Duhamel), 1917
Vie en rose (p Salacrou), 1931
Vie et aventures de Salavin (f Duhamel), from 1920
Vie et l'oeuvre de Semmelweis (Céline), 1936
Vie familiale et sociale des Indiens Nambikwara (Lévi-Strauss), 1948
Vie immédiate (Éluard), 1932
Vie inquiète (v Bourget), 1875
Vie inquiète de Jean Hermelin (f Lacretelle), 1920
Vie matérielle (f Duras), 1987
Vie mode d'emploi (Perec), 1978
Vie, poésies et pensées de Joseph Delorme (v Sainte-Beuve), 1829
Vie tranquille (f Duras), 1944
Vie unanime (v Romains), 1908
Vieille (p Scribe), 1826
Vieille (f Simenon), 1959
Vieille Fille (f Balzac), 1837
Vieille Fille et le mort (f Leduc), 1958
Vieille France (f Martin du Gard), 1933

Vieille granison (f Salmon), 1925
Vieille maitresse (f Barbey d'Aurevilly), 1851
Vieillesse (Beauvoir), 1970
Vierge (Jammes), 1919
Vierge et les sonnets (v Jammes), 1919
Vies imaginaires (f Schwob), 1896
Vieux Garçon et la petite fille (p Scribe), 1822
Vieux Garçons (p Sardou), 1865
Vieux Mari (p Scribe), 1828
Vieux ménage (p Mirbeau), 1901
Vieux Péchés (p Scribe), 1833
Vieux Roi (Gourmont), 1897
View from Afar (Lévi-Strauss), 1985
Vigie de Koat-Ven (f Sue), 1833
Vigneron dans sa vigne (f Renard), 1894
Village aérien (f Verne), 1901
Village in the Tree Tops (f Verne)
Villages illusoires (v Verhaeren), 1895
Ville (p Claudel), 1893
Ville dont le prince est un enfant (p Montherlant), 1951
Ville flottante (f Verne), 1871
Ville noire (f Sand), 1860
Ville ressuscitée (Gourmont), 1882
Villefort (p Dumas père), 1851
Villes à pignons (v Verhaeren), 1909
Villes tentaculaires (v Verhaeren), 1895
Vin blanc de la Villette (f Romains), 1914
Vin de Paris (f Aymé), 1947
Vingt ans après (f Dumas père), 1845
Vingt et un jours d'un neurasthénique (f Mirbeau), 1902
Vingt mille lieues sous les mers (f Verne), 1870
29 degrès à l'ombre (p Labiche), 1873
Vingt-quatre février (p Dumas père), 1850
Viol aux Quat'z'arts (f Simenon), 1925
Violaine la chevelue (p Zola), 1921
Violation de frontières (f Romains), 1951
Violent Ends (f Simenon), 1954
Violon de faïence (f Champfleury), 1862
Violons parfois (p Sagan), 1962
Viou (f Troyat), 1980
Vipers' Tangle (f F. Mauriac), 1933
Virgin Heart (Gourmont), 1921
Virtuous Island (p Giraudoux), 1956
Visages de la vie (v Verhaeren), 1899
Visages radieux (v Claudel), 1946
Visible et l'invisible (Merleau-Ponty), 1964
Vision du passé (Teilhard de Chardin), 1957
Vision of the Past (Teilhard de Chardin), 1966
Visionnaire (f Green), 1934
Visions des souffrances et de la mort de Jésus, fils de Dieu (Jacob), 1928
Visions infernales (Jacob), 1924
Visite à Bedlam (p Scribe), 1826
Visite de noces (p Dumas fils), 1871
Visite en été (p Lacretelle), 1953
Visites aux paysans du Centre (Halévy), 1921
Vitam impendere amori (v Apollinaire), 1917
Vittoria Accoramboni (f Stendhal), 1839
Vivacités du capitaine Tic (p Labiche), 1861
Vivantes cendres, innommées (v Leiris), 1961
Vivants (p Troyat), 1946

Vive Henri IV (p Anouilh), 1977
Vivier (f Troyat), 1935
Vocabulaire (v Cocteau), 1922
Vocalises (v Salmon), 1957
Voeu d'une morte (f Zola), 1866
Voeux (Perec), 1989
Vogue la galère (p Aymé), 1944
Voice (f Pinget), 1982
Voice of Things (v Ponge), 1972
Voices of Silence (Malraux), 1953
Voie des masques (Lévi-Strauss), 1975
Voie royale (f Malraux), 1930
Voix de prison (Lamennais), 1840
Voix du silence (Malraux), 1951
Voix du vieux monde (v Duhamel), 1925
Voix humaine (p Cocteau), 1930
Voix intérieures (v Hugo), 1837
Voix sans personne (p Tardieu), 1956
Voix sans personne (v Tardieu), 1954
Vol à voiles (Cendrars), 1932
Vol de nuit (f Saint-Exupéry), 1931
Vol d'Icare (f Queneau), 1968
Volcan d'or (f Verne), 1906
Volcan en éruption (Gourmont), 1882
Volets verts (f Simenon), 1950
Voleur d'enfants (f Supervielle), 1926
Voleur d'enfants (p Supervielle), 1949
Voleurs de navires (f Simenon), 1927
Voleuse d'amour (f Simenon), 1929
Volière du Père Philippe (p Scribe), 1818
Volontaire (p Feydeau), 1884
Volonté de savoir (Foucault), 1976
Voluptueuses étreintes (f Simenon), 1925
Votre Faust... (p Butor), 1968
Vouivre (f Aymé), 1943
Vous les entendez? (f Sarraute), 1972
Voyage à travers l'impossible (p Verne), 1882
Voyage au bout de la nuit (f Céline), 1932
Voyage au centre de la terre (f Verne), 1864
Voyage autour de ma marmite (p Labiche), 1860
Voyage aux eaux des Pyrénées (Taine), 1855
Voyage aux pays des arbres (f Le Clézio), 1978
Voyage de Hollande (Aragon), 1964
Voyage de Monsieur Perrichon (p Labiche), 1860
Voyage de Patrice Periot (f Duhamel), 1952
Voyage des amants (v Romains), 1920
Voyage d'Horace Pirouelle (f Soupault), 1925
Voyage d'Urien (f Gide), 1893
Voyage en calèche (p Giono), 1947
Voyage en Chine (p Labiche), 1865
Voyage en Espagne (p Gautier), 1843
Voyage en Grande Garabagne (f Michaux), 1936
Voyage en Italie (f Giono), 1954
Voyage en Italie (Taine), 1866
Voyage en orient (Nerval), 1851
Voyage round the World (f Verne), 1876–77
Voyages chez les morts (p Ionesco), 1981
Voyages de l'autre côté (f Le Clézio), 1975
Voyageur de la Toussaint (f Simenon), 1941
Voyageur sans bagage (p Anouilh), 1942
Voyageur sur la terre (f Green), 1927

GENERAL INDEX

All subjects of entries in the *Guide* are entered in the index in **bold type** to indicate that the *Guide* entry itself must be consulted for details of people and topics connected with the indexed writer or movement. The index can then be consulted to discover the whole range of other connections in which such people or topics are mentioned.

There is therefore a reference to Sand under Chopin (no *Guide* entry), but none to Chopin under Sand (*Guide* entry). For persons and topics connected with Sand, the entry in the *Guide* itself has to be consulted. They can then be looked up in the index for their relevance to the subjects of other entries in the *Guide*. Again, therefore, there is a reference under Drumont (no *Guide* entry) to Zola, but none to Drumont under Zola (*Guide* entry) in the index. Drumont's relevance in the context of Zola's life and works is made clear in the Zola *Guide* entry itself. The index makes clear, under Drumont, why he may be of interest to users of the *Guide* and where references to him may be found. By not simply repeating in the index the information given in the relevant *Guide* entries themselves, it has been possible to keep the index to a more manageable length and to prevent its consultation from being more laborious.

Asthma
>and Proust, 504
>and Queneau, 509

Astruc, Gabriel; impresario
>association with Diaghilev, 165

asylum, mental
>Artaud in, 39
>Camille Claudel in, 159, 160
>Vallès in, 677

Aubanel, Théodore (1829–1886); Provençal poet
>friend of Mallarmé, 395
>associated with Mistral, 441
>Maurras's book on, 419

Auber, Esprit (1782–1871); composer
>Scribe wrote opera libretti for, 597–601

Auden, W.H. (1907–1973); British poet who became U.S. citizen
>his views on Cocteau, 170, 171
>influenced by Saint-John Perse, 550

Audiberti, Jacques (1899–1965); poet, novelist, dramatist
>friend of Pieyre de Mandiargues, 491

Auger, Louis-Simon (1772–1829)
>attacked Romantics, 540

Augier, Emile
>**Life, 39–40; Works, 40–41; Publications, 41–42**
>rich from royalties, 7
>knew Mérimée, 425
>contrast Villiers de L'Isle-Adam, 696

August, Prince of Prussia
>romance with Juliette Récamier, 155

Augusta, Empress of Prussia (1811–1890)
>Laforgue, post of reader to, 345

Aumale, Henri-Eugène-Philippe-Louis d'Orléans, duc D'(1822–1897)
>friend and employer of Augier, 40

Aupick, Jacques (1789–1857)
>stepfather of Baudelaire, 71–73

Auric, Georges (1899–1983); composer
>knew Cocteau and Satie, 166–9
>and first night of *Parade*, 166
>knew Radiguet, 511
>and Rue Huyghens studio, 329

L'Aurore—pro-Dreyfus daily paper. Founded in 1897 it went bankrupt in 1904, was saved, supported Clemenceau but steadily lost influence declining from sales of 150,000 to under 7,000 in 1912
>first use of term "intellectual", 98
>Mirbeau wrote on Dreyfus Affair in, 439
>Zola's "J'accuse" published in number of 13 January 1898, 708

Austen, Jane (1775–1817); English novelist
>her style, see Stendhal, 630

"automatic writing", 5
>see Surrealism, 647–9
>and Breton, 119–125
>and Péret, 488
>and Salacrou, 561
>and Soupault, 618

L'Avant-Garde de Normandie—right-wing paper
>Bernanos editor of, 103

L'Avenir—Catholic review, 1830–1832, suppressed by encyclical *Mirari vos* of 15 August 1832
>founded by Lamennais, 358–9
>see Lacordaire, Montalembert, 359
>Lamennais on monarchy in, 554
>Vigny's "Lettre Parisienne" in, 693

Averroës, (1126–1198), Arab doctor and philosopher
>view inherited by Romains, 536

Aymé, Marcel
>**Life, 42; Works, 42–43; Publications, 43**
>contributed to *Je Suis Partout*, 118

Bacciochi, Elisa (1777–1820); sister of Napoleon
>Chateaubriand met, 153

Bachaumont, Louis Petit de (1690–1771); writer and diarist
>Goncourts modelled *Journal* on, 286

Bachelard, Gaston
>**Life, 44; Works, 44–45; Publications, 45**
>attacked by Benda, 98
>Bonnefoy studied with, 112
>Butor's supervisor, 125
>his study of Lautréamont, 364

Bachelin-Deflorenne; publisher
>France worked part-time for, 246
>founded *Le Bibliophile Français Illustré*, 247

Baille, Baptistin; professor
>friend of Zola, 704–9

Baju, Anatole (1861–1903); poet
>founded *Le Décadent* (30 numbers), 650

Baker, Dorothy
>translated by Vian, 689

Baker, Josephine (1906–1975); American singer and dancer
>liaison with Simenon, 607

Bakst, Léon (Lev) (1886–1925); costume and stage designer and painter
>with Ballets Russes, 165

Bakunin, Mikhail (1814–1876); Russian revolutionary
>Barrès wrote about, 68
>saw Sand as leading radical propagandist, 578

"bal anthropométrique"
>Simenon's launch party, 607

Balakirev, Mili (1837–1910); Russian composer
>founded the Group of Five, 167

Balieff, Nikita (1877–1936); cabaret compère
>uncle of Troyat, 671

Ball, Hugo (1886–1927)
>Cabaret Voltaire, and Dada, 189

Ballanche, Pierre Simon (1776–1847); printer, crank, historian, visionary, who worshipped Juliette Récamier from afar, moving to Paris to be near her
>Sand derived pseudo-mysticism from, 578
>article on Senancour, 602

Ballets Russes
>see Diaghilev
>Cocteau's association with, 165–171
>*Nouvelle Revue Française* took little notice of, 473

balloon
>see Nadar
>trip: Maupassant, 407
>story: Verne, 685

788

concentrated in his paintings of straight lines, right angles, and primary colours

"orphism", 30

Le Monde, circulation in 1980, about 600,000. The Lamennais paper lasted only briefly (1836–1837). The 1860 monarchist and ultramontain paper, at first popular, lost over half its circulation before closing in 1871. It was revived in 1883, put at the disposition of the Vatican by Mgr d'Hulst (q.v.), printing 6,000 copies, and amalgamated with *l'Univers* in 1897. Drumont (q.v.) became editor in 1886.

The name was used for a communist weekly from 1928 to 1935. The politically non-aligned national paper which tripled its circulation between 1960 and 1975 has moved to the left

Gourmont articles, 290

Claude Mauriac worked for, 412

Lamennais cut Sand's work in, 573

Monde Dramatique, le—illustrated review

founded by Nerval, 462

Monde Poétique, le

published Heredia, 307

Mondes, les

Cros article on colour photography, 184

Monet, Claude (1840–1926); painter most frequently associated with his sets of paintings of the same generally landscape view in different lights.

Feydeau collected, 225

idol of Louÿs, 386

painted scenes frequented by Maupassant, 405

friend of Mirbeau, 437

see Realism, 512

associated with Zola, 705

Moniteur, le

Gautier worked for, 255

Sainte-Beuve, on Taine in, 653

Moniteur du Calvados, le—provincial paper

Vallès on the Guérins in, 678

Moniteur de la Mode, le

rejected Barbey d'Aurevilly, 62

Murger in staff job, 105

Moniteur Parisien, le

merged with *La Charte de 1830*, 462

Moniteur Universel, le recorded official events from 1814, on 7 March 1815 publishing news of Napoleon's landing on 1 March, known in Paris on 5th. Napoleon was "a rebel and traitor."

The issue of 20 March recorded the king's flight and the arrival of "His Majesty the Emperor." It remained the purveyor of official information, coming 17th with a print-run of 2,000 in 1846. It reported parliamentary speeches and judicial sentences for political offences by newspaper editors, but was simply an official mouthpiece. By 1858 it was printing 16,400 copies, fifth to *Le Siècle* (37,000), *Le Constitutionnel* (26,900), *La Patrie* (24,500), and *La Presse* (21,000). In 1851 the format was enlarged, the price lowered, and literary aspirations become clear (Champfleury, Houssaye, Mérimée, About, Murger, Gautier, Sainte-Beuve qq.v.). Sainte-Beuve was allowed to praise *Madame Bovary* shortly after the failed prosecution.

In 1864 an evening version *Le Petit Moniteur* was launched

as the parent paper became more commercialized. A new official organ, *Le Journal Officiel* was created in 1869. Suppressed during the Commune, the paper never regained its quasi-official position, coming 25th in print-run (14,000) in 1880. After amalgamations it was absorbed with 800 subscribers by *Le Soleil* in 1902

published Banville's letters, 59

Constant's guarantees on the constitution in, 180

published Daudet, 190

Fontanes article praising Chateaubriand, 153

published Flaubert, 234

Mérimée reviewed Salon of 1853 in, 424

published Mérimée and Pushkin, 424, 427

and Romanticism 539

Sainte-Beuve moved to 557

Monnier, Adrienne; publisher and owner of bookshop Aux Amis des Livres, 167

description of Breton, 120

published Vaché's letters, 120

bought Giono poem, 266

Renard let down by, 518

Monnier, Henri (1799–1877); caricaturist and writer

see Augier, 40

described Balzac, 47

drawings of Girardin's papers, 48

cartoons for *Chronique de Paris*, 50

illustrated Balzac, 52

see Realism 512

met Sue at Gudin's studio, 635

Joseph Prudhomme character, 642

monogenesis, doctrine of: see Teilhard de Chardin, 659

Monpou

Music for *Piquillo*, 463

Montaigne, Michel (1533–1592); author of *Les Essais*

misread by Céline, 135

paradox of republican values, see Stendhal, 629

Montalembert, Charles Forbes, Comte de (1810–1870); journalist and politician, liberal Catholic associated with Lamennais until condemnation of *L'Avenir*

went to Rome with Lamennais, 359

at Mme Swetchine's salon, 393

translated Mickiewicz, 559

Montand, Yves (Ivo Livi) (1921–1991); actor, partner of Edith Piaf, Marilyn Monroe, Simone Signoret and Barbra Streisand

friend of Simenon, 608

Monte-Cristo

Dumas's house, 206; also Dumas's schooner, 207

Monte-Cristo, le—monthly paper, 1857–60

published by Dumas, 207

Montesquieu, Charles de Secondat, Baron de la Brède et de (1689–1755); writer

Balzac parodies title, 55

Chateaubriand reminiscent of, 157

model for Anatole France, 251

pioneer of sociology, 500

Sand stayed in Château de la Brède, 569

requirement for moral sense in individual, 666

Montesquiou-Fezensac, Robert de (1855–1921); known for his grotesquely refined style of life.

Cocteau sycophant of, 164

1836, by Armand Dutacq, who at first had wanted to collaborate with Girardin. *Le Siècle*, selling at the same 40-franc subscription as its rival, continuously outsold it, averaging 32,800 copies in 1846 against 24,771 for *Le Constitutionnel* and 22,170 for *La Presse*. In 1861 *Le Siècle* was printing 52,300 copies, its nearest rival only 23,000, its success doubtless due to its popular format and it steady criticism of the administration. The readers appear from the figures to have come from *Le Consitutionnel*, which continued to support the administration. *Le Siècle* had taken from it the supporters of respectable anti-clerical republicanism. What controlled its content was ultimately not principle but shrewd business sense. Like *Le National* and *La Presse* it did not recover from the Franco-Prussian war. From 35,000 in 1870, circulation dropped to 15,000 in 1880, and to 5,000 in 1910. When it ceased publication in 1917, the circulation was 1,000

ISBN 1-55862-086-9

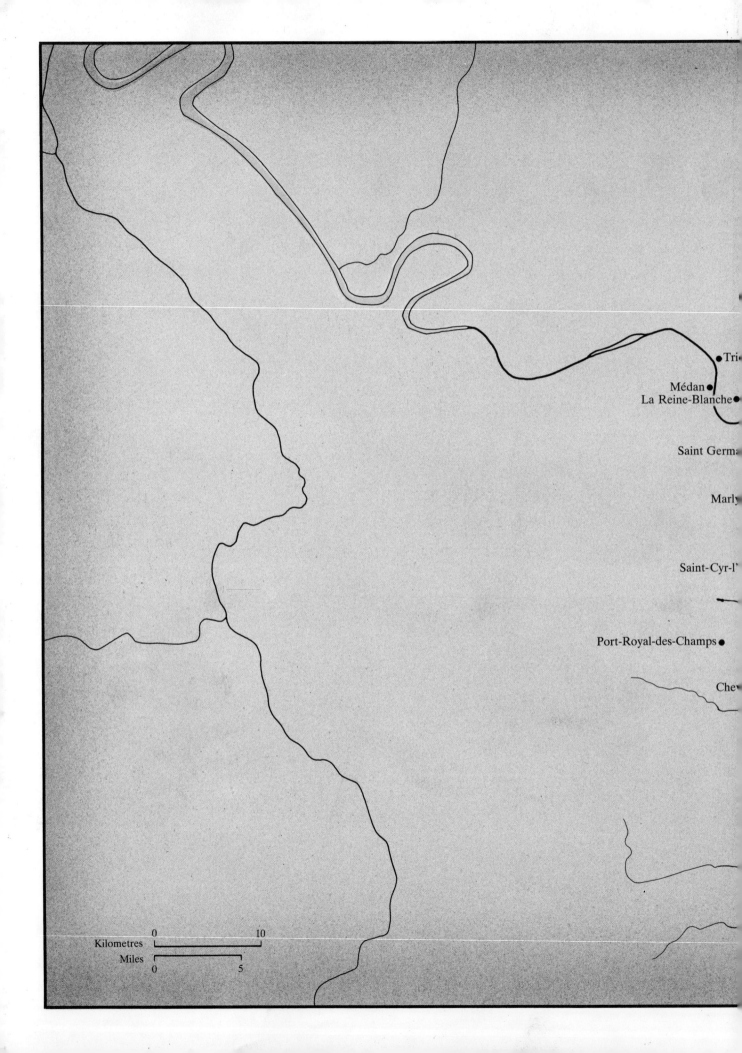

Tri

Médan ●
La Reine-Blanche ●

Saint Germa

Marly

Saint-Cyr-l'

Port-Royal-des-Champs ●

Che

Kilometres
0   10

Miles
0   5